# CHAMBERS'S

# ETYMOLOGICAL DICTIONARY

OF THE

## ENGLISH LANGUAGE

*A NEW AND THOROUGHLY REVISED EDITION*

EDITED BY

ANDREW FINDLATER, M.A., LL.D.

W. & R. CHAMBERS, Limited
LONDON AND EDINBURGH
1900

Edinburgh :
Printed by W. & R. Chambers, Limited.

# CONTENTS.

# PREFACE.

In view of the extraordinary progress which has been made in the historical study of the English Language, it has been found necessary to prepare an entirely New Edition of this Etymological Dictionary. It is confidently hoped that the improvements, which are the result of a careful and exhaustive revision, will greatly increase its efficiency and popularity. The Vocabulary has been enriched by the insertion of a multitude of additional words. The definitions of scientific terms have been carefully verified; and the pronunciation corrected in accordance with the best authorities. The changes in Etymology alone are so great as almost to constitute it a new work. For greater convenience of reference, the arrangement of the words has been made strictly alphabetical throughout.

The Dictionary is intended as a guide in the study and practical use of the English Language; and embraces the MEANINGS of Words, their PRONUNCIATION, and ETYMOLOGY.

**The Vocabulary** contains every English word sanctioned by good authority, with the exception of obsolete and very rare words, and terms exclusively technical. It includes, however, all the obsolete words that occur in the *Bible*, the *Apocrypha*, and the *Book of Common Prayer*. Owing to the wide diffusion of scientific knowledge and the application of scientific discovery to the business of every-day life, many terms that were once purely technical are now entering into the current speech. From this class of words large additions have been made to the Vocabulary.

In the **Definitions** the current meaning of a word is usually put first. It is left to the Etymology to connect the present meaning with the root. But where the word still retains more or less of its original force, the Editor has endeavoured to increase the vividness of the definition by indicating the radical idea in italics. It has been the aim throughout to avoid a distracting multiplicity of definitions—not to pile up unnecessary distinctions, but to emphasise only the real differences in the usage of words.

**The Pronunciation** is exhibited in the simplest possible manner. The correct sound of every word is given by being written anew phonetically, thus obviating the use of a confusing array of marks. The accentuation has also been carefully attended to, and different pronunciations have been given in cases where authorities are divided.

In the **Etymological** part of the work the results of the latest philological research are presented, though necessarily in the briefest possible way. Each word is traced to its origin, whether as belonging to the oldest known form of English, the Anglo-Saxon, or introduced from some sister Teutonic speech, as the Dutch, or borrowed from the classical tongues, either directly, or through the French. Cognate words in other languages, though not in the direct line of descent, are inserted, especially when light is thereby thrown on the primary sense of the word. In thus tracing words to their origin, the aim has been to show that the study of language is one of the greatest interest, that every word has a life of its own, and is not an arbitrary and meaningless thing, but the result of laws of historic growth. It will be seen also that words throw no little light on the history of the men that formed and used them ; and that our vast and complex vocabulary can be traced to a few roots expressing the simplest ideas.

In this department full advantage has been taken of the best French and German works, as also of the labours of the new English school of philologists, who have done so much during the last twenty years to promote the historic and scientific study of our own language. Special acknowledgment of indebtedness is due to Diez, *Etymologisches Wörterbuch der Romanischen Sprachen* (4th ed. 1878) ; to Littré's great work ; to the *Deutsches Wörterbuch* (3d ed. 1878) of Weigand, one of the continuators of Grimm ; and above all to Prof. Skeat, whose Etymological Dictionary is indispensable to every scientific student of the English language. Great assistance has also been obtained from the *Etymologisches Wörterbuch der Englischen Sprache* (2d ed. 1878) of E. Müller ; from the French Etymological Dictionaries of Brachet and Scheler ; from Diefenbach's Gothic Dictionary ; from the works of Morris and Trench ; and from the well-known lectures of Max Müller. As final authorities in their respective languages, the following dictionaries have been used, Liddell and Scott's Greek Lexicon (6th ed.) ; Lewis and Short in Latin ; and the Icelandic Dictionary of Cleasby and Vigfusson.

The **Appendix** contains a Glossary of the obsolete and rare words and meanings in Milton's poetical works ; a copious list of Prefixes and Suffixes, with their signification, derivation, and affinities, as far as ascertained ; a statement of Grimm's Law ; and many useful lists.

The Publishers have only to add that this Dictionary owes its present form to an able staff, including the Rev. A. P. DAVIDSON, M.A., under the superintendence of the late Dr ANDREW FINDLATER.

W. & R. C.

EDINBURGH, 1890.

# EXPLANATIONS TO THE STUDENT.

**The Arrangement of the Words.**—Every word is given in its *alphabetical* order. Each uncompounded verb has its participles, when irregular, placed after it. Exceptional plurals are also given. When a word stands after another, with no meaning given, its meanings can be at once formed from those of the latter, by adding the signification of the affix : thus the meanings of **Darkness** are obtained by prefixing the meaning of ne3s, *state of being*, to those of **Dark**.

**The Pronunciation.**—The Pronunciation is given immediately after each word, by the word being spelled anew. In this new spelling, every consonant used has its ordinary unvarying sound, *no consonant being employed that has more than one sound.* The same sounds are always represented by the same letters, no matter how varied their actual spelling in the language. No consonant used has any mark attached to it, with the one exception of *th*, which is printed in common letters when sounded as in *thick*, but in italics when sounded as in *th*en. *Unmarked vowels* have always their short sounds, as in *lad, led, lid, lot, but, book.* The *marked vowels* are shown in the following line, which is printed at the bottom of each page—

fāte, fär; mē, hėr; mīne; mōte; mūte; mōōn.

Where more than one pronunciation of a word is given, that which is placed first is more accepted.

**The Spelling.**—When more than one form of a word is given, that which is placed first is the more usual spelling.

**The Meanings.**—The current and most important meaning of a word is usually given first. But in some cases, as in **Clerk, Livery, Marshal**, where the force of the word can be made much clearer by tracing its history, the original meaning is first given, and the successive variations of its usage defined.

**The Etymology.**—The Etymology of each word is given after the meanings, within brackets. Where further information regarding a word is given elsewhere, it is so indicated by a reference. It must be noted under the etymology that whenever a word is printed thus: **Ban, Base**, the student is referred to it ; also that the sign — is always to be read as meaning 'derived from.' Examples are generally given of words that are cognate or correspond to the English words ; but it must be remembered that they are inserted merely for illustration. For instance, when an

English word is traced to its Anglo-Saxon form, and then a German word is given, no one should suppose that our English word is derived from the German. German and Anglo-Saxon are alike branches from a common Teutonic stem; and have seldom borrowed from each other. Under each word the force of the prefix is usually given, though not the affix. For fuller explanation in such cases, the student is referred to the list of Prefixes and Affixes in the Appendix.

*∗* The student is recommended at once to master the following List of Abbreviations occurring in the work, which will be found to suggest their own meaning.

## LIST OF ABBREVIATIONS.

| | | |
|---|---|---|
| acc ............according. | freq..........frequentative. | pass...........passive. |
| accus........accusative. | gen...........genitive. | pa.t..........past tense |
| adj...........adjective. | geol .........geology. | perf...........perfect. |
| adv ..........adverb. | geom ........geometry. | perh..........perhaps. |
| agri..........agriculture. | gram........grammar. | pers...........person. |
| alg............algebra. | gun ...........gunnery. | pfx............prefix. |
| anat..........anatomy. | her............heraldry. | phil...........philosophy. |
| arch..........architecture. | hort .........horticulture. | pl.............plural. |
| arith.........arithmetic. | inf ...........infinitive. | poet..........poetical. |
| astr..........astronomy. | int ...........interjection. | poss ..........possessive. |
| B .............Bible. | inten..........intensive. | Pr. Bk........Book of Common |
| book-k .......book-keeping. | jew...........jewellery. |        Prayer. |
| bot............botany. | lit.............literally. | pr.p..........present participle. |
| c..............century. | mas...........masculine. | prep ..........preposition. |
| cf.............compare. | math........mathematics. | pres...........present. |
| chem .........chemistry. | mech.........mechanics. | print..........printing. |
| cog...........cognate. | med...........medicine. | priv...........privative. |
| comp .........comparative. | mil............military. | prob..........probably. |
| conj..........conjunction. | min...........mineralogy. | pron..........pronoun. |
| conn..........connected. | mus...........music. | prov..........provincial. |
| contr.........contraction. | myth.........mythology. | rhet ..........rhetoric. |
| corr...........corruption. | n., ns........noun, nouns. | sig............signifying. |
| demons.......demonstrative. | nat. hist ......natural history. | sing...........singular. |
| Dict..........Dictionary. | naut..........nautical. | superl........superlative. |
| dim...........diminutive. | neg...........negative. | term..........termination. |
| dub...........doubtful. | obs............obsolete. | Test..........Testament. |
| E............English. | opp...........opposed. | theol..........theology. |
| esp ...........especially. | opt ...........optics. | unk ..........unknown. |
| ety ...........etymology. | orig..........originally. | v.i............verb intransitive. |
| fem...........feminine. | p..............participle. | v.t............verb transitive. |
| fig............figuratively. | paint.........painting. | zool ..........zoology. |
| fol............followed. | pa.p..........past participle. | |
| fort..........fortification. | | |

| | | |
|---|---|---|
| Amer........American. | Gael.........Gaelic. | O. Fr........Old French. |
| Ar............Arabic. | Ger...........German. | O. Ger.......Old German. |
| A S...........Anglo-Saxon. | Goth.........Gothic. | Pers..........Persian. |
| Bav..........Bavarian. | Gr............Greek. | Port..........Portuguese. |
| Bohem.......Bohemian. | Heb..........Hebrew. | Prov.........Provençal. |
| Bret..........Breton. | Hind..........Hindustani. | Rom..........Romance. |
| Celt..........Celtic. | Hun..........Hungarian. | Russ..........Russian. |
| Chal..........Chaldean. | Ice............Icelandic. | Sans..........Sanskrit. |
| Corn..........Cornish. | Ir.............Irish. | Scot..........Scottish. |
| Dan...........Danish. | It.............Italian. | Slav..........Slavonic. |
| Dut...........Dutch. | L.............Latin. | Sp............Spanish. |
| E............English. | Lith..........Lithuanian. | Sw...........Swedish. |
| Finn..........Finnish. | M. E .........Middle English. | Teut.........Teutonic. |
| Flem.........Flemish. | Mex..........Mexican. | Turk.........Turkish. |
| Fr............French. | Norm........Norman. | W............Welsh. |
| Fris..........Frisian. | Norw........Norwegian. | |

# CHAMBERS'S

# ETYMOLOGICAL DICTIONARY

## OF THE

## ENGLISH LANGUAGE.

---

## A

**A,** the indefinite article, a broken-down form of **An,** and used before words beginning with the sound of a consonant. [See **An.**]

**A,** used at one time before participles, as in ' She lay a dying.' It is now admitted only colloquially. [Short for A.S. *an*, a dialectic form of *on*, on, in, at. The same word is often used as a prefix. See **Prefixes.**]

**Aback,** a-bak', *adv.* (*naut.*) said of sails pressed backward against the mast by the wind—hence, **Taken aback,** taken by surprise. [A.S. *onbæc.* See **On** and **Back.**]

**Abacus,** ab'a-kus, *n.* a counting-frame or table : (*arch.*) a level tablet on the capital of a column. [L.—Gr. *abax, abakos,* a board for reckoning on.]

**Abaft,** a-baft', *adv.* or *prep., on* the *aft* or hind part of a ship : behind. [Prefix *a,* for A.S. *on,* on, and *bæftan,* after, behind—pfx. *be,* and *æft.* See **Aft.**]

**Abandon,** a-ban'dun, *v.t.* to give up : to desert : to yield (one's self) without restraint. [O. Fr. *bandon,* from the Teut. root *ban,* proclamation, came to mean decree, authorisation, permission ; hence *à bandon* = at will or discretion, *abandonner,* to give up to the will or disposal of some one. See **Ban, Banns.**]

**Abandoned,** a-ban'dund, *adj.* given up, as to a vice : very wicked.—*n.* **Abandonment,** a-ban'-dun-ment, act of abandoning : state of being given up.

**Abase,** a-bās', *v.t.* to cast down : to humble : to degrade.—*n.* **Abasement,** a-bās'ment, state of humiliation. [Fr. *abaisser,* to bring low—L. *ad,* to, and root of **Base,** *adj.*]

**Abash,** a-bash', *v.t.* to confuse with shame or guilt.—*n.* **Abashment,** a-bash'ment, confusion from shame. [O. Fr. *esbahir* (Fr. *ébahir*), *esbahissant,* to be amazed—L. *ex,* out, and int. *bah,* expressive of astonishment.]

**Abate,** a-bāt', *v.t.* to lessen : to mitigate.—*v.i.* to grow less. [Fr. *abattre,* to beat down—L. *ab,* from, and *batere,* popular form of *batuere,* to beat : conn. with **Beat.**]

**Abatement,** a-bāt'ment, *n.* the act of abating : the sum or quantity abated : (*her.*) a mark of dishonour on a coat of arms.

**Abatis, Abattis,** a'bat-is, *n.* (*fort.*) a rampart of trees *felled* and laid side by side, with the branches towards the enemy. [Fr. See **Abate.**]

**Abattoir,** a-bat-wär', *n.* a slaughter-house. [Fr. See ety. of **Abate.**]

## Abhor

**Abba,** ab'a, *n.* in Chaldee and Syriac, a *father.*

**Abbacy,** ab'a-si, *n.* the office of an abbot.

**Abbatial,** ab-bā'shal, **Abbatical,** ab-bat'ik-al, *adj.* pertaining to an abbey.

**Abbess,** ab'es, *n.* the superior of a religious community of women. [*Fem.* of **Abbot.**]

**Abbey,** ab'e, *n.* a monastery of persons of either sex presided over by an abbot or abbess : the church attached to it :—*pl.* **Abb'eys.** [Fr. *abbaye*—L. *abbatia*—**Abba.**]

**Abbot,** ab'ut, *n.* the *father* or head of an abbey. —*fem.* **Abb'ess.** [L. *abbas, abbatis*—**Abba.**]

**Abbreviate,** ab-brē'vi-āt, *v.t.* to make *brief* or short : to abridge. [L. *abbrevio, -atum—ab,* intensive, and *brevis,* short. See **Brief.**]

**Abbreviation,** ab-brē-vi-ā'shun, *n.* a shortening : a part of a word put for the whole.

**Abbreviator,** ab-brē'vi-āt-ur, *n.* one who abbreviates.

**Abdicate,** ab'di-kāt, *v.t.* to renounce or give up (a high office).—*n.* **Abdica'tion.** [L. *ab,* from or off, *dico, -atum,* to proclaim.]

**Abdomen,** ab-dō'men, *n.* the lower part of the belly. [L.]

**Abdominal,** ab-dom'in-al, *adj.* pertaining to the abdomen.

**Abduction,** ab-duk'shun, *n.* the carrying away, esp. of a person by fraud or force. [L. *ab,* from, *duco, ductum,* to draw.]

**Abductor,** ab-dukt'ur, *n.* one guilty of abduction : a muscle that draws away.

**Abeam,** a-bēm', *adv.* (*naut.*) on the beam, or in a line at right angles to a vessel's length. [Pfx. *a* (—A.S. *on,* on), on, and **Beam.**]

**Abed,** a-bed', *adv.* in *bed.* [Prefix *a,* on, and **Bed.**]

**Aberrant,** ab-er'ant, *adj., wandering from* the right or straight path. [L. *ab,* from, *erro,* to wander.]

**Aberration,** ab-ėr-ā'shun, *n.* a wandering from the right path : deviation from truth or rectitude.

**Abet,** a-bet', *v.t.* to incite by encouragement or aid (used chiefly in a bad sense) :—*pr.p.* abett'-ing ; *pa.p.* abett'ed.—*n.* **Abetment,** a-bet'ment. —*n.* **Abettor,** a-bet'ur. [O. Fr. *abeter*—à (—L. *ad,* to). and *beter,* to bait, from root of **Bait.**]

**Abeyance,** a-bā'ans, *n.* a state of suspension or expectation. [Fr.—*à* (—L. *ad,* to), and *bayer,* to gape in expectation, from imitative root *ba,* to gape.]

**Abhor,** ab-hor', *v.t.* to shrink from with horror :

---

**to** detest : to loathe :—*pr.p.* abhorr'ing ; *pa.p.* abhorred'. [L. See Horror.]

**Abhorrence,** ab-hor'ens, *n.* extreme hatred.

**Abhorrent,** ab-hor'ent, *adj.* detesting : repugnant.

**Abhorring,** ab-hor'ing, *n.* (*B.*) object of great hatred.

**Abide,** a-bīd', *v.t.* to *bide* or wait for : to endure : to tolerate.—*v.i.* to remain in a place, dwell or stay :—*pa.t.* and *pa.p.* abōde'.—*adj.* Abid'ing, continual. [A.S. *abidan*—pfx. *a* = Goth. *us* = Ger. *er*, and *bidan*, to wait.] [1 Sam. xxv.]

**Abigail,** ab'i-gāl, *n.* a lady's maid. [From Abigail.

**Ability,** a-bil'i-ti, *n.* quality of being able : power : strength : skill :—*pl.* Abil'ities, the powers of the mind. [M. E. *hability*, Fr. *habileté*—L. *habilitas*—*habilis*, easily handled, fit, apt, able, from *habeo*, to have, hold. See Able.]

**Abject,** ab'jekt, *adj., cast away* : mean : worthless.—*adv.* Ab'jectly. [L. *abjectus*—cast away —*ab*, away, *jacio*, to throw.]

**Abjection,** ab-jek'shun, **Abjectness,** ab'jekt-nes, *n. a mean* or *low state* : baseness.

**Abjure,** ab-jōōr', *v.t.* to renounce on oath or solemnly.—*n.* **Abjuration,** ab-jōōr-ā'shun. [L. *ab*, from, *juro*, *-atum*, to swear.]

**Ablactation,** ab-lak-tā'shun, *n.* a weaning. [L. *ab*, from, *lacto*, to suckle—*lac*, *lactis*, milk.]

**Ablative,** ab'lat-iv, *adj.* used as a *n.* The name of the 6th case of a Latin noun. [L. *ablativus* —*ab*, from, *fero*, *latum*, to take ; as if it indicated taking away, or privation.]

**Ablaze,** a-blāz', *adv., in a blaze* : on fire.

**Able,** ā'bl, *adj.* (*comp.* A'bler ; *superl.* A'blest), having sufficient strength, power, or means to do a thing : skilful.—*adv.* A'bly. [See Ability.]

**Ablution,** ab-lōō'shun, *n.* act of washing, esp. the body, preparatory to religious rites. [L. *ablutio* —*ab*, away, *luo* = *lavo*, to wash.]

**Abnegate,** ab'ne-gāt, *v.t., to deny.* [L. *ab*, away, and *nego*, to deny. See Negation.] [tion.

**Abnegation,** ab-ne-gā'shun, *n.*, denial : renuncia-

**Abnormal,** ab-nor'mal, *adj., not normal* or according to rule : irregular.—*n.* Abnor'mity. [L. *ab*, away from, Normal.]

**Aboard,** a-bōrd', *adv.* or *prep., on board :* in a ship. [Pfx. *a*, on, and Board.]

**Abode,** a-bōd', *n.* a dwelling-place : stay. [Abide.]

**Abode,** a-bōd', *pa.t.* and *pa.p.* of Abide.

**Abolish,** a-bol'ish, *v.t.* to put an end to : to annul. [Fr. *abolir*—L. *aboleo*, *-itum*—*ab*, from, *olo*, *olesco*, to grow—*ab* here reverses the meaning of the simple verb.]

**Abolition,** ab-ol-ish'un, *n.* the act of abolishing.

**Abolitionist,** ab-ol-ish'un-ist, *n.* one who seeks to abolish anything, esp. slavery.

**Abominable,** ab-om'in-a-bl, *adj.* hateful, detestable.—*adv.* Abom'inably.—*n.* Abom'inableness. [See Abominate.]

**Abominate,** ab-om'in-āt, *v.t.* to abhor : to detest extremely. [L. *abominor*, *-atus*—to turn from as of bad omen. See Omen.]

**Abomination,** ab-om-in-ā'shun, *n.* extreme aversion : anything abominable.

**Aboriginal,** ab-o-rij'in-al, *adj.* first, primitive.

**Aborigines,** ab-o-rij'in-ēz, *n.pl.* the *original* inhabitants of a country. [L. See Origin.]

**Abort,** ab-ort', *v.i.* to miscarry in birth. [L. *aborior*, *abortus*—*ab*, *orior*, to rise—*ab* here reverses the meaning.]

**Abortion,** ab-or'shun, *n.* premature delivery : anything that does not reach maturity.

**Abortive,** ab-ort'iv, *adj.* born untimely : unsuccessful : pro lucing nothing.—*adv.* Abort'ively.—*n.* Abort'iveness.

**Abound,** ab-ownd', *v.i.* to overflow, be in great plenty ; (with *in*) to possess in plenty. [L. *abundo*, to overflow as a river, from *unda*, a wave.]

**About,** a-bowt', *prep.* round *on the out* side : around : here and there in : near to : concerning : engaged in.—*adv.* around : nearly : here and there.—**Bring about,** to cause to take place.— **Come about,** to take place.—**Go about,** to prepare to do. [A.S. *abutan*—*a*, on, *be*, by, *utan*, outside.]

**Above,** a-buv', *prep., on the up* side : higher than : more than.—*adv.* overhead : in a higher position, order, or power. [A.S. *abufan*—*a*, on, *be*, by, *ufan*, high, upwards, which is an adv. formed from *uf* = up.] [or table : open.

**Above-board,** a-buv'-bōrd, *adj.* above the board

**Abrade,** ab-rād', *v.t., to scrape* or *rub off.* [L. *ab*, off, *rado*, *rasum*, to scrape.]

**Abrasion,** ab-rā'zhun, *n.* the act of rubbing off.

**Abreast,** a-brest', *adv.* with the *breasts* in a line : side by side : (*naut.*) opposite to. [*a*, on, and Breast.]

**Abridge,** a-brij', *v.t.* to make *brief* or short : to shorten : to epitomise. [Fr. *abréger*—L. *abbreviare.* See Abbreviate.] [mary.

**Abridgment,** a-brij'ment, *n.* contraction : sum-

**Abroad,** a-brawd', *adv.* on the *broad* or open space : out of doors : in another country.

**Abrogate,** ab'ro-gāt, *v.t.* to repeal (a law). [L. *ab*, away, *rogo*, *-atum*, to ask ; because when a law was proposed the people were 'asked' (to sanction or reject it).]

**Abrogation,** ab'ro-gā'shun, *n.* act of repealing.

**Abrupt,** ab-rupt', *adj.* the opposite of gradual, as if *broken off :* sudden : unexpected.—*n.* an abrupt place.—*adv.* Abrupt'ly.—*n.* Abrupt'ness. [L. *abruptus*—*ab*, off, *rumpo*, *ruptum*, to break.]

**Abscess,** ab'ses, *n.* a collection of purulent matter within some tissue of the body. [L. *abscessus*— *abs*, away, *cedo*, *cessum*, to go, to retreat.]

**Abscond,** abs-kond', *v.i.* (*lit.*) *to hide* one's self : to quit the country in order to escape a legal process. [L. *abs*, from or away, *condo*, to hide.]

**Absence,** abs'ens, *n.* the being away or not present : want : inattention.

**Absent,** abs'ent, *adj., being away* : not present : inattentive. [L. *abs*, away from, *ens*, *entis*, being—*sum*, *esse*, to be. See Entity.]

**Absent,** abs-ent', *v.t.* to keep one's self away.

**Absentee,** abs-ent-ē', *n.* one who lives away from his estate or his office.

**Absenteeism,** abs-ent-ē'izm, *n.* the practice of a land-owner living at a distance from his estate.

**Absinth,** ab'sinth, *n.* spirit flavoured with wormwood. [Fr.—L. *absinthium*, wormwood—Gr.]

**Absolute,** ab'so-lūt, *adj.* free from limits or conditions : complete : unlimited : free from mixture : considered without reference to other things : unconditioned, unalterable : unrestricted by constitutional checks (said of a government) : (*gram.*) not immediately dependent.—*adv.* Ab'solutely.—*n.* Ab'soluteness. [L. *absolutus*, pa.p. of *absolvo.* See Absolve.]

**Absolution,** ab-sol-ū'shun, *n.* release from punishment : acquittal : remission of sins by a priest.

**Absolutism,** ab'sol-ūt-izm, *n.* government where the ruler is without restriction.

**Absolve,** ab-zolv', *v.t., to loose* or set free : to pardon : to acquit. [L. *ab*, from, *solvo*, *solutum*, to loose. See Absolve.]

**Absorb,** ab-sorb', *v.t., to suck in* : to swallow up : to engage wholly. [L. *ab*, from, *sorbeo*, *sorptum*, to suck in.]

**Absorbable,** ab-sorb′a-bl, *adj.* that may be absorbed.—*n.* **Absorbabil′ity.**

**Absorbent,** ab-sorb′ent, *adj.* imbibing : swallowing.—*n.* that which absorbs.

**Absorption,** ab-sorp′shun, *n.* the act of absorbing : entire occupation of mind. [absorb.

**Absorptive,** ab-sorpt′iv, *adj.* having power to

**Abstain,** abs-tān′, *v.i.* to *hold* or refrain *from.* [Fr. *abstenir*—L. *abs*, from, *teneo*, to hold. See **Tenable.**]

**Abstemious,** abs-tēm′i-us, *adj.* temperate : sparing in food, drink, or enjoyments.—*adv.* **Abstem′iously.**—*n.* **Abstem′iousness.** [L. *abstemius*—*abs*, from, *temetum*, strong wine.]

**Abstention,** abs-ten′shun, *n.* a refraining.

**Abstergent,** abs-tèrj′ent, *adj.* serving to cleanse.

**Abstersion,** abs-tèr′shun, *n.* act of cleansing by lotions. [L. *abstergeo*, *-tersum*, to wipe away.]

**Abstinence,** abs′tin-ens, *n.* an abstaining or refraining, especially from some indulgence.

**Abstinent,** abs′tin-ent, *adj.* abstaining from : temperate. [See **Abstain.**]

**Abstract,** abs-trakt′, *v.t.*, *to draw away* : to separate : to purloin. [L. *abs*, away from, *traho, tractum*, to draw. See **Trace.**]

**Abstract,** abs′trakt, *adj.* general, as opposed to particular or individual : the opposite of *abstract* is *concrete* : a red colour is an abstract notion, **a** red rose is a concrete notion : an abstract noun is the name of a quality apart from the thing, as redness.—*n.* summary : abridgment : essence. —*adv.* **Abs′tractly.**—*n.* **Abs′tractness.** [L. *abstractus*, as if a quality common to a number of things were drawn away from the things and considered by itself.]

**Abstracted,** abs-trakt′ed, *adj.* absent in mind.— *adv.* **Abstract′edly.**—*n.* **Abstract′edness.**

**Abstraction,** abs-trak′shun, *n.* act of abstracting : state of being abstracted : absence of mind : the operation of the mind by which certain qualities or attributes of an object are considered apart from the rest : a purloining.

**Abstruse,** abs-trōōs′, *adj.* hidden : remote from apprehension : difficult to be understood.— *adv.* **Abstruse′ly.**—*n.* **Abstruse′ness.** [L. *abstrusus*, thrust away (from observation)—*trudo, trusum*, to thrust.]

**Absurd,** ab-surd′, *adj.* obviously unreasonable or false.—*adv.* **Absurd′ly.** [L. *absurdus*—*ab*, from, *surdus*, harsh-sounding, deaf.]

**Absurdity,** ab-surd′i-ti, **Absurdness,** ab-surd′nes, *n.*, *the quality of being absurd* : anything absurd.

**Abundance,** ab-und′ans, *n.* ample sufficiency : great plenty. [See **Abound.**] [**Abund′antly.**

**Abundant,** ab-und′ant, *adj.* plentiful.—*adv.*

**Abuse,** ab-ūz′, *v.t.* to use wrongly : to pervert : to revile : to violate. [L. *ab*, away (from what is right), *utor, usus*, to use.]

**Abuse,** ab-ūs′, *n.* ill use : misapplication : reproach.

**Abusive,** ab-ūs′iv, *adj.* containing or practising *abuse.*—*adv.* **Abus′ively.**—*n.* **Abus′iveness.**

**Abut,** a-but′, *v.i.* to end : to border (on) :—*pr.p.* abutt′ing ; *pa.p.* abutt′ed. [Fr. *aboutir*, from *bout*, the end of anything. See **Butt,** the end.]

**Abutment,** a-but′ment, *n.* that which abuts : (*arch.*) what a limb of an arch ends or rests on.

**Abysm,** a-bizm′, *n.* a form of **Abyss.** [O. Fr. *abysme*, from Lat. *abyssimus*, super. of *abyssus*, bottomless.]

**Abysmal,** a-bizm′al, *adj.* bottomless : unending.

**Abyss,** a-bis′, *n.* a *bottomless* gulf : a deep mass of water. [Gr. *abyssos*, bottomless—*a*, without, *byssos*, bottom.]

**Acacia,** a-kā′shi-a, *n.* a genus of *thorny* leguminous plants with pinnate leaves. [L.—Gr. *akakia* —*akē*, a sharp point.]

**Academic,** ak-ad-em′ik, *n.* a Platonic philosopher : a student in a college. [See **Academy.**]

**Academic,** -al, ak-ad-em′ik, -al, *adj.* of an academy.—*adv.* **Academ′ically.** [academy.

**Academician,** ak-ad-em-ish′yan, *n.* member of an

**Academy,** ak-ad′em-i, *n.* (*orig.*) the school of Plato : a higher school : a society for the promotion of science or art. [Gr. *Akadēmia*, the name of the garden near Athens where Plato taught.]

**Acanthus,** a-kan′thus, *n.* a prickly plant, called bear's breech or brankursine : (*arch.*) an ornament resembling its leaves used in the capitals of the Corinthian and Composite orders. [L.— Gr. *akanthos*—*akē*, a point, *anthos*, a flower— the *prickly* plant.]

**Accede,** ak-sēd′, *v.i.* to agree or assent. [L. *accedo, accessum*, to go near to—*ad*, to, *cedo*, to go. See **Cede.**]

**Accelerate,** ak-sel′èr-āt, *v.t.* to increase the speed of : to hasten the progress of. [L. *accelero, -atum*—*ad*, to, *celer*, swift. See **Celerity.**]

**Acceleration,** ak-sel-èr-ā′shun, *n.* the act of hastening : increase of speed.

**Accelerative,** ak-sel′èr-at-iv, *adj.* quickening.

**Accent,** ak′sent, *n.* modulation of the voice : stress on a syllable or word : a mark used to direct this stress : in poetry, language, words, or expressions in general. [L. *accentus*, a tone or note— *ad*, to, *cano*, to sing.]

**Accent,** ak-sent′, *v.t.* to express or note the accent.

**Accentual,** ak-sent′ū-al, *adj.* relating to accent.

**Accentuate,** ak-sent′ū-āt, *v.t.* to mark or pronounce with accent : to make prominent.—**Accentuation,** ak-sent-ū-ā′shun, *n.* the act of placing or of pronouncing accents.

**Accept,** ak-sept′, *v.t.* to receive : to agree to : to promise to pay : (*B.*) to receive with favour. [L. *accipio, acceptum*—*ad*, to, *capio*, to take.]

**Acceptable,** ak-sept′a-bl, *adj., to be accepted* : pleasing : agreeable.—*adv.* **Accept′ably.**

**Acceptableness,** ak-sept′a-bl-nes, **Acceptability,** ak-sept-a-bil′i-ti, *n., quality of being acceptable.*

**Acceptance,** ak-sept′ans, *n.* a favourable reception : an agreeing to terms : an accepted bill.

**Acceptation,** ak-sept-ā′shun, *n.* a kind reception : the meaning of a word.

**Accepter,** ak-sept′ér, **Acceptor,** ak-sept′ur, *n.* one who accepts.

**Access,** ak-ses′ or ak′ses, *n.* liberty to come to, approach : increase. [See **Accede.**]

**Accessary,** ak′ses-ar-i, same as **Accessory.**

**Accessible,** ak-ses′i-bl, *adj., that may be approached.*—*adv.* **Access′ibly.**—*n.* **Accessibil′ity.**

**Accession,** ak-sesh′un, *n.*, *a coming to* : increase.

**Accessory,** ak′ses-or-i, *adj.* additional : contributing to : aiding.—*n.* anything additional : one who aids or gives countenance to a crime.—*adj.* **Accessor′ial,** relating to an accessory.

**Accidence,** ak′sid-ens, *n.* the part of grammar treating of the inflections of words (because these changes are 'accidentals' of words and not 'essentials').

**Accident,** ak′sid-ent, *n.* that which happens : an unforeseen or unexpected event : chance : an unessential quality or property. [L. *accido*, to fall to, to happen—*ad*, to, *cado*, to fall.]

**Accidental,** ak-sid-ent′al, *adj.* happening by chance : not essential.—*n.* anything not essential.—*adv.* **Accident′ally.**

**Acclaim**, ak-klām', **Acclamation**, ak-klam-ā′shun, *n.* a shout of applause. [L. *acclamo—ad*, to, *clamo, -atum*, to shout. See **Claim**.]

**Acclamatory**, ak-klam′a-tor-i, *adj.* expressing acclamation.

**Acclimate**, ak-klīm′āt, **Acclimatise**, ak-klīm′at-īz, *v.t.* to inure to a foreign *climate*. [Fr. *acclimater*, from *à* and *climat*. See **Climate**.]

**Acclimation**, ak-klīm-ā′shun, **Acclimatation**, ak-klīm-at-ā′shun, **Acclimatisation**, ak-klīm-at-i-zā′shun, *n.* the act of acclimatising : the state of being acclimatised. [The first form of the word is anomalous, the second is that used in French, and the third is that most in use in English.]

**Acclivity**, ak-kliv′i-ti, *n.* a slope upwards, opp. to **Declivity**, a slope downwards. [L. *ad*, to, *clivus*, a slope, from root of *clino*, to slope.]

**Accolade**, ak-ol-ād′, *n.* blow over the neck or shoulder with a sword, given in conferring knighthood. [Fr.—L. *ad*, to, *collum*, neck.]

**Accommodate**, ak-kom′mod-āt, *v.t.* to adapt : to make suitable : to supply : to adjust. [L. *ad*, to, *commodus*, fitting. See **Commodious**.]

**Accommodating**, ak-kom′mod-āt-ing, *p. adj.* affording accommodation : obliging.

**Accommodation**, ak-kom-mod-ā′shun, *n.* convenience : fitness : adjustment : a loan of money.

**Accommodative**, ak-kom′mod-āt-iv, *adj.* furnishing accommodation : obliging.

**Accompaniment**, ak-kum′pan-i-ment, *n.* that which accompanies : instrumental music along with a song.

**Accompanist**, ak-kum′pan-ist, *n.* one who accompanies a singer on an instrument.

**Accompany**, ak-kum′pan-i, *v.t.* to keep *company* with : to attend. [Fr. *accompagner*. See **Company**.]

**Accomplice**, ak-kom′plis, *n.* an associate, esp. in crime. [L. *ad*, to, *complex, -icis*, joined.]

**Accomplish**, ak-kom′plish, *v.t.* to complete : to effect : to fulfil : to equip. [Fr. *accomplir*—L. *ad*, to, *compleo, -plere*, to fill up. See **Complete**.]

**Accomplishable**, ak-kom′plish-a-bl, *adj.* that may be accomplished.

**Accomplished**, ak-kom′plisht, *adj.* complete in acquirements, especially graceful acquirements : polished.

**Accomplishment**, ak-kom′plish-ment, *n.* completion : ornamental acquirement.

**Accord**, ak-kord′, *v.i.* to agree : to be in correspondence.—*v.t.* to grant. [Fr. *accorder*—L. *ad*, to, *cor, cordis*, the heart.]

**Accord**, ak-kord′, *n.* agreement : harmony : (with *own*) spontaneous motion.      [formity.

**Accordance**, ak-kord′ans, *n.* agreement : con-**Accordant**, ak-kord′ant, *adj.* agreeing : corresponding.

**According**, ak-kord′ing, *p.adj.* in accordance : agreeing.—**According as**, an adverbial phrase = in proportion.—**According to**, a prepositional phrase = in accordance with or agreeably to.

**Accordingly**, ak-kord′ing-li, *adv.* in agreement (with what precedes).

**Accordion**, ak-kord′ion, *n.* a small keyed musical instrument with bellows. [From **Accord**.]

**Accost**, ak-kost′, *v.t.* to speak first to : to address. [Fr. *accoster*—L. *ad*, to, *costa*, a side.] [affable.

**Accostable**, ak-kost′a-bl, *adj.* easy of access :

**Accouchement**, ak-kōōsh′mong, *n.* delivery in child-*bed*. [Fr. *à*, and *couche*, a bed. See **Couch**.]

**Accoucheur**, ak-kōō-shèr′, *n.* a man who assists women in childbirth.—*fem.* **Accoucheuse**, ak-kōō-shèz′. [Fr.]

**Account**, ak-kownt′, *v.t.* to reckon : to judge,

value.—*v.i.* (with *for*) to give a reason. [O. Fr. *accomter*—L. *ad*, to, *computare*, to reckon. See **Compute**, **Count**.]      [value : sake.

**Account**, ak-kownt′, *n.* a counting : statement :

**Accountable**, ak-kownt′a-bl, *adj.* liable to account : responsible.—*adv.* **Account′ably**.

**Accountableness**, ak-kownt′a-bl-nes, **Accountability**, ak-kownt-a-bil′i-ti, *n.* liability to give account.      [is skilled in accounts.

**Accountant**, ak-kownt′ant, *n.* one who keeps or

**Accountantship**, ak-kownt′ant-ship, *n.* the employment of an accountant.

**Accoutre**, ak-kōō′tėr, *v.t.* to dress or equip (esp. a warrier) :—*pr.p.* accou′tring ; *pa.p.* accou′tred. [Fr. *accoutrer*—of doubtful origin.]

**Accoutrements**, ak-kōō′tėr-ments, *n.pl.* dress : military equipments.

**Accredit**, ak-kred′it, *v.t.* to give credit, authority, or honour to. [Fr. *accréditer*—L. *ad*, to, *credo, -itum*, to trust. See **Credit**.]      [increase.

**Accrescence**, ak-kres′ens, *n.* gradual growth or

**Accrescent**, ak-kres′ent, *adj., growing* : increasing. [L. *ad*, in addition, *cresco*, to grow.]

**Accretion**, ak-krē′shun, *n.* a growing to : increase.

**Accrue**, ak-krōō′, *v.i.* to spring, come. [Fr. *accroître*, pa.p. *accru*—L. *ad*, to, *cresco*, to grow.]

**Accumbent**, ak-kumb′ent, *adj., lying down* or reclining on a couch. [L. *ad*, to, *cumbo*, to lie.]

**Accumulate**, ak-kūm′ūl-āt, *v.t., to heap* or pile up : to amass.—*v.i.* to increase greatly. [L. *-ad*, to, *cumulus*, a heap.]

**Accumulation**, ak-kūm-ūl-ā′shun, *n.* a heaping up : a heap, mass, or pile.

**Accumulative**, ak-kūm′ūl-āt-iv, *adj.* heaping up.

**Accumulator**, ak-kūm′ūl-āt-ur, *n.* one who accumulates.

**Accuracy**, ak′kūr-a-si, *n.* correctness : exactness.

**Accurate**, ak′kūr-āt, *adj.* done *with care* : exact.— *adv.* **Ac′curately**.—*n.* **-ness**. [L. *ad, cura*, care.]

**Accursed**, ak-kurs′ed, *adj.* subjected to a curse : doomed : extremely wicked. [L. *ad*, and **Curse**.]

**Accusable**, ak-kūz′a-bl, *adj.* that may be accused.

**Accusation**, ak-kūz-ā′shun, *n.* the act of accusing : the charge brought against any one.

**Accusative**, ak-kūz′a-tiv, *adj.* accusing.—*n.* (*gram.*) the case of a noun on which the action of a verb falls (in English, the objective).

**Accusatory**, ak-kūz′a-tor-i, *adj.* containing accusation.

**Accuse**, ak-kūz′, *v.t.* to bring a charge against : to blame. [L. *accuso—ad*, to, *causa*, cause.]

**Accuser**, ak-kūz′ėr, *n.* one who accuses or brings a charge against another.

**Accustom**, ak-kus′tum, *v.t.* to make familiar *by custom* : to habituate. [Fr. *accoutumer*. See **Custom**.]      [habituated.

**Accustomed**, ak-kus′tumd, *p.adj.* usual : frequent :

**Ace**, ās, *n.* the *one* of cards and dice. [Fr.—L. *as*, unity—*as*, Tarentine Doric form of Gr. *heis*, one.]

**Acerbity**, as-ėr′bi-ti, *n.* bitterness : sourness : harshness : severity. [L. *acerbus*, harsh to the taste—*acer*, sharp—root *ak*, sharp.]

**Acetate**, as′et-āt, *n.* a salt of acetic acid which is the sour principle in vinegar.

**Acetic**, as-et′ik, *adj., of vinegar* : sour. [L. *acetum*, vinegar—*aceo*, to be sour.]

**Acetify**, as-et′i-fī, *v.t.* and *v.i.*, *to turn into vinegar*. —*n.* **Acetification**, as-et-i-fi-kā′shun. [L. *acetum*, vinegar, and *facio*, to make.]

**Acetous**, as-ē′tus, *adj.* sour.

**Ache**, āk, *n.* a continued pain.—*v.i.* to be in continued pain :—*pr.p.* āch′ing ; *pa.p.* āched′. [A.S. *ece, æce* ; M. E. *ake*.]

**Achievable**, a-chēv′a-bl, *adj.* that may be achieved.

**Achieve**, a-chēv′, *v.t.*, *to bring to a head* or end : to perform : to accomplish : to gain, win. [Fr. *achever—chef*, the head. See **Chief**.]

**Achievement**, a-chēv′ment, *n.* a performance : an exploit : an escutcheon.

**Achromatic**, a-krōm-at′ik, *adj.* transmitting light *without colour*, as a lens. [Gr. *a*, priv., and *chrōma*, colour.]                    [achromatic.

**Achromatism**, a-krōm′at-izm, *n.* the state of being

**Acicular**, as-ik′ū-lar, *adj.*, *needle-shaped* : slender and sharp-pointed. [L. *acicula*, dim. of *acus*, a needle—root *ak*, sharp.]

**Acid**, as′id, *adj.*, *sharp* : sour.—*n.* a sour substance : (*chem.*) one of a class of substances, usually sour, which turn vegetable dyes to red, and combine with alkalies, metallic oxides, &c. to form salts. [L. *aceo*, to be sour—root *ak*, sharp.]

**Acidifiable**, as-id′i-fī-a-bl, *adj.* capable of being converted into an acid.—*n.* **Acidifica′tion**.

**Acidify**, as-id′i-fī, *v.t.*, *to make acid* : to convert into an acid :—*pr.p.* acid′ifying ; *pa.p.* acid′ified. [L. *acidus*, sour, and *facio*, to make.]

**Acidity**, as-id′i-ti, **Acidness**, as′id-nes, *n.* the quality of being acid or sour.

**Acidulate**, as-id′ū-lāt, *v.t.* to make slightly acid.

**Acidulous**, as-id′ū-lus, *adj.* slightly sour : subacid : containing carbonic acid, as mineral waters. [L. *acidulus*, dim. of *acidus*, sour. See **Acid**.]

**Acknowledge**, ak-nol′ej, *v.t.* to own a *knowledge* of : to admit : to own : to confess. [Pfx. *a* (—A.S. *on*. on). and **Knowledge**.]

**Acknowledgment**, ak-nol′ej-ment, *n.* recognition : admission : confession : thanks : a receipt.

**Acme**, ak′mē, *n.* the top or highest *point* : the crisis, as of a disease. [Gr. *akmē—akē*, a point.]

**Acne**, ak′nē, *n.* a small pimple on the face. [Gr.]

**Acolyte**, ak′o-līt, **Acolyth**, ak′o-lith, *n.* an inferior church officer. [Gr. *akolouthos*, an attendant.]

**Aconite**, ak′o-nīt, *n.* the plant wolf's-bane or monk's-hood : poison. [L. *aconitum*—Gr. *akoniton*.]

**Acorn**, ā′korn, *n.* the seed or fruit of the oak. —*adj.* **A′corned**. [A.S. *œcern* came to be spelled *ac-cern*, *acorn*, from supposing it compounded of *oak* and *kern* or *corn*, seed : *œcern* may be the dim. of *âc*, oak, as Ger. *eichel*, is of *eiche* ; but it is more probably derived from *acer* or *aker*, a field (see **Acre**), and meant primarily 'the fruit of the field.' (Skeat).]

**Acotyledon**, a-kot-i-lē′dun, *n.* a plant *without* distinct *cotyledons* or seed-lobes.—*adj.* **Acotyle′donous**. [Gr. *a*, neg., and *kotylēdōn*. See **Cotyledon**.]

**Acoustic**, a-kowst′ik, *adj.* pertaining to the sense *of hearing* or to the theory of sounds. [Gr. *akoustikos—akouō*, to hear.]

**Acoustics**, a-kowst′iks, *n.* the science of sound.

**Acquaint**, ak-kwānt′, *v.t.* to make or let one to know : to inform.—*p.adj.* **Acquaint′ed**. [O. Fr. *accointer*, Low L. *accognitare*—L. *ad*, to, *cognitus*, known.]

**Acquaintance**, ak-kwānt′ans, *n.* familiar knowledge : a person whom we know.—**Acquaint′anceship**, *n.* familiar knowledge.

**Acquiesce**, ak-kwi-es′, *v.i.*, *to rest* satisfied or without making opposition : to assent. [L. *acquiesco—ad*, and *quies*, rest.]         [submission.

**Acquiescence**, ak-kwi-es′ens, *n.* quiet assent or

**Acquiescent**, ak-kwi-es′ent, *adj.* resting satisfied : easy : submissive.                    [acquired.

**Acquirable**, ak-kwīr′a-bl, *adj.* that may be

**Acquire**, ak-kwīr′, *v.t.* to gain : to attain to. [L. *acquiro*, *-quisitum—ad*, to, and *quero*, to seek —as if, to get *to* something *sought*.]

**Acquirement**, ak-kwīr′ment, *n.* something learned or got by effort, and not a gift of nature.

**Acquisition**, ak-kwiz-ish′un, *n.* the act of acquiring : that which is acquired.

**Acquisitive**, ak-kwiz′it-iv, *adj.* desirous to acquire. —*n.* **Acquis′itiveness**.

**Acquit**, ak-kwit′, *v.t.* to free : to release : to declare innocent :—*pr.p.* acquitt′ing ; *pa.p.* acquitt′ed. [Fr. *acquitter*—L. *ad*, *quiet-*, rest —to give *rest* from an accusation. See **Quit**.]

**Acquittal**, ak-kwit′al, *n.* a judicial discharge from an accusation.

**Acquittance**, ak-kwit′ans, *n.* a discharge from an obligation or debt : a receipt.

**Acre**, ā′kėr, *n.* a measure of land containing 4840 sq. yards. [A.S. *œcer*, Ger. *acker*, L. *ager*, Gr. *agros*, Sans. *ajra*, a field.]

**Acreage**, ā′kėr-āj, *n.* the number of acres in a piece of land.

**Acred**, ā′kėrd, *adj.* possessing acres or land.

**Acrid**, ak′rid, *adj.* biting to the taste : pungent : bitter. [L. *acer*, *acris*, sharp—root *ak*, sharp.]

**Acridity**, a-krid′i-ti, **Acridness**, ak′rid-nes, *n.* quality of being acrid : a sharp, bitter taste.

**Acrimonious**, ak-ri-mōn′i-us, *adj.* sharp, bitter.

**Acrimony**, ak′ri-mun-i, *n.* bitterness of feeling or language. [L. *acrimonia—acer*, sharp.]

**Acrobat**, ak′ro-bat, *n.* a rope-dancer : a tumbler : a vaulter.—*adj.* **Acrobat′ic**. [Gr. *akrobateō*, to walk on tiptoe—*akron*, the top, and *bainō*, to go.]

**Acrogen**, ak′ro-jen, *n.* a plant that *grows at the top* chiefly, as a tree-fern.—*adj.* **Acrog′enous**. [Gr. *akron*, extremity, top, *gen-*, to generate.]

**Acropolis**, a-krop′ol-is, *n.* a citadel, esp. that of Athens. [Gr. *akropolis—akros*, the highest, *polis*, a city.]

**Across**, a-kros′, *prep.* or *adv.*, *cross*-wise : from side to side. [Pfx *a* (—A.S. *on*, on), and **Cross**.]

**Acrostic**, a-kro′stik, *n.* a poem of which, if the first or the last letter of each line be taken in succession, they will spell a name or a sentence. [Gr. *akros*, extreme, and *stichos*, a line.]

**Act**, akt, *v.i.* to exert force or influence : to produce an effect : to behave one's-self.—*v.t.* to perform : to imitate or play the part of.—*n.* something done or doing : an exploit : a law : a part of a play. [L. *ago*, *actum*, Gr. *agō*, to put in motion ; Sans. *aj*, to drive.]

**Acting**, akt′ing, *n.* action : act of performing an assumed or a dramatic part.

**Actinism**, ak′tin-izm, *n.* the chemical force of the sun's *rays*, as distinct from light and heat. [Gr. *aktis*, *aktinos*, a ray.]

**Action**, ak′shun, *n.* a state of acting : a deed : operation : gesture : a battle : a lawsuit.

**Actionable**, ak′shun-a-bl, *adj.* liable to a lawsuit.

**Active**, akt′iv, *adj.* that acts : busy : nimble : (*gram.*) transitive.—*adv.* **Act′ively**.—*ns.* **Activ′ity**, **Act′iveness**.

**Actor**, akt′ur, *n.* one who acts : a stage-player.

**Actress**, ak′tres, *n.* a female stage-player.

**Actual**, akt′ū-al, *adj.* real : existing in fact and now, as opp. to an imaginary or past state of things.—*adv.* **Act′ually**.—*n.* **Actual′ity**.

**Actualise**, akt′ū-al-īz, *v.t.* to make actual.

**Actuary**, akt′ū-ar-i, *n.* a registrar or clerk : one who makes the calculations connected with an insurance office. [L. *actuarius* (*scriba*), an amanuensis, a clerk.]

**Actuate**, akt′ū-āt, *v.t.* to put into or incite to *action* : to influence. [L. *actus*, action. See **Act**.]

**Acumen**, ak-ū′men, *n.*, *sharpness* : quickness of perception : penetration. [L. See **Acute**.]

**Acupressure**, ak-ū-presh′ūr, *n.* a mode of arresting hemorrhage from cut arteries, by inserting *a needle* into the flesh so as *to press* upon the mouth of the artery. [L. *acus*, a needle, and **Pressure**.]

**Acupuncture**, ak-ū-pungkt′ūr, *n.* an operation for relieving pain by *puncturing* the flesh *with* needles. [L. *acus*, a needle, and **Puncture**.]

**Acute**, ak-ūt′, *adj.*, *sharp*-pointed : keen : opp. of dull : shrewd : shrill.—*adv.* **Acutely**, ak-ūt′li. —*n.* **Acute′ness**.—**Acute angle**, an angle less than a right angle.—**Acute disease**, one violent and rapid, as opp. to **Chronic**. [L. *acutus*, pa.p. of *acuo*, to sharpen, from root *ak*, sharp.]

**Adage**, ad′āj, *n.* an old *saying* : a proverb. [L. *adagium*, from *ad*, to, and root of *aio*, to say.]

**Adamant**, ad′a-mant, *n.* a very hard stone: the diamond. [L. and Gr. *adamas*, -*antos*—*a*, neg., and *damaō*, to break, to tame. See **Tame**.]

**Adamantine**, ad-a-man′tin, *adj.* made of or like adamant: that cannot be broken or penetrated.

**Adapt**, ad-apt′, *v.t.*, *to make apt* or fit : to accommodate. [Fr., L. *adaptare*—*ad*, to, and *apto*, to fit.]

**Adaptable**, ad-apt′a-bl, *adj.* that may be adapted. —*n.* **Adaptabil′ity**.

**Adaptation**, ad-apt-ā′shun, *n.* the act of making suitable : fitness.

**Adays**, a-dāz′, *adv.* nowadays : at the present time. [Pfx. *a*, on, and **Days**.]

**Add**, ad, *v.t.* to put (one thing) to (another) : to sum up : with *to*, to increase. [L.—*addo*—*ad*, to, *do*, to put.]

**Addendum**, ad-den′dum, *n.*, *a thing to be added* : an appendix.—*pl.* **Adden′da**. [L. See **Add**.]

**Adder**, ad′ėr, *n.* a kind of serpent. [A.S. *nædre*; Ger. *atter* is for *natter*. *An adder* came by mistake into use for *a nadder*; the reverse mistake is *a newt* for *an ewt* or *eft*.]

**Addict**, ad-dikt′, *v.t.*, to give (one's-self) up to (generally in a bad sense). [L. *addico*, *addictum*—*ad*, to, *dico*, to declare.]

**Addicted**, ad-dikt′ed, *adj.* given up to.—*ns.* **Addict′edness**, **Addic′tion**.

**Addition**, ad-dish′un, *n.* the act of adding : the thing added : the rule in arithmetic for adding numbers together: title, honour.

**Additional**, ad-dish′un-al, *adj.* that is added.

**Addle**, ad′dl, **Addled**, ad′dld, *adj.*, *diseased* : putrid : barren, empty.—**Addle-headed**, **Addle-pated**, having a head or pate with addled brains. [A.S. *adl*, disease, orig. inflammation, from *ad*, a burning : akin to Lat. *æstus*, a glowing heat ; Gr. *aithos*, a burning.]

**Address**, ad-dres′, *v.t.* to direct : to speak or write to : to court : to direct in writing.—*n.* a formal communication in writing : a speech : manners : dexterity : direction of a letter :—*pl.* **Address′es**, attentions of a lover.—**To address one's-self to a task**, to set about it. [Fr. *adresser*. See **Dress**, **Direct**.]

**Adduce**, ad-dūs′, *v.t.* to bring forward : to cite or quote. [L. *adduco*—*ad*, to, and *duco*, to bring.]

**Adducible**, ad-dūs′i-bl, *adj.* that may be adduced.

**Adductor**, ad-dukt′ur, *n.* a muscle which draws one part towards another. [See **Abductor**.]

**Adept**, ad-ept′ or ad′ept, *adj.* completely skilled. —*n.* a proficient. [L. *adeptus* (*artem*), having attained (an art), *pa.p.* of *adipiscor*, to attain—*ad*, to, and *apiscor*, Sans. *ap*, to attain.]

**Adequate**, ad′e-kwāt, *adj.*, *equal to* : proportionate : sufficient.—*adv.* **Ad′equately**. [L. *adæquatus*, made equal—*ad*, to, and *æquus*, equal.]

**Adequateness**, ad′e-kwāt-nes, **Adequacy**, ad′e-kwa-si, *n.* state of being adequate : sufficiency.

**Adhere**, ad-hēr′, *v.i.*, *to stick to* : to remain fixed or attached. [L. *ad*, to, *hæreo*, *hæsum*, to stick.]

**Adherence**, ad-hēr′ens, *n.* state of adhering : steady attachment.

**Adherent**, ad-hēr′ent, *adj.* sticking to.—*n.* one who adheres : a follower : a partisan.

**Adhesion**, ad-hē′zhun, *n.* the act of adhering or sticking to : steady attachment. [See **Adhere**.]

**Adhesive**, ad-hēs′iv, *adj.* sticky : apt to adhere. —*adv.* **Adhes′ively**.—*n.* **Adhes′iveness**.

**Adieu**, a-dū′, *adv.* (I commend you) *to God* : farewell.—*n.* a farewell. [Fr. *à Dieu*, to God.]

**Adipose**, ad′i-pōz, *adj.* fatty. [L. *adeps*, *adipis*, soft fat.]

**Adit**, ad′it, *n.* an opening or passage, esp. into a mine. [L. *aditus*—*ad*, to, *eo*, *itum*, to go.]

**Adjacent**, ad-jās′ent, *adj.*, *lying near to* : contiguous. — *n.* **Adjacency**, ad-jās′en-si. — *adv.* **Adjac′ently**. [L. *ad*, to, *jaceo*, to lie.]

**Adjective**, ad′jekt-iv, *n.* a word *added to* a noun, to qualify it, or, rather perhaps, that *adds* some property to a noun.—*adv.* **Ad′jectively**.—*adj.* **Adjectiv′al**. [L. *adjectivum* (*nomen*), an added (noun)—*adjicio*, -*jectum*, to throw to, to add—*ad*, to, *jacio*, to throw.]

**Adjoin**, ad-join′, *v.i.* to lie next to. [See **Join**.]

**Adjoining**, ad-join′ing, *adj.* joining to : near : adjacent.

**Adjourn**, ad-jurn′, *v.t.* to put off *to* another *day* : to postpone. [Fr. *ajourner*—*ad*, to, and *jour*, day. See **Journal**.]

**Adjournment**, ad-jurn′ment, *n.* the act of adjourning : the interval it causes.

**Adjudge**, ad-juj′, *v.t.* to decide. [See **Judge**.]

**Adjudicate**, ad-jōō′di-kāt, *v.i.* to pronounce judgment.—*ns.* **Adju′dica′tion**, **Adju′dicator**. [See **Judge**.]

**Adjunct**, ad′junkt, *adj.*, *joined* or added *to*.—*n.* the thing joined or added. [L. See **Join**.]

**Adjunctive**, ad-junkt′iv, *adj.* joining.—**Adjunctively**, ad-junkt′iv-li, **Adjunctly**, ad-junkt′li, *adv.* in connection with.

**Adjuration**, ad-jōōr-ā′shun, *n.* the act of adjuring : the charge or oath used in adjuring.

**Adjure**, ad-jōōr′, *v.t.* to charge *on oath* or solemnly. [L.—*ad*, to, *juro*, -*atum*, to swear.]

**Adjust**, ad-just′, *v.t.* to arrange properly : to regulate : to settle. [O. Fr. *ajouster*, Low L. *adjuxtare*, to put side by side—L. *juxta*, near : from root *jug*, seen in L. *jungo*, to join, E. **Yoke**.]

**Adjustment**, ad-just′ment, *n.* arrangement.

**Adjutancy**, ad′joot-ans-i, *n.* the office of an adjutant : assistance.

**Adjutant**, ad′joot-ant, *n.* an officer who *assists* the commanding officer of a garrison or regiment : a large species of stork or crane found in India.— **Adjutant-general**, an officer who performs similar duties for the general of an army. [L. *adjuto* = *adjuvo*—*ad*, to, *juvo*, to assist.]

**Admeasurement**, ad-mezh′ūr-ment, *n.* the same as measurement.

**Administer**, ad-min′is-tėr, *v.t.* to act as server or minister in a performance : to supply : to conduct. [L. *ad*, to, and **Minister**.]

**Administration**, ad-min-is-trā′shun, *n.* The act of administering : the power or party that administers.           [*ministers*.

**Administrative**, ad-min′is-trā-tiv, *adj.*, *that ad-*

**Administrator**, ad-min-is-trā′tur, *n.* one who manages or directs : he who manages the affairs of one dying without making a will.—*fem.* **Administra′trix**.—*n.* **Administra′torship**.

**Admirable**, ad'mir-a-bl, *adj.* worthy of being admired.—*adv.* **Ad'mirably.**—*n.* **Ad'mirableness.**

**Admiral**, ad'mir-al, *n.* a naval officer of the highest rank. [Fr. *amiral*, from Ar. *amir*, a lord, a chief.]

**Admiralty**, ad'mir-al-ti, *n.* the board of commissioners for the administration of naval affairs.

**Admiration**, ad-mir-ā'shun, *n.* the act of admiring : (*obs.*) wonder.

**Admire**, ad-mīr', *v.t.* to have a high opinion of : to love.—*adv.* **Admir'ingly.** [Fr. *admirer*—L. *ad*, at, *miror*, to wonder.]

**Admirer**, ad-mīr'er, *n.* one who admires : a lover.

**Admissible**, ad-mis'i-bl, *adj.* that may be admitted or allowed.—*n.* **Admissibil'ity.**

**Admission**, ad-mish'un, **Admittance**, ad-mit'ans, *n.* the act of admitting : leave to enter.

**Admit**, ad-mit', *v.t.* to allow to enter : to let in : to concede : to be capable of :—*pr.p.* admitt'ing ; *pa.p.* admitt'ed. [L. *admitto*, *-missum*—*ad*, to, *mitto*, to allow to go.]

**Admixture**, ad-miks'tūr, *n.* what is added to the chief ingredient of a mixture.

**Admonish**, ad-mon'ish, *v.t.* to warn : to reprove mildly. [L. *ad*, to, and *moneo*, to put into the mind, akin to Ger. *mahnen*, to remind ; Gr. *menos*, spirit, mind ; Sans. *man*, to think.]

**Admonition**, ad-mon-ish'un, *n.* kind reproof : counsel : advice.

**Admonitory**, ad-mon'i-tor-i, *adj.* containing admonition.

**Ado**, a-dōō', *n.* a *to do* : bustle : trouble. [Contr. of *at do*, a form of the inf. borrowed from the Scandinavian.]

**Adolescence**, ad-o-les'ens, *n.* the period of youth.

**Adolescent**, ad-o-les'ent, *adj.*, *growing to* manhood. [L. *ad*, to, and *olesco*, to grow, allied to *alo*, to nourish.]

**Adopt**, ad-opt', *v.t.* to choose : to take as one's own what is another's, as a child, &c. [L. *adopto*—*ad*, to, and *opto*, to wish, choose.]

**Adoption**, ad-op'shun, *n.* the act of adopting : the state of being adopted.

**Adoptive**, ad-opt'iv, *adj.* that adopts or is adopted.

**Adorable**, ad-ōr'a-bl, *adj.* worthy of being adored.—*adv.* **Ador'ably.**—*n.* **Ador'ableness.**

**Adoration**, ad-ōr-ā'shun, *n.* divine worship: homage.

**Adore**, ad-ōr', *v.t.* to worship : to love intensely.—*adv.* **Ador'ingly.** [L. *ad*, to, *oro*, to speak, to pray. See **Oracle.**]

**Adorer**, ad-ōr'er, *n.* one who adores : a lover.

**Adorn**, ad-orn', *v.t.* to deck or dress. [L. *ad*, to, *orno*, to deck ; Sans. *varna*, colour.] [tion.

**Adornment**, ad-orn'ment, *n.* ornament: decora-

**Adown**, a-down', *adv.* and *prep.* down. [A.S. *of-dune*—*of*, from, *dun*, a hill. See **Down**, a bank.]

**Adrift**, a-drift', *adj.* or *adv.* floating as driven (by the wind) : moving at random. [Lit. 'on drift,' *a* representing A.S. *on*, on. See **Drift.**]

**Adroit**, a-droit', *adj.* dexterous : skilful.—*adv.* **Adroitly**, a-droit'li.—*n.* **Adroit'ness.** [Fr. *à*, *droit*, right—L. *directus*, straight. See **Direct.**]

**Adscititious**, ad-sit-ish'us, *adj.*, *added* or assumed: additional. [L. *adscisco*, *-scitum*, to take or assume—*ad*, to, *scisco*, to inquire—*scio*, to know.]

**Adulation**, ad-ū-lā'shun, *n.* fawning : flattery. [L. *adulor*, *adulatus*, to fawn upon.]

**Adulatory**, ad'ū-la-tor-i, *adj.* flattering.

**Adult**, ad-ult', *adj.*, *grown* : mature.—*n.* a grown-up person [L. *adultus*—*adolesco*, to grow. See **Adolescent.**]

**Adulterate**, ad-ult'er-āt, *v.t.* to corrupt : to make impure (by mixing). [L. *adultero*—*ad*, to, *alter*, other ; as it, to make other than genuine.]

**Adulteration**, ad-ult-er-ā'shun, *n.* the act of adulterating : the state of being adulterated.

**Adulterer**, ad-ult'er-er, *n.* a man guilty of adultery.—*fem.* **Adult'eress.**

**Adulterine** ad-ult'er-in, *adj.* resulting from adultery : spurious.—*n.* the offspring of adultery.

**Adulterous**, ad-ult'er-us, *adj.* guilty of adultery.

**Adultery**, ad-ult'er-i, *n.* violation of the marriage-bed. [See **Adulterate.**]

**Adumbrate**, ad-umbr'āt or ad'-, *v.t.* to give a faint *shadow* of : to exhibit imperfectly.—*n.* **Adumbra'tion.** [L. *ad*, to, *umbra*, a shadow.]

**Advance**, ad-vans', *v.t.* to put forward, or to the *van* : to promote to a higher office : to encourage the progress of : to propose : to supply beforehand.—*v.i.* to move or go forward : to make progress : to rise in rank.—*n.* progress : improvement : a giving beforehand.—**In advance**, beforehand. [Fr. *avancer*—Prov. *avant*, *abans*, before—L. *ab ante*, from before.]

**Advancement**, ad-vans'ment, *n.* promotion : improvement : payment of money in advance.

**Advantage**, ad-vant'āj, *n.* superiority over another : gain or benefit.—*v.t.* to benefit or profit. [Fr. *avantage*, It. *vantaggio*—Fr. *avant*, before. See **Advance.**]

**Advantageous**, ad-vant-ā'jus, *adj.* of advantage : useful.—*adv.* **Advanta'geously.**—*n.* **Advanta'geousness.**

**Advent**, ad'vent, *n.*, *a coming or arrival* : the first or the second coming of Christ : the four weeks before Christmas. [L. *adventus*—*ad*, to, *venio*, to come.]

**Adventitious**, ad-vent-ish'us, *adj.* accidental : foreign.—*adv.* **Adventi'tiously.** [See **Advent.**]

**Adventual**, ad-vent'ū-al, *adj.* relating to Advent.

**Adventure**, ad-vent'ūr, *n.* a risk or chance : a remarkable incident : an enterprise.—*v.i.* to attempt or dare.—*v.t.* to risk or hazard. [O. Fr.—L. *adventurus*, about to come or happen, *fut.p.* of *advenio*. See **Advent.**]

**Adventurer**, ad-vent'ūr-er, *n.* one who engages in hazardous enterprises.—*fem.* **Advent'uress.**

**Adventurous**, ad-vent'ūr-us, **Adventuresome**, ad-vent'ūr-sum, *adj.* enterprising.—*adv.* **Advent'urously.**—*n.* **Advent'urousness.**

**Adverb**, ad'verb, *n.* a word added to a verb, adjective, or other adverb to express some modification of the meaning or an accompanying circumstance. [L. *adverbium*—*ad*, to, *verbum*, a word. It is so called, not because it is added to a *verb*, but because it is a word (*verbum*) joined to, or supplemental of, other words.]

**Adverbial**, ad-verb'i-al, *adj.* pertaining to an adverb.—*adv.* **Adverb'ially.**

**Adversary**, ad'vers-ar-i, *n.* an opponent : an enemy.—**The Adversary**, Satan. [L. *adversarius.* See **Adverse.**]

**Adversative**, ad-vers'a-tiv, *adj.* denoting opposition con:rariety, or variety. [See **Adverse.**]

**Adverse**, ad'vers, *adj.* acting in a contrary direction : opposed to : unfortunate.—*adv.* **Ad'versely.**—*n.* **Ad'verseness.** [L. *adversus*—*ad*, to, and *verto*, *versum*, to turn.]

**Adversity**, ad-vers'i-ti, *n.* adverse circumstances : affliction : misfortune.

**Advert**, ad-vert', *v.i.* (used with *to*) *to turn* the mind (to): to regard or observe. [L. *ad*, to, and *verto*, to turn.]

**Advertence**, ad-vert'ens, **Advertency** ad-vert'-en-si, *n.* attention to : heedfulness : regard.

**Advertise**, ad-vert-īz' or ad'-, *v.t.*, *to turn* attention *to*: to inform : to give public notice of. [Fr., from L. See **Advert.**]

**Advertisement,** ad-vèrt'iz-ment, *n.* the act of advertising or making known : a public notice in a newspaper or periodical.

**Advertiser,** ad-vèrt-iz'èr, *n.* one who advertises : a paper in which advertisements are published.

**Advice,** ad-vīs', *n.* counsel : in *pl.* intelligence. [O. Fr. *advis,* Fr. *avis*—L. *ad visum,* according to what is seen or seems best.]

**Advisable,** ad-vīz'a-bl, *adj.* that may be advised or recommended : prudent : expedient.—*adv.* **Advis'ably.**—*ns.* **Advisabil'ity, Advis'ableness.**

**Advise,** ad-vīz', *v.t.* to give advice or counsel to : to inform.—*v.i.* (— with) to consult :—*pr.p.* advīs'ing ; *pa.p.* advīsed'. [O. Fr. *adviser,* from *advis* or *avis.* See **Advice.**]

**Advised,** ad-vīzd', *adj.* deliberate : cautious.—*adv.* **Advis'edly.**—*n.* **Advisedness,** ad-vīz'ed-nes, deliberate consideration : prudent procedure.

**Adviser,** ad-vīz'èr, *n.* one who advises or gives advice. [See **Advocate.**]

**Advocacy,** ad'vo-ka-si, *n.* a pleading for : defence.

**Advocate,** ad'vo-kāt, *n.* one who pleads the cause of another esp. in a court of law.—*v.t.* to plead in favour of.—*n.* **Advoca'tion.** [L. *advocatus—advoco, -atum—ad,* to, *voco,* to call : to call in (another to help, as in a lawsuit or in sickness).]

**Advowson,** ad-vow'zun, *n.* the right of patronage or presentation to a church benefice. [O. Fr.—Low L. *advocatio,* right of the patron—L. *advocatus,* a patron.]

**Adz, Adze,** adz, *n.* a carpenter's tool consisting of a thin arched blade with its edge at right angles to the handle. [A.S. *adesa.*]

**Ædile,** ē'dil, *n.* See **Edile.**

**Ægis,** ē'jis, *n.* (*orig.*) a shield given by Jupiter to Minerva : anything that protects. [L.—Gr. *aigis.*]

**Æneid,** ē'nē-id, *n.* an epic poem written by Virgil, the hero of which is *Æneas.* [L. *Æneis, -idos.*]

**Æolian,** ē-ō'li-an, *adj.* pertaining to or acted on by the wind. [*Æolus,* the god of the winds.]

**Æon,** ē'on, *n.* a period of time, an age or one of a series of ages, eternity. [Gr. *aiōn.*]

**Aerate,** ā'ér-āt, *v.t.* to put *air* into : to supply with carbonic acid. [L. *aër,* air.]

**Aeration,** ā-ér-ā'shun, *n.* exposure to the air.

**Aerial,** ā-ēr'i-al, *adj.* belonging to the air : inhabiting or existing in the air : elevated, lofty.

**Aerie,** ā'ri or ē'ri, *n.* See **Eyry.**

**Aeriform,** ā'ér-i-form, *adj.* having the *form* or nature of *air* or gas. [L. *aër* and *forma.*]

**Aerolite,** ā'ér-ō-līt, *n.* a meteoric stone. [Gr. *aër,* air, *lithos,* a stone.]

**Aerometer,** ā-ér-om'e-tèr, *n.* an instrument for *measuring* the density of *air* and gases. [Gr. *aër,* and **Meter.**]

**Aeronaut,** ā ér-o-nawt, *n.* one who ascends in a balloon. [Gr. *aër,* air, *nautēs,* sailor.]

**Aeronautics,** ā-ér-o-nawt'iks, *n.* the science or art of *navigating the air* in balloons.

**Aerostatics,** ā-ér-o-stat'iks, *n.* the science *of the equilibrium of air* or of elastic fluids : the science of raising and guiding balloons. [Gr. *aër,* air, *statikos,* relating to equilibrium. See **Statics.**]

**Aerostation,** ā-ér-ō-stā'shun, *n.* the art of raising and guiding balloons.

**Æsthetic,** ēs-thet'ik, **Æsthetical,** ēs-thet'ik-al, *adj.* pertaining to æsthetics.—*adv.* **Æsthet'ically.**

**Æsthetics,** ēs-thet'iks, *n.* the feeling of beauty in objects, the science of taste : the philosophy of the fine arts. [Gr. *aisthētikos,* perceptive—*aisthanomai,* to feel or perceive.] [**Far.**]

**Afar,** a-fär', *adv., at a far* distance. [Pfx. *a,* and

**Affable,** af'fa-bl, *adj.* condescending : easy to speak to.—*adv.* **Af'fably.**—*ns.* **Affabil'ity, Af'fableness.** [Fr.—L. *affabilis—affari,* to speak to—*ad,* to, and *fari,* to speak.]

**Affair,** af-fār', *n., that which is* to be *done* : business : an engagement or battle of minor importance :—*pl.* transactions in general : public concerns. [Fr. *affaire,* O. Fr. *afaire—à* and *faire*—L. *ad,* and *facere,* to do. Cf. E. **Ado.**]

**Affect,** af-fekt', *v.t.,* to *act upon* : to produce a change upon ; to move the feelings. [L. *afficio, affectum—ad,* to, *facio,* to do.]

**Affect,** af-fekt', *v.t.* to strive after : to make a show or pretence of : to love : (*B.*) to pay court to. [L. *affecto,* freq. of *afficio.* See **Affect** above.]

**Affectation,** af-fekt-ā'shun, *n.* a striving after or an attempt to assume what is not natural or real : pretence.

**Affected,** af-fekt'ed, *adj.* touched with a feeling (either for or against): full of affectation : feigned.—*adv.* **Affect'edly.**—*n.* **Affect'edness.**

**Affecting,** af-fekt'ing, *adj.* having power to move the passions : pathetic.—*adv.* **Affect'ingly.**

**Affection,** af-fek'shun, *n.* kindness or love : attachment : an attribute or property. [L. See **Affect.**]

**Affectionate,** af-fek'shun-āt, *adj.* full of affection : loving.—*adv.* **Affec'tionately.**—*n.* **Affec'tionateness.**

**Affectioned,** af-fek'shund, *adj.* (*B.*) disposed.

**Afferent,** af'fèr-ent, *adj.* (*anat.*) bringing *to,* applied to the nerves that convey sensations to the nerve centres. [L. *afferens—ad,* to, and *fero,* to carry.]

**Affiance,** af-fī'ans, *n., faith* pledged *to* : marriage contract : trust.—*v.t.* to pledge faith : to betroth. [O. Fr. *affiance,* It. *affidanza,* confidence—L. *ad,* to, *fides,* faith.]

**Affidavit,** af-fi-dā'vit, *n.* a written declaration *on* oath. [Low L. *affidavit,* 3d pers. sing. perf. of *affido,* to pledge one's faith.]

**Affiliate,** af-fil'i-āt, *v.t.* to receive into a family as a *son,* or into a society as a member. [L. *ad,* to, *filius,* a son.]

**Affiliation,** af-fil-i-ā'shun, *n.* act of receiving into a family or society as a member : (*law*) the assignment of an illegitimate child to its father.

**Affinity,** af-fin'i-ti, *n.* nearness of kin, agreement, or resemblance : relationship by marriage, opposed to consanguinity or relationship by blood : (*chem.*) the peculiar attraction between the atoms of two simple substances that makes them combine to form a compound. [L. *affinitas—affinis,* neighbouring—*ad,* at, *finis,* boundary.]

**Affirm,** af-fèrm', *v.t.* to assert confidently or positively. [L. *affirmo—ad, firmus,* firm. See **Firm.**]

**Affirmable,** af-fèrm'a-bl, *adj.* that may be affirmed.—*n.* **Affirm'ant.**

**Affirmation,** af-fèr-mā'shun, *n.* act of asserting : that which is affirmed : a solemn declaration.

**Affirmative,** af-fèrm'at-iv, *adj.* or *n.* that affirms or asserts.—*adv.* **Affirm'atively.**

**Affix,** af-fiks', *v.t., to fix to* : to add : to attach. [L. *affigo, -fixum—ad,* to, *figo,* to fix. See **Fix.**]

**Affix,** af'fiks, *n.* a syllable or letter put to the end of a word, called also **Postfix, Suffix.**

**Afflatus,** af-flā'tus, *n.* inspiration. [See **Inflation.**]

**Afflict,** af-flikt', *v.t.* to give continued pain, distress, or grief. [L. *ad,* to, *fligo,* to dash—to the ground.]

**Affliction,** af-flik'shun, *n.* distress or its cause.

**Afflictive,** af-flikt'iv, *adj.* causing distress.

**Affluence,** af'floo-ens, *n.* abundance : wealth.

**Affluent**, af'floo-ent, *adj.* abounding : wealthy.— *n.* a stream flowing into a river or lake. [L. *affluo—ad*, to, *fluo*, to flow.]

**Afford**, af-förd', *v.t.* to yield or produce : to be able to sell or to expend. [M. E. *aforthen*, from A.S. *geforthian* or *forthian*, to further or cause to come forth.]

**Affray**, af-frā', *n.* a fight causing *alarm* : a brawl. [Fr. *effrayer*, to frighten ; O. Fr. *esfreer*, to freeze with terror—Low L. *exfrigidare*, to chill. See **Frigid**.]

**Affright**, af-frīt', *v.t.*, *to frighten.—n.* sudden fear. [A.S. *afyrhtan*. See **Fright**.]

**Affront**, af-frunt', *v.t.* to meet *front to front* : to insult openly.—*n.* contemptuous treatment. [Fr. *affronter*—L. *ad*, to, *front-*, the forehead.]

**Affusion**, af-fū'zhun, *n.* the act of *pouring upon* or sprinkling. [L. *ad*, to, *fundo*, *fusum*, to pour.]

**Afield**, a-fēld', *adv.*, *to*, *in*, or *on the field*.

**Afloat**, a-flōt', *adv.* or *adj.* floating : at sea : unfixed.

**Afoot**, a-foot', *adv.*, *on foot*.

**Afore**, a-fōr', *prep.* (*obs.*) before.

**Aforehand**, a-fōr'hand, *adv.* before the regular time of accomplishment : in advance,

**Aforesaid**, a-fōr'sed, *adj.*, *said* or named *before*.

**Aforetime**, a-fōr'tīm, *adv.*, *in former* or past *times*. [root of **Affray**.]

**Afraid**, a-frād', *adj.* struck with fear : timid. [From **Affray**.]

**Afresh**, a-fresh', *adv.* anew. [*a*, on, and **Fresh**.]

**Aft**, aft, *adj.* or *adv.* behind : near or towards the stern of a vessel. [A.S. *æft*, which is short for *æfter*.]

**After**, aft'er, *adj.* behind in place : later in time : more toward the stern of a vessel.—*prep.* behind, in place : later, in time : following, in search of : in imitation of : in proportion to : concerning. —*adv.* subsequently : afterward. [A.S. *æfter*, comp. of *af*, or *of*, the primary meaning being more off, further away ; *-ter* as a comparative affix is seen in L. *al-ter*, E. *o-ther*. See **Of**.]

**Afteract**, aft'er-akt, *n.* an *act after* or subsequent to another.

**Afterbirth**, aft'er-birth, *n.* the placenta and membranes which are expelled from the womb *after the birth*.

**Aftercrop**, aft'er-krop, *n.*, *a crop* coming *after* the first in the same year.

**Aftermath**, aft'er-math, *n.* a second crop of grass. [See **Mow, Meadow**.]

**Aftermost**, aft'er-mōst, *adj.* hindmost. [A.S. *æftemest* ; Goth. *af-tuma*, *-tuma*, being equiv. to L. *-tumus* in *op-tumus*, best. Goth. has also *af-tum-ists* = A.S. *æf-tem-est*, which is thus a double superlative. In *aftermost*, *r* is intrusive and *-most* is not the adv. *most*.] [and evening.

**Afternoon**, aft'er-nōon, *n.* the time between noon

**Afterpiece**, aft'er-pēs, *n.* a farce or other minor *piece* performed *after* a play.

**Afterward**, aft'er-ward, **Afterwards**, aft'er-wardz, *adv.* in *after-time* : later : subsequently. [A.S. *æfter* and *weard*, towards, in direction of.]

**Aga**, ā'ga, *n.* a Turkish *commander* or chief officer. [Turk. *agha*, Pers. *ak*, *aka*, a lord.]

**Again**, a-gen', *adv.* once more : in return : back. [A.S. *on-gean*, again, opposite ; Ger. *ent-gegen*.]

**Against**, a-genst', *prep.* opposite to : in opposition to : in provision for. [Formed from *again*, as *whilst* from *while*.]

**Agape**, a-gāp', *adj.* or *adv.* gaping from wonder, expectation, or attention. [Lit. 'on gape,' from prefix *a* (for A.S. *on*, on), and **Gape**.]

**Agate**, ag'āt, *n.* a precious stone composed of layers of quartz, of different tints. [Gr. *achatēs*, said to be so called because first found near the river Achates in Sicily.]

**Age**, āj, *n.* the ordinary length of human life : the time during which a person or thing has lived or existed : mature years : legal maturity (at 21 years) : a period of time : a generation of men : a century.—*v.i.* to grow old :—*pr.p.* āg'ing ; *pa.p.* āged. [Fr. *âge*, O. Fr. *edage*—L. *ætas* = old L. *ævitas*—L. *ævum*, age ; cog. with E. **Ever**.]

**Aged**, āj'ed, *adj.* advanced in age : having a certain age.—*n.pl.* old people.

**Agency**, āj'en-si, *n.* the office or business : operation or action of an agent.

**Agenda**, aj-end'a, *n.*, *things to be done* : a memorandum-book : a ritual. [L. *agendus*, fut. p. pass. of *ago*, to do.]

**Agent**, āj'ent, *n.* a person or thing that acts or exerts power : one intrusted with the business of another. [L. *ago*, to do. See **Act**.]

**Agglomerate**, ag-glom'ér-āt, *v.t.* to make into *a ball* : to collect into a mass.—*v.i.* to grow into a mass. [L. *glomus, glomeris*, a ball. See **Clew, Globe**.]

**Agglomeration**, ag-glom-ér-ā'shun, *n.* a growing or heaping together : a mass.

**Agglutinate**, ag-gloot'in-āt, *v.t.* to cause to adhere by glue or cement. [L. *agglutino—ad*, to, *gluten*, glue. See **Glue**.]

**Agglutination**, ag-gloot-in-ā'shun, *n.* the act of uniting, as by glue : adhesion of parts.

**Agglutinative**, ag-gloot'in-āt-iv, *adj.* tending to or having power to cause adhesion.

**Aggrandise**, ag'grand-īz, *v.t.*, *to make great* or larger : to make greater in power, rank, or honour. [Fr., from L. *ad*, to, and *grandis*, large.]

**Aggrandisement**, ag-grand-īz'ment, *n.* act of aggrandising : state of being aggrandised.

**Aggravate**, ag'grav-āt, *v.t.* to make worse : to provoke. [L. *ad*, to, *gravis*, heavy. See **Grave**.]

**Aggravation**, ag-grav-ā'shun, *n.* a making worse : any quality or circumstance which makes a thing worse.

**Aggregate**, ag'greg-āt, *v.t.* to collect into a mass : to accumulate. [L. *aggrego, -atum*, to bring together, as a flock—*ad*, to, *grex, gregis*, a flock.]

**Aggregate**, ag'greg-āt, *adj.* formed of parts taken together.—*n.* the sum total.—*adv.* **Ag'gregately**.

**Aggregation**, ag-greg-ā'shun, *n.* act of aggregating : state of being collected together : an aggregate.

**Aggression**, ag-gresh'un, *n.* first act of hostility or injury. [L. *aggredior, -gressus—ad*, to, *gradior*, to step.]

**Aggressive**, ag-gres'iv, *adj.* making the first attack.—*n.* **Aggress'iveness**.

**Aggressor**, ag-gres'ur, *n.* one who attacks first.

**Aggrieve**, ag-grēv', *v.t.* to press *heavily upon* : to pain or injure. [O. Fr. *agrever*, Sp. *agraviar* —L. *ad*, to, and *gravis*, heavy. See **Grief, Grieve**.]

**Aghast**, a-gast', *adj.* stupefied with horror. [Properly *agast* ; M. E. *agasten*, to terrify ; A.S. intens. pfx. *a*, and *gæstan*, to terrify. The primary notion of the root *gæs-* (Goth. *gais-*) is to fix, stick ; to root to the spot with terror. See **Gaze**.]

**Agile**, aj'il, *adj.*, *active* : nimble. [L. *agilis—ago*, to do or act.] [ness.

**Agility**, aj-il'i-ti, *n.* quickness of motion : nimble-

**Agio**, ā′ji-o, *n.* the difference in value between metallic and paper money : discount. [It. *aggio*, *agio*, rate of exchange, same as *agio*, ease, convenience.]

**Agitate**, aj′i-tāt, *v.t.* to keep moving : to stir violently : to discuss. [L. *agito*, freq. of *ago*, to put in motion. See **Act**.]

**Agitation**, aj-i-tā′shun, *n.* commotion : perturbation of mind : discussion. [commotion.

**Agitator**, aj′i-tāt′ur, *n.* one who excites public

**Aglow**, a-glō′, *adj.* very warm : red-hot. [See **Glow**.]

**Agnate**, ag′nāt, *adj.* related on the father's side : allied.—*n.* a relation by the father's side. [L. —*ad*, to, *nascor*, to be born. See **Cognate**.]

**Agnostic**, ag-nos′tik, *n.* one who holds that we *know nothing* of the supernatural.—*n.* **Agnos′-ticism.** [*a*, privative, and Gr. *gnōstikos*, good at knowing. See **Gnostic**.]

**Ago**, a-gō′, **Agone**, a-gon′, *adv., gone:* past : since. [Pa.p. of A.S. *agan*, to pass away—inten. pfx. *a*, and *gan*, to go.]

**Agog**, a-gog′, *adj.* or *adv.* eager. [Ety. doubtful.]

**Agoing**, a-gō′ing, *adv., going on :* current.

**Agonise**, ag′o-nīz, *v.t.* to struggle, suffer *agony.*

**Agonising**, ag′ō-nīz-ing, *adj.* causing *agony.*—*adv.* **Ag′onisingly.**

**Agony**, ag′o-ni, *n.* a violent struggle : extreme suffering. [Gr.—*agōn*, contest.]

**Agrarian**, ag-rā′ri-an, *adj.* relating to *land :* applied especially to Roman laws for the equal distribution of the public lands. [L. *agrarius—ager*, a field. See **Acre**.] [of lands.

**Agrarianism**, ag-rā′ri-an-izm, *n.* an equal division

**Agree**, a-grē′, *v.i.* to be of one mind : to concur : (fol. by *to*) to assent to : (fol. by *with*) to resemble, to suit :—*pa.p.* agreed′. [Fr. *agréer*, to accept kindly—L. *ad*, to, and *gratus*, pleasing.] [*adv.* **Agree′ably.**

**Agreeable**, a-grē′a-bl, *adj.* suitable : pleasant.—

**Agreeableness**, a-grē′a-bl-nes, *n.* suitableness : conformity : quality of pleasing.

**Agreement**, a-grē′ment, *n.* concord : conformity : a bargain or contract. [agriculture.

**Agricultural**, ag-ri-kult′ūr-al, *adj.* relating to

**Agriculture**, ag′ri-kult-ūr, *n.* the art or practice of *cultivating the land.* [L. *agricultura—ager*, a field, *cultura*, cultivation. See **Culture**.]

**Agriculturist**, ag-ri-kult′ūr-ist, *n.* one skilled in agriculture. [on, and **Ground**.]

**Aground**, a-grownd′, *adv.* stranded. [Prefix *a*,

**Ague**, ā′gū, *n.* a fever coming in periodical fits, accompanied with shivering : chilliness. [Fr. *aigu*, sharp—L. *acutus*. See **Acute**.]

**Aguish**, ā′gū-ish, *adj.* having the qualities of an ague : chilly : shivering.

**Ah**, ä, *int.* an exclamation of surprise, joy, pity, complaint, &c. [Fr.—L. ; Ger. *ach*.]

**Aha**, a-hä′, *int.* an exclamation of exultation, pleasure, surprise, or contempt.

**Ahead**, a-hed′, *adv.* further on : in advance : headlong. [Prefix *a*, on, and **Head**.]

**Ahoy**, a-hoi′, *int.* a nautical term used in hailing. [Form of *int.* **Hoy**.]

**Ahull**, a-hul′, *adv.* (*naut.*) with sails furled, and helm lashed, driving before the wind, stern foremost. [*a*, on (—A.S. *on*), and **Hull**.]

**Aid**, ād, *v.t.* to help, assist.—*n.* help : assistance : an auxiliary : subsidy.—*adj.* **Aid′less**. [Fr. *aider* —L. *adjutare—ad*, and *juvo*, *jutum*, to help.]

**Aide-de-camp**, ād′-de-kong, *n.* a military officer who *assists* the general :—*pl.* **Aides-de-camp**. [Fr., assistant of the camp.]

**Aider**, ād′ėr, *n.* one who brings aid : a helper.

**Ail**, āl, *v.t.* to give pain : to trouble.—*v.i.* to feel pain : to be in trouble.—*n.* trouble : indisposition. [A.S. *eglan*, to pain. See **Awe**.]

**Ailment**, āl′ment, *n.* pain : indisposition : disease.

**Aim**, ām, *v.i.* (with *at*) to point at with a weapon : to direct the intention or endeavour.—*v.t.* to point, as a weapon or firearm.—*n.* the pointing of a weapon : the thing pointed at : design : intention. [O. Fr. *esmer*, to reckon—L. *æstimare*, to estimate. See **Estimate**.]

**Aimless**, ām′les, *adj.* without aim.

**Air**, ār, *n.* the fluid we breathe : the atmosphere : a light breeze : a tune : the bearing of a person : —*pl.* affectation.—*v.t.* to expose to the air : to dry : to expose to warm air. [Fr.—L. *aër*—Gr.]

**Air-bed**, ār′-bed, *n.* a bed for the sick, inflated with air.—**Air-cell**, ār′-sel, *n.* a cavity containing air.—**Air-cushion**, ār′-koosh′un, *n.* an airtight cushion, which can be inflated.—**Air-engine**, ār′-en′jin, *n.* an engine put in motion by air expanded by heat.—**Air-gun**, ār′-gun, *n.* a gun which discharges bullets by means of compressed air.—**Airiness**, ār′i-nes, *n.* state of being airy : openness : liveliness.—**Airing**, ār′ing, *n.* exposure to the air or fire : a short excursion in the open air.—**Air-jacket**, ār′-jak′et, *n.* a jacket with air-tight cavities, which being inflated renders a person buoyant in water.—**Airless**, ār′les, *adj.* void of air : not having free communication with the open air.—**Air-pump**, ār′-pump, *n.* an instrument for pumping the air out of a vessel. —**Air-tight**, ār′-tīt, *adj.* so tight as not to admit air.—**Air-vessel**, ār′-ves′el, *n.* a vessel or tube containing air.

**Airy**, ār′i, *adj.* consisting of or relating to air : open to the air : like air : unsubstantial : light of heart : sprightly.—*adv.* **Air′ily.**

**Aisle**, īl, *n.* the *wing* or side of a church : the side passages in a church. [Fr. *aile*, O. Fr. *aisle*—L. *axilla*, *ala*, a wing.]

**Aisled**, īld, *adj.* having aisles.

**Ajar**, a-jär′, *adv.* partly open. [Lit. 'on the turn,' A.S. *on*, on, *cyrr*, a turn. See **Char**, work.]

**Akimbo**, a-kim′bo, *adv.* with hand on hip and elbow *bent* outward. [Pfx. *a*, Celt. *cam*, crooked, with superfluous E. **Bow**.]

**Akin**, a-kin′, *adj.*. *of kin* : related by blood : having the same properties. [Of and **Kin**.]

**Alabaster**, al′a-bas-tėr, *n.* a semi-transparent kind of gypsum or sulphate of lime : the fine limestone deposited as stalagmites and stalactites.—*adj.* made of alabaster. [Gr. *alabastros*, said to be derived from Alabastron, a town in Egypt.]

**Alack**, a-lak′, *int.* an exclamation denoting sorrow. [Prob. from M. E. *lak*, loss. See **Lack**.]

**Alack-a-day**, a-lak′-a-dā, *int.* an exclamation of sadness. [For, 'ah ! a loss to-day.']

**Alacrity**, a-lak′ri-ti, *n.* briskness : cheerful readiness : promptitude. [L. *alacris*, brisk.]

**Alamode**, a-la-mōd′, *adv., according to the mode* or fashion. [Fr. *à la mode*.]

**Alarm**, a-lärm′, *n.* notice of danger : sudden surprise with fear : a mechanical contrivance to arouse from sleep.—*v.t.* to call to arms : to give notice of danger : to fill with dread. [Fr. *alarme* —It. *all′ arme*, to arms—L. *ad*, to, *arma*, arms.]

**Alarmist**, a-lärm′ist, *n.* one who excites alarm : one given to prophesy danger.—*adj.* **Alarm′ist**, alarming.—*adv.* **Alarm′ingly**.

**Alarum**, a-lär′um, *n.* and *v.t.* Same as **Alarm**.

**Alas**, a-las′, *int.* expressive of grief. [Fr. *hélas*— L. *lassus*, wearied.]

**Alb**, alb, *n.* a *white* linen vestment reaching to the feet, worn by priests. [L. *albus*, white.]

**Albatross,** al′ba-tros, *n.* a large, long-winged, web-footed sea-bird, in the Southern Ocean. [Corr. from Span. *alcatraz,* a white pelican.]

**Albeit,** awl-bē′it, *adv.* although: notwithstanding. [Be it all.]

**Albino,** al-bī′no, *n.* a person or animal whose skin and hair are unnaturally *white,* and pupil of the eye red :—*pl.* **Albi′nos.** [It. *albino,* whitish—L. *albus,* white.]

**Album,** al′bum, *n.* among the Romans, a *white* tablet or register : a book for the insertion of portraits, autographs, &c. [L. *albus,* white.]

**Albumen,** al-bū′men, *n.,* the *white* of eggs : a like substance found in animal and vegetable bodies. [L.—*albus,* white.]

**Albuminoid,** al-bū′min-oid, *adj.* like albumen. [Albumen and Gr. *eidos,* form.]     [albumen.

**Albuminous,** al-bū′min-us, *adj.* like or containing

**Alburnum,** al-burn′um, *n.* in trees, the *white* and soft parts of wood between the inner bark and the heart-wood. [L.—*albus,* white.]

**Alcalde,** al-kal′dā, *n., a judge.* [Sp.—Ar. *al-kadi —kadaj,* to judge.]

**Alchemist,** al′kem-ist, *n.* one skilled in alchemy.

**Alchemy, Alchymy,** al′ki-mi, *n.* the infant stage of chemistry, as astrology was of astronomy. A chief pursuit of the alchemists was to transmute the other metals into gold, and to discover the elixir of life. [Ar. *al* = the ; Gr. *cheo,* to pour, to melt, to mix ; hence *chymeia* or *chemeia,* a mixing, and *chymic* or *chemic,* applied to the processes of the laboratory. See **Chemistry.**]

**Alcohol,** al′kō-hol, *n.* pure spirit, a liquid generated by the fermentation of sugar and other saccharine matter, and forming the intoxicating element of fermented liquors. [Ar. *al-kohl—al,* the, *qochl,* fine powder.]

**Alcoholic,** al-kō-hol′ik, *adj.* of or like alcohol.

**Alcoholise,** al′kō-hol-īz, *v.t.* to convert into alcohol : to rectify.

**Alcoholometer,** al-kō-hol-om′e-tèr, *n.* an instrument for ascertaining the strength of spirits. [Alcohol and Meter.]     [article prefixed.

**Alcoran,** al′kō-ran, *n.* **Koran** with the Arabic

**Alcove,** al′kōv or al-kōv′, *n.* a recess in a room : any recess : a shady retreat. [It. *alcova* ; Sp. *alcoba,* a place in a room railed off to hold a bed—Ar. *al-gobah,* a tent.]

**Alder,** awl′dèr, *n.* a tree usually growing in moist ground. [A.S. *alor*; Ger. *eller,* L. *alnus.*]

**Alderman,** awl′dèr-man, *n.* now a civic dignitary next in rank to the mayor.—*adj.* **Alderman′ic.** [A.S. *ealdor* (from *eald,* old), senior, chief : *ealdor-man,* ruler, king, chief magistrate.]

**Aldern,** awl′dèrn, *adj.* made of alder.

**Aldine,** al′dīn, *adj.* applied to books printed by *Aldus* Manutius of Venice, in 16th c.

**Ale,** āl, *n.* a strong *drink* made from malt : a festival, so called from the liquor drunk.—**Ale-berry,** a beverage made from ale.—**Ale-house,** a house in which ale is sold. [A.S. *ealu*; Ice. *öl*; Gael. *ol,* drink.]

**Alee,** a-lē′, *adv., on the lee-*side. [See **Lee.**]

**Alembic,** al-em′bik, *n.* a vessel used by the old chemists in distillation. [Ar. *al,* the, *anbiq*— Gr. *ambiks,* a cup.]

**Alert,** al-èrt′, *adj.* watchful : brisk.—**Upon the alert,** upon the watch.—*n.* **Alert′ness.** [It. *all′ erta,* on the erect—*erto,* L. *erectus,* erect.]

**Alexandrian,** al-egz-an′dri-an, *adj., relating to Alexandria* in Egypt : *relating to Alexander.*

**Alexandrine,** al-egz-an′drin, *n.* a rhyming verse of twelve syllables, so called from its use in an old French poem on *Alexander* the Great.

**Algæ,** al′jē, *n.* (*bot.*) a division of plants, embracing sea-weeds. [L., pl. of *alga,* sea-weed.]

**Algebra,** al′je-bra, *n.* the science of calculating by symbols, thus forming a kind of universal arithmetic. [Sp. from Ar. *al-jabr,* the resetting of anything broken, hence combination.]

**Algebraic, -al,** al-je-brā′ik, -al, *adj.* pertaining to algebra.—**Algebra′ist,** *n.* one skilled in algebra.

**Algum,** al′gum. Same as **Almug.**

**Alias,** ā′li-as, *adv.* otherwise.—*n.* an assumed name. [L. *alias,* at another time, otherwise— *alius,* Gr. *allos,* other.]

**Alibi,** al′i-bī, *n.* the plea, that a person charged with a crime was *in another place* when it was committed. [L.—*alius,* other, *ibi,* there.]

**Alien,** āl′yen, *adj.* foreign : different in nature : adverse to.—*n.* one belonging to another country : one not entitled to the rights of citizenship. [L. *alienus—alius,* other.]

**Alienable,** āl′yen-a-bl, *adj.* capable of being transferred to another.—*n.* **Alienabil′ity.**

**Alienage,** āl′yen-āj, *n.* state of being an alien.

**Alienate,** āl′yen-āt, *v.t.* to transfer a right or title to *another* : to withdraw the affections : to misapply.—*adj.* withdrawn: estranged.—*n.* **Aliena′-tion.** [L. See **Alien.**]

**Alight,** a-līt′, *v.i.* to come down (as from a horse) : to descend : to fall upon. [A.S. *alihtan,* to come down. See **Light,** *v.i.*]

**Alight,** a-līt′, *adj.* on fire : lighted up. [*a,* on, and **Light.** See **Light,** *n.*]

**Align,** a-līn′, *v.t.* to regulate by a line : to arrange in line, as troops. [Fr. *aligner*—L. *ad,* and *linea,* a line.]

**Alignment,** a-līn′ment, *n.* a laying out by a line : the ground-plan of a railway or road.

**Alike,** a-līk′, *adj.* like one another : having resemblance.—*adv.* in the same manner or form : similarly. [A.S. *onlic.* See **Like.**]

**Aliment,** al′i-ment, *n., nourishment* : food. [L. *alimentum—alo,* to nourish.]

**Alimental,** al-i-ment′al, *adj.* supplying food.

**Alimentary,** al-i-ment′ar-i, *adj.* pertaining to aliment: nutritive.—*n.* **Alimenta′tion,** al-i-mentā′shun, the act or state of nourishing or of being nourished.—*n.* (*phren.*) **Alimentiveness,** al-i-ment′iv-nes, desire for food or drink.

**Alimony,** al′i-mun-i, *n.* an allowance for support made to a wife when legally separated from her husband.

**Aliquot,** al′i-kwot, *adj.* such a part of a number as will divide it without a remainder. [L. *aliquot,* some, several—*alius,* other, *quot,* how many.]     [*life.*]

**Alive,** a-līv′, *adj.* in *life* : susceptible. [A.S. *on*

**Alkali,** al′ka-li or -lī, *n.* (*chem.*) a substance which combines with an acid and neutralises it, forming a salt. Potash, soda, and lime are alkalies; they have an acrid taste (that of soap), and turn vegetable blues to green. See **Acid** :—*pl.* **Alkalies.** [Ar. *al-kali,* ashes.]

**Alkalimeter,** al-ka-lim′e-tèr, *n.* an instrument for measuring the strength of alkalies.

**Alkaline,** al′ka-līn or -lin, *adj.* having the properties of an alkali.—*n.* **Alkalin′ity.**

**Alkaloid,** al′ka-loid, *n.* a vegetable principle possessing in some degree alkaline properties.—*adj.* pertaining to or resembling alkali. [Alkali and Gr. *eidos,* form or resemblance.]

**Alkoran,** *n.* same as **Alcoran.**

**All,** awl, *adj.* the whole of : every one of.—*adv.* wholly : completely : entirely.—*n.* the whole : everything.—**All in all,** everything desired.— **All′s one,** it is just the same.—**At all,** in the least degree or to the least extent. [A.S. *eal*, Ger. *all*, Gael. *uile*, W. *oll*.]

**Allah**, al′la, *n.* the Arabic name of the one God. [Ar. *al-ilâh*, 'the worthy to be adored.']

**Allay**, al-lā′, *v.t.* to *lighten*, relieve: to make quiet. [O. Fr. *aleger*—L. *alleviare*—*ad*, and *levis*, light, confused with A.S. *a-lecgan*, to lay down.]

**Allegation**, al-le-gā′shun, *n.* an assertion.

**Allege**, al-lej′, *v.t.* to produce an argument or plea: to assert. [L. *allego*, to send one person to another to confer with him: to mention or bring forward—*ad*, to, and *lego*, *-atum*, to send.]

**Allegiance**, al-lēj′i-ans, *n.* the duty of a subject *to* his *liege* or sovereign. [L. *ad*, to, and **Liege**.]

**Allegoric, -al**, al-le-gor′ik, -al, *adj.* in the form of an allegory: figurative.—*adv.* **Allegor′ically.**

**Allegorise**, al′le-gor-īz, *v.t.* to put in form of an allegory.—*v.i.* to use allegory.

**Allegory**, al′le-gor-i, *n.* a description of one thing under the image of another. [Gr. *allos*, other, and *agoreuō*, to speak.]

**Allegro**, al-lē′grō, *adv.* and *n.* (*mus.*) a word denoting a *brisk* movement. [It.—L. *alacer*, brisk.]                    [leluiah.

**Alleluia, Alleluiah**, al-le-lōō′ya. Same as **Hal-**

**Alleviate**, al-lēv′i-āt, *v.t.* to *make light*: to mitigate.—*n.* **Allevia′tion.** [L. *ad*, *levis*, light.]

**Alley**, al′li, *n.* a walk in a garden: a passage in a city narrower than a street:—*pl.* **All′eys.** [Fr. *allée*, a passage, from *aller*, to go, O. Fr. *aner*, from L. *adnare*, to go to by water. Cf. **Arrive**.]

**All-fools′-day**, awl-fōōlz′-dā, *n.* April first. [From the sportive deceptions practised on that day.]

**All-fours**, awl-fōrz′, *n.pl.* (preceded by *on*) on four legs, or on two hands and two feet.

**All-hail**, awl-hāl′, *int., all health*, a phrase of salutation. [See **Hail**, *int.*]

**All-hallow**, awl-hal′lō, **All-hallows**, awl-hal′lōz, *n.* the day of *all* the *Holy Ones*. See **All-saints.** [**All** and **Hallow.**]

**Alliance**, al-lī′ans, *n.* state of being allied: union by marriage or treaty. [See **Ally.**]

**Alligation**, al-li-gā′shun, *n.* (*arith.*) a rule for finding the price of a compound of ingredients of different values. [L. *alligatio*, a binding together—*ad*, to, and *ligo*, to bind.]

**Alligator**, al′li-gā-tur, *n.* an animal of the crocodile family found in America. [Sp. *el lagarto* —L. *lacerta*, a lizard.]

**Alliteration**, al-lit-ėr-ā′shun, *n.* the recurrence of the same *letter* at the beginning of two or more words following close to each other, as in '*apt* alliteration's artful *aid.*' [Fr.—L. *ad*, to, and *litera*, a letter.]                    [alliteration.

**Alliterative**, al-lit′ėr-ā-tiv, *adj.* pertaining to

**Allocate**, al′lo-kāt, *v.t.*, *to place*: to assign to each his share. [L. *ad*, to, and *locus*, a place.]

**Allocation**, al-lo-kā′shun, *n.* act of allocating: allotment: an allowance made upon an account.

**Allocution**, al-lo-kū′shun, *n.* a formal address, esp. of the Pope to his clergy. [L. *ad*, to, and *loquor*, *locutus*, to speak.]

**Allodial**, al-lō′di-al, *adj.* held independent of a superior: freehold:—opposed to **Feudal.**

**Allodium**, al-lō′di-um, *n.* freehold estate: land held in the possession of the owner without being subject to a feudal superior. [Low L. *allodium*, most prob. from Ice. *aldr*, old age, and *othal*, a homestead; *alda-othal*, a property of ages.]

**Allopathy**, al-lop′a-thi, *n.* a name given by homeopathists to the current or orthodox medical practice.—*adj.* **Allopath′ic.**—*n.* **Allop′-athist.** [See **Homeopathy.**]

**Allot**, al-lot′, *v.t.* to divide as *by lot*: to distribute

in portions: to parcel out:—*pr.p.* allott′ing; *pa.p.* allott′ed. [L. *ad*, to, and **Lot.**]

**Allotment**, al-lot′ment, *n.* the act of allotting: part or share allotted.

**Allotropy**, al-lot′ro-pi, *n.* the property in some elements, as carbon, of existing in more than one form. [Gr. *allos*, another, and *tropos*, form.]

**Allow**, al-low′, *v.t.* to grant: to permit: to acknowledge: to abate. [Fr. *allouer*, to grant— L. *ad*, to, and *loco*, to place.—**Allow**, in the sense of *approve* or *sanction*, as used in *B.* and by old writers, has its root in L. *laudo*, to praise.]

**Allowable**, al-low′a-bl, *adj.* that may be allowed: not forbidden: lawful.—*adv.* **Allow′ably.**—*n.* **Allow′ableness.**

**Allowance**, al-low′ans, *n.* that which is allowed: a stated quantity: abatement.

**Alloy**, al-loi′, *v.t.* to mix one metal with another: to reduce the purity of a metal by mixing a baser one with it.—*n.* a mixture of two or more metals (when mercury is one of the ingredients, it is an **Amalgam**): a baser metal mixed with a finer: anything that deteriorates. [Fr. *aloi*, standard of metals, *aloyer*, It. *allegare*, to alloy —L. *ad legem*, according to law.]

**All-saints′-day**, awl-sānts′-dā, *n.* November 1, a feast of the Roman Catholic Church in honour of *all the saints*. [See **All-hallows.**]

**All-souls′-day**, awl-sōlz′-dā, *n.* the second day of November, a feast of the Roman Catholic Church held to pray for all *souls* in purgatory.

**Allude**, al-lūd′, *v.i.* to mention slightly in passing: to refer to. [L. *ad*, at, *ludo*, *lusum*, to play.]

**Allure**, al-lūr′, *v.t.* to draw on as by a *lure* or bait: to entice. [L. *ad*, to, and **Lure.**]

**Alluring**, al-lūr′ing, *adj.* enticing.—*adv.* **Allur′ingly.**—*n.* **Allure′ment.**

**Allusion**, al-lū′zhun, *n.* an indirect reference.

**Allusive**, al-lūs′iv, *adj.* alluding to: hinting at: referring to indirectly.—*adv.* **Allus′ively.**

**Alluvium**, al-lū′vi-um, *n.* the mass of water-borne matter deposited by rivers on lower lands:— *pl.* **Allu′via.**—*adj.* **Allu′vial.** [L.—*alluo*, to wash to or on—*ad*, and *luo* = *lavo*, to wash.]

**Ally**, al-lī′, *v.t.* to form a relation by marriage, friendship, treaty, or resemblance:—*pa.p.* allīed′. [Fr.—L. *alligo*, *-are*—*ad*, *ligo*, to bind.]

**Ally**, al-lī′, *n.* a confederate: a prince or state united by treaty or league:—*pl.* **Allies′.**

**Almanac**, al′ma-nak, *n.* a register of the days, weeks, and months of the year, &c. [Fr.—Gr. *almenichiaka* (in Eusebius), an Egyptian word, prob. sig. 'daily observation of things.'

**Almighty**, awl-mīt′i, *adj.* possessing all might or power: omnipotent.—**The Almighty**, God.

**Almond**, ä′mund, *n.* the fruit of the almond-tree. [Fr. *amande*—L. *amygdalum*—Gr. *amygdalē*.]

**Almonds**, ä′mundz, *n.pl.* the tonsils or glands of the throat, so called from their resemblance to the fruit of the *almond*-tree.

**Almoner**, al′mun-ėr, *n.* a distributer of *alms*.

**Almonry**, al′mun-ri, *n.* the place where *alms* are distributed.                    [and **Most.**]

**Almost**, awl′mōst, *adv.* nearly. [Prefix *al*, quite,

**Alms**, ämz, *n.* relief given out of pity to the poor. [A.S. *ælmæsse*, through late L., from Gr. *eleëmosynē*—*eleos*, compassion.]

**Alms-deed**, ämz′-dēd, *n.* a charitable deed.

**Alms-house**, ämz′-hows, *n.* a house endowed for the support and lodging of the poor.

**Almug**, al′mug, *n.* a tree or wood mentioned in the Bible, kind uncertain. [Heb.]

**Aloe**, al′ō, *n.* a genus of plants with juicy leaves yielding the gum called aloes. [Gr. *aloē*.]

**Aloes,** al'ōz, *n.* a purgative drug, the juice of several species of aloe.

**Aloft,** a-loft', *adv.* on high : overhead : (*naut.*) above the deck, at the mast-head. [Prefix *a* (—A.S. *on*), on, and **Loft.**]

**Alone,** al-ōn', *adj.* single : solitary.—*adv.* singly, by one's self. [**Al** (for **All**), quite, and **One.**]

**Along,** a-long', *adv.* by or through the length of: lengthwise : throughout : onward : (fol. by *with*) in company of.—*prep.* by the side of : near. [A.S. *andlang*—prefix *and*-, against, and **Long.**]

**Aloof,** a-lōōf', *adv.* at a distance : apart. [Prefix *a* (—A.S. *on*), on, and **Loof.** See **Loof, Luff.**]

**Aloud,** a-lowd', *adv.* with a loud voice : loudly. [From A.S. *on*, on, and *hlyd*, noise, Ger. *laut.* See **Loud.**]

**Alow,** a-lō', *adv.* in a low place :—opp. to **Aloft.**

**Alp,** alp, *n.* a high mountain :—*pl.* **Alps,** specially applied to the lofty mountain-ranges of Switzerland. [L.—Gael. *alp*, a mountain : allied to L. *albus*, white—white with snow.]

**Alpaca,** al-pak'a, *n.* the Peruvian sheep, akin to the llama, having long silken wool : cloth made of its wool. [Peruvian.]

**Alpen-stock,** alp'n-stok, *n.* a long *stick* or staff used by travellers in climbing the *Alps.* [Ger.]

**Alpha,** al'fa, *n.* the first letter of the Greek alphabet : the first or beginning. [Gr. *alpha*—Heb. *aleph*, an ox, the name of the first letter, which in its original figure resembled an ox's head.]

**Alphabet,** al'fa-bet, *n.* the letters of a language arranged in the usual order. [Gr. *alpha, beta*, the first two Greek letters.]

**Alphabetic, -al,** al-fa-bet'ik, -al, *adj.* relating to or in the order of an alphabet.—*adv.* **Alphabet'ically.**

**Alpine,** alp'in or alp'īn, *adj.* pertaining to the Alps, or to any lofty mountains : very high.

**Already,** awl-red'i, *adv.* previously, or before the time specified.

**Also,** awl'so, *adv.* in like manner : further. [*All*, quite, just ; *so*, in that or the same manner.]

**Altar,** awlt'ar, *n.*, *a high place* on which sacrifices were anciently offered : in Christian churches, the communion table : (*fig.*) a place of worship. [L. *altare*—*altus*, high.]

**Altarpiece,** awlt'ar-pēs, *n.* a painting or decorations placed over an altar.

**Alter,** awl'tėr, *v.t.* to make *other* or different : to change.—*v.i.* to become different : to vary. [L. *alter*, other, another—*al* (root of *alius*, other), and the old comparative suffix *-ter* = E. *-ther.*]

**Alterable,** awl'tėr-a-bl, *adj.* that may be altered. —*adv.* **Al'terably.**

**Alteration,** awl-tėr-ā'shun, *n.* change.

**Alterative,** awl'tėr-at-iv, *adj.* having power to alter.—*n.* a medicine that makes a change in the vital functions.

**Altercate,** al'tėr-kāt, *v.i.* to dispute or wrangle. [L. *altercor, -catus*, to bandy words from one to the other (*alter*).] [troversy.

**Altercation,** al-tėr-kā'shun, *n.* contention : con-

**Alternate,** al'tėr-nāt or al-tėr'nāt, *v.t.* to cause to follow by turns or *one after the other.*—*v.i.* to happen by turns : to follow every other or second time. [L. *alter*, other.]

**Alternate,** al-tėr'nāt, *adj.*, *one after the other :* by turns.—*adv.* **Alter'nately.**

**Alternation,** al-tėr-nā'shun, *n.* the act of alternating : interchange.

**Alternative,** al-tėr'nat-iv, *adj.* offering a choice of two things.—*n.* a choice between two things. —*adv.* **Alter'natively.**

**Although,** awl-thō', *conj.* admitting all that : notwithstanding that. [See **Though.**]

**Altitude,** alt'i-tūd, *n.*, *height.* [L. *altitudo*— *altus*, high.]

**Alto,** alt'o, *n.* (*orig.*) the *highest* part sung by males : the lowest voice in women. [It.—L. *altus*, high.]

**Altogether,** awl-too-geth'ėr, *adv.*, *all together :* wholly : completely : without exception.

**Alto-relievo, Alto-rilievo,** alt'o-re-lē'vo, *n.*, *high relief :* figures projected by at least half their thickness from the ground on which they are sculptured. [It. *alto*, high. See **Relief.**]

**Altruism,** al'troo-ism, *n.* the principle of living and acting for the interest of others. [L. *alter*, another.]

**Alum,** al'um, *n.* a mineral salt, the double sulphate of alumina and potash. [L. *alumen.*]

**Alumina, Alumine,** al-ū'min-a, al'ū-min, *n.* one of the earths : the characteristic ingredient of common clay. Alumina is a compound of aluminium and oxygen. [L. *alumen*, alum.]

**Aluminous,** al-ū'min-us, *adj.* containing alum, or alumina.

**Aluminum, Aluminium,** al-ū'min-um, al-ū-min'i-um, *n.* the metallic base of alumina, a metal resembling silver, and remarkable for its lightness.

**Alumnus,** al-um'nus, *n.* one educated at a college is called an alumnus of that college :—*pl.* **Alum'ni.** [L. from *alo*, to nourish.]

**Always, Alway,** awl'wāz, awl'wā, *adv.* through *all ways :* continually : for ever.

**Am,** am, the first person of the verb *To be.* [A.S. *eom* ; Gr. *eimi* ; Lat. *sum* for *esum* ; Sans. *asmi*—*as*, to be.]

**Amain,** a-mān', *adv.*, *with main* or strength : with sudden force. [Pfx. *a* and **Main.**]

**Amalgam,** a-mal'gam, *n.* a compound of mercury with another metal : any soft mixture. [L. and Gr. *malagma*, an emollient—Gr. *malasso*, to soften.]

**Amalgamate,** a-mal'gam-āt, *v.t.* to mix mercury with another metal : to compound.—*v.i.* to unite in an amalgam : to blend.

**Amalgamation,** a-mal-gam-ā'shun, *n.* the blending of different things.

**Amanuensis,** a-man-ū-en'sis, *n.* one who writes to dictation : a copyist : a secretary. [L.—*ab*, from, and *manus*, the hand.]

**Amaranth, -us,** a'mar-anth, -us, *n.* a genus of plants with richly coloured flowers, that last long without withering, as *Love-lies-bleeding.* [Gr. *amarantos*, unfading—*a*, neg., and root *mar*, to waste away ; allied to Lat. *mori*, to die.]

**Amaranthine,** a-mar-anth'in, *adj.* pertaining to amaranth : unfading.

**Amass,** a-mas', *v.t.* to gather in large quantity : to accumulate. [Fr. *amasser*—L. *ad*, to, and *massa*, a mass.]

**Amateur,** am-at-ār', *n.* one who cultivates a particular study or art for the *love* of it, and not professionally. [Fr.—L. *amator*, a lover—*amo*, to love.]

**Amative,** am'at-iv, *adj.*, *relating to love :* amorous. [From L. *amo, -atum*, to love.]

**Amativeness,** am'at-iv-nes, *n.* propensity to love.

**Amatory,** am'at-or-i, *adj.*, *relating to*, or causing *love :* affectionate.

**Amaze,** a-māz', *v.t.* to put the mind *in a maze :* to confound with surprise or wonder.—*n.* astonishment : perplexity. [Prefix *a*, and **Maze.**]

**Amazedness,** a-māz'ed-nes, **Amazement,** a-māz'-

ment, *n.* a feeling of surprise mixed with wonder.

**Amazing**, a-māz′ing, *p.adj.* causing amazement : astonishing.—*adv.* **Amaz′ingly.**

**Amazon**, am′az-on, *n.* one of a fabled nation of female warriors : a masculine woman : a virago. [Ety. dub., perhaps from Gr. *a,* priv., *mazos,* a breast ; they were said to cut off the right breast that they might use their weapons more freely.]

**Amazonian**, am-az-ōn′ian, *adj.* of or like an Amazon : of masculine manners : warlike.

**Ambassador**, am-bas′a-dur, *n.* a diplomatic minister of the highest order sent by one sovereign power to another.—*fem.* **Ambass′adress.**—*adj.* **Ambassador′ial.** [It. *ambasciadore,* L. *ambactus,* derived by Grimm from Goth. *andbahts,* a servant, whence Ger. *amt,* office.]

**Amber**, am′bėr, *n.* a yellowish fossil resin, used in making ornaments. [Fr.—Ar. *anbar.*]

**Ambergris**, am′bėr-grēs, *n.* a fragrant substance, of a *gray* colour, found on the sea-coast of warm countries, and in the intestines of the spermaceti whale. [**Amber** and Fr. *gris,* gray.]

**Ambidexter**, amb′i-deks′tėr, *n.* one who uses *both* hands with equal facility : a double-dealer.—*adj.* **Ambidex′trous.** [L. *ambo,* both, *dexter,* right hand.]

**Ambient**, amb′i-ent. *adj., going round :* surrounding : investing. [L. *ambi,* about, *iens, ientis,* pr.p. of *eo,* to go.]

**Ambiguity**, amb-ig-ū′i-ti, **Ambiguousness**, amb-ig′ū-us-nes, *n.* uncertainty or doubleness of meaning.

**Ambiguous**, amb-ig′ū-us, *adj.* of doubtful signification : equivocal.—*adv.* **Ambig′uously.** [L. *ambiguus—ambigo,* to go about—*ambi,* about, *ago,* to drive.]

**Ambition**, amb-ish′un, *n.* the desire of power, honour, fame, excellence. [L. *ambitio,* the going about, *i.e.,* the canvassing for votes practised by candidates for office in Rome—*ambi,* about, and *eo, itum,* to go.]

**Ambitious**, amb-ish′us, *adj.* full of ambition : desirous of power : aspiring : indicating ambition.—*adv.* **Ambi′tiously.**—*n.* **Ambi′tiousness.**

**Amble**, am′bl, *v.i.* to move as a horse by lifting both legs on each side alternately : to move affectedly.—*n.* a pace of a horse between a trot and a walk. [Fr. *ambler*—L. *ambulo,* to walk about.]

**Ambler**, am′blėr, *n.* a horse that ambles.

**Ambrosia**, am-brō′zhi-a, *n.* the fabled food of the gods, which conferred *immortality* on those who partook of it. [L.—Gr. *ambrosios = ambrotos, immortal—a,* neg., and *brotos,* mortal, for *mrotos,* Sans. *mrita,* dead—*mri* (L. *mori*), to die.] [—*adv.* **Ambro′sially.**

**Ambrosial**, am-brō′zhi-al, *adj.* fragrant : delicious.

**Ambrosian**, am-brō′zhi-an, *adj.* relating to *ambrosia :* relating to *St Ambrose,* bishop of Milan in the 4th century.

**Ambry**, am′bri, *n.* a niche in churches in which the sacred utensils were kept : a cupboard for victuals. [O. Fr. *armarie,* a repository for arms ; Fr. *armoire,* a cupboard—L. *armarium,* a chest for arms—*arma,* arms. ]

**Ambulance**, am′būl-ans, *n.* a carriage which serves as a *movable* hospital for the wounded in battle. [Fr.—L. *ambulans, -antis,* pr.p. of *ambulo,* to walk about.]

**Ambulatory**, am′būl-at-or-i, *adj.* having the power or faculty of walking : moving from place to place, not stationary.—*n.* any part of a

building intended for walking in, as the aisles of a church.

**Ambuscade**, am′busk-ād, *n.* a hiding to attack by surprise : a body of troops in concealment. [Fr. *embuscade*—It. *imboscare,* to lie in ambush—*im,* in, and *bosco,* a wood, from root of **Bush.**]

**Ambush**, am′boosh, *n.* and *v.* same meanings as **Ambuscade.** [O. Fr *embusche.* See **Ambuscade.**]

**Ameer**, a-mēr′, *n.* a title of honour, also of an independent ruler in Mohammedan countries. [Ar. *amir.* See **Admiral.**]

**Ameliorate**, a-mēl′yor-āt, *v.t., to make better :* to improve.—*v.i.* to grow better.—*adj.* **Amel′iorative.**—*n.* **Ameliora′tion.** [L. *ad,* to, and *melior,* better.]

**Amen**, ä′men′, ā′men′, *int.* so let it be ! [Gr.—Heb. *amen,* firm, true.]

**Amenable**, a-mēn′a-bl, *adj.* easy to be led or governed : liable or subject to.—*adv.* **Amen′ably.**—*ns.* **Amenabil′ity, Amen′ableness.** [Fr. *amener,* to lead—*a* = L. *ad,* and *mener,* to lead—Low L. *minare,* to lead, to drive (as cattle)—L. *minari,* to threaten.]

**Amend**, a-mend′, *v.t.* to correct : to improve.—*v.i.* to grow or become better.—*adj.* **Amend′able.** [Fr. *amender* for *emender*—L. *emendo, -are,* to remove a fault—*e, ex,* out of, and *menda,* a fault.] [provement.

**Amendment**, a-mend′ment, *n.* correction : improvement.

**Amends**, a-mendz′, *n.pl.* supply of a loss : compensation.

**Amenity**, am-en′i-ti, *n., pleasantness,* as regards situation, climate, manners, or disposition. [Fr. *aménité*—L. *amœnitas—amœnus,* pleasant, from root of *amo,* to love.]

**Amerce**, a-mėrs′, *v.t.* to punish by a fine. [O. Fr. *amercier,* to impose a fine—L. *merces,* wages, fine.]

**Amercement**, a-mėrs′ment, *n.* a penalty inflicted.

**American**, a-mer′ik-an, *adj., pertaining to America,* especially to the United States.—*n.* a native of America. [From *America,* so called accidentally from Amerigo Vespucci, a navigator who explored part of the continent after its discovery by Columbus.] [American.

**Americanise**, a-mer′ik-an-īz, *v.t.* to render

**Americanism**, a-mer′ik-an-izm, *n.* a word, phrase, or idiom peculiar to America.

**Amethyst**, a′meth-ist, *n.* a bluish-violet variety of quartz of which drinking-cups used to be made, which the ancients supposed *prevented drunkenness.*—*adj.* **Amethyst′ine.** [Gr. *amethystos—a,* neg., *methyō,* to be drunken—*methū,* wine, Eng. *mead,* Sans. *madhu,* sweet.]

**Amiability**, ām-i-a-bil′i-ti, **Amiableness**, ām′i-a-bl-nes, *n.* quality of being amiable, or of exciting love.

**Amiable**, ām′i-a-bl, *adj., lovable :* worthy of love.—*adv.* **A′miably.** [Fr. *amiable,* friendly—L. *amicabilis,* from *amicus,* a friend ; there is a confusion in meaning with Fr. *aimable,* lovable—L. *amabilis—amo,* to love.]

**Amianthus**, a-mi-anth′us, *n.* the finest fibrous variety of *asbestus :* it can be made into cloth which when stained is readily cleansed by fire. [Gr. *amiantos,* unpollutable—*a,* neg., and *miainō,* to soil.]

**Amicable**, am′ik-a-bl, *adj., friendly.*—*adv.* **Am′icably.**—*ns.* **Amicabil′ity, Am′icableness.** [L. *amicabilis—amo,* to love.]

**Amice**, am′is, *n.* a flowing cloak formerly worn by priests and pilgrims : a linen garment worn by priests about the shoulders while celebrating mass. [O. Fr. amis, amict—L. amictus—amicio, to wrap about—amb, about, and jacio, to throw.]

**Amid**, a-mid', **Amidst**, a-midst', prep., in the middle or midst: among.—adv. **Amid'ships**, half-way between the stem and stern of a ship. [Prefix a, on, in, and A.S. mid, middle.]

**Amir**, a-mēr'. Same as **Ameer**.

**Amiss**, a-mis', adj. in error: wrong.—adv. in a faulty manner. [a, on, and Ice. missa, a loss. See **Miss**.]

**Amity**, am'i-ti, n., friendship: good-will. [Fr. amitié—ami—L. amicus, a friend. See **Amicable**.]

**Ammonia**, am-mōn'i-a, n. a pungent gas yielded by smelling-salts, and by burning feathers, &c. [From sal-ammoniac, or smelling-salts, first obtained near the temple of Jupiter Ammon.]

**Ammoniac, -al**, am-mōn'i-ak, -i'ak-al, adj. pertaining to, or having the properties of ammonia.

**Ammonite**, am'mon-īt, n. the fossil shell of an extinct genus of mollusks, so called because they resembled the horns on the statue of Jupiter Ammon, worshipped as a ram.

**Ammunition**, am-mūn-ish'un, n. anything used for munition or defence: military stores, esp. powder, balls, bombs, &c. [L. ad, for, munitio, defence—munio, to defend.]

**Amnesty**, am'nest-i, n. a general pardon of political offenders. [Gr. a-mnestos, not remembered.]

**Amoeba**, a-mēb'a, n. a microscopic animal capable of undergoing many changes of form at will:—pl. **Amœb'æ**. [Gr. ameibō, to change.]

**Among**, a-mung', **Amongst**, a-mungst', prep. of the number of: amidst. [A.S. on-gemang—mængan, to mingle.]

**Amorous**, am'or-us, adj. easily inspired with love: fondly in love: relating to love.—adv. **Am'orously**.—n. **Am'orousness**. [L. amor, love.]

**Amorphous**, a-morf'us, adj. without regular shape, shapeless. [Gr. a, neg., and morphē, form.]

**Amount**, a-mownt', v.i. to mount or rise to: to result in.—n. the whole sum: the effect or result. [O. Fr. amonter, to ascend—L. ad, to, mons, a mountain.]

**Amour**, am-ōōr', n. a love intrigue. [Fr.—L. amor, love.]

**Amphibia**, am-fi'bi-a, **Amphibials** or **Amphibians**, n.pl. animals capable of living both under water and on land.—adj. **Amphi'bious**. [Gr. amphi, both, bios, life.]

**Amphictyonic**, am-fik-ti-on'ik, adj. The Amphictyonic Council was an old Greek assembly composed of deputies from twelve of the leading states. [Gr. amphiktyones, orig. dub.]

**Amphitheatre**, am-fi-thē'a-tér, n. an oval or circular edifice having rows of seats one above another, around an open space, called the arena, in which public spectacles were exhibited: anything like an amphitheatre in form. [Gr. amphi, round about, theatron, a place for seeing—theaomai, to see.]

**Ample**, am'pl, adj. spacious: large enough: liberal.—adv. **Am'ply**.—n. **Am'pleness**. [L. amplus, large.]

**Amplification**, am'pli-fi-kā'shun, n. enlargement.

**Amplify**, am'pli-fī, v.t. to make more copious in expression: to add to. [L. amplus, large, and facio, to make.]

**Amplitude**, am'pli-tūd, n. largeness: the distance from the east point of a horizon at which a heavenly body rises, or from the west point at which it sets.

**Amputate**, am'pūt-āt, v.t. to cut off, as a limb of an animal.—n. **Amputa'tion**. [L. amb, round about, puto, to cut.]

**Amuck**, a-muk', adv. wildly: madly. [Malay, amok, intoxicated or excited to madness.]

**Amulet**, am'ū-let, n. a gem, scroll, or other object carried about the person, as a charm against evil. [L. amulētum, a word of unknown origin; curiously like the mod. Ar. himālah-at, lit. 'a carrier,' often applied to a shoulder-belt, by which a small Koran is hung on the breast.]

**Amuse**, a-mūz', v t. to occupy pleasantly: to beguile with expectation. [Fr. amuser.]

**Amusement**, a-mūz'ment, n. that which amuses: pastime. [entertaining.—adv. **Amus'ingly**.

**Amusing**, a-mūz'ing, adj. affording amusement:

**Amyloid**, am'il-oid, n. a half-gelatinous substance like starch, found in some seeds. [Gr. amylon, the finest flour, starch; lit. 'unground'—a, neg., mylē, a mill, and eidos, form.]

**An**, an, adj., one: the indefinite article, used before words beginning with the sound of a vowel. [A.S. an. See **One**.]

**An**, an, conj. if. [A form of **And**.]

**Ana**, ā'na, a suffix to names of persons or places, denoting a collection of memorable sayings, as Johnsoniana, sayings of Dr Johnson. [The neuter plural termination of L. adjectives in -anus = pertaining to.]

**Anabaptist**, an-a-bapt'ist, n. one who holds that baptism ought to be administered only to adults (by immersion), and therefore that those baptised in infancy ought to be baptised again.—n. **Anabapt'ism**. [Gr. ana, again, baptizō, to dip in water, to baptise.]

**Anachronism**, an-a'kron-izm, n. an error in regard to time, whereby a thing is assigned to an earlier or to a later age than what it belongs to.—adj. **Anachronist'ic**. [Gr. ana, backwards, chronos, time.]

**Anaconda**, an-a-kon'da, n. a large snake, a species of boa, found in South America.

**Anacreontic**, an-a-kre-ont'ik, adj. after the manner of the Greek poet Anacreon: free.

**Anæmia**, an-ēm'i-a, n. a morbid want of blood: the condition of the body after great loss of blood. [Gr. an, neg., haima, blood.]

**Anæsthetic**, an-ēs-thet'ik, adj. producing insensibility.—n. a substance, as chloroform, that produces insensibility. [Gr. a, an, neg., aisthēsis, sensation—aisthanomai, to feel.]

**Anaglyph**, an'a-glif, n. an ornament carved in relief.—adj. **Anaglypt'ic**. [Gr. ana, up, glyphō, to carve.]

**Anagram**, an'a-gram, n. a word or sentence formed by rewriting (in a different order) the letters of another word or sentence: as 'live'—'evil.'—adj. **Anagrammat'ic, -al**. [Gr. ana, again, graphō, to write.]

**Anal**, ān'al, adj. pertaining to or near the anus.

**Analogical**, an-a-loj'ik-al, adj. having, or according to, analogy.

**Analogous**, an-a'log-us, adj. having analogy: bearing some resemblance to: similar.

**Analogue**, an'a-lŏg, n. a word or body bearing analogy to, or resembling another: (anat.) an organ which performs the same function as another, though differing from it in structure. [See **Homologue**.]

**Analogy**, an-a'lŏ-ji, n. an agreement or correspondence in certain respects between things otherwise different: relation in general: likeness. [Gr. ana, according to, and logos, ratio.]

**Analyse**, an'a-līz, v.t. to resolve a whole into its

**elements**: to separate into component parts.— *adj.* **Analys'able.** [Gr. *ana*, up, *lyō*, to loosen.]

**Analysis**, an-a'lis-is, *n.* a resolving or separating a thing into its elements or component parts :—*pl.* **Ana'lyses.** [See **Analyse.**]

**Analyst**, an'al-ist, *n.* one skilled in analysis.

**Analytic, -al**, an-a-lit'ik, -al, *adj.* pertaining to analysis: resolving into first principles.—*adv.* **Analyt'ically.**

**Anapest,** an'a-pest, *n.* (in verse) a foot consisting of three syllables, two short and the third long, or (in Eng.) two unaccented and the third accented, as ap-pre-hend'. [Gr. *anapaistos*, reversed, because it is the dactyl reversed.]

**Anapestic, -al**, an-a-pest'ik, -al, *adj.* pertaining to or consisting of anapests.                      [anarchy.

**Anarchist,** an'ark-ist, *n.* one who promotes

**Anarchy,** an'ark-i, *n.* the *want of government* in a state : political confusion.—*adjs.* **Anarch'ic, Anarch'ical.** [Gr. *a, an*, neg., *archē*, government.]

**Anathema,** an-a'them-a, *n.* (*orig.*) an offering made and *set up* in a temple : an ecclesiastical curse : any person or thing anathematised. [Gr. *ana*, up, *tithēmi*, to set.]          [accursed.

**Anathematise,** an-a'them-at-īz, *v.t.* to pronounce

**Anatomic, -al**, an-a-tom'ik, -al, *adj.* relating to anatomy.

**Anatomise,** an-a'tom-īz, *v.t.* to dissect a body : (*fig.*) to lay open minutely. [From **Anatomy.**]

**Anatomist,** an-a'tom-ist, *n.* one skilled in anatomy.

**Anatomy,** an-a'tom-i, *n.* the art of dissecting any organised body : science of the structure of the body learned by dissection. [Gr. *ana*, up, asunder, *temnō*, to cut.]

**Anbury,** an'ber-i, *n.* a disease in turnips, in which the root becomes divided into a number of parts —hence the popular name **Fingers and Toes.** [From A.S. *ampre*, a crooked swelling vein.]

**Ancestor,** an'ses-tur, *n.* one from whom a person has descended : a forefather.—*fem.* **An'cestress.** —*adj.* **Ances'tral.** [O. Fr. *ancestre*—L. *antecessor*—*ante*, before, *cedo, cessum*, to go.]

**Ancestry,** an'ses-tri, *n.* a line of ancestors: lineage.

**Anchor,** angk'ur, *n.* a hooked iron instrument that holds a ship by sticking into the ground : (*fig.*) anything that gives stability or security. —*v.t.* to fix by an anchor : to fasten.—*v.i.* to cast anchor : to stop, or rest on. [Fr. *ancre*—L. *ancora*—Gr. *angkyra*, from *angkos*, a bend —root *angk*, bent. Conn. with **Angle.**]

**Anchorage,** angk'ur-āj, *n.* ground for anchoring : duty imposed on ships for anchoring.

**Anchoret,** ang'kor-et, **Anchorite,** ang'kor-īt, *n.* one who has withdrawn from the world : a hermit. [Gr. *anachōrētēs*—*ana*, apart, *chōreō*, to go.]

**Anchovy,** an-chō'vi, *n.* a small fish of the herring kind from which a sauce is made. [Sp. and Port. *anchova*; Fr. *anchois.* Of doubtful ety.]

**Ancient,** ān'shent, *adj.* old : belonging to former times.—*n.pl.* **An'cients,** those who lived in remote times : in *B.*, elders.—*adv.* **An'ciently.**— *n.* **An'cientness.** [Fr. *ancien*—Low L. *antianus*, old—L. *ante*, before, prob. conn. with **And.** See **Antique.**]

**Ancient,** ān'shent, *n.* (*obs.*) a *flag* or its bearer: an ensign. [Corr. of Fr. *enseigne.* See **Ensign.**]

**Ancillary,** an'sil-ar-i, *adj.* subservient. [L. *ancilla*, a maid-servant.]

**And,** and, *conj.* signifies addition, and is used to connect words and sentences: in M.E. it was used for *if*. [A.S., and in the other Teut. lang.: prob. allied to L. *ante*, Gr. *anti*, over against.]

**Andante,** an-dan'te, *adj.*, *going* easily : moderately slow : expressive. [It.—*andare*, to go.]

**Andiron,** and'ī-urn, *n.* the iron bars which support the ends of the logs in a wood-fire, or in which a spit turns. [Ety. dub.]

**Anecdotal,** an'ek-dōt-al, **Anecdotical,** an-ek-dot'i-kal, *adj.*, *in the form of an anecdote.*

**Anecdote,** an'ek-dōt, *n.* an incident of private life : a short story. [Gr., not published—*a, an*, neg., and *ekdotos*, published—*ek*, out, and *didōmi*, to give.]

**Anele,** an-ēl', *v.t.* to anoint with *oil* : to administer extreme unction. [A.S. *on-elan*—*on*, on, and *ele*, oil.]

**Anemometer,** a-nem-om'et-ėr, *n.* an instrument for *measuring* the force of the *wind.* [Gr. *anemos*, wind, and **Meter.**]

**Anemone,** a-nem'o-ne, *n.* a plant of the crowfoot family. [Said to be from Gr. *anemos*, **wind**, because some of the species love exposed situations.]

**Aneroid,** an'e-roid, *adj.* noting a barometer by which the pressure of the air is measured *without* the use of *liquid* or quicksilver. [Gr. *a*, neg., *nēros*, wet.]

**Aneurism,** an'ūr-izm, *n.* a soft tumour, arising from the *widening up* or dilatation of an artery. [Gr. *aneurisma*—*ana*, up, *eurys*, wide.]

**Anew,** a-nū', *adv.* afresh : again. [M. E. *of-new* —A.S. *of*, **Of,** and **New.**]

**Angel,** ān'jel, *n.* a divine messenger : a ministering spirit : an old E. coin = 10s., bearing the figure of an *angel.*—*adjs.* **Angelic,** an-jel'ik, **Angel'ical.**—*adv.* **Angel'ically.** [Gr. *angelos*, a messenger.]

**Anger,** ang'ger, *n.* a strong passion excited by injury.—*v.t.* to make angry. [Ice. *angr*; allied to **Anguish.**]

**Angina,** anj-i'na, *n.* applied to diseases in which a sense of *tightening* or suffocation is a prominent symptom. [L. See **Anguish.**]

**Angle,** ang'gl, *n.* a corner : the point where two lines meet : (*geom.*) the inclination of two straight lines which meet, but are not in the same straight line. [Fr.—L *angulus*; cog. with Gr. *angkylos* ; both from root *angk, ak*, to bend, seen also in **Anchor, Ankle.**]

**Angle,** ang'gl, *n.*, *a hook* or *bend* : a fishing-rod with line and hook.—*v.i.* to fish with an angle. —*v.t.* to entice : to try to gain by some artifice. [A.S. *angel*, a hook, allied to **Anchor.**]

**Angler,** ang'glėr, *n.* one who fishes with an angle. —**Angling,** ang'gling, *n.* the art or practice of fishing with an angle.                         [English.]

**Anglican,** ang'glik-an, *adj.*, *English.* [See

**Anglicanism,** ang'glik-an-izm, *n.* attachment to *English* institutions, esp. the English Church: the principles of the English Church.

**Anglicise,** ang'glis-īz, *v.t.* to express in English idiom.                         [peculiarity of language.

**Anglicism,** ang'glis-izm, *n.* an *English* idiom or

**Anglo-,** ang'glo, *pfx.*, *English*—used in composition ; as *Anglo-Saxon*, &c.

**Anglomania,** ang'glo-mān'i-a, *n.*, *a mania for what is English* : an indiscriminate admiration of English institutions.

**Anglo-Saxon,** ang'glo-saks'un, *adj.* applied to the earliest form of the English language ; the term Old English is now preferred by some.

**Angry,** ang'gri, *adj.* excited with anger : inflamed.—**Angrily,** ang'gri-li, *adv.*

**Anguish,** ang'gwish, *n.* excessive pain of body or

mind : agony. [Fr. *angoisse*—L. *angustia*, a strait, straitness—*ango*, to press tightly : to strangle. See **Anger**.]

**Angular**, ang′gū-lar, *adj*. having an angle or corner : (*fig*.) stiff in manner : the opposite of easy or graceful.—*n*. **Angular′ity**.

**Anights**, a-nīts′, *adv*., *of nights*, at night.

**Anile**, an′īl, *adj*. old - womanish : imbecile.—**Anility**, an-il′i-ti, *n*. [L. *anus*, an old woman.]

**Aniline**, an′il-in, *n*. a product of coal-tar, extensively used in dyeing. [*Anil*, an indigo plant, from which also it is made.]

**Animadversion**, an-im-ad-vėr′shun, *n*. criticism, censure, or reproof.

**Animadvert**, an-im-ad-vėrt′, *v.i*. to criticise or censure. [L., to turn the mind to—*animus*, the mind, *ad*, to, and *verto*, to turn.]

**Animal**, an′im-al, *n*. an organised being, having life, sensation, and voluntary motion : it is distinguished from a plant, which is organised and has life, but not sensation or voluntary motion ; the name sometimes implies the absence of the higher faculties peculiar to man.—*adj*. of or belonging to animals : sensual. [L.—*anima*, air, life, Gr. *anemos*, wind—*aō*, *aēmi*, Sans. *an*, to breathe, to blow.]

**Animalcule**, an-im-al′kūl, *n*., *a small animal*, esp. one that cannot be seen by the naked eye.—*pl*. **Animal′cules** or **Animal′cula**. [L. *animalculum*, dim. of *animal*.]

**Animalism**, an′im-al-izm, *n*. the state of being actuated by animal appetites only : sensuality.

**Animate**, an′im-āt, *v.t*. to give life to : to enliven or inspirit.—*adj*. living : possessing animal life. [See **Animal**.]

**Animated**, an′im-āt-ed, *adj*. lively : full of spirit.

**Animation**, an-im-ā′shun, *n*. liveliness : vigour.

**Animism**, an′im-izm, *n*. theory which regards the belief in *spirits*, that appear in dreams, &c., as the germ of religious ideas. [L. *anima*, the soul.]

**Animosity**, an-im-os′i-ti, *n*. bitter hatred : enmity. [L. *animositas*, fullness of spirit. See **Animal**.]

**Animus**, an′im-us, *n*. intention : spirit : prejudice against. [L. *animus*, spirit, soul, as dist. from *anima*, the mere life. See **Animal**.]

**Anise**, an′is, *n*. aromatic plant, the seeds of which are used in making cordials. [Gr. *anison*.]

**Anker**, angk′ėr, *n*. a liquid measure used on the continent, formerly in England, varying from about seven to nine gallons. [Dut.]

**Ankle**, angk′l, *n*. the joint between the foot and leg, forming an *angle* or *bend*. [A.S. *ancleow*, cog. with Ger. *enkel*, and conn. with **Angle**.]

**Anklet**, angk′let, *n*. an ornament for the *ankle*.

**Anna**, an′a, *n*. an Indian coin worth 1½d. sterling.

**Annalist**, an′al-ist, *n*. a writer of annals.

**Annals**, an′alz, *n.pl*. records of events under the *years* in which they happened : year-books. [L. *annales*—*annus*, a year.]

**Anneal**, an-ēl′, *v.t*. to temper glass or metals by subjecting them to great heat and gradually cooling : to heat in order to fix colours on, as glass.—*n*. **Anneal′ing**. [A.S. *anǽlan*, to set on fire—*ǽlan*, to burn.]

**Annelida**, an-el′i-da, *n*. a class of animals having a long body composed of numerous *rings*, as worms, leeches, &c. [L. *annellus*, dim. of *annulus*, a ring.]

**Annex**, an-neks′, *v.t*. to add to the end : to affix.—*n*. something added. [L.—*ad*, to, *necto*, to tie.]

**Annexation**, an-neks-ā′shun, *n*. act of annexing.

**Annihilate**, an-nī′hil-āt, *v.t*. to reduce to *nothing* :

to put out of existence. [L. *ad*, to, *nihil*, nothing.]

**Annihilation**, an-nī-hil-ā′shun, *n*. state of being reduced to nothing : act of destroying.

**Anniversary**, an-ni-vėrs′ar-i, *adj*., *returning* or *happening every year* : annual.—*n*. the day of the year on which an event happened or is celebrated. [L. *annus*, a year, and *verto*, *versum*, to turn.]

**Annotate**, an′not-āt, *v.t*., *to make notes* upon. [L. *annoto*—*ad*, to, *noto*, *-atum*, to mark.]

**Annotation**, an-not-ā′shun, *n*. a note of explanation : comment. [commentator.

**Annotator**, an-not-āt′ur, *n*. a writer of notes : a

**Announce**, an-nowns′, *v.t*. to declare : to give public notice of.—*n*. **Announce′ment**. [Fr. *annoncer*, L. *annunciare*—*ad*, to, *nuncio*, *-are*, to deliver news.]

**Annoy**, an-noi′, *v.t*. to trouble : to vex : to tease :—*pr.p*. **Annoy′ing** ; *pa.p*. **Annoyed′**. [Fr. *ennuyer*, It. *annoiare*—L. *in odio esse*, to be hateful to.]

**Annoyance**, an-noi′ans, *n*. that which annoys.

**Annual**, an′nū-al, *adj*., *yearly* : coming every year : requiring to be renewed every year.—*n*. a plant that lives but one year : a book published yearly.—*adv*. **An′nually**. [L. *annualis*—*annus*, a year.]

**Annuitant**, an-nū′it-ant, *n*. one who receives an annuity. [*yearly*. [L. *annus*, a year.]

**Annuity**, an-nū′i-ti, *n*. a sum of money payable

**Annul**, an-nul′, *v.t*. to make *null*, to reduce *to nothing* : to abolish :—*pr.p*. **Annull′ing** ; *pa.p*. **Annulled′**. [Fr. *annuler*—L. *ad*, to, *nullus*, none.]

**Annular**, an′nūl-ar, *adj*. ring-shaped. [L. *annulus* or *anulus*, a ring—dim. of *anus*, a rounding or ring.] [into rings. [L. See **Annular**.]

**Annulated**, an′nūl-āt-ed, *adj*. formed or divided

**Annunciation**, an-nun-si-ā′shun, *n*. the act of announcing.—**Annunciation-day**, the anniversary of the Angel's salutation to the Virgin Mary, the 25th of March. [L. See **Announce**.]

**Anodyne**, an′o-dīn, *n*. a medicine that allays pain. [Gr. *a*, *an*, neg., and *odynē*, pain.]

**Anoint**, an-oint′, *v.t*., *to smear* with ointment or oil : to consecrate with oil. [O. Fr. *enoindre*—L. *inungo*, *inunctum*—*in*, and *ungo*, to smear.]

**Anointed** (the), an-oint′ed, *n*. the Messiah.

**Anomalous**, an-om′al-us, *adj*. irregular : deviating from rule. [Gr. *anōmalos*—*a*, *an*, neg., and *homalos*, even—*homos*, same.]

**Anomaly**, an-om′al-i, *n*. irregularity : deviation from rule. [See **Anomalous**.]

**Anon**, an-on′, *adv*., *in one* (instant) : immediately.

**Anonymity**, an-on-im′i-ti, *n*. the quality or state of being anonymous.

**Anonymous**, an-on′im-us, *adj*., *wanting a name* : not having the real name of the author.—*adv*. **Anon′ymously**. [Gr. *anōnymos*—*a*, *an*, neg., and *onoma*, name.]

**Another**, an-uth′er, *adj*. not the same : one more : any other. [A.S. *an*, one, and **Other**.]

**Anserine**, an′sėr-īn or -in, *adj*., *relating to* the *goose* or goose-tribe. [L. *anser* ; cog. with E. **Goose** (which see), Sans. *hamsa*.]

**Answer**, an′sėr, *v.t*. to reply to : to satisfy or solve : to suit.—*v.i*. to reply : to be accountable for : to correspond.—*n*. a reply : a solution. [Lit. 'to swear against,' as in a trial by law, from A.S. *and-*, against, *swerian*, to swear.]

**Answerable**, an′sėr-a-bl, *adj*. able to be answered : accountable : suitable : equivalent.—*adv*. **An′swerably**.

**Ant,** ant, *n.* a small insect : the emmet.—*n.* **Ant'-hill,** *the hillock* raised *by* ants to form their nest. [A contr. of **Emmet**—A.S. *æmete.*]

**Antacid,** ant-as'id, *n.* a medicine which counteracts acidity. [Gr. *anti,* against, and **Acid.**]

**Antagonism,** ant-ag'on-izm, *n., a contending* or struggling *against :* opposition. [Gr. *anti,* against—*agōn,* contest. See **Agony.**]

**Antagonist,** ant-ag'on-ist, *n., one who contends* or struggles *with another :* an opponent. [Gr. *antagōnistēs.* See **Antagonism.**]

**Antagonist,** ant-ag'on-ist, **Antagonistic,** antag-on-ist'ik, *adj.* contending against, opposed to.

**Antarctic,** ant-ärkt'ik, *adj., opposite the Arctic :* relating to the south pole or to south polar regions. [Gr. *anti,* opposite, and **Arctic.**]

**Antecedent,** an-te-sēd'ent, *adj., going before* in time : prior.—*n.* that which precedes in time : (*gram.*) the noun or pronoun to which a relative pronoun refers.—*pl.* previous principles, conduct, history, &c.—*adv.* **Anteced'ently.**—*n.* **Anteced'ence.** [L. *ante,* before, *cedens, -entis ;* pr.p. of *cedo, cessum,* to go.] [**room.**

**Antechamber,** an'te-chām-bėr, *n.* [See **Ante-Antedate,** an'te-dāt, *v.t., to date before* the true time : to anticipate. [L. *ante,* before, and **Date.**]

**Antediluvian,** an-te-di-lū'vi-an, *adj.* existing or happening *before the Deluge* or the Flood.—*n.* one who lived before the Flood. [See **Deluge.**]

**Antelope,** an'te-lōp. *n.* a quadruped intermediate between the deer and goat. [Ety. dub.]

**Antemeridian,** an-te-me-ri'di-an, *adj., before mid-day* or noon. [See **Meridian.**]

**Antennæ,** an-ten'ē, *n.pl.* the feelers or horns of insects. [L. *antenna,* the yard or beam of a sail.]

**Antenuptial,** an-te-nupsh'al, *adj., before nuptials* or marriage. [L. *ante,* before, and **Nuptial.**]

**Antepenult,** an-te-pen-ult', *n.* the syllable *before* the *penult* or next ultimate syllable of a word ; the last syllable of a word but two.—*adj.* **Antepenult'imate.** [L. *ante,* before, and **Penult.**]

**Anterior,** an-tē'ri-or, *adj., before,* in time, or place : in front. [L., comp. of *ante,* before.]

**Anteroom,** an te-rōōm, *n., a room before* another : a room leading into a principal apartment. [L. *ante,* before, and **Room.**]

**Anthelmintic,** an-thel-mint'ik, *adj., destroying* or expelling *worms.* [Gr. *anti,* against, and *helmins, helmintos,* a worm.]

**Anthem** an'them, *n.* a piece of sacred music sung in alternate parts : a piece of sacred music set to a passage from Scripture. [A.S. *antefen*—Gr. *antiphōn i—anti,* in return, *p ōnē,* the voice.]

**Anther,** an'thėr, *n.* the top of the stamen in a flower, which contains the pollen or fertilising dust. [Gr. *anthēros,* flowery, blooming.]

**Ant-hill.** See under **Ant.**

**Anthology,** an-thol'oj-i, *n.* (*lit.*) *a gathering* or collection of *flowers :* a collection of poems or choice literary extracts.—*adj.* **Antholog'ical.** [Gr. *anthos,* a flower, *legō,* to gather.]

**Anthracite,** an'thras-īt, *n.* a kind of coal that burns without flame, &c. [Gr. *anthrax,* coal.]

**Anthrax,** an'thraks, *n.* a malignant boil : a splenic fever of sheep and cattle. [L.—Gr. *anthrax,* coal.]

**Anthropoid,** an'throp-oid, *adj., in the form of* or resembling *man.* [Gr. *anthrōpos,* man, *ei os,* form.]

**Anthropology** an-throp-ol'oj-i, *n.* the natural history of man in its widest sense, treating of his relation to the brutes, the different races, &c.—*adj.* **Anthropolog'ical.** [Gr. *anthrōpos,* man, and *logos,* discourse—*iegō,* to say.]

**Anthropomorphism,** an-throp-o-morf'izm, *n.* the representation of the Deity in the *form of man* or with bodily parts : the ascription to the Deity of human affections and passions.—*adj.* **Anthropomorph'ic.** [Gr. *anthrōpos,* man, *morphē,* form.]

**Anthropophagi,** an-throp-of'aj-i, *n.pl., man-eaters,* cannibals.—**Anthropophagous,** an-throp-of'ag-us, *adj.* [Gr. *anthrōpos,* man, *phagō,* to eat.]

**Anthropophagy,** an-throp-of'aj-i, *n.* cannibalism.

**Antic,** ant'ik, *adj.* odd : ridiculous.—*n.* a fantastic figure : a buffoon : a trick. [Fr. *antique*—L. *antiquus,* ancient—*ante,* before. Doublet of **Antique.**]

**Antichrist,** an'ti-krīst, *n.* the great *opposer of Christ* and Christianity. [Gr. *anti,* against, and **Christ.**]

**Antichristian,** an-ti-krist'yan, *adj.* relating to Antichrist : opposed to Christianity.

**Anticipate,** an-tis'ip-āt, *v.t.* to be beforehand with (another person or thing), to forestall or preoccupy : to foresee. [L. *anticipo, -atum—ante,* before, *capio,* to take.]

**Anticipation,** an-tis-ip-ā'shun, *n.* act of anticipating : foretaste : previous notion : expectation.—*adj* **Anti'cipatory.**

**Anticlimax,** an-ti-klim'aks, *n., the opposite of climax :* a sentence in which the ideas become less important towards the close. [Gr. *anti,* against, and **Climax.**]

**Anticlinal,** an-ti-klīn'al, *adj., sloping in opposite directions.*—*n.* (*geol.*) the line from which the strata descend in opposite directions. [Gr. *anti,* against, *klinō,* to lean.]

**Antidote,** an'ti-dōt, *n.* that which is *given against* anything that would produce bad effects : a counter-poison : ( *fig.*) anything that prevents evil.—*adj.* **An'tidotal.** [Gr. *antidotos—anti,* against, *didōmi,* to give.]

**Antimony,** an'ti-mun-i, *n.* a brittle white-coloured metal much used in the arts and in medicine.—*adj.* **Antimōn'ial.** [Ety. dub.]

**Antinomian,** an-ti-nōm'i-an, *n.* one who holds that the law is not a rule of life under the Gospel.—*adj.* against the law : pertaining to the Antinomians.—*n.* **Antinom'ianism.** [Gr. *anti,* against, *nomos,* a law.]

**Antipathy,** an-tip'ath-i, *n.* dislike : repugnance : opposition.—*adj.* **Antipathet'ic.** [Gr. *anti,* against, *pathos,* feeling.]

**Antiphlogistic,** an-ti-floj'ist'ik, *adj., acting against heat,* or inflammation. [Gr. *anti,* against, *phlogiston,* burnt—*phlegō,* to burn.]

**Antiphon,** an'tif-ōn, **Antiphony,** an-tif'ōn-i, *n., alternate chanting* or singing. [Gr. *anti,* in return, and *phōnē,* voice. A doublet of **Anthem.**]

**Antiphonal,** an-tif'ōn-al, *adj* pertaining to antiphony.—*n.* a book of antiphons or anthems.

**Antipodes,** an-tip'od-ēz, *n.pl.* those living on the other side of the globe, and whose *feet* are thus *opposite* to ours.—*adj.* **Antip'odal.** [Gr. *anti,* opposite to, *pous, podos,* a foot.]

**Antipope,** an'ti-pōp, *n.* an opposition pope : a pretender to the papacy. [Gr. *anti,* against, and **Pope.**]

**Antiquary,** an'ti-kwar-i, *n.* one who studies or collects *ancient* things : one skilled in antiquities.—*adj.* **Antiquarian,** an-ti-kwär'i-an.—*n.* **Antiquar'ianism.** [From **Antique.**]

**Antiquated,** an'ti-kwāt-ed, *adj., grown old,* or out of fashion : obsolete.

**Antique**, an-tēk′, *adj.* ancient: old-fashioned.—*n.* anything very old: ancient relics.—*n.* **Antique′ness.** [Fr.—L. *antiquus*, old, ancient—*ante*, before.]

**Antiquity**, an-tik′wi-ti, *n., ancient times:* great age: a relic of the past.

**Antisabbatarian**, an-ti-sab-at-ā′ri-an, *n.* one who *opposes* the observance of the Lord's day with the strictness of the Jewish *Sabbath*. [Gr. *anti*, against, and **Sabbatarian**.]

**Antiscorbutic**, an-ti-skor-būt′ik, *adj.* acting *against* scurvy.—*n.* a remedy for scurvy. [Gr. *anti*, against, and **Scorbutic**.]

**Antiseptic**, an-ti-sept′ik, *adj.* and *n.*, counteracting *putrefaction*. [Gr. *anti*, against, and *sēpō*, to make putrid.]

**Antistrophe**, an-tis′trof-e, *n.* (*poet.*) the stanza of a song alternating with the strophe. [Gr. *anti*, against, and **Strophe**.]

**Antithesis**, an-tith′e-sis, *n.* a figure in which thoughts or words are set in contrast: opposition:—*pl.* **Antith′eses**, -sēz.—*adj.* **Antithet′ic**, -al.—*adv.* **Antithet′ically.** [Gr.—*anti*, against, *tithēmi*, to place.]

**Antitype**, an′ti-tīp, *n.* that which *corresponds to the type:* that which is prefigured by the type. [Gr. *anti*, corresponding to, and **Type**.]

**Antler**, ant′lėr, *n.* the branch of a stag's horn. —*adj.* **Ant′lered.** [Ety. dub.]

**Anus**, ān′us, *n.* the lower orifice of the bowels. [L., for *as-nus*, 'sitting part,' from root *as*, to sit.]

**Anvil**, an′vil, *n.* an iron block on which smiths hammer metal into shape. [A.S. *anfilt, on filt—on fillan*, to strike down or fell. See **Fell**, *v.t.*]

**Anxiety**, ang-zī′e-ti, *n.* state of being anxious.

**Anxious**, angk′shus, *adj.* uneasy regarding something doubtful: solicitous.—*n.* **An′xiousness.**—*adv.* **An′xiously.** [L. *anxius*—*ango*, to press tightly. See **Anger**, **Anguish**.]

**Any**, en′ni, *adj., one* indefinitely: some: whoever.—*adv.* **An′ything** (*B.*), at all.—**An′ywise**, in any way. [A.S. *ænig*—*an*, one.]

**Anywhere**, en′ni-hwȧr, *adv.* in any place.

**Anywhither**, en′ni-hwith-ėr, *adv.* to any place.

**Aonian**, ā-ō′ni-an, *adj.* pertaining to *Aonia* in Greece, or to the Muses supposed to dwell there.

**Aorist**, ā′or-ist, *n.* the name of certain tenses in the Greek verb expressing *indefinite* time.— *adj.* indefinite: undefined. [Gr. *aoristos*, indefinite—*a*, priv., and *horos*, a limit.]

**Aorta**, ā-or′ta, *n.* the great artery that *rises up* from the left ventricle of the heart.—*adjs.* **Aor′tal, Aor′tic.** [Gr. *aortē*—*aeirō*, to raise up.]

**Apace**, a-pās′, *adv.* at a quick *pace:* swiftly: fast. [Prefix *a*, and **Pace**.]

**Apart**, a-pärt′, *adv.* separately: aside. [Fr. *aparte*—L. *a parte*, from the part or side.]

**Apartment**, a-pärt′ment, *n.* a separate room in a house. [Fr. *appartement*, a suite of rooms forming a complete dwelling, through Low L., from L. *ad*, and *partire*, to divide—*pars*, a part.]

**Apathy**, ap′ath-i, *n., want of feeling:* absence of passion: indifference.—*adj.* **Apathet′ic.** [Gr. *a*, priv., *pathos*, feeling.]

**Ape**, āp, *n.* a tailless monkey: a silly imitator.— *v.t.* to imitate, as an ape. [A.S. *apa.* Ger. *affe*.]

**Apeak**, a-pēk′, *adv.* (*naut.*) the anchor is apeak when the cable is drawn so as to bring the ship's bow directly over it. [*a*, on, and **Peak**.]

**Aperient**, a-pē′ri-ent, *adj., opening:* mildly purgative.—*n.* any laxative medicine. [L. *aperio*, to open.]

**Aperture**, a′pėrt-ūr, *n., an opening:* a hole. [L. *apertura*—*aperio*, to open.]

**Apex**, ā′peks, *n., the summit* or point.—*pl.* **Apexes**, ā′peks-ez, **Apices**, ap′i-sēz. [L.]

**Aphelion**, af-ēl′yun, *n.* the point of a planet's orbit farthest *away from the sun.* [Gr. *apo*, from, *hēlios*, the sun.]

**Apheresis**, af-ē′re-sis, *n.* the *taking* of a letter or syllable *from* the beginning of a word. [Gr. —*apo*, from, *haireō*, to take.]

**Aphorism**, af′or-izm, *n.* a brief pithy saying: an adage. [Gr. *aphorizō*, to mark off by boundaries—*apo*, from, and *horos*, a limit.]

**Aphoristic**, -al, af-or-ist′ik, -al, *adj.* in the form of an aphorism.—*adv.* **Aphorist′ically.**

**Apiary**, āp′i-ar-i, *n.* a place where *bees* are kept. [L. *apiarium*—*apis*, a bee.]

**Apiece**, a-pēs′, *adv., in piece:* to each.

**Apish**, āp′ish, *adj.* like an ape: imitative: foppish. —*adv.* **Ap′ishly.**—*n.* **Ap′ishness.**

**Apocalypse**, a-pok′al-ips, *n.* the name of the last book of the New Testament.—*adj.* **Apocalypt′ic, -al.** [Gr., a revelation, an uncovering— *apo*, from, *kalyptō, kalypsō*, to cover.]

**Apocope**, a-pok′op-ē, *n., the cutting off* of the last letter or syllable of a word. [Gr. *apo*, off, *koptō*, to cut.]

**Apocrypha**, a-pok′rif-a, *n.* certain books whose inspiration is not admitted.—*adj.* **Apoc′ryphal.** [Gr., 'things hidden'—*apo*, from, *kryptō*, to hide.]

**Apogee**, ap′o-jē, *n.* the point in the moon's orbit furthest *away from the earth.* [Gr. *apo*, from, *gē*, the earth.]

**Apologetic, -al**, a-pol-oj-et′ik, -al, *adj.* excusing: said or written in defence.—*adv.* **Apologet′ically.**

**Apologetics**, a-pol-oj-et′iks, *n.* branch of theology concerned with the defence of Christianity.

**Apologise**, a-pol′oj-īz, *v.i.* to make excuse.

**Apologist**, a-pol′oj-ist, *n.* one who makes an apology: a defender.

**Apologue**, a′pol-og, *n.* a moral *tale:* a fable. [Fr. —Gr. *apologos*, a fable—*apo*, from, *logos*, speech.]

**Apology**, a-pol′oj-i, *n.* something *spoken* to ward *off* an attack: a defence or justification: an excuse. [Gr.—*apo*, from, *logos*, speech.]

**Apophthegm**, a′po-them, *n.* a form of **Apothegm**.

**Apoplectic, -al**, a-po-plekt′ik, -al, *adj.* of or predisposed to apoplexy.

**Apoplexy**, a′po-pleks-i, *n.* loss of sensation and of motion by a sudden *stroke.* [Gr. *apoplēxia— apo*, from, away, and *plessō*, to strike.]

**Apostasy, Apostacy**, a-post′a-si, *n.* abandonment of one's religion, principles, or party. [Gr. 'a standing away'—*apo*, from, *stasis*, a standing.]

**Apostate**, a-post′āt, *n.* one guilty of apostasy: a renegade.—*adj.* false: traitorous: fallen.— **Apostatise**, a-post′at-īz, *v.i.* to commit apostasy.

**Apostle**, a-pos′l, *n.* one sent to preach the Gospel: specially, one of the twelve disciples of Christ. —**Apostleship**, a-pos′l-ship, *n.* the office or dignity of an apostle.—**Apostolic, -al**, a-pos-tol′ik, -al, *adj.* [Gr., one sent away, *apo*, away, *stellō*, to send.]

**Apostrophe**, a-post′rof-e, *n.* (*rhet.*) a sudden turning away from the subject to address some person or object present or absent: a mark ( ′ ) shewing the omission of a letter. [Gr. *apo*, from, and **Strophe**, a turning.] [apostrophe.

**Apostrophise**, a-post′rof-īz, *v.t.* to address by

**Apothecary**, a-poth′ek-ar-i, *n.* one who dispenses medicine. [Gr. *apothēkē*, a storehouse—*apo*, away, and *tithēmi*, to place.]

**Apothegm**, a′po-them, *n.* a terse pointed remark: an aphorism. [Gr. *apo*, from, out, *phthengomai*, to speak plainly.]

**Apotheosis**, a-po-thē′o-sis, *n.* deification. [Gr.,

a setting aside as a god—*apo*, away from what he was, *theos*, a god.]

**Appal**, ap-pawl', *v.t.* to terrify : to dismay.—*pr.p.* appall'ing ; *pa.p.* appalled'. [Acc. to Skeat, from Celtic *pall*, to weaken, and not from O. Fr. *apalir*, to grow pale.]

**Appanage**, ap'pan-āj, *n.* a provision for younger sons : aliment. [Fr. *apanage*—L. *ad*, and *panis*, bread.]

**Apparatus**, ap-par-āt'us, *n.* things *prepared* or provided : set of instruments or tools. [L. *ad*, to, *paratus*, prepared.]

**Apparel**, ap-par'el, *n.* covering for the body : dress.—*v.t.* to dress, adorn :—*pr.p.* appar'elling or appar'eling ; *pa.p.* appar'elled or appar'eled. [Fr. *appareil*—*pareiller*, to put like to like, to assort or suit—*pareil*, like—L. *par*, equal, like.]

**Apparent**, ap-pār'ent, *adj.* that may be seen : evident : seeming.—*adv.* Appar'ently.—*n.* Appar'entness. [L. *apparens*. See Appear.]

**Apparition**, ap-par-ish'un, *n.*, *an appearance* : something only apparent, not real : a ghost.—*adj.* Appari'tional. [See Appear.]

**Apparitor**, ap-par'it-or, *n.* an officer who attends on a court or on a magistrate to execute orders. [L.—root of Appear.]

**Appeal**, ap-pēl', *v.i.* to call upon, have recourse to : to refer (to a witness or superior authority). —*v.t.* to remove a cause (to another court).—*n.* act of appealing.—*adj.* Appeal'able. [L. *appello*, *-atum*, to address, call by name.]

**Appear**, ap-pēr', *v.i.* to become visible : to be present : to seem, though not real. [L. *appareo*—*ad*, to, *pareo*, *paritum*, to come forth.]

**Appearance**, ap-pēr'ans, *n.* the act of appearing : the thing seen : apparent likeness : arrival : show.

**Appease**, ap-pēz', *v.t.* to pacify : to quiet : to allay.—*adj.* Appeas'able. [Fr. *apaiser*—L. *ad*, to, *pax, pacis*, peace.]

**Appellant**, ap-pel'ant, *n.* one who appeals.

**Appellate**, ap-pel'āt, *adj.* relating to appeals.

**Appellation**, ap-pel-ā'shun, *n.* that by which anything is *called* : a name. [See Appeal.]

**Appellative**, ap-pel'at-iv, *n.* a name common to all of the same kind, as distinguished from a proper name.—*adj.* common to many : general.

**Append**, ap-pend', *v.t.*, *to hang* one thing to another : to add. [L. *ad*, to, *pendo*, to hang.]

**Appendage**, ap-pend'āj, *n.* something appended.

**Appendix**, ap-pend'iks, *n.* something appended or added : a supplement :—*pl.* **Append'ixes**, -iks-ez, **Append'ices**, -is-ez.

**Appertain**, ap-pèr-tān', *v.i.*, *to belong to*. [Fr. from L. *ad*, to, *pertineo*, to belong. See Pertain.]

**Appetence**, ap'pet-ens, **Appetency**, ap'pet-ens-i, *n.*, *a seeking after* : desire, especially sensual desire. [L. *ad*, to, *peto*, to seek.]

**Appetise**, ap'pet-īz, *v.t.* to create or whet appetite.

**Appetiser**, ap'pet-īz ér, *n.* something which whets the appetite.

**Appetite**, ap'pet-īt, *n.* natural *desire* : desire for food : hunger. [Fr., from L. *appetitus*—*appeto*. See Appetence.]

**Applaud**, ap-plawd', *v.t.* to praise by *clapping* the hands : to praise loudly : to extol. [L. *applaudo*—*ad*, to, *plaudo, plausum*, to clap. See Explode.]

**Applause**, ap-plawz', *n.* praise loudly expressed : acclamation.—*adj.* Applaus'ive.

**Apple**, ap'l, *n.* the fruit of the apple-tree.—**The apple of the eye**, the eye-ball. [A.S. *æpl*; the

word is found in all the Teutonic tongues, in the Celtic and the Slavonic.] [used.

**Appliance**, ap-plī'ans, *n.* anything applied : means

**Applicable**, ap'plik-a-bl, *adj.* that may be applied : suitable.—*adv.* **Ap'plicably.**—*ns.* **Applicabil'ity, Ap'plicableness.**

**Applicant**, ap'plik-ant, *n.* one who applies : a petitioner.

**Application**, ap-plik-ā'shun, *n.* the act of applying ; the thing applied : close thought or attention : request : solicitation.

**Apply**, ap-plī', *v.t.* to lay or put to : to employ : to fix the mind on.—*v.i.* to suit or agree : to have recourse to : to make request :—*pr.p.* apply'ing ; *pa.p.* applīed'. [O. Fr. *aplier*, L. *applico*, *-are*—*ad*, to, *plico*, *-atum*, to fold.]

**Appoint**, ap-point', *v.t.* to fix : to settle : to name to an office : to equip. [O. Fr. *apointer*, Prov. *apuntar*, Low L. *appunctare*—L. *ad*, to, *punctum*, a point.]

**Appointment**, ap-point'ment, *n.* settlement : situation : arrangement :—*pl.* equipments.

**Apportion**, ap-pōr'shun, *v.t.*, *to portion out* : to divide in just shares. [L. *ad*, to, and **Portion**.] —*n.* **Appor'tionment.**

**Apposite**, ap'poz-īt, *adj.* adapted : suitable.—*adv.* **Ap'positely.**—*n.* **Ap'positeness.** [L. *appositus*, pa.p. of *appono*, to put to—*ad*, to, *pono*, to put.]

**Apposition**, ap-poz-ish'un, *n.* the act of adding : state of being placed together or against : (*gram.*) the annexing of one noun to another, in the same case or relation, in order to explain or limit the first. [See **Apposite**.]

**Appraise**, ap-prāz', *v.t.*, *to set a price on* : to value with a view to sale. [Fr. *apprécier*, O. Fr. *apreiser*, L. *appretio*, *-are*—*ad*, to, *pretium*, price.]

**Appraisement**, ap-prāz'ment, *n.* a valuation.

**Appraiser**, ap-prāz'ér, *n.* one who values property.

**Appreciate**, ap-prē'shi-āt, *v.t.* (*lit.*) *to set a price on* : to estimate justly—used figuratively.—*adj.* **Appre'ciable.**—*adv.* **Appre'ciably.** [L. *appretiatus*, pa.p. of *appretio*. See **Appraise**.]

**Appreciation**, ap-prē-shi-ā'shun, *n.* the act of setting a value on : just estimation.

**Appreciative**, ap-prē'shi-at-iv, **Appreciatory**, ap-prē'shi-at-or-i, *adj.* implying appreciation.

**Apprehend**, ap-pre-hend', *v.t.*, *to lay hold of* : to seize by authority : to catch the meaning of : to understand : to fear.—*adj.* **Apprehens'ible.** [L. *apprehendo*—*ad*, to, *prehendo*, *-hensum*, to lay hold of, from *præ* and root *hend*, which is for *hed*, the *n* being intrusive, and this akin to English *get*. Compare Gr. *chandanō*—root *chad*, to hold.]

**Apprehension**, ap-pre-hen'shun, *n.* act of apprehending or seizing : arrest : conception : fear.

**Apprehensive**, ap-pre-hens'iv, *adj.* fearful : suspicious.—*n.* **Apprehens'iveness.**

**Apprentice**, ap-prent'is, *n.* (*lit.*) *a learner* : one bound to another to learn a trade or art.—*v.t.* to bind as an apprentice. [Fr. *apprenti*, O. Fr *apprentis*—*apprendre*—L. *apprehendere*, to learn. See **Apprehend**.]

**Apprenticeship**, ap-prent'is-ship, *n.* the state of an apprentice.

**Apprise**, ap-prīz', *v.t.* to give notice : to inform. [Fr. *apprendre*, pa.p. *appris*, to instruct, from root of **Apprehend**.]

**Approach**, ap-prōch', *v.i.*, *to draw near* : to approximate.—*v.t.* to come near to : to re semble.—*n.* a drawing near to : access : a path or avenue.—*adj.* **Approach'able.** [Fr. *ap* *procher*, Low L. *appropiare*—L. *ad*, to, *prope*, near.] [Approve.]

**Approbation**, ap-prob-ā′shun, *n.* approval. [See **Approve**.]

**Appropriate**, ap-prō′pri-āt, *v.t.* to take to one's self *as one's own:* to set apart for a purpose.—*adj.* set apart for a particular purpose : peculiar : suitable.—*adv.* **Appro′priately**.—*n.* **Appro′priateness**. [L. *approprio, -atum*—*ad*, to, *proprius*, one's own. See **Proper**.]

**Appropriation**, ap-prō-pri-ā′shun, *n.* the act of appropriating : application to a particular purpose.

**Approval**, ap-prōōv′al, *n.* the act of approving : approbation.

**Approve**, ap-prōōv′, *v.t.* (*lit.*) to esteem *good*: to be pleased with : to commend : to sanction.—*adv.* **Approv′ingly**. [Fr. *approuver*, Prov. *aprobar*, L. *approbo, -atum*—*ad*, to, and *probo*, to test or try—*probus*, good.]

**Approven**, ap-prōōv′n, old *pa.p.* of **Approve**.

**Approver**, ap-prōōv′ėr, *n.* one who approves : (*law*) an accomplice in crime admitted to give evidence against a prisoner.

**Approximate**, ap-proks′im-āt, *adj.*, *nearest* or *next* : approaching correctness.—*v.t.* to bring near.—*v.i.* to come near, to approach.—*adv.* **Approx′imately**. [L. *approximo, -atum*—*ad*, to, *proximus*, nearest, superlative of *prope*, near. See **Approach**.] [proach.

**Approximation**, ap-proks-im-ā′shun, *n.* an approach.

**Appurtenance**, ap-pur′ten-ans, *n.*, *that which appertains* to an appendage.—*adj.* **Appur′tenant**. [Fr. *appartenance*, O. Fr. *apurtenaunse*, from root of **Appertain**.]

**Apricock**, ā′pri-kok, *n.* old form of **Apricot**.

**Apricot**, ā′pri-kot, *n.* a fruit of the plum kind. [O.E. *apricock*, Fr. *abricot*. The Fr. *abricot* was from Port. *albricoque* = Ar. *al-barquq*. But *barquq* is a corruption of Low Gr. *praikokion*, which is simply the L. *præcoquum* or *præcox*, early ripe. See **Precocious**.]

**April**, ā′pril, *n.* the fourth month of the year, when the earth *opens* to bring forth fruits, &c. [L. *Aprilis* = *aperilis*—*aperio*, to open.]

**Apron**, ā′prun, *n.* a cloth or piece of leather worn before one to protect the dress.—*adj.* **A′proned**. [O. E. and Fr. *naperon*—Fr. *nappe*, cloth, table-cloth, Low L. *napa*, L. *mappa*, a napkin.]

**Apropos**, a-pro-pō′, *adv.*, *to the purpose*: appropriately : in reference to. [Fr. *à propos*. See **Propose**.]

**Apse**, aps, *n.* an *arched* recess at the east end of the choir of a church. [See **Apsis**.]

**Apsidal**, ap′sid-al, *adj.* pertaining to the apsides, or to the apse of a church.

**Apsis**, ap′sis, *n.* one of the two extreme points in the orbit of a planet, one at the greatest, the other at the least distance from the sun :—*pl.* **Ap′sides**. [L. *apsis*—Gr. *hapsis*, a connection, an arch—*haptō*, to connect. See **Apt**.]

**Apt**, apt, *adj.* liable : ready : quick. [L. *aptus*, fit—*apo*, to join ; cog. with Gr. *haptō*.]

**Apteryx**, ap′tėr-iks, *n.* a bird found in New Zealand, wing-less and tail-less. [Gr. *a*, priv., *pteryx*, wing.]

**Aptitude**, apt′i-tūd, *n.* fitness : tendency : readiness.—*adv.* **Apt′ly**.—*n.* **Apt′ness**. [Low L. *aptitudo*—root of **Apt**.]

**Aqua-fortis**, ā′kwa-for′tis, *n.* (*lit.*) *strong water*: nitric acid. [L. *aqua*, water, *fortis*, strong.]

**Aquarium**, a-kwā′ri-um, *n.* a tank or vessel for *water* plants and animals : a public collection of such tanks :—*pl.* **Aqua′riums** or **Aqua′ria**. [L.—*aqua*, water.]

**Aquarius**, a-kwā′ri-us, *n.*, *the water-bearer*, a sign of the zodiac. [L.—*aqua*, water.]

**Aquatic**, a-kwat′ik, *adj.*, *relating to water*: living or growing in water.—**Aquatics**, a-kwat′iks, *n.* amusements on the water, as boating, &c.

**Aqua-vitæ**, ā′kwa-vī′tē, *n.* (*lit.*) *water of life*, a name given to ardent spirits. [L. *aqua*, water, *vitæ*, of life—*vita*, life.]

**Aqueduct**, ak′we-dukt, *n.* an artificial channel for *conveying water*. [L. *aqua*, water—*duco*, *ductum*, to lead.] [water.

**Aqueous**, ā′kwe-us, *adj.* watery : deposited by

**Aquiline**, ak′wil-in or -īn, *adj.* relating *to the eagle:* hooked, like an eagle's beak. [L. *aquila*.]

**Arab**, ar′ab, *n.* a native of *Arabia*: a neglected or homeless boy or girl, usually **Street Arab**.

**Arabesque**, ar′ab-esk, *adj.* after the manner of *Arabian* designs.—*n.* a fantastic painted or sculptured ornament among the Spanish Moors, consisting of foliage and other parts of plants curiously intertwined. [Fr.—It. *arabesco*; -*esco* corresponding to Eng. -*ish*.]

**Arabian**, ar-āb′i-an, *adj.* relating to Arabia.—*n.* a native of Arabia.

**Arabic**, ar′ab-ik, *adj.* relating to Arabia, or to its language.—*n.* the language of Arabia. [L. *Arabicus*.]

**Arable**, ar′a-bl, *adj.* fit *for ploughing* or tillage. [L. *arabilis*—*aro*; cog. with Gr. *aroō*, to plough, A.S. *erian*, E. **Ear**, *v.t.*, Ir. *araim*.]

**Aramaic**, ar-a-mā′ik, **Aramean**, ar-a-mē′an, *adj.* relating to *Aramæa*, the whole of the country to the N.E. of Palestine, or to its language, a branch of the Semitic.

**Arbiter**, är′bit-ėr, *n.* one chosen by parties in controversy to decide between them : a judge having absolute power of decision : an umpire :—*fem.* **Ar′bitress**. [L.—*ar* = *ad*, to, and *bito* (cog. with Gr. *bai-nō*), to go or come ; sig. one who comes to look on, a witness, a judge.]

**Arbitrament**, är-bit′ra-ment, *n.* the decision of an arbiter : determination : choice.

**Arbitrary**, är′bitr-ar-i, *adj.* depending on the will (*as of an arbiter*): not bound by rules : despotic : absolute.—*adv.* **Ar′bitrarily**.—*n.* **Ar′bitrariness**. [to determine.—*n.* Arbitra′tion.

**Arbitrate**, är′bitr-āt, *v.i.* to act *as an arbiter*:

**Arbitrator**, är′bi-trā-tur, *n.* same as **Arbiter**.—*fem.* **Ar′bitratrix**.

**Arboreous**, är-bōr′e-us, *adj.*, *of* or belonging to trees. [L. *arboreus*—*arbor*, a tree.]

**Arborescent**, är-bor-es′ent, *adj.* growing or formed like *a tree*.—*n.* **Arbores′cence**. [L. *arboresco*, to become a tree—*arbor*, a tree.]

**Arboretum**, är-bor-ēt′um, *n.* a place in which specimens of trees and shrubs are cultivated :—*pl.* **Arboret′a**. [L.—*arbor*, a tree.]

**Arboriculture**, är′bor-i-kult′ūr, *n.*, *the culture of trees*, esp. timber-trees.—*adj.* **Arboricul′tural**.—*n.* **Arboricul′turist**. [L. *arbor*, and **Culture**.]

**Arbour**, är′bur, *n.* an inclosed seat in a garden, covered with branches of trees, plants, &c.: a bower. [A corr. of *harbour*, a shelter.]

**Arbute**, är′būt, **Arbutus**, är′būt-us, *n.* the strawberry tree : an evergreen shrub, which bears fruit resembling the strawberry. [L. *arbutus*, akin to *arbor*, tree.]

**Arc**, ärk, *n.* a segment of a circle or other curve. [Fr.—L. *arcus*, a bow.]

**Arcade**, ärk-ād′, *n.* a walk arched over : a long arched gallery, lined with shops on both sides. [Fr.—L. *arcata*, arched. See **Arch**.]

**Arcadian**, ark-ād′i-an, *adj.* pertaining to *Arcadia*, a district in Greece : pastoral : rural.

**Arcanum**, ärk-ān'um, *n.* a secret : a mystery :— *pl.* **Arcan'a**. [L.—*arcanus*, secret, closed—*arca*, a chest.]

**Arch**, ärch, *n.* a construction of stones or other materials, arranged in the line of a curve, so as by mutual pressure to support each other.—*v.t.* to cover with an arch : to bend into the form of an arch. [From Fr. *arc*, as ditch is from dyke —L. *arcus*, a bow.]

**Arch**, ärch, *adj.* cunning : sly : waggish : mirthful : shrewd.—*adv.* **Arch'ly.**—*n.* **Arch'ness.** [A.S. *earg*, timid, slothful ; cog. with Ger. *arg*, mischievous, bad.]

**Arch**, ärch (ärk, before a vowel), *adj.* used as a prefix : *the first* or *chief.* [A.S. *arce*, from Lat. and Gr. *archi-,*—Gr. *archē*, beginning.]

**Archæology**, ärk-e-ol'oj-i, *n.* knowledge of ancient art, customs, &c. : the science of antiquities.—*adj.* **Archæolog'ical.**—*adv.* **Archæolog'ically.** —*n.* **Archæol'ogist.** [Gr. *archaios*, ancient—*archē*, beginning, and *logos*, discourse.]

**Archaic, -al**, ärk-ā'ik, -al, *adj., ancient :* obsolete. [Gr. *archaikos—archaios*, ancient—*archē*, beginning.]                               [word or phrase.

**Archaism**, ärk'ā-izm, *n.* an archaic or obsolete

**Archangel**, ärk-ān'jel, *n.* an angel of the highest order.—*adj.* **Archangel'ic.** [**Arch**, chief, and **Angel.**]

**Archbishop**, ärch-bish'up, *n., a chief bishop :* the bishop of a province as well as of his own diocese.—*n.* **Archbish'opric.** [**Arch**, chief, and **Bishop.**]

**Archdeacon**, ärch-dē'kn, *n., a chief deacon :* the officer having the chief supervision of a diocese or part of it, next under the bishop.—*n.* **Archdea'conry**, *the office*, jurisdiction, or residence *of an archdeacon.*—*n.* **Archdea'conship**, *the office of an archdeacon.* [**Arch**, chief, and **Deacon.**]                             [archbishop.

**Archdiocese**, ärch-dī'o-sēz, *n.* the diocese of an

**Archduke**, ärch-dūk', *n., a chief duke :* a prince of Austria.—*fem.* **Archduch'ess.**—*adj.* **Archdu'cal.**—*ns.* **Archduch'y**, **Archduke'dom**, *the territory of an archduke* or archduchess. [**Arch**, chief, and **Duke.**]

**Archer**, ärch'ér, *n.* one who shoots *with a bow* and arrows :—*fem.* **Arch'eress.** [Fr.—*arc*, L. *arcus*, a bow.]                             [bow.

**Archery**, ärch'ér-i, *n.* the art of shooting with the

**Archetype**, ärk'e-tīp, *n.* the original pattern or model.—*adj.* **Archetyp'al.** [Gr. *archē = archi-,* original, and *typos*, a model.]

**Archidiaconal**, ärk-i-di-ak'on-al, *adj.* pertaining to an archdeacon. [Gr. *archi-* is here taken directly from Greek. See **Archdeacon.**]

**Archiepiscopal**, ärk-i-ep-i'skop-al, *adj.* belonging to an archbishop.—**Archiepis'copacy**, *n.* dignity or province of an archbishop. [See **Episcopal.**]

**Archipelago**, ärk-i-pel'a-gō, *n.* the *chief sea* of the Greeks, or the *Ægean Sea :* a sea abounding in small islands. [Gr. *archi-*, chief, *pelagos*, sea.]

**Architect**, ärk'i-tekt, *n.* one who designs buildings and superintends their erection : a maker. [Gr. *architektōn—archi-*, chief, and *tektōn*, a builder.]

**Architecture**, ärk-i-tekt'ūr, *n., the art* or science of *building :* structure.—*adj.* **Architect'-ural.**

**Architrave**, ärk'i-trāv, *n., the chief beam :* (*arch.*) the lowest division of the entablature resting immediately on the abacus of the column. [It. from Gr. *archi-*, chief, and L. *trabs*, a beam—the chief beam.]

**Archives**, ärk'īvz, *n.* the place in which government records are kept : public records. [Fr.—Gr. *archeion—archē*, government.]       [records.

**Archivist**, ärk'iv-ist, *n.* a keeper of archives or

**Archon**, ärk'on, *n.* one of nine chief magistrates who at one time governed ancient Athens. [Gr. —*archō*, to be first, to rule.]       [arch.

**Archway**, ärch'wā, *n.* a way or passage under an

**Arctic**, ärkt'ik, *adj.* relating to the constellation the Great *Bear*, or to the north. [Gr. *arktos*, a bear.]

**Ardency**, ärd'en-si, *n.* warmth of passion or feeling : eagerness.

**Ardent**, ärd'ent, *adj., burning :* fiery : passionate. —*adv.* **Ard'ently.** [L. *ardens—ardeo*, to burn.]

**Arduous**, ärd'ū-us, *adj.* difficult to accomplish : laborious.—*adv.* **Ard'uously.**—*n.* **Ard'uousness.** [L. *arduus*, high, akin to Celt. *ard*, high, height.]

**Are**, är, the plural of the present indicative of the verb *to be.* [M.E. *ar-en* was the northern form which took the place of A.S. *sindon.* Dan. *er-es*, *ar-en = as-en* ; *er-e = as-e* ; the root is *as-*, to be seen in L. *es-se*, *s-um*, for *es-um.* See **Was.**]

**Area**, ā're-a, *n.* any plane surface or inclosed space : the sunken space around the basement of a building : (*geom.*) the superficial contents of any figure. [L.]

**Arena**, a-rē'na, *n.* an open space strewed with *sand* for combatants : any place of public contest.—*adj.* **Arena'ceous**, sandy. [L. *arena*, sand.]                                          [Areopagus.

**Areopagite**, ar-e-op'aj-īt, *n.* a member of the

**Areopagus**, ar-e-op'ag-us, *n., Mars' Hill*, on which the supreme court of ancient Athens was held : the court itself. [L.—Gr. *Areios pagos*, hill of Ares—or Mars.]

**Argent**, ärj'ent, *adj.* made of, or like silver. [Fr.—L. *argentum*, silver—Gr. *argos*, white.]

**Argillaceous**, ärj-ill-ā'shus, *adj.* of the nature of clay. [L. *argilla*—Gr. *argilos*, white clay—*argos*, white.]

**Argonaut**, är'go-nawt, *n.* one of those who *sailed* in the ship *Argo* in search of the golden fleece. [Gr. *Argo*, and *nautēs*, a sailor.]

**Argosy**, är'go-si, *n.* a large merchant-vessel richly laden. [Prob. from the ship *Argo.* See **Argonaut.**]

**Argue**, ärg'ū, *v.t.* to prove by argument : to discuss.—*v.i.* to offer reasons : to dispute :—*pr.p.* ar'guing ; *pa.p.* ar'gued. [L. *arguo*, to prove—from root of Gr. *argos*, clear, and so = to make clear.]

**Argument**, ärg'ū-ment, *n.* a reason offered as proof : a series of reasons : a discussion : subject of a discourse. [L. *argumentum.* See **Argue.**]

**Argumentation**, ärg-ū-ment-ā'shun, *n.* an arguing or reasoning.—*adj.* **Argument'ative.**—*adv.* **Argument'atively.**—*n.* **Argument'ativeness.**

**Argus**, ärg'us, *n.* a mythological being, said to have had a hundred eyes, some of which were always awake : any very watchful person. [Gr. —*argos*, bright.]

**Arian**, ā'ri-an, *adj., pertaining to Arius* of Alexandria (4th c.), who denied the divinity of Christ.—*n.* one who adheres to the doctrines of Arius : a Unitarian.—**Arianism**, ā'ri-an-izm, *n.* the doctrines of the Arians.

**Arid**, ar'id, *adj., dry :* parched.—*ns.* **Arid'ity**, **Ar'idness.** [L. *aridus.*]

**Aries**, ā'ri-ēz, *n., the Ram*, the first of the signs of the zodiac, which the sun enters on March 21. [L.]

**Aright**, a-rīt', *adv.* in a *right* way : rightly.

**Arise**, a-rīz', *v.i.* to *rise up :* to come into view :

to spring :—*pa.t.* arose, a-rōz′ ; *pa.p.* aris′en. [Prefix *a* (as in **Abide**), and **Rise**.]

**Aristocracy,** ar-is-tok′ras-i, *n.*, *government* by the *best* men or nobles : the nobility or chief persons of a state. [Gr. *aristos*, best, and *kratos*, power.]

**Aristocrat,** ar′is-to-krat or ar-is′-, *n.* one who belongs to or favours an aristocracy : a haughty person.—**Aristocratic, -al,** ar-is-to-krat′ik, -al, *adj.* belonging to aristocracy.—*adv.* **Aristocrat′ically.**

**Aristotelian,** ar-is-to-tē′li-an, *adj.* relating to *Aristotle* or to his philosophy.

**Arithmetic,** ar-ith′met-ik, *n.* the science of *numbers:* the art of reckoning by figures. —*adj.* **Arithmet′ical.**—*adv.* **Arithmet′ically.** [Gr. *arithmētikē (technē*, art), relating to numbers—*arithmos*, number.]　　　[in arithmetic.

**Arithmetician,** ar-ith-me-tish′yan, *n.* one skilled

**Ark,** ärk, *n.* a *chest* or coffer : a large floating vessel. [A.S. *arc*—L. *arca*, a chest—*arceo*, to guard.]

**Arm,** ärm, *n.* the limb extending from the shoulder to the hand : anything projecting from the main body, as an inlet of the sea : (*fig.*) power. —*n.* **Arm′ful.**—*adj.* **Arm′less.**—*n.* **Arm′let,** a bracelet. [A.S.; cog. with L. *armus*, the shoulder-joint, Gr. *harmos*, a joint. From root *ar-*. See **Arms**.]

**Arm,** ärm, *n.* a weapon : a branch of the military service. [Sing. of **Arms**.]

**Arm,** ärm, *v.t.* to furnish with *arms* or weapons : to fortify.—*v.i.* to take arms. [L. *armo*, to arm—*arma*, weapons. See **Arms**.]

**Armada,** ärm-ä′da, *n.* a fleet of *armed* ships. [Sp.—L. *armatus*, armed—*armo*, to arm.]

**Armadillo,** ärm-a-dill′o, *n.* a small quadruped, having its body *armed* with a bony shell :—*pl.* **Armadill′os.** [Sp. dim. of *armado*, armed.]

**Armament,** ärm′a-ment, *n.* forces *armed* or equipped for war : the guns, &c. with which a ship is armed. [L. *armamenta—arma*.]

**Armenian,** ar-mē′ni-an, *adj.* belonging to *Armenia*, a country of Western Asia.—*n.* a native of Armenia.

**Arminian,** ar-min′yan, *adj.* holding the doctrines of *Arminius.*—*n.* a follower of Arminius, a Dutch divine, who denied the Calvinistic doctrine of election.—*n.* **Armin′ianism.**

**Armipotent,** ärm-i′pot-ent, *adj.*, *powerful* in *arms.* [L. *arma*, arms, *potens,-entis*, powerful.]

**Armistice,** ärm′ist-is, *n.* a short suspension of hostilities : a truce. [Fr.—L. *arma*, arms, *sisto*, to stop.]　　　[or to the arms of a family.

**Armorial,** ärm-ōr′i-al, *adj.* belonging to *armour.*

**Armoric,** ar-mor′ik, *n.* the language of the inhabitants of *Armorica*, the ancient name for Brittany. [L. *Armoricus*—Celt. *ar*, on, *mor*, the sea.]

**Armour,** ärm′ur, *n.* defensive arms or dress : plating of ships of war.—*n.* **Arm′our-bearer.** —*adj.* **Arm′our-plated.**

**Armourer,** ärm′ur-ér, *n.* a maker or repairer of, or one who has the charge of armour.

**Armoury,** ärm′ur-i, *n.* the place in which arms are made or kept : a collection of ancient armour.　　　[shoulder.

**Armpit,** ärm′pit, *n.* the pit or hollow under the

**Arms,** ärmz, *n.pl.* weapons of offence and defence : war : hostility : armorial ensigns. [L. *arma*, (*lit.*) ' fittings ;' Gr. *harmona*, the tackling of a ship—root *ar-*, to fit ; conn. with **Arm**, the limb.]

**Army,** ärm′i, *n.* a large body of men *armed* for war and under military command : a host. [Fr. *armée*—L. *armata*.]

**Aroma,** a-rō′ma, *n.* sweet smell : the odorous principle of plants : (*fig.*) flavour of any kind. [Gr.]

**Aromatic,** ar-o-mat′ik, *adj.* fragrant : spicy.

**Arose,** a-rōz′, past tense of **Arise**.

**Around,** a-rownd′, *prep.* on all sides of.—*adv.* on every side : in a circle. [A, on, and **Round**.]

**Arouse,** a-rowz′, *v.t.* Same as **Rouse**.

**Arquebuse, Arquebuss,** är′kwi-bus, *n.* an old-fashioned hand-gun. [Fr. *arquebuse*, from Dut. *haakbus—haak*, hook, and *bus*, box, barrel of a gun ; Ger. *hakenbüchse*.]

**Arrack,** ar′ak, *n.* an ardent spirit used in the East. [Ar. *araq*, juice or sweet.]

**Arraign,** ar-rān′, *v.t.* to call one *to account* : to put a prisoner upon trial : to accuse publicly. —*n.* **Arraign′ment.** [O. Fr. *aragnier*, Fr. *arraisonner*—Low L. *arrationare*—L. *ad*, to, *ratio*, reason.]

**Arrange,** ar-rānj′, *v.t.* to set in a *rank* or row : to put in order : to settle. [Fr. *arranger—à* (—L. *ad*, to), and *ranger*. See **Range**.]

**Arrangement,** ar-rānj′ment, *n.* act of arranging : classification : settlement.

**Arrant,** ar′rant, *adj.* downright, notorious (used in a bad sense). [Corr. of *arghand*, pr.p. of *argh*, the northern form of A.S. *eargian*, to be a coward, Ger. *arg*, bad.]

**Arras,** ar′ras, *n.* tapestry. [From *Arras* in Northern France, where first manufactured.]

**Array,** ar-rā′, *n.* order : dress : equipage.—*v.t.* to put in order : to arrange : to dress, adorn, or equip. [O. Fr. *arroi*, array, equipage—L. *ad*, and a Teut. root, found either in O. Ger. *rat* (Ger. *rath*), counsel, E. **Read**, or in E. **Ready**, Ger. *be-reit*.]

**Arrear,** ar-rēr′, *n.* that which is *in the rear* or *behind :* that which remains unpaid or undone (used mostly in *pl.*). [Fr. *arrière*, behind—L. *ad.* to, *retro*, back, behind.]

**Arrest,** ar-rest′, *v.t.* to stop : to seize : to apprehend by legal authority.—*n.* stoppage : seizure by warrant. [Fr. *arrêter* for *arrester*—L. *ad*, to, *resto*, to stand still.]

**Arrival,** ar-rīv′al, *n.* the act of arriving : persons or things that arrive.

**Arrive,** ar-rīv′, *v.i.* (fol. by *at*) to reach any place : to attain to any object. [Fr. *arriver*— Low L. *adripare*—L. *ad*, to, *ripa*, a bank ; as if, to reach the bank.]

**Arrogance,** ar′rog-ans, **Arrogancy,** ar′rog-ans-i, *n.* undue assumption of importance.

**Arrogant,** ar′rog-ant, *adj.* claiming too much : overbearing.—*adv.* **Ar′rogantly.**

**Arrogate,** ar′rog-āt, *v.t.* to *claim* as one's own : to claim proudly or unduly. [L. *arrogo—ad*, to, *rogo, rogatum*, to ask, to claim.]

**Arrondissement,** ar-ron′dēs-mäng, *n.* a subdivision of a French department. [Fr.—*arrondir*, to make round—L. *ad*, and Fr. *rond*. See **Round**.]

**Arrow,** ar′rō, *n.* a straight, pointed weapon, made to be shot from a bow.—*n.* **Arrow-head,** ar′rō-hed.—**Arrow-headed,** ar′rō-hed′ed, *adj.* shaped like the head of an arrow. [A.S. *arewe ;* Ice. *ör*, akin perhaps to Ice. *örr*, the swift.]

**Arrowroot,** ar′rō-rōōt, *n.* a starch obtained from the roots of certain plants growing chiefly in W. Indies, and much used as food for invalids and children. [Said to be so named because used by the Indians of S. America as an antidote against wounds caused by poisoned arrows.]

**Arrowy,** ar′rō-i, *adj.* of or like arrows.

**Arsenal,** är′se-nal, *n.* a public magazine or manufactory of naval and military stores. [Fr. and Sp. ; from Ar. *dâr*, a house, and *cina'at*, trade.]

**Arsenic**, är'sen-ik, *n.* a mineral poison: a soft, gray-coloured metal. [Gr. *arsēn*, male ; the alchemists fancied some metals male, others female.] [containing arsenic.

**Arsenic, -al**, är-sen'ik, -al, *adj.* composed of or

**Arson**, ärs'on, *n.* the crime of wilfully *burning* houses or other buildings. [O. Fr. *arson*—L. *ardeo*, *arsum*, to burn.]

**Art**, ärt, 2d pers. sing. of the present tense of the verb *to be*. [A.S. *eart*.]

**Art**, ärt, *n.* practical skill guided by rules : the rules and methods of doing certain actions : a profession or trade : contrivance : skill : cunning : artifice. [L. *ars*, *artis*, from root *ar-*, to fit. See **Arm**.]

**Arterialise**, är-tē'ri-al-īz, *v.t.* to make arterial.

**Artery**, är'tėr-i, *n.* a tube or vessel which conveys blood from the heart.—*adj.* **Arte'rial**. [L.—Gr. *artēria*, orig. the windpipe, the bronchiæ, then applied to the arteries : perh. conn. with *artaō*, I fasten to, hang from.]

**Artesian**, är-tē'zhan, *adj.* applied to wells made by boring until water is reached. [From *Artois* (anc. *Artesium*), in the north of France, where these wells are said to have been first made.]

**Artful**, ärt'fool, *adj.* full of art : cunning.—*adv.* **Art'fully.**—*n.* **Art'fulness.**

**Artichoke**, är'ti-chōk, *n.* an eatable plant with large heads, like the cone of the pine. [Fr. *artichaut*, It. *articiocco*, Sp. *alcachofa*—Ar. *alharshaf*.]

**Article**, ärt'i-kl, *n.* a separate element, member, or part of anything : a particular substance : a single clause, or term : (*gram.*) one of the particles, *an* or *a* and *the*.—*v.t.* to draw up or bind by articles. [L. *articulus*, a little joint—*artus*, a joint—root *ar-*, to join.]

**Articular**, är-tik'ūl-ar, *adj.*, *belonging to the joints.* [See **Article**.]

**Articulate**, är-tik'ūl-āt, *adj.* distinct : clear.—*v.t.* to joint: to form into distinct sounds, syllables, or words.—*v.i.* to speak distinctly.—*adv.* **Artic'ulately.**—*n.* **Artic'ulateness.** [L. *articulo*, *-atum*, to furnish with joints, to utter distinctly. See **Article**.]

**Articulation**, är-tik-ūl-ā'shun, *n.*, *a joining*, as of the bones: distinct utterance: a consonant.

**Artifice**, ärt'i-fis, *n.* a contrivance : a trick or fraud. [L. *artificium*—*artifex*, *-ficis*, an artificer—*ars*, *artis*, and *facio*, to make.]

**Artificer**, är-tif'is-er, *n.* a workman : an inventor.

**Artificial**, ärt-i-fish'yal, *adj.*, *made by art* : not natural: cultivated: not indigenous : feigned.—*adv.* **Artific'ially.** [See **Artifice**.]

**Artillerist**, är-til'ėr-ist, *n.* one skilled in artillery or gunnery.

**Artillery**, är-til'ėr-i, *n.* offensive weapons of war, esp. cannon, mortars, &c. : the men who manage them : a branch of the military service : gunnery. [Fr. *artillerie*—O. Fr. *artiller*, to arm ; from a supposed Low L. *artillare*—L. *ars*, *artis*, art.] [artillery.

**Artillery-man**, är-til'ėr-i-man, *n.* a soldier of the

**Artisan**, ärt'i-zan, *n.* one skilled in any *art* or trade : a mechanic. [Fr. *artisan*, It. *artigiano* = L. as if *artitianus*—*artitus*, skilled in the arts—*ars*, *artis*, art.]

**Artist**, ärt'ist, *n.*, *one who practises an art*, esp. one of the fine arts, as painting, sculpture, or architecture. [Fr. *artiste*, Ital. *artista*—L. *ars*, *artis*, art.]

**Artistic, -al**, ärt-ist'ik, -al, *adj.* according to art.

**Artless**, ärt'les, *adj.* guileless : simple.—*n.* **Art'lessness.**

**Aruspicy**, a-rus'pi-si, *n.* divination by inspection of the entrails of beasts. [L. *aruspicium*, orig. dub.]

**Aryan**, ä'ri-an, *adj.* relating to the family of nations otherwise called Indo-European (comprehending the inhabitants of Europe—except the Turks, Magyars, and Finns—and those of Armenia, Persia, and N. Hindustan), or to their languages. [Sans. *arya*, excellent, prob. allied to Gr. *aristos*, the best.]

**As**, az, *adv.* and *conj.* similarly : for example : while : in like manner. [*As* is a corr. of *also*—A.S. *eal-swa*, *al so*, *alse*, *als* ; Ger. *als*. The primary meaning is, just so, quite in that way.]

**As**, *rel. pro.* from the Scand. [O. Ic. *es*, Mod. Ic. *er*. This use of *as* is provincial.]

**Asafetida**, as-a-fet'i-da, *n.*, *fetid asa*, a medicinal gum, having an offensive smell, made from a Persian plant called *asa*.

**Asbestos**, a-sbest'os, *n.* an *incombustible* mineral, a variety of hornblende, of a fine fibrous texture, resembling flax. [Gr. (*lit.*) unquenchable—*a*, neg., *sbestos*, extinguished.]

**Ascend**, as-send', *v.i.*, *to climb* or mount *up* : to rise : to go backwards in the order of time.—*v.t.* to climb or go up on. [L. *ascendo*, *ascensum*—*ad*, and *scando*, to climb, Sans. *skand*, to leap upwards.]

**Ascendant**, as-send'ant, *adj.* superior : above the horizon.—*n.* superiority : (*astrol.*) the part of the ecliptic rising above the horizon at the time of one's birth ; it was supposed to have commanding influence over the person's life, hence the phrase, *in the ascendant*. [ence.

**Ascendency**, as-send'en-si, *n.* controlling influ-

**Ascension**, as-sen'shun, *n.* a rising or going up. [L. *ascensio*—*ascendo*.]

**Ascension-day**, as-sen'shun-dā, *n.* the festival held on Holy Thursday, ten days before Whitsunday, to commemorate Christ's *ascension* to heaven. [ascending : degree of elevation.

**Ascent**, as-sent', *n.* act of ascending : way of

**Ascertain**, as-sėr-tān', *v.t.* to determine : to obtain certain knowledge of.—*adj.* **Ascertain'able.** [O. Fr. *acertainer*. See **Certain**.]

**Ascetic**, as-set'ik, *n.*, *one* rigidly self-denying in religious observances : a strict hermit.—*adj.* excessively rigid : austere : recluse.—*n.* **Asceticism**, as-set'i-sizm. [Gr. *askētēs*, one that uses exercises to train himself.]

**Ascititious**, as-sit-ish'us, *adj.* See **Adscititious**.

**Ascribe**, a-skrīb', *v.t.* to attribute, impute, or assign.—*adj.* **Ascrib'able.** [L. *ascribo*, *-scriptum*—*ad*, to, *scribo*, to write.] [imputing.

**Ascription**, a-skrip'shun, *n.* act of ascribing or

**Ash**, ash, *n.* a well-known timber tree.—*adj.* **Ash'en.** [A.S. *æsc*, Ger. *esche*, Ice. *askr*.]

**Ashamed**, a-shämd', *adj.*, *affected* with shame. [Pa.p. of old verb *ashame*—pfx. *a*, inten., and **Shame**.]

**Ashes**, ash'ez, *n.pl.* the dust or remains of anything burnt : the remains of the human body when burnt : (*fig.*) a dead body. [A.S. *æsce*, Ice. *aska*.]

**Ashlar**, ash'lar, **Ashler**, ash'lėr, *n.* (*lit.*) stones *laid in rows*: hewn or squared stone used in facing a wall, as distinguished from rough, as it comes from the quarry. [Fr. *aisselle*, dim. of *ais*, a plank ; L. *assis*, a plank—*assula*, a little plank, a shingle. Such little wooden boards were used to face walls before stones, and squared stones took the name.]

**Ashore**, a-shōr', *adv.*, *on shore.* [Pfx. *a*, and **Shore**.]

**Ash-Wednesday**, ash-wenz'dā, *n.* the first day of Lent, so called from the Roman Catholic custom of sprinkling *ashes* on the head. [pale.

**Ashy**, ash'i, *adj.* of or like ashes: ash-coloured:

**Aside**, a-sīd', *adv.*, *on* or to one *side:* privately.

**Asinine**, as'in-īn, *adj.* of or like an ass. [See **Ass**.]

**Ask**, ask, *v.t.*, *to seek:* to request, inquire, beg, or question.—*v.i.* to request: to make inquiry. [A.S. *acsian*, *ascian*, Ger. *heischen*, Ice. *æskja*, Sans. *ish*, to desire.]

**Askance**, a-skans', **Askant**, a-skant', *adv.* sideways: awry: obliquely. [O. Fr. *a scanche* ; It. *schiancio*, a slope, from the root of **Slant**.]

**Askew**, a-skū', *adv.* on the **Skew** : awry.

**Aslant**, a-slant', *adj.* or *adv.* on the **Slant** : obliquely.

**Asleep**, a-slēp', *adj.* or *adv.* in *sleep:* sleeping.

**Aslope**, a-slōp', *adj.* or *adv.* on the **Slope**.

**Asp**, asp, **Aspic**, asp'ik, *n.* a very venomous serpent. [Fr.—L. and Gr. *aspis*.]

**Asparagus**, as-par'a-gus, *n.* garden vegetable. [L.—Gr. *asparagos*.]

**Aspect**, as'pekt, *n.* look : view : appearance : position in relation to the points of the compass : the situation of one planet with respect to another, as seen from the earth. [L. *aspectus* —*ad*, at, *specio*, to look.]

**Aspen**, asp'en, *n.* the trembling poplar.—*adj.* made of, or like the aspen. [A.S. *æsp*, Ger. *äspe*.]

**Asperity**, as-per'i-ti, *n. roughness:* harshness. [Fr.—L. *asperitas*—*asper*, rough.]

**Asperse**, as-pèrs', *v.t.* to slander or calumniate. [L. *aspergo*, *-spersum*—*ad*, to, on, *spargo*, to scatter.]

**Aspersion**, as-pèr'shun, *n.* calumny : slander.

**Asphalt**, as-falt', **Asphaltum**, as-falt'um, *n.* a hard, bituminous substance, anciently used as a cement, and now for paving, &c.—*adj.* **Asphalt'ic**. [Gr. *asphaltos*, an Eastern word.]

**Asphodel**, as'fo-del, *n.* a kind of lily. [See **Daffodil**.]

**Asphyxia**, a-sfiks'i-a, *n.* (*lit.*) suspended animation, suffocation.—*adj.* **Asphyx'iated**. [Gr., a stopping of the pulse—*a*, neg., *sphyzō*, to throb.]

**Aspirant**, as-pīr'ant, *n.* one who aspires : a candidate.

**Aspirate**, as'pir-āt, *v.t.* to pronounce with a full breathing, as the letter *h* in *house.*—*n.* a mark of aspiration (`'`) : an aspirated letter.—*n.* **Aspiration**, as-pir-ā'shun, *n.* pronunciation of a letter with a full breathing. [L. *ad*, and *spiro*, to breathe.]

**Aspire**, as-pīr', *v.i.* to desire eagerly : to aim at high things.—*adj.* **Aspir'ing**.—*adv.* **Aspir'ingly**.—**Aspira'tion**, *n.* eager desire. [L. *aspiro*, *-atum*—*ad*, to, *spiro*, to breathe.]

**Asquint**, a-skwint', *adv.* towards the corner of the eye : obliquely. [Pfx. *a*, on, and **Squint**.]

**Ass**, as, *n.* a well-known quadruped of the horse family : (*fig.*) a dull, stupid fellow. [A.S. *assa*. The word, orig. perhaps Semitic, has spread into all the Eur. lang. ; it is a dim. in all but Eng.—L. *as-inus*, Ger. *es-el*.]

**Assafetida**, same as **Asafetida**.

**Assail**, as-sāl', *v.t.* to assault : to attack.—*adj.* **Assail'able**. [Fr. *assaillir*, L. *assilire*—*ad*, upon, and *salio*, to leap.] [attacks.

**Assailant**, as-sāl'ant, *n.* one who assails or

**Assassin**, as-sas'sin, *n.* one who kills by surprise or secretly. [Fr.—Ar. *hashishin*, the followers of an Eastern robber-chief, who fortified themselves for their adventures by *hashish*, an intoxicating drink made from hemp.]

**Assassinate**, as-sas'sin-āt, *v.t.* to murder by surprise or secret assault.

**Assassination**, as-sas-sin-ā'shun, *n.* secret murder.

**Assault**, as-sawlt', *n.* a sudden attack : a storming, as of a town.—*v.t.* to make an assault or attack upon. [Fr. *assaut*, O. Fr. *asalt*—L. *ad*, upon, *saltus*, a leap. See **Assail**.]

**Assay**, as-sā', *v.t.*, *to examine* or *weigh* accurately : to determine the amount of metal in an ore or alloy.—*v.i.* to attempt : to essay.—*n.* the determination of the quantity of metal in an ore or alloy : the thing tested. [See **Essay**.]

**Assegai**, as'se-gā, *n.* a spear or javelin used by the Kaffirs of S. Africa. [Sp. *azagaya*—Ar. *al-khaziq*.] [sons or things.

**Assemblage**, as-sem'blāj, *n.* a collection of per-

**Assemble**, as-sem'bl, *v.t.* to call or bring *to* the *same* place, or together: to collect.—*v.i.* to meet together. [Fr. *assembler*, Low Lat. *assimulare*—L. *ad*, to, *simul*, together, at the same time ; Gr. *homos*, A.S. *sam*, same ; Sans. *sam*, together.]

**Assembly**, as-sem'bli, *n.* a collection of individuals assembled in the same place for any purpose.

**Assent**, as-sent', *v.i.*, *to think with:* agree.—*n.* an agreeing or acquiescence : compliance.—*adv.* **Assent'ingly**. [L.—*ad*, to, *sentio*, to think.]

**Assert**, as-sèrt', *v.t.* to declare strongly: to affirm. [L. *assero*, *assertum*, to lay hold of, declare—*ad*, to, *sero*, to join, knit.]

**Assertion**, as-sèr'shun, *n.* affirmation.

**Assess**, as-ses', *v.t.* to fix the amount of, as a tax : to tax: to fix the value or profits of, for taxation : to estimate.—*adj.* **Assess'able**. [Fr. *asseoir*—L. *assidere*, *assessum*, to sit by, esp. of judges in a court (in Low L. to set, fix a tax), from *ad*, to, *sedeo*, to sit.]

**Assessment**, as-ses'ment, *n.* act of assessing : a valuation for the purpose of taxation : a tax.

**Assessor**, as-ses'or, *n.* a legal adviser who sits beside a magistrate.—*adj.* **Assessorial**, as-ses-ō'ri-al. [See **Assess**.]

**Assets**, as'sets, *n.pl.* the property of a deceased or insolvent person, considered as chargeable for all debts, &c. : the entire property of all sorts belonging to a merchant or to a trading association. [M.E. *aseth*, Fr. *assez*, enough—L. *ad*, to, *satis*, enough.]

**Asseverate**, as-sev'èr-āt, *v.t.* to declare *seriously* or solemnly.—*n.* **Assevera'tion**. [L. *assevero*, *-atum*—*ad*, to, *severus*, serious. See **Severe**.]

**Assiduity**, as-sid-ū'i-ti, *n.* constant application or diligence. [L. *assiduitas*—*assiduus*. See **Assiduous**.]

**Assiduous**, as-sid'ū-us, *adj.* constant or unwearied in application : diligent.—*adv.* **Assid'uously**.—*n.* **Assid'uousness**. [L. *assiduus*, sitting close at—*ad*, to, at, *sedeo*, to sit.]

**Assign**, as-sīn', *v.t.*, *to sign* or *mark out to* one : to allot : to appoint : to allege : to transfer.—*n.* one to whom any property or right is made over. —**Assignable**, as-sīn'a-bl, *adj.* that may be assigned. [Fr. *assigner*—L. *assignare*, to mark out—*ad*, to, *signum*, a mark or sign.]

**Assignation**, as-sig-nā'shun, *n.* an appointment to meet, used chiefly of love-appointments : the making over of anything to another.

**Assignee**, as-sin-ē', *n.* one to whom any right or property is assigned :—*pl.* the trustees of a sequestrated estate.

**Assignment**, as-sīn'ment, *n.* act of assigning : anything assigned : the writing by which a transfer is made.

**Assimilate**, as-sim'il-āt, *v.t.*, *to make similar* or like *to*: to convert into a like substance, as food in our bodies.—*n.* **Assimilation**. [L. *assimilo, -atum—ad*, to, *similis*, like.]

**Assimilative**, as-sim'il-āt-iv. *adj.* having the power or tendency to assimilate.

**Assist**, as-sist', *v.t.* to help. [L. *assisto*, to stand by—*ad*, to, *sisto*, Gr. *histēmi*, to make to stand.]

**Assistance**, as-sist'ans, *n.* help : relief.

**Assistant**, as-sist'ant, *adj.* helping or lending aid. —*n.* one who assists : a helper.

**Assize**, as-sīz', *v.t.*, *to assess* : to set or fix the quantity or price.—*n.* a statute settling the weight, measure, or price of anything :—*pl.* the sessions or sittings of a court held in counties twice a year, at which causes are tried by a judge and jury. [O. Fr. *assise*, an assembly of judges, a set rate—*asseoir*—L. *assideo*.]

**Assizer**, as-sīz'ėr, *n.* an officer who inspects weights and measures.

**Associate**, as-sō'shi-āt, *v.t.* to join with, as a friend or partner : to unite in the same body.—*v.i.* to keep company with : to combine or unite. [L. *associo—ad*, to, *socius*, a companion.]

**Associate**, as-sō'shi-āt. *adj.* joined or connected with.—*n.* one joined or connected with another : a companion, friend, partner, or ally.

**Association**, as-sō-shi-ā'shun, *n.*, *act of associating* : union or combination : a society of persons joined together to promote some object.

**Assoilzie**, as-soil'yē, *v.* to free one accused from a charge ; a Scotch law term, the same as the archaic *assoil*, to absolve from sin, discharge, pardon. [Through Fr. from L. *absolvere*.]

**Assonance**, as'son-ans, *n.* a correspondence *in sound* : in Sp. and Port. poetry, a kind of rhyme, consisting in the coincidence of the vowels of the corresponding syllables, without regard to the consonants. [L. *ad*, to, *sonans*, sounding.]

**Assonant**, as'son-ant, *adj.* resembling in sound.

**Assort**, as-sort', *v.t.* to separate into classes : to arrange.—*v.i.* to agree or be in accordance with. [Fr. *assortir*—L. *ad*, to, *sors*, a lot.]

**Assortment**, as-sort'ment, *n.* act of assorting : quantity or number of things assorted : variety.

**Assuage**, as-swāj', *v.t.* to soften, mitigate, or allay.—*v.i.* to abate or subside. [O. Fr., formed as if from a L. *assuaviare—suavis*, mild.]

**Assuagement**, as-swāj'ment, *n.* abatement : mitigation.                                   [Suasive.]

**Assuasive**, as-swā'siv, *adj.* softening, mild. [See

**Assume**, as-sūm', *v.t.* to take upon one's self : to take for granted : to arrogate : to pretend to possess.—*v.i.* to claim unduly : to be arrogant. [L.—*ad*, to, *sumo, sumptum*, to take.]

**Assuming**. as-sūm'ing, *adj.* haughty : arrogant.

**Assumption**, as-sum'shun, *n.* act of assuming : a supposition. [L. See Assume.]

**Assurance**, ash-shoor'ans, *n.* confidence : feeling of certainty : impudence : positive declaration : insurance, as applied to lives.

**Assure**, ash-shoor', *v.t.* to make *sure* or *secure* : to give confidence : to tell positively : to insure. [Fr. *assurer*—*ad* and *sûr*, sure. See **Sure**.]

**Assured**, ash-shoord', *adj.* certain : without doubt : insured : overbold.—*adv.* **Assur'edly**.— *n.* **Assur'edness**.

**Aster**, as'tėr, *n.* a genus of plants with compound flowers, like little *stars*. [Gr. *astēr*, a star.]

**Asterisk**, as'tėr-isk, *n.* a *star*, used in printing, thus*. [Gr. *asteriskos*, dim. of *astēr*, a star.]

**Astern**, a-stėrn', *adv.* on the *stern*: towards the hinder part of a ship: behind. [See **Stern**, *n.*]

**Asteroid**, as'tėr-oid, *n.* one of the minor planets

revolving between Mars and Jupiter.—*adj.*

**Asteroid'al**. [Gr. *astēr*, a star, *eidos*, form.]

**Asthma**, ast'ma, *n.* a chronic disorder of the organs of respiration. [Gr.—*aō, aēmi*, to breathe hard.]                 [or affected by asthma.]

**Asthmatic**, -al, ast-mat'ik, -al, *adj.* pertaining to

**Astonied**, as-ton'id, *pa.p.* of obs. v. *Astony*.

**Astonish**, as-ton'ish, *v.t.* to impress with sudden surprise or wonder : to amaze. [M. E. *astonien*, due to a confusion of A.S. *stunian* (see **Stun**) and O. Fr. *estonner* (Fr. *étonner*)—Low L. *extonare*—L. *ex*, out, *tonare*, to thunder.]

**Astonishing**, as-ton'ish-ing, *adj.* very wonderful : amazing.—*adv.* **Aston'ishingly**.     [wonder.

**Astonishment**. as-ton'ish-ment, *n.* amazement :

**Astound**, as-townd', *v.t.* to amaze. [M.E. *astonien* ; a doublet of **Astonish**.]

**Astragal**, as'tra-gal, *n.* (*arch.*) a small semicircular moulding or bead encircling a column : a round moulding near the mouth of a cannon. [Gr. *astragalos*, one of the vertebræ, a moulding.]

**Astral**, as'tral, *adj.* belonging to the *stars* : starry. [L. *astrum*, a star ; conn. with **Star**.]

**Astray**, a-strā', *adv.* out of the right way. [Prefix *a*, on, and **Stray**.]

**Astriction**, as-trik'shun, *n.* a *binding* or contraction. [L. See **Astringent**.]

**Astride**, a-strīd', *adv.* with the legs apart, or across. [Pfx. *a*, on, and **Stride**.]

**Astringent**, as-trinj'ent, *adj.*, *binding* : contracting : strengthening.—*n.* a medicine that causes contraction.—*adv.* **Astring'ently**.—*n.* **Astring'ency**. [L. *astringo—ad*, to, *stringo*, to bind.]

**Astrolabe**, as'trō-lāb, *n.* an instrument for measuring the altitudes of the sun or stars at sea, now superseded by Hadley's quadrant and sextant. [Gr. *astron*. a star, *lab, lambano*. I take.]

**Astrologer**, as-trol'o-jėr, *n.* one versed in astrology.

**Astrology**, as-trol'o-ji, *n.* the infant stage of the *science* of the *stars* (now called *Astronomy*) : it was occupied chiefly in foretelling events from the positions of the heavenly bodies.—*adj.* **Astrolog'ic**, -al.—*adv.* **Astrolog'ically**. [Gr. *astrologia—astron*, star, *logos*, knowledge.]

**Astronomer**, as-tron'o-mėr, *n.* one versed in astronomy.

**Astronomy**, as-tron'om-i, *n.* the *laws* or science of the *stars* or heavenly bodies.—*adj.* **Astronom'ic**.—*adv.* **Astronom'ically**. [Gr. *astronomia—astron*, star, *nomos*, a law.]

**Astute**, ast-ūt', *adj.*, *crafty* : cunning : shrewd : sagacious.—*adv.* **Astute'ly**.—*n.* **Astute'ness**. [L. *astutus—astus*, craft, akin perhaps to **Acute**.]

**Asunder**, a-sun'dėr, *adv.* apart : into parts : separately. [Pfx. *a* = on, and **Sunder**.]

**Asylum**, a-sīl'um, *n.* a place of refuge for debtors and for such as were accused of some crime : an institution for the care or relief of the unfortunate, such as the blind or insane : any place of refuge or protection. [L.—Gr. *asylon—a*, priv., *svlē*, right of seizure.]

**Asymptote**, a'sim-tōt, *n.* (*math.*) a line that continually approaches nearer to some curve without ever meeting it.—*adj.* **Asymptot'ical**. [Gr. *asymptōtos*, not coinciding—*a*, not, *syn*, with, *ptōtos*, apt to fall—*piptō*, to fall.]

**At**, at, *prep.* denoting presence, nearness, or relation. [A.S. *æt* ; cog. with Goth. and Ice. *at*, L. *ad* ; Sans. *adhi*, on.]

**Atavism**, at'av-izm, *n.* the recurrence of any peculiarity or disease of an *ancestor* in a later generation. [L. *atavus—avus*, a grandfather.]

**Ate**, āt or et, did eat, *pa.t.* of **Eat**.

**Athanasian**, ath-a-nāz'yan, *adj.* relating to *Athanasius*, or to the creed attributed to him.

**Atheism**, ā'the-izm, *n.* disbelief in the existence of God. [Fr. *athéisme*—Gr. *a*, priv., and *theos*, God.]         [existence of God.

**Atheist**, ā'the-ist, *n.* one who disbelieves in the

**Atheistic, -al**, ā-the-ist'ik, -al, *adj.* relating to or containing atheism.—*adv.* **Atheist'ically.**

**Athenæum, Atheneum**, ath-e-nē'um, *n.* a temple of *Athēna* or Minerva at Athens, in which scholars and poets read their works: a public institution for lectures, reading, &c. [Gr. *Athēnaion*—*Athēna* or *Athēnē*, the goddess Minerva.]

**Athenian**, a-thē'ni-an, *adj., relating to Athens*, the capital of Greece.—*n.* a native of Athens.

**Athirst**, a-thèrst', *adj.*, thirsty: eager for. [A.S. *of*, very, and **Thirst.**]

**Athlete**, ath'lēt, *n., a contender* for victory in feats of strength: one vigorous in body or mind. [Gr. *athlētēs*—*athlos*, contest.]

**Athletic**, ath-let'ik, *adj.* relating to athletics: strong, vigorous.

**Athletics**, ath-let'iks, *n.* the art of wrestling, running, &c. : athletic exercises.

**Athwart**, a-thwawrt', *prep.* across.—*adv.* sidewise: wrongly: perplexingly. [Prefix *a*, on, and **Thwart.**]

**Atlantean**, at-lan-tē'an, *adj., relating to*, or like *Atlas*: strong: gigantic. [See **Atlas.**]

**Atlantes**, at-lan'tēz, *n.pl.* figures of men used instead of columns. [From **Atlas.**]

**Atlantic**, at-lan'tik, *adj.* pertaining to *Atlas*, or to the *Atlantic* Ocean.—*n.* the ocean between Europe, Africa, and America. [From Mount *Atlas*, in the north-west of Africa.]

**Atlas**, at'las, *n.* a collection of maps. [Gr. *Atlas* (the bearer), a god who *bore* the world on his shoulders, and whose figure used to be given on the title-page of atlases—prob. from *a* (euphonic), and *tlaō*, to bear.]

**Atmosphere**, at'mo-sfēr, *n.* the air that surrounds the earth: (*fig.*) any surrounding influence. [Gr. *atmos*, air, *sphaira*, a sphere.]

**Atmospheric, -al**, at-mo-sfer'ik, -al, *adj.* of or depending on the atmosphere.

**Atom**, at'om, *n.* a particle of matter so small that it *cannot be cut* or *divided*: anything very small.—*adjs.* **Atomic**, a-tom'ik, **Atomical**, a-tom'ik-al. [Gr. *atomos*—*a*, not, *temnō*, to cut.]

**Atomism**, at'om-izm, *n.* the doctrine that *atoms* arranged themselves into the universe.

**Atomist**, at'om-ist, *n., one who believes in atomism.*

**Atone**, at-ōn', *v.i.* (with *for*) to give satisfaction or make reparation.—*v.t.* to expiate. [*At* and *one*, as if to set at one, reconcile; the old pronunciation of *one* is here preserved, as in *only*.]

**Atonement**, at-ōn'ment, *n.* the act of atoning: reconciliation: expiation: reparation.

**Atrabiliary**, at-ra-bil'yar-i, *adj.* of a melancholy temperament: hypochondriac. [L. *ater, atra*, black, *bilis*, gall, bile. See **Bile.**]

**Atrocious**, a-trō'shus, *adj.* extremely *cruel* or wicked: heinous. — *adv.* **Atro'ciously.** — *n.* **Atro'ciousness.** [L. *atrox, atrocis*, cruel.]

**Atrocity**, a-tros'i-ti, *n.* shocking wickedness or cruelty.

**Atrophy**, a'trof-i, *n.* a wasting away from want of nourishment owing to some defect in the organs of nutrition. [Gr. *a*, priv., and *trophē*, nourishment.]

**Attach**, at-tach', *v.t.* to bind or fasten: to seize:

to gain over. [Fr. *attacher*, from *à* (—L. *ad*) and **Tack.**]

**Attachable**, at-tach'a-bl, *adj.* that may be attached.

**Attaché**, at-tash-ā', *n.* a young diplomatist attached to the suite of an ambassador. [Fr.]

**Attachment**, at-tach'ment, *n.* a bond of fidelity or affection: the seizure of any one's goods or person by virtue of a legal process.

**Attack**, at-tak', *v.t.* to fall upon violently: to assault: to assail with unfriendly words or writing.—*n.* an assault or onset: severe criticism or calumny. [Fr. *attaquer*. See **Attach**, of which it is a doublet.]

**Attain**, at-tān', *v.t.* to reach or gain by effort: to obtain.—*v.i.* to come or arrive: to reach. [Fr. *atteindre*—L. *attingo, -ere*—*ad*, to, *tango*, to touch.]         [attainable.

**Attainability**, at-tān-a-bil'i-ti, *n.* state of being

**Attainable**, at-tān'a-bl, *adj.* that may be reached. —*n.* **Attain'ableness.**

**Attainder**, at-tān'dèr, *n.* act of attainting : (*law*) loss of civil rights through conviction for high treason. [Fr. *atteindre*, to come to, reach; O. Fr. *attaindre*, to convict, from L. *attingo*. See **Attain.**]

**Attainment**, at-tān'ment, *n.* act of attaining: the thing attained: acquisition.

**Attaint**, at-tānt', *v.t.* to convict: to deprive of rights for being convicted of treason. [See **Attainder, Attain.**]

**Attar of roses.** See **Otto.**

**Attemper**, at-tem'pèr, *v.t.* to mix in due proportion: to modify or moderate: to adapt. [L. *attempero*—*ad*, to, and *tempero*. See **Temper.**]

**Attempt**, at-temt', *v.t., to try* or endeavour: to make an effort or attack upon.—*v.i.* to make an attempt or trial.—*n.* a trial: endeavour or effort. [Fr. *attenter*—L. *attento*—*ad*, and *tempto, tento*, to try—*tendo*, to stretch.]

**Attend**, at-tend', *v.t.* to give heed to : to wait on or accompany: to be present at : to wait for.— *v.i.* to yield attention : to wait. [L. *attendo*— *ad*, to, *tendo*, to stretch.]

**Attendance**, at-tend'ans, *n.* act of attending: presence : the persons attending.

**Attendant**, at-tend'ant, *adj.* giving attendance : accompanying.—*n.* one who attends or accompanies : a servant : what accompanies or follows.

**Attent**, at-tent', *adj.* (*B.*) giving attention.

**Attention**, at-ten'shun, *n.* act of attending : steady application of the mind : heed : care. [L. *attentio*—*attendo*. See **Attend.**]

**Attentive**, at-tent'iv, *adj.* full of attention : mindful.—*adv.* **Attent'ively.**—*n.* **Attent'iveness.**

**Attenuate**, at-ten'ū-āt, *v.t., to make thin* or lean: to break down into finer parts.—*v.i.* to become thin or fine : to grow less. [L. *attenuo, -atum* —*ad*, to, *tenuis*, thin.]

**Attenuate**, at-ten'ū-āt, **Attenuated**, at-ten'ū-āt-ed, *adj.* made thin or slender: made less viscid.—*n.* **Attenuation**, at-ten-ū-ā'shun.

**Attest**, at-test', *v.t., to testify* or *bear witness to*: to affirm : to give proof of, to manifest. [L. *attestor*—*ad*, to, *testis*, a witness.]

**Attestation**, at-test-ā'shun, *n.* act of attesting.

**Attic**, at'ik, *adj., pertaining to Attica* or to Athens : chaste, elegant.—*n.* **Att'icism**, a chaste, elegant expression. [L. *atticus*—Gr.]

**Attic**, at'ik, *n.* (*arch.*) a low story above the cornice that terminates the main part of an elevation : a sky-lighted room in the roof of a house. [Ety. dub.]

**Attire**, at-tīr′, *v.t.* to dress, array, or adorn : to prepare.—*n.* dress : ornamental dress : (*B.*) a woman's head-dress. [O. Fr. *atirer*, from *a* = *ad*, and a Teut. root found in Ger. *zier*, ornament, A.S. *tir*, splendour. See **Tire**, dress.]

**Attitude**, at′ti-tūd, *n.* posture or position : gesture.—*adj.* **Attitud′inal**. [Fr., from It. *attitudine*, a fit position—L. *aptitudo—aptus*, fit.]

**Attitudinise**, at-ti-tūd-in-īz, *v.i.* to assume affected attitudes.

**Attorney**, at-tur′ni, *n.* one legally authorised to act for another : one legally qualified to manage cases in a court of law : a solicitor : a solicitor or attorney prepares cases and does general law business, while a barrister pleads before the courts :—*pl.* **Attor′neys**.—*n.* **Attorney-ship**, at-tur′ni-ship. [O. Fr. *atorné*, Low L. *attornatus—atorno*, to commit business to another—L. *ad*, to, and *torno*, to turn.]

**Attorney-general**, at-tur′ni-jen′ėr-al, *n.* in England, the chief law-officer of the crown, whose duty it is to manage cases in which the crown is interested.

**Attract**, at-trakt′, *v.t.*, *to draw to* or cause to approach : to allure : to entice. [L. *attraho, attractus—ad*, to, *traho*, to draw.]

**Attractable**, at-trakt′a-bl, *adj.*, *that may be attracted*.—*n.* **Attractabil′ity**.

**Attraction**, at-trak′shun, *n.*, *act of attracting* : the force which draws or tends to draw bodies or their particles to each other : that which attracts.

**Attractive**, at-trakt′iv, *adj.*, *having the power of attracting* : alluring.—*advs.* **Attract′ively**, **Attract′ingly**.—*n.* **Attract′iveness**.

**Attribute**, at-trib′ūt, *v.t.* to ascribe, assign, or consider as belonging.—*adj.* **Attrib′utable**. [L. *attribuo, -tributum—ad*, to, *tribuo*, to give.]

**Attribute**, at′trib-ūt, *n.* that which is attributed : that which is inherent in : that which can be predicated of anything : a quality or property.

**Attribution**, at-trib-ū′shun, *n.* act of attributing : that which is attributed : commendation.

**Attributive**, at-trib′ūt-iv, *adj.* expressing an attribute.—*n.* a word denoting an attribute.

**Attrition**, at-trish′un, *n.* the *rubbing* of one thing against another : a wearing by friction. [L. *ad*, and *tero, tritum*, to rub.]

**Attune**, at-tūn′, *v.t.*, *to put in tune* : to make one sound accord with another : to arrange fitly. [L. *ad*, to, and **Tune**.]

**Auburn**, aw′burn, *adj.* reddish brown. [The old meaning was a light yellow, or lightish hue ; Low L. *alburnus*, whitish—L. *albus*, white.]

**Auction**, awk′shun, *n.* a public sale in which one bidder *increases* the price on another, and the articles go to whom he bids highest. [L. *auctio*, an increasing—*augeo, auctum*, to increase.]

**Auctioneer**, awk-shun-ēr′, *n.* one who is licensed to sell by auction.

**Audacious**, aw-dā′shus, *adj.*, *daring* : bold : impudent.—*adv.* **Auda′ciously**.—*ns.* **Auda′ciousness**, **Audacity**, aw-das′i-ti. [Fr. *audacieux*—L. *audax—audeo*, to dare.]

**Audible**, awd′i-bl, *adj.*, *able to be heard*.—*adv.* **Aud′ibly**.—*n.* **Aud′ibleness**. [L. *audibilis—audio*, to hear, conn. with Gr. *ous, ōtos*, the ear.]

**Audience**, awd′i-ens, *n.* the act of hearing : admittance to a hearing : an assembly of hearers.

**Audit**, awd′it, *n.* an examination of accounts by one or more duly authorised persons.—*v.t.* to examine and adjust. [L. *auditus*, a hearing—*audio*, to hear. See **Audible**.]

**Auditor**, awd′it-or, *n.*, *a hearer :* one who audits accounts.—*n.* **Aud′itorship**.

**Auditorium**, awd-it-or′i-um, *n.* in an opera-house, public hall, or the like, the space allotted to the hearers.

**Auditory**, awd′it-or-i, *adj.* relating to the sense of *hearing*.—*n.* an audience : a place where lectures, &c., are heard.

**Augean**, aw-jē′an, *adj.* filthy : difficult. [From *Augeas*, a fabled king of Elis in Greece, whose stalls, containing 3000 cattle, and uncleaned for 30 years, were cleaned by Hercules in one day.]

**Auger**, aw′gėr, *n.* a carpenter's tool used for boring holes in wood. [A corr. of *nauger*, A.S. *nafegar—nafu*, a nave of a wheel, *gar*, a piercer. See **Nave** (of a wheel), **Gore**, a triangular piece.]

**Aught**, awt, *n.* a *whit :* ought : anything : a part. [A.S. *awiht—a*, short for *an*, one, and *wiht*, a wight, a thing.]

**Augment**, awg-ment′, *v.t.* to *increase :* to make larger.—*v.i.* to grow larger. [L. *augmentum*, increase—*augeo*, to increase, Gr. *auxanō*.]

**Augment**, awg′ment, *n.* increase : (*gram.*) a prefix to a word. [addition.

**Augmentation**, awg-ment-ā′shun, *n.* increase :

**Augmentative**, awg-ment′at-iv, *adj.* having the quality or power of augmenting.—*n.* (*gram.*) a word formed from another to express increase of its meaning.

**Augur**, aw′gur, *n.* among the Romans, one who foretold events by observing the flight and the cries of birds : a diviner : a soothsayer.—*v.t.* to foretell from signs.—*v.i.* to guess or conjecture. [L., prob. from *avis*, bird, and root *gar*, in L. *garrire*, to chatter Sans. *gir*, speech.]

**Augury**, aw′gūr-i, *n.* the art or practice of auguring : an omen.—*adj.* **Augural**, aw′gūr-al. [L. *augurium—augur*.]

**August**, aw-gust′, *adj.* venerable : imposing : majestic.—*adv.* **August′ly**.—*n.* **August′ness**. [L. *augustus—augeo*, to increase, honour.]

**August**, aw′gust, *n.* the eighth month of the year, so called after Cæsar *Augustus*, one of the Roman emperors.

**Augustan**, aw-gust′an, *adj.* pertaining to *Augustus* (nephew of Julius Cæsar, and one of the greatest Roman emperors) or to the time in which he lived : classic : refined.

**Augustine**, aw-gust′in, **Augustinian**, aw-gustin′i-an, *n.* one of an order of monks, so called from *St Augustine*.

**Auk**, awk, *n.* a web-footed sea-bird, found in the Northern Seas. [Low L. *alca*, Ice. *alka*.]

**Aulic**, awl′ik, *adj.* pertaining to a royal court. [L. *aulicus—aula*, Gr. *aulē*, a royal court.]

**Aunt**, änt, *n.* a father's or a mother's sister. [O. Fr. *ante*—L. *amita*, a father's sister.]

**Aurelia**, awr-ēl′ya, *n.* the chrysalis of an insect, from its *golden* colour. [L. *aurum*, gold.]

**Aureola**, awr-ē′o-la, **Aureole**, awr′e-ōl, *n.*, *the gold-coloured* light or halo with which painters surround the head of Christ and the saints. [L. *aureolus*, dim. of *aureus*, golden.]

**Auricle**, awr′i-kl, *n.* the external ear :—*pl.* the two ear-like cavities of the heart. [L. *auricula*, dim. of *auris*, the ear.]

**Auricula**, awr-ik′ul-a, *n.* a species of primrose, also called bear's-*ear*, from the shape of its leaf.

**Auricular**, awr-ik′ul-ar, *adj.*, *pertaining to the ear :* known by hearing, or by report.—**Auricular confession**, secret, told in the ear.—*adv.* **Auric′ularly**. [See **Auricle**.]

**Auriculate**, awr-ik′ūl-āt, *adj.*, *ear-shaped*. [Low L. *auriculatus*—L. *auricula*.]

**Auriferous**, awr-if'ĕr-us, *adj.*, *bearing* or *yielding gold*. [L. *aurifer—aurum*, gold, *fero*, to bear.]

**Auriform**, awr'i-form, *adj.*, *ear-shaped*. [L. *auris*, ear, and **Form**.]

**Aurist**, awr'ist, *n.* one skilled in diseases of the *ear*.

**Aurochs**, awr'oks, *n.* the European bison or wild ox. [Ger. *auerochs*, O. Ger. *urohso*—Ger. *ur* (L. *urus*, Gr. *ouros*), a kind of wild ox, and *ochs*, ox.]

**Aurora**, aw-rō'ra, *n.* the dawn: in poetry, the goddess of dawn. [L. for *ausosa;* cog. with Gr. *ēōs;* from a root seen in Sans. *ush*, to burn.]

**Aurora Borealis**, aw-rō'ra bō-rē-ā'lis, *n.*, *the northern aurora* or light: a meteor seen in northern latitudes.—**Aurora Australis**, aws-trā'lis, *n.* a meteor in the S. hemisphere. [L. *borealis*, northern—*boreas*, the north wind. See **Austral**.]

**Auroral**, aw-rō'ral, *adj.* relating to the aurora.

**Auscultation**, aws-kult-ā'shun, *n.* the art of discovering diseases of the lungs and heart by applying the ear to the chest, or to a tube in contact with the chest. [L. *ausculto*, to listen, from *ausicula* for *auricula*. See **Auricle**.]

**Auscultatory**, aws-kult'a-tor-i, *adj.* relating to auscultation.

**Auspice**, aw'spis, *n.* an omen drawn from *observing birds:* augury—generally used in *pl.* **Auspices**, aw'spis-ez, protection: patronage. [Fr. —L. *auspicium—auspex*, *auspicis*, a bird-seer, from *avis*, a bird, *specio*, to observe.]

**Auspicious**, aw-spish'us, *adj.* having good auspices or omens of success: favourable: fortunate.—*adv.* **Auspi'ciously**.—*n.* **Auspi'ciousness**.

**Austere**, aws-tēr', *adj.* harsh: severe: stern.— *adv.* **Austere'ly**. [L. *austerus*—Gr. *austēros—auō*, to dry.]

**Austereness**, aws-tēr'nes, **Austerity**, aws-ter'it-i, *n.* quality of being austere: severity of manners or life: harshness.

**Austral**, aws'tral, *adj.*, *southern*. [L. *australis —auster*, the south wind.]

**Australasian**, aws-tral-ā'shi-an, *adj.*, *pertaining to Australasia*, or the countries that lie to the *south of Asia*.

**Australian**, aws-trā'li-an, *adj.*, *of* or pertaining to *Australia*, a large island between the Indian and Pacific Oceans.—*n.* a native of Australia.

**Austrian**, aws'tri-an, *adj.*, *of* or pertaining to *Austria*, an empire of Central Europe.—*n.* A native of Austria.

**Authentic, -al**, aw-thent'ik, -al, *adj.* having authority or genuineness as if from the *author's own hand:* original: genuine: true.—*adv.* **Authen'tically**. [Gr. *authentēs*, one who does anything with his own hand—*autos*, self.]

**Authenticate**, aw-thent'ik-āt, *v.t.* to make authentic: to prove genuine.

**Authentication**, aw-thent-ik-ā'shun, *n.* act of authenticating: confirmation.

**Authenticity**, aw-thent-is'it-i, *n.* quality of being authentic: genuineness.

**Author**, awth'or, *n.*, *one who originates* or brings into being: a beginner or first mover: the writer of an original book:—*fem.* **Auth'oress**. [Fr. *auteur*, L. *auctor—augeo*, *auctum*, to cause things to increase, to produce.]

**Authorise**, awth'or-īz, *v.t.* to give authority to: to sanction: to establish by authority.—*n.* **Authorisa'tion**.

**Authoritative**, awth-or'it-āt-iv, *adj.* having authority: dictatorial.—*adv.* **Author'itatively**. —*n.* **Author'itativeness**.

**Authority**, awth-or'it-i, *n.* legal power or right: power derived from office or character: weight of testimony: permission:—*pl.* **Author'ities**, precedents: opinions or sayings carrying weight: persons in power. [author.

**Authorship**, awth'or-ship, *n.* state of being an author.

**Autobiographer**, aw-to-bī-og'raf-ėr, *n.* one who writes his own life.

**Autobiography**, aw-to-bī-og'raf-i, *n.*, *the biography* or *life* of a person *written by himself*. —*adjs.* **Autobiograph'ic, Autobiograph'ical**. [Gr. *autos*, one's self, *bios*, life, *graphō*, to write.]

**Autocracy**, aw-tok'ras-i, *n.* an absolute government by one man: despotism. [Gr. *autos*, self, *kratos*, power.]

**Autocrat**, aw'to-krat, *n.* one who rules by *his own power:* an absolute sovereign.—*adj.* **Autocrat'ic**. [Gr. *autokratēs—autos*, self, *kratos*, power.]

**Auto-da-fe**, aw'to-da-fā', *n.* the execution of persons who were condemned by the Inquisition to be burned:—*pl.* **Autos-da-fe**. [Port., from *auto*, L. *actus*, act; *da*, L. *de*, of; and *fe*, L. *fides*, faith—*an act of faith*.]

**Autograph**, aw'to-graf, *n.*, *one's own handwriting:* a signature.—*adj.* **Autograph'ic**. [Gr. *autos*, self, *graphē*, writing.]

**Automatism**, aw-tom'at-izm, *n.* automatic action: power of self-moving.

**Automaton**, aw-tom'a-ton, *n.*, *a self-moving machine*, or one which moves by concealed machinery:—*pl.* **Autom'atons** or **Autom'ata**.— *adjs.* **Automat'ic, Automat'ical**. [Gr. *automatos*, self-moving—*autos*, self, and a stem *mat-*, to strive after, to move.]

**Autonomy**, aw-ton'om-i, *n.* the power or right of *self-government*.—*adj.* **Auton'omous**, self-governing. [Gr.—*autos*, and *nomos*, law.]

**Autopsy**, aw'top-si, *n.*, *personal inspection*, esp. the examination of a body after death. [Gr.— *autos*, self, and *opsis*, sight.]

**Autumn**, aw'tum, *n.* the third season of the year when fruits are gathered in, popularly comprising the months of August, September, and October.—*adj.* **Autum'nal**. [L. *autumnus*, *auctumnus—augeo*, *auctum*, to increase, to produce.]

**Auxiliary**, awg-zil'yar-i, *adj.* helping.—*n.* a helper: an assistant: (*gram.*) a verb that helps to form the moods and tenses of other verbs. [L.—*auxilium*, help—*augeo*, to increase.]

**Avail**, a-vāl', *v.t.* *to be of value* or service to: to benefit.—*v.i.* to be of use: to answer the purpose.—*n.* benefit: profit: service. [Fr.—L. *ad*, to, *valeo*, to be strong, to be worth.]

**Available**, a-vāl'a-bl, *adj.* that one may avail one's self of: profitable: suitable.—*adv.* **Avail'ably**.

**Availableness**, a-vāl'a-bl-nes, **Availability**, a-vāl-a-bil'i-ti, *n.* quality of being available: power in promoting an end in view: validity.

**Avalanche**, av'al-ansh, *n.* a mass of snow and ice sliding down from a mountain: a snow-slip. [Fr.—*avaler*, to slip down—L. *ad*, to, *vallis*, a valley.]

**Avarice**, av'ar-is, *n.* eager desire for wealth: covetousness. [Fr.—L. *avaritia—avarus*, greedy— *aveo*, to pant after.]

**Avaricious**, av-ar-ish'us, *adj.* extremely covetous: greedy.—*adv.* **Avari'ciously**.—*n.* **Avari'ciousness**.

**Avast**, a-väst', *int.* (*naut.*) *hold fast!* stop! [Dut. *houd vast*, hold fast.]

**Avatar**, a-va-tär', *n.*, *the descent* of a Hindu deity in a visible form: incarnation. [Sans.—*ava*, away, down, and *tara*, passage—*tri*, to cross.]

**Avaunt**, a-vawnt', *int.* move on : begone ! [Fr. *avant*, forward—L. *ab*, from, *ante*, before.]

**Ave**, ā′vē, *n.*, *be well* or *happy*: hail, an address or prayer to the Virgin Mary : in full, *Ave Marī'a*. [L. *aveo*, to be well or propitious.]

**Avenge**, a-venj', *v.t.* (*B.*) to inflict punishment for. —*n.* **Avengement**, a-venj'ment. [Fr. *venger* —L. *vindicare*. See **Vengeance**.]

**Avenger**, a-venj'ėr, *n.* one who avenges.

**Avenue**, av'en-ū, *n.* an alley of trees leading to a house : in Amer. a wide street. [Fr., from L. *ad*, to, *venio*, to come.]

**Aver**, a-vėr', *v.t.* to declare *to be true*: to affirm or declare positively :—*pr.p.* averr'ing ; *pa.p.* averred'. [Fr. *avérer*—L. *ad*, and *verus*, true.]

**Average**, av'ér-āj, *n.* the mean value or quantity of a number of values or quantities.—*adj.* containing a mean value.—*v.t.* to fix an average.— *v.i.* to exist in, or form, a mean quantity. [Low L. *averagium*, carrying service due to a lord by his tenants with their *averia* or cattle ; loss, expense in carrying—*averium*, 'havings', goods, cattle—O. Fr. *aver*—L. *habere*, to have ; confused with Dut. *averij*, Fr. *avarie*—Ar. *awar*, damage ; hence a contribution towards damage to a cargo formerly levied on each merchant in proportion to the goods *carried*.]

**Averment**, a-vėr'ment, *n.* positive assertion.

**Averse**, a-vėrs', *adj.* having a disinclination or hatred : disliking.—*adv.* **Averse'ly**.—*n.* **Averse'ness**. [L. *aversus*, turned away, *pa.p.* of *averto*. See **Avert**.]

**Aversion**, a-vėr'shun, *n.* dislike : hatred : the object of dislike. [See **Avert**.]

**Avert**, a-vėrt', *v.t.* to *turn from* or aside : to prevent. [L. *averto*—*ab*, from, *verto*, to turn.]

**Aviary**, ā'vi-ar-i, *n.* a place for keeping *birds*. [L. *aviarium*—*avis*, a bird.]

**Avidity**, a-vid'it-i, *n.* eagerness : greediness. [L. *aviditas*—*avidus*, greedy—*aveo*, to pant after.]

**Avocation**, a-vo-kā'shun, *n.* formerly and properly, a diversion or distraction from one's regular employment : now, one's proper business = **Vocation** : business which calls for one's time and attention. [L. *avocatio*, a calling away—*ab*, from, *voco*, to call.]

**Avoid**, a-void', *v.t.* to try to escape from : to shun. —*adj.* **Avoid'able**. [Pfx. *a* = Fr. *es* = L. *ex*, out, and **Void**.]

**Avoidance**, a-void'ans, *n.* the act of avoiding or shunning : act of annulling.

**Avoirdupois**, av-ér-dū-poiz', *adj.* or *n.* a system of weights in which the lb. equals 16 oz. [Fr. *avoir du pois*, to have (of the) weight—L. *habeo*, to have, *pensum*, that which is weighed.]

**Avouch**, a-vowch', *v.t.* to avow : to assert or own positively. [Fr. *à*, and O. Fr. *vocher*—L. *voco*, to call. See **Vouch**.]

**Avow**, a-vow', *v.t.* to declare openly : to own or confess.—*adv.* **Avow'edly**.—*adj.* **Avow'able**. [Fr. *avouer*, orig. to swear fealty to—L. *ad*, and *votum*, a vow. See **Vow**.]

**Avowal**, a-vow'al, *n.* a positive declaration : a frank confession.

**Await**, a-wāt', *v.t.* to *wait* or look *for*: to be in store for : to attend. [Through Fr. from root of Ger. *wacht*, a watch. See **Wait**.]

**Awake**, a-wāk', *v.t.* to rouse from sleep : to rouse from a state of inaction.—*v.i.* to cease sleeping : to rouse one's self :—*pa.p.* awāked' or awōke'. —*adj.* not asleep : vigilant. [A.S. *awacan*—*a*- (Ger. *er*-, Goth. *us*-, Ice. *or*-), inten. or causal, and *wacan*, to wake.]

**Awaken**, a-wāk'n, *v.t.* and *v.i.* to awake.

**Awakening**, a-wāk'n-ing, *n.* the act of awaking or ceasing to sleep : a revival of religion.

**Award**, a-wawrd', *v.t.* to adjudge : to determine. —*n.* judgment : final decision, esp. of arbitrators. [O. Fr. *eswardeir* or *esgardeir*, from *es* = L. *ex* and a Teutonic root seen in E. **Ward**.]

**Aware**, a-wār', *adj.* wary : informed. [From an A.S. *gewær*, from prefix *ge*- and *wær*, cautious. See **Wary**.]

**Away**, a-wā', *adv.* out of the way : absent.—*int.* begone !—(I cannot) **Away with** = bear or endure : **Away with** (him) = take away : (make) **Away with** = destroy. [A.S. *aweg* —*a*, on, *weg*, way, (*lit.*) ' on one's way.']

**Awe**, aw, *n.* reverential *fear*: dread.—*v.t.* to strike with or influence by fear. [Ice. *agi*, A.S. *ege*, fear ; cog. with Gael. *eaghal*, Gr. *achos*, anguish. From root *ag*-, seen in **Anger**, **Anxious**.]

**Aweary**, a-wē'ri, *n.* weary. [Pfx. *a*, and **Weary**.]

**Awe-struck**, aw'-struk, *adj.* struck or affected with awe.

**Awful**, aw'fool, *adj.* full of awe.—*adv.* **Aw'fully**. —*n.* **Aw'fulness**.

**Awhile**, a-hwīl', *adv.* for some time : for a short time. [Pfx. *a*, and **While**.]

**Awkward**, awk'ward, *adj.* clumsy : ungraceful. —*adv.* **Awk'wardly**.—*n.* **Awk'wardness**. [M. E. *awk*, contrary, wrong, and A.S. *ward*, direction.]

**Awl**, awl, *n.* a pointed instrument for boring small holes in leather. [A.S. *æl*.]

**Awn**, awn, *n.* a scale or husk : beard of corn or grass.—*adjs.* **Awned**, **Awn'less**. [Ice. *ögn*; Ger. *ahne*; from root *ak*-, sharp, seen in **Acute**.]

**Awning**, awn'ing, *n.* a covering to shelter from the sun's rays. [Ety. dub.]

**Awoke**, a-wōk', did awake—*past tense* of **Awake**.

**Awry**, a-rī', *adj.* twisted to one side : crooked : wrong : perverse.—*adv.* unevenly : perversely. [Pfx. *a*, on, and **Wry**.]

**Axe**, aks, *n.* a well-known instrument for hewing or chopping. [A.S. *æx* ; L. *ascia* ; Gr. *axinē*, perhaps from root *ak*-, sharp.]

**Axiom**, aks'yum, *n.* a self-evident truth : a universally received principle in an art or science.—*adjs.* **Axiomat'ic**, **Axiomat'ical**.— *adv.* **Axiomat'ically**. [Gr. *axiōma*—*axioō*, to think worth, to take for granted—*axios*, worth.]

**Axis**, aks'is, *n.* the *axle*, or the line, real or imaginary, on which a body revolves :—*pl.* **Axes**, aks'ēz.—*adj.* **Ax'ial**. [L. *axis*; cf. Gr. *axōn*, Sans. *aksha*, A.S. *eax*.]

**Axle**, aks'l, **Axle-tree**, aks'l-trē, *n.* the pin or rod in the nave of a wheel on which the wheel turns. [Dim. from A.S. *eax*, an axle ; Sw. *axel*.]

**Ay**, **Aye**, ī, *adv.*, *yea*: yes : indeed.—**Aye**, ī, *n.* a vote in the affirmative. [A form of **Yea**.]

**Ayah**, ā'ya, *n.* a native Indian waiting-maid.

**Aye**, ā, *adv.*, *ever*: always : for ever. [Ice. *ei*, ever, A.S. *a*; conn. with **Age**, **Ever**.]

**Ayry**, ā'ri, *n.* a hawk's nest. [See **Eyry**.]

**Azimuth**, az'im-uth, *n.* the arc of the horizon between the meridian of a place and a vertical circle passing through any celestial body. [Ar. *al samt*, the direction. See **Zenith**.]

**Azote**, a-zōt', *n.* nitrogen, so called because it does not sustain animal life.—*adj.* **Azot'ic**. [Gr. *a*, neg., and *zaō*, to live.]

**Azure**, ā'zhur, *adj.* of a faint *blue*: sky-coloured. —*n.* a delicate blue colour : the sky. [Fr. *azur*, corr. of Low L. *lazur*, *lazulum*, *azolum*, blue ; of Pers. origin.]

# B

**Baa**, bä, *n.* the cry of a sheep.—*v.i.* to cry or bleat as a sheep. [From the sound.]

**Babble**, bab'bl, *v.i.* to speak like a *baby*: to talk childishly: to tell secrets.—*v.t.* to prate: to utter. [E.; connected with Dut. *babbelen*, Ger. *babbeln*, Fr. *babiller*, from *ba, ba*, representing the first attempts of a child to speak.]

**Babble**, bab'bl, **Babblement**, bab'bl-ment, **Babbling**, bab'bling, *n.* idle senseless talk.

**Babbler**, bab'blėr, *n.*, *one who babbles*.

**Babe**, bāb, **Baby**, bā'bi, *n.* an infant: child.—*adj.* **Ba'byish.**—*n.* **Ba'byhood.** [*Ba, ba.* See **Babble**.]

**Babel**, bā'bel, *n.* a confused combination of sounds. [From Heb. *Babel* (confusion), where the language of man was confounded.]

**Baboon**, ba-bōōn', *n.* a species of large monkey, having a long face, dog-like tusks, large lips, and a short tail. [Fr. *babouin*; remoter origin dub.]

**Bacchanal**, bak'ka-nal, **Bacchanalian**, bak-ka-nā'li-an, *n.* a worshipper of *Bacchus*: one who indulges in drunken revels.—*adj.* relating to drunken revels. [L. *Bacchus*, Gr. *Bacchos*, the god of wine.]

**Bacchanalia**, bak-ka-nā'li-a, **Bacchanals**, bak-ka-nalz, *n.pl.* orig. feasts in honour of *Bacchus*: drunken revels.

**Bachelor**, bach'el-or, *n.* an unmarried man: one who has taken his first degree at a university.—*ns.* **Bach'elorhood, Bach'elorship.** [O. Fr. *bacheler*, a young man. Ety. disputed; according to Brachet from Low L. *baccalarius*, a farm-servant, originally a cow-herd; from *baccalia*, a herd of cows; and this from *bacca*, Low L. for *vacca*, a cow.]

**Back**, bak, *n.* the hinder part of the body in man, and the upper part in beasts: the hinder part.—*adv.* to the place from which one came: to a former state or condition: behind: in return: again.—*v.t.* to get upon the back of: to help, as if standing at one's back: to put backward.—*v.i.* to move or go back. [A.S. *bæc*, Sw. *bak*, Dan. *bag*.]

**Backbite**, bak'bīt, *v.t.* to speak evil of any one behind his back or in his absence.—*ns.* **Back'biter, Back'biting.**

**Backbone**, bak'bōn, *n.* the bone of the back, the vertebral column.

**Backdoor**, bak'dōr, *n.* a door in the back part of a building.

**Backed**, bakt, *adj.* provided with a back :—used in composition, as Hump-backed.

**Backer**, bak'ėr, *n.* one who backs or supports another in a contest.

**Backgammon**, bak-gam'un, *n.* a game played by two persons on a board with dice and fifteen men or pieces each. [Ety. dub., perhaps A.S. *bæc*, back, and *gamen*, game.]

**Background**, bak'grownd, *n.* ground at the back: a place of obscurity: the space behind the principal figures of a picture.

**Back-handed**, bak'-hand-ed, *adj.* with the hand turned backward (as of a blow): indirect.

**Back-piece**, bak'-pēs, **Back-plate**, bak'-plāt, *n.* a piece or plate of armour for the back.

**Backsheesh, Backshish**, bak'shĕsh, *n.*, *a gift* or *present* of money, in the East. [Pers.]

**Backslide**, bak-slīd', *v.i.* to slide or fall back in faith or morals :—*pa.p.* backslid' or backslidd'en.—*ns.* **Backslid'er, Backslid'ing.**

**Backstairs**, bak'stàrz, *n.pl.* back or private stairs of a house.—*adj.* secret or underhand.

**Backward**, bak'ward, **Backwards**, bak'wardz, *adv.* towards the back: on the back: towards the past: from a better to a worse state. [**Back** and affix **Ward, Wards,** in the direction of.]

**Backward**, bak'ward, *adj.* keeping back: unwilling: slow: late.—*adv.* **Back'wardly.**—*n.* **Back'wardness.**

**Backwoods**, bak'woodz, *n.pl.*, *the forest* or uncultivated part of a country *beyond* the cleared country, as in N. Amer.—*n.* **Backwoods'man.**

**Bacon**, bā'kn, *n.* swine's flesh salted or pickled and dried. [O. Fr.—O. Dutch, *bak*, a pig.]

**Baconian**, bak-ōn'i-an, *adj.* pertaining to Lord Bacon (1561—1626), or to his philosophy, which was *inductive* or based on *experience*.

**Bad**, bad, *adj.* ill or evil: wicked: hurtful :—*comp.* **Worse**; *superl.* **Worst.** [Ety. dub., perhaps from Celt. *baodh*, foolish, wicked.]

**Baddish**, bad'ish, *adj.* somewhat bad: not very good. [**Bad**, and dim. termination *ish*.]

**Bade**, bad, *past tense* of **Bid**.

**Badge**, baj, *n.* a mark or sign by which one is known or distinguished. [Low L. *bagia*, a mark, *baga*, a ring, from a Teut. root, seen in A.S. *beah*, a ring, mark of distinction.]

**Badger**, baj'ėr, *n.* a burrowing animal about the size of a fox, eagerly hunted by dogs.—*v.t.* to pursue with eagerness, as dogs hunt the badger: to pester or worry. [A corr. of *bladger*—O. Fr. *bladier*, Low L. *bladarius*, a corn-dealer, from *bladum*, corn, because the creature was believed to store up corn. Acc. to Diez, *bladum* is from L. *ablatum*, 'carried away.' See **Ablative**.]

**Badinage**, bad'in-äzh, *n.* light playful talk: banter. [Fr. *badinage—badin*, playful or bantering.]

**Badly**, bad'li, *adv.* in a bad manner: not well: imperfectly: wrongly.—*n.* **Bad'ness.**

**Baffle**, baf'fl, *v.t.* to elude or defeat by artifice: to check or make ineffectual. [O. Fr. *béfler*, to deceive, to mock; It. *beffa*, a scoffing.]

**Bag**, bag, *n.* a sack or pouch.—*v.t.* to put into a bag :—*pr.p.* bagg'ing ; *pa.p.* bagged'. [A.S. *bælg*, bag, belly; Celt. *bag, balg*, belly, wallet.]

**Bagatelle**, bag-a-tel', *n.* a trifle : a game played on a board with nine balls and a cue. [Fr. ; It. *bagatella*, a conjurer's trick, a trifle.]

**Baggage**, bag'āj, *n.* the tents, provisions, and other necessaries of an army: traveller's luggage. [Fr. *bagage*—O. Fr. *bagues*, goods or effects ; from Celt. *bag*, a bundle.]

**Baggage**, bag'āj, *n.* a worthless woman: a saucy female. [Fr. *bagasse*, a prostitute.]

**Bagging**, bag'ing, *n.* cloth or material for bags.

**Baggy**, bag'i, *adj.* loose like a bag.

**Bagman**, bag'man, *n.* a commercial traveller.

**Bagnio**, ban'yō, *n.* a house of ill-fame. [It. *bagno* —L. *balneum*, a bath.]

**Bagpipe**, bag'pīp, *n.* a musical wind-instrument, consisting of a leathern bag, which acts as a bellows, and pipes.—*n.* **Bag'piper.** [tempt.

**Bah.** bä, *int.* an exclamation of disgust or con-

**Bail**, bāl, *n.* one who procures the release of an accused person by becoming *guardian* or security for his appearing in court : the security given.—*v t.* to set a person free by giving security for him : to release on the security of another. [O. Fr. *bail*, a guardian, a tutor ; Low L. *baila*, a nurse, from L. *bajulus*, a carrier.]

**Bail**, bāl, *n.* one of the cross pieces on the top of the wicket in cricket. [O. Fr. *bailles*, sticks, a palisade.]

**Bail**, bāl, *v.t.* to clear (a boat) of water with *buckets*. [Dut. *balie*, a tub, Fr. *baille* (whence Diez derives the Dut. word). Also spelled **Bale**.]

**Bailable**, bāl′a-bl, *adj.* admitting of bail.

**Bailie**, bāl′i, *n.* a municipal officer in Scotland corresponding to an alderman. [Fr. *bailli*, land-steward, officer of justice. See **Bailiff**.]

**Bailiff**, bāl′if, *n.* a sheriff's officer: an agent or land-steward. [O. Fr. *baillif* (old form of *bailli*, see **Bailie**); from root of **Bail**.]

**Bailiwick**, bāl′i-wik, *n.* the jurisdiction of a bailiff. [O. Fr. *baillie*, lordship, authority, and A.S. *wíc*—L. *vicus*, a village, station.]

**Bairn**, bārn, *n.* a child. [Scot. *bairn*, A.S. *bearn* —*beran*, to bear.]

**Bait**, bāt, *n.* food put on a hook to allure fish or make them *bite:* any allurement: a refreshment taken on a journey—*v.t.* to set food as a lure: to give refreshment on a journey.—*v.i.* to take refreshment on a journey. [See **Bait**, *v.*]

**Bait**, bāt, *v.t.* to provoke an animal by inciting dogs to *bite* it: to harass. [Ice. *beita*, from root of **Bite**.]

**Baize**, bās, *n.* a coarse woollen cloth. [From pl. of Fr. *baye;* so called from its colour. See **Bay**, *adj.*]

**Bake**, bāk, *v.t.* to dry, harden, or cook by the heat of the sun or of fire: to prepare food in an oven.—*v.i.* to work as a baker. [A.S. *bacan;* cog. with Ger. *backen*, to bake, Gr. *phōgō*, to roast.]　　　　　　　　　　　　[for baking in.

**Bakehouse**, bāk′hows, *n.* a house or place used

**Baker**, bāk′ėr, *n.* one who bakes bread, &c.

**Bakery**, bāk′ėr-i, *n.* a bakehouse.

**Baking**, bāk′ing, *n.* the process by which bread is baked : the quantity baked at one time.

**Balance**, bal′ans, *n.* an instrument for weighing, usually formed of *two dishes* or scales hanging from a beam supported in the middle: act of weighing two things; equality or just proportion of weight or power, as the *balance of power*; the sum required to make the two sides of an account equal, hence the surplus, or the sum due on an account.—*v.t.* to weigh in a balance : to counterpoise : to compare: to settle, as an account.—*v.i.* to have equal weight or power, &c.: to hesitate or fluctuate. [Fr.—L. *bilanx*, having two scales—*bis*, double, *lanx, lancis*, a dish or scale.]

**Balance-sheet**, bal′ans-shēt, *n.* a sheet of paper shewing a summary and balance of accounts.

**Balcony**, balk′on-i, *n.* a platform or gallery outside the window of a room. [It. *balcone;* from O. Ger. *balcho* (Ger. *balken*), a beam, cog. with E. **Balk** in the obs. sense of beam, partition.]

**Bald**, bawld, *adj.* without hair on the head : bare, unadorned.—*adv.***Bald′ly**.—*n.***Bald′ness**. [Orig. 'shining,' 'white,' Celt. *bal*, 'white' spot: or conn. with **Bold**, which in Goth. *balthai*, meant the 'brave,' 'shining,' Ice. *Baldr, Light*god.']

**Balderdash**, bawl′dėr-dash, *n.* idle, senseless talk: anything jumbled together without judgment. [Ety. dub.]　　　　　　　　　　　　　[head.

**Baldhead**, bawld′hed, *n.* a person bald on the

**Baldrick**, bawld′rik, *n.* a warrior's belt. [O. Fr. *baldric*, from O. Ger. *balderich*, girdle.]

**Bale**, bāl, *n.*, *a ball*, bundle, or package of goods. —*v.t.* to make into bales. [See **Ball**.]

**Bale**, bāl, *v.t.* to throw out water. [See **Bail**.]

**Baleen**, bā-lēn′, *n.* the whalebone of commerce. [Fr.—L. *balæna*, whale.]

**Baleful**, bāl′fool, *adj.* full of misery, destructive : full of sorrow, sad.—*adv.* **Bale′fully**. [Obs. E. *bale*, A.S. *bealo*, Ice. *bōl*, woe, evil.]

**Balk**, bawk, *n.* a hinderance or disappointment.— *v.t.* to check, disappoint, or elude. [A.S. *balca*, a heap or ridge, also a beam, a partition; conn. with **Bar**. See **Balcony**.]

**Ball**, bawl, *n.* anything round: a bullet: a well-known game. [Fr. *balle*, Weigand has shown that this is a Romance word, as in It. *palla*—Gr. *pallō*, to swing, akin to *ballō*, to throw.]

**Ball**, bawl, *n.* an entertainment of dancing. [Fr. *bal*—It. and Low L. *ballare*, to dance, from Gr. *ballō*, to throw, the game of ball-throwing having been associated with music and dancing.]

**Ballad**, ball′ad, *n.* a short narrative poem : a popular song. [Fr. *ballade*, It. *ballata*, from *ballare*, to dance ; a song sung in dancing.]

**Balladmonger**, ball′ad-mung-gėr, *n.* a dealer in ballads.

**Ballast**, bal′last, *n.* heavy matter placed in a ship to keep it steady when it has no cargo : that which renders anything steady.—*v.t.* to load with ballast : to make or keep steady. [Dut.; ety. best seen in Dan. *bag-last* or *ballast*, from *bag*, 'behind,' the **Back**, and *last*, load ; a load placed behind or under to steady a ship.]

**Ballet**, ball′ā, *n.* a theatrical exhibition acted chiefly in dancing. [Fr. dim. of *bal*, a dance.]

**Ballista**, ball-is′ta, *n.* a military engine in the form of a cross-bow, used by the ancients for *throwing* heavy arrows, darts, large stones, &c. [L.—Gr. *ballō*, to throw.]

**Balloon**, ball-oon′, *n.* a large bag, made of light material, and filled with a gas lighter than common air, so as to make it ascend. [Fr. *ballon*— *balle*, a ball ; the *on* is augmentative.]

**Ballot**, bal′ut, *n.*, *a little ball* or ticket used in voting: the act of secret voting by putting a ball or ticket into a box.—*v.i.* to vote by ballot: —*pr.p.* ball′oting ; *pa.p.* ball′oted. [Fr. *ballotte*, dim. of *balle*, a ball. See **Ball**.]

**Ball-proof**, bawl′-prōōf, *adj.* proof against balls discharged from firearms.　　　　　　　[dancing.

**Ballroom**, bawl′rōōm, *n.* a room for balls or

**Balm**, bäm, *n.* an aromatic plant : a fragrant and healing ointment obtained from such a plant : anything that heals or soothes pain. [Fr. *baume*, O. Fr. *basme*—L. *balsamum*. See **Balsam**.]

**Balmy**, bäm′i, *adj.* fragrant : soothing : bearing balm.

**Balsam**, bawl′sam, *n.* the name of certain plants : a resinous oily substance flowing from them. [L. *balsamum*—Gr. *balsamon*—Heb. *baal*, a prince, and *schaman*, oil.]

**Balsamic**, bal-sam′ik, *adj.* soothing.

**Baluster**, bal′ust-ėr, *n.* a small pillar used as a support to the rail of a staircase, &c.—*adj.* **Balustered**, bal′ust-ėrd. [Fr. *balustre*—Low L. *balaustium*—Gr. *balaustion*, the flower of the pomegranate ; from the similarity of form.]

**Balustrade**, bal′ust-rād, *n.* a row of balusters joined by a rail.

**Bamboo**, bam-bōō′, *n.* a gigantic Indian reed or grass, with hollow-jointed stem, and of hard texture. [Malay.]　　　　　[found. [Ety. dub.]

**Bamboozle**, bam-bōō′zl, *v.t.* to deceive : to con-

**Ban**, ban, *n.* a proclamation : a denunciation : a curse. [A.S. *ge-bann*, a proclamation, a widely diffused Teut. word, O. Ger. *pannan*, orig. meaning to 'summon to trial.' See **Abandon**.]

**Banana**, ba-nä′na, *n.* a gigantic herbaceous plant, remarkable for its nutritious fruit.

**Band**, band, *n.*, *that which binds* together : a tie. [A.S. *bend*, from *bindan*, to bind. See **Bind**.]

**Band**, band, *n.* a number of persons *bound* together for any common purpose : a body of musicians.—*v.t.* to bind together.—*v.i.* to associate. [Fr. *bande*, from Ger. *band*, bond, thing used in binding—*binden*, E. **Bind**. See **Banner**.]

**Bandage**, band′āj, *n.* a strip of cloth used to bind up a wound or fracture.—*v.t.* to bind with such.

**Bandana, Bandanna**, ban-dan′a, *n.* a kind of silk or cotton coloured handkerchief, originally from India.

**Bandbox**, band′boks, *n.* a thin kind of box for holding bands, caps, &c.

**Bandit**, ban′dit, *n.* an outlaw : a robber :—*pl.* **Ban′dits** or **Banditt′i**. [It. *bandito*—Low L. *bannire, bandire*, to proclaim, from **Ban**.]

**Bandog**, ban′dog, *n.* properly *band-dog*, a large, fierce dog (which, on account of its fierceness, was kept *bound* or chained).

**Bands**, bandz, *n.pl.* a portion of the dress worn by clergymen, barristers, &c.—a relic of the ancient *amice*.

**Bandy**, ban′di, *n.* a club bent at the end for striking a ball : a game at ball with such a club.— *v.t.* to beat to and fro as with a bandy : to toss from one to another (as words), like playing at bandy :—*pa.p.* ban′died. [Fr. *bander*, to bend —Ger. *band*, a tie, string.] [crooked legs.

**Bandy-legged**, ban′di-legd, *adj.* having bandy or

**Bane**, bān, *n.*, *destruction* : death : mischief : poison. [A.S. *bana*, a murderer ; Ice. *bani*, death.] [fully.

**Baneful**, bān′fool, *adj.* destructive.—*adv.* **Bane′-**

**Bang**, bang, *n.* a heavy blow.—*v.t.* to beat : to strike violently. [Ice. *bang*, a hammering ; originally perhaps from the sound.]

**Bang, Bangue**, bang, *n.* an intoxicating drug made from Indian hemp. [Pers. *bang*.]

**Banian**. See **Banyan**.

**Banish**, ban′ish, *v.t.* to condemn to exile : to drive away. [Fr. *bannir*—Low L. *bannire*, to proclaim, from **Ban**, and see **Abandon**.]

**Banishment**, ban′ish-ment, *n.* exile.

**Banister**, ban′ist-ėr, *n.* corruption of **Baluster**.

**Banjo**, ban′jo, *n.* a musical instrument like a fiddle. [Corr. of Fr. *bandore* or *pandore*—L. *pandura*—Gr. *pandoura*.]

**Bank**, bangk, *n.* a mound or ridge of earth : the earthy margin of a river, lake, &c. : rising ground in the sea.—*v.t.* to inclose with a bank. [A.S. *banc* ; Ger. *bank*. Conn. with **Bench** through the idea of ' thing ridged or raised.' ]

**Bank**, bangk, *n.* a place where money is deposited : an institution for the keeping, lending, and exchanging, &c. of money.—*v.t.* to deposit in a bank, as money. [Fr. *banque*—It. *banco*, a bench on which the Italian money-changers displayed their money—Ger. *bank*, E. **Bench**.]

**Banker**, bangk′ėr, *n.* one who keeps a bank : one employed in banking business.

**Banking**, bangk′ing, *n.* the business of a banker. —*adj.* pertaining to a bank.

**Bank-note**, bangk′-nōt, *n.* a note issued by a bank, which passes as money.

**Bankrupt**, bangk′rupt, *n.* one who breaks or fails in business : an insolvent person.—*adj.* insolvent. [**Bank**, a bench, and L. *ruptus*, broken.]

**Bankruptcy**, bangk′rupt-si, *n.* the state of being or act of becoming bankrupt.

**Bank-stock**, bangk′-stok, *n.* a share or shares in the capital stock of a bank.

**Banner**, ban′ėr. *n.* a military standard : a flag or ensign. [Fr. *bannière*, It. *bandiera*—Low L. *bandum*, a standard, from Ger. *band*, a band, a strip of cloth, a waving or fluttering cloth, used as a flag—Ger. *binden*. See **Band, Bind**.]

**Bannered**, ban′ėrd, *adj.* furnished with banners.

**Banneret**, ban′ėr-et, *n.* a higher class of knight, inferior to a baron. [Fr., dim. of **Banner**.]

**Banns**, banz, *n.pl.* a proclamation of marriage. [From **Ban**.]

**Banquet**, bangk′wet, *n.* a feast : any rich treat or entertainment.—*v.t.* to give a feast to.—*v.i.* to fare sumptuously.—*n.* **Banq′uet-house**. [Fr.— It. *banchetto*, dim. of *banco*, a bench or table— Ger. *bank*. See **Bank**, a bench.]

**Banshee**, ban′shē, *n.* a female fairy in Ireland and elsewhere, who usually appears and utters a peculiar shrieking wail before a death in a particular family to which she is attached. [Ir. *bean*, a woman, *sidhe*, a fairy.]

**Bantam**, ban′tam, *n.* a small variety of the common fowl, brought from the East Indies, and supposed to be named from *Bantam* in Java.— *adj.* of the bantam breed.

**Banter**, bant′ėr, *v.t.* to assail with good-humoured raillery : to joke or jest at.—*n.* humorous raillery : jesting. [Ety. dub.]

**Banting**, bant′ing, *n.* a system of diet for reducing superfluous fat. [From W. Banting of London, who recommended it to the public in 1863.]

**Bantling**, bant′ling, *n.* a child. [So called from the *bands* in which it is wrapped.]

**Banyan**, ban′yan, *n.* one belonging to the caste of merchants in India. **Banyan-day**, a day without meat. [Sans. *banij*, a merchant.]

**Banyan**, ban′yan, *n.* the Indian fig-tree whose branches take root and spread over a large area. [So called by the English because the Banyans (merchants) held their markets under it.]

**Baobab**, bā′o-bab, *n.* a large African tree. [W. African.]

**Baptise**, bapt-īz′, *v.t.* to administer baptism to : to christen. [Gr. *baptizō*—*baptō*, to dip in water.]

**Baptism**, bapt′izm, *n.* immersion in or sprinkling with water as a religious ceremony. — *adj.* **Baptism′al**.

**Baptist**, bapt′ist, *n.* one who baptises : one who approves only of adult baptism by immersion.

**Baptistery**, bapt′ist-ėr-i, *n.* a place where baptism is administered.

**Bar**, bär, *n.* a rod of any solid substance : a bolt : a hinderance or obstruction : a bank of sand or other matter at the mouth of a river : the railing that incloses a space in a tavern or in a court of law : any tribunal : the pleaders in a court as distinguished from the judges : a division in music.—*v.t.* to fasten or secure, as with a bar : to hinder or exclude :—*pr.p.* barr′ing ; *pa.p.* barred′. [Fr. *barre*, It. *barra* ; of Celtic origin.]

**Barb**, bärb, *n.* the beard-like jag near the point of an arrow, fish-hook, &c.—*v.t.* to arm with barbs, as an arrow, &c. [Fr.—L. *barba*, a beard.]

**Barb**, bärb, *n.* a swift kind of horse, the breed of which came from Barbary in North Africa.

**Barbacan**, bär′ba-kan, **Barbican**, bär′bi-kan, *n.* an outer work or defence of a castle, esp. before a gate or bridge. [Low L. *barbacana*, prob. from Pers.]

**Barbarian**, bar-bār′i-an, *adj.* uncivilised : savage : without taste or refinement.—*n.* an uncivilised man, a savage : a cruel, brutal man. [L. *barbarus*, Gr. *barbaros—bar, bar*, an imitation of unintelligible sounds—applied by the Greeks (and afterwards the Romans) to those speaking a different language from themselves.]

**Barbaric**, bar-bar′ik, *adj.* foreign : uncivilised.

**Barbarise**, bär′bar-īz, *v.t.* to make barbarous.

**Barbarism**, bär′bar-izm, *n.* savage life : rudeness of manners : an incorrect form of speech.

**Barbarity**, bar-bar′i-ti, *n.* savageness : cruelty.

**Barbarous**, bär′bar-us, *adj.* uncivilised : rude : savage, brutal.—*adv.* **Bar′barously.**—*n.* **Bar′barousness.**

**Barbecue**, bärb′e-kū, *v.t.* to roast whole, as a pig. [Ety. dub.]

**Barbel**, bärb′el. *n.* a fresh-water fish with beard-like appendages at its mouth. [O. Fr. *barbel*—L. *barba*, a beard.]

**Barber**, bärb′ér, *n.* one who shaves beards and dresses hair. [Fr.—L. *barba*, a beard.]

**Barberry**, bär′ber-i, *n.* a thorny shrub with red berries, common in hedges. [Low L. and Sp. *berberis*—Ar. *barbaris*.]

**Barbican**, bär′bi-kan, *n.* Same as **Barbacan**.

**Bard**, bärd, *n.* a poet and singer among the ancient Celts : a poet. [Celtic.]

**Bardic**, bärd′ik, *adj.* pertaining to bards or their poetry.

**Bare**, bār, *adj.* uncovered, naked : poor, scanty : unadorned : mere or by itself.—*v.t.* to strip or uncover.—*adv.* **Bare′ly**—*n.* **Bare′ness.** [A.S. *bær*; Ger. *baar, bar*; Ice. *ber*.]

**Bare**, bār, old *pa.t.* of **Bear.**

**Barefaced**, bär′fāst, *adj.* with the face uncovered : impudent.—*adv.* **Bare′facedly.**—*n.* **Bare′facedness.**

**Bargain**, bär′gin, *n.* a contract or agreement : a favourable transaction.—**Into the bargain**, over : above : besides.—*v.i.* to make a contract or agreement : to chaffer. [Fr. *barguigner*—Low L. *barcaniare* ; acc. to Diez from *barca*, a boat, used in carrying goods about.]

**Barge**, bärj, *n.* a boat used in the unloading of large vessels : a pleasure or state boat. [O. Fr. *barge*—Low L. *bargia*. Prob. a doublet of **Bark**, a barge.]

**Barilla**, bar-il′a, *n.* an alkaline ash obtained by burning several marine plants (that grow chiefly on the east coast of Spain), used for making soap, glass, &c. [Sp.]

**Baritone**, bar′i-tōn. Same as **Barytone.**

**Bark**, bärk, *n.* the noise made by a dog, wolf, &c.—*v.i.* to yelp like a dog : to clamour. [A.S. *beorcan*, probably a variety of *brecan*, to crack, snap. See **Break**.]

**Bark, Barque**, bärk, *n.* a *barge* : a ship of small size : technically, a three-masted vessel with no square sails on her mizzen-mast. [Fr. *barque*—Low L. *barca* ; perh. from Gr. *baris*, a boat.]

**Bark**, bärk, *n.* the outer rind or covering of a tree. —*v.t.* to strip or peel the bark from. [Dan. *bark*, Ice. *börkr*.]

**Barley**, bär′li, *n.* a grain used for food, but chiefly for making malt. [A.S. *bærlic*—*bere* (Scot. *bear*) and *lic* = *lec*, leek, plant ; W. *barllys*—*bara*, bread, *llys*, a plant ; akin to L. *far*, corn—from root of to *bear*.]

**Barley-corn**, bär′li-korn, *n.* a grain of barley : a measure of length = the third part of an inch.

**Barm**, bärm, *n.* froth of beer or other fermenting liquor, used as leaven : yeast. [A.S. *beorma*, Dan. *bärme* ; akin to L. *fermentum*, Eng. *brew*.] [bar of a tavern or beer-shop.

**Barmaid**, bär′mād, *n.* a female who waits at the

**Barmecide**, bär′me-sīd. *adj.* imaginary or pretended. [From a story in the *Arabian Nights*, in which a beggar is entertained by one of the Barmecide princes on an imaginary feast.]

**Barmy**, bärm′i, *adj.* containing barm or yeast.

**Barn**, bärn, *n.* a building in which grain, hay, &c. are stored.—*v.t.* to store in a barn.—*ns.* **Barn-door**, bärn′-dōr, **Barn-yard**, bärn′-yard. [A.S. *berern*, contracted *bern*, from *bere*, barley, *ern*, a house.]

**Barnacle**, bär′na-kl, *n.* a shell-fish which adheres to rocks and the bottoms of ships : a kind of goose. [Ety. dub.]

**Barnacles**, bär′na-klz, *n.* spectacles. [O. Fr. *bericle*, dim. from L. *beryllus*, beryl, crystal ; Ger. *brille*.]

**Barometer**, bar-om′et-ér, *n.* an instrument by which the *weight* of the atmosphere *is measured* and changes of weather indicated.—*adj.* **Barometric.**—*adv.* **Barometrically.** [Gr. *baros*, weight ; *metron*, measure.]

**Baron**, bar′on, *n.* a title of rank next above a baronet and below a viscount, being the lowest in the House of Peers : a title of certain judges : in feudal times, the peers or great lords of the realm. [Fr. *baron* ; in the Romance tongues the word meant a man as opposed to a woman, a strong man, a warrior ; either from Celtic *bar*, a hero, *fear*, a man, or from O. Ger. *bar*, man (O. Ger. *bairan*, E. **Bear**, to carry).]

**Baronage**, bar′on-āj, *n.* the whole body of barons.

**Baroness**, bar′on-es, *n.* a baron's wife.

**Baronet**, bar′on-et, *n.* a title of rank next above a knight and below a baron—the lowest hereditary title in England. [Dim. of **Baron**.]

**Baronetage**, bar′on-et-āj, *n.* the whole body of baronets.

**Baronetcy**, bar′on-et-si, *n.* the rank of baronet.

**Baronial**, bar-ōn′i-al, *adj.* pertaining to a baron or barony.

**Barony**, bar′on-i, *n.* the territory of a baron.

**Barouche**, ba-rōōsh′, *n.* a double-seated four-wheeled carriage with a falling top. [It. *barocio*—L. *birotus*, two-wheeled, from *bis*, twice, *rota*, a wheel.]

**Barque**, bärk, *n.* same as **Bark**, a ship.

**Barrack**, bar′ak, *n.* a hut or building for soldiers, esp. in garrison (generally used in the plural). [Fr. *baraque*, It. *baracca*, a tent ; cf. Celtic *barrachad*, a hut.]

**Barrel**, bar′el, *n.* a round wooden vessel made of *bars* or staves : the quantity which such a vessel contains : anything long and hollow, as the barrel of a gun.—*v.t.* to put in a barrel. [Fr. *baril*—*barre*. See **Bar**.]

**Barren**, bar′en, *adj.* incapable of bearing offspring : unfruitful : dull, stupid.—*n.* **Barr′enness.** [Fr. *bréhaigne*, O. Fr. *baraigne*.]

**Barricade**, bar′ik-ād, *n.* a temporary fortification raised to hinder the advance of an enemy, as in the street fights at Paris.—*v.t.* to obstruct : to fortify. [Fr.—*barre*, a bar. See **Bar**.]

**Barrier**, bar′i-ér, *n.* a defence against attack : a limit or boundary. [Fr. *barrière*.]

**Barrister**, bar′is-tér, *n.* one who is qualified to plead at the *bar* in an English law-court.

**Barrow**, bar′rō, *n.* a small hand or wheel carriage used to bear or convey a load. [A.S. *berewe*—*beran*, to bear.]

**Barrow**, bar′rō, *n.* a mound raised over graves in former times. [A.S. *beorh*—*beorgan*, to protect.]

**Barter**, bär′tér, *v.t.* to give one thing in exchange for another.—*v.i.* to traffic by exchanging.— *n.* traffic by exchange of commodities. [O. Fr. *bareter*.]

**Barytone**, bar′i-tōn, *n.* a deep-toned male voice between bass and tenor. [Gr. *barys*, heavy, deep, and *tonos*, a tone.]

**Basalt**, bas-awlt′, *n.* a hard, dark-coloured rock of igneous origin.—*adj.* **Basalt′ic.** [L. *basaltes* (an African word), a marble found in Ethiopia.]

**Base**, bās, *n.* that on which a thing rests : foot : bottom : foundation : support : the chief ingredient.—*v.t.* to found or place on a base :

—*pr.p.* bās'ing ; *pa.p.* bāsed. [Fr.—L.—Gr. *basis*—*bainō*, to step.]

**Base,** bās, *adj.* low in place, value, estimation, or principle : mean : vile : worthless : (*New Test.*) humble, lowly.—*adv.* **Base'ly.**—*n.* **Base'ness.** [Fr. *bas*—Low L. *bassus*, thick, fat, a vulgar Roman word, found also in name *Bassus*.]

**Base-born,** bās'-bawrn, *adj.* born of low parentage : illegitimate by birth : mean. [tion.

**Baseless,** bās'les, *adj.* without a base or foundation.

**Basement,** bās'ment, *n.* the base or lowest story of a building.

**Base-spirited,** bās'-spir-it-ed, *adj.* mean-spirited.

**Base-string,** bās'-string, *n.* the string of a musical instrument that gives the lowest note.

**Base-viol,** bās'-vī-ol, *n.* Same as **Bass-viol.**

**Bashaw,** ba-shaw', *n.* com. written **Pasha** or **Pacha,** which see.

**Bashful,** bash'fool, *adj.* easily confused : modest : shy : wanting confidence.—*adv.* **Bash'fully.**—*n.* **Bash'fulness.** [From root of **Abash.**]

**Basilica,** baz-il'ik-a, *n.* among the Romans, a large hall used for judicial and commercial purposes, many of which were afterwards converted into Christian churches : a magnificent church built after the plan of the ancient basilica. [L. *basilica,* Gr. *basilike* (*oikia,* a house), belonging to a king, from *basileus,* a king.]

**Basilisk,** baz'il-isk, *n.* a fabulous serpent having a crest on its head like a crown : in modern zoology, a kind of crested lizard. [Gr. *basiliskos,* dim. of *basileus,* a king.]

**Basin,** bās'n, *n.* a wide open vessel or dish : any hollow place containing water, as a dock : the area drained by a river and its tributaries. [Fr. *bassin,* It. *bacino,* Low L. *bacchinus,* perhaps from the Celtic *bac,* a cavity.]

**Basis,** bās'is, *n.* the foundation or that on which a thing rests : the pedestal of a column : the groundwork or first principle :—*pl.* **Bases,** bās'ēz. [See **Base,** foundation.]

**Bask,** bask, *v.i.* to lie in the warmth or sunshine. [From an O. Scand. form of **Bathe.**]

**Basket,** bas'ket, *n.* a vessel made of plaited twigs, rushes, or other flexible materials. [W. *basged*—*basg,* network, plaiting.]

**Basket-hilt,** bas'ket-hilt, *n.* the hilt of a sword with a covering wrought like basket-work to defend the hand from injury.

**Basque,** bask, *adj.* relating to Biscay, a district of Spain, or to the language of its natives.

**Bas-relief,** bä-re-lēf', *n.* Same as **Bass-relief.**

**Bass,** bās, *n.* the *low* or grave part in music.— *adj.* low, deep, grave.—*v.t.* to sound in a deep tone. [See **Base,** low.]

**Bass,** bas, *n.* Same as **Bast,** which see.

**Bassoon,** bas-ōōn', *n.* a musical wind-instrument of a bass or very low note. [It. *bassone,* augment. of *basso,* low, from root of **Base.**]

**Bass-relief,** bas'-re-lēf', *n.* (*sculpture*) figures which do not stand far out from the ground on which they are formed. [It. *basso-rilievo.* See **Base,** low, and **Relief.**]

**Bass-viol,** bās'-vī-ol, *n.* a musical instrument with four strings, used for playing the bass : the violoncello. [See **Bass,** low, and **Viol.**]

**Bast,** bast, *n.* the inner bark of the lime-tree : matting made of it. [A.S. *bæst* ; Dan., Sw., Ger. *bast.*]

**Bastard,** bast'ard, *n.* a child born of parents not married.—*adj.* born out of wedlock : not genuine : false. [Fr. *bâtard* ; O. Fr. *fils de bast,* son of bast, *bast* or *bât* being a coarse saddle for beasts of burden, and indicating contempt.]

**Bastardise,** bast'ard-īz, *v.t.* to prove to be a bastard. [bastard.

**Bastardy,** bast'ard-i, *n.* the state of being a

**Baste,** bāst, *v.t.,* to beat with a stick. [Ice. *beysta,* Dan. *böste,* to beat.]

**Baste,** bāst, *v.t.* to drop fat or butter over meat while roasting. [Ety. unknown.]

**Baste,** bāst, *v.t.,* to sew slightly or with long stitches. [O. Fr. *bastir,* from O. Ger. *bestan,* to sew.]

**Bastille,** bast-ēl', *n.* an old fortress in Paris long used as a state prison, and demolished in 1789. [Fr.—O. Fr. *bastir* (Fr. *bâtir*), to build.]

**Bastinade,** bast-in-ād', **Bastinado,** bast-in-ād'o, *v.t.* to beat with a *baton* or stick, esp. on the soles of the feet (a form of punishment in the East) :—*pr.p.* bastinād'ing or bastinād'oing ; *pa.p.* bastinād'ed or bastinād'oed.—*ns.* **Bastinade', Bastinad'o.** [Sp. *bastonada,* Fr. *bastonnade*—*baston, bâton.* See **Baton.**]

**Bastion,** bast'yun, *n.* a kind of tower at the angles of a fortification. [Fr.—O. Fr. *bastir,* to build.]

**Bat,** bat, *n.* a heavy stick *for beating* or striking : a flat club for striking the ball in cricket : a piece of brick.—*v.i.* to use the bat in cricket : —*pr.p.* batt'ing ; *pa.p.* batt'ed. [Celt. *bat,* the root of *beat,* an imitation of the sound of a blow.]

**Bat,** bat, *n.* an animal with a body like a mouse, but which flies on wings attached to its fore-feet. [M.E. and Scot. *bakke*—Dan. *bakke,* Ice. *letherblaka,* leather-flapper.]

**Batch,** bach, *n.* the quantity of bread *baked* or of anything made at one time. [From **Bake.**]

**Bate,** bāt, *v.t.* and *v.i.* Same as **Abate.**

**Bath,** bäth, *n.* water for plunging the body into : a bathing : a house for bathing :—*pl.* **Baths,** bäthz. [A.S. *bæth* ; cog. with Ger. *bad.*]

**Bath,** bäth, *n.* the largest Jewish liquid measure, containing about 8 gallons. [Heb. 'measured.']

**Bathe,** bāth, *v.t.* to wash as in a *bath* : to wash or moisten with any liquid.—*v.i.* to be or lie in water as in a bath.—*n.* the act of taking a bath. [A.S. *bathian*—*beth.*]

**Bathos,** bā'thos, *n.* a ludicrous *descent* from the elevated to the mean in writing or speech. [Gr. *bathos,* depth, from *bathys,* deep.]

**Bating,** bāt'ing, *prep.,* excepting.

**Batlet,** bat'let, *n.* a wooden mallet used by laundresses for beating clothes. [Dim. of **Bat.**]

**Baton,** bat'on, *n.* a staff or truncheon, esp. of a policeman : a marshal's staff. [Fr. *bâton* —Low L. *basto,* a stick ; of unknown origin.]

**Batrachian,** ba-trā'ki-an, *adj.* of or belonging to the *frog* tribe. [Gr. *batrachos,* a frog.]

**Batsman,** bats'man, *n.* one who wields the bat at cricket, &c.

**Battalion,** bat-al'yun, *n.* in the infantry of a modern army, the tactical unit or unit of command, being a body of soldiers convenient for acting together (numbering from 500 to 1000) ; several companies form a battalion, and one or more battalions a regiment : a body of men drawn up in battle-array. [Fr. ; from root of **Battle.**]

**Batten,** bat'n, *v.i.* to grow fat : to live in luxury.— *v.t.* to fatten : to fertilise or enrich. [Ice. *batna,* to grow better. See **Better.**] [**Baton.**

**Batten,** bat'n, *n.* a piece of board. [Same as

**Batter,** bat'ėr, *v.t.,* to beat with successive blows : to wear with beating or by use : to attack with artillery.—*n.* ingredients beaten along with some liquid into a paste : (*arch.*) a backward slope in the face of a wall. [Fr. *battre,* It. *battere*—L. *battuere* ; conn. with **Beat.**]

**Batter,** bat′ẽr, *n.* one who uses the bat at cricket.

**Battering-ram,** bat′ẽr-ing-ram, *n.* an ancient engine for battering down walls, consisting of a large beam with an iron head like that of a ram, suspended in a frame.

**Battery,** bat′ẽr-i, *n.* a number of cannon with their equipment: the place on which cannon are mounted: the men and horses attending a battery: an instrument used in electric and galvanic experiments: (*law*) an assault by beating or wounding.                    [playing games.

**Batting,** bat′ing, *n.* the management of a bat in

**Battle,** bat′l, *n.* a contest between opposing armies: a fight or encounter.—*v.i.* to join or contend in fight. [Fr. *bataille*—*battre*, to beat. See **Batter.**]

**Battle-axe,** bat′l-aks, *n.* a kind of axe formerly used in battle.

**Battledoor, Battledore,** bat′l-dōr, *n.* a light bat for striking a ball or shuttle-cock. [Sp. *batidor*, a beater, a washing-beetle.]

**Battlement,** bat′l-ment, *n.* a wall or parapet on the top of a building with openings or embrasures, orig. used only on fortifications.—*adj.* **Batt′lemented.** [Prob. from O. Fr. *bastillement*—*bastir*, to build.]

**Battue,** bat-tōō′, *n.* a sporting term: in a battue, the woods are *beaten* and the game driven into one place for the convenience of the shooters. [Fr.—*battre*, to beat.]

**Bauble,** baw′bl, *n.* a trifling piece of finery: a child's plaything. [Fr. *babiole*—It. *babbole*, toys—*babbeo*, a simpleton.]

**Baudric,** bawd′rik. Same as **Baldrick.**

**Bawble,** baw′bl. Same as **Bauble.**

**Bawd,** bawd, *n.* a procurer or procuress of women for lewd purposes.—*n.* **Bawd′ry.** [O. Fr. *baud*, bold, wanton, from root of **Bold.**]

**Bawdy,** bawd′i, *adj.* obscene: unchaste.—*n.* **Bawd′iness.**

**Bawl,** bawl, *v.i.* to shout or cry out loudly.—*n.* a loud cry or bawl. [Ice. *baula*, to bellow.]

**Bay,** bā, *adj.* reddish-brown inclining to chestnut. [Fr. *bai*, It. *bajo*—L. *badius*, chestnut-coloured.]

**Bay,** bā, *n.* the laurel-tree:—*pl.* an honorary garland or crown of victory, orig. of laurel: literary excellence. [Fr. *baie*, a berry—L. *bacca*.]

**Bay,** bā, *n.* an inlet of the sea, an inward bend of the shore. [Fr. *baie*—Low L. *baia*, a harbour; ety. dub. Acc. to Littré from *Baiæ*, name of a town on the Campanian coast.]

**Bay,** bā, *v.i.*, *to bark*, as a dog at his game.—*v.t.* to bark at: to follow with barking.—**At bay,** said of hounds, when the stag turns and checks them, makes them stand and bark. [O. Fr. *abbayer*—L. *ad*, and *baubari*, to yelp.]

**Bayonet,** bā′on-et, *n.* a dagger for fixing on the end of a musket.—*v.t.* to stab with a bayonet. [Fr. *baïonnette*—*Bayonne*, in France, where it was first made.]

**Bays,** bāz, *n.* a garland. See **Bay,** a laurel.

**Bay-salt,** bā′-sawlt, *n.* salt obtained from sea-water by evaporation, esp. from salt-marshes along the coasts of France, &c. [See **Bay,** an inlet.]

**Bay-window,** bā′-win-dō, *n.* a window projecting so as to form a bay or recess within.

**Bazaar, Bazar,** ba-zär′, *n.* an Eastern *market-place* or exchange: a large hall or suite of rooms for the sale of goods. [Arab. *bazar*, a market.]

**Bdellium,** del′i-um, *n.* a kind of gum. [Gr. *bdellion*, from Heb. *bedōlach*.]

**Be,** bē, *v.i.* to live: to exist: to have a certain state or quality:—*pr.p.* bē′ing; *pa.p.* been (*bin*). [A.S. *beon*; Ger. *bin*; Gael. *bi*, to exist; W. *byw*,

to live; Gr. *phuō*, L. *fui*, *fio*, Sans. *bhu*, to be, originally meaning, *to grow*.]

**Beach,** bēch, *n.* the shore of the sea or of a lake, especially when sandy or pebbly: the strand. [Ice. *bakki*, a variety of *bank*.]                         [beach.

**Beached,** bēcht, *adj.* having a beach: driven on a

**Beachy,** bēch′i, *adj.* having a beach or beaches.

**Beacon,** bē′kn, *n.* a fire on an eminence used as a *sign of danger*: anything that warns of danger. —*v.t.* to act as a beacon to: to light up. [A.S. *beacen*, a beacon, a sign; conn. with **Beckon.**]

**Bead,** bēd, *n.* a little ball pierced for stringing, used in counting the prayers recited, also used as an ornament: any small ball. [A.S. *bed*, *gebed*, a prayer, from *biddan*, to pray. See **Bid.**]

**Beadle,** bēd′l, *n.* a messenger or crier of a court: a petty officer of a church, college, parish, &c. [A.S. *bydel*—*beódan*, to proclaim, to bid.]

**Bead-roll,** bēd′-rōl, *n.* among R. Catholics, a *roll* or list of the dead to be prayed for. [See **Bead.**]

**Beadsman,** bēdz′man, *n.* one employed *to pray* for others.—*fem.* **Beads′woman.**

**Beagle,** bē′gl, *n.* a small hound chiefly used in hunting hares. [Ety. unknown.]

**Beak,** bēk, *n.* the bill of a bird: anything pointed or projecting: in the ancient galley, a pointed iron fastened to the prow for piercing the enemy's vessel.—*adj.* **Beak′ed.** [Fr. *bec*—Celt. *beic*, akin to **Peak, Pike.**]

**Beaker,** bēk′ẽr, *n.* a large drinking-bowl or cup. [Ice. *bikarr* (Scot. *bicker*)—Low L. *bicarium*, acc. to Diez from Gr. *bikos*; of Eastern origin.]

**Beam,** bēm, *n.* a large and straight piece of timber or iron forming one of the main supports of a building, ship, &c.: the part of a balance from which the scales hang: the pole of a carriage: a cylinder of wood in a loom: a ray of light. —*v.t.* to send forth light: to shine. [A.S. *beam*, a tree, stock of a tree, a ray of light; Ger. *baum*, a tree; Gr. *phyma*, a growth—*phy-*, to grow.]

**Beamless,** bēm′les, *adj.* without beams: emitting no rays of light.

**Beamy,** bēm′i, *adj.* shining.

**Bean,** bēn, *n.* the name of several kinds of pulse and their seeds. [A.S. *bean*; Ger. *bohne*, W. *ffaen*, L. *faba*.]

**Bear,** bār, *v.t.* to carry or support: to endure: to behave or conduct one's self: to bring forth or produce.—*v.i.* to suffer: to be patient: to press (with *on* or *upon*): to be situated:—*pr.p.* bear′ing; *pa.t.* bōre; *pa.p.* bōrne (but the *pa.p.* when used to mean 'brought forth' is *born*). [A.S. *beran*; Goth. *bairan*, L. *fero*, Gr. *pherō*, Sans. *bhri*.]

**Bear,** bār, *n.* a rough wild quadruped, with long shaggy hair and hooked claws: any brutal or ill-behaved person: (*astron.*) the name of two constellations, the Great and the Little Bear. [A.S. *bera*; Ger. *bär*; L. *fera*, a wild beast, akin to Gr. *thēr*, Æol. *phēr*.]

**Bearable,** bār′a-bl, *adj.* that may be borne or endured.—*adv.* **Bear′ably.**

**Beard,** bērd, *n.* the hair that grows on the chin and adjacent parts: prickles on the ears of corn: the barb of an arrow: the gills of oysters, &c. —*v.t.* to take by the beard: to oppose to the face. [A.S.; W. *barf*, Ger. *bart*, Russ. *boroda*, L. *barba*.]                    [barbed.—*adj.* **Beard′less.**

**Bearded,** bērd′ed, *adj.* having a beard: prickly:

**Bearer,** bār′ẽr, *n.* one who or that which bears, esp. one who assists in carrying a body to the grave: a carrier or messenger.

**Bear-garden,** bār′-gär-dn, *n.* an inclosure where bears are kept: a rude turbulent assembly.

**Bearing**, bār'ing, *n.* behaviour: situation of one object with regard to another: relation.

**Bearish**, bār'ish, *adj.* like a bear.

**Bear's-skin**, bārz'-skin, *n.* the skin of a bear: a shaggy woollen cloth for overcoats. [bears.

**Bear-ward**, bār'-wawrd, *n.* a warden or keeper of

**Beast**, bēst, *n.* an irrational animal, as opposed to man: a four-footed animal: a brutal person. [O. Fr. *beste*, Fr. *bête*—L. *bestia*.]

**Beastings**, bēst'ingz. Same as **Biestings**.

**Beastly**, bēst'li, *adj.* like a beast in actions or behaviour: coarse: obscene.—*n.* **Beast'liness**.

**Beat**, bēt, *v.t., to strike repeatedly :* to break or bruise : to strike, as bushes, in order to rouse game : to thrash : to overcome.—*v.i.* to give strokes repeatedly : to throb: to dash, as a flood or storm :—*pr.p.* beat'ing ; *pa.t.* beat ; *pa.p.* beat'en.—*n.* a stroke : a stroke recurring at intervals, or its sound, as of a watch or the pulse : a round or course : a place of resort.—*adj.* weary : fatigued. [A.S. *beatan*, from root *bat,* imitative of the sound of a sharp blow; hence **Bat, Butt.**]

**Beaten**, bēt'n, *adj.* made smooth or hard by beating or treading: worn by use.

**Beater**, bēt'ėr, *n.* one that beats or strikes : a crushing instrument. [premely happy.

**Beatific, -al**, bē-a-tif'ik, -al, *adj.* making su-

**Beatification**, bē-at-i-fik-ā'shun, *n.* act of beatifying : (*R. C. Church*) a declaration by the pope that a person is blessed in heaven.

**Beatify**, bē-at'i-fī, *v.t., to make blessed* or happy: to bless with eternal happiness in heaven. [L *beatus,* blessed, and *facio,* to make.]

**Beating**, bēt'ing, *n.* the act of striking : chastisement by blows : regular pulsation or throbbing.

**Beatitude**, bē-at'i-tūd, *n.* heavenly happiness, or happiness of the highest kind :—*pl.* sayings of Christ in Matt. v., declaring the possessors of certain virtues to be blessed. [L. *beatitudo—beatus,* blessed.]

**Beau**, bō, *n., a fine, gay* man, fond of dress : a lover :—*pl.* **Beaux** (bōz).—*fem.* **Belle.** [Fr. *beau, bel*—L. *bellus,* fine, gay, a contr. of *benulus,* dim. of *benus, bonus,* good.]

**Beau-ideal**, bō-īd-ē'al, *n., ideal excellence,* or an imaginary standard of perfection.

**Beau-monde**, bō-mongd', *n.* the *gay* or fashionable *world.* [Fr. *beau,* gay, and *monde,* world.]

**Beauteous**, bū'te-us, *adj.* full of beauty : fair : handsome.—*adv.* **Beau'teously.**—*n.* **Beau'teousness.**

**Beautifier**, bū'ti-fī-ėr, *n.* one who or that which beautifies or makes beautiful.

**Beautiful**, bū'ti-fool, *adj.* fair : beauteous.—*adv.* **Beau'tifully.**

**Beautify**, bū'ti-fī, *v.t.* to make beautiful : to grace : to adorn.—*v.i.* to become beautiful, or more beautiful. [**Beauty**, and L. *facio,* to make.]

**Beauty**, bū'ti, *n.* a pleasing assemblage of qualities in a person or object : a particular grace or excellence : a beautiful person. [Fr. *beauté,* from *beau.*] [the face to heighten beauty.

**Beauty-spot**, bū'ti-spot, *n.* a spot or patch put on

**Beaver**, bēv'ėr, *n.* an amphibious quadruped valuable for its fur : the fur of the beaver : a hat made of the beaver's fur: a hat. [A.S. *befer;* Dan. *baever,* Ger. *biber,* Gael. *beabhar,* L. *fiber.*]

**Beaver**, bēv'ėr, *n.* that part of a helmet which covers the face. [So called from a fancied likeness to a child's bib, Fr. *bavière,* from *bave,* slaver.] [quiet.

**Becalm**, be-käm', *v.t.* to make calm, still, or

**Became**, be-kām', *pa.t.* of **Become.**

**Because**, be-kawz', *conj.* for the reason that : on account of : for. [A.S. *be,* by, and **Cause.**]

**Beck**, bek, *n.* a brook. [Ice. *bekkr;* Ger. *bach.*]

**Beck**, bek, *n.* a sign with the finger or head : a nod.—*v.i.* to make such a sign. [A contr. of **Beckon.**]

**Beckon**, bek'n, *v.t.* to nod or make a sign to. [A.S. *beacnian—beacen,* a sign. See **Beacon.**]

**Becloud**, be-klowd', *v.t.* to obscure by clouds.

**Become**, be-kum', *v.i.* to pass from one state to another : to come to be : (fol. by *of* ) to be the fate or end of.—*v.t.* to suit or befit :—*pa.t.* became' ; *pa.p.* become'. [A.S. *becuman*—pfx. *be,* and **Come.**] [—*adv.* Becom'ingly.

**Becoming**, be-kum'ing, *adj.* suitable to : graceful.

**Bed**, bed, *n.* a couch or place to sleep on : a plot in a garden : a place in which anything rests : the channel of a river : (*geol.*) a layer or stratum. —*v.t.* to place in bed : to sow or plant : to lay in layers :—*pr.p.* bedd'ing ; *pa.p.* bedd'ed.—*ns.* **Bed'chamb'er, Bedd'ing.** [A.S. *bed;* Ice. *bedr,* Ger. *bett.*] [any thick and dirty matter.

**Bedaub**, be-dawb', *v.t.* to daub over or smear with

**Bedchair**, bed'chār, *n.* a chair with a movable back to support a sick person as in bed.

**Bedeck**, be-dek', *v.t.* to deck or ornament.

**Bedevil**, be-dev'il, *v.t.* to throw into disorder and confusion, as if by the *devil.*

**Bedew**, be-dū', *v.t.* to moisten gently, as with dew.

**Bedfellow**, bed'fel'ō, *n.* a sharer of the same bed.

**Bedight**, be-dīt', *adj.* adorned. [Pfx. *be,* and **Dight.**]

**Bedim**, be-dim', *v.t.* to make dim or dark.

**Bedizen**, be-dīz'n, *v.t.* to dress gaudily.

**Bedlam**, bed'lam, *n.* an asylum for lunatics : a madhouse : a place of uproar.—*adj.* fit for a madhouse. [Corrupted from *Bethlehem,* the name of a monastery in London, afterwards converted into a madhouse.]

**Bedlamite**, bed'lam-īt, *n.* a madman.

**Bedouin**, bed'oo-in, *n.* the name given to those Arabs who live in tents and lead a nomadic life. [Fr.—Ar. *badawiy,* dwellers in the desert.]

**Bedrench**, be-drensh', *v.t.* to drench or wet thoroughly. [age or sickness.

**Bedrid, -den**, bed'rid, -dn, *adj.* confined to bed by

**Bedroom**, bed'rōōm, *n.* a room in which there is a bed : a sleeping apartment. [bed.

**Bedstead**, bed'sted, *n.* a frame for supporting a

**Bedtick**, bed'tik, *n.* the tick or cover in which feathers, &c. are put for bedding.

**Bee**, bē, *n.* a four-winged insect that makes honey. —*n.* **Bee-line**, the most direct road from one point to another, like the honey-laden bee's way home to the hive. [A.S. *beo;* Ger. *biene.*]

**Bee**, bē, *n.* (*in Amer.*) a social gathering where some work is done in common.

**Beech**, bēch, *n.* a common forest tree with smooth silvery-looking bark, and producing nuts, once eaten by man, now only by pigs.—*adj.* **Beech'en.** [A.S. *bece, boc;* Ger. *buche,* Lat. *fagus,* Gr. *phēgos*—from root of *phagō,* to eat.]

**Bee-eater**, bē'-ėt'ėr, *n.* a bird allied to the kingfisher, which feeds on bees.

**Beef**, bēf, *n.* the flesh of an ox or cow :—*pl.* **Beeves**, used in orig. sense, oxen.—*adj.* consisting of beef. [Fr. *bœuf,* It. *bove*—L. *bos, bovis;* cf. Gr. *bous,* Gael. *bo,* Sans. *go,* A.S. *cu.*]

**Beef-eater**, bēf'-ėt'ėr, *n.* a popular name for a yeoman of the sovereign's guard, also of the warders of the Tower of London. [The obvious ety. is the right one, there being no such form as *buffetier,* as often stated. Cf. A.S. *hláf-aeta,* lit. 'loaf-eater,' a menial servant.]

**Beefsteak**, bēf'stāk, *n.* a steak or slice of beef for broiling. [wits : stupid.

**Beef-witted**, bēf'-wit'ed, *adj.* dull or heavy in

**Beehive**, bē'hīv, *n.* a case for bees to live in.

**Been**, bēn, *pa.p.* of **Be**.

**Beer**, bēr, *n.* a liquor made by fermentation from malted barley and hops. [A.S. *beor*; Fr. *bière*, Ger. *bier*; prob. from root of **Ferment**.]

**Beery**, bēr'i, *adj.* of or affected by beer.

**Beestings**, bēst'ingz. See **Biestings**.

**Beeswax**, bēz'waks, *n.* the wax collected by bees, and used by them in constructing their cells.

**Beet**, bēt, *n.* a plant with a carrot-shaped root, eaten as food, from which sugar is extracted. [A.S. *bete*, Ger. *beete*, Fr. *bette*—L. *beta*.]

**Beetle**, bē'tl, *n.* an insect with hard cases for its wings. [A.S. *bitel*—*bitan*, to bite.]

**Beetle**, bē'tl, *n.* a heavy wooden mallet used to *beat* with.—*v.i.* to jut or hang out like the head of a *beetle* or mallet. [A.S. *bitl*, *bytel*, a mallet —*beatan*, to beat.] [ing or prominent brow.

**Beetle-browed**, bē'tl-browd, *adj.* with overhang-

**Beetroot**, bēt'rōōt, *n.* the root of the beet plant.

**Beeves**, bēvz, *n.pl.* cattle, oxen. [See **Beef**.]

**Befall**, be-fawl', *v.t.* to fall upon or happen to : to betide.—*v.i.* to happen or come to pass :—*pr.p.* befall'ing ; *pa.t.* befell' ; *pa.p.* befall'en. [A.S. *befeallan*. See **Fall**.]

**Befit**, be-fit', *v.t.* to fit, or be suitable to :—*pr.p.* befitt'ing ; *pa.p.* befitt'ed. [Pfx. *be*, and **Fit**.]

**Befool**, be-fōōl', *v.t.* to make a fool of, or deceive.

**Before**, be-fōr', *prep.* at the *fore part*, or in front of : in presence or sight of : previous to : in preference to : superior to.—*adv.* in front : sooner than : hitherto. [A.S. *be-foran*. See **Fore**.]

**Beforehand**, be-fōr'hand, *adv.* before the time : by way of preparation. [favour.

**Befriend**, be-frend', *v.t.* to act as a friend to : to

**Beg**, beg, *v.i.* to ask alms or charity : to live by asking alms.—*v.t.* to ask earnestly : to beseech : to take for granted :—*pr.p.* begg'ing ; *pa.p.* begged'. [A.S. *bed-ec-ian*, contr. *bed'cian*, *beg-gen*, a frequentative, to ask often, from *biddan*, to ask. See **Bead**, **Bid**.]

**Beget**, be-get', *v.t.* to be the father of, to produce or cause : to generate : to produce as an effect, to cause :—*pr.p.* begett'ing ; *pa.t.* begat', begot' ; *pa.p.* begot', begott'en. [A.S. *begitan*, to acquire. See **Get**.]

**Begetter**, be-get'er, *n.* one who begets : a father.

**Beggar**, beg'ar, *n.* one who begs : one who lives by begging.—*v.t.* to reduce to beggary : to exhaust.

**Beggarly**, beg'ar-li, *adj.* poor : mean : contemptible.—*adv.* meanly.—*n.* Begg'arliness.

**Beggary**, beg'ar-i, *n.* extreme poverty.

**Begin**, be-gin', *v.i.* to take rise : to enter on something new : to commence.—*v.t.* to enter on : to commence :—*pr.p.* beginn'ing ; *pa.t.* began' ; *pa.p.* begun'. [A.S. *beginnan* (also *onginnan*), from *be*, and *ginnan*, to begin.]

**Beginner**, be-gin'er, *n.* one who begins : one who is beginning to learn or practise anything.

**Beginning**, be-gin'ing, *n.* origin or commencement : rudiments.

**Begird**, be-gėrd', *v.t.* to gird or bind with a girdle : to surround or encompass :—*pa.t.* begirt', begird'ed ; *pa.p.* begirt'. [See **Gird**.]

**Begirt**, be-gėrt'. *v.t.* Same as **Begird**: also *pa.t.* and *pa.p.* of **Begird**.

**Begone**, be-gon', *int.* (*lit.*) be gone. In **Woebegone**, we have the *pa.p.* of A.S. *began*, to go round, to beset—beset with woe.

**Begot**, be-got', **Begotten**, be-got'n, *pa.p.* of **Beget**.

**Begrime**, be-grīm', *v.t.* to grime or soil deeply.

**Beguile**, be-gīl', *v.t.* to cheat or deceive : to cause to pass unnoticed what may be attended with tedium or pain.—*adv.* Beguil'ingly.—*ns.* Beguile'ment, Beguil'er. [See **Guile**.] [rank.

**Begum**, bē'gum, *n.* a Hindu princess or lady of rank.

**Begun**, be-gun', *pa.p.* of **Begin**.

**Behalf**, be-häf', *n.* favour or benefit : sake, account : part. [A.S. *healf*, half, part ; *on healfe*, on the side of.]

**Behave**, be-hāv', *v.t.* (with *self*) to bear or carry, to conduct.—*v.i.* to conduct one's self : to act. [A.S. *behabban*, to restrain, from *habban*, to have, to use.] [deportment.

**Behaviour**, be-hāv'yur, *n.* conduct : manners or

**Behead**, be-hed', *v.t.* to cut off the head.

**Beheading**, be-hed'ing, *n.* the act of cutting off the head.

**Beheld**, be-held', *pa.t.* and *pa.p.* of **Behold**.

**Behemoth**, bē'he-moth, *n.* an animal described in the book of Job, prob. the hippopotamus. [Heb. 'beasts,' hence 'great beast.']

**Behest**, be-hest', *n.* command : charge. [A.S. *behæs*, vow, from *be*, and *hæs*, command—*hatan*; Goth. *haitan*, to call, to name.]

**Behind**, be-hīnd', *prep.* at the back of : after or coming after : inferior to.—*adv.* at the back, in the rear : backward : past. [A.S. *behindan* ; Ger. *hinten*. See **Hind**.]

**Behindhand**, be-hīnd'hand, *adj.* or *adv.* being behind : tardy, or in arrears.

**Behold**, be-hōld', *v.t.* to look upon : to contemplate.—*v.i.* to look : to fix the attention :—*pa.t.* and *pa.p.* beheld'.—*imp.* or *int.* see ! lo ! observe ! [A.S. *behealden*, to hold, observe—pfx. *be*, and *healdan*, to hold.]

**Beholden**, be-hōld'n, *adj.* bound in gratitude : obliged. [Old *pa.p.* of **Behold**, in its orig. sense.]

**Beholder**, be-hōld'er, *n.* one who beholds : an onlooker. [**Behoove**.

**Behoof**, be-hōōf', *n.* benefit : convenience. [See

**Behoove**, be-hōōv', *v.t.* to be *fit*, *right*, or *necessary* for—now only used impersonally with *it*. [A.S. *behofian*, to be fit, to stand in need of ; connected with **Have**, Ger. *haben*, L. *habeo*, to have, *habilis*, fit, suitable.]

**Being**, bē'ing, *n.* existence : any person or thing existing. [From the pr.p. of **Be**.]

**Belabour**, be-lā'bur, *v.t.* to beat soundly.

**Belated**, be-lāt'ed, *adj.* made too late : benighted.

**Belay**, be-lā', *v.t.* to fasten a rope by winding it round a pin. [Dut. *be-leggen*, cog. with **Lay**, *v.*]

**Belch**, belsh, *v.t.* to throw out wind from the stomach : to eject violently.—*n.* eructation. [A.S. *bealcan*, an imitation of the sound.]

**Beldam**, bel'dam, **Beldame**, bel'dam, *n.* an old woman, esp. an ugly one. [Fr. *bel*, fair (see **Belle**), and **Dame**, orig. fair dame, used ironically.]

**Beleaguer**, be-lēg'er, *v.t.* to lay siege to. [Dut. *belegeren*, to besiege ; conn. with **Belay**.]

**Belfry**, bel'fri, *n.* the part of a steeple or tower in which bells are hung. [Orig. and properly, a watch-tower, from O. Fr. *berfroi*, O. Ger. *bercfrit*—O. Ger. *frid*, a tower, *bergan*, to protect.]

**Belie**, be-lī', *v.t.* to give the lie to : to speak falsely of : to counterfeit :—*pr.p.* bely'ing ; *pa.p.* belied'. [A.S. *be*, and **Lie**.]

**Belief**, be-lēf', *n.* persuasion of the truth of anything : faith : the opinion or doctrine believed.

**Believable**, be-lēv'a-bl, *adj.* that may be believed.

**Believe**, be-lēv', *v.t.* to regard as true : to trust in.—*v.i.* to be firmly persuaded of anything : to exercise faith : to think or suppose.—*adv.* Believ'ingly. [With prefix *be-* for *ge-*, from A.S. *gelyfan*. For root of *lyfan*, see **Leave**, *n.*]

**Believer**, be-lēv'ėr, *n.* one who believes : a professor of Christianity.

**Belike**, be-līk', *adv.* probably : perhaps. [A.S. pfx. *be*, and **Like**.]

**Bell**, bel, *n.* a hollow vessel of metal with a tongue or clapper inside, which when moved : anything bell-shaped.—**Bear the bell**, to be first or superior, in allusion to the bell-wether of a flock, or to the leading horse of a team wearing bells on his collar. [A.S. *bella*, a bell—*bellan*, to sound loudly.]

**Belladonna**, bel-a-don'a, *n.* the plant Deadly Nightshade, used in small doses as a medicine. [It. *bella-donna*, fair lady, from its use as a cosmetic.]

**Belle**, bel, *n.*, *a fine* or handsome *young lady*: a beauty. [Fr., fem. of **Beau**.]

**Belles-lettres**, bel-let'r, *n.* the department of literature, such as poetry and romance, of which the chief aim is to please by its beauty. [Fr. *belle*, fine, *lettres*, learning—*lettre*, L. *litera*, a letter.]                                    [puts up bells.

**Bell-hanger**, bel'-hang'ėr, *n.* one who hangs or

**Bellicose**, bel'ik-ōs, *adj.* contentious. [L. *bellicosus*—*bellum*, war.]

**Bellied**, bel'id, *adj.* swelled out, or prominent, like the belly—used generally in composition.

**Belligerent**, bel-ij'ėr-ent, *adj.*, *carrying on war.*—*n.* a nation engaged in war. [L. *belligero*, to carry on war—*bellum*, war, *gero*, to carry. See **Duel, Jest.**]

**Bellman**, bel'man, *n.* a town-crier, who rings a bell when giving notice of anything.

**Bellow**, bel'ō, *v.i.* to low : to make a loud resounding noise.—*n.* a roaring. [From root of **Bell**.]

**Bellows**, bel'ōz or bel'us, *n.* an instrument to blow with. [A.S. *bælig*, a bag ; Gael. *balg* ; conn. with **Belly, Bag**.]

**Bell-shaped**, bel'-shäpt, *adj.* shaped like a bell.

**Bell-wether**, bel'-we*th*'ėr, *n.* a wether or sheep which leads the flocks with a bell on his neck.

**Belly**, bel'i, *n.* the part of the body between the breast and the thighs.—*v.t.* to swell out : to fill.—*v.i.* to swell :—*pr.p.* bell'ying ; *pa.p.* bell'ied. [From root of **Bag**.]

**Belly-band**, bel'i-band, *n.* a band that goes round the belly of a horse to secure the saddle.

**Bellyful**, bel'i-fool, *n.* as much as fills the belly, a sufficiency.

**Belong**, be-long', *v.i.* to be one's property : to be a part : to pertain : to have residence. [A.S. *langian*, to long after ; cf. Dut. *belangen*.]

**Belonging**, be-long'ing, *n.* that which belongs to one—used generally in the plural.

**Beloved**, be-luvd', *adj.* much loved : very dear.

**Below**, be-lō', *prep.* beneath in place or rank : not worthy of.—*adv.* in a lower place : (*fig.*) on earth or in hell, as opposed to heaven. [*Be*, and **Low**.]

**Belt**, belt, *n.* a *girdle* or band : (*geog.*) a strait.—*v.t.* to surround with a belt : to encircle.—*adj.* **Belt'ed**. [A.S. *belt* ; Ice. *belti*, Gael. *balt*, L. *balteus*, a belt.]

**Belvedere**, bel've-dēr, *n.* (*in Italy*) a pavilion or look-out on the top of a building. [It.—*bello*, beautiful, *vedere*, to see—L. *bellus* and *videre*.]

**Bemoan**, be-mōn', *v.t.* to moan at : to lament.

**Bench**, bensh. *n.* a long *seat* or form : a mechanic's work-table : a judge's seat : the body or assembly of judges.—*v.t.* to place on or furnish with benches. [A.S. *benc* ; cog. with Ger. *bank*, and conn. with E. **Bank**, a ridge of earth.]

**Bencher**, bensh'ėr, *n.* a senior member of an inn of court.

**Bend**, bend, *v.t.* to curve or bow : make crooked : to turn or incline : to subdue.—*v.i.* to be crooked or curved : to lean : to bow in submission :—*pa.p.* bend'ed or bent.—*n.* a curve or crook. [A.S. *bendan*, to bend, from **Band**, a string ; a bow was 'bent' by tightening the *band* or string.]

**Beneath**, be-nēth', *prep.* under, or lower in place : unbecoming.—*adv.* in a lower place : below. [A.S. pfx. *be*, and *neothan*, beneath. See **Nether**.]

**Benedick**, ben'e-dik, **Benedict**, ben'e-dikt, *n.* a newly-married man : also, a bachelor. [From Benedick, a character in Shakespeare's *Much Ado About Nothing*, who begins as a confirmed bachelor and ends by marrying Beatrice.]

**Benedictine**, ben-e-dikt'in, *n.* one of an order of monks named after St Benedict, called also Black Friars from the colour of their dress.

**Benediction**, ben-e-dik'shun, *n.* a blessing : the solemn act of imploring the blessing of God. [L. *benedictio*—*bene*, well, *dico, dictum*, to say.]

**Benedictory**, ben-e-dikt'or-i, *adj.* declaring a benediction : expressing wishes for good.

**Benefaction**, ben-e-fak'shun, *n.* the act of *doing good*: a good deed done or benefit conferred. [L. *benefactio*. See **Benefice**.]

**Benefactor**, ben-e-fak'tor, *n.* one who confers a benefit.—*fem.* **Benefac'tress**.

**Benefice**, ben'e-fis, *n.* an ecclesiastical living. [Fr.—L. *beneficium*, a kindness—*benefacere*, to benefit—*bene*, well, *facio*, to do. In Low L. *beneficium* meant a gift of an estate.]

**Beneficed**, ben'e-fist, *adj.* having a benefice.

**Beneficence**, ben-ef'i-sens, *n.* active goodness: kindness : charity.

**Beneficent**, ben-ef'i-sent, *adj.*, *doing good*: kind : charitable.—*adv.* **Benef'icently**.

**Beneficial**, ben-e-fish'al, *adj.*, *doing good*: useful: advantageous.—*adv.* **Benefic'ially**.

**Beneficiary**, ben-e-fish'i-ar-i, *n.* one who holds a benefice or receives a benefit.—*adj.* holding in gift.

**Benefit**, ben'e-fit, *n.* a favour : advantage : a performance at a theatre, the proceeds of which go to one of the company.—*v.t.* to do good to.—*v.i.* to gain advantage :—*pr.p.* ben'efiting ; *pa.p.* ben'efited. [Fr. *bienfait*—L. *benefactum*.]

**Benevolence**, be-nev'ol-ens, *n.*, *good-will*: disposition to do good : an act of kindness : (*E. Hist.*) a species of tax arbitrarily levied by the sovereign, and represented by him as a gratuity. [L. *benevolentia*—*bene*, well, *volo*, to wish.]

**Benevolent**, be-nev'ol-ent, *adj.*, *well-wishing*: disposed to do good.—*adv.* **Benev'olently**.

**Bengal-light**, ben-gawl'-lit, *n.* a species of firework producing a very vivid blue light, much used for signals by ships.

**Benighted**, be-nīt'ed, *adj.* overtaken by night: involved in darkness : ignorant. [*Be*, and **Night**.]

**Benign**, ben-īn', *adj.* favourable : gracious : kindly. [O. Fr. *benigne*—L. *benignus* = *benigenus*, well-born, of gentle nature—*benus, bonus*, good, and *gen*, root of *gigno*, to produce.]

**Benignant**, ben-ig'nant, *adj.* kind : gracious.—*adv.* **Benig'nantly**. [L. *benignus*.]

**Benignity**, ben-ig'nit-i, *n.* goodness of disposition : kindness : graciousness.

**Benignly**, ben-īn'li, *adv.* kindly : graciously.

**Benison**, ben'i-zn, *n.*, *benediction*, blessing. [O. Fr. *beneiçon*—L. *benedictio*. See **Benediction**.]

**Bent**, bent, *pa.t.* and *pa.p.* of **Bend**.

**Bent**, bent, *n.* leaning or bias : fixed tendency or set of the mind. [From **Bend**.]

**Bent**, bent, *n.* a coarse grass. [A.S. *beonet*.]

**Benumb**, be-num', *v.t.* to make *numb* or torpid.

**Benzine**, ben'zin, *n.* a substance prepared from coal-tar naphtha, used in removing grease stains from cloth. [From **Benzoin**.]

**Benzoin**, ben-zo'in, *n.* a fragrant, medicinal resin, obtained from the Styrax benzoin, a tree of Sumatra. [Of Arab. orig.]

**Bequeath**, be-kwēth', *v.t.* to give or leave by will: to hand down, as to posterity. [A.S. *be*, and *cwethan*, to say, to tell. See **Quoth**.]

**Bequest**, be-kwest', *n.* something bequeathed or left by will: a legacy.

**Bereave**, be-rēv', *v.t.*, *to rob* or make destitute:—*pa.p.* berēaved' or bereft'. [Pfx. *be*, and **Reave**. A.S. *reafian*.]

**Bereavement**, be-rēv'ment, *n.* heavy loss, esp. of friends by death.

**Bereft**, be-reft', *pa.p.* of **Bereave**.

**Bergamot**, ber'ga-mot, *n.* a fragrant oil obtained from the Bergamot pear. [From *Bergamo*, a town of Lombardy in Italy.]

**Berried**, ber'id, *adj.* having berries.

**Berry**, ber'i, *n.* any small juicy fruit. [A.S. *berige*; Ger. *beere*; Dut. *bezie*; Goth. *basi*; Sans. *bhas*, to eat.]

**Berth**, bėrth, *n.* a ship's station at anchor: a room or sleeping-place in a ship: a situation or place of employment. [A form of **Birth**.]

**Beryl**, ber'il, *n.* a precious stone of a greenish colour. [L. and Gr. *beryllus*.]

**Beseech**, be-sēch', *v.t.* to seek or ask from urgently: to implore or entreat:—*pr.p.* beseech'ing; *pa.t.* and *pa.p.* besought (be-sawt').—*adv.* **Beseech'ingly**. [Pfx. *be*, and *secan*, to seek.] [Pfx. *be*, and **Seem**.]

**Beseem**, be-sēm', *v.t.* to be seemly or fit for.

**Beset**, be-set', *v.t.* to surround or inclose: to waylay: to perplex:—*pr.p.* besett'ing; *pa.t.* and *pa.p.* beset'. [A.S. *bi-settan*, to surround.]

**Besetting**, be-set'ing, *adj.* confirmed: habitual.

**Beside**, be-sīd', *prep.*, *by the side of*: over and above: distinct from.—**Beside one's self**, out of one's wits or reason. [A.S. *be*, by, and **Side**.]

**Beside**, be-sīd', **Besides**, be-sīdz', *adv.* moreover: in addition to.

**Besiege**, be-sēj', *v.t.* to lay siege to: to beset with armed forces: to throng round.—*n.* **Besieger**, be-sēj'ėr. [*Be*, and **Siege**.]

**Besmear**, be-smēr', *v.t.* to smear over or daub.

**Besom**, bē'zum, *n.* an implement for sweeping. [A.S. *besem*, *besma*.]

**Besot**, be-sot', *v.t.* to make sottish, dull, or stupid:—*pr.p.* besott'ing; *pa.p.* besott'ed.

**Besought**, be-sawt', *pa.t.* and *pa.p.* of **Beseech**.

**Bespatter**, be-spat'ėr, *v.t.* to spatter or sprinkle with dirt or anything moist: to defame.

**Bespeak**, be-spēk', *v.t.*, *to speak for* or engage beforehand: to betoken. [*Be*, and **Speak**.]

**Best**, best, *adj.* (serves as superl. of **Good**) good in the highest degree: first: highest: most excellent.—*n.* one's utmost endeavour: the highest perfection.—*adv.* (superl. of **Well**) in the highest degree: in the best manner. [A.S. *betst*, *betest*, *best*. See **Better**.]

**Bestead**, be-sted', *p.adj.* situated: treated. [Pfx. *be*, and **Stead**.]

**Bestial**, best'i-al, *adj.* like a beast: vile: sensual. [L. *bestialis*. See **Beast**.]

**Bestialise**, best'i-al-īz, *v.t.* to make like a beast.

**Bestiality**, best-i-al'i-ti, *n.* beastliness.

**Bestir**, be-stėr', *v.t.* to put into lively action.

**Bestow**, be-stō', *v.t.* to stow, place, or put by: to give or confer: to apply. [See **Stow**.]

**Bestowal**, be-stō'al, *n.* act of bestowing: disposal.

**Bestride**, be-strīd', *v.t.* to stride over: to sit or stand across:—*pa.t.* bestrid', bestrōde'; *pa.p.* bestrid', bestridd'en. [See **Stride**.]

**Bestud**, be-stud', *v.t.* to adorn with studs.

**Bet**, bet, *n.* a wager: something staked to be lost or won on certain conditions.—*v.t.* and *i.* to lay or stake, as a bet:—*pr.p.* bett'ing; *pa.t.* and *pa.p.* bet or bett'ed. [Ety. dub.; either A.S. *bad*, a pledge, akin to **Wed**, **Wager**, or a contr. of **Abet**.]

**Betake**, be-tāk', *v.t.* (with *self*) to take one's self to: to apply or have recourse:—*pa.t.* betook'; *pa.p.* betāk'en. [A.S. *be*, and Ice. *taka*, to deliver.]

**Betel**, bē'tl, *n.* the betel-nut, or nut of the areca palm, with lime and the leaves of the Betel-Pepper, is chewed by the Malays as a stimulant. [East. word.]

**Bethink**, be-thingk', *v.t.* to think on or call to mind: to recollect (generally followed by a reflective pronoun).—*v.i.* to consider:—*pa.t.* and *pa.p.* bethought (be-thawt'). [A.S. *bethencan*, Ger. *bedenken*. See **Think**.]

**Betide**, be-tīd', *v.t.*, *to happen to*: to befall. [A.S. pfx. *be*, and *tidan*, to happen. See **Tide**.]

**Betimes**, be-tīmz', *adv.* in good time: seasonably. [Pfx. *be*, and **Time**.]

**Betoken**, be-tō'kn, *v.t.* to shew by a sign: to foreshew. [A.S. *getacnian*. See **Token**.]

**Betook**, be-took', *pa.t.* of **Betake**.

**Betray**, be-trā', *v.t.* to give up treacherously: to disclose in breach of trust: to discover or shew. [Pfx. *be*, and Fr. *trahir*, It. *tradire*—L. *tradere*, to deliver up.]

**Betrayal**, be-trā'al, *n.* act of betraying.

**Betrayer**, be-trā'ėr, *n.* a traitor.

**Betroth**, be-troth', *v.t.* to contract or promise in order to marriage: to affiance. [*Be*, and **Troth** or **Truth**.]

**Betrothal**, be-troth'al, **Betrothment**, be-troth'ment, *n.* an agreement or contract with a view to marriage.

**Better**, bet'ėr, *adj.* (serves as comp. of **Good**) good in a greater degree: preferable: improved.—*adv.* (comp. of **Well**) well in a greater degree: more fully or completely: with greater advantage:—*pl.* superiors.—*v.t.* to make better, to improve: to benefit. [A.S. *bet* (adv.), *betera*, better, Goth. *batiza*, Ger. *besser*; root *bat*, good; it is in all the Teutonic lang. See **Boot**.]

**Better**, bet'ėr, *n.* one who bets.

**Between**, be-twēn', **Betwixt**, be-twikst', *prep.* in the middle of *twain* or *two*: in the middle or intermediate space: from one to another. [A.S. *betweonan*, *betweox*, *betwuxt*—*be*, and *twegen*, *twa*, two, twain.]

**Bevel**, bev'el, *n.* a slant or inclination of a surface: an instrument opening like a pair of compasses for measuring angles.—*adj.* having the form of a bevel: slanting.—*v.t.* to form with a bevel or slant:—*pr.p.* bev'elling; *pa.p.* bev'elled.—**Bevel-gear** (*mech.*), wheels working on each other in different planes, the cogs of the wheels being bevelled or at oblique angles to the shafts. [Fr. *biveau*, an instrument for measuring angles.]

**Beverage**, bev'ėr-āj, *n.*, *drink*: any agreeable liquor for drinking. [O. Fr.; It. *beveraggio*—*bevere*—L. *bibere*, to drink.]

**Bevy**, bev'i, *n.* a brood or flock of birds, especially of quails: a company, esp. of ladies. [It. *beva*, a drink, a company for drinking.]

**Bewail**, be-wāl', *v.t.* to lament. [See **Wail**.]

**Beware**, be-wār′, *v.i.* to be on one's guard : to be suspicious of danger : to take care. [The two words *be ware* run together. See **Wary**.]

**Bewilder**, be-wil′dėr, *v.t.* to perplex or lead astray.—*n.* **Bewil′derment**. [*Be*, and prov. E. *wildern*, a wilderness.]

**Bewitch**, be-wich′, *v.t.* to affect by witchcraft : to fascinate or charm. [See **Witch**.]

**Bewitchery**, be-wich′ėr-i, **Bewitchment**, be-wich′-ment, *n.* fascination.

**Bewitching**, be-wich′ing, *adj.* charming : fascinating.—*adv.* **Bewitch′ingly**.

**Bewray**, be-rā′, *v.t.* (*B.*), *to accuse* : to point out : to betray. [A.S. pfx. *be*, and *wregan*, to accuse.]

**Bey**, bā, *n.* a Turkish *governor* of a town or province. [Turk. *beg*, pronounced *bā*, a governor.]

**Beyond**, be-yond′, *prep.* on the farther side of : farther onward than : out of reach of. [A.S. *be-geond*—pfx. *be*, and *geond*, across, beyond. See **Yon, Yonder**.]

**Bezel**, bez′l, *n.* the part of a ring in which the stone is set. [O. Fr. *bisel*, Fr. *biseau*; of uncertain origin.]

**Bhang**, bang, *n.* Same as **Bang, Bangue**.

**Bias**, bī′as, *n.* a weight on one side of a bowl (in the game of bowling), making it *slope* or turn to one side : a slant or leaning to one side : an inclination of the mind, prejudice.—*v.t.* to cause to turn to one side : to prejudice or prepossess ; *pp.* bī′ased or bī′assed. [Fr. *biais*; prob. L. *bifax*, two-faced—*bis*, twice, *facies*, the face.]

**Bib**, bib, *n.* a cloth put under an infant's chin. [M.E. *bibben*, to imbibe, to tipple, because the cloth imbibes moisture—L. *bibere*, to drink.]

**Bib**, bib, *n.* a fish of the same genus as the cod and haddock, also called the Pout.

**Bibber**, bib′ėr, *n.* a tippler : chiefly used in composition, as (*B.*) wine-bibber. [L. *bibo*, to drink.]

**Bible**, bī′bl, *n.* the sacred writings of the Christian Church, consisting of the Old and New Testaments. [Fr.—L. and Gr. *biblia*, pl. of Gr. *biblion*, a little book, *biblos*, a book, from *byblos*, the papyrus, of which paper was made.]

**Biblical**, bib′lik-al, *adj.* of or relating to the Bible : scriptural.—*adv.* **Bib′lically**.

**Biblicist**, bib′lis-ist, *n.* one versed in biblical learning.

**Bibliographer**, bib-li-og′raf-ėr, *n.* one versed in bibliography or the history of books.—*adj.* **Bibliograph′ic**.

**Bibliography**, bib-li-og′raf-i, *n.*, *the description* or knowledge of *books*, in regard to their authors, subjects, editions, and history. [Gr. *biblion*, a book, *graphō*, to write, describe.]

**Bibliolatry**, bib-li-ol′at-ri, *n.* superstitious reverence for the Bible. [Gr. *biblion*, a book, *latreia*, worship.]

**Bibliology**, bib-li-ol′oj-i, *n.* an account of books : biblical literature, or theology. [Gr. *biblion*, a book, *logos*, discourse.]

**Bibliomania**, bib-li-o-mān′i-a, *n.* a mania for possessing rare and curious books. [Gr. *biblion*, a book, and **Mania**.]

**Bibliomaniac**, bib-li-o-mān′i-ak, *n.* one who has a mania for possessing rare and curious books.

**Bibliopole**, bib′li-o-pōl, **Bibliopolist**, bib-li-op′ol-ist, *n.* a bookseller. [Gr. *biblion*, a book, *pōleō*, to sell.]

**Bibulous**, bib′ū-lus, *adj.*, *drinking* or sucking in : spongy. [L. *bibulus*—*bibo*, to drink.]

**Bicarbonate**, bī-kär′bon-āt, *n.* a carbonate or salt having two equivalents of carbonic acid to one equivalent of base. [L. *bi-* (for *dvi-*, from *duo*, two), twice, and **Carbonate**.]

**Bice**, bīs, *n.* a pale blue or green paint. [Fr. *bis*, *bise*; orig. unknown.]

**Biceps**, bī′seps, *n.* the muscle in front of the arm between the shoulder and elbow. [L. *biceps*, two-headed—*bis*, twice, and *caput*, head.]

**Bicipital**, bī-sip′it-al, *adj.* (*anat.*), *having two heads* or origins. [See **Biceps**.]

**Bicker**, bik′ėr, *v.i.* to contend in a petty way : to quiver : to move quickly and tremulously, as running water. [Acc. to Skeat, *bicker* = *pick-er*, or *peck-er*, to *peck* repeatedly with the *beak*.]

**Bicycle**, bī′sikl, *n.* a velocipede with two wheels, arranged one before the other. [L. *bis*, twice, and Gr. *kyklos*, a circle.]

**Bid**, bid, *v.t.*, *to offer* : to propose : to proclaim : to invite : to command :—*pr.p.* bidd′ing ; *pa.t.* bid or bade ; *pa.p.* bid, bidd′en.—*n.* an offer of a price. [A.S. *beodan*; Goth. *bjudan*, Ger. *bieten*, to offer.]

**Bid**, bid, *v.t.*, *to ask for* : to pray (nearly obs.). [A.S. *biddan*, Goth. *bidjan*; the connection with **Bid**, to command, is dub. See **Bead**.]

**Bidder**, bid′ėr, *n.* one who bids or offers a price.

**Bidding**, bid′ing, *n.* offer : invitation : command.

**Bide**, bīd, *v.t.* and *v.i.* Same as **Abide**, to wait for. [A.S. *bidan*, Goth. *beidan*.]

**Biennial**, bī-en′yal, *adj.* lasting *two years* : happening once in two years.—*n.* a plant that lasts two years.—*adv.* **Bienn′ially**. [L. *biennalis*—*bis*, twice, and *annus*, a year.]

**Bier**, bēr, *n.* a carriage or frame of wood for *bearing* the dead to the grave. [A.S. *bær*; Ger. *bahre*, L. *fer-etrum*. From root of **Bear**, *v.*]

**Biestings**, bēst′ingz, *n.* the first milk from a cow after calving. [A.S. *bysting*; Ger. *biest-milch*.]

**Bifacial**, bī-fā′shyal, *adj.* having *two* like *faces* or opposite surfaces. [L. *bis*, twice, and **Facial**.]

**Bifurcated**, bī-furk′āt-ed, *adj.*, *two-forked* : having two prongs or branches. [L. *bifurcus*—*bis*, twice. *furca*, a fork.]

**Bifurcation**, bī-furk-ā′shun, *n.* a forking or division into two branches.

**Big**, big, *adj.* large or great : pregnant : great in air, mien, or spirit. [M.E. *bigg*, Scot. *bigly*, prob. from Ice. *byggi-ligr*, habitable—*byggja*, to settle, conn. with *bua*, to dwell. From 'habitable' it came to mean 'spacious,' 'large.']

**Bigamist**, big′am-ist, *n.* one who has committed bigamy.

**Bigamy**, big′am-i, *n.* the crime of having two wives or two husbands at once. [Fr.—L. *bis*, twice, and Gr. *gamos*, marriage.]

**Biggin**, big′in, *n.* a child's cap or hood. [Fr. *béguin*, from the cap worn by the *Béguines*, a religious society of women in France.]

**Bight**, bīt, *n.*, *a bend* of the shore, or small bay : a bend or coil of a rope. [Cf. Dan. and Swed. *bugt*, Dut. *bogt*, from root of Goth. *biugan*, A.S. *beogan*, Ger. *biegen*, to bend, Ger. *bow*.]

**Bigness**, big′nes, *n.* bulk, size.

**Bigot**, big′ot, *n.* one blindly and obstinately devoted to a particular creed or party. [Fr. ; variously derived from the oath *By God*, used, acc. to the tale, by the Norman Rollo ; and then a nickname of the Normans : *Béguine*, a religious society of women ; *Visigoth*, a Western Goth ; and Sp. *bigote*, a moustache.]

**Bigoted**, big′ot-ed, *adj.* having the qualities of a bigot.          [especially in religious matters.]

**Bigotry**, big′ot-ri, *n.* blind or excessive zeal,

**Bijou**, be-zhōō′, *n.* a trinket : a jewel : a little box :—*pl.* **Bijoux**, be-zhōō′. [Fr.]

**Bijoutry**, be-zhōō′tri, *n.* jewelry : small articles of virtu.

**Bilateral**, bī-lat'ėr-al, *adj., having two sides.* [L. *bis*, twice, and **Lateral**.]

**Bilberry**, bil'ber-i, *n.* called also **Whortleberry**, a shrub and its berries, which are dark-blue. [Dan. *böllebaer*, ball-berry (cf. **Billiards**); Scot. *blaeberry*; Ger. *blaubeere*.]

**Bilbo**, bil'bō, *n.* a rapier or sword:—*pl.* **Bilboes**, bil'bōz, fetters. [From *Bilboa* in Spain.]

**Bile**, bīl, *n.* a thick yellow bitter fluid secreted by the liver: (*fig.*) ill-humour. [Fr.—L. *bilis*, allied to *fel, fellis*, the gall-bladder.]

**Bilge**, bilj, *n.* the bulging part of a cask: the broadest part of a ship's bottom.—*v.i.* to spring a leak by a fracture in the bilge, as a ship. [See **Bulge, Belly**.]

**Bilge-water**, bilj'-waw'tėr, *n.* the foul water which gathers in the bilge or bottom of a ship.

**Biliary**, bil'yar-i, *adj.* belonging to or conveying bile.

**Bilingual**, bī-ling'wal, *adj.* of or containing *two tongues* or languages. [L. *bilinguis—bis*, twice, *lingua*, tongue.] [bile.

**Bilious**, bil'yus, *adj.* pertaining to or affected by

**Bilk**, bilk, *v.t.* to elude: to cheat. [Perhaps a dim. of **Balk**.]

**Bill**, bil, *n.* a kind of battle-axe: a hatchet with a hooked point for pruning. [A.S. *bil*; Ger. *beil*.]

**Bill**, bil, *n.* the beak of a bird, or anything like it. —*v.i.* to join bills as doves: to caress fondly. [A.S. *bile*, the same word as the preceding, the primary meaning being, a *cutting* implement.]

**Bill**, bil, *n.* an account of money: a draft of a proposed law: a written engagement to pay a sum of money at a fixed date: a placard or advertisement: any written statement of particulars.—**Bill of exchange**, a written order from one person to another, desiring the latter to pay to some specified person a sum of money at a fixed date.—**Bill of lading**, a paper signed by the master of a ship, by which he makes himself responsible for the safe delivery of the goods specified therein.—**Bill of fare**, in a hotel, the list of dishes or articles of food.—**Bill of health**, an official certificate of the state of health on board ship before sailing.—**Bill of mortality**, an official account of the births and deaths occurring within a given time. [(*Lit.*) a sealed paper, from Low L. *billa—bulla*, a seal. See **Bull**, an edict.]

**Billet**, bil'et, *n., a little* note or paper: a ticket assigning quarters to soldiers.—*v.t.* to quarter or lodge, as soldiers. [Fr.—dim. of **Bill**.]

**Billet**, bil'et, *n.* a small *log of wood* used as fuel. [Fr. *billot—bille*, the young stock of a tree, prob. of Celt. orig., perh. allied to **Bole**, the trunk of a tree.]

**Billet-doux**, bil-e-dōō', *n., a sweet note*: a love-letter. [Fr. *billet*, a letter, *doux*, sweet.]

**Billiards**, bil'yardz, *n.* a game played with a cue or mace and balls on a table having pockets at the sides and corners. [Fr. *billard—bille*, a ball.]

**Billingsgate**, bil'ingz-gāt, *n.* foul language like that spoken at Billingsgate (the great fish-market of London).

**Billion**, bil'yun, *n.* a million of millions (1,000,000,000,000); or, according to the French method of numeration, one thousand millions (1,000,000,000). [L. *bis*, twice, and **Million**.]

**Billman**, bil'man, *n.* a soldier armed with a bill.

**Billow**, bil'ō, *n.* a great wave of the sea *swelled* by the wind.—*v.i.* to roll in large waves. [Ice. *bylgja*; Sw. *bölja*, Dan. *bölge*, a wave-root *belg*, to swell. See **Bilge, Bulge**.]

**Billowy**, bil'ō-i, *adj.* swelling into billows.

**Bimana**, bī'man-a, *n.* animals having *two hands*:

a term applied to the highest order of mammalia, of which man is the type and only species. [L. *bis*, twice, and *manus*, the hand.]

**Bimanous**, bī'man-us, *adj.* having *two hands*.

**Bimensal**, bī-mens'al, *adj.* happening once *in two months*: bimonthly. [L. *bis*, and *mensis*, a month.]

**Bimetallism**, bī'met'al-izm, *n.* the system of using a double standard of currency, or one based upon the two metals, gold and silver, instead of on one alone. [A recent coinage, from Gr. *bi*, double, and **Metal**.]

**Bin**, bin, *n.* a place for storing corn, wine. [A.S.]

**Binary**, bī'nar-i, *adj.* composed *of two*: twofold. [L. *binarius—bini*, two by two—*bis*, twice.]

**Bind**, bīnd, *v.t.* to tie or fasten together with a band: to sew a border on: to fasten together (the leaves of a book) and put a cover on: to oblige by oath or agreement or duty: to restrain: to render hard:—*pa.t.* and *pa.p.* bound. [A.S. *bindan*; cog. with Ger. *binden*, Sans. *bandh*. Cf. **Band, Bend,** and **Bundle**.]

**Binder**, bīnd'ėr, *n.* one who binds, as books or sheaves.

**Binding**, bīnd'ing, *adj.* restraining: obligatory.— *n.* the act of binding: anything that binds: the covering of a book.

**Bindweed**, bīnd'wēd, *n.* the convolvulus, a genus of plants so called from their twining or binding.

**Binnacle**, bin'a-kl, *n.* (*naut.*) the box in which on shipboard the compass is kept. [Formerly *bittacle*—Port. *bitacola*—L. *habitaculum*, a dwelling-place—*habito*, to dwell.]

**Binocular**, bin-ok'ūl-ar, *adj.* having *two eyes*: suitable for two eyes. [L. *bis*, and *oculus*, eye.]

**Binomial**, bī-nōm'i-al, *adj.* and *n.* in algebra, a quantity consisting of *two terms* or parts. [L. *bis*, twice, and *nomen*, a name, a term.]

**Biography**, bī-og'raf-i, *n., a written account* or history of *the life* of an individual: the art of writing such accounts.—*n.* **Biog'rapher**, one who writes biography.—*adjs.* **Biograph'ic, Biograph'ical**.—*adv.* **Biograph'ically**. [Gr. *bios*, life, *graphō*, to write.]

**Biology**, bī-ol'oj-i, *n.* the science that treats of life or of organised beings.—*adj.* **Biolog'ical**. [Gr. *bios*, life, *logos*, a discourse.]

**Bipartite**, bi'part-īt or bī-pärt'īt, *adj., divided into two* like *parts.* [L. *bis*, twice, *partitus*, divided—*partio*, to divide.]

**Biped**, bī'ped, *n.* an animal with *two feet*.—*adj.* having two feet. [L. *bipes—bis*, twice, *ped-*, foot.]

**Bipennate**, bī-pen'āt, **Bipennated**, bī-pen'āt-ed, *adj., having two wings*. [L.—*bis, penna*, a wing.]

**Biquadratic**, bī-kwod-rat'ik, *n.* a quantity *twice squared*, or raised to the fourth power. [L. *bis*, twice, and *quadratus*, squared.]

**Birch**, bėrch, *n.* a hardy forest-tree, with smooth, white bark, and very durable wood: a rod for punishment, consisting of a birch twig or twigs. [A.S. *birce*; Ice. *björk*, Sans. *bhurja*.]

**Birch, -en**, bėrch, -'en, *adj.* made of birch.

**Bird**, bėrd, *n.* a general name for feathered animals. —*v.i.* to catch or snare birds. [A.S. *brid*, the young of a bird, a bird: either from root of **Breed** (*bredan*, to breed) or of **Birth** (*beran*, to bear).]

**Bird-fancier**, bėrd'-fan'si-ėr, *n.* one who has a fancy for rearing birds: one who keeps birds for sale. [for catching birds.

**Birdlime**, bėrd'līm, *n.* a sticky substance used

**Bird-of-Paradise**, bėrd-ov-par'a-dīs, *n.* a kind of Eastern bird with splendid plumage.

**Bird's-eye**, bėrdz'-ī, *adj.* seen from above as if by the eye of a flying bird.—*n.* a kind of tobacco.

**Bireme,** bī'rēm, *n.* an ancient vessel with *two* rows of *oars.* [Fr.—L. *biremis—bis,* twice, and *remus,* an oar.]

**Birk,** bérk, *n.* Scotch and prov. E. for **Birch.**

**Birth,** bérth, *n.* a ship's station at anchor. [Same as **Berth.**]

**Birth,** bérth, *n.* the act of *bearing* or bringing forth : the offspring born : dignity of family : origin. [A.S. *beorth,* a birth—*beran,* to bear.]

**Birthright,** bérth'rīt, *n.* the right or privilege to which one is entitled by birth.

**Biscuit,** bis'kit, *n.* hard dry bread in small cakes : a kind of unglazed earthenware. [[*Lit.*] bread *twice* cooked or *baked* (so prepared by the Roman soldiers) ; Fr.—L. *bis,* twice ; Fr. *cuit,* baked—L. *coquo, coctum,* to cook or bake.]

**Bisect,** bī-sekt', *v.t.* to *cut into two* equal parts. [L. *bis,* twice, and *seco, sectum,* to cut.]

**Bisection,** bī-sek'shun, *n.* division into two equal parts.

**Bisexual,** bī-seks'shōō-al, *adj., of both sexes :* (*bot.*) applied to flowers which contain both stamens and pistils within the same envelope. [L. *bis,* twice, and **Sexual.**]

**Bishop,** bish'op, *n.* one of the higher clergy who has charge of a diocese. [A.S. *bisceop*—L. *episcopus*—Gr. *episkopos,* an overseer—*epi,* upon, *skopeō,* to view.]

**Bishopric,** bish'op-rik, *n.* the office and jurisdiction of a bishop : a diocese. [A.S. *ric,* dominion.]

**Bismuth,** biz'muth, *n.* a brittle metal of a reddish-white colour used in the arts and in medicine. [Ger. *bismuth, wissmuth :* orig. unk.]

**Bison,** bī'son, *n.* a large wild animal like the bull, with shaggy hair and a fatty hump on its shoulders. [From L. and Gr.; but prob. of Teutonic origin.]

**Bisque,** bisk, *n.* a species of unglazed porcelain, *twice* passed through the furnace. [Fr., from root of **Biscuit.**]

**Bissextile,** bis-sext'il, *n.* leap-year.—*adj.* pertaining to leap-year. [L. *bis,* twice, and *sextus,* sixth, so called because in every fourth or leap year the *sixth* day before the calends of March, or the 24th February, was reckoned *twice.*]

**Bister, Bistre,** bis'tér. *n.* a *brown* colour made from the soot of wood. [Fr.; orig. unknown.]

**Bisulphate,** bī-sul'fāt, *n., a double sulphate.* [L. *bis,* twice, and **Sulphate.**]

**Bit,** bit, *n.* a bite, a morsel : a small piece : the smallest degree : a small tool for boring : the part of the bridle which the horse holds in his mouth.—*v.t.* to put the bit in the mouth :—*pr.p.* bitt'ing ; *pa.p.* bitt'ed. [From **Bite.**]

**Bitch,** bich, *n.* the female of the dog, wolf, and fox. [A.S. *bicce,* Ice. *bikkia.*]

**Bite,** bīt, *v.t.* to seize or tear with the teeth : to sting or pain : to wound by reproach :—*pa.t.* bit ; *pa.p.* bit or bitt'en.—*n.* a grasp by the teeth : something bitten off : a mouthful.—*n.* **Bit'ing.**—*adj.* **Bit'ing.** [A.S. *bitan ;* Goth. *beitan,* Ice. *bita,* Ger. *beissen ;* akin to L. *fid-,* Sans. *bhid,* to cleave.]

**Bitter,** bit'ér, *adj., biting* or acrid to the taste : sharp : painful.—*n.* any substance having a bitter taste.—*adj.* **Bitt'erish.**—*adv.* **Bitt'erly.** —*n.* **Bitt'erness.** [A.S.—*bitan,* to bite.]

**Bittern,** bit'érn. *n.* a bird of the heron family, said to have been named from the resemblance of its voice to the *lowing of a bull.* [M. E. *bittour*—Fr.—Low L. *butorius* (*bos, taurus*).]

**Bitters,** bit'érz. *n.* a liquid prepared from bitter herbs or roots, and used as a stomachic.

**Bitumen,** bi-tū'men, *n.* a name applied to various inflammable mineral substances, as naphtha, petroleum, asphaltum.—*adj.* **Bitu'minous.** [L.]

**Bivalve,** bī'valv, *n.* an animal having a shell in *two valves* or parts, like the oyster : a seed-vessel of like kind.—*adj.* having two valves.—*adj.* **Bivalv'ular.** [L. *bis,* twice, *valva,* a valve.]

**Bivouac,** biv'oo-ak, *n.* the lying out all night of soldiers in the open air.—*v.i.* to pass the night in the open air :—*pr.p.* biv'ouacking ; *pa.p.* biv'ouacked. [Fr.—Ger. *beiwachen,* to watch beside—*bei,* by, *wachen,* to watch.]

**Bi-weekly,** bī'-wēk'li, *adj.* properly, occurring once in *two weeks,* but usually *twice in every week.* [L. *bis,* twice, and **Week.**]

**Bizarre,** bi-zär', *adj.* odd : fantastic : extravagant. [Fr.—Sp. *bizarro,* high-spirited.]

**Blab,** blab, *v.i.* to talk much : to tell tales.—*v.t.* to tell what ought to be kept secret :—*pr.p.* blabb'ing ; *pa.p.* blabbed. [An imitative word, found in Dan. *blabbre,* Ger. *plappern.*]

**Black,** blak, *adj.* of the darkest colour : without colour : obscure : dismal : sullen : horrible.—*n.* black colour : absence of colour : a negro : mourning.—*v.t.* to make black : to soil or stain.—*adj.* **Black'ish.**—*n.* **Black'ness.** [A.S. *blac, blæc,* black.] [negro.

**Blackamoor,** blak'a-mōōr, *n.,* a *black Moor :* [

**Black-art,** blak'-ärt, *n.* necromancy : magic. [Acc. to Trench, a translation of the Low L. *nigromantia,* substituted erroneously for the Gr. *necromanteia* (see **Necromancy**), as if the first syllable had been L. *niger,* black.]

**Blackball,** blak'bawl, *v.t.* to reject in voting by putting a black ball into a ballot-box.

**Blackberry,** blak'ber-i, *n.* the berry of the bramble. [black colour.

**Blackbird,** blak'bérd, *n.* a species of thrush of a [

**Blackboard,** blak'bōrd, *n.* a board painted black, used in schools for writing, forming figures, &c.

**Black-cattle,** blak'-kat'l, *n.* oxen, bulls, and cows.

**Blackcock,** blak'kok, *n.* a species of grouse, common in the north of England and in Scotland.

**Black-currant,** blak'-kur'ant. *n.* a garden shrub with black fruit used in making preserves.

**Black-death,** blak'-deth, *n.* a name given to the plague of the fourteenth century from the black spots which appeared on the skin.

**Blacken,** blak'n, *v.t.* to make black : to defame.

**Black-flag,** blak'-flag, *n.* the flag of a pirate, from its colour.

**Blackfriar,** blak'frī-ar, *n.* a friar of the Dominican order, so called from his black garments.

**Blackguard,** blag'ärd, *n.* (orig. applied to the lowest menials about a court, who took charge of the pots, kettles, &c.) a low, ill-conducted fellow.—*adj.* low : scurrilous.—*n.* **Black'guard-ism.** [ing leather, &c.

**Blacking,** blak'ing. *n.* a substance used for black- [

**Blacklead,** blak-led', *n.* a *black* mineral used in making pencils, blacking grates, &c.

**Blackleg,** blak'leg, *n.* a low gambling fellow.

**Black-letter,** blak'-let'ér, *n.* the old English (also called Gothic) letter (𝔅𝔩𝔞𝔠𝔨=𝔩𝔢𝔱𝔱𝔢𝔯).

**Blackmail,** blak'māl, *n.* rent or tribute formerly paid to robbers for protection. [**Black** and A.S. *mal,* tribute, toll.]

**Black-rod,** blak'-rod, *n.* the usher of the order of the Garter and of parliament, so called from the black rod which he carries.

**Blacksmith,** blak'smith, *n.* a smith who works in iron, as opposed to one who works in tin.

**Blackthorn,** blak'thorn, *n.* a species of dark-coloured thorn : the sloe.

**Bladder**, blad′ér, *n.* a thin bag distended with liquid or air : the receptacle for the urine. [A.S. *blædr—blawan* ; O. Ger. *blahan, blajan*, to blow ; Ger. *blase*, bladder—*blasen*, to blow ; cf. L. *flat-us*, breath.]

**Blade**, blād, *n.* the leaf or flat part of grass or corn : the cutting part of a knife, sword, &c. : the flat part of an oar : a dashing fellow. [A.S. *blæd* ; Ice. *blad*, Ger. *blatt*.]                [blades.

**Bladed**, blād′ed, *adj.* furnished with a blade or

**Blain**, blān, *n.* a boil or blister. [A.S. *blegen*, a blister, prob. from *blawan*, to blow.]

**Blamable**, blām′a-bl, *adj.* deserving of blame : faulty.—*adv.* **Blam′ably.**—*n.* **Blam′ableness.**

**Blame**, blām, *v.t.* to find fault with : to censure.— *n.* imputation of a fault : crime : censure. [Fr. *blâmer, blasmer*—Gr. *blasphēmeō*, to speak ill. See **Blaspheme.**]

**Blameful**, blām′fool, *adj.* meriting blame : criminal.—*adv.* **Blame′fully.**—*n.* **Blame′fulness.**

**Blameless**, blām′les, *adj.* without blame : guiltless : innocent.—*adv.* **Blame′lessly.**—*n.* **Blame′lessness.**                [blame : culpable.

**Blameworthy**, blām′wur-*th*i, *adj.* worthy of

**Blanch**, blansh, *v.t.* to whiten.—*v.i.* to grow white. [Fr. *blanchir—blanc*, white. See **Blank.**]

**Blanc-mange**, bla-mawngzh′, *n.* a white jelly prepared with milk. [Fr. *blanc*, white, *manger*, food.]

**Bland**, bland, *adj.*, *smooth* : gentle : mild.—*adv.* **Bland′ly.**—*n.* **Bland′ness.** [L. *blandus*, perh. = *mla(n)dus* = E. *mild*.]

**Blandishment**, bland′ish-ment, *n.* act of expressing fondness : flattery : winning expressions or actions. [Fr. *blandissement*, O. Fr. *blandir*, to flatter—L. *blandus*, mild.]

**Blank**, blangk, *adj.* without writing or marks, as in *white* paper : empty : vacant, confused : in poetry, not having rhyme.—*n.* a paper without writing : a ticket having no mark, and therefore valueless : an empty space.—*adv.* **Blank′ly.**— *n.* **Blank′ness.** [Fr. *blanc*, from root of Ger. *blinken*, to glitter—O. H. Ger. *blichen*, Gr. *phlegein*, to shine.]                [without a bullet.

**Blank-cartridge**, blangk′-kär′trij, *n.* a cartridge

**Blanket**, blangk′et, *n.* a white woollen covering for beds : a covering for horses, &c. [Fr. *blanchet*, dim. of *blanc*, from its usual white colour.]

**Blanketing**, blangk′et-ing, *n.* cloth for blankets : the punishment of being tossed in a blanket.

**Blank-verse**, blangk′-vèrs, *n.* verse without rhyme, especially the heroic verse of five feet.

**Blare**, blār, *v.i.* to roar, to sound loudly, as a trumpet.—*n.* roar, noise. [M. E. *blaren*, orig. *blasen*, from A.S. *blæsan*, to blow. See **Blast.**]

**Blaspheme**, blas-fēm′, *v.t.* and *v.i.* to speak impiously of, as of God : to curse and swear.—*n.* **Blasphem′er.** [Gr. *blasphēmeō—blapto*, to hurt, *phemi*, to speak. See **Blame.**]

**Blasphemous**, blas′fem-us, *adj.* containing blasphemy : impious.—*adv.* **Blas′phemously.**

**Blasphemy**, blas′fem-i, *n.* profane speaking : contempt or indignity offered to God.

**Blast**, blast, *n.*, a *blowing* or gust of wind : a forcible stream of air : sound of a wind instrument : an explosion of gunpowder : anything pernicious.—*v.t.* to strike with some pernicious influence : to blight : to affect with sudden violence or calamity : to rend asunder with gunpowder. [A.S. *blæst—blæsan*, to blow ; Ger. *blasen*.]        [nace into which hot air is blown.

**Blast-furnace**, blast′-fur′nās, *n.* a smelting furnace.

**Blasting**, blast′ing, *n.* the separating of masses of stone by means of an explosive substance.

**Blatant**, blāt′ant, *adj.*, *bleating* or bellowing : noisy. [A.S. *blætan*, to bleat.]

**Blaze**, blāz, *n.* a rush of light or of flame : a bursting out or active display.—*v.i.* to burn with a flame : to throw out light. [A.S. *blæse*, a torch, from root of **Blow.**]

**Blaze**, blāz, **Blazon**, blā′zn, *v.t.* to proclaim, to spread abroad.—**To Blaze a tree**, to make a white mark by cutting off a piece of the bark. [Same as **Blare** : **Blazon** is the M. E. *blasen*, with the *n* retained.]

**Blazon**, blā′zn, *v.t.* to make public : to display : to draw or to explain in proper terms, the figures, &c., in armorial bearings.—*n.* the science or rules of coats of arms. [Fr. *blason*, a coat of arms, from root of **Blaze.**]

**Blazonry**, blā′zn-ri, *n.* the art of drawing or of deciphering coats of arms : heraldry.

**Bleach**, blēch, *v.t.* to make *pale* or white : to whiten, as textile fabrics.—*v.i.* to grow white. [A.S. *blacian*, to grow pale, from root of **Bleak.**]

**Bleacher**, blēch′ér, *n.* one who bleaches, or that which bleaches.

**Bleachery**, blēch′ér-i, *n.* a place for bleaching.

**Bleaching**, blēch′ing, *n.* the process of whitening or decolourising cloth.

**Bleak**, blēk, *adj.* colourless : dull and cheerless : cold, unsheltered.—*adv.* **Bleak′ly.**—*n.* **Bleak′ness.** [A.S. *blæc, blāc*, pale, shining ; a different word from *blac* (without accent), black. The root is *blican*, to shine.]

**Bleak**, blēk, *n.* a small white river-fish.

**Blear**, blēr, *adj.* (as in **Blear-eyed**, blēr′-īd) sore or inflamed : dim or blurred with inflammation. [Low Ger. *bleer-oged*, 'blear-eyed.']

**Bleat**, blēt, *v.i.* to cry as a sheep.—*n.* the cry of a sheep. [A.S. *blætan* ; L. *balare*, Gr. *blēchē*, a bleating ; root *bla-* ; formed from the sound.]

**Bleating**, blēt′ing, *n.* the cry of a sheep.

**Bleed**, blēd, *v.i.* to lose blood : to die by slaughter : to issue forth or drop as blood.—*v.t.* to draw blood from :—*pa.t.* and *pa.p.* bled. [A.S. *bledan*. See **Blood.**]

**Bleeding**, blēd′ing, *n.* a discharge of blood : the operation of letting blood.

**Blemish**, blem′ish, *n.* a stain or defect : reproach. —*v.t.* to mark with any deformity : to tarnish : to defame. [Fr. *blême*, pale, O. Fr. *blesmir*, to stain—Ice. *blâman*, livid colour—*blâr*, **Blue.**]

**Blench**, blensh, *v.i.* to shrink or start back : to flinch. [From root of **Blink.**]

**Blend**, blend, *v.t.*, *to mix together* : to confound. —*v.i.* to be mingled or mixed :—*pa.p.* blend′ed and blent.—*n.* **Blend**, a mixture. [A.S. *blandan*.]

**Bless**, bles, *v.t.* to invoke a blessing upon : to make joyous, happy, or prosperous : to wish happiness to : to praise or glorify :—*pa.p.* blessed′ or blest. [A.S. *blessian, bletsian*, to bless ; from *blith-sian* or *blissian*, to be blithe—*blithe*, happy ; or from *blotan*, to kill for sacrifice, to consecrate.]

**Blessed**, bles′ed,        happy : prosperous : happy in heaven.—*adv.* **Bless′edly.**—*n.* **Bless′edness.**

**Blessing**, bles′ing, *n.* a wish or prayer for happiness or success : any means or cause of happiness.

**Blest**, blest, *pa.p.* of **Bless.**

**Blew**, bloō, *pa.t.* of **Blow.**

**Blight**, blīt, *n.* a disease in plants, which blasts or withers them : anything that injures or destroys.—*v.t.* to affect with blight : to blast : to frustrate. [Perh. from A.S. *blæc*, pale, livid.]

**Blind**, blīnd, *adj.* without sight : dark : ignorant or undiscerning : without an opening.—*n.* something to mislead : a window-screen : a shade.—

*v.t.* to make blind : to darken, obscure, or deceive : to dazzle.—*adv.* **Blind′ly.**—*n.* **Blind′ness.** [A.S. *blind*; Ice. *blindr*.]

**Blindfold,** blīnd′fōld, *adj.* having the eyes bandaged, so as not to see : thoughtless : reckless.— *v.t.* to cover the eyes : to mislead. [M. E. *blindfellen,* from A.S. *fyllan, fellan,* to fell or strike down—'struck blind ;' not conn. with *fold.*]

**Blindworm,** blīnd′wurm, *n.* a small reptile, like a snake, having eyes so small as to be supposed blind.

**Blink,** blingk, *v.i.* to glance, twinkle, or wink : to see obscurely, or with the eyes half closed.—*v.t.* to shut out of sight : to avoid or evade.—*n.* a glimpse, glance, or wink. [A.S. *blican,* to glitter ; Dut. *blinken.*] [bad eyes.

**Blinkard,** blingk′ard, *n.* one who blinks or has

**Blinkers,** blingk′érz, *n.* pieces of leather on a horse's bridle which prevent him seeing on the side.

**Bliss,** blis, *n.* the highest happiness. [A.S. *blis— blīthsian, blissian,* to rejoice—*blithe,* joyful.]

**Blissful,** blis′fool, *adj.* happy in the highest degree.—*adv.* **Bliss′fully.**—*n.* **Bliss′fulness.**

**Blister,** blis′tér, *n.* a thin bubble or bladder on the skin, containing watery matter : a pustule : a plaster applied to raise a blister.—*v.t.* to raise a blister. [Dim. of **Blast.**]

**Blistery,** blis′tér-i, *adj.* full of blisters.

**Blithe,** blī*th,* *adj.* happy : gay : sprightly.—*adv.* **Blithe′ly.**—*n.* **Blithe′ness.** [A.S. *blithe,* joyful. See **Bliss.**] [somely.—*n.* **Blithe′someness.**

**Blithesome,** blī*th′*sum, *adj.* joyous.—*adv.* **Blithe′-**

**Bloat,** blōt, *v.t.* to swell or puff out : to dry by smoke (applied to fish).—*v.i.* to swell or dilate : to grow turgid.—*p.adj.* **Bloat′ed.** [Scan., as in Sw. *blota,* to soak, to steep—*blot,* soft.]

**Bloater,** blōt′ér, *n.* a herring partially dried in smoke.

**Block,** blok, *n.* an unshaped mass of wood or stone, &c. : the wood on which criminals are beheaded : (*mech.*) a pulley together with its framework : a piece of wood on which something is formed : a connected group of houses : an obstruction : a blockhead.—*v.t.* to inclose or shut up : to obstruct : to shape. [Widely spread, but acc. to Skeat, of Celt. orig., Gael. *ploc,* O. Ir. *blog,* a fragment. See **Plug.**]

**Blockade,** blok-ād′, *n.* the blocking up of a place by surrounding it with troops or by ships.—*v.t.* to block up by troops or ships.

**Blockhead,** blok′hed, *n.* one with a head like a block, a stupid fellow.

**Blockhouse,** blok′hows, *n.* a small temporary fort generally made of logs.

**Blockish,** blok′ish, *adj.* like a block : stupid : dull.

**Block-tin,** blok′-tin, *n.* tin in the form of blocks or ingots.

**Blonde,** blond, *n.* a person of *fair* complexion with light hair and blue eyes :—opp. to **Brunette.**—*adj.* of a fair complexion : fair. [Fr.]

**Blond-lace,** blond′-lās, *n.* lace made of silk, so called from its colour.

**Blood,** blud, *n.* the red fluid in the arteries and veins of men and animals : kindred, descent : temperament : bloodshed or murder : the juice of anything, esp. if red.—**In hot or cold blood,** under, or free from, excitement or sudden passion.—**Half-blood,** relationship through one parent only. [A.S. *blod*—root *blowan,* to bloom; cog. with O. Fris. *blod,* Ger. *blut.*]

**Bloodheat,** blud′hēt, *n.* heat of the same degree as that of the human blood (about 98° Fahr.).

**Bloodhorse,** blud′hors, *n.* a horse of the purest and most highly prized blood, origin, or stock.

**Bloodhound,** blud′hownd, *n.* a large hound formerly employed in tracking human beings : a blood-thirsty person. [slaughter.

**Bloodshed,** blud′shed, *n.* the shedding of blood :

**Bloodshot,** blud′shot, *adj.* (of the eye) red or inflamed with blood. [derous, cruel.

**Bloody,** blud′i, *adj.* stained with blood : mur-

**Bloody-flux,** blud′i-fluks, *n.* dysentery, in which the discharges from the bowels are mixed with blood. [panied with the discharge of blood.

**Bloody-sweat,** blud′i-swet, *n.* a sweat accom-

**Bloom,** blōōm, *v.i.* to put forth blossoms : to flower : to be in a state of beauty or vigour : to flourish.—*n.* a blossom or flower : the opening of flowers : rosy colour : the prime or highest perfection of anything.—*p.adj.* **Bloom′ing.** [Ice. *blōm,* Goth. *bloma,* from root of A.S. *blōwan,* to bloom, akin to L. *flo-reo,* to flower.]

**Bloomy,** blōōm′i, *adj.* flowery : flourishing.

**Blossom,** blos′om, *n.* a flower-bud, the flower that precedes fruit.—*v.i.* to put forth blossoms or flowers : to flourish and prosper. [A.S. *blōstma,* from root of **Bloom.**]

**Blot,** blot, *n.* a spot or stain : an obliteration, as of something written : a stain in reputation.— *v.t.* to spot or stain : to obliterate or destroy : to disgrace :—*pr.p.* blott′ing ; *pa.p.* blott′ed. [Scand., as in Dan. *plet,* Ice. *blettr,* a spot. Cf. Ger. *platsch,* a splash, and Ice. *blautr,* moist ; L. *fluid-us.*]

**Blotch,** bloch, *n.* a dark spot on the skin : a pustule.—*adj.* **Blotched′.** [Acc. to Skeat, *blotch* = *blatch,* from *black,* as *bleach* from *bleak.*]

**Blotting-paper,** blot′ing-pā′pér, *n.* unsized paper, used for absorbing ink.

**Blouse,** blowz, *n.* a loose outer garment. [Fr.]

**Blow,** blō, *n.* a stroke or knock : a sudden misfortune or calamity. [A.S. *bleovan* is doubtful : found in Dut. *blouwen,* to dress (beat) flax, Ger. *bläuen,* to beat hard, and L. *flig-* in **Inflict, Flagellation.** Derivative **Blue.**]

**Blow,** blō, *v.i.* to bloom or blossom :—*pr.p.* blōw′ing ; *pa.p.* blōwn. [A.S. *blōwan,* Ger. *blühen.* See **Bloom, Blossom.**]

**Blow,** blō, *v.i.* to produce a current of air : to move, as air or the wind.—*v.t.* to drive air upon or into : to drive by a current of air : to sound as a wind instrument :—*pa.t.* blew (blōō) ; *pa.p.* blōwn.—**Blow upon,** to taint, to make stale. [A.S. *blawan ;* Ger. *blähen, blasen ;* L. *flare.*]

**Blowpipe,** blō′pīp, *n.* a pipe through which a current of air is blown on a flame, to increase its heat. [stale, worthless.

**Blown,** blōn, *p.adj.* out of breath, tired : swelled :

**Blowze,** blowz, *n.* a ruddy, fat-faced woman.— *adjs.* **Blowzed′, Blowz′y,** ruddy, or flushed with exercise. [From root of **Blush.**]

**Blubber,** blub′ér, *n.* the fat of whales and other sea animals.—*v.i.* to weep in a noisy manner. [**Blubber, Blabber,** &c., are extensions of *bleb, blob ;* they contain the root idea of 'puffed-up,' and are formed in imitation of the sound of the bubbling or foaming of a liquid.]

**Bludgeon,** blud′jun, *n.* a short stick with a heavy end to strike with. [From root of **Block.**]

**Blue,** blōō, *n.* the colour of the sky when unclouded : one of the seven primary colours.— *adj.* of the colour blue.—*n.* **Blue′ness.** [Found in Ice. *blar,* cog. with Ger. *blau ;* originally meaning *livid,* the colour caused by a **Blow.**]

**Bluebell,** blōō′bel, *n.* a plant that bears blue bell-shaped flowers.

**Bluebook,** blōō′book, *n.* a book containing some official statement, so called from its blue cover.

**Blue-bottle,** blōō'-bot'l, *n.* a plant with blue bottle-shaped flowers that grows among corn : a large blue fly. [guished from a marine.

**Blue-jacket,** blōō-jak'et, *n.* a seaman, as distin-

**Blue-stocking,** blōō'-stok'ing, *n.* a literary lady : applied in Dr Johnson's time to meetings held by ladies for conversation with certain literary men, one of whom always wore blue stockings.

**Bluff,** bluf, *adj.* blustering : outspoken : steep.— *n.* Bluff'ness. [Prob. Dut.]

**Bluff,** bluf, *n.* a high steep bank overlooking the sea or a river. [ness.

**Bluish,** blōō'ish, *adj.* slightly blue.—*n.* Blu'ish-

**Blunder,** blun'dėr, *v.i.* to make a gross mistake, to flounder about.—*n.* a gross mistake. [From root of **Blunt**.]

**Blunderbuss,** blun'dėr-bus, *n.* a short hand-gun, with a wide bore. [Corr. of Dut. *donderbus—donder,* thunder, *bus,* a box, barrel of a gun, a gun ; Ger. *donnerbüchse.*]

**Blunt,** blunt, *adj.* having a dull edge or point : rough, outspoken, dull.—*v.t.* to dull the edge or point : to weaken.—*adj.* Blunt'ish.—*adv.* Blunt'ly.—*n.* Blunt'ness. [Orig. sleepy, dull ; Dan. *blunde,* to slumber, akin to **Blind**.]

**Blur,** blur, *n.* a blot, stain, or spot.—*v.t.* to blot, stain, obscure, or blemish :—*pr.p.* blurr'ing ; *pa.p.* blurred'. [A variety of **Blear**.]

**Blurt,** blurt, *v.t.* to utter suddenly or unadvisedly. [From **Blare**.]

**Blush,** blush, *n.* a red glow on the face caused by shame, modesty, &c. : any reddish colour : sudden appearance.—*v.i.* to shew shame or confusion by growing red in the face : to grow red. [A.S. *blyse,* a blaze. See **Blaze, Blowze.**]

**Bluster,** blus'tėr, *v.i.* to make a noise like a *blast* of wind : to bully or swagger.—*n.* a blast or roaring as of the wind : bullying or boasting language. [An augmentative of **Blast**.]

**Bo,** bō, *int.* a word used to frighten children.

**Boa,** bō'a, *n.* a genus of serpents which includes the largest species of serpents, the **Boa-constrictor** : a long serpent-like piece of fur worn round the neck by ladies. [Perh. conn. with L. *bos,* an ox.]

**Boar,** bōr, *n.* the male of swine. [A.S. *bar.*]

**Board,** bōrd, *n.* a broad and thin strip of timber : a table to put food on : food : a table round which persons meet for some kind of business : any council or authorised body of men, as a school board : the deck of a ship.—*v.t.* to cover with boards : to supply with food at fixed terms : to enter a ship : to attack.—*v.i.* to receive food or take meals. [A.S. *bord,* a board, the side of a ship ; Ice. *bord,* the side of a ship ; found also in Celt. ; conn. either with **Bear** or with **Broad**.] [(food) : one who boards a ship.

**Boarder,** bōrd'ėr, *n.* one who receives board

**Boarding,** bōrd'ing, *n.* the act of covering with boards : the covering itself : act of boarding a ship.

**Boarding-school,** bōrd'ing-skōōl, *n.* a school in which board is given as well as instruction.

**Board-wages,** bōrd'-wāj'ez, *n.* wages allowed to servants to keep themselves in food.

**Boast,** bōst, *v.i.* to talk vaingloriously : to brag. —*v.t.* to brag of : speak proudly or confidently of : to magnify or exalt one's self.—*n.* an expression of pride : a brag : the cause of boasting. [M.E. *bost*—W. *bost,* Gael. *bosd,* a bragging.]

**Boastful,** bōst'fool, *adj.* given to brag.—*adv.* Boast'fully.—*n.* Boast'fulness. [vaunting.

**Boasting,** bōst'ing, *n.* ostentatious display :

**Boat,** bōt, *n.* small open vessel usually moved by oars : a small ship.—*v.i.* to go in a boat. [A.S. *bat* ; Dut. *boot* ; Fr. *bat-eau* ; Gael. *bata.*]

**Boathook,** bōt'hook, *n.* an iron hook fixed to a pole used for pulling or pushing off a boat.

**Boating,** bōt'ing, *n.* the art or practice of sailing in boats. [a boat : a rower.

**Boatman,** bōt'man, *n.* a man who has charge of

**Boatswain,** bōt'swān (colloquially bō'sn), *n.* a petty officer on board ship who looks after the boats, rigging, &c., and calls the seamen to duty. [(*Lit.*) a boat's swain or servant. From A.S. *bátswán*—*bát,* a boat, *swán,* a lad.]

**Bob,** bob, *v.i.* to move quickly up and down, to dangle : to fish with a bob.—*v.t.* to move in a short jerking manner :—*pr.p.* bobb'ing ; *pa.p.* bobbed'.—*n.* a short jerking motion : a slight blow : anything that moves with a bob or swing : a pendant. [Perhaps imitative, like Gael. *bog,* to agitate, *babag, baban,* a tassel.]

**Bobbin,** bob'in, *n.* a small piece of wood on which thread is wound. [Fr. *bobine,* perhaps from Gael. *baban,* a tassel.]

**Bobbinet,** bob-in-et' or bob'in-et, *n.* a kind of fine netted lace made by machines.

**Bobolink,** bob'ō-lingk, *n.* a North American singing bird, found in the northern states in spring and summer. [At first *Bob Lincoln,* from the note of the bird.]

**Bobwig,** bob'wig, *n.* a short wig.

**Bode,** bōd, *v.t.* to portend or prophesy.—*v.i.* to be an omen : to foreshow. [A.S. *bodian,* to announce—*bod,* a message ; allied to **Bid**.]

**Bodice,** bod'is, *n.* a woman's stays, formerly called *bodies,* from fitting close to the body.

**Bodied,** bod'id, *adj.* having a body. [poreal.

**Bodiless,** bod'i-les, *adj.* without a body : incor-

**Bodily,** bod'i-ly, *adj.* relating to the body, esp. as opposed to the mind.

**Bodkin,** bod'kin, *n.,* *a small dagger* : a small instrument for pressing holes or for dressing the hair : a large blunt needle. [Prob. W. *bidog.*]

**Body,** bod'i, *n.* the whole frame of a man or lower animal : the main part of an animal, as distinguished from the limbs : the main part of anything : matter, as opposed to spirit : a mass : a person : a number of persons united by some common tie.—*v.t.* to give form to : to embody : —*pr.p.* bod'ying ; *pa.p.* bod'ied. [A.S. *bodig.*]

**Bodyguard,** bod'i-gärd, *n.* a guard to protect the person, esp. of the sovereign.

**Body-politic,** bod'i-pol'it-ik, *n.* the collective body of the people in its political capacity.

**Bœotian,** be-ō'shyan, *adj.* pertaining to Bœotia in Greece, noted for the dullness of its inhabitants : hence, stupid, dull.

**Bog,** bog, *n.* soft ground : a marsh or quagmire, —*adj.* Bogg'y. [Ir. *bogach* ; Gael. *bog.*]

**Boggle,** bog'l, *v.i.* to stop or hesitate as if at a *bogle* : to make difficulties about a thing.

**Bogle,** bōg'l, *n.* a spectre or goblin. [Scot. *bogle,* a ghost ; W. *bwg,* a goblin. See **Bug**.]

**Bogmoss,** bog'mos, *n.* a genus of moss plants.

**Bogus,** bō'gus, *adj.* counterfeit, spurious. [Amer. cant word, of very doubtful origin.]

**Bohea,** bo-hē', *n.* the lowest quality of blac tea. [Chinese.]

**Bohemian,** bo-hē'mi-an, *n.* and *adj.* applied to persons of loose and irregular habits.—*n.* Bohe'mianism. [Fr. *bohémien,* a gipsy, from the belief that these wanderers came from Bohemia.]

**Boil,** boil, *v.i., to bubble* up from the action of heat : to be hot : to be excited or agitated.—*v.t.* to heat to a boiling state : to cook or dress by boiling. — **Boiling-point,** the temperature at which liquids begin to boil under heat. [O. Fr. *boilir*—L. *bullire—bulla,* a bubble.]

**Boil**, boil, *n.* an inflamed swelling or tumour. [A.S. *byl*; Ger. *beule*; Ice. *bola*, from the root of Bulge.] [anything is boiled.

**Boiler**, boil'ėr, *n.* one who boils : that in which

**Boisterous**, bois'tėr-us, *adj., wild* : noisy : turbulent : stormy.—*adv.* **Bois'terously.**—*n.* **Bois'terousness.** [M.E. *boistous*—W. *bwyst*, wildness.]

**Bold**, bōld, *adj.* daring or courageous : forward or impudent : executed with spirit : striking to the sight : steep or abrupt.—*adv.* **Bold'ly.**—*n.* **Bold'ness.—To make Bold,** to take the liberty, to make free. [A.S., *bald*; O. Ger. *pald*, O. Fr. *baud*, Goth. *balths*, Ice. *ballr*.]

**Bole**, bōl, *n., the round* stem or body of a tree. [Ice. *bolr*, from its round form. Conn. with **Bowl**, a cup, **Bulge**, **Boil**, a swelling, and **Bag**.]

**Boll**, bōl, *n.* one of the *round* heads or seedvessels of flax, poppy, &c. : a pod or capsule : a Scotch dry measure = six imperial bushels, not now legally in use. [A form of **Bowl**, a cup, and sig. 'thing round.'] [*bollen*, to swell.]

**Bolled**, bōld, swollen : podded. [Pa.p. of M.E.

**Bolster**, bōl'stėr, *n.* a long round pillow or cushion : a pad.—*v.t.* to support with a bolster : to hold up. [A.S. *bolster*; from root of **Bowl**.]

**Bolt**, bōlt, *n.* a bar or pin used to fasten a door, &c. : an arrow : a thunderbolt.—*v.t.* to fasten with a bolt : to throw or utter precipitately : to swallow hastily.—*v.i.* to rush away (like a bolt from a bow). [A.S. and Dan. *bolt*, Ger. *bolzen* ; from root of **Bole**, of a tree.]

**Bolt**, bōlt, *v.t.* to sift, to separate the bran from, as flour : to examine by sifting : to sift through coarse cloth. [O. Fr. *bulter*, or *buleter* = *bureter*, from *bure*—Low L. *burra*, a coarse reddishbrown cloth—Gr. *pyrros*, reddish—*pyr* = **Fire**.]

**Bolting-hutch**, bōlt'ing-huch, *n.* a hutch or large box into which flour falls when it is bolted.

**Bolt-upright**, bōlt'-up-rīt', *adv.* upright and straight as a bolt or arrow.

**Bolus**, bō'lus, *n.* a rounded mass of anything : a large pill. [L. *bolus*, Gr. *bōlos*, a lump.]

**Bomb**, bum, *n.* a hollow shell of iron filled with gunpowder, and discharged from a mortar, so as to explode when it falls. [Fr. *bombe*—L. *bombus*, Gr. *bombos*, a humming sound; an imitative word.]

**Bombard**, bum-bärd', *v.t.* to attack with bombs. —*n.* **Bombard'ment.**—*n.* **Bombardier'.**

**Bombasine, Bombazine**, bum-ba-zēn', *n.* a twilled fabric of *silk* and worsted. [Fr. *bombasin*—Low L. *bombacinium*—Gr. *bombyx*, silk. See **Bombast**.]

**Bombast**, bum'bast, *n.* (*orig.*), *cotton* or any soft material used for stuffing garments : inflated or high-sounding language. [Low L. *bombax*, cotton—Gr. *bombyx*, silk.] [flated.

**Bombastic**, bum-bast'ik, *adj.* high-sounding : in-

**Bomb-proof**, bum'-prōōf, *adj.* proof or secure against the force of bombs.

**Bomb-vessel**, bum'-ves-el, *n.* a vessel for carrying the mortars used in bombarding from the sea.

**Bonbon**, bong'bong, *n.* a sweetmeat. [Fr., 'very good'—*bon*, good.]

**Bond**, bond, *n.* that which *binds*, a band : link of connection or union : a writing of obligation to pay a sum or to perform a contract :—*pl.* imprisonment, captivity.—*adj.* bound : in a state of servitude.—*v.t.* to put imported goods in the customs' warehouses till the duties on them are paid. [A.S. ; a variation of *band*—*bindan*, to bind.]

**Bondage**, bond'āj, *n.* state of being bound : captivity : slavery. [O. Fr.—Low L. *bondagium*, a kind of tenure. Acc. to Skeat, this is from A.S. *bonda*, a boor, a householder, from Ice. *bondi* = *buandi*, a tiller, a husbandman.] [duties.

**Bonded**, bond'ed, *p.adj.* secured by bond, as

**Bonding**, bond'ing, *n.* that arrangement by which goods remain in the customs' warehouses till the duties are paid.

**Bondman**, bond'man, *n.* a man slave.—*ns.* **Bond'maid, Bond'woman.** [surety.

**Bondsman**, bondz'man, *n.* a bondman or slave : a

**Bone**, bōn, *n.* a hard substance forming the skeleton of an animal : a piece of the skeleton of an animal.—*v.t.* to take the bones out of, as meat. [A.S. *lan*; Ger. *bein*, Goth. *bain*, bone, leg ; W. *bon*, a stem or stock.]

**Bone-ash**, bōn'-ash, *n.* the remains when bones are burned in an open furnace.

**Bone-black**, bōn'-blak, *n.* the remains when bones are heated in a close vessel.

**Bone-dust**, bōn'-dust, *n.* ground or pulverised bones, used in agriculture.

**Bone-setter**, bōn'-set'ėr, *n.* one whose occupation is to set broken and dislocated bones.

**Bonfire**, bon'fīr, *n.* a large fire in the open air on occasions of public rejoicing, &c. [Orig. a fire in which bones were burnt.]

**Bon-mot**, bong'-mō, *n., a good* or witty saying. [Fr. *bon*, good, *mot*, word.]

**Bonne-bouche**, bon-boosh', *n.* a delicious mouthful. [Fr. *bonne*, good, *bouche*, mouth.]

**Bonnet**, bon'et, *n.* a covering for the head worn by women : a cap.—*p.adj.* **Bonn'eted.** [Fr. —Low L. *bonneta*, orig. the name of a stuff.]

**Bonny**, bon'i, *adj.* beautiful : handsome : gay.— *adv.* **Bonn'ily.** [Fr. *bon*, bonne—L. *bonus*, good ; Celt. *bain*, *baine*, white, fair.]

**Bonus**, bōn'us, *n.* a premium beyond the usual interest for a loan : an extra dividend to shareholders. [L. *bonus*, good.]

**Bony**, bōn'i, *adj.* full of, or consisting of, bones.

**Bonze**, bon'ze, *n.* a Buddhist priest. [Jap. *bozu*, a priest.]

**Booby**, bōōb'i, *n.* a silly or stupid fellow : a waterbird, of the pelican tribe, remarkable for its apparent stupidity. [Sp. *bobo*, a dolt ; O. Fr. *bobu*, stupid—L. *balbus*, stuttering.]

**Book**, book, *n.* a collection of sheets of paper bound together, either printed, written on, or blank : a literary composition : a division of a volume or subject.—*v.t.* to write in a book. [A.S. *boc*, a book, the beech ; Ger. *buche*, the beech, *buch*, a book, because the Teutons first wrote on beechen boards.]

**Book-club**, book'-klub, *n.* an association of persons who buy new books for circulation among themselves. [only with books.—*n.* **Book'ishness.**

**Bookish**, book'ish, *adj.* fond of books : acquainted

**Book-keeping**, book'-kēp'ing, *n.* the art of keeping accounts in a regular and systematic manner.

**Book-learning**, book'-lėrn'ing, *n.* learning got from books, as opposed to practical knowledge.

**Bookplate**, book'plāt, *n.* a label usually pasted inside the cover of a book, bearing the owner's name, crest, or peculiar device.

**Book-post**, book'-pōst, *n.* the department in the Post-office for the transmission of books.

**Bookworm**, book'wurm, *n.* a worm or mite that eats holes in books : a hard reader : one who reads without discrimination or profit.

**Boom**, bōōm, *n.* a pole by which a sail is stretched : a chain or bar stretched across a harbour. [Dut. *boom*, a beam, a tree.]

**Boom**, bōōm, *v.i.* to make a hollow sound or roar.

*—n.* a hollow roar, as of the sea, the cry of the bittern, &c. [From a Low Ger. root found in A.S. *byme,* a trumpet, Dut. *bommen,* to drum ; like **Bomb,** of imitative origin.]

**Boomerang,** boom'e-rang, *n.* a hard-wood missile used by the natives of Australia, shaped like the segment of a circle, and so made that when thrown to a distance it returns towards the thrower [Australian.]

**Boon,** boon, *n.* a petition : a gift or favour. [Ice. *bón,* a prayer ; A.S. *ben.*]

**Boon,** boon, *adj.* (as in *boon* companion) gay, merry or kind. [Fr. *bon*—L. *bonus,* good.]

**Boor,** boor, *n.* a coarse or awkward person. [Dut. *boer* (Ger. *bauer*), a tiller of the soil—Dut. *bou-wen ;* cog. with Ger. *bauen,* A.S. *buan,* to till.]

**Boorish,** boor'ish, *adj.* like a boor : awkward or rude.—*adv.* **Boor'ishly.**—*n.* **Boor'ishness.**

**Boot,** boot, *n.* a covering for the foot and lower part of the leg generally made of leather : an old instrument of torture for the legs : a box or receptacle in a coach :—*n.pl.* the servant in a hotel that cleans the boots.—*v.t.* to put on boots. [Fr. *botte,* a butt, or a boot, from O. Ger. *buten,* a cask. See **Bottle, Butt.**]

**Boot,** boot, *v.t.* to profit or advantage.—*n.* advantage : profit.—**To Boot,** in addition. [A.S. *bot,* compensation, amends, whence *betan,* to amend, to make **Better.**]

**Booth,** booth, *n.* a *hut* or temporary erection formed of slight materials. [Ice. *buth ;* Ger. *bude ;* also Slav. and Celt., as Gael. *both,* hut.]

**Bootjack,** boot'jak, *n.* an instrument for taking off boots. [**Boot** and **Jack.**]

**Bootless,** boot'les, *adj.* without boot or profit : useless.—*adv.* **Boot'lessly.**—*n.* **Boot'lessness.**

**Booty,** boot'i, *n.* spoil taken in war or by force : plunder. [Ice. *byti,* share—*byta,* to divide.]

**Bo-peep,** bo-pep', *n.* a game among children in which one peeps from behind something and cries ' Bo.'

**Boracic,** bo-ras'ik, *adj.* of or relating to borax. —**Boracic acid,** an acid obtained by dissolving borax, and also found native in mineral springs in Italy.

**Borax,** bo'raks, *n.* a mineral salt used for soldering and also in medicine. [Fr.—Ar. *búraq.*]

**Border,** bord'er, *n.* the *edge* or *margin* of anything : the march or boundary of a country : a flower-bed in a garden.—*v.i.* to approach : to be adjacent.—*v.t.* to make or adorn with a border : to bound. [Fr. *bord, bordure ;* from root of **Board.**]

**Borderer,** bord'er-er, *n.* one who dwells on the border of a country.

**Bore,** bor, *v.t.* to pierce so as to form a hole : to weary or annoy.—*n.* a hole made by boring : the size of the cavity of a gun : a person or thing that wearies. [A.S. *borian,* to bore, from *bor,* a borer ; Ger. *bohren ;* allied to L. *foro,* to bore, Gr. *pharynx,* the gullet.]

**Bore,** bor, did bear, *pa.t.* of **Bear.**

**Bore,** bor, *n.* a tidal flood which rushes with great force into the mouths of certain rivers. [Ice. *bára,* a wave or swell, from root of to **Bear** or lift.]

**Boreal,** bo're-al, *adj.* pertaining to the north or the north wind.

**Boreas,** bo're-as, *n.* the north wind. [L. and Gr.]

**Born,** bawrn, *pa.p.* of **Bear,** to bring forth.

**Borne,** born, *pa.p.* of **Bear,** to carry.

**Borough,** bur'o, *n.* a town with a corporation : a town that sends representatives to parliament. [A.S. *burg, burh,* a city, from *beorgan,* Ger. *bergen,* to protect.]

**Boroughmonger,** bur'o-mung'er, *n.* one who buys or sells the patronage of boroughs.

**Borrow,** bor'o, *v.t.* to obtain on loan or trust : to adopt from a foreign source.—*n.* **Borr'ower.** [A.S. *borgian*—*borg, borh,* a pledge, security ; akin to **Borough,** from the notion of security.]

**Boscage,** bosk'aj, *n.* thick foliage : woodland. [Fr. *boscage, bocage*—Low L. *boscus* (hence Fr. *bois*), conn. with Ger. *busch,* E. *bush.*]

**Bosh,** bosh, *n.* used also as *int.,* nonsense, foolish talk or opinions. [Turk. *bosh,* worthless, frequent in Morier's popular novel *Ayesha* (1834).]

**Bosky,** bosk'i, *adj.* woody or bushy : shady.

**Bosom,** booz'um, *n.* the breast of a human being, or the part of the dress which covers it : (*fig.*) the seat of the passions and feelings : the heart : embrace, inclosure, as within the arms : any close or secret receptacle.—*adj.* (in composition) confidential : intimate.—*v.t.* to inclose in the bosom. [A.S. *bosm,* Ger. *busen.*]

**Boss,** bos, *n.* a knob or stud : a raised ornament. —*v.t.* to ornament with bosses. [Fr. *bosse,* It. *bozza,* a swelling, from O. Ger. *bozen,* to beat.]

**Bossy,** bos'i, *adj.* having bosses.

**Botanise,** bot'an-iz, *v.i.* to seek for and collect plants for study.

**Botanist,** bot'an-ist, *n.* one skilled in botany.

**Botany,** bot'a-ni, *n.* the science of plants.—*adj.* **Botan'ic.**—*adv.* **Botan'ically.** [Gr. *botanē,* herb, plant—*boskō,* to feed, L. *vescor,* I feed myself ; perh. cog. with A.S. *weod.*]

**Botch,** boch, *n.,* a *swelling* on the skin : a clumsy patch : ill-finished work.—*v.t.* to patch or mend clumsily : to put together unsuitably or unskilfully. [From root of **Boss.**]

**Botcher,** boch'er, *n.* one who botches.

**Botchy,** boch'i, *adj.* marked with or full of botches.

**Both,** both, *adj.* and *pron., the two :* the one and the other.—*conj.* as well : on the one side. [Ice. *bathi,* Ger. *beide ;* A.S. *bá ;* cf. L. *am-bo,* Gr. *am-phō,* Sans. *ubha,* orig. *ambha.*]

**Bother,** both'er, *v.t.* to perplex or tease. [Perh. from Ir. *buaidhirt,* trouble.]

**Bottle,** bot'l, *n., a bundle* of hay. [Dim. of Fr. *botte,* a bundle, from root of **Boss.**]

**Bottle,** bot'l, *n.* a hollow vessel for holding liquids : the contents of such a vessel.—*v.t.* to inclose in bottles. [Fr. *bouteille,* dim. of *botte,* a vessel for liquids. From root of **Boot, Butt.**]

**Bottled,** bot'ld, *p.adj.* inclosed in bottles : shaped or protuberant like a bottle.

**Bottom,** bot'um, *n.* the lowest part of anything : that on which anything rests or is founded : low land, as in a valley : the keel of a ship, hence the vessel itself.—*v.t.* to found or rest upon.— *adj.* **Bott'omless.** [A.S. *botm ;* Ger. *boden ;* conn. with L. *fundus,* bottom, Gael. *bond, bown,* the sole.]

**Bottomry,** bot'um-ri, *n.* a contract by which money is borrowed on the security of a ship or bottom. [From **Bottom,** a ship.]

**Boudoir,** bood'war, *n.* a lady's private room. [Fr.—*bouder,* to pout, to be sulky.]

**Bough,** bow, *n.* a branch of a tree. [A.S. *bog, boh,* an arm, the shoulder (Ger. *bug,* the shoulder, the bow of a ship)—A.S. *bugan,* to bend.]

**Bought,** bawt, *pa.t.* and *pa.p.* of **Buy.**

**Boulder,** bold'er, *n.* a large stone rounded by the action of water : (*geol.*) a mass of rock transported by natural agencies from its native bed. —*adj.* containing boulders. [Acc. to Wedgwood, from Swed. *bullra,* Dan. *buldre,* to roar like thunder, as large pebbles do.]

**Boulevard,** bool'e-vär, *n.* a promenade, formed by

levelling the old fortifications of a town. [Fr.—Ger. *bollwerk*. See **Bulwark**.]

**Bounce**, bowns, *v.i.* to jump or spring suddenly : to boast, to exaggerate.—*n.* a heavy sudden blow : a leap or spring : a boast : a bold lie. [Dut. *bonzen*, to strike, from *bons*, a blow, from the sound.]      [thing big : a bully : a liar.

**Bouncer**, bowns'ẽr, *n.* one who bounces : something

**Bound**, bownd, *pa.t.* and *pa.p.* of **Bind**.

**Bound**, bownd, *n.* a limit or boundary.—*v.t.* to set bounds to : to limit, restrain, or surround. [O. Fr. *bonne*—Low L. *bodina*—Bret. *bonn*, a boundary.]

**Bound**, bownd, *v.i.* to spring or leap.—*n.* A spring or leap. [Fr. *bondir*, to spring, in O. Fr. to resound—L. *bombita* See **Boom**, the sound.]

**Bound**, bownd, *adj.* ready to go. [Ice. *buinn*, pa.p. of *bua*, to prepare.]

**Boundary**, bownd'a-ri, *n.* a visible bound or limit : border : termination.

**Bounden**, bownd'n, *adj.*, *binding* : required : obligatory. [From **Bind**.]

**Boundless**, bownd'les, *adj.* having no bound or limit : vast.—*n.* **Bound'lessness**.

**Bounteous**, bown'te-us or bown'tyus, **Bountiful**, bown'ti-fool, *adj.* liberal in giving : generous.—*advs.* **Boun'teously**, **Boun'tifully**.—*ns.* **Boun'teousness**, **Boun'tifulness**. [From **Bounty**.]

**Bounty**, bown'ti, *n.* liberality in bestowing gifts : the gift bestowed : money offered as an inducement to enter the army, or as a premium to encourage any branch of industry. [Fr. *bonté*, goodness—L. *bonitas—bonus*, good.]

**Bouquet**, boo'kā, *n.* a bunch of flowers : a nosegay. [Fr.—*bosquet*, dim. of *bois*, a wood—It. *bosco*. See **Boscage**, **Bush**.]

**Bourg**, burg, *n.* Same as **Burgh**, **Borough**.

**Bourgeois**, bur-jois', *n.* a kind of printing type, larger than brevier and smaller than longprimer. [Fr.—perh. from the name of the typefounder.]

**Bourgeoisie**, boorzh-waw'zē, *n.* the middle class of citizens, esp. traders. [From Fr. *bourgeois*, a citizen, from root of **Borough**.]

**Bourgeon**, bur'jun, *v.i.* to put forth sprouts or buds : to grow. [Fr. *bourgeon*, a bud, shoot.]

**Bourn**, **Bourne**, bōrn or bŏŏrn, *n.* a boundary, or a limit. [Fr. *borne*, a limit. See **Bound**.]

**Bourn**, **Bourne**, bōrn or bŏŏrn, *n.* a little stream. [A.S. *burna*, a stream ; Scot. *burn*, a brook ; Goth. *brunna*, a spring.]

**Bourse**, bŏŏrs, *n.* an exchange where merchants meet for business. [Fr. *bourse*. See **Purse**.]

**Bouse**, bŏŏz, *v.i.* to drink deeply. [Dut. *buysen*, to drink deeply—*buis*, a tube or flask ; allied to **Box**.]

**Bout**, bowt, *n.* a turn, trial, or round : an attempt. [Doublet of **Bight** ; from root of **Bow**, to bend.]

**Bovine**, bō'vīn, *adj.* pertaining to cattle. [L. *bos*, *bovis*, Gr. *bous*, an ox or cow.]

**Bow**, bow, *v.t.*, *to bend* or incline towards : to subdue.—*v.i.* to bend the body in saluting a person : to yield.—*n.* a bending of the body in saluting a person : the curving forepart of a ship. [A.S. *bugan*, to bend ; akin to L. *fugio*, to flee, to yield.]

**Bow**, bō, *n.* a *bent* piece of wood for shooting arrows : anything of a bent or curved shape, as the rainbow : the instrument by which the strings of a violin are sounded. [A.S. *boga*.]

**Bowels**, bow'elz, *n.pl.* the interior parts of the body, the entrails : the interior part of anything : (*fig.*) the heart, pity, tenderness. [Fr. *boyau*, O. Fr. *boel*—L. *botellus*, a sausage, also, an intestine.]

**Bower**, bow'ẽr, *n.* an anchor at the bow or forepart of a ship. [From **Bow**.]

**Bower**, bow'ẽr, *n.* a shady inclosure or recess in a garden, an arbour. [A.S. *bur*, a chamber ; Scot. *byre*—root A.S. *búan*, to dwell.]

**Bowery**, bow'ẽr-i, *adj.* containing bowers : shady.

**Bowie-knife**, bō'i-nīf, *n.* a dagger-knife worn in the southern states of America, so named from its inventor, Colonel *Bowie*.

**Bowl**, bōl, *n.* a wooden ball used for rolling along the ground.—*v.t.* and *i.* to play at bowls : to roll along like a bowl : to throw a ball, as in cricket. [Fr. *boule*—L. *bulla*. See **Boll**, *v.*]

**Bowl**, bōl, *n.* a *round* drinking-cup : the round hollow part of anything. [A.S. *bolla*. See **Bole**.]

**Bowlder**, bōld'ẽr, *n.* Same as **Boulder**.

**Bowline**, bō'lin, *n.* (*lit.*) the *line* of the *bow* or *bend* : a rope to keep a sail close to the wind.

**Bowling-green**, bōl'ing-grēn, *n.* a green or grassy plat kept smooth for bowling.

**Bowman**, bō'man, *n.* an archer.

**Bowshot**, bō'shot, *n.* the distance to which an arrow can be shot from a bow.

**Bowsprit**, bō'sprit, *n.* a boom or spar projecting from the bow of a ship. [**Bow** and **Sprit**.]

**Bowstring**, bō'string, *n.* a string with which the Turks strangled offenders.

**Bow-window**, bō'-wind'ō, *n.* a bent or semicircular window.

**Box**, boks, *n.* a tree remarkable for the hardness and smoothness of its wood : a case or receptacle for holding anything : the contents of a box : a small house or lodge : a private seat in a theatre : the driver's seat on a carriage.—*v.t.* to put into or furnish with boxes. [A.S. *box*—L. *buxus*, Gr. *pyxos*, the tree, *pyxis*, a box.]

**Box**, boks, *n.* a blow on the head or ear with the hand.—*v.t.* to strike with the hand or fist.—*v.i.* to fight with the fists. [Dan. *bask*, a sounding blow ; cf. Ger. *pochen*, to strike.]

**Boxen**, boks'n, *adj.* made of or like boxwood.

**Boxing-day**, boks'ing-dā, *n.* in England, the day after Christmas when boxes or presents are given.

**Boxwood**, boks'wood, *n.* wood of the box-tree.

**Boy**, boy, *n.* a male child : a lad.—*n.* **Boy'hood**. —*adj.* **Boy'ish**.—*adv.* **Boy'ishly**.—*n.* **Boy'ishness**. [Fris. *boi*, Dut. *boef*, Ger. *bube*, L. *pupus*.]

**Boycott**, boy'kot, *v.t.* to shut out from all social and commercial intercourse. [From Captain *Boycott*, who was so treated by his neighbours in Ireland in 1881.]

**Brace**, brās, *n.* anything that draws together and holds tightly : a bandage : pair or couple : in printing, a mark connecting two or more words or lines ( } ) :—*pl.* straps for supporting the trousers : ropes for turning the yards of a ship.—*v.t.* to tighten or strengthen. [O. Fr. *brace*, Fr. *bras*, the arm, power—L. *brachium*, Gr. *brachiōn*, the arm, as holding together.]

**Bracelet**, brās'let, *n.* an ornament for the wrist. [Fr., dim. of O. Fr. *brac*. See **Brace**.]

**Brach**, brak, brach, *n.* a dog for the chase. [O. Fr. *brache*, from O. Ger. *bracco*.]

**Brachial**, brak'i-al, *adj.* belonging to the arm. [See **Brace**.]        [From **Brace**.]

**Bracing**, brās'ing, *adj.* giving strength or tone.

**Bracken**, brak'en, *n.* fern. [See **Brake**.]

**Bracket**, brak'et, *n.* a support for something fastened to a wall :—*pl.* in printing, the marks [ ] used to inclose one or more words.—*v.t.* to support by brackets : to inclose by brackets. [Dim. formed from **Brace**.]

**Brackish,** brak'ish, *adj.* saltish : applied to water mixed with salt or with sea-water.—*n.* **Brack'-ishness.** [Dut. *brak,* refuse : conn. with **Wreck.**]

**Bract,** brakt, *n.* an irregularly developed *leaf* at the base of the flower-stalk.—*adj.* **Brac'teal.** [L. *bractea,* a thin plate of metal, gold-leaf.]

**Bradawl,** brad'awl, *n.* an awl to pierce holes. [For inserting *brads,* long, thin nails.]

**Brag,** brag, *v.i.* to boast or bluster :—*pr.p.* bragg'-ing ; *pa.p.* bragged.—*n.* a boast or boasting : the thing boasted of : a game at cards. [Prob. from a root *brag,* found in all the Celtic languages. See **Brave.**]

**Braggadocio,** brag-a-dō'shi-o, *n.* a braggart or boaster : empty boasting. [From *Braggadochio,* a boastful character in Spenser's *Faëry Queen.*]

**Braggart,** brag'art, *adj.* boastful.—*n.* a vain boaster. [O. Fr. *bragard,* vain, bragging, from root of **Brag.**]

**Brahman,** brä'man, **Brahmin,** brä'min, *n.* a person of the highest or priestly caste among the Hindus.—*adjs.* **Brahman'ic, -al, Brahmin'ic, -al.** [From *Brahma,* the Hindu Deity.]

**Brahmanism,** brä'man-izm, **Brahminism,** brä'-min-izm, *n.* one of the religions of India, the worship of Brahma.

**Braid,** brād, *v.t., to plait* or entwine.—*n.* cord, or other texture made by plaiting. [A.S. *bredan, bregdan* ; Ice. *bregda,* to weave.]

**Brain,** brān, *n.* the mass of nervous matter contained in the skull : the seat of the intellect and of sensation : the intellect.—*v.t.* to dash out the brains of. [A.S. *bregen* ; Dut. *brein.*]

**Brainless,** brān'les, *adj.* without brains or understanding : silly.

**Brain-sickness,** brān-sik'nes, *n.* disorder of the brain : giddiness, indiscretion.

**Brake,** brāk, *obs. pa.t.* of **Break.**

**Brake,** brāk, *n.* a fern : a place overgrown with ferns or briers : a thicket. [Low Ger. *brake,* brushwood ; Ger. *brach,* fallow.]

**Brake,** brāk, *n.* an instrument *to break* flax or hemp : a carriage for breaking-in horses : a bit for horses : a contrivance for retarding the motion of a wheel. [From root of **Break.**]

**Braky,** brāk'i, *adj.* full of brakes : thorny : rough.

**Bramble,** bram'bl, *n.* a wild prickly plant bearing black berries : any rough prickly shrub.—*adj.* **Bram'bly.** [A.S. *bremel* ; Dut. *braam,* Ger. *brom.*]

**Bran,** bran, *n., the refuse* of grain : the inner husks of corn sifted from the flour. [Fr. *bran,* bran—Celt. *bran,* bran, refuse.]

**Branch,** bransh, *n.* a shoot or *arm-like* limb of a tree : anything     a branch : any offshoot or subdivision.—*v.t.* to divide into branches.—*v.i.* to spread out as a branch.—*adjs.* **Branch'less, Branch'y.** [Fr. *branche*—Bret. *branc,* an arm ; Low L. *branca,* L. *brachium.* See **Brace.**]

**Branchiæ,** brangk'i-ē, *n.pl., gills.*—*adj.* **Branch-ial,** brangk'i-al. [L.]

**Branchlet,** bransh'let, *n.* a little branch.

**Brand,** brand, *n.* a piece of wood *burning* or partly burned : a mark burned into anything with a hot iron : a sword, so called from its glitter : a mark of infamy.—*v.t.* to burn or mark with a hot iron : to fix a mark of infamy upon. [A.S., from root of **Burn.**]

**Brandish,** brand'ish, *v.t.* to wave or flourish as a *brand* or weapon.—*n.* a waving or flourish. [Fr. *brandir,* from root of **Brand.**]

**Brand-new,** brand'-nū, *adj.* quite new (as if newly from the fire).

**Brandy,** brand'i, *n.* an ardent spirit distilled from wine. [Formerly *brandwine*—Dut. *brandewijn*—*branden,* to burn, to distil, and *wijn,* wine ; cf. Ger. *brantwein.*]

**Bran-new,** bran'-nū, *adj.* Corr. of **Brand-new.**

**Brasier,** brā'zhér, *n.* a pan for holding burning coals. [Fr., from the root of **Brass.**]

**Brass,** bras, *n.* an alloy of copper and zinc : (*fig.*) impudence :—*pl.* monumental plates of brass inlaid on slabs of stone in the pavements of ancient churches. [A.S. *braes* ; Ice. *bras,* solder ; from *brasa,* to harden by fire, Swed. *brasa,* fire.]

**Brass-band,** bras'-band, *n.* a band or company of musicians who perform on brass instruments.

**Brassy,** bras'i, *adj.* of or like brass : impudent.

**Brat,** brat, *n.* a contemptuous name for a child. [A.S. *bratt,* W., Gael. *brat,* a rag ; prov. E. *brat,* a child's pinafore.]

**Bravado,** brav-ä'do, *n.* a display of bravery : a boastful threat :—*pl.* **Brava'does.** [Sp. *bravada,* from root of **Brave.**]

**Brave,** brāv, *adj.* daring, courageous : noble.—*v.t.* to meet boldly : to defy.—*n.* a bully.—*adv.* **Brave'ly.** [Fr. *brave* ; It. and Sp. *bravo ;* from Celt., as in Bret. *braga,* to strut about, Gael. *breagh,* fine. See **Brag.**]

**Bravery,** brāv'èr-i, *n.* courage : heroism : finery.

**Bravo,** brāv'ō, *n.* a daring villain : a hired assassin :—*pl.* **Bravoes,** brāv'ōz. [It. and Sp.]

**Bravo,** brāv'o, *int.* well done : excellent. [It.]

**Bravura,** brāv-ōōr'a, *n.* (*mus.*) a term applied to songs that require great spirit in execution. [It.]

**Brawl,** brawl, *n.* a noisy quarrel.—*v.i.* to quarrel noisily : to murmur or gurgle. [W. *bragal,* to vociferate, which, acc. to Skeat, is a freq. of **Brag.**]

**Brawn,** brawn, *n.* muscle : thick flesh, esp. boar's flesh : muscular strength. [O. Fr. *braon,* from O. Ger. *brato,* flesh (for roasting)—O. Ger. *pratan* (Ger. *braten*), to roast.]

**Brawny,** brawn'i, *adj.* fleshy : muscular : strong.

**Bray,** brā, *v.t., to break,* pound, or grind small. [O. Fr. *breier* (Fr. *broyer*) ; from root of **Break.**]

**Bray,** brā, *n.* the cry of the ass : any harsh grating sound.—*v.i.* to cry like an ass. [Fr. *braire,* Low L. *bragire,* from root of **Brag, Brawl.**]

**Braze,** brāz, *v.t.* to cover or solder with brass.

**Brazen,** brā'zn, *adj.* of or belonging to brass : impudent.—*v.t.* to confront with impudence.

**Brazier,** brā'zhér, *n.* See **Brasier.**

**Breach,** brēch, *n.* a *break* or opening, as in the walls of a fortress : a breaking of law, &c. : a quarrel.—*v.t.* to make a breach or opening. [A.S. *brice,* Fr. *brèche,* from root of **Break.**]

**Bread,** bred, *n.* food made of flour or meal baked : food : livelihood. [A.S. *bread,* from *breotan,* to break ; or from *breowan,* to brew.]

**Bread-fruit-tree,** bred'-frōōt-trē', *n.* a tree of the South Sea Islands, producing a fruit, which when roasted forms a good substitute for bread.

**Breadth,** bredth, *n.* extent from side to side : width. [M.E. *brede,* A.S. *bredu.* See **Broad.**]

**Break,** brāk, *v.t.* to part by force : to shatter : to crush : to tame : to violate : to check by intercepting, as a fall : to interrupt, as silence : to make bankrupt : to divulge.—*v.i.* to part in two : to burst forth : to open or appear, as the morning : to become bankrupt : to fall out, as with a friend :—*pa.t.* brōke ; *pa.p.* brōk'en.—*n.* the state of being broken : an opening : a pause or interruption : the dawn.—**Break cover,** to burst forth from concealment, as game.—**Break down,** to crush, or to come down by breaking : (*fig.*) to give way.—**Break ground,** to commence excavation : (*fig.*) to begin.—**Break the ice** (*fig.*), to get through first difficulties.—**Break a jest**, to utter a jest unexpectedly.—**Break a lance** (*fig.*), enter into a contest with a rival.—**Break upon the wheel**, to punish by stretching a criminal on a wheel, and breaking his bones.—**Break with**, to fall out, as friends. [A.S. *brecan*; Goth. *brikan*, Ger. *brechen*; conn. with L. *frango*, Gr. *rhēg-nūmi*; Gael. *bragh*, a burst.]

**Breakage**, brāk′āj, *n.* a breaking : an allowance for things broken. [the shore.

**Breaker**, brāk′ėr, *n.* a wave broken on rocks or

**Breakfast**, brek′fast, *n.* a break or breaking of a fast : the first meal of the day.—*v.i.* to take breakfast.—*v.t.* to furnish with breakfast.

**Breaking-in**, brāk′ing-in′, *n.* the act of training to labour, as of a horse.                       [broken neck.

**Breakneck**, brāk′nek, *adj.* likely to cause a

**Breakwater**, brāk′waw′tėr, *n.* a barrier at the entrance of a harbour to break the force of the waves.

**Bream**, brēm, *n.* a fresh-water fish of the carp family : a salt-water fish somewhat like it. [Fr. *brême*, for *bresme*—O. Ger. *brahsema*, Ger. *brassen*.]

**Breast**, brest, *n.* the forepart of the human body between the neck and the belly : (*fig.*) conscience, disposition, affections.—*v.t.* to bear the breast against : to oppose manfully. [A.S. *breost*; Ger. *brust*, Dut. *borst*, perh. from the notion of bursting forth, protruding.]

**Breastplate**, brest′plāt, *n.* a plate or piece of armour for the breast : in *B.*, a part of the dress of the Jewish high-priest.

**Breastwork**, brest′wurk, *n.* a defensive work of earth or other materials breast-high.

**Breath**, breth, *n.* the air drawn into and then expelled from the lungs : power of breathing, life : the time occupied by once breathing : a very slight breeze. [A.S. *brǣth*; Ger. *brodem*, steam, breath ; perh. akin to L. *frag-rare*, to smell.]

**Breathe**, brēth, *v.i.* to draw in and expel breath or air from the lungs : to take breath, to rest or pause : to live.—*v.t.* to draw in and expel from the lungs, as air : to infuse : to give out as breath : to utter by the breath or softly : to keep in breath, to exercise.

**Breathing**, brēth′ing, *n.* the act of breathing : aspiration, secret prayer : respite.

**Breathless**, breth′les, *adj.* out of breath : dead. —*n.* **Breath′lessness.**

**Breech**, brēch, *n.* the lower part of the body behind : the hinder part of anything, especially of a gun.—*v.t.* to put into breeches. [See **Breeches**, the garment, in which sense it was first used.]

**Breeches**, brich′ez, *n.pl.* a garment worn by men on the lower part of the body, trousers. [A.S. *brôc*, pl. *brêc*; found in all Teut. lang. ; also Fr. *braies*—L. *braccæ*, which is said to be from the Celt., as in Gael. *briogais*, breeches.]

**Breech-loader**, brēch′-lōd′ėr, *n.* a firearm loaded by introducing the charge at the breech.

**Breed**, brēd, *v.t.* to generate or bring forth : to train or bring up : to cause or occasion.—*v.i.* to be with young : to produce offspring : to be produced or brought forth :—*pa.t.* and *pa.p.* bred.—*n.* that which is bred, progeny or offspring : kind or race. [A.S. *brēdan*, to cherish, keep warm ; Ger. *brüten*, to hatch ; conn. with **Brew**.]

**Breeder**, brēd′ėr, *n.* one who breeds or brings up.

**Breeding**, brēd′ing, *n.* act of producing : education or manners.

**Breeze**, brēz, *n.* a gentle gale ; a wind. [Fr. *brise*, a cool wind ; It. *brezza*.]                      [breezes.

**Breezy**, brēz′i, *adj.* fanned with, or subject to

**Brethren**, bre*th*′ren, *plur.* of **Brother.**

**Breton**, brit′un, *adj.* belonging to Brittany or Bretagne, in France.

**Breve**, brēv, *n.* (*lit.*) *a brief or short note* : the longest note now used in music, ‖○‖. [It. *breve* —L. *brevis*, short. In old church music there were but two notes, the *long* and the *breve* or short. Afterwards the long was disused, and the *breve* became the longest note. It is now little used, the *semibreve* being the longest note.]

**Brevet**, brev′et, *n.* a military commission entitling an officer to take rank above that for which he receives pay. [Fr., a short document—L. *brevis*, short.]

**Breviary**, brēv′i-ar-i, *n.* book containing the daily service of the Roman Catholic Church. [Fr. *bréviaire*—L. *brevis*, short.]

**Brevier**, brev-ēr′, *n.* a small type between bourgeois and minion, orig. used in printing *breviaries.*

**Brevity**, brev′it-i, *n.*, *shortness* : conciseness. [L. *brevitas—brevis*, short.]

**Brew**, brōō, *v.t.* to prepare a liquor, as from malt and other materials : to contrive or plot.—*v.i.* to perform the operation of brewing : to be gathering or forming. [A.S. *breovan*; cf. Ger. *brauen*, which, like Fr. *brasser*, is said to be from Low L. *braxare*, which is perh. from Celt. *brag*, malt.]

**Brewer**, brōō′ėr, *n.* one who brews.

**Brewery**, brōō′ėr-i, *n.* a place for brewing.

**Brewing**, brōō′ing, *n.* the act of making liquor from malt : the quantity brewed at once.

**Bribe**, brīb, *n.* something given to influence unduly the judgment or corrupt the conduct : allurement.—*v.t.* to influence by a bribe. [Fr. *bribe*, a lump of bread—Celt. as in W. *briwo*, to break, *briw*, a fragment.]

**Briber**, brīb′ėr, *n.* one who bribes.      [bribes.

**Bribery**, brīb′ėr-i, *n.* the act of giving or taking

**Brick**, brik, *n.* an oblong or square piece of burned clay : a loaf of bread in the shape of a brick.— *v.t.* to lay or pave with brick. [Fr. *brique*, from root of **Break.**]

**Brickbat**, brik′bat, *n.* a piece of brick. [**Brick** and **Bat**, an implement for striking with.]

**Brick-kiln**, brik′-kil, *n.* a kiln in which bricks are burned.

**Bricklayer**, brik′lā-ėr, *n.* one who lays or builds with bricks.—*n.* **Brick′laying.**

**Bridal**, brīd′al, *n.* a marriage feast : a wedding.— *adj.* belonging to a bride, or a wedding : nuptial. [**Bride**, and **Ale**, a feast.]

**Bride**, brīd, *n.* a woman about to be married : a woman newly married. [A.S. *bryd* ; Ice. *brudr*, Ger. *braut*, a bride ; W. *priod*, one married.]

**Bridecake**, brīd′kāk, *n.* the bride's cake, or cake distributed at a wedding.       [apartment.

**Bride-chamber**, brīd′-chām′bėr, *n.* the nuptial

**Bridegroom**, brīd′grōōm, *n.* a man about to be married : a man newly married.—**Bride′maid, Bride's′maid, Bride′man, Bride's′man,** attendants at a wedding. [A.S. *brydguma—guma*, a man.]

**Bridewell**, brīd′wel, *n.* a house of correction. [From a palace near St Bride's Well in London, afterwards used as a house of correction.]

**Bridge**, brij, *n.* a structure raised across a river, &c. : anything like a bridge.—*v.t.* to build a bridge over. [A.S. *bricg*; Ger. *brücke*, Ice. *bryggja*.]

**Bridle**, brī'dl, *n.* the instrument on a horse's head, by which it is controlled : any curb or restraint.—*v.t.* to put on or manage by a bridle : to check or restrain.—*v.i.* to hold up the head proudly or affectedly. [A.S. *bridel* ; O. Ger. *bridel*, whence Fr. *bride*.]    [horsemen.

**Bridle-path**, brī'dl-päth, *n.* a path or way for

**Brief**, brēf, *adj.*, *short* : concise.—*adv.* **Brief'ly**.—*n.* **Brief'ness**.

**Brief**, brēf, *n.* a *short* account of a client's case for the instruction of counsel : a writ : a short statement of any kind. [Fr. *bref*—L. *brevis*, short.]

**Briefless**, brēf'les, *adj.* without a brief.

**Brier**, brī'ėr, *n.* a prickly shrub : a common name for the wild rose.—*adj.* **Bri'ery**. [M. E. *brere*, —A.S. *brer*, Ir. *briar*, thorn.]

**Brig**, brig, *n.* a two-masted, square-rigged vessel. [Shortened from **Brigantine**.]

**Brigade**, brig-ād', *n.* a body of troops consisting of two or more regiments of infantry or cavalry, and commanded by a general-officer, two or more of which form a division.—*v.t.* to form into brigades. [Fr. *brigade*—It. *brigata*—Low L. *briga*, strife.]

**Brigadier**, brig-a-dēr', **Brigadier-general**, brig-a-dēr'-jen'ėr-al, *n.* a general-officer of the lowest grade, who has command of a brigade.

**Brigand**, brig'and, *n.* a robber or freebooter. [Fr.—It. *brigante*—*briga*, strife.]    [ing.

**Brigandage**, brig'and-āj, *n.* freebooting : plunder-

**Brigandine**, brig'an-dīn, *n.* a coat of mail. [Fr. ; so called because worn by *brigands*.]

**Brigantine**, brig'an-tīn, *n.* a small light vessel or brig. [From **Brigand**, because such a vessel was used by pirates.]

**Bright**, brīt, *adj.*, *shining* : full of light : clear : beautiful : clever : illustrious.—*adv.* **Bright'ly**.—*n.* **Bright'ness**. [A.S. *beorht*, *briht* ; cog. with Goth. *bairhts*, clear, Gr. *phlegō*, L. *flagro*, to flame, *flamma*=*flag-ma*, Sans. *bhraj*, to shine.]

**Brighten**, brīt'n, *v.t.* to make bright or brighter : to make cheerful or joyful : to make illustrious. —*v.i.* to grow bright or brighter : to clear up.

**Brill**, bril, *n.* a fish of the same kind as the turbot, spotted with white. [Corn. *brilli*, mackerel = *brith-el*, dim. of *brith*, speckled, cognate with Gael. *breac*, speckled, a trout. See **Brock**.]

**Brilliant**, bril'yant, *adj.* sparkling : glittering : splendid.—*n.* a diamond of the finest cut.—*adv.* **Brill'iantly**.—*ns.* **Brill'iancy**, **Brill'iantness**. [Fr. *brillant*, pr.p. of *briller*, to shine, which, like Ger. *brille*, an eyeglass, is from Low L. *beryllus*, a beryl.]

**Brim**, brim, *n.* the margin or brink of a river or lake : the upper edge of a vessel.—*v.t.* to fill to the brim.—*v.i.* to be full to the brim :—*pr.p.* brimm'ing ; *pa.p.* brimmed. [A.S. *brim*, surge, surf, the margin of the sea where it sounds ; conn. with O. Ger. *bræmen*, to hum, L. *fremere*, to roar.]

**Brimful**, brim'fool, *adj.* full to the brim.

**Brimmer**, brim'ėr, *n.* a bowl full to the brim or top.

**Brimstone**, brim'stōn, *n.* sulphur. [Lit. *burning stone* ; from A.S. *bryne*, a burning—*byrnan*, to burn, and **Stone** ; cf. Ger. *bernstein*.]

**Brinded**, brin'ded, **Brin'dled**, *adj.* marked with spots or streaks. [See **Brand**.]

**Brine**, brīn, *n.* salt-water : the sea. [A.S. *bryne*, a burning ; applied to salt liquor, from its burning, biting quality.]

**Bring**, bring, *v.t.* to fetch : to carry : to procure : to draw or lead.—*pa.t.* and *pa.p.* brought (brawt).—**Bring about**, to bring to pass, effect.

—**Bring down**, to humble.—**Bring forth**, to give birth to, produce.—**Bring to**, to check the course of, as a ship, by trimming the sails so as to counteract each other. [A.S. *bringan*, to carry, to bring ; allied perh. to **Bear**.]

**Brink**, bringk, *n.* the edge or border of a steep place or of a river. [Dan. *brink*, declivity ; Ice. *bringr*, hillock.]    [sea : salt.

**Briny**, brīn'i, *adj.* pertaining to brine or to the

**Briony**, brī'o-ni, *n.* Same as **Bryony**.

**Brisk**, brisk, *adj.* full of life and spirit : active : effervescing, as liquors.—*adv.* **Brisk'ly**.—*n.* **Brisk'ness**. [W. *brysg*, nimble, *brys*, haste. Other forms are **Frisk**, **Fresh**.]

**Brisket**, brisk'et, *n.* the breast of an animal : the part of the breast next to the ribs. [Fr. *brechet*, *brichet*—W. *brysced*.]

**Bristle**, bris'l, *n.* a short, stiff hair, as of swine. —*v.i.* to stand erect, as bristles. [A.S. *byrst* ; Scot. *birse* ; cog. with Ger. *borste*, Ice. *burst*.]

**Bristly**, bris'li, *adj.* set with bristles : rough.—*n.* **Brist'liness**.

**Britannia-metal**, brit-an'i-a-met'l, *n.* a metallic alloy largely used in the manufacture of spoons, &c.    [or Great Britain : British.

**Britannic**, brit-an'ik, *adj.* pertaining to Britannia

**British**, brit'ish, *adj.* pertaining to Great Britain or its people.

**Briton**, brit'on, *n.* a native of Britain.

**Brittle**, brit'l, *adj.*, *apt to break* : easily broken. —*n.* **Britt'leness**. [A.S. *breotan*, to break.]

**Broach**, brōch, *v.t.* to pierce as a cask, to tap : to open up or begin : to utter. [Fr. *brocher*, to pierce, *broche*, an iron pin—Lat. *brocchus*, a projecting tooth.]

**Broad**, brawd, *adj.* wide : large, free or open : coarse, indelicate.—*adv.* **Broad'ly**.—*n.* **Broad'ness**. [A.S. *brad*, Goth. *braids*.]

**Broad-arrow**, brawd'-ar'ō, *n.* a mark, thus ( ⋏ ) stamped on materials used in the royal dockyards.

**Broadbrim**, brawd'brim, *n.* a hat with a broad brim, such as those worn by Quakers : (*colloq.*) a Quaker.

**Broadcast**, brawd'kast, *adj.* scattered or sown *abroad* by the hand : dispersed widely.—*adv.* by throwing at large from the hand.

**Broad church**, brawd church, *n.* a party in the Church of England holding *broad* or liberal views of Christian doctrine.

**Broadcloth**, brawd'kloth, *n.* a fine kind of woollen fulled cloth, wider than twenty-nine inches.

**Broaden**, brawd'n, *v.t.* to make broad or broader. —*v.i.* to grow broad or extend in breadth.

**Broad-gauge**, brawd'-gāj, *n.* a distance of six or seven feet between the rails of a railway, as distinguished from the narrow gauge of 4 ft. 8½ in.

**Broadside**, brawd'sīd, *n.* the side of a ship : all the guns on one side of a ship of war, or their simultaneous discharge : a sheet of paper printed on one side.    [with a broad blade.

**Broadsword**, brawd'sōrd, *n.* a cutting sword

**Brobdingnagian**, brob-ding-nā'ji-an, *n.* an inhabitant of the fabulous region of Brobdingnag in *Gulliver's Travels*, the people of which were of great stature, hence a gigantic person.—*adj.* gigantic.

**Brocade**, brok-ād', *n.* a silk stuff on which figures are wrought. [It. *broccato*, Fr. *brocart*, from It. *broccare*, Fr. *brocher*, to prick ; from root of **Broach**.]

**Brocaded**, brok-ād'ed, *adj.* woven or worked in the manner of brocade : dressed in brocade.

**Broccoli**, brok'o-li, *n.* a kind of cabbage resembling cauliflower. [It., pl. of *broccolo*, a sprout, dim. of *brocco*, a skewer, a shoot—root of **Broach**.]

**Brochure**, bro-shōōr', *n.* a pamphlet. [Lit. a small book *stitched*, Fr.—*brocher*, to stitch—*broche*, a needle. See **Broach**.]

**Brock**, brok, *n.* a badger, an animal with a black and white streaked face. [From the Celtic, as in Gael. *broc*, a badger, which is from Gael. *breac*, speckled.]

**Brog**, brog, *n.* a pointed steel instrument used by joiners for piercing holes in wood. [Gael. *brog*, a pointed instrument, as an awl; W. *procio*, to stab.]

**Brogue**, brōg, *n.* a stout coarse shoe : a dialect or manner of pronunciation, esp. the Irish. [Ir. and Gael. *brog*, a shoe.]

**Broider**, broid'er, **Broidery**, broid'er-i. Same as **Embroider**, **Embroidery**.

**Broil**, broil, *n.* a noisy quarrel : a confused disturbance. [Fr. *brouiller*, to break out, to rebel, prob. from the Celtic.]

**Broil**, broil. *v.t.* to cook over hot coals.—*v.i.* to be greatly heated. [Ety. dub.]

**Broke**, brōk, *pa.t.* and old *pa.p.* of **Break**.

**Broken**, brō'kn, *p.adj.* rent asunder : infirm : humbled. [From **Break**.]

**Broken-hearted**, brō'kn-härt'ed, *adj.* crushed with grief : greatly depressed in spirit.

**Broker**, brōk'er, *n.* one employed to buy and sell for others. [M. E. *brocour*—A.S. *brucan*, Ger. *brauchen*, to use, to profit.]

**Brokerage**, brōk'er-āj, *n.* the business of a broker : the commission charged by a broker.

**Bromide**, brōm'id, *n.* a combination of bromine with a base.

**Bromine**, brōm'in, *n.* an elementary body closely allied to iodine, so called from its *disagreeable smell.* [Gr. *brōmos*, a disagreeable odour.]

**Bronchiæ**, brongk'i-ā, *n.pl.* a name given to the ramifications of the *windpipe* which carry air into the lungs.—*adj.* **Bronch'ial**. [Gr. *bronchos*, the windpipe.] [bronchiæ.]

**Bronchitis**, brongk-ī'tis, *n.* inflammation of the

**Bronze**, bronz, *n.* a mixture of copper and tin used in various ways since the most ancient times : anything cast in bronze : the colour of bronze : impudence.—*v.t.* to give the appearance of bronze to : to harden. [Fr.—It. *bronzo*; conn. with *bruno*, brown, and root *bren*, to burn.]

**Brooch**, brōch, *n.* an ornamental pin for fastening any article of dress. [Fr. *broche*, a spit. See **Broach**.]

**Brood**, brōōd, *v.i.* to sit upon or cover in order to *breed* or hatch : to cover, as with wings : to think anxiously for a long time.—*v.t.* to mature or cherish with care.—*n.* something bred : offspring : the number hatched at once. [A.S. *brid*, a young one, esp. a young bird, from root of **Breed**.]

**Brood-mare**, brōōd'-mār, *n.* a mare kept for breeding. [breaking forth.]

**Brook**, brook, *n.* a small stream. [A.S. *broc*, water

**Brook**, brook, *v.t.* to bear or endure. [A.S. *brucan*, to use, enjoy ; Ger. *brauchen*, L. *fruor*, *fruc-tus*.]

**Brooklet**, brook'let, *n.* a little brook.

**Broom**, brōōm, *n.* a wild evergreen shrub : a besom made of its twigs. [A.S. *brom*.]

**Broomstick**, brōōm'stik, *n.* the staff or handle of a broom.

**Broth**, broth, *n.* a kind of soup. [A.S. *broth*—*breowan*, to brew ; cf. Fr. *brouet*, O. Ger. *prot*, and Gael. *brod*.]

**Brothel**, broth'el, *n.* a house of ill-fame. [Fr.

*bordel*—O. Fr. *borde*, a hut, from the boards of which it was made.]

**Brother**, bru*th*'er, *n.* a male born of the same parents: any one closely united with or resembling another : a fellow-creature. [A.S. *brōdhor*; cog. with Ger. *bruder*, Gael. *brathair*, Fr. *frère*, L. *frater*. Sans. *bhratri*; from root *bhar*, to bear, and hence brother orig. meant one who *supports* the family after the father's death.]

**Brother-german**, bru*th*'er-jėr'man, *n.* a brother having the same father and mother, in contradistinction to one by the same mother only.

**Brotherhood**, bru*th*'er-hood, *n.* the state of being a brother : an association of men for any purpose.

**Brother-in-law**, bru*th*'er-in-law, *n.* the brother of a husband or wife : a sister's husband.

**Brother-like**, bru*th*'er-līk, **Brotherly**, bru*th*'er-li, *adj.* like a brother : kind : affectionate.

**Brougham**, brōō'am or brōōm, *n.* a one-horse close carriage, either two or four wheeled, named after Lord *Brougham*.

**Brought**, brawt, *pa.t.* and *pa.p.* of **Bring**.

**Brow**, brow, *n.* the ridge over the eyes : the forehead : the edge of a hill. [A.S. *brū* ; Ice. *brun*, Scot. *brae*, a slope ; conn. with Gr. *ophrys*.]

**Browbeat**, brow'bēt, *v.t.* to bear down with stern looks or speech : to bully.

**Brown**, brown, *adj.* of a dark or dusky colour inclining to red or yellow.—*n.* a dark reddish colour.—*v.t.* to make brown or give a brown colour to.—*adj.* **Brown'ish.**—*n.* **Brown'ness**. [A.S. *brun*—A.S. *byrnan*, to burn.]

**Brownie**, brown'i, *n.* in Scotland, a kind of goodnatured domestic spirit.

**Brown-study**, brown'-stud'i, *n.* gloomy reverie : absent-mindedness.

**Browse**, browz, *v.t.* and *v.i.* to feed on the shoots or leaves of plants. [O. Fr. *brouster*(Fr. *brouter*) —*broust*, a sprout ; also Celt. See **Brush**.]

**Bruin**, brōō'in, *n.* a bear, so called from its *brown* colour. [Dut. *bruin*, Ger. *braun*, brown.]

**Bruise**, brōōz, *v.t.*, *to break* or crush : to reduce to small fragments.—*n.* a wound made by anything heavy and blunt. [O. Fr. *bruiser*, from O. Ger. *bresten*, to burst.]

**Bruiser**, brōōz'er, *n.* one that bruises : a boxer.

**Bruit**, brōōt, *n.* something noised abroad : a rumour or report.—*v.t.* to noise abroad : to report. [Fr. *bruit*—Fr. *bruire*; cf. Low L. *brugitus*, Gr. *bruchō*, to roar ; prob. imitative.]

**Brunette**, brōōn-et', *n.* a girl with a *brown* or dark complexion. [Fr. dim. of *brun*, brown.]

**Brunt**, brunt, *n.* the *heat* or shock of an onset or contest : the force of a blow. [Ice. *bruni* ; Ger. *brunst*, heat. See **Burn**.]

**Brush**, brush, *n.* an instrument for removing dust, usually made of bristles, twigs, or feathers : a kind of hair-pencil used by painters : brushwood : a skirmish or encounter : the tail of a fox.—*v.t.* to remove dust, &c. from by sweeping : to touch lightly in passing : (with *off*) remove.—*v.i.* to move over lightly. [Fr. *brosse*, a brush, brushwood—O. Ger. *brusta* (Ger. *bürste*), acc. to Brachet, orig. heather, broom. See **Browse**.]

**Brushwood**, brush'wood, *n.* rough, close bushes : a thicket.

**Brusque**, broosk, *adj.* blunt, abrupt in manner, rude.—*n.* **Brusque'ness**. [Fr. *brusque*, rude. See **Brisk**.]

**Brussels-sprouts**, brus'elz-sprowts, *n.pl.* a variety of the common cabbage with sprouts like miniature cabbages. [From *Brussels*, whence the seeds were imported.]

**Brutal**, brōōt'al, *adj.* like a brute : unfeeling : inhuman.—*adv.* Brut'ally.— *n.* Brutal'ity.

**Brutalise**, brōōt'al-īz, Brut'ify, brōōt'i-fī, *v.t.* to make like a brute, to degrade.

**Brute**, brōōt, *adj.* belonging to the lower animals : irrational : stupid : rude.—*n.* one of the lower animals. [Fr. *brut*—L. *brutus*, dull, irrational.]

**Brutish**, brōōt'ish, *adj.* brutal : (*B.*) unwise.— *adv.* Brut'ishly.—*n.* Brut'ishness.

**Bryony**, brī'o-ni, *n.* a wild climbing plant. [L. *bryonia*, Gr. *bryōnē*, perhaps from *bryō*, to burst forth with, to grow rapidly.]

**Bubble**, bub'l, *n.* a bladder of water blown out with air : anything empty : a cheating scheme. —*v.i.* to rise in bubbles. [Dim. of the imitative word *blob* ; cf. Dut. *bobbel*, L. *bulla*, a bubble.]

**Buccaneer, Bucanier**, buk-an-ēr', *n.* the buccaneers were pirates in the West Indies during the seventeenth century, who plundered the Spaniards chiefly. [Fr. *boucanier*, to smoke meat— Carib *boucan*, a wooden gridiron. The French settlers in the West Indies cooked their meat on a *boucan* after the manner of the natives, and were hence called *boucaniers*.]

**Buck**, buk, *n.* the male of the deer, goat, hare, and rabbit : a dashing young fellow. [A.S. *buc, bucca* ; Ger. *bock*, a he-goat.]

**Buck**, buk, *v.t.* to soak or steep in lye, a process in bleaching.—*n.* lye in which clothes are bleached. [From the Celt., as in Gael. *buac*, cowdung, used in bleaching—*bo*, a cow ; Ger. *beuchen*, &c., from the same source.]

**Bucket**, buk'et, *n.* a vessel for drawing or holding water, &c. [A.S. *buc*, a pitcher ; prob. from Gael. *bucaid*, a bucket.]

**Buckle**, buk'l, *n.* an instrument for fastening shoes and other articles of dress.—*v.t.* to fasten with a buckle : to prepare for action : to engage in close fight.—*v.i.* to bend or bulge out : to engage with zeal. [Fr. *boucle*, the boss of a shield, a ring—Low L. *buccula*, dim. of *bucca*, a cheek.]

**Buckler**, buk'lėr, *n.* a shield with a *buckle* or central boss. [Fr. *bouclier*—Low L. *buccula*.]

**Buckram**, buk'ram, *n.* coarse cloth stiffened with dressing.—*adj.* made of buckram : stiff : precise. [O. Fr. *boqueran*—O. Ger. *boc*, a goat ; such stuff being made orig. of goats' hair.]

**Buckskin**, buk'skin, *n.* a kind of leather :—*pl.* breeches made of buckskin.—*adj.* made of the skin of a buck.

**Buckwheat**, buk'hwēt, *n.* a kind of grain having three-cornered seeds like the kernels of *beech*-nuts. [A.S. *bōc*, beech, and **Wheat** ; Ger. *buch-weizen*—*buche*, beech, *weizen*, corn.]

**Bucolic, -al**, bū-kol'ik, -al, *adj.* pertaining to the tending of cattle : pastoral.—*n.* a pastoral poem. [L. *bucolicus*—Gr. *boukolikos*—*boukolos*, a herdsman, from *bous*, an ox, and perh. the root of L. *colo*, to tend.]

**Bud**, bud, *n.* the first shoot of a tree or plant.— *v.i.* to put forth buds : to begin to grow.—*v.t.* to graft, as a plant, by inserting a bud under the bark of another tree :—*pr.p.* budd'ing ; *pa.p.* budd'ed. [From a Low Ger. root, as in Dut. *bot*, a bud. See **Button**.]

**Buddhism**, bood'izm, *n.* the religion of the greater part of Central and E. Asia, so called from the title of its founder, 'the Buddha,' 'the wise.'

**Buddhist**, bood'ist, *n.* a believer in Buddhism

**Budge**, buj, *v.i.* to move off or stir. [Fr. *bouger* —It. *bulicare*, to boil, to bubble—L. *bullire*.]

**Budget**, buj'et, *n.* a sack with its contents : annual statement of the finances of the British nation made by the Chancellor of the Exchequer. [Fr. *bougette*, dim. of *bouge*, a pouch—L. *bulga*, a word of Gallic origin—root of **Bag**.]

**Buff**, buf, *n.* a leather made from the skin of the buffalo : the colour of buff, a light yellow :—*pl.* a regiment so named from their buff-coloured facings. [Fr. *buffle*, a buffalo.]

**Buffalo**, buf'a-lō, *n.* a large kind of ox, generally wild. [Sp. *bufalo*—L. *bubalus*, Gr. *boubalos*, the wild ox—*bous*, an ox.]

**Buffer**, buf'ėr, *n.* a cushion to deaden the ' buff ' or concussion, as in railway carriages.

**Buffet**, buf'et, *n.* a blow with the fist, a slap.— *v.t.* to strike with the hand or fist : to contend against. [O. Fr. *bufet*—*bufe*, a blow, esp. on the cheek ; conn. with **Puff**, **Buffoon**.]

**Buffet**, buf'et, *n.* a kind of sideboard. [Fr. *buffet* ; orig. unknown.]

**Buffoon**, buf-ōōn', *n.* one who amuses by jests, grimaces, &c. : a clown. [Fr. *bouffon*—It. *buffare*, to jest, (*lit.*) to *puff* out the cheeks.]

**Buffoonery**, buf-ōōn'ėr-i, *n.* the practices of a buffoon : ludicrous or vulgar jesting.

**Bug**, bug, *n.* an object of terror ; applied loosely to certain insects, esp. to one that infests houses and beds. [W. *bwg*, a hobgoblin.]

**Bugbear**, bug'bār, *n.*, *an object of terror*, generally imaginary.—*adj.* causing fright.

**Buggy**, bug'i, *n.* a light one-horse chaise.

**Bugle**, bū'gl, **Bugle-horn**, bū'gl-horn, *n.* a hunting-horn, orig. a buffalo-horn : a keyed horn of rich tone. [O. Fr.—L. *buculus*, dim. of *bos*, an ox.]

**Buhl**, būl, *n.* unburnished gold, brass, or mother-of-pearl worked into patterns for inlaying : furniture ornamented with such. [From Boule, the name of an Italian wood-carver who introduced it into France in the time of Louis XIV.]

**Build**, bild, *v.t.* to erect, as a house : to form or construct.—*v.i.* to depend (on) :—*pa.p.* built or build'ed.—*n.* construction : make. [O. Swed. *bylja*, to build ; Dan. *bol*) ; A.S. *bold*, a house.]

**Builder**, bild'ėr, *n.* one who builds.

**Building**, bild'ing, *n.* the art of erecting houses, &c. : anything built : a house.

**Built**, bilt, *p.adj.* formed or shaped.

**Bulb**, bulb, *n.* an onion-like root.—*v.i.* to form bulbs : to bulge out or swell.—*adjs.* Bulbed, Bul'bous.

**Bulbul**, bool'bool, *n.* the Persian nightingale.

**Bulge**, bulj, *n.* the bilge or widest part of a cask. —*v.i.* to swell out. [A.S. *belgan*, to swell ; Gael. *bolg*, to swell. See **Bilge**, **Belly**, **Bag**, &c.]

**Bulk**, bulk, *n.* magnitude or size : the greater part : (*of a ship*) the whole cargo in the hold. [A form of **Bulge**.]

**Bulkhead**, bulk'hed, *n.* a partition separating one part of a ship between decks from another. [*Bulk* = balk, a beam.]        [*n.* Bulk'iness.

**Bulky**, bulk'i, *adj.* having bulk : of great size.—

**Bull**, bool, *n.* the male of the ox kind : a sign of the zodiac.—*adj.* denoting largeness of size— used in composition, as bull-trout. [From an A.S. word, found only in dim. *bulluca*, a little bull—A.S. *bellan*, to bellow.]

**Bull**, bool, *n.* an edict of the pope which has his seal affixed. [L. *bulla*, a knob, anything rounded by art : later, a leaden seal.]

**Bull**, bool, *n.* a ludicrous blunder in speech. [Perh. in sarcastic allusion to the pope's bulls.]

**Bull-baiting**, bool'-bāt'ing, *n.* the sport of baiting or exciting bulls with dogs. [See **Bait**.]

**Bulldog**, bool'dog, *n.* a kind of dog of great courage, formerly used for baiting bulls.

**Bullet**, bool'et, *n.* a ball of lead for loading small

arms. [Fr. *boulet*, dim. of *boule*, a ball—L. *bulla*. See Bull, an edict.]

**Bulletin**, bool'e-tin, *n.* an official report of public news. [Fr.—It. *bulletino*, dim. of *bulla*, a seal, because issued with the seal or stamp of authority. See Bull, an edict.]

**Bullet-proof**, bool'et-proof, *adj.* proof against bullets.            [amusement in Spain.

**Bullfight**, bool'fīt, *n.* bull-baiting, a popular

**Bullfinch**, bool'finsh, *n.* a species of finch a little larger than the common linnet. [Acc. to Wedgwood, prob. a corr. of *bud-finch*, from its destroying the buds of fruit-trees.]

**Bullion**, bool'yun, *n.* gold and silver regarded simply by weight as merchandise. [Ety. dub.]

**Bullock**, bool'ok, *n.* an ox or castrated bull. [A.S. *bulluca*, a calf or young bull. See Bull.]

**Bull's-eye**, boolz'-ī, *n.* the centre of a target, of a different colour from the rest, and usually round.

**Bulltrout**, bool'trowt, *n.* a *large* kind of trout, nearly allied to the salmon.

**Bully**, bool'i, *n.*, *a blustering*, *noisy*, overbearing fellow.—*v.i.* to bluster.—*v.t.* to threaten in a noisy way:—*pr.p.* bull'ying; *pa.p.* bull'ied. [Dut. *bulderen*, to bluster; Low Ger. *buller-brook*, a noisy blustering fellow.]

**Bulrush**, bool'rush, *n.* a large strong rush, which grows on wet land or in water.

**Bulwark**, bool'wark, *n.* a fortification or rampart: any means of defence or security. [From a Teut. root, seen in Ger. *bollwerk*—root of Bole, trunk of a tree, and Ger. *werk*, work.]

**Bum**, bum, *v.i.* to hum or make a murmuring sound, as a bee:—*pr.p.* bumm'ing; *pa.p.* bummed'. [Bum = boom, from the sound.]

**Bumbailiff**, bum'bāl'if, *n.* an under-bailiff.

**Bumble-bee**, bum'bl-bē, *n.* a large kind of bee that makes a *bumming* or humming noise: the humble-bee. [M. E. *bumble*, freq. of Bum, and Bee.]

**Bumboat**, bum'bōt, *n.* boat for carrying provisions to a ship. [Dut. *bum-boot*, for *bunboot*, a boat with a *bun*, or receptacle for keeping fish alive.]

**Bump**, bump, *v.i.* to make a heavy or loud noise. —*v.t.* to strike with a dull sound: to strike against.—*n.* a dull, heavy blow: a thump: a lump caused by a blow : the noise of the bittern. [W. *pwmpio*, to thump, *pwmp*, a round mass, a bump : from the sound.]

**Bumper**, bump'èr, *n.* a cup or glass filled till the liquor swells over the brim. [A corr. of *bombard*, *bumbard*, a large drinking-vessel.]

**Bumpkin**, bump'kin, *n.* an awkward, clumsy rustic : a clown. [Dut. *boom*, a log, and dim. -kin.]

**Bun**, bun, *n.* a kind of sweet cake. [O. Fr. *bugne*, a kind of fritters, a form of *bigne*, a swelling, and found also in *beignet*, a fritter; cf. Scot. *bannock;* conn. with Bunion and Bunch, the orig. meaning being a *swelling*.]

**Bunch**, bunsh, *n.* a number of things tied together or growing together : a cluster : something in the form of a tuft or knot.—*v.i.* to swell out in a bunch. [O. Sw. and Dan. *bunke*, Ice. *bunki*, a heap—O. Sw. *bunga*, to strike, to swell out.]

**Bunchy**, bunsh'i, *adj.* growing in bunches or like a bunch.

**Bundle**, bun'dl, *n.* a number of things loosely bound together.—*v. t.* to bind or tie into bundles. [A.S. *byndel*—from the root of Bind.]

**Bung**, bung, *n.* the stopper of the hole in a barrel : a large cork.—*v.t.* to stop up with a bung. [Ety. dub.]

**Bungalow**, bung'ga-lō, *n.* a country-house in India. [Pers., ' belonging to Bengal.']

**Bungle**, bung'l, *n.* anything clumsily done : a gross blunder.—*v.i.* to act in a clumsy, awkward manner.—*v.t.* to make or mend clumsily : to manage awkwardly.—*n.* Bungl'er. [Perh. freq. of *bang;* cf. O. Sw. *bunga*, to strike, *bangla*, to work ineffectually.]

**Bunion**, bun'yun, *n.* a lump or inflamed swelling on the ball of the great toe. [From root of Bun.]

**Bunting**, bunt'ing, *n.* a thin woollen stuff of which ships' colours are made : a kind of bird. [Ety. dub.]

**Buoy**, bwoi, *n.* a floating cask or light piece of wood fastened by a rope or chain to indicate shoals, the position of a ship's anchor, &c.—*v.t.* to fix buoys or marks : to keep afloat, bear up, or sustain. [Dut. *boei*, buoy, fetter, through Romance forms (Norman, *boie*), from O. L. *boia*, a collar of leather—L. *bos*, ox.]

**Buoyancy**, bwoi'an-si, *n.* capacity for floating lightly on water or in the air : specific lightness : (*fig.*) lightness of spirit, cheerfulness.

**Buoyant**, bwoi'ant, *adj.* light : cheerful.

**Bur**, **Burr**, bur, *n.* the prickly seed-case or head of certain plants, which sticks to clothes : the rough sound of *r* pronounced in the throat. [Prob. E., but with cognates in many lang., as Swed. *borre*, a sea-urchin, L. *burræ*, trash—from a root signifying rough.]

**Burbot**, bur'bot, *n.* a fresh-water fish, like the eel, having a longish *beard* on its lower jaw. [Fr. *barbote*—L. *barba*, a beard.]

**Burden**, bur'dn, *n.* a load : weight : cargo : that which is grievous, oppressive, or difficult to bear.—*v.t.* to load : to oppress : to encumber. [A.S. *byrthen*—*beran*, to bear.]

**Burden**, bur'dn, *n.* part of a song repeated at the end of every stanza, refrain. [Fr. *bourdon*, a humming tone in music—Low L. *burdo*, a drone or non-working bee.]

**Burdensome**, bur'dn-sum, *adj.* heavy : oppressive.

**Burdock**, bur'dok, *n.* a *dock* with a *bur* or prickly head.

**Bureau**, būr'ō, *n.* a writing-table or chest of drawers, orig. covered with *dark cloth* : a room or office where such a table is used : a department for the transacting of public business :— *pl.* **Bureaux**, būr'ō, **Bureaus**, būr'ōz. [O. Fr. *burel*, coarse russet cloth—L. *burrus*, dark red ; cf. Gr. *pyrrhos*, flame-coloured—*pyr* = Fire.]

**Bureaucracy**, būr-ō'kras-i, *n.* government by *officials* appointed by the ruler, as opposed to self-government or government by parliamentary majority. [Bureau and Gr. *kratō*, to govern.]

**Bureaucratic**, būr-ō-krat'ik, *adj.* relating to, or having the nature of a bureaucracy.

**Burgage**, burg'āj, *n.* a system of tenure in *boroughs*, cities, and towns, by which the citizens hold their lands or tenements.

**Burgamot**, bur'ga-mot, *n.* Same as Bergamot.

**Burgeon**, bur'jun, *v.i.* Same as Bourgeon.

**Burgess**, bur'jes, **Burgher**, burg'èr, *n.* an inhabitant of a *borough:* a citizen or freeman : a magistrate of certain towns.

**Burgh**, bur'ō or burg, *n.*—*adj.* Bur'ghal.

**Burglar**, burg'lar, *n.* one who breaks into a house by night to steal. [Fr. *bourg*, town (—Ger. *burg*, E. Borough), O. Fr. *leres*—L. *latro*, a robber.]

**Burglary**, burg'lar-i, *n.* breaking into a house by night to rob.—*adj.* Burglār'ious.—*adv.* Burglār'iously.

**Burgomaster**, burg'o-mast'èr, *n.* the chief magistrate of a German or a Dutch *burgh*, answering to the English term mayor. [Dut. *burgemeester* —*burg*, and *meester*, a master.]

**Burgundy,** bur'gun-di, *n.* a French wine, so called from *Burgundy,* the district where it is made.

**Burial,** ber'i-al, *n.* the act of placing a dead body in the grave; interment. [A.S. *birgels,* a tomb. See **Bury.**]

**Burin,** būr'in, *n.* a kind of chisel used by engravers. [Fr.; from root of **Bore.**]

**Burke,** burk, *v.t.* to murder, esp. by stifling: hence, (*fig.*) to put an end to quietly. [From *Burke,* an Irishman who committed the crime in order to sell the bodies of his victims for dissection.]

**Burlesque,** bur-lesk', *n.* (*lit.*) a *jesting* or *ridiculing:* a ludicrous representation.—*adj.* jocular: comical.—*v.t.* to turn into burlesque: to ridicule. [Fr.—It. *burlesco:* prob. from Low L. *burra,* a flock of wool, a trifle.]

**Burly,** bur'li, *adj.* bulky and vigorous: boisterous. —*n.* **Bur'liness.** [Prob. Celt., as in Gael. *borr,* a knob, *borrail* = *burly,* swaggering.]

**Burn,** burn, *v.t.* to consume or injure by fire.— *v.i.* to be on fire: to feel excess of heat: to be inflamed with passion:—*pa.p.* burned' or burnt. —*n.* a hurt or mark caused by fire.—**To burn one's fingers,** to suffer from interfering in other's affairs, from embarking in speculations, &c. [A.S. *byrnan;* Ger. *brennen,* to burn; akin to L. *ferveo,* to glow.]

**Burner,** burn'ėr, *n.* the part of a lamp or gas-jet from which the flame arises.

**Burning-glass,** burn'ing-glas, *n.* a glass so formed as to concentrate the sun's rays.

**Burnish,** burn'ish, *v.t.* to polish: to make bright by rubbing.—*n.* polish: lustre. [Fr. *brunir,* to make brown—root of **Brown.**]

**Burnisher,** burn'ish-ėr, *n.* an instrument employed in burnishing.

**Burnt-offering,** burnt'-of'ėr-ing, *n.* something offered and burned upon an altar as a sacrifice.

**Burr,** bur, *n.* Same as **Bur.**

**Burrow,** bur'ō, *n.* a hole in the ground dug by certain animals for *shelter* or *defence.*—*v.i.* to make holes underground as rabbits: to dwell in a concealed place. [A doublet of **Borough**— A.S. *beorgan,* to protect.]

**Bursar,** burs'ar, *n.* one who keeps the *purse,* a treasurer: in Scotland, a student maintained at a university by funds derived from endowment. [Low L. *bursarius*—*bursa,* a purse—Gr. *byrsē,* skin or leather.]      [paid to a *bursar.*

**Bursary,** burs'ar-i, *n.* in Scotland, the allowance

**Burst,** burst, *v.t.* to *break* into pieces: to break open suddenly or by violence.—*v.i.* to fly open or break in pieces: to break forth or away:— *pa.t.* and *pa.p.* burst.—*n.* a sudden outbreak. [A.S. *berstan;* Ger. *bersten,* Gael. *brisd,* to break.]

**Burthen,** bur'*th*n. *n.* and *v.t.* Same as **Burden.**

**Bury,** ber'i, *v.t.* to *hide* in the ground: to place in the grave, as a dead body: to hide or blot out of remembrance:—*pr.p.* bur'ying; *pa.p.* bur'ied. [A.S. *byrgan,* to bury; Ger. *bergen,* to hide.]

**Burying-ground,** ber'i-ing-grownd, **Burying-place,** ber'i-ing-plās, *n.* ground set apart for burying the dead: a graveyard.

**Bush,** boosh, *n.* a shrub thick with branches: anything of bushy tuft-like shape: any wild uncultivated country, esp. at the Cape or in Australia. [M. E. *busk, busch;* from a Teut. root found in Ger. *busch,* Low L. *boscus,* Fr. *bois.*]

**Bush,** boosh, *n.* the metal *box* or lining of any cylinder in which an axle works. [Dut. *bus* —L. *buxus,* the box-tree.]

**Bushel,** boosh'ei, *n.* a dry measure of 8 gallons, for measuring grain, &c. [O. Fr. *boissel,* from the root of **Box.**]

**Bushman,** boosh'man, *n.* a settler in the uncleared land of America or the colonies, a woodsman: one of a savage race in South Africa.

**Bush-ranger,** boosh'-rānj-er, *n.* in Australia, a lawless fellow, often an escaped criminal, who takes to the bush and lives by robbery.

**Bushy,** boosh'i, *adj.* full of bushes: thick and spreading.—*n.* **Bush'iness.**

**Busily,** biz'i-li, *adv.* in a busy manner.

**Business,** biz'nes, *n.* employment: engagement: trade, profession, or occupation: one's concerns or affairs: a matter or affair.

**Busk,** busk, *v.t.* or *v.i.* to prepare: to dress one's self. [Ice. *bua,* to prepare, and *-sk,* contr. of *sik,* the recip. pron. = *self.*]

**Busk,** busk, *n.* the piece of bone, wood, or steel in the front of a woman's stays. [A form of **Bust.**]

**Buskin,** busk'in, *n.* a kind of half-boot with high heels worn in ancient times by actors of tragedy: hence, the tragic drama as distinguished from comedy.—*adj.* **Busk'ined,** dressed in buskins, noting tragedy, tragic. [Ety. dub.]

**Buss,** bus, *n.* a rude or playful kiss.—*v.t.* to kiss, esp. in a rude or playful manner. [M. E. *bass,* prob. from O. Ger. *bussen,* to kiss. but modified by Fr. *baiser,* to kiss, from L. *basium,* a kiss.]

**Bust,** bust, *n.* the human body from the head to the waist: a sculpture representing the upper part of the body. [Fr. *buste*—Low L. *bustum.*]

**Bustard,** bus'tard, *n.* a genus of large, heavy birds, akin to the ostrich family, and of which the Great Bustard is the largest of European land-birds. [Fr. *bistard,* corr. from L. *avis tarda,* slow bird, from the slowness of its flight.]

**Bustle,** bus'l, *v.i.* *to busy one's self:* to be active. —*n.* hurried activity: stir: tumult. [M. E. *buskle,* prob. from A.S. *bysig,* busy.]

**Busy,** biz'i, *adj.* fully employed: active: diligent: meddling.—*v.t.* to make busy: to occupy:— *pr.p.* busying (biz'i-ing); *pa.p.* busied (biz'id).— *adv.* **Bus'ily.** [A.S. *bysig.*]

**Busybody,** biz'i-bod-i, *n.* one busy about others' affairs, a meddling person.

**But,** but, *prep.* or *conj.* without: except: besides: only: yet: still. [A.S. *butan, biutan,* without —*be,* by, and *utan,* out—*near* and yet *outside.*]

**But,** but, *n.* Same as **Butt.**

**Butcher,** booch'ėr, *n.* one whose business is to slaughter animals for food: one who delights in bloody deeds.—*v.t.* to slaughter animals for food: to put to a bloody death, to kill cruelly. [Fr. *boucher,* orig. one who kills he-goats—*bouc,* a he-goat; allied to E. *buck.*]

**Butcher-meat,** booch'ėr-mēt, *n.* the flesh of animals slaughtered by butchers, as distinguished from fish, fowls, and game.

**Butchery,** booch'ėr-i, *n.* great or cruel slaughter: a slaughter-house or shambles.

**Butler,** but'lėr, *n.* a servant who has charge of the liquors, plate, &c. [Norm. Fr. *butuiller,* Fr. *bouteiller*—*bouteille,* a bottle.]

**Butt,** but, *v.i.* and *v.t.,* *to strike* with the head, as a goat, &c.—*n.* the thick and heavy end: a push with the head of an animal: a mark to be shot at: one who is made the object of ridicule. [O. Fr. *boter,* to push, strike, from O. Ger. *bozen.* to strike (see **Beat.**)]

**Butt,** but, *n.* a large *cask:* a wine-butt = 126 gallons, a beer and sherry butt = 108 gallons. [Fr. *botte,* a vessel of leather. See **Boot,** of which it is a doublet. Cf. A.S. *bytte,* a bottle.]

**Butt-end,** but′-end, *n.* the striking or heavy end: the stump. [See **Butt,** to strike.]

**Butter,** but′ér, *n.* an oily substance obtained from cream by churning.—*v.t.* to spread over with butter. [A.S. *buter;* Ger. *butter;* both from L. *butyrum*—Gr. *boutyron*—*bous,* ox, *tyros,* cheese.]

**Buttercup,** but′ér-kup, *n.* a plant of the crow-foot genus, with a *cup*-like flower of a golden yellow, like *butter.*

**Butterfly,** but′ér-flī, *n.* the name of an extensive group of beautiful winged insects, so called perh. from the *butter*-like colour of one of the species.

**Butterine,** but′ér-ēn, *n.* an artificial fatty compound, sold as a substitute for *butter.*

**Buttermilk,** but′ér-milk, *n.* the milk that remains after the butter has been separated from the cream by churning.

**Buttery,** but′ér-i, *n.* a storeroom in a house for provisions, especially liquors. [Fr. *bouteillerie,* lit. 'place for bottles.' See **Butler, Bottle.**]

**Buttock,** but′ok, *n.* the rump or protuberant part of the body behind. [Dim. of **Butt,** end.]

**Button,** but′n, *n.* a knob of metal, bone, &c., used to fasten the dress by means of a button-hole: the knob at the end of a foil.—*v.t.* to fasten by means of buttons. [Fr. *bouton,* any small projection, from *bouter,* to push; cf. W. *botwm,* a button.]

**Buttress,** but′res, *n.* a projecting support built on to the outside of a wall: any support or prop.—*v.t.* to prop or support, as by a buttress. [Prob. from O. Fr. *bretesche,* a battlement.]

**Buxom,** buks′um, *adj.* yielding, elastic: gay, lively, jolly. [M. E. *buhsum,* pliable, obedient —A.S. *búgan,* to bow, yield, and affix *some.*]

**Buy,** bī, *v.t.* to purchase for money: to bribe:—*pr.p.* buy′ing; *pa.t.* and *pa.p.* bought (bawt). [A.S. *bycgan;* Goth. *bugjan.*]

**Buyer,** bī′ér, *n.* one who buys, a purchaser.

**Buzz,** buz, *v.i.* to make a humming noise like bees.—*v.t.* to whisper or spread secretly.—*n.* the noise of bees and flies: a whispered report. [From the sound.]

**Buzzard,** buz′ard, *n.* a bird of prey of the falcon family: a blockhead. [Fr. *busard*—L. *buteo,* a kind of falcon.]

**By,** bī, *prep.* at the side of: near to: through, denoting the agent, cause, means, &c.—*adv.* near: passing near: in presence of: aside, away.—**By and by,** soon, presently.—**By the bye,** by the way, in passing. [A.S. *bí, big;* Ger. *bei,* L. *ambi,* Gr. *amphi,* Sans. *abhi.*]

**By-form,** bī′-form, *n.* a form of a word slightly varying from it. [Prep. **By.**]

**Bygone,** bī′gon, *adj.* past.—*n.* a past event.

**Bylaw,** bī′law, *n.* the law of a city, town, or private corporation: a supplementary law or regulation. [From Ice. *byar-lög,* Dan. *by-lov,* town or municipal law; Scot. *bir-law;* from Ice. *bua,* to dwell. See **Bower.** *By,* town, is a suffix in many place-names. The form *by* in bylaw, esp. in its secondary meaning, is generally confused with the prep.]

**Byname,** bī′nām, *n.* a nickname. [Prep. **By.**]

**Bypath,** bī′päth, *n.* a side path. [Prep. **By.**]

**Byplay,** bī′plā, *n.* a scene carried on, subordinate to, and apart from, the main part of the play. [Prep. **By.**]

**Byroad,** bī′rōd, *n.* a retired sideroad.

**Bystander,** bī′stand′ér, *n.* one who stands by or near one: hence, a looker-on.

**Byway,** bī′wā, *n.* a private and obscure way.

**Byword,** bī′wurd, *n.* a common saying: a proverb.

**Byzant,** biz′ant, **Byzantine,** biz′an-tīn, *n.* a gold coin of the Greek empire, struck at *Byzantium* or Constantinople, valued at £15 sterling.

## C

**Cab,** kab, *n.* short for **Cabriolet.**

**Cab,** kab, *n.* a Hebrew dry measure = nearly 3 pints. [Heb. *kab—kabab,* to hollow.]

**Cabal,** ka-bal′, *n.* a small party united for some secret design : the plot itself.—*v.i.* to form a party for a secret purpose: to plot :—*pr.p.* caball′ing; *pa.p.* caballed′.—*n.* **Caball′er,** a plotter or intriguer. [Fr. *cabale;* from **Cabala.**]

**Cabala,** kab′a-la, *n.* a secret science of the Jewish Rabbis for the interpretation of the hidden sense of Scripture.—*n.* **Cab′alist,** one versed in the cabala. [Chal. *kabbel,* to receive—that is, the mystic interpretation of the Scripture.]

**Cabbage,** kab′āj, *n.* a well-known kitchen vegetable. [Fr. *cabus,* headed (*choux cabus,* a cabbage); from L. *caput,* the head.]

**Cabin,** kab′in, *n.* a *hut* or cottage: a small room, especially in a ship.—*v.t.* to shut up in a cabin. [W. *cab, caban,* a rude little hut.]

**Cabinet,** kab′in-et, *n.* a small room or closet : a case of drawers for articles of value : a private room for consultation—hence **The Cabinet,** the ministers who govern a nation, being in England the leaders of the majority in Parliament.

**Cabinet-maker,** kab′in-et-māk′er, *n.* a *maker of cabinets* and other fine furniture.

**Cable,** kā′bl, *n.* a strong rope or chain which *ties* anything, especially a ship to her anchor. [Fr. —Low L. *caplum,* a halter—*capio,* to hold.]

**Caboose,** ka-bōōs′, *n.* the kitchen or cooking-stove of a ship. [Dut. *kombuis,* a cook's room.]

**Cabriolet,** kab-ri-ō-lā′, *n.* a covered carriage with two or four wheels drawn by one horse. [Fr. *cabriole,* formerly *capriole,* the leap of a kid; the springing motion being implied in the name of the carriage—L. *capra,* a she-goat.]

**Cacao,** ka-kā′o, *n.* the chocolate-tree, from the seeds of which chocolate is made. [Mex. *kakahuatl.*]

**Cachinnation,** kak-in-ā′shun, *n., loud laughter.* [L. *cachino,* to laugh loudly—from the sound.]

**Cackle,** kak′l, *n.* the *sound* made by a *hen* or *goose.*—*v.i.* to make such a sound. [E.; cog. with Dut. *kakelen*—from the sound.]

**Cacophony,** ka-kof′o-ni, *n.* a *bad,* disagreeable *sound :* discord of sounds.—*adj.* **Cacoph′onous.** [Gr. *kakos,* bad, *phōnē,* sound.]

**Cactus,** kak′tus, *n.* an American plant, generally with prickles instead of leaves. [Gr.]

**Cad,** kad, *n.* a low fellow. [Short for **Cadet.**]

**Cadastre,** ka-das′tér, *n.* the *head* survey of the lands of a country : an ordnance survey.—*adj.* **Cadas′tral.** [Fr. — Low L. *capitastrum,* register for a poll-tax—L. *caput,* the head.]

**Cadaverous,** ka-dav′ér-us, *adj.* looking like a *dead body:* sickly-looking. [L. *cadaver,* a dead body—*cado,* to fall dead.]

**Caddy,** kad′i, *n.* a small box for holding tea. [Malay *kati,* the weight of the small packets in which tea is made up.]

**Cade,** kād, *n.* a *barrel* or cask. [L. *cadus,* a cask.]

**Cadence,** kā′dens, *n.* (*lit.*) a *falling:* the *fall* of the voice at the end of a sentence: tone, sound, modulation. [Fr.—L. *cado,* to fall.]

**Cadet,** ka-det′, *n.* the younger or youngest son : in the army, one who serves as a private in order to become an officer: a student in a military school.—n. **Cadet'ship.** [Fr. *cadet*, formerly *capdet*—Low L. *capitettum*, dim. of *caput*, the head. See **Captain.**]

**Cadi,** kä'di, *n.* a judge in Mohammedan countries. [Ar. *kadhi*, a judge.]

**Caducous,** ka-dū'kus, *adj., falling* early, as leaves or flowers. [L. *caducus—cado,* to fall.]

**Cæsura, Cesura,** sē-zū'ra, *n.* a syllable *cut off* at the end of a word after the completion of a foot : a pause in a verse.—*adj.* **Cæsu'ral.** [L.—*cædo, cæsum,* to cut off.]

**Caffeine,** kaf'e-in or kaf-ē'in, *n.* the active principle of coffee and tea. [Fr. *cafeine.* See **Coffee.**]

**Caftan,** kaf'tan, *n.* a Persian or Turkish vest.

**Cage,** kāj, *n.* a place of confinement : a box made of wire and wood for holding birds or small animals. [Fr.—L *cavea,* a hollow place.]

**Cairn,** kärn, *n., a heap of stones,* esp. one raised over a grave. [Celt. *carn.*]

**Caitiff,** kā'tif, *n.* a mean despicable fellow.—*adj.* mean, base. [O. Fr. *caitif* (Fr. *chétif*)—L. *captivus,* a captive—*capio,* to take.]

**Cajole,** ka-jōl', *v.t.* to coax : to cheat by flattery. —*ns.* **Cajoler,** ka-jōl'ėr, **Cajolery,** ka-jōl'ėr-i. [Fr. *cajoler,* O. Fr. *cageoler,* to chatter like a bird in a **Cage.**]

**Cake,** kāk, *n.* a piece of dough that is baked or *cooked* : a small loaf of fine bread : any flattened mass baked hard.—*v.t.* to form into a cake or hard mass.—*v.i.* to become baked or hardened. [Sw. *kaka,* Ger. *kuchen—kochen;* all borrowed from L. *coquo,* to cook.]

**Calabash,** kal'a-bash, *n.* a vessel made of a dried *gourd*-shell : the gourd. [Sp. *calabaza,* the gourd—Ar. *qar aybas,* dried gourd.]

**Calamitous,** kal-am'i-tus, *adj.* making wretched, disastrous.

**Calamity,** kal-am'i-ti, *n.* a great misfortune : affliction. [Fr. *calamité*—L. *calamitas.* Ety. dub.]

**Calamus,** kal'a-mus, *n.* an Indian sweet-scented [grass.

**Calash,** ka-lash', *n.* a light low-*wheeled* carriage with a folding top : a hood worn by ladies to protect their bonnets. [Fr. *calèche*—Ger. *kalesche ;* of Slav. origin, as Bohem. *kolesa,* Russ. *kolo,* a wheel.]

**Calcareous,** kal-kā're-us, *adj.* like or containing *chalk* or *lime.*—*n.* **Calca'reousness.** [L. *calcarius,* from *calx.*]

**Calcine,** kal-sīn' or kal'sīn, *v.t.* to reduce to a *calx* or *chalky* powder by the action of heat.—*v.i.* to become a *calx* or powder by heat.—*n.* **Calcination,** kal-sin-ā'shun.

**Calcium,** kal'si-um, *n.* an elementary substance present in limestone and chalk. [L. *calx,* chalk.]

**Calcography,** kal-kog'ra-fi, *n.* a style of engraving like *chalk-drawing.* — *adj.* **Calcograph'ical.** [L. *calx,* and Gr. *graphē,* writing—*graphō,* to write.]

**Calculate,** kal'kū-lāt, *v.t.* to count or reckon : to adjust.—*v.i.* to make a calculation : to estimate. —*adj.* **Cal'culable.** [L. *calculo,* to reckon by help of little stones—*calculus,* dim. of *calx,* a little stone.]

**Calculation,** kal-kū-lā'shun, *n.* the art or process of calculating : estimate.

**Calculative,** kal'kū-lāt-iv, *adj.* relating to calculation.

**Calculator,** kal'kū-lāt-or, *n.* one who calculates.

**Calculus,** kal'kū-lus, *n.* one of the higher branches of mathematics : a stone-like concretion which forms in certain parts of the body.—*pl.* **Calculi,** kal'kū-lī.

**Caldron,** kawl'dron, *n.* a large kettle for boiling

or *heating* liquids. [L. *caldarium—calidus,* hot—*caleo,* to grow hot.]

**Caledonian,** kal-e-dō'ni-an, *adj.* pertaining to *Caledonia* or Scotland.

**Calendar,** kal'en-dar, *n.* a register of *the months :* an almanac : a list of criminal causes for trial. [L. *calendaris,* relating to the calends—*calendæ.*]

**Calender,** kal'en-dėr, *n.* (a corruption of **Cylinder**) a press consisting of two *rollers* for smoothing and dressing cloth : a person who calenders, properly a calendrer.—*v.t.* to dress in a calender. [Gr. *kylindros—kylindō,* to roll.]

**Calends,** kal'endz, *n.* among the Romans, the first day of each month. [L. *calendæ—calo,* Gr. *kaleō,* to call, because the beginning of the month was proclaimed.]

**Calenture,** kal'en-tūr, *n.* a kind of fever or delirium occurring on board ship in hot climates. [Fr. and Sp.—L. *caleo,* to be hot.]

**Calf,** käf, *n.* the young of the cow and of some other animals : a stupid, cowardly person.—*pl.* **Calves,** kävz. [A.S. *cealf ;* Ger. *kalb,* Goth. *kalbo.*]

**Calf,** käf, *n.* the thick fleshy part of the leg behind. [Ice. *kalfi ;* perh. the same word as the preceding, the root idea being to be *fat, thick.*]

**Calibre, Caliber,** kal'i-bėr, *n.* the size of the bore of a gun : diameter : intellectual capacity. [Fr. *calibre,* the bore of a gun ; It. *calibro.*]

**Calico,** kal'i-kō, *n.* cotton cloth first brought from *Calicut* in the East Indies.

**Calif, Caliph,** kā'lif or kal'if, *n.* the name assumed by the *successors* of Mohammed. [Fr.—Ar. *khalifah,* a successor.]

**Califate, Caliphate,** kal'if-āt, *n.* the office, rank, or government of a calif.

**Caligraphy, Calligraphy,** ka-lig'ra-fi, *n., beautiful* hand-*writing.* [Gr. *kalos,* beautiful (akin to E. *hale*), *graphē,* writing.]

**Calipers,** kal'i-pėrz, **Caliper-compasses,** kal'i-pėr-kum'pas-ez, *n.* compasses with bent legs for measuring the diameter of bodies. [Corr. of **Caliber.**]

**Calisthenics, Callisthenics,** kal-is-then'iks, *n.* exercises for the purpose of promoting *gracefulness* as well as *strength* of body.—*adj.* **Calisthen'ic.** [Gr. *kalos,* beautiful, *sthenos,* strength.]

**Calix.** See **Calyx.**

**Calk,** kawk, *v.t.* to stuff (as if *pressed with the foot*) oakum into the seams of a ship to make it water-tight : to roughen a horse's shoe to keep it from slipping.—*n.* **Calk'er.** [O. Fr. *cauquer* —L. *calcare,* to tread under foot—*calx,* the heel.]

**Call,** kawl, *v.i.* to cry aloud : to make a short visit. —*v.t.* to name : to summon : to appoint or proclaim.—*n.* a summons or invitation : an impulse : a demand : a short visit : a shrill whistle : the cry of a bird. [A.S. *ceallian ;* Ice. *kalla,* Gr. *ger-,* in *gēryein,* to proclaim.]

**Calling,** kawl'ing, *n.* that to which a person is *called* (by a divine voice, as it were) to devote his attention : trade : profession : occupation.

**Callosity,** kal-os'i-ti, *n.* a *hard* swelling on the skin. [L. *callositas—callus,* hard skin.]

**Callous,** kal'us, *adj., hardened :* unfeeling or insensible —*adv.* **Call'ously.** —*n.* **Call'ousness.**

**Callow,** kal'ō, *adj.* not covered with feathers : unfledged. [A.S. *calu ;* Dut. *kaal,* L. *calvus,* bald.]

**Calm,** käm, *adj.* still or quiet : serene, tranquil.— *n.* absence of wind : repose : serenity.—*v.t.* to make *calm* : to quiet.—*adv.* **Calm'ly.**—*n.* **Calm'ness.** [Fr. *calme ;* from Low L. *cauma*—Gr. *kauma,* noonday heat—*kaio,* to burn.]

**Calomel**, kal′ō-mel, *n.* a preparation of mercury much used as a medicine : the *white* sublimate got by the application of heat to a mixture of mercury and corrosive sublimate, which is *black*. [Gr. *kalos*, fair, *melas*, black.]

**Caloric**, ka-lor′ik, *n.*, *heat* : the supposed principle or cause of heat. [L. *calor*, heat—*caleo*, to be hot.]

**Calorific**, kal-or-if′ik, *adj.*, *causing heat* : heating. —*n.* **Calorifica′tion**. [L. *calor*, and *facio*, to make.]

**Calotype**, kal′ō-tīp, *n.* a kind of photography. [Gr. *kalos*, beautiful, *typos*, an image.]

**Caltrop**, kal′trop, *n.* a plant with prickly fruit : an instrument armed with four spikes, formerly strewn in the way of an enemy's cavalry. [A.S. *coltræpe*.]

**Calumet**, kal′ū-met, *n.* a kind of pipe, smoked by the American Indians, regarded as a symbol of peace. [Fr.—L. *calamus*, a reed.]

**Calumniate**, ka-lum′ni-āt, *v.t.* to accuse falsely : to slander.—*v.i.* to spread evil reports.—*ns.* **Calum′niation, Calum′niator**.

**Calumnious**, ka-lum′ni-us, *adj.* of the nature of calumny : slanderous.—*adv.* **Calum′niously**.

**Calumny**, kal′um-ni, *n.* false accusation : slander. [L. *calumnia*—*calvere*, to deceive.]

**Calve**, käv, *v.i.* to bring forth a calf.

**Calvinism**, kal′vin-izm, *n.* the doctrines of *Calvin*, an eminent religious reformer of 16th century.

**Calvinist**, kal′vin-ist, *n.* one who holds the doctrines of *Calvin*.

**Calvinistic**, kal-vin-ist′ik, **Calvinistical**, kal-vin-ist′i-kal, *adj.* pertaining to *Calvin* or Calvinism.

**Calx**, kalks, *n.*, *chalk* or *lime* : the substance of a metal or mineral which remains after being subjected to violent heat.—*pl.* **Calxes**, kalk′sez, or **Calces**, kal′sēz [L. *calx*, a stone, limestone, lime ; allied to Gael. *carraig*, a rock.]

**Calyx**, **Calix**, kal′iks or kā′liks, *n.* the outer *covering* or cup of a flower.—*pl.* **Cal′yxes**, **Cal′yces**, or **Cal′ices**. [L. ; Gr. *kalyx*—*kalyptō*, to cover.]

**Cambric**, kām′brik, *n.* a kind of fine white linen, originally manufactured at *Cambray* in Flanders.

**Came**, kām—did come—*past tense* of **Come**.

**Camel**, kam′el, *n.* an animal of Asia and Africa with one or two humps on its back, used as a beast of burden and for riding. [O. Fr. *camel*, —L. *camelus*—Gr. *kamēlos*—Heb. *gamal*.]

**Camellia**, ka-mel′ya, *n.* a species of evergreen shrubs, natives of China and Japan. [Named from *Camellus*, a Jesuit, said to have brought it from the East.]

**Camelopard**, kam-el′ō-pärd or kam′el-ō-pärd, *n.* the giraffe. [L. *camelopardalis* ; from Gr. *kamēlos*, the camel, and *pardalis*, the panther.]

**Camelot**, kam′lot, *n.* See **Camlet**.

**Cameo**, kam′ē-ō, *n.* a gem or precious stone, carved in relief. [It. *cammeo* ; Fr. *camée*—Low L. *cammæus*, traced by Littré to Gr. *kamnein*, to work.]

**Camera**, kam′ėr-a, **Camera obscura**, kam′ėr-a ob-skū′ra, *n.* an instrument for throwing the images of external objects on a white surface placed within a *dark chamber* or box : used in photography. [L.]

**Camerated**, kam′ėr-āt-ed, *adj.* divided into *chambers* : arched or vaulted.

**Camlet**, kam′let, *n.* a cloth originally made of *camels'* hair, but now chiefly of wool and goats' hair. [Fr.—Low L. *camelotum*—L. *camelus*.]

**Camomile**, **Chamomile**, kam′ō-mīl, *n.* a plant, or its dried flowers, used in medicine. [Gr. *cham-*

*aimēlon*, the earth-apple, from the apple-like smell of its blossoms—*chamai*, on the ground, *mēlon*, an apple.]

**Camp**, kamp, *n.* the ground on which an army pitch their tents : the tents of an army.—*v.i.* to encamp or pitch tents. [Fr. *camp*, a camp—L. *campus*, a plain.]

**Campaign**, kam-pān′, *n.* a large open *field* or *plain* ; the time during which an army keeps the field.—*v.i.* to serve in a campaign. [Fr. *campagne* ; from L. *campania*—*campus*, a field.]

**Campaigner**, kam-pān′ėr, *n.* one who has served several *campaigns*.

**Campaniform**, kam-pan′i-form, **Campanulate**, kam-pan′ū-lāt, *adj., in the form of a bell*, applied to flowers. [It. *campana*, a bell, and *Form.*]

**Campanile**, kam-pan-ē′lā, *n.* Italian name for a church-tower from which bells are hung. [It.—*campana*, a bell, also a kind of balance invented in *Campania*.]

**Campanology**, kam-pan-ol′o-ji, *n.* a *discourse* on, or the science of, *bells* or bell-ringing. [It. *campana*, a bell, and Gr. *logos*, a discourse.]

**Campestral**, kam-pes′tral, *adj.* growing in or pertaining to *fields*. [L. *campestris*, from *campus*.]

**Camp-follower**, kamp-fol′ō-ėr, *n.* any one who follows in the train of an army, but takes no part in battle.

**Camphor** (in *B.*, **Camphire**), kam′for, *n.* the white, solid juice of the laurel-tree of India, China, and Japan, having a bitterish taste and a pleasant smell. [Fr. *camphre*—Low L. *camphora*—Malay *kapur*, chalk.]

**Camphorated**, kam′for-āt-ed, *adj.* impregnated with camphor. [*phor.*]

**Camphoric**, kam-for′ik, *adj.* pertaining to camp-

**Camp-stool**, kamp′-stōōl, *n.* a seat or stool with cross legs, so made as to fold up when not used.

**Can**, kan, *v.i.* to be able : to have sufficient power : —*p.a.t.* **Could**. [A.S. *cunnan*, to know (how to do a thing), to be able, pres. ind. *can* ; Goth. *kunnan*, Ger. *können*, to be able. See **Know**.]

**Can**, kan, *n.* a vessel for holding liquor. [A.S. *canne* ; cf. L. *canna*, a reed. Gr. *kannē*, a reed.]

**Canal**, kan-al′, *n.* an artificial watercourse for navigation : a duct in the body for any of its fluids. [L. *canalis*, a water-pipe ; akin to Sans. *khan*, to dig.] [lying story. [Fr.]

**Canard**, ka-när′ or ka-närd′, *n.* an extravagant or

**Canary**, ka-nā′ri, *n.* a wine from the *Canary* Islands : a bird *sing*. from the Canary Islands.

**Cancel**, kan′sel, *v.t.* to erase or blot out by *crossing with lines* : to annul or suppress :—*pr.p.* can′celling ; *pa.p.* can′celled. [Fr. *canceller*—L. *cancello*, from *cancelli*, railings, lattice-work, dim. of *cancer*.] [or *lines*.

**Cancellated**, kan′sel-āt-ed, *adj.* crossed by *bars*

**Cancer**, kan′sėr, *n.* an eating, spreading tumour or *canker*, supposed to resemble a crab : a sign of the zodiac. [L. *cancer* ; cog. with Gr. *karkinos*, Sans. *karkata*, a crab.]

**Cancerous**, kan′sėr-us, *adj.* of or like a cancer.

**Candelabrum**, kan-de-lā′brum, *n.* a branched and ornamented candlestick.—*pl.* **Candela′bra**. [L.]

**Candid**, kan′did, *adj.* frank, ingenuous : free from prejudice : fair, impartial.—*adv.* **Can′didly**.—*n.* **Can′didness**. [Fr. *candide*—L. *candidus*, white —*candeo*, to shine.]

**Candidate**, kan′di-dāt, *n.* one who offers himself for any office or honour, so called because, at Rome, the applicant used to dress in white.—*ns.* **Can′didature, Can′didateship**. [L. *candidatus*, from *candidus*.]

**Candle**, kan'dl, *n.* wax, tallow, or other like substance surrounding a wick: a light. [A.S. *candel*—L. *candela*, from *candeo*, to glow.]

**Candle-coal**, *n.* the same as **Cannel-coal**.

**Candlemas**, kan'dl-mas, *n.* a festival of the R. Catholic Church in honour of the purification of the Virgin Mary, on the 2d of February, and so called from the number of candles used. [**Candle** and **Mass**.]

**Candlestick**, kan'dl-stik, *n.* an instrument for holding a candle, orig. a *stick* or piece of wood.

**Candour**, kan'dur, *n.* freedom from prejudice or disguise: sincerity: openness. [L. *candor*, whiteness, from *candeo*, to be shining white.]

**Candy**, kan'di, *n.* a sweetmeat made of sugar: anything preserved in sugar.—*v.t.* to preserve or dress with sugar: to congeal or crystallise as sugar.—*v.i.* to become congealed:—*pr.p.* can'dying; *pa.p.* can'died. [Fr. *candi*, from Ar. *qand*, sugar.]

**Cane**, kān, *n.*, *a reed*, as the bamboo, &c.: a walking-stick.—*v.t.* to beat with a cane. [Fr. *canne*—L. *canna*—Gr. *kannē*, a reed.]

**Canine**, ka-nīn', *adj.* like or pertaining to *the dog*. [L. *caninus*, from *canis*, a dog.]

**Canister**, kan'is-tėr, *n.* a box or case, usually of tin: a case containing shot, which bursts on being discharged. [L. *canistrum*, a wicker-basket, Gr. *kanastron*—*kannē*, a reed.]

**Canker**, kang'kėr, *n.* small sores in the mouth: a disease in trees, or in horses' feet: anything that corrupts or consumes.—*v.t.* to eat into, corrupt, or destroy: to infect or pollute.—*v.i.* to grow corrupt: to decay. [Same as L. *cancer*, orig. pronounced *canker*.]                                    [canker.

**Cankerous**, kang'kėr-us, *adj.* corroding like a

**Canker-worm**, kang'kėr-wurm, *n.* a worm that *cankers* or eats into plants.

**Cannel-coal**, kan'el-kōl, **Candle-coal**, kan'dl-kōl, *n.* a very hard, black *coal* that burns without smoke, like a candle. [Prov. *cannel*, candle.]

**Cannibal**, kan'i-bal, *n.* one who eats human flesh.—*adj.* relating to cannibalism. [Span., a corr. of *Caribals* (English *Caribs*), the native name of the W. India islanders, who ate human flesh: prob. changed into a word expressive of their character, from L. *canis*, a dog.]

**Cannibalism**, kan'i-bal-izm, *n.* the practice of eating human flesh.

**Cannon**, kan'un, *n.* a great gun used in war: a particular stroke in billiards. [Fr. *canon*, from L. *canna*, a reed. See **Cane**.]

**Cannonade**, kan-un-ād', *n.* an attack with cannon. —*v.t.* to attack or batter with cannon.

**Cannoneer**, **Cannonier**, kan-un-ēr', *n.* one who manages cannon.

**Cannot**, kan'ot, *v.i.* to be unable. [**Can** and **Not**.]

**Canoe**, ka-nōō', *n.* a boat made of the hollowed trunk of a tree, or of bark or skins. [Sp. *canoa*, which like Fr. *canoe* is from Carib *canaoa*.]

**Cañon**, kan-yun', *n.* a deep gorge or ravine between high and steep banks, worn by water-courses. [Sp., a hollow, from root of **Cannon**.]

**Canon**, kan'un, *n.* a law or rule, esp. in ecclesiastical matters: the genuine books of Scripture, called *the sacred canon*: a dignitary of the Church of England: a list of saints canonised: a large kind of type. [A.S., Fr., from L. *canon*— Gr. *kanōn*, a straight rod—*kanne*, a reed.]

**Canonic**, ka-non'ik, **Canonical**, ka-non'ik-al, *adj.* according to or included in *the canon*: regular: ecclesiastical.—*adv.* Canon'ically.

**Canonicals**, ka-non'ik-alz, *n.* the official dress of the clergy, regulated by the church *canons*.

**Canonicity**, kan-un-is'i-ti. *n.* the state of belonging to the *canon* or genuine books of the Scripture.                    [list of saints.—*n.* Canonisa'tion.

**Canonise**, kan'un-īz, *v.t.* to enrol in the *canon* or

**Canonist**, kan'un-ist, *n.* one versed in the *canon* law.—*adj.* Canonist'ic.

**Canonry**, kan'un-ri, *n.* the benefice of a canon.

**Canopy**, kan'o-pi, *n.* a covering over a throne or bed: a covering of state stretched over the head.—*v.t.* to cover with a canopy:—*pr.p.* can'opying; *pa.p.* can'opied. [Fr. *canapé*, O. Fr. *conopée*—L. *conopeum*—Gr. *kōnōpeion*, a mosquito curtain—*kōnōps*, a mosquito.]

**Canorous**, kan-ō'rus, *adj.*, *musical*: melodious. [L. *canorus*, from *canor*, melody—*cano*, I sing.]

**Cant**, kant, *v.i.* to talk in an affectedly solemn or hypocritical way.—*n.* a hypocritical or affected style of speech: the language peculiar to a sect: odd or peculiar talk of any kind. [Lit. to *sing* or *whine*; L. *canto*, freq. of *cano*, to sing.]

**Cant**, kant, *n.* (orig.) *an edge* or *corner*: an inclination from the level: a toss or jerk.—*v.t.* to turn *on the edge* or *corner*: to tilt or toss suddenly. [Dut. *kant*; Ger. *kante*, a corner.]

**Cantankerous**, kan-tang'kėr-us, *adj.* crossgrained: perverse in temper.—*n.* Cantan'kerousness.

**Cantata**, kan-tä'ta, *n.* a poem set to music, interspersed with recitative. [It.—L. *cantare*, freq. of *cano*, to sing.]

**Canteen**, kan-tēn', *n.* a tin vessel used by soldiers for holding liquors: a barrack-tavern. [Fr. *cantine*—It. *cantina*, a small cellar, dim. of *canto*, a corner.]

**Canter**, kan'tėr, *n.* an easy gallop.—*v.i.* to move at an easy gallop.—*v.t.* to make to canter. [Orig. *Canterbury-gallop*, from the easy pace at which the pilgrims rode to the shrine at Canterbury.]

**Cantharides**, kan-thar'i-dēz, *n.pl.* Spanish flies, used for blistering. [L. *cantharis*, beetle, pl. *cantharides*.]

**Canticle**, kan'ti-kl, *n.* a song:—in *pl.* the Song of Solomon. [L. *canticulum*, dim. of *canticum*.]

**Cantilever**, kan'ti-lēv-ėr, *n.* (*arch.*) a wooden or iron block projecting from a wall to bear mouldings, balconies, and the like. The principle has been applied in the construction of bridges to support enormous weights.

**Canto**, kan'tō, *n.* division of a *song* or poem: the treble or leading melody.

**Canton**, kan'tun, *n.* a small division of territory: also, its inhabitants: a division of a shield or painting.—*v.t.* to divide into cantons: to allot quarters to troops. [Fr., a corner, a division.]

**Cantonal**, kan'tun-al, *adj.* pertaining to or divided into cantons.—*n.* Can'tonment (also pron. Cantōon'ment), the quarters of troops in a town.

**Canvas**, kan'vas, *n.* a coarse cloth made of hemp, used for sails, tents, &c., and for painting on: the sails of a ship. [Fr. *canevas*—L. and Gr. *cannabis* = E. **Hemp**.]

**Canvass**, kan'vas, *v.t.* to sift, examine: to discuss: to solicit votes.—*n.* close examination: a seeking or solicitation.—*n.* Can'vasser. [Lit. to sift through canvas.]

**Cany**, kān'i, *adj.* full of or made of canes.

**Canyon**. Same as **Cañon**.

**Canzonet**, kan-zō-net', *n.* a *little* or *short song*. [It. *canzonetta*, dim. of *canzone*, a song; from L. *canto*—*cano*, to sing.]

**Caoutchouc**, kōō'chook, *n.* the highly elastic juice or gum of a plant which grows in S. America and Asia: India-rubber. [S. American.]

**Cap,** kap, *n.* a *covering* for the head : a *cover* : the *top.—v.t.* to put on a *cap* : to *cover* the end or top :—*pr.p.* capp'ing ; *pa.p.* capped'. [Low L. *cappa*, a cape or cope.]

**Capable,** kāp'a-bl, *adj.* having ability, power, or skill to do : qualified for.—*n.* **Capabil'ity.** [Fr. —L. *capio*, to hold, take or seize.]

**Capacious,** kap-ā'shus, *adj.* including much : roomy : wide : extensive.—*adv.* **Capa'ciously.** —*n.* **Capa'ciousness.** [L. *capax, capacis— capio*, to hold.]

**Capacitate,** kap-as'i-tāt, *v.t., to make capable* : to [qualify.

**Capacity,** kap-as'i-ti, *n.* power of *holding* or *grasping* a thing : room : power of mind : character.

**Caparison,** ka-par'is-un, *n.* the *covering* of a horse : a rich cloth laid over a war-horse.—*v.t.* to *cover* with a cloth, as a horse : to dress very richly. [Fr. *caparaçon*—Sp. *caparazon*, augmentative of *capa*, a cape, cover—Low L. *cappa*.]

**Cape,** kāp, *n.* a *covering* for the shoulders attached to a coat or cloak : a cloak. [O. Fr. *cape*—Low L. *cappa*.]

**Cape,** kāp, *n.* a *head* or point of land running into the sea : a *head*-land. [Fr. *cap*—L. *caput*, the head.]

**Caper,** kā'pėr, *n.* the flower-bud of the caper-bush, used for pickling. [Fr. *câpre*—L. and Gr. *capparis*: from Pers. *kabar*, capers.]

**Caper,** kā'pėr, *v.i.* to leap or skip like *a goat* : to dance in a frolicsome manner.—*n.* a leap : a spring. [It. *capriolare—capriolo*, a kid—L. *caper*, a goat.]

**Capillarity,** kap-il-ar'it-i, *n.* name given to certain effects produced by liquids in contact with *capillary* tubes.

**Capillary,** kap'il-a-ri or ka-pil'a-ri, *adj.* as fine or minute as a *hair* : having a very small bore, as a tube.—*n.* a tube with a bore as fine as a *hair* :—in *pl.* the minute vessels that unite the veins and arteries in animals. [L. *capillaris— capillus*, hair, akin to *caput*, the head, akin to E. **Head.**]

**Capital,** kap'it-al, *adj.* relating to *the head* : involving the loss of the head : chief : principal : important.—*adv.* **Cap'itally.** [Fr.—L. *capitalis —caput*, the head.]

**Capital,** kap'it-al, *n.* the *head* or top part of a column or pillar : the chief or most important thing : the chief city of a country : a large letter : the stock or money for carrying on any business.

**Capitalise,** kap'it-al-īz, *v.t.* to convert into *capital* or money. [or money.

**Capitalist,** kap'it-al-ist, *n.* one who has *capital*

**Capitation,** kap-it-ā'shun, *n.* a numbering of every *head* or individual : a tax on every *head*. [Fr. —Low L. *capitatio—caput*, the head.]

**Capitol,** kap'it-ol, *n.* the temple of Jupiter at Rome, built on the *top* of a hill : in the U.S. the house where Congress meets. [L. *Capitolium —caput*, the head.]

**Capitular,** kap-it'ūl-ar, **Capitulary,** kap-it'ūl-ar-i, *n.* a statute passed in a *chapter* or ecclesiastical court : a member of a chapter.—*adj.* relating to a chapter in a cathedral : belonging to a chapter. —*adv.* **Capit'ularly.** [See **Chapter.**]

**Capitulate,** kap-it'ūl-āt, *v.i.* to yield or surrender on certain conditions or *heads.—n.* **Capitula'- tion.**

**Capon,** kā'pn, *n.* a young cock *cut* or *castrated*. [A.S. *capun*—L. *capo*—Gr. *kapōn—koptō*, to cut. See **Chop.**] [*cape*, a cloak.]

**Capote,** ka-pōt', *n.* a kind of cloak. [Fr., dim. of

**Caprice,** ka-prēs', *n.* a change of humour or opinion without reason : a freak. [Fr. *caprice— *It. *capriccio*; perh. from L. *capra*, a she-goat.]

**Capricious,** ka-prish'us, *adj.* full of *caprice* : changeable.—*adv.* **Capri'ciously.—n.** **Capri'- ciousness.**

**Capricorn,** kap'ri-korn, *n.* one of the signs of the zodiac, like a *horned* goat. [L. *capricornus— caper*, a goat, *cornu*, a horn.]

**Capriole,** kap'ri-ōl, *n.,* a *caper ;* a leap without advancing. [O. Fr. *capriole*—It. *capriola*—L. *caper, capra*, a goat.]

**Capsicum,** kap'si-kum, *n.* a tropical plant, from which cayenne pepper is made. [From L. *capsa*, a case, its berries being contained in pods or capsules—*capio*, to hold.]

**Capsize,** kap-sīz', *v.t.* to upset. [Ety. dub.]

**Capstan,** kap'stan, *n.* an upright machine turned by spokes so as to wind upon it a cable which draws something, generally the anchor, on board ship. [Fr. *cabestan ;* ety. dub.]

**Capsular,** kap'sūl-ar, **Capsulary,** kap'sūl-ar-i, *adj.* hollow like a capsule : pertaining to a capsule.

**Capsule,** kap'sūl, *n.* the seed-vessel of a plant : a small dish. [Fr.—L. *capsula*, dim. of *capsa*, a case—*capio*, to hold.]

**Captain,** kap'tān or kap'tin, *n.* a *head* or chief officer : the commander of a troop of horse, a company of infantry, or a ship : the overseer of a mine. [O. Fr. *capitain*—L. *caput*, the head.]

**Captaincy,** kap'tān-si or kap'tin-si, *n.* the rank or commission of a captain.

**Caption,** kap'shun, *n.* the act of *taking* : an arrest. [L. *captio—capio*, to take.]

**Captious,** kap'shus, *adj.* ready *to catch* at faults or *take* offence : critical : peevish.—*adv.* **Cap'- tiously.—n.** **Cap'tiousness.** [Fr.—L. *captiosus —capto*, to snatch at.]

**Captivate,** kap'tiv-āt, *v.t.* (*lit.*) to *take* or *make captive* : to charm : to engage the affections. [See **Captive.**]

**Captivating,** kap'tiv-āt-ing, *adj.* having power to engage the affections.

**Captive,** kap'tiv, *n.* one *taken* : a prisoner of war : one kept in bondage.—*adj.,* *taken* or *kept* prisoner in war : charmed or subdued by any thing.—*n.* **Captiv'ity.** [L. *captivus—capio, captus.*] [prize.

**Captor,** kap'tor, *n.* one who takes a prisoner or a

**Capture,** kap'tūr, *n.* the act of taking : the thing taken : an arrest.—*v.t.* to take as a prize : to take by force. [Fr. *capture*—L. *captura— capio*, to take.]

**Capuchin,** kap-ū-shēn', *n.* a Franciscan monk, so called from the hood he wears : a *hooded* pigeon. [Fr. *capucin*—It. *cappucino*, a small cowl—Low L. *cappa*. See **Cap, Cape.**]

**Car** (old form **Carr**), kär, *n.* a light vehicle moved on wheels : a railway carriage : (*poetic*) a chariot. [Fr. *char*, O. Fr. *car*, *char*—L. *carrus ;* from Celt. *câr*, allied to Lat. *currus*.]

**Carabine,** kar'a-bīn, **Carbine,** kär'bīn, *n.* a short light musket. [Fr. *carabine*, O. Fr. *calabrin*, a carabineer—*calabre*, a machine for casting stones—Low L. *chadabula*—Gr. *katabolē*, overthrow—*kataballō—kata*, down, and *ballō*, to throw. The name was transferred to the musket after the invention of gunpowder.]

**Carabineer,** kar-a-bin-ēr', **Carbineer,** kär-bin-ēr', *n.* a soldier armed with a carabine.

**Carack,** kar'ak, *n.* a large ship of burden. [Fr. *caraque*, Sp. *carraca ;* perh. from Low L. *carica*, a load—root of **Car.**]

**Caracole,** kar'a-kōl, *n.* the half-*turn* which a horseman makes : a *winding* stair.—*v.i.* to turn half round, as cavalry in wheeling. [Fr. *cara-cole*—Sp. *caracol*, the spiral shell of a snail—Ar. *karkara*, to turn.] [Fr.—Sp. *garrafa*—Ar.]

**Carafe**, ka-raf′, *n.* a water-bottle for the table.

**Carat**, kar′at, *n.* a weight of 4 grains : 1-24th part of pure gold. [Fr.—Ar. *qirat*—Gr. *keration*, a seed or bean used as a weight.]

**Caravan**, kar′a-van, *n.* a company of travellers associated together for security in crossing the deserts in the East : a large close carriage. [Fr. *caravane*—Pers. *kârwân.*]

**Caravansary**, kar-a-van′sa-ri, **Caravansera**, kar-a-van′se-ra, *n.* a kind of unfurnished inn where caravans stop. [Pers. *kârwânsarâi—kârwân*, caravan, *sarâi*, inn.]

**Caravel**, kar′av-el, *n.* a kind of light sailing vessel. [Fr.—It. *caravella*—L. *carabus*—Gr. *karabos*, a barque.]

**Caraway**, kar′a-wā, *n.* a plant with aromatic seeds, used as a tonic and condiment. [Sp. *alcaravea*—Ar. *karviya*—Gr. *karon.*]

**Carbine, Carbineer.** See **Carabine.**

**Carbolic acid**, kar-bol′ik as′id, *n.* an acid produced from *coal*-tar, used as a disinfectant. [L. *carbo*, coal.]

**Carbon**, kär′bon, *n.* an elementary substance, widely diffused, of which pure charcoal is an example. [Fr. *carbone*—L. *carbo*, coal.]

**Carbonaceous**, kär-bon-ā′she-us, **Carbonic**, kär-bon′ik, *adj.* pertaining to or composed of *carbon.*

**Carbonari**, kär-bon-är′i, *n.* members of a secret society in Italy at the beginning of this century. [It. 'charcoal-burners.']

**Carbonate**, kär′bon-āt, *n.* a salt formed by the union of carbonic acid with a base.

**Carbonic**, kär-bon′ik, *adj.* relating to carbon. **Carbonic Acid** is an acid formed of carbon and oxygen, generally gaseous, and evolved by respiration and combustion.

**Carboniferous**, kär-bon-if′ér-us, *adj., producing carbon* or coal. [L. *carbo*, and *fero*, to produce.]

**Carbonise**, kär′bon-īz, *v.t.* to *make* into *carbon.* —*n.* **Carbonisa′tion.**

**Carbuncle**, kär′bung-kl, *n.* a fiery red precious stone : an inflamed ulcer. [L. *carbunculus*, dim. of *carbo*, a coal.]

**Carbuncular**, kär-bung′kū-lar, *adj.* belonging to or resembling a carbuncle : red : inflamed.

**Carcanet**, kär′ka-net, *n.* a collar of jewels. [Fr. —Bret. *kerchen*, the neck.]

**Carcass, Carcase**, kär′kas, *n.* a dead body or corpse : the framework of anything : a kind of bombshell. [Fr. *carcasse*, a skeleton—It. *carcasso*, a quiver, *hull*, hulk—Low L. *tarcasius*— Pers. *tarkash*, a quiver.]

**Card**, kärd, *n.* a piece of pasteboard marked with figures for playing a game, or with a person's address upon it : a note. [Fr. *carte*—L. *charta*, Gr. *chartēs*, paper. **Carte** is a doublet.]

**Card**, kärd, *n.* an instrument for combing wool or flax.—*v.t.* to comb wool, &c. [Fr. *carde*—L. *carduus*, a thistle.]

**Cardiac**, kär′di-ak, **Cardiacal**, kar-dī′ak-al, *adj., belonging to the heart :* cordial, reviving. [L.— Gr. *kardiakos—kardia*, the heart.]

**Cardinal**, kär′din-al, *adj.* denoting that on which a thing *hinges* or depends : principal.—*n.* a dignitary in the R. C. Church next to the pope. [L. *cardinalis—cardo, cardinis*, a hinge.]

**Cardinalate**, kär′din-al-āt, **Cardinalship**, kär′din-al-ship, *n.* the office or dignity of a cardinal.

**Care**, kär, *n., anxiety, heedfulness :* charge, oversight : the object of anxiety.—*v.i.* to be anxious : to be inclined : to have regard. [A.S. *caru;*

Goth. *kara*, sorrow, Ice. *kæra*, to lament, Celt. *car*, care ; allied to L. *carus*, dear.]

**Careen**, ka-rēn′, *v.t.* to lay a ship on her side to repair her *bottom* and *keel.* [Fr. *caréner*— *carène*—L. *carina*, the bottom of a ship, the keel.]

**Careenage**, ka-rēn′āj, *n.* a place where ships are careened : the cost of careening.

**Career**, ka-rēr′, *n.* a racecourse : a race : course of action.—*v.i.* to move or run rapidly. [Fr. *carrière*—O. Fr. *car*, a car. See **Car.**]

**Careful**, kār′fool, *adj., full of care :* heedful : in *B.*, anxious : in Dan. iii. 16, at a loss, puzzled. —*adv.* **Care′fully.**—*n.* **Care′fulness.**

**Careless**, kār′les, *adj., without care :* heedless : unconcerned.—*adv.* **Care′lessly.**—*n.* **Care′lessness.**

**Caress**, ka-res′, *v.t.* to treat with *affection :* to fondle : to embrace.—*n.* any act or expression of affection. [Fr. *caresser*—It. *carezza*, an endearment—Low L. *caritia*—L. *carus*, dear.]

**Caret**, kā′ret, *n.* a mark, ∧, used in writing when a word is left out. [L. *caret*, there is wanting.]

**Cargo**, kär′go, *n.* what a ship *carries :* its load. [Sp., from Celtic root of **Car.**]

**Caricature**, kar-i-ka-tūr′, *n.* a likeness of anything so exaggerated or distorted as to appear ridiculous.—*v.t.* to turn into. ridicule by overdoing a likeness. [It. *caricatura—carricare*, to load, from root of **Car.**] [*tures.*

**Caricaturist**, kar-i-ka-tūr′ist, *n.*, one who *carica-*

**Caries**, kā′ri-ēz, *n., rottenness* or decay of a bone. [L.]

**Cariole**, kar′i-ōl, *n.* a light one-horse carriage, used in Norway. [Fr. *carriole*—root of **Car.**]

**Carious**, kā′ri-us, *adj.* affected with caries.

**Carking**, kärk′ing, *adj.* distressing, causing anxiety. [A.S. *cearc*, care ; allied to **Care.**]

**Carmelite**, kär′mel-īt, *n.* a monk of the order of *Mount Carmel*, in Syria, in the 12th century : a kind of pear.

**Carmine**, kär′mīn, *n.* a *crimson* colour. [Fr. or Sp. *carmin*—Sp. *carmesin*, crimson—*carmes*, cochineal—Ar. *qirmizi*, crimson. Same root as **Crimson.**] [from L. *caro, carnis*, flesh.]

**Carnage**, kär′nāj, *n.* slaughter. [Fr. *carnage*,

**Carnal**, kär′nal, *adj., fleshly :* sensual : unspiritual.—*adv.* **Car′nally.** [L. *carnalis—caro, carnis*, flesh.]

**Carnalist**, kär′nal-ist, *n.* a sensualist : a worldling.

**Carnality**, kar-nal′i-ti, *n.* state of being carnal.

**Carnation**, kar-nā′shun, *n.* flesh-colour : a flesh-coloured flower. [L. *carnatio*, fleshiness.]

**Carnelian**, kar-nē′li-an, *n.* a corr. of **Cornelian**, owing to a supposed ety. from *carneus*, fleshy.

**Carnival**, kär′ni-val, *n.* a feast observed by Roman Catholics just before the fast of Lent : riotous feasting or merriment. [Fr. *carnaval*—It. *carnovale*—Low L. *carnelevamen*, solace of the flesh—*caro, carnis*, flesh, and *levamen*, solace—*levare*, to lighten.] [animals.

**Carnivora**, kar-niv′ō-ra, *n.pl.* order of *flesh-eating*

**Carnivorous**, kar-niv′ō-rus, *adj., flesh-eating.* [L. *caro, carnis*, flesh, *voro*, to eat.]

**Carol**, kar′ol, *n.* a song of joy or praise.—*v.i.* to sing a carol : to sing or warble.—*v.t.* to praise or celebrate in song :—*pr.p.* car′olling ; *pa.p.* car′olled. [O. Fr. *carole* ; It. *carola*, orig. a ring-dance ; ety. dub., either dim. of L. *chorus*, a choral dance, or from Bret. *koroll*, a dance, W. *carol*, a song—root *car*, circular motion.]

**Carotid**, ka-rot′id, *adj.* relating to the two great arteries of the neck. [Gr. *karōtides—karos*, sleep, deep sleep being caused by compression of them.]

fāte, fär ; mē, hèr ; mīne ; mōte ; mūte ; mōōn ; *then.*

**Carousal**, kar-owz′al, *n.* a *carouse*: a feast.

**Carouse**, kar-owz′, *n.* a *drinking-bout*: a noisy revel.—*v.i.* to hold a drinking-bout: to drink freely and noisily. [O. Fr. *carous*, Fr. *carrousse*—Ger. *gar aus*, quite out!—that is, empty the glass.]

**Carp**, kärp, *v.i.* to catch at small faults or errors.—*adv.* **Carp′ingly**. [Ice. *karpa*. to boast, modified in meaning through likeness to L. *carpo*, to pluck, deride.] [lang., also Fr. and It.]

**Carp**, kärp, *n.* a fresh-water fish. [In all Teut.

**Carpenter**, kär′pent-ėr, *n.* a worker in timber as used in building houses, ships, &c.—*n.* **Carpentry**, kär′pent-ri, the trade or work of a carpenter. [Fr. *charpentier*, O. Fr. *carpentier*—Low L. *carpentarius*—*carpentum*, a car, from root of **Car**.]

**Carper**, kärp′ėr, *n.* one who carps or cavils.

**Carpet**, kär′pet, *n.* the woven or felted covering of floors, stairs, &c.—*v.t.* to cover with a carpet:—*pr.p.* and *n.* car′peting; *pa.p.* car′peted. [Fr. *carpette*—Low L. *carpeta*, a coarse fabric made from rags pulled to pieces—L. *carpere*, to pluck.]

**Carriage**, kar′ij, *n.*, *act* or cost of *carrying*: a vehicle for carrying: behaviour: (*B.*) baggage.

**Carrion**, kar′i-un, *n.* the dead and putrid body or *flesh* of any animal.—*adj.* relating to, or feeding on, putrid flesh. [Fr. *carogne*—Low L. *caronia*—L. *caro, carnis*, flesh.]

**Carronade**, kar-un-ād′, *n.* a short cannon of large bore, first made at *Carron* in Scotland.

**Carrot**, kar′ut, *n.* an eatable root of a reddish or yellowish colour. [Fr. *carotte*—L. *carota*.]

**Carroty**, kar′ut-i, *adj.*, *carrot*-coloured.

**Carry**, kar′i, *v.t.* to convey or bear: to lead or transport: to effect: to behave or demean.—*v.i.* to convey or propel as a gun:—*pr.p.* carr′ying; *pa.p.* carr′ied. [O. Fr. *carier*, from root of **Car**.]

**Cart**, kärt, *n.* a vehicle with two wheels for conveying heavy loads.—*v.t.* to convey in a cart. [Celt. *cart*, dim. of **Car**.]

**Cartage**, kärt′āj, *n.* the act or cost of carting.

**Carte**, kärt, *n.* a bill of fare: a term in fencing. [Fr.—L. *charta*, Gr. *chartēs*, paper. See **Card**.]

**Carte-blanche** (-blänsh), *n.* a *white* or blank *card*, with a signature at the foot, which may be filled up at the pleasure of the receiver: unconditional terms. [Fr. *carte*, and *blanche*, white.]

**Carte-de-visite**, -viz-it′, *n.* a photographic portrait pasted on a small *card*.

**Cartel**, kär′tel, *n.* a *paper* of agreement for exchange of prisoners. [Fr. *cartel*—It. *cartello*, dim. from root of **Carte**.]

**Carter**, kärt′ėr, *n.* one who drives a cart.

**Cartesian**, kar-tē′zhi-an, *adj.* relating to the French philosopher *Des Cartes*, or his philosophy.

**Cartilage**, kär′ti-lāj, *n.* a tough, elastic substance, softer than bone: gristle. [Fr.—L. *cartilago*, ety. of which is doubtful.]

**Cartilaginous**, kär-ti-laj′in-us, *adj.* pertaining to or consisting of cartilage: gristly.

**Cartoon**, kär-tōōn′, *n.* a preparatory drawing on strong *paper*, to be transferred to frescoes, tapestry, &c.: any large sketch or design on paper. [Fr. *carton* (It. *cartone*), augmentative of **Carte**.]

**Cartouche**, kär-tōōsh′, *n.* a case for holding cartridges: a case containing bullets to be discharged from a mortar: (*arch.*) an ornament resembling a scroll of paper with the ends rolled up. [Fr.—It. *cartoccio*—L. *charta*, paper.]

**Cartridge**, kär′trij, *n.* a *paper* case containing the charge for a gun. [Corruption of **Cartouche**.]

**Cartulary**, kär′tū-lar-i, *n.* a *register-book* of a monastery, &c.: one who kept the records.

[Low L. *cartularium*—*chartula*, a document—*charta*, paper.]

**Carve**, kärv, *v.t.*, *to cut* into forms, devices, &c.: to make or shape by cutting: to cut up (meat) into slices or pieces: to apportion or distribute.—*v.i.* to exercise the trade of a sculptor. [A.S. *ceorfan*, to cut, to hew; Dut. *kerven*, Ger. *kerben*, to notch. See **Grave**.]

**Carver**, kärv′ėr, *n.* one who carves: a sculptor.

**Caryates**, kar-i-āt′ēz, **Caryatides**, kar-i-at′i-dēz, *n.pl.* (*arch.*) figures of women used instead of columns for supporters. [L. *Caryates*, Gr. *Karyatides*, the women of *Caryæ*, a town in Arcadia.]

**Cascade**, kas-kād′, *n.* a waterfall. [Fr. *cascade*—It. *cascata*, from *cascare*, L. *cado, casus*, to fall.]

**Case**, kās, *n.* a covering, box, or sheath. [Fr. *caisse*, O. Fr. *casse*—L. *capsa*, from *capio*, to receive.]

**Case**, kās, *v.t.* to put in a *case* or box.

**Case**, kās, *n.* that which *falls* or *happens*, event: particular state or condition: subject of question or inquiry: statement of facts: (*gram.*) the inflection of nouns, &c. [Fr. *cas*—L. *casus*, from *cado*, to fall.]

**Casein**, **Caseine**, kā′se-in, *n.* an organic substance, contained in milk and *cheese*. [Fr.—L. *caseus*, cheese.]

**Casemate**, kās′māt, *n.* a bomb-proof chamber or battery in which cannon may be placed to be fired through embrasures. [Fr.; ety. dub.]

**Casement**, kās′ment, *n.* the *case* or frame of a window: a window that opens on hinges: a hollow moulding.

**Cash**, kash, *n.* coin or money: ready-money.—*v.t.* to turn into or exchange for money: to pay money for. [A doublet of **Case**, a box—O. Fr. *casse*, a box or till.]

**Cashier**, kash-ēr′, *n.* a *cash*-keeper: one who has charge of the receiving and paying of money.

**Cashier**, kash-ēr′, *v.t.* to dismiss from a post in disgrace: to discard or put away. [Ger. *cassiren*—Fr. *casser*—L. *cassare*—*cassus*, void, empty.]

**Cashmere**, kash′mēr, *n.* a rich kind of shawl, first made at *Cashmere*, in India.

**Casino**, kas-ē′nō, *n.* a room for public dancing. [It.; from L. *casa*, a cottage.]

**Cask**, kask, *n.* a hollow round vessel for holding liquor, made of staves bound with hoops. [Fr. *casque*, Sp. *casco*, skull, helmet, cask.]

**Casket**, kask′et, *n.*, *a little cask* or case: a small *case* for holding jewels, &c.

**Casque**, **Cask**, kask, *n.* a cover for the head: a helmet. [A doublet of **Cask**.]

**Cassia**, kash′ya, *n.* a species of laurel-tree whose bark is *cut off* on account of its aromatic qualities: wild cinnamon: the senna-tree. [L. *cassia*—Gr. *kasia*; from a Heb. root, to cut.]

**Cassimere**, kas-i-mēr′ (also spelled **Kerseymere**), *n.* a twilled cloth of the finest wools. [Corr. of **Cashmere**.]

**Cassock**, kas′ok, *n.* a vestment worn by clergymen under the gown or surplice. [Fr. *casaque*—It. *casacca*—L. *casa*, a cottage, a covering.]

**Cassowary**, kas′ō-war-i, *n.* an ostrich-like bird, found in the E. Indies. [Malay *kassuwaris*.]

**Cast**, kast, *v.t.*, *to throw* or *fling*: to throw down: to throw together or reckon: to mould or shape.—*v.i.* to warp:—*pa.t.* and *pa.p.* cast.—*n.* act of casting: a throw: the thing thrown: the distance thrown: a motion, turn, or squint, as of the eye: a chance: a mould: the form received from a mould: manner: the assignment of the various parts of a play to the several actors : **the** company of actors to whom such have been assigned. [Scan. ; as Ice. *kasta*, to throw.] [cast.

**Castaway**, kast'a-wā, *n.*, *one cast away*, an outcast.

**Caste**, kast, *n.* one of the classes into which society in India is divided : any class of society which keeps itself apart from the rest. [A name given by the Port. to the classes of people in India, Port. *casta*, breed, race—L. *castus*, pure, unmixed.] [*castle*.

**Castellan**, kas'tel-an, *n.* governor or captain of a

**Castellated**, kas'tel-āt-ed, *adj.* having turrets and battlements like a *castle*. [L. *castellatus*.]

**Caster**, kast'ėr, *n.* a small wheel on the legs of furniture.—in *pl.* small cruets.

**Castigate**, kas'tig-āt, *v.t.*, *to chastise* : to correct: to punish with stripes. [L. *castigo, castigatus*, from *castus*, pure.]

**Castigation**, kas-tig-ā'shun, *n.* act of castigating: chastisement : punishment.

**Castigator**, kas'tig-āt-or, *n.* one who castigates.

**Casting**, kast'ing, *n.* act of casting or moulding: that which is cast : a mould.

**Cast-iron**. See under **Iron**.

**Castle**, kas'l, *n.* a *fortified house* or *fortress*: the residence of a prince or nobleman. [A.S. *castel* —L. *castellum*, dim. of *castrum*, a fortified place : from root *skad*, as E. *shade*.]

**Castor**, kas'tor, *n.* the beaver : a hat made of its fur. [L., Gr. *kastōr* ; cf. Sans. *kasturi*, musk.]

**Castor-oil**, kas'tor-oil, *n.* a medicinal oil obtained from a tropical plant, the *Ricinus communis*. [Ety. dub.]

**Castrate**, kas'trāt, *v.t.* to deprive of the power of generation, to geld : to take from or render imperfect.—*n.* **Castra'tion**. [L. *castrare*.]

**Casual**, kazh'ū-al, *adj.* accidental : unforeseen: occasional. [L. *casualis—casus*. See **Case**.]

**Casualty**, kazh'ū-al-ti, *n.*, *that which falls out*: an accident : a misfortune.

**Casuist**, kazh'ū-ist, *n.* one who studies and resolves *cases* of conscience.

**Casuistic**, kazh-ū-ist'ik, **Casuistical**, kazh-ū-ist'ik-al, *adj.* relating to *cases* of conscience.

**Casuistry**, kazh'ū-ist-ri, *n.* the science or doctrine of *cases* of conscience.

**Cat**, kat, *n.* a common domestic animal. [In Teut., Celt., Slav., Ar., Turk., and Late L.]

**Cataclysm**, kat'a-klizm, *n.* a flood of water : a deluge. [Gr. *kataklysmos—kata*, downward, *klyzein*, to wash or dash.]

**Catacomb**, kat'a-kōm, *n.* a *hollow* or cave *underground* used as a burial-place. [It. *catacomba*, Low L. *catacumba*—Gr. *kata*, downward, and *kymbē*, a hollow, akin to W. *cwm*, a hollow.]

**Catafalque**, kat-a-falk', *n.* a temporary structure of carpentry representing a tomb or cenotaph : a tomb of state. [Fr.—It. *catafalco*—Sp. *catar*, to see, and *falco*, from the Ger. root of **Balcony**. **Scaffold** is a doublet through Fr. *échafaud*.]

**Catalepsy**, kat'a-lep-si, *n.* a disease that seizes suddenly.—*adj.* **Catalep'tic**. [Gr., from *kata*, down, *lambanō, lēpsomai*, to seize.]

**Catalogue**, kat'a-log, *n.* a list of names, books, &c.—*v.t.* to put in a catalogue :—*pr.p.* cat'aloguing ; *pa.p.* cat'alogued. [Fr.—Late Lat.—Gr., from *kata*, down, *logos*, a counting.]

**Catamaran**, kat-a-ma-ran', *n.* a raft of three trees, used by the natives of India and Brazil. [Tamul 'tied logs.']

**Catapult**, kat'a-pult, *n.* anciently a machine for *throwing* stones, arrows, &c.; an instrument used by boys for throwing small stones. [L. *catapulta* —Gr. *katapeltēs—kata*, down, *pallō*, to throw.]

**Cataract**, kat'a-rakt, *n.* a great waterfall ; a disease of the eye which comes on as if a veil fell before the eyes. [Gr. *kata*, down, *arassō*, to dash, to rush.]

**Catarrh**, kat-är', *n.* a discharge of fluid from a mucous membrane, especially of the nose, caused by cold in the head : the cold itself.—*adj.* **Catarrh'al**. [L. *catarrhus*, Gr. *katarrhoos— kata*, down, *rheō*, to flow.]

**Catastrophe**, kat-as'trō-fē, *n.*, *an overturning*: a final event : an unfortunate conclusion : a calamity. [Gr. *kata*, down, *strephō*, to turn.]

**Catcal, Catcall**, kat'kawl, *n.* a squeaking instrument used in theatres to condemn plays.

**Catch**, kach, *v.t.*, *to take hold of* : to seize after pursuit : to trap or insnare : to take a disease by infection.—*v.i.* to be contagious :—*pa.t.* and *pa.p.* caught (kawt).—*n.* seizure : anything that seizes or holds : that which is caught : a sudden advantage taken : a song the parts of which are *caught up* by different voices. [A doublet of **Chase**, from O. Fr. *cachier*—L. *captiare* for *captare*, inten. of *capere*, to take. See **Chase**.]

**Catchpenny**, kach'pen-i, *n.* any worthless thing, esp. a publication, intended merely to gain money.

**Catchpoll**, kach'pōl, *n.* a constable.

**Catchup**, kach'up, **Catsup**, kat'sup, **Ketchup**, kech'up, *n.* a liquor extracted from mushrooms, &c., used as a sauce. [Prob. of E. Indian origin.]

**Catchword**, kach'wurd, *n.* among actors, the last word of the preceding speaker : the first word of a page given at the bottom of the preceding page.

**Catechetic**, kat-e-ket'ik, **Catechetical**, kat-e-ket'ik-al, *adj.*, *relating to a catechism.*—*adv.* **Catechet'ically**.

**Catechise**, kat'e-kīz, *v.t.* to instruct by question and answer : to question : to examine.—*n.* **Cat'echiser**. [Gr. *katēchizō, katēcheō*, to din into the ears—*kata*, down, *ēcheō*, to sound.]

**Catechism**, kat'e-kizm, *n.* a book containing a summary of principles in the form of questions and answers.

**Catechist**, kat'e-kist, *n.* one who catechises.

**Catechumen**, kat-e-kū'men, *n.* one who is *being taught* the rudiments of Christianity. [Gr. *katēchoumenos*, being taught, p. of *katēcheō*, to teach.] [lute : without exception.

**Categorical**, kat-e-gor'ik-al, *adj.* positive : abso-

**Category**, kat'e-gor-i, *n.*, *what may be affirmed* of a class : a class or order. [Gr. *katēgoria—kata*, down, against, *agoreuō*, to harangue, declare.]

**Cater**, kā'tėr, *v.i.* to provide food, entertainment, &c.—*n.* **Ca'terer**. [Lit. to act as a *cater*, the word being orig. a substantive, and spelled *catour* —O. Fr. *acat* (Fr. *achat*), a purchase—Low L. *accaptare*, to buy—L. *ad*, to, *captare*, intensive of *capere*, to take.]

**Caterpillar**, kat'ėr-pil-ar, *n.* a grub that lives upon the leaves of plants. [O. Fr. *chattepeleuse*, a hairy cat—*chatte*, a she-cat, *peleuse* = Lat. *pilosus*, hairy.] [cats.

**Caterwaul**, kat'ėr-wawl, *v.i.* to make a noise like

**Cates**, kāts, *n.pl.* dainty food. [O. E. *acates*— root of **Cater**.]

**Catgut**, kat'gut, *n.* a kind of cord made from the intestines of animals, and used as strings for musical instruments.

**Cathartic**, kath-ärt'ik, **Cathartical**, kath-ärt'ik-al, *adj.* having the power of *cleansing* the stomach and bowels : purgative. [Gr. *kathartikos*, fit for cleansing, from *katharos*, clean.]

**Cathartic**, kath-ärt'ik, *n.* a purgative medicine.

**Cathedral**, kath-ē'dral, *n.* the principal church of

a diocese, in which is the *seat* or throne of a bishop.—*adj.* belonging to a cathedral. [L. *cathedra*—Gr. *kathedra*, a seat.]

**Catholic**, kath'ol-ik, *adj.*, *universal:* general, embracing the *whole* body of Christians : liberal, the opp. of exclusive : the name claimed by its adherents for the Church of Rome as the representative of the church founded by Christ and his apostles : relating to the Roman Catholics.—*n.* an adherent of the Roman Catholic Church. [Gr. *katholikos*, universal—*kata*, throughout, *holos*, the whole.]

**Catholicism**, ka-thol'i-sizm, **Catholicity**, kath-ol-is'it-i, *n.*, *universality ;* liberality or breadth of view : the tenets of the R. Catholic Church.

**Catkin**, kat'kin, *n.* a loose cluster of flowers like a *cat's tail* growing on certain trees, as hazels, &c. [**Cat**, and dim. suffix *-kin*.] [nine lashes.

**Cat-o'-nine-tails**, kat'-ō-nīn'-tālz, *n.* a whip with

**Catoptric**, kat-op'trik, *adj.* relating to *catoptrics*, or vision by reflection. [Gr., from *katoptron*, a mirror—*kata*, against, *optomai*, to see.]

**Catoptrics**, kat-op'triks, *n.sing.* the part of optics which treats of *reflected light*.

**Cat's-paw**, kats'-paw, *n.* the dupe or tool of another : (*naut.*) a light breeze. [From the fable of the monkey who used the paws of the cat to draw the roasting chestnuts out of the fire.]

**Cattle**, kat'l, *n.pl.* beasts of pasture, esp. oxen, bulls, and cows ; sometimes also horses, sheep, &c. [O. Fr. *catel*, *chatel*—Low L. *captale*, orig. capital, property in general, then esp. animals— L. *capitalis*, chief—*caput*, the head, beasts in early times forming the chief part of property.]

**Caucus**, kaw'kus, *n.* a party combination or meeting for influencing elections, esp. in Amer. [Ety. dub. ; perh. a corr. of *calkers'* club, the nickname of a Boston clique about 1760.]

**Caudal**, kaw'dal, *adj.* pertaining to the *tail:* having a tail or something like one. [L. *cauda*.]

**Caudle**, kaw'dl, *n.*, *a warm* drink given to the sick. [O. Fr. *chaudel*—Fr. *chaud*—L. *calidus*, hot.]

**Caught**, kawt, *pa.t.* and *pa.p.* of **Catch**.

**Caul**, kawl, *n.* a net or covering for the head : the membrane covering the head of some infants at their birth. [O. Fr. *cale*, a little cap—Celt. *calla*, a veil, hood.]

**Cauldron**. See **Caldron**.

**Cauliflower**, kaw'li-flow-èr, *n.* a variety of cabbage, the eatable part of which is the flower. [L. *caulis*, cabbage, and **Flower**. See **Cole**.]

**Caulk**. See **Calk**.

**Causal**, kawz'al, *adj.* relating to a *cause* or causes.

**Causality**, kawz-al'it-i, *n.* the working of a *cause:* (*phren.*) the faculty of tracing effects to their causes. [the bringing about of an effect.

**Causation**, kawz-ā'shun, *n., the act of causing:*

**Causative**, kawz'a-tiv, *adj.* producing an effect : causing.—*adv.* **Caus'atively.**

**Cause**, kawz, *n.* that by or through which anything is done : inducement : a legal action.—*v.t.* to produce : to make to exist : to bring about. [Fr. *cause*—L. *causa*.]

**Causeless**, kawz'les, *adj.*, *having 10 cause* or occasion.—*adv.* **Cause'lessly.**—*n* **Cause'lessness.**

**Causeway**, kawz'wā, **Causey**, kawz'e, *n.* a pathway raised and *paved* with stone. [O. Fr. *caucie*, Fr. *chaussée*—L. *calciata*—*calx*, chalk, because built with mortar.]

**Caustic**, kaws'tik, *adj.*, *burning:* severe, cutting. —*n.* a substance that *burns* or wastes away the flesh. [L.—Gr. *kaustikos*—*kaiō*, *kausō*, to burn.]

**Causticity**, kaws-tis'i-ti, *n.* quality of being *caustic*.

**Cauterisation**, kaw-tèr-īz-ā'shun, **Cauterism**, kaw'tèr-izm, **Cautery**, kaw'tèr-i, *n.* a burning with *caustics* or a hot iron.

**Cauterise**, kaw'tèr-īz, *v.t.* to *burn* with a *caustic* or a hot-iron. [Fr. *cautériser*—Gr. *kautēr*, a hot iron—*kaiō*, to burn.]

**Caution**, kaw'shun, *n.* heedfulness : security : warning.—*v.t.* to warn to take care. [Fr.—L. *cautio*—*caveo*, to beware.]

**Cautionary**, kaw'shun-ar-i, *adj.* containing caution : given as a pledge.

**Cautious**, kaw'shus, *adj.* possessing or using caution : watchful : prudent.—*adv.* **Cau'tiously.**— *n.* **Cau'tiousness.**

**Cavalcade**, kav'al-kād, *n.* a train of persons on *horseback*. [Fr.—It. *cavallo*—L. *caballus*, Gr. *kaballēs*, a horse, a nag.]

**Cavalier**, kav-al-ēr', *n.* a knight : a partisan of Charles I.—*adj.* like a *cavalier :* gay : warlike : haughty.—*adv.* **Cavalier'ly.** [Fr.—It. *cavallo*. See **Cavalcade**.] [*rie*—It.]

**Cavalry**, kav'al-ri, *n.*, *horse*-soldiers. [Fr. *cavale*-

**Cave**, kāv, *n.* a *hollow place* in the earth : a den. [Fr.—L. *cavea*—*cavus*, hollow. **Cage** is a doublet.]

**Caveat**, kā've-at, *n.* (*lit.*) *let him take care:* a notice or warning : a notice to stop proceedings in a court. [L.—*caveo*, to take care.]

**Cavendish**, kav'en-dish, *n.* tobacco moistened and pressed into quadrangular cakes.

**Cavern**, kav'ėrn, *n.* a deep *hollow place* in the earth. [L. *caverna*—*cavus*, hollow.]

**Cavernous**, kav'ėr-nus, *adj.*, *hollow:* full of caverns.

**Caviare, Caviar**, kav-i-är', *n.* an article of food made from the salted roes of the sturgeon, &c. [Fr. *caviar*—It. *caviale*—Turk. *haviār*.]

**Cavil**, kav'il, *v.t.* to make empty, trifling objections : to use false arguments :—*pr.p.* cav'illing ; *pa.p.* cav'illed.—*n.* a frivolous objection.—*n.* **Cav'iller.** [O. Fr. *caviller*—L. *cavillor*, to practise jesting—*cavilla*, jesting.]

**Cavity**, kav'it-i, *n.*, *a hollow place:* hollowness : an opening. [L. *cavitas*—*cavus*, hollow.]

**Caw**, kaw, *v.i.* to cry as a crow.—*n.* the cry of a crow.—*n.* **Caw'ing.** [From the sound. See **Chough**.]

**Cazique**, ka-zēk', *n.* a chief in certain parts of America at the time of its discovery. [Span. *cacique*, orig. Haytian.]

**Cease**, sēs, *v.i.*, *to give over:* to stop : to be at an end.—*v.t.* to put an end to. [Fr. *cesser*—L. *cesso*, to give over—*cedo*, to yield, give up.]

**Ceaseless**, sēs'les, *adj.*, *without ceasing:* incessant.—*adv.* **Cease'lessly.**

**Cedar**, sē'dar, *n.* a large evergreen tree remarkable for the durability and fragrance of its wood.—*adj.* made of cedar. [L.—Gr. *kedros*.]

**Cede**, sēd, *v.t.* to yield or give up to another.— *v.i.* to give way. [L. *cedo*, *cessum*, to go away from.]

**Ceil**, sēl, *v.t.* to overlay the inner roof of a room. [See **Ceiling**.]

**Ceiling**, sēl'ing, *n.* the inner roof of a room. [M. E. *syle* or *cyll*, a canopy—Fr. *ciel*, heaven. a canopy, a ceiling—L. *cælum*, the vault of heaven. Cf. Gr. *koilos* = E. **Hollow**.]

**Celandine**, sel'an-dīn, *n.*, *swallow*-wort, a plant of the poppy family, so named because it was supposed to flower when the *swallows* appeared, and to perish when they departed. [O. Fr. *celidoine*—Gr. *chelidonion*—*chelidōn*, a swallow.]

**Celebrate**, sel'e-brāt, *v.t.* to make famous : to

distinguish by solemn ceremonies. [L. *celebro*, -*atum—celeber*, frequented.]

**Celebration**, sel-e-brā'shun, *n.*, *act of celebrating*.

**Celebrity**, sel-eb'ri-ti, *n.* the condition of being *celebrated*: fame. [L. *celebritas—celeber*.]

**Celerity**, sel-er'it-i, *n.* quickness: rapidity of motion. [Fr.—L. *celeritas—celer*, quick—*cello*, Gr. *kellō*, to drive, urge on.]

**Celery**, sel'er-i, *n.* a kitchen vegetable. [Fr. *céleri*—L. and Gr. *selīnon*, parsley.]

**Celestial**, sel-est'yal, *adj.*, *heavenly*: dwelling in heaven: in the visible heavens.—*n.* an inhabitant of heaven.—*adv.* **Celest'ially.** [L. *cælestis—cælum*, heaven; Gr. *koilos*, E. **Hollow.**]

**Celibacy**, sel'i-bas-i or se-lib'as-i, *n.* a *single* life: an unmarried state. [L. *celebs*, single.]

**Celibate**, sel'i-bāt, *adj.*, *pertaining to a single life.—n.* one unmarried.

**Cell**, sel, *n.* a small room: a cave: a small shut cavity. [L. *cella*, conn. with *celare*, to cover.]

**Cellaret**, sel-ar-et', *n.* an ornamental case for holding bottles. [A diminutive of **Cellar**.]

**Cellar**, sel'ar, *n.* a *cell* under ground where stores are kept. [L. *cellarium—cella*.]

**Cellarage**, sel'ar-āj, *n.* space for cellars: cellars: charge for storing in cellars.

**Cellular**, sel'ū-lar, *adj.*, *consisting of* or containing *cells*. [From L. *cellula*, a little cell.]

**Celt**, selt, *n.* a cutting instrument of stone or metal found in ancient barrows. [Founded on *Celte* (translated 'with a chisel'), perh. a misreading for *certe* ('surely'), in the Vulgate, Job xix. 24.]

**Celt**, selt, *n.* one of the *Celts*, an Aryan race, now represented by the Welsh, Irish, and Scottish Highlanders.—*adj.* **Celt'ic.** [L. *Celtæ*; Gr. *Keltoi* or *Keltai*.]

**Cement**, se-ment', *n.* anything that makes two bodies stick together: mortar: a bond of union. [L. *cæmenta*, chips of stone used to fill up in building a wall, *cædimenta—cædo*, to cut off.]

**Cement**, se-ment', *v.t.* to unite with *cement*: to join firmly.

**Cementation**, sem-ent-ā'shun, *n.*, *the act of cementing*: the process by which iron is turned into steel, glass into porcelain, &c.—done by surrounding them with a *cement* or powder and exposing them to heat.

**Cemetery**, sem'e-tėr-i, *n.* a burying-ground. [Low L. *cæmeterium*—Gr. *koimētērion—koimaō*, to lull to sleep.]

**Cenobite**, sen'ō-bīt or sē'nō-bīt, *n.* one of a religious order *living in a community*, in opposition to an **Anchorite**: a monk.—*adjs.* **Cenobit'ic, Cenobit'ical.** [L. *cænobita*—Gr. *koinobios*, from *koinos*, common, and *bios*, life.]

**Cenotaph**, sen'ō-taf, *n.* (*lit.*) *an empty tomb*: a monument to one who is buried elsewhere. [Fr. —L.—Gr. *kenotaphion — kenos*, empty, and *taphos*, a tomb.]

**Censer**, sens'ėr, *n.* a pan in which *incense* is burned. [Fr. *encensoir*—Low L. *incensorium*.]

**Censor**, sen'sor, *n.* in ancient Rome, an officer who kept account of the property of the citizens, imposed taxes, and watched over their morals: in modern times, an officer who examines books or newspapers before they are printed, and whose permission is necessary for their publication: one who *censures* or blames. [L.—*censeo*, to weigh, to estimate.]

**Censorial**, sen-sō'ri-al, *adj.* belonging to a *censor*, or to the correction of public morals.

**Censorious**, sen-sō'ri-us, *adj.* expressing censure: fault-finding.—*adv.* **Censo'riously.**—*n.* **Censo'riousness.**

**Censorship**, sen'sor-ship, *n.* office of censor: time during which he holds office.—**Censorship of the press,** a regulation of certain governments, by which books and newspapers must be examined by officers, whose approval is necessary to their publication.

**Censurable**, sen'shūr-a-bl, *adj.* deserving of *censure*: blamable.—*adv.* **Cen'surably.**—*n.* **Cen'surableness.**

**Censure**, sen'shūr, *n.* an unfavourable *judgment*: blame: reproof.—*v.t.* to blame: to condemn as wrong. [L. *censura*, an opinion, a severe judgment *-censeo*, to estimate or judge.]

**Census**, sen'sus, *n.* an official *enumeration* of the inhabitants of a country. [L. *census*, a register.]

**Cent**, sent, *n.*, *a hundred*: an American coin=the *hundredth part* of a dollar.—**Per cent**, *by the hundred*. [L. *centum*, a hundred.]

**Centage**, sent'āj, *n.* rate *by the hundred*.

**Cental**, sen'tal, *n.* a weight of 100 lbs. proposed for general adoption, legalised in 1878.

**Centaur**, sen'tawr, *n.* a fabulous monster, half-man half-horse. [L.—Gr. *kentauros*; ety. dub.]

**Centenary**, sen'ten-ar-i, *n.* a *hundred*: a *century* or *hundred* years.—*adj.* pertaining to a hundred. —*n.* **Centena'rian**, one a *hundred* years old. [L.—*centeni*, a hundred each—*centum*.]

**Centennial**, sen-ten'i-al, *adj.* happening once in a *hundred years*. [Coined from L. *centum*, and *annus*, a year.]

**Centesimal**, sen-tes'i-mal, *adj.*, *hundredth.*—*adv.* **Centes'imally.** [L. *centesimus—centum*.]

**Centigrade**, sen'ti-grād, *adj.* having a *hundred degrees*: divided into a hundred degrees, as the *centigrade thermometer*, in which freezing-point is zero and boiling-point is 100°. [L. *centum*, and *gradus*, a step, a degree.]

**Centiped**, sen'ti-ped, **Centipede**, sen'ti-pēd, *n.* an insect with a *hundred* or a great many *feet*. [L. *centum*, and *pes*, *pedis*, a foot.]

**Centner**, sent'ner, *n.* a common name on the Continent for a hundredweight.

**Central**, sen'tral, **Centric**, sen'trik, **Centrical**, sen'trik-al, *adjs.*, *relating to*, placed in, or containing *the centre*.—*advs.* **Cen'trally, Cen'trically.** [*n.* **Centralisa'tion.**

**Centralise**, sen'tral-īz, *v.t.* to draw to a *centre*.—

**Centre, Center**, sen'tėr, *n.* the middle point of anything: the middle.—*v.t.* to place on or collect to a centre.—*v.i.* to be placed in the middle :—*pr.p.* cen'tring, cen'tering ; *pa.p.* cen'tred, cen'tered. [Fr.—L. *centrum*—Gr. *kentron*, a sharp point—*kenteō*, to prick.]

**Centrifugal**, sen-trif'ū-gal, *adj.* tending to *flee from the centre*. [L. *centrum*, and *fugio*, to flee from.]

**Centripetal**, sen-trip'et-al, *adj.*, *tending* toward *the centre*. [L. *centrum*, and *peto*, to seek.]

**Centuple**, sen'tū-pl, *adj.*, *hundredfold*. [L. *centuplex—centum*, and *plico*, to fold.]

**Centurion**, sen-tū'ri-on, *n.* among the Romans, the commander of a *hundred* men. [L. *centurio*.]

**Century**, sen'tū-ri, *n.*, *a hundred*, or something consisting of a hundred in number: a hundred years. [L. *centuria—centum*.]

**Cephalic**, se-fal'ik, *adj.* belonging to the *head*. [Gr. *kephalikos—kephalē*, the head.]

**Ceraceous**, se-rā'shus, *adj.*, *of* or *like wax*.

**Ceramic**, se-ram'ik, *adj.*, *pertaining to pottery*. [Gr. *keramos*, potter's earth, and suffix *-ic*.]

**Cere**, sēr, *v.t.* to cover with *wax*.—*ns.* **Cere'cloth, Cere'ment**, a cloth dipped in melted wax in which to wrap a dead body. [L. *cera*; cog. with Gr. *kēros*, Gael. *ceir*, beeswax.]

**Cereal**, sē're-al, *adj.* relating to corn or edible grain.—**Cereals**, sē're-alz, *n.pl.* the grains used as food, such as wheat, barley, &c. [L. *cerealis*—*Ceres*, the goddess of corn or produce.]

**Cerebellum**, ser-e-bel'um, *n.* the hinder and lower part of the brain. [L., dim. of *cerebrum*.]

**Cerebral**, ser'e-bral, *adj.*, *pertaining to the cerebrum*.—*n.* **Cerebra'tion**, action of the brain, conscious or unconscious.

**Cerebrum**, ser'e-brum, *n.* the front and larger part of the brain. [L. *cerebrum*, the brain, of which *cere* = Gr. *kara*, the head, M. E. *hernes*, brains, Scot. *harns*.]

**Ceremonial**, ser-e-mō'ni-al, *adj.* relating to *ceremony*.—*n.* outward form: a system of ceremonies.—*adv.* **Ceremo'nially**.

**Ceremonious**, ser-e-mō'ni-us, *adj.*, *full of ceremony*: particular in observing forms: precise.—*adv.* **Ceremo'niously**.—*ns.* **Ceremo'niousness**.

**Ceremony**, ser'e-mo-ni, *n.* a sacred rite: the outward form, religious or otherwise. [Fr.—L. *cerimonia*, from root *kar*, to make, do.]

**Certain**, sėr'tān or sėr'tin, *adj.* sure: fixed: regular: some: one.—*adv.* **Cer'tainly**.—*ns.* **Cer'tainty**, **Cer'titude**. [Fr. *certain*—L. *certus*, old part. of *cerno*, to decide.]

**Certificate**, sėr-tif'i-kāt, *n.* a written declaration of some fact: a testimonial of character.—*v.t.* to give a certificate.—*n.* **Certifica'tion**. [Fr. *certificat*—L. *certus*, and *facio*.]

**Certify**, sėr'ti-fī, *v.t.*, *to make* known *as certain*: to inform: to declare in writing:—*pr.p.* cer'tifying; *pa.p.* cer'tified. [Fr. *certifier*—L. *certus*, and *facio*, to make.]

**Cerulean**, se-rōō'le-an, *adj.*, *sky-blue*: dark-blue: sea-green. [L. *cœruleus* = *cœluleus*—*cœlum*, the sky.]

**Ceruse**, sē'rōōs, *n.* white-lead, the native carbonate of lead. [Fr.—L. *cerussa*, conn. with *cera*, wax.]

**Cervical**, sėr'vi-kal, *adj.* belonging to the *neck*. [Fr.—L. *cervix*, *cervicis*, the neck.]

**Cervine**, sėr'vīn, *adj.* relating to *deer*. [L. *cervus*, a stag: akin to E. *hart*.]

**Cesarean**, sē-zā're-an, *adj.* the Cesarean operation is taking a child out of the body of its mother *by cutting*. [L. *cædo*, *cæsus*, to cut.]

**Cess**, ses, *n.* a tax.—*v.t.* to impose a tax. [Shortened from **Assess**.]

**Cessation**, ses-ā'shun, *n.* a *ceasing* or stopping: a rest: a pause. [Fr.—L. ; see **Cease**.]

**Cession**, sesh'un, *n.* a yielding up. [Fr.—L. ; see **Cede**.]

**Cesspool**, ses'pōōl, *n.*, *a pool* or hollow in which filthy water collects. [Acc. to **Skeat**, from Celt. *soss-pool*, a pool into which foul messes flow. Cf. Scot. *soss*, a mixed dirty mess.]

**Cestus**, ses'tus, *n.* the girdle of Venus, which had power to awaken love: an ancient boxing-glove loaded with lead or iron. [L.—Gr. *kestos*, a girdle.]

**Cesura.** See **Cæsura**.

**Cetaceous**, set-ā'shus, *adj.* belonging to fishes of the *whale-kind*. [L. *cete*—Gr. *kētos*, any sea-monster.]

**Chace.** See **Chase**.

**Chafe**, chāf, *v.t.*, *to make hot* by rubbing : to fret or wear by rubbing : to cause to fret or rage.—*v.i.* to fret or rage.—*n.* heat caused by rubbing: rage: passion. [Fr. *chauffer*—L. *calefacere*—*caleo*, to be hot, and *facere*, to make.]

**Chafer**, chāf'er, *n.* a kind of beetle. [A.S. *ceafor*.]

**Chaff**, chaf, *n.* the case or covering of grain: empty, worthless matter.—*adjs.* **Chaff'y**, **Chaff'less**. [A.S. *ceaf*; Ger. *kaff*.]

**Chaff**, chaf, *v.t.* to banter.—*n.* **Chaff'ing**. [A corr. of *chafe*.]

**Chaffer**, chaf'er, *v.t.*, *to buy*.—*v.i.* to bargain : to haggle about the price. [M.E. *chapfare*, a bargain, from A.S. *ceap*, price, *faru*, way—a *business proceeding*.]

**Chaffinch**, chaf'insh, *n.* a little song-bird of the finch family. [Said to delight in *chaff*. See **Finch**.]

**Chagrin**, sha-grēn', *n.* that which *wears* or *gnaws* the mind : vexation : ill-humour.—*v.t.* to vex or annoy. [Fr. *chagrin*, shagreen, rough skin used for rasping or polishing wood.]

**Chain**, chān, *n.*, a series of links or rings passing through one another: a number of things coming after each other: anything that binds: a measure of 100 links, 66 feet long.—*v.t.* to bind with or as with a chain. [Fr. *chaîne*—L. *catena*.]

**Chair**, chār, *n.* something *to sit down* upon : a movable seat for one, with a back to it : the seat or office of one in authority.—*v.t.* to carry one publicly in triumph. [Fr. *chaire*—L. *cathedra*—Gr. *kathedra*—*kathezomai*, to sit down.]

**Chaise**, shāz, *n.* a light two-wheeled carriage, for two persons, drawn by one horse. [Fr., a Parisian pronunciation of *chaire*. See **Chair**.]

**Chalcedony**, kal-sed'ō-ni or kal'-, *n.* a variety of quartz of a milk-and-water colour.—*adj.* **Chalcedon'ic**. [From *Chalcedon*, in Asia Minor.]

**Chaldaic**, kal-dā'ik, **Chaldee**, kal'dē, *adj.* relating to *Chaldea*.

**Chaldron**, chawl'drun, *n.* a coal-measure holding 36 bushels. [Fr. *chaudron*. See **Caldron**.]

**Chalice**, chal'is, *n.* a *cup* or *bowl* : a communion-cup.—*adj.* **Chal'iced**. [Fr. *calice*—L. *calix*, *calicis*; Gr. *kylix*, a cup. **Calyx** is a different word, but from the same root.]

**Chalk**, chawk, *n.* the well-known white substance, a carbonate of lime.—*v.t.* to rub or manure with chalk.—*adj.* **Chalk'y**.—*n.* **Chalk'iness**. [A.S. *cealc*, like Fr. *chaux*, O. Fr. *chaulx*, is from L. *calx*, limestone.]

**Challenge**, chal'enj, *v.t.* to call on one to settle a matter by fighting or any kind of contest : to claim as one's own : to accuse : to object to.—*n.* a summons to a contest of any kind : exception to a juror : the demand of a sentry. [O. Fr. *chalenge*, a dispute, a claim—L. *calumnia*, a false accusation—*calui*, *caluere*, to deceive.]

**Chalybeate**, ka-lib'e-āt, *adj.* containing *iron*.—*n.* a water or other liquor containing iron. [Gr. *chalyps*, *chalybos*, steel, so called from the *Chalybes*, a nation in Pontus famous for steel.]

**Chamber**, chām'bėr, *n.* an apartment : the place where an assembly meets : an assembly or body of men met for some purpose, as a chamber of commerce : a hall of justice : the back end of the bore of a gun.—*adj.* **Cham'bered**.—*n.* **Cham'bering**, in *B.*, lewd behaviour. [Fr. *chambre*—L. *camera*—Gr. *kamara*, a vault, a room : akin to Celt. *cam*, crooked.]

**Chamberlain**, chām'bėr-lān or -lin, *n.* an overseer of the private apartments of a monarch or nobleman : treasurer of a corporation.—*n.* **Cham'berlainship**. [O. Fr. *chambrelenc*; O. Ger. *chamerling*—L. *camera*, a chamber, and affix *ling* or *lenc* = E. *ling* in *hireling*.]

**Chameleon**, ka-mēl'yun, *n.* a small lizard famous for changing its colour. [L. *chamæleon*—Gr. *chamaileōn*—*chamai* (= L. *humi*), on the ground, *leōn*, a lion = a dwarf-lion.]

**Chamois**, sham'waw or sha-moi', *n.* a kind of goat : a soft kind of leather originally made from its skin. [Fr.—Ger. *gemse*, a chamois.]

**Chamomile.** See **Camomile.**

**Champ**, champ, *v.i.* to make a snapping noise with the jaws in chewing.—*v.t.* to bite or chew. [Older form *cham*, from Scand., as in Ice. *kiapta*, to chatter, *kiaptr*, the jaw.]

**Champagne**, sham-pān′, *n.* a light sparkling wine from *Champagne*, in France.

**Champaign**, sham-pān′, *adj.*, *level*, open.—*n.* an open, *level country*. [A doublet of **Campaign**, from O. Fr. *champaigne*—L. *campania*, a plain.]

**Champion**, cham′pi-un, *n.* one who fights in single combat for himself or for another : a successful combatant : a hero.—*n.* **Cham′pionship**. [Fr. —Low L. *campio*—Low L. *campus*, a combat— L. *campus*, a plain, a place for games : whence also are borrowed A.S. *camp*, a fight, *cempa*, a warrior, Ger. *kämpfen*, to fight.]

**Chance**, chans, *n.* that which *falls out* or *happens :* an unexpected event : risk : opportunity : possibility of something happening.—*v.t.* to risk.— *v.i.* to happen.—*adj.* happening by chance. [Fr.—Low L. *cadentia*—L. *cado*, to fall.]

**Chancel**, chan′sel, *n.* the part of a church where the altar is placed, formerly inclosed with *lattices* or rails. [O. Fr.—L. *cancelli*, lattices.]

**Chancellor**, chan′sel-or, *n.* the president of a court of *chancery* or other court.—*n.* **Chan′cellorship**. [Fr. *chancelier*—Low L. *cancellarius*, orig. an officer that had charge of records, and stood near the *cancelli* (L.), the crossbars that surrounded the judgment-seat.]

**Chance-medley**, chans′-med-li, *n.* the killing of a person by chance or in self-defence. [*Chance*, a corruption of Fr. *chaude*, hot, *mêlée*, fray, fight.]

**Chancery**, chan′sėr-i, *n.* the highest court of justice next to the parliament, presided over by the Lord High *Chancellor*. [Fr. *chancellerie*.]

**Chandelier**, shan-de-lēr′, *n.* a frame with branches for holding lights. [Fr.—Low L. *candelaria*, a candlestick—L. *candela*, a candle.]

**Chandler**, chand′lėr, *n.* orig. a *candle* maker and dealer : a dealer generally. [Fr. *chandelier*.]

**Chandlery**, chand′lėr-i, *n.* goods sold by a chandler.

**Change**, chānj, *v.t.* to alter or make different : to put or give one thing or person for another : to make to pass from one state to another.—*v.i.* to suffer change.—*n.* alteration or variation of any kind : a shift : variety : small coin : also used as a short term for the Exchange. [Fr. *changer*— Late L. *cambiare*—L. *cambire*, to barter.]

**Changeable**, chānj′a-bl, *adj.* subject or prone to change : fickle : inconstant.—*adv.* **Change′ably**. —*n.* **Change′ableness**.

**Changeful**, chānj′fool, *adj.*, *full of change :* changeable.—*adv.* **Change′fully**.—*n.* **Change′fulness**. [constant.

**Changeless**, chānj′les, *adj.*, *without change :*

**Changeling**, chānj′ling, *n.* a child taken or left in place of another : one apt to change.

**Channel**, chan′el, *n.* the bed of a stream of water : the deeper part of a strait, bay, or harbour : a strait or narrow sea : means of passing or conveying. [O. Fr. *chanel* or *canel*—L. *canalis*.]

**Chant**, chant, *v.t.*, *to sing :* to celebrate in song : to recite in a singing manner.—*n.* song : melody : a kind of sacred music, in which prose is sung. [Fr. *chanter* (It. *cantare*)—L. *canto*—*cano*, to sing.]

**Chanter**, chant′ėr, *n.*, *one who chants :* a chief singer : the tenor or treble pipe of a bagpipe.

**Chanticleer**, chant′i-klēr, *n.* a cock. [M.E. *chaunte-cleer*, from **Chant** and **Clear**.]

**Chantry**, chant′ri, *n.* an endowed chapel in which

masses are *chanted* for the souls of the donors or others. [O. Fr. *chanterie*—*chanter*, to sing.]

**Chaos**, kā′os, *n.* a confused, shapeless mass : disorder : the state of matter before it was reduced to order by the Creator. [L. and Gr. *chaos*— root *ha*, to gape, seen also in Gr. *chainō*, *chaō*, to gape, to yawn.] [disordered.

**Chaotic**, kā-ot′ik, *adj.*, *like chaos :* confused or

**Chap**, chap or chop, *v.t.*, *to cut :* to cleave, split, or crack.—*v.i.* to crack or open in slits :—*pr.p.* chapp′ing ; *pa.p.* chapped′, chapt. [E. ; Dut. *kappen*, Dan. *kappe*, to cut. See **Chip**.]

**Chap**, chap, **Chop**, chop, *n.* a cleft, crack, or chink.

**Chapbook**, chap′book, *n.* a small kind of book or tract, at one time carried about for sale by chapmen.

**Chapel**, chap′el, *n.* place of worship inferior or subordinate to a regular church, or attached to a palace or a private dwelling : a dissenters′ place of worship. [Fr. *chapelle*, O. Fr. *capele*—Low L. *capella*, dim. of *capa*, a cloak or cope : such a small cope was kept in the palaces of kings on which to administer oaths ; the name was transferred to the sanctuary where the capella was kept, and hence to any sanctuary containing relics.—LITTRÉ.] [*chapel*.

**Chapelry**, chap′el-ri, *n.* the jurisdiction of a

**Chaperon**, shap′e-rōn, *n.* a kind of hood or cap : one who attends a lady in public places as a protector.—*v.t.* to attend a lady to public places. [Fr., a large hood or head-dress, and hence a person who affords protection like a hood—*chape*, a hooded cloak—Low L. *cappa*. See **Cape**.]

**Chap-fallen**, chap-fawln. Same as **Chop-fallen**.

**Chapiter**, chap′i-tėr, *n.* the *head* or *capital* of a column. [Fr. *chapitel*—Low L. *capitellum*, dim. of L. *caput*, the head.]

**Chaplain**, chap′lān or chap′lin, *n.* a clergyman attached to a ship of war, a regiment, a public institution, or family.—*ns.* **Chap′laincy**, **Chap′lainship**. [Fr. *chapelain*—Low L. *capellanus* —*capella*. See **Chapel**.]

**Chaplet**, chap′let, *n.* a *garland* or wreath for the head : a rosary. [Fr. *chapelet*, dim. of O. Fr. *chapel*, a hat—Low L. *capa*, a cape.]

**Chapman**, chap′man, *n.* one who buys or sells : a dealer. [A.S. *ceap-man*—*ceap*, trade, and *man*. See **Cheap**.]

**Chaps**, chaps, *n.pl.* the jaws. [N. E. and Scot. *chafts*—Scand., as Ice. *kjaptr*, the jaw. See **Jowl**.]

**Chapt**, chapt, *pa.p.* of **Chap**.

**Chapter**, chap′tėr, *n.*, *a head* or division of a book : a corporation of clergymen belonging to a cathedral or collegiate church : an organised branch of some society or fraternity. [Fr. *chapitre*—L. *capitulum*, dim. of *caput*, the head.]

**Char**, chär, *n.* work done by the day : a turn of work : a job.—*v.i.* to work by the day. [A.S. *cierr*, a turn, space of time—*cyrran*, to turn.]

**Char**, chär, *n.* a *red-bellied* fish or the salmon kind, found in mountain lakes and rivers. [Ir. and Gael. *cear*, red, blood-coloured.]

**Char**, chär, *v.t.* to roast or burn until reduced to *carbon* or *coal*.—*pr.p.* charr′ing ; *pa.p.* charred. [Ety. dub. ; acc. to Skeat, because wood is turned to coal, from **Char**, a *turn* of work.]

**Character**, kar′ak-tėr, *n.* a letter, sign, or figure : the peculiar qualities of a person or thing : description of the qualities of a person or thing : a person with his peculiar qualities. [Fr. *ca* *actère*—L. *character*—Gr. *charaktēr*, from *charassō*, to cut, engrave.]

**Characterise**, kar′ak-tèr-īz, *v.t.* to give a *character* to : to describe by peculiar qualities : to distinguish or designate.—*n.* **Characterisa′tion**. [Gr. *charaktērizō*.]

**Characteristic**, kar-ak-tèr-is′tik, **Characteristical**, kar-ak-tèr-is′tik-al, *adj.* marking or constituting the peculiar nature.—**Characteris′tic**, *n.* that which marks or constitutes the character.—*adv.* **Characteris′tically**. [Gr.]

**Charade**, shar-äd′ or -ād′, *n.* a species of riddle, the subject of which is a word proposed for solution from an enigmatical description of its several syllables and of the whole ; the charade is often acted. [Fr. ; ety. dub.]

**Charcoal**, chär′kōl, *n.*, *coal* made by *charring* or burning wood under turf.

**Charge**, chärj, *v.t.* to *lay on* or *load* : to impose or intrust : to fall upon or attack : to put to the account of : to impute to : to command : to exhort.—*v.i.* to make an onset.—*n.* that which is laid on : cost or price : the load of powder, &c. for a gun : attack or onset : care, custody : the object of care : command : exhortation : accusation. [Fr. *charger*—Low L. *carricare*, to load—L. *carrus*, a wagon. See **Car**, **Cargo**.]

**Chargeable**, chärj′a-bl, *adj.* liable to be *charged* : imputable : blamable : in *B.*, burdensome.—*n.* **Charge′ableness**.—*adv.* **Charge′ably**.

**Charger**, chärj′èr, *n.* a dish capable of holding a heavy *charge* or quantity : a horse used in *charging*, a war-horse.

**Charily**, **Chariness**. See **Chary**.

**Chariot**, char′i-ot, *n.* a four-wheeled pleasure or state carriage : a car used in ancient warfare. [Fr., dim. of *char*, a car, from root of **Car**.]

**Charioteer**, char-i-ot-ér′, *n.* one who drives a chariot.

**Charitable**, char′i-ta-bl, *adj.*, *full of charity* : of or relating to charity : liberal to the poor.—*adv.* **Char′itably**.—*n.* **Char′itableness**.

**Charity**, char′i-ti, *n.* in New Test., universal love : the disposition to think favourably of others, and do them good : almsgiving. [Fr. *charité*—L. *caritas*, from *carus*, dear.]

**Charlatan**, shär′la-tan, *n.* a mere talking pretender : a quack. [Fr.—It. *ciarlatano*—*ciarlare*, to chatter, an imitative word.]

**Charlatanry**, shär′la-tan-ri, *n.* the profession of a *charlatan* : undue or empty pretension : deception.

**Charlock**, chär′lok, *n.* a plant of the mustard family, with yellow flowers, that grows as a weed in cornfields. [A.S. *cerlice*—*cer*, unknown, *lic* = *leek*, a plant.]

**Charm**, chärm, *n.* a spell : something thought to possess hidden power or influence : that which can please irresistibly.—*v.t.* to influence by a charm : to subdue by secret influence : to enchant : to delight : to allure.—*adv.* **Charm′ingly**. [Fr. *charme*—L. *carmen*, a song.] [delights.

**Charmer**, chärm′èr, *n.*, *one who enchants* or

**Charnel**, chär′nel, *adj.* containing *flesh* or carcasses. [Fr. *charnel*—L. *carnalis*—*caro*, *carnis*, flesh.]

**Charnel-house**, chär′nel-hows, *n.* a place where the bones of the dead are deposited.

**Chart**, chärt, *n.* a map of a part of the sea, with its coasts, shoals, &c. for the use of sailors. [L. *charta*, a paper. See **Card**.]

**Charter**, chärt′ér, *n.* a formal written *paper*, conferring or confirming titles, rights, or privileges : a patent : grant : immunity.—*v.t.* to establish by charter : to let or hire, as a ship, on contract. [Fr. *chartre*—L. *chartarium*, archives—*charta*.]

**Charter-party**, chärt′ér-pär-ti, *n.* a mutual charter or contract for the hire of a vessel. [Fr. *chartre-partie*, (*lit.*) a divided charter, as the practice was to divide it in two and give a half to each person.]

**Chartism**, chärt′izm, *n.* the principles of a party who sprung up in Gt. Britain in 1838, and who advocated the people's *charter*—viz. universal suffrage, &c.

**Chartist**, chärt′ist, *n.* one who supports *chartism*.

**Charwoman**, chär-woom′an, *n.* a *woman* who *chars* or does odd work by the day.

**Chary**, chär′i, *adj.* sparing : cautious.—*adv.* **Char′ily**.—*n.* **Char′iness**. [A.S. *cearig*—*cearu*, care.]

**Chase**, chās, *v.t.* to pursue : to hunt : to drive away.—*n.* pursuit : a hunting : that which is hunted : ground abounding in game. [Fr. *chasse.*—Low L. *caciare*—L. *capto*—*capio*, to take.] [chase.]

**Chase**, chās, *v.t.* to *incase* : to emboss. [See **Enchase**.]

**Chase**, chās, *n.* a *case* or frame for holding types : a groove. [Fr. *châsse*, a shrine, a setting—L. *capsa*, a chest. See **Case**.]

**Chaser**, chās′èr, *n.*, *one who chases* : an enchaser.

**Chasm**, kazm, *n.* a *yawning* or *gaping* hollow : a gap or opening : a void space. [Gr. *chasma*, from *chainō*, to gape ; connected with **Chaos**.]

**Chaste**, chāst, *adj.* modest : refined : virtuous : pure in taste and style.—*adv.* **Chaste′ly**. [Fr. *chaste*—L. *castus*, pure.]

**Chasten**, chās′n, *v.t.* to free from faults by punishing : hence, to punish : to correct. [Fr. *châtier*, O. Fr. *chastier*—L. *castigare*—*castus*, pure.]

**Chasteness**, chāst′nes, **Chastity**, chas′ti-ti, *n.*, *purity* of body, conduct, or language.

**Chastise**, chas-tīz′, *v.t.* to inflict punishment upon for the purpose of correction : to reduce to order or to obedience.—*n.* **Chastisement**, chas′tiz-ment.

**Chasuble**, chaz′ū-bl, *n.* the uppermost garment worn by a R. C. priest at mass. [Fr.—Low L. *casubula*, L. *casula*, a mantle, dim. of *casa*, a hut.]

**Chat**, chat, *v.i.* to talk idly or familiarly :—*pr.p* chatt′ing ; *pa.p.* chatt′ed.—*n.* familiar, idle talk. [Short for **Chatter**.]

**Chateau**, sha-tō′, *n.* a *nobleman's castle* : a country-seat. [Fr., O. Fr. *châtel*, *castel*—L. *castellum*, dim. of *castrum*, a fort.]

**Chattel**, chat′l, *n.* any kind of property which is not freehold. [Doublet of **Cattle**.]

**Chatter**, chat′ér, *v.i.* to talk idly or rapidly : to sound as the teeth when one shivers. [From the sound.]

**Chatty**, chat′i, *adj.*, *given to chat* : talkative.

**Cheap**, chēp, *adj.* low in price : of small value.—*adv.* **Cheap′ly**.—*n.* **Cheap′ness**. [Orig. **Good cheap**, *i.e.*, a good bargain ; A.S. *ceap*, price, a bargain ; A.S. *ceapan*, Ice. *kaupa*, Ger. *kaufen*, to buy ; Scot. *coup*—all borrowed from L. *caupo*, a huckster.] [down in price.

**Cheapen**, chēp′n, *v.t.* to *make cheap* : to beat

**Cheat**, chēt, *v.t.* to deceive and defraud.—*n.* a fraud : one who cheats. [A corr. of **Escheat**, the seizure of such property being looked upon as robbery.]

**Check**, chek, *v.t.* to bring to a stand : to restrain or hinder : to rebuke.—*n.* a term *in chess* when one party obliges the other either to move or guard his *king*: anything that checks : a sudden stop : in *B.*, a rebuke. [Fr. *échec* = Pers. *shah*, king—(mind your) king !]—*v.t.* to compare with a counterpart or authority in order to ascertain correctness.—*n.* a mark put against items in a list : a token : an order for money (usually written **Cheque**) : any counter-register used as security : a checkered cloth. [From the practice of the Court of *Exchequer*, where accounts were settled by means of counters on a *checkered* cloth.]

**Check-book**, chek′-book, *n.* a bank-book containing blank checks, for the use of persons having accounts with the bank.

**Checker, Chequer**, chek′ēr, *v.t.* to form into little squares like a *chessboard* or *checker*, by lines or stripes of different colours : to variegate or diversify.—*n.* a chessboard. [Fr. *échiquier*, O. Fr. *eschequier*, a chessboard—*échec*.]

**Checkers**, chek′ērz, *n.pl* a game played by two persons on a *checkered* board ; ..so called **Draughts.**

**Checkmate**, chek′māt, *n.* in chess, a *check* given to the adversary's king when in a position in which it can neither be protected nor moved out of check, so that the game is finished : a complete check : defeat : overthrow.—*v.t.* in chess, to make a movement which ends the game : to defeat. [Fr. *échec et mat* : Ger. *schach-matt*—Pers. *shâh mât*, the king is dead.]

**Cheek**, chēk, *n.* the side of the face below the eye. [A.S. *ceace*, the cheek, jaw.]

**Cheep**, chēp, *v.i.* to chirp, as a young bird. [From the sound, like **Chirp.**]

**Cheer**, chēr, *n.* that which makes the *countenance* glad : joy : a shout : kind treatment : entertainment : fare.—*v.t.* to make the *countenance* glad : to comfort : to encourage : to applaud. [O. Fr. *chiere*, the countenance—Low L. *cara*, the face —Gr. *kara*, the head, face.]

**Cheerful**, chēr′fool, *adj., full of cheer* or good spirits : joyful : lively.—*adv.* **Cheer′fully.**—*n.* **Cheer′fulness.**

**Cheerless**, chēr′les, *adj., without cheer* or comfort : gloomy.—*n.* **Cheer′lessness.**

**Cheery**, chēr′i, *adj., cheerful* : promoting cheerfulness.—*adv.* **Cheer′ily.**—*n.* **Cheer′iness.**

**Cheese**, chēz, *n.* the *curd of milk* pressed into a hard mass. [A.S. *cese, cyse*, curdled milk ; Ger. *käse* ; both from L. *caseus* ; cf. Gael. *caise*.]

**Cheesecake**, chēz′kāk, *n.* a cake made of soft curds, sugar, and butter.                         [cheese.

**Cheesemonger**, chēz′mung′gēr, *n.* a dealer in cheese.

**Cheesy**, chēz′i, *adj.* having the nature of *cheese*.

**Cheetah**, chē′tah, *n.* an eastern animal like the leopard, used in hunting. [Hind. *chîtâ*.]

**Chemic**, kem′ik, **Chemical**, kem′i-kal, *adj., belonging to chemistry.—adv.* **Chem′ically.**

**Chemicals**, kem′ik-alz, *n.pl.* substances used for producing chemical effects.

**Chemise**, she-mēz′, *n.* a lady's shift. [Fr. *chemise*— Low L. *camisia*, a nightgown—Ar. *qamis*, a shirt.]

**Chemisette**, shem-e-zet′, *n.* an under-garment worn by ladies over the *chemise*. [Fr., dim. of *chemise*.]

**Chemist**, kem′ist, *n.* one skilled in *chemistry*.

**Chemistry**, kem′is-tri, formerly **Chymistry**, *n.* the science which treats of the properties of substances both elementary and compound, and of the laws of their combination and action one upon another. [From the ancient **Alchemy**, which see.]

**Cheque, Chequer.** See **Check, Checker.**

**Cherish**, cher′ish, *v.t.* to protect and treat with affection. [Fr. *chérir, chérissant—cher*, dear— L. *carus*.]                                         [known.]

**Cheroot**, she-rōōt′, *n.* a kind of cigar. [Ety. un-

**Cherry**, cher′i, *n.* a small bright-red stone-fruit : the tree that bears it.—*adj.* like a cherry in colour : ruddy. [Fr. *cerise*—Gr. *kerasos*, a cherry-tree. said to be so named from Cerasus, a town in Pontus, from which the cherry was brought by Lucullus.]

**Chert**, chĕrt, *n.* a kind of quartz or flint : hornstone. [Ety. dub.]

**Cherty**, chĕrt′i, *adj., like* or containing *chert*.

**Cherub**, cher′ub, *n.* a celestial spirit : a beautiful child.—*pl.* **Cher′ubs, Cher′ubim, Cher′ubims.** [Heb. *kerub*.]

**Cherubic**, che-rōōb′ik, **Cherubical**, che-rōōb′i-kal, *adj.* pertaining to *cherubs* : angelic.

**Chess**, ches, *n.* a game played by two persons on a board like that used in checkers. [Corr. of **Checks**, the *pl.* of **Check.**]

**Chest**, chest, *n.* a large strong *box* : the part of the body between the neck and the abdomen. [A.S. *cyst*  Scot. *kist*—L. *cista*—Gr. *kistē*.]

**Chestnut, Chesnut**, ches′nut, *n.* a nut or fruit inclosed in a prickly case : the tree that bears it. —*adj.* of a chestnut colour. reddish-brown. [M.E. *chesten-nut*—O. Fr. *chastaigne*—L. *castanea*—Gr. *kastanon*, from *Castana*, in Pontus, where the tree abounded.]

**Cheval-de-frise**, she-val′-de-frēz, *n.* a piece of timber armed with spikes, used to defend a passage or to stop cavalry.—*pl.* **Chevaux-de-frise,** she-vō′-de-frēz. [Fr. *cheval*, horse, *de*, of, *Frise*, Friesland ; a jocular name.]

**Chevalier**, shev-a-lēr′, *n.* a *cavalier* : a knight : a gallant man. [Fr.—*cheval*—L. *caballus*, a hors .]

**Chew**, chōō, *v.t.* to *cut* and bruise with the teeth. [A.S. *ceowan*; Ger. *kauen*: conn. with **Jaw** and **Chaps.**]

**Chiaro-oscuro**, ki-är′ō-os-kōō′rō. See **Clare-obscure.**                            [pipe for smoking.  [Turk.]

**Chibouk, Chibouque**, chi-book′. *n.* a Turkish pipe for smoking.  [Turk.]

**Chicane**, shi-kān′, *v.i.* to use shifts and tricks, to deceive.—*n.* **Chica′nery**, trickery or artifice, esp. in legal proceedings. [Fr. *chicane*, sharp practice at law, through a form *zicanum*, from Low Gr. *tzykanion*, a game at mall—Pers. *tchaugan*.]

**Chiccory.** See **Chicory.**

**Chick**, chik, **Chicken**, chik′en, *n.* the young of fowls, especially of the hen : a child. [A.S. *cicen*. a dim. of *cocc*, a cock.]

**Chicken-hearted**, chik′en-härt′ed, *adj.* as timid *as a chicken* : cowardly.

**Chicken-pox**, chik′en-poks, *n.* mild skin-disease, generally attacking children only.

**Chickling**, chik′ling, *n.* a *little chicken.*

**Chickweed**, chik′wēd, *n.* a low creeping *weed* that *birds* are fond of.

**Chicory, Chiccory**, chik′o-ri, *n., succory*, a carrot-like plant, the root of which when ground is used to adulterate coffee. [Fr. *chicorée*—L. *cichorium*, succory—Gr. *kichōrion*.]

**Chide**, chīd, *v.t.* to scold, rebuke. reprove by words :—*pr.p.* chīd′ing ; *pa.t.* chid, (obs.) chōde ; *pa.p.* chid, chidd′en. [A.S. *cidan*.]

**Chief**, chēf, *adj., head* : principal, highest. first.— *n.* a *head* or principal person : a leader : the principal part or top of anything. [Fr. *chef*— L. *caput*, the head ; Gr. *kephalē*, Sans. *kapala*.]

**Chiefly**, chēf′li, *adv.* in the first place : principally : for the most part.

**Chieftain**, chēf′tān or ′tin, *n.* the *head* of a clan : a leader or commander.—*ns.* **Chief′taincy, Chief′tainship.** [From **Chief**, like **Captain,** which see.]

**Chiffonier**, shif-on-ēr′, *n.* an ornamental cupboard. [Fr., a place for rags—*chiffon*, a rag.]

**Chignon**, shē-nong′, *n.* an artificial arrangement of hair at the back of the head. [Fr., meaning first the nape of the neck, the joints of which are like the links of a chain—*chaînon*, the link of a chain—*chaine*, a chain.]

**Chilblain**, chil′blān, *n.* a *blain* or sore on hands or feet caused by a *chill* or cold. [**Chill** and **Blain**.]

**Child**, chīld, *n.* (*pl.* **Chil′dren**), an infant or very young person : one intimately related to one older : a disciple :—*pl.* offspring : descendants : inhabitants. [A.S. *cild*, from the root *gan-*, to produce, which yields Ger. *kind*, a child.]

**Childbed**, chīld′bed, *n.* the state of a woman brought to *bed* with *child*.

**Childe**, chīld, *n.* a title formerly given to the eldest son of a noble, till admission to knighthood. [Same word as **Child**.]

**Childermas-day**, chil′dėr-mas-dā, *n.* an anniversary in the Church of England, called also Innocents′ Day, held December 28th, to commemorate the slaying of the *children* by Herod. [**Child**, **Mass**, and **Day**.]

**Childhood**, chīld′hood, *n.*, *state* of being a *child*.

**Childish**, chīld′ish, *adj.*, of or *like a child* : silly : trifling.—*adv.* **Child′ishly**.—*n.* **Child′ishness**.

**Childless**, chīld′les, *adj.*, *without children*.

**Childlike**, chīld′līk, *adj.*, *like a child* : becoming a child : docile : innocent.

**Chiliad**, kil′i-ad, *n.* the number 1000 : 1000 of any thing. [Gr.—*chilioi*, 1000.]

**Chill**, chil, *n.*, *coldness* : a cold that causes shivering : anything that damps or disheartens.—*adj.* shivering with cold : slightly cold : opp. of cordial.—*v.t.* to make chill or cold : to blast with cold : to discourage.—*n.* **Chill′ness**. [A.S. *cyle*, coldness, *celan*, to chill. See **Cold**, **Cool**.]

**Chilly**, chil′i, *adj.* somewhat *chill*.—*n.* **Chill′iness**.

**Chime**, chīm, *n.* the harmonious sound of bells or other musical instruments : agreement of sound or of relation :—*pl.* a set of bells.—*v.i.* to sound in harmony : to jingle : to accord or agree.—*v.t.* to strike, or cause to sound in harmony. [M. E. *chimbe*, O. Fr. *cymb⟨r⟩le*—L. *cymbalum*, a cymbal—Gr. *kymbalon*.]

**Chimera**, ki-mē′ra, *n.* a fabulous, fire-spouting monster, with a lion′s head, a serpent′s tail, and a *goat′s* body : any idle or wild fancy. [L. *chimæra*—Gr. *chimaira*, a she-goat.]

**Chimerical**, ki-mer′i-kal, *adj.* of the nature of a *chimera* : wild : fanciful.—*adv.* **Chimer′ically**.

**Chimney**, chim′ni, *n.* a passage for the escape of smoke or heated air. [Fr. *cheminée*—L.*caminus*—Gr. *kamin⟨o⟩s*, a furnace, prob. from *kaiō*, to burn.]

**Chimney-piece**, chim′ni-pēs, *n.* a *piece* or shelf over the *chimney* or fireplace.

**Chimney-shaft**, chim′ni-shaft, *n.* the *shaft* or stalk of a *chimney* which rises above the building.

**Chimpanzee**, chim-pan′zē, *n.* a species of monkey found in Africa. [Prob. native name of the animal.]

**Chin**, chin, *n.* the jutting part of the face, below the mouth. [A.S. *cinn* ; Ger. *kinn*, Gr. *genus*.]

**China**, chīn′a, *n.* a fine kind of earthenware, originally made in *China* : porcelain.

**Chincough**, chin′kof, *n.* a disease attended with *violent fits of coughing* : whooping-cough. [E. ; Scot. *kink-host*, Dut. *kinkhoeste*. See **Chink**, the sound.]

**Chine**, chīn, *n.* the spine or backbone, from its *thorn-like* form : a piece of the backbone of a beast and adjoining parts for cooking. [Fr. *échine*—O. Ger. *skina*, a pin, thorn ; prob. conn. with L. *spina*, a thorn, the spine.]

**Chinese**, chī-nēz′, *adj.* of or belonging to *China*.

**Chink**, chingk, *n.* a *rent* or *cleft* : a narrow opening.—*v.i.* to split or crack. [A.S. *cinu*, a cleft, *cinan*, to split.]

**Chink**, chingk, *n.* the *clink*, as of coins.—*v.i.* to give a sharp sound, as coin. [From the sound.]

**Chintz**, chints, *n.* cotton cloth, printed in five or six *different colours*. [Hind. *chhint*, spotted cotton cloth.]

**Chip**, chip, *v.t.* to *chop* or cut into small pieces : to diminish by cutting away a little at a time :—*pr.p.* chip′ping ; *pa.p.* chipped′.—*n.* a small piece of wood or other substance chopped off. [Dim. of **Chop**.]

**Chirographer**, kī-rog′ra-fėr, **Chirographist**, kī-rog′ra-fist, *n.* one who professes the art of writing.

**Chirography**, kī-rog′ra-fi, *n.* the art of writing or penmanship.—*adj.* **Chirograph′ic**. [Gr. *cheir*, the hand, *graphē*, writing.]

**Chirologist**, kī-rol′o-jist, *n.* one who converses by signs with the hands.

**Chirology**, kī-rol′o-ji, *n.* the art of *discoursing with the hands* or by signs as the deaf and dumb do. [Gr. *cheir*, the hand, *logos*, a discourse.]

**Chiropodist**, kī-rop′o-dist, *n.* a *hand and foot* doctor : one who removes corns, bunions, warts, &c. [Gr. *cheir*, the hand, and *pous*, *podos*, the foot.]

**Chirp**, chėrp, **Chirrup**, chir′up, *n.* the *sharp*, shrill sound of certain birds and insects.—*v.i.* to make such a sound. [From the sound.]

**Chirurgeon**, kī-rur′jun, *n.* old form of **Surgeon**.—*n.* **Chirur′gery**, now **Surgery**.—*adj.* **Chirur′gical**, now **Surgical**. [Fr. *chirurgien*—Gr. *cheirourgos*—*cheir*, the hand, *ergon*, a work.]

**Chisel**, chiz′el, *n.* a tool to cut or hollow out, wood, stone, &c.—*v.t.* to cut, carve, &c. with a chisel :—*pr.p.* chis′elling ; *pa.p.* chis′elled. [O. Fr. *cisel*—Low L. *cisellus*—L. *sicilicula*, dim. of *sicilis*, a sickle, from *seco*, to cut.]

**Chit**, chit, *n.* a baby : a lively or pert young child. [A.S. *cith*, a young tender shoot.]

**Chitchat**, chit′chat, *n.* chatting or idle talk : prattle. [A reduplication of **Chat**.]

**Chivalric**, shiv′al-rik, **Chivalrous**, shiv′al-rus, *adj.*, *pertaining to chivalry* : bold : gallant.—*adv.* **Chiv′alrously**.

**Chivalry**, shiv′al-ri, *n.* the usages and qualifications of *chevaliers* or knights : the system of knighthood : heroic adventures. [Fr. *chevalerie* —*cheval*—L. *caballus*, a horse. See **Cavalry**.]

**Chloral**, klō′ral, *n.* a strongly narcotic substance obtained by the action of chlorine on alcohol. [Word formed by combining *chlor-* in *chlorine*, and *al-* in *alcohol*.]

**Chloric**, klō′rik, *adj.*, *of* or *from chlorine*.

**Chloride**, klō′rid, *n.* a compound of *chlorine* with some other substance. as potash, soda, &c.

**Chlorine**, klō′rin, *n.* a *pale-green* gas, with a disagreeable, suffocating odour. [Gr. *chlōros*, pale-green.]

**Chlorite**, klō′rīt, *n.* a soft mineral of a *greenish* colour, with a soapy feeling when handled.

**Chloroform**, klō′ro-form, *n.* a colourless volatile liquid, much used to induce insensibility. [Orig. a compound of *chlorine* and *formic* acid ; Gr. *chlōros*, and *formic* acid, so called because orig. made from ants, L. *formica*, an ant.]

**Chlorosis**, klor-ō′sis, *n.* a medical name for *green*-sickness. [Gr. *chlōros*, pale-green.]

**Chocolate**, chok′ō-lāt, *n.* a kind of paste made of the pounded seeds of the *Cacao theobroma* : a beverage made by dissolving this paste in hot water. [Sp. *chocolate* ; from Mexican *kakahuatl*. See **Cacao**, **Cocoa**.]

**Choice**, chois, *n.* act or power of *choosing*: the thing chosen: preference: the preferable or best part.—*adj.* worthy of being chosen: select. [Fr. *ch⁀i⁀x—choisir*; from root of **Choose**.]

**Choir**, kwīr, *n.* a *chorus* or band of singers, especially those belonging to a church: the part of a church appropriated to the singers: the part of a cathedral separated from the nave by a rail or screen. [Fr. *chœur*—L. *chorus*—Gr. *choros*.]

**Choke**, chōk, *v.t.* to throttle: to suffocate: to stop or obstruct.—*v.i.* to be choked or suffocated. [Ety. dub.; prob. from the sound.]

**Choke-damp**, chōk'-damp, *n.* carbonic acid gas, so called by miners from its often causing suffocation.

**Choler**, kol'ėr, *n.* the *bile*: anger or irascibility, once supposed to arise from excess of bile. [O. Fr. *cholere*—L., Gr. *cholera*—Gr. *cholē*, bile. Cf. E. **Gall**.]

**Cholera**, kol'ėr-a, *n.* a disease characterised by *bilious* vomiting and purging. [Gr. *cholera—cholē*, bile.] [*cholera.*

**Choleraic**, kol-ėr-ā'ik, *adj., of the nature of*

**Choleric**, kol'ėr-ik, *adj.* full of *choler* or anger: petulant.

**Choose**, chōōz, *v.t.* to take one thing in preference to another: to select.—*v.i.* to will or determine:—*pa.t.* chōse; *pa.p.* chōs'en. [A.S. *ceosan*; cog. with Dut. *kiesen*, Goth. *kiusan*, to choose, and akin to L. *gustare*, to taste.]

**Chop**, chop, *v.t.* to cut with a sudden blow: to cut into small pieces.—*v.i.* to shift suddenly, as the wind:—*pr.p.* chopp'ing; *pa.p.* chopped'. [From a Low-Ger. root found in Dut. *kappen*, also in Ger. *kappen*, to cut; cf. Gr. *koptō*, from a root *skap*, to cut.]

**Chop**, chop, *n.* a *piece chopped off*, esp. of meat.

**Chop**, chop, *v.t.* to exchange or barter: to put one thing in place of another:—*pr.p.* chopp'ing; *pa.p.* chopped'. [M.E. *copen*—O. Dut. *koopen*, to buy. Same root as **Cheap**.]

**Chop**, chop, *n.* the *chap* or jaw, generally used in *pl.* [See **Chaps**.]

**Chop-fallen**, chop'-fawln, *adj.* (*lit.*) having the *chop* or lower jaw *fallen* down: cast-down: dejected.

**Chopper**, chop'ėr, *n.* one who or that which *chops*.

**Chopsticks**, chop'stiks, *n.* two small sticks of wood, ivory, &c., used by the Chinese instead of a fork and knife.

**Choral**, kō'ral, *adj.* belonging to a *chorus* or choir.

**Chord**, kord, *n.* the string of a musical instrument: a combination of tones in harmony: (*geom.*) a straight line joining the extremities of an arc. [L. *chorda*—Gr. *chordē*, an intestine.]

**Chorister**, kor'ist-ėr, *n.* a member of a *choir*.

**Chorus**, kō'rus, *n.* a band of singers and dancers, esp. in the Greek plays: a company of singers: that which is sung by a chorus: the part of a song in which the company join the singer. [L. *chorus*—Gr. *choros*, orig. a dance in a ring.]

**Chose**, chōz, *pa.t.* and obs. *pa.p.* of **Choose**.

**Chosen**, chōz'n, *past participle* of **Choose**.

**Chough**, chuf, *n.* a kind of jackdaw which frequents rocky places and the sea-coast. [A.S. *ceo*: from the cry of the bird—**Caw**.]

**Chouse**, chows, *v.t.* to defraud, cheat, or impose upon.—*n.* one easily cheated: a trick. [Turk. *chiaus*, a messenger or envoy. A *chiaus* sent to England in 1609 committed gross frauds upon the Turkish merchants resident in Britain; hence *chouse*, to act as this *chiaus* did, to defraud.]

**Chrism**, krizm, *n.* consecrated or holy oil: unction. [O. Fr. *chresme*, Fr. *chrême*—Gr. *chrisma*, from *chriō*, *chrisō*, to anoint.]

**Chrismal**, kriz'mal, *adj., pertaining to chrism*.

**Christ**, krīst, *n.* the Anointed, the Messiah. [A.S. *crist*—Gr. *Christos—chriō*, *chrisō*, to anoint.]

**Christen**, kris'n, *v.t.* to baptise in the name of *Christ*: to give a name to. [A.S. *cristnian*, to make a Christian.]

**Christendom**, kris'n-dum, *n.* that part of the world in which Christianity is the received religion: the whole body of Christians. [A.S. *Cristendom—cristen*, a Christian, *dom*, rule, sway.]

**Christian**, krist'yan, *n.* a follower of *Christ*.—*adj.* relating to Christ or his religion.—**Christian name**, the name given when christened, as distinguished from the surname.—*adjs.* **Christ'ianlike**, **Christ'ianly**. [A.S. *cristen*—L. *Christianus*—Gr. *Christos*.]

**Christianise**, krist'yan-īz, *v.t.* to *make Christian*: to convert to Christianity. [*Christ.*

**Christianity**, kris-ti-an'i-ti, *n.* the religion of

**Christmas**, kris'mas, *n.* an annual festival, orig. *a mass*, in memory of the birth of *Christ*, held on the 25th of December. [**Christ** and **Mass**.]

**Christmas-box**, kris'mas-boks, *n.* a *box* containing *Christmas* presents: a Christmas gift.

**Christology**, kris-tol'o-ji, *n.* that branch of theology which treats of the nature and person of Christ. [Gr. *Christos*, and *logos*, a discourse.]

**Chromatic**, krō-mat'ik, *adj.* relating to *colours*: coloured: (*music*) proceeding by semitones.—*n.sing.* **Chromat'ics**, the science of colours. [Gr. *chrōmatikos—chrōma*, colour.]

**Chrome**, krōm, **Chromium**, krō'mi-um, *n.* a metal remarkable for the beautiful *colours* of its compounds.—*adj.* **Chrom'ic**. [Gr. *chrōma*, colour.]

**Chronic**, kron'ik, **Chronical**, kron'ik-al, *adj.* lasting a long *time*: of a disease, deep-seated or long-continued, as opp. to *acute*. [L. *chronicus*, Gr. *chronikos—chronos*, time.]

**Chronicle**, kron'i-kl, *n.* a record of events in the order of *time*: a history.—*v.t.* to record in history.—*n.* **Chron'icler**, a historian.

**Chronology**, kron-ol'o-ji, *n.* the science of dates.—*adjs.* **Chronolog'ic**, **Chronolog'ical**.—*adv.* **Chronolog'ically**.—*ns.* **Chronol'oger**, **Chronol'ogist**. [Gr. *chronos*, time, *logos*, a discourse.]

**Chronometer**, kron-om'e-tėr, *n.* an instrument for *measuring time*: a watch.—*adjs.* **Chronomet'ric**, **Chronomet'rical**. [Gr. *chronos*, and *metron*, a measure.]

**Chrysalis**, kris'a-lis, *n.* the form, often *gold-coloured*, assumed by some insects before they become winged.—*pl.* **Chrysal'ides** (i-dēz).—*adj.* **Chrys'alid**. [Gr. *chrysallis—chrysos*, gold.]

**Chrysanthemum**, kris-an'the-mum, *n.* (*lit.*) *gold-flower*: a genus of composite plants to which belong the corn marigold and ox-eye daisy. [Gr. *chrysos*, gold, *anthemon*, flower.]

**Chrysolite**, kris'o-līt, *n.* a stone of a yellowish colour. [Gr. *chrysos*, and *lithos*, a stone.]

**Chrysoprase**, kris'o-prāz, *n.* a variety of chalcedony: (*B.*) a yellowish-green stone, nature unknown. [Gr. *chrysos*, and *prason*, a leek.]

**Chub**, chub, *n.* a small fat river-fish. [Ety. dub., but same root as **Chubby**.] [**Chubb'iness**.

**Chubby**, chub'i, *adj.* short and thick: plump.—*n.*

**Chuck**, chuk, *n.* the call of a hen: a word of endearment.—*v.i.* to call as a hen. [From the sound—a variety of **Cluck**.]

**Chuck**, chuk, *v.t.* to strike gently, to toss.—*n.* a slight blow. [Fr. *choquer*, to jolt; allied to E. **Shake**.] [chickens: to caress.

**Chuckle**, chuk'l, *v.t.* to call, as a hen does her

**Chuckle**, chuk'l, *v.i.* to laugh in a quiet, suppressed manner, indicating derision or enjoyment. [See **Choke**.]

**Chum**, chum, *n.* a chamber-fellow. [Perh. a mutilation of **Comrade**, or **Chamber-fellow**.]

**Church**, church, *n.* a house set apart for Christian worship: the whole body of Christians: the clergy: any particular sect or denomination of Christians.—*v.t.* to perform with any one the giving of thanks *in church*. [A.S. *circe*; Scot. *kirk*; Ger. *kirche*; all from Gr. *kyriakon*, belonging to the Lord—*Kyrios*, the Lord.]

**Churchman**, church'man, *n.* a clergyman or ecclesiastic: a member of the Church of England.

**Churchwarden**, church-wawr'den, *n.* an officer who represents the interests of a parish or church: a long clay-pipe. [**Church** and **Warden**.]

**Churchyard**, church'yärd, *n.* the *yard* round the *church*, where the dead are buried.

**Churl**, churl, *n.* an ill-bred, surly fellow. [A.S. *ceorl*, a countryman; Ice. *karl*, Ger. *kerl*, a man; Scot. *carl*.]

**Churlish**, churl'ish, *adj.* rude : surly : ill-bred.—*adv.* **Churl'ishly**.—*n.* **Churl'ishness**.

**Churn**, churn, *v.t.* to shake violently, as cream when making butter.—*n.* a vessel in which cream is churned. [Ice. *kirna*, a churn, Dut. and Ger. *kernen*, to churn ; akin to **Kern**-el ; as if to extract the essence or best part.]

**Chuse**, chōōz, *v.t.* a form of **Choose**.

**Chyle**, kīl, *n.* a white fluid drawn from the food while in the intestines.—*adjs.* **Chyla'ceous**, **Chyl'ous**. [Fr.—Gr. *chylos*, juice—*cheō*, to pour.]

**Chylifactive**, kīl-i-fak'tiv, *adj.* having the power to *make chyle*.—*n.* **Chylifac'tion** or **Chylifica'-tion**. [L. *chylus*, and *facio*, to make.]

**Chyme**, kīm, *n.* the pulp to which the food is reduced in the stomach.—*adj.* **Chym'ous**. [Gr. *chymos*, from *cheō*.]

**Chymification**, kīm-i-fi-kā'shun, *n.* the act of being *formed* into *chyme*. [L. *chymus*, and *facio*, to make.]

**Chymist, Chymistry**, now **Chemist, Chemistry**.

**Cicada**, si-kā'da, **Cicala**, si-kā'la, *n.* an insect remarkable for the sound that it produces.

**Cicatrice**, sik'a-tris [Fr.], **Cicatrix**, si-kā'triks [L.], *n.* the scar over a wound after it is healed.

**Cicatrise**, sik'a-trīz, *v.t.* to help the formation of a skin or *cicatrix* on a wound or ulcer by medicines.—*v.i.* to heal. [Fr. *cicatriser*.]

**Cicerone**, sis-e-rō'ne, *n.* one who shews strangers the curiosities of a place: a guide. [It.—L. *Cicero*, the Roman orator.] [*Cicero*.

**Ciceronian**, sis-e-rō'ni-an, *adj.* relating to or like

**Cider**, sī'dėr, *n.* a drink made from apple-juice.—*n.* **Ci'derkin**, an inferior cider. [Fr. *cidre*—L. *sicera*—Gr. *sikera*, strong drink—Heb. *shakar*, to be intoxicated.]

**Ciel, sēl.** See **Ceil**.

**Cigar**, si-gär', *n.* a small roll of *tobacco* for smoking. [Sp. *cigarro*, a kind of tobacco in Cuba.]

**Cigarette**, sig-ar-et', *n.* a *little cigar*: a little finely-cut tobacco rolled in paper for smoking.

**Cilia**, sil'i-a, *n.pl.* hair-like appendages on the edge of a vegetable body, or on an animal organ or animalcule.—*adjs.* **Cil'iary, Cil'iated**, having cilia. [L. *cilium*, pl. *cilia*, eyelids, eyelashes.]

**Cimbric**, sim'brik, *adj.* relating to the *Cimbri*, a tribe originally from the north of Germany.

**Cimeter**, sim'e-tėr. See **Scimitar**.

**Cimmerian**, sim-e'ri-an, *adj.* relating to the *Cimmerii*, a tribe fabled to have lived in perpetual *darkness*: extremely dark.

**Cinchona**, sin-kō'na, *n.* the bark of a tree that grows in Peru, from which **Quinine** is extracted, a valuable medicine for ague : also called Peruvian bark. [Said to be so named from the Countess del *Cinchon*, but prob. from *kinakina*, the native word for bark.]

**Cincture**, singk'tūr, *n.* a *gird'e* or belt : a moulding round a column.—*adj.* **Cinc'tured**, having a cincture. [L. *cinctura*—*cingo*, *cinctus*, to gird.]

**Cinder**, sin'dėr, *n.* the refuse of burned coals: anything charred by fire. [A.S. *sinder*, scoriæ, slag. The *c* instead of *s* is owing to Fr. *cendre*, a wholly unconnected word, which comes from L. *cinis*, *cineris*, ashes.]

**Cindery**, sin'dėr-i, *adj.*, *like* or composed of *cinders*.

**Cinerary**, sin'ėr-ar-i, *adj.* pertaining to *ashes*.

**Cineration**, sin-ėr-ā'shun, *n.* the act of reducing to *ashes*. [L. *cinis*, *cineris*.]

**Cinnabar**, sin'a-bar, *n.* sulphuret of mercury, called vermilion when used as a pigment. [L. *cinnabaris*, Gr. *kinnabari*, a dye, known as dragon's blood, from Pers.]

**Cinnamon**, sin'a-mon, *n.* the spicy bark of a laurel in Ceylon. [L. *cinnamomum*—Heb. *kinnamon*.]

**Cinque**, singk, *n.* the number *five*. [Fr.]

**Cinque-foil**, singk'-foil, *n.* the *five-bladed* clover. [Fr. *cinque*, and *feuille*, L. *folium*, Gr. *phyllon*, a leaf.]

**Cipher**, sī'fėr, *n.* (*arith.*) the character 0 : any of the nine figures: anything of little value: an interweaving of the initials of a name : a secret kind of writing.—*v.i.* to work at arithmetic. [O. Fr. *cifre*, Fr. *chiffre*—Ar. *sifr*, empty.]

**Circassian**, sėr-kash'yan, *adj.* belonging to *Circassia*, a country on the north of Mount Caucasus.

**Circean**, sėr-sē'an, *adj.* relating to the fabled *Circe*, who by magic potions changed her guests into animals : poisonous, delusive, fatal.

**Circle**, sėrk'l, *n.* a plane figure bounded by a line every point of which is equally distant from a point in the middle called the centre : the line which bounds the figure : a ring : a series ending where it began : a company surrounding the principal person.—*v.t.* to move round : to encompass.—*v.i.* to move in a circle. [A.S. *circul*, from L. *circulus*, dim. of *circus*, Gr. *kirkos* or *krikos*, a circle ; allied to A.S. *hring*, a ring—root *kar*, to move in a circle.]

**Circlet**, sėrk'let, *n.* a *little circle*.

**Circuit**, sėr'kit, *n.* the act of *moving round* : that which encircles : a round made in the exercise of a calling, especially the round made by the judges for holding the courts of law. [Fr.—L. *circuitus—circueo*, to go round—*circum*, round, *eo*, *itum*, to go.] [*Circu'itously*.

**Circuitous**, sėr-kū'it-us, *adj.* round about.—*adv.*

**Circular**, sėr'kū-lar, *adj.* round : ending in itself: addressed to a circle of persons.—**Circular notes** are a kind of bank-note issued for the convenience of travellers.—*n.* a note sent round to a circle or number of persons.—*adv.* **Cir'cularly**.—*n.* **Circular'ity**.

**Circulate**, sėr'kū-lāt, *v.t.* to make to go round as *in a circle*: to spread.—*v.i.* to move round : to be spread about. [L. *circulo*, *circulatus*.]

**Circulation**, sėr-kū-lā'shun, *n.* the act of moving *in a circle*, or of going and returning: the money in use at any time in a country.

**Circulatory**, sėr'kū-la-tor-i, *adj.* circular: circulating.

**Circumambient**, sėr-kum-amb'i-ent, *adj.*, *going round about*: surrounding. [L. *circum*, about, *ambio*, to go round—*ambi*, Gr. *amphi*, around, and *eo*, to go.]

**Circumambulate**, sėr-kum-am'būl-āt, *v.i.* to *walk round about.—n.* **Circumambula'tion.** [L. *ambulo, ambulatus,* to walk.]

**Circumcise**, sėr'kum-sīz, *v.t.* to cut off the foreskin according to the Jewish law. [L. *circumcido, circumcisus—cædo,* to cut.]

**Circumcision**, sėr-kum-sizh'un, *n.* the act of circumcising.

**Circumference**, sėr-kum'fėr-ens, *n.* the boundary-line of any round body: the line surrounding anything.—*adj.* **Circumferen'tial.** [L. *fero,* to carry.]        [*circumflex.*]

**Circumflect**, sėr'kum-flekt, *v.t.* to mark with a **Circumflex**, sėr'kum-fleks, *n.* an accent (ʌ) denoting a *rising and falling* of the voice on a vowel or syllable. [L. *flecto, flexus,* to bend.]

**Circumfluent**, sėr-kum'floo-ent, *adj., flowing round about.* [L. *fluens, fluentis,* flowing.]

**Circumfuse**, sėr-kum-fūz', *v.t.* to *pour around.* —*n.* **Circumfu'sion.** [L. *fundo, fusus,* to pour.]

**Circumjacent**, sėr-kum-jā'sent, *adj., lying round:* bordering on every side. [L. *jacens,* lying—*jaceo,* to lie.]

**Circumlocution**, sėr-kum-lō-kū'shun, *n., round-about speaking:* a manner of expression in which more words are used than are necessary.—*adj.* **Circumloc'utory.** [L. *loquor, locutus,* to speak.]

**Circumnavigate**, sėr-kum-nav'i-gāt, *v.t.* to *sail round.—n.* **Circumnaviga'tion.** [See **Navigate.**]        [*who sails round.*]

**Circumnavigator**, sėr-kum-nav'i-gāt-or, *n.,* one

**Circumscribe**, sėr-kum-skrīb', *v.t.* to draw a line round: to inclose within certain limits. [L. *scribo,* to write.]      [*tion:* the line that limits.]

**Circumscription**, sėr-kum-skrip'shun, *n.* limita-

**Circumspect**, sėr'kum-spekt, *adj., looking round on all sides* watchfully: cautious: prudent.—*adv.* **Cir'cumspectly.—n.** **Cir'cumspectness.** [L. *specio, spectum,* to look.]

**Circumspection**, sėr-kum-spek'shun, *n.* watchfulness: caution.

**Circumstance**, sėr'kum-stans, *n.* something attendant upon another thing: an accident or event.—*pl.* the state of one's affairs. [L. *stans, stantis,* standing—*sto,* to stand.]

**Circumstantial**, sėr-kum-stan'shal, *adj.* consisting of details: minute.—*adv.* **Circumstan'tially.—** **Circumstantial evidence,** evidence not positive or direct, but which is gathered indirectly from the circumstances of a case.      [*dentals.*]

**Circumstantials**, sėr-kum-stan'shals, *n.pl.* inci-

**Circumstantiate**, sėr-kum-stan'shi-āt, *v.t.* to *prove by circumstances:* to describe exactly.

**Circumvallation**, sėr-kum-val-ā'shun, *n.* a *surrounding with a wall:* a wall or fortification surrounding a town or fort. [L. *va.lum,* an earthen rampart or wall.]

**Circumvent**, sėr-kum-vent', *v.t.* to *come round* or outwit a person: to deceive or cheat.—*n.* **Circumven'tion.** [L. *venio,* to come.]

**Circumventive**, sėr-kum-vent'iv, *adj.* deceiving by artifices.

**Circumvolution**, sėr-kum-vol-ū'shun, *n.* a turning or rolling round: anything winding or sinuous. [L. *volvo, volutum,* to roll.]

**Circus**, sėr'kus, *n.* a circular building for the exhibition of games: a place for the exhibition of feats of horsemanship. [L. *circus;* cog. with Gr. *kirkos,* A.S. *hring,* a ring.]

**Cirrous**, sir'us, *adj., having a curl* or tendril.

**Cirrus**, sir'us, *n.* the highest form of cloud consisting of curling fibres: (*bot.*) a tendril: (*zool.*) any curled filament. [L., curled hair.]

**Cisalpine**, sis-alp'in or -alp'īn, *adj., on this side* (to

the Romans) *of the Alps,* that is, on the south side. [L. *cis,* on this side, and **Alpine.**]

**Cist**, sist, *n.* a tomb consisting of a stone *chest* covered with stone slabs. [See **Chest, Cyst.**]

**Cistern**, sis'tėrn, *n.* any receptacle for holding water or other liquid: a reservoir. [L. *cisterna,* from *cista,* a chest.]

**Cit**, sit, *n.* shortened from *citizen,* and used as a term of contempt. [See **Citizen.**]

**Citadel**, sit'a-del, *n.* a fortress in or near a city. [It. *cittadella,* dim. of *città,* a city. See **City.**]

**Citation**, sī-tā'shun, *n.* an official *summons* to appear: the act of quoting: the passage or name quoted.

**Cite**, sīt, *v.t.* to *call* or *summon:* to summon to answer in court: to quote: to name. [L. *cito,* to call, intensive of *cieo, cio,* to make to go, to rouse.]

**Cithern**, sith'ėrn, **Cittern**, sit'ėrn, *n.* a musical instrument like the guitar. [A.S. *cytere*—L. *cithara*—Gr. *kithara.* A doublet of **Guitar.**]

**Citizen**, sit'i-zen, *n.* an inhabitant of a *city:* a member of a state: a townsman: a freeman.— *n.* **Cit'izenship,** the rights of a citizen. [M.E. *citesein*—O. Fr. *citeain.* See **City.**]

**Citron**, sit'run, *n.* the fruit of the citron-tree, resembling a lemon. [Fr.—L. *citrus*—Gr. *kitron,* a citron.]

**City**, sit'i, *n.* a large town: a town with a corporation. [Fr. *cité,* a city—L. *civitas,* the state— *civis,* a citizen; akin to L. *quies,* quiet, E. **Hive** and **Home.**]

**Cives**, sīvz, *n.* a plant of the leek and *onion* genus growing in tufts. [Fr. *cive*—L. *cæpa,* an onion.]

**Civet**, siv'et, *n.* a perfume obtained from the civet or civet-cat, a small carnivorous animal of N. Africa. [Fr. *civette*—Ar. *zabad.*]

**Civic**, siv'ik, *adj.* pertaining to a *city* or a citizen. [L. *civicus*—*civis.*]

**Civil**, siv'il, *adj.* pertaining to the community: having the refinement of city-bred people: polite: commercial, not military: lay, not ecclesiastical.—**Civil engineer,** one who plans railways, docks, &c., as opp. to a *military* engineer, or to a *mechanical* engineer, who makes machines, &c.—**Civil list,** now embraces only the expenses of the sovereign's household.— **Civil service,** the paid service of the state, in so far as it is not military or naval.—**Civil war,** a war between citizens of the same state.—*adv.* **Civ'illy.** [L. *civilis*—*civis.*]

**Civilian**, siv-il'yan, *n.* a professor or student of civil law (not canon law): one engaged in civil as distinguished from military and other pursuits.      [*civilised.*]

**Civilisation**, siv-il-i-zā'shun, *n.* the state of being

**Civilise**, siv'il-īz, *v.t.* to reclaim from barbarism: to instruct in arts and refinements.

**Civility**, siv-il'i-ti, *n.* good-breeding: politeness.

**Clack**, klak, *v.i.* to make a *sudden sharp noise* as by striking.—*n.* a sharp sudden sound frequently repeated. [From the sound.]

**Clad**, klad, *pa.t.* and *pa.p.* of **Clothe.**

**Claim**, klām, *v.t.* to *call for:* to demand as a right.—*n.* a demand for something supposed due: right or ground for demanding: the thing claimed. [O. Fr. *claimer*—L. *clamo,* to call out, from *calo,* cog. with Gr. *kaleō,* to call.]

**Claimable**, klām'a-bl, *adj.* that may be *claimed.*

**Claimant**, klām'ant, *n.* one who makes a *claim.*

**Clairvoyance**, klār-voi'ans, *n.* the alleged power of seeing things not present to the senses. [Fr. —*clair*—L. *clarus,* clear, and Fr. *voir*—L. *video,* to see.]

**Clairvoyant**, klār-voi'ant, *n.* one who professes clairvoyance.

**Clam**, klam, *v.t.* to clog with sticky matter:—*pr.p.* clamm'ing; *pa.p.* clammed'. [A.S. *clam*, clay; a variety of *lam*, **Loam**.] [nestly.

**Clamant**, klam'ant, *adj.*, *calling aloud* or ear-

**Clamber**, klam'bėr, *v.i.* to *climb* with difficulty, grasping with the hands and feet. [From root of **Clump**; cf. Ger. *klammern—klemmen*, to squeeze or hold tightly.]

**Clammy**, klam'i, *adj.* sticky: moist and adhesive. —*n.* **Clamm'iness**.

**Clamorous**, klam'or-us, *adj.* noisy: boisterous.—*adv.* **Clam'orously**.—*n.* **Clam'orousness**.

**Clamour**, klam'or, *n.* a loud continuous outcry: uproar.—*v.i.* to cry aloud in demand: to make a loud continuous outcry. [L. *clamor*.]

**Clamp**, klamp, *n.* a piece of timber, iron, &c., used to fasten things together or to strengthen any framework.—*v.t.* to bind with clamps. [From a root, seen in A.S. *clom*, a bond, Dut. *klamp*, a clamp, and akin to E. **Clip**, **Climb**.]

**Clan**, klan, *n.* a *tribe* or collection of families subject to a single chieftain, bearing the same surname, and supposed to have a common ancestor: a clique, sect, or body of persons. [Gael. *clann*, Ir. *clann* or *cland*, offspring, tribe.]

**Clandestine**, klan-des'tin, *adj.*, *concealed* or *hidden*: private: unlawful: sly.—*adv.* **Clandes'tinely**. [L. *clandestinus—clam*, secretly, from root *kal*, seen also in *celo*, to conceal.]

**Clang**, klang, *v.i.* to produce a sharp ringing sound.—*v.t.* to cause to clang.—*n.* a sharp, ringing sound, like that made by metallic substances struck together. [L. *clango*; Ger. *klang*: formed from the sound.]

**Clangour**, klang'gur, *n.* a *clang*: a sharp, shrill, harsh sound. [L. *clangor*.]

**Clank**, klangk, *n.* a sharp sound, less prolonged than a clang, such as is made by a chain.—*v.t.* or *v.i.* to make or cause a clank.

**Clannish**, klan'ish, *adj.* closely united like the members of a *clan*.—*adv.* **Clann'ishly**.—*n.* **Clann'ishness**. [under a chieftain.

**Clanship**, klan'ship, *n.* association of families

**Clansman**, klanz'man, *n.* a member of a *clan*.

**Clap**, klap, *n.* the noise made by the sudden striking together of two things, as the hands: a sudden act or motion: a burst of sound.—*v.t.* to strike together so as to make a noise: to thrust or drive together suddenly: to applaud with the hands.—*v.i.* to strike the hands together: to strike together with noise:—*pr.p.* clapp'ing; *pa.p.* clapped'. [Ice. *klappa*, to pat; Dut. and Ger. *klappen*: formed from the sound.]

**Clapper**, klap'ėr, *n.*, *one who claps*: *that which claps*, as the tongue of a bell.

**Clap-trap**, klap'-trap, *n.* a trick to gain applause.

**Clare-obscure**, klār'-ob-skūr', **Chiaro-oscuro**, ki-är'ō-os-kōō'rō, *n.*, *clear-obscure*: light and shade in painting. [Fr. *clair*—L. *clarus*, clear, and Fr. *obscur*—L. *obscurus*, obscure; It. *chiaro*, clear, *oscuro*, obscure.]

**Claret**, klar'et, *n.* orig. applied to wines of a light or *clear* red colour, but now used in England for the dark-red wines of Bordeaux. [Fr. *clairet* —*clair*—L. *clarus*, clear.] [purifies.

**Clarifier**, klar'i-fī-ėr, *n.* that which *clarifies* or

**Clarify**, klar'i-fī, *v.t.* to *make* clear.—*v.i.* to become clear:—*pr.p.* clar'ifying; *pa.p.* clar'ified.—*n.* **Clarifica'tion**. [L. *clarus*, clear, and *facio*, to make.]

**Clarion**, klar'i-on, *n.* a kind of trumpet whose note is *clear* and shrill. [Fr. *clairon—clair*, clear.]

**Clarionet**, klar'i-on-et, **Clarinet**, klar'i-net, *n.* a wind instrument of music sounded by means of a reed fixed to the mouthpiece. [Fr. *clarinette*, dim. of *clairon*.]

**Clash**, klash, *n.* a loud noise, such as is caused by the striking together of weapons: opposition: contradiction.—*v.i.* to dash noisily together: to meet in opposition: to act in a contrary direction.—*v.t.* to strike noisily against. [Formed from the sound, like Ger. and Sw. *klatsch*.]

**Clasp**, klasp, *n.* a hook for fastening: an embrace. —*v.t.* to fasten with a clasp: to inclose and hold in the hand or arms: to embrace: to twine round. [M. E. *clapse*, from the root of A.S. *clyppan*, to embrace. See **Clip**.]

**Clasper**, klasp'ėr, *n.*, *that which clasps*: the tendril of a plant.

**Clasp-knife**, klasp'-nif, *n.* a *knife*, the blade of which is *clasped* by, or folds into, the handle.

**Class**, klas, *n.* a rank or order of persons or things: a number of students or scholars who are taught together: a scientific division or arrangement. —*v.t.* to form into a class or classes: to arrange methodically. [Fr. *classe*—L. *classis*, orig. a rank or order of the Roman people when *called* together, from a root *kal*-, seen in L. *calare*, *clamare*, to call, Gr. *kaleō*, *klēsis*.]

**Classic**, klas'ik, **Classical**, klas'ik-al, *adj.* of the highest class or rank, especially in literature: originally and chiefly used of the best Greek and Roman writers: (as opp. to romantic) like in style to the authors of Greece and Rome: chaste: refined.—**Class'ics**, *n.pl.* Greek, Roman, and modern writers of the first rank, or their works. —*adv.* **Class'ically**.

**Classicality**, klas-ik-al'i-ti, **Classicalness**, klas'ik-al-nes. *n.* the quality of being *classical*.

**Classification**, klas-i-fi-kā'shun, *n.* act of forming into *classes*.

**Classify**, klas'i-fī, *v.t.* to *make* or form into *classes*: to arrange:—*pr.p.* class'ifying; *pa.p.* class'ified. [L. *classis*, and *facio*, to make.]

**Classman**, klas'man, *n.* one who has gained honours of a certain *class* at the Oxford examinations: opp. to passman.

**Clatter**, klat'ėr, *n.* a repeated confused *rattling noise*: a repetition of abrupt, sharp sounds.— *v.i.* to make rattling sounds: to rattle with the tongue: to talk fast and idly.—*v.t.* to strike so as to produce a rattling. [Acc. to Skeat, *clatter* = *clacker*, a freq. of **Clack**.]

**Clause**, klawz, *n.* a sentence or part of a sentence: an article or part of a contract, will, &c. [Fr. *clause*—L. *clausus—claudo*, to shut, inclose.]

**Clave**, klāv—did cleave—*past tense* of **Cleave**.

**Clavicle**, klav'i-kl, *n.* the collar-bone, so called from its resemblance to a Roman *key*. [Fr. *clavicule*—L. *clavicula*, dim. of *clavis*, a key.]

**Clavicular**, kla-vik'ū-lar, *adj.* pertaining to the clavicle.

**Claw**, klaw, *n.* the hooked nail of a beast or bird: the whole foot of an animal with hooked nails: anything like a claw.—*v.t.* to scratch or tear as with the *claws* or nails: to tickle. [A.S. *clawu*; cog. with Ger. *klaue*: akin to **Cleave**, to stick or hold on.]

**Clay**, klā, *n.* a tenacious ductile earth: earth in general.—*v.t.* to purify with clay, as sugar. [A.S. *clæg*; cog. with Dan. *klæg*, Dut. *klai*, Ger. *klei*: conn. with **Clag**, **Clog**, **Clew**, L. *gluten*, Gr. *glia*, glue; and **Glue**.]

**Clayey**, klā'i, *adj.* consisting of or like *clay*.

**Claymore**, klā'mōr, *n.* a large sword formerly used by the Scottish Highlanders. [Gael. *claid-*

*heamh-mor*—Gael. and Ir. *claidheamh*, sword, and *mor*, great : cf. L. *gladius*, a sword.]

**Clean,** klēn, *adj.* free from stain or whatever defiles : pure : guiltless : neat.—*adv.* quite : entirely : cleverly.—*v.t.* to make clean, or free from dirt.—*n.* **Clean'ness.** [A.S. *clǣne*; W., Gael. *glan*, shine, polish; Ger. *klein*, small.]

**Cleanly,** klen'li, *adj.* clean in habits or person : pure : neat.—*adv.* in a cleanly manner.—*n.* **Clean'liness.**

**Cleanse,** klenz, *v.t.* to make *clean* or pure.

**Clear,** klēr, *adj.* pure, bright, undimmed : free from obstruction or difficulty : plain, distinct : without blemish, defect, drawback, or diminution : conspicuous.—*adv.* in a clear manner : plainly : wholly : quite.—*v.t.* to make clear : to free from obscurity, obstruction, or guilt : to free, acquit, or vindicate : to leap, or pass by or over : to make profit.—*v.i.* to become clear : to grow free, bright, or transparent.—*n.* **Clear'ness.** [Fr. *clair*—L. *clarus*, clear, loud.]

**Clearance,** klēr'ans, *n.*, *act of clearing*: a certificate that a ship has been *cleared* at the customhouse—that is, has satisfied all demands and procured permission to sail.

**Clearing,** klēr'ing, *n.* a tract of land *cleared* of wood, &c., for cultivation.

**Clearing,** klēr'ing, *n.* a method by which banks and railway companies *clear* or arrange certain affairs which mutually concern them.—**Clearing-house,** a place in London where such *clearing* business is done. [tinctly.

**Clearly,** klēr'li, *adv.*, *in a clear manner*: dis-**Cleavage,** klēv'āj, *n.* act or manner of *cleaving* or splitting.

**Cleave,** klēv, *v.t.* to *divide*, to *split*: to separate with violence.—*v.i.* to part asunder : to crack : *pr.p.* cleav'ing; *pa.t.* clōve or cleft; *pa.p.* clov'en or cleft. [A.S. *cleofan*; cog. with Ger. *klieben*.]

**Cleave,** klēv, *v.i.* to *stick* or *adhere*: to unite :—*pr.p.* cleav'ing; *pa.t.* cleaved' or clāve; *pa.p.* cleaved'. [A.S. *clifian*; cog. with Ger. *kleben*, Dut. *kleven*. See **Clay.**]

**Cleaver,** klēv'ėr, *n.* the person or thing *that cleaves*: a butcher's chopper.

**Clef,** klef, *n.* a character in music which determines the *key* or position on the scale of the notes that follow it. [Fr., from L. *clavis*, the root of which is seen also in L. *claudere*, to shut, Gr. *kleis*, a key.]

**Cleft,** kleft, in *B.*, **Clift,** *n.* an opening made by *cleaving* or splitting : a crack, fissure, or chink.

**Clematis,** klem'a-tis, *n.* a creeping plant, called also *virgin's bower* and *traveller's joy.* [Low L.—Gr. *klēmatis*—*klēma*, a twig.]

**Clemency,** klem'en-si, *n.* the quality of being *clement*: mildness : readiness to forgive.

**Clement,** klem'ent, *adj.* mild : gentle : kind : merciful.—*adv.* **Clem'ently.** [Fr.—L. *clemens.*]

**Clench,** klensh. Same as **Clinch.**

**Clepsydra,** klep'si-dra, *n.* an instrument used by the Greeks and Romans for measuring time by the trickling of *water*, as if by *stealth*, through a very small orifice. [L.—Gr. *klepsydra*—*kleptō*, *klepsō*, to steal, *hydōr*, water.]

**Clergy,** klėr'ji, *n.* the body of ministers of religion. [Fr. *clergé*—Low L. *clericia*; from Late L. *clericus*, Gr. *klērikos*, from Gr. *klēros*, a lot, then the clergy : because the Lord was the lot or inheritance of the Levites (Deut. xviii. 2), or because the church was the inheritance of the Lord (1 Peter v. 3), the name being thence applied to the clergy.]

**Clergyman,** klėr'ji-man, *n.* one of the *clergy*, a

man regularly ordained to preach the gospel, and administer its ordinances.

**Cleric,** kler'ik, **Clerical,** kler'ik-al, *adj.* belonging to the *clergy*: pertaining to a *clerk* or writer.

**Clerk,** klärk, *n.* (*orig.*) a *clergyman* or *priest*: a scholar : one who reads the responses in the English Church service : in common use, one employed as a writer or assistant in an office.—*n.* **Clerk'ship.** [A.S. *clerc*, a priest—Late L. *clericus.* See **Clergy.**]

**Clever,** klev'ėr, *adj.* able or dexterous : ingenious : skilfully done.—*adv.* **Clev'erly.**—*n.* **Clev'erness.** [Ety. dub.]

**Clew,** klōō, *n.* a *ball* of thread, or the thread in it : a thread that guides through a labyrinth : anything that solves a mystery : the corner of a sail.—*v.t.* to truss or tie up sails to the yards. [A.S. *cliwe*; prob. akin to L. *glomus*, a ball of thread, and *globus*, a sphere, from root of **Cleave,** to adhere. See **Globe.**]

**Click,** klik, *n.* a short, sharp *clack* or sound : anything that makes such a sound, as a small piece of iron falling into a notched wheel.—*v.i.* to make a light, sharp sound. [Dim. of **Clack.**]

**Client,** klī'ent, *n.* one who employs a lawyer : a dependent.—*n.* **Cli'entship.** [Fr.—L. *cliens*, for *cluens*, one who hears or listens (to advice), from *clueo*, to hear.]

**Cliff,** klif, *n.* a high steep rock : the steep side of a mountain. [Perh. akin to **Climb.**]

**Clift.** Same as **Cleft.**

**Climacteric,** klim-ak'tėr-ik or klim-ak-tėr'ik, *n.* a critical period in human life, in which some great bodily change is supposed to take place, esp. the grand climacteric or sixty-third year.—*adjs.* **Climac'teric, Climacter'ic, Climacter'ical.** [Gr. *klimaktēr*—*klimax*, a ladder.]

**Climate,** klī'māt, *n.* the condition of a country or place with regard to temperature, moisture, &c. [Fr.—L. *clima*, *climatis*—Gr. *klima*, *klimatos*, slope—*klinō*, to make to slope, akin to E. **Lean.**]

**Climatic,** klī-mat'ik, **Climatical,** klī-mat'ik-al, *adj.* relating to, or limited by a *climate*.

**Climatise,** klī'ma-tīz, *v.t.* or *v.i.* See **Acclimatise.**

**Climatology,** klī-ma-tol'o-ji, *n.*, *the science of climates*, or an investigation of the causes on which the climate of a place depends. [Gr. *klima*, and *logos*, discourse.]

**Climax,** klī'maks, *n.* in Rhetoric, the arranging of the particulars of a portion of discourse so as to rise in strength to the last. [Gr. *klimax*, a ladder or staircase—from *klinō*, to slope.]

**Climb,** klīm, *v.i.* or *v.t.* to ascend or mount up by clutching with the hands and feet : to ascend with difficulty. [A.S. *climban*; Ger. *klimmen*; conn. with **Clamber** and **Cleave,** to stick.]

**Clime,** klīm, *n.* a country, region, tract. [A variety of **Climate.**]

**Clinch,** klinsh, *v.t.* to *fasten* or *rivet* a nail : to grasp tightly : to settle or confirm. [Causal form of *klink*, to strike smartly ; Dut. and Ger. *klinken*, to rivet a bolt.] [argument.

**Clincher,** klinsh'ėr, *n.* one that *clinches*; a decisive

**Cling,** kling, *v.i.* to *adhere* or stick close by winding round : to adhere in interest or affection :—*pa.t.* and *pa.p.* clung. [A.S. *clingan*, to shrivel up, to draw together.]

**Clinic,** klin'ik, **Clinical,** klin'ik-al, *adj.* pertaining to a *bed*: (*med.*) applied to instruction given in hospitals at the *bedside* of the patient. [Gr. *klinikos*—*klinē*, a bed, from *klinō*, to recline.]

**Clink,** klingk, *n.* a *ringing* sound made by the striking together of sounding bodies.—*v.t.* to

     fāte, fär ; mē, hėr ; mīne ; mōte ; mūte ; mōōn ; *then.*

cause to make a ringing sound.—*v.i.* to ring or jingle. [A form of **Click** and **Clank**.]

**Clinker**, klink′ér, *n.* the cinder or slag formed in furnaces : brick burned so hard that, when struck, it makes a sharp and ringing sound.

**Clip**, klip, *v.t.* to cut by making the blades of shears meet : to cut off : formerly, to debase the coin by cutting off the edges :—*pr.p.* clipp′ing ; *pa.p.* clipped′. [From the root of Ice. *klippa*, to cut, and allied to A.S. *clyppan*, to embrace, to draw closely.]

**Clip**, klip, *n.* the thing *clipped* off, as the wool that has been shorn off sheep.

**Clipper**, klip′ér, *n.*, *one that clips:* a sharp-built, fast-sailing vessel.

**Clipping**, klip′ing, *n.* the act of cutting, esp. debasing coin by cutting off the edges : the thing clipped off.

**Clique**, klēk, *n.* a group of persons in union for a purpose : a party or faction : a gang :—used generally in a bad sense. [Fr., prob. from root of *click*, and so = a noisy conclave.]

**Cloak**, **Cloke**, klōk, *n.* a loose outer *garment :* a covering : that which conceals : a disguise, pretext.—*v.t.* to clothe with a cloak : to cover : to conceal. [Old Fr. *cloque*—Low L. *cloca*, a bell, also a horseman's cape, because bell-shaped, from root of **Clock**.]

**Clock**, klok, *n.* a machine for measuring time, and which marks the time by the position of its ' hands ' upon the dial-plate, or by the striking of a hammer on a bell. [Word widely diffused, as A.S. *clucga*, Gael. *clog*, Ger. *glocke*, Fr. *cloche*, and all = a bell ; the root is doubtful.]

**Clockwork**, klok′wurk, *n.* the *works* or machinery of a *clock:* machinery like that of a clock.

**Clod**, klod, *n.* a thick round mass or lump, that *cleaves* or *sticks together*, especially of earth or turf : the ground : a stupid fellow :—*pr.p.* clodd′-ing ; *pa.p.* clodd′ed. [A later form of **Clot**.]

**Clodhopper**, klod′hop-ér, *n.* a country-man ; a peasant : a dolt. [**Clod** and **Hopper**.]

**Clodpate**, klod′pāt, **Clodpoll**, klod′pōl, *n.* one with a *head* like a *clod*, a stupid fellow. [**Clod** and **Pate**, **Poll**.]

**Clog**, klog, *v.t.* to accumulate in a mass and cause a stoppage : to obstruct : to encumber :—*pr.p.* clogg′ing ; *pa.p.* clogged′.—*n.* anything hindering motion : an obstruction : a shoe with a wooden sole. [Akin to Scot. *clag*, to cover with mud, *claggy*, sticky ; from root of **Clay**.]

**Cloister**, klois′ter, *n.* a covered arcade forming part of a monastic or collegiate establishment : a place of religious retirement, a monastery or nunnery.—*v.t.* to confine in a cloister : to confine within walls. [O. Fr. *cloistre*, Fr. *cloître* (A.S. *clauster*)—L. *claustrum*—*claudo*, *clausum*, to close, to shut.]

**Cloisteral**, klois′tér-al, **Cloistral**, klois′tral, old form **Claustral**, klaws′tral, *adj.* pertaining to or confined to a *cloister :* secluded.

**Cloistered**, klois′térd, *adj.* dwelling in *cloisters:* solitary : retired from the world.

**Clomb**, klōm, old *past tense* of **Climb**.

**Close**, klōs, *adj., shut up:* with no opening : confined, unventilated : narrow : near, in time or place : compact : crowded : hidden : reserved.—*adv.* in a close manner : nearly : densely.—*n.* an inclosed place : a small inclosed field : a narrow passage of a street.—*adv.* **Close′ly**.—*n.* **Close′-ness.** [Fr. *clos*, shut—*pa.p.* of *clore*, from L. *claudere*, *clausus*, to shut.]

**Close**, klōz, *v.t.* to make *close:* to draw together

and unite : to finish.—*v.i.* to grow together : to come to an end.—*n.* the manner or time of closing : a pause or stop : the end.

**Closet**, kloz′et, *n.* a small private room : a recess off a room.—*v.t.* to shut up in, or take into a closet : to conceal :—*pr.p.* clos′eting ; *pa.p.* clos′eted. [O. Fr. *closet*, dim. of *clos*. See **Close**.]

**Closure**, klōz′ūr, *n.* the act of closing ; that which closes.

**Clot**, klot, *n.* a mass of soft or fluid matter concreted, as blood.—*v.i.* to form into *clots:* to coagulate :—*pr.p.* clott′ing ; *pa.p.* clott′ed. [M.E. *clot*, a clod of earth ; cog. with Ice. *klot*, a ball, Dan. *klode*, a globe ; from root of **Clew**. See **Cleave**, to stick, adhere.]

**Cloth**, kloth, *pl.* **Cloths**, *n.* woven material from which garments or coverings are made : the clerical profession, from their wearing black cloth. [A.S. *clath*, cloth, *clathas*, clothes, garments ; Ger. *kleid*, Ice. *klædi*, a garment.]

**Clothe**, klōth, *v.t.* to cover with *clothes :* to provide with clothes : ( *fig.*) to invest, as with a garment :—*pr.p.* clōth′ing ; *pa.t.* and *pa.p.* clōthed′ or clad.

**Clothes**, klōthz (*colloq.* klōz), *n.pl.* garments or articles of dress. [*cloths* or *clothes*.

**Clothier**, klōth′i-ér, *n.* one who makes or sells

**Clothing**, klōth′ing, *n.*, *clothes:* garments.

**Cloud**, klowd, *n.* a mass of watery vapour floating in the air : ( *fig.*) a great volume of dust or smoke.—*v.t.* to overspread with clouds : to darken : to stain with dark spots or streaks.—*v.i.* to become clouded or darkened. [A.S. *clud*, a hill, then, a cloud, the root idea being a mass or ball. **Clod** and **Clot** are from the same root.]

**Cloudless**, klowd′les, *adj.* unclouded, in any sense.—*adv.* **Cloud′lessly**.

**Cloudlet**, klowd′let, *n.* a *little cloud*.

**Cloudy**, klowd′i, *adj.* darkened with, or consisting of *clouds:* obscure : gloomy : stained with dark spots.—*adv.* **Cloud′ily**.—*n.* **Cloud′iness**.

**Clough**, kluf, *n.* a *cleft* in a rock, or the side of a hill. [A doublet of **Cleft** ; Scot. *cleugh*.]

**Clout**, klowt, *n.* a small piece of cloth : a piece of cloth sewed on clumsily ; a rag.—*v.t.* to *mend with a patch :* to mend clumsily. [A.S. *clut*, from W. *clwt*, a patch.]

**Clove**, klōv, *pa.t.* of **Cleave**, to split.

**Clove**, klōv, *n.* a pungent, aromatic spice, the unexpanded flower-bud (so called from its resemblance to a *nail*) of the clove-tree, a native of the Moluccas. [Sp. *clavo*—L. *clavus*, a nail.]

**Cloven**, klōv′n, *pa.p.* of **Cleave**, to divide, or *adj.* divided : parted.—*adjs.* **Cloven-footed, Cloven-hoofed**, having the foot parted or divided.

**Clove-pink**, klōv′-pingk, *n.* the *clove* gillyflower or carnation *pink*, which has an odour like that of *cloves*.

**Clover**, klōv′ér, *n.* a species of grass in which the leaf is *divided* into three lobes. [A.S. *clæfer*, perh. from *cleofan*, to cleave.]

**Clown**, klown, *n.* a rustic or country-fellow : one with the rough manners of a country-man : a fool or buffoon. [Ety. dub.]

**Clownish**, klown′ish, *adj.* of or like a clown : coarse and awkward : rustic.—*adv.* **Clown′ily**.—*n.* **Clown′ishness**.

**Cloy**, kloi, *v.t.* to fill to loathing : to glut or satiate :—*pr.p.* cloy′ing ; *pa.p.* cloyed′. [O. Fr. *cloyer*, Fr. *clouer*, to drive a nail into, to spike or stop, as a gun, from L. *clavus*, a nail.]

**Club**, klub, *n.* an association of persons for the promotion of a common object, as literature, politics, pleasure, &c.—*v.i.* to *join* together for some common end : to share in a common expense :—*pr.p.* clubb'ing ; *pa.p.* clubbed'. [From root of **Club**, a club being a *clump* of people.]

**Club**, klub, *n.* a heavy tapering stick, *knobby* or *massy* at one end, used to strike with : a cudgel : one of the four suits of cards (called in Sp. *bastos*, cudgels or clubs). [Ice. and Sw. *klubba* ; same root as **Clump**.]

**Club-foot**, klub'-foot, *n.* a short, deformed *foot*, like a *club*.—*adj.* **Club'-foot'ed**.

**Club-law**, klub'-law, *n.* government by violence.

**Club-moss**, klub'-mos, *n.* a *moss* with scaly leaves and stems like a *club*.

**Cluck**, kluk, *n.* the call of a hen to her chickens. —*v.i.* to make the sound of a hen when calling on her chickens. [From the sound, like Dut. *klokken*, Ger. *glucken*, to cluck.]

**Clue.** See **Clew.**

**Clump**, klump, *n.* a thick, short, shapeless piece of anything : a cluster of trees or shrubs. [Prob. E., but cog. with Ger. and Dan. *klump*, a lump ; from root of O. Ger. *klimpfen*, to press together, conn. with **Clamp, Club.**]

**Clumsy**, klum'zi, *adj.* shapeless : ill-made : awkward : ungainly.—*adv.* **Clum'sily.**—*n.* **Clum'siness.** [M. E. *clumsen*, to be stiff or benumbed ; akin to **Clam.**]

**Clung**, klung—did cling—*pa.t.* and *pa.p.* of **Cling**.

**Cluster**, klus'tèr, *n.* a number of things of the same kind growing or joined together : a bunch : a mass.—*v.i.* to grow or gather into clusters.— *v.t.* to collect into clusters. [A.S. *cluster ;* Ice. *klastr*, from the root *klib*, seen in A.S. *clifian*, to adhere.]

**Clutch**, kluch, *v.t.* to *seize* or *grasp.*—*n.* a *grasp* or *grip :* seizure.—*pl.* **Clutch'es**, the hands or paws : cruelty : rapacity. [M. E. *cloche, cloke*, claw, grasp ; Scot. *cleik ;* from root of A.S. *gelæccan*, to catch, whence **Latch**.]

**Clutter**, klut'èr, a form of **Clatter.**

**Clyster**, klis'tèr, *n.* a liquid injected into the intestines to *wash them out*. [Gr.—*klyzō*, to wash out.]

**Coach**, kōch, *n.* a large, close, four-wheeled carriage.—*v.t.* to carry in a *coach*. [Fr. *coche*—L. *concha*, a shell, a boat, a carriage—Gr. *kogkē*, a shell ; or from Hung. *kotschi*.]

**Coadjutor**, kō-ad-jōōt'or, *n.* a *fellow-helper* or assistant : an associate.—*fem.* **Coadjut'rix.**—*n.* **Coadjut'orship.** [L. *co*, with, *adjutor*, a helper—*ad*, to, *juvo*, to help.] [*coagulated.*]

**Coagulable**, kō-ag'u-la-bl, *adj.* capable of being

**Coagulant**, kō-ag'ū-lant, *n.* a substance which causes *coagulation*, as rennet.

**Coagulate**, kō-ag'ū-lāt, *v.t.* to make to curdle or congeal.—*v.i.* to curdle or congeal.—*n.* **Coagula'tion.**—*adj.* **Coag'ulative.** [L. *coagulo—co*, together, *ago*, to drive.]

**Coagulum**, kō-ag'ū-lum, *n.* what is coagulated. [L.]

**Coal**, kōl, *n.* a solid, black, combustible substance used for fuel, dug out of the earth.—*v.i.* to take in coal. [A.S. *col*, cog. with Ice. *kol*, Ger. *kohle ;* conn. with Sw. *kylla*, to kindle.]

**Coalesce**, kō-al-es', *v.i.* to *grow together* or unite into one body : to associate.—*adj.* **Coalesc'ent**, uniting. [L. *coalesco—co*, together, and *alesco*, to grow up, from *alo*, to nourish.] [*union.*]

**Coalescence**, kō-al-es'ens, *n.* act of *coalescing :*

**Coalfield**, kōl'fēld, *n.* a field or district containing coal strata.

**Coalition**, kō-al-ish'un, *n.* act of *coalescing*, or uniting into one body : a union or combination of persons, states, &c. into one : alliance.

**Coalitionist**, kō-al-ish'un-ist, *n.* one of a *coalition*.

**Coaly**, kōl'i, *adj.* of or like *coal*.

**Coarse**, kōrs, *adj.* rough : rude : uncivil : gross. —*adv.* **Coarse'ly.**—*n.* **Coarse'ness.** [Orig. written **Course** ; from being used in the phrase, 'in course,' it came to mean *ordinary, commonplace*.]

**Coast**, kōst, *n.* side or border of land next the sea : the sea-shore : limit or border of a country. —*v.i.* to sail along or near a coast.—*v.t.* to sail by or near to. [Fr. *côte* for *coste*—L. *costa*, a rib, side.] [coast.]

**Coaster**, kōst'èr, *n.* a vessel that sails along the

**Coastguard**, kōst'gärd, *n.* a body of men organised to act as a guard along the coast, orig. intended to prevent smuggling.

**Coastwise**, kōst'wīz, *adv.* along the coast. [**Coast** and **Wise.**]

**Coat**, kōt, *n.* a kind of outer garment : the hair or wool of a beast : vesture or habit : any covering : a membrane or layer : the ground on which ensigns armorial are portrayed, usually called *a coat of arms.*—*v.t.* to cover with a coat or layer. [Fr. *cotte*—Low L. *cottus, cotta*, a tunic ; from root of Ger. *kotze*, a matted covering : akin to **E. cot**, a hut.] [flaps.]

**Coatee**, kōt-ē', *n.* a *little coat :* a coat with short

**Coating**, kōt'ing, *n.* a covering : cloth for coats.

**Coax**, kōks, *v.t.* to persuade by fondling, or flattery : to humour or soothe.—*adv.* **Coax'ingly.** [M. E. *cokes*, a simpleton ; prob. from W. *coeg*, empty, foolish. See **Cog.**]

**Cob**, kob, *n.* a head of maize : a thick strong pony. [W. *cob ;* cf. Dut. *kop*, Ger. *kopf*, the top, head.]

**Cobalt**, kō'bawlt, *n.* a brittle, reddish-gray metal, usually found combined with arsenic and other minerals. [Ger. *kobalt*, from *kobold*, a demon, a nickname given by the German miners, because they supposed it to be a mischievous and hurtful metal ; from Low L. *gobelinus*—Gr. *kobālos*, a goblin.]

**Cobble**, kob'l, *v.t.* to patch up or mend coarsely, as shoes. [O. Fr. *cobler*, to join together, to tie together ; from L. *copulo*, to join.] [shoes.]

**Cobbler**, kob'lèr, *n.* one who *cobbles* or mends

**Coble**, kob'l, *n.* a small fishing-boat. [W. *keubal*, a hollow trunk, a boat.]

**Cobra da capello**, kō'bra da ka-pel'o, *n.* a poisonous snake, native of the East Indies, which dilates the back and sides of the neck so as to resemble a *hood*. [Port. = snake of the hood.]

**Cobweb**, kob'web, *n.* the *spider's web* or net : any snare or device intended to entrap. [A.S. *attorcoppa*, a spider, lit. *poison-head* or tuft, from A.S. *ator*, poison, and *coppa* = W. *cop*, a head, tuft.]

**Cocagne**, kok-ān', *n.* the land of *cookery* or good living : an imaginary country of luxury and delight. [Fr. *cocagne ;* from L. *coquo*, to cook.]

**Cocciferous**, kok-sif'èr-us, *adj., berry-bearing.* [L. *coccus* (—Gr. *kokkos*), a berry, and *fero*, to bear.]

**Cochineal**, koch'i-nēl, *n.* a scarlet dye-stuff consisting of the dried bodies of certain insects gathered from the cactus plant in Mexico, the W. Indies, &c. [Sp. *cochinilla*, dim. of L. *coccinus*—Gr. *kokkos*, a berry, as the cochineal was formerly supposed to be the berry or seed of the plant.]

**Cochleary**, kok'lē-ar-i, **Cochleate**, kok'lē-āt, **Cochleated**, kok'lē-āt-ed, *adj. twisted* like a *snail-shell :* spiral. [L. *cochlea*, snail-shell, screw—Gr. *kochlos*, a shell-fish with a spiral shell.]

**Cock**, kok, *n.* the male of birds, particularly of the domestic fowl: a weathercock: a strutting chief or leader: anything set erect: a tap for liquor.—*v.t.* to set erect or upright: to set up, as the hat.—*v.i.* to strut: to hold up the head. [A.S. *coc*, an imitative word.]

**Cock**, kok, *n.* a small pile of hay. [Swed. *koka*, a lump of earth; Dut. *kogel*, Ger. *kugel*, a ball.]

**Cock**, kok, *n.* part of the lock of a gun. [Ital. *cocca*, a notch, *coccare*, to put the string of a bow into the notch of the arrow; this expression was transferred to firearms—hence, to put a gun on *cock*.]

**Cockade**, kok-ād′, *n.* a knot of ribbons or something similar worn on the hat as a badge. [Fr. *cocarde*—*coq*, perh. from its likeness to the comb of the cock.]

**Cockatoo**, kok-a-tōō′, *n.* a kind of parrot with a crest. [Malay *kakatua*, formed from its cry.]

**Cockatrice**, kok′a-trīs, *n.* a lizard or serpent imagined to be produced from a cock's egg. [The word has nothing to do with *cock*; the O. Fr. *cocatrice* meant a crocodile—Low L. *cocatrix*, a corr. of Low L. *cocodrillus*, a crocodile. See **Crocodile**.]

**Cockboat**, kok′bōt, *n.* a small *boat*. [O. Fr. *coque*, Fr. *coche*, a small boat—L. *concha*, a shell; the word boat is superfluous.]

**Cockchafer**, kok′chāf-ėr, *n.* the May-bug, an insect of a pitchy-black colour, most destructive to vegetation. [Ety. dub.]

**Cocker**, kok′ėr, *v.t.* (*obs.*) *to pamper*, to indulge.

**Cockle**, kok′l, *n.* a troublesome weed among corn, with a purple flower. [A.S. *coccel*—Gael. *cogal*, from *cog*, a husk, a bowl.]

**Cockle**, kok′l, *n.* a shell-fish, having two wrinkled shells, of a heart-shape. [W. *cocs*, cockles, and Gael. *cuach*, a drinking-bowl, dim. *cogan*, a small bowl; compare Fr. *coquille*—Gr. *kongchylion*, *kongchē*, a cockle.]

**Cockloft**, kok′loft, *n.* the room in a house next the roof. [The loft where the cocks roost.]

**Cockney**, kok′ne, *n.* byname for a native of the city of London.—*pl.* **Cock′neys**. [Ety. dub.]

**Cockneydom**, kok′ne-dum, *n.* the region or home of *Cockneys*.

**Cockneyism**, kok′ne-izm, *n.* the dialect or manners of a *Cockney*.

**Cockpit**, kok′pit, *n.* a *pit* or inclosed space where game-*cocks* fought: a room in a ship-of-war for the wounded during an action.

**Cockroach**, kok′rōch. *n.* the common black beetle.

**Cockscomb**, koks′kōm, *n.* the comb or crest on a *cock's* head; the name of three plants.

**Cockswain**, or **Coxswain**, kok′swān (*colloq.* kok′sn), *n.* a seaman who steers a boat, and under the superior officer takes charge of it. [*Cock*, a boat, and *swain*.]

**Cocoa**, kō′kō, *n.* a beverage made from the ground beans of the *cacao* or chocolate tree. [A corr. of *cacao*.]

**Cocoa**, kō′kō, *n.* a palm-tree growing in tropical countries, and producing the cocoa-nut. [Port. and Sp. *coco*, a bugbear: applied to the nut from the three marks at the end of it, which form a grotesque face.]

**Cocoa-nut**, or **Coco-nut**, kō′kō-nut, *n.* the well-known fruit of the cocoa-palm.

**Cocoon**, kō-kōōn′, *n.* the egg-shaped *shell* or covering which the larvæ of silkworms and some other insects spin. [Fr. *cocon*, from *coque*, a shell—L. *concha*, a shell.]

**Cocoonery**, kō-kōōn′ėr-i, *n.* a place for keeping silkworms when feeding and spinning cocoons.

**Coction**, kok′shun, *n.* the act of *boiling*. [L. *coctio*—*coquo*, to boil, to cook.]

**Cod**, kod, **Codfish**, kod′fish, *n.* a species of fish much used as food, found in the northern seas. —**Cod-liver Oil**, a medicinal oil extracted from the fresh liver of the common cod. [Ety. dub.]

**Cod**, kod, *n.* a hu-k, shell, or *pod*, containing seeds. [A.S. *codd*, a small bag; Ice. *koddi*, a cushion.] [boil. [Ety. dub.]

**Coddle**, kod′l, *v.t.* to pamper; to fondle: to par-

**Code**, kōd, *n.* a collection or digest of laws. [Fr. *code*—L. *codex* or *caudex*, the trunk of a tree, a tablet for writing, a set of tablets, a book.]

**Codicil**, kod′i-sil, *n.* a short writing or note added as a supplement to a will.—*adj.* **Codicill′ary**. [L. *codicillus*, dim. of *codex*.]

**Codify**, kod′i-fī, *v.t.* to *put into the form of a code*:—*pr.p.* cod′ifying; *pa.p.* cod′ified.—*n.* **Codifica′tion**. [L. *codex*, a code, and *facio*, to make.]

**Codling**, kod′ling, *n.* a young cod-fish.

**Codling**, kod′ling, **Codlin**, kod′lin, *n.* a hard kind of apple. [Dim of *cod*, a pod.]

**Coefficient**, kō-ef-fish′ent, *n.* that which acts together with another thing: (*math.*) the number or known quantity prefixed as a multiplier to a variable or unknown quantity.—*n.* **Coeffi′ciency**. —*adv.* **Coeffi′ciently**. [L. *co*, together, and **Efficient**.]

**Coerce**, kō-ėrs′, *v.t.* to restrain by force: to compel. [L. *coerceo*—*co*, together, *arceo*, to shut in, conn. with *arca*, a chest.]

**Coercible**, kō-ėrs′i-bl, *adj.* that may be restrained or compelled.—*adv.* **Coerc′ibly**.

**Coercion**, kō-ėr′shun, *n.* the act or process of coercing: restraint.

**Coercive**, kō-ėrs′iv, *adj.* having power to coerce: compelling.—*adv.* **Coerc′ively**.

**Coeval**, kō-ē′val, *adj.*, *of the same age*.—*n.* one of the same age. [L. *co*, together, and *ævum*, age, Gr. *aiōn*.] [sive.

**Co-extensive**, kō-eks-ten′siv, *adj.* equally exten-

**Coffee**, kof′ē, *n.* a drink made from the seeds of the coffee-tree, a native of Arabia. [Turk. *kahveh* —Ar. *qahweh*.]

**Coffer**, kof′ėr, *n.* a *chest* for holding money or treasure. [O. Fr. *cofre* or *cofin*, a chest—L. *cophinus*, a basket—Gr. *kophinos*.]

**Cofferdam**, kof′ėr-dam, *n.* a water-tight barrier or *box* of timber, placed in the bed of a river, &c., to *exclude* the water during the progress of some work. [**Coffer** and **Dam**.]

**Coffin**, kof′in, *n.* the *coffer* or *chest* in which a dead body is inclosed.—*v.t.* to place within a coffin. [The earlier form of **Coffer**.]

**Cog**, kog, *v.t.* to cheat or deceive: to cog dice is to load them so that they may fall in a given way. [W. *coegio*, to make void, to trick—*coeg*, empty.]

**Cog**, kog, *n.* a catch or tooth on a wheel.—*v.t.* to fix teeth in the rim of a wheel:—*pr.p.* cogg′ing; *pa.p.* cogged′. [Acc. to Skeat from Gael. and Ir. *cog*, a mill-cog.]

**Cogency**, kō′jen-si, *n.* power of convincing.

**Cogent**, kō′jent, *adj.*, *driving* or pressing on the mind: powerful: convincing.—*adv.* **Co′gently**. [L. *cogo*—*co*, together, and *ago*, to drive.]

**Cogitate**, koj′i-tāt, *v.i.* to *agitate* or *turn a thing over* in one's mind: to meditate: to ponder. [L. *cogito*, to think deeply—*co*, together, and *agito*, to put a thing in motion.] [tation.

**Cogitation**, koj-i-tā′shun, *n.* deep thought: medi-

**Cogitative**, koj′i-tā-tiv, *adj.* having the power of cogitating or thinking: given to cogitating.

**Cognac, Cogniac,** kŏn'yak, *n.* the best kind of French brandy, so called because much of it is made near the town *Cognac.*

**Cognate,** kog'nāt, *adj., born of the same family:* related to : of the same kind. [L. *cognatus*—*co,* together, and *gnascor, gnatus,* to be born.]

**Cognisable, Cognizable,** kog'niz-abl or kon'-, *adj., that may be known* or understood : that may be judicially investigated. [O. Fr. *cognoissabie.*]

**Cognisance, Cognizance,** kog'ni-zans or kon'-, *n., knowledge* or notice, judicial or private : observation : jurisdiction : that by which one is known, a badge. [O. Fr.—L. *cognosco.*]

**Cognisant, Cognizant,** kog'ni-zant or kon'-, *adj., having cognisance* or knowledge of.

**Cognition,** kog-nish'un, *n.* certain *knowledge.* [L., from *cognosco, cognitum—co,* together, and *nosco, gnosco,* to know.]

**Cognomen,** kog-nō'men, *n.* a surname : the last of the three names of an individual among the Romans, indicating the house or family to which he belonged. [L.—*co,* together, *nomen, gnomen,* a name—*nosco, gnosco,* to know.]

**Cohabit,** kō-hab'it, *v.i.* to dwell together as husband and wife.—*n.* **Cohabita′tion.** [L. *cohabito*—*co,* together, and *habito,* to dwell.]

**Cohere,** kō-hēr′, *v.i.* to *stick together :* to remain in contact : to follow in proper connection. [L. *cohereo—co,* together, and *hereo,* to stick.]

**Coherence,** kō-hēr′ens, **Coherency,** kō-hēr′en-si, *n.* a *sticking together :* a consistent connection between several parts.

**Coherent,** kō-hēr′ent, *adj., sticking together :* connected : consistent.—*adv.* **Coher′ently.**

**Cohesion,** kō-hē′zhun, *n.* the act of *sticking together :* a form of attraction by which particles of bodies of the same nature stick together : logical connection. [L. *cohæsus,* pa.p. of *cohæreo.*]

**Cohesive,** kō-hē′siv, *adj.* having the power of *cohering :* tending to unite into a mass.—*adv.* **Cohe′sively.**—*n.* **Cohe′siveness.**

**Cohort,** kō′hort, *n.* among the Romans, a body of soldiers about 600 in number, forming about a tenth part of a legion : any band of armed men. [Fr.—L. *cohors,* an inclosed place, a multitude inclosed, a company of soldiers. See **Court, Garden, Yard.**]

**Coif,** koif, *n.* a *cap* or covering for the head. [Fr. *coiffe*—Low L. *cofia,* a cap, from O. Ger. *chuppha,* a cap, another form of O. Ger. *chuph,* a cup (Ger. *kopf,* the head) : so that *coif* is a doublet of **Cup.**]

**Coiffure,** koif′ūr, *n.* a head-dress. [Fr.]

**Coign,** koin, *n.* a corner or external angle : a corner-stone : a wedge. [See **Coin.**]

**Coil,** koil, *v.t.* to *gather together,* or wind in rings as a rope, a serpent.—*n.* one of the rings into which a rope is gathered. [O. Fr. *coillir,* Fr. *cueillir*—L. *colligere—col,* together, *legere,* to gather.]

**Coin,** koin, *n.* a piece of metal legally stamped and current as money.—*v.t.* to convert a piece of metal into money : to form, as a medal, by stamping : to make, invent, fabricate. [Fr. *coin,* coin, also the die to stamp money—L. *cuneus,* a wedge. **Coign** is a doublet.]

**Coinage,** koin′āj, *n.* the act or art of *coining :* the pieces of metal coined : invention, fabrication.

**Coincide,** kō-in-sīd′, *v.i.* to *fall in with,* or agree, in opinion : to correspond : to be identical. [L. *co,* together, *incidere—in,* in, *cado,* to fall.]

**Coincidence,** kō-in′si-dens, **Coincidency,** kō-in′si-den-si, *n.* act or condition of *coinciding :* the occurrence of an event at the same time as another event.—*adj.* **Coin′cident.**—*adv.* **Coin′cidently.**

**Coir,** koir, *n.* cocoa-nut fibre for ropes or matting.

**Coke,** kōk, *n.* coal charred and deprived of its volatile matters, for use in furnaces. [Perh. conn. with **Cake.**]

**Colander,** kul′and-ėr, **Cullender,** kul′end-ėr, *n.* a *strainer :* a vessel having small holes in the bottom. [L. *colans, colantis,* pr.p. of *colare,* to strain—*colum,* a strainer.]

**Cold,** kōld, *adj.* the opposite of hot : shivering : without passion or zeal : spiritless : unfriendly : indifferent : reserved.—*n.* absence of heat : the feeling or sensation caused by the absence of heat : a disease caused by cold : catarrh : chillness.—*adv.* **Cold′ly.**—*n.* **Cold′ness.** [A.S. *ceald ;* Scot. *cauld,* Ger. *kalt ;* cog. also with E. *cool,* Ice. *kala,* to freeze, L. *gelidus—gelu,* frost.]

**Coldish,** kōld′ish, *adj., somewhat cold :* cool.

**Cole,** kōl, *n.* a general name for all sorts of cabbage. [A.S. *cawel ;* Ger. *kohl,* Scot. *kail ;* all from L. *colis, caulis,* a stem, especially of cabbage ; cf. Gr. *kaulos.*]

**Coleoptera,** kol-e-op′tėr-a, *n.pl.* an order of insects having two pair of wings, the outer pair being hard or horny, serving as wing-cases for the true wings, as the beetle. [Gr. *koleos,* a sheath, and *pteron,* pl. *ptera,* a wing.]

**Coleopterous,** kol-e-op′tėr-us, *adj., sheath-winged.*

**Colewort,** kōl′wurt, *n.* a species of cole or cabbage. [A.S. *wyrt,* a plant.]

**Colic,** kol′ik, *n.* a disorder of the *colon :* acute pain in the stomach or bowels.

**Coliseum.** See **Colosseum.**

**Collaborator,** kol-ab′ō-rā-tor, *n.* an associate or assistant in labour, particularly literary or scientific. [Coined from L. *col,* with, and *laboro, laboratum,* to labour.]

**Collapse,** kol-aps′, *n.* a falling away or breaking down : any sudden or complete breakdown or prostration.—*v.i.* to fall or break down : to go to ruin. [L. *collapsus—col,* together, and *labor, lapsus,* to slide or fall.]

**Collar,** kol′ar, *n.* something worn round the *neck :* the part of a garment at the neck : a ring : a band.—*v.t.* to seize by the collar : to put on a collar. [Fr. *collier*—L. *collare—collum,* the neck ; akin to A.S. *heals,* Ger. *hals,* the neck.]

**Collar-bone,** kol′ar-bōn, *n.* a bone of the *neck* between the breastbone and the shoulder-blade ; also called the clavicle.

**Collate,** kol-āt′, *v.t.* (*lit.*) to *bring* or *lay together* for comparison : to examine and compare, as books, and esp. old manuscripts : to place in or confer a benefice : to place in order, as the sheets of a book for binding. [L. *collatus,* pa.p. of *confero—con,* together, and *fero,* to bring.]

**Collateral,** kol-at′ėr-al, *adj., side by side :* running parallel or together : not direct : descended from the same ancestor, but not directly, as the children of brothers.—*n.* a collateral relation.—*adv.* **Collat′erally.** [L. *col,* and *latus, lateris,* a side.]

**Collation,** kol-ā′shun, *n., act of collating :* a bringing together, for examination and comparison : presentation to a benefice : a repast between meals.

**Collator,** kol-ā′tor, *n., one who collates* or compares : one who bestows or presents.

**Colleague,** kol′ēg, *n.* a partner, associate, or co-adjutor. [Fr. *collègue*—L. *collega—col,* together, and *lego,* to send on an embassy.]

**Colleague,** kol-ēg′, *v.i.* to join or unite with in the same office:—*pr.p.* colleaguing (kol-ēg′ing); *pa.p.* colleagued (kol-ēgd′).

**Collect,** kol-ekt′, *v.t.* to assemble or bring together: to infer: to compile.—*v.i.* to run together: to accumulate. [L. *colligo, collectus*, from *col*, together, and *lego*, Gr. *legō*, to gather, to choose.]

**Collect,** kol′ekt, *n.* a short and comprehensive prayer in the service of the R. Catholic and Anglican Churches. [Origin of the name dub.]

**Collected,** kol-ekt′ed, *adj., gathered together:* having one's senses gathered together: cool: firm.—*adv.* Collect′edly.—*n.* Collect′edness.

**Collection,** kol-ek′shun, *n., act of collecting:* that which is collected: an assemblage: a heap or mass: a book of selections.

**Collective,** kol-ekt′iv, *adj.* considered as forming one mass or sum: congregated: (*gram.*) expressing a number or multitude.—*adv.* Collect′ively.

**Collector,** kol-ekt′or, *n., one who collects* or gathers.—*ns.* Collec′torate, Collec′torship.

**College,** kol′ej, *n.* (*orig.*) any *collection* or community of men with certain privileges or a common pursuit, as a college of heralds or the college of cardinals: a seminary of learning: a literary, political, or religious institution: the edifice appropriated to a college.—**Collegian,** kol-ē′ji-an, *n.* a member or inhabitant of a *college.* [Fr. *collège*—L. *collegium*, from *col*, and *lego*.]

**Collegiate,** kol-ē′ji-āt, *adj.* pertaining to or resembling a *college:* containing a college, as a town: instituted like a college.

**Collet,** kol′et, *n.* the *collar* of a ring or the part which contains the stone. [Fr.—L. *collum.*]

**Collide,** kol-īd′, *v.i.* to *strike* or dash together. [L. *collido, collisus—col*, together, *lædo*, to strike.] [dub., prob. Celt.]

**Collie, Colly,** kol′i, *n.* a shepherd's dog. [Ety.

**Collier,** kol′yėr, *n.* one who works in a *coal*-mine: a ship that carries coal.

**Colliery,** kol′yėr-i, *n.* a *coal*-mine.

**Collision,** kol-izh′un, *n.* a *striking together:* state of being struck together: conflict: opposition.

**Collocate,** kol′ō-kāt, *v.t.* to *place together:* to place, set, or station. [L. *colloco, collocatus*, from *col*, together, and *loco*, to place.]

**Collocation,** kol-ō-kā′shun, *n., act of collocating:* disposition in place: arrangement. [L. *collocatio.*]

**Collodion,** kol-ō′di-on, *n.* a *gluey* solution of gun-cotton in alcohol and ether, used in surgery and photography. [Gr. *kollōdēs*, from *kolla*, glue, and *eidos*, form, appearance.]

**Collop,** kol′up, *n.* a slice of meat. [From *clop* or *colp*, the sound of a soft lump thrown on a flat surface: Dut. *klop*, It. *colpo*, a blow.]

**Colloquial,** kol-ō′kwi-al, *adj.* pertaining to or used in common conversation.—*adv.* Collo′quially.

**Colloquialism,** kol-ō′kwi-al-izm, *n.* a form of expression, used in familiar talk.

**Colloquy,** kol′ō-kwi, *n.* a *speaking together:* mutual discourse: conversation. [L. *colloquium*, from *col*, together, and *loquor*, to speak.]

**Collude,** kol-ūd′, *v.i.* to play into each other's hand: to act in concert, especially in a fraud. [L. *colludo, collusus*, from *col*, and *ludo*, to play.]

**Collusion,** kol-ū′zhun, *n., act of colluding:* a secret agreement to deceive. [L. *collusio.*]

**Collusive,** kol-ū′ziv, *adj.* fraudulently concerted: deceitful.—*adv.* Collu′sively.—*n.* Collu′siveness.

**Colocynth,** kol′ō-sinth, *n.* the dried and powdered pulp of a kind of cucumber, much used as a purgative. [Gr. *kolokynthis.*]

**Colon,** kō′lon, *n.* the mark ( : ) used to indicate a distinct *member* or clause of a sentence. [Gr. *kōlon*, a limb, member.]

**Colon,** kō′lon, *n.* the lower division of the intestinal canal or large intestine. [Gr. *kōlon*, conn. with *koilos*, hollow.]

**Colonel,** kur′nel, *n.* an officer who has command of a regiment.—*n.* Colonelcy, kur′nel-si, his office or rank. [Fr. (Sp. and O. E. *coronel*): a corr. of It. *colonello*, the leader of a *colonna*, or column—L. *columna*.]

**Colonial,** kol-ō′ni-al, *adj.* pertaining to a *colony.*

**Colonisation,** kol-on-i-zā′shun, *n.* act or practice of *colonising:* state of being colonised.

**Colonise,** kol′on-īz, *v.t.* to plant or establish a *colony* in: to form into a colony.

**Colonist,** kol′on-ist, *n.* an inhabitant of a *colony.*

**Colonnade,** kol-on-ād′, *n.* a *range of columns* placed at regular intervals. [Fr.—L. *columna.*]

**Colony,** kol′on-i, *n.* a body of persons who form a fixed settlement in another country: the settlement so formed. [L. *colonia—colonus*, a husbandman—*colo*, to till.]

**Colophon,** kol′ō-fon, *n.* in early printing, the inscription at the *end* of a book containing the name or date, &c. [L. *colophon*—Gr. *kolophōn*, the top, the finish.]

**Colophony,** kol-of′ō-ni, *n.* the dark-coloured resin got from the distillation of oil of turpentine. [Gr., from *Colophon*, a city of Asia Minor.]

**Colorific,** kul-ur-if′ik, *adj.* containing or producing *colours.* [L. *color*, and *facio*, to make.]

**Colossal,** kol-os′al, *adj., like a colossus:* gigantic.

**Colosseum,** kol-os-ē′um, **Coliseum,** kol-i-sē′um, *n.* Vespasian's amphitheatre at Rome, which was the largest in the world. [L.; from adj. of Gr. *kolossos.*]

**Colossus,** kol-os′us, *n.* a gigantic statue, particularly that of Apollo which stood at the entrance of the harbour of Rhodes. [L.—Gr. *kolossos.*]

**Colour,** kul′ur, *n.* a property of light which causes bodies to have different appearances to the eye: the hue or appearance which bodies present to the eye: appearance of blood in the face: tint: paint: false show: kind.—*pl.* a flag, ensign, or standard: paints.—*v.t.* to put colour on: to stain: to paint: to set in a fair light: to exaggerate.—*v.i.* to shew colour: to blush. [Fr.—L. *color*; akin to *celo*, to cover, conceal.]

**Colourable,** kul′ur-a-bl, *adj.* having a fair appearance: designed to conceal.—*adv.* Col′ourably.

**Colour-blindness,** kul′ur-blīnd′nes, *n.* a defect of the eyesight, by which one is unable to distinguish between colours.

**Colouring,** kul′ur-ing, *n.* any substance used to give *colour:* manner of applying colours: specious appearance.

**Colourist,** kul′ur-ist, *n., one who colours* or paints: one who excels in colouring. [parent.

**Colourless,** kul′ur-les, *adj., without colour:* trans-

**Colour-sergeant,** kul′ur-sär′jent, *n.* the sergeant who guards the colours of a regiment.

**Colportage,** kol′pōrt-āj, *n.* the distribution of books, &c., by *colporteurs.*

**Colporteur,** kol′pōrt-ār, **Colporter,** kol′pōrt-ėr, *n.* a pedler, particularly one who travels for the sale of tracts and religious books. [Fr. *colporteur*, from *col*—L. *collum*, the neck, and *porter* —L. *portare*, to carry.]

**Colt,** kōlt, *n.* a young horse: a foolish young fellow: (*B.*) a young camel or ass. [A.S. *colt*; Sw. *kullt*, a young boar, a stout boy.]

**Colter, Coulter,** kōl'tér, *n.* the foreiron of a plough, that *cuts* through the ground. [A.S. *culter*; from L. *culter*, a knife; Sans. *krit*, to cut.]

**Coltish,** kōlt'ish, *adj., like a colt*: frisky: wanton.

**Colt's-foot,** kōltz-foot, *n.* a plant with large soft leaves once used in medicine.

**Columbary,** kol'um-ba-ri, *n.* a *pigeon-house* or *dovecot.* [L. *columbarium—columba*, a dove.]

**Columbian,** kō-lum'bi-an, *adj.* pertaining to *Columbia*, a name of America. [*Columbia*, America, from *Columbus*, its discoverer.]

**Columbine,** kol'um-bīn, *adj., of or like a dove:* dove-coloured.—*n.* a genus of plants: a kind of violet or dove colour: the heroine in a pantomime. [Fr.—L. *columba*, a dove.]

**Column,** kol'um, *n.* a long, round body, used to support or adorn a building: any upright body or mass like a column: a body of troops drawn up in deep files: a perpendicular row of lines in a book. [L. *columen, columna*, akin to *cel-sus*, high, *collis*, a hill, and Gr. *kolōnē*, a hill.]

**Columnar,** kol-um'nar, *adj.* formed *in columns:* having the form of a column.

**Colure,** kol'ūr, *n.* (*astron.*) one of two great circles supposed to intersect each other at right angles in the poles of the equator, so called because a part is always beneath the horizon. [Gr. *kolouros*, dock-tailed—*kolos*, docked, *oura*, tail.]

**Colza,** kol'za, *n.* a kind of cabbage from the seeds of which is obtained an oil used in lamps. [Dut. *koolzaad*, the 'seed of cabbage.']

**Coma,** kō'ma, *n., deep sleep:* stupor. [Gr.—*koimaō*, to hush to sleep.]

**Comatose,** kō'ma-tōs or kom'-, **Comatous,** kō'ma-tus, *adj., affected with coma:* in a state of stupor from drowsiness: drowsy.

**Comb,** kōm, *n.* a toothed instrument for separating and cleaning hair, wool, flax, &c.; the crest of a cock: the top or crest of a wave or of a hill: a cell for honey.—*v.t.* to separate, arrange, or clean by means of a comb. [A.S. *camb*; Ice. *kambr*, comb, crest.]

**Comb, Combe,** kōm, *n.* a *hollow* among hills: a narrow valley. [W. *cwm*, a hollow.]

**Comb,** kōm, *n.* a dry measure of four bushels. [Ety. dub.]

**Combat,** kom'bat or kum'bat, *v.i.* to contend or struggle with.—*v.t.* to beat against: to act in opposition to: to contest.—*n.* a struggle: a battle or fight. [Fr. *combattre*, to fight—*com*, with, and *battre*, to beat. See **Beat.**]

**Combatant,** kom'bat-ant, *adj.* disposed or inclined to *combat.*—*n.* one who fights or combats.

**Combative,** kom'bat-iv, *adj.* inclined to quarrel or fight.—*n.* **Com'bativeness.**

**Comber,** kōm'ér, *n., one who combs* wool, &c.

**Combination,** kom-bi-nā'shun, *n.* the act of combining: union: a number of persons united for a purpose.

**Combine,** kom-bīn', *v.t.* to *join two together:* to unite intimately.—*v.i.* to come into close union: (*chem.*) to unite and form a new compound. [L. *combinare*, to join—*com*, together, and *bini*, two and two.]

**Combustible,** kom-bust'i-bl, *adj.* that may *take fire and burn:* liable to take fire and burn.—*n.* anything that will take fire and burn. [L. *comburo, combustus*, to consume—*com*, intensive, and *buro, uro*, to burn.]

**Combustibleness,** kom-bust'i-bl-nes, **Combustibility,** kom-bust-i-bil'i-ti, *n.* capable of being burned.

**Combustion,** kom-bust'yun, *n.* a *burning:* the action of fire on combustible substances.

**Come,** kum, *v.i.* to move toward this place (the opp. of *go*): to draw near: to arrive at a certain state or condition: to issue: to happen:—*pr.p.* com'ing; *pa.t.* cāme; *pa.p.* come. [A.S. *cuman*; Ger. *kommen*, to come.]

**Comedian,** kōm-ē'di-an, *n.* one who acts or writes *comedies:* an actor.

**Comedy,** kom'e-di, *n.* a dramatic piece of a pleasant or humorous character, orig. accomp. with dancing and singing. [L. *comœdia*—Gr. *kōmōdia*, a ludicrous spectacle, from *kōmos*, a revel, and *ōdē*, a song.]

**Comely,** kum'li, *adj.* pleasing: graceful: handsome.—*adv.* in a comely manner.—*n.* **Come'liness.** [A.S. *cymlic—cyme*, suitable (from **Come**), and *lic*, like.]

**Comestibles,** kom-est'i-blz, *n.* eatables. [Fr.—L. *comedo*, I eat up.]

**Comet,** kom'et, *n.* a heavenly body with an eccentric orbit and a luminous tail.—*adj.* **Com'etary.** [Gr. *komētēs*, long-haired—*komē*, the hair.]

**Comfit,** kum'fit, **Comfiture,** kum'fit-ūr, *n.* a sweetmeat. [A doubled of **Confect:** from Fr. *confit, confiture*—L. *conficio*, to make up.]

**Comfort,** kum'furt, *v.t.* to relieve from pain or distress: to cheer, revive.—*n.* **Com'forter.** [O. Fr. *conforter*—L. *con*, and *fortis*, strong.]

**Comfort,** kum'furt, *n.* relief: encouragement: ease: quiet enjoyment: freedom from annoyance: whatever gives ease, enjoyment, &c.

**Comfortable,** kum'furt-a-bl, *adj.* imparting or enjoying comfort.—*adv.* **Com'fortably.**

**Comfortless,** kum'furt-les, *adj.* without comfort.

**Comic,** kom'ik, **Comical,** kom'ik-al, *adj.* relating to *comedy:* raising mirth: droll.—*adv.* **Com'ically.**—*ns.* **Comical'ity, Com'icalness.**

**Comitia,** ko-mish'i-a, *n.* among the Romans, the *assemblies* of the people for electing magistrates, passing laws, &c. [L.—*com*, together, *eo, itum*, to go.] [*comitas, -atis—comis*, courteous.]

**Comity,** kom'i-ti, *n., courteousness:* civility. [L.

**Comma,** kom'a, *n.* in punctuation, the point (,) which marks the smallest division of a sentence. [L. *comma*—Gr. *komma*, a section of a sentence, from *koptō*, to cut off.]

**Command,** kom-and', *v.t.* to order: to bid: to exercise supreme authority over: to have within sight, influence, or control.—*v.i.* to have chief authority: to govern.—*n.* an order: authority: message: the ability to overlook or influence: the thing commanded. [Fr. *commander*—L. *commendare*, to commit to one's charge, to order—*com*, and *mandare*, to intrust. A doublet of **Commend.**]

**Commandant,** kom-and-ant', *n.* an officer who has the *command* of a place or of a body of troops.

**Commander,** kom-and'ér, *n., one who commands:* an officer in the navy next in rank under a captain.—*n.* **Command'ership.**

**Commanding,** kom-and'ing, *adj.* fitted to impress or control.—*adv.* **Command'ingly.**

**Commandment,** kom-and'ment, *n.* a *command:* a precept: one of the ten moral laws.

**Commemorate,** kom-em'o-rāt, *v.t.* to call to *remembrance* by a solemn or public act.—*n.* **Commemora'tion.** [L. *commemoratus*, pa.p. of *commemorare*, to remember—*com*, intensive, and *memor*, mindful.]

**Commemorative,** kom-em'o-rā-tiv, *adj.* tending or serving to *commemorate.*

**Commence,** kom-ens', *v.i.* to *begin:* to originate: to take rise.—*v.t.* to begin: to originate: to enter upon. [Fr. *commencer*—L. *com*, and *initiare*, to begin—*in*, into, and *eo*, to go.]

**Commencement**, kom-ens'ment, *n.* the beginning: the thing begun.

**Commend**, kom-end', *v.t.* to give into the charge of: to recommend as worthy: to praise. [L. *commendare*, to intrust. See Command.]

**Commendable**, kom-end'a-bl, *adj.* worthy of being *commended* or praised.—*adv.* **Commend'ably.** —*n.* **Commend'ableness.**

**Commendation**, kom-en-dā'shun, *n.* the *act of commending*: praise: declaration of esteem.

**Commendatory**, kom-end'a-to-ri, *adj., commending*: containing praise or commendation: presenting to favourable notice or reception.

**Commensurable**, kom-en'sū-ra-bl, *adj., having a common measure.*—*adv.* **Commen'surably.**— *ns.* **Commensurabil'ity, Commen'surableness.** [L. *com*, with, and *mensura*, a measure—*metior, mensus*, to measure.]

**Commensurate**, kom-en'sū-rāt, *adj., of the same measure with:* equal in measure or extent: in proportion with.—*adv.* **Commen'surately.**—*ns.* **Commen'surateness, Commensura'tion.**

**Comment**, kom'ent, *n.* a note conveying an illustration or explanation: a remark, observation, criticism.—*v.i.* (or kom-ent') to make critical or explanatory notes.—*ns.* **Com'mentātor, Com'mentor.** [Fr.—L. *commentor*, to reflect upon —*com*, and the root *ment*-, L. *mens*, the Mind.]

**Commentary**, kom'ent-a-ri, *n.* a *comment*, or a book or body of comments.

**Commerce**, kom'ėrs, *n.* interchange of *merchandise* on a large scale *between* nations or individuals: extended trade or traffic: intercourse: fellowship. [Fr. *commerce*—L. *commercium*—*com*, with, and *merx, mercis*, goods, merchandise.]

**Commercial**, kom-ėr'shal, *adj.* pertaining to commerce: mercantile.—*adv.* **Commer'cially.**

**Commination**, kom-in-ā'shun, *n.* a *threat:* a recital of God's threatenings made on Ash-Wednesday in the English Church. [L.—*com*, intensive, and *minor*, to threaten. See Menace.]

**Comminatory**, kom-in'a-tor-i, *adj., threatening* or denouncing punishment.

**Commingle**, kom-ing'gl, *v.t.* to *mingle* or mix with. [L. *com*, together, and Mingle.]

**Comminute**, kom'in-ūt, *v.t.* to reduce to *minute* or small *particles.*—*n.* **Comminu'tion.** [L. *comminuo, -utum*, to break into pieces—*com*, and *minuo*, to make small—root *minus*, less.]

**Commiserate**, kom-iz'ėr-āt, *v.t.* to *feel for the miseries of another:* to pity. [L. *com*, with, and *miseror*, to deplore, from *miser*, wretched.]

**Commiseration**, kom-iz-ėr-ā'shun, *n.* concern for the sufferings of others: pity. [*commissary*.

**Commissarial**, kom-is-ā'ri-al, *adj.* pertaining to a

**Commissariat**, kom-is-ā'ri-at, *n.* the department which is charged with the furnishing of provisions, as for an army: the body of officers in that department: the office of a commissary.

**Commissary**, kom'is-ar-i *n.* one to whom any charge is *committed*: an officer who has the charge of furnishing provisions, &c. to an army. —*n.* **Commissaryship.** [Low L. *commissarius* —L. *committo, commissum*.]

**Commission**, kom-ish'un, *n., act of committing:* that which is committed: a writing conferring certain powers: authority: charge or fee to an agent, &c. for transacting business: one or more persons appointed to perform certain duties.— *v.t.* to give a commission to: to appoint.

**Commissioner**, kom-ish'un-ėr, *n.* one who holds a *commission* to perform some business.

**Commit**, kom-it', *v.t.* to give in charge or trust: to do: to endanger: to pledge:—*pr.p.* com-

mitt'ing; *pa.p.* committ'ed. [L. *committo— com*, with, and *mitto*, to send.]

**Commitment**, kom-it'ment, *n., act of committing:* an order for sending to prison: imprisonment.

**Committal**, kom-it'al, *n.* commitment: a pledge, actual or implied.

**Committee**, kom-it'ē, *n.* one or more persons to whom some special business is *committed* by a court or assembly or other body of men.

**Commix**, kom-iks', *v.t.* to *mix together.*—*v.i.* to mix. [L. *com*, together, and Mix.]

**Commixture**, kom-iks'tūr, *n., act of mixing together:* the state of being mixed: the mass formed by mixing.

**Commode**, kom-ōd', *n.* a small sideboard: a headdress formerly worn by ladies. [Fr.—L. *com-modus*, convenient.]

**Commodious**, kom-ō'di-us, *adj.* suitable or convenient: comfortable.—*adv.* **Commo'diously.**— *n.* **Commo'diousness.** [L. *commodus* (*lit.*, having the same measure, fitting)—*com*, with, *modus*, measure.]

**Commodity**, kom-od'it-i, *n.* a convenience, or that which affords it: an article of traffic. [L. *com-moditas*, from *commodus*.]

**Commodore**, kom'o-dōr, *n.* the *commander* of a squadron or detachment of ships: the *leading* ship of a fleet of merchantmen. [Corr. of Sp. *comendador*—L. *commendo*, in late L. to command.]

**Common**, kom'un, *adj.* belonging equally to more than one: public: general: usual: frequent: easy to be had: of little value: vulgar.—*n.* a tract of open land, used in *common* by the inhabitants of a town, parish, &c.—**Common Pleas**, one of the High Courts of Justice.—**Book of Common Prayer**, the liturgy of the English Church.—*adv.* **Comm'only.**—*n.* **Comm'on-ness.** [Fr. *commun*—L. *communis*—*com*, together, and *munis*, serving, obliging.]

**Commonage**, kom'un-āj, *n.* right of pasturing on a *common*: the right of using anything *in common*.

**Commonalty**, kom'un-al-ti, *n.* the body of *common* people below the rank of nobility.

**Commoner**, kom'un-ėr, *n.* one of the *common* people, as opp. to the nobles: a member of the House of Commons: a student of the second rank in the university of Oxford.

**Commonplace**, kom'un-plās, *n.* a *common topic* or subject: a memorandum: a note.—*adj.* common: hackneyed.—*n.* **Comm'onplace-book**, a note or memorandum book. [Common, and **Place**, a translation of L. *locus*, a place, a topic of discourse.]

**Commons**, kom'unz, *n.pl.* the *common people:* their representatives—*i.e.* the lower House of Parliament or House of Commons: common land: food at a common table.

**Common-sense**, kom'un-sens, *adj.* marked by sound plain good sense.

**Commonweal**, kom'un-wēl, **Commonwealth**, kom'un-welth, *n.* (*lit.*) the *common* or public *well*-being or good: the government in a free state: the public or whole body of the people: a form of government in which the power rests with the people, esp. that in England after the overthrow of Charles I. [See Wealth.]

**Commotion**, kom-ō'shun, *n.* a *violent motion* or *moving:* excited or tumultuous action, physical or mental: agitation: tumult. [L. *commotio— com*, intensive, and *moveo, motus*, to move.]

**Communal**, kom-ūn'al, *adj.* of a *commune*.

**Commune**, kom'ūn, *n.* in France, a territorial

division governed by a mayor. The **Commune** at Paris in 1871 was a revolt against the national government, the principle of the revolt being that each city or district should be ruled independently by its own *commune* or local government. [Fr. *commune*—root of **Common**.]

**Commune,** kom-ūn′, *v.i.* to converse or talk together: to have intercourse. [Fr. *communier*—L. *communico*, from *communis*. See **Common**.]

**Communicable,** kom-ūn′i-ka-bl, *adj.* that may be communicated.—*adv.* **Commun′icably.**

**Communicant,** kom-ūn′i-kant, *n.* one who partakes of The Communion.

**Communicate,** kom-ūn′i-kāt, *v.t.* to give a share of, impart: to reveal: to bestow.—*v.i.* to have something in common with another: to have the means of passing from one to another: to have intercourse: to partake of The Communion. [L. *communico, communicatus*, from *communis*.]

**Communication,** kom-ūn-i-kā′shun, *n.* act of communicating: that which is communicated: intercourse: correspondence.

**Communicative,** kom-ūn′i-kā-tiv, *adj.* inclined to communicate or give information: unreserved. —*n.* **Commun′icativeness.** [ing knowledge.

**Communicatory,** kom-ūn′i-ka-tor-i, *adj.* impart-

**Communion,** kom-ūn′yun, *n.,* act of *communing:* mutual intercourse: fellowship: common possession: interchange of transactions: union in religious service; the body of people who so unite. —**The Communion,** the celebration of the Lord's Supper. [L. *communio*, from *communis*.]

**Communism,** kom′ū-nizm, *n.* a theory or condition of things, according to which private property should be abolished, and all things held in *common.* [principles of *communism.*

**Communist,** kom′ū-nist, *n.* one who holds the

**Community,** kom-ūn′i-ti, *n., common* possession or enjoyment: people having common rights, &c.; the public or people in general.

**Commutable,** kom-ūt′a-bl, *adj.* that may be commuted or exchanged.—*n.* **Commutabil′ity.**

**Commutation,** kom-ū-tā′shun, *n.* the act of *commuting:* change or exchange of one thing for another: the change of a penalty or rate from a greater to a less.

**Commutative,** kom-ūt′a-tiv, *adj.* relating to *exchange:* interchangeable.—*adv.* **Commut′atively.**

**Commute,** kom-ūt′, *v.t.* to *exchange:* to exchange a punishment for one less severe. [L. *commuto*, from *com*, with, and *muto*, to change.]

**Commutual,** kom-ūt′ū-al, *adj.* mutual.

**Compact,** kom-pakt′, *adj., fastened* or *packed together:* firm: close: brief.—*v.t.* to press closely together: to consolidate.—*advs.* **Compact′ly,** **Compact′edly.**—*n.* **Compact′edness.** [Fr.—L. *compactus*, pa.p. of *compingo*—*com*, together, and *pango*, to fasten, fix: akin to E. **Fang**.]

**Compact,** kom′pakt, *n.* a mutual *bargain* or *agreement:* a league, treaty, or union. [L. *compactum*—*compaciscor*, from *com*, with, and *paciscor*, to make a bargain; from root *pango*.]

**Compactness,** kom-pakt′nes, *n.* state of being compact: closeness.

**Companion,** kom-pan′yun, *n.* one who keeps company or frequently associates with another: an associate or partner.—*n.* **Compan′ionship.** [Fr. *compagnon*, from Low L. *companium*, a mess—L. *com*, with, and *panis*, bread.]

**Companionable,** kom-pan′yun-a-bl, *adj., fit to be a companion:* agreeable.—*adv.* **Compan′ionably.** [*companion.*

**Companionless,** kom-pan′yun-les, *adj., without a*

**Company,** kum′pa-ni, *n.* any assembly of persons: a number of persons associated together for trade, &c.: a society: a subdivision of a regiment: the crew of a ship: state of being a companion: fellowship: society.—*v.i.* to associate with. [Fr. *compagnie*. See **Companion**.]

**Comparable,** kom′par-a-bl, *adj.* that may be compared: being of equal regard.—*adv.* **Com′parably.**

**Comparative,** kom-par′a-tiv, *adj.* estimated by *comparing* with something else: not positive or absolute: (*gram.*) expressing more.—*adv.* **Compar′atively.**

**Compare,** kom-pār′, *v.t.* to set things together, to ascertain hcw far they agree or disagree: to liken or represent as similar: (*gram.*) to inflect an adjective.—*v.i.* to hold comparison. [Fr.—L. *comparo*, to match, from *com*, together, and *paro*, to make or esteem equal—*par*, equal.]

**Comparison,** kom-par′i-sun, *n.* the act of *comparing:* comparative estimate: a simile, or figure by which two things are compared: (*gram.*) the inflection of an adjective.

**Compartment,** kom-pärt′ment, *n.* a separate *part* or division of any inclosed space: a subdivision of a carriage. [Fr., from *compartir*, to divide —Lat. *com*, and *partire*, to part.]

**Compass,** kum′pas, *n.* a circuit or circle: space: limit: range: an instrument consisting of a magnetised needle, used to steer ships by, &c.—To *fetch* a **Compass**, to make a circuit, to go round: —*pl.* **Com′passes,** an instrument consisting of two movable legs, for describing circles, &c. [Fr. *compas*, a circle—Low L. *compassus*—L. *com*, together, and *passus*, a step, a way, a route; the mariner's compass goes round in a circle.]

**Compass,** kum′pas, *v.t.* to *pass* or *go round:* to surround or inclose: to besiege: to bring about or obtain: to contrive or plot.

**Compassion,** kom-pash′un, *n.* fellow-feeling, or sorrow for the sufferings of another: pity. [Fr. —L. *compassio*—*com*, with, and *patior, passus*, to suffer.]

**Compassionate,** kom-pash′un-āt, *adj.* inclined to pity or to have mercy upon: merciful.—*v.t.* to have compassion for: to have pity or mercy upon.—*adv.* **Compass′ionately.**—*n.* **Compass′ionateness.**

**Compatibility,** kom-pat-i-bil′it-i, *n.* the *being compatible:* suitability.

**Compatible,** kom-pat′i-bl, *adj., that can bear with:* that suits or agrees with.—*adv.* **Compat′ibly.** [Fr.—L. *com*, with, *patior*, to bear.]

**Compatriot,** kom-pā′tri-ot, *adj., of the same fatherland* or *country.*—*n.* one of the same country. [Fr.—L. *com*, with, and **Patriot**.]

**Compeer,** kom-pēr′, *n., one who is equal to another:* a companion: an associate. [L. *compar*—*com*, with, and **Peer**, from *par*, equal.]

**Compel,** kom-pel′, *v.t.* to *drive* or urge on *forcibly:* to oblige:—*pr.p.* compell′ing; *pa.p.* compelled′.—*adj.* **Compell′able.** [L. *com*, intensive, and *pello, pulsum*, to drive.]

**Compendious,** kom-pen′di-us, *adj.* short: comprehensive.—*adv.* **Compen′diously.**

**Compendium,** kom-pen′di-um, *n.* a shortening or abridgment: a book or treatise containing the substance of a larger one. [L. *compendium*, what is weighed together, or saved (opposed to *dispendium*)—*com*, together, and *pendo*, to weigh.]

**Compensate,** kom-pen′sāt or kom′pen-sāt, *v.t.* to reward suitably for service rendered: to make amends for loss sustained: to recompense: to counterbalance. [L. *com*, intensive, and *penso*, to weigh, freq.-of *pendo*, to weigh.]

**Compensation**, kom-pen-sā'shun, *n*. act of *compensating*: reward for service : amends for loss sustained.

**Compensatory**, kom-pen'sa-tor-i, *adj*. serving for *compensation* : making amends.

**Compete**, kom-pēt', *v.i.* to *seek* or *strive* with others for something : to contend for a prize. [L. *competo*—*com*, together, and *peto*, to seek.]

**Competence**, kom'pe-tens, **Competency**, kom'pe-ten-si, *n*. fitness : sufficiency : legal power or capacity.

**Competent**, kom'pe-tent, *adj*., *suitable* : sufficient : fit : belonging.—*adv*. **Com'petently**. [Fr.—L. *competo*, to strive after together, to agree—*com*, with, and *peto*, to seek.]

**Competition**, kom-pe-tish'un, *n*. the act of *competing* : common strife for the same object.

**Competitive**, kom-pet'i-tiv, *adj*. pertaining to or producing *competition*.

**Competitor**, kom-pet'i-tor, *n*. one who *competes* : a rival or opponent.

**Compilation**, kom-pil-ā'shun, *n*. the act of *compiling*, or the thing compiled : a literary work composed by gathering the materials from various authors.

**Compile**, kom-pīl', *v.t.* to write or compose by collecting the materials from other books : to draw up or collect.—*n*. **Compil'er**. [Fr.—L. *compilo*—*com*, together, and *pilo*, to plunder.]

**Complacence**, kom-plā'sens, **Complacency**, kom-plā'sen-si, *n*. pleasure : satisfaction : civility.

**Complacent**, kom-plā'sent, *adj*. shewing satisfaction : pleased : gratified.—*adv*. **Compla'cently**. [L. *complacens*—*com*, intensive, and *placeo*, to please.]

**Complain**, kom-plān', *v.i.* to express grief, pain, censure : to murmur or express a sense of injury : to accuse. [Fr. *complaindre*—Low L. *complangere*—*com*, intensive, and *plango*, to bewail : (*lit*.) to beat (the breast), Gr. *plēssō*, to strike.]

**Complainant**, kom-plān'ant, *n*. one who *complains* : (*law*) one who raises a suit, a plaintiff.

**Complaint**, kom-plānt', *n*. a *complaining* : an expression of grief : a representation of pains or injuries : a finding fault : the thing complained of.

**Complaisance**, kom'plā-zans or kom-plā-zans', *n*. care or desire to please : an obliging civility. [Fr.]

**Complaisant**, kom'plā-zant or kom-plā-zant', *adj*. desirous of pleasing : obliging.—*adv*. **Complai'santly** or **Complaisant'ly**. [Fr.—*complaire*—L. *complaceo*.]

**Complement**, kom'ple-ment, *n*. that which *completes* or fills up : full number or quantity. [L. *complementum*—*com*, and *pleo*.]

**Complemental**, kom-ple-ment'al, **Complementary**, kom-ple-ment'ar-i, *adj*., *filling up* : supplying a deficiency.

**Complete**, kom-plēt', *v.t.* to *fill up*, finish, or perfect : to accomplish. [L. *compleo*, *completum*, to fill up—*com*, intensive, and *pleo*, to fill.]

**Complete**, kom-plēt', *adj*., *filled up* : free from deficiency : perfect : finished.—*adv*. **Complete'ly**.—*n*. **Complete'ness**.

**Completion**, kom-plē'shun, *n*. the act or state of being *complete* : fulfilment.

**Complex**, kom'pleks, *adj*. composed of more than one, or of many parts : not simple : intricate : difficult.—*adv*. **Com'plexly**.—*n*. **Com'plexness**. [L. *complex*—*com*, together, and root of *plico*, to fold. See **Complicate**.]

**Complexion**, kom-plek'shun, *n*. colour or look of

the skin, esp. of the face : general appearance, temperament, or texture. [Fr.—L. *complexio*, a combination, physical structure of body—*com plector*, *complexus*, to embrace—*plectere*, to plait.]     [on or pertaining to *complexion*.

**Complexional**, kom-plek'shun-al, *adj*. depending

**Complexioned**, kom-plek'shund, *adj*. having a *complexion*, or a certain temperament or state.

**Complexity**, kom-plek'si-ti, *n*. state of being *complex*.               [*ment*.

**Compliance**, kom-plī'ans, *n*. a yielding : agreement.

**Compliant**, kom-plī'ant, *adj*. yielding : civil.—*adv*. **Compli'antly**.             [*plicated*.

**Complicacy**, kom'pli-ka-si, *n*. state of being *complicated*.

**Complicate**, kom'pli-kāt, *v.t.* to *twist* or *plait together* : to render complex : to entangle. [L. *com*, together, and *plico*, *plicatum*, to fold. See **Complex**.]        [blending or entanglement.

**Complication**, kom-pli-kā'shun, *n*. an intricate

**Complicity**, kom-plis'i-ti, *n*. state or condition of being an *accomplice*.

**Compliment**, kom'pli-ment, *n*. an expression of regard : delicate flattery. [Fr. *compliment*, from root of **Comply**. **Complement** is etymologically the same word, but direct from the Lat.]

**Compliment**, kom'pli-ment, *v.t.* to pay a compliment to : to express respect for : to praise : to flatter.            [ing civility or praise.

**Complimentary**, kom-pli-ment'ar-i, *adj*. conveying civility or praise.

**Complot**, kom-plot', *v.i.* to plot together, to conspire :—*pr.p.* complott'ing ; *pa.p.* complott'ed.

**Comply**, kom-plī', *v.i.* to yield to the wishes of another : to agree :—*pr.p.* comply'ing ; *pa.t.* and *pa.p.* complied'. [O. Fr. *complir*, It. *complire*, to fulfil, to suit, to offer courtesies—Lat. *complere*, to fulfil or complete.]

**Component**, kom-pō'nent, *adj*. making up or composing : forming one of the elements of a compound.—*n*. one of the elements of a compound. [L. *com*, together, and *pono*, to place.]

**Comport**, kom-pōrt', *v.i.* to agree, accord, suit.—*v.t.* to bear one's self, to behave. [L. *com*, together, and *porto*, to carry.]         [behaviour.

**Comportment**, kom-pōrt'ment, *n*. deportment.

**Compose**, kom-pōz', *v.t.* to form by putting two or more parts or things together : to place in order : to set at rest : to soothe : to place types in order for printing : to originate or become the author of, as a book. [Fr. *composer*, from L. *cum*, and Fr. *poser*, which is from L. *pausare*, to cease, to rest.]

**Composed**, kom-pōzd', *adj*. settled, quiet, calm.—*adv*. **Compos'edly**.—*n*. **Compos'edness**.

**Composer**, kom-pōz'ér, *n*. one who *composes* or adjusts a thing : a writer, an author, esp. of a piece of music.

**Composite**, kom'poz-it, *adj*., *composed* of two or more distinct parts : (*arch*.) a blending of the Ionic and the Corinthian orders. [L. *compositus*, pa.p. of *componere*, to put together.]

**Composition**, kom-pō-zish'un, *n*. the act of *putting together* : the thing composed, as a work in literature, music, or painting : a coming together or agreement : an agreement whereby payment of part of a debt is taken for the whole.

**Compositor**, kom-poz'i-tor, *n*. one who puts together or sets up types for printing.

**Compost**, kom'pōst, *n*. a mixture for manure : a kind of plaster.       [session : tranquillity.

**Composure**, kom-pō'zhūr, *n*. calmness : self-possession.

**Compound**, kom-pownd', *v.t.* to mix or combine : to settle or adjust by agreement.—*v.i.* to agree, or come to terms : to bargain in the lump. [L. *compono*. See **Composite**.]

**Compound,** kom'pownd, *adj.* mixed or *composed* of a number of parts : not simple.—*n.* a mass made up of a number of parts.

**Comprehend,** kom-pre-hend', *v.t.* to seize or take up with the mind, to understand : to comprise or include. [L. *com*, with, and *prehendo*, from *præ*, before, and an old word *hendo* = Gr. *chandanō*, to hold, comprise ; akin to E. **Get.**]

**Comprehensible,** kom-pre-hen'si-bl, *adj.* capable of being understood.—*adv.* **Comprehen'sibly.**—*ns.* **Comprehensibil'ity, Comprehen'sibleness.**

**Comprehension,** kom-pre-hen'shun, *n.* the act or quality of *comprehending* : power of the mind to understand : (*logic*) the intension of a term or the sum of the qualities implied in the term.

**Comprehensive,** kom-pre-hen'siv, *adj.* having the quality or power of *comprehending* much : extensive : full.—*adv.* **Comprehen'sively.**—*n.* **Comprehen'siveness.**

**Compress,** kom-pres', *v.t.* to *press together :* to force into a narrower space : to condense. [L. *com*, together, and *pressare*, to press—*premo, pressus*, to press.]

**Compress,** kom'pres, *n.* folds of linen, used in surgery to make due *pressure* on any part.

**Compressibility,** kom-pres'i-bil-i-ti, *n.* the property that bodies have of being reduced in bulk by *pressure.*

**Compressible,** kom-pres'i-bl, *adj.* that may be *compressed.*

**Compression,** kom-presh'un, *n.* act of *compressing :* state of being compressed.

**Compressive,** kom-pres'iv, *adj.* able to compress.

**Comprisal,** kom-prīz'al, *n.* the act of *comprising.*

**Comprise,** kom-prīz', *v.t.* to contain, include. [Fr. *compris*, pa.p. of *comprendre*—L. *comprehendere.* See **Comprehend.**]

**Compromise,** kom'prō-mīz, *n.* a settlement of differences by *mutual promise* or concession.—*v.t.* to settle by mutual agreement and concession : to pledge : to involve or bring into question. [Fr. *compromis*—L. *com*, together, and *promitto*, to promise.]

**Comptroll, Comptroller.** See under **Control.**

**Compulsion,** kom-pul'shun, *n.* the act of *compelling :* force : necessity : violence. [See **Compel.**]

**Compulsive,** kom-pul'siv, **Compulsory,** kom-pul'sor-i, *adj.* having power to *compel :* forcing.—*advs.* **Compul'sively, Compul'sorily.**

**Compunction,** kom-pungk'shun, *n.* uneasiness of conscience : remorse. [O. Fr.—L. *compunctio*—*com*, intensive, and *pungo, punctus*, to prick.]

**Compunctious,** kom-pungk'shus, *adj.* feeling or causing *compunction :* repentant : remorseful.

**Computable,** kom-pūt'a-bl, *adj.* that may be *computed* or calculated.

**Computation,** kom-pūt-ā'shun, *n.* act of *computing :* the sum or quantity computed : estimate.

**Compute,** kom-pūt', *v.t.* to calculate : to number. [L. *computo*, from *com*, together, and *puto*, to reckon.]

**Comrade,** kom'rād, *n.* a companion. [Sp. *camarada*, a room-full, a chamber-mate—L. *camera*, a chamber.]

**Con,** kon, a contraction of L. *contra*, against, as in **Pro and con**, for and against.

**Con,** kon, *v.t.* to study carefully : to commit to memory :—*pr.p.* conn'ing ; *pa.p.* conned'. [A.S. *cunnian*, to test, to try to know—from *cunnan*, to know.]

**Concatenate,** kon-kat'e-nāt, *v.t.* to *chain* or *link together :* to connect in a series. [L. *con*, together, and *catena*, a chain.]

**Concatenation,** kon-kat-e-nā'shun, *n.* a series of links united : a series of things depending on each other.

**Concave,** kon'kāv, *adj.* curved, vaulted, or arched, applied to the inner side of any curved line or rounded body, and opposed to *convex*, which is applied to the outside.—*n.* a hollow : an arch or vault. [L. *concavus*, from *con*, intensive, and *cavus*, hollow. See **Cave.**]

**Concavity,** kon-kav'i-ti, *n.* the inner surface of a concave or hollow body.

**Conceal,** kon-sēl', *v.t.* to *hide completely* or *carefully :* to keep secret : to disguise : to keep from telling. [L. *concelo*, from *con*, intens., and *celo*, to hide : akin to A.S. *helan*, to hide.]

**Concealable,** kon-sēl'a-bl, *adj.* that may be *concealed.*

**Concealment,** kon-sēl'ment, *n.* act of *concealing :* secrecy : disguise : hiding-place.

**Concede,** kon-sēd', *v.t.* to *cede* or give up : to quit : to surrender : to admit, to grant.—*v.i.* to admit or grant. [L. *concedo*, from *con*, sig. completeness, and *cedo*, to go, to yield.]

**Conceit,** kon-sēt', *n.* over-estimate of one's self : too favourable opinion of one's own good qualities : a pleasant, fantastical, or affected notion.—**Out of conceit with**, no longer fond of. [Through a Fr. form *conceit*, from L. *conceptus*, pa.p. of *concipio.*]

**Conceited,** kon-sēt'ed, *adj.* having a high opinion of one's self : egotistical.—*adv.* **Conceit'edly.**—*n.* **Conceit'edness.**

**Conceivable,** kon-sēv'a-bl, *adj.* that may be *conceived*, understood, or believed.—*adv.* **Conceiv'ably.**—*n.* **Conceiv'ableness.**

**Conceive,** kon-sēv', *v.t.* to receive into, and form in the womb : to form in the mind : to imagine or think : to understand.—*v.i.* to become pregnant : to think. [O. Fr. *concever*—L. *concipio, conceptum*, from *con*, and *capio*, to take.]

**Concentrate,** kon-sen'trāt, *v.t.* to bring into a closer union, or a narrower compass : to condense. [A lengthened form of **Concentre.**]

**Concentration,** kon-sen-trā'shun, *n.* act of *concentrating :* condensation.

**Concentrative,** kon-sen'tra-tiv, *adj.* tending to concentrate.

**Concentre,** kon-sent'ér, *v.i.* to tend to or meet *in a common centre.*—*v.t.* to bring or direct to a common centre or point :—*pr.p.* concent'ring ; *pa.p.* concent'red or concent'ered. [Fr. *concentrer*—L. *con*, with, and *centrum*, the **Centre.**]

**Concentric,** kon-sen'trik, **Concentrical,** kon-sen'trik-al, *adj.* having a common centre.

**Concept,** kon'sept, *n.* a thing conceived, a notion.

**Conception,** kon-sep'shun, *n.* the act of *conceiving :* the thing conceived : the formation in the mind of an image or idea : a notion.

**Conceptualism,** kon-sep'tū-al-izm, *n.* the doctrine in philosophy that general properties can be conceived in the mind apart from any concrete embodiment.

**Concern,** kon-sérn', *v.t.* to relate or belong to : to affect or interest : to make uneasy.—*n.* that which concerns or belongs to one : interest : regard : anxiety : a business or those connected with it.—*n.* **Concern'ment.** [Fr.—L. *concerno*, from *con*, together, and *cerno*, to sift, to see.]

**Concerned,** kon-sérnd', *adj.* having connection with : interested : anxious.—*adv.* **Concern'edly.**—*n.* **Concern'edness.**

**Concerning,** kon-sérn'ing, *prep.* regarding : pertaining to. [*Pr.p.* of **Concern.**]

**Concert,** kon-sért', *v.t.* to frame or devise together : to arrange, adjust. [Fr. *concerter*—

*con*, together, *certare*, to contend, vie with: acc. to Skeat, from L. *consertus*, joined together.]

**Concert**, kon'sėrt, *n.* union or agreement in any undertaking: harmony: musical harmony: a musical entertainment. [Fr.]

**Concertina**, kon-sėr-tē'na, *n.* a musical instrument, on the principle of the accordion.

**Concerto**, kon-sér'tō, *n.* a piece of music for a *concert.* [It.] [thing conceded: a grant.

**Concession**, kon-sesh'un, *n.* act of *conceding:* the

**Concessive**, kon-ses'iv, *adj.* implying *concession.*

**Concessory**, kon-ses'or-i, *adj.* yielding.

**Conch**, kongk, *n.* a marine *shell.* [L. *concha*—Gr. *kongchē;* Sans. *cankha*, a shell; conn. with **Cockle.**]

**Conchiferous**, kong-kif'ėr-us, *adj., having a shell.* [L. *concha*, and *fero*, to bear.]

**Conchoidal**, kong-koid'al, *adj., shell-like,* applied to the fracture of a mineral. [Gr. *kongchē*, and *eidos*, form.] [*conchology.*

**Conchologist**, kong-kol'o-jist, *n.* one versed in

**Conchology**, kong-kol'o-ji, *n.* the science of shells and of the animals inhabiting them. [Gr. *kong-chē*, and *logos*, a discourse.]

**Conciliate**, kon-sil'i-āt, *v.t.* to gain or win over: to gain the love or good-will of such as have been indifferent or hostile. [L. *concilio, conciliatus,* to bring together—*concilium.* See **Council.**]

**Conciliation**, kon-sil-i-ā'shun, *n.* act of *conciliating.*—*n.* **Conciliator**, kon-sil'i-ā-tor.—*adj.* **Conciliatory**, kon-sil'i-a-tor-i.

**Concise**, kon-sīs', *adj., cut short:* brief.—*adv.* **Concise'ly.**—*n.* **Concise'ness.** [Fr.—L. *concido, concisus,* from *con*, and *cædo*, to cut.]

**Concision**, kon-sizh'un, *n.* (*B.*) circumcision: a faction.

**Conclave**, kon'klāv, *n.* the room in which cardinals meet to elect a pope: the body of cardinals: any close assembly. [L. *conclave*, from *con*, together, and *clavis*, a key.]

**Conclude**, kon-klōōd', *v.t.* to close: to end.—*v.i.* to end: to infer: to form a final judgment. [L. *concludo, conclusus*—*con*, together, and *claudo*, to shut.]

**Conclusion**, kon-klōō'zhun, *n.* act of *concluding:* the end, close, or last part: inference: judgment. [L. *conclusio.*]

**Conclusive**, kon-klōōs'iv, *adj.* final: convincing.—*adv.* **Conclus'ively.**—*n.* **Conclus'iveness.**

**Concoct**, kon-kokt', *v.t.* (*lit.*) to cook or boil *together:* to digest: to prepare or mature. [L. *concoquo, concoctus*—*con*, together, and *coquo*, to cook, to boil.] [ripening: preparation.

**Concoction**, kon-kok'shun, *n.* act of *concocting:*

**Concomitance**, kon-kom'i-tans, **Concomitancy**, kon-kom'i-tan-si, *n.* state of being concomitant.

**Concomitant**, kon-kom'i-tant, *adj., accompanying* or *going along with:* conjoined with.—*n.* he or that which accompanies.—*adv.* **Concom'itantly.** [L. *con*, with, and *comitans*, pr.p. of *comitor*, to accompany—*comes*, a companion.]

**Concord**, kong'kord or kon'-, *n.* state of being of *the same heart* or mind: union: harmony. [Fr. *concorde*—L. *concordia*—*concors*, of the same heart, from *con*, together, and *cor, cordis*, the heart.]

**Concordance**, kon-kord'ans, *n.* agreement: an index or dictionary of the leading words or passages of the Bible, or of any author.

**Concordant**, kon-kord'ant, *adj.* harmonious: united.—*adv.* **Concord'antly.** [L. *concordans*, pr.p. of *concordo*—*concors*, agreeing.]

**Concordat**, kon-kord'at, *n.* an agreement or compact, especially between a temporal sovereign

and the pope. [Fr.—It. *concordato*—L. *concordo*, to agree.]

**Concourse**, kong'kōrs, *n.* an assembly of persons *running* or drawn *together.* [Fr.—L. *concursus.*]

**Concrescence**, kon-kres'ens, *n.* a *growing together.*

**Concrete**, kong'krēt, or kon'-, *adj.* formed into one mass: the opposite of *abstract*, and denoting a particular thing.—*n.* a mass formed by parts growing or sticking together: a mixture of lime, sand, pebbles, &c., used in building.—*adv.* **Concrete'ly.**—*n.* **Concrete'ness.** [L. *concretus*—*con*, together, *cresco, cretum,* to grow.]

**Concrete**, kon-krēt', *v.i.* to unite into a solid mass.

**Concretion**, kon-krē'shun, *n.* a mass concreted: a lump or growth which forms in certain parts of the body, as calculi, &c.

**Concretive**, kon-krēt'iv, *adj., causing* or having power to *concrete.*

**Concubinage**, kon-kū'bin-āj, *n.* state of living together as man and wife without being married.

**Concubine**, kong'kū-bīn, *n.* a woman who cohabits or lives with a man without being married. [Fr.—L. *concubina*—*con*, together, *cubo*, to lie down.]

**Concupiscence**, kon-kū'pis-ens, *n., excessive* or irregular *desire* for unlawful pleasure: lust.—*adj.* **Concu'piscent.** [Fr.—L. *concupiscentia* —*concupisco*—*con*, intensive, *cupio*, to desire.]

**Concur**, kon-kur', *v.i.* to *run together:* to meet in one point: to act together: to agree: to assent to :—*pr.p.* concurr'ing ; *pa.p.* concurred'. [L. *concurro*, from *con*, together, and *curro, cursum*, to run.] [assent.

**Concurrence**, kon-kur'ens, *n.* union : joint action :

**Concurrent**, kon-kur'ent, *adj.* coming, acting, or existing together: united: accompanying.—*adv.* **Concurr'ently.**

**Concussion**, kon-kush'un, *n.* state of being shaken: a violent shock caused by the sudden contact of two bodies: any undue pressure or force exerted upon any one. [L. *concussio*—*concutio*—*con*, intensive, and *quatio*, to shake.]

**Concussive**, kon-kus'iv, *adj.* having the power or quality of *shaking* or compelling.

**Condemn**, kon-dem', *v.t.* to pronounce guilty: to censure or blame: to sentence to punishment: to pronounce unfit for use. [L. *condemno*, from *con*, intensive, and *damno*, to damn. See **Damn.**]

**Condemnable**, kon-dem'na-bl, *adj.* blamable.

**Condemnation**, kon-dem-nā'shun, *n.* state of being condemned: blame: punishment.

**Condemnatory**, kon-dem'na-tor-i, *adj., containing* or implying *condemnation.* [compressed.

**Condensable**, kon-dens'a-bl, *adj.* capable of being

**Condensation**, kon-den-sā'shun, *n.* act of *condensing.*

**Condense**, kon-dens', *v.t.* to compress, or reduce by pressure into smaller compass.—*v.i.* to grow dense. [L. *condenso*—*con*, intensive, *denso*, to make dense. See **Dense.**]

**Condenser**, kon-dens'ėr, *n.* an apparatus for reducing vapours to a liquid form : an appliance for collecting or condensing electricity.

**Condescend**, kon-de-send', *v.i.* to descend willingly from a superior position: to act kindly to inferiors: to deign: to lower one's self. [L. *con*, intensive, and *descendo*, to descend.]

**Condescending**, kon-de-send'ing, *adj.* yielding to inferiors: courteous: obliging.—*adv.* **Condescend'ingly.**

**Condescension**, kon-de-sen'shun, *n.* kindness to inferiors: courtesy.

**Condign**, kon-dīn', *adj.* well merited: adequate (generally said of punishment).—*adv.* **Con-**

**dign'ly.**—*n.* **Condign'ness.** [L. *condignus*—*con*, wholly, *dignus*, worthy.]

**Condiment,** kon'di-ment, *n.* that which is put along with something else to *preserve* or pickle it : seasoning : sauce. [L. *condimentum*—*condio*, to preserve, to pickle.]

**Condition,** kon-dish'un, *n.* state in which things exist : a particular manner of being : quality : rank : temper : a term of a contract : proposal : arrangement.—*v.i.* to make terms.—*v.t.* to agree upon. [L. *conditio*—*condere*, to put together.]

**Conditional,** kon-dish'un-al, *adj.* depending on stipulations or *conditions :* not absolute.—*adv.* **Condi'tionally.**

**Conditioned,** kon-dish'und, *adj.* having a certain *condition,* state, or quality : subject to limitations—the opp. of *absolute.*

**Condole,** kon-dōl', *v.i.* to grieve with another : to sympathise in sorrow. [L. *con*, with, and *doleo*, to grieve.]

**Condolement,** kon-dōl'ment, **Condolence,** kon-dōl'ens, *n.* expression of grief for another's sorrow. [*condonatio.*]

**Condonation,** kon-don-ā'shun, *n., forgiveness.* [L.

**Condone,** kon-dōn', *v.t.* to *forgive.* [L. *con, dono,* to give. See **Donation.**]

**Condor,** kon'dor, *n.* a large vulture found among the Andes of S. America. [Sp. *condor,* from Peruvian *cuntur.*]

**Conduce,** kon-dūs', *v.i.* to *lead* or tend to some end : to contribute. [L. *con,* together, and *duco, ductus,* to lead.]

**Conducible,** kon-dūs'i-bl, **Conducive,** kon-dūs'iv, *adj., leading* or tending : having power to promote.—*advs.* **Conduc'ibly, Conduc'ively.**—*ns.* **Conduc'ibleness, Conduc'iveness.**

**Conduct,** kon-dukt', *v.t.* to *lead* or guide : to direct : to manage : to behave : (*electricity*) to carry or transmit. [See **Conduce.**]

**Conduct,** kon'dukt, *n.* act or method of *leading* or managing : guidance : management : behaviour. [See **Conduce.**]

**Conductible,** kon-dukt'i-bl, *adj.* capable of being *conducted* or transmitted.—*n.* **Conductibil'ity.**

**Conduction,** kon-duk'shun, *n.* act or property of *conducting* or transmitting : transmission by a conductor, as heat.

**Conductive,** kon-dukt'iv, *adj.* having the quality or power of *conducting* or transmitting.

**Conductivity,** kon-duk-tiv'i-ti, *n.* a power that bodies have of transmitting heat and electricity.

**Conductor,** kon-dukt'or, *n.* the person or thing that *conducts :* a leader : a manager : that which has the property of transmitting electricity, heat, &c.—*fem.* **Conduct'ress.**

**Conduit,** kon'dit or kun'-, *n.* a channel or pipe to *lead* or convey water, &c. [Fr. *conduit*—L. *conductus*—*conduco,* to lead.]

**Cone,** kōn, *n.* a solid *pointed* figure with a circular base, as a sugar-loaf : fruit shaped like a cone, as that of the pine, fir, &c. [Fr. *cone*—L. *conus* —Gr. *kōnos,* a peak, a peg ; from a root *ka,* to sharpen ; allied to E. *hone.*]

**Coney.** See **Cony.**

**Confabulate,** kon-fab'ū-lāt, *v.i.* to *talk familiarly together :* to chat.—*n.* **Confabula'tion.** [L. *con,* together, and *fabulor, fabulatus,* to talk—*fabula,* the thing spoken about—*fari,* akin to Gr. *phaō,* and *phēmi,* to speak.]

**Confect,** kon'fekt, **Confection,** kon-fek'shun, *n.* fruit, &c. prepared with sugar : a sweetmeat : a comfit. [L. *conficio, confectus,* to make up together—*con,* together, *facio,* to make.]

**Confectioner,** kon-fek'shun-èr, (*B.*) **Confec'tionary,** *n.* one who makes or sells *confections.*

**Confectionery,** kon-fek'shun-èr-i, *n.* sweetmeats in general : a place for making or selling sweetmeats.

**Confederacy,** kon-fed'ėr-a-si, *n* a league or mutual engagement : persons or states united by a league.

**Confederate,** kon-fed'ėr-āt, *adj., leagued together:* allied.—*n.* one united in a league : an ally : an accomplice.—*v.i.* and *v.t.* to league together or join in a league. [L. *confœderatus,* pa.p. of *confœdero*—*con,* together, *fœdus, fœderis,* a league.]

**Confederation,** kon-fed-ėr-ā'shun, *n.* a league : alliance, especially of princes, states, &c.

**Confer,** kon-fėr', *v.t.* to give or bestow.—*v.i.* to talk or consult together :—*pr.p.* conferr'ing ; *pa.p.* conferred'. [Fr.—L. *confero*—*con,* together, and *fero,* to bring.]

**Conference,** kon'fėr-ens, *n.* an appointed meeting for instruction or discussion.

**Confess,** kon-fes', *v.t.* to *acknowledge fully,* especially something wrong : to own or admit : to make known, as sins to a priest : to hear a confession, as a priest.—*v.i.* to make confession.—*adv.* **Confess'edly.** [Fr. *confesser*—L. *confiteor, confessus*—*con,* sig. completeness, and *fateor*—*fari,* to speak, akin to Gr. *phēmi,* to speak.]

**Confession,** kon-fesh'un, *n.* acknowledgment of a crime or fault : avowal : a statement of one's religious belief : acknowledgment of sin to a priest.

**Confessional,** kon-fesh'un-al, *n.* the seat or inclosed recess where a priest hears *confessions.*

**Confessor,** kon-fes'or, *n.* one who professes the Christian faith : in the R. Catholic Church, a priest who hears *confessions* and grants absolution.

**Confidant,** kon'fi-dant or kon-fi-dant', *n.* one *confided in* or intrusted with secrets : a bosomfriend.—*fem.* **Con'fidante.** [O. Fr., Fr. *confident.*]

**Confide,** kon-fīd', *v.i.* to *trust wholly* or have *faith* in : to rely.—*v.t.* to intrust, or commit to the charge of. [L. *confido*—*con,* sig. completeness, and *fido,* to trust.]

**Confidence,** kon'fi-dens, *n.* firm trust or belief : self-reliance : firmness : boldness.

**Confident,** kon'fi-dent, *adj.* trusting firmly : having full belief : positive : bold.—*adv.* **Con'fidently.**

**Confidential,** kon-fi-den'shal, *adj.* (given) in confidence : admitted to confidence : private.—*adv.* **Confiden'tially.**

**Configuration,** kon-fig-ū-rā'shun, *n.* external *figure* or shape : relative position or aspect, as of planets. [L. *configuratio*—*con,* together, and *figuro,* to form. See **Figure.**]

**Confinable,** kon-fīn'a-bl, *adj.* that may be confined.

**Confine,** kon-fīn', *v.t.* to limit, inclose, imprison. [Fr. *confiner,* to border on, to confine—L. *confinis,* having a common boundary, bordering upon—*con,* with, *finis,* the end or boundary.]

**Confine,** kon'fīn, *n.* border, boundary, or limit—generally used in plural.

**Confinement,** kon-fīn'ment, *n.* state of being shut up : restraint from going abroad by sickness, and esp. of women in childbirth : seclusion.

**Confirm,** kon-fėrm', *v.t.* to strengthen : to fix or establish : to assure : to admit to full communion in the Episcopal Church.—*adj.* **Confirm'able.** [Fr.—L. *confirmo*—*con,* intensive, and root of **Firm.**]

**Confirmation,** kon-fėr-mā'shun, *n.* a making firm

or sure: convincing proof: the rite by which persons are admitted to full communion in the Episcopal Church.                          [firm.

**Confirmative**, kon-ferm'a-tiv, *adj.* tending to con-

**Confirmatory**, kon-ferm'a-tor-i, *adj.* giving additional strength to.

**Confiscate**, kon-fis'kāt or kon'-, *v.t.* to appropriate to the state, as a penalty. [L. *confisco—con*, and *fiscus*, a basket, the public treasury.]

**Confiscate**, kon-fis'kāt or kon'fis-kāt, *adj.* forfeited to the public treasury.—*adj.* **Confis'cable**.—*n.* **Confisca'tion**.

**Confiscator**, kon'fis-kā-tor, *n.* one who confiscates.

**Confiscatory**, kon-fis'ka-tor-i, *adj.* consigning to *confiscation*.

**Conflagration**, kon-fla-grā'shun, *n.* a *great burning* or *fire*. [L. *conflagratio—con*, intensive, and *flagro*, to burn. See **Flagrant**.]

**Conflict**, kon-flikt', *v.i.* to be in opposition: to fight: to contest. [L. *confligo, conflictus*, from *con*, together, and *fligo*, to dash.]

**Conflict**, kon'flikt, *n.* violent collision: a struggle or contest: agony.

**Confluence**, kon'floo-ens, *n.* a *flowing together*: the place of meeting, as of rivers: a concourse.

**Confluent**, kon'floo-ent, *adj., flowing together*: uniting. [L. *confluens*, pr.p. of *confluo, confluxus*, from *con*, together, and *fluo*, to flow.]

**Conflux**, kon'fluks, *n.* a flowing together.

**Conform**, kon-form', *v.t.* to make like or of the same *form with*: to adapt.—*v.z.* to be of the same form: to comply with: to obey. [L. *conformo—con*, with, and *formo—forma*, form.]

**Conformable**, kon-form'a-bl, *adj.* corresponding in *form*: suitable: compliant.—*adv.* **Conform'ably**.

**Conformation**, kon-for-mā'shun, *n.* the manner in which a body is *formed*: shape or structure.

**Conformer**, kon-form'er, **Conformist**, kon-form'-ist, *n.* one who *conforms*, especially with the worship of the Established Church.

**Conformity**, kon-form'i-ti, *n.* likeness: compliance with: consistency.

**Confound**, kon-fownd', *v.t.* to mingle so as to make the parts indistinguishable: to throw into disorder: to perplex: to astonish. [Fr. *confondre*—L. *confundo, confusus—con*, together, and *fundo*, to pour.]

**Confraternity**, kon-fra-ter'ni-ti, *n.* Same as **Fraternity**. [L. *con*, intensive, and **Fraternity**.]

**Confront**, kon-frunt', *v.t.* to stand *front to front*: to face: to oppose: to compare. [Fr. *confronter*—Low L. *confrontare*, from L. *con*, together, and *frons*, the front. See **Front**.]

**Confucian**, kon-fū'shyan, *adj.* of or belonging to *Confucius*, the Chinese philosopher.

**Confuse**, kon-fūz', *v.t.* to *pour* or mix *together* so that things cannot be distinguished: to throw into disorder: to perplex. [A doublet of **Confound**.]

**Confusedly**, kon-fūz'ed-li, *adv.* in a confused manner.                                   [overthrow.

**Confusion**, kon-fū'zhun, *n.* disorder: shame:

**Confute**, kon-fūt', *v.t.* to prove to be false: to repress: to disprove.—*adj.* **Confut'able**.—*n.* **Confuta'tion**. [L. *confuto*, to cool boiling water by pouring in cold—*con*, intensive, and *futis*, a water-vessel, from *fundo*, to pour. See **Futile**.]

**Congé**, kon'jē (formerly written **Congie**), *n.* leave of absence: farewell: parting ceremony.—*v.i.* to take leave: to bow or courtesy. [Fr. (Prov. *comjat*), from L. *commeatus*, a going back and forth, leave of absence—*com*, intensive, and *meo*, to go.]

**Congeal**, kon-jēl', *v.t.* to *cause to freeze*: to change from fluid to solid by cold: to fix, as by cold.—*v.i.* to pass from fluid to solid as by cold.—*adj.* **Congeal'able**. [L. *congelo*, from *con*, and *gelu*, frost.]

**Congealment**, kon-jēl'ment, **Congelation**, kon-jēl-ā'shun, *n.* act or process of *congealing*.

**Congener**, kon'je-ner or kon-jē'ner, *n.* a person or thing of the *same kind* or nature. [L.—*con*, with, and *genus, generis*, Gr. *genos*, kind.]

**Congenial**, kon-jē'ni-al, *adj.* of the *same genius*, spirit, or tastes: kindred, sympathetic: suitable. —*adv.* **Conge'nially**.—*n.* **Congenial'ity**. [L. *con*, with, *genialis*, genial. See **Genial**.]

**Congenital**, kon-jen'i-tal, *adj., begotten* or *born with*, said of diseases or deformities dating from birth. [L. *congenitus*, from *con*, together, *gigno, genitus*, to beget.]                         [*gonggros*.

**Conger**, kong'ger, *n.* a large sea-eel. [L.; Gr.

**Congeries**, kon-jē'ri-ēz, *n.* a collection of particles or small bodies in one mass. [L.—*con*, together, *gero, gestus*, to bring.]

**Congested**, kon-jest'ed, *adj.* affected with an unnatural accumulation of blood.

**Congestion**, kon-jest'yun, *n.* an accumulation of blood in any part of the body: fullness. [L. *congestio*.]                                    [to *congestion*.

**Congestive**, kon-jest'iv, *adj.* indicating or tending

**Conglobate**, kon-glōb'āt, *adj.* formed *together* into a *globe* or ball.—*v.t.* to form into a globe or ball. —*n.* **Congloba'tion**. [L. *con*, together, and *globo, globatus—globus*, a ball, globe. See **Globe**.]

**Conglobulate**, kon-glob'ū-lāt, *v.i.* to gather *into a globule* or small globe. [L. *con*, and *globulus*, dim. of *globus*.]

**Conglomerate**, kon-glom'er-āt, *adj.* gathered *into a clew* or mass.—*v.t.* to gather into a ball.—*n.* a rock composed of pebbles cemented together. [L. *conglomeratus*, pa.p. of *conglomero—con*, together, and *glomus, glomeris*, a clew, akin to *globus*.]                              [being conglomerated.

**Conglomeration**, kon-glom-er-ā'shun, *n.* state of

**Conglutinant**, kon-gloo'tin-ant, *adj.* serving to *glue* or unite: healing.

**Conglutinate**, kon-gloo'tin-āt, *v.t.* to *glue together*: to heal by uniting.—*v.i.* to unite or grow together. [L. *conglutino, conglutinatus—con*, together, and *gluten*, glue. See **Glue**.]

**Conglutination**, kon-gloo-tin-ā'shun, *n.* a joining by means of some sticky substance: healing.

**Conglutinative**, kon-gloo'tin-ā-tiv, *adj.* having power to conglutinate.                          [Chinese.]

**Congou**, kong'goo, *n.* a kind of black tea.

**Congratulate**, kon-grat'ū-lāt, *v.t.* to *wish much joy* to on any fortunate event. [L. *congratulor, congratulatus—con*, intensive, and *gratulor—gratus*, pleasing.]

**Congratulation**, kon-grat-ū-lā'shun, *n.* expression of sympathy or joy on account of good-fortune. —*adj.* **Congrat'ulatory**.

**Congregate**, kong'gre-gāt, *v.t.* to *gather together*: to assemble.—*v.i.* to flock together. [L. *congrego—con*, together, and *grex, gregis*, a flock.]

**Congregation**, kong-gre-gā'shun, *n.* an assembly.

**Congregational**, kong-gre-gā'shun-al, *adj.* pertaining to a *congregation*.

**Congregationalism**, kong-gre-gā'shun-al-izm, *n.* a form of church government in which each *congregation* is independent in the management of its own affairs: also called Independency.

**Congregationalist**, kong-gre-gā'shun-al-ist, *n.* an adherent of *Congregationalism*.

**Congress**, kong'gres, *n.* a *meeting together* or assembly, as of ambassadors, &c., for political purposes: the federal legislature of the United States.—*adj.* **Congress′ional.** [L. *con*, together, and *gradior, gressus*, to step, to go.]

**Congruence,** kong′groo-ens, **Congruency,** kong-groo′en-si, *n.*, *agreement*: suitableness.

**Congruent.** kong′groo-ent, *adj.*, *agreeing*: suitable. [L. *congruo*, to run or meet together, to agree.]

**Congruity,** kong-groo′i-ti, *n.* agreement between things: consistency.

**Congruous,** kong′groo-us, *adj.* suitable: fit: consistent.—*adv.* **Cong′ruously.**—*n.* **Cong′ruousness.**

**Conic,** kon′ik, **Conical,** kon′ik-al, *adj.* having the form of or pertaining to a *cone*.—*adv.* **Con′ically.**

**Conics,** kon′iks, *n.* the part of geometry which treats of the *cone* and its sections.

**Coniferous,** kon-if′er-us, *adj., cone-bearing*, as the fir, &c. [**Cone**, and L. *fero*, to carry.]

**Coniform,** kōn′i-form, *adj.* in the form of a *cone*.

**Conjecture,** kon-jekt′ūr, *n.* an opinion formed on slight or defective evidence : an opinion without proof : a guess : an idea.—*adj.* **Conject′ural.**—*adv.* **Conject′urally.** [L. *conjicio, conjectum*, to throw together—*con*, together, and *jacio*, to throw.]

**Conjecture,** kon-jekt′ūr, *v.t.* to make *conjectures* regarding : to infer on slight evidence : to guess.

**Conjoin,** kon-join′, *v.t.* to *join together.* [Fr. *conjoindre*—L. *con*, together, and *jungo, junctus*, to join. See **Join.**] [—*adv.* **Conjoint′ly.**

**Conjoint,** kon-joint′, *adj.* joined together : united.

**Conjugal,** kon′joo-gal, *adj.* pertaining to the *marriage-tie* or to marriage.—*adv.* **Con′jugally.**—*n.* **Conjugal′ity.** [L. *conjugalis—conjux*, one united to another, a husband or wife—*con*, and *jugum*, a yoke.]

**Conjugate,** kon′joo-gāt, *v.t.* (*gram.*) to give the various inflections or parts of a verb.—*n.* a word agreeing in derivation with another word. [L. *conjugo—con*, together, and *jugum*, that which joins, a yoke.]

**Conjugation,** kon-joo-gā′shun, *n.* a *joining together:* the inflection of the verb : a class of verbs inflected in the same manner.

**Conjunction,** kon-junk′shun, *n., connection*, union : (*gram.*) a word that *connects* sentences, clauses, and words. [L. *conjunctio—con*, and *jungo*.]

**Conjunctive,** kon-junk′tiv, *adj.* closely united : serving to unite : (*gram.*) introduced by a conjunction.—*adv.* **Conjunc′tively.**

**Conjuncture,** kon-junk′tūr, *n.* combination of circumstances : important occasion, crisis.

**Conjuration,** kon-joo-rā′shun, *n.* act of summoning by a sacred name or solemnly : enchantment.

**Conjure,** kon-jōōr′, *v.t.* to call on or summon by a sacred name or in a solemn manner : to implore earnestly.—*n.* **Conjur′er.** [Orig. *v.i.* to *unite under oath*, Fr.—L. *con*, together, and *juro*, to swear.]

**Conjure,** kun′jėr, *v.t.* to compel (a spirit) by incantations : to enchant : to raise up or frame needlessly.—*v.i.* to practise magical arts :—*pr.p.* conjuring (kun′jėr-ing); *pa.p.* conjured (kun′jėrd). [Same word as the preceding.]

**Conjurer,** kun′jėr-ėr, *n.* one who practises magic : an enchanter. [*others.*

**Conjuror,** kon-jōōr′or, *n.* one bound *by oath with*

**Connate,** kon′āt or kon-āt′, *adj., born with* one's self. [L. *con*, with, and *nascor, natus*, to be born.] [*with another.*

**Connatural,** kon-at′ū-ral, *adj.* of the *same nature*

**Connect,** kon-ekt′, *v.t.* to *tie* or *fasten together:* to establish a relation between. [L. *con*, together, and *necto*, to tie.] [*manner.*

**Connectedly,** kon-ekt′ed-li, *adv.* in a connected

**Connection,** kon-ek′shun, *n.* act of *connecting:* that which connects : a body or society held together by a bond : coherence : intercourse.

**Connective,** kon-ekt′iv, *adj.* binding together.—*n.* a word that *connects* sentences or words.—*adv.* **Connect′ively.**

**Connexion,** kon-ek′shun, *n.* Same as **Connection.**

**Connivance,** kon-īv′ans, *n.* voluntary oversight of a fault.

**Connive,** kon-īv′, *v.i.* to *wink* at a fault : to fail by intention to see a fault. [Fr.—L. *conniveo*, to wink.]

**Connoisseur,** kon-is-sār′, *n.* one who *knows well* about a subject : a critical judge. [Fr., from *connoître*—L. *cognosco*, to know—*co*, intensive, and *nosco*, old form *gnosco*, to acquire knowledge.]

**Connoisseurship,** kon-is-ār′ship, *n.* the skill of a connoisseur.

**Connote,** kon-ōt′, *v.t.* to *note* or imply along *with* an object something inherent therein : to include.—*n.* **Connota′tion.**—*adj.* **Connot′ative.** [L. *con*, with, and **Note.**]

**Connubial,** kon-ū′bi-al, *adj.* pertaining to *marriage* or to the married state : nuptial. [L. *con*, and *nubo*, to marry. See **Nuptial.**]

**Conoid,** kōn′oid, *n.* anything *like a cone in form.* —*adjs.* **Con′oid, Conoid′al.** [Gr. *kōnos, eidos*, form.]

**Conquer,** kong′kėr, *v.t.* to gain by force : to overcome or vanquish.—*v.i.* to be victor. [Fr. *conquérir*—L. *conquiro*, to seek after earnestly—*con*, intensive, and *quaero*, to seek.] [*quered.*

**Conquerable,** kong′kėr-a-bl, *adj.* that may be con-

**Conqueror,** kong′kėr-or, *n.* one who conquers.

**Conquest,** kong′kwest, *n.* the act of *conquering:* that which is conquered or acquired by physical or moral force. [O. Fr. *conqueste*, Fr. *conquête* —L. *conquiro, conquisitum.*]

**Consanguineous,** kon-sang-gwin′ē-us, *adj.* related *by blood*: of the same family or descent. [L. *consanguineus—con*, with, and *sanguis*, blood.]

**Consanguinity,** kon-sang-gwin′i-ti, *n.* relationship *by blood*: opposed to *affinity* or relationship by marriage.

**Conscience,** kon′shens, *n.* the *knowledge* of our own acts and feelings as right or wrong : sense of duty : the faculty or principle by which we distinguish right from wrong. [L. *conscientia*, from *conscio*, to know with one's self—*con*, with, and *scio*, to know.]

**Conscientious,** kon-shi-en′shus, *adj.* regulated by a regard to *conscience*: faithful : just.—*adv.* **Conscien′tiously.**—*n.* **Conscien′tiousness.**

**Conscionable,** kon′shun-a-bl, *adj.* governed or regulated by *conscience*.—*adv.* **Con′scionably.**

**Conscious,** kon′shus, *adj.* having the feeling or knowledge : aware.—*adv.* **Con′sciously.**

**Consciousness,** kon′shus-nes, *n.* the knowledge which the mind has of its own acts and feelings.

**Conscript,** kon′skript, *adj., written down*, enrolled, registered.—*n.* one whose name has been enrolled and who is liable to serve as a soldier or sailor. [L. *conscribo, conscriptum*, to write together in a list, to enlist.]

**Conscription,** kon-skrip′shun, *n.* an enrolment of individuals held liable for naval or military service.—*adj.* **Conscrip′tional.**

**Consecrate,** kon′se-krāt, *v.t.* to set apart for a *holy* use : to render holy or venerable.—*n.* **Con′secrater** or **Con′secrator.** [L. *consecro*, to make wholly sacred—*con*, and *sacro*, to set apart as sacred—*sacer*, sacred.]

**Consecration,** kon-se-krā′shun, *n.* the act of devoting to a *sacred* use.

**Consecution**, kon-se-kū'shun, *n.* a train of *conse-quences* or deductions : a series of things that follow one another.

**Consecutive**, kon-sek'ū-tiv, *adj.*, *following* in regular order : succeeding.—*adv.* **Consec'utively.**—*n.* **Consec'utiveness.** [Fr. *consécutif* —L. *con*, and *sequor, secutus*, to follow.]

**Consensus**, kon-sen'sus, *n.* unanimity : agreement.

**Consent**, kon-sent', *v.i.* to *feel* or *think along with* another : to be of the same mind : to agree : to give assent : to yield.—*n.* agreement : accordance with the actions or opinions of another : concurrence. [L. *consentio*, to agree—*con*, with, and *sentio*, to feel, to think.]

**Consentaneous**, kon-sen-tā'ne-us, *adj.*, *agreeable* or accordant to : consistent with.—*adv.* **Consenta'neously.**—*ns.* **Consenta'neousness, Consentane'ity.** [mind or in opinion.

**Consentient**, kon-sen'shi-ent, *adj.*, *agreeing* in

**Consequence**, kon'se-kwens, *n.* that which *follows* or comes *after* : effect : influence : importance. [L. *consequentia*—*con*, with, and *sequor*, to follow.]

**Consequent**, kon'se-kwent, *adj.*, *following* as a natural effect or deduction.—*n.* that which follows : the natural effect of a cause.—*adv.* **Con'sequently.**

**Consequential**, kon-se-kwen'shal, *adj.*, *following* as a result : pretending to importance : pompous. —*adv.* **Consequen'tially.** [of *conserving*.

**Conservant**, kon-sėrv'ant, *adj.* having the power

**Conservation**, kon-sėr-vā'shun, *n.* the act of *conserving* : the keeping entire.

**Conservatism**, kon-sėrv'a-tizm, *n.* the opinions and principles of a Conservative : aversion to change.

**Conservative**, kon-sėrv'a-tiv, *adj.*, *tending*, or having power to *conserve*.—*n.* (*politics*) one who desires to *preserve* the institutions of his country until they can be changed with certainty for the better : one averse to change.

**Conservator**, kon'sėr-vā-tor or kon-sėr-vā'tor, *n.* one who *preserves* from injury or violation.

**Conservatory**, kon-sėrv'a-tor-i, *n.* a place in which things are put for *preservation* : a greenhouse or place in which exotic plants are kept.

**Conserve**, kon-sėrv', *v.t.* to *keep entire* : to retain : to preserve : to preserve in sugar : to pickle.—*n.* **Conserv'er.** [L. *con*, together, and *servo*, to keep.]

**Conserve**, kon'sėrv, *n.* something preserved, as fruits in sugar.—*adj.* **Conserv'able.**

**Consider**, kon-sid'ėr, *v.t.* to look at closely or carefully : to think or deliberate on : to take into account : to attend to : to reward.—*v.i.* to think seriously or carefully : to deliberate. [Fr. —L. *considero*, prob. a word borrowed from augury, meaning to mark out the boundaries of a *templum* (see **Contemplate**) by the stars— *sidus, sideris*, a star.]

**Considerable**, kon-sid'ėr-a-bl, *adj.* worthy of being *considered* : important : more than a little. —*adv.* **Consid'erably.**—*n.* **Consid'erableness.**

**Considerate**, kon-sid'ėr-āt, *adj.* thoughtful : serious : prudent.—*adv.* **Consid'erately.**—*n.* **Considerateness.**

**Consideration**, kon-sid-ėr-ā'shun, *n.* deliberation : importance : motive or reason : compensation : the reason or basis of a compact.

**Consign**, kon-sīn', *v.t.* to give to another formally or under *sign* or *seal* : to transfer : to intrust. —*n.* **Consign'er.** [Fr. *consigner*—L. *consigno*—*con*, with, and *signum*, a sign or seal. See **Sign.**]

**Consignee**, kon-si-nē', *n.* one to whom anything is

consigned or intrusted. [Fr. *consigné*, pa.p. of *consigner*, to consign.]

**Consignment**, kon-sīn'ment, *n.* act of *consigning* : the thing consigned : the writing by which anything is made over.

**Consist**, kon-sist', *v.i.* to be composed : to *co-exist*, *i.e.* to agree. [Fr.—L. *consisto*—*con*, sig. completeness, and *sisto*—*sto*, to stand.]

**Consistence**, kon-sist'ens, **Consistency**, kon-sist'-en-si, *n.* a degree of density : substance : agreement.

**Consistent**, kon-sist'ent, *adj.* fixed : not fluid : agreeing together : uniform.—*adv.* **Consist'ently.**

**Consistory**, kon-sist'or-i, *n.* an assembly or council : a spiritual or ecclesiastical court.—*adj.* **Consisto'rial.** [See **Consist.**]

**Consociation**, kon-sō-shi-ā'shun, *n.*, *companionship with* : association : alliance. [L. *consociatio*—*con*, with, *socius*, a companion.]

**Consolable**, kon-sōl'a-bl, *adj.* that may be *comforted.*

**Consolation**, kon-sol-ā'shun, *n.*, *solace* : alleviation of misery.—*adj.* **Consolatory**, kon-sol'a-tor-i.

**Console**, kon-sōl', *v.t.* to give *solace* or *comfort* : to cheer in distress.—*n.* **Consol'er.** [L. *con*, intensive, and *solor*, to comfort. See **Solace.**]

**Consolidate**, kon-sol'i-dāt, *v.t.* to *make solid* : to form into a compact mass : to unite into one.— *v.i.* to grow solid or firm : to unite. [L. *consolido, consolidatus*—*con*, intensive, and *solidus*, solid.] [or of becoming *solid*.

**Consolidation**, kon-sol-i-dā'shun, *n.* act of *making*

**Consols**, kon'solz, *n.pl.* (short for **Consolidated Annuities**) that part of the British national debt which consists of the 3 per cent. annuities *consolidated* into one fund.

**Consonance**, kon'son-ans, *n.* a state of agreement : agreement or unison of sounds.

**Consonant**, kon'son-ant, *adj.* consistent : suitable. —*n.* an articulation which can be sounded only with a vowel : a letter representing such a sound.—*adj.* **Consonant'al.**—*adv.* **Con'sonantly.** [L. *consonans*, pr.p. of *consono*, to sound with, to harmonise—*con*, with, and *sono*, to sound.]

**Consort**, kon'sort, *n.* one that shares *the same lot with another* : a partner : a companion : a wife or husband : an accompanying ship. [L. *consors*, from *con*, with, and *sors, sortis*, a lot.]

**Consort**, kon-sort', *v.i.* to associate or keep company.

**Conspicuous**, kon-spik'ū-us, *adj.*, *clearly seen* : visible to the eye or mind : prominent.—*adv.* **Conspic'uously.**—*n.* **Conspic'uousness.** [L. *conspicuus*—*conspicio*—*con*, intensive, and *specio*, to look.]

**Conspiracy**, kon-spir'a-si, *n.* a banding together for an evil purpose : a plot : concurrence.

**Conspirator**, kon-spir'a-tor, *n.* a plotter (along with others).

**Conspire**, kon-spīr', *v.i.* to plot or scheme together : to agree : to concur to one end. [L. *conspiro*—*con*, together, and *spiro*, to breathe.]

**Constable**, kun'sta-bl, *n.* formerly, a state-officer of the highest rank : a peace-officer : a policeman.—*n.* **Con'stableship.** [O. Fr. *conestable*, Fr. *connétable*, L. *comes stabuli*, count of the *stabulum*, stable.]

**Constabulary**, kon-stab'ū-lar-i, *adj.* pertaining to *constables* or peace-officers.—*n.* the body of constables. [ableness.

**Constancy**, kon'stan-si, *n.* fixedness : unchange-

**Constant**, kon'stant, *adj.* fixed : unchangeable :

continual: faithful.—*n.* that which remains unchanged. [L. *constans*, from *consto*, to stand firm—*con*, intensive, *sto*, to stand.]

**Constantly**, kon'stant-li, *adv.* firmly: continually.

**Constellation**, kon-stel-ā'shun, *n.* a *group of stars:* an assemblage of beauties or excellencies: (*astrol.*) a particular disposition of the planets. [L. *constellatio*—*con*, together, *stella*, a star.]

**Consternation**, kon-stêr-nā'shun, *n.* terror which throws into confusion: astonishment: horror. [L. *consternatio*—*consterno*, *consternatus*, from *con*, sig. completeness, and *sterno*, to strew, to throw down.]

**Constipate**, kon'stip-āt, *v.t.* to *press closely together:* to stop up: to make costive. [L. *con*, together, and *stipo*, *stipatus*, to pack.]

**Constipation**, kon-stip-ā'shun, *n.* costiveness.

**Constituency**, kon-stit'ū-en-si, *n.* the whole body of voters for a member of parliament.

**Constituent**, kon-stit'ū-ent, *adj.*, *constituting* or forming: essential: elemental.—*n.* an essential or elemental part: one of those who elect a representative, esp. in parliament.

**Constitute**, kon'stit-ūt, *v.t.* to set up: to establish: to form or compose: to appoint. [L. *constituo*, *constitutus*, from *con*, together, and *statuo*, to make to stand, to place—*sto*, to stand.]

**Constitution**, kon-stit-ū'shun, *n.* the natural condition of body or mind: a system of laws and customs: the established form of government: a particular law or usage.

**Constitutional**, kon-stit-ū'shun-al, *adj.* inherent in the natural frame: natural: agreeable to the constitution or frame of government: legal: a **Constitutional Government** is one where the ruler is subject to fixed laws. See **Absolute**.—*n.* a walk for the sake of one's health.—*adv.* **Constitu'tionally.**

**Constitutionalist**, kon-stit-ū'shun-al-ist, **Constitutionist**, kon-sti-tū'shun-ist, *n.* one who favours a *constitutional* government.

**Constitutive**, kon'stit-ūt-iv, *adj.*, *that constitutes* or establishes: having power to enact, &c.

**Constrain**, kon-strān', *v.t.* to urge with irresistible power: to force.—*adj.* **Constrainable**, kon-strān'a-bl.—*adv.* **Constrainedly**, kon-strān'ed-li. [O. Fr. *constraindre*—L. *constringo*, *constrictus*—*con*, together, *stringo*, to press. See **Strain**.]

**Constraint**, kon-strānt', *n.* irresistible force: compulsion: confinement.

**Constrict**, kon-strikt', *v.t.* to *bind* or *press together:* to contract: to cramp. [L. *constringo*, *constrictus*.] [*gether*.

**Constriction**, kon-strik'shun, *n.* a *pressing together*.

**Constrictor**, kon-strikt'or, *n.* that which *draws together:* a serpent which crushes its prey in its folds. [contract. [L. *constringo*.]

**Constringe**, kon-strinj', *v.t.* to *draw together:* to **Constringent**, kon-strinj'ent, *adj.* having the quality of contracting.

**Construct**, kon-strukt', *v.t.* to *build up:* to compile: to put together the parts of a thing: to make: to compose. [L. *construo*, *constructus*, to pile together.]

**Construction**, kon-struk'shun, *n.* anything *piled together*, building: manner of forming: (*gram.*) the arrangement of words in a sentence: interpretation: meaning.

**Constructive**, kon-strukt'iv, *adj.* not direct or expressed, but inferred.—*adv.* **Construct'ively.**

**Constructiveness**, kon-struct'iv-nes, *n.* the faculty of constructing.

**Construe**, kon'strōō, *v.t.* to *set in order:* to exhibit the order or arrangement in another language: to translate: to explain. [L. *construo*, *constructus*, to pile together.]

**Consubstantial**, kon-sub-stan'shal, *adj.* of the *same substance*, nature, or essence.—*n.* **Consubstantial'ity.** [L. *con*, with, and **Substantial**.]

**Consubstantialist**, kon-sub-stan'shal-ist, *n.* one who believes in *consubstantiation*.

**Consubstantiate**, kon-sub-stan'shi-āt, *v.t.* to unite in one common *substance* or nature.

**Consubstantiation**, kon-sub-stan-shi-ā'shun, *n.* state of being of the *same substance:* (*theol.*) the Lutheran doctrine of the actual, *substantial* presence of the body and blood of Christ *with* the bread and wine used at the Lord's Supper. [See **Transubstantiation**.]

**Consuetude**, kon'swe-tūd, *n.* custom.—*adj.* **Con'suetudinary**, also *n.* a ritual of customary devotions. [L. *consuetudo*, custom.]

**Consul**, kon'sul, *n.* among the Romans, one of the two chief-magistrates of the state: one commissioned to reside in a foreign country as an agent for, or representative of, a government. [L.]

**Consular**, kon'sūl-ar, *adj.* pertaining to a *consul*.

**Consulate**, kon'sūl-āt, *n.* the *office*, residence, or jurisdiction of a *consul*. [office, of a *consul*.

**Consulship**, kon'sul-ship, *n.* the *office*, or term of

**Consult**, kon-sult', *v.t.* to ask advice of: to apply to for instruction: to decide or act in favour of.—*v.i.* to consider in company: to take counsel. [L. *consulto*, inten. of *consulo*, to consult.]

**Consultation**, kon-sult-ā'shun, *n.* the act of *consulting:* a meeting for the purpose of consulting.

**Consumable**, kon-sūm'a-bl, *adj.* that can be consumed.

**Consume**, kon-sūm', *v.t.* to destroy by wasting, fire, &c.: to devour: to waste or spend: to exhaust.—*v.i.* to waste away.—*n.* **Consum'er.** [L. *consumo*, to destroy—*con*, sig. completeness, and *sumo*, *sumptus*, to take.]

**Consummate**, kon-sum'āt or kon'-, *v.t.* to raise to the *summit* or *highest point:* to perfect or finish. [L. *consummo*, to perfect—*con*, with, and *summus*, highest, perfect.]

**Consummate**, kon-sum'āt, *adj.* in the *highest degree:* perfect.—*adv.* **Consumm'ately.**

**Consummation**, kon-sum-ā'shun, *n.* act of completing: perfection: close.

**Consumption**, kon-sum'shun, *n.* the act of using up: a disease in the lungs, which gradually *wastes away* the frame = **Phthisis**. [See **Consume**.]

**Consumptive**, kon-sum'tiv, *adj.* having the quality of wasting away: inclined to the disease *consumption*.—*adv.* **Consump'tively.**

**Consumptiveness**, kon-sum'tiv-nes, *n.* a tendency to *consumption*.

**Contact**, kon'takt, *n.* a *close touching:* close union: meeting. [L. *contingo*, *contactum*, to touch—*con*, sig. completeness, and *tango*, to touch—root *tag*-.] [by *contact*.

**Contagion**, kon-tā'jun, *n.* transmission of a disease

**Contagious**, kon-tā'jus, *adj.* that may be communicated by *contact*.—*adv.* **Conta'giously.**—*n.* **Conta'giousness.**

**Contain**, kon-tān', *v.t.* to *hold together:* to comprise, to include: to restrain.—*adj.* **Contain'able**, that may be *contained*. [Fr. *contenir*—L. *contineo*—*con*, together, and *teneo*, to hold.]

**Contaminate**, kon-tam'i-nāt, *v.t.* to defile *by touching* or mixing with: to pollute: to corrupt: to infect. [L. *contamino*—*contamen* = *contagmen*. See **Contact**.]

**Contamination**, kon-tam-i-nā'shun, *n.* pollution.

**Contemn**, kon-tem', *v.t.* to despise: to neglect.—

*n.* **Contem′ner.** [L. *contemno, contemptus,* to value little—*con,* intensive, and *temno,* to slight.]

**Contemplate,** kon-tem′plāt, *v.t.* to consider or look at attentively : to meditate on or study : to intend.—*v.i.* to think seriously : to meditate. [L. *contemplor, contemplatus,* to mark out carefully a *templum* or place for auguries—*con,* sig. completeness, and *templum.* See **Consider** and **Temple.**] [study of a particular subject.

**Contemplation,** kon-tem-plā′shun, *n.* continued

**Contemplative,** kon-tem′pla-tiv, *adj.* given to contemplation.—*adv.* **Contem′platively.**

**Contemporaneous,** kon-tem-po-rā′ne-us, *adj.* living, happening, or being at the *same time.*—*adv.* **Contempora′neously.**—*n.* **Contempora′neousness.** [L. *con,* together, and *temporaneus* —*tempus,* time.]

**Contemporary,** kon-tem′po-rar-i, *adj.* contemporaneous.—*n.* one who lives at the same time.

**Contempt,** kon-tempt′, *n.* scorn : disgrace : (*law*) disobedience of the rules of a court. [See **Contemn.**]

**Contemptible,** kon-tempt′i-bl, *adj.* despicable.— *adv.* **Contempt′ibly.**—*n.* **Contempt′ibleness.**

**Contemptuous,** kon-tempt′ū-us, *adj., full of contempt :* haughty : scornful.—*adv.* **Contempt′uously.**—*n.* **Contempt′uousness.**

**Contend,** kon-tend′, *v.i.* to strive : to struggle in emulation or in opposition : to dispute or debate. [L. *contendo, contentum*—*con,* and *tendo,* to stretch, strain.]

**Content,** kon′tent or kon-tent′, *n.* that which is *contained :* the capacity, measurement, or extent of anything.—*pl.* the things contained : the list of subjects treated of in a book. [See **Contain.**]

**Content,** kon-tent′, *adj.* having the desires limited by present enjoyment : satisfied.—*v.t.* to make *content :* to satisfy the mind : to make quiet : to please.

**Contented,** kon-tent′ed, *adj., content.*—*adv.* **Content′edly.**—*ns.* **Content′edness, Content′ment.**

**Contention,** kon-ten′shun, *n.* a violent straining after any object : strife : debate. [See **Contend.**]

**Contentious,** kon-ten′shus, *adj.* quarrelsome.— *adv.* **Conten′tiously.**—*n.* **Conten′tiousness.**

**Conterminal,** kon-tėr′min-al, **Conterminous,** kon-tėr′min-us, *adj.* having a *common terminus* or boundary. [L. *conterminus,* neighbouring—*con,* together, and *terminus,* a boundary.]

**Contest,** kon-test′, *v.t.* to call in question or make the subject of dispute : to strive for.—*adj.* **Contest′able.** [L. *contestor,* to call to witness—*con,* and *testor,* to be a witness—*testis,* a witness.]

**Contest,** kon′test, *n.* a struggle for superiority : strife : debate.

**Context,** kon′tekst, *n.* something *woven together* or connected : the parts of a discourse or treatise which precede and follow a special passage. [L. *contexo*—*con,* together, *texo, textus,* to weave.]

**Contexture,** kon-tekst′ūr, *n.* the *interweaving* of parts into a whole : system. [close contact.

**Contiguity,** kon-tig-ū′i-ti, *n.* the state of being in

**Contiguous,** kon-tig′ū-us, *adj., touching :* adjoining : near.—*adv.* **Contig′uously.**—*n.* **Contig′uousness.** [L. *contiguus,* from *contingo, contigi,* to touch on all sides—*con,* signifying completeness, *tango,* to touch.]

**Continence,** kon′ti-nens, **Continency,** kon′ti-nen-si, *n.* the restraint imposed by a person upon his desires and passions : chastity. [See **Continent,** *adj.*]

**Continent,** kon′ti-nent, *n.* a large extent of land not broken up by seas : the mainland of Europe : one of the great divisions of the land surface of the globe.—*adj.* **Continent′al.** [L. *continens* = *continuus, holding together,* uninterrupted.]

**Continent,** kon′ti-nent, *adj., holding in* or restraining the indulgence of pleasure, especially of sexual enjoyment : temperate : virtuous.—*adv.* **Con′tinently.** [L. *continens,* moderate—*con*-*tineo*—*con,* together, and *teneo,* to hold.]

**Contingence,** kon-tin′jens, **Contingency,** kon-tin′jen-si, *n.* the quality of being *contingent :* what happens by chance : an accident.

**Contingent,** kon-tin′jent, *adj.* dependent on something else : liable but not certain to happen : accidental.—*n.* an event which is liable but not certain to occur : a share or proportion, especially of soldiers.—*adv.* **Contin′gently.** [L. *contingo,* to touch, to happen.]

**Continual,** kon-tin′ū-al, *adj.* without interruption : unceasing.—*adv.* **Contin′ually.** [See **Continue.**]

**Continuance,** kon-tin′ū-ans, *n.* duration : uninterrupted succession : stay.

**Continuation,** kon-tin-ū-ā′shun, *n.* constant succession : extension.

**Continuative,** kon-tin′ū-ā-tiv, *adj., continuing.*

**Continuator,** kon-tin′ū-ā-tor, *n.* one who *continues* or keeps up a series or succession.

**Continue,** kon-tin′ū, *v.t.* to draw out or prolong : to extend or increase in any way : to unite without break : to persist in.—*v.i.* to remain in the same place or state : to last or endure : to persevere. [Fr. *continuer*—L. *continuus,* joined, connected, from *contineo*—*con,* together, and *teneo,* to hold.]

**Continued,** kon-tin′ūd, *adj.* uninterrupted : unceasing : extended.—*adv.* **Contin′uedly.**

**Continuity,** kon-tin-ū′i-ti, *n.* state of being continuous : uninterrupted connection.

**Continuous,** kon-tin′ū-us, *adj. joined together :* without interruption.—*adv.* **Contin′uously.**

**Contort,** kon-tort′, *v.t.* to *twist* or *turn violently :* to writhe. [L. *con,* intensive, and *torqueo, tortus,* to twist.]

**Contortion,** kon-tor′shun, *n.* a violent twisting.

**Contour,** kon-tōōr′, *n.* the outline : the line which bounds the figure of any object. [Fr. *contour,* from *con,* and *tour,* a turning—L. *tornus,* Gr. *tornos,* a turning-lathe.]

**Contraband,** kon′tra-band, *adj., against* or contrary to *ban* or law : prohibited.—*n.* illegal traffic : prohibition : prohibited goods.—*n.* **Con′trabandist,** a smuggler. [It. *contrabbando*— L. *contra,* against, and Low L. *bandum,* a proclamation. See **Ban.**]

**Contract,** kon-trakt′, *v.t.* to *draw together :* to lessen : to shorten : to acquire : to incur : to bargain for : to betroth.—*v.i.* to shrink : to become less. [L. *contraho, contractus,* from *con,* together, and *traho,* to draw.]

**Contract,** kon′trakt, *n.* an agreement on fixed terms : a bond : a betrothment : the writing containing an agreement. [O. Fr. *contract,* an agreement—L. *contractus,* a compact.]

**Contracted,** kon-trakt′ed, *adj., drawn together :* narrow : mean.—*adv.* **Contract′edly.**—*n.* **Contract′edness.**

**Contractible,** kon-trakt′i-bl, *adj.* capable of being contracted.—*ns.* **Contractibil′ity, Contract′ibleness.**

**Contractile,** kon-trakt′il, *adj.* tending or having power to *contract.*—*n.* **Contractil′ity.**

**Contraction,** kon-trak′shun, *n.* act of *contracting :* a word shortened by rejecting a part of it.

**Contractor,** kon-trakt′or, *n.* one of the parties to a bargain or *agreement :* one who engages to execute work or furnish supplies at a fixed rate.

**Contra-dance**, kon'tra-dans (corruptly **Country-dance**), *n.* a *dance* in which the partners are arranged in *opposite* lines. [Fr. *contre-danse*; from L. *contra*, against, opposite, and **Dance**.]

**Contradict**, kon-tra-dikt', *v.t.* to *speak in opposition to*: to oppose by words : to assert the contrary : to deny. [L. *contradico, contradictus—contra*, against, and *dico*, to speak.]

**Contradiction**, kon-tra-dik'shun, *n.* act of *contradicting*: a speaking against : denial : inconsistency.

**Contradictive**, kon-tra-dikt'iv, **Contradictory**, kon-tra-dikt'or-i, *adj.* affirming the contrary : opposite : inconsistent.—*adv.* **Contradict'orily**.

**Contradistinction**, kon-tra-dis-tink'shun, *n.*, *distinction* by contrast.

**Contradistinctive**, kon-tra-dis-tinkt'iv, *adj.*, *distinguishing* by *opposite* qualities.

**Contradistinguish**, kon-tra-dis-ting'gwish, *v.t.* to *distinguish* or mark the difference by *opposite* qualities. [L. *contra*, against, opposite, and **Distinguish**.]

**Contralto**, kon-tral'tō, *n.* (*music*) *counter-alto*; same as alto or counter-tenor. [See **Alto** and **Counter**.] [sistency.

**Contrariety**, kon-tra-rī'e-ti, *n.* opposition : incon-

**Contrariwise**, kon'tra-ri-wīz, *adv.* on the *contrary way* or side : on the other hand. [**Contrary** and **Ways**.]

**Contrary**, kon'tra-ri, *adj.*, *opposite*: inconsistent : contradictory.—*n.* a thing that is contrary or of opposite qualities.—*n.* **Con'trariness**.—*adv.* **Con'trarily**. [L. *contrarius—contra*, against.]

**Contrast**, kon-trast', *v.i.* to *stand against* or in *opposition* to.—*v.t.* to set in opposition, in order to shew superiority or give effect. [Fr. *contraster—*L. *contra*, opposite to, *stare*, to stand.]

**Contrast**, kon'trast, *n.*, *opposition* or unlikeness in things compared : exhibition of differences.

**Contravallation**, kon-tra-val-ā'shun, *n.* a *fortification* built by besiegers, which is thus *opposed to* that of the besieged. [L. *contra*, opposite to, and *vallo, vallatus*, to fortify—*vallum*, a wall.]

**Contravene**, kon-tra-vēn', *v.t.* to *come against*: to oppose : to hinder. [L. *contra*, against, *venio*, to come.]

**Contravention**, kon-tra-ven'shun, *n.* act of *contravening*: opposition : obstruction.

**Contributary**, kon-trib'ū-tar-i, *adj.* paying a share.

**Contribute**, kon-trib'ūt, *v.t.* to *give along with* others : to give for a common purpose : to pay a share.—*v.i.* to give or bear a part.—*n.* **Contrib'utor**. [L. *con*, along with, *tribuo, tributus*, to give.] [levy.

**Contribution**, kon-trib-ū'shun, *n.* a collection : a

**Contributive**, kon-trib'ū-tiv, **Contributory**, kon-trib'ū-tor-i, *adj.* giving a share : helping.

**Contrite**, kon'trīt, *adj.* broken-hearted for sin : penitent.—*adv.* **Con'tritely**. [L. *contritus—contero—con*, sig. completeness, and *tero*, to bruise.] [remorse.

**Contrition**, kon-trish'un, *n.* deep sorrow for sin :

**Contrivance**, kon-trīv'ans, *n.* act of *contriving*: the thing contrived : invention : artifice.

**Contrive**, kon-trīv', *v.t.* to *find out* or plan : to invent.—*n.* **Contriv'er**. [Fr. *controuver—con*, and *trouver*, to find. See **Trover**.]

**Control**, kon-trōl', *n.* (formerly **Comptroll**), restraint : authority : command.—*v.t.* to check : to restrain : to govern.—*pr.p.* controll'ing ; *pa.p.* controlled'. [Fr. *contrôle*, from *contre-rôle*, a duplicate register, for checking the original. See **Roll**.]

**Controllable**, kon-trōl'a-bl, *adj.* capable of, or subject to *control*.

**Controller, Comptroller**, kon-trōl'ėr, *n.* one who *controls* or checks the accounts of others by keeping a *counter-roll* or register.—*n.* **Controll'ership**.

**Controlment**, kon-trōl'ment, *n.* act or power of *controlling*: state of being controlled : control.

**Controversial**, kon-tro-vėr'shal, *adj.* relating to *controversy*.—*adv.* **Controver'sially**.

**Controversialist**, kon-tro-vėr'shal-ist, *n.* one given to *controversy*.

**Controversy**, kon'tro-vėr-si, *n.* a disputation, discussion, or debate : contest.

**Controvert**, kon'tro-vėrt, *v.t.* to oppose : to argue against : to refute. [L. *contra*, against, and *verto*, to turn.]

**Controvertible**, kon-tro-vėrt'i-bl, *adj.* that may be *controverted*.—*adv.* **Controvert'ibly**.

**Contumacious**, kon-tū-mā'shus, *adj.* opposing lawful authority with contempt : obstinate : stubborn.—*adv.* **Contuma'ciously**.—*n.* **Contuma'ciousness**.

**Contumacy**, kon'tū-ma-si, *n.* obstinate disobedience or resistance : stubbornness. [L. *contumacia—contumax, contumacis*, insolent, from *con*, and root *tem-* in *temno*, to despise, or acc. to Littré from *tumeo*, to swell.]

**Contumelious**, kon-tū-mē'li-us, *adj.* haughtily reproachful : insolent.—*adv.* **Contume'liously**.—*n.* **Contume'liousness**.

**Contumely**, kon'tū-mel-i, *n.* rudeness : insolence : reproach. [L. *contumelia*, which is from the same source as *contumacy*. See **Contumacy**.]

**Contuse**, kon-tūz', *v.t.* to *beat* exceedingly or *bruise* to pieces : to crush. [L. *contundo, contusus—con* and *tundo*, to beat, to bruise.]

**Contusion**, kon-tū'zhun, *n.* act of *bruising*: state of being bruised : a bruise.

**Conundrum**, kon-un'drum, *n.* a sort of riddle containing some odd or fanciful resemblance between things quite unlike. [Ety. unknown.]

**Convalesce**, kon-val-es', *v.i.* to regain health. [L. *con*, and *valesco—valeo*, to be strong.]

**Convalescence**, kon-val-es'ens, *n.* gradual recovery of health and strength.

**Convalescent**, kon-val-es'ent, *adj.* gradually recovering health.—*n.* one recovering health.

**Convection**, kon-vek'shun, *n.* the process of transmission of heat or electricity through liquids or gases by means of currents. [L. *convectio—con*, and *veho*, I carry.]

**Convene**, kon-vēn', *v.i.* to *come together*: to assemble.—*v.t.* to call together. [Fr.—L. *convenio*, from *con*, together, and *venio*, to come.]

**Convener**, kon-vēn'ėr, *n.* one who *convenes* a meeting : the chairman of a committee.

**Convenience**, kon-vēn'yens, **Conveniency**, kon-vēn'yen-si, *n.* suitableness : accommodation.

**Convenient**, kon-vēn'yent, *adj.* suitable : handy : commodious.—*adv.* **Conven'iently**. [L. *conveniens, convenientis*, orig. pr.p. of *convenio*, to come together.]

**Convent**, kon'vent, *n.* an *association* of persons secluded from the world and devoted to a religious life : the house in which they live, a monastery or nunnery. [L. *conventus—convenio*, to come together.]

**Conventicle**, kon-vent'i-kl, *n.* applied in contempt to a meeting for worship of dissenters from the Established Church. [L. *conventiculum*, a secret meeting of monks, dim. of *conventus*.]

**Convention**, kon-ven'shun, *n.* an assembly, esp.

of representatives for some special object : temporary treaty : an agreement. [Fr.—L. *conventio.* See **Convene.**]

**Conventional,** kon-ven'shun-al, *adj.* formed by *convention* : growing out of tacit agreement or custom : customary.—*adv.* **Conven'tionally.**

**Conventionalism,** kon-ven'shun-al-izm, *n.* that which is established by tacit agreement, as a mode of speech, &c.

**Conventionality,** kon-ven-shun-al'i-ti, *n.* state of being *conventional :* that which is established by use or custom.

**Conventual,** kon-vent'ū-al, *adj.* belonging to a *convent.*—*n.* a monk or nun. [L. *conventualis.*]

**Converge,** kon-vėrj', *v.i.* to tend to one point. [L. *con,* together, and *vergo,* to bend, to incline.]

**Convergence,** kon-vėrj'ens, **Convergency,** kon-vėrj'ens-i, *n.* act or quality of tending to one point. [point.

**Convergent,** kon-vėrj'ent, *adj.* tending to one

**Conversable,** kon-vėrs'a-bl, *adj.* disposed to *converse :* sociable.—*adv.* **Convers'ably.** [See **Converse.**

**Conversant,** kon'vėrs-ant, *adj.* acquainted by study : familiar : (*B.*) walking or associating with.

**Conversation,** kon-vėr-sā'shun, *n.* intercourse : talk : familiar discourse : (*B.*) behaviour or deportment.—*adj.* **Conversa'tional.**

**Conversationalist,** kon-vėr-sā'shun-al-ist, *n.* one who excels in *conversation.*

**Conversazione,** kon-vėr-sat-se-ō'ne, *n.* a meeting for *conversation,* particularly on literary subjects. —*pl.* **Conversazio'ni** (-nē). [It.]

**Converse,** kon-vėrs', *v.i.* to have intercourse : to talk familiarly. [Fr.—L. *conversor,* to live with—*con,* intensive, and *verso,* to turn much— *verto,* to turn.] [versation.

**Converse,** kon'vėrs, *n.* familiar intercourse : con-

**Converse,** kon'vėrs, *n.* a proposition *converted* or turned about—*i.e.* one in which the subject and predicate have changed places.—*adj.* reversed in order or relation.—*adv.* **Con'versely.**

**Conversion,** kon-vėr'shun, *n.* change from one thing, state, or religion, to another : change from a wicked to a holy life : appropriation to a special purpose : (*logic*) act of interchanging the terms of a proposition.

**Convert,** kon-vėrt', *v.t.* to *turn round :* to change or turn from one thing, condition, or religion to another : to change from a bad to a good life : to apply to a particular purpose. [L. *converto, conversus—con,* and *verto,* to turn.]

**Convert,** kon'vėrt, *n., one converted :* one who has become religious, or who has changed his religion.

**Convertible,** kon-vėrt'i-bl, *adj.* that may be *converted :* that may be changed one for the other. —*adv.* **Convert'ibly.**—*n.* **Convertibil'ity.**

**Convex,** kon'veks, *adj.* rising into a round form on the outside, the reverse of *concave.*—*adv.* **Con'vexly.** [L. *convexus—conveho—con,* together, and *veho,* to carry.]

**Convexed,** kon-vekst', *adj.* made *convex.*—*adv.* **Convex'edly.** [the outside.

**Convexity,** kon-veks'i-ti, *n.* roundness of form on

**Convey,** kon-vā', *v.t.* (*lit.*) to bring or send on the *way :* to carry : to transmit : to impart.—*adj.* **Conveyable,** kon-vā'a-bl.—*n.* **Convey'er.** [O. Fr. *conveier*—Low L. *conviare,* to conduct—L. *con,* along with, and *via,* a way.]

**Conveyance,** kon-vā'ans, *n.* the instrument or means of *conveying :* (*law*) the act of transferring property : the writing which transfers it.

**Conveyancer,** kon-vā'ans-ėr, *n.* one whose business is the preparation of deeds for the transference of property. [a *conveyancer.*

**Conveyancing,** kon-vā'ans-ing, *n.* the business of

**Convict,** kon-vikt', *v.t.* to prove guilty : to pronounce guilty. [From root of **Convince.**

**Convict,** kon'vikt, *n.* one *convicted* or found guilty of crime, esp. one who has been condemned to penal servitude.

**Conviction,** kon-vik'shun, *n.* act of *convincing* or of *convicting :* strong belief : a proving guilty.

**Convince,** kon-vins', *v.t.* to subdue the mind by evidence : to satisfy as to truth or error : (*B.*) to convict : to refute.—*adj.* **Convin'cible.**—*adv.* **Convin'cingly.** [L. *con,* sig. completeness, and *vinco, victus,* to conquer.]

**Convivial,** kon-viv'i-al, *adj.* feasting in company : relating to a feast : social : jovial.—*adv.* **Conviv'ially.**—*n.* **Convivial'ity.** [L. *convivium,* a living together, a feast—*con,* together, and *vivo,* to live.]

**Convocation,** kon-vo-kā'shun, *n.* act of *convoking :* an assembly, particularly of the clergy of the English Church, or of the heads of a university.

**Convoke,** kon-vōk', *v.t.* to *call together :* to assemble. [L. *con,* together, and *voco, vocatus,* to call.]

**Convolute,** kon'vo-lūt, **Convoluted,** kon'vo-lūt-ed, *adj., rolled together,* or one part on another. [See **Convolve.**]

**Convolution,** kon-vo-lū'shun, *n.* a twisting : a fold.

**Convolve,** kon-volv', *v.t.* to *roll together,* or one part on another. [L. *con,* together, and *volvo, volutus,* to roll.]

**Convolvulus,** kon-vol'vū-lus, *n.* a genus of *twining* or trailing plants, called also bindweed.

**Convoy,** kon-voy', *v.t.* to accompany *on the way* for protection. [Fr. *convoyer,* from root of **Convey.**]

**Convoy,** kon'voy, *n.* the act of *convoying :* protection : that which convoys or is convoyed.

**Convulse,** kon-vuls', *v.t.* to agitate violently : to affect by spasms. [L. *con,* intensive, and *vello, vulsus,* to pluck, to pull.]

**Convulsion,** kon-vul'shun, *n.* a *violent* and involuntary *contortion* of the muscles : commotion.

**Convulsive,** kon-vuls'iv, *adj.* attended with *convulsions :* spasmodic.—*adv.* **Convuls'ively.**—*n.* **Convuls'iveness.**

**Cony, Coney,** kō'ni or kun'i, *n.* a rabbit. [Prob. orig. E. ; *cf.* Dut. *konijn,* Dan. *kanin ;* or, through O. Fr. *connil,* from L. *cuniculus,* a rabbit.]

**Coo,** kōō, *v.i.* to make a noise as a dove : to caress fondly :—*pr.p.* cōō'ing ; *pa.p.* cōōed'. [From the sound.]

**Cook,** kook, *v.t.* to prepare food.—*n.* one whose business is to cook. [A.S. *coc,* a cook (Ger *koch*), borrowed from L. *coquo,* to cook.]

**Cookery,** kook'ėr-i, *n.* the *art* or practice *of cooking.*

**Cool,** kōōl, *adj.* slightly *cold :* free from excitement : calm : not zealous or ardent : indifferent : impudent.—*v.t.* to make cool : to allay or moderate, as heat, excitement, passion, &c.—*v.i.* to grow cool.—*n.* **Cool.**—*adv.* **Cool'ly.** [A.S. *col ;* Ger. *kühl ;* see **Cold** and **Chill.**]

**Cooler,** kōōl'ėr, *n.* anything that *cools.*

**Coolie,** kōōl'i, *n.* a *labourer :* in Hindustan, a porter in general : an Indian or Chinese labourer in other countries. [Hind. *kúli,* a labourer.]

**Coolness,** kōōl'nes, *n.* moderate cold : indifference : want of zeal.

**Coom**, kōōm, *n.* matter that gathers at the naves of wheels : soot that gathers at the mouth of an oven : coaldust. [Conn. with Ger. *kahm*, mould gathered on liquids.]

**Coomb**, kōōm, another form of **Comb** = 4 bushels.

**Coop**, kōōp, *n.* (*lit.*) anything *hollow*, as a *cup*—a tub, cask, or barrel : a box or cage for fowls or small animals.—*v.t.* to confine in a coop : to shut up or confine. [A.S. *cypa*, a basket ; akin to **Cup**.]

**Cooper**, kōōp′ėr, *n.* one who makes *coops*, tubs, casks, &c.

**Cooperage**, kōōp′ėr-āj, *n.* the work, or workshop of a *cooper* : the sum paid for a cooper's work.

**Co-operant**, kō-op′ėr-ant, *adj.* working together.

**Co-operate**, kō-op′ėr-āt, *v.i.* to *work together*.—*n.* **Co-op′erator**. [L. *co*, together, and **Operate**.]

**Co-operation**, kō-op-ėr-ā′shun, *n.* joint operation : the association of a number of persons for the cheaper purchasing of goods, or for carrying on some branch of industry.—*adj.* **Co-op′erative**.

**Co-ordinate**, kō-or′di-nāt, *adj.* holding the *same order* or rank : not subordinate.—*adv.* **Co-or′dinately**. [L. *co*, together, equal, and **Ordinate**.]

**Co-ordination**, kō-or-di-nā′shun, *n.* state of being co-ordinate.

**Coot**, kōōt, *n.* a *short-tailed* water-fowl. [Dut. *koet* ; W. *cwtiar—cwt*, a short tail. See **Cut**.]

**Copal**, kō′pal, *n.* a *resinous* substance used in varnishes. [Sp.—Mexican *copalli*, a general name of resins.]

**Copartner**, kō-pärt′nėr, *n.* a *joint partner*.—*ns.* **Copart′nership**, **Copart′nery**. [L. *co*, together, and **Partner**.]

**Cope**, kōp, *n.* a *covering*, a *cap* or hood : a cloak worn by a priest : anything spread overhead : a coping.—*v.t.* to cover with a cope. [From root of **Cap**.]

**Cope**, kōp, *v.i.* to vie with, especially on equal terms or successfully : to match. [Dut. *koopen*, cog. with A.S. *ceapian*, to bargain. See **Cheap**.]

**Copeck**, kō′pek, *n.* a Russian copper coin equal to 1½ farthings. [Russ.]

**Copestone**, kōp′stōn, **Coping-stone**, kōp′ing-stōn, *n.* the stone which copes or tops a wall. [**Cope**, a covering, and **Stone**.]

**Copier**, kop′i-ėr, **Copyist**, kop′i-ist, *n.* one who copies : an imitator : a plagiarist.

**Coping**, kōp′ing, *n.* the *capping* or covering course of masonry of a wall.

**Copious**, kō′pi-us, *adj.*, *plentiful* : overflowing : not concise.—*adv.* **Co′piously**.—*n.* **Co′piousness**. [O. Fr. *copieux*—L. *copiosus*—*copia*, plenty—*co*, intensive, and *ops*, *opis*, power, property, wealth. See **Opulent**.]

**Copper**, kop′ėr, *n.* a metal of a reddish colour, named from the island of *Cyprus* : a vessel made of copper.—*v.t.* to cover with copper. [Low L. *cuper*—L. *cuprum*, a contr. of *cuprium aes*, 'Cyprian brass,' because the Romans obtained copper in Cyprus.]

**Copperas**, kop′ėr-as, *n.* sulphate of iron or green vitriol. [Fr. *couperose* (It. *copparosa*)—L. *cupri rosa*, rose of copper.]

**Copperish**, kop′ėr-ish, **Coppery**, kop′ėr-i, **Cupreous**, kū′prē-us, *adj.* containing or like *copper*.

**Copperplate**, kop′ėr-plāt, *n.* a *plate* of polished *copper* on which something has been engraved : an impression taken from the plate.

**Coppice**, kop′is, **Copse**, kops, *n.* a wood of small growth for *cutting*. [O. Fr. *copeiz*, wood newly *cut*—*couper*, to cut—Low L. *copare*, to cut.]

**Coprolite**, kop′ro-līt, *n. petrified dung* of animals. [Gr. *kopros*, dung, and *lithos*, a stone.]

**Coptic**, kop′tik, *adj.* pertaining to the *Copts*, the descendants of the ancient Egyptians.

**Copula**, kop′ū-la, *n.* that which *couples* or *joins together* : a bond or tie : (*logic*) the word joining the subject and predicate. [L.—*co*, together, and root *ap*, connected with L. *aptus*, fastened, and Gr. *haptō*, to join.]

**Copulate**, kop′ū-lāt, *v.t.* and *v.i.* to *couple* or *join together* : to come together sexually.

**Copulation**, kop-ū-lā′shun, *n.* act of *copulating*.

**Copulative**, kop′ū-lāt-iv, *adj.*, *uniting*.—*n.* (*gram.*) a conjunction that *unites* ideas as well as words.

**Copy**, kop′i, *n.* one of a number, esp. of books : an imitation from an original pattern : that which is imitated : an original work : manuscript for printing.—*v.t.* to write, paint, &c. after an original : to imitate : to transcribe :—*pa.p.* cop′ied. [Fr. *copie*, from L. *copia*, plenty ; in Low L. a transcript, because by such the original was *multiplied*.]

**Copyhold**, kop′i-hōld, *n.* (*Eng. law*) a species of estate or right of holding land, for which the owner can only shew the *copy* of the rolls originally made by the steward of the lord's court.

**Copyist**. See **Copier**.

**Copyright**, kop′i-rīt, *n.* the exclusive *right* of an author or his heirs to publish for a term of years *copies* of his work, whether a book, painting, engraving, &c.

**Coquet**, ko-ket′, *v.i.* to excite admiration or love, from vanity, or to deceive.—*v.t.* to trifle with in love :—*pr.p.* coquett′ing ; *pa.p.* coquett′ed. [Fr. *coqueter—coquet*, dim. of *coq*, a cock.]

**Coquetry**, ko-ket′ri or kok′et-ri, *n.* act of *coquetting* : attempt to attract admiration, &c., in order to deceive : deceit in love. [Fr. *coquetterie*.]

**Coquette**, ko-ket′, *n.* a vain, trifling woman.

**Coquettish**, ko-ket′ish, *adj.* practising *coquetry* : befitting a coquette.—*adv.* **Coquett′ishly**.—*n.* **Coquett′ishness**. [homer.

**Cor**, kor, *n.* a Hebrew measure, the same as the

**Coracle**, kor′a-kl, *n.* a small oval rowboat used in Wales, made of skins or oilcloth stretched on wicker-work. [W. *corwgl—corwg*, anything round ; Gael. *curach*, a wicker-boat.]

**Coral**, kor′al, *n.* a hard substance of various colours, growing on the bottom of the sea, composed of the skeletons of zoophytes : a child's toy made of coral. [O. Fr. *corallium*—Gr. *korallion*.]

**Coralliferous**, kor-al-if′ėr-us, *adj.* bearing or containing *coral*. [**Coral**, and L. *fero*, to bear.]

**Coralline**, kor′al-in, *adj.* of, like, or containing *coral*.—*n.* a moss-like coral : a coral-like substance.

**Coranach**, kor′a-nak, *n.* a *dirge* or lamentation for the dead, formerly common among the Irish and Scottish Celts. [Ir., a 'dirge.']

**Corban**, kor′ban, *n.* (*lit.*) anything *devoted* to God : a vessel to receive gifts of charity : alms. [Heb. *korban*, an offering, sacrifice.]

**Corbel**, kor′bel, *n.* (*arch.*) an ornament orig. in the form of a *basket*—any ornamented projection supporting a superincumbent weight. [Fr. *corbeille*, from L. *corbicula*, dim. of *corbis*, a basket.]

**Cord**, kord, *n.* (*orig.*) a *chord* : a small rope or thick band of string.—*v.t.* to bind with a cord. [Fr. *corde*—L. *chorda*. See **Chord**.]

**Cordage**, kord′āj, *n.* a quantity of *cords* or ropes.

**Cordelier**, kor-de-lēr′, *n.* a Franciscan friar, so named from the knotted *cord* worn by him as a girdle. [O. Fr. *cordel*, dim. of *corde*, a rope.]

**Cordial**, kor′di-al, *adj.*, *hearty* : with warmth of heart : sincere : affectionate : reviving the heart or spirits.—*n.* anything which revives or com-

forts the heart: a medicine or drink for refreshing the spirits.—*adv.* Cor'dially.—*n.* Cordial'ity.
[Fr.—L. *cor, cordis,* the heart. See Core.]

Cordon, kor'don, *n.* a *cord* or ribbon bestowed as
a badge of honour: (*fort.*) a row of jutting
stones: a line of military posts. [Fr.]

Cordovan, kor'do-van, Cordwain, kord'wān, *n.*
goatskin leather, orig. from *Cordova* in Spain.

Corduroy, kor'du-roy, *n.* thick cotton stuff, corded
or ribbed. [Perh. Fr. *corde du roi,* king's cord.]

Cordwainer, kord'wān-èr, *n.* a worker in *cordovan*
or cordwain: a shoemaker.

Core, kōr, *n.* the *heart:* the inner part of anything, especially of fruit. [O. Fr. *cor*—L. *cor,
cordis,* the heart.]

Corelative, &c. See Correlative.

Coriaceous, kōr-i-ā'shus, *adj., leathery:* of or like
leather. [L. *corium*—Gr. *chorion,* skin. leather.]

Coriander, kōr-i-an'dèr, *n.* an annual plant, the
seeds of which when fresh have a *bug*-like smell,
used as a medicine, spice, &c. [Fr.—L. *cori-
andrum*—Gr. *koriannon, korion,* from *koris,* a
bug.]

Corinthian, ko-rinth'i-an, *adj.* pertaining to
*Corinth,* a city of Greece: pertaining to an
ornate order of Greek architecture.

Cork, kork, *n.* the outer bark of the cork-tree, an
oak found in the south of Europe, &c.: a stopper
made of cork.—*v.t.* to stop with a cork: to stop
up. [Sp. *corcho*—L. *cortex,* bark, rind.]

Cormorant, kor'mo-rant, *n.* a genus of web-footed
seabirds, of great voracity: a glutton. [Fr.
*cormoran* (It. *corvo marino*), from L. *corvus
marinus,* the sea-crow.—Brachet.]

Corn, korn, *n.* a grain or *kernel:* seeds that grow
in ears, as wheat, rye, &c.: *grain* of all kinds.—
*v.t.* to sprinkle with salt in grains.—*n.* Corn'-
field, a field in which corn is growing. [A.S.
*corn;* Goth. *kaurn;* akin to L. *granum.*]

Corn, korn, *n.* (*lit.*) *horn:* a hard, horny excrescence on the toe or foot. [Fr. *corne*—Low L.
*corna*—L. *cornu,* horn, akin to E. Horn.]

Corncrake. Same as Crake.

Cornea, kor'ne-a, *n.* the transparent *horny* membrane which forms the front part of the eye.

Cornel, kor'nel, *n.* the *cornelian*-cherry or dog-
wood-tree, so named from the *horny* or hard
nature of its wood. [O. Fr. *cornille,* Low L.
*corniola, cornolium*—L. *cornu,* a horn.]

Cornelian, kor-nē'li-an, *n.* a precious stone, a
variety of chalcedony. [Fr. *cornaline*—L.
*cornu,* a horn, the stone being so called from the
likeness of its colour to the reddish tint of the
finger-nail.]

Corner, kor'nèr, *n.* a *horn*-like projection: the
point where two lines meet: a secret or confined
place. [O. Fr. *corniere*—L. *cornu.*]

Cornered, kor'nèrd, *adj.* having *corners.*

Corner-stone, kor'nèr-stōn, *n.* the stone which
unites the two walls of a building at a corner:
the principal stone, esp. the corner of the foundation of a building: hence (*fig.*) something of
very great importance, as that upon which other
things rest.

Cornet, kor'net, *n.* (*lit.*) a *little horn:* a horn-
shaped trumpet: formerly, a body of cavalry
accompanied by a cornet-player: formerly, the
lowest rank of commissioned officers in the
British cavalry, corresponding to the present
sub-lieutenant.—*n.* Cor'net-a-pis'ton, a kind of
*cornet* with valves and *pistons.* [Fr. *cornet,*
dim. of *corne,* a horn, trumpet. See Corn,
(*lit.*) horn.]　　　　　　　　　　　　　　[a *cornet.*

Cornetcy, kor'net-si, *n.* the commission or rank of

Cornice, kor'nis, *n.* the highest moulded projection of a wall or column, &c. [Fr.—It.—Low L.
*coronix, coronicis*—Gr. *korōnis,* a curved line,
a flourish; akin to L. *corona.*]

Corniculate, kor-nik'ū-lāt, *adj., horned:* shaped
like a horn. [L. *corniculatus*—*corniculum,*
dim. of *cornu.*]

Cornigerous, kor-nij'èr-us, *adj., bearing horns.*
[L. *cornu,* and *gero,* to bear.]

Corn-laws, korn-lawz, *n.* (in England) laws that
restricted the importation of corn by imposing a
duty, repealed in 1846.

Cornopean, kor-nō'pe-an, *n.* a musical wind-
instrument of the *horn* or trumpet kind. [From
L. *cornu,* a horn.]

Cornucopia, kor-nū-kō'pi-a, *n.* (*lit.*) the *horn of
plenty:* according to the fable, the horn of the
goat that suckled Jupiter, placed among the
stars as an emblem of plenty. [L. *cornu,* and
*copia,* plenty.]

Corolla, ko-rol'a, *n.* the inner covering of a flower
composed of one or more leaves called petals.
[L. *corolla,* dim. of *corona,* a crown.]

Corollary, kor'ol-a-ri, *n.* an inference or deduction
from recognised facts. [L. *corollarium,* a little
garland, a gratuity—*corolla.*]

Coronal, kor'o-nal, Coronary, kor'o-nar-i, *adj.*
pertaining to a *crown,* or to the top of the head.
—Coronal, *n.* a crown or garland: the frontal
bone. [L. *corona,* a crown.]

Coronation, kor-ō-nā'shun, *n.* the act of *crowning*
a sovereign. [L. *coronatio.*]

Coroner, kor'o-nèr, *n.* an officer, appointed by the
*crown,* whose duty is to inquire into the causes
of accidental or suspicious deaths.

Coronet, kor'o-net, *n.* a *small* or inferior *crown*
worn by the nobility: an ornamental head-dress.
—*adj.* Cor'oneted, having or wearing a *coronet.*

Corporal, kor'po-ral, *n.* among infantry, a non-
commissioned or sub-officer next in rank to a
sergeant: in the navy, an officer under a master-
at-arms.—*n.* Cor'poralship. [Fr. *caporal*—It.
*caporale*—*capo,* the head—L. *caput,* the head.]

Corporal, kor'po-ral, *adj.* belonging or relating to
the *body:* having a body: not spiritual.—*n.* the
cloth used in Catholic churches for covering
the elements of the Eucharist.—*adv.* Cor'porally.
[L. *corporalis*—*corpus, corporis,* the body.]

Corporate, kor'po-rāt, *adj.* legally united into a
*body* so as to act as an individual: belonging
to a corporation: united.—*adv.* Cor'porately.—
*n.* Cor'porateness. [L. *corporatus*—*corporo,* to
shape into a body, from *corpus.*]

Corporation, kor-po-rā'shun, *n.* a *body* or society
authorised by law to act as one individual.

Corporeal, kor-pō're-al, *adj.* having a *body* or
substance: material.—*adv.* Corpo'really.—*n.*
Corporeal'ity. [L. *corporeus.*]

Corps, kōr, *n.* a large *body* of soldiers, consisting
of two divisions, and forming a complete army
by itself:—*pl.* Corps, kōrz. [Fr., from L.
*corpus.*]

Corpse, korps, *n.* the dead *body* of a human
being. [O. Fr. *corps,* or *cors,* the body—Lat.
*corpus;* akin to A.S. *hrif.* See Midriff.]

Corpulence, kor'pū-lens, Corpulency, kor'pū-
len-si, *n.* fleshiness of *body:* excessive fatness.

Corpulent, kor'pū-lent, *adj.* having a large *body:*
fleshy or fat.—*adv.* Cor'pulently. [Fr.—L.
*corpulentus*—*corpus,* a body.]

Corpuscle, kor'pus-l, *n.* a minute particle: a
physical atom.—*adj.* Corpus'cular. [L. *corpus-
culum,* a little body, dim. of *corpus,* a body.]

Correct, kor-ekt', *v.t.* to *make right:* to remove

faults: to punish: to counterbalance.—*adj.* made right or straight: free from faults: true.— *adv.* **Correct'ly.**—*n.* **Correct'ness.** [L. *corrigo, correctus—cor,* intensive, *rego,* to rule, set right.]

**Correction,** kor-ek'shun, *n.* amendment: punishment.

**Correctional,** kor-ek'shun-al, **Corrective,** kor-ekt'iv, *adj.* tending, or having the power, to *correct.*—**Correct'ive,** *n.* that which *corrects.*

**Corrector,** kor-ekt'or, *n.* he who, or that which, *corrects.*

**Correlate,** kor'e-lāt, *v.i.* to be *mutually related,* as father and son.—*n.* **Correla'tion.** [Coined from L. *cor,* with, and **Relate.**]

**Correlative,** kor-el'a-tiv, *adj., mutually* or reciprocally *related.*—*n.* person or thing correspondingly *related* to another person or thing.—*adv.* **Correl'atively.**—*n.* **Correl'ativeness.**

**Correspond,** kor-e-spond', *v.i.* to answer, suit: to hold intercourse, especially by sending and receiving letters.—*adv.* **Correspond'ingly.** [Coined from L. *cor,* with, and **Respond.**]

**Correspondence,** kor-e-spond'ens, **Correspondency,** kor-e-spond'en-si, *n.* suitableness: friendly intercourse: communication by means of letters: letters which pass between correspondents.

**Correspondent,** kor-e-spond'ent, *adj.* agreeing with: suitable.—*n.* one with whom intercourse is kept up by letters.—*adv.* **Correspond'ently.**

**Corridor,** kor'i-dōr, *n.* a passage-way or open gallery *running along,* communicating with separate chambers. [Fr.—It. *corridore,* a runner, a running—It. *correre,* to run—L. *curro.*]

**Corrigenda,** kor-i-jen'da, *n.pl.* things to be *corrected.* [reformed, or punished.]

**Corrigible,** kor'i-ji-bl, *adj.* that may be *corrected.*

**Corroborant,** kor-ob'o-rant, **Corroborative,** kor-ob'o-rāt-iv, *adj.* tending to confirm.—*n.* that which corroborates.

**Corroborate,** kor-ob'o-rāt, *v.t.* to confirm: to make more certain. [L. *cor,* intensive, and *roboro, roboratus,* to make strong. See **Robust.**]

**Corroboration,** kor-ob-o-rā'shun, *n.* confirmation.

**Corrode,** kor-ōd', *v.t.* to *gnaw* or eat away by degrees: to rust. [L. *cor,* intensive, *rodo, rosus,* to gnaw.]

**Corrodent,** kor-ōd'ent, *adj.* having the power of *corroding.*—*n.* that which corrodes. [away.

**Corrosion,** kor-ō'zhun, *n.* act of eating or wasting

**Corrosive,** kor-ōs'iv, *adj.* having the quality of eating away.—*n.* that which has the power of corroding.—*adv.* **Corros'ively.**—*n.* **Corros'iveness.** [L. *corrosus.* See **Corrode.**]

**Corrugate,** kor'oo-gāt, *v.t.* to *wrinkle* or draw into folds.—*n.* **Corruga'tion.** [L. *cor,* intensive, *rugo, rugatus,* to wrinkle—*ruga,* a wrinkle.]

**Corrupt,** kor-upt', *v.t.* to make putrid: to defile: to debase: to bribe.—*v.i.* to rot: to lose purity. —*adj.* putrid: depraved: defiled: not genuine: full of errors.—*adv.* **Corrupt'ly.**—*ns.* **Corrupt'ness, Corrupt'er.** [L. *cor,* intensive, and *rumpo, ruptus,* to break.]

**Corruptible,** kor-upt'i-bl, *adj.* liable to be corrupted.—*adv.* **Corrupt'ibly.**—*ns.* **Corruptibil'ity, Corrupt'ibleness.**

**Corruption,** kor-up'shun, *n.* rottenness: putrid matter: impurity: bribery. [of *corrupting.*

**Corruptive,** kor upt'iv, *adj.* having the quality

**Corsair,** kor'sār, *n.* a pirate: a pirate's vessel. [Fr. *corsaire,* one who makes the course or ranges—L. *cursus,* a running—*curro,* to run.]

**Corse,** kors, *n.* a poetic form of **Corpse.**

**Corselet, Corslet,** kors'let, *n.* a piece of armour

for covering the *body.* [Fr. *corselet,* dim. of O. Fr. *cors*—L. *corpus,* the body.]

**Corset,** kor'set, *n.* an article of women's dress laced round the *body:* stays. [Dim. of O. Fr. *cors*—L. *corpus,* the body.]

**Cortege,** kor'tāzh, *n.* a *train* of attendants, orig. applied only to the *court:* a procession. [Fr. —It. *corteggio—corte,* court. See **Court.**]

**Cortes,** kor'tes, *n.* the parliament of Spain and Portugal. [Sp., *pl.* of *corte,* a court.]

**Cortex,** kor'teks, *n.* the *bark* or skin of a plant: a covering.—*adj.* **Cor'tical,** pertaining to *bark:* external. [L. *cortex, corticis,* bark. See **Cork.**]

**Corticate,** kor'ti-kāt, **Corticated,** kor'ti-kāt-ed, *adj.* furnished with *bark;* resembling bark.

**Corundum,** ko-run'dum, *n.* a crystallised mineral of extreme hardness, consisting of pure alumina, used for polishing gems. [Hind. *kurand.*]

**Coruscate,** ko-rus'kāt or kor'-, *v.i.* to *sparkle:* to throw off flashes of light.—*adj.* **Corus'cant,** flashing. [L. *corusco, coruscatus,* to vibrate, glitter—*coruscus.*] [den flash of light.

**Coruscation,** ko-rus-kā'shun, *n.* a glittering: sud-

**Corvette,** kor-vet', *n.* a small *ship* of war, next to a frigate. [Fr.—Port. *corbeta*—L. *corbīta,* a slow-sailing ship, from *corbis,* a basket.]

**Corvine,** kor'vīn, *adj.* pertaining to the *crow.* [L. *corvinus—corvus,* a crow.]

**Corypheus,** kor-i-fē'us, *n.* the chief or leader, esp. the leader of the chorus in the Attic drama. [L.—Gr. *koryphaios—koryphē,* the head.]

**Cosecant,** kō-sē'kant, **Cosine,** kō'sīn, **Cotangent,** kō-tan'jent, *ns.* (*math.*) the secant, sine, or tangent respectively of the complement of an arc or angle of 90°.

**Cosmetic,** koz-met'ik, *adj.* improving beauty, especially that of the complexion.—*n.* a preparation used for beautifying the complexion.—*adv.* **Cosmet'ically.** [Gr. *kosmētikos—kosmeo,* to adorn—*kosmos,* order, ornament.]

**Cosmic,** koz'mik, **Cosmical,** koz'mik-al, *adj.* relating to the *world* or to the universe: (*astron.*) rising or setting with the sun.—*adv.* **Cos'mically.** [Gr. *kosmikos—kosmos.*]

**Cosmogonist,** koz-mog'o-nist, *n.* one who speculates on the origin of the universe.

**Cosmogony,** koz-mog'o-ni, *n.* the science of the *formation of the universe.* [Gr. *kosmogonia— kosmos,* and *gon,* root of *gignomai,* to be born.]

**Cosmographic,** koz-mo-graf'ik, **Cosmographical,** koz-mo-graf'ik-al, *adj.* pertaining to *cosmography.*

**Cosmography,** koz-mog'ra-fi, *n.* (*lit.*) a *description of the world:* the science of the constitution of the universe.—*n.* **Cosmog'rapher.** [Gr. *kosmographia—kosmos,* and *graphō,* to write.]

**Cosmologist,** koz-mol'o-jist, *n.* one versed in cosmology.

**Cosmology,** koz-mol'o-ji, *n.* the *science of the universe:* a treatise on the structure and parts of the system of creation.—*adj.* **Cosmolog'ical.** [Coined from Gr. *kosmos,* and *logos,* discourse.]

**Cosmopolitan,** koz-mo-pol'i-tan, **Cosmopolite,** koz-mop'o-līt, *n.* (*lit.*) a *citizen of the world:* one who can make a home everywhere: one free from local or national prejudices.—*n.* **Cosmopol'itanism.** [Gr. *kosmopolitēs—kosmos,* and *politēs,* a citizen—*polis,* a city.]

**Cosmorama,** koz-mo-rä'ma, *n.* a *view,* or a series of views, of different *parts of the world.*—*adj.* **Cosmoram'ic.** [Gr. *kosmos,* and *horama,* a spectacle—*horaō,* to see.]

**Cosmos,** koz'mos, *n.* the world as an *orderly* or systematic whole, opposed to *chaos.* [Gr.]

**Cossack**, kos'ak, *n.* one of a warlike tribe in the east and south of Russia. [Russ. *Kasake* (of Tartar origin). a light-armed soldier, a robber.]

**Cost**, kost, *v.t.* to bring a certain price : to require to be laid out or suffered :—*pa.t.* and *pa.p.* cost. —*n.* what is laid out, or suffered to obtain anything.—*pl.* expenses of a lawsuit. [Fr. *coûter*, O. Fr. *couster*—L. *constare*, to stand at—*con*, and *stare*, to stand.]

**Costal**, kost'al, *adj.* relating to the *ribs*, or to the side of the body. [L. *costa*, a rib.]

**Costermonger**, kos'tér-mung-gér, *n.* a *seller of costards* or apples and other fruit : an itinerant seller of fruit. [*Costard*, a variety of apple, and **Monger**.]

**Costive**, kos'tiv, *adj.* having the motion of the bowels too slow.—*adv.* **Cos'tively**. [Fr. *constipé*. See **Constipate**.]      [of the bowels.

**Costiveness**, kos'tiv-nes, *n.* slowness in the action

**Costly**, kost'li, *adj.* of *great cost* : high-priced : valuable.—*n.* **Cost'liness.**

**Costume**, kos-tūm', *n.* the manner of dressing prevalent at a particular period or place : dress. [Fr.—It.—Low L. *costuma*—L. *consuetudo*, custom. Doublet of **Custom**.]

**Cot**, kot, *n.* a *small dwelling*, a cottage : a small bed : a sleeping-place on board ship : an inclosure for sheep or cattle. [A.S. *cote*, a cot or den ; a doublet of **Coat**.]     [variety of **Cot**.]

**Cote**, kōt, *n.* an inclosure for sheep, &c. [A

**Cotemporaneous**, kō-tem-po-rā'ne-us, **Cotemporary**, kō-tem'po-rar-i. Same as **Contemporaneous, Contemporary**.

**Coterie**, kō'te-rē, *n.* a number of persons who meet familiarly for social, literary, or other purposes. [Fr. ; orig. a number of peasants clubbed together to obtain a tenure of land from a lord— Low L. *cota*, a hut. See **Cot**.]

**Cotillon, Cotillion**, ko-til'yun, *n.* a brisk dance by eight persons. [Fr.—*cotte*, a petticoat—Low L. *cotta*, a tunic. See **Coat**.]

**Cotquean**, kot'kwēn, *n.* a man who busies himself with women's affairs. [**Cot**, a small house, and *quean*.]

**Cottage**, kot'āj, *n.* a *cot* : formerly applied to a hut or hovel, now to a small neat dwelling.

**Cottager**, kot'āj-ér, *n.* one who dwells in a *cottage*.

**Cottar, Cotter**, kot'ér, *n.* Same as **Cottager**.

**Cotton**, kot'n, *n.* a soft substance like fine wool, got from the pods of the cotton-plant : cloth made of cotton. [Fr. *coton*—Ar. *qutun*.]

**Cotyledon**, kot-i-lē'don, *n.* a *cup-shaped* leaf or lobe in certain plants, forming part of the seed, and on which the growing germ is nourished. [Gr. *kotylēdōn*—*kotylē*, a cup.]

**Cotyledonous**, kot-i-lē'don-us or -led'on-us, *adj.* pertaining to or having *cotyledons* or seed-lobes.

**Couch**, kowch, *v.t.* to *lay down* on a bed, &c. : to arrange in language, to express : to depress or remove a cataract in the eye.—*v.i.* to lie down for the purpose of sleep, concealment, &c. : to bend or stoop in reverence.—**Couch a spear**, to fix it in its rest at the side of the armour. [Fr. *coucher*, to lay or lie down, O. Fr. *colcher* —L. *collocare*, to place—*col*, and *locus*, a place.]

**Couch**, kowch, *n.* any place for rest or sleep : a bed.

**Couchant**, kowch'ant, *adj.* *couching* or lying down with the head raised. [Fr., pr.p. of *coucher*.]      [as the puma. [Brazilian.]

**Cougar**, kōō'gar, *n.* an American animal ; same

**Cough**, kof, *n.* an effort of the lungs to throw off injurious matter, accompanied by a harsh sound, proceeding from the throat.—*v.i.* to make this

effort.—*v.t.* to expel from the throat or lungs by a cough. [From a Low Ger. root found in Dut. *kughen*, to cough, imitative of the sound.]

**Could**, kood, *past tense* of **Can**. [O. E. *coude*, *couth*—A.S. *cuthe* for *cunthe*, was able ; *l* is inserted from the influence of *would* and *should*.]

**Coulter**. See **Colter**.

**Council**, kown'sil, *n.* an assembly *called together* for deliberation or advice. [Fr. *concile*—L. *concilium*—*con*, together, and root *cal*, to call.]

**Councillor**, kown'sil-or, *n.* a member of a *council*.

**Counsel**, kown'sel, *n.*, *consultation* : deliberation : advice : plan : purpose : one who gives counsel, a barrister or advocate.—*v.t.* to give advice : to warn :—*pr.p.* coun'selling ; *pa.p.* coun'selled. [Fr. *conseil*—L. *consilium*, advice—*consulere*, to consult.]

**Counsellor**, kown'sel-or, *n.* one who *counsels* : a barrister.—*n.* **Coun'sellorship**.

**Count**, kownt, *n.* on the continent, a title of nobility equal in rank to an English earl.—*fem.* **Count'ess**, the wife of a *count* or earl. [Fr. *comte*, from L. *comes, comitis*, a companion (of a prince)—*con*, with, and *eo, itum*, to go.]

**Count**, kownt, *v.t.* to number, sum up : to ascribe : esteem : consider.—*v.i.* to add to or increase a number by being counted to it : to depend.—*n.* act of numbering : the number counted : a particular charge in an indictment.—*adj.* **Count'less**. [O. Fr. *cunter*, Fr. *compter*—L. *computare*. See **Compute**.]

**Countenance**, kown'ten-ans, *n.* the face : the expression of the face : appearance.—*v.t.* to favour or approve. [Fr. *contenance*—L. *continentia*, restraint, in late L. demeanour—L. *continere*, to contain. See **Contain**.]

**Counter**, kown'tér, *n.* he who or that which *counts* : that which indicates a number : a piece of metal, &c. used in reckoning : a table on which money is counted or goods laid.

**Counter**, kown'tér, *adv.*, *against* : in opposition. —*adj.* contrary : opposite. [L. *contra*, against.]

**Counteract**, kown-tér-akt', *v.t.* to *act counter* or in opposition to : to hinder or defeat.—*n.* **Counterac'tion**.

**Counteractive**, kown-tér-akt'iv, *adj.* tending to *counteract*.—*n.* one who or that which counteracts.—*adv.* **Counteract'ively**.

**Counterbalance**, kown-tér-bal'ans, *v.t.* to *balance* by weight on the *opposite* side : to act against with equal weight, power, or influence.

**Counterbalance**, kown'tér-bal-ans, *n.* an equal weight, power, or agency working in opposition.

**Counterfeit**, kown'tér-fit, *v.t.* to imitate : to copy without authority : to forge. [Fr. *contrefait*, from *contrefaire*, to imitate—L. *contra*, against, *facere*, to do, to make.]

**Counterfeit**, kown'tér-fit, *n.* something false or copied, or that pretends to be true and original. —*adj.* pretended : made in imitation of : forged : false.

**Counterfoil**, kown'tér-foil, *n.* the corresponding part of a tally or check. [**Counter** and **Foil**.]

**Countermand**, kown-tér-mand', *v.t.* to give a *command in opposition* to every already given : to revoke. [Fr. *contremander*—L. *contra*, against, and *mando*, to order.]

**Countermand**, kown'tér-mand, *n.* a revocation of a former order.—*adj.* **Countermand'able**.

**Countermarch**, kown-tér-märch', *v.i.* to march back or in a direction contrary to a former one.

**Countermarch**, kown'tér-märch, *n.* a marching backward or in a direction different from a former one : (*mil.*) an evolution by which a body of men change front, and still retain the same men in the front rank : change of measures.

**Counterpane,** kown'tĕr-pān, *n.* a coverlet for a *bed, stitched* or woven in squares. [A corr. of O. Fr. *contrepointe,* which is a corr. of *coulte-pointe*—L. *culcita puncta,* a stitched pillow or cover. See **Quilt.**]

**Counterpart,** kown'tĕr-pärt, *n.* the part that answers to another part : that which fits into or completes another, having the qualities which the other lacks, and so an opposite.

**Counterpoint,** kown'tĕr-point, *n.* the older form of **Counterpane.**

**Counterpoint,** kown'tĕr-point, *n.* (*music*) written harmony which originally consisted of *points* placed *opposite* to each other : the setting of a harmony of one or more parts to a melody : the art of composition. [Fr. *contrepoint*—*contre,* against, and *point,* a point. See **Counter** and **Point.**]

**Counterpoise,** kown-tĕr-poiz', *v.t.* to *poise* or weigh *against* or on the opposite side : to act in opposition to with equal effect.—*n.* **Coun'terpoise,** an equally heavy weight in the other scale. [**Counter** and **Poise.**]

**Counterscarp,** kown'tĕr-skärp, *n.* (*fort.*) the side of the ditch nearest to the besiegers and *opposite* to the *scarp.* [**Counter** and **Scarp.**]

**Countersign,** kown'tĕr-sīn, *v.t.* to *sign* on the *opposite side* of a writing : to sign in addition to the signature of a superior, to attest the authenticity of a writing.—*n.* a military private *sign* or word, which must be given in order to pass a sentry : a counter-signature. [**Counter** and **Sign.**]     [*countersigned* to a writing.]

**Counter-signature,** kown'tĕr-sig'na-tūr, *n.* a name

**Counter-tenor,** kown'tĕr-ten'or, *n.* name applied to alto, when sung by a male voice (so called, because a *contrast* to tenor).

**Countervail,** kown-tĕr-vāl', *v.t.* to be of *avail against* : to act against with equal effect : to be of equal value to. [**Counter** and **Avail.**]

**Countess.** See under **Count.**

**Country,** kun'tri, *n.* a rural region as distinct from a town : a tract of land : the land in which one was born, or in which one resides.—*adj.* belonging to the country : rustic : rude. [Fr. *contrée* —Low L. *contrata, contrada,* an extension of L. *contra,* over against. It was a name adapted by the German settlers in Gaul as a translation of Ger. *gegend,* region (from *gegen,* over against).]

**Country-dance.** See **Contra-dance.**

**Countryman,** kun'tri-man, *n.* one who lives in the *country* : a farmer : one born in the same country with another.

**County,** kown'ti, *n.* (*orig.*) the province ruled by a *count* : a portion of a country separated for the administration of justice : a shire.

**Couple,** kup'l, *n.* two of a kind *joined together,* or connected : two : a pair.—*v.t.* to join together : to unite. [Fr., from L. *copula.* See **Copula.**]

**Couplet,** kup'let, *n.,* *two* lines of verse that rhyme with each other.

**Coupling,** kup'ling, *n.* that which connects.

**Coupon,** kōō'pong, *n.* an interest warrant attached to transferable bonds, which is *cut off* when presented for payment. [Fr.—*couper,* to cut off.]

**Courage,** kur'āj, *n.* the quality that enables men to meet dangers without fear : bravery : spirit. [Fr. *courage,* from L. *cor,* the heart.]

**Courageous,** kur-ā'jus, *adj., full of courage :* brave.—*adv.* **Coura'geously.**—*n.* **Coura'geousness.**

**Courier,** kōō'ri-ĕr, *n.* a *runner* : a messenger : a state servant or messenger : a travelling attendant. [Fr., from *courir*—L. *currere,* to run.]

**Course,** kōrs, *n.* the *act of running* : the road or track on which one runs : the direction pursued : a voyage : a race : regular progress from point to point : method of procedure : conduct : a part of a meal served at one time. [Fr. *cours*— L. *cursus,* from *curro, cursum,* to run.]

**Course,** kōrs, *v.t.* to *run,* chase, or hunt after,— *v.i.* to move with speed as in a race or hunt.

**Courser,** kōrs'ĕr, *n.* a *runner* : a swift horse : one who courses or hunts.

**Coursing,** kōrs'ing, *n., hunting* with greyhounds.

**Court,** kōrt, *n.* a *space inclosed* : a space surrounded by houses : the palace of a sovereign : the body of persons who form his suite or council : attention : civility, as to pay court : (*law*) the hall of justice : the judges and officials who preside there : any body of persons assembled to decide causes, whether civil, military, or ecclesiastical.—*v.t.* to pay attentions to : to woo : to solicit : to seek.—*n.* **Court'yard,** a court or inclosure near a house. [Fr. *cour,* O. Fr. *cort*— Low L. *cortis,* a courtyard—L. *cors, cohors,* an inclosure ; akin to Gr. *chortos,* an inclosed place, L. *hortus,* a garden. See **Yard.**]

**Courteous,** kurt'yus, *adj.* of *court-like* manners : polite : respectful : obliging.—*adv.* **Court'eously.** —*n.* **Court'eousness.**

**Courtesan, Courtezan,** kurt'e-zan, *n.* a fashionable prostitute. [Sp. *cortesana*—*corte,* court. See **Court.**]

**Courtesy,** kurt'e-si, *n., courtliness :* elegance of manner : an act of civility or respect.

**Courtesy,** kurt'si, *n.* the gesture of salutation or respect performed by women by slightly depressing the body and bending the knees.—*v.i.* to make a courtesy :—*pr.p.* court'esying ; *pa.p.* court'esied. [O. Fr. *cortoisie.* See **Court.**]

**Courtier,** kōrt'yĕr, *n.* one who frequents *courts* or palaces : one who courts or flatters.

**Courtly,** kōrt'li, *adj.* having manners *like* those of a *court* : elegant.—*n.* **Court'liness.**

**Court-martial,** kōrt'-mär'shal, *n.* a *court* held by officers of the *army* or *navy* for the trial of offences against military or naval laws.—*pl.* **Courts-mar'tial.**

**Court-plaster,** kōrt'-plas'tĕr, *n.* sticking *plaster* made of silk, orig. applied as patches on the face by ladies at *court.*

**Courtship,** kōrt'ship, *n.* the act of wooing with intention to marry.

**Cousin,** kuz'n, *n.* formerly, a kinsman generally : now, the son or daughter of an uncle or aunt.— **Cousin-german,** a first-cousin. [Fr.—L. *consobrinus*—*con,* sig. connection, and *sobrinus* for *sororinus,* applied to the children of sisters— *soror,* a sister.]

**Cove,** kōv, *n.* a small inlet of the sea : a bay.— *v.t.* to overarch, and thus form a hollow. [A.S. *cofa,* a chamber ; Ice. *kofi,* a shed ; not to be confused with *cave* or *alcove.*]

**Covenant,** kuv'e-nant, *n.* a mutual agreement : the writing containing the agreement.—*v.i.* to enter into an agreement : to contract or bargain. [O. Fr.—L. *con,* together, and *venio,* to come.]

**Covenanter,** kuv-e-nant'ĕr, *n.* one who signed or adhered to the Scottish National Covenant of 1638.

**Cover,** kuv'ĕr, *v.t.* to hide : to clothe : to shelter : to brood or sit on : to be sufficient for, as to cover expense.—*n.* that which covers or protects : (*hunting*) the retreat of a fox or hare.

[Fr. *couvrir* (It. *coprire*)—L. *cooperire*—*con*, and *operio*, to cover.]

**Covering**, kuv'ẽr-ing, *n.* anything that *covers*.

**Coverlet**, kuv'ẽr-let, *n.* a *bedcover*. [Fr. *couvre-lit*, from *couvre*, and *lit*—L. *lectum*, a bed.]

**Covert**, kuv'ẽrt, *adj.*, *covered* : concealed : secret. —*n.* a place that covers or affords protection.

**Covertly**, kuv'ẽrt-li, *adv.* in a *covered* or concealed manner.

**Coverture**, kuv'ẽr-tūr, *n.*, *covering*, shelter, defence : (*law*) the condition of a married woman.

**Covet**, kuv'et, *v.t.* or *v.i.* to *desire* or wish for *eagerly* : to wish for what is unlawful.—*adj.* **Cov'etable**. [O. Fr. *coveiter*, Fr. *convoiter*; It. *cubitare*—L. *cupidus*, desirous—*cupio*, to desire.]

**Covetous**, kuv'et-us, *adj.* inordinately *desirous* : avaricious.—*adv.* **Cov'etously.**—*n.* **Cov'etousness.**

**Covey**, kuv'i, *n.* a *brood* or *hatch* of birds : a small flock of birds—said of game. [Fr. *couvée* —*couvé*, pa.p. of *couver*, to hatch—L. *cubo*, to lie down.]

**Cow**, kow, *n.* the female of the bull. [A.S. *cu*; Ger. *kuh*, Sans. *go* : from its cry.]

**Cow**, kow, *v.t.* to *subdue*, *keep under* : to dishearten. [Ice. *kuga*, Dan. *kue*, to subdue, to keep under.]

**Coward**, kow'ard, *n.* one who *turns tail* : one without courage. [O. Fr. *couard*, It. *codardo*— L. *cauda*, a tail.]

**Coward**, kow'ard, **Cowardly**, kow'ard-li, *adj.* afraid of danger : timid : mean.—*adv.* **Cow'ardly.**—*n.* **Cow'ardliness.** [timidity.

**Cowardice**, kow'ard-is, *n.* want of courage :

**Cower**, kow'ẽr, *v.i.* to sink down, generally through fear : to crouch. [Cf. Ice. *kura*, Dan. *kure*, to lie quiet.]

**Cowl**, kowl, *n.* a *cap* or *hood* : a monk's hood : a cover for a chimney. [A.S. *cufle*; Ice. *cofl*: akin to L. *cucullus*, hood.]

**Cowled**, kowld, *adj.* wearing a *cowl*.

**Cowpox**, kow'poks, *n.* a disease which appears in *pox* or pimples on the teats of the *cow*, the matter from which is used for **Vaccination**.

**Cowry**, kow'ri, *n.* a small shell used as money in the E. Indies and in Africa. [Hind. *kauri*.]

**Cowslip**, kow'slip, *n.* a species of primrose which appears early in spring in moist places. [A.S. *ku-slyppe*, a word of doubtful meaning.]

**Cowtree**, kow'trē, *n.* a tree that produces a nourishing fluid resembling milk.

**Coxcomb**, koks'kōm, *n.* a strip of red cloth notched like a cock's comb, which professional fools used to wear : a fool : a fop. [Corr. of **Cockscomb**.]

**Coxswain**. See **Cockswain**.

**Coy**, koy, *adj.* modest : bashful : shy.—*adv.* **Coy'ly.**—*n.* **Coy'ness.** [Fr. *coi*; from L. *quietus*, quiet.] [ishly.—*n.* **Coy'ishness**.

**Coyish**, koy'ish, *adj.*, somewhat *coy*.—*adv.* **Coy'-**

**Coz**, kuz, *n.* a contraction of **Cousin**.

**Cozen**, kuz'n, *v.t.* to flatter : to cheat.—*n.* **Coz'ener**. [From Fr. *cousiner*, to claim kindred for one's own advantage, play the parasite—*cousin*, a cousin.] [deceit.

**Cozenage**, kuz'n-āj, *n.* the practice of *cheating* :

**Cozy**, kō'zi, *adj.* snug : comfortable.—*adv.* **Co'zily.** [Fr. *causer*, to chat : prob. fr. Ger. *kosen*, to caress.]

**Crab**, krab, *n.* a common shell-fish having ten legs, the front pair terminating in claws : a sign in the zodiac. [A.S. *crabba*; Ger. *krabbe*.]

**Crab**, krab, *n.* a wild *bitter* apple. [Perh. because it pinches, like a *crab*.]

**Crabbed**, krab'ed, *adj.* ill-natured : peevish :

harsh : rough : difficult, perplexing. —*adv.* **Crabb'edly.**—*n.* **Crabb'edness**.

**Crack**, krak, *v.i.* to utter a sharp sudden sound : to split.—*v.t.* to produce a sudden noise : to break into chinks : to split : to break partially or wholly.—*n.* a sudden sharp splitting sound : a chink : a flaw. [A.S. *cearcian*, to crack : Dut. *krak*, Gael. *cnac*; like **Creak**, **Croak**, &c., from the sound.]

**Cracker**, krak'ẽr, *n.* the person or thing which *cracks* : a noisy firework : a hard biscuit.

**Crackle**, krak'l, *v.i.* to give out *slight* but *frequent cracks*.—*n.* **Crack'ling**, the rind of roasted pork.

**Cracknel**, krak'nel, *n.* a hard, *brittle* biscuit.

**Cradle**, krā'dl, *n.* a bed or crib in which children are rocked : (*fig.*) infancy : a frame in which anything is imbedded : a case for a broken limb : a frame under a ship for launching it.—*v.t.* to lay or rock in a cradle. [A.S. *cradol*, borrowed from Gael. *creathall*, a cradle, a grate; akin to L. *craticula*, dim. of *crates*, a crate, and to E. **Hurdle.** See **Crate**.]

**Craft**, kraft, *n.* cunning : dexterity : art : trade : small ships. [A.S. *craeft*; Ger. *kraft*, power, energy ; from root of **Cramp**.] [or trade.

**Craftsman**, krafts'man, *n.* one engaged in a *craft*

**Crafty**, kraft'i, *adj.* having *craft* or skill : cunning : deceitful.—*adv.* **Craft'ily.**—*n.* **Craft'iness**.

**Crag**, krag, *n.* a rough, steep rock or point : (*geol.*) a bed of gravel mixed with shells. [Gael. *creag*, W. *craig*, a rock, which is short for *car-eg*, a dim. from root *car*, a rock, whence also *carn* = E. **Cairn**.]

**Cragged**, krag'ed, **Craggy**, krag'i, *adj.*, *full of crags* or broken rocks : rough : rugged.—*ns.* **Cragg'edness**, **Cragg'iness**.

**Crake**, krāk, **Corn'crake**, *n.* the landrail, a migratory bird which lives much among grass, corn, &c. [So named from its cry.]

**Cram**, kram, *v.t.* to press close : to stuff : to fill to superfluity.—*v.i.* to eat greedily :—*pr.p.* cramm'-ing ; *pa.p.* crammed'.—*n.* **Cramm'er**, one who prepares students for examination by *cramming* them with the required knowledge. [A.S. *crammian*; Ice. *kremja*, to squeeze ; Dan. *kramme*, to crumple, crush.]

**Cramp**, kramp, *n.* a painful spasmodic contraction of muscles : restraint : a piece of iron bent at the ends, for holding together wood, stone, &c.— *v.t.* to affect with spasms : to confine : to hinder : to fasten with a crampiron. [E.; Ger. *krampf*, conn. with **Clamp**.]

**Crampfish**, kramp'fish, *n.* the torpedo, because it causes *spasms* when touched.

**Cranberry**, kran'ber-i, *n.* a red, sour *berry* growing on a stalk resembling the neck of a *crane*, much used for tarts, &c.

**Cranch**, kranch. Same as **Crunch**.

**Crane**, krān, *n.* a large wading bird, with long legs, neck, and bill : a bent pipe for drawing liquor out of a cask, a machine for raising heavy weights —both named from their likeness to the bird. [A.S. *cran*; Ger. *kranich*, W. *garan*; Gr. *geranos*, L. *grus*, a crane, from the sound ; cf. **Garrulous**.]

**Cranial**, krā'ni-al, *adj.* pertaining to the *cranium*.

**Craniologist**, krā-ni-ol'o-jist, *n.* one skilled in craniology.

**Craniology**, krā-ni-ol'o-ji, *n.* the study of *skulls* : phrenology.—*adj.* **Craniolog'ical**. [Low L. *cranium*, a skull, and Gr. *logos*, a discourse.]

**Cranium**, krā'ni-um, *n.* the skull : the bones inclosing the brain. [Low L. *cranium*—Gr. *kranion*, from *karē*, the head.]

**Crank**, krangk, *n.* a *crook* or *bend:* a bend on an axis for communicating motion : a twisting or conceit in speech. [From an E. root *krank*, seen also in Dut. *kronkelen*, *krinkelen*, to curl, twist, bend ; also in E. **Cringe**, **Crinkle**.]

**Crank**, krangk, **Crankle**, krangk′l, **Crinkle**, kringk′l, *v.t.* to form with short turns or wrinkles.—*v.i.* to bend, turn, wind, or wrinkle.

**Crank**, krangk, **Cranky**, krangk′i, *adj.* weak : (*naut.*) liable to be upset. [From the notion of bending ; cf. Ger. *krank*, sick.]

**Crankle**, krangk′l, **Crinkle**, kringk′l, *n.* a turn, winding, or wrinkle.

**Crankness**, krangk′nes, *n.* liability to be upset.

**Crannog**, kran′og, *n.* the name given in Scotland and Ireland to a fortified island (partly natural and partly artificial) in a lake, used as a dwelling-place and place of refuge among the early inhabitants.

**Cranny**, kran′i, *n.* (*lit.*) a *rent:* a chink : a secret place. [Fr. *cran*, a notch—L. *crena*, a notch.]

**Crape**, krāp, *n.* a thin transparent *crisp* or crimpled silk stuff, usually black, used in mourning. [Fr. *crêpe*, O. Fr. *crespe*—L. *crispus*, crisp.]

**Crapulence**, krap′ū-lens, *n.* sickness caused by intemperance.—*adj.* **Crap′ulous**, **Crap′ulent**. [Fr. *crapule*—L. *crapula*, intoxication.]

**Crash**, krash, *n.* a noise as of things breaking or being *crushed* by falling.—*v.i.* to make a noise as of things falling and breaking. [Formed from the sound. See **Crush**.]

**Crasis**, krā′sis, *n.* (*gram.*) the *mingling* or contraction of two vowels into one long vowel, or into a diphthong. [Gr. *krasis—kerannūmi*, to mix.]

**Crass**, kras, *adj., gross :* thick : coarse. [L. *crassus*.]

**Crassament**, kras′a-ment, *n.* the *gross* or thick part of a fluid, esp. blood. [L. *crassamentum*—*crassus*.]

**Crassitude**, kras′i-tūd, *n.* grossness : coarseness.

**Cratch**, krach, *n.* a crib to hold hay for cattle, a manger. [Fr. *crèche*, a manger ; from a Teut. root, of which E. **Crib** is an example.]

**Crate**, krāt, *n.*, *wicker-work :* a case made of rods wattled together, and used for packing crockery in. [L. *crates*, a hurdle. See **Cradle**.]

**Crater**, krāt′ėr, *n.* the *bowl*-shaped mouth of a volcano. [L. *crater*—Gr. *kratēr*, a large bowl for mixing wine, from *kerannūmi*, to mix.]

**Craunch**, kranch. A form of **Crunch**.

**Cravat**, kra-vat′, *n.* a kind of neckcloth worn by men, introduced into France in 1636 from the *Cravates* or *Croatians*. [Fr. *cravate*, a corruption of *Croat*.]

**Crave**, krāv, *v.t.* to beg earnestly : to beseech : to demand or require : to long for. [A.S. *crafian*, to crave.]

**Craven**, krāv′n, *n.* a coward : a spiritless fellow.—*adj.* cowardly : spiritless.—*adv.* **Crav′enly**.—*n.* **Crav′enness**. [Orig. *cravant*, or *cravand*, *craving* quarter or mercy when vanquished.]

**Craving**, krāv′ing, *n.* a strong desire.

**Craw**, kraw, *n.* the *crop*, *throat*, or first stomach of fowls. [Dan. *kroe* ; Ger. *kragen* ; Scot. *craig*, the neck.]

**Crawfish**. See **Crayfish**.

**Crawl**, krawl, *v.i.* to *creep* or move on : to move feebly or slowly. [Ice. *krafla*, Dan. *kravle* ; Ger. *krabbeln*, to creep.]

**Crayfish**, krā′fish, **Crawfish**, kraw′fish, *n.* a small species of *crab* or lobster, found in fresh water. [A corr. of Fr. *écrevisse*, from O. Ger. *krebiz*, a crab ; not a compound of **Fish**.]

**Crayon**, krā′on, *n.* a pencil made of *chalk* or pipeclay, variously coloured, used for drawing : a drawing done with crayons. [Fr. *crayon—craie*, chalk, from L. *creta*, chalk.]

**Craze**, krāz, *v.t.* to weaken : to derange (applied to the intellect).—*adv.* **Craz′edly**. [Ice. *krasa*, to crackle, from which also is derived Fr. *écraser*, to crush, shatter ; akin to **Crash**.]

**Crazy**, krāz′i, *adj.* feeble : crack-brained : insane.—*adv.* **Craz′ily**.—*n.* **Craz′iness**.

**Creak**, krēk, *v.i.* to make a sharp, *cracking*, grating *sound*, as of a hinge, &c. [E. ; O. Fr. *criquer*, is from the same Teut. root ; conn. with **Crack**.]

**Cream**, krēm, *n.* the oily substance which forms on milk : the best part of anything.—*v.t.* to take off the cream.—*v.i.* to gather or form cream. [Fr. *crème*—Low L. *crema* ; perh. allied to A.S. *reám*, Ger. *rahm*, which had prob. initial *h*.]

**Cream-faced**, krēm′-fāst, *adj.*, *pale-faced* either naturally or through fear : coward-looking.

**Creamy**, krēm′i, *adj.*, *full of* or like *cream:* gathering like cream.—*n.* **Cream′iness**.

**Crease**, krēs, *n.* a mark made by folding or doubling anything.—*v.t.* to make creases in anything. [Bret. *kriz*, a wrinkle ; perh. akin to L. *crispus*.]

**Crease**, **Creese**, krēs, *n.* a Malay dagger. [The Malay word.]

**Creasote**. See **Creosote**.

**Create**, krē-āt′, *v.t.* to bring into being or form out of nothing : to beget : to form : to invest with a new form, office, or character : to produce. [L. *creo*, *creatus* ; cog. with Gr. *krainō*, to accomplish, to fulfil ; Sans. *kri*, to make.]

**Creatin**, krē′a-tin, *n.* a crystallisable substance found in the *flesh* or muscular tissue of animals. [Gr. *kreas*, flesh.]

**Creation**, krē-ā′shun, *n.* the act of *creating*, esp. the universe : that which is created, the world, the universe. [L. *creatio*.]

**Creative**, krē-ā′tiv, *adj.* having power to *create:* that creates.—*adv.* **Crea′tively**.—*n.* **Crea′tiveness**.

**Creator**, krē-ā′tor, *n.* he who creates : a maker.— **The Creator**, the Supreme Being, God.

**Creature**, krē′tūr, *n.* whatever has been *created*, animate or inanimate : esp. every animated being, an animal, a man : a term of contempt or endearment : a dependent. [O. Fr.—L. *creatura*.]

**Credence**, krē′dens, *n.* *belief:* trust : the small table beside the altar on which the bread and wine are placed before being consecrated. [Low L. *credentia*—*credent*-, believing, pr.p. of *credo*.]

**Credent**, krē′dent, *adj.* easy of belief.

**Credential**, krē-den′shal, *adj.* giving a title to *belief* or credit.—*n.* that which entitles to credit or confidence.—*pl.* esp. the letters by which one claims confidence or authority among strangers.

**Credible**, kred′i-bl, *adj.* that may be believed.—*ns.* **Credibil′ity**, **Cred′ibleness**.—*adv.* **Cred′ibly**.

**Credit**, kred′it, *n.*, *belief:* esteem : reputation : honour : good character : sale on trust : time allowed for payment : the side of an account on which payments received are entered.—*v.t.* to *believe:* to trust : to sell or lend to on trust : to enter on the credit side of an account : to set to the credit of. [L. *creditus—credo*.]

**Creditable**, kred′it-a-bl, *adj.* trustworthy : bringing credit or honour.—*n.* **Cred′itableness**.—*adv.* **Cred′itably**.     [a debt is due.

**Creditor**, kred′it-or, *n.* (*commerce*) one to whom

**Credulity**, kre-dū′li-ti, *n.*, *credulousness:* disposition to believe on insufficient evidence.

**Credulous**, kred'ū-lus, *adj., easy of belief:* apt to believe without sufficient evidence : unsuspecting.—*adv.* **Cred'ulously.**—*n.* **Cred'ulousness.**

**Creed**, krēd, *n.* a summary of the articles of religious *belief*. [L. *credo*, I believe, the first word of the Apostles' Creed ; akin to Sans. *çraddha*, faith.]

**Creek**, krēk, *n.* a small inlet or bay of the sea or a river : any *turn* or *winding*. [A.S. *crecca* ; cog. with Dut. *kreek ;* Ice. *kriki*, a corner—orig. a *bend*.]

**Creeky**, krēk'i, *adj.* full of creeks : winding. [Gael.]

**Creel**, krēl, *n.* a basket, esp. an angler's basket. [Gael.]

**Creep**, krēp, *v.i.* to move on the belly, like a snake : to move slowly : to grow along the ground or on supports, as a vine : to fawn :—*pr.p.* creep'ing ; *pa.t.* and *pa.p.* crept. [A.S. *creopan ;* Dut. *kruipen*.]        [small climbing birds.

**Creeper**, krēp'ėr, *n.* a creeping plant : a genus of **Crease.** See **Crease.**

**Cremation**, krem-ā'shun, *n.* act of *burning*, esp. of the dead. [L. *crematio*, from *cremo*, to burn.]

**Cremona**, krem-ō'na, *n.* a superior kind of violin made at *Cremona* in Italy.

**Crenate**, krē'nāt, **Crenated**, krē'nāt-ed, *adj.* (*bot.*) having the edge *notched*. [L. *crena*, a notch.]

**Crenelated**, kre-nel-āt'ed, *adj.* furnished with *notches* in a parapet to fire through : indented : battlemented. [Low L. *crenellare*, to indent —*crenellus*, a battlement—L. *crena*, a notch.]

**Creole**, krē'ōl, *n.* strictly applied to an inhabitant of S. America or W. Indies born in the country and of pure European blood : one born in tropical America of any colour, but of a race not native to it. [Fr. *créole*—Sp. *criollo*, contr. of *criadillo*, 'a little nursling,' dim. of *criado*—*criar*, lit. to create, also to bring up, to nurse—L. *creare*.]

**Creosote**, krē'o-sōt, **Creasote**, krē'a-sōt, *n.* an oily, colourless liquid distilled from woodtar, and having the quality of *preserving flesh* from corruption. [Gr. *kreas*, *kreōs*, flesh, and *sōtēr*, a preserver, from *sōzō*, to save.]

**Crepitate**, krep'i-tāt, *v.i.* to *crackle*, as salt when suddenly heated. [L. *crepito*, *crepitatus*, frequentative of *crepo*, to crack, rattle.]

**Crepitation**, krep-i-tā'shun, *n.* a repeated snapping noise.

**Crept**, krept, *pa.t.* and *pa.p.* of **Creep**.

**Crepuscular**, kre-pus'kū-lar, **Crepusculous**, krepus'kū-lus, *adj.* of or pertaining to *twilight*.

**Crepuscule**, kre-pus'kūl, **Crepuscle**, kre-pus'l, *n.*, *twilight*. [L. *crepusculum*—*creper*, dusky, obscure.]

**Crescendo**, kres-en'dō, *adv.* with an *increasing* volume of sound, a musical term whose sign is <

**Crescent**, kres'ent, *adj.*, *increasing*.—*n.* the moon as she *increases* towards half-moon : a figure like the crescent moon, as that on the Turkish standard : the standard itself : the Turkish power : a range of buildings in curved form. [L. *crescens*, *crescentis*, pr.p. of *cresco*, to grow.]

**Cress**, kres, *n.* the name of several species of plants like the watercress, which grow in moist places, and have pungent leaves used as a salad. [A.S. *cærse*, *cresse* ; cog. with Dut. *kers*, Ger. *kresse*.]

**Cresset**, kres'et, *n.* a cruse, jar, or open lamp filled with combustible material, placed on a beacon, lighthouse, &c. [Fr. *creuset*. See **Crock**, **Cruse**.]

**Crest**, krest, *n.* the comb or tuft on the head of a cock and other birds : a plume of feathers or other ornament on the top of a helmet : (*her.*) a figure placed over a coat of arms.—*v.t.* to

furnish with, or serve for, a crest. [O. Fr. *creste*—L. *crista*.]

**Crest-fallen**, krest'-fawln, *adj.* dejected : heartless.

**Crestless**, krest'les, *adj.* without a crest : not of high birth.

**Cretaceous**, krē-tā'shus, *adj.* composed of or like *chalk*. [L. *crētaceus*, from *creta*, chalk.]

**Cretin**, krē'tin, *n.* one of a class of idiots found in deep valleys, esp. among the Alps, and generally afflicted with goitre. [Ety. dub.]

**Cretinism**, krē'tin-izm, *n.* the condition of a cretin.

**Crevasse**, krev-as', *n.* a *crack* or split, esp. applied to a cleft in a glacier. [Fr. *crevasse*—*crever*, to burst, rive—L. *crepare*, to creak, crack.]

**Crevice**, krev'is, *n.* a *crack* or rent : a narrow opening. [A doublet of **Crevasse**.]

**Crew**, krōō, *n.* a company, in a bad or contemptuous sense : a ship's company. [Ice. *kru*, a multitude ; Sw. *kry*, to swarm.]

**Crew**, krōō—did crow—*past tense* of **Crow**.

**Crewel**, krōō'el, *n.* a kind of embroidery. [Cf. **Clew**.]

**Crib**, krib, *n.* the rack or manger of a stable : a stall for oxen : a child's bed : a small cottage : (*colloq.*) a literal translation of the classics, which schoolboys use unfairly in preparing their lessons. —*v.t.* to put away in a crib, confine, pilfer :— *pr.p.* crib'bing ; *pa.p.* cribbed'. [A.S. *crib ;* Ger. *krippe*.]

**Cribbage**, krib'āj, *n.* a game at cards in which the dealer makes up a third hand to himself partly by *cribbing* or taking from his opponent.

**Cribble**, krib'l, *n.* a coarse screen or *sieve*, used for sand, gravel, or corn : coarse flour or meal. —*v.t.* to sift or riddle. [L. *cribellum*, dim. of *cribrum*, a sieve.]

**Crick**, krik, *n.* a spasm or cramp, esp. of the neck. [A doublet of **Creek**.]

**Cricket**, krik'et, *n.* a genus of insects allied to grasshoppers, which make a chirping noise with their wing-covers. [Fr. *criquet*, from Teut. root of **Creak**.]

**Cricket**, krik'et, *n.* a game with bat and ball.— *v.i.* to play at cricket. [A.S. *cricc*, a staff ; the game was at first played with a club or staff.]

**Cricketer**, krik'et-ėr, *n.* one who plays at cricket.

**Cried**, krīd, *pa.t.* and *pa.p.* of **Cry**.

**Crime**, krīm, *n.* a violation of law : offence : sin. [Fr.—L. *crimen*.]

**Criminal**, krim'in-al, *adj.* relating to *crime* : guilty of crime : violating laws.—*n.* one guilty of crime.—*adv.* **Crim'inally.**

**Criminality**, krim-in-al'i-ti, *n.* guiltiness.

**Criminate**, krim'in-āt, *v.t.* to accuse.—*adj.* **Crim'inatory**.              [*ing* : accusation.

**Crimination**, krim-in-ā'shun, *n.* act of *criminat-*

**Crimp**, krimp, *adj.* made crisp or brittle.—*v.t.* to wrinkle : to plait : to make crisp : to seize or decoy.—*n.* one who decoys another into the naval or military service. [A dim. of *cramp ;* Dut. *krimpen*, to shrink.]

**Crimple**, krimp'l, *v.t.* to contract or draw together : to plait : to curl. [Dim. of **Crimp**.]

**Crimson**, krim'zn, *n.* a deep red colour, tinged with blue : red in general.—*adj.* of a deep red colour.—*v.t.* to dye crimson.—*v.i.* to become crimson : to blush. [O. E. *crimosyn*—O. Fr. *cramoisin ;* from Ar. *kermes* (= Sans. *krimi*, L. *vermis*, E. *worm*), the cochineal insect, from which it is made.]

**Cringe**, krinj, *v.i.* to *bend* : to crouch with servility : to submit : to fawn : to flatter. [A.S. *crincan*, *cringan*, to face ; connected with **Crank**, weak.]

**Cringeling**, krinj'ling, *n.* one who *cringes.*

**Crinite**, krī'nīt, *adj., hairy* : (*bot.*) resembling a tuft of hair. [L. *crinitus,* provided with hair—*crinis,* hair.]

**Crinkle.** See under **Crank** and **Crankle.**

**Crinoline**, krin'o-lin, *n.* a lady's stiff petticoat, originally made of *haircloth,* but afterwards expanded by hoops, &c. [Fr. *crin*—L. *crinis,* hair, and *lin*—L. *linum,* flax.]

**Cripple**, krip'l, *n.* a lame person.—*adj.* lame.—*v.t.* to make lame : to deprive of the power of exertion. [From root of **Creep.**]

**Crisis**, krī'sis, *n.* point or time for deciding anything—that is, when it must either terminate or take a new course : the decisive moment.—*pl.* **Crises,** krī'sēz. [Gr. *krisis,* from *krinō,* to separate.]

**Crisp**, krisp, *adj., curled* : so dry as to be crumbled easily : brittle.—*v.t.* to curl or twist : to make wavy.—*adv.* **Crisp'ly.**—*n.* **Crisp'ness.** [L. *crispus.*]

**Crispy**, krisp'i, *adj., curled* or curly : brittle.

**Criterion**, krī-tē'ri-on, *n.* a *means* or standard of *judging* : a test : a rule :—*pl.* **Crite'ria.** [Gr., from *kritēs,* a judge—*krinō.*]

**Critic**, krit'ik, *n.* a judge in literature, the fine arts, &c. : a fault-finder. [Gr. *kritikos*—*krinō.*]

**Critical**, krit'ik-al, *adj.* relating to criticism : skilled in judging literary and other productions : discriminating : captious : decisive.—*adv.* **Crit'ically.**—*n.* **Crit'icalness** [censure.

**Criticise**, krit'i-sīz, *v.t.* to pass judgment on : to **Criticism**, krit'i-sizm, *n.* the art of judging, esp. in literature or the fine arts : a critical judgment or observation.

**Critique**, kri-tēk', *n.* a *criticism* or critical examination of any production : a review. [Fr.]

**Croak**, krōk, *v.i.* to utter a low rough sound as a frog or raven : to grumble : to forebode evil.—*n.* the sound of a frog or raven.—*n.* **Croak'er.** [From the sound. Cf. **Crake, Crow,** and L. *graculus,* a jackdaw.]

**Crochet**, krō'shā, *n.* fancy knitting made by means of a *small hook.* [Fr. *crochet,* a little crook, a hook—*croc,* from root of **Crook.**]

**Crock**, krok, *n.* a narrow-necked earthen vessel or pitcher : a cup. [A.S. *croc;* Ger. *krug;* perh. of Celt. origin, as in W. *crochan,* a pot, Gael. *krog,* a pitcher ; akin to **Crag,** and giving the notion of hardness.]

**Crockery**, krok'ėr-i, *n.* earthenware : vessels formed of baked clay.

**Crocodile**, krok'o-dīl, *n.* a large amphibious reptile inhabiting the large rivers of Asia and Africa. [Fr.—L. *crocodilus*—Gr. *krokodeilos,* a lizard ; so called from its resemblance to a lizard.]

**Crocus**, krō'kus, *n.* a well-known flower. [L. *crocus*—Gr. *krokos;* prob. of Eastern origin, as Heb. *karkom,* saffron.]

**Croft**, kroft, *n.* a small piece of arable land adjoining a dwelling : a kind of small farm.—*n.* **Croft'er.** [A.S. *croft;* perh. from Gael. *croit,* a croft.]

**Cromlech**, krom'lek, *n.* a circle of standing stones, often called a Druidical circle. [W. *cromlech*—*crom,* curved, circular, and *llech,* a stone.]

**Crone**, krōn, *n.* an old woman, usually in contempt. [Perh. Celt., as in Ir. *crion,* withered, old.] [From **Crone.**]

**Crony**, krōn'i, *n.* an old and intimate companion.

**Crook**, krook, *n.* a bend, anything bent : a staff bent at the end, as a shepherd's or bishop's : an artifice or trick.—*v.t.* to bend or form into a hook : to turn from the straight line or from what is right.—*v.i.* to bend or be bent. [From a root common to Teut. and Celt., as W. *crwg,* a hook, Ice. *krokr,* Dut. *kroke,* a fold or wrinkle.]

**Crooked**, krook'ed, *adj., bent like a crook* : not straight : deviating from rectitude, perverse.—*adv.* **Crook'edly.**—*n.* **Crook'edness.**

**Crop**, krop, *n.* all the produce of a field of grain: anything gathered or cropped : the craw of a bird.—*v.t.* to cut off the top or ends : to cut short or close : to mow, reap, or gather :—*pr.p.* cropp'ing ; *pa.p.* cropped'.—**Crop out,** *v.i.* to appear above the surface : to come to light. [A.S. *crop,* the top shoot of a plant ; any protuberance, as the crop of a bird ; Dut. *crop,* a bird's crop.]

**Croquet**, krō'kā, *n.* a game in which two or more players try to drive wooden balls, by means of long-handled mallets, through a series of arches set in the ground. [Ety. unknown.]

**Crosier**, krō'zhėr, *n.* a staff with a *crook* at the top carried before bishops on solemn occasions. [O. Fr. *croce,* a crosier—Fr. *croc,* a crook, hook, from root of **Crook.**]

**Cross**, kros, *n.* a *gibbet* on which malefactors were *hung,* consisting of two pieces of timber, one placed crosswise on the other, either thus † or ✕ ; the instrument on which Christ suffered, and thus the symbol of the Christian religion : the sufferings of Christ : anything that crosses or thwarts : adversity or affliction in general : a crossing or mixing of breeds, esp. of cattle.—*v.t.* to mark with a cross : to lay one body or draw one line across another : to cancel by drawing cross lines : to pass from side to side : to obstruct : to thwart : to interfere with.—*v.i.* to lie or be athwart : to move or pass from place to place. [O. Fr. *crois,* Fr. *croix*—L. *crux,* orig. an upright post to which latterly a cross-piece was added ; conn. with **Crook** by Gael. *crocan,* a hook, *croch,* hung ; Ir. *crochaim,* to hang, *croch,* a gallows.]

**Cross**, kros, *adj., lying across* : transverse : oblique : opposite : adverse : ill-tempered : interchanged.—*adv.* **Cross'ly.**—*n.* **Cross'ness.**

**Crossbill**, kros'bil, *n.* a genus of birds resembling bullfinches, linnets, &c. with the mandibles of the *bill* crossing each other near the points.

**Crossbow**, kros'bō, *n.* a weapon for shooting arrows, formed of a *bow* placed *crosswise* on a stock.

**Crossbun**, kros'bun, *n.* a *bun* marked with the form of a *cross,* eaten on Good-Friday.

**Cross-examine**, kros-egz-am'in, *v.t.* to test the evidence of a witness by subjecting him to an examination by the opposite party.—*n.* **Cross-examina'tion.**

**Cross-grained**, kros'-grānd, *adj.* having the *grain* or fibres *crossed* or intertwined : perverse : contrary : untractable.

**Crossing**, kros'ing, *n.* act of going *across* : a thwarting : a place for passing from one side to the other.

**Crosslet**, kros'let, *n.* a *little cross.* [examine.

**Cross-question**, kros'-kwest-yun, *v.t.* to cross-

**Crosstrees**, kros'trēz, *n.* pieces of timber placed *across* the upper end of the lower-masts and top-masts of a ship.

**Crossway**, kros'wā, *n.* a *way* that *crosses* another.

**Crosswise**, kros'wīz, *adv.* in the form of a cross : across.

**Crotchet**, kroch'et, *n.* a note in music, equal to half a minim, ♩ : a *crooked* or perverse fancy : a whim or conceit. [Fr. *crochet,* diminutive of *croc,* a hook. See **Crochet.**]

**Crotchety**, kroch'et-i, *adj.* having *crotchets* or peculiarities : whimsical.

**Croton**, krō'ton, *n.* a genus of tropical plants, producing a brownish-yellow oil, having a hot biting taste. [Gr. *krotōn*, a tick or mite, which the seed of the plant resembles.]

**Crouch**, krowch, *v.i.* to squat or lie close to the ground : to cringe : to fawn. [A form of Crook.]

**Croup**, krōōp, *n.* a severe disease in the throat of children, accompanied by a hoarse cough. [A.S. *hropan*, to cry ; Scot. *roup*, *croup*, hoarseness : from the sound.]

**Croup**, krōōp, *n.* the rump of a fowl : the buttocks of a horse : the place behind the saddle. [Fr. *croupe*, a protuberance ; allied to Crop.]

**Croupier**, krōō'pi-èr, *n.* one who sits at the *croup* or lower end of the table as assistant-chairman at a public dinner : a vice-president : he who watches the cards and collects money at a gaming-table.

**Crow**, krō, *n.* a large bird, generally black, which utters a *croaking* sound : the cry of a cock : a boast.—*v.i.* to *croak* : to cry as a cock, in joy or defiance : to boast : to swagger :—*pa.t.* crew (krōō) or crowed ; *pa.p.* crowed'. [A.S. *crawe*, a crow : from the sound.]

**Crowbar**, krō'bär, *n.* a large iron *bar* with a claw like the beak of a *crow*.

**Crowd**, krowd, *n.* a number of persons or things closely *pressed* together, without order : the rabble : multitude.—*v.t.* to gather into a lump or crowd : to fill by pressing or driving together. —*v.i.* to press together in numbers : to swarm. [A.S. *creodan*, to crowd, press.]

**Crowfoot**, krō'foot, *n.* a common weed, the flower of which is like a *crow's foot*.

**Crown**, krown, *n.* the diadem or state-cap of royalty : regal power : honour : reward : the top of anything, esp. of the head : completion : accomplishment : a 5s. piece stamped with a *crown*.—*v.t.* to cover or invest with a crown : to invest with royal dignity : to adorn : to dignify : to complete.—*adj.* Crown'less. [Fr. *couronne*—L. *corona* ; cog. with Gr. *korōnos*, curved ; W. *crwn*, Gael. *cruinn*, round.]

**Crown-glass**, krown'-glas, *n.* a kind of window-*glass* formed in *circular* plates or discs.

**Crown-prince**, krown'-prins, *n.* the *prince* who succeeds to the *crown*.

**Crow's-foot**, krōz'-foot, *n.* wrinkles produced by age, spreading out in the shape of a crow's foot from the corners of the eyes : (*mil.*) a caltrop.

**Crucial**, krōō'shi-al, *adj.* testing, searching, from the practice of marking a testing instance with a *cross* to draw attention to it. [Fr. *crucial*, from L. *crux, crucis*, a cross. See Cross.]

**Crucible**, krōō'si-bl, *n.* an *earthen pot* for melting ores, metals, &c. [Low L. *crucibulum*, from root of Crock ; erroneously supposed to be conn. with L. *crux*.]

**Cruciferous**, krōō-sif'èr-us, *adj.* (*bot.*) bearing four petals in the form of a *cross*. [L. *crux*, and *fero*, to bear.]      [Christ *fixed* to the *cross*.

**Crucifix**, krōō'si-fiks, *n.* a figure or picture of Christ on the *cross*.

**Crucifixion**, krōō-si-fik'shun, *n.* death on the *cross*, especially that of Christ.        [*cross*.

**Cruciform**, krōō'si-form, *adj.* in the *form* of a *cross*.

**Crucify**, krōō'si-fī, *v.t.* to put to death by *fixing* the hands and feet to a *cross* : to subdue completely : to mortify :—*pa.p.* cruc'ified. [Fr. *crucifier*—L. *crucifigo, crucifixus*—*crux*, and *figo*, to fix.]

**Crude**, krōōd, *adj.* *raw*, unprepared : not reduced to order or form : unfinished : undigested : imma-

ture.—*adv.* Crude'ly.—*n.* Crude'ness. [L. *crudus*, raw. See Raw.]     [which is crude.

**Crudity**, krōōd'i-ti, *n.* rawness : unripeness : that

**Cruel**, krōō'el, *adj.* disposed to inflict pain, or pleased at suffering : void of pity, merciless, savage.—*adv.* Cru'elly.—*n.* Cru'elty. [Fr. *cruel*—L. *crudelis*. From root of Crude.]

**Cruet**, krōō'et, *n.* a *small jar* or phial for sauces and condiments. [Acc. to Skeat, prob. formed from Dut. *kruik*, a jar = E. Crock ; and acc. to E. Müller, dim. of O. Fr. *cruye* (mod. Fr. *cruche, cruchette*, a jar), from root of Crock.]

**Cruise**, krōōz, *v.i.* to sail to and fro : to rove on the sea.—*n.* a sailing to and fro : a voyage in various directions in search of an enemy, or for the protection of vessels.—*n.* Cruis'er. [Dut. *kruisen*, to cross—*kruis*, a cross—O. Fr. *crois*—L. *crux*.]

**Cruise**, krōōz, *n.* a small bottle. Same as Cruse.

**Crumb**, krum, *n.* a *small bit* or morsel of bread : the soft part of bread. [A.S. *cruma* ; Ger. *krume* ; allied to Crimp.]

**Crumbcloth**, krum'kloth, *n.* a *cloth* laid under a table to receive falling *crumbs*, and keep the carpet clean.

**Crumble**, krum'bl, *v.t.* to break into *crumbs*.—*v.i.* to fall into small pieces : to decay : to perish. [Orig. dim. of Crumb ; Dut. *kruimelen* ; Ger. *krümeln*.]

**Crumby, Crummy**, krum'i, *adj., in crumbs* : soft.

**Crump**, krump, *adj.* crooked : wrinkled. [A.S. *crumb* ; Ger. *krumm* ; Scot. *crummy*, a cow with a crumpled horn. From the root of Cramp, Crimp.]      [cake or muffin.

**Crumpet**, krum'pet, *n.* a kind of *crumby* or soft

**Crumple**, krump'l, *v.t.* to mark with or draw into folds or wrinkles : to crease.—*v.i.* to become wrinkled : to contract or shrink. [Freq. of Cramp.]

**Crunch**, krunch, *v.t.* to crush with the teeth : to chew anything hard, and so make a noise. [From the sound ; cf. Fr. *grincer*.]

**Crupper**, krup'èr, *n.* a strap of leather fastened to the saddle and passing under the horse's tail to keep the saddle in its place. [Fr. *croupière*—*croupe*, the Croup of a horse.]

**Crural**, krōō'ral, *adj.* belonging to or shaped like a *leg*. [L. *cruralis*, from *crus, cruris*, the leg.]

**Crusade**, kroo-sād', *n.* a military expedition under the banner of the *cross* to recover the Holy Land from the Turks : any daring or romantic undertaking. [Fr. *croisade*—Prov. *crozada*—*croz*, a cross. See Cross.]        [*crusade*.

**Crusader**, kroo-sād'èr, *n.* one engaged in a

**Cruse**, krōōz, *n.* an *earthen pot* : a small cup or bottle. [Fr. ; Ice. *krus* : also allied to Crock.]

**Crush**, krush, *v.t.* to break or bruise : to squeeze together : to beat down or overwhelm : to subdue : to ruin.—*n.* a violent squeezing. [O. Fr. *cruisir*, from a Scan. root seen in Sw. *krysta*, whose oldest form appears in Goth. *kriustan*, to grind the teeth, formed from the sound. See Crash and Craze.]

**Crust**, krust, *n.* the *hard rind* or outside coating of anything : the outer part of bread : covering of a pie, &c. : (*geol.*) the solid exterior of the earth.—*v.t.* to cover with a crust or hard case. —*v.i.* to gather into a hard crust. [O. Fr.— L. *crusta* ; perh. conn. with Gr. *kryos*, icy cold.]

**Crustacea**, krus-tā'shi-a, *n.pl.* a class of animals whose bodies are covered with a *crust-like* shell covering, such as lobsters, shrimps, and crabs.

**Crustacean**, krus-tā'shi-an, *n.* one of the *Crustacea*.

**Crustaceous**, krus-tā′shi-us, **Crustacean**, krus-tā′-shi-an, *adj.* pertaining to the *Crustacea*, or shellfish.

**Crustated**, krus-tāt′ed, *adj.* covered with a *crust*.

**Crustation**, krus-tā′shun, *n.* an adherent crust.

**Crusty**, krust′i, *adj.* of the nature of or *having a crust*: having a hard or harsh exterior: hard: snappy: surly.—*adv.* **Crust′ily.**—*n.* **Crust′iness.**

**Crutch**, kruch, *n.* a staff with a *cross*-piece at the head to place under the arm of a lame person: any support like a crutch. [From root of **Crook**; perh. modified by L. *crux*, a cross.]

**Cry**, krī, *v.i.* to utter a *shrill loud sound*, esp. one expressive of pain or grief: to lament: to weep: to bawl.—*v.t.* to utter loudly: to proclaim or make public:—*pa.t.* and *pa.p.* cried′.—*n.* any loud sound: particular sound uttered by an animal: bawling: lamentation: weeping: prayer: clamour:—*pl.* **Cries.**—*n.* **Cri′er.** [Fr. *crier* (It. *gridare*)—L. *quiritare*, to scream —freq. of L. *queri*, to lament.]

**Crypt**, kript, *n.* an underground cell or chapel, esp. one used for *burial*. [L. *crypta*—Gr. *kryptē*—*kryptō*, to conceal. Doublet of **Grot.**]

**Cryptogamia**, krip-to-gā′mi-a, *n.* the class of flowerless plants, or those which have their *fructification concealed*. [Gr. *kryptos*, concealed, and *gamos*, marriage.]

**Cryptogamic**, krip-to-gam′ik, **Cryptogamous**, krip-tog′a-mus, *adj.* pertaining to the *Cryptogamia*.

**Crystal**, kris′tal, *n.* a superior kind of glass: (*chem.*) a piece of matter which has assumed a definite geometrical form, with plane faces. [O. Fr. *cristal*—L. *crystallum*, from Gr. *krystallos*, ice—*kryos*, icy cold; akin to **Crust.**]

**Crystal**, kris′tal, **Crystalline**, kris′tal-īn or -in, *adj.* consisting of or like *crystal* in clearness, &c. [*crystallising.*

**Crystallisation**, kris-tal-iz-ā′shun, *n.* the act of

**Crystallise**, kris′tal-īz, *v.t.* to *reduce to* the form of a *crystal*.—*v.i.* to assume a crystalline form.

**Crystallography**, kris-tal-og′ra-fi, *n.* the *science* of *crystallisation*. [Gr. *krystallos*, and *graphō*, to write.]

**Cub**, kub, *n.* the young of certain animals, as foxes, &c.: a whelp: a young boy or girl (in contempt).—*v.* to bring forth young:—*pr.p.* cubb′ing: *pa.p.* cubbed′. [Prob. Celt., as Ir. *cuib*, a whelp, from *cu*, a dog.]

**Cubature**, kūb′a-tūr, *n.* the act of finding the solid or *cubic* content of a body: the result thus found.

**Cube**, kūb, *n.* a solid body having six equal square faces, a solid square: the third power of a number, as $-2 \times 2 \times 2 = 8$.—*v.t.* to raise to the third power. [Fr. *cube*—L. *cubus*—Gr. *kybos*, a die.]

**Cubic**, kūb′ik, **Cubical**, kūb′ik-al, *adj.* pertaining to a *cube*.—*adv.* **Cub′ically.**

**Cubiform**, kūb′i-form, *adj.* in the *form* of a *cube*.

**Cubit**, kūb′it, *n.* a measure employed by the ancients, equal to the length of the arm from the *elbow* to the tip of the middle-finger, varying from 18 to 22 inches. [L. *cubitus* (*lit.*) a *bend*; akin to L. *cubare*, to lie down: also to **Cup.**]

**Cuboid**, kūb′oid, **Cuboidal**, kūb-oid′al, *adj.* resembling a *cube in shape*. [Gr. *kyboeidēs*, from *kybos*, a die, and *eidos*, form.]

**Cuckold**, kuk′old, *n.* a man whose wife has proved unfaithful.—*v.t.* to wrong a husband by unchastity. [O. Fr. *coucuol* (Mod. Fr. *cocu*)—*coucou*, a cuckoo—L. *cuculus*.]

**Cuckoo**, koo′kōō, *n.* a bird which cries *cuckoo*, remarkable for laying its eggs in the nests of

other birds. [Fr. *coucou*—L. *cuculus*, from the sound. Cf. **Cock, Cockatoo.**]

**Cucumber**, kū′kum-bėr, *n.* a creeping plant, with large oblong fruit used as a salad and pickle. [L. *cucumis, cucumeris*.]

**Cud**, kud, *n.* the food brought from the first stomach of a ruminating animal back into the mouth and *chewed* again. [Like **Quid**, what is chewed, from A.S. *ceowan*, to chew.]

**Cuddle**, kud′l, *v.t.* to hug: to embrace: to fondle. —*v.i.* to lie close and snug together.—*n.* a close embrace. [Acc. to Skeat, a freq. of M.E. *couth*, well known, familiar. See **Uncouth.**]

**Cuddy**, kud′i, *n.* a small cabin or cookroom, generally in the forepart of a boat or lighter: in large vessels, applied to the officers' cabin under the poopdeck. [Fr. *cahute*; Dut. *kajuit*; Ger. *kajūte*.]

**Cudgel**, kud′jel, *n.* a heavy staff: a club.—*v.t.* to beat with a cudgel:—*pr.p.* cud′gelling; *pa.p.* cud′gelled. [W. *cogyl*, a club.]

**Cudweed**, kud′wēd, *n.* the popular name for many species of plants covered with a *cottony* down. [Probably corrupted from *cotton-weed*.]

**Cue**, kū, *n.* a *queue*, or *tail*-like twist of hair formerly worn at the back of the head: a rod used in playing billiards: the *last* words of an actor's speech serving as a hint to the next speaker: any hint: the part one has to play. [Fr. *queue* —L. *cauda*, a tail.]

**Cuff**, kuf, *n.* a *stroke* with the open hand.—*v.t.* to strike with the open hand. [From a Scan. root seen in Sw. *kuffa*, to knock.]

**Cuff**, kuf, *n.* the end of the sleeve near the wrist: a covering for the wrist. [Prob. cog. with **Coif.**]

**Cuirass**, kwi-ras′ or kwē′-, *n.* a defensive covering for the breast orig. made of *leather*, afterwards of iron fastened with straps and buckles, &c. [Fr. *cuirasse*—Low L. *coratia*—L. *corium*, skin, leather; whence Fr. *cuir*.] [*cuirass.*

**Cuirassier**, kwi-ras-ēr′, *n.* a soldier armed with a

**Culdee**, kul′dē, *n.* one of a Celtic fraternity of monks who formerly lived in Scotland, Ireland, and Wales. [Ir. *ceile de*, 'servant of God.' See **Gillie.**]

**Culinary**, kū′lin-ar-i, *adj.* pertaining to the *kitchen* or to cookery: used in the kitchen. [L. *culinarius*—*culina*, a kitchen.]

**Cull**, kul, *v.t.* to select: to pick out. [Fr. *cueillir*, to gather—L. *colligo*—*col*, together, and *lego*, to gather. A doublet of **Collect.**]

**Cullender.** See **Colander.**

**Cullion**, kul′yun, *n.* a wretch: a cowardly fellow. [Fr. *couillon*, a dastard, a poltroon (It. *coglione*)—L. *coleus*, a leather bag, the scrotum.]

**Cully**, kul′i, *n.* (a contr. of **Cullion**) a mean dupe. —*v.t.* to deceive meanly.—*pa.p.* cull′ied.

**Culm**, kulm, *n.* the *stalk* or stem of corn or of grasses. [L. *culmus*, a stalk or stem. Cog. with **Haulm.**]

**Culmiferous**, kul-mif′ėr-us, *adj.*, *bearing stalks* or stems. [L. *culmus*, a stalk, and *fero*, to bear.]

**Culminate**, kul′min-āt, *v.i.* to *come to the top*: (*astron.*) to be vertical or at the highest point of altitude: to reach the highest point. [Coined, as if from a Low L. *culmino*, from L. *culmen*, properly *columen*, a summit. See **Column.**]

**Culmination**, kul-min-ā′shun, *n.* act of culminating: the top or highest point: (*astron.*) transit or passage of a body across the meridian or highest point for the day.

**Culpability**, kul-pa-bil′i-ti, **Culpableness**, kul′pa-bl-nes, *n.* liability to blame.

**Culpable**, kul′pa-bl, *adj.* faulty, criminal.—*adv.*

**Cul′pably.** [O. Fr.—L. *culpabilis,* worthy of blame—*culpa,* a fault.]

**Culprit,** kul′prit, *n.* one *culpable* or in *fault:* a criminal: in Eng. law, a prisoner accused, but not tried. [For *culpate,* from old law L. *culpatus,* a person accused.]

**Cult,** kult, *n.* a system of religious belief, *worship.* [L. *cultus*—*colo, cultus,* to worship.]

**Cultivate,** kul′ti-vāt, *v.t.* to *till* or produce by tillage: to prepare for crops: to devote attention to: to civilise or refine.—*n.* **Cul′tivator.** [Low L. *cultivo, cultivatus*—L. *colo, cultus,* to till, to worship.]

**Cultivation,** kul-ti-vā′shun, *n.* the art or practice of cultivating: civilisation: refinement.

**Culture,** kul′tūr, *n., cultivation:* the state of being cultivated: advancement or refinement the result of cultivation.—*v.t.* to cultivate: to improve. [L. *cultura.*]

**Culver,** kul′vėr, **Culverin,** kul′vėr-in, *n.* an ancient cannon, so called from its long, thin, *serpent-like* shape, or from its being ornamented with the figures of serpents. [Fr. *coulevrine,* from *couleuvre*—L. *coluber,* a serpent.]

**Culvert,** kul′vėrt, *n.* an arched water-course, &c. [Prob. from Fr. *couler,* to flow—L. *colare*—*colum,* a strainer.]

**Cumber,** kum′bėr, *v.t.* to trouble or hinder with something useless: to retard, perplex, trouble. [O. Fr. *combrer,* to hinder—Low L. *combrus,* a heap; corr. of L. *cumulus,* a heap.]

**Cumbersome,** kum′bėr-sum, *adj.* troublesome.

**Cumbrance,** kum′brans, *n.* encumbrance.

**Cumbrous,** kum′brus, *adj.* hindering: obstructing: heavy: giving trouble.—*adv.* **Cum′brously.** —*n.* **Cum′brousness.**

**Cumin, Cummin,** kum′in *n.* a plant, the seeds which are valuable for their carminative qualities. [L. *cuminum,* through the Gr. *kyminon,* from Heb. *kammōn.*]

**Cumulate,** kūm′ū-lat, *v.t.* to *heap together:* to accumulate. [L. *cumulo, -atum*—*cumulus,* a heap.]           [lation.

**Cumulation,** kūm′ū-lā-shun. Same as **Accumu-**

**Cumulative,** kūm′ū-lā-tiv, *adj.* increasing by successive additions.]

**Cumulus,** kū′mū-lus, *n.* a species of cloud.

**Cuneal,** kū′ne-al, **Cuneate,** kū′ne-āt, *adj.* of the form of a *wedge.* [L. *cuneus,* a wedge.]

**Cuneiform,** kū-nē′i-form, **Cuniform,** kū′ni-form, *adj.* wedge-shaped—specially applied to the old Babylonian and Assyrian writing, of which the characters have a *wedge-shape.*

**Cunning,** kun′ing, *adj., knowing:* skilful: artful: crafty.—*n.* knowledge: skill: faculty of using stratagem to accomplish a purpose.—*adv.* **Cunn′ingly.** [A.S. *cunnan,* to know.]

**Cup,** kup, *n.* a vessel used to contain liquid : a drinking-vessel: the liquid contained in a cup: that which we must receive or undergo: afflictions: blessings.—*v.t.* to extract blood from the body by means of cupping-glasses from which the air has been exhausted:—*pr.p.* cupp′ing; *pa.p.* cupped′. [A.S. *cuppe,* Fr. *coupe,* It. *coppa,* a cup, the head; all from L. *cupa, cuppa,* a tub, a drinking-vessel.]

**Cupboard,** kup′bŏrd or kub′urd, *n.* a place for keeping victuals, dishes, &c. [**Cup,** and **Board,** a table or shelf.]

**Cupid,** kū′pid, *n.* the god of love. [L. *Cupido*—

**Cupidity,** kū-pid′i-ti, *n., eager desire for:* covetousness: lust after. [L. *cupiditas*—*cupidus,* desirous.]

**Cupola,** kū′po-la, *n.* a *cup-shaped* vault on the

---

summit of a tower: a dome. [It. : dim. of Low L. *cupa,* a cup—L. *cupa,* a tub. See **Cup.**]

**Cupreous.** See under **Copperish.**

**Cur,** kur, *n.* a worthless, degenerate dog: a churlish fellow.—*adj.* **Curr′ish.** [Dut. *korre,* Dan. *kurre,* to whir; from its growling.]

**Curable,** kūr′a-bl, *adj.* that may be *cured.*—*n.* **Curabil′ity.**

**Curaçoa,** koo-ra-sō′, *n.* a liqueur so named from the island of Curaçoa in the West Indies, where it was first made. [benefice *of a curate.*

**Curacy,** kūr′a-si, *n.* the *office,* employment, or

**Curate,** kūr′āt, *n.* one who has the *cure* or *care* of souls, so in Pr. Bk. : an inferior clergyman in the Church of England who assists a rector or vicar in the discharge of his duties. [Low L. *curatus,* from L. *cura,* care.]

**Curative,** kūr′a-tiv, *adj.* tending to cure.

**Curator,** kūr-ā′tor, *n.* one who has the *care* of anything : a superintendent : one appointed by law as guardian.

**Curb,** kurb, *v.t.* to *bend* to one's will : to subdue : to restrain or check: to furnish with or guide by a curb.—*n.* that which curbs: a check or hindrance : a chain or strap attached to the bit of a bridle for restraining the horse. [Fr. *courber,* from L. *curvus,* crooked, bent.]

**Curbstone,** kurb′stŏn, *n.* a *stone* placed edgeways against earth or stone work to *check* it.

**Curd,** kurd, *n.,* milk thickened or coagulated : the cheese part of milk, as distinguished from the whey. [Celt., as in Gael. *gruth,* Ir. *cruth,* curd, *cruthaim,* I milk.]

**Curdle,** kurd′l, *v.i.* to *turn into curd:* to congeal : to thicken.—*v.t.* to cause to turn into curd, or to congeal.

**Curdy,** kurd′i, *adj.* like or full of *curd.*

**Cure,** kūr, *n.* care of souls or spiritual charge: care of the sick : act of healing : that which heals : a remedy.—*v.t.* to heal : to preserve, as by drying, salting, &c. :—*pr.p.* cūr′ing ; *pa.p.* cūred′. [O. Fr. *cure*—L. *cura,* solicitude, care ; not of the same origin as **Care.**]

**Cureless,** kūr′les, *adj.* that cannot be cured.

**Curfew,** kur′fū, *n.* (*lit.*) *cover-fire:* in feudal times the ringing of a bell at eight o'clock, as a signal to *cover* or put out all *fires* and lights. [Fr. *couvrefeu,* from *couvrir,* to cover, and *feu,* fire, from L. *focus.*]

**Curiosity,** kūr-i-os′i-ti, *n., state* or quality *of being curious:* inquisitiveness: that which is curious : anything rare or unusual.

**Curious,** kūr′i-us, *adj.* anxious to learn : inquisitive : shewing great care or nicety: skilfully made : singular : rare.—*adv.* **Cur′iously.**—*n.* **Cur′iousness.** [Fr. *curieux*—L. *curiosus*—*cura.*]

**Curl,** kurl, *v.t.* to twist into ringlets: to coil.—*v.i.* to shrink into ringlets : to rise in undulations: to writhe : to ripple : to play at the game of curling.—*n.* a ringlet of hair, or what is like it : a wave, bending, or twist. [Orig. *crull* ; Dut. *krullen,* Dan. *krolle,* to curl.]

**Curlew,** kur′lū, *n.* one of the wading-birds, having a very long slender bill and legs, and a short tail. [Fr. *corlieu;* probably from its cry.]

**Curling,** kurl′ing, *n.* a game, common in Scotland, consisting in hurling heavy stones along a sheet of ice, like playing at bowls.

**Curly,** kurl′i, *adj., having curls :* full of curls.— *n.* **Curl′iness.**

**Curmudgeon,** kur-muj′un, *n.* an avaricious, ill-natured fellow : a miser.—*adj.* **Curmud′geonly.** [O. E. *cornmudgin,* sig. *corn-hoarding,* from

---

*corn* and *mudge* or *mug*, or *mooch*, to hide or hoard; seen in *muglard*, a miser; from O. Fr. *mucer*, Fr. *musser*, to conceal.]

**Currant**, kur'ant, *n.* a small kind of raisin or dried grape, imported from the Levant : the fruit of several garden shrubs. [From *Corinth*, in Greece.]

**Currency**, kur'en-si, *n.* circulation : that which circulates, as the money of a country : general estimation.

**Current**, kur'ent, *adj.*, *running* or *flowing* : passing from person to person : generally received : now passing : present.—*n.* a *running* or *flowing* : a stream : a portion of water or air moving in a certain direction : course.—*adv.* **Curr'ently**. [L. *currens, currentis*—*curro, cursus*, to run.]

**Curricle**, kur'i-kl, *n.* a two-wheeled open chaise, drawn by two horses abreast : a chariot. [L. *curriculum*, from *curro*.]

**Curriculum**, kur-ik'ū-lum, *n.* a course, esp. the course of study at a university. [L.]

**Currier**, kur'i-èr, *n.* one who *curries* or dresses tanned leather.

**Curry**, kur'i, *n.* a kind of sauce or seasoning much used in India and elsewhere, and compounded of pepper, ginger, and other spices : a stew mixed with curry-powder. [Pers. *khūrdi*, broth, juicy meats, from *khūrdan*, to eat.]

**Curry**, kur'i, *v.t.* to dress leather : to rub down and dress a horse : to beat : to scratch :—*pr.p.* curry'ing ; *pa.p.* curr'ied.—**To curry favour** (corr. of **Curry favell**), to rub down a horse, *favell* being a common old name for a horse), to seek favour by flattery. [Fr. *corroyer*—*corroi*, O. Fr. *conroi*; from a Teut. root present in Ice. *reidhi*, tackle, Dan. *rede*, to set in order, E. *ready*. See **Ready**.]

**Curse**, kurs, *v.t.* to invoke or wish evil upon : to devote to perdition : to vex or torment.—*v.i.* to utter imprecations : to swear.—*n.* the invocation or wishing of evil or harm upon : evil invoked on another : torment.—*n.* **Curs'er**. [A.S. *cursian*—*curs*, a curse, perh. from Sw. and Dan. *kors*, a cross, which is derived from O. Fr. *crois*. See **Cross**.]

**Cursed**, kurs'ed, *adj.* under a *curse* : deserving a curse : blasted by a curse : hateful.

**Cursive**, kur'siv, *adj.*, *running*, as applied to handwriting : flowing. [L. *curro, cursus*, to run.]

**Cursory**, kur'sor-i, *adj.* hasty : superficial : careless.—*adv.* **Cur'sorily**. [L. *curro*.]

**Curt**, kurt, *adj.*, *short* : concise.—*adv.* **Curt'ly**.— *n.* **Curt'ness**. [L. *curtus*, shortened ; Sans. *krit*, to cut, separate.]

**Curtail**, kur-tāl', *v.t.* to *cut short* : to cut off a part : to abridge :—*pr.p.* curtail'ing ; *pa.p.* curtailed'. [Old spelling *curtal*, O. Fr. *courtault*, It. *cortaldo*—L. *curtus*.]

**Curtain**, kur'tin, *n.* drapery hung round and inclosing a bed, &c. : the part of a rampart between two bastions.—*v.t.* to inclose or furnish with curtains. [Fr. *courtine*—Low L. *cortina*; from L. *cors, cortis*, a place inclosed, a court.]

**Curtsy**, kurt'si. Same as **Courtesy**, the gesture.

**Curule**, kū'rool, *adj.* applied to a chair in which the higher Roman magistrates had a right to sit. [L. *currus*, a chariot—*curro*, to run.]

**Curvature**, kur'va-tūr, *n.* a *curving* or *bending* : the continual bending or the amount of bending from a straight line. [L. *curvatura*.]

**Curve**, kurv, *n.* anything *bent* : a bent line : an arch.—*v.t.* to bend : to form into a curve. [L. *curvus*, crooked. See **Circle**.]

**Curvet**, kurv'et, *n.* a certain leap of a horse in which he gives his body a *curve* : a leap or frolic.—*v.i.* to leap in curvets : to leap : to frisk : —*pr.p.* curv'eting ; *pa.p.* curv'eted.

**Curvilinear**, kur-vi-lin'i-ar, **Curvilineal**, kur-vi-lin'i-al, *adj.* bounded by *curved lines*. [L. *curvus*, and *linea*, a line.]

**Cushat**, koosh'at, *n.* the ringdove or wood-pigeon. [Prov. E. *cowshot*; from A.S. *cusceote*.]

**Cushion**, koosh'un, *n.* a case filled with some soft, elastic stuff, for resting on : a pillow.—*v.t.* to seat on or furnish with a cushion. [Fr. *coussin*, It. *cuscino*, from L. *culcitinum*, dim. of *culcita*, mattress. See **Counterpane** and **Quilt**.]

**Cusp**, kusp, *n.* a *point* : the point or horn of the moon, &c. [L. *cuspis*, a point.]

**Cuspidate**, kus'pi-dāt, **Cuspidated**, kus'pi-dāt-ed, *adj.* (*bot.*) having a sharp end or *point*. [L. *cuspidatus*—*cuspis*.]

**Custard**, kus'tard, *n.* a composition of milk, eggs, &c. sweetened and flavoured. [Once spelled *custade*, a corr. of *crustade*, a pie with crust ; from O. Fr. *croustade*—L. *crustatus*, crusted. See **Crust**.]

**Custard-apple**, kus'tard-ap'l, *n.* the *fruit* of a W. Indian tree, having an eatable pulp, *like a custard*.

**Custodial**, kus-tō'di-al, *adj.* pertaining to *custody*.

**Custodian**, kus-tō'di-an, *n.* one who has *custody*, or care, esp. of some public building.

**Custody**, kus'to-di, *n.* a *watching* or *guarding* : care : security : imprisonment. [L. *custodia*, from *custos, custodis*, a watcher or keeper.]

**Custom**, kus'tum, *n.* what one is wont to do : usage : frequent repetition of the same act : a frequenting of a shop to buy goods : regular trade or business : a tax on goods.—*pl.* duties imposed on imports and exports. [O. Fr. *custume, costume*; from L. *consuetudo*—*consuesco, consuetus*, to accustom.]

**Customary**, kus'tum-ar-i, *adj.* according to use and wont : holding or held by custom.—*adv.* **Cus'tomarily**.—*n.* **Cus'tomariness**.

**Customer**, kus'tum-èr, *n.* one *accustomed* to frequent a certain place of business : a buyer.

**Custom-house**, kus'tum-hows, *n.* the place where *customs* or duties on exports and imports are collected.

**Cut**, kut, *v.t.* to make an incision : to cleave or pass through : to divide : to carve or hew : to wound or hurt : to affect deeply : to castrate :—*pr.p.* cutt'ing ; *pa.t.* and *pa.p.* cut.—*n.* a cleaving or dividing : a stroke or blow : an incision or wound : a piece cut off : an engraved block, or the picture from it : manner of cutting, or fashion.—**A short cut**, a short or near passage. [W. *cwtau*, to shorten, *cwtt*, a little piece ; Ir. *cntaich*, to curtail.]

**Cutaneous**, kū-tā'ne-us, *adj.* belonging to the *skin*.

**Cuticle**, kū'ti-kl, *n.* the outermost or thin skin. [L. *cuticula*, dim. of *cutis*, the skin, E. **Hide**.]

**Cutlass**, kut'las, *n.* a broad curving sword with one edge. [Fr. *coutelas*, from L. *cultellus*, dim. of *culter*, a ploughshare, a knife.]

**Cutler**, kut'lèr, *n.* one who makes or sells *knives*. [Fr. *coutelier*, from root of **Cutlass**.]

**Cutlery**, kut'lèr-i, *n.* the *business of a cutler* : edged or cutting instruments in general.

**Cutlet**, kut'let, *n.* a slice of meat cut off for cooking, esp. of mutton or veal, generally the rib and the meat belonging to it. [Fr. *côtelette*, dim. of *côte*, from L. *costa*, a rib. See **Coast**.]

**Cutter**, kut'èr, *n.* the *person* or *thing that cuts* : a small swift vessel with one mast and sharp bows that *cut* the water.

**Cutting,** kut′ing, *n.* a *dividing* or lopping off : an incision : a piece cut off : a twig.

**Cuttle,** kut′l, **Cuttle-fish,** kut′l-fish, *n.* a kind of mollusc, remarkable for its power of ejecting a black inky liquid. [A.S. *cudele ;* origin dub.]

**Cut-water,** kut′-waw′tėr, *n.* the forepart of a ship's prow.

**Cycle,** sī′kl, *n.* a period of time in which events happen in a certain order, and which constantly repeats itself : an imaginary circle or orbit in the heavens. [Gr. *kyklos,* a circle ; akin to **Circle.**]

**Cyclic,** sī′klik, **Cyclical,** sī′klik-al, *adj.* pertaining to or containing a *cycle.*

**Cycloid,** sī′kloid, *n.* a figure *like a circle :* a curve made by a point in a circle, when the circle is rolled along a straight line.—*adj.* **Cycloid′al.** [Gr. *kyklos,* and *eidos,* form.]

**Cyclone,** sī′klōn, *n.* a *circular* or rotatory storm. [Coined from Gr. *kyklōn,* pr.p. of *kykloō,* to whirl round—*kyklos.*]

**Cyclopædia, Cyclopedia,** sī-klō-pē′di-a, *n.* the *circle* or compass of human *knowledge :* a work containing information on every department, or on a particular department of knowledge.— *adj.* **Cycloped′ic.** [Gr. *kyklos,* a circle, and *paideia,* learning.]

**Cyclopean,** sī-klō-pē′an, *adj.* of or like the *Cyclopes,* a fabled race of giants with one *circular eye* in the middle of the forehead : giant-like : vast. [Gr. *kyklōpeios—kyklōps—kyklos,* a circle, and *ōps,* an eye.]

**Cygnet,** sig′net, *n.* a *young swan.* [Acc. to Diez, dim. of Fr. *cygne,* whose old form *cisne* (Sp. *cisne,* a swan) is from Low L. *cecinus,* and is not connected with L. *cygnus,* Gr. *kyknos,* a swan.]

**Cylinder,** sil′in-dėr, *n.* a solid circular or *roller*-like body, whose ends are equal parallel circles. [Gr. *kylindros,* from *kylindō,* to roll.]

**Cylindric,** si-lin′drik, **Cylindrical,** si-lin′drik-al, *adj.* having the form or properties of a *cylinder.*

**Cymbal,** sim′bal, *n.* a *hollow* brass, basin-like, musical instrument, beaten together in pairs. [L. *cymbalum,* from Gr. *kymbalon—kymbē,* the hollow of a vessel ; akin to E. **Hump.**]

**Cynic,** sin′ik, **Cynical,** sin′ik-al, *adj., dog-like :* surly : snarling : austere : misanthropic.—*adv.* **Cyn′ically.** [Gr. *kynikos,* dog-like, from *kyōn, kynos,* a dog ; akin to L. *can-is,* E. **Hound.**]

**Cynic,** sin′ik, *n.* one of a sect of ancient philosophers, so called from their morose and contemptuous views : a morose man : a snarler.

**Cynicism,** sin′i-sizm, *n., surliness :* contempt for human nature : heartlessness, misanthropy.

**Cynosure,** sin′o-shōōr, or sī′-, *n.* the *dog's tail,* a constellation containing the north-star : hence, anything that strongly attracts attention. [Gr. *kyōn, kynos,* a dog, *oura,* a tail.]

**Cypress,** sī′pres, *n.* an evergreen tree whose branches used to be carried at funerals : hence, a symbol of death. [Fr. *cyprès*—L. *cupressus*— Gr. *kyparissos.*]

**Cyst,** sist, *n.* (*lit.*) a *chest :* a bag in animal bodies containing morbid matter. [From root of **Chest.**]

**Czar,** zär, **Tsar,** tsär, *n.* the emperor of Russia.— *fem.* **Czarina,** zä-rē′na, the empress of Russia. [Russ. *tsare,* a king ; its conn. with Ger. *kaiser,* L. *cæsar,* a king or emperor, is doubtful.]

**Czarevitch,** zär′e-vitch, **Cesarevitch,** sē-zär′e-vitch, *n.* the eldest *son* of the *czar.*—*fem.* **Czarevna,** zär-ev′na, his consort. [Russ. *tsare,* a czar, and *vitz* (pronounced *vitch*), descended from.]

# D

**Dab,** dab, *v.t.* to strike gently with something soft or moist :—*pr.p.* dabb′ing ; *pa.p.* dabbed′. —*n.* a gentle blow : a small lump of anything soft or moist : a small flat fish like a flounder, but with a rough back. [E. ; from a Teut. root present in O. Dut. *dabben,* to pinch, Ger. *tappe,* a pat. E. **Tap** is a doublet. See also **Dub.**]

**Dab,** dab, *n.* an expert person. [Prob. a corr. of **Adept.**]

**Dabble,** dab′l, *v.t.* to *wet* by little *dabs* or strokes : to spatter.—*v.i.* to play in water with hands or feet : to do anything in a trifling way. [Freq. of **Dab.**]

**Dabbler,** dab′lėr, *n.* one who *dabbles* or does things in a superficial, trifling way.

**Dabchick,** dab′chik, *n.* a *small* water-*fowl* that dives or *dabbles* in the water.

**Dace,** dās, **Dare,** dār, **Dart,** därt, *n.* a small river fish, so called from the *quickness* of its motions. [M.E. *darce*—O. Fr. *dars*—Low L. *dardus,* a dart or javelin (Fr. *dard,* a dart or a dace)].

**Dactyl,** dak′til, *n.* in Latin and Greek poetry, a foot of three syllables, one long followed by two short, so called from its likeness to the joints of a *finger :* in English, a foot of three syllables, with the first accented, as *mér*rily. [L. *dactylus*—Gr. *daktylos,* a finger. See **Digit.**]

**Dactylic,** dak-til′ik, *adj.* relating to or consisting chiefly of *dactyls.*

**Dactylology,** dak-til-ol′o-ji, *n.* the art of *talking* with the *fingers,* like the deaf and dumb. [Gr. *daktylos,* and *logos,* discourse—*legō,* to speak.]

**Dad,** dad, **Daddy,** dad′i, *n., father,* a word used by children. [W. *tad ;* Gr. *tata,* Sans. *tata.*]

**Dado,** dā′do, *n.* the solid block or *cube* forming the body of a pedestal : wainscoting round the lower part of a wall. [It.—L. *datus* (*talus,* a die, being understood), given or thrown forth— *dare,* to give. Doublet **Die.**]

**Daffodil,** daf′o-dil, **Daffodilly,** daf′o-dil-i, *n.* a yellow flower of the lily tribe, also called King's spear. [M.E. *affodille*—O. Fr. *asphodile*—Gr. and L. *asphodelus ;* the *d* is prefixed accidentally.]

**Dagger,** dag′ėr, *n.* a short sword for stabbing : a mark of reference (†). [W. *dagr,* Ir. *daigear,* Fr. *dague,* It. *daga.*]

**Daggle,** dag′l, *v.t.* and *v.i.* to *wet* or grow wet by dragging on the wet ground. [Freq. of prov. E. *dag,* to sprinkle with water, from a Scand. root seen in Sw. *dagg,* E. **Dew.**]

**Daguerreotype,** da-ger′o-tīp, *n.* a method of taking sun-pictures on metal plates : a picture thus produced. [Fr., from *Daguerre,* the inventor, and **Type.**]

**Dahlia,** dāl′i-a, *n.* a garden plant with a large beautiful flower. [From *Dahl,* a Swedish botanist.]

**Daily,** dā′li, *adj.* and *adv.* every day.

**Dainty,** dān′ti, *adj.* pleasant to the palate : delicate : fastidious.—*n.* that which is dainty, a delicacy.—*adv.* **Dain′tily.**—*n.* **Dain′tiness.** [M.E. *deintee,* anything worthy or costly—O. Fr. *daintié,* worthiness—L. *dignitas.* See **Dignity.**]

**Dairy,** dā′ri, *n.* the place where milk is kept, and butter and cheese made : an establishment for the supply of milk. [M.E. *dey,* dairymaid—Ice. *deigja,* a dairymaid ; orig. a kneader of **Dough,** in Ice. *deig ;* or from a root sig. to milk. See **Dug.**]

**Dais,** dā′is, *n.* a raised floor at the upper end of the dining-hall where the high *table* stood ; a raised floor with a seat and canopy. [O. Fr. *dais*—Low L. *discus*, a table—L. *discus*, a quoit—Gr. *diskos*. See **Dish, Disc**.]

**Daisied**, dā′zid, *adj*. covered with *daisies*.

**Daisy**, dā′zi, *n*. (*lit.*) the *day's eye*, a common spring flower, so called from its *sun*-like appearance. [A.S. *dæges ege*, day's eye, the sun.]

**Dale**, dāl, **Dell**, del, *n*. the low ground between hills: the valley through which a river flows.—*n*. **Dales′man**. [A.S. *dæl*; Scand. *dal*, Ger. *thal*, orig. meaning 'cleft.' See **Deal, Dell**.]

**Dalliance**, dal′i-ans, *n*., *dallying*, toying, or trifling: interchange of embraces: delay.

**Dally**, dal′i, *v.i.* to lose time by idleness or trifling: to play:—*pa.p.* dall′ied. [A.S. *dol*, foolish; Ger. *dahlen*, to trifle: perh. conn. with **Dwell**.]

**Dam**, dam, *n*. an embankment to restrain water.—*v.t.* to keep back water by a bank or other obstruction:—*pr.p.* damm′ing; *pa.p.* dammed′. [E., and in all the Teut. tongues.]

**Dam**, dam, *n*. a *mother*, applied to quadrupeds. [A form of **Dame**.]

**Damage**, dam′āj, *n*., *hurt, injury, loss*: the value of what is lost.—*pl.* compensation for loss or injury.—*v.t.* to harm, injure.—*v.i.* to take injury. [O. Fr. *damage* (Fr. *dommage*), from L. *damnum*, loss, injury.]      [*damaged*.

**Damageable**, dam′āj-a-bl, *adj*. capable of being

**Damask**, dam′ask, *n*. figured stuff orig. of silk, now of linen, cotton, or wool.—*v.t.* to flower or variegate, as cloth.—*adj.* of a red colour, like that of a damask rose. [From *Damascus*, in Syria, where it was orig. made.]

**Dame**, dām, *n*. the *mistress* of a house: a matron : a noble lady. [Fr. *dame*—L. *domina*, a mistress, *fem.* of *dominus*, a master. Doublet, **Dam**, a mother. See **Dominate**.]

**Damn**, dam, *v.t.* to censure or *condemn*: to sentence to eternal punishment.—*n*. an oath : a curse. [Fr. *damner*—L. *damnare*, to condemn, from *damnum*, loss, penalty.]

**Damnable**, dam′na-bl, *adj*., *deserving* or tending to *damnation*: hateful: pernicious.—*adv.* **Dam′nably**.—*n*. **Dam′nableness**. [Late L. *damnabilis*.]

**Damnation**, dam-nā′shun, *n*. (*theol.*) the punishment of the impenitent in the future state : eternal punishment. [L. *damnatio*.]

**Damnatory**, dam′na-tor-i, *adj*. containing sentence of condemnation. [L. *damnatorius*.]

**Damp**, damp, *n.*, *vapour, mist*: moist air : lowness of spirits.—*pl.* dangerous vapours in mines, &c.—*v.t.* to wet slightly : to chill : to discourage : to check : to make dull.—*adj.* moist : foggy.—*adv.* **Damp′ly**.—*n*. **Damp′ness**. [E. ; akin to Dut. *damp*, Ger. *dampf*, vapour.]

**Damper**, damp′ėr, *n*. that which checks or moderates : (*Australia*) a kind of hastily-baked bread.

**Damsel**, dam′zel, *n*. a *little dame* or lady : a young unmarried woman : a girl. [Fr. *demoiselle*, O. Fr. *damoisel*, a page—Low L. *domicellus*, dim. of *dominus*, a lord.]

**Damson**, dam′zn, *n*. a small black plum. [Shortened from *Damascene*—*Damascus*. See **Damask**.]

**Dance**, dans, *v.i.* to move with measured steps to music.—*v.t.* to make to dance or jump.—*n*. the movement of one or more persons with measured steps to music. [Fr. *danser*, from O. Ger. *danson*, to draw along, Ger. *tanzen*.]

**Dancer**, dans′ėr, *n*. one who practises *dancing*.

**Dancing**, dans′ing, *n*. the act or art of moving in the *dance*.

**Dandelion**, dan-de-lī′un, *n*. a common plant with a yellow flower, so called from the jagged *tooth-*like edges of its leaf. [Fr. *dent de lion*, tooth of the lion.]

**Dandle**, dan′dl, *v.t.* to *play with*: to fondle or toss in the arms, as a baby. [E. ; cog. with Ger. *tändeln*—*tand*, a toy; allied to Scot. *dander*, to go about idly, to trifle.]

**Dandriff, Dandruff**, dand′ruf, *n*. a scaly *scurf* which grows on the head, esp. under the hair and beard. [W. *ton*, surface, skin, and *drwg*, bad.]

**Dandy**, dan′di, *n*. a foppish, *silly fellow*: one who pays much attention to dress. [Perh. from Fr. *dandin*, a ninny ; and prob. from root of **Dandle**.]

**Dane**, dān, *n*. a native of *Denmark*.

**Danger**, dān′jėr, *n*. a hazard or risk : insecurity. [O. Fr. *dangier*, absolute power (of a feudal lord), hence power to hurt—Low L. *dominium*, feudal authority—L. *dominus*, a lord. See **Dungeon**.]

**Dangerous**, dān′jėr-us, *adj*. full of danger: unsafe : insecure.—*adv.* **Dan′gerously**.

**Dangle**, dang′gl, *v.i.* to hang loosely or with a *swinging motion*: to follow any one about.—*v.t.* to make to dangle. [From a Scand. root, found in Ice. *dingla*, to swing to and fro, freq. of Ding, to throw, push.]

**Dangler**, dang′glėr, *n*. one who *dangles* about others, especially about women.

**Danish**, dān′ish, *adj*. belonging to *Denmark*.

**Dank**, dangk, *adj*. moist, wet. [Perh. conn. with Dew. See also **Daggle**.]

**Dapper**, dap′ėr, *adj*. quick : little and active : neat : spruce. [Dut. *dapper*, brave ; Ger. *tapfer*, quick, brave.]

**Dapple**, dap′l, *adj*. marked with spots.—*v.t.* to variegate with spots. [See **Dimple**.]

**Dare**, dār, *v.i.* to be bold enough: to venture :—*pa.t.* durst.—*v.t.* to challenge: to defy. [A.S. *dear, durran*; Goth. *daursan*: akin to Gr. *tharreō*, Sans. *dhrish*, to be bold.]

**Dare**, dār. Same as **Dace**.

**Daring**, dār′ing, *adj*., *bold* : courageous : fearless.—*n*. boldness.—*adv.* **Dar′ingly**.

**Dark**, därk, *adj*. without light: black or somewhat black : gloomy : difficult to understand : unenlightened : secret.—*n*. absence of light: obscurity : a state of ignorance.—*adv.* **Dark′ly**.—*n*. **Dark′ness**. [A.S. *deorc*.]

**Darken**, därk′n, *v.t.* to make *dark*: to render ignorant : to sully.—*v.i.* to grow dark or darker.

**Darkish**, därk′ish, *adj*. somewhat dark : dusky.

**Darkling**, därk′ling, *adj*. being in the *dark* (poet.).

**Darksome**, därk′sum, *adj.*, *dark*: gloomy (poet.)

**Darling**, där′ling, *n*. a *little dear*: one dearly beloved : a favourite. [**Dear**, and *ling*.]

**Darn**, därn, *v.t.* to mend a hole by imitating the texture of the stuff.—*n*. the place darned. [W. *darn*, a piece, a patch.]     [Ety. dub.]

**Darnel**, där′nel, *n*. a weed of the ryegrass genus.

**Dart**, därt, *n*. a pointed weapon for throwing with the hand : anything that pierces.—*v.t.* to hurl suddenly : to send or shoot forth.—*v.i.* to start or shoot forth rapidly.—*adv.* **Dart′ingly**. [O. Fr. *dart* : from a Low Ger. root.]

**Dart**. See **Dace**.

**Darwinism**, där′-win-ism, *n*. the theory of the origin of species propounded by C. Darwin.—*adj.* **Dar-win′ian**.

**Dash**, dash, *v.t.* to throw violently : to break by throwing together : to throw water suddenly : to bespatter : to destroy or frustrate : to mix or adulterate.—*v.i.* to strike against : to break against, as water : to rush with violence.—*n.* a violent striking : a rushing or violent onset : a blow : a mark (—) at a break in a sentence : a slight admixture. [Dan. *daske*, to slap.]

**Dashing**, dash'ing, *adj.* rushing : reckless : hasty and rash : gallant.—*adv.* **Dash'ingly**.

**Dastard**, das'tard, *n.* a cowardly fellow.—*adj.* shrinking from danger ; cowardly.—*adj.* and *adv.* **Das'tardly**.—*ns.* **Das'tardness, Das'tardliness**. [From a Scand. stem *dast* = E. *dazed*, and Fr. suffix -*ard*. See **Daze**.]

**Data**, dā'ta, *n.pl.* facts given or admitted from which other facts may be deduced.—*sing.* **Da'tum**. [L. *datum*, *data*, given—*do*, to give.]

**Date**, dāt, *n.* the time when a letter is given or written : the time of any event : a stipulated time.—*v.t.* to affix the date to.—*v.i.* to reckon : to begin. [Fr. *date*—L. *datum*.]

**Date**, dāt, *n.* the fruit of the date-palm, so called from its fancied resemblance to the *finger*. [Fr. *datte*—L. *dactylus*—Gr. *daktylos*, a finger.]

**Dative**, dāt'iv, *adj.* that is given or appointed.—*n.* the *dative* case, the oblique case of nouns, &c. which follows verbs or other parts of speech that express *giving* or some act directed to the object—generally indicated in English by *to* or *for*. [L. *dativus*.]

**Datum**, dā'tum, *n.* See **Data**.

**Daub**, dawb, *v.t.* to smear : to paint coarsely.—*n.* a coarse painting.—**Dauber**, dawb'ėr, *n.* one who *daubs* : a coarse painter. [O. Fr. *dauber*, to plaster—L. *dealbare*, to whitewash—*de*, down, and *albus*, white.]

**Daughter**, daw'tėr, *n.* a female child : a female descendant.—*n.* **Daugh'ter-in-law**, a son's wife. [A.S. *dohtor* ; Scot. *dochter*, Ger. *tochter*, Gr. *thygatēr*, Sans. *duhitri*, from *duh* or *dhugh*, to milk—as if 'the milkmaid.' See **Dug**.]

**Daughterly**, daw'tėr-li, *adj.*, *like* or becoming a *daughter*.—*n.* **Daugh'terliness**.

**Daunt**, dänt, or dawnt, *v.t.* to frighten : to discourage. [O. Fr. *danter*, Fr. *dompter*—L. *domito*—*domo*, Gr. *damaō*, to tame : conn. with **Tame**.]

**Dauntless**, dänt'les, *adj.* not to be *daunted*.—*adv.* **Daunt'lessly**.—*n.* **Daunt'lessness**.

**Dauphin**, daw'fin, *n.* formerly a name given to the eldest son of the king of France.—*fem.* **Dau'phiness**, the dauphin's wife. [O. Fr. *daulphin*, Fr. *dauphin*—L *delphinus*, a dolphin. *Dauphin* was the proper name of the lords of Viennois, who had taken for their crest three dolphins. When Viennois (Dauphiné) was ceded to the crown of France, the name became the title of the king's eldest son.]

**Davit**, dāv'it, *n.* a spar projecting from a ship, used as a crane for hoisting the anchor clear of the vessel.—*pl.* pieces of timber or iron, projecting over a ship's side or stern, having tackle to raise a boat by. [Fr. *davier*, a forceps.]

**Daw**, daw, *n.* a bird of the crow kind : a jackdaw. [From its cry.]

**Dawdle**, daw'dl, *v.i.* to waste time by trifling : to act or move slowly.—*n.* **Daw'dler**. [Allied to **Dandle** and **Dandy**.]

**Dawn**, dawn, *v.i.* to become *day* : to begin to grow light : to begin to appear.—*n.* daybreak : beginning. [A.S. *dagian*, day.]

**Day**, dā, *n.* the time of light : the time from morning till night : twenty-four hours, the time the earth takes to make a revolution on her axis. [A.S. *dæg* ; Ger. *tag*, from an unknown root, not conn. with L. *dies*.]

**Daybook**, dā'book, *n.* a *book* in which merchants, &c. enter the transactions of every *day*.

**Daybreak**, dā'brāk, *n.* the *breaking of day*, or first appearance of light. [while awake.

**Daydream**, dā'drēm, *n.* a *dreaming* or musing

**Day-lily**, dā'-lil'i, *n.* a *lily* that blooms during the *day* or for a day only.

**Daysman**, dāz'man, *n.* one who appoints a *day* to hear a cause : an umpire.

**Dayspring**, dā'spring, *n.* the *springing of day* :

**Daystar**, dā'stär, *n.* the *star* which ushers in the *day* : the morning-star.

**Daze**, dāz, *v.t.* (*obs.*) to render dull or stupid. [Ice. *dasa*, to be breathless or exhausted ; conn. with A.S. *dwæs*, foolish.]

**Dazzle**, daz'l, *v.t.* to *daze* or overpower with any strong light.—*adv.* **Dazz'lingly**. [Freq. of **Daze**.]

**Deacon**, dē'kn, *n.* in Episcopal churches the order of clergy under priests : in some Presbyterian churches, an officer under the elders : in Congregational and some other churches, the principal lay official : in Scot. the master of an incorporated company.—*fem.* **Dea'coness**.—*ns.* **Dea'conship, Dea'conry**. [L. *diaconus*—Gr. *diakonos*, a servant.]

**Dead**, ded, *adj.* deprived of life : that never had life : deathlike : useless : dull : cold and cheerless : without vegetation : perfect.—**Dead-drunk**, completely drunk ; **Dead-language**, one no longer spoken ; **Dead-letter**, a letter undelivered and unclaimed at the post-office ; **Dead-lights**, storm-shutters for a cabin window ; **Dead-lock**, a position of matters when they have become so complicated that they are at a complete standstill and progress is impossible ; **Dead-march**, a piece of solemn music played at funeral processions, especially of soldiers ; **Dead-reckoning**, an estimation of a ship's place, simply by the log-book ; **Dead-weight**, a heavy or oppressive burden.—*adv.* **Dead'ly**.—*n.* **Dead'ness**. [A.S. *dead* ; Goth. *dauths*, Ger. *todt*, from root of *die*.] [those who are dead.

**Dead**, ded, *n.* the time of greatest *stillness*.—*n.pl.*

**Deaden**, ded'n, *v.t.* to make *dead* : to deprive partly of vigour or sensation : to blunt : to lessen.

**Deadly**, ded'li, *adj.*, *causing death* : fatal : implacable.—*n.* **Dead'liness**.

**Deaf**, def, *adj.*, *dull* of hearing : unable to hear at all : not willing to hear : inattentive.—*adv.* **Deaf'ly**.—*n.* **Deaf'ness**. [A.S. *deaf* ; Dut. *doof*, Ger. *taub*.]

**Deafen**, def'n, *v.t.* to *make deaf*, partly or altogether : to stun : to render impervious to sound.

**Deaf-mute**, def'-mūt, *n.* one who is both *deaf* and *mute* or dumb.

**Deal**, dēl, *n.* a *portion* : an indefinite quantity : a large quantity : the act of dividing cards : one of the divisions or boards into which a piece of timber is cut : a fir or pine board. [A.S. *dæl* ; Ger. *theil*, a part or division.]

**Deal**, dēl, *v.t.* to *divide*, to *distribute* : to throw about.—*v.i.* to transact business : to act : to distribute cards :—*pa.t.* and *pa.p.* dealt (delt). [A.S. *dælan*—*dæl* ; Ger. *theilen*—*theil*.]

**Dealer**, dēl'ėr, *n.* one who *deals* : a trader.

**Dealing**, dēl'ing, *n.* manner of acting towards others : intercourse of trade.

**Dean**, dēn, *n.* a dignitary in cathedral and collegiate churches who presides over the other clergy : the president of the faculty in a college.—*ns.* **Dean'ship, Dean'ery**, the *office* of a dean : a dean's house. [O. Fr. *deien*—L. *decanus*, a chief of ten—*decem*, ten.]

**Dear**, dēr, *adj.* high in price : costly : scarce : highly valued : beloved.—*n.* one who is dear or beloved.—*adv.* **Dear′ly.**—*n.* **Dear′ness.** [A.S. *deore*; Ger. *theuer*, O. Ger. *tiuri*, precious.]

**Dearth**, dėrth, *n.*, *dearness, high price:* scarcity: want: famine: barrenness.

**Death**, deth, *n.* state of *being dead:* extinction of life: manner of dying: mortality.—*n.* **Death′-bed,** the last illness. [A.S. *death*; Ger. *tod.*]

**Debar**, de-bär′, *v.t.* to *bar out from:* to exclude: to hinder:—*pr.p.* debarr′ing; *pa.p.* debarred′. [L. *de*, from, and **Bar.**]

**Debark**, de-bärk′, *v.t.* or *v.i.* to land *from a bark,* ship, or boat: to disembark. [Fr. *débarquer*—*des* = L. *dis*, away, and **Barque**, a ship.]

**Debarkation, Debarcation,** de-bärk-ā′shun, *n.* the act of *debarking* or disembarking.

**Debase**, de-bās′, *v.t.* to lower: to make mean or of less value: to adulterate. [L. *de*, down, and **Base**, low.]

**Debasement**, de-bās′ment, *n.* degradation.

**Debasing**, de-bās′ing, *adj.* tending to *lower* or degrade.—*adv.* **Debas′ingly.**

**Debatable**, de-bāt′a-bl, *adj.* liable to be disputed.

**Debate**, de-bāt′, *n.* a contention in words or argument.—*v.t.* to contend for in argument.—*v.i.* to deliberate: to join in debate.—*n.* **Debat′er.** [Fr. *de*, and *battre*, to beat. See **Beat.**]

**Debauch**, de-bawch′, *v.t.* to lead away from duty or allegiance: to corrupt with lewdness.—*v.i.* to indulge in revelry.—*n.* a fit of intemperance or debauchery. [Fr. *débaucher*—*des* = L. *dis*, and a word *bauche*, a workshop, of unknown origin.]      [*bauchery*: a libertine.

**Debauchee**, deb′o-shē, *n.* one given up to *de-*

**Debauchery**, de-bawch′ėr-i, *n.* corruption of fidelity: seduction from duty: excessive intemperance: habitual lewdness.

**Debenture**, de-bent′ūr, *n.* an acknowledgment of a *debt:* a deed of mortgage given by a railway or other company for borrowed money: a certificate entitling an exporter of imported goods to a drawback or repayment of the duty paid on their importation. [L. *debentur*, there are due, 3d person pl. passive of *debeo*, to owe.]

**Debilitate**, de-bil′i-tāt, *v.t.* to *make weak:* to impair the strength of. [L. *debilito, debilitatus* —*debilis*, weak—*de*, not, *habilis*, able. See **Ability.**]

**Debility**, de-bil′i-ti, *n.*, *weakness* and languor: a weak action of the animal functions.

**Debit**, deb′it, *n.* a *debt* or something due: an entry on the debtor side of an account.—*v.t.* to charge with debt: to enter on the debit or debtor side of an account. [L. *debitum*, what is due, from *debeo*, to owe.]

**Debonair**, deb-o-nār′, *adj.* of *good air* or appearance and manners: elegant: courteous. [Fr. *de*, of, *bon*, good, *air*, appearance, manner.]

**Debouch**, de-bōōsh′, *v.i.* to march out *from a narrow pass* or confined place. [Fr. *déboucher* —*de*, from, *bouche*, the mouth—L. *bucca*, the cheek.]        [river or strait.

**Debouchure**, dā-bōō-shōōr′, *n.* the *mouth* of a

**Debris**, de-brē′, *n.*, *bruised* or *broken* pieces of anything, esp. of rock: rubbish: ruins. [Fr., from *briser*, akin to **Bruise.**]

**Debt**, det, *n.* what one *owes* to another: what one becomes liable to do or suffer. [L. *debitum*.]

**Debtor**, det′ur, *n.* one who *owes* a debt: the side of an account on which *debts* are charged. [L. *debitor.*]

**Debut**, de-bu′ (*u* sounded as in Scot. *gude*), *n.* a beginning or first attempt: a first appearance before the public, as of an actor, &c. [Fr. *début*, a first stroke—*de*, from, *but*, aim, mark.]

**Decade** or **Decad**, dek′ad or dek′ād, *n.* an aggregate of *ten.* [Fr. *décade*—Gr. *dekas*—*deka*, ten.]

**Decadence**, de-kā′dens, **Decadency**, de-kā′den-si, *n.*, *state of decay.* [Fr.—Low L. *decadentia*, from *de*, down, and Low L. *cadentia*—L. *cado*, to fall. See **Cadence, Decay.**]

**Decagon**, dek′a-gon, *n.* a plane figure of *ten angles* and sides. [Gr. *deka*, and *gēnia*, an angle: akin to **Knee.**]

**Decahedron**, dek-a-hē′dron, *n.* a solid figure having *ten bases* or sides. [Gr. *deka*, and *hedra*, a seat.]

**Decalogue**, dek′a-log, *n.* the *ten commandments.* [Gr. *deka*, ten, *logos*, a discourse, a proposition.]

**Decamp**, de-kamp′, *v.i.* (*lit.*) to *go from* or shift a *camp:* to go away, esp. secretly. [Fr. *décamper*—Fr. *de* = L. *dis*, away, and *camp.* See **Camp.**]

**Decampment**, de-kamp′ment, *n.*, *shifting a camp:* a marching off. [Fr. *décampement.*]

**Decanal**, dek′an-al, *adj.* pertaining to a *deanery.*

**Decant**, de-kant′, *v.t.* to pour off, leaving sediment: to pour from one vessel into another. [Fr. *décanter*—*de*, from, and **Cant**, a side or corner.]

**Decanter**, de-kant′ėr, *n.* a *vessel* for holding *decanted* liquor: an ornamental bottle.

**Decapitate**, de-kap′i-tāt, *v.t.* to take the *head from:* to behead. [Low L. *decapitare*—L. *de*, from, and *caput, capitis*, the head.]

**Decapitation**, de-kap-i-tā′shun, *n.* the act of *beheading.*

**Decapod**, dek′a-pod, *n.* one of the shellfish which have *ten feet* or claws, as the crab. [Gr. *deka*, ten, and *pous, podos*, a foot.]

**Decarbonise**, de-kär′bon-īz, *v.t.* to deprive of *carbon.* [*De*, from, and **Carbon.**]

**Decastyle**, dek′a-stīl, *n.* a portico with *ten styles* or *columns* in front. [Gr. *deka*, ten, *stylos*, a column.]

**Decasyllabic**, dek-a-sil-ab′ik, *adj.* having *ten syllables.* [Fr. *décasyllabique*—Gr. *deka*, ten, *syllabē*, a syllable.]

**Decay**, de-kā′, *v.i.* to *fall away from* a state of health or excellence: to waste away.—*n.* a falling into a worse or less perfect state: a passing away. [O. Fr. *decaer*—L. *de*, from, *cadere*, to fall.]

**Decease**, de-sēs′, *v.i.* to *cease* to live: to die.—*n.* death. [O. Fr. *deces*—L. *decessus*—*de*, away, *cedo, cessus*, to go.]

**Deceit**, de-sēt′, *n.* act of *deceiving:* anything intended to mislead another. [Through Fr. from L. *deceptus.*]

**Deceitful**, de-sēt′fool, *adj.* full of *deceit:* disposed or tending to deceive: insincere.—*adv.* **Deceit′-fully.**—*n.* **Deceit′fulness.**

**Deceivable**, de-sēv′a-bl, *adj.* that may be *deceived:* exposed to imposture.—*n.* **Deceiv′ableness.**—*adv.* **Deceiv′ably.**

**Deceive**, de-sēv′, *v.t.* to mislead or cause to err: to cheat: to disappoint.—*n.* **Deceiv′er.** [Fr. *décevoir*—L. *decipere, deceptus*—*de*, from, *capere*, to take, catch.]

**December**, de-sem′bėr, *n.* the *tenth month* among the Romans, who began their year with March: with us, the twelfth month of the year. [L. *decem*, ten.]

**Decemvir**, de-sem′vir, *n.* one of *ten magistrates* who at one time had absolute power in Rome:—*pl.* **Decem′virs** or (L.) **Decemviri**, dē-sem′vi-rī. [L. *decem*, ten, and *vir*, a man.]

**Decemvirate**, de-sem′vir-āt, *n.* a body of *ten men* in office: the term of office of decemvirs.

---

**Decency**, de'sen-si, *n.* becomingness : modesty. [L. *decentia*. See **Decent**.]

**Decennary**, de-sen'ar-i, *n.* a period of *ten years*. [L. *decem*, ten, and *annus*, a year.]

**Decennial**, de-sen'i-al, *adj.* consisting of, or happening every *ten years*.

**Decent**, de'sent, *adj.*, *becoming* : seemly : proper : modest : moderate : tolerable.—*adv.* **De'cently**. [L. *decens*, *decentis*, pr.p. of *decet*, it is becoming.]

**Decentralise**, de-sen'tral-īz, *v.t.* to withdraw from the centre. [L. *de*, priv., and **Centralise**.]

**Deception**, de-sep'shun, *n.* act of *deceiving* : the means by which it is sought to deceive. [L. *deceptio*.]

**Deceptive**, de-sep'tiv, *adj.* tending to *deceive.*—*adv.* **Decep'tively**.—*n.* **Decep'tiveness**.

**Decide**, de-sīd', *v.t.* to determine : to end : to settle. [Fr. *décider*—L. *decidere*—*de*, away, *cædo*, to cut.]

**Decided**, de-sīd'ed, *adj.*, *determined* : clear, unmistakable : resolute.—*adv.* **Decid'edly**.

**Deciduous**, de-sid'ū-us, *adj.*, *falling off* : that fall in autumn, as leaves : not permanent.—*n.* **Decid'uousness**. [L. *deciduus*—*decido*, from *de*, *cado*, to fall.]

**Decimal**, des'i-mal, *adj.* numbered or proceeding *by tens*.—*n.* a fraction having ten or some power of ten for its denominator.—**Decimal system** is the French system of weights or measures, the principle of which is that it multiplies and divides *by ten*.—*adv.* **Dec'imally**. [Fr.—Low L. *decimalis*—*decem*, ten.]

**Decimate**, des'i-māt, *v.t.* to *take the tenth* part of : to put to death every tenth man.—*n.* **Dec'imator**. [L. *decimo*, *decimatus*—*decimus*, tenth.]

**Decimation**, des-i-mā'shun, *n.* a military punishment, by which every tenth man was selected by lot and put to death, or otherwise punished.

**Decipher**, de-sī'fer, *v.t.* to *un-cipher* or read secret writing : to make out what is unintelligible or obscure. [L. *de*, negative, and **Cipher**.]

**Decipherable**, de-sī'fer-a-bl, *adj.* that may be *deciphered*. [determination : settlement.

**Decision**, de-sizh'un, *n.* the act of *deciding* :

**Decisive**, de-sī'siv, *adj.* having the power of *deciding* : final : positive.—*adv.* **Deci'sively**.—*n.* **Deci'siveness**.

**Deck**, dek, *v.t.* to *cover* : to clothe : to adorn : to furnish with a deck, as a vessel.—*n.* a covering : the floor or covering of a ship. [Dut. *dekken*, to cover ; Ger. *decken* ; akin to L. *tego*. See **Thatch**.]

**Decker**, dek'er, *n.* the person or thing *that decks* : a vessel which has a deck or decks, used chiefly in composition, as a three-decker, a ship with three decks.

**Declaim**, de-klām', *v.i.* to make a set or rhetorical speech : to harangue.—*ns.* **Declaim'ant**, **Declaim'er**. [Fr.—L. *declamo*—*de*, intensive, *clamo*, to cry out.]

**Declamation**, dek-la-mā'shun, *n.* act of *declaiming* : a set speech in public : display in speaking.

**Declamatory**, de-klam'a-tor-i, *adj.* relating to *declamation* : appealing to the passions : noisy and rhetorical merely.

**Declaration**, dek-la-rā'shun, *n.* act of *declaring* : that which is declared : a written affirmation.

**Declarative**, de-klar'a-tiv, **Declaratory**, de-klar'a-tor-i, *adj.* explanatory.—*advs.* **Declar'atively**, **Declar'atorily**.

**Declare**, de-klār', *v.t.* to make known : to shew *plainly* to others by words : to assert.—*v.i.* to

make a statement. [Fr. *déclarer*, from L. *declaro*, *declaratus*—*de*, sig. completeness, *clarus*, clear.]

**Declension**, de-klen'shun, *n.* a falling off : decay : descent : (*gram.*) change of termination for the oblique cases. [See **Decline**.]

**Declinable**, de-klīn'a-bl, *adj.* having inflection for the oblique cases.

**Declination**, dek-lin-a'shun, *n.* act of *declining* : deviation : decay : (*astr.*) the distance from the celestial equator.

**Decline**, de-klīn', *v.i.* to *bend* or *turn away from* (a straight line) : to deviate : to refuse : to bend down : to fail or decay : to draw to an end.— *v.t.* to bend down : to turn away from : to refuse : to avoid : (*gram.*) to give the changes of a word in the oblique cases.—*n.* a falling off : deviation : decay : a gradual sinking of the bodily faculties, consumption. [Fr. *décliner*— L. *de*, down, away from, *clino*, to bend. See **Lean**.]

**Declivity**, de-kliv'i-ti, *n.* a place that *declines* or slopes *downward*, opp. of **Acclivity** : inclination downward : a gradual descent. [L. *declivitas*—*de*, downward, *clivus*, sloping, akin to *clino*.]

**Decoct**, de-kokt', *v.t.* to digest by heat. [L. *decoquo*, *decoctus*—*de*, *coquo*, to cook.]

**Decoction**, de-kok'shun, *n.* an extract of anything got by *boiling*.—*adj.* **Decoc'tive**.

**Decollate**, de-kol'āt, *v.t.* to behead. [L. *decollo* —*de*, from, *collum*, the neck.] [ing.

**Decollation**, de-kol-ā'shun, *n.* the act of *behead*-

**Decolorant**, de-kul'ur-ant, *n.* a substance that bleaches or *removes colour.*

**Decoloration**, de-kul'ur-ā-shun, *n.* the *removal* or absence of *colour.*

**Decolour**, de-kul'ur, **Decolourise**, de-kul'ur-īz, *v.t.* to deprive of *colour*. [Fr. *décolorer*—L. *decoloro*—*de*, from, *color*, colour.]

**Decomposable**, de-kom-pōz'a-bl, *adj.* that may be *decomposed*.

**Decompose**, de-kom-pōz', *v.t.* to *separate* the parts *composing* anything : to resolve into original elements. [L. *de*, sig. separation, and **Compose**.]

**Decomposition**, de-kom-po-zish'un, *n.* act of decomposing : decay or dissolution.

**Decompound**, de-kom-pownd', *v.t.* to *compound again* : to compound things already compounded ; also, to divide a thing into its constituent parts.—*adj.* compounded a second time. —*adj.* **Decompound'able**. [L. *de*, intensive, and **Compound**.]

**Decorate**, dek'o-rāt, *v.t.* to *ornament*, to beautify. [L. *decoro*, *decoratus*—*decus*, what is becoming, ornament, from *decet*, it is becoming.]

**Decoration**, dek-o-rā'shun, *n.* ornament : anything that heightens beauty. [to adorn.

**Decorative**, dek'o-rā-tiv, *adj.* adorning : suited

**Decorator**, dek'o-rā-tor, *n.* one who decorates.

**Decorous**, de-kō'rus, *adj.*, *becoming* : suitable : proper : decent.—*adv.* **Deco'rously**. [L. *decorus*.]

**Decorticate**, de-kor'ti-kāt, *v.t.* to deprive of the *bark*, husk, or peel.—*n.* **Decortica'tion**. [L. *decortico*, *decorticatus*—*de*, from, and *cortex*, bark.]

**Decorum**, de-kō'rum, *n.* that which is *becoming* in outward appearance : propriety of conduct : decency. [L., neuter of *decorus*, becoming.]

**Decoy**, de-koy', *v.t.* to allure, entice : to entrap : to lure into a trap or snare.—*n.* anything intended to allure into a snare. [L. *de*, down, and O. Fr. *coy*, quiet; as if to quiet down. See Coy.]

**Decrease**, de-krēs′, *v.i.* to *grow* or become *less*.— *v.t.* to make less: to lessen gradually.—*n.* a growing less: loss.—*adv.* **Decreas′ingly**. [O. Fr. *decrois*, a decrease, from L. *decresco*—*de*, from, and *cresco*, to grow.]

**Decree**, de-krē′, *n.* an order by one in authority: an established law: a predetermined purpose.— *v.t.* to decide or determine by sentence in law: to appoint.—*v.i.* to make a decree :—*pr.p.* de-cree′ing; *pa.p.* decreed′. [Fr.—L. *decretum*—*decerno*, to decide.]

**Decrement**, dek′re-ment, *n.* the quantity lost by *decrease*. [L. *decrementum*—*decresco*.]

**Decrepit**, de-krep′it, *adj.* worn out by the infir-mities of old age : in the last stage of decay. [L. *decrepitus*, noiseless, very old—*de*, not, *crepitus*, a noise.]

**Decrepitate**, de-krep′i-tāt, *v.i.* to *crackle*, as salts, when heated.—*v.t.* to roast so as to cause a con-tinual crackling.—*n.* **Decrepita′tion**. [L. *de*, inten., *crepito*, to rattle much, freq. of *crepo*.]

**Decrepitude**, de-krep′i-tūd, *n.* state of *being de-crepit* or worn out with age.

**Decrescent**, de-kres′ent, *adj.*, *becoming* gradually *less*. [L.]

**Decretal**, de-krē′tal, *adj.* pertaining to a *decree*. —*n.* a decree, esp. of the pope : a book contain-ing decrees : a collection of the pope's decrees. [L. *decretalis*—*decretum*.]     [*decree*.

**Decretive** de-krē′tiv, *adj.* having the force of a **Decretory**, dek′re-tor-i, *adj.* established by a *decree*: determining: judicial.

**Decrial**, de-krī′al, *n.* a *crying down*: clamorous condemnation.

**Decry**, de-krī′, *v.t.* to *cry down*: to condemn : to blame :—*pa.p.* decried′. [Fr. *de*(*s*) = L. *dis*, and *crier*, to cry. See **Cry**.]

**Decumbence**, de-kum′bens, **Decumbency**, de-kum′ben-si, *n.* the act or posture of *lying down*.

**Decumbent**, de-kum′bent, *adj.*, *lying down* : re-clining on the ground.—*adv.* **Decum′bently**. [L. *decumbens*—*de*, down, and *cumbo*, for *cubo*, to lie.]

**Decuple**, dek′ū-pl, *adj.*, *tenfold*.—*n.* a number ten times repeated.—*v.t.* to make tenfold. [Fr. *décuple*—L. *decem*, ten, and *plico*, to fold.]

**Decurrent**, de-kur′ent, *adj.*, *running* or extend-ing *downward*.—*adv.* **Decur′rently**. [L. *de-currens*—*de*, down, *curro*, *cursum*, to run.]

**Decussate**, de-kus′āt, *v.t.* to cross in the form of an X : to cross, as lines, &c.—*adj.* crossed : arranged in pairs which cross each other.—*n.* **Decussa′tion**. [L. *decusso*, *decussatus*—*decus-sis*, a coin of *ten asses* (*decem asses*) marked with X, the symbol of ten. See **Ace**.]

**Dedicate**, ded′i-kāt, *v.t.* to set apart and conse-crate to some sacred purpose : to devote wholly or chiefly : to inscribe to any one. [L. *dedico*, *dedicatus*—*de*, down, *dico*, to declare.]

**Dedication**, ded-i-kā′shun, *n.* the act of *dedicat-ing*: an address to a patron, prefixed to a book.          [*dedication*.

**Dedicatory**, ded′i-kā-tor-i, *adj.* serving as a

**Deduce**, de-dūs′, *v.t.* to *draw from*: to infer a truth or opinion from what precedes or from premises. [L. *de*, from, *duco*, *ductum* to lead.]

**Deducible** de-dūs′i-bl, *adj.* that may be deduced or inferred.          [to subtract.

**Deduct**, de-dukt′, *v.t.* to *take from*: to separate :

**Deduction**, de-duk′shun, *n.* (1) the act of *deduc-ing*: that which is deduced : reasoning from a general to a particular proposition. [From

**Deduce**.] (2) the act of *deducting*: that which is deducted : abatement. [From **Deduct**.]

**Deductive**, de-dukt′iv, *adj.*, *that is*, or may be *deduced* from premises.—*adv.* **Deduct′ively**.

**Deed**, dēd, *n.* something *done* : an act: an ex-ploit : a legal transaction : the written evidence of it. [A.S. *dæd*—*don*, to do; Ger. *that*—*thun*, to do. See **Do**.]        [deeds.

**Deedless**, dēd′les, *adj.* not having performed

**Deem**, dēm, *v.t.* or *v.i.* to *judge*: to think : to believe. [A.S. *deman*, to form a judgment—*dom*, judgment. See **Doom**.]

**Deep**, dēp, *adj.* extending far down or far from the outside : difficult to understand : secret : wise and penetrating : cunning : very still : pro-found : intense : sunk low : low or grave.—*n.* that which is deep : the sea : anything profound or incomprehensible.—*adv.* to a great depth : profoundly.—*adv.* **Deep′ly**.—*n.* **Deep′ness**. [A.S. *deop*; Ger. *tief*; akin to **Dip**, **Dive**.]

**Deepen**, dēp′n, *v.t.* to *make deeper* in any sense : to increase.—*v.i.* to become deeper.

**Deer**, dēr, *n.* a quadruped of several species, as the stag, reindeer, &c. ; in M. E. any kind of animal. [A.S. *deor*; Ger. *thier*, Gr. *thēr*, L. *fera*, a wild beast.]

**Deer-stalker**, dēr′-stawk′ėr, *n.* one who practises deer-stalking.

**Deer-stalking**, dēr′-stawk′ing, *n.* the hunting of *deer* by *stalking*, or stealing upon them una-wares. [See **Stalk**, to walk.]

**Deface**, de-fās′, *v.t.* to *destroy* or mar the *face* or external appearance of, to disfigure : to obliter-ate. [O. Fr. *desfacer*—*des* = L. *dis*, away, and *face*, from L. *facies*.]

**Defacement**, de-fās′ment, *n.* act of *defacing*: injury to form or appearance : that which de-faces.

**Defalcate**, de-fal′kāt, *v.t.* to deduct a part of, used chiefly of money, &c. : to embezzle money held on trust. [Low L. *difalco*, *difalcatus*, to cut away—L. *dif-* = *dis-*, off, and *falx*, *falcis*, a sickle. See **Falchion**.]

**Defalcation**, def-al-kā′shun, *n.* a diminution : a deficit of funds instrusted to one's care.

**Defamation**, def-a-mā′shun, *n.* the act of *defam-ing*: calumny : slander.

**Defamatory**, de-fam′a-tor-i, *adj.* containing *de-famation*: injurious to reputation : calumnious.

**Defame**, de-fām′, *v.t.* to *take away* or destroy the good *fame* or reputation of : to speak evil of. [O. Fr. *defamer*—L. *diffamare*—*dis*, away, detraction, and *fama*, report. See **Fame**.]

**Default**, de-fawlt′, *n.* a *fault*, *failing*, or *failure*: defect : neglect to do what duty or law requires : offence.—*v.i.* to fail through neglect of duty : to fail to appear in court when called upon. [O. Fr. *defaute*, and *default*—*de* = L. *dis*, in-tensive, and *faute*. See **Fault**.]

**Defaulter**, de-fawlt′ėr, *n.* one who fails to account for money instrusted to his care.

**Defeasance**, de-fēz′ans, *n.* (*law*) a condition annexed to a deed, which, being performed, renders the deed void. [Norm. *defaisance*—Fr. *défaisant*, pr.p. of *défaire*, to undo.]

**Defeasible**, de-fēz′i-bl. *adj.* that may be *defeated* or annulled.—*n.* **Defeas′ibleness**.

**Defeat**, de-fēt′, *v.t.* to frustrate : to overcome : to ruin.—*n.* a frustration of plans : overthrow, as of an army in battle. [Fr. *défaite*—*défaire*, to undo—*dé* = L. *dis*, asunder, and Fr. *faire*, L. *facere*, to do.]

**Defecate**, def′e-kāt, *v.t.* to *clear from dregs* or impurities : to purify from extraneous matter.

[L. *defæco, defæcatus,* to cleanse—*de,* from, *fæx, fæcis,* dregs.]      [away impurities.

**Defecation,** def-e-kā'shun, *n.* the act of clearing

**Defect,** de-fekt', *n.* a *deficiency*: a want: imperfection: blemish: fault. [L. *deficio, defectus,* to fail or be wanting—*de,* neg., and *facio,* to do.]

**Defectible,** de-fekt'i-bl, *adj.* liable to imperfection.        [duty: revolt.

**Defection,** de-fek'shun, *n.* a *falling away from*

**Defective,** de-fekt'iv, *adj.* having *defect*: wanting in some necessary quality: insufficient.—*adv.* **Defect'ively.**—*n.* **Defect'iveness.**

**Defence,** de-fens', *n.* a *defending*: that which defends: protection: vindication: (*law*) a defendant's plea.—**Defenc'ed,** *pa.p.* (*B.*) fortified.

**Defenceless,** de-fens'les, *adj.* without defence.—*adv.* **Defence'lessly.**—*n.* **Defence'lessness.**

**Defend,** de-fend', *v.t.* (*lit.*) to *fend* or *ward off*: to keep off anything hurtful: to guard or protect: to maintain against attack: (*law*) to resist as a claim: to contest.—*n.* **Defend'er.** [L. *defendo, defensus,* to ward off—*de,* off, and obs. *fendo,* to strike.]       [defended.

**Defendable,** de-fend'a-bl, *adj.* that may be

**Defendant,** de-fend'ant, *n.* a *defender*: (*law*) a person accused or sued.

**Defensible,** de-fens'i-bl, *adj.* that may be *defended.*—*n.* **Defensibil'ity.**

**Defensive,** de-fens'iv, *adj.* serving to *defend*: in a state or posture of defence.—*n.* that which defends: posture of defence.—*adv.* **Defens'-ively.**

**Defer,** de-fėr', *v.t.* to *put off* to another time: to delay—*pr.p.* deferr'ing; *pa.p.* deferred'. [L. *differo—dis,* asunder, *fero,* to bear, carry.]

**Defer,** de-fėr', *v.i.* to yield to the wishes or opinions of another, or to authority.—*v.t.* to submit to or lay before—*pr.p.* deferr'ing; *pa.p.* deferred'. [L. *defero—de,* down, and *fero,* to bear.]

**Deference,** def'ėr-ens, *n.* a *deferring* or yielding in judgment or opinion: regard: submission.

**Deferential,** def-ėr-en'shal, *adj.* expressing *deference* or respect.—*adv.* **Deferen'tially.**

**Defiance,** de-fī'ans, *n.* the act of *defying*: a challenge to combat: contempt of opposition.

**Deficiency,** de-fish'en-si, *n.* defect.

**Deficient,** de-fish'ent, *adj.* wanting.

**Deficit,** def'i-sit, *n.,* *deficiency,* esp. of revenue, as compared with expenditure. [L., it is wanting, 3d per. sing. of *deficio.*]

**Defile,** de-fīl', *v.i.* to march off in *file* or line, or file by file.—*n.* a long narrow pass or way, in which troops can march only in *file,* or with a narrow front. [Fr. *défiler*—L. *dis,* and *filum,* a thread. See **File.**]

**Defile,** de-fīl', *v.t.* to make *foul*: to pollute or corrupt: to violate.—*n.* **Defil'er.** [L. *de,* and A.S. *fylan, gefylan,* to pollute.]      [ness.

**Defilement,** de-fīl'ment, *n.* act of *defiling*: foul-

**Definable,** de-fīn'a-bl, *adj.* that may be *defined.*

**Define,** de-fīn', *v.t.* to *fix* the *bounds* or limits of: to determine with precision: to describe accurately: to fix the meaning of. [Fr.—L. *definio, definitus,* to set bounds to—*de,* and *finis,* a limit.]

**Definite,** def'i-nit, *adj., defined*: having distinct limits: fixed: exact: clear.—*adv.* **Def'initely.** —*n.* **Def'initeness.**

**Definition,** def-i-nish'un, *n.* a *defining*: a description of a thing by its properties: an explanation of the exact meaning of a word, term, or phrase.

**Definitive,** de-fin'i-tiv, *adj., defining* or limiting:

positive: final.—*n.* (*gram.*) an adjective used to limit the extent of the signification of a noun. —*adv.* **Defin'itively.**

**Deflagrate,** def'la-grāt, *v.i.* or *v.t.* to *burn down*: to burn with suddenness and sparkling.—*n.*

**Deflagra'tion.** [L. *deflagro—de,* down, and *flagro,* to burn.]

**Deflagrator,** def'la-grā-tor, *n.* a galvanic instrument for producing *rapid combustion.*

**Deflect,** de-flekt', *v.i.* or *v.t.* to *turn aside*: to swerve or deviate from a right line or proper course. [L. *de,* from, and *flecto,* to bend, turn.]

**Deflection,** de-flek'shun, *n.* a *turning aside*: deviation.

**Deflorate,** de-flō'rāt, *adj., past the flowering state,* as an anther after it has shed its pollen.

**Defloration,** def-lo-rā'shun, *n.* the act of *deflouring.*

**Deflour,** de-flowr', *v.t.* to *deflower* or deprive of *flowers*: to deprive of original grace and beauty: to ravish.—*n.* **Deflour'er.** [Fr. *défleurir*—L. *defloro,* to strip flowers off—*de,* priv., and *flos, floris,* a flower.]

**Deflower.** Same as **Deflour.**

**Defluxion,** de-fluk'shun, *n.* a discharge of fluid matter in the body. [L. *defluxio—de,* down, and *fluo, fluxum,* to flow.]

**Defoliation,** de-fō-li-ā'shun, *n.* the *falling off* of *leaves*: the time of shedding leaves. [Low L. *defolio, defoliatum*—*de,* off, *folium,* a leaf.]

**Deforce,** de-fōrs', *v.t.* (*law*) to keep out of possession *by force.*—*n.* **Deforce'ment.** [Fr. *de* = L. *dis,* and **Force.**]

**Deform,** de-form', *v.t.* to *alter* or injure the *form of*: to disfigure. [L. *deformis,* ugly—*de,* from, and *forma,* form, beauty.]

**Deformation,** def-or-mā'shun, *n.* act of *deforming.*

**Deformity,** de-form'i-ti, *n.* state of being *deformed*: want of proper form: ugliness: disfigurement: anything that destroys beauty.

**Defraud,** de-frawd', *v.t.* to deprive of by *fraud*: to withhold wrongfully: to cheat or deceive. [L. *defraudo—de,* from, and *fraus, fraudis,* fraud.]

**Defray,** de-frā', *v.t.* to discharge the *expenses* of anything: to pay:—*pr.p.* defray'ing; *pa.p.* defrayed'.—*ns.* **Defray'ment, Defray'al.** [Fr. *défrayer—dé,* and *frais,* expense—Low L. *fractum,* breakage, damage, expense.]

**Deft,** deft, *adj.* handy, clever.—*adv.* **Deft'ly.**— *n.* **Deft'ness.** [A.S. *dæft,* convenient, fitting.]

**Defunct,** de-funkt', *adj.* having *finished* the course of life, dead.—*n.* a dead person. [L. *defungor, defunctus,* to finish—*de,* and *fungor,* to perform.]

**Defy,** de-fī', *v.t.* to challenge: to brave:—*pr.p.* defy'ing; *pa.p.* defied'.—*n.* **Defi'er.** [Fr. *défier* —Low L. *diffidare,* to renounce faith or allegiance—L. *dis,* asunder, and *fido,* to trust—*fides,* faith.]

**Degeneracy,** de-jen'ėr-a-si, **Degeneration,** de-jen-ėr-ā'shun, *n.* the act or process of becoming *degenerate*: the state of being degenerate.

**Degenerate,** de-jen'ėr-āt, *adj.* having departed *from* the high qualities of race or *kind*: become base.—*adv.* **Degen'erately.**—*n.* **Degen'erateness.** [L. *degeneratus,* from *degenero,* to depart from its kind—*de,* from, down, *genus, generis,* kind.]      [state: to be or to grow worse.

**Degenerate,** de-jen'ėr-āt, *v.i.* to fall from a nobler

**Degenerative,** de-jen'ėr-ā-tiv, *adj.,* tending or causing to *degenerate.*

**Deglutition,** deg-lōō-tish'un, *n.* the act or power of *swallowing.* [Fr.—L. *de,* down, and *glutio,* to swallow. See **Glut.**]

**Degradation**, deg-ra-dā'shun, *n.* disgrace.

**Degrade**, de-grād', *v.t.* to *lower in grade* or rank: to deprive of office or dignity: to lower in character or value: to disgrace. [Fr. *dégrader*—L. *de*, down, and *gradus*, a step. See **Grade**.]

**Degree**, de-grē', *n.* a *grade* or *step*: position: rank: extent: a mark of distinction conferred by universities: the 360th part of a circle: 60 geographical miles. [Fr. *degré*—L. *de*, and *gradus*, a step.] [capsules of a plant.

**Dehiscence**, de-his'ens, *n.* the *opening* of the

**Dehiscent**, de-his'ent, *adj.*, *gaping* or opening, as the capsules of plants. [L. *dehiscens*, pr.p. of *dehisco*—de, intensive, and *hisco*, to gape.]

**Deicide**, dē'i-sīd, *n.* the *killing of a god*: the putting to death of Jesus Christ. [From a supposed L. form *deicidium*—*deus*, and *cædo*, to cut, to kill.]

**Deification**, dē-i-fi-kā'shun, *n.* the act of *deifying*.

**Deiform**, dē'i-form, *adj.* having the *form* of a god.

**Deify**, dē'i-fī, *v.t.* to exalt to the rank of a god: to worship as a deity:—*pr.p.* dēify'ing; *pa.p.* dēified'. [Fr. *déifier*—L. *deificare*—*deus*, and *facere*, to make.]

**Deign**, dān, *v.i.* to condescend.—*v.t.* to give: to allow. [Fr. *daigner*—L. *dignor*, to think worthy—*dignus*, worthy.] [*déisme*.]

**Deism**, dē'izm, *n.* the creed of a *deist*. [Fr.

**Deist**, dē'ist, *n.* one who believes in the existence of *God* but not in revealed religion.—*adj.* Deist'-ical. [Fr. *déiste*—L. *deus*, god.]

**Deity**, dē'i-ti, *n.* the *divinity*: godhead: a god or goddess: the Supreme Being. [Fr.—Low L. *deitas*—L. *deus*, god; Sans. *deva*—*div*, to shine.]

**Deject**, de-jekt', *v.t.* to *cast down* the countenance or spirits of. [L. *dejicio*, *dejectus*—*de*, down, and *jacio*, to cast.]

**Dejected**, de-jekt'ed, *adj.*, *cast down*: dispirited.—*adv.* Deject'edly.—*n.* Deject'edness.

**Dejection**, de-jek'shun, *n.* lowness of spirits.

**Delation**, de-lā'shun, *n.* (*law*) act of charging with a crime. [L. *defero*, *delatum*, to bring a report against, to inform—*de*, intensive, and *fero*, to bear.]

**Delay**, de-lā', *v.t.* to *put off* to another time: to defer: to hinder or retard.—*v.i.* to pause, linger, or put off time.—*n.* a putting off or deferring: a lingering: hinderance:—*pr.p.* delay'ing; *pa.p.* delayed'. [Fr. *délai*—L. *dilatio*, a putting off—*differo*, *dilatum*—*dis*, apart, and *fero*, to carry. See **Defer**.] [See **Delete**.]

**Deleble**, del'e-bl, *adj.* that can be *blotted out*.

**Delectable**, de-lekt'a-bl, *adj.*, *delightful*: pleasing.—*n.* Delect'ableness.—*adv.* Delect'ably. [Fr.—L. *delectabilis*—*delecto*, to delight. See **Delight**.]

**Delectation**, de-lek-tā'shun, *n.* delight.

**Delegate**, del'e-gāt, *v.t.* to send as a *legate* or representative: to intrust or commit to.—*n.* one who is delegated: a deputy or representative.—*adj.* delegated, deputed. [L. *de*, away, and *lego*, *legatus*, to send as ambassador. See **Legate**.] [gated.

**Delegation**, del-e-gā'shun, *n.* the persons dele-

**Delete**, de-lēt', *v.t.* to *blot out*: to erase: to destroy.—*n.* Dele'tion. [L. *deleo*, *deletum*, to blot out.]

**Deleterious**, del-e-tē'ri-us, *adj.* tending to *destroy* life: hurtful or destructive: poisonous.—*n.* Delete'riousness. [Gr. *dēlētērios*, hurtful—*dēleomai*, to hurt.]

**Delf**, delf, *n.* a kind of earthenware made at *Delft*, in Holland.

**Deliberate**, de-lib'ér-āt, *v.t.* to *weigh well* in one's mind.—*v.i.* to consider the reasons for and against: to reflect upon: to discuss. [L. *delibero*, *deliberatum*—*de*, intensive, and *libro*, to weigh—*libra*, a balance.]

**Deliberate**, de-lib'ér-āt, *adj.* well considered: considering carefully: slow in determining.—*adv.* Delib'erately.—*n.* Delib'erateness.

**Deliberation**, de-lib-ér-ā'shun, *n.* the act of *deliberating*: mature reflection: calmness: coolness.

**Deliberative**, de-lib'er-a-tiv, *adj.* proceeding or acting by deliberation.—*adv.* Delib'eratively.

**Delicacy**, del'i-ka-si, *n.* state or quality of *being delicate*: anything delicate or dainty. [Fr. *délicatesse*—L. *delicatus*.]

**Delicate**, del'i-kāt, *adj.* pleasing to the senses, esp. the taste: dainty: nicely discriminating or perceptive: of a fine, slight texture or constitution: tender, frail: requiring nice handling: refined in manners, gentle, polite, considerate.—*n.pl.* Del'icates, (*B.*) delicacies.—*adv.* Del'i-cately, in a delicate manner: (*B.*) luxuriously.—*n.* Del'icateness, state of being delicate: (*B.*) delicacy, luxury. [L. *delicatus*—*deliciæ*, allurements, luxury—*delicio*—*de*, intensive, and *lacio*, to entice.]

**Delicious**, de-lish'us, *adj.* full of *delicacies*: highly pleasing to the senses: affording exquisite pleasure.—*n.* Deli'ciousness. [L. *deliciosus*—*deliciæ*.]

**Deliciously**, de-lish'us-li, *adv.* in a *delicious manner*: (*B.*) luxuriously.

**Delight**, de-līt', *v.t.* to please highly.—*v.i.* to have or take great pleasure: to be greatly pleased.—*n.* a high degree of pleasure: extreme satisfaction: that which gives great pleasure. [O. E. *delite*; from O. Fr. *deliter*—L. *delectare*, intensive of *delicio*. See **Delicate**.]

**Delightful**, de-līt'fool, **Delight'some**, -sum, *adj.*, *full of delight*.—*adv.* Delight'fully.—*n.* Delight'fulness.

**Delineate**, de-lin'e-āt, *v.t.* to mark out with *lines*: to represent by a sketch or picture: to portray: to describe accurately in words. [L. *delineo*, *delineatum*—*de*, down, and *linea*, a line. See **Line**.]

**Delineation**, de-lin-e-ā'shun, *n.* the act of *delineating*: a sketch, representation, or description.

**Delineator**, de-lin'e-ā-tor, *n.* one who *delineates*.

**Delinquency**, de-ling'kwen-si, *n.*, *failure* in or omission of duty: a fault: a crime.

**Delinquent**, de-ling'kwent, *adj.*, *leaving* one's duty: failing in duty.—*n.* one who fails in or *leaves* his duty: a transgressor: a criminal.—*adv.* Delin'quently. [L. *delinquens*, *-entis*, pr.p. of *delinquo*—*de*, intensive, and *linquo*, to leave.]

**Deliquesce**, del-i-kwes', *v.i.* to melt and *become liquid* by absorbing moisture, as certain salts, &c. [L. *deliquesco*, to melt away—*de*, intensive, and *liquesco*, to become fluid—*liqueo*, to be fluid.]

**Deliquescent**, del-i-kwes'ent, *adj.*, *becoming liquid* in the atmosphere.—*n.* Deliquesc'ence.

**Delirious**, de-lir'i-us, *adj.* wandering in mind: light-headed: insane.—*adv.* Delir'iously.—*n.* Delir'iousness. [L. *delirus*, one that goes out of the furrow in ploughing—*de*, from, and *lira*, a furrow.]

**Delirium**, de-lir'i-um, *n.* state of *being delirious*: strong excitement: wild enthusiasm.—**Delirium Tremens**, a name generally applied to delirium produced by excessive drinking, and marked by

fāte, fär; mē, hér; mīne; mōte; mūte; mōōn; *then.*

convulsive or *trembling* symptoms. [L. *delirium* (see **Delirious**), and *tremens*, pr.p. of *tremo*, to tremble.]          [*cealed:* retirement.

**Delitescence,** del-i-tes'ens, *n.* state of *being concealed.*

**Delitescent,** del-i-tes'ent, *adj., lying hid* or concealed (*e.g.* the germs of an infectious disease). [L. *delitescens,* pr.p. of *delitesco—de,* from, and *latesco—lateo,* to lie hid.]

**Deliver,** de-liv'er, *v.t.* to *liberate* or *set free* from restraint or danger: to rescue from evil or fear: to give up, or part with: to communicate: to pronounce: to give forth, as a blow, &c.: to relieve a woman in childbirth.—*n.* **Deliv'erer.** [Fr. *délivrer*—L. *de,* from, and *liberare,* to set free—*liber,* free.]

**Deliverance,** de-liv'er-ans, *n.* act of *delivering* or freeing: state of being delivered: freedom.

**Delivery,** de-liv'er-i, *n.* the act of *delivering:* a giving up: the act or manner of speaking in public: the act of giving birth.

**Dell.**   See **Dale.**

**Delta,** del'ta, *n.* the fourth letter of the Greek alphabet, the capital form of which is Δ; a tract of land of like shape formed at the mouth of a river. [Gr., from Heb. *daleth,* a door (of a tent).]

**Deltoid,** del'toid, *adj.* of the form of the Greek Δ; triangular. [Gr. *deltoeidēs—delta,* and *eidos,* form.]

**Delude,** de-lūd', *v.t.* to *play* or impose *upon:* to deceive: to cheat. [L. *deludo,* to play, make sport of—*de,* down, *ludo, lusus,* to play.]

**Deluge,** del'ūj, *n.* a great overflow of water: a flood, esp. that in the days of Noah.—*v.t.* to inundate: to overwhelm as with water. [Fr.—L. *diluvium—diluo—dis,* away, *luo = lavo,* to wash.]

**Delusion,** de-lū'zhun, *n.* the act of *deluding:* the state of being deluded: a false belief: error.

**Delusive,** de-lū'siv, **Delusory,** de-lū'sor-i, *adj.,* apt or tending to *delude:* deceptive.—*adv.* **Delu'sively.**—*n.* **Delu'siveness.**

**Delve,** delv, *v.t.* to *dig* with a spade.—*n.* **Delv'er.** [A.S. *delfan,* to dig; conn. with **Dale, Dell.**]

**Demagnetise,** de-mag'net-īz, *v.t.* to deprive of *magnetic power.* [L. *de,* priv., and **Magnetise.**]

**Demagogue,** dem'a-gog, *n.* a *leader of the people:* a popular and factious orator. [Gr. *dēmagōgos—dēmos,* the people, *agōgos,* leading—*agō,* to lead.]                              [**Domain.**

**Domain,** de-mān', **Demesne,** de-mēn', *n.* forms of

**Demand,** de-mand', *v.t.* to claim: to ask earnestly or authoritatively: to call for: to question.—*n.* the asking for what is due: an asking for with authority: a claim: earnest inquiry. [Fr.—L. *demando,* to give in charge—Low L. *demando,* to demand—*de,* from, and *mando,* to put into one's charge.]          [demanded.

**Demandable,** de-mand'a-bl, *adj.* that may be

**Demandant,** de-mand'ant, *n.* one who demands: a plaintiff.

**Demarcation, Demarkation,** de-mark-ā'shun, *n.* the act of *marking off* or setting bounds to: division: a fixed limit. [Fr. *démarquer,* to mark off—*dé,* off, and *marquer,* to mark. See **Mark.**]

**Demean,** de-mēn', *v.t.* (with *self*) to conduct: to behave. [Fr. *démener*—*de,* intensive, and *mener,* to lead—Low L. *minare,* to drive cattle, L. *minor,* to threaten.]

**Demean,** de-mēn', *v.t.* to *make mean:* to lower. [L. *de,* and **Mean.**]

**Demeanour,** de-mēn'ur, *n.* behaviour: bearing.

**Demented,** de-ment'ed, *adj., out of one's mind:*

deprived of reason. [L. *demens, dementis,* out of one's mind—*de,* from, and *mens,* the mind.]

**Demerit,** de-mer'it, *n.* ill-desert: fault: crime. [L. *de,* want of, and **Merit.**]

**Demesne.**   See **Domain.**

**Demigod,** dem'i-god, *n., half a god:* one whose nature is partly divine. [Fr. *demi,* half, and **God.**]

**Demise,** de-mīz, *n., laying down*—hence, a transferring: the death of a sovereign or a distinguished person: a transfer of the crown or of an estate to a successor.—*v.t.* to send down to a successor: to bequeath by will. [O. Fr. *démise,* pa.p. of *démettre,* to lay down—L. *dimittere,* to send away—L. *dis,* aside and *mittere, missus,* to send.]

**Demi-semiquaver,** dem'i-sem'i-kwā-vėr, *n.* (*music*) a note equal in time to the *half* of a *semiquaver.* [Fr. *demi,* half, and **Semiquaver.**]

**Demission,** de-mish'un, *n.* a *lowering* or *letting down:* degradation: humiliation. [L. *demissio.*]

**Democracy,** de-mok'ra-si, *n.* a form of *government* in which the supreme power is vested *in the people* collectively. [Gr. *dēmokratia—dēmos,* the people, and *krateō,* to rule—*kratos,* strength; akin to E. **Hard.**]

**Democrat,** dem'o-krat, *n.* one who adheres to or promotes *democracy.*

**Democratic,** dem-o-krat'ik, **Democratical,** dem-o-krat'i-kal, *adj.* relating to *democracy.*—*adv.* **Democrat'ically.**

**Demolish,** de-mol'ish, *v.t.* to reduce to a shapeless *heap:* to destroy, ruin. [Fr. *démolir*—L. *demolior,* to throw or pull down—*de,* down, and *molior,* to move, to hurl—*moles,* a heap.]

**Demolition,** dem-o-lish'un, *n.* the act of pulling down: ruin: destruction.

**Demon,** dē'mon, *n.* (*myth.*) a *spirit* holding a place between man and the gods: an evil spirit, a devil. [L. *dæmon*—Gr. *daimōn,* a spirit, genius.]

**Demoniac,** de-mō'ni-ak, **Demoniacal,** de-mō-nī'-ak-al, *adj.* pertaining to or like *demons* or evil spirits: influenced by demons.—*adv.* **Demoni'acally.**

**Demoniac,** de-mō'ni-ak, *n.* a human being possessed by a *demon* or evil spirit.

**Demonolatry,** dē-mon-ol'a-tri, *n.* the *worship of demons.* [Gr. *daimōn,* and *latreia,* worship.]

**Demonologist,** dē-mon-ol'o-jist, *n.* a *writer on demonology.*

**Demonology,** dē-mon-ol'o-ji, *n.* a *discourse on demons* and their agency.—*adjs.* **Demonolog'ic, Demonolog'ical.** [Gr. *daimōn, logos,* a discourse.]

**Demonstrable,** de-mon'stra-bl, *adj.* that may be *demonstrated.*—*n.* **Demon'strableness.**—*adv.* **Demon'strably.**

**Demonstrate,** de-mon'strāt, *v.t.* to *shew* or point out *clearly:* to prove with certainty. [L. *demonstro—de,* intensive, and *monstro,* to shew. See **Monster.**]

**Demonstration,** dem-on-strā'shun, *n.* a pointing out: proof beyond doubt: expression of the feelings by outward signs: show: a feigned movement of troops in war.

**Demonstrative,** de-mon'stra-tiv, *adj.* making evident: proving with certainty: given to the manifestation of one's feelings.—*adv.* **Demon'stratively.**—*n.* **Demon'strativeness.**

**Demonstrator,** dem'on-strā-tor, *n.* one who proves beyond doubt: one who teaches: (*anat.*) one who teaches anatomy from the dissected parts.

**Demoralisation,** de-mor-al-i-zā′shun, *n.* act of *demoralising:* corruption or subversion of morals.

**Demoralise,** de-mor′al-īz, *v.t.* to *bring down* or corrupt *in morals:* to lower the *morale*—that is, to deprive of spirit and confidence. [Fr. *démoraliser*—L. *de*, down, and Fr. *morale*, morals. See **Moral**.]

**Demotic,** de-mot′ik, *adj.* pertaining to *the people:* popular. [Gr. *dēmos*, the people.]

**Demulcent,** de-mul′sent, *adj. soothing.* [L. *demulcens*—*de*, and *mulceo*, to stroke, to soothe.]

**Demur,** de-mur′, *v.i.* to hesitate from uncertainty or before difficulty: to object :—*pr.p.* demurr′ing; *pa.p.* demurred′.—*n.* a stop: pause, hesitation. [Fr. *demeurer*—L. *demoror*, to loiter, linger—*de*, intensive, and *moror*, to delay—*mora*, delay.]

**Demure,** de-mūr′, *adj.* sober: staid: modest: affectedly modest: making a show of gravity.—*adv.* **Demure′ly.**—*n.* **Demure′ness.** [O. Fr. *de* (*bons*) *murs*, of good manners, Fr. *mœurs*—L. *mores*, manners.]

**Demurrage,** de-mur′āj, *n.* an allowance made to the owner of a trading vessel for undue *delay* or *detention* in port.

**Demurrer,** de-mur′er, *n.* one who demurs: (*law*) an exception by one party in a suit to the sufficiency in point of law of the case of the opposite party.

**Demy,** de-mī′, *n.* a size of paper 22½ by 17½ inches. [Fr. *demi*—L. *dimidium*, half—*dis*, through, and *medius*, the middle.]

**Demy,** de-mī′, *n.* a scholar of Magdalen College, Oxford. [Ety. same as above.]

**Den,** den, *n.* the hollow lair of a wild beast: a cave: provin., a narrow valley. [A.S. *denn*, a cave, and *denu*, a valley.]

**Denary,** den′ar-i, *adj.* containing *ten.*—*n.* the number ten. [L. *denarius*—*deni*, ten at a time —*decem*, ten.]

**Denationalise,** de-nash′un-al-īz, *v.t.* to deprive of *national* rights. [L. *de*, priv. and **Nationalise.**]

**Denaturalise,** de-nat′ū-ral-īz, *v.t.* to make *unnatural:* to deprive of acquired citizenship in a foreign country. [L. *de*, priv., and **Naturalise.**]

**Dendroid,** den′droid, *adj.* having the *form* of a *tree.* [Gr. *dendron*, a tree, and *eidos*, form.]

**Dendrology,** den-drol′o-ji, *n.* a *treatise on trees:* the natural history of trees. [Gr. *dendron*, and *logos*, a discourse.]

**Deniable,** de-nī′a-bl, *adj.* that may be *denied.*

**Denial,** de-nī′al, *n.* act of *denying* or *saying no:* contradiction: refusal: rejection.

**Denizen,** den′i-zn, *n.* an inhabitant: one admitted to the rights of a citizen.—*v.t.* to make a denizen of, or admit to residence: to enfranchise: to provide with occupants.—*n.* **Den′izenship.** [O. Fr. *deinzein*—*deinz*, *dens*, Fr. *dans*, within—L. *de intus*, from within.]

**Denominate,** de-nom′in-āt, *v.t.* to give a *name* to: to call: to designate. [L. *de*, and *nomino*, *nominatum*, to name—*nomen*, a name.]

**Denomination,** de-nom-in-ā′shun, *n.* the act of *naming:* a name or title : a collection of individuals called by the same name : a sect.

**Denominational,** de-nom-in-ā′shun-al, *adj.* belonging to a *denomination* or sect.

**Denominationalism,** de-nom-in-ā′shun-al-izm, *n.* a *denominational* or class *spirit* or policy: devotion to the interests of a sect.

**Denominative,** de-nom′in-āt-iv, *adj.* giving or having a title.—*adv.* **Denom′inatively.**

**Denominator,** de-nom′in-āt-or, *n.* he who or that which gives a *name:* (*arith.*) the lower number in a vulgar fraction, which *names* the parts into which the integer is divided.

**Denote,** de-nōt′, *v.t.* to *note* or *mark off:* to indicate by a sign: to signify or mean: (*log.*) to indicate the objects comprehended in a class. —*n.* **Denota′tion.** [L. *denoto*—*de*, intensive, and *noto*, to mark—*nota*, a mark or sign. See **Note**.]

**Denouement,** de-nōō′mong, *n.* the *unravelling* of a plot or story: the issue, event, or outcome. [Fr. *dénouer*, to untie—*de*, priv., and *nouer*, to tie—L. *nodus*, a knot.]

**Denounce,** de-nowns′, *v.t.* to inform against or accuse publicly. [Fr. *dénoncer*—L. *denuncio*—*de*, intensive, and *nuncio*, to announce.]

**Denouncement,** de-nowns′ment. Same as **Denunciation.**

**Dense,** dens, *adj., thick:* close: compact.—*adv.* **Dense′ly.**—*n.* **Dense′ness.** [L. *densus*, thick.]

**Density,** dens′i-ti, *n.* the quality of being *dense:* the proportion of mass to bulk or volume.

**Dent,** dent, *n.* a small hollow made by the pressure or blow of a harder body on a softer.—*v.t.* to make a mark by means of a blow. [A variety of **Dint.**]

**Dental,** den′tal, *adj.* belonging to the *teeth:* produced by the aid of the teeth.—*n.* an articulation or letter pronounced chiefly with the teeth. [L. *dens, dentis*, a tooth. See **Tooth**.]

**Dentate,** den′tāt, **Dentated,** den′tāt-ed, *adj. toothed:* notched : set as with teeth.

**Denticle,** den′ti-kl, *n.* a *small tooth.*—*adj.* **Denticulate,** den-tik′ū-lāt.—*n.* **Denticula′tion.** [L. *denticulus,* dim. of *dens*, a tooth.]

**Dentifrice,** den′ti-fris, *n.* a substance used in *rubbing* or cleaning the *teeth.* [L. *dentifricium,* from *dens*, and *frico*, to rub.]

**Dentist,** den′tist, *n.* one who *cures* diseases of the *teeth*, or inserts artificial teeth.

**Dentistry,** den′tist-ri, *n.* the business of a *dentist.*

**Dentition,** den-tish′un, *n.* the *cutting* or growing of *teeth:* the conformation or arrangement of the teeth. [L., from *dentio*, to cut teeth—*dens.*]

**Denudation,** den-ū-dā′shun, *n.* a making *nude* or *bare:* (*geol.*) the wearing away of rocks by water and atmospheric action, whereby the underlying rocks are laid *bare.*

**Denude,** de-nūd′, *v.t.* to make *nude* or *naked:* to lay bare. [L. *denudo*—*de*, intensive, and *nudo*, to make naked—*nudus*, naked. See **Nude, Naked.**]

**Denunciate,** de-nun′shi-āt. Same as **Denounce.**

**Denunciation,** de-nun-shi-ā′shun or -si-ā′-, *n.* the act of *denouncing:* a threat. [*nounces.*]

**Denunciator,** de-nun′shi-ā-tor, *n.* one who *denounces.*

**Denunciatory,** de-nun′shi-a-tor-i, *adj.* containing a *denunciation:* threatening.

**Deny,** de-nī′, *v.t.* to gainsay or declare not to be true: to reject: to disown :—*pr.p.* deny′ing; *pa.p.* denied′. [Fr. *denier*—L. *de-nego*—*de*, intensive, and *nego*, to say no. See **Negation.**]

**Deodorise,** de-ō′dor-īz, *v.t.* to take the *odour* or smell *from.* [L. *de*, from, and root of **Odour.**]

**Deoxidate,** de-oks′i-dāt, **Deoxidise,** de-oks′i-dīz, *v.t.* to take *oxygen from,* or reduce from the state of an *oxide.*—*n.* **Deoxida′tion.** [L. *de*, from, and **Oxidate, Oxidise.**]

**Depart,** de-pärt′, *v.i.* to *part from:* to go away: to quit or leave: to die. [Fr. *départir*—L. *de*, from, and *partior*, to part, to divide. See **Part.**]

**Department,** de-pärt′ment, *n.* that which is *parted* or separated : a part or portion : a separate part of business or duty: a section of the administration: a division of a country, esp. of France.—*adj.* **Department'al.**

**Departure**, de-pärt'ūr, *n.* act of *departing*: a going away from a place: deviation: death.

**Depend**, de-pend', *v.i.* to *hang down* or *from*: to be sustained by or connected with anything: to rest. [Fr. *dépendre*—L. *dependeo*—*de*, from, and *pendeo*, to hang.]

**Dependence**, de-pend'ens, **Dependency,** de-pend'en-si, *n.* state of being *dependent*: connection: reliance: trust: that on which one depends: colony.

**Dependent,** de-pend'ent, *n.* one who *depends on*, relies on, or is sustained by another. [Fr.]

**Dependent,** de-pend'ent, *adj.*, *depending*: relying or resting on: subject to: subordinate.—*adv.* **Depend'ently.** [L.]

**Depict,** de-pikt', *v.t.* to *picture* or *paint* carefully: to make a likeness of: to describe minutely. [L. *depingo, depictus*—*de,* intensive, and *pingo,* to paint.]

**Depilatory,** de-pil'a-tor-i, *adj., taking hair off.*—*n.* an application for taking off hair. [Fr.—L. *depilo*—*de,* off, and *pilus,* hair. See **Pile.**]

**Depletion,** de-plē'shun, *n.* the lessening of the quantity of blood in the vessels. [L. *depleo, depletus*—*de,* negative, and *pleo,* to fill. See **Fill, Full.**]

**Deplorable,** de-plōr'a-bl, *adj.* lamentable: sad.—*n.* **Deplor'ableness.**—*adv.* **Deplor'ably.**

**Deplore,** de-plōr', *v.t.* to feel or express deep grief for: to lament.—*adv.* **Deplor'ingly.** [Fr.—L. *deploro*—*de,* intensive, and *ploro,* to weep.]

**Deploy,** de-ploy', *v.t.* to *unfold:* to open out or extend.—*v.i.* to open: to extend from column into line, as a body of troops. [Fr. *déployer*—*des* (= L. *dis*), apart, and *ployer* (= L. *plico*), to fold. Doublet of **Display.** See **Ply.**]

**Deplume,** de-plōōm', *v.t.* to take the *plumes* or *feathers from.*—*n.* **Depluma'tion.** [L. *de,* from, and *pluma,* a feather.]

**Depolarise,** de-pō'lar-īz, *v.t.* to deprive of *polarity.*—*n.* **Depolarisa'tion.** [L. *de,* from, and **Polarise.**]

**Depone,** de-pōn', *v.t.* to testify upon oath. [L. *depono,* to lay down—*de,* down, and *pono,* to place.]

**Deponent,** de-pō'nent, *adj.* (*gram.*) applied to verbs with a passive form that *lay down* or lose the passive signification.—*n.* one who gives evidence in a court of justice. [L., *pr.p.* of *depono.*]

**Depopulate,** de-pop'ū-lāt, *v.t.* to deprive of population, to dispeople.—*v.i.* to become dispeopled.—*n.* **Depop'ulator.** [L. *depopulor, depopulatus*—*de,* inten., and *populor,* to spread over a country. said of a hostile *people* (L. *populus*), hence to ravage, to destroy.]

**Depopulation,** de-pop-ū-lā'shun, *n.* act of *depopulating:* havoc: destruction.

**Deport,** de-pōrt', *v.t.* to *carry off:* to transport: to exile: to behave. [L. *deporto*—*de,* away, and *porto, portatus,* to carry.]

**Deportation,** de-pōrt-ā'shun, *n.* act of *deporting:* state of being deported or exiled: banishment.

**Deportment,** de-pōrt'ment, *n.* carriage: behaviour.

**Deposable,** de-pōz'a-bl, *adj.* that may be *deposed.*

**Deposal,** de-pōz'al, *n.* act of *deposing.*

**Depose,** de-pōz', *v.t.* to *put down* from a throne or high station: to degrade [Fr. *déposer*—*de,* and *poser,* to place—L. *pausare,* to pause; Low L., to place. See **Pause, Pose.**]

**Deposit,** de-poz'it, *v.t.* to *put* or *set down:* to place:

to lay up or past: to intrust.—*n.* that which is deposited or put down: (*geol.*) rocks produced by denudation or *laying down* of other formations: something intrusted to another's care, esp. money put in a bank: a pledge.—*n.* **Depos'itor.** [L. *depositus,* placed—*depono,* from *de,* and *pono,* to put or set down.]

**Depositary,** de-poz'i-tar-i, *n.* a *person* with whom anything is *deposited,* or left for safe keeping: a guardian.

**Deposition,** dep-o-zish'un, *n.* act of *deposing:* act of *deponing:* evidence given in a court of justice: removal: act of *depositing:* what is deposited, sediment. [thing is *deposited.*

**Depository.** de-poz'i-tor-i, *n.* a *place* where anything is *deposited.*

**Depot,** de-pō' or dē'pō, *n.* a place of *deposit:* a storehouse; a military station where stores are kept and recruits trained: the headquarters of a regiment. [Fr. *dépôt*—L. *depositum*—*depono.* The *n.* **Deposit** is a doublet.]

**Depravation,** dep-ra-vā'shun, *n.* act of *depraving:* state of being depraved: depravity.

**Deprave,** de-prāv', *v.t.* to make *bad* or worse: to corrupt. [Fr.—L. *depravo*—*de,* intensive, and *pravus,* crooked, bad.]

**Depraved,** de-prāvd', *adj.* corrupt: abandoned.—*adv.* **Deprav'edly.**—*n.* **Deprav'edness.**

**Depravity,** de-prav'i-ti, *n.* a vitiated or corrupt state of moral character: extreme wickedness: corruption.

**Deprecate,** dep're-kāt, *v.t.* to try to ward *off* by *prayer:* to desire earnestly the removal of: to regret deeply.—*adv.* **Dep'recatingly.** [L. *deprecor, deprecatus*—*de,* away, and *precor,* to pray. See **Pray.**] [evil: entreaty.

**Deprecation,** dep-re-kā'shun, *n.* a *praying* against

**Deprecative,** dep're-kā-tiv, **Deprecatory,** dep're-kā-tor-i, *adj.* tending to avert evil by *prayer;* having the form of prayer.

**Depreciate,** de-prē'shi-āt, *v.t.* to lower the *worth* of: to undervalue: to disparage.—*v.i.* to fall in value. [L. *depretio, depretiatus*—*de,* down, and *pretium,* price. See **Price.**]

**Depreciation,** de-prē-shi-ā'shun, *n.* the falling of *value:* disparagement.

**Depreciative,** de-prē'shi-ā-tiv, **Depreciatory,** de-prē'shi-ā-tor-i, *adj.* tending to *depreciate* or lower.

**Depredate,** dep're-dāt, *v.t.* to *plunder* or *prey upon:* to rob: to lay waste: to devour. [L. *deprædor, deprædatus*—*de,* intensive, and *prædor*—*præda,* plunder. See **Prey.**]

**Depredation,** dep-re-dā'shun, *n.* act of *depredating* or plundering: state of being depredated.

**Depredator,** dep're-dā-tor, *n.* a *plunderer,* a robber.—*adj.* **Dep'redatory.**

**Depress,** de-pres', *v.t.* to *press down:* to let down: to lower: to humble: to dispirit or cast a gloom over.—*adv.* **Depress'ingly.** [L. *de-primo, depressus*—*de,* down, and *premo,* to press.]

**Depression,** de-presh'un, *n.*. a falling in or sinking: a hollow: abasement: dejection.

**Depressive,** de-pres'iv, *adj.* able or tending to *depress.*—*n.* **Depress'or.**

**Deprivation,** de-pri-vā'shun, *n.* act of *depriving:* state of being deprived: loss: bereavement.

**Deprive,** de-prīv', *v.t.* to *take away from* one his *own:* to take from: to dispossess: to bereave. [L. *de,* from, and *privo,* to deprive—*privus,* one's own.]

**Depth,** depth, *n., deepness:* the measure of deepness down or inwards: a deep place: the sea: the middle. as *depth of winter:* abstruseness: extent of sagacity and penetration.—*adj.* **Depth'-less,** having no depth. [See **Deep.**]

**Deputation,** dep-ū-tā'shun, *n.* act of *deputing:* the person or persons deputed or appointed to transact business for another.

**Depute,** de-pūt', *v.t.* to appoint or send, as a substitute or agent: to send with a special commission. [Fr.—L. *deputo,* to cut off, Late L. to select.]

**Deputy,** dep'ū-ti, *n.* one *deputed* or appointed to act for another: a delegate or representative.

**Derange,** de-rānj', *v.t.* to put *out of place* or order: to disorder. [Fr. *déranger—dé* (L. *dis*), asunder, and *ranger,* to rank. See **Range, Rank.**]

**Derangement,** de-rānj'ment, *n.* disorder: insanity.

**Derelict,** der'e-likt, *adj.,* entirely relinquished or forsaken: abandoned.—*n.* anything forsaken or abandoned. [L. *derelinquo, derelictus—de,* intensive, and *linquo,* to leave. See **Leave.**]

**Dereliction,** der-e-lik'shun, *n.* act of *forsaking:* an entire forsaking: state of being abandoned.

**Deride,** de-rīd', *v.t.* to *laugh at:* to mock.—*n.* **Derid'er.**—*adv.* **Derid'ingly.** [L. *derideo—de,* intensive, and *rideo,* to laugh.]

**Derision,** de-rizh'un, *n.* act of *deriding:* mockery: a laughing-stock. [*sively.*

**Derisive,** de-rī'siv, *adj.* mocking.—*adv.* **Deri'-**

**Derivable,** de-rīv'a-bl, *adj.* capable of being *derived.*—*adv.* **Deriv'ably.**

**Derivation,** der-i-vā'shun, *n.* act of *deriving:* a drawing off or from: the tracing of a word to its original root: that which is derived.

**Derivative,** de-riv'a-tiv, *adj., derived,* or taken from something else: not radical or original.—*n.* that which is derived: a word taken or formed from another word.—*adv.* **Deriv'atively.**

**Derive,** de-rīv', *v.t.* to draw from, as water *from a river:* to take or receive from a source or origin: to infer: (*etym.*) to trace a word to its root. [L. *derivo—de,* down from, and *rivus,* a river.] [the skin—*derō,* to flay.]

**Derm,** dèrm, *n.* the *skin.* [Gr. *derma, dermatos,*

**Dermal,** dèrm'al, *adj.* pertaining to the *skin:* consisting of skin.

**Dermatology,** dèr-ma-tol'o-ji, *n.* the branch of physiology which treats of the *skin.* [Gr. *derma,* and *logos,* a discourse.]

**Derogate,** der'o-gāt, *v.i.* to lessen by taking away: to detract. [L. *derogo,* to repeal part of a law—*de,* down from, and *rogo,* to propose a law. See **Abrogate.**]

**Derogation,** der-o-gā'shun, *n.* a taking from: detraction: depreciation.

**Derogatory,** de-rog'a-tor-i, *adj.* detracting: injurious.—*adv.* **Derog'atorily.**—*n.* **Derog'atoriness.**

**Dervis, Dervish,** dèr'vis, dèr'vish, *n.* among Mohammedans, a class of monks who profess extreme *poverty,* and lead an austere life. [Pers. *derwêsh,* poor.]

**Descant,** des'kant, *n.* (*lit.*) a *part song:* a discourse or disquisition in several parts, or under several 'heads': a discourse. [O. Fr. *descant—* L. *dis,* apart, and *cantus,* a song—*canto,* to sing.] [comment.

**Descant,** des-kant', *v.i.* to discourse at length: to

**Descend,** de-send', *v.i.* to *climb down:* to pass from a higher to a lower place or condition: to fall upon or invade: to be derived.—*v.t.* to go down upon. [Fr. *descendre—*L. *descendo—de,* down, and *scando,* to climb.]

**Descendant,** de-send'ant, *n.* one who *descends,* as offspring from an ancestor. [Fr.]

**Descendent,** de-send'ent, *adj., descending* or *going down:* proceeding from an ancestor. [L.]

**Descendible,** de-send'i-bl, *adj.* that may *descend* or be descended.

**Descension,** de-sen'shun, *n.* act of *descending:* a falling or sinking.—*adj.* **Descen'sional.**

**Descent,** de-sent', *n.* act of *descending:* motion or progress downward: slope: a falling upon or invasion: derivation from an ancestor.

**Describable,** de-skrīb'a-bl, *adj.* capable of being *described.*

**Describe,** de-skrīb', *v.t.* to trace out or delineate: to give an account of. [L. *describo—de,* down, and *scribo, scriptus,* to write.]

**Description,** de-skrip'shun, *n.* act of *describing:* an account of anything in words: definition: sort, class, or kind.

**Descriptive,** de-skrip'tiv, *adj.* containing description.—*adv.* **Descrip'tively.**—*n.* **Descrip'tiveness.**

**Descry,** de-skrī', *v.t.* to discover by the eye: to espy:—*pr.p.* descry'ing; *pa.p.* descried'. [O. Fr. *descrire* for *descrivre*—L. *describo.* It is a doublet of **Describe.**]

**Desecrate,** des'e-krāt, *v.t.* to divert *from a sacred purpose:* to profane. [L. *desecro—de,* away from, and *sacro,* to make sacred—*sacer,* sacred.]

**Desecration,** des-e-krā'shun, *n.* act of *desecrating:* profanation.

**Desert,** de-zėrt', *n.* the reward or punishment *deserved:* claim to reward: merit.

**Desert,** de-zėrt', *v.t.* to leave: to forsake.—*v.i.* to run away: to quit a service, as the army, without permission. [L. *desero, desertus—de,* negative, and *sero,* to bind.]

**Desert,** dez'ėrt, *adj., deserted:* forsaken: desolate: uncultivated.—*n.* a desolate or barren place: a wilderness: a solitude.

**Deserter,** de-zėrt'ėr, *n.* one who *deserts* or quits a service without permission.

**Desertion,** de-zėr'shun, *n.* act of *deserting:* state of being deserted.

**Deserve,** de-zėrv', *v.t.* to earn *by service:* to merit.—*v.i.* to be worthy of reward. [L. *deservio—de,* intensive, and *servio,* to serve.]

**Deservedly,** de-zėrv'ed-li, *adv.* according to *desert:* justly. [—*adv.* **Deserv'ingly.**

**Deserving,** de-zėrv'ing, *adj., worthy.*—*n.* desert.

**Deshabille,** des-a-bil', *n.* an *undress:* a careless toilet. [Fr. *déshabillé,* undressed—*des,* L. *dis* = *un,* not, and *habiller,* to dress.]

**Desiccant,** de-sik'ant, **Desiccative,** de-sik'at-iv, *adj., drying:* having the power of drying.—*n.* an application that tends to dry up sores.

**Desiccate,** de-sik'āt, *v.t.* to *dry up.*—*v.i.* to grow dry. [L. *desicco,* to dry up—*de,* and *siccus,* dry.]

**Desiccation,** des-ik-ā'shun, *n.* the act of *desiccating:* state of being desiccated.

**Desiderate,** de-sid'ėr-āt, *v.t.* to long for or earnestly *desire* a thing: to want or miss. [L. *desidero, desideratum*—from root of **Consider.** A doublet of **Desire.**]

**Desideratum,** de-sid-ėr-ā'tum, *n.* something desired or much wanted:—*pl.* **Desiderata,** de-sid-ėr-ā'ta. [L., pa.p. of *desidero.*]

**Design,** de-sīn' or de-zīn', *v.t.* to *mark out:* to draw: to form a plan of: to contrive: to intend.—*n.* a drawing or sketch: a plan in outline: a plan or scheme formed in the mind: plot: intention.—*adj.* **Design'able.** [Fr.—L. *designo—de,* and *signum,* a mark.]

**Designate,** des'ig-nāt, *v.t.* to *mark out* so as to make known: to shew: to name.—*n.* **Des'ignator.**

**Designation**, des-ig-nā′shun, *n.* a showing or pointing out : name : title.

**Designedly**, de-sīn′ed-li, *adv.* by *design* : intentionally. [or patterns : a plotter.

**Designer**, de-sīn′ėr, *n.* one who furnishes designs

**Designing**, de-sīn′ing, *adj.* artful : scheming : deceitful.—*n.* the art of making designs or patterns.

**Desirable**, de-zīr′a-bl, *adj.* worthy of *desire* : pleasing : agreeable.—*adv.* **Desir′ably.**—*n.* **Desir′ableness.**

**Desire**, de-zīr′, *v.t.* to *long for* the possession of : to wish for : to request, ask : (*B.*) to regret.—*n.* an earnest longing for : eagerness to obtain : a prayer or request : the object desired : lust. [Fr. *désirer*—L. *desiderare*. See **Desiderate**.]

**Desirous**, de-zīr′us, *adj.* full of *desire* : anxious to obtain : eager.

**Desist**, de-sist′, *v.i.* to stop : to forbear. [L. *desisto*—*de*, away, and *sisto*, to cause to stand.]

**Desk**, desk, *n.* a sloping *table* for the use of writers or readers : a pulpit. {A.S. *disc*, a table, plate —L. *discus*. It is a variant of **Dish** and **Disc**.]

**Desolate**, des′o-lāt, *v.t.* to *make solitary* : to deprive of inhabitants : to lay waste.—*adj.* solitary : destitute of inhabitants : laid waste.—*adv.* **Des′olately.**—*n.* **Des′olateness.** [L. *desolo*, *desolatus*—*de*, intensive, and *solo*, to make alone —*solus*, alone.] [a place desolated.

**Desolation**, des-o-lā′shun, *n.* waste : destruction :

**Despair**, de-spār′, *v.i.* to be *without hope* : to despond.—*n.* want of hope : utter hopelessness : that which causes despair.—*adv.* **Despair′ingly.** [O. Fr. *desperer* and *despoirer*—L. *despero*—*de*, privative, and *spero*, to hope.]

**Despatch**, de-spach′, *v.t.* to send away hastily : to send out of the world : to put to death : to dispose of : to perform speedily.—*n.* a sending away in haste : dismissal : rapid performance : haste : that which is despatched, as a message. [O. Fr. *despeecher*, acc. to Littré, from Low L. *dispedicare*, to remove obstacles (*pedica*, a fetter), the opp. of *impedicare*. See **Impeach**.]

**Desperado**, des-pėr-ā′dō, *n.* a *desperate fellow* : one reckless of danger : a madman :—*pl.* **Despera′does.** [Sp. *desesperado*—L. *desperatus*.]

**Desperate**, des′pėr-āt, *adj.* in a state of *despair* : hopeless : beyond hope : fearless of danger : rash : furious.—*adv.* **Des′perately.**—*n.* **Des′perateness.** [disregard of danger : fury.

**Desperation**, des-pėr-ā′shun, *n.* state of despair :

**Despicable**, des′pi-ka-bl, *adj.* deserving to be *despised* : contemptible : worthless.—*n.* **Des′picableness.**—*adv.* **Des′picably.**

**Despight**, de-spīt′, an old form of **Despite**.

**Despise**, de-spīz′, *v.t.* to *look down upon* with contempt : to scorn. [L. *despicio*—*de*, down, *specio*, to look.]

**Despite**, de-spīt′, *n.* a *looking down upon* with contempt : violent malice or hatred.—*prep.* in *spite of* : notwithstanding. [Fr. *dépit*, O. Fr. *despit* —L. *despectus*—*despicio*.]

**Despiteful**, de-spīt′fool, *adj.* full of *despite* or spite.—*adv.* **Despite′fully.**—*n.* **Despite′fulness.**

**Despoil**, de-spoil′, *v.t.* to *spoil completely* : to strip : to bereave : to rob.—*ns.* **Despoil′er**, **Despolia′tion**. [O. Fr. *despoiller*—L. *despoliare*—*de*, inten., and root of **Spoil**.]

**Despond**, de-spond′, *v.i.* to lose hope or courage : to despair.—*adv.* **Despond′ingly.** [L. *despondeo*—*de*, away, and *spondeo*, to promise.]

**Despondence**, de-spond′ens, **Despondency**, de-spond′en-si, *n.* state of being without hope : dejection.

**Despondent**, de-spond′ent, *adj.*, *desponding* : without courage or hope : sad.—*adv.* **Despond′ently.**

**Despot**, des′pot, *n.* one invested with absolute power : a tyrant. [Gr. *des-potēs*—*des*, origin unknown, and root *pot*, found in L. *potis*, able, Gr. *posis*, a husband, Sans. *pati*, lord.]

**Despotic**, des-pot′ik, **Despotical**, des-pot′ik-al, *adj.* pertaining to or like a *despot* : having absolute power : tyrannical.—*adv.* **Despot′ically.**

**Despotism**, des′pot-izm, *n.* absolute power.

**Despumate**, des′pū-māt or de-spū′-, *v.i.* to *throw off in foam* or scum. [L. *despumo*, *despumatus* —*de*, off, and *spuma*, foam.]

**Desquamation**, des-kwa-mā′shun, *n.* a *scaling off* : the separation of the cuticle or skin in scales. [L. *desquamo*, *desquamatus*—*de*, off, and *squama*, a scale.]

**Dessert**, dez-ėrt′, *n.* fruits, confections, &c. served at the close of an entertainment after the rest has been taken away. [Fr.—*desservir*, to clear the table—pfx. *des*, away, and *servir*, to serve—L. *servio*.]

**Destemper**, des-tem′pėr, **Distemper**, dis-tem′pėr, *n.* a coarse mode of painting, in which the colours are *tempered* or mixed in a watery glue, chiefly used in scene-painting and in staining paper for walls. [Fr. *détrempe*—*dé*, L. *dis*, and *tremper* for *temprer*—L. *temperare*, to temper.]

**Destination**, des-ti-nā′shun, *n.* the purpose or end to which anything is *destined* or appointed : end : purpose : design : fate : place to which one is going.

**Destine**, des′tin, *v.t.* to ordain or appoint to a certain use or state : to fix : to doom. [Fr.— L. *destino*—*de*, intensive, and root *sta*, in *sto*, *stare*, to stand, and allied to Gr. *histanō*, *histēmi*, to make to stand, E. **Stand**.]

**Destiny**, des′ti-ni, *n.* the purpose or end to which any person or thing is *destined* or appointed : unavoidable fate : necessity.

**Destitute**, des′ti-tūt, *adj.*, *left alone* : forsaken : in want, needy. [L. *destituo*, *destitutus*—*de*, away, and *statuo*, to place.]

**Destitution**, des-ti-tū′shun, *n.* state of being *destitute* : poverty.

**Destroy**, de-stroy′, *v.t.* to *unbuild* or *pull down* : to overturn : to ruin : to put an end to :—*pr.p.* destroy′ing ; *pa.p.* destroyed′. [O. Fr. *destruire* (Fr. *détruire*)—L. *destruo*, *destructum* —*de*, down, and *struo*, to build.]

**Destroyer**, de-stroy′ėr, *n.* one who *destroys*.

**Destructible**, de-struk′ti-bl, *adj.* liable to be *destroyed*.—*n.* **Destructibil′ity.**

**Destruction**, de-struk′shun, *n.* act of *destroying* : overthrow : ruin : death.

**Destructive**, de-struk′tiv, *adj.* causing *destruction* : mischievous : ruinous : deadly.—*adv.* **Destruc′tively.**—*n.* **Destruc′tiveness.**

**Desudation**, des-ū-dā′shun, *n.* a *violent sweating* : an eruption of small pimples on children. [L. *de*, intensive, and *sudo*, to sweat.]

**Desuetude**, des′we-tūd, *n.*, *disuse* : discontinuance of custom, habit, or practice. [L. *desuetudo* —*de*, negative, and *suesco*, to become used.]

**Desultory**, des′ul-tor-i, *adj.*, *jumping from* one thing to another : without rational or logical connection : rambling : hasty : loose.—*adv.* **Des′ultorily.**—*n.* **Des′ultoriness.** [L. *desultorius*—*de*, from, and *salio*, to jump.]

**Detach**, de-tach′, *v.t.* to *untack* or *unfasten* : to take from or separate : to withdraw. [Fr. *détacher*—*dé*, from, and root of **Attach**.]

**Detachment**, de-tach′ment, *n.* state of being

separated : that which is detached, as a body of troops.

**Detail**, de-tāl′, *v.t.* to relate minutely : to enumerate : to set apart for a particular service.—*n.* (dē′tāl or de-tāl′) a small part : a minute and particular account. [Fr. *détailler*—*de*, inten., and *tailler*, to cut. See Tailor, Tally.]

**Detain**, de-tān′, *v.t.* to *hold from* or back : to stop : to keep. [Fr. *détenir*—L. *detineo*—*de*, from, and *teneo*, to hold.]

**Detainer**, de-tān′ėr, *n.* one who *detains* : (*law*) the holding of what belongs to another.

**Detainment**, de-tān-ment, *n.* Same as **Detention**.

**Detect**, de-tekt′, *v.t.* (*lit.*) to *uncover*—hence to *discover* : to find out. [L. *de*, neg., and *tego, tectus*, to cover.]                       [*tected*.

**Detectable**, de-tekt′a-bl, *adj.* that may be *de*-

**Detecter, Detector**, de-tekt′ėr, -or, *n.* one who *detects*.                                    [hidden.

**Detection**, de-tek′shun, *n.* discovery of something

**Detective**, de-tekt′iv, *adj.* employed in detecting.—*n.* a policeman employed secretly to *detect* crime.

**Detention**, de-ten′shun, *n.* act of *detaining* : state of being detained : confinement : delay.

**Deter**, de-tėr′, *v.t.* to *frighten from* : to hinder or prevent :—*pr.p.* deter′ring ; *pa.p.* deterred′. [L. *deterreo*—*de*, from, and *terreo*, to frighten.]

**Deterge**, de-tėrj′, *v.t.* to *wipe off* : to cleanse (as a wound). [L. *detergeo, detersus*—*de*, off, and *tergeo*, to wipe.]        [—*n.* that which cleanses.

**Detergent**, de-tėrj′ent, *adj.* *cleansing* : purging.

**Deteriorate**, de-tē′ri-o-rāt, *v.t.* to *bring down* or *make worse*.—*v.i.* to grow worse. [L. *deterior*, worse—obs. *deter*, lower—*de*, down ; cf. *in-ter-ior*.]                             [growing worse.

**Deterioration**, de-tē-ri-o-rā′shun, *n.* the state of

**Determinable**, de-tėr′min-a-bl, *adj.* capable of being *determined*, decided on, or finished.

**Determinate**, de-tėr′min-āt, *adj.*, *determined* or limited : fixed : decisive.—*adv.* Deter′minately.

**Determination**, de-tėr-min-ā′shun, *n.* that which is *determined* or resolved on : end : direction to a certain end : resolution : purpose : decision.

**Determinative**, de-tėr′min-ā-tiv, *adj.* that *determines*, limits, or defines.

**Determine**, de-tėr′min, *v.t.* to *put terms* or *bounds to* : to limit : to fix or settle the form or character of : to influence : to put an end to : to resolve on : to define. [L. *determino, determinatus*—*de*, priv., and *terminus*, a boundary.]

**Determined**, de-tėr′mind, *adj.* firm in purpose : fixed : resolute.—*adv.* Deter′minedly.

**Deterrent**, de-tėr′ent, *adj.* serving to *deter*.—*n.* anything that deters or prevents.       [Deterge.]

**Detersion**, de-tėr′shun, *n.* act of *cleansing*. [See

**Detersive**, de-tėr′siv, *n.* Same as **Detergent**.

**Detest**, de-test′, *v.t.* to hate intensely. [L. *detestor*—*de*, intensive, and *testor*, to call to witness, execrate—*testis*, a witness.]

**Detestable**, de-test′a-bl, *adj.* worthy of being *detested* : extremely hateful : abominable.—*adv.* Detest′ably.—*n.* Detest′ableness.

**Detestation**, de-test-ā′shun, *n.* extreme hatred.

**Dethrone**, de-thrōn′, *v.t.* to remove *from a throne* : to divest of royal authority. [L. *de*, from, and **Throne**.]                    [*a throne* : deposition.

**Dethronement**, de-thrōn′ment, *n.* removal *from*

**Detonate**, det′o-nāt, *v.i.* to explode.—*v.t.* to cause to explode. [L. *detono*—*de*, down, and *tono*, to thunder.]

**Detonation**, det-o-nā′shun, *n.* a *sudden explosion*.

**Detour**, de-tōōr′, *n.* a winding : a circuitous way. [Fr. *dé*, for L. *dis*, asunder, and *tour*, a turning. See **Turn**.]

**Detract**, de-trakt′, *v.t.* to *take away from* the credit or reputation of : to defame : to abuse.—*ns.* Detract′er. Detract′or—*adv.* Detract′ingly. [L.—*de*, from, and *traho*, to draw.]

**Detraction**, de-trak′shun, *n.* depreciation : slander.

**Detractory**, de-trakt′or-i, *adj.* tending to detract : derogatory.

**Detrain**, de-trān′, *v.t.* to take out of a railway *train*, as troops.

**Detriment**, det′ri-ment, *n.* a *rubbing off* or wearing away : damage : loss. [L. *detrimentum*—*de*, off, and *tero, tritus*, to rub.]

**Detrimental**, det-ri-ment′al, *adj.* injurious.

**Detrition**, de-trish′un, *n.* a *wearing away*.

**Detritus**, de-trī′tus, *n.* a mass of substance gradually *rubbed* or *worn off* solid bodies—smaller than debris. [L.—*de*, off, and *tero, tritus*, to rub.]

**Detrude**, de-trōōd′, *v.t.* to *thrust down*. [L. *de*, down, and *trudo*, to thrust.]

**Detruncate**, de-trung′kāt, *v.t.* to cut *off* from the *trunk* : to lop off : to shorten. [L. *de*, off, and *trunco*, to lop—*truncus*, a trunk.]        [off.

**Detruncation**, de-trung-kā′shun, *n.* act of lopping

**Detrusion**, de-trōō′zhun, *n.* a *thrusting down*.

**Deuce**, dūs, *n.* a card or die with *two* spots. [Fr. *deux*, two—L. *duo*, two.]

**Deuce, Deuse**, dūs, *n.* the evil one : the devil. [O. Fr. *deus*, O God—L. *deus*, God. 'It is merely a Norman oath vulgarised' (Skeat).]

**Deuterogamy**, dū-tėr-og′a-mi, *n.*, *second marriage*, esp. of the clergy, after the death of the first wife. [Gr. *deuteros*, second, and *gamos*, marriage.]

**Deuteronomy**, dū-tėr-on′o-mi or du′tėr-on-o-mi, *n.* the fifth book of the Pentateuch, which contains the *second* giving of the *law* by Moses. [Gr. *deuteros*, second, and *nomos*, law.]

**Devastate**, dev′as-tāt, *v.t.* to *lay waste* : to plunder. [L. *de*, intensive, and *vasto*, to lay waste.]

**Devastation**, dev-as-tā′shun, *n.* act of *devastating* : state of being devastated : waste : desolation.

**Develop**, de-vel′op, *v.t.* to unroll : to unfold : to lay open by degrees.—*v.i.* to grow into : to open out :—*pr.p.* devel′oping ; *pa.p.* devel′oped. [Fr. *développer*, opp. of *envelopper* ; both perh. from a Teut. root found in E. Lap, to wrap. See Lap, Envelope.]

**Development**, de-vel′op-ment, *n.* a gradual unfolding : a gradual growth.

**Deviate**, dē′vi-āt, *v.i.* to go *from the way* : to turn aside from a certain course : to err. [L. *de*, from, *via*, a way.]

**Deviation**, dē-vi-ā′shun, *n.* a going out of the way : a turning aside : error.

**Device**, de-vīs′, *n.* that which is *devised* or designed : contrivance : power of devising : genius : (*her.*) the emblem borne upon a shield. [Fr. *devise*. See Devise.]

**Devil**, dev′l, *n.* (*lit.*) the *slanderer* or *accuser* : Satan : any evil spirit : a very wicked person.—*v.t.* (*cookery*) to pepper excessively. [A.S. *deofol, aioful*—L. *diabolus*—Gr. *diabolos*, from *diaballō*, to throw across, to slander, from *dia*, across, and *ballō*, to throw.]

**Devilish**, dev′l-ish, *adj.* of or like the *devil* : excessively bad.—*adv.* Dev′ilishly.—*n.* Dev′ilishness.                    [extreme wickedness.

**Devilry**, dev′il-ri, *n.* conduct worthy of the *devil* :

**Devious**, dē′vi-us, *adj.* from or out of the *way* : erring.—*adv.* De′viously.—*n.* De′viousness. [See Deviate.]

**Devise**, de-vīz′, *v.t.* to imagine : to scheme : to contrive : to give by will : to bequeath.—*n.* act of bequeathing : a will : property bequeathed by will. [Fr. *deviser*—Low L. *divisa*, a division of goods, a bound or mark of division, a mark, a device—L. *divido, divisus*, to divide.] [trives.

**Deviser**, de-vīz′ėr, *n.* one who *devises* or con-

**Devisor**, de-vīz′or, *n.* one who *devises* or bequeaths by will.

**Devoid**, de-void′, *adj., quite void :* destitute : free from. [L. *de*, intensive, and Void.]

**Devoir**, dev-wawr′, *n.* what *is due*, duty : service : an act of civility. [Fr.—L. *debeo*, to owe.]

**Devolution**, dev-o-lū′shun, *n.* a passing from one person to another. [See Devolve.]

**Devolve**, de-volv′, *v.t.* to *roll down :* to hand down : to deliver over.—*v.i.* to roll down : to fall or pass over. [L. *de*, down, *volvo, volutus*, to roll.]

**Devonian**, de-vō′ni-an, *adj.* noting a system of geological strata which abound in Devonshire, originally called Old Red Sandstone.

**Devote**, de-vōt′, *v.t.* to *vow :* to set apart or dedicate by solemn act : to doom : to give up wholly. [L. *devoveo, devotus*—*de*, away, and *voveo*, to vow.]

**Devoted**, de-vōt′ed, *adj.* given up to, as by a vow : strongly attached : zealous.—*adv.* Devot′edly.—*n.* Devot′edness.

**Devotee**, dev-o-tē′, *n.* one wholly or superstitiously *devoted*, esp. to religion : a bigot.

**Devotion**, de-vō′shun, *n.* consecration : giving up of the mind to the worship of God : piety : prayer : strong affection or attachment : ardour.

**Devotional**, de-vō′shun-al, *adj.* pertaining or suitable to *devotion.*—*adv.* Devo′tionally.

**Devour**, de-vowr′, *v.t.* to *swallow greedily :* to eat up : to consume or waste with violence or wantonness : to destroy.—*n.* Devour′er. [Fr. *dévorer*—L. *devoro*—*de*, intensive, and *voro*, to swallow. See Voracious.]

**Devout**, de-vowt′, *adj.* given up to religious thoughts and exercises : pious : solemn.—*adv.* Devout′ly.—*n.* Devout′ness. [Fr. *dévot*—L. *devotus*. See Devote.]

**Dew**, dū, *n., moisture* deposited from the air in minute specks upon the surface of objects.—*v.t.* to wet with dew : to moisten.—*n.* Dew′drop. [A.S. *deaw*, akin to Ice. *dögg*, Ger. *thau*, dew.]

**Dewlap**, dū′lap, *n.* the loose flesh about the throat of oxen, which *laps* or licks the *dew* in grazing.

**Dewpoint**, dū′point, *n.* the *point* or temperature at which *dew* begins to form.

**Dewy**, dū′i, *adj.* like *dew :* moist with dew.

**Dexter**, deks′tėr, *adj.* on the *right-hand* side : right. [L. *dexter ;* Gr. *dexios*, Sans. *dakshina*, on the right, on the south.]

**Dexterity**, deks-ter′i-ti, *n., right-handedness :* cleverness : readiness and skill : adroitness.

**Dexterous**, deks′tėr-us, *adj., right-handed :* adroit : subtle.—*adv.* Dex′terously.—*n.* Dex′terousness.

**Dextral**, deks′tral, *adj., right*, as opposed to left.

**Dey**, dā, *n.* a governor of Algiers before the French conquest. [Turk. *dāi*, orig. a maternal uncle, a familiar title of the chief of the Janizaries, often promoted to the above post.]

**Diabetes**, dī-a-bē′tēz, *n.* a disease marked by a morbid and excessive *discharge* of urine. [Gr., from *dia*, through, and *bainō*, to go.]

**Diabetic**, dī-a-bet′ik, *adj.* pertaining to *diabetes.*

**Diabolic**, dī-a-bol′ik, **Diabolical**, dī-a-bol′ik-al, *adj., devilish.*—*adv.* Diabol′ically. [L.—Gr. *diabolikos*, from *diabolos*, the devil. See Devil.]

**Diaconal**, dī-ak′o-nal, *adj.* pertaining to a *deacon.*

**Diaconate**, dī-ak′o-nāt, *n.* the office of a *deacon.*

**Diacritic**, dī-a-krit′ik, **Diacritical**, dī-a-krit′ik-al, *adj., distinguishing between.* [Gr.—*dia*, between, and *krinō*, to distinguish. See Critic.]

**Diadem**, dī′a-dem, *n.* a *band* or fillet worn *round* the head as a badge of royalty : a crown : royalty. [Gr. *diadēma*—*dia*, round, and *deō*, to bind.]

**Diademed**, dī′a-demd, *adj.* wearing a diadem.

**Diæresis, Dieresis**, dī-ėr′e-sis, *n.* a mark (··) placed over one of two vowels to shew that each is to be pronounced separately, as in *aërial.*—*pl.* Diær′eses, Dier′eses. [Gr.—*dia*, apart, and *haireō*, to take.]

**Diagnosis**, dī-ag-nō′sis, *n.* the *distinguishing* a disease by means of its symptoms : a brief description :—*pl.* Diagno′ses. [Gr.—*dia*, between, and *ginōskō*, to know.]

**Diagnostic**, dī-ag-nos′tik, *adj., distinguishing :* characteristic.—*n.* that by which anything is known : a symptom.

**Diagonal**, dī-ag′o-nal, *adj., through the corners,* or *from angle to* an opposite *angle* of a four or many sided figure.—*n.* a straight line so drawn.—*adv.* Diag′onally. [L. *diagonalis*, from Gr. *diagōnios*—*dia*, through, and *gōnia*, a corner.]

**Diagram**, dī′a-gram, *n.* a figure or plan drawn to illustrate any statement.—*adj.* Diagrammat′ic. [Gr. *diagramma*—*dia*, round, and *graphō*, to write, delineate.]

**Diagraph**, dī′a-graf, *n.* an instrument used in perspective *drawing.*

**Dial**, dī′al, *n.* an instrument for shewing the time of *day* by the sun's shadow : the face of a watch or clock. [Low L. *dialis*, daily—L. *dies*, a day.]

**Dialect**, dī′a-lekt, *n.* a variety or form of a language peculiar to a district. [Gr. *dialektos*, speech, manner of speech, peculiarity of speech —*dia*, between, and *legō*, to choose, to speak.]

**Dialectic**, dī-a-lek′tik, **Dialectical**, dī-a-lek′tik-al, *adj.* pertaining to *dialect* or to discourse : pertaining to *dialectics :* logical.—*n.* same as Dialectics.—*adv.* Dialec′tically. [Gr. *dialektikos.*]

**Dialectician**, dī-a-lek-tish′an, *n.* one skilled in *dialectics*, a logician.

**Dialectics**, dī-a-lek′tiks, *n.pl.* art of *discussing :* that branch of logic which teaches the rules and modes of reasoning. [Gr. *dialektikē* (*technē*, art, being understood), art of discussing by questioning, logic.]

**Dialist**, dī′al-ist, *n.* a maker of dials : one skilled in dialling.—**Dialling**, dī′al-ing, *n.* the art of constructing dials. [of, a *dialogue.*

**Dialogist**, dī-al′o-jist, *n.* a speaker in, or writer

**Dialogistic**, dī-al-o-jist′ik, **Dialogistical**, dī-al-o-jist′ik-al, *adj.* in the form of a *dialogue.*

**Dialogue**, dī′a-log, *n., conversation between* two or more persons, esp. of a formal or imaginary nature. [Fr.—L. *dialogus*—Gr. *dialogos*, a conversation—*dialegomai*, to discourse. See Dialect.]

**Dialysis**, dī-al′i-sis, *n.* (*chem.*) the separation of substances by diffusion through a membranous septum or partition : diæresis :—*pl.* Dialyses, dī-al′i-sēz.—*adj.* Dialyt′ic. [Gr. *dialysis*—*dia*, asunder, and *lyō*, to loose.]

**Diamagnetic**, dī-a-mag-net′ik, *adj., cross-magnetic :* applied to any substance, such as a rod of bismuth or glass, which, when suspended between the poles of a magnet, arranges itself *across* the line joining the poles (a rod of iron or of sealing-wax so held arranges itself *parallel* to the line joining the poles, and is said to be *paramagnetic*). [Gr. *dia*, through, across, and *magnētis*, a magnet.]

**Diameter**, dī-am'e-tėr, *n.* the *measure through* or *across:* a straight line passing through the centre of a circle or other figure, terminated at both ends by the circumference. [Gr. *diametros* —*dia*, through, and *metrein*, to measure.]

**Diametrical**, dī-a-met'rik-al, *adj.* in the direction of a diameter : direct.—*adv.* **Diamet'rically.**

**Diamond**, dī'a-mond, *n.* the most valuable of all gems and the hardest of all substances : a four-sided figure with two obtuse and two acute angles : one of the smallest kinds of English printing type. [Fr. *diamant*, a corr. of Gr. *adamas, adamantos*, adamant. See **Adamant**; also **Daunt** and **Tame**.]

**Diapason**, dī-a-pā'zon, *n.* a whole octave : the concord of the first and last notes of the scale. [Gr. *dia*, through, and *pasōn*, genitive pl. of *pas*, all—part of the Gr. phrase, *dia pasōn chordōn symphōnia*, concord *through all* the notes.]

**Diaper**, dī'a-pėr, *n.* linen cloth woven in figures, used for towels, &c.—*v.t.* to variegate with figures, as diaper. [Fr. *diapré*, O. Fr. *diaspre*; from root of **Jasper**.]

**Diaphaneity**, dī-a-fa-nē'i-ti, *n.* quality of being *diaphanous*: power of transmitting light.

**Diaphanous**, dī-af'a-nus, *adj.*, *shining* or appearing *through*, transparent : clear.—*adv.* **Diaph'anously.** [Gr. *diaphanēs*—*dia*, through, and *phainō*, to shew, shine. See **Phantom**.]

**Diaphoretic**, dī-a-fo-ret'ik, *adj.* promoting perspiration.—*n.* a medicine that increases perspiration. [Gr. *diaphoreo*, to carry off—*dia*, through, and *pherō*, to bear.]

**Diaphragm**, dī'a-fram, *n.* a thin *partition* or dividing membrane : the muscle which separates the chest from the abdomen : called also the midriff. [Gr. *diaphragma*—*dia*, across, *phrag-nymi*, to fence.]

**Diaphragmatic**, dī-a-frag-mat'ik, *adj.* pertaining to the diaphragm.

**Diarist**, dī'a-rist, *n.* one who keeps a *diary*.

**Diarrhœa**, dī-a-rē'a, *n.* a persistent purging or looseness of the bowels. [Gr. *diarrhoia*—*dia*, through, and *rheō*, to flow.]

**Diarrhœtic**, dī-a-ret'ik, *adj.* producing diarrhœa.

**Diary**, dī'a-ri, *n.* a *daily* record : a journal. [L. *diarium*, from *dies*, a day. See **Dial**.]

**Diastole**, dī-as'to-lē, *n.*, *dilation* of the heart, auricles, and arteries ; opposed to **Systole** or contraction of the same : the making a short syllable long. [Gr. *diastolē*—*dia*, asunder, and *stellō*, to place.]

**Diathermal**, dī-a-thėr'mal, *adj.* letting *heat through*, permeable by radiating heat. [Gr. *dia*, through, and *thermē*, heat.]

**Diatonic**, dī-a-ton'ik, *adj.* proceeding *by tones*, as the natural scale in music.—*adv.* **Diaton'ically.** [Gr., from *dia*, through, and *tonos*, tone.]

**Diatribe**, dī'a-trīb, *n.* a continued discourse or disputation : an invective harangue. [Gr. *dia-tribē*, a wearing away of time : a discussion—*dia*, through, and *tribō*, to rub.]

**Dibber**, dib'ėr, **Dibble**, dib'l, *n.* a pointed tool used for *dabbing* or pricking holes to put seed or plants in.

**Dibble**, dib'l, *v.t.* to plant with a dibble.—*v.i.* to make holes : to dip as in angling. [Freq. of *dib*, a form of **Dip**.]

**Dice**, pl. of **Die**, for gaming.

**Dicephalous**, dī-sef'a-lus, *adj.*, *two-headed*. [Gr. *dikephalos*—*dis*, two, and *kephalē*, a head.]

**Dichotomy**, dī-kot'o-mi, *n.* a *division* into two

parts.—*adj.* **Dichot'omous.** [Gr., from *dicha*, in two, and *temno*, to cut.]

**Dickey, Dicky**, dik'i, *n.* a seat behind a carriage. [Ety. dub.]

**Dicotyledon**, dī-kot-i-lē'don, *n.* a plant having *two seed-lobes.* [Gr. *dis*, two, and **Cotyledon**.]

**Dicotyledonous**, dī-kot-i-lē'don-us, *adj.* having *two cotyledons* or seed-lobes.

**Dictate**, dik'tāt, *v.t.* to *tell* another what to say or write : to communicate with authority : to point out : to command.—*n.* an order, rule, or direction : impulse. [L. *dicto, dictatus*, freq. of *dico*, to say, to speak.] [*dictating*.]

**Dictation**, dik-tā'shun, *n.* act, art, or practice of

**Dictator**, dik-tā'tor, *n.* one invested for a time with absolute authority.

**Dictatorial**, dik-ta-tō'ri-al, *adj.* like a *dictator:* absolute : authoritative.—*adv.* **Dictato'rially.**

**Dictatorship**, dik-tā'tor-ship, *n.* the office of a *dictator:* term of a dictator's office.

**Diction**, dik'shun, *n.* a *saying* or speaking : manner of speaking or expression : choice of words : style. [L. *dictio*, from *dico, dictus*, to say ; akin to Gr. *deiknymi*, to shew.]

**Dictionary**, dik'shun-a-ri, *n.* a book containing the *words* of a language alphabetically arranged, with their meanings, &c. : a work containing information on any department of knowledge, alphabetically arranged. [Fr. *dictionnaire*.]

**Dictum**, dik'tum, *n.*, *something said* : a saying : an authoritative saying :—*pl.* **Dic'ta.** [L.]

**Did**, did—*past tense* of **Do.**

**Didactic**, di-dak'tik, **Didactical**, di-dak'tik-al, *adj.* fitted or intended to *teach* : instructive : preceptive.—*adv.* **Didac'tically.** [Gr. *didaktikos—didaskō*, for *di-dak-sko*, to teach ; akin to L. *doc-eo*, to teach, *disc-o*, to learn.]

**Didapper**, did'ap-ėr, *n.* a water-bird that is constantly *dipping* or diving under water, also called the *dab*chick (orig. *dap*chick). [A compound of *dive* and *dapper* (which is a variant of *dipper*). See **Dip** and **Dive**.]

**Die**, dī, *v.i.* to lose life : to perish : to wither : to languish : to become insensible :—*pr.p.* dying ; *pa.t.* and *pa.p.* died (dīd). [From a Scand. root seen in Ice. *deyja*, Dan. *dö*, Scot. *dee*, akin to O. Ger. *touwi-an*, whence Ger. *todt*. The A.S. word is *steorfan*, whence our *starve*.]

**Die**, dī, *n.* a small cube used in gaming the being *thrown* from a box : any small cubical body : hazard :—*pl.* **Dice**, dīs. [Fr. *dé, det*, Prov. *dat*, It. *dado*, from Low L. *dadus*—L. *datus*, given or cast (*talus*, a piece of bone used in play, being understood). Doublets, **Dado, Date**.]

**Die**, dī, *n.* a stamp for impressing coin, &c. : the cubical part of a pedestal :—*pl.* **Dies**, dīz.

**Diet**, dī'et, *n.* mode of *living* with especial reference to food : food prescribed by a physician : allowance of provision.—*v.t.* to furnish with food.—*v.i.* to eat : to take food according to rule. [Fr. *diète*, Low L. *diæta*—Gr. *diaita*, mode of living, diet.]

**Diet**, dī'et, *n.* an assembly of princes and delegates, the chief national council in several countries in Europe. [Low L. *diæta*—Gr. *diaita;* or acc. to Littré, from L. *dies*, a (set) day, with which usuage cf. Ger. *tag*, a day, *reichstag.*]

**Dietary**, dī'et-a-ri, *adj.* pertaining to *diet* or the rules of diet.—*n.* course of diet : allowance of food, especially in large institutions.

**Dietetic**, dī-et-et'ik, **Dietetical**, dī-et-et'ik-al, *adj.* pertaining to *diet*.—*n.* **Dietet'ics**, rules for regulating diet.—*adv.* **Dietet'ically.** [Fr. *diététique*, from Gr. *diaitētikos*.]

fāte, fär ; mē, hėr ; mīne ; mōte ; mūte ; mōōn ; *then.*

**Differ,** dif'ėr, *v.i.* to disagree : to strive : to be unlike, distinct, or various :—*pr.p.* diff'ering ; *pa.p.* diff'ered. [L. *differo*—*dif* (= *dis*), apart, *fero,* to bear. See **Bear,** to carry.]

**Difference,** dif'ėr-ens, *n.* the quality distinguishing one thing from another : a contention or quarrel : the point in dispute : the excess of one quantity or number over another.

**Different,** dif'ėr-ent, *adj.* distinct : separate : unlike : not the same.—*adv.* **Diff'erently.** [Fr.—L. *differens, differentis,* pr.p. of *differo.*]

**Differential,** dif-ėr-en'shal, *adj.* creating a *difference*: (*math.*) pertaining to a quantity or difference infinitely small.

**Difficult,** dif'i-kult, *adj.* not *easy*: hard to be done : requiring labour and pains : hard to please : not easily persuaded.—*adv.* **Diff'i-cultly.** [L. *difficilis*—*dif* (= *dis*), negative, and *facilis,* easy.]

**Difficulty,** dif'i-kul-ti, *n.* laboriousness : obstacle : objection : that which cannot be easily understood or believed : embarrassment of affairs. [Fr. *difficulté*—L. *difficultas* = *difficilitas.* See **Difficult.**]

**Diffidence,** dif'i-dens, *n.* want of confidence : want of self-reliance : modesty : bashfulness. [L.]

**Diffident,** dif'i-dent, *adj., wanting faith* in : *distrustful* of one's self : modest : bashful.—*adv.* **Diff'idently.** [L., pr.p. of *diffido,* to distrust—*dif* (= *dis*), negative, *fido,* to trust—*fides,* faith.]

**Diffuse,** dif-ūz', *v.t.* to *pour out all around*: to send out in all directions : to scatter : to circulate : to publish.—*n.* **Diffus'er.** [L. *diffundo, diffusus*—*dif* (= *dis*), asunder, *fundo,* to pour out.]

**Diffuse,** dif-ūs', *adj., diffused*: widely spread : wordy : not concise.—*adv.* **Diffuse'ly.**—*n.* **Diffuse'ness.**

**Diffused,** dif-ūzd', *pa.p.* and *adj., spread widely*: loose.—*adv.* **Diffus'edly.**—*n.* **Diffus'edness.**

**Diffusible,** dif-ūz'i-bl, *adj.* that may be *diffused.*—*n.* **Diffusibil'ity** [abroad : extension.

**Diffusion,** dif-ū'zhun, *n.* a spreading or scattering

**Diffusive,** dif-ūs'iv, *adj.* extending : spreading widely.—*adv.* **Diffus'ively.**—*n.* **Diffus'iveness.**

**Dig,** dig, *v.t.* to turn up the earth : to cultivate with a spade :—*pr.p.* digg'ing ; *pa.t.* and *pa.p.* dug, (*B.*) digged'.—*n.* **Digg'er.** [A.S. *dician* —*dic,* a ditch. See **Dike, Ditch.**]

**Digastric,** dī-gas'trik, *adj., double-bellied,* or fleshy at each end, applied to one of the muscles of the lower jaw. [Gr. *di,* double, *gastēr,* the belly.]

**Digest,** di-jest', *v.t.* to dissolve food in the stomach : to soften by heat and moisture : to distribute and arrange : to prepare or classify in the mind : to think over.—*v.i.* to be dissolved in the stomach : to be softened by heat and moisture.—*n.* **Digest'er.** [L. *digero, digestus,* to carry asunder, or dissolve—*di* (= *dis*), asunder, and *gero,* to bear.]

**Digest,** dī'jest, *n.* a body of laws collected and arranged, esp. the Justinian code of civil laws. [L. *digesta,* neut. pl. of *digestus,* pa.p. of *digero,* to carry apart, to arrange.]

**Digestible,** di-jest'i-bl, *adj.* that may be *digested.*—*n.* **Digestibil'ity.**

**Digestion,** di-jest'yun, *n.* the *dissolving* of the food in the stomach : orderly arrangement : exposing to slow heat, &c. [L. *digestio.*]

**Digestive,** di-jest'iv, *adj.* promoting *digestion.*

**Dight,** dīt, *adj.* disposed, adorned. [A.S. *dihtan,* to arrange, prescribe, from L. *dictare,* to dictate, whence Ger. *dichten,* to write poetry.]

**Digit,** dij'it, *n.* (*lit.*) a *finger*: a finger's breadth

or ¾ inch : from the habit of counting on the fingers, any one of the nine figures : the twelfth part of the diameter of the sun or moon. [L. *digitus,* a finger or toe, akin to Gr. *daktylos*; acc. to Curtius, from the root *dek,* seen in Gr. *dechomai,* to receive.]

**Digital,** dij'it-al, *adj.* pertaining to the *fingers.* [L. *digitalis*—*digitus.*]

**Digitate,** dij'i-tāt, **Digitated,** dij'i-tāt-ed, *adj.* consisting of several *finger-like* sections.—*n.* **Digita'tion.** [L. *digitatus,* having fingers—*digitus.*]

**Digitigrade,** dij'i-ti-grād, *adj., walking* on the *toes.*—*n.* an animal that walks on its toes, as the lion. [L. *digitus,* and *gradior,* to step, to walk.]

**Dignified,** dig'ni-fīd, *adj.* marked with *dignity*: exalted : noble : grave.

**Dignify,** dig'ni-fī, *v.t.* to invest with honour : to exalt :—*pr.p.* dig'nifying ; *pa.p.* dig'nified. [Low L. *dignifico*—*dignus,* worthy, *facio,* to make.]

**Dignitary,** dig'ni-tar-i, *n.* one in a *dignified* position : one who holds an ecclesiastical rank above a priest or canon. [Fr. *dignitaire*—L. *dignitas.*]

**Dignity,** dig'ni-ti, *n.* the state of being *worthy* or *dignified*: elevation of mind or character : grandeur of mien : elevation in rank, place, &c. : degree of excellence : preferment : high office. [Fr. *dignité*—L. *dignitas*—*dignus,* worthy ; akin to **Decent, Decorous.**]

**Digraph,** dī'graf, *n.* two letters expressing but one sound, as *ph* in *digraph.* [Gr. *di,* twice, *graphē,* a mark, a character—*graphō,* to write.]

**Digress,** di-gres', *v.i.* to *step aside* or go from the main subject : to introduce irrelevant matter. [L. *digredior, digressus*—*di,* aside, *gradior,* to step. See **Grade.**]

**Digression,** di-gresh'un, *n.* a going from the main point : a part of a discourse not upon the main subject.

**Digressional,** di-gresh'un-al, **Digressive,** di-gres'iv, *adj.* departing from the main subject.—*adv.* **Digress'ively.**

**Dike,** dīk, *n.* a trench or the earth dug out and thrown up : a ditch : a mound raised to prevent inundation : (*geol.*) a wall-like mass of igneous rock in the fissures of stratified rocks.—*v.t.* to surround with a dike or bank. [A.S. *dic*; Dut. *dijk,* Ger. *teich,* a pond ; Gr. *teichos,* a wall or rampart ; akin to **Dough.** See **Dig**; also **Ditch.**]

**Dilacerate,** di-las'ėr-āt, *v.t.* to *rend* or *tear asunder.*—*n.* **Dilac'eration.** [L.—*di,* asunder, and **Lacerate.**]

**Dilapidate,** di-lap'i-dāt, *v.t.* to pull *stone from stone*: to lay waste : to suffer to go to ruin.—*n.* **Dilap'idator.** [L. *dilapido*—*di,* asunder, *lapis, lapidis,* a stone.]

**Dilapidation,** di-lap-i-dā'shun, *n.* the state of ruin : impairing of church property by an incumbent.

**Dilatable,** di-lāt'a-bl, *adj.* that may be *dilated* or expanded.—*n.* **Dilatabil'ity.**

**Dilatation,** dil-a-tā'shun, **Dilation,** di-lā'shun, *n.* expansion.

**Dilate,** di-lāt', *v.t.* to *spread out* in all directions : to enlarge : the opp. of **Contract.**—*v.i.* to widen : to swell out : to speak at length.—*n.* **Dilat'er.** [L. *dilatus* (used as pa.p. of *differo*), from *di* (= *dis*, apart), and *latus* = *tlatus* (Gr. *tlētos,* borne, suffered), from root of *tollo.* See **Tolerate.**]

**Dilatory,** dil'a-tor-i, *adj.* slow : given to procrastination : loitering : tending to delay.—*adv.*

**Dil'atorily.**—_n._ **Dil'atoriness.** [L. _dilatorius_, extending or putting off (time). See **Dilate**.]

**Dilemma**, di-lem'a, _n._ an argument in which the opponent is _caught_ between _two_ difficulties : a state of matters in which it is difficult to determine what course to pursue. [L.—Gr. _dilēmma_ —_di_, twice, double, _lēmma_, anything received —_lambanō_, to take, to seize.]

**Dilettante**, dil-et-an'te, _n._ one who loves the fine arts, but in a superficial way and without serious purpose :—_pl._ **Dilettan'ti** (-tē).—_n._ **Dilettan'teism.** [It., pr.p. of _dilettare_, to take delight in—L. _delectare_, to delight.]

**Diligence**, dil'i-jens, _n._ steady application : industry : a French stage-coach.

**Diligent**, dil'i-jent, _adj._ steady and earnest in application : industrious.—_adv._ **Dil'igently.** [Fr.—pr.p. of L. _diligo_, to choose, to love.]

**Dill**, dil, _n._ a plant, the seeds of which are used in medicine. [A.S. _dile_ ; Ger. and Sw. _dill_.]

**Diluent**, dil'ū-ent, _adj._, _diluting_.—_n._ that which dilutes.

**Dilute**, di-lūt', _v.t._ to make thinner or more liquid : to diminish the strength, flavour, &c. of, by mixing, esp. with water.—_adj._ diminished in strength by mixing with water.—_n._ **Dilu'tion.** [L. _diluo_, _dilutus_—_di_, away from, _luo_, to wash.]

**Diluvial**, di-lū'vi-al, **Diluvian**, di-lū'vi-an, _adj._ pertaining to a _flood_, esp. that in the time of Noah : caused by a deluge.

**Diluvialist**, di-lū'vi-al-ist, _n._ one who explains geological phenomena by _The Flood_.

**Diluvium**, di-lū'vj-um, _n._ an inundation or flood : (_geol._) a deposit of sand, gravel, &c. made by the former action of the sea. [L. _diluvium_— _diluo._ See **Deluge**.]

**Dim**, dim, _adj._ not bright or distinct : obscure : mysterious : not seeing clearly.—_adj._ **Dimm'ish**, somewhat dim.—_adv._ **Dim'ly.**—_n._ **Dim'ness.** [A.S. _dim_ ; akin to Ice. _dimmr_, dark, and Ger. _dämmerung_, twilight.]

**Dim**, dim, _v.t._ to make dark : to obscure :—_pr.p._ dimm'ing ; _pa.p._ dimmed'.

**Dime**, dīm, _n._ the _tenth_ part of an American dollar. [Fr., orig. _disme_, from L. _decima_ (_pars_, a part, being understood), a tenth part.]

**Dimension**, di-men'shun, _n._ usually in _pl._, _measure_ in length, breadth, and thickness : extent : size. [Fr.—L. _dimensio_—_dimetior_, _dimensus_ —_di_ (= _dis_), apart, _metior_, to measure.]

**Dimeter**, dim'e-tér, _adj._ containing _two metres_ or _measures_.—_n._ a verse of two measures. [L.— Gr. _dimetros_—_di_, twice, _metron_, a measure.]

**Diminish**, di-min'ish, _v.t._ to _make less_ : to take a part from : to degrade.—_v.i._ to grow or appear less : to subside.—_adj._ **Dimin'ishable.** [Coined from L. _di_ (= _dis_), apart, and E. **Minish**.]

**Diminuendo**, di-min-ū-en'dō, _adv._ (_lit._) to be _diminished_ : (_mus._) a direction to let the sound die away, marked thus >. [It.—L. _diminuendus_, fut. p. pass. of _diminuo_, _diminutus_, to lessen.]

**Diminution**, dim-i-nū'shun, _n._ a _lessening_ : degradation.

**Diminutive**, di-min'ū-tiv, _adj._ of a _diminished_ size : small : contracted.—_n._ (_gram._) a word formed from another to express a little one of the kind.—_adv._ **Dimin'utively.**—_n._ **Dimin'utiveness.**

**Dimissory**, dim'is-or-i or di-mis'-, _adj._, _sending away_ or giving leave to depart to another jurisdiction. [L. _dimissorius_—_dimitto_, _dimissus_.]

**Dimity**, dim'i-ti, _n._ a kind of stout white cotton cloth, striped or figured in the loom by weaving

with _two threads_. [Through the L., from Gr. _dimitos_—_di_, twice, _mitos_, a thread.]

**Dimorphism**, dī-mor'fizm, _n._ (_bot._) a state in which _two forms_ of flower are produced by the same species : the property of crystallising in _two forms_. [Gr. _di_, twice, _morphē_, form.]

**Dimorphous**, dī-mor'fus, _adj._ having the property of dimorphism.

**Dimple**, dim'pl, _n._ a _small hollow_: a small natural depression on the face.—_v.i._ to form dimples. —_v.t._ to mark with dimples. [Dim. of _dip_, with inserted _m_. Another dim. is **Dapple**.]

**Dimply**, dim'pli, _adj._ full of _dimples_.

**Din**, din, _n._ a loud continued noise.—_v.t._ to strike with a continued or confused noise : to annoy with clamour :—_pr.p._ dinn'ing ; _pa.p._ dinned'. [A.S. _dyne_ ; akin to Ice. _dynr_, noise.]

**Dine**, dīn, _v.i._ to take dinner.—_v.t._ to give a dinner to. [O. Fr. _disner_ (Fr. _dîner_)—Low L. _disnare_ : perh. from _decænare_—L. _de_, intensive, and _cæno_, to dine.]

**Ding**, ding, _v.t._ to _throw_ or _dash violently_: to urge or enforce.—_v.i._ to ring or sound. [E. ; cf. Scot. _ding_, Ice. _dengja_, to hammer, Sw. _dänga_, to bang.]

**Dingdong**, ding'dong, _n._ the sound of bells ringing : monotony : sameness.

**Dingle**, ding'gl, _n._ a _little hollow_ : a narrow hollow between hills :=_dimble_ or _dimple_, a little dip or depression. [See **Dimple** and **Dip**.]

**Dingle-dangle**, ding'gl-dang'gl, _adv._ hanging loose : swinging backwards and forwards. [See under **Dangle**.]

**Dingo**, ding'go, _n._ the native dog of Australia.

**Dingy**, din'ji, _adj._ of a _dim_ or dark colour : dull : soiled.—_n._ **Din'giness.** [Acc. to Skeat = _dungy_, _i.e._ dirty.]

**Dinner**, din'ér, _n._ the chief meal of the day : a feast. [O. Fr. _disner._ See **Dine**.]

**Dinornis**, dī-nor'nis, _n._ a genus of large extinct birds, the bones of which are found in New Zealand. [Gr. _deinos_, terrible, and _ornis_, a bird.]

**Dinotherium**, dī-no-thē'ri-um, _n._ an extinct animal of huge size, with elephant-like tusks. [Gr. _deinos_, terrible, and _thērion_, a beast.]

**Dint**, dint, _n._ (_orig._) a _blow_ or _stroke_: the mark left by a blow : force, power. [A.S. _dynt_, a blow ; Scot. _dunt_, a blow with a dull sound, Ice. _dyntr._]

**Diocesan**, dī-os'es-an or dī'ō-sē-san, _adj._ pertaining to a _diocese._—_n._ a bishop as regards his diocese.

**Diocese**, dī'ō-sēs, _n._ the circuit or extent of a bishop's jurisdiction. [Gr. _dioikēsis_—_dioikeō_, to keep house—_di_, for _dia_, sig. completeness, _oikeō_, to manage a household—_oikos_, a house.]

**Diœcious**, dī-ēshi-us, _adj._ (_bot._) having male flowers on one plant, and female on another. [Gr. _di_, twice, and _oikos_, a house.]

**Dioptric**, dī-op'trik, **Dioptrical**, dī-op'trik-al, _adj._ pertaining to dioptrics. [Gr.—_di_, through, and root _op-_, which appears in _opsomai_, fut. of _horaō_, to see.]

**Dioptrics**, dī-op'triks, _n.pl._ the science of the properties of light in passing through different mediums.

**Diorama**, dī-o-rä'ma, _n._ an exhibition of pictures, illuminated, and _viewed through_ an opening in the wall of a darkened chamber.—_adj._ **Dioram'ic.** [Gr. _di_, through, / _oraō_, to see.]

**Dip**, dip, _v.t._ to _dive_ or plunge into any liquid for a moment.—_v.i._ to sink : to enter slightly : to look cursorily : to incline downwards :—_pr.p._ dipp'ing ; _pa.p._ dipped'.—_n._ inclination downwards : a sloping. [A.S. _dyppan_ ; Dan. _dyppe_ ;

Ger. *taufen*, to immerse; related to **Deep** and **Dive**.]

**Dipchick,** dip'chik, *n.* Same as **Dabchick.**

**Dipetalous,** dī-pet'a-lus, *adj.* having *two petals.* [Gr. *di*, twice, and **Petal** ]

**Diphtheria,** dif-thē'ri-a, *n.* a throat disease in which the air-passages become covered with a *leather-like* membrane.—*adj.* **Diphtherit'ic.** [Gr. *diphthera*, leather.]

**Diphthong,** dif'thong or dip'thong, *n.*, *two* vowel-*sounds* pronounced as one syllable. [Fr. *diphthongue*—Gr. *diphthongos*, with two sounds—Gr. *di*, twice, *phthongos*, a sound.]

**Diphthongal,** dif-thong'gal or dip-thong'gal, *adj.* relating to a *diphthong.*—*adv.* **Diphthong'ally.**

**Diploma,** di-plō'ma, *n.* a writing conferring some honour or privilege. [L. *diploma*, from Gr. *diplōma*, a letter folded double—*diploos*, double.]

**Diplomacy,** di-plō'ma-si, *n.* the art of negotiation, esp. of treaties between states: political skill.

**Diplomat,** di-plō'mat, *n.* a *diplomatist.*

**Diplomatic,** dip-lō-mat'ik, **Diplomatical,** dip-lō-mat'ik-al, *adj.* pertaining to *diplomacy*: skilful in negotiation.—*adv.* **Diplomat'ically.**

**Diplomatic,** dip-lō-mat'ik, *n.* a minister at a foreign court.—*pl.* the science of deciphering ancient writings, as diplomas, &c. [Fr. *diplomatique*.] [*diplomacy.*

**Diplomatist,** di-plō'ma-tist, *n.* one skilled in

**Dipper,** dip'ér, *n.* a bird that finds its food by *dipping* or diving into streams or lakes.

**Dipsas,** dip'sas, *n.* an Asiatic and American tree-snake whose bite is said to cause intense *thirst.* [Gr. *dipsas—dipsos*, thirst.]

**Dipsomania,** dip-sō-mā'ni-a, *n.* an insane or irresistible craving for alcoholic stimulants. [Gr. *dipsa*, thirst, and *mania*, madness.]

**Dipteral,** dip'tér-al, **Dipterous,** dip'tér-us, *adj.* having *two wings.* [Gr. *di*, twice, *pteron*, a wing.]

**Dipteran,** dip'tér-an, *n.* an insect having only *two wings*, as the house-fly.—*pl.* **Dip'terans** or **Dip'tera.**

**Diptych,** dip'tik, *n.* a double-folding writing tablet: a register of bishops, saints, &c. [Gr. *diptychos—di*, and *ptyssō*, to fold.]

**Dire,** dīr, *adj.* dreadful: calamitous in a high degree. [L. *dirus*, perhaps akin to Gr. *deidō*, to fear.]

**Direct,** di-rekt', *adj.* quite *straight*: straightforward: in the line of descent: outspoken: sincere.—*v.t.* to keep or lay quite straight: to point or aim straightly or correctly: to point out the proper course to: to guide: to order: to mark with the name and residence of a person. —*adv.* **Direct'ly.**—*n.* **Direct'ness.** [L. *dirigo*, *directus—di*, completely, and *rego*, to rule, to make straight.]

**Direction,** di-rek'shun, *n.* aim at a certain point: the line or course in which anything moves: guidance: command: the body of persons who guide or manage a matter: the written name and residence of a person. [ency to direct.

**Directive,** di-rekt'iv, *adj.* having power or tend-

**Director,** di-rekt'or, *n.* one who directs: a manager or governor: a counsellor: part of a machine or instrument which guides its motion. —*fem.* **Direct'ress** or **Direct'rix.**

**Directorate,** di-rekt'or-āt, **Directorship,** di-rekt'or-ship, *n.* the office of, or a body of *directors.*

**Directorial,** di-rek-tō'ri-al, *adj.* pertaining to *directors*: giving direction.

**Directory,** di-rekt'or-i, *adj.* containing *directions*: guiding.—*n.* a *body of directions*: a

guide: a book with the names and residences of the inhabitants of a place: a body of directors.

**Direful,** dīr'fool, *adj.* old and poetic form. Same as **Dire.**—*adv.* **Dire'fully.**—*n.* **Dire'fulness.**

**Dirge,** dérj, *n.* a funeral song or hymn. [Contracted from *dirige*, the first word of a Latin funeral hymn, from *dirigo*, to direct.]

**Dirk,** dérk, *n.* a dagger or poniard. [Scot. *durk*; from the Celtic, as in Ir. *duirc*.]

**Dirt,** dért, *n.*, *dung, excrement*: any filthy substance. [A.S. *gedritan*; Ice. *drit*, excrement.]

**Dirty,** dért'i, *adj.* defiled with *dirt*: foul: filthy: mean.—*v.t.* to soil with dirt: to sully:—*pr.p.* dirt'ying; *pa.p.* dirt'ied.—*adv.* **Dirt'ily.**—*n.* **Dirt'iness.** [of legal qualification.

**Disability,** dis-a-bil'i-ti, *n.* want of power: want

**Disable,** dis-ā'bl, *v.t.* to *make unable*: to deprive of power: to weaken: to disqualify. [L. *dis*, privative, and **Able.**]

**Disabuse,** dis-ab-ūz', *v.t.* to *free from abuse* or mistake: to undeceive: to set right. [L. *dis*, privative, and **Abuse.**]

**Disadvantage,** dis-ad-vant'āj, *n.* want of advantage: what is unfavourable to one's interest: loss: injury. [L. *dis*, and **Advantage.**]

**Disadvantageous,** dis-ad-vant-ā'jus, *adj.* attended with disadvantage: unfavourable.—*adv.* **Disadvanta'geously.**

**Disaffect,** dis-af-fekt', *v.t.* to *take away* the *affection* of: to make discontented or unfriendly:—*pa.p.* and *adj.* **Disaffect'ed,** ill-disposed, disloyal.—*adv.* **Disaffect'edly.**—*n.* **Disaffect'edness.** [L. *dis*, privative, and **Affect.**]

**Disaffection,** dis-af-fek'shun, *n.* state of being *disaffected*: want of affection or friendliness: disloyalty: hostility: ill-will.

**Disaffirm,** dis-af-férm', *v.t.* to deny (what has been *affirmed*): to contradict. [L. *dis*, negative, and **Affirm.**]

**Disafforest,** dis-af-for'est, *v.t.* to *deprive* of the privilege of *forest* laws. [L. *dis*, privative, and Low L. *afforestare*, to make into a forest. See **Forest.**]

**Disagree,** dis-a-grē', *v.i.* to differ or be at variance: to dissent. [L. *dis*, negative, and **Agree.**]

**Disagreeable,** dis-a-grē'a-bl, *adj.* not agreeable: unpleasant: offensive.—*adv.* **Disagree'ably.**—*n.* **Disagree'ableness.**

**Disagreement,** dis-a-grē'ment, *n.* want of agreement: difference: unsuitableness: dispute.

**Disallow,** dis-al-low', *v.t.* not to allow: to refuse permission to: to deny the authority of: to reject. [L. *dis*, negative, and **Allow.**]

**Disallowable,** dis-al-low'a-bl, *adj.* not allowable.

**Disallowance,** dis-al-low'ans, *n.* refusal to permit.

**Disannul,** dis-an-nul', *v.t.* to annul completely.—*ns.* **Disannul'ment, Disannull'ing.** [L. *dis*, intensive, and **Annul.**]

**Disappear,** dis-ap-pēr', *v.i.* to vanish from sight. [L. *dis*, negative, and **Appear.**]

**Disappearance,** dis-ap-pēr'ans, *n.* a ceasing to appear: removal from sight.

**Disappoint,** dis-ap-point', *v.t.* to deprive one of what he expected: to frustrate. [L. *dis*, negative, and **Appoint.**]

**Disappointment,** dis-ap-point'ment, *n.* the defeat of one's hopes: miscarriage: frustration.

**Disapprobation,** dis-ap-prob-ā'shun, **Disapproval,** dis-ap-prōōv'al, *n.* censure: dislike.

**Disapprove,** dis-ap-prōōv', *v.t.* to give an unfavourable opinion of: to reject.—*adv.* **Disapprov'ingly.** [L. *dis*, negative, and **Approve.**]

**Disarm,** diz-ärm', *v.t.* to deprive of arms: to render defenceless: to quell: to render harmless.—*n.* **Disarm'ament.** [L. *dis*, privative, and **Arm.**]

**Disarrange**, dis-a-rānj', *v.t.* to undo the arrangement of: to disorder.—*n.* **Disarrange'ment.** [L. *dis*, privative, and **Arrange.**]

**Disarray**, dis-a-rā', *v.t.* to break the array of: to throw into disorder: to strip of array or dress. —*n.* want of array or order: undress. [L. *dis*, privative, and **Array.**]

**Disassociate**, dis-as-sō'shi-āt, *v.t.* to disconnect things *associated*. [L. *dis*, privative, and **Associate.**]

**Disaster**, diz-as'tèr, *n.* an adverse or unfortunate event: a misfortune: calamity. [Fr. *désastre*—*des* (=L. *dis*), negative, and *astre*, a star, (good) fortune—L. *astrum*, a star.]

**Disastrous**, diz-as'trus, *adj.*, *ill-starred*: unpropitious: unfortunate.—*adv.* **Disas'trously.**

**Disavow**, dis-a-vow', *v.t.* to disclaim: to disown: to deny. [L. *dis*, negative, and **Avow.**]

**Disavowal**, dis-a-vow'al, *n.* act of *disavowing*: rejection: denial.

**Disband**, dis-band', *v.t.* to break up a band: to disperse.—*v.i.* to break up. [L. *dis*, privative, and **Band.**]

**Disbandment**, dis-band'ment, *n.* act of disbanding.

**Disbar**, dis-bär', *v.t.* to expel a barrister from the bar. [L. *dis*, privative, and **Bar.**]

**Disbelief**, dis-be-lēf', *n.* want of belief.

**Disbelieve**, dis-be-lēv', *v.t.* to refuse belief or credit to. [L. *dis*, neg., and **Believe.**]

**Disbeliever**, dis-be-lēv'èr, *n.* one who disbelieves.

**Disburden**, dis-bur'dn, **Disburthen**, dis-bur'*th*n, *v.t.* to unburden or rid of a burden: to free. [L. *dis*, privative, and **Burden.**]

**Disburse**, dis-burs', *v.t.* to take from the *purse*: to pay out. [O. Fr. *desbourser*—*des* (=L. *dis*), a part, and *bourse*, a purse.]

**Disbursement**, dis-burs'ment, *n.* a paying out: that which is paid out.

**Disc, Disk**, disk, *n.* the face of a round plate: the face of a celestial body. [A.S. *disc*—L. *discus* —Gr. *diskos*, a round plate, a quoit, from *dikein*, to cast. See **Desk, Dish.**]

**Discard**, dis-kärd', *v.t.* to throw away, as useless, said of *cards*: to cast off: to discharge: to reject. [L. *dis*, away, and **Card.**]

**Discern**, diz-èrn', *v.t.* to distinguish clearly by the eye or understanding: to judge. [L. *dis*, thoroughly, and *cerno*, to sift, perceive.]

**Discerner**, diz-èrn'èr, *n.* a person or thing that discerns.

**Discernible**, dis-èrn'i-bl, *adj.* that may be *perceived*: distinguishable.—*adv.* **Discern'ibly.**

**Discernment**, diz-èrn'ment, *n.* power or faculty of discriminating: judgment.

**Discharge**, dis-chärj', *v.t.* to free from a *charge*: to unload or remove the *cargo*: to set free: to acquit: to dismiss: to fire, as a gun: to let out or emit.—*n.* act of discharging: unloading: acquittance: dismissal: that which is discharged. —*n.* **Discharg'er.** [L. *dis*, priv., and **Charge.**]

**Disciple**, dis-ī'pl, *n.* a *learner*: one who professes to receive instruction from another: one who follows or believes in the doctrine of another: a follower.—*n.* **Disci'pleship.** [Fr.—L. *discipulus*, from *disco*, to learn; akin to *doceo*, to teach.]

**Disciplinable**, dis'i-plin-a-bl, *adj.* capable of training or instruction. [forces rigid rule.

**Disciplinarian**, dis'i-plin-ā'ri-an, *n.* one who enDisciplinary, dis'i-plin-ar-i, *adj.* pertaining to or intended for *discipline*.

**Discipline**, dis'i-plin, *n.*, *instruction*: training, or mode of life in accordance with rules: subjec-tion to control: order: severe training: mortification: punishment.—*v.t.* to subject to discipline: to train: to educate: to bring under control: to chastise. [L. *disciplina*, from *discipulus*.]

**Disclaim**, dis-klām', *v.t.* to renounce claim to: to refuse to acknowledge: to reject. [L. *dis*, privative, and **Claim.**] [or renunciation.

**Disclaimer**, dis-klām'èr, *n.* a denial, disavowal,

**Disclose**, dis-klōz', *v.t.* to *unclose*: to open: to lay open: to bring to light: to reveal. [L. *dis*, negative, and **Close.**]

**Disclosure**, dis-klō'zhür, *n.* act of *disclosing*: a bringing to light or revealing: that which is disclosed or revealed.

**Discoid, Discoidal**, dis-koid'al, *adj.* having the *form* of a *disc*. [Gr. *diskos*, and *eidos*, form.]

**Discoloration**, dis-kul-èr-ā'shun, *n.* act of *discolouring*: state of being discoloured: stain.

**Discolour**, dis-kul'èr, *v.t.* to take away colour from: to change the natural colour of: to alter the appearance of. [L. *dis*, priv., and **Colour.**]

**Discomfit**, dis-kum'fit, *v.t.* to disconcert, to balk: to defeat or rout:—*pr.p.* discom'fiting; *pa.p.* discom'fited. [O. Fr. *desconfit*, pa.p. of *desconfire*—L. *dis*, sig. the opposite, and *conficio*, to prepare—*con*, thoroughly, *facio*, to make.]

**Discomfiture**, dis-kum'fit-ūr, *n.* frustration, defeat.

**Discomfort**, dis-kum'furt, *n.* want of comfort: uneasiness: pain.—*v.t.* to deprive of comfort: to make uneasy: to pain: to grieve. [L. *dis*, privative, and **Comfort.**]

**Discommend**, dis-kom-end', *v.t.* to blame. [L. *dis*, privative, and **Commend.**]

**Discommon**, dis-kom'un, *v.t.* to deprive of the right of *common*. [L. *dis*, privative, and **Common.**]

**Discompose**, dis-kom-pōz', *v.t.* to deprive of composure: to disarrange, to disorder: to disturb. [L. *dis*, privative, and **Compose.**]

**Discomposure**, dis-kom-pō'zhür, *n.* disorder: agitation.

**Disconcert**, dis-kon-sèrt', *v.t.* to deprive of harmony or agreement: to disturb: to frustrate: to defeat. [L. *dis*, privative, and **Concert.**]

**Disconnect**, dis-kon-ekt', *v.t.* to separate or disjoin.—*n.* **Disconnec'tion.** [L. *dis*, privative, and **Connect.**]

**Disconsolate**, dis-kon'sō-lāt, *adj.* without consolation or comfort: hopeless: sad.—*adv.* **Discon'solately.**—*n.* **Discon'solateness.** [L. *dis*, privative, and *consolor, consolatus*, to console.]

**Discontent**, dis-kon-tent', *adj.* not content: dissatisfied: uneasy.—*n.* want of content: dissatisfaction: uneasiness.—*v.t.* to deprive of content: to make uneasy. [L. *dis*, neg., and **Content.**]

**Discontented**, dis-kon-tent'ed, *adj.* discontent.—*adv.* **Discontent'edly.**—*n.* **Discontent'edness.**

**Discontentment**, dis-kon-tent'ment, *n.* the opp. of contentment: uneasiness.

**Discontinuance**, dis-kon-tin'ū-ans, **Discontinuation**, dis-kon-tin-ū-ā'shun, *n.* a breaking off or ceasing.

**Discontinue**, dis-kon-tin'ū, *v.t.* to cease to continue: to put an end to: to leave off: to stop.— *v.i.* to cease: to be separated from. [L. *dis*, negative, and **Continue.**]

**Discord**, dis'kord, *n.* opp. of concord: disagreement, strife: difference or contrariety of qualities: a union of inharmonious sounds. [L. *dis*, apart, and *cor, cordis*, the heart.]

**Discordance**, dis-kord'ans, **Discordancy**, dis-kord'an-si, *n.* disagreement.

**Discordant**, dis-kord'ant, *adj.* without concord or

agreement : inconsistent : jarring.—*adv.* **Dis-cord'antly.**

**Discount,** dis'kownt, *n.* a sum taken from the *count* or reckoning : a sum returned to the payer of an account : a deduction made for interest in advancing money on a bill. [L. *dis*, privative, and **Count.**]

**Discount,** dis-kownt', *v.t.* to allow discount : to advance money on, deducting discount.—*v.i.* to practise discounting. [discounted.]

**Discountable,** dis-kownt'a-bl, *adj.* that may be

**Discountenance,** dis-kown'ten-ans, *v.t.* to put out of countenance : to abash : to refuse countenance or support to : to discourage.—*n.* cold treatment : disapprobation. [L. *dis*, privative, and **Countenance.**]

**Discourage,** dis-kur'āj, *v.t.* to take away the courage of : to dishearten : to seek to check by shewing disfavour to. [L. *dis*, privative, and **Courage.**]

**Discouragement,** dis-kur'āj-ment, *n.* act of discouraging : that which discourages : dejection.

**Discourse,** dis-kōrs', *n.* speech or language generally : conversation : a treatise : a sermon.—*v.i.* to talk or converse : to reason : to treat formally.—*v.t.* to utter or give forth. [Fr. *discours* —L. *discursus*—*dis*, to and fro, *curro*, to run.]

**Discourteous,** dis-kurt'yus, *adj.* wanting in good manners : uncivil : rude.—*adv.* **Discourt'eously.** —*n.* **Discourt'eousness.** [L. *dis*, negative, and **Courteous.**] [incivility.

**Discourtesy,** dis-kurt'e-si, *n.* want of courtesy :

**Discous,** disk'us, *adj.*, *disc-like* : broad : flat.

**Discover,** dis-kuv'ėr, *v.t.* to uncover : to lay open or expose : to make known : to find out : to espy.—*n.* **Discov'erer.** [L. *dis*, negative, and **Cover.**] [found out.

**Discoverable,** dis-kuv'ėr-a-bl, *adj.* that may be

**Discovery,** dis-kuv'ėr-i, *n.* act of finding out : the thing discovered : revelation.

**Discredit,** dis-kred'it, *n.* want of credit : bad credit : ill repute : disgrace.—*v.t.* to refuse credit to, or belief in : to deprive of credibility : to deprive of credit : to disgrace. [L. *dis*, privative, and **Credit.**]

**Discreditable,** dis-kred'it-a-bl, *adj.* not creditable : disgraceful.—*adv.* **Discred'itably.**

**Discreet,** dis-krēt', *adj.* having discernment : wary : circumspect : prudent.—*adv.* **Discreet'ly.** —*n.* **Discreet'ness.** [L. *discretus*—*discerno*, to separate, to perceive. See **Discern.**]

**Discrepance,** dis'krep-ans or dis-krep'ans, **Discrepancy,** dis'krep-an-si or dis-krep'an-si, *n.* disagreement.

**Discrepant,** dis'krep-ant or dis-krep'ant, *adj.* disagreeing : different. [L. *dis*, different, and *crepans*, pr.p. of *crepo*, to sound.]

**Discrete,** dis-krēt' or dis'krēt, *adj.*, *separate* : distinct : disjunctive :—opp. of concrete. [A doublet of **Discreet.**]

**Discretion,** dis-kresh'un, *n.* quality of being *discreet* : prudence : liberty to act at pleasure.

**Discretional,** dis-kresh'un-al, **Discretionary,** dis-kresh'un-ar-i, *adj.* left to discretion : unrestrained.—*advs.* **Discre'tionally, Discre'tionarily.** [junctive.—*adv.* **Discret'ively.**

**Discretive,** dis-krēt'iv, *adj.*, *separating* : dis-

**Discriminate,** dis-krim'i-nāt, *v.t.* to note the difference : to distinguish : to select from others.— *v.i.* to make a difference or distinction : to distinguish.—*adv.* **Discrim'inately.** [L. *discrimino*—*discrimen*, *discriminis*, that which separates, from root of **Discern.**]

**Discrimination,** dis-krim-i-nā'shun, *n.* act or quality of distinguishing : acuteness, discernment, judgment.

**Discriminative,** dis-krim'i-na-tiv, *adj.* that marks a difference : characteristic : observing distinctions.—*adv.* **Discrim'inatively.**

**Discrown,** dis-krown', *v.t.* to deprive of a crown. [L. *dis*, privative, and **Crown.**]

**Discursion,** dis-kur'shun, *n.* desultory talk : act of discoursing or reasoning.

**Discursive,** dis-kur'siv, *adj.*, *running from* one thing to another : roving, desultory : proceeding regularly from premises to conclusion.—*adv.* **Discur'sively.** [See **Discourse.**]

**Discuss,** dis-kus', *v.t.* to break up or disperse : to examine in detail, or by disputation : to debate : to sift. [L. *discutio*, *discussus*—*dis*, asunder, and *quatio*, to shake.]

**Discussion,** dis-kush'un, *n.* debate : (*surg.*) dispersion of a tumour.

**Discussive,** dis-kus'iv, **Discutient,** dis-kū'shi-ent, *adj.* able or tending to *discuss* or disperse tumours.

**Disdain,** dis-dān', *v.t.* to think *unworthy* : to reject as unworthy or unsuitable : to scorn.— *n.* a feeling of scorn or aversion : haughtiness. [O. Fr. *desdaigner*—L. *dedignor*—*de*, privative, and *dignus*, worthy.]

**Disdainful,** dis-dān'fool, *adj.* full of disdain : haughty : scornful.—*adv.* **Disdain'fully.**—*n.* **Disdain'fulness.**

**Disease,** diz-ēz', *n.* (*lit.*) *want of ease*, hence pain : disorder or want of health in mind or body : ailment : cause of pain. [L. *dis*, privative, and **Ease.**] [Diseas'edness.

**Diseased,** diz-ēzd', *adj.* affected with disease.—*n.*

**Disedge,** dis-ej', *v.t.* (*Shak.*) to deprive of the edge : to blunt : to dull. [L. *dis*, privative, and **Edge.**]

**Disembark,** dis-em-bärk', *v.t.* to land what has been embarked : to take out of a ship : to land. —*v.i.* to quit a ship : to land. [L. *dis*, privative, and **Embark.**]

**Disembarkation,** dis-em-bär-kā'shun, **Disembarkment,** dis-em-bärk'ment, *n.* a landing from a ship.

**Disembarrass,** dis-em-bär'as, *v.t.* to free from embarrassment or perplexity. [L. *dis*, privative, and **Embarrass.**]

**Disembody,** dis-em-bod'i, *v.t.* to take away from or out of the *body* : to discharge from military service or array. [L. *dis*, priv., and **Embody.**]

**Disembogue,** dis-em-bōg', *v.t.* to discharge *at the mouth* as a stream.—*n.* **Disembogue'ment.** [Sp. *desembocar*—L. *dis*, asunder, and *bucca*, a cheek, the mouth.]

**Disembowel,** dis-em-bow'el, *v.t.* to take out the bowels. [L. *dis*, intensive, and **Embowel.**]

**Disembroil,** dis-em-broil', *v.t.* to free from *broil* or confusion. [L. *dis*, priv., and **Embroil.**]

**Disenchant,** dis-en-chant', *v.t.* to free from enchantment.—*n.* **Disenchant'ment.** [L. *dis*, privative, and **Enchant.**]

**Disencumber,** dis-en-kum'bėr, *v.t.* to free from encumbrance : to disburden.—*n.* **Disencum'brance.** [L. *dis*, privative, and **Encumber.**]

**Disendow,** dis-en-dow', *v.t.* to take away the endowment of.—*n.* **Disendow'ment.** [L. *dis*, privative, and **Endow.**]

**Disengage,** dis-en-gāj', *v.t.* to separate or free from being engaged : to separate : to set free : to release. [L. *dis*, privative, and **Engage.**]

**Disengagement,** dis-en-gāj'ment, *n.* act of disengaging : state of being disengaged : release : leisure.

**Disennoble**, dis-en-nŏ'bl, *v.t.* to deprive of what ennobles: to degrade. [L. *dis*, priv., and **Ennoble**.]

**Disentangle**, dis-en-tang'gl, *v.t.* to free from entanglement or disorder : to unravel : to disengage or set free.—*n.* **Disentang'lement**. [L. *dis*, privative, and **Entangle**.]

**Disenthral**. Same as **Disinthral**.

**Disenthrone**, dis-en-thrōn', *v.t.* to *dethrone*. [L. *dis*, privative, and **Enthrone**.]

**Disentitle**, dis-en-tī'tl, *v.t.* to deprive of title. [L. *dis*, privative, and **Entitle**.]

**Disentomb**, dis-en-tōōm', *v.t.* to take out from a tomb. [L. *dis*, privative, and **Entomb**.]

**Disentrance**, dis-en-trans', *v.t.* to awaken from a trance or deep sleep: to arouse from a reverie. [L. *dis*, privative, and **Entrance**.]

**Disestablish**, dis-es-tab'lish, *v.t.* to take away what has been established or settled, esp. applied to the church as established by law.—*n.* **Disestab'lishment**. [L. *dis*, privative, and **Establish**.]

**Disesteem**, dis-es-tēm', *n.* want of esteem: disregard.—*v.t.* to disapprove : to dislike.—*n.* **Disestima'tion**. [L. *dis*, privative, and **Esteem**.]

**Disfavour**, dis-fā'vur, *n.* want of favour: displeasure : dislike.—*v.t.* to withhold favour from : to disapprove. [L. *dis*, privative, and **Favour**.]

**Disfiguration**, dis-fig-ūr-ā'shun, **Disfigurement**, dis-fig'ūr-ment, *n.* defacement of beauty.

**Disfigure**, dis-fig'ūr, *v.t.* to spoil the *figure of* : to change to a worse form : to spoil the beauty of : to deform. [L. *dis*, privative, and **Figure**.]

**Disfranchise**, dis-fran'chiz, *v.t.* to deprive of a *franchise*, or of rights and privileges, esp. that of voting for a M.P.—*n.* **Disfranchisement**, dis-fran'chiz-ment. [L. *dis*, priv., and **Franchise**.]

**Disgorge**, dis-gorj', *v.t.* to discharge from the *gorge* or *throat* : to vomit : to throw out with violence : to give up what has been seized.—*n.* **Disgorge'ment**. [L. *dis*, negative, and **Gorge**.]

**Disgrace**, dis-grās', *n.* state of being out of *grace* or favour, or of being dishonoured : cause of shame : dishonour.—*v.t.* to put out of favour : to bring disgrace or shame upon. [L. *dis*, privative, and **Grace**.]

**Disgraceful**, dis-grās'fool, *adj.* bringing disgrace: causing shame: dishonourable.—*adv.* **Disgrace'fully**.—*n.* **Disgrace'fulness**.

**Disguise**, dis-gīz', *v.t.* to change the *guise* or appearance of : to conceal by a dress intended to deceive, or by a counterfeit manner and appearance.—*n.* a dress intended to conceal the wearer : a false appearance.—*ns.* **Disguis'er**, **Disguise'ment**. [L. *dis*, privative, and **Guise**.]

**Disgust**, diz-gust' or dis-, *n.* loathing : strong dislike.—*v.t.* to excite disgust in : to offend the taste of : to displease. [O. Fr. *desgouster—des* (= L. *dis*), and *goust* = L. *gustus*, taste.]

**Disgusting**, diz-gust'ing or dis-, **Disgustful**, diz-gust'fool, *adj.* causing disgust : loathsome : hateful.—*adv.* **Disgust'ingly**.

**Dish**, dish, *n.* a *plate* : a vessel in which food is served : the food in a dish : a particular kind of food.—*v.t.* to put in a dish, for table. [A.S. *disc*, a plate, a dish, a table—L. *discus*. Doublets, **Disc** and **Desk**.]

**Dishabille** dis-a-bil'. Same as **Deshabille**.

**Dishearten**, dis-härt'n, *v.t.* to deprive of *heart*, courage, or spirits : to discourage : to depress. [L. *dis*, privative, and **Heart**.]

**Dishevel** di-shev'el, *v.t.* to disorder the *hair* : to cause the hair to hang loose.—*v.i.* to spread in disorder :—*pr.p.* dishev'elling ; *pa p.* dishev'elled.

O. Fr. *descheveler—des*, and *chevel*, hair—L. *dis*, in different directions, *capillus*, the hair.]

**Dishonest**, diz-on'est, *adj.* not honest : wanting integrity : disposed to cheat : insincere.—*adv.* **Dishon'estly**. [L. *dis*, negative, and **Honest**.]

**Dishonesty**, diz-on'es-ti, *n.* want of honesty or integrity : faithlessness : a disposition to cheat.

**Dishonour**, diz-on'ur, *n.* want of honour : disgrace : shame : reproach.—*v.t.* to deprive of honour : to disgrace : to cause shame to : to seduce : to degrade : to refuse the payment of, as a bill.—*n.* **Dishon'ourer**. [L. *dis*, privative, and **Honour**.]

**Dishonourable**, diz-on'ur-abl, *adj.* having no sense of honour : disgraceful.—*adv.* **Dishon'ourably**. [inclination : unwillingness.

**Disinclination**, dis-in-kli-nā'shun, *n.* want of

**Disincline**, dis-in-klīn', *v.t.* to turn away *inclination* from : to excite the dislike or aversion of. [L. *dis*, priv., and **Incline**.] [averse.

**Disinclined**, dis-in-klīnd', *adj.* not inclined :

**Disincorporate**, dis-in-kor'por-āt, *v.t.* to deprive of *corporate* rights. [L. *dis*, privative, and **Incorporate**.]

**Disinfect**, dis-in-fekt', *v.t.* to free from *infection*.—*n.* **Disinfec'tion**. [L. *dis*, privative, and **Infect**.]

**Disinfectant**, dis-in-fekt'ant, *n.* anything that destroys the causes of *infection*.

**Disingenuous**, dis-in-jen'ū-us, *adj.* not ingenuous : not frank or open : crafty.—*adv.* **Disingen'uously**.—*n.* **Disingen'uousness**. [L. *dis*, negative, and **Ingenuous**.]

**Disinherit**, dis-in-her'it, *v.t.* to cut off from *hereditary* rights : to deprive of an inheritance.—*n.* **Disinher'itance**. [L. *dis*, privative, and **Inherit**.]

**Disintegrate**, dis-in'te-grāt or diz-, *v.t.* to separate into *integrant* parts.—*adj.* **Disin'tegrable**.—*n.* **Disintegra'tion**. [L. *dis*, negative, and **Integrate**.]

**Disinter**, dis-in-tér', *v.t.* to take out of a grave : to bring from obscurity into view.—*n.* **Disinter'ment**. [L. *dis*, negative, and **Inter**.]

**Disinterested**, dis-in'tér-est-ed, *adj.* not interested or influenced by private feelings or considerations : impartial.—*adv.* **Disin'terestedly**.—*n.* **Disin'terestedness**. [L. *dis*, negative, and **Interested**.]

**Disinthral**, dis-in-thrawl', *v.t.* to set free from *thraldom* or oppression. [L. *dis*, negative, and **Inthral**.]

**Disjoin**, dis-join' or diz-, *v.t.* to separate what has been joined. [L. *dis*, negative, and **Join**.]

**Disjoint**, dis-joint', *v.t.* to put out of joint : to separate united parts : to break the natural order or relations of things : to make incoherent.—*n.* **Disjoint'edness**.

**Disjunct**, dis-jungkt', *adj.*, *disjoined*. [L. *disjunctus*, pa.p. of *disjungo—dis*, negative, and *jungo*, to join.]

**Disjunction**, dis-junk'shun, *n.* the act of *disjoining* : disunion : separation.

**Disjunctive**, dis-jungkt'iv, *adj.*, *disjoining* : tending to separate : (*gram.*) uniting sentences but disjoining the sense, or rather, marking an adverse sense.—*n.* a word which disjoins.—*adv.* **Disjunct'ively**. [L. *disjunctivus*.]

**Disk**. Same as **Disc**.

**Dislike**, dis-līk', *v.t.* to be displeased with : to disapprove of : to have an aversion to.—*n.* disinclination : aversion : distaste : disapproval. [L. *dis*, negative, and **Like** ; the genuine Eng. word is **Mislike**.]

**Dislocate**, dis-lō-kāt, *v.t.* to *displace*: to put out of joint. [L. *dis*, negative, and **Locate**.]

**Dislocation**, dis-lō-kā'shun, *n.* a dislocated joint: displacement: (*geol.*) a 'fault,' or displacement of stratified rocks.

**Dislodge**, dis-loj', *v.t.* to drive from a *lodgment* or place of rest: to drive from a place of hiding or of defence.—*v.i.* to go away.—*n.* **Dislodg'ment**. [L. *dis*, privative, and **Lodge**.]

**Disloyal**, dis-loy'al, *adj.* not loyal: false to one's sovereign: faithless: treacherous.—*adv.* **Disloy'ally**.—*n.* **Disloy'alty**. [L. *dis*, negative, and **Loyal**.]

**Dismal**, diz'mal, *adj.* gloomy: dreary: sorrowful: full of horror.—*adv.* **Dis'mally**. [Ety. unknown.]

**Dismantle**, dis-man'tl, *v.t.* to strip: to deprive of furniture, &c. so as to render useless: of a fortified town, to raze the fortifications. [L. *dis*, privative, and **Mantle**.]

**Dismask**, dis-mask', *v.t.* to strip a mask from: to remove a disguise from: to uncover. [L. *dis*, privative, and **Mask**.]

**Dismast**, dis-mast', *v.t.* to deprive of a mast or masts. [L. *dis*, privative, and **Mast**.]

**Dismay**, dis-mā', *v.t.* to terrify: to discourage.—*n.* loss of strength and courage through fear. [A hybrid word, from O. Fr. *desmayer—des* (= L. *dis*), and O. Ger. *magan* = A.S. *magan*, to have might or power. See **May**.]

**Dismember**, dis-mem'bėr, *v.t.* to divide member from member: to separate a limb from the body: to disjoint: to tear to pieces.—*n.* **Dismem'berment**. [L. *dis*, asunder, and **Member**.]

**Dismiss**, dis-mis', *v.t.* to *send away*: to despatch: to discard: to remove from office or employment. [L. *dimitto, dimissus—di*, away from, and *mitto*, to send.]

**Dismissal**, dis-mis'al, **Dismission**, dis-mish'un, *n.* act of sending away: discharge from office or employment.

**Dismount**, dis-mownt', *v.i.* to come down: to come off a horse.—*v.t.* to throw or bring down from any elevated place: to throw off their carriages, as cannon: to unhorse. [L. *dis*, negative, and **Mount**.]

**Disobedience**, dis-o-bē'di-ens, *n.* neglect or refusal to *obey*. [See **Obedience**.]

**Disobedient**, dis-o-bē'di-ent, *adj.* neglecting or refusing to *obey*. [See **Obedient**.]

**Disobey**, dis-o-bā', *v.t.* to neglect or refuse to obey or do what is commanded. [O. Fr. *desobeir—des* (= L. *dis*), and *obeir*, to obey.]

**Disoblige**, dis-o-blīj', *v.t.* to offend by an act of unkindness or incivility: to do something against the wishes of another: to injure slightly. [L. *dis*, negative, and **Oblige**.]

**Disobliging**, dis-o-blīj'ing, *adj.* not obliging: not careful to attend to the wishes of others: unaccommodating: unkind.—*adv.* **Disoblig'ingly**.

**Disorder**, dis-or'dėr, *n.* want of order: confusion: disturbance: breach of the peace: disease.—*v.t.* to throw out of order: to disarrange: to disturb: to produce disease. [Fr. *des* (= L. *dis*), privative, and **Order**.]

**Disorderly**, dis-or'dėr-li, *adj.* out of order: in confusion: irregular: lawless.—*adv.* without order: confusedly: in a lawless manner.

**Disorganise**, dis-or'gan-īz, *v.t.* to destroy the *organic* structure of: to break up a union of parts: to throw into disorder.—*n.* **Disorganisa'tion**. [L. *dis*, negative, and **Organise**.]

**Disown**, diz-ōn', *v.t.* to refuse to own or acknowledge as belonging to one's self: to deny: to renounce. [L. *dis*, negative, and **Own**.]

**Disparage**, dis-par'aj, *v.t.* to dishonour by comparison with what is inferior: to lower in rank or estimation.—*n.* **Dispar'ager**. [O. Fr. *desparager—des* (= L. *dis*), negative, and Low L. *paragium*, equality of birth—L. *par*, equal.]

**Disparagement**, dis-par'aj-ment, *n.* injurious comparison with what is inferior: indignity.

**Disparagingly**, dis-par'aj-ing-li, *adv* in a manner to *disparage* or dishonour.

**Disparity**, dis-par'i-ti, *n.*, inequality. [L. *dis*, negative, and **Parity**.]

**Dispark**, dis-pärk', *v.t.* to throw open inclosed ground. [A hybrid word, from L. *dis*, negative, and **Park**.]

**Dispart**, dis-pärt', *v.t.* to part asunder: to divide, to separate.—*v.i.* to separate.—*n.* the difference between the thickness of metal at the breech and the mouth of a gun. [L. *dis*, asunder, and **Part**.]

**Dispassion**, dis-pash'un, *n.* freedom from *passion*: a calm state of mind. [L. *dis*, negative, and **Passion**.]

**Dispassionate**, dis-pash'un-āt, *adj.* free from *passion*: unmoved by feelings: cool: impartial.—*adv.* **Dispass'ionately**.

**Dispatch**. Same as **Despatch**.

**Dispel**, dis-pel', *v.t.* to *drive away*: to cause to disappear: to banish :—*pr.p.* dispell'ing ; *pa.p.* dispelled'. [L. *dispello—dis*, away from, *pello*, to drive.]

**Dispensable**, dis-pens'a-bl, *adj.* that may be *dispensed*, or dispensed with.—*n.* **Dispens'ableness**.

**Dispensary**, dis-pens'ar-i, *n.* a place where medicines are *dispensed*, especially to the poor, gratis.

**Dispensation**, dis-pen-sā'shun, *n.* the act of *dispensing* or dealing out: the dealing of God with his creatures: the distribution of good and evil in the divine government: license or permission to neglect a rule.

**Dispensative**, dis-pens'a-tiv, **Dispensatory**, dis-pens'a-tor-i, *adj.* granting *dispensation*.—*advs.* **Dispens'atively**, **Dispens'atorily**. [L. *dispensativus, dispensatorius*.]

**Dispense**, dis-pens', *v.t.* to *weigh* or deal out in portions: to distribute: to administer.—**Dispense with**, to permit the want of: to do without.—*n.* **Dispens'er**. [Fr. *dispenser*—L. *dis*, asunder, and *penso*, intensive of *pendo*, to weigh.]

**Dispeople**, dis-pē'pl, *v.t.* to empty of *people* or inhabitants. [L. *dis*, privative, and **People**.]

**Dispermous**, dī-spėrm'us, *adj.* having only *two* seeds. [Gr. *di*, twofold, *sperma*, a seed.]

**Disperse**, dis-pėrs', *v.t.* to *scatter* in all directions: to spread: to diffuse: to drive asunder: to cause to vanish.—*v.i.* to separate: to vanish.—*n.* **Dispers'er**. [L. *dispergo, dispersus—di*, asunder, apart, *spargo*, to scatter.]

**Dispersion**, dis-pėr'shun, *n.* a *scattering*: (*med.*) the removal of inflammation: (*optics*) the separation of light into its different rays.

**Dispersive**, dis-pėrs'iv, *adj.* tending to *disperse*.

**Dispirit**, dis-pir'it, *v.t.* to dishearten: to discourage. [L. *dis*, privative, and **Spirit**.]

**Displace**, dis-plās', *v.t.* to put out of place: to disarrange: to remove from a state, office, or dignity.—*n.* **Displace'ment**, the quantity of water displaced by a ship afloat, and whose weight equals that of the displacing body. [O. Fr. *desplacer*—L. *dis*, privative, and **Place**.]

**Displant**, dis-plant', *v.t.* to remove anything from where it has been *planted* or placed: to drive from an abode. [L. *dis*, privative, and **Plant**.]

**Display**, dis-plā', *v.t.* to *unfold* or spread out : to exhibit : to set out ostentatiously.—*n.* a displaying or unfolding : exhibition : ostentatious show.—*n.* **Display'er**. [O. Fr. *desployer—des* (= L. *dis*), negative, and *ployer*, same as *plier*—L. *plico*, to fold. Doublet, **Deploy**. See **Ply**.]

**Displease**, dis-plēz', *v.t.* to offend : to make angry in a slight degree : to be disagreeable to.—*v.i.* to raise aversion. [L. *dis*, negative, and **Please**.]

**Displeasure**, dis-plezh'ūr, *n.* the feeling of one who is offended : anger : cause of irritation.

**Displume**, dis-plōōm', *v.t.* to deprive of *plumes* or feathers. [L. *dis*, privative, and **Plume**.]

**Dispone**, dis-pōn', *v.t.* (*law*) to make over to another : to convey legally. [L. *dispono*, to arrange.]

**Disport**, dis-pōrt', *v.i.* to divert, amuse, enjoy one's self : to move in gaiety.—*v.t.* to amuse. [O. Fr. *desporter* (with *se*), to carry one's self away from one's work, to amuse one's self, from *des* (= L. *dis*), and *porter*—L. *portare*, to carry, as it were from serious matters. See **Sport**.]

**Disposable**, dis-pōz'a-bl, *adj.* free to be used : not already engaged. [See **Dispose**.]

**Disposal**, dis-pōz'al, *n.* the act of *disposing*: order : arrangement : management : right of bestowing.

**Dispose**, dis-pōz', *v.t.* to arrange : to distribute : to apply to a particular purpose : to bestow : to incline.—**To dispose of**, to apply to any purpose : to part with : to place in any condition.—*n.* **Dispos'er**. [Fr. *disposer*—L. *dis*, asunder, and Fr. *poser*, to place. See **Pose**, *n.*]

**Disposition**, dis-po-zish'un, *n.* arrangement : natural tendency : temper : (*New Test.*) ministry, ministration : (*Scots law*) a giving over to another = (*English*) conveyance or assignment. [Fr.—L., from *dis*, apart, *pono*, to place.]

**Dispossess**, dis-poz-zes', *v.t.* to put out of possession. [L. *d's*, privative, and **Possess**.]

**Dispraise**, dis-prāz', *n.* blame : reproach : dishonour.—*v.t.* to blame : to censure. [L. *dis*, negative, and **Praise**.]

**Dispread**, dis-pred', *v.t.* to *spread* in different ways.—*v.i.* to spread out : to expand. [L. *dis*, asunder, and **Spread**.]

**Disproof**, dis-prōōf', *n.* a *disproving*: refutation.

**Disproportion**, dis-pro-pōr'shun, *n.* want of *proportion*, symmetry, or suitableness of parts : inequality.—*v.t.* to make unsuitable in form or size, &c. [L. *dis*, privative, and **Proportion**.]

**Disproportionable**, dis-pro-pōr'shun-a-bl, **Disproportional**, dis-pro-pōr'shun-al, *adj.* not having *proportion* or symmetry of parts : unsuitable : unequal. —*advs.* **Dispropor'tionably**, **Dispropor'tionally**.

**Disproportionate**, dis-pro-pōr'shun-āt, *adj.* not *proportioned* : unsymmetrical : unsuitable to something else in some respect.—*adv.* **Dispropor'tionately**.—*n.* **Dispropor'tionateness**.

**Disprove**, dis-prōōv', *v.t.* to *prove* to be *false* : to refute. [L. *dis*, negative, and **Prove**.]

**Disputable**, dis'pū-ta-bl, *adj.* that may be *disputed* : of doubtful certainty.—*adv.* **Dis'putably**.—*n.* **Dis'putableness**.

**Disputant**, dis'pū-tant, **Disputer**, dis-pūt'ér, *n.* one who *disputes* or argues : one given to dispute. [ment : an exercise in debate.

**Disputation**, dis-pū-tā'shun, *n.* a contest in argu-

**Disputatious**, dis-pū-tā'shus, **Disputative**, dis-pūt'a-tiv, *adj.* inclined to *dispute*, cavil, or controvert.—*adv.* **Disputa'tiously**.—*n.* **Disputa'tiousness**.

**Dispute**, dis-pūt', *v.t.* to make a subject of argument : to contend for : to oppose by argument :

to call in question.—*v.i.* to argue : to debate.—*n.* a contest with words : an argument : a debate. [Fr. *disputer*—L. *disputare*—*dis*, apart, and *puto*, to think.]

**Disqualify**, dis-kwol'i-fī, *v.t.* to *deprive* of the *qualities* necessary for any purpose : to make unfit : to disable.—*n.* **Disqualifica'tion**. [L. *dis*, privative, and **Qualify**.]

**Disquiet**, dis-kwī'et, *n.* want of *quiet* : uneasiness, restlessness : anxiety.—*v.t.* to render unquiet : to make uneasy : to disturb. [L. *dis*, privative, and **Quiet**.]

**Disquietude**, dis-kwī'et-ūd, *n.* state of *disquiet*.

**Disquisition**, dis-kwi-zish'un, *n.* a *careful* and formal *inquiry* into any matter by arguments, &c. : an elaborate essay.—*adj.* **Disquisi'tional**. [L. *disquisitio—disquiro*, *disquisitus—dis*, intensive, *quæro*, to seek.]

**Disregard**, dis-re-gärd', *v.t.* to pay no attention to.—*n.* want of *attention* : neglect : slight. [L. *dis*, negative, and **Regard**.]

**Disregardful**, dis-re-gärd'fool, *adj.* neglectful : careless : heedless.—*adv.* **Disregard'fully**.

**Disrelish**, dis-rel'ish, *v.t.* to *relish*: to dislike the taste of : to dislike.—*n.* distaste : dislike : some degree of disgust. [L. *dis*, negative, and **Relish**.]

**Disrepair**, dis-re-pär', *n.* state of being *out of repair*. [L. *dis*, negative, and **Repair**.]

**Disreputable**, dis-rep'ū-ta-bl, *adj.* in *bad repute* : discreditable : disgraceful.—*adv.* **Disrep'utably**.

**Disrepute**, dis-re-pūt', **Disreputation**, dis-rep-ū-tā'shun, *n.* ill *character* : discredit. [L. *dis*, negative, and **Repute**.]

**Disrespect**, dis-re-spekt', *n.* want of respect or reverence : incivility. [L. *dis*, negative, and **Respect**.]

**Disrespectful**, dis-re-spekt'fool, *adj.* shewing disrespect : irreverent : uncivil.—*adv.* **Disrespect'-fully**.

**Disrobe**, dis-rōb', *v.t.* to deprive of a *robe* : to undress : to uncover. [L. *dis*, priv., and **Robe**.]

**Disroot**, dis-rōōt', *v.t.* to tear up by the roots.

**Disruption**, dis-rup'shun, *n.* the act of *breaking asunder :* the act of bursting and rending : breach. [L. *disruptio—dirumpo*, *diruptus—dis*, asunder, and *rumpo*, to break.]

**Dissatisfaction**, dis-sat-is-fak'shun, *n.* state of being dissatisfied : discontent : uneasiness.

**Dissatisfactory**, dis-sat-is-fak'tor-i, *adj.* causing dissatisfaction : unable to give content.

**Dissatisfied**, dis-sat'is-fīd, *adj.* not satisfied : discontented : not pleased.

**Dissatisfy**, dis-sat'is-fī, *v.t.* not to satisfy : to make discontented : to displease. [L. *dis*, negative, and **Satisfy**.]

**Dissect**, dis-sekt', *v.t.* to *cut asunder :* to cut into parts for the purpose of minute examination : to divide and examine.—*adj.* **Dissect'ible**. [L. *disseco*, *dissectus—dis*, asunder, in pieces, *seco*, to cut.]

**Dissection**, dis-sek'shun, *n.* the *act* or the art of *cutting in pieces* a plant or animal in order to ascertain the structure of its parts : anatomy.

**Dissector**, dis-sekt'or, *n.* one who dissects.

**Dissemble**, dis-sem'bl, *v.t.* to represent a thing as *unlike* what it actually is : to put an untrue *semblance* or appearance upon : to disguise.—*v.i.* to assume a false appearance : to play the hypocrite.—*n.* **Dissem'bler**. [O. Fr. *dissembler*, from L. *dissimulo—dissimilis*, unlike—*dis*, negative, and *similis*, like.]

**Disseminate**, dis-sem'i-nāt, *v.t.* to *sow* or scatter *abroad :* to propagate : to diffuse.—*ns.* **Dis-**

**semina'tion, Dissem'inator.** [L. *dissemino, disseminatus—dis,* asunder, and *semino,* to sow —*semen, seminis,* seed.]

**Dissension,** dis-sen'shun, *n.* disagreement in opinion : discord : strife.

**Dissent,** dis-sent', *v.i.* to *think differently* : to disagree in opinion : to differ.—*n.* the act of dissenting : difference of opinion : a differing or separation from an established church. [L. *dissentio, dissensus—dis,* apart from, *sentio,* to think. See **Sense.**]

**Dissenter,** dis-sent'ėr, *n.* one who separates from the service and worship of an established church.

**Dissentient,** dis-sen'shent, *adj., dissenting :* declaring dissent : disagreeing.—*n.* one who disagrees : one who declares his dissent. [L. *dissentiens, dissentientis,* pr.p. of *dissentio.*]

**Dissertation,** dis-ėr-tā'shun, *n.* a formal discourse : a treatise.—*adj.* **Disserta'tional.** [L. *dissertatio—disserto,* intensive of *dissero,* to debate, to discuss—*dis,* and *sero,* to put in a row, to join.] [*sertations :* a debater.

**Dissertator,** dis'ėr-tā-tor, *n.* one who writes *dis-*

**Disserve,** dis-sėrv', *v.t.* to do the opposite of *serving :* to injure. [L. *dis,* negative, and **Serve.**]

**Disservice,** dis-sėrv'is, *n.* injury : mischief.

**Disserviceable,** dis-sėrv'is-a-bl, *adj.* not serviceable or useful : injurious : mischievous.

**Dissever,** dis-sev'ėr, *v.t.* to *sever :* to part in two : to separate : to disunite.—*n.* **Dissev'erance,** a dissevering or parting. [L. *dis,* intensive, and **Sever.**]

**Dissident,** dis'i-dent, *adj.* dissenting : not agreeing.—*n.* a dissenter. [L. *dissidens, dissidentis,* pr.p. of *dissideo—dis,* apart, and *sedeo,* to sit.]

**Dissilient,** dis-sil'yent, *adj.,* leaping asunder or bursting open with elastic force.—*n.* **Dissil'ience.** [L. *dissiliens, -entis—dis,* asunder, *salio,* to leap.]

**Dissimilar,** dis-sim'i-lar, *adj.* not similar : unlike in any respect : of different sorts.—*adv.* **Dissim'ilarly.** [L. *dis,* negative, and **Similar.**]

**Dissimilarity,** dis-sim-i-lar'i-ti, **Dissimilitude,** dis-si-mil'i-tūd, *n., unlikeness :* want of resemblance.

**Dissimulation,** dis-sim-ū-lā'shun, *n.* the act of *dissembling :* a hiding under a false appearance : false pretension : hypocrisy.

**Dissipate,** dis'i-pāt, *v.t.* to *throw apart* or *spread abroad :* to scatter : to squander : to waste.— *v.i.* to separate and disappear : to waste away. [L. *dissipo, -atus—dis,* asunder, and obs. *supo,* which appears in *insipo,* to throw into.]

**Dissipation,** dis-i-pā'shun, *n.* dispersion : state of being dispersed : scattered attention : a dissolute course of life.

**Dissociate,** dis-sō'shi-āt, *v.t.* to *separate from* a *society* or company : to disunite.—*n.* **Disso'ciation.** [L. *dis,* asunder, and *socio,* to unite. See **Social.**]

**Dissoluble,** dis'ol-ū-bl, *adj., dissolvable.*—*n.* **Dissolubil'ity,** capacity of being *dissolved.*

**Dissolute,** dis'ol-ūt, *adj., loose,* esp. in morals : lewd : licentious.—*adv.* **Diss'olutely.**—*n.* **Diss'-oluteness.** [See **Dissolve.**]

**Dissolution,** dis-ol-ū'shun, *n.* the breaking up of an assembly : change from a solid to a liquid state : a melting : separation of a body into its original elements : decomposition : destruction : death. [*dissolved* or melted.

**Dissolvable,** diz-zolv'a-bl, *adj.* capable of being **Dissolve,** diz-zolv', *v.t.* to *loose asunder :* to separ-

ate or break up : to melt : to destroy.—*v.i.* to break up : to waste away : to crumble : to melt. [L. *dis,* asunder, and *solvo, solutus,* to loose.]

**Dissolvent,** diz-zolv'ent, *adj.* having power to *dissolve* or melt.—*n.* that which can dissolve or melt. [L., pr.p. of *dissolvo.* See **Dissolve.**]

**Dissonance,** dis'o-nans, *n., disagreement of sound :* want of harmony : discord : disagreement.

**Dissonant,** dis'o-nant, *adj., not agreeing* in *sound :* without concord or harmony : disagreeing. [L. *dis,* apart, *sonans, -antis,* pr.p. of *sono,* to sound.]

**Dissuade,** dis-swād', *v.t.* to *advise against :* to try to divert from anything by advice or persuasion. [L. *dis,* against, and *suadeo, suasus,* to advise.]

**Dissuasion,** dis-swā'zhun, *n.* act of *dissuading :* advice against anything. [See **Dissuade.**]

**Dissuasive,** dis-swā'ziv, *adj.* tending to *dissuade.* —*n.* that which tends to dissuade.—*adv.* **Dissua'sively.**

**Dissyllabic,** dis-sil-lab'ik, *adj.* of *two syllables.*

**Dissyllable,** dis-sil'a-bl, *n.* a word of only *two syllables.* [Gr. *dis,* twice, and **Syllable.**]

**Distaff,** dis'taf, *n.* the *staff* or stick which holds the *bunch* of flax, tow, or wool in spinning. [A.S. *distæf,* compounded of *dis* = Low Ger. *diesse,* the bunch of flax on the staff ; and *stæf* = E. **Staff.** See **Dizen.**]

**Distain,** dis-tān', *v.t.* to stain : to sully. [O. Fr. *desteindre,* to take away the colour of—L. *dis,* privative, and *tingo,* to stain. See **Stain.**]

**Distance,** dis'tans, *n.* space or interval between : remoteness : opposition : reserve of manner.— *v.t.* to place at a distance : to leave at a distance behind. [See **Distant.**]

**Distant,** dis'tant, *adj.* remote, in time, place, or connection : not obvious : indistinct : reserved in manner.—*adv.* **Dis'tantly.** [L. *distans— dis,* apart, and *stans, stantis,* pr.p. of *sto,* to stand.]

**Distaste,** dis-tāst', *n., oppositeness* or aversion of *taste :* dislike of food : dislike : disgust.—*v.t.* to disrelish : to dislike : to loathe. [L. *dis,* negative, and **Taste.**]

**Distasteful,** dis-tāst'fool, *adj.* producing *distaste :* unpleasant to the taste : offensive.—*adv.* **Distaste'fully.**—*n.* **Distaste'fulness.**

**Distemper,** *n.* a kind of painting. See **Destemper.**

**Distemper,** dis-tem'pėr, *n.* a morbid or disorderly state of body or mind : disease, esp. of animals : ill-humour.—*v.t.* to derange the temper : to disorder or disease. [L. *dis,* negative, and **Temper.**]

**Distend,** dis-tend', *v.t.* to *stretch asunder* or in all directions : to swell.—*v.i.* to swell. [L. *dis,* asunder, and *tendo, tensus* or *tentus,* to stretch.]

**Distensible,** dis-ten'si-bl, *adj.* that may be *stretched.*

**Distensive,** dis-ten'siv, *adj., distending,* or capable of being stretched.

**Distention, Distension,** dis-ten'shun, *n.* act of distending or stretching : state of being stretched : breadth.

**Distich,** dis'tik, *n.* a *couple of lines* or *verses,* making complete sense : a couplet. [Gr. *distichos—dis,* twice, and *stichos,* a line, verse.]

**Distil,** dis-til', *v.i.* to fall in *drops :* to flow gently : to use a still.—*v.t.* to let or cause to fall in drops : to convert a liquid into vapour by heat, and then to condense it again : to extract the spirit or essential oil from anything by evaporation and condensation:—*pr.p.* distill'ing : *pa.p.* distilled'. [Fr. *distiller*—L. *de*, down, and *stillo*, to drop—*stilla*, a drop.]

**Distillation**, dis-til-ā'shun, *n.* act or process of *distilling:* that which is distilled.   [tion.

**Distillatory**, dis-til'a-tor-i, *adj.* of or for distilla-

**Distiller**, dis-til'ėr, *n.* one who distils.

**Distillery**, dis-til'ėr-i, *n.* a place for distilling.

**Distinct**, dis-tingkt', *adj.* separate : different : well-defined : clear.—*adv.* **Distinct'ly.**—*n.* **Distinct'ness.** [See **Distinguish**.]

**Distinction** dis-tingk'shun, *n.* separation or division : that which distinguishes : difference : eminence.

**Distinctive**, dis-tingkt'iv, *adj.* marking or expressing *difference.*—*adv.* **Distinct'ively.**—*n.* **Distinct'iveness.**

**Distinguish.** dis-ting'gwish, *v.t.* to *mark off*, set apart : to recognise by characteristic qualities : to discern critically : to separate by a mark of honour : to make eminent or known.—*v.i.* to make or shew distinctions or differences. [L. *distinguo, distinctus*—*dis*, asunder, and *stinguo*, to prick, conn. with Gr. *stizō*, to mark, to prick. See **Sting**.]

**Distinguishable**, dis-ting'gwish-a-bl, *adj.* that may be capable of being *distinguished.*—*adv.* **Disting'uishably.**

**Distort**, dis-tort', *v.t.* to *twist* or turn a *different way:* to force out of the natural or regular shape or direction : to turn aside from the true meaning : to pervert. [L. *dis*, asunder, and *torqueo, tortus*, to twist.]

**Distortion**, dis-tor'shun, *n.* a twisting out of regular shape : crookedness : perversion.

**Distract**, dis-trakt', *v.t.* to *draw in different directions*—applied to the mind or attention : to confuse : to harass : to render crazy.—*adj.* **Distract'ed.**—*adv.* **Distract'edly.** [L. *dis*, asunder, and *traho, tractus*, to draw.]

**Distraction**, dis-trak'shun, *n.* state of being *distracted* : perplexity : agitation : madness.

**Distrain**, dis-trān', *v.t.* to seize, esp. goods, for debt.—*v.i.* to seize the goods of a debtor. [O. Fr. *destraindre*, from L. *dis*, asunder, and *stringo*, to draw tight.]

**Distrainer**, dis-trān'ėr, **Distrainor**, dis-trān'or, *n.* one who distrains or seizes goods for debt.

**Distraint**, dis-trānt', *n.*, seizure of goods for debt.

**Distraught**, dis-trawt', *adj.* distracted : perplexed. [See **Distract**.]

**Distress**, dis-tres', *n.* extreme pain : that which causes suffering : calamity : misfortune : a state of danger : act of distraining goods.—*v.t.* to afflict with pain or suffering : to harass : to grieve : to distrain. [O. Fr. *destresse*; from L. *distringo, districtus*, to pull asunder, in late L. to punish.]

**Distressful**, dis-tres'fool, *adj.* full of distress : calamitous.—*adv.* **Distress'fully.**

**Distributable**, dis-trib'ū-ta-bl, *adj.* that may be *divided.*

**Distribute**, dis-trib'ūt, *v.t.* to *divide* amongst several : to deal out or allot : to classify. [L. *distribuo*—*dis*, asunder, *tribuo, tributus*, to allot.]        [or deals out.

**Distributer**, dis-trib'ū-tėr, *n.* one who distributes

**Distribution**, dis-tri-bū'shun, *n.* allotment : classification

**Distributive**, dis-trib'ū-tiv, *adj.* that distributes, separates, or divides.—*adv.* **Distrib'utively.**

**District**, dis'trikt, *n.* (*orig.*) the territory within which a superior had a right to *distrain* or otherwise exercise authority : a portion of terri-

tory defined or undefined : a region. [L. *districtus*—*distringo*, to draw tight.]

**Distrust**, dis-trust', *n.* want of trust : want of faith or confidence : doubt.—*v.t.* to have no trust in : to disbelieve : to doubt. [L. *dis*, privative, and **Trust**.]

**Distrustful**, dis-trust'fool, *adj.* full of distrust : apt to distrust : suspicious.—*adv.* **Distrust'fully.**—*n.* **Distrust'fulness.**

**Disturb**, dis-turb', *v.t.* to throw into confusion : to agitate : to disquiet : to interrupt.—*n.* **Disturb'er.** [L. *dis*, asunder, and *turbo*, to agitate—*turba*, a crowd.]

**Disturbance**, dis-turb'ans, *n.*, *agitation :* tumult : interruption : perplexity.

**Disunion**, dis-ūn'yun, *n.*, *want of union:* breaking up of union or concord : separation.

**Disunite**, dis-ū-nīt', *v.t.* to separate what is *united:* to sever or sunder.—*v.i.* to fall asunder : to part. [L. *dis*, privative, and **Unite**.]

**Disusage**, dis-ūz'āj, *n.* gradual cessation of *use* or custom. [L. *dis*, privative, and **Usage**.]

**Disuse**, dis-ūs', *n.* cessation or giving up of *use* or custom. [L. *dis*, privative, and **Use**.]

**Disuse**, dis-ūz', *v.t.* to cease to *use* or practise.

**Ditch**, dich, *n.* a trench *dug* in the ground : any long narrow receptacle for water.—*v.i.* to make a ditch or ditches.—*v.t.* to dig a ditch in or around : to drain by ditches. [A corr. of **Dike**.]

**Ditcher**, dich'ėr, *n.* a *ditch*-maker.

**Ditheism**, dī'thē-izm, *n.* the doctrine of the existence of *two gods*. [Gr. *di*, two, and *theos*, a god.]

**Dithyramb**, dith'i-ram, **Dithyrambus**, dith-i-ram'bus, *n.* an ancient Greek hymn sung in honour of Bacchus : a short poem of a like character. [Gr. *Dithyrambos*, whose origin is unknown.]

**Dithyrambic**, dith-i-ram'bik, *adj.* of or like a *dithyramb:* wild and boisterous.

**Dittany**, dit'a-ni, *n.* a genus of aromatic perennial plants, formerly much used medicinally as a tonic. [L. *dictamnus*, Gr. *diktamnos*—*Diktē*, a mountain in Crete, where the plant grows abundantly.]

**Ditto**, dit'ō, contracted **Do.**, *n.* that which has been *said:* the same thing.—*adv.* as before, or aforesaid : in like manner. [It. *detto*—L. *dictum*, said, pa.p. of *dico*, to say.]

**Ditty**, dit'i, *n.* a song : a little poem to be sung. [O. Fr. *dite*—L. *dictatum*, neuter of *dictatus*, perf.p. of *dicto*, to dictate.]

**Diuretic**, dī-ū-ret'ik, *adj.* tending to excite the *passing through* or discharge of *urine.*—*n.* a medicine causing this discharge. [Fr.—Gr. *diourētikos*—*dia*, through, and *ouron*, urine.]

**Diurnal**, dī-ur'nal, *adj.*, *daily :* relating to or performed in a day.—*n.* in the R. C. Church, a breviary with daily services.—*adv.* **Diur'nally.** [L. *diurnus*—*dies*, a day. See **Journal**.]

**Divan**, di-van', *n.* the Turkish council of state : a court of justice : used poetically of any council or assembly : a council-chamber with cushioned seats : a sofa : a smoking-room : a collection of poems. [Arab. and Pers. *díwán*, a tribunal.]

**Divaricate**, dī-var'i-kāt, *v.i.* to part into two branches, to fork : to diverge.—*v.t.* to divide into two branches.—*n.* **Divarica'tion.** [L. *divarico, divaricatus*—*dis*, asunder, and *varico*, to spread the legs—*varus*, bent apart.]

**Dive**, dīv, *v.i.* to *dip* or plunge into water : to plunge or go deeply into any matter. [A.S. *dufan;* Ice. *dyfa.* See **Dip**.]

**Diver**, dīv'ėr, *n.* one who *dives :* a bird very expert at diving.

**Diverge**, di-vèrj', *v.i.* to incline or *turn asunder*: to tend from a common point in different directions.—*adv.* **Diverg'ingly**. [L. *dis*, asunder, *vergo*, to incline.]

**Divergence**, di-vèrj'ens, **Divergency**, di-vèrj'en-si, *n.* a going apart: tendency to recede from one point.     [receding from one point.

**Divergent**, di-vèrj'ent, *adj* tending to *diverge*:

**Divers**, dī'vèrz, *adj.* sundry: several: more than one: (*b.*) same as **Diverse**. [See **Divert**.]

**Diverse**, dī'vèrs or dī-vèrs', *adj.* different: unlike: multiform: various.—*adv.* **Di'versely** or **Diverse'ly**. [See **Divert**.]

**Diversify**, di-vèr'si-fī, *v.t.* to *make diverse* or different: to give variety to:—*pr.p.* diver'sifying; *pa.p.* diver'sified.—*n.* **Diversifica'tion**. [L. *diversus*, and *facio*, to make.]

**Diversion**, di-vèr'shun, *n.* act of *diverting* or turning aside: that which diverts: amusement, recreation: something done to turn the attention of an enemy from the principal point of attack.    [difference: unlikeness: variety.

**Diversity**, di-vèr'si-ti, *n.* state of being *diverse*:

**Divert**, di-vèrt', *v.t.* to *turn aside*: to change the direction of: to turn the mind from business or study: to amuse.—*adj.* **Divert'ing**.—*adv.* **Divert'ingly**. [L. *diverto, diversus—dis*, aside, and *verto*, to turn.]

**Divest**, di-vest', *v.t.* to strip or deprive of anything. [L. *dis*, priv., and *vestio*, to clothe—*vestis*, a garment.]

**Divide**, di-vīd', *v.t.* to *part asunder*: to part among, to allot, &c.: to set at variance: to separate into two parts (as in voting).—*v.i.* to part or open: to break friendship: to vote by separating into two bodies.—*adv.* **Divid'edly**. [L. *divido, divisus—dis*, asunder, and root *vid*, to separate.]

**Dividend**, div'i-dend, *n.* that which is to be *divided*: the share of a sum divided that falls to each individual. [L. *dividendum—divido*.]

**Divider**, di-vīd'èr, *n.* he or that which divides.

**Divination**, div'i-nā-shun, *n.* the act or practice of *divining*: prediction: conjecture.

**Divine**, di-vīn', *adj.* belonging to or proceeding from *God*: devoted to God's service: holy: sacred: excellent in the highest degree.—*n.* one skilled in divine things: a minister of the gospel: a theologian.—*v.t.* to foresee or foretell as if divinely inspired: to guess or make out.—*v.i.* to profess or practise divination: to have forebodings.—*adv.* **Divine'ly**. [L. *divinus*, from *divus, deus*, a god.]

**Diviner**, di-vīn'èr, *n.* one who *divines* or professes divination: a conjecturer.

**Diving-bell**, dīv'ing-bel, *n.* a hollow vessel orig. *bell-shaped*, air-tight except at the bottom, in which one may descend into and work under water. [See **Dive**.

**Divining-rod**, di-vīn'ing-rod, *n.* a rod usually of hazel used by those professing to discover water or metals under ground.

**Divinity**, di-vin'i-ti, *n.* godhead: the nature or essence of God: God: a celestial being: any god: the science of divine things: theology. [See **Divine**.]

**Divisibility**, di-viz-i-bil'i-ti, *n.* quality of being divisible or separable.

**Divisible**, di-viz'i-bl, *adj.* capable of being *divided* or separated.—*adv.* **Divis'ibly**.

**Division**, di-vizh'un, *n.* act of *dividing*: state of being divided: that which divides: a partition: a barrier: the portion divided or separated: separation: difference in opinion, &c.: dis-

union: (*arith.*) the rule or process of finding how many times one number is contained in another.

**Divisional**, di-vizh'un-al, *adj.* pertaining to or marking a *division* or separation.

**Divisive**, di-vī'ziv, *adj.* forming *division* or separation: creating discord.

**Divisor**, di-vī'zor, *n.* (*arith.*) the number which *divides* the dividend.

**Divorce**, di-vōrs', *n.* the legal *separation* of husband and wife: the sentence by which a marriage is dissolved.—*v.t.* to separate: to sunder: to dissolve the marriage-contract of: to put away.—*n.* **Divorc'er**. [Fr.—L. *divortium—divortere*, another form of *divertere*. See **Divert**.]

**Divorcement**, di-vōrs'ment, *n.* (*B.*) divorce.

**Divulge**, di-vulj', *v.t.* to spread abroad among the *vulgar* or the *people*: to make public: to reveal. [L. *dis*, among, and *vulgus*, the common people. See **Folk**.]

**Divulsion**, di-vul'shun, *n.* act of *pulling* or rending *asunder* or away. [L. *dis*, asunder, and *vello, vulsus*, to pull.]

**Divulsive**, di-vul'siv, *adj.* tending to *pull asunder*.

**Dizen**, dī'zn or diz'n, *v.t.* (*obs.*) to dress: to deck: to dress gaudily. [Orig. to put a bunch of flax on the distaff, from an E. form found also in Low Ger. *diesse*, the bunch of flax on the distaff. See **Distaff**.]

**Dizziness**, diz'i-nes, *n.* giddiness.

**Dizzy**, diz'i, *adj.*, *dazed*: giddy: confused: causing giddiness: unthinking: heedless.—*v.t.* to make dizzy: to confuse. [A.S. *dysig*, foolish, silly; O. Dut. *duysigh*; Dan. *dösig*, drowsy; conn. with E. **Daze**, **Doze**.]

**Do**, dōō, *v.t.* to perform any action: to bring about or effect: to accomplish or finish: to prepare: to put or bring into any form or state. —To do on, to don or put on: to do off, to doff or put off: to do away, to remove or destroy: to be done for, to be defeated or ruined.—*v.i.* to act or behave:—*pr.p.* do'ing; *pa.t.* did; *pa.p.* done (dun). [A.S. *don*; Dut. *doen*, Ger. *thun*; conn. with Gr. *tithemi*, to put, place.]

**Do**, dōō, *v.i.* to fare or get on, as to health: to succeed: to suit or avail. [Prov. E. *dow*, to avail, to be worth; from A.S. *dugan*, to be worth; Ger. *taugen*, to be strong, to be worth. See **Doughty**.]

**Docile**, dō'sīl or dos'il, *adj.*, *teachable*: ready to learn: easily managed. [L. *docilis—doceo*, to teach.]

**Docility**, do-sil'i-ti, *n.*, *teachableness*: aptness.

**Dock**, dok, *n.* a troublesome weed with large leaves and a long root, difficult to eradicate. [A.S. *docce*; prob. from Gael. *dogha*, a burdock; perhaps allied to Gr. *daukos*, a kind of carrot.]

**Dock**, dok, *v.t.* to *cut short*: to curtail: to cut off: to clip.—*n.* the part of a tail left after clipping. [W. *tociaw*, to cut short; cf. Ice. *dockr*, a stumpy tail.]

**Dock**, dok, *n.* an inclosure or artificial basin near a harbour or river, for the reception of vessels: the box in court where the accused stands.—*v.t.* to place in a dock. [O. Dut. *dokke*; perh. from Low L. *doga*, a canal—Gr. *dochē*, a receptacle —*dechomai* to receive.]

**Dockage**, dok'āj, *n.* a charge for the use of a *dock*.

**Docket** dok'et, *n.* a summary of a larger writing: a bill or ticket affixed to anything: a label: a list or register of cases in court.—*v.t.* to make a summary of the heads of a writing: to enter in a book: to mark the contents of papers on the back:—*pr.p.* dock'eting; *pa.p.* dock'eted. [Dim. of **Dock**, to curtail.]

**Dockyard**, dok'yärd, *n.* a *yard* or store near a *dock*, where ships are built and naval stores kept.

**Doctor**, dok'tur, *n.* one who has received from a university the highest degree in a faculty: a physician.—*adj.* **Doc'toral.** [L. (*lit.*) *a teacher*—*doceo*, to teach.]

**Doctorate**, dok'tur-āt, *n.* a *doctor's* degree.

**Doctrinal**, dok'trin-al, *adj.* relating to or containing *doctrine*: relating to the act of teaching.—*adv.* **Doc'trinally.**

**Doctrine**, dok'trin, *n.* a thing *taught*: a principle of belief: what the Scriptures teach on any subject: (*B.*) act or manner of teaching. [See **Doctor.**]

**Document**, dok'ū-ment, *n.* a paper containing information or the proof of anything. [L. *documentum*—*doceo*, to teach.]

**Documental**, dok-ū-ment'al, **Documentary**, dok-ū-ment'ar-i, *adj.* relating to or found in *documents.*

**Dodecagon**, dō-dek'a-gon, *n.* a plane figure having *twelve* equal *angles* and sides. [Gr. *dōdeka*, twelve, and *gōnia*, an angle.]

**Dodecahedron**, dō-dek-a-hē'dron, *n.* a solid figure, having *twelve* equal pentagonal *bases* or faces. [Gr. *dōdeka*, twelve, and *hedra*, a base, a side.]

**Dodge**, doj, *v.i.* to start aside or shift about: to evade or use mean tricks: to shuffle or quibble.—*v.t.* to evade by a sudden shift of place.—*n.* an evasion: a trick: a quibble.—*n.* **Dodg'er.** [Ety. dub.]

**Dodo**, dō'dō, *n.* a large, clumsy bird, now extinct, once found in Mauritius and Madagascar. [Port. *doudo*, silly.]

**Doe**, dō, *n.* the female of the fallow-deer or buck. [A.S. *da*; Dan. *daa*, a deer.]

**Does**, duz, third pers. sing. pres. ind. of **Do.**

**Doeskin**, dō'skin, *n.* the skin of a doe: a twilled cloth, named from its likeness to the skin of a doe.

**Doff**, dof, *v.t.* to *do* or take *off*: to rid one's self of. [A contr. of *do off*.]

**Dog**, dog, *n.* a domestic quadruped: a term of contempt: one of two constellations of stars: an andiron: an iron hook for holding logs of wood.—*v.t.* to follow as a *dog*: to follow and watch constantly: to worry with importunity:—*pr.p.* dogg'ing; *pa.p.* dogged'.—*n.* **Dogg'er.** [Not in A.S.; Dut. *dog*, a mastiff; Ger. *dogge, docke.*]

**Dog-brier**, dog'-brī'ėr, *n.* the *brier dog*rose.

**Dogcart**, dog'kärt, *n.* a one-horse *carriage* for sportsmen, so called from dogs being carried inside. [very cheap.]

**Dogcheap**, dog'chēp, *adj., cheap* as *dog's*-meat:

**Dogday**, dog'dā, *n.* one of the *days* when the *Dogstar* rises and sets with the sun, between the end of July and the beginning of September.

**Doge**, dōj, *n.* formerly the chief-magistrate in Venice and Genoa. [It., prov. for *duce* = E. *duke*—L. *dux*, a leader—*duco*, to lead.]

**Dogfish**, dog'fish, *n.* a species of British shark, so named from their habit of following their prey like *dogs* hunting in packs.

**Dogged**, dog'ed, *adj.* surly like an angry *dog*: sullen: obstinate.—*adv.* **Dogg'edly.**—*n.* **Dogg'edness.**

**Doggerel**, dog'ėr-el, *n.* irregular measures in burlesque poetry, so named in contempt: worthless verses.—*adj.* irregular: mean. [From **Dog.**]

**Doggish**, dog'ish, *adj.* like a *dog*: churlish: brutal.—*adv.* **Dogg'ishly.**—*n.* **Dogg'ishness.**

**Dogma**, dog'ma, *n.* a settled opinion: a principle or tenet: a doctrine laid down with authority.

[Gr., an opinion, from *dokeō*, to think, allied to L. *decet.* See **Decent.**]

**Dogmatic**, dog-mat'ik, **Dogmatical**, dog-mat'-ik-al, *adj.* pertaining to a *dogma*: asserting a thing as if it were a dogma: asserting positively: overbearing.—*adv.* **Dogmat'ically.**

**Dogmatise**, dog'ma-tīz, *v.i.* to state one's opinion *dogmatically* or arrogantly.—*n.* **Dog'matiser**

**Dogmatism**, dog'ma-tizm, *n., dogmatic* or positive assertion of opinion.

**Dogmatist**, dog'ma-tist, *n.* one who makes positive assertions.

**Dogrose**, dog'rōz, *n.* the *rose* of the *dog*-brier.

**Dog's-ear**, dogz'-ėr, *n.* the corner of the leaf of a book turned down, like a *dog's ear.*—*v.t.* to turn down the corners of leaves:—*pa.p.* dog's'-eared.

**Dogstar**, dog'stär, *n.* Sirius, a *star* of the first magnitude, whose rising and setting with the sun gave name to the *dog*days.

**Doily**, doi'li, *n.* a small napkin used at dessert. [Prob. from Dut. *dwaal* = E. *towel.*]

**Doings**, dōō'ingz, *n.pl., things done*, events: behaviour.

**Doit**, doit, *n.* a small Dutch coin worth about half a farthing: a thing of little or no value. [Dut. *duit.* Origin dub.]

**Dole**, dōl, *v.t.* to *deal out* in small portions.—*n.* a share distributed: something given in charity: a small portion. [From root of **Deal**, to divide.]

**Dole**, dōl, *n.* (*obs.*) *pain: grief:* heaviness at heart. [O. Fr. *doel*, Fr. *deuil*, grief—L. *doleo*, to feel pain.]

**Doleful**, dōl'fool, *adj.* full of *dole* or grief: melancholy.—*adv.* **Dole'fully.**—*n.* **Dole'fulness.**

**Dolesome**, dōl'sum, *adj.* dismal.—*adv.* **Dole'-somely.**

**Doll**, dol, *n.* a puppet or toy-baby for a child. [Dut. *dollen*, to sport, O. Dut. *dol*, a whipping-top; cf. *dol*, mad; or perh. familiar for *Dorothy.*]

**Dollar**, dol'ar, *n.* a silver coin of the United States, worth 100 cents, or about 4*s.* 2*d.* sterling. [Ger., short for *Joachimsthaler*, because first coined at the silver mines in Joachimsthal (Joachim's dale) in Bohemia.

**Dolmen**, dol'men, *n.* a *stone table:* an ancient structure of two or more unhewn stones placed erect in the earth and supporting a large stone. [Celtic *daul*, table, *maen*, a stone.]

**Dolomite**, dol'o-mīt, *n.* a magnesian limestone, so called from the French geologist *Dolomieu.*

**Dolor, Dolour**, dō'lor, *n., pain: grief:* anguish. [L.]

**Dolorific**, dol-or-if'ik, *adj., causing* or expressing *dolor*, pain, or grief. [L. *dolor, facio*, to make.]

**Dolorous**, dol'or-us, *adj.* full of *dolor*, pain, or grief: doleful.—*adv.* **Dol'orously.** [L. *dolorosus.*]

**Dolphin**, dol'fin, *n.* an animal of the whale kind, found in all seas, about 8 or 10 feet long: the coryphene, a fish about 5 feet in length, noted for the brilliancy of its colours when dying. [O. Fr. *daulphin*—L. *delphinus.*]

**Dolt**, dōlt, *n.* a *dull* or stupid fellow. [Dolt = *dulled* or blunted. See **Dull.**]

**Doltish**, dōlt'ish, *adj.* dull: stupid.—*adv.* **Dolt'-ishly.**—*n.* **Dolt'ishness.**

**Domain**, do-mān', *n.* what one is *master of* or has *dominion* over: an estate: territory. [Fr. *domaine*—L. *dominium, dominus*, a master.]

**Dome**, dōm, *n.* a structure raised above the roof of large buildings, usually hemispherical: a large *cupola*: a cathedral: (*poet.*) a building.—*adj.* **Domed'**, having a dome. [Fr. *dôme*, It. *duomo*, first meant a town-hall or public building; then the cupola on such a building; It. *duomo* and Ger. *dom* are applied to the principal church of a place with or without a cupola. —Gr. and L. *domus*, a house, a temple—Gr. *demo*, to build.]

**Domesday-** or **Doomsday-book**, dōōmz'dā-book, *n.* a *book* compiled by order of William the Conqueror, containing a survey of all the lands in England, their value, owners, &c.; so called from its authority in *doom* or judgment on the matters contained in it.

**Domestic**, do-mes'tik, *adj.* belonging to the *house*: remaining much at home, private: tame: not foreign.—*n.* a servant in the house.—*adv.* Domes'tically.—*n.* Domestic'ity. [L. *domesticus* —*domus*, a house.]

**Domesticate**, do-mes'tik-āt, *v.t.* to make *domestic* or familiar: to tame.—*n.* Domestica'tion.

**Domicile**, dom'i-sil, *n.* a *house*: an abode.—*v.t.* to establish a fixed residence.—*adj.* Domicil'iary. [L. *domicilium*—*domus*, a house.]

**Domiciliate**, do-mi-sil'yāt, *v.t.* to establish in a permanent residence.—*n.* Domicilia'tion.

**Dominant**, dom'in-ant, *adj.* prevailing: predominant.—*n.* (*music*) the fifth note of the scale in its relation to the first and third. [L. *dominans, -antis*, pr.p. of *dominor*, to be master.]

**Dominate**, dom'in-āt, *v.t.* to be *lord* over: to govern: to prevail over. [L. *dominor*, to be master—*dominus*, lord—*domare*=E. **Tame**.]

**Domination**, dom-in-ā'shun, *n.*, *government*: absolute authority: tyranny. [L. *dominatio*.]

**Dominative**, dom'in-a-tiv, *adj.*, *governing*: arbitrary. [command haughtily.

**Domineer**, dom-in-ēr', *v.i.* to *rule* arbitrarily: to

**Dominical**, do-min'ik-al, *adj.* belonging to Our *Lord*, as the Lord's Prayer, the Lord's Day. [L. *dominicus*—*dominus*, lord, master.]

**Dominican**, do-min'i-kan, *adj.* belonging to St *Dominic* or to the Dominicans.—*n.* a friar or monk of the order of St Dominic, founded early in the thirteenth century.

**Dominion**, do-min'yun, *n.*, *lordship*: highest power and authority: control: the country or persons governed.—*pl.* (*B.*) angelic and powerful spirits.

**Domino**, dom'i-no, *n.* a cape with a hood worn by a *master* or by a priest: a long cloak of black silk, with a hood, used for disguise.—*pl.* Dom'inoes (-nōz), the name of a game, so called because the pieces are (partly) coloured black. [Sp. *domine*, a master or teacher.]

**Don**, don, *n.* a Spanish title, corresponding to English Sir, formerly applied only to noblemen, now to all classes.—*fem.* Donn'a. [Sp., from L. *dominus*.]

**Don**, don, *v.t.* to *do* or put *on*: to assume:—*pr.p.* donn'ing; *pa.p.* donned'. [A contr. of *do on*.]

**Donation**, do-nā'shun, *n.* act of *giving*: that which is given, a gift of money or goods: (*law*) the act by which a person freely transfers his title to anything to another. [L. *donatio*—*dono*, *donatum*—*donum*, a gift—*do*, to give.]

**Donative**, don'a-tiv, *n.* a *gift*: a gratuity: a benefice presented by the founder or patron without reference to the bishop.—*adj.* vested or vesting by donation. [L. *donativum*.]

**Done**, dun, *pa.p.* of Do.

**Donee**, do-nē', *n.* one who receives a *gift*.

**Donjon**, dun'jun, *n.* a strong central tower in ancient castles, to which the garrison retreated when hard pressed. [Fr., from Low L. *domjio* = *domnio* for Low L. *dominio* (= L. *dominium*, dominion), because the tower *dominated* over the rest. See **Dungeon**.]

**Donkey**, dong'ke, *n.* the ass. [= *Dun-ik-ie*, a double dim. of **Dun**, from its colour.]

**Donor**, dō'nor, *n.* a *giver*: a benefactor.

**Doom**, dōōm, *n.*, *judgment*: condemnation: destiny: ruin: final judgment.—*v.t.* to pronounce judgment on: to sentence: to condemn:—*pr.p.* dōōm'ing; *pa.p.* dōōmed'. [A.S. *dom*, judgment: allied to Gr. *themis*, justice.]

**Doomsday**, dōōmz'dā, *n.* the *day of doom*, the day when the world will be judged.

**Door**, dōr, *n.* the usual entrance into a house or into a room: the wooden frame on hinges closing up the entrance: a means of approach or access. [A.S. *duru*; Gr. *thura*, L. *fores* (pl.), a door, allied to Sans. *dvar*, an opening, from a root meaning to blow.]

**Doquet**, dok'et, a form of **Docket**.

**Dor, Dorr**, dor, *n.* a species of beetle, so called from its *droning* sound. [A.S. *dora*, a drone, locust.]

**Doree**, do-rē' or dōr'ā, *n.* a fish of a *golden-yellow* colour, called also **Dory** and **John Doree**. [**Doree** is the Fr. *dorée*, from verb *dorer*, to gild —L. *deaurare*, to gild—*de*, of, with, and *aurum*, gold. John is simply the ordinary name.]

**Doric**, dor'ik, *adj.* belonging to *Doris* in Greece: denoting one of the Grecian orders of architecture: a dialect of the Greek language distinguished by the use of broad vowel sounds: any dialect having this character, as Scotch. [Fr. *dorique*, from L. *Doricus*—Gr. *Dōris*.]

**Dormancy**, dor'man-si, *n.* quiescence.

**Dormant**, dor'mant, *adj.*, *sleeping*: at rest: not used: in a sleeping posture: (*arch.*) leaning.— *n.* a crossbeam: a joist. [Fr., pr.p. of *dormir*, from L. *dormio*, to sleep.]

**Dormer-window**, dor'mer-win'dō, *n.* a vertical window, esp. of a *sleeping*-room (formerly called *dormer*), on the sloping roof of a house. [Fr. *dormir*, to sleep.]

**Dormitory**, dor'mi-tor-i, *n.* a large *sleeping*-chamber with many beds. [L. *dormitorium*—*dormio*, to sleep.]

**Dormouse**, dor'mows (*pl.* Dor'mice), *n.* a gnawing animal, intermediate between the squirrel and the rat, so called because torpid in winter. [Prob. from a Prov. E. *dor*, to sleep, and **Mouse**.]

**Dorsal**, dor'sal, *adj.* pertaining or belonging to the *back*. [L. *dorsum*, the back.]

**Dory**. See **Doree**.

**Dose**, dōs, *n.* the quantity of medicine *given* to be taken at one time: a portion: anything disagreeable that must be taken.—*v.t.* to order or give in doses: to give anything nauseous to. [Fr., from Gr. *dosis*, a giving—*didōmi*, to give.]

**Dost**, dust, second pers. sing. pres. ind. of Do.

**Dot**, dot, *n.* any small mark made with a pen or sharp point.—*v.t.* to mark with dots: to diversify with objects.—*v.i.* to form dots:—*pr.p.* dott'ing; *pa.p.* dott'ed. [Ety. dub.]

**Dotage**, dōt'āj, *n.* a doting: childishness of old age: excessive fondness.

**Dotal**, dō'tal, *adj.* pertaining to *dowry* or to dower. [L. *dotalis*—*dos, dotis*, a dowry.]

**Dotard**, dōt'ard, *n.* one who *dotes*: one shewing the weakness of old age, or excessive fondness.

**Dotation**, do-tā'shun, *n.* the act of bestowing a *dowry* on a woman: an endowment. [Low L. *dotatio*.]

**Dote**, dōt, *v.i.* to be weakly affectionate: to shew excessive love.—*adv.* Dot'ingly. [E.; Dut. *doten*, to be silly, Scot. *doitet*, stupid; Fr. *radoter*, to rave, is from the same root.]

---

fāte, fär; mē, hėr; mīne; mōte; mūte; mōōn; *th*en.　　137

**Doth**, duth, third pers. sing. pres. ind. of **Do**.

**Double**, dub'l, *adj.*, *twofold*: twice as much: two of a sort together: in pairs: acting two parts, insincere.—*adv.* **Doub'ly**. [Fr.—L. *duplus—duo*, two, and *plus*, akin to *plenus*, full]

**Double**, dub'l, *v.t.* to multiply by *two*: to fold.—*v.i.* to increase to twice the quantity: to wind in running.—*n.* twice as much: a duplicate: one's wraith or apparition: a trick.

**Double-bass**, dub'l-bās, *n.* the lowest-toned musical instrument of the violin form.

**Double-dealing**, dub'l-dēl'ing, *n.* insincere dealing: duplicity.

**Double-entry**, dub'l-en'tri, *n.* book-keeping in which *two entries* are made of every transaction.

**Doubleness**, dub'l-nes, *n.* duplicity.

**Doublet**, dub'let, *n.* a pair: an inner garment: name given to words that are really the same, but vary somewhat in spelling and signification, as *desk*, *disc* and *dish*, *describe* and *descry*. [O. Fr., dim. of *double*.]

**Doubloon**, dub-lōōn', *n.* a Sp. gold coin, so called because it is *double* the value of a pistole.

**Doubt**, dowt, *v.i.* to waver in opinion: to be uncertain: to hesitate: to suspect.—*v.t.* to hold in doubt: to distrust. [O. Fr. *doubter—*L. *dubito*, from root *dub* in *dubius*, doubtful.]

**Doubt**, dowt, *n.* uncertainty of mind: suspicion: fear: a thing doubted or questioned.—*n.* **Doubt'er**.—*adv.* **Doubt'ingly**.]

**Doubtful**, dowt'fool, *adj.* full of doubt: undetermined: not clear: not secure: suspicious: not confident.—*adv.* **Doubt'fully**.—*n.* **Doubt'fulness**. [tainly.—*adv.* **Doubt'lessly**.]

**Doubtless**, dowt'les, *adv.* without doubt: cer-

**Douceur**, dōō-sėr', *n.* sweetness of manner: something intended to please, a present or a bribe. [Fr., from *doux*, *douce—*L. *dulcis*, sweet.]

**Douche**, dōōsh, *n.* a jet of water *directed* upon the body from a pipe. [Fr.—It. *doccia*, a water-pipe, from L. *duco*, to lead.]

**Dough**, dō, *n.* a mass of flour or meal moistened and kneaded, but not baked. [A.S. *dah*; Ger. *teig*, Ice. *deig*, dough, from a root found in Goth. *deigan*, to knead: conn. with **Dike**, and with L. *fi(n)go*, to mould.]

**Doughty**, dow'ti, *adj.*, *able*, *strong*: brave. [A.S. *dyhtig*, valiant—*dugan*, to be strong; Ger. *tüchtig*, solid, able—*taugen*, to be strong. See **Do**, far to get or get on.]

**Doughy**, dō'i, *adj.* like *dough*: soft.

**Douse**, dows, *v.t.* to plunge into water: to slacken suddenly, as a sail.—*v.i.* to fall suddenly into water. [Ety. unknown.]

**Dove**, duv, *n.* a pigeon: a word of endearment. [A.S. *duva—dūfan*, to dive; perh. from its habit of ducking the head.]

**Dovecot**, duv'kot, **Dovecote**, duv'kōt, *n.* a small cot or a box in which pigeons breed.

**Dovelet**, duv'let, *n.* a young or small *dove*.

**Dovetail**, duv'tāl, *n.* a mode of fastening boards together by fitting pieces shaped like a *dove's tail* spread out into corresponding cavities.—*v.t.* to fit one thing into another.

**Dowable**, dow'a-bl, *adj.* that may be *endowed*: entitled to *dower*.

**Dowager**, dow'a-jėr, *n.* a widow with a *dower* or jointure: a title given to a widow to distinguish her from the wife of her husband's heir. [O. Fr. *douagiere—*Low L. *dotar:um—*L. *dotare*, to endow. See **Dower**.]

**Dower**, dow'ėr, *n.* a jointure, that part of the husband's property which his widow enjoys during her life—sometimes used for **Dowry**.—*adjs.*

**Dow'ered**, furnished with dower, **Dow'erless**, without dower. [Fr. *douaire—*Low L. *doarium*, *dotarium—*L. *doto*, to endow—*dos*, *dotis*, a dowry—*do*, Gr. *di-dō-mi*, to give.]

**Dowlas**, dow'las, *n.* a coarse linen cloth. [Fr. *douilleux—douille*, soft—L. *ductilis*, pliant—*duco*, to draw.]

**Down**, down, *n.* the soft hair under the feathers of fowls: the hairy covering of the seeds of certain plants: anything which soothes or invites to repose. [From root of Ice. *dunn*, Ger. *dunst*, vapour, dust. See **Dust**.]

**Down**, down, *n.* a bank of sand thrown up by the sea.—*pl.* a tract of hilly land, used for pasturing sheep. [A.S. *dun*, a hill (cog. with *tun*, a fort), found in all the Teut. and Romance languages: prob. from Celt. *dun*, which is found in many names of places, as Dunkeld.]

**Down**, down, *adv.* from a higher to a lower position: on the ground: from earlier to later times.—*prep.* along a descent: from a higher to a lower position or state. [A corr. of M.E. *a-down*, *adun—*A.S. *of dune*, 'from the hill'—A.S. *dun*, a hill. See **Down**, a bank of sand.]

**Downcast**, down'kast, *adj.*, *cast* or bent *downward*: dejected: sad. [reputation: ruin.

**Downfall**, down'fal, *n.* sudden loss of rank or

**Downhearted**, down'hart-ed, *adj.* dejected in spirits. [easy.

**Downhill**, down'hil, *adj.* descending: sloping:

**Downright**, down'rīt, *adj.* plain: open: artless: unceremonious.—*adv.* **Down'right**.

**Downward**, down'ward, **Downwards**, down'wardz, *adv.* in a *direction down*: towards a lower place or condition: from the source: from a time more ancient. [A.S. *adunweard—adun*, *weard*. direction. See **Down**, *adv.*]

**Downward**, down'ward, *adj.* moving or tending *down* (in any sense).

**Downy**, down'i, *adj.* covered with or made of *down*: like down: soft: soothing.

**Dowry**, dow'ri, *n.* the property which a woman brings to her husband at marriage—sometimes used for **Dower**. [Orig. *dower-y*. See **Dower**.]

**Doxology**, doks-ol'o-ji, *n.* a hymn expressing praise and honour to God. [Gr. *doxologia—doxologos*, giving glory—*doxa*, praise—*dokeō*, to think, and *legō*, to speak.]

**Doze**, dōz, *v.i.* to *sleep lightly* or to be half asleep: to be in a dull or stupefied state.—*v.t.* (with *away*) to spend in drowsiness.—*n.* a short light sleep.—*n.* **Doz'er**. [From a Scand. root, seen in Ice. *dusa*, Dan. *döse*, to dose; A.S. *dwaes*, dull; akin to **Dizzy**.]

**Dozen**, duz'n, *adj.*, *two and ten* or twelve.—*n.* a collection of twelve articles. [Fr. *douzaine—*L. *duodecim—duo*, two, and *decem*, ten.]

**Drab**, drab, *n.* a low, sluttish woman: a prostitute.—*v.i.* to associate with bad women. [Gael. and Ir. 'slut,' orig. a stain, closely akin to Gael. and Ir. *drabh*, grains of malt, which answers to E. **Draff**.]

**Drab**, drab, *n.* thick, strong gray *cloth*: a gray or dull brown colour, perh. from the muddy colour of undyed wool. [Fr. *drap*, cloth. See **Drape**.]

**Drabble**, drab'l, *v.t.* to besmear with mud and water. [Freq. form, from root of **Drab**, a low woman.]

**Drachm**, dram. *n.* See **Dram**. [Gr. *drachmē*, from *drassomai*, to grasp with the hand.]

**Draff**, draf, *n.* (*lit.*) *dregs*, waste matter: the refuse of malt that has been brewed from.—*adjs.* **Draff'ish**, **Draff'y**, worthless. [Prob. E., cog. with Scand. *draf*, and with Gael. and Ir. *drabh*.]

**Draft,** draft, *n.* anything *drawn*: a selection of men from an army, &c. : an order for the payment of money : lines drawn for a plan : a rough sketch : the depth to which a vessel sinks in water. [A corr. of **Draught.**]

**Draft,** draft, *v.t.* to *draw* an outline of : to compose and write : to draw off : to detach.

**Drafts,** drafts, *n.* a game. See **Draughts.**

**Draftsman,** drafts′man, *n.* one who *draws* plans or designs.

**Drag,** drag, *v.t.* to *draw* by force : to draw slowly : to pull roughly and violently : to explore with a dragnet.—*v.i.* to hang so as to trail on the ground : to be forcibly drawn along : to move slowly and heavily :—*pr.p.* drag′ging ; *pa.p.* dragged′. [A.S. *dragan* ; Ger. *tragen*, represented in all the Teut. tongues. Acc. to Curtius, nowise connected with L. *traho*.]

**Drag,** drag, *n.* a net or hook for *dragging* along to catch things under water : a heavy harrow : a low car or cart : a contrivance for retarding carriage wheels in going down slopes : any obstacle to progress. [See **Drag,** *v.*]

**Draggle,** drag′l, *v.t.* or *v.i.* to make or become wet and dirty by *dragging* along the ground. [Freq. of **Draw.** Doublet, **Drawl.**]

**Dragnet,** drag′net, *n.* a *net* to be dragged or *drawn* along the bottom of water to catch fish.

**Dragoman,** drag′o-man, *n.* an interpreter, in Eastern countries:—*pl.* **Drag′omans.** [Sp., from Ar. *tarjumān—tardjama*, to interpret. See **Targum.**]

**Dragon,** drag′un, *n.* a fabulous winged serpent : the constellation Draco : a fierce person : the flying lizard of the E. Indies.—*adjs.* **Drag′-onish, Drag′onlike.** [Fr.—L. *draco, draconis* —Gr. *drakōn*, (*lit.*) 'the sharp-sighted,' from *e-drak-on*, aorist of *derk-omai*, to look.]

**Dragonet,** drag′un-et, *n.* a little *dragon* : a genus of fishes of the goby family, two species of which are found on the coast of England.

**Dragon-fly,** drag′un-flī, *n.* an insect with a long body and brilliant colours.

**Dragonnade,** drag-on-ād′, *n.* the persecution of French Protestants under Louis XIV. and his successor by an armed force, usually of *dragoons:* abandonment of a place to the violence of soldiers. [Fr., from *dragon*, dragoon.]

**Dragon's-blood,** drag′unz-blud, *n.* the red juice of several trees in S. America and the E. Indies, used for colouring.

**Dragoon,** dra-gōōn′, *n.* formerly a soldier trained to fight either on horseback or on foot, now applied only to a kind of cavalry.—*v.t.* to give up to the rage of soldiers : to compel by violent measures. [Sp., prob. so called from having orig. a dragon (L. *draco*) on their standard. See **Dragon.**]

**Dragoonade,** drag-ōōn-ād′. Same as **Dragonnade.**

**Drain,** drān, *v.t.* to *draw off* by degrees : to filter : to clear of water by drains : to make dry : to exhaust.—*v.i.* to flow off gradually.—*n.* a watercourse : a ditch : a sewer.—*adj.* **Drain′able.** [A.S. *drehnigean,* of which *dreh* = *drag,* or else through *dreg,* from the same root.]

**Drainage,** drān′āj, *n.* the *drawing off* of water by rivers or other channels : the system of drains in a town.

**Drainer,** drān′er, *n.* a utensil on which articles are placed to *drain.*

**Drake,** drāk, *n.* the male of the *duck.* [Lit. 'duck-king,' being a contr. of A.S. *end-rake* or *ened-rake,* of which *ened* is cog. with Ice. *önd,* Dan. *and,* Ger. *ente,* L. *anas, anatis* ; and

*rake* is the same as Goth. *reiks,* ruling, *reiki,* rule, and *ric*(*k*), in *bishop-ric, Frede-rick.*]

**Dram,** dram, *n.* a contraction of **Drachm** : $\frac{1}{16}$th of an oz. avoirdupois : formerly, with apothecaries, $\frac{1}{8}$th of an oz. : as much raw spirits as is drunk at once. [Through Fr. and L., from Gr. *drachmē,* (1) a small weight = 66 gr. ; (2) a coin = 9$\frac{3}{4}$d.— *drassomai,* to grasp ; a handful, a pinch.]

**Drama,** dram′a or drä′ma, *n.* a representation of *actions* in human life : a series of deeply interesting events : a composition intended to be represented on the stage : dramatic literature. [L.—Gr. *drama, dramatos—draō,* to do.]

**Dramatic,** dra-mat′ik, **Dramatical,** dra-mat′ik-al, *adj.* belonging to the *drama* : appropriate to or in the form of a drama.—*adv.* **Dramat′ically.**

**Dramatise,** dram′a-tīz, *v.t.* to compose or turn into the form of a *drama* or play. [Gr. *dramatizō.* See **Drama.**]

**Dramatist,** dram′a-tist, *n.* a writer of plays.

**Drank,** drangk—*past tense* of **Drink.**

**Drape,** drāp, *v.t.* to cover with *cloth.* [Fr. *drap,* cloth. From a Teut. root.]

**Draper,** drāp′er, *n.* one who deals in *drapery* or cloth. [Fr. *drapier—drap.*]

**Drapery,** drāp′er-i, *n.* *cloth* goods : hangings of any kind : (*art*) the representation of the dress of human figures. [Fr. *draperie—drap.*]

**Drastic,** dras′tik, *adj., active,* powerful.—*n.* a medicine that purges quickly or thoroughly. [Gr. *drastikos—draō,* to act, to do.]

**Draught,** draft, *n.* act of *drawing*: force needed to draw : the act of drinking : the quantity drunk at a time : outline of a picture : that which is taken in a net by drawing ; a chosen detachment of men : a current of air : the depth to which a ship sinks in the water.—*v.t.* more commonly **Draft,** *to draw out.* [From A.S. *dragan,* to draw. See **Drag,** *v.* and **Draw.**]

**Draught,** draft, **Draught′house,** *n.* (*B.*) a privy.

**Draughts,** drafts, *n.* a game in which two persons make alternate moves (in O. E. *draughts*), on a checkered board, called the **Draught′board,** with pieces called **Draughts′men.**

**Draughtsman,** drafts′man, *n.* See **Draftsman.**

**Drave,** drāv, old *pa.t.* of **Drive.**

**Draw,** draw, *v.t.* to pull along : to bring forcibly towards one : to entice : to inhale : to take out : to deduce : to lengthen : to make a picture of, by lines drawn : to describe : to require a depth of water for floating.—*v.i.* to pull : to practise drawing : to move : to approach :—*pa.t.* drew (drōō) ; *pa.p.* drawn.—*n.* the act of drawing : anything drawn.—*adj.* **Draw′able.—To draw on,** to lead on : to ask or obtain payment by a written bill or *draft.*—**To draw up,** to form in regular order. [A later form of **Drag.**]

**Drawback,** draw′bak, *n.* a *drawing* or receiving *back* some part of the duty on goods on their exportation : any loss of advantage.

**Drawbridge,** draw′brij, *n.* a *bridge* that can be *drawn* up or let down at pleasure.

**Drawee,** draw-ē′, *n.* the person on whom a bill of exchange is *drawn.*

**Drawer,** draw′er, *n.* he or that which *draws:* a thing drawn out, like the sliding box in a case.— *pl.* a close under-garment for the lower limbs.

**Drawing,** draw′ing, *n.* the art of representing objects by lines *drawn,* shading, &c. : a picture : the distribution of prizes, as at a lottery.

**Drawing-room,** draw′ing-rōōm, *n.* (*orig.*) a *withdrawing room*: a room to which the company withdraws after dinner : a reception of company in it.

## Drawl

**Drawl**, drawl, *v.i.* to speak in a slow, lengthened tone.—*v.t.* to utter words in a slow and sleepy manner.—*n.* a slow, lengthened utterance of the voice.—*adv.* **Drawl'ingly**.—*n.* **Drawl'ingness**. [Freq. of **Draw**. Doublet, **Draggle**.]

**Draw-well**, draw'-wel, *n.* a *well* from which water is *drawn* up by a bucket and apparatus.

**Dray**, drā, *n.* a low strong cart for heavy goods, which is *dragged* or *drawn*. [A.S. *dræge*, a drag, from *dragan*. See **Drag**, *v.*]

**Dread**, dred, *n. fear:* awe : the objects that excite fear.—*adj.* exciting great fear or awe.—*v.t.* (*Pr. Bk.*) to *fear* with reverence : to regard with terror. [A.S. *on-drædan*, to fear; Ice. *ondreda*, O. Ger. *tratan*, to be afraid.]

**Dreadful**, dred'fool, *adj.* (*orig.*) full of dread : producing great fear or awe : terrible.—*adv.* **Dread'-fully**.—*n.* **Dread'fulness**.

**Dreadless**, dred'les, *adj.* free from dread : intrepid.—*adv.* **Dread'lessly**.—*n.* **Dread'less-ness**.

**Dream**, drēm, *n.* a train of thoughts and fancies during sleep, a vision : something only imaginary. [A.S. *dream* means rejoicing, music; in M.E. the two meanings of music, mirth, and of dreaming occur ; Dut. *droom*, Ger. *traum*, a dream.]

**Dream**, drēm, *v.i.* to fancy things during sleep : to think idly.—*v.t.* to see in, or as in a dream : —*pa.t.* and *pa.p.* dreamed' or dreamt (dremt).—*n.* **Dream'er**.—*adv.* **Dream'ingly**.

**Dreamy**, drēm'i, *adj.* full of dreams : appropriate to dreams : dreamlike.—*n.* **Dream'iness**.

**Drear**, drēr, **Dreary**, drēr'i, *adj* gloomy : cheerless.—*adv.* **Drear'ily**.—*n.* **Drear'iness**. [A.S. *dreorig*, bloody—*dreoran*, to fall, become weak ; Ger. *traurig*—*trauern*, to mourn.]

**Dredge**, drej, *n.* an instrument for *dragging :* a dragnet for catching oysters, &c. : a machine for taking up mud from a harbour or other water.—*v.t.* to gather with a dredge : to deepen with a dredge. [O. Fr. *drege*; from a Teut. root found in Dut. *dragen*, E. *drag*.]

**Dredge**, drej, *v.t.* to sprinkle flour on meat while roasting.—*n.* **Dredg'er**, a utensil for dredging. [Fr. *dragée*, mixed grain for horses, through Prov. and It., from Gr. *tragēmata*, dried fruits, things nice to eat—*e-trag-on*, aorist of *trōgō*, to eat.]

**Dredger**, drej'ér, *n.* one who fishes with a *dredge :* a dredging-machine.

**Dreggy**, dreg'i, *adj.* containing *dregs :* muddy : foul.—*ns.* **Dregg'iness**, **Dregg'ishness**.

**Dregs**, dregz, *n.pl.* impurities in liquor that fall to the bottom, the grounds : dross : the vilest part of anything. [Ice. *dregg—draga*, to draw.]

**Drench**, drensh, *v.t.* to fill with *drink* or liquid : to wet thoroughly : to physic by force.—*n.* a draught : a dose of physic forced down the throat. [A.S. *drencan*, to give to drink, from *drincan*, to drink. See **Drink**.]

**Dress**, dres, *v.t.* to put *straight* or in order : to put clothes upon : to prepare : to cook : to trim : to deck : to cleanse a sore.—*pa.t.* and *pa.p.* dressed' or drest.—*n.* the covering or ornament of the body : a lady's gown : style of dress. [Fr. *dresser*, to make straight, to prepare, from L. *dirigo, directum*, to direct.]

**Dresser**, dres'ér, *n.* one who dresses : a table on which meat is *dressed* or prepared for use.

**Dressing**, dres'ing, *n.*, *dress* or clothes : manure given to land : matter used to give stiffness and gloss to cloth : the bandage, &c. applied to a sore : an ornamental moulding.

## Dromedary

**Dressing-case**, dres'ing-kās, *n.* a *case* of articles used in *dressing* one's self.

**Dressy**, dres'i, *adj.* showy in or fond of *dress*.

**Drew**, drōō—did draw—*pa.t.* of **Draw**.

**Dribble**, drib'l, *v.i.* to fall in small *drops :* to drop quickly : to slaver, as a child or an idiot.—*v.t.* to let fall in drops.—*n.* **Dribb'ler**. [Dim. of **Drip**.] [a small quantity.

**Dribblet**, **Driblet**, drib'let, *n.* a *very small drop :*

**Drift**, drift, *n.* a heap of matter *driven* together, as snow : the direction in which a thing is driven : the object aimed at : the meaning of words used.—*v.t.* to drive into heaps, as snow. —*v.i.* to be floated along : to be driven into heaps. [See **Drive**.]

**Driftless**, drift'les, *adj.* without drift or aim.

**Driftwood**, drift'wood, *n.*, *wood drifted* by water.

**Drill**, dril, *v.t.* to pierce through with a revolving borer (this implies tremor, and connects **Drill** with **Thrill**).—*n.* an instrument that bores.

**Drill**, dril, *v.t.* to exercise, *e.g.* soldiers or pupils. —*n.* the exercising of soldiers. [Perh. Fr. *drille*, a foot-soldier, from O. Ger. *drigil*, a servant. See **Thrall**.]

**Drill**, dril, *n.* a *row* or furrow to put seed into in sowing.—*v.t.* to sow in rows. [W. *rhill*, a row.]

**Drilling**, dril'ing, *n.* a coarse linen or cotton cloth, used for trousers. [Ger. *drillich*—L. *trilix*, made of three threads, L. *tres*, and *licium*, a thread of the warp.] [*drilling* holes in metals.

**Drillpress**, dril'pres, *n.* a *press* or machine for

**Drill-sergeant**, dril'-sär'jent, *n.* a *sergeant* or non-commissioned officer who *drills* soldiers.

**Drily**. See **Dry**, *adj.*

**Drink**, dringk, *v.t.* to swallow, as a liquid : to take in through the senses.—*v.i.* to swallow a liquid : to take intoxicating liquors to excess : —*pr.p.* drink'ing ; *pa.t.* drank ; *pa.p.* drunk.—*n.* something to be drunk : intoxicating liquor.—*adj.* **Drinkable**, dringk'a-bl.—*n.* **Drink'able-ness**.—*n.* **Drinker**, dringk'ér, a tippler. [A.S. *drincan*; Ger. *trinken*.]

**Drink-offering**, dringk'-ofér-ing, *n.* a Jewish *offering of wine*, &c. in their religious services.

**Drip**, drip, *v.i.* to fall in *drops :* to let fall drops.—*v.t.* to let fall in drops :—*pr.p.* dripp'ing ; *pa.p.* dripped'.—*n.* a falling in drops : that which falls in drops : the edge of a roof. [A.S. *drypan*. **Drop** and **Drip** are from the same root.]

**Dripping**, drip'ing, *n.* that which falls in *drops*, as fat from meat in roasting.

**Drive**, drīv, *v.t.* to force along : to hurry one on : to guide, as horses drawing a carriage.—*v.i.* to press forward with violence : to be forced along : to go in a carriage : to tend towards a point : —*pr.p.* drīv'ing ; *pa.t.* drōve ; *pa.p.* driv'en.—*n.* an excursion in a carriage : a road for driving on.—*n.* **Driv'er**. [A.S. *drīfan*, to drive ; Ger. *treiben*, to push.]

**Drivel**, driv'l, *v.i.* to slaver or let spittle *dribble*, like a child : to be foolish : to speak like an idiot :—*pr.p.* driv'elling ; *pa.p.* driv'elled.—*n.* slaver : nonsense.—*n.* **Driv'eller**, a fool. [A form of **Dribble**.]

**Drizzle**, driz'l, *v.i.* to rain in small drops.—*n.* a small, light rain.—*adj.* **Drizz'ly**. [Freq. of M.E. *dreosen*, A.S. *dreosan*, to fall.]

**Droll**, drōl, *adj.* odd : amusing : laughable.—*n.* one who excites mirth : a jester.—*v.i.* to practise drollery : to jest.—*adj.* **Droll'ish**, somewhat droll.—*n.* **Droll'ery**. [Fr. *drôle*; from the Teut., as in Dut. and Ger. *drollig*, funny.]

**Dromedary**, drum'e-dar-i, *n.* the Arabian camel, which has one hump on its back ; so named from its *speed*. [Low L. *dromedarius*, from Gr. *dromas*, *dromados*, running—root *drem*, to run.]

**Drone**, drōn, *n.* the male of the honey-bee: one who lives on the labour of others, like the drone-bee: a lazy, idle fellow. [A.S. *dran*, the bee; Dut. and Ger. *drone*, Sans. *druna*, Gr. *anthrēnē*, Dan. *drone*, din, a rumbling noise.]

**Drone**, drōn, *v.i.* to make a low droning sound.

**Drone**, drōn, *n.* the largest tube of the bagpipe. [From the sound.]

**Dronish**, drōn'ish, *adj.* like a *drone*: lazy, idle.—*adv.* **Dron'ishly**.—*n.* **Dron'ishness**.

**Droop**, drōōp, *v.i.* to sink or hang down: to grow weak or faint: to decline. [A form of **Drop**.]

**Drop**, drop, *n.* a small particle of liquid which falls at one time: a very small quantity of liquid: anything hanging like a drop: anything arranged to drop.—*n.* **Drop'let**, a little drop. [A.S. *dropa*, a drop; Dut. *drop*.]

**Drop**, drop, *v.i.* to fall in small particles: to let drops fall: to fall suddenly: to come to an end: to fall or sink lower.—*v.t.* to let fall in drops: to let fall: to let go, or dismiss: to utter casually: to lower:—*pr.p.* dropp'ing; *pa.p.* dropped'. [A.S. *dropian—dropa;* Ger. *tropfen*, akin to *triefen*, to drop, to trickle.]

**Dropsical**, drop'sik-al, *adj.* pertaining to, resembling, or affected with *dropsy*.—*n.* **Drop'sicalness**.

**Dropsy**, drop'si, *n.* an unnatural collection of *water* in any part of the body. [Corr. from *hydropsy*—Fr. *hydropisie*—L. *hydropisis*—Gr. *hydrops—hydōr*, water.]

**Drosky**, dros'ki, *n.* a low four-wheeled open carriage, much used in Russia. [Russ. *drojki*.]

**Dross**, dros, *n.* the scum which metals throw off when melting: waste matter: refuse: rust. [A.S. *dros*, from *dreosan*, to fall; Ger. *druse*, ore decayed by the weather.]

**Drossy**, dros'i, *adj.* like dross: impure: worthless.—*n.* **Dross'iness**.

**Drought**, drowt, *n.*, *dryness:* want of rain or of water: thirst. [A.S. *drugoth*, dryness—*dryge*.]

**Droughty**, drowt'i, *adj.* full of *drought:* very dry: wanting rain, thirsty.—*n.* **Drought'iness**.

**Drouth**, drowth, *n.* Same as **Drought**.

**Drove**, drōv, *pa.t.* of **Drive**. [animals, *driven*.

**Drove**, drōv, *n.* a number of cattle, or other

**Drover**, drōv'ėr, *n.* one who *drives* cattle.

**Drown**, drown, *v.t.* to *drench* or sink in water: to kill by placing under water: to overpower: to extinguish.—*v.i.* to be suffocated in water. [A.S. *druncnian*, to drown—*druncen*, pa.p. of *drincen*, to drink. See **Drench**.]

**Drowse**, drowz, *v.i.* to nod the head, as when heavy with sleep: to look heavy and dull.—*v.t.* to make heavy with sleep: to stupefy. [A.S. *drusian*, to be sluggish; Dut. *droosen*, to fall asleep.]      [Drows'ily.—*n.* **Drows'iness**.

**Drowsy**, drowz'i, *adj.*, *sleepy:* heavy: dull.—*adv.*

**Drub**, drub, *v.t.* to *strike:* to beat or thrash:—*pr.p.* drubb'ing; *pa.p.* drubbed'.—*n.* a blow. [Prov. E. *drab*, from A.S. *drepan;* Ice. *drep*.]

**Drudge**, druj, *v.i.* to work hard: to do very mean work.—*n.* one who works hard: a slave: a menial servant.—*adv.* **Drudg'ingly**. [Perh. Celt. as in Ir. *drugaire*, a drudge.]

**Drudgery**, druj'ėr-i, *n.* the work of a *drudge:* hard or humble labour.

**Drug**, drug, *n.* any substance used in medicine, or in dyeing: an article that sells slowly, like medicines.—*v.t.* to mix or season with drugs: to dose to excess.—*v.i.* to prescribe drugs or medicines:—*pr.p.* drugg'ing; *pa.p.* drugged'.

[Fr. *drogue*, from Dut. *droog*, dry; as if applied orig. to dried herbs. See **Dry**.]

**Drugget**, drug'et, *n.* a *coarse* woollen cloth, used as a protection for carpets. [Fr. *droguet*, dim. of *drogue*, drug, trash.]

**Druggist**, drug'ist, *n.* one who deals in *drugs*.

**Druid**, drōō'id, *n.* a *priest* among the ancient Celts of Britain, Gaul, and Germany, who worshipped under *oak-trees.*—*fem.* **Dru'idess**.—*adj.* **Druid'ical**. [Gael. *druidh*, W. *derwydd;* Littré accepts the ety. from Celt. *derw*, an oak, which is from the same root as Gr. *drys*, an oak.]

**Druidism**, drōō'id-izm, *n.* the doctrines which the *Druids* taught: the ceremonies they practised.

**Drum**, drum, *n.* a cylindrical musical instrument: anything shaped like a drum: the tympanum or middle portion of the ear: (*arch.*) the upright part of a cupola: (*mech.*) a revolving cylinder. [Perh. E.; from a Teut. root found in Dut. *trom*, Ger. *trommel*, a drum; an imitative word.]

**Drum**, drum, *n.* formerly a large and tumultuous evening-party. [Said to be so called, because rival hostesses vied with each other in *beating up* crowds of guests.]

**Drum**, drum, *v.i.* to beat a drum: to beat with the fingers.—*v.t.* to drum out, to expel:—*pr.p.* drumm'ing; *pa.p.* drummed'.—*n.* **Drumm'er**.

**Drumhead**, drum'hed, *n.* the head of a drum: the top part of a capstan.

**Drum-major**, drum'-mā'jėr, *n.* the *major* or chief *drummer* of a regiment. [the *drum* is beat.

**Drumstick**, drum'stik, *n.* the *stick* with which

**Drunk**, drungk, *pa.p.* of **Drink**.

**Drunk**, drungk, *adj.* intoxicated: saturated.

**Drunkard**, drungk'ard, *n.* one who frequently *drinks* to excess.

**Drunken**, drungk'n, *adj.* given to excessive drinking: resulting from intoxication.

**Drunkenness**, drungk'n-nes, *n.* excessive drinking, intoxication: habitual intemperance.

**Drupaceous**, drōō-pā'shus, *adj.* producing or pertaining to *drupes* or stone-fruits.

**Drupe**, drōōp, *n.* a fleshy fruit containing a stone, as the plum, &c. [Fr.—L. *drupa*—Gr. *druppa*, an over-ripe olive, from *drys*, a tree, and *pepto*, to cook, to ripen.]

**Dry**, drī, *adj.* free from moisture: deficient in moisture: without sap: not green: not giving milk: thirsty: uninteresting: frigid, precise.—*adv.* **Dry'ly** or **Dri'ly**.—*n.* **Dry'ness**. [A.S. *dryge;* Dut. *droog*, cf. Ger. *trocken*.]

**Dry**, drī, *v.t.* to free from water or moisture: to exhaust.—*v.i.* to become dry: to become free from juice: to evaporate entirely:—*pr.p.* dry'ing; *pa.p.* dried'.—*n.* **Dri'er**.

**Dryad**, drī'ad, *n.* (*Greek myth.*) a nymph of the woods. [Gr. *dryades*, pl., from *drys*, a tree.]

**Dry-goods**, drī'-goodz, *n.pl.* drapery, &c. as distinguished from groceries.

**Dry-nurse**, drī'-nurs, *n.* a *nurse* who feeds a child *without milk* from the breast.

**Dry-rot**, drī'-rot, *n.* a decay of timber, caused by fungi which reduce it to a *dry*, brittle mass.

**Drysalter**, drī-sawlt'ėr, *n.* a dealer in *salted* or *dry meats*, pickles, &c.: or in gums, dyes, drugs, &c.

**Drysaltery**, drī-sawlt'ėr-i, *n.* the articles kept by a *drysalter:* the business of a drysalter.

**Dual**, dū'al, *adj.* consisting of *two*. [L., from *duo*, two.]      [one good, the other evil.

**Dualism**, dū'al-izm, *n.* the doctrine of *two* gods,

**Dualist**, dū'al-ist, *n.* a believer in dualism.

**Duality**, dū-al'it-i, *n.*, *doubleness:* state of being double.

**Dub**, dub, *v.t.* to confer knighthood by *striking*

the shoulder with a sword : to confer any dignity :—*pr.p.* dubb'ing ; *pa.p.* dubbed'. [From a Teut. root, seen in A.S. *dubban*, Ice. *dubba*, to strike ; akin to **Dab.**]

**Dubiety**, dū-bī′e-ti, *n.* doubtfulness.

**Dubious**, dū′bi-us, *adj.*, *doubtful* : undetermined : causing doubt : of uncertain event or issue.—*adv.* **Du′biously.**—*n.* **Du′biousness.** [L. *dubius*, from *duo*, two. See **Doubt.**]

**Ducal**, dūk′al, *adj.* pertaining to a *duke* or duke-

**Ducat**, duk′at, *n.* (*orig.*) a coin struck by a *duke* : a coin worth, when silver, 4s. 6d. ; when gold, twice as much. [Fr. *ducat*—It. *ducato*—Low L. *ducatus*, a duchy—*dux*, a leader. See **Duke.**]

**Duchess**, duch′es, *n.* the consort or widow of a *duke* : a lady who possesses a duchy in her own right. [Fr. *duchesse*—*duc*—L. *dux*, a leader.]

**Duchy**, duch′i, *n.* the territory of a *duke*, a duke-dom. [Fr. *duché—duc*.]

**Duck**, duk, *n.* a kind of coarse *cloth* for small sails, sacking, &c. [Dut. *doek*, linen cloth ; Ger. *tuch*.]

**Duck**, duk, *v.t.* to dip for a moment in water.—*v.i.* to dip or dive : to lower the head suddenly.—*n.* a well-known water-bird, so named from its *ducking* or dipping its head : a dipping or stooping of the head : a pet, darling. [E. ; from a root found also in Low Ger. *ducken*, Dut. *duiken*, to stoop ; Ger. *tauchen*, to dip, *tauch-ente*, the duck. **Dip, Dive, Dove**, are parallel forms.]

**Ducking-stool**, duk′ing-stōōl, *n.* a stool or chair in which scolds were formerly tied and *ducked* in the water as a punishment.

**Duckling**, duk′ling, *n.* a young *duck*.

**Duct**, dukt, *n.* a tube *conveying* fluids in animal bodies or plants. [L. *ductus—duco*, to lead.]

**Ductile**, duk′til, *adj.* easily led : yielding : capable of being *drawn* out into wires or threads. [L. *ductilis—duco*, *ductus*, to lead.]

**Ductility**, duk-til′i-ti, *n.* capacity of being *drawn* out without breaking. [*dygen*, anger.]

**Dudgeon**, duj′un, *n.* resentment : grudge. [W.

**Dudgeon**, duj′un, *n.* the haft of a dagger : a small dagger. [Ety. unknown.]

**Due**, dū, *adj.*, *owed* : that ought to be paid or done to another : proper : appointed.—*adv.* exactly : directly.—*n.* that which is owed : what one has a right to : perquisite : fee or tribute. [Fr. *dû*, pa.p. of *devoir*, L. *debeo*, to owe.]

**Duel**, dū′el, *n.* a combat between *two* persons : single combat to decide a quarrel.—*v.i.* to fight in single combat :—*pr.p.* dū′elling ; *pa.p.* dū′elled.—*n.* **Du′eller** or **Du′ellist.** [It. *duello*, from L. *duellum*, the orig. form of *bellum—duo*, two.]

**Duelling**, dū′el-ing, *n.* fighting in a *duel* : the practice of fighting in single combat.

**Duenna**, dū-en′a, *n.* an old lady who acts as guardian to a younger. [Sp., a form of **Donna.**]

**Duet**, dū-et′, **Duetto**, dū-et′o, *n.* a piece of music for *two*. [It. *duetto*—L. *duo*, two.]

**Duffel**, duf′l, *n.* a thick, coarse woollen cloth, with a nap. [Prob. from *Duffel*, a town in Belgium.]

**Dug**, dug, *n.* the nipple of the pap, esp. applied to that of a cow or other beast. [Cf. Sw. *dägga*, Dan. *dægge*, to suckle a child. See **Dairy.**]

**Dug**, dug, *pa.t.* and *pa.p.* of **Dig.**

**Dugong**, dū-gong′, *n.* a kind of herb-eating whale, from 8 to 20 feet long, found in Indian seas. The fable of the mermaid is said to be founded on this animal. [Malayan *dúyóng*.]

**Duke**, dūk, *n.* (*lit.*) a *leader*, (*B.*) a chieftain : the highest order of nobility next below the Prince of Wales : (*on the continent*) a sovereign prince.

[Fr. *duc*—L. *dux*, *ducis*, a leader—*duco*, to lead ; akin to A.S. *teohan* (see **Tow**), Ger. *ziehen*, to draw or lead ; A.S. *heretoga*, army-leader, Ger. *herzog*, now = E. *duke*.]

**Dukedom**, dūk′dum, *n.* the title, rank, or territories of a *duke*. [**Duke**, and A.S. *dom*, dominion.]

**Dulcet**, duls′et, *adj.*, *sweet* to the taste, or to the ear : melodious, harmonious. [Old Fr. *dolcet*, dim. of *dols* = *doux*—L. *dulcis*, sweet.]

**Dulcifluous**, dul-sif′loo-us, *adj.*, *flowing sweetly*. [L. *dulcis*, and *fluo*, to flow.]

**Dulcimer**, dul′si-mér, *n.* a musical instrument played by striking brass wires with small rods : a Jewish musical instrument, acc. to Gesenius, a double pipe with a bag. [Sp. *dulcemele*—L. *dulce melos*, a sweet song—*dulcis*, sweet ; *melos* = Gr. *melos*, a song.]

**Dull**, dul, *adj.* slow of hearing, of learning, or of understanding : insensible : without life or spirit : slow of motion : drowsy : sleepy : sad : downcast : cheerless : not bright or clear : cloudy : dim, obscure : obtuse : blunt.—*adv.* **Dul′ly.**—*n.* **Dull′ness** or **Dul′ness.** [A.S. *dwal*, *dol—dwelan*, to lead astray ; Dut. *dol*, mad—*dolen*, to wander, to rave ; Ger. *toll*, mad.]

**Dull**, dul, *v.t.* to make *dull* : to make stupid : to blunt : to damp : to cloud.—*v.i.* to become dull.

**Dullard**, dul′ard, *n.* a *dull* and stupid *person* : a dunce. [weak suffix.]

**Dull-sighted**, dul′-sīt′ed, *adj.* having *dull* or

**Dull-witted**, dul′-wit′ed, *adj.* not smart : heavy.

**Duly**, dū′li, *adv.* properly : fitly : at the proper time.

**Dumb**, dum, *adj.* without the power of speech : silent : soundless.—*n.* **Dumb′ness.** [A.S. *dumb* ; Ger. *dumm*, stupid, Dut. *dom*.]

**Dumb-bells**, dum′-belz, *n.pl.* weights swung in the hands for exercise. [pantomime.

**Dumb-show**, dum′-shō, *n.* gesture without words :

**Dumfound**, dum′fownd, *v.t.* to strike dumb : to confuse greatly.

**Dummy**, dum′i, *n.* one who is *dumb* : a sham package in a shop : the fourth or exposed hand when three persons play at whist.

**Dumpish**, dump′ish, *adj.* given to *dumps* : depressed in spirits.—*adv.* **Dump′ishly.**—*n.* **Dump′ishness.**

**Dumpling**, dump′ling, *n.* a kind of thick pudding or mass of paste. [Dim. of *dump*, in **Dumpy.**]

**Dumps**, dumps, *n.pl.* dullness or gloominess of mind : ill-humour. [From a Teut. root, seen in Sw. *dumpin*, Ger. *dumpf*, gloomy, E. **Damp.**]

**Dumpy**, dump′i, *adj.* short and thick. [From a prov. form *dump*, a clumsy piece.]

**Dun**, dun, *adj.* of a *dark* colour, partly brown and black. [A.S. *dun*—W. *dwn*, dusky, Gael. *don*, brown.]

**Dun**, dun, *v.t.* to demand a debt with *din* or noise : to urge for payment :—*pr.p.* dunn′ing ; *pa.p.* dunned′.—*n.* one who *duns* : a demand for payment. [A S. *dynnan*, Ice. *dynia*, to make a noise, to clamour.]

**Dunce**, duns, *n.* one slow at learning : a stupid person.—*adjs.* **Dunc′ish**, **Dunce′like**. [*Duns* (Scotus), the leader of the schoolmen, from him called *Dunses*, who opposed classical studies on the revival of learning ; hence any opposer of learning. Duns Scotus was a native of Duns in Berwickshire, or of Dunston in Northumberland, whence his name.]

**Dune**, dūn, *n.* a low hill of sand on the seashore. [An earlier form of **Down**, a hill.]

**Dung**, dung, *n.* the excrement of animals : refuse

litter mixed with excrement.—*v.t.* to manure with dung. — *v.i.* to void excrement. — *adj.* **Dung′y.** [A.S. *dung*: Ger. *dung, dünger.*]

**Dungeon,** dun′jun, *n.* (*orig.*) the principal tower of a castle : a close, dark prison : a cell under ground. [A doublet of **Donjon.**]

**Dunghill,** dung′hil, *n.* a hill or heap of dung : any mean situation.

**Dunlin,** dun′lin, *n.* a kind of sandpiper, so called from its frequenting the *dunes* and *pools* by the seaside. [Gael. *dun,* hill, and *linne,* a pool.]

**Dunnish,** dun′ish, *adj.* somewhat dun.

**Duo,** dū′o, *n.* a song in *two* parts. [L. *duo,* two.]

**Duodecennial,** dū-o-de-sen′i-al, *adj.* occurring every *twelve years.* [L. *duodecim,* twelve, and *annus,* a year.]

**Duodecimal,** dū-o-des′i-mal, *adj.* computed by *twelves* : twelfth.—*pl.* a rule of arithmetic in which the denominations rise by twelve. [L. *duodecim,* twelve—*duo,* two, and *decem,* ten.]

**Duodecimo,** dū-o-des′i-mo, *adj.* formed of sheets folded so as to make *twelve* leaves.—*n.* a book of such sheets—usually written 12mo.

**Duodecuple,** dū-o-dek′ū-pl, *adj.*, *twelvefold* : consisting of twelve. [L. *duodecim, plico,* to fold.]

**Duodenum,** dū-o-dē′num, *n.* the first portion of the small intestines, so called because about *twelve* fingers' breadth in length.—*adj.* **Duo-de′nal.** [L. *duodeni,* twelve each.]

**Dup,** dup, *v.t.* (*obs.*) to undo a door. [From **Do** and **Up.** Cf. **Don** and **Doff.**]

**Dupe,** dūp, *n.* one *easily cheated* : one who is deceived or misled.—*v.t.* to deceive : to trick.—*adj.* **Dup′able.** [Fr. *dupe* ; of uncertain origin.]

**Duple,** dū′pl, *adj.*, *double* : twofold. [L. *duplex, duplicis,* twofold, from *duo,* two, and *plico,* to fold. Cf. **Complex.**]

**Duplicate,** dū′plik-āt, *adj.*, *double* : twofold.—*n.* another thing of the same kind : a copy or transcript.—*v.t.* to double : to fold.—*n.* **Duplica′tion.** [L. *duplico, duplicatus—duplex.*]

**Duplicity,** dū-plis′it-i, *n.*, *doubleness* : insincerity of heart or speech : deceit. [L. *duplicitas—duplex.*]

**Durability,** dūr-a-bil′it-i, *n.* quality of being *durable* : power of resisting decay.

**Durable,** dūr′a-bl, *adj.* able to *last* or *endure* : hardy : permanent.—*adv.* **Dur′ably.**—*n.* **Dur′ableness.** [L. *durabilis—duro,* to last.]

**Durance,** dūr′ans, *n., continuance* : imprisonment : duress. [L. *durans,* pr.p. of *duro.*]

**Duration,** dū-rā′shun, *n., continuance in time* : time indefinitely : power of continuance. [L. *duratus,* pa.p. of *duro.*]

**Durbar,** dur′bar, *n.* an audience-chamber : a reception or levee, esp. a reception of native princes held by the Viceroy of India. [Pers. *dar-bar,* a prince's court, (*lit.*) a *door* of *admittance.*] [Fr. *durer*—L. *duro—durus,* hard.]

**Dure,** dūr, *v.i.* (*obs.*) to endure, last, or continue.

**Duress,** dūr′es or dūr-es′, *n.* constraint : imprisonment : (*E. law*) the plea of compulsion by one who has failed in an obligation or committed a crime. [O. Fr. *duresce*—L *duritia—durus,* hard ]

**During,** dūr′ing, *prep.* for the time a thing *lasts.* [Orig. pr.p. of *obs.* **Dure,** to last.]

**Durst,** durst, *pa.t.* of **Dare,** to venture. [A.S. *dorste.* pa.t. of *dear,* to dare.]

**Dusk,** dusk, *adj.* darkish : of a dark colour.—*n.* twilight : partial darkness : darkness of colour. —*adv* **Dusk′ly.**—*n.* **Dusk′ness.** [From an older form of A.S. *deorc,* whence E. **Dark** ; cf. Sw. *dusk,* dull weather.]

**Duskish,** dusk′ish, *adj.* rather dusky : slightly dark or black.—*adv.* **Dusk′ishly.**—*n.* **Dusk′-ishness.**

**Dusky,** dusk′i, *adj.* partially dark or obscure : dark-coloured : sad : gloomy.—*adv.* **Dusk′ily.** —*n.* **Dusk′iness.**

**Dust,** dust, *n.* fine particles of anything like *smoke* or *vapour* : powder : earth : the grave, where the body becomes *dust* : a mean condition.—*v.t.* to free from dust : to sprinkle with dust. [A.S. *dust* ; Ger. *dunst,* vapour.]

**Duster,** dust′ėr, *n.* a cloth or brush for removing *dust.*

**Dusty,** dust′i, *adj.* covered or sprinkled with *dust* : like dust.—*n.* **Dust′iness.**

**Dutch,** duch, *adj.* belonging to Holland, or its people—in old writers rather applied to the *Germans.* [Ger. *deutsch* (*lit.*) belonging to the *people*—O. Ger. *diut-isk,* of which *-isk* = the E. suffix *-ish,* and *diut* = A.S. *theod,* Goth. *thiuda,* a nation. See **Teutonic.**]

**Duteous,** dū′te-us, *adj.* devoted to *duty* : obedient. —*adv.* **Du′teously.**—*n.* **Du′teousness.**

**Dutiful,** dū′ti-fool, *adj.* attentive to *duty* : respectful : expressive of a sense of duty.—*adv.* **Du′tifully.**—*n.* **Du′tifulness.**

**Duty,** dū′ti, *n.* that which is *due* : what one is bound by any obligation to do : obedience : military service : respect or regard : one's proper business : tax on goods. [Formed from O. Fr. *deu* or *due* (mod. Fr. *dû*), and suffix *-ty.* See **Due.**]

**Duumvirate,** dū-um′vi-rāt, *n.* the union of *two men* in the same office : a form of government in ancient Rome. [L. *duo,* two, and *vir,* a man.]

**Dwale,** dwāl, *n.* (*bot.*) deadly nightshade, which poisons, dulls, or *stupefies* : (*her.*) a black colour. [A.S. *dwala,* error, hence stupefaction, from *dwal* or *dol.* See **Dull** and **Dwell.**]

**Dwarf,** dwawrf, *n.* an animal or plant that does not reach the ordinary height : a diminutive man.—*v.t.* to hinder from growing. [A.S. *dweorg* = Dut. and Scand. *dwẽrg,* Ger. *zwerg.*]

**Dwarfish,** dwawrf′ish, *adj.* like a dwarf : very small : despicable.—*adv.* **Dwarf′ishly.**—*n.* **Dwarf′ishness.**

**Dwell,** dwel, *v.i.* to abide in a place : to inhabit : to rest the attention : to continue long :—*pr.p.* dwell′ing ; *pa.t.* and *pa.p.* dwelled′ or dwelt.— *n.* **Dwell′er.** [A.S. *dwelan,* to cause to wander, to delay, from *dwal* or *dol,* the original form of E. **Dull.**] [habitation : continuance.

**Dwelling,** dwel′ing, *n.* the place where one dwells :

**Dwindle,** dwin′dl, *v.i.* to grow less : to grow feeble : to become degenerate.—*v.t.* to lessen. [Dim. of *dwine,* from A.S. *dwinan,* to fade = Ice. *dvina,* Dan. *tvine,* to pine away : akin to A.S. *swindan,* Ger. *schwinden.* See **Swoon.**]

**Dye,** dī, *v.t.* to stain : to give a new colour to :— *pr.p.* dye′ing ; *pa.p.* dyed′.—*n.* colour : tinge : stain : a colouring liquid. [A.S. *deagan,* to dye, from *deag* or *deah,* colour.] [cloth, &c.

**Dyeing,** dī′ing, *n.* the art or trade of *colouring*

**Dyer,** dī′er, *n.* one whose trade is to *dye* cloth, &c.

**Dyestuffs,** dī′stufs, *n.pl.* material used in dyeing.

**Dying,** dī′ing, *pr.p.* of **Die.**—*adj.* destined for death, mortal : occurring immediately before death, as dying words : supporting a dying person, as a dying bed : pertaining to death.— *n.* death. [See **Die,** *v.*]

**Dyke.** Same as **Dike.**

**Dynamic,** di-nam′ik, **Dynamical,** di-nam′ik-al, *adj.* relating to *force*: relating to the effects of forces in nature.—*adv.* **Dynam′ically.** [Gr. *dynamikos—dynamis,* power—*dynamai,* to be able.]

**Dynamics**, di-nam′iks, *n.sing.* the science which investigates the action of *force*.

**Dynamite**, din′a-mīt, *n.* a *powerful* explosive agent, consisting of absorbent matter, as porous silica, saturated with nitro-glycerine. [Gr. *dynamis.*]

**Dynamometer**, din-am-om′e-tėr, *n.* an instrument for *measuring effort* exerted, esp. the work done by a machine. [Gr. *dynamis*, power, and *metron*, a measure.]

**Dynasty**, din′as-ti or dī′nas-ti, *n.* a succession of kings of the same family.—*adj.* **Dynas′tic**, belonging to a dynasty. [Gr. *dynasteia*—*dynastēs*, a lord—*dynamai*, to be able.]

**Dysentery**, dis en-ter-i, *n.* a disease of the *entrails* or bowels, attended with pain and a discharge of mucus and blood.—*adj.* **Dysenter′ic**. [Gr. *dysenteria*, from *dys*, ill, *entera*, the entrails.]

**Dyspepsy**, dis-pep′si, **Dispepsia**, dis-pep′si-a, *n.*, *difficult digestion:* indigestion. [Gr. *dyspepsia*—*dys*, hard, difficult, and *pessō*, *pepsō*, to digest.]

**Dyspeptic**, dis-pep′tik, *adj.* afflicted with, pertaining to, or arising from *indigestion*.—*n.* a person afflicted with dyspepsy.

# E

**Each**, ēch, *adj.*, *every one* in any number separately considered. [A.S. *ælc* = ā-ge-lic, from *â* (= *aye*), prefix *ge*, and *lic*, like, *i.e.* aye-like.]

**Eager**, ē′gėr, *adj.* excited by desire : ardent to do or obtain : earnest.—*adv.* **Eag′erly**.—*n.* **Eag′erness**. [M. E. *egre*—Fr. *aigre*, from L. *acer*, *acris*, sharp—root *ak*, sharp. See **Acrid**.]

**Eagle**, ē′gl, *n.* a large bird of prey : a military standard, carrying the figure of an eagle : a gold coin of the United States, worth ten dollars. [Fr. *aigle*, from L. *aquila*, from root *ac*, sharp, swift.]           [discerning.

**Eagle-eyed**, ē′gl-īd, *adj.* having a piercing eye :

**Eaglet**, ē′glet, *n.* a young or small eagle.

**Eagre**, ē′gėr, *n.* rise of the tide in a river; same as **Bore**. [A.S. *egor*, water, sea.]

**Ear**, ēr, *n.* a spike, as of corn.—*v.i.* to put forth ears, as corn. [A.S. *ear*; Ger. *ähre*.]

**Ear**, ēr, *v.t.* (*obs.*) to *plough* or till. [A.S. *erian*; L. *aro*, Gr. *aroō*—root *ar*, to plough.]

**Ear**, ēr, *n.* the organ of hearing or the external part merely : the sense or power of hearing : the faculty of distinguishing sounds : attention : anything like an ear.—*adjs.* **Eared′**, having ears; **Ear′less**, wanting ears. [A.S. *eare*; L. *auris*, Ger. *ohr*.]

**Earache**, ēr′āk, *n.* an *ache* or pain in the *ear*.

**Eardrop**, ēr′drop, **Earring**, ēr′ring, *n.* a *ring* or ornament *drooping* or hanging from the *ear*.

**Eardrum**, ēr′drum, *n.* the *drum* or middle cavity of the *ear*. [See **Tympanum**.]

**Earing**, ēr′ing, *n.* (*obs.*) *ploughing*.

**Earl**, ėrl, *n.* an English nobleman ranking between a marquis and a viscount.—*fem.* **Count′ess**. [A.S. *eorl*, a warrior, hero; Ice. *jarl*.]

**Earldom**, ėrl′dum, *n.* the dominion or dignity of an *earl*. [**Earl**, and A.S. *dom*, power.]

**Early**, ėr′li, *adj.* in good season : at or near the beginning of the day.—*adv.* soon.—*n.* **Ear′liness**. [A.S. *ærlice*—*ær*, before.]

**Earmark**, ēr′märk, *n.* a *mark* on a sheep's *ear*.

**Earn**, ėrn, *v.t.* to *gain by labour* : to acquire : to deserve. [A.S. *earnian*, to earn; cog. with O. Ger. *arin*, to reap; Ger. *ernte*: Goth. *asans*, harvest].

**Earnest**, ėr′nest, *adj.* shewing strong desire : de-

termined : eager to obtain : intent : sincere.—*n.* seriousness : reality.—*adv.* **Ear′nestly**.—*n.* **Ear′nestness**. [A.S. *eornest*, seriousness ; Dut. *ernst*, Ger. *ernst*, ardour, zeal.]

**Earnest**, ėr′nest, *n.* money given in token of a bargain made : a pledge : first-fruits. [W. *ernes*, an earnest, pledge-money, akin to Gael. *earlas*, whence Scot. *arles*. Perh. like Fr. *arrabón* and L. *arrha*, from Heb. *'erabon*.]

**Earnings**, ėr′ningz, *n.pl.* what one has *earned*: money saved.

**Earshot**, ēr′shot, *n.* hearing-distance.

**Earth**, ėrth, *n.* the matter on the surface of the globe : soil : dry land, as opposed to sea : the world : the people of this world. [A.S. *eorthe*; Ger. *erde*; allied to Gr. *era*.]

**Earth**, ėrth, *v.t.* to hide or cause to hide in the *earth*: to bury.—*v.i.* to burrow.

**Earthborn**, ėrth′bawrn, *adj.*, *born* from the *earth*.

**Earthbound**, ėrth′bownd, *adj.*, *bound* or held by the *earth*, as a tree.

**Earthen**, ėrth′n, *adj.* made of *earth* or clay : earthly : frail.—*n.* **Earth′enware**, crockery.

**Earthflax**, ėrth′flaks, *n.* asbestos.

**Earthling**, ėrth′ling, *n.* a dweller on the *earth*.

**Earthly**, ėrth′li, *adj.* belonging to the *earth*: vile : worldly.—*n.* **Earth′liness**.

**Earthly-minded**, ėrth′li-mīnd′ed, *adj.* having the *mind* intent on *earthly* things.

**Earthnut**, ėrth′nut, *n.* the popular name of certain tuberous roots growing underground.

**Earthquake**, ėrth′kwāk, *n.* a *quaking* or shaking of the earth : a heaving of the ground.

**Earthward**, ėrth′ward, *adv.*, *toward the earth*.

**Earthwork**, ėrth′wurk, *n.* the removing of earth in making railways, &c. : a fortification of earth.

**Earthworm**, ėrth′wurm, *n.* the common worm : a mean, niggardly person.

**Earthy**, ėrth′i, *adj.* consisting of, relating to, or resembling earth : inhabiting the earth : gross : unrefined.—*n.* **Earth′iness**.     [*hearing*.

**Ear-trumpet**, ēr′-trump′et, *n.* a *tube* to aid in

**Earwax**, ēr′waks, *n.* a *waxy* substance secreted by the glands of the *ear* into the outer passage.

**Earwig**, ēr′wig, *n.* a common insect with forceps at its tail, incorrectly supposed to *creep* into the brain through the *ear* : one who gains the ear of another by stealth for a bad end. [A.S. *eorwicga*; *eor* being **Ear**, and *wicga*, from *wegan*, to carry, akin to L. *veho*.]

**Ear-witness**, ēr′-wit′nes, *n.* a *witness* that can testify from his own *hearing* : one who hears a thing.

**Ease**, ēz, *n.* freedom from pain or disturbance : rest from work : quiet : freedom from difficulty : naturalness. [Fr. *aise*; same in L. *agio*.]

**Ease**, ēz, *v.t.* to free from pain, trouble, or anxiety : to relieve : to calm.

**Easel**, ēz′l, *n.* the frame on which painters support their pictures while painting. [Dut. *ezel*, or Ger. *esel*, an ass, dim. of stem *as*. See **Ass**.]

**Easement**, ēz′ment, *n.* relief : assistance : support.

**East**, ēst, *n.* that part of the heavens where the sun first shines or rises : one of the four cardinal points of the compass : the countries to the east of Europe.—*adj.* toward the rising of the sun. [A.S. *east*; Ger. *ost*; akin to Gr. *ēōs*, the dawn; Sans. *ushas*, the dawn—*ush*, to burn.]

**Easter**, ēst′ėr, *n.* a Christian festival commemorating the resurrection of Christ, held on the Sunday after Good-Friday. [A.S. *Eastor*, from *Eastre*, a goddess whose festival was held in April.]

**Easterling**, ēst′ėr-ling, *n.* a native of a country

lying to the *east* of us, esp. a trader from the shores of the Baltic. [See **Sterling**.]

**Easterly**, ēst′ėr-li, *adj.* coming from the *eastward* : looking toward the east.—*adv.* on the east : toward the east.

**Eastern**, ēst′ėrn, *adj.* toward the *east* : connected with the East : dwelling in the East.

**Eastward**, ēst′ward, *adv.* toward the *east*.

**Easy**, ēz′i, *adj.* at *ease* : free from pain : tranquil : unconstrained : giving ease : not difficult : yielding : not straitened.—*adv.* **Eas′ily**.—*n.* **Eas′iness**.

**Eat**, ēt, *v.t.* to chew and swallow : to consume : to corrode.—*v.i.* to take food :—*pr.p.* eat′ing : *pa.t.* āte (āt or et) ; *pa.p.* eaten (ēt′n) or (*obs.*) eat (et).—*n.* **Eat′er**. [A.S. *etan* ; Ger. *essen*, L. *edo*, *esse*, Gr. *edō*, Sans. *ad*, to eat.]

**Eatable**, ēt′a-bl, *adj.* fit to be eaten.—*n.* anything used as food.

**Eaves**, ēvz, *n.pl.* the edge of the roof projecting over the wall. [A.S. *efese*, the clipt edge of thatch.]

**Eavesdrop**, ēvz′drop, *n.* the water which falls in *drops* from the *eaves* of a house.—*v.i.* to stand under the eaves or near the windows of a house to listen.—*n.* **Eaves′dropper**, one who thus listens : one who tries to overhear private conversation.

**Ebb**, eb, *n.* the going back or retiring of the tide : a decline or decay.—*v.i.* to flow back : to sink : to decay. [A.S. *ebba* ; Ger. *ebbe*, from the same root as *even*.]

**Ebb-tide**, eb-tīd, *n.* the ebbing or retiring tide.

**Ebon**, eb′on, *adj.* made of *ebony* : black as ebony.

**Ebony**, eb′on-i, *n.* a kind of wood almost as heavy and hard as *stone*, usually black, admitting of a fine polish. [Fr. *ébène*—L. *ebenus*—Gr. *ebenos*, from Heb. *hobnim*, pl. of *hobni*, *obni*—*eben*, a stone.]

**Ebriety**, e-brī′e-ti, *n.*, *drunkenness*. [Fr. *ébrieté*—L. *ebrietas*, from *ebrius*, drunk.]

**Ebullient**, e-bul′yent, *adj.*, *boiling up* or *over*. [L. *ebulliens*, *-entis*—*e*, out, and *bullio*, to boil.]

**Ebullition**, eb-ul-lish′un, *n.* act of *boiling* : agitation : a display of feeling : an outbreak.

**Ecarté**, ā-kär′tā, *n.* a game at cards played by two, in which the cards may be *discarded* or exchanged for others. [Fr.—*e*, out, *carte*, a card. See **Card**.]

**Eccentric**, ek-sen′trik, **Eccentrical**, ek-sen′trik-al, *adj.* departing *from* the *centre* : not having the same centre as another, said of circles : out of the usual course : not conforming to common rules : odd.—*adv.* **Eccen′trically**. [Gr. *ek*, out of, and *kentron*, the centre. See **Centre**.]

**Eccentric**, ek-sen′trik, *n.* a circle not having the same *centre* as another : (*mech.*) a wheel having its axis out of the centre.

**Eccentricity**, ek-sen-tris′it-i, *n.* the distance of the centre of a planet's orbit *from* the *centre* of the sun : singularity of conduct : oddness.

**Ecclesiastes**, ek-klē-zi-as′tēz, *n.* one of the books of the Old Testament. [Gr., *lit.* a preacher.]

**Ecclesiastic**, ek-klē-zi-as′tik, **Ecclesiastical**, ek-klē-zi-as′tik-al, *adj.* belonging to the *church*.—*n.* **Ecclesias′tic**, one consecrated to the church, a priest, a clergyman. [Low L.—Gr. *ekklēsiastikos*, from *ekklēsia*, an assembly called out, the church—*ek*, out, and *kaleō*, to call.]

**Ecclesiasticus**, ek-klē-zi-as′tik-us, *n.* a book of the Apocrypha. [L.—Gr., *lit.* a preacher.]

**Ecclesiology**, ek-klē-zi-ol′o-ji, *n.* the *science* of building and decorating *churches*. [Gr. *ekklēsia*, a church, *logos*, a discourse.]

**Echo**, ek′ō, *n.*—*pl.* **Echoes**, ek′ōz, the repetition of a *sound* from some object.—*v.i.* to reflect sound : to be sounded back : to resound.—*v.t.* to send back the sound of : to repeat a thing said :—*pr.p.* ech′ōing ; *pa.p.* ech′ōed. [L. *echo* —Gr. *ēchō*, a sound.]

**Eclaircissement**, ek-lār′sis-mong, *n.* the act of *clearing* up anything : explanation. [Fr.— *éclaircir*, pr.p. *éclaircissant*, from *é* = L. *ex*, out, and *clair*—L. *clarus*, clear.]

**Eclat**, e-klä′, *n.* a striking effect : applause : splendour. [Fr. *éclat*, from O. Fr. *esclater*, to break, to shine ; from the Teut. root of Ger. *schleissen*, to break ; cog. with E. *slit*.]

**Eclectic**, ek-lek′tik, *adj.*, *electing* or *choosing out* : picking out.—*n.* one who selects opinions from different systems.—*adv.* **Eclec′tically**. [Gr. *eklektikos*—*ek*, out, *legō*, to choose.]

**Eclecticism**, ek-lek′ti-sizm, *n.* the practice of an eclectic : the doctrine of the Eclectics, certain philosophers who profess to choose from all systems the parts they think true.

**Eclipse**, e-klips′, *n.* the interception of the light of one celestial body by another : loss of brilliancy : darkness.—*v.t.* to hide a luminous body wholly or in part : to darken : to throw into the shade, surpass. [Fr.—L. *eclipsis*—Gr. *ekleipsis* —*ekleipō*, to fail—*ek*, out, *leipō*, to leave.]

**Ecliptic**, e-klip′tik, *n.* the line in which *eclipses* take place, the apparent path of the sun round the earth : a great circle on the globe corresponding to the celestial ecliptic.—*adj.* pertaining to the ecliptic. [Gr. *ekleiptikos*.]

**Eclogue**, ek′log, *n.* a pastoral poem. [L. *ecloga*— Gr. *eklogē*, a *selection*, esp. of poems—*ek*, and *legō*, to choose. See **Eclectic**.]

**Economic**, ek-o-nom′ik, **Economical**, ek-o-nom′- ik-al, *adj.* pertaining to economy : frugal : careful.—*adv.* **Econom′ically**.

**Economics**, ek-o-nom′iks, *n. sing.* the science of *household management* : political economy.

**Economise**, ek-on′o-mīz, *v.i.* to manage with economy : to spend money carefully : to save. —*v.t.* to use prudently : to spend with frugality.

**Economist**, ek-on′o-mist, *n.* one who is economical : one who studies political economy.

**Economy**, ek-on′o-mi, *n.* the *management* of a *household* or of money matters : a frugal and judicious expenditure of money : a system of rules or ceremonies : regular operations, as of nature. [L. *œconomia*—Gr. *oikonomia*—*oikos*, a house, and *nomos*, a law.]

**Ecstasy**, ek′sta-si, *n.* an extraordinary state of feeling, in which the mind *stands out of* or is detached from sensible things : excessive joy : enthusiasm. [Gr. *ekstasis*—*ek*, aside, *histēmi*, to make to stand.]

**Ecstatic**, ek-stat′ik, **Ecstatical**, ek-stat′i-cal, *adj.* causing *ecstasy* : amounting to ecstasy ; rapturous.—*adv.* **Ecstat′ically**.

**Ecumenic**, ek-ū-men′ik, **Ecumenical**, ek-ū-men′- ik-al, *adj.* belonging to the whole *inhabited world* : general. [L. *œcumenicus*, from Gr. *oikoumenē* (*gē*), the inhabited (world)—*oikeō*, to inhabit.]

**Eczema**, ek′zē-ma, *n.* an eruptive disease of the skin. [Gr. from *ekzeō*, I boil out, -*ek*, out, *zeō*, I boil.]

**Edacious**, e-dā′shus, *adj.* given to eating : gluttonous.—*adv.* **Eda′ciously**.—*n.* **Edacity**, e-das′- it-i. [L. *edax*, *edacis*—*edo*, to eat.]

**Edda**, ed′a, *n.* the name of two Scandinavian books, the one a collection of ancient mythological and heroic songs, the other a prose composition of the same kind. [Ice. 'great-grandmother,' a name given with good reason to a collection of old and venerable traditions.]

**Eddy**, ed'i, *n.* a *current* of water or air running back, contrary to the main stream, thus causing a circular motion : a whirlpool : a whirlwind.—*v.i.* to move round and round :—*pr.p.* edd'ying ; *pa.p.* edd'ied. [Either from an A.S. *ed*, back, present as *t-* in *twit*, or from Ice. *ida*, a whirlpool—*id*, back ; but the two roots are identical.]

**Edematose**, ē-dem'a-tōs, **Edematous**, ē-dem'a-tus, *adj.*, *swelling* with watery humour : dropsical. [Gr. *oidēma*, a swelling—*oideō*, to swell.]

**Eden**, ē'den, *n.* the garden where Adam and Eve lived : a paradise. [Heb. *eden*, delight, pleasure.]

**Edentate**, e-den'tāt, **Edentated**, e-den'tāt-ed, *adj.*, *without teeth* : wanting front teeth. [L. *edentatus*—*e*, neg., and *dens*, *dentis*, a tooth.]

**Edge**, ej, *n.* the *border* of anything : the brink : the cutting side of an instrument : something that wounds or cuts : sharpness of mind or appetite : keenness.—*v.t.* to put an edge on : to place a border on : to exasperate : to urge on : to move by little and little.—*v.i.* to move sideways. [M.E. *egge*—A.S. *ecg* ; Ger. *ecke*, L. *acies*—root *ak*, sharp.]

**Edgetool**, ej'tōol, *n.* a *tool* with a sharp *edge*.

**Edgewise**, ej'wīz, *adv.* in the direction of the *edge* : sideways. [Edge, and Wise—A.S. *wisa*, manner.]

**Edging**, ej'ing, *n.* that which forms the *edge* : a border : fringe.

**Edible**, ed'i-bl, *adj.* fit to be *eaten*. [L. *edo*, to eat.]

**Edict**, ē'dikt, *n.* something *spoken* or *proclaimed* by authority : an order issued by a king or lawgiver. [L. *edictum*—*e*, out, and *dico*, *dictum*, to say.]

**Edification**, ed-i-fi-kā'shun, *n.* instruction : progress in knowledge or in goodness.

**Edifice**, ed'i-fis, *n.* a large *building* or house.

**Edify**, ed'i-fī, *v.t.* to *build up* in knowledge and goodness: to improve the mind :—*pr.p.* ed'ifying ; *pa.p.* ed'ified.—*n.* Ed'ifyer. [Fr. *édifier*—L. *ædifico*—*ædes*, a house, and *facio*, to make.]

**Edifying**, ed'i-fī-ing, *adj.* instructive : improving.—*adv.* Ed'ifyingly.

**Edile**, ē'dīl, *n.* a Roman magistrate who had the charge of public *buildings* and works.—*n.* E'dileship. [L. *ædilis*—*ædes*, a building.]

**Edit**, ed'it, *v.t.* to *give out*, as a book : to superintend the publication of : to prepare for publication. [L. *edo*, *editum*—*e*, out, and *do*, to give.]

**Edition**, e-dish'un, *n.* the *publication* of a book : the number of copies of a book printed at a time.

**Editor**, ed'i-tur, *n.* one who *edits* a book or journal.—*fem.* Ed'itress.—*adj.* Editorial, ed-i-tō'ri-al.—*adv.* Edito'rially.—*n.* Ed'itorship.

**Educate**, ed ū-kāt, *v.t.* to *educe* or *draw out* the mental powers of, as a child : to train : to teach : to cultivate any power.—*n.* Ed'ucator. [L. *educo*, *educatus*.]

**Education**, ed-ū-kā'shun, *n.* the *bringing up* or training, as of a child : instruction : strengthening of the powers of body or mind.—*adj.* Edu-ca'tional.

**Educationist**, ed-ū-kā'shun-ist, *n.* one skilled in methods of *educating* or teaching : one who promotes education.

**Educe**, e-dūs', *v.t.* to *lead* or *draw out* : to extract : to cause to appear. [L. *educo*, *eductum*—*e*, and *duco*, to lead.]

**Educible**, e-dūs'i-bl, *adj.* that may be *educed* or brought out and shewn.

**Eduction**, e-duk'shun, *n.* the act of educing.

**Eductor**, e-duk'tor, *n.* he or that which *educes*.

**Eel**, ēl, *n.* a well-known fish, with a slimy body, living chiefly in mud. [A.S. *æl* ; Ger. *aal* ; akin to L. *anguilla*, dim. of *anguis*, a snake.]

**E'en**, ēn, a contraction of Even.

**E'er**, ār, a contraction of Ever.

**Efface**, ef-fās', *v.t.* to destroy the *face* or *surface* of a thing : to blot or rub out : to wear away.—*n.* Efface'ment. [Fr. *effacer*—L. *ef = ex*, from, and *facies*, the face.]

**Effaceable**, ef-fās'a-bl, *adj.* that can be *rubbed out*.

**Effect**, ef-fekt', *n.* the result of an action : impression produced : reality : the consequence intended :—*pl.* goods : property.—*v.t.* to produce : to accomplish. [L. *efficio*, *effectum*, to accomplish—*ef*, out, and *facio*, to do or make.]

**Effectible**, ef-fekt'i-bl, *adj.* that may be effected.

**Effection**, ef-fek'shun, *n.* a *doing* : creation : (geom.) the construction of a proposition.

**Effective**, ef-fek'tiv, *adj.* having power to effect : causing something : powerful : serviceable.—*adv.* Effec'tively.—*n.* Effec'tiveness.

**Effectual**, ef-fek'tū-al, *adj.* producing an effect : successful in producing the desired result.—*adv.* Effec'tually.

**Effectuate**, ef-fek'tū-āt, *v.t.* to accomplish.

**Effeminacy**, ef-fem'in-a-si, *n.* the possession of a *womanish* softness or weakness : indulgence in unmanly pleasures.

**Effeminate**, ef-fem'in-āt, *adj.*, *womanish* : unmanly : weak : cowardly : voluptuous.—*v.t.* to make womanish : to unman : to weaken.—*v.i.* to become effeminate.—*adv.* Effem'inately.—*n.* Effem'inateness. [L. *effeminatus*, pa.p. of *effemino*, to make womanish—*e*, sig. change, and *femina*, a woman.]

**Effendi**, ef-fen'di, *n.* a Turkish title of distinction. [Turk.; from modern Gr. *aphentēs*—Gr. *authentēs*, an absolute master.]

**Effervesce**, ef-fer-ves', *v.i.* to *boil up* : to bubble and hiss : to froth up.—*adj.* Effervesc'ible. [L. *effervesco*—*ef*, intensive, and *ferveo*, to boil. See Fervent.]

**Effervescent**, ef-fer-ves'ent, *adj.*, *boiling* or bubbling from the disengagement of gas.—*n.* Effervesc'ence.

**Effete**, ef-fēt', *adj.* exhausted : worn out with age. [L. *effetus*, weakened by having brought forth young—*ef*, out, *fetus*, a bringing forth young.]

**Efficacious**, ef-fi-kā'shus, *adj.* able to produce the result intended.—*adv.* Effica'ciously.—*n.* Effica'ciousness. [L. *efficax*—*efficio*.]

**Efficacy**, ef'fi-ka-si, *n.* virtue : energy.

**Efficience**, ef-fish'ens, **Efficiency**, ef-fish'n-si, *n.* power to produce the result intended.

**Efficient**, ef-fish'ent, *adj.* capable of producing the desired result : effective.—*n.* the person or thing that effects.—*adv.* Effic'iently. [L. *efficiens*, *-entis*, pr.p. of *efficio*.]

**Effigy**, ef'fi-ji, *n.* a *likeness* or *figure* of a person : the head or impression on a coin : resemblance. [L. *effigies*—*effingo*—*ef*, inten., *fingo*, to form.]

**Effloresce**, ef-flo-res', *v.i.* to *blossom* forth : (chem.) to become covered with a white dust: to form minute crystals. [L.—*ef*, forth, *floresco*, to begin to blossom—*floreo*—*flos*, a flower.]

**Efflorescence**, ef-flo-res'ens, *n.* production of *flowers* : the time of flowering : a redness of the skin : the formation of a white powder on the surface of bodies, or of minute crystals.

**Efflorescent**, ef-flo-res'ent, *adj.* forming a white dust on the surface : shooting into white threads. [L. *efflorescens*, *-entis*, pr.p. of *efflo-resco*.]

**Effluence**, ef'floo-ens, *n.* a *flowing out:* that which flows from any body : issue.

**Effluent**, ef'floo-ent, *adj., flowing out.—n.* a stream that *flows out of* another stream or lake. [L. *effluens, -entis,* pr.p. of *effluo—ef* (= *ex*), out, *fluo,* to flow.]

**Effluvium**, ef-floo'vi-um, *n.* minute particles that *flow out* from bodies : disagreeable vapours rising from decaying matter :—*pl.* **Effluvia**, ef-floo'vi-a.—*adj.* **Efflu'vial**. [L.—*effluo.*]

**Efflux**, ef'fluks, *n.* act of *flowing out:* that which flows out. [L. *effluo, effluxum.*]

**Effort**, ef'fort, *n.* a *putting forth* of *strength:* attempt : struggle. [L. *ef* (= *ex*), out, forth, and *fortis,* strong.]

**Effrontery**, ef-frunt'èr-i, *n.* shamelessness : impudence. [O. Fr.—L. *effrons, effrontis—ef* (= *ex*), forth, and *frons, frontis,* the forehead. See **Front.**]

**Effulgence**, ef-ful'jens, *n.* great lustre or brightness : a flood of light.

**Effulgent**, ef-ful'jent, *adj., shining forth:* extremely bright : splendid.—*adv.* **Efful'gently**. [L. *effulgens, -entis—ef* (= *ex*), out, and *fulgeo,* to shine.]

**Effuse**, ef-fūz', *v.t.* to *pour out:* to pour forth, as words : to shed. [L. *effundo, effusus—ef* (= *ex*), out, and *fundo,* to pour.]

**Effusion**, ef-fū'zhun, *n.* act of *pouring out:* that which is poured out or forth.

**Effusive**, ef-fū'ziv, *adj., pouring forth* abundantly : gushing.—*adv.* **Effu'sively.—n.** **Effu'siveness**.

**Eft**, eft, *n.* a kind of lizard : a newt. [A.S. *efete,* perh. akin to Gr. *ophis,* a serpent, Sans. *apada,* a reptile—*a,* neg., and *pad,* a foot. See **Newt.**]

**Egg**, eg, *n.* an oval body laid by birds and certain other animals, from which their young are produced : anything shaped like an egg. [A.S. *æg;* cog. with Ice. *egg,* Ger. *ei,* L. *ovum,* Gr. *ōon.* See **Oval.**]

**Egg**, eg, *v.t.* to instigate. [Ice. *eggja—egg,* an edge ; cog. with A.S. *ecg.* See **Edge.**]

**Eglantine**, eg'lan-tīn, *n.* a name given to the sweetbrier, and some other species of rose, whose branches are covered with *sharp prickles*. [Fr. *églantine,* formerly *aiglantier,* from an O. Fr. form *aiglent—*as if from a L. *aculentus,* prickly—*aculeus,* dim. of *acus,* a needle—root *ak,* sharp.]

**Egoism**, ē'go-izm or eg'-, *n.* an excessive love of *one's self:* the doctrine of the Egoists. [L. *ego,* I.]

**Egoist**, ē'go-ist or eg'-, *n.* one who thinks too much of himself : one of a class of philosophers who doubt everything but their own existence.

**Egotise**, ē'got-īz or eg'-, *v.i.* to talk much of *one's self*.

**Egotism**, ē'got-izm or eg'-, *n.* a frequent use of the pronoun *I:* speaking much of one's self : self-exaltation.

**Egotist**, ē'got-ist or eg'-, *n.* one full of egotism.

**Egotistic**, ē-got-ist'ik or eg', **Egotistical**, ē-got-ist'ik-al or eg-, *adj.* shewing *egotism:* self-important : conceited.—*adv.* **Egotist'ically**.

**Egregious**, e-grē'ji-us, *adj.* prominent : distinguished, in a bad sense.—*adv.* **Egre'giously**.—*n.* **Egre'giousness**. [L. *egregius,* chosen out of the flock—*e,* out of, *grex, gregis,* a flock. Cf. **Gregarious.**]

**Egress**, ē'gres, *n.* act of *going out:* departure : the power or right to depart. [L. *egredior, egressus—e,* out, forth, and *gradior,* to go. Cf. **Grade.**]

**Egyptian**, ē-jip'shi-an, *adj.* belonging to *Egypt.* —*n.* a native of Egypt : a gypsy. [L. *Ægyptius* —*Ægyptus,* Egypt, Gr. *Aigyptos.*]

**Egyptology**, ē-jip-tol'o-ji, *n.* the science of Egyptian antiquities.—*n.* **Egyptol'ogist**. [Egypt, and Gr. *logos,* discourse.]

**Eh**, ā, *int.* expressing inquiry or slight surprise.

**Eider**, ī'dèr, **Eider-duck**, ī'dèr-duk, *n.* a kind of seaduck, found chiefly in northern regions, and sought after for its fine down. [Ice. *ædr,* an eider-duck.]  [*duck.*]

**Eider-down**, ī'dèr-down, *n.* the *down* of the *eider-*

**Eidograph**, ī'do-graf, *n.* an instrument for *copying drawings*. [Gr. *eidos,* form, and *grapho,* to write.]

**Eight**, āt, *adj.* twice four.—*n.* the figure (8) denoting eight. [A.S. *eahta;* Scot. *aucht,* Ger. *acht,* Gael. *ochd,* L. *octo,* Gr. *oktō,* Sans. *ashtan.*]

**Eighteen**, āt'ēn, *adj.* and *n., eight* and *ten:* twice nine. [Orig. *eight-teen.*]  [decimo.

**Eighteenmo**, āt'ēn-mō, *adj.* and *n.* See **Octo-**

**Eighteenth**, āt'ēnth, *adj.* and *n.* next in order after the seventeenth.

**Eightfold**, āt'fōld, *adj.* eight times any quantity. —*n.* an eighth part. [Orig. *eight-th.*]

**Eighth**, āt'th, *adj.* next in order after the seventh.

**Eighthly**, āt'th-li, *adv.* in the eighth place.

**Eightieth**, āt'i-eth, *adj.* and *n.* the eighth tenth : next after the seventy-ninth.

**Eighty**, āt'i, *adj.* and *n., eight* times *ten:* fourscore. [A.S. *eahta,* and *tig,* ten.]

**Either**, ē'thèr or ī'thèr, *adj.* or *pron.* the one or the other : one of two : (*B.*) each of two.—*conj.* correlative to **Or**: (*B.*) or. [A.S. *æther,* a contr. of *æghwether* = *â,* aye, the prefix *ge,* and *hwæther,* E. **Whether**. See also **Each**.]

**Ejaculate**, e-jak'ū-lāt, *v.t.* to utter with suddenness.—*v.i.* to utter ejaculations. [L. *e,* out, and *jaculor, jaculatus—jacio,* to throw.]

**Ejaculation**, e-jak-ū-lā'shun, *n.* an uttering suddenly : what is so uttered.

**Ejaculatory**, e-jak'ū-lā-tor-i, *adj.* uttered in short, earnest sentences.

**Eject**, e-jekt', *v.t.* to *cast out:* to dismiss : to dispossess of : to expel. [L. *ejicio, ejectus—e,* out, *jacio,* to throw.]

**Ejection**, e-jek'shun, *n.* discharge : expulsion : state of being ejected : vomiting : that which is ejected.

**Ejectment**, e-jekt'ment, *n.* expulsion : dispossession : (*law*) an action for the recovery of the possession of land.

**Ejector**, e-jekt'or, *n.* one who ejects or dispossesses another of his land.

**Eke**, ek, *v.t.* to *add to* or *increase:* to lengthen. [A.S. *ecan,* akin to L. *augeo,* to increase ; also to *vigeo,* to be vigorous, and E. **Wax**.]

**Eke**, ek, *adv.* in addition to : likewise. [A.S. *eac;* Ger. *auch;* from root of **Eke**, *v.t.*]

**Elaborate**, e-lab'or-āt, *v.t.* to *labour on:* to produce with labour : to take pains with : to improve by successive operations. [L. *e,* intensive, and *laboro, laboratus,* to labour—*labor,* labour.]

**Elaborate**, e-lab'or-āt, *adj., wrought with labour:* done with fullness and exactness : highly finished. —*adv.* **Elab'orately.—n.** **Elab'orateness**.

**Elaboration**, e-lab-or-ā'shun, *n.* act of elaborating : refinement : the process by which substances are formed in the organs of animals or plants.

**Eland**, ē'land, *n.* the South African antelope, resembling the *elk* in having a protuberance on the larynx. [Dut. ; Ger. *elend,* the elk.]

**Elapse**, e-laps', *v.i.* to *slip* or glide *away:* to pass silently, as time. [L. *e*, out, away, and *labor*, *lapsus*, to slide. See **Lapse**.]

**Elastic**, e-las'tik, *adj.* having a tendency to recover the original form : springy : able to recover quickly a former state or condition after a shock.—*adv.* **Elas'tically.** [Coined from Gr. *elaō*, *elaunō*, fut. *elasō*, to drive ; akin to L. *alacer*, *alacris*, brisk.]

**Elasticity**, e-las-tis'it-i, *n.* springiness : power to recover from depression.

**Elate**, e-lāt', *adj.*, *lifted up :* puffed up with success.—*v.t.* to raise or exalt : to elevate : to make proud.—*adv.* **Elat'edly.**—*n.* **Elat'edness.** [L. *elatus—e*, up, out, and *latus*, from root of *tollo*. Cf. **Dilate** and **Tolerate**.]

**Elation**, e-lā'shun, *n.* pride resulting from success : a puffing up of the mind.

**Elbow**, el'bō, *n.* the joint where the *arm bows* or bends : any sharp turn or bend.—*v.t.* to push with the elbow : to encroach on. [A.S. *elboga—eln* = L. *ulna*, the arm, *boga*, a bow or bend —*bugan*, to bend. See **Ell** ; also **Bow**, *n.* and *v.t.*]

**Elbow-room**, el'bō-rōōm, *n.*, *room* to extend the *elbows :* space enough for moving or acting.

**Eld**, eld, *n.* old age, antiquity. [A.S. *æld*, from *eald*, old. See **Old**.]

**Elder**, eld'ér, *n.* a small tree with a spongy pith, bearing useful purple berries. [A.S. *ellern* ; it is perh. the same as **Alder**.]

**Elder**, eld'ér, *adj.* older : having lived a longer time : prior in origin.—*n.* one who is older : an ancestor : one advanced to office on account of age : one of the office-bearers in the Presbyterian Church. [A.S. *yldra*, comp. of *eald*, old. [Cf. **Alderman** and **Old**.] [on old age.

**Elderly**, eld'ér-li, *adj.* somewhat old : bordering

**Eldership**, eld'ér-ship, *n.* state of being older : the office of an elder. [superl. of *eald*.]

**Eldest**, eld'est, *adj.* oldest. [A.S. *yldesta*]

**Elect**, e-lekt', *v.t.* to *choose out :* to *select* for any office or purpose : to select by vote. [L. *eligo*, *electus—e*, out, *lego*, to choose.]

**Elect**, e-lekt', *adj.*, *chosen :* taken by preference from among others : chosen for an office but not yet in it.—*n.* one chosen or set apart.—**The elect** (*theol.*), those chosen by God for salvation.

**Election**, e-lek's un, *n.* the act of electing or *choosing:* the public choice of a person for office : freewill : (*theol.*) the predetermination of certain persons as objects of divine mercy : (*B.*) those who are elected.

**Electioneering**, e-lek-shun-ēr'ing, *n.* (also used as *adj.*) the soliciting of votes and other business of an election.

**Elective**, e-lekt'iv, *adj.* pertaining to, dependent on, or exerting the power of *choice.*—*adv.* **Elect'ively.**

**Elector**, e-lekt'or, *n.* one who *elects :* one who has a vote at an election : the title formerly belonging to those princes and archbishops of the German Empire who had the right to elect the Emperor.—*fem.* **Elect'ress.**

**Electoral**, e-lekt'or-al, *adj.* pertaining to elections or to electors : consisting of electors.

**Electorate**, e-lekt'or-āt, *n.* the dignity or the territory of an elector.

**Electric**, e-lek'trik, **Electrical**, e-lek'trik-al, *adj.* having the property of attracting and repelling light bodies when rubbed : pertaining to or produced by electricity.—*n.* any electric substance : a non-conductor of electricity, as amber, glass, &c.—*adv.* **Elec'trically.** [L. *electrum*—Gr. *ēlektron*, amber, in which the above property was first observed.]

**Electrician**, e-lek-trish'yan, *n.* one who studies, or is versed in, the science of *electricity*.

**Electricity**, e-lek-tris'i-ti, *n.* the property of attracting and repelling light bodies : the science which investigates the phenomena and laws of this property. [See **Electric**.]

**Electrify**, e-lek'tri-fī, *v.t.* to communicate electricity to : to excite suddenly : to astonish :—*pa.p.* elec'trified.—*adj.* **Elec'trifiable.**—*n.* **Elec'trifica'tion.** [L. *electrum*, *facio*, to make.]

**Electro-dynamics**, e-lek'tro-di-nam'iks, *n.* the branch of physics which treats of the action of electricity.

**Electro-kinetics**, e-lek'tro-kin-et'iks, *n.* that branch of science which treats of electricity in motion. [See **Kinetics**.]

**Electrolysis**, e-lek-trol'i-sis, *n.* the process of chemical *decomposition* by electricity. [Gr. *ēlektron*, *lysis*, dissolving—*lyō*, to loose, dissolve.]

**Electro-magnetism**, e-lek'tro-mag'net-izm, *n.* a branch of science which treats of the relation of electricity to magnetism.

**Electro-metallurgy**, e-lek'tro-met'al-ur-ji, *n.* a name given to certain processes by which electricity is applied to the working of metals, as in electroplating and electrotyping.

**Electrometer**, e-lek-trom'e-tér, *n.* an instrument for *measuring* the quantity of *electricity*. [Gr. *ēlektron*, and *metron*, a measure.]

**Electroplate**, e-lek'tro-plāt, *v.t.* to *plate* or cover with a coating of metal *by electricity*.

**Electroscope**, e-lek'tro-skōp, *n.* an instrument for detecting the presence of electricity in a body and the nature of it. [Gr. *ēlektron*, and *skopeō*, to examine.]

**Electro-statics**, e-lek'tro-stat'iks, *n.* that branch of science which treats of electricity *at rest*. [Gr. *ēlektron*, and **Statics**.]

**Electrotype**, e-lek'tro-tīp, *n.* the art of copying an engraving or *type* on a metal deposited by electricity.

**Electuary**, e-lek'tū-ar-i, *n.* a composition of medicinal powders with honey or sugar. [Low L. *electuarium*, a medicine that dissolves in the mouth—Gr. *ekleikton—ekleichō*, to lick up.]

**Eleemosynary**, e-le-mos'i-nar-i, *adj.* relating to *charity* or almsgiving : given in charity. [Gr. *eleēmosynē*, compassionateness, alms—*eleos*, pity. See **Alms**.]

**Elegance**, el'e-gans, **Elegancy**, el'e-gans-i, *n.* the state or quality of being elegant : the beauty of propriety : neatness : refinement : that which is elegant. [Fr., from L. *elegantia—elegans*.]

**Elegant**, el'e-gant, *adj.* pleasing to good taste : graceful : neat : refined : nice : richly ornamental.—*adv.* **El'egantly.** [Fr.—L. *elegans*, *-antis—eligo*, to choose.]

**Elegiac**, el-e-jī'ak or el-ē'ji-ak, *adj.* belonging to *elegy :* mournful : used in elegies.—*n.* elegiac verse.—*adj.* **Elegiacal**, el-e-jī'ak-al. [L.—Gr. *elegeiakos—elegos*, a lament.]

**Elegist**, el'e-jist, *n.* a writer of *elegies*.

**Elegy**, el'e-ji, *n.* a song of *mourning*, a lament : a funeral-song. [Fr.—L.—Gr. *elegos*, a lament.]

**Element**, el'e-ment, *n.* a first principle : one of the essential parts of anything : an ingredient : the proper state or sphere of any thing or being :—*pl.* the rudiments of anything : (*chem.*) the simple bodies that have not been decomposed : among the ancients, fire, air, earth, and water, supposed to be the constituents of all things : the bread and wine used at the Communion. [L. *elementum*, pl. *elementa*, first principles.]

**Elemental,** el-e-ment'al, *adj.* pertaining to elements or first principles : belonging to or produced by elements or the elements.—*adv.* **Element'ally.**

**Elementary,** el-e-ment'ar-i, *adj.* of a single element : primary : uncompounded : pertaining to the elements : treating of first principles.

**Elephant,** el'e-fant, *n.* the largest quadruped, having a very thick skin, a trunk, and two ivory tusks. [Fr.—L. *elephas, elephantis*—Gr. *elephas*—Heb. *eleph, aleph,* an ox. See **Alpha.**]

**Elephantiasis,** el-e-fant-I'a-sis, *n.* a disease in which the legs become thick like the *elephant's.* [Gr.—*elephas.*]

**Elephantine,** el-e-fan'tin, *adj.* pertaining to the elephant : like an elephant : very large.

**Elevate,** el'e-vāt, *v.t.* to *raise* to a higher position : to raise in mind and feelings : to improve : to cheer. [L. *elevo, elevatus*—*e,* out, up, *levo,* to raise—*levis,* light. See **Light,** *adj.*]

**Elevation,** el-e-vā'shun, *n.* the act of elevating or raising, or the state of being raised : exaltation : an elevated place or station : a rising ground : height : (*arch.*) a geometrical view of the side of a building : (*gun.*) the angle made by the line of direction of a gun with the plane of the horizon.

**Elevator,** el'e-vā-tor, *n.* the person or thing that lifts up : a machine for raising grain, &c. to a higher floor : a muscle raising a part of the body.

**Elevatory,** el'e-vā-tor-i, *adj.* able or tending to raise.

**Eleven,** e-lev'n, *adj.* ten and one.—*n.* the number 11. [A.S. *en(d)luf-on,* of which (*d* being excrescent, and -*on,* a dative pl. suffix) *en* = A.S. *an,* E. **One,** and -*luf* (or -*lif*) is prob. the root *tak,* ten, successively weakened to *dak, lik, lip,* and *lif;* cf. the Goth. *ain-lif.*]

**Eleventh,** e-lev'nth, *adj.* and *n.* the next after the tenth. [A.S. *endlyfta.*]

**Elf,** elf, *n.* a little spirit formerly believed to haunt woods and wild places : a dwarf :—*pl.* **Elves,** elvz. [A.S. *ælf;* Ger. *elf.*]

**Elfin,** elf'in, *adj.* of or relating to *elves.*—*n.* a *little elf*: a child. [Dim. of **Elf.**]                    [guised.

**Elfish,** elf'ish, **Elvan,** elv'an, *adj.* elf-like : dis-

**Elicit,** e-lis'it, *v.t.* to entice or *draw out*: to bring to light : to deduce. [L. *elicio, elicitus*—*e,* out, *lacio,* to entice. Cf. **Lace.**]

**Elide,** e-līd', *v.t.* to *strike out* or cut off, as a syllable. [L. *elido, elisus*—*e,* out, *lædo,* to strike. Cf. **Lesion.**]

**Eligibility,** el-i-ji-bil'i-ti, *n.* fitness to be elected or *chosen*: the state of being preferable to something else : desirableness.

**Eligible,** el'i-ji-bl, *adj.* fit or worthy to be *chosen*: legally qualified : desirable.—*n.* **El'igibleness,** same as **Eligibil'ity.**—*adv.* **El'igibly.** [Fr.—L. *eligo.* See **Elect,** *v.t.*]

**Eliminate,** e-lim'in-āt, *v.t.* to leave out of consideration.—*n.* **Elimina'tion.** [L. *elimino, eliminatus,* to turn out of doors—*e,* out, *limen, liminis,* a threshold.]

**Elision,** e-lizh'un, *n.* the *cutting off* or suppression of a vowel or syllable. [See **Elide.**]

**Elite,** ā-lēt', *n.* a *chosen* or *select* part : the best of anything. [Fr.—L. *electa* (*pars,* a part, understood). See **Elect,** *v.t.*]

**Elixir,** e-liks'ér, *n.* a liquor once supposed to have the power of prolonging life or of transmuting metals : the quintessence of anything : a substance which invigorates : (*med.*) a compound tincture. [Ar. *al-iksir,* the philosopher's stone, from *al-,* the, and *âksir,* quintessence.]

**Elizabethan,** e-liz-a-bēth'an or e-liz'-, *adj.* pertaining to Queen Elizabeth or her time.

**Elk,** elk, *n.* the largest species of deer, found in the North of Europe and in North America. [From the Scand., Ice. *elgr,* Sw. *elg;* O. Ger. *elch;* L. *alces,* Gr. *alkē.*]

**Ell,** el, *n.* a measure of length orig. taken from the *arm*: a cloth measure equal to 1¼ yds. [A.S. *eln,* Dut. and Ger. *elle,* L. *ulna,* Gr. *ōlenē,* the *el*-bow, the arm. See **Elbow.**]

**Ellipse,** el-lips', *n.* an oval : (*geom.*) a figure produced by the section of a cone by a plane passing obliquely through the opposite sides. [L. *ellipsis*—Gr. *elleipsis* (*lit.*) a defect, so called because its plane forms with the base of the cone a *less* angle than that of the parabola.]

**Ellipsis,** el-lip'sis, *n.* (*gram.*) a figure of syntax by which a word or words are *left out* and implied.—*pl.* **Ellipses,** el-lip'sēz. [L.—Gr. *elleipsis*—*en,* in, and *leipō,* to leave. Cf. **Eclipse.**]

**Ellipsoid,** el-lip'soid, *n.* (*math.*) a surface, every plane section of which is an ellipse. [Gr. *elleipsis,* and *eidos,* form.]

**Elliptic,** el-lip'tik, **Elliptical,** el-lip'tik-al, *adj.* pertaining to an *ellipse*: oval : pertaining to *ellipsis*: having a part understood.—*adv.* **Elliptically.** [Gr. *elleiptikos*—*elleipsis.*]

**Elm,** elm, *n.* a well-known forest tree. [A.S. *elm;* Ger. *ulme,* L. *ulmus.*]

**Elmy,** elm'i, *adj.* abounding with elms.

**Elocution,** el-o-kū'shun, *n.* style or manner of *speaking*: utterance.—*adj.* **Elocu'tionary.** [Fr. —L. *elocutio*—*eloquor, elocutus*—*e,* out, and *loquor,* to speak.]

**Elocutionist,** el-o-kū'shun-ist, *n.* one versed in elocution : a teacher of elocution.

**Eloge,** ā-lōzh', **Elogium,** e-lō'ji-um, *n.* a funeral *oration*: a panegyric. [Fr. *éloge*—L. *elogium,* a short statement, an inscription on a tomb—L. *e,* inten., and Gr *logos,* discourse.]

**Elongate,** e-long'gāt, *v.t.* to make *longer*: to extend. [Low L. *elongo, elongatus*—*e,* out, and *longus,* long.]

**Elongation,** e-long-gā'shun, *n.* act of *lengthening out*: state of being lengthened : distance.

**Elope,** e-lōp', *v.i.* to escape privately, said esp. of a woman, either married or unmarried, who runs away with a lover. [Prob. a corr. of Dut. *ont-loopen,* to run away, from *ont-* (Ger. *ent-*), away, and *loopen* = E. leap. See **Leap.**]

**Elopement,** e-lōp'ment, *n.* a secret departure, esp. of a woman with a man.

**Eloquence,** el'o-kwens, *n.* the *utterance* of strong emotion in correct, appropriate, expressive, and fluent language : the art which produces fine speaking : persuasive speech.

**Eloquent,** el'o-kwent, *adj.* having the power of *speaking* with fluency, elegance, and power : containing eloquence : persuasive.—*adv.* **El'o-quently.** [L. *eloquens, -entis,* pr.p. of *eloquor.* See **Elocution.**]

**Else,** els, *pron.* other.—*adv.* otherwise : besides : except that mentioned. [A.S. *elles.* otherwise—orig. gen. of *el,* other; cf. O. Ger. *alles* or *elles.* See **Alias.**]                                  [other places.

**Elsewhere,** els'hwār, *adv.* in another place : in

**Elucidate,** e-lū'si-dāt, *v.t.* to make *lucid* or clear : to throw light upon : to explain : to illustrate.—*ns.* **Elucida'tion, Elu'cidator.** [Low L. *elucido, elucidatus*—*e,* intensive, and *lucidus,* clear. See **Lucid.**]

**Elucidative,** e-lū'si-dā-tiv, **Elucidatory,** e-lū'si-dā-tor-i, *adj.* making *lucid* or clear : explanatory.

**Elude,** e-lūd', *v.t.* to avoid or escape by stratagem : to baffle. [L. *eludo, elusus*—*e,* out, *ludo,* to play.]

**Elusion**, e-lū'zhun, *n.* act of *eluding*: escape by artifice: evasion.

**Elusive**, e-lū'siv, *adj.* practising *elusion*: deceptive.—*adv.* **Elu'sively**.

**Elusory**, e-lū'sor-i, *adj.* tending to *elude* or cheat: evasive: deceitful.

**Elutriate**, e-lū'tri-āt, *v.t.* to separate (by *washing out* with water) the lighter from the heavier parts of ores, pigments, &c.—*n.* **Elutria'tion**. [L. *elutrio, elutriatus*, to wash out, to decant—*eluo* —*e*, out, and *luo*, to wash.]

**Elvan, Elves**. See under **Elfish, Elf**.

**Elysian**, e-lizh'i-an, *adj.* pertaining to Elysium: exceedingly delightful.

**Elysium**, e-lizh'i-um, *n.* (*myth.*) the abode of the blessed after death: any delightful place. [L. —Gr. *ēlysion* (*pedion*), the Elysian (plain).]

**Emaciate**, e-mā'shi-āt, *v.t.* to make *meagre* or *lean*: to deprive of flesh: to waste.—*v.i.* to become lean: to waste away. [L. *emacio, emaciatus*—*e*, intensive, *macio*, to make lean— *maci-es*, leanness. See **Meagre**.]

**Emaciation**, e-mā-shi-ā'shun, *n.* the condition of becoming emaciated or lean: leanness.

**Emanate**, em'a-nāt, *v.i.* to *flow out* or *from*: to proceed from some source: to arise. [L. *emano, emanatus*—*e*, out from, *mano*, to flow.]

**Emanation**, em-a-nā'shun, *n.* a *flowing out* from a source: that which issues or proceeds from some source.—*adj.* **Em'anative**.

**Emancipate**, e-man'si-pāt, *v.t.* to set free from servitude: to free from restraint or bondage of any kind.—*n.* **Eman'cipator**. [L. *e*, away from, and *mancipare*, to transfer property— *manceps, mancipis*, one who gets or acquires property, (*lit.*) who *takes* by the *hand*, from *manus*, the hand, *capio*, to take.]

**Emancipation**, e-man-si-pā'shun, *n.* the act of setting free from bondage or disability of any kind: the state of being set free.

**Emancipationist**, e-man-si-pā'shun-ist, *n.* an advocate of the emancipation of slaves.

**Emasculate**, e-mas'kū-lāt, *v.t.* to *deprive of* the properties of a *male*: to castrate: to deprive of *masculine* vigour: to render effeminate.—*n.* **Emascula'tion**. [Low L. *emasculo, emasculatus* —*e*, priv., and *masculus*, dim. of *mas*, a male.]

**Embalm**, em-bäm', *v.t.* to preserve from decay by aromatic drugs, as a dead body: to perfume: to preserve with care and affection.— *ns.* **Embalm'er, Embalm'ing**. [Fr. *embaumer*, from *em*, in, and *baume*. See **Balm**.]

**Embank**, em-bangk', *v.t.* to inclose or defend with a *bank* or dike. [Coined from *em*, in, and **Bank**.]

**Embankment**, em-bangk'ment, *n.* the act of embanking: a bank or mound.

**Embarcation**. Same as **Embarkation**.

**Embargo**, em-bär'gō, *n.* a prohibition of ships to leave port: a stoppage of trade for a short time by authority:—*pl.* **Embar'goes**.—*v.t.* to lay an embargo on:—*pr.p.* embar'gōing; *pa.p.* embar'gōed. [Sp.—*embargar*, to impede, to restrain —Sp. *em*, in, and *barra*, a bar. See **Barricade**, and **Embarrass**.]

**Embark**, em-bärk', *v.t.* to put on board a *bark* or ship: to engage in any affair.—*v.i.* to go on board ship: to engage in a business: to enlist. [Fr. *embarquer*, from *em*, in, and *barque*. See **Bark**, a barge.]

**Embarkation**, em-bär-kā'shun, *n.* a putting or going on board: that which is embarked.

**Embarrass**, em-bar'as, *v.t.* to encumber: to involve in difficulty, esp. in money-matters: to perplex: (*lit.*) to put a *bar* or difficulty *in the way of*.

[Fr. *embarrasser*—Fr. *em*, in, and (through Prov. *barras*) Fr. *barre*, a bar. See **Bar**.]

**Embarrassment**, em-bar'as-ment, *n.* perplexity or confusion: difficulties in money-matters.

**Embassy**, em'bas-i, *n.* the charge or function of an *ambassador*: the person or persons sent on an embassy. [Low L. *ambascia*. See **Ambassador**.]

**Embattle**, em-bat'l, *v.t.* to furnish with battlements. [*Em* and O. Fr. *bastiller*, from the same root as **Battlement, Bastille**, and **Baste**, to sew. The form of this word is due to a confusion with E. **Battle**.]

**Embattle**, em-bat'l, *v.t.* to range in order of *battle*. [Coined from *em*, in, and **Battle**.]

**Embay**, em-bā', *v.t.* to inclose in a *bay*: to landlock. [*Em*, in, into, and **Bay**.]

**Embed**. Same as **Imbed**.

**Embellish**, em-bel'ish, *v.t.* to make *beautiful* with ornaments: to decorate: to make graceful: to illustrate pictorially, as a book.—*n.* **Embell'isher**. [Fr. *embellir, embellissant*— *em*, in, *bel, beau*, beautiful. See **Beau**.]

**Embellishment**, em-bel'ish-ment, *n.* act of embellishing or adorning: decoration: ornament.

**Ember-days**, em'bėr-dāz, *n.pl.* in R. Catholic and English Church, three Fast-days in each quarter. [A.S. *ymbrine*, orig. sig. a *running round* or circuit—*ymbe*, round (Ger. *um*, L. *ambi*-), and *ryne*, a running, from *rinnan*, to run.]

**Embers**, em'bėrz, *n.pl.* red-hot ashes: the smouldering remains of a fire. [A.S. *emyrian*; Ice. *eimyrja*. The *b* is excrescent.]

**Embezzle**, em-bez'l, *v.t.* to waste or dissipate: to appropriate fraudulently what has been intrusted. —*n.* **Embezz'ler**. [Perh. from root of **Imbecile**, the primary sense being to weaken, waste; (*obs.*) *bezzle*, to squander, is the same word, the first syllable being dropped.]

**Embezzlement**, em-bez'l-ment, *n.* fraudulent appropriation of another's property by the person to whom it was intrusted.

**Embitter**. See **Imbitter**.

**Emblazon**, em-blā'zn, *v.t.* to deck in *blazing* colours: (*her.*) to *blazon* or adorn with figures. —*n.* **Embla'zonment**, an emblazoning. [*Em* and **Blazon**.]

**Emblazonry**, em-blā'zn-ri, *n.* the art of emblazoning or adorning: devices on shields.

**Emblem**, em'blem, *n.* a picture representing to the mind something different from itself: a type or symbol. [Lit. something *inserted* in a surface as ornament; Fr. *emblème*—L. *emblēma*, inlaid work—Gr.—*em* (= *en*), in, *ballō*, to lay, to cast.]

**Emblematic**, em-blem-at'ik, **Emblematical**, em-blem-at'ik-al, *adj.* pertaining to or containing *emblems*: representing.—*adv.* **Emblemat'ically**.

**Embloom**, em-blōōm', *v.t.* to cover or enrich with *bloom*. [*Em*, in, and **Bloom**.]

**Embodiment**, em-bod'i-ment, *n.* act of embodying: state of being embodied.

**Embody**, em-bod'i, *v.t.* to form into a *body*: to make corporeal: to make tangible.—*v.i.* to unite in a body or mass. [*Em*, in, and **Body**.]

**Emboguing**, em-bōg'ing, *n.* the *mouth* of a river. [See **Disembogue**.]

**Embolden**, em-bōld'n, *v.t.* to make *bold* or courageous. [*Em*, to make, and **Bold**.]

**Embolism**, em'bo-lizm, *n.* the *insertion* of days, months, or years in an account of time to produce regularity: (*med.*) the presence of obstructing clots in the blood-vessels.—*adjs.* **Embolism'al, Embolism'ic**. [Fr.—Gr. *embolismos* —*emballō*, to cast in. See **Emblem**.]

**Emborder**, em-bord´ėr, *v.t.* to *border*.

**Embosom**, em-booz´um, *v.t.* to take into the *bosom*: to receive into the affections: to inclose or surround. [*Em*, in, into, and **Bosom**.]

**Emboss**, em-bos´, *v.t.* to form *bosses* or protuberances upon: to ornament with raised-work.—*n.* **Emboss´er**. [*Em*, in, into, and **Boss**.]

**Embossment**, em-bos´ment,´ *n.* a prominence like a *boss*: raised-work.

**Embouchure**, em-boo-shōōr´, *n.* the *mouth* of a river, of a cannon, &c. : the mouth-hole of a wind musical instrument. [Fr.—*em-boucher*, to put to the mouth. See **Debouch, Debouchure**.]

**Embow**, em-bō´, *v.t., v.i.* to *bow* or arch. [*Em* and **Bow**.]

**Embowel**, em-bow´el, *v.t.* properly, to inclose in something else; but also used for *disembowel*, to remove the entrails from:—*pr.p.* embow´elling ; *pa.p.* embow´elled.—*n.* **Embow´elment**. [*Em*, in, into, and **Bowel**.]

**Embower**, em-bow´ėr, *v.t.* to place in a *bower*: to shelter, as with trees. [*Em*, in, and **Bower**.]

**Embrace**, em-brās´, *v.t.* to take in the *arms*: to press to the bosom with affection: to take eagerly or willingly : to comprise : to admit or receive.—*v.i.* to join in an embrace.—*n.* an embracing : fond pressure in the arms. [O. Fr. *embracer* (mod. Fr. *embrasser*)—*em*, L. *in*, in, into, and *bras*—L. *brachium*, an arm. See **Brace**.]

**Embrasure**, em-brā´zhūr, *n.* a door or window with the sides slanted on the inside : an opening in a wall for cannon. [Fr., properly, an opening through which a gun may be fired—*embraser*, to set on fire, from the O. Ger. *bras*, fire. See **Brasier** and **Brass**.]

**Embrocate**, em´bro-kāt, *v.t.* to *moisten* and rub, as a sore with a lotion. [Low L. *embroco*, *embrocatus*, from Gr. *embrochē*, a lotion—*em*—*brechō*, to soak in—*em* (= *en*), in, into, *brechō*, to wet.]

**Embrocation**, em-bro-kā´shun, *n.* act of embrocating : the lotion used.

**Embroider**, em-broid´ėr, *v.t.* to ornament with designs in needle-work, orig. on the *border*.—*n.* **Embroid´erer**. [*Em*, on, and Fr. *broder*, another form of *border—bord*, edge. See **Border**.]

**Embroidery**, em-broid´ėr-i, *n.* the act or art of embroidering : ornamental needle-work : variegation or diversity : artificial ornaments.

**Embroil**, em-broil´, *v.t.* to involve in a *broil*, or in perplexity : to entangle : to distract : to throw into confusion. [Fr. *embrouiller—em*, in, and *brouiller*, to break out. See **Broil**, *n.*]

**Embroilment**, em-broil´ment, *n.* a state of perplexity or confusion : disturbance.

**Embryo**, em´bri-ō, **Embryon**, em´bri-on, *n.* the young of an animal in its earliest stages of development : the part of a seed which forms the future plant : the beginning of anything :—*pl.* **Em´bryos, Em´bryons**.—*adj.*, also **Embryon´ic**, of or relating to anything in an imperfect state : rudimentary. [Fr.—Gr.—*em* (= *en*), in, and *bryon*, neuter of pr.p. of *bryō*, to swell.]

**Embryology**, em-bri-ol´oj-i, *n.* science of the embryo or fetus of animals.—*n.* **Embryol´ogist**.

**Emendation**, em-en-dā´shun, *n.* a mending or removal of an *error* or fault : correction. [L. *emendatio—emendo, emendatus—e*, out, away, and *mendum*, a fault. See **Amend**.]

**Emendator**, em´en-dā-tor, *n.* a corrector of errors in writings : one who corrects or improves.

**Emendatory**, e-men´da-tor-i, *adj.* mending or contributing to correction.

**Emerald**, em´ėr-ald, *n.* a precious stone of a green colour : a small printing-type. [Fr. *émeraude* (O. Fr. *esmeralde*)—L. *smaragdus*—Gr. *smaragdos*.]

**Emerge**, e-mėrj´, *v.i.* to *rise out of*: to issue or come forth : to reappear after being concealed : to come into view. [L. *emergo, emersus—e*, out of, *mergo*, to plunge.]

**Emergence**, e-mėr´jens, **Emergency**, e-mėr´jen-si, *n.* act of emerging : sudden appearance : an unexpected occurrence : pressing necessity.

**Emergent**, e-mėr´jent, *adj.* emerging : suddenly appearing : arising unexpectedly : urgent.—*adv.* **Emer´gently**. [L. *emergens, -entis*, pr.p. of *emergo*.]

**Emerods**, em´e-rodz, *n.pl.* (*B.*) now **Hemorrhoids**.

**Emersion**, e-mėr´shun, *n.* act of *emerging*: (*astr.*) the reappearance of a heavenly body after being eclipsed by another or by the sun's brightness.

**Emery**, em´ėr-i, *n.* a very hard mineral, used as powder for *polishing*, &c. [Fr. *émeri, émeril*—It. *smeriglio*—Gr. *smēris—smaō*, to smear.]

**Emetic**, e-met´ik, *adj.* causing *vomiting*.—*n.* a medicine that causes vomiting. [Through L., from Gr. *emetikos—emeō*, to vomit. See **Vomit**.]

**Emeu**. Same as **Emu**.

**Emigrant**, em´i-grant, *adj.* emigrating or having emigrated.—*n.* one who emigrates. [L. *emigrans, -antis*, pr.p. of *emigro*.]

**Emigrate**, em´i-grāt, *v.i.* to *migrate* or remove from one's native country to another.—*n.* **Emigra´tion**. [L. *emigro, emigratus—e*, from, *migro*, to remove.]

**Eminence**, em´i-nens, *n.* a part *eminent* or rising above the rest : a rising-ground : height : distinction : a title of honour.

**Eminent**, em´i-nent, *adj., rising above* others : conspicuous : distinguished : exalted in rank or office.—*adv.* **Em´inently**. [L. *eminens, -entis*, pr.p. of *emineo—e*, out, *mineo*, to project.]

**Emir**, ē´mir, *n.* a Turkish title given esp. to descendants of Mohammed. [Ar. *amir*; cog. with Heb. *amar*, to command. Doublet, **Ameer**.]

**Emissary**, em´is-ar-i, *n.* one *sent out* on a secret mission : a spy : an underground channel by which the water of a lake escapes.—*adj.* same as **Emissory**. [L. *emissarius—emitto*.]

**Emission**, e-mish´un, *n.* the act of emitting : that which is issued at one time. [*Emissus—emitto*.]

**Emissory**, e-mis´or-i, *adj.* (*anat.*) conveying excretions from the body. [*Emissus—emitto*.]

**Emit**, e-mit´, *v.t.* to *send out*: to throw or give out ; to issue :—*pr.p.* emit´ting ; *pa.p.* emit´ted. [L. *emitto, emissus—e*, out of, *mitto*, to send.]

**Emmet**, em´et, *n.* the ant. [A.S. *æmete*; cog. with Ger. *ameise*; perh. also with Ger. *emsig*, diligent, Ice. *amr*, work. **Ant** is a contr.]

**Emolliate**, e-mol´i-āt, *v.t.* to *soften*: to render effeminate. [L. *emollio, emollitus—e*, intensive, and *mollio*, to soften—*mollis*, soft.]

**Emollient**, e-mol´yent, *adj., softening*: making supple.—*n.* (*med.*) a substance used to soften the tissues. [L. *emolliens, -entis*, pr.p. of *emollio*.]

**Emolument**, e-mol´ū-ment, *n.* advantage : profit arising from employment, as salary or fees. [Fr.—L. *emolumentum*, for *emolimentum—emolior*, to work out—*e*, sig. completeness, and *molior*, to exert one's self, to toil ; or from L. *emolere—e*, and *molere*, to grind, thus sig. first, the produce of a mill, then, any profit.]

**Emotion**, e-mō´shun, *n.* a *moving* of the feelings : agitation of mind. [L. *emotio—emoveo, emotus*, to stir up, agitate—*e*, forth, and *moveo*, to move.]

**Emotional,** e-mō′shun-al, *adj.* pertaining to emotion.

**Empale,** em-pāl′, *v.t.* to fence in with *pales* or stakes : to shut in : to put to death by spitting on a stake.—*n.* **Empale′ment.** [*Em,* in, on, and **Pale,** a stake.]

**Empannel.** Same as **Impannel.**

**Empark.** Same as **Impark.**

**Emperor,** em′për-or, *n.* one ruling an empire.—*fem.* **Em′press.** [Fr. *empereur*—L. *imperator* (fem. *imperatrix*), a commander—*impero,* to command.]

**Emphasis,** em′fa-sis, *n.* stress of the voice on particular words or syllables to make the meaning *clear* : impressiveness of expression or weight of thought :—*pl.* **Em′phases,** -sēz. [Gr.—*em* (= *en*), in, into, and *phasis—phaō, phainō,* to shew, to make clear. See **Phase.**]

**Emphasise,** em′fa-sīz, *v.t.* to make *emphatic.*

**Emphatic,** em-fat′ik, **Emphatical,** em-fat′ik-al, *adj.* uttered with or requiring *emphasis* : forcible : impressive.—*adv.* **Emphat′ically.** [Gr. *empha(n)tikos—emphasis.*]

**Empire,** em′pīr, *n.* supreme control or dominion : the territory under the dominion of an emperor. [Fr.—L. *imperium—impero,* to command.]

**Empiric,** em-pir′ik, **Empirical,** em-pir′ik-al, *adj.* resting on *trial* or experiment : known only by experience. [Fr.—L. *empiricus,* from Gr. *empeirikos* = *empeiros—em,* in, and *peira,* a trial.]

**Empiric,** em-pir′ik, *n.* one who makes *trials* or experiments : one whose knowledge is got from experience only : a quack.—*adv.* **Empir′ically.**

**Empiricism,** em-pir′i-sizm, *n.* ( *phil.* ) the system which, rejecting all *à priori* knowledge, rests solely on experience and induction : dependence of a physician on his *experience* alone without a regular medical education : the practice of medicine without a regular education : quackery.

**Employ,** em-ploy′, *v.t.* to occupy the time or attention of : to use as a means or agent.—*n.* a poetical form of **Employment.**—*n.* **Employ′er.** [Fr. *employer*—L. *implicare,* to infold—*in,* in, and *plico,* to fold. **Imply** and **Implicate** are parallel forms.]

**Employé,** em-ploy′ā, *n.* one who is *employed.* [Fr. *employé,* pa.p. of *employer.* See **Employ.**]

**Employment,** em-ploy′ment, *n.* act of employing : that which engages or occupies : occupation.

**Emporium,** em-pō′ri-um, *n.* a place to which goods are extensively collected from various parts for sale : a great mart. [L.—Gr. *emporion* —*emporos,* a trader—*em* (= *en*), in, and *poros,* a way. See **Fare.**] [and **Power.**]

**Empower,** em-pow′ėr, *v.t.* to give power to. [*Em*

**Empress.** See **Emperor.**

**Emptiness,** em′ti-nes, *n.* state of being empty : want of substance : unsatisfactoriness.

**Empty,** em′ti, *adj.* having nothing in it : unfurnished : without effect : unsatisfactory : wanting substance.—*v.t.* to make empty : to deprive of contents.—*v.i.* to become empty : to discharge its contents—*pa.p.* em′ptied. [A.S. *æmtig,* empty—*æmta,* leisure, rest. The *p* is excrescent.]

**Empurple,** em-pur′pl, *v.t.* to dye or tinge *purple.* [*Em* and **Purple.**]

**Empyema,** em-pi-ē′ma, *n.* a collection of *pus* in the chest. [Gr.—*em* (= *en*), in, and *pyon,* pus.]

**Empyreal,** em-pir′e-al, *adj.* formed of pure *fire* or light : pertaining to the highest and purest region of heaven. [Coined from Gr. *empyros,* in fire—*em* (= *en*), in, and *pyr,* fire. See **Fire.**]

**Empyrean,** em-pi-rē′an, *adj.,* *empyreal.*—*n.* the highest heaven, where the pure element of *fire* was supposed by the ancients to subsist.

**Emu,** ē′mū, *n.* the Australian ostrich. [Port. ′ ostrich.′]

**Emulate,** em′ū-lāt, *v.t.* to *strive* to equal or excel : to imitate, with a view to equal or excel : to rival.—*n.* **Em′ulator.** [L. *æmulor, æmulatus* —*æmulus,* striving with.]

**Emulation,** em-ū-lā′shun, *n.* act of emulating or attempting to equal or excel : rivalry : competition : contest : ( *B.* ) sinful rivalry.

**Emulative,** em′ū-lā-tiv, *adj.* inclined to emulation. rivalry, or competition.

**Emulous,** em′ū-lus, *adj.* eager to emulate : desirous of like excellence with another : engaged in competition or rivalry.—*adv.* **Em′ulously.**

**Emulsion,** e-mul′shun, *n.* a white liquid prepared by mixing oil and water by means of another substance that combines with both. [Fr. —L. *emulgeo, emulsus,* to milk out—*e,* out, and *mulgeo,* to milk. See **Milk.**]

**Emulsive,** e-mul′siv, *adj.* milk-like : softening : yielding a milk-like substance. [See **Emulsion.**]

**Enable,** en-ā′bl, *v.t.* to make able : to give power, strength, or authority to. [*En,* to make, and **Able.**]

**Enact,** en-akt′, *v.t.* to perform : to act the part of : to establish by law. [*En,* to make, and **Act.**]

**Enactive,** en-akt′iv, *adj.* having power to enact.

**Enactment,** en-akt′ment, *n.* the passing of a bill into law : that which is enacted : a law.

**Enallage,** en-al′a-jē, *n.* (*gram.*) the *exchange* of one case, mood, or tense for another. [Gr. —*en,* and *allasso,* to make other—*allos,* another.]

**Enamel,** en-am′el, *n.* a substance like glass, which is *melted* and used for inlaying jewellery, &c. : any smooth hard coating, esp. that of the teeth : anything enamelled.—*v.t.* to coat with or paint in enamel : to form a glossy surface upon, like enamel :—*pr.p.* enam′elling ; *pa.p.* enam′elled. —*n.* **Enam′eller.** [Fr. *en* (= L. *in*), in, and M. E. *amel*—O. Fr. *esmail* (now *émail*), from a Teut. root, which appears in Ger. *schmelz, schmelzen,* E. **Smelt, Melt.**]

**Enamour,** en-am′ur, *v.t.* to inflame with *love* : to charm. [Fr. *en,* to make, and *amour*—L. *amor,* love.]

**Enarthrosis,** en-ar-thrō′sis, *n.* (*anat.*) a *joint* of ′ ball-and-socket′ form, allowing motion in all directions. [Gr.—*en,* in, and *arthroō, arthrōsō,* to fasten by a joint—*arthron,* a joint.]

**Encage,** en-kāj′, *v.t.* to shut up in a *cage.* [*En,* in, and **Cage.**]

**Encamp,** en-kamp′, *v.t.* to form into a *camp.*— *v.i.* to pitch tents ; to halt on a march. [*En,* in, and **Camp.**]

**Encampment,** en-kamp′ment, *n.* the act of encamping : the place where an army or company is encamped : a camp.

**Encase.** Same as **Incase.**

**Encaustic,** en-kaws′tik, *adj., burned in* or done by heat.—*n.* an ancient method of painting in melted wax. [Fr.—Gr.—*engkaio, engkausō— en,* in, and *kaio,* to burn. Cf. **Ink** and **Calm.**]

**Encave,** en-kāv′, *v.t.* to hide in a *cave.* [*En,* in, and **Cave.**]

**Enceinte,** äng-sengt′, *n.* ( *fort.* ) an *inclosure,* the wall or rampart which surrounds a place. [Fr. —*enceindre,* to surround—L. *in,* in, and *cingo, cinctus,* to gird.]

**Enceinte,** äng-sengt′, *adj.* pregnant, with child. [Fr.—L. *incincta,* girt about—*incingo, cinctus,* to gird in, gird about—*in,* and *cingo.* Cf. **Cincture.**]

**Enchain**, en-chān′, *v.t.* to put in *chains*: to hold fast: to link together.—*n.* **Enchain′ment**. [Fr. *enchaîner—en*, and *chaîne*, a chain—L. *catena*.]

**Enchant**, en-chant′, *v.t.* to act on by *songs* or rhymed formulas of sorcery: to charm: to delight in a high degree. [Fr. *enchanter*—L. *incantare*, to sing a magic formula over—*in*, on, *canto*, to sing. See **Chant**.]

**Enchanter**, en-chant′ėr, *n.* one who enchants: a sorcerer or magician: one who charms or delights.—*fem.* **Enchant′ress**.

**Enchantment**, en-chant′ment, *n.* act of enchanting: use of magic arts: that which enchants.

**Enchase**, en-chās′, *v.t.* to fix in a border: to adorn with raised or embossed work. [Fr. *enchâsser—en*, in, *châssis*, *caisse*, a case. See **Case**, *n.*, also **Case**, a covering. **Chase**, *v.t.* is a contr.]

**Encircle**, en-sėrk′l, *v.t.* to inclose *in* a *circle*: to embrace: to pass around. [*En*, in, and **Circle**.]

**Enclave**, äng′-klāv, *n.* a territory entirely inclosed within the territories of another power. [Fr.—L. *in*, and *clavus*, a key.]

**Enclitic**, en-klit′ik, *adj.* that *inclines* or *leans upon.—n.* (*gram.*) a word or particle which always follows another word, and is so united with it as to seem a part of it. [Gr. *engklitikos —en*, in, *klinō*, to bend, cog. with E. **Lean**.]

**Enclose**, en-klōz′. Same as **Inclose**.

**Encomiast**, en-kō′mi-ast, *n.* one who *praises*, or one who utters or writes encomiums. [Gr. *eng-kōmiastēs—engkōmion*.]

**Encomiastic**, en-kō-mi-as′tik, **Encomiastical**, en-kō-mi-as′tik-al, *adj.* containing *encomiums* or praise: bestowing praise.—*adv.* **Encomias′tically**. [Gr. *engkōmiastikos—engkōmion*.]

**Encomium**, en-kō′mi-um, *n.* high *commendation: —pl.* **Enco′miums**. [L.—Gr. *engkōmion*, a song of praise—*en*, in, *kōmos*, festivity.]

**Encompass**, en-kum′pas, *v.t.* to *compass* or go round: to surround or inclose.—*n.* **Encom′pass-ment**. [*En*, in, and **Compass**.]

**Encore**, äng-kōr′, *adv.* again: once more.—*v.t.* to call for a repetition of. [Fr. (It. *ancora*)—L. (*in*) *hanc horam*, till this hour, hence = still.]

**Encounter**, en-kownt′ėr, *v.t.* to run *counter* to or *against:* to meet face to face, esp. unexpectedly: to meet in contest: to oppose.—*n.* a meeting unexpectedly: an interview: a fight. [O. Fr. *encontrer*—L. *in*, in, and *contra*, against.]

**Encourage**, en-kur′āj, *v.t.* to put *courage* in: to inspire with spirit or hope: to incite.—*n.* **Encour′ager**.—*adv.* **Encour′agingly**. [Fr. *encourager—en*, to make, and *courage*. See **Courage**.]

**Encouragement**, en-kur′āj-ment, *n.* act of encouraging: that which encourages or incites.

**Encrinal**, en-krī′nal, **Encrinic**, en-krin′ik, **Encrinit′ic**, Encrinit′ical, *adj.* relating to or containing *encrinites*.

**Encrinite**, en′kri-nīt, *n.* the stone-*lily:* a fossilised animal on a long stem or stalk, with a *lily*-shaped head. [Gr. *en*, in, and *krinon*, a lily.]

**Encroach**, en-krōch′, *v.i.* to seize on the rights of others: to intrude: to trespass.—*n.* **Encroach′er**. —*adv.* **Encroach′ingly**. [Formed from Fr. *en*, and *croc*, a hook; cf. *accrocher* (*ad* and *crocher*), to hook up. See **Crochet**, **Crotchet**, and **Crook**.]

**Encroachment**, en-krōch′ment, *n.* act of encroaching: that which is taken by encroaching.

**Encrust**, en-krust′. Same as **Incrust**.

**Encumber**, en-kum′bėr, *v.t.* to impede the motion of, with something *cumbrous:* to embarrass: to load with debts. [Fr. *encombrer*, from *en-* and *combrer*. See **Cumber**.]

**Encumbrance**, en-kum′brans, *n.* that which encumbers or hinders: a legal claim on an estate.

**Encyclical**, en-sik′lik-al, *adj.* sent *round* to many persons or places, as an *encyclical* letter of the Pope. [Gr. *engkyklios—en*, in, and *kyklos*, a circle.] [Same as **Cyclopædia**.

**Encyclopædia**, **Encyclopedia**, en-sī-klo-pē′di-a, *n.*

**Encyclopedian**, en-sī-klo-pē′di-an, *adj.* embracing the whole *circle* of *learning*.

**Encyclopedic**, en-sī-klo-ped′ik, **Encyclopedical**, en-sī-klo-ped′ik-al, *adj.* pertaining to an encyclopedia.

**Encyclopedist**, en-sī-klo-pē′dist, *n.* the compiler or one who assists in the compilation of an encyclopedia. [bag. [*En*, in, and **Cyst**.]

**Encysted**, en-sist′ed, *adj.* inclosed in a *cyst* or

**End**, end, *n.* the last point or portion: termination or close: death: consequence: object aimed at: a fragment.—*v.t.* to bring to an end: to destroy.—*v.i.* to come to an end: to cease. [A.S. *ende*; Ger. and Dan. *ende*, Goth. *andeis*; Sans. *anta*; also akin to L. prefix *ante-* and Gr. *anti-*.]

**Endamage**, en-dam′āj, *v.t.* (*B.*) same as **Damage**.

**Endanger**, en-dan′jėr, *v.t.* to place in *danger:* to expose to loss or injury. [*En*, in, and **Danger**.]

**Endear**, en-dēr′, *v.t.* to make *dear* or more dear. [*En*, to make, and **Dear**.]

**Endearment**, en-dēr′ment, *n.* act of endearing: state of being endeared: that which excites or increases affection.

**Endeavour**, en-dev′ur, *v.i.* to strive to accomplish an object: to attempt or try.—*v.t.* (*Pr. Bk.*) to exert.—*n.* an exertion of power towards some object: attempt or trial. [Fr. *en devoir—en*, in (with force of 'to do' or 'make,' as in *en-amour*, *en-courage*), and *devoir*, duty. See **Devoir**.] [agon.

**Endecagon**, en-dek′a-gon, *n.* Same as **Hendec-**

**Endemic**, en-dem′ik, **Endemical**, en-dem′ik-al, **Endemial**, en-dē′mi-al, *adj.* peculiar to a *people* or a *district*, as a disease.—*n.* a disease of an endemic character.—*adv.* **Endem′ically**. [Gr. *endēmios—en*, in, and *dēmos*, a people, a district.]

**Ending**, end′ing, *n.* termination: (*gram.*) the terminating syllable or letter of a word.

**Endive**, en′div, *n.* a plant of the same genus as chicory, used as a salad. [Fr.—L. *intubus*.]

**Endless**, end′les, *adj.* without end: continual: everlasting: objectless.—*adv.* **End′lessly**.—*n.* **End′lessness**.

**Endocardium**, en-do-kar′di-um, *n.* the *lining* membrane of the *heart*.—*n.* **Endocarditis**, en-do-kar-dī′tis, disease thereof. [Gr. *endon*, within, and *kardia*, the heart. See **Heart**.]

**Endogen**, en′do-jen, *n.* a plant that *grows from within*, or by additions to the inside of the stem, as the *palm, grasses*, &c. [Gr. *endon*, within, and *gen*, root of *gignomai*, to be produced.]

**Endogenous**, en-doj′e-nus, *adj.* increasing like *endogens*, or by internal growth.

**Endorse**, en-dors′. Same as **Indorse**.

**Endow**, en-dow′, *v.t.* to give a *dowry* or marriage-portion to: to settle a permanent provision on: to enrich with any gift or faculty.—*n.* **Endow′er**. [Fr. *en* (= L. *in*), and *douer*, to endow—L. *doto*. See **Dower**.]

**Endowment**, en-dow′ment, *n.* act of endowing: that which is settled on any person or institution: a quality or faculty bestowed on any one.

**Endue**, en-dū′, an older form of **Endow**.

**Endurable**, en-dūr′a-bl, *adj.* that can be endured or borne.—*adv.* **Endur′ably**.—*n.* **Endur′ableness**.

**Endurance,** en-dūr'ans, *n.* state of enduring or bearing: continuance: a suffering patiently without sinking: patience.

**Endure,** en-dūr', *v.t.* to remain firm under: to bear without sinking.—*v.i.* to remain firm: to last. [Fr. *endurer—en* (= L. *in*), and *durer*, to last. See **Dure.**]

**Endwise,** end'wīz, *adv.*, *end ways:* on the end: with the end forward. [**End** and **Wise.**]

**Enema,** e-nē'ma or en'e-ma, *n.* a liquid medicine *thrown into* the rectum: an injection. [Gr.—*eniēmi*, to send in—*en*, in, and *hiēmi*, to send.]

**Enemy,** en'e-mi, *n.* one who hates or dislikes: a foe: a hostile army. [O. Fr. *enemi* (mod. Fr. *ennemi*)—L. *inimicus—in*, negative, and *amicus*, a friend. See **Amicable, Amity.**]

**Energetic,** en-ér-jet'ik, **Energetical,** en-ér-jet'ik-al, *adj.* having or shewing *energy:* active: forcible: effective.—*adv.* **Energet'ically.** [Gr. *energētikos.*]

**Energy,** en'ér-ji, *n.* power of doing *work:* power exerted: vigorous operation: strength. [Gr. *energeia—en*, in, and *ergon*, work; akin to E. **Work.**]

**Enervate,** en-ér'vāt, *v.t.* to deprive of *nerve*, strength, or courage: to weaken.—*n.* **Enervation,** en-ér-vā'shun. [L. *enervo, enervatus—e*, out of, and *nervus*, a nerve. See **Nerve.**]

**Enfeeble,** en-fē'bl, *v.t.* to make feeble: to deprive of strength, to weaken. [Fr. *en* (= L. *in*), causative, and E. **Feeble.**]

**Enfeeblement,** en-fē'bl-ment, *n.* act of enfeebling or weakening: weakness.

**Enfeoff,** en-fef', *v.t.* to give a *fief* or *feud* to: to invest with a possession *in fee.* [Fr. *en* (= L. *in*), and **Feoff.**]

**Enfeoffment,** en-fef'ment, *n.* act of enfeoffing: the deed which invests with the fee of an estate.

**Enfilade,** en-fi-lād', *n.* a *line*, or straight passage: a situation or a body open from end to end.—*v.t.* to rake with shot through the whole length of a line. [Fr. *enfiler—en* (= L. *in*), and *fil*, a thread. See **File**, a line or wire.]

**Enforce,** en-fōrs', *v.t.* to gain by force: to give force to: to put in force: to give effect to: to urge. [O. Fr. *enforcer—en* (= L. *in*), and *force.* See **Force.**]

**Enforcement,** en-fōrs'ment, *n.* act of enforcing: compulsion: a giving effect to: that which enforces.

**Enfranchise,** en-fran'chiz, *v.t.* to give a franchise or political privileges to. [Fr. *en* (= L. *in*), and E. **Franchise.**]

**Enfranchisement,** en-fran'chiz-ment, *n.* act of enfranchising: admission to civil or political privileges.

**Engage,** en-gāj', *v.t.* to bind by a *gage* or pledge: to render liable: to gain for service: to enlist: to gain over: to win: to occupy: to enter into contest with.—*v.i.* to pledge one's word: to become bound: to take a part: to enter into conflict. [Fr. *engager—en gage*, in pledge. See **Gage.**]

**Engagement,** en-gāj'ment, *n.* act of engaging: state of being engaged: that which engages: promise: employment: a fight or battle.

**Engaging,** en-gāj'ing, *adj.* winning: attractive. —*adv.* **Engag'ingly.**

**Engender,** en-jen'dér, *v.t.* to *gender* or beget: to breed: to sow the seeds of: to produce.—*v.i.* to be caused or produced. [Fr. *engendrer*—L. *ingenerare—in*, and *genero*, to generate. See **Genus** and **Gender.**]

**Engine,** en'jin, *n.* a complex and powerful machine,

esp. a p.ime mover: a military machine: anything used to effect a purpose. [Fr. *engin*—L. *ingenium*, skill. See **Ingenious.**]

**Engineer,** en-jin-ēr', *n.* an *engine-maker* or manager: one who directs military works and engines: a civil engineer, one who superintends the construction of *public* works. [Orig. *enginer.*]

**Engineering,** en-jin-ēr'ing, *n.* the art or profession of an *engineer.* [**Gird.**]

**Engird,** en-gérd', *v.t.* to *gird round.* [*En* and **English,** ing'glish, *adj.* belonging to *England* or its inhabitants.—*n.* the language or the people of England. [A.S. *Englisc*, from *Engle, Angle*, from the Angles who settled in Britain.]

**Engraft.** See **Ingraft.**

**Engrain,** en-grān'. Same as **Ingrain.**

**Engrave,** en-grāv', *v.t.* to cut out with a *graver* a representation of anything on wood, steel, &c.: to imprint: to impress deeply.—*n.* **Engrav'er.** [Fr. *en* (= L. *in*), and E. **Grave.**]

**Engraving,** en-grāv'ing, *n.* act or art of cutting designs on metal, wood, or stone: an impression taken from an engraved plate: a print.

**Engross,** en-grōs', *v.t.* to occupy wholly, monopolise: to copy a writing in a *large* hand or in distinct characters.—*n.* **Engross'er.** [From Fr. *en gros*, in large. See **Gross.**]

**Engrossment,** en-grōs'ment, *n.* act of engrossing: that which has been engrossed: a fair copy.

**Engulf.** See **Ingulf.**

**Enhance,** en-hans', *v.t.* to raise or heighten: to add to: to increase. [Prov. *enansar—enans*, forward, formed from L. *in ante*, before. See **Advance.**]

**Enhancement,** en-hans'ment, *n.* act of enhancing: state of being enhanced: increase: aggravation.

**Enigma,** en-ig'ma, *n.* a statement with a *hidden* meaning to be guessed: anything very obscure: a riddle. [L. *ænigma*—Gr. *ainigma, ainigmatos*—*ainissomai*, to speak darkly—*ainos*, a tale.]

**Enigmatic,** en-ig-mat'ik, **Enigmatical,** en-ig-mat'ik-al, *adj.* relating to, containing, or resembling an *enigma:* obscure: puzzling.—*adv.* **Enigmat'ically.**

**Enigmatise,** en-ig'ma-tīz, *v.i.* to utter or deal in *riddles.* [*tises.*

**Enigmatist,** en-ig'ma-tist, *n.* one who *enigma-***Enjoin,** en-join', *v.t.* to lay upon, as an order: to order or direct with authority or urgency. [Fr. *enjoindre*—L. *injungere—in*, and *jungo*, to **Join.**]

**Enjoy,** en-joy', *v.t.* to *joy* or delight in: to feel or perceive with pleasure: to possess or use with satisfaction or delight. [Fr. *en* (= L. *in*), and *joie.* See **Joy.**]

**Enjoyment,** en-joy'ment, *n.* state or condition of enjoying: satisfactory possession or use of anything: pleasure: happiness.

**Enkindle,** en-kin'dl, *v.t.* to *kindle* or set on fire: to rouse. [Fr. *en* (= L. *in*), and E. **Kindle.**]

**Enlarge,** en-lärj', *v.t.* to make *larger*: to increase in size or quantity: to expand: to amplify or spread out discourse: (*B.*) to set at large or free. —*v.i.* to grow large or larger: to be diffuse in speaking or writing: to expatiate. [Fr. *en* (= L. *in*), and E. **Large.**]

**Enlargement,** en-lärj'ment, *n.* act of enlarging: state of being enlarged: increase: extension: diffuseness of speech or writing: a setting at large: release.

**Enlighten,** en-līt'n, *v.t.* to *lighten* or shed light on: to make clear to the mind: to impart knowledge to: to elevate by knowledge or religion. [Fr. *en* (= L. *in*), and E. **Lighten**.]

**Enlightenment**, en-līt'n-ment, *n.* act of enlightening: state of being enlightened.

**Enlist**, en-list', *v.t.* to enrol: to engage in public service: to employ in advancing an object.—*v.i.* to engage in public service: to enter heartily into a cause. [Fr. *en* (= L. *in*), and *liste*, E. **List**.]

**Enlistment**, en-list'ment, *n.* act of enlisting: state of being enlisted.

**Enliven**, en-līv'n, *v.t.* to put *life* into: to excite or make active: to make sprightly or cheerful: to animate.—*n.* **Enliv'ener**. [Fr. *en* (= L. *in*), and E. **Life**. See also **Live**.]

**Enmity**, en'mi-ti, *n.* the quality of being an *enemy*: unfriendliness: ill-will: hostility. [Fr. *inimitié*, from *en*— (L. *in*-, negative), and *amitié*, amity. See **Amity**.]

**Ennoble**, en-nō'bl, *v.t.* to make *noble*: to elevate: to raise to nobility. [Fr. *ennoblir*—Fr. *en* (= L. *in*), and *noble*, E. **Noble**.]

**Ennui**, äng-nwē', *n.* a feeling of weariness or disgust from satiety, &c. [Fr. *ennui*—O. Fr. *anoi*—L. *in o.tio habui*, (*lit.*) 'I hold in hatred,' *i.e.* I am tired of. See **Annoy**.]

**Enormity**, e-nor'mi-ti, *n.* state or quality of being *enormous*: that which is enormous: a great crime: great wickedness.

**Enormous**, e-nor'mus, *adj.* excessive: atrocious.—*adv.* **Enor'mously**. [L. *enormis*—*e*, out of, and *norma*, rule. See **Normal**.]

**Enough**, e-nuf', *adj.* sufficient: giving content: satisfying want.—*adv.* sufficiently.—*n.* sufficiency: as much as satisfies desire or want. [A.S. *ge-noh, ge-nog*; Goth. *ga-nohs*; Ger. *ge-nug*; Ice. *g-nog-r*.] [used as its plural.

**Enow**, e-now', *adj.* Same as **Enough**, but often

**Enquire**. See **Inquire**.

**Enrage**, en-rāj', *v.t.* to make angry or furious. [Fr. *enrager*—*en* (= L. *in*), and *rage*, E. **Rage**.]

**Enrapture**, en-rap'tūr, *v.t.* to put in *rapture*: to transport with pleasure or delight. [Fr. *en* (= L. *in*), and E. **Rapture**.]

**Enrich**, en-rich', *v.t.* to make *rich*: to fertilise: to adorn. [Fr. *enrichir*—*en* (= L. *in*), and *riche*, E. **Rich**.] [that which enriches.

**Enrichment**, en-rich'ment, *n.* act of enriching:

**Enrol**, en-rōl', *v.t.* to insert in a *roll* or register: to record: to leave in writing:—*pr.p.* enroll'ing; *pa.p.* enrolled'. [Fr.—*en*, and *rolle*, E. **Roll**.]

**Enrolment**, en-rōl'ment, *n.* act of enrolling: that in which anything is enrolled: a register.

**Ensample**, en-sam'pl, *n.* a corr. of **Example**.

**Ensconce**, en-skons', *v.t.* to cover or protect, as with a *sconce* or fort: to hide safely. [Fr. *en* (= L. *in*), and E. **Sconce**.]

**Enshrine**, en-shrīn', *v.t.* to inclose in or as in a *shrine*: to preserve with affection. [Fr. *en* (= L. *in*), and E. **Shrine**.]

**Enshroud**, en-shrowd', *v.t.* to cover with a *shroud*: to cover up. [Fr. *en* (= L. *in*), and E. **Shroud**.]

**Ensign**, en'sīn, *n.* the *sign* or flag distinguishing a nation or a regiment: formerly the junior subaltern rank of commissioned officers of the British infantry, so called from bearing the colours. [Fr. *enseigne*—L. *insignia*, pl. of *insigne*, a distinctive mark—*in*, on, *signum*, a mark.]

**Ensigncy**, en'sīn-si, **Ensignship**, en'sīn-ship, *n.* the rank or commission of an *ensign* in the army.

**Ensilage**, en'sil-āj, *n.* the storing of green fodder, &c., in pits. [Fr.—*en*, and Sp. *silo*—L.—Gr. *siros*, pit for keeping corn in.]

**Enslave**, en-slāv', *v.t.* to make a *slave* of: to sub-

ject to the influence of. [Fr. *en* (= L. *in*), to make, and E. **Slave**.]

**Enslavement**, en-slāv'ment, *n.* act of enslaving: state of being enslaved: slavery: bondage.

**Ensnare**. Same as **Insnare**.

**Enstamp**, en-stamp', *v.t.* to mark as with a *stamp*. [Fr. *en* (= L. *in*), and **Stamp**.]

**Ensue**, en-sū', *v.i.* to *follow*: to succeed or come after: to result from: (*B.*) *v.t.* to follow after:—*pr.p.* ensū'ing; *pa.p.* ensūed'. [O. Fr. *ensuir* (Fr. *ensuivre*)—L. *in*, after, and *sequor*, to follow. See **Sue**.]

**Ensure**. Same as **Insure**.

**Entablature**, en-tab'la-tūr, **Entablement**, en-tā'bl-ment, *n.* (*arch.*) the superstructure, consisting of the architrave, frieze, and cornice, that surmounts the columns, and rests upon their capitals. [Fr. *entablement*, O. Fr. *entablature*, from L. *in*, in the manner of, *tabula*, a table.]

**Entail**, en-tāl', *v.t.* to *cut off* an estate from the heirs-general, and settle it on a particular heir or series of heirs: to bring on as an inevitable consequence:—*pr.p.* entail'ing; *pa.p.* entailed'. —*n.* an estate entailed: the rule of descent of an estate. [Fr. *entailler*, to cut into—*en*, in, into, and *tailler*, to cut—L. *talea*, a twig or cutting. See **Tally**.]

**Entailment**, en-tāl'ment, *n.* act of entailing: state of being entailed.

**Entangle**, en-tang'gl, *v.t.* to twist into a *tangle*, or so as not to be easily separated: to involve in complications: to perplex: to insnare. [Fr. *en* (= L. *in*), and E. **Tangle**.]

**Entanglement**, en-tang'gl-ment, *n.* state of being entangled: a confused state: perplexity.

**Enter**, en'tèr, *v.i.* to *go* or *come in*: to penetrate: to engage in: to form a part of.—*v.t.* to come or go into: to join or engage in: to begin: to put into: to enrol or record. [Fr. *entrer*—L. *intrare*, to go into—*in*, in, and a root *tar*, to cross, which appears in L. *trans*, across.]

**Enteric**, en-ter'ik, *adj.* belonging to the *intestines*. [Gr. *enterikos*—*enteron*, intestine.]

**Enteritis**, en-te-rī'tis, *n.* inflammation of the *intestines*.

**Enterprise**, en'tèr-prīz, *n.* that which is *taken hold of, entered on*, or attempted: a bold or dangerous undertaking: an adventure: daring. [Fr. *entrepris*, pa.p. of *entreprendre*—*entre*, in, into, and *prendre*, to seize—L. *prehendo*.]

**Enterprising**, en'tèr-prīz-ing, *adj.* forward in *undertaking*: adventurous.—*adv.* **En'terprisingly**.

**Entertain**, en-tèr-tān', *v.t.* to receive and treat hospitably: to hold the attention of and amuse by conversation: to receive and take into consideration: to keep or hold in the mind.—*n.* **Entertain'er**.—*adv.* **Entertain'ingly**. [Fr. *entretenir*—*entre*, among, and *tenir*—L. *teneo*, to hold.]

**Entertainment**, en-tèr-tān'ment, *n.* act of entertaining: hospitality at table: that which entertains: the provisions of the table: a banquet: amusement: a performance which delights.

**Enthral**. Same as **Inthral**.

**Enthrone**, en-thrōn', *v.t.* to place on a *throne*: to exalt to the seat of royalty: to instal as a bishop. [O. Fr. *enthroner*, from Fr. *en*, and *trône*—Gr. *thronos*, a throne.]

**Enthronement**, en-thrōn'ment, *n.* the act of enthroning or of being enthroned.

**Enthronisation**, en-thrōn-i-zā'shun, *n.* the *enthronement* of a bishop.

**Enthusiasm**, en-thū′zi-azm, *n.* intense interest: passionate zeal. [Gr. *enthousiasmos*, a god-inspired zeal—*enthousiazō*, to be inspired by a god—*en*, in, and *theos*, a god.]

**Enthusiast**, en-thū′zi-ast, *n.* one inspired by *enthusiasm*: one who admires or loves intensely.

**Enthusiastic**, en-thū-zi-as′tik, **Enthusiastical**, en-thū-zi-as′tik-al, *adj.* filled with *enthusiasm*: zealous: ardent.—*adv.* Enthusias′tically.

**Entice**, en-tīs′, *v.t.* to induce by exciting hope or desire: to tempt: to lead astray.—*adv.* Entic′ingly.—*n.* Entic′er. [O. Fr. *enticer*, *enticher*, to taint, the root of which is uncertain.]

**Enticeable**, en-tīs′a-bl, *adj.* capable of being enticed.

**Enticement**, en-tīs′ment, *n.* act of enticing: that which entices or tempts: allurement.

**Entire**, en-tīr′, *adj.* whole: complete: unmingled.—*adv.* Entire′ly.—*n.* Entire′ness. [Fr. *entier*—L. *integer*, whole, from *in*, not, and *tago*, *tango*, to touch.]

**Entirety**, en-tīr′ti, *n.* completeness: the whole.

**Entitle**, en-tī′tl, *v.t.* to give a *title* to: to style: to give a claim to. [Fr. *en* (= L. *in*), and Title. See Title.]

**Entity**, en′ti-ti, *n.*, *being:* existence: a real substance. [Formed by adding suffix -*ty* to L. *ens*, *entis*, being—*esse*, to be.]

**Entomb**, en-tōōm′, *v.t.* to place in a *tomb*, to bury. [En and Tomb.]

**Entombment**, en-tōōm′ment, *n.* burial.

**Entomologist**, en-to-mol′o-jist, *n.* one learned in entomology.

**Entomology**, en-to-mol′o-ji, *n.* the *science* which treats of *insects*.—*adjs.* Entomolog′ic, Entomolog′ical.—*adv.* Entomolog′ically. [Gr. *entoma*, insects, (*lit.*) animals cut into—*tomos*, cutting—*temnō*, to cut, and *logos*, a discourse.]

**Entozoa**, en-to-zō′a (*sing.* Entozō′on), *n.pl.* animals that live *inside* of other *animals*. [Gr. *entos*, within, and *zōon*, an animal.]

**Entrails**, en′trālz, *n.pl.* the *internal* parts of an animal's body, the bowels. [Fr. *entrailles*—Low L. *intralia*, corr. of *interanea*, neut. pl. of *interaneus*, inward—*inter*, within.]

**Entrain**, en-trān′, *v.t.* to put into a *train*, said of troops by railway.

**Entrance**, en′trans, *n.* act of entering: power or right to enter: the place for entering, the door: the beginning. [L. *intrans*, pr.p. of *intrare*.]

**Entrance**, en-trans′, *v.t.* to put into a *trance:* to fill with rapturous delight. [En, in, and Trance.]

**Entrancement**, en-trans′ment, *n.* state of *trance* or of excessive joy.

**Entrap**, en-trap′, *v.t.* to catch as in a *trap:* to insnare: to entangle. [En and Trap.]

**Entreat**, en-trēt′, *v.t.* (*orig.*) to *treat*, to deal with—so in *B.:* to ask earnestly: to pray for.—*v.i.* to pray. [En and Treat.]     [prayer.

**Entreaty**, en-trēt′i, *n.* act of entreating: earnest

**Entrench.** Same as Intrench.

**Entrust.** Same as Intrust.

**Entry**, en′tri, *n.* act of entering: a passage into: act of committing to writing: the thing entered or written: (*law*) the taking possession of.

**Entwine**, en-twīn′, *v.t.* to *twine*. [En and Twine.]     [and Twist.

**Entwist**, en-twist′, *v.t.* to *twist* round. [En

**Enumerate**, e-nū′mer-āt, *v.t.* to count the *number* of: to name over. [L. *e*, out, and *numero*, *numeratus*, to number. See Number.]

**Enumeration**, e-nū-mer-ā′shun, *n.* act of *numbering:* a detailed account: a summing up.

**Enunciate**, e-nun′si (or -shi) -āt, *v.t.* to state for-

mally: to pronounce distinctly.—*n.* Enun′ciator, one who enunciates. [L. *enuncio*, *enunciatum—e*, and *nuncio*, to tell—*nuncius*, a messenger.]

**Enunciation**, e-nun-si (or -shi) -ā′shun, *n.* act of enunciating: manner of uttering or pronouncing: a distinct statement or declaration : the words in which a proposition is expressed.

**Enunciative**, e-nun′si (or shi) -āt-iv, **Enunciatory**, e-nun′si (or shi) -āt-or-i, *adj.* containing *enunciation* or utterance: declarative.

**Envelop**, en-vel′up, *v.t.* to *roll* or *fold in:* to cover by wrapping: to surround entirely: to hide. [Fr. *envelopper;* the origin of the word is obscure, but may perh. be found in the Teut. root of M. E. *wlappen*, L. *lap.*]

**Envelope**, en′vel-ōp or äng′vel-ōp, *n.* that which *envelops*, wraps, or covers, esp. the cover of a letter.     [covering on all sides.

**Envelopment**, en-vel′op-ment, *n.* a *wrapping* or

**Envenom**, en-ven′um, *v.t.* to put *venom into:* to poison: to taint with bitterness or malice. [En, in, and Venom.]

**Enviable**, en′vi-a-bl, *adj.* that excites *envy:* capable of awakening desire to possess.—*adv.* En′viably.

**Envious**, en′vi-us, *adj.* feeling *envy:* directed by envy.—*adv.* En′viously.—*n.* En′viousness.

**Environ**, en-vī′run, *v.t.* to *surround:* to encircle: to invest :—*pr.p.* envī′roning ; *pa.p.* envī′roned.—*n.* Envi′ronment, a surrounding. [Fr. *environner—environ*, around—*virer*, to turn round, from root of Veer.]

**Environs**, en′vi-runz or en-vī′, *n.pl.* the places that *environ:* the outskirts of a city: neighbourhood.

**Envoy**, en′voy, *n.* a messenger, esp. one sent to transact business with a foreign government: a diplomatic minister of the second order.—*n.* En′voyship. [Fr. *envoyé—envoyer*, to send—*en*, on, and *voie*—L. *via*, a way.]

**Envy**, en′vi, *v.t.* to *look upon* with a grudging eye: to hate on account of prosperity :—*pr.p.* en′vying ; *pa.p.* en′vied.—*n.* pain at the sight of another's success : a wicked desire to supplant one : (*B.*) ill-will. [Fr. *envie*—L. *invidia—in*, on, and *video*, to look.]

**Envying**, en′vi-ing, *n.* (*B.*) envy, ill-will.

**Enwrap.** See Inwrap.

**Eocene**, ē′o-sēn, *adj.* (*geol.*) first in time of the three subdivisions of the tertiary formation. [Gr. *ēos*, daybreak, *kainos*, recent.]

**Eolian**, ē-ō′li-an, **Eolic**, ē-ol′ik, *adj.* belonging to *Æolia*, in Asia Minor, or to the Greek dialect of *Æolia:* pertaining to *Æolus*, god of the winds.

**Epact**, ē′pakt, *n.* the moon's age at the end of the year : the excess of the solar month or year above the lunar. [Gr. *epaktos*, brought on—*epi*, on, *agō*, to bring.]

**Epaulet**, ep-awl-et′, *n.* a *shoulder-piece:* a badge of a military or naval officer, now disused in the British army. [Fr. *épaulette—épaule*, the shoulder—*spatula*, a blade, in Late L. the shoulder, dim. of *spatha*—Gr. *spathē*, a blade.]

**Epergne**, e-pėrn′, *n.* an ornamental stand for a large dish for the centre of a table. [Fr. *épargne*, saving—*épargner*, to save : of uncertain origin.]

**Epha**, **Ephah**, ē′fa, *n.* a Hebrew measure for dry goods = 3 E. pecks and 3 pints. [Heb.—Coptic.]

**Ephemera**, ef-em′er-a, *n.* a fly that lives one *day* only: the Mayfly, a genus of short-lived insects : a fever of one day's continuance only. [Gr. *ephēmeros*, living a day—*epi*, for, and *hēmera*, a day.]

**Ephemeral**, ef-em'er-al, *adj.* existing only for a *day* : daily : short-lived.

**Ephemeris**, ef-em'er-is, *n.* an account of *daily* transactions : a journal : an astronomical almanac : —*pl.* **Ephemerides**, ef-e-mer'i-dēz.

**Ephemerist**, ef-em'er-ist, *n.* one who studies the *daily* motions of the planets.

**Ephod**, ef'od, *n.* a kind of linen surplice worn by the Jewish priests. [Heb.—*aphad*, to put on.]

**Epic**, ep'ik, *adj.* applied to a poem which recounts a great event in an elevated style.—*n.* an epic or heroic poem. [L. *epicus*—Gr. *epikos*—*epos*, a word.]

**Epicene**, ep'i-sēn, *adj.* or *n.*, *common* to both sexes : (*gram.*) of either gender. [Gr. *epikoinos* —*epi*, and *koinos*, common. See **Cenobite**.]

**Epicure**, ep'i-kūr, *n.* a follower of *Epicurus*, a Greek philosopher, who taught that pleasure was the chief good : one given to sensual enjoyment : one devoted to the luxuries of the table. [L. *Epicurus*—Gr. *Epikouros*.]

**Epicurean**, ep-i-kū-rē'an, *adj.* pertaining to *Epicurus* : given to luxury.—*n.* a follower of Epicurus : one given to the luxuries of the table.

**Epicureanism**, ep-i-kū-rē'an-izm, *n.* the doctrine of *Epicurus* : attachment to these doctrines.

**Epicurism**, ep'i-kūr-izm, *n.* the doctrines of *Epicurus* : luxury : sensual enjoyment.

**Epicycle**, ep'i-sī-kl, *n.* a circle having its *centre on* the circumference of a greater circle, on which it moves. [Gr. *epi*, upon, *kyklos*, a circle.]

**Epidemic**, ep-i-dem'ik, **Epidemical**, ep-i-dem'ik-al, *adj.* affecting a *whole people* : general.—*n.* a disease falling on great numbers.—*adv.* **Epidem'ically.** [Gr. *epidēmos*, general —*epi*, among, and *dēmos*, the people.]

**Epidermis**, ep-i-dėr'mis, *n.* that which lies *on the* true *skin* : the cuticle or outer skin of animals. —*adjs.* **Epider'mic**, **Epider'mal.** [Gr. *epidermis*—*epi*, upon, and *derma*, the skin.]

**Epigastric**, ep-i-gas'trik, *adj.* relating to the *epigastrium*, or upper part of the abdomen. [Gr. *epi*, upon, and *gastēr*, the stomach.]

**Epiglottis**, ep-i-glot'is, *n.* the cartilage at the root of the tongue that falls *upon the glottis*, or opening of the larynx. [Gr.—*epi*, upon, and **Glottis**.]

**Epigram**, ep'i-gram, *n.* (*in anc. times*) first a poetic inscription, then a short or pointed poem : a short poem on one subject ending with a witty or sarcastic thought : any concise and pointed or sarcastic saying. [Through Fr. and L., from Gr. *epigramma*, *epigrammatos*—*epi*, upon, and *gramma*, a writing, from *graphō*, to write.]

**Epigrammatic**, ep-i-gram-mat'ik, **Epigrammatical**, ep-i-gram-mat'ik-al, *adj.* relating to or dealing in *epigrams* : like an epigram : concise and pointed.—*adv.* **Epigrammat'ically.**

**Epigrammatise**, ep-i-gram'at-īz, *v.t.* to make an *epigram*.—**Epigrammatist**, ep-i-gram'at-ist, *n.* one who writes *epigrams*.

**Epigraph**, ep'i-graf, *n.* a *writing*, esp. on a building : a citation or motto at the commencement of a book or its parts. [Gr. *epi-graphē*—*epi*, upon, and *graphō*, to write.]

**Epilepsy**, ep'i-lep-si, *n.* a disease of the brain attended by convulsions, which *seizes on one suddenly*, causing him to fall.—*adj.* **Epilep'tic.** [Gr. *epilepsia*—*epi*, upon, and *lambanō*, *lēpsomai*, to seize, Sans. *labh*, to get.]

**Epilogue**, ep'i-log, *n.* a speech or short poem at the end of a play.—*adj.* **Epilog'ical**, -loj'. [Through Fr. and L., from Gr. *epilogos*, conclusion—*epi*, upon, and *legō*, to speak.]

**Epiphany**, e-pif'an-i, *n.* a church festival cele-

brated on Jan. 6, in commemoration of the *appearance* of Christ to the wise men of the East. [Gr. *epiphaneia*, appearance—*epi*, and *phainō*, to shew, from *phaō*, to shine.]

**Episcopacy**, e-pis'ko-pas-i, *n.* the government of the church by *bishops*. [L. *episcopatus*—Gr. *episkopos*, an overseer, a bishop. See **Bishop.**]

**Episcopal**, e-pis'ko-pal, *adj.* governed by *bishops* : belonging to or vested in bishops.—*adv.* **Epis'copally.**

**Episcopalian**, e-pis-ko-pā'li-an, *adj.* belonging to *bishops*, or government by bishops.—*n.* one who belongs to the Episcopal Church.

**Episcopalianism**, e-pis-ko-pā'li-an-izm, *n.*, *episcopalian* government and doctrine.

**Episcopate**, e-pis'ko-pāt, *n.* a *bishopric* : the office of a bishop : the order of bishops.

**Episode**, ep'i-sōd, *n.* a story *coming in* or introduced into a narrative or poem to give variety : an interesting incident. [Gr. *epeisodion*—*epi*, upon, *eisodos*, a coming in—*eis*, into, *hodos*, a way.]

**Episodial**, e-pi-sō'di-al, **Episodic**, e-pi-sod'ik, **Episodical**, e-pi-sod'ik-al, *adj.* pertaining to or contained in an *episode*: brought in as a digression. [*episode*: incidentally.]

**Episodically**, e-pi-sod'ik-al-i, *adv.* by way of **Epistle**, e-pis'l, *n.* a writing *sent* to one, a letter. [O. Fr. *epistle*—L. *epistola*—Gr. *epistolē*—*epi*, and *stellō*, to send.]

**Epistolary**, e-pis'to-lar-i, *adj.* pertaining to or consisting of *epistles* or letters : suitable to an epistle : contained in letters.

**Epistolic**, e-pis-tol'ik, **Epistolical**, e-is-tol'ik-al, *adj.* pertaining to *epistles* or letters : designating the method of representing ideas by letters and words.

**Epitaph**, ep'i-taf, *n.* an inscription *upon a tomb.* —*adjs.* **Epitaph'ian**, **Epitaph'ic.** [Gr. *epitaphion*—*epi*, upon, and *taphos*, a tomb.]

**Epithalamium**, ep-i-tha-lā'mi-um, *n.* a song in celebration of a *marriage*. [Gr. *epithalamion*—*epi*, upon, *thalamos*, a bedchamber, marriage.]

**Epithet**, ep'i-thet, *n.* an adjective expressing some real quality of the thing to which it is applied, or an attribute expressing some quality ascribed to it. [Gr. *epithetos*, added—*epi*, on, and *tithēmi*, to place.]

**Epithetic**, ep-i-thet'ik, *adj.* pertaining to an epithet : abounding with epithets.

**Epitome**, e-pit'o-me, *n.* an abridgment or short summary of anything, as of a book. [Gr.—*epi*, and *temnō*, to cut.]

**Epitomise**, e-pit'o-mīz, *v.t.* to make an *epitome* of : to shorten : to condense.

**Epitomiser**, e-pit'o-mīz-ėr, **Epitomist**, e-pit'o-mist, *n.* one who *epitomises* or abridges.

**Epoch**, ep'ok or ē'-, *n.* a point of time *fixed* or made remarkable by some great event from which events are reckoned : a period remarkable for important events. [Gr. *epochē*—*epechō*, to stop—*epi*, upon, and *echō*, to hold.]

**Epode**, ep'ōd, *n.* a kind of lyric poem in which a longer verse is followed by a shorter one.—*adj.* **Epod'ic.** [Gr. *ehōdos*—*epi*, on, and *ōdē*, an ode or song. See **Ode.**]

**Eponym**, **Eponyme**, ep'o-nim, *n.* a name, as of a country or people, derived from that of an individual.—*adj.* **Epon'ymous.** [Gr. *epi*, upon, to, and *onoma*, name.]

**Epopee**, ep'o-pē, *n.* the writing of *epic* poetry : an epic poem : the subject of an epic. [Fr.—Gr. *epopoiia*—*epos*, a word, an epic poem, *poieō*, to make.]

**Equability**, ē-kwa-bil′i-ti, *n.* state or condition of being *equable* or not variable.

**Equable**, ē′kwa-bl, *adj.*, *equal* and uniform: smooth: not variable.—*adv.* **E′quably.** [L. *æquabilis.*]

**Equal**, ē′kwal, *adj.*, *one* or the same in regard to any quality: adequate: in just proportion: fit: equable: uniform: equitable: evenly balanced: just.—*n.* one of the same age, rank, &c.—*v.t.* to be or to make equal to:—*pr.p.* ē′qualling; *pa.p.* ē′qualled.—*adv.* **E′qually.** [L. *æqualis*—*æquus*, equal; Sans. *ēka*, one.]

**Equalisation**, ē-kwal-i-zā′shun, *n.* the act of making *equal*: state of being equalised.

**Equalise**, ē′kwal-īz, *v.t.* to make *equal.*

**Equality**, ē-kwol′i-ti, *n.* the condition of being *equal*: sameness: evenness. [L. *æqualitas.*]

**Equanimity**, ē-kwa-nim′i-ti, *n.*, *equality* or evenness *of mind* or temper. [L. *æquanimitas*—*æquus*, equal, and *animus*, the mind.]

**Equation**, ē-kwā′shun, *n.* (*alg.*) a statement of the *equality* of two quantities: reduction to a mean proportion.

**Equator**, ē-kwā′tor, *n.* (*geog.*) a great circle passing round the middle of the globe, and dividing it into two *equal* parts: (*astr.*) the equinoctial.—*adj.* **Equato′rial.**

**Equery, Equerry**, ek′we-ri or ek-wer′i, *n.* one who has the charge of *horses*: in England, an officer under the sovereign's Master of the Horse. [Fr. *écurie*—Low L. *scuria*, a stable—O. Ger. *skiura* (Ger. *schauer*), shelter, a shed.]

**Equestrian**, e-kwes′tri-an, *adj.* pertaining to *horses* or *horsemanship*: on horseback.—*n.* one who rides on horseback. [L. *equester*, *equestris*—*eques*, a horseman—*equus.*]

**Equiangular**, ē-kwi-ang′gū-lar, *adj.* consisting of or having *equal angles.* [L. *æquus*, equal, and **Angular.**]

**Equidistant**, ē-kwi-dis′tant, *adj.*, *equally distant* from.—*adv.* **Equidis′tantly.** [L. *æquus*, equal, and **Distant.**]

**Equilateral**, ē-kwi-lat′ėr-al, *adj.* having all the *sides equal.* [L. *æquus*, equal, and **Lateral.**]

**Equilibrate**, ē-kwi-lī′brāt, *v.t.* to *balance* two scales *equally.*—*n.* **Equilibra′tion.** [L. *æquus*, equal, and **Librate.**]

**Equilibrium**, ē-kwi-lib′ri-um, *n.*, *equal balancing*: equality of weight or force: level position. [L. *æquus*, and *libra*, a balance.]

**Equimultiple**, ē-kwi-mul′ti-pl, *adj.*, *multiplied* by the same or an *equal* number.—*n.* a number multiplied by the same number as another. [L. *æquus*, equal, and **Multiple.**]

**Equine**, ē′kwīn, **Equinal**, e-kwīn′al, *adj.* pertaining to a *horse* or horses. [L. *equinus*—*equus.*]

**Equinoctial**, ē-kwi-nok′shal, *adj.* pertaining to the *equinoxes*, the time of the equinoxes, or to the regions about the equator.—*n.* a great circle in the heavens corresponding to the equator of the earth, so called because when the sun crosses it the days and *nights* are *equal.*

**Equinoctially**, ē-kwi-nok′shal-i, *adv.* in the direction of the equinox.

**Equinox**, ē′kwi-noks, *n.* the time when the sun crosses the equator, making the *night equal* in length to the day, about 21st March and 23d Sept. [L. *æquus*, equal, and *nox*, *noctis*, night.]

**Equip**, e-kwip′, *v.t.* to *fit out*: to furnish with everything needed for any service or work:—*pr.p.* equipp′ing; *pa.p.* equipped′. [Fr. *équiper* for *esquiper*, to attire; from a Teut. root, found in O. Ger. *skif*, Ger. *schiff*, E. *ship* and *shape*; also Ice. *skipa*, to set in order.]

**Equipage**, ek′wi-pāj, *n.* that with which one is *equipped*: furniture required for any service, as armour of a soldier, &c.; a carriage and attendants, retinue.—*adj.* **Eq′uipaged**, furnished with an equipage.

**Equipment**, e-kwip′ment, *n.* the act of equipping: the state of being equipped: things used in equipping or furnishing.

**Equipoise**, ē′kwi-poiz, *n.*, *equality of weight* or force: the state of a balance when the two weights are equal. [L. *æquus*, equal, and **Poise.**]

**Equipollent**, ē-kwi-pol′ent, *adj.* having *equal power* or force: equivalent.—*n.* **Equipol′lence.** [L. *æquus*, equal, and *pollens*, *pollentis*, pr.p. of *polleo*, to be able.]

**Equiponderant**, ē-kwi-pon′dėr-ant, *adj.*, *equal* in *weight*.—*n.* **Equipon′derance.** [L. *æquus*, equal, and *pondus*, *ponderis*, weight.]

**Equiponderate**, ē-kwi-pon′dėr-āt, *v.i.* to be *equal* in *weight*: to balance.

**Equitable**, ek′wi-ta-bl, *adj.* possessing or exhibiting *equity*: held or exercised in equity.—*adv.* **Eq′uitably.**—*n.* **Eq′uitableness.**

**Equitation**, ek-wi-tā′shun, *n.* the art of riding on *horse*back. [L. *equito*, to ride—*equus*, a horse.]

**Equity**, ek′wi-ti, *n.* right as founded on the laws of nature: fairness: justice. [Fr. *équité*—L. *æquitas* —*æquus*, equal.]

**Equivalent**, e-kwiv′a-lent, *adj.*, *equal* in *value*, *power*, effect, meaning, &c.—*n.* a thing equal in value, &c.—*adv.* **Equiv′alently.**—*n.* **Equiv′alence.** [Fr.—L. *æquus*, equal, and *valens*, *valentis*, pr.p. of *valeo*, to be strong.]

**Equivocal**, e-kwiv′ō-kal, *adj.*, *meaning equally* two or more things: of doubtful meaning: capable of a double explanation.—*adv.* **Equiv′ocally.**—*n.* **Equiv′ocalness.** [L. *æquus*, equal, and *vox*, *vocis*, the voice, a word.]

**Equivocate**, e-kwiv′ō-kāt, *v.i.* to use *equivocal* or doubtful *words* in order to mislead.

**Equivocation**, e-kwiv-ō-kā′shun, *n.* act of equivocating or using ambiguous words to mislead.— *n.* **Equiv′ocator.**

**Era**, ē′ra, *n.* a series of *years* reckoned from a particular point. [Late L. *æra*, a number, hence a space of time, orig. ' counters,' pieces of copper used in counting, being the neuter pl. of *æs*, *æris*, copper.]

**Eradicate**, e-rad′i-kāt, *v.t.* to pull up by the *roots*: to destroy. [L. *eradico*, to root out—*e*, and *radix*, *radicis*, a root.]

**Eradication**, e-rad-i-kā′shun, *n.* the act of eradicating: state of being eradicated.

**Erase**, e-rās′, *v.t.* to *rub* or *scrape out*: to efface: to destroy.—*adj.* **Eras′able.**—*n.* **Eras′er.** [L. *erado*—*e*, out, and *rado*, *rasus*, to scrape.]

**Erasion**, e-rā′zhun, **Erasement**, e-rāz′ment, **Erasure**, e-rā′zhōōr, *n.* the act of erasing: a rubbing out: the place where something written has been rubbed out.

**Erastian**, e-rast′yan, *n.* a follower of Thomas *Erastus*, a Swiss physician, who maintained that the church is wholly dependent on the state for its existence and authority.—*adj.* relating to the Erastians or their doctrines.

**Erastianism**, e-rast′yan-izm, *n.* principles of the *Erastians*: control of the church by the state.

**Ere**, ār, *adv.*, *before*: sooner than.—*prep.* before. [A.S. *ær*; Goth. *air*, soon.]

**Erect**, e-rekt′, *v.t.* to set *upright*: to raise: to build: to exalt: to establish. [L. *erectus*, from *erigo*, to set upright—*e*, out, and *rego*, to make straight.]

**Erect**, e-rekt′, *adj.*, *upright*: directed upward:

unshaken : bold.—*adv.* **Erect′ly.**—*n.* **Erect′-ness.**

**Erection,** e-rek′shun, *n.* act of erecting or raising : state of being erected : exaltation : anything erected : a building of any kind.

**Eremite,** er′e-mīt, *n.* now **Hermit.**

**Ermine,** ėr′min, *n.* a northern animal of the weasel tribe, valued for its fur ; its white fur, an emblem of the purity of judges and magistrates, whose robes are lined with it.—*adj.* **Er′mined,** adorned with ermine. [O. Fr. *ermine* (Fr. *hermine*) ; from L. (*mus*) *Armenius,* lit. mouse of *Armenia,* whence it was brought to Rome : but acc. to Skeat from O. Ger. *harmin* (Ger. *hermelin*), ermine-fur.]     [*rosus,* to gnaw.]

**Erode,** e-rōd′, *v.t.* to *eat away.* [L. *e,* and *rodo,*

**Erosion,** e-rō′zhun, *n.* the act of eroding or eating away : the state of being eaten away.

**Erosive,** e-rō′siv, *adj.* having the property of eroding or eating away.

**Erotic,** e-rot′ik, **Erotical,** e-rot′ik-al, *adj.* pertaining to *love.* [Gr. *erōtikos—erōs, erōtos,* love.]

**Err,** er, *v.i.* to *wander* from the right way : to go astray : to mistake : to sin. [Fr. *errer—*L. *erro,* to stray ; cog. with Ger. *irren,* and *irre,* astray.]

**Errand,** er′and, *n.* a *message* : a commission to say or do something. [A.S. *ærende* ; Ice. *eyrendi* ; acc. to Max Müller, from root *ar,* to plough, to work, *ende* being the pr.p. suffix.]

**Errant,** er′ant, *adj.,* erring or wandering : roving : wild. [L. *errans, errantis,* pr.p. of *erro.*]

**Errantry,** er′ant-ri, *n.* an *errant* or wandering state : a rambling about like a knight-errant.

**Erratic,** er-at′ik, **Erratical,** er-at′ik-al, *adj., wandering :* having no certain course : not stationary.—*adv.* **Errat′ically.**

**Erratum,** er-ā′tum, *n.* an *error* in writing or printing :—*pl.* **Errata,** er-ā′ta. [L.—*erro,* to stray.]

**Erroneous,** er-ō′ne-us, *adj., wandering :* erring : full of *error :* wrong : mistaken.—*adv.* **Erro′neously.**—*n.* **Erro′neousness.**

**Error,** er′or, *n.* a *wandering* or deviation from truth, right, &c. : a blunder or mistake : a fault : sin. [L.—*erro,* to wander.]

**Erse,** ėrs, *n.* corr. of *Irish,* the name given by the Lowland Scots to the language of the people of the W. Highlands, as being of Irish origin.

**Erst,** ėrst, *adv., first :* at first : formerly. [A.S. *ærest,* superl. of *ær.* See **Ere.**]

**Erubescent,** er-ōō-bes′ent, *adj., growing red :* red or reddish : blushing.—*n.* **Erubesc′ence.** [L. *erubescens, -entis,* pr.p. of *erubesco,* to grow red —*e,* out, very much, and *rubesco—rubere,* to be red. See **Ruby.**]

**Eructation,** er-uk-tā′shun, *n.* the act of *belching* or rejecting wind from the stomach : a violent ejection of wind or other matter from the earth. [L. *eructo, eructatus—e,* and *ructo,* to belch forth ; cog. with Gr. *ereugomai,* to vomit, aorist *e-rug-on.*]

**Erudite,** er′ū-dīt, *adj.* learned.—*adv.* **Er′uditely.** [L. *erudio, eruditus,* to free from rudeness—*e,* from, and *rudis,* rude.]

**Erudition,** er-ū-di′shun, *n.* state of being *erudite* or learned : knowledge gained by study : learning, esp. in literature.

**Eruginous,** e-rōō′jin-us, *adj.* resembling the *rust* of *copper* or brass : rusty. [L. *eruginosus—ærugo,* rust of copper—*æs, æris,* metal, copper.]

**Erupted,** e-rupt′ed, *adj.* suddenly and forcibly *thrown out,* as lava from a volcano.

**Eruption,** e-rup′shun, *n.* a *breaking* or bursting

*forth :* that which bursts forth : a breaking out of spots on the skin. [L. *eruptio—erumpo, eruptus—e,* out, and *rumpo,* to break.]

**Eruptive,** e-rupt′iv, *adj., breaking forth :* attended by or producing eruption : produced by eruption.

**Erysipelas,** er-i-sip′e-las, *n.* an inflammatory disease, generally in the face, marked by a bright *redness* of the *skin.* [Gr.—*e-ryth-ros,* red, and *pella,* skin. See **Red** and **Pell.**]

**Escalade,** es-ka-lād′ or es-′, *n.* the *scaling* of the walls of a fortress by means of *ladders.*—*v.t.* to *scale :* to mount and enter by means of ladders. [Fr.—Sp. *escalado—escala,* a ladder—L. *scala.*]

**Escalop,** es-kol′up. Same as **Scallop.**

**Escapade,** es-ka-pād′, *n.* a mischievous freak.

**Escape,** es-kāp′, *v.t.* to flee from : to pass unobserved : to evade.—*v.i.* to flee and become safe from danger : to be passed without harm. —*n.* act of escaping : flight from danger or from prison. [O. Fr. *escaper* (Fr. *échapper*)—L. *ex cappa,* lit. 'out of one's cape or cloak.' See **Cape.**]

**Escapement,** es-kāp′ment, *n.* part of a timepiece connecting the wheelwork with the pendulum or balance, and allowing a tooth to *escape* at each vibration.

**Escarp,** es-kärp′, *v.t.* to make into a *scarp* or sudden slope.—*n.* a scarp or steep slope : (*fort.*) the side of the ditch next the rampart. [Fr. *escarper,* to cut down steep, from root of **Scarp.**]

**Escarpment,** es-kärp′ment, *n.* the precipitous side of any hill or rock : (*fort.*) same as **Escarp.**

**Eschalot,** esh-a-lot′, *n.* a kind of small onion, formerly found at *Ascalon* in Palestine. [O. Fr. *eschalote*—L. *Ascalonius,* of Ascalon.]

**Eschatology,** es-ka-tol′o-ji, *n.* (*theol.*) the doctrine of the *last* or final things, as death, judgment, the state after death. [Gr. *eschatos,* last, and *logos,* a discourse.]

**Escheat,** es-chēt′, *n.* property which *falls* to the state for want of an heir, or by forfeiture.—*v.i.* to *fall* to the lord of the manor or to the state. [O. Fr. *escheat—escheoir* (Mod. Fr. *échoir*)—Low L. *excadere*—L. *ex,* out, and *cado,* to fall.]

**Eschew,** es-chōō′, *v.t.* to *shun :* to flee from. [O. Fr. *eschever,* cog. with Ger. *scheuen,* to shy at.]

**Escort,** es′kort, *n.* a *guide :* an attendant : a guard : a body of armed men as a guard. [Fr. *escorte*—It. *scorta,* a guide—*scorgere,* to guide —L. *ex,* and *corrigere,* to set right.]

**Escort,** es-kort′, *v.t.* to attend as a guard.

**Escritoire,** es-kri-twor′, *n.* a *writing-desk.* [O. Fr. *escriptoire,* Fr. *écritoire*—Low L. *scriptorium—scribo, scriptum,* to write.]

**Esculapian,** es-kū-lā′pi-an, *adj.* pertaining to *Esculapius,* and hence—to the art of healing. [*Æsculapius,* the god of the healing art.]

**Esculent,** es′kū-lent, *adj., eatable :* fit to be used for food by man.—*n.* something that is eatable. [L. *esculentus,* eatable—*esca,* food—*edo,* to eat.]

**Escutcheon,** es-kuch′un, *n.* a *shield* on which a coat of arms is represented : a family shield : the part of a vessel's stern bearing her name. —*adj.* **Escutch′eoned** ('und), having an escutcheon. [O. Fr. *escusson*—L. *scutum,* a shield. Cf. **Esquire.**]

**Esophagus** or **Œsophagus,** ē-sof′a-gus, *n.* the passage through which *food is carried* to the stomach, the gullet. [L.—Gr. *oisophagus—oisō,* fut. of *pherō,* to carry, and *phagō,* to eat.]

**Esoteric,** es-o-ter′ik, *adj., inner :* secret : mysterious : (*phil.*) taught to a select few :—opposed to **Exoteric.**—*adv.* **Esoter′ically.** [Gr. *esōterikos—esōteros,* inner, a comp. form from *esō,* within—*es* (=*eis*), into.]

**Espalier**, es-pal'yėr, *n.* a lattice-work of wood on which to train fruit-trees : a row of trees so trained. [Fr.—It. *spalliera*, a support for the shoulders—*spalla*, a shoulder—*spatula*, a blade. Cf. **Epaulet**.]

**Esparto**, es-pär'to, *n.* a strong kind of grass found in the south of Europe, esp. in Spain, used for making baskets, cordage, paper, &c. [Sp.]

**Especial**, es-pesh'al, *adj., special :* particular : principal : distinguished.—*adv.* **Espec'ially.** [O. Fr.—L. *specialis.* See **Special, Species.**]

**Espionage**, es'pi-on-āj, *n.* practice or employment of *spies.* [Fr. *espionnage*—*espion*, a spy.]

**Esplanade**, es-pla-nād', *n.* a *plane* or *level* space between a citadel and the first houses of the town : any space for walking or driving in. [Fr. —*esplaner*, to lay level—L. *explano*—*ex*, out, and *plano*—*planus*, flat. See **Plain** and **Explain.**]

**Espousal**, es-powz'al, *n.* the act of espousing or betrothing : the taking upon one's self, as a cause :—*pl.* a contract or mutual promise of marriage. [Fr. *espousailles.* See **Espouse.**]

**Espouse**, es-powz', *v.t.* to give as *spouse* or *betrothed :* to give in marriage : to take as spouse : to wed : to take with a view to maintain : to embrace, as a cause.—*n.* **Espous'er.** [O. Fr. *espouser*, Fr. *épouser*—L. *spondeo, sponsus*, to promise solemnly.]

**Espy**, es-pī', *v.t.* to *see at a distance* : to *spy* or catch sight of : to observe : to discover unexpectedly. [O. Fr. *espier*, from root of **Spy.**]

**Esquire**, es-kwīr' or es'kwīr, *n.* (*orig.*) a *squire* or *shield-bearer*: an attendant on a knight : a title of dignity next below a knight : a title given to younger sons of noblemen, &c. : a general title of respect in addressing letters. [O. Fr. *escuyer* (Fr. *écuyer*), from *escu*, now *écu* —L. *scutum*, a shield.]

**Essay**, es'ā, *n.* a *trial :* an experiment : a written composition less elaborate than a treatise.— *v.t.* es-sā', to *try :* to attempt : to make experiment of :—*pr.p.* essay'ing ; *pa.p.* essayed'. [Fr. *essai*—L. *exagium*—Gr. *exagion*, a weighing—*exagō*, to lead out, export merchandise— *ex*, out, and *agō*, to lead.] [of *essays.*]

**Essayer**, es-sā'ėr, **Essayist**, es'ā-ist, *n.* a writer

**Essence**, es'ens, *n.* the inner distinctive nature of anything : the qualities which make any object what it is : a being : the extracted virtues of any drug : the solution in spirits of wine of a volatile or essential oil : a perfume. [Fr.—L. *essentia*—*essens, essentis*, old pr.p. of *esse*, from root *as*, to be ; Sans. *as*, to be. See **Are.**]

**Essential**, es-sen'shal, *adj.* relating to or containing the *essence :* necessary to the existence of a thing : indispensable or important in the highest degree : highly rectified : pure.—*n.* something essential or necessary : a leading principle.— *adv.* **Essen'tially.**

**Essentiality**, es-sen-shi-al'i-ti, *n.* the quality of being essential : an essential part.

**Establish**, es-tab'lish, *v.t.* to settle or fix : to ordain : to found : to set up (in business).—*n.* **Estab'lisher.** [O. Fr. *establir*, pr.p. *establissant*—L. *stabilire*—*stabilis*, firm—*sto*, to stand.]

**Establishment**, es-tab'lish-ment, *n.* act of establishing : fixed state : that which is established : a permanent civil or military force : one's residence and style of living : the church established by law.

**Estate**, es-tāt', *n.* condition or rank : property, esp. landed property : fortune : an order or class of men in the body-politic :—*pl.* dominions :

possessions : the legislature—king, lords, and commons. [O. Fr. *estat* (Fr. *état*)—L. *status*, a standing, from *sto*, to stand.]

**Esteem**, es-tēm', *v.t.* to set a high *estimate* or value on : to regard with respect or friendship : to consider or think.—*n.* high estimation or value : favourable regard. [Fr. *estimer*—L. *æstimo.* Cf. **Estimate.**] [thetics.]

**Esthetic, Esthetics.** Same as **Æsthetic, Æs-**

**Estimable**, es'tim-a-bl, *adj.* that can be *estimated* or *valued :* worthy of esteem : deserving our good opinion.—*adv.* **Es'timably.**

**Estimate**, es'tim-āt, *v.t.* to judge of the worth of a thing : to calculate. [L. *æstimo, æstimatus*, to value. **Esteem** and **Aim** are parallel forms.]

**Estimate**, es'tim-āt, *n.* a *valuing* in the mind : judgment or opinion of the worth or size of anything : a rough calculation.

**Estimation**, es-tim-ā'shun, *n.* act of estimating : a reckoning of value : esteem, honour.

**Estrange**, es-tränj', *v.t.* to make *strange* : to alienate : to divert from its original use or possessor.—*n.* **Estrange'ment.** [O. Fr. *estranger*, from root of **Strange.**]

**Estuary**, es'tū-ar-i, *n.* a narrow passage, as the mouth of a river, where the tide meets the current, so called from the *boiling* or foaming caused by their meeting. [L. *æstuarium*, from *æstuo, æstuare*, to boil up—*æstus*, a burning.]

**Etch**, ech, *v.t.* or *v.i.* to make designs on metal, glass, &c. by *eating out* the lines with an acid. [Ger. *ätzen*, to corrode by acid ; from same root as Ger. *essen.* See **Eat.**]

**Etching**, ech'ing, *n.* the act or art of etching or engraving : the impression from an etched plate.

**Eternal**, ē-tėr'nal, *adj.* without beginning or end of existence : everlasting : ceaseless : unchangeable.—*n.* **The Eternal**, an appellation of God. —*adv.* **Eter'nally.** [Fr. *éternel*—L.' *æternus, æviternus*—*ævum*—Gr. *aiōn*, a period of time, an age. See **Age.**]

**Eternise**, ē-tėr'nīz, *v.t.* to make *eternal :* to immortalise. [Fr. *éterniser.*]

**Eternity**, ē-tėr'ni-ti, *n.* eternal *duration :* the state or time after death. [Fr. *éternité*—L. *æternitas.*]

**Etesian**, e-tē'zhan, *adj.* periodical : blowing at stated seasons, as certain winds. [Fr. *étésien*— L. *etesius*—Gr. *etēsios*, annual—*etos*, a year.]

**Ether**, ē'thėr, *n.* the clear, upper air : the subtile medium supposed to fill all space : a light, volatile, inflammable fluid. [L.—Gr. *aithēr*, from *aithō*, to light up.]

**Ethereal**, e-thē're-al, *adj.* consisting of *ether ;* heavenly : spirit-like.—*adv.* **Ethe'really.**

**Etherealise**, e-thē're-al-īz, *v.t.* to convert into *ether*, or the fluid ether : to render spirit-like.

**Etherise**, ē'thėr-īz, *v.t.* to convert into *ether :* to stupefy with ether.

**Ethic**, eth'ik, **Ethical**, eth'ik-al, *adj.* relating to *morals :* treating of morality or duty.—*adv.* **Eth'ically.** [Gr. *ēthikos*—*ēthos*, custom.]

**Ethics**, eth'iks, *n. sing.* the science of duty : a system of principles and rules of duty.

**Ethiopian**, ē-thi-ō'pi-an, **Ethiopic**, ē-thi-op'ik, *adj.* pertaining to *Ethiopia*, a name given to the countries south of Egypt inhabited by the *negro* races. [Gr. *Aithiops*, sunburnt, Ethiopian—*aithō*, to burn, and *ōps*, the face.]

**Ethnic**, eth'nik, **Ethnical**, eth'nik-al, *adj.* concerning *nations* or races : pertaining to the heathen. [L.—Gr.—*ethnos*, a nation.]

**Ethnography**, eth-nog'ra-fi, *n.* a *description* of the *nations* or races of the earth.—*n.* **Ethnog'-**

rapher.—*adj.* **Ethnograph′ic.** [Gr. *ethnos*, and *graphō*, to describe.]

**Ethnology,** eth-nol′o-ji, *n.* the *science* that treats of the *varieties of the human race.*—*n.* **Eth′nol′ogist.**—*adj.* **Ethnolog′ical.**—*adv.* **Ethnolog′ically.** [Gr. *ethnos*, and *logos*, an account —*legō*, to speak.]

**Etiolate,** ē-ti-o-lāt′, *v.t.* (*med.* and *bot.*), to cause to grow pale, from want of light and fresh air.—*v.i.* to become pale from disease or absence of light.—*n.* **Etiola′tion.** [Fr. *étioler*, from *éteule*, stubble—L. *stipula*, a stalk, stubble, and therefore to blanch like stubble.]

**Etiology,** ē-ti-ol′o-ji, *n.* the *science of causes*, esp. of disease. [Gr. *aitia*, a cause, and *logos*, an account—*legō*, to speak.]

**Etiquette,** et-i-ket′, *n.* forms of ceremony or decorum : ceremony. [Fr. See **Ticket.**]

**Etymologist,** et-i-mol′o-jist, *n.* one skilled in or who writes on *etymology.*

**Etymology,** et-i-mol′o-ji, *n.* an *account* of the *etymons* or true origin of words : the science that treats of the origin and history of words : the part of grammar relating to inflection.—*adj.* **Etymolog′ical.**—*adv.* **Etymolog′ically.** [Fr. —L.—Gr.—*etymon*, and *logos*, an account.]

**Etymon,** et′i-mon, *n.* the *true* origin of a word : an original root : the genuine or literal sense of a word. [Gr.—*etymos*, *eteos*, true.]

**Eucalyptus,** ū-kal-ip′tus, *n.* the 'gum-tree,' a large evergreen, native of Australia, which is very beneficial in destroying the miasma of malarious districts. [Coined from Gr. *eu*, well, and *kalyptos*, folded round—*kalyptō*, to cover.]

**Eucharist,** ū′ka-rist, *n.* the sacrament of the Lord's Supper.—*adjs.* **Eucharist′ic, Eucharist′ical.** [Gr. *eucharistia*, thanksgiving—*eu*, well, and *charizomai*, to shew favour—*charis*, grace, thanks. Cog. with E. **Yearn.**]

**Eulogic,** ū-loj′ik, **Eulogical,** ū-loj′ik-al, *adj.* containing *eulogy* or praise.—*adv.* **Eulog′ically.**

**Eulogise,** ū′lo-jīz, *v.t.* to speak well of : to praise.

**Eulogist,** ū′lo-jist, *n.* one who *praises* or extols another.—*adj.* **Eulogist′ic,** full of praise.—*adv.* **Eulogist′ically.**

**Eulogium,** ū-lō′ji-um, **Eulogy,** ū′lo-ji, *n.* a *speaking well of* : a speech or writing in praise of. [Late L.—Gr. *eulogion* (classical, *eulogia*)—*eu*, well, and *logos*, a speaking.]

**Eunuch,** ū′nuk, *n.* a castrated man ; eunuchs were employed as *chamberlains* in the East, and often had great influence as chief *ministers* of the kings. [Gr. *eunouchos*—*eunē*, a couch, and *echō*, to have charge of.]                    [*eunuch.*

**Eunuchism,** ū′nuk-izm, *n.* the state of being a

**Eupepsy,** ū-pep′si, *n., good digestion :*—opposed to **Dyspepsy.**—*adj.* **Eupep′tic,** having good digestion. [Gr. *eupepsia*—*eu*, well, and *pepsis*, digestion, from *pessō*, *peptō*, to digest.]

**Euphemism,** ū′fem-izm, *n.* a soft or pleasing term employed to express what is disagreeable.—*adj.* **Euphemist′ic.** [Gr. *euphēmismos*—*eu*, well, and *phēmi*, to speak.]

**Euphonic,** ū-fon′ik, **Euphonical,** ′ik-al, **Euphonious,** ū-fō′ni-us, *adj.* pertaining to *euphony:* agreeable in sound.—*adv.* **Eupho′niously.**

**Euphonise,** ū′fon-īz, *v.t.* to make *euphonious.*

**Euphony,** ū′fo-ni, *n.* an *agreeable sound:* a pleasing, easy pronunciation. [Gr. *euphōnia*—*eu*, well, and *phōnē*, sound.]

**Euphrasy,** ū′fra-zi, *n.* (*bot.*) the plant eyebright, formerly regarded as beneficial in disorders of the eyes. [Gr. *euphrasia*, delight, from *euphrainō*, to cheer—*eu*, well, *phrēn*, the heart.]

**Euphuism,** ū′fū-izm, *n.* an affectation of excessive refinement of language : a high-flown expression.—*n.* **Eu′phuist.**—*adj.* **Euphuist′ic.** [From *Euphues*, a book by John Lyly in the time of Queen Elizabeth, which brought the style into vogue—Gr. *euphyēs*, graceful—*eu*, well, *phyē*, growth—*phyomai*, to grow.]

**Eurasian,** ū-rā′zi-an, *n.* a descendant of a European on the one side, and an Asian on the other. [A contr. of *European* and *Asian.*]

**Euroclydon,** ū-rok′li-don, *n.* a tempestuous *south-east wind* raising great *waves* in the Mediterranean Sea. [Gr., from *euros*, the south-east wind, and *klydōn*, a wave, from *klyzō*, to dash over.]

**European,** ū-ro-pē′an, *adj.* belonging to *Europe.*—*n.* a native or inhabitant of Europe.

**Eurythmy,** ū′rith-mi, *n.* just proportion or symmetry in anything. [Gr. *eurythmia*—*eu*, well, and *rhythmos*, measured motion.]

**Euthanasia,** ū-than-ā′zi-a, **Euthanasy,** ū-than′-a-si, *n.* an *easy*, pleasant mode of *death.* [Gr. *euthanasia*—*eu*, well, and *thanatos*, death.]

**Evacuate,** e-vak′ū-āt, *v.t.* to *throw out* the contents of : to discharge : to withdraw from. [L. *e*, out, *vacuo*, *vacuatus*, to empty—*vaco*, to be empty.]

**Evacuation,** e-vak-ū-ā′shun, *n.* act of emptying out : a withdrawing from : that which is discharged.

**Evacuator,** e-vak′ū-āt-or, *n.* one who evacuates : (*law*) one who nullifies or makes void.

**Evade,** e-vād′, *v.t.* to escape artfully : to avoid cunningly. [L. *evado*—*e*, out, *vado*, to go.]

**Evanescent,** ev-an-es′ent, *adj.* fleeting : imperceptible.—*adv.* **Evanesc′ently.**—*n.* **Evanesc′ence.** [L. *evanescens*, *-entis*—*e*, and *vanesco*, to vanish—*vanus*, empty.]

**Evangel,** ē-van′jel, *n.* (*poet.*) good news, esp. the gospel.

**Evangelic,** ē-van-jel′ik, **Evangelical,** ē-van-jel′-ik-al, *adj.* belonging to or consisting of *good tidings:* relating to the four gospels : according to the doctrine of the gospel : maintaining the truth taught in the gospel.—*adv.* **Evangel′ically.**—*n.* **Evangel′icalness.** [L. *evangelicus* —Gr. *euanggelikos*—*eu*, well, and *anggellō*, to bring news.]

**Evangelicism,** ē-van-jel′i-sizm, **Evangelicalism,** ē-van-jel′ik-al-izm, *n., evangelical* principles.

**Evangelisation,** ē-van-jel-i-zā′shun, *n.* act of evangelising or proclaiming the gospel.

**Evangelise,** ē-van′jel-īz, *v.t.* to make known the *good news:* to make acquainted with the gospel. —*v.i.* to preach the gospel from place to place.

**Evangelist,** ē-van′jel-ist, *n.* one who evangelises : one of the four writers of the gospels : an assistant of the apostles : one authorised to preach.

**Evaporable,** e-vap′or-a-bl, *adj.* able to be evaporated or converted into *vapour.*

**Evaporate,** e-vap′or-āt, *v.i.* to fly off in *vapour:* to pass into an invisible state.—*v.t.* to convert into steam or gas. [L. *e*, off, *vaporo*, *-atum*—*vapor*, vapour.]

**Evaporation,** e-vap-or-ā′shun, *n.* act of evaporating or passing off in steam or gas.

**Evasion,** e-vā′zhun, *n.* act of *evading* or eluding : an attempt to escape the force of an argument or accusation : an excuse.

**Evasive,** e-vā′siv, *adj.* that *evades* or seeks to evade : not straightforward : shuffling.—*adv.* **Eva′sively.**—*n.* **Eva′siveness.**

**Eve,** ēv, **Even,** ēv′n, *n.* (*poet.*) evening : the night before a day of note : the time just preceding a great event. [A.S. *æfen;* Dut. *avond;* Ger. *abend,* the sinking of the day, from *ab,* down.]

**Even,** ēv'n, *adj., equal : level:* uniform : parallel : equal on both sides : not odd, able to be divided by 2 without a remainder.—*adv.* **Ev'enly.**—*n.* **Ev'enness.** [A.S. *efen;* Dut. *even;* Ger. *eben* —*ebenen,* to make smooth: perh. allied to L. *æquus,* equal.]

**Even,** ēv'n, *v.t.* to make even or smooth.—*adv.* exactly so : indeed : so much as : still.

**Even-handed,** ēv'n-hand'ed, *adj.* with an *equal,* fair, or impartial *hand:* just.

**Evening,** ēv'ning, *n.* the close of the daytime : the decline or end of life. [A.S. *æfenung,* from *æfen.*] [or calm *mind:* equable.

**Even-minded,** ēv'n-mīnd'ed, *adj.* having an *even*

**Evensong,** ēv'n-song, *n.* the *evening* service in church, so called because formerly chanted or *sung.*

**Event,** e-vent', *n.* that which *comes out* or happens : the result : any incident or occurrence. [L. *eventus*—*evenio*—*e,* out, and *venio,* to come.]

**Eventful,** e-vent'fool, *adj., full* or fruitful of *events.*

**Eventide,** ēv'n-tīd, *n.* the *tide* or time of *evening.*

**Eventual,** e-vent'ū-al, *adj.* happening as a consequence, ultimate or final.—*adv.* **Event'ually,** finally : at length.

**Ever,** ev'ėr, *adv.* always : eternally : at any time : in any degree. [A.S. *æfre,* always ; from A.S. *awa,* ever, which is cog. with Goth. *aiws,* L. *ævum,* Gr. *aiōn.* See also **Age, Aye, Never.**]

**Evergreen,** ev'ėr-grēn, *adj. ever* or always *green.* —*n.* a plant that remains green all the year.

**Everlasting,** ev-ėr-last'ing, *adj.* endless : eternal. —*n.* eternity.—*adv.* **Everlast'ingly.**—*n.* **Everlast'ingness.** [nally.

**Evermore,** ev-ėr-mōr', *adv.* unceasingly : eternally. [nally.

**Every,** ev'ėr-i, *adj., each one* of a number : all taken separately. [A.S. *æfre,* ever, and *ælc,* each.]

**Everywhere,** ev'ėr-i-hwār, *adv.* in *every* place.

**Evict,** e-vikt', *v.t.* to dispossess by law : to expel from. [L. *evictus,* pa.p. of *evinco,* to overcome. See **Evince.**]

**Eviction,** e-vik'shun, *n.* the act of evicting from house or lands : the lawful recovery of lands.

**Evidence,** ev'i-dens, *n.* that which makes evident : proof or testimony : a witness.—*v.t.* to render evident : to prove.

**Evident,** ev'i-dent, *adj.* that is *visible* or can be *seen :* clear to the mind : obvious.—*adv.* **Ev'idently** (*New Test.*) visibly. [L. *evidens, -entis* —*e* and *video,* to see.]

**Evidential,** ev-i-den'shal, *adj.* furnishing *evidence:* tending to prove.—*adv.* **Eviden'tially.**

**Evil,** ē'vl, *adj.* wicked : mischievous : unfortunate. —*adv.* in an evil manner : badly.—*n.* that which produces unhappiness or calamity : harm : wickedness : depravity. [A.S. *yfel;* Dut. *euvel,* Ger. *übel.* Ill is a doublet.]

**Ev'l doer,** ē'vl-dōō'ėr, *n.* one who does evil.

**Evil-eye,** ē'vl-ī, *n.* a supposed power to cause *evil* or harm by the *look* of the *eye.*

**Evil-favouredness,** ē'vl-fā'vurd-nes, *n.* (*B.*) ugliness : deformity. [malicious : wicked.

**Evil-minded,** ē'vl-mīnd'ed, *adj.* inclined to evil :

**Evil-speaking,** ē'vl-spēk'ing, *n.* the speaking of evil : slander. [does evil.

**Evil-worker,** ē'vl-wurk'ėr, *n.* one who works or

**Evince,** e-vins', *v.t.* to prove beyond doubt : to shew clearly : to make evident. [L. *evinco*—*e,* inten., and *vinco,* to overcome.]

**Evincible,** e-vins'i-bl, *adj.* that may be *evinced* or made evident.—*adv.* **Evinc'ibly.**

**Evincive,** e-vins'iv, *adj.* tending to *evince,* prove, or demonstrate.

**Eviscerate,** e-vis'ėr-āt, *v.t.* to tear out the *viscera* or *bowels.*—*n.* **Eviscera'tion.** [L. *e,* out, and *viscera,* the bowels.]

**Evoke,** e-vōk', *v.t.* to *call out :* to draw out or bring forth. [L. *evoco*—*e,* out, and *voco,* to call.]

**Evolution,** ev-o-lū'shun, *n.* the act of *unrolling* or *unfolding:* gradual working out or development : a series of things unfolded : the doctrine according to which higher forms of life have gradually arisen out of lower : (*arith.* and *alg.*) the extraction of roots : the orderly movements of a body of troops or of ships of war.—*adj.* **Evolu'tionary,** pertaining to evolution.

**Evolutionist,** ev-o-lū'shun-ist, *n.* one skilled in *evolutions* or military movements : one who believes in *evolution* as a principle in science or philosophy.

**Evolve,** e-volv', *v.t.* to *roll out* or unroll : to disclose : to develop : to unravel.—*v.i.* to disclose itself. [L. *evolvo*—*e,* out, and *volvo,* to roll.]

**Evulsion,** e-vul'shun, *n.* a *plucking out* by force. [L. *e,* out, and *vello, vulsus,* to pluck.]

**Ewe,** ū, *n.* a female sheep. [A.S. *eowu;* L. *ovis,* Gr. *oïs,* Sans. *avi,* a sheep.]

**Ewer,** ū'ėr, *n.* a large jug placed on a washstand to hold *water.* [O. Fr. *euwier,* Fr. *évier*—L. *aquarium*—*aqua,* water, whence also Fr. *eau.*]

**Exacerbate,** egz-as'ėr-bāt, *v.t.* to *imbitter :* to provoke : to render more violent or severe, as a disease. [L. *exacerbo, exacerbatus*—*ex,* and *acerbo,* from *acerbus,* bitter. See **Acerbity.**]

**Exacerbation,** egz-as-ėr-bā'shun, **Exacerbescence,** egz-as-ėr-bes'ens, *n.* increase of irritation or violence, esp. the increase of a fever or disease.

**Exact,** egz-akt', *adj.* precise : careful : punctual : true : certain or demonstrable.—*adv.* **Exact'ly.** —*n.* **Exact'ness.** [L. *exactus,* pa.p. of *exigo,* to drive out, to measure—*ex,* and *ago,* to drive, to do.]

**Exact,** egz-akt', *v.t.* to *force from:* to compel full payment of : to make great demands or to demand urgently: to extort.—*v.i.* to practise extortion. [See **Exact,** *adj.*]

**Exaction,** egz-ak'shun, *n.* the act of exacting or demanding strictly : an oppressive demand : that which is exacted, as excessive work or tribute.

**Exaggerate,** egz-aj'ėr-āt, *v.t.* to magnify unduly : to represent too strongly. [L. *exaggero, exaggeratus*—*ex, aggero,* to heap up—*agger,* a heap.]

**Exaggeration,** egz-aj-ėr-ā'shun, *n.* extravagant representation : a statement in excess of the truth.

**Exaggerative,** egz-aj'ėr-āt-iv, **Exaggeratory,** egz-aj'ėr-a-tor-i, *adj.* containing exaggeration or tending to exaggerate.

**Exalt,** egz-awlt', *v.t.* to raise very *high :* to elevate to a higher position : to elate or fill with the joy of success : to praise or extol : (*chem.*) to refine or subtilise.—*n.* **Exalt'edness.** [L. *exalto*—*ex,* and *altus,* grown great by nourishing, high, from *alo,* to nourish ; Gr. *althō,* to cause to grow.] [or dignity : high estate.

**Exaltation,** egz-awlt-ā'shun, *n.* elevation in rank

**Examination,** egz-am-i-nā'shun, *n.* careful search or inquiry : trial.

**Examine,** egz-am'in, *v.t.* to test : to inquire into : to question. [L. *examen* (= *exagmen*), the tongue of a balance. From the root of **Exact.**]

**Examiner,** egz-am'in-ėr, *n.* one who examines.

**Example,** egz-am'pl, *n.* that which is *taken out*

as a specimen of the rest, or as an illustration of a rule, &c. : the person or thing to be imitated or avoided : a pattern : a warning : a former instance : a precedent. [Fr.—L. *exemplum—eximo*, to take out—*ex*, out of, and *emo*, *emptus*, to take.]

**Exasperate**, egz-as′pèr-āt, *v.t.* to make very *rough* or angry : to irritate in a high degree. [L. *ex*, intensive, and *aspero*, to make rough—*asper*, rough.]

**Exasperation**, egz-as-pèr-ā′shun, *n.* act of irritating : state of being exasperated : provocation : rage : aggravation.

**Excavate**, eks′ka-vāt, *v.t.* to *hollow* or scoop out. [L. *excavo—ex*, out, *cavus*, hollow.]

**Excavation**, eks-ka-vā′shun, *n.* act of excavating : a hollow or cavity made by excavating.

**Excavator**, eks′ka-vā-tor, *n.* one who excavates.

**Exceed**, ek-sēd′, *v.t.* to *go beyond* the limit or measure of : to surpass or excel.—*v.i.* to go beyond a given or proper limit. [L. *ex*, beyond, and *cedo, cessum*, to go.]

**Exceeding** (*obs.*), ek-sēd′ing, **Exceedingly**, ek-sēd′ing-li, *adv.* very much : greatly.

**Excel**, ek-sel′, *v.t.* to *rise beyond* : to exceed : to surpass.—*v.i.* to have good qualities in a high degree : to perform very meritorious actions : to be superior :—*pr.p.* excell′ing ; *pa.p.* excelled′. [L. *excello—ex*, out, up, and a root *cello*, same as Gr. *kellō*, to drive, to urge.]

**Excellence**, ek′sel-ens, **Excellency**, ek′sel-en-si, *n.* great merit : any excellent quality : worth : greatness : a title of honour given to persons high in rank or office. [Fr.—L. *excellentia—excellens*, rising above, distinguishing one′s self.]

**Excellent**, ek′sel-ent, *adj.* surpassing others in some good quality : of great virtue, worth, &c. : superior : valuable.—*adv.* Ex′cellently. [Fr.—L. *excellens, -entis—excello.*]

**Except**, ek-sept′, *v.t.* to *take* or *leave out* : to exclude.—*v.i.* to object. [L. *excipio, exceptus—ex*, out, and *capio*, to take.]

**Except**, ek-sept′, **Excepting**, ek-sept′ing, *prep., leaving out* : excluding : but.

**Exception**, ek-sep′shun, *n.* that which is excepted : exclusion : objection : offence.

**Exceptionable**, ek-sep′shun-a-bl, *adj.* objectionable.

**Exceptional**, ek-sep′shun-al, *adj.* peculiar.

**Exceptive**, ek-sept′iv, *adj.* including, making, or being an *exception.*

**Exceptor**, ek-sept′or, *n.* one who excepts or objects.

**Excerpt**, ek-sèrpt′, *n.* a passage *picked out* or selected from a book, an extract. [L. *excerptum*, pa.p. of *excerpo—ex*, out, and *carpo*, to pick.]

**Excess**, ek-ses′, *n.* a *going beyond* what is usual or proper : intemperance : that which exceeds : the degree by which one thing exceeds another. [L. *excessus—excedo, excessus*, to go beyond.]

**Excessive**, ek-ses′iv, *adj.* beyond what is right and proper : immoderate : violent.—*adv.* Excess′ively.—*n.* Excess′iveness.

**Exchange**, eks-chānj′, *v.t.* to give or leave one place or thing for another : to give and take mutually : to barter. [Fr. *échanger—ex*, from, and root of **Change**.]

**Exchange**, eks-chānj′, *n.* the giving and taking one thing for another : barter : the thing exchanged : process by which accounts between distant parties are settled by bills instead of money : the difference between the value of money in different places : the place where merchants, &c. meet for business.

**Exchangeable**, eks-chānj′a-bl, *adj.* that may be exchanged.—*n.* **Exchangeabil′ity**.

**Exchanger**, eks-chānj′ér, *n.* one who exchanges or practises exchange : (*B.*) a money-changer, a banker.

**Exchequer**, eks-chek′ér, *n.* a superior court which had formerly to do only with the revenue, but now also with common law, so named from the *checkered* cloth which formerly covered the table, and on which the accounts were reckoned.—*v.t.* to proceed against a person in the Court of Exchequer. [From root of **Check, Checker**.]

**Excise**, ek-sīz′, *n.* a tax on certain home commodities and on licenses for certain trades.—*v.t.* to subject to excise duty. [O. Dut. *aksiis*—Fr. *assis*, assessments—*assise*, an assize, at which the tax was fixed. See **Assess** and **Assize**.]

**Exciseman**, ek-sīz′man, *n.* an officer charged with collecting the *excise.*

**Excision**, ek-sizh′un, *n.* a *cutting out* or off of any kind : extirpation. [Fr.—L., from *excido*. to cut out—*ex*, out, and *cædo*, to cut. See **Concise**.]

**Excitable**, ek-sīt′a-bl, *adj.* capable of being, or easily excited.—*n.* **Excitabil′ity**.

**Excitant**, ek-sīt′ant or ek′sit-ant, *n.* that which excites or rouses the vital activity of the body : a stimulant.

**Excitation**, ek-sit-ā′shun, *n.* act of exciting.

**Excitative**, ek-sīt′a-tiv, **Excitatory**, ek-sīt′a-tor-i, *adj.* tending to excite.

**Excite**, ek-sīt′, *v.t.* to call into activity : to stir up : to rouse : to irritate.—*n.* **Excit′er**. [L. *ex*, out, and root of **Cite**.] [excites.

**Excitement**, ek-sīt′ment, *n.* agitation : that which

**Exclaim**, eks-klām′, *v.i.* to *cry out* : to utter or speak vehemently. [Fr. *exclamer*—L. *exclamo*—*ex*, out, *clamo*, to shout.]

**Exclamation**, eks-kla-mā′shun, *n.* vehement utterance : outcry : an uttered expression of surprise, and the like : the mark expressing this (!) : an interjection.

**Exclamatory**, eks-klam′a-tor-i, *adj.* containing or expressing exclamation.

**Exclude**, eks-klood′, *v.t.* to *close* or *shut out* : to thrust out : to hinder from entrance : to hinder from participation : to except. [L. *excludo—ex*, out, and *claudo*, to shut.]

**Exclusion**, eks-kloo′zhun, *n.* a shutting or putting out : ejection : exception.

**Exclusionist**, eks-kloo′zhun-ist, *n.* one who *excludes*, or would exclude another from a privilege.

**Exclusive**, eks-kloo′siv, *adj.* able or tending to *exclude* : debarring from participation : sole : not taking into account.—*n.* one of a number who exclude others from their society.—*adv.* Exclu′sively.—*n.* **Exclu′siveness**.

**Excogitate**, eks-koj′i-tāt, *v.t.* to discover by *thinking* : to think earnestly or laboriously. [L. *excogito, -atus—ex*, out, and *cogito*, to think.]

**Excogitation**, eks-koj-i-tā′shun, *n.* laborious thinking : invention : contrivance.

**Excommunicate**, eks-kom-ūn′i-kāt, *v.t.* to *put out of* or expel from the *communion* of the church : to deprive of church privileges. [L. *ex*, out of, and **Communicate**.]

**Excommunication**, eks-kom-ūn-i-kā′shun, *n.* act of expelling from the communion of a church.

**Excoriate**, eks-kō′ri-āt, *v.t.* to strip the *skin from.* [L. *excorio, -atus—ex*, from, *corium*, the skin.]

**Excrement**, eks′kre-ment, *n.* useless matter discharged from the animal system : dung.—*adj.* **Excrement′al**. [L. *excrementum—excerno, excretus*, to separate.]

**Excrementitious**, eks-kre-men-tish′us, *adj.* pertaining to, consisting of, or containing *excrement*.

**Excrescence**, eks-kres'ens, *n.* that which *grows out* unnaturally from anything else : an outbreak : a wart or tumour : a superfluous part. [Fr.—L.—*excresco*—*ex*, out, and *cresco*, to grow.] [superfluous.

**Excrescent**, eks-kres'ent, *adj.*, *growing out* :

**Excrete**, eks-krēt', *v.t.* to *separate from*, or discharge : to eject. [L. *ex*, from, and *cerno*, *cretus*, to separate.]

**Excretion**, eks-krē'shun, *n.* act of excreting matter from the animal system : that which is excreted.—*adj.* **Excre'tive**, able to excrete.

**Excretory**, eks-krē'tor-i, *adj.* having the quality of excreting.—*n.* a duct or vessel that helps to receive and excrete matter.

**Excruciate**, eks-krōō'shi-āt, *v.t.* to *torture* as if on a *cross* : to rack. [L. *ex*, out, and *crucio*, *cruciatus*, to crucify—*crux*, *crucis*, a cross.]

**Excruciation**, eks-krōō-shi-ā'shun, *n.* torture : vexation.

**Exculpate**, eks-kul'pāt, *v.t.* to clear *from* the charge of a *fault* or crime : to absolve : to vindicate.—*n.* **Exculpa'tion**. [L. *exculpo*, *exculpatus*—*ex*, from, *culpa*, a fault.]

**Exculpatory**, eks-kul'pa-tor-i, *adj.* exculpating or freeing from the charge of fault or crime.

**Excursion**, eks-kur'shun, *n.* a going forth : an expedition : a trip for pleasure or health : a wandering from the main subject : a digression. [L. *excursio*—*ex*, out, and *curro*, *cursum*, to run.]

**Excursionist**, eks-kur'shun-ist, *n.* one who goes on an excursion or pleasure-trip.

**Excursive**, eks-kur'siv, *adj.* rambling : deviating.—*adv.* **Excur'sively**.—*n.* **Excur'siveness**.

**Excursus**, eks-kur'sus, *n.* a dissertation on some particular point appended to a book or chapter.

**Excusable**, eks-kūz'a-bl, *adj.* admitting of justification. [taining excuse.

**Excusatory**, eks-kūz'a-tor-i, *adj.* making or con-

**Excuse**, eks-kūz', *v.t.* to free from blame or guilt : to forgive : to free from an obligation : to release : to make an apology or ask pardon for. [L. *excuso*—*ex*, from, *causor*, to plead—*causa*, a cause, an accusation.] [of a fault.

**Excuse**, eks-kūs', a plea offered in extenuation

**Execrable**, eks'e-kra-bl, *adj.* deserving execration : detestable : accursed.—*adv.* **Ex'ecrably**.

**Execrate**, eks'e-krāt, *v.t.* to curse : to denounce evil against : to detest utterly. [L. *exsecror*, *-atus*, to curse—*ex*, from, and *sacer*, sacred.]

**Execration**, eks-e-krā'shun, *n.* act of execrating : a curse pronounced : that which is execrated.

**Execute**, eks'e-kūt, *v.t.* to perform : to give effect to : to carry into effect the sentence of the law : to put to death by law.—*n.* **Ex'ecuter**. [Fr. *exécuter*—L. *exsequor*, *exsecutus*—*ex*, out, and *sequor*, to follow.]

**Execution**, eks-e-kū'shun, *n.* act of executing or performing : accomplishment : completion : carrying into effect the sentence of a court of law : the warrant for so doing.

**Executioner**, eks-e-kū'shun-ėr, *n.* one who executes : esp. one who inflicts capital punishment.

**Executive**, egz-ek'ū-tiv, *adj.* designed or fitted to execute : active : qualifying for or pertaining to the execution of the law.—*adv.* **Exec'utively**. [Fr. *exécutif*.]

**Executive**, egz-ek'ū-tiv, *n.* the power or authority in government that carries the laws into effect : the persons who administer the government.

**Executor**, egz-ek'ū-tor, *n.* one who executes or performs : the person appointed to see a will carried into effect.—*fem.* **Exec'utrix**.—*n.* **Exec'utorship**.

**Executory**, egz-ek'ū-tor-i, *adj.* executing official duties : designed to be carried into effect.

**Exegesis**, eks-e-jē'sis, *n.* the science of *interpretation*, esp. of the Scriptures. [Gr. *exēgēsis*—*exēgeomai*, to explain—*ex*, out, and *hēgeomai*, to guide—*ago*, to lead.]

**Exegetic**, eks-e-jet'ik, **Exegetical**, eks-e-jet'ik-al, *adj.* pertaining to exegesis : explanatory.—*adv.* **Exeget'ically**.—*n.sing.* **Exeget'ics**, the science of exegesis. [Gr. See Exegesis.]

**Exemplar**, egz-em'plar, *n.* a person or thing to be imitated : the ideal model of an artist. [Fr. *exemplaire*—L. *exemplar*—*exemplum*. See Example.]

**Exemplary**, egz'em-plar-i, *adj.* worthy of imitation or notice : commendable.—*adv.* **Ex'emplarily**. [See Exemplar.]

**Exemplification**, egz-em-pli-fi-kā'shun, *n.* act of exemplifying : that which exemplifies : a copy or transcript.

**Exemplify**, egz-em'pli-fī, *v.t.* to illustrate by *example* : to make an attested copy of : to prove by an attested copy :—*pr.p.* exem'plifying ; *pa.p.* exem'plified. [L. *exemplum*, and *facio*, to do or make.]

**Exempt**, egz-emt', *v.t.* to free, or grant immunity from.—*adj.* taken out : not liable to : released. [Fr.—L. *eximo*, *exemptus*—*ex*, out, and *emo*, to take, to buy. Cf. Example.]

**Exemption**, egz-em'shun, *n.* act of exempting : state of being exempt : freedom from any service, duty, &c. : immunity. [Fr.—L. *exemptio*.]

**Exequies**, eks'e-kwiz, *n.pl.* a funeral procession : the ceremonies of burial. [L. *exsequiæ*—*ex*, out, *sequor*, to follow.]

**Exercise**, eks'ėr-sīz, *n.* a putting in practice : exertion of the body for health or amusement : discipline : a lesson or task. [Fr. *exercice*—L. *exercitium*—L. *exerceo*, *-citus*—*ex*, out, and *arceo*, to drive.]

**Exercise**, eks'ėr-sīz, *v.t.* to train by use : to improve by practice : to afflict : to put in practice : to use.

**Exert**, egz-ėrt', *v.t.* to bring into active operation : to do or perform. [L. *exsero*, *exsertus*—*ex*, out, and *sero*, to put together. See Series.]

**Exertion**, egz-ėr'shun, *n.* a bringing into active operation : effort : attempt.

**Exfoliate**, eks-fō'li-āt, *v.i.* to come off in scales.—*n.* **Exfolia'tion**. [L. *exfolio*, *exfoliatus*—*ex*, off, and *folium*, a leaf. See Foliage.]

**Exhalation**, egz-hal-ā'shun, *n.* act or process of exhaling : evaporation : that which is exhaled : vapour : steam. [L. *exhalatio*—*exhalo*, *-atus*.]

**Exhale**, egz-hāl', *v.t.* to emit or send out as vapour : to evaporate.—*v.i.* to rise or be given off as vapour. [Fr. *exhaler*—L. *exhalare*—*ex*, out, *halo*, *halatus*, to breathe.]

**Exhaust**, egz-hawst', *v.t.* to *draw out* the whole of : to use the whole strength of : to wear or tire out : to treat of or develop completely. [L. *exhaurio*, *exhaustus*—*ex*, out, and *haurio*, to draw.] [tied : consumed : tired out.

**Exhausted**, egz-hawst'ed, *adj.* drawn out : emp-

**Exhauster**, egz-hawst'ėr, *n.* he who or that which exhausts. [hausted.

**Exhaustible**, egz-hawst'i-bl, *adj.* that may be ex-

**Exhaustion**, egz-hawst'yun, *n.* act of exhausting or consuming : state of being exhausted : extreme fatigue.

**Exhaustive**, egz-hawst'iv, *adj.* tending to exhaust.

**Exhaustless**, egz-hawst'les, *adj.* that cannot be exhausted.

**Exhibit**, egz-hib'it, *v.t.* to *hold forth* or present

to view: to present formally or publicly.—*ns.*
**Exhib'iter, Exhib'itor.** [L. *exhibeo, exhibitus*
—*ex*, out, *habeo, habitus,* to have or hold.]
**Exhibition,** eks-hi-bish'un, *n.* presentation to
view: display: a public show, esp. of works of
art, manufactures, &c.: that which is exhibited:
an allowance or bounty to scholars in a university. [Fr.—L. *exhibitio.*]
**Exhibitioner,** eks-hi-bish'un-èr, *n.* one who enjoys
an exhibition or allowance at a university.
**Exhibitory,** egz-hib'it-or-i, *adj.* exhibiting.
**Exhilarant,** egz-hil'a-rant, *adj.* exhilarating:
exciting joy, mirth, or pleasure.
**Exhilarate,** egz-hil'a-rāt, *v.t.* to make *hilarious*
or merry: to enliven: to cheer. [L. *exhilaro,*
*exhilaratus*—*ex,* intensive, *hilaris,* cheerful.]
**Exhilarating,** egz-hil'a-rāt-ing, *adj.* cheering:
gladdening.—*adv.* Exhil'aratingly.
**Exhilaration,** egz-hil-a-rā'shun, *n.* state of being
exhilarated: joyousness.
**Exhort,** egz-hort', *v.t.* to *urge strongly* to good
deeds, esp. by words or advice: to animate: to
advise or warn. [Fr. *exhorter*—L. *exhortor,*
*-atus*—*ex,* inten., *hortor,* to urge.]
**Exhortation,** eks-hor-tā'shun, *n.* act or practice
of exhorting to laudable deeds: language intended to exhort: counsel. [L. *exhortatio.*]
**Exhortative,** egz-hort'a-tiv, **Exhortatory,** egz-
hort'a-tor-i, *adj.* tending to exhort or advise.
**Exhumation,** eks-hū-mā'shun, *n.* act of exhum-
ing: disinterment.
**Exhume,** eks-hūm', *v.t.* to take *out of* the *ground,*
or place of burial: to disinter. [L. *ex,* out of,
*humus,* the ground. See **Humble.**]
**Exigence,** eks'i-jens, **Exigency,** eks'i-jen-si, *n.*
pressing necessity: emergency: distress.
**Exigent,** eks'i-jent, *adj. pressing:* demanding
immediate attention or action. [L. *exigens,*
*-ntis*—*exigo*—*ex,* out, *ago,* to drive.]
**Exiguous,** eks-ig'ū-us, *adj.* small: slender. [L.]
**Exile,** eks'īl, *n.* state of being sent *out of* one's
native *country ;* expulsion from home: banishment: one away from his native country.—*v.t.*
to expel from one's native country, to banish.
[Fr. *exil*—L. *exsilium,* banishment, *exsul,* an
exile—*ex,* out of, and *solum,* soil, land.]
**Exility,** eks-il'i-ti, *n.* slenderness, smallness. [L.
*exilis,* slender, contr. for *exigilis.* See **Exigent.**]
**Exist,** egz-ist', *v.i.* to have an actual being: to
live: to continue to be. [L. *existo, exsisto*—*ex,*
out, and *sisto,* to make to stand.]
**Existence,** egz-ist'ens, *n.* state of existing or being:
continued being: life: anything that exists: a
being. [L. *existens, -entis,* pr.p. of *existo.*]
**Existent,** egz-ist'ent, *adj.* having being.
**Exit,** eks'it, *n.* (*orig.*) a direction in playbooks to
an actor to *go off* the stage: the departure of a
player from the stage: any departure: a way
of departure: a passage out: a quitting of the
world's stage, or life: death. [L. *exit,* he goes
out, *exeo,* to go out—*ex,* out, and *eo, itum,* to go.]
**Exodus,** eks'o-dus, *n.* a *going out* or departure,
esp. that of the Israelites from Egypt: the
second book of the Old Testament narrating this
event. [L.—Gr. *exodos*—*ex,* out, *hodos,* a way.]
**Exogamy,** eks-og'am-i, *n.* the practice of *marrying* only *outside* of one's own tribe. [Gr. *exō,*
out, and *gamos,* marriage.]
**Exogen,** eks'o-jen, *n.* a plant belonging to the
great class that increases by layers *growing* on
the *outside* of the wood. [Gr. *exō,* outside, and
*gen,* root of *gignomai,* to be produced.]
**Exogenous,** eks-oj'e-nus, *adj.* growing by successive additions to the outside.

**Exonerate,** egz-on'ér-āt, *v.t.* to free *from* the
*burden* of blame or obligation: to acquit. [L.
*exonero, -atus*—*ex,* from, *onus, oneris,* burden.]
**Exoneration,** egz-on-ér-ā'shun, *n.* act of exoner-
ating or freeing from a charge or blame.
**Exonerative,** egz-on'ér-a-tiv, *adj.* freeing from a
burden or obligation.
**Exorbitance,** egz-or'bi-tans, **Exorbitancy,** egz-
or'bi-tan-si, *n.* state or quality of being exorbitant: extravagance: enormity.
**Exorbitant,** egz-or'bi-tant, *adj.* going beyond the
usual limits: excessive.—*adv.* Exor'bitantly.
[Fr.—L. *exorbitans, -ntis,* pr.p. of *exorbito*—
*ex,* out of, and *orbita,* a track—*orbis,* a circle.]
**Exorcise,** eks'or-sīz, *v.t.* to adjure by some holy
name: to call forth or drive away, as a spirit:
to deliver from the influence of an evil spirit.
[Through Late L., from Gr. *exorkizō*—*ex,* out,
*horkizō,* to bind by an oath—*horkos,* an oath.]
**Exorciser,** eks'or-sīz-èr, **Exorcist,** eks'or-sist, *n.*
one who exorcises or pretends to expel evil
spirits by adjurations. [Fr. *exorciste*—Gr. *exor-
kistēs.*]
**Exorcism,** eks'or-sizm, *n.* act of exorcising or expelling evil spirits by certain ceremonies. [Fr.
*exorcisme*—Gr. *exorkismos.*]
**Exordial,** egz-or'di-al, *adj.* pertaining to the
exordium.
**Exordium,** egz-or'di-um, *n.* the *introductory* part
of a discourse or composition. [L.—*exordior,*
to begin a web—*ex,* out, and *ordior,* to begin,
to weave.]
**Exostosis,** eks-os-tō'sis, *n.* (*anat.*) morbid enlargement of a bone. [Gr. *ex,* out of, and
*osteon,* a bone.]
**Exoteric,** eks-o-ter'ik, **Exoterical,** eks-o-ter'ik-al,
*adj.* external: fit to be communicated to the
public or multitude:—opposed to **Esoteric.**—*n.*
**Exoter'icism.** [Gr. *exōterikos*—comp. formed
from *exō,* without.]
**Exotic,** egz-ot'ik, **Exotical,** egz-ot'ik-al, *adj.* introduced from a foreign country:—the opposite
of **Indigenous.**—*n.* anything of foreign origin:
something not native to a country, as a plant,
[L.—Gr. *exōtikos*—*exō,* outward.]
**Expand,** eks-pand', *v.t.* to *spread out:* to open or
lay open: to enlarge in bulk or surface.—*v.i.* to
become opened: to enlarge. [L. *expando*—*ex,*
out, and *pando, pansus,* to spread.]
**Expanse,** eks-pans', *n.* a wide extent of space or
body: the firmament.
**Expansible,** eks-pans'i-bl, *adj.* capable of being
expanded or extended.—*n.* Expansibil'ity.—
*adv.* Expans'ibly.
**Expansion,** eks-pan'shun, *n.* act of expanding:
state of being expanded: enlargement: that
which is expanded: immensity.
**Expansive,** eks-pans'iv, *adj.* widely extended:
diffusive.—*adv.* Expans'ively.—*n.* Expans'iveness.
**Expatiate,** eks-pā'shi-āt, *v.i.* to range at large:
to enlarge in discourse, argument, or writing.
[L. *expatior, -atus*—*ex,* out of, and *spatior,*
to roam—*spatium,* space.]
**Expatiation,** eks-pā-shi-ā'shun, *n.* act of expatiat-
ing or enlarging in discourse.
**Expatriate,** eks-pā'tri-āt, *v.t.* to send *out of* one's
*fatherland* or native country: to banish or exile.
[Low L. *expatrio, -atus*—*ex,* out of, *patria,*
fatherland—*pater, patris,* a father.]
**Expatriation,** eks-pā-tri-ā'shun, *n.* act of expatri-
ating: exile, voluntary or compulsory.
**Expect,** eks-pekt', *v.t.* to wait for: to look forward to as something about to happen: to

anticipate : to hope. [L. *exspecto*, *-atus—ex*, out. and *specto*, inten. of *specio*, to look.]

**Expectance**, eks-pekt'ans, **Expectancy**, eks-pekt'an-si. *n.* act or state of expecting : that which is expected : hope.

**Expectant**, eks-pekt'ant, *adj.* looking or waiting for.—*n.* one who expects : one who is looking or waiting for some benefit.

**Expectation**, eks-pek-tā'shun, *n.* act or state of expecting, or of looking forward to as about to happen : prospect of future good : that which is expected : the ground or qualities for anticipating future benefits or excellence : promise : the value of something expected. [expectation.

**Expectingly**, eks-pekt'ing-li, *adv.* in a state of

**Expectorant**, eks-pek'to-rant, *adj.* tending to promote expectoration.—*n.* a medicine which promotes expectoration. [See **Expectorate**.]

**Expectorate**, eks-pek'to-rāt, *v.t.* to expel *from* the *breast* or lungs, by coughing, &c. : to spit forth.—*v.i.* to discharge or eject phlegm from the throat. [L. *expectoro, expectoratus—ex*, out of, from, and *pectus, pectoris*, the breast.]

**Expectoration**, eks-pek-to-rā'shun, *n.* act of expectorating : that which is expectorated : spittle.

**Expectorative**, eks-pek'to-ra-tiv, *adj.* having the quality of promoting expectoration.

**Expedience**, eks-pē'di-ens, **Expediency**, ex-pē'di-en-si. *n.* fitness : desirableness : self-interest.

**Expedient**, eks-pē'di-ent, *adj.* suitable : advisable. —*n.* that which serves to promote : means suitable to an end : contrivance.—*adv.* **Expe'diently.** [L. *expediens—expedio*, to set free.]

**Expedite**, eks'pe-dīt, *v.t.* to free from impediments to hasten : to send forth.—*adj.* free from impediment : quick : prompt.—*adv.* **Ex'peditely.** [L. *expedio, -itus—ex*, out, and *pes, pedis*, a foot.]

**Expedition**, eks-pe-dish'un, *n.* speed : any undertaking by a number of persons : a hostile march or voyage : those who form an expedition. [L. *expeditio*.]

**Expeditious**, eks-pe-dish'us, *adj.* characterised by expedition or rapidity : speedy : prompt.—*adv.* **Expedi'tiously.**

**Expel**, eks-pel', *v.t.* to *drive out* from or cut off connection with a society : to banish :—*pr.p.* expell'ing ; *pa.p.* expelled'. [L. *expello, expulsus—ex*, out, and *pello*, to drive.]

**Expend**, eks-pend', *v.t.* to lay out : to employ or consume in any way : to spend. [L. *expendo—ex*, out, and *pendo, pensum*, to weigh.]

**Expenditure**, eks-pend'i-tūr, *n.* act of expending or laying out : that which is expended : money spent. [*law*] the costs of a lawsuit.

**Expense**, eks-pens', *n.* outlay : cost :—*pl.* (*Scots*

**Expensive**, eks-pens'iv, *adj.* causing or requiring much expense : extravagant.—*adv.* **Expensively.**—*n.* **Expens'iveness.**

**Experience**, eks-pē'ri-ens, *n.*, *thorough trial* of : practical acquaintance with any matter gained by trial : repeated trial : long and varied observation, personal or general : wisdom derived from the changes and trials of life.—*v.t.* to make trial of, or practical acquaintance with : to prove or know by use : to suffer. [Fr.—L. *experientia*, from *experior—ex*, intensive, and old verb *perior*, to try.]

**Experienced**, eks-pē'ri-enst, *adj.* taught by experience : skilful : wise.

**Experiential**, eks-pē-ri-en'shal, *adj.* pertaining to or derived from experience.

**Experiment**, eks-per'i-ment, *n.* a *trial* : something done to *prove* some theory, or to discover something unknown.—*v.i.* to make an experiment or trial : to search by trial. [L. *experimentum*, from *experior*, to try thoroughly.]

**Experimental**, eks-per-i-ment'al, *adj.* founded on or known by experiment : taught by experiment or experience.—*adv.* **Experiment'ally.**

**Experimentalist**, eks-per-i-ment'al-ist, **Experimentist**, eks-per'i-ment-ist, *n.* one who makes *experiments.*

**Expert**, eks-pėrt', *adj.* taught by practice : having a familiar knowledge : having a facility of performance : skilful, adroit.—*n.* eks'pėrt or eks-pėrt', one who is expert or skilled in any art or science : a scientific or professional witness.—*adv.* **Expert'ly.**—*n.* **Expert'ness.** [Fr.—L. *expertus—experior*, to try thoroughly.]

**Expiable**, eks'pi-a-bl, *adj.* capable of being expiated, atoned for, or done away.

**Expiate**, eks'pi-āt, *v.t.* to make complete atonement for : to make satisfaction or reparation for. [L. *expio, expiatus—ex*, intensive, and *pio*, to appease, atone for—*pius*, pious.]

**Expiation**, eks-pi-ā'shun, *n.* act of expiating or atoning for : the means by which atonement is made : atonement. [L. *expiatio*.]

**Expiator**, eks'pi-ā-tor, *n.* one who expiates.

**Expiatory**, eks'pi-a-tor-i, *adj.* having the power to make expiation or atonement.

**Expirable**, eks-pīr'a-bl, *adj.* that may expire or come to an end.

**Expiration**, eks-pir-ā'shun, *n.* a breathing out : death : end : that which is expired. [L. *exspiratio*.]

**Expiratory**, eks-pī'ra-tor-i, *adj.* pertaining to expiration, or the emission of the breath.

**Expire**, eks-pīr', *v.t.* to *breathe out* : to emit or throw out from the lungs : to emit in minute particles.—*v.i.* to breathe out the breath or life : to die : to come to an end. [L. *ex*, out, and *spiro*, to breathe.]

**Expiry**, eks'pīr-i, *n.* the end or termination : expiration.

**Expiscate**, eks-pis'kāt, *v.t.* to *fish out* or ascertain by artful means. [L. *expiscor, expiscatus—ex*, out, and *piscor*, to fish—*piscis*, a fish.]

**Explain**, eks-plān', *v.t.* to make plain or intelligible : to unfold and illustrate the meaning of : to expound. [O. Fr. *explaner*—L. *explano—ex*, out, *plano—planus*, plain.]

**Explainable**, eks-plān'a-bl, *adj.* that may be explained or cleared up.

**Explanation**, eks-plan-ā'shun, *n.* act of explaining or clearing from obscurity : that which explains or clears up : the meaning or sense given to anything : a mutual clearing up of matters.

**Explanatory**, eks-plan'a-tor-i, *adj.* serving to explain or clear up : containing explanations.

**Expletive**, eks'ple-tiv, *adj.*, *filling out* : added for ornament or merely to fill up.—*n.* a word or syllable inserted for ornament or to fill up a vacancy. [L. *expletivus—ex*, out, *pleo*, to fill.]

**Expletory**, eks'ple-tor-i, *adj.* serving to *fill up* : expletive.

**Explicable**, eks'pli-ka-bl, *adj.* capable of being explicated or explained. [L. *explicabilis*.]

**Explicate**, eks'pli-kāt, *v.t.* to *fold out* or unfold : to lay open or explain the meaning of. [L. *explico, explicatus* or *explicitus—ex*, out, *plico*, to fold.]

**Explication**, eks-pli-kā'shun, *n.* act of explicating or explaining : explanation. [L. *explicatio*.]

**Explicative**, eks'pli-kā-tiv, **Explicatory**, eks'pli-kā-tor-i, *adj.* serving to explicate or explain.

**Explicit**, eks-plis'it, *adj.* not implied merely, but distinctly stated : plain in language : clear : unreserved.—*adv.* **Explic'itly.**—*n.* **Explic'itness.** [L. *explicitus*, from *explico*.]

**Explode**, eks-plōd', *v.t.* to cry down, as an actor : to bring into disrepute, and reject.—*v.i.* to burst with a loud report. [L. *explodo—ex*, out, and *plaudo*, to clap the hands.]

**Exploit**, eks-ploit', *n.* a deed or achievement, esp. an heroic one : a feat.—*v.* to work up, utilise.—*n.* **Exploita'tion**, the act of successfully applying industry to any object, as the working of mines, &c. [Fr. *exploit*—L. *explicitum*, ended, achieved.]

**Exploration**, eks-plo-rā'shun, *n.* act of exploring, or searching thoroughly. [See **Explore**.]

**Exploratory**, eks-plor'a-tor-i, *adj.* serving to explore : searching out.

**Explore**, eks-plōr', *v.t.* to search through for the purpose of discovery : to examine thoroughly. [Fr.—L. *exploro, exploratus*, to search out—*ex*, out, and *ploro*, to make to flow, to weep.]

**Explorer**, eks-plōr'ėr, *n.* one who explores.

**Explosion**, eks-plō'zhun, *n.* act of exploding : a sudden violent burst with a loud report.

**Explosive**, eks-plō'siv, *adj.* liable to or causing explosion : bursting out with violence and noise.—*adv.* **Explo'sively.**

**Exponent**, eks-pō'nent, *n.* he or that which points out, or represents : (*alg.*) a figure which shews how often a quantity is to be multiplied by itself, as $a^3$ : an index. [L. *exponens—ex*, out, and *pono*, to place.]

**Exponential**, eks-po-nen'shal, *adj.* (*alg.*) pertaining to or involving *exponents*.

**Export**, eks-pōrt', *v.t.* to carry or send *out* of a country, as goods in commerce.—*n.* **Export'er.** [L. *exporto—ex*, out of, and *porto*, to carry. See **Port**.]

**Export**, eks'pōrt, *n.* act of exporting : that which is exported : a commodity which is or may be sent from one country to another, in traffic.

**Exportable**, eks-pōrt'a-bl, *adj.* that may be exported.

**Exportation**, eks-pōr-tā'shun, *n.* act of exporting, or of conveying goods from one country to another. [See **Export**, *v.t.*]

**Expose**, eks-pōz', *v.t.* to *place* or *lay forth* to view : to deprive of cover, protection, or shelter : to make bare : to explain : to make liable to : to disclose.—*n.* **Expos'er.** [Fr. *exposer*—L. *ex*, out, and Fr. *poser*, to place. See **Pose**, *n.*]

**Exposition**, eks-po-zish'un, *n.* act of exposing, or laying open : a setting out to public view : a public exhibition : act of *expounding*, or laying open of the meaning of an author : explanation.

**Expositor**, eks-pozʹi-tor, *n.* one who or that which *expounds* or explains : an interpreter.

**Expository**, eks-pozʹi-tor-i, *adj.* serving to *expound* or explain : explanatory.

**Expostulate**, eks-post'ū-lāt, *v.i.* to reason earnestly with a person on some impropriety of his conduct : to remonstrate.—*n.* **Expost'ulator**. [L. *expostulo, expostulatus—ex*, intensive, and *postulo*, to demand.]

**Expostulation**, eks-post-ū-lā'shun, *n.* act of expostulating, or reasoning earnestly with a person against his conduct : remonstrance.

**Expostulatory**, eks-post'ū-la-tor-i, *adj.* containing expostulation.

**Exposure**, eks-pō'zhūr, *n.* act of exposing or laying open or bare : state of being laid open or bare : openness to danger : position with regard to the sun, influence of climate, &c.

**Expound**, eks-pownd', *v.t.* to *expose*, or lay open the meaning of : to explain. [Ō. Fr. *espondre*—L. *expono—ex*, and *pono*, to place.]

**Expounder**, eks-pownd'ėr, *n.* one who expounds : an interpreter.

**Express**, eks-pres', *v.t.* to *press* or force *out* : to represent or make known by a likeness or by words : to declare : to designate. [L. *ex*, out, and **Press**.]

**Express**, eks-pres', *adj.* pressed or clearly brought out : exactly representing : directly stated : explicit : clear : intended or sent for a particular purpose.—*n.* a messenger or conveyance sent on a special errand : a regular and quick conveyance.—*adj.* **Express'ible.** *adv.* **Express'ly.**

**Expression**, eks-presh'un, *n.* act of expressing or forcing out by pressure : act of representing or giving utterance to : faithful and vivid representation by language, art, the features, &c. : that which is expressed : look : feature : the manner in which anything is expressed : tone of voice or sound in music.—*adj.* **Express'ionless.**

**Expressive**, eks-pres'iv, *adj.* serving to express or indicate : full of expression : vividly representing : significant.—*adv.* **Express'ively.**—*n.* **Express'iveness.**

**Expulsion**, eks-pul'shun, *n.* banishment. [L. *expulsio*. See **Expel**.]     [*expel*.

**Expulsive**, eks-pul'siv, *adj.* able or serving to

**Expunge**, eks-punj', *v.t.* to wipe out : to efface. [L. *ex*, out, and *pungo*, to prick.]

**Expurgate**, eks-pur'gāt or eks'pur-, *v.t.* to *purge out* or render *pure :* to purify from anything noxious or erroneous. [L. *expurgo, expurgatus—ex*, out, and *purgo*, to purge or purify, from *purus*, pure.]     [gating or purifying.

**Expurgation**, eks-pur-gā'shun, *n.* act of expur-

**Expurgator**, eks'pur-gā-tor or eks-pur'ga-tor, *n.* one who expurgates or purifies.

**Expurgatory**, eks-pur'ga-tor-i, *adj.* serving to expurgate or purify.

**Exquisite**, eks'kwi-zit, *adj.* of superior quality : excellent : of delicate perception or close discrimination : not easily satisfied : fastidious : exceeding, extreme, as pain.—*n.* one exquisitely nice or refined in dress : a fop.—*adv.* **Ex'quisitely.**—*n.* **Ex'quisiteness.** [L. *exquisitus—ex*, out, and *quero, quæsitus*, to seek.]

**Exsanguious**, eks-sang'gwi-us, **Exsanguinous**, eks-sang'gwin-us, *adj.* : *without blood* or red blood. [L. *ex*, priv., and *sanguis, sanguinis*, blood.]     [*scindo*, to cut.]

**Exscind**, ek-sind', *v.t.* to *cut off*. [L. *ex*, off, and

**Extant**, eks'tant, *adj.*, *standing out*, or above the rest : still standing or existing. [L. *exstans, -antis—ex*, out, and *sto*, to stand.]

**Extasy.** Same as **Ecstasy**.

**Extatic.** Same as **Ecstatic**.

**Extemporaneous**, eks-tem-po-rā'ne-us, **Extemporary**, eks-tem'po-rar-i, *adj.* done on the spur of the moment : done without preparation : off-hand.—*adv.* **Extempora'neously.** [L. *extemporaneus—ex*, and *tempus, temporis*, time.]

**Extempore**, eks-tem'po-re, *adv.* on the spur of the moment : without preparation : suddenly. [L. *ex tempore—ex*, out of, and *tempus, temporis*, time.]

**Extemporise**, eks-tem'po-rīz, *v.i.* to speak *extempore* or without previous preparation : to discourse without notes : to speak off-hand.

**Extend**, eks--tend', *v.t.* to *stretch out :* to prolong in any direction : to enlarge : to widen : to hold out : to bestow or impart.—*v.i.* to stretch : to be continued in length or breadth. [L. *extendo, extentus—ex*, out, *tendo, tensum*, to stretch.]

**Extensible**, eks-tens'i-bl, **Extensile**, eks-tens'īl, *adj.* that may be *extended*.—*n.* **Extens'ibility.**

**Extension**, eks-ten'shun, *n.* a stretching out, prolongation, or enlargement: that property of a body by which it occupies a portion of space.

**Extensive**, eks-tens'iv, *adj.* large: comprehensive.—*adv.* **Extens'ively.**—*n.* **Extens'iveness.**

**Extent**, eks-tent', *n.* the space or degree to which a thing is *extended*: bulk: compass.

**Extenuate**, eks-ten'ū-āt, *v.t.* to *lessen* or diminish: to weaken the force of: to palliate.—*n.* **Exten'uator.** [L. *extenuo, extenuatus—ex*, intensive, and *tenuo*, from *tenuis*, thin.]

**Extenuating**, eks-ten'ū-āt-ing, *adj.* lessening: palliating.—*adv.* **Exten'uatingly.**

**Extenuation**, eks-ten-ū-ā'shun, *n.* act of representing anything as less wrong or criminal than it is: palliation: mitigation.

**Extenuatory**, eks-ten'ū-a-tor-i, *adj.* tending to extenuate [extenuate.

**Exterior**, eks-tē'ri-or, *adj.*, *outer*: outward: on or from the outside: foreign.—*n.* outward part or surface: outward form or deportment: appearance. [L. *exterior*, comp. of *exter*, outward, from *ex*, out.]

**Exterminate**, eks-tėr'mi-nāt, *v.t.* to destroy utterly: to put an end to: to root out.—*n.* **Exter'minator.** [L. *extermino, exterminatus—ex*, out of, and *terminus*, a boundary.]

**Extermination**, eks-tėr-mi-nā'shun, *n.* complete destruction or extirpation.

**Exterminatory**, eks-tėr'mi-na-tor-i, *adj.* serving or tending to exterminate.

**External**, eks-tėr'nal, *adj.*, *exterior, outward*: that may be seen: apparent: not innate or intrinsic: derived from without: accidental: foreign.—*adv.* **Exter'nally.** [L. *externus—exter.*] [outward forms or ceremonies.

**Externals**, eks-tėr'nalz, *n.pl.* the *outward parts*:

**Extinct**, eks-tinkt', *adj.* put out: no longer existing: dead. [See **Extinguish.**]

**Extinction**, eks-tingk'shun, *n.* a quenching or destroying: destruction: suppression.

**Extinguish**, eks-ting'gwish, *v.t.* to *quench*: to destroy: to obscure by superior splendour.—*adj.* **Exting'uishable.** [L. *exstinguo, exstinctus—ex*, out, and *stinguo*, to quench, to prick, from root *stig*, to prick.]

**Extinguisher**, eks-ting'gwish-ėr, *n.* a small hollow conical instrument for putting out a candle.

**Extirpate**, eks-tėr'pāt, *v.t.* to *root out*: to destroy totally: to exterminate.—*n.* **Extir'pator.** [L. *exstirpo, exstirpatus—ex*, out, and *stirps*, a root.] [total destruction.

**Extirpation**, eks-tėr-pā'shun, *n.* extermination:

**Extol**, eks-tol', *v.t.* to magnify: to praise:—*pr.p.* extoll'ing; *pap.* extolled'. [L. *extollo—ex*, up, *tollo*, to lift or raise.]

**Extorsive**, eks-tors'iv, *adj.* serving or tending to *extort*.—*adv.* **Extors'ively.**

**Extort**, eks-tort', *v.t.* to gain or draw from by compulsion or violence. [L. *extorqueo, extortus—ex*, out, and *torqueo*, to twist.]

**Extortion**, eks-tor'shun, *n.* illegal or oppressive exaction: that which is extorted.

**Extortionary**, eks-tor'shun-ar-i, *adj.* pertaining to or implying extortion.

**Extortionate**, eks-tor'shun-āt, *adj.* oppressive.

**Extortioner**, eks-tor'shun-ėr, *n.* one who practises extortion.

**Extra**, eks'tra, *adj.*, *beyond* or more than is necessary: extraordinary: additional. [L. *extra*, beyond, outside of, contracted from *extera—exter—ex*, out, and root *tar*, to cross.]

**Extract**, eks-trakt', *v.t.* to *draw out* by force or otherwise: to choose out or select: to find out:

to distil.—*adj.* **Extract'ible.** [L. *extraho, extractus—ex*, out, and *traho*, to draw.]

**Extract**, eks'trakt, *n.* anything drawn from a substance by heat, distillation, &c. as an essence: a passage taken from a book or writing.

**Extraction**, eks-trak'shun, *n.* act of extracting or drawing out: derivation from a stock or family: birth: lineage: that which is extracted.

**Extractive**, eks-trakt'iv, *adj.* tending or serving to extract.—*n.* an extract. [extracts.

**Extractor**, eks-trakt'or, *n.* he who or that which

**Extradition**, eks-tra-dish'un, *n.* a *delivering up* by one government to another of fugitives from justice. [L. *ex*, from, and *traditio—trado, traditus*, to deliver up.]

**Extra-judicial**, eks'tra-jōō-dish'al, *adj.*, *out* of the proper court, or *beyond* the usual course of *legal* proceeding. [**Extra** and **Judicial.**]

**Extra-mundane**, eks'tra-mun'dān, *adj.*, *beyond* the material *world*. [**Extra** and **Mundane.**]

**Extra-mural**, eks'tra-mū'ral, *adj.* without or *beyond* the *walls*. [**Extra** and **Mural.**]

**Extraneous**, eks-trān'yus, *adj.* external: foreign: not belonging to or dependent on a thing: not essential.—*adv.* **Extran'eously.** [L. *extraneus*, from *extra*. See **Extra.**]

**Extraordinaries**, eks-tror'di-nar-iz, *n.pl.* things that *exceed* the usual *order*, kind, or method.

**Extraordinary**, eks-tror'di-nar-i, *adj.*, *beyond ordinary*: not usual or regular: wonderful: special.—*adv.* **Extraor'dinarily.** [**Extra** and **Ordinary.**]

**Extravagance**, eks-trav'a-gans, *n.* irregularity: excess: lavish expenditure.

**Extravagant**, eks-trav'a-gant, *adj.*, *wandering beyond* bounds: irregular: unrestrained: excessive: profuse in expenses: wasteful.—*adv.* **Extrav'agantly.** [L. *extra*, beyond, and *vagans, -antis*, pr.p. of *vagor*, to wander.]

**Extravaganza**, eks-trav-a-gan'za, *n.* an *extravagant* or wild and irregular piece of music. [It.]

**Extravasate**, eks-trav'a-sāt, *v.t.* to let *out* of the proper *vessels*, as blood. [L. *extra*, out of, and *vas*, a vessel.]

**Extreme**, eks-trēm', *adj.*, *outermost*: most remote: last: highest in degree: greatest: most violent: most urgent.—*n.* the utmost point or verge: end: utmost or highest limit or degree: great necessity.—*adv.* **Extreme'ly.** [Fr. *extrême*—L. *extremus*, superl. of *exter*, on the outside, outward.]

**Extremity**, eks-trem'i-ti, *n.* the utmost limit, point, or portion: the highest degree: greatest necessity, emergency, or distress. [Fr. *extrémité*—L. *extremitas*.]

**Extricate**, eks'tri-kāt, *v.t.* to free *from hinderances* or perplexities: to disentangle: to emit.—*adj.* **Ex'tricable.** [L. *extrico, extricatus—ex*, out, *tricæ*, trifles, hinderances.]

**Extrication**, eks-tri-kā'shun, *n.* disentanglement: act of sending out or evolving.

**Extrinsic**, eks-trin'sik, **Extrinsical**, eks-trin'sik-al, *adj.* on the *outside* or *outward*: external: not contained in or belonging to a body: foreign: not essential:—opposed to **Intrinsic.**—*adv.* **Extrin'sically.** [Fr.—L. *extrinsecus—exter*, outward, and *secus*, from the same root as *sequor*, to follow.]

**Extrude**, eks-trōōd', *v.t.* to *force* or urge *out*: to expel: to drive off. [L. *extrudo, extrusus—ex*, out, and *trudo*, to thrust.]

**Extrusion**, eks-trōō'zhun, *n.* act of extruding, thrusting, or throwing out: expulsion.

**Exuberance,** eks-ū'bĕr-ans, **Exuberancy,** eks-ū'-bĕr-an-si, *n.* an overflowing quantity : richness : superfluousness.

**Exuberant,** eks-ū'bĕr-ant, *adj.* plenteous : overflowing : superfluous.—*adv.* **Exu'berantly.** [L. *exuberans,* pr.p. of *exubero*—*ex,* intensive, and *uber,* rich, abundant.]

**Exudation,** eks-ū-dā'shun, *n.* act of exuding or discharging through pores : the sweat, &c. exuded.

**Exude,** eks-ūd', *v.t.* to discharge by *sweating* : to discharge through pores or incisions, as sweat, moisture, &c.—*v.i.* to flow out of a body through the pores. [L. *ex,* out, *sudo,* to sweat.]

**Exult,** egz-ult', *v.i.* to rejoice exceedingly : to triumph.—*adv.* **Exult'ingly.** [L. *exsulto,* from *exsilio*—*ex,* out or up, and *salio,* to leap.]

**Exultant,** egz-ult'ant, *adj., exulting* : triumphant. [L. *exsultans.*]

**Exultation,** egz-ul-tā'shun, *n.* lively joy at any advantage gained : rapturous delight : transport. [L. *exsultatio.*]

**Exuviæ,** eks-ū'vi-ē, *n.pl., cast-off* skins, shells, or other coverings of animals : (*geol.*) fossil shells and other remains of animals. [L., from *exuo,* to draw or put off.]

**Eyalet,** ī'a-let, *n.* a division of the Turkish empire. [From an Arab. word sig. government. **Vilayet** is a doublet.]

**Eye,** ī, *n.* the organ of sight or vision, more correctly the globe or movable part of it : the power of seeing : sight : regard : aim : keenness of perception : anything resembling an eye, as the hole of a needle, loop or ring for a hook, &c.—*v.t.* to look on : to observe narrowly :—*pr.p.* ey'ing or eye'ing ; *pa.p.* eyed' (īd).—*n.* **Eye'-shot,** the reach or range of sight of the eye. [A.S. *eage ;* Goth. *augo ;* Ger. *auge ;* Slav. *oko ;* allied to Gr. *okos, osse,* the two eyes, connected with *ossomai,* to see ; L. *oculus,* Sans. *aksha.*]

**Eyeball,** ī'bawl, *n.* the *ball,* globe, or apple of the *eye.*

**Eyebright,** ī'brīt, *n.* a beautiful little plant of the genus Euphrasia, formerly used as a remedy for diseases of the *eye.* [the *eye.*

**Eyebrow,** ī'brow, *n.* the *brow* or hairy arch above

**Eyelash,** ī'lash, *n.* the line of hairs that edges the eyelid. [**Eye** and **Lash.**]

**Eyeless,** ī'les, *adj.* without eyes or sight.

**Eyelet,** ī'let, **Eyelet-hole,** ī'let-hōl, *n.* a *small eye* or *hole* to receive a lace or cord, as in garments, sails, &c. [Fr. *œillet,* dim. of *œil,* an eye.]

**Eyelid,** ī'lid, *n.* the *lid* or cover of the *eye :* the portion of movable skin by means of which the eye is opened or closed at pleasure.

**Eye-service,** ī'-sĕr'vis, *n., service* performed only under the *eye* or inspection of an employer.

**Eyesight,** ī'sīt, *n.* power of seeing : view : observation. [sight to the *eye.*

**Eyesore,** ī'sōr, *n.* anything that is *sore* or offen-

**Eyetooth,** ī'tōōth, *n.* a *tooth* in the upper jaw next the grinders, with a long fang pointing towards the *eye.* [done.

**Eye-witness,** ī'-wit'nes, *n.* one who *sees* a thing

**Eyre,** ār, *n.* a *journey* or circuit : a court of itinerant justices : justices in eyre formerly corresponded to our present justices of assize. [O. Fr. *eire,* journey, from L. *iter,* a way, a journey —*eo, itum,* to go.]

**Eyry, Eyrie, Aerie,** ē're or ā're, *n.* a place where birds of prey construct their nests and hatch their eggs : a brood of eagles or hawks. [Fr. *aire,* from Ger. *aar,* an eagle ; cog. with Ice. *ari,* an eagle.]

# F

**Fable,** fā'bl, *n.* a feigned story or *tale* intended to instruct or amuse : the plot or series of events in an epic or dramatic poem : fiction : a falsehood.—*v.t.* to feign : to invent. [Fr. *fable*—L. *fabula,* from *fari,* to speak.]

**Fabric,** fab'rik or fā'brik, *n., workmanship* : texture : anything framed by art and labour : building : manufactured cloth : any system of connected parts. [Fr.—L. *fabrica*—*faber,* a worker in hard materials—*facio,* to make.]

**Fabricate,** fab'ri-kāt, *v.t.* to put together by art and labour : to manufacture : to produce : to devise falsely.—*n.* **Fab'ricator.** [L. *fabrico, fabricatus,* from *fabrica.* See **Fabric.**]

**Fabrication,** fab-ri-kā'shun, *n.* construction : manufacture : that which is fabricated or invented : a story : a falsehood.

**Fabulise,** fab'ū-līz, *v.t.* to write *fables,* or to speak in fables.

**Fabulist,** fab'ū-list, *n.* one who invents *fables.*

**Fabulous,** fab'ū-lus, *adj.* feigned, as a *fable :* related in fable : false.—*adv.* **Fab'ulously.** [L. *fabulosus.*]

**Façade,** fa-sād', *n.* the *face* or *front* of a building. [Fr., from It. *facciata,* the front of a building, *faccia,* the face—L. *facies.* See **Face.**]

**Face,** fās, *n.* the visible forepart of the head : the outside make or appearance : front : cast of features : look : boldness : presence : (*B.*) anger or favour. [Fr. *face*—L. *facies,* form, face—*facio,* to make, akin to Gr. *phainō,* to cause to appear.]

**Face,** fās, *v.t.* to meet in the *face* or in front : to stand opposite to : to resist : to put an additional face or surface on : to cover in front.—*v.i.* to turn the face. [of a corpse.

**Facecloth,** fās'kloth, *n.* a cloth laid over the face

**Facet,** fas'et, *n.* a *little face :* a small surface, as of a crystal. [Fr. *facette,* dim. of *face.*]

**Facetiæ,** fa-sē'shi-ē, *n.pl. witty* or humorous sayings or writings. [L.—*facetus,* merry, witty.]

**Facetious,** fa-sē'shus, *adj.* witty, humorous, jocose.—*adv.* **Face'tiously.**—*n.* **Face'tiousness.** [Fr., from L. *facetiæ.*]

**Facial,** fā'shal, *adj.* of or relating to the *face.*—*adv.* **Fa'cially.**

**Facile,** fas'il, *adj.* *easily* persuaded : yielding : easy of access : courteous : easy. [Fr., from L. *facilis,* that may be done, easy, from *facio,* to do.] [difficulty.

**Facilitate,** fa-sil'i-tāt, *v.t.* to make *easy :* to lessen

**Facility,** fa-sil'i-ti, *n.* quality of being *facile* or *easily done :* dexterity : easiness to be persuaded : pliancy : easiness of access : affability.—*pl.* **Facil'ities,** means that render anything easy to be done. [Fr.—L. *facilitas.*]

**Facing,** fās'ing, *n.* a covering in front for ornament or protection.

**Fac-simile,** fak-sim'i-le, *n.* an exact copy. [L. *fac,* contr. of *factum,* made—*facio,* to make, and *similis,* like.]

**Fact,** fakt, *n.* a *deed* or anything *done :* anything that comes to pass : reality : truth : the assertion of a thing done. [L. *factum,* from *facio,* to make.]

**Faction,** fak'shun, *n.* a company of persons associated or *acting* together, mostly used in a bad sense : a contentious party in a state or society : dissension. [L. *factio,* from *facio,* to do.]

**Factious,** fak'shus, *adj.* turbulent : disloyal.—*adv.* **Fac'tiously.**—*n.* **Fac'tiousness.** [L. *factiosus*—*factio.*]

---

**Factitious**, fak-tish′us, *adj.*, *made* by art, in opposition to what is natural.—*adv.* **Facti′tiously.** [L. *factitius*, from *facio*, to make.]

**Factor**, fak′tor, *n.* a *doer* or transactor of business for another : one who buys and sells goods for another, on commission : one of two or more quantities which, multiplied together, form a product.—*n.* **Fac′torship.** [L., from *facio*.]

**Factorage**, fak′tor-āj, *n.* the fees or commission of a factor.

**Factorial**, fak-tō′ri-al, *adj.* pertaining to or consisting in a *factory*.

**Factory**, fak′tor-i, *n.* a manufactory : a trading settlement in a distant country, as the factory of the East India Company at Calcutta.

**Factotum**, fak-tō′tum, *n.* a person employed to *do all* kinds of work. [L. *facio*, and *totus*, all.]

**Faculty**, fak′ul-ti, *n.*, *facility* or power to *act* : an original power of the mind : personal quality or endowment : right, authority, or privilege to act : license : a body of men to whom any privilege is granted : the professors constituting a department in a university : the members of a profession. [Fr.—L. *facultas*—*facilis*, easy.]

**Fad**, fad, *n.* a weak hobby. [Fr. *fade*, insipid. See under **Fade**.]

**Fade**, fād, *v.i.* to lose strength, freshness, or colour gradually.—*adj.* **Fade′less.** [Fr. *fade*, insipid, from L. *fatuus*, silly, insipid.]

**Fæces** or **Feces**, fē′sēz, *n.pl.*, *grounds*: sediment after infusion or distillation : excrement. [L., pl. of *fæx*, *fæcis*, grounds.]

**Fag**, fag, *v.i.* to become weary or tired out : to work as a fag :—*pr.p.* fagg′ing ; *pa.p.* fagged′.—*n.* one who labours like a drudge : a school-boy forced to do menial offices for one older. [Ety. dub. ; perh. a corr. of **Flag**, to droop, which see.]

**Fag-end**, fag′-end, *n.* the *end* of a web of cloth that *flags* or hangs loose : the untwisted end of a rope : the refuse or meaner part of a thing.

**Fagot** or **Faggot**, fag′ut, *n.* a *bundle of sticks* used for fuel : a stick : anything like a fagot : a soldier numbered on the muster-roll, but not really existing : a voter who has obtained his vote expressly for party purposes.—*adj.* got up for a purpose, as in **Fagot vote.** [Fr. *fagot*, a bundle of sticks, perh. from L. *fax*, a torch.]

**Fahrenheit**, fa′ren-hīt, *n.* the name applied to a thermometer, the freezing-point of which is marked at 32. and the boiling-point at 212 degrees. [Named from the inventor, a German.]

**Faience**, fā′yens, *n.* a fine kind of painted pottery. [From *Faenza* in Italy, where first made.]

**Fail**, fāl, *v.i.* to *fall* short or be wanting : to fall away : to decay : to die : to miss : to be disappointed or baffled : to be unable to pay one's debts.—*v.t.* to be wanting to : not to be sufficient for :—*pr.p.* fail′ing ; *pa.p.* failed′. [Fr. *faillir* —L. *fallo* ; conn. with Gr. *sphallō*, to cause to fall, deceive, A.S. *feallan*, to fall.]

**Failing**, fāl′ing, *n.* a fault, weakness : a foible.

**Failure**, fāl′ūr, *n.* a falling short, or cessation : omission : decay : bankruptcy.

**Fain**, fān, *adj.* glad or *joyful*: inclined : content or compelled to accept, for want of better.—*adv.* gladly. [A.S. *fægen*, joyful ; Ice. *feginn*, glad.]

**Faint**, fānt, *adj.* wanting in strength : fading : lacking distinctness : not bright or forcible : weak in spirit : lacking courage : depressed : done in a feeble way.—*v.i.* to become feeble or weak : to lose strength, colour, &c. : to swoon : to fade or decay : to vanish : to lose courage or spirit : to become depressed.—*adv.* **Faint′ly.** [Used of anything that cannot bear trial or proof, from

Fr. *feint* (*feindre*), feigned, unreal—L. *fingere*, to feign or dissemble. See **Feign**.]

**Faintish**, fānt′ish, *adj.*, *somewhat* or slightly *faint*.—*n.* **Faint′ishness.**

**Faintness**, fānt′nes, *n.* want of strength : feebleness of colour, light, &c. : dejection.

**Fair**, fār, *adj.*, *bright* : *clear* : free from blemish : pure : pleasing to the eye : beautiful : free from a dark hue : of a light shade : free from clouds or rain : favourable : unobstructed : open : prosperous : frank : impartial : pleasing : hopeful : moderate.—*adv.* **Fair′ly.**—*n.* **Fair′ness.** [A.S. *fæger*; Ice. *fagr*, bright, Dan. *feir*.] [female sex.

**Fair**, fār, *n.* a *fair woman*.—**The Fair**, *n.pl.* the

**Fair**, fār, *n.* a stated market. [O. Fr. *feire*, from L. *feria*, or *feriæ*, holidays, conn. with *festus*, festive. See **Feast**.]

**Fairy**, fār′i, *n.* an imaginary being, said to assume a human form, and to influence the *fate* of man. [O. Fr. *faerie*, enchantment—Fr. *fée*. See **Fay**, which would have been the correct form, *fairy* being properly an abstract word.]

**Fairy**, fār′i, *adj.* of or belonging to *fairies*.

**Fairyland**, fār′i-land, *n.* the imaginary country of the fairies.

**Faith**, fāth, *n.*, *trust* or *confidence* in any person : belief in the statement of another : belief in the truth of revealed religion : confidence and trust in God : reliance on Christ as the Saviour : that which is believed : any system of religious belief : fidelity to promises : honesty : word or honour pledged. [M.E. *feith*, *feyth*, *fey*—O. Fr. *feid*—L. *fides*—*fido*, to trust ; connected with Gr. *peithō*, to persuade.]

**Faithful**, fāth′fool, *adj.* full of faith, believing : firm in adherence to promises, duty, allegiance, &c.: loyal : conformable to truth : worthy of belief : true. **The Faithful**, believers.—*adv.* **Faith′fully.**—*n.* **Faith′fulness.**

**Faithless**, fāth′les, *adj.* without faith or belief : not believing, esp. in God or Christianity : not adhering to promises, allegiance, or duty : delusive.—*adv.* **Faith′lessly.**—*n.* **Faith′lessness.**

**Fakir**, fā′kèr or fa-kēr′, *n.* a member of a religious order of mendicants in India and the neighbouring countries. [Ar. *fakhar*, poor.]

**Falcate**, fal′kāt, **Falcated**, fal′kāt-ed, *adj.* (*astr.* and *bot.*) bent like a *sickle*, as the crescent moon, and certain leaves. [L. *falcatus*, from *falx*, a sickle.]

**Falchion**, fawl′shun, *n.* a short crooked sword, *falcated* or bent somewhat like a sickle. [It. *falcione*—Low L. *falcio*, from L. *falx*, a sickle.]

**Falcon**, fawl′kn, *n.* a bird of prey formerly trained to the pursuit of game. [Fr. *faucon*—L. *falco*, from *falx*, a hook or sickle ; the bird being so called from its hooked claws.]

**Falconer**, faw′kn-èr, *n.* one who sports with, or who breeds and trains *falcons* or hawks for taking wild-fowl. [Fr. *fauconnier*.]

**Falconry**, faw′kn-ri, *n.* the art of training or hunting with *falcons*. [Fr. *fauconnerie*.]

**Faldstool**, fawld′stōōl, *n.* a *folding* or camp *stool*: a kind of stool for the king to kneel on at his coronation : a bishop's seat within the altar : a small desk at which the litany is sung or said. [From Low L. *faldistolium*—O. H. Ger. *faldan* (Ger. *falten*), to fold, and *stual* (Ger. *stuhl*), stool, seat, or throne ; Fr. *fauteuil* is from the same source.]

**Fall**, fawl, *v.i.* to *drop down* : to descend by the force of gravity : to become prostrate : (*of a river*) to discharge itself : to sink as if dead : to vanish : to die away : to lose strength : to decline in power, wealth, value, or reputation : to sink into sin : to depart from the faith : to become dejected : to pass gently into any state : to befall : to issue : to enter upon with haste or vehemence : to rush : —*pr.p.* fall'ing ; *pa.t.* fell ; *pa.p.* fallen (faw'ln). [A.S. *feallan ;* Ger. *fallen ;* connected with L. *fallo,* to deceive, Gr. *sphallō,* to cause to fall, Sans. *sphal,* to tremble. See **Fail.**]

**Fall,** fawl, *n.* the *act of falling,* in any of its senses : descent by gravity : a dropping down : overthrow : death : descent from a better to a worse position : slope or declivity : descent of water : a cascade : length of a fall : outlet of a river : decrease in value : a sinking of the voice : the time when the leaves fall, autumn : that which falls : a lapse into sin, especially that of Adam and Eve, called **The Fall :**—*pl.* (*Apocrypha*) death, overthrow.

**Fallacious,** fal-lā'shus, *adj.* calculated to *deceive* or mislead : not well founded : causing disappointment : delusive.—*adv.* **Falla'ciously.**—*n.* **Falla'ciousness.** [L. *fallaciosus.*]

**Fallacy,** fal'a-si, *n.* something *fallacious :* deceptive appearance : an apparently genuine but really illogical argument. [Fr. *fallace,* deceit— L. *fallacia,* from *fallax,* deceptive, *fallo,* to deceive.]

**Fallibility,** fal-i-bil'i-ti, *n.* liability to err.

**Fallible,** fal'i-bl, *adj.* liable to error or mistake.— *adv.* **Fall'ibly.** [Low L. *fallibilis,* from *fallo.*]

**Fallow,** fal'ō, *adj.* left untilled or unsowed for a time.—*n.* land that has lain a year or more untilled or unsown after having been ploughed.— *v.t.* to plough land without seeding it. [Orig. yellow or reddish yellow, and applied to land unsown or left bare of a crop, from its reddish colour ; from A.S. *fealo ;* Ger. *falb, fahl ;* allied to L. *pallidus,* Gr. *polios,* livid, Sans. *palita,* gray. *Fallow* is an extension of *fal-* = *pal-* in *pale.*]

**Fallow-deer,** fal'ō-dēr, *n.* a species of deer smaller than the red-deer, with broad flat antlers, and of a *yellowish*-brown colour.      [untilled.

**Fallowness,** fal'ō-nes, *n.* state of being *fallow* or

**False,** fawls, *adj., deceptive* or *deceiving :* untruthful : unfaithful to obligations : untrue : not genuine or real : hypocritical : not well founded. —*adv.* **False'ly.**—*n.* **False'ness.** [O. Fr. *fals* (*faux*)—L. *falsus,* pa.p. of *fallo,* to deceive. See **Fail, Fall, Fallacious.**]

**Falsehood,** fawls'hood, *n.* state or quality of *being false :* want of truth : want of honesty : deceitfulness : false appearance : an untrue statement : a lie. [**False,** and *hood,* A.S. *had,* state.]

**Falsetto,** fawl-set'o, *n.* a *false* or artificial voice : a range of voice beyond the natural compass. [It. *falsetto,* from root of **False.**]

**Falsification,** fawls-i-fi-kā'shun, *n.* the act of *making false :* the giving to a thing the appearance of something which it is not.

**Falsifier,** fawls'i-fī-ér, *n.* one who *falsifies* or gives to a thing a false appearance.

**Falsify,** fawls'i-fī, *v.t.* to forge or counterfeit : to prove untrustworthy : to break by falsehood :— *pr.p.* fals'ifying ; *pa.p.* fals'ified. [L. *falsus,* false, and *facio,* to make.]

**Falsity,** fawls'i-ti, *n.* quality of being *false* : a false assertion. [L. *falsitas,* from *falsus,* false.]

**Falter,** fawl'tér, *v.i.* to fail or stutter in speech : to tremble or totter : to be feeble or irresolute. [Lit., to be at fault ; from root of **Fault** ; cf. Span. *faltar,* It. *faltare,* to be deficient.]

**Falteringly,** fawl'tér-ing-li, *adv.* in a *faltering* or hesitating *manner.*

**Fame,** fām, *n.* public report or rumour : **renown** or celebrity, good or bad. [Fr.—L. *fama,* from *fari,* to speak ; Gr. *phēmē,* from *phēmi,* to say, make known, Sans. *bhāsh,* to speak, A.S. *bannan,* to proclaim.]

**Famed,** fāmd, *adj.* renowned.

**Familiar,** fa-mil'yar, *adj.* well acquainted or intimate : shewing the manner of an intimate : free : having a thorough knowledge of : well known or understood.—*n.* one well or long acquainted : a demon supposed to attend at call.—*adv.* **Famil'iarly.** [L. *familiaris,* from *familia,* a family.]

**Familiarise,** fa-mil'yar-īz, *v.t.* to make thoroughly acquainted : to accustom : to make easy by practice or study.

**Familiarity,** fa-mil-ye-ar'i-ti, *n.* intimate acquaintanceship : freedom from constraint. [L. *familiaritas.*]

**Family,** fam'i-li, *n.* the household, or all those who live in one house under one head : the descendants of one common progenitor : race : honourable or noble descent : a group of animals, plants, languages, &c. more comprehensive than a genus. [Fr.—L. *familia—famulus,* a servant.]

**Famine,** fam'in, *n.* general scarcity of food. [Fr., through an unrecorded Low L. *famina,* from L. *fames,* hunger.]

**Famish,** fam'ish, *v.t.* to starve.—*v.i.* to die or suffer extreme hunger or thirst : to suffer from exposure.

**Famishment,** fam'ish-ment, *n.* starvation.

**Famous,** fā'mus, *adj.* renowned : noted.—*adv.* **Fa'mously.** [L. *famosus,* from *fama.*]

**Fan,** fan, *n.* a broad, flat instrument used by ladies to cool themselves : anything of this form, as for winnowing grain, &c. : a small sail to keep a windmill to the wind.—*v.t.* to cool with a fan : to winnow : to ventilate :—*pr.p.* fann'ing ; *pa.p.* fanned'. [A.S. *fann,* Fr. *van,* both from L. *vannus,* a fan.]

**Fanatic,** fa-nat'ik, **Fanatical,** fa-nat'ik-al, *adj.* extravagantly or unreasonably zealous, esp. in religion : excessively enthusiastic.—*adv.* **Fanat'ically.** [Fr.—L. *fanaticus,* from *fanum,* a temple ; it meant first belonging to a temple ; then, inspired by a god, enthusiastic, madly enthusiastic. See **Fane.**]

**Fanatic,** fa-nat'ik, *n.* a person frantically or excessively enthusiastic, esp. on religious subjects.

**Fanaticism,** fa-nat'i-sizm, *n.* wild and excessive religious enthusiasm.

**Fanciful,** fan'si-fool, *adj.* guided or created by fancy : imaginative : whimsical : wild.—*adv.* **Fan'cifully.**—*n.* **Fan'cifulness.**

**Fancy,** fan'si, *n.* that faculty of the mind by which it recalls, represents, or *makes to appear* past images or impressions : an image or representation thus formed in the mind : an unreasonable or capricious opinion : a whim : capricious inclination or liking.—*adj.* pleasing to, or guided by fancy or caprice.—**Fancy-ball,** *n.* a ball at which fancy dresses in various characters are worn —**The Fancy,** *n.pl.* sporting characters generally. [Contracted from *fantasy,* Fr. *fantasie,* through L., from Gr. *phantasi :*—Gr. *phantazō,* to make visible—*phainō,* to bring to light, to shew, Sans. *bhā,* to shine.]

**Fancy,** fan'si, *v.t.* to portray in the mind : to imagine : to have a fancy or liking for : to be pleased with :—*pr.p.* fan'cying ; *pa.p.* fan'cied.

**Fandango,** fan-dan'go, *n.* an old Spanish dance. [Sp.]

---

**Fane**, fān, *n.* a temple. [L. *fanum*, from *fari*, to speak, to dedicate.]

**Fanfare**, fan'fār, *n.* a flourish of trumpets on entering the lists: a boast: a bravado. [Fr. *fanfare* —Sp. *fanfarria*, which is from Arab. *farfar*, loquacious.]

**Fanfaron**, fan'fa-ron, *n.* one who uses *fanfare* or bravado: a bully. [Fr., from *fanfare*.]

**Fanfaronade**, fan-far-on-ād', *n.* vain boasting: bluster. [Fr. *fanfaronnade*, from *fanfare*.]

**Fang**, fang, *n.* the tooth of a ravenous beast: a claw or talon. [A.S. *fang*, from *fon*, to seize; Ger. *fangen*, to catch.]

**Fanged**, fangd, *adj.* having *fangs*, clutches, or anything resembling them.

**Fanlight**, fan'līt, *n.* a *window* resembling in form an open *fan*.

**Fanner**, fan'ér, *n.* a machine with revolving fans, used for winnowing grain, &c.

**Fanpalm**, fan'pām, *n.* a species of *palm* 60 or 70 ft. high, with *fan*-shaped leaves, used for umbrellas, tents, &c.

**Fantasia**, fan-tä'zi-a, *n.* a *fanciful* or *fantastic* musical composition, not governed by the ordinary musical rules. [It., from Gr. *phantasia*. See **Fancy**.]

**Fantastic**, fan-tas'tik, **Fantastical**, fan-tas'tik-al, *adj.*, *fanciful*: not real: capricious: whimsical: wild.—*adv.* **Fantas'tically**.

**Fantasy**, fan'ta-si, *n.* old form of **Fancy**.

**Far**, fär, *adj.* remote: more distant of two: remote from or contrary to purpose or design.—*adv.* to a great distance in time, space, or proportion: remotely: considerably or in great part: very much: to a great height: to a certain point, degree, or distance. [A.S. *feor*; Dut. *ver*, *verre*; Ice. *fiarri*; Ger. *fahren*, to go.] allied to Gr. *porrō*, at a distance, *pro*, before, Sans. *pra*, before, and also to E. **Fare**.

**Farce**, färs, *n.* a style of comedy, *stuffed* with low humour and extravagant wit: ridiculous or empty show. [Fr. *farce*, the stuffing in meat, from L. *farcio*, to stuff.]

**Farcical**, färs'i-kal, *adj.* of or relating to a *farce*: ludicrous.—*adv.* **Farc'ically**.

**Fardel**, fär'del, *n.* a pack or bundle. [O. Fr. *fardel*, Fr. *fardeau*, dim. of *farde*, a burden, of which ety. dub.]

**Fare**, fār, *v.i.* to *get on* or succeed : to happen well or ill to : to feed.—*n.* (*orig.*) a *course* or *passage*: the price of passage: food or provisions for the table. [A.S. *faran*; Ger. *fahren*, to go.]

**Farewell**, fār-wel' or fär'-, *int.* may you *fare well!* an affectionate prayer for safety or success.—*n.* well-wishing at parting : the act of departure.—*adj.* parting: final.

**Far-fetched**, fär'-fecht, *adj.*, *fetched* or brought from *far*, or from a remote place: forced, unnatural.

**Farina**, fa-rī'na, *n.*, *ground corn:* meal: starch: pollen of plants. [L.—*far*, a sort of grain, akin to E. **Barley**.]

**Farinaceous**, far-in-ā'shus, *adj.* mealy.

**Farm**, färm, *n.* land let or rented for cultivation or pasturage, with the necessary buildings. [A.S. *feorm*, goods, entertainment, from Low L. *firma*, a feast, tribute, also a contract, an oath—L. *firmus*, firm, durable. **Farm** is therefore a doublet of **Firm**.]

**Farm**, färm, *v.t.* to let out as lands to a tenant: to take on lease : to grant certain rights in return for a portion of what they yield, as to farm the taxes: to cultivate, as land.

**Farmer**, färm'ér, *n.* one who *farms* or cultivates land : the tenant of a farm: one who collects taxes, &c. for a certain rate per cent.—*n.* **Farm'ing**, the business of cultivating land.

**Faro**, fār'o, *n.* a game of chance played with cards. [Said to be so called because king Pharaoh was formerly represented on one of the cards.]

**Farrago**, far-rā'gō, *n.* a confused mass. [L.—*far*, a sort of grain.]

**Farrier**, far'i-ér, *n.* one who shoes horses : one who cures the diseases of horses. [O. Fr. *ferrier*, through Low L. *ferrarius*, from L. *ferrum*, iron.]

**Farriery**, far'i-ér-i, *n.* the art of curing the diseases of cattle.

**Farrow**, far'o, *n.* a litter of *pigs*.—*v.* to bring forth pigs. [A.S. *fearh*, a pig ; Dan. *fare*, to farrow ; Ger. *ferkel*, allied to L. *porcus*, pig, *verres*, boar.]

**Farther**, fär'*th*ér, *adj.* (comp. of **Far**) *more far* or distant : tending to a greater distance: longer: additional.—*adv.* at or to a greater distance : more remotely : beyond : moreover. [A rather recent form, comp. of **Far**, the euphonic *th* being inserted from the analogy of **Further**.]

**Farthest**, fär'*th*est, *adj.* (superl. of **Far**) *most far*, distant, or remote.—*adv.* at or to the greatest distance. [Superl. of **Far**, coined from the analogy of **Furthest**.]

**Farthing**, fär'*th*ing, *n.* the *fourth* of a penny : (*New Test.*) = 2 farthings, sometimes ⅛ of our farthing. [A.S. *feorthling*, *feorthing*, a fourth part—*feorth*, fourth, and dim. *ing* or *ling*—*feor*, four.]

**Farthingale**, fär'*th*ing-gāl, *n.* a kind of crinoline made of whalebone for distending the dress, introduced by Queen Elizabeth. [Fr. *vertugade*, O. Fr. *verdugalle*—Sp. *verdugado*, hooped—*verdugo*, a rod, a young shoot—*verde*, green—L. *viridis*, green.]

**Fasces**, fas'ēz, *n.pl.* (*Roman antiquities*) a *bundle* of rods with an axe in the middle, borne before the Roman magistrates as a badge of their authority. [L. *fascis*, a bundle.]

**Fascicle**, fas'i-kl, *n.* a *little bundle*: (*bot.*) a close cluster, with the flowers much crowded together, as in the sweet-william. [L. *fasciculus*, dim. of *fascis*.]

**Fascicular**, fas-sik'ū-lar, **Fasciculate**, fas-sik'ū-lāt, *adj.* united as *in a bundle*.

**Fascinate**, fas'i-nāt, *v.t.* to fix or control by the glance: to charm: to enchant. [L. *fascino*, *-atus* ; prob. allied to Gr. *baskainō*, to bewitch.]

**Fascination**, fas-i-nā'shun, *n.* the act of charming: supposed power to harm by looks or spells: mysterious attractive power exerted by a man's words or manner : irresistible power of alluring. [L. *fascinatio*.]

**Fascine**, fas-sēn', *n.* a *fagot* or *bundle* of rods, used in fort. to raise batteries, fill ditches, &c. [Fr.—L. *fascina*—*fascis*, a bundle.]

**Fashion**, fash'un, *n.* the *make* or cut of a thing: form or pattern : prevailing mode or shape of dress : a prevailing custom : manner: genteel society : (*New Test.*) appearance.—*v.t.* to make: to mould according to a pattern : to suit or adapt.—*n.* **Fash'ioner**. [Fr. *façon*—L. *factio*—*facio*, to make.]

**Fashionable**, fash'un-a-bl, *adj.* made according to prevailing *fashion*: prevailing or in use at any period : observant of the fashion in dress or living : genteel : moving in high society.—*adv.* **Fash'ionably**.—*n.* **Fash'ionableness**.

**Fast**, fast, *adj.* firm : fixed : steadfast.—*adv.* firmly : soundly or sound (asleep).—**Fast by**, close to. [A.S. *fæst* ; Ger. *fest* ; allied to *fassen*, to seize.]

**Fast**, fast, *adj.* quick : rash : dissipated.—*adv.* swiftly : in rapid succession : extravagantly. [A special use of *fast*, firm, derived from the Scand., in the sense of urgent or pressing.]

**Fast**, fast, *v.i.* to keep from food : to go hungry : to abstain from food in whole or part, as a religious duty.—*n.* abstinence from food : special abstinence enjoined by the church : the day of fasting.—*ns.* **Fast′er**, one who fasts ; **Fast′ing**, religious abstinence ; **Fast′-day**, a day of religious fasting. [A.S. *fæstan*, to fast ; Ger. *fasten*, Goth. *fastan*, to keep ; allied with **Fast**, firm, in the sense of making firm or strict.]

**Fasten**, fas′n, *v.t.* to make *fast* or tight : to fix securely : to attach firmly one thing to another. —*v.i.* to fix itself.—*n.* **Fas′tening**, that which fastens.

**Fastidious**, fas-tid′i-us, *adj.* affecting superior taste : over-nice : difficult to please.—*adv.* **Fastid′iously.**—*n.* **Fastid′iousness.** [L. *fastidiosus* —*fastidium*, loathing—*fastus*, pride, and *tædium*, loathing.]

**Fastness**, fast′nes, *n.* fixedness : a stronghold, fortress, castle.

**Fat**, fat, *adj.* plump, fleshy : fruitful : gross.—*n.* an oily substance under the skin : solid animal oil : the richest part of anything.—*v.t.* to make fat.—*v.i.* to grow fat :—*pr.p.* fatt′ing ; *pa.p.* fatt′ed. [A.S. *fæt* ; Ger. *fett*.]

**Fat**, fat, *n.* a vat. See **Vat.**

**Fatal**, fāt′al, *adj.* belonging to or appointed by *fate :* causing ruin or death : mortal : calamitous.—*adv.* **Fat′ally.**

**Fatalism**, fāt′al-izm, *n.* the doctrine that all events are subject to *fate*, and happen by unavoidable necessity.—*n.* **Fat′alist**, one who believes in *fatalism*.—*adj.* **Fat′alistic**, belonging to or partaking of *fatalism*.

**Fatality**, fat-al′i-ti, *n.* the state of being *fatal* or unavoidable : the decree of fate : fixed tendency to disaster or death : mortality.

**Fate**, fāt, *n.* inevitable destiny or necessity : appointed lot : ill-fortune : doom : final issue. [L. *fatum*, a prediction—*fatus*, spoken—*fari*, to speak.]

**Fated**, fāt′ed, *adj.* doomed : destined.

**Fates**, fāts, *n.pl.* the three goddesses of *fate*, Clotho, Lachesis, and Atropos, who were supposed to determine the birth, life, and death of men.

**Father**, fā′thèr, *n.* a male parent : an ancestor or forefather : a contriver or originator : a title of respect : an ecclesiastical writer of the early centuries : the first Person of the Trinity.—*v.t.* to adopt : to ascribe to one as his offspring or production. [A.S. *faeder* ; Ger. *vater*, L. *pater*, Gr. *patēr*, Sans. *pitri*, from root *pa*, to feed.]

**Fatherhood**, fā′thèr-hood, *n.* state of being a *father :* fatherly authority.

**Father-in-law**, fā′thèr-in-law, *n.* the father of one's husband or wife. [*fathers*.

**Fatherland**, fā′thèr-land, *n.* the *land* of one's

**Fatherless**, fā′thèr-les, *adj.* destitute of a living *father :* without a known author.—*n.* **Fa′therlessness.**

**Fatherly**, fā′thèr-li, *adj.* like a *father* in affection and care : paternal.—*n.* **Fa′therliness.**

**Fathom**, fath′um, *n.* the distance between the extremities of both arms *extended* or *held out :* a nautical measure = 6 feet.—*v.t.* to try the depth of : to comprehend or get to the bottom of.— *adjs.* **Fath′omable, Fath′omless.** [A.S. *faethm ;* Dut. *vadem*, Ger. *faden ;* cf. L. *pateo*, Gr. *petannymi*, to stretch.]

**Fatigue**, fa-tēg′, *n.*, *weariness* from labour of body or of mind : toil : military work, distinct from the use of arms.—*v.t.* to reduce to a state of weariness : to exhaust one's strength : to harass :—*pr.p.* fatigu′ing ; *pa.p.* fatigued′. [Fr., from L. *fatigo*, to weary.]          [slaughter.

**Fatling**, fat′ling, *n.* a *young* animal *fattened* for

**Fatness**, fat′nes, *n.* quality or state of being fat : fullness of flesh : richness : fertility : that which makes fertile.

**Fatten**, fat′n, *v.t.* to *make fat* or fleshy : to make fertile.—*v.i.* to grow fat.—*ns.* **Fatt′ener**, he who or that which fattens ; **Fatt′ening**, the process of making fat : state of growing fat.

**Fatty**, fat′i, *adj.* containing fat or having the qualities of fat.—*n.* **Fatt′iness.**          [imbecility.

**Fatuity**, fa-tū′i-ti, *n.* the being feeble in intellect :

**Fatuous**, fat′ū-us, *adj.* silly : without reality : deceptive, like the *ignis-fatuus*. [L. *fatuus*, foolish.]

**Fauces**, faw′sēz, *n.pl.* the upper part of the throat from the root of the tongue to the entrance of the gullet. [L.]

**Faucet**, faw′set, *n.* a pipe inserted in a barrel to draw liquid. [Fr. *fausset—fausser*, to falsify, to pierce—L. *falsus*. See **False.**]

**Faugh**, faw, *int.* an exclamation of contempt or disgust. [Prob. from the sound.]

**Fault**, fawlt, *n.* a failing : error : blemish : a slight offence : (*geol.* and *min.*) a displacement of strata or veins. [Fr. *faute*—L. *fallo*, to deceive.]

**Faultless**, fawlt′les, *adj.* without *fault* or *defect.* —*adv.* **Fault′lessly.**—*n.* **Fault′lessness.**

**Faulty**, fawlt′i, *adj.* imperfect : guilty of a fault : blamable.—*adv.* **Fault′ily.**—*n.* **Fault′iness.**

**Faun**, fawn, *n.* a rural deity among the Romans— the *protector* of shepherds and agriculture. [L. *faunus*, from *faveo*, *fautum*, to favour.]

**Fauna**, fawn′a, *n.pl.* the animals native to any region or epoch, so called because protected by the *Fauns.*

**Favour**, fā′vur, *n.* a *regarding kindly :* countenance : good-will : a kind deed : an act of grace or lenity : a knot of white ribbons worn at a wedding.—*v.t.* to regard with good-will : to be on the side of : to treat indulgently : to afford advantage to.—*n.* **Fa′vourer.** [Fr.—L. *favor— faveo*, to favour, befriend.]

**Favourable**, fā′vur-a-bl, *adj.* friendly : propitious : conducive to : advantageous.—*adv.* **Fa′vourably.**—*n.* **Fa′vourableness.**

**Favourite**, fā′vur-it, *n.* a person or thing regarded with *favour :* one unduly loved.—*adj.* esteemed, beloved, preferred.—*n.* **Fa′vouritism**, the practice of favouring or shewing partiality.

**Fawn**, fawn, *n.* a young deer.—*adj.* resembling a fawn in colour.—*v.i.* to bring forth a fawn. [Fr. *faon*, through an unrecorded Low L. *fœtonus*, an extension of L. *fœtus*, offspring.]

**Fawn**, fawn, *v.i.* to cringe : to flatter in a servile way (followed by *upon*).—*n.* a servile cringe or bow : mean flattery.—*n.* **Fawn′er**, one who flatters to gain favour.—*adv.* **Fawn′ingly.** [M.E. *faunen ;* from Ice. *fagna*, to rejoice, conn. with A.S. *fegen*, glad.]

**Fay**, fā, *n.* a fairy. [Fr. *fée*—Low L. *fata*, a fairy—L. *fatum*, fate. See **Fate.**]

**Fealty**, fē′al-ti or fēl′ti, *n.* the oath sworn by the vassal to be *faithful* to his feudal lord : loyalty. [O. Fr. *fealte*—L. *fidelitas—fidelis*, faithful —*fido*, to trust.]

**Fear**, fēr, *n.* a painful emotion excited by danger : apprehension of danger or pain : alarm : the object of fear : (*B.*) deep reverence : piety towards God.—*v.t.* to regard with fear : to expect with alarm : (*B.*) to stand in awe of : to venerate : (*obs.*) to terrify : to make afraid. [A.S. *fær*; Ger. *gefahr*, Ice. *far*, harm, mischief.]

**Fearful,** fēr′fool, *adj.* timorous : exciting intense fear : terrible.—*adv.* **Fear′fully.**—*n.* **Fear′fulness.**

**Fearless,** fēr′les, *adj.* without *fear* : daring : brave. —*adv.* **Fear′lessly.**—*n.* **Fear′lessness.**

**Feasible,** fēz′i-bl, *adj.* practicable.—*adv.* **Feas′ibly.**—*ns.* **Feas′ibleness, Feasibil′ity.** [Fr. *faisable*, that can be done—*faire*, *faisant*—L. *facere*, to do, to make.]

**Feast,** fēst, *n.* a day of unusual solemnity or joy : a rich and abundant repast : rich enjoyment for the mind or heart.—*v.i.* to hold a feast : to eat sumptuously : to receive intense delight.—*v.t.* to entertain sumptuously.—*n.* **Feast′er.** [O. Fr. *feste* (Fr. *fête*)—L. *festum*, a holiday, *festus*, solemn, festal.]

**Feat,** fēt, *n.* a deed manifesting extraordinary strength, skill, or courage. [Fr. *fait*, O. Fr. *faict*—L. *factus*, done—L. *facio*, to do, to make.]

**Feather,** feth′ėr, *n.* one of the growths which form the covering of a bird : a feather-like ornament.—*v.t.* to furnish or adorn with feathers.—**To feather an oar,** to bring it out of the water in a flat or horizontal position. [A.S. *fether*; Ger. *feder* : conn. with L. *penna* (= *petna*), Gr. *pteron*, Sans. *patra—pat*, to fly.]

**Feathery,** feth′ėr-i, *adj.* pertaining to, resembling, or covered with *feathers*.

**Feature,** fēt′ūr, *n.* the marks by which anything is recognised : the prominent traits of anything : the cast of the face :—*pl.* the countenance.—*adjs.* **Feat′ured,** with features well marked ; **Feat′ureless,** destitute of distinct features. [O. Fr. *faiture*—L. *factura*, *facturus*, fut. part. of *facio*, to make.]

**Febrifuge,** feb′ri-fūj, *n.* a medicine for *removing* fever. [L. *febris*, and *fugo*, to put to flight.]

**Febrile,** fē′bril or feb′ril, *adj.* pertaining to *fever* : feverish. [Fr. *fébrile*, from L. *febris*, fever.]

**February,** feb′roo-ar-i, *n.* the second month of the year. [L. *Februarius* (*mensis*), the month of expiation, because on this month the great Roman feast of expiation was held—*februa*, the festival of expiation.]

**Fecal,** fē′kal, *adj.* relating to, consisting of fæces. **Feces.** See **Fæces.**

**Feculent,** fek′ū-lent, *adj.* containing *fæces* or sediment : muddy : foul.—*n.* **Fec′ulence** or **Fec′ulency.**

**Fecund,** fek′und, *adj., fruitful* : fertile : prolific. [L. *fecundus*—obs. *feo*, to bring forth.]

**Fecundate,** fek′und-āt, *v.t.* to make fruitful : to impregnate.

**Fecundation,** fek-un-dā′shun, *n.* the act of impregnating : the state of being impregnated.

**Fecundity,** fek-und′i-ti, *n.* fruitfulness : prolificness in female animals.

**Fed,** fed, *pa.t.* and *pa.p.* of **Feed.**

**Federal,** fed′ėr-al, *adj.* pertaining to or consisting of a *treaty* or *covenant* : founded upon mutual agreement.—A **Federal** union or government is one in which several states, while independent in home affairs, combine for national or general purposes, as in the United States and Switzerland. In American civil war, **Federal** was the name given to the party of the North which defended the Union against the Confederate separatists of the South. [Fr *fédéral*—L. *fœdus, fœderis*, a treaty, akin to *fido*, to trust.]

**Federalist,** fed′ėr-al-ist, *n.* a supporter of a *federal* constitution or union.—*n.* **Fed′eralism,** the principles or cause maintained by federalists.

**Federate,** fed′ėr-āt, *adj.* united by league : confederated.—*adj.* **Fed′erative,** uniting in league.

**Fee,** fē, *n.* price paid for services, as to a lawyer or physician : recompense : a grant of land for feudal service : an unconditional inheritance (often termed *fee simple*) : possession : ownership.—*v.t.* to pay a fee to : to hire :—*pr.p.* fee′ing ; *pa.p.* feed′. [A.S. *feoh*, cattle, property ; a special kind of property, property in land ; Ger. *vieh*, Ice. *fe*; allied to L. *pecus*, cattle, *pecunia*, money.]

**Feeble,** fē′bl, *adj.* weak : wanting in strength of body : shewing weakness or incapacity : faint : dull.—*adv.* **Fee′bly.**—*n.* **Fee′bleness.** [O. Fr. *foible*, for *floible*—L. *flebilis*, lamentable, from *fleo, flere*, to weep.]    [irresolute.

**Feeble-minded,** fē′bl-mīnd′ed, *adj.* weak-minded :

**Feed,** fēd, *v.t.* to give *food* to : to nourish : to furnish with necessary material : to foster.—*v.i.* to take food : to nourish one's self by eating : —*pr.p.* feed′ing ; *pa.t.* and *pa.p.* fed.—*n.* an allowance of provender given to cattle.—*n.* **Feed′er,** he who feeds or that which supplies. [A.S. *fedan*, to feed, nourish—*foda*, food.]

**Feel,** fēl, *v.t.* to perceive by the touch : to handle : to be conscious of : to be keenly sensible of : to have an inward persuasion of.—*v.i.* to know by the touch : to have the emotions excited : to produce a certain sensation when touched, as to feel hard or hot :—*pr.p.* feel′ing ; *pa.t.* and *pa.p.* felt. [A.S. *felan*, to feel ; Ger. *fühlen* ; akin to L. *palpare*.]

**Feeler,** fēl′ėr, *n.* a remark cautiously dropped to sound the opinions of others :—*pl.* jointed fibres in the heads of insects, &c. possessed of a delicate sense of touch, termed *antennæ*.

**Feeling,** fēl′ing, *n.* the sense of touch : perception of objects by touch : consciousness of pleasure or pain : tenderness : emotion :—*pl.* the affections or passions.—*adj.* expressive of great sensibility or tenderness : easily affected.—*adv.* **Feel′ingly.**

**Feet,** fēt, plural of **Foot.**

**Feign,** fān, *v.t.* to invent : to imagine : to make a show or pretence of.—*adv.* **Feign′edly.**—*n.* **Feign′edness.** [Fr. *feindre*, pr.p. *feignant*, to feign—L. *fingo, fictum*, to form.]

**Feint,** fānt, *n.* a false appearance : a pretence : a mock-assault : a deceptive movement in fencing. [Fr. *feint*, pa.p. of *feindre*. See **Feign.**]

**Feldspar,** feld′spär, **Feldspath,** feld′spath, *n.* a crystalline mineral found in granite, &c. [*Field spar*—Ger. *feld*, a field, *spath*, spar. See **Spar.**]

**Feldspathic,** feld-spath′ik, *adj.* pertaining to or consisting of *feldspar*.

**Felicitate,** fe-lis′i-tāt, *v.t.* to express joy or pleasure to : to congratulate. [L. *felicitas*, from *felix, felicis*, happy.]    [tating or congratulating.

**Felicitation,** fe-lis-i-tā′shun, *n.* the act of _felici-

**Felicitous,** fe-lis′i-tus, *adj.* happy : prosperous : delightful : appropriate.—*adv.* **Felic′itously.**

**Felicity,** fe-lis′i-ti, *n.* happiness : delight : a blessing : a happy event.

**Feline,** fē′līn, *adj.* pertaining to the *cat* or the cat-kind : like a cat. [L. *felinus—feles*, a cat.]

**Fell,** fel, *n.* a barren or stony hill. [Ice.]

**Fell,** fel, *pa.t.* of **Fall.**

**Fell,** fel, *v.t.* to cause to fall : to bring to the ground : to cut down. [A.S. *fellan*, causal form of *feallan*, to fall. See **Fall.**]    [*pella*.]

**Fell,** fel, *n.* a skin. [A.S. *fel*; cf. L. *pellis*, Gr.

**Fell**, fel, *adj.* cruel : fierce : bloody.—*n.* **Fell'-ness**.—*adv.* **Fell'ly**. [A.S. *fel*; Dut. *fel*, which appears also in O. Fr. *fel*.]

**Feller**, fel'ér, *n.* a cutter of wood.

**Felloe**. See **Felly**, *n.*

**Fellow**, fel'ō, *n.* an associate : a companion and equal : one of a pair, a mate : a member of a university who enjoys a fellowship : a member of a scientific or other society : a worthless person. [M.E. *felawe*—Ice. *félagi*, a partner in goods, from *fe* (Ger. *vieh*), cattle, property, and *lag*, a laying together, a law ; cf. E. *fee*, and *law*.]    [fellows or equals : sympathy.

**Fellow-feeling**, fel'ō-fēl'ing, *n.* feeling between

**Fellowship**, fel'ō-ship, *n.* the state of being a *fellow* or partner : friendly intercourse : communion : an association : an endowment in a university for the support of graduates called *fellows*: the position and income of a fellow : (*arith.*) the proportional division of profit and loss among partners.

**Felly**, fel'i, **Felloe**, fel'ō, *n.* one of the curved pieces in the circumference of · wheel. [A.S. *felgu*; Ger. *felge*.]

**Felon**, fel'on, *n.* one guilty of felony : a convict : a wicked person.—*adj.* wicked or cruel. [Fr.—Low L. *fello*, a traitor, which is prob. from the Celtic.]

**Felonious**, fe-lō'ni-us, *adj.* wicked : depraved : done with the deliberate intention to commit crime.—*adv.* **Felo'niously**.

**Felony**, fel'on-i, *n.* (*orig.*) a crime punished by total forfeiture of lands, &c. : a crime punishable by imprisonment or death.

**Felspar**. Same as **Feldspar**.

**Felt**, felt, *pa.t.* and *pa.p.* of **Feel**.

**Felt**, felt, *n.* cloth made of *wool* united without weaving.—*v.t.* to make into felt : to cover with felt. [Ger. *filz*, woollen cloth, allied to Gr. *pilos*, wool wrought into felt, L. *pileus*, a felt-hat.]    [*felt.*

**Felting**, felt'ing, *n.* the art or process of making

**Felucca**, fe-luk'a, *n.* a boat with oars and broad three-cornered sails, used in the Mediterranean. [It. *feluca*, which, like Fr. *felouque*, is from Ar. *fulk*, a ship.]

**Female**, fē'māl, *adj.* of the sex that *produces* young : pertaining to females : (*bot.*) having a pistil or fruit-bearing organ.—*n.* one of the female sex. [Fr. *femelle*—L. *femella*, a young female ; dim. of *femina*—obs. *feo*, to bring forth.]

**Feminine**, fem'i-nin, *adj.* pertaining to women : tender, delicate : womanly : (*gram.*) the gender denoting females.—*adv.* **Fem'ininely**. [See **Female**.]

**Femoral**, fem'o-ral, *adj.* belonging to the *thigh*. [L. *femoralis*—*femur*, *femoris*, the thigh.]

**Fen**, fen, *n.* a kind of low marshy land often or partially covered with water : a morass or bog. —*adjs.* **Fenn'y**, **Fenn'ish** [A.S. *fen*; Ice. *fen*, Goth. *fani*, mud.]

**Fence**, fens, *n.* a wall or hedge for inclosing animals or for protecting land ; the art of fencing : defence.—*v.t.* to inclose with a fence : to fortify.—*v.i.* to practise fencing. [Abbrev. of **Defence**.]

**Fencible**, fens'i-bl, *adj.* capable of being *fenced* or defended.—*n.pl.* **Fen'cibles**, volunteer regiments raised for local defence during a special crisis : militia enlisted for home service.

**Fencing**, fens'ing, *adj.* defending or guarding.— *n.* the act of erecting a fence : the art of attack and defence with a sword or other weapon.—*n.* **Fenc'er**, one who practises fencing with a sword.

**Fend**, fend, *v.t.* to ward off : to shut out. [Merely an abbrev. of **Defend**—L. obs. *fendo*, root of *defendo*, to fend or ward off.]

**Fender**, fend'ér, *n.* a metal guard before a fire to confine the ashes : a protection for a ship's side. [From **Fend**.]

**Fenestral**, fe-nes'tral, *adj.* belonging to *windows*. [L. *fenestralis*—*fenestra*, a window, allied to Gr. *phainō*, to shine.]

**Fenian**, fē'ne-an, *n.* applied to an association of Irishmen for the overthrow of the English government in Ireland.—*n.* **Fe'nianism**. [Prob. from the *Finna*, an ancient Irish militia.]

**Fennel**, fen'el, *n.* a fragrant plant with yellow flowers. [A.S. *finol*; Ger. *fenchel*—L. *fœniculum*, fennel, from *fenum*, hay.]

**Feoff**, fef, *n.* a *fief*.—*v.t.* to grant possession of a fief or property in land.—*ns.* **Feoff'ment**, the *gift* of a *fief* or feoff ; **Feoff'er**, he who grants the *fief*. [O. Fr. *feoffer* or *fiefer*—O. Fr. *fief*.]

**Feretory**, fer'e-tor-i, *n.* a place in a church for a bier. [L. *feretrum*—*fero*, Gr. *pherō*, to bear.]

**Ferine**, fē'rin, *adj.* pertaining to or like a *wild beast* : savage. [L. *ferinus*—*fera*, a wild beast—*ferus*, wild, akin to Gr. *thēr*, Ger. *thier*, a beast.]

**Ferment**, fér'ment, *n.* what excites fermentation, as yeast, leaven : internal motion amongst the parts of a fluid : agitation : tumult. [L. *fermentum*, for *fervimentum*—*ferveo*, to boil.]

**Ferment**, fer-ment', *v.t.* to excite fermentation : to inflame.—*v.i.* to rise and swell by the action of fermentation : to work, used of wine, &c. : to be in excited action : to be stirred with anger.

**Fermentable**, fer-men't-a-bl, *adj.* capable of fermentation.—*n.* **Fermentabil'ity**.

**Fermentation**, fér-ment-ā'shun, *n.* the act or process of *fermenting* : the change which takes place in liquids exposed to air · the kind of spontaneous decomposition which produces alcohol : restless action of the mind or feelings.

**Fermentative**, fer-ment'a-tiv, *adj.* causing or consisting in fermentation.—*n.* **Ferment'ativeness**.

**Fern**, fern, *n.* a plant which becomes a tree in the tropics with feather-like leaves. [A.S. *fearn*; Ger. *farn*.]    [*ferns.*

**Forny**, férn'i, *adj.*, full of or overgrown with

**Ferocious**, fe-rō'shus, *adj.* savage, fierce : cruel. —*adv.* **Fero'ciously**.—*n.* **Fero'ciousness**. [Fr. and It. *feroce*—L. *ferox*, wild—*ferus*, wild.]

**Ferocity**, fe ros'i-ti, *n.* savage cruelty of disposition : untamed fierceness.

**Ferreous**, fer e-us, *adj.* pertaining to or made of iron. [L. *ferreus*—*ferrum*, iron.]

**Ferret**, fer'et, *n.* ribbon woven from spun-silk. [Corr. from Ital. *fioretto*—L. *flos*, *floris*, a flower ; the ribbon being prob. so called from some flowering-work upon it.]

**Ferret**, fer'et, *n.* a tame animal of the weasel kind employed in unearthing rabbits. [Fr. *furet*, a ferret, prob. from L. *fur*, a thief.]

**Ferret**, fer'et, *v.t* to search out carefully and minutely like a *ferret* : to drive out by patient effort :—*pr.p.* ferr'eting ; *pa.p.* ferr'eted.

**Ferriferous**, fer-rif'ér-us, *adj.*, *bearing* or yielding iron. [L. *ferrum*, iron, and *fero*, to bear.]

**Ferruginous**, fer-rōō'jin-us, *adj.* of the colour of *iron-rust* : impregnated with iron. [L. *ferrugineus*—*ferrugo*, iron-rust—*ferrum*.]

**Ferrule**, fer'ōōl, *n.* a metal *ring* on a staff, &c. to keep it from splitting. [Fr. *virole*, L. *viriola*, a bracelet—*viere*, to bind.]

**Ferry**, fer'i, *v.t.* to *carry* or convey over a water

in a boat:—*pr.p.* ferr'ying; *pa.p.* ferr'ied.—*n.* a place where one may be rowed across a water: the right of conveying passengers: the ferry-boat. [A.S. *ferian*, to convey, *faran*, to go; Ger. *fähre*, a ferry—*fahren*, to go, to carry.]

**Fertile**, fèr'til, *adj.* able to *bear* or produce abundantly: rich in resources: inventive.—*adv.* **Fer'tilely.** [Fr.—L. *fertilis—fero*, to bear.]

**Fertilise**, fèr'til-īz, *v.t.* to make *fertile* or fruitful: to enrich.

**Fertility**, fèr-til'i-ti, *n.* fruitfulness: richness: abundance.

**Ferule**, fer'ōōl, *n.* a rod used for *striking* children in punishment. [L. *ferula*, a cane—*ferio*, to strike.]

**Fervency**, fèr'ven-si, *n.* state of being *fervent*: heat of mind: eagerness: warmth of devotion.

**Fervent**, fèr'vent, *adj.* ardent: zealous: warm in feeling.—*adv.* **Fer'vently.** [L. *ferveo*, to boil, akin to Gr. *therō*, to heat, E. and Ger. *warm*, Sans. *gharma*, heat.]

**Fervid**, fèr'vid, *adj.* very hot: having burning desire or emotion: zealous.—*adv.* **Fer'vidly.**—*n.* **Fer'vidness.** [L. *fervidus.*]

**Fervour**, fèr'vur, *n.* heat: heat of mind: zeal.

**Festal**, fes'tal, *adj.* pertaining to a *feast* or *holiday*: joyous: gay.—*adv.* **Fes'tally.**

**Fester**, fes'tèr, *v.i.* to corrupt or rankle: to suppurate: to become malignant.—*v.t.* to cause to fester.—*n.* a wound discharging corrupt matter. [Ety. unknown.]

**Festival**, fes'ti-val, *n.* a joyful celebration: a feast.

**Festive**, fes'tiv, *adj.* festal: mirthful.—*adv.* **Fes'tively.** [L. *festivus—festus.*]

**Festivity**, fes-tiv'i-ti, *n.* social mirth at a *feast*: joyfulness: gaiety.

**Festoon**, fes-tōōn', *n.* a garland suspended between two points: (*arch.*) an ornament like a wreath of flowers, &c.—*v.t.* to adorn with festoons. [Fr. *feston*, from L. *festum.*]

**Fetch**, fech, *v.t.* to bring: to go and get: to obtain as its price: to accomplish in any way: to reach or attain.—*v.i.* to turn: (*naut.*) to arrive at. [A.S. *fetian*, to fetch, from root of **Foot**; Ger. *fassen*, to seize.]

**Fetch**, fech, *n.* a trick. [From **Fetch**, *v.t.*, the meaning being, something that one goes to find, a thing contrived.]

**Fetch**, fech, **Fetch-candle**, fech'-kan'dl, *n.* the apparition of a living person: a nocturnal light, as of a moving candle, supposed to portend a death. [Prob. from Norwegian *Vætte-lys*, the Vætt's or goblin's candle = ignis-fatuus.]

**Fête**, fāt, *n.* a *festival* or *feast*: a holiday.—*v.t.* to entertain at a feast. [Fr.—L. *festum.*]

**Fetich**, fē'tish, *n.* an object, either natural or artificial, considered as possessing divine power, and worshipped, as in W. Africa. [Fr. *fétiche*—Port. *feitiço*, magic; a name given by the Port. to the gods of W. Africa—Port. *feitiço*, artificial—L. *factitius—facere*, to make.]

**Fetichism**, fē'tish-izm, **Feticism**, fē'tis-izm, *n.* the worship of a *fetich*: a belief in charms.

**Fetid**, fet'id or fē'tid, *adj.*, *stinking*: having a strong offensive odour.—*n.* **Fet'idness.** [L. *fætidus—fæteo*, to stink.]

**Fetlock**, fet'lok, *n.* a tuft of hair that grows behind on horses' feet: the part where this hair grows. [From root of **Foot** and **Lock**, as in **Lock** of hair.]

**Fetter**, fet'ėr, *n.* a chain or shackle for the *feet*: anything that restrains:—used chiefly in *pl.*—*v.t.* to put fetters on: to restrain. [A.S. *fetor*—*fet*, feet.]

**Fettered**, fet'ėrd, *adj.* bound by *fetters*: (*zool.*) applied to the feet of animals which bend backward and seem unfit for walking.

**Fetus, Fœtus**, fē'tus, *n.* the young of animals in the egg or in the womb, after its parts are distinctly formed, until its birth. [L., from obs. *feo*, to bring forth.]

**Feu**, fū, *n.* (*in Scotland*) a tenure where the vassal, in place of military services, makes a return in grain or in money: a sale of land for a stipulated annual payment, esp. for building on. [Low L. *feudum*—root of **Fee.**]

**Feuar**, fū'ar, *n.* (*in Scotland*) one who holds real estate in consideration of a payment called *feu-duty.*

**Feud**, fūd, *n.* a deadly quarrel between tribes or families: a bloody strife. [A.S. *fæhdh—fah*, hostile; Ger. *fehde.*]

**Feud**, fūd, *n.* a *fief* or land held on condition of service.—*adj.* **Feud'al**, pertaining to *feuds* or fiefs: belonging to feudalism. [Low L. *feudum*, from root of **Fee.**]

**Feudalism**, fūd'al-izm, *n.* the system, during the middle ages, by which vassals held lands from lords-superior on condition of military service.

**Feudatory**, fūd'at-or-i, *adj.* holding lands or power by a feudal tenure.

**Fever**, fē'vėr, *n.* a disease marked by great bodily *heat* and quickening of pulse: extreme excitement of the passions: a painful degree of anxiety.—*v.t.* to put into a fever.—*v.i.* to become fevered. [Fr. *fièvre*—L. *febris—ferveo*, to be hot; or from root of Ger. *beben*, to tremble, Gr. *phobos*, fear.]

**Feverish**, fē'vėr-ish, *adj.* slightly fevered: indicating fever: fidgety: fickle.—*adv.* **Fe'verishly.**—*n.* **Fe'verishness.**

**Few**, fū, *adj.*, *small* in number: not many.—*n.* **Few'ness.** [A.S. *fea*, plur. *feave*; Goth. *favs*; Fr. *peu*; L. *paucus*, small.]

**Fiars**, fī'arz, *n.pl.* (*in Scotland*) the prices of grain legally fixed for the year, to regulate the payment of stipend, rent, and prices not expressly agreed upon. [From the root of **Fee.**]

**Fiasco**, fi-as'ko, *n.* a failure in a musical performance: a failure of any kind. [It. *fiasco*, bottle, like Fr. *flacon*, Ger. *flasche*, perh. from L. *vasculum*, a little vessel, *vas*, a vessel; why it came to be used in the sense of failure, does not appear.]

**Fiat**, fī'at, *n.* a formal or solemn command: a decree. [L. 3d pers. sing. pres. subj. of *fio*, passive of *facio*, to do.]

**Fib**, fib, *n.* something said falsely: a soft expression for a lie.—*v.i.* to tell a fib or lie: to speak falsely:—*pr.p.* fibb'ing; *pa.p.* fibbed'. [An abbrev. of **Fable.**]

**Fibre**, fī'bėr, *n.* one of the small *threads* composing the parts of animals or vegetables: any fine thread, or thread-like substance.—*adjs.* **Fi'bred**, having fibres; **Fi'breless**, having no fibres. [Fr.—L. *fibra*, a thread.]

**Fibril**, fī'bril, *n.* a *small fibre*: one of the extremely minute threads composing an animal fibre. [Low L. *fibrilla*, dim. of L. *fibra.*]

**Fibrillous**, fī-bril'us, *adj.* formed of small fibres.

**Fibrine**, fī'brin, *n.* an organic compound, composed of thready *fibres*, found in animals and plants.

**Fibrous**, fī'brus, *adj.* composed of or containing *fibres.*—*n.* **Fi'brousness.**

**Fickle**, fik'l, *adj.* inconstant: changeable.—*n.* **Fick'leness.** [A.S. *ficol*; Ger. *ficken*, to move quickly to and fro; cf. **Fidget.**]

**Fictile**, fik'til, *adj.* used or fashioned by the potter. [L. *fictilis—fingo*, to form or fashion.]

**Fiction**, fik'shun, *n.* a feigned or false story : a falsehood : romance. [Fr.—L. *fictio—fictus*, pa.p. of *fingo*.] [forged.—*adv.* Ficti'tiously.

**Fictitious**, fik-tish'us, *adj.* imaginary : not real :

**Fiddle**, fid'l, *n.* a stringed instrument of music, called also a violin.—*v.t.* or *v.i.* to play on a fiddle :—*pr.p.* fidd'ling ; *pa.p.* fidd'led.—*n.* **Fiddler**. [A.S. *fithele* ; Ger. *fiedel*. See **Violin**.]

**Fidelity**, fi-del'i-ti, *n.* faithful performance of duty : honesty : firm adherence. [L. *fidelitas—fidelis*, faithful—*fido*, to trust.]

**Fidget**, fij'et, *v.i.* to be unable to rest : to move uneasily :—*pr.p.* fidg'eting ; *pa.p.* fidg'eted.— *n.* irregular motion : restlessness :—*pl.* general nervous restlessness, with a desire of changing the position. [Ice. *fika*, to climb up nimbly ; Ger. *ficken*, to move to and fro ; conn. with **Fickle**.] [etiness.

**Fidgety**, fij'et-i, *adj.* restless : uneasy.—*n.* **Fidg'**-

**Fiducial**, fi-dū'shi-al, *adj.* shewing *confidence* or reliance : of the nature of a trust.—*adv.* **Fidu'cially**. [L. *fiducia*, confidence, from *fido*, to trust.]

**Fiduciary**, fi-dū'shi-ar-i, *adj.*, *confident* : unwavering : held in trust.—*n.* one who holds anything in trust : (*theol.*) one who depends for salvation on faith without works, an Antinomian. [L. *fiduciarius—fiducia*.]

**Fie**, fī, *int.* denoting disapprobation or disgust. [Ger. *pfui !* Fr. *fi !* the sound instinctively made in presence of a bad smell.]

**Fief**, fēf, *n.* land held of a superior in *fee* or on condition of military service : a feud. [Fr.— Low L. *feudum*.]

**Field**, fēld, *n.* country or open country in general : a piece of ground inclosed for tillage or pasture : the locality of a battle : the battle itself : room for action of any kind : a wide expanse : (*her.*) the surface of a shield : the background on which figures are drawn. [A.S. and Ger. *feld* ; Dut. *veld*, the open country ; cf. E. *fell*, a hill.] [fields.

**Fieldbook**, fēld'book, *n.* a book used in surveying

**Field-day**, fēld'-dā, *n.* a day when troops are drawn out for instruction in field exercises.]

**Fieldfare**, fēld'fār, *n.* a species of thrush, having a reddish-yellow throat and breast spotted with black. [A.S. *feldefare—feld*, a field, and *faran*, to fare, travel over.]

**Field-marshal**, fēld'-mär'shal, *n.* an officer of the highest rank in the army. [See **Marshal**.]

**Field-officer**, fēld'-of'i-sėr, *n.* a military officer above the rank of captain, and below that of general. [artillery used in the field of battle.

**Fieldpiece**, fēld'pēs, *n.* a cannon or piece of

**Fieldtrain**, fēld'trān, *n.* a department of the Royal Artillery responsible for the safety and supply of ammunition during war.

**Fieldworks**, fēld'wurks, *n.pl.* temporary works thrown up by troops in the field, either for protection or to cover an attack upon a stronghold.

**Fiend**, fēnd, *n.* the devil : one actuated by the most intense wickedness or hate. [A.S. *feond*, pr.p. of *feon*, to hate ; Ger. *feind*, Dut. *vijand*.]

**Fiendish**, fēnd'ish, *adj.* like a *fiend*: malicious.— *n.* **Fiend'ishness**.

**Fierce**, fērs, *adj.*, *ferocious*: violent : angry.— *adv.* **Fierce'ly**.—*n.* **Fierce'ness**. [O. Fr. *fers*, *fiers*—L. *ferus*, wild, savage.]

**Fiery**, fīr'i or fī'ėr-i, *adj.* ardent : impetuous : irritable.—*n.* **Fi'eriness**.

**Fife**, fīf, *n.* a small *pipe* used as a wind-instrument for military music, an octave higher than the flute.—*v i.* to play on the fife.—*n.* **Fif'er**, one who plays on a fife. [Fr. *fifre*, Ger. *pfeife*, both, acc. to Littré, from L. *pipare*, to peep, to chirp. See **Pipe**.]

**Fifteen**, fif'tēn, *adj.* and *n.* five and ten. [A.S. *fíftyne—fíf*, five, *tyn*, ten.]

**Fifteenth**, fif'tēnth, *adj.* the fifth after the tenth : being one of fifteen equal parts.—*n.* a fifteenth part. [A.S. *fífteotha—fíf*, five, *teotha*, tenth.]

**Fifth**, fifth, *adj.* next after the fourth.—*n.* one of five equal parts. [A.S. *fífta*.]

**Fifthly**, fifth'li, *adv.* in the fifth place.

**Fiftieth**, fif'ti-eth, *adj.* the ordinal of fifty.—*n.* a fiftieth part. [A.S. *fíftigotha*.]

**Fifty**, fif'ti, *adj.* and *n.* five tens or five times ten. [A.S. *fíftig—fíf*, five, *tig*, ten.]

**Fig**, fig, *n.* the *fig-tree* or its fruit, growing in warm climates : a thing of little consequence. [Fr. *figue*, which, like A.S. *fíc*, Ger. *feige*, is from L. *ficus*, a fig.]

**Fight**, fīt, *v.i.* to strive with : to contend in war or in single combat.—*v.t.* to engage in conflict with :—*pr.p.* fight'ing ; *pa.t.* and *pa.p.* fought (fawt).—*n.* a struggle : a combat : a battle or engagement.—*n.* **Fight'er**. [A.S. *feohtan* ; Ger. *fechten* ; prob. conn. with L. *pugnus*, the fist, Gr. *pux*, with clenched fist.]

**Fighting**, fīt'ing, *adj.* engaged in or fit for war.— *n.* the act of fighting or contending.

**Figment**, fig'ment, *n.* a fabrication or invention. [L. *figmentum—fingo*, to form.]

**Figuration**, fig-ū-rā'shun, *n.* act of giving *figure* or form : (*music*) mixture of chords and discords.

**Figurative**, fig'ū-ra-tiv, *adj.* (*rhet.*) representing by, containing or abounding in *figures*: metaphorical : flowery : typical.—*adv.* **Fig'uratively**.

**Figure**, fig'ūr, *n.* the *form* of anything in outline : the representation of anything in drawing, &c. : a drawing : a design : a statue : appearance : a character denoting a number : value or price : (*rhet.*) a deviation from the ordinary mode of expression, in which words are changed from their literal signification or usage : (*logic*) the form of a syllogism with respect to the position of the middle term : steps in a dance : a type or emblem. [Fr.—L. *figura*, from root of *fingo*, to form.]

**Figure**, fig'ūr, *v.t.* to *form* or shape : to make an image of : to mark with figures or designs : to imagine : to symbolise : to foreshew : to note by figures.—*v.i.* to make figures : to appear as a distinguished person.—*adj.* **Fig'urable**.

**Figured**, fig'ūrd, *adj.* marked or adorned with *figures*.

**Figurehead**, fig'ūr-hed, *n.* the figure or bust on the head or prow of a ship.

**Filament**, fil'a-ment, *n.* a slender or thread-like object : a fibre. [Fr.—L. *filum*, a thread.]

**Filamentous**, fil-a-ment'us, *adj.*, *thread*-like.

**Filanders**, fil'an-dėrz, *n.pl.* a disease in hawks consisting of *filaments* of blood, also of small *thread*-like worms. [Fr. *filandres*—L. *filum*.]

**Filature**, fil'a-tūr, *n.* the reeling of silk, or the place where it is done. [Fr.—L. *filum*, a thread.]

**Filbert**, fil'bert, *n.* the fruit or nut of the cultivated hazel. [Prob. so called from St Philibert, whose day fell in the nutting season, Aug. 22 (old style) ; so in German it is Lambertsnuss, St Lambert's nut.]

**Filch**, filch, *v.t.* to steal : to pilfer. [*Filch* stands for *filk*, formed from M.E. *felen*, to hide, by adding *k*, as *talk* from *tell*, *stalk* from *steal*, perh. from Ice. *fela*, to hide or bury; cf. **Pilch**.]

**Filcher**, filch′ér, *n.* a thief.

**File**, fīl, *n.* a line or wire on which papers are placed in order: the papers so placed: a roll or list: a line of soldiers ranged behind one another.—*v.t.* to put upon a file: to arrange in an orderly manner: to put among the records of a court: to bring before a court.—*v.i.* to march in a file. [Fr. *file*, from L. *filum*, a thread.]

**File**, fīl, *n.* a steel instrument with sharp-edged furrows for smoothing or rasping metals, &c.:—*v.t.* to cut or smooth with, or as with a file. [A.S. *feol*; Ger. *feile*; Bohem. *pila*, a saw, *pilnijk*, a file; allied to L. *polio*, to polish.]

**Filial**, fil′yal, *adj.* pertaining to or becoming a *son* or *daughter*: bearing the relation of a child.—*adv.* **Fi′lially.** [L. *filius*, a son, *filia*, a daughter.]

**Filiate**, fil′i-āt, *v.t.* Same as **Affiliate**.

**Filiation**, fil-i-ā′shun, *n.* Same as **Affiliation**.

**Filibuster, Filibuster**, fil′i-bus-tér, *n.* a lawless military or piratical adventurer, as in the W. Indies: a buccaneer. [Sp. *filibuster*, Sp. *filibote*, *flibote*, a small, fast-sailing vessel, from E. *flyboat*.]

**Filiform**, fil′i-form, *adj.* having the *form* of a *filament*: long and slender. [L. *filum* and **Form**.]

**Filigree**, fil′i-grē, *n.* extremely fine *thread*-like network, containing *beads*: ornamental work of gold and silver wire. [Sp. *filigrana*—L. *filum*, and *granum* a grain or bead.]

**Filing**, fīl′ing, *n.* a particle rubbed off with a *file*.

**Fill**, fil, *v.t.* to make *full*: to put into until all the space is occupied: to supply abundantly: to satisfy: to glut: to perform the duties of: to supply a vacant office.—*v.i.* to become full: to become satiated.—*n.* as much as fills or satisfies: a full supply.—*n.* **Fill′er**, he who or that which fills. [A.S. *fyllan*, *fullian*—*full*, full; Ger. *füllen*. See **Full**.]

**Fillet**, fil′et, *n.* a *little string* or band, esp. to tie round the head: something tied up with a fillet, as meat: the fleshy part of the thigh of meat, esp. of veal: (*arch.*) a small space or band used along with mouldings.—*v.t.* to bind or adorn with a fillet:—*pr.p.* fill′eting; *pa.p.* fill′eted. [Fr. *filet*, dim. of *fil*, from L. *filum*, a thread.]

**Fillibeg, Philibeg**, fil′i-beg *n.* the kilt, the dress or petticoat reaching nearly to the knees, worn by the Highlanders of Scotland. [Gael. *filleadh-beag*—*filleadh*, plait, fold, and *beag*, little.]

**Fillip**, fil′ip, *v.t.* to strike with the nail of the finger, forced from the ball of the thumb with a sudden jerk:—*pr.p.* fill′iping; *pa.p.* fill′iped.—*n.* a jerk of the finger suddenly let go from the thumb. [Formed from the sound.]

**Filly**, fil′i, *n.* a young mare: a lively, wanton girl. [Dim. of *foal*, formed by adding suffix *y*, and modifying the vowel. See **Foal**.]

**Film**, film, *n.* a *thin skin* or membrane: a very slender thread.—*v.t.* to cover with a film, or thin skin.—*adj.* **Film′y**, composed of *film* or membranes.—*n.* **Film′iness**. [A.S., formed by adding suffix *-m* to the root of E. *fell*. a skin, present also in Goth. *filleins*, leathern.]

**Filter**, fil′tér, *n.* a substance through which liquors are strained.—*v.t.* to purify liquor by a filter.—*v.i.* to pass through a filter: to percolate. [Fr. *filtre*—Low L. *filtrum*, felt, from Ger. root of **Felt**, which see.]

**Filth**, filth, *n.*, *foul* matter: anything that de-

files, physically or morally. [A.S. *fyldh—fûl*, foul. See **Foul**.]

**Filthy**, filth′i, *adj.* foul: unclean: impure.—*adv.* **Filth′ily**.—*n.* **Filth′iness**.

**Filtrate**, fil′trāt, *v.t.* to *filter* or percolate. [*ing*.

**Filtration**, fil-trā′shun, *n.* act or process of *filter-*

**Fimbriate**, fim′bri-āt, **Fimbriated**, fim′bri-āt-ed, *adj.* having *fibres* on the margin: fringed. [L. *fimbriatus—fimbriæ*, fibres—from root of **Fibre**.]

**Fimbriate**, fim′bri-āt, *v.t.* to *fringe*: to hem.

**Fin**, fin, *n.* the organ by which a fish balances itself and swims. [A.S. *fin*; L. *pinna*, a fin.]

**Finable**, fīn′a-bl, *adj.* liable to a *fine*.

**Final**, fī′nal, *adj.* last: decisive: respecting the end or motive.—A **Final cause** is the last end or purpose for which things were made, and the doctrine of *final causes* teaches that all things were made on a plan or for a purpose.—*adv.* **Fi′nally**. [Fr.—L. *finalis—finis*, an end.]

**Finale**, fe-nä′lā, *n.* the *end*: the last passage in a piece of music: the concluding piece in a concert. [It. *finale*, final—L. *finis*.]

**Finality**, fī-nal′i-ti, *n.* state of being *final*: completeness or conclusiveness.

**Finance**, fi-nans′, *n.* money affairs or revenue, esp. of a ruler or state: public money: the art of managing or administering the public money. [Fr.—Low L. *financia*—Low L. *finare*, to pay a fine—*finis*. See **Fine**, *n.*]

**Financial**, fi-nan′shal, *adj.* pertaining to finance.—*adv.* **Finan′cially**.

**Financier**, fi-nan′sér, *n.* one skilled in finance: an officer who administers the public revenue.

**Finch**, finsh, *n.* the name of several species of birds, many of them excellent singers [A.S. *finc*; Ger. *fink*; allied to W. *pinc*, a chaffinch, also smart, gay.]

**Find**, fīnd, *v.t.* to come upon or meet with: to discover or arrive at: to perceive: to experience: to supply:—*pr.p.* find′ing; *pa.t.* and *pa.p.* found.—*n.* **Find′er**. [A.S. *findan*; Ger. *finden*.]

**Fine**, fīn, *adj.* excellent: beautiful: not coarse or heavy: subtle: thin: slender: exquisite: nice: delicate: overdone: showy: splendid.—The **Fine arts**, as painting and music, are those in which the love of the beautiful and fineness of taste are chiefly concerned; opp. to the *useful* or *industrial arts*.—*v.t.* to make fine: to refine: to purify.—*adv.* **Fine′ly**.—*n.* **Fine′ness**. [Fr.—L. *finitus*, finished, from *finio*, to finish, *finis*, an end.]

**Fine**, fīn, *n.* a composition: a sum of money imposed as a punishment.—**In fine**, in conclusion.—*v.t.* to impose a fine on: to punish by fine. [From the Law Lat. *finis*, a fine, a payment which *ends* or *concludes* a strife—L. *finis*, an end.]

**Finer**, fīn′ér, *n.* Same as **Refiner**.

**Finery**, fīn′ér-i, *n.* splendour: fine or showy things: a place where anything is fined or refined: a furnace for making iron malleable.

**Finesse**, fi-nes′, *n.* subtilty of contrivance: artifice.—*v.i.* to use artifice. [Fr., from root of **Fine**.]

**Finger**, fing′gér, *n.* one of the five extreme parts of the hand: a finger's breadth: skill in the use of the hand or fingers.—*v.t.* to handle or perform with the fingers: to pilfer.—*v.i.* to use the fingers on a musical instrument. [A.S., Ger., Dan., from root of **Fang**.]

**Finger-board**, fing′gér-bōrd, *n.* the *board*, or part of a musical instrument, on which the keys for the *fingers* are placed.

**Fingered**, fing′gėrd, *adj.* having fingers, or anything like fingers.

**Fingering**, fing′gėr-ing, *n.* act or manner of touching with the *fingers*, esp. a musical instrument.

**Finger-post**, fing′gėr-pōst, *n.* a *post* with a *finger* pointing, for directing passengers to the road.

**Finial**, fin′i-al, *n.* the bunch of foliage, &c. at the top of a pinnacle : the pinnacle itself. [From L. *finio—finis.*]

**Finical**, fin′i-kal, *adj.* affectedly *fine* or precise in trifles : nice : foppish.—*adv.* **Fin′ically.**

**Fining**, fīn′ing, *n.* process of refining or purifying.

**Finis**, fī′nis, *n.* the end : conclusion. [L.]

**Finish**, fin′ish, *v.t.* to end or complete the making of anything : to perfect : to give the last touches to.—*n.* that which finishes or completes : last touch : the last coat of plaster to a wall. [Fr. *finir, finissant,* L. *finire—finis,* an end.]

**Finisher**, fin′ish-ėr, *n.* one who finishes, completes, or perfects.

**Finite**, fī′nīt, *adj.* having an *end* or limit :—opp. to Infinite.—*adv.* **Fi′nitely.**—*n.* **Fi′niteness.** [L. *finitus,* pa.p. of *finio.*]

**Finny**, fin′i, *adj.* furnished with *fins.*

**Fiord**, fyord, *n.* name given in Scandinavia to a long, narrow, rock-bound strait or inlet. [Norw.]

**Fir**, fėr, *n.* the name of several species of cone-bearing, resinous trees, valuable for their timber. [A.S. *furh;* Ice. *fura,* Ger. *föhre,* W. *pyr,* L. *quercus.*]

**Fire**, fīr, *n.* the heat and light caused by burning : flame : anything burning, as fuel in a grate, &c. : a conflagration : torture by burning : severe trial : anything inflaming or provoking : ardour of passion : vigour : brightness of fancy : enthusiasm : sexual love. [A.S., Sw., and Dan. *fyr;* Ger. *feuer;* Gr. *pyr;* allied to Sans. *pâvana,* pure, also fire.]

**Fire**, fīr, *v.t.* to set on fire ; to inflame : to irritate : to animate : to cause the explosion of : to discharge.—*v.i.* to take fire : to be or become irritated or inflamed : to discharge firearms.

**Firearms**, fīr′ärmz, *n.pl.* arms or weapons which are discharged by fire exploding gunpowder.

**Fireball**, fīr′bawl, *n.* a ball filled with combustibles to be thrown among enemies : a meteor.

**Firebox**, fīr′boks, *n.* the box or chamber of a steam-engine, in which the fire is placed.

**Firebrand**, fīr′brand, *n.* a brand or piece of wood on fire : one who inflames the passions of others.

**Firebrick**, fīr′brik, *n.* a brick so made as to resist the action of fire.

**Fire-brigade**, fīr′-brig-ād′, *n.* a brigade or company of men for extinguishing fires or conflagrations.

**Fireclay**, fīr′klā, *n.* a kind of clay, capable of resisting fire, used in making firebricks.

**Firecock**, fīr′kok, *n.* a cock or spout to let out water for extinguishing fires.

**Firedamp**, fīr′damp, *n.* a gas, carburetted hydrogen, in coal-mines, apt to take fire.

**Fire-engine**, fīr′-en′jin, *n.* an engine or forcing-pump used to extinguish fires with water.

**Fire-escape**, fīr′-es-kāp′, *n.* a machine used to enable people to escape from fires.

**Firefly**, fīr′flī, *n.* a winged luminous fly which emits a bright light like a firespark.

**Firelock**, fīr′lok, *n.* a gun in which the fire is caused by a lock with steel and flint.

**Fireman**, fīr′man, *n.* a man whose business it is to assist in extinguishing fires : a man who tends the fires, as of a steam-engine.

**Fireplace**, fīr′plās, *n.* the place in a house appropriated to the fire : a hearth.

**Fireplug**, fīr′plug, *n.* a plug placed in a pipe which supplies water in case of fire.

**Fireproof**, fīr′prŏŏf, *adj.* proof against fire.

**Fireship**, fīr′ship, *n.* a ship filled with combustibles, to set an enemy's vessels on fire.

**Fireside**, fīr′sīd, *n.* the side of the fireplace : the hearth : home. [bears a high degree of heat.

**Firestone**, fīr′stōn, *n.* a kind of sandstone that

**Fireworks**, fīr′wurks, *n.pl.* artificial works or preparations of gunpowder, sulphur, &c. to be fired chiefly for display or amusement.

**Fire-worship**, fīr′-wur′ship, *n.* the worship of fire, chiefly by the Parsees in Persia and India.—*n.* **Fire′-wor′shipper.** [guns : firewood : fuel.

**Firing**, fīr′ing, *n.* a putting *fire* to or discharge of

**Firkin**, fėr′kin, *n.* a measure equal to the *fourth* part of a barrel : 9 gallons : 56 lbs. of butter. [O. Dut. *vier,* four, and the dim. suffix -*kin.*]

**Firm**, fėrm, *adj.* fixed : compact : strong : not easily moved or disturbed : unshaken : resolute : decided.—*adv.* **Firm′ly.**—*n.* **Firm′ness.** [Fr. *ferme;* L. *firmus;* allied to Sans. *dhri,* to bear, to support.]

**Firm**, fėrm, *n.* the title under which a company transacts business : a business house or partnership. [It. *firma,* from L. *firmus.*]

**Firmament**, fėr′ma-ment, *n.* the *solid* sphere in which the stars were supposed to have been fixed : the sky. [Fr.—L. *firmamentum—firmus,* firm or solid ; the ancients believed that the firmament was solid.]

**Firmamental**, fėr-ma-ment′al, *adj.* pertaining to the firmament : celestial.

**Firman**, fėr′man, *n.* any decree emanating from the Turkish government. [Pers. *firmân;* Sans. *pramâna,* measure, decision.]

**First**, fėrst, *adj., foremost :* preceding all others in place, time, or degree : most eminent : chief. —*adv.* before anything else, in time, space, rank, &c. [A.S. *fyrst;* Ice. *fyrstr;* the superl. of *fore* by adding -*st.*]

**First-born**, fėrst′-bawrn, *adj.* born first.—*n.* the first in the order of birth : the eldest child.

**First-fruit**, fėrst′-frŏŏt, **First-fruits**, fėrst′-frŏŏts, *n.* the fruits first gathered in a season : the first profits or effects of anything.

**Firstling**, fėrst′ling, *n.* the first produce or offspring, esp. of animals. [First and dim. *ling.*]

**First-rate**, fėrst′-rāt, *adj.* of the first or highest rate or excellence : pre-eminent in quality, size, or estimation.

**Firth**, fėrth. Same as Frith.

**Fisc**, fisk, *n.* the state treasury : the public revenue. [Fr. *fisc*—L. *fiscus,* a basket or purse, the treasury.]

**Fiscal**, fisk′al, *adj.* pertaining to the public treasury or revenue.—*n.* a treasurer : (*in Scotland*) an officer who prosecutes in petty criminal cases.

**Fish**, fish. *n.* an animal that lives in water, and breathes through gills : the flesh of fish :—*pl.* **Fish** or **Fishes.**—*v.t.* to search for fish : to search by sweeping : to draw out or up : to seek to obtain by artifice. [A.S. *fisc;* Ger. *fisch;* Ice. *fiskr;* Goth. *fisks;* L. *piscis;* Gr. *ichthys;* Gael. *iasg.*]

**Fisher**, fish′ėr, **Fisherman**, fish′ėr-man, *n.* one who fishes, or whose occupation is to catch fish.

**Fishery**, fish′ėr-i, *n.* the business of catching fish : a place for catching fish.

**Fishing**, fish′ing. *adj.* used in fishery.—*n.* the art or practice of catching fish.

**Fishmonger**, fish′mung-gėr, *n.* a dealer in fish. (**Fish** and **Monger.**)

---

**Fishy**, fish′i, *adj.* consisting of fish : like a fish : abounding in fish.—*n.* **Fish′iness.**

**Fissile**, fis′il, *adj.* that may be *cleft* or split in the direction of the grain. [L. *fissilis*, from *findo*, to cleave.]

**Fission**, fish′un, *n.* a *cleaving* or breaking up into two parts. [L. *fissio—findo, fissum*, to cleave.]

**Fissiparous**, fis-sip′a-rus, *adj.*, *propagated* by spontaneous *fission* into minute parts. [L. *fissus*, pa.p. of *findo*, and *pario*, to bring forth.]

**Fissirostral**, fis-i-ros′tral, *adj.* having a deeply *cleft* or gaping *beak*, as swallows, &c. [L. *fissus*, and *rostrum*, a beak.]

**Fissure**, fish′ūr, *n.* a narrow opening or chasm. [Fr.—L. *fissura*, from *findo, fissus*, to cleave.]

**Fist**, fist, *n.* the closed or clenched hand, orig. as used for striking. [A.S. *fyst*; Ger. *faust*; Russ. *piaste*; allied to L. *pugnus*, a fist, Gr. *pux*, with clenched fist.]

**Fistula**, fist′ū-la, *n.* a deep, narrow, *pipe*-like, sinuous ulcer. [L. *fistula*, a pipe.]

**Fistular**, fist′ū-lar, *adj.* hollow like a *pipe*.

**Fistulous**, fist′ū-lus, *adj.* of the nature or form of a *fistula*.

**Fit**, fit, *adj.* adapted to any particular end or standard : qualified : convenient : proper.—*v.t.* to make fit or suitable : to suit one thing to another : to be adapted to : to qualify.—*v.i.* to be suitable or becoming :—*pr.p.* fitt′ing; *pa.p.* fitt′ed.—*adv.* **Fit′ly.**—*n.* **Fit′ness.** [Ice. *fitja*, to knit together; Goth. *fetjan*, to adorn.]

**Fit**, fit, *n.* a sudden attack by convulsions, as apoplexy, epilepsy, &c. : convulsion or paroxysm : a temporary attack of anything, as laughter, &c. : a sudden effort or motion : a passing humour. [A.S. *fit*, a song; Ice. *fet*, a foot; Sans. *pada*, a step, a verse of a poem. The orig. sense was a foot or step, then a part of a poem, a bout of fighting, and lastly, a sudden attack of pain. Cf. *fetch, foot, fit* (above).]

**Fitch**, fich, *n* now **Vetch**: (*B.*) in Isaiah, the black poppy, with a seed like cummin : in Ezekiel, a kind of bearded wheat, spelt. [See **Vetch**.]

**Fitchet**, fich′et, **Fitchew**, fich′ōō, *n.* a polecat. [O. Fr. *fissau*, froom root of Dut. *vies*, nasty.]

**Fitful**, fit′fool, *adj.* marked by sudden impulses : spasmodic.—*adv.* **Fit′fully.**—*n.* **Fit′fulness.**

**Fitter**, fit′er, *n.* he who or that which makes *fit*.

**Fitting**, fit′ing, *adj.* fit : appropriate.—*n.* anything used in fitting up, esp. in *pl.*—*adv.* **Fitt′ingly.**

**Fitz**, fits, *n.* (a prefix), *son of :* used in England, esp. of the illegitimate sons of kings and princes. [Norman Fr. *fiz*, Fr. *fils*—L. *filius*; cf. Russ. suffix *vitz*, a son.]

**Five**, fīv, *adj.* and *n.* four and one. [A.S. *fíf*; Ger. *fünf*; Goth. *fimf*; W. *pump*; L. *quinque*; Gr. *pente, pempe*; Sans. *panchan*.]

**Fivefold**, fīv′fōld, *adj.* five times folded or repeated : in fives.

**Fives**, fīvz, *n.pl.* a game with a ball played against a wall, so named because three *fives* or 15 are counted to the game.

**Fix**, fiks, *v.t.* to make firm or fast : to establish : to drive into : to settle : to direct steadily : to deprive of volatility.—*v.i.* to settle or remain permanently : to become firm : to congeal. [Fr. —L. *figo, fixus*; Gr. *pēgnumi*; conn. with Sans. *pac*, to bind.]

**Fixation**, fiks-ā′shun, *n.* act of fixing or state of being fixed : steadiness : firmness : state in which a body does not evaporate.

**Fixed**, fikst, *adj.* settled : not apt to evaporate.— *adv.* **Fix′edly.**—*n.* **Fix′edness.**

**Fixity**, fiks′i-ti, *n.* fixedness.

**Fixture**, fiks′tūr, *n.* what is *fixed* to anything, as to land or to a house : a fixed article of furniture.

**Fizz**, fiz, **Fizzle**, fiz′l, *v.i.* to make a hissing sound. [Formed from the sound.]

**Flabby**, flab′i, *adj.* easily moved or shaken : soft and yielding : hanging loose.—*n.* **Flabb′iness.** [From **Flap**.]

**Flaccid**, flak′sid, *adj.*, *flabby : lax :* easily yielding to pressure : soft and weak.—*adv.* **Flac′cidly.** [O. Fr.—L. *flaccidus—flaccus*, flabby; conn. with **Flap**.]

**Flaccidness**, flak′sid-nes, **Flaccidity**, flak-sid′i-ti, *n.* laxness : want of firmness.

**Flag**, flag, *v.i.* to grow languid or spiritless :— *pr.p.* flagg′ing; *pa.p.* flagged′. [From a root which is found in A.S. *flacor*, flying, roving; Ice. *flaka*, to flap; Ger. *flackern*, to flutter.]

**Flag**, flag, *n.* a water-plant. [So called from its waving in the wind. From root of *v.* **Flag**.]

**Flag**, flag, *n.* the ensign of a ship or of troops : a banner. [Dan. *flag*, Ger. *flagge*; from root of *v.* **Flag**, and so called from its fluttering in the wind.]

**Flag**, flag, **Flagstone**, flag′stōn, *n.* a *stone* that separates in *flakes* or layers : a flat stone used for paving. [A form of *flake*; Ice. *flaga*, a flag or slab.]

**Flagellant**, flaj′el-ant, *n.* one who *scourges* himself in religious discipline.

**Flagellate**, flaj′el-āt, *v.t.* to *whip* or scourge.— *n.* **Flagella′tion.** [L. *flagello, flagellatus—flagellum*, dim. of *flagrum*, a whip.]

**Flageolet**, flaj′o-let, *n.* a small wind-instrument like a *flute*. [Fr., dim. of O. Fr. *flageol*, a pipe—Low L. *flautiolus—flauta*, a flute. See **Flute**.]

**Flaggy**, flag′i, *adj.* flexible : weak : full of the plant flag.—*n.* **Flagg′iness.**

**Flagitious**, fla-jish′us, *adj.* grossly wicked : guilty of enormous crimes.—*adv.* **Flagi′tiously.**—*n.* **Flagi′tiousness.** [L. *flagitiosus—flagitium*, anything disgraceful done in the heat of passion —root *flag*, in *flagro*, to burn.]

**Flagon**, flag′un, *n.* a drinking *vessel* with a narrow neck. [Fr. *flacon* for *flascon*—Low L. *flasco*. See **Flask**.]

**Flagrant**, flā′grant, *adj.* glaring : notorious : enormous.—*adv.* **Fla′grantly.**—*n.* **Fla′grancy.** [L. *flagrans, flagrantis*, pr.p. of *flagro*, to flame.]

**Flagship**, flag′ship, *n.* the *ship* in which an admiral sails, and which carries his flag.

**Flail**, flāl, *n.* a wooden instrument for *beating* or thrashing corn. [O. Fr. *flael*—L. *flagellum*, a scourge.]

**Flake**, flāk, *n.* a small layer or film : a very small loose mass, as of snow or wool.—*v.t.* to form into flakes. [Scand.; Norw. *flak*, a slice, Ice. *flagna*, to flake off.] [*n.* **Flak′iness.**

**Flaky**, flāk′i, *adj.* consisting of *flakes* or layers.—

**Flambeau**, flam′bō, *n.* a *flaming* torch :—*pl.* **Flam′beaux** (-bō). [Fr.—*flambe*—L. *flamma*.]

**Flamboyant**, flam-boy′ant, *adj.* (*arch.*) with waving or *flame*-like tracery. [Pr.p. of Fr. *flamboyer*, to blaze—*flamber*.]

**Flame**, flām, *n.* the gleam or blaze of a fire: rage : ardour of temper : vigour of thought : warmth of affection : love.—*v.i.* to burn as flame : to break out in passion.—*adj.* **Flame′less.** [Fr. *flamme*, from L. *flamma*, for *flagma—flag*, root of *flagro*, to burn; Gr. *phleg*, Sans. *bhrag*, to shine.]

**Flamen**, flā′men, *n.* (*in ancient Rome*) a priest devoted to one particular god. [L., same as *filamen*, perh. from *filum*, a fillet of wool, as a flamen wore a fillet round his head.]

**Flaming**, flām'ing, *adj.* red : gaudy : violent.—*adv.* **Flam'ingly.**

**Flamingo**, fla-ming'gō, *n.* a tropical bird of a *flaming* or bright-red colour, with long legs and neck. [Sp. *flamenco*—L. *flamma*, a flame.]

**Flammiferous**, flam-if'ėr-us, *adj.* producing flame. [L. *flamma*, and *fero*, to bear, produce.]

**Flange**, flanj, *n.* a raised edge or *flank* on the rim of a wheel, as of a railway carriage.—*adj.* **Flanged'.** [Corr. of **Flank**.]

**Flank**, flangk, *n.* the side of an animal from the ribs to the thigh : the side of anything, esp. of an army or fleet.—*v.t.* to attack or pass round the side of.—*v.i.* to be posted on the side : to touch. [Fr. *flanc*, perh. from L. *flaccus*, flabby, the flank being the weak part of the body. See **Flaccid**.]

**Flanker**, flank'ėr, *n.* a fortification which commands the *flank* of an assailing force.—*v.t.* to defend by flankers : to attack sideways.

**Flannel**, flan'el, *n.* a soft *woollen* cloth of loose texture.—*adj.* **Flann'eled.** [Orig. *flannen*—W. *gwlanen*, wool.]

**Flap**, flap, *n.* the blow or motion of a broad loose object : anything broad and flexible hanging loose, as the tail of a coat.—*v.t.* to beat or move with a flap.—*v.i.* to move, as wings : to hang like a flap :—*pr.p.* flapp'ing ; *pa.p.* flapped'.—*n.* **Flap'per.** [From the sound, conn. with **Flabby**, **Flaccid**, **Flag**.]

**Flare**, flār, *v.i.* to burn with a glaring, unsteady light : to glitter or flash.—*n.* an unsteady, offensive light. [From a root found in Norw. *flara*, Swed. *flasa*, to blaze.]

**Flash**, flash, *n.* a momentary gleam of light : a sudden burst, as of merriment : a short transient state.—*v.i.* to break forth, as a sudden light : to break out into intellectual brilliancy : to burst out into violence.—*v.t.* to cause to flash. [From the root of Swed. *flasa*, to blaze ; cf. Ice. *flasa*, to rush ; allied to *flare* and *flush*.]

**Flashy**, flash'i, *adj.* dazzling for a moment : showy but empty.—*adv.* **Flash'ily.**—*n.* **Flash'iness.**]

**Flask**, flask, *n.* a narrow-necked *vessel* for holding liquids : a bottle. [A.S. *flasc* ; Ger. *flasche* ; Fr. *flasque*, *flacon*, *flascon* ; Low L. *flasca* ; all perh. from L. *vasculum*, a little vessel, *vas*, a vessel. See **Fiasco**.]

**Flat**, flat, *adj.* smooth : level : wanting points of prominence and interest : monotonous : dejected : (*music*) opposite of sharp.—*n.* a level plain : a tract covered by shallow water : something broad : a story or floor of a house : (*music*) a character (♭) which lowers a note a semitone.—*adv.* **Flat'ly.**—*n.* **Flat'ness.** [From a Teut. root found in Ice. *flatr*, flat, Swed. *flat* ; cf. Dut. *vlak*, Ger. *flach*.] [flat.

**Flatten**, flat'n, *v.t.* to make flat.—*v.i.* to become

**Flatter**, flat'ėr, *v.t.* to soothe with praise and servile attentions : to please with false hopes.—*n.* **Flatt'erer.** [Fr. *flatter* ; orig. dub., perh. from *flat*, in the sense of making smooth by a gentle caress, or from root *flak* or *plag*, to pat.]

**Flattering**, flat'ėr-ing, *adj.* uttering false praise : pleasing to pride or vanity.—*adv.* **Flatt'eringly.**

**Flattery**, flat'ėr-i, *n.* false praise.

**Flattish**, flat'ish, *adj.* somewhat flat.

**Flatulence**, flat'ū-lens, **Flatulency**, flat'ū-len-si, *n.* windiness : air generated in a weak stomach. [See **Flatulent**.]

**Flatulent**, flat'ū-lent, *adj.* affected with air in the stomach : apt to generate wind in the stomach : empty : vain.—*adv.* **Flat'ulently.** [Fr.—Low L. *flatulentus*—L. *flo*, *flatus*, to blow.]

**Flatus**, flā'tus, *n.* a puff of wind : air generated in the stomach or any cavity of the body. [L.]

**Flatwise**, flat'wīz, *adj.* or *adv.*, *flatways* or with the flat side downward.

**Flaunt**, flänt or flawnt, *v.i.* to *fly* or wave in the wind : to move ostentatiously : to carry a saucy appearance.—*n.* anything displayed for show. [Prob. from a contr. of A.S. *fleogan*, *fleon*, to fly.]

**Flautist**. See **Fluter**.

**Flavorous**, flā'vur-us, *adj.* of a pleasant *flavour*.

**Flavour**, flā'vur, *n.* that quality of anything which affects the *smell* or the palate.—*v.t.* to impart flavour to.—*adj.* **Fla'vourless.** [Fr. *flairer*—L. *fragro*, to smell.]

**Flaw**, flaw, *n.* a *break*, a *crack* : a defect.—*v.t.* to crack or break.—*adj.* **Flaw'less.** [Ice. *flaga*, a fragment ; W. *flaw*, a splinter.]

**Flawy**, flaw'i, *adj.* full of *flaws* or cracks : faulty.

**Flax**, flaks, *n.* the fibres of a plant which are woven into linen cloth : the flax-plant. [A.S. *fleax* ; Ger. *flachs*.]

**Flaxen**, flaks'n, *adj.* made of or resembling *flax* : fair, long, and flowing.

**Flay**, flā, *v.t.* to strip off the skin :—*pr.p.* flay'ing ; *pa.p.* flayed'.—*n.* **Flay'er.** [A.S. *flean* ; Ice. *flaga*, to cut turfs. See **Flake**.]

**Flea**, flē, *n.* a well-known troublesome insect. [A.S. *flea*—*fleohan* ; cf. Ger. *floh*, Dut. *vloo*, Russ. *blocha*.]

**Fleam**, flēm, *n.* an instrument for bleeding cattle. [Fr. *flamme*—Gr. *phlebotomon*, a lancet—*phleps*, *phlebos*, a vein, and *tom* or *tam*, the base of *temnō*, to cut.]

**Fleck**, flek, *n.* a spot or speckle : a little bit of a thing. [Ice. *flekkr*, a spot, *flekka*, to stain ; Ger. *fleck*, a spot.]

**Fleck**, flek, **Flecker**, flek'ėr, *v.t.* to *spot* or speckle : to streak. [See **Fleck**, *n.*]

**Flection**. Same as **Flexion**.

**Fled**, fled, *pa.t.* and *pa.p.* of **Flee**.

**Fledge**, flej, *v.t.* to furnish with feathers or wings. [A.S. *fleogan*, Ger. *fliegen*, to fly.]

**Fledgling**, flej'ling, *n.* a *little* bird just *fledged*.

**Flee**, flē, *v.i.* to run away, as from danger.—*v.t.* to keep at a distance from :—*pr.p.* flee'ing ; *pa.t.* and *pa.p.* fled. [A.S. *fleohan*, contracted *fleon*, akin to *fleogan*, to fly ; Ger. *fliehen*, akin to *fliegen*, to fly. See **Fly**.]

**Fleece**, flēs, *n.* the coat of wool shorn from a sheep at one time.—*v.t.* to clip wool from : to plunder : to cover, as with wool.—*adj.* **Fleece'less.** [A.S. *flys* ; Dut. *vlies*, Ger. *fliess*.]

**Fleeced**, flēst, *adj.* having a fleece.

**Fleecer**, flēs'ėr, *n.* one who strips or plunders.

**Fleecy**, flēs'i, *adj.* covered with wool : woolly.

**Fleer**, flēr, *v.t.* or *v.i.* to make wry faces in contempt, to mock.—*n.* mockery. [From a root found in Norw. *flira*, Swed. *flissa*, to titter.]

**Fleet**, flēt, *n.* a number of ships in company, esp. ships of war : a division of the navy, commanded by an admiral. [A.S. *fleot*, *flota*, a ship—*fleotan*, to float ; conn. with Ice. *floti*, Dut. *vloot*, Ger. *flotte*.]

**Fleet**, flēt, *v.i.* to pass swiftly :—*pr.p.* fleet'ing ; *pa.p.* fleet'ed.—*adj.* swift : nimble : fleeting or transient.—*adv.* **Fleet'ly.**—*n.* **Fleet'ness.** [A.S. *fleotan*, to float.] [rary.—*adv.* **Fleet'ingly.**

**Fleeting**, flēt'ing, *adj.* passing quickly : tempo-

**Flemish,** flem'ish, *adj.* of or belonging to the *Flemings* or people of Flanders.

**Flense,** flens, *v.t.* to cut up the blubber of, as a whale. [Dan. *flense*, Scot. *flinch*.]

**Flesh,** flesh, *n.* the soft substance which covers the bones of animals : animal food : the bodies of beasts and birds, not fish : the body, not the soul : animals or animal nature : mankind : bodily appetites : the present life : the soft substance of fruit : the part of a fruit fit to be eaten. [A.S. *flæsc ;* cog. forms in all the Teut. lang.]

**Flesh,** flesh, *v.t.* to train to an appetite for flesh, as dogs for hunting : to accustom : to glut : to use upon flesh, as a sword, esp. for the first time.

**Fleshed,** flesht, *adj.* having flesh : fat.

**Fleshless,** flesh'les, *adj.* without flesh : lean.

**Fleshly,** flesh'li, *adj.* corporeal : carnal : not spiritual.—*n.* **Flesh'liness.**

**Fleshy,** flesh'i, *adj.* fat : pulpy : plump.—*adv.* **Flesh'ily.**—*n.* **Flesh'iness.**

**Fleur-de-lis,** floor'-de-lē', *n.* the flower of the lily :—*pl.* **Fleurs'-de-lis'.** [Fr., *lis* being for L. *lilium,* a lily.]

**Flew,** floo, *past tense of* **Fly.**    [be persuaded.

**Flexibility,** fleks-i-bil'i-ti, *n.* pliancy : easiness to

**Flexible,** fleks'i-bl, **Flexile,** fleks'il, *adj.* easily *bent :* pliant : docile.—*n.* **Flex'ibleness.**—*adv.* **Flex'ibly.** [Fr.—L. *flexibilis, flexilis—flecto, flexum,* to bend.]      [—*flecto.*]

**Flexion,** flek'shun, *n.* a bend : a fold. [L. *flexio*

**Flexor,** fleks'or, *n.* a muscle which *bends* a joint.

**Flexuous,** fleks'ū-us, **Flexuose,** fleks'ū-ōs, *adj.* full of windings and turnings : variable.

**Flexure,** fleks'ūr, *n.* a bend or turning : (*math.*) the curving of a line or surface : the bending of loaded beams. [L. *flexura.* See **Flexible.**]

**Flicker,** flik'er, *v.i.* to *flutter* and move the wings, as a bird : to burn unsteadily, as a flame. [A.S. *flicerian ;* cf. Ice. *flökra,* Dut. *flikkeren.*]

**Flier, Flyer,** flī'er, *n.* one who *flies* or flees : a fly-wheel.

**Flight,** flīt, *n.* a passing through the air : a soaring : excursion : a sally : a series of steps : a flock of birds flying together : the birds produced in the same season : a volley or shower : act of fleeing : hasty removal. [A.S. *flyht—fleogan.*]

**Flighty,** flīt'i, *adj.* fanciful : changeable : giddy.—*adv.* **Flight'ily**—*n.* **Flight'iness.**

**Flimsy,** flim'zi, *adj.* thin : without solidity, strength, or reason : weak.—*n.* **Flim'siness.**

**Flinch,** flinsh, *v.i.* to shrink back : to fail.—*n.* **Flinch'er.**—*adv.* **Flinch'ingly.** [M.E. *flecchen* —Fr. *fléchir*—L. *flectere,* to bend.]

**Fling,** fling, *v.t.* to *strike* or throw from the hand : to dart : to send forth : to scatter.—*v.i.* to act in a violent and irregular manner : to upbraid : to sneer :—*pr.p.* fling'ing ; *pa.t.* and *pa.p.* flung. —*n.* a cast or throw : a taunt. [Scot. *fling,* to strike with the foot, as a horse ; cf. Ice. *flengja ;* O. Sw. *flenga,* to strike.]

**Flint,** flint, *n.* a very hard kind of stone, formerly used for striking fire : anything proverbially hard. [A.S. *flint ;* Dan. *flint ;* Gr. *plinthos,* a brick.]      [hard : cruel.—*n.* **Flint'iness.**

**Flinty,** flint'i, *adj.* consisting of or like flint :

**Flip,** flip, *n.* a hot drink of beer and spirits sweetened. [Ety. unknown.]

**Flippancy,** flip'an-si, **Flippantness,** flip'ant-nes, *n.* pert fluency of speech : pertness.

**Flippant,** flip'ant, *adj.* quick and pert of speech : thoughtless.—*adv.* **Flipp'antly.** [Prov. E. *flip,* to move quickly : prob. from the sound of a slight quick blow.]

**Flirt,** flėrt, *v.i.* to trifle with love : to play at

courtship.—*n.* a pert, giddy girl. [A.S. *fleardian,* to trifle—*fleard,* a foolish thing.]

**Flirtation,** flėrt-ā'snun, *n.* the act of flirting.

**Flit,** flit, *v.i.* to remove from place to place : to flutter on the wing : to fly quickly : to be unsteady or easily moved :—*pr.p.* flitt'ing ; *pa.p.* flitt'ed. [From a Teut. root found in Swed. *flytta,* Ice. *flyta.*]

**Flitch,** flich, *n.* the side of a hog salted and cured. [A.S. *flicce ;* Prov. E. *flick,* bacon.]

**Flittings,** flit'ingz, *n.pl.* (*Pr. Bk.*) wanderings.

**Float,** flōt, *v.i.* to *flow* or swim on a liquid : to be buoyed up : to move lightly and irregularly.— *v.t.* to cause to swim : to cover with water.—*n.* anything swimming on water : a raft : the cork on a fishing-line.—*n.* **Float'er.**—*adj.* **Float'able.** [A.S. *fleotan, flotan,* to float. See **Fleet,** *n.,* and **Flow.**]      [*ing* on rivers or on the sea.

**Floatage, Flotage,** flōt'āj, *n.* things found *float-*

**Floating,** flōt'ing, *adj.* swimming : not fixed : circulating.—*adv.* **Float'ingly.**

**Flocculent,** flok'ū-lent, *adj.* adhering in *locks* or flakes.—*n.* **Flocc'ulence.** [See **Flock,** a lock of wool.]

**Flock,** flok, *n.* a *flight* of *birds* sitting on the ground : a company : a Christian congregation. —*v.i.* to gather in flocks or in crowds. [A.S. *flocc,* a flock, a company, *flyg,* a flying—*fleogan,* to fly.]      [*floccus,* a lock of wool.]

**Flock,** flok, *n.* a lock of wool. [O. Fr. *floc*—L.

**Floe,** flō, *n.* a field of floating ice. [Dan. *iis-flage,* ice-*floe.* See **Flake.**]

**Flog,** flog, *v.t.* to beat or strike : to lash : to chastise with blows :—*pr.p.* flogg'ing ; *pa.p.* flogged'. [A late word ; perhaps a school-boy's abbrev. from L. *flagellare,* to whip.]

**Flood,** flud, *n.* a great *flow* of water : a river, so in *B.:* an inundation : a deluge : the rise or flow of the tide : any great quantity.—*v.t.* to overflow : to inundate :—*pr.p.* flood'ing ; *pa.p.* flood'ed.—**The Flood,** the deluge in the days of Noah. [A.S. *flod ;* Scand. *flod,* Ger. *fluth.* Cog. with **Flow.**]

**Floodgate,** flud'gāt, *n.* a *gate* for letting water *flow* through, or to prevent it : an opening or passage : an obstruction.

**Flooding,** flud'ing, *n.* an extraordinary flow of blood from the uterus.      [which the *tide* rises.

**Floodmark,** flud'märk, *n.* the *mark* or line to

**Floor,** flōr, *n.* the part of a room on which we stand : a platform : the rooms in a house on the same level, a story.—*v.t.* to furnish with a floor. [A.S. *flor ;* Dut. *vloer,* a flat surface, Ger. *flur,* flat land, W. *llawr.*]

**Floorcloth,** flōr'kloth, *n.* a covering for floors made of canvas oil-painted on both sides.

**Flooring,** flōr'ing, *n.* material for floors : a platform.

**Flora,** flō'ra, *n.pl.* the whole of the plants of a particular country : a catalogue of plants. [L.— *flos, floris,* a flower.]

**Floral,** flō'ral, *adj.* pertaining to *Flora* or to *flowers :* (*bot.*) containing the flower.

**Florescence,** flo-res'ens, *n.* a bursting into *flower:* (*bot.*) the time when plants flower. [L. *florescens,* pr.p. of *floresco,* to begin to blossom—*floreo,* to blossom—*flos,* a flower.]

**Floret,** flō'ret, *n.* a *little flower:* (*bot.*) a separate little flower of an aggregate flower.

**Floriculture,** flō'ri-kul-tūr, *n.* the culture of *flowers* or plants.—*adj.* **Floricul'tural.**—*n.* **Floricul'turist,** a florist. [L. *flos, floris,* a flower, and **Culture.**]

**Florid,** flor'id, *adj.* bright in colour : flushed with red : containing flowers of rhetoric or lively figures : richly ornamental.—*adv.* **Flor′idly.**—*n.* **Flor′idness.** [L. *floridus*—*flos*.]

**Floriferous,** flo-rif′ĕr-us, *adj., bearing* or producing *flowers.* [L. *flos, floris,* and *fero,* to bear.]

**Floriform,** flō′ri-form, *adj.* flower-shaped. [L. *flos,* and **Form.**]

**Florin,** flor′in, *n.* (*orig.*) a Florentine coin stamped with the *lily flower,* the national badge of Florence : a silver coin, the value of the English florin being 2s. [Fr., from It. *fiorino*—*fiore,* a lily—L. *flos.*]

**Florist,** flōr′ist, *n.* a cultivator of *flowers :* one who writes an account of plants.

**Floscular,** flos′kū-lar, **Flosculous,** flos′kū-lus, *adj.* composed of many *floscules* or tubular florets.

**Floscule,** flos′kūl, *n.* a *floret* of an aggregate flower. [L. *flosculus,* dim. of *flos,* a flower.]

**Floss,** flos, *n.* the *loose* downy or silky substance in the husks of certain plants, as the bean : portions of silk broken off in unwinding it.—*adj.* **Floss′y.** [It. *floscio*—L. *fluxus,* loose—*fluo,* to flow.]

**Floss-silk,** flos′-silk, *n.* an inferior kind of *silk* made from *floss,* or ravelled fragments of fibre.

**Flotage.** Same as **Floatage.**

**Flotilla,** flo-til′a, *n.* a fleet of small ships. [Sp., dim. of *flota,* Fr. *flotte,* a fleet.]

**Flotsam,** flot′sam, **Flotson,** flot′son, *n.* goods lost by shipwreck, and found *floating* on the sea. [See **Jetsam.**]

**Flounce,** flowns, *v.i.* to move abruptly or impatiently : to plunge and struggle.—*n.* an impatient gesture. [O. Sw. *flunsa,* Dut. *plonzen,* to plunge in water.]

**Flounce,** flowns, *n.* a *plaited* strip or border sewed to the skirt of a dress.—*v.t.* to furnish with flounces. [Fr. *froncis,* a plait ; prob. from Low L. *frontiare,* to wrinkle the brow—L. *frons, frontis,* the brow.]

**Flounder,** flown′dĕr, *v.i.* to struggle with violent motion. [From a Low Ger. root found in Dut. *flodderen.*]

**Flounder,** flown′dĕr, *n.* a small flat fish, generally found in the sea near the mouths of rivers. [Ger. *flunder,* Sw. *flundra.*]

**Flour,** flowr, *n.* the finely-ground meal of wheat or other grain : the fine soft powder of any substance.—*v.t.* to reduce into or sprinkle with flour. [Fr. *fleur* (*de farine,* of meal), fine flour —L. *flos, floris,* a flower.]

**Flourish,** flur′ish, *v.i.* to thrive luxuriantly : to be prosperous : to use copious and flowery language : to make ornamental strokes with the pen.— **Flourished** = lived (L. *floruit*).—*v.t.* to adorn with flourishes or ornaments : to swing about by way of show or triumph. [M. E. *florisshen*—Fr. *fleurir,* from L. *florescere,* to blossom—*flos.*]

**Flourish,** flur′ish, *n.* decoration : showy splendour : a figure made by a bold stroke of the pen : the waving of a weapon or other thing : a parade of words : a musical prelude.

**Flourishing,** flur′ish-ing, *adj.* thriving : prosperous : making a show.—*adv.* **Flour′ishingly.**

**Flout,** flowt, *v.t.* or *v.i.* to *jeer,* mock, or insult : to treat with contempt.—*n.* a mock : an insult. [O. Dut. *fluyten* (Dut. *fluiten*), to play the flute, to jeer.]

**Flow,** flō, *v.i.* to run, as water : to rise, as the tide : to move in a stream, as air : to glide smoothly : to circulate, as the blood : to abound : to hang loose and waving : (*B.*) to melt.—*v.t.* to cover with water. [A.S. *flowan* ; Ger. *fliessen,* akin to L. *pluo,* to rain, Gr. *phleō,* to swim, Sans. *plu,* to swim.]

**Flow,** flō, *n.* a stream or current : the setting in of the tide from the ocean : abundance : copiousness : free expression.

**Flower,** flow′ĕr, *n.* the *blossom* of a plant : the best of anything : the prime of life : the person or thing most distinguished : a figure of speech.— *v.t.* to adorn with figures of flowers.—*v.i.* to blossom : to flourish. [O. Fr. *flour,* Fr. *fleur* —L. *flos, floris,* akin to **Blow, Bloom.**]

**Flower-bud,** flow′ĕr-bud, *n.* a bud with the unopened flower.

**Floweret,** flow′ĕr-et, *n.* a *little flower :* a floret.

**Flowerless,** flow′ĕr-les, *adj.* (*bot.*) having no flowers.

**Flowers,** flō′ĕrz, *n.pl.* (*B.*) in Leviticus, menstrual discharges. [Fr. *fleur*—L. *flos,* a flower.]

**Flowery,** flow′ĕr-i, *adj.* full of or adorned with flowers : highly embellished with figurative style, florid.—*n.* **Flow′eriness.**

**Flowing,** flō′ing, *adj.* moving as a fluid : fluent or smooth.—*adv.* **Flow′ingly.**—*n.* **Flow′ingness.**

**Flown,** flōn, *pa.p.* of **Fly.**

**Fluctuate,** fluk′tū-āt, *v.i.* to float backward and forward : to roll hither and thither : to be irresolute. [L. *fluctuo, fluctuatus*—*fluctus,* a wave —*fluo,* to flow. See **Flow.**]

**Fluctuation,** fluk-tū-ā′shun, *n.* a rising and falling, like a *wave :* motion hither and thither : agitation : unsteadiness.

**Flue,** flōō, *n.* a smoke-pipe or small chimney. [Corr. of *flute*—O. Fr. *fleute.* See **Flute.**]

**Fluency,** flōō′en-si, *n.* readiness or rapidity of utterance : volubility.

**Fluent,** flōō′ent, *adj.* ready in the use of words : voluble.—*adv.* **Flu′ently.** [L. *fluens, fluentis,* pr.p. of *fluo,* to flow.]

**Fluid,** flōō′id, *adj.* that *flows,* as water : liquid or gaseous.—*n.* a liquid, not a solid.

**Fluidity,** flōō-id′i-ti, **Fluidness,** flōō′id-nes, *n.* a liquid or gaseous state.

**Fluke,** flōōk, *n.* a flounder : a parasitic worm in sheep, so called because like a miniature flounder. [A.S. *floc,* a flounder.]

**Fluke,** flōōk, *n.* the part of an anchor which fastens in the ground. [Akin to Ger. *pflug,* a plough, Ice. *fleika,* to tear.]

**Flume,** flōōm, *n.* the channel for the water that drives a mill-wheel. [A.S. *flum,* a stream ; from L. *flumen,* a river—*fluo,* to flow.]

**Flummery,** flum′ĕr-i, *n.* an *acid* jelly made from the husks of oats, the Scotch sowens : anything insipid : empty compliment. [W. *llymry*—*llymrig,* harsh, raw—*llym,* sharp, severe.]

**Flung,** flung, *pa.t.* and *pa.p.* of **Fling.**

**Flunky** or **Flunkey,** flung′ki, *n.* a livery servant : a footman : a mean, cringing fellow.—*n.* **Flun′kyism.** [Prob. from Fr. *flanquer,* to run along by the *side* of ; cf. *henchman.* See **Flank.**]

**Fluor,** flōō′or, *n.* a beautiful mineral, often crystallised, and usually called **Flu′or-spar.**—*adj.* **Fluor′ic.** [A name given by the alchemists to all mineral acids because of their *fluidity,* from L. *fluo,* to flow.]

**Fluorine,** flōō′or-in, *n.* an elementary substance allied to chlorine, obtained chiefly from *fluor.*

**Flurry,** flur′i, *n.* a sudden blast or gust : agitation : bustle.—*v.t.* to agitate :—*pr.p.* flurr′ying ; *pa.p.* flurr′ied. [Perhaps conn. with **Flutter, Flit.**]

**Flush,** flush, *n.* a *flow* of blood to the face causing redness : sudden impulse : bloom : abundance.—*v.i.* to flow suddenly : to come in haste : to become red in the face.—*v.t.* to wash with flowing water : to make red in the face : to excite with joy. [Prob. through O. Fr. *flus*, Fr. *flux*, from L. *flux—fluo*, to flow.]

**Flush**, flush, *adj.* fresh and vigorous : abounding : having the surface level with the adjacent surface. [Prob. same as above.]

**Fluster**, flus′tėr, *n. hurrying*, confusion : heat.—*v.i.* to bustle : to be agitated.—*v.t.* to make hot and confused. [Perh. from Scand. *flaustr*, hurry, and conn. with **Flutter**.]

**Flute**, floot, *n.* a musical pipe with finger-holes and keys sounded by *blowing* : a channel, as on a pillar, called also **Flut′ing**.—*v.i.* to play the flute.—*v.t.* to form flutes or channels in. [Fr., O. Fr. *flaute*, It. *flauto*, from L. *flo*, *flatum*, to blow.] [*player*.

**Fluter**, floot′ėr, **Flautist**, flawt′ist, *n.* a flute-

**Flutter**, flut′ėr, *v.i.* to move or flap the wings without flying or with short flights : to move about with bustle : to vibrate : to be in agitation or in uncertainty.—*v.t.* to throw into disorder.—*n.* quick, irregular motion : agitation : confusion. [A.S. *flotorian*, to float about, from *flot*, the sea ; cf. Ger. *flattern*, Low Ger. *fluttern*.]

**Fluvial**, floo′vi-al, **Fluviatic**, floo-vi-at′ik, *adj.* of or belonging to *rivers* : growing or living in streams or ponds. [L. *fluvialis*, *fluviaticus—fluvius*, a river—*fluo*, to flow.]

**Flux**, fluks, *n.* act of *flowing* : the motion of a fluid : a flow of matter : quick succession : that which flows, as the tide : matter discharged : state of being liquid.—*v.t.* to melt. [Fr.—L. *fluxus—fluo*, to flow.]

**Fluxation**, fluks-ā′shun, *n.* the act of *fluxing* or passing away and giving place to another.

**Fluxible**, fluks′i-bl, *adj.* that may be *fluxed* or melted.—*n.* **Fluxibil′ity**.

**Fluxion**, fluk′shun, *n.* a flowing or discharge : a difference or variation.

**Fly**, flī, *v.i.* to move through the air on wings : to move swiftly : to pass away : to flee : to burst : to flutter.—*v.t.* to avoid, flee from : to cause to fly, as a kite—*pr.p.* fly′ing ; *pa.t.* flew (floo) ; *pa.p.* flown (flōn).—*n.* a small insect with two transparent wings, esp. the common house-fly : a fish-hook dressed with silk, &c. in imitation of a fly : a light double-seated carriage : (*mech.*) a fly-wheel. [A.S. *fleogan* ; Ger. *fliegen* ; from a root *flug*, an extension of *flu*, which is conn. with root *plu*, to swim. Thus **Fly** is akin to **Flow**.]

**Flyblow**, flī′blō, *n.* the *egg* of a *fly*.—*adj.* **Flyblown**, flī′blōn, tainted with the eggs which produce maggots. [Prov. E. *blots*, eggs of maggots.] [used on canals.

**Flyboat**, flī′bōt, *n.* a long narrow *swift boat*

**Fly-catcher**, flī′-kach′ėr, *n.* a small bird, so called from its *catching flies* while on the wing.

**Fly-fish**, flī′-fish, *v.i.* to *fish* with *flies*, natural or artificial, as bait.—*n.* **Fly′-fish′ing**.

**Flying-fish**, flī′ing-fish, *n.* a *fish* which can leap from the water and sustain itself in the air for a short time, by its long pectoral fins, as if *flying*.

**Flying-squirrel**, flī′ing-skwir′el, *n.* a *squirrel* in S. Asia and N. America, which has a broad fold of skin between its fore and hind legs, by which it can take great leaps in the air, as if *flying*. [and end of a book.

**Flyleaf**, flī′lēf, *n.* a blank *leaf* at the beginning

**Flywheel**, flī′hwēl, *n.* a heavy *wheel* applied to machinery to equalise the effect of the moving power.

**Foal**, fōl, *n.* the young of a mare or of a she-ass.—*v.i.* and *v.t.* to bring forth a foal. [A.S. *fola* ; Ger. *fohlen*, Gr. *pōlos* : L. *pullus*, prob. contr. of

*puellus*, dim. of *puer*, a boy, Sans. *putra*, a son, from root *pu*, to beget.]

**Foam**, fōm, *n., froth* : the bubbles which rise on the surface of liquors.—*v.i.* to gather foam : to be in a rage.—*v.t.* (*B.*) (with *out*) : to throw out with rage or violence.—*adv.* **Foam′ingly**.—*adj.* **Foam′less**, without foam. [A.S. *fam* ; Ger. *feim*, akin to L. *spuma—spuo*, to spit ; Sans. *phena*, froth.]

**Foamy**, fōm′i, *adj.* frothy.

**Fob**, fob, *n.* a small *pocket* for a watch. [From a Low Ger. root, found only in Prov. Ger. *fuppe*, a pocket.]

**Focal**, fō′kal, *adj.* of or belonging to a *focus*.

**Focalise**, fō′kal-īz, *v.t.* to bring to a *focus* : to concentrate.

**Focus**, fō′kus, *n.* (*optics*) a point in which the rays of light meet after reflection or refraction, and cause great heat : any central point :—*pl.* **Fo′cuses** and **Foci** (fō′sī).—*v.t.* to bring to a focus ; *pp.* fo′cussed. [L. *focus*, a hearth.]

**Fodder**, fod′ėr, *n., food* for cattle, as hay and straw.—*v.t.* to supply with fodder. [A.S. *foder—foda*, food.]

**Foe**, fō, *n.* an enemy : an ill-wisher. [A.S. *fah-fian*, *fiogan*, to hate. See **Feud**, a quarrel.]

**Foeman**, fō′man, *n.* an enemy in war.—*pl.* **Foe′men**.

**Fœtus**, fē′tus. See **Fetus**.

**Fog**, fog, *n.* a thick mist : watery vapour rising from either land or water. [Dan. *sne-fog*, thick falling snow ; Ice. *fok*, a snow-drift.]

**Fog**, fog, **Foggage**, fog′āj, *n.* grass which grows in autumn after the hay is cut. [Perh. of Celt. origin, as in W. *fwg*, dry grass, Scot. *fog*, moss.]

**Fogbank**, fog′bangk, *n.* a dense mass of *fog* sometimes seen at sea appearing like a *bank* of land.

**Foggy**, fog′i, *adj.* misty : damp : clouded in mind, stupid.—*adv.* **Fogg′ily**.—*n.* **Fogg′iness**.

**Fog-signal**, fog-sig′nal, *n.* an audible signal used on board ship, &c. during a fog, when visible signals cease to be of use.

**Fogy**, fō′gi, *n.* a dull old fellow : a person with antiquated notions. [Ety. unknown.]

**Foh**, fō, *int.* an exclamation of abhorrence or contempt. [A form of **Faugh**.]

**Foible**, foi′bl, *n.* a *weak* point in one's character : a failing. [O. Fr. *foible*, weak. See **Feeble**.]

**Foil**, foil, *v.t.* to defeat : to puzzle : to disappoint : —*pr.p.* foil′ing ; *pa.p.* foiled′.—*n.* failure after success seemed certain : defeat. [Fr. *fouler*, to stamp or crush—Low L. *fullare—fullo*, a fuller of cloth. See **Fuller**.]

**Foil**, foil, *n.* a blunt sword used in fencing. [So called because blunted or *foiled*.]

**Foil**, foil, *n.* a *leaf* or thin plate of metal, as tin-foil : a thin leaf of metal put under precious stones to increase their lustre or change their colour : anything that serves to set off something else. [Fr. *feuille*—L. *folium*, a leaf.]

**Foist**, foist, *v.t.* to bring in by stealth : to insert wrongfully : to pass off as genuine.—*n.* **Foist′er**. [Orig. to break wind in a noiseless manner, and so to introduce stealthily something afterwards felt to be disagreeable, from Dut. *vysten*, to fizzle, cog. with E. **Fizz**.]

**Fold**, fōld, *n.* the *doubling* of any flexible substance : a part laid over on another : that which infolds : an inclosure for sheep : a flock of sheep : the Church.—*v.t.* to lay one part over another : to inclose : to inclose in a fold. [A.S. *fald—fealdan*, to fold ; Scot. *fauld*, Ger. *falte*, akin to L. -*plex*, in *duplex*, double, Gr. -*ploos*, in *diploos*, double.]       [in **Tenfold.**

**Fold**, in composition with numerals = times, as

**Foldage**, fōld′āj, *n.* the right of *folding* sheep.

**Folding**, fōld′ing, *adj.* that may be folded or doubled.—*n.* a fold or plait : the keeping of sheep in inclosures on arable land.

**Foliaceous**, fō-li-ā′shus, *adj.* pertaining to or consisting of *leaves* or laminæ. [L. *foliaceus—folium*, a leaf.]

**Foliage**, fō′li-āj, *n.*, *leaves* : a cluster of leaves. [Fr. *feuillage—feuille*—L. *folium*, a leaf.]

**Foliaged**, fō′li-ājd, *adj.* worked like *foliage*.

**Foliate**, fō′li-āt, *v.t.* (*orig.*) to beat into a *leaf* : to cover with leaf-metal.

**Foliated**, fō′li-āt-ed, *adj.* (*min.*) consisting of plates or thin layers.

**Foliation**, fō-li-ā′shun, *n.* the leafing, esp. of plants.

**Foliferous**, fo-lif′ėr-us, *adj.*, *bearing* or producing *leaves*. [L. *folium*, a leaf, and *fero*, to bear.]

**Folio**, fō′li-ō, *n.* a sheet of paper once folded : a book of such sheets : (*book-k.*) a page in an account-book, or two opposite pages numbered as one.—*adj.* pertaining to or containing paper only once folded. [Abl. of L. *folium*, the leaf of a tree, a *leaf* or sheet of paper.]

**Foliole**, fō′li-ōl, *n.* (*bot.*) a single *leaflet* of a compound leaf. [Fr., dim. of L. *folium*.]

**Folious**, fō′li-us, *adj.*, *leafy* : (*bot.*) having leaves mixed with the flowers.

**Folk**, fōk, *n.* the people : certain people :—*gen.* used in *pl.* **Folk** or **Folks** (fōks). [A.S. *folc* ; Ger. *volk* ; akin perh. to E. *full*, Ger. *voll*, full.]

**Folkland**, fōk′land, *n.* among the Anglo-Saxons, public land as distinguished from boc-land (book-land), *i.e.* land granted to private persons by a written charter.

**Folklore**, fōk′lōr, *n.*, *lore* or knowledge of the ancient customs, superstitions, &c. of the *folk* or people. [The name was first suggested by W. J. Thoms ('Ambrose Merton') in 1846.

**Folkmote**, fōk′mōt, *n.* an assembly of the people among the Anglo-Saxons.

**Follicle**, fol′i-kl, *n.* a *little bag*: (*anat.*) a gland : (*bot.*) a seed-vessel. [Fr.—L. *folliculus*, dim. of *follis*, a wind ball or bag.]

**Follow**, fol′ō, *v.t.* to go after or behind : to pursue : to attend : to imitate : to obey : to adopt, as an opinion : to keep the eye or mind fixed on : to pursue, as an object of desire : to result from : (*B.*) to strive to obtain.—*v.i.* to come after another : to result.—**To follow on** (*B.*), to continue endeavours. [A.S. *fylcgan*, perh. from A.S. *folc*, folk, a crowd. Ger. *folgen*.]

**Follower**, fol′ō-ėr, *n.* one who comes after : a copier : a disciple.

**Following**, fol′ō-ing, *adj.* coming next after.

**Folly**, fol′i, *n.* silliness or weakness of mind : a foolish act : criminal weakness : (*B.*) sin. [Fr. *folie—fol*, foolish. See **Fool.**]

**Foment**, fo-ment′, *v.t.* to bathe with *warm* water : to encourage.—*n.* **Foment′er.** [Fr.—L. *fomento—fomentum* for *fovimentum—foveo*, to warm.]

**Fomentation**, fo-men-tā′shun, *n.* a bathing with warm water : a lotion applied hot : encouragement.

**Fond**, fond, *adj.*, *foolishly* tender and loving : weakly indulgent : very affectionate. — *adv.* **Fond′ly.**—*n.* **Fond′ness.** [For *fonned*, pa.p. of M. E. *fonnen*, to act foolishly, *fon*, a fool ; from Ice. *fana*, to be foolish.—**Fond of**, relishing highly.]       [caress.—*n.* **Fond′ler.**

**Fondle**, fond′l, *v.t.* to treat with *fondness*: to

**Fondling**, fond′ling, *n.* the person or thing *fondled.*

**Font**, font, **Fount**, fownt, *n.* a complete assortment of types of one sort, with all that is necessary for printing in that kind of letter. [Fr. *fonte—fondre*—L. *fundere*, to cast. See **Found.**]

**Font**, font, *n.* a basin for water in baptism. [L. *fons*, a fountain.]

**Food**, fōōd, *n.* what one *feeds* on : that which being digested nourishes the body ; whatever promotes growth. — *adj.* **Food′less**, without food. [A.S. *foda*, from a root *pa*, to nourish.]

**Fool**, fōōl, *n.* one who acts stupidly : a person of weak mind : a jester : (*B.*) a wicked person.—*v.t.* to deceive : to treat with contempt.—*v.i.* to play the fool : to trifle. [O. Fr. *fol* (Fr. *fou*), It. *folle*—L. *follis*, an air-bag, a grimace made by puffing out the cheeks.]       [folly.

**Foolery**, fōōl′ér-i, *n.* an act of folly : habitual

**Fool-hardy**, fōōl′-härd′i, *adj.*, *foolishly hardy* or bold : rash or incautious.—*n.* **Fool′-har′diness.**

**Foolish**, fōōl′ish, *adj.* weak in intellect : wanting discretion : ridiculous : marked with folly : deserving ridicule : (*B.*) sinful, disregarding God's laws.—*adv.* **Fool′ishly.**—*n.* **Fool′ishness.**

**Foolscap**, fōōlz′kap, *n.* paper of a certain size, so called from having originally borne the watermark of a *fool's cap* and bells.

**Fool's-errand**, fōōlz′-er′and, *n.* a silly or fruitless enterprise : search for what cannot be found.

**Foot**, foot, *n.* that part of its body on which an animal stands or walks : the lower part or base : a measure = 12 in. (*orig.*) the length of a man's foot : foot-soldiers : a division of a line of poetry :—*pl.* **Feet** (fēt).—*v.i.* to dance : to walk : —*pr.p.* foot′ing ; *pa.p.* foot′ed. [A.S. *fot*, pl. *fet* ; Ger. *fuss*, L. *pes, pedis*, Gr. *pous, podos*, Sans. *pad*, from root *pad*, to go.]

**Football**, foot′bawl, *n.* a large ball for kicking about in sport : play with this ball.

**Footboy**, foot′boy, *n.* an attendant in livery.

**Footbridge**, foot′brij, *n.* a narrow bridge for foot-passengers.       [ground : a footstep.

**Footfall**, foot′fawl, *n.* a setting the foot on the

**Foot-guards**, foot′-gärdz, *n.pl.* guards that serve on foot, the élite of the British foot-soldiers.

**Foothold**, foot′hōld, *n.* space on which to plant the feet : that which sustains the feet.

**Footing**, foot′ing, *n.* place for the foot to rest on : firm foundation : position : settlement : tread : dance : plain cotton lace.

**Footlight**, foot′līt, *n.* one of a row of lights in front of and on a level with the stage in a theatre, &c.

**Footman**, foot′man, *n.* (*orig.* and *B.*) a soldier who serves on foot : a runner : a servant or attendant in livery :—*pl.* **Foot′men.**

**Footmark**, foot′märk, **Footprint**, foot′print, *n.* the mark or print of a foot : a track.

**Footpad**, foot′pad, *n.* a highwayman or robber on *foot*, who frequents public *paths* or roads. [**Foot**, and **Pad**, a path.]       [travels on foot.

**Foot-passenger**, foot′-pas′en-jér, *n.* one who

**Foot-pound**, foot′-pownd, *n.* the force needed to raise one *pound* weight the height of one *foot*—the usual unit in measuring mechanical force.

**Footrot**, foot′rot, *n.* a rot or ulcer in the feet of sheep.       [in length.

**Footrule**, foot′rōōl, *n.* a rule or measure a foot

**Foot-soldier**, foot′-sōl′jér, *n.* a soldier that serves on foot.       [the foot of and supporting a leaf.

**Footstalk**, foot′stawk, *n.* (*bot.*) the little stalk at

**Footstall**, foot′stawl, *n.* a woman's stirrup. [**Foot**, and Prov. E. *stall*, a case for the finger.]

**Footstep**, foot′step, *n.* the step or impression of

the foot : a track : trace of a course pursued :—
*pl.* **Foot'steps**, course : example.

**Fop**, fop, *n.* an affected dandy. [Dut. *foppen*, to
cheat, mock, *fopper*, a wag.]

**Fopling**, fop'ling, *n.* a vain affected person.

**Foppery**, fop'ėr-i, *n.* vanity in dress or manners :
affectation : folly.

**Foppish**, fop'ish, *adj.* vain and showy in dress :
affectedly refined in manners.—*adv.* **Fopp'ishly.**
—*n.* **Fopp'ishness.**

**For**, for, *prep.* in the place of : for the sake of : on
account of : in the direction of : with respect to :
beneficial to : in quest of : notwithstanding, in
spite of : in recompense of : during.—**As for**, as
far as concerns. [A.S. *for*; Ger. *für*, *vor*,
akin to L. and Gr. *pro*, Sans. *pra*, before in place
or time.]

**For**, for, *conj.* the word by which a reason is introduced : because : on the account that.—**For all**
(*New Test.*), notwithstanding.—**For to** (*B.*), in
order to.

**Forage**, for'aj, *n.*, *fodder*, or food for horses and
cattle : provisions : the act of foraging.—*v.i.* to
go about and forcibly carry off food for horses
and cattle, as soldiers.—*v.t.* to plunder.—*n.*
**For'ager.** [Fr. *fourrage*—Low L. *foragium*—
*fodrum*, which is from a Teut. root found in
Ger. *futter*, E. *fodder*, O. Dan. *foder*. See
**Fodder, Foray.**]

**Foramen**, fo-rā'men, *n.* a small opening :—*pl.*
**Foramina**, fo-ram'i-na. [L.—*foro*, to pierce.]

**Foraminated**, fo-ram'i-nāt-ed, **Foraminous**, fo-
ram'i-nus, *adj.* pierced with small holes : porous.

**Forasmuch**, for'az-much, *conj.* because that.

**Foray**, for'ā, *n.* a sudden incursion into an enemy's
country. [A Lowland Scotch form of **Forage.**]

**Forbade**, for-bad', *pa.t.* of **Forbid.**

**Forbear**, for-bār', *v.i.* to keep one's self in check :
to abstain.—*v.t.* to abstain from : to avoid voluntarily : to spare, to withhold. [*For-*, prefix,
away, and **Bear.** See list of Prefixes.]

**Forbearance**, for-bār'ans, *n.* exercise of patience :
command of temper : clemency.

**Forbearing**, for-bār'ing, *adj.* long - suffering :
patient.—*adv.* **Forbear'ingly.**

**Forbid**, for-bid', *v.t.* to prohibit : to command not
to do. [*For-*, prefix, away, and **Bid.**]

**Forbidden**, for-bid'n, *adj.* prohibited : unlawful.

**Forbidding**, for-bid'ing, *adj.* repulsive : raising
dislike : unpleasant.

**Force**, fōrs, *n.* strength, power, energy : efficacy :
validity : influence : vehemence : violence : coercion or compulsion : military or naval strength
(often in plural) : an armament : (*mech.*) that
which produces or tends to produce a change in
a body's state of rest or motion. [Fr.—Low L.
*forcia*, *fortia*—L. *fortis*, strong.]

**Force**, fōrs, *v.t.* to draw or push by main strength :
to compel : to constrain : to compel by strength
of evidence : to take by violence : to ravish :
(*hort.*) to cause to grow or ripen rapidly.

**Force**, fōrs, **Foss**, fos, *n.* a waterfall. [Scand., as
in Ice. *foss*, formerly *fors*.]

**Force**, fōrs, *v.t.* (*cookery*) to *stuff*, as a fowl. [A
corr. of **Farce.**]

**Forced**, fōrst, *p.* and *adj.* accomplished by great
effort, as a forced march : strained, excessive,
unnatural.

**Forceful**, fōrs'fool, *adj.* full of force or might :
driven or acting with power.—*adv.* **Force'fully.**

**Forceless**, fōrs'les, *adj.* weak.

**Forcemeat**, fōrs'mēt, *n.*, *meat* chopped fine and
highly seasoned, used as a *stuffing* or alone.

**Forceps**, for'seps, *n.* a pair of tongs, pincers, or

pliers for *holding* anything *hot* or otherwise
difficult to be held with the hand. [L. *formus*,
hot, and *capio*, to hold.]

**Forcepump**, fōrs'pump, **Forc'ing-pump**, *n.* a
*pump* which *forces* the water through a sidepipe.

**Forcible**, fōrs'i-bl, *adj.* active : impetuous : done
by force : efficacious : impressive.—*n.* **Forc'ibleness.**—*adv.* **Forc'ibly.**

**Forcing**, fōrs'ing, *n.* (*hort.*) the art of hastening
the growth of plants.

**Forcipated**, for'si-pāt-ed, *adj.* formed and opening
like a *forceps.* [L.—*forceps*, *forcipis.*]

**Ford**, förd, *n.* a place where water may be crossed
on foot.—*v.t.* to cross water on foot.—*adj.*
**Ford'able.** [A.S. *faran*, to go; Ger. *furt-
fahren*, to go on foot : akin to Gr. *poros*—root of
*peraō*, to cross, and to E. **Fare, Ferry**, and **Far.**]

**Fore**, fōr, *adj.*, *in front of* : advanced in position :
coming first.—*adv.* at the front : in the first
part : previously. [A.S., radically the same as
**For**, *prep.* But both must be carefully distinguished from prefix *for-* (Ger. *ver-* in *vergessen*,
L. *per*). See list of Prefixes.]

**Forearm**, fōr'ärm, *n.* the forepart of the arm, or
that between the elbow and the wrist.

**Forearm**, fōr-ärm', *v.t.* to arm or prepare beforehand.

**Forebode**, fōr-bōd', *v.t.* to feel a secret sense of
something future, esp. of evil.—*n.* **Forebod'er.**
[See **Bode.**] [evil.

**Forebodement**, fōr-bōd'ment, *n.* feeling of coming

**Foreboding**, fōr-bōd'ing, *n.* a *boding* or perception
*beforehand* : apprehension of coming evil.

**Forecast**, fōr-kast', *v.t.* to contrive or reckon
*beforehand* : to foresee.—*v.i.* to form schemes
beforehand.—*n.* **Forecast'er.** [See **Cast.**]

**Forecast**, fōr'kast, *n.* a previous contrivance :
foresight.

**Forecastle**, fōr'kas-l or fok'sl, *n.* a foredeck, raised
above the maindeck : more commonly the fore-
part of the ship under the maindeck, the quarters
of the crew : (*orig.*) that part of the upper deck
of a ship *before* the foremast, so called from the
small turret or *castle* near the prow in ancient
vessels.

**Foreclose**, fōr-klōz', *v.t.* to preclude : to prevent : to
stop. [Fr. *forclos*, pa.p. of *forclore*, to exclude
—L. *foris*, outside, and *claudo*, *clausus*, to shut.]

**Foreclosure**, fōr-klōz'ūr, *n.* a *foreclosing* : (*law*)
the depriving a mortgager of the right of redeeming a mortgaged estate. [time.

**Foredate**, fōr-dāt', *v.t.* to *date before* the true

**Foredeck**, fōr'dek, *n.* the *fore*part of a *deck* or
ship. [that is forward.

**Fore-end**, fōr'-end, *n.* the end that goes first or

**Forefather**, fōr'fā-thėr, *n.* an ancestor. [**Fore**,
and **Father.**]

**Forefend**, fōr-fend', *v.t.* to ward off, avert. [Pro-
perly *forfend*, from the prefix *for-*, and *-fend*, an
abbrev. of *defend*. See prefix *For-*.]

**Forefinger**, fōr'fing-gėr, *n.* the finger before the
others, or next the thumb.

**Forefoot**, fōr'foot, *n.* one of the feet of an animal
in front or next the head.

**Forefront**, fōr'front, *n.* the front or foremost part.

**Forego**, fōr-gō', *v.t.* to go before. precede : chiefly
used in its *pr.p.* forego'ing and *pa p.* foregone'.—
*n.* **Forego'er.**—A **foregone conclusion** is a conclusion come to before the examination of the evidence. [**Fore**, and **Go.**]

**Forego**, fōr-gō', *v.t.* to give up : to forbear the use
of. [Should have been *forgo*, A.S. *forgan*, to
pass over, from the A.S. prefix *for-*, away, and
*gan*, to go. See prefix *For-*.]

**Foreground**, fōr'grownd, _n._ the _ground_ or space which seems to lie _before_ the figures in a picture.

**Forehand**, fōr'hand, _n._ the part of a horse which is in front of its rider.—_adj._ taken in _hand_ or done _before_ needed.

**Forehanded**, fōr'hand-ed, _adj._, forehand : seasonable : formed in the foreparts.

**Forehead**, fōr'hed, _n._ the _fore_part of the _head_ above the eyes, the brow.

**Foreign**, for'in, _adj._ belonging to another country : from abroad : not belonging to, unconnected : not appropriate. [Fr. _forain_—Low L. _foraneus_ —_foras_, out of doors. See Door.]

**Foreigner**, for'in-èr, _n._ a native of another country.

**Forejudge**, fōr-juj', _v.t._ to judge before hearing the facts and proof. [foresee.

**Foreknow**, fōr-nō', _v.t._ to know beforehand : to

**Foreknowledge**, fōr-nol'ej, _n._ knowledge of a thing before it happens.

**Foreland**, fōr'land, _n._ a point of land running forward into the sea.

**Forelock**, fōr'lok, _n._ the lock of hair on the forehead : to take by the **Forelock**, to seize promptly.

**Foreman**, fōr'man, _n._ the first or chief man : an overseer.—_pl._ Fore'men.

**Foremast**, fōr'mast, _n._ the _mast_ that is _fore_ or _in front_, or next the bow of a ship.

**Forementioned**, fōr-men'shund, _adj._ mentioned before in a writing or discourse.

**Foremost**, fōr'mōst, _adj._ (superl. of Fore), _first_ in place : most advanced : first in rank or dignity. [A.S. _forma_, first, superl. of _fore_, and superl. suffix _-st_. It is, therefore, a double superl. ; the old and correct form was _formest_, which was wrongly divided _for-mest_ instead of _form-est_, and the final _-mest_ was mistaken for _-most_.]

**Forenamed**, fōr'nāmd, _adj._ mentioned before.

**Forenoon**, fōr'nōōn, _n._ the part of the day before noon or mid-day. [it happens.

**Forenotice**, fōr-nō'tis, _n._ notice of anything before

**Forensic**, fo-ren'sik, _adj._ belonging to courts of law, held by the Romans in the _forum ;_ used in law pleading. [L. _forensis—forum_, market-place, akin to _fores_. See Foreign and Door.]

**Fore-ordain**, fōr-or-dān', _v.t._ to arrange or appoint beforehand : to predestinate : to predetermine.— _n._ Fore-ordina'tion.

**Forepart**, fōr'pärt, _n._ the part before the rest : the front : the beginning : (_B._) the bow of a ship.

**Forerank**, fōr'rangk, _n._ the rank which is before all the others : the front. [precede.

**Forerun**, fōr-run', _v.t._ to run or come before : to

**Forerunner**, fōr-run'èr, _n._ a runner or messenger sent before : a sign that something is to follow.

**Foresail**, fōr'sāl, _n._ a _sail_ attached to the _fore_-yard on the foremast. [hand.

**Foresee**, fōr-sē', _v.t._ or _v.i._ to see or know before-

**Foreshadow**, fōr-shad'ō, _v.t._ to shadow or typify beforehand. [a ship.

**Foreship**, fōr'ship, _n._ (_B._) the bow or _fore_part of

**Foreshore**, fōr'shōr, _n._ the part immediately before the shore : the sloping part of a shore included between the high and low water marks.

**Foreshorten**, fōr-short'n, _v.t._ (_in a picture_) to represent the _shortened_ appearance of an object projecting _forward._—_n._ Foreshortening (_in painting_), the representation of the _shortened_ appearance of an object projecting _forward._

**Foreshow**, fōr-shō', _v.t._ to shew or represent beforehand : to predict.

**Foreside**, fōr'sīd, _n._ the side towards the front.

**Foresight**, fōr'sīt, _n._ act of foreseeing : wise forethought, prudence. [glans penis.

**Foreskin**, fōr'skin, _n._ the skin that covers the

**Forest**, for'est, _n._ a large uncultivated tract of land covered with trees and underwood : woody ground and rude pasture.—_adj._ pertaining to a forest : silvan : rustic.—_v.t._ to cover with trees. [O. Fr. _forest_, Fr. _forêt_—Low L. _foresta_, which in mediæval writers is the open wood, as opposed to the _parcus_ (park) or walled-in wood—_forestis_, out of, not shut—L. _foris_, out of doors—_fores_, doors. See Foreign and Door.]

**Forestall**, fōr-stawl', _v.t._ to buy goods _before_ they are brought to _stall_ or market : to anticipate.

**Forester**, for'est-èr, _n._ one who has charge of a _forest :_ an inhabitant of a forest.

**Foretaste**, fōr-tāst', _v.t._ to taste before possession : to anticipate. [pation.

**Foretaste**, fōr'tāst, _n._ a taste beforehand : antici-

**Foretell**, fōr-tel', _v.t._ to tell before : to prophesy. —_v.i._ to utter prophecy.—_n._ Foretell'er.

**Forethought**, fōr'thawt, _n._ thought or care for the future : provident care. [hand.

**Foretoken**, fōr'tō-kn, _n._ a token or sign before-

**Foretoken**, fōr-tō'kn, _v.t._ to signify beforehand.

**Foretooth**, fōr'tōōth, _n._ a tooth in the forepart of the mouth :—_pl._ Foreteeth, fōr'tēth.

**Foretop**, fōr'top, _n._ (_naut._) the platform at the head of the foremast.

**Foretopmast**, fōr-top'mast, _n._ in a ship, the _mast_ erected at the top of the _foremast_, and at the top of which is the **Foretop-gall'ant-mast.**

**Forever**, for-ev'ér, _adv._ for ever, for all time to come : to eternity : through endless ages.

**Forewarn**, fōr-wawrn', _v.t._ to warn beforehand : to give previous notice.—_n._ Forewarn'ing, warning beforehand.

**Forfeit**, for'fit, _v.t._ to lose the right to by some fault or crime :—_pr.p._ for'feiting ; _pa.p._ for'-feited.—_n._ that which is forfeited : a penalty for a crime : a fine : something deposited and redeemable.—_adj._ For'feitable. (Fr. _forfaire_, _forfait_—Low L. _forisfacere, forisfactum_, to do beyond what is permitted, to offend—_foris_, out of doors, beyond, _facere_, to do.]

**Forfeiture**, for'fit-ūr, _n._ act of _forfeiting :_ state of being forfeited : the thing forfeited.

**Forgat**, for-gat'—forgot—old _pa.t._ of Forget.

**Forge**, fōrj, _n._ the workshop of a _faber_ or workman in hard materials : a furnace, esp. one in which iron is heated : a smithy : a place where anything is shaped or made.—_v.t._ to form by heating and hammering : to form : to make falsely : to fabricate : to counterfeit.—_v.i._ to commit forgery. [Fr. _forge_, Prov. _farga_—L. _fabrica_— _faber_, a workman.] [guilty of forgery.

**Forger**, fōrj'èr, _n._ one who forges or makes : one

**Forgery**, fōrj'ér-i, _n._ fraudulently making or altering any writing : that which is forged or counterfeited.

**Forget**, for-get', _v.t._ to _lose_ or put _away_ from the memory : to neglect :—_pr.p._ forgett'ing ; _pa.t._ forgot' ; _pa.p._ forgot', forgott'en. [A.S. _forgitan_ —_for-_, prefix, away, and _gitan_, to get.]

**Forgetful**, for-get'fool, _adj._ apt to forget : inattentive.—_adv._ Forget'fully.—_n._ Forget'fulness.

**Forget-me-not**, for-get'-me-not', _n._ a small herb with beautiful blue flowers, regarded as the emblem of _friendship :_ a keepsake.

**Forgive**, for-giv', _v.t._ to pardon : to overlook an offence or debt. [A.S. _forgifan—for-_, prefix, away, and _gifan_, to give ; cf. Ger. _ver-geben_.]

**Forgiveness**, for-giv'nes, _n._ pardon : remission : disposition to pardon.

**Forgiving**, for-giv'ing, _adj._ ready to pardon : merciful : compassionate.

**Fork**, fork, _n._ an instrument with two or more

prongs at the end: one of the points or divisions of anything fork-like:—in *pl.* the branches into which a road or river divides, also the point of separation.—*v.i.* to divide into two branches, as a road or tree: to shoot into blades, as corn.—*v.t.* to form as a fork: to pitch with a fork. [A.S. *forc*—L. *furca.*]

**Forked,** fork′ed, **Forky,** fork′i, *adj.* shaped like a *fork.*—*adv.* **Fork′edly.**—*ns.* **Fork′edness, Fork′iness.**

**Forlorn,** for-lorn′, *adj.* quite lost: forsaken: wretched. [A.S. *forloren,* pa.p. of *forleosan,* to lose—*for,* away, and *leosan,* to lose; Ger. *verloren,* pa.p. of *verlieren,* to lose.]

**Forlorn-hope,** for-lorn′-hōp, *n.* a body of soldiers selected for some service of uncommon danger. [From the Dut. *verloren hoop,* the *forlorn* or *lost troop.* See **Hope.**]

**Form,** form, *n.* shape of a body: the boundary-line of an object: a model: a mould: mode of arrangement: order: regularity: system, as of government: beauty or elegance: established practice: ceremony: (*print.*) the type from which an impression is to be taken arranged and secured in a chase: (*in the fol. senses pron.* fōrm) a long seat, a bench: (*in schools*) the pupils on a form, a class: the bed of a hare, which takes its shape from the animal's body. [Fr. *forme*—L. *forma*—*fero,* to bear, like *facies,* appearance, from *facio,* to make.]

**Form,** form, *v.t.* to give *form* or shape to: to make: to contrive: to settle, as an opinion: to combine: to go to make up: to establish: (*gram.*) to make by derivation.—*v.i.* to assume a form.

**Formal,** form′al, *adj.* according to *form* or established mode: ceremonious: methodical: having the form only: having the power of making a thing what it is: essential: proper.—*adv.* **Form′ally.**           [external *forms* of religion.

**Formalism,** form′al-izm, *n.* a resting in the mere **Formalist,** form′al-ist, *n.* one who is content with the mere *forms* of religion.

**Formality,** for-mal′i-ti, *n.* the precise observance of forms or ceremonies: established order. [L. *formalitas*—*forma.*]

**Formation,** for-mā′shun, *n.* a making or producing: structure: (*geol.*) a group of strata belonging to one period. [L. *formatio.*]

**Formative,** form′a-tiv, *adj.* giving *form*: (*gram.*) serving to form, not radical.—*n.* a derivative. [Fr. *formatif*—*formo, formatus,* to shape.]

**Former,** form′ėr, *adj.* (comp. of **Fore**) before in time or order: past: first mentioned. [A.S. *forma,* first, superl. of *fore,* and comp. suffix *-er.*]

**Former,** form′ėr, *n.* one who *forms* or makes.

**Formerly,** form′ėr-li, *adv.* in *former* times: heretofore.

**Formic,** for′mik, *adj.* pertaining to *ants,* as formic acid, originally obtained from ants. [L. *formica,* an ant.]

**Formicate,** for′mi-kāt, *adj.* resembling an ant.

**Formication,** for-mi-kā′shun, *n.* a sensation like that of *ants* creeping on the skin. [L. *formicatio*—*formicare,* to creep like an ant—*formica.*]

**Formidable,** for′mi-da-bl, *adj.* causing *fear*: adapted to excite fear.—*adv.* **For′midably.**—*n.* **For′midableness.** [Fr.—L. *formidabilis*—*formido,* fear.]

**Formula,** form′ū-la, *n.* a prescribed form: a formal statement of doctrines: (*math.*) a general expression for solving problems: (*chem.*) a set of symbols expressing the components of a body:

—*pl.* **Formulæ,** form′ū-lē, **Form′ulas.** [L., dim. of *forma.*]

**Formulary,** form′ū-lar-i, *n.* a *formula*: a book of formulæ or precedents.—*adj.* prescribed: ritual. [Fr. *formulaire*—L. *formula.*]

**Formulate,** form′ū-lāt, **Formulise,** form′ū-līz, *v.t.* to reduce to or express in a formula: to state or express in a clear or definite form.

**Fornicate,** for′ni-kāt, **Fornicated,** for′ni-kāt-ed, *adj.,* arched: (*bot.*) arching over. [L. *fornicor, fornicatus—fornix,* an arch.]

**Fornicate,** for′ni-kāt, *v.i.* to commit lewdness: to have unlawful sexual intercourse. [L. *fornicor, fornicatus—fornix,* an arch, a vault, a brothel.]

**Fornication,** for-ni-kā′shun, *n.* sexual intercourse between unmarried persons: (*B.*) adultery, incest, and frequently idolatry.

**Fornicator,** for′ni-kā-tor, *n.* an unmarried person guilty of lewdness:—*fem.* **Fornicatress,** for′ni-kā-tres. [L. *fornicator,* and *fornicatrix*—*fornicor.*]

**Forsake,** for-sāk′, *v.t.* to desert: to abandon:—*pr.p.* forsāk′ing; *pa.t.* forsook′; *pa.p.* forsāk′en. [A.S. *forsacan*—*for,* away, and O. E. *sake,* dispute, strife—A.S. *sacan,* to strive. See **Sake.**]

**Forsooth,** for-sōōth′, *adv., for* or in *sooth* or truth: certainly. [A.S. *for sothe,* for truth, *sothe* being the dat. of *soth.* See **Sooth.**]

**Forswear,** for-swār′, *v.t.* to deny upon oath.—(*B.*) **To forswear one's self,** to swear falsely, to commit perjury. [*For-,* away, and **Swear.**]

**Fort,** fōrt, *n.* a small fortress. [Fr.—L. *fortis,* strong.]

**Fortalice,** fort′al-is, *n.* a *small* outwork of a *fortification.* [O. Fr. *fortelesce*—Low L. *fortalitia*—*fortis.*]

**Forte,** fōrt, *n.* one's strong point, that in which one excels. [Same as below.]

**Forte,** for′tā, *adv.* (*mus.*) strongly, with emphasis, loud. [It. *forte*—L. *fortis.*]

**Forth,** fōrth, *adv., before* or *forward* in place or order: in advance: onward in time: out into view: abroad: (*B.*) out. [A.S. *forth*; Dut. *voort,* forward, Ger. *fort,* on, further, radically the same as **For, Fore.**]

**Forthcoming,** fōrth′kum-ing, *adj.* just *coming forth*: about to appear.            [out delay.

**Forthwith,** fōrth-with′, *adv.* immediately: with-

**Fortieth,** for′ti-eth, *adj.* the *fourth tenth.*—*n.* a fortieth part. [A.S. *feowertigotha.*]

**Fortification,** for-ti-fi-kā′shun, *n.* the art of strengthening a military position by means of defensive works: that which fortifies.

**Fortify,** for′ti-fī, *v.t.* to *strengthen* against attack with forts, &c.: to invigorate: to confirm:—*pa.p.* for′tifïed.—*n.* **For′tifier.** [Fr. *fortifier*—Low L. *fortificare*—*fortis,* strong, *facio,* to make.]

**Fortissimo,** for-tis′i-mō, *adv.* (*mus.*) *very strong* or loud. [It., superl. of *forte.* See **Forte,** *adv.*]

**Fortitude,** for′ti-tūd, *n.* that strength of mind which enables one to meet danger or endure pain with calmness. [L. *fortitudo*—*fortis.*]

**Fortnight,** fort′nīt, *n.* two weeks or fourteen days. [Contr. of *fourteen nights.*]            [fortnight.

**Fortnightly,** fort′nīt-li, *adj.* and *adv.* once a

**Fortress,** for′tres, *n.* a *fortified place*: a defence. [Fr. *forteresse,* another form of *fortelesce,* which see under **Fortalice.**]

**Fortuitous,** for-tū′i-tus, *adj.* happening by chance or accident.—*adv.* **Fortu′itously.**—*ns.* **Fortu′itousness, Fortu′ity.** [L. *fortuitus,* casual.]

**Fortunate,** for′tū-nāt, *adj.* happening by *good-fortune*: lucky.—*adv.* **For′tunately.**

**Fortune,** for'tūn, *n.* whatever comes *by lot* or *chance*: luck: the arbitrary ordering of events: the lot that falls to one in life: success: wealth. [Fr.—L. *fortuna,* a lengthened form of *fors, fortis,* chance, from *fero,* to bear, and lit. meaning, that which is produced.]

**Fortune-hunter,** for'tūn-hunt'ėr, *n.* a man who *hunts* for a marriage with a woman of *fortune.*

**Fortuneless,** for'tūn-les, *adj.* without a fortune: luckless.

**Fortune-teller,** for'tūn-tel'ėr, *n.* one who pretends to foretell one's fortune.—*n.* **For'tune-tell'ing.**

**Forty,** for'ti, *adj.* and *n.* four times ten. [A.S. *feowertig—feower,* four, *tig,* ten.]

**Forum,** fō'rum, *n.* (*fig.*) a market-place, esp. the market-place in Rome, where public business was transacted and justice dispensed: the courts of law as opp. to the Parliament. [L., akin to *foras,* out of doors. See **Door** and **Foreign.**]

**Forward,** for'ward, **Forwards,** for'wardz, *adv., towards* what is *before* or in front: onward: progressively. [A.S. *foreweard—fore,* fore, and *weard,* sig. direction. *Forwards*—M.E. *forwardes.* was orig. the gen. form (cf. Ger. *vorwärts*).]

**Forward,** for'ward, *adj.* near or at the *fore*part: in advance of something else: ready: too ready: presumptuous: earnest: early ripe.—*adv.* **For'wardly.**—*n.* **For'wardness.**

**Forward,** for'ward, *v.t.* to help on, to quicken: to send on.—*n.* **For'warder.**

**Fosse, Foss,** fos, *n.* (*fort.*) a moat or trench in front of a fortified place. [Fr. *fosse,* L. *fossa—fodio, fossum,* to dig.]

**Fossil,** fos'il, *n.* the petrified remains of an animal or vegetable found imbedded in the strata of the earth's crust.—*adj.* in the condition of a fossil. [Fr. *fossile,* L. *fossilis—fodio,* to dig; so called because obtained by digging.]

**Fossiliferous,** fos-il-if'ėr-us, *adj.* bearing or containing *fossils.* [L. *fossilis,* and *fero,* to bear.]

**Fossilise,** fos'il-īz, *v.t.* to convert into a *fossil.*—*v.i.* to be changed into a stony or fossil state.—*n.* **Fossilisa'tion,** a changing into a fossil.

**Fossilist,** fos'il-ist, *n.* one skilled in *fossils.* [ing.

**Fossorial,** fos-ōr'i-al, *adj.* (*zool.*) digging, burrow-

**Foster,** fos'tėr, *v.t.* to bring up or nurse: to encourage.—*n.* **Fos'terer.** [A.S. *fostrian,* to nourish, *fostre* a nurse, *fostor* (= *fod-stor*), food. See **Food.**]

**Foster-brother,** fos'tėr-bru*th*'ėr, *n.* a male child, *fostered* or brought up with another of different parents.

**Foster-child,** fos'tėr-chīld, *n.* a *child nursed* or brought up by one who is not its parent.

**Foster-parent,** fos'tėr-pā'rent, *n.* one who *rears* a child in the place of its *parent.*

**Fougasse,** foo-gas', *n.* (*mil.*) a small mine, from six to twelve feet underground. [Fr.—L. *focus,* hearth, fire.]

**Fought,** fawt, *pa.t.* and *pa.p.* of **Fight.**

**Foul,** fowl, *adj.* filthy: loathsome: profane: impure: stormy: unfair: running against: entangled.—*adv.* **Foul'ly.**—*n.* **Foul'ness.** [A.S. *ful,* akin to Scand. *ful,* Ger. *faul,* Goth. *fuls;* all from root *pu,* to stink. See **Putrid.**]

**Foul,** fowl, *v.t.* to make *foul:* to soil.—*v.i.* to come into collision:—*pr.p.* foul'ing; *pa.p.* fouled'.

**Foul-mouthed,** fowl'-mow*th*d, *adj.* addicted to the use of *foul* or profane language.

**Foumart,** foo'märt, *n.* the polecat. [From A.S. *ful,* foul, and Fr. *marte* or *martre,* a marten. See **Foul** and **Marten.**]

**Found,** *pa.t.* and *pa.p.* of **Find.**

**Found,** fownd, *v.t.* to lay the *bottom* or *foundation* of: to establish on a basis: to originate: to endow. [Fr. *fonder*—L. *fundo, fundatus,* to found—*fundus,* the bottom. See **Bottom.**]

**Found,** fownd, *v.t.* to form by *melting* and *pouring* into a mould: to cast. [Fr. *fondre*—L. *fundo, fusus,* to pour. Cf. **Fuse.**]

**Foundation,** fownd-ā'shun, *n.* the act of founding: the base of a building: the groundwork or basis: a permanent *fund* for the support of anything.—*n.* **Founda'tioner,** one supported from the funds or *foundation* of an institution.

**Founder,** fownd'ėr, *n.* one who melts and casts metal, as a brassfounder.

**Founder,** fownd'ėr, *n.* one who *founds,* establishes, or originates: an endower.—*fem.* **Found'ress.**

**Founder,** fownd'ėr, *v.i.* to go to the *bottom*: to fill with water and sink.—*v.t.* to disable by injuring the feet, of a horse. [Fr. *fondre—fond*—L. *fundus,* the bottom.]

**Founding,** fownd'ing, *n.* metal-*casting.*

**Foundling,** fownd'ling, *n.* a *little* child *found* deserted.

**Foundry,** fownd'ri, **Foundery,** fownd'ėr-i, *n.* the art of *founding* or casting: the house where founding is carried on.

**Fount,** fownt, **Fountain,** fownt'ān, *n.* a spring of water, natural or artificial: the structure for a jet of water: the source of anything. [Fr. *fontaine,* O. Fr. *font*—Low L. *fontana—fontanus,* adj., from L. *fons, fontis,* a spring—*fundo,* to pour.]

**Fountain-head,** fownt'ān-hed, *n.* the *head* or source of a *fountain*: the beginning.

**Four,** fōr, *adj.* and *n.* two and two. [A.S. *feower;* Ger. *vier,* Goth. *fidvor,* L. *quatuor,* Gr. *tettares, pisures,* Sans. *chatvar.*]

**Fourfold,** fōr'fold, *adj.* folded four times: multiplied four times. [**Four** and **Fold.**]

**Four-footed,** fōr'-foot'ed, *adj.* having four feet.

**Fourscore,** fōr'skōr, *adj.* four times a score—80.

**Foursquare,** fōr'skwār, *adj.* having four equal sides and angles: square.

**Fourteen,** fōr'tēn, *adj.* and *n.* four and ten.

**Fourteenth,** fōr'tēnth, *adj.* and *n.* fourth or the fourth after the tenth. [A.S. *feowerteotha—feower* and *teotha,* tenth.]

**Fourth,** fōrth, *adj.* next after the third.—*n.* one of four equal parts.—*adv.* **Fourth'ly.** [A.S. *feortha.*]

**Fowl,** fowl, *n.* a bird: a bird of the barn-door or poultry kind, a cock or hen: the flesh of fowl:—*pl.* **Fowls** or **Fowl.**—*v.i.* to kill fowls by shooting or snaring.—*n.* **Fowl'er,** a sportsman who takes wild-fowl. [A.S. *fugel;* Ger. *vogel,* Ice. *fugl*: connection with A.S. *fleogan,* E. *fly,* &c. is improbable.] [small-shot, used in *fowling.*

**Fowling-piece,** fowl'ing-pēs, *n.* a light *gun* for

**Fox,** foks, *n.* an animal of the dog family, noted for cunning: any one notorious for cunning. [A.S.; Ger. *fuchs.*]

**Foxglove,** foks'gluv, *n.* a biennial plant with *glove-like* flowers, whose leaves are used as a soothing medicine. [A.S. *foxes glofa*; cf. Norw. *revhanskje,* foxglove, from *rev,* a fox.]

**Foxhound,** foks'hownd, *n.* a hound used for chasing foxes.

**Foxy,** foks'i, *adj.* of foxes: cunning: (*paint.*) having too much of the reddish-brown or fox-colour.

**Fracas,** fra-kä', *n.* uproar: a noisy quarrel. [Fr. from *fracasser,* to break—It. *fracassare—fra,* among, and *cassare,* Fr. *casser,* to break—L. *quassare,* to shake.]

**Fraction,** frak'shun, *n.* a fragment or very small

piece : (*arith.*) any part of a unit. [Fr.—L. *fractio*—*frango, fractus*, to break, from root *frag*, whence Gr. *rhēgnumi*, to break.]

**Fractional**, frak'shun-al, *adj.* belonging to or containing a *fraction* or fractions.

**Fractious**, frak'shus, *adj.* ready to *break out* in a passion : cross.—*adv.* **Frac'tiously.**—*n.* **Frac'tiousness.** [See Fraction.]

**Fracture**, frak'tūr, *n.* the breaking of any hard body : a breach or part broken.—*v.t.* to break through.

**Fragile**, fraj'il, *adj., easily broken* : frail : delicate. [L. *fragilis*—from *frango*, to break.]

**Fragility**, fra-jil'i-ti, *n.* the state of being *fragile*.

**Fragment**, frag'ment, *n.* a piece *broken off* : an unfinished portion.—*adj.* **Fragment'al.** [See Fraction.]     [fragments or pieces : broken.

**Fragmentary**, frag'ment-ar-i, *adj.* consisting of

**Fragrance**, frā'grans, *n.* pleasantness of *smell* or perfume : sweet or grateful influence.

**Fragrant**, frā'grant, *adj.* sweet-scented.—*adv.* **Fra'grantly.** [L. *fragrans, fragrantis*, pr.p. of *fragro*, to smell.]

**Frail**, frāl, *adj.* wanting in strength or firmness : weak.—*n.* **Frail'ness.** [Fr. *frêle*; from L. *fragilis.* See Fragile.]

**Frailty**, frāl'ti, *n.* weakness : infirmity.

**Frame**, frām, *v.t.* to form : to shape : to construct by fitting the parts to each other : to plan : to constitute : to put a border on : (*B.*) to contrive. [A.S. *fremman*, to promote or make—*fram*, forward, strong, excellent; conn. with Ger. *fromm*, kind, pious, Goth. *fruma*, first, L. *primus.*]

**Frame**, frām, *n.* the form : a putting together of parts : a case made to inclose or support anything : the skeleton : state of mind.

**Framer**, frām'er, *n.* he who forms or constructs : one who makes frames for pictures, &c.

**Framework**, frām'wurk, *n.* the *work* that forms the *frame* : the skeleton or outline of anything.

**Framing**, frām'ing, *n.* the act of constructing : a frame or setting.

**Franc**, frangk, *n.* a silver coin orig. used in *France*, now also in Belgium, &c., equal to 10d. sterling.

**Franchise**, fran'chiz, *n.* a privilege or right granted : the right of voting for a member of Parliament. [Fr., from *franc, franche*, free.]

**Franchise**, fran'chiz, *v.t.* to enfranchise : to give one the franchise.

**Franciscan**, fran-sis'kan, *adj.* belonging to the order of *St Francis* in the R. C. Church.—*n.* a monk of this order. [L. *Franciscus*, Francis.]

**Frangible**, fran'ji-bl, *adj.* easily broken.—*n.* **Frangibil'ity.** [See Fraction.]

**Frank**, frangk, *adj.* open or candid in expression. —*v.t.* to send free of expense, as a letter. —*adv.* **Frank'ly** (*New Test.*) gratuitously.—*n.* **Frank'ness.** [Fr. *franc*—Low L. *francus*—O. Ger. *franko*, one of the tribe called Franks, a free man.]

**Frankincense**, frangk'in-sens, *n.* a sweet-smelling vegetable resin issuing from a tree in Arabia, and used in sacrifices. [O. Fr. *franc encens*, pure incense. See Frank and Incense.]

**Franklin**, frangk'lin, *n.* an old English freeholder. [O. Fr. *frankeleyn*, from root of Frank.]

**Frantic**, fran'tik, *adj.* mad, furious : wild.—*adv.* **Fran'tically.** [Fr. *frénétique*—L. *phreneticus* —Gr. *phrenētikos*, mad, suffering from *phrenītis* or inflammation of the brain—Gr. *phrēn*, the heart, mind. See Frenzy.]

**Fraternal**, fra-ter'nal, *adj.* belonging to a *brother* or *brethren* : becoming brothers.—*adv.* **Frater'-** nally. [Fr.—Low L. *fraternalis*—*frater*, a brother, akin to E. *brother*, Gr. *phratēr*, a clansman : Sans. *bhratri.*]

**Fraternisation**, fra-ter-niz-ā'shun, *n.* the associating as *brethren*.

**Fraternise**, frat'er-nīz, *v.i.* to associate as *brothers* : to seek brotherly fellowship.—*n.* **Frat'erniser.**

**Fraternity**, fra-ter'ni-ti, *n.* the state of being *brethren* : a society formed on a principle of brotherhood. [Fr.—L. *fraternitas.*]

**Fratricide**, frat'ri-sīd, *n.* one who *kills* his *brother* : the murder of a brother.—*adj.* **Frat'ricidal.** [Fr.—L. *frater, fratris*, and *cædo*, to kill.]

**Fraud**, frawd, *n.* deceit : imposture : a deceptive trick. [Fr.—L. *fraus, fraudis*, fraud.]

**Fraudful**, frawd'fool, *adj.* deceptive : treacherous.—*adv.* **Fraud'fully.**

**Fraudless**, frawd'les, *adj.* without fraud.

**Fraudulence**, frawd'ū-lens, **Fraudulency**, frawd'-ū-len-si, *n.* the being dishonest or deceitful.

**Fraudulent**, frawd'ū-lent, *adj.* using, containing, or obtained by *fraud* : dishonest.—*adv.* **Fraud'ulently.** [O. Fr.—L. *fraudulentus.*]

**Fraught**, frawt, *adj.*, *freighted* : *laden* : filled. [Swed. *frakta*, to load ; allied to Dut. *vracht*, a cargo, Ger. *frachten*, to load.]

**Fray**, frā, *n.* an affray.—*v.t.* (*B.*) to frighten. [See Affray.]      [*frayer*—L. *fricare*, to rub.]

**Fray**, frā, *v.t.* to wear off by *rubbing.* [Fr.

**Freak**, frēk, *n.* a sudden caprice or fancy : sport. [A.S. *frec*, bold, rash ; Ger. *frech*, Ice. *frekr.*]

**Freak**, frēk, *v.t.* to spot or streak : to variegate. [From a root found in Ice. *freknur*, Dan. *fregne*, which in pl. = Freckles.]

**Freakish**, frēk'ish, *adj.* apt to change the mind suddenly : capricious —*adv.* **Freak'ishly.**—*n.* **Freak'ishness.** [See Freak, *n.*]

**Freckle**, frek'l, *v.t.* to spot : to colour with spots. —*n.* a yellowish spot on the skin : any small spot.—*adj.* **Freck'ly**, full of freckles. [Dim. of Freak, *v.t.*]

**Free**, frē, *adj.* not bound : at liberty : not under arbitrary government : set at liberty : guiltless : frank : lavish : not attached : exempt (fol. by *from*) : having a franchise (fol. by *of*) : gratuitous : idiomatic, as a translation.—*adv.* **Free'ly.** —*n.* **Free'ness.** [A.S. *freo* ; Ger. *frei*, Ice. *fri.*]

**Free**, frē, *v.t.* to set at liberty : to deliver from what confines : to rid (fol. by *from* or *of*) :— *pr.p.* free'ing ; *pa.p.* freed'.

**Free-agency**, frē-ā'jen-si, *n.* state or power of *acting freely*, or without necessity or constraint upon the will.—*n.* **Free'-a'gent.**

**Freebooter**, frē'boot-er, *n.* one who roves about *freely* in search of *booty* : a plunderer. [See Booty.]

**Freedman**, frēd'man, *n.* a *man* who has been a slave, and has been *freed* or set free.

**Freedom**, frē'dum, *n.* liberty : frankness : separation : privileges connected with a city : improper familiarity : license.

**Free-hand**, frē'-hand, *adj.* applied to drawing by the unguided hand.        [liberal.

**Free-handed**, frē'-hand'ed, *adj.* open-handed :

**Free-hearted**, frē'-härt'ed, *adj.* open-hearted : liberal.

**Freehold**, frē'hōld, *n.* a property *held free* of duty except to the king.—*n.* **Free'holder**, one who possesses a freehold.

**Freeman**, frē'man, *n.* a man who is free or enjoys liberty : one who holds a particular franchise or privilege :—*pl.* **Free'men.**

**Freemason**, frē'mā-sn, *n.* one of an association orig. of *masons* or builders in stone who were *freed* from the laws that regulated common labourers. and now composed of persons united for social enjoyment and mutual assistance —*n.* **Freema'sonry,** the institutions, practices, &c. of freemasons.

**Freestone.** frē'stōn, *n.* stone composed of sand or grit. [So called because it can be *freely* cut ]

**Freethinker,** frē thingk-ėr, *n.* one who professes to be *free* from common modes of *thinking* in religion : one who discards revelation.—*n.* **Free'-thinking,** the habit of mind of a freethinker.

**Free-trade,** frē'-trād, *n.,* *free* or unrestricted *trade :* free interchange of commodities.

**Free-will,** frē'-wil, *n.,* *freedom* of the *will* from restraint : liberty of choice.—*adj* spontaneous.

**Freeze,** frēz, *v.i.* to become ice or like a solid body. —*v.t.* to harden into ice : to cause to shiver, as with terror :—*pr.p.* freez'ing ; *pa.t.* frōze ; *pa p.* frōz'en. [A.S. *freosan ;* Dut. *vriezen,* Ger. *frieren,* to freeze.]

**Freezing-point,** frēz'ing-point, *n.* the temperature at which water freezes, marked 32° on the Fahrenheit thermometer, and 0° on the Centigrade.

**Freight,** frāt, *n.* the lading or cargo, esp. of a ship : the charge for transporting goods by water.—*v.t.* to load a ship.—*n.* **Freight'age,** money paid for freight.—*n.* **Freight'er,** one who freights a vessel. [A late form of *Fraught,* from Fr. *fret*—O. Ger. *freht* (Ger. *fracht*) ]

**French,** frensh, *adj.* belonging to *France* or its people.—*n.* the people or language of France

**Frenzy,** fren'zi, *n.* violent excitement approaching to madness: mania.—*adj.* **Fren'zied, Fren'zical,** partaking of frenzy. [Through Fr. and L., from Late Gr. *phrenēsis* = Gr. *phrenītis,* inflammation of the brain—*phrēn,* the heart, the mind.]

**Frequency,** frē'kwen-si, *n.* repeated occurrence of anything

**Frequent,** frē'kwent. *adj.* coming or occurring often.—*adv.* **Fre'quently.**—*n.* **Fre'quentness.** [L *frequens, frequentis,* allied to the root of **Farce.**]

**Frequent,** frē-kwent', *v.t.* to visit often.—*n.* **Frequent'er.**

**Frequentation,** frē-kwent-ā'shun, *n.* the act of visiting often.

**Frequentative,** frē-kwent'a-tiv, *adj.* (*gram.*) denoting the *frequent* repetition of an action.—*n.* (*gram.*) a verb expressing this repetition.

**Fresco.** fres'kō, *n.* a painting executed on plaster while wet or *fresh.*—*v.t.* to paint in fresco :— *pr.p.* fres'cōing ; *pa.p.* fres cōed. [It. *fresco,* fresh. See **Fresh.**]

**Fresh,** fresh, *adj.* in a state of activity and health : new and strong : recently produced or obtained : untried : having renewed vigour : healthy : not salt.—*adv.* **Fresh'ly.**—*n.* **Fresh'ness.** [A.S. *fersc ;* cog with Dut. *versch,* Ger. *frisch,* O. Ger. *frisg,* from which come Fr. *frais, fraîche,* It. *fresco.*]

**Freshen,** fresh'n, *v.t.* to make *fresh :* to take the saltness from.—*v.i.* to grow fresh : to grow brisk or strong.

**Freshet,** fresh'et, *n.* a pool or stream of fresh water : the sudden overflow of a river from rain or melted snow. [From **Fresh,** with dim. suffix *-et.*]

**Freshman,** fresh'man, *n.* one in the rudiments of knowledge, esp. a university student in his first year.

**Fret,** fret, *v.t.* to wear away by rubbing : to eat into : to vex.—*v.i.* to wear away : to vex one's self : to be peevish :—*pr.p.* frett'ing ; *pa.p.* frett'ed.—*n.* agitation of the surface of a liquid :

irritation : ill-humour. [A.S. *fretan,* to gnaw—*for-,* intensive prefix, and *etan,* to eat.]

**Fret,** fret (*B.*) *pa.p.* of **Fret,** to wear away.

**Fret,** fret, *n.* the *worn* side of the bank of a river. [From **Fret,** to wear away.]

**Fret,** fret, *v.t.* to ornament with raised-work : to variegate :—*pr.p.* frett'ing ; *pa.p.* frett'ed. [A.S. *fraetwian,* Goth. *fratvian,* to adorn.]

**Fret,** fret, *n.* (*lit.*) the interlacing of bars or fillets of *iron :* (*arch.*) an ornament consisting of small fillets intersecting each other at right angles : (*her.*) bars crossed and interlaced.—*adj.* **Frett'ed,** ornamented with frets. [O. Fr. *frete,* a ferrule —It. *ferrata,* the grating of a window—L. *ferrum,* iron.]

**Fret,** fret, *n.* a short wire on the finger-board of a guitar or other instrument.—*v.t.* to furnish with frets. [Prob. the same word as the above.]

**Fretful,** fret'fool, *adj.* ready to fret : peevish.— *adv.* **Fret'fully.**—*n.* **Fret'fulness.**

**Fretting,** fret'ing, *adj., wearing out :* vexing.— *n.* peevishness. [raised-work.

**Fretwork,** fret'wurk, *n.* work adorned with frets :

**Friable,** frī'a-bl, *adj.* apt to *crumble :* easily reduced to powder.—*ns.* **Fri'ableness, Friabil'-ity.** [Fr.—L. *friabilis—frio, friatum,* to crumble.]

**Friar,** frī'ar, *n.* a *brother* or member of certain religious orders in the R. C. Church. [Fr. *frère,* L. *frater,* a brother. See **Brother.**] [*friars.*

**Friary,** frī'ar-i, *n.* a monastery or residence of

**Fribble,** frib'l, *v.i* to *trifle.*—*n* a trifler. [Perh. from Fr. *frivole*—L. *frivolus,* trifling.]

**Fricassee,** frik-as-sē', *n.* a dish made of fowls cut into pieces and cooked in sauce. *v.t.* to dress as a fricassee :—*pr.p.* fricassee'ing ; *pa.p.* fricasseed'. [Fr. *fricassée fricasser,* of which the orig. is unknown ; perh. from *frico, fricare,* to rub.]

**Friction,** frik'shun, *n.* the act of *rubbing :* (*mech.*) the resistance to a body from the surface on which it moves.—*n.pl.* **Fric'tion-wheels,** wheels that lessen friction. [Fr.—L. *frictio—frico, frictum,* to rub ]

**Friday,** frī'dā, *n.* the sixth day of the week. [A.S. *Frigedaeg*—*Frig,* Ice. *Frigg,* the wife of the god Odin, and *daeg,* day.]

**Friend,** frend, *n.* one *loving* or attached to another : an intimate acquaintance ; a favourer : one of a society so called. [A.S. *freond,* pr.p. of *freon,* to love.]

**Friendless,** frend'les. *adj.* without friends : destitute.—*n.* **Friend'lessness.**

**Friendly,** frend'li, *adj.* like a friend : having the disposition of a friend : favourable.—*n.* **Friend'-liness.** [esteem : friendly assistance.

**Friendship,** frend'ship, *n.* attachment from mutual

**Frieze,** frēz, *n.* a coarse woollen cloth with a nap on one side.—*adj.* **Friezed',** having a nap. [Fr. *frise ;* prob. from Dut. *Vriesland,* Friesland, whence the cloth came ]

**Frieze,** frēz, *n.* (*arch.*) the part of the entablature of a column between the architrave and cornice, often ornamented with figures. [Fr. ; of dub. origin.]

**Frigate,** frig'āt, *n.* a quick-sailing ship-of-war of second-rate power. [Fr. *frégate*—It. *fregata ;* of dub origin.]

**Frigate-bird,** frig'āt-bėrd, *n.* a large tropical seabird, with very long wings, prob. named from its *rapid flight.*

**Frigatoon,** frig-a-tōōn', *n.* a small Venetian vessel.

**Fright,** frīt, *n.* sudden fear : terror. [A.S. *fyrhtu,* akin to Ger. *furcht,* fear.]

**Fright**, frīt, **Frighten**, frīt'n, *v.t.* to make afraid : to alarm.

**Frightful**, frīt'fool, *adj.* full of what causes fear : terrible : shocking.—*adv.* **Fright'fully.**—*n.* **Fright'fulness.**

**Frigid**, frij'id, *adj.* frozen or stiffened with *cold* : cold : without spirit or feeling : unanimated. —*adv.* **Frig'idly.**—*n.* **Frig'idness.** [L. *frigidus* —*frigeo,* to be cold—*frigus,* cold ; akin to Gr. *rhigos,* cold. See Freeze.]

**Frigidity**, frij-id'i-ti, *n.* coldness : coldness of affection : want of animation.

**Frigorific**, frig-or-if'ik, *adj.,* *causing cold.* [L. *frigus, frigoris,* cold, and *facio,* to cause.]

**Frill**, fril, *v.i.* to ruffle, as a hawk its feathers, when *shivering*—*v.t.* to furnish with a frill. [O. Fr. *friller,* to shiver—O. Fr. *frilleux,* chilly —L. *frigidulus,* somewhat cold—*frigidus.* See Frigid.] [of linen.

**Frill**, fril, *n.* a ruffle : a ruffled or crimped edging

**Fringe**, frinj, *n.,* *loose threads* forming a border : the extremity.—*v.t.* to adorn with fringe : to border.—*adj.* **Fringe'less.** [Fr. *frange* (cf. Wal. *frimbie, fimbrie*)—L. *fimbria,* threads, fibres, akin to *fibra,* a fibre.]

**Fringy**, frinj'i, *adj.* ornamented with *fringes.*

**Frippery**, frip'er-i, *n.,* *worn-out* clothes : the place where old clothes are sold : useless trifles. [Fr. *friperie*—*friper,* to wear ; of doubtful origin.]

**Frisk**, frisk, *v.i.* to gambol : to leap playfully.— *n.* a frolic.—*n.* **Frisk'er.** [O. Fr. *frisque* ; Low L. *friscus*—root of Ger. *frisch.* See Fresh.]

**Frisket**, frisk'et, *n.* (*print.*) the light frame which holds a sheet of paper before it is laid on the form for impression, so called from the *quickness* of its motion. [Fr. *frisquette*—O. Fr. *frisque.*]

**Frisky**, frisk'i, *adj.* lively : jumping with gaiety : frolicsome.—*adv.* **Frisk'ily.**—*n.* **Frisk'iness.**

**Frith**, frith, **Firth**, fẽrth, *n.* a narrow inlet of the sea, esp. at the mouth of a river. [From Ice. *fiörthr*; cf. Dan. and Norw. *fiord* ; conn. with *fare* and *ford,* L. *portus,* Gr. *porthmos.*]

**Fritter**, frit'ẽr, *n.* a piece of meat *fried* : a kind of pancake : a fragment.—*v.t.* to break into fragments : to waste away by degrees. [Fr. *friture* —*frire,* to fry—L. *frigere, frictum,* to fry.]

**Frivolity**, fri-vol'i-ti, *n.* acts or habits of trifling : levity.

**Frivolous**, friv'ol-us, *adj.* trifling : slight : silly. —*adv.* **Friv'olously.**—*n.* **Friv'olousness.** [L. *frivolus,* which orig. seems to have meant *rubbed away*—L. *friare, fricare,* to rub.]

**Frizz** or **Friz**, friz, *v.t.* to *curl* : to render rough and tangled.—*n.* a curl. [Fr. *friser,* to curl ; perh. from root of **Frieze,** the cloth, and so meaning to raise the nap on cloth.]

**Frizzle**, friz'l, *v.t.* to form in small short curls. [Dim. of Frizz.]

**Fro**, frō, *adv., from* : back or backward. [A shortened form of *from*; but perh. directly derived from Ice. *fra,* from.]

**Frock**, frok, *n.* a monk's cowl : a loose upper garment worn by men : a gown worn by females. [Fr. *froc,* a monk's cowl—Low L. *frocus*—L. *floccus,* a flock of wool ; or more prob. (acc. to Brachet and Littré) from Low L. *hrocus*—O. Ger. *hroch* (Ger. *rock*), a coat.]

**Frocked**, frokt, *adj.* clothed in a frock.

**Frog**, frog, *n.* an ornamental fastening or tasselled button for a *frock* or cloak. [From root of Frock.]

**Frog**, frog, *n.* an amphibious reptile, with webbed feet, remarkable for its rapid swimming and leaping : a soft, horny substance, in the middle of a horse's foot, so called from its likeness to the leg of a frog. [A.S. *froga, frosc* ; cog. with Ice. *froskr*; Ger. *frosch,* Dan. *frö.*]

**Frolic**, frol'ik, *adj.* merry : pranky.—*n.* gaiety : a wild prank : a merry-making.—*v.i.* to play wild pranks or merry tricks : to gambol :—*pr.p.* frol'icking ; *pa.p.* frol'icked. [Dut. *vrolijk,* merry, from a root preserved in Ger. *froh,* and suffix *-lijk* (= E. *like, ly*) ; cf. Ger. *fröhlich,* joyful, gay.]

**Frolicsome**, frol'ik-sum, *adj.* gay : sportive.—*n.* **Frol'icsomeness.**

**From**, from, *prep., forth* : out of, as from a source : away : at a distance : springing out of : by reason of. [A.S. ; akin to Goth. *fram,* Ice. *fram* and *fra,* Dan. *frem,* forth, forwards.]

**Frond**, frond, *n.* a *leafy* branch or stalk, esp. the fern. [L. *frons, frondis,* a leaf.]

**Frondescence**, fron-des'ens, *n.* act of putting forth *leaves* : the season for putting forth leaves. [L. *frondescens*—*frondesco,* to grow leafy.]

**Frondiferous**, fron-dif'ẽr-us, *adj., bearing* or producing *fronds.* [L. *frons,* and *fero,* to bear.]

**Front**, frunt, *n.* the *forehead* : the whole face : the forepart of anything : the most conspicuous part : boldness : impudence.—**In front of,** before.—*adj.* of, relating to, or in the front.—*v.t.* to stand in front of or opposite : to oppose face to face.— *v.i.* to stand in front or foremost : to turn the front or face in any direction. [Fr.—L. *frons, frontis,* the forehead ; allied to Brow.]

**Frontage**, frunt'āj, *n.* the *front* part of a building.

**Frontal**, front'al, *adj.* of or belonging to the *front* or forehead.—*n.* a front-piece : something worn on the forehead or face : (*arch.*) a pediment over a door or window. [Fr.—L. *frontale*— *frons,* a front ornament for horses.]

**Fronted**, frunt'ed, *adj.* formed with a *front.*

**Frontier**, front'ēr, *n.* that part of a country which *fronts* another : the boundary of a territory.— *adj.* lying on the frontier : bordering. [Fr. *frontière,* from L. *frons.*]

**Frontispiece**, front'i-spēs, *n.* the principal front or face of a building : a figure or engraving in front of a book. [Fr.—Low L. *frontispicium*— *frons,* and *specio,* to see ; not conn. with Piece.]

**Frontless**, frunt'les, *adj.* void of shame or modesty.

**Frontlet**, frunt'let, *n.* a *little* band worn on the *front* or forehead. [Dim. of Front.]

**Frost**, frost, *n.* the state of the atmosphere in which water *freezes* : frozen dew, also called *hoar-frost.*—*v.t.* to cover with anything resembling hoar-frost. [A.S. *forst*—*freosan* ; cf. Ger. *frost,* Goth. *frius.*]

**Frost-bite**, frost'-bīt, *n.* the freezing or depression of vitality in a part of the body by exposure to cold. [by frost.

**Frost-bitten**, frost'-bit'n, *adj.* bitten or affected

**Frost-bound**, frost'-bownd, *adj.* bound or confined by frost.

**Frosting**, frost'ing, *n.* the composition, resembling hoar-*frost,* used to cover cake, &c.

**Frost-nail**, frost'-nāl, *n.* a *nail* driven into a horseshoe to prevent the horse from slipping on *ice.*

**Frost-work**, frost'-wurk, *n., work* resembling hoar-*frost* on shrubs.

**Frosty**, frost'i, *adj.* producing or containing *frost* : chill in affection : frost-like.—*adv.* **Frost'ily.**— *n.* **Frost'iness.**

**Froth**, froth, *n.* the foam on liquids caused by boiling, or any agitation : fig., an empty show in speech : any light matter.—*v.t.* to cause froth on.—*v.i.* to throw up froth. [Scand., as in Ice. *fraud, froda,* Dan. *fraade,* Swed. *fragda.*]

**Frothy,** froth'i, *adj.* full of *froth* or foam : empty : unsubstantial.—*adv.* **Froth'ily.**—*n.* **Froth'iness.**

**Frounce,** frowns, *v.i.* (*obs.*) to frown or wrinkle the *brow.*—*v.t.* to plait : to curl : to wrinkle up : to frown.—*n.* a plait or curl. [Fr. *froncer*—L. *frons, frontis,* the brow. See **Flounce,** *n.,* of which it is an older form.]

**Froward,** frō'ward, *adj.* self-willed : perverse : unreasonable :—opp. to **Toward.**—*adv.* **Fro'wardly.**—*n.* **Fro'wardness.** [Scand. Eng. for A.S. *from,* away, averse, and affix *-ward.*]

**Frown,** frown, *v.i.* to wrinkle the brow, as in anger : to look angry.—*v.t.* to repel by a frown.—*n.* a wrinkling or contraction of the brow in displeasure, &c. : a stern look.—*adv.* **Frown'ingly.** [From a Fr. *frogner* in *se refrogner,* to knit the brow ; orig. unknown.]

**Frowsy,** frow'si, *adj.* fetid : ill-scented : dingy.

**Frozen,** frōz'n, *pa.p.* of **Freeze.**

**Fructescence,** fruk-tes'ens, *n.* the time for the ripening of *fruit.* [Fr., from L. *fructesco,* to bear fruit—*fructus,* fruit.]

**Fructiferous,** fruk-tif'er-us, *adj.,* bearing *fruit.* [L. *fructifer*—*fructus,* and *fero,* to bear.]

**Fructification,** fruk-ti-fi-kā'shun, *n.* act of *fructifying,* or producing fruit : (*bot.*) all the parts that compose the flower and fruit.

**Fructify,** fruk'ti-fī, *v.t.* to make *fruitful* : to fertilise.—*v.i.* to bear fruit. [L. *fructifico*—*fructus,* and *facio,* to make.]

**Frugal,** frōō'gal, *adj.* economical in the use of means : thrifty.—*adv.* **Fru'gally.** [Fr.—L. *frugalis*—*frugi,* temperate, fit for food—*frux, frugis,* fruit.]                      [thrift.

**Frugality,** frōō-gal'i-ti, *n.* prudent economy :

**Frugiferous,** frōō-jif'er-us, *adj.,* fruit-bearing. [L. *frux, frugis,* fruit, and *fero,* to bear.]

**Frugivorous,** frōō-jiv'o-rus, *adj.,* feeding on fruits or seeds. [L. *frux, frugis,* and *voro,* to eat.]

**Fruit,** frōōt, *n.* the produce of the earth, which supplies the wants of men and animals : the part of a plant which contains the seed : the offspring of animals : product, consequence, effect, advantage. [O. Fr. *fruict,* Fr. *fruit*—L. *fructus,* from *fruor, fructus,* to enjoy.]

**Fruitage,** frōōt'āj, *n., fruit* collectively : fruits.

**Fruiterer,** frōōt'er-ėr, *n.* one who deals in *fruit.*

**Fruitery,** frōōt'er-i, *n.* a place for storing *fruit* : fruitage.

**Fruitful,** frōōt'fool, *adj.* producing fruit abundantly : productive.—*adv.* **Fruit'fully.**—*n.* **Fruit'fulness.**

**Fruition,** frōō-ish'un, *n., enjoyment* : use or possession of anything, esp. accompanied with pleasure. [O. Fr. *fruition,* from L. *fruor,* to enjoy.]

**Fruitless,** frōōt'les, *adj.* barren : without profit : useless.—*adv.* **Fruit'lessly.**—*n.* **Fruit'lessness.**

**Frumentaceous,** frōō-men-tā'shus, *adj.* made of or resembling wheat or other grain. [L. *frumentaceus*—*frumentum,* for *frugimentum,* corn—*frux, frugis,* fruit.]

**Frumenty,** frōō'men-ti, **Furmenty,** fur'men-ti, *n.* food made of wheat boiled in milk. [O. Fr. *froumenté,* wheat boiled—*froument*—L. *frumentum.*]

**Frush,** frush, *n.* the *frog* of a horse's foot : a disease in that part of a horse's foot. [Ger. *frosch.* See **Frog,** a reptile.]

**Frustrate,** frus'trāt, *v.t.* to make *vain* or *of no effect* : to bring to nothing : to defeat. [L. *frustro, frustratus*—*frustra,* without effect, in vain.]

**Frustrate,** frus'trāt (*obs.*) *pa.p.* of **Frustrate.**

**Frustration,** frus-trā'shun, *n.* disappointment : defeat. [L. *frustratio.*]

**Frustum,** frus'tum, *n.* a *piece* or slice of a solid body : the part of a cone, which remains when the top is cut off by a plane parallel to the base. [L. *frustum,* a piece, a bit.]

**Frutescent,** frōō-tes'ent, *adj.* becoming *shrubby,* or like a shrub. [L. *frutex, fruticis,* a shrub.]

**Fruticose,** frōō'ti-kōs, **Fruticous,** frōō'ti-kus, *adj., shrub-like* : shrubby. [L. *fruticosus*—*frutex.*]

**Fry,** frī, *v.t.* to dress food with oil or fat in a pan over the fire :—*pr.p.* fry'ing ; *pa.p.* fried.—*v.i.* to undergo the action of heat in a frying-pan : to simmer.—*n.* a dish of anything fried. [Fr. *frire*—L. *frigo ;* cf. Gr. *phrygō,* Sans. *bhrij,* to fry.]

**Fry,** frī, *n.* a swarm of fishes just spawned : a number of small things. [Fr. *frai, frayer,* act of fertilising in fishes, from L. *fricare,* to rub ; but cf. Goth. *fraiv,* Ice. *frio,* seed, egg.]

**Fuchsia,** fū'shi-a, *n.* a plant with long pendulous red flowers, originally natives of S. America. [Named after *Leonard Fuchs,* a German botanist of the 16th century.]

**Fudge,** fuj, *int.* stuff : nonsense : an exclamation of contempt. [From the sound ; cf. Prov. Fr. *fuche,* Ger. *futsch.*]

**Fuel,** fū'el, *n.* anything that feeds a *fire* : whatever supports heat, excitement, or energy. [O. Fr. *fouaille*—Low L. *foallia,* fuel—Low L. *focale*—L. *focus,* a fireplace.]

**Fugacious,** fū-gā'shus, *adj.* apt to *flee away* : fleeting.—*ns.* **Fuga'ciousness, Fugac'ity.** [L. *fugax, fugacis,* from *fugio* ; Gr. *pheugō,* to flee, Sans. *bhuj,* to bend.]

**Fugitive,** fūj'i-tiv, *adj.* apt to *flee away* : uncertain : volatile : perishable : temporary.—*n.* one who flees or has fled from his station or country : one hard to be caught.—*adv.* **Fug'itively.**—*n.* **Fug'itiveness.** [Fr.—L. *fugitivus,* from *fugio,* to flee.]

**Fugleman,** fū'gl-man, *n.* (*lit.*) a *wing-man,* a soldier who stands before a company at drill as an example. [Ger. *flügelmann,* the leader of a wing or file—*flügel,* a wing.]

**Fugue,** fūg, *n.* (*mus.*) a composition in which the parts *follow* or *pursue* one another at certain distances. [Fr.—It. *fuga,* from L. *fuga,* flight.]

**Fuguist,** fūg'ist, *n.* one who writes or plays *fugues.*

**Fulcrum,** ful'krum, *n.* (*mech.*) the *prop* or fixed point on which a lever moves : a prop :—*pl.* **Ful'cra** or **Ful'crums.** [L. *fulcrum,* a prop, from *fulcio,* to prop.]

**Fulfil,** fool-fil', *v.t.* to complete : to accomplish : to carry into effect :—*pr.p.* fulfill'ing ; *pa.p.* fulfilled'.—*n.* **Fulfill'er.**

**Fulfilment,** fool-fil'ment, *n.* full performance : completion : accomplishment.

**Fulgent,** ful'jent, *adj., shining* : bright : dazzling.—*adv.* **Ful'gently.**—*n.* **Ful'gency.** [L. *fulgens, -entis,* pr.p. of *fulgeo,* to flash, to shine.]

**Fuliginous,** fū-lij'i-nus, *adj.* sooty : smoky. [L. *fuliginosus*—*fuligo,* soot.]

**Full,** fool, *adj.* having all it can contain : having no empty space : abundantly supplied or furnished : abounding : containing the whole matter : complete : perfect : strong : clear.—*n.* complete measure : highest degree : the whole : time of full-moon.—*n.* **Full'ness** or **Ful'ness.** [A.S. *full ;* Goth. *fulls,* Ice. *fullr,* Ger. *voll,* L. *plenus,* Gr. *pleos.* See **Fill.**]

**Full,** fool, *adv.* quite to the same degree : with the whole effect : completely.

**Full,** fool, *v.t.* (*obs.*) to bleach or whiten cloth.—*n.* **Full'er,** a bleacher or cleanser of cloth.

[Through A.S. *fullian*, to whiten as a fuller, from L. *fullo*, a fuller.]

**Full**, fool, *v.t.* to press or pound cloth in a mill : to scour and thicken in a mill.—*n.* **Full'er.** [Through Fr. *fouler*, to full or thicken cloth, from L. *fullo*, a cloth-fuller.]

**Full-blown,** fool'-blōn, *adj.* blown or fully expanded, as a flower.

**Full-bottomed,** fool'-bot'umd, *adj.* having a full or large bottom, as a wig.

**Fuller's-earth,** fool'erz-ėrth, *n.* a soft *earth* or clay, capable of absorbing grease, used in *fulling* or bleaching cloth.

**Full-faced,** fool'-fāst, *adj.* having a full or broad face.

**Full-hearted,** fool'-härt'ed, *adj.* full of heart or courage : elated.

**Full-orbed,** fool'-orbd, *adj.* having the orb or disc fully illuminated, as the full-moon : round.

**Fully,** fool'li, *adv.* completely : entirely.

**Fulmar,** ful'mar, *n.* a species of petrel inhabiting the Shetland Isles and other northern regions, valuable for its down, feathers, and oil. [Named from the *foul* smell of its oil. See **Foumart.**]

**Fulminate,** ful'min-āt, *v.i.* to thunder or make a loud noise : to issue decrees with violence.—*v.t.* to cause to explode : to send forth, as a denunciation. [Lit. to hurl *lightning*, L. *fulmino*, *fulminatus*—*fulmen* (for *fulgimen*), lightning—*fulgeo*, to shine.]

**Fulminate,** ful'min-āt, *n.* a compound of fulminic acid with mercury, &c.

**Fulmination,** ful-min-ā'shun, *n.* act of fulminating, thundering, or issuing forth : a chemical explosion : a denunciation.

**Fulminic,** ful-min'ik, *adj.* pertaining to an acid used in preparing explosive compounds.

**Fulsome,** ful'sum, *adj.* cloying : nauseous : offensive : gross : disgustingly fawning.—*adv.* **Ful'somely.**—*n.* **Ful'someness.** [A.S. *ful*, full, in the sense of producing satiety, and then disgust, and affix -*some*.]

**Fulvous,** ful'vus, **Fulvid,** ful'vid, *adj.* deep or dull yellow : tawny. [L. *fulvus*, deep yellow, tawny.]

**Fumarole,** fūm'a-rōl, *n.* a *smoke*-hole in a volcano or sulphur-mine. [It. *fumarola*—L. *fumus*.]

**Fumble,** fum'bl, *v.i.* to grope about awkwardly : to do anything awkwardly : to handle much.—*v.t.* to manage awkwardly.—*n.* **Fum'bler.** [From Dut. *fommelen*, to fumble or grabble ; cf. Dan. *famle*, Ice. *falma*, to grope about ; all come from the root of A.S. *folm*, the palm of the hand. Cf. **Palm.**]

**Fume,** fūm, *n.*, *smoke* or vapour : any volatile matter : heat of mind, rage : anything unsubstantial, vain conceit.—*v.i.* to smoke : to throw off vapour : to be in a rage. [Fr.—L. *fumus*, smoke, from root *dhū*, to blow, whence **Dust.**]

**Fumiferous,** fūm-if'ėr-us, *adj.* producing *fumes* or smoke. [L. *fumifer*—*fumus*, and *fero*, to bear, to produce.]

**Fumigate,** fūm'i-gāt, *v.t.* to expose to *smoke* or gas, esp. for disinfecting : to perfume. [L. *fumigo*, *fumigatus*—*fumus*, and -*ig* = -*ag*, the base of *ago*, to drive.]

**Fumigation,** fūm-i-gā'shun, *n.* act of fumigating or of applying purifying smoke, &c. to.

**Fumitory,** fūm'i-to-ri, *n.* a plant of a disagreeable smell. [O Fr. *fume-terre*, earth-smoke—L. *fumus*, smoke, and *terra*, earth.]

**Fumous,** fūm'us, **Fumy,** fūm'i, *adj.* producing *fumes.*

**Fun,** fun, *n.* merriment : sport. [Ety. dub. ; not

an old word ; acc. to Skeat, prob. imported from the Irish, in which occurs *fonn*, delight.]

**Funambulate,** fū-nam'bū-lāt, *v.i.* to *walk* or dance on a *rope*.—*n.* **Funambula'tion.** [Sp.—L. *funis*, a rope, and *ambulo*, to walk. See **Amble.**]

**Funambulist,** fū-nam'bū-list, *n.* a *rope*-dancer.

**Function,** fungk'shun, *n.* the *doing* of a thing : duty peculiar to any office or profession : the peculiar office of any part of the body or mind : power : (*math.*) a quantity so connected with another that any change in the one changes the other. [O. Fr.—L. *functio*, from *fungor*, *functus*, to perform.]

**Functional,** fungk'shun-al, *adj.* pertaining to or performed by *functions* :—opp. to **Organic** or **Structural.**—*adv.* **Func'tionally.**

**Functionary,** fungk'shun-ar-i, *n.* one who discharges any *function* or duty : one who holds an office.

**Fund,** fund, *n.* a sum of money on which some enterprise is founded or expense supported : a supply or source of money : a store laid up : supply :—*pl.* permanent debts due by a government and paying interest.—*v.t.* to form a debt into a stock charged with interest : to place money in a fund. [Fr. *fond*, from L. *fundus*, the bottom. See **Found,** to lay the *bottom* of.]

**Fundament,** fund'a-ment, *n.* the lower part or seat of the body. [Fr.—L. *fundamentum*, from *fundus.*]

**Fundamental,** fun-da-ment'al, *adj.* pertaining to or serving for the foundation : essential : important.—*n.* that which serves as a foundation or groundwork : an essential.—*adv.* **Fundamentally.**

**Funeral,** fū'nėr-al, *n.*, *burial* : the ceremony, &c. connected with burial.—*adj.* pertaining to or used at a burial. [Low L. *funeralis*—L. *funus*, *funeris*, a funeral procession.]

**Funereal,** fū-nē're-al, *adj.* pertaining to or suiting a *funeral* : dismal : mournful. [L. *funereus.*]

**Fungoid,** fung'goid, *adj.* resembling a *mushroom.* [L. *fungus*, and Gr. *eidos*, appearance.]

**Fungous,** fung'gus, *adj.* of or like *fungus* : soft : spongy : growing suddenly : ephemeral.

**Fungus,** fung'gus, *n.* (*lit.*) a *spongy* plant : an order of plants including *mushrooms*, toadstools, mould, &c. : proud-flesh formed on wounds :—*pl.* **Fungi,** fun'jī, or **Funguses,** fung'gus-ez. [L. *fungus*, a mushroom—Gr. *sphonggos*, *sponggos*, a sponge.]

**Funicle,** fū'ni-kl, *n.* a small *cord* or ligature : a fibre. [L. *funiculus*, dim. of *funis*, a cord or rope.]        [*funicle.*

**Funicular,** fū-nik'ū-lar, *adj.* consisting of a

**Funnel,** fun'el, *n.* a tube or passage for the escape of smoke, &c. : an instrument for pouring fluids into close vessels, as bottles, &c. [Ety. dub. ; perh. from W. *ffynel*, air-hole—*ffwn*, breath ; or from L. *in-fundibulum*—*fundo*, to pour.] [**Ily.**

**Funny,** fun'i, *adj.* full of fun : droll.—*adv.* **Funn'-**

**Fur,** fur, *n.* the short fine hair of certain animals : their skins with the fur prepared for garments : a fur-like coating on the tongue, the interior of boilers, &c.—*v.t.* to line with fur : to cover with morbid fur-like matter :—*pr.p.* furr'ing ; *pa.p.* furred'. [O. Fr. *fourre*, Fr. *fourreau* (cf. Sp. *forro*, It. *fodero*, lining)—Teut. root found in Goth. *fodr.* Ger. *futter*, a case or sheath.]

**Furbelow,** fur'be-lō, *n.* (*lit.*) a *plait* or *flounce* : the fringed border of a gown or petticoat. [Fr., It., and Sp. *falbala*, of unknown origin. The word simulates an English form—*fur-below.*]

**Furbish,** fur′bish, *v.t.* to *purify* or polish: to *rub* up until bright. [Fr. *fourbir*—O. Ger. *furban,* to purify.]

**Furcate,** fur′kāt, *adj. forked:* branching like the prongs of a fork. [L., from *furca,* a fork.]

**Furcation,** fur-kā′shun, *n.* a *forking* or branching out.

**Furfuraceous,** fur-fū-rā′shus, *adj., branny:* scaly: scurfy. [L. *furfuraceus*—*furfur,* bran.]

**Furious,** fū′ri-us, *adj.* full of fury: violent.—*adv.* **Fu′riously.**—*n.* **Fu′riousness.** [Fr. *furieux*—L. *furiosus*—*furia,* rage. See **Fury.**]

**Furl,** furl, *v.t.* to draw or roll up, as a sail. [Contr. of obs. *furdle,* from **Fardel,** *n.*]

**Furlong,** fur′long, *n.* 40 poles: one ⅛th of a mile. [A.S. *furlang,* lit. the 'length of a furrow'—*furh,* furrow, *lang,* long.]

**Furlough,** fur′lō, *n., leave* of absence.—*v.t.* to grant leave of absence. [From Dut. *verlof,* where *ver* = E. *for-,* intensive, and *lof* = E. *leave;* cog. Ger. *verlaub*—root of *erlauben,* to give leave to.]

**Furmenty.** See **Frumenty.**

**Furnace,** fur′nās, *n.* an *oven* or inclosed fireplace for melting ores and other purposes: a time or place of grievous affliction or torment. [Fr. *fournaise*—L. *fornax*—*furnus,* an oven.]

**Furnish,** fur′nish, *v.t.* to *fit up* or supply *completely,* or with what is necessary: to equip.—*n.* **Fur′nisher.** [Fr. *fournir*—O. Ger. *frumjan,* to do, to perfect.]

**Furniture,** fur′ni-tūr, *n.* movables either for use or ornament, with which a house is equipped: equipage: decorations. [Fr. *fourniture.*]

**Furrier,** fur′i-ėr, *n.* a dealer in *furs* and fur-goods.

**Furriery,** fur′i-ėr-i, *n., furs* in general: trade in furs.

**Furrow,** fur′ō, *n.* the trench made by a plough: any trench or groove: a wrinkle on the face.—*v.t.* to form furrows in: to groove: to wrinkle. [A.S. *furh;* cog. with Ger. *furche;* and cf. L. *porca,* a sow, a ridge.]

**Furry,** fur′i, *adj.* consisting of, covered with, or dressed in *fur.*

**Further,** fur′thėr, *adv.* to a greater distance or degree: in addition.—*adj.* more distant: additional. [A.S. *furthur,* either a comp. of *furth* (= forth), or more prob. of *fore,* with comp. suffix *-thor* or *-thur,* which corresponds to Goth. *-thar* = Gr. *-ter* (in *proteros*) = Sans. *-tara.* Cf. **After.**]

**Further,** fur′thėr, *v.t.* to help *forward,* promote. [A.S. *fyrthran.*]

**Furtherance,** fur′thėr-ans, *n.* a helping forward.

**Furthermore,** fur′thėr-mōr, *adv.* in addition to what has been said, moreover, besides.

**Furthermost,** fur′thėr-mōst, *adj., most further:* most remote.

**Furthest,** fur′thest, *adv.* at the greatest distance.—*adj.* most distant. [A superl. either of *furth* (= forth), or more prob. of *fore.* See **Further.**]

**Furtive,** fur′tiv, *adj.* stealthy: secret.—*adv.* **Fur′tively.** [Fr.—L. *furtivus*—*fur,* a thief.]

**Fury,** fū′ri, *n., rage:* violent passion: madness: *(myth.)* one of the three goddesses of vengeance: hence, a passionate, violent woman. [Fr. *furie*—L. *furia*—*furo,* to be angry.]

**Furze,** furz, *n.* the whin or gorse, a prickly evergreen bush with beautiful yellow flowers, so called from the likeness of its spines to those of the *fir*-tree. [A.S. *fyrs;* cog. with Gael. *preas,* a brier.]

**Furzy,** furz′i, *adj.* overgrown with *furze.*

**Fuscous,** fus′kus, *adj.* brown: dingy. [L. *fuscus,* akin to *furvus* (for *fus-vus*).]

**Fuse,** fūz, *v.t.* to *melt:* to liquefy by heat.—*v.i.* to be melted: to be reduced to a liquid. [L. *fundo, fusum,* to melt.]

**Fuse,** fūz, *n.* a tube filled with *combustible* matter for firing mines, discharging shells, &c. [A corr. of **Fusil.**]

**Fusee,** fū-zē′, *n.* a match or cigar light: a fuse: a fusil.

**Fusee,** fū-zē′, *n.* the *spindle* in a watch or clock on which the chain is wound. [Fr. *fusée,* a spindleful, from L. *fusus,* a spindle.]

**Fusel-oil,** fū′zel-oil, *n.* a nauseous oil in spirits distilled from potatoes, barley, &c. [Ger. *fusel,* bad spirits.]              [—*n.* **Fusibil′ity.**

**Fusible,** fūz′i-bl, *adj.* that may be *fused* or melted.

**Fusil,** fūz′il, *n.* a light *musket* or firelock. [Fr. *fusil,* a flint, musket, same as It. *focile*—Low L. *focile,* steel (to strike fire with), dim. of *focus,* a fireplace.]

**Fusilade,** fūz′il-ād, *n.* a simultaneous discharge of *firearms.*—*v.t.* to shoot down by a simultaneous discharge of firearms. [Fr.—*fusil,* a musket.]

**Fusilier, Fusileer,** fū-zil-ēr′, *n.* (*orig.*) a soldier armed with a *fusil,* but now armed like other infantry.

**Fusing-point,** fūz′ing-point, *n.* the temperature at which any solid substance is *fused*—that is, becomes liquid.

**Fusion,** fū′zhun, *n.* act of melting: the state of fluidity from heat: a close union of things, as if melted together.

**Fuss,** fus, *n.* a bustle or tumult: haste, flurry.—*adj.* **Fuss′y.**—*adv.* **Fuss′ily.** [A.S. *fus,* ready, prompt to find—*fundian,* to strive after—*findan,* to find.]

**Fustet,** fus′tet, *n.* the wood of the Venice sumach: a dyestuff. [Fr. *fustet,* dim. of O. Fr. *fust*—L. *fustis,* a stick, in Low L. a tree.]

**Fustian,** fust′yan, *n.* a kind of coarse, twilled cotton cloth: a pompous and unnatural style of writing or speaking: bombast.—*adj.* made of fustian: bombastic. [O. Fr. *fustaine,* Fr. *futaine*—It. *fustagno*—Low L. *fustaneum,* from Fostat (a suburb of Cairo) in Egypt, where first made.]

**Fustic,** fus′tik, *n.* the wood of a W. Indian tree, used as a dyestuff. [Fr. *fustoc*—L. *fustis.*]

**Fustigation,** fus-ti-gā′shun, *n.* a beating with a *stick.* [L. *fustigo, fustigatus,* to beat with a stick—*fustis,* a stick.]

**Fusty,** fust′i, *adj.* (*lit.*) smelling of the *wood* of the cask, as wine: ill-smelling.—*n.* **Fust′iness.** [O. Fr. *fust,* wood or a cask—L. *fustis.*]

**Futile,** fū′til, *adj.* useless: unavailing: trifling.—*adv.* **Fu′tilely.** [Fr.—L. *futilis*—*fud,* root of *fundo,* to pour.]

**Futility,** fū-til′i-ti, *n.* uselessness.

**Futtocks,** fut′uks, *n.pl.* a curved timber forming part of one of the ribs of a ship. [Perh. corrupted from *foot-hooks.*]

**Future,** fūt′ūr, *adj., about to be:* that is to come: (*gram.*) expressing what will be.—*n.* time to come. [L. *futurus,* fut. p. of *esse,* to be.]

**Futurity,** fūt-ūr′i-ti, *n.* time *to come:* an event or state of being yet to come.

**Fuzz,** fuz, *v.i.* to fly off in minute particles with a *fizzing* sound like water from hot iron.—*n.* fine light particles, as dust.—*n.* **Fuzz′ball,** a kind of fungus, whose head is full of a fine dust. [Akin to **Fizz;** Ger. *pfuschen,* to fizz.]

**Fȳ,** fī, *int.* Same as **Fie.**

# G

**Gabardine, Gaberdine,** gab-ar-dēn' or gab'ar-din, *n.* a coarse frock or loose upper garment : a mean dress. [Sp. *gabardina*—Sp. *gaban,* a kind of greatcoat, of which ety. dub.]

**Gabble,** gab'l, *v.i.* to talk inarticulately : to chatter : to cackle like geese.—*ns.* **Gabb'ler, Gabb'ling.** [Prob. from Ice. *gabba ;* cf. Fr. *gaber,* Dut. *gabberen,* to joke, and many other forms, which are all imitative.]

**Gabion,** gā'bi-un, *n. (fort.)* a bottomless basket of wicker-work filled with earth, used for shelter from the enemy's fire. [Fr.—It. *gabbione,* a large cage—*gabbia*—L. *cavea,* a hollow place—*cavus,* hollow.]                    [thrown up as a defence.

**Gabionnade,** gā-bi-un-ād', *n.* a line of *gabions*

**Gable,** gā'bl, *n. (arch.)* the triangular part of an exterior wall of a building between the top of the side-walls and the slopes of the roof. [Perh. of Celt. origin, as in Ir. *gabhal,* a fork or gable ; cf. Ger. *giebel,* a gable, *gabel,* a fork.]

**Gablet,** gā'blet, *n.* a *small gable* or canopy.

**Gaby,** gā'bi, *n.* a simpleton. [From a Scand. root seen in Ice. *gapi—gapa,* to gape. See **Gape.**]

**Gad,** gad, *n.* a wedge of steel : a graver : a rod or stick. [Prob. from Scand. *gaddr,* a goad, and cog. with A.S. *gad,* a goad.]

**Gad,** gad, *v.i.* to rove about restlessly, like cattle stung by the *gadfly :—pr.p.* gadd'ing ; *pa.p.* gadd'ed.

**Gadfly,** gad'flī, *n.* a fly which pierces the skin of cattle in order to deposit its eggs. [From **Gad,** *n.* and **Fly.**]

**Gaelic,** gā'lik, *adj.* pertaining to the *Gaels* or Scottish Highlanders.—*n.* the northern or *Ga-dhelic* branch of the Celtic family of languages, embracing the Irish, the Highland-Scottish, and the **Manx:** (more commonly) the Highland-Scottish dialect. [Prob. originally a Celtic word, of which the Latinised form is *Gallus.* The O. Ger. word *walh* or *walah* (E. *Welsh*), applied by the Teutons to their neighbours, is not found till the 8th cent., and is merely a form of L. *Gallus,* a Gaul, a stranger or foreigner. See **Welsh.**]

**Gaff,** gaf, *n.* a boat-hook or fishing-spear : a kind of boom or yard. [Fr. *gaffe,* from a Celt. root found in Irish *gaf,* a hook—root *gabh,* to take ; allied to L. *capio,* E. **Have.**]

**Gaffer,** gaf'èr, *n. (orig.)* a word of respect applied to an old man, now expressive of familiarity or contempt. [Contr. of *gramfer,* the West of England form of **Grandfather.** See **Gammer.**]

**Gag,** gag, *v.t.* to forcibly stop the mouth : to silence :—*pr.p.* gagg'ing ; *pa.p.* gagged'.—*n.* something thrust into the mouth or put over it to enforce silence. [Ety. dub. ; prob. imitative.]

**Gage,** gāj, *n.* a *pledge* : security for the fulfilment of a promise : something thrown down as a challenge, as a glove.—*v.t.* to bind by pledge or security. [Fr. *gage—gager,* to wager—Low L. *vadium,* which is either from L. *vas, vadis,* a pledge, or from a Teut. root found in Goth. *vadi,* A.S. *wed,* a pledge, Ger. *wette,* a bet ; the two roots, however, are cog. See **Bet.**]

**Gage,** gāj, *v.t.* to measure. Same as **Gauge.**

**Gaiety,** gā'e-ti, *n.* merriment : finery : show.

**Gaily,** gā-li, *adv.* in a gay manner. See **Gay.**

**Gain,** gān, *v.t.* to obtain by effort : to earn : to be successful in : to draw to one's own party : to reach : *(New Test.)* to escape.—*n.* that which is gained : profit :—opp. to **Loss.** [M.E. *gainen,* to profit, from the Scand., in Ice. *gagn,* Dan.

*gavn,* gain. The word is quite independent of Fr. *gagner,* with which it has been confused.]

**Gainer,** gān'èr, *n.* one who *gains* profit, &c.

**Gainful,** gān'fool, *adj.* productive of wealth : advantageous.—*adv.* **Gain'fully.**—*n.* **Gain'fulness.**        [or acquired by labour or enterprise.

**Gainings,** gān'ingz, *n.pl.* what have been *gained*

**Gainless,** gān'les, *adj.* unprofitable.—*n.* **Gain'-lessness.**

**Gainsay,** gān'sā or gān-sā', *v.t.* to *say* something *against :* to deny : to dispute.—*n.* **Gain'sayer** *(B.),* an opposer. [A.S. *gegn,* against, and **Say.**]

**Gairish.** See **Garish.**                       [*gata,* a way.]

**Gait,** gāt, *n., way* or manner of walking. [Ice.

**Gaiter,** gāt'èr, *n.* a covering of cloth fitting down upon the shoe. [Fr. *guêtre, guestre.*]

**Gala,** gā'la, *n., show :* splendour : festivity, as a *gala-day.* [Fr. *gala,* show—It. *gala,* finery ; from a Teut. root found in A.S. *gal,* merry.]

**Galaxy,** gal'ak-si, *n.* the *Milky-*Way, or the luminous band of stars stretching across the heavens : any splendid assemblage. [Through Fr. and L., from Gr. *galaxias—gala, galaktos,* akin to L. *lac, lactis,* milk.]

**Galbanum,** gal'ban-um, **Galban,** gal'ban, *n.* a resinous juice obtained from an Eastern plant, used in med. and in the arts, and by the Jews in the preparation of the sacred incense. [L.—Gr. *chalbanē*—Heb. *chelbenah,* from *cheleb,* fat.]

**Gale,** gāl, *n.* a strong wind between a stiff breeze and a storm. [Prob. from Scand., as in Dan. *gal,* mad, Norw. *galen,* raging.]

**Gale,** gāl, *n.* the wild myrtle, a shrub found in bogs. [Prov. E.—A.S. *gagel ;* Scot. *gaul,* Dut. *gagel.*]

**Galeated,** gā'le-āt-ed, *adj., helmeted :* having a flower like a helmet, as the monk's-hood. [L. *galeatus—galea,* a helmet.]

**Galena,** ga-lē'na, *n.* native sulphuret of lead. [L. *galena,* lead-ore—Gr. *galēnē,* calmness : so called from its supposed efficacy in allaying disease.]

**Galiot, Galliot,** gal'i-ut, *n.* a *small galley* or brigantine : a Dutch vessel carrying a mainmast, a mizzen-mast, and a large gaff-mainsail. [Fr., dim. of *galée,* a galley.]

**Gall,** gawl, *n.* the greenish-*yellow* fluid secreted from the liver, called bile : bitterness : malignity. [A.S. *gealla,* gall ; allied to Ger. *galle,* Gr. *cholē,* L. *fel*—all from the same root as E. *yellow,* Ger. *gelb,* L. *helvus.*]

**Gall,** gawl, *v.t.* to fret or hurt the skin by rubbing : to annoy : to enrage.—*n.* a wound caused by rubbing. [O. Fr. *galle,* a fretting of the skin—L. *callus,* hard thick skin.]

**Gall,** gawl, **Gall-nut,** gawl'-nut, *n.* a light nut-like ball which certain insects produce on the oak-tree, used in dyeing. [Fr. *galle*—L. *galla,* oak-apple, gall-nut.]

**Gallant,** gal'ant, *adj. (orig.)* gay, splendid, magnificent *(B.):* brave : noble.—*adv.* **Gall'antly.** —*n.* **Gall'antness.** [Fr. *galant ;* It. *galante—gala.* See **Gala.**]

**Gallant,** gal-ant', *adj.* courteous or attentive to ladies : like a *gallant* or brave man.—*n.* a man of fashion : a suitor : a seducer.—*v.t.* to attend or wait on, as a lady.

**Gallantry,** gal'ant-ri, *n.* bravery : intrepidity : attention or devotion to ladies, often in a bad sense.

**Galleon,** gal'i-un, *n.* a large Spanish vessel with lofty stem and stern. [Sp. *galeon*—Low L. *galea ;* cf. **Galley.**]

**Gallery,** gal'èr-i, *n.* a balcony surrounded by rails : a long passage : the upper floor of seats in a church or theatre : a room for the exhibition of works of art : (*fort.*) a covered passage cut through the earth or masonry. [Fr. *galerie*—It. *galleria*—Low L. *galeria*, an ornamental hall : perhaps from **Gala**.]

**Galley**, gal′i, *n.* a long, low-built ship with one deck, propelled by oars : (*on board ship*) the place where the cooking is done : a kind of boat attached to a ship-of-war : (*print.*) the frame which receives the type from the composing-stick. [O. Fr. *galée*—Low L. *galea;* origin unknown.]

**Galley-slave**, gal′i-slāv, *n.* one condemned for crime to work like a *slave* at the oar of a *galley*.

**Galliard**, gal′yard, *n.* a lively dance. [From the Sp. *gallardo*, lively, gay.]

**Gallic**, gal′ik, *adj.* pertaining to *Gaul* or France. [L. *Gallicus*—*Gallia*, Gaul.]

**Gallic Acid**, gal′ik as′id, *n.* a crystalline substance obtained from *gall*-nuts, mango seeds, &c.

**Gallicism**, gal′i-sizm, *n.* a mode of speech peculiar to the *French:* a French idiom.

**Galligaskins**, gal-i-gas′kinz, *n.pl.* large, open hose or trousers : leggings worn by sportsmen. [Prob. a corr. of Fr. *Greguesques*, Grecians.]

**Gallinaceous**, gal-in-ā′shus, *adj.* pertaining to the order of birds to which the domestic fowl, pheasant, &c. belong. [L. *gallina*, a hen—*gallus*, a cock.]

**Galliot.** See **Galiot**.

**Gallipot**, gal′i-pot, *n.* a small glazed pot for containing medicine. [Corr. of O. Dut. *gleypot*, a glazed pot—Dut. *gleis*, glazed.]

**Gallon**, gal′un, *n.* the standard measure of capacity = 4 quarts. [O. Fr. *gallon* (Fr. *jale*), a bowl.]

**Galloon**, ga-lōōn′, *n.* a kind of lace : a narrow ribbon made of silk or worsted, or of both. [Sp. *galon*—*gala*, finery.]

**Gallop**, gal′up, *v.i.* to *leap* in running : to ride at a galloping pace.—*n.* the pace at which a horse runs when the forefeet are lifted together and the hindfeet together : a quick dance (*in this sense pron.* gal-op′). [Fr. *galoper*, from a Teut. root found in Goth. *gahlaupan*, Ger. *laufen*, A.S. *gehleapan*, to leap.]

**Gallopade**, gal-up-ād′, *n.* a quick kind of dance—then, the music appropriate to it.—*v.i.* to perform a gallopade. [Fr.]

**Galloway**, gal′o-wā, *n.* a small strong horse orig. from *Galloway* in Scotland.

**Gallows**, gal′us, *n.* an instrument on which criminals are executed by hanging. [A.S. *galga;* Ger. *galgen.*]

**Galoche, Galosh**, ga-losh′, *n.* a shoe or slipper worn over another in wet weather. [Fr. *galoche*, of which ety. dub. : either from L. *gallica*, a slipper, from *Gallicus*, pertaining to Gaul, or from L. *calopedia*, a wooden shoe—Gr. *kalopodion*, dim. of *kalopous, kalapous*, a shoemaker's last—*kālon*, wood, and *pous*, the foot.]

**Galvanic**, gal-van′ik, *adj.* belonging to or exhibiting *galvanism*.

**Galvanise**, gal′van-īz, *v.t.* to affect with *galvanism.*—*n.* **Gal′vanist**, one skilled in galvanism.

**Galvanism**, gal′van-izm, *n.* a branch of the science of electricity, which treats of electric currents produced by chemical agents. [From *Galvani* of Bologna, the discoverer, 1737–98.]

**Galvanometer**, gal-van-om′et-ėr, *n.* an instrument for *measuring* the strength of galvanic currents. [*Galvani*, and Gr. *metron*, a measure.]

**Gambado**, gam-bā′dō, *n.* a leather covering for the *legs* to defend them from mud in riding. [It. *gamba*, the leg.]

**Gamble**, gam′bl, *v.i.* to play for money in *games* of chance.—*v.t.* to squander away.—*n.* **Gam′bler**.

**Gamboge**, gam-bōōj′ or gam-bōj′, *n.* a yellow gum-resin used as a pigment and in medicine. [So named from *Cambodia*, in Asia, where it is obtained.]

**Gambol**, gam′bol, *v.i.* to leap or skip : to frisk or dance in sport.—*pr.p.* gam′boling ; *pa.p.* gam′boled.—*n.* a skipping : playfulness. [Fr. *gambade*, a gambol, from *gambe*, old form of Fr. *jambe*, the leg—Low L. *gamba*, a thigh.]

**Game**, gām, *n.*, *sport* of any kind : an exercise for amusement : the stake in a game : wild animals protected by law and hunted by sportsmen. [A.S. *gamen*, play ; cog. with Ice. *gaman*, Dan. *gammen*, O. Ger. *gaman*, mirth, joy.]

**Game**, gām, *v.i.* to play at any game : to play for money, to gamble.—*n.* **Gam′ing**, the practice of playing for money.

**Gamecock**, gām′kok, *n.* a cock trained to fight.

**Gamekeeper**, gām′kēp-ėr, *n.* one who keeps or has the care of game.

**Game-laws**, gām′-lawz, *n.pl.* laws relating to the protection of certain animals called game.

**Gamesome**, gām′sum, *adj.* playful.

**Gamester**, gām′stėr, *n.* one viciously addicted to *gaming* or playing for money : a gambler.

**Gammer**, gam′ėr, *n.* an old woman—the correlative of **Gaffer**. [Contr. of *grammer*, the West of England form of **Grandmother**. See **Gaffer**.]

**Gammon**, gam′un, *n.* the leg or thigh of a hog pickled and smoked or dried.—*v.t.* to cure, as bacon :—*pr.p.* gamm′oning ; *pa.p.* gamm′oned. [O. Fr. *gambon*, old form of *jambon*, a ham.]

**Gammon**, gam′un, *n.* a hoax : nonsense.—*v.t.* to hoax, impose upon. [A.S. *gamen*, a game. See **Game**.]

**Gamut**, gam′ut, *n.* the musical scale : the scale or compass of wind instruments. [So called from the Gr. *gamma*, which stood first in the scale invented by Guy of Arezzo, and thus gave its name to the whole scale ; and L. *ut*, the syllable used in singing the first note of the scale.]

**Gander**, gan′dėr, *n.* the male of the goose. [A.S. *gandra*, from older form *ganra*, with inserted *d*. See **Goose**.]

**Gang**, gang, *n.* a number of persons *going together* or associated for a certain purpose, usually in a bad sense. [A.S.—*gangan*, to go.]

**Gangboard**, gang′bōrd, *n.* a *board* or plank on which passengers may *go* or walk into or out of a ship.

**Gangliac**, gang′gli-ak, **Ganglionic**, gang-gli-on′ik, *adj.* pertaining to a *ganglion*.

**Ganglion**, gang′gli-on, *n.* a *tumour* in the sheath of a tendon : an enlargement in the course of a nerve :—*pl.* **Gang′lia** or **Gang′lions**. [Gr.]

**Gangrene**, gang′grēn, *n.* loss of vitality in some part of the body : the first stage in mortification.—*v.t.* to mortify.—*v.i.* to become putrid. [Fr.—L. *gangræna*—Gr. *ganggraina*, from *grainō*, to gnaw.]

**Gangrenous**, gang′gren-us, *adj.* mortified.

**Gangway**, gang′wā, *n.* a passage or *way* by which to *go* into or out of any place, esp. a ship : (*naut.*) a narrow platform of planks along the upper part of a ship's side. [A.S. *gang*, and **Way**.]

**Gannet**, gan′et, *n.* a web-footed fowl found in the northern seas. [A.S. *ganot*, a sea-fowl, from root of **Gander**.]

**Ganoid**, gan′oid, *n.* one of an order of fishes having *shining* scales, enamelled and angular, as the sturgeon. [Gr. *ganos*, splendour, *eidos*, form.]

**Gant'let**, *n.* a glove. Same as **Gauntlet**.

**Gantlet**, gant'let, **Gantlope**, gant'lōp, *n.* a punishment consisting in driving a criminal through a *lane* formed by two files of men, who each strike him as he passes—said to have been introduced by Gustavus Adolphus of Sweden. [Sw. *gatlopp—gata* (E. *gate*), a street, a line of soldiers, *lopp* (E. *leap*), course.]

**Gaol, Jail,** jāl, *n.* a prison.—*n.* **Gaol'er, Jail'er,** one who has charge of a *gaol* or of prisoners, called also a turnkey. [O. Fr. *gaiole,* Fr. *geôle* —Low L. *gabiola,* a cage, dim. of Low L. *gabia,* a cage, which is a corr. of *cavea,* a cage, coop, lit. a hollow place—L. *cavus,* hollow. See **Cage.**]

**Gap,** gap, *n.* an *opening* made by rupture or parting: a cleft: a passage. [From **Gape.**]

**Gape,** gāp, *v.i.* to open the mouth wide: to yawn: to stare with open mouth: to be open, like a gap.—*n.* act of gaping: width of the mouth when opened. [A.S. *geapan,* to gape; Ice. *gapa,* to open.]

**Gaper,** gāp'ėr, *n.* one who gapes.

**Gap-toothed,** gap'-tōōtht, *adj.* having *gaps* or interstices between the *teeth.*

**Gar,** gär, **Garfish,** gär'fish, *n.* a long, slender fish with a *pointed* head. [A.S. *gar,* a dart.]

**Garb,** gärb, *n.* fashion of dress: external appearance. [O. Fr., from O. Ger. *garawi,* preparation, dress. O. Ger. *garo,* ready; cf. A.S. *gearu,* ready, E. **Yare.**]

**Garbage,** gär'bāj, *n.* refuse, as the bowels of an animal. [Prob. from **Garble.**]

**Garble,** gär'bl, *v.t.* to select out of a book or writing what may serve our own purpose, in a bad sense: to mutilate or corrupt.—*n.* **Gar'bler,** one who *garbles* or selects. [O. Fr.—Sp. *garbillar,* to sift—*garbillo,* a sieve; of dub. origin.]

**Garden,** gär'dn, *n.* a piece of ground on which flowers, &c. are cultivated.—*v.i.* to work in a garden : to practise gardening. [O. Fr. *gardin,* Fr. *jardin,* from root of Ger. *garten,* A.S. *geard.* E. *yard,* Goth. *gards.*]

**Gardening,** gär'dn-ing, *n.* the art of laying out and cultivating gardens.—*n.* **Gar'dener,** one who cultivates or has charge of a garden.

**Gargle,** gär'gl, *v.t.* to make a liquid gurgle or bubble in the throat without swallowing it : to wash the throat, preventing the liquid from going down by expelling air against it.—*n.* a preparation for washing the throat. [Fr. *gargouiller—gargouille,* the weasand or throat. See **Gargoyle.**]

**Gargoyle,** gär'goil, *n.* a projecting spout, conveying the water from the roof-gutters of buildings, often representing human or other figures. [Fr. *gargouille,* the throat, mouth of a spout, dim. from root *garg* or *gorg* in **Gorge.**]

**Garish,** gär'ish, *adj.* showy : gaudy.—*adv.* **Gar'ishly.**—*n.* **Gar'ishness.** [O. E. *gare,* to stare ; a form of M. E. *gasen,* whence **Gaze,** which see.]

**Garland,** gär'land, *n.* a wreath of flowers or leaves : a name for a book of extracts in prose or poetry.—*v.t.* to deck with a garland. [O. Fr. *garlande* ; origin doubtful.]

**Garlic,** gär'lik, *n.* a bulbous-rooted plant having a pungent taste, used as seasoning.—*adj.* **Gar'licky,** like garlic. ['Spear-leek' or 'spearplant,' from the shape of its leaves, from A.S. *garleac—gar,* a spear, and *leac,* a leek, plant.]

**Garment,** gär'ment, *n.* any article of clothing, as a coat or gown. [O. Fr. *garniment—garnir,* to furnish.]

**Garner,** gär'nėr, *n.* a granary or place where *grain* is stored up.—*v.t.* to store as in a garner. [O. Fr. *gernier* (Fr. *grenier*)—L. *granaria,* a granary—*granum,* a grain. See **Granary.**]

**Garnet,** gär'net, *n.* a precious stone resembling the *grains* or seeds of the *pomegranate* : (*naut.*) a sort of tackle fixed to the mainstay in ships. [Fr. *grenat*—L. (*pomum*) *granatum,* grained (apple), the pomegranate—*granum,* a grain.]

**Garnish,** gär'nish, *v.t.* to *furnish* : to adorn : to surround with ornaments, as a dish. [Fr. *garnir,* to furnish, old form *guarnir, warnir,* to warn, defend—from a Teut. root found in A.S. *warnian,* Ger. *warnen.* E. *warn.*]

**Garnish,** gär'nish, **Garnishment,** gär'nish-ment, *n.* that which garnishes or embellishes : ornament.

**Garnisher,** gär'nish-ėr, *n.* one who garnishes.

**Garniture,** gär'nit-ūr, *n.,* furniture : ornament.

**Garret,** gar'et, *n.* a room next the roof of a house. [O. Fr. *garite,* a place of safety—O. Fr. *garir,* Fr. *guérir,* from a Teut. root found in Ger. *wehren,* Goth. *varjan,* A.S. *warian,* to defend, E. *wary, warn.*] [a poor author.

**Garreteer,** gar-et-ēr', *n.* one who lives in a *garret* :

**Garrison,** gar'i-sn, *n.* a supply of soldiers for guarding a fortress : a fortified place.—*v.t.* to furnish a fortress with troops : to defend by fortresses manned with troops. [Fr. *garnison—garnir,* to furnish. See **Garnish.**]

**Garrotte,** gar-rot', **Garrote,** gar-rōt', *n.* a Spanish mode of strangling criminals with a cord placed over the neck and twisted tight by a *stick* : the brass collar afterwards used in strangling.—*v.t.* to strangle by a brass collar tightened by a screw, whose point enters the spinal marrow : to suddenly render insensible by semi-strangulation, and then to rob:—*pr.p.* garrott'ing, garrōt'ing ; *pa.p.* garrott'ed, garrōt'ed. [Sp. *garrote,* a cudgel, a packing-stick ; of uncertain origin.]

**Garrotter,** gar-rot'ėr, **Garroter,** gar-rōt'ėr, *n.* one who garrottes.

**Garrulity,** gar-ūl'i-ti, **Garrulousness,** gar'ū-lus-nes, *n.* talkativeness : loquacity.

**Garrulous,** gar'ū-lus, *adj.* talkative. [L. *garrulus*—root of *garrio,* to chatter.]

**Garter,** gär'tėr, *n.* a string or band used to tie the stocking to the *leg* : the badge of the highest order of knighthood in Great Britain, called the Order of the Garter.—*v.t.* to bind with a garter. [Norm. Fr. *gartier,* Fr. *jarretières—jarret,* the ham of the leg, from Bret. *gar* (W. *gar*), the shank of the leg.]

**Gas,** gas, *n.* fluid in the form of air : any kind of air, esp. that obtained from coal, used in lighting houses.—*pl.* **Gas'es.** [A word invented by Van Helmont, a chemist of Flanders, 1577—1644 ; the form of the word was prob. suggested by Flem. *geest,* Ger. *geist,* spirit.]

**Gasalier,** gas-a-lēr', *n.* a hanging frame with branches for *gas-jets.*

**Gasconade,** gas-kon-ād', *n.* a boasting or bragging like a Gascon : bravado.—*v.i.* to brag or boast.—*ns.* **Gasconad'ing, Gasconad'er.** [*Gascon,* a native of Gascony in France—a province whose inhabitants are noted for boasting.]

**Gaseous,** gāz'e-us, *adj.* in the form of *gas* or air.

**Gas-fitter,** gas'-fit'ėr, *n.* one who fits up the pipes and brackets for *gas-lighting.*

**Gash,** gash, *v.t.* to make a deep hack or cut into anything, esp. into flesh.—*n.* a deep, open wound. [Ety. dub.]

**Gasify,** gas'i-fī, *v.t.* to convert into *gas* :—*pr.p.* gas'ifying ; *pa.p.* gas'ified.—*n.* **Gasifica'tion.** [**Gas,** and L. *facio,* to make.]

**Gasometer**, gaz-om'et-ėr, *n.* an instrument for *measuring gas* : a place for holding gas. [**Gas**, and Gr. *metron*, a measure.]

**Gasp**, gasp, *v.i.* to gape in order to catch breath : to breathe laboriously or convulsively. — *n.* the act of opening the mouth to catch the breath : a painful catching of the breath. [Ice. *geispa*, to yawn ; thus *gaspa* stands for *gapsa*, an extension of Ice. *gapa*, to gape ; hence **Gasp** is etymologically a freq. of **Gape**.]

**Gastric**, gas'trik, *adj.* belonging to the *belly* or stomach. [Gr. *gastēr*, the belly.]

**Gastronomy**, gas-tron'om-i, *n.* the art or science of good eating. [Gr. *gastēr*, and *nomos*, a rule.]

**Gat**, gat (*B.*) *pa.t.* of **Get**.

**Gate**, gāt, *n.* a passage into a city, inclosure, or any large building : a frame in the entrance into any inclosure : an entrance. [A.S. *geat*, a way, a gate ; cog. forms exist in all the Teut. languages.]

**Gated**, gāt'ed, *adj.* furnished with gates.

**Gateway**, gāt'wā, *n.* the way through a gate : a gate itself.

**Gather**, gath'ėr, *v.t.* to collect : to acquire : to plait : to learn by inference. — *v.i.* to assemble or muster : to increase : to suppurate. — *n.* a plait or fold in cloth, made by drawing the thread through. [A.S. *gaderian* — A.S. *gaed*, company.] [gleaner.

**Gatherer**, gath'ėr-ėr, *n.* one who collects : a

**Gathering**, gath'ėr-ing, *n.* a crowd or assembly : a tumour or collection of matter.

**Gaucho**, gā-ŏ'chō, *n.* a native of the La Plata pampas of Spanish descent, noted for their marvellous horsemanship.

**Gaudy**, gawd'i, *adj.* showy : gay. — *adv.* **Gaud'ily**. — *n.* **Gaud'iness**, showiness. [M. E. *gaude*, an ornament : from L. *gaudium*, joy — *gaudere*.]

**Gauge**, gāj, *n.* a *measuring-rod* : a standard of measure : estimate. — *v.t.* to measure the contents of any vessel : to estimate ability. [O. Fr. *gauger* — *gauge*, a liquid measure, old form of *jauge*, a measuring-rod — Low L. *gaugia*.]

**Gauger**, gāj'ėr, *n.* an excise officer whose business is to *gauge* or measure the contents of casks.

**Gauging**, gāj'ing, *n.* the art of *measuring* casks containing excisable liquors.

**Gaul**, gawl, *n.* a name of ancient France : an inhabitant of Gaul. — *adj.* **Gaul'ish**. [L. *Gallia*.]

**Gaunt**, gänt, *adj.* thin : of a pinched appearance. — *adv.* **Gaunt'ly**. — *n.* **Gaunt'ness** [Ety. dub.]

**Gauntlet**, gänt'let, *n.* the iron *glove* of armour, formerly thrown down in challenge : a long glove covering the wrist. [Fr. *gantelet* — *gant*, from a Teut. root ; cf. Ice. *vöttr*, a glove, Dan. *vante*.]

**Gauze**, gawz, *n.* a thin, transparent fabric, orig. of silk, now of any fine hard-spun fibre. — *adj.* **Gauz'y**, like gauze. [Fr. *gaze* — *Gaza* in Palestine, whence it was first brought.]

**Gave**, gāv, *pa.t.* of **Give**.

**Gavelkind**, gav'el-kīnd, *n.* tenure by which lands descend from the father to all the sons in equal portions. [Celt. ; Ir. *gabhail*, a tenure, *cine*, a race.]

**Gavotte**, ga-vot', *n.* a lively kind of dance, somewhat like a country-dance, orig. a dance of the *Gavotes*, the people of *Gap*, in the Upper Alps.

**Gawk**, gawk, *n.* a cuckoo : a simpleton : a tall, awkward fellow. — *adj.* **Gawk'y**, like a cuckoo, awkward. [A.S. *geac* : Scot. *gowk*, Ger. *gauch*, cuckoo, a simpleton. See **Cuckoo**.]

**Gay**, gā, *adj.*, lively : bright : sportive, merry : showy. — *adv.* **Gai'ly** or **Gay'ly**. [Fr. *gai* ; prob. from root of Ger. *jähe*, quick, lively.]

**Gayety**, gā'e-ti, *n.* Same as **Gaiety**.

**Gaze**, gāz, *v.i.* to look fixedly. — *n.* a fixed look : a look of prolonged attention : the object gazed at. [From a Scand. root preserved in Swed. *gasa*, to stare ; akin to the Goth. base *gais*. See **Aghast** and **Ghastly**.]

**Gazelle, Gazel**, ga-zel', *n.* a small species of antelope with beautiful dark eyes, found in Arabia and N. Africa. [Fr. — Ar. *ghazal*, a wild-goat.]

**Gazette**, ga-zet', *n.* a newspaper : the official newspaper. — *v.t.* to publish in a gazette :— *pr.p.* gazett'ing ; *pa.p.* gazett'ed. [Fr. — It. *gazzetta*, a Venetian coin worth about ¾d., the sum charged for a reading of the first Venetian newspaper, a written sheet which appeared about the middle of the 16th century during the war with Soliman II.; or from It. *gazzetta*, in the sense of a magpie = a chatterer.]

**Gazetteer**, gaz-et-ēr', *n.* (*orig.*) a writer for a *gazette* : a geographical dictionary.

**Gazing-stock**, gāz'ing-stok, *n.* something *stuck up to be gazed at* : a person exposed to public view as an object of curiosity or contempt.

**Gear**, gēr, *n.* dress : harness : tackle : (*mech.*) connection by means of toothed wheels. — *v.t.* to put in gear, as machinery. [A.S. *gearwe*, preparation — *gearu*, ready. **Yare** is a doublet : also **Garb**.] [toothed wheels and pinions.

**Gearing**, gēr'ing, *n.* harness : (*mech.*) a train of

**Geese**, plural of **Goose**.

**Gehenna**, ge-hen'a, *n.* (*lit.*) the *valley of Hinnom*, near Jerusalem, in which the Israelites sacrificed their children to Moloch, and to which, at a later time, the refuse of the city was conveyed to be slowly burnt — hence (*New Test.*) hell. [L. — Heb. *Ge*, valley of, and *Hinnom*.]

**Gelatin, Gelatine**, jel'a-tin, *n.* an animal substance which dissolves in hot water and forms a *jelly* when cold. [Fr. — L. *gelo, gelatum*, to freeze — *gelu*, frost.]

**Gelatinate**, je-lat'in-āt, **Gelatinise**, je-lat'in-īz, *v.t.* to make into *gelatine* or jelly. — *v.i.* to be converted into gelatine or jelly. — *n.* **Gelatina'tion**. [into *jelly*.

**Gelatinous**, je-lat'in-us, *adj.* resembling or formed

**Geld**, geld, *v.t.* to emasculate or castrate : to deprive of anything essential : to deprive of anything obscene or objectionable. — *n.* **Geld'er**. [Scand., as in Ice. *gelda*, Dan. *gilde*. See **Cullion**.] [animal, especially a horse.

**Gelding**, geld'ing, *n.* act of castrating : a castrated

**Gelid**, jel'id, *adj.*, icy cold : cold. — *adv.* **Gel'idly**. — *ns.* **Gel'idness, Gelid'ity**. [L. *gelidus* — *gelu*.]

**Gem**, jem, *n.* (*lit.*) *leaf-bud* : any precious stone, esp. when cut : anything extremely valuable or attractive. — *v.t.* to adorn with gems :— *pr.p.* gemm'ing ; *pa.p.* gemmed'. [Fr. *gemme* — L. *gemma*, a bud ; allied to Gr. *gemō*, to be full.]

**Gemini**, jem'i-nī, *n.pl.* the *twins*, a constellation containing the two bright stars Castor and Pollux. [L., pl. of *geminus*, twin-born, for *genminus* — *gen*, root of *gigno*, to beget.]

**Geminous**, jem'in-us, *adj.* (*bot.*) *double*, in pairs.

**Gemmate**, jem'āt, *adj.* (*bot.*) having *buds*. [L. *gemmatus*, pa.p. of *gemmo*, to bud — *gemma*.]

**Gemmation**, jem-mā'shun, *n.* (*bot.*) act or time of *budding* : arrangement of buds on the stalk.

**Gemmiferous**, jem-mif'ėr-us, *adj.*, *producing buds*. [L. *gemmifer* — *gemma*, and *fero*, to bear.]

**Gemmiparous**, jem-mip'ar-us, *adj.* (*zool.*) *reproducing by buds* growing on the body. [L. *gemma*, a bud, *pario*, to bring forth.]

**Gemmule**, jem'ūl, *n.* a *little gem* or leaf-bud. [Fr. — L. *gemmula*, dim. of *gemma*.]

---

fāte, fär ; mē, hėr ; mīne ; mōte ; mūte ; mōōn ; *then*.       199

**Gender**, jen'der, *v.t.* to *beget.—v.i.* (*B.*) to copulate. [An abbrev. of **Engender.**]

**Gender**, jen'der, *n. kind*, esp. with regard to sex : (*gram.*) the distinction of nouns acc. to sex. [Fr. *genre*—L. *genus, generis*, a kind, kin.]

**Genealogical**, jen-e-a-loj'ik-al, *adj.* pertaining to or exhibiting the *genealogy* or pedigree of families or persons.—*adv.* **Genealog'ically.**

**Genealogist**, jen-e-al'o-jist, *n.* one who studies or traces *genealogies* or descents.

**Genealogy**, jen-e-al'o-ji, *n., history* of the descent of *families* : the pedigree of a particular person or family. [Fr.—L.—Gr. *genealogia—genea*, birth, descent, and *-logia*, an account—*legein*, to speak of. See **Genus** and **Logic.**]

**Genera.** See **Genus.**

**General**, jen'er-al, *adj.* relating to a *genus* or whole class : including many species : not special : not restricted : common : prevalent : public : loose : vague. [Fr.—L. *generalis—genus.*]

**General**, jen'er-al, *n.* the whole or chief part : an officer who is head over a whole department : a military officer who commands a body of men not less than a brigade : the chief commander of an army in service : in the R. C. Church, the head of a religious order, responsible only to the Pope.

**Generalisation**, jen-er-al-i-zā'shun, *n.* act of generalising or of comprehending under a common name several objects resembling each other in some part of their nature.

**Generalise**, jen'er-al-īz, *v.t.* to make general : to reduce to or include under a *genus* or general term : to infer from one or a few the nature of a whole class. [Fr. *généraliser—général.*]

**Generalissimo**, jen-er-al-is'i-mo, *n.* the *chief general* or commander of an army of two or more divisions, or of separate armies. [It.]

**Generality**, jen-er-al'i-ti, *n.* state of being *general* or of including particulars : the main part : the greatest part. [Fr.—L. *generalitas.*]

**Generally**, jen'er-al-i, *adv.* in general : commonly : extensively : most frequently : in a general way : without detail : (*B.*) collectively, together : (*Pr. Bk.*) without restriction or limitation.]

**Generalship**, jen'er-al-ship, *n.* the office or skill of a *general* or military officer : military skill.

**Generant**, jen'er-ant, *n.* the power that *generates* or produces. [L., pr.p. of *genero*, to generate.]

**Generate**, jen'er-āt, *v.t.* to produce one's *kind* : to bring into life : to originate. [L. *genero, generatus—genus*, a kind.]

**Generation**, jen-er-ā'shun, *n.* a producing or originating : that which is generated : a single stage in natural descent : the people of the same age or period : race :—*pl.* (*B.*) genealogy, history. [Fr.—L. *generatio.*]

**Generative**, jen'er-ā-tiv, *adj.* having the power of generating or producing : prolific.

**Generator**, jen'er-ā-tor, *n.* begetter or producer : the principal sound in music. [L.]

**Generic**, je-ner'ik, **Generical**, je-ner'ik-al, *adj.* marking or comprehending a *genus.—adv.* **Gener'ically.** [Fr. *générique.*]

**Generosity**, jen-er-os'i-ti, *n.* nobleness or liberality of nature. [Fr. *générosité*—L. *generositas.*]

**Generous**, jen'er-us, *adj.* of a noble nature : courageous : liberal : invigorating in its nature, as wine.—*adv.* **Gen'erously.—n.** **Gen'erousness.** [Lit. and orig. of a high or noble *genus* or family. O. Fr.—L. *generosus—genus*, birth.]

**Genesis**, jen'e-sis, *n., generation, creation*, or production : the first book of the *Bible*, so called from its containing an account of the *Creation.* [L. and Gr.—Gr. *gignomai*—obs. *genō*, to beget.]

**Genet.** Same as **Jennet.**

**Genet**, jen'et, *n.* a carnivorous animal, allied to the civet, of a gray colour, marked with black or brown, a native of Africa, Asia, and S. Europe. [Fr. *genette*—Sp. *gineta* : of Eastern origin.]

**Geneva**, je-nē'va, *n.* a spirit distilled from grain and flavoured with *juniper*-berries, also called Hollands. [Fr. *genièvre*—L. *juniperus*, the juniper ; corrupted to *Geneva* by confusion with the town of that name. See **Gin.**]

**Genial**, jē'ni-al, *adj.* cheering : merry : kindly : sympathetic : healthful.—*adv.* **Ge'nially.** [Fr.—L. *genialis*, from *genius*, the spirit of social enjoyment.]

**Geniality**, jē-ni-al'i-ti, **Genialness**, jē'ni-al-nes, *n.* quality of being *genial :* gaiety : cheerfulness.

**Geniculate**, je-nik'ū-lāt, **Geniculated**, je-nik'ū-lāt-ed, *adj.* (*bot.*) bent abruptly like the *knee :* jointed : knotted.—*n.* **Genicula'tion.** [L. *geniculatus—geniculum*, a little knee—*genu*, the knee.]

**Genital**, jen'i-tal, *adj.* belonging to *generation*, or the act of producing. [Fr.—L. *genitalis—gigno, genitus*, to beget. See **Genus.**] [*generation.*

**Genitals**, jen'i-talz, *n.pl.* the exterior organs of

**Genitive**, jen'i-tiv, *adj.* (*gram.*) applied to a case properly denoting the class or kind to which a thing belongs, represented in modern English by the Possessive case. [L. *genitivus* (*gigno, genitus*, to beget), as if indicating origin, a mistranslation of Gr. *genikos—genos*, a class.]

**Genius**, jē'ni-us or jēn'yus, *n.* a good or evil spirit, supposed by the ancients to preside over every person, place, and thing, and esp. to preside over a man's destiny from his *birth :—pl.* **Genii**, jē'ni-ī. [L. *genius—gigno, genitus*, to beget, produce. See **Genus.**]

**Genius**, jēn'yus or jē'ni-us, *n.* the special *inborn* faculty of any individual : special taste or disposition qualifying for a particular employment : superior inborn power of mind : a man having such power of mind : peculiar constitution or character of anything :—*pl.* **Geniuses**, jēn'yus-ez.

**Gennet.** Same as **Jennet.**

**Genre-painting**, zhongr-pānt'ing, *n.* (*paint.*) the general name applied to all compositions with figures that are not specifically landscapes or historical paintings. [Fr. *genre*, kind, sort—L. *genus.* Cf. **Gender.**]

**Gent**, jent, *n.* familiar abbrev. of **Gentleman :** one who apes the gentleman.

**Genteel**, jen-tēl', *adj.* well-bred : graceful in manners or in form.—*adv.* **Genteel'ly.—n.** **Genteel'ness**, same as **Gentility.** [Lit. belonging to a noble race or family, from Fr. *gentil*—L. *gentilis—gens*, a Roman clan or family—*gen*, root of Gr. *gignomai*, to beget. See **Genus.**]

**Gentian**, jen'shan, *n.* a plant the root of which is used in medicine, said to have been brought into use by *Gentius*, king of Illyria, conquered by the Romans in 167 B.C.

**Gentile**, jen'tīl, *n.* (*B.*) any one not a Jew : a heathen.—*adj.* belonging to any nation but the Jews : (*gram.*) denoting a race or country. [L. *gentilis—gens*, a nation ; the Jews spoke of those who did not acknowledge their religion as *the nations.*]

**Gentility**, jen-til'i-ti, *n.* good *birth* or extraction : good-breeding : politeness of manners.

**Gentle**, jen'tl, *adj.* well-born : mild and refined in manners : mild in disposition : amiable : soothing. —*adv.* **Gent'ly.—n.** **Gent'leness.** [Fr.—L. *gentilis.* See **Genteel.**]

**Gentle**, jen'tl, *n.* the maggot of the blue-bottle used as bait in angling. [Ety. dub.]

**Gentlefolks,** jen'tl-fōks, *n.pl., folk of good family* or above the vulgar. [See **Folk**]

**Gentleman,** jen'tl-man, *n.* a *man* of *gentle* or good birth : one who without a title wears a coat of arms : more gen. every man above the rank of yeoman, including the nobility : one above the trading classes : a man of refined manners : an officer of the royal household :—in *pl.* a word of address :—*pl.* **Gen'tlemen** :—*fem.* **Gen'tlewoman.**

**Gentlemanlike,** jen'tl-man-līk, **Gentlemanly,** jen'tl-man-li, *adj.* well-bred, refined, generous. —*n.* **Gen'tlemanliness.**

**Gentry,** jen'tri, *n.* the class of people between the nobility and the vulgar. [M. E. *gentrie* is a corr. of an older form *gentrise,* from O. Fr. *genterise, gentilise,* which was formed from adj. *gentil,* gentle, like *noblesse* from *noble.*]

**Genuflection, Genuflexion,** jen-ū-flek'shun, *n.* act of *bending the knee,* esp. in worship. [Fr.—L. *genu,* the knee, *flexio,* a bending—*flecto, flexum,* to bend.]

**Genuine,** jen'ū-in, *adj.* natural, not spurious or adulterated : real : pure.—*adv.* **Gen'uinely.**—*n.* **Gen'uineness.** [Fr. ; L. *genuinus — gigno, genitus,* to beget, to be born.]

**Genus,** jē'nus, *n.* a group consisting of a number of species having common marks or characteristics : (*log.*) a class of objects comprehending several subordinate species:—*pl.* **Genera,** jen'ėr-a. [L. *genus, ge. :ris,* birth ; cog. with Gr. *genos— gignomai,* obs. *genō,* Sans. *jan,* to beget, E. **Kin.**]

**Geocentric,** jē-o-sen'trik, **Geocentrical,** jē-o-sen'-trik-al, *adj.* having the *earth* for its *centre* : (*astr.*) as seen or measured from the earth.— *adv.* **Geocen'trically.** [Gr. *gē,* the earth, and *kentron,* a centre.]

**Geode,** jē'ōd, *n.* (*min.*) a rounded nodule of stone with a hollow interior. [Gr. *geōdēs,* earth-like, earthen—*gē,* earth, *eidos,* form.]

**Geodesic,** jē-o-des'ik, **Geodesical,** jē-o-des'ik-al, **Geodetic,** jē-o-det'ik, **Geodetical,** jē-o-det'ik-al, *adj.* pertaining to or determined by geodesy.

**Geodesy,** je-od'e-si, *n.* a science whose object is to measure the earth and its parts on a large scale. [Fr. *géodesie*—Gr. *geōdaisia*—*gē,* the earth, *daiō,* to divide.]

**Geognosy,** je-og'no-si, *n.* a branch of geology which explains the actual mineral structure of the earth without inquiring into its history or the mode of its formation.—*n.* **Geog'nost.**—*adj.* **Geognost'ic.** [Fr. *géognosie*—Gr. *gē,* the earth, and *gnōsis,* knowledge—*gignōskō,* to know.]

**Geogony,** je-og'o-ni, *n.* the doctrine of the *production* or *formation* of the *earth.*—*adj.* **Geogon'ic.** [Fr. *géogonie*—Gr. *gē,* the earth, *gonē,* generation—*genō, gignomai,* to be born, produced.]

**Geographer,** je-og'ra-fėr, *n.* one who is versed in, or who writes on geography.

**Geographic,** jē-o-graf'ik, **Geographical,** jē-o-graf'ik-al, *adj.* relating to geography.—*adv.* **Geograph'ically.**

**Geography,** je-og'ra-fi, *n.* the science which *describes* the surface of the *earth* and its inhabitants : a book containing a description of the earth. [Fr.—L.—Gr. *geōgraphia*—*gē,* the earth, *graphē,* a description—*graphō,* to write, to describe.]

**Geological,** jē-o-loj'ik-al, *adj.* pertaining to geology. —*adv.* **Geolog'ically.** [Fr. *géologique.*]

**Geologise,** je-ol'o-jīz, *v.i.* to study geology.

**Geologist,** je-ol'o-jist, *n.* one versed in geology.

**Geology,** je-ol'o-ji, *n.* the *science* that treats **of** the structure and history of the *earth,* of the changes it has undergone, and their causes, and of the plants and animals imbedded in its crust. [Fr. *géologie*—Gr. *gē,* the earth, *logos,* a discourse.] [mancy.]

**Geomancer,** jē'o-man-sėr, *n.* one skilled in geo-

**Geomancy,** jē'o-man-si, *n., divination* by figures or lines drawn on the *earth.* [Fr. *géomancie*— Gr. *gē,* the earth, and *manteia,* divination.]

**Geomantic,** jē-o-man'tik, *adj.* pertaining to geomancy.

**Geometer,** je-om'e-tėr, **Geometrician,** je-om'e-trish-yan, *n.* one skilled in geometry.

**Geometric,** jē-o-met'rik, **Geometrical,** jē-o-met'-rik-al, *adj.* pertaining to geometry : according to or done by geometry.—*adv.* **Geomet'rically.**

**Geometry,** je-om'e-tri, *n.* the science of measurement : that branch of mathematics which treats of magnitude and its relations. [Fr.—L.—Gr. *geōmetria*—*geōmetreō,* to measure land—*gē,* the earth, *metreō,* to measure.]

**Geoponic,** jē-o-pon'ik, **Geoponical,** jē-o-pon'ik-al, *adj.* pertaining to *tilling* the *earth* or to agriculture. [Fr. *géoponique*—Gr. *geōponikos*—*gē,* the earth, *ponos,* labour—*penomai,* to labour.]

**Georama,** jē-o-rä'ma or jē-o-rä'ma, *n.* a spherical chamber with a general *view* of the *earth* on its inner surface. [Gr. *gē,* the earth, *horama,* a view—*horaō,* to see.]

**Georgian,** jorj'i-an, *adj.* relating to the reigns of the four *Georges,* kings of Great Britain.

**Georgic,** jorj'ik, **Georgical,** jorj'ik-al, *adj.* relating to *agriculture* or rustic affairs. [L. *georgicus,* Gr. *geōrgikos*—*geōrgia,* agriculture—*gē,* the earth, and *ergon,* a work.]

**Georgic,** jorj'ik, *n.* a poem on *husbandry.*

**Gerah,** gē'ra, *n.* (*B.*) the smallest Hebrew weight and coin, $\frac{1}{20}$ of a shekel, and worth about 1½d. [Heb. *gerah,* a bean.]

**Geranium,** je-rā'ni-um, *n.* a genus of plants with seed-vessels like a *crane's bill.* [L.—Gr. *geranion*—*geranos,* a crane.]

**Gerfalcon,** jėr'faw-kn, *n.* Same as **Gyrfalcon.**

**Germ,** jėrm, *n.* rudimentary form of a living thing, whether a plant or animal : (*bot.*) the seed-bud of a plant : a shoot : that from which anything springs, the origin : a first principle. [Fr. *germe* —L. *germen,* a bud.]

**German,** jėr'man, **Germane,** jėr-mān', *adj.* of the first degree, as *cousins-german* : closely allied. [Fr.—L. *germanus,* prob. for *germin-anus— germen,* bud, origin.]

**German,** jėr'man, *n.* a native of Germany : the German language:—*pl.* **Ger'mans.**—*adj.* of or from Germany. [L. *Germani,* variously given as meaning 'the shouters,' from Celt. *gairm,* a loud cry ; 'neighbours,' *i.e.* to the Gauls, from the Celtic ; and 'the war-men,' from Ger. *wehr* = Fr. *guerre,* war.]

**German-silver,** jėr'man-sil'vėr, *n.* an alloy of copper, nickel, and zinc, white like silver, and first made in *Germany.*

**Germen,** jėrm'en, *n.* Same as **Germ.**

**Germinal,** jėrm'in-al, *adj.* pertaining to a *germ.*

**Germinant,** jėrm'in-ant, *adj.* *sprouting* : sending forth germs or buds.

**Germinate,** jėrm'in-āt, *v.i.* to spring from a *germ*: to begin to grow.—*n.* **Germina'tion.** [L. *germino, germinatus—germen.*]

**Gerund,** jer'und, *n.* a part of the Latin verb expressing the *carrying on* of the action of the verb.—*adj.* **Gerund'ial.** [L. *gerundium—gero,* to bear, to carry.]

**Gestation**, jes-tā′shun, *n.* the act of *carrying* the young in the womb : the state or condition in which the young is so carried. [Fr.—L. *gestatio—gesto*, *gestatum*, to carry—*gero*, to bear.]

**Gestatory**, jes′ta-tor-i, *adj.* pertaining to *gestation* or carrying : that may be carried.

**Gestic**, jes′tik, *adj.* pertaining to bodil*y* action or motion. [L. *gestus*—carriage, motion—*gero*.]

**Gesticulate**, jes-tik′ū-lāt, *v.i.* to make gestures or motions when speaking : to play antic tricks. [L. *gesticulor*, *gesticulatus—gesticulus*, dim. of *gestus*, a gesture—*gero*, to carry.]

**Gesticulation**, jes-tik-ū-lā′shun, *n.* act of making *gestures* in speaking : a gesture : antic tricks.

**Gesticulator**, jes-tik′ū-lāt-or, *n.* one who gesticulates or makes gestures.

**Gesticulatory**, jes-tik′ū-lā-tor-i, *adj.* representing or abounding in *gesticulations* or gestures.

**Gesture**, jes′tūr, *n.* a *bearing*, position, or movement of the body : an action expressive of sentiment or passion. [From fut.p. of L. *gero*, to carry.]

**Get**, get, *v.t.* to obtain : to beget offspring : to learn : to persuade : (*B.*) to betake, to carry.—*v.i.* to arrive or put one's self in any place, state, or condition : to become :—*pr.p.* gett′ing ; *pa.t.* got ; *pa.p.* got, (*obs.*) gott′en.—**Get at**, to reach : **Get off**, to escape : **Get on**, to proc-ed, advance : **Get over**, to surmount : **Get through**, to finish : **Get up**, to arise, to ascend. [A.S. *gitan*, to get ; allied to *chad*, root of Gr. *chandanō*, and *hed*, root of L. *pre-hendo*, to seize.]

**Getter**, get′ėr, *n.* one who *gets* or obtains.

**Getting**, get′ing, *n.* a gaining : anything gained.

**Gewgaw**, gū′gaw, *n.* a toy : a bauble.—*adj.* showy without value. [Acc. to Skeat, a reduplicated form of A.S. *gifan*, to give ; preserved also in Northern E., as *giff-gaff*, interchange of intercourse.]      [Ice. *geysa*, to gush.]

**Geyser**, gī′sėr, *n.* a boiling spring, as in Iceland.

**Ghastly**, gast′li, *adj.* deathlike : hideous.—*n.* **Ghast′liness**. [A.S. *gǣstlic*, terrible, from *gaist*, an extended form of the base *gais*, and *-lic* (= *like*, *-ly*). See **Aghast** and **Gaze**.]

**Ghaut**, gawt, *n.* (*in India*) a mountain-pass : a chain of mountains : landing-stairs for bathers on the sides of a river or tank. [Hind. *ghat*, a passage or gateway.]

**Ghee**, ghē, *n.* clarified butter, made in India, esp. from buffaloes' milk. [The Indian name.]

**Gherkin**, gėr′kin, *n.* a small cucumber used for pickling. [Dut. *agurkje*, a gherkin ; a word of Eastern origin, as in Pers. *khiyâr*.]

**Ghost**, gōst, *n.* (*lit.*) breath, spirit: the soul of man : a spirit appearing after death.—*adj.* **Ghost′like.—To give up the ghost** (*B.*), to die. [A.S. *gast* ; Ger. *geist*.]

**Ghostly**, gōst′li, *adj.*, *spiritual* : religious : pertaining to apparitions.—*n.* **Ghost′liness**.

**Ghoul**, gōōl, *n.* a *demon* supposed to feed on the dead. [Pers. *ghol*, a mountain demon.]

**Giant**, jī′ant, *n* a man of extraordinary size : a person of extraordinary powers.—*fem.* **Gi′antess**.—*adj.* gigantic. [Fr. *géant*—L. *gigas*—Gr. *gigas*, *gigantos*, of which ety. uncertain.]

**Giaour**, jowr, *n.* infidel, term applied by the Turks to all who are not of their own religion. [Pers. *gawr*.]

**Gibberish**, gib′ėr-ish, *n.* rapid, *gabbling* talk : unmeaning words.—*adj.* unmeaning. [Obsolete *gibber*, to gabble or jabber. See **Gabble**.]

**Gibbet**, jib′et, *n.* a gallows : the projecting beam of a crane.—*v.t.* to expose on a gibbet, to execute. [Fr. *gibet* ; origin unknown.]

**Gibbon**, gib′un, *n.* a kind of long-armed ape, native of the East Indies.

**Gibbose**, gib-bōs′, *adj.*, *humped :* having one or more elevations. [Fr. *gibbeux*—L. *gibbosus—gibbus*, a hump.]

**Gibbous**, gib′us, *adj.*, *hump-backed :* swelling, convex, as the moon when nearly full.—*adv.* **Gibb′ously**.—*n.* **Gibb′ousness**.

**Gibe**, jīb, *v.t.* to sneer at : to taunt.—*n.* a scoff or taunt : contempt.—*adv.* **Gib′ingly**. [From Scand., as in Ice. *geipa*, to talk nonsense.]

**Giblets**, jib′lets, *n.pl.* the internal eatable parts of a fowl, taken out before cooking it.—*adj.* **Gib′let**, made of giblets. [O. Fr. *gibelet* ; origin unknown ; not a dim. of *gibier*, game.]

**Giddy**, gid′i, *adj.* unsteady, dizzy : that causes giddiness : whirling : inconstant : thoughtless.—*adv.* **Gidd′ily**.—*n.* **Gidd′iness**. [A.S. *gyddian*, to sing, be merry. [See **Gyrfalcon**.]

**Gier-eagle**, jēr′ē-gl, *n.* (*B.*) a species of eagle.

**Gift**, gift, *n.* a thing *given* : a bribe : a quality bestowed by nature : the act of giving—*v.t.* to endow with any power or faculty. [See **Give**.]

**Gifted**, gift′ed, *adj.* endowed by nature.

**Gig**, gig, *n.* a light, two-wheeled carriage : a long, light boat. [Found in Ice. *gigja*, a fiddle (Fr. *gigue*, a lively dance), and properly meaning a 'thing that moves lightly.']

**Gigantic**, jī-gan′tik, *adj.* suitable to a *giant* : enormous.—*adv.* **Gigan′tically**.

**Giggle**, gig′l, *v.i.* to laugh with short catches of the breath, or in a silly manner.—*n.* a laugh of this kind.—*n.* **Gigg′ler**. [From the sound.]

**Gigot**, jig′ut, *n.* a leg of mutton. [Fr.—O. Fr. *gigue*, a leg ; a word of unknown origin. There is another *gigue*, an old stringed instrument.]

**Gild**, gild, *v.t.* to cover or overlay with *gold* : to cover with any gold-like substance : to adorn with lustre—*pr.p.* gild′ing ; *pa.t.* and *pa.p.* gild′ed or gilt. [A.S. *gyldan—gold*. See **Gold**.]

**Gilder**, gild′ėr, *n.* one whose trade is to gild or cover articles with a thin coating of gold.

**Gilding**, gild′ing, *n.* act or trade of a gilder : gold laid on any surface for ornament.

**Gill**, gil, *n.* (*pl.* the breathing organs in fishes and certain other aquatic animals : the flap below the bill of a fowl. [Scand., as in Dan. *giælle*, a gill, Swed. *gäl*.]

**Gill**, jil, *n.* a measure = ¼ pint. [O. Fr. *gelle* ; cf. Low L. *gillo*, a flask ; allied to Fr. *jale*, a large bowl, E. *gallon*. See **Gallon**.]

**Gill**, jil, *n.* ground-ivy : beer flavoured with ground-ivy. [From *Gillian* or *Juliana* (from *Julius*), a female name, contracted *Gill*, *Jill*.]

**Gillie**, gil′y, gil′i, *n.* a youth, a man-servant. [Gael. *gille*, a lad, Ir. *ceile*. See **Culdee**.]

**Gillyflower**, jil′i-flow-ėr, *n.* popular name for stock, wallflower, &c., so called from its clove-like smell. [Fr. *giroflée*—Gr. *karyophyllon*, the clove-tree—*karyon*, a nut *phyllon*, a leaf.]

**Gilt**, gilt, *adj.* gilded.—*adj.* **Gilt-edged**, having gilded edges, as the leaves of a book.

**Gilt**, gilt. *pa.t.* and *pa.p.* of **Gild**.

**Gimbals**, gim′balz, *n.pl.*, *two rings* for suspending the mariner's compass so as to keep it always horizontal. [L. *gemelli*, twins.]

**Gimblet**. Same as **Gimlet**.      [Ety. dub.]

**Gimcrack**, jim′krak, *n.* a toy : a trivial mechanism.

**Gimlet**, gim′let, *n.* a small tool for boring holes by *wimbling* or turning it with the hand.—*v.t.* to pierce with a gimlet : (*naut.*) to turn round (an anchor) as if turning a gimlet. [Fr. *gibelet*, *gimbelet*, from a Teut. root, whence also E **Wimble**.]

**Gimp**, gimp, *n.* a kind of trimming, &c. of silk, woollen, or cotton twist. [Fr. *guimpe*, from O. Ger. *wimpal*, a light robe ; E. *wimple*.]

**Gin**, jin, *n.* Same as **Geneva**, of which it is a contraction.

**Gin**, jin, *n.* the name of a variety of machines, esp. one with pulleys for raising weights, &c. : a pump worked by rotary sails : a trap or snare (*B.*).—*v.t.* to trap or snare : to clear cotton of its seeds by a machine :—*pr.p.* ginn'ing ; *pa.p.* ginned'. [Contr. from **Engine** ; but in the sense of *snare*, it is derived from Scand., Ice. *ginna*, to deceive.]

**Ginger**, jin'ėr, *n.* the root of a plant in the E. and W. Indies, with a hot and spicy taste, so called from being *shaped* like a *horn*. [Old form in M. E. *gingivere*—O. Fr. *gingibre*—L. *zingiber*—Gr. *zingiberis*—Sans. *çringa-vera*—*çringa*, horn, *vera*, shape.]      [flavoured with ginger.

**Gingerbeer**, jin'jer-bēr, *n.* an effervescent drink

**Gingerbread**, jin'jer-bred, *n.* sweet bread flavoured with ginger.

**Gingerly**, jin'jer-li, *adv.* with soft steps : cautiously. [From a Scand. root, seen in Swed. *gingla*, to totter.]

**Gingham**, ging'ham, *n.* a kind of cotton cloth. [Fr. *guingan*, acc. to Littré, a corr. of *Guingamp*, a town in Brittany, where such stuffs are made.]

**Gingle**, jing'l. Same as **Jingle**.

**Gipsy, Gypsey, Gypsy**, jip'si, *n.* one of a wandering race, originally from India, now scattered over Europe : a reproachful name for one with a dark complexion : a sly, tricking woman. [Lit. *Egyptian*, because supposed to come from Egypt, M. E. *Gyptian*.]

**Giraffe**, ji-raf' or zhi-raf', *n.* the camelopard, an African quadruped with remarkably long neck and legs. [Fr.—Sp. *girafa*—Ar. *zaraf*.]

**Gird**, gėrd, *v.t.* to bind round : to make fast by binding : to surround : to clothe :—*pa.t.* and *pa.p.* gird'ed or girt. [A.S. *gyrdan* ; akin to Ger. *gürten* ; from a root *gard*, whence also E. **Garden** and **Yard**.]

**Girder**, gėrd'ėr, *n.* one who or that which *girds* : one of the principal pieces of timber in a floor binding the others together : (*engineering*) any simple or compound beam sustaining a weight, and supported at both ends.

**Girdle**, gėrd'l, *n.* that which *girds* or encircles, esp. a band for the waist : an inclosure : (*jew.*) a horizontal line surrounding a stone.—*v.t.* to bind as with a girdle : to inclose : to make a circular incision, as through the bark of a tree to kill it. [A.S. *gyrdel*—*gyrdan*, to gird.]

**Girl**, gėrl, *n.* a female child : a young woman. [Prob. from O. Ger. *gōr*, a child, with suffix -*l* = -*la*.]

**Girlhood**, gėrl'hood, *n.* the state of being a *girl*.

**Girlish**, gėrl'ish, *adj.* of or like a *girl*.—*adv.* **Girl'ishly** —*n.* **Girl'ishness**.

**Girt, Girth**, gėrth, *n.* belly-band of a saddle : measure round the waist.

**Girt**, gėrt, *v.t.* to *gird*.

**Gist**, jist, *n.* the main point or pith of a matter. [The word in this sense comes from an old French proverb, ' I know where the hare *lies*' (O. Fr. *gist*, Fr. *gît*), *i.e.* I know the main point —Fr. *gésir*, to lie—L. *jacēre*.]

**Give**, giv, *v.t.* to bestow : to impart : to yield : to grant : to permit : to afford : to furnish : to pay or render, as thanks : to pronounce, as a decision : to shew, as a result : to apply, as one's self : to allow or admit.—*v.i.* to yield to pressure : to

begin to melt : to grow soft :—*pr.p.* giv'ing ; *pa.t.* gāve ; *pa.p.* given (giv'n).—**Give chase**, to pursue : **Give forth**, to emit, to publish : **Give in**, to yield : **Give out**, to report, to emit : **Give over**, to cease : **Give place**, to give way, to yield : **Give up**, to abandon. [A.S. *gifan* ; Ger. *geben*, Goth. *giban*, from a Teut. root *gab*, to give.]

**Giver**, giv'ėr, *n.* one who gives or bestows.

**Gizzard**, giz'ard, *n.* the muscular stomach of a fowl or bird. [M. E. *giser*, Fr. *gésier*—L. *gigerium*, used only in pl. *gigeria*, the cooked entrails of poultry.]

**Glabrous**, glā'brus, *adj.*, *smooth* : having no hairs or any unevenness. [L. *glaber*, smooth ; akin to *glubo*, to peel, Gr. *glaphō*, to carve.]

**Glacial**, glā'shi-al, *adj.*, *icy* : frozen : pertaining to ice or its action, esp. to glaciers. [Fr.—L. *glacialis*—*glacies*, ice.]

**Glacier**, glā'shėr or glas'i-ėr, *n.* a field or, more properly, a slowly moving river of *ice*, such as is found in the hollows and on the slopes of lofty mountains. [Fr.—*glace*, ice—L. *glacies*, ice.]

**Glacis**, glā'sis or glā-sēs', *n.* a gentle slope : (*fort.*) a smooth sloping bank. [Fr.—O. Fr. *glacier*, to slide—*glace*, ice.]

**Glad**, glad, *adj.* pleased : cheerful : bright : giving pleasure.—*v.t.* to make glad :—*pr.p.* gladd'ing ; *pa.p.* gladd'ed.—*adv.* **Glad'ly**.—*n.* **Glad'ness**. [A.S. *glæd* ; Ger. *glatt*, smooth, Ice. *glathr*, bright, Dan. *glad* : the root meant ' shining,' and is found also in **Glade**.]      [animate.

**Gladden**, glad'n, *v.t.* to make glad : to cheer : to

**Glade**, glād, *n.* an open space in a wood. [Scand., as in Norw. *glette*, a clear spot among clouds, Ice. *glita*, to shine, *glathr*, bright ; the original sense being, a ' bright opening.' See **Glad**.]

**Gladiate**, glad'i-āt, *adj.*, *sword-shaped*. [L. *gladius*, a sword.]

**Gladiator**, glad'i-ā-tor, *n.* in ancient Rome, a professional combatant with men or beasts in the arena. [L. (*lit.*) a *swordsman*—*gladius*, a sword.]

**Gladiatorial**, glad-i-a-tōr'i-al, **Gladiatory**, glad'-i-ā-tor-i, *adj.* relating to gladiators or prizefighting.

**Gladiole**, glad'i-ōl, **Gladiolus**, gla-dī'o-lus, *n.* the plant sword-lily. [L. *gladiolus*, dim. of *gladius*.]

**Gladsome**, glad'sum, *adj.*, *glad* : joyous : gay.—*adv.* **Glad'somely**.—*n.* **Glad'someness**.

**Glair**, glār, *n.* the *clear* part of an egg used as varnish : any viscous, transparent substance.—*v.t.* to varnish with white of egg.—*adjs.* **Glair'y**, **Glar'eous**. [Fr. *glaire*—Low L. *clara ovi*, white of egg—L. *clarus*, clear. See **Clear**.]

**Glaive**, glāv, *n.* Same as **Glave**.

**Glamour**, glam'ėr, *n.* the supposed influence of a charm on the eyes, making them see things as fairer than they are. [Scotch ; Ice. *glam*, dimness of sight.]

**Glance**, glans, *n.* a sudden shoot of light : a darting of the eye : a momentary view.—*v.i.* to dart a ray of light or splendour : to snatch a momentary view : to fly off obliquely : to make a passing allusion.—*adv.* **Glanc'ingly**. [From a Teut. root found in Swed. *glans*, Dut. *glans*, Ger. *glanz*, lustre, and allied to obs. E. *glint*, E. *glitter*, *glass*.]

**Gland**, gland, *n.* a fleshy organ of the body which secretes some substance from the blood : (*bot.*) a small cellular spot which secretes oil or aroma. [Fr. *glande*—L. *glans*, *glandis*, an acorn ; from the likeness of shape to an acorn.]

**Glandered**, gland'ėrd, *adj.* affected with glanders.

**Glanders,** gland′ėrz, *n.* (*in horses*) a disease of the *glands* of the lower jaw and of the mucous membrane.

**Glandiferous,** gland-if′ėr-us, *adj., bearing acorns* or nuts. [L. *glandifer—glans, glandis,* and *fero,* to bear.]

**Glandiform,** gland′i-form, *adj.* resembling a *gland* : nut-shaped. [L. *glans,* and *forma,* form.]

**Glandular,** gland′ū-lar, **Glandulous,** gland′ū-lus, *adj.* containing, consisting of, or pertaining to *glands.*

**Glandule,** gland′ūl, *n.* a *small gland.*

**Glare,** glār, *n.* a clear, dazzling light : overpowering lustre : a piercing look.—*v.i.* to shine with a clear, dazzling light : to be ostentatiously splendid : to look with piercing eyes. [Perh. from A.S. *glær,* a pellucid substance, amber ; akin to **Glass.**]

**Glaring,** glār′ing, *adj.* bright and dazzling : barefaced : notorious.—*adv.* **Glar′ingly.**—*n.* **Glar′ingness.**

**Glass,** glas, *n.* the hard, brittle, transparent substance in windows : anything made of glass, esp. a drinking-vessel, a mirror, &c. :—*pl.* spectacles : the quantity of liquid a glass holds.—*adj.* made of glass.—*v.t.* to case in glass.—*adj.* **Glass′like.** [A.S. *glæs* ; widely diffused in the Teut. languages, and from a Teut. base *gal,* to shine, seen also in **Glow, Gleam, Glad, Glance,** and **Glare.**]

**Glass-blower,** glas′-blō′ėr, *n.* one who *blows* and fashions *glass.*

**Glasswort,** glas′wurt, *n.* a *plant* so called from its yielding soda, used in making *glass.* [**Glass,** and A.S. *wyrt,* a plant.]

**Glassy,** glas′i, *adj.* made of or like *glass.*—*adv.* **Glass′ily.**—*n.* **Glass′iness.**

**Glaucoma,** glawk-ō′ma, *n.* a disease of the eye, marked by the green colour of the pupil. [See **Glaucous.**]

**Glaucous,** glaw′kus, *adj.* sea-green : grayish blue : (*bot.*) covered with a fine green bloom. [L. *glaucus,* bluish—Gr. *glaukos,* blue or gray, orig. gleaming, akin to *glausso,* to shine.]

**Glave,** glāv, *n.* a sword. [Fr.—L. *gladius* (= *cladius,* akin to *clades*). See **Claymore.**]

**Glaze,** glāz, *v.t.* to furnish or cover with *glass :* to cover with a thin surface of or resembling glass : to give a glassy surface to.—*n.* the glassy coating put upon pottery : any shining exterior. [M. E. *glasen*—**Glass.**]

**Glazier,** glā′zi-ėr, *n.* one whose trade is to set *glass* in window-frames, &c. [For *glaz-er* ; like *law-y-er* for *law-er.*]

**Glazing,** glāz′ing, *n.* the act or art of setting *glass :* the art of covering with a vitreous substance : (*paint.*) semi-transparent colours put thinly over others to modify the effect.

**Gleam,** glēm, *v.i.* to *glow* or *shine :* to flash.—*n.* a small stream of light : a beam : brightness. [A.S. *glæm,* gleam, brightness ; akin to **Glass, Glow.**]

**Gleamy,** glēm′i, *adj.* casting *beams* or rays of light.

**Glean,** glēn, *v.t.* to gather in *handfuls* the corn left by the reapers : to collect what is thinly scattered.—*v.i.* to gather after a reaper.—*n.* that which is gleaned : the act of gleaning.—*ns.* **Glean′er, Glean′ing.** [O. Fr. *glener*=Fr. *glaner,* through Low L. forms, from A.S. *gelm,* a handful.]

**Glebe,** glēb, *n.* the land belonging to a parish church or ecclesiastical benefice : (*mining*) a piece of earth containing ore. [Fr.—L. *gleba,* a clod, soil. Cf. **Globe.**]

**Glebous,** glēb′us, **Gleby,** glēb′i, *adj., cloddy,* turfy. [L. *glebosus—gleba.*]

**Glede,** glēd, *n.* (*B.*) the common kite, a rapacious bird. [A.S. *glida,* 'the glider,' akin to *glidan,* to glide.]

**Glee,** glē, *n.* joy : mirth and gaiety : (*mus.*) a song or catch in parts. [A.S. *gleo,* mirth, song ; Ice. *gly.*]

**Gleeful,** glē′fool, *adj.* merry.

**Gleeman,** glē′man, *n.* a minstrel. [See **Glee.**]

**Gleet,** glēt, *n.* a glairy discharge from a mucous surface.—*adj.* **Gleet′y.** [From root of **Glide.**]

**Glen,** glen, *n.* a narrow valley worn by a river : a depression between hills. [Celt., as in Gael. and Ir. *gleann,* W. *glyn.*]

**Glib,** glib, *adj.* moving easily : voluble.—*adv.* **Glib′ly.**—*n.* **Glib′ness.** [A contr. of Dut. *glibberig,* slippery.]

**Glide,** glīd, *v.i.* to slide smoothly and easily : to flow gently : to pass rapidly.—*n.* act of gliding.—*adv.* **Glid′ingly.** [A.S. *glidan,* to slip, to slide ; Ger. *gleiten,* to move smoothly, closely akin to **Glad.**]

**Glimmer,** glim′ėr, *v.i.* to burn or appear faintly.—*n.* a faint light : feeble rays of light : (*min.*) mica. [From a Teut. root, found in Dan. and Ger. *glimmer,* of which the base is seen in **Gleam.**]

**Glimmering,** glim′ėr-ing, *n.* Same as **Glimmer,** *n.*

**Glimpse,** glimps, *n.* a short *gleam :* a weak light : transient lustre : a hurried view : fleeting enjoyment : the exhibition of a faint resemblance.—*v.i.* to appear by glimpses. [M. E. *glimsen,* to glimpse—*glim.* See **Glimmer.**]

**Glisten,** glis′n, **Glister,** glis′tėr, *v.i.* to *glitter* or *sparkle* with light : to shine. [From base *glis-,* to shine, with excrescent *-t* ; cf. Dut. *glinsteren.* See **Glitter.**]

**Glitter,** glit′ėr, *v.i.* to glisten, to sparkle with light : to be splendid : to be showy.—*n.* lustre : brilliancy. [Scand., as in Ice. *glitra,* to glisten, Ice. *glit,* glitter ; closely akin to **Glisten, Glister,** &c.]

**Glittering,** glit′ėr-ing, *adj., shining :* splendid : brilliant.—*adv.* **Glitt′eringly.**

**Gloaming,** glōm′ing, *n.* twilight, dusk. [A.S. *glomung,* Scot. *gloamin,* akin to **Gloom.**]

**Gloat,** glōt, *v.i.* to look eagerly, in a bad sense : to view with joy. [Scand., as in Ice. *glotta,* to grin.]

**Globate,** glōb′āt, *adj.* like a *globe :* circular. [L. *globo, globatus,* to form into a ball—*globus.*]

**Globe,** glōb, *n.* a *ball :* a round body, a sphere : the earth : a sphere representing the earth (terrestrial globe) or the heavens (celestial globe). [Fr.—L. *globus ;* akin to *gleba,* a clod.]

**Globose,** glob-ōs′, **Globous,** glōb′us, *adj.* globular.—*n.* **Globo′sity.**

**Globular,** glob′ū-lar, **Globulous,** glob′ū-lus, *adj.* like a *globe :* spherical.—*adv.* **Glob′ularly.**—*n.* **Globular′ity.**

**Globule,** glob′ūl, *n.* a *little globe* or round particle.

**Glome,** glōm, *n.* (*bot.*) a globular head of flowers. [L. *glomus*=*globus,* and conn. with **Clump, Lump.**]

**Glomerate,** glom′ėr-āt, *v.t.* to gather into a *ball :* to collect into a spherical mass.—*adj* growing in rounded or massive forms : conglomerate. [L. *glomero, -atus—glomus, glomeris,* a clue of yarn.]

**Glomeration,** glom-ėr-ā′shun, *n.* act of gathering into a *ball :* a body formed into a ball.

**Gloom,** glōm, *n.* partial darkness : cloudiness : heaviness of mind, sadness : hopelessness : sullenness.—*v.i.* to be sullen or dejected: to be cloudy or obscure. [A.S. *glom*, gloom; Prov. Ger. *glumm*, gloomy, E. **Glum.**]

**Gloomy**, glōōm'i, *adj.* dim or obscure: dimly lighted: sad, melancholy.—*adv.* **Gloom'ily**.—*n.* **Gloom'iness**.

**Glorify**, glō'ri-fī, *v.t.* to make *glorious*: to honour: to exalt to glory or happiness: to ascribe honour to, to worship:—*pa.p.* glō'rified.—*n.* **Glorifica'-tion.** [L. *gloria*, and *facio*, to make.]

**Glorious**, glō'ri-us, *adj.* noble, splendid: conferring renown.—*adv.* **Glo'riously**.—*n.* **Glo'rious-ness.** [L. *gloriosus*.]

**Glory**, glō'ri, *n.* renown: honour: the occasion of praise: an object of pride: excellency: splendour: brightness: circle of rays surrounding the head of a saint: (*B.*) the presence of God: the manifestation of God to the blessed in heaven: heaven.—*v.i.* to boast: to be proud of anything: to exult:—*pa.p.* glō'ried. [Fr.—L. *gloria* (for *cloria*), akin to *clarus*, from root of L. *clu-eo*, Gr. *klu-o*, to be famed; E. **Loud.**]

**Gloss**, glos, *n.*, *brightness* or lustre, as from a polished surface: external show.—*v.t.* to give a superficial lustre to: to render plausible: to palliate. [Ice. *glossi*, brightness, *gloa*, to glow. See **Glass.**]

**Gloss**, glos, *n.* a remark to explain a subject: a comment.—*v.i.* to comment or make explanatory remarks. [L. *glossa*, a word requiring explanation—Gr. *glōssa*, the tongue.]

**Glossarial**, glos-ā'ri-al, *adj.* relating to a glossary: containing explanation.

**Glossarist**, glos'ar-ist, *n.* a writer of a glossary.

**Glossary**, glos'ar-i, *n.* a vocabulary of words requiring special explanation. [From Gr. *glōssa*.]

**Glossator**, glos-ā'tor, *n.* a writer of *glosses* or comments: a commentator.

**Glossography**, glos-og'raf-i, *n.* the *writing* of *glossaries* or comments.—*n.* **Glossog'rapher**.—*adj.* **Glossograph'ical**. [Gr. *glōssa*, and *graphō*, to write.]

**Glossology**, glos-ol'o-ji, *n.* the science of language: the knowledge of the definition of technical terms.—*n.* **Glossol'ogist**.—*adj.* **Glossolog'ical**. [Gr. *glōssa*, and *logos*, a discourse.]

**Glossy**, glos'i, *adj.* smooth and shining: highly polished.—*adv.* **Gloss'ily**.—*n.* **Gloss'iness**.

**Glottis**, glot'is, *n.* the opening of the larynx or entrance to the windpipe.—*adj.* **Glott'al**. [Gr. *glōttis—glōssa*, the tongue.]

**Glottology**, glot-ol'o-ji, *n.* the science of language, comparative philology. [Gr. *glōtta*, Attic for *glōssa*, and *logos*, a discourse.]

**Glove**, gluv, *n.* a cover for the hand, with a sheath for each finger.—*v.t.* to cover with or as with a glove. [A.S. *glof* (= *ge-lof*); allied to Scot. *loof*, Ice. *lofi*, palm of the hand.]

**Glover**, gluv'ėr, *n.* one who makes or sells *gloves*.

**Glow**, glō, *v.i.* to shine with an intense heat: to feel great heat of body: to be flushed: to feel the heat of passion: to be ardent.—*n.* shining or white heat: unusual warmth: brightness of colour: vehemence of passion. [A.S. *glowan*, to glow, as a fire; Ger. *glühen*, Ice. *gloa*, to glow.]

**Glow-worm**, glō'-wurm, *n.* the female of a certain *insect*, which *glows* or shines in the dark.

**Gloze**, glōz, *v.i.* to give a false meaning to: to flatter: to wheedle.—*v.t.* to palliate by specious explanation. [M. E. *glosen*, to make glosses, from M. E. *glose*, a gloss. See **Gloss** a remark.]

**Glucose**, glōō-kōs', *n.* the peculiar kind of *sugar* in the juice of fruits. [Gr. *glykys*, sweet.]

**Glue**, glōō, *n.* a sticky substance obtained by boiling to a jelly the skins, hoofs, &c. of animals.—*v.t.* to join with glue:—*pr.p.* glū'ing; *pa.p.* glūed'. [Fr. *glu*—Low L. *glus*, *glutis—gluo*, to draw together.] [—*n.* **Glu'eyness**.

**Gluey**, glōō'i, *adj.* containing glue: *sticky*: viscous.

**Glum**, glum, *adj.* frowning: sullen: gloomy. [From root of **Gloom.**]

**Glume**, glōōm, *n.* the *husk* or floral covering of grain and grasses.—*adj.* **Gluma'ceous**. [L. *gluma*, husk—*glubo*, to peel off bark.]

**Glut**, glut, *v.t.* to swallow greedily: to feast to satiety: to supply in excess:—*pr.p.* glutt'ing; *pa.p.* glutt'ed.—*n.* that which is gorged: more than enough: anything that obstructs the passage. [L. *glutio*—root *glu*, akin to Sans. *gri*, to devour, and L. *gula*, and *gurgulio*, the throat: from the sound of swallowing.]

**Gluten**, glōō'ten, *n.* the viscid, sticky substance seen in the dough of wheaten bread. [L. *gluten*, the same as *glus*. See **Glue.**]

**Glutinate**, glōō'tin-āt, *v.t.* to unite, as with *glue*.—*n.* **Glutina'tion**. [L. *glutino*, *glutinatum—gluten*.]

**Glutinative**, glōō'tin-ā-tiv, *adj.* having the quality of *gluing* or cementing: tenacious.

**Glutinous**, glōō'tin-us, *adj.*, *gluey*: tenacious: (*bot.*) covered, as a leaf, with slimy moisture.—*n.* **Glu'tinousness**.

**Glutton**, glut'n, *n.* one who eats to excess: a carnivorous quadruped in northern regions, once thought very voracious. [Fr. *glouton*—L. *gluto*, from L. root of **Glut.**] [*glutton*.

**Gluttonise**, glut'n-īz, *v.i.* to eat to excess, like a

**Gluttonous**, glut'n-us, **Gluttonish**, glut'n-ish, *adj.* given to, or consisting in *gluttony*.—*adv.* **Glutt'onously**.

**Gluttony**, glut'n-i, *n.* excess in eating.

**Glycerine**, glis'ėr-in, *n.* a colourless, viscid liquid of a *sweet* taste. [Fr.—Gr. *glykeros* = *glykys*, sweet.]

**Glyph**, glif, *n.* (*arch.*) an ornamental *sunken* channel or fluting, usually vertical. [Gr. *glyphē—glyphō*, to hollow out, carve.]

**Glyphography**, glif-og'raf-i, *n.* a process of taking a *raised* copy of a *drawing* by electrotype.—*adj.* **Glyphograph'ic**. [Gr. *glypho*, to carve, engrave, and *graphē*, drawing—*graphō*, to write.]

**Glyptic**, glip'tik, *adj.* pertaining to *carving* on stone, &c.: (*min.*) figured.—**Glyp'tics**, *n.sing.* the art of engraving, esp. on precious stones.

**Glyptodon**, glip'tod-on, *n.* a fossil animal of S. America with fluted teeth. [Gr. *glyptos*, carved, and *odous*, *odontos*, tooth.]

**Glyptography**, glip-tog'raf-i, *n.* a description of the art of *engraving* on precious stones.—*adj.* **Glyptograph'ic**. [Gr. *glyptos*, carved, and *graphō*, to write.]

**Gnar**, när, *v.i.* to snarl or growl. [From a Teut. root found in Ger. *knurren*, Dan. *knurre*, to growl; formed from the sound.]

**Gnarl**, närl, *v.i.* to snarl or growl. [Freq. of **Gnar.**]

**Gnarl**, närl, *n.* a twisted knot in wood.—*adj.* **Gnarled**, knotty, twisted. [From a Teut. root, as in Ger. *knorren*, Dan. *knort*, a knot, gnarl, and prob. akin to *gnarl* in the sense of pressing close together.]

**Gnash**, nash, *v.t.* to strike the *teeth* together in rage or pain.—*v.i.* to grind the teeth. [From the sound.] [irritating bite. [A.S. *gnæt*.]

**Gnat**, nat, *n.* a small winged insect with an

**Gnaw**, naw, *v.t.* to bite so as to make a noise with the teeth: to bite off by degrees: to bite in agony or rage: (*fig.*) to torment.—*v.i.* to use the teeth in biting. [A.S. *gnagan*; cf. Dut. *knagen*, Ice. *naga*, Prov. E. *nag*, to tease, worry.]

**Gneiss**, nīs, *n.* (*geol.*) a species of stratified rock composed of quartz, felspar, and mica. [Ger. *gneiss*, a name used by the Saxon miners, of unknown origin.]

**Gneissoid**, nīs'oid, *adj.* having some of the *characters of gneiss.* [**Gneiss**, and Gr. *eidos*, form.]

**Gnome**, nōm, *n.* a sententious saying.—*adj.* **Gnom'ic**. [Gr. *gnomē*, an opinion—*gnōnai*, *gignōskō*, to know.]

**Gnome**, nōm, *n.* a kind of sprite, said to preside over the inner parts of the earth and its treasures : a dwarf or goblin. [Fr.—a word traced by Littré to Paracelsus, and perh. formed from Gr. *gnōmē*, intelligence, because it was supposed these spirits could reveal the treasures of the earth.]

**Gnomon**, nō'mon, *n.* the pin of a dial, whose shadow points to the hour : the index of the hour-circle of a globe : (*geom.*) a parallelogram minus one of the parallelograms about its diagonal. [Gr. *gnōmōn*, an interpreter—*gnōnai*, to know.]

**Gnomonic**, nō-mon'ik, **Gnomonical**, nō-mon'ik-al, *adj.* pertaining to the art of dialling.—*adv.* **Gnomon'ically**.—*n.sing.* **Gnomon'ics**, the art of dialling.

**Gnostic**, nos'tik, *n.* one of a sect in the beginning of the Christian era who pretended that they alone had a true *knowledge* of religion.—*adj.* pertaining to the Gnostics or their doctrines. [Gr. *gnōstikos*, good at knowing—*gignōskō*, to know.]

**Gnosticism**, nos'ti-sizm, *n.* the doctrines of the *Gnostics.*

**Gnu**, nū, *n.* a kind of antelope in S. Africa, resembling the horse and ox. [Hottentot, *gnu.*]

**Go**, gō, *v.i.* to pass from one place to another : to be in motion : to proceed : to walk : to depart from : to lead in any direction : to extend : to tend : to be about to do : to pass in report : to pass, as in payment : to be accounted in value : to happen in a particular way : to turn out : to fare :—*pr.p.* gō'ing ; *pa.t.* went ; *pa.p.* gone (gon).—**Go about** (*B.*), to set one's self about : to seek : to endeavour.—**Go beyond** (*B.*), to overreach.—**Go to**, *int.* (*B.*) come now ! [A.S. *gan, gangan* ; Ger. *gehen*, Dan. *gaa.*]

**Goad**, gōd, *n.* a sharp-pointed stick, often shod with iron, for driving oxen : a stimulus.—*v.t.* to drive with a goad : to urge forward. [A.S. *gad*, a goad.]

**Goal**, gōl, *n.* a mark set up to bound a race : the winning-post ; also the starting-post : the two upright posts between which the ball is kicked in the game of football : an end or aim. [Fr. *gaule*, a pole ; prob. of Teut. origin, as Fris. *walu*, a staff, Goth. *walus* ; but acc. to Littré from L. *vallus*, a stake.]

**Goat**, gōt, *n.* the well-known quadruped, allied to the sheep. [A.S. *gat* ; Ger. *geiss*—obs. and prov. Ger. *geissen = gehen*, to go ; like Gr. *aix*, a goat—*aïssō*, to leap : akin to L. *hædus*.]

**Goatmoth**, gōt'moth, *n.* one of the largest of British *moths*, which has a *goatlike* odour.

**Goat's'-beard**, -bērd, **Goat's'-rue**, -rōō, **Goat's'-stones**, -stōnz, **Goat's'-thorn**, -thorn, *n.* names of plants.

**Goatsucker**, gōt'suk-ėr, *n.* a kind of swallow erroneously thought to *suck goats.*

**Go-between**, gō'-be-twēn', *n.* one who is agent between two parties.

**Gobbet**, gob'et, *n.* a *mouthful* : a little lump [Fr. *gobet*—Gael. *gob*, the mouth, from the sound.]

**Gobble**, gob'l, *v.t.* to swallow in lumps : to swallow hastily.—*v.i.* to make a noise in the throat, as a turkey. [Fr. *gober*, to devour, with E. suffix -*le*—a Celt. word *gob*, the mouth, which has also passed into prov. E.]

**Gobelin**, gob'e-lin, *n.* a rich French tapestry. [From the Gobelins, Flemish dyers settled in Paris in the 16th century.]

**Goblet**, gob'let, *n.* a large drinking *cup* without a handle. [Fr. *gobelet*, dim. of Low L. *gubellus*, which again is a dim. of L. *cupa*, a cask. See **Cup**.]

**Goblin**, gob'lin, *n.* a frightful phantom : a fairy. [Fr. *goblin*—Low L. *gobelinus*—Gr. *kobālos*, a mischievous spirit. See **Cobalt**.]

**Goby**, gō'bi, *n.* a genus of small sea-fishes, which build nests of seaweed. [L. *gobius*—Gr. *kōbios.*]

**Go-by**, gō'-bī, *n.* a going by without notice : escape by artifice : evasion.

**Go-cart**, gō'-kärt, *n.* a *cart* or contrivance for teaching children to *go* or walk.

**God**, god, *n.* the Supreme Being : the Creator and Preserver of the world : an object of worship, an idol : (*B.*) a ruler.—*fem.* **Godd'ess**. [A.S. *god* ; Ger. *gott*, Goth. *guth*, Dut. *god*, and in all the other Teut. languages ; all from a Teut. root *gutha*, God, and quite distinct from *good* ; perh. conn. with Pers. *khoda*, lord, and Sans. *gudha*, secret.]

**Godfather**, god'fä-*th*ėr, *n.* a man who, at a child's baptism, engages to be its *father* in relation to *God* or its religious training.—*fem.* **God'mother**.—*ns.* **God'child**, **God'-daughter**, **God'son**.

**Godhead**, god'hed, *n.* state of being a god : deity : divine nature. [**God**, and **Head**, which see in list of Affixes.]

**Godless**, god'les, *adj.* living without God : impious : atheistical.—*adv.* **God'lessly**.—*n.* **God'lessness**.

**Godlike**, god'līk, *adj.* like God : divine.

**Godly**, god'li, *adj.* like God in character : pious : according to God's law.—*advs.* **God'ly**, **God'lily**.—*n.* **God'liness**. [**God**, and *ly = like*.]

**Godmother**. See **Godfather**.

**Godsend**, god'send, *n.* an unexpected piece of good-fortune. [**God** and **Send**.]

**Godson**, god'sun, *n.* See **Godfather**.

**Godspeed**, god'spēd, *n.* for *good speed* or success. [Cf. A.S. *gōd-spēdig*, successful.]

**Godward**, god'wawrd, *adv.*, *toward God*. [**God**, and A.S. *weard*, L. *versus*, sig. direction.]

**Godwit**, god'wit, *n.* a bird with a long bill and long slender legs, that frequents marshes. [Perh. from A.S. *god*, good, and *wiht*, creature.]

**Goer**, gō'ėr, *n.* one who or that which goes : a horse, considered in reference to his gait.

**Goggle**, gog'l, *v.i.* to strain or roll the eyes.—*adj.* rolling : staring : prominent.—*n.* a stare, or affected rolling of the eye :—*pl.* spectacles with projecting eye-tubes : blinds for shying horses. [Prob. freq. of Celt. *gog*, to move slightly ; *gog*, a nod.]

**Going**, gō'ing, *n.* the act of moving : departure : (*B.*) course of life, behaviour.—**Going forth**, *n.* (*B.*) an outlet.—**Goings** or **goings out**, *n.* (*B.*) utmost extremity : departures or journeyings.

**Goitre, Goiter**, goi'tėr, *n.* a tumour on the fore-part of the throat, being an enlargement of one of the glands. [Fr. *gottre*—L. *guttur*, the throat. Cf. **Cretin**.] [*goitre.*

**Goitred, Goitered**, goi'tėrd, *adj.* affected with *goitre.*

**Goitrous**, goi'trus, *adj.* pertaining to *goitre.*

**Gold**, gōld, *n.* one of the precious metals much used for coin : money, riches : yellow, gold colour. [A.S. ; also in most Aryan languages, **as**

Ice. *gull*, Ger. *gold*, Goth. *gul-th*, Russ. *zla-to*, Gr. *chry-sos*, Sans. *hirana*—all from a primary form *ghar-ta*, from a root *ghar*, to be yellow, from which also *green*, *yellow*, are derived.]

**Gold-beater**, gōld'-bēt'ėr, *n.* one whose trade is to beat gold into gold-leaf.—*n.* **Gold'-beat'ing.**

**Gold-dust**, gōld'-dust, *n.* gold in dust or very fine particles, as it is sometimes found in rivers.

**Golden**, gōld'n, *adj.* made of gold: of the colour of gold: bright: most valuable: happy: highly favourable. [A.S. *gylden*—*gold*.]

**Goldfinch**, gōld'finsh, *n.* a singing-bird or *finch* with *gold*-coloured wings.

**Goldfish**, gōld'fish, *n.* a small *gold*-coloured *fish*, native to China, kept in this country in glass globes and ponds.

**Gold-leaf**, gōld'-lēf, *n.* gold beaten extremely thin, or into leaves, and used for gilding.

**Goldsmith**, gōld'smith, *n.* a smith or worker in gold and silver.

**Goldylocks**, gōld'i-loks, *n.* a plant with *yellow* flowers, like *locks* of hair: wood crowfoot.

**Golf**, golf, *n.* a game played with a *club* and ball, in which he who drives the ball into a series of small holes in the ground with fewest strokes is the winner. [From name of a Dut. game—Dut. *kolf*, a club: cf. Ger. *kolbe*, Ice. *kolfr*. See **Club**.]

**Golosh**, go-losh', *n.* Same as **Galoche**.

**Gondola**, gon'do-la, *n.* a long, narrow pleasure-boat used at Venice. [It., a dim. of *gonda*—Gr. *kondy*, a drinking-vessel, said to be a Pers. word.]

**Gondolier**, gon-do-lēr', *n.* one who rows a *gondola*.

**Gone**, gon, *pa.p.* of **Go**.

**Gonfalon**, gon'fa-lon, *n.* an ensign or standard with streamers.—*n.* **Gon'falonier**, one who bears the foregoing. [Fr.—It. *gonfalone*.]

**Gong**, gong, *n.* a musical instrument of circular form, made of bronze, producing, when struck with a wooden mallet, a loud sound. [Malay.]

**Gonorrhea**, gon-or-rē'a, *n.* an inflammatory discharge of mucus from the membrane of the urethra. [Gr. *gonorrhoia*—*gonē*, that which begets, and *rheō*, to flow.]

**Good**, good, *adj.* having qualities, whether physical or moral, desirable or suitable to the end proposed: promoting success, welfare, or happiness: virtuous: pious: kind: benevolent: proper: fit: competent: sufficient: valid: sound: serviceable: beneficial: real: serious, as in *good earnest*: not small, considerable, as in *good deal*: full, complete, as *measure*: unblemished, honourable, as in *good name*:—*comp.* **Bett'er**: *superl.* **Best.**—**As good as**, the same as, no less than. [A.S. *gōd*; closely akin to Dut. *goed*, Ger. *gut*, Ice. *gothr*, Goth. *gods*.]

**Good**, good, *n.* that which promotes happiness, success. &c.:—opposed to **Evil**: prosperity: welfare: advantage. temporal or spiritual: moral qualities: virtue: (*B.*) possessions:—*pl.* household furniture: movable property: merchandise.

**Good**, good, *int.* well! right!

**Good-breeding**, good-brēd'ing, *n.* polite manners formed by a *good breeding* or education.

**Good-bye**, good-bī', *n.* or *int.* contracted from *God be with you*: farewell, a form of address at parting.

**Good-day**, good-dā', *n., int.* a common salutation, a contr. of *I wish you a good day.* [panion.

**Good-fellow**, good-fel'o, *n.* a jolly or boon companion.

**Good-fellowship**, good-fel o-ship, *n.* merry or pleasant company: conviviality. [See **Fellow**.]

**Good-Friday**, good-fri'dā, *n.* a fast, in memory of our Lord's crucifixion, held on the *Friday* of Passion-week.

**Good-humour**, good-yōō'mur, *n.* a *good* or cheerful temper, from the old idea that temper depended on the *humours* of the body.—*adj.* **Good-hu'moured.**—*adv.* **Good-hu'mouredly.**

**Goodly**, good'li, *adj., good-like*; good-looking: fine: excellent:—*comp.* **Good'lier**; *superl.* **Good'-liest.**—*n.* **Good'liness.**

**Goodman**, good-man', *n.* (*B.*) the *man* or master of the house; the co-relative to it is **Goodwife.**

**Good-nature**, good-nā'tūr, *n.* natural goodness and mildness of disposition.—*adj.* **Good-na'tured.**—*adv.* **Good-na'turedly.** [lence.

**Goodness**, good'nes, *n.* virtue: excellence: benevo-

**Good-night**, good-nīt', *n., int.* a common salutation, a contr. of *I wish you a good night.*

**Good-speed**, good-spēd', *n.* a contr. of *I wish you good speed.* [Cf. **Speed** and **Godspeed.**]

**Good-will**, good-wil', *n.* benevolence: well-wishing: the custom of any business or trade.

**Goose**, gōōs, *n.* a web-footed animal like a duck, but larger and stronger: a tailor's smoothing-iron, from the likeness of the handle to the neck of a goose: a stupid silly person:—*pl.* **Geese.** [A.S. *gos* (from older form *gans*); akin to Ice. *gas* (also for *gans*), Ger. *gans*, L. *anser* (= *hans-er*), Gr. *chēn*, Sans. *hamsa*, Russ. *gus'*; from base *ghan-*, root *gha-*, to gape (whence **Gannet, Gander,** and **Yawn**), with *s* added.]

**Gooseberry**, gōōz'ber-i, *n.* the berry or fruit of a shrub of the same name. [*Goose-* is for *grose-* or *groise-*, which appears in O. Fr. *groisele*, a gooseberry, Scot. *grosart*, and is from the O. Ger. *krus* (Ger. *kraus*), crisp, curled, from the hairs with which the coarser varieties are covered.]

**Goose-grass**, gōōs'-gras, *n.* a common creeping plant, a favourite food of the *goose.*

**Goose-quill**, gōōs'-kwil, *n.* one of the quills or large wing-feathers of a goose, used as pens.

**Goosery**, gōōs'ėr-i, *n.* a place for keeping *geese.*

**Gopher**, gō'ėr, *n.* (*B.*) a kind of wood, prob. fir. [The Heb. word.]

**Gorcock**, gor'kok, *n.* the moorcock or red grouse. [*Gor* is either derived from **Gorse**, furze; or it may be from its cry.]

**Gorcrow**, gor'krō, *n.* the *gore* or carrion *crow.* [A.S *gor*, filth, carrion, and **Crow**.]

**Gordian**, gord'yan, *adj.* intricate: difficult. [The *Gordian knot* was a knot so tied by Gordius, king of Phrygia, that no one could untie it.]

**Gore**, gōr, *n.* clotted blood: blood. [A.S. *gor*, blood, dung, dirt; akin to Sw. *gorr*, Ice. *garn-ir*, *gorn*, guts; L. *hira*, gut.]

**Gore**, gōr, *n.* a *triangular* piece let into a garment to widen it: a triangular piece of land.—*v.t.* to shape like or furnish with gores: to pierce with anything pointed, as a spear or horns. [A.S. *gara*, a pointed triangular piece of land—*gar*, a spear with triangular blade.]

**Gorge**, gorj, *n.* the throat: a narrow pass among hills: (*fort.*) the entrance to an outwork. —*v.t.* to swallow greedily: to glut.—*v.i.* to feed. [Fr.—L. *gurges*. a whirlpool; from its gaping appearance or voracity, applied to the gullet; akin to Sans. *gar-gar-a*, whirlpool.]

**Gorgeous**, gor'jus, *adj.* showy: splendid.—*adv.* **Gor'geously**—*n.* **Gor'geousness.** [O. Fr. *gor-gias*, beautiful, gaudy—*gorgias*, a ruff, Fr. *gorge*, the throat. See **Gorge**.]

**Gorget**, gor'jet. *n.* a piece of armour for the *throat*: a military ornament round the neck. [O. Fr. *gorgette*—Fr. *gorge*. See **Gorge**.]

**Gorgon**, gor'gun, *n.* a fabled monster of so horrible an aspect that every one who looked on it was turned to stone : anything very ugly. [L. *gorgon*—Gr. *gorgō-gorgos*, grim.]

**Gorgon**, gor′gun, **Gorgonean, Gorgonian**, gor-gō′ni-an, *adj.* like a *gorgon* : very ugly or terrific.

**Gorilla**, gor-il′a, *n.* the largest of the monkey tribe, found on the west coast of tropical Africa. [The African word.]

**Gormand.** Older form of **Gourmand**.

**Gormandise**, gor′mand-īz, *v.i.* to eat like a *gor-mand*.—*n.* **Gor′mandiser**.

**Gormandising**, gor′mand-īz-ing, *n.* the act or habit of eating like a *gormand* or voraciously.

**Gorse**, gors, *n.* a prickly shrub growing on waste places, the furze or whin. [A.S. *gorst*, furze.]

**Gory**, gōr′i, *adj.* covered with *gore* : bloody.

**Goshawk**, gos′hawk, *n.* a short-winged hawk, once used for hunting *wild-geese* and other fowl. [A.S. *gos*, goose, *hafuc*, hawk.]

**Gosling**, goz′ling, *n.* a young goose. [A.S. *gos*, goose, *ling*, little.]

**Gospel**, gos′pel, *n.* the Christian revelation : the narrative of the life of Christ, as related by Matthew, Mark, Luke, or John : a system of religious truth. [A.S. *godspell* ; commonly derived from A.S. *gōd*, good, and *spell*, story, and so a translation of Gr. *eu-anggelion*, good news ; but more prob. from *god*, God, and *spell*, a narrative, God-story ; so also the Ice. is *guth-spjall*, God-story, and not *gōth-spjall*, good-story ; and the O. Ger. was *got* (God) -*spel*, not *guot* (good) -*spel*.]

**Gossamer**, gos′a-mėr, *n.* very fine spider-threads which float in the air or form webs on bushes in fine weather. [M. E. *gossomer*, perh. formed from *god* and *summer*—M. E. *samare*—Romance *samarra*, the skirt of a mantua, from the legend that it is the shreds of the Virgin Mary's shroud which she cast away when she was taken up to heaven ; Skeat thinks it is formed of *goose* and *summer*, of which *summer* may (as in Ger. *mädchen-sommer*) mean 'summer-film.']

**Gossip**, gos′ip, *n.* a familiar acquaintance : one who runs about telling and hearing news : idle talk.—*v.i.* to run about telling idle tales : to talk much : to chat.—*n.* **Goss′ipry.**—*adj.* **Goss′ipy.** [Orig. a sponsor in baptism, or one *related* in the service of *God ;* M. E. *gossib* (earlier form, *godsib*)—**God**, and *sib*, peace, relationship ; cf. Ger. *sippe*, Ice. *sif*, affinity, Scot. *sib*, related.]

**Got, Gotten.** See under **Get**.

**Goth**, goth, *n.* one of an ancient Germanic nation : a rude or uncivilised person, a barbarian. [A.S. *Geatas*, L. *Gothi*, Gr. *Gothoi*, Goth. *Guthans*, the Goths.]

**Gothamite**, goth′a-mīt, or **Gothamist**, goth′a-mist, *n.* a simpleton : a wiseacre. [Orig. 'man of Gotham,' a village of Nottinghamshire, which got a reputation for foolish blundering.]

**Gothic**, goth′ik, *adj.* belonging to the *Goths* or their language : barbarous : romantic : denoting a style of architecture with high-pointed arches, clustered columns, &c. [Applied to architecture as a term of reproach at the time of the Renascence.] [bring back to barbarism.

**Gothicise**, goth′i-sīz, *v.t.* to make *Gothic* : to

**Gothicism**, goth′i-sizm, *n.* a *Gothic* idiom or style of building : rudeness of manners.

**Gouge**, gōōj or gowj, *n.* a chisel, with a hollow blade, for cutting grooves or holes.—*v.t.* to scoop out, as with a gouge : to force out, as the eye with the thumb. [Fr.—Low L. *guvia*, a kind of chisel.]

**Gourd**, gōrd or gōōrd, *n.* a large fleshy fruit : the

rind of a gourd used as a drinking-cup : the gourd plant. [Fr. *cougourde*—L. *cucurbita*, a gourd.]

**Gourmand**, gōōr′mand, *n.* one who eats greedily : a glutton.—*adj.* voracious : gluttonous. [Fr. *gourmand*, a glutton ; origin unknown.]

**Gout**, gowt, *n.* a disease of the smaller joints, and esp. of the great toe. [Fr. *goutte*—L. *gutta*, a drop, because the disease was supposed to be caused by a humour settling on the joints in drops.]

**Gout**, gōō, *n.* taste : relish. [Fr.—L. *gustus*, taste : akin to Gr. *geuō*, to make to taste.]

**Gouty**, gowt′i, *adj.* relating to *gout* : diseased with or subject to gout.—*adv.* **Gout′ily.**—*n.* **Gout′iness.**

**Govern**, guv′ėrn, *v.t.* to direct : to control : to rule with authority : (*gram.*) to determine the mood, tense, or case of.—*v.i.* to exercise authority : to administer the laws.—*adj.* **Gov′ernable.** [Fr. *gouverner* (It. *governare*)—L. *guberno*, to steer a ship, to rule, borrowed from Gr. *kybernaō*, akin to Gr. *kybē*, head.]

**Governance**, guv′ėr-nans, *n.*, *government* : control : direction.

**Governante**, guv-ėr-nant′ or guv′-, *n.* The same as **Governess**. [Fr.—*gouvernant*, pr.p. of *gouverner*.]

**Governess**, guv′ėr-nes, *n.* a lady who has charge of the instruction of young ladies : a tutoress. [O. Fr. *governesse*—L. *gubernatrix*—*guberno*.]

**Government**, guv′ėrn-ment, *n.* a ruling or managing : control : system of governing : the persons authorised to administer the laws : the territory over which sovereign power extends : (*gram.*) the power of one word in determining the form of another.—*adj.* of or pursued by government. [Fr. *gouvernement*—*gouverner*.]

**Governmental**, guv-ėrn-ment′al, *adj.* pertaining to or sanctioned by *government*.

**Governor**, guv′ėrn-ur, *n.* a ruler : one invested with supreme authority : a tutor : (*machinery*) a regulator, or contrivance for maintaining uniform velocity with a varying resistance : (*B.*) a pilot. —*n.* **Gov′ernorship.**

**Gowan**, gow′an, *n.* the wild daisy. [Celt., as in Ir. and Gael. *gugan*, bud, daisy.]

**Gown**, gown, *n.* a woman's upper garment : a long loose robe worn by professional men. [W. *gwn*, akin to *gwnio*, to stitch.]

**Gowned**, gownd, *adj.* dressed in a *gown*.

**Gownman**, gown′man, **Gownsman**, gownz′man, *n.* one whose professional habit is a *gown*, as a divine or lawyer, and esp. a member of an English university.

**Grab**, grab (vulgar) *v.t.* to *seize* or grasp suddenly : —*pr.p.* grabb′ing ; *pa.p.* grabbed′. [From same root as **Grapple, Grasp, Grip.** Cf. Sw. *grabba*, to grasp, Ger. *greifen*, to seize.]

**Grabble**, grab′l, *v.i.* to grope. [Freq. of **Grab**.]

**Grace**, grās, *n.* easy elegance in form or manner : what adorns and commends to favour : adornment, embellishment : favour : mercy, pardon : the undeserved kindness and mercy of God : divine influence : eternal life or salvation : a short prayer at meat : the title of a duke or an archbishop :—*pl.* (with *good*) favour, friendship : (*myth.*) the three sister goddesses in whom beauty was deified.—*v.t.* to mark with favour : to adorn.—**Days of Grace**, three days allowed for the payment of a note or bill of exchange, after being due acc. to its date. [Fr.—L. *gratia*, favour—*gratus*, agreeable ; akin to Gr. *charis*, grace.] [**Grace′fully.**—*n.* **Grace′fulness.**

**Graceful**, grās′fool, *adj.* elegant and easy.—*adv.*

**Graceless**, grās′les, *adj.* wanting grace or excellence : depraved : wicked.—*adv.* **Grace′lessly.** —*n.* **Grace′lessness.**

**Gracious**, grā′shus, *adj.* abounding in grace or kindness : benevolent : proceeding from divine favour : acceptable.—*adv.* **Gra′ciously.**—*n.* **Gra′ciousness.**

**Gradation**, gra-dā′shun, *n.* a rising *step by step* : progress from one degree or state to another : state of being arranged in ranks : (*mus.*) a diatonic succession of chords : (*paint.*) the gradual blending of tints.—*adj.* **Grada′tional.** [Fr.—L. *gradatio*, a rising by steps—*gradus*, a step.]         [*tions* or stages.

**Gradationed**, gra-dā′shund, *adj.* formed by *grada-*

**Grade**, grād, *n.* a *degree* or *step* in rank or dignity : the degree of slope on a road. [Fr.—L. *gradus*, a step—*gradior*, to step, to go.]

**Gradient**, grā′di-ent, *adj.* gradually rising : rising with a regular slope.—*n.* the degree of slope on a road or railway : the difference in the height of the barometer between one place and another place at some distance : an incline. [L. *gradiens, -entis*, pr.p. of *gradior*, to step.]

**Gradual**, grad′ū-al, *adj.* advancing by *grades* or degrees : regular and slow.—*adv.* **Grad′ually.** —*n.* **Gradual′ity.**

**Gradual**, grad′ū-al, **Grail**, grāl, *n.* in the Roman Church, the portion of the mass between the epistle and the gospel, formerly always sung from the *steps* of the altar : the book containing such anthems. [Low L. *graduale* (or *gradale*) —L. *gradus*, a step. **Grail** is from O. Fr. *greel—graduale.*]

**Graduate**, grad′ū-āt, *v.t.* to divide into regular intervals : to mark with *degrees* : to proportion. —*v.i.* to pass by *grades* or degrees : to pass through a university course and receive a degree. —*n.* one admitted to a degree in a college, university, or society.—*n.* **Gradua′tion.** [Low L. *graduatus*—L. *gradus*, a step, a degree.]

**Graduator**, grad′ū-ā-tor, *n.* a mathematical instrument for *graduating* or dividing lines into regular intervals.

**Gradus**, grā′dus, *n.* a dictionary of Greek or Latin prosody. [Contr. of *gradus ad Parnassum*, a step or stair to Parnassus, the abode of the Muses.]

**Graff**, *n.* and *v.* (*B.*) old form of **Graft**.

**Graft**, graft, *n.* a small branch used in grafting. —*v.t.* to make an incision in a tree or plant, and insert in it a small branch of another : to insert in something anything not belonging to it.—*v.i.* to insert cuttings into a tree.—*n.* **Graft′er.** [Orig. **Graff**—O. Fr. *graffe* (Fr. *greffe*)—L. *graphium*, a style or pencil (which the inserted slip resembled)—Gr. *graphō*, to write.]

**ɫrail**, See **Gradual**.

**ɫrail**, grāl, *n.* (*in medieval legend*) the Holy Cup in which Christ celebrated the Lord's Supper. [Orig. the *San Graal*, 'Holy Dish' (not *Sang Real*, 'Holy Blood'), in which it is said Joseph of Arimathea collected our Lord's blood ; from O. Fr. *graal* or *greal*, a flat dish—Low L. *gradale*, prob. a corr. of *cratella*, dim. of *crater*, a bowl. Cf. **Crater**.]

**Grain**, grān, *n.* a single small hard seed : (collectively) the seeds of certain plants which form the chief food of man : a minute particle : a very small quantity : the smallest British weight : the arrangement of the particles or fibres of anything, as stone or wood : texture : the dye made from cochineal insects, which, in the prepared ·state, resembles *grains* of seed : hence to **Dye in**

**grain** is to dye deeply, also, to dye in the wool. —*v.t.* to paint in imitation of wood. [Fr.—L. *granum*, seed, which is akin to E. **Corn**.]

**Grained**, grānd, *adj.* rough, as if covered with *grains*.         [the *grain* of wood.

**Grainer**, grān′ér, *n.* one who paints in imitation of

**Grallatorial**, gral-a-tōr′i-al, **Grallatory**, gral′a-tor-i, *adj.* of or relating to the *grallatores* or wading birds, as the crane, stork, &c. [L. *grallator*, one walking on stilts—*grallæ*, stilts, contr. of *gradulæ*, dim. of *gradus*, a step— *gradior*, to step.]

**Gram**, **Gramme**, gram, *n.* a French unit of weight, equal to 15·432 English grains. [Gr. *gramma*, a letter, a small weight.]

**Gramineal**, gra-min′e-al, **Gramineous**, gra-min′e-us, *adj.* like or pertaining to *grass* : grassy. [L. *gramineus—gramen, -inis*, grass. See **Grass**.]

**Graminifolious**, gram-in-i-fō′li-us, *adj.* bearing *leaves*. [L. *gramen*, and *folium*, a leaf.]

**Graminivorous**, gram-in-iv′o-rus, *adj., feeding* or subsisting on *grass* and herbs. [L. *gramen, graminis*, grass, and *voro*, to eat greedily.]

**Grammar**, gram′ar, *n.* the science of the right use of language : a book which teaches grammar : any elementary work. [Fr. *grammaire* ; from Low L. *gramma*, a letter, with the termination *-arius*—Gr. *gramma*, a letter—*graphō*, to write.]

**Grammarian**, gram-mā′ri-an, *n.* one versed in, or who teaches *grammar*. [Fr. *grammairien*.]

**Grammar-school**, gram′ar-skōōl, *n.* a *school* in which *grammar* is taught : a higher school, in which Latin and Greek are taught.

**Grammatic**, gram-mat′ik, **Grammatical**, gram-mat′ik-al, *adj.* belonging to or according to the rules of *grammar*.—*adv.* **Grammat′ically.** [Fr.—L. *grammaticus*—Gr. *grammatikos*— *gramma, grammatos*, a letter.]

**Grammaticise**, gram-mat′i-sīz, *v.t.* to make grammatical.—*v.i.* to act the grammarian.

**Grampus**, gram′pus, *n.* a large voracious fish of the Dolphin family, common in Arctic seas and on British coasts. [A corr., through It., Port., or Sp., of the L. *grandis piscis*, great fish.]

**Granary**, gran′ar-i, *n.* a storehouse for *grain* or thrashed corn. [L. *granaria—granum*.]

**Grand**, grand, *adj.* of great size, extent, power, or dignity : splendid : illustrious : noble : sublime : chief : of the second degree of parentage or descent, as **Grand′father**, a father or mother's father, **Grand′child**, a son or daughter's child ; so **Grand′mother**, **Grand′son**, **Grand′daughter**, &c.—**Grand-ju′ry**, a jury that decides whether there is sufficient evidence to put an accused person on trial.—*adv.* **Grand′ly.**—*n.* **Grand′ness.** [Fr. *grand*—L. *grandis*, great.]

**Grandam**, gran′dam, *n.* an old dame or woman : a grandmother. [**Grand** and **Dam**, a mother.]

**Grandee**, gran-dē′, *n.* a Spanish nobleman of the first *rank* : a man of high rank or station.—*n.* **Grandee′ship.** [Sp.—L. *grandis*, great.]

**Grandeur**, grand′ūr, *n.* vastness : splendour of appearance : loftiness of thought or deportment. [Fr., from *grand*, great. See **Grand**.]

**Grandiloquent**, gran-dil′o-kwent, *adj.* speaking *grandly* or bombastically : pompous.—*adv.* **Grandil′oquently.**—*n.* **Grandil′oquence.** [L. *grandis*, and *loquor*, to speak.]

**Grand-master**, grand′-mas-tér, *n.* title of the head of the religious orders of knighthood (Hospitallers, Templars, and Teutonic Knights) : the head, for the time being, of the Freemasons.

**Grandsire**, grand′sīr, *n.* a grandfather : any ancestor. [See **Grand**.]

---

**Grange**, grānj, *n.* a farmhouse with its stables and other buildings. [Fr. *grange*, barn—Low L. *granea*—L. *granum*, grain.]

**Granite**, gran'it, *n.* an igneous crystalline rock, composed of *grains* of quartz, feldspar, and mica, and of a whitish, grayish, or reddish colour. [It. *granito*, granite, grained—L. *granum*, grain.] [of, or like *granite*.

**Granitic**, gran-it'ik, *adj.* pertaining to, consisting

**Granitiform**, gran-it'i-form, **Granitoid**, gran'i-toid, *adj.* of the *form* of or resembling *granite*.

**Granivorous**, gran-iv'or-us, *adj.*, *eating grain:* feeding on seeds. [L. *granum*, and *voro*, to eat.]

**Grant**, grant, *v.t.* to bestow or give over : to give possession of : to admit as true what is not yet proved : to concede. [M. E. *graunten*, *graunt*; O. Fr. *graanter*, *craanter*, *creanter*, to promise, as if from a Low L. *credento*—L. *credo*, to believe.]

**Grant**, grant, *n.* a bestowing : something bestowed, an allowance : a gift : a transfer or conveyance by deed or writing.

**Grantee**, grant-ē', *n.* the person to whom a *grant*, gift, or conveyance is made.

**Grantor**, grant'or, *n.* the person by whom a *grant* or conveyance is made

**Granular**, gran'ū-lar, **Granulary**, gran'ū-lar-i, *adj.* consisting of or like *grains*.—*adv.* **Gran'ularly.**

**Granulate**, gran'ū-lāt, *v.t.* to form or break into *grains* or small masses : to make rough on the surface.—*v.i.* to be formed into grains.—*adj.* granular : having the surface covered with small elevations. [Formed from **Granule.**]

**Granulation**, gran-ū-lā'shun, *n.* act of forming into *grains*, esp. of metals by pouring them through a sieve into water while hot :—*pl.* the grain-like bodies which form in sores when healing.

**Granule**, gran'ūl, *n.* a *little grain.* [L. *granulum*, dim. of *granum*. See **Grain.**] [ticles.

**Granulous**, gran'ū-lus, *adj.* full of *grains* or par-

**Grape**, grāp, *n.* the fruit of the vine : a mangy tumour on the legs of horses : grapeshot. [O. Fr. *grappe*, a clu-ter of grapes, which came in E. to mean a single berry ; from O. Ger. *chrappo*, a hook. It properly meant a hook, then clustered fruit, hooked on, attached to, a stem (Brachet).]

**Grapery**, grāp'er-i, *n.* a place where *grapes* are grown

**Grapeshot**, grāp'shot, *n.*, *shot* or small iron balls *clustered* or piled on circular plates round an iron pin, and which scatter on being fired.

**Graphic**, graf'ik, **Graphical**, graf'ik-al, *adj.* pertaining to *writing*, describing, or delineating : picturesquely described.—*adv.* **Graph'ically.** [L. *graphicus*—Gr. *graphikos*—*graphō*, to write.]

**Graphite**, graf'īt, *n.* a mineral, commonly called blacklead or plumbago (though containing no lead) largely used in making pencils. [Gr. *graphō.*]

**Grapnel**, grap'nel, *n.* a small anchor with several claws or arms : a grappling-iron. [Fr. *grappin*; O. Fr. *grappil*; from root of **Grapple.**]

**Grapple**, grap'l, *v.t.* to grıpe or seize : to lay fast hold of.—*v.i.* to contend in close fight. [Dim. of **Grab.**]

**Grappling-iron**, grap'ling-ī'urn, *n.* a large grapnel formerly used for seizing hostile ships in naval engagements

**Grapy**, grāp'i, *adj.* made of or like *grapes*.

**Grasp**, grasp, *v.t.* to seize and hold by clasping with the fingers or arms : to catch at.—*v.i.* to endeavour to seize : to catch (followed by *at*).—*n.* gripe of the hand : reach of the arms : power

of seizure. [M. E. *graspen* = *grapsen.* See **Grope** and **Grapple.**]

**Grass**, gras, *n.* common herbage : an order of plants with long, narrow leaves, and tubular stem, including wheat, rye, oats, &c.—*v.t.* to cover with grass. [A.S. *gærs, græs*; Ice., Ger., Dut., and Goth. *gras*; prob. allied to *green* and *grow.*]

**Grasshopper**, gras'hop-er, *n.* a *hopping* insect that feeds on *grass*, allied to the locust.

**Grass-plot**, gras-plot, *n.* a *plot* of *grassy* ground.

**Grassy**, gras'i, *adj.* covered with or resembling *grass :* green.—*n.* **Grass'iness.**

**Grate**, grā:, *n.* a framework composed of bars with interstices, esp. one of iron bars for holding coals while burning. [Low L. *grata*, a grate, hurdle, lattice—from L. *crates*, a hurdle. See **Crate.**]

**Grate**, grāt, *v.t.* to rub hard or wear away with anything rough : to make a harsh sound : to irritate or offend. [Fr. *gratter;* through Low L., from O. Ger. *chrazon* (Ger. *kratzen*), to scratch, akin to Sw. *kratta.*]

**Grated**, grāt'ed, *adj.* having a *grate* or grating.

**Grateful**, grāt'fool, *adj.* causing *pleasure :* acceptable : delightful : thankful : having a due sense of benefits.—*adv.* **Grate'fully.**—*n.* **Grate'fulness.** [O. Fr. *grat*—L. *gratus*, pleasing, thankful, and **Full.** See **Grace.**]

**Grater**, grāt'er, *n.* an instrument with a rough surface for *grating* or rubbing down a body.

**Gratification**, grat-i-fi-kā'shun, *n.* a pleasing or indulging : that which gratifies : delight. [L. *gratificatio.*]

**Gratify**, grat'i-fī, *v.t.* to do what is *agreeable* to : to please : to soothe : to indulge :—*pa.p.* grat'ified.—*n.* **Grat'ifier.** [Fr.—L. *gratificor*—*gratus*, and *facio*, to make.]

**Grating**, grāt'ing, *n.* the *bars* of a *grate* : a partition or frame of bars.

**Grating**, grāt'ing, *adj.* rubbing hard on the feelings : harsh : irritating.—*adv.* **Grat'ingly.**

**Gratis**, grā'tis, *adv.* for nothing : without payment or recompense. [L. contr. of *gratiis*, ablative *pl.* of *gratia*, favour—*gratus.*]

**Gratitude**, grat-i-tūd, *n.* warm and friendly feeling towards a benefactor : thankfulness. [Fr.—Low L. *gratitudo.*]

**Gratuitous**, gra-tū'i-tus, *adj.*, *done* or *given gratis* or for nothing : voluntary : without reason, ground, or proof.—*adv.* **Gratu'itously.** [L. *gratuitus*—*gratus.*]

**Gratuity**, gra-tū'i-ti, *n.* a present : an acknowledgment of service, generally pecuniary. [Fr. —Low L. *gratuitas*—L. *gratus.*]

**Gratulate**, grat'ū-lāt, *v.t.* to **Congratulate.**

**Gratulation**, grat-ū-lā'shun, *n.* **Congratulation.**

**Gratulatory**, grat'ū-la-tor-i, *adj.* **Congratulatory.**

**Gravamen**, grav-ā'men, *n.* grievance : substantial ground of complaint or accusation. [L.—*gravis*, heavy.]

**Grave**, grāv, *v.t.* to carve or cut, on a hard substance : to engrave.—*v.i.* to engrave :—*pa.p.* grāved' or grāv'en.—*n.* a pit graved or dug out, esp. one in which to bury the dead : any place of burial : (*fig.*) death : destruction. [A.S. *grafan;* cog. with Dut. *graven* (whence Fr. *graver*), Ger. *graben*, Goth. *graban;* Gr. *graphō*, to grave, scratch, L. *scribere*, to write, *scrobs*, a ditch.]

**Grave**, grāv, *v.t.* to smear with *graves* or *greaves*, a mixture of tallow, rosin, &c. boiled together. [See **Greaves.**]

**Grave**, grāv, *adj.* (*fig.*) weighty : of importance :

serious: not gay: sober: solemn: (*mus.*) not acute: low.—*adv.* **Grave'ly.**—*n.* **Grave'ness.** [Fr.—L. *gravis*; Sans. *guru*.]

**Gravel**, grav'el, *n.* small stones often intermixed with sand: small collections of gravelly matter in the kidneys or bladder.—*v.t.* to cover with gravel: to puzzle:—*pr.p.* grav'elling; *pa.p.* grav'elled.—*adj.* **Grav'elly.** [O. Fr. *gravelle*—Fr. *grève* or *grave*, a sandy shore; prob. Celt., as in Bret. *grouan*, sand, W. *gro*, pebbles.]

**Graver**, grāv'èr, *n.* an engraver: a tool for engraving on hard substances.

**Graves.** Same as **Greaves**, tallow-drippings.

**Gravid**, grav'id, *adj.*, *heavy*, esp. as being with child: pregnant. [L. *gravidus*—*gravis*, heavy.]

**Graving**, grāv'ing, *n.* act of *graving* or cutting out on hard substances: that which is graved or cut out: carved-work: act of cleaning a ship's bottom.—*n.* **Grav'ing-dock**, a dock into which ships are taken to be graved.

**Gravitate**, grav'i-tāt, *v.i.* to be acted on by *gravity*: to tend towards the earth. [From L. *gravis*, heavy.]

**Gravitation**, grav-i-tā'shun, *n.* act of gravitating: the tendency of all bodies to attract each other.

**Gravity**, grav'i-ti, *n.* weightiness: the tendency of matter to attract and be attracted, thus causing weight: state of being grave or sober: relative importance: (*mus.*) lowness of a note. [Fr. *gravité*—L. *gravitas*—*gravis*, heavy.]

**Gravy**, grāv'i, *n.* the juices from meat while cooking. [Prob. orig. an adj. formed from **Greaves**, the dregs of tallow.]

**Gray**, grā, *adj.* of a white colour mixed with black: ash-coloured: (*fig.*) aged.—*n.* a gray colour: an animal of a grayish colour, as a horse, &c.—*n.* **Gray'ness.** [A.S. *graeg*; allied to Ger. *grau*, and L. *ravus*, tawny.]

**Graybeard**, grā'bèrd, *n.* one with a gray beard, hence, an old man: a coarse earthenware vessel for holding liquors.

**Grayish**, grā'ish, *adj.* somewhat gray.

**Grayling**, grā'ling, *n.* a silvery *gray* fish of the salmon family, but with a smaller mouth and teeth, and larger scales.

**Graystone**, grā'stōn, *n.* a grayish or greenish volcanic rock allied to basalt.

**Graywacke**, grā'wak-e, *n.* a kind of sandstone, consisting of rounded pebbles and sand firmly united together. [Ger. *grauwacke*—*grau*, gray, and **Wacke**.]

**Graze**, grāz, *v.t.* to eat or feed on grass: to feed with grass.—*v.i.* to eat grass: to supply grass. [From **Grass**.]

**Graze**, grāz, *v.t.* to pass lightly along the surface. —*n.* **Graz'er**, an animal which grazes. [Ety. dub.: perh. only a special use of **Graze** above: perh. coined from *rase* (Fr. *raser*), the form of the word being modified by confusing it with *graze* (the above word). See **Rase**.]

**Grazier**, grā'zhèr, *n.* one who *grazes* or pastures cattle and rears them for the market. [For *graz-er*—**Grass**.]

**Grease**, grēs, *n.* soft thick animal *fat*: oily matter of any kind: an inflammation in the heels of a horse, marked by swelling. &c.—*v.t.* (sometimes pron. grēz) to smear with grease. [Fr. *graisse*, from *gras*, fat—L. *crassus*, gross, thick.]

**Greasy**, grē'zi or grēs'i, *adj.* of or like *grease* or oil: smeared with grease: smooth: fat.—*adv.* **Greas'ily.**—*n.* **Greas'iness.**

**Great**, grāt, *adj.* large: long-continued: superior: distinguished: highly gifted: noble: mighty: sublime: of high rank: chief: proud: weighty:

indicating one degree more remote in the direct line of descent, as **Great'-grand'father. Great'-grand'son.**—*adv.* **Great'ly.**—*n.* **Great'ness.** [A.S.: Dut. *groot*, Ger. *gross*; perh. allied to **Grand, Gross, Grow.**]

**Greatcoat**, grāt'kōt, *n.* an overcoat.

**Great-hearted**, grāt'-härt'ed, *adj.* having a great or noble heart: high-spirited: noble.

**Greaves**, grēvz, *n.pl.* the sediment of melted tallow, pressed into cakes for dogs' food. [Sw. *grevar*, leavings of tallow, Ger. *griebe*.]

**Greaves**, grēvz, *n.pl.* ancient armour for the *legs*, of leather, &c. [O. Fr. *grèves*, from *grève*, the shin-bone.]

**Grebe**, grēb, *n.* an aquatic bird, having a long conical beak, short wings, and no tail. [Fr. *grèbe*; from the Celtic, as in Bret. *krib*, a comb, W. *crib*, crest, one species having a crest.]

**Grecian**, grē'shan, *adj.* pertaining to *Greece.*—*n.* a native of Greece: one well versed in the Greek language and literature: (*B.*) a Jew who spoke Greek. [A.S. and Fr. *Grec*—L. *Graecus*—Gr. *Graikos*.]

**Grecise**, grē'sīz, *v.t.* to make *Grecian*: to translate into Greek.—*v.i.* to speak Greek.       [guage.

**Grecism**, grē'sizm, *n.* an idiom of the *Greek* lan-

**Greed**, grēd, *n.* an eager desire or longing: covetousness. [See **Greedy**.]

**Greedy**, grēd'i, *adj.* having a voracious appetite: covetous: eagerly desirous.—*adv.* **Greed'ily.**—*n.* **Greed'iness.** [A.S. *graedig*, Dut. *gretig*, Goth. *gredags*, hungry; Sans. *gridhnu* (from *v. gridh*, to be greedy).]

**Greek**, grēk, *adj.* Grecian.—*n.* a Grecian: the language of Greece: (*B.*) a Greek by race, or more frequently a Gentile as opposed to a Jew.

**Greek-fire**, grēk'-fīr, *n.* a combustible substance inextinguishable by water, used by the *Greeks* of the Byzantine empire against the Saracens.

**Green**, grēn, *adj.* of the colour of *growing*-plants: growing: vigorous: new: unripe: inexperienced: young.—*n.* the colour of growing-plants: a small green or grassy plat:—*pl.* fresh leaves: wreaths: the leaves of green vegetables for food, &c.—*n.* **Green'ness.** [A.S. *grene*; Ger. *grün*, Dut. *groen*, green, Ice. *gränn*, allied to **Grow**.]

**Greenback**, grēn'bak, *n.* popular name for the paper money first issued by the United States in 1862.

**Green-cloth**, grēn'-kloth, *n.* formerly, a court for regulating the affairs of the royal household, and which had power to punish offenders within the palace, and 200 yds. beyond the gates, so called from the *green cloth* on the table round which it sat. [tables, as grasses, turnips, &c.

**Green-crop**, grēn'-krop, *n.* a crop of green vege-

**Greenery**, grēn'èr-i, *n.* green plants: verdure.

**Greengage**, grēn'gāj, *n.* a *green* and very sweet variety of the plum. [Latter part of the word obscure.]

**Greengrocer**, grēn'grō-sèr, *n.* a grocer or dealer who retails greens, or fresh vegetables and fruits.

**Greenhorn**, grēn'horn, *n.* a raw, inexperienced youth.

**Greenhouse**, grēn'hows, *n.* a house to shelter tender plants from the cold weather.

**Greenish**, grēn'ish, *adj.* somewhat green.—*n.* **Green'ishness.**

**Greenroom**, grēn'rōōm, *n.* the retiring-*room* of actors in a theatre, which originally had the walls coloured *green.*

**Greensand**, grēn'sand, *n.* a *sandstone* in which *green* specks of iron occur.

**Green-sickness.** grēn'-sik'nes, *n.* chlorosis, a disease of young females characterised by general languor and a pale or *green*ish colour of skin.

**Greenstone**, grēn′stōn, *n.* a variety of trap-*rock* of a *green* colour.

**Greet**, grēt, *v.t.* to salute or address with kind wishes : to send kind wishes to : to congratulate. —*v.i.* to meet and salute :—*pr.p.* greet′ing ; *pa.p.* greet′ed. [A.S. *grētan*, to go to meet ; Dut. *groeten*, Ger. *grüssen*, to salute.]

**Greeting**, grēt′ing, *n.* expression of kindness or joy : salutation.

**Gregarious**, gre-gā′ri-us, *adj.* associating or living in *flocks* or herds.—*adv.* **Grega′riously.**—*n.* **Grega′riousness.** [L. *gregarius*—*grex*, *gregis*, a flock.]

**Gregorian**, gre-gō′ri-an, *adj.* belonging to or established by Pope *Gregory* ; as the Gregorian chant or tones, introduced by Gregory I. (6th cent.), and the calendar, reformed by Gregory XIII. (16th cent.)

**Grenade**, gre-nād′, *n.* a small shell of iron or glass, filled with powder and bits of iron, and thrown from the hand, so called from its resembling a pomegranate. [Fr.—Sp. *granada*—L. *granatum*, a pomegranate—*granum*, a grain.]

**Grenadier**, gren-a-dēr′, *n.* (*orig.*) a soldier who threw *grenades* : formerly, a member of the first company of every battalion of foot.

**Grew**, grōō, *past tense* of **Grow.**

**Grey**, grā. Same as **Gray.**

**Greyhound**, grā′hownd, *n.* a swift hunting *hound*, of slender form, great length of limb and muzzle, and great keenness of sight. [Ice. *greyhundr* —Ice. *grey*, a dog, and *hundr* (E. *hound*), a hound.]

**Griddle**, grid′l, *n.* a flat iron plate for baking cakes. [W. *greidell*—*greidio*, to scorch or singe ; Gael. *greidil*, Scot. *girdle*.]

**Gridiron**, grid′ī-urn, *n.* a frame of iron bars for broiling flesh or fish over the fire. [M. E. *gredire*, a griddle, and from the same Celtic root as *griddle* ; but the termin. *-ire* became identified with M. E. *ire*, iron.]

**Grief**, grēf, *n.*, *heaviness* of heart : sorrow : regret : mourning : cause of sorrow : affliction : (*B.*) bodily as well as mental pain. [Fr. *grief*—*grever*, to burden—L. *gravo*, to grieve—*gravis*, heavy.] [hardship : injury : grief.

**Grievance**, grēv′ans, *n.* cause of *grief* : burden :

**Grieve**, grēv, *v.t.* to cause *grief* or pain of mind to : to make sorrowful : to vex : (*B.*) also, to inflict bodily pain.—*v.i.* to feel grief : to mourn.

**Grievous**, grēv′us, *adj.* causing or full of *grief* : burdensome : painful : heinous : atrocious : hurtful.—*n.* **Griev′ousness.**        [(*B.*) severely.

**Grievously**, grēv′us-li, *adv.* in a *grievous* manner :

**Griffin**, grif′in, **Griffon.** grif′un, *n.* an imaginary animal, with the body and legs of a lion, and the *crooked beak* and wings of an eagle. [Fr. *griffon* —L. and Gr. *gryps*—Gr. *grypos*, hook-nosed.]

**Grig**, grig, *n.* a small *lively* eel, the sand-eel. [Prov. E. *grig*, a cricket : from its wriggling motion.]

**Grill**, gril, *v.t.* to broil on a gridiron : to torment. [Fr. *griller*—*gril*, a gridiron—L. *craticula*, dim. of *crates*, a grate.]

**Grilse**, grils, *n.* a young salmon on its first return from salt water. [Sw. *graalax*, a gray salmon.]

**Grim**, grim, *adj.* of forbidding aspect : ferocious : ghastly : sullen.—*adv.* **Grim′ly.**—*n.* **Grim′ness.** [A.S. *grim* ; Ger. *grimmig*—*grimm*, fury, Dut. *grimmig*, Ice. *grimmr*.]

**Grimace**, gri-mās′, *n.* a distortion of the face, in jest, &c. : a smirk. [Fr., of uncertain orig., perh.

from root of Ice. and A.S. *grima*, a mask or phantom.]        [torted.

**Grimaced**, gri-māsd′, *adj.* with a *grimace* : dis-

**Grimalkin**, gri-mal′kin, *n.* an old cat. [*Gray*, and *malkin*, a dirty drab, a hare, a dim. of Moll or Mary.]

**Grime**, grīm, *n.* ingrained dirt.—*v.t.* to soil deeply. [From a Teut. root found in Dan. *grim*, soot, Fris. *grime*, a dark spot on the face.]

**Grimy**, grīm′i, *adj.* full of *grime* : foul.

**Grin**, grin, *v.i.* to set the teeth together and withdraw the lips.—*v.t.* to express by grinning :— *pr.p.* grinn′ing ; *pa.p.* grinned′.—*n.* act of grinning. [A.S. *grennian* ; Ice. *grenja*, Ger. *greinen*, Dut. *grijnen*, to grumble, Sc. *girn* ; allied to E. *groan*, Fr. *grogner*.]

**Grind**, grīnd, *v.t.* to reduce to powder by friction : to wear down or sharpen by rubbing : to rub together : to oppress or harass.—*v.i.* to be moved or rubbed together :—*pr.p.* grīnd′ing ; *pa.t.* and *pa.p.* ground. [A.S. *grindan.*]

**Grinder**, grīnd′ėr, *n.* he or that which *grinds* : a double or jaw tooth that *grinds* food.

**Grindstone**, grīnd′stōn, *n.* a circular revolving *stone* for *grinding* or sharpening tools.

**Grip**, grip, **Gripe**, grīp, *n.*, *grasp* or firm hold with the hand, &c. : oppression : pinching distress :— *pl.* **Gripes**, severe pains in the bowels. [See **Gripe**, *v.*]

**Gripe**, grīp, *v.t.* to grasp with the hand : to seize and hold fast : to squeeze : to give pain to the bowels.—**Grip′ing**, *part. adj.* avaricious : of a pain that catches or seizes acutely. [A.S. *gripan* ; Ice. *gripa*, Ger. *greifen*, Dut. *grijpen* : allied to **Grab**.]

**Grisette**, gri-zet′, *n.* a gay young Frenchwoman of the lower class. [Fr. *grisette*, a gray gown, which used to be worn by that class—*gris*, gray.]

**Grisled**, griz′ld. Same as **Grizzled.**

**Grisly**, griz′li, *adj.* frightful : hideous. [A.S. *gryslic*, *agrisan*, to dread ; Ger. *grässlich*, *grieseln*, to shudder.]

**Grist**, grist, *n.* corn for *grinding* at one time : supply : profit. [A.S. *grist*, *gerst*, a grinding ; from root of **Grind**.

**Gristle**, gris′l, *n.* a soft, elastic substance in animal bodies, also called cartilage. [A.S. *gristel* ; a dim. of *grist* and *grind*, because one must crunch it in eating.]        [*n.* **Grist′liness.**

**Gristly**, gris′li, *adj.* consisting of or like *gristle.*—

**Grit**, grit, *n.* the coarse part of meal : gravel : a kind of hard sandstone :—*pl.* oats coarsely ground, groats. [A.S. *greot*, *grytt* ; Dut. *grut*, groats, Ger. *gries*, gravel, akin to *groat*, *grout*.]

**Gritty**, grit′i, *adj.* consisting of or having *grits* or hard particles.—*n.* **Gritt′iness.**

**Grizzle**, griz′l, *n.* a *gray* colour. [Fr. *gris*, gray— O. Ger. *gris*, gray, Ger. *greis*.]

**Grizzled**, griz′ld, *adj.*, *gray*, or mixed with gray.

**Grizzly**, griz′li, *adj.* of a *gray* colour.

**Groan**, grōn, *v.i.* to utter a moaning sound in distress : (*fig.*) to be afflicted.—*n.* a deep moaning sound as of distress : a sound of disapprobation. [A.S. *granian.*]        [any low rumbling sound.

**Groaning**, grōn′ing, *n.* a deep moan as of pain :

**Groat**, grawt or grōt, *n.* an old English coin = 4d. [O. Low Ger. *grote*, a coin of Bremen ; like Dut. *groot* = great, so called because greater than the copper coins formerly in use (Skeat) ; Ger. *groschen*—Low L. *grossus*, thick.]

**Groats**, grawts or grōts, *n.pl.* the grain of oats deprived of the husks. [A.S. *grut*, coarse meal.]

**Grocer**, grōs′ėr, *n.* a dealer in tea, sugar, &c. [Fr. *grossier*, from root of **Gross** ; the word, formerly *grosser*, orig. meant one who sold whole-sale.]      [articles sold by *grocers*.

**Grocery**, grōs′ėr-i, *n.* (generally used in *pl*)

**Grog**, grog, *n.* a mixture of spirit and cold water. [Derived from 'Old Grog,' a nickname given by the sailors to Admiral Vernon, who first introduced it, because he used, in bad weather, to wear a grogram cloak.]

**Grogram**, grog′ram, *n.* a kind of cloth made of silk and mohair, of a *coarse grain* or texture. [O. Fr. *gros-grain*, of a coarse grain or texture. See **Gross** and **Grain**.]

**Groin**, groin, *n.* the part of the body just where the legs begin to *divide*: (*arch*.) the angular curve formed by the crossing of two arches. [Ice. *grein*, division, branch—*greina*, to divide; Sw. *gren*, branch, space between the legs; Scot. *graine, grane*, the branch of a tree or river.]

**Groined**, groind, *adj.* having *groins* or angular curves made by the intersection of two arches.

**Groom**, grōōm, *n.* one who has the charge of horses : a title of several officers of the royal household : a bridegroom.—*v.t.* to tend, as a horse.—*n.* **Grooms′man**, attendant on a bridegroom at his marriage. [Ety. dub. ; prob. from A.S. *guma* (in bride*groom*), a man, which is allied to Goth. *guma*, Ice. *gumi*, L. *homo*.]

**Groove**, grōōv, *n.* a furrow, or long hollow, such as is cut with a tool.—*v.t.* to grave or cut a groove or furrow in. [A.S. *grof, graf*—*grafan*, to dig ; Ger. *grube*—*graben*, to dig; Dut. *groeve*, a furrow, pit ; from root of **Grave**.]

**Grope**, grōp, *v.i.* (orig.) to *gripe* or *feel* with the *hands* : to search or attempt to find something, as if blind or in the dark.—*v.t.* to search by feeling, as in the dark. [A.S. *grapian*, to seize, handle ; allied to **Grab, Gripe**.]

**Gropingly**, grōp′ing-li, *adv.* in a *groping* manner.

**Grosbeak.** Same as **Grossbeak**.

**Gross**, grōs, *adj.* coarse : rough : dense : palpable : whole : coarse in mind : stupid : sensual : obscene.—*n.* the main bulk : the whole taken together : a *great* hundred, *i.e.* twelve dozen.—*adv.* **Gross′ly**.—*n.* **Gross′ness**. [Fr. *gros*—Low L. *grossus*—L. *crassus*.]

**Grossbeak**, grōs′bēk, *n.* a genus of birds with a *thick* strong convex *beak*. [**Gross** and **Beak**.]

**Grot**, grot, **Grotto**, grot′ō, *n.* a cave : a place of shade, for pleasure, made like a cave :—*pl.* **Grots, Grottos**. [Fr. *grotte*—L. *crypta* ; thus a doublet of **Crypt** ; *grotto* is the It. form.]

**Grotesque**, grō-tesk′, *adj.* extravagantly formed : ludicrous.—*n.* (*art*) extravagant ornament, containing animals, plants, &c. not really existing.—*adv.* **Grotesque′ly**.—*n.* **Grotesque′ness**. [Fr. *grotesque*—It. *grottesca*—*grotto*; because old *grottos* were commonly adorned with quaint and extravagant paintings.]

**Grotto.** See **Grot**.

**Ground**, grownd, *pa.t.* and *pa.p.* of **Grind**.

**Ground**, grownd, *n.* the surface of the earth : a portion of the earth's surface : land : field : the floor, &c. : position : field or place of action : (*lit.* or *fig.*) that on which something is raised : foundation : reason : (*art*) the surface on which the figures are represented. [A.S. *grund* ; cog. with Ger. Dan. and Sw. *grund*, Ice. *grunnr*, Goth. *grundus* ; prob. conn. with *grind*, and orig. meaning 'ground small.']

**Ground**, grownd, *v.t.* to fix on a foundation or principle : to instruct in first principles.—*v.i.* to strike the bottom, and remain fixed.

**Groundage**, grownd′āj, *n.* the tax paid by a ship for the *ground* or space occupied while in port.

**Ground-floor**, grownd′-flōr, *n.* the floor of a house on a level with the street or exterior ground.

**Ground-ivy**, grownd′-ī′vi, *n.* a plant which creeps along the *ground*, like *ivy*.

**Groundless**, grownd′les, *adj.* without ground, foundation, or reason.—*adv.* **Ground′lessly**.—*n.* **Ground′lessness**.

**Groundling**, grownd′ling, *n.* a *small* fish which keeps near the bottom of the water : a spectator in the pit of a theatre. [Both formed from **Ground** and double dim. -*ling*.]

**Ground-nut**, grownd′-nut, *n.* a term applied to the *fruit* of some plants and the root of others found in the *ground*.

**Ground-plan**, grownd′-plan, *n.*, *plan* of the horizontal section of the lowest or *ground* story of a building.

**Ground-plot**, grownd′-plot, *n.* the plot of ground on which a building stands.

**Ground-rent**, grownd′-rent, *n.*, *rent* paid to a landlord for liberty to build on his *ground*.

**Grounds**, grownds, *n. pl.* dregs of drink : sediment at the bottom of liquors. [Gael. and Ir. *grunndas* ; conn. with **Ground**.]

**Groundsel**, grownd′sel, *n.* an annual plant, about a foot high, with small yellow flowers. [A.S. *grundswelige*—*grund*, ground, and *swelgan*, to swallow ; therefore lit. *ground-swallower*.]

**Ground-swell**, grownd′-swel, *n.* a broad, deep *swell* or undulation of the ocean, proceeding from a distant storm.

**Groundwork**, grownd′wurk, *n.* the *work* which forms the *ground* or foundation of anything : the basis : the essential part : the first principle.

**Group**, grōōp, *n.* a number of persons or things together : (*art*) an assemblage of persons, animals, or things, forming a whole.—*v.t.* to form into a group or groups. [Fr. *groupe*—It. *groppo*, a bunch, knot ; from a root found in Ger. *kropf*, a protuberance.]

**Grouping**, grōōp′ing, *n.* (*art*) the act of disposing and arranging figures or objects in *groups*.

**Grouse**, grows, *n.* the heathcock or moorfowl, a bird with a short curved bill, short legs, and feathered feet, which frequents moors and hills. [Prob. formed from the older *grice* (on the analogy of *mouse, mice*)—O. Fr. *griesche*, of unknown origin.]

**Grout**, growt, *n.* coarse meal : the sediment of liquor : lees : a thin coarse mortar : a fine plaster for finishing ceilings. [A.S. *grut*, coarse meal ; cog. with Dut. *grut*, Ice. *grautr*, porridge, Ger. *grütze*, groats.]

**Grove**, grōv, *n.* a wood of small size, generally of a pleasant or ornamental character : an avenue of trees. [A.S. *graf*, a grove, a lane cut among trees—*grafan*, to dig. See **Grave, Groove**.]

**Grovel**, grov′el, *v.i.* to crawl on the earth : to be mean :—*pr.p.* grov′elling ; *pa.p.* grov′elled.—*n.* **Grov′eller**. [Perh. from Ice. *grufla*, to grovel, from *grufa*, as in *grufa nidr*, to stoop down. See **Grab, Grope**.]

**Grow**, grō, *v.i.* to become enlarged by a natural process : to advance towards maturity : to increase in size : to develop : to become greater in any way : to extend : to improve : to pass from one state to another : to become.—*v.t.* to cause to grow : to cultivate :—*pa.t.* grew (grōō) ; *pa.p.* grown.—*n.* **Grow′er**. [A.S. *growan*; Ice. *groa* ; conn. with *green*.]

**Growl**, growl, *v.i.* to utter a deep, murmuring sound, like a dog : to grumble surlily.—*v.t.* to express by growling.—*n.* **Growl′er**. [Dut. and Ger. *grollen*, to be angry, to roar ; allied to Gr.

*gryllizō*, to grunt, *gryllos*, a pig : from the sound. See **Grudge** and **Grunt**.]

**Growl**, growl, *n.* a murmuring, snarling sound, as of an angry dog.

**Growth**, grōth, *n.* a *growing*: gradual increase : progress : development : that which has grown : product.

**Grub**, grub, *v.i.* to dig in the dirt : to be occupied meanly.—*v.t.* to dig or root out of the ground (generally followed by *up*):—*pr.p.* grubb'ing ; *pa.b.* grubbed'. [Ety. dub. ; but prob. allied to **Grab**, **Gripe**.]

**Grub**, grub, *n.* the larva of the beetle, moth, &c. [Same word as above.]

**Grubber**, grub'ėr, *n.* he or that which *grubs :* an instrument for digging up the roots of trees, &c.

**Grub-street**, grub'-strėt, *n.* a street in London inhabited by shabby literary men.—*adj.* applied to any mean literary production.

**Grudge**, gruj, *v.t.* to murmur at: to look upon with envy : to give or take unwillingly.—*v.i.* to shew discontent.—*n.* secret enmity or envy : an old cause of quarrel. [M. E. *grucchen*, *gruggen* —O. Fr. *groucher*, *groucer*, *gruger*, from an imitative root *gru*, which is found in Gr. *gry*, the grunt of a pig, also in *growl*, *grunt*.]

**Grudgingly**, gruj'ing-li, *adv.* unwillingly.

**Gruel**, grōō'el, *n.* a thin food, made by boiling *groats* or oatmeal in water. [O. Fr. *gruel* (Fr. *gruau*), groats—Low L. *grutellum*, dim. of *grutum*, meal—O. Ger. *grut*, groats, A.S.*grut*.]

**Gruesome**, grōō'sum, *adj.* horrible : fearful. [Scan. ; cog. with Ger. *grausam*.]

**Gruff**, gruf, *adj.* rough, stern, or abrupt in manner: churlish.—*adv.* **Gruff'ly**.—*n.* **Gruff'ness**. [Dut. *grof* ; cog. with Sw. *grof*, Dan. *grov*, Ger. *grob*, coarse ; prob. imitative.]

**Grumble**, grum'bl, *v.i.* to murmur with discontent: to growl: to rumble.—*n.* **Grum'bler**.— *adv.* **Grum'blingly**. [Fr. *grommeler ;* from O. Ger. *grummeln*.]

**Grume**, grōōm. *n.* a thick consistence of fluid : a clot as of blood. [O. Fr. *grume*, a knot, a bunch (Fr. *grumeau*, a clot of blood)—L. *grumus*, a little heap.]

**Grumous**, grōōm'us, *adj.* thick : clotted.

**Grumpy**, grum'pi, *adj.* surly : dissatisfied : melancholic. [From same root as **Grumble**.]

**Grunt**, grunt, *v.i.* to make a sound like a pig.— *n.* a short, guttural sound, as of a hog.—*n.* **Grunt'er**. [Like words are found in most European languages ; all from the sound. See **Growl** and **Grudge**.]

**Guaiacum**, gwā'ya-kum, *n.* a genus of trees in the W. Indies, that yield a greenish resin used in medicine. [Sp. *guayaco*, from a Haytian word.]

**Guano**, goo-ā'nō or gwā'nō, *n.* the long-accumulated *dung* of certain seafowl, found on certain coasts and islands, esp. about S. America, much used for manure. [Sp. *guano* or *huano*, from Peruvian *huanu*, dung.]

**Guarantee**, gar-an-tē', **Guaranty**, gar'an-ti, *n.* a warrant or surety : a contract to see performed what another has undertaken : the person who makes such a contract.—*v t.* to undertake that another shall perform certain engagements: to make sure :—*pr.p.* guarantee'ing ; *pa.p.* guaranteed'. [O. Fr. *garantie*, *guarantie*, *pa.p.* of *garantir*, to warrant—*garant*, warrant. See **Warrant**.]

**Guard**, gärd, *v.t.* to *ward*, watch, or take care of : to protect from danger.—*v.i.* to watch : to be wary.—*n.* that which guards from danger : a man or body of men stationed to protect : one who has charge of a coach or railway-train : state of caution : posture of defence : part of the hilt of a sword : a watch-chain :—*pl.* troops attached to the person of a sovereign. [O. Fr. *garder*, *guarder*—O. Ger. *warten ;* cog. with E. *ward*.]　　　　[turned towards the beholder.

**Guardant**, gär'dant, *adj.* (*her.*) having the face

**Guarded**, gärd'ed, *adj.* wary : cautious : uttered with caution.—*adv.* **Guard'edly**.—*n.* **Guard'- edness**.

**Guardian**, gärd'yan, *n.* one who guards or takes care of : (*law*) one who has the care of an orphan minor.—*adj.* protecting.—*n.* **Guard'ianship**.　　　　[modation of *guards*.

**Guardroom**, gärd'rōōm, *n.* a room for the accom-

**Guardship**, gärd'ship, *n.* a *ship* of war that *guards* or superintends marine affairs in a harbour.

**Guardsman**, gärds'man, *n.* a soldier of the *guards*.

**Guava**, gwä'va, *n.* a genus of trees and shrubs, of tropical America, with yellow, pear-shaped fruit which is made into jelly. [Sp. *guayaba ;* of W. Indian origin.]

**Gudgeon**, guj'un, *n.* a small fresh-water fish, allied to the carp, easily caught—hence, any one easily cheated. [Fr. *goujon*—L. *gobio*—Gr. *kōbios*. See **Goby**.]

**Guelder-rose**, gel'dėr-rōz, *n.* a tree with large white ball-shaped flowers. [So called from Gueldres in Holland—also called *snowball-tree*.]

**Guerdon**, gėr'dun, *n.* a *reward* or recompense. [O. Fr. *guerdon*, *guerredon* (It. *guidardone*)— Low L. *widerdonum*, corr. from O. Ger. *widar- lon*, A.S. *widherlean—widher* (same as with in E. *withstand*), against, *lean* (same as E. *loan*), reward ; or more prob. the latter part of the word is from L. *donum*, a gift.]

**Guerilla**, **Guerrilla**, gėr-ril'a, *n.* a mode of harassing an army by small bands adopted by the Spaniards against the French in the Peninsular War : a member of such a band.—*adj.* conducted by or conducting petty warfare. [Sp. *guerrilla*, dim. of *guerra* (Fr. *guerre*)—O. Ger. *werra*, war. See **War**.]

**Guess**, ges, *v.t.* to form an opinion on uncertain knowledge.—*v.i.* to judge on uncertain knowledge : to conjecture rightly. [M. E. *gessen ;* cog. with Dut. *gissen ;* Dan. *gisse*, Ice. *giska*, for *git-ska—geta*, to get, think, A.S. *gitan*, whence E. **Get**. See also **Forget**.]

**Guess**, ges, *n.* judgment or opinion without sufficient evidence or grounds.

**Guesswork**, ges'wurk, *n.*, *work* done by *guess*.

**Guest**, gest, *n.* a visitor received and entertained. [A.S. *gæst*, *gest ;* allied to Dut. and Ger. *gast*, L. *hostis*, stranger, enemy. Cf. **Host**, an army.]

**Guest-chamber**, gest'-chām'bėr, *n.* (*B.*) a *chamber* or room for the accommodation of *guests*.

**Guffaw**, guf-faw', *n.* a loud laugh. [From the sound.]

**Guidance**, gīd'ans, *n.* direction : government.

**Guide**, gīd, *v.t.* to lead or direct : to regulate : to influence.—*n.* he who or that which guides : one who directs another in his course of life : a soldier or other person employed to obtain information for an army. [Fr. *guider ;* prob. from a Teut. root, as in A.S. *witan*, to know, observe, *wis*, wise, Ger. *weisen*, to shew, and so conn. with *wit* and *wise*.]　　　　[tourists.

**Guidebook**, gīd'book, *n.* a book of information for

**Guidepost**, gīd'pōst, *n.* a post erected at a roadside, to guide the traveller.

**Guild**, gild, *n.* (*orig.*) an association in a town where *payment* was made for mutual support and protection : an association of men for mutual aid : a corporation.—**Guild'hall**, *n.* the hall of a *guild* or corporation, esp. in London. [A.S. *gild*, money, *gildan*, to pay : it is the same word as **Gold** and **Gild**.]

**Guile**, gīl, *n.* wile, jugglery : cunning : deceit. [O. Fr. *guille*, deceit ; from a Teut. root, as in A.S *wil*, Ice *vel*, a trick. See **Wile**.]

**Guileful**, gīl'fool, *adj.* crafty : deceitful.—*adv.* **Guile'fully.**—*n.* **Guile'fulness.**

**Guileless**, gīl'les, *adj.* without deceit : artless.—*adv.* **Guile'lessly.**—*n.* **Guile'lessness.**

**Guillemot**, gil'e-mot, *n.* a genus of marine birds having a pointed bill and very short tail [Fr.]

**Guillotine**, gil'ō-tēn, *n.* an instrument for beheading—consisting of an upright frame down which a sharp heavy axe descends on the neck of the victim—adopted during the French Revolution, and named after *Guillotin*, a physician, who first proposed its adoption.—*v.t.* to *behead* with the *guillotine.*

**Guilt**, gilt, *n.* punishable conduct : the state of having broken a law : crime. [Orig. a *payment* or *fine* for an offence ; A.S. *gylt*, guilt—*gildan*, to pay, to atone.]

**Guiltless**, gilt'les, *adj.* free from crime : innocent. —*adv.* **Guilt'lessly.**—*n.* **Guilt'lessness.**

**Guilty**, gilt'i, *adj.* justly chargeable with a crime : wicked.—**Guilty of** (sometimes in *B.*), deserving.—*adv.* **Guilt'ily.**—*n.* **Guilt'iness.** [A.S. *gyltig*.]

**Guinea** gin'i, *n.* an English gold coin, no longer used = 21s., so called because first made of gold brought from *Guinea*, in Africa.

**Guinea-fowl**, gin'i-fowl, **Guinea-hen**, gin'i-hen, *n.* a fowl like the turkey, of a dark-gray colour, with white spots, originally from Guinea, in Africa.

**Guinea-pig**, gin'i-pig, *n.* a small S. American animal, belonging to the Rodentia, and somewhat resembling a small pig. [Prob. a mistake for *Guiana-pig.*]

**Guise**, gīz, *n.*, manner, behaviour : external appearance : dress. [Fr. *guise*; from O. Ger. *wisa* (Ger. *weise*), a way. guise, which is cog. with A.S. *wis*, wise, *wisa*, cause, manner, E. *wise*, guide.]     [mas mummer.

**Guiser**, gīz'èr, *n.* a person in *disguise* : a Christ-

**Guitar**, gi-tär', *n.* a musical stringed instrument like the violin in shape, but larger, and played upon with the fingers. [Fr. *guitare;* from L. *cithara*—Gr. *kithara*, a lyre or lute. See **Cithern**.]

**Gules**, gūlz. *n.* (*her.*) a *red* colour, marked in engraved figures by perpendicular lines. [Fr. *gueules;* of doubtful origin : acc. to Brachet, from Pers. *ghul*, a rose ; but acc. to other authorities, it is from Fr. *gueule*—L. *gula*, the throat, prob. from the colour of the open mouth of the heraldic lion.]

**Gulf**, gulf, *n.* a hollow or indentation in the sea-coast : a deep place in the earth : an abyss : a whirlpool : anything insatiable. [Fr. *golfe*—Late Gr. *kolphos*, Gr. *kolpos*, the bosom, a fold, a gulf.]

**Gulfy**, gulf'i, *adj.* full of *gulfs* or whirlpools.

**Gull**, gul, *n.* a web-footed sea-fowl, named from its *wailing* cry. [Corn. *gullan*, W. *gwylan*, Bret. *gwelan*—Bret. *gwela*, to weep, to cry.]

**Gull**, gul. *v.t.* to beguile : to deceive.—*n.* a trick : one easily cheated. [Same word as *gull*, a sea-fowl, the bird being thought stupid.]

**Gullet**, gul'et, *n.* the throat : the passage in the neck by which food is taken into the stomach. [Fr. *goulet*, the gullet, dim. of O. Fr. *goule*, Fr. *gueule*—L. *gula*, the throat.]

**Gullible**, gul'i-bl, *adj.* easily *gulled* or deceived.—*n.* **Gullibil'ity.**

**Gully**, gul'i, *n.* a gullet or channel worn by running-water.—*v.t.* to wear a gully or channel in. [A form of **Gullet**.]

**Gulp**, gulp, *v.t.* to swallow eagerly or in large draughts. [Dut. *gulpen*, to swallow eagerly, from Dut. *gulp*, a great draught.]

**Gum**, gum, *n.* the flesh of the jaws which surrounds the teeth. [A.S. *goma*; Ice. *gomr*, Ger. *gaumen*, roof of the mouth, palate.]

**Gum**, gum, *n.* a substance which exudes from certain trees, and hardens on the surface.—*v.t.* to smear or unite with gum :—*pr.p.* gumm'ing ; *pa.p.* gummed'. [Fr. *gomme*—L. *gummi*—Gr. *kommi.*]

**Gummiferous**, gum-if'èr-us, *adj. producing gum.* [L. *gummi*, and *fero*, to bear, to produce.]

**Gummous**, gum'us, **Gummy**, gum'i. *adj.* consisting of or resembling *gum* : producing or covered with gum.—*n.* **Gumm'iness.** [L. *gummosus.*]

**Gun**, gun, *n.* a firearm or weapon, from which balls or other projectiles are discharged, usually by means of gunpowder : now, generally applied to cannon. [Ety. dub. ; perh. from W. *gwn*, a bowl, gun.]     [a gun.

**Gun-barrel**, gun'-bar'el, *n.* the barrel or tube of

**Gunboat**, gun'bōt, *n.* a boat or small vessel of light draught, fitted to carry one or more guns.

**Gun-carriage**, gun'-kar'ij, *n.* a carriage on which a gun or cannon is supported.

**Gun-cotton**, gun'-kot'n, *n.* cotton rendered highly explosive like gunpowder.     [by a ship of war.

**Gunnage**, gun'āj, *n.* the number of *guns* carried

**Gunner**, gun'èr, *n.* one who works a gun or cannon : (*naut.*) a petty officer who has charge of the *ordnance* on board ship.

**Gunnery**, gun'èr-i, *n.* the art of managing *guns*, or the science of artillery.

**Gunny**, gun'i, *n.* a strong coarse cloth manufactured in India from jute, and used as sacking. [Prob. a native word.]

**Gunpowder**, gun'pow-dèr. *n.* an explosive powder used for guns and firearms.

**Gunshot**, gun'shot, *n.* the distance to which *shot* can be thrown from a *gun*.—*adj.* caused by the *shot* of a *gun.*

**Gunsmith**, gun'smith, *n.* a smith or workman who makes or repairs guns or small-arms.

**Gunstock**, gun'stok, *n.* the *stock* or piece of wood on which the barrel of a *gun* is fixed.

**Gunwale**, gun'el, *n.* the *wale* or upper edge of a ship's side next to the bulwarks, so called because the upper *guns* are pointed from it. [See **Wale**.]

**Gurgle**, gur'gl, *v.i.* to flow in an irregular noisy current, as water from a bottle : to make a bubbling sound. [Through an It. *gorgogliare*, from the same root as **Gorge**; cf. **Gargle**.]

**Gurnet**, gur'net, **Gurnard**, gur'nard, *n.* a kind of fish. [Supposed to be so called from the sound it makes when taken out of the water; from O. Fr. *gournauld*—Fr. *grogner*, to grunt—L. *grunnio*, to grunt.]

**Gush**, gush, *v.i.* to flow out with violence or copiously.—*n.* that which flows out : a violent issue of a fluid. [From a Teut. root found in Ice. *gusa*, to gush, A.S. *geotan*, Ger. *giessen*, akin to Gr. *cheō*, to pour ]

**Gushing**, gush'ing, *adj.* rushing forth with violence, as a liquid : flowing copiously : effusive.—*adv.* **Gush'ingly.**

**Gusset**, gus'et, *n.* the piece of cloth in a shirt which covers the armpit : an angular piece of cloth inserted in a garment to strengthen some part of it. [Fr. *gousset*, armpit, gusset—*gousse*, It. *guscio*, a pod, husk ; from the fancied likeness of the armpit to the hollow husk of a bean or pea.]

**Gust**, gust, *n.* a sudden blast of wind : a violent burst of passion. [Ice. *gustr*, blast, from root of **Gush**.]

**Gust**, gust, **Gusto**, gust'ō, *n.* sense of pleasure of *tasting* : relish : gratification. [L. *gustus*, taste ; akin to Gr. *geuō*, to make to taste.]

**Gustatory**, gust'a-tor-i, *adj.* pertaining to, or tending to please the *taste*. [Gust'iness.]

**Gusty**, gust'i, *adj.* stormy : tempestuous.—*n.*

**Gut**, gut, *n.* the intestinal canal.—*v.t.* to take out the bowels of : to plunder :—*pr.p.* gutt'ing ; *pa.p.* gutt'ed. [A.S. *gut*, the orig. sense being *channel* ; cf. A.S. *geotan*, to pour, Prov. E. *gut*, a drain, O. Dut. *gote*, a channel.]

**Gutta-percha**, gut'a-pèrch'a, *n.* the solidified juice of various trees in the Malayan Islands. [Malay *gatah*, *guttah*, gum, *percha*, the tree producing it.]

**Gutter**, gut'ér, *n.* a channel at the eaves of a roof for conveying away the *drops* : a channel for water.—*v.t.* to cut or form into small hollows.—*v.i.* to become hollowed : to run down in drops, as a candle. [Fr. *gouttière*—*goutte*—L. *gutta*, a drop.]

**Guttural**, gut'ur-al, *adj.* pertaining to the *throat* : formed in the throat.—*n.* (*gram.*) a letter pronounced in the throat.—*adv.* **Gutt'urally.** [L. *guttur*, the throat.]

**Guy**, gī, *n.* (*naut.*) a rope to *guide* or steady any suspended weight. [Sp. *guia*, a guide ; from the same source as **Guide**.]

**Guy**, gī, *n.* an effigy of Guy Fawkes, dressed up grotesquely on the day of the Gunpowder plot : an odd figure.

**Guzzle**, guz'l, *v.i.* to eat and drink with haste and greediness.—*v.t.* to swallow with exceeding relish.—*n.* **Guzz'ler.** [O. Fr. *des-gouziller*, to swallow down—*gosier*, the throat.]

**Gymnasium**, jim-nā'zi-um, *n.* (*orig.*) a place where athletic exercises were practised *naked* : a school for gymnastics : a school for the higher branches of literature and science :—*pl.* **Gymnasia**, jim-nā'zi-a. [L.—Gr. *gymnasion*—*gymnazō*, to exercise—*gymnos*, naked.]

**Gymnast**, jim'nast, *n.* one who teaches or practises *gymnastics*. [Fr. *gymnaste*—Gr. *gymnastēs*.]

**Gymnastic**, jim-nas'tik, **Gymnastical**, jim-nas'tik-al, *adj.* pertaining to athletic exercises.—*n.pl.* used as *sing.* **Gymnas'tics**, athletic exercises : the art of performing athletic exercises.—*adv.* **Gymnas'tically.** [L. *gymnasticus*—Gr. *gymnastikos*, relating to gymnastics. See **Gymnasium**.]

**Gymnosophist**, jim-nos'of-ist, *n.* one of a sect of Indian philosophers who lived an ascetic life and went *naked*. [Gr. *gymnos*, naked, *sophos*, wise.]

**Gynarchy**, jin'är-ki, *n.*, *government* by a *female*. [Gr. *gynē*, a woman, *archē*, rule.]

**Gynecocracy**, jin-e-kok'ra-si, **Gyneocrasy**, jin-e-ok'ra-si, *n.*, *government* by *women*. [Gr. *gynē*, a woman, *krateō*, to rule.]

**Gyp**, jip, *n.* at Cambridge, a college servant.

**Gypseous**, jip'se-us, *adj.* of or resembling *gypsum*.

**Gypsum**, jip'sum, *n.* sulphate of lime ; when calcined it is plaster of Paris. [L.—Gr. *gypsos*, chalk.]

**Gypsy.** See **Gipsy**.

**Gyrate**, jī'rāt, *v.i.* to whirl round a central point :

to move spirally.—*adj.* (*bot.*) winding round. [L. *gyro*, *gyratum*, to move in a circle.]

**Gyration**, jī-rā'shun, *n.* act of whirling round a central point : a spiral motion.

**Gyratory**, jī'ra-tor-i, *adj.* moving in a circle.

**Gyre**, jīr, *n.* a circular motion. [L. *gyrus*—Gr. *gyros*, a ring, round.]

**Gyrfalcon**, **Gierfalcon**, jèr'faw-kn, *n.* a large *falcon*, found in the northern regions of both the Old and New Worlds. [Low L. *gyrofalco* ; from Ger. *geier* (O. Ger. *giri*, voracious), a vulture, and *falke*, falcon.]

**Gyromancy**, jī'ro-man-si, *n.*, *divination* by walking in a *circle*. [Gr. *gyros*, a circle, and *manteia*, divination.]

**Gyroscope**, jī'ro-skōp, *n.* an instrument shewing to the eye the effects of *rotation*. [Gr. *gyros*, and *skopeō*, to see.]

**Gyve**, jīv, *n.* a fetter, esp. one to confine the legs —used commonly in pl.—*v.t.* to fetter. [W. *gefyn*, fetters.]

# H

**Ha**, hä, *int.* denoting surprise, joy, or grief ; and, when repeated, laughter. [From the sound.]

**Habeas-corpus**, hā'be-as-kor'pus, *n.* a writ to a jailer to produce the body of one detained in prison, and to state the reasons of such detention, that the court may judge of their sufficiency. [Lit. *have the body*, from L. *habeo*, to have, and *corpus*, the body.]

**Haberdasher**, hab'ér-dash-ér, *n.* a seller of smallwares, as ribbons, tape, &c. [O. Fr. *hapertas* ; of uncertain origin.] [a haberdasher.]

**Haberdashery**, hab'ér-dash-ér-i, *n.* goods sold by

**Habergeon**, ha-bèr'je-un, *n.* a piece of armour to defend the neck and breast. [Fr. *haubergeon*, dim. of O. Fr. *hauberc*. See **Hauberk**.]

**Habiliment**, ha-bil'i-ment, *n.* a garment :—*pl.* clothing, dress. [Fr. *habillement*—*habiller*, to dress—L. *habilis*, fit, ready—*habeo*.]

**Habit**, hab'it, *n.* ordinary course of conduct : tendency to perform certain actions : general condition or tendency, as of the body : practice : custom : outward appearance, dress : a garment, esp. a tight-fitting dress, with a skirt, worn by ladies on horseback.—*v.t.* to dress :—*pr.p.* hab'iting ; *pa.p.* hab'ited. [Fr.—L. *habitus*, state, dress—*habeo*, to have, to be in a condition.]

**Habitable**, hab'it-a-bl, *adj.* that may be dwelt in.—*adv.* **Hab'itably.**—*n.* **Hab'itableness.** [Fr.—L. *habitabilis*—*habito*, *habitatus*, to inhabit, freq. of *habeo*, to have.]

**Habitat**, hab'it-at, *n.* (*nat. hist.* and *bot.*) the natural abode or locality of an animal or plant. [3d pers. sing. pres. ind. of L. *habito*.]

**Habitation**, hab-i-tā'shun, *n.* act of inhabiting or dwelling : a dwelling or residence. [Fr.—L. *habitatio*—*habito*.]

**Habitual**, ha-bit'ū-al, *adj.* formed or acquired by *habit* or frequent use : customary.—*adv.* **Habit'ually.** [Low L. *habitualis*—L. *habitus*.]

**Habituate**, ha-bit'ū-āt, *v.t.* to cause to acquire a *habit* : to accustom. [L. *habituo*, *habituatum* —*habitus*, held in a state or condition.]

**Habitude**, hab'i-tūd, *n.* tendency from acquiring a *habit* : usual manner. [L. *habitudo*—*habeo*.]

**Hack**, hak, *v.t.* to cut : to chop or mangle : to notch. —*n.* a cut made by hacking.—**Hacking cough**, a broken, troublesome cough. [A.S. *haccan* ; Dut. *hakken*, and Ger. *hacken*. See **Hash**.]

**Hack**, hak, *n.* a hackney, esp. a poor and jaded one : any person overworked on hire : a literary drudge.—*adj.* hackney, hired.—*v.t.* to offer for hire : to use roughly. [Contr. of **Hackney** ; cf. **Cab.**]

**Hackle**, hak'l, *n.* an instrument with *hooks* or iron teeth for sorting hemp or flax : any flimsy substance unspun : a feather in a cock's neck : a hook and fly for angling, dressed with this feather. [Dut. *hekel,* dim of *haak,* a hook ; akin to Ger. *hechel—haken,* E. **Hook.**]

**Hackle**, hak'l, *v.t.* to dress with a hackle, as flax : to tear rudely asunder.

**Hackly**, hak'li, *adj.* rough and broken, as if *hacked* or chopped : (*min.*) covered with sharp points.

**Hackney**, hak'ni, *n.* a horse for general use, esp. for hire.—*v.t.* to carry in a hackney-coach : to use much : to make commonplace. [Fr. *haquenée* —Dut. *hakke-nei,* an ambling nag ; prob. from *hakken* (E. **Hack,** to cut), and *negge* (E. **Nag,** a small horse).]

**Hackney, Hackneyed,** hak'nid, *adj.* let out for hire : devoted to common use : much used. [for hire.

**Hackney-coach**, hak'ni-kōch, *n.* a coach let out

**Had**, *pa.t.* and *pa.p.* of **Have** : (*B.*) = held, Acts xxv. 26. [Contr. from A.S. *hǽfed, hǽfd* = haved.]

**Haddock**, had'uk, *n.* a sea-fish of the cod family. [Ety. dub. ; cf. W. *hadog,* prolific—*had,* seed ; perh. from Low L. *gadus,* cod—Gr. *gados,* and dim. termination *ock.*]

**Hades**, hā'dēz, *n.* the unseen world : the abode of the dead. [Gr. *haidēs, hadēs*—prob. from *a,* priv., and *idein,* to see, ' The Unseen.']

**Hæmal, Hæmatite,** &c. See **Hemal, Hematite.**

**Hæmoglobin**, hē-mo-glob'in, *n.* the colouring matter of the blood. [Gr. *haima,* blood, L. *globus,* a round body.]

**Hæmorrhage**, &c. See **Hemorrhage.**

**Haft**, haft, *n.* a handle. [A.S. *hæft,* from the root of *have* ; cog. with Dut. and Ger. *heft.*]

**Hag**, hag, *n.* an ugly old woman : (*orig.*) a witch. [Shortened from A.S. *hæg-tesse,* a witch or fury ; Ger. and Dan. *hexe* ; perh. conn. with Ice. *hagr,* wise, or with A.S. *haga,* a hedge, because witches were thought to frequent bushes.]

**Haggard**, hag'ard, *adj., wild,* applied to an untrained hawk. [Fr.—Ger. *hager,* lean—*hag,* a thicket.]

**Haggard**, hag'ard, *adj.* lean : hollow-eyed.—*adv.* **Hagg'ardly.** [Lit. ' hag-like.' See **Hag.**]

**Haggis**, hag'is, *n.* a Scotch dish made of different parts of sheep or lamb *chopped* up with suet, onions, oatmeal, &c., and boiled in a sheep's maw. [Scot. *hag,* to chop, E. **Hack** ; cf. Fr. *hachis,* from *hacher.*] [ishly.

**Haggish**, hag'ish, *adj.* hag-like.—*adv.* **Hagg'-**

**Haggle**, hag'l, *v.t.* to cut unskilfully : to mangle. [Freq. of **Hack,** to cut.]

**Haggle**, hag'l, *v.i.* to be slow and hard in making a bargain : to stick at trifles.—*n.* **Hagg'ler.** [Prob. same as above.]

**Hagiographa**, hag- or hā-ji-og'raf-a, **Hagiography,** hag- or hā-ji-og'raf-i, *n.pl.* the last of the three Jewish divisions of the Old Testament, comprehending the books of Psalms, Proverbs, Job, Daniel, Ezra, Nehemiah, Ruth, Esther, Chron., Cant., Lament., Eccles.—*adj.* **Hagiog'raphal.** [Gr. *hagiographa* (*biblia*)—*hagios,* holy, *graphō,* to write.]

**Hagiographer**, hag- or hā-ji-og'raf-ėr, *n.* one of the writers of the *Hagiographa,* a sacred writer.

**Hagiology**, hag- or hā-ji-ol'oj-i, *n.* history of saints. [Gr. *hagios,* holy, and *logos,* discourse.]

**Hah**, hä, *int.* Same as **Ha.**

**Haha**, hahä', *n.* Same as **Hawhaw.**

**Hail**, hāl, *int.* or *imp.* (*lit.*) may you be in *health.* [Ice. *heill,* hale, healthy, much used in greeting. See **Hale, Healthy, Heal,** and **Whole.**]

**Hail**, hāl, *v.t.* to greet : to call to, at a distance : to address one passing. [Same word as above.]

**Hail**, hāl, *n.* frozen rain or particles of ice falling from the clouds.—*v.t.* to rain hail. [M. E. *hawel* —A.S. *hagal ;* Ger. *hagel,* and in most other Teut. languages.] [like *hail.*

**Hailstone**, hāl'sho., *n.* small *shot* which scatters

**Hailstone**, hāl'stōn, *n.* a single *stone* or ball of *hail.*

**Hair**, hār, *n.* a filament growing from the skin of an animal : the whole mass of hairs which forms a covering for the head or the whole body : (*bot.*) minute hair-like processes on the cuticle of plants : anything very small and fine.—*adj.* **Hair'less.** [A.S. *hær,* a common Teut. word.]

**Hairbreadth**, hār'bredth, **Hair's-breadth,** hārz'-bredth, *n.* the *breadth* of a *hair :* a very small distance.

**Haircloth**, hār'kloth, *n.* cloth made partly or entirely of hair. [of a few fine *hairs.*

**Hair-pencil**, hār'pen'sil, *n.* an artist's brush made

**Hair-powder**, hār'pow'dėr, *n.* a white powder for dusting the hair. [minute distinctions.

**Hair-splitting**, hār'-split'ing, *n.* the art of making

**Hairspring**, hār'spring, *n.* a very fine *hair*like *spring* on the balance-wheel of a watch.

**Hairstroke**, hār'strōk, *n.* in writing, a *stroke* or line as fine as a *hair.*

**Hair-trigger**, hār'-trig'ėr, *n.* a trigger which discharges a gun or pistol by a hairlike spring.

**Hairworm**, hār'wurm, *n.* a worm, like a horsehair, which lives in the bodies of certain insects.

**Hairy**, hār'i, *adj.* of or resembling *hair :* covered with hair.—*n.* **Hair'iness.**

**Hake**, hāk, **Hakot**, hak'ut, *n.* a sea-fish of the cod family. [Lit. the ' *hooked* fish,' A.S. *hacod,* Norw. *hake-fisk,* Ger. *hecht,* a pike.]

**Halberd**, hal'bėrd, *n.* a *poleaxe :* a weapon consisting of an *axe* and heavy dagger fixed on a *pole.* [Fr. *hallebarde*—O. Ger. *helmbarte* (Ger. *hellebarte*), the long-handled axe, from O. Ger. *halm,* a handle, *barte,* an axe.]

**Halberdier**, hal-bėrd-ēr', *n.* one armed with a halberd.

**Halcyon**, hal'si-un, *n.* the kingfisher, a bird that was once believed to make a floating nest on the sea, which remained calm while it was hatching. —*adj.* calm : peaceful : happy.—Hence **Halcyondays,** a time of peace and happiness. [L.—Gr. *alkyōn, halkyōn ;* the fancied ety., with which the fable is associated, is from *hals,* the sea, and *kyō,* to conceive, to br d ; true ety. dub., prob. correctly spelt *alkyon* without an aspirate, and conn. with *alcedo,* the true L. name for the bird.]

**Hale**, hāl, *adj., healthy :* robust : sound of body. [M.E. *heil*—Ice. *heill ;* cog. with **Whole.**]

**Hale**, hāl, *v.t.* to drag. [A variant of **Haul.**]

**Half**, häf (*pl.* **Halves,** hävz), *n.* one of two equal parts.—*adj.* having or consisting of one of two equal parts : being in part : incomplete, as measures.—*adv.* in an equal part or degree : in part : imperfectly. [A.S. *healf, half ;* the word is found in all the Teut. languages ; there is also a parallel form *healf,* sig. *side* or *part,* which may have been the original meaning. See **Behalf.**]

**Half-blood**, häf'-blud, *n.* relation between those who are of the same father or mother, but not of both.

**Half-blooded**, häf'-blud'ed, **Half-breed,** häf'-brēd, *adj.* produced from a male and female of *different* blood or *breeds.*

**Half-bred**, häf'-bred, *adj.*, *half* or not well *bred* or trained : wanting in refinement.

**Half-brother**, häf'-bruth'ér, **Half-sister**, häf'-sis'-tér, *n.* a *brother* or *sister* by one parent only.

**Half-caste**, häf'-kast, *n.* a person one of whose parents belongs to a Hindu *caste*, and the other is a European.

**Half-cock**, häf'-kok, *n.* the position of the *cock* of a gun when retained by the first notch.

**Half-moon**, häf'-mōōn, *n.* the *moon* at the quarters when but *half* of it is illuminated : anything semicircular.  [military officers.

**Half-pay**, häf'-pā, *n.* reduced pay. as of naval or

**Halfpenny** (*pl.* **Halfpence**, häf'pens or hā'pens), *n.* a copper coin worth *half* a *penny*: the value of half a penny.—*n.* **Half'penny-worth**, the *worth* or value of a *halfpenny*.

**Half-tint**, häf'-tint, *n.* an intermediate tint.

**Half-way**, häf'-wā, *adv.* at half the way or distance : imperfectly.—*adj.* equally distant from two points.  [intellect : silly.

**Half-witted**, häf'-wit'ed, *adj.* weak in *wit* or

**Half-yearly**, häf'-yēr'li, *adj.* occurring at every *half-year* or twice in a year.—*adv.* twice in a year.

**Halibut**, hal'i-but, *n.* the largest kind of flat-fishes. [M. E. *hali*, holy, and *butte.* a flounder, plaice, the fish being much eaten on fast- or holy-days ; cf. Dut. *heilbot*, Ger. *heilbutt.*]

**Hall**, hawl, *n.* a large room or passage at the entrance of a house : a large chamber for public business : an edifice in which courts of justice are held : a manor-house (so called because courts of justice used to be held in them) : the edifice of a college : at Oxford, an unendowed college : at Cambridge, a college. [A.S. *heal*, a word found in most Teut. languages, which has passed also into Fr. *halle*, from the root of A.S. *helan*, to cover ; allied to L. *cella* ; not conn with L. *aula*.]

**Halleluiah**, **Hallelujah**, hal-e-lōō'ya, *n.* an expression of praise. [Heb. ' Praise ye Jehovah,' *halelu*, praise ye, and *Jah*, Jehovah, God.]

**Halliard**. See **Halyard**.

**Hall-mark**, hawl'-märk, *n.* the *mark* made on plate at Goldsmiths' *Hall* to shew its purity.

**Halloo**, hal-lōō', *int.*, *n.* a hunting cry : a cry to draw attention.—*v.i.* to cry after dogs : to raise an outcry.—*v.t.* to encourage or chase with shouts. [From the sound, like A.S. *ealá*, Fr. *halle !* Ger. *halloh*.]

**Hallow**, hal'ō, *v.t.* to make *holy*: to set apart for religious use: to reverence. [A.S. *halgian*, *haligan*—*halig*, holy ; conn. with **Hale**, **Heal**, **Holy**, **Whole**.] [Hallows or All-Saints'-Day.

**Halloween**, hal'ō-ēn, *n.* the evening before All-

**Hallowmas**, hal'ō-mas, *n.* the *mass* or feast of *All-Hallows*. [Hallow and Mass.]

**Hallucination**, hal-lū-sin-ā'shun, *n.* error : delusion : (*med.*) perception of things that do not exist. [L. *hallucinatio*—*hallucinor*, *alucinor*, *-atum*, to wander in mind.]

**Hallucinatory**, hal-lū'sin-a-tor-i, *adj.* partaking of or tending to produce *hallucination*.

**Halo**, hā'lō, *n.* a luminous *circle* round the sun or moon, caused by the refraction of light through mist : (*paint.*) the bright ring round the heads of holy persons :—*pl.* **Halos**, hā'lōz. [L. *halos*—Gr. *halōs*, a round thrashing-floor.]

**Halser**, hawz'ér, *n.* See **Hawser**.

**Halt**, hawlt, *v.t.* (*mil.*) to cause to cease marching.—*v.i.* to stop from going on : (*mil.*) to stop in a march : to limp : (*B.*) to be in doubt : to hesitate : to walk lamely.—*adj.* lame.—*n.* a

stopping : (*mil.*) a stop in marching. [A.S. *healt* ; Ice. *haltr*, Dan. and Swed. *halt*.]

**Halter**, hawlt'ér, *n.* a head-rope for holding and leading a horse : a rope for hanging criminals : a strong strap or cord.—*v.t.* to catch or bind with a rope. [A.S. *healfter* ; Ger. *halfter* ; the root is uncertain.]

**Halting**, hawlt'ing, *adj.* holding back : stopping : limping.—*adv.* **Halt'ingly**.   [parts.

**Halve**, häv, *v.t.* to divide into *halves* or two equal

**Halved**, hävd, *adj.* divided into *halves* : (*bot.*) appearing as if one side were cut away.

**Halyard**, **Halliard**, hal'yard, *n.* (*naut.*) a rope by which *yards*, sails, &c. are *hauled* or hoisted. [See **Yard** and **Hale**, *v.*]

**Ham**, ham, *n.* the hind part or inner *bend* of the knee : the thigh of an animal, esp. of a hog salted and dried. [A.S. *hamm* ; Ger. *hamme*, O. Ger. *hamma*, from root *ham* or *kam*, to bend, Celt. *cam*, crooked, bent.]

**Hamadryad**, ham'a-drī-ad, *n.* (*myth.*) a dryad or wood-nymph, who lived and died *along with* the *tree* in which she dwelt :—*pl.* **Ham'adryads** and **Hamadry'ades** (-ēz). [Gr. *hamadryas*—*hama*, together, *drys*, a tree.]

**Hamitic**, ham-it'ik, *adj.* pertaining to *Ham*, a son of Noah, or to his descendants.

**Hamlet**, ham'let, *n.* a cluster of houses in the country : a small village. [O. Fr. *hamel* (Fr. *hameau*), and dim. affix *-et*—from the O. Ger. *cham*, Ger. *heim*, A.S. *ham*, a dwelling ; E. *home* ; conn. also with Gr. *kōmē*, a village. See **Home**.]

**Hammer**, ham'ér, *n.* a tool for *beating*, or driving nails : anything like a hammer, as the part of a clock that strikes the bell : the baton of an auctioneer.—*v.t.* to drive or shape with a hammer : to contrive by intellectual labour. [A.S. *hamor* ; Ger. *hammer*, Ice. *hamarr*.]

**Hammercloth**, ham'ér-kloth, *n.* the *cloth* which covers a coach-box. [An adaptation of Dut. *hemel*, heaven, a covering ; Ger. *himmel* (Skeat).]

**Hammerman**, ham'ér-man, *n.* a man who hammers.

**Hammock**, ham'uk, *n.* a piece of strong cloth or netting suspended by the corners, and used as a bed by sailors. [*Hamaca*, an American Indian word, meaning a net.]

**Hamper**, ham'pér, *v.t.* to impede or perplex : to shackle.—*n.* a chain or fetter. [A corr. through M. E. *hamelen* and obs. *hamble* from A.S. *hamelian*, to maim, the root of which is seen in Goth. *hanfs*, maimed, Scot. *hummel* cow, *i.e.* maimed, deprived of its horns.]

**Hamper**, ham'pér, *n.* a large *basket* for conveying goods.—*v.t.* to put in a hamper. [Contr. from **Hanaper**.]

**Hamster**, ham'stér, *n.* a species of rat provided with cheek-pouches. [Ger.]

**Hamstring**, ham'string, *n.* the *string* or tendon of the *ham*.—*v.t.* to lame by cutting the hamstring.

**Hanaper**, han'a-pér, *n.* a large strong basket for packing goods, esp. crockery : (*orig.*) a royal treasure-basket : a treasury or exchequer. [Low L. *hanaperium*, a large vessel for keeping cups in —O. Fr. *hanap*, a drinking-cup—O. Ger. *hnapf*, Ger. *napf*, A.S. *hnæp*, a bowl.]

**Hand**, hand, *n.* the extremity of the arm below the wrist : that which does the duty of a hand by pointing, as the hand of a clock : the forefoot of a horse : a measure of four inches : an agent or workman : performance : power or manner of performing : skill : possession : style of handwriting : side : direction.—*v.t.* to give with the hand : to lead or conduct : (*naut.*) to furl, as sails.—*n.* Hand'er.—Hand down, to transmit in succession.—Hand over head, rashly. —Hand to mouth, without thought for the future, precariously.—Off Hand or Out of Hand, immediately.—To bear a Hand, make haste to help. [A.S. *hand*; found in all the Teut. languages, and perh. from the base of A.S. *hentan*, Goth. *hinthan*, to seize.]

Hand-barrow, hand'-bar'ō, *n.* a *barrow*, without a wheel, carried by the *hands* of men.

Handbill, hand'bil, *n.* a *bill* or pruning-hook used in the hand : a *bill* or loose sheet, with some announcement.

Handbook, hand'book, *n.* a *manual* or *book* of reference for the *hand* : a guide-book for travellers.

Handbreadth, hand'bredth, *n.* the *breadth* of a *hand* : a palm. [*hand*.

Handcart, hand'kärt, *n.* a small *cart* drawn by

Handcuff, hand'kuf, *n.* a *cuff* or fetter for the *hand*. —*v.t.* to put handcuffs on :—*pr.p.* hand'cuffing ; *pa.p.* hand'cuffed (-kuft). [A.S. *handcosp*, *handcops*—hand, and *cosp*, a fetter, the latter being modified by confusion with Cuff.]

Handful, hand'fool, *n.* as much as *fills* the *hand* : a small number or quantity :—*pl.* Hand'fuls.

Hand-gallop, hand'-gal'up, *n.* an easy *gallop*, in which the speed of the horse is restrained by the *hand* pressing the bridle.

Handglass, hand'glas, *n.* a *glass* or small glazed frame used to protect plants, able to be lifted by the *hand*. [thrown by the hand.

Hand-grenade, hand'-gre-nād', *n.* a *grenade* to be

Handicap, hand'i-kap, *n.* a race in which the horses carry different weights, or are placed at different distances, or start at different times, so that all shall have, as nearly as possible, an equal chance of winning. [Orig. applied to a method of settling a bargain or exchange by arbitration, in which each of the parties exchanging put his *hand* containing money into a *cap*, while the terms of the award were being stated, the award being settled only if money was found in the hands of both when the arbiter called 'Draw.']

Handicraft, hand'i-kraft, *n.* a *craft*, trade, or work performed by the *hand*.

Handicraftsman, hand'i-krafts-man, *n.* a *man* skilled in a *handicraft* or manual occupation.

Handiwork, Handywork, hand'i-wurk, *n.* work done by the *hands* : work of skill or wisdom. [A.S. *handgeweorc*—hand, hand, and *geweorc*, another form of *weorc*, work.]

Handkerchief, hang'kėr-chif, *n.* a piece of cloth for wiping the nose, &c. : a neckerchief. [Hand and Kerchief.]

Handle, hand'l, *v.t.* to touch, hold, or use with the *hand* : to make familiar by frequent touching : to manage : to discuss : to practise.—*v.i.* to use the hands. [A S. *handlian*, from Hand.]

Handle, hand'l, *n.* that part of anything held in the *hand* : (*fig.*) that of which use is made : a tool.

Handless, hand'les, *adj.* without hands.

Handmaid, hand'mād, Handmaiden, hand'mād-n, *n.* a female servant.

Handsel, hand'sel, *n.* money for something sold given into the *hands* of another : the first sale or using of anything : a first instalment or earnest : a new-year's gift.—*v.t.* to give a handsel : to use or do anything the first time. [A.S. *handselen*, a giving into hands—hand, and *sellan*, to give, whence E. *sell*.]

Handsome, hand'sum or han'sum, *adj.* good-looking : with dignity : liberal or noble : generous : ample.—*adv.* Hand'somely.—*n.* Hand'someness. [Hand, and affix *some*; Dut. *handzaam*, easily handled.]

Handspike, hand'spīk, *n.* a *spike* or bar used with the *hand* as a lever.

Handstaves, hand'stāvz, *n.pl.* (*B.*) staves for the *hand*, probably javelins.

Handwriting, hand'rīt-ing. *n.* the style of *writing* peculiar to each *hand* or person : writing.

Handy, hand'i, *adj.* dexterous : ready to the hand : convenient : near. [A.S. *hendig*, from Hand ; Dut. *handig*, Dan. *hændig*.]

Handywork. Same as Handiwork.

Hang, hang, *v.t.* to hook or fix to some high point : to suspend : to decorate with pictures, &c. as a wall : to put to death by suspending, and choking.—*v.i.* to be hanging so as to allow of free motion : to lean, or rest for support : to drag : to hover or impend : to be in suspense : to linger : —*pr.p.* hang'ing ; *pa.t.* and *pa.p.* hanged or hung. [A.S. *hangian*, causal form of *hon*, pa.p. *hangen*; Dut. and Ger. *hangen*, Goth. *hahan*.]

Hanger, hang'ėr, *n.* that on which anything is hung : a short sword, curved near the point.

Hanger-on, hang'ėr-on, *n.* one who *hangs on* or sticks to a person or place : an importunate acquaintance : a dependent.

Hanging, hang'ing, *adj.* deserving death by *hanging*.—*n.* death by the halter : that which is hung, as drapery, &c. :—used chiefly in *pl.*— Hang-dog *adj.* like a fellow that deserves hanging, as in 'a hang-dog look.'

Hangman, hang'man, *n.* a public executioner.

Hank, hangk, *n.* (*lit.*) that by which anything is *hung* or fastened : two or more skeins of thread tied together. [Ice. *hanki*, cord ; Ger. *henkel*, a handle, *henken*, to hang ; from root of Hang.]

Hanker, hangk'ėr, *v.i.* to long for with eagerness and uneasiness : to linger about. [A freq. of Hang, in the sense of to hang on ; cf. Dut. *hunkeren*.]

Hanseatic, han-se-at'ik, *adj.* pertaining to the *Hanse* cities in Germany, which *leagued* together for protection about the 12th century. [O. Fr. *hanse*, league—O. Ger. *hansa*, troop, association.]

Hansom-cab, han'sum-kab, *n.* a light two-wheeled *cab* or carriage with the driver's seat raised behind. [From the name of the inventor.]

Hap, hap, *n.* chance : fortune : accident. [Ice. *happ*, good-luck.]

Hap-hazard, hap'-haz'ard, *n.* that which happens by *hazard* : chance, accident. [Hap'lessly.

Hapless, hap'les, *adj.* unlucky : unhappy.—*adv.*

Haply, hap'li, *adv.* by *hap*, chance, or accident : perhaps : it may be.

Happen, hap'n, *v.i.* to fall out : to take place.

Happy, hap'i, *adj.* lucky, successful : possessing or enjoying pleasure or good : secure of good : furnishing enjoyment : dexterous.—*adv.* Happ'-ily.—*n.* Happ'iness [See Hap.]

Harangue, ha-rang', *n.* a loud speech addressed to a multitude : a popular, pompous address.—*v.i.* to deliver a harangue.—*v.t.* to address by a harangue :—*pr.p.* haranguing (-rang'ing) ; *pa.p.* harangued (-rangd').—*n.* Harang'uer. [Fr., from O. Ger. *hring* (Ger. *ring*, A.S. *hring*), a ring, a ring of people assembled.]

Harass, har'as, *v.t.* to fatigue : to annoy or torment.—*n.* Har'asser. [Fr. *harasser*; prob. from O. Fr. *harer*, to incite a dog, from the cry *har*, made in inciting a dog to attack ]

Harbinger, här'bin-jėr, *n.* (*orig.*) one who goes

forward to provide *harbour* or lodging : a fore-runner.—*v.t.* to precede, as a harbinger. [M. E. *herbergeour*—O. Fr. *herberge* (Fr. *auberge*)—O. Ger. *hereberga*. See **Harbour**.]

**Harbour**, här′bur, *n.* any refuge or shelter : a port for ships.—*v.t.* to lodge or entertain : to protect : to possess or indulge, as thoughts.—*v.i.* to take shelter.—*adj.* **Har′bourless**. [M. E. *herberwe ;* prob. through O. Fr. *herberge* from O. Ger. *hereberga*, a military encampment, from *heri* (Ger. *heer*), and *bergan*, to shelter ; a similar form occurs in Ice.]

**Harbourage**, här′bur-āj, *n.* place of *harbour* or shelter : entertainment.                    [entertains.

**Harbourer**, här′bur-ér, *n.* one who harbours or

**Harbour-master**, här′bur-mas′tèr, *n.* the *master* or public officer ..ho has charge of a *harbour*.

**Hard**, härd, *adj.* not easily penetrated : firm : solid : difficult to understand or accomplish : difficult to bear : painful : unjust : difficult to please : unfeeling : severe : stiff : constrained. —*adv.* with urgency : with difficulty : close, near, as in **Hard by ; Hard-a-lee**, *i.e.* close to the lee-side, &c. : earnestly : forcibly.—**To die hard**, to die only after a desperate struggle for life.—*n.* **Hard′ness** (*B.*), sometimes hardship. [A.S. *heard ;* Dut. *hard*, Ger. *hart*, Goth. *hardus ;* allied to Gr. *kratys*, strong.]

**Harden**, härd′n, *v.t.* to make *hard* or *harder :* to make firm : to strengthen : to confirm in wickedness : to make insensible.—*v.i.* to become hard or harder, either *lit.* or *fig.*—*n.* **Hard′ener**. [A.S. *heardian*. See **Hard**.]

**Hardened**, härd′nd, *adj.* made *hard*, unfeeling.

**Hard-favoured**, härd′-fā′vurd, *adj.* having coarse features.

**Hard-featured**, härd′-fēt′ūrd, *adj.* of *hard*, coarse, or forbidding *features*.

**Hard-fisted**, härd′-fist′ed, *adj.* having *hard* or strong *fists* or hands : close-fisted : niggardly.

**Hard-handed**, härd′-hand′ed, *adj.* having *hard* or tough *hands :* rough : severe.                [gent.

**Hard-headed**, härd′-hed′ed, *adj.* shrewd, intelli-

**Hard-hearted**, härd′-härt′ed, *adj.* having a *hard* or unfeeling *heart :* cruel.—*n.* **Hard′-heart′ed-ness**.

**Hardihood, Hardiness**. See **Hardy**.

**Hardish**, härd′ish, *adj.* somewhat *hard*.

**Hardly**, härd′li, *adv.* with difficulty : scarcely, not quite : severely, harshly.

**Hard-mouthed**, härd′-mow*th*d, *adj.* having a *mouth hard* or insensible to the bit : not easily managed.

**Hards**, härdz, *n.pl.* coarse or refuse flax.

**Hardship**, härd′ship, *n.* a *hard state*, or that which is hard to bear, as toil, injury, &c.

**Hard-visaged**, härd′-viz′ājd, *adj.* of a *hard*, coarse, or forbidding *visage*.

**Hardware**, härd′wār, *n.* trade name for all sorts of articles made of the baser metals, such as iron or copper. [**Hard** and **Ware**.]

**Hardy**, härd′i, *adj.* daring, brave, resolute : confident : impudent : able to bear cold, exposure, or fatigue.—*adv.* **Hard′ily**.—*ns.* **Hard′ihood, Hard′iness**. [Fr. *hardi*—O. Ger. *harti* (Ger. *hart*) : A.S. *heard*, hard. See **Hard**.]

**Hare**, här, *n.* a common and very timid animal, with a divided upper lip and long hind-legs, which runs swiftly by leaps. [A.S. *hara ;* Dan. and Sw. *hare*, Ger. *hase ;* Sans. *çaça—çaç*, to jump.]

**Harebell**, här′bel, *n.* a plant with blue bell-shaped flowers. [**Hare** and **Bell** ; a fanciful name.]

**Harebrained**, här′brānd, *adj.* having a wild,

scared *brain* like that of a *hare :* giddy : heedless.

**Harelip**, här′lip, *n.* a fissure in one or both *lips*, generally the upper, like that of a *hare*.—*adj.* **Hare′lipped**.

**Harem**, hā′rem, *n.* the portion of a house allotted to females in the East, *forbidden* to all males except the husband : the collection of wives belonging to one man. [Ar. *haram*, anything forbidden—*harama*, to forbid.]

**Haricot**, har′i-kō, *n.* small pieces of mutton, partly boiled, and then fried with vegetables : the kidney-bean. [Fr. *haricot*, a stew, a kidney-bean, so called because used in a stew : of unknown origin.]

**Hark**, härk, *int.* or *imp.*, hearken, listen. [Contr. of **Hearken**.]                    [substance.

**Harl**, härl, *n.* the skin of flax : any filamentous

**Harlequin**, här′le-kwin or -kin, *n.* the leading character in a pantomime, in a tight spangled dress, with a wand, by means of which he is supposed to be invisible and to play tricks : a buffoon. [Fr. *harlequin, arlequin ;* It. *arlecchino ;* ety. unknown.]

**Harlequinade**, här′le-kwin- or -kin-ād′, *n.* exhibitions of *harlequins :* the portion of a pantomime in which the harlequin plays a chief part. [Fr.]

**Harlot**, här′lot, *n.* a woman who prostitutes her body for hire.—*adj.* wanton : lewd. [O. Fr. *arlot, herlot ;* origin dub., perh. from Ger. *kerl*, A.S. *ceorl*, the word being orig. used for a person of either sex, and in the sense of *fellow*, a *rogue*.]

**Harlotry**, här′lot-ri, *n.* trade or practice of being a *harlot* or prostitute : prostitution.

**Harm**, härm, *n.* injury : moral wrong.—*v.t.* to injure. [A.S. *hearm ;* Ger. *harm*, conn. with *gram*, grief.]

**Harmattan**, har-mat′an, *n.* a hot, dry, noxious wind which blows periodically from the interior of Africa. [Arab.]

**Harmful**, härm′fool, *adj.* injurious, hurtful.—*adv.* **Harm′fully**.—*n.* **Harm′fulness**.

**Harmless**, härm′les, *adj.* not injurious : unharmed. —*adv.* **Harm′lessly**.—*n.* **Harm′lessness**.

**Harmonic**, har-mon′ik, **Harmonical**, har-mon′ik-al, *adj.* pertaining to *harmony :* musical : concordant : recurring periodically.—**Harmonic Proportion**, proportion in which the first is to the third as the difference between the first and second is to the difference between the second and third, as in the three numbers 2, 3, and 6.—*adv.* **Harmon′ically**.

**Harmonics**, har-mon′iks, *n.pl.* used as *sing.* the science of *harmony* or of musical sounds :—as *pl.* consonances, the component sounds included in what appears to the ear to be a single sound.

**Harmonious**, har-mō′ni-us, *adj.* having *harmony :* symmetrical : concordant.—*adv.* **Harmo′niously**.—*n.* **Harmo′niousness**.

**Harmonise**, här′mon-īz, *v.i.* to be in *harmony :* to agree.—*v.t.* to make in harmony : to cause to agree : (*mus.*) to provide parts to.—*n.* **Harmonis′er**.                    [*mony :* a musical composer.

**Harmonist**, här′mon-ist, *n.* one skilled in *har-*

**Harmonium**, har-mō′ni-um, *n.* a musical wind-instrument with keys, so called from its *harmonious* sound.

**Harmony**, här′mo-ni, *n.* a *fitting* together of parts so as to form a connected whole : (*mus.*) a combination of accordant sounds heard at the same time : concord : a book with parallel passages regarding the same event. [Fr.—L.—Gr. *harmonia—harmos*, a fitting—*arō*, to fit.]

**Harness**, här′nes, *n.* formerly, the armour of a

man or horse: the equipments of a horse.—*v.t.* to equip with armour: to put the harness on a horse. [Fr. *harnais;* from the Celt., as in Low Bret. *harnez,* old iron, also armour, from Bret. *houarn,* iron; W. *haiarn,* Gael. *iarunn;* conn. with E. *iron,* Ger. *eisen,* &c.]

**Harp,** härp, *n.* a triangular musical instrument with strings struck by the fingers.—*v.i.* to play on the harp: to dwell tediously upon anything. [A.S. *hearpe;* Dan. *harpe,* Ger. *harfe.*]

**Harper,** härp'ér, **Harp'ist,** härp'ist, *n.* a player on the *harp.*

**Harpoon,** här-pōōn', *n.* a dart for striking and killing whales.—*v.t.* to strike with the harpoon. [Dut. *harpoen*—Fr. *harpon;* origin uncertain, perh. from O. Ger. *har/an,* to seize.]

**Harpooner,** här-pōōn'ér, **Harponeer,** här-pon-ēr', *n.* one who uses a harpoon.

**Harpsichord,** härp'si-kord, *n.* an old-fashioned keyed musical instrument strung with *chords* or wires, like a *harp.* [O. Fr. *harpe-chorde.* See **Harp** and **Chord.**]

**Harpy,** här'pi, *n.* (*myth.*) a hideous rapacious monster, half bird and half woman: a species of eagle: an extortioner. [Gr., pl. *harpyiai,* 'snatchers,' symbols of the storm-wind—*harpazō,* to seize.]

**Harquebus, Harquebuss, Harquebuss,** här'kwi-   [bus, *n.* Same as **Arquebuse.**

**Harridan,** har'i-dan, *n.* a worn-out strumpet. [Another form of O. Fr. *haridelle,* a lean horse, a jade, ety. unknown.]

**Harrier,** har'i-ér, *n.* a *hare*-hound, a dog with a keen smell, for hunting hares. [Formed like *graz-i-er.*]

**Harrier,** har'i-ér, *n.* a kind of hawk so named from its *harrying* or destroying small animals.

**Harrow,** har'ō, *n.* a frame of wood or iron toothed with spikes for tearing and breaking the soil, &c. —*v.t.* to draw a harrow over: to harass: to tear. —*adj.* **Harr'owing,** acutely distressing to the mind.—*adv.* **Harr'owingly.** [A.S. *hyrwe,* a harrow; Dan. *harv,* a harrow.]

**Harry,** har'i, *v.t.* to plunder: to ravage: to destroy: to harass:—*pr.p.* harr'ying; *pa.p.* harr'ied. [A.S. *hergian,* from root of A.S. *here,* gen. *herg-es,* an army; Ger. *heer.*]

**Harsh,** härsh, *adj.* rough: bitter: jarring: abusive: severe.—*adv.* **Harsh'ly.**—*n.* **Harsh'ness.** [M. E. *harsk;* from a root found in Dan. *harsk,* rancid, Ger. *harsch,* hard.]

**Hart,** härt, *n.* the stag or male deer:—*fem.* **Hind.** [Lit. 'a *horned* animal,' from A.S. *heort;* Dut. *hert,* Ger. *hirsch;* conn. with L. *cervus,* W. *carw,* a stag, also with Gr. *keras,* E. *horn.*]

**Hartshorn,** härts'horn, *n.* a solution of ammonia, orig. a decoction of the shavings of a *hart's horn.*

**Hartstongue,** härts'tung, *n.* a species of fern shaped like the *tongue* of a *hart.*

**Harum-scarum,** hä'rum-skä'rum, *adj.* flighty: rash. [Prob. compounded of an obs. v. *h re,* to affright, and **Scare.**]

**Harvest,** här'vest, *n.* the time of gathering in the *crops* or *fruits:* the crops gathered in: fruits: the product of any labour: consequences.—*v.t.* to reap and gather in. [A.S. *haerfest;* Ger. *herbst,* Dut. *herfst;* conn. with L. *carpo,* to gather fruit, Gr. *karpos,* fruit.]

**Harvester,** här'vest-ér, *n.* a reaper in *harvest.*

**Harvest-home,** här'vest-hōm, *n.* the feast held at the bringing *home* of the *harvest.*    [harvest.

**Harvest-man,** här'vest-man, *n.* (*B.*) a reaper in *harvest.*

**Harvest-moon,** här'vest-mōōn, *n.* the *moon* about the full in *harvest,* when it rises nearly at the same hour for several days.

**Harvest-queen,** här'vest-kwēn, *n.* an image of Ceres, the *queen* or goddess of fruits, in ancient times carried about on the last day of *harvest.*

**Has,** haz, 2d pers. sing. pres. ind. of **Have.**

**Hash,** hash, *v.t.* to hack: to mince: to chop small.—*n.* that which is hashed: a mixed dish of meat and vegetables in small pieces: a mixture and preparation of old matter. [Fr. *hacher*—Ger. *hacken;* same root as E. *hack.*]

**Hashish,** hash'ésh, *n.* name given to the leaves of the Indian hemp, from which a strongly intoxicating preparation is made. [Ar.]

**Hasp,** hasp, *n.* a clasp: the clasp of a padlock.—*v.t.* to fasten with a hasp. [A.S. *hæpse;* Dan. and Ger. *haspe.*]

**Hassock,** has'uk, *n.* a thick mat for kneeling on in church. [W. *hesgog,* sedgy, *hesg,* sedge, rushes; from being made of coarse grass.]

**Hast,** hast, 2d pers. sing. pres. ind. of **Have.**

**Hastate,** hast'āt, **Hastated,** hast'āt-ed, *adj.* (*bot.*) shaped like a *spear.* [L. *hastatus*—*hasta,* a spear.]

**Haste,** hāst, *n.* speed: quickness: rashness: vehemence. [From a Teut. root, seen in Sw., Dan., and Ger. *hast,* whence also Fr. *hâte.* See **Hate.**]

**Haste,** hāst, **Hasten,** hās'n, *v.t.* to put to speed: to hurry on: to drive forward.—*v.i.* to move with speed: to be in a hurry:—*pr.p.* hāst'ing, hastening (hās'ning); *pa.p.* hāst'ed, hastened (hās'nd).

**Hastiness,** hāst'i-nes, *n.* hurry: rashness: irritability.     [passionate.—*adv.* **Hast'ily.**

**Hasty,** hāst'i, *adj.* speedy: quick: rash: eager:

**Hat,** hat, *n.* a covering for the head: the dignity of a cardinal, so named from his red hat. [A.S. *hæt;* Dan. *hat,* Ice. *hattr;* conn. with Sans. *chhad,* to cover.]

**Hatable,** hāt'a-bl, *adj.* deserving to be hated.

**Hatch,** hach, *n.* a door with an opening over it, a wicket or door made of cross bars: the covering of a hatchway. [North E. *heck,* from A.S. *haca,* the bar of a door; Dut. *hek,* a gate.]

**Hatch,** hach, *v.t.* to produce, especially from eggs, by incubation: to originate: to plot.—*v.i.* to produce young: to be advancing towards maturity.—*n.* act of hatching: brood hatched. [Lit. to produce young by sitting in a hatch or coop, a hatch being anything made of cross bars of wood (Skeat), and hence the same word as **Hatch,** a door.]

**Hatch,** hach, *v.t.* to shade by minute lines crossing each other in drawing and engraving.—*n.* **Hatch'ing,** the mode of so shading. [Fr. *hacher,* to chop, from root of **Hack.**]

**Hatchel,** hach'el, *n.* Same as **Hackle.**

**Hatchet,** hach'et, *n.* a small axe. [Fr. *hachette.* See **Hatch,** to shade.]

**Hatchment,** hach'ment, *n.* the escutcheon of a dead person placed in front of the house, &c. [Corrupted from **Achievement.**]

**Hatchway,** hach'wā, *n.* the opening in a ship's deck into the hold or from one deck to another.

**Hate,** hāt, *v.t.* to dislike intensely.—*n.* extreme dislike: hatred.—*n.* **Hat'er.** [A.S. *hatian,* to hate; Ger. *hassen,* Fr. *haïr;* conn. with L. *odisse,* and Gr. *kēdō,* to vex. **Hate** is from the same root as **Haste,** and orig. meant to pursue, then to persecute, to dislike greatly.]

**Hateful,** hāt'fool, *adj.* exciting hate: odious: detestable: feeling or manifesting hate.—*adv.* **Hate'fully.**—*n.* **Hate'fulness.**     [lignity.

**Hatred,** hāt'red, *n.* extreme dislike: enmity: malignity.

**Hatted,** hat'ed, *adj.* covered with a hat.

**Hatter,** hat'ér, *n.* one who makes or sells hats.

**Hatti-sheriff,** hat'i-sher'if, *n.* a Turkish decree of the highest authority. [Ar., 'noble writing.']

**Hauberk,** haw′bėrk, *n.* a coat of mail formed of rings interwoven. [O. Fr. *hauberc*—O. Ger. *halsberge*—*hals*, the neck, and *bergan*, to protect.]

**Haughty,** hawt′i, *adj.* proud : arrogant : contemptuous.—*adv.* **Haught′ily**.—*n.* **Haught′iness.** [M. E. *hautein*—O. Fr. *hautain*, *haut*, high—L. *altus*, high.]

**Haul,** hawl, *v.t.* to drag : to pull with violence.—*n.* a pulling : a draught, as of fishes.—*n.* **Haul′er.** [A.S. *holian*, to get ; Ger. *holen*, Dut. *halen*, to fetch or draw.]

**Haulage,** hawl′āj, *n.* act of *hauling :* charge for hauling or pulling a ship or boat.

**Haulm, Haum,** hawm, *n.* straw : stubble. [A.S. *healm ;* Dut. *halm*, Russ. *soloma*, Fr. *chaume*, L. *calamus*, Gr. *kalamos*, a reed.]

**Haunch,** hänsh, *n.* the part between the last rib and the thigh : the hip. [Fr. *hanche*—O. Ger. *ancha*, the leg, of the same root as **Ankle**.]

**Haunt,** hänt, *v.t.* to frequent : to follow importunately : to inhabit or visit as a ghost.—*v.i.* to be much about : to appear or visit frequently.—*n.* a place much resorted to. [Fr. *hanter ;* acc. to Littré, a corr. of L. *habitare*.]

**Hautboy,** hō′boi, *n.* a *high*-toned *wooden* wind-instrument, of a tapering tube, and having holes and keys, also called **Oboe** (ō′bo-i) : a large kind of strawberry. [Fr. *hautbois*—*haut*, high, *bois*, wood ; It. *oboe*—L. *altus*, high, and Low L. *boscus*, a bush. See **Bush**.]

**Have,** hav, *v.t.* to own or possess : to hold : to regard : to obtain : to bear or beget : to effect : to be affected by :—*pr.p.* hav′ing ; *pa.t.* and *pa.p.* had. [A.S. *habban ;* Ger. *haben*, Dan. *have ;* allied to L. *capio*, to take, Gr. *kōpē*, a handle.]

**Haven,** hā′vn, *n.* an inlet of the sea, or mouth of a river, where ships can get good and safe anchorage : any place of safety : an asylum. [A.S. *hæfene ;* Dut. *haven*, Ger. *hafen*, Ice. *höfn*, Fr. *havre*, O. Fr. *havle ;* from Teut. base *hab* in **Have**.]

**Haversack,** hav′ėr-sak, *n.* a bag of strong linen for a soldier's provisions. [Lit. 'oat-sack,' Fr. *havresac*—Ger. *habersack*—*haber* or *hafer*, Dan. *havre*, prov. E. *haver*, oats, and **Sack**.]

**Havoc,** hav′uk, *n.* general waste or *destruction :* devastation.—*v.t.* to lay waste.—*int.* an ancient hunting or war cry. [Ety. dub. ; cf. A.S. *hafoc*, a hawk, and W. *hafog*, destruction, which prob. is derived from the E.]

**Haw,** haw, *n.* (*orig.*) a hedge or inclosure : the berry of the hawthorn. [A.S. *haga*, a yard or inclosure ; Dut. *haag*, a hedge, Ice. *hagi*, a field. See **Hedge**.]

**Haw,** haw, *v.i.* to speak with a *haw* or hesitation.—*n.* a hesitation in speech. [Formed from the sound.]

**Hawfinch,** haw′finsh, *n.* a species of grossbeak, a very shy bird, with variegated plumage, living chiefly in forests. [See **Haw**, a hedge.]

**Hawhaw,** haw-haw′, *n.* a sunk fence, or a ditch not seen till close upon it. [Reduplication of **Haw**, a hedge.]

**Hawk,** hawk, *n.* the name of several birds of prey allied to the falcons. [A.S. *hafoc ;* Dut. *havik*, Ger. *habicht*, Ice. *haukr ;* from Teut. root *hab*, to seize, seen in E. **Have**.]

**Hawk,** hawk, *v.i.* to hunt birds with hawks trained for the purpose : to attack on the wing.—*n.* **Hawk′er.**

**Hawk,** hawk, *v.i.* to force up matter from the throat.—*n.* the effort to do this. [W. *hochi ;* Scot. *haugh ;* formed from the sound.]

**Hawk,** hawk, *v.t.* to carry about for sale : to cry for sale. [See **Hawker**.]

**Hawker,** hawk′ėr, *n.* one who carries about goods for sale on his back, a peddler. [From an O. Low Ger. root found in O. Dut. *heukeren*, to hawk, and Ger. *höker*, a hawker ; conn. with **Huckster**.]

**Hawse,** hawz, *n.* the situation of the cables in front of a ship's bow when she has two anchors out forward :—*pl.* the holes in a ship's bow through which the cables pass. [M. E. *hals*, A.S. *hals* or *heals*, the neck, applied to the corresponding part of a ship ; Ice. and Ger. *hals*.]

**Hawseholes,** hawz′hōlz. See **Hawse**.

**Hawser, Halser,** hawz′ėr, *n.* a small cable : a large towline. [From *hawse*, meaning orig. the rope which passes through the hawses at the bow of a ship.]

**Hawthorn,** haw′thorn, *n.* the *hedge* or white *thorn*, a shrub with shining leaves, and small red fruit called *haws*, much used for hedges.

**Hay,** hā, *n.* grass after it is *cut* down and dried. [A.S. *heg*, *hig ;* Ger. *heu*, Ice. *hey ;* from root of **Hew**.] [in the field.

**Haycock,** hā′kok, *n.* a *cock* or conical pile of *hay*

**Hay-fever,** hā-fē′vėr, *n.* an ailment in time of haymaking marked by excessive irritation of the nose, throat, &c., and accompanied with violent sneezing. [and drying grass for hay.

**Haymaker,** hā′māk-ėr, *n.* one employed in cutting

**Hazard,** haz′ard, *n.* a game or throw at dice : chance : accident : risk.—*v.t.* to expose to chance : to risk. [Fr. *hasard ;* prob. through the Sp. from Arab. *al zar*, the die ; but Littré prefers to derive it from Hazart, a castle in Syria where the game was discovered during the crusades.]

**Hazardous,** haz′ard-us, *adj.* dangerous : perilous : uncertain.—*adv.* **Haz′ardously.**

**Haze,** hāz, *n.* vapour which renders the air thick : obscurity. [Ety. dub.]

**Hazel,** hā′zl, *n.* a well-known tree or shrub.—*adj.* pertaining to the hazel : of a light-brown colour, like a hazel-nut. [A.S. *hæsel ;* Ger. *hasel*, L. *corulus* (for *costulus*). [*nut.*

**Hazelly,** hā′zel-i, *adj.* light-brown like the *hazel*-

**Hazel-nut,** hā′zl-nut, *n.* the *nut* of the hazel-tree.

**Hazy,** hāz′i, *adj.* thick with *haze*.—*n.* **Haz′iness.**

**He,** hē, *pron.* of the third person : the male person named before : any one.—*adj.* male. [A.S. *he ;* Dut. *hij*, Ice. *hann*.]

**Head,** hed, *n.* the uppermost or foremost part of an animal's body : the brain : the understanding : a chief or leader : the place of honour or command : the front : an individual : a topic or chief point of a discourse : the source or spring : height of the source of water : highest point of anything : a cape : strength. [A.S. *heafod ;* Ger. *haupt*, L. *caput*, Gr. *kephalē*.]

**Head,** hed, *v.t.* to act as a head to, to lead or govern : to go in front of : to commence : to check : (*naut.*) to be contrary.—*v.i.* to grow to a head : to originate.

**Headache,** hed′āk, *n.* an ache or pain in the head.

**Headband,** hed′band, *n.* a band or fillet for the head : the band at each end of a book.

**Head-dress,** hed′-dres, *n.* an ornamental dress or covering for the head, worn by women.

**Headgear,** hed′gēr, *n.* gear, covering, or ornament of the head.

**Headiness.** See under **Heady**. [*head.*

**Heading,** hed′ing, *n.* that which stands at the

**Headland,** hed′land, *n.* a point of *land* running out into the sea, like a *head*, a cape.

**Headless**, hed'les, *adj.* without a head.

**Headlong**, hed'long, *adv.* with the *head* first: without thought, rashly: precipitately.—*adj.* rash: precipitous, steep. [**Head** and adv. termination -*inga*, *linga*, seen also in **Darkling**, **Sidelong**, and in **Learn-ing**.] [vanced.

**Headmost**, hed'mōst, *adj.*, *most ahead* or ad-

**Headpiece**, hed'pēs, *n.* a *piece* of armour for the *head*, a helmet.

**Headquarters**, hed'kwor-tèrz, *n.* the *quarters* or residence of a *commander-in-chief* or general.

**Headsman**, hedz'man, *n.* a *man* who cuts off *heads*, an executioner.

**Headstall**, hed'stawl, *n.* the part of a bridle round the head. [From **Stall**, a place or receptacle.]

**Headstone**, hed'stōn, *n.* the principal *stone* of a building: the corner-stone: the stone at the head of a grave.

**Headstrong**, hed'strong, *adj.* self-willed: violent.

**Headway**, hed'wā, *n.* the *way* or distance gone *ahead* or advanced: motion of an advancing ship. [against a ship's *head*.

**Headwind**, hed'wind, *n.* a *wind* blowing right

**Heady**, hed'i, *adj.* affecting the *head* or the brain: intoxicating: inflamed: rash.—*adv.* **Head'ily**. —*n.* **Head'iness**.

**Heal**, hēl, *v.t.* to make *whole* and healthy: to cure: to remove or subdue: to restore to soundness: (*B.*) often, to forgive.—*v.i.* to grow sound:—*pr.p.* heal'ing; *pa.p.* healed'.—*n.* **Heal'er**. [A.S. *hælan*, as Hæland, the Healer, Saviour; from A.S. *hál*, whole; Ger. *heil*. **Whole** is simply another form of the A.S. root. See **Hail**, **Hale**.]

**Healing**, hēl'ing, *n.* the act or process by which anything is *healed* or cured.—*adj.* tending to cure: mild.—*adv.* **Heal'ingly**.

**Health**, helth, *n.*, *wholeness* or soundness of body: soundness and vigour of mind: (*B.*) salvation, or divine favour. [A.S. *hælth—hál*, whole.]

**Healthful**, helth'fool, *adj.* full of or enjoying *health*: indicating health: wholesome: salutary. —*adv.* **Health'fully**.—*n.* **Health'fulness**.

**Healthless**, helth'les, *adj.* sickly, ailing.—*n.* **Health'lessness**.

**Healthy**, helth'i, *adj.* in a state of good *health*: conducive to health: sound: vigorous.—*adv.* **Health'ily**.—*n.* **Health'iness**.

**Heap**, hēp, *n.* a pile or mass heaved or thrown together: a collection: (*B.*) a ruin.—*v.t.* to throw in a heap or pile: to amass: to pile above the top:—*pr.p.* heap'ing; *pa.p.* heaped'. [A.S. *heap*; Ice. *hopr*, Ger. *haufe*.]

**Hear**, hēr, *v.t.* to perceive by the ear: to listen to: to grant or obey: to answer favourably: to attend to: to try judicially.—*v.i.* to have the sense of hearing: to listen: to be told:—*pr.p.* hear'ing; *pa.t.* and *pa.p.* heard (hèrd).—*n.* **Hear'er**. [A.S. *hyran*; Ice. *heyra*, Ger. *hören*, Goth. *hausjan*.]

**Hearing**, hēr'ing, *n.* act of perceiving by the ear: the sense of perceiving sound: opportunity to be heard: reach of the ear.

**Hearken**, härk'n, *v.i.* to *hear* attentively: to listen: to grant. [A.S. *hyrcnian*, from **Hear**; O. Dut. *harcken*, Ger. *horchen*.] [port.

**Hearsay**, hēr'sā, *n.* common talk: rumour: re-

**Hearse**, hèrs, *n.* (*orig.*) a triangular framework for holding candles at a church service, and esp. at a funeral service: a carriage in which the dead are conveyed to the grave. [Fr. *herse*, It. *erpice*—L. *hirpex*, *hirpicis*, a harrow, which, from its triangular shape, gave rise to the derived meanings.]

**Heart**, härt, *n.* the organ that circulates the blood: the vital, inner, or chief part of anything: the seat of the affections, &c., esp. love: courage: vigour: secret meaning or design: that which resembles a heart. [A.S. *heorte*; Dut. *hart*, Ger. *herz*; cog. with L. *cor*, *cordis*, Gr. *kardia*, *kēr*, Sans. *hrid*.]

**Heartache**, härt'āk, *n.* sorrow: anguish.

**Heart-breaking**, härt'-brāk'ing, *adj.* crushing with grief or sorrow. [or grieved.

**Heart-broken**, härt'-brōk'n, *adj.* intensely afflicted

**Heartburn**, härt'burn, *n.* a disease of the stomach causing a *burning*, acrid feeling near the *heart*.

**Heartburning**, härt'burn-ing, *n.* discontent: secret enmity.

**Heartease**, härt'ēz, *n.*, *ease* of mind: quiet.

**Hearten**, härt'n, *v.t.* to encourage.

**Heartfelt**, härt'felt, *adj.*, felt deeply.

**Hearth**, härth, *n.* the part of the floor on which the fire is made: the fireside: the house itself. [A.S. *heorth*; Ger. *herd*.]

**Hearthstone**, härth'stōn, *n.* the stone of the hearth.

**Heartless**, härt'les, *adj.* without heart, courage, or feeling.—*adv.* **Heart'lessly**—*n.* **Heart'lessness**.

**Heartlet**, härt'let, *n.* a *little heart*.

**Heart-rending**, härt'-rend'ing, *adj.* deeply afflictive: agonising.

**Heart's-ease**, härts'-ēz, *n.* a common name for the pansy, a species of violet, an infusion of which was once thought to *ease* the lovesick *heart*.

**Heartsick**, härt'sik, *adj.* pained in mind: depressed.—*n.* **Heart'sickness**.

**Heartwhole**, härt'hōl, *adj.*, *whole* at *heart*: unmoved in the affections or spirits.

**Hearty**, härt'i, *adj.* full of or proceeding from the heart: warm: genuine: strong: healthy.—*adv.* **Heart'ily**.—*n.* **Heart'iness**.

**Heat**, hēt, *n.* that which excites the sensation of warmth: sensation of warmth: a warm temperature: the warmest period, as the heat of the day: indication of warmth, flush, redness: excitement: a single course in a race: animation. —*v.t.* to make hot: to agitate.—*v.i.* to become hot:—*pr.p.* heat'ing; *pa.p.* heat'ed. [A.S. *hæto*, which is from adj. *hát*, hot: conn. with Ger. *hitze*, Goth. *heito*, Ice. *hita*. See **Hot**.]

**Heater**, hēt'èr, *n.* one who or that which heats.

**Heath**, hēth, *n.* a barren open country: a small evergreen shrub with beautiful flowers, that grows on heaths. [A.S. *hæth*; Ger. *heide*, Goth. *haithi*, a waste.]

**Heathen**, hē'thn, *n.* an unbeliever when Christianity prevailed in cities alone: an inhabitant of an unchristian country: a pagan: an irreligious person.—*adj.* pagan, irreligious [Lit. a dweller on the *heath* or open country, A.S. *hæthen*, a heathen; Dut. and Ger. *heiden*. See **Heath**, and cf. **Pagan**.]

**Heathendom**, hē'thn-dum, *n.* those regions of the world where *heathenism* prevails.

**Heathenise**, hē'thn-īz, *v.t.* to make *heathen*.

**Heathenish**, hē'thn-ish, *adj.* relating to the *heathen*: rude: uncivilised: cruel.—*adv.* **Hea'-thenishly**.—*n.* **Hea'thenishness**.

**Heathenism**, hē'thn-izm, *n.* the religious system of the *heathens*: paganism: barbarism.

**Heather**, heth'èr, *n.* a small evergreen shrub, growing on *heaths*.—*adj.* **Heath'ery**. [A Northern E. form, appearing to be nothing more than *heath er* = inhabitant of the heath (Skeat).]

**Heathy**, hēth'i, *adj.* abounding with heath.

**Heave**, hēv, *v.t.* to lift up: to throw: to cause to swell: to force from the breast.—*v.i.* to be raised: to rise and fall: to try to vomit:—*pr.p.*

heav′ing ; *pa.t.* and *pa.p.* heaved′ or (*naut.*) hōve. —*n.* an effort upward : a throw : a swelling : an effort to vomit. [A.S. *hebban ;* Ger. *heben,* Goth. *hafjan,* to lift.]

**Heaven,** hev′n, *n.* the arch of sky overhanging the earth : the air : the dwelling-place of the Deity and the blessed : supreme happiness. [A.S. *heofon ;* O. Ice. *hifinn ;* origin doubtful, though conn. by some with *heave,* and so meaning the 'heaved' or 'lifted up.']

**Heavenly,** hev′n-li, *adj.* of or inhabiting *heaven :* celestial : pure : supremely blessed : very excellent.—*adv.* in a manner like that of heaven : by the influence of heaven.—*n.* Heav′enliness.

**Heavenly-minded,** hev′n-li-mīnd′ed, *adj.* having the *mind* placed upon *heavenly* things : pure.— *n.* Heav′enly-mind′edness.

**Heavenward,** hev′n-ward, **Heavenwards,** hev′n-wardz, *adv.,* * *ward* or in the direction of *heaven.* [Heaven, and *ward,* sig. direction.]

**Heave-offering,** hēv′-of′ēr-ing, *n.* a Jewish *offering heaved* or moved up and down by the priest.

**Heaver,** hēv′ẽr, *n.* one who or that which heaves.

**Heavy,** hev′i, *adj.* weighty : not easy to bear : oppressive : afflicted : inactive : inclined to slumber : violent : loud : not easily digested, as food : miry, as soil : having strength, as liquor : dark with clouds : gloomy : expensive : (*B.*) sad.— *adv.,* also **Heav′ily.**—*n.* **Heav′iness.** [A.S. *hefig—hebban,* to heave, and so meaning *hard to heave ;* O. Ger. *hepig, hebig.*]

**Hebdomadal,** heb-dom′a-dal, **Hebdomadary,** heb-dom′a-dar-i, *adj.* occurring every *seven days :* weekly. [L. *hebdomadalis*—Gr. *hebdomas,* a period of seven days—*hepta,* seven.]

**Hebdomadary,** heb-dom′a-dar-i, *n.* a member of a chapter or convent whose *week* it is to officiate in the choir, &c.

**Hebraic,** hē-brā′ik, **Hebraical,** hē-brā′ik-al, *adj.* relating to the *Hebrews,* or to their language.

**Hebraically,** hē-brā′ik-al-i, *adv.* after the manner of the *Hebrew* language : from right to left.

**Hebraise,** hē′bra-īz, *v.t.* to turn into *Hebrew.*

**Hebraism,** hē′bra-izm, *n.* a *Hebrew* idiom.

**Hebraist,** hē′bra-ist, *n.* one skilled in *Hebrew.*

**Hebraistic,** hē-bra-ist′ik, *adj.* of or like *Hebrew.*

**Hebrew,** hē′brōō, *n.* one of the descendants of Abraham, who emigrated *from beyond the Euphrates* into Palestine : an Isrælite, a Jew : the language of the Hebrews.—*adj.* relating to the Hebrews. [Fr. *Hébreu*—L. *Hebræus*—Gr. *Hebraios*—Heb *ibhri,* a stranger from the other side of the Euphrates—*ebher,* the region on the other side—*abar,* to pass over.]

**Hecatomb,** hek′a-tōōm or -tom, *n.* among the Greeks and Romans, a sacrifice of a *hundred oxen :* any large number of victims. [Gr. *hekatombē*—*hekaton,* a hundred, and *bous,* an ox.]

**Heckle,** hek′l. Same as **Hackle.**

**Hectic,** hek′tik, **Hectical,** hek′tik-al, *adj.* pertaining to the constitution or *habit* of body : affected with hectic fever.—*adv.* **Hec′tically.** [Fr.—Gr. *hektikos,* habitual—*hexis,* habit.]

**Hectic,** hek′tik, *n.* a *habitual* or remittent fever, usually associated with consumption.

**Hector,** hek′tor, *n.* a bully : one who annoys.—*v.t.* to treat insolently : to annoy.—*v.i.* to play the bully. [From *Hector,* the famous Trojan leader.]

**Hedge,** hej, *n.* a thicket of bushes : a fence round a field, &c.—*v.t.* to inclose with a hedge : to obstruct : to surround : to guard. [A.S. *hege ;* Dut. *hegge,* Ice. *heggr.*]

**Hedgebill,** hej′bil, **Hedging-bill,** hej′ing-bil, *n.* a *bill* or hatchet for dressing *hedges.*

**Hedgeborn,** hej′bawrn, *adj.* of low birth, as if *born* by a *hedge* or in the woods : low : obscure.

**Hedgehog,** hej′hog, *n.* a small prickly-backed quadruped, so called from its living in *hedges* and bushes, and its resemblance to a *hog* or pig.

**Hedger,** hej′ẽr, *n.* one who dresses *hedges.*

**Hedgerow,** hej′rō, *n.* a *row* of trees or shrubs for *hedging* fields.

**Hedgeschool,** hej′skōōl, *n.* an open-air *school* kept by the side of a *hedge,* in Ireland.

**Hedge-sparrow,** hej′-spar′ō, *n.* a little singing bird, like a *sparrow,* which frequents *hedges.*

**Heed,** hēd, *v.t.* to observe : to look after : to attend to.—*n.* notice : caution : attention. [A.S. *hedan ;* Dut. *hoeden,* Ger. *hüten.*]

**Heedful,** hēd′fool, *adj.* attentive : cautious.—*adv.* **Heed′fully.**—*n.* **Heed′fulness.**

**Heedless,** hēd′les, *adj.* inattentive : careless.— *adv.* **Heed′lessly.**—*n.* **Heed′lessness.**

**Heel,** hēl, *n.* the part of the foot projecting behind : the whole foot (esp. of beasts) : the covering of the heel : a spur : the hinder part of anything.— *v.t.* to use the heel : to furnish with heels. [A.S. *hela ;* Dut. *hiel ;* prob. conn. with L. *calx,* Gr. *lax,* the heel.]

**Heel,** hēl, *v.i.* to *incline :* to lean on one side, as a ship. [A.S. *hyldan ;* Ice. *halla,* to incline.]

**Heelpiece,** hēl′pēs, *n.* a *piece* or cover for the *heel.*

**Heft,** heft. Same as **Haft.**

**Hegemony,** he-jem′o-ni, *n., leadership.*—*adj.* **Hegemon′ic.** [Gr. *hēgemonia*—*hēgemōn,* leader —*hēgeisthai,* to go before.]

**Hegira, Hejira,** he-jī′ra, *n.* the *flight* of Mohammed from Mecca, July 16, 622 A.D., from which is dated the Mohammedan era : any flight. [Ar. *hijrah,* flight.]

**Heifer,** hef′ẽr, *n.* a young cow. [A.S. *heahfore ;* acc. to Skeat from A.S. *heah,* high, and *fear,* an ox, and so meaning a *full-grown ox.*]

**Heigh-ho,** hī′-hō, *int.* an exclamation expressive of weariness. [Imitative.]

**Height,** hīt, *n.* the condition of being *high :* distance upwards : that which is elevated, a hill : elevation in rank or excellence : utmost degree. [Corr. of *highth*—A.S. *heahthu*—*heah,* high. See **High.**]

**Heighten,** hīt′n, *v.t.* to make *higher :* to advance or improve : to make brighter or more prominent.

**Heinous,** hā′nus, *adj.* wicked in a high degree : enormous : atrocious.—*adv.* **Hei′nously.** — *n.* **Hei′nousness.** [O. Fr. *haïnos,* Fr. *haineux*— *haine,* hate, from *hair,* to hate, from an O. Ger. root, found in Ger. *hassen,* Goth. *hatyan,* to hate. See **Hate.**]

**Heir,** ār, *n.* one who inherits anything after the death of the owner : one entitled to anything after the present possessor.—*fem.* **Heiress** (ār′es). —*ns.* **Heir′dom, Heir′ship.** [O. Fr. *heir*—L. *heres,* an heir, allied to L. *herus,* a master, and Gr. *cheir,* the hand, from a root *ghar,* to seize.]

**Heir-apparent,** ār-ap-pār′ent, *n.* the one *apparently* or acknowledged to be *heir.*

**Heirless,** ār′les, *adj.* without an heir.

**Heirloom,** ār′lōōm, *n.* any piece of *furniture* or personal property which descends to the *heir.* [Heir and *loom*—M. E. *lome*—A.S. *loma, geloma,* furniture. See **Loom,** *n.*]

**Heir-presumptive,** ār-pre-zump′tiv, *n.* one who is *presumed* to be or would be *heir* if no nearer relative should be born.

**Hejira.** See **Hegira.**

**Held,** *pa.t.* and *pa.p.* of **Hold.**

**Heliacal,** he-lī′ak-al, *adj.* relating to the *sun :*

(*astr.*) emerging from the light of the sun or falling into it.—*adv.* Heli'acally. [Gr. *hēliakos—hēlios*, the sun.]

Helical, hel'ik-al, *adj.* spiral.—*adv.* Hel'ically.

Heliocentric, hē-li-o-sen'trik, Heliocentrical, hē-li-o-sen'trik-al, *adj.* (*astr.*) as seen from the *sun's centre*.—*adv.* Heliocen'trically. [From Gr. *hēlios*, the sun, *kentron*, the centre.]

Heliograph, hē'li-o-graf, *n.* an apparatus for telegraphing by means of the sun's rays.

Heliography, hē-li-og'ra-fi, *n.* the art of taking *pictures* by *sunlight*, photography : the art of signalling by flashing the rays of the sun.—*adj.* Heliograph'ical.—*n.* Heliog'rapher. [Gr. *hēlios*, the sun, *graphē*, a painting—*graphō*, to grave.]

Heliolater, hē-li-ol'a-tėr, *n.* a *worshipper* of the *sun.* [Gr. *hēlios*, the sun, *latris*, a servant.]

Heliolatry, hē-li-ol'a-tri, *n.*, *worship* of the *sun.* [Gr. *hēlios*, the sun, *latreia*, service, worship.]

Heliometer, hē-li-om'e-tėr, *n.* an instrument for *measuring* the apparent diameter of the *sun* or other heavenly body. [Gr. *hēlios*, and *metron*, a measure.]

Helioscope, hē'li-o-skōp, *n.* a telescope for *viewing* the *sun* without dazzling the eyes.—*adj.* Helioscop'ic. [Fr. *hélioscope*—Gr. *hēlios*, the sun, *skopeō*, to look, to spy.]

Heliostat, hē'li-o-stat, *n.* an instrument by means of which a beam of sunlight is reflected in an invariable direction. [Gr. *hēlios*, and *statos*, fixed.]

Heliotrope, hē'li-o-trōp, *n.* a plant whose flowers are said always to *turn* round to the *sun* : (*min.*) a bloodstone, a variety of chalcedony of a dark-green colour variegated with red : an instrument for signalling by flashing the sun's rays. [Fr.—L.—Gr. *hēliotropion*—*hēlios*, the sun, *tropos*, a turn—*trepō*, to turn.]

Heliotype, hē'li-o-tīp, *n.* a photograph. [Gr. *hēlios*, the sun, and *typos*, an impression.]

Helispheric, hel-i-sfer'ik, Helispherical, hel-i-sfer'ik-al, *adj.*, *winding* spirally round a *sphere.*

Helix, hē'liks, *n.* a spiral, as of wire in a coil : (*zool.*) the snail or its shell : the external part of the ear :—*pl.* Helices, hel'i-sēz. [L.—Gr. *helix—helissō*, to turn round.]

Hell, hel, *n.* the place or state of punishment of the wicked after death : the abode of evil spirits : the powers of hell : any place of vice or misery : a gambling-house. [A.S. *hel, helle* ; Ice. *hel*, Ger. *hölle* (O. Ger. *hella*). From *Hel* (Scand.), *Hell* (A.S.), or *Hella* (O. Ger.), the Teut. d-dess of death, whose name again is from a Teut. root seen in A.S. *helan*, to hide, Ger. *hehlen*, cog. with L. *cel-are*, to hide.]

Hellebore, hel'e-bōr, *n.* a plant used in medicine, anciently used as a cure for insanity. [Fr. *hellé-bore*—L. *helleborus*—Gr. *helleboros*.]

Hellenic, hel-len'ik or hel-lē'nik, Hellenian, hel-lē'ni-an, *adj.* pertaining to the *Hellenes* or Greeks : Grecian. [Gr. *Hellēnios, Hellēnikos —Hellēnes*, a name ultimately given to all the Greeks—*Hellēn*, the son of Deucalion, the Greek Noah.]

Hellenise, hel'en-īz, *v.i.* to use the Greek language. [Gr. *hellēnizō—Hellēn*.]

Hellenism, hel'en-izm, *n.* a Greek idiom. [Fr. *Hellénisme*—Gr. *Hellēnismos*.]

Hellenist, hel'en-ist, *n.* one skilled in the *Greek language* : a Jew who used the Greek language as his mother-tongue. [Gr. *Hellēnistēs*.]

Hellenistic, hel-en-ist'ik, Hellenistical, hel-en-ist'ik-al, *adj.* pertaining to the *Hellenists* : Greek with Hebrew idioms.—*adv.* Hellenist'ically.

Hellhound, hel'hownd, *n.* a *hound* of *hell* : an agent of hell.

Hellish, hel'ish, *adj.* pertaining to or like *hell* : very wicked.—*adv.* Hell'ishly.—*n.* Hell'ishness.

Helm, helm, *n.* the instrument by which a ship is steered : the station of management or government. [A.S. *helma* ; Ice. *hjalm*, a rudder, Ger. *helm*, a handle ; allied to *helve*.]

Helm, helm, Helmet, hel'met, *n.* a *covering* of armour for the head : (*bot.*) the hooded upper lip of certain flowers. [A.S.—*helan*, to cover ; Ger. *helm*, a covering, helmet. *Helmet* is from the O. Fr. *healmet*, dim. of *healme*, the O. Fr. form of the same word.]

Helmed, helmd', Helmeted, hel'met-ed, *adj.* furnished with a *helmet.*

Helminthic, hel-min'thik, *adj.* pertaining to *worms* : expelling worms.—*n.* a medicine for expelling worms. [From Gr. *helmins, helmin-thos*, a worm—*heileō, helissō*, to wriggle.]

Helminthoid, hel'min-thoid, *adj.* worm-shaped. [Gr. *helmins*, and *eidos*, form.]

Helminthology, hel-min-thol'o-ji, *n.* the *science* or natural history of *worms.* *adj.* Helmintho-log'ical.—*n.* Helminthol'ogist. [From Gr. *helmins*, and *logos*, a discourse.]

Helmsman, helmz'man, *n.* the *man* at the helm.

Helot, hel'ot or hē'lot, *n.* a *slave*, among the Spartans. [Gr. ; said to be derived from *Helos*, a town in Greece, reduced to slavery by the Spartans.]

Helotism, hel'ot-izm or hē'lot-izm, *n.* the condition of the *Helots* in ancient Sparta : slavery.

Helotry, hel'ot-ri or hē'lot-ri, *n.* the whole body of the *Helots* : any class of slaves.

Help, help, *v.t.* to support : to assist : to give means for doing anything : to remedy : to prevent.—*v.i.* to give assistance : to contribute :—*pa.p.* helped', (*B.*) hōlp'en.—*n.* means or strength given to another for a purpose : assistance : relief : one who assists : (*Amer.*) a hired man or woman. [A.S. *helpan* ; Goth. *hilpan*, Ice. *hialpa*, Ger. *helfen*, to aid, assist.]

Helper, help'ėr, *n.* one who helps : an assistant.

Helpful, help'fool, *adj.* giving help : useful.—*n.* Help'fulness.

Helpless, help'les, *adj.* without help or power in one's self : wanting assistance.—*adv.* Help'-lessly.—*n.* Help'lessness.

Helpmate, help'māt, *n.* a *mate* or companion who *helps* : an assistant : a partner : a wife. [Formed on a misconception of the phrase *an help meet* in Gen. ii. 18, 20.]

Helter-skelter, hel'ter-skel'ter, *adv.* in a confused hurry : tumultuously. [Imitative.]

Helve, helv, *n.* a *handle* : the handle of an axe or hatchet.—*v.t.* to furnish with a handle, as an axe. [A.S. *hielf, helfe*, a handle ; O. Dut. *helve.*]

Helvetic, hel-vet'ik, *adj.* pertaining to Switzerland. [L.—*Helvetia*, L. name of Switzerland.]

Hem, hem, *n.* the *border* of a garment doubled down and sewed.—*v.t.* to form a hem on : to edge :—*pr.p.* hemm'ing ; *pa.p.* hemmed'.—Hem in, to surround. [A.S. *hem*, a border ; Ger. *hamme*, a fence, Fris. *hämel*, an edge.]

Hem, hem, *n.* (*int.*) a sort of half cough to draw attention.—*v.i.* to utter the sound *hem* !—*pr.p.* hemm'ing ; *pa.p.* hemmed'. [From the sound.]

Hemal, hē'mal, *adj.* relating to the *blood* or blood-vessels. [Gr. *haima*, blood.]

Hematine, hem'a-tin, *n.* the red colouring matter in the *blood.* [Fr.—Gr. *haima*, blood.]

Hematite, hem'a-tīt, *n.* (*min.*) a valuable ore of iron, sometimes of a reddish-brown colour, with a *blood* red streak.—*adj.* **Hematit'ic.** [L.— Gr. *haimatitēs*, blood-like—*haima, haimatos*, blood.]

**Hemiptera,** hem-ip'tèr-a. *n.* an order of insects, having four wings, the two anterior of which are scarcely perceptible. [Gr. *hēmi*, half (cog. with Lat. *semi*), and *pteron*, a wing.]

**Hemisphere,** hem'i-sfēr, *n.* a *half-sphere :* half of the globe, or a map of it. [Gr. *hēmisphairion—hēmi*, half, and *sphaira*, a sphere.]

**Hemispheric,** hem-i-sfer'ik, **Hemispherical,** hem-i-sfer'ik-al, *adj.* pertaining to a *hemisphere.*

**Hemistich,** hem'i-stik, *n., half a line*, or an incomplete line in poetry. [L. *hemistichium*—Gr. *hēmistichion—hēmi*, half, *stichos*, a line.]

**Hemistichal** he-mis'tik-al, *adj.* pertaining to or written in *hemistichs.*

**Hemlock,** hem'lok, *n.* a poisonous plant used in medicine. [A.S. *hemlic—leac*, a plant, a **Leek**, the first syllable being of unknown origin. Cf. **Charlock** and **Garlic.**]

**Hemorrhage,** hem'or-āj, *n.* a *bursting* or flowing of *blood.*—*adj.* **Hemorrhagic** (hem-or-aj'ik). [Gr. *haimorrhagia—haima*, blood, *rhēgnymi*, to burst.]

**Hemorrhoids,** hem'or-oidz, *n.pl.* painful tubercles around the margin of the anus, from which *blood* occasionally *flows.*—*adj.* **Hemorrhoid'al.** [Gr. *haimorrhoides—haima*, blood, *rheō*, to flow.]

**Hemp,** hemp, *n.* a plant with a fibrous bark used for cordage, coarse cloth, &c. : the fibrous rind prepared for spinning.—*adjs.* **Hemp'en,** made of *hemp ;* **Hemp'y,** like hemp. [A.S. *hænep*, Ice. *hampr ;* borrowed early from L. *cannabis*—Gr. *kannabis*, which is considered to be of Eastern origin, from Sans. *çana*, hemp. Cf. **Canvas.**]

**Hen,** hen, *n.* the female of any bird, esp. of the domestic f wl. [A.S. *henn*, akin to Ger. *henne*, Ice. *hæna*, the fem. forms respectively of A.S. *hana*, Ger. *hahn*, Ice. *hani*, the male of birds, a cock ; orig. the singer or crier, akin to L. *cano*, to sing.]

**Henbane,** hen'bān, *n.* a plant which is a *bane* or poison to domestic *fowls :* the stinking nightshade, used in medicine for opium.

**Hence** hens, *adv., from* this place or time : in the future : from this cause or reason : from this origin.—*int.* away ! begone ! [M. E. *hennes, henen*—A.S. *heonan*, from the base of **He** ; Ger. *hinnen, hin*, hence ; so L. *hinc*, hence—*hic*, this.]

**Henceforth,** hens-fōrth' or hens'-, **Henceforward,** hens-for'ward, *adv.* from this time *forth* or *forward.*

**Henchman,** hensh'man, *n.* a servant : a page. [Usually derived from *haunch-man*, cf. **Flunkey ;** perh., however, from A.S. *hengest*, a horse, Ger. *hengst*, and *man*, and meaning a groom (Skeat).]

**Hencoop,** hen'kōop, *n.* a coop or large cage for domestic fowls.

**Hendecagon,** hen-dek'a-gon, *n.* a plane figure of *eleven angles* and eleven sides. [Fr. *hendécagone*—Gr. *hendeka.* eleven, *gōnia*, an angle.]

**Hendecasyllable,** hen-dek'a-sil'a-bl, *n.* a metrical line of *eleven syllables.*—*adj.* **Hendec'asyllab'ic.** [Gr. *hendeka*, eleven, *syllabē*, a syllable.]

**Hendiadys,** hen-dī'a-dis, *n.* a figure in which *one* and the same notion is presented in *two* expressions. [Gr. *Hen dia dyoin*, one thing by means of two.]

**Hen-harrier,** hen'-har'i-èr. *n.* a species of falcon, the common harrier. [See **Harrier**, a hawk.]

**Henna,** hen'a *n.* a pigment used in the East for dyeing the nails and hair [Ar. *hinna*, the shrub from whose leaves it is made.]

**Henpecked,** hen'pekt, *adj.* weakly subject to his wife, as a cock *pecked* by the hen.

**Hep,** hep, *n.* See **Hip**, the fruit of the dogrose.

**Hepatic,** hep-at'ik, **Hepatical,** hep-at'ik-al, *adj.* pertaining to the *liver :* liver-coloured. [L. *hepaticus*—Gr. *hēpar, hēpatos*, the liver.]

**Hepatitis,** hep-a-tī'tis, *n.* inflammation of the *liver.* [Gr. *hēpar, hēpatos*, the liver.]

**Hepatoscopy,** hep-a-tos'kop-i, *n.* divination by *inspection* of the *livers* of animals. [Gr. *hēpatoskopia*—*hēpar, hēpatos*, liver, *skopeō*, to inspect.]

**Heptade,** hep'tad, *n.* the sum or number of *seven.* [Fr.—Gr. *heptas, heptados—hepta*, seven.]

**Heptaglot,** hep'ta-glot, *adj.* in *seven languages.* —*n.* a book in seven languages. [Gr. *heptaglōttos—hepta*, seven, *glōtta, glōssa*, tongue, language.]

**Heptagon,** hep'ta-gon, *n.* a plane figure with *seven angles* and seven sides.—*adj.* **Heptag'onal.** [Gr. *heptagōnos*, seven-cornered—*hepta*, and *gōnia*, an angle.]

**Heptahedron,** hep-ta-hē'dron, *n.* a solid figure with *seven bases* or sides. [Gr. *hepta*, seven, *hedra*, a seat, a base.]

**Heptarchy,** hep'tär-ki, *n.* a *government* by *seven* persons : the country governed by seven : a period in the Saxon history of England (a use of the word now disapproved by historians).—*adj.* **Heptar'chic.** [Gr. *hepta*, seven, *archē*, sovereignty.]

**Her,** hėr, *pron.* objective and possessive case of **She.**—*adj.* belonging to a female. [M. E. *here* —A.S. *hire*, genitive and dative sing. of *heo*, she.]

**Herald,** her'ald, *n.* in ancient times, an officer who made public proclamations and arranged ceremonies : in medieval times, an officer who had charge of all the etiquette of chivalry, keeping a register of the genealogies and armorial bearings of the nobles : an officer whose duty is to read proclamations, to blazon the arms of the nobility, &c. : a proclaimer : a forerunner.—*v.t.* to introduce, as by a herald : to proclaim. [O. Fr. *heralt :* of Ger. origin, O. Ger. *hari* (A.S. *here*, Ger. *heer*), an army, and *wald = walt*, strength, sway. See **Wield, Valid.**]

**Heraldic,** her-al'dik, *adj.* of or relating to *heralds* or *heraldry.*—*adv.* **Heral'dically.**

**Heraldry,** her'ald-ri, *n.* the art or office of a *herald :* the science of recording genealogies and blazoning coats of arms.

**Herb,** hėrb or ėrb, *n.* a plant the stem of which dies every year, as distinguished from a tree or shrub which has a permanent stem.—*adj.* **Herb'less.** [Fr. *herbe*—L. *herba*, akin to Gr. *phorbē*, pasture—*pherbō*, to feed, to nourish.]

**Herbaceous,** hėr-bā'shus, *adj.* pertaining to or of the nature of *herbs :* (*bot.*) having a soft stem that dies to the root annually. [L. *herbaceus.*]

**Herbage,** hėrb'āj or ėrb'āj, *n.* green food for cattle : pasture : herbs collectively.

**Herbal,** hėrb'al, *adj.* per aining to *herbs.*—*n.* a book containing a classification and description of plants : a collection of preserved plants.

**Herbalist,** hėrb'al-ist, *n.* one who makes collections of *herbs* or plants : one skilled in plants.

**Herbarium,** hėr-bā'ri-um, *n.* a classified collection of preserved *herbs* or plants.—*pl.* **Herba'riums** and **Herba'ria.** [Low L.—L. *herba.*]

**Herbescent,** hėr-bes'ent, *adj., growing* into herbs, becoming herbaceous. [L. *herbescens, -entis*, pr.p. of *herbesco*, to grow into herbs.]

**Herbivorous,** hėr-biv'or-us, *adj., eating* or living on *herbaceous plants.* [L. *herba, voro*, to devour.]

**Herborisation**, hèrb-or-i-zā′shun, *n.* the seeking for *plants* : (*min.*) the figure of plants.

**Herborise**, hèrb′o-rīz, *v.i.* to search for *plants* : to botanise.—*v.t.* to form plant-like figures in, as in minerals. [Fr. *herboriser*, for *herbariser*—L. *herba.*]

**Herculean**, hèr-kū′le-an, *adj.* extremely difficult or dangerous, such as might have been done by *Hercules*, a Greek hero famous for his strength : of extraordinary strength and size.

**Herd**, hèrd, *n.* a number of beasts feeding together, and watched or tended : any collection of beasts, as distinguished from a flock : a company of people, in contempt : the rabble.—*v.i.* to run in herds.—*v.t.* to tend, as a herdsman. [A.S. *heord, herd* ; cognate words are found in all the Teut. languages.]

**Herd**, hèrd. *n.* one who tends a herd. [A.S. *heorde, hirde,* from *heord* or *herd,* a herd of beasts ; Ger. *hirt.*]

**Herdsman**, hèrdz′man (*B.,* **Herd′man**), *n.* a *man* employed to *herd* or tend cattle.]

**Here**, hēr, *adv.* in *this* place : in the present life or state.—**Here′about,** *adv.* about this place.—**Hereaft′er,** *adv.* after this, in some future time or state.—*n.* a future state.—**Here and There,** *adv.* in this place, and then in that : thinly : irregularly.—**Hereby′,** *adv.* by this.—**Herein′,** *adv.* in this.—**Hereof′,** *adv.* of this.—**Heretofore′,** *adv.* before this time : formerly.—**Hereunto′,** *adv.* to this point or time.—**Hereupon′,** *adv.* on this : in consequence of this.—**Herewith′,** *adv.* with this. [A.S. *her;* Ger. *hier,* from the demonstrative stem *hi-.* See Her, and cf. **Who, Where.**]

**Hereditable**, he-red′it-a-bl, *adj.* that may be inherited. [heritèd.

**Hereditament**, her-e-dit′a-ment, *n.* all property of whatever kind that may pass to an heir.

**Hereditary**, he-red′i-tar-i, *adj.* descending by *inheritance* : transmitted from parents to their offspring.—*adv.* **Hered′itarily.** [L. *hereditarius—hereditas,* the state of an heir—*heres,* an heir.]

**Heredity**, he-red′i-ti, *n.* the transmission of qualities from the parents or ancestors to their offspring.

**Heresiarch**, her′e-si-ärk or he-rē′zi-ärk, *n.* a leader in heresy, a chief among heretics. [Gr. *hairesis,* heresy, and *archos,* a leader—*archō,* to lead.]

**Heresy**, her′e-si, *n.* an opinion *adopted* in opposition to the usual belief, esp. in theology : heterodoxy. [Fr. *hérésie*—L. *hæresis*—Gr. *hairesis—haireō,* to take or choose.]

**Heretic**, her′e-tik, *n.* the upholder of a *heresy.*— *adj.* **Heret′ical.**—*adv.* **Heret′ically.** [Gr. *hairetikos,* able to choose, heretical.] [Here.

**Hereby, Hereunto, Herewith,** &c. See under

**Heriot**, her′i-ot, *n.* a tribute of *munitions of war* anciently given to the lord of the manor on the decease of a tenant : a duty paid to the lord of the manor on the decease of a tenant. [A.S. *heregeatu,* a military preparation—*here,* army, *geatwe,* apparatus.]

**Heritable**, her′it-abl. *adj.* that may be *inherited.* —**Heritable Property** (*Scotch law*) real property, as opposed to movable property, or chattels.—**Heritable Security,** same as English mortgage. [O. Fr *heritable, hereditable*—Low L. *hereditabilis*—L. *hereditas.*]

**Heritage**, her′it-āj, *n.* that which is *inherited* : (*B.*) the children (of God). [Fr.—Low L. *heritagium, hæreditagium*—L. *hereditas.*]

**Heritor**, her′it-or, *n.* (*in Scotland*) a landholder in a parish. [Low L. *heritator,* for *hæreditator*— L. *hereditas.*]

**Hermaphrodism**, hèr-maf′rod-izm, **Hermaphrod-**

**itism**, hèr-maf′rod-it-izm, *n.* the union of the two sexes in one body.

**Hermaphrodite**, hèr-maf′rod-īt, *n.* an animal or a plant in which the two sexes are united : an abnormal individual in whom are united the properties of both sexes.—*adj.* uniting the distinctions of both sexes. [L.—Gr. *Hermaphroditos,* the son of *Hermēs* and *Aphroditē,* who, when bathing, grew together with the nymph Salmacis into one person.]

**Hermaphroditic**, hèr-maf-rod-it′ik, **Hermaphroditical**, hèr-maf-rod-it′ik-al, *adj.* pertaining to a hermaphrodite : partaking of both sexes.

**Hermeneutic**, hèr-me-nū′tik, **Hermeneutical,** hèr-me-nū′tik-al, *adj., interpreting* : explanatory.— *adv.* **Hermeneu′tically.**—*n. sing.* **Hermeneu′tics,** the science of interpretation, esp. of the Scriptures. [Gr. *hermēneutikos—hermēneuō,* an interpreter, from *Hermēs,* Mercury, the god of art and eloquence.]

**Hermetic**, hèr-met′ik, **Hermetical,** hèr-met′ik-al, *adj.* belonging in any way to the beliefs current in the middle ages under the name of *Hermes,* the Thrice Great : belonging to magic or alchemy, magical : perfectly close.—*adv.* **Hermet′ically.** —**Hermet′ically sealed,** closed completely, said of a glass vessel, the opening of which is closed by melting the glass. [From *Hermēs Trismegistos,* Hermes ' the thrice-greatest,' the Gr. name for the Egyptian god Thoth. who was god of science, esp. alchemy, and whose magic seal was held by medieval alchemists to make vessels and treasures inaccessible.]

**Hermit**, hèr′mit, *n.* one who retires from society and lives in *solitude* or in the *desert.* [M. E. *eremite,* through Fr. and L. from Gr. *'erēmitēs —erēmos,* solitary, desert.]

**Hermitage**, hèr′mit-āj, *n.* the dwelling of a *hermit* : a retired abode : a kind of wine, so called from *Hermitage,* a district of France.

**Hern.** Same as Heron.

**Hernia**, hèr′ni-a, *n.* a rupture, esp. of the abdomen.—*adj.* **Her′nial.** [L.]

**Hero**, hē′rō, *n.* (*orig.*) a *warrior,* a demigod : a man of distinguished bravery : any illustrious person : the principal figure in any history or work of fiction.—*fem.* **Heroine,** her′o-in. [Through Fr. and L. from Gr. *hērōs* ; akin to L. *vir,* A.S. *wer,* a man, Sans. *vira,* a hero.]

**Herodians**, he-rō′di-ans, *n.pl.* a party among the Jews, taking their name from *Herod,* as being his especial partisans.

**Heroic**, he-rō′ik, **Heroical,** he-rō′ik-al, *adj.* becoming a *hero* : courageous : illustrious : designating the style of verse in which the exploits of heroes are celebrated.—*n.* a heroic verse.—*adv.* **Hero′ically.**

**Heroi-comic**, her′o-i-kom′ik, **Heroi-comical,** her′-o-i-kom′ik-al, *adj.* consisting of a mixture of *heroic* and *comic* : designating the high burlesque. [courage : boldness.

**Heroism**, her′o-izm, *n.* the qualities of a *hero* :

**Heron**, her′un, *n.* a large screaming water-fowl, with long legs and neck.—*n.* **Her′onry,** a place where herons breed. [Fr.—O. Ger. *heigro,* cog. with A.S. *hragra,* Ice. *hegri,* all imitative of its croak.]

**Heronshaw**, her′un-shaw, *n.* a *young heron.* [Properly, *heronsewe* (root- unknown), which was confounded with the old form *hernshaw,* a heronry, from **Heron,** and *shaw,* a wood.]

**Hero-worship** hē′ro-wur′ship, *n.* the *worship* of *heroes* : excessive admiration of great men.

**Herpes**, hèr′pēz, *n.* a kind of skin disease. [So

called from its *creeping* over the skin, from Gr. *herpēs, herpō*, to creep.]

**Herring**, her´ing, *n.* a common small sea-fish found moving in great shoals or *multitudes*. [A.S. *hæring* (Ger. *häring*)—*here* (Ger. *heer*), an army or multitude ; or perh. corr. from L. *haiec*, fish-pickle.]

**Hers**, hèrz, *pron.* possessive of **She**.

**Herse**. Same as **Hearse**.

**Herself**, hèr-self´, *pron.* the emphatic form of **She** in the nominative or objective case : in her real character : having the command of her faculties : sane. [**Her** and **Self**.]

**Hesitancy**, hez´i-tan-si, **Hesitation**, hez-i-tā´shun, *n.* wavering : doubt : stammering.

**Hesitate**, hez´i-tāt, *v.i.* to stop in making a decision : to be in doubt : to stammer.—*adv.* **Hes´itatingly**. [L. *hæsito, hæsitatum*, freq. of *hæreo hæsum*, to stick, adhere.]

**Hesper**, hes´pèr, **Hesperus**, hes´pèr-us, *n.* the *evening*-star or Venus. [L. and Gr. *hesperos*, evening, al∼o L. *vesper*.] [west.

**Hesperian**, hes-pē´ri-an, *adj.* of *Hesperus* or the

**Heterocercal**, het-er-o-sèr´kal, *adj.* having the upper fork of the *tail different from* or longer than the lower, as the shark :—opposed to **Homocercal**. [Gr. *heteros*, different from, and *kerkos*, the tail.]

**Heteroclite**, het´er-o-klīt, **Heteroclitic**, het-er-o-klit´ik. **Heteroclitical**, het-er-o-klit-ik-al, *adj.*, *irregularly inflected*: irregular. [Gr. *heteroklitos—heteros*, other, and *klitos*, inflected—*klinō*, to inflect.]

**Heteroclite**, het´er-o-klīt, *n.* (*gram.*) a word *irregularly inflected*: anything irregular.

**Heterodox**, het´er-o-doks, *adj.* holding an *opinion other* or different from the established one, esp. in theology : heretical. [Gr. *heterodoxos—heteros*, other, *doxa*, an opinion—*dokeō*, to think.]

**Heterodoxy**, het´er-o-doks-i, *n.* heresy.

**Heterogeneous**, het-er-o-jēn´e-us, **Heterogeneal**, het-er-o-jēn´e-al, *adj.* of *another race* or *kind*: dissimilar :—opposed to **Homogeneous**.—*adv.* **Heterogen´eously**.—*ns.* **Heterogene´ity, Heterogen´eousness**. [Gr. *heterogenēs—heteros*, other, *genos*, a kind.] [Cossacks. [Russ.]

**Hetman**, het´man, *n.* the chief or general of the

**Hew**, hū, *v.t.* to cut with any sharp instrument : to cut in pieces : to shape :—*pa p.* hewed´ or hewn. [A.S. *heawan* ; Ger. *hauen*.]

**Hewer**, hū´èr, *n.* one who *hews*.

**Hexagon**, heks´a-gon, *n.* a plane figure with *six angles* and sides.—*adj.* **Hexag´onal**.—*adv.* **Hexag´onally**. [Gr. *hexagōnon — hex*, six, *gōnia*, an angle.]

**Hexahedron**, heks-a-hē´dron, *n.* a cube, a regular solid with *six* sides or faces, each of these being a square.—*adj.* **Hexahe´dral**. [Gr. *hex*, six, *hed-ra*, a base.]

**Hexameter**, heks-am´et-èr, *n.* a verse of *six measures* or feet.—*adj.* having *six metrical* feet. [L.—Gr. *hex*, six, *metron*, a measure.]

**Hexapla**, heks´a-pla, *n.* an edition of the Scriptures in *six* different versions, esp. that prepared by Origen of Alexandria.—*adj.* **Hex´aplar**. [Gr. *hexaplous*, sixfold.]

**Hexapod**, heks´a-pod, *n.* an animal with *six feet*. [Gr. *hexapous, -podos—hex*, six, *pous*, a foot.]

**Hexastich**, heks´a-stik, *n.* a poem of *six lines* or *verses*. [Gr. *hexastichos—hex*, six, *stichos*, a line.]

**Hexastyle**, heks´a-stīl, *n.* a building with *six pillars*. [Gr. *hexastylos—hex*, six, *stylos*, a pillar.]

**Hey**, hā, *int.* expressive of joy or interrogation. [From the sound, like Ger. *hei*.]

**Heyday**, hā´dā, *int.* expressive of frolic, exultation, or wonder. [Ger. *heida*, or Dut. *hei daar*, (Ger.) *da*, (Dut.) *daar* = **There**.]

**Heyday**, hā´dā, *n.* the wild gaiety of youth. [For *high day* ; M. E. *hey-day*.]

**Hiatus**, hī-ā´tus, *n.* a *gap* : an opening : a defect : (*gram.*) a concurrence of vowel sounds in two successive syllables. [L., from *hio*, to gape ; Gr. *chainō*, to gape ; from root *cha*, the sound produced by gaping.]

**Hibernal**, hī-bėr´nal, *adj.* belonging to *winter* : wintry. [Fr.—L. *hibernalis—hiems*, Gr. *cheima*, winter, Sans. *hima*, snow.]

**Hibernate**, hī´bèr-nāt, *v.i.* to pass the winter in sleep or torpor.—*n.* **Hiberna´tion**, the state of torpor in which many animals pass the winter. [L. *hiberno, hibernatum—hiberna*, winter-quarters.]

**Hibernian**, hī-bėr´ni-an, *adj.* relating to *Hibernia* or Ireland.—*n.* an Irishman. [From L. *Hibernia*, Gr. *Iouernia*, Ireland.]

**Hibernianism**, hī-bėr´ni-an-izm, **Hibernicism**, hī-bėr´ni-sizm, *n.* an Irish idiom or peculiarity.

**Hiccough, Hiccup, Hickup**, hik´up, *n.* a sudden and involuntary kind of cough.—*v.i.* to have a cough of this kind :—*pr.p.* hiccoughing (hik´up-ing) ; *pa.p.* hiccoughed (hik´upt). [Imitative ; there are similar words in many languages, as Dut. *hik*, Dan. *hikke*, Bret. *hik*.]

**Hickory**, hik´or-i, *n.* the name of several American nut-bearing trees. [Ety. unknown.]

**Hid, Hidden**. See **Hide**.

**Hidalgo**, hi-dal´gō, *n.* a Spanish nobleman of the lowest class. [Sp. *hijo de algo*, the son of something, *i.e.*, of a good house, and without mixture of Moorish or Jewish blood.]

**Hidden**, hid´n, *adj.* concealed : unknown.

**Hide**, hīd, *v.t.* to conceal : to keep in safety.—*v.i.* to lie concealed :—*pa.t.* hid ; *pa.p.* hidd´en, hid. [A.S. *hydan*, to hide ; allied to Gr. *keuthō*, and perh. to L. *custos* (= *cud-tos*), a protector.]

**Hide**, hīd, *n.* the skin of an animal.—*v.t.* to flog or whip. [A.S. *hyd* ; Ger. *haut*, allied to L. *cutis*, Gr. *skutos*.]

**Hide**, hīd, *n.* an old measure of land varying from 60 to 120 acres. [A.S. *hīd*, contracted for *higid* = *hiwisc*, both words meaning as much land as could support a family, and so conn. with A.S. *hiwan*, domestics. See **Hive**.]

**Hidebound**, hīd´bownd, *adj.* having the *hide* closely bound to the body, as in animals : in trees, having the bark so close that it impedes the growth.

**Hideous**, hid´e-us, *adj.* frightful : horrible : ghastly.—*adv.* **Hid´eously**.—*n.* **Hid´eousness**. [Fr *hideux*—O. Fr. *hide, hisde*, dread ; perh. from L. *hispidus*, rough, rude.]

**Hiding**, hīd´ing, *n.* a place of concealment.

**Hie**, hī, *v i.* to hasten :—*pr.p.* hie´ing ; *pa.p.* hied´. [A.S. *higian*, to hasten.]

**Hierarch**, hī´èr-ärk, *n.* a *ruler* in *sacred* matters. —*adj.* **Hi´erarchal**. [Gr. *hierarchēs—hieros*, sacred, *archō*, to rule.]

**Hierarchy**, hī´èr-ärk-i, *n.*, *rule* in *sacred* matters : persons that so rule : the body of the clergy : a government by priests.—*adj.* **Hierarch´ical**.

**Hieratic**, hī-èr-at´ik, *adj.*, *sacred*: relating to priests. [L. *hieraticus*—Gr. *hieratikos*.]

**Hieroglyph**, hī´èr-o-glif, **Hieroglyphic**, hī-èr-o-glif´ik, *n.* the *sacred characters* of the ancient Egyptian language : picture-writing, or writing in which figures of objects are employed instead of conventional signs, like the alphabet : any symbolical figure.—*adjs.* **Hieroglyph´ic, Hiero-**

---

glyph'ical.—*adv.* **Hieroglyph'ically.** [Gr. *hieroglyphikon—hieros,* sacred, *glyphō,* to carve.]

**Hieroglyphist,** hī-ēr-o-glif'ist, *n.* one skilled in reading *hieroglyphics.*

**Hierographic,** hī-ēr-o-graf'ik, **Hierographical,** hī-ēr-o-graf'ik-al, *adj.* pertaining to *sacred writing.* [Gr. *hierographikos—hieros,* sacred, and *graphikos,* from *graphō,* to write.]

**Hierology,** hī-ēr-ol'o-ji, *n.* the *science* which treats of *sacred* matters, especially sacred writing and inscriptions. [Gr. *hierologia—hieros,* sacred, and *logos,* a discourse or treatise.]

**Hierophant,** hī'ēr-o-fant, *n.* one who *shews* or reveals *sacred* things : a priest. [Gr. *hierophantēs—hieros,* sacred, *phainō,* to shew.]

**Higgle,** hig'l, *v.i.* to *hawk* about provisions for sale : to make difficulty in bargaining : to chaffer. —*n.* **Higg'ler.** [A form of **Haggle,** and **Hawk,** to sell.]

**High,** hī, *adj.* elevated : lofty : tall : eminent in anything : exalted in rank : dignified : chief : noble : ostentatious : arrogant : proud : strong : powerful : angry : loud : violent : tempestuous : excellent : far advanced : difficult : dear : remote in time.—*adv.* aloft : eminently : powerfully : profoundly.—*adv.* **High'ly.** [A.S. *heah* ; Goth. *hauhs,* Ice. *har,* Ger. *hoch.*]

**High-admiral,** hī'-ad'mi-ral, *n.* a *high* or *chief admiral* of a fleet.

**High-altar,** hī'-awl'tar, *n.* the principal altar in a church

**High-bailiff,** hī'-bāl'if, *n.* an officer who serves writs, &c. in certain franchises, exempt from the ordinary supervision of the sheriff.

**High-born,** hī'-bawrn, *adj.* of *high* or noble *birth.*

**High-bred,** hī'-bred, *adj.* of *high* or noble *breed,* training, or family.

**High-church,** hī'-church, *n.* a party within the Church of England, who exalt the authority and jurisdiction of the church, and attach great importance to ecclesiastical dignities, ordinances, and ceremonies.—*ns.* **High'church'man, High'church'ism.** [or glaring *colour.*

**High-coloured,** hī'-kul'urd, *adj.* having a strong

**High-day,** hī'-dā, *n.* a holiday : (*B.*) broad daylight. [pampered.—*n.* **High'feed'ing.**

**High-fed,** hī'-fed. *adj.,* *fed highly* or luxuriously :

**Highflier,** hī'flī-ēr, *n.* one who *flies high,* or runs into extravagance of opinion or action.—*adj.* **High'fly'ing.** [turgid.

**High-flown,** hī'-flōn, *adj.* extravagant : elevated :

**High-handed,** hī'-hand'ed, *adj.* overbearing : violent. [*high* or full of courage.

**High-hearted,** hī'-härt'ed, *adj.* with the *heart*

**Highland,** hī'land, *n.* a mountainous district.

**Highlander,** hī'land-ēr, *n.* an inhabitant of a mountainous region. [occasions.

**High-mass,** hī'-mas, *n.* the *mass* read on *high*

**High-minded,** hī'-mīnd'ed, *adj.* having a *high,* proud, or arrogant *mind* : having honourable pride : magnanimous.—*n.* **High'mind'edness.**

**Highness,** hī'nes, *n.* the state of being *high* : dignity of rank : a title of honour given to princes.

**High-place,** hī'-plās, *n.* (*B.*) an eminence on which unlawful worship was performed by the Jews.

**High-pressure,** hī'-presh'ūr, *adj.* applied to a steam-engine in which the steam is raised to a *high* temperature, so that the *pressure* may exceed that of the atmosphere.

**High-priest,** hī'-prēst, *n.* a *chief priest.*

**High-principled,** hī'-prin'si-pld, *adj.* of *high,* noble, or strict *principle.*

**High-proof,** hī'-prōōf, *adj., proved* to contain *much* alcohol : highly rectified.

**High-road,** hī'-rōd, *n.* one of the public or chief *roads.*

**High-seasoned,** hī'-sē'znd, *adj.* made *rich* or piquant with spices or other *seasoning.*

**High-souled,** hī'-sōld, *adj.* having a *high* or lofty *soul* or spirit. [ostentatious.

**High-sounding,** hī'-sownd'ing, *adj.* pompous :

**High-spirited,** hī'-spir'it-ed, *adj.* having a *high spirit* or natural fire : bold : daring : irascible.

**Hight,** hīt, a *pass. verb,* used in the third pers. sing., he was or is called or named. [A.S. *hatan,* to be called—*hatan,* to call ; Ger. *heissen.*]

**High-tasted,** hī'-tast'ed, *adj.* having a *strong* piquant *taste* or relish.

**High-treason,** hī'-trē'zn, *n.* treason against the sovereign or state, being the highest civil offence.

**High-water,** hī'-waw'tēr, *n.* the time at which the *tide* is *highest :* the greatest elevation of the tide.

**Highway,** hī'wā, *n.* a *high* or public *way* or road.

**Highwayman,** hī'wā-man, *n.* a robber who attacks people on the public *way.*

**High-wrought,** hī'-rawt, *adj. wrought* with *exquisite* skill : highly finished.

**Hilarious,** hi-lā'ri-us, *adj.* gay : very merry. [L. *hilaris*—Gr. *hilaros—hilaos,* kindly, gay, cheerful.] [ment.

**Hilarity,** hi-lar'i-ti, *n.* gaiety : pleasurable excite-

**Hilary,** hil'ar-i, *adj.* the name applied to one of the four terms of the law-courts of England, from 11th to 31st January, so called from *St Hilary,* whose festival is Jan. 13.

**Hill,** hil, *n.* a *high* mass of land, less than a mountain. [A.S. *hyll ;* allied to L. *collis,* a hill, and root *cel* in *celsus,* high, Gr. *kolōnos,* a hill.]

**Hillock,** hil'uk, *n.* a small hill.

**Hilly,** hil'i, *adj.* full of hills.—*n.* **Hill'iness.**

**Hilt,** hilt, *n.* the handle, esp. of a sword. [A.S. *hilt* ; Dut. *hilte,* O. Ger. *helza ;* not conn. with **Hold.**]

**Hilted,** hilt'ed, *adj.* having a hilt.

**Him,** him, *pron.* the objective case of **He.** [A.S. *he,* dative *him,* acc. *hine.*]

**Himself,** him-self', *pron.* the emphatic and reflective form of **He** and **Him** : it also expresses the proper character or state of mind of a person.

**Hin,** hin, *n.* a Hebrew liquid measure, containing about 6 English quarts. [Heb.]

**Hind,** hīnd, *n.* the female of the stag. [A.S. *hind ;* Ger. *hinde,* hindin, O. Ger. *hinda,* hinta.]

**Hind,** hīnd, *n.* a farm-servant, a ploughman, a peasant. [Lit. a *domestic,* from A.S. *hina, hiwan,* domestics—*hiw,* a house. See **Hive.**]

**Hind,** hīnd, *adj.* placed in the rear : pertaining to the part *behind :* backward : opposed to **Fore.** [A.S. *hindan,* from the base *hi,* seen also in **He, Hence,** and **Hither.**]

**Hinder,** hīnd'ēr, *adj.* comparative of **Hind,** but used in the same significations.

**Hinder,** hin'dēr, *v.t.* to put or keep *behind :* to stop, or prevent progress : to embarrass.—*v.i.* to raise obstacles. [A.S. *hindrian ;* Ger. *hindern ;* from **Hind,** adj.]

**Hinderance,** hin'dēr-ans, **Hindrance,** hin'drans, *n.* act of hindering : that which hinders : obstacle.

**Hindermost,** hīnd'ēr-mōst. **Hindmost,** hīnd'mōst, *adj.* superlative of **Hind** ; furthest behind. [For *-most,* see **Aftermost** and **Foremost.**]

**Hindi,** hin'dē, *n.* one of the languages of Aryan stock now spoken in North-India. [Pers. *Hind,* 'India.']

**Hindoostanee.** See **Hindustani.**

**Hindrance.** See **Hinderance.**

**Hindu, Hindoo,** hin'dōō, *n.* a native of *Hindustan :* now more properly applied to native Indian believers in Brahmanism, as opp. to Mohammedans, &c. [Lit. a dweller on the banks of the river *Sindhu*, Sans. for Indus.]

**Hinduism, Hindooism,** hin′dōō-izm, *n.* the religion and customs of the Hindus.

**Hindustani,** hin-uōō-stan′ē, *n.* a dialect of Hindi, also called **Urdu** ('language of the camp,' Turk. *urdū* or *ordū,* 'camp'), being likewise the chief official and commercial language of India.

**Hinge,** hinj, *n.* the hook or joint on which a door or lid *hangs :* that on which anything depends or turns.—*v.t.* to furnish with hinges : to bend.—*v.i.* to hang or turn as on a hinge :—*pr.p.* hing′ing ; *pa.p.* hinged′. [M. E. *henge,* from M. E. *hengen,* to hang, which, according to Skeat, is of Scand. origin, as in Ice. *henja,* to hang, but cog. with A.S. *hangian.*]

**Hinny,** hin′i, *n.* the produce of a stallion and a she-ass. [L. *hinnus*—Gr. *hinnos, ginnos,* a mule.]

**Hint,** hint, *n.* a distant allusion : slight mention : insinuation.—*v.t.* to bring to mind by a slight mention or remote allusion : to allude to.—*v.i.* to make an indirect or remote allusion : to allude. [Lit. *a thing taken,* from A.S. *hentan,* to seize, and so allied to *hunt* and *hand.*]

**Hip,** hip, *n.* the haunch or fleshy part of the thigh. —*v.t.* to sprain the hip :—*pr.p.* hipp′ing ; *pa.p.* hipped′. [A.S. *hype ;* Goth. *hups,* Ger. *hüfte.*]

**Hip,** hip, **Hep,** hep, *n.* the fruit of the wild brier or dogrose. [M. E. *hepe ;* from A.S. *heope.*]

**Hippish,** hip′ish, *adj.* somewhat hypochondriac. [A familiar corr. of **Hypochondriac.**]

**Hippocampus,** hip′o-kam-pus, *n.* a genus of fishes with head and neck somewhat like those of a *horse,* and a long, tapering tail which they can *twist* round anything. [Gr. *hippokampos*— *hippos,* a horse, *kampē,* a turning.]

**Hippocentaur,** hip-o-sent′awr, *n.* Same as **Centaur.** [Gr. *hippos,* a horse, and **Centaur.**]

**Hippodrome,** hip′o-drōm, *n.* a race*course* for *horses* and chariots : an equestrian circus. [Gr. *hippodromos*—*hippos,* a horse. *dromos,* a course.]

**Hippogriff,** hip′o-grif, *n.* a fabulous winged animal, half *horse* and half *griffin.* [Fr. *hippogriffe*—Gr. *hippos,* a horse, and *gryps,* a griffin.]

**Hippopathology,** hip-o-pa-thol′o-ji, *n.* the *pathology* of the *horse ;* the science of veterinary medicine. [Gr. *hippos,* a horse, and **Pathology.**]

**Hippophagous,** hip-pof′a-gus, *adj., horse-eating.* [Gr. *hippos,* a horse, and *phagō,* to eat.]

**Hippophagy,** hip-pof′a-ji, *n.* the act or practice of *feeding* on *horse*-flesh.—*n.* **Hippoph′agist**

**Hippopotamus,** hip-o-pot′a-mus, *n.* the *river*-*horse*—an African quadruped, one of the largest existing, of aquatic habits, having a very thick skin, short legs, and a large head and muzzle. [L.—Gr. *hippopotamos*—*hippos,* and *potamos,* a river.]

**Hippuric,** hip-ū′rik, *adj.* denoting an acid obtained from the *urine* of *horses.* [Fr. *hippurique*—Gr. *hippos,* a horse, and *ouron,* urine.]

**Hire,** hīr. *n., wages* for service : the price paid for the use of anything.—*v.t.* to procure the use or services of, at a price : to engage for wages : to let for compensation : to bribe.—*n.* **Hir′er.** [A.S. *hyr,* wages, *hyrian,* to hire ; Ger. *heuer,* Dut. *huur,* Dan. *hyre.*]

**Hireling,** hīr′ling, *n.* a *hired servant* : a mercenary : a prostitute. [A.S. *hyrling.*]

**Hires,** hīrz (*B.*), *n.* plural of **Hire,** not now used.

**Hirsute,** hir-sūt′, *adj., hairy :* rough : shaggy : (*bot.*) having long, stiffish hairs. [L. *hirsutus*— *hirsus, hirtus,* rough. hairy, shaggy.]

**His,** hiz, *pron.* possessive form of **He** : (*B.*) used

for *its.* [A.S. *his,* possessive of *he,* and orig. of *it.*]

**Hispid,** his′pid, *adj.* (*bot.*) rough with or having strong *hairs* or bristles. [L. *hispidus.*]

**Hiss,** his, *v.i* to make a sound like the letter *s,* as the goose, serpent, &c. : to express contempt, &c. by hissing.—*v.t.* to condemn by hissing. [A.S. *hysian ;* formed from the sound.]

**Hiss,** his, *n.* the sound of the letter *s,* an expression of disapprobation, contempt, &c.

**Hissing,** his′ing, *n.* the *noise* of a *hiss :* object of hissing : object or occasion of contempt.

**Hist,** hist, *int.* demanding silence and attention : *hush !* silence ! [Formed from the sound.]

**Histology,** his-tol′o-ji, *n.* the *science* which treats of the minute *structure* of animal and vegetable tissue. [Gr. *histos,* beam of a loom, web, texture —*histēmi,* to make to stand (the beam in the Gr. loom was upright), and *logos,* a discourse.]

**Historian,** his-tō′ri-an, *n.* a *writer* of *history.*

**Historic,** his-tor′ik, **Historical,** his-tor′ik-al, *adj.* pertaining to history : containing history : derived from history.—*adv.* **Histor′ically.**

**Historiette,** his-tor-i-et′, *n.* a short history or story. [Fr.]

**Historiographer,** his-tō-ri-og′ra-fēr, *n.* a *writer* of *history :* a professed or official historian.

**Historiography,** his-tō-ri-og′ra-fi, *n.* the art or employment of *writing history.* [Gr. *historiographia*—*historia,* and *graphō,* to write.]

**History,** his′to-ri, *n.* an account of an event : a systematic account of the origin and progress of a nation : the knowledge of facts, events, &c. [L. and Gr. *historia*—Gr. *historeō,* to learn by inquiry—*histōr,* knowing, learned. from the root *id-,* in *eidenai,* to know, which is found also in L. *videre,* Sans. *vid,* E. *wit.*]

**Histrionic,** his-tri-on′ik, **Histrionical,** his-tri-on′-ik-al, *adj.* relating to the *stage* or *stage-players :* befitting a theatre.—*adv.* **Histrion′ically.** [L. *istrionicus*—*histrio,* Etruscan, primary form *hister,* a player.]

**Histrionism,** his′tri-o-nizm, *n.* the *acts* or practice of *stage-playing,* or of pantomime.

**Hit,** hit, *v.t.* to *light* on that which is aimed at : to touch or strike : to reach : to suit.—*v.i.* to come in contact : to chance luckily : to succeed : —*pr.p.* hitt′ing ; *pa.t.* and *pa.p.* hit.—*n.* **Hitt′er.** [Ice. *hitta,* to light on, to find ; perh. allied to L. *cado,* to fall.]

**Hit,** hit, *n.* a *lighting upon :* a lucky chance : a stroke : a happy turn of thought or expression.

**Hitch,** hich, *v.i.* to move by jerks, as if caught by a hook : to be caught by a hook : to be caught or fall into.—*v.t.* to hook : to catch.—*n.* a jerk : a catch or anything that holds : an obstacle : a sudden halt (*naut.*) a knot or noose. [Ety. dub.]

**Hither,** hi*th*′ēr, *adv., to this place.*—*adj.* toward the speaker : nearer. [A.S. *hither, hider,* from the Teut. base *hi* and affix *-ter,* as in **Af-ter, Whe-ther** ; Goth. *hidre,* Ice. *hedhra.* See **He.**]

**Hithermost,** hi*th*′ēr-mōst, *adj.* nearest on this side.

**Hitherto,** hi*th*′ēr-tōō, *adv., to this place* or time : as yet. [*place.*]

**Hitherward,** hi*th*′ēr-ward, *adv., towards this*

**Hive,** hīv, *n* a swarm of bees in a box or basket : the habitation of bees : any busy company.—*v.t.* to collect into a hive : to lay up in store.—*v.i.* to take shelter together : to reside in a body.—*n.* **Hiv′er.** [Lit. a *house* or *family,* from A.S. *hiw,* a house, *hiwan,* domestics ; conn. with Goth. *heiv,* Ice. *hiu,* family.]

**Ho, Hoa,** hō, *int.* a call to excite attention : hold ! stop ! [Formed from the sound.]

**Hoar**, hōr, *adj.*, *white* or grayish-white, esp. with age or frost.—*n.* hoariness. [A.S. *har*, hoary, gray; Ice. *harr*.]

**Hoard**, hōrd, *n.* a *store*: a hidden stock: a treasure.—*v.t.* to store: to amass and deposit in secret.—*v.i.* to store up: to collect and form a hoard.—*n.* **Hoard'er**. [A.S. *hord*; Ice. *hodd*, Ger. *hort*; from the same root as *house*.]

**Hoard**, hōrd, *Hoarding*, hōrd'ing, *n.* a *hurdle* or fence inclosing a house and materials while builders are at work. [O. Fr. *horde*; Dut. *horde*, a hurdle; same root as **Hurdle**.]

**Hoar-frost**, hōr'-frost, *n.*, *white frost*: the white particles formed by the freezing of dew.

**Hoarhound, Horehound**, hōr'hownd, *n.* a plant of a *whitish* or downy appearance, used as a tonic. [M. E. *horehune*—A.S. *harhune*, from *har*, hoar or white, and *hune* (acc. to Skeat, meaning 'strong-scented'); cf. L. *cunila*, Gr. *konile*, wild marjoram.]

**Hoarse**, hōrs, *adj.* having a harsh, grating voice, as from a cold: harsh: discordant.—*adv.* **Hoarse'ly**.—*n.* **Hoarse'ness**. [A.S. *has*; Ice. *hass*, Dut. *heesch*, Ger. *heiser*, hoarse.]

**Hoary**, hōr'i, *adj.*, *white* or gray with age: (*bot.*) covered with short, dense, whitish hairs.—*n.* **Hoar'iness**. [See **Hoar.**]

**Hoax**, hōks, *n.* a deceptive trick: a practical joke.—*v.t.* to deceive: to play a trick upon for sport, or without malice.—*n.* **Hoax'er**. [Corr. of *hocus*. See **Hocus-pocus.**]

**Hob**, hob. *n.* the projecting nave of a wheel: the flat part of a grate, orig. the raised stones between which the embers were confined. [Ger. *hub*, a heaving; W. *hob*, a projection. See **Hump.**]

**Hob**, hob, *n.* a clownish fellow: a rustic: a fairy. [A corr. of *Robin*, which again is a Fr. corr. of *Robert*.]

**Hobble**, hob'l, *v.i.* to walk with a limp: to walk awkwardly: to move irregularly.—*v.t.* to fasten loosely the legs of.—*n.* an awkward, limping gait: a difficulty.—*n.* **Hobb'ler**.—*adv.* **Hobb'lingly**. [Freq. of **Hop.**]

**Hobbledehoy**, hobl-de-hoi', *n.* a stripling, neither man nor boy. [Ety. unknown.]

**Hobby**, hob'i, *Hobby-horse*, hob'i-hors, *n.* a strong, active horse: a pacing horse: a stick or figure of a horse on which boys ride: a subject on which one is constantly setting off: a favourite pursuit. [O. Fr. *hobin*, Dan. *hoppe*, a mare; cog. with **Hop.**]      [*hobereau.*]

**Hobby**, hob'i, *n.* a small species of falcon. [O. Fr.

**Hobgoblin**, hob-gob'lin, *n.* a fairy: a frightful apparition. [**Hob**, **Robin**, and **Goblin**.]

**Hobnail**, hob'nāl, *n.* a *nail* with a thick, strong *head*, used in the shoes of horses, and sometimes of men: a clownish fellow, so called from the hobnails in his shoes.—*adj.* **Hob'nailed**. [From **Hob**, a projecting head.]

**Hobnob**, hob'nob, *adv.*, *have* or *not have*, a familiar invitation to drink. [A.S. *habban*, to have, and *nabban*, not to have.]

**Hock**, hok, *n.* and *v.* See **Hough.**

**Hock**, hok, *n.* properly, the wine produced at *Hochheim*, in Germany: now applied to all white Rhine wines.

**Hockey**, hok'i, *Hookey*, hook'i, *n.* a game at ball played with a club or *hooked* stick.

**Hockle**, hok'l, *v.t.* to hamstring. [See **Hough.**]

**Hocus-pocus**, hō'kus-pō'kus, *n.* a juggler: a juggler's trick.—*v.t.* (also **To Hocus**) to cheat:—*pr.p.* ho'cussing; *pa.p.* ho'cussed. [The meaningless gibberish of a juggler; there is no ground for the ordinary etymologies.]

**Hod**, hod, *n.* a kind of trough borne on the shoulder, for carrying bricks and mortar. [Fr. *hotte*, a basket carried on the back; of Teut. origin, and prob. cog. with E. **Hut.**]

**Hoddengray**, hodn'grā, *n.* coarse cloth made of undyed wool. [Said to be from **Holden**, and **Gray**.]

**Hodgepodge**, hoj'poj, *n.* See **Hotchpotch.**

**Hodman**, hod'man, *n.* a *man* who carries a *hod:* a mason's labourer.

**Hodometer**, ho-dom'e-tėr, *n.* an instrument attached to the axle of a vehicle to register the revolutions of the wheels. [Gr. *hodos*, a way, and *metron*, a measure.]

**Hoe**, hō, *n.* an instrument for *hewing* or digging up weeds, and loosening the earth.—*v.t.* to cut or clean with a hoe: to weed.—*v.i.* to use a hoe:—*pr.p.* hoe'ing; *pa.p.* hoed'.—*n.* **Ho'er**. [Fr. *houe* - O. Ger. *houwa* (Ger. *haue*), a hoe, from O. Ger. *houwan*, to strike, E. **Eew.**]

**Hog**, hog, *n.* a general name for swine: a castrated boar: a pig.—*v.t.* to cut short the hair of:—*pr.p.* hogg'ing; *pa.p.* hogged'. [W. *hwch*; Bret. *hoc'h*, *houc'h*, swine—*houc'ha*, to grunt.]

**Hoggerel**, hog'ėr-el (in Scot. **Hogg**), *n.* a young sheep of the second year. [D. *hokkeling*, a beast of one year old, from being fed in the *hok* or pen.]

**Hogget**, hog'et, *n.* a boar of the second year: a sheep or colt after it has passed its first year.

**Hoggish**, hog'ish, *adj.* resembling a hog: brutish: filthy: selfish.—*adv.* **Hogg'ishly**.—*n.* **Hogg'ishness**.

**Hogmanay**, hog-ma-nā', *n.* (*in Scot.*) the old name for the last day of the year. [Ety. unknown.]

**Hog-ringer**, hog'-ring'ėr, *n.* one who puts *rings* into the snouts of *hogs*.

**Hogshead**, hogz'hed, *n.* a measure of capacity = 52½ imperial gallons, or 63 old wine gallons; of **Claret** = 46 gallons; of **Beer** = 54 gallons; of tobacco (*in United States*) varies from 750 to 1200 lbs.: a large cask. [Corr. of O. Dut. *okshoofd*, ox-head; the cask perh. was so called from an ox's head having been branded upon it.]

**Hog's-lard**, hogz'-lärd, *n.* the melted fat of the *hog*.

**Holden**, hoi'dn, *n.* a romping, ill-bred girl: a flirt.—*adj.* rude, rustic: bold.—*v.i.* to romp indelicately. [M. E. *hoydon*—O. Dut. *heyden*, a clownish person, a form of **Heathen.**]

**Hoist**, hoist, *v.t.* to *lift*: to raise with tackle: to heave.—*n.* act of lifting: the height of a sail: an apparatus for lifting heavy bodies to the upper stories of a building. [Formerly *hoise* or *hoyse*, from O. Dut. *hyssen*, Dut. *hijschen*, to hoist.]

**Hoity-toity**, hoi'ti-toi'ti, *int.* an exclamation of surprise or disapprobation.—*adj.* giddy, flighty, gay, noisy. [Like *hut* and *tut*, interjections, expressive of disapprobation.]

**Hold**, hōld, *v.t.* to *keep* possession of or authority over: to sustain: to defend: to occupy: to derive title to: to bind: to confine: to restrain: to continue: to persist in: to contain: to celebrate: to esteem.—*v.i.* to remain fixed: to be true or unfailing: to continue unbroken or unsubdued: to adhere: to derive right:—*pr.p.* hōld'ing; *pa.t.* held; *pa.p.* held (*obs.* hōld'en).—**To hold over**, to keep possession of land or a house beyond the term of agreement.—**Hold of** (*Pr. Bk.*) to regard.—*n.* **Hold'er**. [A.S. *healdan*; O Ger. *haltan*, Goth. *haldan*, Dan. *holdie*, to keep.]

**Hold**, hōld, *n.*, *act* or manner of *holding*: seizure: power of seizing: something for support: a place of confinement: custody: a fortified place:

(*mus.*) a mark over a rest or note, indicating that it is to be prolonged.

**Hold**, hōld, *n.* the interior cavity of a ship between the floor and the lower deck, used for the cargo. [Dut. *hol*, a cavity or hole, with excrescent *d*. See **Hole**.]

**Holden**, hōld'n (*B.*) old *pa.p.* of **Hold**.

**Holdfast**, hōld'fast, *n.* that which *holds fast*: a long nail : a catch.

**Holding**, hōld'ing, *n.* anything *held*: a farm *held* of a superior : hold : influence : (*Scots law*) tenure.

**Hole**, hōl, *n.* a *hollow* place : a cavity : an opening in a solid body : a pit : a subterfuge : a means of escape.—*v.t.* to form holes in : to drive into a hole.—*v.i.* to go into a hole. [A.S. *hol*, a hole, cavern ; Dut. *hol*, Dan. *hul*, Ger. *hohl*, hollow ; conn. with Gr. *koilos*, hollow.]

**Holibut**. See **Halibut**.

**Holiday**, hol'i-dā, *n.* (*orig.*) *holy-day* (which see) : a day of amusement.

**Holily**. See **Holy**.

**Holiness**, hō'li-nes, *n.* state of being holy : religious goodness : sanctity : a title of the pope.

**Holla**, hol'a, **Hollo, Holloa**, hol'ō or hol-lō', *int.*, *ho, there* : attend : (*naut.*) the usual response to **Ahoy**.—*n.* a loud shout.—*v.i.* to cry loudly to one at a distance. [Ger. *holla* is from Fr. *holà—ho*, and *là*—L. *illac*, there ; the other forms are due to confusion with **Halloo**.] [*Holland*.

**Holland**, hol'and, *n.* a kind of linen first made in

**Hollands**, hol'andz, *n.* gin made in *Holland*.

**Hollow**, hol'ō, *adj.* vacant : not solid : containing an empty space : sunken : unsound : insincere.—*n.* a hole : a cavity : a depression in a body : any vacuity : a groove : a channel.—*v.t.* to make a hole in : to make hollow by digging : to excavate. [A.S. *holh*, a hollow place—A.S. *hol*, E. **Hole**.]

**Hollow-eyed**, hol'ō-īd, *adj.* having *sunken eyes*.

**Hollow-hearted**, hol ō-härt'ed, *adj.* having a *hollow* or untrue *heart* : faithless : treacherous.

**Hollowness**, hol'ō-nes, *n.* the state of being hollow : cavity : insincerity : treachery.

**Hollow-ware**, hol'ō-wār, *n.* trade name for *hollow* articles of iron, as pots and kettles.

**Holly**, hol'i, *n.* an evergreen shrub having prickly leaves and scarlet or yellow berries. [M. E. *holin*—A.S. *holegn*, the holly ; cog. with W. *celyn*, Ir. *cuileann*.]

**Hollyhock**, hol'i-hok, *n.* a kind of *mallow*, brought into Europe from the *Holy* Land. [M. E. *holi-hoc—holi*, holy, and A.S. *hoc*, mallows ; W. *hocys*.]

**Holm**, hōlm or hōm, *n.* a river-islet : rich flat land near a river. [A.S. *holm*, a mound ; in various Teut. tongues.]

**Holm-oak**, hōlm'- or hōm'-ōk, *n.* the ilex or evergreen oak, so called from some resemblance to the holly. [*Holm-* is a corr. of *holin*, the M. E. form of *holly*, which see.]

**Holocaust**, hol'ō-kawst, *n.* a *burnt* sacrifice, in which the *whole* of the victim was consumed. [L.—Gr. *holokauston—holos*, whole, and *kaustos*, burnt.]

**Holograph**, hol'ō-graf, *n.* a document *wholly written* by the person from whom it proceeds.—*adj.* **Holograph'ic**. [Gr.—*holos*, whole, and *graphō*. to write.]

**Holometer**, hol-om'et-ėr, *n.* an instrument for taking *all* kinds of *measures*. [Fr. *holomètre*—Gr. *holos*, whole, and *metron*, measure.]

**Holpen**, hōlp'n. old *pa.p.* of **Help**.

**Holster**, hōl'stėr, *n.* the leathern case carried by a horseman at the forepart of the saddle for *covering* a pistol.—*adj.* **Hol'stered**. [Acc. to Skeat, from Dut. *holster*, a pistol-case—*hullen*, to cover, which is cog. with A.S. *helan*, to cover.]

**Holt**, hōlt, *n.* a *wood* or woody hill : a hole, or other place of security, esp a deep hole in a river, where there is protection for fish. [A.S. *holt*, a wood ; Ice. *holt*, a copse, Ger. *holz*.]

**Holus-bolus**, hōl'us-bō'lus, *n.* *adv.* all at a gulp : altogether. [A vulgarism, formed from *whole*, and *bolus*, a pill.]

**Holy**, hō'li, *adj.* perfect in a moral sense : pure in heart : religious : set apart to a sacred use.—*adv.* **Ho'lily**. [A.S. *halig*, lit. whole, perfect ; healthy—*hal*, sound, whole ; conn. with **Hail**, **Heal**, **Whole**.]

**Holy-day**, hō'li-dā, *n.* a *holy day* : a religious festival : a day for the commemoration of some event.

**Holy Ghost**, hō'li gōst, **Holy Spirit**, hō'li spir'it, *n.* the third person of the Trinity. [**Holy** and A.S. *gást*. See **Ghost**.]

**Holy-office**, hō'li-of'is, *n.* the *holy tribunal*: the Inquisition. [**Holy** and **Office**.]

**Holy One**, hō'li wun, *n.* the *one* who is *holy*, by way of emphasis : God : Christ : one separated to the service of God.

**Holy orders**, hō'li or'dėrs, *n.* ordination to the rank of minister in holy things : the Christian ministry. [**Holy** and **Orders**.]

**Holy-rood**, hō'li-rōōd, *n.* the *holy cross*, in R. Cath. churches, over the entrance to the chancel. [**Holy** and **Rood**.]

**Holy Spirit**. See **Holy Ghost**.

**Holystone**, hō'li-stōn, *n.* a *stone* used by seamen for cleaning the decks.—*v.t.* to scrub with a holystone.

**Holy-Thursday**, hō'li-thurz'dā, *n.* the day on which the ascension of our Saviour is commemorated, ten days before Whitsuntide.

**Holy-water**, hō'li-waw'tėr, *n.*, *water consecrated* by the priest for sprinkling persons and things.

**Holy-week**, hō'li-wēk, *n.* the *week* before Easter, kept *holy* to commemorate our Lord's passion.

**Holy-writ**, hō'li-rit, *n.* the *holy writings*: the Scriptures.

**Homage**, hom'āj, *n.* the submission and service which a tenant promised to his feudal superior, in these words, *homo vester devenio*, I become your *man* ; the act of fealty : respect paid by external action : reverence directed to the Supreme Being : devout affection. [Fr. *hommage* —Low L. *homaticum*—L. *homo*, a man.]

**Home**, hōm, *n.* one's *house* or country : place of constant residence : the seat, as of war.—*adj.* pertaining to one's dwelling or country : domestic : close : severe.—*adv.* to one's habitation or country : close : closely : to the point.—*adj.* **Home'less**.—*n.* **Home'lessness**. [A.S. *ham* ; Dut. and Ger. *heim*, Goth. *haims* ; from a root *ki*, to rest, which appears also in Gr. *keimai*, to lie, *kōmē*, a village, L. *civis*, a citizen, E. *hive*.]

**Home-bred**, hōm'-bred, *adj.* bred at *home* : native : domestic : plain : unpolished.

**Home-farm**, hōm'-färm, *n.* the *farm* near the *home* or mansion of a gentleman.

**Home-felt**, hōm'-felt, *adj.*, *felt* in one's own *breast* : inward : private.

**Homely**, hōm'li, *adj.* pertaining to *home* : familiar : plain : rude.—*n.* **Home'liness**.—*adv.* **Home'-** lily. [the south coast of England

**Homelyn**, hom'el-in, *n.* a species of ray, found on

**Home-made**, hōm'-mād, *adj.*, *made* at *home* : made in one's own country : plain.

**Homeopathic**, hō-me-o-path'ik, *adj.* of or per-

fāte, fär ; mē, hėr ; mīne ; mōte : mūte : mōōn ; *then*.

taining to *homeopathy.—adv.* **Homeopath'-**
**ically.** [lieves in or practises *homeopathy.*
**Homeopathist,** hō-me-op'a-thist, *n.* one who be-
**Homeopathy,** hō-me-op'a-thi, *n.* the system of
curing diseases by small quantities of those
drugs which excite *symptoms similar* to those
of the disease. [Lit. *similar feeling* or affection, from Gr. *homoiopatheia—homoios,* like,
*pathos,* feeling.]
**Homer,** hō'mėr, *n.* a Hebrew measure containing
as a liquid measure about 2 barrels, as a dry
measure 8 bushels. [Heb. *chomer,* a heap—
*chamar,* to swell up.]
**Homeric,** hō-mer'ik, *adj.* pertaining to *Homer,*
the great poet of Greece : pertaining to or resembling the poetry of Homer.
**Home-Rule,** hōm'-rōōl, *n.* (*in Ireland*) a form of
home government claimed by the league so
called, the chief feature of it being a separate
parliament for the management of internal
affairs.
**Homesick,** hōm'sik, *adj.,* *sick* or grieved at separation from *home.—n.* **Home'-sick'ness.**
**Homespun,** hōm'spun, *adj.,* *spun* or wrought at
*home :* not made in foreign countries : plain :
inelegant.—*n.* cloth made at home.
**Homestall,** hōm'stawl, **Homestead,** hōm'sted, *n.*
the *place* of a mansion-house : the inclosures
immediately connected with it : original station.
[**Home** and **Stall** and **Stead.**]
**Homestead.** See under **Homestall.**
**Homeward,** hōm'ward, *adv.,* *toward home :*
toward one's habitation or country.—*adj.* in the
direction of home. [**Home,** and *ward,* sig.
direction.]
**Homeward-bound,** hōm'ward-bownd, *adj.,* *bound
homeward* or to one's native land. [See **Bound,**
*adj.*]
**Homewards,** hōm'wardz, *adv.,* *toward home.*
**Homicidal,** hom'i-sīd-al, *adj.* pertaining to homicide : murderous : bloody.
**Homicide,** hom'i-sīd, *n.,* *manslaughter* : one who
kills another. [Fr.—L. *homicidium—homo,* a
man, and *cædo,* to kill.]
**Homiletics,** hom-i-let'iks, *n.sing.* the science
which treats of *homilies,* and the best mode of
preparing and delivering them.—*adjs.* **Homilet'ic,**
**Homilet'ical.** [gregation.
**Homilist,** hom'i-list, *n.* one who preaches to a con-
**Homily,** hom'i-li, *n.* a plain sermon preached to a
mixed assembly : a serious discourse. [Gr.
*homilia,* an assembly, a sermon—*homōs,* the
same, cog. with E. **Same,** and *ilē,* a crowd.]
**Hominy,** hom'i-ni, *n.* maize hulled, or hulled and
crushed, boiled with water. [American Indian,
*auhuminea,* parched corn.]
**Hommock,** hom'uk, *n.* a hillock or small conical
eminence. [A dim. of **Hump.**]
**Homocentric,** hō-mo-sen'trik, *adj.* having the
*same centre.* [Fr. *homocentrique—*Gr. *homo-
kentros—homos,* the same, and *kentron,* centre.]
**Homocercal,** hō-mo-sėr'kal, *adj.* having the upper
fork of the *tail similar to* the lower one, as the
herring. [Gr. *homos,* the same, *kerkos,* tail.]
**Homœopathy,** &c. See **Homeopathy.**
**Homogeneal,** hō-mo-jē'ni-al, **Homogeneous,** hō-
mo-jē'ni-us, *adj.* of the *same kind* or nature :
having the constituent elements all similar.—*ns.*
**Homoge'neousness, Homogene'ity.** [Gr. *homo-
genēs—homos,* one, same, and *genos,* kind.]
**Homologate,** hō-mol'o-gāt, *v.t.* to *say* the *same :*
to agree : to approve : to allow.—*n.* **Homologa'-**
**tion.** [Low L. *homologo, homologatum—*Gr.
*homologeō—homos,* the same, and *legō,* to say.]

**Homologous,** hō-mol'o-gus, *adj.* agreeing : corresponding in relative position, proportion, value,
or structure. [Gr. *homologos—homos,* the same,
and *logos—legō,* to say.]
**Homologue,** hom'o-log, *n.* that which is homologous to something else, as the same organ in
different animals under its various forms and
functions.
**Homology,** hō-mol'o-ji, *n.* the quality of being
*homologous ;* affinity of structure, and not of
form or use.—*adj.* **Homolog'ical.**
**Homonym,** hom'o-nim, *n.* a word having the same
sound as another, but a different meaning. [Fr.
*homonyme—*Gr. *homōnymos—homos,* the same,
and *onoma,* name.]
**Homonymous,** hō-mon'i-mus, *adj.* having the
*same name :* having different significations :
ambiguous : equivocal.—*adv.* **Homon'ymously.**
**Homonymy,** hō-mon'i-mi, *n.* sameness of *name,*
with difference of meaning : ambiguity : equivocation. [Fr. *homonymie—*Gr. *homōnymia.*]
**Homophone,** hom'o-fōn, *n.* a letter or character
having the *same sound* as another. [Gr. *homos,*
the same, and *phōnē,* sound.]
**Homophonous,** hō-mof'o-nus, *adj.* having the *same
sound.—n.* **Homoph'ony.**
**Homoptera,** hom-op'tėr-a, *n.* an order of insects
having two pair of *wings uniform* throughout.
—*adj.* **Homop'terous.** [Gr. *homos,* the same,
uniform, and *pteron,* a wing.]
**Homotype,** hom'o-tīp, *n.* that which has the *same*
fundamental *type* of structure with something
else. [Gr. *homos,* the same, and *typos,* type.]
**Hone,** hōn, *n.* a stone of a fine grit for *sharpening*
instruments.—*v.t.* to sharpen as on a hone.
[A.S. *han* ; Ice. *hein* ; allied to Gr. *kōnos,* a cone.
Sans. *çana,* a whetstone ; from a root *ka,* to
sharpen. See **Cone.**]
**Honest,** on'est, *adj.* full of *honour :* just : the opp.
of thievish, free from fraud : frank : chaste :
(*B.*) also, honourable.—*adv.* **Hon'estly.** [L.
*honestus—honor.*]
**Honesty,** on'es-ti, *n.* the state of being honest :
integrity : candour : a small flowering plant so
called from its *transparent* seed-pouch : (*B.*)
becoming deportment.
**Honey,** hun'i, *n.* a sweet, thick fluid collected by
bees from the flowers of plants : anything sweet
like honey.—*v.t.* to sweeten : to make agreeable :—*pr.p.* hon'eying ; *pa.p.* hon'eyed (-'id).
[A.S. *hunig* ; Ger. *honig,* Ice. *hunang.*]
**Honeybear,** hun'i-bār, *n.* a South American carnivorous mammal about the size of a cat, with
a long protrusive tongue, which he uses to rob
the nests of wild bees.
**Honey-buzzard,** hun'i-buz'ard, *n.* a genus of
*buzzards* or falcons, so called from their feeding
on *bees,* wasps, &c.
**Honeycomb,** hun'i-kōm, *n.* a *comb* or mass of
waxy cells formed by bees, in which they store
their *honey :* anything like a honeycomb.—*adj.*
**Hon'eycombed** (-kōmd), formed like a honeycomb. [**Honey,** and **Comb,** a hollow cell.]
**Honeydew,** hun'i-dū, *n.* a sugary secretion from
the leaves of plants in hot weather : a fine sort
of tobacco moistened with molasses.
**Honeyed, Honied,** hun'id, *adj.* covered with
*honey :* sweet.
**Honeymoon,** hun'i-mōōn, **Hon'eymonth,** -munth,
*n.* the *honey* or sweet *moon* or *month,* the first
month after marriage.
**Honey-mouthed,** hun'i-mowth̄d, *adj.* having a
*honeyed mouth* or speech : soft or smooth in
speech.

**Honeysuckle**, hun′i-suk-l, *n.* a climbing shrub with beautiful cream-coloured flowers, so named because *honey* is readily *sucked* from the flower. [A.S. *hunig-sucle*.]

**Honey-tongued**, hun′i-tungd, *adj.* having a *honeyed tongue* or speech : soft in speech.

**Honied.** Same as **Honeyed.**

**Honorarium**, hon-ur-ā′ri-um, *n.* a voluntary fee paid to a professional man for his services. [L. *honorarium* (*donum*), honorary (gift.]

**Honorary**, on′ur-ar-i, *adj.*, *conferring honour :* holding a title or office without performing services or receiving a reward.—*n.* a fee. [L. *honorarius*—*honor*.]

**Honour**, on′ur, *n.* the *esteem* due or paid to worth : respect : high estimation : veneration, said of God : that which rightfully attracts esteem : exalted rank : distinction : excellence of character : nobleness of mind : any special virtue much esteemed : any mark of esteem : a title of respect :—*pl.* privileges of rank or birth : civilities paid : the four highest cards in card-playing : academic prizes or distinctions.—*adj.* **Hon′ourless.** [L. *honor*.]

**Honour**, on′ur, *v.t.* to hold in high *esteem :* to respect : to adore : to exalt : to accept and pay when due.—*adj.* **Hon′oured.**

**Honourable**, on′ur-a-bl, *adj.* worthy of honour : illustrious : actuated by principles of honour : conferring honour : becoming men of exalted station : a title of distinction.—*adv.* **Hon′ourably.**

**Honourableness**, on′ur-a-bl-nes, *n.* eminence : conformity to the principles of honour : fairness.

**Hood**, hood, *n.* a covering for the head : anything resembling a hood : an ornamental fold at the back of an academic gown.—*v.t.* to cover with a hood : to blind.—*adj.* **Hood′ed.** [A.S. *hod*; Dut. *hoed*, Ger. *hut*, conn. with **Heed.**]

**Hoodwink**, hood′wingk, *v.t.* (*lit.*) to make one *wink* by covering the eyes with a *hood :* to blindfold : to deceive. [**Hood** and **Wink**.]

**Hoof**, hoof, *n.* the horny substance on the feet of certain animals, as horses, &c. : a hoofed animal :—*pl.* **Hoofs** or **Hooves.**—*adj.* **Hoofed′.** [A.S. *hof*; Ger. *huf*, Sans. *çapha*.]

**Hook**, hook, *n.* a piece of metal bent into a curve, so as to catch or hold anything : a snare : an instrument for cutting grain. [A.S. *hoc*; Dut. *haak*, Ger. *haken*, allied to Gr. *kyklos*, a circle.]

**Hook**, hook, *v.t.* to catch or hold with a hook : to draw as with a hook : to insnare.—*v.i.* to bend : to be curved.—*adj.* **Hooked′.—By hook or by crook**, one way or the other.

**Hookah**, hoō′ka, *n.* a pipe in which the smoke is made to pass through water. [Ar. *huqqa*.]

**Hook-nosed**, hook′-nōzd, *adj.* having a hooked or curved nose.

**Hooky**, hook′i, *adj.* full of or pertaining to *hooks.*

**Hoop**, hoōp, *n.* a pliant strip of wood or metal formed into a *ring* or band, for holding toge her the staves of casks, &c. : something resembling a hoop : a ring :—*pl.* elastic materials used to expand the skirt of a lady's dress.—*v.t.* to bind with hoops : to encircle. [Akin to Dut. *hoep*; cf. Ice. *hop*, a bay, from its round form.]

**Hoop**, hoōp, *v.i.* to call out. Same as **Whoop.**

**Hooper**, hoōp′ér, *n.* one who *hoops* casks : a cooper.

**Hooping-cough.** See under **Whoop.**

**Hoopoe**, hoōp′ō **Hoopoo**, hoōp′oō, *n.* a bird with a large crest. [L. *upupa*, Gr. *epops*—imitative.]

**Hoot**, hoōt, *v.i.* to shout in contempt : to cry like an owl.—*v.t.* to drive with cries of contempt. —*n.* a scornful cry. [An imitative word ; cf.

Scand. *hut*, begone ; Fr. *huer*, to call ; W. *hwt*, off with it.]

**Hop**, hop, *v.i.* to leap on one leg : to spring : to walk lame : to limp :—*pr.p.* hopp′ing ; *pa.t.* and *pa.p.* hopped′.—*n.* a leap on one leg : a jump : a spring. [A.S. *hoppian*, to dance ; Ger. *hüpfen.*]

**Hop**, hop, *n.* a plant with a long twining stalk, the bitter cones of which are much used in brewing and in medicine.—*v.t.* to mix with hops. - *v.i.* to gather hops :—*pr.p.* hopp′ing ; *pa.t.* and *pa.p.* hopped′. [Dut. *hop*; Ger. *hopfen.*]

**Hopbind**, hop′bīnd (corr. into *hopbine*), *n.* the stalk of the hop. [-*bind* expresses the clinging of the stalk to its support ; cf. **Bindweed.**]

**Hope**, hōp, *v.i.* to cherish a desire of good with expectation of obtaining it : to place confidence (in).—*v.t.* to desire with expectation or with belief in the prospect of obtaining. [A.S. *hopian*; Dut. *h*<sub></sub>*pen*, Ger. *hoffen*, perhaps akin to L. *cup-io*, to desire.]

**Hope**, hōp, *n.* a desire of some good, with expectation of obtaining it : confidence : anticipation : he who or that which furnishes ground of expectation : that which is hoped for. [A.S. *hopa*; Ger. *hoff-nung*.]

**Hope**, hōp, *n.* troop, only in the phrase *forlorn-hope*. [Dut. *verloren hoop*—*hoop*, a band of men, E. **Heap.** See also **Forlorn.**]

**Hopeful**, hōp′fool, *adj.* full of hope : having qualities which excite hope : promising good or success.—*adv.* **Hope′fully.**—*n.* **Hope′fulness**

**Hopeless**, hōp′les, *adj.* without hope : giving no ground to expect good or success : desperate.—*adv.* **Hope′lessly.**—*n.* **Hope′lessness.**

**Hopper**, hop′ér, *n.* one who *hops :* a wooden trough through which grain passes into a mill, so called from its *hopping* or shaking motion : a vessel in which seedcorn is carried for sowing.

**Hopple**, hop′l, *v.t.* to tie the feet close together to prevent *hopping* or running.—*n.* chiefly in *pl.*, a fetter for horses, &c. when left to graze. [Freq. of **Hop.**]

**Hopscotch**, hop′skoch, *n.* a game in which children *hop* over lines *scotched* or traced on the ground.

**Hopvine**, hop′vīn, *n.* the stalk or stem of the hop. [See **Vine**, and cf. **Hopbind.**]

**Horal**, hōr′al, *adj.* relating to an *hour.*

**Horary**, hōr′ar-i, *adj.* pertaining to an *hour :* noting the hours : hourly : continuing an hour.

**Horde**, hōrd, *n.* a migratory or wandering tribe or clan. [Fr.—Turk. *ordû*, camp—Pers. *ôrdû*, court, camp, horde of Tatars.]

**Horehound.** See **Hoarhound.**

**Horizon**, ho-rī′zun, *n.* the circle *bounding* the view where the earth and sky appear to meet. [Fr. —L.—Gr. *horizōn* (*kyklos*), bounding (circle), *horizō*, to bound—*horos*, a limit.]

**Horizontal**, hor-i-zon′tal, *adj.* pertaining to the *horizon :* parallel to the horizon : level : near the horizon.—*adv.* **Horizon′tally.**—*n.* **Horizontal′ity.**

**Horn**, horn, *n.* the hard substance projecting from the heads of certain animals, as oxen, &c. : something made of or like a horn : a symbol of strength : (*mus.*) a wind-instrument consisting of a coiled brass tube.—*v.t.* to furnish with horns.—*adj.* **Horned′.** [A.S. *horn :* Scand. and Ger. *horn*, Celt. *corn*, L. *cornu*, Gr. *keras*.]

**Hornbill**, horn′bil, *n.* a bird about the size of the turkey, having a *horny* excrescence on its *bill.*

**Hornblende**, horn′blend, *n.* a mineral of various colours, found in granite and other igneous rocks that contain quartz. [Ger., from *horn*, horn, from the shape of its crystals, and -*blende*— *blenden*, to dazzle, from its glittering appearance.]

**Hornbook**, horn'book, *n.* a first *book* for children, which formerly consisted of a single leaf set in a frame, with a thin plate of transparent *horn* in front to preserve it.

**Horned-owl.** See **Hornowl**.

**Hornet**, horn'et, *n.* a species of wasp, so called from its antennæ or *horns*. [A.S. *hyrnet*, dim. of *horn*.]

**Hornfoot**, horn'foot, *adj.* having a hoof or *horn* on the *foot*.

**Horning**, horn'ing, *n.* appearance of the moon when in its crescent form.

**Hornowl**, horn'owl, **Horned-owl**, hornd'-owl, *n.* a species of *owl*, so called from two tufts of feathers on its head, like *horns*.

**Hornpipe**, horn'pīp, *n.* a Welsh musical instrument, consisting of a wooden *pipe*, with a *horn* at each end : a lively air : a lively dance.

**Hornstone**, horn'stōn, *n.* a *stone* much like flint, but more brittle. [**Horn** and **Stone**.]

**Hornwork**, horn'wurk, *n.* ( *fort.*) an out*work* having angular points or *horns*, and composed of two demi-bastions joined by a curtain.

**Horny**, horn'i, *adj.* like horn : hard : callous.

**Horography**, hor-og'ra-fi, *n.* the art of constructing dials or instruments for *indicating* the *hours*. [Gr. *hōra*, an hour, and *graphō*, to describe.]

**Horologe**, hor'o-loj, *n.* any instrument for *telling* the *hours*. [O. Fr. *horologe* (Fr. *horloge*)— L. *horologium*—Gr. *hōrologion*—*hōra*, an hour, and *legō*, to tell.]

**Horology**, hor-ol'o-ji, *n.* the science which treats of the construction of machines for *telling* the *hours.—adj.* **Horolog'ical**.

**Horometry**, hor-om'et-ri, *n.* the art or practice of *measuring time.—adj.* **Horomet'rical**. [Gr. *hōra*, an hour, and *metron*, a measure.]

**Horoscope**, hor'o-skōp, *n.* an *observation* of the heavens at the *hour* of a person's birth, by which the astrologer predicted the events of his life : a representation of the heavens for this purpose. [Fr.—L.—Gr. *hōroskopos*—*hōra*, an hour, and *skopeō*, to observe.]

**Horoscopy**, hor-os'kop-i, *n.* the art of predicting the events of a person's life from his *horoscope* : aspect of the stars at the time of birth.—*adj.* **Horoscop'ic.** *n.* **Horos'copist**, an astrologer.

**Horrent**, hor'ent, *adj.* standing on end, as bristles. [L. *horrens, -entis*, pr.p. of *horreo*, to bristle.]

**Horrible**, hor'i-bl, *adj.* causing or tending to cause *horror* : dreadful : awful : terrific.—*adv.* **Horr'ibly.**—*n.* **Horr'ibleness.** [L. *horribilis*— *horreo*.]

**Horrid**, hor'id, *adj.* fitted to produce horror : shocking offensive—*adv.* **Horr'idly.**—*n.* **Horr'idness.** [L. *horridus*, orig. *bristling*—*horreo*. See **Horror**.]

**Horrific**, hor-rif'ik, *adj.* exciting *horror* : frightful.

**Horrify**, hor'i-fī *v.t.* to strike with *horror* :—*pa.p.* horr'ified. [L. *horror*, and *facio*, to make.]

**Horror**, hor'ur, *n.* a shuddering : excessive fear : that which excites horror. [Lit. ' a bristling,' as of hair, L. —*horreo*, to bristle, to shudder.]

**Horse**, hors, *n.* a well-known quadruped · (*collectively*) cavalry : that by which something is supported.—*v.t.* to mount on a horse : to provide with a horse : to sit astride : to carry on the back.—*v.i.* to get on horseback. [A.S. *hors*, Ice. *hross*, O. Ger. *hros* (Ger. *ross*), perh. akin to Sans. *hresh*, to neigh, but more prob. conn. with L. *curro, cursus*, to run ; cf. **Courser**.]

**Horseblock**, hors'blok, *n.* a *block* or stage **by** which to mount or dismount from a *horse*.

**Horseboat**, hors'bōt, *n.* a boat for carrying horses.

**Horse-breaker**, hors'-brāk'ėr, **Horse-tamer**, hors'-tām'ėr, *n.* one whose business is to *break* or tame *horses*, or to teach them to draw or carry.

**Horse-chestnut**, hors'-ches'nut, *n.* a large variety of chestnut, prob. so called from its coarseness contrasted with the edible chestnut : the tree that produces it. [See **Chestnut.**]

**Horsefly**, hors'flī, *n.* a large *fly* that stings horses.

**Horse-guards**, hors'-gärdz, *n.* horse-soldiers employed as guards : the 3d heavy cavalry regiment of the British army, forming part of the household troops : ( *formerly*) the official residence in London of the commander-in-chief of the British army.

**Horsehoe**, hors'hō, **Horserake**, hors'rāk, &c. *n.* a *hoe, rake*, &c. drawn by *horses*.

**Horselaugh**, hors'läf, *n.* a harsh, boisterous laugh. [**Hoarse** and **Laugh.**]

**Horseleech**, hors'lēch, *n.* a large species of *leech*, so named from its fastening on *horses* when wading in the water. [between two *horses*.]

**Horse-litter**, hors'-lit'ėr, *n.* a *litter* or bed borne

**Horseman**, hors'man, *n.* a rider on horseback : a mounted soldier.

**Horsemanship**, hors'man-ship, *n.* the art of riding, and of training and managing horses.

**Horse-power**, hors'-pow'ėr, *n.* the *power* a *horse* can exert, or its equivalent = that required to raise 33,000 lbs. avoirdupois one foot per minute : a standard for estimating the power of steam-engines.

**Horserace**, hors'rās, *n.* a race by horses.

**Horseracing**, hors'rās-ing, *n.* the practice of racing or running horses in matches.

**Horse-radish**, hors'-rad'ish, *n.* a plant with a pungent *root*, used in medicine and as a salad. [So named from a notion of its being wholesome for *horses*.]

**Horseshoe**, hors'shoō, *n.* a shoe for horses, consisting of a curved piece of iron : anything shaped like a horseshoe.

**Horsetail**, hors'tāl, *n.* a genus of leafless plants with hollow rush-like stems, so called from their likeness to a *horse's tail*.

**Horse-trainer**, hors'-trān'ėr, *n.* one who *trains* horses for racing, &c.

**Horsewhip**, hors'hwip, *n.* a whip for driving horses.—*v.t.* to strike with a horsewhip : to lash.

**Hortative**, hort'a-tiv, **Hortatory**, hort'a-tor-i, *adj.*, *inciting* : encouraging : giving advice. [L. *hortor, hortatus*, to incite.]

**Horticultural**, hor-ti-kul'tūr-al, *adj.* pertaining to the *culture* of *gardens*.

**Horticulture**, hor'ti-kul-tūr, *n.* the art of *cultivating gardens*. [L. *hortus*, a garden, and **Culture.**]

**Horticulturist**, hor-ti-kul'tūr-ist, *n.* one versed in the art of *cultivating gardens*.

**Hosanna**, hō-zan'a, *n* an exclamation of praise to God, or a prayer for blessings. [Lit. ' save, I pray thee,' Gr. *hōsanna*—Heb. *hoshiahnna*— *yasha, hoshia*, to save, and *na*, I pray thee.]

**Hose**, hōz, *n.* a covering for the legs or feet : stockings : socks : a flexible pipe for conveying fluids, so called from its shape :—*pl.* **Hose** ; (*B.*) **Hos'en.** [A.S. *hosa* ; Dut. *hoos*, Ger. *hose*.]

**Hosier**, hō'zhi-ėr, *n.* one who deals in *hose*, or stockings and socks, &c.

**Hosiery**, hō'zhi-ėr-i, *n.*, *hose* in general.

**Hospice**, hos′pēs, *n.* an Alpine convent where travellers are treated as *guests*. [Fr., from L. *hospitium—hospes*, a stranger who is treated as a guest, one who treats another as his guest.]

**Hospitable**, hos′pit-abl, *adj.* pertaining to a *host* or *guest :* entertaining strangers and guests kindly and without reward : shewing kindness.—*adv.* **Hos′pitably.**—*n.* **Hos′pitableness.**

**Hospital**, hos′pit-al or os′-, *n.* a building for the reception and treatment of the old, sick, &c., or for the support and education of the young. [Orig. a place for the entertainment of *strangers* or *guests*, from O. Fr. *hospital*—Low L. *hospitale—hospes*, a guest. See **Hospice**.]

**Hospitality**, hos-pi-tal′it-i, *n.* the practice of one who is *hospitable :* friendly welcome and entertainment of guests.

**Hospitaller**, hos′pit-al-ėr, *n.* one of a charitable brotherhood for the care of the sick in hospitals : one of an order of knights, commonly called Knights of St John, who during the Crusades built a hospital for pilgrims at Jerusalem.

**Hospodar**, hos′po-där, *n.* ( *formerly* ) the title of the princes of Moldavia and Wallachia. [Slav.]

**Host**, hōst, *n.* one who entertains a *stranger* or *guest* at his house without reward : an innkeeper.—*fem.* **Host′ess.** [O. Fr. *hoste*—L. *hospes*.]

**Host**, hōst, *n.* an army : a large multitude. [Orig. an *enemy ;* O. Fr. *host*—L. *hostis*, an enemy.]

**Host**, hōst, *n.* in the R. Cath. Church, the consecrated bread of the Eucharist, in which Christ is *offered*. [L. *hostia*, a victim—*hostio*, to strike.]

**Hostage**, hos′tāj, *n.* one remaining with the enemy as a pledge for the fulfilment of the conditions of a treaty. [O. Fr. *hostage*, Fr. *ôtage* —Low L. *obsidaticus—obses, obsidis*, a hostage.]

**Hostel**, hos′tel, **Hostelry**, hos′tel-ri, *n.* an inn. [O. Fr. *hostel, hostellerie.* See **Hotel**.]

**Hostile**, hos′til, *adj.* belonging to an *enemy :* shewing enmity : warlike : adverse.—*adv.* **Hos′tilely.** [L. *hostilis—hostis.*]

**Hostility**, hos-til′it-i, *n.* enmity :—*pl.* **Hostil′ities,** acts of warfare.

**Hostler**, os′lėr, *n.* he who has the care of horses at an inn. [Orig. one who kept a house for strangers, O. Fr. *hostelier—hostel—*L. *hospes.*]

**Hot**, hot, *adj.* having heat : very warm : fiery : pungent : animated : ardent in temper : violent : passionate : lustful.—*adv.* **Hot′ly.**—*n.* **Hot′ness.** [A.S. *hat ;* Ger. *heiss*, Sw. *het.* See **Heat**.]

**Hotbed**, hot′bed, *n.* a glass-covered *bed heated* for bringing forward plants rapidly : any place favourable to rapid growth.

**Hotblast**, hot′blast, *n.* a blast of *heated air* blown into a furnace to raise the heat.

**Hot-blooded**, hot′-blud′ed, *adj.* having hot blood : high-spirited : irritable.

**Hotchpotch**, hoch′poch, **Hotchpot**, hoch′pot, **Hodgepodge**, hoj′poj, *n.* a confused mass of ingredients *shaken* or mixed together in the same *pot.* [Fr. *hochepot—hocher*, to shake, and *pot*, a pot—O. Dut. *hutsen*, to shake, and Dut. *pot*, a pot. See **Hustle** and **Pot**.]

**Hotel**, hō-tel′, *n.* a superior house for the accommodation of *strangers :* an inn : in France also a palace. [M. E. *hostel*—O. Fr. *hostel* (Fr. *hôtel*)—L. *hospitalia*, guest-chambers—*hospes.* See **Hospital**.]

**Hot-headed**, hot′-hed′ed, *adj.* hot in the head : having warm passions : violent : impetuous.

**Hothouse**, hot′hows, *n.* a *house* kept *hot* for the rearing of tender plants.

**Hotpress**, hot′pres, *v.t.* to *press* paper, &c. between *hot* plates to produce a glossy surface.

**Hotspur**, hot′spur, *n.* one pressing his steed with *spurs* as in *hot* haste : a violent, rash man.

**Hottentot**, hot′n-tot, *n.* a native of the Cape of Good Hope : a brutish individual. [Dut., because the language of the S. Africans seemed to the first Dutch settlers to sound like a repetition of the syllables *hot* and *tot ;* Dut. *en* = and.]

**Houdah.** See **Howdah**.

**Hough**, hok, **Hock**, hok, *n.* the joint on the hind-leg of a quadruped, between the knee and fetlock, corresponding to the ankle-joint in man : in man, the back part of the knee-joint : the ham.—*v.t.* to hamstring :—*pr.p.* hough′ing ; *pa.p.* houghed (hokt′). [A.S. *hoh*, the heel.]

**Hound**, hownd, *n.* a dog used in hunting.—*v.t.* to set on in chase : to hunt : to urge on. [Orig. the *dog* generally, from A.S. *hund :* akin to Gr. *kyōn, kynos,* L. *canis,* Sans. *çvan.*]

**Houndfish.** Same as **Dogfish**.

**Hound's-tongue**, howndz′-tung, *n.* a plant, so called from the shape of its leaves. [A.S. *hundestunge.*]

**Hour**, owr, *n.* 60 min. or the 24th part of a day : the time indicated by a clock, &c. : a time or occasion :—*pl.* (*myth.*) the goddesses of the seasons and the *hours :* in the R. Cath. Church, prayers to be said at certain *hours*. [Orig. a definite space of time fixed by natural laws ; O. Fr. *hore,* Fr. *heure*—L. *hora*—Gr. *hōra.* See **Year**.]

**Hourglass**, owr′glas, *n.* an instrument for measuring the *hours* by the running of sand from one *glass* vessel into another.

**Houri**, how′ri, *n.* a nymph of the Mohammedan paradise. [Pers. *huri—hura,* a black-eyed girl.]

**Hourly**, owr′li, *adj.* happening or done every *hour :* frequent.—*adv.* every hour : frequently.

**Hourplate**, owr′plāt, *n.* the *plate* of a timepiece on which the *hours* are marked : the dial.

**House**, hows, *n.* a building for dwelling in : a dwelling-place : an inn : household affairs : a family : kindred : a trading establishment : one of the estates of the legislature : (*astrol.*) the twelfth part of the heavens :—*pl.* **Houses** (howz′ez). [A.S. *hus ;* Goth. *hus,* Ger. *haus.*]

**House**, howz, *v.t.* to protect by covering : to shelter : to store.—*v.i.* to take shelter : to reside.

**Housebreaker**, hows′brāk-ėr, *n.* one who *breaks* open and enters a *house* for the purpose of stealing.—*n.* **House′breaking.**

**Household**, hows′hōld, *n.* those who are held together in the same *house*, and compose a family. —**The Household**, the royal domestic establishment.—*adj.* pertaining to the house and family. —**Household Troops**, six regiments whose peculiar duty is to attend the sovereign and defend the metropolis. [of a *house.*]

**Householder**, hows′hōld-ėr, *n.* the *holder* or tenant

**Housekeeper**, hows′kēp-ėr, *n.* a female servant who *keeps* or has the chief care of the *house.*

**Housekeeping**, hows′kēp-ing, *n.* the *keeping* or management of a *house* or of domestic affairs : hospitality.—*adj.* domestic.

**Houseless**, hows′les, *adj.* without a house or home : having no shelter.

**Housemaid**, hows′mād, *n.* a *maid* employed to keep a *house* clean, &c.

**House-steward**, hows′-stū′ard, *n.* a *steward* who manages the *household* affairs of a great family.

**House-surgeon**, hows′-sur′jun, *n.* the *surgeon* or medical officer in a hospital who resides in the *house.*

**House-warming**, hows'-wawrm'ing, *n.* an entertainment given when a family enters a new *house*, as if to *warm* it.

**Housewife**, hows'wif, *n.* the mistress of a *house*: a female domestic manager.—*adj.* **House'wifely**.

**Housewife**, huz'if, *n.* a small case for articles of female work, properly spelt **Hussif**, which see.

**Housewifery**, hows'wif-ri, *n.* business of a *housewife*.

**Housing**, howz'ing, *n.* an ornamental *covering* for a horse: a saddle-cloth:—*pl.* the trappings of a horse. [Fr. *housse*; prob. from O. Ger. *hulst*, a covering—*hullen*, to cover. Cf. **Holster**, **Husk**.]

**Hove**, *pa.t.* and *pa.p.* of **Heave**.

**Hovel**, huv'el, *n.* a small or mean *dwelling*: a shed.—*v.t.* to put in a hovel: to shelter:—*pa.p.* hov'elling; *pa.p.* hov'elled. [Dim. of A.S. *hof*, a dwelling.]

**Hover**, hov'er or huv'er, *v.i.* to remain aloft flapping the wings: to wait in suspense: to move about near. [Prob. from A.S. *hof*, and therefore lit. to *dwell*; O. Fris. *hovia*, to receive into one's house; cf. W. *hofian*, to hang over.]

**How**, how, *adv., in what* manner: to what extent: for what reason: by what means: from what cause: in what condition: (*New Test.*) sometimes = that. [A.S. *hu, hwu*, from the interrogative *wha*, who, as L. *qui*, how, from *quis*, who.] [withstanding: yet: however.

**Howbeit**, how-bē'it, *conj., be it how* it may: not-

**Howdah, Houdah**, how'da, *n.* a seat fixed on an elephant's back. [Ar. *hawdaj*.]

**However**, how-ev'er, *adv.* and *conj.* in *whatever* manner or degree: nevertheless: at all events. [**How, Ever**.]

**Howitzer**, how'its-ér, *n.* a short, light cannon, used for *throwing* shells. [Ger. *haubitze*, orig. *haufnitz*—Bohem. *haufnice*, a sling.]

**Howker**, how'kér, *n.* a Dutch vessel with two masts: a fishing-boat with one mast used on the Irish coast. [Dut. *hoeker*.]

**Howl**, howl, *v.i.* to yell or cry, as a wolf or dog: to utter a long, loud, whining sound: to wail: to roar.—*v.t.* to utter with outcry:—*pr.p.* howl'-ing; *pa.p.* howled'.—*n.* a loud, prolonged cry of distress: a mournful cry. [O. Fr. *huller*; from L. *ululare*, to shriek or howl—*ulula*, an owl; conn. with Gr. *hulaō*, Ger. *heulen*, E. *owl*.]

**Howlet**, how'let. Same as **Owlet**.

**Howsoever**, how-so-ev'ér, *adv.* in *what* way *soever*: although: however.

**Hoy**, hoi, *n.* a large one-decked boat, commonly rigged as a sloop. [Dut. *heu*, Flem. *hui*.]

**Hoy**, hoi, *int., ho!* stop! [From the sound.]

**Hub**, hub, *n.* the *projecting* nave of a wheel: a projection on a wheel for the insertion of a pin: the hilt of a weapon: a mark at which quoits, &c. are cast. [A form of **Hob**.]

**Hubble-bubble**, hub'l-bub'l, *n.* a kind of tobacco-pipe, used in the E. Indies, in which the smoke is drawn through water with a bubbling sound.

**Hubbub**, hub'ub, *n.* a confused sound of many voices: riot: uproar. [Either from the repetition of *hoop, whoop* (which see), or in imitation of the confused noise of numerous voices, like *mur-mur* in Latin. Cf. **Barbarian**.]

**Huckaback**, huk'a-bak, *n.* a coarse variety of table-linen, having raised figures on it. [Perh. because sold by hucksters with their goods on their back.]

**Huckle**, huk'l, *n.* a hunch: the hip. [Dim. of **Huck**, a Prov. E. form of **Hook**, from its bent or jointed appearance.]

**Huckle-backed**, huk'l-bakt, **Huck-shouldered**,

huk-shōl'dérd, *adj.* having the back or shoulders round like a hunch.

**Huckle-bone**, huk'l-bōn, *n.* the hipbone.

**Huckster**, huk'stér, *n.* a retailer of small wares, a hawker or peddler: a mean, trickish fellow.—*fem.* **Huck'stress**.—*v.i.* to deal in small articles. [Orig. and properly a fem. form of an O. Low Ger. root, of which *hawker* is the masculine. This root is found in Dut. *heuker*, a retailer, from O. Dut. *hucken*, to stoop or bow, and conn. with Ice. *huka*, to sit on one's hams (whence E. **Hug**); Ger. *hucke*, the bent back. See **Hawker**, **Hook**, **Huckle**.]

**Huddle**, hud'l, *v.t.* to put up things confusedly: to hurry in disorder: to crowd.—*v.t.* to throw or crowd together in confusion: to put on hastily.—*n.* a crowd: tumult: confusion. [M. E. *hodren*; perh. conn. with root of **Hide**, to conceal, and so orig. meaning to crowd together for concealment or shelter.]

**Hudibrastic**, hū-di-bras'tik, *adj.* similar in style to *Hudibras*, a satire by Butler, 1612-80; doggerel.

**Hue**, hū, *n.* appearance: colour: tint: dye.—*adj.* **Hue'less**. [A.S. *hiw, heow*; Goth. *hiwi*, Swed. *hy*, appearance, complexion.]

**Hue**, hū, *n.* a shouting.—**Hue and cry**, the old practice of pursuing felons with loud *hooting* and *crying*. [Fr. *huer*, of imitative origin; cf. W. *hwa*, to hoot.]

**Huff**, huf, *n.* sudden anger or arrogance: a fit of disappointment or anger: a boaster.—*v.t.* to swell: to bully: to remove a 'man' from the board for not capturing pieces open to him, as in draughts.—*v.i.* to swell: to bluster. [An imitative word, the idea of 'puffing' or 'blowing' being present in it.]

**Huffish**, huf'ish, *adj.* given to *huff*: insolent: arrogant.—*adv.* **Huff'ishly**.—*n.* **Huff'ishness**.

**Huffy**, huf'i, *adj.* given to *huff*: puffed up: petulant.—*n.* **Huff'iness**.

**Hug**, hug, *v.t.* to embrace closely and fondly: to congratulate (one's self): (*naut.*) to keep close to.—*v.i.* to crowd together:—*pr.p.* hugg'ing; *pa.p.* hugged'.—*n.* a close and fond embrace: a particular grip in wrestling. [Scand., orig. to squat or cower together, as in Ice. *huka*, to sit on one's hams. See **Huckster**.]

**Huge**, hūj, *adj.* (comp. **Hug'er**) superl. **Hug'est**) having great dimensions, especially *height*; enormous: monstrous: (*B.*) large in number.—*adv.* **Huge'ly**.—*n.* **Huge'ness**. [M. E. *huge*; formed by dropping *a* (supposed article) from O. Fr. *ahuge*, the root of which may prob. be found in Dut. *hoog*, Ger. *hoch*, E. **High**.]

**Hugger-mugger**, hug'ér-mug'ér, *n.* secrecy: confusion. [Perh. a rhyming extension of **Hug**.]

**Huguenot**, hū'ge-not or -nō, *n.* the name formerly given in France to an adherent of the Reformation. [15 false etymologies have been given of this name, which most authorities now regard as a dim. of Fr. *Hugues*, Hugh, the name of some one of the French Calvinists, and afterwards applied as a nickname to them all.]

**Hulk**, hulk, *n.* the body of a ship: an old ship unfit for service: anything unwieldy—often confounded in meaning with **Hull**, the body of a ship:—*pl.* **The Hulks**, old ships used as prisons. [Orig. a large merchant-ship, from Low L. *hulka*—Gr. *holkas*, a ship which is towed—*helkō*, to draw.]

**Hull**, hul, *n.* the *husk* or outer *covering* of anything.—*v.t.* to strip off the hull: to husk. [A.S. *hulu*, a husk, as of corn—*helan*, to cover; Ger. *hülle*, a covering, *hehlen*, to cover.]

**Hull**, hul, *n.* the frame or body of a ship.—*v.t.* to pierce the hull (as with a cannon-ball).—*v.i.* to float or drive on the water, as a mere hull. [Same word as above, perh. modified in meaning by confusion with Dut. *hol*, a ship's hold, or with **Hulk**.]

**Hully**, hul'i, *adj.* having *husks* or pods.

**Hum**, hum, *v.i.* to make a buzzing sound like bees: to utter a low, droning sound: to supply an interval in speaking by an audible sound.—*v.t.* to sing in a low tone :—*pr.p.* humm'ing ; *pa.p.* hummed'.—*n.* the noise of bees and some other insects : any low, dull noise.—*int.* a sound with a pause implying doubt. [An imitative word ; cf. Ger. *hummen, humsen* ; Dut. *hommelen*.]

**Human**, hū'man, *adj.* belonging or pertaining to *man* or *mankind* : having the qualities of a man.—*adv.* **Hu'manly**. [Fr.—L. *humanus*—*homo*, a human being.]

**Humane**, hū-mān', *adj.* having the feelings proper to *man*: kind: tender: merciful.—*adv.* **Humane'ly**.

**Humanise**, hū'man-īz, *v.t.* to render *human* or *humane* : to soften.—*v.i.* to become humane or civilised.

**Humanist**, hū'man-ist, *n.* a student of polite literature : at the Renascence, a student of Greek and Roman literature : a student of human nature. [L. (*literæ*) *humaniores*, polite (literature).]

**Humanitarian**, hū-man-i-tā'ri-an, *n.* one who denies Christ's divinity, and holds him to be a mere *man*.—*adj.* of or belonging to humanity, benevolent.

**Humanity**, hū-man'it-i, *n.* the nature peculiar to a *human* being : the kind feelings of man : benevolence : tenderness : mankind collectively : —*pl.* **Human'ities**. in Scotland, grammar, rhetoric, Latin, Greek, and poetry, so called from their *humanising* effects.—**Professor of Humanity**, in Scotch universities, the Professor of Latin. [Fr.—L. *humanitas*—*humanus*.]

**Humankind**, hū'man-kīnd, *n.* the *human* species.

**Humble**, hum'bl, um'bl, *adj.* low : meek : modest.—*v.t.* to bring down to the ground : to lower : to mortify : to degrade.—*n.* **Hum'bleness**.—*adv.* **Hum'bly**. [Lit. 'on the ground,' from Fr.—L. *humilis*, low—*humus*, the ground.]

**Humble-bee**, hum'bl-bē, *n.* the *humming-bee* : a genus of social bees which construct their hives under ground. [*Hum-b-le* is a freq. of **Hum**.]

**Humbug**, hum'bug, *n.* an imposition under fair pretences : one who imposes.—*v.t.* to deceive : to hoax :—*pr.p.* hum'bugging ; *pa.p.* hum'-bugged. [Orig. a false alarm, a bugbear, from **Hum** and **Bug**, a frightful object. Approbation in public places was formerly expressed by *humming*, which in slang E. came to be conn. with anything flattering, deceiving, false.]

**Humdrum**, hum'drum, *adj.* dull : droning : monotonous.—*n.* a stupid fellow. [Compound of **Hum** and **Drum**.]

**Humectant**, hū-mek'tant, *adj.* pertaining to remedies supposed to increase the *fluidity* of the blood. [L. *humectans*—*humeo*, to be moist.]

**Humective**, hū-mek'tiv, *adj.* having the power to *moisten*.

**Humeral**, hū'mėr-al, *adj.* belonging to the *shoulder* [Fr.—L. *humerus*, the shoulder.]

**Humerus**, hū'mėr-us, *n.* the arm from the shoulder to the elbow : the bone of the upper arm. [L. 'the shoulder.']

**Humhum**, hum'hum, *n.* a kind of plain, coarse cotton cloth used in E. Indies. [?]

**Humic**, hū'mik, *adj.* denoting an acid formed by the action of alkalies on *humus*.

**Humid**, hū'mid, *adj., moist*: damp : rather wet.—*n.* **Hu'midness**. [L. *humidus*—*humeo*, to be moist.] [degree of wetness.]

**Humidity**, hū-mid'i-ti, *n.* moisture : a moderate

**Humiliate**, hū-mil'i-āt, *v.t.* to make *humble* : to depress : to lower in condition. [L. *humilio, -ātum*.]

**Humiliation**, hū-mil-i-ā'shun, *n.* the act of *humiliating* : abasement : mortification.

**Humility**, hū-mil'i-ti, *n.* the state or quality of being *humble*: lowliness of mind : modesty. [Fr. *humilité*—L. *humilitas*.]

**Humming-bird**, hum'ing-bėrd, *n.* a tropical bird, of brilliant plumage and rapid flight, so called from the *humming* sound of its wings.

**Hummock**, hum'uk. Same as **Hommock**.

**Humoral**, ū'mur-al, *adj.* pertaining to or proceeding from the *humours*.

**Humoralism**, ū'mur-al-izm, *n.* the state of being *humoral*: the doctrine that diseases have their seat in the humours.—*n.* **Hu'moralist**, one who favours the doctrine of humoralism.

**Humorist**, ū'mur-ist, *n.* one whose conduct and conversation are regulated by *humour* or caprice: one who studies or portrays the humours of people.

**Humorless**, ū'mur-les, *adj.* without *humour*.

**Humorous**, ū'mur-us, *adj.* governed by *humour* : capricious : irregular : full of humour : exciting laughter.—*adv.* **Hu'morously**.—*n.* **Hu'morousness**.

**Humour**, ū'mur, *n.* the *moisture* or fluids of animal bodies : an animal fluid in an unhealthy state : state of mind (because once thought to depend on the humours of the body) : disposition : caprice : a mental quality which delights in ludicrous and mirthful ideas.—*v.t.* to go in with the humour of : to gratify by compliance. [O. Fr. *humor* (Fr. *humeur*)—L. *humor*—*humeo*, to be moist.]

**Hump**, hump, *n.* a lump or hunch upon the back. [Prob. a form of **Heap** ; a Low Ger. word, as in Dut. *homp*; cf. Gr. *kȳphos*, a hump, Sans. *kubja*, humpbacked ; allied to **Hunch**.]

**Humpback**, hump'bak, *n.* a *back* with a *hump* or hunch : a person with a humpback.—*adj.* **Hump'-backed**, having a humpback.

**Humus**, hū'mus, **Humine**, hū'min, *n.* a brown or black powder in rich soils, formed by the action of air on animal or vegetable matter. [Lit. the 'ground, soil ;' L., akin to Gr. *chamai*, on the ground.]

**Hunch**, hunsh, *n.* a hump, esp. on the back : a lump.—**Hunch'back**, *n.* one with a *hunch* or hump on his *back*—**Hunch'backed**, *adj.* having a humpback. [The nasalised form of **Hook** ; cog. with Ger. *hucke*, the bent back ; cf. Scot. to *hunker* down, to sit on one's heels with the knees bent up towards the chin.]

**Hundred**, hun'dred, *n.* the number of ten times ten : a division of a county in England, orig. supposed to contain a *hundred* families. [A.S. *hundred*—old form *hund*, a hundred, with the superfluous addition of *red* or *ræd* (E. *rate*), a reckoning : cogs. of A.S. *hund* are O. Ger. *hunt*, Goth. *hu.d*, W. *cant*, Gael. *ciad*, Lat. *cent-um*, Gr. *he-kat-on*, Sans. *çata*, a hundred.]

**Hundredfold**, hun'dred-fōld, *adj., folded* a *hundred* times, multiplied by a hundred.

**Hundredth**, hun'dred*th*, *adj.* coming last or forming one of a *hundred*.—*n.* one of a hundred.

**Hundredweight**, hun'dred-wāt, *n.* a *weight* the

twentieth part of a ton, or 112 lbs. **avoirdupois**; orig. a *hundred* lbs., abbreviated *cwt.* (*c.* standing for L. *centum*, *wt.* for weight).

**Hung,** *pa t.* and *pa.p.* of Hang.

**Hunger,** hung'gėr, *n.* desire for food : strong desire for anything.—*v.i.* to crave food : to long for. [A.S. *hungor* (n.), *hyngran* (v.) ; corresponding words are found in all the Teut. languages.]

**Hunger-bitten,** hung'gėr-bit'n, *adj.* bitten, pained, or weakened by hunger.

**Hungry,** hung'gri, *adj.* having eager desire : greedy : lean : poor.—*adv* **Hung'rily.**

**Hunks,** hungks, *n.sing.* a covetous man : a miser.

**Hunt,** hunt, *v.t.* to chase wild animals for prey or sport : to search for : to pursue.—*v.i.* to go out in pursuit of game : to search.—*n.* a chase of wild animals : search : an association of huntsmen.—**Hunt down,** to destroy by persecution or violence.—**Hunt out, up, after,** to search for, seek. [A.S. *huntian*; A.S. *hentan*, to seize, Goth. *hinthan*; from the same root is E. *hand.*] [in the chase.—*fem.* Hunt'ress.

**Hunter,** hunt'ėr, *n.* one who hunts : a horse used

**Hunting-box,** hunt'ing-boks, **Hunting-seat,** hunt'ing-sēt, *n.* a temporary *residence* for *hunting*.

**Huntsman,** hunts'man, *n.* one who hunts : a servant who manages the hounds during the chase.

**Huntsmanship,** hunts'man-ship, *n.* the qualifications of a *huntsman*.

**Hurdle,** hur'dl, *n.* a frame of twigs or sticks interlaced : (*agri.*) a movable frame of timber or iron for gates, &c.—*v.t.* to inclose with hurdles. [A.S. *hyrdel*; Ger. *hürde*, Goth. *haurds*, a wicker-gate, L. *crates.* See Cradle and Crate.]

**Hurdy-gurdy,** hur'di-gur'di, *n.* a musical stringed instrument, like a rude violin, the notes of which are produced by the friction of a wheel. [Prob. a rhyming imitation of its sound.]

**Hurl,** hurl, *v.i.* to make a noise by throwing : to move rapidly : to whirl.—*v.t.* to throw with violence : to utter with vehemence.—*n.* act of hurling, tumult, confusion.—*n.* Hurl'er. [Contr. of Hurtle, which see.]

**Hurly-burly,** hur'li-bur'li, *n.* tumult : confusion. [*Hurly* is from O. Fr. *hurler*, to yell, orig. *huller*, whence E. Howl. *Burly* is simply a rhyming addition.]

**Hurrah, Hurra,** hoor-rä', *int.* an exclamation of excitement or joy.—*n.* and *v.i.* [Dan. and Swed. *hurra.*]

**Hurricane,** hur'ri-kān, *n.* a storm with extreme violence and sudden changes of the wind, common in the E. and W. Indies. [Sp. *huracan*; from an American-Indian word, prob. imitative of the rushing of the wind.]

**Hurry,** hur'i, *v.t.* to urge forward: to hasten.—*v.i.* to move or act with haste :—*pa.p.* hurr'ied. —*n.* a driving forward: haste : tumult.—*adv.* **Hurr'yingly.** [An imitative word, to which correspond O. Swed. *hurra*, to whirl round, and other Scand. forms.]

**Hurry-skurry,** hur'i-skur'i, *n.* confusion and bustle. [Hurry, with the rhyming addition *skurry.*]

**Hurt,** hurt, *v.t.* to cause bodily pain to : to damage : to wound, as the feelings :—*pa.t.* and *pa.p.* hurt.—*n.* a wound : injury. [Lit. to *butt* or *thrust* like a ram, O. Fr. *hurter* (Fr. *heurter*), to knock, to run against ; prob. from the Celtic, as in W. *hwrdd*, a thrust, the butt of a ram, Corn. *hordh*, a ram.]

**Hurtful,** hurt'fool, *adj.* causing hurt or loss : mischievous.—*adv.* Hurt'fully.—*n.* Hurt'fulness.

**Hurtle,** hurt'l, *v.t.* to dash against : to move vio-

lently : to clash : to rattle. [Freq. of Hurt in its original sense.]

**Hurtless,** hurt'les, *adj.* without hurt or injury, harmless.—*adv.* Hurt'lessly.—*n.* Hurt'lessness.

**Husband,** huz'band, *n.* a married man : (*B.*) a man to whom a woman is betrothed : one who manages affairs with prudence : (*naut.*) the owner of a ship who manages its concerns in person.—*v.t.* to supply with a husband : to manage with economy. [M. E. *husbonde*—A.S. *husbonda,* Ice. *husbondi—hus,* a house, and Ice. *bondi,* for *buandi,* inhabiting, pr.p. of Ice. *bua* to dwell, akin to Ger. *bauen,* to till. See Bondage.]

**Husbandman,** huz'band-man, *n.* a working farmer : one who labours in tillage.

**Husbandry,** huz'band-ri, *n.* the business of a farmer : tillage : economical management : thrift.

**Hush,** hush, *int.* or *imp.* silence ! be still !—*adj.* silent : quiet.—*v.t.* to make quiet. [Imitative. Cf. Hist and Whist.]

**Hush-money,** hush'-mun'i, *n., money* given as a bribe to *hush* or make one keep silent.

**Husk,** husk, *n.* the dry, thin *covering* of certain fruits and seeds.—*v.t.* to remove the husks from. [*Hulsk* with the *l* dropped, from M. E. *hulen* (with suffix -*sk*)—*helan,* to cover ; cf. Ger. *hülse,* Dut. *hulse,* &c., in all of which the *l* has been retained.] [of husks.

**Husked,** huskt', *adj.* covered with a *husk* : stripped

**Husking,** husk'ing, *n.* the stripping of *husks*.

**Husky,** husk'i, *adj.* hoarse, as the voice : rough in sound.—*adv.* Husk'ily.—*n.* Husk'iness. [A corr. of *husty,* from M. E. *host* (Scot. *host,* a cough) —A.S. *hwosta,* a cough ; cog. with Ger. *husten.*]

**Hussar,** hooz-zär', *n.* (*orig.*) a soldier of the national cavalry of Hungary : a light-armed cavalry soldier. [Hun. *huszar—husz,* twenty, because at one time in Hungary one cavalry soldier used to be levied from every twenty families.]

**Hussif,** huz'if, *n.* a case for needles, thread, &c., used in sewing. [Ice. *husi,* a case—*hus,* a house. The -*f* was added through confusion with Housewife.] [Contr. of Housewife.]

**Hussy,** huz'i, *n.* a pert girl : a worthless female.

**Hustings,** hus'tingz, *n. sing.* the principal court of the City of London : (*formerly*) the booths where the votes were taken at an election of a M.P., or the platform from which the candidates gave their addresses. [A.S. *husting,* a council, but a Scand. word, and used in speaking of the Danes—Ice. *husthing—hus,* a house, and *thing,* an assembly ; cogs. E. House and Thing.]

**Hustle,** hus'l, *v.t.* to shake or push together : to crowd with violence. [O. Dut. *hutsen, hutselen,* to shake to and fro. See Hotchpotch.]

**Hut,** hut, *n.* a small or mean house : (*mil.*) a small temporary dwelling.—*v.t.* (*mil.*) to place in huts, as quarters :—*pr.p.* hutt'ing; *pa.p.* hutt'ed. [Fr. *hutte*—O. Ger. *hutta* (Ger. *hütte*).]

**Hutch,** huch, *n.* a *box,* a *chest* : a coop for rabbits. [Fr. *huche,* a chest; from Low L. *hutica,* a box.]

**Huzza,** hooz-zä', *int.* and *n.* hurrah ! a shout of joy or approbation.—*v.t.* to attend with shouts of joy.—*v.i.* to utter shouts of joy or acclamation :—*pr.p.* huzza'ing ; *pa.p.* huzzaed (-zäd'). [Ger. *hussa :* the same as Hurrah.]

**Hyacinth,** hī'a-sinth, *n.* (*myth.*) a flower which sprang from the blood of *Hyakinthos* [Gr.], a youth killed by Apollo with a quoit : a bulbousrooted flower of a great variety of colours : a precious stone, the *jacinth.* [Doublet, Jacinth.]

**Hyacinthine,** hī-a-sinth'in, *adj.* consisting of or resembling *hyacinth* : curling like the hyacinth.

**Hyades,** hī'a-dēz, **Hyads,** hī'adz, *n.* a cluster of

five stars in the constellation of the Bull, supposed by the ancients to bring *rain* when they rose with the sun. [Gr. *hyades—hyein*, to rain.]

**Hyæna.** See **Hyena**.

**Hyaline,** hī′a-lin, *adj., glassy :* consisting of or like glass. [Gr. *hyalinos—hyalos*, glass, probably an Egyptian word meaning a transparent stone.]

**Hybernate,** &c. See **Hibernate,** &c.

**Hybrid,** hī′brid, *n.* an animal or plant produced from two different species : a mongrel : a mule : a word formed of elements from different languages. [Lit. something *unnatural*, from L. *hibrida*, a mongrel, perh. from Gr. *hybris, hybridos*, outrage, insult.]

**Hybrid,** hī′brid. **Hybridous,** hib′rid-us, *adj.* produced from different species : mongrel.

**Hybridism,** hī′brid-izm, **Hybridity,** hib-rid′i-ti, *n.* state of being *hybrid*.

**Hydatid,** hid′a-tid, *n.* a *watery* cyst or vesicle sometimes found in animal bodies. [Gr. *hydatis,* a watery vesicle—*hydōr, hydatos,* water.]

**Hydra,** hī′dra, *n.* (*myth.*) a *water*-serpent with many heads, which when cut off were succeeded by others : any manifold evil : a genus of freshwater polypes remarkable for their power of being multiplied by being cut or divided. [L.—Gr. *hydra—hydōr,* water, akin to Sans. *udras,* an otter, also to E. **Otter.**]

**Hydrangea,** hī-dran′je-a, *n.* a genus of shrubby plants with large heads of showy flowers, natives of China and Japan. [Lit. the 'water-vessel ;' so called from the *cup*-shaped seed-vessel. Coined from Gr. *hydōr,* water, and *anggeion,* vessel.]

**Hydrant,** hī′drant, *n.* a machine for discharging *water :* a water-plug. [Gr. *hydōr,* water.]

**Hydraulic,** hī-drawl′ik, **Hydraulical,** hī-drawl′-ik-al, *adj.* relating to hydraulics : conveying water : worked by water.—*adv.* **Hydraul′ically.** [Lit. 'belonging to a water-organ' or water-pipe, from Gr. *hydōr,* water, *aulos,* a pipe.]

**Hydraulics,** hī-drawl′iks, *n.pl.* used as *sing.* the science of hydrodynamics in its practical application to *water-pipes,* &c.

**Hydrocephalus,** hī-dro-sef′a-lus, *n., water* in the *head :* dropsy of the brain. [Gr. *hydōr,* water, *kephalē,* the head.]

**Hydrodynamics,** hī-dro-di-nam′iks, *n.pl.* used as *sing.* the science that treats of the motions and equilibrium of a material system partly or wholly fluid, called **Hydrostatics** when the system is in equilibrium, **Hydrokinetics** when it is not.—*adjs.* **Hydrodynam′ic, Hydrodynam′-ical.** [Gr. *hydōr,* water, and **Dynamics.**]

**Hydrogen,** hī′dro-jen, *n.* a gas which in combination with oxygen *produces water,* an elementary gaseous substance, the lightest of all known substances, and very inflammable.—*adj.* **Hydrog′-enous** [A word coined by Cavendish (1766) from Gr. *hydōr,* water, and *gen-naō,* to produce.]

**Hydrographer,** hī-drog′ra-fėr, *n.* a *describer* of *waters* or seas : a maker of sea-charts.

**Hydrography,** hī-drog′ra-fi, *n.* the art of measuring and *describing* the size and position of *waters* or seas : the art of making sea-charts.—*adjs.* **Hydrograph′ic, Hydrograph′ical.**—*adv.* **Hydrograph′ically.** [Gr. *hydōr,* water, *graphō,* to write.]

**Hydrokinetics,** hī-dro-ki-net′iks, *n.pl.* used as *sing* a branch of **Hydrodynamics,** which see. [Gr. *hydōr,* water, and see **Kinetics.**]

**Hydrology,** hī-drol′o-ji, *n.* the *science* which treats of *water.* [Gr. *hydōr,* water, *logos,* a discourse.]

**Hydrometer,** hī-drom′et-ėr, *n.* an instrument for measuring the specific gravity of *liquids,* also the strength of spirituous liquors.—*adjs.* **Hydromet′ric, Hydromet′rical.**—*n.* **Hydrom′-etry.** [Gr. *hydōr, metron,* a measure.]

**Hydropathist,** hī-drop′a-thist, *n.* one who practises *hydropathy.*

**Hydropathy,** hī-drop′a-thi, *n.* the treatment of *diseaṡe* by cold *water.—adjs.* **Hydropath′ic, Hydropath′ical.—***adv.***Hydropath′ically.** [Gr. *hydōr,* water, and *pathos,* suffering, from *pascho, pathein,* to suffer.]

**Hydrophobia,** hī-dro-fō′bi-a, *n.* an unnatural *dread* of *water,* a symptom of a disease resulting from the bite of a mad animal, hence the disease itself.—*adj.* **Hydrophob′ic.** [Gr. *hydōr,* water, and *phobos,* fear.]

**Hydropsy,** hī′drop-si, *n.* Same as **Dropsy.**

**Hydrostatics,** hī-dro-stat′iks, *n.pl.* used as *sing.* a branch of **Hydrodynamics,** which see.—*adjs.* **Hydrostat′ic, Hydrostat′ical.—***adv.***Hydro-stat′ically.** [Gr. *hydōr,* water, and **Statics.**]

**Hyemal,** hī-ē′mal, *adj.* belonging to *winter :* done during winter. [L. *hiemalis—hiems,* winter. See **Hibernal.**]

**Hyena, Hyæna,** hī-ēn′a, *n.* a bristly-maned quadruped of the dog kind, so named from its likeness to the *sow.* [L.—Gr. *hyaina* (*lit.*) ' sow-like '—*hys,* a sow.]

**Hygeian,** hī-je′an, *adj.* relating to *health* and its preservation. [Gr. *hygieia,* health, the goddess of health, *hygiēs,* healthy—root *hyg,* Sans. *ug,* L. *veg, vig.*]

**Hygiene,** hī′ji-ēn, **Hygienics,** hī-ji-en′iks, **Hygienism,** hī′ji-en-izm, *n.* the *science* which treats of the preservation of health—*adj.* **Hygien′ic.** [Fr.]

**Hygienist,** hī′ji-en-ist, *n.* one skilled in *hygiene.*

**Hygrometer,** hī-grom′et-ėr, *n.* an instrument for *measuring* the *moisture* in the atmosphere. [Gr. *hygros,* wet, *metron,* a measure.]

**Hygrometry,** hī-grom′et-ri, *n.* the art of *measuring* the *moisture* in the atmosphere, and of bodies generally.—*adjs.* **Hygromet′ric, Hygro-met′rical.**

**Hygroscope,** hī′gro-skōp, *n.* an instrument for *shewing* the *moisture* in the atmosphere.—*adj.* **Hygroscop′ic.** [Gr. *hygros, skopeō,* to view.]

**Hymen,** hī′men, *n.* (*myth.*) the god of marriage : marriage.—*adjs.* **Hymene′al, Hymene′an.** [L., Gr. *hymēn,* perh. conn. with Gr. *hymnos,* a festive song, a hymn.]

**Hymn,** him, *n.* a song of praise.—*v.t.* to celebrate in song : to worship by hymns.—*v.i.* to sing in praise or adoration. [L. *hymnus*—Gr. *hymnos.*]

**Hymnic,** him′nik, *adj.* relating to *hymns.*

**Hymnologist,** him-nol′o-jist, *n.* one skilled in *hymnology :* a writer of hymns.

**Hymnology,** him-nol′o-ji, *n.* the *science* which treats of *hymns :* a collection of hymns. [Gr. *hymnos,* a hymn, *logos,* a discourse.]

**Hypallage,** hī-pal′a-je, *n.* an *interchange :* in rhetoric, a figure in which the relations of things in a sentence are mutually interchanged, but without obscuring the sense, as *he covered his hat with his head,* instead of *he covered his head with his hat.* [Fr.—L., Gr., from *hypal-lassō,* to interchange—*hypo,* under, and *allassō,* to change.]

**Hyperbaton,** hī-pėr′ba-ton, *n.* (*rhet.*) a figure by which words are transposed from their natural order. [Gr. a 'transposition,' from *hyperbainō*—*hyper,* beyond, and *bainō,* to go.]

**Hyperbola,** hī-pėr′bo-la, *n.* (*geom.*) one of the conic sections or curves formed when the intersecting plane makes a greater angle with the

---

base than the side of the cone makes.—*adjs.*
**Hyperbol'ic, Hyperbol'ical.**—*adv.* **Hyperbol'i-
cally.** [L. (*lit.*) a 'throwing beyond'—Gr.
*hyperbolē*, from *hyperballō—hyper*, beyond,
*ballō*, to throw.]

**Hyperbole,** hī-pėr'bo-lē, *n.* a rhetorical figure
which produces a vivid impression by representing things as much greater or less than they
really are : an exaggeration.—*adjs.* **Hyperbol'ic, Hyperbol'ical.**—*adv.* **Hyperbol'ically.**
[A doublet of the above.]

**Hyperbolise,** hī-pėr'bol-īz, *v.t.* to represent hyperbolically.—*v.i.* to speak hyperbolically or with
exaggeration.—*n.* **Hyper'bolism.**

**Hyperborean,** hī-pėr-bō're-an, *adj.* belonging to
the *extreme north.*—*n.* an inhabitant of the extreme north. [Gr. *hyperboreos—hyper*, beyond,
and *Boreas*, the north wind.]

**Hypercritic,** hī-pėr-krit'ik, *n.* one who is *over-
critical.*—*adjs.* **Hypercrit'ic, Hypercrit'ical,**
*over-critical.*—*adv.* **Hypercrit'ically.**—*n.* **Hypercrit'icism.** [Gr. *hyper*, over, and **Critic.**]

**Hypermetrical,** hī-pėr-met'rik-al, *adj.*, *beyond*
or exceeding the ordinary *metre* of a line :
having a syllable too much. [Gr. *hyper*, and
**Metrical.**]

**Hyperphysical,** hī-pėr-fiz'ik-al, *adj.* beyond physical laws : supernatural.

**Hypertrophy,** hī-pėr'tro-fi, *n.*, *over-nourishment :*
the state of an organ, or part of the body
when it grows too large from over-nourishment.
[From Gr. *hyper*, and *trophē*, nourishment—
*trephō*, to nourish.]

**Hyphen,** hī'fen, *n.* a short stroke (-) joining two
syllables or words. [Gr. *hypo*, under, *hen*, one.]

**Hypnotism,** hip'no-tizm, *n.* a sleep-like condition
induced by artificial means : a nervous sleep
like the condition under mesmerism. [Coined in
1843 from Gr. *hypnos*, sleep.]

**Hypochondria,** hip-o-kon'dri-a, *n.* a nervous
malady, often arising from indigestion, and tor-
menting the patient with imaginary fears. [L.,
Gr., from *hypo*, under, *chondros*, a cartilage, because the disease was supposed to have its seat
in the parts *under the cartilage* of the breast.]

**Hypochondriac,** hip-o-kon'dri-ak, *adj.* relating
to or affected with *hypochondria :* melancholy.—
*n.* one suffering from hypochondria.

**Hypocrisy,** hi-pok'ri-si, *n.* a feigning to be what
one is not : concealment of true character. [Lit.
'the acting of a part on the stage,' from Gr.
*hypokrisis—hypokrinomai*, to play on the stage,
from *hypo*, under, *krinō*, to decide.]

**Hypocrite,** hip'o-krit, *n.* one who practises hypocrisy.—*adj.* **Hypocrit'ic**, practising hypocrisy.—
*adv.* **Hypocrit'ically.** [Lit. 'an actor, Fr.—L.,
Gr. *hypokritēs.*]

**Hypogastric,** hip-o-gas'trik, *adj.* belonging to the
*lower* part of the *abdomen.* [Gr. *hypo*, under,
*gastēr*, the belly.]

**Hypostasis,** hī-pos'ta-sis, *n.* a substance : the
essence or personality of the three divisions of
the Godhead.—*adjs.* **Hypostat'ic, Hypostat'-
ical.**—*adv.* **Hypostat'ically.** [Lit. a 'standing
under,' L., Gr. *hypostasis—hyphistēmi—hypo*,
under, *histēmi*, to make to stand.]

**Hypotenuse,** hī-pot'en-ūs or hip-, **Hypothenuse,**
hī-poth'en-ūs, *n.* the side of a right-angled triangle
opposite to the right angle. [Fr.—Gr. *hypotei-
nousa* (*grammē*), (*lit.*) (a line) 'which stretches
under'—*hypo*, under, *teinō*, to stretch.]

**Hypothec.** hī-poth'ek, *n.* in Scotch law, a *security*
in favour of a creditor over the property of his
debtor, while the property continues in the

debtor's possession. [Fr.—L. *hypotheca*—Gr.
*hypothēkē*, a pledge.]

**Hypothecate,** hī-poth'e-kāt, *v.t.* to *place* or assign
anything as security *under* an arrangement : to
mortgage.—*n.* **Hypotheca'tion.** [Low L. *hypo-
theco, hypothecatum—hypotheca*, a pledge, from
Gr. *hypothēkē—hypo*, under, *tithēmi*, to place.]

**Hypothesis,** hī-poth'e-sis, *n.* a supposition : a proposition assumed for the sake of argument : a
theory to be proved or disproved by reference to
facts : a provisional explanation of anything.
[Lit. 'that which is placed under,' Gr. *hypo*,
under, *tithēmi*, to place.]

**Hypothetic,** hī-po-thet'ik, **Hypothetical,** hī-po-
thet'ik-al, *adj.* belonging to a *hypothesis :* conditional.—*adv.* **Hypothet'ically.** [Gr. *hypo-
thetikos.*]

**Hyson,** hī'son, *n.* a very fine sort of green tea.
[Chinese 'first crop.']

**Hyssop,** his'up, *n.* an aromatic plant. [Fr.—L.
*hyssopum*—Gr. *hyssōpos*—Heb. *ezobh.*]

**Hysteric,** his-ter'ik, **Hysterical,** his-ter'ik-al, *adj.*
resulting from the *womb :* convulsive : affected
with hysterics.—*adv.* **Hyster'ically.** [L. *hys-
tericus*—Gr. *hysterikos—hystera*, the womb.]

**Hysterics,** his-ter'iks, **Hysteria,** his-tēr'i-a, *n.*
a disease resulting from an affection of the
*womb*, causing nervous or convulsive fits.

**Hysteron-proteron,** his'ter-on-prot'er-on, *n.* a
figure of speech in which what should follow
comes first : an inversion. [Gr. (*lit.*) 'the last
first.']

# I

**I,** ī, *pron.* the nominative case singular of the first
personal pronoun : the word used by a speaker or
writer in mentioning himself. [M. E. *ich*, A.S.
*ic* ; Ger. *ich*, Ice. *ek*, L. *ego*, Gr. *egō*, Sans. *aham*.]

**Iambic,** ī-am'bik, **Iambus,** ī-am'bus, *n.* a metrical
foot of two syllables, the first short and the
second long, as in L. *fĭdēs* ; or the first unaccented and the second accented, as in *deduce'*.
[L. *iambus*—Gr. *iambos*, from *iaptō*, to assail,
this metre being first used by writers of satire.]

**Iambic,** ī-am'bik, *adj.* consisting of *iambics.*

**Ibex,** ī'beks, *n.* a genus of goats, inhabiting the
Alps and other mountainous regions. [L.]

**Ibis,** ī'bis, *n.* a genus of wading birds like the
stork, one species of which was worshipped by
the ancient Egyptians. [L., Gr., an Egyptian
word.]

**Icarian,** ī-kā'ri-an, *adj.* belonging to *Icarus :* adventurous or unfortunate in flight. [L. *Icarius*
—Gr. *Ikarios—Ikaros*, who fell into the sea on
his flight from Crete, his waxen wings being
melted by the sun.]

**Ice,** īs, *n.* water congealed by freezing : concreted
sugar.—*v.t.* to cover with ice : to freeze : to
cover with concreted sugar :—*pr.p.* īc'ing ; *pa.p.*
īced'. [A.S. *is* ; Ger. *eis*, Ice., Dan. *is.*]

**Iceberg,** īs'bėrg, *n.* a *mountain* or huge mass of
floating *ice.* [From Scand. or Dut., the latter
part *berg* = mountain.]

**Iceblink,** īs'blingk, *n.* the *blink* or light reflected
from *ice* near the horizon.

**Iceboat,** īs'bōt, *n.* a *boat* used for forcing a passage through or being dragged over *ice.*

**Icebound,** īs'bownd, *adj.*, *bound*, surrounded, or
fixed in with *ice.*

**Icecream,** īs'krēm, **Iced-cream,** īst'-krēm, *n.*,
*cream* sweetened or flavoured, and artificially
*frozen.*

**Icefield,** īs'fēld, *n.* a large *field* or sheet of *ice.*

**Icefloat**, īs′flōt, **Icefloe**, īs′flō, *n.* a large mass of *floating ice*.

**Icehouse**, īs′hows, *n.* a *house* for preserving *ice*.

**Iceland-moss**, īs′land-mos, *n.* a lichen found in the northern parts of the world, esp. in Iceland and Norway. and valuable as a medicine and as an article of diet.

**Icepack**, īs′pak, *n.* drifting *ice packed* together.

**Iceplant**, īs′plant, *n.* a *plant* whose leaves glisten in the sun as if covered with *ice*.

**Ichneumon**, ik-nū′mun, *n.* a small carnivorous animal in Egypt, famed for destroying the crocodile's eggs : an insect which lays its eggs on the larvæ of other insects. [Gr. (*lit.*) the 'hunter,' from *ichneuō*, to hunt after—*ichnos*, a track.]

**Ichnography**, ik-nog′raf-i, *n.* a *tracing out* : (*arch.*) a ground-plan of a work or building.— *adjs.* **Ichnograph′ic, Ichnograph′ical**.—*adv.* **Ichnograph′ically**. [Gr. *ichnographia—ichnos*, a track, *graphō*, to grave.]

**Ichnology**, ik-nol′oj-i. *n., footprint lore* : the science of fossil footprints. [Gr. *ichnos*, a track, a footprint, and *logos*, discourse ]

**Ichor**, ī′kor, *n.* (*myth.*) the ethereal juice in the veins of the gods : a watery humour : colourless matter from an ulcer.—*adj.* **I′chorous**. [Gr. *ichōr*, akin to Sans. *sich*, to sprinkle, Ger. *seihen*, to filter.]

**Ichthyography**, ik-thi-og′ra-fi, *n.* a *description* of or treatise on *fishes*. [Gr. *ichthys, ichthyos*, a fish. *graphō*, to write.]

**Ichthyolite**, ik′thi-o-līt, *n.* a *fish* turned into *stone*, a fossil fish : the impression of a fish in a rock. [Gr. *ichthys*, a fish, and *lithos*, a stone.]

**Ichthyology**, ik-thi ol′o-ji, *n.* the branch of zoology that treats of *fishes*.—*adj.* **Ichthyolog′ical**.— *n.* **Ichthyol′ogist**, one skilled in ichthyology. [Gr. *ichthys*, a fish, *logos*, discourse, science.]

**Ichthyophagous**, ik-thi-of′a-gus, *adj., eating* or subsisting on *fish*. [Gr. *ichthys*, a fish, *phagō*, to eat.]

**Ichthyosaurus**, ik-thi-o-sawr′us, *n.* the *fish-lizard*, a genus of extinct marine reptiles, uniting some of the characteristics of the Saurians with those of fishes. [Gr. *ichthys*, a fish, *sauros*, a lizard.]

**Icicle**, īs′i-kl, *n.* a hanging point of *ice* formed by the freezing of dropping water. [A.S. *ísgicel*, for *isesgicel* ; *ises* being the gen. of *ís*, ice, and *gicel*, a dim. of a Celt. word sig. ice (Ir. *aigh*). Cf. Ice. *jökull*, icicle, also a dim.]

**Icily, Iciness**. See **Icy**.      [sugar.

**Icing**, īs′ing, *n.* a covering of *ice* or concreted

**Iconoclasm**, ī-kon′o-klazm, *n.* act of *breaking images*.—*adj.* **Iconoclast′ic**, *image-breaking* : pertaining to iconoclasm.

**Iconoclast**, ī-kon′o-klast. *n.* a *breaker* of *images*, one opposed to idol-worship. [Coined from Gr. *eikōn*, an image, and *klastēs*, a breaker—*klaō*, to break.]

**Iconology**, ī-kon-ol′o-ji, *n.* the *doctrine* of *images*, especially with reference to worship. [Gr. *eikōn*, and *logos*, science, discourse.]

**Icosahedral**, ī-kos-a-hē′dral, *adj.* having *twenty* equal *sides* or faces.

**Icosahedron**, ī-kos-a-hē′dron, *n.* (*geom.*) a solid having *twenty* equal *sides* or faces. [Gr. *eikosi*, twenty, *hedra*, base—*hed-*, root of *hezomai*, E. **Sit**.]

**Icy**, īs′i, *adj.* composed of, abounding in, or like *ice* : frosty : cold : chilling : without warmth of affection.—*adv* **Ic′ily**.—*n.* **Ic′iness**.

**Idea**, ī-dē′a, *n.* an *image* of a thing formed by the mind : a notion : thought : opinion. [L.—Gr. *idea—idein*, to see : akin to **Wit**.]

**Ideal**, ī-dē′al, *adj.* existing in *idea* : mental : existing in imagination only : the highest and best conceivable, the perfect, as opp. to the real, the imperfect.—*n.* the highest conception of anything.—*adv.* **Ide′ally**.

**Idealisation**, ī-dē-al-ī-zā′shun, *n.* act of forming in idea, or of raising to the highest conception.

**Idealise**, ī-dē′al-īz, *v.t.* to form in *idea* : to raise to the highest conception.—*v.i.* to form ideas.

**Idealism**, ī-dē′al-izm, *n.* the doctrine that in external perceptions the objects immediately known are *ideas* : any system that considers thought or the *idea* as the ground either of knowledge or existence : tendency towards the highest conceivable perfection, love for or search after the best and highest.      [of *idealism*.

**Idealist**, ī-dē′al-ist, *n.* one who holds the doctrine

**Idealistic**, ī-dē-al-ist′ik, *adj.* pertaining to *idealists* or to idealism.

**Ideality**, ī-dē-al′i-ti, *n., ideal state* : ability and disposition to form ideals of beauty and perfection.

**Identical**, ī-den tik-al, *adj.* the very *same* : not different.—*adv.* **Iden′tically**.—*n.* **Iden′ticalness**, identity. [L. as if *identicus—idem*, the same.]

**Identify**, ī-den′ti-fī, *v.t.* to make to be the *same* : to ascertain or prove to be the same :—*pa.p.* **Iden′tified**.—*n.* **Identifica′tion**. [Fr. *identifier* (It. *identificare*)—L. as if *identicus—idem*, the same, and *facio*, to make.]

**Identity**, ī-den′ti-ti, *n.* state of being the *same* : sameness. [Fr.—Low L. *identitas*—L. *idem*, the same.]

**Ideographic**, id-e-o-graf′ik, **Ideographical**, -′ik-al, *adj.* representing *ideas* by *pictures* instead of words. [Gr. *idea*, idea, *graphō*, to write.]

**Ideology**, ī-de-ol′o-ji, *n.* the *science* of *ideas*, metaphysics. [Gr. *idea*, and *logos*, discourse.]

**Ides**, īdz, *n.sing.* in ancient Rome, the 15th day of March, May, July, Oct., and the 13th of the other months. [Fr.—L. *idus*, origin doubtful, said to be Etruscan.]

**Idiocrasy**, id-i-ok′ra-si, *n.* Same as **Idiosyncrasy**. [Fr.—Gr. *idiokrasia—idios*, peculiar, and *krasis*. See **Crasis**.]      [an *idiot* : imbecility : folly.

**Idiocy**, id′i-o-si, **Idiotcy**, id′i-ut-si, *n.* state of being

**Idiom**, id′i-um, *n.* a mode of expression *peculiar* to a language. [Fr.—L.—Gr. *idiōma*, peculiarity - *idioō*, make one's own—*idios*, one's own.]

**Idiomatic**, id-i-o-mat′ik, **Idiomatical**, id-i-o-mat′-ik-al, *adj.* conformed or pertaining to the *idioms* of a language.—*adv.* **Idiomat′ically**. [Gr. *idiōmatikos—idiōma. idiōmatos*, peculiarity.]

**Idiopathic**, id-i-o-path′ik. *adj.* (*med.*) primary, not depending on or preceded by another disease.— *adv.* **Idiopath′ically**.

**Idiopathy**, id-i-op′a-thi, *n.* a *peculiar affection* or state : (*med.*) a primary disease, one not occasioned by another. [Gr. *idios*, peculiar, *pathos*, suffering—*pathein*, to suffer.]

**Idiosyncrasy**, id-i-o-sin′kra-si, *n., peculiarity* of *temperament* or constitution : any characteristic of a person.—*adj.* **Idiosyncrat′ic**. [Gr. *idios*, one's own, peculiar. and *syncrasis*, a mixing together—*syn*, together, and *krasis*, a mixing. See **Crasis**.]

**Idiot**, id′i-ut, *n.* one deficient in intellect : a foolish or unwise person. [Fr.—L. *idiota*—Gr. *idiōtēs*, orig. a 'private man,' then an ignorant, rude person—*idios*, one's own, peculiar.]

**Idiotcy**. Same as **Idiocy**.

**Idiotic**, id-i-ot′ik, **Idiotical**, id-i-ot′ik-al, *adj.* pertaining to or like an *idiot* : foolish.—*adv.* **Idiot′ically**.

**Idiotism**, id′i-ut-izm, *n.* an idiom. [L.—Gr.—

*idiōtizō*, to put into common or current language—*idiōtēs*. See **Idiot.**]

**Idle**, ī′dl, *adj.* vain : trifling : unemployed : averse to labour : not occupied : useless : unimportant : unedifying.—*v.t.* to spend in idleness.—*ns.* **I′dler, I′dleness**—*adv.* **I′dly.** [A.S. *idel ;* Dut. *ijdel.* Ger. *eitel,* conn. with Gr. *itharos,* clear, *aithēr,* upper air, from *aitho,* burn. The orig. sense was prob. ' clear ;' then pure, mere, sheer ; than vain, unimportant (Skeat).]

**Idol**, ī′dul, *n.* a figure : an image of some object of worship : a person or thing too much loved or honoured. [L. *idolum*—Gr. *eidōlon*—*eidos,* that which is seen—*idein,* to see. See **Wit.**]

**Idolater**, ī-dol′a-tėr, *n.* a *worshipper* of *idols :* a great admirer.—*fem.* **Idol′atress.** [Fr. *idolâtre,* corr. of L.—Gr. *eidōlolatrēs*—*eidōlon,* idol, *latrēs,* worshipper.]      [to adore.

**Idolatrise**, ī-dol′a-trīz, *v.i.* to *worship* as an *idol :*
**Idolatrous**, ī-dol′a-trus, *adj.* pertaining to *idolatry.*—*adv.* **Idol′atrously.**      [cessive love.

**Idolatry**, ī-dol′a-tri, *n.* the *worship* of *idols :* ex-
**Idolise**, ī′dul-īz, *v.t.* to make an *idol* of, for worship : to love to excess.—*n.* **Idolis′er.**

**Idyl, Idyll**, ī′dil, *n.* a short pictorial poem, chiefly on pastoral subjects : a narrative poem. [L. *idyllium*—Gr. *eidyllion,* dim. of *eidos,* image—*eidōmai,* to seem. See **Wit.**]

**Idyllic**, ī-dil′ik, *adj.* of or belonging to *idyls.*

**If**, if, *conj.* an expression of doubt : whether : in case that : supposing that. [A.S. *gif ;* cog. with Dut. *of,* Ice. *ef,* if, *efa,* to doubt ; O. Ger. *ibu, ipu,* dative case of *iba,* a condition.]

**Igneous**, ig′ne-us, *adj.* pertaining to, consisting of, or like *fire :* (*geol.*) produced by the action of fire. [L. *igneus*—*ignis,* fire, cog. with Sans. *agni.*]      [L. *ignescens*—*ignis.*]

**Ignescent**, ig-nes′ent, *adj.* emitting sparks of fire.

**Ignis-fatuus**, ig′nis-fat′ū-us, *n.* a light which misleads travellers, often seen over marshy places, of which the cause is not well understood, also called ' Will-o′-the-wisp ' :—*pl.* **Ignes-fatui,** ig′-nēz-fat′ū-ī. [L. *ignis,* fire, *fatuus,* foolish.]

**Ignite**, ig-nīt′, *v.t.* to set on *fire,* to kindle : to render luminous with heat.—*v.i.* to take fire : to burn. [See **Ignition.**]

**Ignitible**, ig-nīt′i-bl, *adj.* that may be ignited.

**Ignition**, ig-nish′un, *n.* act of setting on *fire :* state of being kindled, and esp. of being made red-hot. [Fr., coined from L. *ignio, ignitus,* to set on fire—*ignis,* fire.]

**Ignoble**, ig-nō′bl, *adj.* of low birth : mean or worthless : dishonourable.—*adv.* **Igno′bly.**—*n.* **Igno′bleness.** [Fr.—L. *ignobilis*—*in,* not, *gnobilis, nobilis,* noble.]

**Ignominious**, ig-nō-min′i-us, *adj.* dishonourable : marked with ignominy : contemptible : mean.—*adv.* **Ignomin′iously.**—*n.* **Ignomin′iousness.**

**Ignominy**, ig′nō-min-i, *n.* the *loss* of one's *good name :* public disgrace : infamy. [Fr.—L. *ig-nominia*—*in,* not, *gnomen, nomen,* name. See **Name.**]

**Ignoramus**, ig-nō-rā′mus, *n.* an ignorant person, esp. one making a pretence to knowledge :—*pl.* **Ignora′muses.** [L. ' we are ignorant,' 1st pers. pl. pres. ind. of *ignoro.*]

**Ignorance**, ig′nō-rans, *n.* state of being ignorant : want of knowledge :—*pl.* in Litany, sins committed through ignorance. [Fr.—L. *ignorantia.*]

**Ignorant**, ig′nō-rant, *adj.* without knowledge : uninstructed : unacquainted with.—*adv.* **Igno′-rantly.** [Fr.—L. *ignorans, -antis,* pr.p. of *ignoro.* See **Ignore.**]

**Ignore**, ig-nōr′, *v.t.* wilfully to disregard : to set aside. [Fr.—L. *ignoro,* not to know—*in,* not, and *gno-,* root-of (*g*)*nosco,* to know. See **Know.**]

**Iguana**, i-gwä′na, *n.* a genus of tropical lizards, having a large dewlap under the throat. [Sp., said to be a Haytian word.]

**Ilex**, ī′leks, *n.* the scientific name for **Holly** (which see) : the evergreen or holm oak. [L.]

**Iliac**, il′i-ak, *adj.* pertaining to the lower intestines. [Fr., through a Low L. *iliacus*—*ilia,* the flanks, the groin.]

**Iliad**, il′i-ad, *n.* an epic poem by Homer, giving an account of the destruction of *Ilium* or ancient Troy. [L. *Ilias, Iliadis*—Gr. *Ilias, Iliados* (*poiēsis,* a poem), belonging to **Ilium,** the city of *Ilos,* its founder.]

**Ilk**, ilk, *adj.* the same. [Scot., from A.S. *ylc,* from *y-* or *i-* (base of **He**), and *lic* = like.]

**Ill**, il, *adj.* (comp. **worse :** superl. **worst**) evil, bad : contrary to good : wicked : producing evil : unfortunate : unfavourable : sick : diseased : improper : incorrect : cross, as temper.—*adv.* not well : not rightly : with difficulty.—*n.* evil : wickedness : misfortune.—**Ill,** when compounded with other words, expresses badness of quality or condition. [From Ice. *illr,* a contr. of the word which appears in A.S. *yfel,* E. **Evil.**]

**Illapse**, il-laps′, *n.* a *sliding in :* the entrance of one thing into another. [L. *illapsus*—*illabor*—*in,* into, *labor,* to slip, to slide.]

**Illation**, il-lā′shun, *n.* act of *inferring* from premises or reasons : inference : conclusion. [Fr.—L. *illatio,* a bringing in a logical inference—*infero, illatum*—*in,* in, into, *fero,* to bear.]

**Illative**, il′la-tiv, *adj.* denoting an *inference :* that may be inferred.—*adv.* **Il′latively.**

**Ill-blood**, il′-blud, *n.* ill feeling : resentment.

**Ill-bred**, il′-bred, *adj.* badly bred, or educated : uncivil.—*n.* **Ill-breed′ing.**

**Illegal**, il-lē′gal, *adj.* contrary to *law.*—*adv.* **Ille′-gally.** [Fr.—L. *in,* not ; see **Legal.**]

**Illegalise**, il-lē′gal-īz, *v.t.* to render *unlawful.*

**Illegality**, il-le-gal′i-ti, *n.* the quality or condition of being illegal.

**Illegible**, il-lej′i-bl, *adj.* that cannot be *read :* indistinct.—*adv.* **Illeg′ibly.**—*ns.* **Illeg′ibleness, Illegibil′ity.** [Fr.—L. *in,* not ; see **Legible.**]

**Illegitimate**, il-le-jit′i-māt, *adj., not* according to *law :* not born in wedlock : not properly inferred or reasoned : not genuine.—*adv.* **Illegit′imately.**—*n.* **Illegit′imacy.** [L. *in,* not ; see **Legitimate.**]      [ugly.

**Ill-favoured,** il-fā′vurd, *adj.* ill-looking : deformed :
**Illiberal,** il-lib′er-al, *adj.* niggardly : mean.—*adv.* **Illib′erally.**—*n.* **Illiberal′ity.** [Fr.—L. *in,* not, and **Liberal.**]

**Illicit,** il-lis′it, *adj., not allowable :* unlawful : unlicensed.—*adv.* **Illic′itly.**—*n.* **Illic′itness.** [Fr.—L. *illicitus*—*in,* not, and *licitus,* pa.p. of *liceo.* to be allowable. See **License.**]

**Illimitable,** il-lim′it-a-bl, *adj.* that cannot be *bounded :* infinite.—*adv.* **Illim′itably.**—*n.* **Illim′-itableness.** [L. *in,* not, and **Limitable.**]

**Illision,** il-lizh′un, *n.* the act of *dashing* or *striking against.* [L. *illisio*—*illido,* to strike against—*in,* in, upon, *læd*, to dash, to strike.]

**Illiteracy,** il-lit′ėr-a-si, *n.* state of being illiterate : want of learning.

**Illiterate,** il-lit′ėr-āt, *adj., not learned :* uninstructed : ignorant.—*adv.* **Illit′erately.**—*n.* **Il-lit′erateness.** [L. *in,* not, and **Literate.**]

**Ill-natured,** il-nā′tūrd, *adj.* of an ill nature or temper : cross : peevish.—*adv.* **Ill-na′turedly.**

**Illness,** il′nes, *n.* sickness : disease.

**Illogical,** il-loj′i-kal, *adj.* contrary to the rules of logic.—*adv.* **Illog'ically.**—*n.* **Illog'icalness.** [L. *in*, not, and **Logical.**]

**Ill-starred**, il'-stärd, *adj.* born (according to an ancient superstition) under the influence of an *unlucky star*: unlucky.

**Illude**, il-lūd', *v.t.* to *play upon* by artifice: to deceive. [L. *illudo*, *illusum—in*, upon, *ludo*, to play.]

**Illume.** See **Illumine.**

**Illuminate**, il-lū'min-āt, *v.t.* to light up: to enlighten: to illustrate: to adorn with ornamental lettering or illustrations.—*adj.* enlightened. [L. *illumino*, *illuminatus—in*, in, upon, and *lumino*, to cast light—*lumen* (= *lucimen*)—*luceo.* to shine, light.]

**Illuminati**, il-lū-min-ā'tī, *n.pl.* the *enlightened*, a name given to various sects, and esp. to a society of German Freethinkers at the end of last century.

**Illumination**, il-lū-min-ā'shun, *n.* act of *giving light*: that which gives light: splendour: brightness: a display of lights: adorning of books with coloured lettering or illustrations: (*B.*) enlightening influence, inspiration.

**Illuminative**, il-lū'min-ā-tiv, *adj.* tending to *give light*: illustrative or explanatory.

**Illuminator**, il-lū'min-ā-tor, *n.* one who illuminates, especially one who is employed in adorning books with coloured letters and illustrations.

**Illumine**, il-lū'min, **Illume**, il-lūm', *v.t.* to make luminous or bright: to enlighten: to adorn.

**Illusion**, il-lū'zhun, *n.* a *playing upon*: a mocking: deceptive appearance: false show: error. [Fr. See **Illude.**]

**Illusive**, il-lū'siv, **Illusory**, il-lū'sor-i, *adj., deceiving* by false appearances: false.—*adv.* **Illu'sively.**—*n.* **Illu'siveness.**

**Illustrate**, il-lus'trāt, *v.t.* to make distinguished: to make clear to the mind: to explain: to explain and adorn by pictures.—*n.* **Illus'trator.** [L. *illustro*, *illustratum*, to light up—*illustris.* See **Illustrious.**]

**Illustration**, il-lus-trā'shun, *n.* act of making *lustrous* or clear: act of explaining: that which illustrates: a picture or diagram.

**Illustrative**, il-lus'tra-tiv, *adj.* having the quality of *making clear* or explaining.—*adv.* **Illus'tratively.**

**Illustrious**, il-lus'tri-us, *adj.* morally bright, distinguished: noble: conspicuous: conferring honour.—*adv.* **Illus'triously.**—*n.* **Illus trious ness.** [L. *illustris*, prob. for *illucestris—in*, in, and *lux, lucis*, light.]

**Ill-will**, il-wil', *n.* unkind feeling: enmity.

**Image**, im'āj, *n.* likeness: a statue: an idol: a representation in the mind, an idea: a picture in the imagination: (*optics*) the figure of any object formed by rays of light.—*v.t.* to form an image of: to form a likeness of in the mind. [Fr.—L. *imago*, an image, from root of *imitor*, to imitate. See **Imitate.**]

**Imagery**, im'a-jèr-i or im'āj-ri, *n.* (*orig.*) *images* in general: the work of the imagination: mental pictures: figures of speech.

**Imaginable**, im-aj'in-a-bl, *adj.* that may be imagined.—*adv.* **Imag'inably.**—*n.* **Imag'inableness.**

**Imaginary**, im-aj'in-ar-i, *adj.* existing only in the *imagin tion*: not real: (*alg.*) impossible.

**Imagination**, im-aj-in-ā'shun, *n.* act of imagining: the faculty of forming images in the mind: that which is imagined: contrivance. [See **Imagine.**]

**Imaginative**, im-aj'in-a-tiv, *adj.* full of imagina-

tion: given to imagining: proceeding from the imagination.—*n.* **Imag'inativeness.**

**Imagine**, im-aj'in, *v.t.* to *form* an *image* of in the mind: to conceive: to think: (*B.*) to contrive or devise.—*v.i.* to form mental images: to conceive.—*n.* **Imag'iner.** [Fr.—L. *imagino—imago*, an image.]

**Imago**, i-mā'gō, *n.* the last or perfect state of insect life, when the case covering it is dropped, and the inclosed *image* or being comes forth. [L.]

**Iman**, i-man', **Imam**, i-mam', **Imaum**, i-mawm', *n.* a Mohammedan priest: a Mohammedan prince with both temporal and spiritual authority. [Ar. *Imam*, chief.]

**Imbank**, im-bangk'. Same as **Embank.**

**Imbecile**, im'be-sēl, *adj.* without strength either of body or of mind: feeble.—*n.* one destitute of strength, either of mind or body. [Fr. *imbécile*—L. *imbecillus*; origin unknown. See **Embezzle.**]

**Imbecility**, im-be-sil'i-ti, *n.* state of being imbecile: weakness of body or mind.

**Imbed**, im-bed', *v.t.* to lay, as *in* a *bed*: to place in a mass of matter. [E. **In** (= *into*) and **Bed.**]

**Imbibe**, im-bīb', *v.t.* to *drink in*: to absorb: to receive into the mind.—*n.* **Imbib'er.** [Fr.—L. *imbibo—in*, in, into, and *bibo*, to drink.]

**Imbitter**, im-bit'ér, *v.t.* to make *bitter*: to render more violent: to render unhappy.—*n.* **Imbitt'erer.** [E. **In** and **Bitter.**]

**Imbody**, im-bod'i. Same as **Embody.**

**Imborder**, im-bor'dèr, *v.t.* to *border.*

**Imbosom**, im-booz'um. Same as **Embosom.**

**Imbricate**, im'bri-kāt, **Imbricated**, im'bri-kāt-ed, *adj.* bent like a *gutter-tile*: (*bot.*) overlapping each other like tiles on a roof. [L. *imbricatus*, pa.p. of *imbrico*, to cover with tiles—*imbrex*, a gutter-tile—*imber*, a shower.]

**Imbrication**, im-bri-kā'shun, *n.* a concave indenture as of a *tile*: an overlapping of the edges.

**Imbroglio**, im-brōl'yo, *n.* an intricate plot in a romance or drama: a perplexing state of matters: a complicated misunderstanding. [It.]

**Imbrown**, im-brown', *v.t.* to make *brown*: to darken: to obscure. [E. **In** and **Brown.**]

**Imbrue**, im-brōō', *v.t.* to wet or moisten: to soak: to drench; causal of *imbibe.* [O. Fr. *embruer* —O. Fr. *bevre* (Fr. *boire*)—L. *bibere*, to drink.]

**Imbue**, im-bū', *v.t.* to *cause* to *drink*: to moisten: to tinge deeply: to cause to imbibe, as the mind. [L. *imbuo—in*, and root of *bibo*, to drink: akin to Gr. *pi, po*, root of *pino*, Sans. *pa*, to drink.]

**Imitable**, im'it-a-bl, *adj.* that may be imitated or copied: worthy of imitation.—*n.* **Imitabil'ity.**

**Imitate**, im'i-tāt, *v.t.* to *copy*, to strive to be the same as: to produce a likeness of.—*n.* **Im'itator.** [L. *imitor*, *imitatus*, ety. unknown.]

**Imitation**, im-i-tā'shun, *n.* act of imitating: that which is produced as a copy, a likeness.

**Imitative**, im'i-tāt-iv, *adj.* inclined to imitate: formed after a model.—*adv.* **Im'itatively.**

**Immaculate**, im-mak'ū-lāt, *adj.*, *spotless*: unsta:ned: pure.—*adv.* **Immac'ulately.**—*n.* **Immac'ulateness.**—**Immaculate Conception** the R. Cath. doctrine that the Virgin Mary was born without original sin. [L. *immaculatus—in*, not, and *maculo*, to stain—*macula*, a spot.]

**Immanent**, im'a-nent, *adj., remaining within*: inherent. [L. *immanens*, *-entis*, pr.p. of *immaneo—in*, in or near. *maneo*, to remain.]

**Immaterial**, im-a-tē'ri-al, *adj., not* consisting of *matter*: incorporeal: unimportant.—*adv.* **Immate'rially.**—*v.* **Immate'rialise.** [Fr.—L. *in*, not, and **Material.**]

**Immaterialism**, im-a-tē'ri-al-izm, *n.* the doctrine

that there is *no material* substance.—*n.* **Imma-te'rialist,** one who believes in this.

**Immateriality,** im-a-tē-ri-al'i-ti, *n.* the quality of being immaterial or of not consisting of matter.

**Immature,** im-a-tūr', **Immatured,** im-a-tūrd', *adj.* not *ripe* : not perfect : come before the natural time.—*adv.* **Immature'ly.**—*ns.* **Imma-ture'ness, Immaturity.** [L. *in,* not, and **Mature.**]

**Immeasurable,** im-mezh'ūr-a-bl, *adj.* that cannot be measured.—*adv.* **Immeas'urably.**—*n.* **Im-meas'urableness.** [Fr.—L. *in,* not, and **Meas-urable.**]

**Immediate,** im-mē'di-āt, *adj.* with *nothing* in the *middle* between two objects : not acting by second causes : direct : present : without delay. —*adv.* **Imme'diately.**—*n.* **Imme'diateness.** [Fr.—Low L. *immediatus—in,* not, and *medius,* the middle.]

**Immemorial,** im-me-mō'ri-al, *adj.* beyond the reach of *memory.*—*adv.* **Immemo'rially.** [Fr. —L. *in,* not, and **Memorial.**]

**Immense,** im-mens', *adj.* that cannot be *measured* : vast in extent : very large.—*adv.* **Immense'ly.** —*n.* **Immense'ness.** [Fr.—L. *immensus—in,* not, *mensus,* pa.p. of *metior,* to measure.]

**Immensity,** im-mens'it-i, *n.* an extent *not* to be *measured* : infinity : greatness.

**Immensurable,** im-mens'ūr-a-bl, *adj.* that cannot be *measured.*—*n.* **Immensurabil'ity.** [Fr.—L. *in,* not, and *mensurabilis—metior.*]

**Immerge,** im-mėrj', *v.t.* to plunge something *into.* [L. *in,* into, and *mergo, mersus* to plunge.]

**Immerse,** im-mėrs', *v.t.* to *immerge* or plunge something into : to engage deeply : to overwhelm.

**Immersion,** im-mėr'shun, *n.* act of immersing or plunging into : state of being dipped into : state of being deeply engaged.

**Immethodical,** im-me-thod'ik-al, *adj.* without method or order : irregular.—*adv.* **Immethod'-ically.** [L. *in,* not, and **Methodical.**]

**Immigrant,** im'i-grant, *n.* one who immigrates.

**Immigrate,** im'i-grāt, *v.i.* to *migrate* or remove *into* a country. [L. *immigro—in,* into, and *migro, migratum,* to remove.]

**Immigration,** im-i-grā'shun, *n.* act of immigrating.

**Imminent,** im'i-nent, *adj.* near at hand : threaten-ing : impending.—*adv.* **Imm'inently.**—*n.* **Imm'-inence.** [L. *imminens, -entis—in,* upon, *mineo,* to project.]

**Immission,** im-mish'un, *n.* act of *immitting.*

**Immit,** im-mit', *v.t.* to *send into* : to inject :—*pr.p.* immitt'ing ; *pa.p.* immitt'ed. [L. *immitto—in,* into, *mitto, missus,* to send.]

**Immobility,** im-mo-bil'i-ti, *n.* the being *immov-able.* [Fr.—L. *in,* not, and **Mobility.**]

**Immoderate,** im-mod'ėr-āt, *adj.* exceeding proper bounds.—*adv.* **Immod'erately.** [L. *in,* not, and **Moderate.**]

**Immodest,** im-mod'est, *adj.* wanting restraint : impudent : wanting shame or delicacy.—*adv.* **Immod'estly.**—*n.* **Immod'esty,** *want of mod-esty.* [Fr.—L. *in,* not, and **Modest.**]

**Immolate,** im'o-lāt, *v.t.* to offer in sacrifice. [Lit. 'to sprinkle meal on a victim,' L. *immolo, immo-latus—in,* upon, *mola,* meal.]    [a sacrifice.

**Immolation,** im-o-lā'shun, *n.* act of immolating.

**Immoral,** im-mor'al, *adj.* inconsistent with what is right : wicked.—*adv.* **Immor'ally.** [Fr.—L. *in,* not, and **Moral.**]

**Immorality,** im-mor-al'i-ti, *n.* quality of being im-moral : an immoral act or practice.

**Immortal,** im-mor'tal, *adj.* exempt from death : imperishable : never to be forgotten (as a name,

poem, &c.).—*n.* one who will never cease to exist.—*adv.* **Immor'tally.** [Fr.—L. *in,* not, and **Mortal.**]

**Immortalise,** im-mor'tal-īz, *v.t.* to make immortal.

**Immortality,** im-mor-tal'i-ti, *n.* quality of being immortal : exemption from death or oblivion.

**Immortelle,** im-mor-tel', *n.* the flower commonly called *everlasting.* [Fr. (*fleur*) *immortelle,* immortal (flower).]

**Immovable,** im-mōōv'a-bl, *adj.* steadfast : un-alterable : that cannot be impressed or made to fall.—*adv.* **Immov'ably.**—*ns.* **Immov'ableness, Immovabil'ity.** [Fr.—L. *in,* not, and **Movable.**]

**Immovables,** im-mōōv'a-blz, *n.pl.* fixtures, &c., *not movable* by a tenant.

**Immunity,** im-mūn'i-ti, *n., freedom* from any *obligation* or *duty* : privilege. [Fr.—L. *im-munitas—in,* not, *munis,* serving, obliging.]

**Immure,** im-mūr', *v.t.* to *wall in* : to shut up : to imprison. [Fr.—L. *in,* in, and *murus,* a wall.]

**Immutability,** im-mūt-a-bil'i-ti, **Immutableness,** im-mūt'a-bl-nes, *n.* unchangeableness.

**Immutable,** im-mūt'a-bl, *adj.* unchangeable.—*adv.* **Immut'ably.** [Fr.—L. *in,* not, and **Mut-able.**]

**Imp,** imp, *n.* a little devil or wicked spirit.—*v.t.* (*falconry*) to mend a broken or defective wing by inserting a feather : to qualify for flight.—*adj.* **Imp'ish,** like an imp : fiendish. [Lit. and orig. a *graft, offspring* ; from Low L. *impotus,* a graft—Gr. *emphytos,* ingrafted—*en,* and root *phy-,* to grow ; akin to **Be.**]

**Impact,** im'pakt, *n. a striking against* : collision : the blow of a body in motion *impinging* on another body : the impulse resulting from col-lision.—**Impact',** *v.t.* to press firmly together. [L. *impactus,* pa.p. of *impingo.* See **Impinge.**]

**Impair,** im-pār', *v.t.* to *make worse* : to diminish in quantity, value, or strength : to injure : to weaken. [M. E. *empeiren*—O. Fr. *empeirer* (Fr. *empirer*), from L. *im (in),* inten-ive, and Low L. *pejorare,* to make worse—L. *pejor,* worse.]    [palement.

**Impale, Impalement.** Same as **Empale, Em-**

**Impalpable,** im-pal'pa-bl, *adj.* not perceivable by touch : not coarse : not easily understood.—*adv.* **Impal'pably**—*n.* **Impalpabil'ity.** [Fr.—L. *in,* not, and **Palpable.**]

**Impanel, Impannel,** im-pan'l, *v.t.* to enter the names of a jury in a list, or *on* a piece of parch-ment called a *panel* :—*pr.p.* impan'elling ; *pa.p.* impan'elled. [L. *in,* in, and **Panel.**]

**Imparity,** im-par'i-ti, *n., want of parity* or equality : indivisibility into equal parts. [L. *in,* not. and **Parity.**]

**Impark,** im-pärk', *v.t.* to *inclose* for a *park* : to shut up. [L. *in,* in, and **Park.**]

**Impart,** im-pärt', *v.t.* to bestow a *part* of : to give : to communicate : to make known.—*v.i.* to give a part. [O. Fr.—L. *impartio—in,* on, and *pars, partis,* a part.]

**Impartial,** im-pär'shal, *adj.* not favouring one more than another : just.—*adv.* **Impar'tially.** [Fr.—L. *in,* not, and **Partial.**]

**Impartiality,** im-pär-shi-al'i-ti, *n.* quality of being impartial : freedom from bias.

**Impartible,** im-pärt'i-bl, *adj.* capable of being imparted.—*n.* **Impartibil'ity.** [From **Impart.**]

**Impartible,** im-pärt'i-bl, *adj.* not partible : indi-visible.—*n.* **Impartibil'ity.** [L. *in,* not, and **Partible.**]

**Impassable,** im-pas'a-bl, *adj.* not capable of being passed.—*adv* **Impass'ably.**—*ns.* **Impassabil'-ity, Impass'ableness.** [L. *in,* not, **Passable.**]

**Impassible**, im-pas′i-bl, *adj.* incapable of passion or feeling.—*ns.* **Impassibil′ity**, **Impass′ibleness**, quality of being impassible. [Fr.—L. *impassibilis—in*, not, and *patior, passus*, to suffer.]

**Impassioned**, im-pash′und, **Impassionate**, im-pash′un-āt, *adj.* moved by strong passion or feeling : animated : excited. [L. *in*, intensive, and **Passion**.]

**Impassive**, im-pas′iv, *adj.* not susceptible of pain or feeling.—*adv.* **Impass′ively**.—*n.* **Impass′iveness**.

**Impatient**, im-pā′shent, *adj.* not able to endure or to wait : fretful : restless.—*adv.* **Impa′tiently**.—*n.* **Impa′tience**, want of patience.

**Impawn**, im-pawn′, *v.t.* to *pawn* or deposit as security. [L. *in*, intensive, and **Pawn**.]

**Impeach**, im-pēch′, *v.t.* to charge with a crime : to cite before a court for official misconduct : to call in question.—*n.* **Impeach′ment**, an accusation presented by the House of Commons to the House of Lords, as the supreme court of criminal jurisdiction. [Lit. 'to hinder,' Fr. *empêcher* (It. *impacciare*) ; either from L. *impingere*, to strike against, or *impedicare*, to fetter. See **Impinge** and **Impede**.]

**Impeachable**, im-pēch′a-bl, *adj.* liable to impeachment : chargeable with a crime.

**Impearl**, im-pėrl′, *v.t.* to adorn with or as with *pearls* : to make like pearls. [L. *in*, in, and **Pearl**.]

**Impeccable**, im-pek′a-bl, *adj.* not liable to sin.—*ns.* **Impeccabil′ity**, **Impecc′ancy**. [L. *in*, not, and **Peccable**.]

**Impecunious**, im-pe-kū′ni-us, *adj.* having *no money* : poor.—*n.* **Impecunios′ity**. [L. *in*, priv., and *pecunia*, money.]

**Impede**, im-pēd′, *v.t.* to hinder or obstruct. [Lit. 'to entangle the feet,' from L. *impedio—in*, in, and *pes, pedis*, a foot.]

**Impediment**, im-ped′i-ment, *n.* that which impedes : hinderance : a defect preventing fluent speech.

**Impeditive**. im-ped′i-tiv, *adj.* causing *hinderance*.

**Impel**, im-pel′, *v.t.* to *drive* or urge forward : to excite to action : to instigate :—*pr.p.* impell′ing ; *pa.p.* impelled′.—*n.* **Impell′er**. [L. *impello, impulsus—in*, on, and *pello*, to drive.]

**Impellent**, im-pel′ent, *adj.* having the quality of impelling or driving on.—*n.* a power that impels.

**Impend**, im-pend′, *v.i.* to *hang over* : to threaten : to be near. [L. *in*, on, and *pendeo*, to hang.]

**Impendent**, im-pend′ent, **Impending**, im-pend′ing, *adj.*, *hanging over* : ready to act or happen.

**Impenetrable**, im-pen′e-tra-bl, *adj.* incapable of being pierced : preventing another body from occupying the same space at the same time : not to be impressed in mind or heart.—*adv.* **Impen′etrably**.—*n.* **Impen′etrability**, quality of being impenetrable. [Fr.—L. *in*, not, and **Penetrable**.]

**Impenitent**, im-pen′i-tent, *adj.* not repenting of sin.—*n.* one who does not repent : a hardened sinner.—*adv.* **Impen′itently**.—*n.* **Impen′itence**. [Fr.—L. *in*, not. and **Penitent**.]

**Impennate**, im-pen′āt, **Impennous**, im-pen′us, *adj.* wingless : having very short wings useless for flight. [L. *in*, not, and **Pennate**.]

**Imperative**, im-per′a-tiv, *adj.* expressive of *command* : authoritative : obligatory.—*adv.* **Imper′atively**. [Fr.—L. *imperativus—impero*, to command—*in*, and *paro*, to prepare.]

**Imperceptible**, im-pėr-sep′ti-bl, *adj.* not discernible : insensible : minute.—*ns.* **Impercep′tibleness**, **Imperceptibil′ity**.—*adv.* **Impercep′tibly**. [L. *in*, not, and **Perceptible**.]

**Imperfect**, im-pėr′fekt, *adj.* incomplete : defective : not fulfilling its design : liable to err.—*ns.* **Imper′fectness**, **Imperfec′tion**.—*adv.* **Imper′fectly**. [Fr.—L. *in*, not, and **Perfect**.]

**Imperforable**, im-pėr′for-a-bl, *adj.* that cannot be perforated or bored through.

**Imperforate**, im-pėr′fo-rāt, **Imperforated**, im-pėr′fo-rāt-ed, *adj.* not pierced through : having no opening.—*n.* **Imperfora′tion**. [L. *in*, not, and **Perforate**.]

**Imperial**, im-pē′ri-al, *adj.* pertaining to an *empire* or to an emperor : sovereign : supreme : of superior size or excellence.—*n.* a tuft of hair on the lower lip : a kind of dome, as in Moorish buildings : an outside seat on a diligence.—*adv.* **Impe′rially**. [Fr.—L. *imperialis—imperium*, sovereignty. See **Empire**.]

**Imperialism**, im-pē′ri-al-izm, *n.* the power or authority of an *emperor* : the spirit of empire.

**Imperialist**, im-pē′ri-al-ist, *n.* one who belongs to an *emperor* : a soldier or partisan of an emperor.

**Imperiality**, im-pē-ri-al′i-ti, *n.* imperial power, right, or privilege.

**Imperil**, im-per′il, *v.t.* to put *in peril* : to endanger. [L. *in*, in, and **Peril**.]

**Imperious**, im-pē′ri-us, *adj.* assuming *command* : haughty : tyrannical : authoritative.—*adv.* **Impe′riously**.—*n.* **Impe′riousness**. [L. *imperiosus*.]

**Imperishable**, im-per′ish-a-bl, *adj.* indestructible : everlasting.—*ns.* **Imper′ishableness**, **Imperishabil′ity**.—*adv.* **Imper′ishably**. [Fr.—L. *in* = not, and **Perishable**.]

**Impermeable**, im-pėr′me-a-bl, *adj.* not permitting passage : impenetrable.—*ns.* **Impermeabil′ity**, **Imper′meableness**.—*adv.* **Imper′meably**. [Fr.—L. *in*, not, and **Permeable**.]

**Impersonal**, im-pėr′sun-al, *adj.* not representing a person : not having personality : (*gram.*) not varied acc. to the persons.—*adv.* **Imper′sonally**.—*n.* **Impersonal′ity**. [Fr.—L. *in*, not, and **Personal**.]

**Impersonate**, im-pėr′sun-āt, *v.t.* to invest with personality or the bodily substance of a person : to ascribe the qualities of a person to : to personify.—*n.* **Impersona′tion**. [L. *in*, in, and **Personate**.]

**Impersuasible**, im-pėr-swā′zi-bl, *adj.* not to be moved by persuasion or argument. [L. *in*, not, and **Persuasible**.]

**Impertinence**, im-pėr′ti-nens, *n.* that which is impertinent, out of place, or of no weight : intrusion : impudence.

**Impertinent**, im-pėr′ti-nent, *adj.* not *pertaining* to the matter in hand : trifling : intrusive : saucy : impudent.—*adv.* **Imper′tinently**. [Fr.—L. *in*. not, and **Pertinent**.]

**Imperturbable**, im-pėr-tur′ba-bl, *adj.* that cannot be disturbed or agitated : permanently quiet.—*n.* **Imperturbabil′ity**. [L. *imperturbabilis—in*, not, and *perturbo*, to disturb.]

**Imperturbation**, im-pėr-tur-bā′shun, *n.* freedom from agitation of mind.

**Impervious**, im-pėr′vi-a-bl, **Impervious**, im-pėr′vi-us, *adj.* not to be penetrated.—*ns.* **Imper′viableness**, **Imperviabil′ity**, **Imper′viousness**.—*adv.* **Imper′viously**. [L. *in*, not, and **Pervious**.]

**Impetigo**, im-pe-tī′go, *n.* a skin disease characterised by thickly-set clusters of pustules. [L. *impeto*, to attack.]

**Impetuous**, im-pet′ū-us, *adj.* rushing upon with *impetus* or violence : vehement in feeling : furious : passionate.—*ns.* **Impet′uousness**, **Impetuos′ity**.—*adv.* **Impet′uously**.

**Impetus**, im′pe-tus, *n.* an attack : assault : force

or quantity of motion : violent tendency to any point : activity. [L.—*in*, and *peto*, to fall upon.]

**Impiety.** See **Impiousness.**

**Impinge,** im-pinj´, *v.i* to *strike* or fall *against*: to touch upon. [L. *impingo*—*in*, against, and *pango*, to strike.]

**Impingement,** im-pinj´ment, *n.* act of impinging.

**Impingent,** im-pinj´ent, *adj.* striking against.

**Impious,** im pi-us, *adj.* irreverent : wanting in veneration for God : profane.—*adv.* **Im piously.** [Fr.—L. *in*, not, and **Pious.**]

**Impiousness,** im′pi-us-nes, **Impiety,** im-pī′e-ti, *n.* want of piety : irreverence towards God : neglect of the divine precepts.

**Implacable,** im-plăk′a-bl, *adj.* not to be appeased : inexorable : irreconcilable.—*adv.* **Impla cably.** —*ns.* **Impla′cableness, Implacabil′ity.** [Fr.— L. *in*, not and **Placable.**]

**Implant,** im-plant′, *v.t.* to *plant* or fix *into* : to plant in order to grow : to insert : to infuse. [Fr. —L. *in*, into, and **Plant.**]

**Implantation,** im-plan-tā′shun, *n.* the act of implanting or infixing, esp. in the mind or heart.

**Implead,** im-plēd′, *v.t.* to put *in* or urge a *plea* : to prosecute a suit at law.—*n.* **Implead′er.** [Fr. —L. *in*, in, and **Plead.**]

**Implement,** im′ple-ment, *n.* a tool or instrument of labour.—*v.t.* to give effect to. [Low L. *implementum*, an accomplishing—L. *im-pleo*, to fill, to discharge ; akin to *ple-nus*. See **Full.**]

**Impletion,** im-plē′shun, *n.* a filling : the state of being full. [From *impleo*. See **Implement.**]

**Implex,** im′pleks, *adj.* not simple : complicated. [L. *implexus*—*implecto*—*in*, into, and *plecto*, akin to Gr. *plekō*, to twine.]

**Implicate,** im′pli-kāt, *v.t.* to *infold* : to involve : to entangle. [L. *implico, implicatus, implicitus* —*im* (= *in*), in, and *plica*, a fold. See **Ply. Imply** and **Employ** are doublets.]

**Implication,** im-pli-kā′shun, *n.* the act of implicating : entanglement : that which is implied.

**Implicative,** im′pli-kā-tiv, *adj.* tending to implicate.—*adv.* **Im′plicatively.**

**Implicit,** im-plis′it, *adj.* implied : resting on or trusting another : relying entirely.—*adv.* **Implic′itly.**—*n.* **Implic′itness.** [Lit. *infolded*, from L. *implicitus*—*implico.* See **Implicate.**]

**Implore,** im-plōr′, *v.t.* to ask earnestly : to beg. [Fr.—L. *imploro*—*in*, and *ploro*, to weep aloud.]

**Imploringly,** im-plōr′ing-li, *adv.* in an imploring or very earnest manner.

**Imply,** im-plī′, *v.t.* to include in reality : to mean : to signify :—*pa.p.* implied′. [Lit. to *infold*—L. *implico.* Cf. **Implicate.**]

**Impolicy,** im-pol′i-si, *n.* imprudence.

**Impolite,** im-po-līt′, *adj.* of unpolished manners : uncivil.—*adv.* **Impolite′ly.**—*n.* **Impolite′ness.** [L. *in*, not, and **Polite.**]

**Impolitic,** im-pol′i-tik. *adj.* imprudent : unwise : inexpedient.—*adv.* **Impol′iticly.** [L. *in*, not, and **Politic.**]

**Imponderable,** im-pon′dėr-a-bl, *adj.* not able to be weighed : without sensible weight.—**Impon′derables,** *n.pl.* fluids *without* sensible *weight*, the old general name given to heat, light, electricity, and magnetism, when they were supposed to be material.—*ns.* **Impon′derableness, Imponderabil′ity.** [L. *in*, not, and **Ponder-able.**] [derable.]

**Imponderous,** im-pon′dėr-us. Same as **Impon-**

**Import,** im-pōrt′, *v.t.* to *carry into* : to bring from abroad : to convey, as a word : to signify : to be of consequence to : to interest. [Fr.—L. *importo, -atus*—*in*, in, and *porto*, to carry.]

**Import,** im′pōrt, *n.* that which is brought from abroad : meaning : importance : tendency.

**Importable,** im-pōrt′a-bl, *adj.* that may be imported or brought into a country : (*obs.*) not to be borne or endured : insupportable.

**Important,** im-port′ant, *adj.* of great import or consequence : momentous.—*adv.* **Import′antly.** —*n.* **Import′ance.**

**Importation,** im-por-tā′shun, *n.* the act of importing : the commodities imported.

**Importer,** im-pōrt′ėr, *n.* one who brings in goods from abroad.

**Importunate,** im-port′ū-nāt, *adj.* troublesomely urgent : over-pressing in request.—*adv.* **Import′-unately.**—*n.* **Import′unateness.** [Coined from the word following.]

**Importune,** im-por-tūn′, *v.t.* to urge with *troublesome* application : to press urgently. [In M. E. an adj., and sig. 'troublesome,' through the Fr., from L. *importunus*, orig. 'difficult of access,' from *in*, not, and *portus*, a harbour. Cf. **Opportune.**]

**Importunity,** im-por-tūn′i-ti, *n.* the quality of being importunate : urgent request. [L. *importunitas*.]           [posed or laid on.

**Imposable,** im-pōz′a-bl, *adj.* capable of being im-

**Impose,** im-pōz′, *v.t.* to *place upon* : to lay on : to enjoin or command : to put over by authority or force : to obtrude unfairly : to palm off.—*v.i.* to mislead or deceive [Fr. *imposer*—*im* (= L. *in*), on, and *poser*, to place. See **Pose.**]

**Imposing,** im-pōz′ing, *adj.* commanding : adapted to impress forcibly. *adv.* **Impos′ingly.**

**Imposition,** im-po-zish′un, *n.* a *laying on* : laying on of hands in ordination : a tax, a burden : a deception. [Fr.—L.—*impono, impositus*, to lay on—*in*, on, and *pono*, to place.]

**Impossible,** im-pos′i-bl, *adj.* that which cannot be done : that cannot exist : absurd.—*n.* **Impossibil′ity.** [Fr.—L. *in*, not, and **Possible.**]

**Impost,** im′pōst, *n.* a tax, esp. on imports : (*arch.*) that part of a pillar in vaults and arches on which the weight of the building is laid. [O. Fr. *impost*, Fr. *impôt*—L. *impono*, to lay on.]

**Imposthumate,** im-pos′tūm-āt, *v.i.* to form an imposthume or abscess. *v.t.* to affect with an imposthume.—*n.* **Imposthuma′tion,** the act of forming an abscess : an abscess.

**Imposthume,** im-pos′tūm, *n.* an abscess : a gathering or corrupt matter in a cavity in the tissues. [A corr. of L. *apostema*—Gr. *aphistēmi*, to separate—*apo*, away, *histēmi*, to make to stand.]

**Impostor,** im-pos′tur, *n.* one who practises imposition or fraud. [L.—*impono*, to lay on.]

**Imposture,** im-pos′tūr, *n.* imposition or fraud.

**Impotent,** im′po-tent, *adj.* powerless : unable : imbecile : useless : wanting the power of self-restraint.—*adv.* **Impotently.**—*ns.* **Im′potence, Im′potency.** [Fr.—L. *in*, not, and **Potent.**]

**Impound,** im-pownd′, *v.t.* to confine, as in a *pound* : to restrain within limits : to take possession of. —*n.* **Impound′age,** the act of impounding cattle. [E **In** and **Pound,** an inclosure.]

**Impoverish,** im-pov′ėr-ish, *v.t.* to make *poor* : to exhaust the resources (as of a nation), or fertility (as of the soil).—*n.* **Impov′erishment.** [A corr. of *appovriss-ant*, pr.p. of O. Fr. *appovrir* (Fr. *appauvrir*)—Fr. prefix *ap-* (= L. *ad*), towards, and O. Fr. *povre* (Fr. *pauvre*), poor—L. *pauper*.]

**Impracticable,** im-prak′tik-a-bl, *adj.* not able to be done : unmanageable : stubborn.—*adv.* **Imprac′-ticably.**—*ns.* **Imprac′ticability, Imprac′tic-ableness.** [L. *in*, not, and **Practicable.**]

**Imprecate,** im′pre-kāt, *v.t.* (*lit.*) to *pray* for good

or evil *upon*: to curse.—*n.* **Impreca'tion**, the act of imprecating: a curse. [L. *imprecor, imprecatus—in*, upon, *precor, precatum*, to pray.]

**Imprecatory**, im'pre-kā-tor-i, *adj.* cursing.

**Impregnable**, im-preg'na-bl, *adj.* that cannot be *taken* or seized: that cannot be moved or shaken: invincible.—*adv.* **Impreg'nably**.—*n.* **Impregnabil'ity**. [Fr. *imprenable*—L. *in*, not, and *prehendo*, to take. See **Get**.]

**Impregnate**, im-preg'nāt, *v.t.* to make *pregnant*: to come into contact with an ovum, so as to cause it to germinate: to impart the particles or qualities of one thing to another. [Low L. *imprægno, -atus—in*, and *prægnans*, pregnant. See **Pregnant**.]

**Impregnation**, im-preg-nā'shun, *n.* the act of impregnating: that with which anything is impregnated.

**Impress**, im-pres', *v.t* to *press upon*: to mark by pressure: to produce by pressure: to stamp: to fix deeply (in the mind): to force into service, esp. the public service.—*n.* **Im'press**, that which is made by pressure: stamp, likeness: device, motto. [L. *in*, in, *premo, pressus*, to press.]

**Impressible**, im-pres'i-bl, *adj.* capable of being impressed or made to feel: susceptible.—*adv.* **Impress'ibly**.—*n.* **Impressibil'ity**.

**Impression**, im-presh'un, *n.* the act of impressing: that which is produced by pressure: a single edition of a book: the effect of any object on the mind: idea: slight remembrance.—*adj.* **Impress'ionable**, able to receive an impression.

**Impressive**, im-pres'iv, *adj.* capable of making an impression on the mind: solemn.—*adv.* **Impress'ively**.—*n.* **Impress'iveness**.

**Impressment**, im-pres'ment, *n.* the act of impressing or seizing for service, esp. in the navy. [A word coined from *press*, in **Pressgang**.]

**Imprimatur**, im-pri-mā'tur, *n.* a license to print a book, &c. [Lit. 'let it be printed;' from L. *imprimo—in*, on, and *premo*, to press.]

**Imprint**, im-print', *v.t.* to *print in* or *upon*: to print: to stamp: to impress: to fix in the mind.—*n.* **Im'print**, that which is *imprinted*: the name of the publisher, time and place of publication of a book, &c. printed on the title-page: also the printer's name on the back of the title-page, and at the end of the book. [L. *in*, in or upon, and **Print**.]

**Imprison**, im-priz'n, *v.t.* to put *in prison*: to shut up: to confine or restrain.—*n.* **Impris'onment**, the act of imprisoning or state of being imprisoned: confinement or restraint. [Fr.—L. *in*, into, and **Prison**.]

**Improbable**, im-prob'a-bl, *adj.* unlikely.—*adv.* **Improb'ably**.—*n.* **Improbabil'ity**. [Fr.—L. *in*, not, and **Probable**.]

**Improbity**, im-prob'i-ti, *n.* want of *probity* or integrity: dishonesty. [L. *in*, not, and **Probity**.]

**Impromptu**, im-promp'tū, *adj.*, *prompt, ready*: off-hand.—*adv.* readily.—*n.* a short witty saying expressed at the moment: any composition produced at the moment. [Fr.—L.—*in*, and *promptus*, readiness. See **Prompt**.]

**Improper**, im-prop'ér, *adj.* not suitable: unfit: unbecoming: incorrect: wrong.—*adv.* **Improp'erly**. [Fr.—L. *in*, not, and **Proper**.]

**Impropriate**, im-prō'pri-āt, *v.t.* (*lit.*) to *appropriate* to private use: to place ecclesiastical property in the hands of a layman.—*n.* **Impropria'tion**, the act of appropriating: the property impropriated. [L. *in*, in. and *proprio, propriatum*, to appropriate—*proprius*, one's own, proper.]

**Impropriety**, im-pro-prī'e-ti, *n.* that which is improper or unsuitable: want of propriety or fitness. [L. *in*, not, and **Propriety**.]

**Improvable**, im-prōōv'a-bl, *adj.* able to be improved: capable of being used to advantage.—*adv.* **Improv'ably**.—*ns.* **Improvabil'ity**, **Improv'ableness**.

**Improve**, im-prōōv', *v.t.* to make better: to advance in value or excellence: to correct: to employ to good purpose.—*v.i.* to grow better: to make progress: to increase: to rise (as prices).—*n.* **Improv'er**. [Prefix *in-* and O. Fr. *prover*—L. *probare*, to try, to consider as good.]

**Improvement**, im-prōōv'ment, *n.* the act of improving: advancement or progress: increase, addition, or alteration: the turning to good account: instruction.

**Improvident**, im-prov'i-dent, *adj.* not provident or prudent: wanting foresight: thoughtless.—*adv.* **Improv'idently**.—*n.* **Improv'idence**. [L. *in*, not, and **Provident**.] [ing manner.

**Improvingly**, im-prōōv'ing-li, *adv.* in an improv-

**Improvisate**, im-prov'i-sāt, **Improvise**, im-pro-vīz', *v.t.* to compose and recite, esp. in verse, *without preparation*: to bring about on a sudden: to do anything off-hand.—*n.* **Improvis'er**. [Fr. *improviser*—It. *improvisare*—L. *in*, not, and *provisus*, foreseen. See **Provide**.]

**Improvisation**, im-prov-i-sā'shun, *n.* act of improvising: that which is improvised.

**Improvisatore**, im-pro-viz-a-tō'rā, *n.* one who improvises: one who composes and recites verses without preparation:—*pl.* **Improvisato'ri** (-rē). [It. See **Improvisate**.]

**Imprudent**, im-prōō'dent, *adj.* wanting foresight or discretion: incautious: inconsiderate.—*adv.* **Impru'dently**.—*n.* **Impru'dence**. [Fr.—L. *in*, not, and **Prudent**.]

**Impudent**, im'pū-dent, *adj.*, *wanting shame* or modesty: brazen-faced: bold: rude: insolent.—*adv.* **Im'pudently**.—*n.* **Im'pudence**. [Fr.—L. *in*, not, *pudens, -entis*, from *pudeo*, to be ashamed.]

**Impugn**, im-pūn', *v.t.* to oppose: to attack by words or arguments: to call in question.—*n.* **Impugn'er**. [Fr.—L. *impugno—in*, against, *pugno*, to fight.]

**Impugnable**, im-pūn'a-bl, *adj.* able to be impugned or called in question.

**Impulse**, im'puls, **Impulsion**, im-pul'shun, *n.* the act of *impelling* or driving on: effect of an impelling force force suddenly communicated: influence on the mind. [From **Impel**.]

**Impulsive**, im-puls'iv, *adj.* having the power of *impelling* or driving on: actuated by mental impulse: (*mech.*) acting by impulse: not continuous.—*adv.* **Impuls'ively**.—*n.* **Impuls'iveness**.

**Impunity**, im-pūn'i-ti, *n.* freedom or safety from punishment: exemption from injury or loss. [Fr.—L. *impunitas—in*, not, *pœna*, punishment.]

**Impure**, im-pūr', *adj.* mixed with other substances: defiled by sin: unholy: unchaste: unclean.—*adv.* **Impure'ly**.—*ns.* **Impur'ity**, **Impure'ness**, quality of being impure. [Fr.—L. *in*, not, **Pure**.]

**Impurple**, im-pur'pl. Same as **Empurple**.

**Imputable**, im-pūt'a-bl, *adj.* capable of being imputed or charged: attributable.—*adv.* **Imput'ably**.—*ns.* **Imput'ableness**, **Imputabil'ity**.

**Imputation**, im-pū-tā'shun, *n.* act of imputing or charging: censure: reproach: the reckoning as belonging to. [puted.—*adv.* **Imput'atively**.

**Imputative**, im-pūt'a-tiv, *adj.* that may be im-

**Impute**, im-pūt', *v.t.* to reckon as belonging to—

fāte, fär; mē, hèr; mīne; mōte; mūte; mōōn; *then*.

in a bad sense : to charge.—*n.* **Imput'er.** [Fr. *imputer*—L. *imputo*, *-atum*—*in*, and *puto*, to reckon.]

**In,** in, *prep.* denotes presence or situation in place, time, or circumstances—within, during : by or through.—*adv.* within : not out. [A.S. *in* ; Dut., Ger., and Goth. *in*, Scand. *i* ; W. *yn*, Ir. *in* ; L. *in*, Gr. *en* ; Sans. *ana.*]

**Inability,** in-a-bil'i-ti, *n.* want of sufficient power : incapacity. [Fr.—L. *in*, not, and **Ability.**]

**Inaccessible,** in-ak-ses'i-bl, *adj.* not to be reached, obtained, or approached.—*adv.* **Inaccess'ibly.**—*ns.* **Inaccess'ibility, Inaccess'ibleness.** [Fr.—L. *in*, not, and **Accessible.**] [mistake.

**Inaccuracy,** in-ak'kūr-a-si, *n.* want of exactness :

**Inaccurate,** in-ak'kūr-āt, *adj.* not exact or correct : erroneous.—*adv.* **Inac'curately.** [L. *in*, not, and **Accurate.**]

**Inaction,** in-ak'shun, *n.* want of action : idleness : rest. [Fr.—L. *in*, not, and **Action.**]

**Inactive,** in-akt'iv, *adj.* having no power to move : idle : lazy : (*chem.*) not shewing any action.—*adv.* **Inact'ively.** [L. *in*, not, and **Active.**]

**Inactivity,** in-akt-iv'i-ti, *n.* want of activity : inertness : idleness. [L. *in*, not, and **Activity.**]

**Inadequate,** in-ad'e-kwāt, *adj.* insufficient.—*adv.* **Inad'equately.**—*ns.* **Inad'equacy, Inad'equateness,** insufficiency. [L. *in*, not, **Adequate.**]

**Inadmissible,** in-ad-mis'i-bl, *adj.* not admissible or allowable.—*n.* **Inadmissibil'ity.** [Fr.—L. *in*, not, **Admissible.**]

**Inadvertence,** in-ad-vèrt'ens, **Inadvertency,** in-ad-vèrt'en-si, *n.* lack of advertence or attention : negligence : oversight.

**Inadvertent,** in-ad-vèrt'ent, *adj.* inattentive.—*adv.* **Inadvert'ently.** [L. *in*, not, **Advertent.**]

**Inalienable,** in-āl'yen-a-bl, *adj.* not capable of being transferred.—*n.* **Inal'ienableness.** [Fr.—L. *in*, not, **Alienable.**]

**Inamorato,** in-am-o-rä'tō, *n.* one who is enamoured or in love :—*pl.* **Inamora'ti** (-tē). [It. See **Enamour.**]

**Inane,** in-ān', *adj., empty :* void : void of intelligence : useless. [L. *inanis.*]

**Inanimate,** in-an'im-āt, *adj.* without animation or life : dead. [L. *in*, not, **Animate.**]

**Inanimation,** in-an-im-ā'shun, *n.* want of animation : lifelessness. [L. *in*, not, and **Animation.**]

**Inanition,** in-a-nish'un, *n.* state of being inane : emptiness : exhaustion from want of food. [Fr., from root of **Inane.**]

**Inanity,** in-an'i-ti, *n* empty space : senselessness.

**Inapplicable,** in-ap'plik-a-bl, *adj.* not applicable or suitable.—*n.* **Inapplicabil'ity.** [L. *in*, not, **Applicable.**]

**Inapplication,** in-ap-plik-ā'shun, *n.* want of application or attention. [L. *in*, not, **Application.**]

**Inapposite,** in-ap'poz-it, *adj.* not apposite or suitable.—*adv.* **Inap'positely.** [L. *in*, not, **Apposite.**]

**Inappreciable,** in-ap-prē'shi-a-bl, *adj.* not appreciable or able to be valued. [L. *in*, not, **Appreciable.**]

**Inapproachable,** in-ap-prōch'a-bl, *adj.* inaccessible. [L. *in*, not, **Approachable.**]

**Inappropriate,** in-ap-prō'pri-āt, *adj.* not suitable.—*adv.* **Inappro'priately.**—*n.* **Inappro'priateness.** [L. *in*, not, **Appropriate.**]

**Inapt,** in-apt', *adj.* not *apt :* unfit.—*adv.* **Inapt'ly.**—*n.* **Inapt'itude,** unfitness. [L. *in*, not, **Apt.**]

**Inarching,** in-ärch'ing, *n.* a method of grafting by which branches are united together, generally in

the form of an arch, before being separated from the original stem. [L. *in*, and **Arch.**]

**Inarticulate,** in-är-tik'ūl-āt, *adj.* not distinct : (*zool.*) not jointed.—*adv.* **Inartic'ulately.**—*ns.* **Inartic'ulateness, Inarticula'tion,** indistinctness of sounds in speaking. [L. *in*, not, and **Articulate.**]

**Inartificial,** in-ärt-i-fish'yal, *adj.* not done by art : simple.—*adv.* **Inartific'ially.** [L. *in*, not, **Artificial.**]

**Inasmuch,** in-az-much', *adv.* since : seeing that : this being the case. [**In, As,** and **Much.**]

**Inattention,** in-at-ten'shun, *n.* want of attention : neglect : heedlessness. [Fr.—L. *in*, not, **Attention.**] [attent'ively.

**Inattentive,** in-at-tent'iv, *adj.* careless.—*adv.* **In-**

**Inaudible,** in-awd'i-bl, *adj.* not able to be heard.—*adv.* **Inaud'ibly.**—*ns.* **Inaudibil'ity, Inaud'-ibleness.** [L. *in*, not, and **Audible.**]

**Inaugural,** in-aw'gūr-al, *adj.* pertaining to, done, or pronounced at an *inauguration.*

**Inaugurate,** in-aw'gūr-āt, *v.t.* to induct into an office in a formal manner : to cause to begin : to make a public exhibition of for the first time. [L. *inauguro*, *-atum.* See **Augur.**]

**Inauguration,** in-aw-gūr-ā'shun, *n.* act of inaugurating (in its different meanings).

**Inaugurator,** in-aw'gūr-ā-tor, *n.* one who inaugurates.

**Inauspicious,** in-aw-spish'us, *adj.* not auspicious : ill-omened : unlucky.—*adv.* **Inauspi'ciously.**—*n.* **Inauspi'ciousness.** [L. *in*, not, and **Auspicious.**]

**Inborn,** in'bawrn, *adj., born in* or *with :* implanted by nature. [E. **In** and **Born.**]

**Inbreathe,** in'brēth, *v.t.* to *breathe into.* [E. **In** and **Breathe.**] [natural.

**Inbred,** in'bred, *adj., bred within :* innate :

**Inbreed,** in-brēd', *v.t.* to *breed* or generate *within.* [E. **In** and **Breed.**]

**Inca,** ing'ka, *n.* a name given to the ancient kings and princes of Peru :—*pl.* **Incas,** ing'kaz.

**Incage,** in-kāj'. Same as **Encage.**

**Incalculable,** in-kal'kū-la-bl, *adj.* not calculable or able to be reckoned.—*adv.* **Incal'culably.** [L. *in*, not, **Calculable.**]

**Incandescent,** in-kan-des'ent, *adj.* white or glowing with heat.—*n.* **Incandes'cence,** a white-heat. [L. *incandescens*—*in*, and *candesco*, inceptive of *candeo*, to glow. Cf. **Candle.**]

**Incantation,** in-kan-tā'shun, *n.* a magical charm uttered by *singing :* enchantment. [L. *incantatio*, from root of **Enchant.**]

**Incapable,** in-kāp'a-bl, *adj.* not capable : insufficient : unable : disqualified.—*adv.* **Incap'ably.**—*n.* **Incapabil'ity.** [Fr.—L. *in*, not, and **Capable.**]

**Incapacious,** in-kap-ā'shus, *adj.* not capacious or large : narrow. [L. *in*, not, and **Capacious.**]

**Incapacitate,** in-kap-as'i-tāt, *v.t.* to deprive of capacity : to make incapable : to disqualify. [L. *in*, not, and **Capacitate.**]

**Incapacity,** in-kap-as'i-ti, *n.* want of capacity or power of mind : inability : disqualification. [Fr.—L. *in*, not, and **Capacity.** See **Capacious.**]

**Incarcerate,** in-kär'ser-āt, *v.t.* to *imprison :* to confine.—*n.* **Incarcera'tion,** imprisonment. [L. *in*, and *carcer-o*, *-atus*—*carcer*, a prison, a word of doubtful origin.]

**Incarnadine,** in-kär'na-din, *v.t.* to dye of a red colour. [Fr., from root of **Incarnate.**]

**Incarnate,** in-kär'nāt, *v.t.* to embody in *flesh.*—*adj.* invested with flesh. [Low L. *incarn-o*, *-atus*—*in*, and *caro, carnis,* flesh. Cf. **Carnal.**]

**Incarnation,** in-kär-nā'shun, *n.* act of embodying in flesh: act of taking a human body and the nature of a man: an incarnate form: manifestation: (*surg.*) the process of healing, or forming new flesh.

**Incarnative,** in-kär'na-tiv, *adj.* causing new flesh to grow.—*n.* a medicine which causes new flesh to grow.

**Incase,** in-kās', *v.t.* to put *in* a *case:* to surround with something solid. [Fr. *encaisser*—L. *in*, in, and **Case.**]

**Incasement,** in-kās'ment, *n.* act of inclosing with a *case:* an inclosing substance.

**Incautious,** in-kaw'shus, *adj.* not cautious or careful.—*adv.* **Incau'tiously.**—*n.* **Incau'tiousness,** want of caution. [L. *in.* not, and **Cautious.**]

**Incendiary,** in-sen'di-ar-i, *n.* one that sets *fire* to a building, &c. maliciously: one who promotes quarrels.—*adj.* wilfully setting fire to: relating to incendiarism: tending to excite sedition or quarrels.—*n.* **Incen'diarism.** [L. *incendiarius*—*incendium*, a burning—*incendo, incensus*, to kindle, allied to *candeo* to glow.]

**Incense,** in-sens', *v.t.* to inflame with anger. [See above word.]

**Incense,** in'sens, *n.* odour of spices burned in religious rites: the materials so burned. [Fr. *encens*—L. *incensum,* what is burned. See **Incendiary.**]

**Incentive,** in-sent'iv, *adj.* inciting: encouraging. —*n.* that which incites to action or moves the mind: motive. [L. *incentivus,* striking up a tune, hence provocative, from *incino*—*in,* and *cano,* to sing. Cf **Chant, Enchant.**]

**Inception,** in-sep'shun, *n.* a beginning.—*adj.* **Incep'tive,** beginning or marking the beginning. [L. *incipio, inceptus,* to begin—*in,* on, and *capio,* to seize.]

**Incertitude,** in-sèr'ti-tūd, *n.* want of certainty: doubtfulness. [From L. *incertus—in,* not, and *certus,* certain.]

**Incessant,** in-ses'ant, *adj.* not ceasing: uninterrupted: continual.—*adv.* **Incess'antly.** [L. *incess-ans, -antis—in,* not, and *cesso,* to cease.]

**Incest,** in'sest, *n.* sexual intercourse within the prohibited degrees of kindred. [Fr. *inceste*—L. *incestus,* unchaste—*in,* not, and *castus,* chaste. Cf. **Chaste.**]

**Incestuous,** in-sest'ū-us, *adj.* guilty of incest.—*adv.* **Incest'uously.**

**Inch,** insh, *n.* the *twelfth* part of a foot: proverbially, a small distance or degree.—**By inches,** by slow degrees. [A.S. *ynce,* an inch —L. *uncia,* the twelfth part of anything, an inch, also an ounce (twelfth of a pound). Doublet **Ounce.**]

**Inch,** insh, **Inched,** insht, *adj.* containing inches.

**Inchoate,** in'kō-āt, *adj.* only *begun:* unfinished.— *n.* **Inchoa'tion,** beginning.—*adj.* **Incho'ative,** inceptive. [L. *inchoo, inchoatus,* to begin.]

**Incidence,** in'si-dens, *n.* a *falling upon:* the meeting of one body with another.—**Angle of Incidence,** the angle at which a ray of light or radiant heat falls upon a surface. [See **Incident.**]

**Incident,** in'si-dent, *adj., falling upon:* fortuitous: liable to occur: naturally belonging.—*n.* that which *falls out* or happens: an event: a subordinate action: an episode. [Fr.—L. *incidens.*]

**Incidental,** in-si-dent'al, *adj., falling out:* coming without design: occasional: accidental.—*adv.* **Incident'ally.**—*n.* **Incident'alness.**

**Incipient,** in-sip'i-ent, *adj.* beginning.—*adv.* **Incip'iently.** — *ns.* **Incip'ience, Incip'iency.** [Pr.p. of L. *incipio.* See **Inception.**]

**Incircle,** in-sèrk'l. Same as **Encircle.**

**Incise,** in-sīz', *v.t.* to *cut into:* to cut or gash: to engrave. [Fr. *inciser*—L. *incīdo, incisus—in,* into, and *cædo,* to cut. Cf. **Cæsura** and **Excision.**]

**Incision,** in-sizh'un, *n.* the act of *cutting into* a substance: a cut: a gash.

**Incisive,** in-sī'siv, *adj.* having the quality of cutting into, or penetrating as with a sharp instrument: trenchant: acute: sarcastic. [Fr. *incisif*—L. *incisus.*] [**Inci'sory.** [L.]

**Incisor,** in-sī'zor, *n. a cutting* or fore tooth.—*adj.*

**Incitation,** in-si-tā'shun, *n.* the act of inciting or rousing: that which stimulates to action: an incentive. [Fr.—L. See **Incite.**]

**Incite,** in-sīt', *v.t.* to *rouse:* to move the mind to action: to encourage: to goad.—*adv.* **Incit'ingly.**—*n.* **Incit'er.** [Fr.—L. *incito—in,* and *cito,* to rouse—*cieo,* to put in motion ]

**Incitement,** in-sīt'ment. Same as **Incitation.**

**Incivility,** in-si-vil'i-ti, *n.* want of civility or courtesy: impoliteness: disrespect: an act of discourtesy (in this sense has a *pl.,* **Incivil'ities**). [L. *in,* not, and **Civility.**]

**Inclement,** in-klem'ent, *adj.* unmerciful: stormy: very cold.—*adv.* **Inclem'ently.**—*n.* **Inclem'ency.** [Fr.—L. *in,* not, and **Clement.**]

**Inclinable,** in-klīn'a-bl, *adj.* that may be *inclined* or *bent towards:* leaning: tending: somewhat disposed.—*n.* **Inclin'ableness.**

**Inclination,** in-kli-nā'shun, *n.* the act of *inclining* or *bending towards:* tendency: natural aptness: favourable disposition: affection: act of bowing: angle between two lines or planes.

**Incline,** in-klīn', *v.i.* to *lean towards:* to deviate from a line toward an object: to be disposed: to have some desire.—*v.t.* to cause to bend towards: to give a leaning to: to dispose: to bend.—*n.* an inclined plane: a regular ascent or descent. [Fr.—L. *inclino—in,* towards, *clino;* cog. with Gr. *klinō,* to bend, and E. *lean.*]

**Inclose,** in-klōz', *v.t.* to *close* or *shut in:* to confine: to surround: to put within a case: to fence. [Fr.—L. *includo, inclusus—in,* in, and *claudo,* to shut.]

**Inclosure,** in-klō'zhūr, *n.* act of inclosing: state of being inclosed: that which is inclosed: a space fenced off: that which incloses: a barrier.

**Include,** in-klood', *v.t.* to *close* or *shut in:* to embrace within limits: to contain: to comprehend. [L. *includo, inclusus—in,* in, and *claudo,* to shut. See **Close.**]

**Inclusion,** in-kloo'zhun, *n.* act of including.

**Inclusive,** in-kloo'siv, *adj., shutting in:* inclosing: comprehending the stated limit or extremes. —*adv.* **Inclu'sively.**

**Incognisable, Incognizable,** in-kog'niz-a-bl or in-kon'iz-a-bl, *adj.* that cannot be known or distinguished. [Prefix *in,* not, **Cognisable.**]

**Incognito,** in-kog'ni-tō, *adj., unknown:* disguised. —*adv.* in concealment: in a disguise: under an assumed title. [It.—L. *incognitus—in,* not, and *cognitus,* known—*cognosco,* to know.]

**Incoherence,** in-kō-hēr'ens, *n.* want of coherence or connection: looseness of parts: want of connection: incongruity. [Fr.—L. *in,* not, and **Coherence.**]

**Incoherent,** in-kō-hēr'ent, *adj.* not connected: loose: incongruous.—*adv.* **Incoher'ently.**

**Incombustible,** in-kom-bust'i-bl, *adj.* incapable of being consumed by fire.—*ns.* **Incombustibil'ity, Incombust'ibleness.**—*adv.* **Incombust'ibly.** [L. *in,* not, and **Combustible.**]

**Income,** in'kum, *n.* the gain, profit, or interest

resulting from anything : revenue. [E. **In** and **Come**.]

**Incommensurable,** in-kom-en'sū-ra-bl, *adj.* having no common measure.—*ns.* Incommensurabil′ity, Incommen′surableness.—*adv.* Incommen′surably. [Fr.—L. *in*, not, and **Commensurable**.]

**Incommensurate,** in-kom-en'sū-rāt, *adj.* not admitting of a common measure : not adequate : unequal.—*adv.* Incommen′surately.

**Incommode,** in-kom-ōd′, *v.t.* to cause trouble or inconvenience to : to annoy : to molest. [Fr.—L. *incommodo*—*incommodus*, inconvenient—*in*, not, and *commodus*. See **Commodious**.]

**Incommodious,** in-kom-ō′di-us, *adj.* inconvenient : annoying.—*n.* Incommo′diousness.—*adv.* Incommo′diously. [L. *in*, not, and **Commodious**.]

**Incommunicable,** in-kom-ūn′i-ka-bl, *adj.* that cannot be communicated or imparted to others. —*ns.* Incommunicabil′ity, Incommun′icableness.—*adv.* Incommun′icably. [Fr.—L. *in*, not, and **Communicable**.]

**Incommunicative,** in-kom-ūn′i-kā-tiv, *adj.* not disposed to hold communion with : unsocial.— *adv.* Incommun′icatively.

**Incommutable,** in-kom-ūt′a-bl, *adj.* that cannot be commuted or exchanged.—*ns.* Incommutabil′ity, Incommut′ableness.—*adv.* Incommut′ably. [Fr.—L. *in*, not, and **Commutable**.]

**Incomparable,** in-kom′par-a-bl, *adj.* matchless.— *n.* Incom′parableness.—*adv.* Incom′parably. [Fr.—L. *in*, not, and **Comparable**.]

**Incompatible,** in-kom-pat′i-bl, *adj.* not consistent : contradictory :—*pl.* things which cannot co-exist. —*n.* Incompatibil′ity.—*adv.* Incompat′ibly. [Fr.—L. *in*, not, and **Compatible**.]

**Incompetence,** in-kom′pe-tens, **Incompetency,** in-kom′pe-ten-si, *n.* state of being incompetent : want of sufficient power : want of suitable means : insufficiency.

**Incompetent,** in-kom′pe-tent, *adj.* wanting adequate powers : wanting the proper qualifications : insufficient.—*adv* Incom′petently. [Fr.—L. *in*, not, and **Competent**.]

**Incomplete,** in-kom-plēt′, *adj.* imperfect.—*n.* Incomplete′ness.—*adv.* Incomplete′ly. [L. *in*, not, and **Complete**.]

**Incompliant,** in-kom-plī′ant, **Incompliable,** in-kom-plī′a-bl, *adj.* not disposed to comply : unyielding to request.—*n.* Incompli′ance.—*adv.* Incompli′antly. [L. *in*, not, and **Compliant**.]

**Incomprehensible,** in-kom-pre-hen′si-bl, *adj.* (*Pr. Bk.*) not to be comprehended, or contained within limits : not capable of being understood : inconceivable.—*ns.* Incomprehensibil′ity, Incomprehen′sibleness, Incomprehen′sion.—*adv.* Incomprehen′sibly. [Fr.—L. *in*, not, and **Comprehensible**.]

**Incomprehensive,** in-kom-pre-hen′siv, *adj.* limited.—*n.* Incomprehen′siveness.

**Incompressible,** in-kom-pres′i-bl, *adj.* not to be compressed into smaller bulk.—*n.* Incompressibil′ity. [L. *in*, not, and **Compressible**.]

**Incomputable,** in-kom-pūt′a-bl, *adj.* that cannot be computed or reckoned. [L. *in*, not, and **Computable**.]

**Inconceivable,** in-kon-sēv′a-bl, *adj.* that cannot be conceived by the mind : incomprehensible.— *n.* Inconceiv′ableness.—*adv.* Inconceiv′ably. [Fr.—L. *in*, not, and **Conceivable**.]

**Inconclusive,** in-kon-klōōs′iv, *adj.* not settling a point in debate.—*adv.* Inconclus′ively.—*n.* Inconclus′iveness. [L. *in*, not, and **Conclusive**.]

**Incondensable,** in-kon-dens′a-bl, *adj.* not to be

condensed or made more dense or compact.—*n.* Incondensabil′ity. [L. *in*, not, **Condensable**.]

**Incongenial,** in-kon-jē′ni-al, *adj.* unsuitable : unsympathetic.—*n.* Inconge′niality. [See **Congenial**.]

**Incongruous,** in-kong′grōō-us, *adj.* inconsistent : unsuitable.—*n.* Incongru′ity.—*adv.* Incon′gruously. [L. *in*, not, and **Congruous**.]

**Inconsequent,** in-kon′se-kwent, *adj.* not following from the premises.—*n.* Incon′sequence. [L. *in*, not, and **Consequent**.]

**Inconsequential,** in-kon-se-kwen′shal, *adj.* not regularly following from the premises.—*adv.* Inconsequen′tially.

**Inconsiderable,** in-kon-sid′ėr-a-bl, *adj.* not worthy of notice : unimportant.—*adv.* Inconsid′erably. [Fr.—L. *in*, not, and **Considerable**.]

**Inconsiderate,** in-kon-sid′ėr-āt, *adj.* not considerate : thoughtless : inattentive.—*adv.* Inconsid′erately.—*n.* Inconsid′erateness.

**Inconsistent,** in-kon-sist′ent, *adj.* not consistent : not suitable or agreeing with : contrary : not uniform : irreconcilable.—*ns.* Inconsist′ence, Inconsist′ency.—*adv.* Inconsist′ently. [L. *in*, not, and **Consistent**.]

**Inconsolable,** in-kon-sōl′a-bl, *adj.* not to be comforted.—*adv.* Inconsol′ably. [Fr.—L. *in*, not, and **Consolable**.]

**Inconspicuous,** in-kon-spik′ū-us, *adj.* not conspicuous : scarcely discernible.—*adv.* Inconspic′uously.—*n.* Inconspic′uousness.

**Inconstant,** in-kon′stant, *adj.* subject to change : fickle.—*n.* Incon′stancy.—*adv.* Incon′stantly. [Fr.—L. *in*, not, and **Constant**.]

**Inconsumable,** in-kon-sūm′a-bl, *adj.* that cannot be consumed or wasted. [L. *in*, not, **Consumable**.]

**Incontestable,** in-kon-test′a-bl, *adj.* too clear to be called in question : undeniable.—*adv.* Incontest′ably. [Fr.—L. *in*, not, and **Contestable**.]

**Incontinent,** in-kon′ti-nent, *adj.* not restraining the passions or appetites : unchaste.—*ns.* Incon′tinence, Incon′tinency.—*adv.* Incon′tinently. [Fr.—L. *in*, not, and **Continent**.]

**Incontinently,** in-kon′ti-nent-li, *adv.* immediately. [Same root as above.]

**Incontrollable,** in-kon-trōl′a-bl, *adj.* that cannot be controlled.—*adv.* Incontroll′ably. [L. *in*, not, and **Controllable**.]

**Incontrovertible,** in-kon-tro-vèrt′i-bl, *adj.* too clear to be called in question.—*n.* Incontrovertibil′ity.—*adv.* Incontrovert′ibly. [L. *in*, not, and **Controvertible**.]

**Inconvenience,** in-kon-vēn′yens, **Inconveniency,** in-kon-vēn′yen-si, *n.* the being inconvenient : want of convenience : that which causes trouble or uneasiness.—*v.t.* Inconven′ience, to trouble or incommode.

**Inconvenient,** in-kon-vēn′yent, *adj.* unsuitable : causing trouble or uneasiness : increasing difficulty : incommodious.—*adv.* Inconven′iently. [Fr.—L. *in*, not, and **Convenient**.]

**Inconvertible,** in-kon-vèrt′i-bl, *adj.* that cannot be changed.—*n.* Inconvertibil′ity. [L. *in*, not, and **Convertible**.]

**Inconvincible,** in-kon-vins′i-bl, *adj.* not capable of conviction.—*adv.* Inconvinc′ibly. [L. *in*, not, and **Convincible**.]

**Incorporate,** in-kor′po-rāt, *v.t.* to form *into a body* : to combine into one mass : to unite : to form into a corporation.—*v.i.* to unite into one mass : to become part of another body.—*adj.* united in one body : mixed. [L. *incorporo, -atum*—*in*, into, *corporo*, to furnish with a body. See **Corporate**.]

**Incorporation**, in-kor-po-rā'shun, *n.* act of incorporating : state of being incorporated : formation of a legal or political body : an association.

**Incorporeal**, in-kor-pō'rē-al, *adj.* not having a body : spiritual.—*adv.* **Incorpo'really.** [L. *in*, not, and **Corporeal.**]

**Incorrect**, in-kor-ekt', *adj.* containing faults : not accurate : not according to the rules of duty.—*adv.* **Incorrect'ly.**—*n.* **Incorrect'ness.** [Fr.—L. *in*, not, and **Correct.**]

**Incorrigible**, in-kor'i-ji-bl, *adj.* bad beyond correction or reform.—*ns.* **Incorr'igibleness, Incorrigibil'ity.**—*adv.* **Incorr'igibly.**

**Incorrodible**, in-kor-ōd'i-bl, *adj.* not able to be rusted. [L. *in*, not, and **Corrodible.**]

**Incorrupt**, in-kor-upt', *adj.* sound : pure : not depraved : not to be tempted by bribes.—*adv.* **Incorrupt'ly.** [L. *in*, not, and **Corrupt.**]

**Incorruptible**, in-kor-upt'i-bl, *adj.* not capable of decay : that cannot be bribed : inflexibly just.—*adv.* **Incorrupt'ibly.**—*n.* **Incorrupt'ibleness.**

**Incorruption**, in-kor-up'shun. *n.* state of being incorrupt or exempt from corruption.

**Incorruptness**, in-kor-upt'nes, *n.* a being exempt from corruption or decay : purity of mind.

**Incrassate**, in-kras'āt, *v.t.* to *make thick.*—*v.i.* (*med.*) to become thicker.—*adj.* made thick or fat : (*bot.*) thickened towards the flower.—*n.* **Incrassa'tion.** [L. *incrasso*, *-atum*—*in*, into, *crasso*, to make thick—*crassus*, thick. See **Crass.**]

**Incrassative**, in-kras'a-tiv, *adj.*, *thickening.*—*n.* that which has power to thicken.

**Increase**, in-krēs', *v.i.* to *grow* in size : to become greater : to advance.—*v.t.* to make greater : to advance : to extend : to aggravate.—**In'crease**, *n.* growth : addition to the original stock : profit : produce : progeny. [Through Norm. Fr. from L. *incresco*—*in*, in, *cresco*, to grow.]

**Incredible**, in-kred'i-bl, *adj.* surpassing belief.—*adv.* **Incred'ibly.**—*n.* **Incredibil'ity.** [Fr.—L. *in*, not, and **Credible.** See **Creed.**]

**Incredulous**, in-kred'ū-lus, *adj.* hard of belief.—*adv.* **Incred'ulously.**—*n.* **Incredu'lity.**

**Increment**, in'kre-ment, *n.* act of *increasing* or becoming greater : growth : that by which anything is increased : (*math.*) the finite increase of a variable quantity : (*rhet.*) an adding of particulars without climax, see 2 Peter i. 5–7. [L. *incrementum*—*incresco.* See **Increase.**]

**Increscent**, in-kres'ent, *adj.* increasing : growing. [L. *in*, and **Crescent.**]

**Incriminate**, in-krim'in-āt. Same as **Criminate.**

**Incrust**, in-krust', *v.t.* to cover with a *crust* or hard case : to form a crust on the surface of. [Fr.—L. *incrust-o*, *-atus*—*in*, on, and *crusta.* See **Crust.**]

**Incrustation**, in-krus-tā'shun. *n.* act of incrusting : a crust or layer of anything on the surface of a body : an inlaying of marble, mosaic, &c.

**Incubate**, in'kū-bāt, *v.i.* to *sit on* eggs to hatch them. [L. *incubo*, *-atum*—*in*, upon, *cubo*, to lie down.]

**Incubation**, in-kū-bā'shun, *n.* the act of sitting on eggs to hatch them : (*med.*) the period between the implanting of a disease and its development.

**Incubator**, in'kū-bā-tor, *n.* a machine for hatching eggs by artificial heat.

**Incubus**, in'kū-bus, *n.* a sensation during sleep as of a weight *lying on* the breast, nightmare : any oppressive or stupefying influence :—*pl.* **In'cubuses, Incubi** (in'kū-bī). [L.—*incubo.*]

**Inculcate**, in-kul'kāt, *v.t.* to enforce by frequent admonitions or repetitions.—*n.* **Incul'cator.**

[Lit. to *tread* or *press in :* L. *inculco*, *inculcatum* —*in*, into, *calco*, to tread—*calx*, the heel.]

**Inculcation**, in-kul-kā'shun, *n.* act of impressing by frequent admonitions.

**Inculpable**, in-kul'pa-bl, *adj.* blameless.—*adv.* **Incul'pably** [L. *in*, not, and **Culpable.**]

**Inculpate**, in-kul'pāt, *v.t.* to bring into *blame :* to censure.—*n.* **Inculpa'tion.** [Low L. *inculpo*, *inculpatum*—L. *in*, into, *culpa*, a fault.]

**Inculpatory**, in-kul'pa-tor-i, *adj.* imputing blame.

**Incumbency**, in-kum'ben-si, *n.* a *lying* or *resting on :* the holding of an office : an ecclesiastical benefice. [See **Incumbent.**]

**Incumbent**, in-kum'bent, *adj.* or *lying* or *resting on :* lying on as a duty : indispensable.—*n.* one who holds an ecclesiastical benefice (in England or Ireland).—*adv.* **Incum'bently.** [L. *incumbens*, *-entis*, pr.p. of *incumbo*, *incubo*, to lie upon. See **Incubate.**] [**Encumbrance.**

**Incumber, Incumbrance.** Same as **Encumber,**

**Incunabula**, in-kū-nab'u-la, *n.pl.* books printed in the early period of the art, before the year 1500. [L. *incunabula*, (*lit.*) ' swaddling-clothes,' hence ' beginnings.']

**Incur**, in-kur', *v.t.* to become liable to : to bring on :—*pr.p.* incurr'ing ; *pa.p.* incurred'. [Lit. to *run into*, to *fall upon ;* L. *incurro*, *incursum*—*in*, into. *curro*, to run.]

**Incurable**, in-kūr'a-bl, *adj.* not admitting of correction.—*n.* one beyond cure.—*ns.* **Incur'ableness, Incurabil'ity.**—*adv.* **Incur'ably.** [Fr.—L. *in*, not, and **Curable.**]

**Incursion**, in-kur'shun, *n.* a hostile inroad. [Fr. —L. *incursio*—*incurro.*]

**Incursive**, in-kur'siv, *adj.* pertaining to or making an incursion or inroad.

**Incurvate**, in-kur'vāt, *v.t.* to *curve* or *bend.*—*adj.* curved inward.—*n.* **Incurva'tion.** [L. *incurvo*, *incurvatum*—*in*, in, and *curvus*, bent. See **Curve.**]

**Indebted**, in-det'ed, *adj.* being *in debt :* obliged by something received.—*n.* **Indebt'edness.** [Fr. —L. *in*, in, and **Debt.**]

**Indecent**, in-dē'sent, *adj.* offensive to common modesty.—*adv.* **Inde'cently.**—*n.* **Inde'cency.** [Fr.—L. *in*, not, and **Decent.**]

**Indecision**, in-de-sizh'un, *n.* want of decision or resolution : hesitation. [Fr.—L. *in*, not, and **Decision.**]

**Indecisive**, in-de-sī'siv, *adj.* unsettled : wavering. —*adv.* **Indeci'sively.**—*n.* **Indeci'siveness.**

**Indeclinable**, in-de-klīn'a-bl, *adj.* (*gram.*) not varied by inflection.—*adv.* **Indeclin'ably.** [L. *in*, not, and **Declinable.**]

**Indecomposable**, in-de-kom-pōz'a-bl, *adj.* that cannot be decomposed. [L. *in*, not, **Decomposable.**]

**Indecorous**, in-de-kō'rus, *adj.* not becoming : violating good manners.—*adv.* **Indeco'rously.** [L. *in*, not, and **Decorous.**]

**Indecorum**, in-de-kō'rum, *n.* want of decorum or propriety of conduct. [L. *in*, not, and **Decorum.**]

**Indeed**, in-dēd', *adv.* in fact : in truth : in reality. [E. **In** and **Deed.**]

**Indefatigable**, in-de-fat'i-ga-bl, *adj.* that cannot be fatigued or wearied out : unremitting in effort : persevering.—*adv.* **Indefat'igably.**—*n.* **Indefat'igableness.** [Fr.—L. *indefatigabilis* —*in*, not, *de*, down, and *fatigo*, to tire.]

**Indefeasible**, in-de-fēz'i-bl, *adj.* not to be defeated or made void.—*adv.* **Indefeas'ibly.**—*n.* **Indefeas'ibility.** [Fr.—L. *in*, not, and **Defeasible.**]

**Indefectible**, in-de-fekt'i-bl, *adj.* incapable of defect : unfailing. [L. *in*, not, and **Defectible.**]

**Indefensible**, in-de-fens'i-bl, *adj.* that cannot be

fāte, fär ; mē, hėr ; mīne ; mōte ; mūte ; mōōn ; *then.*

maintained or justified.—*adv.* **Indefens′ibly.** [L. *in*, not, and **Defensible.**]

**Indefinable**, in-de-fīn′a-bl, *adj.* that cannot be defined.—*adv.* **Indefin′ably.** [L. *in*, not, and **Definable.**]

**Indefinite**, in-def′i-nit, *adj.* not limited : not precise or certain.—*adv.* **Indef′initely.**—*n.* **Indef′initeness.** [L. *in*, not, and **Definite.**]

**Indelible**, in-del′i-bl, *adj.* that cannot be blotted out or effaced.—*adv.* **Indel′ibly.**—*n.* **Indel′ibility.** [Fr.—L. *in*, not, and *delebilis*—*deleo*, to destroy.]

**Indelicacy**, in-del′i-ka-si, *n.* want of delicacy or refinement of taste and manners : rudeness.

**Indelicate**, in-del′i-kāt, *adj.* offensive to good manners or purity of mind : coarse.—*adv.* **Indel′icately.** [Fr.—L. *in*, not, and **Delicate.**]

**Indemnification**, in-dem-ni-fi-kā′shun, *n.* act of indemnifying : that which indemnifies.

**Indemnify**, in-dem′ni-fī, *v.t.* to make good for damage done : to save harmless :—*pa.p.* indem′-nified. [Fr.—L. *indemnis*, unharmed—*in*, not, and *damnum*, loss ; and *facio*, to make.]

**Indemnity**, in-dem′ni-ti, *n.* security from damage, loss, or punishment : compensation for loss or injury. [Fr.—L. *indemnitas*.]

**Indemonstrable**, in-de-mon′stra-bl, *adj.* that cannot be demonstrated or proved. [L. *in*, not, and **Demonstrable.**]

**Indent**, in-dent′, *v.t.* to cut into points like teeth : to notch : (*print.*) to begin further in from the margin than the rest of a paragraph.—*n.* a cut or notch in the margin : a recess like a notch. [Low L. *indento*—L. *in*, *dens*, *dentis*, a tooth.]

**Indentation**, in-den-tā′shun, *n.* act of indenting or notching : notch : recess.

**Indenture**, in-dent′ūr, *n.* a written agreement between two or more parties : a contract.—*v.t.* to bind by indentures : to indent. [Indentures were originally duplicates *indented* so as to correspond to each other.]

**Independent**, in-de-pend′ent, *adj.* not dependent or relying on others : not subordinate : not subject to bias : affording a comfortable livelihood : belonging to the Independents.—*adv.* **Independ′ently.**—*ns.* **Independ′ence. Independ′ency.** [L. *in*, not, and **Dependent.**]

**Independent**, in-de-pend′ent, *n.* one who in ecclesiastical affairs holds that every congregation is *independent* of every other and subject to no superior authority.

**Indescribable**, in-de-skrīb′a-bl, *adj.* that cannot be described. [L. *in*, not, and **Describable.**]

**Indestructible**, in-de-struk′ti-bl, *adj.* that cannot be destroyed.—*adv.* **Indestruc′tibly.**—*n.* **Indestructibil′ity.** [L. *in*, not, and **Destructible.**]

**Indeterminable**, in-de-tèr′min-a-bl, *adj.* not to be ascertained or fixed.—*adv.* **Indeter′minably.** [L. *in* not, and **Determinable.**]

**Indeterminate**, in-de-tèr′min-āt, *adj.* not determinate or fixed : uncertain.—*adv.* **Indeter′minately.**

**Indetermination**, in-de-tèr-min-ā′shun, *n.* want of determination : a wavering state of the mind : want of fixed direction. [mined : unsettled.

**Undetermined**, in-de-tèr′mind, *adj.* not deter-

**Index**, in′deks, *n.* (*pl.* **Indexes**, in′deks-ez, and in *math.*, **Indices**, in′di-sēz), anything that *indicates* or *points out* : a hand that directs to anything, as the hour of the day, &c. : the forefinger : alphabetical list of subjects treated of in a book : (*math.*) the exponent of a power.—*v.t.* to provide with or place in an index. [L. *index*, *indicis*—*indico*, to shew ]

**Indiaman**, in′di-a-man or ind′ya-man, *n.* a large ship employed in trade with *India*.

**Indian**, in′di-an, *adj.* belonging to the *Indies*, East or West, or to the aborigines of America. —*n.* a native of the Indies : an aboriginal of America.—**Indian corn**, maize, so called because brought from W. Indies.—**Indian file**, following one another in single file, like Indians through a wood.—**Indian ink**, a substance used in water-colours, composed of lampblack and animal glue, orig. used in *India*, or rather in China.—**Indian** or **India rubber**, caoutchouc, so named from its *rubbing* out pencil-marks. [From the river *Indus*, and applied by mistake to the W. Indies by their first discoverers, who thought they had arrived at India. See Hindu.]

**Indicate**, in′di-kāt, *v.t.* to *point out*: to shew. [L. *indico*, *-atum*—*in*, and *dico*, to proclaim.]

**Indication**, in-di-kā′shun, *n.* act of indicating : that which indicates.

**Indicative**, in-dik′a-tiv, *adj., pointing out*: giving intimation of : (*gram.*) applied to the mood of the verb which indicates, i.e. affirms or denies. —*adv.* **Indic′atively.**

**Indicator**, in′di-kā-tor, *n.* one who indicates : an instrument on a steam-engine to shew the pressure.—*adj.* **In′dicatory**, shewing.

**Indict**, in-dīt′, *v.t.* to charge with a crime formally or in writing, esp. by a grand-jury. [L. *in*, and *dicto*, freq. of *dico*, to say.]

**Indictable**, in-dīt′a-bl, *adj.* liable to be indicted.

**Indiction**, in-dik′shun, *n.* (*lit.*) a *proclamation* : a cycle of fifteen years, instituted by Constantine the Great. [L. *indictio*.]

**Indictment**, in-dīt′ment, *n.* the written accusation against one who is to be tried by jury.

**Indifferent**, in-dif′er-ent, *adj.* without importance : of a middle quality : neutral : unconcerned.—*ns.* **Indiff′erence, Indiff′erency.** [Lit. 'without a difference ;' L. *in*, not, and **Different.**]

**Indifferentism**, in-dif′er-ent-izm, *n.* indifference, esp. in matters of belief : unconcern.

**Indifferently**, in-dif′er-ent-li, *adv.* in an indifferent manner : tolerably, passably : (*Pr. Bk*) without distinction, impartially. [poverty.

**Indigence**, in′di-jens, *n., want* of means : extreme

**Indigenous**, in-dij′en-us, *adj., native* born or originating in : produced naturally in a country. [L. *indigenus*—*indu* or *in*, in, and *gen*, root of *gigno*, to produce.]

**Indigent**, in′di-jent, *adj., in need* of anything : destitute of means of subsistence : poor.—*adv.* **In′digently.** [Fr.—L. *indigens*, *-entis*, pr.p. of *indigeo*—*indu* or *in*, in, and *egeo*, to need.]

**Indigested**, in-di-jes′ted, *adj.* not digested : unarranged : not methodised. [L. *in*, not, and **Digested.** See **Digest.**]

**Indigestible**, in-di-jest′i-bl, *adj.* not digestible : not easily digested : not to be received or patiently endured.—*adv.* **Indigest′ibly.**

**Indigestion**, in-di-jest′yun, *n.* want of digestion : painful digestion. [L. *in*, not, and **Digestion.**]

**Indignant**, in-dig′nant, *adj.* affected with anger and disdain.—*adv.* **Indig′nantly.** [Lit. 'considering as unworthy' or 'improper,' from L. *indignans*, *-antis*, pr.p. of *indignor*—*in*, not, *dignus*, worthy.]

**Indignation**, in-dig-nā′shun, *n.* the feeling caused by what is *unworthy* or base : anger mixed with contempt. [Fr.—L. *indignatio*.]

**Indignity**, in-dig′ni-ti, *n.* unmerited contemptuous treatment : incivility with contempt or insult. [Lit. 'unworthiness,' Fr.—L. *indignitas*.]

**Indigo**, in'di-go, *n.* a blue dye obtained from the stalks of the indigo or *Indian* plant. [Fr.—Sp. *indico*—L. *indicum*, from *Iudicus*, Indian.]

**Indirect**, in-di-rekt', *adj.* not direct or straight : not tending to a result by the plainest course : not straightforward or honest.—*adv.* **Indirect'ly.** —*n.* **Indirect'ness.** [Fr.—L. *in*, not, and Direct.]

**Indiscernible**, in-diz-ern'i-bl, *adj.* not discernible. —*adv.* **Indiscern'ibly.** [L. *in*, not, and **Discernible.**]

**Indiscoverable**, in-dis-kuv'er-a-bl, *adj.* not discoverable. [L. *in*, not, and **Discoverable.**]

**Indiscreet**, in-dis-krēt', *adj.* not discreet : imprudent : injudicious.—*adv.* **Indiscreet'ly.**—*n.* **Indiscreet'ness.** [Fr.—L. *in*, not, and **Discreet.**]

**Indiscretion**, in-dis-kresh'un, *n.* want of discretion : rashness : an indiscreet act.

**Indiscriminate**, in-dis-krim'i-nāt, *adj.* not distinguishing : confused.—*adv.* **Indiscrim'inately.** [L. *in*, not, and **Discriminate.**]

**Indispensable**, in-dis-pens'a-bl, *adj.* that cannot be dispensed with : absolutely necessary.—*adv.* **Indispens'ably.**—*n.* **Indispens'ableness.** [L. *in*, not, and **Dispensable.**]

**Indispose**, in-dis-pōz', *v.t.* to render *indisposed* or unfit : to make averse to. [Fr.—L. *in*, not, and **Dispose.**]

**Indisposed**, in-dis-pōzd', *adj.* averse : disinclined : slightly disordered in health.—*n.* **Indispos'edness.**

**Indisposition**, in-dis-po-zish'un, *n.* state of being indisposed : disinclination : slight illness.

**Indisputable**, in-dis'pū-ta-bl, *adj.* too evident to be called in question : certain.—*adv.* **Indis'putably.**—*n.* **Indis'putableness.** [Fr.—L. *in*, not, and **Disputable.**]

**Indissoluble**, in-dis'ol-ū-bl, *adj.* that cannot be broken or violated : inseparable : binding for ever. —*adv.* **Indiss'olubly.**—*ns.* **Indiss'olubleness, Indissolubil'ity.** [Fr.—L. *in*, not, and **Dissoluble.**]

**Indistinct**, in-dis-tingkt', *adj.* not plainly marked : confused : not clear to the mind.—*adv.* **Indistinct'ly.**—*n.* **Indistinct'ness.** [L. *in*, not, and **Distinct**.]

**Indistinguishable**, in-dis-ting'gwish-a-bl, *adj.* that cannot be distinguished.—*adv.* **Indistin'guishably.**

**Indite**, in-dīt', *v.t.* to *dictate* what is to be uttered or written : to compose or write.—*ns.* **Indit'er, Indite'ment.** [O. Fr. *enditer, endicter*, from root of **Indict.**]

**Individual**, in-di-vid'ū-al, *adj.* not *divided* : subsisting as one : pertaining to one only.—*n.* a single person, animal, plant, or thing.—*adv.* **Individ'ually.** [L. *individuus*, and suffix *-al*—*in*, not, *dividuus*, divisible—*divido*, to divide.]

**Individualise**, in-di-vid'ū-al-īz, *v t.* to distinguish each *individual* from all others : to particularise. —*n.* **Individualisa'tion.**

**Individualism**, in-di-vid'ū-al-izm, *n.* the state of regard to *individual* interests instead of those of society at large.

**Individuality**, in-di-vid-ū-al'it-i, *n.* separate and distinct existence : oneness : distinctive character.

**Individuate**, in-di-vid'ū-āt, *v.t.* to *individualise* : to make single.—*n.* **Individua'tion.**

**Indivisible**, in-di-viz'i-bl, *adj.* not divisible.—*n.* (*math.*) an indefinitely small quantity.—*adv.* **Indivis'ibly.**—*n.* **Indivis'ibleness.** [Fr.—L. *in*, not, and **Divisible.**]

**Indocile**, in-dō'sil or in-dos'il, *adj.* not docile : not disposed to be instructed.—*n.* **Indocil'ity.** [Fr. —L. *in*, not, and **Docile.**]

**Indoctrinate**, in-dok'trin-āt, *v.t.* to instruct in any *doctrine* : to imbue with any opinion.—*n.* **Indoctrina'tion.** [L. *in*, into, *doctrina*, doctrine. See **Doctrine.**]

**Indolent**, in'do-lent, *adj.* indisposed to activity. —*adv.* **In'dolently.**—*n.* **In'dolence.** [Lit. and orig. 'free from pain' or 'trouble,' from L. *in*, not, *dolens, -entis*, pr.p. of *doleo*, to suffer pain.]

**Indomitable**, in-dom'it-a-bl, *adj.* that cannot be *tamed* : not to be subdued.—*adv.* **Indom'itably.** [L. *indomitus*, untamed—*in*, not, *domo*, to tame.]

**Indorse**, in-dors', *v.t.* to write *upon* the *back* of : to assign by writing on the back of : to give one's sanction to.—*n.* **Indors'er.** [Through an old form *endosse*, from Fr. *endosser*—Low L. *indorso*—L. *in*, upon, *dorsum*, the back.]

**Indorsee**, in-dor-sē', *n.* the person to whom a bill, &c. is assigned by indorsement.

**Indorsement**, in-dors'ment, *n.* act of writing on the *back* of a bill, &c. in order to transfer it : that which is written on a bill, &c. : sanction given to anything.

**Indubious**, in-dū'bi-us, *adj.* not dubious : certain. [L. *in*, not, and **Dubious.**]

**Indubitable**, in-dū'bit-a-bl, *adj.* that cannot be *doubted* : too plain to be called in question : certain.—*adv.* **Indu'bitably.**—*n.* **Indu'bitableness.** [Fr.—L. *indubitabilis*—*in*, not, *dubito*, to doubt. See **Doubt.**]

**Induce**, in-dūs', *v.t.* to prevail on : to cause : (*physics*) to cause, as an electric state, by mere proximity of surfaces.—*n.* **Induc'er.** [L. *induco, inductum*—*in*, into, *duco*, to lead.]

**Inducement**, in-dūs'ment, *n.* that which induces or causes : (*law*) a statement of facts introducing other important facts.

**Inducible**, in-dūs'i-bl, *adj.* that may be induced : offered by induction.

**Induct**, in-dukt', *v.t.* (*lit.*) to *bring in* : to introduce : to put in possession, as of a benefice.—*n.* **Induct'or.** [See **Induce.**]

**Inductile**, in-duk'til, *adj.* that cannot be drawn out into wire or threads.—*n.* **Inductil'ity.**

**Induction**, in-duk'shun, *n.* introduction to an office, especially of a clergyman : the act or process of reasoning from particulars to generals : (*physics*) the production by one body of an opposite electric state in another by proximity.—*adj.* **Induc'tional.** [See **Induce.**]

**Inductive**, in-duk'tiv, *adj.*, *leading* or *drawing* : leading to inferences : proceeding by induction in reasoning.—*adv.* **Induc'tively.**

**Indue**, in-dū', *v.t.* to *put on*, as clothes : to invest or clothe with : to supply with :—*pr.p.* indū'ing ; *pa.p.* indūed'.—*n.* **Indue'ment.** [L. *induo, -duere*, to put on.]

**Indue**, in-dū', *v.t.* a corr. of **Endue** (which see), which has been very generally confused with **Indue**, to invest with.

**Indulge**, in-dulj', *v.t.* to yield to the wishes of : to allow, as a favour : not to restrain, as the will, &c.—*v.i.* to allow one's self.—*n.* **Indulg'er.** [See **Indulgent.**]

**Indulgence**, in-dul'jens, *n.* permission : gratification : in R. Catholic Church, a remission, to a repentant sinner, of punishment which would otherwise await him in purgatory. [Fr.]

**Indulgent**, in-dul'jent, *adj.* yielding to the wishes of others : compliant : not severe.—*adv.* **Indul'gently.** [Fr.—L. *indulgens, -entis*, pr.p. of *indulgeo*, which perh. is from *in*, towards, and *dulcis*, sweet.]

**Indurate**, in'dū-rāt, *v.t.* to *harden*, as the feelings.—*v.i.* to grow hard : to harden.—*n.* **In-**

**dura'tion.** [L. *induro, induratum—in*, in, *duro*, to harden—*durus*, hard.]

**Indusial**, in-dū'zi-al, *adj.* (*geol.*) composed of *indusia*, or the petrified larva-cases of insects.

**Indusium**, in-dū'zi-um, *n.* (*bot.*) a sort of hairy cup inclosing the stigma of a flower : the scale covering the fruit-spot of ferns. [Lit. 'an under garment ;' L.—*induo*.]

**Industrial**, in-dus'tri-al, *adj.* relating to or consisting in industry.—*adv.* **Indus'trially.**

**Indust_ialism**, in-dus'tri-al-izm, *n.* devotion to labour or industrial pursuits : that system or condition of society in which industrial labour is the chief and most characteristic feature, opp. to feudalism and the military spirit.

**Industrious**, in-dus'tri-us, *adj.* diligent or active in one's labour : laborious : diligent in a particular pursuit.—*adv.* **Indus'triously.** [Fr.—L. : perh. from *indu*, old form of *in*, within, and *struo*, to build up, to arrange.]

**Industry**, in'dus-tri, *n.* quality of being industrious : steady application to labour : habitual diligence.

**Indwelling**, in'dwel-ing, *adj., dwelling within.*— *n.* residence within, or in the heart or soul. [E. **In**, within, and **Dwelling.**]

**Inebriate**, in-ē'bri-āt, *v.t.* to *make drunk* : to intoxicate. [L. *inebri*, *inebriatum—in*, inten., *ebrio*, to make drunk—*ebrius*, drunk. See **Ebriety.**]

**Inebriation**, in-ē-bri-ā'shun, **Inebriety**, in-e-brī'e-ti, *n.* drunkenness : intoxication.

**Inedited**, in-ed'it-ed, *adj.* not edited : unpublished. [L *in*, not, and **Edited.**]

**Ineffable**, in-ef'a-bl, *adj.* that cannot be spoken or described.—*adv.* **Ineff'ably.**—*n.* **Ineff'ableness.** [Fr.—L. *ineffabilis—in*, not, *effabilis—effor*, to speak, to utter—*ef*, for *ex*, out, *fari*, to speak.]

**Ineffaceable**, in-ef-fās'a-bl, *adj.* that cannot be rubbed out.—*adv.* **Ineffface'ably.** [Fr.—L. *in*, not, and **Effaceable.**]

**Ineffective**, in-ef-fek'tiv, *adj.* inefficient : useless. —*adv.* **Ineffec'tively.** [L. *in*, not, and **Effective.**]

**Ineffectual**, in-ef-fek'tū-al, *adj.* fruitless.—*adv.* **Ineffec'tually.**—*n.* **Ineffec'tualness.**

**Inefficacious**, in-ef-fi-kā'shus, *adj.* not having power to produce an effect.—*adv.* **Ineffica'ciously.**

**Inefficacy**, in-ef'fi-ka-si, *n.* want of efficacy or power to produce effect.

**Inefficient**, in-ef-fish'ent, *adj.* effecting nothing. —*adv.* **Ineffic'iently.**—*n.* **Ineffic'iency.**

**Inelegance**, in-el'e-gans, **Inelegancy**, in-el'e-gan-si, *n.* want of elegance : want of beauty or polish.

**Inelegant**, in-el'e-gant, *adj.* wanting in beauty, refinement, or ornament.—*adv.* **Inel'egantly.** [L. *in*, not, and **Elegant.**]

**Ineligible**, in-el'i-ji-bl, *adj.* not capable or worthy of being chosen.—*adv.* **Inel'igibly.**—*n.* **Ineligibil'ity.** [Fr.—L. *in*, not, and **Eligible.**]

**Ineloquent**, in-el'o-kwent, *adj.* not fluent or persuasive. [Fr.—L. *in*, not, and **Eloquent.**]

**Inept**, in-ept', *adj.* not *apt* or fit : unsuitable : foolish : inexpert.—*adv.* **Inept'ly.**—*n.* **Inept'itude.** [Fr.—L. *ineptus—in*, not, *aptus*, apt. See **Apt.**]

**Inequality**, in-e-kwol'i-ti, *n.* want of equality : difference : inadequacy : incompetency : unevenness : dissimilarity. [Fr.—L. *in*, not, and **Equality.**]

**Inequitable**, in-ek wi-ta-bl, *adj.* unfair, unjust. [L. *in*, not, and **Equitable.**]

**Ineradicable**, in-e-rad'i-ka-bl, *adj.* not able to be eradicated or rooted out.—*adv.* **Inerad'icably.** [L. *in*, not, and root of **Eradicate.**]

**Inert**, in-ėrt', *adj.* dull : senseless : inactive : slow : without the power of moving itself, or of active resistance to motion : powerless.—*adv.* **Inert'ly.**—*n.* **Inert'ness.** [Lit. without *art* or skill, from L. *iners, inertis—in*, not, and *ars, artis*, art. See **Art.**]

**Inertia**, in-ėr'shi-a, *n., inertness :* the inherent property of matter by which it tends to remain for ever at rest when still, and in motion when moving.

**Inessential**, in-es-sen'shal, *adj.* not essential or necessary. [L. *in*, not, and **Essential.**]

**Inestimable**, in-es'tim-a-bl, *adj.* not able to be estimated or valued : priceless.—*adv.* **Ines'timably.** [Fr.—L. *in*, not, and **Estimable.**]

**Inevitable**, in-ev'it-a-bl. *adj.* not able to be evaded or avoided : that cannot be escaped : irresistible.—*adv.* **Inev'itably.**—*n.* **Inev'itableness.** [Fr.—L. *inevitabilis—in*, not, and *evitabilis*, avoidable—*evito*, to avoid—*e*, out of, and *vito*, to avoid.]

**Inexact**, in-egz-akt', *adj.* not precisely correct or true.—*n.* **Inexact'ness.** [L. *in*, not, and **Exact**.]

**Inexcusable**, in-eks-kūz'a-bl, *adj.* not justifiable : unpardonable.—*adv.* **Inexcus'ably.**—*n.* **Inexcus'ableness.** [Fr.—L. *in*, not, and **Excusable.**]

**Inexhausted**, in-egz-hawst'ed, *adj.* not exhausted or spent. [L. *in*, not, and **Exhausted.**]

**Inexhaustible**, in-egz-hawst'i-bl, *adj.* not able to be exhausted or spent : unfailing.—*adv.* **Inexhaust'ibly.**—*n.* **Inexhaustibil'ity.**

**Inexorable**, in-egz'or-a-bl, *adj.* not to be moved by entreaty : unrelenting : unalterable.—*adv.* **Inex'orably.**—*ns.* **Inex'orableness, Inexorabil'ity.** [Fr.—L. *inexorabilis—in*, not, and *exorabilis*, from *exoro—ex*, and *oro*, to entreat, from *os, oris*, the mouth.]

**Inexpedient**, in-eks-pē'di-ent, *adj.* not tending to promote any end : unfit : inconvenient.—*adv.* **Inexpe'diently.**—*ns.* **Inexpe'dience, Inexpe'diency.** [Fr.—L. *in*, not, and **Expedient.**]

**Inexpensive**, in-eks-pens'iv, *adj.* of slight expense.

**Inexperience**, in-eks-pē'ri-ens, *n.* want of experience. [Fr.—L. *in*, not, and **Experience.**]

**Inexperienced**, in-eks-pē'ri-enst, *adj.* not having experience : unskilled or unpractised.

**Inexpert**, in-eks-pėrt', *adj.* unskilled.—*n.* **Inexpert'ness.** [L. *in*, not, and **Expert.**]

**Inexpiable**, in-eks'pi-a-bl, *adj.* not able to be expiated or atoned for.—*adv.* **Inex'piably.**—*n.* **Inex'piableness.** [Fr.—L. *in*, not, and **Expiable.**]

**Inexplicable**, in-eks'pli-ka-bl, *adj.* that cannot be explained : unintelligible.—*adv.* **Inex'plicably.** —*ns.* **Inexplicabil'ity, Inex'plicableness.** [Fr.—L. *in*, not, and **Explicable.**]

**Inexplicit**, in-eks-plis'it, *adj.* not clear. [L. *in*, not, and **Explicit.**]

**Inexpressible**, in-eks-pres'i-bl, *adj.* that cannot be expressed : unutterable : indescribable.—*adv.* **Inexpress'ibly.** [L. *in*, not, **Expressible.**]

**Inexpressive**, in-eks-pres'iv. *adj.* not expressive or significant.—*n.* **Inexpress'iveness.**

**Inextinguishable**, in-eks-ting'gwish-a-bl, *adj.* that cannot be extinguished, quenched, or destroyed.—*adv.* **Inextin'guishably.** [Prefix *in-*, not, and **Extinguishable.**]

**Inextricable**, in-eks'tri-ka-bl, *adj.* not able to be extricated or disentangled.—*adv.* **Inex'tricably.** [Fr.—L. *in*, not, and **Extricable.**]

**Infallible**, in-fal′i-bl, *adj.* incapable of error : trustworthy : certain.—*adv.* **Infall′ibly**.—*n.* **Infallibil′ity**. [Fr.—L. *in*, not, and **Fallible**.]

**Infamous**, in′fa-mus, *adj.*, *of ill fame* or bad report : having a reputation of the worst kind : publicly branded with guilt : notoriously vile : disgraceful.—*adv.* **In′famously**. [Prefix *in-*, not, and **Famous**.]

**Infamy**, in′fa-mi, *n.*, *ill fame* or repute : public disgrace : extreme vileness.

**Infancy**, in′fan-si, *n.* the state or time of being an *infant* : childhood : the beginning of anything.

**Infant**, in′fant, *n.* a babe : (*Eng. law*) a person under 21 years of age.—*adj.* belonging to infants or to infancy : tender : intended for infants. [L. *infans, -antis*, that cannot speak—*in*, not, and *fans*, pr.p. of *fari*, to speak, Gr. *phēmi*. See **Fame**.]

**Infanta**, in-fan′ta, *n.* a title given to a daughter of the kings of Spain and Portugal, except the heiress-apparent. [Sp., from root of **Infant**.]

**Infante**, in-fan′tā, *n.* a title given to any son of the kings of Spain and Portugal except the heir-apparent. [Sp., from root of **Infant**.]

**Infanticide**, in-fant′i-sīd, *n.*, *infant* or child *murder:* the murderer of an infant.—*adj.* **Infant′icidal**. [Fr.—L. *infanticidium—infans*, and *cædo*, to kill ]

**Infantile**, in′fant-īl or -il, **Infantine**, in′fant-īn or -in, *adj.* pertaining to *infancy* or to an infant.

**Infantry**, in′fant-ri, *n.* foot-soldiers. [Fr. *infanterie*—It. *infanteria—infante, fante*, a child, a servant, a foot-soldier, foot-soldiers being formerly the servants and followers of knights.]

**Infatuate**, in-fat′ū-āt, *v.t.* to make *foolish:* to affect with folly : to deprive of judgment : to inspire with foolish passion : to stupefy.—*n.* **Infatua′tion**. [L. *infatuo, -atum—in*, and *fatuus*, foolish.]

**Infatuate**, in-fat′ū-āt, *adj.*, *infatuated* or foolish.

**Infect**, in-fekt′, *v.t.* to taint, especially with disease : to corrupt : to poison. [Lit. ' to dip anything into,' from Fr. *infect*—L. *inficio, infectum—in*, into, and *facio*, to make.]

**Infection**, in-fek′shun, *n.* act of infecting : that which infects or taints.

**Infectious**, in-fek′shus, **Infective**, in-fek′tiv, *adj.* having the quality of infecting : corrupting : apt to spread.—*adv.* **Infec′tiously**.—*n.* **Infec′tiousness**.

**Infelicitous**, in-fe-lis′i-tus, *adj.* not felicitous or happy. [L. *in*, not, and **Felicitous**.]

**Infelicity**, in-fe-lis′i-ti, *n.* want of felicity or happiness : misery : misfortune : unfavourableness.

**Infer**, in-fėr′, *v.t.* to deduce : to derive, as a consequence :—*pr.p.* inferr′ing ; *pa.p.* inferred′. [Fr.—L. *infero—in*, into, and *fero*, to bring.]

**Inferable**, in-fėr′a-bl, **Inferrible**, in-fėr′i-bl, *adj.* that may be inferred or deduced.

**Inference**, in′fėr-ens, *n.* that which is inferred or deduced : conclusion : consequence.

**Inferential**, in-fėr-en′shal, *adj.* deducible or deduced by inference.—*adv.* **Inferen′tially**.

**Inferior**, in-fē′ri-ur, *adj.*, *lower* in any respect : subordinate : secondary.—*n.* one lower in rank or station : one younger than another. [Fr.—L. *inferior*, comp. of *inferus*, low.]

**Inferiority**, in-fē-ri-or′i-ti, *n.* the state of being inferior : a lower position in any respect.

**Infernal**, in-fėr′nal, *adj.* belonging to the *lower* regions or hell : resembling or suitable to hell : devilish.—*adv.* **Infer′nally**. [Fr.—L. *infernus—inferus*.]

**Infertile**, in-fėr′til, *adj.* not productive : barren.—*n.* **Infertil′ity**. [L. *in*, not, and **Fertile**.]

**Infest**, in-fest′, *v.t.* to disturb : to harass. [Fr.—L. *infesto*, from *infestus*, hostile, from *in* and an old verb *fendere*, to strike, found in *of-fendere, de-fendere*.]

**Infidel**, in′fi-del, *adj.*, *unbelieving:* sceptical : disbelieving Christianity : heathen.—*n.* one who withholds belief, esp. from Christianity. [Fr.—L. *infidelis—in*, not, *fidelis*, faithful—*fides*, faith.]

**Infidelity**, in-fi-del′i-ti, *n.*, *want of faith* or belief : disbelief in Christianity : unfaithfulness, esp. to the marriage contract : treachery.

**Infiltrate**, in-fil′trāt, *v.t.* to enter a substance by *filtration*, or through its pores.—*n.* **Infiltra′tion**, the process of infiltrating, or the substance infiltrated. [L. *in*, in, and **Filtrate**.]

**Infinite**, in′fin-it, *adj.* without end or limit : without bounds : (*math.*) either greater or smaller than any quantity that can be assigned.—*adv.* **In′finitely**.—*n.* **In′finite**, that which is infinite : the Infinite Being or God. [L. *in*, not, and **Finite**.]

**Infinitesimal**, in-fin-i-tes′im-al, *adj.* infinitely small.—*n.* an infinitely small quantity.—*adv.* **Infinites′imally**.

**Infinitive**, in-fin′it-iv, *adj.* (*lit.*) *unlimited*, unrestricted : (*gram.*) the mood of the verb which expresses the idea without person or number.—*adv.* **Infin′itively**. [Fr.—L. *infinitivus*.]

**Infinitude**, in-fin′i-tūd, **Infinity**, in-fin′i-ti, *n.* boundlessness : immensity : countless or indefinite number.

**Infirm**, in-fėrm′, *adj.* not strong : feeble : sickly : weak : not solid : irresolute : imbecile. [L. *in*, not, and **Firm**.]

**Infirmary**, in-fėrm′ar-i, *n.* a hospital or place for the *infirm*. [Low L. *infirmaria*.]

**Infirmity**, in-fėrm′it-i, *n.* disease : failing : defect : imbecility.

**Infix**, in-fiks′, *v.t. to fix in:* to drive or fasten in : to set in by piercing. [L. *in*, in, and **Fix**.]

**Inflame**, in-flām′, *v.t. to cause to flame:* to cause to burn : to excite : to increase : to exasperate.—*v.i.* to become hot, painful, or angry. [Fr.—L. *in*, into, and **Flame**.]

**Inflammable**, in-flam′a-bl, *adj.* that may be burned : combustible : easily kindled.—*n.* **Inflammabil′ity**.—*adv.* **Inflamm′ably**.

**Inflammation**, in-flam-ā′shun, *n.* state of being in flame : heat of a part of the body, with pain and swelling : violent excitement : heat.

**Inflammatory**, in-flam′a-tor-i, *adj.* tending to *inflame:* inflaming : exciting.

**Inflate**, in-flāt′, *v.t.* to swell with air : to puff up.—*adv.* **Inflat′ingly**. [L. *inflo, inflatum—in*, into, and *flo*, to blow, with which it is cog.]

**Inflation**, in-flā′shun, *n.* state of being puffed up.

**Inflatus**, in-flā′tus, *n.* a *blowing* or breathing *into:* inspiration. [L.]

**Inflect**, in-flekt′, *v.t.* to *bend in:* to turn from a direct line or course : to modulate, as the voice : (*gram.*) to vary in the terminations. [L. *inflecto—in*, in, and *flecto, flexum*, to bend.]

**Inflection**, in-flek′shun, *n.* a *bending* or deviation : modulation of the voice : (*gram.*) the varying in termination.—*adj.* **Inflec′tional**.

**Inflective**, in-flekt′iv, *adj.* subject to inflection.

**Inflexed**, in-flekst′, *adj.*, *bent inward:* bent : turned.

**Inflexible**, in-fleks′i-bl, *adj.* that cannot be bent : unyielding : unbending.—*ns.* **Inflexibil′ity**, **Inflex′ibleness**.—*adv.* **Inflex′ibly**. [Fr.—L. *in*, not, **Flexible**.]

**Inflexion.** Same as **Inflection**.

**Inflexure**, in-fleks'ūr, *n.* a *bend* or fold.

**Inflict**, in-flikt', *v.t.* to lay on : to impose, as punishment. [Lit. 'to strike against,' L. *in*, against, and *fligo*, to strike.]

**Infliction**, in-flik'shun, *n.* act of inflicting or imposing : punishment applied.

**Inflictive**, in-flikt'iv, *adj.* tending or able to inflict.

**Inflorescence**, in-flor-es'ens, *n.* character or mode of flowering of a plant. [Fr.—L. *inflorescens—infloresco*, to begin to blossom. See **Florescence**.]

**Influence**, in'floo-ens, *n.* power exerted on men or things : power in operation : authority.—*v.t.* to affect : to move : to direct. [Orig. a term in astrology, the power or virtue supposed to flow from planets upon men and things ; Fr.—Low L. *influentia*—L. *in*, into, and *fluo*, to flow.]

**Influential**, in-floo-en'shal, *adj.* having or exerting influence or power over.—*adv.* **Influen'tially**.

**Influenza**, in-floo-en'za, *n.* a severe epidemic catarrh, accompanied with weakening fever. [It.—L., a by-form of **Influence**, which see.]

**Influx**, in'fluks, *n.* a *flowing in* : infusion : abundant accession. [L. *influxus—influo*.]

**Infold**, in-fōld', *v.t.* to inwrap : to involve : to embrace. [E. **In**, into, and **Fold**.]

**Inform**, in-form', *v.t.* to give *form* to : to animate or give life to : to impart knowledge to : to tell. [Fr.—L. *in*, into, and **Form**.]

**Informal**, in-form'al, *adj.* not in proper form : irregular.—*adv.* **Inform'ally**.—*n.* **Informal'ity**. [L. *in*, not, and **Formal**.]

**Informant**, in-form'ant, *n.* one who informs or gives intelligence.

**Information**, in-for-mā'shun, *n.* intelligence given : knowledge : an accusation given to a magistrate or court.

**Informer**, in-form'ėr, *n.* one who informs against another for the breaking of a law.

**Infraction**, in-frak'shun, *n.* violation, esp. of law. [Fr.—L. *infractio—in*, in, and *frango, fractus*, to break. See **Fraction**.]

**Infrangible**, in-fran'ji-bl, *adj.* that cannot be broken : not to be violated.—*ns.* **Infrangibil'ity**, **Infran'gibleness**. [See **Infraction**.]

**Infrequent**, in-frē'kwent, *adj.* seldom occurring : rare : uncommon.—*adv.* **Infre'quently**.—*n.* **Infre'quency**. [L. *in*, not, and **Frequent**.]

**Infringe**, in-frinj', *v.t.* to violate, esp. law : to neglect to obey. [Lit. to 'break into,' from L. *infringo—in*, and *frango*.] [non-fulfilment.

**Infringement**, in-frinj'ment, *n.* breach : violation :

**Infuriate**, in-fū'ri-āt, *v.t.* to enrage : to madden. [L. *in*, and *furio, -atum*, to madden—*furo*, to rave.]

**Infuse**, in-fūz', *v.t.* to *pour into* : to inspire with : to introduce : to steep in liquor without boiling. [Fr.—L. *in*, into, *fundo, fusum*, to pour.]

**Infusible**, in-fūz'i-bl, *adj.* that cannot be dissolved or melted. [L. *in*, not, and **Fusible**.]

**Infusion**, in-fū'zhun, *n.* the pouring of water, whether boiling or not, over any substance, in order to extract its active qualities : a solution in water of an organic, esp. a vegetable substance : the liquor so obtained : inspiration : instilling.

**Infusoria**, in-fū-sō'ri-a, *n.pl.* microscopic animalcula found in *infusions* of animal or vegetable material exposed to the atmosphere. [L.]

**Infusorial**, in-fū-sō'ri-al, **Infusory**, in-fū'sor-i, *adj.* composed of or containing infusoria.

**Ingathering**, in'gāth-ėr-ing, *n.* the collecting and securing of the fruits of the earth : harvest. [E. **In** and **Gathering**.]

**Ingenious**, in-jē'ni-us, *adj.* of good natural abilities : skilful in inventing : shewing ingenuity : witty.—*adv.* **Inge'niously**.—*n.* **Inge'niousness**. [Fr.—L. *ingeniosus—ingenium*, mother-wit, from *in*, and *gen*, root of *gigno*, to beget.]

**Ingenuity**, in-jen-ū'i-ti, *n.* power of ready invention : facility in combining ideas : curiousness in design. [Orig. meant 'ingenuousness ;' L. *ingenuitas—ingenuus*.]

**Ingenuous**, in-jen'ū-us, *adj.* frank : honourable : free from deception.—*adv.* **Ingen'uously**.—*n.* **Ingen'uousness**. [Lit. 'free-born, of good birth ;' L. *ingenuus*.]

**Inglorious**, in-glō'ri-us, *adj.* not glorious ; without honour : shameful.—*adv.* **Inglo'riously**.—*n.* **Inglo'riousness**. [Fr.—L. *in*, not, and **Glorious**.]

**Ingot**, in'got, *n.* a mass of unwrought metal, esp. gold or silver, cast in a mould. [Lit. 'something poured in,' from A.S. *in*, in, and *goten*, pa.p. of *geotan*, to pour ; cog. with Ger. *giessen*, Goth. *gjutan*, and L. *fun-do, fud-i*, to pour. The Ger. *ein-guss* is an exact parallel to *ingot*.]

**Ingraft**, in-graft', *v.t.* to *graft* or insert a shoot of one tree *into* another : to introduce something foreign : to fix deeply. [Fr.—L. *in*, into, and **Graft**.]

**Ingraftment**, in-graft'ment, *n.*, *ingrafting* : the thing ingrafted : a scion.

**Ingrain**, in-grān', *v.t.* (*orig.*) to dye *in grain* (meaning *with grain*), that is, cochineal : hence, to dye of a fast or lasting colour : to dye in the raw state : to infix deeply. [L. *in*, into, and see **Grain**.] [*gratus*.

**Ingrate**, in'grāt, *adj.* unthankful. [Fr.—L. *in-*

**Ingratiate**, in-grā'shi-āt, *v.t.* to commend to *grace* or *favour* (used reflexively, and followed by *with*) : to secure the good-will of another. [L. *in*, into, and *gratia*, favour. See **Grace**.]

**Ingratitude**, in-grat'i-tūd, *n.* unthankfulness : the return of evil for good. [Fr.—L. *in*, not, and **Gratitude**.]

**Ingredient**, in-grē'di-ent, *n.* that which *enters into* a compound : a component part of anything. [Fr.—L. *ingrediens, -entis*, pr.p. of *ingredior—in*, into, and *gradior*, to walk, to enter. See **Grade** and **Ingress**.]

**Ingress**, in'gres, *n.*, *entrance* : power, right, or means of entrance. [L. *ingressus—ingredior*.]

**Inguinal**, ing'gwin-al, *adj.* relating to the *groin*. [L. *inguinalis—inguen, inguinis*, the groin.]

**Ingulf**, in-gulf', *v.t.* to swallow up wholly, as *in a gulf* : to cast into a gulf : to overwhelm.—*n.* **Ingulf'ment**. [E. **In** and **Gulf**.]

**Ingurgitate**, in-gur'ji-tāt, *v.t.* to swallow up greedily, as in a *gulf*. [L. *ingurgito, -atum—in*, into, and *gurges*, a gulf, whirlpool.]

**Inhabit**, in-hab'it, *v.t.* to dwell in : to occupy. [Fr.—L., from *in*, in, and *habito*, to have frequently, to dwell—*habeo*, to have. Cf. **Habit**.]

**Inhabitable**, in-hab'it-a-bl, *adj.* that may be inhabited. [Late L. *inhabitabilis*.]

**Inhabitant**, in-hab'it-ant, **Inhab'iter** (*B.*), *n.* one who inhabits : a resident. [L. *inhabitans*.]

**Inhalation**, in-ha-lā'shun, *n.* the drawing into the lungs, as air, or fumes.

**Inhale**, in-hāl', *v.t.* to *draw in* the *breath* : to draw into the lungs, as air.—*n.* **Inhal'er**. [L. *inhalo*, to breathe upon—*in*, upon, and *halo*, to breathe.]

**Inharmonious**, in-har-mō'ni-us, *adj.* discordant : unmusical.—*adv.* **Inharmo'niously**.—*n.* **Inharmo'niousness**. [Prefix *in-*, not, **Harmonious**.]

**Inhere**, in-hēr', *v.i.* to *stick fast* : to remain firm in. [L. *inhæreo—in*, and *hæreo*, to stick.]

**Inherence**, in-hēr'ens, **Inherency**, in-hēr'en-si, *n.* a *sticking fast* : existence in something else : a fixed state of being in another body or substance.

**Inherent**, in-hēr'ent, *adj.*, *sticking fast* : existing in and inseparable from something else : innate : natural.—*adv.* **Inher'ently.** [L. *inhærens.*]

**Inherit**, in-her'it, *v.t.* to *take as heir* or by descent from an ancestor : to possess.—*v.i.* to enjoy, as property. [L. *in*, and Fr. *hériter*—L. *heredito*, to inherit. See **Heir.**]

**Inheritable.** Same as **Heritable.**

**Inheritance**, in-her'it-ans, *n.* that which is or may be inherited : an estate derived from an ancestor : hereditary descent : natural gift : possession.

**Inheritor**, in-her'it-or, *n.* one who inherits or may inherit : an heir.—*fem.* **Inher'itress, Inher'itrix.**

**Inhesion**, in-hē'zhun. Same as **Inherence.**

**Inhibit**, in-hib'it, *v.t.* to *hold in* or back : to keep back : to check. [L. *inhibeo*, *-hibitum*—*in*, in, and *habeo*, to have, to hold. Cf. **Habit.**]

**Inhibition**, in-hi-bish'un, *n.* the act of inhibiting or restraining : the state of being inhibited : prohibition : a writ from a higher court to an inferior judge to stay proceedings.

**Inhibitory**, in-hib'it-or-i, *adj.* prohibitory.

**Inhospitable**, in-hos'pit-a-bl, *adj.* affording no kindness to strangers.—*adv.* **Inhos'pitably.**—*n.* **Inhos'pitableness.** [Fr.—L. *in*, not, and **Hospitable.**] [tality or courtesy to strangers.

**Inhospitality.** in-hos-pi-tal'i-ti, *n.* want of hospi-

**Inhuman**, in-hū'man, *adj.* barbarous : cruel : unfeeling.—*adv.* **Inhu'manly.** [Fr.—L. *in*, not, and **Human.**]

**Inhumanity**, in-hū-man'i-ti, *n.* the state of being inhuman : barbarity : cruelty.

**Inhumation**, in-hū-mā'shun, *n.* the act of inhuming or depositing in the ground : burial.

**Inhume**, in-hūm', *v.t.* to inter. [Fr.—L. *inhumo* —*in*, in, and *humus*, the ground.]

**Inimical**, in-im'i-kal, *adj.* like an *enemy*, *not friendly* : contrary : repugnant.—*adv.* **Inim'ically.** [L. *inimicalis*—*inimicus*—*in*, not, and *amicus*, friendly—*amo*, to love.]

**Inimitable**, in-im'it-a-bl, *adj.* that cannot be imitated : surpassingly excellent.—*adv.* **Inim'itably.** [Fr.—L. *in*, not, and **Imitable.**]

**Iniquitous**, in-ik'wi-tus, *adj.* unjust : unreasonable : wicked.—*adv.* **Iniq'uitously.**

**Iniquity**, in-ik'wi-ti, *n.* want of equity or fairness : injustice : wickedness : a crime. [Fr.—L. *iniquitas*—*iniquus*, unequal—*in*, not, and *æquus*, equal or fair.]

**Initial**, in-ish'al, *adj.* commencing : placed at the beginning.—*n.* the letter beginning a word, esp. a name.—*v.t.* to put the initials of one's name to. [L. *initialis*—*initium*, a beginning, *ineo*, *initus* —*in*, into, *eo*, *itum*, to go.]

**Initiate**, in-ish'i-āt, *v.t.* to make a *beginning* : to instruct in principles : to acquaint with : to introduce into a new state or society.—*v.i.* to perform the first act or rite.—*n.* one who is initiated.— *adj.* fresh : unpractised. [See **Initial.**]

**Initiation**, in-ish-i-ā'shun, *n.* act or process of initiating or acquainting one with principles before unknown : act of admitting to any society, by instructing in its rules and ceremonies.

**Initiative**, in-ish'i-a-tiv, *adj.* serving to initiate : introductory.—*n.* an introductory step.

**Initiatory**, in-ish'i-a-tor-i, *adj.* tending to initiate : introductory.—*n.* introductory rite.

**Inject**, in-jekt', *v.t.* to *throw into* : to cast on. [L. *injicio*, *injectum*—*in*, into, *jacio*, to throw.]

**Injection**, in-jek'shun, *n.* act of injecting or throwing in or into : the act of filling the vessels of an animal body with any liquid : a liquid to be injected into any part of the body.

**Injudicial**, in-joo-dish'al, *adj.* not according to law-forms. [L. *in*, not, and **Judicial.**]

**Injudicious**, in-joo-dish'us, *adj.* void of or wanting in judgment : inconsiderate.—*adv.* **Injudi'ciously.**—*n.* **Injudi'ciousness.** [Fr.—L. *in*, not, and **Judicious.**]

**Injunction**, in-jungk'shun, *n.* act of *enjoining* or commanding : an order : a precept : exhortation : a writ of prohibition granted by a court of equity. [L. *injunctio*—*in*, and *jungo*, *junctum*, to join.]

**Injure**, in'joor, *v.t.* to act with *injustice* or contrary to law : to wrong : to damage : to annoy. [Fr. *injurier*—L. *injurior*—*injuria*, injury—*in*, not, and *jus*, *juris*, law.]

**Injurious**, in-jōō'ri-us, *adj.* tending to injure : unjust : wrongful : mischievous : damaging reputation.—*adv.* **Inju'riously.**—*n.* **Inju'riousness.**

**Injury**, in'joor-i, *n.* that which injures : wrong : mischief : annoyance : (*Pr. Bk.*) insult, offence.

**Injustice**, in-jus'tis, *n.* violation or withholding of another's rights or dues : wrong : iniquity. [Fr. —L. *injustitia*, *in*, not, and **Justice.**]

**Ink**, ingk, *n.* a coloured fluid used in writing, printing, &c.—*v.t.* to daub with ink. [O. Fr. *enque* (Fr. *encre*)—L. *encaustum*, the purplered ink used by the later Roman emperors—Gr. *engkauston*—*engkaiō*, to burn in. See **Encaustic.**]

**Inkholder**, ingk'hōld-ėr, **Inkstand**, ingk'stand, *n.* a vessel for *holding ink.*

**Inkhorn**, ingk'horn, *n.* (*obs.*) an *ink*holder, formerly of *horn* : a portable case for ink, &c.

**Inking-roller**, ingk'ing-rōl'ėr, *n.* a *roller* covered with a composition for *inking* printing types.

**Inking-table**, ingk'ing-tā'bl, *n.* a *table* or flat surface used for supplying the inking-roller with *ink* during the process of printing.

**Inkling**, ingk'ling, *n.* a *hint* or whisper : intimation. [From the M. E. verb to *inkle* (for *im-k-le*, cog. with Ice. *ym-ta*, to mutter, from *ym-r*, a humming sound), a freq. formed from an imitative base -*um* (Sw. *hum*, E. **Hum**.)]

**Inky**, ingk'i, *adj.* consisting of or resembling ink : blackened with ink.—*n.* **Ink'iness.**

**Inlaid**, in-lād', *pa.p.* of **Inlay.**

**Inland**, in'land, *n.* the interior part of a country. —*adj.* remote from the sea : carried on or produced within a country : confined to a country. [A.S. *inland*, a domain—*in*, and *land*.]

**Inlander**, in'land-ėr, *n.* one who lives inland.

**Inlay**, in-lā', *v.t.* to ornament by *laying in* or inserting pieces of metal, ivory, &c. : —*pa.p.* **Inlaid'.**—*n.* pieces of metal, ivory, &c. for inlaying. —*ns.* **Inlay'ing, Inlay'er.** [E. **In** and **Lay.**]

**Inlet**, in'let, *n.* a passage by which one is *let in* : place of ingress : a small bay. [E. **In** and **Let.**]

**Inly**, in'li, *adj.* : *inward* : secret.—*adv.*, *inwardly* : in the heart. [A.S. *inlic*—*in*, and *lic*, like.]

**Inmate**, in'māt, *n.* one who lodges in the same house with another : a lodger : one received into a hospital, &c. [**In** and **Mate.**]

**Inmost.** See **Innermost.**

**Inn**, in, *n.* a house for the lodging and entertainment of travellers : a hotel : (*B.*) a lodging.— **Inns of Court**, four societies in London for students-at-law, qualifying them to be called to the bar. [A.S. *in*, *inn*, an inn, house—*in*, *inn*, within, from the prep. *in*, in ; Ice. *inni*, a house, *inni*, within.]

**Innate**, in'āt or in-nāt', *adj.*, *inborn* : natural : inherent.—*n.* **Inn'ateness.**—*adv.* **Inn'ately.** [L. *innatus*—*innascor*—*in*, in, *nascor*, to be born.]

**Innavigable,** in-nav'i-ga-bl, *adj.* impassable by ships.—*adv.* **Innav'igably.** [Fr.—L. *in,* not, and **Navigable.**]     [terior. [A.S.]

**Inner,** in'er, *adj.* (comp. of **In**), *further in :* in—

**Innermost,** in'er-mōst, **inmost,** in'mōst, *adj.* (superl. of **In**), *furthest in :* most remote from the outward part. [A.S. *innemest ;* for the termination *-most,* see **Aftermost, Foremost.**]

**Innerve,** in-érv', *v.t.* to supply with force or *nervous* energy.—*n.* **Innerva'tion,** special mode of activity inherent in the nervous structure : nervous activity. [Fr.—L. *in,* in, and **Nerve.**]

**Inning,** in'ing, *n.* the *in*gathering of grain : turn for using the bat in cricket (in this sense used only in the pl.) :—*pl.* lands recovered from the sea. [A verbal noun from old verb to *inn,* i.e. to house corn, which is from noun **Inn.**]

**Innkeeper,** in'kēp-ér, *n.* one who keeps an inn.

**Innocence,** in'o-sens, **Innocency,** in'o-sen-si, *n.* harmlessness : blamelessness : purity : integrity.

**Innocent,** in'o-sent, *adj.* not *hurtful :* inoffensive : blameless : pure : lawful.—*n.* one free from harm or fault.—*adv.* **Inn'ocently.** [Fr.— L. *innocens, -entis—in,* not, and *noceo,* to hurt. Cf. **Noxious.**]

**Innocuous,** in-nok'ū-us, *adj.* not *hurtful :* harmless in effects.—*adv.* **Innoc'uously.**—*n.* **Innoc'-uousness.** [L. *innocuus.*]

**Innovate,** in'o-vāt, *v.t.* to *introduce* something *new.*—*v.i.* to introduce novelties : to make changes.—*ns.* **Inn'ovator, Innova'tion.** [L. *innovo, -novatum—in,* and *novus,* new.]

**Innoxious.** Same as **Innocuous.**—*adv.* **Innox'-iously.** [L. *in,* not, and **Noxious.**]

**Innuendo,** in-ū-en'dō, *n.* a side-hint : an indirect reference or intimation. [Lit. a suggestion conveyed *by a nod ;* L. ; it is the gerund ablative of *innuo—in,* and *nuo,* to nod.]

**Innumerable,** in-nū'mér-a-bl, *adj.* that cannot be numbered : countless.—*adv.* **Innu'merably.**— *n.* **Innu'merableness.** [Fr.—L. *in,* not, and **Numerable.**]

**Innutrition,** in-nū-trish'un, *n.* want of nutrition : failure of nourishment.

**Innutritious,** in-nū-trish'us, *adj.* not nutritious : without nourishment. [L. *in,* not, **Nutritious.**]

**Inobservant,** in-ob-zérv'ant, *adj.* not observant : heedless. [L. *in,* not, and **Observant.**]

**Inobtrusive,** in-ob-trōō'siv, *adj.* not obtrusive.— *adv.* **Inobtru'sively.**—*n.* **Inobtru'siveness.** [L. *in,* not, and **Obtrusive.**]

**Inoculate,** in-ok'ū-lāt, *v.t.* to *insert* an *eye* or *bud :* to ingraft : to communicate disease by inserting matter in the skin.—*v.i.* to propagate by budding : to practise inoculation. [L. *inoculo, -atum—in,* into, and *oculus,* an eye. See **Ocular.**]

**Inoculation,** in-ok-ū-lā'shun, *n.* act or practice of *inoculating :* insertion of the buds of one plant into another : the communicating of disease by inserting matter in the skin.

**Inodorous,** in-ō'dur-us, *adj.* without smell. [L. *in,* not, and **Odorous.**]

**Inoffensive,** in-of-fen'siv, *adj.* giving no offence : harmless.—*adv.* **Inoffen'sively.**—*n.* **Inoffen'-siveness.** [Fr.—L. *in,* not, and **Offensive.**]

**Inofficial,** in-of-fish'al, *adj.* not proceeding from the proper officer : without the usual forms of authority.—*adv.* **Inoffic'ially.** [Fr.—L. *in,* not, and **Official.**]

**Inoperative,** in-op'ér-a-tiv, *adj.* not in action : producing no effect. [Fr.—L. *in,* not, and **Operative.**]

**Inopportune,** in-op-por-tūn', *adj.* unseasonable in time.—*adv.* **Inopportune'ly.** [Fr.—L. *in,* not, and **Opportune.**]

**Inordinate,** in-or'di-nāt, *adj.* beyond usual bounds : irregular : immoderate.—*adv.* **Inor'dinately.**— *n.* **Inor'dinateness.** [L. *in,* not, and **Ordinate.**]

**Inordination,** in-or-di-nā'shun, *n.* deviation from rule : irregularity.

**Inorganic,** in-or-gan'ik, *adj.* without life or organisation, as minerals, &c.—*adv.* **Inorgan'ically.** [Fr.—L. *in,* not, and **Organic.**]    [ganic.

**Inorganised,** in-or'gan-īzd, *adj.* Same as **Inor-**

**Inosculate,** in-os'kū-lāt, *v.t.* and *v.i.* to unite by mouths or ducts, as two vessels in an animal body : to blend.—*n.* **Inoscula'tion.** [L. *in,* and *osculor, -atum,* to kiss.]

**Inquest,** in'kwest, *n.* act of inquiring : search : judicial inquiry : a jury for inquiring into any matter, esp. any case of violent or sudden death. [O. Fr. *enqueste ;* see **Inquire.** Doublet **Inquiry.**]

**Inquietude,** in-kwī'et-ūd, *n.* disturbance or uneasiness of body or mind. [Fr.—L. *in,* not, and **Quietude.**]

**Inquire,** in-kwīr', *v.i.* to ask a question : to make an investigation.—*v.t.* to ask about : to make an examination regarding.—*n.* **Inquir'er.** [L. *in-quiro—in,* and *quæro, quæsitum,* to seek.]

**Inquiring,** in-kwīr'ing, *adj.* given to inquiry.— *adv.* **Inquir'ingly.**

**Inquiry,** in-kwī'ri, *n.* act of inquiring : search for knowledge : investigation : a question. [Doublet **Inquest.**]

**Inquisition,** in-kwi-zish'un, *n.* an *inquiring* or searching for : investigation : judicial inquiry : a tribunal in some Catholic countries for examining and punishing heretics. [Fr.—L. *inquisitio ;* see **Inquire.**]

**Inquisitional,** in-kwi-zish'un-al, *adj.* making inquiry : relating to the Inquisition.

**Inquisitive,** in-kwiz'i-tiv, *adj., searching into :* apt to ask questions : curious.—*adv.* **Inquis'i-tively.**—*n.* **Inquis'itiveness.**

**Inquisitor,** in-kwiz'i-tur, *n.* one who *inquires :* an official inquirer : a member of the Court of Inquisition.—*adj.* **Inquisito'rial.**—*adv.* **Inquisi-to'rially.** [L.]

**Inroad,** in'rōd, *n.* a *riding into* an enemy's country : a sudden or desultory invasion : attack : encroachment. [E. **In,** into, and **Road.**]

**Insalivation,** in-sal-i-vā'shun, *n.* the process of mixing the food with the *saliva.*

**Insalubrious,** in-sa-lōō'bri-us, *adj.* not healthful : unwholesome.—*n.* **Insalu'brity.** [L. *in,* not, and **Salubrious.**]

**Insane,** in-sān', *adj.* not *sane* or of *sound mind :* mad : pertaining to insane persons : utterly unwise.—*adv.* **Insane'ly.** [L. *in,* not, and **Sane.**]

**Insanity,** in-san'i-ti, *n.* want of sanity : state of being insane : madness.

**Insatiable,** in-sā'shi-a-bl, **Insatiate,** in-sā'shi-āt, *adj.* that cannot be satiated or satisfied.—*adv.* **Insa'tiably.**—*ns.* **Insa'tiableness, Insatiabil'-ity.** [Fr.—L. *in,* not, and **Satiable, Satiate.**]

**Inscribe,** in-skrīb', *v.t.* to *write upon :* to engrave, as on a monument : to address : to imprint deeply : *(geom.)* to draw one figure within another.—*n.* **Inscrib'er.** [L. *inscribo, inscrip-tus—in,* upon, and *scribo,* to write.]

**Inscription,** in-skrip'shun, *n.* a *writing upon :* that which is inscribed : title : dedication of a book to a person. [See **Inscribe.**]

**Inscriptive,** in-skrip'tiv, *adj.* bearing an inscription : of the character of an inscription.

**Inscrutable,** in-skrōōt'a-bl, *adj.* that cannot be

scrutinised or *searched into* and understood : inexplicable.—*adv.* Inscrut′ably.—*ns.* Inscrut-abil′ity, Inscrut′ableness. [Fr.—L. *inscruta-bilis—in*, not, and *scrutor*, to search into.]

Insect, in′sekt, *n.* a small animal, as a wasp or fly, with a body as if *cut in* the middle, or divided into sections : anything small or contemptible.—*adj.* like an insect : small : mean. [Fr.—L. *insectum*, pa.p. of *inseco—in*, into, and *seco*, to cut.] [insect.

Insectile, in-sek′til, *adj.* having the nature of an

Insection, in-sek′shun, *n.* a *cutting in* : incision.

Insectivorous, in-sek-tiv′or-us, *adj.*, *devouring* or living on *insects*. [L. *insectum*, and *voro*, to devour.]

Insecure, in-se-kūr′, *adj.* apprehensive of danger or loss : exposed to danger or loss.—*adv.* Inse-cure′ly.—*n.* Insecur′ity. [L. *in*, not, and Secure.]

Insensate, in-sen′sāt, *adj.* void of sense : wanting sensibility : stupid. [L. *insensatus—in*, not, and *sensatus*, from *sensus*, feeling.]

Insensible, in-sen′si-bl, *adj.* not having feeling : callous : dull : imperceptible by the senses.—*adv.* Insen′sibly.—*n.* Insensibil′ity. [Fr.—L. *in*, not, and Sensible.]

Insentient, in-sen′shi-ent, *adj.* not having perception. [L. *in*, not, and Sentient.]

Inseparable, in-sep′ar-a-bl, *adj.* that cannot be separated.—*adv.* Insep′arably.—*ns.* Insep′ar-ableness, Inseparabil′ity. [Fr.—L. *in*, not, and Separable.]

Insert, in-sèrt′, *v.t.* to introduce into : to put in or among. [L. *in*, and *sero*, *sertum*, to join.]

Insertion, in-sèr′shun, *n.* act of inserting : condition of being inserted : that which is inserted.

Insessorial, in-ses-sō′ri-al, *adj.* having feet (as birds) formed for *perching* or climbing *on* trees. [L. *insessor*, from *insideo*, *insessum—in*, on, and *sedeo*, to sit.]

Inseverable, in-sev′èr-a-bl, *adj.* that cannot be severed or separated. [L. *in*, not, and Sever-able.] [*sheath*. [E. In and Sheathe.]

Insheathe, in-shēth′, *v.t.* to *put* or hide in a

Inshore, in-shōr′, *adv.*, *on* or near the *shore*. [E. In and Shore.]

Inshrine, in-shrīn′. Same as Enshrine.

Insiccation, in-sik-kā′shun, *n.* act of *drying in*. [L. *in*, in, and *sicco*, *siccatum*, to dry.]

Inside, in′sīd, *n.* the *side* or part *within*.—*adj.* being within : interior.—*adv.* or *prep.* within the sides of : in the interior of. [E. In and Side.]

Insidious, in-sid′i-us, *adj.* watching an opportunity to insnare : intended to entrap : treacherous.—*adv.* Insid′iously.—*n.* Insid′iousness. [Lit. ' sitting in wait,' from Fr.—L. *insidiosus—insidiæ*, an ambush—*insideo—in*, *sedeo*, to sit.]

Insight, in′sīt, *n.*, *sight into* : view of the interior : thorough knowledge or skill : power of acute observation. [E. In and Sight.]

Insignia, in-sig′ni-a, *n.pl.*, *signs* or badges of office or honour : marks by which anything is known. [L., pl. of *insigne*, from *in*, and *signum*, a mark.]

Insignificant, in-sig-nif′i-kant, *adj.* destitute of meaning : without effect : unimportant : petty. —*adv.* Insignif′icantly.—*ns.* Insignif′icance, Insignif′icancy. [L. *in*, not, and Significant.]

Insignificative, in-sig-nif′i-ka-tiv, *adj.* not significative or expressing by external signs.

Insincere, in-sin-sēr′, *adj.* deceitful : dissembling : not to be trusted : unsound.—*adv.* Insincere′ly. —*n.* Insincer′ity. [Fr.—L. *in*, not, and Sincere.]

Insinuate, in-sin′ū-āt, *v.t.* to introduce gently or artfully : to hint, esp. a fault : to work into

favour.—*v.i.* to creep or flow in : to enter gently : to obtain access by flattery or stealth.—*n.* In-sin′uator. [L. *insinuo*, *-atum—in*, and *sinus*, a curve, bosom.]

Insinuating, in-sin′ū-āt-ing, *adj.* tending to insinuate or enter gently : insensibly winning confidence.—*adv.* Insin′uatingly.

Insinuation, in-sin-ū-ā′shun, *n.* act of insinuating : power of insinuating : that which is insinuated : a hint, esp. conveying an indirect imputation.

Insinuative, in-sin′ū-ā-tiv, *adj.*, *insinuating* or stealing on the confidence : using insinuations.

Insipid, in-sip′id, *adj.*, *tasteless* : wanting spirit or animation : dull.—*adv.* Insip′idly.—*ns.* In-sip′idness, Insipid′ity, want of taste. [Fr.—L. *insipidus—in*, not, *sapidus*, well-tasted—*sapio*, to taste.]

Insist, in-sist′, *v.i.* to dwell on in discourse : to persist in pressing.—*n.* Insist′ence. [Fr.—L. *in*, upon, *sisto*, to stand.]

Insnare, in-snār′, *v.t.* to catch in a *snare* : to entrap : to take by deceit : to entangle. [E. In and Snare.]

Insobriety, in-so-brī′e-ti, *n.* want of sobriety : intemperance. [Prefix *in-*, not, and Sobriety.]

Insolate, in′so-lāt, *v.t.* to expose to the sun's rays. —*n.* Insola′tion. [L. *in*, in, and *sol*, the sun.]

Insolent, in′so-lent, *adj.* haughty and contemptuous : insulting : rude.—*adv.* In′solently.—*n.* In′solence. [Lit. ' unusual,' Fr.—L. *insolens—in*, not, *solens*, pr.p. of *soleo*, to be accustomed.]

Insolidity, in-so-lid′i-ti, *n.* want of solidity : weakness. [Prefix *in-*, not, and Solidity.]

Insoluble, in-sol′ū-bl, *adj.* not capable of being dissolved : not to be solved or explained.—*ns.* Insolubil′ity, Insol′ubleness. [Fr.—L. *in*, not, and Soluble.]

Insolvable, in-solv′a-bl, *adj.* not solvable : not to be explained. [L. *in*, not, and Solvable.]

Insolvent, in-solv′ent, *adj.* not able to pay one's debts : pertaining to insolvent persons.—*n.* one who is unable to pay his debts.—*n.* Insolv′ency. [L. *in*, not, and Solvent.]

Insomnia, in-som′ni-a, *n.* sleeplessness.—*adj.* In-som′nious. [L. *insomnis*, sleepless.]

Insomuch, in-so-much′, *adv.* to such a degree : so. [In, So, Much.]

Inspan, in-span′, *v.t.* to yoke draught-oxen or horses to a vehicle. [E. In, and Span, a yoke of oxen.]

Inspect, in-spekt′, *v.t.* to *look into* : to examine : to look at narrowly : to superintend. [L. *in-specto*, freq. of *inspicio*, *inspectum—in*, into, and *specio*, to look or see.]

Inspection, in-spek′shun, *n.* the act of inspecting or looking into : careful or official examination.

Inspector, in-spekt′ur, *n.* one who *looks into* or oversees : an examining officer : a superintendent. —*n.* Inspect′orship, the office of an inspector.

Inspirable, in-spīr′a-bl, *adj.* able to be inhaled.

Inspiration, in-spi-rā′shun, *n.* the act of inspiring or *breathing into* : a breath : the divine influence by which the sacred writers were instructed : superior elevating or exciting influence.

Inspiratory, in-spīr′a-tor-i or in′spir-a-tor-i, *adj.* belonging to or aiding inspiration or inhalation.

Inspire, in-spīr′, *v.t.* to *breathe into* : to draw or inhale into the lungs : to infuse by breathing, or as if by breathing : to infuse into the mind : to instruct by divine influence : to instruct or affect with a superior influence.—*v.i.* to draw in the breath.—*n.* Inspir′er. [Fr.—L. *inspiro—in*, into, and *spiro*, to breathe.]

Inspirit, in-spir′it, *v.t.* to infuse spirit into : to give new life to : to invigorate : to encourage. **[In and Spirit.]**

**Inspissate**, in-spis′āt, *v.t.* to *thicken* by the evaporation of moisture, as the juices of plants.—*n.* **Inspissa′tion.** [L. *inspisso*, *-atum—in*, and *spissus*, thick.]

**Instability**, in-sta-bil′i-ti, *n.* want of stability or steadiness : want of firmness : inconstancy : fickleness : mutability. [Fr.—L. *in*, not, and **Stability.**]

**Install, Instal,** in-stawl′, *v.t.* to place *in* a *stall* or seat : to place in an office or order : to invest with any charge or office with the customary ceremonies. [Fr.—Low L.—L. *in*, in, and Low L. *stallum*, a stall or seat—O. Ger. *stal* (Ger. *stall*, E. **Stall**).]

**Installation**, in-stal-ā′shun, *n.* the act of installing or placing in an office with ceremonies.

**Instalment**, in-stawl′ment, *n.* the act of installing : one of the parts of a sum paid at various times : that which is produced at stated periods.

**Instance**, in′stans, *n.* quality of being *instant* or urgent : solicitation : occurrence : occasion : example.—*v.t.* to mention as an example or case in point. [Fr.—L. *instantia—instans.*]

**Instant**, in′stant, *adj.* pressing, urgent : immediate : quick : without delay : present, current, as the passing month.—*n.* the present moment of time : any moment or point of time.—*adv.* **In′stantly**, on the instant or moment : immediately : (*B.*) importunately, zealously. [L. *instans*, *-antis*, pr.p. of *insto*, to stand upon—*in*, upon, *sto*, to stand.]

**Instantaneous**, in-stan-tān′e-us, *adj.* done in an instant : momentary : occurring or acting at once : very quickly.—*adv.* **Instantan′eously.**

**Instanter**, in-stan′ter, *adv.* immediately. [L. See **Instant.**]    [install. **[In and State.]**

**Instate**, in-stāt′, *v.t.* to put in possession : to

**Instead**, in-sted′, *adv.*, *in* the *stead*, place, or room of. [M. E. *in stede*—A.S. *on stede*, in the place. See **Stead.**]

**Instep**, in′step, *n.* the prominent upper part of the human foot near its junction with the leg : in horses, the hindleg from the ham to the pastern joint. [Prob. from **In** and **Stoop**, as if sig. the 'in-bend' (Skeat).]

**Instigate**, in′sti-gāt, *v.t.* to urge on : to set on : to incite. [L. *instigo—in*, and root *stig*, Gr. *stizō*, Sans. *tij*, to prick. See **Stigma** and **Sting**.]

**Instigation**, in-sti-gā′shun, *n.* the act of instigating or inciting : impulse, esp. to evil.

**Instigator**, in′sti-gāt-ur, *n.* an inciter to ill.

**Instil**, in-stil′, *v.t.* to *drop into*: to infuse slowly into the mind :—*pr.p.* instill′ing ; *pa.p.* instilled′. [Fr.—L. *instillo—in*, and *stillo*, to drop. See **Distil.**]

**Instillation**, in-stil-ā′shun, **Instilment**, in-stil′-ment, *n.* the act of instilling or pouring in by drops : the act of infusing slowly into the mind : that which is instilled or infused.

**Instinct**, in′stingkt, *n.* impulse : an involuntary or unreasoning prompting to action : the natural impulse by which animals are guided apparently independent of reason or experience. [L. *instinctus*, from *instinguo*, to instigate—*in*, and *stinguo—stig*.]     [moved : animated.

**Instinct**, in-stingkt′, *adj.*, *instigated* or incited :

**Instinctive**, in-stingkt′iv, *adj.* prompted by instinct : involuntary : acting according to or determined by natural impulse.—*adv.* **Instinct′-ively.**

**Institute**, in′sti-tūt, *v.t.* to set up in : to erect : to originate : to establish : to appoint : to com-

mence : to educate.—*n.* anything instituted or formally established : established law : precept or principle : a book of precepts or principles : an institution : a literary and philosophical society. [Lit. to 'cause' to 'stand up,' L. *instituo —in*, and *statuo*, to cause to stand—*sto*, to stand.]

**Institution**, in-sti-tū′shun, *n.* the act of instituting or establishing : that which is instituted or established : foundation : established order : enactment : a society established for some object : that which institutes or instructs : a system of principles or rules.

**Institutional**, in-sti-tū′shun-al, **Institutionary**, in-sti-tū′shun-ar-i, *adj.* belonging to an institution : instituted by authority : elementary.

**Institutist**, in′sti-tūt-ist, *n.* a writer of institutes or elementary rules.

**Institutive**, in′sti-tūt-iv, *adj.* able or tending to institute or establish : depending on an institution.

**Instruct**, in-strukt′, *v.t.* to prepare : to inform : to teach : to order or command.—*n.* **Instruct′or** : —*fem.* **Instruct′ress.** [Lit. to 'put in order,' L. *instruo*, *instructum—in*, and *struo*, to pile up, to set in order.]     [structed.

**Instructible**, in-strukt′i-bl, *adj.* able to be in-

**Instruction**, in-struk′shun, *n.* the act of instructing or teaching : information : command.

**Instructive**, in-strukt′iv, *adj.* containing instruction or information : conveying knowledge.— *adv.* **Instruct′ively.**—*n.* **Instruct′iveness.**

**Instrument**, in′stroo-ment, *n.* a tool or utensil : a machine producing musical sounds : a writing containing a contract : one who or that which is made a means. [Lit. 'that which instructs' or 'builds up,' Fr.—L. *instrumentum—instruo.* See **Instruct.**]

**Instrumental**, in-stroo-ment′al, *adj.* acting as an instrument or means : serving to promote an object : helpful : belonging to or produced by musical instruments.—*adv.* **Instrument′ally.**— *n.* **Instrumental′ity**, agency.

**Instrumentalist**, in-stroo-ment′al-ist, *n.* one who plays on a musical instrument.

**Instrumentation**, in-stroo-men-tā′shun, *n.* (*music*) the arrangement of a composition for performance by different instruments : the playing upon musical instruments.

**Insubjection**, in-sub-jek′shun, *n.* want of subjection or obedience. [Prefix *in-*, not, and **Subjection.**]

**Insubordinate**, in-sub-or′din-āt, *adj.* not subordinate or submissive : disobedient.—*n.* **Insubordina′tion.** [*In*, not, and **Subordinate.**]

**Insufferable**, in-suf′er-a-bl, *adj.* that cannot be suffered or endured : unbearable : detestable.— *adv.* **Insuff′erably.** [*In*, not, and **Sufferable.**]

**Insufficient**, in-suf-fish′ent, *adj.* not sufficient : deficient : unfit : incapable.—*adv.* **Insuffi′ciently.** —*n.* **Insuffi′ciency.** [*In*, not, and **Sufficient.**]

**Insular**, in′sū-lar, *adj.* belonging to an *island* : surrounded by water.—*adv.* **In′sularly.**—*n.* **Insular′ity**, the state of being insular. [Fr.— L. *insularis—insula*, an island. See **Isle.**]

**Insulate**, in′sū-lāt, *v.t.* to place in a detached situation : to prevent connection or communication : (*electricity*) to separate by a non-conductor. —*n.* **Insula′tion.** [Lit. to make an *island* of : from L. *insula.*]

**Insulator**, in′sū-lāt-ur, *n.* one who or that which insulates : a non-conductor of electricity.

**Insult**, in-sult′, *v.t.* to treat with indignity or contempt : to abuse : to affront.—*n.* **In′sult**, *n.* abuse : affront : contumely. [Fr.—L. *insulto—insilio*, to spring at—*in*, upon, and *salio*, to leap.]

**Insultingly,** in-sult'ing-li, *adv.* in an insulting or insolent manner.

**Insuperable,** in-sū'pėr-a-bl, *adj.* that cannot be *passed over :* insurmountable : unconquerable.—*adv.* Insu'perably.—*n.* Insuperabil'ity. [Fr.—L. *insuperabilis—in,* not, *superabilis—supero,* to pass over —*super,* above.]

**Insupportable,** in-sup-pōrt'a-bl, *adj.* not supportable or able to be supported or endured : unbearable : insufferable.—*adv.* Insupport'ably.—*n.* Insupport'ableness. [Fr.—L. *in,* not, and Supportable.]

**Insuppressible,** in-sup-pres'i-bl, *adj.* not to be suppressed or concealed. [L. *in,* not, and Suppressible.]

**Insurable,** in-shōōr'a-bl, *adj.* that may be insured.

**Insurance,** in-shōōr'ans, *n.* the act of insuring, or a contract by which one party undertakes for a payment or premium to guarantee another against risk or loss : the premium so paid.

**Insure,** in-shōōr', *v.t.* to *make sure* or secure : to contract for a premium to make good a loss, as from fire, &c. or to pay a certain sum on a certain event, as death.—*v.i.* to practise making insurance. [Fr.—L. *in,* intensive, and Sure.]

**Insurer,** in-shōōr'ėr, *n.* one who insures.

**Insurgency,** in-sur'jen-si, *n.* a *rising up* or *against :* insurrection : rebellion.

**Insurgent,** in-sur'jent, *adj., rising up* or *against :* rising in opposition to authority : rebellious.—*n.* one who rises in opposition to established authority : a rebel. [L. *insurgens, -entis—insurgo,* to rise upon—*in,* upon, and *surgo,* to rise.]

**Insurmountable,** in-sur-mownt'a-bl, *adj.* not surmountable : that cannot be overcome.—*adv.* Insurmount'ably. [Fr.—L. *in,* not, and Surmountable.]

**Insurrection,** in-sur-rek'shun, *n.* a *rising up* or *against :* open and active opposition to the execution of the law : a rebellion.—*adjs.* Insurrec'tional, Insurrec'tionary. [L. *insurrectio—insurgo.* See Insurgent.]

**Insurrectionist,** in-sur-rek'shun-ist, *n.* one who favours or takes part in an *insurrection.*

**Insusceptible,** in-sus-sep'ti-bl, *adj.* not susceptible : not capable of feeling or of being affected. —*n.* Insusceptibil'ity. [L. *in,* not, and Susceptible.]

**Intact,** in-takt', *adj., untouched :* uninjured. [L. *intactus—in,* not, *tango, tactus,* to touch. See Tangent and Tact.]

**Intactible,** in-takt'i-bl, *adj.* = Intangible.

**Intagliated,** in-tal'yāt-ed, *adj.* formed in *intaglio :* engraved.

**Intaglio,** in-tal'yō, *n.* a figure *cut into* any substance : a stone or gem in which the design is hollowed out, the opposite of a cameo. [It.—*intagliare—in,* into, *tagliare,* to cut—Low L. *taleo,* to cut twigs—L. *talea,* a rod, twig. See Tally and Detail.]

**Intangible,** in-tan'ji-bl, *adj.* not tangible or perceptible to touch.—*ns.* Intan'gibleness, Intangibil'ity.—*adv.* Intan'gibly. [See Intact.]

**Integer,** in'te-jėr, *n.* that which is left *untouched* or undiminished, a whole : (*arith.*) a whole number. [L.—*in,* not, and *tag,* root of *tango,* to touch. Doublet Entire.]

**Integral,** in'te-gral, *adj., entire* or *whole :* not fractional.—*n.* a whole : the whole as made up of its parts.—*adv.* In'tegrally.—*n.* Integral calculus, a branch of the higher mathematics.

**Integrant,** in'te-grant, *adj.* making part of a *whole :* necessary to form an integer or an entire thing. [L. *integrans, -antis,* pr.p. of *integro.*]

**Integrate,** in'te-grāt, *v.t.* to make up as a *whole :* to make entire : to renew.—*n.* Integra'tion. [L. *integro, integratum—integer.* See Integer.]

**Integrity,** in-teg'ri-ti, *n.* (*lit.*) *entireness, wholeness :* the unimpaired state of anything : uprightness : honesty : purity. [See Integer.]

**Integument,** in-teg'ū-ment, *n.* the external protective *covering* of a plant or animal.—*adj.* Integument'ary. [L. *integumentum—intego —in,* upon, *tego,* to cover.]

**Intellect,** in'tel-lekt, *n.* the mind, in reference to its rational powers : the thinking principle. [Fr. —L. *intellectus—intelligo,* to choose between—*inter,* between, *lego,* to choose.]

**Intellection,** in-tel-lek'shun, *n.* the act of *understanding :* (*phil.*) apprehension or perception.

**Intellective,** in-tel-lekt'iv, *adj.* able to *understand :* produced or perceived by the understanding.

**Intellectual,** in-tel-lekt'ū-al, *adj.* of or relating to the intellect or mind : perceived or performed by the intellect : having the power of understanding. —*adv.* Intellect'ually.

**Intellectualism,** in-tel-lekt'ū-al-ism, *n.* system of doctrines concerning the intellect : the culture of the intellect.

**Intellectualist,** in-tel-lekt'ū-al-ist, *n.* one who overrates the human *intellect.*

**Intelligence,** in-tel'i-jens, *n., intellectual* skill or knowledge : information communicated : news : a spiritual being.

**Intelligent,** in-tel'i-jent, *adj.* having *intellect :* endowed with the faculty of reason : well-informed.— *adv.* Intel'ligently. [L. *intelligens, -entis,* pr.p. of *intelligo.*]

**Intelligential,** in-tel-i-jen'shal, *adj.* pertaining to the intelligence : consisting of spiritual being.

**Intelligible,** in-tel'i-ji-bl, *adj.* that may be *understood :* clear.—*adv.* Intell'igibly.—*ns.* Intell'i-gibleness, Intelligibil'ity.

**Intemperance,** in-tem'pėr-ans, *n.* want of due restraint : excess of any kind : habitual indulgence in intoxicating liquor. [Fr.—L. *in,* not, and Temperance.]

**Intemperate,** in-tem'pėr-āt, *adj.* indulging to excess any appetite or passion : given to an immoderate use of intoxicating liquors : passionate : exceeding the usual degree.—*adv.* Intem'perately.—*n.* Intem'perateness.

**Intend,** in-tend', *v.t.* to fix the mind upon : to design : to purpose.—*v.i.* to have a design : to purpose. [Orig. 'to stretch' out or forth, M. E. *entend*—Fr. *entendre*—L. *intendo, intentum* and *intensum—in,* towards, *tendo,* to stretch.]

**Intendant,** in-tend'ant, *n.* an officer who *superintends.*—*n.* Intend'ancy, his office.

**Intended,** in-tend'ed, *adj.* purposed : betrothed. —*n.* an affianced lover.

**Intense,** in-tens', *adj.* closely strained : extreme in degree : very severe.—*adv.* Intense'ly.—*ns.* Intense'ness, Intens'ity. [See Intend.]

**Intensify,** in-tens'i-fī, *v.t.* to make more intense. —*v.i.* to become intense : *pa.p.* intens'ified.

**Intension,** in-ten'shun, *n.* a *straining* or bending : increase of intensity : (*logic*) the sum of the qualities implied by a general name.

**Intensive,** in-tens'iv, *adj., stretched :* admitting of increase of degree : unremitted : serving to intensify : (*gram.*) giving force or emphasis.— *adv.* Intens'ively.—*n.* Intens'iveness.

**Intent,** in-tent', *adj.* having the mind *intense* or bent on : fixed with close attention : diligently applied.—*n.* the thing aimed at or intended : a design : meaning.—*adv.* Intent′ly.—*n.* Intent′-ness. [See Intend.]

Intention, in-ten′shun, *n.* (*lit.*) a *stretching* of the mind towards any object : fixed direction of mind : the object aimed at : design : purpose. Intentional, in-ten′shun-al, Intentioned, in-ten′shund, *adj., with intention :* intended : designed.—Well (or Ill) Intentioned, having good (or ill) designs.—*adv.* Inten′tionally.

Inter, in-tėr′, *v.t.* to bury :—*pr.p.* interr′ing; *pa.p.* interred′. [Fr. *enterrer*—Low L. *interro*—L. *in*, into, *terra*, the earth.]

Interaction, in-tėr-ak′shun, *n.*, *action between* bodies, mutual action. [L. *inter*, between, and Action.]

Intercalary, in-tėr′kal-ar-i, Intercalar, in-tėr′-kal-ar, *adj.* inserted between others.

Intercalate, in-tėr′kal-āt, *v.t.* to insert between, as a day in a calendar.—*n.* Intercala′tion. [L. *intercalo, -atum*—*inter*, between, *calo*, to call. See Calends.]

Intercede, in-tėr-sēd′, *v.t.* to act as peacemaker between two : to plead for one.—*n.* Interced′er. [Fr.—L. *intercedo, -cessum*—*inter*, between, *cedo*, to go. See Cede.]

Intercedent, in-tėr-sēd′ent, *adj.* going between : pleading for.—*adv.* Interced′ently.

Intercellular, in-tėr-sel′ū-lar, *adj.* lying *between* cells. [L. *inter*, between, and Cellular.]

Intercept, in-tėr-sept′, *v.t.* to stop and *seize* on its passage : to obstruct, check : to interrupt communication with : to cut off : (*math.*) to take or comprehend between.—*ns.* Intercept′er, Intercept′or, Intercep′tion.—*adj.* Intercept′ive. [Fr.—L. *intercipio, -ceptum*—*inter*, between, *capio*, to seize.] [or pleading for another.

Intercession, in-tėr-sesh′un, *n.* act of interceding

Intercessional, in-tėr-sesh′un-al, *adj.* containing intercession or pleading for others.

Intercessor, in-tėr-ses′ur, *n.* one who *goes between :* one who reconciles two enemies : one who pleads for another : a bishop who acts during a vacancy in a see.—*adj.* Intercesso′rial.

Intercessory, in-tėr-ses′or-i, *adj.* interceding.

Interchange, in-tėr-chānj′, *v.t.* to give and take mutually : to exchange : to succeed alternately.—*n.* mutual exchange : alternate succession. [Fr.—L. *inter*, between, and Change.]

Interchangeable, in-tėr-chānj′a-bl, *adj.* that may be interchanged : following each other in alternate succession.—*adv.* Interchange′ably.—*ns.* Interchange′ableness, Interchangeabil′ity.

Intercipient, in-tėr-sip′i-ent, *adj., intercepting.*—*n.* the person or thing that intercepts. [L. *intercipiens, -entis, pr.p.* of *intercipio.*]

Interclude, in-tėr-klōōd′, *v.t.* to *shut* out from anything by something *coming between :* to intercept : to cut off.—*n.* Interclu′sion. [L. *intercludo*—*inter*, between, *claudo*, to shut.]

Intercolonial, in-tėr-kol-ō′ni-al, *adj.* pertaining to the relation existing between colonies. [L. *inter*, between, and Colonial.]

Intercolumniation, in-tėr-ko-lum-ni-ā′shun, *n.* (*arch.*) the distance *between* columns, measured from the lower part of their shafts. [L. *inter*, between, and root of Column.]

Intercommune, in-tėr-kom-ūn′, *v.t.* to *commune between* or *together.* [L. *inter*, between, and Commune.]

Intercommunicable, in-tėr-kom-ūn′i-ka-bl, *adj.* that may be *communicated between* or mutually.

Intercommunicate, in-tėr-kom-ūn′i-kāt, *v.t.* to *communicate between* or mutually.—*n.* Intercommunica′tion.

Intercommunion, in-tėr-kom-ūn′yun, *n.*, *communion between* or mutual communion.

Intercommunity, in-tėr-kom-ūn′i-ti, *n.* mutual communication : reciprocal intercourse.

Intercostal, in-tėr-kost′al, *adj.* (*anat.*) lying *between* the ribs. [Fr.—L. *inter*, between, and Costal.]

Intercourse, in′tėr-kōrs, *n.* connection by dealings : communication : commerce : communion. [Fr.—L. *inter*, between, and Course.]

Intercurrent, in-tėr-kur′ent, *adj., running between :* intervening.—*n.* Intercurr′ence. [L. *inter*, between, and Current.]

Interdependence, in-tėr-de-pend′ens, *n.* mutual dependence : dependence of parts one on another. [L. *inter*, between, and Dependence.]

Interdict, in-tėr-dikt′, *v.t.* to prohibit : to forbid : to forbid communion.—*n.* Interdic′tion. [L. *interdico, -dictum*—*inter*, between, and *dico*, to say, pronounce.]

Interdict, in′tėr-dikt, *n.* prohibition : a prohibitory decree : a prohibition of the Pope restraining the clergy from performing divine service.

Interdictive, in-tėr-dikt′iv, Interdictory, in-tėr-dikt′or-i, *adj.* containing interdiction : prohibitory.

Interest, in′tėr-est, *n.* advantage : premium paid for the use of money (in Compound Interest, the interest of each period is added to its principal, and the amount forms a new principal for the next period) : any increase : concern : special attention : influence over others : share : participation. [O. Fr. *interest* (Fr. *intérêt*)—L. *interest*, it is profitable, it *concerns*—*inter*, between, and *esse*, to be. See Essence.]

Interest, in′tėr-est, *v.t.* to engage the attention : to awaken concern in : to excite (in behalf of another). [From obs. *interess*—O. Fr. *interesser*, to concern—L. *interesse.*]

Interested, in′tėr-est-ed, *adj.* having an *interest* or concern : liable to be affected.—*adv.* In′terestedly.

Interesting, in′tėr-est-ing, *adj.* engaging the attention or regard : exciting emotion or passion.—*adv.* In′terestingly.

Interfere, in-tėr-fēr′, *v.i.* to come in collision : to intermeddle : to interpose : to act reciprocally—said of waves, rays of light, &c.—*ns.* Interfer′er, Interfer′ence. [Lit. 'to strike between,' through O. Fr., from L. *inter*, between, and *ferio*, to strike.]

Interfluent, in-tėr′floo-ent, Interfluous, in-tėr′floo-us, *adj., flowing between.* [L. *interfluens*, —*inter*, between, and *fluo*, to flow.]

Interfoliaceous, in-tėr-fō-li-ā′shus, *adj.* placed *between leaves.* [L. *inter*, between, Foliaceous.]

Interfretted, in-tėr-fret′ed, *adj., fretted between* or interlaced. [L. *inter*, between, and Fretted.]

Interfused, in-tėr-fūzd′, *adj., poured* or spread *between.* [L. *interfusus*—*inter*, between, and *fundo*, to pour.] [ing *between.*

Interfusion, in-tėr-fū′zhun, *n.* a *pouring* or spread-

Interim, in′tėr-im, *n.* time *between* or intervening : the mean time. [L.—*inter*, between.]

Interior, in-tē′ri-ur, *adj., inner :* internal : remote from the frontier or coast : inland.—*n.* the inside of anything : the inland part of a country.—*adv.* Inte′riorly. [L.—comp. of *interus*, inward.] [a space or region between others.

Interjacency, in-tėr-jā′sen-si, *n.* a *lying between.*

Interjacent, in-tėr-jā′sent, *adj., lying between :* intervening. [L. *inter*, between, and *jaceo*, to lie.]

Interject, in-tėr-jekt′, *v.t.* to *throw between :* to

insert.—*v.i.* to throw one's self between. [L. *inter*, between, and *jacto*, freq. of *jacio*, to throw.]

**Interjection**, in-tėr-jek′shun, *n.* a *throwing between:* (*gram.*) a word thrown in to express emotion.—*adj.* **Interjec′tional.** [Fr.—L. *interjectio.*]

**Interjunction**, in-tėr-jungk′shun, *n.* a *junction* or joining *between.* [L. *inter*, between, and **Junction.**]

**Interknit**, in-tėr-nit′, *v.t.* to *knit together:* to unite closely. [L. *inter*, between, and **Knit.**]

**Interlace**, in-tėr-lās′, *v.t.* to *lace together:* to unite : to insert one thing within another : to intermix.—*n.* **Interlace′ment.** [L. *inter*, between, and **Lace.**]

**Interlard**, in-tėr-lärd′, *v.t.* to mix in, as fat with lean : to diversify by mixture. [L. *inter*, between, and **Lard.**]

**Interlay**, in-tėr-lā′, *v.t.* to lay among or between. [L. *inter*, between, and **Lay.**]

**Interleave**, in-tėr-lēv′, *v.t.* to put a *leaf between:* to insert blank leaves in a book. [L. *inter*, and **Leaf.**]

**Interline**, in-tėr-līn′, *v.t.* to write in alternate lines : to write between lines. [L. *inter*, between, and **Line.**]

**Interlinear**, in-tėr-lin′e-ar, *adj.* written *between lines.* [L. *inter*, between, and **Linear.**]

**Interlineation**, in-tėr-lin-e-ā′shun, *n.* act of interlining : that which is interlined. [L. *inter*, between, and **Line.**]

**Interlink**, in-tėr-lingk′, *v.t.* to connect by uniting links. [L. *inter*, between, and **Link.**]

**Interlobular**, in-tėr-lob′ū-lar, *adj.* being *between lobes.* [L. *inter*, between, and **Lobular.**]

**Interlocation**, in-tėr-lo-kā′shun, *n.* a *placing between.* [L. *inter*, between, and **Location.**]

**Interlocution**, in-tėr-lo-kū′shun, *n.* conference : an intermediate decree before final decision. [Fr.—L. *interlocutio*, from *interloquor*—*inter*, between, and *loquor, locutus,* to speak.]

**Interlocutor**, in-tėr-lok′ū-tur, *n.* one who *speaks between* or in dialogue : (*Scotch law*) an intermediate decree before final decision.—*adj.* **Interloc′utory.**

**Interlope**, in-tėr-lōp′, *v.t.* to intrude into any matter in which one has no fair concern.—*n.* **Interlop′er.** [L. *inter*, between, and Dut. *loopen*, to run ; Scot. *loup* ; E. *leap.*]

**Interlude**, in′tėr-lōōd, *n.* a short dramatic performance or *play between* the play and afterpiece, or between the acts of a play : a short piece of music played between the parts of a song. [From L. *inter*, between, *ludus*, play.] **Interluded**, in-tėr-lōōd′ed, *adj.* inserted as an interlude : having interludes.

**Interlunar**, in-tėr-lōō′nar, **Interlunary**, in-tėr-lōō′nar-i, *adj.* belonging to the time when the *moon*, about to change, is invisible. [Lit. 'between the moons;' L. *inter*, between, and **Lunar.**]

**Intermarry**, in-tėr-mar′i, *v.i.* to *marry between* or *among:* to marry reciprocally or take one and give another in marriage.—*n.* **Intermarr′iage.**

**Intermaxillary**, in-tėr-maks′il-ar-i, *adj.* situated betw the *jawbones.* [L. *inter*, between, and **Maxillary.**]

**Intermeddle**, in-tėr-med′l, *v.i.* to *meddle* or mix *with:* to interpose or interfere improperly.—*n.* **Intermedd′ler.** [Fr.—L. *inter*, among, **Meddle.**]

**Intermediate**, in-tėr-mē′di-āt, **Intermediary**, in-tėr-mē′di-ar-i, **Intermedial**, in-tėr-mē′di-al, *adjs.* in the *middle between:* intervening.—*adv.* **Interme′diately.** [L. *inter*, between, and **Mediate, Mediary, Medial.**]

**Intermedium**, in-tėr-mē′di-um, *n.* a *medium between:* an intervening agent or instrument.

**Interment**, in-tėr′ment, *n.* burial. [From **Inter.**]

**Intermigration**, in-tėr-mi-grā′shun, *n.* reciprocal migration. [L. *inter*, among, and **Migration.**]

**Interminable**, in-tėr′min-a-bl, **Interminate**, in-tėr′min-āt, *adj., without termination* or limit : boundless : endless.—*adv.* **Inter′minably.**—*n.* **Inter′minableness.** [L. *interminabilis*—*in*, not, and *terminus*, a boundary.]

**Intermingle**, in-tėr-ming′gl, *v.t.* or *v.i.* to *mingle* or mix *together.* [L. *inter*, among, **Mingle.**]

**Intermission**, in-tėr-mish′un, *n.* act of intermitting : interval : pause.—*adj.* **Intermiss′ive**, coming at intervals.

**Intermit**, in-tėr-mit′, *v.t.* to cause to cease for a time : to interrupt. [L. *intermitto, -missum—inter*, between, and *mitto*, to cause to go.]

**Intermittent**, in-tėr-mit′ent, *adj., intermitting* or ceasing at intervals, as a fever.—*adv.* **Intermitt′ingly.**

**Intermix**, in-tėr-miks′, *v.t.* or *v.i.* to *mix among* or together. [L. *inter*, among, and **Mix.**]

**Intermixture**, in-tėr-miks′tūr, *n.* a mass formed by mixture : something intermixed.

**Intermundane**, in-tėr-mun′dān, *adj., between worlds.* [L. *inter*, between, and **Mundane.**]

**Intermural**, in-tėr-mū′ral, *adj.* lying *between walls.* [L. *inter*, between, and **Mural.**]

**Intermuscular**, in-tėr-mus′kū-lar, *adj. between* the *muscles.* [L. *inter*, between, and **Muscular.**]

**Intermutation**, in-tėr-mū-tā′shun, *n., mutual change:* interchange. [L. *inter*, between, and **Mutation.**]

**Intern**, in-tėrn′, *v.t.* (*mil.*) to disarm and quarter in a neutral country such troops as have taken refuge within its frontier. [Fr. *interner.* See **Internal.**]

**Internal**, in-tėr′nal, *adj.* being in the *interior:* domestic, as opposed to foreign : intrinsic : pertaining to the heart :—opposed to **External.**—*adv.* **Inter′nally.** [L. *internus—inter*, within.]

**International**, in-tėr-nash′un-al, *adj.* pertaining to the relations *between nations.*—*adv.* **Interna′tionally.** [L. *inter*, between, and **National.**]

**Internecine**, in-tėr-nē′sīn, *adj., mutually destructive:* deadly. [L. *interneco—inter*, between, and *neco*, to kill, akin to Sans. root *nak.*]

**Internode**, in′tėr-nōd, *n.* (*bot.*) the space *between* two *nodes* or points of the stem from which the leaves arise.—*adj.* **Interno′dial.** [L. *internodium*, from *inter*, between, and *nodus*, a knot.]

**Internuncio**, in-tėr-nun′shi-ō, *n.* a messenger *between* two parties : the Pope's representative at republics and small courts.—*adj.* **Internun′cial.** [Sp.—L. *internuncius—inter*, between, and *nuncius*, a messenger.]

**Interoceanic**, in-tėr-ō-she-an′ik, *adj., between oceans.* [L. *inter*, between, and **Oceanic.**]

**Interocular**, in-tėr-ok′ū-lar, *adj., between* the *eyes.* [L. *inter*, between, and **Ocular.**]

**Interosseal**, in-tėr-os′e-al, **Interosseus**, in-tėr-os′e-us, *adj.* situated *between bones.* [L. *inter*, between, and **Osseal, Osseous.**]

**Interpellation**, in-tėr-pel-ā′shun, *n.* a question raised during the course of a debate : interruption : intercession : a summons : an earnest address.—*v.t.* **Inter′pellate**, to question. [Fr.—L. *interpellatio*, from *interpello, interpellatum*, to disturb by speaking—*inter*, between, and *pello*, to drive.]

**Interpetalary**, in-tėr-pet′al-ar-i, *adj.* (*bot.*) *between* the *petals.* [L. *inter*, between, and **Petal.**]

**Interpetiolar**, in-tèr-pet′i-o-lar, *adj.* (*bot.*) *between* the *petioles*. [L. *inter*, between, and **Petiole**.]

**Interpilaster**, in-tèr-pi-las′tèr, *n.* (*arch.*) space *between* two *pilasters*. [L. *inter*, between, and **Pilaster**.]

**Interplanetary**, in-tèr-plan′et-ar-i, *adj.*, *between* the *planets*. [L. *inter*, between, and **Planet**.]

**Interplead**, in-tèr-plēd′, *v.i.* (*law*) to *plead* or discuss a point, happening *between* or incidentally, before the principal cause can be tried.

**Interpleader**, in-tèr-plēd′ér, *n.* one who interpleads : (*law*) a bill in equity to determine to which of the parties a suit, debt, or rent is due.

**Interpledge**, in-tèr-plej′, *v.t.* to *pledge mutually :* to give and take a pledge. [L. *inter*, between, mutually, and **Pledge**.]

**Interpolate**, in-tèr′po-lāt, *v.t.* to insert unfairly, as a spurious word or passage in a book or manuscript : to corrupt : (*math.*) to fill up the intermediate terms of a series.—*ns.* **Inter′polator**, **Interpola′tion**. [L. *interpolo*, *interpolatum*, from *inter*, between, and *polio*, to polish.]

**Interposal**, in-tèr-pōz′al. Same as **Interposition**.

**Interpose**, in-tèr-pōz′, *v.t.* to *place between :* to thrust in : to offer, as aid or services.—*v.i.* to come between : to mediate : to put in by way of interruption : to interfere.—*n.* **Interpos′er**. [Fr. —L. *inter*, between, and Fr. *poser*, to place. See **Pose**, *n.*]

**Interposition**, in-tèr-pō-zish′un, *n.* act of interposing : intervention : mediation : anything interposed. [Fr.—*inter*, and **Position**.]

**Interpret**, in-tèr′pret, *v.t.* to explain the meaning of : to translate into intelligible or familiar terms. [Fr.—L. *interpretor*, -*pretatus*—*interpres*, from *inter*, between, the last part of the word being of uncertain origin.]                    [terpretation.

**Interpretable**, in-tèr′pret-a-bl, *adj.* capable of in-

**Interpretation**, in-tèr-pre-tā′shun, *n.* act of interpreting : the sense given by an interpreter : the power of explaining.

**Interpretative**, in-tèr′pre-tā-tiv, *adj.* collected by or containing interpretation.—*adv.* **Inter′pretatively**.

**Interpreter**, in-tèr′pret-ér, *n.* one who explains *between* two parties : an expounder : a translator.

**Interregnum**, in-tèr-reg′num, *n.* the time *between* two *reigns :* the time between the cessation of one and the establishment of another government. [L. *inter*, between, *regnum*, rule.]

**Interrex**, in′tèr-reks, *n.* one who rules during an interregnum : a regent. [L. *inter*, between, and *rex*, a king.]

**Interrogate**, in-tèr′o-gāt, *v.t.* to question : to examine by asking questions.—*v.i.* to ask questions : to inquire.—*n.* **Interr′ogator**. [L. *inter-rogo*, *interrogatum*, from *inter*, between, and *rogo*, to ask.]

**Interrogation**, in-tèr-o-gā′shun, *n.* act of interrogating : a question put : the mark of a question (?), orig. the first and last letters of L. *quæstio*, a question.

**Interrogative**, in-tèr-rog′a-tiv, *adj.* denoting a question : expressed as a question.—*n.* a word used in asking a question.—*adv.* **Interrog′atively**.

**Interrogatory**, in-tèr-rog′a-tor-i, *n.* a question or inquiry.—*adj.* expressing a question.

**Interrupt**, in-tèr-rupt′, *v.t.* to *break in between :* to stop or hinder by breaking in upon : to divide : to break continuity. [L. *interrumpo—inter*, between, and *rumpo*, *ruptum*, to break.]

**Interruptedly**, in-tèr-rup′ted-li, *adv.* with interruptions.

**Interruption**, in-tèr-rup′shun, *n.* act of interrupting : hinderance : cessation.

**Interruptive**, in-tèr-rup′tiv, *adj.* tending to interrupt.—*adv.* **Interrup′tively**.

**Interscapular**, in-tèr-ska′pū-lar, *adj.* (*anat.*) between the *shoulder-blades*. [L. *inter*, between, and **Scapular**.]

**Interscribe**, in-tèr-skrīb′, *v.t.* to *write between*. [L. *interscribo—inter*, between, and *scribo*, to write.]                    [parts : crossing.

**Intersecant**, in-tèr-sē′kant, *adj.* dividing into

**Intersect**, in-tèr-sekt′, *v.t.* to *cut between* or asunder : to cut or cross mutually : to divide into parts.—*v.i.* to cross each other. [L. *inter*, between, and *seco*, *sectum*, to cut.]

**Intersection**, in-tèr-sek′shun, *n.*, *intersecting :* (*geom.*) the point or line in which two lines or two planes cut each other.

**Intersperse**, in-tèr-spèrs′, *v.t.* to *scatter* or set *here and there*.—*n.* **Intersper′sion**. [L. *interspergo*, *interspersum—inter*, among, *spargo*, to scatter, akin to Gr. *speirō*, to sow.]

**Interstellar**, in-tèr-stel′ar, **Interstellary**, in-tèr-stel′ar-i, *adj.* situated beyond the solar system or *among* the *stars :* in the intervals *between* the *stars*. [L. *inter*, between, and *stella*, a star.]

**Interstice**, in-tèr-stis or in-tèr′stis, *n.* a small *space between* things closely set, or between the parts which compose a body.—*adj.* **Interstit′ial**. [Fr. —L. *interstitium—inter*, between, and *sisto*, *stitum*, to stand.]

**Interstratified**, in-tèr-strat′i-fīd, *adj.*, *stratified between* other bodies. [L. *inter*, between, and **Stratified**.]

**Intertexture**, in-tèr-teks′tūr, *n.* a being *interwoven*. [L. *inter*, between, and **Texture**.]

**Intertropical**, in-tèr-trop′ik-al, *adj.*, *between* the *tropics*. [L. *inter*, between, and **Tropical**.]

**Intertwine**, in-tèr-twīn′, *v.t.* to *twine* or twist *together*.—*v.i.* to be twisted together : to become mutually involved.—*adv.* **Intertwin′ingly**. [L. *inter*, together, and **Twine**.]

**Intertwist**, in-tèr-twist′, *v.t.* to *twist together*.—*adv.* **Intertwist′ingly**. [L. *inter*, together, and **Twist**.]

**Interval**, in′tèr-val, *n.* time or *space between :* the distance between two given sounds in music. [Lit. the *space between* the *rampart* of a camp and the soldiers' tents, Fr.—L. *intervallum—inter*, between, and *vallum*, a rampart.]

**Intervene**, in-tèr-vēn′, *v.i.* to *come* or be *between :* to occur between points of time : to happen so as to interrupt : to interpose.—*v.t.* to separate. [Fr.—L. *inter*, between, and *venio*, to come.]

**Intervention**, in-tèr-ven′shun, *n.*, *intervening :* interference : mediation : interposition.

**Interview**, in′tèr-vū, *n.* a *mutual view* or sight : a meeting : a conference.—*v.t.* (*in America*) to visit a notable or notorious person with a view to publishing a report of his conversation. [Fr. *entrevue*—L. *inter*, between, and **View**.]

**Intervital**, in-tèr-vī′tal, *adj.*, *between lives*, between death and resurrection. [L. *inter*, between, and *vita*, life.]

**Interweave**, in-tèr-wēv′, *v.t.* to *weave together :* to intermingle. [L. *inter*, together, and **Weave**.]

**Intestacy**, in-tes′ta-sy, *n.* the state of one dying without having made a valid will.

**Intestate**, in-tes′tāt, *adj.* dying *without* having made a valid *will :* not disposed of by will.—*n.* a person who dies without making a valid will. [L. *intestatus—in*, not, and *testatus—testor*, to make a will.]

**Intestinal,** in-tes'tin-al, *adj.* pertaining to the intestines of an animal body.

**Intestine,** in-tes'tin, *adj., internal:* contained in the animal body : domestic : not foreign.—*n.* (usually in *pl.*) the part of the alimentary canal that lies between the stomach and the anus. [Fr. —L. *intestinus—intus,* within, on the inside.]

**Inthral,** in-thrawl', *v.t.* to bring *into thraldom* or bondage : to enslave : to shackle :—*pr.p.* inthrall'ing ; *pa.p.* inthralled'. [E. In, into, and Thrall.]       [or enslaving : slavery.

**Inthralment,** in-thrawl'ment, *n.* act of inthralling

**Intimacy,** in'ti-ma-si, *n.* state of being intimate : close familiarity.

**Intimate,** in'ti-māt, *adj., innermost:* internal : close : closely acquainted : familiar.—*n.* a familiar friend : an associate.—*adv.* In'timately. [L. *intimus,* innermost—*intus,* within.]

**Intimate,** in'ti-māt, *v.t.* to hint : to announce. [Lit. to make one *intimate with,* L. *intimo, -atum—intus.*]       [announcement.

**Intimation,** in-ti-mā'shun, *n.* obscure notice : hint :

**Intimidate,** in-tim'i-dāt, *v.t.* to make timid or fearful : to dispirit. [L. *in,* and *timidus,* fearful —*timeo,* to fear.]

**Intimidation,** in-tim-i-dā'shun, *n.* act of intimidating : state of being intimidated.

**Intituled,** in-tit'ūld.   Same as **Entitled.**

**Into,** in'too, *prep.* noting passage inwards : noting the passage of a thing from one state to another : (*B.*) often used for **Unto.** [Lit. coming *to* and going *in,* In and To.]

**Intolerable,** in-tol'er-a-bl, *adj.* that cannot be endured.—*n.* Intol'erableness.—*adv.* Intol'erably. [Fr.—L. *in,* not, and Tolerable.]

**Intolerant,** in-tol'er-ant, *adj.* not able or willing to endure : not enduring difference of opinion : persecuting.—*n.* one opposed to toleration.—*adv.* Intol'erantly.—*ns.* Intol'erance, Intolera'tion. [L. *in,* not, and Tolerant.]

**Intomb,** in-tōōm'.   Same as **Entomb.**

**Intonate,** in'ton-āt, *v.i.* to sound forth : to sound the notes of a musical scale : to modulate the voice. [Low L. *intono, -atum—*L. *in tonum,* according to tone.   See Tone.]

**Intonation,** in-to-nā'shun, *n.* act or manner of sounding musical notes : modulation of the voice.

**Intone,** in-tōn', *v.i.* to utter *in tones* : to give forth a low protracted sound.—*v.t.* to chant : to read (the church service) in a singing, recitative manner. [See Intonate.]

**Intorsion,** in-tor'shun, *n.* a *twisting,* winding, or bending. [L. *in,* and Torsion.]

**Intoxicate,** in-toks'i-kāt, *v t* to make drunk : to excite to enthusiasm or madness. [Lit. to *drug* or poison, from Low L. *intoxico, -atum—toxicum—*Gr. *toxikon,* a poison in which arrows were dipped—*toxon,* an arrow.]

**Intoxication,** in-toks-i-kā'shun, *n.* state of being drunk : high excitement or elation.

**Intractable,** in-trakt'a-bl, *adj.* unmanageable : obstinate.—*ns.* Intractabil'ity, Intract'ableness.—*adv.* Intract'ably. [Fr.—L. *in,* not, Tractable.]

**Intramural,** in-tra-mū'ral, *adj., within the walls,* as of a city. [L. *intra,* within, and Mural.]

**Intransitive,** in-tran'si-tiv, *adj.* not passing over or indicating passing over : (*gram.*) representing action confined to the agent.—*adv.* Intran'sitively. [L. *in,* not, and Transitive.]

**Intransmissible,** in-trans-mis'i-bl, *adj.* that cannot be transmitted. [L. *in,* not, and Transmissible.]

**Intransmutable,** in-trans-mūt'a-bl, *adj.* that cannot be changed into another substance.—*n.* Intransmutabil'ity. [L. *in,* not, Transmutable.]

**Intrant,** in'trant, *adj., entering:* penetrating.—*n.* one who enters, esp. on some public duty. [L. *intrans, -antis—intro,* to enter.   See Enter.]

**Intrench,** in-trensh', *v.t.* to dig a *trench around :* to fortify with a ditch and parapet : to furrow.— *v.i.* to encroach. [E. In and Trench.]

**Intrenchment,** in-trensh'ment, *n.* act of intrenching : a trench : a ditch and parapet for defence : any protection or defence : an encroachment.

**Intrepid,** in-trep'id, *adj.* without trepidation or fear : undaunted : brave.—*n.* Intrepid'ity, firm, unshaken courage.—*adv.* Intrep'idly. [L. *in-trepidus—in,* not, and root of Trepidation.]

**Intricate,** in'tri-kāt, *adj.* involved : entangled : perplexed.—*ns.* In'tricacy, In'tricateness.—*adv.* In'tricately. [L. *intricatus—in,* and *tricor,* to make difficulties—*tricæ,* hinderances.]

**Intrigue,** in-trēg', *n.* a complex plot : a private or party scheme : the plot of a play or romance : secret illicit love.—*v.i.* to form a plot or scheme : to carry on illicit love :—*pr.p.* intrigu'ing ; *pa.p.* intrigued'. [Fr. *intriguer—*root of Intricate.]

**Intriguer,** in-trēg'er, *n.* one who intrigues, or pursues an object by secret artifices.

**Intrinsic,** in-trin'sik, **Intrinsical,** in-trin'sik-al, *adj.* inward : essential : genuine : inherent.—*n.* Intrinsical'ity.—*adv.* Intrin'sically. [Fr.— L. *intrinsecus—intra,* within, and *secus,* following.]

**Introduce,** in-tro-dūs', *v.t.* to *lead* or *bring in :* to conduct into a place : formally to make known or acquainted : to bring into notice or practice : to commence : to preface. [L. *introduco, ductum—intro,* within, *duco,* to lead.   See Duke.]

**Introduction,** in-tro-duk'shun, *n.* act of conducting into : act of making persons known to each other : act of bringing into notice or practice : preliminary matter to the main thoughts of a book : a treatise introductory to a science or course of study. [See Introduce.]

**Introductory,** in-tro-duk'tor-i, **Introductive,** in-tro-duk'tiv, *adj.* serving to *introduce :* preliminary : prefatory.—*adv.* Introduc'torily.

**Intromission,** in-tro-mish'un, *n. sending within* or *into :* (*Scot. law*) intermeddling with another's goods. [See Intromit.]

**Intromit,** in-tro-mit', *v.t.* to *send within :* to admit : to permit to enter :—*pr.p.* intromitt'ing ; *pa.p.* intromitt'ed. [L. *intro,* within, *mitto, missum,* to send.]

**Introspection,** in-tro-spek'shun, *n. a sight of the inside* or *interior :* self-examination.—*adj.* Introspec'tive. [L. *intro,* within, *specio,* to see.]

**Introvert,** in-tro-vèrt', *v.t.* to *turn inward.* [L. *intro,* within, and *verto,* to turn.]

**Intrude,** in-trōōd', *v.i.* to *thrust* one's self *in :* to enter uninvited or unwelcome.—*v.t.* to force in.—*n.* Intrud'er. [L. *in,* in, *trudo,* to thrust.]

**Intrusion,** in-trōō'zhun, *n.* act of *intruding* or of entering into a place without welcome or invitation : encroachment.

**Intrusive,** in-trōō'siv, *adj.* tending or apt to *intrude :* entering without welcome or right.— *adv.* Intru'sively.—*n.* Intru'siveness.

**Intrust,** in-trust', *v.t.* to give *in trust :* to commit to another, trusting his fidelity. [E. In, in, and Trust.]

**Intuition,** in-tū-ish'un, *n.* the power of the mind by which it immediately perceives the truth of things without reasoning or analysis : a truth so perceived.—*adj.* Intui'tional. [Lit. a *looking* *upon* or *into*, L. *in*, into or upon, and *tuitio—tueor, tuitus*, to look. See **Tuition** and **Tutor**.]

**Intuitive**, in-tū'i-tiv, *adj.*, *perceived* or perceiving *by intuition*: received or known by simple inspection.—*adv.* **Intu'itively**.

**Intumescence**, in-tū-mes'ens, *n.* the action of *swelling*: a swelling: a tumid state. [Fr.—L. *in*, and *tumesco, -cens—tumeo*, to swell.]

**Intwine**, in-twīn'. Same as **Entwine**. [In and **Twine**.]          [**Twist**.]

**Intwist**, in-twist'. Same as **Entwist**. [In and

**Inumbrate**, in-um'brāt, *v.t.* to cast a *shadow upon*: to shade. [L. *inumbro, inumbratum—in*, and *umbro*, to shade—*umbra*, a shadow.]

**Inundate**, in-un'dāt or in'-, *v.t.* to *flow upon* or over *in waves* (said of water): to flood: to fill with an overflowing abundance.—*n.* **Inunda'tion**, act of inundating: a flood: an overflowing. [L., from *inundo, -atum—in*, and *undo*, to rise in waves—*unda*, a wave.]

**Inure**, in-ūr', *v.t.* to *use* or practise *habitually*: to accustom: to harden.—*v.i.* (*law*) to come into use or effect: to serve to the use or benefit of. [From *in*, and an old word *ure* (used in the phrase 'to put in ure'—*i.e.* in operation), which is from O. Fr. *ovre, eure* (Fr. *œuvre*, work)—L. *opera*, work; the same word *ure* is found in *manure*, which see.]

**Inurement**, in-ūr'ment, *n.* act of inuring: practice.

**Inurn**, in-urn', *v.t.* to place in an *urn*: to entomb, to bury. [L. *in*, in, and **Urn**.]

**Inutility**, in-ū-til'i-ti, *n.* want of utility: uselessness: unprofitableness. [Fr.—L. *in*, not, and **Utility**.]

**Invade**, in-vād', *v.t.* to enter a country as an enemy: to attack: to encroach upon: to violate: to seize or fall upon.—*n.* **Invad'er**. [Fr.—L. *invado, invasum—in*, and *vado*, to go. See **Wade**.]

**Invalid**, in'va-lid, *adj.* not valid or strong: infirm: sick.—*n.* one who is weak: a sickly person: one disabled for active service, esp. a soldier or sailor.—*v.t.* to make invalid or affect with disease: to enrol on the list of invalids. [Fr. *invalide*—L. *invalidus—in*, not, and *validus*, strong. See **Valid**.]

**Invalid**, in-val'id, *adj.* not sound: weak: without value, weight. or cogency: having no effect: void: null. [Fr.—L. *in*, not, and **Valid**.]

**Invalidate**, in-val'id-āt, *v.t.* to render invalid: to weaken or destroy the force of.—*n.* **Invalida'tion**.         [want of force.

**Invalidity**, in-val-id'i-ti, *n.* want of cogency:

**Invaluable**, in-val'ū-a-bl, *adj.* that cannot be valued: priceless.—*adv.* **Inval'uably**. [Fr.—L. *in*, not, and **Valuable**.]

**Invariable**, in-vā'ri-a-bl, *adj.* not variable: without variation or change: unalterable: constantly in the same state.—*adv.* **Inva'riably**.—*n.* **Inva'riableness**. [Fr.—L. *in*, not, and **Variable**.]

**Invasion**, in-vā'zhun, *n.* the act of *invading*: an attack: an incursion: an attack on the rights of another: an encroachment: a violation. [See **Invade**.]    [*sive*: infringing another's rights.

**Invasive**, in-vā'siv, *adj.* making invasion: aggres-

**Invective**, in-vek'tiv, *n.* a severe or reproachful accusation *brought against* any one: an attack with words: a violent utterance of censure: sarcasm or satire.—*adj.* railing: abusive: satirical. [See **Inveigh**.]

**Inveigh**, in-vā', *v.i.* to attack with words: to rail against: to revile. [Lit. to *carry* or bring *against*, L. *inveho, invectum—in*, and *veho*, to carry. See **Vehicle**.]

**Inveigle**, in-vē'gl, *v.t.* to entice: to seduce: to wheedle. [Ety. dub.; prob. a corr. of Fr. *aveugle*, blind—L. *ab*, without, *oculus*, the eye; therefore perh. (*lit.*) 'to hoodwink.']

**Inveiglement**, in-vē'gl-ment, *n.* an enticing: an enticement.

**Invent**, in-vent', *v.t.* to devise or contrive: to make: to frame: to fabricate: to forge. [Lit. *to come upon*: Fr.—L. *invenio, inventum—in*, upon, and *venio*, to come.]

**Invention**, in-ven'shun, *n.* that which is *invented*: contrivance: a deceit: power or faculty of inventing: ability displayed by any invention or effort of the imagination.

**Inventive**, in-vent'iv, *adj.* able to *invent*: ready in contrivance.—*adv.* **Invent'ively**.—*n.* **Invent'iveness**.

**Inventor, Inventer**, in-vent'ur, *n.* one who *invents* or finds out something new:—*fem.* **Invent'ress**.

**Inventory**, in'ven-tor-i, *n.* a catalogue of furniture, goods, &c.—*v.t.* to make an inventory or catalogue of. [Fr. *inventaire*—L. *inventarium*, a list of the *things found*. See **Invent**.]

**Inverse**, in-vèrs', *adj.*, *inverted*: in the reverse or contrary order: opposite.—*adv.* **Inverse'ly**.

**Inversion**, in-vèr'shun, *n.* the act of *inverting*: the state of being inverted: a change of order or position.

**Invert**, in-vèrt', *v.t.* to *turn in* or *about*: to turn upside down: to reverse: to change the customary order or position. [L. *inverto, inversum—in*, and *verto*, to turn. See **Verse**.]

**Invertebral**, in-vèr'te-bral, **Invertebrate**, in-vèr'te-brāt, *adj.* without a vertebral column or backbone.—*n.* **Invert'ebrate**, an animal destitute of a skull and vertebral column. [L. *in*, not, and **Vertebrate**.]      [contrary manner.

**Invertedly**, in-vèrt'ed-li, *adv.* in an inverted or

**Invest**, in-vest', *v.t.* to put *vesture on*: to dress: to confer or give: to place in office or authority: to adorn: to surround: to block up: to lay siege to: to place, as property in business: to lay out money on. [L. *investio, -itum—in*, on, and *vestio*, to clothe. See **Vest**.]

**Investigable**, in-vest'i-ga-bl, *adj.* able to be investigated or searched out.

**Investigate**, in-vest'i-gāt, *v.t.* (*lit.*) to trace the *vestiges* or tracks of: to search into: to inquire into with care and accuracy. [L. *investigo, -atum—in*. and *vestigo*, to track. See **Vestige**.]

**Investigation**, in-vest-i-gā'shun, *n.* act of investigating or examining into: research: study.

**Investigative**, in-vest'i-gā-tiv, **Investigatory**, in-vest'i-gā-tor-i, *adj.* promoting or given to investigation.      [gates or examines into.

**Investigator**, in-vest'i-gā-tur, *n.* one who investi-

**Investiture**, in-vest'i-tūr, *n.* the act or the right of *investing* or putting in possession.

**Investment**, in-vest'ment, *n.* the act of investing: a blockade: the act of surrounding or besieging: laying out money on: that in which anything is invested.

**Inveterate**, in-vet'èr-āt, *adj.* firmly established by long continuance: deep-rooted: violent.—*adv.* **Invet'erately**.—*ns.* **Invet'erateness, Invet'eracy**, firmness produced by long use or continuance. [L. *grown old*, L. *invetero, -atum*, to grow old—*in*, and *vetus, veteris*, old. See **Veteran**.]

**Invidious**, in-vid'i-us, *adj.* likely to incur or provoke ill-will: likely to excite envy, enviable.—*adv.* **Invid'iously**.—*n.* **Invid'iousness**. [L. *invidiosus—invidia*. See **Envy**.]

**Invigorate**, in-vig'or-āt, *v.t.* to give *vigour* to: to strengthen : to animate.—*n*. **Invigora′tion**, the act or state of being invigorated. [L. *in*, in, and **Vigour**.]

**Invincible**, in-vin′si-bl, *adj*. that cannot be overcome : insuperable.—*adv*. **Invin′cibly**.—*ns*. **Invin′cibleness, Invincibil′ity**. [Fr.—L. *in*, not, and **Vincible**.]

**Inviolable**, in-vī′ol-a-bl, *adj*. that cannot be profaned : that cannot be injured.—*adv*. **Invī′olably**.—*n*. **Inviolabil′ity**. [Fr.—L. *in*, not, and **Violable**.]

**Inviolate**, in-vī′ō-lāt, **Inviolated**, in-vī′ō-lāt-ed, *adj*. not violated : unprofaned : uninjured. [L.]

**Invisible**, in-viz′i-bl, *adj*. not visible or capable of being seen.—*adv*. **Invis′ibly**.—*ns*. **Invisibil′ity, Invis′ibleness**. [Fr.—L. *in*, not, and **Visible**.]

**Invitation**, in-vit-ā′shun, *n*. the act of inviting : an asking or solicitation.

**Invite**, in-vīt′, *v.t*. to ask : to summon : to allure : to attract.—*v.i*. to ask in invitation.—*n*. **Invit′er**. [Fr.—L. *invito, -atum*.] [tempting manner.

**Invitingly**, in-vīt′ing-li, *adv*. in an inviting or **Invocate**, in′vo-kāt, *v.t*. to invoke or *call on* solemnly or with prayer : to implore. [See **Invoke**.]

**Invocation**, in-vo-kā′shun, *n*. the act or the form of invocating or addressing in prayer : a call or summons, especially a judicial order.

**Invoice**, in′vois *n*. a letter of advice of the *despatch* of goods, with particulars of their price and quantity.—*v.t*. to make an invoice of. [Prob. a corr. of *envois*, English plur. of Fr. *envoi*. See **Envoy**.]

**Invoke**, in-vōk′, *v.t*. to *call upon* earnestly or solemnly : to implore assistance : to address in prayer. [Fr.—L. *invoco, -atum—in*, on, *voco*, to call, conn. with *vox, vocis*, the voice.]

**Involucre**, in-vo-lū′kėr, *n*. (*bot*.) a group of bracts in the form of a whorl around an expanded flower or umbel. [Lit. an *envelope* or *wrapper*, L. *involucrum—involvo*. See **Involve**.]

**Involuntary**, in-vol′un-tar-i, *adj*. not voluntary : not having the power of will or choice : not done willingly : not chosen.—*n*. **Invol′untariness**.—*adv*. **Invol′untarily**. [L. *in*, not, **Voluntary**.]

**Involute**, in′vo-lūt, *n*. that which is *involved* or rolled inward : a curve traced by the end of a string unwinding itself from another curve.

**Involute**, in′vo-lūt, **Involuted**, in′vo-lūt-ed, *adj*. (*bot*.) *rolled* spirally inward : (*conchology*) turned inward. [See **Involve**.]

**Involution**, in-vo-lū′shun, *n*. the action of *involving* : state of being involved or entangled : (*arith*.) act or process of raising a quantity to any given power.

**Involve**, in-volv′, *v.t*. to wrap up : to envelop : to implicate : to include : to complicate : to overwhelm : to catch : (*arith*.) to multiply a quantity into itself any given number of times. [Fr.—L. *involvo—in*, upon, *volvo, volutum*, to roll.]

**Involvement**, in-volv′ment, *n*. act of involving : state of being involved or entangled.

**Invulnerable**, in-vul′nėr-a-bl, *adj*. that cannot be wounded.—*ns*. **Invulnerabil′ity, Invul′nerableness**.—*adv*. **Invul′nerably**. [Fr.—L. *in*, not, and **Vulnerable**.]

**Inward**, in′ward, *adj*. placed or being *within* : internal : seated in the mind or soul : (*B*.) intimate.—*n.pl*. (*B*.) the intestines.—*adv*. toward the inside : toward the interior : into the mind or thoughts. [A.S. *inneweard—in*, and *ward*, direction.]

**Inwardly**, in′ward-li, *adv*. in the parts *within* : in the heart : privately : toward the centre.

**Inwards**, in′wardz, *adv*. Same as **Inward**.

**Inweave**, in-wēv′, *v.t*. to *weave into* : to entwine : to complicate. [E. **In** and **Weave**.]

**Inwrap**, in-rap′, *v.t*. to *cover* by *wrapping* : to perplex : to transport. [E. **In** and **Wrap**.]

**Inwreathe**, in-rēth′, *v.t*. to encircle as with a *wreath*, or the form of a wreath. [E. **In** and **Wreathe**.]

**Inwrought**, in-rawt′, *adj*., *wrought in* or among other things : adorned with figures. [E. **In** and **Wrought**. See **Work**.]

**Iodate**, ī′o-dāt, *n*. a combination of iodic acid with a salifiable base. [simple body.

**Iodide**, ī′o-did, *n*. a combination of iodine with a **Iodine**, ī′o-din, *n*. one of the elementary bodies, so named from the *violet colour* of its vapour. —*adj*. **Iod′ic**. [Gr. *ioeidēs*, violet-coloured—*ion*, a violet, and *eidos*, form, appearance.]

**Iolite**, ī′o-līt, *n*. a transparent gem which presents a *violet-blue* colour when looked at in a certain direction. [Gr. *ion*, a violet, and *lithos*, a stone.]

**Ionic**, ī-on′ik, *adj*. relating to *Ionia* in Greece : denoting an order in architecture distinguished by the ram's horn volute of its capital.

**Iota**, ī-ō′ta, *n*. a jot : a very small quantity or degree. [Gr., the smallest letter in the alphabet, corresponding to the English *i*. See **Jot**.]

**Ipecacuanha**, ip-e-kak-ū-an′a, *n*. a West Indian plant, whose root affords a useful emetic. [Brazilian, *roadside-sick-making* (plant).]

**Irascible**, ī-ras′i-bl, *adj*. susceptible of *ire* or anger : easily provoked : irritable.—*n*. **Irascibil′ity**.—*adv*. **Iras′cibly**. [Fr.—L. *irascibilis—irascor*, to be angry—*ira*.]

**Irate**, ī-rāt′, *adj*. enraged : angry. [L. *iratus*, pa.p. of *irascor*, to be angry.] [L. *ira*.]

**Ire**, īr, *n*., *anger* : rage : keen resentment. [Fr.—

**Ireful**, īr′fool, *adj*., *full of ire* or wrath : resentful.—*adv*. **Ire′fully**.

**Iridescent**, ir-i-des′ent, **Irisated**, ī′ris-āt-ed, *adj*. coloured like the *iris* or rainbow.—*n*. **Irides′cence**. [See **Iris**.]

**Iris**, ī′ris, *n*. the rainbow : an appearance resembling the rainbow : the contractile curtain perforated by the pupil, and forming the coloured part of the eye : the fleur-de-lis or flagflower :—*pl*. **I′rises**. [L. *iris, iridis*—Gr. *iris, iridos*, the messenger of the gods, the rainbow.]

**Irish**, ī′rish, *adj*. relating to or produced in *Ireland*.—*n*. language of the Irish, a form of Celtic : —*pl*. the natives or inhabitants of Ireland.

**Iritis**, ī-rī′tis, *n*. inflammation of the *iris* of the eye.

**Irk**, ėrk, *v.t*. to weary : to trouble : to distress (now used only impersonally). [From a Teut. root found in A.S. *weorcsum*, painful, Sw. *yrka*, to urge, press ; L. *urgere*. See **Urge**.]

**Irksome**, ėrk′sum, *adj*. causing uneasiness : tedious : unpleasant.—*adv*. **Irk′somely**.—*n*. **Irk′someness**.

**Iron**, ī′urn, *n*. the most common and useful of the metals : an instrument or utensil made of iron : strength :—*pl*. fetters : chains.—*adj*. formed of iron : resembling iron : rude : stern : fast-binding : not to be broken : robust : dull of understanding.—*v.t*. to smooth with an iron instrument : to arm with iron : to fetter.—**Cast-iron**, a compound of iron and carbon, obtained directly from iron ore by smelting. [A.S. *iren* ; Ger. *eisen*, Ice. *jarn*, W. *haiarn*.]

**Ironbound**, ī′urn-bownd, *adj*., *bound* with *iron* : rugged, as a coast.

**Ironclad**, ī′urn-klad, *adj*., *clad* in *iron* : covered or protected with iron.—*n*. a vessel defended by iron plates.

**Iron**-founder, ī′urn-fownd′ẻr, *n.* one who *founds* or makes castings in *iron*.

**Iron-foundry**, ī′urn-fownd′ri, *n.* a place where *iron* is *founded* or cast.

**Irongray**, ī′urn-grā, *adj.* of a *gray* colour, like that of *iron* freshly cut or broken.—*n.* this colour. [hard as *iron.*

**Iron-handed**, ī′urn-hand′ed, *adj.* having *hands* hard as *iron* : cruel.

**Iron-hearted**, ī′urn-härt′ed, *adj.* having a *heart* hard as *iron* : cruel.

**Ironical**, ī-ron′ik-al, *adj.* meaning the opposite of what is expressed : satirical.—*adv.* **Iron′ically.** [See **Irony**.] [prietor of *iron*works.

**Iron-master**, ī′urn-mäs′tẻr, *n.* a *master* or pro-

**Ironmonger**, ī′urn-mung-gẻr, *n.* a *monger* or dealer in articles made of *iron.*

**Ironmongery**, ī′urn-mung-gẻr-i, *n.* a general name for articles made of *iron :* hardware.

**Ironmould**, ī′urn-mōld, *n.* the spot left on wet cloth after touching rusty *iron.* [See **Mould**, dust or earth.]

**Ironware**, ī′urn-wār, *n.*, *wares* or goods of *iron.*

**Ironwood**, ī′urn-wood, *n.* applied to the timber of various trees on account of their hardness.

**Ironwork**, ī′urn-wurk, *n.* the parts of a building, &c. made of *iron :* anything of iron : a furnace where iron is smelted, or a foundry, &c. where it is made into heavy work.

**Irony**, ī′urn-i, *adj.*, *made*, consisting, or partaking of *iron :* like iron : hard.

**Irony**, ī′urn-i, *n.* a mode of speech conveying the opposite of what is meant : satire. [Fr.—L. *ironia*, Gr. *eirōneia*, dissimulation—*eirōn*, a dissembler—*eirō*, to talk.]

**Irradiance**, ir-rā′di-ans, **Irradiancy**, ir-rā′di-an-si, *n.* the throwing of rays of light on (any object) : that which irradiates or is irradiated : beams of light emitted : splendour.

**Irradiant**, ir-rā′di-ant, *adj.*, *irradiating* or shedding beams of light.

**Irradiate**, ir-rā′di-āt, *v.t.* to *dart rays* of light *upon* or *into :* to adorn with lustre : to decorate with shining ornaments : to animate with light or heat : to illuminate the understanding.—*v.i.* to emit rays : to shine.—*adj.* adorned with rays of light or with lustre. [L. *irradio, irradiatum—in*, on, and **Radiate**.]

**Irradiation**, ir-rā-di-ā′shun, *n.* act of *irradiating* or emitting beams of light : that which is irradiated : brightness : intellectual light.

**Irrational**, ir-rash′un-al, *adj.* void of reason or understanding : absurd.—*n.* **Irrational′ity.**—*adv.* **Irra′tionally.** [L. *in*, not, and **Rational**.]

**Irreclaimable**, ir-re-klām′a-bl, *adj.* that cannot be reclaimed or reformed : incorrigible.—*adv.* **Irreclaim′ably.** [Fr.—L. *in*, not, and **Reclaimable**.]

**Irreconcilable**, ir-rek-on-sīl′a-bl, *adj.* incapable of being brought back to a state of friendship : inconsistent.—*n.* **Irreconcil′ableness.**—*adv.* **Irreconcil′ably.** [Fr.—L. *in*, not, and **Reconcilable**.]

**Irrecoverable**, ir-re-kuv′ẻr-a-bl, *adj.* irretrievable. —*n.* **Irrecov′erableness.**—*adv.* **Irrecov′erably.** [Fr.—L. *in*, not, and **Recoverable**.]

**Irredeemable**, ir-re-dēm′a-bl, *adj.* not redeemable : not subject to be paid at the nominal value.—*ns.* **Irredeem′ableness**, **Irredeemabil′ity.**—*adv.* **Irredeem′ably.** [Prefix *in-*, not, and **Redeemable**.]

**Irreducible**, ir-re-dūs′i-bl, *adj.* that cannot be reduced or brought from one form or state to another.—*n.* **Irreduc′ibleness.**—*adv.* **Irreduc′ibly.** [L. *in*, not, and **Reducible**.]

**Irreflective**, ir-re-flekt′iv, *adj.* not reflective. [L. *in*, not, and **Reflective**.]

**Irrefragable**, ir-ref′ra-ga-bl, *adj.* that cannot be refuted or overthrown : unanswerable.—*ns.* **Irrefragabil′ity**, **Irref′ragableness.**—*adv.* **Irref′ragably.** [Lit. *that cannot be broken or bent*, from Fr.—L. *in*, not, *re*, backwards, and *frag*, root of *frango*, to break.]

**Irrefutable**, ir-re-fūt′a-bl or ir-ref′ū-ta-bl, *adj.* that cannot be refuted or proved false.—*adv.* **Irrefut′ably** or **Irref′utably.** [Fr.—L. *in*, not, and **Refutable**.]

**Irregular**, ir-reg′ū-lar, *adj.* not according to rule : unnatural : unsystematic : vicious : (*gram.*) departing from the ordinary rules in its inflection : variable : not symmetrical.—*n.* a soldier not in regular service.—*adv.* **Irreg′ularly.** [L. *in*, not, and **Regular**.]

**Irregularity**, ir-reg-ū-lar′i-ti, *n.* state of being irregular : deviation from a straight line, or from rule : departure from method or order : vice.

**Irrelative**, ir-rel′a-tiv, *adj.* not relative : unconnected.—*adv.* **Irrel′atively.** [L. *in*, not, and **Relative**.]

**Irrelevant**, ir-rel′e-vant, *adj.* not bearing directly on the matter in hand.—*n.* **Irrel′evancy.**—*adv.* **Irrel′evantly.** [Prefix *in-*, not, and **Relevant**.]

**Irreligion**, ir-re-lij′un, *n.* want of religion.

**Irreligious**, ir-re-lij′us, *adj.* destitute of religion : ungodly.—*adv.* **Irrelig′iously.**—*n.* **Irrelig′iousness.** [Fr.—L. *in*, not, and **Religious**.]

**Irremediable**, ir-re-mē′di-a-bl, *adj.* that cannot be remedied or redressed.—*n.* **Irreme′diableness.** —*adv.* **Irreme′diably.** [Fr.—L. *in*, not, and **Remediable**.]

**Irremissible**, ir-re-mis′i-bl, *adj.* not to be remitted or forgiven.—*n.* **Irremiss′ibleness.** [Fr.—L. *in*, not, and **Remissible**.]

**Irremovable**, ir-re-mōōv′a-bl, *adj.* not removable : steadfast.—*ns.* **Irremovabil′ity**, **Irremov′ableness.**—*adv.* **Irremov′ably.** [Prefix *in-*, not, and **Removable**.]

**Irreparable**, ir-rep′ar-a-bl, *adj.* that cannot be recovered.—*n.* **Irrep′arableness.**—*adv.* **Irrep′arably.** [Fr.—L. *in*, not, and **Reparable**.]

**Irrepealable**, ir-re-pēl′a-bl, *adj.* that cannot be repealed or annulled.—*adv.* **Irrepeal′ably.** [L. *in*, not, and **Repealable**.]

**Irreprehensible**, ir-rep-re-hens′i-bl, *adj.* that cannot be blamed.—*adv.* **Irreprehens′ibly.**—*n.* **Irreprehens′ibleness.** [Fr.—L. *in*, not, and **Reprehensible**.]

**Irrepressible**, ir-re-pres′i-bl, *adj.* not to be restrained.—*adv.* **Irrepress′ibly.** [Fr.—L. *in*, not, and **Repressible**.]

**Irreproachable**, ir-re-prōch′a-bl, *adj.* free from blame : upright : innocent.—*adv.* **Irreproach′ably.** [Fr.—L. *in*, not, and **Reproachable**.]

**Irreprovable**, ir-re-prōōv′a-bl, *adj.* blameless.— *adv.* **Irreprov′ably.**—*n.* **Irreprov′ableness.** [Fr.—L. *in*, not, and **Reprovable**.]

**Irresistance**, ir-re-zist′ans, *n.* want of resistance : passive submission. [L. *in*, not, **Resistance**.]

**Irresistible**, ir-re-zist′i-bl, *adj.* not to be opposed with success.—*adv.* **Irresist′ibly.**—*ns.* **Irresist′ibleness**, **Irresistibil′ity.**

**Irresolute**, ir-rez′o-lūt, *adj.* not firm in purpose. —*adv.* **Irres′olutely.** [L. *in*, not, and **Resolute**.]

**Irresoluteness**, ir-rez′o-lūt-nes, **Irresolution**, ir-rez-o-lū′shun, *n.* want of resolution, or of firm determination of purpose.

**Irresolvable**, ir-re-zolv′a-bl, *adj.* that cannot be resolved. [L. *in*, not, and **Resolvable**.]

**Irrespective**, ir-re-spekt′iv, *adj.* not having regard

to.—*adv.* Irrespect'ively. [Fr.—L. *in*, not, and Respective.]

Irresponsible, ir-re-spons'i-bl, *adj.* not responsible or liable to answer (for).—*adv.* Irrespons'ibly.—*n.* Irresponsibil'ity. [L. *in*, not, Responsible.]

Irretrievable, ir-re-trēv'a-bl, *adj.* not to be recovered or repaired.—*adv.* Irretriev'ably.—*n.* Irretriev'ableness. [Fr.—L. *in*, not, and Retrievable.]

Irreverence, ir-rev'ėr-ens, *n.* want of reverence or veneration : want of due regard for the character and authority of the Supreme Being.

Irreverent, ir-rev'ėr-ent, *adj.* not reverent : proceeding from irreverence.—*adv.* Irrev'erently. [Fr.—L. *in*, not, and Reverent.]

Irreversible, ir-re-vėrs'i-bl, *adj.* not reversible : that cannot be recalled or annulled.—*adv.* Irrevers'ibly.—*n.* Irrevers'ibleness. [L. *in*, not, and Reversible.]

Irrevocable, ir-rev'o-ka-bl, *adj.* that cannot be recalled.—*adv.* Irrev'ocably.—*n.* Irrev'ocableness. [Fr.—L. *in*, not, and Revocable.]

Irrigate, ir'i-gāt, *v.t.* to *water* : to wet or moisten : to cause water to flow upon. [L. *irrigo, -atum—in*, upon, *rigo*, to wet ; akin to Ger. *regen*, E. *rain*.]

Irrigation, ir-i-gā'shun, *n.* act of watering, esp. of watering lands artificially.

Irriguous, ir-rig'ū-us, *adj., watered :* wet : moist.

Irrision, ir-rizh'un, *n.* act of *laughing at* another. [Fr.—L. *irrisio—in*, against, *rideo, risum*, to laugh.]

Irritability, ir-i-ta-bil'i-ti, *n.* the quality of being easily irritated : the peculiar susceptibility to stimuli possessed by the living tissues.

Irritable, ir'i-ta-bl, *adj.* that may be irritated : easily provoked : (*med.*) susceptible of excitement or irritation.—*adv.* Irr'itably.—*n.* Irr'itableness. [L. *irritabilis.* See Irritate.]

Irritant, ir'i-tant, *adj., irritating.*—*n.* that which causes irritation. [L. *irritans, -antis*, pr.p. of *irrito.*]

Irritate, ir'i-tāt, *v.t.* to make angry : to provoke : to excite heat and redness in. [L. *irrito, -atum*, prob. freq. of *irrio*, to snarl, as a dog.]

Irritation, ir-i-tā'shun, *n.* act of irritating or exciting : excitement : (*med.*) a vitiated state of sensation or action.

Irritative, ir'i-tāt-iv, Irritatory, ir'i-ta-tor-i, *adj.* tending to irritate or excite : accompanied with or caused by irritation.

Irruption, ir-rup'shun, *n.* a *breaking* or bursting *in :* a sudden invasion or incursion. [Fr.—L. *irruptio—in*, and *rumpo, ruptum*, to break.]

Irruptive, ir-rupt'iv, *adj., rushing suddenly in* or upon.—*adv.* Irrupt'ively.

Is, iz, third person sing. pres. of Be. [A.S. *is* ; Ger. *ist*, L. *est*, Gr. *esti*, Sans. *asti—as*, to be.]

Isagon, I'sa-gon, *n.* a figure having *equal angles.* [Fr. *isagone—*Gr. *isos*, equal, *gonia*, an angle.]

Ischiadic, isk-i-ad'ik, Ischiatic, isk-i-at'ik, *adj.* relating to the region of the *hip.* [Fr.—L.—Gr., from *is-chion*, the hip-joint.]

Isinglass, I'zing-glas, *n.* a glutinous substance, chiefly prepared from the air-*bladders* of the *sturgeon.* [A corr. of Dut. *huizenblas—huizen*, a kind of sturgeon, *blas*, a bladder ; Ger. *hausenblase.* See Bladder.]

Islam, iz'lam, Islamism, iz'lam-izm, *n.* the Mohammedan religion.—*adj.* Islamit'ic. [Lit. complete *submission to the will of God*, from Ar. *islam—salama*, to submit to God.]

Island, I'land, *n.* land surrounded with water : a large floating mass. [M. E. *iland*, A.S. *igland —ig*, an island, and *land*, land ; Dut. and Ger.

*eiland*, Ice. *eyland*, Swed. and Dan. *öland*. A.S. *ig =* Ice. *ey*, Swed. and Dan. *ö*, and is from a root which appears in A.S. *ea*, L. *aqua*, water, so that it orig. means *water-land.* The *s* in island is due to a confusion with *isle*, from L. *insula.*]

Islander, I'land-ėr, *n.* an inhabitant of an island.

Isle, īl, *n.* an island. [M. E. *ile, yle—*O. Fr. *isle* (Fr. *île*)—L. *insula*, considered to be so called because lying *in salo*, in the main sea, L. *salum* being akin to Gr. *salos*, the main sea, while both are allied to E. *swell*, Ger. *schwellen*, and mean the ' swelling ' or ' billowing,' the high sea ; Celt. *innis, ennis*, Scot. *inch.*]

Islet, I'let, *n.* a little isle.

Isocheimal, I-so-kī'mal, Isocheimenal, I-so-kī'-men-al, *adj.* having the same mean winter temperature. [Lit. *having equal winters*, Gr. *isos*, equal, *cheima*, winter.]

Isochromatic, I-so-krō-mat'ik, *adj.* (*optics*) having the *same colour.* [Gr. *isos*, equal, and *chrōma*, colour.]

Isochronal, I-sok'ron-al, Isochronous, I-sok'ron-us, *adj.* of *equal time :* performed in equal times. [Gr. *isochronos—isos*, equal, *chronos*, time.]

Isochronism, I-sok'ron-izm, *n.* the quality of being isochronous or done in equal times.

Isolate, I'so-lāt, is'o-lāt, or iz'-, *v.t.* to place in a detached situation, like an *island.*—*n.* Isola'tion. [It. *isolare—isola—*L. *insula*, an island.]

Isomeric, I-so-mėr'ik, *adj.* applied to compounds which are made up of the same elements in the same proportions, but having different properties. —*n.* Isom'erism. [Lit. *having equal parts*, Gr. *isos*, equal, *meros*, part.]

Isometric, I-so-met'rik, Isometrical, I-so-met'-rik-al, *adj.* having *equality* of *measure.* [Gr. *isos*, equal, *metron*, measure.]

Isomorphism, I-so-morf'izm, *n.* the property of being isomorphous.

Isomorphous, I-so-morf'us, *adj.* having the same crystalline form, but composed of different elements. [Gr. *isos*, equal, and *morphē*, form.]

Isonomy, I-son'o-mi, *n.*, *equal law*, rights, or privileges [Gr. *isonomia—isos*, equal, *nomos*, law—*nemō*, to deal out, distribute.]

Isosceles, I-sos'e-lēz, *adj.* (*geom.*) having two equal sides, as a triangle. [Lit. *having equal legs*, Gr. *isoskelēs—isos*, equal, *skelos*, a leg.]

Isotheral, I-soth'ėr-al, *adj.* having the same mean summer temperature. [Lit. *having equal summers*, Gr. *isos*, equal, *theros*, summer—*therō*, to be warm.]

Isothermal, I-so-thėr'mal, *adj.* having an *equal* degree of *heat.* [Fr. *isotherme—*Gr. *isos*, equal, *thermē*, heat—*thermos*, hot.]

Isotonic, I-so-ton'ik, *adj.* having *equal tones.* [Gr. *isos*, equal, *tonos*, tone.]

Israelite, iz'ra-el-īt, *n.* a descendant of *Israel* or Jacob : a Jew. [Gr. *Israelitēs— Israēl*, Heb. *Yisrael*, contender, soldier of God—*sara*, to fight, and *El*, God.]

Israelitic, iz-ra-el-it'ik, Israelitish, iz'ra-el-īt-ish, *adj.* pertaining to the Israelites or Jews.

Issue, ish'ū, *v.i.* to *go*, flow, or come *out :* to proceed, as from a source : to spring : to be produced : (*law*) to come to a point in fact or law : to terminate.—*v.t.* to send out : to put into circulation : to give out for use.—*n.* Iss'uer. [Fr. *issue—*O. Fr. *issir*, to go or flow out—L. *exire—ex*, out, *ire*, to go.]

Issue, ish'ū, *n.* a *going* or flowing *out :* act of sending out : that which flows or passes out : fruit of the body, children : produce, profits :

circulation, as of bank-notes : publication, **as of** a book : a giving out for use : ultimate result, consequence : (*law*) the question of fact submitted to a jury : (*med.*) an ulcer produced artificially.

**Issueless**, ish′ōō-les, *adj.* without issue : childless.

**Isthmus**, ist′mus, *n.* a neck of land connecting two larger portions of land. [L.—Gr. *isthmos*, a passage, an isthmus, allied to *ithma*, a step, from root of *eimi*, to go.]

**It**, it, *pron.* the thing spoken of or referred to. [M. E. and A.S. *hit*, neut. of *he* ; Ice. *hit*, Dut. *het*, Goth. *ita* ; akin to L. *id*, Sans. *i*, pronominal root = here. The *t* is an old neuter suffix, as in *tha-t*, *wha-t*, and cognate with *d* in L. *illu-d*, *istu-d*, *quo-d*.]

**Italian**, i-tal′yan, **Italic**, i-tal′ik, *adj.* of or relating to *Italy* or its people.—*n.* a native of Italy : the language of Italy. [It. *Italiano*, *Italico*—L. *Italia*—Gr. *italos*, a bull, L. *vitulus*, a calf.]

**Italianise**, i-tal′yan-īz, *v.t.* to make Italian.—*v.i.* to play the Italian : to speak Italian.

**Italicise**, i-tal′i-sīz, *v.t.* to print in Italics.

**Italics**, i-tal′iks, *n.pl.* a kind of types which *slope to the right* (as in the last four words), so called because first used by an Italian printer, Aldo Manuzio, about 1500.

**Itch**, ich, *n.* an uneasy, irritating sensation in the skin : an eruptive disease in the skin, caused by a parasitic animal : a constant teasing desire.—*v.i.* to have an uneasy, irritating sensation in the skin : to have a constant, teasing desire. [A.S. *gictha*, *gicenes*, an itching—*giccan*, to itch ; Scot. *youk*, *yuck*, Ger. *jücken*, to itch.]

**Itchy**, ich′i, *adj.* pertaining to or affected with itch.

**Item**, ī′tem, *adv.* (*lit.*) *likewise* : also.—*n.* a separate article or particular.—*v.t.* to make a note of. [L.—*id*, that, akin to Sans. *i:tham*, thus.]

**Iterate**, it′ėr-āt, *v.t.* to do *again* : to repeat, in modern usage replaced by the verb *reiterate*. —*n.* **Itera′tion**, repetition. [L. *itero*, *-atum*—*iterum* (*is*, this, and comparative affix *terum*), beyond this, again ; akin to Sans. *itara*, other.]

**Iterative**, it′ėr-āt-iv, *adj.*, *repeating*. [L. *iterativus*.]

**Itinerant**, ī-tin′ėr-ant, *adj.*, *making journeys* from place to place : travelling.—*n.* one who travels from place to place, esp. a preacher : a wanderer.—*adv.* **Itin′erantly.**—*ns.* **Itin′eracy, Itin′erancy.** [L. *itinerans*, *-antis*, part. of obs. v. *itinero*, to travel—L. *iter*, *itineris*, a journey—*eo*, *itum*, to go.]

**Itinerary**, ī-tin′ėr-ar-i, *adj.*, *travelling:* done on a journey.—*n.* a book of travels : a guide-book for travellers : a rough sketch and description of the country through which troops are to march. [L. *itinerarius*—*iter.*]

**Itinerate**, ī-tin′ėr-āt, *v.i.* to *travel* from place to place, esp. for the purpose of preaching or lecturing. [L. *itinero*—*iter*, *itineris*—*eo*, *itum*, to go.]

**Its**, its, *poss. pron.*, the possessive of **It.** [The old form was *his*, *its* not being older than the end of the 16th century. *Its* does not occur in the English Bible of 1611, or in Spenser, rarely in Shakspeare, and is not common until the time of Dryden.]

**Itself**, it-self′, *pron.* the neuter reciprocal pronoun, applied to things. [**It** and **Self.**]

**Ivied, Ivyed**, ī′vid, **Ivy-mantled**, ī′vi-man′tld, *adj.* overgrown or *mantled* with *ivy*.

**Ivory**, ī′vo-ri, *n.* the hard, white substance composing the tusks of the **e**lephant and of the

sea-horse.—*adj.* made of or resembling **ivory.** [O. Fr. *ivurie*, Fr. *ivoire*—L. *ebur*, *eboris*, ivory —O. Egyptian *ebou*, Sans. *ibha*, an elephant.]

**Ivory-black**, ī′vo-ri-blak, *n.* a *black* powder, orig. made from burnt *ivory*, but now from bone.

**Ivory-nut**, ī′vo-ri-nut, *n.* the *nut* of a species of palm, containing a substance like *ivory*.

**Ivy**, ī′vi, *n.* a creeping evergreen plant on trees and walls. [A.S. *ifig* ; O. Ger. *ebah* ; prob. conn. with L. *apium*, parsley.]

# J

**Jabber**, jab′ėr, *v.i.* to *gabble* or talk rapidly and indistinctly : to chatter.—*v.t.* to utter indistinctly : —*pr.p.* jabb′ering ; *pa.p.* jabb′ered.—*n.* rapid indistinct speaking.—*n.* **Jabb′erer.** [From root of **Gabble.**]

**Jacinth**, jā′sinth, *n.* (*B.*) a precious stone, a *red* variety of zircon, now called hyacinth : a dark-purple colour. [Contr. of **Hyacinth.**]

**Jack**, jak, *n.* used as a familiar name or diminutive of *John* : a saucy or paltry fellow : a sailor : any instrument serving to supply the place of a boy or helper, as a bootjack for taking off boots, a contrivance for turning a spit, a screw for raising heavy weights : the male of some animals : a young pike : a support to saw wood on : a miner′s wedge : a flag displayed from the bowsprit of a ship : a coat of mail. [Fr. *Jacques*, the most common name in France, hence used as a substitute for John, the most common name in England ; but it is really = *James* or *Jacob*—L. *Jacobus*. See **Jacobin.**]

**Jack, Jak**, jak, *n.* a tree of the E. Indies of the same genus as the bread-fruit-tree.

**Jackal**, jak′awl, *n.* a wild, gregarious animal closely allied to the dog. [Pers. *shaghal* ; Sans. *çrigāla.*]

**Jackanapes**, jak′a-nāps, *n.* an impudent fellow : a coxcomb. [For Jack o′ apes, being one who exhibited monkeys, with an *n* inserted to avoid the hiatus.]

**Jackass**, jak′as, *n.* the *male* of the *ass* : a blockhead. [**Jack** = the male, and **Ass.**]

**Jackboots**, jak′bōōts, *n.pl.* large *boots* reaching above the knee, to protect the leg, formerly worn by cavalry, and covered with plates of iron. [**Jack** = coat of mail, and **Boots.**]

**Jackdaw**, jak′daw, *n.* a species of crow. [**Jack** and **Daw.**]

**Jacket**, jak′et, *n.* a *short coat*. [O. Fr. *jaquette*, a jacket, or sleeveless coat, a dim. of O. Fr. *jaque*, a coat of mail.]

**Jacketed**, jak′et-ed, *adj.* wearing a *jacket*.

**Jackscrew**, jak′skrōō, *n.* a *screw* for raising heavy weights. [**Jack** and **Screw.**]

**Jacobin**, jak′o-bin, *n.* one of an order of monks, so named from their orig. establishment in the *Rue St Jacques* (St James′s Street), Paris ; one of a society of revolutionists in France, so called from their meeting in a *Jacobin* convent : a demagogue : a *hooded* pigeon. [Fr.—L. *Jacobus*, James—Gr. *Jacōbos*—Heb. *Ja′akob.*]

**Jacobinical**, jak-o-bin′i-kal, *adj.* pertaining to the *Jacobins* or revolutionists of France : holding revolutionary principles.

**Jacobinism**, jak′o-bin-izm, *n.* the principles of the *Jacobins* or French revolutionists.

**Jacobite**, jak′o-bīt, *n.* an adherent of *James* II. and his descendants.—*adj.* of or belonging to the Jacobites.—*adj.* **Jacobit′ical.**—*n.* **Jac′obitism.**

**Jacob's-ladder**, jā′kobs-lad′ėr, *n.* (*naut.*) a ladder made of ropes with wooden steps : a garden plant with large blue flowers. [From the ladder which Jacob saw in his dream.]

**Jacquerie**, zhak′e-rē, *n.* name given to the revolt of the French peasants in the 14th century. [From Jaques (Bonhomme), Jack (Goodfellow), a name applied in derision to the peasants.]

**Jade**, jād, *n.* a tired horse : a worthless nag : a woman—in contempt or irony.—*v.t.* to tire : to harass. [Ety. dub. ; Sc. *yad, yaud.*]

**Jade**, jād, *n.* a dark-green stone used for ornamental purposes. [Fr.—Sp. *ijada*, the flank—L. *ilia.* It was believed to cure pain of the side.]

**Jag**, jag, *n.* a *notch* : a ragged protuberance : (*bot.*) a cleft or division.—*v.t.* to cut into notches :—*pr.p.* jagg′ing ; *pa.p.* jagged. [Celt. *gag*, a cleft.]       [**Jagg′edly.**—*n.* **Jagg′edness.**

**Jagged**, jag′ed, *adj., notched* : rough-edged.—*adv.*

**Jagger**, jag′ėr, *n.* a brass wheel with a *notched* edge for cutting cakes, &c. into ornamental forms.              [uneven.

**Jaggy**, jag′i, *adj., notched* : set with teeth :

**Jaguar**, jag′ū-är or jag-wär′, *n.* a powerful beast of prey, allied to the leopard, found in South America. [Braz. *janouara*.]

**Jah**, jä, *n.* Jehovah. [Heb.]

**Jail, Jailer.** Same as **Gaol, Gaoler.**

**Jalap**, jal′ap, *n.* the purgative root of a plant first brought from *Jalapa* or *Xalapa*, in Mexico.

**Jam**, jam, *n.* a conserve of fruit boiled with sugar. [Ety. dub. ; perh. from *jam*, to squeeze.]

**Jam**, jam, *v.t.* to press or squeeze tight :—*pr.p.* jamm′ing ; *pa.p.* jammed′. [From the same root as *champ*.]

**Jamb**, jam, *n.* the sidepiece or post of a door, fireplace, &c. [Fr. *jambe*, O. Fr. *gambe*, It. *gamba*, a leg—Celt. *cam*, bent.]

**Jangle**, jang′l, *v.i.* to sound discordantly as in *wrangling* : to wrangle or quarrel.—*v.t.* to cause to sound harshly.—*n.* discordant sound : contention.—*ns.* **Jang′ler, Jang′ling.** [O. Fr. *jangler*, from the sound, like **Jingle** and **Chink.**]

**Janitor**, jan′i-tor, *n.* a doorkeeper : a porter :—*fem.* **Jan′itrix.** [L., from *janua*, a door.]

**Janizary**, jan′i-zar-i, **Janissary**, jan′i-sar-i, *n.* a soldier of the old Turkish foot-guards, formed originally of a tribute of children taken from Christian subjects.—*adj.* **Janiza′rian.** [Fr. *Janissaire*—Turk. *yeni*, new, and *askari*, a soldier.]

**Jantily, Jantiness, Janty.** See **Jaunty,** &c.

**January**, jan′ū-ar-i, *n.* the first month of the year, dedicated by the Romans to *Janus*, the god of the sun. [L. *Januarius*—*Janus*, the sun-god.]

**Japan**, ja-pan′, *v.t.* to varnish after the manner of the Japanese or people of *Japan* : to make black and glossy :—*pr.p.* japann′ing ; *pa.p.* japanned′.—*n.* work japanned : the varnish or lacquer used in japanning.—*n.* **Japann′er.**

**Jar**, jär, *v.i.* to make a harsh discordant sound : to quarrel : to be inconsistent.—*v.t.* to shake :—*pr.p.* jarr′ing ; *pa.p.* jarred′.—*n.* a harsh rattling sound : clash of interests or opinions : discord.—*adv.* **Jarr′ingly.** [From an imitative Teut. root, *kar*, found also in **Care**, and conn. with **Jargon**, and L. *garrire*, to prattle.]

**Jar**, jär, *n.* an earthen or glass bottle with a wide mouth : a measure. [Fr. *jarre*—Pers. *jarrah*, a water-pot.]

**Jargon**, jär′gun, *n.* confused talk : slang. [Fr. *jargon.* See **Jar**, to quarrel.]

**Jargonelle**, jär-go-nel′, *n.* a kind of pear. [Fr.]

**Jasmine**, jas′min, **Jessamine**, jes′a-min, *n.* a

genus of plants, many species of which have very fragrant flowers. [Ar. and Pers. *jâsmin.*]

**Jasper**, jas′pėr, *n.* a precious stone, being a hard siliceous mineral of various colours. [Fr. *jaspe* —L. and Gr. *iaspis*—Arab. *yasb.*]

**Jaundice**, jän′dis, *n.* a disease, characterised by a *yellowness* of the eyes, skin, &c. caused by bile. [Fr. *jaunisse*, from *jaune*, yellow—L. *galbanus*, yellowish, *galbus*, yellow.]      [prejudiced.

**Jaundiced**, jän′dist, *adj.* affected with jaundice :

**Jaunt**, jänt, *v.i.* to go from place to place : to make an excursion.—*n.* an excursion : a ramble. [Old form *jaunce*—O. Fr. *jancer*, to stir (a horse).]

**Jaunting**, jänt′ing, *adj., strolling* : making an excursion.

**Jaunty, Janty**, jänt′i, *adj.* airy : showy : dashing : finical.—*adv.* **Jaunt′ily.**—*n.* **Jaunt′iness.** [From **Jaunt.**]

**Javelin**, jav′lin, *n.* a *spear* about six feet long, anciently used by both infantry and cavalry. [Fr. *javeline*, of uncertain origin.]

**Jaw**, jaw, *n.* the bones of the mouth in which the teeth are set : the mouth : anything like a jaw. [Old spelling *chaw*, akin to **Chew.**]

**Jawbone**, jaw′bōn, *n.* the *bone* of the *jaw*, in which the teeth are set.

**Jawed**, jawd, *adj.* having *jaws* : denoting the appearance of the jaws, as lantern-jawed.

**Jawfall**, jaw′fawl, *n.* a falling of the jaw : (*fig.*) depression of spirits. [**Jaw** and **Fall.**]

**Jay**, jā, *n.* a bird of the crow family with *gay* plumage. [O. Fr. *jay*, Fr. *geai* ; from root of **Gay.**]

**Jealous**, jel′us, *adj.* suspicious of or incensed at rivalry : anxious to defend the honour of.—*adv.* **Jeal′ously.**—*n.* **Jeal′ousy.** [Fr. *jaloux*—L. *zelus*—Gr. *zēlos*, emulation.]

**Jean**, jān, *n.* a twilled cotton cloth. [From *Jaen*, in Spain.]

**Jeer**, jēr, *v.t.* to make sport of : to treat with derision.—*v.i.* to scoff : to deride : to make a mock of.—*n.* a railing remark : biting jest : mockery.—*adv.* **Jeer′ingly.** [Acc. to Skeat, from the Dut. phrase *den gek scheeren*, lit. *to shear the fool*, to mock, the words *gek scheeren* being run together, and corr. into *jeer.*]

**Jehovah**, je-hō′va, *n.* the eternal or self-existent *Being*, the chief Hebrew name of the Deity. [Heb. *Yehovah*, from *hayah*, to be.]

**Jejune**, je-jōōn′, *adj.* empty : void of interest : barren.—*adv.* **Jejune′ly.**—*n.* **Jejune′ness.** [L. *jejunus*, abstaining from food, hungry.]

**Jejunum**, je-jōō′num, *n.* a part of the smaller intestine, so called because generally found *empty* after death. [L.—*jejunus.*]

**Jellied**, jel′id, *adj.* in the state of *jelly.*

**Jelly**, jel′i, *n.* anything gelatinous : the juice of fruit boiled with sugar. [Anything *congealed* or *frozen*, Fr. *gelée*, from *geler*—L. *gelo*, to freeze.]      *jelly.* [**Jelly** and **Fish.**]

**Jelly-fish**, jel′i-fish, *n.* marine radiate animals like

**Jennet**, also spelt **Gennet, Genet**, jen′et, *n.* a small Spanish horse. [Fr. *genet*—Sp. *ginete*, a nag, orig. a horse-soldier : of Moorish origin.]

**Jenneting**, jen′et-ing, *n.* a kind of early apple. [?]

**Jenny**, jen′i, *n.* a *gin* or machine for spinning. [From root of **Gin**, a machine.]

**Jeopard**, jep′ard, **Jeopardise**, jep′ard-īz, *v.t.* to put in jeopardy.

**Jeopardous**, jep′ard-us, *adj.* exposed to danger or loss.—*adv.* **Jeop′ardously.**

**Jeopardy**, jep′ard-i, *n.* hazard, danger. [Fr. *jeu parti*, lit. a *divided game*, one in which the chances are even—Low L. *jocus partitus*—

L. *jocus*, a game, *partitus*, divided—*partior*, to divide.]

**Jerboa**, jėr′bō-a or jėr-bō′a, *n.* a genus of small rodent quadrupeds, remarkable for the length of their hindlegs and their power of jumping. [Ar. *yerbôa, yarbūa*.]

**Jeremiad**, jer-e-mī′ad, *n.* a *lamentation*: a tale of grief: a doleful story. [From *Jeremiah*, the prophet, author of the book of *Lamentations*.]

**Jerfalcon.** Same as **Gyrfalcon**.

**Jerk**, jėrk, *v.t.* to throw with a quick effort: to give a sudden movement.—*n.* a short, sudden movement: a striking against with a sudden motion. [Orig. *to strike*, Scot. *yerk*, by-forms being *jert* and *gird*, and conn. with *yard*, a rod.]

**Jerked-beef**, jėrkt′-bēf, *n.*, *beef* cut into thin pieces and dried in the sun. [Chilian *charqui*.]

**Jerkin**, jėr′kin, *n.* a jacket, a short coat or close waistcoat. [Dut., dim. of *jurk*, a frock.]

**Jersey**, jėr′zi, *n.* the finest part of wool: combed wool: a kind of close-fitting woollen shirt worn in rowing, &c. [From the island *Jersey*.]

**Jerusalem Artichoke**, je-rōō′sa-lem är′ti-chōk, *n.* a plant of the same genus as the common sunflower, the roots of which are used as food. [A corr. of It. *girasole* (L. *gyrare*, to turn, and *sol*, the sun), sunflower, and **Artichoke**, from the similarity in flavour of its root to that of this plant.]

**Jess**, jes, *n.* a short strap round the legs of a hawk, by which she is held and *let go*. [Lit. a *throw*, O. Fr. *ject—jecter*, to throw—L. *jactare*, to throw.]

**Jessamine**, jes′a-min. See **Jasmine**.

**Jesse**, jes′i, *n.* a large branched candlestick used in churches. [From its likeness to the genealogical tree of *Jesse*, the father of David, formerly hung up in churches.]

**Jessed**, jest, *adj.* having *jesses* on.

**Jest**, jest, *n.* something ludicrous: joke: fun: something uttered in sport: object of laughter.—*v.i.* to make a jest or merriment.—*adv.* **Jest′ingly.** [Orig. a *deed*, a *story*, M. E. *geste*—O. Fr. *geste*—L. *gestum*—*gero*, to do.]

**Jester**, jest′ėr, *n.* one who jests: a buffoon. [Orig. a *story-teller*.]

**Jesuit**, jez′ū-it, *n.* one of the Society of *Jesus*, founded in 1534 by Ignatius Loyola, the members of which are reputedly celebrated for craftiness: a crafty person.—*adjs.* **Jesuit′ic, Jesuit′ical.**—*adv.* **Jesuit′ically.**

**Jesuitism**, jez′ū-it-izm, *n.* the principles and practices of the *Jesuits*: cunning: deceit.

**Jesus**, jē′zus, *n.* the Saviour of mankind. [Gr. *Iēsous*—Heb. *Joshua—Jehoshua*, help of Jehovah, the Saviour—*yasha*, to save.]

**Jet**, jet, *n.* a mineral very compact and black used for ornaments. [Fr. *jaiet*—L., Gr. *gagatēs*, from *Gagas*, a town and river in Lycia, in Asia Minor, where it was obtained.]

**Jet**, jet, *v.i.* to *throw* or *shoot* forward: to jut.—*v.t.* to emit in a stream:—*pr.p.* jett′ing; *pa.p.* jett′ed. [Fr. *jeter*—L. *jacto*, freq. of *jacio*, to throw.]

**Jet**, jet, *n.* a spouting stream: a short pipe emitting a flame of gas. [Fr., It. *geto*—L. *jactus*, from *jacio*, to throw.]

**Jet-black**, jet′-blak, *adj.*, *black* as jet, the deepest [black colour.]

**Jetsam**, jet′sam, **Jetson**, jet′sun, **Jettison**, jet′i-sun, *n.* the *throwing* of goods overboard in a case of great peril to lighten a vessel: the goods so thrown away which remain under water.

**Jetty**, jet′i, *adj.* made of *jet*, or black as jet.—*n.* **Jett′iness.**

**Jetty**, jet′i, *n.* a projection: a kind of pier. [Fr. *jetée*, thrown out—*jeter*.]

**Jew**, jōō, *n.* an inhabitant of Judea: a Hebrew or Israelite:—*fem.* **Jew′ess.** [O. Fr. *Juis*—L. *Judæus*, Gr. *Ioudaios—Ioudaia*, Judea.]

**Jewel**, jōō′el, *n.* an ornament of dress: a precious stone: anything highly valued.—*v.t.* to dress or adorn with jewels: to fit with a jewel:—*pr.p.* jew′elling; *pa.p.* jew′elled. [O. Fr. *jouel*, Fr. *joyau*; either a dim. of Fr. *joie*, joy, from L. *gaudium*, joy—*gaudeo*, to rejoice (see **Joy**), or derived through Low L. *jocale*, from L. *jocari*, to jest.]

**Jeweller**, jōō′el-ėr, *n.* one who makes or deals in jewels. [in general.]

**Jewelry**, jōō′el-ri, **Jewellery**, jōō′el-ėr-i, *n.*, *jewels* [Jews.]

**Jewish**, jōō′ish, *adj.* belonging to the Jews.—*adv.* **Jew′ishly.**—*n.* **Jew′ishness.**

**Jewry**, jōō′ri, *n.*, *Judea*: a district inhabited by Jews.

**Jew's-harp**, jōōz′-härp, *n.* a small *harp*-shaped musical instrument played between the teeth by striking a spring with the finger. [From **Jew**, and **Harp**; a name prob. given in derision.]

**Jib**, jib, *n.* a triangular sail borne in front of the foremast in a ship, so called from its *shifting* of itself.—*v.t.* to shift a boom sail from one tack to the other.—*v.i.* to move restively. [Dan. *gibbe*, Dut. *gijpen*, to turn suddenly.]

**Jib-boom**, jib′-bōōm, *n.* a *boom* or extension of the bowsprit, on which the *jib* is spread.

**Jibe.** Same as **Gibe**.

**Jig**, jig, *n.* a quick, lively tune: a quick dance suited to the tune.—*v.i.* to dance a jig:—*pr.p.* jig′ging; *pa.p.* jigged′. [Fr. *gigue*, a stringed instrument—Ger. *geige*; conn. with **Gig**.]

**Jilt**, jilt, *n.* a woman who encourages a lover and then neglects or rejects him: a flirt.—*v.t.* to encourage and then disappoint in love. [Scot. *jillet*, dim. of *Jill* (L. *Juliana—Julius*), a female name, used in contempt.]

**Jingle**, jing′l, *n.* a *jangling* or clinking sound: that which makes a rattling sound: a correspondence of sounds.—*v.i.* to sound with a jingle. [Formed from the sound, like **Jangle**.]

**Jingoism**, jing′ō-izm, *n.* nickname for a phase of the military spirit in England. [Jingo is said to be the Basque name for ' lord.']

**Job**, job, *n.* a sudden stroke or stab with a pointed instrument like a *beak*.—*v.t.* to strike or stab suddenly:—*pr.p.* jobb′ing; *pa.p.* jobbed′. [Gael. *gob*, W. *gyb*, a beak; conn. with **Gobble, Job**.]

**Job**, job, *n.* any piece of work, esp. of a *trifling* or temporary nature: any undertaking with a view to profit: a mean transaction, in which private gain is sought under pretence of public service.—*v.i.* to work at jobs: to buy and sell, as a broker: to hire or let out for a short time, esp. horses. [Lit. 'a lump' or ' portion,' and formerly spelt *gob*, M. E. *gobet*—O. Fr. *gob*, a mouthful; from the same Celtic root as **Gobble**.]

**Jobber**, job′ėr, *n.* one who *jobs*: one who buys and sells, as a broker: one who turns official actions to private advantage: one who engages in a mean, lucrative affair.

**Jobbery**, job′ėr-i, *n.*, *jobbing*: unfair means employed to procure some private end.

**Jockey**, jok′i, *n.* a man (orig. a boy) who rides horses in a race: a horsedealer: one who takes undue advantage in business.—*v.t.* to jostle by riding against: to cheat. [Dim. of *Jock*, northern E. for *Jack*, which see.]

**Jockeyism**, jok′i-izm, **Jockeyship**, jok′i-ship, *n.* the art or practice of a jockey.

**Jocose**, je-kōs′, *adj.* full of *jokes*: humorous:

merry.—*adv.* **Jocose'ly.**—*n.* **Jocose'ness.** [L. *jocosus—jocus,* a joke. See **Joke.**]

**Jocular,** jok'ū-lar, *adj.* given to *jokes:* humorous: droll: laughable.—*adv.* **Joc'ularly.**—*n.* **Jocular'ity.** [L. *jocularis—jocus.*]

**Jocund,** jok'und, *adj.* in a *jocose* humour: merry: cheerful: pleasant.—*adv.* **Joc'undly.**—*n.* **Joc'und'ity.** [L. *jocundus—jocus.*]

**Jog,** jog, *v.t.* to *shock* or *shake:* to push with the elbow or hand.—*v.i.* to move by small shocks: to travel slowly:—*pr.p.* jog'ging; *pa.p.* jogged'.— *n.* a slight shake: a push. [A weakened form of **Shock.**]

**Joggle,** jog'l, *v.t.* to *jog* or shake slightly: to jostle.—*v.i.* to shake:—*pr.p.* jog'ling; *pa.p.* jog'led. [Dim. of **Jog.**]

**Jogtrot,** jog'trot, *n.* a slow *jogging trot.*

**John Doree.** See **Doree.**

**Join,** join, *v.t.* to connect: to unite: to associate: to add or annex.—*v.i.* to be connected with: to grow together: to be in close contact: to unite (with). [Fr. *joindre,* It. *giugnere*—L. *jungere, junctum:* conn. with Gr. *zeugnūmi,* Sans. *yuj,* to join. See **Yoke.**] [carpenter.

**Joiner,** join'ér, *n.* one who *joins* or unites: a

**Joinery,** join'ér-i, *n.* the art of the *joiner.*

**Joint,** joint, *n.* a *joining:* the place where two or more things join: a knot: a hinge: a seam: the place where two bones are joined (*cook.*) the part of the limb of an animal cut off at the joint.— *adj.* joined, united, or combined: shared among more than one.—*v.t.* to unite by joints: to fit closely: to provide with joints: to cut into joints, as an animal.—*v.i.* to fit like joints. [Fr., O. Fr. *joinct*—Fr. *joindre.* See **Join.**]

**Jointly,** joint'li, *adv.* in a joint manner: unitedly or in combination: together. [company.

**Joint-stock,** joint'-stok, *n., stock* held *jointly* or in

**Jointure,** joint'ūr, *n.* property *joined* to or settled on a woman at marriage to be enjoyed after her husband's death.—*v.t.* to settle a jointure upon. [Fr., O. Fr. *joincture*—L. *junctura.* See **Join.**]

**Jointuress,** joint'ūr-es, **Jointress,** joint'res, *n.* a woman on whom a *jointure* is settled.

**Joist,** joist, *n.* the timbers to which the boards of a floor or the laths of a ceiling are nailed.—*v.t.* to fit with joists. [Lit. 'that on which anything lies,' Scot. *geist*—O. Fr. *giste,* from Fr. *gésir*—L. *jacere,* to lie. See **Gist.**]

**Joke,** jōk, *n.* a *jest:* a witticism: something witty or sportive: anything said or done to excite a laugh.—*v.t.* to cast jokes at: to banter: to make merry with.—*v.i.* to jest: to be merry: to make sport. [L. *jocus.*]

**Joker,** jōk'ér, *n.* one who jokes or jests.

**Jokingly,** jōk'ing-li, *adv.* in a joking manner.

**Jole,** another form of **Jowl.**

**Jollification,** jol-i-fi-kā'shun, *n.* a *making jolly:* noisy festivity and merriment. [**Jolly,** and L. *facio,* to make.]

**Jolly,** jol'i, *adj., merry:* expressing or exciting mirth: comely, robust.—*adv.* **Joll'ily.**—*ns.* **Joll'ity, Joll'iness.** [Fr. *joli*—Ice. *jol,* a Christmas feast, E. *yule.*]

**Jollyboat,** jol'i-bōt, *n.* a small boat belonging to a ship. [**Jolly** (a corr. of Dan. *jolle,* a boat, a yawl) and **Boat.** See **Yawl.**]

**Jolt,** jōlt, *v.i.* to shake with sudden jerks.—*v.t.* to shake with a sudden shock.—*n.* a sudden jerk. [Old form *joll,* prob. conn. with **Jowl,** and so orig. meaning to knock one head against another, as in the phrase *jolthead.*]

**Joltingly,** jōlt'ing-li. *adv.* in a jolting manner.

**Jonquil,** jon'kwil, **Jonquille,** jon-kwēl', *n.* a name

given to certain species of narcissus with *rush*-like leaves. [Fr. *jonquille*—L. *juncus,* a rush.]

**Joss-stick,** jos'-stik, *n.* in China, a stick of gum burned as incense to their gods. [Chinese *joss,* a god.]

**Jostle,** jos'l, *v.t.* to *joust* or strike against: to drive against. [Freq. of **Joust.**]

**Jot,** jot, *n.* the least quantity assignable.—*v.t.* to set down briefly: to make a memorandum of :— *pr.p.* jott'ing; *pa.p.* jott'ed. [L.—Gr. *iōta*— Heb. *yod,* the smallest letter in the alphabet, E. *i.*]

**Jotting,** jot'ing, *n.* a memorandum.

**Journal,** jur'nal, *n.* a *diurnal* or daily register or diary: a book containing an account of each day's transactions: a newspaper published daily or otherwise: a magazine: the transactions of any society. [Fr.—L. *diurnalis.* See **Diurnal.**]

**Journalism,** jur'nal-izm, *n.* the keeping of a *journal:* the profession of conducting public journals.

**Journalist,** jur'nal-ist, *n.* one who writes for or conducts a *journal* or newspaper.

**Journalistic,** jur-nal-ist'ik, *adj.* pertaining to *journals* or newspapers, or to *journalism.*

**Journey,** jur'ni, *n.* any travel: tour: excursion. —*v.i.* to travel :—*pr.p.* jour'neying; *pa.p.* jour'neyed (-nid). [Lit. *a day's travel,* Fr. *journée* —*jour,* It. *giorno,* a day—L. *diurnus.*]

**Journeyman,** jur'ni-man, *n.* one who works by the *day:* any hired workman: one whose apprenticeship is completed.

**Joust,** just or jōōst, *n.* the encounter of two knights on horseback at a tournament.—*v.i.* to run in the tilt. [Lit. *a coming together,* O. Fr. *jouste, juste*—L. *juxta,* nigh to.]

**Jovial,** jō'vi-al, *adj.* joyous: full of mirth and happiness. —*adv.* **Jo'vially.**—*ns.* **Jovial'ity, Jo'vialness.** [L. *Jovialis*—*Jupiter, Jovis,* Jupiter, the star, which, according to the old astrology, had a happy influence on human affairs.]

**Jowl, Jole,** jōl, *n.* the *jaw* or cheek. [M. E. forms are *choul, chaul,* corr. from *chavel,* and this again from A.S. *ceafl,* the jaw.]

**Joy,** joy, *n.* gladness: rapture: mirth: the cause of joy.—*v.i.* to *rejoice:* to be glad: to exult :— *pr.p.* joy'ing; *pa.p.* joyed'. [Fr. *joie,* It. *gioja* —L. *gaudium—gaudeo,* to rejoice, allied to Gr. *gētheō.*]

**Joyful,** joy'fool, *adj.* full of joy: very glad, happy, or merry.—*adv.* **Joy'fully.**—*n.* **Joy'fulness.**

**Joyless,** joy'les, *adj.* without joy: not giving joy. —*adv.* **Joy'lessly.**—*n.* **Joy'lessness.**

**Joyous,** joy'us, *adj.* full of joy, happiness, or merriment.—*adv.* **Joy'ously.**—*n.* **Joy'ousness.**

**Jubilant,** jōō'bi-lant, *adj.* shouting for joy: rejoicing: uttering songs of triumph. [L. *jubilo,* to shout for joy. Not conn. with **Jubilee.**]

**Jubilate,** jōō-bi-lā'te, *n.* the 3d Sunday after Easter, so called because the Church Service began on that day with the 66th Psalm, '*Jubilate* Deo,' &c. [From root of **Jubilant.**]

**Jubilation,** jōō-bi-lā'shun, *n.* a shouting for joy: the declaration of triumph. [See **Jubilant.**]

**Jubilee,** jōō'bi-lē, *n.* the year of release among the Jews every fiftieth year, proclaimed by the sound of a *trumpet:* any season of great public joy and festivity. [Fr. *jubilé*—L. *jubilæus*— Heb. *yobel,* a trumpet, the sound of a trumpet.]

**Judaic,** jōō-dā'ik, **Judaical,** jōō-dā'ik-al, *adj.* pertaining to the *Jews.*—*adv.* **Juda'ically.** [L. *Judaicus*—*Juda,* Judah, one of the sons of Israel.]

**Judaise**, joo'da-īz, *v.i.* to conform to or practise *Judaism*.

**Judaism**, joo'da-izm, *n.* the doctrines and rites of the *Jews*: conformity to the Jewish rites.

**Judean**, joo-dē'an, *adj.* belonging to *Judea.—n.* a native of Judea.

**Judge**, juj, *v.i.* to point out or declare what is *just* or *law*: to hear and decide: to pass sentence: to compare facts to determine the truth: to form or pass an opinion: to distinguish.—*v.t.* to hear and determine authoritatively: to sentence: to be censorious towards: to consider: (*B.*) to condemn. [Fr. *juger—L. judico—jus*, law, and *dico*, to say.]

**Judge**, juj, *n.* one who *judges*: a civil officer who hears and settles any cause: an arbitrator: one who can decide upon the merit of anything: in Jewish history, a magistrate having civil and military powers:—*pl.* title of 7th book of the Old Testament. [Fr. *juge*, L. *judex—judico*.]

**Judgeship**, juj'ship, *n.* the office of a *judge*.

**Judgment**, juj'ment, *n.* act of *judging*: the comparing of ideas, to elicit truth: faculty by which this is done, the reason: opinion formed: taste: sentence: condemnation: doom.

**Judgment-day**, juj'ment-dā, *n.* the *day* on which God will pronounce final *judgment* on mankind.

**Judgment-seat**, juj'ment-sēt, *n.*, *seat* or bench in a court from which *judgment* is pronounced.

**Judicable**, joo'di-ka-bl, *adj.* that may be *judged* or *tried.* [L. *judicabilis.*] [*judge.*

**Judicative**, joo'di-kā-tiv, *adj.* having power to

**Judicatory**, joo'di-kā-tor-i, *adj.* pertaining to a *judge*: distributing justice.—*n.* distribution of justice: a tribunal.

**Judicature**, joo'di-kā-tūr, *n.* profession of a *judge*: power or system of dispensing justice by legal trial: jurisdiction: a tribunal.

**Judicial**, joo-dish'al, *adj.* pertaining to a *judge* or court: practised in, or proceeding from a court of justice: established by statute.—*adv.* **Judi'cially.** [O. Fr.—L. *judicialis.*]

**Judiciary**, joo-dish'i-ar-i, *n.* the *judges* taken collectively.—*adj.* pertaining to the courts of law: passing judgment. [L. *judiciarius.*]

**Judicious**, joo-dish'us, *adj.* according to sound *judgment*: possessing sound judgment: discreet.—*n.* **Judi'ciousness.**—*adv.* **Judi'ciously.**

**Jug**, jug, *n.* a large vessel with a swelling body and narrow mouth for liquors.—*v.t.* to boil or stew as in a jug:—*pr.p.* jugg'ing; *pa.p.* jugged'. [Prob. a familiar equivalent of Joan or Jenny, and jocularly applied to a drinking-vessel; cf. Jack and Gill in a like sense.]

**Jug**, jug, *v.i.* to utter the sound *jug*, as certain birds, esp. the nightingale. [From the sound.]

**Juggle**, jug'l, *v.i.* to *joke* or *jest*: to amuse by sleight-of-hand: to conjure: to practise artifice or imposture.—*n.* a trick by sleight-of-hand: an imposture. [O. Fr. *jongler—L. joculor*, to jest —*jocus*, a jest.]

**Juggler**, jug'lėr, *n.* one who performs tricks by sleight-of-hand: a trickish fellow. [M. E. *jogelour—*Fr. *jongleur—L. joculator*, a jester.]

**Jugglery**, jug'lėr-i, *n.* art or tricks of a *juggler*: legerdemain: trickery.

**Jugular**, joo'gū-lar, *adj.* pertaining to the *collarbone*, which *joins* the neck and shoulders.—*n.* one of the large veins on each side of the neck. [L. *jugulum*, the collar-bone—*jungo*, to join.]

**Juice**, joos, *n.* the sap of vegetables: the fluid part of animal bodies.—*adj.* **Juice'less.** [Fr.—L. *jus*, lit. *mixture.*]

**Juicy**, joos'i, *adj., full of juice.—n.* **Juic'iness.**

**Jujube**, joo'joob, *n.* a genus of spiny shrubs or small trees, the fruit of which is dried as a sweetmeat: a lozenge made of sugar and gum. [Fr.—L. *zizyphus—*Gr. *zizyphon—*Pers. *zizfun*, the jujube-tree.]

**Julep**, joo'lep, **Julap**, joo'lap, *n.* a pleasant liquid medicine in which other nauseous medicines are taken. [Lit. *rose-water*, Fr.—Ar. *julab—*Pers. *gul*, rose, *âb*, water.]

**Julian**, jool'yan, *adj.* noting the old account of time established by *Julius* Cæsar, and used from 46 B.C. till 1752.

**July**, joo-lī', *n.* the seventh month of the year, so called from Caius *Julius* Cæsar, who was born in this month.

**Jumble**, jum'bl, *v.t.* to mix confusedly: to throw together without order.—*v.i.* to be mixed together confusedly: to be agitated.—*n.* a confused mixture. [M. E. *jombre*, prob. a freq. of **Jump**, in the sense of to stamp or shake about.]

**Jumblingly**, jum'bling-li, *adv.* in a *jumbled* or confused manner.

**Jump**, jump, *v.i.* to spring upward, or forward, or both: to bound: to pass to as by a leap.—*v.t.* to pass by a leap: to skip over:—*pr.p.* jump'ing; *pa.p.* jumped'.—*n.* act of jumping: a bound. [From a Teut. root seen in Sw. *gumpa*, O. Ger. *gumpen*, to jump.]

**Junction**, jungk'shun, *n.* a *joining*, a union or combination: place or point of union. [See **Join**.]

**Juncture**, jungk'tūr, *n.* a *joining*, a union: a critical or important point of time. [L. *junctura*.]

**June**, joon, *n.* the sixth month, orig. of 26 days, but since Julius Cæsar's time of 30. [L. *Junius*, the name of the sixth month, and also of a Roman gens or clan, prob. from root of L. *juvenis*, junior, Sans. *juwan*, young, and so = the month of *growth*.]

**Jungle**, jung'gl, *n.* land covered with thick brushwood, &c.—*adj.* **Jung'ly.** [Sans. *jangala*, desert.]

**Junior**, joon'yur, *adj., younger*: less advanced.— *n.* one younger or less advanced. [Contr. of L. *juvenior*, younger—*juvenis*, young.]

**Juniority**, joo-ni-or'i-ti, **Juniorship**, joo'ni-ur-ship, *n.* state of being *junior*.

**Juniper**, joo'ni-pėr, *n.* an evergreen shrub, the berries of which are used in making gin. [L. *juniperus—juvenis*, young, and *pario*, to bring forth; lit. *young-bearing*, from its evergreen appearance.]

**Junk**, jungk, *n.* a Chinese vessel, having three masts. [Port. *junco—*Chinese *chw'an*, a boat.]

**Junk**, jungk, *n.* pieces of old cordage, used for making mats, &c. and when picked to pieces forming oakum for the seams of ships: salt meat supplied to vessels for long voyages, so called because it becomes as hard as old rope. [L. *juncus*, a rush, of which ropes used to be made.]

**Junket**, jung'ket, *n.* any sweetmeat, so called from being carried in little baskets made of *rushes*: a stolen entertainment.—*v.i.* to feast in secret.—*v.t.* to feast:—*pr.p.* jun'keting; *pa.p.* jun'keted. [It. *giuncata—L. juncus*, a rush.]

**Junta**, jun'ta, *n.* a body of men *joined* or united: a Spanish grand council of state. [Sp., a fem. form of **Junto**.]

**Junto**, jun'to, *n.* a body of men *joined* or united for some secret intrigue: a confederacy: a cabal or faction:—*pl.* **Jun'tos**. [Sp.—L. *junctus—jungo*.]

**Jupiter**, joo'pi-tėr, *n.* the chief god among the Romans: the largest, and, next to Venus, the brightest of the planets. [Contr. from *Jovis pater* or *Diespiter*, 'Jove-father' or 'Heaven-father,' from *Jovis* (= Gr. *Zeus*, Sans. *Dyaus*, A.S. *Tiw*, O. High Ger. *Zio*, L. *dies*, *divum*, and sig. light, heaven), and *pater*, father.]

**Juridical**, jōō-rid′ik-al, *adj.* relating to the distribution of *justice* : pertaining to a judge : used in courts of law.—*adv.* **Jurid′ically.** [L. *juridicus—jus*, *juris*, law, and *dico*, to declare.]

**Jurisconsult**, jōō-ris-kon′sult, *n.* one who is *consulted* on the *law* : a lawyer who gives opinions on cases put to him : a jurist. [L. *jus*, *juris*, law, and *consultus—consulo*, to consult.]

**Jurisdiction**, jōō-ris-dik′shun, *n.* the *distribution* of *justice* : legal authority : extent of power : district over which any authority extends.—*adj.* **Jurisdic′tional.** [Fr.—L. *jurisdictio*. See **Just** and **Diction.**]

**Jurisprudence**, jōō-ris-prōō′dens, *n.* the *science* or *knowledge of law.* [Fr.—L. *jurisprudentia— jus*, *juris*, law, and *prudentia*, knowledge. See **Just** and **Prudence.**]

**Jurist**, jōō′rist, *n.* one who professes or is versed in the science of *law*, especially the Roman or civil law : a civilian. [Fr. *juriste*.]

**Juror**, jōō′rur, **Juryman**, jōō′ri-man, *n.* one who serves on a *jury*. [Fr. *jureur*.]

**Jury**, jōō′ri, *n.* a body of not less than twelve men, selected and *sworn*, as prescribed by law, to declare the truth on evidence before them : a committee for deciding prizes at a public exhibition. [Fr. *juré*, sworn—*jurer*—L. *juro*, to swear.]

**Jurymast**, jōō′ri-mäst, *n.* a temporary *mast* erected in a ship instead of one lost or destroyed. [Ety. dub., by some thought to be an abbrev. of *injury-mast.*] [for one lost.

**Jury-rudder**, jōō′ri-rud′ėr, *n.* a temporary *rudder*

**Just**, *n.* a tilt. Same as **Joust.**

**Just**, just, *adj.*, *lawful* : upright : exact : regular : true : righteous.—*adv.* accurately : barely. [Fr. —L. *justus—jus*, law.]

**Justice**, jus′tis, *n.* quality of being *just* : integrity : impartiality : desert : retribution : a judge : a magistrate. [Fr.—L. *justitia*.]

**Justiceship**, jus′tis-ship, *n.* office or dignity of a *justice* or judge.

**Justiciary**, jus-tish′i-ar-i, **Justiciar**, jus-tish′i-ar, *n.* an administrator of *justice* : a chief-justice.

**Justifiable**, jus-ti-fī′a-bl, *adj.* that may be justified or defended.—*n.* **Justifi′ableness.**—*adv.* **Justifi′ably.**

**Justification**, jus-ti-fi-kā′shun, *n.* vindication : absolution : a plea of sufficient reason for.

**Justificative**, jus′ti-fi-kā-tiv, **Justificatory**, jus′ti-fi-kā-tor-i, *adj.* having power to justify.

**Justifier**, jus′ti-fī-ėr, *n.* one who defends, or vindicates : he who pardons and absolves from guilt and punishment.

**Justify**, jus′ti-fī, *v.t.* to make *just* : to prove or shew to be just or right : to vindicate : to absolve :—*pr.p.* jus′tifying : *pa.p.* jus′tified. [Fr. —L. *justifico—justus*, just, and *facio*, to make.]

**Justle**, *v.t.* Same as **Jostle.**

**Justly**, just′li, *adv.* in a just manner : equitably : uprightly : accurately : by right. [ness.

**Justness**, just′nes, *n.* equity : propriety : exact-

**Jut**, jut, *v.i.* to shoot forward : to project :—*pr.p.* jutt′ing ; *pa.p.* jutt′ed. [A form of **Jet.**]

**Jute**, jōōt, *n.* the fibre of an Indian plant resembling hemp, used in the manufacture of coarse bags, mats, &c. [Orissa *jhot*, Sans. *jhat.*]

**Juvenescent**, jōō-ven-es′ent, *adj.* becoming young. —*n.* **Juvenes′cence.** [L. *juvenescens— juvenesco*, to grow young.]

**Juvenile**, jōō′ve-nīl or -nil, *adj.*, *young* : pertaining or suited to youth : puerile.—*ns.* **Ju′venileness, Juvenil′ity.** [Fr.—L. *juvenilis—juvenis*, young : akin to Sans. *juwan*, young, and *djuna*, sportive.]

**Juxtaposition**, juks-ta-po-zish′un, *n.* a *placing* or being *placed near* : contiguity. [L. *juxta*, near, and **Position.**]

## K

**Kaffir**, kaf′ir, *n.* one of a native race of S.E. Africa. [Ar. *Kafir*, unbeliever.]

**Kail, Kale**, kāl, *n.* a cabbage with open curled leaves. [The Northern E. form of **Cole.**]

**Kaleidoscope**, ka-lī′do-skōp, *n.* an optical toy in which we *see* an endless variety of *beautiful* colours and *forms*. [Gr. *kalos*, beautiful, *eidos*, form, and *skopeō*, to see.] [**Calends.**

**Kalendar, Kalends.** Same as **Calendar, Calends.**

**Kamptulicon**, kamp-tu′li-kon, *n.* a floorcloth made of ground cork and caoutchouc. [Gr. *kamptō*, to bend.]

**Kangaroo**, kang-gar-ōō′, *n.* an Australian quadruped, remarkable for the length of its hindlegs and its power of leaping. [The native name.]

**Kedge**, kej, *n.* a small anchor for keeping a ship steady and for warping the ship.—*v.t.* to move by means of a kedge, to warp.—*n.* **Kedg′er**, a kedge. [Ice. *kaggi*, a cask fixed to an anchor as a buoy.]

**Keel**, kēl, *n.* the part of a ship extending along the bottom from stem to stern, and supporting the whole frame : a low flat-bottomed boat : (*bot.*) the lowest petals of the corolla of a papilionaceous flower.—*v.t.* or *v.i.* to plough with a keel, to navigate : to turn keel upwards. [A.S. *ceol*, a ship ; Ger. and Dut. *kiel* ; prob. confused with Ice. *kiölr*, the keel of a ship.]

**Keelage**, kēl′āj, *n.* dues for a *keel* or ship in port.

**Keeled**, kēld, *adj.* (*bot.*) *keel-shaped* : having a prominence on the back.

**Keelhaul**, kēl′hawl, *v.t.* to punish by *hauling* under the *keel* of a ship by ropes from the one side to the other : to treat a subordinate in a galling manner.

**Keelson, Kelson**, kel′sun, *n.* an inner keel placed right over the outer keel of a ship, and securely fastened thereto. [Swed. *kölsvin*, Norw. *kjölsvill*, the latter syllable = Ger. *schwelle*, E. **Sill.**]

**Keen**, kēn, *adj.* eager : sharp, having a fine edge : piercing : acute of mind : penetrating.—*adv.* **Keen′ly.**—*n.* **Keen′ness.** [A.S. *cene* ; Ger. *kühn*, bold ; Ice. *kænn*, wise. It is from the same root as *ken* and *can*, the orig. sense being *able* or *knowing.*]

**Keep**, kēp, *v.t.* to have the care of : to guard : to maintain : to have in one's service : to remain in : to adhere to : to practise : not to lose : to maintain hold upon : to restrain from departure : to preserve in a certain state.—*v.i.* to remain in any position or state : to last or endure : to adhere :—*pr.p.* keep′ing ; *pa.t.* and *pa.p.* kept.— *n.* that which keeps or protects : the innermost and strongest part of a castle, the donjon : a stronghold.—*n.* **Keep′er.**—*n.* **Keep′ership**, office of a keeper. [A.S. *cepan*, orig. to traffic, hence to store up, keep—*ceap*, price. See **Cheap.**]

**Keeping**, kēp′ing, *n.* care : just proportion, harmony : (*paint.*) due proportion of light and shade.

**Keepsake**, kēp′sāk, *n.* something given to be *kept* for the *sake* of the giver. [a cask.]

**Keg**, keg, *n.* a small *cask* or barrel. [Ice. *kaggi*,

**Kelp**, kelp, *n.* the calcined ashes of seaweed, once used in making glass. [Ety. unknown.]

**Kelpie, Kelpy**, kel′pi, *n.* a water-sprite in the form of a horse. [Ety. dub.]

**Kelson.** Same as **Keelson**.

**Ken**, ken, *v.t.* to *know:* to see and recognise at a distance.—*n.* reach of knowledge or sight. [Ice. *kenna*, orig. to cause to know. See **Can** and **Know**.]

**Kendal-green**, ken′dal-grēn, *n.*, *green* cloth made at *Kendal* in Westmoreland.

**Kennel**, ken′el, *n.* a house for *dogs:* a pack of hounds : the hole of a fox, &c. : a haunt.—*v.t.* to keep in a kennel.—*v.i.* to live in a kennel :—*pr.p.* kenn′elling ; *pa.p.* kenn′elled. [Norm. Fr. *kenil*, Fr. *chenil*—L. *canīle*—*canis*, a dog.]

**Kennel**, ken′el, *n.* the water-course of a street : a gutter. [A form of **Canal**.]

**Kennel-coal.** Same as **Cannel-coal**.

**Kept**, *past tense* and *past participle* of **Keep**.

**Kerbstone**, kėrb′stōn, *n.* a form of **Curbstone**.

**Kerchief**, kėr′chif, *n.* (*orig.*) a square piece of cloth worn by women to *cover* the *head:* any loose cloth used in dress. [M. E. *couerchef*, Fr. *couvrechef*—*couvrir*, to cover, *chef*, the head. See **Cover** and **Chief**.]

**Kern.** See **Quern**.       [*cearn*, a man.]

**Kern, Kerne**, kėrn, *n.* an Irish foot-soldier. [Ir.

**Kernel**, kėrn′el, *n.* anything in a husk or shell : the substance in the shell of a nut : the seed of a pulpy fruit. [Lit. *a grain of corn*, A.S. *cyrnel*, from A.S. *corn*, grain, and dim. suffix -*el; Ger. *kern*, a grain. See **Corn** and **Grain**.]

**Kernelly**, kėrn′el-i, *adj.* full of or resembling kernels.

**Kerosene**, ker′o-sēn, *n.* an oil obtained from bituminous coal, used for lamps, &c. [Gr. *kēros*, wax.]

**Kersey**, kėr′zi, *n.* a coarse woollen cloth. [Perh. from Kersey in Suffolk, where a woollen trade was once carried on.]

**Kerseymere**, kėr-zi-mėr′ or kėr′-, *n.* a twilled cloth of the finest wools. [A corr. of **Cassimere**, **Cashmere**.]

**Kestrel**, kes′trel, *n.* a small species of falcon like the sparrow-hawk. [Fr. *cresserelle*, of unknown origin.]

**Ketch**, kech, *n.* a small two-masted vessel, generally used as a yacht or as a bomb-vessel. [Corr. from Turk. *qaiq*, a boat, skiff, whence also Fr. *caïque*.]

**Ketchup.** Same as **Catchup**.

**Kettle**, ket′l, *n.* a vessel of metal, for heating or boiling liquids. [A.S. *cetel;* Ger. *kessel*, Goth. *katils;* all conn. with and perh. borrowed from L. *catillus*, dim. of *catinus*, a deep cooking-vessel.]

**Kettledrum**, ket′l-drum, *n.* a *drum* made of a metal vessel like a *kettle*, and covered with parchment : a tea-party. [See **Drum**.]

**Key**, kē, *n.* an instrument for shutting or opening a lock : that by which something is screwed or turned : (*arch.*) the middle stone of an arch : a piece of wood let into another piece crosswise to prevent warping : (*mus.*) one of the small levers in musical instruments for producing notes : the fundamental note of a piece of music : that which explains a mystery : a book containing answers to exercises, &c. [A.S. *cæg*, a key ; O. Fris. *kei, kai*.]

**Keyboard**, kē′bōrd, *n.* the *keys* or levers in a piano or organ arranged along a flat *board*.

**Keyhole**, kē′hōl, *n.* the *hole* in which a *key* of a door, &c. is inserted.

**Keynote**, kē′nōt, *n.* the *key* or fundamental *note* of a piece of music.

**Keystone**, kē′stōn, *n.* the same as **Key**, in *arch.*

**Khan**, kan, *n.* in N. Asia, a prince or chief: in Persia, a governor.—*n.* **Khan′ate**, the dominion or jurisdiction of a khan. [Pers. *khan*, lord or prince, which is a modification of a Tartar word.]

**Khedive**, ked′iv, *n.* the title of the ruler of Egypt. [Persian *khidīv*, prince or sovereign.]

**Kibe**, kīb, *n.* a chilblain. [W. *cibwst*, from *cib*, a cup, expressive of the swollen or rounded appearance of the disease, and *gwst*, a disease.]

**Kick**, kik, *v.t.* to hit with the *foot*.—*v.i.* to thrust out the foot with violence : to shew opposition. —*n.* a blow with the foot. [M. E. *kiken*—W. *cicio*—*cic*, the foot.]

**Kickshaw**, kik′shaw, *n.*, *something* uncommon or fantastical that has no name : (*cook.*) a fantastical dish. [Corr. of Fr. *quelque chose*, something.]

**Kid**, kid, *n.* a young goat.—*v.t.* or *v.i.* to bring forth a goat :—*pr.p.* kidd′ing ; *pa.p.* kidd′ed. [Scand., as in Ice. *kidh;* Ger. *kitze*, a young goat.]

**Kidling**, kid′ling, *n.* a young kid.

**Kidnap**, kid′nap, *v.t.* to steal, as a human being :—*pr.p.* kid′napping ; *pa.t.* and *pa.p.* kid′napped. —*n.* **Kid′napper**. [Vulgar *kid* (see **Kid**), a child, and vulgar *nab*, to steal.]

**Kidney**, kid′ni, *n.* one of two flattened glands, on each side of the loins, which secrete the urine. [M. E. *kidnere*—A.S. *cwid*, Scot. *kyte*, Ice. *kvidr*, the womb, the belly, and Ice. *nyra*, Ger. *niere*, a kidney.]       [like a *kidney*.

**Kidneybean**, kid′ni-bēn, *n.* a kind of *bean* shaped

**Kilderkin**, kil′dėr-kin, *n.* a *small* barrel : a liquid measure of 18 gallons. [Old Dut. *kindeken, kinneken*, Scot. *kinken*, dim. of Dut. *kind*, a child.]

**Kill**, kil, *v.t.* to put to death : to slay.—*n.* **Kill′er**. [M. E. *killen* or *cullen*—Ice. *kolla*, to hit on the head—*kollr*, the head ; or perh. a doublet of **Quell**.]

**Kiln**, kil, *n.* a large oven in which corn, bricks, &c. are dried : bricks piled for burning.—*v.t.* **Kiln′-dry**, to dry in a kiln. [A.S. *cyln;* Ice. *kylna*, a drying-house for corn : acc. to Skeat from L. *culina*, a kitchen.]

**Kilogramme**, kil′o-gram, *n.* a French measure of weight, equal to 1000 grammes, or 2¼ lbs. avoirdupois. [Lit. 1000 *grammes*, Gr. *chilioi*, 1000, and **Gramme**.]

**Kilometre**, kil′o-mē-tr, *n.* a French measure, being 1000 metres, or nearly ⅝ of a mile. [Fr.— Gr. *chilioi*, 1000, and **Metre**.]

**Kilt**, kilt, *n.* a kind of short petticoat worn by the Highlandmen of Scotland. [Northern E. *kilt*, to tuck up, from Dan. *kilte*, to tuck up, cf. Ice. *kilting*, a skirt.]

**Kin**, kin, *n.* persons of the same *family* : relatives : relationship : affinity. [A.S. *cyn* : Ice. *kyn*, Goth. *kuni*, family, race, from a root *gan*, to beget, found in L. *genus*, Gr. *genos*. See **Genus**, also **Kind, Kindred, King**.]

**Kind**, kīnd, *n.* those of a *kin*, a *race:* sort or species : nature : style : character : produce, as distinguished from money.—*adj.* having the feelings natural for those of the same family : disposed to do good to others.—*n.* **Kind′ness**.— *adj.* **Kind′-hearted**. [A.S. *cynd*—*cyn*, kin. See **Kin**.]

**Kindle**, kin′dl, *v.t.* to set fire to : to light : to inflame, as the passions : to provoke : to excite to action.—*v.i.* to take fire : to begin to be excited : to be roused.—*n.* **Kin′dler**. [Ice.

*kynda,* to set fire to, *kyndyll,* a torch, conn. with **Candle.**]

**Kindly,** kīnd′li, *adj.* (*orig.*) belonging to the *kind* or *race :* natural : benevolent.—*adv.* **Kind′ly.**—*n.* **Kind′liness.**

**Kindred,** kin′dred, *n.* (*lit.*) state of being of the same *family :* relatives : relationship :—*pl.* (*B.*) families.—*adj.* related : congenial. [M. E. *kinrede*—A.S. *cyn,* kin, and the suffix *-ræden,* expressing mode or condition.]

**Kine,** kīn, *n.pl.* (*B.*) cows. [M. E. *ky-en,* a doubled plur. of A.S. *cū,* a cow, the plur. of which is *cy ;* cf. Scotch *kye.*]

**Kinematics,** kin-i-mat′iks, *n.* the science of pure motion without reference to force.—*adj.* **Kine-mat′ical.** [Gr. *kinēma, -atos,* motion—*kineō,* to move.]

**Kinetics,** ki-net′iks, *n.* the science of motion viewed with reference to its causes.—*adj.* **Ki-net′ic.** [Gr. *kinētikos,* putting in motion—*kineō,* to move.]

**King,** king, *n.* the chief ruler of a nation : a monarch : a card having the picture of a king : the most important piece in chess.—*fem.* **Queen.**—*adjs.* **King′less, King′like.** [A.S. *cyning*—*cyn,* a tribe ; Sans *janaka,* father—root *gan,* to beget, therefore meaning 'father,' the father of a tribe, the 'king of his own kin ;' but acc. to Skeat, *cyning* = *cyn* (as above) and suffix *-ing,* meaning 'belonging to,' 'son of' the 'tribe,' the elected chief of the people. See **Kin.**]

**King-at-arms,** king-at-ärmz′, *n.* one of the three chief officers of the Heralds' College.

**Kingcrab,** king′krab, *n.* the *chief* or largest of the *crab* genus, most common in the Molucca Islands.

**Kingcraft,** king′kraft, *n.* the art of governing, mostly in a bad sense. [meadow crowfoot.

**Kingcup,** king′kup, *n.* the buttercup or upright

**Kingdom,** king′dum, *n.* the *state* or attributes of a *king :* the territory of a king : government : a region : one of the three grand divisions of Nat. Hist., as the animal, vegetable, or mineral.

**Kingfisher,** king′fish-ėr, *n.* a bird with very brilliant or *kingly* plumage, which feeds on *fish,* the halcyon. [golden-crested wren.

**Kinglet,** king′let, *n.* a little or petty king : the

**Kingly,** king′li, *adj.* belonging or suitable to a king : royal : noble.—*adv.* **King′ly.**—*n.* **King′-liness.**

**King's Bench,** kingz′ bensh, *n.* the *bench* or seat of the *king :* one of the high courts of law, so called because the king used to sit there, called Queen's Bench during a queen's reign.—**King's counsel,** an honorary rank of barristers.—**King's evidence,** a criminal allowed to become a witness against an accomplice.

**King's-evil,** kingz′-ē′vl, *n.* a scrofulous disease or *evil* formerly supposed to be healed by the touch of the *king.* [related to one another.

**Kinsfolk,** kinz′fōk, *n., folk* or people *kindred* or

**Kinsman,** kinz′man, *n.* a *man* of the same *kin* or race with another.—*fem.* **Kins′woman.**

**Kiosk,** ki-osk′, *n.* an Eastern garden pavilion. [Turk. *kieuchk.*]

**Kipper,** kip′ėr, *n.* a salmon in the state of *spawning :* a salmon split open, seasoned, and dried.—*v.t.* to cure or preserve, as a salmon. [Lit. *spawner*—Dut. *kippen,* to hatch, to seize ; Norw. *kippa.*] [E. form of Church.]

**Kirk,** kėrk, *n.* in Scotland, a *church.* [A Northern

**Kirtle,** kėr′tl, *n.* a sort of gown or outer petticoat : a mantle. [A.S. *cyrtel ;* Dan. *kiortel ;* Ice. *kyrtill :* perh. conn. with **Skirt** and **Shirt.**]

**Kiss,** kis, *v.t.* to salute by touching with the lips :

to treat with fondness : to touch gently.—*v.i.* to salute with the lips.—*n.* a salute with the lips.—*n.* **Kiss′er.** [A.S. *cyssan,* to kiss, *coss,* a kiss ; Ger. *küssen,* Dan. *kys ;* allied to **Choose.**]

**Kit,** kit, *n.* a small wooden tub : a soldier's outfit. [Dut. *kit, kitte,* a hooped beer-can.]

**Kit,** kit, *n.* a small pocket violin. [Contracted from A.S. *cytere ;* see **Cithern ; Guitar.**]

**Kitcat,** kit′kat, *adj.* the name of a London club in the reign of Queen Anne, which met at the house of Christopher *Kat :* a portrait 28 by 36 inches in size, so called from the portraits of the *Kitcat Club* painted by Sir G. Kneller.

**Kitchen,** kich′en, *n.* a room where food is *cooked :* a utensil with a stove for dressing food, &c. [A.S. *cicen ;* Ger. *küche,* Fr. *cuisine,* all from L. *coquina*—*coquor,* to cook.]

**Kitchen-garden,** kich′en-gär′dn, *n.* a *garden* where vegetables are cultivated for the *kitchen.*

**Kitchen-maid,** kich′en-mād, *n.* a *maid* or servant whose work is in the *kitchen.*

**Kite,** kīt, *n.* a rapacious bird of the hawk kind : a rapacious person : a paper toy for flying in the air. [A.S. *cyta ;* cf. W. *cûd,* Bret. *kidel,* a hawk.]

**Kitten,** kit′n, *n.* a young cat.—*v.i.* to bring forth young cats. [M. E. *kyton,* dim. of **Cat,** Scot. *kitling ;* L. *catulus,* a whelp.]

**Kleptomania,** klep-to-mā′ni-a, *n.* a *mania for stealing :* a morbid impulse to secrete things. [Gr. *kleptō,* to steal, and *mania,* madness.]

**Klick.** Same as **Click.**

**Knack,** nak, *n.* a petty contrivance : a toy : a nice trick : dexterity. [Orig. an imitative word ; cf. Gael. *cnac,* Dut. *knak,* a crack, Ger. *knacken,* to crack.]

**Knacker,** nak′ėr, *n.* a dealer in old horses and dog's-meat. [From Ice. *knakkr,* a saddle.]

**Knag,** nag, *n.* a knot in wood : a peg. [From a root found in Dan. *knag,* Ger. *knagge,* Ir. and Gael. *cnag,* a knot in wood, a knob.]

**Knaggy,** nag′i, *adj., knotty :* rugged.

**Knap,** nap, (obs.) *v.t.* to snap or break with a snapping noise :—*pr.p.* knapp′ing ; *pa.p.* knapped′. [Perh. from Dut. *knappen,* to crack or crush ; but cf. Celtic root *cnap.*]

**Knapsack,** nap′sak, *n.* a provision-sack : a case for necessaries borne by soldiers and travellers. [Dut. *knappen,* to crack, eat, and *zak,* a sack.]

**Knave,** nāv, *n.* a false, deceitful fellow : a villain : a card bearing the picture of a servant or soldier.—*n.* **Knav′ery,** dishonesty. [A.S. *cnafa, cnapa,* a boy, a youth, Ger. *knabe, knappe,* Gael. *knapach.*] [*adv.* **Knav′ishly.**

**Knavish,** nāv′ish, *adj.* fraudulent : villainous.—

**Knead,** nēd, *v.t.* to work and press together into a mass, as flour into dough.—*n.* **Knead′er.** [A.S. *cnedan ;* Ice. *knoda,* Ger. *kneten,* to knead.] [*kneading.*

**Kneading-trough,** nēd′ing-truf, *n.* a *trough* for

**Knee,** nē, *n.* the joint between the thigh and shin bones : a piece of timber like a bent knee. [A.S. *cneow, cneo ;* Ger. *knie,* L. *genu,* Gr. *gonu,* Sans. *jānu.*]

**Kneed,** nēd, *adj., having knees :* (*bot.*) having angular joints like the knee.

**Kneel,** nēl, *v.i.* to bend the *knee :* to rest or fall on the knee :—*pa.t.* and *pa.p.* kneeled′, knelt. [Formed from **Knee.**]

**Knell,** nel, *n.* the stroke of a bell : the sound of a bell at a death or funeral.—*v.i.* to sound as a bell : toll. [A.S. *cnyllan,* to beat noisily ; Sw. and Ger. *knall,* loud noise ; Ice. *gnella,* to scream, Low L. *nola,* a bell.]

**Knew**, nū, *past tense* of **Know**.

**Knickerbockers**, nik-ẽr-bok'ẽrz, *n.pl.* loose breeches gathered in at the knee. [From the wide-breeched Dutchmen in 'Knickerbocker's' (Washington Irving's) humorous *History of New York*.]

**Knick-knack**, nik'-nak, *n.* a trifle or toy. [A doubling of **Knack**.]

**Knife**, nīf, *n.* an instrument for cutting : a sword or dagger :—*pl.* **Knives**, nīvz. [A.S. *cnif*; Ger. *kneif*, knife, *kneifen*, to nip.]

**Knife-edge**, nīf'-ej, *n.* (*mech.*) a sharp piece of steel like a *knife's edge* serving as the axis of a balance, &c.

**Knight**, nīt, *n.* a man-at-arms : champion : one admitted in feudal times to a certain military rank : the rank of gentlemen next below baronets : a piece used in the game of chess.—*v.t.* to create a knight.—*adj.* and *adv.* **Knight'ly**. —**Knight of the Shire**, a member of parliament for a county. [Lit. a *youth*, a *servant*, A.S. *cniht*; Ger. and Dut. *knecht*, Dan. *knegt*, a servant.]

**Knight-errant**, nīt-ẽr'ant, *n.* a knight who travelled in search of adventures.—*n.* **Knighterr'antry**.

**Knighthood**, nīt'hood, *n.* the character or privilege of a *knight* : the order or fraternity of knights.                    [the royal household.

**Knight-marshal**, nīt-mär'shal, *n.* an officer of

**Knight-service**, nīt-sẽr'vis, *n.* tenure by a *knight* on condition of military *service*.

**Knit**, nit, *v.t.* to form into a *knot* : to tie together : to unite into network by needles : to cause to grow together : to unite closely : to draw together, to contract.—*v.i.* to interweave with needles : to grow together :—*pr.p.* knitt'ing ; *pa.t.* and *pa.p.* knit or knit.—*n.* **Knitt'er**. [A.S. *cnyttan*; from A.S. *cnotta*, a knot.]

**Knitting**, nit'ing, *n.* the work of a *knitter* : union, junction : the network formed by knitting.

**Knives**, plural of **Knife**.

**Knob**, nob, *n.* a hard *protuberance* : a hard swelling : a round ball. [A later form of **Knop**.]

**Knobbed**, nobd, *adj.* containing or set with *knobs*.

**Knobby**, nob'i, *adj.* full of *knobs* : knotty.—*n.* **Knobb'iness**.

**Knock**, nok, *v.i.* to *strike* with something hard or heavy : to drive or be driven against : to strike for admittance : to rap.—*v.t.* to strike : to drive against.—*n.* a sudden stroke : a rap. [A.S. *cnucian*—Gael. and Ir. *cnag*, a crack ; Ger. *knacken*, to crack or snap, like **Knack** and **Crack**, orig. imitative of the sound.]

**Knocker**, nok'ẽr, *n.* the hammer suspended by a door for making a *knock*.

**Knock-kneed**, nok'-nēd, *adj.* having *knees* that *knock* or touch in walking. [**Knock** and **Knee**.]

**Knoll**, nōl, *n.* a round hillock : the top of a hill. [A.S. *cnol*; Ger. *knollen*, a knob, lump ; perh. a dim. of Gael. *cnoc*, a hill.]

**Knoll**, nōl. Same as **Knell**.

**Knop**, nop, *n.* (*B.*) a knob, a bud. [A.S. *cnæp*; Dut. *knop*, Ger. *knopf*; conn. with and perh. derived from the Celt., as Gael. *cnap*.]

**Knot**, not, *n.* a wading bird much resembling a snipe, said in Drayton's *Polyolbion* to be named from king *Canute*, with whom it was a favourite article of food.

**Knot**, not, *n.* anything confusedly fastened or twisted, as threads, &c. : a figure the lines of which are interlaced : a bond of union : a difficulty : a cluster : the part of a tree where a branch shoots out : an epaulet : pad for supporting burdens carried on the head : (*naut.*) à division of the log-line, a mile.—*v.t.* to tie in a knot : to unite closely.—*v.i.* to form knots or joints : to knit knots for a fringe :—*pr.p.* knott'ing ; *pa.t.* and *pa.p.* knott'ed. [A.S. *cnotta*; Ger. *knoten*, Dan. *knude*, L. *nodus* for *gnodus*.]

**Knot-grass**, not'-gras, *n.* a common weed or *grass*, so called from the joints or *knots* of its stem.

**Knotty**, not'i, *adj.* containing *knots* : hard, rugged : difficult, intricate.—*n.* **Knott'iness**.

**Knout**, nowt, *n.* a whip formerly used as an instrument of punishment in Russia : punishment inflicted by the knout. [Russ. *knute*.]

**Know**, nō, *v.t.* to be informed of : to be assured of : to be acquainted with : to recognise : (*B.*) to approve :—*pr.p.* knōw'ing ; *pa.t.* knew (nū) ; *pa.p.* known (nōn).—*n.* **Know'ableness**. [A.S. *cnawan*; Ice. *kna*, Russ. *znate*, L. *nosco* for *gnosco*, Gr. *gignōskō*, Sans. *jna*.]

**Knowing**, nō'ing, *adj.* intelligent : skilful : cunning.—*adv.* **Know'ingly**.

**Knowledge**, nol'ej, *n.* assured belief : that which is known : information, instruction : enlightenment, learning : practical skill. [M. E. *knowleche*, where -*leche* is the Northern form of the suffix in *wed-lock*, being A.S. *lac*, gift, sport. See **Lark**, a game.]

**Knuckle**, nuk'l, *n.* projecting joint of the fingers : (*cook.*) the knee-joint of a calf or pig.—*v.i.* to bend the fingers : to yield. [M. E. *knokil*; prob. from a (not found) A.S. form, like Dut. and Dan. *knokel*.]

**Kobold**, kō'bold, *n.* Same as **Goblin**.

**Kopeck**, kō'pek, *n.* a Russian copper coin = ⅜d.

**Koran**, kō'ran, *n.* the Mohammedan Scriptures : Alcoran. [Lit. *reading*, the *book*—Ar. *quran*, reading—root *qara-a*, he read.]

**Kraal**, kräl, *n.* a Hottentot village or hut, so named by the Dutch settlers from the huts being arranged like a *coral*, or string of beads.

**Kraken**, krä'ken, *n.* a fabled sea-animal of enormous size. [Scand.]

**Kreatin, Kreosote**. See **Creatin, Creosote**.

**Kreese**. See **Crease**, a Malay dagger.

**Kyanise**, kī'an-īz, *v.t.* to preserve wood from dry-rot by immersing it in a solution of corrosive sublimate. [*Kyan*, the inventor.]

**Kyrie**, kir'i-ē, *n.* (*lit.*) *O Lord*: the first word of all masses : (*music*) a part of a mass. [Voc. case of Gr. *kyrios*, Lord.]

**Kythe**, kīth (Scot.), *v.t.* to make known.—*v.i.* to shew one's self, to appear. [Scot.—A.S. *cythan*, to make known. See **Uncouth**.]

# L

**La**, lä, *int.*, *lo!* see! behold! ah! indeed! [A.S.]

**Labarum**, lab'a-rum, *n.* a Roman military standard, adopted as the imperial standard after Constantine's conversion. It bore the Greek letters XP (Chr), joined in a monogram, to signify the name of Christ. [Gr.]

**Label**, lā'bel, *n.* a small slip of writing affixed to anything to denote its contents, ownership, &c.: (*law*) a paper annexed to a will, as a codicil : (*her.*) a fillet with pendants : (*arch.*) the dripstone over a Gothic window or doorway arch.— *v.t.* to affix a label to :—*pr.p.* lā'belling ; *pa.t.* and *pa.p.* lā'belled. [O. Fr. *label* (Fr. *lambeau*); perh. from O. Ger. *lappen* (Ger. *lappen*).]

**Labellum**, la-bel'um, *n.* the lower petal of a flower, esp. an orchis. [L. dim. of *labium*, a lip.]

**Labial**, lā'bi-al, *adj.* pertaining to the *lips* : formed by the lips.—*n.* a sound formed by the lips: a letter representing such a sound as *b, p.*—*adv.* **La′bially.** [Fr.—L. *labium*, a lip. See **Lip.**]

**Labiate,** lā′bi-āt, **Labiated,** lā′bi-āt-ed, *adj.* (*bot.*) having two unequal divisions, as in the monopetalous corolla of the mints. [See **Labial.**]

**Labiodental,** lā-bi-o-dent′al, *adj.* pronounced both by the *lips* and *teeth.* [L. *labium*, a lip, **Dental.**]

**Laboratory,** lab′or-a-tor-i, *n.* a chemist's *workroom:* a place where scientific experiments are systematically carried on: a place for the manufacture of arms and war-material: a place where anything is prepared for use. [L. *laborare*—*labor,* work.]

**Laborious,** la-bō′ri-us, *adj.* full of *labour:* toilsome: wearisome: devoted to labour: industrious.—*adv.* Labo′riously.—*n.* Labo′riousness. [Fr. *laborieux*—L. *laboriosus*—*labor.*]

**Labour,** lā′bur, *n.* toil or exertion, esp. when fatiguing: work: pains: duties: a task requiring hard work: the pangs of childbirth.—*v.i.* to undergo labour: to work: to take pains: to be oppressed: to move slowly: to be in travail: (*naut.*) to pitch and roll heavily. [Fr. *labeur*—L. *labor.*]      [or effort in the execution.

**Laboured,** lā′burd, *adj.* bearing marks of *labour*

**Labourer,** lā′bur-èr, *n.* one who *labours:* one who does work requiring little skill.

**Laburnum,** la-bur′num, *n.* a small tree with beautiful yellow flowers, a native of the Alps. [L.]

**Labyrinth,** lab′i-rinth, *n.* (*orig.*) a building consisting of halls connected by intricate *passages:* a place full of inextricable windings: an inexplicable difficulty: (*anat.*) the cavities of the internal ear. [Fr. *labyrinthe*—L. *labyrinthus*—Gr. *labyrinthos;* akin to *laura*, a passage.]

**Labyrinthian,** lab-i-rinth′i-an, **Labyrinthine,** lab-i-rinth′in, *adj.* pertaining to or like a *labyrinth:* winding: intricate: perplexing.

**Labyrinthiform,** lab-i-rinth′i-form, *adj.* having the *form* of a *labyrinth:* intricate.

**Lac,** lak, *n.* the term used in the E. Indies for 100,000, primarily applied to money. At the exchange of 2s. for the rupee, a lac = £10,000. [Hind. *lak,* Sans. *laksha,* 100,000, a mark.]

**Lac,** lak, *n.* a resinous substance, produced on trees in the East by the lac insect, used in *dyeing.* [Pers. *lak;* Sans. *laksha—ranj,* to dye.]

**Lace,** lās, *n.* a plaited string for fastening: an ornamental fabric of fine thread curiously woven. —*v.t.* to fasten with a lace: to adorn with lace. [Fr. *lacer,* to lace—L. *laqueus,* a noose.]

**Lacerable,** las′ėr-a-bl, *adj.* that may be *lacerated* or torn.

**Lacerate,** las′ėr-āt, *v.t.* to *tear:* to rend: to wound: to afflict. [L. *lacero, -atum,* to tear—*lacer,* torn; akin to Gr. *lakis* and *rakos,* a rent.]

**Laceration,** las-ėr-ā′shun, *n.* act of *lacerating* or tearing: the rent or breach made by tearing.

**Lacerative,** las′ėr-ā-tiv, *adj.* tearing: having power to tear.

**Lachrymal,** lak′ri-mal, *adj.* pertaining to *tears:* secreting or conveying tears.—*n.* same as **Lachrymatory.** [L. *lachryma* (properly *lacrima*), a tear; akin to Gr. *dakru,* E. **Tear.**]

**Lachrymary,** lak′ri-mar-i, *adj.* containing *tears.*

**Lachrymatory,** lak′ri-mā-tor-i, *n.* a vessel anciently interred with a deceased person, symbolising the *tears* shed for his loss. [Low L. *lacrymatorium—lachryma.*]

**Lachrymose,** lak′ri-mōs, *adj.* full of *tears:* generating or shedding tears.—*adv.* Lach′rymosely.

**Lacing,** lās′ing, *n.* a fastening with a *lace* or cord through eyelet-holes: a cord used in fastening.

**Lack,** lak, *v.t.* and *v.i.* to *want:* to be in want: to be destitute of.—*n.* want: destitution. [From an O. Low Ger. root found in Dut. *lak,* blemish; Ice. *lakr,* defective; akin to **Lax** and **Slack.**]

**Lackadaisical,** lak-a-dā′zi-kal, *adj.* affectedly pensive, sentimental. [*Alack-a-day.* See **Alack.**]

**Lack-a-day,** lak-a-dā′, *int.* See **Alack-a-day.**

**Lacker.** See **Lacquer.**

**Lackey,** lak′i, *n.* a menial attendant: a footman or footboy.—*v.t.* and *v.i.* to pay servile attendance: to act as a footman. [O. Fr. *laquay,* Fr. *laquais*—Sp. *lacayo,* a lackey; of uncertain origin, perh. Arab.]

**Laconic,** la-kon′ik, **Laconical,** la-kon′ik-al, *adj.* expressing in few words after the manner of the *Lacones* or *Spartans:* concise: pithy.—*adv.* **Lacon′ically.** [L.—Gr. *Lakōnikos—Lakōn,* a Laconian.]

**Laconism,** lak′on-izm, **Laconicism,** la-kon′i-sizm, *n.* a *laconic* or concise style: a short, pithy phrase.

**Lacquer, Lacker,** lak′ėr, *n.* a varnish made of *lac* and alcohol.—*v.t.* to cover with lacquer: to varnish. [Fr. *laque*—**Lac.**]

**Lacquerer,** lak′ėr-ėr, *n.* one who varnishes or covers with *lacquer.*

**Lactation,** lak-tā′shun, *n.* the act of giving *milk:* the period of suckling. [See **Lacteal.**]

**Lacteal,** lak′te-al, *adj.* pertaining to or resembling *milk:* conveying chyle.—*n.* one of the absorbent vessels of the intestines which convey the chyle to the thoracic ducts. [L. *lac, lactis,* akin to Gr. *gala, galaktos,* milk.]

**Lactescent,** lak-tes′ent, *adj.* turning to *milk:* producing milk or white juice: milky.—*n.* Lactes′cence. [L. *lactesco,* to turn to milk—*lac.*]

**Lactic,** lak′tik, *adj.* pertaining to *milk.*—**Lactic Acid,** an acid obtained from milk.

**Lactiferous,** lak-tif′er-us, *adj.* producing *milk* or white juice. [L. *lac,* and *fero,* to bear.]

**Lacuna,** la-kū′na, *n.* a gap or hiatus. [L.]

**Lacustral,** la-kus′tral, **Lacustrine,** la-kus′trin, *adj.* pertaining to *lakes.* [From L. *lacus,* a lake.]

**Lad,** lad, *n.* a boy: a youth.—*fem.* **Lass.** [W. *llawd;* Ir. *lath,* a youth, champion, perh. cognate with Goth. *lauths,* from *liudan,* to grow, and so akin to Ger. *lode* or *latte,* a shoot.]

**Ladanum,** lad′a-num, *n.* a resinous exudation from the leaves of a shrub growing round the Mediterranean. [L.—Gr. *lēdanon*—Pers. *ladan.* See **Laudanum.**]

**Ladder,** lad′ėr, *n.* a frame made with steps placed between two upright pieces, by which one may ascend a building, &c.: anything by which one ascends: a gradual rise. [A.S. *hlæder;* O. Ger. *hleitra,* Ger. *leiter.*]

**Lade,** lād, *v.t.* a form of **Load.** [See **Load.**]

**Lade,** lād, *v.t.* to throw in or out, as a fluid, with a ladle or dipper. [A.S. *hladan.*]

**Laden,** lād′n, *adj., laded* or loaded: oppressed.

**Lading,** lād′ing, *n.* that which *lades* or *loads:* load: cargo: freight. [See **Load.**]

**Ladle,** lād′l, *n.* a large spoon for *lading* or lifting out liquid from a vessel: the receptacle of a millwheel which receives the water that turns it. [See **Lade,** to throw in or out.]

**Lady,** lā′di, *n.* the mistress of a house: a wife: a title of the wives of knights, and all degrees above them, and of the daughters of earls and all higher ranks: a title of complaisance to any woman of refined manners. [A.S. *hlæf-dige—hlæf,* a loaf, bread, and *dægee,* a kneader, and thus lit. *a bread-kneader,* or = *hlâfweardige* {*i.e.* loaf-keeper, bread-distributer, see **Ward**, and thus a contr. fem. of **Lord**.]

**Ladybird**, lā'di-bėrd, *n.* a genus of little beetles, usually of a brilliant red or yellow colour, called also *Ladybug, Ladycow*. [Lit. ' Our *Lady's' bug*; **Lady** = Virgin Mary, and **Bird**, a corruption of **Bug**.]

**Lady-chapel**, lā'di-chap'el, *n.* a *chapel* dedicated to ' Our *Lady*,' the Virgin Mary.

**Ladyday**, lā'di-dā, *n.* the 25th March, the day of the Annunciation of ' Our *Lady*,' the Virgin Mary. [varieties of British *ferns*.]

**Ladyfern**, lā'di-fėrn, *n.* one of the prettiest

**Ladylike**, lā'di-līk, *adj.*, *like a lady* in manners : soft, delicate. [sweetheart.

**Ladylove**, lā'di-luv, *n.* a *lady* or woman *loved* : a

**Ladyship**, lā'di-ship, *n.* the title of a *lady*.

**Lag**, lag, *adj.*, *slack* : *sluggish* : coming behind.— *n.* he who or that which comes behind : the fag-end.—*v.i.* to move or walk slowly : to loiter :— *pr.p.* lagg'ing ; *pa.p.* lagged'. [From the Celt., as in W. *llag*, loose, sluggish, Gael. *lag*, feeble ; akin to Gr. *lagaros*, slack, L. *laxus*, loose.]

**Laggard**, lag'ard, *adj.*, *lagging* : slow : backward.

**Laggard**, lag'ard, **Lagger**, lag'er, *n.* one who *lags* or stays behind : a loiterer : an idler.

**Laggingly**, lag'ing-li, *adv.* in a *lagging* manner.

**Lagoon, Lagune**, la-gōōn'. *n.* a shallow *lake* or pond into which the sea flows. [It. *laguna*—L. *lacuna*, from root of **Lake**.]

**Laic, Laical.** See **Lay**, *adj.*

**Laid**, *pa.t.* and *pa.p.* of **Lay**.

**Lain**, *pa.p.* of **Lie**, to rest.

**Lair**, lār, *n.* a *lying-place*, esp. the den or retreat of a wild beast. [A.S. *leger*, a couch—*licgan*, to lie down ; Dut. *leger*, Ger. *lager*.]

**Laity**, lā'i-ti, *n.* the *people* as distinct from the clergy. [See **Lay, Laic**.]

**Lake**, lāk, *n.* a colour like *lac*, generally of a deep red. [Fr. *laque*. See **Lac**, a resinous substance.]

**Lake**, lāk, *n.* a large body of water within land.— **Lake dwellings** were settlements in prehistoric times, which were built on piles driven into a lake, and of which many remains have been discovered in late years. [A.S. *lac*—L. *lacus*, akin to Gr. *lakkos*, a pit, a pond.]

**Lakelet**, lāk'let, *n.* a little lake.

**Lakh**, *n.* See **Lac**, term used for 100,000.

**Laky**, lāk'i, *adj.* pertaining to a *lake* or *lakes*.

**Lama**, *n.* an animal. See **Llama**.

**Lama**, lā'ma, *n.* a Buddhist priest in Tibet. [Tib. *llama*, spiritual teacher or lord.]

**Lamaism**, lā'ma-izm, *n.* the religion prevailing in Tibet and Mongolia, a development of Buddhism, the object of worship being the Grand Lama.

**Lamb**, lam, *n.* the young of a sheep : one innocent and gentle as a lamb : the Saviour of the world. —*v.i.* to bring forth young, as sheep. [A.S.]

**Lambent**, lam'bent, *adj.* moving about as if *licking*, or touching lightly : playing about : gliding over : flickering. [L. *lambens*—*lambo*, to lick.]

**Lambkin**, lam'kin, *n.* a *little lamb*.

**Lamblike**, lam'līk, *adj.* like a *lamb* : gentle.

**Lame**, lām, *adj.* disabled in the limbs : hobbling : unsatisfactory : imperfect.—*v.t.* to make lame : to cripple : to render imperfect.—*adv.* Lame'ly. —*n.* Lame'ness. [A.S. *lama*, lame ; Ice. *lami*, broken, enfeebled, from *lama*, to break.]

**Lament**, la-ment', *v.i.* to utter grief *in outcries* : to wail : to mourn.—*v.t.* to mourn for : to deplore : —*n.* sorrow expressed in cries : an elegy or mournful ballad. [Fr. *lamenter*—L. *lamentor*, akin to *clamo*, to cry out.]

**Lamentable**, lam'ent-a-bl, *adj.* deserving or expressing sorrow : sad : pitiful, despicable.—*adv.* **Lam'entably**.

**Lamentation**, lam-en-tā'shun, *n.* act of *lamenting* : audible expression of grief : wailing :—*pl.* (*B.*) a book of Jeremiah, so called from its contents. [*tion.*

**Lamentingly**, la-ment'ing-li, *adv.*, *with lamenta-*

**Lamina**, lam'i-na, *n.* a *thin plate* : a thin layer or coat lying over another :—*pl.* **Laminæ**, lam'i-nē. —*adj.* **Lam'inable.** [L.]

**Laminar**, lam'i-nar, *adj.* in *laminæ* or thin plates : consisting of or resembling thin plates.

**Laminate**, lam'i-nāt, **Laminated**, lam'i-nāt-ed, *adj.* in *laminæ* or thin plates : consisting of scales or layers, one over another.—*n.* **Lamina'-tion**, the arrangement of stratified rocks in thin *laminæ* or layers.

**Laminiferous**, lam-in-if'er-us, *adj.* consisting of laminæ or layers. [L. *lamina*, and *fero*, to bear.]

**Lamish**, lām'ish, *adj.* a little *lame* : hobbling.

**Lammas**, lam'as, *n.*, *loaf-mass* or feast of first-fruits, on 1st August. [A.S. *hlaf-mæsse* and *hlammæsse*—*hlaf*, loaf, and *mæsse*, feast.]

**Lamp**, lamp, *n.* a vessel for burning oil with a wick, and so giving *light* : a light of any kind. [Fr. *lampe*—Gr. *lampas*—*lampō*, to shine.]

**Lampblack**, lamp'blak, *n.* the *black* substance formed by the smoke of a *lamp* : a fine soot formed of the smoke of pitch, &c.]

**Lampoon**, lam-pōōn', *n.* a personal satire in writing : low censure.—*v.t.* to assail with personal satire : to satirise :—*pr.p.* lampōōn'ing ; *pa.p.* lampōōned'. [O. Fr. *lampon*, orig. a drinking-song, with the refrain *lampons* = let us drink— *lamper* (or *laper*, to lap), to drink.]

**Lampooner**, lam-pōōn'er, *n.* one who writes a *lampoon*, or abuses with personal satire.

**Lampoonry**, lam-pōōn'ri, *n.* practice of *lampooning* : written personal abuse or satire.

**Lamprey**, lam'pre, *n.* a genus of cartilaginous fishes resembling the eel, so called from their attaching themselves to rocks or stones by their mouths. [Fr. *lamproie*—Low L. *lampreda*, *lampetra*—L. *lambo*, to lick, and *petra*, rock.]

**Lance**, lans, *n.* a long shaft of wood, with a spear-head, and bearing a small flag.—*v.t.* to pierce with a lance : to open with a lancet. [Fr.—L. *lancea*, akin to Gr. *longchē*, a lance.]

**Lance-corporal**, lans'-kor'po-ral, *n.* a soldier doing the duties of a corporal.

**Lanceolate**, lan'se-o-lāt, **Lanceolated**, lan'se-o-lāt-ed, *adj.* (*bot.*) having the form of a *lance*-head : tapering toward both ends. [L. *lanceolatus*— *lanceola*, dim. of *lancea*.]

**Lancer**, lan'sėr, *n.* name given to a kind of cavalry armed with a *lance* :—*pl.* a kind of dance.

**Lancet**, lan'set, *n.* a surgical instrument used for opening veins, &c. : a high and narrow window, pointed like a lance. [Fr. *lancette*, dim. of *lance*.]

**Lanch.** Same as **Launch.**

**Land**, land, *n.* earth, the solid portion of the surface of the globe : a country : a district : soil : real estate : a nation or people.—*v.t.* to set on land or on shore.—*v.i.* to come on land or on shore. [A.S. ; found in all the Teut. languages.]

**Landau**, lan'daw, *n.* a coach or carriage with a top which may be opened and thrown back, so called from *Landau* in Germany.

**Landbreeze**, land'brēz, *n.* a *breeze* setting from the *land* towards the sea.

**Landcrab**, land'krab, *n.* a family of *crabs* which live much or chiefly on *land*.

**Landflood**, land′flud, *n.* a *flooding* or overflowing of *land* by water : inundation.

**Landforce**, land′fōrs, *n.* a military *force* serving on *land*, as distinguished from a naval force.

**Landgrave**, land′grāv, *n.* a German earl.—*ns.* **Landgra′viate**, the territory of a landgrave, **Landgravine**, land′gra-vēn, the wife of a landgrave. [Lit. ‘land-earl,’ Land, and Ger. *graf*, earl, fem. *grä′fin*.]

**Landholder**, land′hōld-ėr, *n.* a *holder* or proprietor of *land*.

**Landing**, land′ing, *n.* act of *going on land* from a vessel : a place for getting on shore : the level part of a staircase between the flights of steps. — *adj.* relating to the unloading of a vessel's cargo.

**Landlady**, land′lā-di, *n.* a *lady* or woman who has property in *lands* or houses : the mistress of an inn or lodging-house.

**Landlock**, land′lok, *v.t.* to *lock* or inclose by *land*.

**Landlord**. land′lord, *n.* the *lord* or owner of *land* or houses : the master of an inn or lodging-house.                                      [used by sailors.]

**Land-lubber**, land′-lub′ėr, *n.* a landsman, a term

**Landmark**, land′märk, *n.* anything serving to *mark* the boundaries of *land* : any object on land that serves as a guide to seamen.

**Landrail**, land′rāl, *n.* the crake or corncrake, so named from its cry. [Land and Rail.]

**Landscape**, land′skāp, *n.* the *shape* or appearance of that portion of *land* which the eye can at once view : the aspect of a country, or a picture representing it. [Borrowed from the Dutch artists, Dut. *landschap*, lit. the *form* or *fashion* of the *land*, from *land* and *-schap*, a suffix = A.S. *-scipe*, and the mod. E. *-ship*.]

**Landslip**, land′slip, *n.* a portion of land that falls down, generally from the side of a hill, usually due to the undermining effect of water.

**Landsman**, landz′man, **Landman**, land′man, *n.* a *man* who lives or serves on *land* : one inexperienced in seafaring.

**Land-steward**, land′-stū′ard, *n.* a *steward* or person who manages a *landed* estate.

**Land-tax**, land′-taks, *n.* a *tax* upon *land*.

**Land-waiter**, land′-wāt′ėr, *n.* a custom-house officer who *waits* or attends on the *landing* of goods from ships. [Land and Waiter.]

**Landward**, land′ward, *adv.* towards the *land*.— *adj.* lying toward the land, away from the sea-coast : situated in or forming part of the country, as opposed to the town : rural.

**Lane**, lān, *n.* an *open* space between corn-fields, hedges, &c. : a narrow passage or road : a narrow street. [A.S. *lane ;* Scot. *loan*, North E. *lonnin*, Dut. *laan*.]

**Language**, lang′gwāj, *n.* that which is spoken by the *tongue* : human speech : speech peculiar to a nation : style or expression peculiar to an individual : diction : any manner of expressing thought. [Fr. *langage—langue*—L. *lingua* (old form *dingua*), the tongue, akin to L. *lingo*, Gr. *leichō*, Sans. *lih*, to lick.]

**Languid**, lang′gwid, *adj.*, *slack* or feeble : flagging : exhausted : sluggish : spiritless.—*adv.* **Lan′guidly**.—*n.* **Lan′guidness**. [L. *languidus* —*langueo*, to be weak, conn. with Lag.]

**Languish**, lang′gwish, *v.i.* to become *languid* or enfeebled : to lose strength and animation : to pine : to become dull, as of trade. [Fr. *languir* —L. *languesco—langueo*.]

**Languishingly**, lang′gwish-ing-li, *adv.* in a languishing, weak, dull, or tender manner.

**Languishment**, lang′gwish-ment, *n.* the act or state of *languishing* : tenderness of look.

**Languor**, lang′gwur, *n.* state of being *languid* or faint : dullness : listlessness : softness.

**Laniard**. Same as Lanyard.

**Laniferous**, lan-if′ėr-us, **Lanigerous**, lan-ij′ėr-us, *adj.*, *wool-bearing*. [L. *lanifer*, *laniger—lana*, wool, and *fero*, *gero*, to bear.]

**Lank**, langk, *adj.* (*lit.*) *faint* or *weak*: languid or drooping : soft or loose : thin.—*adv.* **Lank′ly**. —*n.* **Lank′ness**. [A.S. *hlanc ;* Dut. *slank*, Ger. *schlank*, slender, conn. with Lag and Slack.]

**Lansquenet**, lans′ke-net, *n.* a German foot-soldier : a game at cards. [Fr.—Ger. *landsknecht*—*land*, country, and *knecht*, a soldier.]

**Lantern**, lant′ėrn, *n.* a case for holding or carrying a light : a drum-shaped erection surmounting a dome to give light and to crown the fabric : the upper square cage which illuminates a corridor or gallery.—*v.t.* to furnish with a lantern. [Fr. *lanterne*—L. *lanterna*—Gr. *lamptēr*— *lampō*, to give light.]

**Lanthorn**, *n.* an obsolete spelling of Lantern, arising from the use of horn for the sides of lanterns.

**Lanyard**, **Laniard**, lan′yard, *n.* the lanyards are short ropes used on board ship for fastening or stretching. [Fr. *lanière*, perh. from L. *lanarius*, made of wool—*lana*, wool.]

**Lap**, lap, *v.t.* or *v.i.* to *lick up* with the tongue :— *pr.p.* lapp′ing ; *pa.t.* and *pa.p.* lapped. [A.S. *lapian ;* Fr. *laper*, Gr. *laptō*, allied to L. *lambo*, Sans. *lih*, to lick.]

**Lap**, lap, *n.* the *loose* or overhanging *flap* of anything : the part of the clothes lying on the knees when a person sits down : the part of the body thus covered : a fold.—*v.t.* to lay over or on.—*v.i.* to be spread on or over : to be turned over or upon. [A.S. *læppa*, a loosely hanging part ; Ice. *lapa*, to hang loose, Ger. *lappen*, anything hanging loose ; conn. with Flap.]

**Lap**, lap, *v.t.* to wrap, fold, involve. [M. E. *wlappen*, being a form of Wrap. See Envelope.]

**Lapel**, la-pel′, *n.* the part of the breast of a coat which folds over like a *lap*.—*adj.* **Lapelled**. [Dim. of Lap.]

**Lapful**, lap′fool, *n.* as much as *fills* a *lap*.

**Lapidary**, lap′i-dar-i, *adj.* pertaining to the cutting of *stones*.—*n.* a cutter of stones, especially precious stones : a dealer in precious stones. [L. *lapidarius—lapis*, *lapidis*, a stone.]

**Lapidescent**, lap-id-es′ent, *adj.* becoming *stone*: having the quality of petrifying or turning to stone.—*n.* **Lapides′cence**. [L. *lapidesco*, to become stone.]

**Lapidify**, la-pid′i-fi, *v.t.* to make into *stone*.—*v.i.* to turn into stone :—*pr.p.* lapid′ifying ; *pa.p.* lapid′ified.—*n.* **Lapidifica′tion**. [L. *lapis*, and *facio*, to make.]

**Lapidist**, lap′id-ist, *n.* Same as Lapidary.

**Lapper**, lap′ėr, *n.* one who *laps*, wraps, or folds.

**Lappet**, lap′et, *n.* a *little lap* or flap.—*adj.* **Lapp′eted**. [Dim. of Lap.]

**Lapse**, laps, *v.i.* to *slip* or glide : to pass by degrees : to fall from the faith or from virtue : to fail in duty : to pass to another proprietor by the negligence of a patron, &c. : to become void.—*n.* a *slipping* or *falling*: a failing in duty : a fault : a gliding, a passing. [L. *labor*, *lapsus*, to slip or fall, akin to Lap and Flap.]

**Lapwing**, lap′wing, *n.* the name of a bird of the plover family, also called peewit, from its peculiar cry. [M. E. *lappewinke*—A.S. *hleape-wince—hleapan*, to leap or run, and root of *wink*, which like Ger. *wanken* orig. meant to move from side to side : the name is descriptive of the movement of the bird.]

**Lar,** lär, *n.* among the ancient Romans, a household god, supposed to be animated by the soul of a deceased ancestor :—*pl.* **Lares,** lā'rēz. [L.]

**Larboard,** lär'bōrd, *n.* an obsolete naval term for the *left side* of a *ship* looking from the stern, now, by command of the Admiralty, substituted by the term *port,* to prevent the mistakes caused by its resemblance in sound to *starboard.*—*adj.* pertaining to the larboard side. [Ety. dub.]

**Larcenist,** lär'sen-ist, *n.* one who commits *larceny* : a thief.

**Larceny,** lär'sen-i, *n.* the legal term in England and Ireland for stealing : theft. [Fr. *larcin*— L. *latrocinium*—*latro,* Gr. *latris,* a robber.]

**Larch,** lärch, *n.* a cone-bearing kind of pine-tree. [L. and Gr. *larix.*]

**Lard,** lärd, *n.* the melted *fat* of swine.—*v.t.* to smear with lard : to stuff with bacon or pork : to fatten : to mix with anything. [Fr.—L. *laridum* or *lardum*; akin to Gr. *larinos,* fat—*laros,* sweet or dainty.]

**Lardaceous,** lärd-ā'shus, *adj.* of or like *lard.*

**Larder,** lärd'ér, *n.* a room or place where meat, &c. is kept. [Lit. a place where *lard* is kept.]

**Lardy,** lärd'i, *adj.* containing *lard* : full of lard.

**Large,** lärj, *adj.* great in size : extensive : bulky : wide : long : abundant.—*adv.* **Large'ly.**—*n.* **Large'ness.**—**At large,** without restraint or confinement : fully. [Fr.—L. *largus.*]

**Large-hearted,** lärj'-härt'ed, *adj.* having a *large heart* or liberal disposition : generous.

**Largess,** lärj'es, *n.* a present or donation. [Fr. *largesse*—L. *largitio*—*largior,* to give freely— *largus.*]

**Lariat,** lär'i-at, *n.* a lasso. [Sp.]

**Lark,** lärk, *n.* a well-known singing-bird.—*v.t.* to catch larks. [Scot. and M. E. *laverock*—A.S. *lawerce*; Dut. *leeuwerik, lercke,* Ger. *lerche.*]

**Lark,** lärk, *n.* a game, frolic. [A.S. *lac,* which appears as suffix in know-*ledge,* and wed-*lock.*]

**Larkspur,** lärk'spur, *n.* a plant with showy flowers.

**Larum,** lar'um, *n., alarm :* a noise giving notice of danger. [A contr. of **Alarm.**]

**Larva,** lär'va, *n.* an insect in its first stage after issuing from the egg, *i.e.* in the caterpillar state : —*pl.* **Larvae** (lär'vē).—*adj.* **Lar'val.** [L. *larva,* a spectre, a mask, a fanciful name applied to the caterpillar, because it hides as in a *mask* its higher life.]          [*larynx.*]

**Laryngitis,** lar-in-jī'tis, *n.* inflammation of the

**Laryngoscope,** la-ring'go-skōp, *n.* a kind of reflecting mirror for examining the *larynx* and the throat. [Gr. *larynx,* and *skopeo,* to behold.]

**Larynx,** lar'ingks or lär'ingks, *n.* the upper part of the windpipe : the throat.—*adjs.* **Laryn'geal, Laryn'gean.** [Gr. *larynx, laryngos.*]

**Lascar,** las'kar, *n.* a native East Indian sailor. [Hind.—Pers. *lashkar,* an army, from which *lashkari,* a camp-follower.]

**Lascivious,** las-siv'i-us, *adj.* lustful : tending to produce lustful emotions.—*adv.* **Lasciv'iously.** —*n.* **Lasciv'iousness.** [L. *lascivus*; Sans. *lash,* to desire.]

**Lash,** lash, *n.* a *thong* or cord : the flexible part of a whip : a stroke with a whip or anything pliant : a stroke of satire, a sharp retort.—*v.t.* to strike with a lash : to whip : to dash against : to fasten or secure with a rope or cord : to censure severely : to scourge with sarcasm or satire.—*v.i.* to use the whip : to attack severely. [From a Teut. root, seen in O. Low

Ger. *laske,* a flap, Ger. *lasche,* a stripe or flap, influenced perh. by Fr. forms from L. *laqueus,* a snare, and *laxus,* loose.]

**Lasher,** lash'ér, *n.* one who *lashes* or whips.

**Lashing,** lash'ing, *n.* a whipping with a *lash :* a chastisement : a rope for making anything fast.

**Lass,** las, *n.* (*fem.* of **Lad**), a girl, esp. a country girl. [Prob. a contr. of *laddess,* formed from **Lad**; or directly from W. *llodes,* fem. of *llawd,* a **Lad.**]

**Lassitude,** las'i-tūd, *n., faintness :* weakness : weariness : languor. [Fr. — L. *lassitudo*— *lassus,* faint ; akin to **Languid.**]

**Lasso,** las'ō, *n.* a rope with a *noose* for catching wild horses, &c. :—*pl.* **Lass'os.**—*v.t.* to catch with the lasso :—*pr.p.* lass'ōing ; *pa.p.* lass'ōed. [Port. *laço,* Sp. *lazo*—L. *laqueus,* a noose. See **Latch.**]

**Last,** last, *n.* a wooden mould of the foot on which boots and shoes are made.—*v.t.* to fit with a last. [A.S. *last,* Goth. *laists,* a footmark.]

**Last,** last, *v.i.* to continue, endure. [Same word as above, and lit. meaning to follow a trace or footmark, and so to follow out, to continue.]

**Last,** last, *n.* a weight generally estimated at 4000 lbs., but varying in different articles : a ship's cargo. [A.S. *hlæst*—*hladan,* to load ; Ger. *last,* Ice. *hlass.*]

**Last,** last, *adj., latest :* coming after all the others : final : next before the present : utmost : meanest. —*adv.* **Last, Last'ly.** [A contr. of **Latest.**]

**Lastingly,** last'ing-li, *adv.* in a *lasting* or enduring manner.

**Latch,** lach, *n.* a small piece of wood or iron to fasten a door.—*v.t.* to fasten with a latch. [A.S. *læccan,* to catch ; akin to L. *laqueus.* See **Lace.**]      [a shoe. [Dim. of **Latch.**]

**Latchet,** lach'et, *n.* a *lace* or buckle for fastening

**Latchkey,** lach'kē, *n.* a *key* to raise the *latch* of a door.

**Late,** lāt, *adj.* (comp. **Lat'er** ; superl. **Lat'est**), slow, tardy : behindhand : coming after the expected time : long delayed : far advanced towards the close : last in any place or character : deceased : departed : out of office : not long past.—*advs.* **Late, Late'ly.**—*n.* **Late'ness,** state of being late. [A.S. *læt,* slow ; Dut. *laat,* Ice. *latr,* Ger. *lass,* weary ; L. *lassus,* tired.]

**Lateen,** la-tēn', *adj.* applied to a triangular sail, common in the Mediterranean. [Lit. *Latin* or *Roman* sails, Fr.—L. *Latinus,* Latin.]

**Latency,** lā'ten-si, *n.* state of being *latent.*

**Latent,** lā'tent, *adj., lying hid :* concealed : not visible or apparent : not making itself known by its effects.—*adv.* **La'tently.** [L. *latens,* pr.p. of *lateo,* to lie hid ; akin to Gr. *lanthanō,* to hide.]

**Lateral,** lat'er-al, *adj.* belonging to the *side :* proceeding from or in the direction of the side.— *adv.* **Lat'erally.** [L. *lateralis*—*latus, lateris,* a side.]

**Lateritious,** lat-èr-ish'us, *adj., brick*-coloured. [L. *lateritius*—*later, lateris,* a brick.]

**Lath,** läth, *n.* a thin cleft slip of wood used in slating, plastering, &c. :—*pl.* **Laths** (läthz).— *v.t.* to cover with laths. [A.S. *lættu*; Dut. *lat,* Ger. *latte,* a lath, W. *llath,* a rod.]

**Lathe,** lāth, *n.* a machine for turning and shaping articles of wood, metal, &c. [Ice. *löth,* root uncertain.]

**Lather,** la*th*'er, *n.* a *foam* or froth made with water and soap : froth from sweat.—*v.t.* to spread over with lather.—*v.i.* to form a lather : to become frothy. [A.S. *leathor,* lather ; Ice. *lödr,* foam of the sea.]

**Latin,** lat'in, *adj.* pertaining to Latin or to the

Latins or Romans : written or spoken in Latin. —*n.* the language of the ancient Romans. [L. *Latinus*, belonging to *Latium*, the district in which Rome was built.]

**Latinise**, lat'in-īz, *v.t.* to give *Latin* terminations to.—*v.i.* to use words or phrases from the Latin.

**Latinism**, lat'in-izm, *n.* a *Latin* idiom.

**Latinist**, lat'in-ist, *n.* one skilled in *Latin*.

**Latinity**, la-tin'i-ti, *n.* purity of *Latin* style : the Latin tongue, style, or idiom.

**Latish**, lāt'ish, *adj.* somewhat *late*.

**Latitude**, lat'i-tūd, *n.* the distance of a place north or south from the equator : the angular distance of a celestial body from the ecliptic : fig. extent of signification : freedom from restraint : scope. [Fr.—L. *latitudo*, -*inis*—*latus*, broad.]

**Latitudinal**, lat-i-tūd'i-nal, *adj.* pertaining to *latitude* : in the direction of latitude.

**Latitudinarian**, lat-i-tūd-i-nā'ri-an, *adj.*, *broad* or *liberal*, esp. in religious belief : not orthodox : lax : not restricted by ordinary rules or limits. —*n.* one who in principle or practice departs from orthodox rule.—*n.* **Latitudina'rianism**.

**Latitudinous**, lat-i-tūd'i-nus, *adj.* having *latitude* or large extent.

**Latrine**, lat'rin, *n.* a place of convenience for soldiers in camp or barracks. [Fr.—L. *lavatrina* —*lavo*, to wash.]

**Latten**, lat'en, *n.* brass or bronze used for crosses : sheet tin, tinned iron-plate. [O. Fr. *laton*, Fr. *laiton*; from Fr. *latte*, a lath, the metal being wrought into thin plates. See **Lath**.]

**Latter**, lat'ér, *adj.*, *later* : coming or existing after : mentioned the last of two : modern : recent. [An irreg. comp. of **Late**.]

**Latterly**, lat'ér-li, *adv.* in *latter* time : of late.

**Lattice**, lat'is, *n.* a network of crossed *laths* or bars, called also **Latt'ice-work** : anything of lattice-work, as a window.—*v.t.* to form into open-work : to furnish with a lattice. [Fr. *lattis* —*latte*, a lath, from Ger. *latte*, cog. with E. **Lath**.]

**Laud**, lawd, *v.t.* to *praise* in words, or with singing : to celebrate.—*n.* **Laud'er**. [L. *laudo*— *laus*, *laudis*, praise, probably akin to Gr. *kluō*, Sans. *çru*, to hear.]

**Laudable**, lawd'a-bl, *adj.* worthy of being *praised*. —*adv.* **Laud'ably**.—*n.* **Laud'ableness**.

**Laudanum**, lawd'a-num, *n.* a preparation of opium : tincture of opium. [Orig. the same word as **Ladanum**, transferred to a different drug.]

**Laudatory**, lawd'a-tor-i, *adj.* containing *praise* : expressing praise.—*n.* that which contains praise.

**Laugh**, läf, *v.i.* to make the noise shewing or caused by mirth : to be gay or lively.—*n.* the sound caused by merriment.—**Laugh at**, to ridicule. [A.S. *hlihan*; Ger. *lachen*, Goth. *hlahjan*; prob. from the sound.]

**Laughable**, läf'a-bl, *adj.* fitted to cause *laughter* : ludicrous.—*adv.* **Laugh'ably**.—*n.* **Laugh'ableness**. [*laughter*, called nitrous oxide.

**Laughing-gas**, läf'ing-gas, *n.* a *gas* which excites

**Laughingly**, läf'ing-li, *adv.* in a *laughing* or merry way : with laughter.

**Laughing-stock**, läf'ing-stok, *n.* an object of ridicule, like something *stuck* up to be *laughed* at.

**Laughter**, läf'tér, *n.* act or noise of *laughing*.

**Launch**, **Lanch**, länsh, *v.t.* to throw as a *lance* or spear : to send forth : to cause to slide into the water.—*v.i.* to go forth, as a ship into the water : to expatiate in language.—*n.* act of launching or moving a ship into the water : the largest boat carried by a man-of-war. [Fr. *lancer*— *lance*, a lance. See **Lance**.]

**Launder**, lawn'dér, *n.* (*mining*) a trough used in washing ore. [Orig. a *washerwoman*, M. E. *lavandre*—Fr. *lavandière*—L. *lavare*.]

**Laundress**, lawn'dres, *n.* a *washerwoman*.

**Laundry**, lawn'dri, *n.* a place or room where clothes are *washed* and dressed. [See **Lave**.]

**Laureate**, law're-āt, *adj.* crowned with *laurel*.— *n.* one crowned with laurel : the poet-laureate or court poet.—*v.t.* to crown with laurel, in token of literary merit : to confer a degree upon. [See **Laurel**.]

**Laureateship**, law're-āt-ship, *n.* office of a *laureate*.

**Laureation**, law-re-ā'shun, *n.* act of *laureating* or conferring a degree.

**Laurel**, law'rel, *n.* the *bay-tree*, used by the ancients for making honorary wreaths. [Fr. *laurier*—L. *laurus*.]

**Laurelled**, law'reld, *adj.* crowned with *laurel*.

**Lava**, lä'va or lā'va, *n.* the melted matter discharged from a burning mountain, and that *flows* down its sides. [It. *lava*, a stream—L. *lavare*, to wash.]

**Lavatory**, lav'a-tor-i, *n.* a place for *washing* : a place where gold is got by washing. [See **Lave**.]

**Lave**, läv, *v.t.* and *v.i.* to *wash* : to bathe. [Fr. *laver*—L. *lavo*, *lavatum*, akin to Gr. *louō*, to wash.]

**Lave**, läv, *v.t.* (obs. and prov.) to lift or lade or throw out (as water from a boat). [Perh. Fr. *lever*—L. *levo*, to lift.]

**Lavender**, lav'en-dér, *n.* an odoriferous plant, so called from its being laid with newly *washed* clothes. [Fr. *lavande*. See **Lave**.]

**Laver**, lā'vér, *n.* a large vessel for *laving* or washing.

**Lavish**, lav'ish, *v.t.* to expend profusely : to waste. —*adj.* lavishing or bestowing profusely : prodigal : extravagant : wild : unrestrained.—*adv.* **Lav'ishly**. [From **Lave**, to throw out.]

**Lavishment**, lav'ish-ment, **Lavishness**, lav'ishnes, *n.* state of being *lavish* : profusion : prodigality.

**Law**, law, *n.* a rule of action *laid down* or established by authority : edict of a government : statute : the rules of a community or state : a rule or principle of science or art : the whole jurisprudence or the science of law : established usage : that which rules : conformity to law : that which is lawful : a theoretical principle educed from practice or observation : (*theol.*) the Mosaic code or the books containing it : (*B.*) the word of God, the Old Testament. [M. E. *lawe*— A.S. *lagu*, *lah*, from *lecgan*, to lay, or *licgan*, to lie ; Ice. *lag*; akin to L. *lex*, law, Gr. *legō*, to lay.]

**Lawful**, law'fool, *adj.* according to *law* : legal : constituted by law : rightful.—*adv.* **Law'fully**. —*n.* **Law'fulness**.

**Lawgiver**, law'giv-ér, *n.* one who *gives* or enacts *laws* : a legislator. [**Law** and **Giver**.]

**Lawless**, law'les, *adj.* unrestrained by *law* : illegal.—*adv.* **Law'lessly**.—*n.* **Law'lessness**.

**Lawmonger**, law'mung-ger, *n.* a *monger* or low dealer in *law*.

**Lawn**, lawn, *n.* a sort of fine *linen* or cambric.— *adj.* made of lawn. [Prob. Fr. *linon*—L. *linum*, modified perh. by confusion with L. *lana*, wool. See **Linen**.]

**Lawn**, lawn, *n.* an *open space* between woods : a space of ground covered with grass, generally in front of or around a house or mansion. [M. E. *laund*—O. Fr. *lande*, from Ger. *land* (see **Land**), or from Bret. *lann*.]

**Lawn-tennis**, lawn'-ten'is, *n.* a kind of tennis generally played on an open *lawn*.

**Lawsuit**, law'sūt, *n.* a *suit* or process in *law*.

**Lawyer**, law'yėr, *n.* one versed in or who practises *law* : (*B.*) a Jewish divine or expounder of the law. [**Law**, and suffix *-yer*.]

**Lax**, laks, *adj.*, *slack* : *loose* : soft, flabby : not crowded : not strict in discipline or morals : loose in the bowels.—*adv.* **Lax'ly**. [L. *laxus*, loose, *laxo*, *-atum*, to unloose ; prob. akin to **Languid**.]

**Laxation**, laks-ā'shun, *n.* act of *loosening* : state of being loose or slackened.

**Laxative**, laks'a-tiv, *adj.* having the power of *loosening* the bowels.—*n.* a purgative or aperient medicine.—*n.* **Lax'ativeness**. [Fr. *laxatif*— L. *laxo*.]

**Laxity**, laks'i-ti, **Laxness**, laks'nes, *n.* state or quality of being *lax* : want of exactness.

**Lay**, *pa.t.* of **Lie**, to lay one's self down.

**Lay**, lā, *v.t.* to cause to *lie down* : to place or set down : to beat down : to spread on a surface : to calm : to appease : to wager : to bring forth : to impose : to charge : to present.—*v.i.* to produce eggs : *pr.p.* lāy'ing ; *pa.t.* and *pa.p.* laid.—**Lay to** (*Pr. Bk.*) to apply with vigour. [It is the causal of *lie*, from A.S. *lecgan* ; Ice. *leggja*, Ger. *legen* ; Gr. *legō*. See **Lie**.]

**Lay**, lā, *n.* a *song* : a lyric or narrative poem. [O. Fr. *lai*, of Celtic origin, as W. *llais*, a sound, Gael. *laoidh*, a verse, sacred poem ; perh. conn. with Ger. *lied*.]

**Lay**, lā, **Laic**, lā'ik, **Laical**, lā'ik-al, *adj.* pertaining to the *people* : not clerical. [Fr. *lai*—L. *laicus*—Gr. *laikos*—*laos*, the people.]

**Layer**, lā'ėr, *n.* a bed or stratum : a shoot laid for propagation. [See **Lay**, *v.t.*]      [*layers*.]

**Layering**, lā'ėr-ing, *n.* the propagation of plants by

**Lay-figure**, lā'-fig'ūr, or **Layman**, lā'man, *n.* a wooden figure used by artists to represent the human body, and which serves as a model for attitude and drapery. [Dut. *leeman*, a jointed image—*ledt*, *lid*, a joint.]

**Layman**, lā'man, *n.* one of the *laity* : a non-professional man. [See **Lay**, **Laic**.]

**Lazar**, lā'zar, *n.* one afflicted with a filthy and pestilential disease like *Lazarus*, the beggar. [Fr. *lazare*, from *Lazarus* of the parable in Luke xvi.]

**Lazaretto**, laz-a-ret'o, **Lazaret**, laz'a-ret, *n.* a public hospital for diseased persons, esp. for such as have infectious disorders. [It. *lazzeretto* ; Fr. *lazaret*. See **Lazar**.]

**Lazar-house**, lā'zar-hows, *n.* a *lazaretto* : a hospital for quarantine. [**Lazar** and **House**.]

**Lazarlike**, lā'zar-līk, *adj.* like a *lazar* : full of sores : leprous.

**Lazy**, lā'zi, *adj.* disinclined to exertion : averse to labour : sluggish : tedious.—*adv.* **La'zily**.—*n.* **La'ziness**, state or quality of being lazy. [M. E. *lasche*—O. Fr. *lasche* (Fr. *lâche*), slack, weak, base—L. *laxus*, loose.]

**Lazzaroni**, laz-a-rō'ni, *n.* name given to the lowest classes in Naples, who used to live an idle out-cast life. [It., from Lazarus.]

**Lea** or **Ley**, lē (obs. **Lay**), *n.* a meadow : grass-land, pasturage. [A.S. *leah* ; cf. prov. Ger. *lohe*, *loh*, found also in place-names, as Water-loo = water-lea.]

**Lead**, led, *n.* a well-known metal of a bluish-white colour : the plummet for sounding at sea : a thin plate of lead separating lines of type :—*pl.* a flat roof covered with lead.—*v.t.* to cover or fit with lead : (*print.*) to separate lines with leads.— *n.* **Lead-pois'oning**, poisoning by the absorption

and diffusion of lead in the system. [A.S. ; Ger. *loth*.]

**Lead**, lēd, *v.t.* to shew the *way* by going first : to guide by the hand : to direct : to precede : to allure.—*v.i.* to go before and shew the way : to have a tendency : to exercise dominion :—*pr.p.* lead'ing ; *pa.t.* and *pa.p.* led.—*n.* first place : precedence : direction : guidance. [A.S. *lædan*, to make to go, causal form of *lídan*, to go ; Ice. *leida*, Ger. *leiten*, to lead.]

**Leaden**, led'n, *adj.* made of *lead* : heavy : dull.

**Leader**, lēd'ėr, *n.* one who *leads* or goes first : a chief : the leading editorial article in a news-paper : principal wheel in any machinery.

**Leadership**, lēd'ėr-ship, *n.* state or condition of a *leader* or conductor.

**Leading-strings**, lēd'ing-stringz, *n.pl.*, *strings* used to *lead* children when beginning to walk.

**Lead-pencil**, led'-pen'sil, *n.* a *pencil* or instrument for drawing, &c. made of black*lead*.

**Leaf**, lēf, *n.* one of the thin, flat parts of plants : anything beaten thin like a leaf : two pages of a book : one side of a window-shutter, &c. :—*pl.* **Leaves**, lēvz.—*v.i.* to shoot out or produce leaves :—*pr.p.* leaf'ing ; *pa.p.* leafed'. [A.S. ; Ger. *laub*, Dut. *loof*, a leaf.]

**Leafage**, lēf'āj, *n.*, *leaves* collectively : abundance of leaves : season of leaves or leafing.

**Leafless**, lēf'les, *adj.* destitute of *leaves*.

**Leaflet**, lēf'let, *n.* a *little leaf*.

**Leafy**, lēf'i, *adj.* full of *leaves*.—*n.* **Leaf'iness**.

**League**, lēg, *n.* a distance of about three English miles, but varying greatly in different countries. —A **Sea-league** contains 3½ Eng. miles nearly. [Fr. *lieue*—L. *leuca*, a Gallic mile of 1500 Roman paces ; from the Celt., as in Bret. *leo*, Gael. *leig*, a league.]

**League**, lēg, *n.* a *bond* or alliance : union for the promotion of mutual interest.—*v.i.* to form a league : to unite for mutual interest :—*pr.p.* leag'uing ; *pa.t.* and *pa.p.* leagued'. [Fr. *ligue*— Low L. *liga*—L. *ligo*, to bind.]

**Leaguer**, lēg'ėr, *n.* a camp, esp. of a besieging army. [Dut. *leger*, a lair. See **Beleaguer**.]

**Leak**, lēk, *n.* a crack or hole in a vessel through which liquid may pass : the oozing of any fluid through an opening.—*v.i.* to let any fluid into or out of a vessel through a leak. [Ice. *leka*, Dut. *lekken*, to drip.]

**Leakage**, lēk'āj, *n.* a *leaking* : that which enters or escapes by leaking : an allowance for leaking.

**Leaky**, lēk'i, *adj.* having a *leak* or *leaks* : letting any liquid in or out.—*n.* **Leak'iness**.

**Leal**, lēl, *adj.* true-hearted, faithful. [M. E. *lel*— Norm. Fr. *leal*, same as **Loyal**.]

**Lean**, lēn, *v.i.* to *incline* or *bend* : to turn from a straight line : to rest against : to incline towards : —*pr.p.* lean'ing ; *pa.t.* and *pa.p.* leaned' or leant (lent). [A.S. *hlínian* and causal form *hlǽnan* ; Dut. *leunen* ; akin to Gr. *klinō*, L. *in-clino*, to bend.]

**Lean**, lēn, *adj.* thin, wanting flesh : not fat.—*n.* flesh without fat.—*adv.* **Lean'ly**.—*n.* **Lean'ness**. [A.S. *hlæne* ; Low Ger. *leen* ; from **Lean**, to bend, from want of substance or support.]

**Leap**, lēp, *v.i.* to move with *springs* or *bounds* : to spring upward or forward : to jump : to rush with vehemence.—*v.t.* to spring or bound over :—*pr.p.* leap'ing ; *pa.t.* leaped' or leapt (lept) ; *pa.p.* leaped', rarely leapt.—*n.* act of leaping : bound : space passed by leaping : sudden transition. [A.S. *hleapan* ; Ice. *hlaupa*, to spring, Ger. *laufen*, to run.]      [over another like a *frog*.

**Leap-frog**, lēp'-frog, *n.* a play in which one boy

**Leap-year**, lēp′-yēr, *n.* every fourth *year* which *leaps* forward or adds one day in February, a year of 366 days.

**Learn**, lėrn, *v.t.* to acquire knowledge of, to get to know: to gain power of performing.—*v.i.* to gain knowledge: to improve by example. [A.S. *leornian*; Ger. *lernen*.]

**Learned**, lėrn′ed, *adj.* having *learning*: versed in literature, &c.: skilful.—*adv.* **Learn′edly**.—*n.* **Learn′edness**.

**Learner**, lėrn′ėr, *n.* one who *learns*: one who is yet in the rudiments of any subject.

**Learning**, lėrn′ing, *n.* what is *learned*: knowledge: scholarship: skill in languages or science.

**Lease**, lēs, *n.* a *letting* of tenements for a term of years: the contract for such letting: any tenure.—*v.t.* to let for a term of years:—*pr.p.* leas′ing; *pa.t.* and *pa.p.* leased′. [O. Fr. *lesser*, Fr. *laisser*, to let, leave, relinquish—L. *laxo*, to loose, *laxus*, loose.]

**Leasehold**, lēs′hōld, *adj.*, *held* by *lease* or contract.—*n.* a tenure held by lease.

**Leash**, lēsh, *n.* a *lash* or *line* by which a hawk or hound is held: a brace and a half, three.—*v.t.* to hold by a leash: to bind. [O. Fr. *lesse*, Fr. *laisse*, a thong to hold a dog by, a thong held *loosely*—L. *laxus*, loose.]

**Leasing**, lēz′ing, *n.* (*B.*) *falsehood*: lies. [A.S. *leasung*—*leas*, false, loose, Goth. *laus*, Ice. *los*.]

**Least**, lēst, *adj.* (serves as superl. of **Little**), *little* beyond all others: smallest.—*adv.* in the smallest or lowest degree. [A.S. *lǽst*, contr. from *lǽsest*, from root of **Less**.]

**Leather**, *leth′ėr*, *n.* the prepared skin of an animal.—*adj.* consisting of leather. [A.S. *lether*, leather; Dut. and Ger. *leder*.]

**Leathern**, *leth′ėrn*, *adj.* made or consisting of *leather*. [tough.

**Leathery**, *leth′ėr-i*, *adj.* resembling *leather*:

**Leave**, lēv, *n.*, *permission*: liberty granted: formal parting of friends: farewell. [A.S. *leaf*; Ice. *leyfa*, to permit; conn. with **Lief**, **Love**, **Believe**, **Furlough**.]

**Leave**, lēv, *v.t.* to allow to remain: to abandon, resign: to depart from: to have remaining at death: to bequeath: to refer for decision.—*v.i.* to desist: to cease:—*pr.p.* leav′ing; *pa.t.* and *pa.p.* left. [A.S. *lǽfan*; Ice. *leifa*, L. *linquo*, Gr. *leipō*, to leave. The primary meaning is to *let remain*; the root is seen in A.S. *lifian*, Ice. *lifa*, to be remaining, to **Live**, also in Ger. *bleiben* (= be-*leiben*), to remain.]

**Leaved**, lēvd, *adj.* furnished with *leaves*: having a leaf, or made with leaves or folds.

**Leaven**, lev′n, *n.* the ferment which makes dough *rise* in a spongy form: anything that makes a general change, whether good or bad.—*v.t.* to raise with leaven: to taint. [Fr. *levain*—L. *levamen*—*levo*, to raise—*levis*, light.]

**Leaves**, lēvz, *pl.* of **Leaf**.

**Leavings**, lēv′ingz, *n.pl.*, *things left*: relics: refuse.

**Lecher**, lech′ėr, *n.* a man addicted to lewdness. [Fr. *lécheur*—*lécher*, to lick; from O. Ger. *lecchon*, Ger. *lecken*, E. **Lick**; L. *ligurio*, to lick up what is dainty.]

**Lecherous**, lech′ėr-us, *adj.* lustful: provoking lust.—*adv.* **Lech′erously**.—*ns.* **Lech′erousness**, **Lech′ery**.

**Lectern**, lek′tėrn, *n.* a reading-desk in churches from which the Scripture lessons are read. [Corr. from Low L. *lectrinum*, a reading-desk—Low L. *lectrum*, a pulpit—Gr. *lektron*, a couch, and so a support for a book.]

**Lection**, lek′shun, *n.* a *reading*: a variety in a

manuscript or book: a portion of Scripture read a divine service. [L. *lectio*—*lego*, *lectum*, to read.]

**Lectionary**, lek′shun-ar-i, *n.* the R. Catholic service-book, containing *lections* or portions of Scripture. [in the ancient churches.

**Lector**, lek′tor, *n.* a *reader*: a reader of Scripture

**Lecture**, lek′tūr, *n.* a discourse on any subject: a formal reproof.—*v.t.* to instruct by discourses: to instruct authoritatively: to reprove.—*v.i.* to give a lecture or lectures. [See **Lection**.]

**Lecturer**, lek′tūr-ėr, *n.* one who *lectures*: one who instructs by giving set discourses.

**Lectureship**, lek′tūr-ship, *n.* the office of a *lecturer*.

**Lecturn**, lek′turn, **Lettern**, let′ėrn, *n.* Same as **Lectern**.

**Led**, led, *pa.t.* and *pa.p.* of **Lead**, to shew the way.

**Ledge**, lej, *n.* a shelf on which articles may be *laid*: that which resembles such a shelf: a ridge or shelf of rocks: a layer: a small moulding. [A.S. *lecgan*, to lay. See **Lay**, *v.t.*]

**Ledger**, lej′ėr, *n.* the principal book of accounts among merchants, in which the entries in all the other books are *laid up* or entered.

**Ledger-line**. See **Leger-line**.

**Ledgy**, lej′i, *adj.* abounding in ledges.

**Lee**, lē, *n.* the part toward which the wind blows.—*adj.* as in **Lee-side**, the sheltered side of a ship: **Lee-shore**, the shore opposite to the leeside of a ship. [Lit. a *sheltered place*, A.S. *hleow*, shelter; Ice. *hle*, Low Ger. *lee*; cf. Goth. *hlija*, a tent, prov. E. *lew*, a shelter.]

**Leech**, lēch, *n.* a *physician*: a blood-sucking worm.—*v.t.* to apply leeches to. [A.S. *læce*; Goth. *lekeis*, a physician, found also in Celt. and Slav. languages.]

**Leek**, lēk, *n.* a kind of onion: the national emblem of Wales. [A.S. *leac*, a leek, a plant, which is present also in **Char-lock**, **Gar-lic**, **Hem-lock**.]

**Leer**, lēr, *n.* a sly, sidelong look.—*v.i.* to look askance: to look archly or obliquely. [A.S. *hleor*, face, cheek; Ice. *hlyr*.]

**Leeringly**, lēr′ing-li, *adv.* with a *leering* look.

**Lees**, lēz, *n.pl.* sediment or dregs that settle at the bottom of liquor. [Fr. *lie*, ety. dub.]

**Leet**, lēt, *n.* (*Scot.*) a selected list of candidates for an office.

**Leeward**, lē′ward, *adj.* pertaining to or in the direction of the *lee*, or the part toward which the wind blows.—*adv.* toward the lee.

**Leeway**, lē′wā, *n.* the *way* or distance a ship is driven to *leeward* of her true course. [**Lee** and **Way**.]

**Left**, left, *pa.t.* and *pa.p.* of **Leave**.

**Left**, left, *adj.* the *weaker* as opposed to the stronger, hence right: being on the left side.—*n.* the side opposite to the right. [M. E. *lift*, *luft*, prob. a contr. of *lefed*, p. of A.S. *lēfan*, to weaken—*lēf*, weak; Dut. *loof*, weak.]

**Left-handed**, left-hand′ed, *adj.* having the *left* hand stronger and readier than the right: awkward: unlucky.—*ns.* **Left-hand′edness**, **Left-hand′iness**, awkwardness.

**Leg**, leg, *n.* one of the limbs by which animals walk: a long, slender support of anything, as of a table.—*adj.* **Legged′**, having legs. [Ice. *leggr*, a stalk, Dan. *läg*, Sw. *lägg*.]

**Legacy**, leg′a-si, *n.* that which is *left* to one by *will*: a bequest of personal property. [L. as if *legatia*, for *legatum*—*lego*, to leave by will.]

**Legacy-hunter**, leg′a-si hunt′ėr, *n.* one who *hunts* after *legacies* by courting those likely to leave them.

**Legal**, lē′gal, *adj.* pertaining to or according to

*law* : lawful : created by law.—*adv.* **Le′gally.**—*n.* **Legal′ity.** [Fr.—L. *legalis*—*lex, legis*, law.]

**Legalise**, lē′gal-īz, *v.t.* to make *legal* or lawful : to authorise : to sanction.

**Legate**, leg′āt, *n.* an ambassador, esp. from the Pope.—*n.* **Leg′ateship**, the office of a legate. [Fr. *légat*, It. *legato*—L. *legatus*—*lego*, to send with a commission.]

**Legatee**, leg-a-tē′, *n.* one to whom a *legacy* is left.

**Legatine**, leg′a-tīn, *adj.* of or relating to a *legate*.

**Legation**, le-gā′shun, *n.* the person or persons sent as *legates* or ambassadors : a deputation.

**Legend**, lej′end or lē′-, *n.* a marvellous or romantic story from early times : the motto on a coat of arms, medal, or coin. [Fr.—Low L. *legenda*, a book of chronicles of the saints *read* at matins —L. *legendus*, to be read—*lego*, to read.]

**Legendary**, lej′end-ar-i, *n.* a book of *legends* : one who relates legends.—*adj.* consisting of legends : romantic : fabulous.

**Legerdemain**, lej-ėr-de-mān′, *n.*, *lightness* or *nimbleness of hand* : sleight-of-hand : jugglery. [O. Fr. *legier* (Fr. *léger*) *de main*, 'light of hand' —L. as if *leviarius*—*levis*, light, and Fr. *de*, of, *main*, L. *manus*, hand.]

**Leger-line**, lej′ėr-līn, *n.* (*mus.*) one of the short lines added above or below the staff to extend its compass. [Fr. *léger*, light, and **Line.**]

**Legging**, leg′ing, *n.* a covering for the *leg*.

**Legible**, lej′i-bl, *adj.* that may be *read* : clear and distinct : that may be understood.—*adv.* **Leg′ibly.**—*ns.* **Leg′ibleness, Legibil′ity.** [L. *legibilis*—*lego*.]

**Legion**, lē′jun, *n.* in ancient Rome, a body of soldiers of from three to six thousand : a military force : a great number. [Fr.—L. *legio*—*lego*, to choose, to levy.]

**Legionary**, lē′jun-ar-i, *adj.* relating to or consisting of a *legion* or legions : containing a great number.—*n.* a soldier of a legion. [L. *legionarius*.]

**Legislate**, lej′is-lāt, *v.i.* to *bring* forward, propose, or make *laws*.—*n.* **Legisla′tion.** [L. *lex, legis*, law, *fero, latum*, to bear, propose.]

**Legislative**, lej′is-lāt-iv, *adj.*, *giving* or *enacting laws* : pertaining to legislation.

**Legislator**, lej′is-lā-tor, *n.* one who *makes laws* : a lawgiver.—*fem.* **Leg′islatress.**

**Legislature**, lej′is-lāt-ūr, *n.* the body of men in a state who have the power of *making laws*.

**Legist**, lē′jist, *n.* one skilled in the laws. [Fr. *légiste*—Low L. *legista*—L. *lex*.]

**Legitimacy**, le-jit′i-ma-si, *n.* state of being *legitimate* or according to law : lawfulness of birth : genuineness : regular deduction.

**Legitimate**, le-jit′i-māt, *adj.* lawful : lawfully begotten : genuine : fairly deduced : following by natural sequence : authorised by usage.—*v.t.* to make lawful : to give the rights of a legitimate child to an illegitimate one.—*adv.* **Legit′imately.** [Low L. *legitimo, -atum*—L. *lex*.]

**Legitimation**, le-jit-i-mā′shun, *n.* act of rendering *legitimate*, esp. of conferring the privileges of lawful birth.

**Legitimist**, le-jit′i-mist, *n.* one who supports *legitimate* authority : in France, an adherent of the Bourbons deposed in 1830.

**Legless**, leg′les, *adj.* without legs.

**Legume**, leg′ūm, **Legumen**, le-gū′men, *n.* (*bot.*) a seed-vessel which splits into two valves, having the seeds attached to the ventral suture only : a pod, as of the pea, bean, &c. :—*pl.* **Legu′mens, Legu′mina.** [Fr.—L. *legumen*—*lego*, to gather ; so called because *gathered* for food.]

**Leguminous**, le-gū′min-us, *adj.* bearing *legumes* as seed-vessels : consisting of pulse.

**Leisure**, lē′zhōōr or lezh′-, *n.* time free from employment : freedom from occupation.—*adj.* unoccupied. [M. E. *leyser*—O. Fr. *leisir*, 'to be permitted'—L. *licet*, it is permitted.]

**Leisurely**, lē′zhōōr-li, *adj.* done at *leisure* : slow : deliberate.—*adv.* in a leisurely manner.

**Leman**, lē′man, *n.* a sweetheart. [M. E. *lemman*, earlier form *leofmon*—A.S. *leof*, loved, and **Man.**]

**Lemma**, lem′a, *n.* (*math.*) a proposition demonstrated for the purpose of being used in a subsequent proposition. [L.—Gr. *lēmma*—*lambanō*, to receive, assume.]

**Lemming**, lem′ing, *n.* a species of rat in northern countries, remarkable for migrating southward in great numbers. [Norw. *lemming*, Sw. *lemel*, Lap. *loumik*.]

**Lemon**, lem′un, *n.* an oval fruit, resembling the orange, with an acid pulp : the tree that bears lemons. [Fr. *limon*—Pers. *limun*.]

**Lemonade**, lem-un-ād′, *n.* a drink made of *lemon-juice*, water, and sugar.

**Lemur**, lē′mur, *n.* an animal in Madagascar, allied to the monkey, which goes about at night, whence its name. [L. *lemur*, a ghost.]

**Lend**, lend, *v.t.* to give for a short time something to be returned : to afford or grant, in general : to let for hire :—*pr.p.* lend′ing ; *pa.t.* and *pa.p.* lent.—*n.* **Lend′er.** [M. E. *lenen*—A.S. *lænan* ; Ger. *leihen*. See **Loan.**]

**Length**, length, *n.* quality of being *long* : extent from end to end : the longest measure of anything : long continuance : detail. [A.S. *length* —*lang*, long.]

**Lengthen**, length′n, *v.t.* to increase in *length* : to draw out.—*v.i.* to grow longer.

**Lengthwise**, length′wīz, *adv.* in the *way* or direction of the *length*. [For **Lengthways.**]

**Lengthy**, length′i, *adj.* of great *length* : rather long.—*adv.* **Length′ily.**—*n.* **Length′iness.**

**Lenient**, lē′ni-ent, *adj.*, *softening* or *mitigating* : mild : merciful.—*n.* (*med.*) that which softens : an emollient.—*n.* **Le′niency.** [L. *leniens, -entis*, pr.p. of *lenio*, to soften—*lenis*, soft.]

**Lenitive**, len′it-iv, *adj.*, *softening* or *mitigating* : laxative.—*n.* (*med.*) an application for easing pain : a mild purgative.

**Lenity**, len′i-ti, *n.* mildness : clemency.

**Lens**, lenz, *n.* (*optics*) a piece of glass or other transparent substance with one or both sides convex, so called from its likeness to a *lentil* seed : the crystalline humour of the eye. [L. *lens, lentis*, the lentil.]

**Lent**, lent, *n.* a fast of forty days, observed in commemoration of the fast of our Saviour, beginning with Ash-Wednesday and continuing till Easter. [M. E. *lenten*—A.S. *lencten*, the spring : Dut. *lente*, Ger. *lenz* ; acc. to some derived from root of **Long**, because in spring the days grow *long*.]

**Lenten**, lent′en, *adj.* relating to or used in *Lent* : sparing.

**Lenticular**, len-tik′ū-lar, **Lentiform**, len′ti-form, *adj.* resembling a *lens* or *lentil* seed : double-convex.—*adv.* **Lentic′ularly.** [L. *lenticularis* —*lenticula*, dim. of *lens*, a lentil.]

**Lentil**, len′til, *n.* an annual plant, common near the Mediterranean, bearing pulse used for food. [Fr. *lentille*—L. *lens, lentis*, the lentil.]

**Lentisk**, len′tisk, *n.* the mastic-tree. [Fr. *lentisque* —L. *lentiscus*—*lentus*, sticky ; so called from the stickiness of its gum.] [Lentisk.]

**Lentous**, len′tus, *adj.*, *sticky* : viscid. [See

**Leo,** lē′ō, *n.* (*astr.*) the *Lion*, the fifth sign of the zodiac. [L.]

**Leonine,** lē′o-nīn, *adj.* of or like a *lion*.

**Leonine,** lē′o-nīn, *adj.* a kind of Latin verse which rhymes at the middle and end, much in use among the Latin hymn-writers of the Middle Ages. [Said to be named from Leoninus, a canon in Paris in the 12th century; or from Pope Leo II., who was a lover of music.]

**Leopard,** lep′ard, *n.* an animal of the cat-kind, with a spotted skin. [O. Fr.—L. *leopardus*—Gr. *leopardos*—*leōn*, lion, *pardos*, pard; because supposed by the ancients to be a mongrel between the pard or panther and lioness.]

**Leper,** lep′ėr, *n.* one affected with leprosy, which covers the skin with *scales*. [L.—Gr. *lepra*, leprosy—*lepros*, scaly—*lepos*, a scale—*lepō*, to peel off.]

**Lepidoptera,** lep-i-dop′tėr-a, *n.pl.* an order of insects, with four *wings* covered with very fine *scales* like powder, as the butterfly, moth, &c. [Gr. *lepis*, *lepidos*, a scale, *pteron*, a wing.]

**Lepidopteral,** lep-i-dop′tėr-al, **Lepidopterous,** lep-i-dop′tėr-us, *adj.* pertaining to the *lepidoptera*.

**Leporine,** lep′o-rīn, *adj.* pertaining to or resembling the *hare*. [L. *leporinus*—*lepus*, *leporis*, the hare.]    [by *scales* or scurfy scabs.

**Leprosy,** lep′ro-si, *n.* a disease of the skin marked

**Leprous,** lep′rus, *adj.* affected with *leprosy*.—*adv.* **Lep′rously.**—*n.* **Lep′rousness.** [See Leper.]

**Lesion,** lē′zhun, *n.* a *hurt*: (*med.*) an injury or wound. [Fr.—L. *lœsio*—*lœdo*, *lœsum*, to hurt.]

**Less,** les, *adj.* (serves as comp. of **Litt′le**), diminished: smaller.—*adv.* not so much: in a lower degree.—*n.* a smaller portion: (*B.*) the inferior or younger. [A.S. *lœs*, *lœssa*; comparative form from a root *las*, feeble, found also in Goth. *lasivs*, weak, Ice. *las*, weakness, and which is not conn. with the root of *little*.]

**Lessee,** les-sē′, *n.* one to whom a *lease* is granted.

**Lessen,** les′n, *v.t.* to make *less*, in any sense: to weaken: to degrade.—*v.i.* to become less.

**Lesser,** les′ėr, *adj.* (*B.*) *less*: smaller: inferior. [A double comp., formed from **Less**.]

**Lesson,** les′n, *n.* a portion of Scripture *read* in divine service: that which a pupil learns at a time: a precept or doctrine inculcated: instruction derived from experience: severe lecture. [Fr. *leçon*—L. *lectio*—*lego*, to gather, to read. See **Lection**.]

**Lessor,** les′or, *n.* one who grants a *lease*.

**Lest,** lest, *conj.* that not: for fear that. [From the A.S. phrase *thy lœs the* (that the less = L. *quóminus*), the first word being dropped, while the third joined to the second made *lesthe*, *leste*. See **Less**.]

**Let,** let, *v.t.* to *slacken* or *loose restraint upon*: to give leave or power to: to allow, permit, suffer: to grant to a tenant or hirer:—*pr.p.* lett′ing; *pa.t.* and *pa.p.* let. [A.S. *lœtan*, to permit—*lœt*, Ice. *latr*, slow, lazy, slack; Ger. *lassen*, Fr. *laisser*, to let, permit. See **Late**.]

**Let,** let, *v.t.* (*B.*) to prevent: to hinder.—*n.* (*law*) hinderance, obstruction: delay. [A.S. *lettan*, to make late—*lœt*, slow, slack, being same root as above.]

**Lethal,** lē′thal, *adj.*, *death-dealing*, *blotting out*: deadly: mortal. [L. *lethalis*—*lethum*, *letum*, death; akin to *leo*, simple form of *deleo*, to blot out, or to Sans. *li*, to melt, dissolve.]

**Lethargic,** le-thär′jik, **Lethargical,** le-thär′jik-al, *adj.* pertaining to *lethargy*: unnaturally sleepy:

dull.—*adv.* **Lethar′gically.** [L. *lethargicus* —Gr. *lethargikos*.]

**Lethargy,** leth′ar-ji, *n.* heavy unnatural slumber: dullness. [Fr.—L.—Gr. *lēthargia*, drowsy forgetfulness—*lēthē*, forgetfulness.]

**Lethe,** lē′the, *n.* (*myth.*) one of the rivers of hell said to cause *forgetfulness* of the past to all who drank of its waters: oblivion. [Gr.—*lēthō*, old form of *lanthanō*, to forget.]

**Lethean,** le-thē′an, *adj.*, *of Lethe*: oblivious.

**Lethiferous,** le-thif′ėr-us, *adj.*, *carrying death*: deadly. [L. *lethifer*—*lethum*, death, and *fero*, to bear.]

**Letter,** let′ėr, *n.* a conventional mark to express a sound: a written or printed message: literal meaning: a printing-type:—*pl.* learning.—*v.t.* to stamp letters upon.—*n.* **Lett′erer.** [Fr. *lettre*—L. *litera*—*lino*, *litum*, to smear; so called because *smeared* or scrawled on parchment.]

**Lettered,** let′ėrd, *adj.* marked with *letters*: educated: versed in literature: belonging to learning.    [or casts *letters* or types.

**Letter-founder,** let′ėr-fownd′ėr, *n.* one who *founds*

**Lettering,** let′ėr-ing, *n.* the act of *impressing letters*: the letters impressed.

**Lett′er-of-cred′it,** *n.* a *letter* authorising *credit* or cash to a certain sum to be paid to the bearer.—

**Lett′er-of-marque** (märk), *n.* a commission given to a private ship by a government to make reprisals on the vessels of another state. [See **Marque**.]

**Letterpress,** let′ėr-pres, *n.*, *letters impressed* or matter printed from type, as distinguished from engraving.

**Letters-patent,** let′ėrz-pā′tent, *n.* a writing conferring a patent or authorising a person to enjoy some privilege, so called because written on *open* sheets of parchment. [See **Patent**.]

**Lettuce,** let′is, *n.* a plant containing a *milky* white juice, the leaves of which are used as a salad. [O. Fr. *laictuce*, Fr. *laitue*—L. *lactuca*—*lac*, milk.]

**Levant,** le-vant′, *n.* the point where the sun *rises*: the East: the coasts of the Mediterranean east of Italy.—*adj.* **Lev′ant** or **Lē′vant**, eastern. [It. *levante*—L. *levare*, to raise.]

**Levanter,** le-vant′ėr, *n.* a strong easterly wind in the *Levant* or eastern part of the Mediterranean.

**Levantine,** le-vant′in, *adj.* belonging to the *Levant*.

**Levee,** lev′ē, *n.* a morning assembly of visitors: an assembly received by a sovereign or other great personage. [Fr. *levée*, a rising—*lever*.]

**Level,** lev′el, *n.* a horizontal line or surface: a surface without inequalities: proper position: usual elevation: state of equality: the line of direction: an instrument for shewing the horizontal.—*adj.* horizontal: even, smooth: even with anything else: in the same line or plane: equal in position or dignity.—*v.t.* to make horizontal: to make flat or smooth: to make equal: to take aim:—*pr.p.* lev′elling; *pa.t.* and *pa.p.* lev′elled. [O. Fr. *livel*, *liveau* (Fr. *niveau*)—L. *libella*, a plummet, from *libra*, a level, a balance.]

**Leveller,** lev′el-ėr, *n.* one who *levels* or makes equal.

**Levelling,** lev′el-ing, *n.* the act of making uneven surfaces level: the process of finding the differences in level between different points on the surface of the earth.    [or equal.

**Levelness,** lev′el-nes, *n.* state of being *level*, even,

**Lever,** lē′vėr, *n.* a bar of metal or other substance turning on a support called the fulcrum or prop, for raising weights. [Lit. *that which lifts* or *raises*, Fr. *lévier*—*lever*—L. *levo*, to raise.]

**Leverage**, lē′vėr-āj, *n.* the mechanical *power* gained by the use of the *lever*.

**Leveret**, lev′ėr-et, *n.* a *young hare*: a hare in its first year. [O. Fr. *levrault*, Fr. *lièvre*—L. *lepus, leporis*, a hare.]

**Leviable**, lev′i-a-bl, *adj.* able to be *levied* or assessed and collected.

**Leviathan**, le-vī′a-than, *n.* (*B.*) a huge aquatic animal, described in the book of Job: anything of huge size. [Heb. *liv′yâthân*—*lv′yah*, a wreath, Ar. *lawa′*, to bend or twist; so called from its twisting itself in folds.]

**Levigate**, lev′i-gāt, *v.t.* to make *smooth*: to grind to a fine, impalpable powder.—*n.* **Leviga′tion**. [L. *levigo, levigatum*—*levis*, Gr. *leios*, smooth, akin to **Level**.]

**Levitation**, lev-i-tā′shun, *n.* act of rendering *light*. [L. *levis*, light.]

**Levite**, lē′vīt, *n.* a descendant of *Levi*: an inferior priest of the ancient Jewish Church.—*adjs.* **Levit′ic, Levit′ical**.—*adv.* **Levit′ically**. [Heb. *Levi*, a son of Jacob, whose descendants were priests.]

**Leviticus**, le-vit′i-kus, *n.* the name of one of the books of the Old Testament, so called from its containing the laws, &c. relating to the *Levites.*

**Levity**, lev′it-i, *n.*, *lightness* of weight: lightness of temper or conduct: thoughtlessness: disposition to trifle: vanity. [L. *levitas*—*levis*, light.]

**Levy**, lev′i, *v.t.* to *raise*: to collect by authority, as an army or a tax:—*pr.p.* lev′ying; *pa.t.* and *pa.p.* lev′ied.—*n.* the act of collecting by authority: the troops so collected. [Fr. *lever*—L. *levo*, to make light or raise—*levis*, light.]

**Lewd**, lūd or lōōd, *adj.* ignorant, vicious, or bad, so in *B.*: lustful: licentious: unchaste: debauched.—*adv.* **Lewd′ly**.—*n.* **Lewd′ness**. [A.S. *læwed*, lay, belonging to the laity, either the *pa.p.* of the verb *læwan*, to weaken, and so meaning weak, simple, untaught, or from *leod*, the people. See **Laity**.]

**Lexicographer**, leks-i-kog′ra-fėr, *n.* one skilled in *lexicography* or the art of compiling dictionaries.

**Lexicography**, leks-i-kog′ra-fi, *n.* the art of *writing a dictionary.*—*adjs.* **Lexicograph′ic, Lexicograph′ical**. [Gr. *lexikon*, and *graphō*, to write.]

**Lexicologist**, leks-i-kol′o-jist, *n.* one skilled in *lexicology.*

**Lexicology**, leks-i-kol′o-ji, *n.* that branch of philology which treats of the proper signification and use of words. [Gr. *lexis*, and *logos*, a discourse or treatise.]

**Lexicon**, leks′i-kon, *n.* a *word-book* or dictionary. —*adj.* **Lex′ical**, belonging to a lexicon. [Gr. *lexikon*—*lexis*, a word—*legō*, to speak.]

**Ley**, lē, *n.* Same as **Lea**.

**Liability**, lī-a-bil′i-ti, *n.* state of being *liable* or responsible.

**Liable**, lī′a-bl, *adj.* able to be *bound* or obliged: responsible: tending: subject: exposed. [Fr. *lier*—L. *ligare*, to bind.]

**Liaison**, lē′a-zong, *n.* union, or bond of union: connection, esp. an illicit intimacy between a man and woman. [Fr.—*lier*, from L. *ligare*, to bind.]

**Liar**, lī′ar, *n.* one who *lies* or utters falsehood.

**Lias**, lī′as, *n.* (*geol.*) a formation of argillaceous limestone, &c. underlying the oolitic system.— *adj.* **Liassic**, lī-as′ik, pertaining to the *lias* formation. [Fr., of uncertain origin, perh. from Bret. *liach*, a stone.]

**Libation**, lī-bā′shun, *n.* the *pouring forth* wine or other liquid in honour of a deity: the liquid poured. [L. *libatio*—*libo*, Gr. *leibō*, to pour.]

**Libel**, lī′bel, *n.* a written accusation: any malicious defamatory publication: (*law*) the statement of a plaintiff's grounds of complaint against a defendant.—*v.t.* to defame by a libel: to satirise unfairly: (*law*) to proceed against by producing a written complaint:—*pr.p.* lī′belling; *pa.t.* and *pa.p.* lī′belled. [Lit. a ' little book,' from L. *libellus*, dim. of *liber*, a book.]

**Libeller**, lī′bel-ėr, *n.* one who defames by *libels.*

**Libellous**, lī′bel-us, *adj.* containing a *libel:* defamatory.—*adv.* **Li′bellously**.

**Liberal**, lib′ėr-al, *adj.* becoming a gentleman: generous: noble-minded: candid: free: free from restraint: general, extensive.—*n.* one who advocates greater freedom in political institutions.—*adv.* **Lib′erally**. [Lit. ' belonging or suitable to a free-born man,' Fr.—L. *liberalis*—*liber*, free, doing as one pleases—*libet, lubet*, to please, akin to Gr. *eleutheros*, free, Sans. *lubh*, to desire. See **Lief, Love**.]

**Liberalise**, lib′ėr-al-īz, *v.t.* to make *liberal*, or enlightened: to enlarge.

**Liberalism**, lib′ėr-al-izm, *n.* the principles of a *liberal* in politics or religion.

**Liberality**, lib-ėr-al′i-ti, *n.* the quality of being *liberal:* generosity: largeness or nobleness of mind: candour: impartiality.

**Liberate**, lib′ėr-āt, *v.t.* to set *free:* to release from restraint, confinement, or bondage.—*n.* **Libera′tion**. [L. *libero, liberatum*.] [frees.

**Liberator**, lib′ėr-āt-or, *n.* one who *liberates* or

**Libertine**, lib′ėr-tin or -tīn, *n.* formerly, one who professed *free* opinions, esp. in religion: one who leads a licentious life, a rake or debauchee. —*adj.* belonging to a freedman: unrestrained: licentious. [L. *libertinus*, a *freedman*.]

**Libertinism**, lib′ėr-tin-izm, *n.* the conduct of a *libertine:* licentiousness of opinion or practice: lewdness or debauchery.

**Liberty**, lib′ėr-ti, *n.* freedom to do as one pleases: freedom from restraint: the unrestrained enjoyment of natural rights: privilege: exemption: leave: relaxation of restraint: the bounds within which certain privileges are enjoyed: freedom of speech or action beyond ordinary civility. [Fr.—L. *libertas.*]

**Libidinous**, li-bid′in-us, *adj., lustful:* given to the indulgence of the animal passions.—*adv.* **Libid′inously**.—*n.* **Libid′inousness**. [Fr.—L. *libidinosus*—*libido*, desire, lust—*lubet.*]

**Libra**, lī′bra, *n.* the *balance*, a sign of the zodiac. [L.]

**Librarian**, lī-brā′ri-an, *n.* the keeper of a library. —*n.* **Libra′rianship**. [L. *librarius*, a transcriber of books.]

**Library**, lī′brar-i, *n.* a building or room containing a collection of *books* : a collection of books. [L. *librarium*—*liber*, a book.]

**Librate**, lī′brāt, *v.t.* to poise: to balance.—*v.i.* to move slightly, as a balance: to be poised.—*n.* **Libra′tion**, balancing: a state of equipoise: a slight swinging motion. [L. *libro, libratum*—*libra*, a level, a balance. See under **Level**.]

**Libratory**, lī′bra-tor-i, *adj.* swaying like a *balance.*

**Libretto**, li-bret′o, *n.* a *book* of the words of an opera or other musical composition. [It., dim. of *libro*—L. *liber*, a book.]

**Lice**, līs, *plural* of **Louse**.

**License, Licence**, lī′sens, *n.* a being *allowed:* leave: grant of permission: the document by which authority is conferred: excess or abuse of freedom.—**Li′cense**, *v.t.* to grant license to: to authorise or permit. [Fr.—L. *licentia—licet*, to be allowed.]

**Licenser**, lī'sens-ėr, *n.* one who grants *license* or permission : one authorised to license.

**Licentiate**, lī-sen'shi-āt, *n.* one who has a *license* or grant of permission to exercise a profession.

**Licentious**, lī-sen'shus, *adj.* indulging in excessive freedom : given to the indulgence of the animal passions : dissolute.—*adv.* Licen'tiously. —*n.* Licen'tiousness. [Fr.—L. *licentiosus.*]

**Lichen**, lī'ken or lich'en, *n.* one of an order of cellular flowerless plants : an eruption on the skin. [L.—Gr. *leichēn*, from *leichō*, Sans. *lih*, to lick ; from its licking up or encroaching on the soil. See **Lick.**]

**Lichgate**, lich'gāt, *n.* a churchyard *gate* with a porch to rest the bier under. [M. E. *lich*—A.S. *lic* (Ger. *leiche*, Goth. *leik*, a corpse), and **Gate.** See **Like,** *adj.*]

**Lichwake**, lich'wāk, *n.* the *wake* or watch held over a *dead body.* [M. E. *lich*, a body, a corpse (see **Like,** *adj.*), and **Wake.**]

**Lick**, lik, *v.t.* to pass the tongue over : to take in by the tongue : to lap.—*n.* Lick'er. [A.S. *liccian* ; Ger. *lecken*, L. *lingo*, Gr. *leichō*, Sans. *lih.* See **Tongue** and **Language.**]

**Lickerish**, lik'ėr-ish, *adj.* dainty : eager to taste or enjoy. [From **Lick.**]

**Lickspittle**, lik'spit-l, *n.* a mean, servile dependent.

**Licorice.** Same as **Liquorice.**

**Lictor**, lik'tor, *n.* an officer who attended the Roman magistrates, bearing an axe and bundle of rods. [L., conn. with *ligare*, to bind.]

**Lid**, lid, *n.* a *cover :* that which *shuts* a vessel : the cover of the eye. [A.S. *hlid ;* Dut. *lid ;* akin to L. *clivus*, Gr. *klinō*, E. **Lean.**]

**Lie**, lī, *n.* anything meant to deceive : an intentional violation of truth : anything that misleads. —*v.i.* to utter falsehood with an intention to deceive : to make a false representation :—*pr.p.* ly'ing ; *pa.t.* and *pa.p.* lied'. [A.S. *leogan* (*lyga*, a falsehood), prov. E. *lig ;* Dut. *liegen*, Goth. *liugan*, Ger. *lügen*, to lie. Cf. Lett. *leeks*, 'crooked,' and L. *ob-liqu-us*, slanting.]

**Lie**, lī, *v.i.* to rest in a reclining posture : to lean : to press upon : to be situated : to abide : to consist : (*law*) to be sustainable :—*pr.p.* ly'ing ; *pa.t.* lay ; *pa.p.* lain, (*B.*) lī'en.—*ns.* Li'er, Lie-a-bed, one who lies long in the morning (also *adj.*).—**To lie in**, to be in childbed. [A.S. *licgan ;* Ger. *liegen ;* Goth. *ligan ;* Ice. *liggja ;* Ir. *luighim ;* Gr. *lechos*, a bed, L. *lectus.*]

**Lief**, lēf, *adj.* (*poetry*) *loved, dear.*—*adv.* lovingly : willingly, now chiefly used in the phrase, 'I had as lief.' [A.S. *leof ;* Ger. *lieb*, loved.]

**Liege**, lēj, *adj.* true, faithful : subject : under a feudal tenure : sovereign or having lieges.—*n.* one under a feudal tenure : a vassal : a lord or superior or one who has lieges. [Fr. *lige*, which prob. is derived from O. Ger. *ledec*, Ger. *ledig*, free, unfettered. The word was orig. applied to the *free* bands in the German tribes that overturned the Roman empire. But as the free bands settled on the conquered territory and formed the Feudal System, the meaning of the word gradually changed ; thus it orig. meant ' free,' then ' true to their chief,' ' loyal,' ' bound ' by a feudal tenure ; but the sense of ' bound ' was also due to confusion with L. *ligatus*, bound.]

**Lien**, lī'en or lē'en, *n.* (*law*) a right in one to retain the property of another to pay a claim. [Fr., tie, band—L. *ligamen—ligo*, to bind.]

**Lien**, lī'en (*B.*) *pa.p.* of **Lie**, to lie down.

**Lieth**, lī'eth (*B.*) 3d pers. sing. of **Lie**, to lie down.

**Lieu**, lū, *n., place,* stead. [Fr.—L. *locus*, place.]

**Lieutenancy**, lef-ten'an-si, *n., office* or *commission* of a *lieutenant :* the body of lieutenants.

**Lieutenant**, lef-ten'ant, *n.* an officer *holding* the *place of another* in his absence : a commissioned officer in the army next below a captain, or in the navy next below a commander : one holding a place next in rank to a superior, as in the compounds lieutenant-colonel, lieutenant-general. [Fr., from *lieu*, a place, and *tenant*, holding— *tenir*, to hold. See **Lieu** and **Tenant.**]

**Life**, līf, *n.* state of *living :* animate existence : union of soul and body : the period between birth and death : present state of existence : manner of living : moral conduct : animation : a living being : system of animal nature : social state : human affairs : narrative of a life : eternal happiness, also He who bestows it : a quickening principle in a moral sense :—*pl.* **Lives**, līvz. [A.S., Ice., and Sw. *lif ;* Dut. *liif*, body, life ; Ger. *leben*, to live. See **Live.**]

**Life-assurance**, līf'-ash-shōōr'ans. Same as **Life-insurance.**

**Lifeboat**, līf'bōt, *n.* a *boat* of peculiar construction for saving shipwrecked persons.

**Life-estate**, līf'-es-tāt', *n.* an *estate* held during the *life* of the possessor.

**Life-guard**, līf'-gärd, *n.* a *guard* of the *life* or person : a guard of a prince or other dignitary.

**Lifehold**, līf'hōld, *n.* land *held* by lease for *life.*

**Life-insurance**, līf'-in-shōōr'ans, *n.* a contract by which a sum of money is *insured* to be paid at the close of a person's *life.* [**Life** and **Insurance.**]

**Lifeless**, līf'les, *adj.* dead : without vigour : insipid : sluggish.—*adv.* Life'lessly.—*n.* Life'lessness.

**Lifelong**, līf'long, *adj.* during the *length* of a *life.*

**Life-preserver**, līf'-pre-zėrv'ėr, *n.* an invention for the preservation of life, in cases of fire or shipwreck : a cane with a loaded head.

**Liferent**, līf'rent, *n.* a *rent* that continues for *life.*

**Lift**, lift, *v.t.* to bring to a higher position : to elevate : to elate : to take and carry away.—*v.i.* to try to raise.—*n.* act of *lifting :* that which is to be raised : that which assists to lift. [Lit. 'to raise into the *air*,' from M. E. *lift* or *luft*, the air, sky. It is simply a form of **Loft**, which see.]

**Ligament**, lig'a-ment, *n.* anything that *binds :* (*anat.*) the membrane connecting the movable bones : a bond of union. [Fr.—L. *ligamentum* —*ligo, ligatum*, to bind.]

**Ligamental**, lig-a-ment'al, **Ligamentous**, lig-a-ment'us, *adj.* composing or resembling a *ligament.* [being bound.

**Ligation**, li-gā'shun, *n.* act of *binding :* state of

**Ligature**, lig'a-tūr, *n.* anything that *binds :* a bandage : (*mus.*) a line connecting notes : (*print.*) a type of two letters : (*med.*) a cord for tying the blood-vessels, &c. [See **Ligament.**]

**Light**, līt, *n.* that which *shines* or is *brilliant :* the agent by which objects are rendered visible : the power of vision : day : dawn of day : that which gives light, as the sun, a candle : the illuminated part of a picture : (*fig.*) mental or spiritual illumination : enlightenment : knowledge : public view : point of view : a conspicuous person : an aperture for admitting light : (*B.*) prosperity, favour.—*adj.* not dark : bright : whitish. —*v.t.* to give light to : to set fire to : to attend with a light :—*pr.p.* light'ing ; *pa.t.* and *pa.p.* light'ed or lit.—*n.* Light'er. [A.S. *leoht, lyht ;* Ger. *licht*, Goth. *liuhath*, W. *llug*, L. *lux*, light, Gr. *leukos ;* akin to Sans. *lok, loch*, to see, to shine, *ruch*, to shine.]

**Light,** lĭt, *adj.* not heavy : easily suffered or performed : easily digested : not heavily armed : active : not heavily burdened : unimportant : not dense or copious : gentle : easily influenced : gay, lively : amusing : unchaste : not of legal weight : loose, sandy : (*B.*) idle, worthless.— *adv.* Light'ly, cheaply : (*B.*) easily, carelessly. —*n.* Light'ness (*B.*) levity, fickleness. [A.S. *leoht ;* Ger. *leicht,* Ice. *lettr ;* L. *levis,* Gr. *elachys ;* akin to Sans. *laghu,* light.]

**Light,** lĭt, *v.i.* (followed by *on, upon*) to stoop from flight : to settle : to rest : to come to by chance : (fol. by *down, from*) to descend, to alight :—*pr.p.* light'ing ; *pa.t.* and *pa.p.* light'ed or lit. [From **Light,** not heavy, as 'to light from a horse,' to relieve him of his burden.]

**Lighten,** lĭt'n, *v.t.* to make *light* or *clear* : (*fig.*) to illuminate with knowledge : (*B.*) to free from trouble.—*v.i.* to shine like lightning : to flash : to become less dark.                    [to alleviate : to cheer.

**Lighten,** lĭt'n, *v.t.* to make *lighter* or less heavy : **Lighten upon,** *v.i.* (*Pr. Bk.*) to alight or descend upon.

**Lighter,** lĭt'ėr, *n.* a large open boat used in *lightening* (unloading) and loading ships.—*n.* **Light'-erman.**

**Lighterage,** lĭt'ėr-āj, *n.* price paid for unloading ships by *lighters :* the act of thus unloading.

**Light-fingered,** lĭt'-fing'gėrd, *adj., light* or active with one's *fingers :* thievish.

**Light-headed,** lĭt'-hed'ed, *adj.* giddy in the head : thoughtless : unsteady. [**Light** and **Head.**]

**Light-hearted,** lĭt'-härt'ed, *adj., light* or merry of *heart :* free from anxiety : cheerful.—*adv.* **Light'-heart'edly.**—*n.* **Light'-heart'edness.**

**Lighthorse,** lĭt'hors, *n., light-armed cavalry.*

**Lighthouse,** lĭt'hows, *n.* a tower or *house* with a *light* at the top to guide mariners at night.

**Light-infantry,** lĭt'-in'fant-ri, *n., infantry lightly* or not heavily armed.

**Light-minded,** lĭt'-mīnd'ed, *adj.* having a *light* or unsteady *mind :* not considerate.

**Lightning,** lĭt'ning, *n.* the electric flash usually followed by thunder.

**Lightning-rod,** lĭt'ning-rod, *n.* a metallic *rod* for protecting buildings from *lightning.*

**Lights,** lĭts, *n.pl.* the lungs of animals. [So called from their *light* weight.]

**Lightsome,** lĭt'sum, *adj., light,* gay, lively, cheering.—*n.* **Light'someness.**

**Lign-aloes,** lĭn-al'ōz, **Lignaloes,** lig-nal'ōz, *n.* (*B.*) *aloes-wood.* [L. *lignum,* wood, and **Aloes.**]

**Ligneous,** lig'ne-us, *adj., wooden : woody :* made of wood. [L. *ligneus—lignum,* wood.]

**Ligniferous,** lig-nif'ėr-us, *adj., producing wood,* [L. *lignum,* wood, and *fero,* to bear.]

**Lignify,** lig'ni-fī, *v.t.* to turn into *wood.*—*v.i.* to become wood or woody :—*pr.p.* lig'nifying ; *pa.p.* lig'nified.—*n.* **Lignifica'tion.** [Fr. *lignifier*— L. *lignum,* wood, and *facio,* to make.]

**Lignine,** lig'nin, *n.* pure *woody* fibre.

**Lignite,** lig'nīt, *n.* coal retaining the texture of *wood.*—*adj.* **Lignit'ic.**

**Lignum-vitæ,** lig'num-vē'tā, *n.* popular name of a South American tree with very hard wood.

**Ligule,** lig'ūl, *n.* (*bot.*) the flat part of the leaf of a grass : a strap-shaped petal in certain flowers. [Lit. 'a little tongue,' L. *ligula,* dim. of *lingua,* a tongue.]                              [Gr. *ligurion.*]

**Ligure,** lī'gūr or lig'ūr, *n.* (*B.*) a precious stone.

**Like,** līk, *adj.* equal in quantity, quality, or degree : similar : likely.—*n.* the like thing or person : an exact resemblance : a liking.—*adv.* in the same manner : probably. [A.S. *lic,* oftener

*ge-lic,* Ice. *likr,* Dut. *ge-lijk,* Ger. *gleich* (= *ge-leich*). Acc. to Bopp, the simple forms, as in Ice., A.S., &c. are abbreviations of the full form, as seen in Goth. *ga-leik-s ;* Goth. *leik,* A.S. *lic* means body, shape (see **Lichgate**), and *ga-, ge-* = with, L. *cum ;* so that *ge-lic* means 'having body or shape in common with another' = L. *conformis.* A.S. *lic* appears in the suffix *-ly* (godly), and the same root may be traced in L. *ta-li-s,* Gr. *tē-lik-os.*]

**Like,** līk, *v.t.* to be *pleased with :* to approve : to enjoy : (*obs.*) to please. [Orig. the verb meant 'to be pleasing,' and was used impersonally, as 'it likes me,' *i.e.* it pleases me, A.S. *lician,* to be pleasing—*lic,* like, similar, conformable, suitable, pleasing.]

**Likely,** līk'li, *adj., like* the thing required : credible : probable : having reason to expect.—*adv.* probably.—*ns.* **Like'liness, Like'lihood.**

**Likely,** līk'li, *adj.* that may be *liked :* pleasing.

**Liken,** līk'n, *v.t.* to represent as *like* or similar : to compare.

**Likeness,** līk'nes, *n.* resemblance ; one who resembles another : that which resembles : a portrait or picture : effigy.

**Likewise,** līk'wīz, *adv.* in *like wise* or manner : also : moreover : too. [**Like,** *adj.* and **Wise.**]

**Liking,** līk'ing, *n.* state of being *pleased with :* inclination : satisfaction in : (*B.*) condition, plight. —*adj.* (*B.*), as in **Good-liking, Well-liking,** in good condition.                      [the Pers. *lilaj.*]

**Lilac,** lī'lak, *n.* a pretty flowering shrub. [Sp.—

**Liliaceous,** lil-i-ā'shus, *adj.* pertaining to *lilies.*

**Lilied,** lil'id, *adj.* adorned with *lilies.*

**Lilliputian,** lil-i-pū'shi-an, *n.* an inhabitant of the island of Lilliput, described by Swift in his *Gulliver's Travels :* a person of small size, a dwarf.—*adj.* of small size : dwarfish.

**Lilt,** lilt, *v.i.* to do anything cleverly or quickly, as to hop about : to sing, dance, or play merrily. —*n.* a cheerful song or air. [Ety. dub.]

**Lily,** lil'i, *n.* a bulbous plant, with showy and fragrant flowers.—**Lily of the Valley,** a well-known and much-loved flower of the lily genus. [A.S. *lilie*—L. *lilium*—Gr. *leirion,* lily.]

**Limb,** lim, *n.* a jointed part in animals : a projecting part : a branch of a tree.—*v.t.* to supply with limbs : to tear off the limbs. [A.S. *lim ;* perh. from A.S. *lemian* (hence **Lame**), to break, and so orig. '*a part broken off, fragment.*']

**Limb,** lim, *n.* an edge or border, as of the sun, &c. : the edge of a sextant, &c. [L. *limbus.*]

**Limber,** lim'bėr, *n.* the part of a gun-carriage consisting of two wheels and a shaft to which the horses are attached.—*v.t.* to attach to the limbers, as a gun. [Prov. E. *limbers,* shafts—Ice. *limar,* boughs, cart-shafts orig. being only boughs of trees ; cf. **Limb,** a branch of a tree.]

**Limber,** lim'bėr, *adj.* pliant, flexible. [See **Limp,** *adj.*]

**Limbo,** lim'bo, **Limbus,** lim'bus, *n.* in the creed of the R. Cath. Church, a place on the *borders* of hell, in which the souls of the pious who died before the time of Christ await his coming, and where the souls of unbaptised infants remain : a place of confinement. [It. *limbo,* L. *limbus,* border.]

**Lime,** līm, *n.* any *slimy* or *gluey* material : bird-lime : the white caustic earth from limestone, and used for cement.—*v.t.* to cover with lime : to cement : to manure with lime : to insnare. [A.S. *lim ;* cog. with Ger. *leim,* glue, L. *limus,* slime ; from a base *li* seen in L. *li-nere,* to smear, and Sans. *li,* to be viscous.]

**Lime,** līm, *n.* a kind of citron or *lemon* tree and its fruit. [Fr. See **Lemon.**]

**Lime-juice,** līm'-jūs, *n.* the acid juice of the lime, used at sea as a specific against scurvy.

**Limekiln,** līm'kil, *n.* a *kiln* or furnace in which limestone is burned to *lime.*

**Limestone,** līm'stōn, *n., stone* from which lime is procured by burning.

**Lime-tree,** līm'-trē, *n.* the linden-tree, common in Europe, with heart-shaped leaves and panicles of yellowish flowers. [*Lime* is a corr. of *line*, and *line* of *lind*, which is = linden-tree. See **Linden.**]       [*lime.*

**Limetwig,** līm'twig, *n.* a *twig* smeared with bird-

**Limit,** lim'it, *n.* boundary : utmost extent : restriction.—*v.t.* to confine within bounds : to restrain. [Fr.—L. *limes, limitis—limus*, transverse.]      [bounded, or restrained.

**Limitable,** lim'it-a-bl, *adj.* that may be *limited.*

**Limitary,** lim'it-ar-i, *adj.* placed at the boundary, as a guard, &c. : confined within limits.

**Limitation,** lim-it-ā'shun, *n.* the act of *limiting*, bounding, or restraining : the state of being limited, bounded, or restrained : restriction.

**Limited,** lim'it-ed, *adj.* within *limits* : narrow : restricted.—**Limited Liability,** in a joint-stock company, means that the members are liable only in a fixed proportion to each share.—*adv.* **Lim'itedly.**—*n.* **Lim'itedness.**

**Limitless,** lim'it-les, *adj.* having no *limits* : boundless : immense : infinite.

**Limn,** lim, *v.t.* (*orig.*) to *illuminate* with ornamental letters, &c. : to draw or paint, esp. in water-colours. [Contr. of Fr. *enluminer*—L. *illumino*, from root of **Luminary.**]

**Limner,** lim'nèr, *n.* one who *limns*, or paints on paper or parchment : a portrait-painter.

**Limous,** līm'us, *adj., gluey* : *slimy* : muddy. [See **Lime,** any slimy material.]

**Limp,** limp, *adj.* wanting stiffness, flexible : weak, flaccid. [A nasalised form of **Lap**, seen also in W. *llibin, lleipr*, drooping, Ice. *limpa*, weakness.]

**Limp,** limp, *v.i.* to halt : to walk lamely.—*n.* act of limping : a halt. [A.S. *limp-healt*, lame ; O. Ger. *limphin*, to limp : prob. a form of **Lame.**]

**Limpet,** lim'pet, *n.* a small shell-fish, which clings to *bare rocks.* [Prob. through the Fr., from L. and Gr. *lepas*, a limpet—Gr. *lepas*, a bare rock —*lepō*, to peel.]

**Limpid,** lim'pid, *adj., clear* : shining : transparent : pure.—*ns.* **Limpid'ity, Lim'pidness.** [Fr.—L. *limpidus*, perh. a form of *liquidus.* See **Liquid.**]

**Limpingly,** limp'ing-li, *adv.* in a limping manner.

**Limy,** līm'i, *adj., glutinous* : sticky : containing, resembling, or having the qualities of *lime.*

**Linchpin,** linsh'pin, *n.* a *pin* used to keep the wheel of a carriage on the *axle-tree.* [A.S. *lynis*, an axle-tree ; cog. with Dut. *luns*, O. Ger. *lun*, peg, bolt, and **Pin.**]

**Linden,** lin'den, *n.* the lime-tree. [A.S., Sw., Ice. *lind*, Ger. *linde*, O. Ger. *linta.*]

**Line,** līn, *n.* a *thread* of *linen* or *flax* : a slender cord : (*math.*) that which has length without breadth or thickness : an extended stroke : a straight row : a cord extended to direct any operations : outline : a series, succession of : a mark or lineament, hence a characteristic : a row : a rank : a verse : a short letter or note : a trench, in *pl.* military works of defence : limit : method : the equator : lineage : direction : occupation : the regular infantry of an army : the twelfth part of an inch. [L. *līnea—līnum*, flax.]

**Line,** līn, *v.t.* to mark out with *lines* : to cover with

lines : to place along by the side of for guarding : by a guard within or by anything added.

**Line,** līn, *v.t.* to cover on the inside with *linen* or other material : to cover.

**Lineage,** lin'e-āj, *n.* descendants in a *line* from a common progenitor : race : family.

**Lineal,** lin'e-al, *adj.* of or belonging to a *line* : composed of lines : in the direction of a line : descended in a direct line from an ancestor.— *adv.* **Lin'eally.**

**Lineament,** lin'e-a-ment, *n.* feature : distinguishing mark in the form, esp. of the face. [Lit. 'a drawing ;' Fr.—L. *lineo*, to draw a line.]

**Linear,** lin'e-ar, *adj.* of or belonging to a *line* : consisting of or having the form of lines : straight.—*adv.* **Lin'early.**

**Lineation,** lin-e-ā'shun, *n.* Same as **Delineation.**

**Linen,** lin'en, *n.* cloth made of *lint* or *flax* : underclothing, particularly that made of linen.—*adj.* made of flax : resembling linen cloth. [Properly an *adj.* with suffix *-en*—A.S. *lin*—L. *linum*, flax ; Gr. *linon*.]

**Liner,** līn'èr, *n.* a vessel belonging to a regular *line* or series of packets.

**Ling,** ling, *n.* a fish resembling the cod, so called from its *lengthened* form. [A.S. *lang*, long.]

**Ling,** ling, *n.* heather. [Ice. *lyng*.]

**Linger,** ling'gèr, *v.i.* to remain *long* in any state : to loiter : to hesitate. [A.S. *lengan*, to protract—*lang*, long.]

**Lingering,** ling'gèr-ing, *adj., lengthened out* in time : protracted.—*n.* a remaining long.

**Linget, Lingot,** ling'get, ling'got, *n.* Same as **Ingot.** [Fr. *lingot*, from root of **Ingot.**]

**Linguadental,** ling-gwa-den'tal, *adj.* uttered by the joint action of the *tongue* and *teeth*, as of the letters *d* and *l.*—*n.* a sound thus produced. [L. *lingua*, the tongue, and **Dental.**]

**Lingual,** ling'gwal, *adj.* pertaining to the *tongue.* —*n.* a letter pronounced mainly by the tongue, as *l.*—*adv.* **Lin'gually.** [From L. *lingua* (old form *dingua*), the tongue.]      [*languages.*

**Linguist,** ling'gwist, *n.* one skilled in *tongues* or

**Linguistic,** ling-gwist'ik, **Linguistical,** ling-gwist'-ik-al, *adj.* pertaining to languages and the affinities of languages.

**Linguistics,** ling-gwist'iks, *n.sing.* the science of *languages* and words, the general or comparative study of languages.

**Liniment,** lin'i-ment, *n.* a kind of thin ointment. [L. *linimentum—lino*, to besmear.]

**Lining,** līn'ing, *n.* act of drawing *lines* upon, or of marking with lines : an inside covering.

**Link,** lingk, *n.* something *bent* so as to form a *joint* : a ring of a chain : anything connecting : a single part of a series.—*v.t.* to connect as by a link : to join in confederacy : to unite in a series. —*v.i.* to be connected. [A.S. *hlence* ; Ice. *hlekkr*, Ger. *gelenk* (*lenken*, to bend).]

**Link,** lingk, *n.* a *light* or torch of pitch and tow. —*n.* **Link'boy,** boy who carries such to light travellers. [Prob. corr. from Dut. *lont*, a gunner's match of tow ; Scot. *lunt*, Dan. *lunte*.]

**Links,** lingks, *n.pl.* a stretch of flat or gently undulating ground along a sea-shore, on which the game of golf is played. [Scotch.]

**Linnæan, Linnean,** lin-nē'an, *adj.* pertaining to *Linnæus*, the Latinised form of the name of Linné, the celebrated Swedish botanist (1707 –78), or to the artificial system of classification introduced by him into Botany.

**Linnet,** lin'et, *n.* a small singing-bird, so called from feeding on the seed of *flax.* [Fr. *linot—lin*, flax—L. *linum.* See **Linen.**]

**Linoleum**, lin-ō′le-um, *n.* a preparation used as a floorcloth, *linseed*-oil being greatly used in the making of it. [L. *linum*, flax, *oleum*, oil.]

**Linseed**, lin′sēd, **Lintseed**, lint′sēd, *n.*, *lint* or *flax seed*. [From **Lint**.]

**Linseed-cake**, lin′sēd-kāk, *n.* the *cake* remaining when the oil is pressed out of *lint* or *flax seed*.

**Linseed-oil**, lin′sēd-oil, *n.*, *oil* from *flax-seed*.

**Linsey-woolsey**, lin′ze-wool′ze, *adj.* made of *linen* and *wool* mixed : mean : of unsuitable parts.— *n.* a thin coarse stuff of linen and wool mixed.

**Linstock**, lin′stok, *n.* a staff to hold a lighted match for firing cannon. [Also *lintstock*, *lint* being a mistaken form of *lunt*, due to confusion with *lint*, scraped linen, from Dut. *lontstok— lont*, a match, and *stok*, a stick. See **Link**.]

**Lint**, lint, *n.*, *flax* : linen scraped into a soft woolly substance to lay on wounds. [See **Linen**.]

**Lintel**, lin′tel, *n.* the piece of timber or stone over a doorway : the headpiece of a door or case-ment. [O. Fr. *lintel* (Fr. *linteau*)—Low L. *lintellus* for *limitellus*, dim. of L. *limes*, a boundary, border. See **Limit**.]

**Lion**, lī′un, *n.* a large and fierce quadruped, remarkable for its roar : (*astr.*) Leo, a sign of the zodiac : any object of interest.—*fem.* **Li′oness**. [O. Fr. *lion*—L. *leo*—Gr. *leōn* ; Ger. *löwe* ; A.S. *leo*, borrowed directly from L.]

**Lion-hearted**, lī′un-härt′ed, *adj.* having the *heart* or courage of a *lion*. [interest.

**Lionise**, lī′un-īz, *v.t.* to treat as a *lion* or object of

**Lip**, lip, *n.* the muscular border in front of the teeth by which things are taken into the mouth : the edge of anything. [A.S. *lippe* ; Dut. *lip*, Ger. *lippe*, L. *labium*, akin to L. *lambo*, E. *lap*, expressive of the sound of lapping.]

**Lipped**, lipt, *adj.* having *lips* : having a raised or rounded edge like the lip.

**Liquation**, li-kwā′shun, *n.* the act of making *liquid* or melting : the capacity of being melted. [L. *liquo*, *liquatum*, to make liquid, to melt.]

**Liquefaction**, lik-we-fak′shun, *n.* the *act* or process of *making liquid*: the state of being melted.

**Liquefy**, lik′we-fī, *v.t.* to make *liquid*: to dissolve. —*v.i.* to become liquid :—*pa.t.* and *pa.p.* liq′uē-fīed. [L. *liquefacio—liqueo*, to be fluid or liquid, and *facio*, to make.]

**Liquescent**, li-kwes′ent, *adj.*, *becoming liquid*: melting.—*n.* **Liques′cency**. [L. *liquescens*, *-entis*, pr.p. of *liquesco*, to become liquid—*liqueo*.]

**Liqueur**, lik-ėr′, *n.* a flavoured spirit : a cordial. [Fr.]

**Liquid**, lik′wid, *adj.*, *flowing*: fluid : soft : smooth : clear.—*n.* a flowing substance : a letter of a smooth flowing sound, as *l* and *r*, in *pla*, *pra*.— *ns.* **Liquid′ity**, **Liq′uidness**. [L. *liquidus*, fluid, clear—*liqueo*, to be fluid or liquid.]

**Liquidate**, lik′wi-dāt, *v.t.* to make *clear*, esp. to *clear* or settle an account : to arrange or wind up the affairs of a bankrupt estate. [See **Liquid**.]

**Liquidation**, lik-wi-dā′shun, *n.* the clearing up of money affairs, esp. the adjustment of the affairs of a bankrupt estate.

**Liquidator**, lik-wi-dāt′or, *n.* one engaged in a liquidation.

**Liquor**, lik′ur, *n.* anything *liquid*: strong drink.

**Liquorice**, lik′ur-is, *n.* a plant with a *sweet root* which is used for medicinal purposes. [Through an O. Fr. form, from L. *liquiritia*, a corr. of Gr. *glykyrrhiza—glykys*, sweet, and *rhiza*, root.]

**Lisp**, lisp, *v.i.* to speak with the tongue against the upper teeth or gums, as in pronouncing *th* for *s* or *z* : to articulate as a child : to utter imper-fectly.—*v.t.* to pronounce with a lisp.—*n.* the

act or habit of lisping. [A.S. *wlisp*, lisping ; Dut. *lispen*, Ger. *lispeln* ; from the sound.]

**Lisping**, lisp′ing, *adj.* pronouncing with a *lisp*.— *n.* the act of speaking with a lisp.—*adv.* **Lisp′-ingly**.

**Lissome**, lis′um, *adj.* Same as **Lithesome**.

**List**, list, *n.* a stripe or border of cloth. [A.S. ; Ice. *lista*, Ger. *leiste*, border.]

**List**, list, *n.* an edge or border : a catalogue or roll.—*v.t.* to place in a list or catalogue : to engage for the public service, as soldiers. [Orig. a strip, as of parchment, hence a roll, a list of names, Fr. *liste*—O. Ger. *lista*, Ger. *leiste*, stripe, border ; A.S. *list*, and orig. the same word as the above.]

**List**, list, *n.* a line inclosing a piece of ground, esp. for combat :—*pl.* **Lists**, the ground inclosed for a contest.—**To enter the lists**, to engage in contest. [Fr. *lice*, It. *lizza*—Low L. *licia*, barriers ; of unknown origin.]

**List**, list, *v.i.* to have *pleasure* : to desire : to like or please : to choose. [A.S. *lystan*, to desire—*lust*, pleasure ; Dut. and Ger. *lust*, pleasure.]

**List**, list, *v.t.* or *v.i.* dim. of **Listen**.

**Listen**, lis′n, *v.t.* to *hear* or attend to.—*v.i.* to *give ear* or hearken : to follow advice. [A.S. *hlistan—hlyst*, hearing, from *hlust*, the ear ; Ice. *hlusta*, L. *cluo*, Gr. *kluō*, to hear, W. *clust*, an ear. See **Loud**.]

**Listener**, lis′n-ėr, *n.* one who *listens* or hearkens.

**Listless**, list′les, *adj.* having no *desire* or wish : careless : uninterested : weary : indolent.—*adv.* **List′lessly**.—*n.* **List′lessness**. [From **Lust** and suffix *-less*.] [to alight.

**Lit**, *pa.t.* and *pa.p.* of **Light**, to lighten, and **Light**,

**Litany**, lit′a-ni, *n.* a *praying*: a form of suppli-cation in public worship. [Fr.—L. *litania*—Gr. *litaneia—litē*, a prayer.]

**Literal**, lit′ėr-al, *adj.* according to the *letter*: plain : not figurative or metaphorical : following the letter or exact meaning, word for word.— *adv.* **Lit′erally**.—*n.* **Lit′eralness**. [Fr.—L. *literalis—litera*, a letter.]

**Literary**, lit′ėr-ar-i, *adj.* belonging to *letters* or *learning*: pertaining to men of letters : derived from learning : skilled in learning : consisting of written or printed compositions. [L. *literarius*.]

**Literate**, lit′ėr-āt, *adj.* acquainted with *letters* or *learning*: learned.—*n.* one educated but not having taken a university degree. [L. *literatus*.]

**Literati**, lit-ėr-ā′tī, *n.pl.* men of *letters*, the learned.

**Literature**, lit′ėr-a-tūr, *n.* the *science of letters* or what is written : the whole body of literary com-positions in any language, or on a given subject : all literary productions except those relating to positive science and art, usually confined, how-ever, to the belles-lettres. [Fr.—L. *literatura— litera*.]

**Litharge**, lith′arj, *n.* the semi-vitrified oxide of lead separated from silver in refining. [Lit. ' stone-silver,' Fr.—Gr. *lithargyros—lithos*, a stone, and *argyros*, silver.]

**Lithe**, lī*th*, *adj.* easily bent, flexible, active.— *n.* **Lithe′ness**. [A.S. *lithe* (for *linthe*) ; Ger. *ge-lind*, Ice. *linr*, akin to L. *lenis*, soft, tender.]

**Lithesome**, lī*th*′sum, *adj.*, lithe, supple, nimble. —*n.* **Lithe′someness**.

**Lithograph**, lith′o-graf, *v.t.* to *write* or engrave on *stone* and transfer to paper by printing.—*n.* a print from stone. [Gr. *lithos*, a stone, and *graphō*, to write.] [the art of *lithography*.

**Lithographer**, lith-og′ra-fėr, *n.* one who practises **Lithographic**, lith-o-graf′ik, **Lithographical**, lith-o-graf'ik-al, *adj.* belonging to *lithography.* —*adv.* Lithograph'ically.

Lithography, lith-og'raf-i, *n.* the art of *writing* or engraving on *stone* and printing therefrom.

Lithology, lith-ol'o-ji, *n.* a department of geology *treating* of the structure of *rocks.*—*adj.* Litholog'ical.—*n.* Lithol'ogist, one skilled in lithology. [Gr. *lithos,* a stone, and *logos,* discourse.]

Lithophyte, lith'o-fīt, *n.* an animal production apparently both *stone* and *plant,* as coral. [Gr. *lithos,* stone, *phyton,* plant—*phyō,* to grow.]

Lithotomy, lith-ot'o-mi, *n.* the operation of *cutting* for *stone* in the bladder.—*n.* Lithot'omist, one who practises lithotomy. [Gr. *lithos,* a stone, and *tomē,* a cutting—*temnō,* to cut.]

Lithotripsy, lith-ot'rip-si, Lithotrity, lith-ot'ri-ti, *n.* the operation of *breaking* a *stone* in the bladder. [Gr. *lithos,* stone, and *tribo,* cog. with L. *tero,* to grind.]

Litigable, lit'i-ga-bl, *adj.* that may be contested in law.

Litigant, lit'i-gant, *adj.* contending at law: engaged in a lawsuit.—*n.* a person engaged in a lawsuit.

Litigate, lit'i-gāt, *v.t.* to *contest* in law.—*v.i.* to carry on a lawsuit.—*n.* Litiga'tion. [L. *litigo,* *-atum—lis, litis,* a strife, and *ago,* to do.]

Litigious, li-tij'yus, *adj.* inclined to engage in lawsuits: subject to contention.—*adv.* Litig'iously. —*n.* Litig'iousness.

Litmus, lit'mus, *n.* a purple dye obtained from certain lichens; known also as turnsole. [For *lakmose*—Dut. *lakmoes—lak,* lac, and *moes,* pulp.]

Litotes, lit'o-tēz or lī'-, *n.* (*rhet.*) a softening of a statement for *simplicity* and sometimes for emphasis. [Gr. *litotēs,* simplicity—*litos,* plain.]

Litre, lē'tr, *n.* a French liquid measure, about 1¾ E. pints.

Litter, lit'ėr, *n.* a heap of straw, &c. for animals to lie upon: materials for a bed: any scattered collection of objects, esp. of little value: a vehicle containing a bed for carrying about: a brood of small quadrupeds.—*v.t.* to cover or supply with litter: to scatter carelessly about: to give birth to (said of small animals).—*v.i.* to produce a litter or brood. [Fr. *litière*—Low L. *lectaria*—L. *lectus,* a bed, from root of Lie.]

Little, lit'l, *adj.* (comp. Less; superl. Least) small in quantity or extent: weak, poor: brief.—*n.* that which is small in quantity or extent: a small space.—*adv.* in a small quantity or degree: not much.—*n.* Litt'leness. [A.S. *lytel;* Ice. *litill,* O. Ger. *luzil,* Goth. *leitils.*]

Littoral, lit'or-al, *adj.* belonging to the *sea-shore.* —*n.* the strip of land along the shore. [L. *littus, -oris,* the shore.]        [*liturgies.*]

Liturgics, li-tur'jiks, *n.* the doctrine or theory of Liturgist, lit'ur-jist, *n.* one who adheres to or has a knowledge of *liturgies.*

Liturgy, lit'ur-ji, *n.* the form of service or established ritual of a church.—*adjs.* Litur'gic, Litur'gical. [Fr.—Gr. *leitourgia*—*leitos,* public —*laos,* the people, and *ergō,* to work, do.]

Live, liv, *v.i.* to have life: to continue in life: to be exempt from death: to last: to subsist: to enjoy life, to be in a state of happiness: to be nourished or supported: to dwell.—*v.t.* to spend: to act in conformity to:—*pr.p.* liv'ing; *pa.t.* and *pa.p.* lived'.—*n.* Liv'er. [A.S. *lifian, lybban;* Dut. *leven,* Ger. *leben;* orig. meaning to *remain,* to *continue.* See Leave, *v.t.*]

Live, līv, *adj.* having *life:* alive, not dead:

active: containing fire: burning: vivid.— -Lived, līvd, used in compounds, as Long-lived.

Livelihood, līv'li-hood, *n.* means of *living:* support. [For M. E. *liflode, liflade,* from A.S. *lif,* life, and *lad,* a leading, way, lit., *life-leading.*]

Livelong, liv'long, *adj.* that *lives* or lasts *long.*

Lively, līv'li, *adj.* having or shewing life: vigorous, active: sprightly: spirited: strong: vivid. —*adv.* vivaciously, vigorously.—*n.* Live'liness.

Liver, liv'ėr, *n.* the largest gland in the body, which secretes the bile. [A.S. *lifer;* Ger. *leber,* Ice. *lifr.*]        [*overgrown liver.*]

Liver-grown, liv'ėr-grōn, *adj.* having a swelled or Liveried, liv'ėr-id, *adj.* having or wearing a *livery.*

Liverwort, liv'ėr-wurt, *n.* Iceland-moss. [From A.S. *wurt,* plant.]

Livery, liv'ėr-i, *n.* (*orig.*) the distinctive dress worn by the household of a king or nobleman, so called because *delivered* or given at regular periods: the uniform worn by servants: a dress peculiar to certain persons or things, as in the trade-guilds of London: any characteristic dress: the being kept and fed at a certain rate, as horses at livery: the whole body of liverymen in London. [Fr. *livrée*—*livrer*—Low L. *libero,* to give or hand over. See Deliver.]

Liveryman, liv'ėr-i-man, *n.* a man who wears a *livery:* a freeman of the city of London entitled to wear the livery and enjoy other privileges of his Company.

Livery-stable, liv'ėr-i-stā'bl, *n.* a *stable* where horses are kept at *livery.*    [reared on a farm.

Livestock, līv'stok, *n.* the animals employed or Livid, liv'id, *adj.* black and blue: of a lead colour: discoloured.—*n.* Liv'idness. [Fr.—L. *lividus*— *liveo,* to be of a lead colour, or black and blue.]

Living, liv'ing, *adj.* having *life:* active, lively: producing action or vigour: running or flowing. —*n.* means of subsistence: a property: the benefice of a clergyman.—The Living, those alive.

Livre, lē'vr, *n.* an old French coin, about the value of a franc, by which it was superseded. [Fr. —L. *libra,* a pound.]

Lizard, liz'ard, *n.* a genus of four-footed scaly reptiles. [Fr. *lézard,* It. *lucerta*—L. *lacerta.*]

Llama, lä'ma or lä'ma, *n.* a small species of camel peculiar to South America. [Peruvian.]

Llano, lan'o, *n.* one of the vast steppes or plains in the northern part of South America:—*pl.* Llan'os. [Sp., from L. *planus,* plain.]

Lloyd's, loidz, *n.* a part of the London Royal Exchange frequented by ship-owners, underwriters, &c. to obtain shipping intelligence, and transact marine insurance. [So called from their orig. meeting at *Lloyd's* Coffee-house.]

Lo, lō, *int.* look: see: behold. [A.S. *la,* an imitative word.]        [*loche,* Sp. *loja.*]

Loach, Loche, lōch, *n.* a small river-fish. [Fr.

Load, lōd, *v.t.* to *lade* or burden: to put on as much as can be carried: to heap on: to put on overmuch: to confer or give in great abundance: to charge, as a gun.—*n.* a lading or burden: as much as can be carried at once: freight or cargo: a measure: any large quantity borne: a quantity sustained with difficulty: that which burdens or grieves: a weight or encumbrance. [A.S. *hladan,* to load.]

Loading, lōd'ing, *n.* the act of *loading* or *lading:* a charge, cargo, or lading.

Loadstar. Same as Lodestar.

Loadstone. Same as Lodestone.

Loaf, lōf, *n.* a regularly shaped mass of bread: a mass of sugar: any lump:—*pl.* Loaves (lōvz). [A.S. *hlaf;* Goth. *hlaifs,* Ger. *laib,* Russ. *khlieb.*]

fāte, fär; mē, hėr; mīne; mōte; mūte; mōōn; *then.*

**Loaf**, lōf, *v.i.* to loiter, pass time idly.—*n.* **Loaf'er.** [Prov. Ger. *lōfen*, Ger. *laufen*, to run about.]

**Loaf-sugar**, lōf'-shoog'ar, *n.* refined *sugar* in the form of a *loaf* or cone.

**Loam**, lōm, *n.* a muddy soil, of clay, sand, and animal and vegetable matter.—*v.t.* to cover with loam. [A.S. *lam;* Ger. *lehm*, akin to E. **Lime.**]

**Loamy**, lōm'i, *adj.* consisting of or resembling *loam.*

**Loan**, lōn, *n.* anything *lent:* the act of lending: permission to use: money lent for interest. —*v.t.* to lend. [A.S. *læn;* Ice. *lan*, Dan. *laan*, cf. Ger. *lehen*, a fief.]

**Loath** or **Loth**, lōth, *adj.* disliking: reluctant, unwilling.—*adv.* **Loath'ly.**—*n.* **Loath'ness.** [A.S. *lath;* Ger. *leiden*, to suffer.]

**Loathe**, lōth, *v.t.* to dislike greatly, to feel disgust at. [A.S. *lathian.*]

**Loathful**, lōth'fool, *adj.* full of loathing, hate, or abhorrence: exciting loathing or disgust.

**Loathing**, lōth'ing, *n.* extreme hate or disgust: abhorrence.—*adj.* hating.—*adv.* **Loath'ingly.**

**Loathsome**, lōth'sum, *adj.* exciting loathing or abhorrence: detestable.—*adv.* **Loath'somely.**— *n.* **Loath'someness.**

**Loaves**, lōvz, *n., pl.* of **Loaf.**

**Lobate**, lōb'āt, **Lobed**, lōbd', *adj.* having or consisting of *lobes.*

**Lobby**, lob'i, *n.* a small hall or waiting-room: a passage serving as a common entrance to several apartments. [Low L. *lobia*—O. Ger. *loube*, Ger. *laube*, a portico, arbour—*laub*, E. *leaf.* See **Lodge.**]

**Lobe**, lōb, *n.* the lower part of the ear: (*anat.*) a division of the lungs, brain, &c.: (*bot.*) a division of a leaf.—*adj.* **Lob'ular.** [Fr., prob. through Low L. from Gr. *lobos;* akin to **Lap**, to fold.]

**Lobelet**, lōb'let, **Lobule**, lob'ūl, *n.* a *small lobe.*

**Lobelia**, lob-ē'li-a, *n.* an ornamental flower, the roots of which are used in medicine. [*Lobel*, a Flemish botanist.]

**Lobster**, lob'stėr, *n.* a shellfish with large claws, used for food. [A.S. *loppestre, lopystre;* a corr. of L. *locusta*, a lobster.]

**Lobworm**, lob'wurm, *n.* a large worm used as bait. [So called from its clumsy form. See **Lubbard.**]

**Local**, lō'kal, *adj.* of or belonging to a *place:* confined to a spot or district.—*adv.* **Lo'cally.** [Fr. —L. *localis*—*locus*, a place.]

**Localise**, lō'kal-īz, *v.t.* to make *local:* to put into a place.—*n.* **Localisa'tion.** [tion>: district.

**Locality**, lō-kal'i-ti, *n.* existence in a *place:* position.

**Locate**, lō-kāt' or lō'kāt, *v.t.* to *place:* to set in a particular position: to designate the place of.

**Location**, lō-kā'shun, *n.* act of locating or placing: situation: (*law*) a leasing on rent.

**Locative**, lō'ka-tiv, *adj.* (*gram.*) indicating *place.*

**Loch**, loch, *n.* a lake or arm of the sea. [Gael. and Ir. *loch*, W. *llwch*, L. *lacus*, E. **Lake.**]

**Loche**, *n.* See **Loach.**

**Lock**, lok, *n.* an instrument to fasten doors, &c.: an inclosure in a canal for raising or lowering boats: the part of a firearm by which it is discharged: a grapple in wrestling: a state of being immovable: any narrow confined place.—*v.t.* to fasten with a *lock:* to fasten so as to impede motion: to shut up: to close fast: to embrace closely: to furnish with locks.—*v.i.* to become fast: to unite closely. [A.S. *loca*, a lock; Ice. *loka*, a bolt, Ger. *loch*, a dungeon.]

**Lock**, lok, *n.* a tuft or ringlet of hair: a flock of wool, &c. [A.S. *locc;* Ice. *lokkr*, Ger. *locke*, a lock.]

**Lockage**, lok'āj, *n.* the *locks* of a canal: the difference in their levels, the materials used for them, and the tolls paid for passing through them.

**Locker**, lok'ėr, *n.* any closed place that may be *locked.*

**Locket**, lok'et, *n.* a *small lock:* a little ornamental case of gold or silver, usually containing a miniature.

**Lock-jaw**, lok'-jaw, **Locked-jaw**, lokt'-jaw, *n.* a contraction of the muscles of the *jaw* by which its motion is suspended. [**Lock** and **Jaw.**]

**Lock-keeper**, lok'-kēp'ėr, *n.* one who *keeps* or attends the *locks* of a canal.

**Lockram**, lok'ram, *n.* a kind of coarse linen, so called from *Locrenan*, in Bretagne, where it is made. [mends *locks.*

**Locksmith**, lok'smith, *n.* a *smith* who makes and

**Lockstitch**, lok'stich, *n.* a *stitch* formed by the *locking* of two threads together.

**Lockup**, lok'up, *n.* a place for *locking up* or confining persons for a short time.

**Locomotion**, lō-ko-mō'shun, *n.* act or power of *moving* from *place* to *place.*

**Locomotive**, lō-ko-mō'tiv or lō'-, *adj., moving* from *place* to *place:* capable of or assisting in locomotion.—*n.* a *locomotive* machine: a railway engine.—*n.* **Locomotiv'ity.** [L. *locus*, a place, and *moveo, motum*, to move.]

**Loculous**, lok'ū-lus, *adj.* (*bot.*) divided internally into *cells.* [L. *loculus*, a cell, dim. of *locus.*]

**Locus**, lō'kus, *n., place:* (*math.*) the curve described by a point, or the surface generated by a line, moving in a given manner. [L.]

**Locust**, lō'kust, *n.* a migratory winged insect, in shape like the grasshopper, highly destructive to vegetation: a name of several plants and trees. [L. *locusta.*]

**Lode**, lōd, *n.* (*mining*) a *course* or vein containing metallic ore. [A.S. *lād*, a course—*lithan*, to lead. See **Lead**, to shew the way.]

**Lodestar**, lōd'stär, *n.* the *star* that *leads* or guides: the pole-star.

**Lodestone**, lōd'stōn, *n.* a *stone* or ore of iron that *leads* or attracts other pieces of iron. [Made up of **Lode** and **Stone**. See **Magnet.**]

**Lodge**, loj, *n.* a small house in a park (*B.*, a hut): the cottage of a gatekeeper: a retreat: a secret association, also the place of meeting.—*v.t.* to furnish with a temporary dwelling: to infix, to settle: to drive to covert: to lay flat, as grain. —*v.i.* to reside: to rest: to dwell for a time (*B.*, to pass the night): to lie flat, as grain. [Fr. *loge*, from root of **Lobby.**]

**Lodger**, loj'ėr, *n.* one who *lodges* or lives at board or in a hired room: one who stays in any place for a time.

**Lodging**, loj'ing, *n.* temporary habitation: a room or rooms hired in the house of another (often in *pl.*): harbour.

**Lodgment**, loj'ment, *n.*, act of *lodging*, or state of being lodged: accumulation of something that remains at rest: (*mil.*) the occupation of a position by a besieging party, and the works thrown up to maintain it.

**Loft**, loft, *n.* the room or space immediately under a roof: a gallery in a hall or church: (*B.*) an upper room. [From the Scand., as in Ice. *lopt* (pronounced *loft*), the sky or air, an upper room; A.S. *lyft*, Ger. *luft*, the air. See **Lift.**]

**Lofty**, loft'i, *adj.* high in position, character, sentiment, or diction: high: stately: haughty.— *adv.* **Loft'ily.**—*n.* **Loft'iness.**

**Log**, log, *n.* a Hebrew liquid measure = $\frac{3}{4}$ or $\frac{5}{6}$ of a pint. [Heb., a basin—*lug*, to be hollow.]

**Log**, log, *n.* a bulky piece of wood : (*naut.*) a piece of wood, with a line, for measuring the speed of a ship. [Scand., as in Ice. *lag*, Dan. *log*.]

**Logarithm**, log´a-rithm, *n.* (of a number) the power to which another given number must be raised in order that it may equal the former number. [Lit. 'the number of the ratios,' Gr. *logos*, ratio, and *arithmos*, number.]

**Logarithmic**, log-a-rith´mik, **Logarithmical**, log-a-rith´mik-al, *adj.* pertaining to or consisting of logarithms.—*adv.* **Logarith´mically.**

**Logboard**, log´bōrd, **Logbook**, log´book, *ns.* (*naut.*) a *board* and *book* on which the *log*-reckoning is kept.

**Log-cabin**, log´-kab´in, **Loghouse**, log´hows, **Log-hut**, log´hut, *ns.* a *cabin*, *house*, or *hut* built of *logs*.

**Loggerhead**, log´ėr-hed, *n.* a *blockhead* : a dunce : (*naut.*) a round piece of timber, in a whale-boat, over which the line is passed : a species of sea-turtle :—*pl.* quarrel : dispute. [**Log**, a piece of wood, and **Head**.]

**Logic**, loj´ik, *n.* the science and art of *reasoning* correctly : the science of the necessary laws of thought. [Gr. *logikē*, from *logos*, speech, reason.]

**Logical**, loj´ik-al, *adj.* according to the rules of logic : skilled in logic : discriminating.—*adv.* **Log´ically.**

**Logician**, lo-jish´an, *n.* one skilled in logic.

**Logistic**, lo-jis´tik, **Logistical**, lo-jis´tik-al, *adj.* (*lit.*) skilled in *calculating* : (*math.*) made on the scale of sixty. [Gr. *logistikos*—*logizomai*, to calculate—*logos*, a number.]

**Logline**, log´līn, *n.* the *line* fastened to the *log*, and marked for finding the speed of a vessel.

**Logography**, lo-gog´ra-fi, *n.* a method of printing with whole words cast in a single type. [Gr. *logographia*, word-writing—*logos*, word, and *graphō*, to write.]

**Logomachy**, lo-gom´a-ki, *n.*, *contention* about *words* or in words merely. [Gr. *logomachia*—*logos*, word, and *machē*, fight.]

**Logreel**, log´rēl, *n.* a *reel* for the *log*line.

**Logwood**, log´wood, *n.* a red *wood* much used in dyeing. [**Log** and **Wood**.]

**Loin**, loin, *n.* the back of a beast cut for food :—*pl.* the reins, or the lower part of the back. [O. Fr. *logne*, Fr. *longe*, loin—L: *lumbus*, loin.]

**Loiter**, loi´tėr, *v.i.* to delay : to be slow in moving : to linger.—*n.* **Loi´terer.** [Dut. *leuteren*, to trifle ; Ger. *lottern*, to waver ; from root of **Lout**.]

**Loll**, lol, *v.i.* to lie lazily about, to lounge : to hang out from the mouth.—*v.t.* to thrust out (the tongue). [M. E. *lollen*, prob. from O. Dut. *lollen*, to sit over the fire ; Ice. *lalla*, to move slowly. See **Lull**.]

**Lollards**, lol´ards, *n.pl.* a sect of reformers in Germany, arising about 1300 A.D. : the followers of Wycliffe in England. [Prob. from Low Ger. *lollen*, to sing, to hum, the name having arisen from the manner of singing peculiar to them ; cf. **Lull**.]

**Lone**, lōn, **Lonely**, lōn´li, *adj.*, *alone* : having no company : solitary : retired : standing by itself.—*n.* **Lone´liness.** [Contraction of **Alone**.]

**Lonesome**, lōn´sum, *adj.* solitary : dismal.—*adv.* **Lone´somely.**—*n.* **Lone´someness.**

**Long**, long, *adj.* (comp. **Long´er** ; superl. **Long´est**) extended : not short : extended in time : slow in coming : tedious : far-reaching.—*adv.* to a great extent in space or time : through the whole : all along.—*v.i.* to desire earnestly : to have an eager appetite.—*adv.* **Long´ingly.** [A.S. *lang* ;

found in all the Teut. languages, as in Ger. *lang*, also in L. *longus*.]

**Longboat**, long´bōt, *n.* the *longest boat* of a ship.

**Longeval**, lon-jē´val, **Longevous**, lon-jē´vus, *adj.* of *long* or great *age*. [L. *longus*, long, *ævum*, age.]

**Longevity**, lon-jev´i-ti, *n.*, *long life* : old age.

**Longimanous**, lon-jim´a-nus, *adj.*, *long-handed*. [L. *longus*, long, and *manus*, a hand.]

**Longish**, long´ish, *adj.* somewhat long.

**Longitude**, lon´ji-tūd, *n.* distance of a place east or west of a given meridian : distance in degrees from the vernal equinox, on the ecliptic. [Lit. 'length,' Fr.—L. *longitudo*.]

**Longitudinal**, lon-ji-tūd´i-nal, *adj.* pertaining to longitude or length : extending lengthwise.—*adv.* **Longitud´inally.**

**Long-measure**, long´-mezh´ūr, *n.* the *measure* of *length*.

**Longrun**, long´run, *n.* the *long* or whole *run* or course of events : the ultimate result.

**Longshore-man**, long´shōr-man, *n.* a *man* employed *along* the *shore* or about wharfs in loading and unloading vessels.

**Long-sighted**, long´-sīt´ed, *adj.* able to *see* at a *long* distance : sagacious.—*n.* **Long´-sight´ed-ness.**

**Long-stop**, long´-stop, *n.* (*cricket*) one whose duty is to stand behind the wicket-keeper and *stop* balls sent a *long* distance.

**Long-suffering**, long´-suf´ėr-ing, *adj.*, *suffering* or enduring *long*.—*n.*, *long* endurance or patience.

**Long-vacation**, long´-va-kā´shun, *n.* (*law*), in autumn, the period during which judicial proceedings are intermitted. [See **Loo**.]

**Loo**, lōō, *n.* a game at cards.—*v.t.* to beat in the game of loo :—*pr.p.* lōō´ing ; *pa.p.* lōōed´. [Formerly *lanterloo*—Fr. *lanturelu*, nonsense, fudge, a game at cards, orig. the refrain of a famous vaudeville of the time of Cardinal Richelieu.]

**Loof**, lōōf, *n.* the after-part of a ship's bow where the planks begin to curve in towards the cut-water. [See **Luff**.]

**Look**, look, *v.i.* to turn the eye toward so as to *see*: to direct the attention to : to watch : to seem : to face, as a house : (*B.*) to expect.—*v.t.* to express by a look : to influence by look.—**Look after**, to attend to or take care of : (*B.*) to expect.—**Look into**, to inspect closely.—**Look on**, to regard, view, think.—**Look out**, to watch : to select.—**Look to**, to take care of : to depend on.—**Look through**, to penetrate with the eye or the understanding.—*n.* **Look´er-on.** [A.S. *locian*, to see ; O. Ger. *luogen*.]

**Look**, look, *n.* the act of looking or seeing : sight : air of the face : appearance.

**Look**, look, *imp.* or *int.* see : behold.

**Looking**, look´ing, *n.*, *seeing* : search or searching.—**Look´ing-for**, (*B.*) expectation.—**Look´ing-glass**, a *glass* which reflects the image of the person *looking* into it, a mirror.

**Lookout**, look´owt, *n.* a careful *looking out* or watching for : an elevated place from which to observe : one engaged in watching.

**Loom**, lōōm, *n.* the frame or machine for weaving cloth : the handle of an oar, or the part within the rowlock. [A.S. *geloma*, furniture, utensils.]

**Loom**, lōōm, *v.i.* to *shine* or appear above the horizon : to appear larger than the real size, as in a mist : to be seen at a distance in the mind's ye, as something in the future. [A.S. *leomian*, to shine—*leoma*, a beam of light. Allied to **Light**.]

**Looming**, lōōm´ing, *n.* the indistinct and magnified

# Loon

Louver

appearance of objects seen in certain states of the atmosphere : mirage.

**Loon,** lōōn, *n.* a low fellow, a rascal. [O. Dut. *loen.*]

**Loon** (also **Loom**), lōōn, *n.* a genus of web-footed aquatic birds, with short wings, and legs placed very far back, also called *Divers* from their expertness in diving. [Ice. *lomr*, prob. influenced by *loon*, as above, from their awkward manner of walking.]

**Loop,** lōōp, *n.* a doubling of a cord through which another may pass : an ornamental doubling in fringes.—*v.t.* to fasten or ornament with loops. [Prob. from Celt. *lub*, a bend, a fold.]

**Loop,** lōōp, **Loophole,** lōōp′hōl, *n.* a small *hole* in a wall, &c. through which small-arms may be fired : a means of escape.—*adj.* **Loop′holed.**

**Loopers,** lōōp′ėrz, *n.pl.* the caterpillars of certain moths, which move by drawing up the hindpart of their body to the head, thus forming a *loop.*

**Loose,** lōōs, *adj.*, *slack*, *free* : unbound : not confined : not compact : not strict : unrestrained : licentious : inattentive.—*adv.* **Loose′ly.**—*n.* **Loose′ness.**—**Break loose,** to escape from confinement.—**Let loose,** to set at liberty. [A.S. *leas*, loose, weak ; from the same root as **Loose,** *v.t.* and **Lose,** seen also in Goth. *laus*, Ger. *los*, loose.]

**Loose,** lōōs, *v.t.* to *free from* any fastening : to release : to relax.—*v.i.* (*B.*) to set sail. [A.S. *losian* ; Ger. *lösen*, Goth. *lausjan*, to loose. From root of **Lose.**]

**Loosen,** lōōs′n, *v.t.* to make *loose* : to relax anything tied or rigid : to make less dense : to open, as the bowels.—*v.i.* to become loose : to become less tight.

**Loot,** lōōt, *n.* act of plundering, esp. in a conquered city : plunder.—*v.t.* or *v.i.* to plunder. [Hindi *lut*—Sans. *lotra, loptra*, stolen goods.]

**Lop,** lop, *v.t.* to cut off the top or extreme parts of, esp. of a tree : to curtail by cutting away the superfluous parts :—*pr.p.* **lopp′ing** ; *pa.t.* and *pa.p.* **lopped′.**—*n.* twigs and small branches of trees cut off. [Dut. *lubben*, to cut ; perhaps connected with **Leaf.**]

**Loquacious,** lo-kwā′shus, *adj.*, *talkative.*—*adv.* **Loqua′ciously.**—*ns.* **Loqua′ciousness, Loquac′ity,** talkativeness. [L. *loquax, -acis*—*loquor*, to speak.]

**Lord,** lawrd, *n.* a master : a superior : a husband : a ruler : the proprietor of a manor : a baron : a peer of the realm : the son of a duke or marquis, or the eldest son of an earl : a bishop, esp. if a member of parliament : (*B.*) the Supreme Being, Jehovah (when printed in capitals).—*v.t.* to raise to the peerage.—*v.i.* to act the lord : to tyrannise.—**Lord's-day,** the first day of the week.—**Lord's-supper,** the sacrament of the communion, instituted at our *Lord's* last *supper.* [M. E. *loverd, laverd*—A.S. *hlaford*—*hlaf*, a loaf, bread, and either *weard*, warder, or *ord*, origin.]

**Lordling,** lawrd′ling, *n.* a *little lord* : a would-be lord.

**Lordly,** lawrd′li, *adj.*, *like*, becoming or pertaining to a *lord* : dignified : haughty : tyrannical.—*adv.* **Lord′ly.**—*n.* **Lord′liness.**

**Lordship,** lawrd′ship, *n.* state or condition of being a *lord* : the territory belonging to a lord : dominion : authority.

**Lore,** lōr, *n.* that which is *learned* or *taught* : doctrine : learning. [A.S. *lar*, from root of **learn.**]

**Lorica,** lo-rī′ka, *n.* in ancient Rome, a cuirass made of *thongs.* [L.—*lorum*, a thong.]

**Loricate,** lor′i-kāt, *v.t.* to furnish with a *lorica* or

coat-of-mail : to plate or coat over. [L. *lorico, -atum*—*lorica.*]

**Lorication,** lor-i-kā′shun, *n.* a coating or crusting over, as with plates of mail. [L. *loricatio.*]

**Loriot,** lō′ri-ut, *n.* the *oriole.* [Fr. *le*, the, and *oriol*—L. *aureolus*, dim. of *aureus*, golden—*aurum*, gold. See **Oriole.**]

**Lorry,** lor′i, *n.* a four-wheeled wagon without sides. [Perh. from prov. E. *lurry*, to pull or lug.]

**Lory,** lō′ri, *n.* a small bird allied to the parrot. [Malay *luri.*]

**Lose,** lōōz, *v.t.* the opposite of keep or gain : to be deprived of : to mislay : to waste, as time : to miss : to bewilder : to cause to perish : to ruin : to suffer waste:—*pr.p.* **losing** (lōōz′ing); *pa.t.* and *pa.p.* **lost.**—*adj.* **Los′able.**—*n.* **Los′er.** [A.S. *losian*—*leosan* ; cog. with Ger. ver-*lieren*, to lose, Gr. *luo*, to loose ; perh. akin to **Less.** See **Loose.**] [ingly.

**Losing,** lōōz′ing, *adj.* causing *loss.*—*adv.* **Los′-**

**Loss,** los, *n.* the act of *losing* : injury : destruction : defeat : that which is lost : waste. [A.S. *los*—*leosan*, to lose. See **Lose.**]

**Lost,** lost, *adj.* parted with : no longer possessed : missing : thrown away : squandered : ruined.

**Lot,** lot, *n.* one's fate in the future : that which falls to any one as his fortune : that which decides by chance : a separate portion.—*v.t.* to allot : to separate into lots : to catalogue :—*pr.p.* **lott′ing** ; *pa.p.* **lott′ed.** [A.S. *hlot*, a lot, *hleotan*, to cast lots ; Ice. *hlutr*, lot, *hljota*, to cast lots.]

**Lote,** lōt, **Lotus,** lō′tus, **Lotos,** lō′tos, *n.* the water-lily of Egypt : a tree in N. Africa, fabled to make strangers who ate of its fruit forget their home : a genus of leguminous plants.—**Lo′tus-eat′er,** *n.* an *eater* of the *lotus* : one given up to sloth. [L. *lotus*—Gr. *lotos.*]

**Loth,** lōth, *adj.* Same as **Loath.**

**Lotion,** lō′shun, *n.* (*med.*) a fluid for external application to a wound, bruise, &c. [Fr.—L. *lotio*—*lavo, lotum*, to wash.]

**Lottery,** lot′ėr-i, *n.* a distribution of prizes by *lot* or chance : a game of chance.

**Lotus,** *n.* See **Lote.**

**Loud,** lowd, *adj.* making a great sound : striking the ear with great force : noisy : clamorous.—*adv.* **Loud, Loud′ly.**—*n.* **Loud′ness.** [Lit. 'heard,' A.S. *hlud* ; Ice. *hliod*, Ger. *laut*, sound ; L. *inclytus*, much heard of, Gr. *klytos*, heard—*klyō*, Sans. *kru*, to hear.]

**Lough,** loch, *n.* The Irish form of **Loch.**

**Louis-d'or,** lōō′e-dōr′, *n.* a French gold coin, superseded in 1795 by the 20-franc piece. [Fr. *Louis*, king's name, and *or*—L. *aurum*, gold.]

**Lounge,** lownj, *v.i.* to recline at one's ease : to move about listlessly.—*n.* the act or state of lounging : an idle stroll : a place for lounging : a kind of sofa.—*n.* **Loung′er.** [Fr. *longis*, one that is long in doing anything, formed (but with a pun on L. *longus*, long) from L. *Longius* or *Longinus*, the legendary name of the centurion who pierced the body of Christ.]

**Louse,** lows, *n.* a common wingless parasitic insect :—*pl.* **Lice** (līs). [A.S. *lus*, pl. *lys* ; Ger. *laus* ; from the root of Goth. *liusan*, to destroy, to devour.] [**Lous′iness.**

**Lousy,** lowz′i, *adj.* swarming with *lice.*—*n.*

**Lout,** lowt, *n.* a clown : a mean, awkward fellow. [From old verb *lout*—A.S. *lutan*, to stoop.]

**Loutish,** lowt′ish, *adj.* clownish : awkward and clumsy.—*adv.* **Lout′ishly.**—*n.* **Lout′ishness.**

**Louver, Louvre,** lōō′vėr, *n.* an opening in the roofs of ancient houses serving for a *skylight*, often in the form of a turret or small lantern.—

fāte, fär ; mē, hėr ; mīne ; mōte ; mūte ; mōōn ; *then.*

297

**Louver-window**, an open window in a church tower, crossed by a series of sloping boards. [O. Fr. *louvert* for *l'ouvert*, the open space. See Overt.]

**Lovable**, luv'a-bl, *adj.* worthy of love : amiable.

**Love**, luv, *n.* fondness : an affection of the mind caused by that which delights : pre-eminent kindness : benevolence : reverential regard : devoted attachment to one of the opposite sex : the object of affection : the god of love, Cupid : nothing, in billiards and some other games.—*v.t.* to be fond of : to regard with affection : to delight in with exclusive affection : to regard with benevolence. [A.S. *lufu*, love ; Ger. *liebe* ; akin to L. *libet*, *lubet*, to please, Sans. *lubh*, to desire.]

**Lovebird**, luv'berd, *n.* a genus of small *birds* of the parrot tribe, so called from their *love* or attachment to each other.     [token of *love*.

**Loveknot**, luv'not, *n.* an intricate *knot*, used as a

**Lovelock**, luv'lok, *n.* a *lock* or curl of hair hanging at the ear, worn by men of fashion in the reigns of Elizabeth and James I.

**Lovelorn**, luv'lorn, *adj.* forsaken by one's *love*. [See Forlorn.]

**Lovely**, luv'li, *adj.* exciting love or admiration : amiable : pleasing : delightful.—*n.* Love'liness.

**Lover**, luv'er, *n.* one who *loves*, esp. one in love with a person of the opposite sex : one who is fond of anything : (*B.*) a friend.

**Loving**, luv'ing, *adj.* having love or kindness : affectionate : fond : expressing love.—*adv.* Lov'ingly.—*n.* Lov'ingness.

**Loving-kindness**, luv'ing-kīnd'nes, *n.*, *kindness* full of *love* : tender regard : mercy : favour.

**Low**, lō, *v.i.* to make the loud noise of oxen : to bellow. [A.S. *hlowan* ; Dut. *loeijen* : formed from the sound.]

**Low**, lō, *adj.* (*comp.* Low'er ; *superl.* Low'est), *lying* on an inferior place or position : not high : deep : shallow : small : moderate : cheap : dejected : mean : plain : in poor circumstances : humble.—*adv.* not aloft : cheaply : meanly : in subjection, poverty, or disgrace : in times near our own : not loudly : (*astr.*) near the equator. —*n.* Low'ness. [Ice. *lagr*, Dut. *laag*, low ; allied to A.S. *licgan*, to lie.]

**Low-church**, lō'-church, *n.* a party within the Church of England who do not attach any great importance to ecclesiastical constitutions, ordinances, and forms :—opposed to **High-church**.

**Lower**, lō'er, *v.t.* to *bring low* : to depress : to degrade : to diminish.—*v.i.* to fall : to sink : to grow less.

**Lower**, low'er, *v.i.* to gather and appear gloomy, as the clouds : to threaten a storm : to frown. [M. E. *louren*—Dut. *loeren*, to frown ; or from M. E. *lure*, *lere*, the cheek, allied to A.S. *hleor*, and thus another form of Leer.]

**Lowering**, lō'er-ing, *n.* the act of bringing low or reducing.—*adj.* letting down : sinking : degrading.

**Lowering**, low'er-ing, *adj.*, *looking sullen* : appearing dark and threatening.—*adv.* Low'eringly.

**Lowermost**, lō'er-mōst, *adj.* lowest. [See Foremost.]

**Lowing**, lō'ing, *adj.* bellowing, or making the loud noise of oxen.—*n.* the bellowing or cry of cattle.

**Lowland**, lō'land, *n.*, *land low* with respect to higher land.—*n.* Low'lander, a native of lowlands.

**Lowly**, lō'li, *adj.* of a *low* or humble mind : not high : meek : modest.—*n.* Low'liness.

**Low-pressure**, lō'-presh'ur, *adj.* employing or exerting a *low* degree of *pressure* (viz., less than

50 lbs. to the sq. inch), said of steam and steam-engines.

**Low-spirited**, lō'-spir'it-ed, *adj.* having the *spirits low* or cast down : not lively : sad.—*n.* Low'-spir'itedness.          [*tide* at ebb.

**Low-water**, lō'-waw'ter, *n.* the *lowest* point of the

**Loyal**, loy'al, *adj.* faithful to one's sovereign : obedient : true to a lover.—*adv.* Loy'ally.—*n.* Loy'alty. [Orig. faithful to *law*, Fr.—L. *legalis*, pertaining to the law—*lex*, *legis*, law.]

**Loyalist**, loy'al-ist, *n.* a *loyal* adherent of his sovereign, esp. in English history, a partisan of the Stuarts : in the American war, one that sided with the British troops.

**Lozenge**, loz'enj, *n.* an oblique-angled parallelogram or a rhombus : a small cake of flavoured sugar, orig. lozenge or diamond shaped : (*her.*) the rhomb-shaped figure in which the arms of maids, widows, and deceased persons are borne. [Fr. *losange*, of uncertain origin.]

**Lubber**, lub'er, **Lubbard**, lub'ard, *n.* an awkward, clumsy fellow : a lazy, sturdy fellow.—*adj.* and *adv.* Lubb'erly. [W. *llob*, a dolt, *llabbi*, a stripling, perh. conn. with *lleipr*, flabby.]

**Lubricate**, lōō'bri-kāt, *v.t.* to make smooth or *slippery*.—*ns.* Lu'bricator, Lubrica'tion, Lu'bricant. [L. *lubrico*, *-atum*—*lubricus*, slippery.]

**Lubricity**, lōō-bris'i-ti, *n.*, *slipperiness* : smoothness : instability : lewdness.

**Luce**, loos, *n.* a fresh-water fish, the pike. [O. Fr. *lus*—L. *lucius*.]

**Lucent**, lōō'sent, *adj.*, *shining* : bright. [L. *lucens*—*luceo*, to shine—*lux*, *lucis*, light.]

**Lucerne**, lōō-sern', *n.* a well-known fodder-plant. [Fr. *luzerne*, from the Gael. *llysian*, a plant.]

**Lucid**, lōō'sid, *adj.*, *shining* : transparent : easily understood : intellectually bright : not darkened with madness.—*adv.* Lu'cidly.—*ns.* Lucid'ity, Lu'cidness. [L. *lucidus*—*lux*, *lucis*, light.]

**Lucifer**, lōō'si-fer, *n.* (*lit.*) *light-bringer* : the planet Venus when it appears as the morning-star : Satan : a match of wood tipped with a combustible substance which is ignited by friction. [L. *lux*, *lucis*, light, and *fero*, to bring.]

**Luck**, luk, *n.* fortune, good or bad : chance : lot : good fortune. [From a Low Ger. root, seen in Dut. *luk*, also in Ger. *glück*, prosperity, fortune.]

**Luckless**, luk'les, *adj.* without good-luck : unhappy.—*adv.* Luck'lessly.—*n.* Luck'lessness.

**Lucky**, luk'i, *adj.* having good-luck : fortunate : auspicious.—*adv.* Luck'ily.—*n.* Luck'iness.

**Lucrative**, lōō'kra-tiv, *adj.* bringing *lucre* or gain : profitable.—*adv.* Lu'cratively.

**Lucre**, lōō'ker, *n.*, *gain* (esp. sordid gain) : profit : advantage. [Fr.—L. *lucrum*, gain, akin to Gr. *leia*, booty, Ir. *luach*, wages, Ger. *lohn*, pay, Sans. *lotra* for *loptra*, booty. See Loot.]

**Lucubrate**, lōō'kū-brāt, *v.i.* to work or study by lamp*light* or at night. [L. *lucubro*, *atum*—*lux*.]

**Lucubration**, lōō-kū-brā'shun, *n.* study by lamp-*light* : that which is composed by night : any composition produced in retirement.

**Lucubratory**, lōō'kū-brā-tor-i, *adj.* composed by candle-*light*.

**Luculent**, lōō'kū-lent, *adj.* lucid : clear : transparent : evident. [L. *luculentus*—*lux*.]

**Ludicrous**, lōō'di-krus, *adj.* that serves for *sport* : adapted to excite laughter : laughable : comic. —*adv.* Lu'dicrously.—*n.* Lu'dicrousness. [L. *ludicrus*—*ludo*, to play.]

**Luff**, luf, *n.* the *windward* side of a ship : the act of sailing a ship close to the wind : the loof.— *v.i.* to turn a ship towards the wind. [Orig. the palm of the hand (Scot. *loof*), then a fixed paddle (like the palm of the hand) attached to a ship's side, and which being placed to suit the wind, gave its name to the windward side of a ship : found in M. E. *lof*, which is cog. with and (in this sense) perh. borrowed from Dut. *loef*.]

**Lug**, lug, *v.t.* to *pull* along : to drag : to pull with difficulty :—*pr.p.* lugging ; *pa.t.* and *pa.p.* lugged'. [From a Scand. root, found in Sw. *lugga*, to pull by the hair—*lugg*, the forelock ; from a base *luk*, to pull, present in Scot. *lug*, the ear.]

**Luggage**, lug'āj, *n.* the trunks and other baggage of a traveller, so called from their being *lugged* or dragged along.

**Lugger**, lug'ẽr, *n.* a small vessel with two or three masts, a running bowsprit, and long or *lug* sails.

**Lugsail**, lug'sāl, *n.* a square *sail* bent upon a yard that *hangs* obliquely to the mast.

**Lugubrious**, loo-gū'bri-us, *adj.*, *mournful* : sorrowful.—*adv.* Lugu'briously. [L. *lugubris*—*lugeo*, to mourn.]

**Lugworm**, lug'wurm, *n.* a sluggish *worm* found in the sand on the sea-shore, much used for bait by fishermen, also called Lob'worm. [From root of Lag, Log, and Worm.]

**Lukewarm**, look'wawrm, *adj.*, *partially* or moderately *warm* : indifferent.—*n.* Luke'warmness. [M. E. *leuk*, *luke*, an extension of *lew*, cog. with the A.S. *hleo*, the source of Lee, or from A.S. *wlæc*, warm ; cf. Dut. *leuk*, Ger. *lau*.]

**Lull**, lul, *v.t.* to soothe : to compose : to quiet.—*v.i.* to become calm : to subside.—*n.* a season of calm. [Scand., as in Sw. *lulla* ; an imitative word, like Ger. *lallen*, Gr. *laleo*.] [sleep.

**Lullaby**, lul'a-bi, *n.* a song to *lull* children to

**Lumbago**, lum-bā'gō, *n.* a rheumatic pain in the *loins* and small of the back. [L.—*lumbus*, a loin.]

**Lumbar**, lum'bar, **Lumbal**, lum'bal, *adj.* pertaining to or near the *loins*. [See Lumbago.]

**Lumber**, lum'bẽr, *n.* anything cumbersome or useless : timber sawed or split for use.—*v.t.* to fill with lumber : to heap together in confusion. [Fr.—Ger. *Langbart* ; the *lumber*-room being orig. the *Lombard*-room or place where the Lombards, the mediæval bankers and pawnbrokers, stored their pledges.]

**Lumber**, lum'bẽr, *v.i.* to move heavily and laboriously. [From a Scand. root seen in prov. Sw. *lomra*, to resound, Ice. *hljomr*, a sound.]

**Lumbering**, lum'bẽr-ing, *adj.* filling with *lumber* : putting in confusion (See Lumber, *n.*) : moving heavily. (See Lumber, *v.i.*)

**Luminary**, loo'min-ar-i, *n.* any body which gives *light*, esp. one of the heavenly bodies : one who illustrates any subject or instructs mankind. [L *lumen*, *luminis*, light—*luceo*, to shine.]

**Luminiferous**, loo-min-if'er-us, *adj.*, *transmitting light*. [L. *lumen*, *luminis*, light—*fero*, to carry.]

**Luminous**, loo'min-us, *adj.* giving *light* : shining : illuminated : clear : lucid.—*adv.* Lu'minously. —*ns.* Lu'minousness, Luminos'ity.

**Lump**, lump, *n.* a small shapeless mass : the whole together : the gross.—*v.t.* to throw into a confused mass : to take in the gross. [From a Scand. root seen in Norw. *lump*, Dut. *lomp*.]

**Lumper**, lump'ẽr, *n.* a labourer employed in the lading or unlading of ships. [From Lump, *v.t.*]

**Lumpfish**, lump'fish, *n.* a clumsy sea-fish with a short, deep, and thick body and head, and a ridge on its back, also called Lump'sucker, from the power of its *sucker*. [Lump and Fish.]

**Lumping**, lump'ing, *adj.* in a *lump* : heavy : bulky.

**Lumpish**, lump'ish, *adj.* like a *lump* : heavy :

gross : dull.—*adv.* Lump'ishly.—*n.* Lump'ishness.

**Lumpy**, lump'i, *adj.* full of lumps.

**Lunacy**, loo'na-si, *n.* a kind of madness formerly supposed to be affected by the *moon* : insanity.

**Lunar**, loon'ar, **Lunary**, loon'ar-i, *adj.* belonging to the *moon* : measured by the revolutions of the moon : caused by the moon : like the moon. —**Lunar caustic**, fused crystals of nitrate of silver, applied to ulcers, &c. [L. *lunaris*—*luna*, the moon—*luceo*, to shine.]

**Lunate**, loon'āt, **Lunated**, loon'āt-ed, *adj.* formed like a half-*moon* : crescent-shaped.

**Lunatic**, loo'na-tik, *adj.* affected with *lunacy*.—*n.* a person so affected : a madman.

**Lunation**, loo-nā'shun, *n.* the time between two revolutions of the *moon* : a lunar month.

**Lunch**, lunsh, **Luncheon**, lunsh'un, *n.* a slight repast between breakfast and dinner.—*v.i.* to take a lunch. [Our word *lunch* is a contr. of *luncheon*, and the latter is prob. from prov. E. *lunch*, a lump of bread, which again is simply a form of Lump.]

**Lune**, loon, *n.* anything in the shape of a half-*moon*. [Fr. *lune*—L. *luna*.]

**Lunette**, loo-net', *n.* a *little moon* : (*fort.*) a detached bastion : a hole in a concave ceiling to admit light : a watch-glass flattened more than usual in the centre. [Fr., dim. of *lune*.]

**Lung**, lung, *n.* one of the organs of breathing, so called from its *light* or spongy texture.—*adj.* **Lunged**. [A.S. *lungan*, the lungs ; from a root seen in Sans. *laghu*, light.]

**Lunge**, lunj, *n.* a sudden thrust in fencing.—*v.i.* to give such a thrust. [A clipped form of Fr. *allonger*, to lengthen—L. *ad*, and *longus*, long, the arm being extended in delivering a thrust.]

**Lungwort**, lung'wurt, *n.* an herb with purple flowers, so called from a fancied likeness of its spotted leaves to the *lungs* : a lichen that grows on tree trunks. [Lung, and A.S. *wurt*, plant.]

**Lupine**, loo'pīn, *adj.* like a *wolf* : wolfish. [L. *lupinus*—*lupus*, Gr. *lykos*, a wolf.]

**Lupine**, loo'pin, *n.* a kind of flowering pulse. [Fr. —L. *lupinus*, same word as the above.]

**Lupus**, loo'pus, *n.* a malignant corroding skindisease, often affecting the nose. [L. *lupus*, a wolf ; so called from its eating away the flesh.]

**Lurch**, lurch, **To leave in the**, to leave in a difficult situation, or without help. [O. Fr. *lourche*, a game at tables, also used when one party gains every point before the other makes one.]

**Lurch**, lurch, *v.i.* to evade by stooping, to lurk : to roll or pitch suddenly to one side (as a ship). —*n.* a sudden roll of a ship to one side. [From root of Lurk.]

**Lurcher**, lurch'ẽr, *n.* one who *lurks* or lies in wait : one who watches to steal, or to betray or entrap : a dog for game (a cross between the greyhound and collie).

**Lure**, loor, *n.* any enticement : bait, decoy.—*v.t.* to entice. [Orig. an object dressed up like a bird to entice a hawk back, O. Fr. *loerre*, Fr. *leurre*—Ger. *luder*, bait.] [L. *luridus*.]

**Lurid**, loo'rid, *adj.* ghastly pale : wan : gloomy.

**Lurk**, lurk, *v.i.* to lie in wait : to be concealed. [Prob. from Scand., as in Sw. *lurka*.] [sight.

**Lurking**, lurk'ing, *adj.* lying hid : keeping out of

**Luscious**, lush'us, *adj.* sweet in a great degree : delightful : fulsome as flattery.—*adv.* **Lus'ciously**.—*n.* Lus'ciousness. [Old form *lushious*, from Lusty.]

**Lush**, lush, *adj.* rich and juicy, said of grass. [A contr. of *lushious*, old form of Luscious.]

**Lust**, lust, *n.* longing desire : eagerness to possess : carnal appetite : (*B.*) any violent or depraved desire.—*v.i.* to desire eagerly : to have carnal desire : to have depraved desires. [A.S. *lust*, orig. meaning pleasure ; found in all the Teut. languages. See List, to have pleasure in.]

**Lustful**, lust'fool, *adj.* having lust : inciting to lust : sensual.—*adv.* Lust'fully.—*n.* Lust'fulness.

**Lustral**, lus'tral, *adj.* relating to or used in *lustration* or purification. See Lustre, a period.]

**Lustration**, lus-trā'shun, *n.* a *purification by sacrifice* : act of purifying. [L.—*lustro*, to purify—*lustrum*. See Lustre, a period.]

**Lustre**, lus'tėr, *n.* brightness : splendour : (*fig.*) renown : a candlestick ornamented with pendants of cut-glass. [Fr. ; either from L. *lustro*, to purify—*lustrum* (see below), or from the root of L. *luceo*, to shine.]

**Lustre**, lus'tėr, **Lustrum**, lus'trum, *n.* a period of five years : (*orig.*) the solemn offering for the *purification* of the Roman people' made by one of the censors at the conclusion of the census, taken every five years. [L. *lustrum*—*luo*, to wash, to purify.]

**Lustreless**, lus'tėr-les, *adj.* destitute of lustre.

**Lustring**, lus'tring, *n.* a kind of *glossy* silk cloth. [Fr. *lustrine*—It. *lustrino*. See Lustre, brightness.] [ous.—*adv.* Lus'trously.

**Lustrous**, lus'trus, *adj.* bright : shining : lumin-

**Lusty**, lust'i, *adj.* vigorous : healthful : stout : bulky.—*adv.* Lust'ily.—*ns.* Lust'ihood, Lust'iness. [From Lust, meaning pleasure.]

**Lutarious**, lōō-tā'ri-us, *adj.* of or like *mud*. [See Lute, composition like clay.]

**Lute**, lōōt, *n.* a stringed instrument of music like the guitar.—*ns.* Lut'er, Lut'ist, a player on a lute. [O. Fr. *leut*, Fr. *luth* ; like Ger. *laute*, from Ar. *al-'ud*—*al*, the, and *ud*, wood, the lute.]

**Lute**, lōōt, **Luting**, lōōt'ing, *n.* a composition like clay for making vessels air-tight, or protecting them when exposed to fire.—*v.t.* to close or coat with lute.—*n.* Luta'tion. [Lit. *mud*, what is *washed* down, L. *lutum*, from *luo*, to wash.]

**Lutestring**, lōōt'string, *n.* the *string* of a *lute*.

**Lutestring**, *n.* a lustrous silk. [A blunder for Lustring.]

**Lutheran**, lōō'thėr-an, *adj.* pertaining to Luther, the German Protestant reformer (1483-1546), or to his doctrines : a follower of Luther.—*n.* Lu'theranism, his doctrines.

**Luxate**, luks'āt, *v.t.* to put out of joint : to displace.—*n.* Luxa'tion, a dislocation. [L. *luxo*, *luxatum*—*luxus*, Gr. *loxos*, slanting.]

**Luxuriant**, lug-zū'ri-ant, *adj.* exuberant in growth : overabundant.—*adv.* Luxu'riantly.—*ns.* Luxu'riance, Luxu'riancy.

**Luxuriate**, lug-zū'ri-āt, *v.i.* to be luxuriant : to grow exuberantly : to live luxuriously : to expatiate with delight.

**Luxurious**, lug-zū'ri-us, *adj.* given to luxury : administering to luxury : furnished with luxuries : softening by pleasure.—*adv.* Luxu'riously.—*n.* Luxu'riousness.

**Luxury**, luks'ū-ri or luk'shū-ri, *n.* free indulgence in rich diet or costly dress or equipage : anything delightful : a dainty. [Lit. 'excess, extravagance,' from L. *luxuria*, luxury—*luxus*, excess.]

**Lycanthropy**, lī-kan'thro-pi, *n.* a form of madness, in which the patient imagines himself to be a wolf. [Gr. *lykos*, a wolf, and *anthrōpos*, a man.]

**Lyceum**, lī-sē'um, *n.* a place devoted to instruction by lectures : an association for literary im-

provement. [Orig. the place where Aristotle the Greek philosopher taught, L.—Gr. *lykeion*, from the temple of Apollo *Lykeios*, the Wolf-Slayer—*lykos*, a wolf.]

**Lychgate**. Same as Lichgate.

**Lye**, lī, *n.* a mixture of ashes and water for washing. [A.S. *leah*; Ger. *lauge*; allied to *lavo*, to wash.]

**Lying**, lī'ing, *adj.* addicted to telling *lies*.—*n.* the habit of telling lies.—*adv.* Ly'ingly.

**Lymph**, limf, *n.* water : a colourless nutritive fluid in animal bodies. [L. *lympha*.]

**Lymphatic**, lim-fat'ik, *adj.* pertaining to *lymph*. —*n.* a vessel which conveys the *lymph*.

**Lynch**, linch, *v.t.* to judge and punish without the usual forms of law. [From *Lynch*, a farmer in N. Carolina, who so acted.]

**Lynch-law**, linch'-law, *n.* (*Amer.*) a kind of summary justice exercised by the people in cases where the regular law is thought inadequate.

**Lynx**, lingks, *n.* a wild animal of the cat-kind noted for its sharp sight. [L. and Gr. *lynx*; prob. from Gr. *lykē*, light, and so called from its bright eyes.]

**Lynx-eyed**, lingks'-īd, *adj.* sharp-sighted like the *lynx*. [Lynx and Eye.]

**Lyon Court**, lī'un kōrt, *n.* the Heralds' College of Scotland, the head of which is the Lyon King-at-arms. [From the heraldic lion (O. Fr. *lyon*) of Scotland.]

**Lyrate**, lī'rāt, *adj.* (*bot.*) lyre-shaped.

**Lyre**, līr, *n.* a musical instrument like the harp, anciently used as an accompaniment to poetry : *Lyra*, one of the northern constellations.—*n.* Lyr'ist, a player on the lyre or harp. [Fr.—L. *lyra*—Gr.]

**Lyrebird**, līr'bėrd, *n.* an Australian *bird* about the size of a pheasant, having the 16 tail-feathers of the male arranged in the form of a *lyre*.

**Lyric**, lir'ik, **Lyrical**, lir'ik-al, *adj.* pertaining to the *lyre* : fitted to be sung to the lyre : written in stanzas : said of poetry which. expresses the individual emotions of the poet : that composes lyrics.—*n.* Lyr'ic, a *lyric* poem.

## M

**Mab**, mab, *n.* the queen of the fairies. [W. *mab*, a male child.]

**Macadamise**, mak-ad'am-īz, *v.t.* to cover, as a road, with small broken stones, so as to form a smooth, hard surface.—*n.* Macadamisa'tion. [From *Macadam*, the inventor, 1756-1836.]

**Macaroni**, mak-a-rō'ni, *n.* a preparation of wheat-flour in long slender tubes : a medley : something fanciful and extravagant : a fool : a fop. [O. It. *maccaroni*—*maccare*, to crush, prob. from the root of Macerate.]

**Macaronic**, mak-a-ron'ik, *adj.* pertaining to or like a *macaroni*, medley, or fool : trifling : affected : consisting of modern words Latinised, or Latin words modernised, intermixed with genuine Latin words.—*n.* a jumble : a macaronic composition.

**Macaroon**, mak-a-rōōn', *n.* a sweet biscuit made chiefly of almonds and sugar. [Fr.—It. *macarone*, sing. of Macaroni.]

**Macassar-oil**, ma-kas'ar-oil, *n.* an oil much used for the hair, imported from India and other Eastern countries. [So called because orig. exported from *Macassar*, the Dutch capital of the island of Celebes.]

**Macaw**, ma-kaw', *n.* a genus of large and beautiful birds of tropical America, closely allied to the parrots. [Said to be the native name in the W. India Islands.]

**Mace**, mās, *n.* a staff used as an ensign of authority : the heavier rod used in billiards : formerly, a weapon of offence, consisting of a staff headed with a heavy spiked ball of iron. [O. Fr. *mace* (Fr. *masse*)—obs. L. *matea*, whence L. dim. *mateola*, a mallet.]

**Mace**, mās, *n.* a spice, the second coat of the nutmeg. [Fr. *macis*—L. *macer*—Gr. *maker* ; cf. Sans. *makar-anda*, nectar of a flower.]

**Macer**, mās′ér, *n.* a mace-bearer.

**Macerate**, mas′ér-āt, *v.t.* to steep : to soften by steeping. [L. *macero*, *-atus*, to steep.]

**Maceration**, mas-ér-ā′shun, *n.* act of softening by steeping : mortification of the flesh by fasting and other austerities.

**Machiavelian**, mak-i-a-vēl′yan, *adj.* politically cunning : crafty : perfidious.—*n.* one who imitates Machiavel.—*n.* **Machiavel′ianism**. [Lit. 'pertaining to *Machiavel*,' a Florentine statesman and political writer (1469–1527), who expounded a peculiar system of statecraft.]

**Machicolation**, mach-i-ko-lā′shun, *n.* (*arch.*) a projecting parapet with apertures for *pouring* molten *substances* upon assailants.—*adj.* **Machic′olated**, having *machicolations*. [Fr. *machecoulis*, from *mèche*, a match, and *couler*, to flow—L. *colo*, to filter.]

**Machinate**, mak′i-nāt, *v.t.* to contrive skilfully : to form a plot or scheme. [L. *machinor*, *-atus* —*machina*. See **Machine**.]

**Machination**, mak-i-nā′shun, *n.* act of *machinating* or contriving a scheme for executing some purpose, esp. an evil one : an artful design deliberately formed.

**Machinator**, mak′i-nā-tur, *n.* one who *machinates*.

**Machine**, ma-shēn′, *n.* any artificial means or contrivance : an instrument formed by combining two or more of the mechanical powers : an engine : (*fig.*) supernatural agency in a poem : one who can do only what he is told. [Fr.—L. *machina*—Gr. *mēchanē*, akin to *mēch-os*, contrivance, and to the root of **May**, *v.i.* to be able, and **Make**.]

**Machinery**, ma-shēn′ér-i, *n.*, *machines* in general : the parts of a machine : means for keeping in action : supernatural agency in a poem.

**Machinist**, ma-shēn′ist, *n.* a constructor of *machines* : one well versed in machinery : one who works a machine.

**Mackerel**, mak′ér-el, *n.* a sea-fish largely used for food. [O. Fr. *makerel* (Fr. *maquereau*), prob. from L. *macula*, a stain, and so meaning the 'spotted' one.]

**Mackintosh**, mak′in-tosh, *n.* a waterproof overcoat. [From *Mackintosh*, the inventor.]

**Macrocosm**, mak′ro-kozm, *n.* the whole universe : —opposed to **Microcosm**. [Lit. the 'great world,' Gr. *makros*, long, great, and *kosmos*, the world.]

**Macula**, mak′ū-la, *n.* a *spot*, as on the skin, or on the surface of the sun, moon, or planets :—*pl.* **Maculæ**, mak′ū-lē. [L.]

**Maculate**, mak′ū-lāt, *v.t.* to *spot*, to defile.—*n.* **Macula′tion**, act of *spotting*, a spot. [L. *maculo*, *-atus*—*macula*, a spot.]

**Mad**, mad, *adj.* (*comp.* **Madd′er** ; *superl.* **Madd′est**) disordered in intellect : insane : proceeding from madness : troubled in mind : excited with any violent passion or appetite : furious with anger.—*adv.* **Mad′ly**.—*n.* **Mad′ness**. [Prob. lit. 'hurt,' 'weakened,' A.S. *ge-mæd* ; cog. with O. Sax. *ge-med*, foolish, Ice. *meidd-r*, hurt.]

**Madam**, mad′am, *n.* a courteous form of address to a lady : a lady. [Fr. *madame*—ma, my—L. *mea*, and Fr. *dame*, lady—L. *domina*.]

**Madcap**, mad′kap, *n.* a wild, rash, hot-headed person. [**Mad** and **Cap**.]

**Madden**, mad′n, *v.t.* to *make mad* : to enrage.—*v.i.* to *become mad* : to act as one mad.

**Madder**, mad′ér, *n.* a plant whose root affords a red dye. [A.S. *mædere* ; cog. with Ice. *madhra*, and Dut. *meed*, madder.]

**Made**, mād, *pa.t.* and *pa.p.* of **Make**.

**Made continually** (*Pr. Bk.*) established for ever.

**Madeira**, ma-dē′ra, *n.* a rich wine produced in *Madeira*.

**Mademoiselle**, mad-mwa-zel′, *n.* a courteous form of address to a young lady : Miss. [Fr. *ma*, my, and *demoiselle*. See **Damsel**.]

**Madhouse**, mad′hows, *n.* a house for *mad* persons.

**Madman**, mad′man, *n.* a maniac.

**Madonna, Madona**, ma-don′a, *n.* a name given to the Virgin Mary, especially as represented in art. [It. *madonna*, lit. 'my lady'—L. *mea domina*.]

**Madrepore**, mad′re-pōr, *n.* the common coral. [Lit. 'mother-stone,' Fr.—It., from *madre*, mother, and *-pora*—Gr. *pōros*, tufa.]

**Madrigal**, mad′ri-gal, *n.* (*mus.*) an elaborate vocal composition in five or six parts : a short poem expressing a graceful and tender thought. [Lit. 'pastoral,' It. *madrigale*, from *mandra*, a sheepfold—L. and Gr. *mandra*, a fold ; the affix *-gal* —L. *-calis*.]

**Madwort**, mad′wurt, *n.* a *plant* believed to cure canine *madness*. [From A.S. *wurt*, plant.]

**Maelstrom**, māl′strom, *n.* a celebrated whirlpool off the coast of Norway. [Norw. 'grinding stream.']

**Magazine**, mag-a-zēn′, *n.* a storehouse : a receptacle for military stores : the gunpowder-room in a ship : a pamphlet published periodically, containing miscellaneous compositions. [Fr. *magasin*—It. *magazzino*—Ar. *makhzan*, a storehouse.]

**Magdalen**, mag′da-len, *n.* a reformed prostitute. [From Mary Magdalene of Scripture.]

**Magenta**, ma-jen′ta, *n.* a delicate pink colour. [From the battle of Magenta in N. Italy, 1859.]

**Maggot**, mag′ut, *n.* a worm or grub : a whim.—*adj.* **Magg′oty**, full of *maggots*. [Lit. 'something bred,' W. *maceiad*, akin to *magiaid*, worms—*magu*, to breed.]

**Magi**, mā′jī, *n.pl.* priests of the Persians : the Wise Men of the East. [L.—Gr. *magos*, orig. a title equivalent to 'Reverend,' 'Doctor,' given by the Akkadians, the primitive inhabitants of Chaldea, to their wise men, whose learning was chiefly in what we should now call astrology and magical arts. The word is found in cuneiform inscriptions ; it was adopted by the Semitic inhabitants of Babylon, and from them by the Persians and Greeks.]

**Magian**, mā′ji-an, *adj.* pertaining to the *Magi*.—*n.* one of the Magi.—*n.* **Ma′gianism**, the philosophy or doctrines of the *Magi*.

**Magic**, maj′ik, *n.* the science of the *Magi* : the pretended art of producing marvellous results contrary to nature, generally by evoking spirits : enchantment : sorcery. [Fr. See **Magi**.]

**Magic**, maj′ik, **Magical**, maj′ik-al, *adj.* pertaining to, used in, or done by *magic* : imposing or startling in performance.—*adv.* **Mag′ically**.—**Magic-Lantern**, an optical instrument which produces striking effects by throwing a magnified image of a picture on a screen.

**Magician**, ma-jish′an, *n.* one skilled in *magic*.

**Magisterial**, maj-is-tē′ri-al, *adj.* pertaining or suitable to a *master*: authoritative: proud: dignified.—*adv.* **Magiste′rially.**—*n.* **Magiste′rialness.** [L. *magisterius—magister*, a master —*mag*, root of L. *mag-nus*, great. See **May**, *v.i.* to be able.]

**Magistracy**, maj′is-tra-si, *n.* the office or dignity of a *magistrate*: the body of magistrates.

**Magistrate**, maj′is-trāt, *n.* a public civil officer: a justice of the peace.—*adj.* **Magistrat′ic.** [Fr.—L. *magistratus, magister.* See **Magisterial.**]

**Magna Charta**, mag′na kär′ta, *n.* the *Great Charter* obtained from King John, 1215 A.D. [L.]

**Magnanimity**, mag-na-nim′i-ti, *n.*, *greatness* of *soul*: mental elevation or dignity: generosity. [Fr.—L. *magnanimitas—magnus*, great, and *animus*, the mind.]

**Magnanimous**, mag-nan′i-mus, *adj.*, *great-souled*: elevated in soul or sentiment: noble or honourable: brave: unselfish.—*adv.* **Magnan′i-mously.** [L.]

**Magnate**, mag′nāt, *n.* a *great man*: a noble: a man of rank or wealth. [Fr. *magnat*, a title of nobles of Hungary and Poland—L. *magnas, magnatis*, a prince—*magnus*, great.]

**Magnesia**, mag-nē′shi-a or -si-a, *n.* the single oxide of magnesium, occurring as a light, white powder. [So called from some resemblance to the **Magnet** or ‘Magnesian’ stone.]

**Magnesian**, mag-nē′shi-an or -si-an, *adj.* belonging to, containing, or resembling *magnesia.*

**Magnesium**, mag-nē′shi-um or -si-um, *n.* the metallic base of *magnesia.*

**Magnet**, mag′net, *n.* the lodestone, an iron ore which attracts iron, and, when freely suspended, points to the poles: a bar or piece of steel to which the properties of the lodestone have been imparted. [Through O. Fr., from L. *magnes*, a magnet—Gr. *magnēs*, properly ‘Magnesian’ stone, from *Magnesia*, a town in Lydia or Thessaly.]

**Magnetic**, mag-net′ik, **Magnetical**, mag-net′ik-al, *adj.* pertaining to the *magnet*: having the properties of the magnet: attractive.—*adv.* **Magnet′ically.**

**Magnetise**, mag′net-īz, *v.t.* to render *magnetic*: to attract as if by a magnet.—*v.i.* to become magnetic. [which imparts *magnetism.*]

**Magnetiser**, mag′net-īz-ėr, *n.* one who or that

**Magnetism**, mag′net-izm, *n.* the cause of the attractive power of the *magnet*: attraction: the science which treats of the properties of the magnet. [*ism.*

**Magnetist**, mag′net-ist, *n.* one skilled in *magnet-*

**Magnific**, mag-nif′ik, **Magnifical**, mag-nif′ik-al, *adj.* great: splendid: noble. [L. *magnificus— magnus*, great, and *facio*, to do.]

**Magnificat**, mag-nif′i-kat, *n.* the song of the Virgin Mary, Luke i. 46-55, beginning in the Latin Vulgate with this word. [L. ‘ (my soul) doth magnify,’ 3d pers. sing. pres. ind. of *magnifico.*]

**Magnificent**, mag-nif′i-sent, *adj.* grand: noble: pompous: displaying grandeur.—*adv.* **Magnif′i-cently.**—*n.* **Magnif′icence.** [Lit. ‘doing great things.’ See **Magnify.**]

**Magnify**, mag′ni-fī, *v.t.* to *make great* or greater: to enlarge: to increase the apparent dimensions of: to exaggerate: to praise highly:—*pa.p.* mag′nified. [Fr.—L. *magnifico.* See **Magnific**.]

**Magniloquent**, mag-nil′o-kwent, *adj.*, *speaking* in a *grand* or pompous style: bombastic.—*adv.* **Magnil′oquently.**—*n.* **Magnil′oquence.** [L., from *magnus*, great, and *loquor*, to speak.]

**Magnitude**, mag′ni-tūd, *n.*, *greatness*: size: extent: importance. [L. *magnitudo—magnus.*]

**Magnolia**, mag-nōl′i-a or -ya, *n.* a species of trees of beautiful flower and foliage found chiefly in N. America. [Named after *Pierre Magnol*, once professor of botany at Montpellier.]

**Magnum**, mag′num, *n.* a bottle holding two quarts. [L.]

**Magpie**, mag′pī, *n.* a chattering bird, of a genus allied to the crow, with *pied* or *coloured* feathers. [*Mag*, a familiar contr. of Margaret (cf. *Robin-Redbreast, Jenny-Wren*), and **Pie**, from L. *pica*, a magpie, from *pingo, pictum*, to paint.]

**Mahogany**, ma-hog′a-ni, *n.* a tree of tropical America: its wood, of great value for making furniture. [*Mahogon*, the native South American name.]

**Mahomedan, Mahometan.** See **Mohammedan.**

**Maid**, mād, **Maiden**, mād′n, *n.* an unmarried woman, esp. a young one: a virgin: a female servant. [A.S. *mæden, mægden—mæg* or *mæge*, a ‘may,’ a maid—root *mag*. See **May**, *v.i.* to be able.]

**Maiden**, mād′n, *n.* a maid: in Scotland, a machine like the guillotine, formerly used for a like purpose.—*adj.* pertaining to a virgin or young woman: consisting of maidens: (*fig.*) unpolluted: fresh: new: unused: first.

**Maidenhair**, mād′n-hār, *n.* a name given to a fern, from the fine hair-like stalks of its fronds.

**Maidenhood**, mād′n-hood, **Maidenhead**, mād′n-hed, *n.* the state of being a *maid*: virginity: purity: freshness.

**Maidenly**, mād′n-li, *adj., maiden-like*: becoming a maiden: gentle: modest.—*n.* **Maid′enliness.**

**Mail**, māl, *n.* defensive armour for the body formed of steel rings or network: armour generally.—*v.t.* to clothe in mail. [Fr. *maille* (It. *maglia*) —L. *macula*, a spot or a mesh.]

**Mail**, māl, *n.* a *bag* for the conveyance of letters, &c.: the contents of such a bag: the person or the carriage by which the mail is conveyed. [Fr. *malle*, a trunk, a mail—O. Ger. *malaha*, a sack; akin to Gael. *mala*, a sack.]

**Maim**, mām, *n. a bruise*: an injury: a lameness: the deprivation of any essential part.—*v.t.* to bruise: to disfigure: to injure: to lame or cripple: to render defective. [O. Fr. *mehaing*, a bruise or defect, of uncertain origin.]

**Maimedness**, mām′ed-nes, *n.* the state of being *maimed* or injured.

**Main**, mān, *n.* might: strength. [A.S. *mægen— mag*, root of **May**, *v.i.* to be able.]

**Main**, mān, *adj.* chief, principal: first in importance: leading.—*n.* the chief or principal part: the ocean or main sea: a continent or a larger island as compared with a smaller.—*adv.* **Main′ly**, chiefly, principally. [O. Fr. *maine* or *magne*, great—*magnus*, great.]

**Maindeck**, mān′dek, *n.* the *principal* deck of a ship. So in other compounds, **Main′mast, Main′sail, Main′spring, Main′stay, Main′top, Main′yard.**

**Mainland**, mān′land, *n.* the *principal* or larger *land*, as opposed to a smaller portion.

**Maintain**, men-tān′, *v.t.* to keep in any state: to keep possession of: to carry on: to keep up: to support: to make good: to support by argument: to affirm: to defend.—*v.i.* to affirm, as a position: to assert. [Fr. *maintenir*—L. *manu tenēre*, to hold in the hand—*manus*, a hand, and *teneo*, to hold.] [ported or defended.

**Maintainable**, men-tān′a-bl, *adj.* that can be supported or defended.

**Maintenance**, mān′ten-ans, *n.* the act of *main-*

*taining*, supporting, or defending : continuance : the means of support : defence, protection.

**Maize**, māz, *n.* a plant, and its fruit, called also Indian corn or wheat. [Sp. *maiz* (Fr. *maïs*)—Haitian *mahiz*, *mahis*.]

**Majestic**, ma-jes′tik, *adj.* having or exhibiting *majesty* : stately : sublime.

**Majesty**, maj′es-ti, *n.*, *greatness* : grandeur : dignity : elevation of manner or style : a title of kings and other sovereigns. [Fr. *majesté*—L. *majestas*—*majus*, comp. of *mag-nus*, great.]

**Majolica**, ma-jol′i-ka, *n.* name applied to painted or enamelled earthenware. [So called from the island of Majorca, where it was first made.]

**Major**, mā′jur, *adj.*, *greater* : (*logic*) the term of a syllogism which forms the predicate of the conclusion.—*n.* a person of full age (21 years) : an officer in rank between a captain and a lieutenant-colonel.—**Major-General**, mā′jur-jen′ėral, *n.* an officer in the army next in rank below a lieutenant-general. [L., comp. of *mag-nus*, great.]

**Majorate**, mā′jur-āt, **Majorship**, mā′jur-ship, *n.* the office or rank of *major* : majority.

**Major-domo**, mā′jur-dō′mo, *n.* an official who has the general management in a large household : a general steward : a chief minister. [Sp. *mayor-domo*, a house-steward—L. *major*, greater, and *domus*, a house.]

**Majority**, ma-jor′i-ti, *n.* the greater number : the amount between the greater and the less number : full age (at 21) : the office or rank of major.

**Make**, māk, *v.t.* to fashion, frame, or form : to produce : to bring about : to perform : to force : to render : to represent, or cause to appear to be : to turn : to occasion : to bring into any state or condition : to establish : to prepare : to obtain : to ascertain : to arrive in sight of, to reach : (*B.*) to be occupied with, to do.— *v.i.* to tend or move : to contribute : (*B.*) to feign or pretend—*pa.t.* and *pa.p.* māde.— **Make away**, to put out of the way, to destroy. —**Make for**, to move toward : to tend to the advantage of, so in *B.*—**Make of**, to understand by : to effect : to esteem.—**Make out**, to discover : to prove : to furnish : to succeed.—**Make over**, to transfer.—**Make up**, to approach : to become friendly.—**Make up for**, to compensate. [A.S. *macian*, cog. with Ger. *machen*, A.S. and Goth. *magan*, all from *mag*, root of L. *mag-nus*, Gr. *meg-as*, great. See **May**, *v.i.* to be able, and **Match**, *v.*]

**Make**, māk, *n.* form or shape : structure, texture.

**Maker**, māk′ėr, *n.* one who *makes* : the Creator.

**Makeshift**, māk′shift, *n.* that which serves a *shift* or *turn* : a temporary expedient.

**Makeweight**, māk′wāt, *n.* that which is thrown into a scale to *make* up the *weight* : something of little value added to supply a deficiency.

**Malachite**, mal′a-kīt, *n.* a *green-coloured* mineral, composed essentially of carbonate of copper, much used for inlaid-work. [Formed from Gr. *malachē*, a mallow, a plant of a green colour.]

**Maladjustment**, mal-ad-just′ment, *n.* a *bad* or wrong *adjustment*. [Fr. *mal*—L. *malus*, bad, and **Adjustment**.]

**Maladministration**, mal-ad-min-is-trā′shun, *n.* bad management, esp. of public affairs. [Fr. *mal*—L. *malus*, bad, and **Administration**.]

**Malady**, mal′a-di, *n.*, *illness* : disease, bodily or mental. [Fr. *maladie*—*malade*, sick—L. *male habitus*, in ill condition—*male*, badly, and *habitus*, pa.p. of *habeo*, have, hold.]

**Malapert**, mal′a-pėrt, *adj.* saucy : impudent.— *adv.* **Mal′apertly**.—*n.* **Mal′apertness**. [O. Fr. *mal*—L. *malus*, bad, and *apert*, well-bred—L. *apertus*, open. See **Aperient**.]

**Malaria**, ma-lā′ri-a, *n.* the noxious exhalations of marshy districts, producing fever, &c. : miasma. —*adjs.* **Mala′rious**, **Mala′rial**. ['Bad air ;' It. *mala aria*—L. *malus*, bad, and *aër*. See **Air**.]

**Malconformation**, mal-kon-for-mā′shun, *n.*, *bad conformation* or form : imperfection or disproportion of parts. [Fr. *mal*—L. *malus*, bad, and **Conformation**.]

**Malcontent, Malecontent**, mal′kon-tent, *adj.* discontented, dissatisfied, esp. in political matters.—*n.* one who is discontented.—*n.* **Malcontent′edness**. [Fr.—L. *male*, ill, and Fr. *content*. See **Content**.]

**Male**, māl, *adj.*, *masculine* : pertaining to the sex that begets (not bears) young : (*bot.*) bearing stamens.—*n.* one of the male sex : a he-animal : a stamen-bearing plant. [Fr. *mâle*—L. *masculus*, male—*mas* (for *man-s*), a male, cog. with **Man**.]

**Malediction**, mal-e-dik′shun, *n.*, *evil-speaking* : denunciation of evil : curse : execration or imprecation. [Fr.—L. *maledictio*—*male*, badly, *dico*, *dictus*, to speak.]

**Malefactor**, mal′e-fak-tur or mal-e-fak′tur, *n.* an *evil-doer* : a criminal. [L., from *male*, badly, and *factor*, a doer—*facio*, to do.]

**Malevolent**, mal-ev′o-lent, *adj.*, *wishing evil* : ill-disposed towards others : envious : malicious.— *adv.* **Malev′olently**.—*n.* **Malev′olence**. [L. *male*, badly, *volens*, pr.p. of *volo*, to wish.]

**Malformation**, mal-for-mā′shun, *n.*, *bad* or wrong *formation* : irregular or anomalous structure. [Fr. *mal*—L. *malus*, bad, and **Formation**.]

**Malice**, mal′is, *n.* (*lit.*) *badness*—so in *B.* : ill-will : spite : disposition to harm others : deliberate mischief. [Fr.—L. *malitia*—*malus*, bad, orig. dirty, black = Gr. *melas*.]

**Malicious**, ma-lish′us, *adj.* bearing ill-will or spite : prompted by hatred or ill-will : with mischievous intentions.—*adv.* **Malic′iously**.—*n.* **Malic′iousness**. [See **Malice**.]

**Malign**, ma-līn′, *adj.* of an evil nature or disposition towards others : malicious : unfavourable.— *v.t.* (*orig.*) to treat with *malice* : to speak evil of. —*adv.* **Malign′ly**.—*n.* **Malign′er**. [Fr. *malin*, fem. *maligne*—L. *malignus*, for *maligenus*, of evil disposition—*malus*, bad, and *gen*, root of **Genus**.]

**Malignant**, ma-lig′nant, *adj.*, *malign* : acting *maliciously* : actuated by extreme enmity : tending to destroy life.—*n.* (*Eng. Hist.*) a name applied by the Puritan party to one who had fought for Charles I. in the Civil War.—*adv.* **Malig′nantly**.—*n.* **Malig′nancy**, state or quality of being *malignant*. [L. *malignans*, pr.p. of *maligno*, to act maliciously. See **Malign**.]

**Malignity**, ma-lig′ni-ti, *n.* extreme malevolence : virulence : deadly quality.

**Malinger**, ma-ling′gėr, *v.i.* to feign sickness in order to avoid duty. [Fr. *malingre*, sickly, from *mal*, badly—L. *malus*, bad, and O. Fr. *heingre*, emaciated—L. *æger*, sick.]

**Malison**, mal′i-zn, *n.* a curse—opposed to **Benison**. [O. Fr., a doublet of **Malediction**; cf. **Benison** and **Benediction**.]

**Mall**, mawl or mal, *n.* a large wooden beetle or hammer. *v.t.* to beat with a *mall* or something heavy : to bruise. [Fr. *mail*—L. *malleus*, prob. akin to Ice. *Mjöl-nir*, Thor's hammer.]

**Mall**, mal or mel, *n.* (*orig.*) a place for playing in

with *malls* or mallets and balls : a level shaded walk : a public walk. [Contr. through O. Fr. of O. Ital. *palamaglio*—It. *palla*, a ball, and *maglio*, a mace, or hammer.]

**Mallard**, mal′ard, *n.* a drake : the common duck in its wild state. [O. Fr. *malard* (Fr. *malart*) —*mâle*, male, and suffix -*ard*.]

**Malleable**, mal′e-a-bl, *adj.* that may be *malleated* or beaten out by hammering.—*ns.* **Mall′eableness, Malleabil′ity**, quality of being *malleable*. [O. Fr. See **Malleate**.]

**Malleate**, mal′e-āt, *v.t.* to *hammer:* to extend by hammering.—*n.* **Mallea′tion.** [L. *malleus*. See **Mall**, a hammer.]

**Mallet**, mal′et, *n.* a wooden hammer. [Dim. of **Mall**, a hammer.]

**Mallow**, mal′ō, **Mallows**, mal′ōz, *n.* a plant having *soft downy* leaves and *relaxing* properties. [A.S. *malwe* (Ger. *malve*) : borrowed from L. *malua*, akin to Gr. *malachē*, from *malassō*, to make soft.]

**Malmsey**, mäm′ze, *n.* a sort of grape : a strong and sweet wine. [Orig. *malvesie*—Fr. *malvoisie*, from *Malvasia* in the Morea.]

**Malpractice**, mal-prak′tis, *n.* evil practice or conduct : practice contrary to established rules. [L. *male*, evil, and **Practice**.]

**Malt**, mawlt, *n.* barley or other grain steeped in water, allowed to sprout, and dried in a kiln.— *v.t.* to make into malt.—*v.i.* to become malt.— *adj.* containing or made with malt. [A.S. *mealt*, pa.t. of *meltan* (see **Melt**) : cog. with Ice. *malt*, Ger. *malz*. See also **Mild**.]

**Maltreat**, mal-trēt′, *v.t.* to abuse : to use roughly or unkindly.—*n.* **Maltreat′ment.** [Fr. *maltraiter*—L. *male*, ill, and *tractare*. See **Treat**.]

**Maltster**, mawlt′ster, *n.* one whose trade or occupation it is to make *malt*. [-*ster* was up to the end of the 13th century a fem. affix. Cf. **Spinster**.]

**Malvaceous**, mal-vā′shus, *adj.* (*bot.*) pertaining to *mallows*. [See **Mallow**.]

**Malversation**, mal-vėr-sā′shun, *n.* fraudulent artifices : corruption in office. [Fr. ; from L. *male*, badly, and *versor*, *versatus*, to turn or occupy one's self.]

**Mamaluke**, mam′a-lōōk, **Mameluke**, mam′e-lōōk, *n.* (formerly) one of a force of light horse in Egypt formed of Circassian slaves. [Fr. *Mameluc*—Ar. *mamlûk*, a purchased slave—*malaka*, to possess.]

**Mamma**, mam-mä′, *n.*, *mother*—used chiefly by young children. [*Ma-ma*, a repetition of *ma*, the first syllable a child naturally utters.]

**Mammal**, mam′al, *n.* (*zool.*) one of the *mammalia* : —*pl.* **Mammals**, mam′alz. [See **Mammalia**.]

**Mammalia**, mam-mā′li-a, *n.pl.* (*zool.*) the whole class of animals that suckle their young.—*adj.* **Mamma′lian** [Formed from L. *mammalis* (neut. pl. *mammalia*), belonging to the breast —L. *mamma*, the breast.]

**Mammalogy**, mam-mal′o-ji, *n.* the *science* of *mammals*. [**Mammal**, and *logos*, discourse.]

**Mammifer**, mam′i-fėr, *n.* an animal having *breasts* or *paps*.—*adj.* **Mammif′erous.** [L. *mamma*, breast, and *fero*, to bear.]

**Mammillary**, mam-il′ar-i or mam′il-ar-i, *adj.* pertaining to or resembling the *breasts*. [L., from *mammilla*, dim. of *mamma*, breast.]

**Mammillated**, mam′il-lāt-ed, *adj.* having *small nipples* or *paps*, or little globes like nipples.

**Mammon**, mam′un, *n.*, *riches :* the god of riches. [L. *mammona*—Gr. *mamōnas*—Syriac *mamōnā*, riches.]

**Mammonist**, mam′un-ist, **Mammonite**, mam′un-īt, *n.* one devoted to *mammon* or riches : a worldling.

**Mammoth**, mam′uth, *n.* an extinct species of elephant.—*adj.* resembling the mammoth in size : very large. [Russ. *mamant′*, from Tartar *mamma*, the earth, because believed by the Tartars to have worked its way in the *earth* like a mole.]

**Man**, man, *n.* a human being : mankind : a grown-up male : a male attendant : one possessing a distinctively masculine character : a husband : a piece used in playing chess or draughts :—*pl.* **Men**.—*v.t.* to supply with men : to strengthen or fortify :—*pr.p.* mann′ing ; *pa.t.* and *pa.p.* manned′. [Lit. ' the *thinking* animal,' A.S. *mann*—root *man*, to think ; cog. with Ger. and Goth. *man*, Ice. *madhr* (for *mannr*). See **Mind**.]

**Manacle**, man′a-kl, *n.* a *handcuff*.—*v.t.* to put manacles on : to restrain the use of the limbs or natural powers. [Through O. Fr., from L. *manicula*, dim. of *manica*, a sleeve—*manus*, the hand.]

**Manage**, man′āj, *v.t.* to conduct with economy : to control : to wield : to handle : to have under command : to contrive : to train, as a horse.— *v.i.* to conduct affairs.—*n.* **Man′ager**. [Fr. *manége*, the managing of a horse—It. *maneggio* (*lit.*) a handling—L. *manus*, the hand.]

**Manageable**, man′āj-a-bl, *adj.* that can be *managed :* governable.—*n.* **Man′ageableness.**

**Management**, man′āj-ment, *n.* manner of directing or using anything : administration : skilful treatment.

**Manatee**, man-a-tē′, *n.* an aquatic animal, also called the sea-cow or Dugong (which see). [Sp. *manati*—West Indian.]                    [white bread.

**Manchet**, man′chet, *n.* a small loaf or cake of fine

**Man-child**, man′-chīld, *n.* a *male child*.

**Mandarin**, man-da-rēn′, *n.* a European name for a Chinese official, whether civil or military. [Port. *mandarin*—Malayan *mantri*, counsellor —Sans. *mantra*, counsel—root *man*. See **Man**.]

**Mandatary**, man′da-tar-i, **Mandatory**, man′da-tor-i, *n.* one to whom a *mandate* is given.

**Mandate**, man′dāt, *n.* a charge : an authoritative command : a rescript of the Pope. [Lit. ' something put into one's hands,' Fr. *mandat*—L. *mandatum*, from *mando*—*manus*, the hand, and *do*, to give.]

**Mandatory**, man′da-tor-i, *adj.* containing a *mandate* or command : preceptive : directory.

**Mandible**, man′di-bl, *n.* (*zool.*) a jaw.—*adj.* **Mandib′ular**, relating to the jaw. [Lit. ' that which chews,' L. *mandibula*—*mando*, to chew.]

**Mandrake**, man′drāk, *n.* a narcotic plant. [A corr. of A.S. *mandragora*, through L., from Gr. *mandragoras*.]

**Mandrel**, man′drel, *n.* the revolving shank to which turners fix their work in the lathe. [A corr. of Fr. *mandrin ;* prob. through Low L. from Gr. *mandra,* an inclosed space. See **Madrigal**.]

**Mandrill**, man′drill, *n.* a large kind of baboon. [Fr.]

**Mane**, mān, *n.* the long hair flowing from the neck of some quadrupeds, as the horse and lion. [Ice. *mön ;* cog. with Ger. *mähne*.]

**Manege**, man-äzh′, *n.* the *managing* of horses : the art of horsemanship or of training horses : a riding-school. [Fr. See **Manage**.]

**Manful**, man′fool, *adj.* full of *manliness :* bold : courageous.—*adv.* **Man′fully**.—*n.* **Man′fulness.**

**Manganese**, mang-ga-nēz′ or mang′ga-nēz, *n.* a

hard and brittle metal of a reddish-white colour.
—*adj.* **Mangane′sian.** [O. Fr. *manganese*, a material used in making glass—It.]

**Mange**, mānj, *n.* the scab or itch which *eats* the skin of domestic animals. [From the *adj.* **Mangy.**]

**Mangel-wurzel**, mang′gl-wur′zl, **Mangold-wur′zel**, mang′gold-wur′zl, *n.* a plant of the beet kind cultivated as food for cattle. [Lit. ‘beet-root,’ Ger. *mangold*, beet, and *wurzel*, root.]

**Manger**, mānj′ėr, *n.* an *eating*-trough for horses and cattle. [Fr. *mangeoire*—*manger*, to eat —L. *manducus*, a glutton—*mando*, to chew.]

**Mangle**, mang′gl, *v.t.* to cut and bruise: to tear in cutting: to mutilate: to take by piecemeal.— *n.* **Mang′ler.** [Freq. of M. E. *manken*, to mutilate—A.S. *mancian*—L. *mancus*, maimed.]

**Mangle**, mang′gl, *n.* a rolling-press for smoothing linen.—*v.t.* to smooth with a mangle : to calender.—*n.* **Mang′ler.** Dut. *mangelen*, to roll with a rolling-pin (It. *mangano*, a calender), through Low L., from Gr. *mangganon*, the axis of a pulley.]

**Mango**, mang′gō, *n.* the fruit of the mango-tree of the East Indies : a green musk-melon pickled. [Malay *mangga*.]

**Mangrove**, man′grōv, *n.* a tree of the E. and W. Indies, whose bark is used for tanning. [Malayan.]

**Mangy**, mānj′i, *adj.* scabby.—*n.* **Mang′iness.** [Anglicised form of Fr. *mangé*, eaten, pa.p. of *manger*, to eat. See E. **Mange.**]

**Manhood**, man′hood, *n.* state of being a *man* : manly quality : human nature.

**Mania**, mā′ni-a, *n.* violent madness : insanity : excessive or unreasonable desire. [L.—Gr. *mania*—root *man*, to think.]

**Maniac**, mā′ni-ak, *n.* one affected with *mania* : a madman.—*adj.* **Maniacal**, ma-nī′a-kal. [Fr. *maniaque*—**Mania.**]

**Manifest**, man′i-fest, *adj.* clear : apparent : evident.—*v.t.* to make manifest : to shew plainly : to put beyond doubt : to reveal or declare.—*adv.* **Man′ifestly.**—*n.* **Man′ifestness**, state of being *manifest*. [Lit. ‘hand-struck,’ *i.e.* palpable, Fr.—L. *manifestus*—*manus*, the hand, and *-festus*, pa.p. of obs. *fendo*, to dash against.]

**Manifest**, man′i-fest, *n.* a list or invoice of a ship's cargo to be *exhibited* at the custom-house.

**Manifestable**, man-i-fest′a-bl, **Manifestible**, man-i-fest′i-bl, *adj.* that can be *manifested*.

**Manifestation**, man-i-fest-ā′shun, *n.* act of disclosing : display : revelation.

**Manifesto**, man-i-fest′ō, *n.* a public written declaration of the intentions of a sovereign or state. [It.—L. See **Manifest**, *adj.*]

**Manifold**, man′i-fōld, *adj.* various in kind or quality : many in number : multiplied.—*adv.* **Man′ifoldly.** [A.S. *manig-feald*. See **Many** and **Fold.**]

**Manikin**, man′i-kin, *n.* (*orig.*) a *little man* : a pasteboard model, exhibiting the different parts and organs of the human body. [O. Dut. *mann-ek-en*, a double dim. of *man*, E. **Man.**]

**Maniple**, man′i-pl, *n.* a company of foot-soldiers in the Roman army : a kind of scarf worn by a R. Cath. priest on the left arm, a stole.—*adj.* **Manip′ular.** [Lit. a ‘handful,’ L. *manipulus* —*manus*, the hand, *pleo*, to fill.]

**Manipulate**, ma-nip′ū-lāt, *v.t.* to *work with the hands.*—*v.i.* to use the hands, esp. in scientific experiments : to handle or manage. [Low L. *manipulo*, *manipulatum*.]

**Manipulation**, ma-nip-ū-lā′shun, *n.* act of manipu-

*lating* or working by hand : use of the hands, in a skilful manner, in science or art.

**Manipulative**, ma-nip′ū-lāt-iv, **Manipulatory**, ma-nip′ū-la-tor-i, *adj.* done by *manipulation.*

**Manipulator**, ma-nip′ū-lāt-ur, *n.* one who *manipulates* or works with the hand.

**Mankind**, man-kīnd′, *n.* the *kind* or race of *man.*

**Manly**, man′li, *adj.*, *manlike* : becoming a man : brave : dignified : noble : pertaining to manhood : not childish or womanish.—*n.* **Man′liness.**

**Manna**, man′a, *n.* the food supplied to the Israelites in the wilderness of Arabia : a sweetish exudation from many trees, as the ash of Sicily. [Heb. *man hu*, what is it ? or from *man*, a gift.]

**Manner**, man′ėr, *n.* mode of action : way of performing anything : method : fashion : peculiar deportment : habit : custom : style of writing or thought : sort : style :—*pl.* morals : behaviour : deportment : respectful deportment.—**In a′manner**, to a certain degree.—**In or with the manner**, (*B.*) in the very act, ‘manner’ here being a corr. of *manuopere*, as in the legal phrase, *cum manuopere captus*. [Fr. *manière*—*main*—L. *manus*, the hand.]

**Mannerism**, man′ėr-izm, *n.* peculiarity of manner, esp. in literary composition, becoming wearisome by its sameness.—*n.* **Mann′erist**, one addicted to *mannerism.*

**Mannerly**, man′ėr-li, *adj.* shewing good-*manners* : decent in deportment : complaisant : not rude.— *adv.* with good *manners* : civilly : respectfully : without rudeness.—*n.* **Mann′erliness.**

**Manœuvre**, ma-nōō′vėr or ma-nū′-, *n.* a piece of ~~dexterous~~ management : stratagem : an adroit movement in military or naval tactics.—*v.t.* to perform a manœuvre : to manage with art : to change the position of troops or ships.—*n.* **Manœu′vrer.** [Lit. ‘hand-work,’ Fr.—*main*— L. *manus*, the hand, and *œuvre*—L. *opera*, work. See **Manure.**]　　　　　　　[a warrior.

**Man-of-war**, man-of-wawr′, *n.* a ship-of-war : (*B.*).

**Manor**, man′or, *n.* the land belonging to a nobleman, or so much as he formerly kept for his own use : jurisdiction of a court baron. [Fr. *manoir* —L. *maneo*, *mansum*, to stay. See **Mansion.**]

**Manor-house**, man′or-hows, **Manor-seat**, man′or-sēt, *n.* the *house* or *seat* belonging to a *manor.*

**Manorial**, ma-nō′ri-al, *adj.* pertaining to a *manor.*

**Manse**, mans, *n.* the residence of a clergyman (Scot.). [Low L. *mansa*, a farm—*maneo*, *mansus*, to remain.]

**Mansion**, man′shun, *n.* a house, esp. one of some size : a manor-house. [Lit. ‘a resting-place,’ so in *B.*; O. Fr.—L. *mansio*, *-onis*, akin to Gr. *meno*, to remain.]

**Mansion-house**, man′shun-hows, *n.* a *mansion* : the official residence of the Lord Mayor of London. [**Mansion** and **House.**]

**Manslaughter**, man′slaw-tėr, *n.* the *slaying* of a *man* : (*law*) the killing of any one unlawfully, but without malice or premeditation. [**Man** and **Slaughter.**]

**Manslayer**, man′slā-ėr, *n.* one who *slays* a *man.*

**Mantel**, man′tl, *n.* the shelf over a fireplace (which in old fireplaces was formed like a *hood*, to intercept the smoke) : a narrow shelf or slab above a fireplace : also **Man′tel-piece, Man′tel-shelf.** [Doublet of **Mantle.**]

**Mantelet.** See **Mantlet.**

**Mantle**, man′tl, *n.* a covering : a kind of cloak or loose outer garment : (*zool.*) the thin fleshy membrane lining the shell of a mollusk.—*v.t.* to cover, as with a mantle : to hide : to disguise.—*v.i.* to expand or spread like a mantle :

to revel: to joy: to froth: to rush to the face and impart a crimson glow, as blood. [O. Fr. *mantel*, Fr. *manteau*—L. *mantellum*, a napkin.]

**Mantlet**, man′tlet, **Mantelet**, man′tel-et, *n.* a small cloak for women : (*fort.*) a movable parapet to protect pioneers. [Dim. of **Mantle**.]

**Mantling**, man′tling, *n.* (*her.*) the representation of a *mantle*, or the drapery of a coat-of-arms.

**Mantua**, man′tū-a, *n.* a lady's *cloak* or *mantle* : a lady's gown.—*n.* **Man′tua-mak′er**, a *maker* of *mantuas* or ladies' dresses. [Prob. arose through confusion of Fr. *manteau* (It. *manto*), with *Mantua*, in Italy.]

**Manual**, man′ū-al, *adj.* pertaining to the *hand* : done, made, or used by the hand.—*adv.* **Man′ually.** [L. *manualis*—*manus*, the hand.]

**Manual**, man′ū-al, *n.* a *hand*book : a *handy* compendium of a large subject or treatise : the service-book of the Roman Catholic Church.

**Manufactory**, man-ū-fakt′or-i, *n.* a *factory* or place where goods are *manufactured*.

**Manufacture**, man-ū-fakt′ūr, *v.t.* to make from raw materials by any means into a form suitable for use.—*v.i.* to be occupied in manufactures.—*n.* the process of manufacturing : anything manufactured. — *adj.* **Manufact′ural.** [Lit. 'to make by the hand,' Fr.—L. *manus*, the hand, and *factura*, a making, from *facio*, *factum*, to make.] [*manufactures.*

**Manufacturer**, man-ū-fakt′ūr-ėr, *n.* one who **Manumission**, man-ū-mish′un, *n.* act of *manumitting* or freeing from slavery.

**Manumit**, man-ū-mit′, *v.t.* to release from slavery : to set free, as a slave :—*pr.p.* manūmit′ing ; *pa.t.* and *pa.p.* manūmit′ted. [Lit. 'to send away or free from one's hand or power,' L. *manumitto*—*manus*, the hand, and *mitto*, *missum*, to send.]

**Manure**, man-ūr′, *v.t.* to enrich land with any fertilising substance.—*n.* any substance used for fertilising land.—*n.* **Manur′er.** [Orig. 'to work with the hand,' contr. of Fr. *manœuvrer*. See **Manœuvre.**] [of manure on land.

**Manuring**, man-ūr′ing, *n.* a dressing or spreading

**Manuscript**, man′ū-skript, *adj.*, *written* by the *hand*.—*n.* a book or paper written by the hand. [L. *manus*, the hand, *scribo*, *scriptum*, to write.]

**Manx**, manks, *n.* the language of the Isle of *Man*, a dialect of the Celtic.—*adj.* pertaining to the Isle of Man or its inhabitants.

**Many**, men′i, *adj.*—comp. **More** (mōr) ; superl. **Most** (mōst)—comprising a great number of individuals : not few : numerous.—*n.* many persons : a great number : the people. [A.S. *manig*; cog. forms are found in all the Teut. languages ; allied to L. *magnus*.]

**Map**, map, *n.* a representation of the surface of the earth, or of part of it on any plane surface : a representation of the celestial sphere.—*v.t.* to draw, as the figure of any portion of land : to describe clearly :—*pr.p.* map′ping ; *pa.t.* and *pa.p.* mapped′. [L. *mappa*, a napkin, a painted cloth, orig. a Punic word.]

**Maple**, mā′pl, *n.* a tree of several species, from one of which, the rock-maple, sugar is made. [A.S. *mapul*, maple.]

**Mar**, mär, *v.t.* to injure by cutting off a part, or by wounding : to damage : to interrupt : to disfigure :—*pr.p.* mar′ring ; *pa.t.* and *pa.p.* marred′. [A.S. *merran*, *mirran*, from a widely diffused Aryan root *mar*, to crush, bruise, found in L. *molo*, to grind, *morior*, to die, Gr. *mar-ainō*, to wither, Sans. *mri*, to die ; also in E. **Meal**, **Mill**. See **Mortal**.]

**Maranatha**, mar-a-nā′tha or mar-a-nath′a, *n.* (*lit.*) *our Lord cometh* to take vengeance, part of a Jewish curse. [Syriac.]

**Maraud**, ma-rawd′, *v.i.* to *rove* in quest of plunder. [Fr. *marauder*—*maraud*, vagabond, rogue.]

**Marauder**, ma-rawd′ėr, *n.* one who roves in quest of booty or plunder.

**Maravedi**, mar-a-vē′dī, *n.* the smallest copper coin of Spain. [Sp.—Arab. *Murabitin*, the dynasty of the Almoravides.]

**Marble**, mär′bl, *n.* any species of limestone taking a high polish : that which is made of marble, as a work of art, or a little ball used by boys in play.—*adj.* made of marble : veined like marble : hard : insensible.—*v.t.* to stain or vein like marble.—*n.* **Mar′bler.** [Lit. 'the sparkling stone,' Fr. *marbre*—L. *marmor*; cog. with Gr. *marmaros*, from *marmairō*, to sparkle, flash.]

**Marbly**, mär′bli, *adv.* in the manner of *marble*.

**Marcescent**, mar-ses′ent, *adj.* (*bot.*) withering, decaying. [L. *marcescens*, *-entis*, pr.p. of *marcesco*—*marceo*, to fade.]

**March**, märch, *n.* the third month of the year, named from *Mars*, the god of war. [L. *Martius* (*mensis*), (the month) of *Mars*.]

**March**, märch, *n.* a border : frontier of a territory : —used chiefly in *pl.* **March′es.** [A.S. *mearc*; doublet of **Mark**.]

**March**, märch, *v.i.* to move in order, as soldiers : to walk in a grave or stately manner.—*v.t.* to cause to march.—*n.* the movement of troops : regular advance : a piece of music fitted for marching to : the distance passed over. [Fr. *marcher*. Ety. dub. ; acc. to Scheler, prob. from L. *marcus*, a hammer (cf. 'to *beat* time') ; others suggest root of **March**, a frontier.]

**Marchioness**, mär′shun-es, *n.*, *fem.* of **Marquis.**

**Mare**, mār, *n.* the female of the horse. [A.S. *mere*, fem. of *mearh*, a horse ; cog. with Ger. *mähre*, Ice. *mar*, W. *march*, a horse.]

**Mareschal**, mär′shal. Same as **Marshal.**

**Marge**, märj, *n.* edge, brink. [Fr.—L. *margo*. See **Margin.**]

**Margin**, mär′jin, *n.* an *edge*, *border*; the blank edge on the page of a book. [L. *margo*, *marginis*; cog. with E. **Mark**.]

**Marginal**, mär′jin-al, *adj.* pertaining to a *margin* : placed in the margin.—*adv.* **Mar′ginally.**

**Marginate**, mär′jin-āt, **Marginated**, mär′jin-āt-ed, *adj.* having a *margin*. [L. *marginatus*, pa.p. of *margino*, to border.]

**Margrave**, mär′grāv, *n.* (*orig.*) a *lord* or keeper of the *marches* : a German nobleman of the same rank as an English marquis.—*fem.* **Margravine**, mär′gra-vēn. [Dut. *markgraaf* (Ger. *markgraf*)—*mark*, a border, and *graaf*, a count, which is cog. with Ger. *graf*, A.S. *gerefa*, E. **Reeve** and **She-riff.** See **March**, a border.]

**Marigold**, mar′i-gōld, *n.* a plant bearing a *yellow* flower. [From the Virgin *Mary*, and **Gold**, because of its yellow colour.]

**Marine**, ma-rēn′, *adj.* of or belonging to the *sea* : done at sea : representing the sea : near the sea. —*n.* a soldier serving on shipboard : the whole navy of a country or state : naval affairs. [Fr.— L. *marinus*—*mare*, sea ; akin to E. **Mere.**]

**Mariner**, mar′i-nėr, *n.* a *seaman* or sailor : one who assists in navigating ships. [Fr. *marinier.*]

**Mariolatry**, mā-ri-ol′a-tri, *n.* the *worship* of the Virgin *Mary*. [Formed from L. *Maria*, Mary, and Gr. *latreia*, worship.]

**Marish**, mar′ish, *n.* (*B.*). Same as **Marsh.**

**Marital**, mar′i-tal, *adj.* pertaining to a husband.

[Fr.—L. *maritalis*—*maritus*, a husband—*mas, maris*, a male. See **Male**.]

**Maritime**, mar'i-tim, *adj.* pertaining to the *sea* : relating to navigation or naval affairs : situated near the sea : having a navy and naval commerce. [L. *maritimus*—*mare*. See **Marine**.]

**Marjoram**, mär'jo-ram, *n.* an aromatic plant used as a seasoning in cookery. [Fr. *marjolaine*—Low L. *majoraca*—L. *amaracus*—Gr. *amarakos;* prob. an Eastern word.]

**Mark**, märk, *n.* a visible sign : any object serving as a guide : that by which anything is known : badge : a trace : proof : any visible effect : symptom : a thing aimed at : a character made by one who cannot write : distinction.—*v.t.* to make a mark on anything : to impress with a sign : to take notice of : to regard.—*v.i.* to take particular notice.—*n.* **Mark'er**, one who marks the score at games, as billiards. [A.S. *mearc*, a boundary ; found in all the Teut. languages, as Ger. *mark*, and Goth. *marka*; also akin to L. *margo*, and perh. to Sans. *marga*, a trace.]

**Mark**, märk, *n.* an obsolete English coin = 13s. 4d. : a coin of the present German Empire = one shilling : a silver coin of Hamburg = 1s. 4d. [A.S. *marc*, another form of the above word.]

**Market**, mär'ket, *n.* a public place for the purposes of buying and selling : the time for the market : sale : rate of sale : value.—*v.i.* to deal at a market : to buy and sell. [Through the O. Fr. (Fr. *marché*, It. *mercato*), from L. *mercatus*, trade, a market—*merx*, merchandise.]

**Marketable**, mär'ket-a-bl, *adj.* fit for the *market:* saleable.—*n.* **Mar'ketableness**.

**Market-cross**, mär'ket-kros, *n.* a *cross* anciently set up where a *market* was held.

**Market-town**, mär'ket-town, *n.* a *town* having the privilege of holding a public *market*.

**Marking-ink**, märk'ing-ingk, *n.* indelible *ink*, used for *marking* clothes.

**Marksman**, märks'man, *n., one* good at hitting a *mark:* one who shoots well. [**Mark** and **Man**.]

**Marl**, märl, *n.* a fat or rich earth or clay often used as manure.—*v.t.* to cover or manure with marl. [O. Fr. *marle* (Fr. *marne*), from a Low L. dim. of L. *marga*, marl.]

**Marlaceous**, märl-ā'shus, *adj.* having the qualities of or resembling *marl*.

**arline**, mär'lin, *n.* a small line for winding round a rope—*v.t.* **Marline**, mär'lin, **Marl**, märl, to *bind* or wind round with marline. [Dut. *marlijn, marling*—*marren*, to bind, E. **Moor** (a ship), and *lijn, lien*, a rope, E. **Line**.]

**Marlinespike**, mär'lin-spīk, *n.* an iron tool, like a *spike*, for separating the strands of a rope.

**Marlite**, mär'līt, *n.* a variety of *marl*.—*adj.* **Marlit'ic**.

**Marly**, märl'i, *adj.* having the qualities of or resembling *marl:* abounding in marl.

**Marmalade**, mär'ma-lād, *n.* a jam or preserve generally of oranges, orig. of *quinces*. [Fr., from Port. *marmelada*—*marmêlo*, a quince, L. *melimelum*, Gr. *melimēlon*, a sweet apple, an apple grafted on a quince—*meli*, honey, *mēlon*, an apple.]

**Marmoraceous**, mar-mo-rā'shus, *adj.* belonging to or like *marble*. [From L. *marmor*, marble.]

**Marmoreal**, mar-mō're-al, **Marmorean**, mar-mō're-an, *adj.* belonging to or like *marble :* made of marble. [L. *marmoreus*.]

**Marmoset**, mär'mo-zet, *n.* a small variety of American monkey. [Fr. *marmouset*, a little grotesque figure (hence applied to an ape), a figure in marble—L. *marmor*, marble.]

**Marmot**, mär'mot, *n.* a rodent animal, about the size of a rabbit, which inhabits the higher parts of the Alps and Pyrenees. [Lit. ' the mountain mouse,' It. *marmotto*—L. *mus, muris*, a mouse, and *mons, montis*, a mountain.]

**Maroon**, ma-rōōn', *adj.* brownish crimson. [Lit. 'chestnut-coloured,' Fr. *marron*, a chestnut—It. *marrone*.]

**Maroon**, ma-rōōn', *n.* a fugitive slave living *on the mountains*, in the W. Indies.—*v.t.* to put on shore on a desolate island. [Fr. *marron*, a shortened form of Sp. *cimarron*, wild—*cima*, a mountain-summit.]

**Marque**, märk, *n.* a license to pass the *marches* or limits of a country to make reprisals : a ship commissioned for making captures. [Fr., from root of **Mark** and **March**.]

**Marquee**, mär-kē', *n.* a large field-tent. [Fr. *marquise*, acc. to Littré, orig. a marchioness's tent. See **Marquess**.]

**Marquis**, mär'kwis, **Marquess**, mär'kwes, *n.* (*orig.*) an officer who guarded the *marches* or frontiers of a kingdom : a title of nobility next below that of a duke.—*fem.* **Mar'chioness**. [Fr. (It. *marchese*), from the root of **March**, **Mark**, a frontier.]                    [of a *marquis*.

**Marquisate**, mär'kwis-āt, *n.* the dignity or lordship

**Marriage**, mar'ij, *n.* the ceremony by which a man and woman become husband and wife : the union of a man and woman as husband and wife. [See **Marry**.]

**Marriageable**, mar'ij-a-bl, *adj.* suitable for *marriage ;* capable of union.—*n.* **Marr'iageableness**.

**Marrow**, mar'ō, *n.* the soft, fatty matter in the cavities of the bones : the pith of certain plants : the essence or best part.—*adj.* **Marr'owy**. [A.S. *mearh;* Ice. *mergr*, Ger. *mark*, W. *mer*.]

**Marrow-bone**, mar'ō-bōn, *n.* a *bone* containing marrow.                    [resembling *marrow*.

**Marrowish**, mar'ō-ish, *adj.* of the nature of or

**Marry**, mar'i, *v.t.* to take for husband or wife : to unite in matrimony.—*v.i.* to enter into the married state : to take a husband or a wife :—*pr.p.* marr'ying ; *pa.t.* and *pa.p.* marr'ied. [Fr. *marier*—L. *marito*—*maritus*, a husband—*mas, maris*, a male. See **Male**.]

**Marsala**, mar'sä-la, *n.* a light wine resembling sherry, from *Marsala* in Sicily.

**Marseillaise**, mar'säl-yāz, *n.* the French revolutionary hymn, first sung by men of Marseilles brought to Paris to aid in the Revolution in 1792.

**Marsh**, märsh, *n.* a tract of low *wet land :* a morass, swamp, or fen.—*adj.* pertaining to wet or boggy places. [A.S. *mersc*, for *mer-isc*, as if 'mere-ish,' full of *meres*. See **Mere**, a pool.]

**Marshal**, mär'shal, *n.* (*orig.*) a title given to various officers, who had the care of horses, esp. those of a prince : a title of honour applied to the holder of various high offices : the chief officer who regulated combats in the lists : a master of ceremonies : a pursuivant or harbinger : a herald : in France, an officer of the highest military rank : in the United States, the civil officer of a district, corresponding to the sheriff of a county in England.—*v.t.* to arrange in order : to lead, as a herald :—*pr.p.* mar'shalling ; *pa.t.* and *pa.p.* mar'shalled. [Lit. 'horse-servant,' Fr. *maréchal;* from O. Ger. *marah*, a horse, and *schalh* (Ger. *schalk*), a servant.]

**Marshaller**, mär'shal-ėr, *n.* one who *marshals* or arranges in order.

**Marshalship**, mär'shal-ship, *n.* office of *marshal*.

**Marsh-mallow**, märsh'-mal'ō, *n.* a species of mallow common in meadows and marshes.

**Marshy,** märsh′i, *adj.* pertaining to or produced in *marshes:* abounding in marshes.—*n.* **Marsh′iness.**

**Marsupial,** mar-sū′pi-al, *adj.* carrying young in a *pouch.*—*n.* a marsupial animal. [L. *marsupium*—Gr. *marsupion*, a pouch.]

**Mart,** märt, *n.* a *market* or place of trade. [A contraction of **Market.**]

**Martello,** mar-tel′o, *n.* a circular fort erected to protect a coast. [Orig. a tower (on the Italian coast), from which warning against pirates was given by striking a bell with a *hammer*, It. *martello*, a hammer—L. *martellus*, dim. of *marcus*, a hammer.]

**Marten,** mär′ten, *n.* a destructive kind of weasel valued for its fur. [Fr. *martre*, also *marte*—Low L. *marturis*, from a Teut. root seen in Ger. *marder*, and A.S. *mearth*, a marten.]

**Martial,** mär′shal, *adj.* belonging to *Mars*, the god of war: belonging to war: warlike: brave.—*adv.* **Mar′tially.** [Fr.—L. *martialis*—*Mars, Martis.*]

**Martin,** mär′tin, **Martinet,** mär′tin-et, *n.* a bird of the swallow kind. [Named after *St Martin.*]

**Martinet,** mär′tin-et, *n.* a strict disciplinarian. [From *Martinet*, a very strict officer in the army of Louis XIV. of France.]

**Martingale,** mär′tin-gāl or -gal, **Martingal,** mär′tin-gal, *n.* a strap fastened to a horse's girth to hold his head down: in ships, a short spar under the bowsprit. [Fr., a kind of breeches, so called from *Martigues* in Provence, where they were worn.]

**Martinmas,** mär′tin-mas, *n.* the *mass* or feast of *St Martin:* 11th November. [See **Mass.**]

**Martlet,** märt′let, *n.* martin, the bird. [From Fr. *martinet*, dim. of **Martin.**]

**Martyr,** mär′ter, *n.* one who by his death bears *witness* to the truth: one who suffers for his belief.—*v.t.* to put to death for one's belief. [A.S., L., Gr., a witness, from the same root as **Memory.**]

**Martyrdom,** mär′ter-dum, *n.* the sufferings or death of a martyr.

**Martyrology,** mär-ter-ol′o-ji, *n.* a *history* of *martyrs:* a discourse on martyrdom.—*n.* **Martyrol′ogist.** [Martyr, and Gr. *logos*, a discourse.]

**Marvel,** mär′vel, *n.* a *wonder:* anything astonishing or wonderful.—*v.i.* to wonder: to feel astonishment :—*pr.p.* mar′velling ; *pa.t.* and *pa.p.* mar′velled. [Fr. *merveille*—L. *mirabilis*, wonderful—*miror*, to wonder.]

**Marvellous,** mär′vel-us, *adj.* astonishing : beyond belief : improbable.—*adv.* **Mar′vellously.**—*n.* **Mar′vellousness.**

**Marybud,** mā′ri-bud, *n.* the marigold.

**Masculine,** mas′kū-lin, *adj.* having the qualities of a man : resembling a man : robust : bold : expressing the male gender.—*adv.* **Mas′culinely.**—*n.* **Mas′culineness.** [Fr.—L. *masculinus*—*masculus*, male—*mas*, a male.]

**Mash,** mash, *v.t.* to beat into a *mixed* mass : to bruise : in brewing, to mix malt and hot water together.—*n.* a mixture of ingredients beaten together : in brewing, a mixture of crushed malt and hot water. [Prob. from root of **Mix.**]

**Mashy,** mash′i, *adj.* of the nature of a mash.

**Mask, Masque,** mask, *n.* anything disguising or concealing the face : anything that disguises : a pretence : a masquerade : a dramatic performance in which the actors appear masked.—*v.t.* to cover the face with a mask : to disguise : to hide.—*v.i.* to join in a mask or masquerade : to be disguised in any way : to revel. [Fr. *masque*

—Sp. *mascara*, Ar. *maskharat*, a jester, man in masquerade.]

**Masker,** mask′er, *n.* one who wears a *mask.*

**Mason,** mā′sn, *n.* one who *cuts*, prepares, and lays stones : a builder in stone : a freemason. [Fr. *maçon*—Low L. *macio*; cf. O. Ger. *meizan*, to hew, cut, from which are Ger. *messer*, a knife, *stein-metz*, a stone-mason.]

**Masonic,** ma-son′ik, *adj.* relating to *freemasonry.*

**Masonry,** mā′sn-ri, *n.* the craft of a *mason :* the work of a mason : the art of building in stone : freemasonry.

**Masque.** See **Mask.**

**Masquerade,** mask-er-ād′, *n.* an assembly of persons wearing *masks*, generally at a ball : disguise.—*v.t.* to put into disguise.—*v.i.* to join in a masquerade : to go in disguise. [Fr. *mascarade.* See **Mask.**]        [*mask :* one disguised

**Masquerader,** mask-er-ād′er, *n.* one wearing a

**Mass,** mas, *n.* a lump of matter : a quantity : a collected body : the gross body : magnitude : the principal part or main body : quantity of matter in any body.—*v.t.* to form into a mass : to assemble in masses. [Fr. *masse*—L. *massa*—Gr. *maza*—*massō*, to squeeze together.]

**Mass,** mas, *n.* the celebration of the Lord's Supper in R. Cath. churches. [Fr. *messe*, It. *messa*, said to be from the Latin words *ite, missa est* (*ecclesia*), 'go, the congregation is dismissed,' said at the close of the service.]

**Massacre,** mas′a-ker, *n.* indiscriminate *killing* or slaughter, esp. with cruelty : carnage.—*v.t.* to kill with violence and cruelty : to slaughter. [Fr. ; from the Teut., as in Low Ger. *matsken*, to cut, Ger. *metz-ger*, a butcher.]

**Massive,** mas′iv, *adj.* bulky : weighty.—*adv.* **Mass′ively.**—*n.* **Mass′iveness.**

**Massy,** mas′i, *adj.*, *massive.*—*n.* **Mass′iness.**

**Mast,** mast, *n.* a long upright pole for sustaining the yards, rigging, &c. in a ship.—*v.t.* to supply with a mast or masts. [A.S. *mæst*, the stem of a tree ; Ger. *mast*, Fr. *mât.*]

**Mast,** mast, *n.* the fruit of the oak, beech, chestnut, and other forest trees, on which swine *feed :* nuts, acorns. [A.S. *mæst ;* Ger. *mast*, whence *mästen*, to feed ; akin to **Meat.**]

**Master,** mas′ter, *n.* one who commands : a lord or owner : a leader or ruler : a teacher : an employer : the commander of a merchant-ship : the officer who navigates a ship-of-war under the captain : a degree in universities : one eminently skilled in anything : the common title of address to a young gentleman.—*adj.* belonging to a master, chief, principal.—*v.t.* to become master of : to overcome : to become skilful in : to execute with skill. [O. Fr. *maistre* (Fr. *maître*)—L. *magister*, from *mag*, root of *magnus*, great.]

**Mas′ter,** in many compounds = chief, as in **Mas′ter-build′er, Mas′ter-ma′son,** &c.

**Masterhand,** mas′ter-hand, *n.* the *hand* of a *master :* a person highly skilled.

**Masterkey,** mas′ter-kē, *n.* a *key* that *masters* or opens many locks : a clue out of difficulties.

**Masterless,** mas′ter-les, *adj.* without a *master* or owner : ungoverned : unsubdued.

**Masterly,** mas′ter-li, *adj.* like a *master :* with the skill of a master : skilful : excellent.—*adv.* with the skill of a master.

**Masterpiece,** mas′ter-pēs, *n.* a *piece* or work worthy of a *master :* a work of superior skill : chief excellence.

**Mastership,** mas′ter-ship, *n.* the office of *master :* rule or dominion : superiority.

**Masterstroke,** mas′ter-strōk, *n.* a *stroke* or performance worthy of a *master:* superior performance.

**Mastery**, mas'tėr-i, *n.* the power or authority of a *master:* dominion: victory: superiority: the attainment of superior power or skill.

**Mastic, Mastich**, mas'tik, *n.* a species of gumresin from the lentisk-tree: a cement from mastic: the tree producing mastic. [Fr.—L. *mastiche*—Gr. *mastichē*—*masaomai*, to chew; so called because it is chewed in the East.]

**Masticate**, mas'ti-kāt, *v.t.* to *chew:* to grind with the teeth.—*adj.* Mas'ticable.—*n.* Mastica'tion. [L. *mastico*, -*atum*—*mastiche*. See Mastic.]

**Masticatory**, mas'ti-ka-tor-i, *adj.*, *chewing:* adapted for chewing.—*n.* (*med.*) a substance to be chewed to increase the saliva.

**Mastiff**, mas'tif, *n.* a large and strong variety of dog much used as a watchdog. [M. E. and O. Fr. *mestif* (Fr. *mâtin*)—Low L. *masnada*, a family—L. *mansio*, a house. See Mansion.]

**Mastodon**, mas'to-don, *n.* an extinct animal, resembling the elephant, with *nipple-like* projections on its *teeth*. [Gr. *mastos*, the breast of a woman, *odous, odontos*, a tooth.]

**Mat**, mat, *n.* a texture of sedge, &c. for cleaning the feet on: a web of rope-yarn.—*v.t.* to cover with mats: to interweave: to entangle:—*pr.p.* matt'ing; *pa.t.* and *pa.p.* matt'ed. [A.S. *meatta* —L. *matta*.]

**Matadore**, mat'a-dōr, *n.* the man who *kills* the bull in bull-fights. [Sp. *matador*—*matar*, to kill—L. *macto*, to kill, to honour by sacrifice— *mactus*, honoured, from root *mag* in *magnus*.]

**Match**, mach, *n.* a piece of inflammable material used for obtaining fire easily: a prepared rope for firing artillery, &c. : a lucifer. [Fr. *mèche* —Low L. *myxus*—Gr. *myxa*, the snuff or wick of a lamp, discharge from the nose (which the snuff of a wick resembles), from root of Mucus.]

**Match**, mach, *n.* anything which agrees with or suits another thing: an equal: one able to cope with another: a contest or game: a marriage: one to be gained in marriage.—*v.i.* to be of the same make, size, &c.—*v.t.* to be equal to: to be able to compete with: to find an equal to: to set against as equal: to suit: to give in marriage.— *n.* Match'er. [A.S. *mæca, gemæca*, earlier *maca*, a mate, a wife. See Make and Mate.]

**Matchless**, mach'les, *adj.* having *no match* or equal.—*adv.* Match'lessly.—*n.* Match'lessness.

**Matchlock**, mach'lok, *n.* the *lock* of a musket containing a *match* for firing it: a musket so fired.

**Mate**, māt, *n.* a companion: an equal: the male or female of animals that go in pairs: in a merchant-ship, the second in command: an assistant.—*v.t.* to be equal to: to match: to marry. [A.S. *ge-maca*, lit. 'having *make* or shape in common with another;' Ice. *maki*, an equal, from the same root as Make. See Match, and cf. Like.]　　　　　　　　　　　[**mate**.

**Mate**, māt, *n.* and *v.t.* in chess. Same as Check-

**Mateless**, māt'les, *adj.* without a *mate* or companion.

**Material**, ma-tē'ri-al, *adj.* consisting of *matter:* corporeal, not spiritual: substantial: essential: important.—*n.* esp. in *pl.* that out of which anything is to be made.—*adv.* Mate'rially.—*ns.* Mate'rialness, Material'ity. [Fr.—L. *materialis*—*materia*.]

**Materialise**, ma-tē'ri-al-īz, *v.t.* to render *material:* to reduce to or regard as matter: to occupy with material interests.

**Materialism**, ma-tē'ri-al-izm, *n.* the doctrine that

denies the independent existence of spirit, and maintains that there is but one substance—viz. *matter.*

**Materialist**, ma-tē'ri-al-ist, *n.* one who holds the doctrine of *materialism.*

**Materialistic**, ma-tē-ri-al-ist'ik, **Materialistical**, ma-tē-ri-al-ist'ik-al, *adj.* pertaining to *materialism.*

**Maternal**, ma-tėr'nal, *adj.* belonging to a *mother:* motherly.—*adv.* Mater'nally. [Fr. *maternel*, It. *maternale*—L. *maternus*—*mater*, mother.]

**Maternity**, ma-tėr'ni-ti, *n.* the *state*, character, or relation of a *mother.*

**Mathematic**, math-e-mat'ik, **Mathematical**, math-e-mat'ik-al, *adj.* pertaining to or done by *mathematics:* very accurate.—*adv.* Mathemat'ically.

**Mathematician**, math-e-ma-tish'an, *n.* one versed in *mathematics*. [L. *mathematicus*.]

**Mathematics**, math-e-mat'iks, *n.sing.* the science of number and space, and of all their relations. [Fr. *mathématiques*—L. *mathematica* —Gr. *mathēmatikē* (*epistēmē*, skill, knowledge), relating to learning or science—*mathēma*—*manthanō*, to learn.]

**Matin**, mat'in, *adj.*, *morning:* used in the morning.—*n.* in *pl.* morning prayers or service: in R. Cath. Church, the earliest canonical hours of prayer. [Fr.—L. *matutinus*, belonging to the morning—*Matuta*, the goddess of the morning, prob. akin to *maturus*, early. See Mature.]

**Matrice**, mat'ris or mat'ris, *n.* Same as Matrix.

**Matricide**, mat'ri-sīd, *n.* a *murderer* of his *mother:* the murder of one's mother.—*adj.* Mat'ricidal. [Fr.—L. *matricida*, one who kills his mother, *matricidium*, the killing of a mother—*mater*, mother, *cædo*, to kill.]

**Matriculate**, ma-trik'ū-lāt, *v.t.* to admit to membership by entering one's name in a register, esp. in a college: to enter a university by being enrolled as a student.—*n.* one admitted to membership in a society.—*n.* Matricula'tion. [L. *matricula*, a register, dim. of *matrix*.]

**Matrimonial**, mat-ri-mō'ni-al, *adj.* relating to or derived from *marriage.*—*adv.* Matrimo'nially.

**Matrimony**, mat'ri-mun-i, *n.* marriage: the state of marriage. [O. Fr. *matrimonie*—L. *matrimonium*—*mater*.]

**Matrix**, mā'triks or mat'riks, *n.* (*anat.*) the cavity in which an animal is formed before its birth, the womb: the cavity in which anything is formed, a mould: (*mining*) substances in which minerals are found imbedded: (*dyeing*) the five simple colours (black, white, blue, red, and yellow) from which all the others are formed: —*pl.* Matrices, mā'tri-sez or mat'ri-sez. [Fr.— L. *matrix, -icis*—*mater*, mother.]

**Matron**, mā'trun, *n.* an elderly married woman: an elderly lady: a female superintendent in a hospital. [Fr.—L. *matrona*, a married lady— *mater*, mother.]

**Matronage**, mā'trun-āj, **Matronhood**, mā'trunhood, *n.* state of a *matron.*

**Matronal**, mā'trun-al or mat'run-al, *adj.* pertaining or suitable to a *matron:* motherly: grave.

**Matronise**, mā'trun-īz or mat'-, *v.t.* to render *matronly:* to attend a lady to public places, as protector.

**Matronly**, mā'trun-li, *adj.* like, becoming, or belonging to a *matron:* elderly: sedate.

**Matter**, mat'ėr, *n.* fluid in abscesses or on festering sores, pus. [An application of the word below.]

**Matter**, mat'ėr, *n.* that which occupies space, and

with which we become acquainted by our bodily senses : that out of which anything is made : the subject or thing treated of : that with which one has to do : cause of a thing : thing of consequence : importance : indefinite amount.—*v.i.* to be of importance : to signify :—*pr.p.* matt'ering ; *pa.p.* matt'ered. — *adj.* **Matt'erless.**— **Matter-of-fact,** *adj.* adhering to the *matter of fact :* not fanciful : dry. [Lit. '*building* stuff,' Fr. *matière*—L. *materia*, from a root *ma*, to measure, to build or construct ; akin to **Mother.**]

**Matting,** mat'ing, *n.* a covering with *mats :* a texture like a mat, but larger : material for mats.

**Mattock,** mat'uk, *n.* a kind of *pickaxe* having the iron ends broad instead of pointed. [A.S. *mattuc*—W. *madog.*]

**Mattress,** mat'res, *n.* a sort of quilted bed stuffed with wool, horse-hair, &c. [O. Fr. *materas* (Fr. *matelas*)—Ar. *matrah.*]

**Maturate,** mat'ū-rāt, *v.t.* to make *mature :* (*med.*) to promote the suppuration of.—*v.i.* (*med.*) to suppurate perfectly.—*n.* **Matura'tion.** [L. *maturo—maturus*, ripe.]

**Maturative,** mat'ū-rāt-iv, *adj.*, *maturing* or ripening : (*med.*) promoting suppuration.—*n.* a medicine promoting suppuration.

**Mature,** ma-tūr', *adj.*, *grown to its full size :* perfected : ripe : (*med.*) come to suppuration : fully digested, as a plan.—*v.t.* to ripen : to bring to perfection : to prepare for use.—*v.i.* to become ripe : to become payable, as a bill.—*adv.* **Mature'ly.**—*n.* **Mature'ness.** [L. *maturus*, ripe.]

**Maturescent,** mat-ū-res'ent, *adj.*, *becoming ripe :* approaching maturity. [L. *maturesco*, to become ripe—*maturus.*]

**Maturity,** ma-tūr'i-ti, *n.* ripeness : a state of completeness. [L. *maturitas—maturus*, ripe.]

**Matutinal,** mat-ū-tī'nal, **Matutine,** mat'ū-tīn, *adj.* pertaining to the *morning :* early. [L. *matutinalis, matutinus.* See **Matin.**]

**Maudlin,** mawd'lin, *adj.* silly, as if half drunk : sickly sentimental. [Contr. from M. E. *Maudeleyne*, which comes through O. Fr. and L. from Gr. *Magdalēnē*, the orig. sense being 'shedding tears of penitence,' hence 'with eyes red and swollen with weeping,' like Mary Magdalene.]

**Mauger, Maugre,** maw'gėr, *prep.* in spite of. [Lit. '*not agreeable to*' or 'against one's will,' Fr. *malgré*—L. *male gratum—male*, badly, *gratum*, agreeable.]

**Maul,** mawl. Same as **Mall,** to beat with a mall.

**Maulstick,** mawl'stik, *n.* a *stick* used by *painters* to steady their hand when working. [Ger. *malerstock—maler*, painter, and *stock*, stick.]

**Maunder,** mawn'dėr, *v.i.* to grumble : to mutter. [Fr. *mendier*, to beg—L. *mendicare.* See **Mendicant.**]

**Maundy-Thursday,** mawn'di-thurz'dā, *n.* the *Thursday* in Passion-week, when royal charity is distributed to the poor at Whitehall. [M. E. *maundee*, a command—O. Fr. *mande* (Fr. *mandé*)—L. *mandatum*, command, *i.e.* the 'new Commandment,' to love one another, mentioned in John xiii. 34.]

**Mausolean,** maw-so-lē'an, *adj.* pertaining to a *mausoleum :* monumental.

**Mausoleum,** maw-so-lē'um, *n.* a magnificent tomb or monument. [L.—Gr. *Mausōleion*, from Mausolus, king of Caria, to whom his widow erected a splendid tomb.]

**Mauve,** mawv, *n.* a beautiful purple dye extracted from coal-tar, so called from its likeness in colour to the flowers of the *mallow :* this colour. [Fr.—L. *malva*, the mallow.]

**Mavis,** mā'vis, *n.* the song-thrush. [Fr. *mauvis ;* prob. from Bret. *milfid*, a mavis.]

**Maw,** maw, *n.* the stomach, esp. in the lower animals : the craw, in birds. [A.S. *maga ;* Ger. *magen.*]

**Mawkish,** mawk'ish, *adj.* loathsome, disgusting, as anything beginning to breed *mawks* or maggots.—*adv.* **Mawk'ishly.**—*n.* **Mawk'ishness.** [With suffix -*ish* from M. E. *mauk*, from same root as **Maggot.**]

**Mawworm,** maw'wurm, *n.* a *worm* that infests the *stomach*, the threadworm. [See **Maw.**]

**Maxillar,** maks'il-ar, **Maxillary,** maks'il-ar-i, *adj.* pertaining to the *jawbone* or jaw. [L. *maxillaris—maxilla*, jawbone, dim. from root of **Macerate.**]

**Maxim,** maks'im, *n.* a general principle, usually of a practical nature : a proverb. [Fr. *maxime* —L. *maxima* (*sententia*, an opinion), superl. of *magnus*, great.]

**Maximum,** maks'i-mum, *adj.* the *greatest.*—*n.* the greatest number, quantity, or degree : (*math.*) the value of a variable when it ceases to increase and begins to decrease :—*pl.* **Max'ima.** [L., superl. of *magnus*, great.]

**May,** mā, *v.i.* to be *able :* to be allowed : to be free to act : to be possible : to be by chance : *pa.t.* might (mīt). [A.S. *mæg*, pr.t. of *mugan*, to be able, pa.t. *meahte, mihte ;* cog. with Goth. *magan*, Ger. *mögen ;* also with L. *mag-nus*, great, Gr. *mech-anē*, contrivance ; all from a root *mag* or *magh*, to have power.]

**May,** mā, *n.* the fifth month of the year : the early or gay part of life.—*v.i.* to gather May (prov. E. the blossom of the hawthorn, which blooms in May) :—*pr.p.* May'ing. [Fr. *Mai*—L. *Maius* (*mensis*, a month), sacred to Maia, the mother of Mercury ; prob. from root *mag*, Sans. *mah*, to grow, and so May = the month of growth.]

**Mayday,** mā'dā, *n.* the first *day* of *May.*

**May-flower,** mā'-flow'ėr, *n.* the hawthorn, which *blooms in May.*        [*pears in May.*

**Mayfly,** mā'flī, *n.* an ephemeral *fly* which appears in *May.*

**Mayor,** mā'ur, *n.* the chief magistrate of a city or borough.—*n.* **May'oress,** the wife of a mayor. [Fr. *maire*—L. *major*, comp. of *magnus*, great.]

**Mayoralty,** mā'ur-al-ti, **Mayorship,** mā'ur-ship, *n.* the office of a mayor.

**Maypole,** mā'pōl, *n.* a *pole* erected for dancing round on *Mayday.*

**May-queen,** mā'-kwēn, *n.* a young woman crowned with flowers as *queen* on *Mayday.*

**Maze,** māz, *n.* a place full of intricate windings : confusion of thought : perplexity.—*v.t.* to bewilder : to confuse. [Prov. E. to *maze*, to wander, as if stupefied, from the Scand., as in Ice. *masa*, to jabber.]

**Mazurka,** ma-zōōr'ka, *n.* a lively Polish dance, or music such as is played to it.

**Mazy,** māz'i, *adj.* full of *mazes* or windi..gs : intricate.—*adv.* **Maz'ily.**—*n.* **Maz'iness.**

**Me,** mē, *personal pron.* the objective case of **I.** [A.S. ; L., Gr. *me*, Sans. *mâ.*]

**Mead,** mēd, *n.*, *honey* and water fermented and flavoured. [A.S. *medo ;* a word common to the Aryan languages, as Ger. *meth*, W. *medd*, mead, Gr. *methu*, strong drink, Sans. *madhu*, sweet, honey (which was the chief ingredient of the drink).]

**Mead,** mēd, **Meadow,** med'ō, *n.* a place where grass is *mown* or cut down : a rich pastureground. [A.S. *mæd—mawan*, to mow ; Ger. *mahd*, a mowing, Swiss *matt*, a meadow. See **Mow,** to cut down.]

**Meadowy**, med'ō-i, *adj.* containing *meadows*.

**Meagre, Meager**, mē'gėr, *adj.*, *lean*: poor: barren: scanty: without strength.—*adv.* **Mea'grely.**—*n.* **Mea'greness.** [Fr. *maigre*—L. *macer*, lean; cog. with Ger. *mager*.]

**Meal**, mēl, *n.* the food taken at one time: the act or the time of taking food. [A.S. *mæl*, time, portion of time; Dut. *maal*, Ger. *mahl*.]

**Meal**, mēl, *n.* grain *ground* to powder. [A.S. *melu*; Ger. *mehl*, Dut. *meel*, meal, from the root of Goth. *malan*, L. *molo*, to grind.]

**Mealy**, mēl'i, *adj.* resembling *meal*: besprinkled as with meal.—*n.* **Meal'iness.**

**Mealy-mouthed**, mēl'i-mowthd, *adj.* smooth-tongued: unwilling to state the truth in plain terms.

**Mean**, mēn, *adj.* low in rank or birth: base: sordid: low in worth or estimation: poor: humble.—*adv.* **Mean'ly.**—*n.* **Mean'ness.** [A.S. *mæne*, wicked; perh. conn. with A.S. *gemæne*, Ger. *gemein*, common, Goth. *gamains*, unclean.]

**Mean**, mēn, *adj.*, *middle*: coming between: moderate.—*n.* the middle point, quantity, value, or degree: instrument:—*pl.* income: estate: instrument. [O. Fr. *meien* (Fr. *moyen*)—L. *medianus*, enlarged form of *medius*; cog. with Gr. *mesos*, Sans. *madhya*, middle.]

**Mean**, mēn, *v t.* to have in the *mind* or thoughts: to intend: to signify.—*v.i.* to have in the mind: to have meaning:—*pr.p.* mean'ing; *pa.t.* and *pa.p.* meant (ment). [A.S. *mænan*; Ger. *meinen*, to think; from a root *man*, found also in **Man** and **Mind**.]

**Meander**, mē-an'dėr, *n.* a *winding* course: a maze: perplexity.—*v.i.* to flow or run in a winding course: to be intricate.—*v.t.* to wind or flow round. [L.—Gr., the name of a *winding* river in Asia Minor.]

**Meandering**, mē-an'dėr-ing, *adj.*, *winding* in a course.—*n.* a winding course.

**Meaning**, mēn'ing, *n.* that which is in the *mind* or thoughts: signification: the sense intended: purpose.—*adj.* significant.—*adv.* **Mean'ingly.** [See **Mean**, *v.t.*]

**Meaningless**, mēn'ing-les, *adj.* without meaning.

**Meanly, Meanness.** See **Mean**, low in rank.

**Meant**, *pa.t.* and *pa.p.* of **Mean**, to have in the mind.        [with *measles.*

**Measled**, mē'zld, **Measly**, mē'zli, *adj.* infected with measles.

**Measles**, mē'zlz, *n.sing.* a contagious fever accompanied with small red *spots* upon the skin. [Dut. *maselen*, measles, from *masa*, a spot, cog. with O. Ger. *masa*, a spot, Ger. *masern*, measles.]

**Measurable**, mezh'ūr-a-bl, *adj.* that may be *measured* or computed: moderate: in small quantity or extent.—*adv.* **Meas'urably.**

**Measure**, mezh'ūr, *n.* that by which extent is ascertained or expressed: the extent of anything: a rule by which anything is adjusted: proportion: a stated quantity: degree: extent: moderation: means to an end: metre: musical time.—*v.t.* to ascertain the dimensions of: to adjust: to mark out: to allot.—*v.i.* to have a certain extent: to be equal or uniform. [Fr. *mesure*—L. *mensura*, a measure—*metior*, to measure, akin to Gr. *metron*, a measure, Sans. root *mâ*, *mâd*, to measure.]

**Measured**, mezh'ūrd, *adj.* of a certain *measure*: equal: uniform: steady: restricted.

**Measureless**, mezh'ūr-les, *adj.* boundless: immense.

**Measurement**, mezh'ūr-ment, *n.* the act of *measuring*: quantity found by measuring.

**Meat**, mēt, *n.* anything eaten as food: the flesh of animals used as food. [A.S. *mete*; Goth. *mats*, food, Dut. *met*, Dan. *mad*; prob. from a root seen in L. *mando*, to chew, as in **Mandible**.]

**Meat-offering**, mēt'-of'ėr-ing, *n.* a Jewish offering of *meat* or food in their religious services.

**Mechanic**, me-kan'ik, **Mechanical**, me-kan'ik-al, *adj.* pertaining to *machines* or *mechanics*: constructed according to the laws of mechanics: acting by physical power: done by a machine: pertaining to artisans: done simply by force of habit: vulgar.—*n.* **Mechan'ic**, one engaged in a mechanical trade: an artisan.—*adv.* **Mechan'ically.** [O. Fr.—L. *mechanicus*; Gr. *mēchanikos*—*mēchanē*—*mēchos*, a contrivance.]

**Mechanician**, mek-an-ish'an, **Mechanist**, mek'an-ist, *n.* a *machine-maker*: one skilled in mechanics.

**Mechanics**, me-kan'iks, *n.* the science which treats of *machines*: the science which determines the effect produced by forces on a body.

**Mechanism**, mek'an-izm, *n.* the construction of a *machine*: the arrangement and action of its parts, by which it produces a given result.

**Medal**, med'al, *n.* a piece of *metal* in the form of a coin bearing some device or inscription: a reward of merit. [Fr. *médaille*—It. *medaglia*; through a Low L. form *medalla* or *medalia*, a small coin, from L. *metallum*, a metal. See **Metal**.]

**Medallic**, me-dal'ik, *adj.* pertaining to *medals*.

**Medallion**, me-dal'yun, *n.* a large antique *medal*: a bass-relief of a round form: an ornament of a circular form, in which a portrait or hair is inclosed. [See **Medal**.]

**Medallist, Medalist**, med'al-ist, *n.* one skilled in *medals*: an engraver of medals: one who has gained a medal.

**Meddle**, med'l, *v.i.* to interfere officiously (*with* or *in*): to have to do (*with*). [O. Fr. *medler*, a corr. of *mesler* (Fr. *mêler*)—Low L. *misculare* —L. *misceo*, to mix.]

**Meddler**, med'lėr, *n.* one who meddles or interferes with matters in which he has no concern.

**Meddlesome**, med'l-sum, *adj.* given to meddling. —*n.* **Medd'lesomeness.**

**Meddling**, med'ling, *adj.* interfering in the concerns of others: officious.—*n.* officious interposition.

**Mediæval.** Same as **Medieval.**

**Medial**, mē'di-al, *adj.* noting a mean or average. [Low L. *medialis*—L. *medius*, middle, cog. with root of **Mid**.]

**Mediate**, mē'di-āt, *adj.*, *middle*: between two extremes: acting by or as a means.—*v.i.* to interpose between parties as a friend of each: to intercede.—*v.t.* to effect by mediation.—*adv.* **Me'diately.**—*n.* **Me'diateness.** [Low L. *mediatus*—L. *medius*. Cf. **Medial**.]

**Mediation**, mē-di-ā'shun, *n.* the act of mediating or interposing: entreaty for another.

**Mediatise**, mē'di-a-tīz, *v.t.* to annex as a smaller state to a larger neighbouring one.

**Mediator**, mē'di-āt-ur, *n.* one who mediates or interposes between parties at variance.

**Mediatorial**, mē-di-a-tō'ri-al, *adj.* belonging to a mediator or intercessor.—*adv.* **Mediato'rially.**

**Medic**, med'ik, *n.* a genus of leguminous plants, with leaves like those of clover. [L. *medica*— Gr. *mēdikē* (*poa*), lit. 'median' (grass), orig. brought from *Media*, in Asia.]

**Medicable**, med'i-ka-bl, *adj.* that may be healed.

**Medical**, med'i-kal, *adj.* relating to the art of *healing* diseases: containing that which heals: intended to promote the study of medicine.— *adv.* **Med'ically.** [Low L. *medicalis*—L. *medi-*

*cus*, pertaining to healing, a physician—*medeor*, to heal.]

**Medicament**, med′i-ka-ment, *n.* a medicine or *healing* application.

**Medicate**, med′i-kāt, *v.t.* to treat with medicine : to impregnate with anything medicinal. [L. *medico*, to heal—*medicus*. See **Medical**.]

**Medicated**, med′i-kāt-ed, *adj.* tinctured or impregnated with medicine.

**Medication**, med-i-kā′shun, *n.* the act or process of *medicating* or of tincturing with medicinal substances : the use of medicine.

**Medicative**, med′i-kā-tiv, *adj.*, *healing* : tending to heal.

**Medicinal**, me-dis′in-al, *adj.* relating to *medicine* : fitted to cure or lessen disease or pain.—*adv.* **Medic′inally.**

**Medicine**, med′i-sin or med′sin, *n.* anything applied for the *cure* or lessening of disease or pain. [Fr.—L. *medicina*—*medicus*. See **Medical**.]

**Medieval**, **Mediæval**, mē-di-ē′val, *adj.* relating to the *middle ages*. [L. *medius*, middle, and *ævum*, an age. See **Medial** and **Age**.]

**Medievalist**, **Mediævalist**, mē-di-ē′val-ist, *n.* one versed in the history of the *middle ages*.

**Mediocre**, mē′di-ō-kėr, *adj.*, *middling* : moderate. [Fr.—L. *mediocris*—*medius*, middle.]

**Mediocrity**, mē-di-ok′ri-ti, *n.* a *middle state* or *condition* : a moderate degree.

**Meditate**, med′i-tāt, *v.i.* to consider thoughtfully : to purpose.—*v.t.* to think on : to revolve in the mind : to intend. [L. *meditor*, a freq. form from root *med*, seen in L. *mederi* and Gr. *manthanō*, to learn.] [planned.

**Meditated**, med′i-tāt-ed, *adj.* thought of :

**Meditation**, med-i-tā′shun, *n.* the act of *meditating* : deep thought : serious contemplation.

**Meditative**, med′i-tāt-iv, *adj.* given to *meditation* : expressing design.—*adv.* **Med′itatively.** —*n.* **Med′itativeness.**

**Mediterranean**, med-i-ter-rā′ne-an, **Mediterraneous**, med-i-ter-rā′ne-us, *adj.* situated in the *middle* of the *earth* or *land* : inland.—**Mediterranean Sea**, so called from being, as it were, in the *middle* of the *land* of the Old World. [L., from *medius*, middle, and *terra*, earth, land.]

**Medium**, mē′di-um, *n.* the *middle* : the middle place or degree : anything intervening : means or instrument : the substance in which bodies exist, or through which they move : in spiritualism, the person through whom spirits are alleged to make their communications :—*pl.* **Me′diums** or **Me′dia**. [L. See **Medial** and **Mid**.]

**Medlar**, med′lar, *n.* a small tree, common in Britain and Europe, with fruit like a pear. [O. Fr. *meslier*, a medlar-tree—L. *mespilum*—Gr. *mespilon*.]

**Medley**, med′li, *n.* a mingled and confused mass : a miscellany. [Orig. pa.p. of O. Fr. *medler*, to mix, thus the same word with mod. Fr. *mêlée*. See **Meddle**.]

**Medullar**, me-dul′ar, **Medullary**, me-dul′ar-i, *adj.* consisting of or resembling *marrow* or pith. [L. *medullaris*—*medulla*, marrow—*medius*, middle.]

**Medusa**, me-dū′sa, *n.* (*myth.*) one of the Gorgons, whose head, cut off by Perseus and placed in the ægis of Minerva, had the power of turning beholders into stone : the name given to the common kinds of jelly-fishes, prob. from the likeness of their tentacles to the snakes on Medusa's head :—*pl.* **Medu′sæ**. [Gr. *medousa*, fem. of *medōn*, a ruler—*medō*, to rule.]

**Meed**, mēd, *n.* *wages* : reward : that which is bestowed for merit. [A.S. *med*; cog. with Goth.

*mizdo*, reward, Ger. *miethe*, hire ; allied to Gr. *misthos*, hire, wages.]

**Meek**, mēk, *adj.*, *mild* : gentle : submissive.—*adv.* **Meek′ly.**—*n.* **Meek′ness.** [Ice. *mjukr*, Dut. *muik*, Dan. *myg*.]

**Meerschaum**, mēr′shawm, *n.* a fine white clay used for making tobacco-pipes, so called because once supposed to be the petrified *scum* or *foam* of the *sea*. [Ger. *meer*, the sea (E. **Mere**), and *schaum*, foam (E. **Scum**).]

**Meet**, mēt, *adj.* fitting : qualified : adapted.— *adv.* **Meet′ly.**—*n.* **Meet′ness.** [A.S. *ge-met*, fit —*metan*, to measure. See **Mete**.]

**Meet**, mēt, *v.t.* to come face to face : to encounter : to find : to receive, as a welcome.—*v.i.* to come together : to assemble : to have an encounter : —*pa.t.* and *pa.p.* met.—*n.* a meeting, as of huntsmen. [A.S. *metan*, to meet—*mot*, *ge-mot*, a meeting. Cf. **Moot**.]

**Meeting**, mēt′ing, *n.* an interview : an assembly.

**Meeting-house**, mēt′ing-hows, *n.* a *house* or building where people, esp. dissenters, *meet* for public worship.

**Megalosaurus**, meg-a-lo-saw′rus, *n.* the *great saurian* or lizard, a gigantic fossil found in England. [Gr. *megas*, *megalē*, great, *sauros*, a lizard.]

**Megatherium**, meg-a-thē′ri-um, *n.* a gigantic fossil quadruped found in the pampas of S. America. [Gr. *megas*, great, *thērion*, wild beast.]

**Megrim**, mē′grim, *n.* a pain affecting *one half* of the *head* or face. [Fr. *migraine*, corr. of Gr. *hēmicrania*—*hēmi*, half, and *kranion*, the skull. See **Cranium**.]

**Meiocene.** Same as **Miocene.**

**Meiosis**, mī-ō′sis, *n.* (*rhet.*) a species of hyperbole representing a thing as *less* than it is. [Gr. *meiōsis*—*meio-ō*, to lessen.]

**Melancholic**, mel′an-kol-ik or -kol′ik, *adj.* affected with melancholy : dejected : mournful.

**Melancholy**, mel′an-kol-i, *n.* a disease causing gloomy groundless fears, and general depression of spirits, so called because it was supposed to be occasioned by an excess of *black bile* : dejection.—*adj.* gloomy : producing grief. [Fr. —L. *melancholia*—Gr. *melangcholia*—*melan*, black, and *cholē*, bile, E. **Gall**.]

**Meliorate**, mē′li-or-āt, *v.t.* to make *better* : to improve. [L. *melioro*, *-atus*, to make better— *melior*, better.]

**Melioration**, mē-li-or-ā′shun, *n.* the act of *making better* : improvement.

**Mellay**, mel′ā, *n.* confusion. [Fr. *mêlée*. See **Medley**.]

**Melliferous**, mel-if′ėr-us, *adj.*, *honey-producing*. [L. *mel*, honey, and *fero*, to produce.]

**Mellifluent**, mel-if′lōō-ent, **Mellifluous**, mel-if′-lōō-us, *adj.*, *flowing* with *honey* or sweetness : smooth.—*adv.* **Mellif′luently**, **Mellif′luously.** —*n.* **Mellif′luence.** [L. *mel*, and *fluens*—*fluo*, to flow.]

**Mellow**, mel′ō, *adj.*, *soft* and ripe : well matured : soft to the touch.—*v.t.* to soften by ripeness or age : to mature.—*v.i.* to become soft : to be matured. [A.S. *mearu*, soft, cog. with Dut. *murw* and *mollig*, L. *mollis*, Gr. *malakos*. See **Marrow**.]

**Mellowness**, mel′ō-nes, *n.*, *softness* : maturity.

**Mellowy**, mel′ō-i, *adj.*, *soft* : oily.

**Melodious**, me-lō′di-us, *adj.* full of *melody* : harmonious.—*adv.* **Melo′diously.**—*n.* **Melo′diousness.**

**Melodrama**, mel-o-dram′a, **Melodrame**, mel′o-dram, *n.* a kind of sensational drama, formerly largely intermixed with *songs*. [Gr. *melos*, a song, and *drama*, a drama.]

**Melodramatic**, mel-o-dra-mat′ik, *adj.* of the nature of melodrama : overstrained : sensational.

**Melodramatist**, mel-o-dram′a-tist, *n.* one skilled in melodramas, or who prepares them.

**Melody**, mel′o-di, *n.* an air or tune : music : an agreeable succession of a single series of musical sounds, as distinguished from 'harmony' or the concord of a succession of simultaneous sounds. —*n.* **Mel′odist**. [Fr.—L.—Gr. *melōdia*—*melos*, a song, and *ōdē*, a lay.]

**Melon**, mel′un, *n.* a kind of cucumber and its fruit, which resembles an *apple*. [Fr.—L. *melo* —Gr. *mēlon*, an apple.]

**Melt**, melt, *v.t.* to make liquid, to dissolve : to soften : to waste away.—*v.i.* to become liquid : to dissolve : to become tender or mild : to lose substance : to be discouraged. [A.S. *meltan*, prob. conn. with **Marrow**, **Mellow**.]

**Melting**, melt′ing, *n.* the act of making liquid or of dissolving : the act of softening or rendering tender.—*adv.* **Melt′ingly**.

**Member**, mem′ber, *n.* a limb of an animal : a clause : one of a community : a representative in a legislative body : (*B.*, in *pl.*) the appetites and passions.—*adj.* **Mem′bered**, having limbs. [Fr. *membre*—L. *membrum*.]

**Membership**, mem′ber-ship, *n.* the state of being a *member* or one of a society : a community.

**Membrane**, mem′brān, *n.* the thin tissue which covers the *members* or parts of the body : the film containing the seeds of a plant. [Fr.—L. *membrana*—*membrum*.]

**Membraneous**, mem-brān′e-us, **Membranous**, mem′bran-us, **Membranaceous**, mem-bran-ā′-shus, *adj.* relating to, consisting of, or like a *membrane*.

**Memento**, me-men′tō, *n.* a suggestion or notice to awaken memory :—*pl.* **Memen′tos**. [L. imper. of *memini*, to remember, from root of **Mention**.]

**Memoir**, mem′wor or me-moir′, *n.* a familiar notice of anything as *remembered* by the writer : a short biographical sketch : a record of researches on any subject : the transactions of a society. [Fr. *mémoire*—L. *memoria*, memory—*memor*, mindful, akin to Sans. root *smri*, to remember.]

**Memorable**, mem′or-a-bl, *adj.* deserving to be *remembered* : remarkable.—*adv.* **Mem′orably**.

**Memorandum**, mem-or-an′dum, *n.* something to be *remembered* : a note to assist the memory :— *pl.* **Memoran′dums**, **Memoran′da**.

**Memorial**, me-mō′ri-al, *adj.* bringing to *memory* : contained in memory.—*n.* that which serves to keep in remembrance : a monument : a note to help the memory : a written statement with a petition, laid before a legislative or other body : (*B.*) memory.

**Memorialise**, me-mō′ri-al-īz, *v.t.* to present a *memorial* to : to petition by memorial.

**Memorialist**, me-mō′ri-al-ist, *n.* one who writes, signs, or presents a *memorial*.

**Memory**, mem′o-ri, *n.* a having or keeping in the *mind* : the faculty of the mind by which it retains the knowledge of previous thoughts or events : retention : remembrance. [See **Memoir**.]

**Men**, *plural* of **Man**.

**Menace**, men′ās, *v.t.* to threaten.—*n.* a threat or threatening. [Fr.—L. *minor*, to threaten— *minæ*, the overhanging points of a wall.]

**Menacing**, men′ās-ing, *adj.* overhanging : threatening.—*adv.* **Men′acingly**.

**Menagerie**, **Menagery**, men-äzh′e-ri or men-aj′-èr-i, *n.* a place for *managing* and keeping wild animals : a collection of such animals. [Fr., from root of **Manage**.]

**Mend**, mend, *v.t.* to remove a *fault* : to repair : to correct, improve—*v.i.* to grow better.—*n.* **Mend′er**. [Short for **Amend**.]

**Mendacious**, men-dā′shus, *adj.*, *lying* : false.— *adv.* **Menda′ciously**. [L. *mendax, mendacis*— *mentior*, to lie.]

**Mendacity**, men-das′i-ti, *n.*, *lying* : falsehood.

**Mendicancy**, men′di-kan-si, *n.* the state of being a *mendicant* or beggar : beggary.

**Mendicant**, men′di-kant, *adj.* poor to beggary : practising beggary.—*n.* one who is in extreme want, a beggar : one of the begging fraternity of the R. Cath. Church. [L. *mendicans, -antis*, pr.p. of *mendico*, to beg—*mendicus*, a beggar, perh. conn. with L. *menda*, a want.]

**Mendicity**, men-dis′i-ti, *n.* the state of being a *mendicant* or beggar : the life of a beggar.

**Mending**, mend′ing, *n.* the act of repairing.

**Menial**, mē′ni-al, *adj.* servile : low.—*n.* a domestic servant : one performing servile work : a person of servile disposition. [Orig. an adj. from M. E. *meine*, a household, through O. Fr. from Low L. *mansion-ata, maisnada*—L. *mansio, -onis*. See **Mansion**.]

**Meningitis**, men-in-jī′tis, *n.* inflammation of the membranes of the brain. [Gr. *mēninx, mēning-gos*, a membrane.]

**Meniver**, men′i-vèr, **Minever**, **Miniver**, min′i-vèr, *n.* the ermine : its fur. [O. Fr. *menu ver—menu*, small—L. *minutus*, and *vair*, fur—L. *varius*, changing, mottled.]

**Menses**, men′sēz, *n.pl.* the *monthly* discharge from the womb. [L. *mensis*, a month.]

**Menstrual**, men′strōō-al, *adj.*, *monthly* : belonging to a menstruum. [L. *menstrualis*.]

**Menstruant**, men′strōō-ant, *adj.* subject to *menses*. [L. *menstruans, -antis*, pr.p. of *menstruo*.]

**Menstruate**, men′strōō-āt, *v.i.* to discharge the *menses*.—*n.* **Men′struation**. [L. *menstruo, -atum*.] [ing to menses. [L. *menstruus*.]

**Menstruous**, men′strōō-us, *adj.* having or belong-

**Menstruum**, men′strōō-um, *n.* a solvent or dissolving substance :—*pl.* **Men′strua**, the menses. [L., from a fancy of the old chemists that dissolvents could be prepared only at certain stages of the moon.]

**Mensurable**, mens′ū-ra-bl, *adj.* that can be *measured* : measurable.—*n.* **Mensurabil′ity**, quality of being mensurable. [L. *mensura-bilis—mensuro*, to measure. See **Measure**.]

**Mensural**, mens′ū-ral, *adj.* pertaining to *measure*.

**Mensuration**, mens-ū-rā′shun, *n.* the act, process, or art of *measuring* : art of finding the length, area, or volume of bodies : the result of measuring.

**Mental**, men′tal, *adj.* pertaining to the *mind* : intellectual.—*adv.* **Men′tally**. [From L. *mens, mentis*, the mind—Sans. root *man*, to think.]

**Mention**, men′shun, *n.* a brief notice or remark : a hint.—*v.t.* to notice briefly : to remark : to name.—*adj.* **Men′tionable**. [L. *mentio, mentionis*, from root *men*, Sans. *man*, to think.]

**Mentor**, men′tor, *n.* a wise and faithful counsellor or monitor.—*adj.* **Mentor′ial**. [From Gr. *Men-tōr*, the friend of Ulysses—root of **Mental**.]

**Menu**, men′oo, *n.* list of things composing a repast. [Lit. 'detailed,' 'minute,' Fr.—L. *minutus*, small. See **Minute**.]

**Mephistophelean**, mef-is-tof-ē′le-an, *adj.* cynical, sceptical, malicious. [From *Mephistopheles*, a character in Goethe's *Faust*.]

**Mephitic**, me-fit′ik, *adj.* pertaining to *mephitis* : offensive to the smell : noxious : pestilential.

**Mephitis**, me-fī'tis, **Mephitism**, mef'i-tizm, *n.* a foul, pestilential exhalation from the ground. [L. *mephitis.*]

**Mercantile**, mėr'kan-tīl, *adj.* pertaining to *merchants*: commercial. [Fr. and It.—Low L. *mercantilis*—L. *mercans, -antis*, pr.p. of *mercor*, to trade—*merx, mercis*, merchandise—*mereo*, to gain.]

**Mercenary**, mėr'se-nar-i, *adj.* hired for money: actuated by the hope of reward: greedy of gain: sold or done for money.—*n.* one who is hired: a soldier hired into foreign service. [Fr.—L. *mercenarius—merces*, hire.]

**Mercer**, mėr'sėr, *n.* a *merchant* in silks and woollen cloths. [Fr. *mercier*, from root of **Merchant**.]

**Mercery**, mėr'sėr-i, *n.* the trade of a *mercer*: the goods of a mercer.

**Merchandise**, mėr'chand-īz, *n.* the goods of a *merchant*: anything traded in. [Fr. *marchandise —marchand*, a merchant.]

**Merchant**, mėr'chant, *n.* one who carries on *trade*, esp. on a large scale: one who buys and sells goods: a trader.—*adj.* pertaining to trade or merchandise. [Fr. *marchand*—L. *mercans, -antis*, pr.p. of *mercor*, to trade.]

**Merchantman**, mėr'chant-man, *n.* a trading-ship: (*B.*) a merchant:—*pl.* **Mer'chantmen.** [**Merchant** and **Man**.]

**Merciful**, mėr'si-fool, *adj.* full of or exercising *mercy*: willing to pity and spare: compassionate: tender: humane.—*adv.* **Mer'cifully.**—*n.* **Mer'-cifulness.**

**Merciless**, mėr'si-les, *adj.* without *mercy*: unfeeling: hard-hearted: unsparing: cruel.—*adv.* **Mer'cilessly.**—*n.* **Mer'cilessness**, want of mercy.

**Mercurial**, mėr-kū'ri-al, *adj.* having the qualities said to belong to the god *Mercury*: active: sprightly: containing or consisting of mercury. [L. *mercurialis.* See **Mercury**.]

**Mercurialise**, mėr-kū'ri-al-īz, *v.t.* to make *mercurial*: (*med.*) to affect with mercury: to expose to the vapour of mercury.

**Mercury**, mėr'kū-ri, *n.*, the *god of merchandise* and eloquence, and the messenger of the gods: the planet nearest the sun: a white, liquid metal, also called quicksilver: a messenger: a newspaper. [Fr.—L. *Mercurius—merx, mercis*, merchandise. See **Merchant**.]

**Mercy**, mėr'si, *n.* a forgiving disposition: clemency: leniency: tenderness: an act of mercy. [Fr. *merci*, grace, favour—L. *merces, mercedis*, pay, reward, in Low L. also pity, favour.]

**Mercy-seat**, mėr'si-sēt, *n.* (*lit.*) the *seat* or place of *mercy*: the covering of the Jewish Ark of the Covenant: the throne of God.

**Mere**, mēr, *n.* a pool or lake. [A.S. *mere*; Ger. and Dut. *meer*; akin to L. *mare*, the sea, Fr. *mer*, and *mare*, pool; prob. conn. with Sans. *maru*, desert, *mri*, to die, and with the root of **Mortal**. See **Marsh** and **Marine**.]

**Mere**, mēr, *adj.* unmixed: pure: only this and nothing else: alone: absolute.—*adv.* **Mere'ly**, purely, simply: only: thus and no other way: solely. [L. *merus*, unmixed (of wine).]

**Mere**, mēr, *n.* a boundary. [A.S. *mære, ge-mare*.]

**Merestead**, mēr'sted, *n.* the land within the boundaries of a farm. [From **Mere**, a boundary, and **Stead**.]

**Meretricious**, mer-e-trish'us, *adj.* alluring by false show: gaudy and deceitful: false.—*adv.* **Meretri'ciously.**—*n.* **Meretri'ciousness.** [L. *meretricius—meretrix, meretricis*, a harlot—*mereo*, to earn. See **Mercantile**.]

**Merganser**, mer-gan'sėr, *n.* a *diving* bird or seaduck. [L. *mergus*, a diver, and *anser*, a goose.]

**Merge**, mėrj, *v.t.* to dip or plunge in: to sink: to cause to be swallowed up.—*v.i.* to be swallowed up, or lost.—*n.* **Merg'er** a merging. [L. *mergo, mersum*, akin to Sans. *majj*, to dive, to sink.]

**Meridian**, me-rid'i-an, *adj.* pertaining to *mid-day*: being on the meridian or at mid-day: raised to the highest point.—*n.*, *mid-day*: the highest point, as of success: an imaginary circle on the earth's surface passing through the poles and any given place: (*astr.*) an imaginary circle, passing through the poles of the heavens, and the zenith of the spectator, which the sun crosses at mid-day. [Fr.—L. *meridianus*, pertaining to mid-day, from *meridies* (corr. for *medidies*), mid-day—*medius*, middle, and *dies*, day.]

**Meridional**, me-rid'i-un-al, *adj.* pertaining to the *meridian*: southern: having a southern aspect. —*adv.* **Merid'ionally**, in the direction of the meridian.—*n.* **Meridional'ity.** [Fr.—L. *meridionalis.*]

**Merino**, me-rē'no, *n.* a variety of sheep having very fine wool, orig. from Spain: a fabric of merino wool.—*adj.* belonging to the merino sheep or their wool. [Sp., and meaning 'moving from pasture to pasture'—*merino*, inspector of sheepwalks—Low L. *majorinus*, from root of **Major**.]

**Merit**, mer'it, *n.* excellence that *deserves* honour or reward: worth: value: that which is earned. —*v.t.* to earn: to have a right to claim as reward: to deserve. [Fr.—L. *meritum—mereo, meritum*, to obtain as a lot or portion, to deserve; cf. Gr. *meiromai*, to divide. See **Mercantile**.]

**Meritorious**, mer-i-tō'ri-us, *adj.* possessing *merit* or desert: deserving of reward, honour, or praise. —*adv.* **Merito'riously.**—*n.* **Merito'riousness.**

**Merk**, mėrk, *n.* an old Scotch silver coin worth 13s. 4d. Scots, or 13½d. sterling. [Same word as English *mark*.]

**Merle**, mėrl, *n.* the blackbird. [Fr.—L. *merula.*]

**Merlin**, mėr'lin, *n.* a species of small hawk: a wizard. [Fr. *émerillon*, prob. same as **Merle**.]

**Merlon**, mėr'lon, *n.* (*fort.*) the part of a parapet which lies between two embrasures. [Fr.; ety. dub.]

**Mermaid**, mėr'mād, *n.*, *maid* of the *sea*, a fabled marine animal, having the upper part like a woman and the lower like a fish—*masc.* **Mer'-man.** [A.S. *mere*, a lake (influenced by Fr. *mer*, the sea), and *mægd*, a maid.]

**Merriment**, mer'i-ment, **Merriness**, mer'i-nes, *n.* gaiety with laughter and noise: mirth: hilarity.

**Merry**, mer'i, *adj.*, *sportive*: cheerful: noisily gay: causing laughter: lively.—*adv.* **Merr'ily.** [A.S. *mear*, from the Celtic, as in Gael. and Ir. *mear*, from *mir*, to sport. See **Mirth**.]

**Merry-andrew**, mer'i-an'drōō, *n.* a buffoon: one who attends a mountebank or quack doctor. [**Merry**, and perhaps *Andrew* Borde, a physician in the time of Henry VIII., noted for his facetious sayings.] [tainment, a festival.

**Merry-making**, mer'i-māk'ing, *n.* a merry enter-

**Merry-thought**, mer'i-thawt, *n.* the forked bone of a fowl's breast, which two persons pull at in play, the one who breaks off the longer part being thought likely to be first married. [**Merry** and **Thought**.]

**Mersion**, mėr'shun, *n.* Same as **Immersion.**

**Meseems**, me-sēmz', *v.impers.* it seems to me (used only in poetry). [**Me**, the dative of I, and **Seems** used impersonally.]

**Mesembryanthemum**, me-zem-bri-an'the-mum,

*n.* a genus of succulent plants, mostly belonging to South Africa. [Gr. *mesēmbria*, mid-day—*mesos*, middle, *hēmera*, day, and *anthēma—antheō*, to blossom, so called because their flowers usually expand at mid-day.]

**Mesentery**, mes'en-tèr-i or mez'-, *n.* a membrane in the cavity of the abdomen, attached to the vertebræ, and serving to support the intestines.— *adj.* **Mesenter'ic** [L.—Gr. *mesenteron—mesos*, middle, *enteron*, intestines—*entos*, within.

**Mesh**, mesh, *n.* the opening between the threads of a net : network.—*v.t.* to catch in a net.— *adj.* **Mesh'y**, formed like network. [M. E. *maske*—A.S. *max*, a net : Ger. *masche*.]

**Mesmeric**, mez-mèr'ik, **Mesmerical**, mez-mèr'-ik-al, *adj.* of or relating to mesmerism.

**Mesmerise**, mez'mèr-īz, *v.t.* to induce an extraordinary state of the nervous system, in which the operator is supposed to control the actions of the subject.—*n.* **Mes'meriser** or **Mes'merist**, one who mesmerises. [From *Mesmer*, a German physician (1733–1815), who brought mesmerism into notice.]

**Mesmerism**, mez'mèr-izm, *n.* art of *mesmerising*.

**Mesne**, mēn, *adj.*, *intermediate:* applied to a writ issued between the beginning and end of a suit. [Norm. Fr. *mesne*, middle.]

**Mess**, mes, *n.* a *mixture* disagreeable to the sight or taste : a medley: disorder: confusion. [A form of **Mash**.]

**Mess**, mes, *n.* a dish or quantity of food *served up* at one time : a number of persons who eat together, esp. in the army and navy.—*v.t.* to supply with a mess.—*v.i.* to eat of a mess : to eat at a common table. [O. Fr. *mes* (Fr. *mets*), a dish, a course at table—L. *mitto, missum*, to send, in Low L. to place.]

**Message**, mes'āj, *n.* any communication *sent* from one to another : an errand : an official communication. [Fr.—Low L. *missaticum*, from *mitto, missus*, to send.]

**Messenger**, mes'en-jèr, *n.* the bearer of a *message:* a forerunner : (*law*) an officer who executes summonses, called *messenger-at-arms*.

**Messiah**, mes-sī'a, **Messias**, mes-sī'as, *n.* the *anointed one*, the *Christ*.—*n.* **Messi'ahship**. [Heb. *mashiach—mashach*, to anoint.]

**Messianic**, mes-si-an'ik, *adj.* relating to the Messiah.      [table. [**Mess** and **Mate**.]

**Messmate**, mes'māt, *n.* one who eats at the same

**Messuage**, mes'wāj, *n.* (*law*) a *dwelling* and offices with the adjoining lands appropriated to the use of the household. [O. F].—Low L. *messuagium*—L. *mansa*, pa.p. of *maneo*, to remain. See **Mansion**.]

**Mestee**, mes-tē', *n.* the offspring of a white person and a quadroon. [West Indian.]

**Mestizo**, mes-tēz'o, *n.* the offspring of a Spaniard or Creole and a native American Indian. [Sp.—L. *mixtus—misceo*, to mix.]

**Met**, *pa.t.* and *pa.p.* of **Meet**.

**Metacarpal**, met-a-kär'pal, *adj.* pertaining to the part of the hand between the *wrist* and the fingers. [Gr. *meta*, after, and *karpos*, wrist.]

**Metachronism**, me-tak'ron-izm, *n.* the placing of an event *after* its real *time*. [Fr.—Gr. *meta—chronos—meta*, beyond, and *chronos*, time.]

**Metage**, mēt'āj, *n.*, *measurement* of coal : price of measurement. [See **Mete**.]

**Metal**, met'al, *n.* a solid, shining, opaque body, such as gold, &c. : broken stone used for macadamised roads. [Fr.—L. *metallum*—Gr. *metallon*, a mine, a metal, prob. from *metallaō*, to search after. Cf. **Mettle**.]

**Metallic**, me-tal'ik, *adj.* pertaining to or like a *metal:* consisting of metal. [L. *metallicus*.]

**Metalliferous**, met-al-if'ér-us, *adj.*, *producing* or yielding *metals*. [L. *metallifer—metallum*, metal, and *fero*, to bear, to produce.]

**Metalliform**, me-tal'i-form, *adj.* having the *form* of *metals* : like metal.

**Metalline**, met'al-īn, *adj.* pertaining to a *metal:* consisting of or impregnated with metal.

**Metallise**, met'al-īz, *v.t.* to form into *metal:* to give to a substance its metallic properties.—*n.* **Metallisa'tion**.      [skilled in metals.

**Metallist**, met'al-ist, *n.* a worker in *metals* : one

**Metalloid**, met'al-oid, *n.* that which has a *form* or appearance like a *metal* : usually, any of the non-metallic inflammable bodies, as sulphur, phosphorus, &c. [Gr. *metallon*, a metal, and *eidos*, form.]

**Metalloid**, met'al-oid, **Metalloidal**, met-al-oid'al, *adj.* pertaining to the metalloids.

**Metallurgist**, met'al-ur-jist, *n.* one who *works metals* : one skilled in metallurgy.

**Metallurgy**, met'al-ur-ji, *n.* the art of *working metals* : the art of separating metals from their ores.—*adj.* **Metallur'gic**, pertaining to *metallurgy*. [Gr. *metallon*, a metal, *ergon*, work.]

**Metamorphic**, met-a-mor'fik, *adj.* subject to *change of form* : (*geol.*) applied to rocks, which, though of aqueous origin, have been greatly altered by heat.—*n.* **Metamor'phism**, state or quality of being *metamorphic*.

**Metamorphose**, met-a-mor'fōz, *v.t.* to *change* into another *form*: to transform. [Gr. *metamorphoō*—*meta*, expressing change, *morphē*, form.]

**Metamorphosis**, met-a-mor'fo-sis, *n.*, *change of form* or *shape* : transformation : the change living beings undergo in the course of their growth : *pl.* **Metamor'phoses**.

**Metaphor**, met'a-fur, *n.* (*rhet.*) a transference (of meaning) : the putting of one thing for another which it only resembles, as when *knowledge* is called a *lamp*, or *words* are said to be *bitter*. [Fr.—Gr. *metaphora—metapherō—meta*, over, *pherō*, to carry.]

**Metaphoric**, met-a-for'ik, **Metaphorical**, met-a-for'i-kal, *adj.* pertaining to or containing *metaphor* : figurative.—*adv.* **Metaphor'ically**.

**Metaphrase**, met'a-frāz, *n.* a *translation* from one language into another *word for word*. [Gr. *metaphrasis — meta*, denoting change, and *phrasis*, a speaking—*phrazō*, to speak.]

**Metaphrast**, met'a-frast, *n.* one who translates word for word.—*adj.* **Metaphras'tic**.

**Metaphysical**, met-a-fiz'ik-al, *adj.* pertaining to *metaphysics* : abstract.—*adv.* **Metaphys'ically**.

**Metaphysician**, met-a-fi-zish'an, *n.* one versed in *metaphysics*.

**Metaphysics**, met-a-fiz'iks, *n.sing.* the science which investigates the first principles of nature and thought : ontology or the science of being. [So called from certain works of Aristotle which *followed* or were studied *after* his *physics*— Gr. *meta*, after, and *physika*, physics, from *physis*, nature.]

**Metatarsal**, met-a-tär'sal, *adj.* belonging to the front part of the foot, just behind the toes. [Gr. *meta*, beyond, and *tarsos*, the flat of the foot.]

**Metathesis**, me-tath'es-is, *n.* (*gram.*) *transposition* of the letters of a word. [Gr.—*metatithēmi*, to transpose—*meta*, over, *tithēmi*, to place.]

**Metayer**, me-tā'yèr, *n.* a farmer who pays, instead of other rent, a *half*, or other fixed proportion, of the crops. [Fr.—Low L. *medietarius—*L. *medietas*, the half—*medius*, middle.]

**Mete**, mēt, *v.t.* to measure. [A.S. *metan*; Ger. *messen*, Goth. *mitan*, L. *metior*, Sans. *mâ*.]

**Metempsychosis**, me-temp-si-kō'sis, *n.* the *transmigration* of the *soul* after death into some other body:—*pl.* **Metempsycho'ses**. [Gr.—*meta*, expressing change, and *empsychōsis*, an animating —*en*, in, *psychē*, soul.]

**Meteor**, mē'te-or, *n.* a body which, in passing through the earth's atmosphere, becomes incandescent and luminous, as a shooting-star or fireball: formerly used of any appearance in the atmosphere, as clouds, rain : (*fig.*) anything that transiently dazzles or strikes with wonder. [Lit. 'that which is suspended in the air,' Gr. *meteōron*—*meta*, beyond, and *eōra*, anything suspended, from *aeirō*, to lift.]

**Meteoric**, mē-te-or'ik, *adj.* pertaining to or consisting of *meteors :* proceeding from a meteor : influenced by the weather.

**Meteorolite**, mē-te-or'o-līt, **Meteorite**, mē'te-or-īt, *n.* a *meteoric* stone. [Gr. *meteōros*, *lithos*, stone.]

**Meteorologist**, mē-te-or-ol'o-jist, *n.* one skilled in *meteorology*.

**Meteorology**, mē-te-or-ol'o-ji, *n.* the science which treats of the atmosphere and its phenomena, esp. of the weather.—*adjs.* **Meteorolog'ic**, **Meteorolog'ical**. [Gr. *meteōros*, and *logos*, discourse.]

**Meter**, mē'ter, *n.* one who or that which measures, esp. an apparatus for measuring gas. [See **Metre**.]        [*meting* or measuring.

**Meteyard**, mē'tyärd, *n.* (*B.*) a *yard* or rod for **Metheglin**, meth-eg'lin, *n.* mead, a fermented liquor made from honey. [W. *meddyglyn*, from *medd*, mead, and *llyn*, liquor.]

**Methinks**, me-thingks', (*B.*) **Methink'eth**, *v.impers.*, *it seems to me :* I think :—*pa.t.* **Methought**, mē-thawt'. [A.S. *me thynceth*—*me*, dative of I, and *thyncan*, to seem (impersonal). Not from *thencan*, to think. Cf. Ger. *dünken*, to seem.]

**Method**, meth'ud, *n.* the mode or rule of accomplishing an end: orderly procedure: manner : arrangement : system : rule : classification. [Lit. 'the way after anything,' Fr.—L. *methodus*— Gr. *methodos*—*meta*, after, and *hodos*, a way.]

**Methodic**, me-thod'ik, **Methodical**, me-thod'ik-al, *adj.* arranged with *method :* disposed in a just and natural manner: formal.—*adv.* **Method'ically**.        [to dispose in due order.

**Methodise**, meth'ud-īz, *v.t.* to reduce to *method :*

**Methodism**, meth'ud-izm, *n.* the principles and practice of the *Methodists*.

**Methodist**, meth'ud-ist, *n.* (*orig.*) one who observes *method :* one of a sect of Christians founded by John Wesley (1703–1791), noted for the strictness of its discipline : one strict or formal in religion. [The name first applied in 1729, in derision, by their fellow-students at Oxford, to John Wesley and his associates.]

**Methodistic**, meth-ud-ist'ik, **Methodistical**, meth-ud-ist'ik-al, *adj.* resembling the *Methodists :* strict in religious matters.—*adv.* **Methodist'ically**.

**Methought**. See **Methinks**.

**Methylated spirit**, meth'il-āt-ed spir'it, *n.* a mixture of pure alcohol with 10 per cent. of naphtha or wood-spirit, to prevent people drinking it.

**Metonic**, me-ton'ik, *adj.* pertaining to the lunar cycle of nineteen years. [From *Meton*, an Athenian, the discoverer, about 430 B.C.]

**Metonymic**, met-o-nim'ik, **Metonymical**, met-o-nim'ik-al, *adj.* used by way of *metonymy*.—*adv.* **Metonym'ically**.

**Metonymy**, me-ton'i-mi or met'o-nim-i, *n.* (*rhet.*)

a trope in which one word is put for another related to it, as the effect for the cause. [Lit. ' a change of name,' L.—Gr. *metōnymia*—*meta*, expressing change, and *onoma*, a name.]

**Metre**, mē'ter, *n.* poetical *measure* or arrangement of syllables : rhythm : verse : a French measure of length equal to nearly 39½ inches. [Fr.—L. *metrum*—Gr. *metron*. See **Mete**.]

**Metric**, met'rik, **Metrical**, met'rik-al, *adj.* pertaining to *metre* or to metrology : consisting of verses. The **Metrical** system is the French system of weights and measures, which is founded on the French *mètre* ; it divides or multiplies by *ten*, and is therefore a *decimal* system.— *adv.* **Met'rically**.

**Metrology**, me-trol'o-ji, *n.* the *science* of weights and *measures*. [Gr. *metron*, measure, and *logos*, discourse.]

**Metronome**, met'ro-nōm, *n.* an instrument which *measures* musical time. [Gr. *metron*, measure, and *nemō*, to distribute.]

**Metronomy**, me-tron'o-mi, *n.* measurement of time by a *metronome*.

**Metropolis**, me-trop'o-lis, *n.* the chief city or capital of a country: (properly) the chief cathedral city, as Canterbury of England :—*pl.* **Metrop'olises**. [Lit. 'mother-city,' L.—Gr. *mētēr*, mother—*polis*, a city.]

**Metropolitan**, met-ro-pol'it-an, *adj.* belonging to a *metropolis :* pertaining to the mother-church. —*n.* (*orig.*) the bishop of a *metropolis* or chief city : the bishop who presides over the other bishops of a province. [L. *metropolitanus*. See **Metropolis**.]

**Mettle**, met'l, *n.* ardour or keenness of temperament : spirit : sprightliness : courage. [A metaphor from the *metal* of a blade.]

**Mettled**, met'ld, **Mettlesome**, met'l-sum, *adj.* high-spirited : ardent.

**Mew**, mū, *n.* a sea-fowl : a gull. [A.S. *mæw*; cog. with Dut. *meeuw*, Ice. *már*, Ger. *mōwe*— all imitative.]        [Imitative.]

**Mew**, mū, *v.i.* to cry as a cat.—*n.* the cry of a cat.

**Mew**, mū, *v.t.* to shed or cast : to confine, as in a cage.—*v.i.* to change : to cast the feathers : to moult.—*n.* a place for *mewing* or confining : a cage for hawks while mewing : generally in *pl.* a stable, because the royal stables were built where the king's hawks were *mewed* or confined : a place of confinement. [Fr. *mue*, a changing, esp. of the coat or skin—*muer*, to mew—L. *muto*, to change.]

**Miasm**, mī'azm, **Miasma**, mī-az'ma, *n.* infectious matter floating in the air arising from putrefying bodies :—*pl.* **Mi'asms**, **Miasmata**, mī-az'ma-ta. [Gr. *miasma*—*miainō*, to stain.]

**Miasmal**, mī-az'mal, **Miasmatic**, mī-az-mat'ik, *adj.* pertaining to or containing *miasma*.

**Mica**, mī'ka, *n.* a glittering mineral which cleaves into thin transparent plates, sometimes used as glass.—*adj.* **Mica'ceous**. [L. *mica*, a crumb.]

**Mice**, mīs, *pl.* of **Mouse**.

**Michaelmas**, mik'el-mas. *n.* the *mass* or *feast* of St *Michael*, a R. Cath. festival celebrated Sept. 29.

**Microcosm**, mī'kro-kozm, *n.* man, who was regarded by ancient philosophers as a model or *epitome* of the *universe*.—*adjs.* **Microcos'mic**, **Microcos'mical**, pertaining to the *microcosm*. [Lit. the 'little world,' Fr.—L.—Gr., from *mikros*, little ; *kosmos*, world.]

**Micrography**, mī-krog'ra-fi, *n.* the *description* of *small* or microscopic objects. [Gr. *mikros*, little, and *graphō*, to write.]

**Micrometer**, mī-krom′e-tėr, *n.* an instrument used with a telescope or microscope for *measuring* very *small* spaces.—*adj.* **Micromet′rical.** [Gr. *mikros*, little, and *metron*, measure.]

**Microphone**, mī′kro-fōn, *n.* an instrument which, by means of an electric current, renders the *faintest sounds* distinctly audible. [Gr. *mikros*, little, and *phōnē*, sound.]

**Microscope**, mī′kro-skōp, *n.* an optical instrument for *viewing small* or minute objects.—*n.* **Micros′-copy.** [Gr. *mikros*, little, and *skopeō*, to look at.]

**Microscopic**, mī-kro-skop′ik, **Microscopical**, mī-kro-skop′ik-al, *adj.* pertaining to a *microscope* : made by or resembling a microscope : visible only by the aid of a microscope.—*adv.* **Micro-scop′ically.** [use of the microscope.

**Microscopist**, mī′kro-skōp-ist, *n.* one skilled in the

**Mid**, mid, *adj.*, *middle* : situated between extremes. [A.S. *mid*, *midd*; cog. with Ger. *mitte* and *mittel*, L. *medius*, Gr. *mesos*, Sans. *madhya*.]

**Mid-day**, mid′-dā, *n.* the *middle* of the *day* : noon.

**Midden**, mid′en, *n.* a heap of ashes or dung. [From Scand., as Dan. *mödding—mög*, dung; cf. **Mud** and **Muck**.]

**Middle**, mid′l, *adj.* equally distant from the extremes : intermediate : intervening.—*n.* the middle point or part : midst : central portion. [A.S. *middel—mid* (see **Mid**) ; cog. with Dut. *middel*, Ger. *mittel*.]

**Middle-man**, mid′l-man, *n.* one who stands in the *middle* between two persons : an agent between two parties : in Ireland, one who rents land of proprietors in large tracts, and lets it in portions to the peasantry.—*n.* **Middle-Ages**, the period from the overthrow of the Roman Empire in the 5th century to the Revival of Learning at the end of the 15th century.—*adjs.* **Middlemost**, **Midmost**, (*B.*) nearest the middle.—*n.* **Middle-passage**, in the slave-trade, the voyage across the Atlantic from Africa.—*n.* **Middle term** (*logic*) that term of a syllogism with which the two extremes are separately compared.

**Middling**, mid′ling, *adj.* of *middle* rate, state, size, or quality : about equally distant from the extremes : moderate.

**Midge**, mij, *n.* the common name of several species of small dipterous insects, resembling gnats, but having a shorter proboscis. [A.S. *micge*, cog. with Ger. *mücke*, a gnat, and Dut. *mug*.]

**Midland**, mid′land, *adj.* in the *middle* of or surrounded by *land* : distant from the coast : inland.

**Midnight**, mid′nīt, *n.* the *middle* of the *night* : twelve o'clock at night.—*adj.* being at midnight : dark as midnight.

**Midrib**, mid′rib, *n.* (*bot.*) the continuation of the leaf-stalk to the point of a leaf.

**Midriff**, mid′rif, *n.* the diaphragm. [Lit. the 'middle of the belly,' A.S. *mid*, middle, and *hrif*, the belly.]    [*ship.*—*adv.* **Mid′ships**.

**Midship**, mid′ship, *adj.* being in the *middle* of a

**Midshipman**, mid′ship-man, *n.* a naval cadet or officer whose rank is *intermediate* between the common seamen and the superior officers.

**Midst**, midst, *n.* the *middle*.—*adv.* in the middle. [From the M. E. phrase *in midde-s*, in the midst, with excrescent *t* (cf. *whil-s-t*). See **Mid**.]

**Midsummer**, mid′sum-ėr, *n.* the *middle* of *summer* : the summer solstice about the 21st of June.

**Midway**, mid′wā, *n.* the *middle* of the *way* or distance.—*adj.* being in the middle of the way or distance.—*adv.* half-way.

**Midwife**, mid′wīf, *n.* a woman who assists others in childbirth :—*pl.* **Midwives** (mid′wīvz). [Lit.

'helping-woman,' A.S. *mid*, together with (cog. with Ger. *mit*, Gr. *met-a*), and *wif*, woman.]

**Midwifery**, mid′wif-ri or mid′wif-ri, *n.* art or practice of a *midwife* or accoucheuse.

**Midwinter**, mid′win-tėr, *n.* the *middle* of *winter* : the winter solstice (21st December), or the time about it.

**Mien**, mēn, *n.* the look or appearance, esp. of the face : manner : bearing. [Fr. *mine—mener*, to lead, conduct ; Prov. *se menar*, to behave one's self—L. *mino*, in Low L., to drive cattle. See **Amenable** and **Demeanour**.]

**Might**, mīt, *pa.t.* of **May**.

**Might**, mīt, *n.*, *power* : ability : strength : energy or intensity of purpose or feeling.—**Might and Main**, utmost strength. [A.S. *meaht*, *miht*; Goth. *mahts*, Ger. *macht*; from root of **May**.]

**Mightiness**, mīt′i-nes, *n.* power : greatness : a title of dignity : excellency.

**Mighty**, mīt′i, *adj.* having great power : strong : valiant : very great : important : exhibiting might : wonderful.—*adv.* **Might′ily**.

**Mignonette**, min-yo-net′, *n.* an annual plant, bearing sweet-scented flowers. [Fr., dim. of *mignon*, darling. See **Minion**.]

**Migrate**, mī′grāt, *v.i.* to remove for residence from one country to another. [L. *migro*, *migratus*, akin to *meo*, to go.]

**Migration**, mī-grā′shun, *n.* a change of abode from one country or climate to another. [Fr.—L.]

**Migratory**, mī′gra-tor-i, *adj.*, *migrating* or accustomed to migrate : wandering.    [**Milk**.]

**Milch**, milch, *adj.* giving *milk*. [Another form of

**Mild**, mīld, *adj.* gentle in temper and disposition : not sharp or bitter : acting gently : gently and pleasantly affecting the senses : soft : calm.—*adv.* **Mild′ly**.—*n.* **Mild′ness**. [A.S. *milde*, mild, merciful ; a word common to the Teut. languages, as Ger. *mild*, Ice. *mildr*, gracious, &c.]

**Mildew**, mil′dū, *n.* a disease on plants, marked by the growth on them of minute fungi.—*v.t.* to taint with mildew. [A.S. *mele-deáw*, prob. sig. 'honey-dew ;' *mele-* being prob. cog. with L. *mel*, honey, Gr. *meli*. See **Dew**.]

**Mile**, mīl, *n.* 1760 yards. [A.S. *mil*; Fr. *mille*; both a contr. of L. *mille passuum*, a thousand paces, the Roman mile.]

**Mileage**, mīl′āj, *n.* fees paid by the *mile* for travel or conveyance : length in miles.

**Milestone**, mīl′stōn, *n.* a *stone* set to mark the distance of a *mile*.

**Milfoil**, mil′foil, *n.* the herb yarrow, remarkable for the numerous divisions of its leaf. [L. *mille-folium—mille*, thousand, and *folium*, a leaf.]

**Miliary**, mil′yar-i, *adj.* resembling a *millet-seed* : attended with an eruption of small red pimples, like millet-seeds, as fever. [L. *milium*.]

**Militant**, mil′i-tant, *adj.* fighting : engaged in warfare. [L. *militans*, *-antis*, pr.p. of *milito*.]

**Militarism**, mil′i-tar-izm, *n.* an excess of the *military* spirit.

**Military**, mil′i-tar-i, *adj.* pertaining to *soldiers* or warfare : warlike : becoming a soldier : engaged in the profession of arms : derived from service as a soldier.—*n.* soldiery : the army. [L. *militaris—miles*, a soldier.]

**Militate**, mil′i-tāt, *v.i.* (*lit.*) to be a *soldier*, to fight : to contend : to stand opposed.

**Militia**, mi-lish′a, *n.* a body of men enrolled and drilled as soldiers, but only liable to home service. [L. *militia*, warfare, soldiery—*miles*, *militis*.]    [the *militia* force.

**Militiaman**, mi-lish′a-man, *n.* a *man* or soldier in

**Milk**, milk, *v.t.* to squeeze or draw milk from : to

supply with milk.—*n.* a white fluid secreted by female mammals for the nourishment of their young : a milk-like juice of certain plants.—*n.* **Milk'er.** [A.S. *meolc,* milk ; Ger. *milch,* milk, L. *mulgeo,* to milk ; orig. meaning to 'stroke,' 'squeeze,' as in Sans. *marj,* to rub, stroke.]

**Milk-fever,** milk'-fē'vėr, *n.* a fever accompanying the secretion of milk after bearing.

**Milkmaid,** milk'mād, *n.* a woman who milks : a dairymaid.

**Milksop,** milk'sop, *n.* a piece of bread *sopped* or soaked in *milk :* an effeminate, silly fellow.

**Milk-tree,** milk'-trē, *n.* a *tree* yielding a *milk*-like, nourishing juice, as the cow-tree of S. America.

**Milky,** milk'i, *adj.* made of, full of, like, or yielding *milk :* soft : gentle.—*adv.* **Milk'ily.**— *n.* **Milk'iness.**—*n.* **Milk'y-way** (*astr.*) a broad, luminous or *whitish* zone in the sky, supposed to be the light of innumerable fixed stars.

**Mill,** mil, *n.* a machine for *grinding* any substance, as grain, by crushing it between two hard, rough surfaces : a place where grinding or manufacture of some kind is carried on.—*v.t.* to grind : to press or stamp in a mill : to stamp, as coin : to clean, as cloth. [A.S. *miln,* which, like Ger. *mühle,* is from L. *mola,* a mill—*molo,* to grind, akin to Sans. *mrid,* to bruise. See **Mar.**]

**Millcog,** mil'kog, *n.* a *cog* of a *mill*wheel.

**Milldam,** mil'dam, **Millpond,** mil'pond, *n.* a *dam* or *pond* to hold water for driving a *mill.*

**Millenarian,** mil-le-nā'ri-an, *adj.* lasting a *thousand years :* pertaining to the millennium.—*n.* one believing in the millennium.—*ns.* **Millena'rianism, Mil'lenarism,** the doctrine of millenarians.

**Millenary,** mil'e-nar-i, *adj.* consisting of a *thousand.*—*n.* a thousand years. [L. *millenarius* —*milleni,* a thousand each—*mille,* a thousand.]

**Millennial,** mil-len'i-al, *adj.* pertaining to a *thousand years :* pertaining to the millennium.

**Millennianism,** mil-len'i-an-izm, **Millennarism,** mil-len'i-ar-izm, *n.* belief in the *millennium.*— *n.* **Millenn'ialist,** a believer in the millennium.

**Millennium,** mil-len'i-um, *n.* a *thousand years :* the thousand years during which, as some believe, Christ will personally reign on the earth. [L. *mille,* a thousand, *annus,* a year.]

**Milleped,** mil'e-ped, *n.* a small worm-like animal, with an immense number of legs.—*pl.* **Mill'e-pedes** (-pedz). [L. *millepeda*—*mille,* a thousand, and *pes, pedis,* a foot.]

**Miller,** mil'ėr, *n.* one who attends a *corn-mill.*

**Miller's-thumb,** mil'ėrz-thum, *n.* a small fresh-water fish with a large, broad, and rounded head like a *miller's thumb,* the river bull-head.

**Millesimal,** mil-les'im-al, *adj., thousandth :* consisting of thousandth parts.—*adv.* **Milles'imally.** [L. *millesimus*—*mille,* a thousand.]

**Millet,** mil'et, *n.* a grass yielding grain used for food. [Fr. *millet*—L. *milium :* from *mille,* a thousand, from the number of its seeds.]

**Milliard,** mil'yard, *n.* a thousand millions. [Fr.— L. *mille,* a thousand.]

**Milliner,** mil'in-ėr, *n.* one who makes head-dresses, bonnets, &c. for women. [Prob. from *Milaner,* a trader in Milan wares, esp. female finery.]

**Millinery,** mil'in-ėr-i, *n.* the articles *made* or *sold* by *milliners.*

**Milling,** mil'ing, *n.* the act of passing through a *mill :* the act of fulling cloth : the process of indenting coin on the edge.

**Million,** mil'yun, *n.* a *thousand thousands* (1,000,000) : a very great number. [Fr.—Low L. *millio*—L. *mille,* a thousand.]

**Millionaire,** mil'yun-ār, *n.* a man worth a *million* of money or enormously rich. [Fr.]

**Millionary,** mil'yun-ar-i, *adj.* pertaining to or consisting of *millions.*

**Millionth,** mil'yunth, *adj.* or *n.* the ten hundred thousandth.

**Millrace,** mil'rās, *n.* the *current* of water that turns a *mill*wheel, or the canal in which it runs.

**Millstone,** mil'stōn, *n.* one of the two *stones* used in a *mill* for grinding corn.

**Millstone-grit,** mil'stōn-grit, *n.* (*geol.*) a hard *gritty* variety of sandstone suitable for *millstones.*

**Millwright,** mil'rīt, *n.* a *wright* or mechanic who builds and repairs *mills.*

**Milt,** milt, *n.* the soft roe of fishes : (*anat.*) the spleen.—*v.t.* to impregnate, as the spawn of the female fish.—*n.* **Milt'er,** a male fish. [A.S. *milte :* Ger. *milz ;* from the root of **Melt,** or corr. from **Milk,** as in Sw. *mjölk,* milk, *mjölke,* milt of fishes, and Ger. *milch,* milk, milt of fishes.]

**Mime,** mīm, *n.* a kind of farce, in which scenes from actual life were represented by action and gesture : an actor in such a farce. [Gr. *mimos.*]

**Mimetic,** mī-met'ik, **Mimetical,** mī-met'ik-al, *adj.* apt to *mimic* or *imitate.* [Gr. *mimētikos*— *mimos,* an imitator ; cf. L. *i-mi-to,* to imitate.]

**Mimic,** mim'ik, **Mimical,** mim'ik-al, *adj., imitative :* apt to copy : consisting of ludicrous imitation : miniature.

**Mimic,** mim'ik, *v.t.* to *imitate* for sport :—*pr.p.* mim'icking ; *pa.p.* mim'icked.—*n.* one who mimics or imitates : a buffoon : a servile imitator. [*mimics.*

**Mimicry,** mim'ik-ri, *n.* act or practice of one who

**Mimosa,** mi-mō'za, *n.* a genus of leguminous plants, including the sensitive plant, said to be so called from its *imitating* animal sensibility. [From Gr. *mimos,* an imitator ; cf. L. *i-mi-to.*]

**Mina,** mī'na, *n.* (*B.*) a weight of money valued at fifty shekels. [L. *mina,* Gr. *mna.*]

**Minaret,** min'a-ret, *n.* a turret on a Mohammedan mosque, from which the people are summoned to prayers. [Sp. *minarete*—Ar. *manarat,* light-house—*nar,* fire.]

**Minatory,** min'a-tor-i, *adj.* threatening : menacing. [L. *minor, minatus,* to threaten.]

**Mince,** mins, *v.t.* to cut into *small* pieces : to chop fine : to *diminish* or suppress a part in speaking : to pronounce affectedly.—*v.i.* to walk with affected nicety : to speak affectedly :—*pr.p.* minc'ing ; *pa.p.* minced (minst'). [A.S. *minsian* —*min,* small ; prob. from same Teut. base as Fr. *mince,* thin.]

**Minced-pie,** minst'-pī, **Mince-pie,** mins'-pī, *n.* a *pie* made with *minced* meat, &c.

**Mincing,** mins'ing, *adj.* not giving fully : speaking or walking with affected nicety.—*adv.* **Minc'ingly.**

**Mind,** mīnd, *n.* the faculty by which we *think,* &c. : the understanding : the whole spiritual nature : choice : intention : thoughts or sentiments : belief : remembrance : (*B.*) disposition. —*v.t.* (*orig.*) to *remind :* to attend to : to obey : (*Scotch*) to remember.—*v.i.* (*B.*) to remember. [A.S. *ge-mynd*—*munan,* to think ; Ger. *meinen,* to think ; L. *mens,* the mind, Gr. *menos,* mind, Sans. *manas,* mind, all from root *man,* to think.]

**Minded,** mīnd'ed, *adj.* having a *mind :* disposed : determined.—*n.* **Mind'edness.**

**Mindful,** mīnd'fool, *adj., bearing in mind :* attentive : observant.—*adv.* **Mind'fully.**—*n.* **Mind'fulness.**

**Mindless,** mīnd'les, *adj.* without *mind :* stupid.

**Mine,** mīn, *adj. pron.* belonging to *m : my.*
[A.S. *min;* Ger. *mein.* See **Me, My.**]

**Mine,** mīn, *v.t.* to dig for metals : to excavate : to
dig underground in order to overturn a wall : to
destroy by secret means.—*n.* a place from which
metals are dug : an excavation dug under a
fortification to blow it up with gunpowder : a
rich source of wealth. [Lit. to 'lead' or form
a passage underground, Fr. *miner*—Low L.
*minare,* to lead, drive (cattle) by threats—L.
*minor,* to threaten--*minæ,* threats. See **Amenable** and **Menace.**]

**Miner,** mīn′ėr, *n.* one who digs in a *mine.*

**Mineral,** min′ėr-al, *n.* an inorganic substance
found in the earth or at its surface : any substance containing a metal.—*adj.* relating to
minerals : impregnated with minerals, as water :
a term applied to inorganic substances. [Fr.—
Low L. *minerale—minera,* a mine. See **Mine.**]

**Mineralise,** min′ėr-al-īz, *v.t.* to make into a
*mineral :* to give the properties of a mineral to :
to impregnate with mineral matter.—*v.i.* to collect minerals.—*n.* **Mineralisa′tion.**

**Mineralist,** min′ėr-al-ist, *n.* one versed in or employed about *minerals.*

**Mineralogical,** min-ėr-al-oj′ik-al, *adj.* pertaining
to *mineralogy.*—*adv.* **Mineralog′ically.**

**Mineralogist,** min-ėr-al′o-jist, *n.* one versed in
mineralogy.

**Mineralogy,** min-ėr-al′o-ji, *n.* the *science* of *minerals :* the art of describing and classifying
minerals. [**Mineral,** and Gr. *logos,* discourse,
science.]

**Minever,** min′e-vėr, *n.* Same as **Meniver.**

**Mingle,** ming′gl, *v.t.* to mix : to unite into one
mass : to confuse : to join in mutual intercourse.
—*v.i.* to be mixed or confused.—*n.* **Ming′ler.**
[A.S. *mengan;* Dut. *mengelen,* Ger. *mengen ;*
conn. with **Among, Many.**]

**Mingling,** ming′gling, *n., mixture :* a mixing or
blending together.—*adv.* **Ming′lingly.**

**Miniature,** min′i-a-tūr or min′i-tūr, *n.* a painting
on a small scale : a small or reduced copy of
anything.—*adj.* on a small scale : minute.—
*v.t.* to represent on a small scale. [Fr.—It.
*miniatura,* a painting like those used to ornament manuscripts—*minio,* to write with red
lead—L. *minium,* vermilion.]

**Minikin,** min′i-kin, *n.* a *little darling :* a small
sort of pin.—*adj.* small. [Dim. of **Minion.**]

**Minim,** min′im, *n.* (*med.*) the smallest liquid
measure, a drop, 1/60 drachm : (*mus.*) a note
♩ equal to two crotchets. [Fr. *minime*—L.
*minimus,* the least, the smallest.]

**Minimise,** min′i-mīz, *v.t.* to reduce to the *smallest*
possible proportion : to diminish. [From **Minim.**]

**Minimum,** min′i-mum, *n.* the *least* quantity or
degree possible : a trifle :—*pl.* **Min′ima.** [L.]

**Mining,** mīn′ing, *n.* the art of forming or working
*mines.*

**Minion,** min′yun, *n.* a *darling,* a *favourite,* esp.
of a prince : a flatterer : (*print.*) a small kind of
type. [Fr. *mignon,* a darling—O. Ger. *minni,
minne,* love, from the root of **Man** and **Mind.**]

**Minish,** min′ish, *v.t.* (*B.*) to make *little* or *less :*
to diminish. [Fr. *menuiser,* to cut small, said of
a carpenter—L. *minuo,* to lessen—*minor,* less.
See **Minor.**]

**Minister,** min′is-tėr, *n.* a servant : one serving at
the altar : a clergyman : one transacting business under another : one intrusted with the
management of state affairs : the representative

of a government at a foreign court.—*v.i.* to
attend, as a servant : to perform duties : to give
things needful.—*v.t.* to furnish :—*pr.p.* min′istering ; *pa.p.* min′istered. [L.—*minor,* less.
See **Minor.** See **Magistrate.**]

**Ministerial,** min-is-tē′ri-al, *adj.* pertaining to attendance as a *servant :* acting under superior
authority : pertaining to the office of a minister :
clerical : executive.—*adv.* **Ministe′rially.**

**Ministerialist,** min-is-tē′ri-al-ist, *n.* one who supports ministers or the government.

**Ministrant,** min′is-trant, *adj.* administering : attendant. [L. *ministrans, -antis,* pr.p. of *ministro,* to minister—*minister.*]

**Ministration,** min-is-trā′shun, *n.* act of *ministering* or performing service : office or service of a
minister. [L. *ministratio—ministro.*]

**Ministrative,** min′is-trāt-iv, *adj.* serving to aid or
assist.

**Ministry,** min′is-tri, *n.* act of ministering : service :
office or duties of a minister : the clergy : the
clerical profession : the body of ministers of state.

**Miniver.** Same as **Meniver.**

**Mink,** mingk, *n.* a small quadruped of the weasel
kind, valued for its fur. [A form of **Minx.**]

**Minnow,** min′ō, *n.* a very *small* fresh-water fish :
the young of larger fish. [A.S. *myne,* prob.
from A.S. *min,* small, and therefore from the
same root as **Mince** and **Minute.**]

**Minor,** mī′nor, *adj., smaller :* less : inferior in importance, degree, bulk, &c. : inconsiderable :
lower : (*music*) lower by a semitone : (*logic*) the
term of a syllogism which forms the subject of
the conclusion.—*n.* a person under age (21 years).
[L.—root *min,* small.]

**Minorite,** mī′nor-īt, *n.* name for the Franciscan
friars, adopted in humility by St Francis the
founder. [L. *Fratres Minores,* 'lesser brethren.']

**Minority,** mi-nor′i-ti, *n.* the being under age : the
smaller number :—opposed to **Majority.**

**Minotaur,** min′o-tawr, *n.* the *bull* of *Minos,* a
fabulous monster, half man half bull. [L. *minotaurus—Minos,* an ancient king of Crete, and
*taurus,* a bull.]

**Minster,** min′stėr, *n.* the church of a *monastery*
or one to which a monastery has been attached :
sometimes, a cathedral church. [A.S. *mynster*
—L. *monasterium,* a monastery. See **Monastery.**]

**Minstrel,** min′strel, *n.* one who *ministered* to the
amusement of the rich by music or jesting : one
of an order of men who sang to the harp verses
composed by themselves or others : a musician.
[O. Fr. *menestrel*—Low L. *ministralis,* from
L. *minister.* See **Minister.**]

**Minstrelsy,** min′strel-si, *n.* the art or occupation
of a *minstrel :* the collective body of minstrels :
a body of song : instrumental music.

**Mint,** mint, *n.* the place where money is coined by
authority : a place where anything is invented
or fabricated : any source of abundant supply.—
*v.t.* to coin : to invent. [A.S. *mynet,* money—
L. *monēta* (the 'warning' one), a surname of
Juno, in whose temple at Rome money was
coined—*moneo,* to remind.]

**Mint,** mint, *n.* an aromatic plant producing a
highly odoriferous oil. [A.S. *minte*—L. *mentha*
—Gr. *mintha.*]

**Mintage,** mint′āj, *n.* that which is *minted* or
*coined :* the duty paid for coining. [inventor.]

**Minter,** mint′ėr, *n.* one who *mints* or coins : an

**Minuend,** min′ū-end, *n.* the number to be *lessened*
by subtraction. [L. *minuendum—minuo,* to
lessen, from root of **Minor.**]

---

fāte, fär ; mē, hėr ; mīne ; mōte ; mūte ; mōōn ; *then.*　　　　　319

**Minuet**, min′ū-et, *n.* a slow, graceful dance with *short* steps: the tune regulating such a dance. [Fr. *menuet*—*menu*, small—root of **Minor**.]

**Minus**, mī′nus, *adj.*, *less*: the sign (−) before quantities requiring to be subtracted. [L., neuter of *minor*, less.]

**Minute**, min-ūt′, *adj.* very *small*: extremely slender or little: of small consequence: slight: attentive to small things: particular: exact.—*adv.* **Minute′ly.**—*n.* **Minute′ness.** [Fr.—L. *minutus*, pa.p. of *minuo*, to lessen.]

**Minute**, min′it or -ut, *n.* the sixtieth part of an hour: the sixtieth part of a degree: an indefinitely small space of time: a brief jotting or note:—*pl.* a brief report of the proceedings of a meeting.—*v.t.* to make a brief jotting or note of anything. [Same word as above, and lit. sig. a 'small portion' of time.]

**Minute-book**, min′it-book, *n.* a *book* containing *minutes* or short notes.

**Minute-glass**, min′it-glas, *n.* a *glass* the sand of which measures a *minute* in running.

**Minute-gun**, min′it-gun, *n.* a *gun* discharged every *minute*, as a signal of distress or mourning.

**Minute-hand**, min′it-hand, *n.* the *hand* that points to the *minutes* on a clock or watch.

**Minutiæ**, mi-nū′shi-ē, *n.pl.*, *minute* or small *things*: the smallest particulars or details. [L.]

**Minx**, mingks, *n.* a pert young girl: a she-puppy: a mink. [Contr. of **Minikin**.]

**Miocene**, mī′o-sēn, *adj.* (*geol.*) *less recent*, applied to the middle division of the tertiary strata. [Gr. *meiōn*, less, and *kainos*, recent.]

**Miracle**, mir′a-kl, *n.* anything *wonderful*: a prodigy: anything beyond human power, and deviating from the common action of the laws of nature: a supernatural event. [Fr.—L. *miraculum*, from *miror, miratus*, to wonder.]

**Miraculous**, mi-rak′ū-lus, *adj.* of the nature of a *miracle*: done by supernatural power: very wonderful: able to perform miracles.—*adv.* **Mirac′ulously.**—*n.* **Mirac′ulousness.**

**Mirage**, mi-räzh′, *n.* an optical illusion by which objects are seen double as if reflected in a *mirror*, or appear as if suspended in the air. [Fr., from root of **Mirror**.]

**Mire**, mīr, *n.* deep mud.—*v.t.* to plunge and fix in mire: to soil with mud.—*v.i.* to sink in mud. [Ice. *myri*, marsh; Dut. *moer*, mud, bog.]

**Mirror**, mir′ur, *n.* a looking-glass: any polished substance in which objects may be seen: a pattern.—*v.t.* to reflect as in a mirror:—*pr.p.* mirr′oring; *pa.p.* mirr′ored. [Fr. *miroir*—L. *miror, -atus*, to wonder at.]

**Mirth**, mėrth, *n.*, *merriness*: pleasure: delight: noisy gaiety: jollity: laughter. [A.S. *myrth*, from Gael. *mireadh*—*mir*, to sport. See **Merry**.]

**Mirthful**, mėrth′fool, *adj.*, *full of mirth* or merriment: merry: jovial.—*adv.* **Mirth′fully.**—*n.* **Mirth′fulness.**

**Miry**, mī′ri, *adj.* consisting of or abounding in *mire*: covered with mire.—*n.* **Mi′riness.**

**Mis-**. This prefix has two sources; it is either A.S. from root of verb to **Miss**; or it stands for Fr. *mes-*, from L. *minus*, less; in both cases the meaning is 'wrong,' 'ill.' Where the prefix is Fr., it is so noted. See list of Prefixes.

**Misadventure**, mis-ad-ven′tūr, *n.* an unfortunate adventure: ill-luck: disaster. [Fr. *mes-*, ill, and **Adventure**.] [directed.

**Misadvised**, mis-ad-vīzd′, *adj.* ill-advised, ill-

**Misalliance**, mis-al-lī′ans, *n.* a bad or improper alliance or association. [Fr. *mes-*.]

**Misanthrope**, mis′an-thrōp, **Misanthropist**, mis-an′thro-pist, *n.* a *hater* of *mankind*. [Fr.—Gr. *misanthrōpos*—*miseō*, to hate, *anthrōpos*, a man.]

**Misanthropic**, mis-an-throp′ik, **Misanthropical**, mis-an-throp′ik-al, *adj.* hating mankind.—*adv.* **Misanthrop′ically.** [kind.

**Misanthropy**, mis-an′thro-pi, *n.* hatred to man-

**Misapply**, mis-ap-plī′, *v.t.* to apply amiss or wrongly.—*n.* **Misapplica′tion.**

**Misapprehend**, mis-ap-pre-hend′, *v.t.* to apprehend wrongly.—*n.* **Misapprehen′sion.**

**Misappropriate**, mis-ap-prō′pri-āt, *v.t.* to appropriate wrongly.—*n.* **Misappropria′tion.**

**Misarrange**, mis-ar-rānj′, *v.t.* to arrange wrongly. —*n.* **Misarrange′ment.**

**Misbecome**, mis-be-kum′, *v.t.* not to suit or befit.

**Misbehave**, mis-be-hāv′, *v.i.* to behave ill or improperly.—*n.* **Misbehav′iour.**

**Misbelieve**, mis-be-lēv′, *v.t.* to believe wrongly or falsely.—*ns.* **Misbelief′, Misbeliev′er.**

**Miscalculate**, mis-kal′kū-lāt, *v.t.* to calculate wrongly.—*n.* **Miscalcula′tion.**

**Miscall**, mis-kawl′, *v.t.* to call by a wrong name: to abuse or revile.

**Miscarriage**, mis-kar′ij, *n.* the act of miscarrying: failure: ill-conduct: the act of bringing forth young prematurely.

**Miscarry**, mis-kar′i, *v.i.* to carry badly: to be unsuccessful: to fail of the intended effect: to bring forth, as young, prematurely.

**Miscellaneous**, mis-sel-lān′i-us, *adj.*, *mixed* or mingled: consisting of several kinds.—*adv.* **Miscellan′eously.**—*n.* **Miscellan′eousness.** [L. *miscellaneus*—*misceo*, to mix. See **Mix**.]

**Miscellany**, mis′el-an-i or mis-el′an-i, *n.* a *mixture* of various kinds: a collection of writings on different subjects.—*n.* **Miscell′anist**, a writer of miscellanies.

**Mischance**, mis-chans′, *n.* ill-luck: mishap, misfortune: calamity. [Fr. *mes-*.]

**Mischief**, mis′chif, *n.* that which *ends ill*: an ill consequence: evil: injury: damage. [O. Fr. *meschef*, from *mes-*, ill, and *chef*—L. *caput*, the head.]

**Mischievous**, mis′chiv-us, *adj.* causing *mischief*: injurious: prone to mischief.—*adv.* **Mis′chievously.**—*n.* **Mis′chievousness.**

**Miscible**, mis′si-bl, *adj.* that may be *mixed*. [Fr. —L. *misceo*, to mix.]

**Misconceive**, mis-kon-sēv′, *v.t.* to conceive wrongly: to mistake.—*v.i.* to have a wrong conception of anything.—*n.* **Misconcep′tion.**

**Misconduct**, mis-kon′dukt, *n.* bad conduct.—*v.t.* **Misconduct′**, to conduct badly.

**Misconstrue**, mis-kon′strōō, *v.t.* to construe or interpret wrongly.—*n.* **Misconstruc′tion.**

**Miscount**, mis-kownt′, *v.t.* to count wrongly.—*n.* a wrong counting. [Fr. *mes-*.]

**Miscreant**, mis′kre-ant, *n.* formerly, a *misbeliever*: an infidel: a vile or unprincipled fellow. [O. Fr. *mescreant*—*mes-*, and L. *credens, -entis*, pr.p. of *credo*, to believe.]

**Misdate**, mis-dāt′, *n.* a wrong date.—*v.t.* to date wrongly or erroneously.

**Misdeed**, mis-dēd′, *n.* a bad deed: fault: crime.

**Misdemeanour**, mis-de-mēn′ur, *n.* ill demeanour: bad conduct: a petty crime. [Misdirec′tion.

**Misdirect**, mis-di-rekt′, *v.t.* to direct wrongly.—*n.*

**Misdo**, mis-dōō′, *v.t.* to do wrongly: to commit a crime or fault.—*n.* **Misdo′er.**

**Misemploy**, mis-em-ploy′, *v.t.* to employ wrongly or amiss: to misuse.

**Miser**, mī′zėr, *n.* an extremely covetous person: a niggard: one whose chief pleasure is the hoarding of wealth. [L. *miser*, wretched or miserable.]

**Miserable**, miz'ėr-a-bl, *adj.*, *wretched* or exceedingly unhappy: causing misery: very poor or mean: worthless: despicable: barren.—*adv.* **Mis'erably.**—*n.* **Mis'erableness.** [Fr.—L. *miserabilis*—*miser*.]

**Miserere**, miz-e-rē're, *n.* in R. Cath. Church, the 51st psalm, beginning with this word, and usually appointed for penitential acts: a musical composition adapted to this psalm. [L. 2d pers. sing. imperative of *misereor*, to have mercy, to pity—*miser*, wretched.] [sordid: niggardly.

**Miserly**, mī'zėr-li, *adj.* excessively covetous:

**Misery**, miz'ėr-i, *n.*, *wretchedness*: great unhappiness: extreme pain of body or mind. [O. Fr. *miserie*—L. *miseria.* See **Miser**.]

**Misfortune**, mis-for'tūn, *n.* ill-fortune: an evil accident: calamity.

**Misgive**, mis-giv', *v.i.* to fail, as the heart.—*n.* **Misgiv'ing**, a failing of confidence: mistrust.

**Misgotten**, mis-got'n, *adj.* wrongly gotten: unjustly obtained.

**Misgovern**, mis-guv'ėrn, *v.t.* to govern ill.—*n.* **Misgov'ernment.**

**Misguide**, mis-gīd', *v.t.* to guide wrongly: to lead into error.—*n.* **Misguid'ance.**

**Mishap**, mis-hap', *n.*, *ill-hap* or chance: accident: ill-luck: misfortune.

**Misimprove**, mis-im-prōōv', *v.t.* to apply to a bad purpose: to abuse: to misuse.—*n.* **Misimprove'ment.**

**Misinform**, mis-in-form', *v.t.* to inform or tell incorrectly.—*ns.* **Misinforma'tion, Misinform'er.**

**Misinterpret**, mis-in-tėr'pret, *v.t.* to interpret wrongly.—*ns.* **Misinterpreta'tion, Misinter'preter.** [fitly.

**Misjoin**, mis-join', *v.t.* to join improperly or unfitly.

**Misjoinder**, mis-join'dėr, *n.* (*law*) an *incorrect union* of parties or of causes of action in a suit.

**Misjudge**, mis-juj', *v.t.* and *v.i.* to judge wrongly. —*n.* **Misjudg'ment.**

**Mislay**, mis-lā', *v.t.* to lay in a wrong place or in a place not remembered: to lose.

**Misle**, miz'l. See **Mizzle.**

**Mislead**, mis-lēd', *v.t.* to lead wrong: to guide into error: to cause to mistake.

**Misletoe.** See **Mistletoe.**

**Mismanage**, mis-man'āj, *v.t.* to manage or conduct ill.—*n.* **Misman'agement.** [name.

**Misname**, mis-nām', *v.t.* to call by the wrong

**Misnomer**, mis-nō'mėr, *n.* a *misnaming*: a wrong name. [O. Fr., from Fr. *mes-*, and *nommer*—L. *nomino*, to name. See **Nominate.**]

**Misogamist**, mis-og'a-mist, *n.* a *hater of marriage.*—*n.* **Misog'amy.** [Gr. *miseō*, to hate, and *gamos*, marriage.]

**Misogynist**, mis-oj'i-nist, *n.* a *woman-hater.*—*n.* **Misog'yny.** [Gr. *miseō*, to hate, and *gynē*, a woman.]

**Misplace**, mis-plās', *v.t.* to put in a wrong place: to set on an improper object.—*n.* **Misplace'ment.** [mistake in printing.

**Misprint**, mis-print', *v.t.* to print wrong.—*n.* a

**Misprision**, mis-prizh'un, *n.* (*law*) oversight, neglect, contempt. [Fr. See **Misprize.**]

**Misprize**, mis-prīz', *v.t.* to slight or undervalue. [Fr. *mes-*, and **Prize.**]

**Mispronounce**, mis-pro-nowns', *v.t.* to pronounce incorrectly.

**Mispronunciation**, mis-pro-nun-si-ā'shun, *n.* wrong or improper pronunciation.

**Misquote**, mis-kwōt', *v.t.* to quote wrongly.—*n.* **Misquota'tion**, a wrong quotation.

**Misreckon**, mis-rek'n, *v.t.* to reckon or compute wrongly.—*n.* **Misreck'oning.**

**Misrepresent**, mis-rep-re-zent', *v.t.* to represent incorrectly.—*n.* **Misrepresenta'tion.**

**Misrule**, mis-rōōl', *n.* wrong or unjust rule: disorder: tumult.

**Miss**, mis, *n.* a title of address of an unmarried female: a young woman or girl:—*pl.* **Miss'es.** [Contracted from **Mistress.**]

**Miss**, mis, *v.t.* to fail to hit, reach, find, or keep: to omit: to fail to have: to discover the absence of: to feel the want of.—*v.i.* to fail to hit or obtain.—*n.* a deviation from the mark. [A.S. *missan;* Dut. *missen*, to miss, Ice. *missa*, to lose.]

**Missal**, mis'al, *n.* the Roman Catholic *mass-book.* [Low L. *missale*, from *missa*, mass. See **Mass.**]

**Missel**, miz'l, **Missel-bird**, miz'l-bėrd, *n.* the largest of the European thrushes, which feeds on the berries of the *mistletoe.*

**Missel, Misseltoe.** See **Mistletoe.**

**Misshape**, mis-shāp', *v.t.* to shape ill: to deform.

**Missile**, mis'il, *adj.* that may be *thrown* from the hand or any instrument.—*n.* a weapon *thrown* by the hand. [L. *missilis*—*mitto*, *missum*, to send, throw.]

**Missing**, mis'ing, *adj.* absent from the place where it was expected to be found: lost: wanting. [See **Miss**, *v.t.*]

**Mission**, mish'un, *n.* a *sending*: a being sent with certain powers, esp. to propagate religion: persons sent on a mission: an embassy: a station or association of missionaries: duty on which one is sent: purpose of life. [L. *missio.*]

**Missionary**, mish'un-ar-i, *n.* one sent upon a *mission* to propagate religion.—*adj.* pertaining to missions. [Fr. *missionnaire.*]

**Missive**, mis'iv, *adj.* that may be *sent*: intended to be thrown or hurled.—*n.* that which is sent, as a letter. [Fr.—L. *missus.* See **Missile.**]

**Misspell**, mis-spel', *v.t.* to spell wrongly.—*n.* **Misspell'ing**, a wrong spelling.

**Misspend**, mis-spend', *v.t.* to spend ill: to waste or squander:—*pa.t.* and *pa.p.* misspent'.

**Misstate**, mis-stāt', *v.t.* to state wrongly or falsely. —*n.* **Misstate'ment.**

**Mist**, mist, *n.* watery vapour in the atmosphere: rain falling in very fine drops. [A.S. *mist*, darkness; cog. with Ice. *mistr*, *mist*, Dut. *mist*.]

**Mistake**, mis-tāk', *v.t.* to understand wrongly: to take one thing or person for another.—*v.i.* to err in opinion or judgment.—*n.* a taking or understanding wrongly: an error.—*adj.* **Mistak'able.**

**Mistaken**, mis-tāk'n, *adj.*, *taken* or understood *incorrectly*: guilty of a mistake: erroneous: incorrect.—*adv.* **Mistak'enly.**

**Mister**, mis'tėr, *n.* sir: a title of address to a man, written **Mr.** [A corr. of **Master**, through the influence of **Mistress.**]

**Misterm**, mis-tėrm', *v.t.* to term or name wrongly.

**Mistime**, mis-tīm', *v.t.* to time wrongly.

**Mistiness.** See **Misty.**

**Mistitle**, mis-tī'tl, *v.t.* to call by a wrong *title.*

**Mistletoe, Misletoe**, or **Misseltoe**, miz'l-tō, *n.* a parasitic evergreen plant, sometimes found on the apple and oak. [A.S. *mistel-tan* (Ice. *mistel-teinn*)—*mistel*, mistletoe (as in Sw. and Ger.), and A.S. *tan*, twig (Ice. *teinn*); *mistel* is a dim. of *mist*, a root which in Ger. means 'dung,' the connection prob. being through the slime in the berries.]

**Mistranslate**, mis-trans-lāt', *v.t.* to translate incorrectly.—*n.* **Mistransla'tion.**

**Mistress**, mis'tres, *n.* (*fem.* of **Master**), a woman having power or ownership: the female head of a family, school, &c.: a woman well skilled in anything : a woman loved : a concubine : (*fem.* of **Mister**) a form of address (usually written **Mrs** and pronounced **Missis**). [O. Fr. *maistresse* (Fr. *maîtresse*), from root of **Master**.]

**Mistrust**, mis-trust', *n.* want of trust or confidence. —*v.t.* to regard with suspicion : to doubt.

**Mistrustful**, mis-trust'fool, *adj.* full of mistrust. —*adv.* **Mistrust'fully**.—*n.* **Mistrust'fulness**.

**Misty**, mist'i. *adj.* full of *mist* : dim : obscure.— *adv.* **Mist'ily**.—*n.* **Mist'iness**.

**Misunderstand**, mis-un-dėr-stand', *v.t.* to understand wrongly : to take in a wrong sense.

**Misunderstanding**, mis-un-dėr-stand'ing, *n.* a misconception : a slight disagreement or difference.

**Misuse**, mis-ūz', *v.t.* to misapply : to treat ill : to abuse.—*n.* **Misuse**, -ūs', improper use : application to a bad purpose.

**Mite**, mīt, *n.* a very *small* insect, which generally breeds in cheese. [Lit. 'the biter,' A.S. *mite*—root *mit-*, to cut small.]

**Mite**, mīt, *n.* the *minutest* or smallest of coins, about ⅓ of a farthing : anything very small : a very little quantity. [O. Dut. *mijt*, a small coin. From same root as above.]

**Mitigable**, mit'i-gabl, *adj.* that can be mitigated.

**Mitigate**, mit'i-gāt, *v.t.* to alleviate : to soften in severity : to temper : to reduce in amount (as evil). [L. *mitigo*, *-atus*—*mitis*, soft, mild.]

**Mitigation**, mit-i-gā'shun, *n.* act of mitigating : alleviation : abatement.

**Mitigative**, mit'i-gāt-iv, *adj.* tending to mitigate : soothing.

**Mitigator**, mit'i-gāt-or, *n.* one who mitigates.

**Mitrailleuse**, mit-ral-yāz', *n.* a breech-loading gun, consisting of several barrels, which are discharged almost simultaneously. [Fr. *mitrailler*, to fire with grapeshot—*mitraille*, grapeshot, small shot, broken pieces of metal, from O. Fr. *mite*, a small coin, from same root as **Mite**.]

**Mitral**, mī'tral, *adj.* of or resembling a *mitre*. [Fr.]

**Mitre**, mī'tėr, *n.* a *head-dress* or crown of archbishops and bishops, and sometimes of abbots : fig. episcopal dignity : (*arch.*) a junction of two pieces, as of moulding, at an angle of 45°.—*v.t.* to adorn with a mitre : to unite at an angle of 45° : [Fr.—L. *mitra*—Gr. *mitra*, belt, fillet, headdress, perh. akin to *mitos*, thread.]

**Mitriform**, mit'ri-form, *adj.* having the form of a mitre : (*bot.*) conical, and somewhat dilated at the base. [**Mitre** and **Form**.]

**Mitt**, mit, short for **Mitten**.

**Mitten**, mit'n, *n.* a kind of glove for winter use, without a separate cover for each finger : a glove for the hand and wrist, but not the fingers. [Fr. *mitaine*, perh. from O. Ger. *mittamo* (from root of **Mid**), half, and so properly 'half-glove.']

**Mittimus**, mit'i-mus, *n.* (*law*) a warrant granted for *sending* to prison a person charged with a crime : a writ by which a record is transferred out of one court into another. [L., 'we send'— *mitto*, to send.]

**Mity**, mīt'i, *adj.* full of *mites* or insects.

**Mix**, miks, *v.t.* to unite two or more things into one mass : to mingle : to associate.—*v.i.* to become mixed : to be joined : to associate.—*n.* **Mix'er**. [A.S. *miscan* ; cog. with Ger. *mischen*, L. *misceo*, Gr. *mignymi*, *misgō*, Sans. *miçr*.]

**Mixture**, miks'tūr, *n.* act of mixing or state of being mixed : a mass or compound formed by mixing : (*chem.*) a composition in which the ingredients retain their properties. [L. *mixtura*.]

**Mizzen**, miz'n, *n.* in a three-masted vessel, the hindmost of the fore-and-aft sails, lying along

the *middle* of the ship.—*adj.* belonging to the mizzen : nearest the stern. [Fr. *misaine*—It. *mezzana*—Low L. *medianus*—L. *medius*, the middle.] [the *mizzen*.

**Mizzen-mast**, miz'n-mast, *n.* the mast that bears

**Mizzle**, miz'l, *v.i.* to rain in small drops.—*n.* fine rain. [For *mist-le*, freq. from **Mist**.]

**Mnemonic**, nē-mon'ik, **Mnemonical**, nē-mon'ik-al, *adj.* assisting the *memory*. [Gr. *mnēmonikos* —*mnēmōn*, mindful—*mnaomai*, to remember.]

**Mnemonics**, nē-mon'iks, *n.* the art or science of assisting the *memory*.

**Moa**, mō'a, *n.* a large wingless bird of New Zealand, now extinct or nearly so. [Native name.]

**Moan**, mōn, *v.i.* to make a low sound of grief or pain : to lament audibly.—*v.t.* to lament.—*n.* audible expression of pain. [A.S. *mænan*.]

**Moat**, mōt, *n.* a deep trench round a castle or fortified place, sometimes filled with water.— *v.t.* to surround with a moat.—*adj.* **Moat'ed**. [O. Fr. *mote*, a mound, also a trench (cf. **Dike** and **Ditch**) ; of uncertain origin.]

**Mob**, mob, *n.* the *mobile* or fickle common people : the vulgar : a disorderly crowd : a riotous assembly.—*v.t.* to attack in a disorderly crowd :— *pr.p.* mobb'ing ; *pa.p.* mobbed'. [Contr. for L. *mobile* (*vulgus*), the fickle (multitude) ; *mobile* is for *movibile*, from *moveo*, to move.]

**Mob** or **Mob-cap**, mob, *n.* a kind of cap. [O. Dut. *mop* ; prob. akin to **Muff** and **Muffle**.]

**Mobile**, mō'bil or mō-bēl', *adj.* that can be *moved* or excited.—*n.* **Mobil'ity**, quality of being mobile. [Fr., from root of **Mob**.]

**Mobilise**, mob'i-līz, *v.t.* to call into active service, as troops.—*n.* **Mobilisa'tion**. [Fr. *mobiliser*.]

**Mobocracy**, mob-ok'ra-si, *n.* rule or ascendency exercised by the mob. [**Mob**, and Gr. *krateo*, to rule.]

**Moccasin** or **Mocassin**, mok'a-sin, *n.* a shoe of deerskin or other soft leather, worn by the North American Indians. [A native word.]

**Mock**, mok, *v.t.* to laugh at : to make sport of : to mimic in ridicule : to disappoint the hopes of : to deceive.—*n.* ridicule : a sneer.—*adj.* imitating reality, but not real : false.—*n.* **Mock'er**.— *adv.* **Mock'ingly**. [Fr. *moquer* ; from a Teut. root seen in Ger. *mucken*, to mutter ; of imitative origin.]

**Mockery**, mok'ėr-i, **Mocking**, mok'ing, *n.* derision : ridicule : subject of laughter or sport : vain imitation : false show. [Fr. *moquerie*— *moquer*.]

**Mock-heroic**, mok-he-rō'ik, *adj.* mocking the heroic, or actions or characters of heroes.

**Mocking-bird**, mok'ing-bėrd, *n.* a bird of North America, of the thrush family, which *mocks* or imitates the notes of birds and other sounds.

**Modal**, mō'dal, *adj.* relating to *mode* or form : consisting of mode only : (*logic*) indicating some mode of expression.—*adv.* **Mo'dally**.—*n.* **Modal'ity**. [See **Mode**.]

**Modalist**, mō'dal-ist, *n.* (*theol.*) one of a class who consider the three persons of the Godhead as only *modes* of being, and not as distinct persons.

**Mode**, mōd, *n.* rule : custom : form : manner of existing : that which exists only as a quality of substance. [Fr.—L. *modus*, a measure ; cog. with Gr. *mēdos*, plan, from root *mad* (**Mete**), an extension of root *ma*, to measure (cf. **Moon**).]

**Model**, mod'el, *n.* something to shew the *mode* or way : something to be copied : a pattern : a mould : an imitation of something on a smaller scale : something worthy of imitation.—*v.t.* to form after a model: to shape: to make a model or copy of: to form in some soft material.—*v.i.* to practise modelling:—*pr.p.* mod'elling; *pa.p.* mod'elled.—*n.* Mod'eller. [Fr. *modèle*—L. *modulus*, dim. of *modus*, a measure.]

**Modelling**, mod'el-ing, *n.* the act or art of making a *model* of something, a branch of sculpture.

**Moderate**, mod'ėr-āt, *v.t.* to keep within *measure* or bounds: to regulate: to reduce in intensity: to make temperate or reasonable: to pacify: to decide as a moderator.—*v.i.* to become less violent or intense: to preside as a moderator.—*adj.* kept within *measure* or bounds: not excessive or extreme: temperate: of middle rate.—*adv.* Mod'erately.—*n.* Mod'erateness. [L. *moderor, -atus—modus*, a measure.]

**Moderation**, mod-ėr-ā'shun, *n.* act of moderating: state of being moderated or moderate: freedom from excess: calmness of mind.

**Moderatism**, mod'ėr-a-tizm, *n.* moderate opinions in religion or politics.

**Moderato**, mod-ėr-ä'to, *adv.* (*mus.*) with *moderate* quickness. [It.]

**Moderator**, mod'ėr-ā-tor, *n.* one who or that which *moderates* or restrains: a president or chairman, esp. in Presbyterian Church courts.—*n.* Mod'eratorship. [L.]

**Modern**, mod'ėrn, *adj.*, *limited* to the *present* or recent *time*: not ancient.—*n.* one of modern times:—*pl.* the nations after the Greeks and Romans, who are called the ancients.—*adv.* Mod'ernly.—*n.* Mod'ernness. [Fr.—L. *modernus—modo*, just now, (*lit.*) 'with a limit' (of time); orig. ablative of *modus*. See Mode.]

**Modernise**, mod'ėrn-īz, *v.t.* to render modern: to adapt to the present time.—*n.* Mod'erniser.

**Modernism**, mod'ėrn-izm, *n.* modern practice: something of modern origin. [*moderns*.

**Modernist**, mod'ėrn-ist, *n.* an admirer of the

**Modest**, mod'est, *adj.* restrained by a due sense of propriety: not forward: decent: chaste: pure and delicate, as thoughts or language: moderate.—*adv.* Mod'estly. [Fr.—L. *modestus*, within due bounds—*modus*, a measure.]

**Modesty**, mod'est-i, *n.* absence of presumption: decency: chastity: purity: moderation. [Fr. *modestie*—L. *modestia*.]

**Modicum**, mod'i-kum, *n.* something of a *moderate* size: a little. [L., neut. of *modicus*, moderate—*modus*. See Mode.]

**Modification**, mod-i-fi-kā'shun, *n.* act of modifying: changed shape or condition. [Fr.—L. *modificatio*.]

**Modify**, mod'i-fī, *v.t.* to make or set *bounds* to: to moderate: to change the form of: to vary.—*n.* Mod'ifier.—*adj.* Modifi'able. [Fr. *modifier*—L. *modifico, -atus—modus*, a measure, and *facio*, to make.]

**Modish**, mō'dish, *adj.* according to or in the *mode*, *i.e.* the fashion: fashionable.—*adv.* Mo'dishly.—*n.* Mo'dishness.

**Modist**, mō'dist, *n.* one who follows the *mode* or fashion.—**Modiste**, mo-dēst', *n.* one who makes dresses according to the fashionable *mode*. [Fr.]

**Modulate**, mod'ū-lāt, *v.t.* to *measure*, to regulate: to vary or inflect, as sounds: (*mus.*) to change the key or mode.—*v.i.* to pass from one key into another. [L. *modulor, -atus—modulus*, a little measure, dim. of *modus*.]

**Modulation**, mod-ū-lā'shun, *n.* the act of modulating: state of being modulated: (*mus.*) the changing of the keynote and the alteration of the original scale by the introduction of a new sharp or flat.

**Modulator**, mod'ū-lāt-or, *n.* one who or that which *modulates*: a chart in the Tonic Sol-fa musical notation on which the *modulations* or transitions from one scale to another are indicated by the relative position of the notes.

**Module**, mod'ūl, *n.* (*arch.*) a *measure* for regulating the proportion of columns: a model. [Fr.—L. *modulus*.]

**Modulus**, mod'ū-lus, *n.* (*math.*) a constant multiplier in a function of a variable, by which the function is adapted to a particular base.

**Mohair**, mō'hār, *n.* the fine silken hair of the Angora goat of Asia Minor: cloth made of mohair. [O. Fr. *mouaire* (Fr. *moire*)—Ar. *mukhayyar*. Doublet Moire.]

**Mohammedan**, mo-ham'ed-an, *adj.* pertaining to Mohammed or to his religion.—*n.* a follower of Mohammed: one who professes Mohammedanism: also written **Mahom'etan, Mahom'edan**. [*Mohammed*, the great prophet of Arabia, born about 570—Ar. *muhammad*, praiseworthy—*hamd*, praise.]

**Mohammedanise**, mo-ham'ed-an-īz, *v.t.* to convert to, or make conformable to Mohammedanism.

**Mohammedanism**, mo-ham'ed-an-izm, **Mohammedism**, mo-ham'ed-izm, *n.* the religion of Mohammed, contained in the Koran.

**Mohur**, mō'hur, *n.* in British India, a gold coin = fifteen rupees or 30s. [The Pers. word.]

**Moidore**, moi'dōr, *n.* a disused gold coin of Portugal, worth 27s. [Port. *moeda d'ouro*—L. *moneta de auro*, money of gold.]

**Moiety**, moi'e-ti, *n.*, *half*: one of two equal parts. [Fr. *moitié*—L. *medietas, -tatis*, middle, half—*medius*, middle.]

**Moil**, moil, *v.t.* to daub with dirt.—*v.i.* to toil or labour: to drudge. [O. Fr. *moiler* (Fr. *mouiller*), to wet—L. *mollis*, soft. See Mollify.]

**Moire**, mwor, *n.* watered silk. [Fr. See Mohair.]

**Moist**, moist, *adj.*, *damp*: humid: juicy: containing water or other liquid.—*n.* Moist'ness. [O. Fr. *moiste* (Fr. *moite*)—L. *musteus*, fresh, sappy—*mustum*, juice of grapes, new wine.]

**Moisten**, mois'n, *v.t.* to make moist or *damp*: to wet slightly.

**Moisture**, moist'ūr, *n.*, *moistness*: that which moistens or makes slightly wet: a small quantity of any liquid.

**Molar**, mō'lar, *adj.*, *grinding*, as a *mill*: used for grinding.—*n.* a grinding tooth, which is double. [L. *molaris—mola*, a mill—*molo*, to grind.]

**Molasses**, mo-las'ez, *n.sing.* a kind of syrup that drains from sugar during the process of manufacture: treacle. [Port. *melaço* (Fr. *mélasse*)—L. *mell-aceus*, honey-like—*mel, mellis*, honey.]

**Mole**, mōl, *n.* a permanent dark-brown *spot* or *mark* on the human skin. [A.S. *mal*; cog. with Scand. and Ger. *maal*, and prob. also with L. *mac-ula*, a spot.]

**Mole**, mōl, *n.* a small animal, with very small eyes and soft fur, which burrows in the ground and *casts up* little heaps of mould.—*ns.* Mole'cast, Mole'hill, a little hill or heap of earth cast up by a mole.—*adj.* Mole'-eyed, having eyes like those of a mole: seeing imperfectly.—*n.* Mole'track, the track made by a mole burrowing. [Short for the older *mold-warp* = mould-caster—M. E. *molde* (E. Mould), and *werpen* (E. Warp).]

**Mole**, mōl, *n.* a breakwater. [Fr.—L. *moles*, a huge mass.]

**Mole-cricket**, mōl'-krik'et, *n.* a burrowing insect like a cricket, with forelegs like those of a mole.

**Molecular**, mo-lek'ū-lar, *adj.* belonging to or consisting of *molecules*.—*n.* **Molecular'ity**.

**Molecule**, mol'e-kūl, *n.* one of the minute particles of which matter is composed. [Fr., a dim. coined from L. *moles*, a mass.]

**Molerat**, mōl'rat, *n.* a *rat*-like animal, which burrows like a *mole*.

**Moleskin**, mōl'skin, *n.* a superior kind of fustian, or coarse twilled cotton cloth, so called from its being soft like the *skin* of a *mole*.

**Molest**, mo-lest', *v.t.* to *trouble*, disturb, or annoy.—*n.* **Molest'er**.—*adj.* **Molest'ful**. [Fr. *molester*—L. *molesto*—*molestus*, troublesome—*moles*, a mass, a difficulty.]

**Molestation**, mol-es-tā'shun, *n.* act of molesting: state of being molested: annoyance.

**Mollient**, mol'yent, *adj.* serving to *soften*: assuaging. [L. *mollis*, soft. See **Emollient**.]

**Mollification**, mol-i-fi-kā'shun, *n.* act of mollifying: state of being mollified: mitigation.

**Mollify**, mol'i-fī, *v.t.* to make *soft* or tender: to assuage: to calm or pacify:—*pa.p.* moll'ified.—*adj.* **Moll'ifiable**.—*n.* **Moll'ifier**. [Fr.—L. *mollifico*—*mollis*, soft, and *facio*, to make.]

**Mollusc, Mollusk**, mol'usk, *n.* one of the **Mollus'ca**, those animals which have a *soft* inarticulate fleshy body, as the snail and all shellfish:—*pl.* **Moll'uscs, Moll'usks**, or **Mollus'ca**. [Fr., from L. *molluscus*, softish—*mollis*, soft.]

**Molluscan**, mol-us'kan, **Molluscous**, mol-us'kus, *adj.* of or like *molluscs*.—*n.* **Mollus'can**, a mollusc.

**Molten**, mōlt'n, *adj.*, *melted*: made of melted metal. [Old *pa.p.* of **Melt**.]

**Moment**, mō'ment, *n.* *moving* cause or force: importance in effect: value: the smallest portion of time in which a movement can be made: an instant: (*mech.*) the moment of a force about a point is the product of the force and the perpendicular on its line of action from the point. [Fr.—L. *momentum*, for *movimentum*—*moveo*, to move.]

**Momentary**, mō'ment-ar-i, *adj.* lasting for a *moment*: done in a moment.—*adv.* **Mo'mentarily**.—*n.* **Mo'mentariness**.

**Momently**, mō'ment-li, *adv.* for a *moment*: in a moment: every moment.

**Momentous**, mō-ment'us, *adj.* of *moment* or importance: of great consequence.—*adv.* **Moment'ously**.—*n.* **Moment'ousness**.

**Momentum**, mō-ment'um, *n.* the quantity of *motion* in a body, which is measured by the product of the mass and the velocity of the moving body:—*pl.* **Moment'a**.

**Monachal**, mon'ak-al, *adj.* living *alone*: pertaining to monks or to a monastic life. [See **Monastery**.]       [of being a monk.

**Monachism**, mon'ak-izm, *n.*, *monastic* life: state

**Monad**, mon'ad, *n.* an ultimate atom or simple unextended point: a *simple*, primary element assumed by Leibnitz and other philosophers: (*zool.*) one of the simplest of animalcules. [L. *monas*, *-adis*—Gr. *monas*, *-ados*—*monos*, alone.]

**Monadelphian**, mon-a-del'fi-an, **Monadelphous**, mon-a-del'fus, *adj.* (*bot.*) having the stamens united into *one brotherhood* or body by the filaments. [Gr. *monos*, alone, *adelphos*, a brother.]

**Monadic**, mon-ad'ik, **Monadical**, mon-ad'ik-al, *adj.* being or resembling a *monad*.

**Monandrian**, mon-an'dri-an, **Monandrous**, mon-an'drus, *adj.* (*bot.*) having only *one* stamen or *male* organ. [Gr. *monos*, and *anēr*, *andros*, a male.]

**Monarch**, mon'ark, *n.* *sole* or supreme *ruler*: a sovereign: the chief of its kind.—*adj.* supreme: superior to others. [Fr. *monarque*, through L., from Gr. *monarchēs*—*monos*, alone, *archē*, rule.]

**Monarchal**, mon-ärk'al, *adj.* pertaining to a monarch: regal.

**Monarchic**, mon-ärk'ik, **Monarchical**, mon-ärk'ik-al, *adj.* relating to a monarch or monarchy: vested in a single ruler.

**Monarchise**, mon'ark-īz, *v.t.* to rule over, as a monarch: to convert into a monarchy.

**Monarchist**, mon'ark-ist, *n.* an advocate of monarchy.       [*monarch*: a kingdom.

**Monarchy**, mon'ark-i, *n.* government headed by a

**Monastery**, mon'as-tèr-i, *n.* a house for monks: an abbey: a convent. [L. *monasterium*—Gr. *monastērion*—*monastēs*, a monk—*monos*, alone.]

**Monastic**, mon-as'tik, **Monastical**, mon-as'tik-al, *adj.* pertaining to *monasteries*, monks, and nuns: recluse: solitary.—*adv.* **Monas'tically**.

**Monastic**, mon-as'tik, *n.* a monk.

**Monasticism**, mon-as'ti-sizm, *n.* monastic life.

**Monday**, mun'dā, *n.* the day sacred to the *moon*: the second day of the week. [**Moon** and **Day**.]

**Monetary**, mun'e-tar-i, *adj.* relating to *money* or moneyed affairs: consisting of money.

**Money**, mun'i, *n.* coin: pieces of stamped metal used in commerce: any currency used as the equivalent of money: wealth:—*pl.* **Mon'eys**. [Fr. *monnaie*—L. *moneta*, from root of **Mint**.]

**Money-broker**, mun'i-brōk'ér, **Money-changer**, mun'i-chānj'ér, *n.* a broker who deals in money or exchanges.

**Moneyed**, mun'id, *adj.* having money: rich in money: consisting in money.

**Moneyless**, mun'i-les, *adj.* destitute of money.

**Monger**, mung'gér, *n.* a *trader*: a dealer, used chiefly in composition, sometimes in a depreciatory sense.—*v.t.* to trade or deal in. [A.S. *mangere*—*mang*, a mixture, allied to *manig*, **Many**. Cf. Ice. *mangari*—*manga*, to trade, and perh. L. *mango*, a trader.]

**Mongrel**, mung'grel, *adj.* of a *mixed* breed.—*n.* an animal of a mixed breed. [A contracted dim. from a root seen in A.S. *mangian*, later *mengan*, to mix. See **Mingle** and **Monger**.]

**Monition**, mon-ish'un, *n.* a reminding or *admonishing*: warning: notice. [L. *monitio*—*moneo*, *-itum*, to remind—root *man*, to think.]

**Monitive**, mon'i-tiv, *adj.* conveying admonition.

**Monitor**, mon'i-tor, *n.* one who *admonishes*: an adviser: an instructor: a pupil who assists a schoolmaster:—*fem.* **Mon'itress**—*n.* **Mon'itorship**. [See **Monition**.]

**Monitorial**, mon-i-tō'ri-al, *adj.* relating to a *monitor*: performed or taught by a monitor.—*adv.* **Monito'rially**.

**Monitory**, mon'i-tor-i, *adj.* reminding or *admonishing*: giving admonition or warning.

**Monk**, mungk, *n.* formerly, one who retired *alone* to the desert to lead a religious life: one of a religious community living in a monastery. [A.S. *munec*—L. *monachus*—Gr. *monachos*—*monos*, alone.]

**Monkey**, mungk'i, *n.* a *name of contempt*, esp. for a mischievous person: the order of mammalia next to man, having their feet developed like hands: an ape:—*pl.* **Monk'eys**. [O. It. *monicchio*, dim. of O. It. *monna*, nickname for an old woman, an ape, contr. of It. *madonna*, mistress. See **Madonna**.]

**Monkish**, mungk'ish, *adj.* pertaining to a *monk*: like a monk: monastic.

**Monk's-hood**, mungks'-hood, *n.* the aconite, a poisonous plant with a flower like a *monk's hood*.

**Monochord,** mon′o-kord, *n.* a musical instrument of *one chord* or string. [Gr. *monos*, alone, and **Chord.**]

**Monochromatic,** mon-o-krō-mat′ik, *adj.* of *one colour* only. [Gr. *monos*, and **Chromatic.**]

**Monocotyledon,** mon-o-kot-i-lē′don, *n.* a plant with only *one cotyledon.—adj.* **Monocotyle′donous.** [Gr. *monos*, alone, and **Cotyledon.**]

**Monocular,** mon-ok′ū-lar, **Monoculous,** mon-ok′ū-lus, *adj.* with *one eye* only. [Gr. *monos*, and **Ocular.**]

**Monodist,** mon′o-dist, *n.* one who writes *monodies.*

**Monody,** mon′o-di, *n.* a mournful *ode* or poem in which a *single* mourner bewails.—*adj.* **Monod′ical.** [Gr. *monos*, single, and **Ode.**]

**Monogamy,** mon-og′a-mi, *n.*, *marriage* to *one* wife only: the state of such marriage.—*adj.* **Monog′amous.**—*n.* **Monog′amist.** [Gr. *monos*, one, *gamos*, marriage.]

**Monogram,** mon′o-gram, *n.* a character or cipher of several letters interwoven or written into *one.* [Gr. *monos*, alone, *gramma*, a letter.]

**Monograph,** mon′o-graf, *n.* a paper or treatise *written* on *one* particular subject or a branch of it. [Gr. *monos*, alone, and *graphō*, to write.]

**Monographer,** mon-og′ra-fèr, **Monographist,** mon-og′ra-fist, *n.* a writer of *monographs.*

**Monographic,** mon-o-graf′ik, **Monographical,** mon-o-graf′i-kal, *adj.* pertaining to a *monograph :* drawn in lines without colours.

**Monography,** mon-og′ra-fi, *n.* a representation by *one* means only, as lines : an outline drawing.

**Monogynian,** mon-o-jin′i-an, **Monogynous,** mon-oj′i-nus, *adj.* (*bot.*) having only *one* pistil or *female* organ. [Gr. *monos*, alone, and *gynē*, a female.]

**Monolith,** mon′o-lith, *n.* a pillar, or column, of a *single stone.—adjs.* **Monolith′ic, Monolith′al.** [Gr. *monos*, alone, and *lithos*, stone.]

**Monologue,** mon′o-log, *n.* a *speech* uttered by *one* person : soliloquy : a poem, &c. for a single performer. [Fr.—Gr. *monos*, alone, and *logos*, speech.]

**Monomania,** mon-o-mā′ni-a, *n.*, *madness* confined to *one* subject, or one faculty of the mind. [Gr. *monos*, alone, and *mania*, madness.]

**Monomaniac,** mon-o-mā′ni-ak, *adj.* affected with *monomania.—n.* one affected with monomania.

**Monome,** mon′ōm, **Monomial,** mon-ō′mi-al, *n.* an algebraic expression of *one term* only : a series of factors of single terms.—*adj.* **Mono′mial.** [Gr. *monos*, alone, and *nomē*, division.]

**Monophyllous,** mon-of′il-us or mon-o-fil′us, *adj.* having a *leaf* of but *one* piece. [Gr. *monos*, alone, *phyllon*, a leaf.]

**Monopolise,** mon-op′o-līz, *v.t.* to obtain possession of anything so as to be the *only seller* of it : to engross the whole of.—*ns.* **Monop′oliser, Monop′olist,** one who monopolises.

**Monopoly,** mon-op′o-li, *n.* the *sole* power of *dealing* in anything : exclusive command or possession : (*law*) a grant from the crown to an individual for the sole dealing in anything. [L. *monopolium*—Gr. *monos*, alone, and *pōleō*, to sell.]

**Monospermous,** mon-o-spèrm′us, *adj.* (*bot.*) having *one seed* only. [Gr. *monos*, alone, *sperma*, seed.]

**Monostich,** mon′o-stik, *n.* a poem complete in *one verse.* [Gr. *monos*, alone, *stichos*, verse.]

**Monostrophic,** mon-o-strof′ik, *adj.* having but *one strophe :* not varied in measure. [Gr. *monos*, alone, *strophē*, a strophe.]

**Monosyllabic,** mon-o-sil-lab′ik, *adj.* consisting of *one syllable,* or of words of one syllable.

**Monosyllable,** mon-o-sil′la-bl, *n.* a word of *one syllable.* [Fr.—L.—Gr. *monos*, alone, *syllabē*, a syllable.]

**Monotheism,** mon-o-thē′izm, *n.* the belief in only *one God.* [Gr. *monos*, alone, and *theos*, God.]

**Monotheist,** mon′o-thē-ist, *n.* one who believes that there is but *one God.—adj.* **Monotheist′ic.**

**Monotone,** mon′o-tōn, *n.* a *single,* unvaried *tone* or sound : a succession of sounds having the same pitch. [Gr. *monos*, alone, and *tonos*, a tone, note.]

**Monotonous,** mon-ot′o-nus, *adj.* uttered in *one* unvaried *tone :* marked by dull uniformity.—*adv.* **Monot′onously.**

**Monotony,** mon-ot′o-ni, *n.* dull *uniformity* of *tone* or sound : (*fig.*) irksome sameness or want of variety.

**Monsoon,** mon-sōōn′, *n.* a *periodical* wind of the Indian Ocean, which blows from the S.W. from April to October, and from the N.E. the rest of the year : similar winds elsewhere. [Through Fr. or It. from Malay *musim*—Ar. *mawsim*, a time, a season.]

**Monster,** mon′stèr, *n.* anything out of the usual course of nature : a prodigy : anything horrible from ugliness or wickedness. [Lit. a warning or portent, Fr.—L. *monstrum*, a divine omen or warning, a bad omen, a monster—*moneo*, to warn, admonish—root *man*, to think. See **Man, Mind.**]

**Monstrance,** mon′strans, *n.* in the R. Cath. Church, the utensil in which the consecrated wafer is *shewn* to the congregation. [Fr.—L. *monstro*, to shew—*monstrum*, an omen.]

**Monstrosity,** mon-stros′i-ti, *n.* state of being *monstrous :* an unnatural production.

**Monstrous,** mon′strus, *adj.* out of the common course of nature : enormous : wonderful : horrible.—*adv.* **Mon′strously.**

**Month,** munth, *n.* the period of one revolution of the *moon* (now distinguished as a 'lunar' month) : one of the twelve parts of the year (a 'calendar' month). [A.S. *monath*—*mona,* the moon. See **Moon.**]

**Monthly,** munth′li, *adj.* performed in a month : happening or published once a month.—*n.* a monthly publication.—*adv.* once a month : in every month.

**Monument,** mon′ū-ment, *n.* anything that perpetuates the memory of a person or event : a record. [Fr.—L. *monumentum*—*moneo,* to remind—root *man,* to think.]

**Monumental,** mon-ū-ment′al, *adj.* of or relating to a *monument* or tomb : serving as a monument : memorial.—*adv.* **Monument′ally.**

**Mood,** mōōd, *n.* fashion : manner : (*gram.*) a form of verbal inflection to express the *mode* or manner of action or being : (*logic*) the form of the syllogism as determined by the quantity and quality of its three constituent propositions : (*mus.*) the arrangement of the intervals in the scale, as major and minor. [Same as **Mode.**]

**Mood,** mōōd, *n.* disposition of mind : temporary state of the mind : anger : heat of temper. [A.S. *mod,* mind, disposition ; found in all the Teut. languages, and orig. sig. 'courage' (Ger. *muth*).]

**Moody,** mōōd′i, *adj.* indulging *moods :* out of humour : angry : sad : gloomy.—*adv.* **Mood′ily.** —*n.* **Mood′iness,** quality of being moody : peevishness. [See **Mood,** disposition of mind.]

**Moon,** mōōn, *n.* the secondary planet or satellite which revolves round the earth : a satellite revolving about any other planet : a month : (*fort.*) a moon-shaped outwork. [Lit. the 'measurer' (of time), A.S. *mona ;* found in all the Teut.

languages, also in O. Slav. *menso*, L. *mensis*, Gr. *mēnē*, Sans. *mas-a*, and all from root *ma*, to measure.]

**Moonbeam**, moōn'bēm, *n.* a beam from the moon.

**Moonless**, moōn'les, *adj.* destitute of moonlight.

**Moonlight**, moōn'līt, *adj.* lighted by the moon: occurring during moonlight.—*n.* the light of the moon. [**Moon** and **Light**.]

**Moonshee**, moōn'shē, *n.* a Mohammedan professor or teacher of languages, so called in India. [Arab.]

**Moonshine**, moōn'shīn, *n.* the shining of the moon : (*fig.*) show without reality.

**Moonstruck**, moōn'struk, *adj.* (*lit.*) struck or affected by the moon : lunatic.

**Moor**, moōr, *n.* an extensive waste covered with heath, and having a poor, peaty soil : a heath. [A.S. *mor*; Dut. *moer*, Ice. *mor*, peat, turf, moor. See **Mire** and **Moss**.]

**Moor**, moōr, *v.t.* to fasten a ship by cable and anchor.—*v.i.* to be fastened by cables or chains. [Dut. *marren*, to tie, allied to A.S. *merran*, O. Ger. *marrjan*, to mar, to hinder.]

**Moor**, moōr, *n.* a native of N. Africa, of a *dark* complexion. [Fr. *more*, *maure*—L. *maurus*—Gr. *mauros*, black.]

**Moorage**, moōr'āj, *n.* a place for *mooring*.

**Moorcock**, moōr'kok, **Moorfowl**, moōr'fowl, *n.* the red grouse or heath*cock* found in *moors*.

**Moorhen**, moōr'hen, *n.* the *moor* or water *hen*.

**Mooring**, moōr'ing, *n.*, *act of mooring* : that which serves to moor or confine a ship : in *pl.* the place or condition of a ship thus moored.

**Moorish**, moōr'ish, **Moory**, moōr'i, *adj.* resembling a *moor* : sterile : marshy : boggy.

**Moorish**, moōr'ish, *adj.* belonging to the *Moors*.

**Moorland**, moōr'land, *n.* a tract of heath-covered and marshy land.

**Moose**, moōs, *n.* the largest deer of America, resembling the European elk. [Indian.]

**Moot**, moōt, *v.t.* to propose for discussion : to discuss : argue for practice.—*adj.* discussed or debated. [A.S. *motian—mot*, an assembly, akin to *metan*, to meet. See **Meet**, to come face to face.]            [debated.

**Mootable**, moōt'a-bl, *adj.* that can be *mooted* or

**Moot-case**, moōt'-kās, **Moot-point**, moōt'-point, *n.* a *case*, *point*, or question to be *mooted* or debated : an unsettled question.

**Moot-court**, moōt'-kort, *n.* a meeting or *court* for *mooting* or arguing supposed cases.

**Mop**, mop, *n.* an instrument for washing floors, made of cloth, &c. fastened to a handle.—*v.t.* to rub or wipe with a mop :—*pr.p.* mopp'ing ; *pa.t.* and *pa.p.* mopped'. [Either Celt. as in W. *mop*, *mopa*, a mop ; or through Fr. *mappe*, from L. *mappa*, a napkin, from which also **Map** and **Napkin**.]

**Mope**, mōp, *v.i.* to be silent and dispirited : to be dull or stupid.—*adv.* Mop'ingly. [Dut. *moppen*, to pout, sulk.]               [ishness.

**Mopish**, mōp'ish, *adj.* dull : spiritless.—*n.* Mop'-

**Moppet**, mop'et, *n.* a doll or rags like a *mop*.

**Moraine**, mo-rān', *n.* (*geol.*) a line of block and gravel found at the bases and edges of glaciers. [Fr.; from the Teut., as in Prov. Ger. *mur*, stones broken off.]

**Moral**, mor'al, *adj.* of or belonging to the *manners* or conduct of men : conformed to right : virtuous : capable of moral action : subject to the moral law : instructing with regard to morals : supported by evidence of reason or probability. —*n.* in *pl.* manners : the doctrine or practice of the duties of life : moral philosophy or ethics :

conduct : in *sing.* the practical lesson given by anything. [Fr.—L. *moralis—mos*, *moris*, manner, custom.]

**Morale**, mo-räl', *n.* the *moral* condition : mental state as regards spirit and confidence, esp. of a body of men. [Fr.]

**Moralise**, mor'al-īz, *v.t.* to apply to a *moral* purpose : to explain in a moral sense.—*v.i.* to speak or write on moral subjects : to make moral reflections.—*n.* Mor'aliser. [Fr. *moraliser*.]

**Moralist**, mor'al-ist, *n.* one who teaches morals : one who practises moral duties : one who prides himself on his morality.

**Morality**, mo-ral'i-ti, *n.* quality of being *moral*: the quality of an action which renders it right or wrong : the practice of moral duties : virtue : the doctrine which treats of moral actions : ethics : a kind of moral allegorical play. [Fr.—L. *moralitas*.]

**Morally**, mor'al-i, *adv.* in a *moral* manner.

**Morass**, mo-ras', *n.* a tract of soft, wet ground : a marsh. [Dut. *moer-as*, for *moer-asch*, (*lit.*) 'moor-ish,' adj. from *moer*, mire. See **Moor**.]

**Moravian**, mo-rā'vi-an, *adj.* pertaining to *Moravia* or to the *Moravians* or United Brethren.—*n.* one of the United Brethren, a Protestant religious sect, orig. from *Moravia*, in Austria.

**Morbid**, mor'bid, *adj.*, *diseased*, sickly : not healthful.—*adv.* Mor'bidly.—*n.* Mor'bidness, sickliness. [Fr.—L. *morbidus—morbus*, disease ; akin to *mor-ior*, to die. See **Mortal**.]

**Morbific**, mor-bif'ik, *adj.* causing *disease*. [Coined from L. *morbus*, disease, and *facio*, to make.]

**Mordacious**, mor-dā'shus, *adj.* given to *biting*: biting : (*fig.*) sarcastic : severe.—*adv.* Morda'ciously. [L. *mordax*, *mordacis*, from *mordeo*, to bite.]

**Mordacity**, mor-das'i-ti, *n.* quality of being mordacious. [Fr.—L. *mordacitas—mordax*.]

**Mordant**, mor'dant, *adj.* (*lit.*) *biting into* : serving to fix colours.—*n.* any substance, as alum, used to give permanency or brilliancy to dyes : matter to make gold-leaf adhere. [Fr., pr.p. of *mordre* —L. *mordeo*, to bite.]

**More**, mōr, *adj.* (serves as *comp.* of **Many** and **Much**), *greater*, so in *B.* : additional : other besides.—*adv.* to a greater degree : again : longer.—*n.* a greater thing : something further or in addition.—*superl.* **Most**, mōst. [A.S. *mara* (Ice. *meiri*)—root *mag*, identical with Sans. *mah* (= *magh*), to grow. See **May**, **Main**.]

**Moreen**, mo-rēn', *n.* a stout woollen stuff, used for curtains, &c. [A form of **Mohair**.]

**Morel**. See **Moril**.

**Moreover**, mōr-ō'ver, *adv.*, *more over* or beyond what has been said : further : besides : also.

**Moresque**, mo-resk', *adj.* done after the manner of the *Moors*.—*n.* a kind of ornamentation, same as arabesque. [Fr. ; It. *moresco*.]

**Morganatic**, mor-gan-at'ik, *adj.* noting a marriage of a man with a woman of inferior rank, in which neither the latter nor her children enjoy the rank or inherit the possessions of her husband, though the children are legitimate. [Low L. *morganatica*, a gift from a bridegroom to his bride ; from Ger. *morgen*, morning, used for *morgengabe*, the gift given by a husband to his wife.]

**Moribund**, mor'i-bund, *adj.*, *about to die*. [L. *moribundus—morior*, to die.]

**Moril**, mor'il, *n.* a mushroom abounding with little holes. [Fr. *morille* ; prob. from Fr. *more*, black, because it turns black in cooking. See **Moor**, a native of N. Africa.]

**Morion**, mō'ri-un, *n.* an open helmet, without visor

or beaver. [Fr. (It. *morione*), prob. from Sp. *morrion*—*morra*, crown of the head.]

**Morisco**, mo-ris′ko, **Morisk**, mo-risk′, *n.* the *Moorish* language: a Moorish dance or dancer.

**Mormon**, mor′mon, *n.* one of a religious sect in the United States, founded in 1830 by Joseph Smith, who made an addition to the Bible, called the *Book of Mormon*, from Mormon, its alleged author.—*n.* **Mor′monism** (-izm), the doctrines of this sect.

**Morn**, morn, *n.* the first part of the day: morning. [Contr. of M. E. *morwen*—A.S. *morgen*, cog. with Ger. *morgen*, Ice. *morgun*, Goth. *maurgins;* a doublet of **Morrow**.]

**Morning**, morn′ing, *n.* the first part of the day: an early part.—*adj.* pertaining to the morning: done or being in the morning. [Contr. of *morwen-ing*. See **Morn**.]

**Morocco**, mo-rok′o, *n.* a fine kind of leather of goat or sheep skin, first brought from *Morocco.*

**Morose**, mō-rōs′, *adj.* of a sour temper: gloomy: severe.—*adv.* **Morose′ly**.—*n.* **Morose′ness**, quality of being morose. [L. *morosus*, peevish, fretful—*mos, moris*, (*orig.*) self-will, hence manner, way of life. See **Moral**.]

**Morphia**, mor′fi-a, **Morphine**, mor′fin, *n.* the *narcotic* principle of opium. [Coined from Gr. *Morpheus*, god of dreams, (*lit.*) 'the fashioner,' from *morphē*, shape.]

**Morphology**, mor-fol′o-ji, *n.* the *science* of the *forms* assumed by plants and animals. [Gr. *morphē*, form, and *logos*, a discourse.]

**Morris, Morrice**, mor′is, **Morris-dance**, mor′is-dans, *n.* a *Moorish* dance: a dance in which bells, rattles, tambours, &c. are introduced. [Sp. *mor-isco*, (*lit.*) 'Moor-ish'—Sp. *moro*, a Moor.]

**Morrow**, mor′o, *n.* the day following the present: to-morrow: the next following day. [M. E. *morwe*, for *morwen*. See its doublet **Morn**.]

**Morse**, mors, *n.* the walrus or sea-horse. See **Walrus**. [Russ. *morjs*.]

**Morsel**, mor′sel, *n.* a *bite* or mouthful: a small piece of food: a small quantity. [O. Fr. *morcel* (Fr. *morceau*, It. *morsello*), dim. from L. *morsus*, from *mordeo, morsum*, to bite. See **Mordacious**.]

**Mortal**, mor′tal, *adj.* liable to *die:* causing death: deadly: fatal: punishable with death: extreme, violent: belonging to man, who is mortal.—*adv.* **Mor′tally**. [O. Fr. *mortal*—L. *mortalis*—*mors, mortis*, death, akin to Gr. *brotos* (for *mrotos*, see **Ambrosia**), and Sans. *mri*, to die.]

**Mortality**, mor-tal′i-ti, *n.* condition of being *mortal:* death: frequency or number of deaths: the human race. [L. *mortalitas*.]

**Mortar**, mor′tar, *n.* a vessel in which substances are *pounded* with a pestle: a piece of ordnance, resembling a mortar, for throwing shells, &c.: a cement of lime, sand, and water. [A.S. *mortere*—L. *mortarium*, from root of **Mar**.]

**Mortgage**, mor′gāj, *n.* a conveyance of property, as security for a debt, which is lost or becomes *dead* to the debtor if the money is not paid on a certain day: the state of being pledged.—*v.t.* to pledge, as security for a debt.—*n.* **Mort′gager**. [Fr.—*mort*, dead—L. *mortuus*, and *gage*, a pledge. See **Gage**, a pledge.]

**Mortgagee**, mor-gā-jē′, *n.* one to whom a *mortgage* is made or given.

**Mortiferous**, mor-tif′ėr-us, *adj.*, *death-bringing:* fatal. [L. *mors*, death, and *fero*, to bring.]

**Mortification**, mor-ti-fi-kā′shun, *n.* act of *mortifying* or state of being mortified: the death of one part of an animal body: subjection of the passions and appetites by bodily severities: humiliation: vexation: that which mortifies or vexes: (*Scotch law*) a bequest to some institution.

**Mortify**, mor′ti-fī, *v.t.* to *make dead:* to destroy the vital functions of: to subdue by severities and penance: to vex: to humble.—*v.i.* to lose vitality, to gangrene: to be subdued:—*pa.t.* and *pa.p.* mor′tified. [Fr.—L. *mortifico*, to cause death to—*mors*, death, and *facio*, to make.]

**Mortifying**, mor′ti-fī-ing, *adj.* tending to *mortify* or humble: humiliating: vexing.

**Mortise**, mor′tis, *n.* a cavity cut into a piece of timber to receive the tenon, another piece made to fit it.—*v.t.* to cut a mortise in: to join by a mortise and tenon. [Fr. *mortaise;* ety. unknown.]

**Mortmain**, mort′mān, *n.* the transfer of property to a corporation, which is said to be a *dead hand*, or one that can never part with it again. [Fr. *mort*, dead, and *main*—L. *manus*, the hand.]

**Mortuary**, mort′ū-ar-i, *adj.* belonging to the burial of the *dead.*—*n.* a burial-place: a gift claimed by the minister of a parish on the death of a parishioner. [Low L. *mortuarium*, from L. *mortuarius*.]

**Mosaic**, mō-zā′ik, **Mosaic-work**, mō-zā′ik-wurk, *n.* a kind of work in which designs are formed by small pieces of coloured marble, glass, &c. cemented on a ground of stucco, or inlaid upon metal.—*adj.* **Mosa′ic**, relating to or composed of mosaic.—*adv.* **Mosa′ically**. [Fr. *mosaïque* (It. *mosaico*)—L. *museum* or *musivum* (*opus*), mosaic (work)—Gr. *mouseios*, belonging to the Muses. See **Muse**.]

**Mosaic**, mō-zā′ik, *adj.* pertaining to *Moses*, the great Jewish lawgiver.

**Moschatel**, mos′ka-tel, *n.* a plant, with pale-green flowers and a *musky* smell. [Fr. *moscatelline*—Low L. *moschatellina*—*muscus*, musk.]

**Moselle**, mo-zel′, *n.* a white wine from the district of the *Moselle.*

**Moslem**, moz′lem, *n.* a Mussulman or Mohammedan.—*adj.* of or belonging to the Mohammedans. [Ar. *muslim*—*salama*, to submit (to God). Doublet **Mussulman**. See **Islam**.]

**Mosque**, mosk, *n.* a Mohammedan place of *worship*. [Fr.—Sp. *mezquita*—Ar. *masjid*—*sajada*, to bend, to adore.]

**Mosquito**, mos-kē′to, *n.* a biting gnat common in tropical countries:—*pl.* **Mosqui′toes**. [Sp., dim. of *mosca*, a fly—L. *musca*.]

**Moss**, mos, *n.* a family of cryptogamic plants with a branching stem and narrow, simple leaves: a piece of ground covered with moss: a bog.—*v.t.* to cover with moss. [A.S. *meos;* cog. with Dut. *mos*, Ger. *moos*, and L. *muscus*.]

**Mossland**, mos′land, *n.*, *land* abounding in *moss* or peat-bogs.

**Moss-rose**, mos′-rōz, *n.* a variety of *rose* having a *moss*-like growth on the calyx.

**Moss-trooper**, mos′-trōōp′ėr, *n.* one of the *troopers* or bandits that used to infest the *mosses* between England and Scotland.

**Mossy**, mos′i, *adj.* overgrown or abounding with *moss*.—*n.* **Moss′iness**.

**Most**, mōst, *adj.* (superl. of **More**), *greatest:* excelling in number.—*adv.* in the highest degree. —*n.* the greatest number or quantity.—*adv.* **Most′ly**. [A.S. *mǣst*, cog. with Ger. *meist*. See **More**.]

**Mote**, mōt, *n.* a particle of *dust:* a spot or speck: anything small. [A.S. *mot;* ety. unknown.]

**Motet**, mo-tet′, *n.* a short piece of sacred music. [Fr.—It. *mottetto*, dim. of *motto*. See **Motto**.]

**Moth**, moth, *n.* a family of insects like butter-flies, seen mostly at night : the larva of this insect which gnaws cloth : that which eats away gradually and silently.—*v.t.* **Moth'-eat**, to prey upon, as a *moth eats* a garment. [A.S. *moththe*; cog. with Ger. *motte*, also with A.S. *madhu*, a bug, Ger. *made*.] [moths.

**Moth-eaten**, moth'-ēt'n, *adj.* eaten or cut by

**Mother**, mu*th*'ėr, *n.* a female parent, esp. of the human race : a matron : that which has produced anything.—*adj.* received by birth, as it were from one's mother : natural : acting the part of a mother : originating.—*v.t.* to adopt as a son or daughter.—*n.* **Moth'er-in-law**, the mother of one's husband or wife.—*n.* **Moth'er-of-pearl**, the internal layer of the shells of several molluscs, esp. of the pearl-oyster, so called because *pro-ducing the pearl.* [M. E. *moder*—A.S. *moder*, cog. with Dut. *moeder*, Ice. *modhir*, Ger. *mutter*, Ir. and Gael. *mathair*, Russ. *mate*, L. *mater*, Gr. *mētēr*, Sans. *mata*, *matri*, all from the Aryan root *ma*, to measure, to manage, from which also **Matter** and **Mete**.]

**Mother**, mu*th*'ėr, *n.* dregs or sediment, as of vinegar. [A form of **Mud**.] [mother.

**Motherhood**, mu*th*'ėr-hood, *n.* state of being a

**Motherless**, mu*th*'ėr-les, *adj.* without a mother.

**Motherly**, mu*th*'ėr-li, *adj.* pertaining to or becom-ing a *mother*: parental : tender.—*n.* **Moth'erli-ness**.

**Moth-hunter**, moth'-hunt'ėr, *n.* a little kind of swallow which *hunts moths*, &c., called also the goatsucker.

**Mothy**, moth'i, *adj.* full of moths.

**Motion**, mō'shun, *n.* the act or state of *moving* : a single movement : change of posture : gait : power of motion : excitement of the mind : proposal made, esp. in an assembly :—in *pl.* (*B.*) impulses. —*v.i.* to make a significant movement. [Fr.— L. *motio*, *-onis*—*moveo*, *motum*, to move.]

**Motionless**, mō'shun-les, *adj.* without motion.

**Motive**, mō'tiv, *adj.* causing *motion* : having power to move.—*n.* that which moves, or excites to action : inducement : reason. [M. E. *motif*— Fr., through Low L., from *moveo*, *motus*, to move.]

**Motivity**, mō-tiv'it-i, *n.* power of producing *motion* : the quality of being influenced by motion.

**Motley**, mot'li, *adj.* covered with spots of different colours : consisting of different colours : com-posed of various parts. [Lit. 'curdled,' M. E. *mottelee*, through O. Fr., from an unknown O. Ger. root seen in Bavarian *matte*, curds.]

**Motor**, mō'tor, *n.* a *mover*: that which gives motion. [See **Motive**.]

**Motory**, mō'tor-i, *adj.* giving motion.

**Mottled**, mot'ld, *adj.* marked with spots of various colours, or shades of colour. [From **Motley**.]

**Motto**, mot'ō, *n.* a sentence or phrase prefixed to anything intimating the subject of it : a phrase attached to a device :—*pl.* **Mottoes** (mot'ōz). [It.—Low L. *muttum*—*muttio*, to mutter. See **Mutter**.]

**Mould**, mōld, *n.* dust : soil rich in decayed matter : the matter of which anything is composed : a minute fungus which grows on bodies in a damp atmosphere, so named from often growing on mould.—*v.t.* to cover with mould or soil : to cause to become mouldy.—*v.i.* to become mouldy. [A.S. *molde*; Ger. *mull*, Goth. *mulda*; akin to Goth. *malan*, L. *molo*, to grind.]

**Mould**, mōld, *n.* a hollow form in which anything is cast : a pattern : the form received from a mould : character.—*v.t.* to form in a mould : to

knead, as dough.—*n.* **Mould'er**. [Fr. *moule*— L. *modulus*. See **Model**.]

**Mouldable**, mōld'a-bl, *adj.* that may be moulded.

**Moulder**, mōld'ėr, *v.i.* to crumble to *mould*: to waste away gradually.—*v.t.* to turn to dust.

**Moulding**, mōld'ing, *n.* anything *moulded* : (*arch.*) an ornamental projection beyond a wall, &c.

**Mouldwarp**, mōld'worp, *n.* the mole, which *casts up* little heaps of *mould*. [See **Mole**.]

**Mouldy**, mōld'i, *adj.* overgrown with *mould*.—*n.* **Mould'iness**.

**Moult**, mōlt, *v.i.* to *change* or cast the feathers, &c. as birds, &c. [Formed with intrusive *l* from L. *mutare*, to change.]

**Moulting**, mōlt'ing, *n.* the act or process of *moult-ing* or casting feathers, skin, &c.

**Mound**, mownd, *n.* (*fort.*) an artificial bank of earth or stone : an artificial mount : a natural hillock.—*v.t.* to fortify with a mound. [A.S. *mund*, a defence ; O. Ger. *munt*, defence ; akin to L. *mons*, a mount.]

**Mount**, mownt, *n.* ground rising above the level of the surrounding country : a hill : an ornamental mound : (*B.*) a bulwark for offence or defence.— *v.i.* to project or rise up : to be of great eleva-tion.—*v.t.* to raise aloft : to climb : to get upon, as a horse : to put on horseback : to put upon something, to arrange or set in fitting order.— *n.* **Mount'er**. [A.S. *munt*—L. *mons*, *montis*, a mountain, from root of *-mineo*, as in *emineo*, to project.] [or ascended.

**Mountable**, mownt'a-bl, *adj.* that may be *mounted*

**Mountain**, mownt'ān or -'in, *n.* a high hill : any-thing very large.—*adj.* of or relating to a mount-ain : growing or dwelling on a mountain.—*n.* **Mount'ain-ash**, the rowan-tree, with bunches of red berries, common on mountains.—*n.* **Mount'-ain-limestone** (*geol.*) a series of limestone strata separating the old red sandstone from the coal-measures. [Fr. *montagne*—Low L. *montanea*, a mountain—L. *mons*, *montis*.]

**Mountaineer**, mownt-ān-ēr' or -in-ēr', *n.* an in-habitant of a *mountain*: a rustic.

**Mountainous**, mownt'ān-us or -'in-us, *adj.* full of *mountains*: large as a mountain : huge.

**Mountebank**, mownt'e-bank, *n.* a quack-doctor who boasts of his skill and his medicines : a boastful pretender. [It. *montambanco*—*mon-tare*, to mount, *in*, on, upon, and *banco*, a bench. See **Bank**, a place for depositing money.]

**Mounting**, mownt'ing, *n.* the act of *mounting* or embellishing, as the setting of a gem, &c.

**Mourn**, mōrn, *v.i.* to grieve : to be sorrowful : to wear mourning.—*v.t.* to grieve for : to utter in a sorrowful manner.—*n.* **Mourn'er**. [A.S. *mur-nan*, *meornan*; O. Ger. *mornen*, to grieve, whence Fr. *morne*, dull, sad.]

**Mournful**, mōrn'fool, *adj.*, *mourning*: causing or expressing sorrow : feeling grief.—*adv.* **Mourn'-fully**.—*n.* **Mourn'fulness**.

**Mourning**, mōrn'ing, *adj.*, *grieving*: lamenting. —*n.* the act of expressing grief : the dress of mourners.—*adv.* **Mourn'ingly**.

**Mouse**, mows, *n.* a little rodent animal found in houses and in the fields :—*pl.* **Mice** (mīs).— *n.* **Mouse'ear**, a name of several plants with soft leaves shaped like a mouse's ear.—*n.* **Mouse'tail**, a small plant with a spike of seed-vessels very like the tail of a mouse. [Lit. 'the stealing animal,' A.S. *mus*, pl. *mys*; Ger. *maus*, L. and Gr. *mus*, Sans. *musha*, a rat or mouse ; from root *mus*, to steal, seen in Sans. *mush*, to steal.]

**Mouse**, mowz, *v.i.* to catch *mice*: to watch for slily.—*n.* **Mous'er**.

**Moustache,** moos-tash′. Same as **Mustache.**

**Mouth,** mowth, *n.* the opening in the head of an animal by which it eats and utters sound : opening or entrance, as of a bottle, river, &c. : the instrument of speaking : a speaker :—*pl.* **Mouths** (mou*thz*). [A.S. *muth*; found in all the Teut. languages, as in Ger. *mund,* Dut. *mond.*]

**Mouth,** mow*th, v.t.* to utter with a voice overloud or swelling.—*n.* **Mouth′er,** an affected speaker.

**Mouthed,** mow*thd, adj.* having a mouth.

**Mouthful,** mowth′fool, *n.* as much as fills the mouth : a small quantity :—*pl.* **Mouth′fuls.**

**Mouthless,** mowth′les, *adj.* without a mouth.

**Mouthpiece,** mowth′pēs, *n.* the *piece* of a musical instrument for the *mouth :* one who speaks for others.

**Movable,** mōōv′a-bl, *adj.* that may be *moved,* lifted, &c. : not fixed : changing from one time to another.—*adv.* **Mov′ably.**—*ns.* **Mov′ableness, Movabil′ity.**

**Movables,** mōōv′a-blz, *n.pl.* (*law*) such articles of property as may be *moved,* as furniture, &c.

**Move,** mōōv, *v.t.* to cause to change place or posture : to set in motion : to impel : to excite to action : to persuade : to instigate : to arouse : to provoke : to touch the feelings of : to propose or bring before an assembly : to recommend.—*v.i.* to go from one place to another : to change place or posture : to walk : to change residence : to make a motion as in an assembly.—*n.* the act of moving : a movement, esp. at chess.—*n.* **Mov′er.** [Fr. *mouvoir*—L. *moveo,* to move.]

**Movement,** mōōv′ment, *n.* act or manner of *moving :* change of position : motion of the mind, emotion : the wheel-work of a clock or watch : (*mus.*) a part having the same time.

**Moving,** mōōv′ing, *adj.* causing *motion :* changing position : affecting the feelings : pathetic.—*adv.* **Mov′ingly.**

**Mow,** mō, *n.* a pile of hay or corn in sheaves laid up in a barn.—*v.t.* to lay hay or sheaves of grain in a heap :—*pr.p.* mow′ing ; *pa.t.* mowed′ ; *pa.p.* mowed′ or mown. [A.S. *muga,* a heap ; Ice. *muga,* a swath in mowing.]

**Mow,** mō, *v.t.* to cut down with a scythe : to cut down in great numbers :—*pr.p.* mow′ing ; *pa.t.* mowed′ ; *pa.p.* mowed′ or mown. [A.S. *mawan* ; Ger. *mähen*; allied to L. *meto,* to mow.]

**Mowed,** mōd, **Mown,** mōn, *adj.* cut down with a scythe : cleared of grass with a scythe, as land.

**Mower,** mō′er, *n.* one who mows or cuts grass.

**Mowing,** mō′ing, *n.* the art of cutting down with a scythe : land from which grass is cut.

**Much,** much, *adj., great* in quantity : long in duration.—*adv.* to a great degree : by far : often or long : almost.—*n.* a great quantity : a strange thing. [Through old forms *michel, muchel,* from A.S. *mic-el ;* Ice. *mjök,* Goth. *mikils,* Gr. *meg-as,* L. *mag-nus.*]

**Mucid,** mū′sid, *adj.* like *mucus :* slimy.—*n.* **Mu′cidness.**

**Mucilage,** mū′si-lāj, *n.* a *slimy* substance like *mucus,* found in certain vegetables : gum.

**Mucilaginous,** mū-si-laj′in-us, *adj.* pertaining to or secreting *mucilage :* slimy.

**Muck,** muk, *n., dung :* a mass of decayed vegetable matter : anything low and filthy.—*v.t.* to manure with muck. [Scand., as in Ice. *myki,* Dan. *mög,* dung.]

**Muck,** mistaken form of **Amuck.**

**Mucky,** muk′i, *adj.* consisting of muck : nasty, filthy.—*n.* **Muck′iness.**

**Mucous,** mū′kus, *adj.* like *mucus :* slimy : viscous.

**Mucus,** mū′kus, *n.* the slimy fluid from the nose :

the slimy fluid on all the interior canals of the body to moisten them. [L.—*mungo,* Gr. *apo-myssō,* to blow the nose ; Sans. *much,* to loosen.]

**Mud,** mud, *n.* wet, soft earth.—*v.t.* to bury in mud : to dirty : to stir the sediment in, as in liquors. [Low Ger. *mudde,* Dut. *modder.*]

**Muddle,** mud′l, *v.t.* to render *muddy* or foul, as water : to confuse, especially with liquor.

**Muddy,** mud′i, *adj.* foul with *mud :* containing mud : covered with mud : confused : stupid.—*v.t.* to dirty : to render dull :—*pa.t.* and *pa.p.* mudd′ied.—*adv.* **Mudd′ily.**—*n.* **Mudd′iness.**

**Muddy-headed,** mud′i-hed′ed, *adj.* having a *muddy* or dull *head* or understanding.

**Muezzin,** mū-ez′in, *n.* the Mohammedan official attached to a mosque, whose duty is to announce the hours of prayer. [Arab.]

**Muff,** muf, *n.* a warm, soft cover for the hands in winter, usually of fur or dressed skins. [From a Teut. root, seen in Ger. *muff,* a muff, Dut. *mof,* a sleeve.]

**Muff,** muf, *n.* a stupid, silly fellow. [Prob. from prov. E. *moffle,* to mumble, do anything ineffectually.]

**Muffin,** muf′in, *n.* a *soft,* light, spongy cake. [Prob. from **Muff,** on account of its softness.]

**Muffle,** muf′l, *v.t.* to wrap up as with a *muff :* to blindfold : to cover up so as to render sound dull : to cover from the weather. [Fr. *moufler* —*moufle,* a muff, prob. from the root of **Muff.**]

**Muffler,** muf′lėr, *n.* a cover that *muffles* the face.

**Mufti,** muf′ti, *n.* a doctor or official expounder of Mohammedan law in Turkey. [Ar.]

**Mug,** mug, *n.* a kind of earthen or metal *cup* for liquor. [Ir. *mugan,* a mug, *mucog,* a cup.]

**Muggy,** mug′i, **Muggish,** mug′ish, *adj., foggy :* close and damp. [Ice. *mugga,* dark, thick weather.]

**Mulatto,** mū-lat′ō, *n.* the offspring of black and white parents.—*fem.* **Mulat′tress.** [Lit. one of a mixed breed *like* a *mule,* Sp. *mulato—mulo,* a mule.]

**Mulberry,** mul′ber-i, *n.* the *berry* of a tree : the tree itself, the leaves of which form the food of the silkworm. [*Mul-* is A.S. *mor-* or *mur-* (as in A.S. *mor-beam,* a mulberry, where *beam* = tree), from L. *morus* ; cog. with Gr. *mŏron,* a mulberry : and **Berry.**]

**Mulct,** mulkt, *n.* a *fine :* a penalty.—*v.t.* to fine. [L. *mulcto,* to fine.]

**Mulctuary,** mulk′tū-ar-i, *adj.* imposing a *fine.*

**Mule,** mūl, *n.* the offspring of the horse and ass : an instrument for cotton-spinning : an obstinate person. [A.S. *mul*—L. *mulus,* a mule.]

**Muleteer,** mūl-et-ēr′, *n.* one who drives *mules.*

**Mulish,** mūl′ish, *adj.* like a *mule :* sullen : obstinate.—*adv.* **Mul′ishly.**—*n.* **Mul′ishness.**

**Mull,** mul, *v.t.* to warm, spice, and sweeten (wine, ale, &c.). [From **Mulled,** *adj.*]

**Mullagatawny,** mul-a-ga-taw′ni, *n.* an East Indian curry-soup.

**Mulled,** muld, *adj.* heated, sweetened, and spiced (as wine, &c.). [M. E. *mold-ale,* Scot. *mulde-mete,* a funeral banquet, where *molde* = Scot. *mools,* E. **Mould,** the earth of the grave, and *ale* = feast (cf. **Bridal**).]

**Mullet,** mul′et, *n.* a genus of fishes nearly cylindrical in form, highly esteemed for the table. [Fr. *mulet*—L. *mullus.*]

**Mullion,** mul′yun, *n.* an upright division between the lights of windows, &c. in a Gothic arch.—*v.t.* to shape into divisions by mullions. [M. E. *munion,* ety. dub., either from **Fr.** *meneau,* a mullion, of unknown origin, or from Fr.

*moignon*, a stump, as of an arm or branch, which is perh. derived from L. *mancus*, maimed.]

**Multangular**, mult-ang'gul-ar, *adj.* having *many angles* or corners. [L. *multus*, many, and **Angular**.]

**Multifarious**, mul-ti-fā'ri-us, *adj.* having *great diversity :* manifold.—*adv.* **Multifa'riously.** [L. *multus*, many, and *varius*, diverse.]

**Multiform**, mul'ti-form, *adj.* having *many forms.* —*n.* **Multiform'ity.** [L. *multus*, many, and **Form.**]

**Multilateral**, mul-ti-lat'ėr-al, *adj.* having *many sides.* [L. *multus*, many, and **Lateral.**]

**Multilineal**, mul-ti-lin'e-al, *adj.* having *many lines.* [L. *multus*, many, and **Lineal.**]

**Multiped**, mul'ti-ped, *n.* an insect having *many feet.* [L. *multus*, many, and *pes, pedis*, foot.]

**Multiple**, mul'ti-pl, *adj.* having *many folds* or parts : repeated many times.—*n.* a number or quantity which contains another an exact number of times. [L. *multiplex—multus*, many, and *plico*, to fold.]

**Multiplex**, mul'ti-pleks, *adj.* having *many folds :* manifold.

**Multipliable**, mul'ti-plī-a-bl, *adj.* that may be multiplied.

**Multiplicand**, mul'ti-pli-kand, *n.* a number or quantity to be *multiplied* by another.

**Multiplication**, mul-ti-pli-kā'shun, *n.* the act of *multiplying :* the rule or operation by which any given number or quantity is multiplied.

**Multiplicative**, mul'ti-pli-kāt-iv, *adj.* tending to *multiply :* having the power to multiply.

**Multiplicity**, mul-ti-plis'i-ti, *n.* the state of being *multiplied* or various : a great number.

**Multiplier**, mul'ti-plī-ėr, *n.* one who or that which *multiplies* or increases : the number or quantity by which another is multiplied.

**Multiply**, mul'ti-plī, *v.t.* to *fold* or increase *many* times : to make more numerous : to repeat any given number or quantity as often as there are units in another number.—*v.i.* to increase :— *pr.p.* mul'tiplying ; *pa.t.* and *pa.p.* mul'tiplied. [Fr.—L. *multiplex*. See **Multiple.**]

**Multitude**, mul'ti-tūd, *n.* the state of being *many :* a great number of individuals : a crowd : the vulgar or common people. [Fr.—L. *multitudo —multus*, many.]

**Multitudinous**, mul-ti-tūd'i-nus, *adj.* consisting of or having the appearance of a *multitude.*

**Mum**, mum, *adj.* silent.—*n.* silence.—*int.* be silent. [Cf. L. and Gr. *mu*, the least possible sound made with the lips ; of imitative origin.]

**Mum**, mum, *n.* a sort of beer made in Germany. [Orig. brewed by a German named *Mumme.*]

**Mumble**, mum'bl, *v.i.* to utter the sound *mum* in speaking : to speak indistinctly : to chew softly : to eat with the lips close :—*v.t.* to utter indistinctly or imperfectly : to mouth gently. [See **Mum.**]

**Mumbler**, mum'blėr, *n.* one who *mumbles* or speaks with a low, indistinct voice.

**Mumbling**, mum'bling, *adj.* uttering with a low, indistinct voice : chewing softly.—*adv.* **Mum'-blingly.**

**Mumm**, mum, *v.t.* to mask : to make diversion in disguise. [O. Dut. *mommen*, to mask, *mom*, a mask ; cf. Low Ger. *mummeln*, to mask, whence Ger. *vermummen*, to mask.]

**Mummer**, mum'ėr, *n.* one who *mumms* or makes diversion in disguise : a masker : a buffoon.

**Mummery**, mum'ėr-i, *n., masking :* diversion.

**Mummify**, mum'i-fī, *v.t.* to make into a mummy : to embalm and dry as a mummy :—*pr.p.*

mumm'ifying ; *pa.p.* mumm'ified.—*n.* **Mummifica'tion.** [**Mummy**, and *facio*, to make.]

**Mumming**, mum'ing, *n.* the sports of *mummers.* —*adj.* pertaining to the sports of mummers.

**Mummy**, mum'i, *n.* a human body preserved by the Egyptian art of embalming, in which *wax*, spices, &c. were employed.—*v.t.* to embalm and dry as a mummy :—*pr.p.* mumm'ying ; *pa.p.* mumm'ied. [Fr.—It. *mummia*—Ar. and Pers. *mumayim*, a mummy—Pers. *mum*, wax.]

**Mump**, mump, *v.t.* or *v.i.* to *mumble* or move the lips with the mouth almost closed : to nibble : to cheat : to play the beggar. [Form of **Mum.**]

**Mumper**, mump'ėr, *n.* one who *mumps :* an old cant term for a beggar.

**Mumpish**, mump'ish, *adj.* having *mumps :* dull : sullen.—*adv.* **Mump'ishly.**—*n.* **Mump'ishness**.

**Mumps**, mumps, *n.* a swelling of the glands of the neck, accompanied with difficulty of speaking. [From **Mump.**]

**Munch**, munsh, *v.t.* or *v.i.* to *chew* with shut mouth. [M. E. *monchen*, from an imitative root, or from Fr. *manger*, It. *mangiare*—L. *manducare*, to chew.]

**Muncher**, munsh'ėr, *n.* one who *munches.*

**Mundane**, mun'dān, *adj.* belonging to the *world :* terrestrial.—*adv.* **Mun'danely.** [Fr.—L. *mundanus—mundus*, the world—*mundus*, ordered, adorned ; akin to Sans. *mand*, to adorn.]

**Municipal**, mū-nis'i-pal, *adj.* pertaining to a corporation or city. [Fr.—L. *municipalis*, from *municipium*, a free town—*munia*, official duties, and *capio*, to take.]

**Municipality**, mū-nis-i-pal'i-ti, *n.* a *municipal* district : in France, a division of the country.

**Munificence**, mū-nif'i-sens, *n.* quality of being munificent : bountifulness. [Fr.—L. *munificentia—munus*, a duty, present, and *facio*, to make.]

**Munificent**, mū-nif'i-sent, *adj.* very liberal in giving : generous : bountiful.—*adv.* **Munif'i-cently.**

**Muniment**, mū'ni-ment, *n.* that whioh *fortifies :* that which defends : a stronghold : place or means of defence : defence : (*law*) a record *fortifying* a claim : title-deeds. [Fr.—L. *munimentum*, from *munio, munitum*, to fortify— *mœnia*, walls.]

**Munition**, mū-nish'un, *n.* materials used in war : military stores of all kinds : (*B.*) stronghold, fortress. [Fr.—L. *munitio.*]

**Munnion**, mun'yun. Same as **Mullion**.

**Mural**, mū'ral, *adj.* pertaining to or like a *wall :* steep. [Fr.—L. *muralis*, from *murus*, a wall ; akin to *mœnia*, walls, and *munio*, to fortify.]

**Murder**, mur'dėr, *n.* the *act of putting* a person *to death*, intentionally and from malice.—*v.t.* to commit murder : to destroy : to put an end to. [A.S. *morthor*, from *morth*, death ; Ger. *mord*, Goth. *maurthr ;* akin to L. *mors, mortis*, death, and Sans. *mri*, to die.]

**Murderer**, mur'dėr-ėr, *n.* one who *murders*, or is guilty of murder.—*fem.* **Mur'deress**.

**Murderous**, mur'dėr-us, *adj.* guilty of *murder :* consisting in or fond of murder : bloody : cruel. —*adv.* **Mur'derously.**

**Murex**, mū'reks, *n.* a shellfish, from which the Tyrian purple dye was obtained. [L.]

**Muriatic**, mū-ri-at'ik, *adj.* pertaining to or obtained from sea-salt. [L. *muriaticus—muria*, brine.]

**Muricate**, mū'ri-kāt, **Muricated**, mū'ri-kāt-ed, *adj.* (*bot.*) armed with *sharp points* or prickles. [L. *muricatus*, from *murex, muricis*, a pointed rock or stone.]

**Muriform**, mū′ri-form, *adj.* (*bot.*) *resembling* the bricks *in a wall*. [L. *murus*, a wall, *forma*, shape.]

**Murky**, murk′i, *adj.*, *dark*: obscure: gloomy.—*adv.* **Murk′ily.**—*n.* **Murk′iness.** [A.S. *murc*; Ice. *myrkr*, Dan. and Sw. *mörk*.]

**Murmur**, mur′mur, *n.* a low, indistinct sound, like that of running water: a complaint in a low, muttering voice.—*v.i.* to utter a murmur: to grumble:—*pr.p.* mur′muring; *pa.t.* and *pa.p.* mur′mured.—*n.* **Mur′murer.** [Fr.—L., formed from the sound.]

**Murmurous**, mur′mur-us, *adj.* attended with *murmurs*: exciting murmur.

**Murrain**, mur′rān or -′rin, *n.* an infectious and *fatal* disease among cattle. [O. Fr. *morine*, a dead carcass—L. *morior*, to die. See **Mortal.**]

**Murrion**, mur′ri-un. Same as **Morion.**

**Muscadel**, mus′ka-del, **Muscadine**, mus′ka-dīn, **Muscat**, mus′kat, **Muscatel**, mus′ka-tel, *n.* a rich, spicy wine: also the grape producing it: a fragrant and delicious pear. [O. Fr. *muscadel*—It. *moscadello, moscatello*, dim. of *muscato*, smelling like musk—L. *muscus*, musk. See **Musk.**]

**Muscle**, mus′l, *n.* the fleshy parts of an animal body by which it moves. [Fr.—L. *musculus*, dim. of *mus*, a mouse, hence a muscle, from its appearance under the skin.]

**Muscle, Mussel**, mus′l, *n.* a marine bivalve shellfish, used for food. [A.S. *muscle*: Ger. *muschel*, Fr. *moule*: all from L. *musculus*.]

**Muscoid**, mus′koid, *adj.* (*bot.*) *moss-like*.—*n.* a moss-like, flowerless plant. [A hybrid, from L. *muscus*, moss, and Gr. *eidos*, form.]

**Muscular**, mus′kū-lar, *adj.* pertaining to a *muscle*: consisting of muscles: brawny: strong: vigorous.—*adv.* **Mus′cularly.**—*n.* **Muscular′ity**, state of being muscular.

**Muse**, mūz, *v.i.* to study in silence: to be absent-minded: to meditate.—*n.* deep thought: contemplation: absence of mind.—*adv.* **Mus′ingly.** —*n.* **Mus′er.** [Fr. *muser*, to loiter, to trifle; It. *musare*; acc. to Diez from O. Fr. *muse*, Fr. *museau*, the mouth, snout of an animal; from a dog snuffing idly about. See **Muzzle.**]

**Muse**, mūz, *n.* one of the nine goddesses of poetry, music, and the other liberal arts. [Fr.— L. *musa*—Gr. *mousa*, prob. from *maō*, to invent.]

**Museum**, mū-zē′um, *n.* a collection of natural, scientific, or other curiosities, or of works of art. [L.—Gr. *mouseion*. See **Muse.**]

**Mush**, mush, *n.* Indian meal boiled in water. [Ger. *mus*, pap, any thick preparation of fruit.]

**Mushroom**, mush′rōōm, *n.* the common name of certain fungi, esp. such as are edible: (*fig.*) one who rises suddenly from a low condition: an upstart. [Fr. *mousseron*, through *mousse*, moss —O. Ger. *mos*, Ger. *moos*.]

**Music**, mū′zik, *n.* melody or harmony: the science which treats of harmony: the art of combining sounds so as to please the ear: a musical composition. [Fr. *musique*—L. *musica*—Gr. *mousikē* (*technē*, art)—*mousa*, a **Muse.**]

**Musical**, mū′zik-al, *adj.* pertaining to or producing *music*: pleasing to the ear: melodious.—*adv.* **Mu′sically.**—*n.* **Mu′sicalness.** [Fr.]

**Musician**, mū-zish′an, *n.* one skilled in *music*: a performer of music. [Fr. *musicien*.]

**Musk**, musk, *n.* a strong perfume, obtained from the male musk-deer: a hornless deer, in Tibet and Nepaul, yielding musk.—*v.t.* to perfume with musk. [Fr. *musc*—L. *muscus*, Gr. *moschos* —Pers. *musk*.]

**Musk′-apple, Musk′-cat, Musk′-mel′on, Musk′-rose**, &c., so called from their *musky* odour.

**Musket**, mus′ket, *n.* formerly, the common hand-gun of soldiers. [Fr. *mousquet*, a musket, formerly a hawk—It. *mosquetto*—L. *musca*, a fly; many of the old guns had fancy names derived from birds and other animals.]

**Musketeer**, mus-ket-ēr′, *n.* a soldier armed with a *musket*. [Fr. *mousquetaire*.]

**Musketoon**, mus-ket-ōōn′, *n.* a short *musket*: one armed with a musketoon. [Fr. *mousgueton*.]

**Musketry**, mus′ket-ri, *n.*, *muskets* in general: practice with muskets. [Fr. *mousqueterie*.]

**Musk-ox**, musk′-oks, *n.* a small animal of the ox family inhabiting the northern parts of America, the flesh of which has a strong *musky* smell.

**Musk-rat**, musk′-rat, *n.* an animal of the shrew family, so named from the strong *musky* odour of its skin.

**Musky**, musk′i, *adj.* having the odour of musk.—*adv.* **Musk′ily.**—*n.* **Musk′iness.**

**Muslin**, muz′lin, *n.* a fine thin kind of cotton cloth with a downy nap. [Fr. *mousseline*—It. *mussolino*: said to be from *Mosul* in Mesopotamia.]

**Muslinet**, muz′lin-et, *n.* a coarse kind of muslin.

**Musquito.** Same as **Mosquito.**

**Mussel.** See **Muscle**, a shellfish.

**Mussulman**, mus′ul-man, *n.* a *Moslem* or Mohammedan:—*pl.* **Muss′ulmans** (-manz). [Low L. *mussulmanus*—Ar. *moslemûna*, pl. of *moslem*.]

**Must**, must, *v.i.* to be obliged physically or morally. [A.S. *mot, moste*; Ger. *müssen*.]

**Must**, must, *n.* wine pressed from the grape, but not fermented. [A.S., Ice. and Ger. *most*; all from L. *mustum*, from *mustus*, new, fresh.]

**Mustache, Mustachio**, mus-täsh′yo, *n.* the beard upon the upper lip. [Fr. *moustache*, It. *mostaccio*; from Gr. *mustax, mustakos*, the upper lip.]                                    [tachios.

**Mustachioed**, mus-täsh′yōd, *adj.* having mus-

**Mustard**, mus′tard, *n.* a plant with a pungent taste: the seed ground and used as a condiment. [O. Fr. *moustarde*, Fr. *moutarde*—O. Fr. *moust*, Fr. *moût*—L. *mustum*, must, orig. used in preparing it.]

**Muster**, mus′tėr, *v.t.* to assemble, as troops for duty or inspection: to gather.—*v.i.* to be gathered together, as troops.—*n.* an assembling of troops: a register of troops mustered: assemblage: collected show.—**Pass muster**, to pass inspection uncensured. [O. Fr. *mostrer*—Fr. *montrer*—L. *monstro*, to shew. See **Monster.**]

**Muster-master**, mus′tėr-mas′tėr, *n.* the *master* of the *muster*, or who takes an account of troops, their arms, &c.

**Muster-roll**, mus′tėr-rōl, *n.* a roll or register of the officers and men in each company, troop, or regiment.

**Musty**, must′i, *adj.*, *mouldy*: spoiled by damp: sour: foul.—*adv.* **Must′ily.**—*n.* **Must′iness.** [M. E. *must*, to be mouldy, from the base of L. *mucidus*, mouldy, from *mucus*. See **Mucus.**]

**Mutable**, mū′ta-bl, *adj.* that may be *changed*: subject to change: inconstant.—*adv.* **Mu′tably.** —*ns.* **Mutabil′ity, Mu′tableness**, quality of being mutable. [L. *mutabilis*—*muto, mutatum*, to change—*moveo, motum*, to move.]

**Mutation**, mū-tā′shun, *n.* act or process of *changing*: change: alteration.

**Mute**, mūt, *adj.* incapable of speaking: dumb: silent: unpronounced.—*n.* one mute or dumb: one who remains silent: a person stationed by undertakers at the door of a house at a funeral: (*gram.*) a letter having no sound without the

**Mute,** mūt, *v.i.* to dung, as birds. [O. Fr. *mutir; esmeut,* dung; conn. with E. *smelt* or *melt.*]

**Mutilate,** mū'ti-lāt, *v.t.* to *maim*: to cut off: to remove a material part of.—*n.* **Mu'tilator,** one who mutilates. [L. *mutilo—mutilus,* maimed, Gr. *mutilos, mitulos,* curtailed, hornless.]

**Mutilation,** mū-ti-lā'shun, *n.* act of mutilating: deprivation of a limb or essential part.

**Mutineer,** mū-ti-nēr', *n.* one guilty of *mutiny.*

**Mutinous,** mū'ti-nus, *adj.* disposed to *mutiny*: seditious.—*adv.* **Mu'tinously.**—*n.* **Mu'tinousness.**

**Mutiny,** mū'ti-ni, *v.i.* to rise against authority in military or naval service: to revolt against rightful authority:—*pr.p.* mū'tinying; *pa.t.* and *pa.p.* mū'tinied.—*n.* insurrection, esp. naval or military: tumult: strife. [Fr. *mutiner—mutin,* riotous—Fr. *meute—*L. *motus,* rising, insurrection, from *moveo, motum,* to move.]

**Mutter,** mut'ėr, *v.i.* to utter words in a low voice: to murmur: to sound with a low, rumbling noise. —*v.t.* to utter indistinctly.—*n.* **Mutt'erer.** [Prob. imitative, like Prov. Ger. *muttern*; L. *mutio.*]

**Mutton,** mut'n, *n.* the flesh of sheep. [Fr. *mouton,* a sheep—Low L. *multo,* which is prob. from the Celt., as Bret. *maoud,* W. *mollt,* a wether, sheep; or acc. to Diez, from L. *mutilus,* mutilated. See **Mutilate.**]

**Mutton-chop,** mut'n-chop, *n.* a rib of *mutton chopped* at the small end. [**Mutton** and **Chop.**]

**Mutual,** mū'tū-al, *adj., interchanged*: in return: given and received.—*adv.* **Mu'tually.**—*n.* **Mutual'ity.** [Fr. *mutuel—*L. *mutuus—muto,* to change.]

**Muzzle,** muz'l, *n.* the projecting mouth, lips, and nose of an animal: a fastening for the mouth to prevent biting: the extreme end of a gun, &c.— *v.t.* to put a muzzle on: to restrain from biting: to keep from hurting. [O. Fr. *musel,* Fr. *museau,* prob. from L. *morsus,* a bite—*mordeo,* to bite.]

**My** (when emphatic or distinct), mī, (otherwise) me, *poss. adj.* belonging to me. [Contr. of **Mine.**]

**Mycology,** mī-kol'o-ji, *n.* the science treating of the fungi or mushrooms. [Gr. *mykes,* fungus, and *logos,* discourse.]

**Myopy,** mī'o-pi, *n.* shortness or nearness of sight. —*adj.* **Myop'ic.** [Gr.—*myō,* to close, and *ōps,* the eye.]

**Myriad,** mir'i-ad, *n.* any immense number. [Gr. *myrias, myriados,* a ten thousand, allied to W. *mawr,* great, more, *myrdd,* an infinity.]

**Myriapod,** mir'i-a-pod, *n.* a worm-shaped articulate animal with many jointed legs. [Gr. *myrioi,* ten thousand, and *pous, podos,* foot.]

**Myrmidon,** mėr'mi-don, *n.* (*orig.*) one of a tribe of warriors who accompanied Achilles: one of a ruffianly band under a daring leader. [L. and Gr., derived, acc. to the fable, from *n.yrmēx,* an ant.]

**Myrrh,** mėr, *n.* a bitter aromatic, transparent gum, exuded from the bark of a shrub in Arabia. [Fr. *myrrhe—*L. and Gr. *myrrha—*Ar. *murr,* from *marra,* to be bitter.]

**Myrtle,** mėr'tl, *n.* an evergreen shrub with beautiful and fragrant leaves. [Fr. *myrtil,* dim. of *myrte—*L. and Gr. *myrtus—*Gr. *myron,* any sweet juice.]

**Myself,** mī-self' or me-self', *pron., I* or *me,* in person—used for the sake of emphasis and also as the reciprocal of *me.* [**My** and **Self.**]

**Mysterious,** mis-tē'ri-us, *adj.* containing *mystery*: obscure: secret: incomprehensible.—*adv.* **Myste'riously.**—*n.* **Myste'riousness.**

**Mystery,** mis'tėr-i, *n.* a *secret* doctrine: anything very obscure: that which is beyond human comprehension: anything artfully made difficult. [M. E. *mysterie,* from L. *mysterium—*Gr. *mystērion—mystēs,* one initiated—*mueō,* to initiate into mysteries—*muō,* to close the eyes—root *mu,* close. See **Mute,** dumb.]

**Mystery,** mis'tėr-i, *n.* a trade, handicraft: a kind of rude drama of a religious nature (so called because acted by craftsmen). [M. E. *mistere,* corr. from O. Fr. *mestier,* Fr. *métier—*L. *ministerium—minister.* Prop. spelt *mistery*; the spelling *mystery* is due to confusion with the above word. See **Minister.**]

**Mystic,** mis'tik, **Mystical,** mis'tik-al, *adj.* relating to or containing *mystery*: sacredly obscure or secret: involving a secret meaning: allegorical: belonging to mysticism.—*adv.* **Mys'tically.** [L. *mysticus—*Gr. *mystikos.* See **Mystery,** a secret doctrine.]

**Mystic,** mis'tik, *n.* one of a sect professing to have direct intercourse with the Spirit of God who revealed *mysteries* to them.

**Mysticism,** mis'ti-sizm, *n.* the doctrine of the *mystics*: obscurity of doctrine.

**Mystify,** mis'ti-fī, *v.t.* to make *mysterious,* obscure, or secret: to involve in mystery:—*pr.p.* mys'tifying; *pa.t.* and *pa.p.* mys'tified.—*n.* **Mystifica'tion.** [Fr. *mystifier,* from Gr. *mystēs,* and L. *facio,* to make.]

**Myth,** mith, *n.* a fable: a legend: a fabulous narrative founded on a remote event, esp. those made in the early period of a people's existence. [Gr. *mythos.*]

**Mythic,** mith'ik, **Mythical,** mith'ik-al, *adj.* relating to *myths*: fabulous.—*adv.* **Myth'ically.** [Gr. *mythikos.*]

**Mythologic,** mith-o-loj'ik, **Mythological,** mith-o-loj'ik-al. *adj.* relating to *mythology*: fabulous. —*adv.* **Mytholog'ically.**

**Mythologist,** mith-ol'o-jist, *n.* one versed in or who writes on *mythology.*

**Mythology,** mith-ol'o-ji, *n.* a system of myths: a treatise regarding myths: the science of myths. [Fr.—Gr. *mythologia—mythos,* and *logos,* a treatise.]

## N

**Nabob,** nā'bob, *n.* a *deputy* or governor under the Mogul empire: a European who has enriched himself in the East: any man of great wealth. [Corr. of Hindi *naiwâb,* a deputy; from Ar. *nawwab,* governors.]

**Nacre,** nā'kr, *n.* a white brilliant matter which forms the interior of several shells. [Fr.—Pers. *nigar,* painting.]

**Nadir,** nā'dir, *n.* the point of the heavens directly opposite and *corresponding* to the zenith. [Ar. *nadîr, nazir,* from *nazara,* to be like.]

**Nag,** nag, *n.* a horse, but particularly a small one. [Prob., with intrusive initial *n,* from Dan. *ög,* cog. with O. Saxon *ehu* (cf. L. *equa,* a mare).]

**Naiad,** nā'yad, *n.* a *water-nymph* or female deity, fabled to preside over rivers and springs. [L. and Gr. *naias, naiados,* from *naō,* to flow.]

**Nail,** nāl, *n.* the horny scale at the end of the human fingers and toes: the claw of a bird or

**other** animal : a pointed spike of metal for fastening wood : a measure of length (2¼ inches). —*v.t.* to fasten with nails. [A.S. *nægel* ; Ger. *nagel* ; allied to L. *unguis*, Gr. *o-nyx*, Sans. *nakha* ; all from a root seen in E. **Gnaw**, and sig. to pierce.]

**Nailer**, nāl′ėr, *n.* one whose trade is to make nails.

**Nailery**, nāl′ėr-i, *n.* a place where nails are made.

**Naïve**, nä′ēv, *adj.* with natural or unaffected simplicity : artless : ingenuous.—*adv.* **Na′ïvely.**—*n.* **Naïveté**, nä′ēv-tā. [Fr. *naïf*, *naïve*—L. *nativus*, native, innate, from *nascor*, *natus*, to be born.]

**Naked**, nā′ked, *adj.* uncovered : exposed : unarmed : defenceless : unconcealed : plain or evident : without addition or ornament : simple : artless : (*bot.*) without the usual covering.—*adv.* **Na′kedly.**—*n.* **Na′kedness.** [A.S. *nacod* ; Ger. *nackt*, Sans. *nagna*, L. *nudus*, naked ; all from a root found in M. E. *naken*, to lay bare.]

**Namby-pamby**, nam′bi-pam′bi, *adj.* weakly sentimental or affectedly pretty. [From first name of Ambrose Philips, an affected E. poet of the beginning of the 18th century.]

**Name**, nām, *n.* that by which a person or thing *is known* or called : a designation : reputed character : reputation : fame : celebrity : remembrance : a race or family : appearance : authority : behalf : assumed character of another : (*gram.*) a noun.—*v.t.* to give a name to : to designate : to speak of by name : to nominate.—*n.* **Nam′er.** [A.S. *nama* ; Ger. *name* ; L. *nomen*—*nosco*, to know ; Gr. *onoma* for *ognoma*, from *gna*, root of *gignōskō*, to know ; Sans. *nâman*—*jna*, to know.]

**Nameless**, nām′les, *adj.* without a name : undistinguished.—*adv.* **Name′lessly.**—*n.* **Name′lessness.**

**Namely**, nām′li, *adv.* by *name* : that is to say.

**Namesake**, nām′sāk, *n.* one bearing the same name as another for his *sake*. [**Name** and **Sake**.] [first made at *Nankin* in China.

**Nankeen**, nan-kēn′, *n.* a buff-coloured cotton cloth

**Nap**, nap, *n.* a short sleep.—*v.i.* to take a short sleep : to feel drowsy and secure :—*pr.p.* napp′ing ; *pa.p.* napped′ [A.S. *hnæppian*, to nap, orig. to nod ; cf. Ger. *nicken*, to nod.]

**Nap**, nap, *n.* the woolly substance on the surface of cloth : the downy covering of plants.—*adj.* **Napp′y.** [A.S. *hnoppa*, nap, a form of *cnæp*, a top, knob. See **Knob.**]

**Nape**, nāp, *n.* the *knob* or projecting joint of the neck behind. [A.S. *cnæp*, the top of anything, W. *cnap*, a knob. See **Knob.**]

**Napery**, nāp′ėr-i, *n.* linen, esp. for the table. [O. Fr. *naperie*—Fr. *nappe*, a table-cloth—Low L. *napa*, corr. from L. *mappa*, a napkin.]

**Naphtha**, nap′tha or naf′tha, *n.* a clear, inflammable liquid distilled from coal-tar : rock-oil. [L.—Gr.—Ar. *naft*.]

**Naphthaline**, nap′tha-lin or naf′-, *n.* a grayish-white, inflammable substance formed in the distillation of coal.

**Napkin**, nap′kin, *n.* a cloth for wiping the hands : a handkerchief. [Dim of Fr. *nappe*. See **Napery**.]

**Napless**, nap′les, *adj.* without nap : threadbare.

**Narcissus**, nar-sis′us, *n.* a genus of flowering plants comprising the daffodils, &c. having *narcotic* properties. [L.—Gr. *narkissos*—*narkē*, torpor.]

**Narcotic**, nar-kot′ik, *adj.* producing *torpor*, sleep, or deadness.—*n.* a medicine producing sleep or stupor.—*adv.* **Narcot′ically.** [Fr.—Gr. *narkē*, torpor.]

**Nard.** närd, *n.* an aromatic plant usually called **Spikenard** : an unguent prepared from it.—*adj.* **Nard′ine.** [Fr.—L. *nardus*—Gr. *nardos*—Pers. *nard*—Sans. *nalada*, from Sans. *nal*, to smell.]

**Narrate**, na-rāt′ or nar′-, *v.t.* to tell or recite : to give an account of.—*n.* **Narra′tion.** [Fr.—L. *narro*, *narratum*—*gnarus*, knewing—root *gna*.]

**Narrative**, nar′a-tiv, *adj.*, *narrating* : giving an account of any occurrence : inclined to narration : story-telling.—*n.* that which is narrated : a continued account of any occurrence : story.

**Narrow**, nar′ō, *adj.* of little breadth or extent : limited : contracted in mind : bigoted : not liberal : selfish : within a small distance : close : accurate : careful.—*n.* (oftener used in the *pl.*) a narrow passage, channel, or strait.—*v.t.* to make narrow : to contract or confine.—*v.i.* to become narrow.—*adv.* **Narr′owly.**—*n.* **Narr′owness.** [A.S. *nearu*, *nearo* ; not conn. with *near*, but prob. with *nerve*, *snare*.]

**Narrow-minded**, nar′ō-mīnd′ed, *adj.* of a *narrow* or illiberal *mind*.—*n.* **Narr′ow-mind′edness.**

**Narwhal**, när′hwal, **Narwal**, när′wal, *n.* the sea-unicorn, a mammal of the whale family with one large projecting tusk. [Dan. *narhval*—Ice. *nâhvalr*, either 'nose-whale' (*na-* for *nas-*, nose) or 'corpse-whale,' from the creature's pallid colour [Ice. *nâr* for *nar-*, corpse). See **Whale**.]

**Nasal**, nāz′al, *adj.* belonging to the *nose* : affected by or sounded through the nose.—*n.* a letter or sound uttered through the nose. [Fr., from L. *nasus*, the nose. See **Nose**.] [sound.

**Nasalise**, nā′zal-īz, *v.t.* to render *nasal*, as a

**Nascent**, nas′ent, *adj.*, *springing up* : arising : beginning to exist or grow. [L. *nascens*, *-entis*, pr.p. of *nascor*, *natus*, to be born, to spring up.]

**Nasturtium**, nas-tur′shi-um, *n.* a kind of cress with a pungent taste. [Lit. 'nose-tormenting,' L., from *nasus*, the nose, and *torqueo*, *tortum*, to twist, torment.]

**Nasty**, nas′ti, *adj.* dirty : filthy : obscene : nauseous.—*adv.* **Nas′tily.**—*n.* **Nas′tiness.** [Old form *nasky*—A.S. *hnesce*, soft ; cf. prov. Swed. *snaskig*, nasty, from *snaska*, to eat like a pig.]

**Natal**, nā′tal, *adj.* pertaining to *birth* : native. [Fr.—L. *natalis*—*nascor*, *natus*, to be born.]

**Natation**, na-tā′shun, *n.* swimming. [L. *natatio* —*nato*, to swim.]

**Natatory**, nā′ta-tor-i, *adj.* pertaining to swimming.

**Nation**, nā′shun, *n.* those *born* of the same stock : the people inhabiting the same country, or under the same government : a race : a great number. [Fr.—L. *nascor*, *natus*, to be born.]

**National**, nash′un-al, *adj.* pertaining to a *nation* : public : general : attached to one's own country. —*adv.* **Na′tionally.**—*n.* **Na′tionalness.**

**Nationalise**, nash′un-al-īz, *v.t.* to make *national*.

**Nationalism**, nash′un-al-izm, **Nationality**, nash-un-al′i-ti, *n.* the being attached to one's country : national character.—*n.* **Na′tionalist.**

**Native**, nā′tiv, *adj.* from or by *birth* : produced by nature : pertaining to the time or place of birth : original.—*n.* one born in any place : an original inhabitant.—*adv.* **Na′tively.**—*n.* **Na′tiveness.** [Fr.—L. *nativus*. See **Natal**.]

**Nativity**, na-tiv′i-ti, *n.* state of being *born* : time, place, and manner of birth : state or place of being produced : a horoscope.—**The Nativity**, the birthday of the Saviour.

**Natron**, nā′trun, *n.* an impure native carbonate of soda, the *nitre* of the Bible. [Fr.—L. *nitrum* —Gr. *nitron*.] [**Adder**.]

**Natterjack**, nat′ėr-jak, *n.* a species of toad. [See

**Natty**, nat′i, *adj.* trim, spruce. [Allied to **Neat**.]

**Natural,** nat′ū-ral, *adj.* pertaining to, produced by, or according to *nature*: inborn: not far-fetched: not acquired: tender: unaffected: illegitimate: (*music*) according to the usual diatonic scale.—*n.* an idiot: (*music*) a character (♮) which removes the effect of a preceding sharp or flat.—*adv.* Nat′urally.—*n.* Nat′uralness.—**Natural History,** originally the description of all that is in nature, now used of the sciences that deal with the earth and its productions—botany, zoology, and mineralogy, especially zoology.—**Natural Philosophy,** the science of nature, of the physical properties of bodies: physics.—**Natural Theology,** the body of theological truths discoverable by reason without revelation.

**Naturalise,** nat′ū-ral-īz, *v.t.* to make *natural* or familiar: to adapt to a different climate: to invest with the privileges of natural-born subjects.—*n.* Naturalisa′tion.

**Naturalism,** nat′ū-ral-izm, *n.* mere state of *nature*.

**Naturalist,** nat′ū-ral-ist, *n.* one who studies *nature*, more particularly animated nature.

**Nature,** nā′tūr, *n.* the power which creates and which presides over the material world: the established order of things: the universe: the essential qualities of anything: constitution: species: character: natural disposition: conformity to that which is natural: a mind, or character: nakedness. [Fr.—L. *natura—nascor, natus,* to be born—*gna,* a form of root *gen* = Gr. *gen,* to be born.]

**Naught,** nawt, *n., no-whit,* nothing.—*adv.* in no degree.—*adj.* of no value or account: worthless: bad. [A.S. *naht, na-wiht—na,* not, *wiht,* whit, anything.]

**Naughty,** nawt′i, *adj.* bad: mischievous: perverse.—*adv.* Naught′ily.—*n.* Naught′iness.

**Nausea,** naw′she-a, *n.* any sickness of the stomach, with a propensity to vomit: loathing. [L.—Gr. *nausia,* sea-sickness—*naus,* a ship.]

**Nauseate,** naw′she-āt, *v.i.* to *feel nausea:* to become squeamish: to feel disgust.—*v.t.* to loathe: to strike with disgust.

**Nauseous,** naw′she-us, *adj.* producing *nausea:* disgusting: loathsome.—*adv.* Nau′seously.—*n.* Nau′seousness.

**Nautical,** naw′tik-al, *adj.* pertaining to *ships,* sailors, or navigation: naval: marine.—*adv.* Nau′tically. [L. *nauticus*—Gr. *nautikos—naus;* cog. with which are Sans. *nau,* L. *navis,* a ship, A.S. *naca,* Ger. *nachen,* a boat.]

**Nautilus,** naw′ti-lus, *n.* a kind of shellfish furnished with a membrane which was once believed to enable it to sail like a *ship:—pl.* Nau′tiluses or Nau′tili. [L.—Gr. *nautilos.*]

**Naval,** nā′val, *adj.* pertaining to *ships:* consisting of ships: marine: nautical: belonging to the navy. [Fr.—L. *navalis—navis,* a ship.]

**Nave,** nāv, *n.* the middle or body of a church, distinct from the aisles or wings, so called from the resemblance of the roof to the hull of a *ship,* or because the church of Christ was often likened to a ship. [Fr. *nef*—L. *navis,* a ship. See **Nautical.**]

**Nave,** nāv, *n.* the hub or piece of wood, &c. in the centre of a wheel, through which the axle passes. [A.S. *nafu,* nave; cf. Dut. *naaf,* Ger. *nabe;* Sans. *nabhi,* nave, navel—prob. from *nabh,* to burst.]

**Navel,** nāv′l, *n.* the mark or depression in the centre of the lower part of the abdomen, at first, a *small projection.* [Dim. of **Nave,** a hub.]

**Navigable,** nav′i-ga-bl, *adj.* that may be passed by *ships* or vessels.—*n.* Nav′igableness.—*adv.* Nav′igably.

**Navigate,** nav′i-gāt, *v.t.* to steer or *manage a ship* in sailing: to sail on.—*v.i.* to go in a vessel or ship: to sail. [L. *navigo, -atum—navis,* a ship, and *ago,* to drive.]

**Navigation,** nav-i-gā′shun, *n.* the act, science, or art of sailing *ships.*

**Navigator,** nav′i-gāt-or, *n.* one who navigates or sails: one who directs the course of a ship.

**Navvy,** nav′i, *n.* (*orig.*) a labourer on canals for internal *navigation:* a labourer. [A contraction of **Navigator.**]

**Navy,** nā′vi, *n.* a fleet of *ships:* the whole of the ships-of-war of a nation: the officers and men belonging to the war-ships of a nation. [O. Fr. —L. *navis,* a ship.]

**Nay,** nā, *adv., no:* not only so: yet more.—*n.* denial. [M. E.—Ice. *nei,* Dan. *nei;* cog. with **No.**]

**Nazarene,** naz′ar-ēn, *n.* a follower of Jesus of Nazareth, originally used of Christians in contempt: one belonging to the early Christian sect of the Nazarenes. [From *Nazareth,* the town.]

**Nazarite,** naz′ar-īt, *n.* a Jew who vowed to abstain from strong drink, &c. [Heb. *nazar,* to consecrate.]      [tice of a *Nazarite.*

**Nazaritism,** naz′ar-īt-izm, *n.* the vow and prac-

**Naze,** nāz, *n.* a headland or cape. [Scand., as in Dan. *næs;* a doublet of **Ness.**]

**Neap,** nēp, *adj.* low, applied to the lowest tides. —*n.* a neap-tide. [A.S. *nep,* orig. *hnēp;* Dan. *knap,* Ice. *neppr,* scanty. From verb **Nip.**]

**Neaped,** nēpt, *adj.* left in the *neap*-tide or aground.

**Near,** nēr, *adj., nigh:* not far distant: intimate: dear: close to anything followed or imitated: direct: stingy.—*adv.* at a little distance: almost. —*v.t.* to approach: to come nearer to. [A.S. *near,* nearer, comp. of *neah,* nigh, now used as a positive; Ice. *nær;* Ger. *näher.* See **Nigh.**]

**Nearly,** nēr′li, *adv.* at no great distance: closely: intimately: pressingly: almost: stingily.

**Nearness,** nēr′nes, *n.* the state of being *near:* closeness: intimacy: close alliance: stinginess.

**Near-sighted,** nēr′-sīt′ed, *adj., seeing* only when *near:* short-sighted.—*n.* Near′-sight′edness.

**Neat,** nēt, *adj.* belonging to the bovine genus.— *n.* black-cattle: an ox or cow. [A.S. *neat,* cattle, a beast—*neotan, niotan,* to use, employ; Ice. *njotan,* Ger. *geniessen,* to enjoy; Scot. *nowt,* black-cattle.]

**Neat,** nēt, *adj.* trim: tidy: without mixture or adulteration.—*adv.* Neat′ly.—*n.* Neat′ness. [Fr. *net*—L. *nitidus,* shining—*niteo,* to shine: or perh. conn. with A.S. *neōd, neōdlice,* pretty.]

**Neatherd,** nēt′hèrd, *n.* one who *herds* or has the care of *neat* or cattle.

**Neb,** neb, *n.* the beak of a bird: the nose. [A.S. *nebb,* the face; cog. with Dut. *neb,* beak. The word orig. had an initial *s* like Dut. *sneb,* Ger. *schnabel,* and is conn. with **Snap, Snip.**]

**Nebula,** neb′ū-la, *n.* a *little cloud:* a faint, misty appearance in the heavens produced either by a group of stars too distant to be seen singly, or by diffused gaseous matter:—*pl.* Neb′ulæ. [L.; Gr. *nephelē,* cloud, mist.]

**Nebular,** neb′ū-lar, *adj.* pertaining to *nebulæ.*

**Nebulose,** neb′ū-lōs, **Nebulous,** neb′ū-lus, *adj.* misty, hazy, vague: relating to or having the appearance of a nebula.—*n.* Nebulos′ity.

**Necessary,** nes′es-sar-i, *adj.* needful: unavoidable: indispensable: not free.—*n.* a requisite— used chiefly in *pl.*—*adv.* Nec′essarily. [Fr.—

L. *necessarius*, which is either from root *nac*, seen in L. *nanciscor*, to obtain, Gr. *ēnegka*, to bear, or from *ne*, not, and *cedo, cessum*, to yield.]

**Necessitarian,** ne-ses-si-tā´ri-an, **Necessarian,** nes-es-sā´ri-an, *n.* one who holds the doctrine of *necessity*, denying freedom of will.

**Necessitate,** ne-ses´i-tāt, *v.t.* to make *necessary*: to render unavoidable: to compel. [L. *necessitas*.]

**Necessitous,** ne-ses´it-us, *adj.*, *in necessity*: very poor: destitute.—*adv.* **Necess´itously.**—*n.* **Necess´itousness.**

**Necessity,** ne-ses´i-ti, *n.* that which is *necessary* or unavoidable: compulsion: need: poverty.

**Neck,** nek, *n.* the part of an animal's body between the head and trunk: a long narrow part. [A.S. *hnecca*; Ger. *nacken*; prob. from root *angk*, to bend, as in **Anchor, Angle,** Sans. *ac, anc*, to bend.] [the *neck* by men.

**Neckcloth,** nek´kloth, *n.* a piece of *cloth* worn on

**Necked,** nekt, *adj.* having a neck.

**Neckerchief,** nek´ėr-chif, *n.* a *kerchief* for the *neck.*

**Necklace,** nek´lās, *n.* a *lace* or string of beads or precious stones worn on the *neck* by women.

**Necktie,** nek´tī, *n.* a *tie* or cloth for the *neck.*

**Neckverse,** nek´vėrs, *n.* the verse formerly read to entitle the person to benefit of clergy—said to be the first of the 51st Psalm.

**Necrologic,** nek-ro-loj´ik, **Necrological,** nek-ro-loj´ik-al, *adj.* pertaining to *necrology.*

**Necrologist,** nek-rol´o-jist, *n.* one who gives an account of *deaths.*

**Necrology,** nek-rol´o-ji, *n.* an *account* of the *dead*: a register of deaths. [Gr. *nekros*, dead, and *logos*, a discourse.]

**Necromancer,** nek´ro-man-sėr, *n.* one who practises necromancy: a sorcerer.

**Necromancy,** nek´ro-man-si, *n.* the art of *revealing future events* by communication with the *dead*: enchantment. [Gr. *nekromanteia*—*nekros*, and *manteia*, a prophesying—*mantis*, a prophet. For the mediæval spelling, *nigromancy*, see **Black-art**.]

**Necromantic,** nek-ro-man´tik, **Necromantical,** nek-ro-man´tik-al, *adj.* pertaining to necromancy: performed by necromancy.—*adv.* **Necroman´tically.**

**Necropolis,** nek-rop´o-lis, *n.* a cemetery. [Lit. 'a city of the dead,' Gr. *nekros*, and *polis*, a city.]

**Nectar,** nek´tar, *n.* the red wine or drink of the gods: a delicious beverage: the honey of the glands of plants. [L.—Gr. *nektar*; ety. dub.]

**Nectareal,** nek-tā´re-al, **Nectarean,** nek-tā´re-an, *adj.* pertaining to or resembling *nectar*: delicious.

**Nectared,** nek´tard, *adj.* imbued with *nectar*: mingled or abounding with nectar.

**Nectareous,** nek-tā´re-us, *adj.* pertaining to, containing, or resembling *nectar*: delicious.

**Nectarine,** nek´ta-rin, *adj.* sweet as *nectar.*—*n.* a variety of peach with a smooth fruit.

**Nectarous,** nek´tar-us, *adj.* sweet as *nectar.*

**Nectary,** nek´tar-i, *n.* the part of a flower which secretes the *nectar* or honey.

**Need,** nēd, *n.*, *necessity*: a state that requires relief: want.—*v.t.* to have occasion for: to want.—*n.* **Need´er.** [A.S. *nyd, nead*; Dut. *nood*, Ger. *noth*, Goth. *nauths*, orig. prob. sig. 'compulsion.']

**Needful,** nēd´fool, *adj.* full of *need*, needy: necessary: requisite.—*adv.* **Need´fully.**—*n.* **Need´fulness.**

**Needle,** nēd´l, *n.* a small, sharp-pointed steel

instrument, with an eye for a thread: anything like a needle, as the magnet of a compass. [A.S. *nædel*; Ice. *nal*, Ger. *nadel*; conn. with Ger. *nähen*, to sew, L. *nere*, Gr. *neein*, to spin.]

**Needlebook,** nēd´l-book, *n.* a number of pieces of cloth, arranged like a book, for holding needles.

**Needleful,** nēd´l-fool, *n.* as much thread as *fills* a needle.

**Needle-gun,** nēd´l-gun, *n.* a *gun* or rifle loaded at the breech with a cartridge containing powder and exploded by the prick of a needle.

**Needless,** nēd´les, *adj.*, *not needed*: unnecessary.—*adv.* **Need´lessly.**—*n.* **Need´lessness.**

**Needlewoman,** nēd´l-woom-an, *n.* a woman who makes her living by her needle, a seamstress.

**Needlework,** nēd´l-wurk, *n.* work done with a needle: the business of a seamstress.

**Needs,** nēdz, *adv.*, *of necessity*: indispensably. [A.S. *nedes*, of necessity, gen. of *nead*. See **Need.**] [**Need´ily.**—*n.* **Need´iness.**

**Needy,** nēd´i, *adj.* being in *need*: very poor.—*adv.*

**Ne´er,** nār, *adv.* contraction of **Never.**

**Neesing,** nēz´ing, *n.* (*B.*) old form of **Sneezing.**

**Nefarious,** ne-fā´ri-us, *adj.* impious: wicked in the extreme: villainous.—*adv.* **Nefa´riously.**—*n.* **Nefa´riousness.** [L. *nefarius*, contrary to divine law—*ne*, not, *fas*, divine law, prob. from *fari*, to speak.]

**Negation,** ne-gā´shun, *n.* act of *saying no*: denial: (*logic*) the absence of certain qualities in anything. [L. *negatio—nego, -atum*, to say no—*nec*, not, *aio*, to say yes.]

**Negative,** neg´a-tiv, *adj.* that *denies*: implying absence: that stops or restrains: (*logic*) denying the connection between a subject and predicate: (*algebra*) noting a quantity to be subtracted.—*n.* a proposition by which something is denied: (*gram.*) a word that denies.—*v.t.* to prove the contrary: to reject by vote.—*adv.* **Neg´atively.**—*n.* **Neg´ativeness.** [L. *negativus—nego*, to deny.]

**Neglect,** neg-lekt´, *v.t.* not to care for: to disregard: to omit by carelessness.—*n.* disregard: slight: omission. [L. *negligo, neglectum—nec*, not, *lego*, to gather, pick up.]

**Neglectful,** neg-lekt´fool, *adj.* careless: accustomed to omit or neglect things: slighting.—*adv.* **Neglect´fully.**—*n.* **Neglect´fulness.**

**Negligee,** neg-li-zhā´, *n.* easy undress: a plain, loose gown: a necklace, usually of red coral. [Fr. *négligé—négliger*, to neglect.]

**Negligence,** neg´li-jens, *n.* quality of being *negligent*: habitual neglect: carelessness: omission of duty. [Fr.—L. *negligentia—negligens, -entis*, pr.p. of *negligo*. See **Neglect.**]

**Negligent,** neg´li-jent, *adj.*, *neglecting*: careless: inattentive.—*adv.* **Neg´ligently.**

**Negotiable,** ne-gō´shi-a-bl, *adj.* that may be *negotiated* or transacted.—*n.* **Negotiabil´ity.**

**Negotiate,** ne-gō´shi-āt, *v.i.* to carry on *business*: to bargain: to hold intercourse for the purpose of mutual arrangement.—*v.t.* to arrange for by agreement: to pass, as a bill: to sell.—*n.* **Nego´tiator.** [L. *negotior, -atus—negotium*, business—*nec*, not, *otium*, leisure.]

**Negotiation,** ne-gō-shi-ā´shun, *n.* act of negotiating: the treating with another on business.

**Negotiatory,** ne-gō´shi-a-tor-i, *adj.* of or pertaining to *negotiation.*

**Negro,** nē´grō, *n.* one of the black race in Africa:—*fem.* **Ne´gress.** [Sp. *negro*—L. *niger*, black.]

**Negrohead,** nē´grō-hed, *n.* tobacco soaked in molasses and pressed into cakes, so called from its *blackness.*

**Negus**, nē′gus, *n.* a beverage of hot wine, water, sugar, nutmeg, and lemon-juice. [Said to be so called from Colonel *Negus*, its first maker, in the reign of Queen Anne.]

**Neigh**, nā, *v.i.* to utter the cry of a horse:— *pr.p.* neigh′ing ; *pa.t.* and *pa.p.* neighed′ (nād). —*n.* the cry of a horse. [A.S. *hnǣgan* ; Ice. *hneggja*, Scot. *nicher ;* from the sound. See **Nag.**]

**Neighbour**, nā′bur, *n.* a person who *dwells near* another.—*adj.* (*B.*) neighbouring.—*v.i.* to live near each other.—*v.t.* to be near to. [A.S. *neahbur, neahgebur*—A.S. *neah*, near, *gebur* or *bur*, a farmer. See **Boor.**]

**Neighbourhood**, nā′bur-hood, *n.* state of being neighbours : adjoining district.

**Neighbouring**, nā′bur-ing, *adj.* being *near*.

**Neighbourly**, nā′bur-li, *adj.* like or becoming a neighbour : friendly : social.—*adv.* **Neigh′-bourly.**—*n.* **Neigh′bourliness.**

**Neither**, nē′thèr or nī′thèr, *adj.*, *pron.*, or *conj.*, *not either.* [A.S. *nawther*, contr. of *ne-hwæther*—*na*, no, and *hwæther*, whether. Doublet **Nor.**]

**Nemesis**, nem′e-sis, *n.* (*myth.*) the goddess of *vengeance :* retributive justice. [Gr. *nemō*, to distribute.]

**Neolithic**, ne-o-lith′ik, *adj.* applied to the more *recent* of two divisions of the *stone* age, the other being **Palæolithic.** [Gr. *neos*, new, *lithos*, a stone.]

**Neologic**, ne-o-loj′ik, **Neological**, ne-o-loj′ik-al, *adj.* pertaining to *neology :* using new words.

**Neologise**, ne-ol′o-jīz, *v.i.* to introduce *new words.*

**Neologism**, ne-ol′o-jism, *n.* a *new word* or doctrine.

**Neologist**, ne-ol′o-jist, *n.* an *innovator* in *language :* an innovator in theology.

**Neology**, ne-ol′o-ji, *n.* the introduction of *new words* into a language : a new word or phrase : (*theol.*) new doctrines, esp. German rationalism. [Gr. *neos*, new, and *logos*, word.]

**Neophyte**, nē′o-fīt, *n.* a new convert : in R. Cath. Church, one newly admitted to the priesthood or to a monastery : a novice.—*adj.* newly entered on office. [L. *neophytus*—Gr. *neos*, new, *phytos*, grown—*phyō*, to produce.]

**Neozoic**, nē-o-zō′ik, *adj.* denoting all rocks from the Trias down to the most *recent formations*, as opposed to **Paleozoic.** [Gr. *neos*, new, *zoē*, life.]

**Nepenthe**, ne-pen′thē, **Nepenthes**, ne-pen′thēz, *n.* (*med.*) a drug that relieves pain : a genus of plants having a cup or pitcher attached to the leaf, often filled with a sweetish liquid, the pitcher plant. [Gr. *nēpenthēs*, removing sorrow —*nē*, priv., and *penthos*, grief, sorrow.]

**Nephew**, nev′ū or nef′ū, *n.* (*orig.*) a *grandson*—so in New Test.; the son of a brother or sister : —*fem.* **Niece.** [Fr. *neveu*—L. *nepos, nepotis*, grandson, nephew ; cog. with Sans. *napat*, Gr. *anepsios*, cousin, A.S. *nefa*, a nephew.]

**Nephralgia**, ne-fral′ji-a, **Nephralgy**, ne-fral′ji, *n.*, *pain* or disease of the *kidneys.* [Gr. *nephroi*, kidneys, *algos*, pain.]

**Nephrite**, nef′rīt, *n.* scientific name for **Jade**, a mineral used as a charm against *kidney* disease.

**Nephritic**, ne-frit′ik, **Nephritical**, ne-frit′ik-al, *adj.* pertaining to the *kidneys :* affected with a disease of the *kidneys :* relieving diseases of the kidneys.—*n.* **Nephrit′ic**, a medicine for the cure of diseases of the kidneys.

**Nephritis**, ne-frī′tis, *n.* inflammation of the kidneys.

**Nepotism**, nep′o-tizm, *n.* undue favouritism to one's relations, as in the bestowal of patronage.

—*n.* **Nep′otist**, one who practises nepotism. [L. *nepos, nepotis*, a grandson, nephew, descendant.]

**Neptune**, nep′tūn, *n.* (*myth.*) the god of the sea : (*astr.*) a large planet discovered in 1846. [L. *Neptunus*, from a root seen in Gr. *nipho*, L. *nimbus*, Zend *nápita*, wet, Sans. *nepa*, water.]

**Neptunian**, nep-tū′ni-an, *adj.* pertaining to the *sea :* formed by water : (*geol.*) applied to stratified rocks or to those due mainly to the agency of water, as opposed to Plutonic or igneous.

**Nereid**, nē′re-id, *n.* (*myth.*) a *sea-nymph*, one of the daughters of the sea-god Nereus, who attended Neptune riding on sea-horses : (*zool.*) a genus of marine worms like long myriapods. [L. *Nereis*—Gr. *Nēreis, -idos*—*Nēreus*, a sea-god ; akin to *neō*, to swim, *naō*, to flow, and Sans. *nara*, water.]

**Nerve**, nèrv, *n.* (*orig.*) a *tendon* or *sinew :* physical strength : firmness : courage : (*anat.*) one of the fibres which convey sensation from all parts of the body to the brain : (*bot.*) one of the fibres in the leaves of plants.—*v.t.* to give strength or vigour to : courage. [Fr.—L. *nervus ;* Gr. *neuron*, a sinew ; orig. form was with initial *s*, as in E. **Snare**, Ger. *schnur*, a lace or tie.]

**Nerveless**, nèrv′les, *adj.* without *nerve* or strength.

**Nervine**, nèrv′in, *adj.* acting on the *nerves :* quieting nervous excitement.—*n.* a medicine that soothes nervous excitement. [L. *nervinus.*]

**Nervous**, nèrv′us, *adj.* having *nerve :* sinewy : strong : vigorous : pertaining to the nerves : having the nerves easily excited or weak.—*adv.* **Nerv′ously.**—*n.* **Nerv′ousness**—**Nerv′ous sys′tem** (*anat.*) the brain, spinal chord, and nerves collectively. [Fr. *nerveux*—L. *nervosus.*]

**Nervous**, nèrv′us, **Nervose**, nèr-vōs′, **Nerved**, nèrvd′, *adj.* (*bot.*) having parallel fibres or veins.

**Nescience**, nesh′ens, *n.* want of knowledge. [L. *nescientia*—*nescio*, to be ignorant—*ne*, not, and *scio*, to know.]

**Ness**, nes, *n.* a promontory or headland. [A.S. *næs*, promontory ; a doublet of **Naze**, and prob. conn. with **Nose.**]

**Nest**, nest, *n.* the bed formed by a bird for hatching her young : the place in which the eggs of any animal are laid and hatched : a comfortable residence : the abode of a large number, often in a bad sense : a number of boxes each inside the next larger.—*v.i.* to build and occupy a nest. [A.S. *nest ;* Ger. *nest*, Gael. *nead ;* akin to L. *nidus*, for *nisdus*, Sans. *nida.*]

**Nestle**, nes′l, *v.i.* to lie close or snug as in a *nest :* to settle comfortably.—*v.t.* to cherish, as a bird her young. [A.S. *nestlian*—*nest.*]

**Nestling**, nest′ling, *adj.* being in the *nest*, newly hatched.—*n.* a young bird in the nest.

**Nestorian**, nes-tō′ri-an, *adj.* pertaining to the doctrine of *Nestorius*, patriarch of Constantinople : resembling *Nestor*, the aged warrior and counsellor mentioned in Homer : experienced : wise.

**Net**, net, *n.* an instrument of twine knotted into meshes for catching birds, fishes, &c. : anything like a net : a snare : a difficulty.—*v.t.* to form as network : to take with a net.—*v.i.* to form network :—*pr.p.* nett′ing ; *pa.t.* and *pa.p.* nett′ed. [A.S. *net, nett ;* Dan. *net*, Ger. *netz ;* ety. dub.]

**Net**, net, *adj.* clear of all charges or deductions : opposed to gross.—*v.t.* to produce as clear profit :—*pr.p.* nett′ing ; *pa.t.* and *pa.p.* nett′ed. [A.S. *nett*, another form of **Neat.**]

**Nether**, neth′er, *adj.*, *beneath* another, lower : infernal. [A.S. *neothera*, a comp. adj. due to adv. *nither*, downward ; Ger. *nieder*, low.]

**Nethermost**, neth′er-mōst, *adj.*, *most beneath*,

lowest. [A.S., a corr. of *nithemesta*, a doubled superl. of *nither*. For suffix *-most*, see After-most, Foremost.]

**Nethinim**, neth'in-im, *n.pl.* (*B.*) men *given* to the Levites to assist them. [Heb. *nathan*, to give.]

**Netting**, net'ing, *n.* act of forming *network*: a piece of network.

**Nettle**, net'l, *n.* a common plant covered with hairs which sting sharply.—*v.t.* to fret, as a nettle does the skin: to irritate. [A.S. *netele*; by some taken from same root as *needle*; more probably from Teut. base meaning 'scratch,' and akin to Gr. *knidē*, nettle. See also Nit.]

**Nettlerash**, net'l-rash, *n.* a kind of fever charac-terised by a *rash* or eruption on the skin like that caused by the sting of a *nettle*.

**Network**, net'wurk, *n.* a piece of *work* or a fabric formed like a *net*.

**Neural**, nū'ral, *adj.* pertaining to the *nerves*. [Gr. *neuron*, a nerve. See Nerve.]

**Neuralgia**, nū-ral'ji-a, **Neuralgy**, nū-ral'ji, *n.* *pain* in the *nerves*. [Gr. *neuron*, and *algos*, pain.]

**Neuralgic**, nū-ral'jik, *adj.* pertaining to *neuralgia*.

**Neurology**, nū-rol'o-ji, *n.* the *science* of the *nerves*. —*adj.* **Neurolog'ical.**—*n.* **Neurol'ogist**, a writer on neurology. [Gr. *neuron*, and *logos*, science.]

**Neuroptera**, nū-rop'tèr-a, *n.pl.* an order of insects which have generally four *wings* reticulated with many *nerves*. [Gr. *neuron*, nerve, *ptera*, pl. of *pteron*, a wing.]

**Neuropteral**, nū-rop'tèr-al, **Neuropterous**, nū-rop'tèr-us, *adj.*, *nerve-winged*: belonging to the neuroptera.

**Neurotic**, nū-rot'ik, *adj.* relating to or seated in the *nerves*.—*n.* a disease of the nerves: a medi-cine useful for diseases of the nerves.

**Neurotomy**, nū-rot'om-i, *n.* the *cutting* or dissec-tion of a nerve. [Gr. *neuron*, a nerve, and *tomē*, cutting.]

**Neuter**, nū'tèr, *adj.*, *neither*: taking no part with either side: (*gram.*) neither masculine nor feminine: (*bot.*) without stamens or pistils: (*zool.*) without sex.—*n.* one taking no part in a contest: (*bot.*) a plant having neither stamens nor pistils: (*zool.*) a sexless animal, esp. the working bee. [L.—*ne*, not, *uter*, either.]

**Neutral**, nū'tral, *adj.* being *neuter*, indifferent: unbiased: neither very good nor very bad: (*chem.*) neither acid nor alkaline.—*n.* a person or nation that takes no part in a contest.—*adv.* **Neu'trally.**—*n.* **Neutral'ity.** [L. *neutralis*—*neuter*, neither.]

**Neutralise**, nū'tral-īz, *v.t.* to render *neutral* or indifferent: to render of no effect.—*ns.* **Neu'traliser, Neutralisa'tion.**

**Never**, nev'èr, *adv.*, *not ever*: at no time: in no degree: not. [A.S. *næfre*—*ne*, not, and *æfre*, ever.]

**Nevertheless**, nev-èr-*th*e-les', *adv.*, *never* or *not the less*: notwithstanding: in spite of that. [Lit. 'never less on that account;' *the* = *thi*, the old instrumental case of *that*.]

**New**, nū, *adj.* lately made: having happened lately: recent: not before seen or known: strange: recently commenced: not of an ancient family: modern: as at first: unaccustomed: fresh from anything: uncultivated or recently cultivated.—*adv.* **New'ly.**—*n.* **New'ness.** [A.S. *niwe, neowe*; cog. with Ger. *neu*, Ir. *nuadh*, L. *novus*, Gr. *neos*, Sans. *nava*. Same as Now.]

**Newel**, nū'el, *n.* (*arch.*) the upright post about which the steps of a circular staircase wind. [O. Fr. *nual* (Fr. *noyau*), stone of fruit—L.

*nucalis*, like a nut—*nux*, *nucis*, a nut. See Nucleus.]

**Newfangled**, nū-fang'gld, *adj.* fond of new things: newly devised.—*n.* **Newfang'ledness.** [Corr. from Mid. E. *newefangel*—*new*, and the root of **Fang**, thus meaning 'ready to seize.']

**New-fashioned**, nū-fash'und, *adj.* newly fashioned: lately come into fashion.

**Newish**, nū'ish, *adj.* somewhat *new*: nearly new.

**News**, nūz, *n. sing.* something *new*: recent ac-count: fresh information of something that has just happened: intelligence.

**Newsboy**, nūz'boy, **Newsman**, nuz'man, *n.* a *boy* or *man* who delivers or sells *news*papers.

**Newsletter**, nūz'let-èr, *n.* an occasional *letter* or printed sheet containing *news*, the predecessor of the regular newspaper.

**Newsmonger**, nūz'mung-gėr, *n.* one who *deals* in *news*: one who spends much time in hearing and telling news. [**News** and **Monger.**]

**Newspaper**, nūz'pā-pèr, *n.* a *paper* published periodically for circulating *news*, &c.

**Newsroom**, nūz'rōōm, *n.* a *room* for the reading of *news*papers, magazines, &c.

**New-style**, nū'-stīl, *n.* the Gregorian as opposed to the Julian method of reckoning the calendar.

**Newsvender, Newsvendor**, nūz'vend'èr, *n.* a *vender* or seller of *news*papers.

**Newt**, nūt, *n.* a genus of amphibious animals like small lizards. [Formed with initial *n*, borrowed from the article *an*, from *ewt*—A.S. *efeta*.]

**Newtonian**, nū-tō'ni-an, *adj.* relating to, formed, or discovered by Sir Isaac *Newton*, the cele-brated philosopher, 1642–1727.

**New-year's-day**, nū'-yèrz-dā, *n.* the first *day* of the *new year*. [**New, Year,** and **Day.**]

**Next**, nekst, *adj.* (superl. of **Nigh**), nearest in place, time, &c.—*adv.* nearest or immediately after. [A.S. *neahst, nyhst*, superl. of *neah*, near; Ger. *nächst*. See **Near.**]

**Nexus**, nek'sus, *n.* a tie or connecting principle. [L., from *necto*, to bind.]

**Nib**, nib, *n.* something small and pointed: a point, esp. of a pen.—*adj.* **Nibbed'**, having a nib. [Same as **Neb.**]

**Nibble**, nib'l, *v.t.* to bite by small *nips*: to eat by little at a time.—*v.i.* to bite: to find fault.—*n.* **Nibb'ler.** [Freq. of **Nip**; but some connect it with **Nib.**]

**Nice**, nīs, *adj.* foolishly particular: hard to please: fastidious: requiring refinement of apprehen-sion or delicacy of treatment: exact: deli-cate: dainty: agreeable: delightful.—*adv.* **Nice'ly.** [O. Fr. *nice*, foolish, simple; from L. *nescius*, ignorant—*ne*, not, and *scio*, to know.]

**Nicene**, nī'sēn, *adj.* pertaining to the town of Nice or Nicæa, in Asia Minor, esp. in reference to an œcumenical council held there in 325, at which was drawn up a confession of faith, out of which the present Nicene Creed has grown.

**Niceness**, nīs'nes, *n.* exactness, scrupulousness: pleasantness.

**Nicety**, nīs'e-ti, *n.* quality of being *nice*: delicate management: exactness of treatment: delicacy of perception: fastidiousness: that which is delicate to the taste: a delicacy.

**Niche**, nich, *n.* a recess in a wall for a statue, &c. [Lit. a 'shell-like' recess, Fr.; from It. *nicchia*, a niche, *nicchio*, a shell—L. *mytilus*, *mitulus*, a sea-muscle. Cf. **Napery**, from L. *mappa*.]

**Niched**, nicht, *adj.* placed in a *niche*.

**Nick**, nik, *n.* a *notch* cut into something: a score for keeping an account: the precise moment of time.—*v.t.* to cut in notches : to hit the precise time. [Another spelling of **Nock**, old form of **Notch**.]

**Nick**, nik, *n.* the devil. [A.S. *nicor*, a water-spirit ; Ice. *nykr*, Ger. *nix*, *nixe*.]

**Nickel**, nik'el, *n.* a grayish-white metal, very malleable and ductile. [Sw. and Ger. ; from Sw. *kopparnickel*, Ger. *kupfernickel*, copper of Nick or *Nicholas*, because it was thought to be a *base* ore of *copper*.] [knack.]

**Nicknack**, nik'nak, *n.* a trifle. [Same as **Knick-**

**Nickname**, nik'nām, *n.* a name given in contempt or sportive familiarity.—*v.t.* to give a nickname to. [M. E. *neke-name*, with intrusive initial *n* from *eke-name*, surname ; from **Eke** and **Name**. Cf. Swed. *öknamn*, Dan. *ögenavn*.]

**Nicotian**, ni-kō'shi-an, *adj.* pertaining to tobacco, from *Nicot*, who introduced it into France in 1560.

**Nicotine**, nik'o-tin, *n.* a poisonous liquid forming the active principle of the tobacco plant.

**Nidification**, nid-i-fi-kā'shun, *n.* the act of *building* a *nest*, and the hatching and rearing of the young. [L. *nidus*, a nest, and *facio*, to make.]

**Niece**, nēs, *n.* (fem. of **Nephew**) the daughter of a brother or sister. [Fr. *nièce*—L. *neptis*, a granddaughter, niece, fem. of *nepos, nepotis*, a nephew.]

**Niggard**, nig'ard, *n.* a parsimonious person : a miser. [Ice. *hnöggr*, stingy ; Ger. *genau*, close, strict.]

**Niggard**, nig'ard, **Niggardly**, nig'ard-li, *adj.* having the qualities of a *niggard* : miserly.—*adv.* **Nigg'ardly**.—*n* **Nigg'ardliness**.

**Nigh**, nī, *adj.*, *near* : not distant : not remote in time, &c. : close.—*adv.* near : almost.—*prep.* near to : not distant from. [A.S. *neah, neh* ; Ice. *na*, Ger. *nahe*, Goth. *nehv*. See **Near**.]

**Night**, nīt, *n.* the time from sunset to sunrise : darkness : intellectual and moral darkness : a state of adversity : death. [A.S. *niht* ; Ger. *nacht*, Goth. *nahts* ; L. *nox*, Gr. *nux*, Sans. *nakta* ; all from a root *nak*, sig. to fail, disappear, found in Sans. *naç*, to disappear, L. *necare*, to kill, Gr. *nekus*, a corpse.]

**Nightcap**, nīt'kap, *n.* a *cap* worn at *night* in bed —so **Night'dress**, **Night'gown**, **Night'shirt**.

**Nightfall**, nīt'fawl, *n.* the *fall* or beginning of the *night*.

**Nightingale**, nīt'in-gāl, *n.* a small bird celebrated for its *singing* at *night*. [A.S. *nihtegale*—*niht*, night, and *galan*, to sing ; Ger. *nachtigall*.]

**Nightjar**, nīt'jär, **Nightchurr**, nīt'chur, *n.* the goatsucker, so called from its coming out at *night* and its *jarring* noise.

**Nightless**, nīt'les, *adj.* having no *night*.

**Nightly**, nīt'li, *adj.* done by *night* : done every night.—*adv.* by *night* : every night.

**Nightmare**, nīt'mār, *n.* a dreadful dream accompanied with pressure on the breast, and a feeling of powerlessness of motion or speech. [A.S. *niht*, night, and *mara*, a nightmare ; O. H. Ger. *mara*, incubus, Ice. *mara*, nightmare.]

**Nightpiece**, nīt'pēs, *n.* a *piece* of painting representing a *night*scene : a painting to be seen best by candle-light.

**Nightshade**, nīt'shād, *n.* a name of several plants having narcotic properties, often found in damp *shady* woods. [**Night** and **Shade**.]

**Night-walker**, nīt'-wawk'ér, *n.* one who *walks* in his sleep at *night* : one who walks about at night for bad purposes.

**Nightward**, nīt'ward, *adj.*, *toward* night.

**Nightwatch**, nīt'woch, *n.* a *watch* or guard at *night* : time of watch in the night.

**Nigrescent**, nī-gres'ent, *adj.*, *growing black* or

dark: approaching to blackness. [L. *nigrescens*, pr.p. of *nigresco*, to grow black—*niger*, black.]

**Nihilism**, nī'hi-lizm, *n.* belief in *nothing*, extreme scepticism : in Russia, the system of certain socialists, most of whom seek to overturn all the existing institutions of society in order to build it up anew on different principles. [Name given by their opponents, from L. *nihil*, nothing.]

**Nihilists**, nī'hi-lists, *n.* those who profess nihilism.

**Nil**, nil, *n.* nothing. [L. contr. of *nihil*.]

**Nimble**, nim'bl, *adj.* light and quick in motion : active : swift.—*adv.* **Nim'bly**.—*n.* **Nim'bleness**. [A.S. *numol*, capable, quick at catching, from *niman* (Ger. *nehmen*), to take.]

**Nimbus**, nim'bus, *n.* the raincloud : (*paint.*) the circle of rays round the heads of saints, &c. [L.]

**Nincompoop**, nin'kom-poop, *n.* a simpleton. [Corruption of L. *non compos* (*mentis*), not of sound mind.]

**Nine**, nīn, *adj.* and *n.* eight and one. [A.S. *nigon* ; Dut. *negen*, Goth. *niun*, L. *novem*, Gr. *ennea*, Sans. *navan*.] [repeated.]

**Ninefold**, nīn'fōld, *adj.*, *nine* times *folded* or

**Nineholes**, nīn'hōlz, *n.* a game in which a ball is to be bowled into *nine holes* in the ground.

**Ninepins**, nīn'pinz, *n.* skittles, so called from *nine pins* being used.

**Nineteen**, nīn'tēn, *adj.* and *n.*, *nine* and *ten*. [A.S. *nigontyne*—*nigon*, nine, *tyn*, ten.]

**Nineteenth**, nīn'tēnth, *adj.* the *ninth* after the *tenth* : being one of nineteen equal parts.—*n.* a nineteenth part. [A.S. *nigonteotha*—*nigon*, nine, *teotha*, tenth.]

**Ninetieth**, nīn'ti-eth, *adj.* the last of *ninety* : next after the eighty-ninth.—*n.* a ninetieth part.

**Ninety**, nīn'ti, *adj.* and *n.*, *nine tens* or nine times ten. [A.S. *nigon*, nine, and *tig*, ten.]

**Ninny**, nin'i, *n.* a simpleton : a fool. [It. *ninno*, child ; Sp. *nino*, infant ; imitated from the lullaby, *ninna-nanna*, for singing a child to sleep.]

**Ninth**, nīnth, *adj.* the last of *nine* : next after the 8th.—*n.* one of nine equal parts. [A.S. *nigotha*.]

**Ninthly**, nīnth'li, *adv.* in the *ninth* place.

**Nip**, nip, *v.t.* to *pinch* : to cut off the edge : to check the growth or vigour of : to destroy :—pr.p. nipp'ing ; *pa.t.* and *pa.p.* nipped'.—*n.* a pinch : a seizing or closing in upon : a cutting off the end : a blast : destruction by frost.—*adv.* **Nipp'ingly**. [From root of **Knife** ; found also in Dut. *knijpen*, Ger. *kneipen*, to pinch.]

**Nipper**, nip'ér, *n.* he or that which *nips* : one of the 4 fore-teeth of a horse :—in *pl.* small pincers.

**Nipple**, nip'l, *n.* the pap by which milk is drawn from the breasts of females : a teat : a small projection with an orifice, as the nipple of a gun. [A dim. of **Neb** or **Nib**.]

**Nit**, nit, *n.* the egg of a louse or other small insect. —*adj.* **Nit'ty**, full of nits. [A.S. *hnitu* ; Ice. *nitr*, Ger. *niss*.]

**Nitrate**, nī'trāt, *n.* a salt of *nitric* acid.—*adj.* **Ni'trated**, combined with nitric acid. [Fr.—L. *nitratus*.]

**Nitre**, nī'tér, *n.* the nitrate of potash, also called saltpetre.—**Cubic Nitre**, nitrate of soda, so called because it crystallises in cubes. [Fr.—L. *nitrum*—Gr. *nitron*, natron, potash, soda—Ar. *nitrun, natrun*.]

**Nitric**, nī'trik, *adj.* pertaining to, containing, or resembling nitre.

**Nitrify**, nī'tri-fī, *v.t.* to convert into *nitre*.—*v.i.* to become nitre :—pr.p. nī'trifying ; *pa.t.* and *pa.p.* nī'trified.—*n.* **Nitrifica'tion**. [L. *nitrum*, and *facio*, to make.]

**Nitrite,** nī'trīt, *n.* a salt of *nitrous* acid.

**Nitrogen,** nī'tro-jen, *n.* a gas forming nearly four-fifths of common air, so called from its being an essential constituent of *nitre.—adj.* **Nitrog'-enous.** [Gr. *nitron*, and *gennaō*, to generate.]

**Nitro-glycerine,** nī'tro-glis'ėr-in, *n.* an explosive compound produced by the action of *nitric* and sulphuric acids on *glycerine.* [*nitre.*

**Nitrous,** nī'trus, *adj.* resembling or containing **Nitry,** nī'tri, *adj.* of or producing *nitre.* [*nitre.*]

**No,** nō, *adj., not* any : not one : none. [Short for **None.**]

**No,** nō, *adv.* the word of refusal or denial. [A.S. *na,* compounded of *ne,* not, and *á,* ever ; O. Ger. *ni* ; Goth. *ni,* Sans. *na.*]

**Noachian,** nō-ā'ki-an, *adj.* pertaining to *Noah* the patriarch, or to his time.

**Nob,** nob, *n.* a superior sort of person. [A familiar contr. of **Nobleman.**]

**Nobility,** no-bil'i-ti, *n.* the quality of being *noble* : rank : dignity : excellence : greatness : antiquity of family : descent from noble ancestors : the peerage.

**Noble,** nō'bl, *adj.* illustrious : exalted in rank : of high birth : magnificent : generous : excellent. *—n.* a person of exalted rank : a peer : an obs. gold coin = 6s. 8d. sterling.*—adv.* **No'bly.** [Fr. *—*L. *nobilis,* obs. *gnobilis—nosco* (*gnosco*), to know.]

**Nobleman,** nō'bl-man, *n.* a man who is noble or of rank : a peer : one above a commoner.

**Nobleness,** nō'bl-nes, *n.* the quality of being noble : dignity : greatness : ingenuousness : worth. [a person of no account.

**Nobody,** nō'bod-i, *n.* no body or person : no one :

**Nocturn,** nok'turn, *n.* a religious service at *night.* [Fr. *nocturne—*L. *nocturnus—nox, noctis,* night.]

**Nocturnal,** nok-tur'nal, *adj.* pertaining to *night* : happening by night : nightly.*—n.* an instrument for observations in the night.*—adv.* **Noctur'-nally.**

**Nod,** nod, *v.i.* to give a quick forward motion of the head : to bend the head in assent : to salute by a quick motion of the head : to let the head drop in weariness.*—v.t.* to incline : to signify by a nod*—pr.p.* nodd'ing ; *pa.t.* and *pa.p.* nodd'ed.*—n.* a bending forward of the head quickly : a slight bow : a command. [From a Teut. root found in prov. Ger. *notteln,* to wag, Ice. *hnjotha,* to hammer ; cf. **Nudge.**]

**Nodal,** nōd'al, *adj.* pertaining to *nodes.* [See **Node.**]

**Nodated,** nōd-āt'ed, *adj., knotted.* [See **Node.**]

**Nodding,** nod'ing, *adj.* inclining the head quickly : indicating by a nod. [See **Nod.**]

**Noddle,** nod'l, *n.* properly, the *projecting* part at the back of the head : the head. [A dim. from root of **Knot** ; cf. O. Dut. *knodde,* a knob.]

**Noddy,** nod'i, *n.* one whose *head nods* from weakness : a stupid fellow : a sea-fowl, so called from the *stupidity* with which it allows itself to be taken. [See **Nod.**]

**Node,** nōd, *n.* a *knot* : a knob : (*astr.*) one of the two points at which the orbit of a planet intersects the ecliptic : (*bot.*) the joint of a stem : the plot of a piece in poetry. [L. *nodus* (for *gnodus*), allied to **Knot.**]

**Nodose,** nōd'ōs, *adj.* full of *knots* : having knots or swelling joints : knotty.

**Nodule,** nod'ūl, *n.* a little *knot* : a small lump.

**Noggin,** nog'in, *n.* a small mug or wooden cup. [Ir. *noigin,* Gael. *noigean.*]

**Noise,** noiz, *n.* sound of any kind : any over-loud or excessive sound, 'din : frequent or public talk.*—v.t.* to spread by rumour.*—v.i.* to sound loud. [Fr. *noise,* quarrel, Provençal *nausa ;* prob. from L. *nausea,* disgust, annoyance ; but possibly from L. *noxa,* that which hurts—*noceo,* to hurt.]

**Noiseless,** noiz'les, *adj.* without noise : silent.*—adv.* **Noise'lessly.—***n.* **Noise'lessness.**

**Noisome,** noi'sum, *adj.* injurious to health : disgusting.*—adv.* **Noi'somely.—***n.* **Noi'someness.**

**Noisy,** noiz'i, *adj.* making a loud *noise* or sound : clamorous : turbulent.*—adv.* **Nois'ily.—***n.* **Nois'-iness.**

**Nomad, Nomade,** nom'ad or nō'mad, *n.* one of a tribe that wanders about in quest of game, or of pasture. [Gr. *nomas, nomados—nomos,* pasture—*nemō,* to deal out, to drive to pasture.]

**Nomadic,** no-mad'ik, *adj.* of or for the *feeding* of cattle : pastoral : pertaining to the life of nomads : rude.*—adv.* **Nomad'ically.**

**Nomenclator,** nō'men-klā-tor, *n.* one who *gives names* to things.*—fem.* **No'menclatress.** [L.— *nomen,* a name, and *calo,* Gr. *kalō,* to call.]

**Nomenclature,** nō'men-klā-tūr, *n.* a system of naming : a list of names : a *calling* by *name* : the peculiar terms of a science.

**Nominal,** nom'in-al, *adj.* pertaining to a *name* : existing only in name : having a name.*—adv.* **Nom'inally.** [L. *nominalis—nomen, -inis,* a name.]

**Nominalism,** nom'in-al-izm, *n.* the doctrine that general terms have no corresponding reality either in or out of the mind, being mere words. [From L. *nomen,* a name.]

**Nominalist,** nom'in-al-ist, *n.* one of a sect of philosophers who held the doctrine of nominalism.

**Nominate,** nom'in-āt, *v.t.* to *name* : to appoint : to propose by name. [L. *nomino, -atum,* to name—*nomen.*]

**Nomination,** nom-in-ā'shun, *n.* the act or power of nominating : state of being nominated.

**Nominative,** nom'in-a-tiv, *adj., naming* : (*gram.*) applied to the case of the subject.*—n.* the naming case, the case of the subject.

**Nominator,** nom'in-āt-or, *n.* one who nominates.

**Nominee,** nom-in-ē', *n.* one *nominated* by another : one on whose life depends an annuity or lease : one to whom the holder of a copyhold estate surrenders his interest.

**Non,** non, *adv., not,* a Latin word used as a prefix, as in **Non-appear'ance, Non-attend'ance, Non-compli'ance.**

**Nonage,** non'āj, *n.* the state of being *not of age* : the time of life before a person becomes legally of age : minority.*—adj.* **Non'aged.** [L. *non,* not, and **Age.**]

**Nonagenarian,** non-a-je-nā'ri-an, *n.* one *ninety* years old. [L. *nonagenarius,* containing ninety *—nonaginta,* ninety—*novem,* nine.]

**Nonce,** nons, *n.* (only in phrase 'for the nonce') the present time, occasion. [The substantive has arisen by mistake from ' for the nones,' originally *for then ones,* meaning simply ' for the once ;' the *n* belongs to the dative of the article.]

**Non-commissioned,** non-kom-ish'und, *adj. not* having a *commission,* as an officer in the army or navy below the rank of lieutenant.

**Non-conductor,** non-kon-dukt'or, *n.* a substance which does *not conduct* or transmit certain properties or conditions, as heat or electricity.

**Nonconforming,** non-kon-form'ing, *adj., not conforming,* especially to an established church.

**Nonconformist,** non-kon-form'ist, *n.* one who does

*not conform:* especially one who refused to conform to the established church at the restoration of Charles II.

**Nonconformity,** non-kon-form′i-ti, *n.* want of *conformity,* esp. to the established church.

**Non-content,** non′-con-tent or non-kon-tent′, *n.* one *not content:* in House of Lords, one giving a negative vote.

**Nondescript,** non′de-skript, *adj.* novel : odd.—*n.* anything *not* yet *described* or classed : a person or thing not easily described or classed. [L. *non,* not, and *descriptus,* described. See **Describe.**]

**None,** nun, *adj.* and *pron., not one :* not any : not the smallest part. [A.S. *nan—ne,* not, and *an,* one.]

**Nonentity,** non-en′ti-ti, *n.* want of *entity* or being : a thing not existing.

**Nones,** nōnz, *n.sing.* in the Roman calendar, the *ninth* day before the ides—the 5th of Jan., Feb., April, June, Aug., Sept., Nov., Dec., and the 7th of the other months : in R. Cath. Church, a season of prayer observed at *noon.* [L. *nonæ—nonus* for *novenus,* ninth—*novem,* nine.]

**Nonesuch,** nun′such, *n.* a thing like which there is *none such :* an extraordinary thing.

**Nonjuring,** non-jōōr′ing, *adj., not swearing* allegiance. [L. *non,* not, and *juro,* to swear.]

**Nonjuror,** non-jōōr′or or non′jōōr-or, *n.* one who would *not swear* allegiance to the government of England at the Revolution of 1688.

**Nonpareil,** non-pa-rel′, *n.* a person or thing *without an equal:* unequalled excellence : a rich kind of apple : a small printing type.—*adj.* without an equal : matchless. [Fr.—*non,* not, and *pareil,* equal—Low L. *pariculus,* dim. of *par,* equal.]

**Nonplus,** non′plus, *n.* a state in which *no more* can be done or said : great difficulty.—*v.t.* to throw into complete perplexity : to puzzle :—*pr.p.* non′plusing or non′plussing ; *pa.t.* and *pa.p.* non′plused or non′plussed. [L. *non,* not, and *plus,* more.]

**Nonsense,** non′sens, *n.* that which has *no sense :* language without meaning : absurdity : trifles. [L. *non,* not, and **Sense.**]

**Nonsensical,** non-sens′ik-al, *adj., without sense :* absurd.—*adv.* **Nonsens′ically.**—*n.* **Nonsens′-icalness.**

**Nonsuit,** non′sūt, *n.* a *withdrawal* of a *suit* at law, either voluntarily or by the judgment of the court.—*v.t.* to record that a plaintiff drops his suit. [L. *non,* not, and **Suit.**]

**Noodle,** nōō′dl, *n.* a simpleton, a blockhead. [See **Noddy.**]

**Nook,** nōōk, *n.* a *corner:* a narrow place formed by an angle : a recess : a secluded retreat. [Scot. *neuk ;* from Gael., Ir. *niuc.*]

**Noon,** nōōn, *n.* (*orig.*) the *ninth* hour of the day, or three o'clock P.M.: afterwards (the church service for the ninth hour being shifted to mid-day) mid-day : twelve o'clock : middle : height.—*adj.* belonging to mid-day : meridional. [A.S. *non-tid* (noontide)—L. *nona* (*hora*), the ninth (hour). See its doublet **Nones.**]

**Noonday,** nōōn′dā, *n.* mid-day.—*adj.* pertaining to mid-day : meridional.

**Noontide,** nōōn′tīd, *n.* the tide or time of noon : mid-day.—*adj.* pertaining to noon : meridional.

**Noose,** nōōz or nōōs, *n.* a running *knot* which ties the firmer the closer it is drawn.—*v.t.* to tie or catch in a noose. [Prob. from O. Fr. *nous,* plur. of *nou* (Fr. *nœud*)—L. *nodus,* knot.]

**Nor,** nor, *conj.* a particle marking the second or subsequent part of a negative proposition :—cor-

relative to **Neither** or **Not.** [Contr. from *nother,* a form of **Neither.**]

**Normal,** nor′mal, *adj.* according to *rule:* regular : analogical : perpendicular.—*n.* a perpendicular. —*adv.* **Nor′mally.** [L. *normalis—norma,* a rule.]

**Norman,** nor′man, *n.* a native or inhabitant of Normandy.—*adj.* pertaining to the Normans or to Normandy. [The invading *Northmen* from Scandinavia gave their name to Normandy.]

**Norse,** nors, *adj.* pertaining to ancient Scandinavia.—*n.* the language of ancient Scandinavia. [Norw. *Norsk* (= *Northisk*), from **North.**]

**North,** north, *n.* the point opposite the sun at noon : one of the four cardinal points of the horizon. [A.S. *north ;* found in most Teut. tongues, as in Ice. *northr,* Ger. *nord.*]

**North-east,** north-ēst′, *n.* the point between the north and east, equidistant from each.—*adj.* belonging to or from the north-east.

**North-easterly,** north-ēst′ér-li, *adj.* toward or coming from the north-east.

**North-eastern,** north-ēs′tèrn, *adj.* belonging to the north-east : being in the north-east, or in that direction. [the north-east.

**North-eastward,** north-ēst′ward, *adv.* towards

**Northerly,** north′ér-li, *adj.* being toward the north : from the north.—*adv.* toward or from the north.

**Northern,** north′érn, *adj.* pertaining to the north : being in the north or in the direction towards it. —*n.* an inhabitant of the north.

**Northernmost,** north′érn-mōst, **Northmost,** north′-mōst, *adj.* situate at the point furthest north.

**North-star,** north′-stär, *n.* the north polar star.

**Northward,** north′ward, **Northwardly,** north′-ward-li, *adj.* being toward the north.—*adv.* (also **North′wards**) toward the north.

**North-west,** north-west′, *n.* the point between the north and west, equidistant from each.—*adj.* pertaining to or from the north-west.

**North-westerly,** north-west′ér-li, *adj.* toward or from the north-west.

**North-western,** north-west′érn, *adj.* pertaining to or being in the north-west or in that direction.

**Norwegian,** nor-wē′ji-an, *adj.* pertaining to *Norway.*—*n.* a native of Norway.

**Nose,** nōz, *n.* the organ of smell : the power of smelling : sagacity.—*v.t.* to smell : to oppose rudely to the face : to sound through the nose. [A.S. *nosu ;* Ice. *nös,* Ger. *nase,* L. *nasus,* Sans. *nâsâ.*]

**Nosebag,** nōz′bag, *n.* a *bag* for a horse's *nose,* containing oats, &c. [**Nose** and **Bag.**]

**Nosegay,** nōz′gā, *n.* a bunch of fragrant flowers : a posy or bouquet. [From **Nose** and **Gay,** *adj.*]

**Noseless,** nōz′les, *adj.* without a nose.

**Nosology,** nos-ol′o-ji, *n.* the *science* of *diseases:* the branch of medicine which treats of the classification and nomenclature of diseases.—*adj.* **Nosolog′ical.**—*n.* **Nosol′ogist.** [Gr. *nosos,* a disease, and *logos,* a discourse, an account.]

**Nostril,** nos′tril, *n.* one of the *holes* of the *nose.* [M. E. *nosethirl*—A.S. *nosthyrl—nos,* for *nosu,* the nose, and *thyrel,* an opening. Cf. **Drill,** to pierce, and **Thrill.**]

**Nostrum,** nos′trum, *n.* a medicine the composition of which is kept secret : a quack or patent medicine. [L. (*lit.*) ' our own,' from *nos,* we.]

**Not,** not, *adv.* a word expressing denial, negation, or refusal. [Same as **Naught,** from A.S. *ne,* and *wiht,* a whit.] [notable person or thing.

**Notability,** nōt-a-bil′i-ti, *n.* the being *notable:* a

**Notable,** nōt′a-bl, *adj.* worthy of being *known* or

*noted:* remarkable: memorable: distinguished: notorious.—*n.* a person or thing worthy of note.—*adv.* Not'ably.—*n.* Not'ableness.

Notary, nōt'ar-i, *n.* in ancient Rome, one who took *notes*, a shorthand writer: an officer authorised to certify deeds or other writings.—*adj.* Nota'rial.—*adv.* Nota'rially. [L. *notarius.*]

Notation, nō-tā'shun, *n.* a *noting* or marking: the act or practice of recording by marks or symbols: a system of signs or symbols. [L. *notatio*—*noto, notatum,* to mark.]

Notch, noch, *n.* a *nick* cut in anything: an indentation.—*v.t.* to cut a hollow into. [From a Teut. root, found also in O. Dut. *nock.* See Nick, a notch.]

Note, nōt, *n.* that by which a person or thing is *known:* a mark or sign: a brief explanation: a short remark: a memorandum: a short letter: a diplomatic paper: (*mus.*) a mark representing a sound, also the sound itself: a paper acknowledging a debt and promising payment, as a bank-note, a note of hand: notice, heed, observation: reputation: fame.—*v.t.* to make a note of: to notice: to attend to: to record in writing: to furnish with notes. [Fr.,—L. *nota,* from *gna,* root of *nosco, notum,* to know.]

Noted, nōt'ed, *adj., marked:* well known: celebrated: eminent: notorious.—*adv.* Not'edly.

Noteless, nōt'les, *adj.* not attracting notice.

Noteworthy, nōt'wur-*th*i, *adj.* worthy of note or notice.

Nothing, nuth'ing, *n., no thing:* non-existence: absence or negation of being: no part or degree: a low condition: no value or use: not anything of importance, a trifle: utter insignificance, no difficulty or trouble: no magnitude: a cipher.—*adv.* in no degree: not at all.—*n.* Noth'ingness.

Notice, nōt'is, *n.* act of *noting:* attention: observation: information: warning: a writing containing information: public intimation: civility or respectful treatment: remark.—*v.t.* to mark or see: to regard or attend to: to mention, or make observations upon: to treat with civility. [Fr.,—L. *notitia*—*nosco, notum,* to know.]

Noticeable, nōt'is-a-bl, *adj.* able to be *noticed:* worthy of observation.—*adv.* Not'iceably.

Notification, nōt-i-fi-kā'shun, *n.* the act of notifying: the notice given: the paper containing the notice. [See Notify.]

Notify, nōt'i-fī, *v.t.* to *make known:* to declare: to *give notice* or information of:—*pa.t.* and *pa.p.* nōt'ified. [Fr.,—L. *notifico, -atum—notus,* known, and *facio,* to make.]

Notion, nō'shun, *n.* a conception: opinion: belief: judgment. [Fr.,—L. *notio—nosco, notum,* to know.]    [*notion:* ideal: fanciful.

Notional, nō'shun-al, *adj.* of the nature of a

Notoriety, nō-to-rī'e-ti or no-, *n.* state of being *notorious:* publicity: public exposure.

Notorious, no-tō'ri-us, *adj.* publicly *known* (now used in a bad sense): infamous.—*adv.* Noto'riously.—*n.* Noto'riousness. [Low L. *notorius*—*noto, notatum,* to mark—*nosco.*]

Notwithstanding, not-with-stand'ing, *conj.* and *prep.* (this) *not standing against* or opposing: nevertheless: however. [Not and Withstanding, *pr.p.* of Withstand.]

Nought, nawt, *n., not anything:* nothing.—*adv.* in no degree.—Set at nought, to despise. [Same as Naught.]

Noun, nown, *n.* (*gram.*) the *name* of anything. [O. Fr. *non* (Fr. *nom*)—L. *nomen.* See Name.]

Nourish, nur'ish, *v.t.* to *suckle:* to feed or bring up: to support: to encourage: to cherish: to educate.—*n.* Nour'isher.—*adj.* Nour'ishable, able to be nourished. [Fr. *nourrir*—L. *nutrio.*]

Nourishment, nur'ish-ment, *n.* the act of *nourishing* or the state of being nourished: that which nourishes: food: nutriment.

Novel, nov'el, *adj., new:* unusual: strange.—*n.* that which is new: a fictitious tale: a romance. [O. Fr. *novel* (Fr. *nouveau*)—L. *novellus—novus.*]

Novelette, nov-el-et', *n.* a small novel.

Novelist, nov'el-ist, *n.* a novel-writer. [Orig. an introducer of *new* things.]    [strange.

Novelty, nov'el-ti, *n., newness:* anything new or

November, nō-vem'bėr, *n.* the eleventh month of our year. [The *ninth* month of the Roman year; L., from *novem,* nine.]

Novennial, nō-ven'yal, *adj.* done every *ninth* year. [L. *novennis—novem,* nine, *annus,* a year.]

Novice, nov'is, *n.* one *new* in anything: a beginner: one newly received into the church: an inmate of a convent or nunnery who has not yet taken the vow. [Fr.,—L. *novitius—novus,* new.]

Novitiate, nō-vish'i-āt, *n.* the state of being a *novice:* the period of being a novice: a novice. [Low L. *novitiatus.*]

Now, now, *adv.* at the present time: at this time or a little before.—*conj.* but: after this: things being so.—*n.* the present time.—Now—now, at one time, at another time. [A.S. *nu;* Ger. *nun,* L. *nunc,* Gr. *nun,* Sans. *nu,* a doublet of New.]

Nowadays, now'a-dāz, *adv.* in days now present.

Noway, nō'wā, Noways, nō'wāz, *adv.* in no way. manner, or degree.

Nowhere, nō'hwār, *adv.* in no where or place.

Nowise, nō'wīz, *adv.* in *no way* or degree.

Noxious, nok'shus, *adj., hurtful:* unwholesome: injurious: destructive: poisonous.—*adv.* Nox'iously.—*n.* Nox'iousness. [L. *noxius—noxa,* hurt—*noceo,* to hurt.]

Nozzle, noz'l, *n.* a *little nose:* the snout: the extremity of anything: an extremity with an orifice. [Dim. of Nose.]

Nuance, nōō-äns', *n.* a delicate degree or *shade* of difference perceived by any of the senses, or by the intellect. [Through Fr. from L. *nubes,* a cloud.]

Nucleated, nū'kle-āt-ed, *adj.* having a *nucleus.*

Nucleus, nū'kle-us, *n.* the central mass round which matter gathers: (*astr.*) the head of a comet :—*pl.* Nuclei (nū'kle-ī). [Lit. 'the kernel of a nut,' L. from *nux, nucis,* a nut.]

Nude, nūd, *adj., naked:* bare: void.—*adv.* Nude'ly. [L. *nudus.* See Naked.]

Nudge, nuj, *n.* a gentle push.—*v.t.* to push gently. [Akin to Knock, Knuckle. Cf. Dan. *knuge.*]

Nudity, nūd'i-ti, *n., nakedness* :—*pl.* naked parts: figures divested of drapery.

Nugatory, nū'ga-tor-i, *adj., trifling:* vain: insignificant: of no power: ineffectual. [L. *nugatorius—nugæ,* jokes, trifles.]

Nugget, nug'et, *n.* a lump or mass, as of a metal. [A corruption of Ingot.]

Nuisance, nū'sans, *n.* that which *annoys* or hurts: that which troubles: that which is offensive. [Fr.,—L. *noceo,* to hurt.]

Null, nul, *adj.* of *no* force: void: invalid. [L. *nullus,* not any, from *ne,* not, and *ullus,* any.]

Nullify, nul'i-fī, *v.t.* to *make null:* to annul: to render void :—*pr.p.* null'ifying; *pa.t.* and *pa.p.* null'ified.—*n.* Nullifica'tion. [L. *nullifico, -atum—nullus,* and *facio,* to make.]

Nullity, nul'i-ti, *n.* the state of being *null* or void: nothingness: want of existence, force, or efficacy.

Numb, num, *adj.* deprived of sensation or motion: stupefied: motionless.—*v.t.* to make numb: to deaden: to render motionless :—*pr.p.* numbing (num'ing); *pa.p.* numbed (numd').—*n.* **Numb'-ness.** [A.S. *numen*, pa.p. of *niman*, to take; so Ice. *numinn*, bereft.]

**Number,** num'bėr, *n.* that by which things are counted or computed: a collection of things: more than one: a unit in counting: a numerical figure: the measure of multiplicity: sounds distributed into harmonies: metre, verse, esp. in *pl.*: (*gram.*) the difference in words to express singular or plural.—*pl.* the 4th book of the Old Test. from its having the numbers of the Israelites.—*v.t.* to count: to reckon as one of a multitude: to mark with a number: to amount to.—*n.* **Num'berer.** [Fr. *nombre*—L. *numerus*, akin to Gr. *nomos*, that which is distributed—*nemō*, to distribute.]

**Numberless,** num'bėr-les, *adj.* without number: more than can be counted.

**Numerable,** nū'mėr-a-bl, *adj.* that may be *numbered* or counted.—*adv.* **Nu'merably.**—*ns.* **Nu'merableness, Numerabil'ity.** [L. *numerabilis*.]

**Numeral,** nū'mėr-al, *adj.* pertaining to or consisting of *number*.—*n.* a figure used to express a number, as 1, 2, 3, &c. [L. *numeralis*—*numerus*.]

**Numerary,** nū'mėr-ar-i, *adj.*, *belonging* to a certain *number*. [Fr. *numéraire*—Low L. *numerarius*.]

**Numerate,** nū'mėr-āt, *v.t.* (*orig.*) to *enumerate*, to *number*: to point off and read, as figures.

**Numeration,** nū-mėr-ā'shun, *n.* act of *numbering*: the art of reading numbers.

**Numerator,** nū'mėr-ā-tor, *n.* one who *numbers*: the upper number of a vulgar fraction, which expresses the number of fractional parts taken.

**Numeric,** nū-mer'ik, **Numerical,** nū-mer'ik-al, *adj.* belonging to, or consisting in *number*: the same both in number and kind.—*adv.* **Numer'ically.**

**Numerous,** nū'mėr-us, *adj.* great in number: being many.—*adv.* **Nu'merously.**—*n.* **Nu'merousness.**

**Numismatic,** nū-mis-mat'ik, *adj.* pertaining to *money*, coins, or medals. [L. *numisma*—Gr. *nomisma*, current coin—*nomizō*, to use commonly—*nomos*, custom.]

**Numismatics,** nū-mis-mat'iks, *n.sing.* the *science* of *coins* and medals.

**Numismatology,** nū-mis-ma-tol'o-ji, *n.* the *science* of *coins* and medals in relation to history.—*n.* **Numismatol'ogist,** one versed in numismatology. [L. *numisma*—Gr. *nomisma*, and *logos*, science.]

**Nummulite,** num'ū-līt, *n.* (*geol.*) a *fossil* shell resembling a *coin.* [L. *nummus*, a coin, and Gr. *lithos*, a stone.] [Numb and Skull.]

**Numskull,** num'skul, *n.* a blockhead. [From **Numb** and **Skull.**]

**Nun,** nun, *n.* in R. Cath. Church, a female who devotes herself to celibacy and seclusion: (*zool.*) a kind of pigeon with the feathers on its head like the hood of a nun. [A.S. *nunna*—Low L. *nunna, nonna,* a nun, an old maiden lady, the orig. sig. being 'mother;' cf. Gr. *nannē,* aunt, Sans. *nana,* a child's word for 'mother.']

**Nunciature,** nun'shi-a-tūr, *n.* the *office* of a *nuncio.*

**Nuncio,** nun'shi-o, *n.* an ambassador from the Pope to an emperor or king. [It.—L. *nuncius,* a messenger, one who brings news; prob. a contr. of *noventius,* from an obs. verb *novere,* to make new, *novus,* new.]

**Nuncupative,** nun-kū'pa-tiv or nun'kū-pā-tiv, **Nuncupatory,** nun-kū'pa-tor-i, *adj., declaring publicly* or solemnly: (*law*) verbal, not written. [Fr. *nuncupatif*—Low L. *nuncupativus,* nom-

inal—L. *nuncupare,* to call by name—prob. from *nomen,* name, *capio,* to take.]

**Nunnery,** nun'ėr-i, *n.* a house for *nuns.*

**Nuptial,** nup'shal, *adj.* pertaining to *marriage*: done at a marriage: constituting marriage.—*n.pl.* **Nup'tials,** marriage: wedding ceremony. [Fr.—L. *nuptialis*—*nuptiæ,* marriage—*nubo, nuptum,* to veil, to marry.]

**Nurse,** nurs, *n.* a woman who *nourishes* an infant: a mother, while her infant is at the breast: one who has the care of infants or of the sick: (*hort.*) a shrub or tree which protects a young plant.—*v.t.* to tend, as an infant, or a sick person: to bring up: to manage with care and economy. [O. Fr. *nurrice* (Fr. *nourrice*)—L. *nutrix*—*nutrio,* to suckle, to nourish.]

**Nursery,** nurs'ėr-i, *n.* place for nursing: an apartment for young children: a place where the growth of anything is promoted: (*hort.*) a piece of ground where plants are reared. [father.

**Nursing-father,** nurs'ing-fā'thėr, *n.* (*B.*) a foster-**Nursling,** nurs'ling, *n.* that which is *nursed*: an infant. [**Nurse,** and dim. *ling.*]

**Nurture,** nurt'ūr, *n.* act of *nursing* or nourishing: nourishment: education: instruction.—*v.t.* to nourish: to bring up: to educate.—*n.* **Nurt'urer.** [Fr. *nourriture*—Low L. *nutritura*—L. *nutrio,* to nourish.]

**Nut,** nut, *n.* the fruit of certain trees, consisting of a kernel in a hard shell: a small block of metal for screwing on the end of a bolt.—*v.i.* to gather nuts:—*pr.p.* nut'ting; *pa.p.* nut'ted. [A.S. *hnutu*; Ice. *hnot,* Dut. *noot,* Ger. *nuss.*]

**Nutant,** nū'tant, *adj.*, *nodding*: (*bot.*) having the top bent downward. [L. *nuto,* to nod.]

**Nutation,** nū-tā'shun, *n.* a *nodding*: (*astr.*) a periodical vibratory motion of the earth's axis: (*bot.*) the turning of flowers towards the sun.

**Nut-brown,** nut'-brown, *adj., brown,* like a ripe old *nut.*

**Nutcracker,** nut'krak-ėr, *n.* an instrument for *cracking* nuts: a bird in Europe and N. Asia which feeds on *nuts,* berries, and insects.

**Nuthatch,** nut'hach, *n.* a small climbing bird which feeds on *nuts* and insects, called also **Nut'jobber, Nut'pecker.** [M. E. *nuthake,* hacker of nuts.]

**Nutmeg,** nut'meg, *n.* the aromatic kernel of an E. Indian tree. [M. E. *notemuge,* a hybrid word formed from **Nut** and O. Fr. *muge,* musk —L. *muscus,* musk. See **Musk.**]

**Nutria,** nū'tri-a, *n.* the fur of the coypu, a kind of beaver, in S. America. [Sp. *nutria, nutra* —Gr. *enudris,* an otter.]

**Nutrient,** nū'tri-ent, *adj., nourishing.*—*n.* anything nourishing. [L. *nutrio,* to nourish.]

**Nutriment,** nū'tri-ment, *n.* that which *nourishes*: food. [L. *nutrimentum*—*nutrio,* to nourish.]

**Nutrimental,** nū-tri-ment'al, *adj.* having the quality of *nutriment* or food: nutritious.

**Nutrition,** nū-trish'un, *n.* act of *nourishing*: process of promoting the growth of bodies.

**Nutritious,** nū-trish'us, *adj., nourishing*: promoting growth.—*adv.* **Nutri'tiously.**—*n.* **Nutri'tiousness.**

**Nutritive,** nū'tri-tiv, *adj., nourishing.*—*adv.* **Nu'tritively.**—*n.* **Nu'tritiveness.**

**Nux vomica,** nuks vom'ik-a, *n.* the fruit of an E. Indian tree, from which the powerful poison known as strychnine is obtained. [L. *nux,* a nut, and *vomica,* from *vomo,* to vomit.]

**Nuzzle,** nuz'l, *v.i.* to poke about with the *nose,* like a swine. [A freq. verb from **Nose.**]

**Nyctalopia,** nik-ta-lō'pi-a, **Nyctalopy,** nik'ta-lō-pi, *n.* a diseased state of vision, in which objects are seen only at night or in the dusk. [Gr. *nyktalōpia—nyktalōps*, seeing by night only—*nyx, nyktos*, night, *ōps*, vision.]

**Nyctalops**, nik′ta-lops, *n.* one affected with *nyctalopy.*

**Nylghau**, nil′gaw, *n.* a large species of antelope, in N. Hindustan, the males of which are of a *bluish* colour. [Pers. *nil-gaw—nil*, blue, *gaw*, ox, cow.]

**Nymph**, nimf, *n.* a maiden : (*myth.*) one of the beautiful goddesses who inhabited every region of the earth and waters.—*adj.* **Nymph′-like.** [Fr.—L. *nympha*—Gr. *nymphē*, a bride, lit. 'a veiled one (like L. *nupta*), from same root as Gr. *nephos*, a cloud.]

**Nymph**, nimf, **Nympha**, nimf′a, *n.* the pupa or chrysalis of an insect :—*pl.* **Nymphæ** (nimf′ē).

**Nymphean**, nim-fē′an, *adj.* pertaining to or inhabited by *nymphs.*

**Nymphical**, nimf′ik-al, *adj.* pertaining to *nymphs.*

**Nympholepsy**, nimf′o-lep-si, *n.* a species of madness which seized those who had seen nymphs. [Gr. *nymphē*, a nymph, and *lambanō, lepsomai*, to seize.]

# O

**O**, ō, *int.* an exclamation of wonder, pain, grief, &c.

**Oaf**, ōf, *n.* a foolish child left by the fairies in place of another : a dolt, an idiot. [A form of **Elf.**]

**Oak**, ōk, *n.* a tree of many species, the most famous of which is the British oak, so valuable for its timber. [A.S. *ac*; Ice. *eik*, Ger. *eiche*.]

**Oakapple**, ōk′ap-l, *n.* a spongy substance on the leaves of the *oak*, caused by insects, so called from its likeness to a small *apple*, called also **Oak′leaf-gall.**

**Oaken**, ōk′n, *adj.* consisting or made of *oak.*

**Oakling**, ōk′ling, *n.* a *young oak.*

**Oakum**, ōk′um, *n.* old ropes untwisted and teased into loose hemp for calking the seams of ships. [A.S. *acumba, æcemba—cemb*, that which is combed—*cemban*, to **Comb.**]

**Oar**, ōr, *n.* a light pole with a flat end for rowing boats.—*v.t.* to impel by rowing.—*v.i.* to row. [A.S. *ar*; cog. with Gr. *er-essein*, to row, *amph-ēr-ēs*, two-oared.]

**Oared**, ōrd, *adj.* furnished with *oars.*

**Oarsman**, ōrz′man, *n.* one who rows with an oar.

**Oasis**, ō′a-sis or ō-ā′sis, *n.* a fertile spot in a sandy desert :—*pl.* **Oases** (ō′a-sēz or ō-ā′sēz). [L.—Gr. *oasis*; from Coptic *ouahe*, a resting-place or dwelling.]

**Oat**, ōt (oftener in *pl.* **Oats**, ōts), *n.* a well-known grassy plant, the seeds of which are much used as food : its seeds.—*n.* **Oat′cake**, a thin broad *cake* made of oatmeal. [A.S. *ata*, oat.]

**Oaten**, ōt′n, *adj.* consisting of an *oat* stem or straw : made of oatmeal.

**Oath**, ōth, *n.* a solemn statement with an appeal to God as witness, and a calling for his vengeance in case of falsehood or failure :—*pl.* **Oaths** (ō*th*z). [A.S. *ath*; Ger. *eid*, Ice. *eidhr*.]

**Oatmeal**, ōt′mēl, *n.* meal made of oats.

**Obduracy**, ob′dū-ras-i, *n.* state of being *obdurate* : invincible hardness of heart.

**Obdurate**, ob′dū-rāt, *adj.* hardened in heart or feelings : stubborn.—*adv.* **Ob′durately.**—*n.* **Ob′durateness.** [L. *obduratus*, pa.p. of *obduro* —*ob*, against, *duro*, to harden—*durus*, hard.]

**Obedience**, ō-bē′di-ens, *n.* state of being *obedient* : compliance with what is required : dutifulness.

**Obedient**, ō-bē′di-ent, *adj.* willing to *obey* : dutiful.—*adv.* **Obe′diently.** [Fr.—L. *obedio*.]

**Obeisance**, ō-bā′sans, *n.*, *obedience* : a bow or act of reverence. [Fr. *obéissance—obéissant*, pr.p. of *obéir*, to obey.]

**Obelisk**, ob′e-lisk, *n.* a tall, four-sided tapering pillar, cut off at the top like a flat pyramid : (*print.*) a dagger (†). [Through Fr. and L., from Gr. *obeliskos*, dim. of *obelos, belos*, a dart —*ballō*, to throw.]

**Obese**, ō-bēs′, *adj.* fat : fleshy. [L. *obesus—ob*, and *edo, esum*, to eat.]

**Obeseness**, ō-bēs′nes, **Obesity**, ō-bes′it-i, *n.*, *fatness* : abnormal fatness.

**Obey**, ō-bā′, *v.t.* to do as told : to be ruled by : to yield to.—*v.i.* (*B.*) to yield obedience (followed by *to*).—*n.* **Obey′er.** [Fr. *obéir*—L. *obedio* —*ob*, against, towards, *audio*, to hear.]

**Obeyingly**, ō-bā′ing-li, *adv.*, *obediently.*

**Obfuscate**, ob-fus′kāt, *v.t.* to darken : to confuse. —*n.* **Obfusca′tion.** [L. *obfusco, obfuscatum*— *ob*, intan., and *fuscus*, dark.]

**Obit**, ō′bit or ob′it, *n.*, *death* : funeral solemnities : an anniversary mass for the repose of a departed soul. [Fr.—L. *obitus—obeo*, to go to meet—*ob*, against, *eo*, to go.]

**Obitual**, ō-bit′ū-al, *adj.* pertaining to *obits.*

**Obituary**, ō-bit′ū-ar-i, *adj.* relating to the *death* of a person.—*n.* a *register of deaths* (*orig.*) in a monastery : an account of a deceased person or notice of his death.

**Object**, ob-jekt′, *v.t.* to offer in opposition : to oppose.—*v.i.* to oppose.—*n.* **Object′or.** [Fr.— L. *objecto*, a freq. of *objicio, -jectum—ob*, in the way of, and *jacio*, to throw.]

**Object**, ob′jekt, *n.* anything set or *thrown* before the mind : that which is sought for : end : motive : (*gram.*) that which follows a transitive verb.

**Object-glass**, ob′jekt-glas, *n.* the *glass* at the end of a telescope or microscope next the *object.*

**Objection**, ob-jek′shun, *n.* act of *objecting* : anything in opposition : argument against.

**Objectionable**, ob-jek′shun-a-bl, *adj.* that may be *objected* to.

**Objective**, ob-jekt′iv, *adj.* relating to an *object* : being exterior to the mind : as opp. to *subjective*, that which is real or which exists in nature, in contrast with what is ideal or exists merely in the thought of the individual : (*gram.*) belonging to the case of the object.—*n.* (*gram.*) the case of the object : (*war*) the point to which the operations of an army are directed.—*adv.* **Objectively.**

**Objectiveness**, ob-jekt′iv-nes, **Objectivity**, ob-jek-tiv′i-ti, *n.* state of being *objective.*

**Objurgation**, ob-jur-gā′shun, *n.* a blaming : reproof : reprehension. [Fr.—L.—*ob*, against, and *jurgare*, to sue at law, to quarrel with—*jus*, law, and *ago*, to drive.] [blame or reproof.

**Objurgatory**, ob-jur′ga-tor-i, *adj.* expressing

**Oblate**, ob-lāt′, *adj.* flattened at opposite sides or poles : shaped like an orange.—*n.* **Oblate′-ness.** [L. *oblatus*, pa.p. of *offero*, to carry forward, to offer—*ob*, against, and *fero*, to bring.]

**Oblation**, ob-lā′shun, *n.* anything *offered* in worship or sacred service : an offering. [Fr.—L. *oblatio*.]

**Obligation**, ob-li-gā′shun, *n.* act of *obliging* : that which binds : any act which binds one to do something for another : state of being indebted for a favour : (*law*) a bond containing a penalty on failure.

**Obligatory,** ob'li-gā-tor-i, *adj., binding: impos-*
ing duty.—*adv.* **Ob'ligatorily.**—*n.* **Ob'ligatori-**
**ness.**

**Oblige,** ō-blīj', *v.t.* to *bind* or constrain : to bind
by some favour rendered, hence to do a favour
to. [Fr.—L. *obligo, obligatum—ob,* and *ligo,* to
bind.]     [another is *obliged* or bound.

**Obligee,** ob-li-jē', *n.* (*law*) the person to whom

**Obliging,** ō-blīj'ing, *adj.* disposed to *oblige* or confer favours.—*adv.* **Oblig'ingly.**—*n.* **Oblig'ing-**
**ness.**

**Obligor,** ob-li-gor', *n.* (*law*) the *person* who *binds*
*himself* to another.

**Oblique,** ob-lēk', *adj., slanting:* not perpendicular : not parallel : not straightforward : obscure : (*geom.*) not a right angle : (*gram.*)
denoting any case except the nominative.—*adv.*
**Oblique'ly.** [Fr.—L. *obliquus—ob,* and *liquis,*
bent, slanting.]

**Obliqueness,** ob-lēk'nes, **Obliquity,** ob-lik'wi-ti,
*n.* state of being *oblique* : a slanting direction :
error or wrong : irregularity.

**Obliterate,** ob-lit'ér-āt, *v.t.* to blot out : to wear
out : to destroy : to reduce to a very low state.
[L. *oblitero, -atum—ob,* over, and *litera,* a letter.
See **Letter.**]

**Obliteration,** ob-lit-ér-ā'shun, *n.* act of obliterat-
ing : a blotting or wearing out : extinction.

**Oblivion,** ob-liv'i-un, *n.* act of *forgetting* or state
of being forgot : remission of punishment.
[Fr.—L. *oblivio, oblivionis—obliviscor,* to forget,
from root of *livere,* to become *dark;* hence, to
have the mind darkened, to forget.]

**Oblivious,** ob-liv'i-us, *adj., forgetful:* causing forgetfulness.—*adv.* **Obliv'iously.**—*n.* **Obliv'ious-**
**ness.**

**Oblong,** ob'long, *adj., long* in one way : longer
than broad.—*n.* (*geom.*) a rectangle longer than
broad : any oblong figure. [Fr.—L. *ob,* over,
and *longus,* long.]

**Obloquy,** ob'lo-kwi, *n.* a *speaking against :* reproachful language : censure : calumny. [L.
*obloquium—ob,* against, and *loquor,* to speak.]

**Obnoxious,** ob-nok'shus, *adj., liable* to *hurt* or
punishment : blameworthy : offensive : subject :
answerable.—*adv.* **Obnox'iously.**—*n.* **Obnox'-**
**iousness.** [L. *obnoxius—ob,* before, and *noxa,*
hurt. See **Noxious.**]

**Oboe.** See **Hautboy.**

**Obolus,** ob'o-lus, *n.* in ancient Greece, a small
coin, worth rather more than three-halfpence ;
also a weight, the sixth part of a drachma. [Gr.
*obelos,* a spit, from the coin being marked with a
spit, or from iron or copper *nails* being used in
ancient barter.]

**Obscene,** ob-sēn', *adj.* offensive to chastity:
unchaste : indecent : disgusting.—*adv.* **Ob-**
**scene'ly.** [L. *obscenus;* perh. from *ob* and
*cænum,* filth, or (with meaning of 'unlucky')
from *scævus,* left-handed, unlucky.]

**Obsceneness,** ob-sēn'nes, **Obscenity,** ob-sen'i-ti,
*n.* quality of being *obscene :* lewdness.

**Obscurant,** ob-skūr'ant, *n.* one who obscures : a
writer who opposes the progress of modern
enlightenment.

**Obscurantism,** ob-skūr'ant-izm, *n.* the doctrine or
principles of an obscurant.

**Obscuration,** ob-skūr-ā'shun, *n.* the act of *obscur-*
*ing* or state of being obscured.

**Obscure,** ob-skūr', *adj. dark:* not distinct : not
easily understood : not clear or legible : unknown : humble : living in darkness.—*adv.*
**Obscure'ly.** [Fr.—L. *obscurus,* akin to Sans.
*sku,* to cover.]

**Obscure,** ob-skūr', *v.t.* to *darken:* to make less
plain. [*obscure:* unintelligibleness : humility.

**Obscurity,** ob-skūr'i-ti, *n.* state or quality of being

**Obsequies,** ob'se-kwiz, *n.* funeral rites and solemnities. [Lit. 'a following,' Fr. *obsèques—*L.
*obsequiæ—ob,* and *sequor,* to follow.]

**Obsequious,** ob-sē'kwi-us, *adj.* compliant to
excess: meanly condescending.—*adv.* **Obse'-**
**quiously.**—*n.* **Obse'quiousness.** [See **Ob-**
**sequies.**]

**Observable,** ob-zèrv'a-bl, *adj.* that may be *ob-*
*served* or noticed : worthy of observation.—*adv.*
**Observ'ably.**—*n.* **Observ'ableness.**

**Observance,** ob-zèrv'ans, *n.* act of *observing:*
performance : attention : that which is to be
observed : rule of practice. [Fr.—L. *observantia.*]

**Observant,** ob-zèrv'ant, *adj., observing :* taking
notice : adhering to : carefully attentive.—*adv.*
**Observ'antly.**

**Observation,** ob-zèr-vā'shun, *n.* act of *observing:*
attention : as distinguished from *experiment,* the
act of recognising and noting phenomena as
they occur in nature : that which is observed :
a remark : performance.

**Observational,** ob-zèr-vā'shun-al, *adj.* consisting
of or containing *observations* or remarks.

**Observer,** ob'zèrv-ā-tor, *n.* one who *observes :*
a remarker.

**Observatory,** ob-zèrv'a-tor-i, *n.* a place for making
astronomical and physical *observations.*

**Observe,** ob-zèrv', *v.t.* to *keep in view:* to notice :
to regard attentively : to remark : to comply
with : to keep religiously : (*B.*) to keep or guard.
—*v.i.* to take notice : to attend : to remark.—
*n.* **Observ'er.** [Fr.—L. *observo, -atum—ob,* and
*servo,* to heed, keep.]

**Observing,** ob-zèrv'ing, *adj.* habitually taking
notice : attentive.—*adv.* **Observ'ingly.**

**Obsidian,** ob-sid'i-an, *n.* a glass produced by
volcanoes. [So called from *Obsidius,* who, acc.
to Pliny, discovered it in Ethiopia.]

**Obsolescent,** ob-so-les'ent, *adj., going out of* use.
[L. *obsolescens, -entis,* pr.p. of *obsolesco, obso-*
*letum—ob,* and *soleo,* to be wont.]

**Obsolete,** ob'so-lēt, *adj., gone out of use:* antiquated : (*zool.*) obscure : rudimental.—*n.* **Ob'so-**
**leteness.**

**Obstacle,** ob'sta-kl, *n.* anything that *stands in*
*the way* of or hinders progress : obstruction.
[Fr.—L. *obstaculum—ob,* in the way of, *sto,* to
stand.]

**Obstetric,** ob-stet'rik, **Obstetrical,** ob-stet'rik-al,
*adj.* pertaining to midwifery. [L. *obstetricius*
—*obstetrix, -icis,* a midwife, a female that stands
before or near—*ob,* before, and *sto,* to stand.]

**Obstetrics,** ob-stet'riks, *n.sing.* the science of
midwifery.

**Obstinacy,** ob'sti-nas-i, **Obstinateness,** ob'sti-
nāt-nes, *n.* the being obstinate : excess of firmness : stubbornness : fixedness that yields with
difficulty.

**Obstinate,** ob'sti-nāt, *adj.* blindly or excessively
firm : unyielding : stubborn : not easily subdued.
—*adv.* **Ob'stinately.** [L. *obstino, -atum—ob,*
in the way of, *sto,* to stand.]

**Obstreperous,** ob-strep'ér-us, *adj., making* a loud
*noise:* clamorous : noisy.—*adv.* **Obstrep'er-**
**ously.** [L. *obstreperus—ob,* and *strepere,* to
make a noise.]

**Obstruct,** ob-strukt', *v.t.* to block up : to hinder
from passing : to retard. [L. *ob,* in the way of,
*struo, structum,* to pile up.]

**Obstruction,** ob-struk'shun, *n.* act of obstructing :
that which obstructs : obstacle : impediment.

**Obstructive,** ob-strukt'iv, *adj.* tending to obstruct : hindering.—*adv.* **Obstruct'ively.**

**Obstruent,** ob'stroo-ent, *adj., obstructing :* blocking up.—*n.* (*med.*) anything that obstructs in the body. [L. *obstruens, -entis,* pr.p. of *obstruo.*]

**Obtain,** ob-tān', *v.t.* to *lay hold of :* to hold : to procure by effort : to gain.—*v.i.* to be established : to continue in use : to become held or prevalent : to subsist : (rare) to succeed. [Fr.—L. *obtineo* —*ob,* and *teneo,* to hold.]

**Obtainable,** ob-tān'a-bl, *adj.* that may be obtained, procured, or acquired.

**Obtrude,** ob-trōōd', *v.t.* to *thrust in upon* when not wanted : to urge upon against the will of.— *v.i.* to thrust or be thrust upon. [L. *obtrudo*— *ob,* and *trudo, trusum,* to thrust.]

**Obtruding,** ob-trōōd'ing, **Obtrusion,** ob-trōō'zhun, *n.* a thrusting in or upon against the will of.

**Obtrusive,** ob-trōō'siv, *adj.* disposed to obtrude or thrust one's self among others.—*adv.* **Obtrus'-ively.**

**Obtuse,** ob-tūs', *adj., blunt :* not pointed : stupid : not shrill : (*geom.*) greater than a right angle. —*adv.* **Obtuse'ly.**—*n.* **Obtuse'ness.** [Fr.—L. *obtusus*—*obtundo,* to blunt—*ob,* against, *tundo,* to beat.]

**Obverse,** ob-vèrs', *adj., turned towards* one : bearing the face : (*bot.*) having the base narrower than the top.—*adv.* **Obverse'ly.** [L. *obversus*— *ob,* towards, and *verto,* to turn.]

**Obverse,** ob'vèrs, *n.* the side of a coin containing the head or principal symbol :—opposed to **Re-verse.**

**Obviate,** ob'vi-āt, *v.t.* to remove, as difficulties. [L. *obvio—ob,* in the way of, and *vio, viatum,* to go—*via,* a way.]

**Obvious,** ob'vi-us, *adj., meeting in the way :* evident.—*adv.* **Ob'viously.**—*n.* **Ob'viousness.** [L. *obvius.*]

**Obvolute,** ob'vo-lūt, **Obvoluted,** ob'vo-lūt-ed, *adj., rolled* or *turned in :* (*bot.*) arranged so as alternately to overlap. [L. *obvolutus*—*ob,* and *volvo, volutum,* to roll.]

**Occasion,** ok-kā'zhun, *n.* occurrence : opportunity : requirement.—*v.t.* to cause : to influence. [Fr. —L. *occasio—occido—ob,* in the way of, and *cado, casum,* to fall.]

**Occasional,** ok-kā'zhun-al, *adj., falling* in the *way* or *happening :* occurring only at times : resulting from accident : produced on some special event.—*adv.* **Occa'sionally.**

**Occident,** ok'si-dent, *n.* the western quarter of the hemisphere where the sun *goes down* or sets : the west.—*adj.* **Occident'al,** noting the quarter where the sun goes down or sets : western.—*adv.* **Occident'ally.** [Fr.—L. *occidens, -entis,* pr.p. of *occido,* to fall down.]

**Occipital,** ok-sip'it-al, *adj.* pertaining to the *occi-put* or back part of the head.

**Occiput,** ok'si-put, *n.* the *back* part of the *head* or skull. [L.—*ob,* over against, *caput,* head.]

**Occult,** ok-kult', *adj., covered over :* hidden : secret : unknown.—*adv.* **Occult'ly.**—*ns.* **Occult'-ism,** the science of the unknown, **Occult'ness.** [Fr.—L. *occulto,* to hide—*occulo,* to cover over —*ob,* over, and *cal,* root of *celo,* to conceal, *clam,* secretly ; Gr. *kryptō, kalyptō,* to hide, E. **Hull,** a husk.]

**Occultation,** ok-kul-tā'shun, *n.* a *concealing,* esp. of one of the heavenly bodies by another.

**Occupancy,** ok'ū-pan-si, *n.* the act of occupying, or of taking or holding possession : possession.

**Occupant,** ok'ū-pant, *n.* one who takes or has possession.

**Occupation,** ok-ū-pā'shun, *n.* the act of occupying or taking possession : possession : employment.

**Occupier,** ok'ū-pī-ér, *n.* an occupant : (*B.*) a trader.

**Occupy,** ok'ū-pī, *v.t.* to *take* or *seize :* to hold possession of : to cover or fill : to employ : (*B.*) to use : to trade with.—*v.i.* to hold possession : (*B.*) to trade :—*pa.t.* and *pa.p.* occ'ŭpied. [Fr. —L. *occupo, -atum—ob,* and *capio,* to take.]

**Occur,** ok-kur', *v.i.* to come or be presented to the mind : to happen : to appear : to be found here and there :—*pr.p.* occur'ring ; *pa.p.* occurred'. [Fr.—L. *occurro—ob,* towards, and *curro,* to run.]

**Occurrence,** ok-kur'ens, *n.* anything that *occurs :* [an event : occasional presentation.

**Occurrent,** ok-kur'ent, *n.* (*B.*) an occurrence or chance.—*adj.* (*B.*) coming in the way.

**Ocean,** ō'shun, *n.* the vast expanse of salt water that covers the greater part of the surface of the globe : also, one of its five great divisions : any immense expanse.—*adj.* pertaining to the great sea. [Fr.—L. *oceanus*—Gr. *ōkeanos,* perh. from *ōkys,* swift, and *naō,* to flow.]

**Oceanic,** ō-she-an'ik, *adj.* pertaining to the *ocean :* found or formed in the ocean.

**Ocelot,** ō'se-lot, *n.* the name of several species of animals in the tropical parts of S. America allied to the leopard, but much smaller. [Mex. *ocelotl.*]

**Ochlocracy,** ok-lok'ra-si, *n., mob-rule :* a government by the populace.—*adjs.* **Ochlocrat'ic, Ochlocrat'ical.**—*adv.* **Ochlocrat'ically.** [Gr. *ochlokratia—ochlos,* the mob, and *kratos,* rule.]

**Ochraceous,** ō-krā'shus, *adj.* of an *ochre* colour.

**Ochre,** ō'kèr, *n.* a fine clay, mostly *pale yellow.* [Fr.—L. *ochra*—Gr. *ōchra—ōchros,* pale yellow ; Sans. *hari,* yellow.]

**Ochreous,** ō'kre-us, **Ochry,** ō'kri, *adj.* consisting of, containing, or resembling *ochre.*

**Octagon,** ok'ta-gon, *n.* a plane figure of eight sides and *eight angles.*—*adj.* **Octag'onal.** [Gr. *oktō,* eight, and *gōnia,* an angle.]

**Octahedron,** ok-ta-hē'dron, *n.* a solid figure with *eight* equal sides, each of which is an equilateral triangle.—*adj.* **Octahe'dral.** [Gr. *oktō,* and *hedra,* a base.]

**Octangular,** ok-tang'gul-ar, *adj.* having *eight angles.* [L. *octo,* eight, and **Angular.**]

**Octant,** ok'tant, *n.* the *eighth* part of a circle : the aspect of two planets when 45°, or ⅛ of a circle, apart. [L. *octans, octantis—octo,* eight.]

**Octave,** ok'tāv, *adj., eight :* consisting of eight. —*n.* an eighth : that which consists of eight : the eighth day inclusive after a church festival : the eight days following a festival inclusive : (*mus.*) an eighth, or an interval of twelve semitones. [Fr.—L. *octavus,* eighth—*octo,* eight.]

**Octavo,** ok-tā'vō, *adj.* having *eight* leaves to the sheet.—*n.* a book having *eight* leaves to the sheet, contracted 8vo :—*pl.* **Octa'vos.**

**October,** ok-tō'bèr, *n.* the *eighth* month of the Roman year, which began in March, but the tenth in our calendar. [L. *octo,* eight.]

**Octodecimo,** ok-to-des'i-mō, *adj.* having *eighteen* leaves to the sheet, contracted 18mo. [L. *octo-decim,* eighteen—*octo,* eight, and *decem,* ten.]

**Octogenarian,** ok-to-jen-ā'ri-an, **Octogenary,** ok-toj'en-ar-i, *n.* one who is *eighty* years old.

**Octogenary,** ok-toj'en-ar-i, *adj.* of *eighty* years of age. [L. *octogenarius—octogeni,* eighty each.]

**Octopod,** ok'to-pod, **Octopus,** ok'to-pus, *n.* a mollusc having a round purse-like body and *eight* arms. [Gr. *oktō,* eight, and *pous, podos,* foot.]

**Octoroon,** ok-to-rōōn', *n.* the offspring of a quadroon and a white person. [From L. *octo,* eight.]

**Octosyllabic**, ok-to-sil-lab′ik, *adj.* consisting of *eight syllables*. [L. *octo*, eight, and **Syllabic**.]

**Ocular**, ok′ū-lar, *adj.* pertaining to the *eye* : formed in or known by the eye : received by actual sight.—*adv.* **Oc′ularly.** [L. *ocularius—oculus*, Gr. *okkos*, akin to E. **Eye**, Sans. *aksha*, eye.]

**Oculist**, ok′ū-list, *n.* one skilled in *eye* diseases.

**Odalisque**, ō′dal-isk, *n.* a female slave in a Turkish harem. [Fr.—Turk. *oda*, a chamber.]

**Odd**, od, *adj.* not paired with another : not even : left over after a round number has been taken : not exactly divisible by two : strange : unusual : trifling.—*adv.* **Odd′ly.**—*n.* **Odd′ness.** [From the Scand., as in Ice. *oddi*, a triangle (which has a third or *odd* angle and side), hence metaphorically, an odd number—Ice. *oddr*, a point ; conn. with A.S. *ord*, a point, beginning (as perh. in Lord), and Ger. *ort*, a place.]

**Oddfellow**, od′fel-ō, *n.* one of a secret benevolent society called Oddfellows. [**Odd** and **Fellow**.]

**Oddity**, od′i-ti, *n.* the state of being *odd* or singular : strangeness : a singular person or thing.

**Odds**, odz, *n.*, *inequality :* difference in favour of one against another : more than an even wager : advantage : dispute : scraps, miscellaneous pieces, as in the phrase ' odds and ends' (lit. ' points ' and ends). [From **Odd**.]

**Ode**, ōd, *n.* a *song :* a poem written to be set to music. [Fr.—L. *ode, oda*—Gr. *ōdē*, contracted from *aoidē—aeidō*, to sing.]

**Odious**, ō′di-us, *adj.*, *hateful :* offensive : repulsive : hated.—*adv.* **O′diously.**—*n.* **O′diousness.** [Fr. See **Odium**.]

**Odium**, ō′di-um, *n.*, *hatred :* offensiveness : quality of provoking hate. [L.—*odi*, to hate.]

**Odometer**, od-om′et-ėr, *n.* an instrument for measuring the distance passed over by a carriage by marking the number of revolutions of the wheel. [Gr. *nodos*, a way, and *metron*, a measure.]

**Odontology**, ō-don-tol′o-ji, *n.* the *science* of the *teeth*. [Gr. *odons, odontos*, a tooth, and *logos*, discourse, science.]

**Odoriferous**, ō-dur-if′ėr-us, *adj.*, *bearing odours :* diffusing fragrance : perfumed.—*adv.* **Odorif′erously.** [L. *odoriferus—odor*, and *fero*, to bear.]

**Odorous**, ō′dur-us, *adj.* emitting an *odour* or scent : sweet-smelling : fragrant.—*adv.* **O′dorously.**

**Odour**, ō′dur, *n.*, *smell :* perfume : estimation. [Fr.—L. *odor*—root *od*, found in Gr. *ozō*, to smell.]

**Odourless**, ō′dur-les, *adj.* without odour.

**O′er**, ōr, contracted from **Over**.

**Œsophagus**. See **Esophagus**.

**Of**, ov, *prep.* from or out from : belonging to : out of : among : proceeding from, so in the Litany and Nicene Creed : owing to : concerning : (*B.* and *Pr. Bk.*) sometimes = by, from, on, or over. [A.S. *of ;* found in all the Teutonic languages, as Ger. *ab*, also in L. *ab*, Gr. *apo*, Sans. *apa*, away from.]

**Of purpose** (*B.*) intentionally.

**Off**, of, *adv.* from : away from : on the opposite side of a question : not on.—*adj.* most distant : on the opposite or further side.—*prep.* not on.—*int.* away ! depart ! [Same as **Of**, differently used.]

**Offal**, of′al, *n.* waste meat : the part of an animal unfit for use : refuse : anything worthless. [**Off** and **Fall**.]

**Offence**, of-fens′, *n.* any cause of anger or displeasure : an injury : a crime : a sin : affront : assault.

**Offend**, of-fend′, *v.t.* to displease or make angry :

to affront : (*B.*) to cause to sin.—*v.i.* to sin : to cause anger : (*B.*) to be made to sin. [Fr.—L. *ob*, against, and *fendo*, akin to Sans. *han*, to strike.] [a trespasser : a criminal.

**Offender**, of-fend′ėr, *n.* one who *offends* or injures :

**Offensive**, of-fens′iv, *adj.* causing *offence :* displeasing : injurious : used in attack : making the first attack.—*n.* the act of the attacking party : the posture of one who attacks.—*adv.* **Offens′ively.**—*n.* **Offens′iveness.** [Fr. *offensif*—L. *offendo, offensum—ob*, and *fendo*.]

**Offer**, of′ėr, *v.t.* to *bring to* or *before :* to make a proposal to : to lay before : to present to the mind : to attempt : to propose to give : to present in worship.—*v.i.* to present itself : to be at hand : to declare a willingness.—*n.* act of offering : first advance : that which is offered : proposal made.—*n.* **Off′erer.** [L. *offerre—ob*, towards, *fero, ferre*, to bring.]

**Offerable**, of′ėr-a-bl, *adj.* that may be offered.

**Offering**, of′ėr-ing, *n.* that which is offered : (*B.*) that which is offered on an altar : a sacrifice :—*pl.* in Church of England, certain dues payable at Easter.

**Offertory**, of′ėr-tor-i, *n.* in English Church, that part of the liturgy where the people's *offerings* are made : in R. Cath. Church, an anthem chanted during the first part of the mass.

**Off-hand**, of′hand, *adv.* at once : without hesitating.

**Office**, of′is, *n.* settled duty or employment : business : act of good or ill : act of worship : formulary of devotion : peculiar use : a place for business : a benefice with no jurisdiction attached :—*pl.* the apartments ᴐ a house in which the domestics discharge their duties. [Lit. *a rendering* of *aid*, Fr.—L. *officium—opis*, aid.]

**Office-bearer**, of′is-bār′ėr, *n.* one who holds office.

**Officer**, of′i-sėr, *n.* one who holds an office : a person who performs some public office.—*v.t.* to furnish with officers : to command, as officers.

**Official**, of-fish′al, *adj.* pertaining to an *office :* depending on the proper office or authority : done by authority.—*n.* one who holds an office : a subordinate public officer : the deputy of a bishop, &c.—*adv.* **Offi′cially.** [O. Fr.—L. *officialis—officium*.]

**Officiate**, of-fish′i-āt, *v.i.* to perform the duties of an office : to perform official duties for another.

**Officinal**, of-fis′in-al or of-i-sī′nal, *adj.* belonging to or used in a *shop :* denoting an approved medicine kept prepared by apothecaries. [Fr.—L. *officina*, a workshop, contr. from *ofificina—opifex, -icis—opus*, work, *facio*, to do.]

**Officious**, of-fish′us, *adj.* too forward in offering services : overkind : intermeddling.—*adv.* **Offi′ciously.**—*n.* **Offi′ciousness.** [Fr.—L. *officiosus—officium*.]

**Offing**, of′ing, *n.* a part of the sea with deep water *off* from the shore.

**Offscouring**, of′skowr-ing, *n.* matter *scoured off :* refuse : anything vile or despised.

**Offset**, of′set, *n.* in accounts, a sum or value *set off* against another as an equivalent : a young shoot or bulb : a terrace on a hillside : (*arch.*) a horizontal ledge on the face of a wall : in *surveying*, a perpendicular from the main line to an outlying point.—*v.t.* in accounts, to place against as an equivalent.

**Offshoot**, of′shōōt, *n.* that which *shoots off* the parent stem : anything growing out of another.

**Offspring**, of′spring, *n.* that which *springs from* another, a child, or children : issue : production of any kind.

**Oft**, oft, **Often**, of'n, *adv.*, *frequently*: many times. —*adj.* **Often** (*B.*) frequent. [A.S.; Ger. *oft*, Goth. *ufta*.]

**Oftenness**, of'n-nes, *n.* frequency.

**Ofttimes**, oft'tīmz, **Oftentimes**, of'n-tīmz, *adv.*, *many times*: frequently. [Oft and *Times.*]

**Ogee**, ō-jē', *n.* a wave-like moulding with the convex part upwards. [Fr. *ogive*.]

**Ogham**, og'am, *n.* a peculiar kind of writing practised by the ancient Irish: its characters.

**Ogle**, ō'gl, *v.t.* to look at fondly with side glances. —*v.i.* to practise ogling.—*ns.* **O'gler**, **O'gling**. [Dut. *oogen*—*ooge*, the eye: cf. Ger. *äugeln*.]

**Ogre**, ō'gėr, *n.* a man-eating monster or giant of fairy tales.—*fem.* **O'gress**.—*adj.* **O'greish**, like an ogre in character or appearance. [Fr. *ogre*— Sp. *ogro*—L. *orcus*, the lower world, the god of the dead; cf. A.S. *orc*, a demon.]

**Oh**, ō, *int.* denoting surprise, pain, sorrow, &c.

**Oil**, oil, *n.* the juice from the fruit of the *olive-tree*: any greasy liquid.—*v.t.* to smear or anoint with oil. [O. Fr. *oile* (Fr. *huile*)—L. *oleum*— Gr. *elaion*—*elaia*, the olive.]

**Oilbag**, oil'bag, *n.* a bag or cyst in animals containing oil.

**Oilcake**, oil'kāk, *n.* a cake made of flax seed from which the oil has been pressed out.

**Oilcloth**, oil'kloth, *n.* a painted floorcloth.

**Oil-colour**, oil'-kul'ur, *n.* a colouring substance mixed with oil.

**Oilnut**, oil'nut, *n.* the butter-nut of N. America.

**Oil-painting**, oil'-pānt'ing, *n.* a picture painted in oil-colours: the art of painting in oil-colours.

**Oily**, oil'i, *adj.* consisting of, containing, or having the qualities of oil: greasy.—*n.* **Oil'iness**.

**Ointment**, oint'ment, *n.* anything used in anointing: (*med.*) any greasy substance applied to diseased or wounded parts: (*B.*) a perfume. [O. Fr. *oignement*, ointment, Fr. *oindre*, to anoint—L. *unguentum*—*ungo*, to smear.]

**Old**, ōld, *adj.* advanced in years: having been long in existence: decayed by time: out of date: ancient: having the age or duration of: long practised.—*n.* **Old'ness**.—**Old style** (often written with a date O. S.), the mode of reckoning time before 1752, according to the Julian calendar or year of 365¼ days. [A.S. *eald; Ger. alt*, from a root seen in Goth. *alan*, to nourish, L. *alo* (hence *adultus*), to nourish.]

**Olden**, ōld'n, *adj., old*: ancient.

**Oleaginous**, ō-le-aj'in-us, *adj., oily*: (*bot.*) fleshy and oily.—*n.* **Oleag'inousness**. [L. *oleaginus* —*oleum*, oil.]

**Oleander**, ō-le-an'dėr, *n.* an evergreen shrub with beautiful flowers. [Fr., being a corr. of **Rhodo-dendron**.]

**Oleaster**, ō-le-as'tėr, *n.* the wild olive. [L.—*olea*, an olive-tree, from Gr. *elaia*.]

**Oleiferous**, ō-le-if'ėr-us, *adj., producing oil*, as seeds. [L. *oleum*, oil, and *fero*, to bear.]

**Oleograph**, ō'le-o-graf, *n.* a *print* in *oil*-colours to imitate an oil-painting. [L. *oleum*, oil, and Gr. *graphō*, to write, draw.]

**Olfactory**, ol-fak'tor-i, *adj.* pertaining to or used in *smelling*. [L. *olfacto*, to smell—*oleo*, to smell —root of *odor*, smell, *facio*, to do or make.]

**Oligarch**, ol'i-gärk, *n.* a member of an *oligarchy*.

**Oligarchal**, ol-i-gärk'al, **Oligarchical**, ol-i-gärk'-ik-al, *adj.* pertaining to an *oligarchy*.

**Oligarchy**, ol'i-gärk-i, *n., government* by a *few*: a state governed by a few. [Fr.—Gr., from *oligos*, few, *archē*, rule.]

**Olio**, ō'li-ō, *n.* a dish of different sorts of meat and vegetables boiled together: a mixture: (*music*) a medley: a literary miscellany. [Sp. *olla*—L. *olla*, a pot.]

**Olivaceous**, ol-i-vā'shus, *adj., olive-coloured*: olive-green. [Fr.—L. *oliva*.]

**Olive**, ol'iv, *n.* a tree cultivated round the Mediterranean for its oily fruit: its fruit: peace, of which the olive was the emblem: a colour like the unripe olive. [Fr.—L. *oliva*.]

**Olla-podrida**, ol'la-po-drē'da, *n.* a mixed stew or hash of meat and vegetables in common use in Spain: any incongruous mixture or miscellaneous collection. [Sp., lit. 'putrid or rotten pot'—L. *olla*, a pot, and *puter*, putrid.]

**Olympiad**, ō-lim'pi-ad, *n.* in ancient Greece, a period of four years, being the interval between the *Olympic games*, used in reckoning time (the date of the 1st Olympiad is 776 B.C.). [Gr. *olympias, -ados*, belonging to *Olympia*, a district in Elis in ancient Greece.]

**Olympian**, ō-lim'pi-an, **Olympic**, ō-lim'pik, *adj.* pertaining to *Olympia*, where the Olympic games were celebrated, or to *Mt. Olympus*, the fabled seat of the gods.—**Olym'pics, Olym'pic Games**, games celebrated every four years, dedicated to Olympian Jupiter.

**Ombre**, om'bėr, *n.* a game of cards usually played by three persons. [Fr.—Sp. *hombre*—L. *homo*, a man.]

**Omega**, ō'meg-a or o-mē'ga, *n.* (*lit.*) the *great O*, the last letter of the Greek alphabet: (*B.*) the end. [Gr. *ō mega*, the great or long *O*.]

**Omelet**, **Omelette**, om'e-let, *n.* a pancake chiefly of eggs. [Fr. *omelette*, of which the O. Fr. is *amelette*, which through the form *alemette* is traced to *alemelle*, the O. Fr. form of Fr. *alumelle*, a thin plate, a corr. (with the prep. *à*) of *lamelle*, dim. of *lame*—L. *lamina*, a thin plate.]

**Omen**, ō'men, *n.* a sign of some future event. [L. for *osmen*, that which is uttered by the mouth, L. *os;* or for *ausmen*, 'that which is heard'— *audio*, to hear.]

**Omened**, ō'mend, *adj.* containing *omens*.

**Omer**, ō'mėr, *n.* a Hebrew dry measure containing 1/10 part of a homer. [See **Homer**.]

**Ominous**, om'in-us, *adj.* pertaining to or containing an *omen*: foreboding evil: inauspicious.— *adv.* **Om'inously**.—*n.* **Om'inousness**.

**Omissible**, ō-mis'i-bl, *adj.* that may be omitted.

**Omission**, ō-mish'un, *n.* act of *omitting*: the neglect or failure to do something required: that which is left out. [Fr.—L. *omissio*.]

**Omissive**, ō-mis'iv, *adj., omitting* or leaving out.

**Omit**, ō-mit', *v.t.* to leave out: to neglect: to fail:—*pr.p.* omitt'ing; *pa.t.* and *pa.p.* omitt'ed. [L. *omitto*, *omissum*—*ob*, away, *mitto*, to send.]

**Omnibus**, om'ni-bus, *n.* a large four-wheeled vehicle for conveying passengers, chiefly used in towns:—*pl.* **Om'nibuses**. [Lit. 'something for all,' L. dative pl. of *omnis*, all.]

**Omnifarious**, om-ni-fā'ri-us, *adj.* of *all varieties* or kinds. [L. *omnifarius*—*omnis*, all, and *varius*, various.]

**Omniferous**, om-nif'ėr-us, *adj., bearing* or producing *all* kinds. [L. *omnifer*—*omnis*, *fero*, to bear.] [nip'o-ten-si, *n.* unlimited power.

**Omnipotence**, om-nip'o-tens, **Omnipotency**, om-

**Omnipotent**, om-nip'o-tent, *adj., all-powerful*: possessing unlimited power.—*n.* **The Omnipotent**, God.—*adv.* **Omnip'otently**. [Fr.—L. *omnipotens*—*omnis*, all, and **Potent**.]

**Omnipresent**, om-ni-pres'ent, *adj., present everywhere*.—*n.* **Omnipres'ence**. [L. *omnis*, and **Present**.]

**Omniscient**, om-nish'ent, *adj.*, *all-knowing*: all-seeing: infinitely wise.—*adv.* **Omnis'ciently.**—*n.* **Omnis'cience.** [L. *omnis*, all, and *sciens, scientis*, knowing—*scio*, to know.]

**Omnium-gatherum**, om'ni-um-*gath*'ér-um, *n.* a miscellaneous collection of things or persons. [L. *omnium*, of all, gen. pl. of *omnis*, all, and a slang Latinised form of E. *gather*.]

**Omnivorous**, om-niv'or-us, *adj.*, *all-devouring*: (*zool.*) feeding on both animal and vegetable food. [L. *omnivorus—omnis*, all, and *voro*, to devour.]

**Omphalic**, om-fal'ik, *adj.* pertaining to the *navel*. [Gr. *omphalikos—omphalos*, the navel.]

**On**, on, *prep.* in contact with the upper part of: to and towards the surface of: upon or acting by contact with: not off: at or near: at or during: in addition to: toward, for: at the peril of: in consequence: immediately after: (*B.*) off.—*adv.* above, or next beyond: forward, in succession: in continuance: not off.—*int.* go on! proceed! [A.S. *on*, which with the cog. Dut. *aan*, Ice. *á* (= *an*), Ger. *an*, and Gr. *ana*, is from an Aryan pronominal base *ana*; whence also is prep. **In**.]

**Onager**, on'a-jèr, *n.* the *wild ass* of Central Asia. [L.—Gr. *onagros*, for *onos agrios—onos*, an ass, *agrios*, living in the fields—*agros*, a field.]

**Once**, ons, *n.* Same as **Ounce**, the animal.

**Once**, wuns, *adv.* a single time: at a former time.—*n.* one time. [M. E. *ones*—A.S. *anes*, orig. the gen. of *an*, one, used as an adv. See **Nonce**.]

**One**, wun, *pron.* a person (spoken of indefinitely), as in the phrase **One says**. [Merely a special use of the numeral *one*: hence nowise conn. with Fr.—L. *homo*, a man.]

**One**, wun, *adj.* single in number: single: undivided: the same.—**At one**, of one mind. [M. E. *oon*—A.S. *an*; cog. with Ice. *einn*, Ger. *ein*, Goth. *ains*; also with L. *unus* and W. *un*.]

**Oneness**, wun'nes, *n.* singleness: unity.

**Onerary**, on'ér-ar-i, *adj.* fitted or intended for carrying *burdens*: comprising burdens. [L. *onerarius—onus, oneris*, a burden.]

**Onerous**, on'ér-us, *adj.*, *burdensome*: oppressive.—*adv.* **On'erously.** [L. *onerosus—onus*.]

**Onesided**, wun'sīd-ed, *adj.* limited to one side: partial.—*n.* **Onesid'edness.**              [duct : event.

**Ongoing**, on'gō-ing, *n.* a going on : course of con-

**Onion**, un'yun, *n.* a common plant, with a bulbous root. [Fr. *oignon*—L. *unio, -onis—unus*, one.]

**Only**, ōn'li, *adj.* (*lit.*) *one-like*: single: this above all others: alone.—*adv.* in one manner: for one purpose: singly: merely: barely. [A.S. *anlic* (adj.)—*an*, one, and *lic*, like.]

**Onomatopœia**, on-o-mat-o-pē'ya, *n.* the formation of a word with resemblance in sound to that of the thing signified: such a word itself, also the use of such a word, as 'click,' 'cuckoo.'—*adj.* **Onomatopoet'ic.** [Lit. 'name-making,' Gr. *onoma, -atos*, a name, *poieō*, to make.]

**Onset**, on'set, *n.* violent attack : assault : a storming. [**On** and **Set**.]

**Onslaught**, on'slawt, *n.* an attack or onset : assault. [A.S. *on*, on, and *sleaht*, a stroke. See **Slaughter**.]

**Ontology**, on-tol'o-ji, *n.* the *science* that treats of the principles of pure *being*: metaphysics.—*adjs.* **Ontolog'ical**, **Ontolog'ical.**—*adv.* **Ontolog'ically.**—*n.* **Ontol'ogist**, one versed in ontology. [Gr. *ōn, ontos*, being pr.p. of *eimi* (Sans. *as*), to be, and *logos*, discourse.]

**Onward**, on'ward, *adj.*, *going on*: advancing: advanced.—*adv.* toward a point *on* or in front: forward. [**On**, and **Ward**, direction.]

**Onwards**, on'wardz, *adv.* Same as **Onward**.

**Onyx**, on'iks, *n.* (*min.*) an agate formed of layers of chalcedony of different colours, used for making cameos, so called from its likeness to the *nail* in colour. [L.—Gr. *o-nyx, o-nych-os*, a fingernail. See **Nail**.]

**Oolite**, ō'o-līt, *n.* (*geol.*) a seafish of the Dory family, composed of grains like the *eggs* or roe of a fish.—*adj.* **Oolit'ic.** [Fr. *oolithe*, from Gr. *ōon*, an egg, and *lithos*, stone. See **Oval**.]

**Ooze**, ōōz, *n.* soft mud: gentle flow: the liquor of a tan vat.—*v.i.* to flow gently: to percolate, as a liquid through pores. [M. E. *wose*—A.S. *wase*, mud; akin to A.S. *wos*, juice, and Ice. *vas*, moisture.]

**Oozy**, ōōz'i, *adj.* resembling *ooze*: slimy.

**Opacity**, o-pas'i-ti, *n.* opaqueness: obscurity. [See **Opaque**.]

**Opah**, ō'pa, *n.* a seafish of the Dory family, also called kingfish. [Ety. unknown.]

**Opal**, ō'pal, *n.* a precious stone of a milky hue, remarkable for its changing colours. [Fr. *opale*—L. *opalus*.]

**Opalescent**, ō-pal-es'ent, *adj.* reflecting a milky or pearly light from the interior.

**Opaque**, ō-pāk', *adj.*, *shady*: *dark*: not transparent. [Fr.—L. *opacus*.]

**Opaqueness**, ō-pāk'nes, *n.* quality of being *opaque*: want of transparency.

**Ope**, ōp, *v.t.* and *v.i.* (*poetry*) short for **Open**.

**Open**, ō'pn, *adj.* not shut: free of access: free from trees: not fenced: not drawn together: not frozen up: not frosty: free to be used, &c.: public: without reserve: frank: easily understood: generous: liberal: clear: unbalanced, as an account: attentive: free to be discussed.—*v.t.* to make open: to bring to view: to explain: to begin.—*v.i.* to become open: to unclose: to be unclosed: to begin to appear: to begin.—*adv.* **O'penly.**—*ns.* **O'penness**, **O'pener.** [A.S. *open*, from *up*, up; like the cog. Dut. *open* (from *op*), Ice. *opinn* (from *upp*), and Ger. *offen* (from *auf*). See **Up**.]    [hand: generous: liberal.

**Open-handed**, ō'pn-hand'ed, *adj.* with an open

**Open-hearted**, ō'pn-härt'ed, *adj.* with an open heart: frank: generous.

**Opening**, ō'pn-ing, *n.* an open place: a breach: an aperture: beginning: first appearance: opportunity.                [*opera*. See **Operate**.]

**Opera**, op'er-a, *n.* a musical drama. [It.—L.

**Opera-bouffe**, op'er-a-bōōf, *n.* a comic opera. [Fr.—It. *opera-buffa*. See **Buffoon**.]

**Opera-glass**, op'er-a-glas, *n.* a small *glass* or telescope for use at *operas*, theatres, &c.

**Operate**, op'er-āt, *v.i.* to *work*: to exert strength: to produce any effect: to exert moral power: (*med.*) to take effect upon the human system: (*surgery*) to perform some unusual act upon the body with the hand or an instrument.—*v.t.* to effect: to produce by agency. [L. *operor, -atus*—*opera*, work, closely conn. with *opus, operis*, work (Sans. *apas*).]

**Operatic**, op-er-at'ik, **Operatical**, op-er-at'ik-al, *adj.* pertaining to or resembling the *opera*.

**Operation**, op-er-ā'shun, *n.* act or process of operating: agency: influence: method of working: action or movements: surgical performance.

**Operative**, op'er-a-tiv, *adj.* having the power of operating or acting: exerting force: producing effects.—*n.* a workman in a manufactory: a labourer.—*adv.* **Op'eratively.**

**Operator**, op'er-ā-tor, *n.* one who or that which operates or produces an effect.

**Operculum**, ō-per'kū-lum, *n.* (*bot.*) a *cover* or lid:

(*zool.*) the plate over the entrance of a shell : the apparatus which protects the gills of fishes :—*pl.* **Oper'cula.**—*adj.* **Oper'cular,** belonging to the operculum.—*adjs.* **Oper'culate, Oper'culated,** having an operculum. [L., from *operio*, to cover.]       [drama. [It., dim. of **Opera.**]

**Operetta,** op-ėr-et'a, *n.* a short, light musical

**Operose,** op'ėr-ōs, *adj., laborious* : tedious.—*adv.* **Op'erosely.**—*n.* **Op'eroseness.** [See **Operate.**]

**Ophicleide,** of'i-klīd, *n.* a large bass trumpet, with a deep pitch. [Fr. ; coined from Gr. *ophis*, a serpent, and *kleis, kleidos*, a key.]

**Ophidian,** of-id'i-an, **Ophidious,** of-id'i-us, *adj.* pertaining to *serpents*. [Gr. *ophis*, a serpent, erroneously supposed to have gen. *ophidos*.]

**Ophthalmia,** of-thal'mi-a, **Ophthalmy,** of'thal-mi, *n.* inflammation of the *eye*. [Gr.—*ophthalmos*, eye, from root of **Optics.**]       [*eye*.

**Ophthalmic,** of-thal'mik, *adj.* pertaining to the

**Ophthalmoscope,** of-thal'mo-skōp, *n.* an instrument for *examining* the interior of the *eye*. [Gr. *ophthalmos*, eye, and *skopeō*, look at.]

**Opiate,** ō'pi-āt, *n.* any medicine that contains *opium*, and induces sleep : that which induces rest.—*adj.* inducing sleep : causing rest.

**Opiated,** ō'pi-āt-ed, *adj.* mixed with *opiates* : under the influence of opiates.

**Opine,** o-pīn', *v.i.* to be of opinion : to judge : to suppose. [Fr. *opiner*—L. *opinor*, to think.]

**Opinion,** ō-pin'yun, *n.* a conviction on probable evidence : judgment : notion : estimation. [L.]

**Opinionated,** ō-pin'yun-āt-ed, *adj.* firmly adhering to one's own *opinions*.

**Opinionative,** ō-pin'yun-āt-iv, *adj.* unduly attached to one's own *opinions* : stubborn.—*adv.* **Opin'ionatively.**—*n.* **Opin'ionativeness.**

**Opium,** ō'pi-um, *n.* the narcotic *juice* of the white poppy. [L.—Gr. *opion*, dim. from *opos*, sap.]

**Opossum,** o-pos'um, *n.* an American quadruped with a prehensile tail, the female having a pouch in which she carries her young. [West Indian.]

**Oppidan,** op'i-dan, *n.* at Eton, a student who boards in the *town*, not in the college. [Orig. a townsman, L. *oppidanus*—*oppidum*, a town.]

**Opponent,** op-pō'nent, *adj., opposing* : situated in front : adverse.—*n.* one who opposes, esp. in argument : an adversary.

**Opportune,** op-por-tūn', *adj.* present at a proper time : timely : convenient.—*adv.* **Opportune'ly.**—*ns.* **Opportune'ness ; Opportun'ist,** a politician who waits for events before declaring his opinions. [Fr.—L. *opportunus*—*ob*, before, and *portus*, a harbour.]

**Opportunity,** op-por-tūn'i-ti, *n.* an *opportune* or convenient time : occasion.

**Opposable,** op-pōz'a-bl, *adj.* that may be *opposed*.

**Oppose,** op-pōz', *v.t.* to *place before* or in the way of : to set against : to place as an obstacle : to resist : to check : to compete with.—*v.i.* to make objection.—*n.* **Oppos'er.** [Fr.—L. *ob*, and Fr. *poser*, to place. See **Pose,** *n.*]

**Opposite,** op'o-zit, *adj., placed over against* : standing in front : contrasted with : adverse : contrary.—*n.* that which is opposed or contrary : an opponent.—*adv.* **Opp'ositely.**—*n.* **Opp'ositeness.** [Fr.—L. *oppositus*—*ob*, against, and *pono*, to place.]

**Opposition,** op-o-zish'un, *n.* state of being placed over against : standing over against : repugnance : contrariety : act of opposing : resistance : that which opposes : obstacle : the party that opposes the ministry or existing administration : (*astron.*) the situation of heavenly bodies when 180 degrees apart. [See **Opposite.**]

**Oppress,** op-pres', *v.t.* to use severely : to burden : to lie heavy upon : to constrain : to overpower. [Fr.—L. *opprimo, oppressus*—*ob*, against, and *premo*, to press.]

**Oppression,** op-presh'un, *n.* act of oppressing : severity : cruelty : state of being oppressed : misery : hardship : injustice : dullness. [Fr.—L.]

**Oppressive,** op-pres'iv, *adj.* tending to oppress : over-burdensome : unjustly severe : heavy : overpowering.—*adv.* **Oppress'ively.**—*n.* **Oppress'iveness.**

**Oppressor,** op-pres'er, *n.* one who oppresses.

**Opprobrious,** op-prō'bri-us, *adj.* expressive of *opprobrium* : reproachful : infamous : despised.—*adv.* **Oppro'briously.**—*n.* **Oppro'briousness.**

**Opprobrium,** op-prō'bri-um, *n., reproach* with contempt or disdain : disgrace : infamy. [L. *ob*, against, *probrum*, reproach—perhaps contracted from *prohibrum*—*prohibeo*, to prohibit.]

**Oppugn,** op-pūn', *v.t.* to *fight against* : to oppose : to resist.—*n.* **Oppugn'er.** [Fr.—L. *oppugno*, to fight against—*ob*, against, and *pugna*, a fight. See **Pugilism.**]

**Optative,** op'ta-tiv or op-tā'tiv, *adj.* expressing *desire* or *wish*.—*n.* (*gram.*) a mood of the verb expressing wish.—*adv.* **Op'tatively.** [L. *optativus*, from *opto, optatum*, to wish.]

**Optic,** op'tik, **Optical,** op'tik-al, *adj.* relating to *sight*, or to optics.—*adv.* **Op'tically.** [Fr. *optique*—Gr. *optikos*—root *op* or *ok*, seen in Gr. *op-somai*, I shall see, and L. *oc-ulus*, eye. See **Eye.**]

**Optician,** op-tish'an, *n.* one skilled in *optics* : one who makes or sells optical instruments.

**Optics,** op'tiks, *n.sing.* the science of the nature and laws of vision and light.

**Optimism,** op'tim-izm, *n.* the doctrine that everything is ordered for the *best* :—opp. to **Pessimism.** [L. *optimus*, best.]

**Optimist,** op'tim-ist, *n.* one who holds that everything is ordered for the best.

**Option,** op'shun, *n.* act of *choosing* : power of choosing or wishing : wish. [L. *optio, optionis*.]

**Optional,** op'shun-al, *adj.* left to one's *option* or choice.—*adv.* **Op'tionally.**

**Opulence,** op'ū-lens, *n., means* : riches : wealth.

**Opulent,** op'ū-lent, *adj.* wealthy.—*adv.* **Op'ulently.** [Fr.—L. *op-ulentus*—*ob*, base of L. pl. *op-es*, wealth—root *ap*, to obtain.]

**Or,** or, *conj.* marking an alternative, and sometimes opposition. [Short for *other*, modern E. **Either.**]—*prep.* (*B.*) before. [In this sense a corr. of **Ere.**]

**Or,** or, *n.* (*heraldry*) gold. [Fr.—L. *aurum*, gold.]

**Oracle,** or'a-kl, *n.* the answer *spoken* or uttered by the gods : the place where responses were given, and the deities supposed to give them : one famed for wisdom : a wise decision : (*B.*) the sanctuary :—*pl.* the revelations made to the prophets. [Fr.—L. *ora-cu-lum*, double dim. from *oro*, to speak—*os, oris*, the mouth.]

**Oracular,** ō-rak'ū-lar, *adj.* delivering *oracles* : resembling oracles : grave : venerable : equivocal : obscure.—*adv.* **Orac'ularly.**—*n.* **Orac'ularness.**

**Oral,** ō'ral, *adj.* uttered by the *mouth* : spoken.—*adv.* **O'rally.** [L. *os, oris*, the mouth.]

**Orang,** ō-rang', *n.* a kind of ape resembling *man*, found in Borneo and Sumatra. [Malay, 'man.']

**Orange,** or'anj, *n.* a tree with a delightful gold-coloured fruit : its fruit : a colour composed of red and yellow.—*adj.* pertaining to an orange : orange-coloured. [Fr.—It. *arancio*—Pers. *naranj*, the *n* being dropped ; it was thought to come from L. *aurum*, gold, hence Low L. *aurantium*.]

**Orangeman**, or'anj-man, *n.* a member **of** a secret society instituted in Ireland in 1795 to uphold Protestantism, so called from William of *Orange*.

**Orangery**, or'anj-ėr-i, *n.* a plantation of *orange*-trees.

**Orang-outang**, ō-rang'-ōō-tang', **Orang-utan**, ō-rang'-ōō-tan', *n.* the Indian or red orang. [Malay, 'wild man.']

**Oration**, o-rā'shun, *n.* a public *speech* of a formal character. [Fr.—L. *oratio*, from *oro*, to speak, pray.]

**Orator**, or'a-tor, *n.* a public *speaker*: a man of eloquence :—*fem.* **Or'atress**, **Or'atrix.**

**Oratorical**, or-a-tor'ik-al, *adj.* pertaining to *oratory*: becoming an orator.—*adv.* **Orator'ically.**

**Oratorio**, or-a-tō'ri-ō, *n.* a kind of musical drama, usually founded on a Scriptural subject. [It. So called because they originated among the priests of the *Oratory*.]

**Oratory**, or'a-tor-i, *n.* the art of *speaking* well, or so as to please and persuade, esp. publicly : the exercise of eloquence : an apartment or building for private worship. [See under **Oration**.]

**Orb**, orb, *n.* a *circle* : a sphere : a celestial body : a wheel : any rolling body : the eye.—*v.t.* to surround : to form into an orb. [L. *orbis*, a circle.]

**Orbed**, orbd, *adj.* in the form of an *orb* : circular.

**Orbicular**, or-bik'ū-lar, *adj.* having the form of an *orb* : spherical : round.—*adv.* **Orbic'ularly.**—*n.* **Orbic'ularness.** [From L. *orbiculus*, dim. of *orbis*.]

**Orbiculate**, or-bik'ū-lāt, **Orbiculated** or-bik'ū-lāt-ed, *adj.* in the form of an *orb*.—*n.* **Orbicula'tion.**

**Orbit**, or'bit, *n.* the path described by a celestial body in the heavens : the bony cavity for the eyeball : the skin round the eye. [L. *orbita—orbis*, a ring or circle.]

**Orbital**, or'bit-al, *adj.* pertaining to an *orbit*.

**Orchard**, orch'ard, *n.* a garden of fruit-trees, esp. apple-trees. [A.S. *orceard*—older form *ortgeard*. See **Wort**, a plant, and **Yard**.]

**Orchestra**, or'kes-tra, *n.* in the Greek theatre, the place where the chorus *danced :* the part of a theatre for the musicians : the performers in an orchestra. [L.—Gr. *orchēstra—orcheomai*, to dance.]

**Orchestral**, or'kes-tral or or-kes'-, *adj.* pertaining to an *orchestra :* performed in an orchestra.

**Orchid**, or'kid, *n.* an orchidaceous plant.

**Orchidaceous**, or-ki-dā'shus, *adj.* relating to a natural order of plants with beautiful fragrant flowers. [Gr. *orchis*, a testicle, which its root resembles in shape.]

**Orchis**, or'kis, *n.* a genus of orchidaceous plants.

**Ordain**, or-dān', *v.t.* to put in *order :* to appoint : to regulate : to set in an office : to invest with ministerial functions. [O. Fr. *ordener* (Fr. *ordonner*)—L. *ordino*, *ordinatus—ordo*. See **Order**.]

**Ordeal**, or'de-al, *n.* a *dealing* out or giving of just judgment : an ancient form of trial by lot, fire, water, &c.: any severe trial or examination. [A.S. *or-del*, *or-dal ;* cog. with Dut. *oor-deel*, judgment, Ger. *ur-theil ;* the prefix *or-* (Dut. *oor-*, Ger. *ur-*) sig. out, and *-deal* being the same word as **Deal** and **Dole**.]

**Order**, or'dėr, *n.* regular arrangement : method : proper state : rule : regular government : command : a class : a society of persons : a religious fraternity : a scientific division of objects : (*arch.*) a system of the parts of columns :—*pl.* the Christian ministry.—*v.t.* to arrange : to conduct : to command.—*v.i.* to give command. [M. E. *ordre*—Fr. *ordre*—L. *ordo*, -*inis*.]

**Ordering**, or'dėr-ing, *n.* arrangement : management. [orderly.

**Orderless**, or'dėr-les, *adj.* without order : disorderly.

**Orderly**, or'dėr-li, *adj.* in *order :* regular : well regulated : quiet : being on duty.—*adv.* regularly : methodically.—*n.* a soldier who attends on a superior, esp. for carrying official messages.—*n.* **Or'derliness.**

**Ordinal**, or'din-al, *adj.* shewing *order* or succession.—*n.* a number noting order : a ritual for ordination.

**Ordinance**, or'din-ans, *n.* that which is *ordained* by authority : a law : an established rite. [See **Ordain**, doublet **Ordnance**.]

**Ordinary**, or'din-ar-i, *adj.* according to the common *order :* usual : of common rank : plain : of little merit.—*n.* an established judge of ecclesiastical causes : settled establishment : actual office : a bishop : a place where meals are provided at fixed charges.—*adv.* **Or'dinarily.**

**Ordinate**, or'din-āt, *adj.* in *order :* regular.—*n.* a straight line in a curve terminated on both sides by the curve and bisected by the diameter.—*adv.* **Or'dinately.** [See **Ordain**.]

**Ordination**, or-din-ā'shun, *n.* the act of *ordaining :* established order. [See **Ordain**.]

**Ordnance**, ord'nans, *n.* (*orig.*) any *arrangement*, disposition, or equipment : great guns : artillery. [See **Ordinance**.]

**Ordure**, or'dūr, *n.*, *dirt :* dung : excrement. [Fr.—O. Fr. *ord*, foul—L. *horridus*, rough.]

**Ore**, ōr, *n.* metal in its unreduced state : metal mixed with earthy and other substances. [A.S. *ōr*, another form of *ar*, brass, cog. with Ice. *eir*, Goth. *aiz*, L. *æs*, *ær-is*, bronze.]

**Organ**, or'gan, *n.* an instrument or means by which anything is *done :* that by which a natural operation is carried on : a musical instrument with pipes, bellows, and keys : the medium of communication. [Fr. *organe*—L. *organum*—Gr. *organon*, akin to *ergon*. See **Work**.]

**Organic**, or-gan'ik, **Organical**, or-gan'ik-al, *adj.* pertaining to an *organ* : consisting of or containing organs : produced by the organs : instrumental.—*adv.* **Organ'ically.**

**Organisable**, or-gan-īz'a-bl, *adj.* that may be organised or arranged.

**Organisation**, or-gan-i-zā'shun, *n.* the act of organising : the state of being organised.

**Organise**, or'gan-īz, *v.t.* to supply with *organs :* to form, as an organised body : to arrange.

**Organism**, or'gan-izm, *n.* organic structure : a living being. [organ.

**Organist**, or'gan-ist, *n.* one who plays on the

**Orgasm**, or'gasm, *n.* immoderate excitement or action. [Gr. *orgasmos*, *orgao*, I swell.]

**Orgies**, or'jiz, *n.pl.* (*orig.*) ceremonies observed in the worship of Bacchus, distinguished by furious revelry : any drunken nocturnal rites or revelry. [Fr.—L. *orgia*, secret rites—Gr., closely akin to *ergon*, work. See **Organ** and **Work**.]

**Oriel**, ō'ri-el, *n.* (*orig.*) a chamber or apartment : a window that juts out so as to form a small apartment. [O. Fr. *oriol*, a porch, a corridor—Low L. *oriolum*, a highly ornamented recess—L. *aureolus*, gilded—*aurum*, gold. See **Oriole**.]

**Orient**, ō'ri-ent, *adj.*, *rising*, as the sun : eastern : shining.—*n.* the part where the sun *rises :* the east. [L. *oriens*, -*entis*, pr.p. of *orior*, to rise.]

**Oriental**, ō-ri-ent'al, *adj.* eastern : pertaining to, in, or from the east.—*n.* a native of the east.

**Orientalism**, ō-ri-ent'al-izm, *n.* oriental doctrine.

**Orientalist**, ō-ri-ent'al-ist, *n.* one versed in **the** eastern languages : an oriental.

**Orifice**, or'i-fis, *n.* something *made* like a *mouth*

or opening. [Fr—L. *orificium—os, oris*, mouth, and *facio*, to make.]

**Oriflamme**, or'i-flam, *n.* a little banner of red silk with many points streaming like *flames*, borne on a *gilt* staff, the ancient royal standard of France. [Fr.—Low L. *auriflamma*, a little banner—L. *aurum*, gold, *flamma*, a flame.]

**Origan**, or'i-gan, **Origanum**, o-rig'a-num, *n.* wild marjoram. [Lit. 'mountain-pride,' Fr. *origan*—L. *origanum*—Gr. *origanon—oros*, mountain, *ganos*, pride, beauty.]

**Origin**, or'i-jin, *n.* the *rising* or first existence of anything : that from which anything first proceeds : cause : derivation. [Fr. *origine*—L. *origo, originis—orior*, to rise.]

**Original**, o-rij'in-al, *adj.* pertaining to the *origin* : first in order or existence : not copied : not translated : having the power to originate, as thought. —*n.* origin : first copy : the precise language used by a writer : an untranslated tongue.—*adv.* **Orig'inally**. [Fr.—L. *originalis—origo*.]

**Originality**, o-rij-in-al'it-i, *n.* quality or state of being *original* or of originating ideas.

**Originate**, o-rij'in-āt, *v.t.* to give *origin* to : to bring into existence.—*v.i.* to have origin : to begin.—*n.* **Orig'inator**. [It. *originare*—L. *origo*.]

**Origination**, o-rij'in-ā'shun, *n.* act of originating or of coming into existence : mode of production.

**Oriole**, ōr'i-ōl, *n.* the *golden* thrush. [O. Fr. *oriol*—L. *aureolus*, dim. of *aureus*, golden—*aurum*, gold. Cf. **Oriel**.]

**Orion**, o-rī'on, *n.* (*astr.*) one of the constellations. [*Orion* (*myth.*), a giant placed among the stars at his death.]

**Orison**, or'i-zun, *n.* a *prayer*. [O. Fr. *orison* (Fr. *oraison*)—L. *oratio, -onis—oro*, to pray. See **Oral**.]

**Orlop**, or'lop, *n.* the deck of a ship where the cables, &c. are stowed : the under-deck of a ship-of-the-line. [Lit. a 'running over,' Dut. *overloop*, the upper-deck—*overlopen*, to run over.]

**Ormolu**, or-mo-lōō', *n.* a kind of brass like gold from the quantity of copper in it. [Lit. 'beaten gold,' Fr. *or*—L. *aurum*, gold, and *moulu*, pa.p. of *moudre*, to grind—L. *molo*, to grind.]

**Ornament**, or'na-ment, *n.* anything that adds grace or beauty : additional beauty :—*pl.* (*Pr. Bk.*) all the articles used in the services of the church.—*v.t.* to adorn : to furnish with ornaments. [Fr. *ornement*—L. *orna-mentum—orno*, to adorn.]

**Ornamental**, or-na-ment'al, *adj.* serving to *adorn* or beautify.—*adv.* **Ornament'ally**.

**Ornamentation**, or-na-men-tā'shun, *n.* act or art of ornamenting : (*arch.*) ornamental work.

**Ornate**, or-nāt', *adj.* *ornamented* : decorated.— *adv.* **Ornate'ly**.—*n.* **Ornate'ness**. [L. *ornatus*, pa.p. of *orno*.]

**Ornithological**, or-ni-tho-loj'ik-al, *adj.* pertaining to ornithology.—*adv.* **Ornitholog'ically**.

**Ornithology**, or-ni-thol'o-ji, *n.* the *science of birds*. —*n.* **Ornithol'ogist**, one versed in ornithology. [Gr. *ornis, ornithos*, a bird (cog. with A.S. *earn*, eagle), and *logos*, science.]

**Ornithomancy**, or-nith'o-man-si or or'nith-, *n.*, divination by *birds*, their flight, &c. [Gr. *ornis, ornithos*, bird, *manteia*, divination.]

**Ornithorhynchus**, or-ni-tho-ring'kus, *n.* an animal in Australia, with a body like an otter and a snout like the bill of a duck, also called Duck-bill. [Lit. 'bird-snout,' Gr. *ornis, ornithos*, bird, *rhynchos*, snout.]

**Orography**, or-og'ra-fi, *n.* the description of moun-tains.—*adj.* **Orograph'ic, Orograph'ical**. [Gr. *oros*, a mountain, and *graphō*, to describe.]

**Orology**. Same as **Orography**.

**Orphan**, or'fan, *n.* a child *bereft* of father or mother, or of both.—*adj.* bereft of parents. [Gr. *orphanos*, akin to L. *orbus*, bereaved.]

**Orphanage**, or'fan-āj, *n.* the state of an *orphan* : a house for orphans.

**Orphean**, or-fē'an or or'fe-an, *adj.* pertaining to *Orpheus* : (*myth.*) a poet who had the power of moving inanimate objects by the music of his lyre.

**Orpiment**, or'pi-ment, *n.* yellow sulphuret of arsenic, used for the *gold* or *yellow paint* called king's yellow. [Fr.—L. *auripigmentum—aurum*, gold, *pigmentum*, paint.]

**Orpin**, or'pin, *n.* a deep *gold* or yellow colour.

**Orpine**, or'pin, *n.* a plant with *gold* or purplish-rose coloured flowers. [Fr. *orpin*, from *or*—L. *aurum*, and Fr. *peindre*. See **Paint**.]

**Orrery**, or'ér-i, *n.* an apparatus for illustrating, by balls mounted on rods, the size, positions, motions, &c. of the heavenly bodies [From the Earl of *Orrery*, for whom one of the first was made.]

**Orris**, or'is, *n.* a species of *iris* in the south of Europe, the dried root of which has a smell of violets, used in perfumery. [Prob. a corruption of **Iris**.]

**Ort**, ort, *n.* a fragment, esp. one left from a meal : usually *pl.* [Low Ger. *ort*, refuse of fodder, Scot. *ort* or *wort*.]

**Orthodox**, or'tho-doks, *adj.*, *sound* in *doctrine* : believing the received or established opinions, esp. in religion : according to the received doctrine.—*adv.* **Or'thodoxly**. [Through Fr. and Late L. from Gr. *orthodoxos—orthos*, right, *doxa*, opinion—*dokeō*, to seem.]

**Orthodoxy**, or'tho-doks-i, *n.*, *soundness* of *opinion* or doctrine : belief in the commonly accepted opinions, esp. in religion. [Gr. *orthodoxia*. See **Orthodox**.]

**Orthoepy**, or'tho-e-pi, *n.* (*gram.*) *correct* pronunciation of *words*.—*adj.* **Orthoep'ical**.—*n.* **Or'thoepist**, one versed in orthoepy. [Gr. *orthos*, right, *epos*, a word.]

**Orthogon**, or'tho-gon, *n.* (*geom.*) a figure with all its angles *right angles*.—*adj.* **Orthog'onal**, rectangular. [Gr. *orthos*, right, *gōnia*, angle.]

**Orthographer**, or-thog'ra-fér, *n.* one who *spells* words *correctly*.

**Orthographic**, or-tho-graf'ik, **Orthographical**, or-tho-graf'ik-al, *adj.* pertaining or according to *orthography* : spelt correctly.—*adv.* **Ortho-graph'ically**.

**Orthography**, or-thog'ra-fi, *n.* (*gram.*) the correct spelling of words. [Gr. *orthographia—orthos*, right, *graphō*, to write.]

**Orthoptera**, or-thop'tér-a, *n.* an order of insects with uniform wing-covers, that overlap at the top when shut, under which are the true wings, which fold lengthwise like a fan. [Lit. 'straight wings,' Gr. *orthos*, straight, *ptera*, pl. of *pteron*, wing.] [the *orthoptera*.

**Orthopterous**, or-thop'tér-us, *adj.* pertaining to

**Ortolan**, ort'o-lan, *n.* a kind of bunting, common in Europe, and considered a great delicacy. [Lit. 'the frequenter of gardens,' Fr.—It. *ortolano*—L. *hortolanus*, belonging to gardens—*hortulus*, dim. of *hortus*, a garden. See **Court** and **Yard**, a place inclosed.]

**Oscillate**, os'il-lāt, *v.i.* to move backwards and forwards : to fluctuate between certain limits. [L. *oscillo, -atus*, to swing—*oscillum*, a swing.]

**Oscillation,** os-il-lā'shun, *n.* act of oscillating : a swinging like a pendulum. [Fr.—L. *oscillatio.*]

**Oscillatory,** os'il-la-tor-i, *adj., swinging.*

**Osculant,** os'kū-lant, *adj., kissing* : adhering closely. [L. *osculans, -antis,* pr.p. of *osculor.*]

**Osculate,** os'kū-lāt, *v.t.* to *kiss* : to touch, as two curves.—*n.* Oscula'tion. [L. *osculor, -atum—osculum,* a little mouth, a kiss, dim. of *os,* mouth.]

**Osculatory,** os'kū-la-tor-i, *adj.* of or pertaining to *kissing* : (*geom.*) having the same curvature at the point of contact.

**Osier,** ō'zhi-ėr, *n.* the water-willow, used in making baskets.—*adj.* made of or like osiers. [Fr. ; perh. from Gr. *oisos ;* akin to L. *vitex.*]

**Osiered,** ō'zhi-ėrd, *adj.* adorned with *willows.*

**Osmium,** oz'mi-um, *n.* a gray-coloured metal found with platinum, the oxide of which has a disagreeable *smell.* [Low L.—Gr. *osmē,* smell, orig. *od-mē,* conn. with root of **Odour.**]

**Osnaburg,** oz'na-burg, *n.* a coarse kind of linen, originally brought from *Osnaburg* in Germany.

**Osprey, Ospray,** os'prā, *n.* the fish-hawk, a species of eagle very common on the coast of N. America. [Corr. from **Ossifrage,** which see.]

**Osseous,** os'e-us, *adj., bony* : composed of or resembling bone. [L. *osseus—os, ossis,* bone.]

**Ossicle,** os'i-kl, *n.* a *small bone.* [Dim. of *os.*]

**Ossiferous,** os-sif'ėr-us, *adj.* producing *bone* : (*geol.*) containing bones. [L. *os,* and *fero,* to bear.]

**Ossification,** os-si-fi-kā'shun, *n.* the *change* or state of being changed into a *bony* substance.

**Ossifrage,** os'i-frāj, *n.* the sea or bald eagle, common in the United States : (*B.*) the bearded vulture, the largest of European birds. [Lit. 'the bone-breaker,' L. *ossifragus,* breaking bones —*os,* and *frag,* root of *frango, fractum,* to break.]

**Ossify,** os'i-fī, *v.t.* to make into *bone* or into a bone-like substance.—*v.i.* to become bone :— *pa.p.* oss'ified. [L. *ossifico—os,* and *facio,* to make.]

**Ossivorous,** os-siv'or-us, *adj., devouring* or feeding on *bones.* [L. *os,* and *voro,* to devour.]

**Ossuary,** os'ū-ar-i, *n.* a place where the *bones* of the dead are deposited : a charnel-house.

**Ostensible,** os-tens'i-bl, *adj.* that may be *shown* : declared : apparent.—*adv.* Ostens'ibly.—*n.* Ostensibil'ity. [L. *ostendo, ostensum,* to show.]

**Ostensive,** os-tens'iv, *adj., showing* : exhibiting. —*adv.* Ostens'ively.

**Ostentation,** os-ten-tā'shun, *n.* act of *making a display* : ambitious display : boasting. [Fr.— L. *ostendo,* to show.]

**Ostentatious,** os-ten-tā'shus, *adj.* given to show : fond of self-display : intended for display.—*adv.* Ostenta'tiously.—*n.* Ostenta'tiousness.

**Osteological,** os-te-o-loj'ik-al, *adj.* pertaining to osteology.—*adv.* Osteolog'ically.

**Osteology,** os-te-ol'o-ji, *n.* the *science* of the *bones,* that part of anatomy which treats of the bones. —*ns.* Osteol'oger, Osteol'ogist, one versed in osteology. [Gr. *osteon,* bone, *logos,* science.]

**Ostler,** os'lėr. Same as **Hostler.**

**Ostracise,** os'tra-sīz, *v.t.* in ancient Greece, to banish by the vote of the people written on a *potsherd* : to banish from society. [Gr. *ostrakizō—ostrakon,* a potsherd, orig. a shell. Cf. **Osseous** and **Oyster.**]

**Ostracism,** os'tra-sizm, *n.* banishment by *ostracising.* [Gr. *ostrakismos—ostrakizō.*]

**Ostrich,** os'trich, *n.* the largest of birds, found in Africa, remarkable for its speed in running, and prized for its feathers. [O. Fr. *ostruche* (Fr.

*autruche*)—L. *avis-, struthio,* ostrich—Gr. *strouthos,* little bird, *megas strouthos,* the large bird, the ostrich. Cf. **Bustard.**]

**Otacoustic,** ot-a-kows'tik, *adj.* assisting the sense of *hearing.*—*n.* (also **Otacous'ticon**) an instrument to assist the hearing. [Gr. *akoustikos,* relating to hearing—*akouō,* to hear—*ous, ōtos,* ear.]

**Other,** uth'ėr, *adj.* and *pron.* different, not the same : additional : second of two. [A.S. *other ;* cog. with Goth. *anthar,* Ger. *ander,* Sans. *antara,* L. *alter.*]

**Otherwise,** uth'ėr-wīz, *adv.* in *another way* or manner : by other causes : in other respects.

**Otiose,** ō'shi-ōs, *adj.* be'ing at *ease* : unoccupied : lazy. [L. *otiosus—otium,* rest.]

**Otitis,** o-tī'tis, *n.* inflammation of the internal ear. [From Gr. *ous, ōtos,* the ear.]

**Otoscope,** o'to-skōp, *n.* an instrument for *exploring* the *ear.* [Gr. *ous, ōtos,* the ear, and *skopeo,* to look at.]

**Otter,** ot'ėr, *n.* a large kind of weasel living entirely on fish. [Lit. the 'water-animal,' A.S. *otor, oter ;* cog. with Dut. and Ger. *otter,* Ice. *otr,* akin to *uddr,* water, Gr. *hydra,* E. **Water.**]

**Otto,** ot'o, **Ottar,** ot'ar, (better spelt) **Attar,** at'ar, *n.* a fragrant oil obtained from certain flowers, esp. the rose. [Ar. *'itr—'atira,* to smell sweetly.]

**Ottoman,** ot'o-man, *adj.* pertaining to the Turkish Empire, founded by *Othman* or Osman in 1299.—*n.* a Turk : a low, stuffed seat without a back, first used in Turkey. [The Fr. form.]

**Oubliette,** ōō-bli-et', *n.* a dungeon with no opening but at the top. [Lit. 'a place where one is *forgotten,*' Fr., from *oublier,* to forget—L. *obliviscor.*]

**Ouch,** owch, *n.* the socket of a precious stone. [O. Fr. *nouche, nosche ;* from O. Ger. *nusche,* a clasp.]

**Ought,** *n.* Same as **Aught.**

**Ought,** awt, *v.i.* to be under obligation : to be proper or necessary. [Lit. 'owed,' pa.t. of **Owe.**]

**Ounce,** owns, *n.* the *twelfth part* of a pound troy = 480 grains : $\frac{1}{16}$ of a pound avoirdupois = 437½ troy grains. [A.S. *ynce,* $\frac{1}{12}$ of a foot, an inch ; Fr. *once*—L. *uncia,* the twelfth part of anything. See **Inch.**]

**Ounce,** owns, *n.* a feline carnivorous animal of Asia, allied to the leopard. [Fr. *once,* prob. nasalised form of Pers. *yuz.*]

**Our,** owr, *adj.* and *pron.* pertaining or belonging to *us.* [A.S. *ure* for *usere,* gen. pl. of 1st pers. pron. See **Us.**]

**Ourang-outang.** Same as **Orang-outang.**

**Ours,** owrz, *pron.* possessive of **We.**

**Ourself,** owr-self', *pron., myself* (in the regal style) :—*pl.* **Ourselves** (-selvz'), we, not others : us.

**Ousel,** ōō'zl, *n.* a kind of thrush. [A.S. *osle* (short for *amsele*) ; cog. with Ger. *amsel.*]

**Oust,** owst, *v.t.* to eject or expel. [O. Fr. *oster* (Fr. *ōter*), to remove ; acc. to Diez, from L. *haurio, haustus,* to draw (water). Cf. **Exhaust.**]

**Ouster,** owst'ėr, *n.* (*law*) ejection : dispossession.

**Out,** owt, *adv.* without, not within : gone forth : abroad : in a state of discovery : in a state of exhaustion, extinction, &c. : completely : freely : forcibly : at a loss : unsheltered : uncovered.— *int.* away ! begone !—**Out of course,** out of order.—**Out of hand,** instantly. [A.S. *ute, ut ;* cog. with Ice. and Goth. *ut,* Ger. *aus,* Sans. *ud.*]

---

uncover—*de* = un-, and *operio*, to cover acc. to Littré, from L. *operire*, to cover, confounded in meaning with *aperire*, to open.]

**Overtake,** ō-vėr-tāk', *v.t.* to come up with: to catch: to come upon.

**Overtask,** ō-vėr-task', *v.t.* to task overmuch: to impose too heavy a task on.

**Overtax,** ō-vėr-taks', *v.t.* to tax overmuch.

**Overthrow,** ō-vėr-thrō', *v.t.* to throw down: to upset: to bring to an end: to demolish: to defeat utterly.—*n.* **O'verthrow,** act of overthrowing or state of being overthrown: ruin: defeat.

**Overtop,** ō-vėr-top', *v.t.* to rise over the top of: to surpass: to obscure.            [beyond capital.

**Overtrade,** ō-vėr-trād', *v.i.* to trade overmuch or

**Overture,** ō'vėr-tūr, *n.* (*orig.*) an opening, disclosure: a proposal: (*music*) a piece introductory to a greater piece or ballet.—*v.t.* to lay an overture or proposal before. [Fr. *ouverture.*]

**Overturn,** ō-vėr-turn', *v.t.* to throw down: to subvert: to ruin.—*n.* **O'verturn,** state of being overturned.

**Overvalue,** ō-vėr-val'ū, *v.t.* to value overmuch.

**Overweening,** ō-vėr-wēn'ing, *adj.,* *weening* or thinking *too highly*: conceited: vain. [A.S. *oferwenan.* See **Ween.**]

**Overweigh,** ō-vėr-wā', *v.t.* to outweigh.

**Overweight,** ō-vėr-wāt', *n.* weight beyond what is required or is just.

**Overwhelm,** ō-vėr-hwelm', *v.t.* to overspread and crush by something heavy or strong: to immerse and bear down: to overcome.

**Overwise,** ō-vėr-wīz', *adj.* wise overmuch: affectedly wise.—*adv.* **Overwise'ly.**

**Overwork,** ō-vėr-wurk', *v.t.* and *v.i.* to work overmuch or beyond the strength: to tire.—*n.* **O'verwork,** *excess of work*: excessive labour.

**Overworn,** ō-vėr-wōrn', *adj.* worn out: subdued by toil: spoiled by use.

**Overwrought,** ō-vėr-rawt', *pa.p.* of **Overwork,** wrought overmuch: worked all. over.

**Oviferous,** ō-vif'ėr-us, *adj., egg-bearing.* [L. *ovum,* egg, and *fero,* to bear.]

**Oviform,** ō'vi-form, *adj.* having the *form* of an *oval* or egg. [L. *ovum,* egg, and **Form.**]

**Oviparous,** ō-vip'a-rus, *adj., bringing forth eggs.* [L. *ovum,* egg, and *pario,* to bring forth.]

**Ovoid,** ō'void, **Ovoidal,** ō-void'al, *adj., oval* or *egg shaped.* [L. *ovum,* egg, and Gr. *eidos,* form.]

**Ovum,** ō'vum, *n.* an egg: (*anat.*) the body in which after impregnation the development of the fetus takes place:—*pl.* **O'va.** [L.]

**Owe,** ō, *v.t.* to possess what belongs to another: to be bound to pay: to be obliged for. [A.S. *agan;* Ice. *eiga,* O. Ger. *eigan,* to possess.]

**Owing,** ō'ing, *adj.* due: ascribable to: imputable to.

**Owl,** owl, *n.* a nocturnal carnivorous bird, noted for its *howling* or hooting noise. [A.S. *ule;* Ger. *eule,* L. *ulula,* Sans. *uluka,* from the sound.]

**Owlet,** owl'et, *n.* a *little owl.* [Dim. of **Owl.**]

**Owlish,** owl'ish, *adj.* like an *owl.*

**Own,** ōn, *v.t.* to grant: concede: acknowledge. [A.S. *unnan,* to grant, cog. with Ger. *gönnen,* to grant.]

**Own,** ōn, *v.t., to possess:* to have a rightful title to. [A.S. *agnian,* with addition of causal suffix —*agen,* one's own. See **Own,** *adj.*]

**Own,** ōn, *adj., possessed:* belonging to: peculiar. [A.S. *agen,* pa.p. of *agan,* to possess, cog. with Ger. *eigen,* Ice, *eiginn,* one's own.]

**Owner,** ōn'ėr, *n.* one who *owns* or possesses.—*n.* **Own'ership.**

**Ox,** oks, *n.* a ruminant quadruped of the bovine family: the male of the cow, esp. when castrated: —*pl.* **Oxen,** oks'n, used for both male and female. [A.S. *oxa,* pl. *oxan;* Ice. *uxi;* Ger. *ochs,* Goth. *auhsa,* Sans. *ukshan.*]

**Oxalic,** oks-al'ik, *adj.* pertaining to or obtained from sorrel.

**Oxalis,** oks'a-lis, *n.* wood-*sorrel:* (*bot.*) a genus of plants having an *acid* taste. [Gr., from *oxys,* acid.]

**Oxeye,** oks'ī, *n.* a common plant in meadows, so called because its flower is like the eye of an ox.

**Oxeyed,** oks'īd, *adj.* having large full eyes like those of an ox.                          [oxen.

**Oxfly,** oks'flī, *n.* a fly hatched under the skin of

**Oxidation,** oks-id-ā'shun, **Oxidisement,** oks-id-īz'ment, *n.* act or process of *oxidising.*

**Oxide,** oks'id, *n.* a compound of *oxygen* and a base destitute of acid properties.

**Oxidisable,** oks-id-īz'a-bl, *adj.* capable of being *oxidised.*

**Oxidise,** oks'id-īz, *v.t.* to convert into an *oxide.*— *v.i.* to become an oxide.—*n.* **Oxidis'er.**

**Oxygen,** oks'i-jen, *n.* a gas without taste, colour, or smell, forming part of the air, water, &c. and supporting life and combustion. [Lit. 'that which generates acids,' from Gr. *oxys,* sharp, acid, and *gennaō,* to generate.]

**Oxygenate,** oks'ij-en-āt, *v.t.* to unite or cause to unite with *oxygen.*—*n.* **Oxygena'tion,** act of oxygenating.

**Oxygenise,** oks'ij-en-īz. Same as **Oxygenate.**

**Oxygenous,** oks-ij'en-us, *adj.* pertaining to or obtained from *oxygen.*

**Oxymel,** oks'i-mel, *n.* a mixture of vinegar and honey. [Lit. 'sour honey,' Gr. *oxys,* sour, *meli,* honey.]

**Oxytone,** oks'i-tōn, *adj.* having an *acute sound:* having the acute accent on the last syllable. [Gr. *oxys,* sharp, and *tonos,* tone, accent.]

**Oyer,** ō'yer, *n.* (*lit.*) a *hearing:* (*law*) a commission which confers the power of hearing and determining treasons, &c. [Norm. Fr. *oyer* (Fr. *ouir*)—L. *audire,* to hear.]

**Oyez, Oyes,** ō'yes, *int.* (*lit.*) *hear ye:* the introductory call of a public crier for attention. [Norm. Fr., 2d. pers. pl. imperative of *oyer.*]

**Oyster,** ois'tėr, *n.* a well-known bivalve shell-fish. [O. Fr. *oistre* (Fr. *huître*)—L. *ostrea*—Gr. *ostreon,* an oyster—*osteon,* a bone.]

**Ozone,** ō'zōn, *n.* name given to a modification of oxygen, when affected by electric discharges, marked by a peculiar *smell.* [Gr. *ozō,* to smell.]

# P

**Pabular,** pab'ū-lar, *adj.* pertaining to *food.*

**Pabulum,** pab'ū-lum, *n., food:* provender: fuel. [L.—*pa-sco, pa-vi,* to feed. See **Pastor.**]

**Paca,** pä'ka, *n.* a genus of rodent animals belonging to South America. [Port., the native name.]

**Pace,** pās, *n.* a *stride:* (*mil.*) the space left between the feet in one step, measured from heel to heel, and varying from 30 to 36 inches: a *step:* space between the feet in ordinary walking, 2½ feet: gait: rate of motion (of a man or beast): mode of stepping in horses in which the legs on the same side are lifted together: amble.—*v.t.* to measure by steps: to cause to progress: to regulate in motion.—*v.i.* to walk: to walk slowly: to amble.—*n.* **Pacer,** pās'ėr. [Fr. *pas*—L. *passus* —*pando, passus,* to stretch.]

**Pacha, Pachalic.** See **Pasha, Pashalic.**

**Pachyderm,** pak'i-dėrm, *n.* one of an order of non-ruminant, hoofed mammals, distinguished for the *thickness* of their *skin*, as the elephant:—*pl.* **Pach′yderms** or **Pachyderm′ata**. [Gr. *pachys*, thick, (*lit.*) firm, from root *pak*, and *derma*, *dermatos*, skin. See **Pack**.]

**Pachydermatous**, pak-i-dėrm′a-tus, *adj.* relating to a *pachyderm*, or of the order of pachyderms.

**Pacific**, pa-sif′ik, *adj.*, *peace-making* : appeasing : mild : tranquil.—*n.* the ocean between Asia and America, so called because found *peaceful* by its discoverer Magellan, after weathering Cape Horn.—*adv.* **Pacif′ically**. [See **Pacify**.]

**Pacification**, pas-if-i-kā′shun, *n.* the act of *making peace* between parties at variance.

**Pacificator**, pa-sif′i-kā-tor, **Pacifier**, pas′i-fī-ėr, *n.* a *peacemaker*.—*adj.* **Pacif′icatory**.

**Pacify**, pas′i-fī, *v.t.* to make peaceful : to appease : to calm : to soothe. [Fr. *pacifier*—L. *pacifico*—*pax*, *pacis*, peace, and *facio*, to make. See **Peace**.]

**Pack**, pak, *n.* (*lit.*) that which is *bound up* together : a bundle : a burden : a complete set of cards : a number of hounds hunting, or kept together : a number of persons combined for bad purposes : any great number.—*v.t.* to press together and fasten up : to place in close order : to select persons for some unjust object.—*n.* **Pack′er**. [From a root found in Ger. *pack* and Celt. *pac*, and conn. with L. *pango*, Sans. *paç*, to bind. Cf. **Pact**.]

**Package**, pak′āj, *n.* something *packed* : a bundle [or bale.

**Packet**, pak′et, *n.* a *small package* : a despatch vessel, so called from its carrying the packets of letters : a vessel plying regularly between ports.—*v.t.* to bind in a packet or parcel.

**Packhorse**, pak′hors, *n.* a horse formerly used to carry goods in panniers.

**Packing**, pak′ing, *n.* the act of putting in *packs* or tying up for carriage : material for packing.

**Packing-sheet**, pak′ing-shēt, *n.* a coarse cloth for packing or covering goods.

**Packman**, pak′man, *n.* a pedler or man who carries a pack. [burdens.

**Pack-saddle**, pak′-sad′l, *n.* a saddle for packs or

**Packthread**, pak′thred, *n.* a coarse thread used to sew up packages.

**Pact**, pakt, **Paction**, pak′shun, *n.* that which is *fixed* or agreed on : a contract. [L. *pactum*—*paciscor*, *pactus*, to make a contract—root *pak*, to bind. Cf. **Pack**, **Peace**.]

**Pad**, pad, *n.* a thief on the high-*road* (more commonly **Footpad**) : a roadster, an easy-paced horse.—*v.i.* to walk on foot : to rob on foot :—*pr.p.* padd′ing ; *pa.t.* and *pa.p.* padd′ed. [Dut. *pad*, a path, cog. with E. **Path**.]

**Pad**, pad, *n.* anything stuffed with a soft material : a soft saddle, cushion, &c. : a package of some soft material for writing upon.—*v.t.* to stuff with anything soft : to fix colours in cloth :—*pr.p.* padd′ing ; *pa.t.* and *pa.p.* padd′ed. [A variant of **Pod**, and orig. sig. 'a bag.']

**Padding**, pad′ing, *n.* the soft stuffing of a saddle, &c. : superfluous matter introduced into a book or article in order to make it of the length desired.

**Paddle**, pad′l, *v.i.* to dabble in water with the *feet* : to finger : to beat the water as with the feet, to row.—*v.t.* to move with an oar or paddle. —*n.* a short, broad, spoon-shaped oar, used for moving canoes : the blade of an oar : one of the boards at the circumference of a paddle-wheel : (*B.*) a little spade. [For **Pattle**, a freq. form of **Pat**.]

**Paddle-wheel**, pad′l-hwēl, *n.* the wheel used in paddling or propelling steam-vessels.

**Paddock**, pad′uk, *n.* a toad or frog. [Dim. of M. E. *padde*, a toad—Ice. *padda*.]

**Paddock**, pad′uk, *n.* a *small park* under pasture, immediately adjoining the stables of a domain. [A.S. *pearroc*, a park—*sparran* (Ger. *sperren*), to shut (obs. E. 'to spar'). Doublet **Park**.]

**Paddockstool**, pad′uk-stōōl, *n.* a *toadstool*.

**Paddy**, pad′i, *n.* rice in the husk. [E. Indian.]

**Padlock**, pad′lok, *n.* a lock with a link to pass through a staple or eye.—*v.t.* to fasten with a padlock. [Ety. unknown.]

**Pæan**, pē′an, *n.* (*orig.*) a song in honour of Apollo : a song of triumph. [L.—Gr. *Paian* or *Paiōn*, an epithet of Apollo. See **Peony**.]

**Pædobaptism**, **Pædobaptist**. See **Pedobaptism**, **Pedobaptist**.

**Pagan**, pā′gan, *n.* a heathen.—*adj.* heathen. [L. *paganus*, a countryman, rustic, then a heathen, because the country-people were later in being converted than the people of the towns —*pagus*, a district (regarded as having fixed boundaries)—*pango*, to fix. See **Pact**.]

**Paganise**, pā′gan-īz, *v.t.* to render *pagan* or heathen : to convert to paganism.

**Paganish**, pā′gan-ish, *adj.* heathenish.

**Paganism**, pā′gan-izm, *n.* heathenism.

**Page**, pāj, *n.* a boy attending on a person of distinction. [Fr. *page* ; acc. to Littré, prob. from Low L. *pagensis*, a peasant—L. *pagus*, a village (cf. **Pagan**, **Peasant**) ; acc. to Diez, through the It. from Gr. *paidion*, dim. of *pais*, *paidos*, a boy.]

**Page**, pāj, *n.* one side of a leaf : (*orig.*) a leaf of a book, so called because leaves were *fastened* together to form a book :—*pl.* writings.—*v.t.* to number the pages of. [Fr.—L. *pagina*, a thing fastened—*pag*, root of *pa-n-go*, to fasten.]

**Pageant**, paj′ant or pā′-, *n.* a showy exhibition : a spectacle : a fleeting show : (*orig.*) a scaffold for the purpose of scenic exhibition.—*adj.* showy : pompous. [M. E. *pagent* (with excrescent -*t* as in *ancient*, *pheasant*), from an older form *pagen* or *pagin*—Low L. *pagina*, a stage, something framed or compacted—L. *pagina*—*pango*, to fix. See **Page**, one side of a leaf.]

**Pageantry**, paj′an-tri or pā′jan-tri, *n.* ostentatious display : pompous exhibition or spectacle.

**Pagination**, paj-i-nā′shun, *n.* the act of paging a book : the figures that indicate the number of pages. [See **Page**, one side of a leaf.]

**Pagoda**, pa-gō′da, *n.* an *idol-house* : an Indian idol : its temple. [Port., a corr. of Pers. *but-kadah*, an idol-temple.]

**Paid**, pād, *pa.t.* and *pa.p.* of **Pay**.

**Paideutics**, pā-dū′tiks, *n.sing.* the science or theory of *teaching*. [Gr. *paideutike*—*paideuō*, to teach—*pais*, *paidos*, a child.]

**Pail**, pāl, *n.* an open vessel of wood, &c. for holding or carrying liquids. [O. Fr. *paele*—L. *patella*, a pan, dim. of *patera*—*pateo*, to be open.]

**Pailful**, pāl′fool, *n.* as much as *fills* a pail.

**Paillasse**, pal-yas′ = **Palliasse**, which see.

**Pain**, pān, *n.* bodily suffering : anguish :—*pl.* labour : the throes of childbirth.—*v.t.* to distress : to torment : to grieve. [Fr. *peine*—L. *pœna*, satisfaction, penalty, punishment, cog. with Gr. *poinē*, penalty.]

**Pained**, pānd, *adj.* (*B.*) in pain, in labour.

**Painful**, pān′fool, *adj.* full of pain : causing pain : distressing : difficult. — *adv.* **Pain′fully**. — *n.* **Pain′fulness**.

**Painless**, pān′les, *adj.* without pain.—*adv.* **Pain′-lessly**.—*n.* **Pain′lessness**. [or care.

**Painstaker**, pānz′tāk-ėr, *n.* one who takes pains

**Painstaking**, pānz′tāk-ing, *adj.* taking pains or care : laborious : diligent.—*n.* labour : diligence.

**Paint**, pānt, *v.t.* to *colour* : to represent in colours : to describe.—*v.i.* to practise painting : to lay colours on the face.—*n.* a colouring substance. [*Paint*, O. Fr. pa.p. of Fr. *peindre*, to paint—L. *pingo, pictus*, to paint, cog. with Gr. *poikilos*, variegated, Sans. *pinj*, to colour.]

**Painter**, pānt′ėr, *n.* one whose employment is to paint : one skilled in painting.

**Painter**, pānt′ėr, *n.* a rope used to fasten a boat. [A corr. of M. E. *panter*, a fowler's noose, through O. Fr., from L. *panther*, a hunting-net —Gr. *panthēros*, catching all—*pan*, neut. of *pas*, every, and *thēr*, wild beast, E. **Deer**.]

**Painting**, pānt′ing, *n.* the act or employment of laying on *colours* : the act of representing objects by colours : a picture : vivid description in words.

**Pair**, pār, *n.* two things *equal*, or suited to each other, or used together : a couple : a man and his wife.—*v.t.* to join in couples.—*v.i.* to be joined in couples : to fit as a counterpart.—**Pair off**, to go *off* in *pairs* : to make an arrangement with one of an opposite opinion by which the votes of both are withheld. [Fr. *paire*, a couple —*pair*, like—L. *par*, equal. It was orig. not confined to *two*, but was applied to a *set* of like or *equal* things, as a *pair* of cards.]

**Palace**, pal′ās, *n.* a royal house : a house eminently splendid : a bishop's official residence. [Fr. *palais*—L. *Palatium*, the Roman emperor's residence on the *l'alatine* Hill at Rome.]

**Paladin**, pal′a-din, *n.* a knight of Charlemagne's household : a knight-errant, generally. [Fr.— It. *paladino*—L. *palatinus*, belonging to the palace. See **Palatine**.]

**Palæography**, pā-lē-og′ra-fi, *n.* study of *ancient writings* and modes of writing. [Gr. *palaios*, ancient, and *graphō*, to write.]

**Palæolithic**, pā-lē-o-lith′ik, *adj.* applied to the older division of the prehistoric Stone Age. [Gr. *palaios*, old, and *lithos*, stone.]

**Palæology**, pā-lē-ol′o-ji, *n.* a *discourse* or treatise on *antiquities* : archæology.—*n.* **Palæol′ogist**. [Gr. *palaios*, ancient, and *logos*, discourse.]

**Palæontology**, pā-lē-on-tol′o-ji, *n.* the *science* of the *ancient life* of the earth, or of its fossil remains.—*adj.* **Palæontolog′ical**.—*n.* **Palæontol′ogist**. [Gr. *palaios*, ancient, *ōn, ontos*, being, *logos*, discourse.]

**Palæozoic**, pā-lē-o-zō′ik, *adj.* denoting the lowest strata of the fossiliferous rocks, so called because they contain the *earliest* forms of *life*. [Gr. *palaios*, ancient, and *zoē*, life.]

**Palanquin**, **Palankeen**, pal-an-kēn′, *n.* a light covered carriage used in China, &c. for a single person, and borne on the shoulders of men. [Hind. *palang*, a bed—Sans. *paryanka*, a bed.]

**Palatable**, pal′at-a-bl, *adj.* agreeable to the palate or taste : savoury.—*adv.* **Pal′atably**.

**Palatal**, pal′at-al, *adj.* pertaining to the palate : uttered by aid of the palate.—*n.* a letter pronounced chiefly by the aid of the palate.

**Palate**, pal′āt, *n.* the roof of the mouth touched by the food : taste : relish. [O. Fr. *palat*—L. *palatum*.]          [royal : magnificent.

**Palatial**, pa-lā′shi-al, *adj.* pertaining to a *palace* :

**Palatinate**, pal-at′in-āt, *n.* province of a *palatine*.

**Palatine**, pal′a-tin, *adj.* pertaining to a *palace*, originally applied to officers of the royal household : possessing royal privileges.—*n.* a noble invested with royal privileges : a subject of a palatinate. [Fr.—L. *palatinus*. See **Palace**.]

**Palaver**, pal-ā′vėr, *n.* idle talk : talk intended to deceive : a public conference. [Port. *palavra*— L. *parabola*, a parable—Gr. See **Parable**.]

**Pale**, pāl, *n.* a narrow piece of wood used in inclosing grounds : anything that incloses : any inclosure : limit : district.—*v.t.* to inclose with stakes : to encompass. [Fr. *pal*—L. *palus*, a stake, for *pag-lus*—root *pag* (= *pak*), to fix. Doublet **Pole**. See **Pack**.]

**Pale**, pāl, *adj.* not ruddy or fresh of colour : wan : of a faint lustre : dim.—*v.t.* to make pale.—*v.i.* to turn pale.—*adv.* **Pale′ly**.—*n.* **Pale′ness**. [Fr.—L. *pallidus*, pale ; akin to Sans. *palita*, gray, and E. **Fallow**. Doublet **Pallid**.]

**Paleography**, &c. See **Palæography**, &c.

**Palestra**, pa-les′tra, *n.* a *wrestling* school. [L.— Gr. *palaistra*—*palē*, wrestling.]

**Palestric**, pa-les′trik, **Palestrical**, pa-les′trik-al, *adj.* pertaining to *wrestling*.

**Paletot**, pal′e-tō, *n.* a loose overcoat. [Fr., corr. of O. Dut. *palts-rock* (*lit.*) a 'palace-coat,' a court dress, *pals* being = Ger. *pfalz*—L. *palatium*, and O. Dut. *roc* = Ger. *rock*, O. Ger. *hroch*, from which prob. E. **Frock**.]

**Palette**, pal′et, *n.* a little oval board on which a painter mixes his colours. [Fr.—It. *paletta*, dim. of *pala*, a spade—L. *pala*, a spade.]

**Palfrey**, pal′fri, *n.* a saddle-horse, esp. for a lady. [Fr. *palefroi*—Low L. *paraveredus*, prob. from Gr. *para*, beside, extra, and Low L. *veredus*, a posthorse.]

**Palimpsest**, pal′imp-sest, *n.* a manuscript which has been written upon twice, the first writing having been *rubbed* off to make room for the second. [Gr. *palimpsēston*, rubbed a second time—*palin*, again, and *psēstos*, rubbed.]

**Palindrome**, pal′in-drōm, *n.* a word, verse, or sentence that reads the same either backward or forward, as *madam*. [Gr. *palindromia*—*palin*, back, and *dromos*, a running.]

**Paling**, pāl′ing, *n.*, *pales* in general : a fence of pales : an inclosure.

**Palinode**, pal′in-ōd, *n.* a song or poem retracting a former one : a recantation. [Fr.—L.—Gr., from *palin*, back, and *ōdē*, a song. See **Ode**.]

**Palisade**, pal-i-sād′, *n.* a fence of pointed *pales* or stakes firmly fixed in the ground.—*v.t.* to surround with a palisade. [Fr. *palissade*, from L. *palus*, a stake.]

**Palish**, pāl′ish, *adj.* somewhat pale or wan.

**Pall**, pawl, *n.* a *cloak* or *mantle* : a kind of scarf worn by the Pope, and sent by him to archbishops : the cloth over a coffin at a funeral. [A.S. *pæll*, purple cloth—L. *palla*, a mantle, a curtain, conn. with *pallium*, a cloak.]

**Pall**, pawl, *v.i.* to become vapid : to lose strength, life, spirit, or taste.—*v.t.* to make vapid or insipid : to dispirit or depress : to cloy. [W. *pallu*, to fail, *pall*, loss of energy, failure.]

**Palladium**, pal-lā′di-um, *n.* a statue of *Pallas*, on the preservation of which the safety of ancient Troy was supposed to depend : any safeguard : a rare metal found with platinum. [L.—Gr. *palladion*—*Pallas, Pallados*, Pallas or Minerva.]

**Pallet**, pal′et, *n.* a palette : the shaping tool used by potters : an instrument for spreading goldleaf. [Another form of **Palette**.]

**Pallet**, pal′et, *n.* a mattress, or couch, properly a mattress of *straw*. [Prov. Fr. *paillet*, dim. of Fr. *paille*, straw. See **Palliasse**.]

**Palliasse**, pal-yas′, *n.* a small bed, orig. made of *chaff* or straw : an under mattress of straw. [Fr. *paill-asse—paille*, straw—L. *palea*, chaff. Cf. **Pallet**, a mattress, &c.]

**Palliate**, pal′i-āt, *v.t.* to *cloak* or excuse : to

extenuate: to soften by favourable representations. [L. *palliatus*, cloaked—*pallium*.]

Palliation, pal-i-ā′shun, *n.* act of palliating or
excusing: extenuation: mitigation.

Palliative, pal′i-ā-tiv, *adj.* serving to palliate or
extenuate: mitigating.

Pallid, pal′id, *adj.*, *pale*: having little colour:
wan. [L. *pallidus*. See Pale, *adj.* which is a
doublet.]

Pall-mall, pel-mel′, *n.* an old game, in which a
*ball* was driven through an iron ring with a
*mallet*: a street in London where the game
used to be played. [O. Fr. *pale-maille*—It.
*pallamaglio*—*palla*—O. Ger. *palla* (Ger. *ball*),
E. Ball, and *maglio*—L. *malleus*, a hammer.
See Mall.]

Pallor, pal′or, *n.* quality or state of being *pallid*
or *pale*: paleness. [L.—*pallere*, to be pale,
conn. with root of Pale.]

Palm, päm, *n.* the inner part of the hand: a
tropical branchless tree of many varieties, bearing at the summit large leaves like the *palm*
of the hand, borne in token of victory or rejoicing: (*fig.*) triumph or victory.—*v.t.* to stroke
with the palm or hand: to conceal in the palm of
the hand: (esp. with *off*) to impose by fraud.
[Fr. *paume*—L. *palma*; cog. with Gr. *palamē*,
A.S. *folm*.]

Palmary, pal′ma-ri, *adj.* worthy of the *palm*:
pre-eminent. [L. *palma*, a palm.]

Palmate, pal′māt, Palmated, pal′māt-ed, *adj.*
shaped like the *palm* of the hand: entirely
webbed, as feet. [L. *palmatus*—*palma*. See
Palm.]

Palmer, päm′ėr, *n.* a pilgrim from the Holy Land,
distinguished by his carrying a branch of *palm*.

Palmer-worm, päm′ėr-wurm, *n.* (*B.*) a hairy
*worm* which wanders like a *palmer*, devouring
leaves, &c.

Palmetto, pal-met′o, *n.* a name for several fan-
*palms*. [Sp.—L. *palma*.]

Palmhouse, päm′hows, *n.* a glass *house* for raising *palms* and other tropical plants.

Palmiped, pal′mi-ped, *adj.* (*lit.*) *palm-footed*:
web-footed.—*n.* a web-footed or swimming bird.
[L. *palma*, palm of the hand, and *pes*, *pedis*, the
foot.]

Palmister, pal′mis-tėr, *n.* one who tells fortunes
by the lines of the *palm* of the hand.—*n.* Pal′-
mistry.

Palm-Sunday, päm′-sun′dā, *n.* the *Sunday* before
Easter, the day our Saviour entered Jerusalem,
when *palm* branches were strewed in his way.

Palmy, päm′i, *adj.* bearing *palms*: flourishing:
victorious.

Palpability, pal-pa-bil′i-ti, Palpableness, pal′pa-
bl-nes, *n.* quality of being palpable: obviousness.

Palpable, pal′pa-bl, *adj.* that can be felt: readily
perceived: obvious: gross.—*adv.* Pal′pably.
[Fr.—L. *palpabilis*—*palpo*, *palpatus*, to touch
softly.]

Palpitate, pal′pi-tāt, *v.i.* to move often and
quickly: to beat rapidly: to throb. [L. *palpito*,
*-atus*, freq. of *palpo*. See Palpable.]

Palpitation, pal-pi-tā′shun, *n.* act of palpitating:
irregular or violent action of the heart, caused
by excitement, excessive exertion, or disease.

Palsy, pawl′zi, *n.* paralysis.—*v.t.* to affect with
palsy: to deprive of action or energy: to paralyse:—*pa.p.* pal′sied. [A corr. of Fr. *paralysie*
—Gr. *paralysis*. See Paralysis.]

Palter, pawl′tėr, *v.i.* to trifle: to dodge: to shuffle:
to equivocate. [Prob. lit. to 'deal meanly,' to
'haggle over trifles,' from root of Paltry.]

Paltry, pawl′tri, *adj.* mean: vile: worthless.—
*adv.* Pal′trily.—*n.* Pal′triness. [From a Teut.
root seen in Dan. *pialter*, rags, and in Low Ger.
*paltrig*, ragged.]

Paludal, pal-ū′dal, Paludinous, pal-ū′din-us, *adj.*
pertaining to *marshes*: marshy. [From L.
*palus*, *paludis*, a marsh.]

Pampas, pam′paz, *n.pl.* vast *plains* in S. America.
[Peruvian *pampa*, a field, plain.]

Pamper, pam′pėr, *v.t.* to feed luxuriously or to the
full: to glut.—*n.* Pam′perer. [A freq. from
*pamp*, a nasalised form of Pap; conn. with Low
Ger. *pampen*—*pampe*, pap made of meal.]

Pamphlet, pam′flet, *n.* a small book consisting of
one or more sheets stitched together. [Ety.
dub.: acc. to Skeat, perh. through Fr. from
*Pamphila*, a female writer of *epitomes* in the
1st century: others suggest Fr. *paume*, the
palm of the hand, and *feuillet*, a leaf.]

Pamphleteer, pam-flet-ēr′, *n.* a writer of pamphlets.

Pamphleteering, pam-flet-ēr′ing, *adj.* writing
pamphlets.—*n.* the writing of pamphlets.

Pan, pan, *n.* a broad shallow vessel for domestic
use: the part of a firelock which holds the priming. [A.S. *panne*—through the Celt., from L.
*patina*, whence also are Ger. *pfanne*, Ice.
*panna*.]

Panacea, pan-a-sē′a, *n.* an *all-healing* remedy: a
universal medicine. [Gr. *panakeia*—*pas*, *pan*,
all, and *akeomai*, to heal.]

Pancake, pan′kāk, *n.* a thin *cake* of eggs, flour,
sugar, and milk fried in a *pan*.

Pancreas, pan′kre-as, *n.* a fleshy gland (commonly
called the 'sweetbread') situated under and behind the stomach, secreting a saliva-like fluid
which assists digestion in the intestines.—*adj.*
Pancreat′ic, pertaining to the pancreas. [Lit.
'all flesh,' Gr. *pas*, *pan*, all, and *kreas*, flesh.]

Pandect, pan′dekt, *n.* a treatise *containing* the
*whole* of any science:—*pl.* the digest of Roman
or civil law made by command of the Emperor
Justinian. [L.—Gr. *pandectes*—*pas*, *pan*, all,
and *dek-*, root of *dechomai*, to take, receive.]

Pandemonium, pan-de-mō′ni-um, *n.* the great
hall of demons or evil spirits, described by Milton. [Lit. 'the place of all the demons,' Gr.
*pas*, *pan*, all, and *daimōn*, a demon.]

Pander, pan′dėr, *n.* one who procures for another
the means of gratifying his passions: a pimp.
—*v.t.* to play the pander for.—*v.i.* to act as a
pander: to minister to the passions. [From
*Pandarus*, the pimp in the story of Troilus and
Cressida.]

Pandit. See Pundit.

Pandour, pan′dōor, *n.* a Hungarian foot-soldier in
the Austrian service. [From *Pandur*, a village
in Hungary, where they were orig. raised.]

Pane, pān, *n.* a patch, esp. in variegated work: a
plate of glass. [Fr. *pan*, a lappet, pane—L.
*pannus*, a cloth, a rag, akin to Gr. *pēnos*, the
woof, and E. Vane. See also Panel.]

Paned, pānd, *adj.* composed of panes or small
squares: variegated.

Panegyric, pan-e-jir′ik, *n.* an oration or eulogy in
praise of some person or event: an encomium.—
*adjs.* Panegyr′ic, Panegyr′ical.—*adv.* Pane-
gyr′ically. [Through L., from Gr. *panēgyrikos*,
fit for a national festival or 'gathering' of a
'whole' nation, as at the Olympic games—*pas*,
*pan*, all, and *agyris*, a gathering.]

Panegyrise, pan′e-jir-īz, *v.t.* to write or pronounce a panegyric on: to praise highly.—*n.*
Panegyr′ist.

**Panel** or **Pannel**, pan′el, n. (arch.) a compartment with raised margins : a board with a surrounding frame : a thin board on which a picture is painted : (law) a schedule containing the names of those summoned to serve as jurors : the jury : (Scots law) a prisoner at the bar.—v.t. to furnish with panels :—pr.p. pan′elling ; pa.p. pan′elled.—n. Pan′elling, panel-work. [Lit. 'a piece,' orig. 'a piece of cloth,' O. Fr.—Low L. panellus, dim. of L. pannus, a cloth, a rag. Cf. **Impanel**, and see **Pane**.]

**Pang**, pang, n. a violent momentary pain : a paroxysm of extreme sorrow : a throe. [A form of **Prong**, prob. modified by confusion with Fr. poing, a fist—L. pugnus, the fist.]

**Panic**, pan′ik, n. extreme or sudden fright.—adj. of the nature of a panic : extreme or sudden : imaginary. [Orig. an adj. ; Gr. panikon (deima), 'panic' (fear), from panikos, belonging to Pan, god of the woods, to whom sudden frights were ascribed.]

**Panicle**, pan′i-kl, n. (lit.) a tuft on plants : (bot.) a form of inflorescence in which the cluster is irregularly branched, as in oats. [L. panicula, double dim. of panus, thread wound on a bobbin, akin to L. pannus, and Gr. pēnos. See **Pane**.]

**Panic-stricken**, pan′ik-strik′en, **Panic-struck**, pan′ik-struk, adj., struck with a panic or sudden fear.

**Paniculate**, pan-ik′ū-lāt, **Paniculated**, pan-ik′ū-lāt-ed, adj. furnished with, arranged in, or like panicles.

**Pannel**. Same as **Panel**.

**Pannier**, pan′yėr or pan′i-ėr, n. one of two baskets slung across a horse, for carrying light produce to market : (arch.) a corbel. [Fr. panier—L. panarium, a bread-basket, from panis, bread—root pa, to feed. See **Pantry**.]

**Panoplied**, pan′o-plid, adj. dressed in panoply : completely armed.

**Panoply**, pan′o-pli, n., complete armour : a full suit of armour. [Gr. panoplia—pas, pan, all, and hopla (pl.), arms.]

**Panorama**, pan-o-rä′ma or -rä′ma, n. a picture representing a number of scenes unrolled and made to pass before the spectator.—adj. **Panoram′ic**. [Gr. pan, all, and horama, a view, from horaō, to see.]

**Pansy**, pan′zi, n. a species of violet, heart's-ease. [Fr. pensée—penser, to think, from L. penso, to weigh, to ponder. See **Pensive**, and cf. **Forget-me-not**.]

**Pant**, pant, v.i. to breathe hard : to gasp : to throb : to desire ardently. [Imitative ; or a nasalised form of **Pat**, v.t.]

**Pantagraph**, pan′ta-graf, n. an instrument for copying drawings, esp. on a different scale from the original. [Gr. pan, everything, and graphō, to write.]

**Pantaloon**, pan-ta-lōōn′, n. in pantomimes, a ridiculous character, a buffoon : (orig.) a ridiculous character in Italian comedy, also a garment worn by him, consisting of breeches and stockings all in one piece :—pl. a kind of trousers. [Fr. pantalon—It. pantalone, from Pantaleone (Gr. 'all-lion'), the patron saint of Venice, and a common Christian name among the Venetians, wherefore it was applied to them as a nickname by the other Italians.]

**Pantheism**, pan′the-izm, n. the doctrine that nature or the universe is God. [Gr. pan, all, and **Theism**.]

**Pantheist**, pan′the-ist, n. a believer in pantheism.—adjs. **Pantheist′ic**, **Pantheist′ical**.

**Pantheon**, pan′the-on or -thē′on, n. a temple dedicated to all the gods : a complete mythology. [L. panthēon—Gr. pantheion (hieron), (a temple) common to all gods. Cf. **Pantheism**.]

**Panther**, pan′thėr, n. a fierce spotted carnivorous quadruped, found in Asia and Africa. [Fr. panthère—L. panthera—Gr. panthēr.]

**Pantomime**, pan′to-mīm, n. one who expresses his meaning by mute action : a representation or an entertainment in dumb-show.—adj. representing only by mute action.—adjs. **Pantomim′ic**, **Pantomim′ical**.—adv. **Pantomim′ically**. [Fr.—L.—Gr. pantomimos, imitator of all—pas, pantos, all, and mimos, an imitator.]

**Pantomimist**, pan′to-mīm-ist, n. an actor in a pantomime.

**Pantry**, pan′tri, n. a room or closet for provisions. [Fr. paneterie, a place where bread is distributed, through the Low L., from L. panis, bread—root pa, to nourish. See **Paternal**.]

**Pap**, pap, n. soft food for infants : pulp of fruit : support or nourishment.—adj. **Papp′y**. [From the first cries of infants for food.]

**Pap**, pap, n. a nipple or teat. [Of the same origin with **Pap** and **Papa**.]

**Papa**, pa-pä′, n. father. [A reduplication of one of the first utterances of a child.]

**Papacy**, pā′pa-si, n. the office of the Pope : the authority of the Pope : Popery : the Popes, as a body. [Low L. papatia—papa, a father.]

**Papal**, pā′pal, adj. belonging or relating to the Pope or to Popery : Popish.—adv. **Pa′pally**.

**Papaveraceous**, pap-av-er-ā′shus, adj. of or like the poppy. [L. papaver, the poppy.]

**Paper**, pā′pėr, n. the substance on which we commonly write and print : a piece of paper : a document : a newspaper : an essay or literary contribution, generally brief : paper-money : paper-hangings.—adj. consisting or made of paper.—v.t. to cover with paper : to fold in paper. [A docked form of **Papyrus**.]

**Paper-credit**, pā′pėr-kred′it, n. the system of dealing on credit by means of acknowledgments of indebtedness written on paper.

**Paper-hanger**, pā′pėr-hang′ėr, n. one who hangs paper on the walls of rooms, &c.

**Paper-hangings**, pā′pėr-hang′ingz, n.pl., paper for hanging on or covering walls.

**Papering**, pā′pėr-ing, n. the operation of covering or hanging with paper : the paper itself.

**Paper-money**, pā′pėr-mun′i, n. printed and authorised papers issued by banks and circulated in place of coin or money.

**Paper-reed**, pā′pėr-rēd, n. (B.) the papyrus.

**Paper-stainer**, pā′pėr-stān′ėr, n. one who stains or prepares paper-hangings. [**Paper** and **Stainer**.]

**Papier-maché**, pap′yä-mä′shä, n. pulped paper moulded into forms, and japanned. [Fr. (lit.) 'paper mashed' or 'chewed :' papier, from **Papyrus**; mâché is pa.p. of Fr. mâcher, to chew —L. masticare. See **Masticate**.]

**Papilionaceous**, pa-pil-yo-nā′shus, adj. (bot.) having a winged corolla somewhat like a butterfly, as the bean, pea, &c. [From L. papilio, -onis, a butterfly. Cf. **Pavilion**.]

**Papilla**, pa-pil′a, n. one of the minute elevations on the skin, esp. on the upper surface of the tongue and on the tips of the fingers, and in which the nerves terminate : (bot.) a nipple-like protuberance :—pl. **Papill′æ**. [L., a small pustule or nipple, dim. of papula, itself a dim. from base pap, to swell. Cf. **Pimple**.]

**Papillary**, pap′il-ar-i or pa-pil′ar-i, **Papillous**,

**pap′il-us,** *adj.* belonging to or like *pimples,* nipples, or teats : warty.

**Papillote,** pap′il-ōt, *n.* a curl-paper. [Fr., from *papillot,* old form of *papillon,* butterfly—L. *papilio.*]

**Papist,** pā′pist, *n.* an adherent of the *Pope*: a Roman Catholic.—*adjs.* **Papist′ic, Papist′ical,** pertaining to *Popery,* or to the Church of Rome, its doctrines, &c.—*adv.* **Papist′ically.**

**Pappous,** pap′us, **Pappose,** pap-ōs′, *adj.* provided with *down.* [L. *pappus*—Gr. *pappos,* down.]

**Papular,** pap′ū-lar, **Papulous,** pap′ū-lus,, **Papulose,** pap′ū-lōs, *adj.* full of *pimples.* [From L. *papula,* a pimple.]

**Papyrus,** pa-pī′rus, *n.* an Egyptian reed, from the inner rind (called *byblos*) of which the ancients made their paper : a manuscript on papyrus :—*pl.* **Papy′rī.** [L.—Gr. *papyros.* Cf. **Bible.**]

**Par,** pär, *n.* state of *equality* : equal value : equality of nominal and market value : equality of condition. [L. *par,* equal.]

**Parable,** par′a-bl, *n.* a comparison : a fable or allegory in which some fact or doctrine is illustrated. [Lit. a 'placing beside,' Gr. *parabolē—paraballō,* to compare—*para,* beside, *ballō,* to throw. Parallel forms, **Parabola, Parole, Palaver,** and **Parley.**]

**Parabola,** par-ab′o-la, *n.* (*geom.*) a conic section formed by the intersection of the cone with a plane *parallel to one side.* [Gr. *parabolē.* See **Parable.**]

**Parabolic,** par-a-bol′ik, **Parabolical,** par-a-bol′ik-al, *adj.* expressed by a *parable* : belonging to or of the form of a parabola.—*adv.* **Parabol′ically.**

**Parachute,** par′a-shōōt, *n.* an apparatus resembling a huge umbrella for descending safely from a balloon. [Fr., for *par′ à chute* (*lit.*) 'that which *parries* against falling,' from Fr. *parer* (see **Parry**), and *chute,* a fall.]

**Paraclete,** par′a-klēt, *n.* the Holy Ghost. [Lit. 'one *called* to stand *beside* one,' an 'advocate,' through L., from Gr. *paraklētos—para,* beside, *kaleō,* call.]

**Parade,** par-ād′, *n.* the arrangement of troops for display or inspection : the place where such a display takes place : military display : pompous display.—*v.t.* to shew off : to marshal in military order.—*v.i.* to walk about as if for show : to pass in military order : to march in procession. [Lit. a '*preparation* for exhibition,' Fr.—Sp. *parada—parar,* to halt—L. *paro, paratus,* to prepare.]

**Paradigm,** par′a-dim, *n.* an example : model : (*gram.*) an example of the inflection of a word.—*adjs.* **Paradigmat′ic, Paradigmat′ical,** consisting of or resembling paradigms.—*adv.* **Paradigmat′ically.** [Fr.—L.—Gr. *paradeigma—para,* beside, and *deiknymi,* to shew.]

**Paradise,** par′a-dīs, *n.* the garden of Eden : heaven : any place or state of blissful delights.—*adj.* **Paradisi′acal.—Bird of Paradise,** a family of Eastern birds closely allied to the crow, remarkable for the splendour of their plumage. [Fr. *paradis*—L. *paradisus*—Gr. *paradeisos,* a park or pleasure-ground, an Oriental word, prob. Persian.]

**Paradox,** par′a-doks, *n.* that which is contrary to received opinion, or that which is apparently absurd but really true. [Through Fr. and L., from Gr. *paradoxon—para,* contrary to, and *doxa,* an opinion.]

**Paradoxical,** par-a-doks′ik-al, *adj.* of the nature of a paradox : inclined to paradoxes.—*adv.* **Paradox′ically.**—*n.* **Paradox′icalness.**

**Paraffine, Paraffin,** par′af-fin, *n.* a white crystal-line substance, obtained from shale, &c., so named from its slight tendency to combine with other bodies. [Fr.—L. *parum,* little, and *affinis,* allied.]

**Paragoge,** par-a-gō′je, *n.* the addition of a letter or syllable to the end of a word.—*adjs.* **Paragogic,** par-a-goj′ik, **Paragog′ical.** [L.—Gr., from *para,* beyond, and *agō,* to lead.]

**Paragon,** par′a-gon, *n.* a pattern or model *with which comparisons are made* : something supremely excellent. [O. Fr., from Sp. compound prep. *para con,* in comparison with.]

**Paragraph,** par′a-graf, *n.* a distinct part of a discourse or writing : a short passage, or a collection of sentences with unity of purpose.—*adj.* **Paragraph′ic, Paragraph′ical.** [Lit. that which is 'written beside' the text to shew division, as the mark ¶, the reversed initial of this word, Fr.—Low L.—Gr. *paragraphos—para,* beside, *graphō,* to write.]

**Paraleipsis,** par-a-līp′sis, *n.* (*rhet.*) a figure by which one fixes attention on a subject by pretending to neglect it. [Gr., from *paraleipō,* to leave on one side—*para,* beside, and *leipō,* to leave.]

**Parallax,** par′a-laks, *n.* an apparent *change* in the position of an object caused by change of position in the observer : (*astr.*) the difference between the apparent and real place of a celestial object.—*adjs.* **Parallac′tic, Parallac′tical.** [Gr. *parallaxis—para,* beside, and *allassō,* to change—*allos,* another.]

**Parallel,** par′al-lel, *adj.* side by side : (*geom.*) extended in the same direction and equidistant in all parts : with the same direction or tendency : running in accordance with : resembling in all essential points : like or similar.—*n.* a line always equidistant from another : a line marking latitude : likeness : a comparison : counterpart : (*mil.*) in *pl.* the trenches, generally dug parallel with the outline of the fortress.—*v.t.* to place so as to be parallel : to correspond to :—*pr.p.* par′alleling or par′allelling ; *pa.p.* par′alleled or par′allelled. [Lit. 'beside one another,' Fr.—L. *parallelus*—Gr. *parallēlos—para,* beside, *allēlōn,* of one another—*allos,* another.]

**Parallelepiped,** par-al-lel-e-pī′ped, **Parallelepip′edon,** improperly **Parallelopiped, Parallelopipedon,** *n.* a regular solid bounded by six plane *parallel surfaces.* [L.—Gr. *parallēlepipedon—parallēlos,* and *epipedon,* a plane surface—*epi,* on, and *pedon,* the ground.]

**Parallelism,** par′al-lel-izm, *n.* state of being parallel : resemblance : comparison.

**Parallelogram,** par-al-lel′o-gram, *n.* a plane four-sided *figure,* the opposite sides of which are *parallel* and equal. [Fr.—L.—Gr. *parallēlos,* and *gramma,* a line—*graphō,* to write.]

**Paralogism,** par-al′o-jism, *n., reasoning beside* or from the point : a conclusion unwarranted by the premises. [Fr.—L.—Gr. *paralogismos—para,* beside, beyond, and *logismos,* from *logos,* discourse, reason.]

**Paralyse,** par′a-līz, *v.t.* to strike with paralysis or palsy : to make useless : to deaden : to exhaust. [Fr.—L.—Gr. *paralyō, paralysō—para,* indicating derangement, and *lyō,* to loosen.]

**Paralysis,** par-al′i-sis, *n.* a loss of the power of motion or sensation in any part of the body : palsy. [L.—Gr.—*para,* beside, and *lyō,* to loosen. Doublet **Palsy.**]

**Paralytic,** par-a-lit′ik, *adj.* afflicted with or inclined to *paralysis.—n.* one affected with paralysis. [Fr.—L. *paralyticus*—Gr. *paralytikos.*]

**Paramagnetic**, par-a-mag-net′ik, *adj.* See under **Diamagnetic**.

**Paramatta**, par-a-mat′a, *n.* a fabric like merino made of worsted and cotton. [From *Paramatta*, a town in New South Wales.]

**Paramount**, par′a-mownt, *adj.* superior to all others : chief : of the highest importance.—*n.* the chief. [O. Fr. *par amont* (*lit.*) 'by that which is *upwards*,' i.e. at the top, *par* being the L. prep. *per*. For *amont*, see **Amount**.]

**Paramour**, par′a-mōōr, *n.* a lover, one beloved (now used in a bad sense). [Fr. *par amour*, by or with love—L. *per amorem*. See **Amour**.]

**Parapet**, par′a-pet, *n.* a rampart breast-high : a breast-high wall on a bridge, &c.—*adj.* **Par′apeted**, having a parapet. [Lit. a *protection* for the *breast*, Fr.—It. *parapetto*—It. *para-re*, to adorn, to protect—L. *parare*, to prepare (see **Parry**), and It. *petto*—L. *pectus*, the breast (see **Pectoral**). Cf. **Parasol**.]

**Paraphernalia**, par-a-fėr-nāl′i-a, *n.pl.* that which a bride brings *over* and *above* her *dowry* : the clothes, jewels, &c. which a wife possesses beyond her dowry in her own right : ornaments of dress generally : trappings. [L. *parapherna*—Gr., from *para*, beyond, and *phernē*, a dowry—*pherō*, to bring. E. **Bear**, *v.t.*]

**Paraphrase**, par′a-frāz, *n.* a saying of the same thing in other words : an explanation of a passage : a loose or free translation.—*v.t.* to say the same thing in other words : to render more fully : to interpret or translate freely.—*v.i.* to make a paraphrase. [Fr.—L.—Gr. *paraphrasis*—*para*, beside, and *phrasis*, a speaking—*phrazō*, to speak. See **Phrase**.]

**Paraphrast**, par′a-frast, *n.* one who paraphrases.

**Paraphrastic**, par-a-frast′ik, **Paraphrastical**, par-a-frast′ik-al, *adj.* of the nature of a *paraphrase* : clear and ample in explanation : free, loose, diffuse.—*adv.* **Paraphrast′ically**.

**Parasite**, par′a-sīt, *n.* one who frequents another's table : a hanger-on : (*bot.*) a plant nourished by the juices of another : (*zool.*) an animal which lives on another.—*n.* **Par′asitism**. [Lit. 'one who *feeds with* another,' Fr.—L. *parasītus*—Gr. *parasitos*—*para*, beside, and *sitos*, corn, food.]

**Parasitic**, par-a-sit′ik, **Parasitical**, par-a-sit′ik-al, *adj.* like a parasite : fawning : living on other plants or animals.—*adv.* **Parasit′ically**.

**Parasol**, par′a-sol, *n.* a small umbrella used as a shade *from the sun*. [Fr.—It. *parasole*—*parare*, to hold or keep off—L. *paro*, to prepare, and *sol, solis*, the sun. See **Parapet** and **Parry**.]

**Parboil**, pär′boil, *v.t.* to *boil* in *part*. [**Part** and **Boil**.]

**Parcel**, pär′sel, *n.* a *little part* : a portion : a quantity : a package.—*v.t.* to divide into portions :—*pr.p.* par′celling ; *pa.t.* and *pa.p.* par′celled. [Fr. *parcelle* (It. *particella*)—L. *particula*, dim. of *pars, partis*, a part.]

**Parch**, pärch, *v.t.* to burn slightly : to scorch.—*v.i.* to be scorched : to become very dry. [?]

**Parched**, pärcht, *adj.* scorched.—*adv.* **Parch′edly**.—*n.* **Parch′edness**.

**Parchment**, pärch′ment, *n.* the skin of a sheep or goat prepared for writing on. [Fr. *parchemin*—L. *pergamena* (*charta*, paper), from Gr. *Pergamos*, in Asia Minor, where it was invented.]

**Pard**, pärd, *n.* the panther : the leopard : in poetry, any spotted animal. [L. *pardus*—Gr. *pardos*, the panther, the leopard.]

**Pardon**, pär′dn, *v.t.* to *forgive* : to remit the penalty of.—*n.* forgiveness : remission of a penalty or punishment.—*n.* **Par′doner**. [Lit. to *give up*, Fr. *pardonner*—Low L. *perdonare*—L. *per*, through, away (= E. *for*), *dono, donare*, to give.]

**Pardonable**, pär′dn-a-bl, *adj.* that may be *pardoned* : excusable.—*adv.* **Par′donably**.—*n.* **Par′donableness**.

**Pare**, pār, *v.t.* to cut or shave off : to diminish by littles. [Lit. to *prepare* or *make ready*, Fr. *parer*—L. *paro*, to prepare.]

**Paregoric**, par-e-gor′ik, *adj., soothing* : assuaging pain.—*n.* a medicine that assuages pain, tincture of opium. [L.—Gr. *parēgorikos*—*parēgoreō*, to soothe ; properly, to exhort—*para*, beside, and *agoreuo*, to address an assembly.]

**Parent**, pār′ent, *n.* one who *begets* or brings forth : a father or mother : that which produces, a cause. [Fr., kinsman—L. *parens*, for *pariens*, *-entis*, pr.p. of *pario*, to beget, bring forth.]

**Parentage**, pār′ent-āj, *n., birth* : extraction : descent.

**Parental**, pa-rent′al, *adj.* pertaining to or becoming *parents* : affectionate : tender.—*adv.* **Parent′ally**.

**Parenthesis**, pa-ren′the-sis, *n.* a word, phrase, or sentence *put in* or inserted in another grammatically complete without it :—*pl.* the marks ( ) used to shew this :—*pl.* **Paren′theses** (-sēz). [Gr.—*para*, beside, *en*, in, *thesis*, a placing.]

**Parenthetic**, par-en-thet′ik, **Parenthetical**, par-en-thet′ik-al, *adj.* expressed in a *parenthesis* : using parentheses.—*adv.* **Parenthet′ically**.

**Parhelion**, par-hē′li-un, *n.* a bright light sometimes seen *near* the *sun* :—*pl.* **Parhe′lia**. [Gr. *para*, beside, near, *hēlios*, the sun.]

**Pariah**, pär′i-a or pā′-, *n.* in Hindustan, one who has lost his caste : an outcast. [Tamul *pareyer*.]

**Parian**, pār′i-an, *adj.* pertaining to or found in the island of *Paros*, in the Ægean Sea.

**Parietal**, pa-rī′et-al, *adj.* pertaining to *walls* : (*anat.*) forming the sides or walls : (*bot.*) growing from the inner lining or wall of another organ. [L. *parietalis*—*paries, parietis*, a wall.]

**Paring**, pār′ing, *n.* that which is *pared* off : rind : the cutting off the surface of grass land for tillage.

**Parish**, par′ish, *n.* a district under one pastor : an ecclesiastical district having officers of its own and supporting its own poor.—*adj.* belonging or relating to a parish : employed or supported by the parish. [Lit. a number of *dwellings near* one another, Fr. *paroisse*—L. *parœcia*—Gr. *paroikia*—*paroikos*, dwelling beside or near—*para*, beside, near, *oikos*, a dwelling.]

**Parishioner**, par-ish′un-ėr, *n.* one who belongs to or is connected with a *parish*. [M. E. *parisshen* (with *-er* added)—O. Fr. *paroissien*. See **Parish**.]

**Parity**, par′i-ti, *n.* state of being *equal* : resemblance : analogy. [Fr. *parité*—L. *paritas*—*par*.]

**Park**, pärk, *n.* an inclosure : a tract surrounding a mansion : a piece of ground inclosed for recreation : (*mil.*) a space in an encampment occupied by the artillery ; hence, a collection of artillery, or stores in an encampment.—*v.t.* to inclose : to bring together in a body, as artillery. [A.S. *pearroc* (see **Paddock**, a small park), prob. modified by Fr. *parc* ; further ety. obscure.]

**Parlance**, pär′lans, *n., speaking* : conversation : idiom of conversation. [Fr.—*parlant*, pr.p. of *parler*, to speak. See next word.]

**Parley**, pär′li, *v.i.* to speak with another : to confer : to treat with an enemy.—*n.* talk : a conference with an enemy in war. [Lit. 'to *throw* words *together*,' Fr. *parler*—L. *parabola*

—Gr. *parabolē*, a parable, speech, word. See Parable.]

**Parliament**, pär′li-ment, *n.* meeting for consultation : the legislature of the nation, consisting of the sovereign, lords, and commons. [Lit. 'a parleying or speaking,' Fr. *parlement—parler*.]

**Parliamentarian**, pär-li-men-tā′ri-an, *adj.* adhering to the *Parliament* in opposition to Charles I.

**Parliamentary**, pär-li-ment′ar-i, *adj.* pertaining to *parliament* : enacted or done by parliament : according to the rules of legislative bodies.

**Parlour**, pär′lur, *n.* an ordinary sitting-room : (*orig.*) a room in a monastery for *conversation*. [Fr. *parloir—parler*, to speak.]

**Parochial**, par-ō′ki-al, *adj.* of or relating to a *parish.—adv.* **Paro′chially.—Parochial Board** (in Scotland), the board in each parish which is charged with the relief of the poor. [L. *parochialis—parochia*, a variant of *parœcia*. See Parish.]    [*parishes.*

**Parochialise**, par-ō′ki-al-īz, *v.t.* to form into

**Parody**, par′o-di, *n.* a caricature of a poem made by applying its words and ideas with a burlesque effect.—*v.t.* to apply in parody :—*pa.p.* par′odied.—*n.* **Par′odist**, one who writes a parody. [L.—Gr. *parōdia—para*, beside, *ōdē*, an ode or song.]

**Parole**, par-ōl′, *n.* word of mouth : (*mil.*) word of honour (esp. by a prisoner of war, to fulfil certain conditions) : the daily password in camp or garrison.—*adj.* given by word of mouth. [Fr. —L. *parabola*, a parable, a speech, a saying. See Parable.]

**Paronomasia**, par-o-no-mā′zhi-a, *n.* a rhetorical figure in which words similar in sound are set in opposition or antithesis. [Gr.—*parōnymos*. See Paronymous.]

**Paronyme**, par′o-nim, *n.* a *paronymous* word.

**Paronymous**, par-on′i-mus, *adj.* formed by a slight *change* of word or *name* : derived from the same root : having the same sound, but different in spelling and meaning. [Gr. *para*, beside, *onoma*, E. Name.]

**Paroquet**, par′o-ket, *n.* a small kind of parrot found in tropical countries. [Lit. 'little Peter,' Fr. *perroquet—Pierrot*, dim. of *Pierre*, Peter.]

**Paroxysm**, par′oks-izm, *n.* a fit of *acute* pain occurring at intervals : a fit of passion : any sudden violent action. [Fr.—L.—Gr. *paroxysmos—para*, beyond—*oxys*, sharp.]

**Paroxysmal**, par-oks-iz′mal, *adj.* pertaining to or occurring in *paroxysms*.

**Parquetry**, par′ket-ri, *n.* figured inlaid woodwork for floors. [Fr., from *parquet*, an inlaid floor, dim. of *parc*, an inclosure. See Park.]

**Parr**, pär, *n.* a young salmon. [Ety. unknown.]

**Parrakeet**, par-a-kēt, *n.* Same as Paroquet.

**Parricidal**, par-ri-sīd′al, *adj.* pertaining to or committing *parricide*.

**Parricide**, par′ri-sīd, *n.* the *murderer* of a *father* or mother : the murder of a parent : the murder of any one to whom reverence is due. [Fr.—L. *parricida* (for *patri-cida*)—*pater, patris*, father, and *cædo*, to slay.]

**Parrot**, par′ut, *n.* one of a family of tropical birds, with brilliant plumage and a hooked bill, remarkable for their faculty of imitating the human voice. [Contr. of Fr. *perroquet*. See Paroquet.]

**Parry**, par′i, *v.t.* to *ward* or *keep off* : to turn aside :—*pa.t.* and *pa.p.* par′ried. [Fr. *parer* (It. *parare*)—L. *paro*, to prepare, keep off.]

**Parse**, pärs, *v.t.* (*gram.*) to tell the *parts* of speech of a sentence and their relations.—*n.* **Pars′ing.** [L. *pars* (*orationis*), a part of speech.]

**Parsee**, pär′sē or par-sē′, *n.* one of the adherents

of the ancient Persian religion, now settled in India. [Per. *Pársi*, a Persian—*Pars*, Persia.]

**Parsimonious**, pär-si-mō′ni-us, *adj. sparing* in the use of money : frugal to excess : covetous. —*adv.* **Parsimo′niously.**—*n.* **Parsimo′niousness.**

**Parsimony**, pär′si-mun-i, *n., sparingness* in the spending of money : frugality : niggardliness. [Fr.—L. *parsimonia, parcimonia—parco*, to spare.]

**Parsley**, pärs′li, *n.* a bright-green pot-herb. [Fr. *persil*—L. *petroselinum*—Gr. *petroselinon— petros*, a rock, *selinon*, a kind of parsley. See Celery.]

**Parsnip, Parsnep**, pärs′nip, *n.* an edible plant with a carrot-like root. [O. Fr. *pastenaque*—L. *pastinaca—pastinum*, a dibble.]

**Parson**, pär′sn, *n.* the priest or incumbent of a parish : a clergyman. [O. Fr. *persone*, a parson, from L. *persona*, a character, person, which in Low L. had the sense of rank, dignity, and so was applied to a clergyman. See Person.]

**Parsonage**, pär′sn-āj, *n.* (*orig.*) the benefice of a *parish* : the residence of the incumbent of a parish.

**Part**, pärt, *n.* a portion : a quantity or number making up with others a larger quantity or number : a fraction : a member : a proportional quantity : share : interest : side or party : action : (*math.*) a quantity which taken a certain number of times will equal a larger quantity : (*music*) one of the melodies of a harmony :—*pl.* qualities : talents.—*v.t.* to divide : to make into parts : to put or keep asunder.—*v.i.* to be separated : to be torn asunder : to have a part or share.—**Part of speech** (*gram.*), one of the classes of words.—**In good-part, In bad-part**, favourably, unfavourably. [Fr.—L. *pars, partis*.]

**Partake**, par-tāk′, *v.i.* to *take* or have a *part* : to have something of the properties, &c. : to be admitted.—*v.t.* to have a part in : to share.—*n.* **Partak′er.**    [combination in an evil design.

**Partaking**, par-tāk′ing, *n.* a *sharing* : (*law*) a

**Parterre**, par-tär′, *n.* a system of plots with spaces of turf or gravel for walks. [Fr.—L. *per terram*, along the ground.]

**Partial**, pär′shal, *adj.* relating to a *part* only : not total or entire : inclined to favour one party : having a preference : (*bot.*) subordinate.—*adv.* **Par′tially.** [Fr.—Low L. *partialis*—L. *pars*.]

**Partiality**, pär-shi-al′it-i, *n.* quality of being *partial* or inclined to favour one party or side : liking for one thing more than others.

**Partible**, pärt′i-bl, *adj.* that may be parted : separable.—*n.* **Partibil′ity.**

**Participant**, par-tis′i-pant, *adj., participating* : sharing.—*n.* a partaker.—*adv.* **Partic′ipantly.**

**Participate**, par-tis′i-pāt, *v.i.* to *partake* : to have a share.—*n.* **Participa′tion.** [L. *participo, -atum—pars*, and *capio*, to take.]

**Participial**, par-ti-sip′i-al, *adj.* having the nature of a *participle* : formed from a participle.—*adv.* **Particip′ially.**

**Participle**, pär′ti-si-pl, *n.* a word *partaking* of the nature of both adjective and verb. [L. *participium—particeps*, sharing—*pars*, and *capio*, to take.]

**Particle**, pär′ti-kl, *n.* a *little part* : a very small portion : (*physics*) the minutest part into which a body can be divided : (*gram.*) an indeclinable word, or a word that cannot be used alone : in R. Cath. Church, a crumb of consecrated bread, also the 'smaller breads' used in the communion of the laity. [Fr.—L. *particula*, dim. of *pars*, *partis*.]

**Particular**, par-tik'ū-lar, *adj*. relating to a *particle*: pertaining to a single person or thing: individual: special: worthy of special attention: concerned with things single or distinct: exact: nice in taste: precise.—*n*. a distinct or minute part: a single point: a single instance:—*pl*. details. —**In particular**, specially, distinctly. [Fr.—L. *particularis—particula*.]

**Particularise**, par-tik'ū-lar-īz, *v.t*. to mention the *particulars* of: to enumerate in detail.—*v.i*. to mention or attend to single things or minute details.

**Particularity**, par-tik-ū-lar'i-ti, *n*. quality of being *particular*: minuteness of detail: a single act or case: something peculiar or singular.

**Particularly**, par-tik'ū-lar-li, *adv*. (*B.*), in detail.

**Parting**, pärt'ing, *adj*. putting *apart*: sep·rating: departing: given at parting.—*n*. the act of parting: a division: (*geol.*) a fissure in strata.

**Partisan**, pär'ti-zan, *n*. an adherent of a *party* or faction.—*adj*. adhering to a party.—*n*. **Par'tisanship**. [Fr.—It. *partigiano*—L. *partior*. See **Party**.]

**Partisan**, pär'ti-zan, *n*. a kind of halberd. [Fr. *pertuisane*, which is perh. from O. Ger. *partâ*, *barte*, a battle-axe, seen in **Halberd**.]

**Partite**, pär'tīt, *adj*. (*bot.*), *parted* nearly to the base. [L. *partitus*, pa.p. of *partior*, to divide —*pars*.]

**Partition**, par-tish'un, *n*. act of *parting* or dividing: state of being divided: separate part: that which divides: a wall between apartments: the place where separation is made.—*v.t*. to divide into shares: to divide into **parts by walls**. [Fr.—L. *partitio—partior*.]

**Partitive**, pär'ti-tiv, *adj*., *parting*: dividing: distributive.—*n*. (*gram.*) a word denoting a part or partition.—*adv*. **Par'titively**.

**Partlet**, pärt'let, *n*. a ruff or band worn by women: a hen, from ruffling the feathers round its neck. [Dim. of **Part**.]

**Partly**, pärt'li, *adv*. in part: in some degree.

**Partner**, pärt'nèr, *n*. a sharer: an associate: one who dances with another: a husband or wife.

**Partnership**, pärt'nèr-ship, *n*. state of being a partner: a contract between persons engaged in any business.

**Partook**, par-took', *past tense* of **Partake**.

**Partridge**, pär'trij, *n*. a genus of gallinaceous birds preserved for game. [Fr. *perdrix*—L. *perdix, perdicis*—Gr. *perdix*.]

**Partridge-wood**, pär'trij-wood, *n*. a hard variegated *wood*, from Brazil and the W. Indies, used in cabinet-work.

**Part-song**, pärt'song, *n*. a song sung in parts.

**Parturient**, par-tū'ri-ent, *adj*., *bringing* or about to bring *forth* young. [L. *parturiens*, *-entis*, pr.p. of *parturio—pario*, to bring forth.]

**Parturition**, par-tū-rish'un, *n*. act of *bringing forth*. [Fr.—L. *parturitio—parturio*.]

**Party**, pär'ti, *n*. a *part* of a greater number of persons: a faction: a company met for a particular purpose: an assembly: one concerned in any affair: a single individual spoken of: (*mil.*) a detachment.—*adj*. belonging to a party and not to the whole: consisting of different parties, parts, or things: (*her.*) parted or divided. [Fr. *parti*—O. Fr. *partir*—L. *partior*, to divide, from *pars*, a part.]

**Party-coloured**, pär'ti-kul'urd, *adj.*, *coloured* differently at different *parts*.

**Parvenu**, pär've-nōō, *n*. an *upstart*: one newly risen into notice or power. [Fr., pa.p. of *parvenir*—L. *pervenio*, to arrive at—*per*, quite to, *venio*, to come.]

**Parvis**, pär'vis, *n*. a porch: a schoolroom over a church porch. [O. Fr.—Low L. *paravisus*, corr. of Gr. *paradeisos*. See **Paradise**.]

**Pasch**, pask, *n*. the Jewish *passover*: Easter.— **Pasch of the Cross**, Good-Friday. [A.S. *pascha*—L.—Gr.—Heb. *pesach*, the Passover— *pasach*, to pass over.]

**Paschal**, pas'kal, *adj*. pertaining to the *Pasch* or Passover, or to Easter.

**Pasha, Pacha**, pä'sha or pash-ä', *n*. a title of Turkish officers who are governors of provinces or hold high naval and military commands. [Per. *basha*, a corr. of *padshah—pad*, protecting, and *shah*, king.]

**Pashalic**, pa-shäl'ik, *n*. the jurisdiction of a pasha.

**Pasque-flower, Pasch-flower**, pask'-flow'èr, *n*. a kind of anemone, which flowers about *Easter*.

**Pasquin**, pas'kwin, **Pasquinade**, pas'kwin-ād, *n*. a lampoon or satire.—*v.t*. or *v.i*. to lampoon or satirise. [*Pasquino*, a tailor in Rome in 15th cent. remarkable for his sarcastic humour.]

**Pass**, pas, *v.i*. to *pace* or walk onward: to move from one place to another: to travel: to go from one state to another: to change: to circulate: to be regarded: to go by: to go unheeded or neglected: to elapse, as time: to be finished: to move away: to disappear: (*B.*) to pass away: to go through inspection: to be approved: to happen: to fall, as by inheritance: to flow through: to thrust, as with a sword: to run, as a road:—*pa.p.* passed and past. [Fr. *passer*, It. *passare*—L. *passus*, a step. See **Pace**.]

**Pass**, pas, *v.t*. to go by, over, beyond, through, &c.: to spend: to omit, to disregard: to surpass: to enact, or to be enacted by: to cause to move: to send: to transfer: to give forth: to cause to go by: to approve: to give circulation to: (*fencing*) to thrust.—**Come to pass**, to happen.

**Pass**, pas, *n*. that through which one *passes*: a narrow passage: a narrow defile: a passport: state or condition: (*fencing*) a thrust.—*n*. **Pass'-book**, a book that *passes* between a trader and his customer, in which credit purchases are entered.—*n*. **Pass'key**, a *key* enabling one to *pass* or enter a house: a *key* for opening several locks.—*n*. **Pass'word**, (*mil.*) a private *word* enabling one to *pass* or enter a camp, by which a friend is distinguished from a stranger.

**Passable**, pas'a-bl, *adj*. that may be *passed*, travelled, or navigated: that may bear inspection: tolerable.—*n*. **Pass'ableness**.—*adv*. **Pass'ably**.

**Passage**, pas'āj, *n*. act of *passing*: journey: course: time occupied in passing: way: entrance: enactment of a law: right of passing: occurrence: a single clause or part of a book, &c.: (*B.*) a mountain-pass: ford of a river: (*zool.*) migratory habits.

**Passant**, pas'ant, *adj*. (*her.*) walking (said of an animal). [Fr. See **Pass**, *v.i.*]

**Passenger**, pas'en-jèr, *n*. one who *passes*: one who travels in some public conveyance. [Fr. *passager*, with inserted *n*, as in *messenger*, *porringer*, *nightingale*.]

**Passer**, pas'èr, *n*. one who *passes*.—*n*. **Pass'er-by**, one who *passes by* or near.

**Passerine**, pas'èr-in, *adj*. relating to the *passeres*, an order of birds of which the *sparrow* is the type. [L. *passer*, a sparrow.]

**Passing**, pas'ing, *adj*., *going by*: surpassing.— *adv*. exceedingly.—*n*. **Pass'ing-bell**, a *bell* tolled immediately after a person's death, orig.

to invite prayers for the soul *passing* into eternity.

**Passion,** pash'un, *n.* strong *feeling* or agitation of mind, esp. rage : ardent love : eager desire : state of the soul when receiving an impression : endurance of an effect, as opposed to action : the *sufferings,* esp. the death of Christ : —*pl.* excited conditions of mind. [Fr.—L. *passio, passionis—passus,* pa.p. of *patior,* to suffer. See **Patient** and **Passive.**]

**Passionate,** pash'un-āt, *adj.* moved by *passion* : easily moved to anger : intense.—*adv.* **Pas'sionately.**—*n.* **Pas'sionateness.**

**Passion-flower,** pash'un-flow'ér, *n.* a *flower* so called from a fancied resemblance to a crown of thorns, the emblem of Christ's *passion.*

**Passionless,** pash'un-les, *adj.* free from passion : not easily excited to anger.

**Passion-play,** pash'un-plā, *n.* a religious drama representing the *passion* of Christ.

**Passion-week,** pash'un-wēk, *n.* name commonly given in England to Holy-week (as being the *week* of Christ's *passion* or suffering, that is, his trial and crucifixion) ; but, according to proper rubrical usage, the week preceding Holy-week. [See **Holy-week.**]

**Passive,** pas'iv, *adj., suffering* : unresisting : not acting : (*gram.*) expressing the suffering of an action.—*adv.* **Pass'ively.**—*n.* **Pass'iveness.** [Fr.—L. *passivus—patior.* See **Passion.**]

**Passivity,** pas-iv'i-ti, *n., passiveness* : inactivity : (*physics*) tendency of a body to preserve a given state, either of motion or rest.

**Passman,** pas'man, *n.* one who gains only an ordinary degree or *pass* at the Oxford examinations.

**Passover,** pas'ō-vér, *n.* an annual feast of the Jews, to commemorate the destroying angel's *passing over* the houses of the Israelites when he slew the first-born of the Egyptians.

**Passport,** pas'pōrt, *n.* a written warrant granting permission to travel in a foreign country : (*orig.*) permission to *pass* out of *port* or through the gates. [**Pass,** and L. *portus,* a harbour, or *porta,* a gate.]

**Past,** past, *pa.p.* of **Pass.**—*adj.* gone by : elapsed : ended : in time already passed.—*prep.* farther than : out of reach of : no longer capable of.—*adv.* by.—**The past,** that which has passed, esp. time.

**Paste,** pāst, *n.* dough prepared for pies, &c. : a cement of flour and water : anything mixed up to a viscous consistency : a fine kind of glass for making artificial gems.—*v.t.* to fasten with paste.—*n.* **Paste'board,** a stiff *board* made of sheets of paper *pasted* together, &c. [O. Fr. *paste* (Fr. *pâte*)—Late L. *pesta*—Gr. *pastē,* a mess of food—*pastos,* besprinkled with salt—*passo,* to sprinkle.]

**Pastel,** pas'tel, **Pastil,** pas'til, *n.* (*paint.*) a roll of coloured paste, used for a crayon : a medicated lozenge. [Fr. *pastel*—It. *pastello*—L. *pastillus,* a small loaf, dim. of *pastus,* food—*pasco, pastus,* to feed. Doublet **Pastille.**]

**Pastern,** pas'tern, *n.* the part of a horse's foot from the fetlock to the hoof, where the shackle is fastened. [O. Fr. *pasturon* (Fr. *pâturon*)—O. Fr. *pasture,* pasture, a tether (for a horse at pasture).]

**Pastille,** pas-tēl', *n.* a small cone of charcoal and aromatic substances, burnt to perfume a room : a small aromatic pill. [Fr.—L. *pastillus,* a small loaf ; a doublet of **Pastel.**]

**Pastime,** pas'tīm, *n.* that which serves to *pass* away the *time* : amusement : recreation.

**Pastor,** pas'tur, *n.* a *shepherd :* a clergyman. [L., from *pastus,* to feed, pa.p. of *pasco,* to feed.]

**Pastoral,** pas'tur-al, *adj.* relating to *shepherds* or shepherd life : rustic : relating to the pastor of a church : addressed to the clergy of a diocese. —*n.* a poem which professes to delineate the scenery and life of the country : a pastoral letter or address : (*mus.*) a simple melody.

**Pastorate,** pas'tur-āt, **Pastorship,** pas'tur-ship, *n.* the office of a pastor.

**Pastorly,** pas'tur-li, *adj.* becoming a pastor.

**Pastry,** pāst'ri, *n.* articles of fancy-bread, chiefly of *paste* or dough : crust of pies : act or art of making articles of paste.—*n.* **Past'rycook,** one who *cooks* or sells *pastry.* [From **Paste.**]

**Pasturable,** past'ūr-a-bl, *adj.* that can be pastured : fit for pasture.        [cattle : pasture.

**Pasturage,** past'ūr-āj, *n.* the business of feeding

**Pasture,** past'ūr, *n.* grass for grazing : ground covered with grass for grazing.—*v.t.* to feed on pasture : to supply with grass.—*v.i.* to feed on pasture : to graze. [O. Fr. *pasture* (Fr. *pâture*) —L. *pastura—pasco, pastum.*]

**Pasty,** pāst'i, *adj.* like *paste.*—*n.* a small pie of crust raised without a dish.

**Pat,** pat, *n.* a light, quick blow, as with the hand. —*v.t.* to strike gently : to tap :—*pr.p.* patt'ing ; *pa.t.* and *pa.p.* patt'ed. [From the sound.]

**Pat,** pat, *n.* a small lump of butter. [Celt., as **Ir.** *pait,* a lump.]

**Pat,** pat, *adj.* fitly : at the right time or place. [An application of **Pat,** a light blow.]

**Patch,** pach, *v.t.* to mend with a piece : to repair clumsily : to make up of pieces : to make hastily. —*n.* a piece sewed or put on : anything like a patch : a small piece of ground : a plot. [Low Ger. *patschen* ; prob. conn. with **Piece.**]

**Patchouli,** pa-chōō'li, *n.* the highly odoriferous dried branches of an Eastern shrub, 1½–2 ft. high : the perfume distilled from these. [Lit. ' the gum-leaf ;' Tamil, *patchei,* gum, and *elei,* a leaf.]

**Patchwork,** pach'wurk, *n., work* formed of *patches* or pieces sewed together : a thing patched up or clumsily executed. [**Patch** and **Work.**]

**Pate,** pāt, *n.* the crown of the head : the head. [Through O. Fr., from Ger. *platte,* a plate (whence Low L. *platta,* a priest's tonsure).]

**Paten,** pat'en, *n.* the plate for the bread in the Eucharist. [Fr.—L. *patina,* a plate—Gr. *patanē.* See **Pan.**]

**Patent,** pā'tent or pat'ent, *adj., open* : conspicuous : public : protected by a patent : (*bot.*) expanding.—*n.* an official document, *open,* but sealed at the foot, conferring an exclusive right or privilege, as a title of nobility, or the sole right for a term of years to the proceeds of an invention.—*v.t.* **Pat'ent,** to grant or secure by patent. [Fr.—L. *patens, patentis,* pr.p. of *pateo.*]        [being patented.

**Patentable,** pā' or pat'ent-a-bl, *adj.* capable of

**Patentee,** pā-tent-ē' or pat-ent-ē', *n.* one who holds a *patent.*

**Paternal,** pa-tér'nal, *adj.,* fatherly : shewing the disposition of a father : hereditary.—*adv.* **Paternally.** [Fr. *paternel*—Low L. *paternalis* —L. *paternus—pater* (Gr. *patēr*), a father—root *pa,* to guard, to feed ; akin to Sans. *pa,* to protect, and E. **Food.** See **Father.**]

**Paternity,** pa-tér'ni-ti, *n.* the relation of a *father* to his offspring : origination or authorship. [Fr.—L. *paternitas, fatherly* feeling.]

**Paternoster,** pat-ér-nos'tér or pā'tér-nos-tér, *n.* the Lord's Prayer. [L. *Pater noster,* ' Our

Father,' the first two words of the Lord's Prayer in Latin.]

**Path,** päth, *n.* a way : track : road : course of action or conduct :—*pl.* **Paths,** päthz. [A.S. *peth, path ; * akin to Ger. *pfad,* Gr. *patos,* L. *pons, pontis,* a bridge, and Sans. *patha,* a path.]

**Pathetic,** pa-thet′ik, *adj.* affecting the tender emotions : touching.—**The Pathetic,** the style or manner fitted to excite emotion.—*adv.* **Pathet′-ically.**—*n.* **Pathet′icalness.** [Gr. *pathētikos.*]

**Pathless,** path′les, *adj.* without a *path* : untrodden.

**Pathology,** pa-thol′o-ji, *n.* science of diseases.—*n.* **Pathol′ogist,** one versed in pathology.—*adjs.* **Patholog′ic, Patholog′ical.**—*adv.* **Patholog′-ically.** [Fr.—Gr. *pathos,* suffering, *logos,* discourse.]

**Pathos,** pā′thos, *n.* that which raises the tender emotions : the expression of deep feeling. [Gr., from root *path,* in *e-path-on,* 2 aorist of *paschō,* to suffer, feel ; akin to Sans. *badh,* to suffer, to pain.]

**Pathway,** päth′wā, *n.* a *path* or *way* : a footpath : course of action. [**Path** and **Way.**]

**Patience,** pā′shens, *n.* quality of being patient or calmly enduring. [Fr.—L. *patientia—patiens.* See **Patient.**]

**Patient,** pā′shent, *adj.* sustaining pain, &c. without repining : not easily provoked : persevering : expecting with calmness.—*n.* one who bears or suffers : a person under medical treatment.—*adv.* **Pa′tiently.** [Fr.—L. *patiens, -entis,* pr.p. of *patior,* to bear ; akin to root of **Pathos.**]

**Patin, Patine,** pat′in, *n.* Same as **Paten.**

**Patois,** pat-waw′ or pat′-, *n.* a vulgar dialect. [Fr., orig. *patrois—*L. *patriensis,* indigenous, native *—patria,* one's native country.]

**Patriarch,** pā′tri-ärk, *n.* one who governs his family by paternal right : (*B.*) one of the early heads of families from Abraham to Jacob and his sons : in Eastern churches, a dignitary superior to an archbishop. [O. Fr.—L.—Gr. *patriarchēs—patria,* lineage—*patēr,* a father, and *archē,* a beginning. See **Paternal** and **Archaic.**]

**Patriarchal,** pā-tri-ärk′al, **Patriarchic,** pā-tri-ärk′ik, *adj.* belonging or subject to a patriarch.

**Patriarchate,** pā-tri-ärk′āt, *n.* the office or jurisdiction of a patriarch or church dignitary : the residence of a patriarch.                [patriarch.

**Patriarchism,** pā′tri-ärk-izm, *n.* government by a

**Patrician,** pa-trish′an, *n.* a nobleman in ancient Rome, being a descendant of the *fathers* or first Roman senators : a nobleman.—*adj.* pertaining to a patrician or nobleman : noble. [L. *patricius—pater, patris,* a father. See **Paternal.**]

**Patrimonial,** pat-ri-mō′ni-al, *adj.* pertaining to a patrimony : inherited from ancestors.—*adv.* **Patrimo′nially.**

**Patrimony,** pat′ri-mun-i, *n.* a right or estate inherited from a *father* or one's ancestors : a church estate or revenue. [Fr. *patrimoine—*L. *patrimonium—pater, patris,* a father. See **Paternal.**]

**Patriot,** pā′tri-ot, *n.* one who truly loves and serves his *fatherland.* [Fr.—Low L.—Gr. *patriōtēs—patrios,* of one's father or fatherland—*patēr,* a father. See **Paternal.**]

**Patriotic,** pā-tri-ot′ik, *adj.* like a *patriot* : actuated by a love of one's country : directed to the public welfare.—*adv.* **Patriot′ically.** [Gr.]

**Patriotism,** pā′tri-ot-izm, *n.* quality of being patriotic : love of one's country.

**Patristic,** pa-tris′tik, **Patristical,** pa-tris′tik-al, *adj.* pertaining to the *fathers* of the Christian

Church. [Fr., coined from L. *pater, patris,* a father. See **Father** and **Paternal.**]

**Patrol,** pa-trōl′, *v.i.* to go the rounds in a camp or garrison.—*v.t.* to pass round as a sentry :—*pr.p.* **patrōll′ing ; ** *pa.t.* and *pa.p.* **patrōlled′.**—*n.* the marching round of a guard in the night : the guard which makes a patrol. [Fr. *patrouille,* a patrol, *patrouiller,* to march in the mud, through a form *patouiller,* from *patte,* the paw or foot of a beast, which is from Teut. root *pat,* found in Ger. *patsche,* little hand.]

**Patron,** pā′trun, *n.* a protector : one who countenances : one who has the gift of a benefice :—*fem.* **Patroness,** pā′trun-es. [Fr.—L. *patronus* (*lit.*) one acting as a *father—pater, patris,* a father. See **Paternal. Doublet Pattern.**]

**Patronage,** pat′run-āj or pā′, *n.* the support of a patron : guardianship of saints : the right of bestowing offices, privileges, or church benefices.

**Patroness,** pā′trun-es, *fem.* of **Patron.**

**Patronise,** pat′run-īz or pā′, *v.t.* to act as patron toward : to support : to assume the air of a patron to.—*n.* **Pat′roniser.**—*adv.* **Pat′ronisingly.**

**Patronymic,** pat-ro-nim′ik, **Patronymical,** pat-ro-nim′ik-al, *adj.* derived from the *name* of a *father* or ancestor. [Gr. *patēr,* a father, *onoma,* a name.]                [one's *father* or ancestor.

**Patronymic,** pat-ro-nim′ik, *n.* a name taken from

**Patten,** pat′en, *n.* a wooden sole with an iron ring worn under the shoe to keep it from the wet : the base of a pillar. [Fr. *patin,* a skate, clog—*patte.* See **Patrol.**]

**Patter,** pat′ér, *v.i.* to *pat* or strike often, as hail :—*pr.p.* **patt′ering ; ** *pa.t.* and *pa.p.* **patt′ered.** [A freq. of **Pat.**]

**Pattern,** pat′érn, *n.* a person or thing to be copied : a model : an example : style of ornamental work : anything to serve as a guide in forming objects. [Fr. *patron,* a protector ; also a pattern, sample. **Doublet Patron.**]

**Patty,** pat′i, *n.* a *little pie.* [Fr. *pâté.* See **Paste.**]

**Paucity,** paw′sit-i, *n., fewness :* smallness of number or quantity. [Fr.—L. *paucitas—paucus,* few ; akin to **Pause.**]

**Pauline,** paw′līn, *adj.* of the Apostle *Paul.*

**Paunch,** pawnsh or pänsh, *n.* the belly : the first and largest stomach of a ruminant.—*v.t.* to pierce or rip the belly of : to eviscerate. [O. Fr. *panche,* Fr. *panse—*L. *pantex, panticis.*]

**Pauper,** paw′pér, *n.* a *poor* person : one supported by charity or some public provision. [L.]

**Pauperise,** paw′pér-īz, *v.t.* to reduce to pauperism.—*n.* **Pauperisa′tion.**

**Pauperism,** paw′pér-izm, *n.* state of being a pauper.

**Pause,** pawz, *n.* a *ceasing* : a temporary stop : cessation caused by doubt : suspense : a mark for suspending the voice : (*music*) a mark showing continuance of a note or rest.—*v.i.* to make a pause. [Fr.—L. *pausa—*Gr. *pausis,* from *pauō,* to cause to cease. **Doublet Pose.**]

**Pausingly,** pawz′ing-li, *adv., with pauses :* by breaks.

**Pave,** pāv, *v.t.* to lay down stone, &c. to form a level surface for walking on : to prepare, as a way or passage.—**To pave the way,** to prepare the way for.—*ns.* **Pav′er, Pav′ier.** [Fr. *paver* —L. *pavio ;* cog. with Gr. *paiō,* to beat.]

**Pavement,** pāv′ment, *n.* a paved causeway or floor : that with which anything is paved. [L. *pavimentum.*]

**Pavilion,** pa-vil′yun, *n.* a tent : an ornamental building often turreted or domed : (*mil.*) a tent raised on posts.—*v.t.* to furnish with pavilions. [Lit. that which is spread out like the wings of a *butterfly;* Fr. *pavillon*—L. *papilio*, a butterfly, a tent.]

**Pavior**, pāv′yur, *n.* one whose trade is to *pave*.

**Paw**, paw, *n.* the *foot* of a beast of prey having claws: the hand, used in contempt.—*v.i.* to draw the forefoot along the ground like a horse.—*v.t.* to scrape with the forefoot: to handle with the paws: to handle roughly: to flatter. [Perh. Celtic, as W. *pawen*, a paw; but it is also a Teut. word.]

**Pawed**, pawd, *adj.* having paws: broad-footed.

**Pawky**, pawk′i, *adj.* sly, arch, shrewd. [Scot. *paik*, a trick.]

**Pawl**, pawl, *n.* a short bar used to prevent the recoil of a windlass, &c.: a catch. [W. *pawl*, a stake, conn. with L. *palus*, a stake. See **Pale**, *n.*]

**Pawn**, pawn, *n.* something given as security for the repayment of money.—*v.t.* to give in pledge. [Fr. *pan*—L. *pannus*, a rag, cloth, a thing left in pledge, because a piece of clothing was a convenient thing to leave in pledge.]

**Pawn**, pawn, *n.* a common piece in chess. [O. Fr. *paon*, a foot-soldier—Low L. *pedo, pedonis*, a foot-soldier, from L. *pes, pedis*, the foot.]

**Pawnbroker**, pawn′brōk-ėr, *n.* a *broker* who lends money on *pawns* or pledges.

**Pawner**, pawn′ėr, *n.* one who gives a *pawn* or pledge as security for money borrowed.

**Paxwax**, paks′waks, *n.* the strong tendon in the neck of animals. [Orig. *fax-wax*—A.S. *feax, fex*, hair, and *weaxan*, to grow.]

**Pay**, pā, *v.t.* to discharge a debt: to requite with what is deserved: to reward: to punish.—*v.i.* to recompense:—*pa.t.* and *pa.p.* paid.—*n.* that which satisfies: money given for service: salary, wages.—*n.* **Pay′er.**—**Pay off**, to discharge: to take revenge upon: to requite.—**Pay out**, to cause to run out, as rope. [Fr. *payer*—L. *pacare*, to appease, from base of *pax, pacis*, peace. See **Peace**.]

**Pay**, pā, *v.t.* (*naut.*, and in the proverb 'the devil to pay') to smear with tar, pitch, &c. [From L. *picare*, to pitch, prob. through Sp. *pega*.]

**Payable**, pā′a-bl, *adj.* that may be paid: that ought to be paid.

**Payee**, pā-ē′, *n.* one to whom money is *paid*.

**Paymaster**, pā′mas-tėr, *n.* the *master* who *pays*: an officer in the army or navy whose duty it is to pay soldiers, &c.

**Payment**, pā′ment, *n.* the act of *paying*: that which is paid: recompense: reward.

**Paynim**, **Painim**, pā′nim, *n.* a pagan. [Orig. and properly, *paynim* was not a man, but a country, and = 'heathendom,' from O. Fr. *paienisme*, paganism—L. *paganismus*—*paganus*, a pagan. See **Pagan**.]

**Pea**, pē, *n.* a common vegetable:—def. *pl.* **Peas**: indef. *pl.* **Pease**. [M. E. *pese*, pl. *pesen* and *peses*—A.S. *pisa*, pl. *pisan*—L. *pisum*, Gr. *pison*, from a root seen in Sans. *pish*, to bruise. Pea is erroneously formed, the *s* of the root being mistaken for the sign of the plural.]

**Peace**, pēs, *n.* a state of quiet: freedom from disturbance: freedom from war: friendliness: calm: rest: harmony: silence.—*int.* silence, hist!—**Hold one's peace**, to be silent. [O. Fr. *pais* (Fr. *paix*)—L. *pax, pacis*, from root *pac-*, to bind, seen in *pac-iscor*, to make a contract. Cf. **Pact**.]

**Peaceable**, pēs′a-bl, *adj.* disposed to peace: quiet: tranquil.—*adv.* **Peace′ably.**—*n.* **Peace′ableness.**

**Peaceful**, pēs′fool, *adj.* full of peace: quiet: tran-

quil: calm: serene.—*adv.* **Peace′fully.**—*n.* **Peace′fulness.**

**Peacemaker**, pēs′māk-ėr, *n.* one who *makes* or produces *peace*. [**Peace** and **Maker**.]

**Peace-offering**, pēs′-of′ėr-ing, *n.* an *offering* propitiating *peace*: among the Jews, an offering to God, either in gratitude for past or petition for future mercies: satisfaction to an offended person.

**Peace-officer**, pēs′-of′is-ėr, *n.* an *officer* whose duty it is to preserve the *peace*: a police-officer.

**Peace-party**, pēs′-pär′ti, *n.* a political *party* advocating the preservation of *peace*.

**Peach**, pēch, *n.* a tree with delicious fruit.—*adj.* **Peach′y.** [Fr. *pêche* (It. *persica, pesca*)—L. *Persicum (malum)*, the Persian (apple), from *Persicus*, belonging to Persia.]

**Peach-coloured**, pēch′-kul′urd, *adj.* of the *colour* of a *peach* blossom, pale red.

**Peacock**, pē′kok, *n.* a large gallinaceous bird remarkable for the beauty of its plumage, named from its cry:—*fem.* **Pea′hen**. [Pea- is from A.S. *pawe*—L. *pavo*—Gr. *taōs*—(acc. to Max Müller) Pers. *tawus*—O. Tamil *tokei, togei*. See also **Cock**.]

**Pea-jacket**, pē′-jak′et, *n.* a coarse thick jacket worn esp. by seamen. [Pea- is from Dut. *pij* (*pron.* pī), a coat of coarse thick cloth; and **Jacket**.]

**Peak**, pēk, *n.* a *point*: the pointed end of anything: the top of a mountain: (*naut.*) the upper outer corner of a sail extended by a gaff or yard, also the extremity of the gaff. [Celt. See **Beak**, **Pike**.]

**Peaked**, pēkt, *adj.*, *pointed*: ending in a point.

**Peakish**, pēk′ish, *adj.*, having peaks.

**Peal**, pēl, *n.* a loud sound: a set of bells tuned to each other: the changes rung upon a set of bells.—*v.i.* to resound like a bell: to utter or give forth loud or solemn sounds.—*v.t.* to assail with noise: to celebrate. [Short for **Appeal**.]

**Pean**. See **Pæan**.

**Pear**, pār, *n.* a common fruit: the tree. [A.S. *pera* or *peru*—L. *pirum*, a pear (whence also Fr. *poire*).]

**Pearl**, pėrl, *n.* a well-known shining gem, found in several shellfish, but most in the mother-of-pearl oyster: anything round and clear: anything very precious: a jewel: a white speck or film on the eye: (*print.*) the smallest type except diamond.—*adj.* made of or belonging to pearls.—*v.t.* to adorn with pearls. [Fr. *perle*, acc. to Diez, prob. either a corr. of L. *pirula*, a dim. of *pirum*, a pear (see **Pear**), or of L. *pilula*, dim. of *pila*, a ball.]

**Pearl-ash**, pėrl′-ash, *n.* a purer carbonate of potash, obtained by calcining potashes, so called from its *pearly*-white colour.

**Pearly**, pėrl′i, *adj.* containing or resembling *pearls*: clear: pure: transparent.—*n.* **Pearl′iness.**

**Peasant**, pez′ant, *n.* a *countryman*: a rustic: one whose occupation is rural labour.—*adj.* of or relating to peasants: rustic: rural. [O. Fr. *paisant* (with excrescent *-t*), Mod. Fr. *paysan* —*pays*—L. *pagus*, a district, a country. See **Pagan**.]

**Peasantry**, pez′ant-ri, *n.pl.* the body of peasants or tillers of the soil: rustics: labourers.

**Pease**, pēz, *indef. pl.* of **Pea**.

**Peat**, pēt, *n.* decayed vegetable matter like turf, cut out of boggy places, dried for fuel.—*adj.* **Peat′y.** [True form *beat*, as in Devonshire; from M. E. *beten*, to mend a fire—A.S. *betan*, to make better—*bot*, advantage. See **Boot**, *v.t.*]

**Pebble,** peb'l, *n.* a small roundish ball or stone: transparent and colourless rock-crystal. [A.S. *papol(-stan),* a pebble(-stone); akin to L. *papula,* a pustule.]

**Pebbled,** peb'ld, **Pebbly,** peb'li, *adj.* full of pebbles.

**Peccable,** pek'a-bl, *adj.* liable to sin.—*n.* **Peccabil'ity.** [L. *peccabilis—pecco, -atum,* to sin.]

**Peccadillo,** pek-a-dil'lo, *n.* a *little* or trifling *sin:* a petty fault:—*pl.* **Peccadil'los.** [Sp. *pecadillo,* dim. of *pecado—*L. *peccatum,* a sin.]

**Peccant,** pek'ant, *adj.,* sinning: transgressing: guilty: morbid: offensive: bad.—*adv.* **Pecc'antly.**—*n.* **Pecc'ancy.** [L. *peccans, -antis,* pr.p. of *pecco.*]

**Peccary,** pek'ar-i, *n.* a hog-like quadruped of South America. [The S. American word.]

**Peck,** pek, *n.* a dry measure = 2 gallons, or ⅓ of a bushel. [M. E. *pekke,* prob. from *peck,* 'to pick up,' formerly an indefinite quantity.]

**Peck,** pek, *v.t.* to strike with the *beak:* to pick up with the beak: to eat: to strike with anything pointed: to strike with repeated blows.—*adj.* **Peck'ish,** hungry. [A later form of **Pick.**]

**Pecker,** pek'er, *n.* that which pecks: a woodpecker.

**Pectinal,** pek'tin-al, *adj.* of a *comb:* having bones like the teeth of a comb. [L. *pecten, pectinis,* a comb.]

**Pectinate,** pek'tin-āt, **Pectinated,** pek'tin-āt-ed, *adj.* resembling the teeth of a *comb.*—*adv.* **Pec'tinately.**—*n.* **Pectina'tion,** the state of being pectinated.

**Pectoral,** pek'tor-al, *adj.* relating to the *breast* or chest.—*n.* a pectoral fin: a medicine for the chest. —*adv.* **Pec'torally.** [Fr.—L. *pectoralis—pectus, pectoris,* the breast.]

**Peculate,** pek'ū-lāt, *v.t.* to embezzle: to steal.—*ns.* **Pecula'tion, Pec'ulator.** [L. *peculor, peculatus,* from *peculium,* private property, akin to *pecunia,* money. See **Pecuniary.**]

**Peculiar,** pe-kūl'yar, *adj.* one's own: appropriate: particular: strange.—*adv.* **Pecul'iarly.**—*n.* **Peculiarity,** pe-kūl-i-ar'it-i. [Fr.—L. *peculiaris —peculium,* private property. Cf. **Peculate.**]

**Pecuniary,** pe-kū'ni-ar-i, *adj.* relating to *money.* —*adv.* **Pecu'niarily.** [Fr.—L. *pecuniarius—pecunia,* money—*pecu,* which appears in L. *pecua* (pl.), cattle of all kinds, cattle forming the wealth of early races; akin to E. **Fee.**]

**Pedagogic,** ped-a-goj'ik, **Pedagogical,** ped-a-goj'ik-al, *adj.* relating to *teaching.*

**Pedagogics,** ped-a-goj'iks, **Pedagogy,** ped'a-goj-i, *n.* the science of *teaching.*

**Pedagogue,** ped'a-gog, *n.* a teacher: a pedant. [Lit. a *leader of a boy* to and from school, Fr. —L.—Gr. *paidagōgos—pais, paidos,* a boy, *agōgos,* a leader—*agō,* to lead.]

**Pedal,** ped'al or pē'dal, *adj.* pertaining to a *foot.* —*n.* in musical instruments, a lever moved by the foot. [L. *pedalis—pes, pedis,* the foot, E. **Foot.**]

**Pedant,** ped'ant, *n.* one making a vain and useless display of learning. [Fr.—It. *pedante,* which was prob. formed from Gr. *paideuō,* to instruct, from *pais, paidos,* a boy. See **Pedagogue.**]

**Pedantic,** ped-ant'ik, **Pedantical,** ped-ant'ik-al, *adj.* vainly displaying knowledge.

**Pedantry,** ped'ant-ri, *n.* vain and useless display of learning.

**Peddle,** ped'l, *v.i.* to travel about with a *basket* or bundle of goods, esp. small-wares, for sale: to be busy about trifles.—*v.t.* to retail in very small quantities.—*n.* **Pedd'ler.** [See **Pedlar.**]

**Peddlery,** ped'ler-i, *n.* the trade of a peddler: the wares sold by a peddler.

**Peddling,** ped'ling, *n.* the trade of a peddler.

**Pedestal,** ped'es-tal, *n.* the *foot* or base of a pillar, &c. [Sp.—It. *piedestallo—*L. *pes, pedis,* the foot, and *'t. stallo,* a place. See **Stall.**]

**Pedestrian,** pe-des'tri-an, *adj.* going on *foot:* performed on foot.—*n.* one journeying on foot: an expert walker. [L. *pedestris—pes, pedis.*]

**Pedestrianism,** pe-des'tri-an-izm, *n.* a going on *foot:* walking: the practice of a pedestrian.

**Pedicel,** ped'i-sel, **Pedicle,** ped'i-kl, *n.* the *little foot*stalk by which a leaf or fruit is fixed on the tree. [Fr. *pédicelle—*L. *pediculus,* dim. of *pes, pedis,* the foot.]

**Pedigree,** ped'i-grē, *n.* a register of descent from ancestors: lineage: genealogy. [Ety. dub.: Wedgwood gives Fr. *pied de gres,* a tree of degrees, *pied* being technically used in the sense of 'tree;' Skeat suggests Fr. *pied de grue,* crane's-foot, from the crane's foot used in drawing out a pedigree.]

**Pediment,** ped'i-ment, *n.* (*arch.*) a triangular or circular ornament, which finishes the fronts of buildings, and serves as a decoration over gates. —*adj.* **Pediment'al.** [Ety. dub., perh. conn. with L. *pes, pedis,* the foot.]

**Pedlar, Pedler, Peddler,** ped'ler, *n.* a hawker or petty chapman.—*n.* **Pedlary, Pedlery,** a pedlar's small wares: his employment. [Older form *peddar* or *pedder,* one who carries wares in a *ped,* prov. E. for basket, and prob. same as **Pad.**]

**Pedobaptism,** pē-do-bap'tizm, *n., infant baptism.* [Gr. *pais, paidos,* a child, and **Baptism.**]

**Pedobaptist,** pē-do-bap'tist, *n.* one who believes in *infant baptism.*

**Pedometer,** ped-om'et-er, *n.* an instrument, somewhat like a watch, by which the steps of a pedestrian are registered, and thus the distance he walks is measured. [L. *pes, pedis,* a foot, and Gr. *metron,* a measure.]

**Peduncle,** pē-dung'kl, *n.* same as **Pedicel.**—*adjs.* **Pedun'cular, Pedun'culate, Pedun'culated.** [Fr. *pedoncule—*Low L. *pedunculus—*L. *pes, pedis,* the foot.]

**Peel,** pēl, *v.t.* to strip off the skin or bark: to bare.—*v.i.* to come off, as the skin.—*n.* the skin, rind, or bark. [Fr. *peler,* to unskin, from L. *pilo,* to deprive of hair, from *pilus,* a hair, cr from *pellis,* a skin, E. **Fell.**] [a stake, a fort.]

**Peel,** pēl, *n.* a small Border fortress. [Celt. *pill,*

**Peel,** pēl, *n.* a baker's wooden shovel: a fireshovel. [Fr. *pelle—*L. *pāla,* a spade.]

**Peel,** pēl, *v.t.* to plunder: to pillage. [Same as **Pill,** *v.*]

**Peep,** pēp, *v.i.* to chirp, or cry as a chicken. [Fr. *piper—*L. *pipare,* an imitative word.]

**Peep,** pēp, *v.i.* to look through a narrow space: to look slyly or closely: to begin to appear.—*n.* a sly look: a beginning to appear. [Same as the above word, Fr. *piper,* sig. to chirp like a bird (said of a bird-catcher), then to beguile, whence *peep =* to look out slyly.]

**Peeper,** pēp'er, *n.* one that peeps: a chicken just breaking the shell.

**Peer,** pēr, *n.* an *equal:* an associate: a nobleman: a member of the House of Lords:—*fem.* **Peer'ess.** [O. Fr. (Fr. *pair*)—L. *par, paris,* equal.]

**Peer,** pēr, *v.i.* to appear.

**Peer,** pēr, *v.i.* to look narrowly: to peep:—*pa.t.* and *pa.p.* peered. [M. E. *piren—*Low Ger. *piren,* orig. *plüren,* to draw the eyelids together.] [the body of peers.]

**Peerage,** pēr'āj, *n.* the rank or dignity of a peer:

---

**Peerless**, pēr′les, *adj.* having no peer or equal : matchless.—*adv.* **Peer′lessly.**—*n.* **Peer′lessness.**

**Peevish**, pēv′ish, *adj.* habitually fretful : easily annoyed : hard to please.—*adv.* **Peev′ishly.**—*n.* **Peev′ishness.** [Prob. imitative of the puling of fretful infants.]

**Peewit.** Same as **Pewit**.

**Peg**, peg, *n.* a wooden *pin* for fastening boards, &c. : one of the pins of a musical instrument.—*v.t.* to fasten with a peg :—*pr.p.* peg′ging ; *pa.t.* and *pa.p.* pegged. [Scand., as in Dan. *pig*, a spike.]

**Pegged**, pegd, *adj.* fastened or supplied with pegs.

**Pegtop**, peg′top, *n.* a child's plaything for spinning.

**Pekoe**, pē′kō, *n.* a scented black tea. [Chinese.]

**Pelagian**, pe-lā′ji-an, *n.* one who holds the views of *Pelagius*, a British monk of the 4th century, in respect to original sin.—*adj.* pertaining to Pelagius and his doctrines.—*n.* **Pela′gianism,** the doctrines of Pelagius.

**Pelargonium**, pel-ar-gō′ni-um, *n.* a vast genus of beautiful flowering plants. [From Gr. *pelargos*, stork, the fruit resembling a stork's beak.]

**Pelf**, pelf, *n.* riches (in a bad sense) : money. [O. Fr. *pelfre*, booty, of unknown origin ; allied to **Pilfer**.]

**Pelican**, pel′i-kan, *n.* a large water-fowl, having an enormous bill of the shape of an *axe*. [Fr.—L. *pelicanus*—Gr. *pelikan—pelekus*, an axe.]

**Pelisse**, pe-lēs′, *n.* (*orig.*) a *furred* coat or robe, now a silk habit worn by ladies. [Fr.—L. *pellis*, a skin.]

**Pell**, pel, *n.* a *skin* or *hide* : a roll of parchment. [O. Fr. *pel*, Fr. *peau*—L. *pellis*, a skin or hide.]

**Pellet**, pel′et, *n.* a little *ball*, as of lint or wax. [Fr. *pelote*—L. *pila*, a ball to play with.]

**Pelleted**, pel′et-ed, *adj.* consisting of pellets : pelted, as with bullets.

**Pellicle**, pel′i-kl, *n.* a *thin skin* or film : the film which gathers on liquors.—*adj.* **Pellic′ular.**

**Pell-mell**, pel-mel′, *adv.* mixed confusedly : promiscuously. [O. Fr. *pesle-mesle* (Fr. *pêle-mêle*) -*mesle* being from O. Fr. *mesler* (Fr. *mêler*), to mix—Low L. *misculo*—L. *misceo* ; and *pesle*, a rhyming addition, perh. influenced by Fr. *pelle*, shovel.]

**Pellucid**, pel-lōō′sid, *adj.* perfectly clear : transparent.—*adv.* **Pellu′cidly.**—*n.* **Pellu′cidness.** [Fr.—L. *pellucidus—per*, perfectly, and *lucidus*, clear—*luceo*, to shine.] [hawk all torn.

**Pelt**, pelt, *n.* a raw *hide* : the quarry or prey of a

**Pelt**, pelt, *v.t.* to strike with *pellets*, or with something thrown : to throw or cast.—*n.* a blow from a pellet, or from something thrown. [See **Pellet**.]

**Pelting**, pelt′ing, *n.* an assault with a *pellet*, or with anything thrown. [furs.

**Peltry**, pelt′ri, *n.* the *skins* of furred animals :

**Pelvis**, pel′vis, *n.* the *basin* or bony cavity forming the lower part of the abdomen. [L.]

**Pemmican, Pemican**, pem′i-kan, *n.* (*orig.*) a N. American Indian preparation, consisting of lean venison, dried, pounded, and pressed into cakes, now used in Arctic expeditions.

**Pen**, pen, *v.t.* to shut up : to confine in a small inclosure :—*pr.p.* penn′ing ; *pa.t.* and *pa.p.* penned or pent.—*n.* a small inclosure : a coop. [A.S. *pennan*, to shut up.]

**Pen**, pen, *n.* an instrument used for writing, formerly of the *feather* of a bird, but now of steel, &c.—*v.t.* to write :—*pr.p.* penn′ing ; *pa.t.* and *pa.p.* penned. [Fr. *penne*—L. *penna*, old forms,

*pesna, petna,* a feather—root *pat*, to fly. See **Feather, Find.**]

**Penal**, pē′nal, *adj.* pertaining to *punishment* : incurring or denouncing punishment : used for punishment.—*adv.* **Pe′nally.** [Fr.—L. *pœnalis* —*pœna*, akin to Gr. *poinē*, punishment.]

**Penalty**, pen′al-ti, *n., punishment* : personal or pecuniary punishment : a fine.

**Penance**, pen′ans, *n.* in the R. C. Church, the *punishment* borne by a penitent. [O. Fr. See **Penitence**.]

**Penates**, pe-nā′tēs, *n.pl.* the tutelary household deities of ancient Rome. [L., from root *pen* in L. *penitus*, within, *penetralia*, the inner part of anything.]

**Pence**, pens, *n.* plural of **Penny**, which see.

**Penchant**, päng′shäng, *n.* inclination : decided taste. [Fr., pr.p. of *pencher*, to incline, through a form *pendicare*, from L. *pendeo*, to hang.]

**Pencil**, pen′sil, *n.* a small hairbrush for laying on colours : any pointed instrument for writing or drawing without ink : a collection of rays of light converging to a point : the art of painting or drawing.—*v.t.* to write, sketch, or mark with a pencil : to paint or draw :—*pr.p.* pen′cilling ; *pa.t.* and *pa.p.* pen′cilled. [O. Fr. *pincel*, Fr. *pinceau*—L. *penicillum*, a painter's brush, dim. of *penis*, a tail.]

**Pencilled**, pen′sild, *adj.* written or marked with a pencil : having pencils of rays : radiated : (*bot.*) marked with fine lines, as with a pencil.

**Pencilling**, pen′sil-ing, *n.* the art of writing, sketching, or marking with a pencil : a sketch.

**Pendant**, pend′ant, *n.* anything *hanging*, especially for ornament : an earring : a long narrow flag, at the head of the principal mast in a royal ship. [Fr.—*pendant*, pr.p. of *pendre*, to hang— L. *pendens, -entis*—pr.p. of *pendeo*, to hang.]

**Pendence**, pend′ens, **Pendency**, pend′en-si, *n.* a *hanging* in suspense : state of being undecided.

**Pendent**, pend′ent, *adj., hanging* : projecting : supported above the ground or base.—*adv.* **Pend′ently.** [Latinised form of Fr. adj. *pendant*. See **Pendant**.]

**Pending**, pend′ing, *adj., hanging* : remaining undecided : not terminated.—*prep.* during. [Anglicised form of Fr. adj. *pendant*. [See **Pendant**.]

**Pendulous**, pend′ū-lus, *adj., hanging* : swinging. —*adv.* **Pend′ulously.**—*ns.* **Pend′ulousness, Pendulos′ity.** [L. *pendulus—pendeo*, to hang.]

**Pendulum**, pend′ū-lum, *n.* any weight so *hung* or suspended from a fixed point as to swing freely. [L., neut. of *pendulus*, hanging.]

**Penetrable**, pen′e-tra-bl, *adj.* that may be penetrated or pierced by another body : capable of having the mind affected.—*n.* **Penetrabil′ity.**

**Penetrate**, pen′e-trāt, *v.t.* to thrust into the *inside* : to pierce into : to affect the feelings : to understand : to find out.—*v.i.* to make way : to pass inwards. [L. *penetro, -atum*—root *pen*, within. See **Penates**.]

**Penetrating**, pen′e-trāt-ing, *adj., piercing* or entering : sharp : subtle : acute : discerning.

**Penetration**, pen-e-trā′shun, *n.* the act of penetrating or entering : acuteness : discernment.

**Penetrative**, pen′e-trāt-iv, *adj.* tending to penetrate : piercing : sagacious : affecting the mind.

**Penguin**, pen′gwin, **Pinguin**, pin′gwin, *n.* an aquatic bird in the southern hemisphere. [Ety. dub., acc. to some from L. *pinguis*, fat, acc. to others from W. *pen*, head, and *gwen*, white.]

**Peninsula**, pen-in′sū-la, *n.* land so surrounded by water as to be *almost an island*. [L.—*pœne*, almost, *insula*, an island. See **Insular**.]

**Peninsular**, pen-in'sū-lar, *adj.* pertaining to a peninsula : in the form of a peninsula : inhabiting a peninsula.       [sorrow for sin.

**Penitence**, pen'i-tens, *n.* state of being penitent :

**Penitent**, pen'i-tent, *adj.* suffering *pain* or sorrow for sin : contrite : repentant.—*n.* one grieved for sin : one under penance.—*adv.* **Pen'itently**. [Fr.—L. *pœnitens, -entis—pœniteo,* to cause to repent—*pœna,* punishment.]

**Penitential**, pen-i-ten'shal, *adj.* pertaining to or expressive of *penitence*.—*n.* a book of rules relating to penance.—*adv.* **Peniten'tially**.

**Penitentiary**, pen-i-ten'shar-i, *adj.* relating to *penance :* penitential.—*n.* a penitent : an office at the court of Rome for secret bulls, &c. : a place for penance : a house of correction for offenders.     [and mending quill *pens.*

**Penknife**, pen'nīf, *n.* a small *knife* orig. for making

**Penman**, pen'man, *n.* a *man* skilled in the use of the *pen :* an author.

**Penmanship**, pen'man-ship, *n.* the use of the pen in writing : art of writing : manner of writing.

**Pennant**, pen'ant, **Pennon**, pen'un, *n.* a small flag : a banner : a long narrow piece of bunting at the mast-heads of war-ships. [*Pennant* is formed from *pennon,* with excrescent *t ; pennon* is Fr. *pennon*—L. *penna,* a wing, feather.]

**Pennate**, pen'āt, **Pennated**, pen'āt-ed, *adj., winged :* (*bot.*) same as **Pinnate**. [L. *pennatus* —*penna,* feather, wing.]     [out money : poor.

**Penniless**, pen'i-les, *adj.* without a penny : with-

**Pennon**. See **Pennant**.

**Penny**, pen'i, *n.* a copper coin, orig. silver = $\frac{1}{12}$ of a shilling, or four farthings : a small sum : money in general : (*New Test.*) a silver coin = 7½d. :—*pl.* **Pennies** (pen'iz), denoting the number of coins, **Pence** (pens), the amount of pennies in value. [A.S. *pening, penig ;* the oldest form is *pending,* where *pend* = E. *pawn,* Ger. *pfand,* Dut. *pand,* a pledge, all which are from L. *pannus,* a rag, a piece of cloth. See **Pawn**, something given as security.]

**Penny-a-liner**, pen'i-a-līn'ér, *n.* one who writes for a public journal at so much a line : a writer for pay.

**Pennyroyal**, pen'i-roy-al, *n.* a species of mint. [Corr. from old form *pulial,* which is traced through O. Fr. to L. *puleium regium,* the plant pennyroyal—*pulex,* a flea ; it was thought to be a protection from fleas.]

**Pennyweight**, pen'i-wāt, *n.* twenty-four grains of troy weight. [Lit. *the weight of a silver penny.*]

**Pennyworth**, pen'i-wurth, *n.* a *penny's worth* of anything : a good bargain.

**Pensile**, pen'sīl, *adj., hanging :* suspended.—*n.* **Pen'sileness**. [O. Fr. *pensil*—L. *pensilis—pendeo,* to hang.]

**Pension**, pen'shun, *n.* a stated allowance to a person for past services : a sum paid to a clergyman in place of tithes.—*v.t.* to grant a pension to. [Fr.—L. *pensio—pendo, pensum,* to weigh, pay, akin to *pendeo,* to hang.]

**Pensionary**, pen'shun-ar-i, *adj.* receiving a *pension :* consisting of a pension.—*n.* one who receives a pension : a chief magistrate of a Dutch town.

**Pensioner**, pen'shun-ér, *n.* one who receives a *pension :* a dependent.

**Pensive**, pen'siv, *adj.* thoughtful : reflecting : expressing thoughtfulness with sadness.—*adv.* **Pen'sively**.—*n.* **Pen'siveness**. [Lit. 'weighing in the mind,' Fr.—from L. *penso,* to weigh—*pendo.*]

**Pent**, *pa.t.* and *pa.p.* of **Pen**, to shut up.

**Pentachord**, pen'ta-kord, *n.* a musical instrument with *five strings.* [Gr. *pentachordos,* five-stringed—*pente,* five, *chordē,* string.]

**Pentagon**, pen'ta-gon, *n.* (*geom.*) a plane figure having *five angles* and five sides.—*adj.* **Pentag'onal**. [Gr. *pentagōnon—pente,* five, *gōnia,* angle.]

**Pentahedron**, pen-ta-hē'dron, *n.* (*geom.*) a solid figure having *five* equal *bases* or sides.—*adj.* **Pentahe'dral**, having five equal sides. [Gr. *pente,* five, and *hedra,* seat, base.]

**Pentameter**, pen-tam'e-tér, *n.* a verse of *five measures* or feet.—*adj.* having five feet. [Gr. *pentametros—pente,* five, and *metron,* a measure.]

**Pentangular**, pen-tang'gul-ar, *adj.* having *five angles.* [Gr. *pente,* five, and **Angular**.]

**Pentarchy**, pen'tär-ki, *n., government* by *five persons.* [Gr. *pente,* five, *archē,* rule.]

**Pentateuch**, pen'ta-tūk, *n.* the first *five books* of the Old Testament. [Gr. *Pentateuchos—pente,* five, and *teuchos,* a tool, in late Gr. a book, from *teuchō,* to prepare.]     [the *Pentateuch.*

**Pentateuchal**, pen-ta-tūk'al, *adj.* pertaining to

**Pentecost**, pen'te-kost, *n.* a Jewish festival on the *fiftieth* day after the Passover, in commemoration of the giving of the Law : Whitsuntide. [Gr. *pentēkostē (hēmera),* the fiftieth (day).]

**Pentecostal**, pen-te-kost'al, *adj.* pertaining to *Pentecost.*

**Penthouse**, pent'hows, *n.* a shed projecting from or adjoining a main building. [Lit. 'an appendage' or 'out-building,' a corr. of *pentice,* which is from Fr. *appentis*—L. *appendicium,* an appendage. See **Append**.]

**Pentroof**, pent'rōōf, *n.* a roof with a slope on one side only. [A hybrid word, from Fr. *pente,* a slope—*pendre,* to hang, and E. **Roof**.]

**Penult**, pe-nult' or pē'nult, **Penultima**, pe-nult'-i-ma, *n.* the syllable last but one. [L. *penultima—pæne,* almost, *ultimus,* last.]

**Penultimate**, pe-nult'i-māt, *adj.* last but one.—*n.* the penult. [See under **Penult**.]

**Penumbra**, pe-num'bra, *n.* a *partial shadow* round the perfect shadow of an eclipse : the part of a picture where the light and shade blend. [L. *pæne,* almost, and *umbra,* shade.]

**Penurious**, pen-ū'ri-us, *adj.* showing *penury* or scarcity : not bountiful : sordid : miserly.—*adv.* **Penu'riously**.—*n.* **Penu'riousness**.

**Penury**, pen'ū-ri, *n., want :* absence of means or resources : poverty. [Fr.—L. *penuria,* akin to Gr. *peina,* hunger.]

**Peony**, pē'o-ni, *n.* a plant having beautiful crimson flowers. [O. Fr. *pione* (Fr. *pivoine*)—L. *pæonia,* healing, the plant being thought to have healing virtues—Gr. *Paiōn,* the physician of the gods.]

**People**, pē'pl, *n.* persons generally : an indefinite number : inhabitants : a nation : the vulgar : the populace :—*pl.* **Peoples** (pē'plz), races, tribes.—*v.t.* to stock with people or inhabitants. [Fr. *peuple*—L. *populus,* prob. reduplicated from root of *plebs,* people, Gr. *polys,* E. **Full**.]

**Pepper**, pep'ér, *n.* a plant and its fruit, with a hot, pungent taste.—*v.t.* to sprinkle with pepper. [A.S. *pipor*—L. *piper*—Gr. *peperi*—Sans. *pippala.*]

**Peppercorn**, pep'ér-korn, *n.* the *corn* or berry of the *pepper* plant : something of little value.

**Peppermint**, pep'ér-mint, *n.* a species of *mint,* aromatic and pungent like *pepper :* a liquor distilled from the plant.

**Peppery**, pep'ér-i, *adj.* possessing the qualities of *pepper :* hot : pungent.

**Pepsine**, pep'sin, *n.* one of the essential constituents of the gastric juice, which aids in *digestion*. [Fr.—Gr. *pepsis*, digestion—*peptō*, *pessō*, to cook, digest.]

**Peptic**, pep'tik, *adj.* relating to or promoting *digestion*. [Gr. *peptikos*—*peptō*, to digest.]

**Peradventure**, per-ad-vent'ūr, *adv.* by *adventure*: by chance: perhaps. [L. *per*, by, Adventure.]

**Perambulate**, per-am'būl-āt, *v.t.* to *walk through* or over: to pass through to survey. [L. *perambulo*, *-atum*—*per*, through, and *ambulo*, to walk.]

**Perambulation**, per-am-būl-ā'shun, *n.* act of *perambulating*: the district within which a person has the right of inspection.

**Perambulator**, per-am'būl-āt-or, *n.* one who *perambulates*: an instrument for measuring distances on roads: a light carriage for a child.

**Perceivable**, per-sēv'a-bl, *adj.* same as **Perceptible.**—*adv.* **Perceiv'ably**, same as **Perceptibly.**

**Perceive**, per-sēv', *v.t.* to obtain knowledge through the senses; to see: to understand: to discern.—*n.* **Perceiv'er.** [O. Fr. *percever* (Fr. *apercevoir*)—L. *percipio*, *perceptum*—*per*, perfectly, and *capio*, to take.]

**Percentage**, per-sent'āj, *n.* rate per cent., or *by the hundred*. [See **Cent.**]

**Perceptible**, per-sept'i-bl, *adj.* that can be *perceived*: that may be known: discernible.—*adv.* **Percept'ibly.**—*n.* **Perceptibil'ity**, quality of being perceptible.

**Perception**, per-sep'shun, *n.* act of *perceiving*: discernment: (*phil.*) the faculty of perceiving: the evidence of external objects by our senses.

**Perceptive**, per-sept'iv, *adj.* having the power of *perceiving* or discerning.—*n.* **Perceptiv'ity**, quality of being perceptive.

**Perch**, pėrch, *n.* a genus of fishes, so called from their *dusky* colour. [Fr. *perche*—L. *perca*—Gr. *perkē*, from *perkos*, dark-coloured, spotted.]

**Perch**, pėrch, *n.* a *rod* on which birds roost: a measure = $5\frac{1}{2}$ yds.: a square measure = $30\frac{1}{4}$ square yards.—*v.i.* to sit or roost on a perch: to settle.—*v.t.* to place, as on a perch. [Fr. *perche*—L. *pertica*, a long staff, a rod.]

**Perchance**, per-chans', *adv.* by *chance*: perhaps. [Fr. *par cas*, from L. *per*, by, and L. root of **Chance.**]

**Percher**, pėrch'ėr, *n.* a bird that perches on trees.

**Percipient**, per-sip'i-ent, *adj.*, *perceiving*: having the faculty of perception.—*n.* one who perceives.

**Percolate**, pėr'ko-lāt, *v.t.* to *strain through*: to filter.—*v.i.* to filter. [L. *percolo*, *-atum*—*per*, through, *colo*, to strain.]

**Percolation**, pėr-ko-lā'shun, *n.* act of filtering.

**Percolator**, pėr'ko-lā-tor, *n.* a filtering vessel.

**Percussion**, per-kush'un, *n.* the *striking* of one body against another: collision, or the shock produced by it: impression of sound on the ear: (*med.*) the tapping upon the body to find the condition of an internal organ by the sounds. [L. *percussio*—*percutio*, *percussum*—*per*, thoroughly, and *quatio*, to shake, strike.]

**Percussive**, per-kus'iv, *adj.*, *striking* against.

**Perdition**, per-dish'un, *n.* utter loss or ruin: the utter loss of happiness in a future state. [Lit. a 'being put utterly away,' Fr.—L. *perditio*—*perdo*, *perditum*—*per*, entirely, and *do*, Sans. *dha*, to put.]

**Peregrinate**, per'e-grin-āt, *v.i.* to travel *through the country*: to travel about: to live in a foreign country. [L. *peregrinor*, *-atum*—*peregrinus*, foreign—*pereger*, away from home, probably from *per*, through, *ager*, a field, territory.]

**Peregrination**, per-e-grin-ā'shun, *n.* act of peregrinating or travelling about. [Fr.]

**Peregrinator**, per'e-grin-ā-tor, *n.* one who travels about.

**Peremptory**, per'emp-tor-i, *adj.*, *preventing* debate: authoritative: dogmatical.—*adv.* **Peremptorily.**—*n.* **Per'emptoriness.** [Fr.—L. *peremptorius*, from *perimo*, *peremptum*—*per*, entirely, and *emo*, to take.]

**Perennial**, per-en'i-al, *adj.* lasting *through* the *year*: perpetual: (*bot.*) lasting more than two years.—*adv.* **Perenn'ially.** [L. *perennis*—*per*, through, and *annus*, a year.]

**Perfect**, pėr'fekt, *adj.*, *done thoroughly* or *completely*: completed: not defective: unblemished: possessing every moral excellence: completely skilled or acquainted: (*gram.*) expressing an act completed.—*v.t.* (or per-fekt') to make perfect or complete: to finish.—*n.* **Per'fecter.** [Fr.—L. *perfectus*, pa.p. of *perficio*—*per*, thoroughly, and *facio*, to do.]

**Perfectible**, per-fekt'i-bl, *adj.* that may be made perfect.—*n.* **Perfectibil'ity**, quality of being perfectible.

**Perfection**, per-fek'shun, *n.* state of being perfect: a perfect quality or acquirement.

**Perfectionist**, per-fek'shun-ist, *n.* one who pretends to be perfect: an enthusiast in religion or politics.—*n.* **Perfec'tionism.**

**Perfective**, per-fekt'iv, *adj.* tending to make perfect.—*adv.* **Perfect'ively.**

**Perfectly**, pėr'fekt-li, *adv.* in a perfect manner: completely: exactly.

**Perfectness**, pėr'fekt-nes, *n.* state or quality of being perfect: consummate excellence.

**Perfidious**, per-fid'i-us, *adj.* faithless: unfaithful: violating trust or confidence: treacherous.—*adv.* **Perfid'iously.**—*n.* **Perfid'iousness.** [L. *perfidiosus*—*perfidia*, faithlessness.]

**Perfidy**, pėr'fi-di, *n.*, *faithlessness*: treachery. [L. *perfidia*—*perfidus*, faithless—*per*, away from, *fides*, faith.]

**Perfoliate**, per-fō'li-āt, *adj.* (*bot.*) having the stem as it were passing *through the leaf*, having the leaf round the stem at the base. [L. *per*, through, *folium*, a leaf.]

**Perforate**, pėr'fo-rāt, *v.t.* to *bore through*: to pierce: to make a hole through. [L. *perforo*, *-atum*—*per*, through, *foro*, to bore, akin to **Bore.**]

**Perforation**, pėr-fo-rā'shun, *n.* act of boring or piercing through: a hole through anything.

**Perforator**, pėr'fo-rāt-or, *n.* an instrument for perforating or boring.

**Perforce**, per-fōrs', *adv.* by *force*: violently: of necessity. [L. *per*, by, and **Force.**]

**Perform**, per-form', *v.t.* to do *thoroughly*: to carry out: to achieve: to act.—*v.i.* to do: to act a part: to play, as on a musical instrument. [Fr. *parfournir*, from *par* = L. *per*, and *fournir*, to furnish. See **Furnish.**]

**Performable**, per-form'a-bl, *adj.* capable of being performed: practicable.

**Performance**, per-form'ans, *n.* act of performing: carrying out of something: something done: public execution of anything: an act or action.

**Performer**, per-form'ėr, *n.* one who performs, esp. one who makes a public exhibition of his skill.

**Perfume**, pėr'fūm or per-fūm', *n.* odorous *smoke*: sweet-smelling scent: anything which yields a sweet odour.—*v.t.* **Perfume'**, to fill with a pleasant odour: to scent. [Fr. *parfum*—L. *per*, through, *fumus*, smoke.]

**Perfumer,** per-fūm′ėr, *n.* one who or that which perfumes : one who trades in perfumes.

**Perfumery,** per-fūm′ėr-i, *n.* perfumes in general : the art of preparing perfumes.

**Perfunctory,** per-fungk′tor-i, *adj.* carelessly performed : negligent : slight.—*adv.* **Perfunc′torily.**—*n.* **Perfunc′toriness.** [L. *perfunctorius—perfunctus*, pa.p. of *perfungor*, to execute—*per*, thoroughly, and *fungor*. See **Function.**]

**Perhaps,** per-haps′, *adv.* it may be : possibly. [Lit. ′by haps′ or ′chances,′ L. *per*, by, and *haps*, pl. of **Hap.**]

**Peri,** pē′ri, *n.* in Persian mythology, a female elf or fairy. [Lit. ′winged,′ Pers. *pari*, conn. with root of **Feather.**]

**Perianth,** per′i-anth, *n.* (*bot.*) the floral envelope of those plants in which the calyx and corolla are not easily distinguished. [Gr. *peri*, around, about, and *anthos*, a flower.]

**Pericardium,** per-i-kärd′i-um, *n.* (*anat.*) the sac which *surrounds* the *heart*.—*adjs.* **Pericard′iac, Pericard′ial, Pericard′ian.** [Late L.—Gr. *perikardion—peri*, around, *kardia*, E. **Heart.**]

**Pericarp,** per′i-kärp, *n.* (*bot.*), the *covering*, shell, or rind of *fruits* : a seed-vessel.—*adj.* **Pericarp′ial.** [Gr. *perikarpion—peri*, around, *karpos*, fruit. See **Harvest.**]

**Pericranium,** per-i-krā′ni-um, *n.* (*anat.*) the membrane that *surrounds* the *cranium*. [Late L.—Gr. *perikranion—peri*, around, *kranion*, the skull. See **Cranium.**]

**Perigee,** per′i-jē, *n.* (*astr.*) the point of the moon′s orbit *nearest* the *earth*. [From Gr. *peri*, near, *gē*, the earth.]

**Perihelion,** per-i-hē′li-on, **Perihelium,** per-i-hē′li-um, *n.* the point of the orbit of a planet or comet *nearest* to the *sun* :—opposed to **Aphelion.** [Gr. *peri*, near, *hēlios*, the sun.]

**Peril,** per′il, *n.* exposure to danger : danger.—*v.t.* to expose to danger :—*pr.p.* per′illing ; *pa.t.* and *pa.p.* per′illed. [Lit. a ′trial passed through,′ Fr. *péril*—L. *periculum*—root of *peritus*, tried, *experior*, to try : akin to Gr. *peiraō*, to try, *peraō*, to pass through, cog. with **Fare.**]

**Perilous,** per′il-us, *adj.* full of peril : dangerous.—*adv.* **Per′ilously.**—*n.* **Per′ilousness.**

**Perimeter,** per-im′e-tėr, *n.* (*geom.*) the circuit or boundary of any plane figure, or sum of all its sides.—*adj.* **Perimet′rical,** pertaining to the perimeter. [Lit. the ′measure round about,′ Gr. *perimetros—peri*, around, *metron*, measure.]

**Period,** pē′ri-ud, *n.* the time in which anything is performed : (*astr.*) the time occupied by a body in its revolution : a stated and recurring interval of time : a series of years : length of duration : the time at which anything ends : conclusion : (*gram.*) a mark at the end of a sentence ( . ) : (*rhet.*) a complete sentence. See **Date, Epoch, Era.** [Lit. a ′going round,′ a ′circuit,′ Fr. *période*—L. *periodus*—Gr. *periodos*, a going round—*peri*, around, *hodos*, a way.]

**Periodic,** pē-ri-od′ik, **Periodical,** pē-ri-od′ik-al, *adj.* pertaining to a period : happening by revolution : occurring at regular intervals : pertaining to periodicals.—*adv.* **Period′ically.**

**Periodical,** pē-ri-od′ik-al, *n.* a magazine or other publication which appears in parts at regular *periods*.—*n.* **Period′icalist,** one who writes in a periodical. [periodic.

**Periodicity,** pē-ri-o-dis′it-i, *n.* state of being

**Peripatetic,** per-i-pa-tet′ik, *adj.* pertaining to the philosophy of Aristotle, who taught while *walking up and down* in the Lyceum at Athens.—*n.*

an adherent of the philosophy of Aristotle : one accustomed or obliged to walk.—*n.* **Peripatet′icism,** the philosophy of Aristotle. [Gr. *peripatētikos—peri*, about, *pateō*, to walk ; cog. with E. **Path.**]

**Periphery,** per-if′ėr-i, *n.* (*geom.*) the circumference of a circle or any figure.—*adj.* **Periph′eral.** [Lit. ′that which is carried round,′ L.—Gr. *peri*, around, *pherō*, to carry ; cog. with E. **Bear.**]

**Periphrase,** per′i-frāz, **Periphrasis,** per-if′ra-sis, *n.* a *roundabout* way of *speaking* : the use of more words than are necessary to express an idea : (*rhet.*) a figure employed to avoid a trite expression.—*v.t.* or *v.i.* **Per′iphrase,** to use circumlocution. [L.—Gr. *periphrasis—peri*, round, about, *phrasis*, a speaking. See **Phrase.**]

**Periphrastic,** per-i-fras′tik, **Periphras′tical,** *adj.* containing or expressed by *periphrasis* or circumlocution.—*adv.* **Periphras′tically.** [Gr.]

**Perish,** per′ish, *v.i.* to *pass away completely* : to waste away : to decay : to lose life : to be destroyed : to be ruined or lost. [M. E. *perisshen*—Fr. *périr*, pr.p. *périssant*—L. *perire*, to perish—*per*, completely, ′to the bad,′ *ire*, to go.]

**Perishable,** per′ish-a-bl, *adj.* that may perish : subject to speedy decay.—*adv.* **Per′ishably.**—*n.* **Per′ishableness.**

**Peristyle,** per′i-stīl, *n.* a range of *columns round* a building or square : a court, square, &c. with columns on three sides. [L. *peristylium*—Gr. *peristylon—peri*, around, *stylos*, a column.]

**Periwig,** per′i-wig, *n.* a *peruke* or small wig, usually shortened to **Wig.** [O. Dut. *peruyk*—Fr. *perruque*, a peruke. See **Peruke.**]

**Periwinkle,** per′i-wingk-l, *n.* a genus of *binding* or creeping evergreen plants, growing in woods. [M. E. *peruenke*, through A.S. *peruincæ*, from L. *pervinca*, called also *vinca-pervinca*, conn. with *vincio*, to bind.]

**Periwinkle,** per′i-wingk-l, *n.* a small univalve mollusc. [Corrupted by confusion with preceding from A.S. *pinewincla—wincle*, a whelk ; prov. E. *pin-patch*, prob. because eaten with a pin.]

**Perjure,** pėr′joor, *v.t.* to *swear falsely* (followed by a reciprocal pronoun).—*n.* **Per′jurer.** [Fr.—L. *perjuro—per* (same as E. *for-* in **Forswear**), and *juro*, to swear.]

**Perjury,** pėr′jur-i, *n.* false swearing : (*law*) the act of wilfully giving false evidence on an oath. [L. *perjurium*.]

**Perk,** pėrk, *adj.* trim, spruce.—*v.t.* to make smart or trim.—*v.i.* to hold up the head with smartness. [W. *perc, pert*, trim, smart. See **Pert.**]

**Permanence,** pėr′ma-nens, **Per′manency,** -nen-si, *n.* state or quality of being permanent : continuance in the same state : duration.

**Permanent,** pėr′ma-nent, *adj.* lasting : durable.—*adv.* **Per′manently.** [Fr.—L. *permanens, -entis*, pr.p. of *permaneo—per*, through, *maneo*, to continue.]

**Permeable,** pėr′me-a-bl, *adj.* that may be permeated.—*adv.* **Per′meably.**—*n.* **Permeabil′ity.** [Fr.—L. *permeabilis*.]

**Permeate,** pėr′me-āt, *v.t.* to *pass through* the pores of : to penetrate and pass through.—*n.* **Permea′tion.** [L. *per*, through, *meo*, to go.]

**Permissible,** per-mis′i-bl, *adj.* that may be permitted : allowable.—*adv.* **Permiss′ibly.**

**Permission,** per-mish′un, *n.* act of permitting : liberty granted : allowance. [Fr.—L. *permissio*.]

**Permissive,** per-mis′iv, *adj.* granting permission or liberty : allowing : granted.—*adv.* **Permiss′ively.**

**Permit**, per-mit', *v.t.* to give leave to : to allow : to afford means :—*pr.p.* permitt'ing ; *pa.t.* and *pa.p.* permitt'ed.—*n.* **Per'mit**, *permission*, esp. from a custom-house officer to remove goods. [L. *permitto, -missus,* to let pass through—*per,* through, *mitto,* to send.]

**Permutable**, per-mūt'a-bl, *adj.* mutable or that may be *changed* one for another.—*adv.* **Permut'ably**.—*n.* **Permut'ableness**. [L. *permutabilis*—*per,* through, *muto,* to change.]

**Permutation**, pėr-mū-tā'shun, *n.* act of *changing one thing for another* : (*math.*) the arrangement of things or letters in every possible order. [Fr.—L.]

**Pernicious**, per-nish'us, *adj., killing utterly* : hurtful : destructive : highly injurious.—*adv.* **Perni'ciously**.—*n.* **Perni'ciousness**. [Fr.—L. *per,* completely, and *nex, necis,* death by violence.]

**Peroration**, per-o-rā'shun, *n.* the conclusion of a speech. [Fr.—L. *peroratio*—*peroro,* to bring a speech to an end—*per,* through, *oro,* to speak—*os, oris,* the mouth.]

**Perpendicular**, pėr-pen-dik'ū-lar, *adj.* exactly upright : extending in a straight line toward the centre of the earth : (*geom.*) at right angles to a given line or surface.—*n.* a perpendicular line or plane.—*adv.* **Perpendic'ularly**.—*n.* **Perpendicular'ity**, state of being perpendicular. [Fr.—L. *perpendicularis*—*perpendiculum,* a plumbline—*per,* through, and *pendo,* to weigh.]

**Perpetrate**, pėr'pe-trāt, *v.t.* to perform or commit (usually in a bad sense).—*n.* **Per'petrator**. [L. *perpetro, -atum*—*per,* thoroughly, and *patro,* to perform, from root of **Potent**.]

**Perpetration**, pėr-pe-trā'shun, *n.* act of perpetrating or committing a crime : the thing being petrated.

**Perpetual**, per-pet'ū-al, *adj.* never ceasing : everlasting : not temporary.—*adv.* **Perpet'ually**. [Fr. *perpétuel*—L. *perpetuus,* continuous—*per,* through, and root *pet,* to go. See **Path**.]

**Perpetuate**, per-pet'ū-āt, *v.t.* to make *perpetual* : to preserve from extinction or oblivion. [L.]

**Perpetuation**, per-pet-ū-ā'shun, *n.* act of perpetuating or preserving from oblivion.

**Perpetuity**, pėr-pet-ū'i-ti, *n.* state of being perpetual : endless duration : duration for an indefinite period : something perpetual : the sum paid for a perpetual annuity. [Fr.—L.]

**Perplex**, per-pleks', *v.t.* to make difficult to be understood : to embarrass : to puzzle : to tease with suspense or doubt. [Fr.—L. *perplexus,* entangled—*per,* completely, and *plexus,* involved, pa.p. of *plecto.* See **Plait**.]

**Perplexity**, per-pleks'i-ti, *n.* state of being perplexed : intricacy : embarrassment : doubt.

**Perquisite**, pėr'kwi-zit, *n.* an allowance granted more than the settled wages : a fee allowed by law to an officer for a specific service. [Lit. 'anything sought for diligently,' L. *perquisitum,* from *perquiro*—*per,* thoroughly, *quero,* to ask.]

**Perry**, per'i, *n.* the fermented juice of *pears*. [Fr. *poiré,* from *poire,* a pear—L. *pirum.* See **Pear**.]

**Persecute**, pėr'se-kūt, *v.t.* to *pursue* so as to injure or annoy : to harass : to annoy or punish, esp. for religious or political opinions.—*n.* **Per'secutor**. [Fr. *persécuter*—L. *persequor, persecutus*—*per,* thoroughly, and *sequor,* to follow.]

**Persecution**, pėr-se-kū'shun, *n.* act or practice of persecuting : state of being persecuted.

**Perseverance**, pėr-se-vēr'ans, *n.* act or state of persevering. [L. *perseverantia*.]

**Persevere**, pėr-se-vēr', *v.i.* to persist in anything :

to pursue anything steadily.—*adv.* **Persever'ingly**. [Fr.—L. *persevero*—*perseverus,* very strict—*per,* very, *severus,* strict. See **Severe**.]

**Persiflage**, pėr'si-fläzh, *n.* a frivolous way of talking or treating any subject : banter. [Fr.—*persifler,* to banter—L. *per,* through, and Fr. *siffler*—L. *sibilare,* to whistle, to hiss.]

**Persist**, per-sist', *v.i.* to *stand throughout* or something begun : to continue in any course : to persevere.—*adv.* **Persist'ingly**. [Fr.—L. *persisto*—*per,* through, and *sisto,* to cause to stand —*sto,* to stand.]

**Persistence, Persistency**, per-sist'ens, per-sist'en-si, *n.* quality of being persistent : perseverance : obstinacy : duration.

**Persistent**, per-sist'ent, *adj., persisting* : tenacious : fixed : (*bot.*) remaining till or after the fruit is ripe.—*adv.* **Persist'ently**.

**Person**, pėr'sun, *n.* character represented, as on the stage : character : an individual : a living soul : the outward appearance, &c. : body : (*gram.*) a distinction in form, according as the subject of the verb is the person speaking, spoken to, or spoken of.—**In person**, by one's self, not by a representative. [Fr.—L. *persōna,* a mask, esp. that used by players, which covered the whole head, and was varied acc. to the *character* represented, perh. from *persōno, -atus*—*per,* through, and *sono,* to sound, from the voice of the actor *sounding* through the large-mouthed mask.]

**Personable**, pėr'sun-a-bl, *adj.* having a well-formed body or *person* : of good appearance.

**Personage**, pėr'sun-āj, *n.* a *person* : character represented : an individual of eminence.

**Personal**, pėr'sun-al, *adj.* belonging to a *person* : peculiar to a person or his private concerns : pertaining to the external appearance : done in person : applying offensively to one's character : (*gram.*) denoting the person.

**Personality**, pėr-sun-al'i-ti, *n.* that which constitutes distinction of *person* : individuality : a personal remark or reflection.

**Personally**, pėr'sun-al-li, *adv.* in a personal or direct manner : in person : individually.

**Personalty**, pėr'sun-al-ti, *n.* (*law*) *personal* estate or all sorts of movable property.

**Personate**, pėr'sun-āt, *v.t.* to assume the *person* or character of : to represent : to counterfeit : to feign.—*ns.* **Persona'tion, Per'sonator**.

**Personify**, per-son'i-fī, *v.t.* (*rhet.*) to ascribe to any inanimate object the qualities of a person : —*pa.t.* and *pa.p.* person'i-fīed.—*n.* **Personifica'tion**.

**Perspective**, per-spekt'iv, *n.* a view, vista : the art of delineating objects on a plane surface as they appear to the eye : a picture in perspective.—*adj.* pertaining or according to perspective. [Fr.—L. *perspicio, perspectus*—*per,* through, and *specio,* to look.]

**Perspectively**, per-spekt'iv-li, *adv.* according to the rules of perspective.

**Perspicacious**, pėr-spi-kā'shus, *adj.* of clear or acute understanding.—*adv.* **Perspica'ciously**. —*n.* **Perspica'ciousness**. [L. *perspicax, perspicacis*—*perspicio,* to see through.]

**Perspicacity**, pėr-spi-kas'i-ti, *n.* state of being *perspicacious* or acute in discerning.

**Perspicuity**, pėr-spi-kū'i-ti, *n.* state of being *perspicuous* : clearness : freedom from obscurity.

**Perspicuous**, per-spik'ū-us, *adj.* clear to the mind : not obscure in any way : evident.—*adv.* **Perspic'uously**.—*n.* **Perspic'uousness**. [L. *perspicuus,* from *perspicio,* to see through.]

**Perspiration**, pėr-spi-rā'shun, *n.* act of perspiring: that which is perspired: sweat. [Fr.—L.]

**Perspiratory**, per-spīr'a-to-ri, *adj.* pertaining to or causing perspiration.

**Perspire**, per-spīr', *v.i.* and *v.t.* to emit through the pores of the skin: to sweat. [Lit. to *breathe through*, L. *perspiro*, *-atus—per*, through, and *spiro*, to breathe.]

**Persuade**, per-swād', *v.t.* to influence successfully by argument, advice, &c.: to bring to any particular opinion: to convince.—*n.* **Persuad'er.** [Fr.—L. *persuadeo*, *-suasum—per*, thoroughly, and *suadeo*, to advise.]

**Persuasible**, per-swā'si-bl, *adj.* capable of being *persuaded*.—*ns.* **Persua'sibleness, Persuasibil'ity.**

**Persuasion**, per-swā'zhun, *n.* act of *persuading*: state of being persuaded: settled opinion: a creed: a party adhering to a creed.

**Persuasive**, per-swā'siv, *adj.* having the power to *persuade*: influencing the mind or passions.—*adv.* **Persua'sively.**—*n.* **Persua'siveness.**

**Pert**, pėrt, *adj.* forward: saucy: impertinent.—*adv.* **Pert'ly.**—*n.* **Pert'ness.** [A form of **Perk.**]

**Pertain**, per-tān', *v.i.* to belong: to relate (to). [O. Fr. *partenir*—L. *pertineo—per*, thoroughly, and *teneo*, to hold.]

**Pertinacious**, pėr-ti-nā'shus, *adj.*, *thoroughly tenacious*: holding obstinately to an opinion or purpose: obstinate.—*adv.* **Pertina'ciously.**—*n.* **Pertina'ciousness.** [Fr.—L. *pertinax*, *-acis—per*, thoroughly, and *tenax*, tenacious—*teneo*, to hold.]

**Pertinacity**, pėr-ti-nas'i-ti, *n.* quality of being *pertinacious* or unyielding: obstinacy.

**Pertinence**, pėr'ti-nens, **Pertinency**, pėr'ti-nen-si, *n.* state of being *pertinent*: appositeness: fitness.

**Pertinent**, pėr'ti-nent, *adj.*, *pertaining* or related to a subject: fitting or appropriate.—*adv.* **Per'tinently.**

**Perturb**, per-turb', *v.t.* to disturb greatly: to agitate. [Fr.—L. *perturbo*, *-atus—per*, thoroughly, and *turbo*, disturb—*turba*, a crowd. See **Turbid.**]

**Perturbation**, pėr-tur-bā'shun, *n.* state of being *perturbed*: disquiet of mind: (*astr.*) a deviation of a heavenly body from its normal orbit.

**Peruke**, per'ook or per-rūk', *n.* an artificial cap of *hair*: a periwig. [Fr. *perruque*—It. *parrucca* (Sp. *peluca*)—L. *pilus*, hair. Doublets, **Periwig, Wig.**] [ing: examination: study.

**Perusal**, per-ūz'al or per-ōōz'al, *n.* the act of perus-

**Peruse**, per-ūz' or per-ōōz', *v.t.* to read attentively: to examine.—*n.* **Perus'er.** [Formed from **L.** *per* and **Use**, *v.t.*]

**Peruvian**, per-ōō'vi-an, *adj.* pertaining to *Peru* in S. America.—*n.* a native of Peru.

**Pervade**, per-vād', *v.t.* to *go through* or penetrate: to spread all over. [L. *pervado*, *pervasum—per*, through, and *vado*, to go: conn. with **Wade.**]

**Pervasive**, per-vās'iv, *adj.* tending or having power to *pervade*.

**Perverse**, per-vėrs', *adj.*, *perverted* or turned aside: obstinate in the wrong: stubborn: vexatious.—*ns.* **Perverse'ness, Pervers'ity.**—*adv.* **Perverse'ly.**

**Perversion**, per-vėr'shun, *n.* the act of *perverting*: a diverting from the true object: a turning from truth or propriety: misapplication.

**Pervert**, per-vėrt', *v.t.* to *turn wrong* or from the right course: to change from its true use: to corrupt: to turn from truth or virtue.—*n.* **Pervert'er.** [Fr. *pervertir*—L. *perverto—per*, thoroughly, 'to the bad,' and *verto, versus*, to turn.]

**Pervertible**, per-vėrt'i-bl, *adj.* able to be perverted.

**Pervious**, pėr'vi-us, *adj.* penetrable.—*adv.* **Per'viously.**—*n.* **Per'viousness.** [Lit. 'affording a *way through*,' L. *pervius—per*, through, via, a way.]

**Pessimist**, pes'i-mist, *n.* one who complains of everything being for the *worst*:—opposed to **Optimist.**—*n.* **Pess'imism.** [From L. *pessimus*, worst.]

**Pest**, pest, *n.* a deadly *disease*: a plague: anything destructive. [Fr. *peste*—L. *pestis*, a contagious disease.]

**Pester**, pes'tėr, *v.t.* to disturb, to annoy. [Short for *impester*, O. Fr. *empestrer* (Fr. *empêtrer*), to entangle, from *in*, in, and Low L. *pastorium*, the foot-shackle of a horse at pasture—L. *pastus*, pa.p. of *pasco*, to feed.]

**Pesthouse**, pest'hows, *n.* a *house* or hospital for persons afflicted with any *pest* or contagious disease.

**Pestiferous**, pest-if'ėr-us, *adj.*, *bearing pestilence*: pestilent.—*adv.* **Pestif'erously.** [L. *pestis*, and *fero*, E. **Bear.**] [disease.

**Pestilence**, pest'i-lens, *n.* any contagious deadly

**Pestilent**, pest'i-lent, *adj.* producing *pestilence*: hurtful to health and life: mischievous: corrupt: troublesome.—*adv.* **Pestilently.** [Fr.—L.]

**Pestilential**, pest-i-len'shal, *adj.* of the nature of *pestilence*: producing pestilence: destructive.—*adv.* **Pestilen'tially.**

**Pestle**, pes'l or pest'l, *n.* an instrument for *pounding* anything in a mortar.—*v.t.* and *v.i.* to pound with a pestle. [O. Fr. *pestel*—L. *pistillum*, a pounder, from *pinso, pistum*, to pound.]

**Pet**, pet, *n.* any animal tame and fondled: a word of endearment often used to young children.—*v.t.* to treat as a pet: to fondle:—*pr.p.* pett'ing; *pa.t.* and *pa.p.* pett'ed. [Celt., as Ir. *peat*, Gael. *peata*.]

**Pet**, pet, *n.* a sudden fit of peevishness or slight passion. [From the above word.]

**Petal**, pet'al, *n.* a flower-*leaf*. [Gr. *petalon*, a leaf, neuter of *petalos*, spread out, from root of *peta-nnymi*, to spread out. Cf. **Fathom.**]

**Petaled**, pet'ald, **Petalous**, pet'al-us, *adj.* having petals or flower-leaves.

**Petaline**, pet'al-in, *adj.* pertaining to or resembling a petal: attached to a petal.

**Petaloid**, pet'al-oid, *adj.* having the *form* of a petal. [**Petal,** and Gr. *eidos*, form.]

**Petard**, pe-tärd', *n.* an engine of war, used to break down barriers, &c. by *explosion*. [Fr.—*péter*, to crack or explode—L. *pedo*, cog. with Gr. *perdō*, Sans. *pard*, and Ger. *furzen*.]

**Peter-pence**, pē'tėr-pens, *n.* an annual tax of a silver *penny*, formerly paid by the English to the Pope as successor of St *Peter*.

**Petiole**, pet'i-ōl, *n.* the *footstalk* of a leaf. [Fr.—L. *petiolus*, a little foot—*pes, pedis*, E. **Foot.**]

**Petition**, pe-tish'un, *n.* a request: a prayer: a supplication.—*v.t.* to present a petition to: to supplicate. [Fr.—L. *petitio—peto, petitus*, to fall on, to ask—*pat*, to fall. See **Pen**, *n.*]

**Petitionary**, pe-tish'un-ar-i, *adj.* containing a petition: supplicatory. [petition or prayer.

**Petitioner**, pe-tish'un-ėr, *n.* one who offers a

**Petitioning**, pe-tish'un-ing, *n.* the act of presenting a petition: entreaty: solicitation.

**Petre.** Same as **Saltpetre.**

**Petrean**, pe-trē'an, *adj.* pertaining to *rock*. [L. *petræus*, Gr. *petraios*—L., Gr. *petra*, a rock.]

**Petrel**, pet′rel, *n.* a genus of ocean birds, which appear during flight sometimes to touch the surface of the waves with their feet, prob. so called in allusion to St *Peter's* walking on the sea. [Fr.]

**Petrescent**, pe-tres′ent, *adj.* growing into or becoming *stone.*—*n.* Petres′cence

**Petrifaction**, pet-ri-fak′shun, *n.* the act of turning into *stone:* the state of being turned into stone: that which is made stone.

**Petrifactive**, pet-ri-fakt′iv, **Petrific**, pe-trif′ik, *adj.* having the power to change into stone.

**Petrify**, pet′ri-fī, *v.t.* to turn into *stone:* to make callous: to fix in amazement.—*v.i.* to become stone, or hard like stone:—*pa.t.* and *pa.p.* pet′rified. [L. *petra*, a rock—Gr., and *facio, factus*, to make.]

**Petroleum**, pe-trō′le-um, *n.* a liquid inflammable substance issuing from certain rocks. [Lit. 'rock-oil,' L. *petra*, rock—Gr., and *oleum*, oil. See Oil.]

**Petrous**, pē′trus, *adj.* like *stone:* hard.

**Petted**, pet′ed, *adj.* treated as a pet: indulged.

**Petticoat**, pet′i-kōt, *n.* a *little coat:* a loose under garment worn by females. [Petty and Coat.]

**Petticoated**, pet′i-kōt-ed, *adj.* wearing a petticoat.

**Pettifogger**, pet′i-fog-ėr, *n.* a lawyer who *practises* only in *petty* or paltry cases. [Petty, and prov. E. *fog*, to resort to mean contrivances.]

**Pettifoggery**, pet′i-fog-ėr-i, *n.* the practice of a pettifogger: mean tricks: quibbles.

**Pettish**, pet′ish, *adj.* shewing a *pet:* peevish: fretful.—*adv.* Pett′ishly.—*n.* Pett′ishness.

**Petty**, pet′i, *adj., small:* inconsiderable: contemptible.—*adv.* Pett′ily.—*n.* Pett′iness.— [M. E. *petit*—Fr. *petit:* cf. W. *pitw*, small.]

**Petulance**, pet′ū-lans, **Petulancy**, pet′ū-lan-si, *n.* forwardness: impudence: sauciness: peevishness: wantonness.

**Petulant**, pet′ū-lant, *adj., falling upon* or assailing saucily: forward: impudent: peevish.— *adv.* Pet′ulantly. [L. *petulans, -antis*—obs. *petulo*, dim. of *peto*, to fall upon.]

**Pew**, pū, *n.* an inclosed seat in a church. [O. Fr. *pui*, a raised place—L. *podium*, a projecting seat in the amphitheatre for the emperor, &c.— Gr. *podion*, orig. a footstool—*pous, podos*, E. Foot.]

**Pewit**, pē′wit, **Pewet**, pē′wet, *n.* the lapwing, a bird with a black head and crest, common in moors. [From its cry. Cf. Dut. *piewit* or *kiewit*.]

**Pewter**, pū′tėr, *n.* an alloy of tin and antimony with lead or with copper: vessels made of pewter. —*adj.* made of pewter. [O. Fr. *peutre* (It. *peltro*), from a Teut. root, found in Ice. *pjatr*, E. Spelter.]

**Pewterer**, pū′tėr-ėr, *n.* one who works in pewter.

**Phaeton**, fā′e-tun, *n.* a kind of open pleasure-carriage on four wheels, named after *Phaëthon*, the fabled son of Helios, the sun, whose chariot he attempted to drive: the tropic bird.

**Phalanx**, fal′angks or fā′-, *n.* a line of battle: a square battalion of heavy armed infantry drawn up in ranks and files close and deep: any compact body of men:—*pl.* Phalan′ges, the small bones of the fingers and toes. [L.—Gr. *phalangks*.]

**Phanerogamous**, fan-ėr-og′am-us, *adj.* having visible flowers (as opposed to the Cryptogamia).

**Phantasm**, fant′azm, *n.* a vain, airy *appearance:* a fancied vision: a spectre:—*pl.* Phant′asms, Phantas′mata. [Gr. *phantasma—phantazō*, to make visible—*phainō*, to bring to light—*pha-ō*, to shine.]

**Phantasmagoria**, fant-az-ma-gō′ri-a, *n.* a gather-

*ing* of *appearances* or figures upon a flat surface by a magic-lantern. [Gr. *phantasma* (see Phantasm), an appearance, and *agora*, an assembly—*ageirō*, to gather.]

**Phantastic, Phantasy.** See Fantastic, Fantasy.

**Phantom.** Same as Phantasm. [O. Fr. *fantosme*—Gr.]

**Pharisaic**, far-i-sā′ik, **Pharisaical**, far-i-sā′ik-al, *adj.* pertaining to or like the *Pharisees:* hypocritical.—*adv.* Pharisa′ically.—*n.* Pharisa′icalness.

**Pharisaism**, far′i-sā-izm, **Phariseeism**, far′i-sē-izm, *n.* the practice and opinions of the *Pharisees:* strict observance of outward forms in religion without the spirit of it: hypocrisy.

**Pharisee**, far′i-sē, *n.* one of a religious school among the Jews, marked by their strict observance of the law and of religious ordinances. [Lit. 'one *separate*,' L. *pharisæus*—Gr. *pharisaios*—Heb. *parash*, to separate.]

**Pharmaceutic**, fär-ma-sūt′ik, **Pharmaceutical**, fär-ma-sūt′ik-al, *adj.* pertaining to the knowledge or art of *pharmacy.*—*adv.* Pharmaceut′ically.

**Pharm₂ceutics**, fär-ma-sūt′iks, *n.sing.* the science of preparing *medicines.*

**Pharmaceutist**, fär-ma-sūt′ist, *n.* one who practises *pharmacy.*

**Pharmacopœia**, fär-ma-ko-pē′ya, *n.* a book containing directions for the *preparation of medicines.* [Gr. *pharmakon*, and *poieō*, to make.]

**Pharmacy**, fär′ma-si, *n.* the art of preparing and mixing medicines. [Fr. *pharmacie*—L., Gr. *pharmakon*, a drug.]

**Pharos**, fā′ros, *n.* a lighthouse or beacon, so named from the famous lighthouse on the island of *Pharos* in the Bay of Alexandria.

**Pharynx**, far′ingks, *n.* the *cleft* or cavity forming the upper part of the gullet.—*adj.* Pharyn′geal. [Late L.—Gr. *pharyngks.* See Bore, *v.*]

**Phase**, fāz, **Phasis**, fās′is, *n.* an *appearance:* the illuminated surface exhibited by a planet: the particular state at any time of a phenomenon which undergoes a periodic change:—*pl.* Phas′es. [Gr. *phasis*, from the root *pha-*, to shine. See Phantasm.]

**Pheasant**, fez′ant, *n.* a gallinaceous bird abundant in Britain, and highly valued as food. [Lit. 'the *Phasian* bird,' Fr. *faisan* (with excrescent -*t*) —L. *Phasiana* (*avis*, bird, being understood) —Gr. *Phasianos*, of Phasis, a river flowing into the eastern part of the Black Sea, whence the bird was brought to Europe.] [ants.

**Pheasantry**, fez′ant-ri, *n.* an inclosure for pheas-

**Phœnix, Phoenix**, fē′niks, *n.* a fabulous bird said to exist 500 years single and to rise again from its own ashes; hence, the emblem of immortality. [L. *phœnix*—Gr. *phoinix.*]

**Phenomenal**, fen-om′en-al, *adj.* pertaining to a phenomenon.—*adv.* Phenom′enally.

**Phenomenon**, fen-om′en-on, *n.* an *appearance:* something as it is perceived (not necessarily as 't really is): an observed result: a remarkable or unusual appearance:—*pl.* Phenom′ena. [Gr. *phainomenon—phainō*, to shew. See Phantasm.]

**Phial**, fī′al, *n.* a small glass vessel or bottle. [L. *phiala*—Gr. *phialē.* Cf. Vial.]

**Philander**, fi-lan′dėr, *v.i.* to make love: to flirt or coquet. [Gr. *philandros*, loving men—*philos*, dear—*philō*, to love, and *anēr, andros*, a man.]

**Philanthropic**, fil-an-throp′ik, **Philanthropical**, fil-an-throp′ik-al, *adj., loving mankind:* shewing philanthropy: benevolent.—*adv.* Philan′throp′ically.

**Philanthropist**, fil-an'thro-pist, *n.* one who *loves* and wishes to serve *mankind*.

**Philanthropy**, fil-an'thro-pi, *n.*, *love of mankind:* good-will towards all men. [L.—Gr. *philanthrōpia—philos*, loving, *anthrōpos*, a man.]

**Philharmonic**, fil-har-mon'ik, *adj.*, *loving harmony* or music. [Gr. *philos*, loving, *harmonia*, harmony.]

**Philibeg.** See **Fillibeg.**

**Philippic**, fil-ip'ik, *n.* one of the orations of Demosthenes against *Philip* of Macedon : a discourse full of invective. [L.—Gr.]

**Philistine**, fil'is-tin, *n.* one of the ancient inhabitants of South-western Palestine, enemies of the Israelites : name applied by German students to shopkeepers and others not conn. with the university : a person without liberal ideas, an uncultured person.—*n.* Phil'istinism

**Philologist**, fil-ol'o-jist, *n.* one versed in *philology.*

**Philology**, fil-ol'o-ji, *n.* the science of language : the study of etymology, grammar, rhetoric, and literary criticism : (*orig.*) the study of the classical languages of Greece and Rome.—*adj.* **Philolog'ic, Philolog'ical.**—*adv.* **Philolog'ically.** [L.—Gr. *philologia* (*lit.*) love of talking—*philologos*, fond of words—*philos*, loving, *logos*, discourse, from *legō*, to speak.]

**Philomath**, fil'o-math, *n.* a lover of learning.—*adjs.* **Philomath'ic, -al.** [Gr. *philomathēs*, fond of learning—*philos*, loving, and *e-math-on*, 2 aorist of *manthanō*, to learn.]

**Philomel**, fil'o-mel, **Philomela**, fil-o-mē'la, *n.* the nightingale. [Gr. *Philomēla*, daughter of Pandion, king of Athens, fabled to have been changed into a nightingale.]

**Philoprogenitiveness**, fil-o-pro-jen'i-tiv-nes, *n.* (*phrenology*) the instinctive love of offspring. [A hybrid word, from Gr. *philos*, loving, and L. *progenies*, progeny.]

**Philosopher**, fil-os'o-fer, *n.* a *lover of wisdom* : one versed in or devoted to philosophy : one who acts calmly and rationally. [Fr.—L.—Gr. *philosophos—philos*, a lover, *sophos*, wise.]

**Philosophic**, fil-o-sof'ik, **Philosophical**, fil-o-sof'ik-al, *adj.* pertaining or according to philosophy : skilled in or given to philosophy : rational : calm. —*adv.* **Philosoph'ically.** [L. *philosophicus.*]

**Philosophise**, fil-os'o-fīz, *v.i.* to reason *like a philosopher.*

**Philosophism**, fil-os'o-fizm, *n.* would-be philosophy. —*n.* **Philos'ophist.**—*adj.* **Philosophist'ic.**

**Philosophy**, fil-os'o-fi, *n.* the knowledge of the causes of all phenomena : the collection of general laws or principles belonging to any department of knowledge : reasoning : a particular philosophical system. [Lit. 'the love of wisdom,' Fr.—L.—Gr. *philosophia—philos*, loving, *sophia*, wisdom ]

**Philtre, Philter**, fil'tėr, *n.* a charm or spell to excite *love.* [Fr. *philtre*—L. *philtrum*—Gr. *philtron—philos*, loving, *-tron*, denoting the agent.]

**Phlebotomy**, fle-bot'o-mi, *n.* act of letting blood. [Lit. 'vein-cutting,' Fr.—L.—Gr., from *phleps, phlebos*, a vein, and *tomos*, a cutting.]

**Phlegm**, flem, *n.* the thick, slimy matter secreted in the throat, and discharged by coughing : sluggishness : indifference. [Fr.—L.—Gr. *phlegma, phlegmatos*, a flame, inflammation—*phleg-ō*, to burn ; like L. *flam-ma* (for *flag-ma—flag-*, as in L. *flag-rare*, to burn), whence **Flame.**]

**Phlegmatic**, fleg-mat'ik, **Phlegmatical**, fleg-mat'ik-al, *adj.* abounding in or generating *phlegm* : cold : sluggish : not easily excited.—*adv.* **Phlegmat'ically.** [Gr. *phlegmatikos—phlegma.*]

**Phlogiston**, flo-jis'ton, *n.* the imaginary principle of fire, supposed by Stahl to be fixed in combustible bodies.—*adj.* **Phlogis'tic.** [Gr.]

**Phlox**, floks, *n.* a well-known garden plant, so called from its colour. [Gr. 'a flame'—*phlegō*, to burn. See **Phlegm.**]

**Phocine**, fō'sin, *adj.* pertaining to the *seal* family. [L. *phoca*—Gr. *phōkē*, a seal.]

**Phœnix.** Same as **Phenix.**

**Phonetic**, fo-net'ik, **Phonetical**, fo-net'ik-al, *adj.* pertaining to or according to the *sound* of the voice : representing the separate elementary sounds : vocal.—*n.sing.* **Phonet'ics**, the science of *sounds*, esp. of the human voice.—*adv.* **Phonet'ically.** [Gr. *phōnetikos—phōnē*, a sound.]

**Phonic**, fon'ik, *adj.* pertaining to *sound.*—*n.sing.* **Phon'ics**, the science of sound, acoustics.

**Phonograph**, fō'no-graf, *n.* an instrument by which articulate speech or other *sounds* can be *recorded* by indentations on tinfoil, and mechanically reproduced at will from the record, almost in the original tones. [Gr. *phōnē*, sound, and *graphō*, to write.]

**Phonographer**, fo-nog'ra-fėr, **Phonographist**, fo-nog'ra-fist, *n.* one versed in phonography.

**Phonography**, fo-nog'ra-fi, *n.* the art of representing spoken *sounds*, each by a distinct *character* : phonetic shorthand.—*adjs.* **Phonograph'ic, -al.** —*adv.* **Phonograph'ically.**

**Phonology**, fo-nol'o-ji, *n.* the *science* of the elementary spoken *sounds* : phonetics.—*adj.* **Phonolog'ical.**—*n.* **Phonol'ogist**, one versed in phonology. [Gr. *phōnē*, sound, *logos*, discourse.]

**Phonotype**, fō'no-tīp, *n.* a *type* or sign representing a *sound.* [Gr. *phōnē*, sound, *typos*, type.]

**Phonotypy**, fo-not'ip-i, *n.* the art of representing *sounds* by *types* or distinct characters.

**Phosphate**, fos'fāt, *n.* a salt formed by the combination of phosphoric acid with a base.

**Phosphoresce**, fos-for-es', *v.i.* to shine in the dark like phosphorus.

**Phosphorescent**, fos-for-es'ent, *adj.* shining in the dark like phosphorus.—*n.* **Phosphores'cence.**

**Phosphoric**, fos-for'ik, **Phosphorous**, fos'for-us, *adj.* pertaining to or obtained from phosphorus.

**Phosphorus**, fos'for-us, *n.* the morning-star : a yellowish substance, like wax, inflammable and luminous in the dark. [L.—Gr. *phōsphoros*, light-bearer—*phōs*, light, and *phoros*, bearing, from *pherō*, E. **Bear.**]

**Phosphuret**, fos'fū-ret, *n.* a compound of phosphorus with a metal.—*adj.* **Phos'phuretted**, combined with phosphorus. [phosphorus.]

**Photograph**, fō'to-graf, *n.* a picture produced by

**Photographer**, fo-tog'ra-fėr, **Photographist**, fo-tog'ra-fist, *n.* one who practises photography.

**Photographic**, fō-to-graf'ik, **Photographical**, fō-to-graf'ik-al, *adj.* pertaining to or done by photography.—*adv.* **Photograph'ically.**

**Photography**, fo-tog'raf-i, *n.* the art of producing pictures by the action of *light* on chemically prepared surfaces. [Gr. *phōs, phōtos*, light, *graphō*, to draw.]

**Photometer**, fo-tom'et-ėr, *n.* an instrument for *measuring* the intensity of *light.* [Gr. *phōs, phōtos*, light, *metron*, a measure.]

**Photophone**, fō'to-fōn, *n.* an apparatus for transmitting articulate *speech* to a distance along a beam of *light.* [Gr. *phōs, phōtos*, light, and *phōnē*, sound.]

**Photosphere**, fō'to-sfēr, *n.* the luminous envelope round the sun's globe, which is the source of *light.* [Gr. *phōs, phōtos*, light, and **Sphere.**]

**Phrase**, frāz, *n.* a part of a sentence : a short

pithy expression: a form of speech: (*music*) a short clause or portion of a sentence.—*v.t.* to express in words: to style. [Fr.—L.—Gr. *phrasis*—*phrazō*, to speak.]

**Phraseologic**, frā-ze-o-loj′ik, **Phraseological**, frā-ze-o-loj′ik-al, *adj.* pertaining to phraseology: consisting of phrases.—*adv.* **Phraseolog′ically.**

**Phraseology**, frā-ze-ol′o-ji, *n.* style or manner of expression or use of *phrases:* peculiarities of diction: a collection of phrases in a language. [Gr. *phrasis*, *phraseōs*, phrase, *logos*, science.]

**Phrenologist**, fren-ol′o-jist, *n.* one who believes or is versed in *phrenology.*

**Phrenology**, fren-ol′o-ji, *n.* the theory of Gall and his followers, which connects the mental faculties with certain parts of the brain, and professes to discover the character from an examination of the skull.—*adj.* **Phrenolog′ical.** —*adv.* **Phrenolog′ically.** [Gr. *phrēn*, *phrenos*, mind, *logos*, science.]

**Phthisic**, tiz′ik, **Phthisical**, tiz′ik-al, *adj.* pertaining to or having *phthisis.*

**Phthisis**, thī′sis, *n.* consumption of the lungs. [L.—Gr. *phthiō*, to waste away.]

**Phylactery**, fi-lak′tér-i, *n.* among the Jews, a slip of parchment inscribed with passages of Scripture, worn on the left arm and forehead. —*adjs.* **Phylacter′ic, Phylacter′ical.** [Lit. a charm to *protect* from danger, L.—Gr. *phylak-tērion*, *phylaktēr*, a guard—*phylassō*, to guard.]

**Phylloxera**, fil-ok′ser-a, *n.* a genus of insects destructive to vines. [Gr. *phyllon*, a leaf, and *zēros*, dry, withered.]

**Physic**, fiz′ik, *n.* the science of medicine: the art of healing: a medicine.—*v.t.* to give medicine to:—*pr.p.* phys′icking; *pa.t.* and *pa.p.* phys′-icked. [From the Fr. of the Middle Ages (mod. Fr. *physique* is the same as E. *physics*)—Gr. *physikē*, natural, physical (as medical men were then the only naturalists)—Gr. *phy-sis*, nature, from the same root as E. **Be.**]

**Physical**, fiz′ik-al, *adj.* pertaining to *nature* or natural objects: pertaining to material things: known to the senses: pertaining to the body. —*adv.* **Phys′ically.** [Gr. *physikos*—*physis*, nature. See **Physics.**]

**Physician**, fi-zish′an, *n.* one skilled in the use of physic or the art of healing: one who prescribes remedies for diseases. [versed in physics.

**Physicist**, fiz′i-sist, *n.* a *student of nature:* one

**Physics**, fiz′iks, *n.pl.* used as *sing.* (*orig.*) equivalent to **Physical Science,** *i.e.* the science of the order of nature: usually sig. (as distinguished from chemistry) study of matter and the general properties of matter as affected by energy—also called natural philosophy. [L. *physica*, Gr. *physikē* (*theōria*, theory)—*physis*, nature.]

**Physiognomy**, fiz-i-og′no-mi or fiz-i-on′o-mi, *n.* the art of knowing a man's disposition from his features: expression of countenance: the face. —*adjs.* **Physiognom′ic, Physiognom′ical.**— *adv.* **Physiognom′ically.**—*n.sing.* **Physiog-nom′ics,** same as **Physiognomy.**—*n.* **Physiog′-nomist.** [For *physiognomony*—Gr. *physiognō-monia*—*physis*, nature, *gnōmōn*, one who indicates or interprets—*gnōnai*, to know.]

**Physiography**, fiz-i-og′ra-fi, *n.* a *description* of *nature*, esp. in its external aspects: an introduction to the study of nature. [Gr. *physis*, nature, and *graphō*, to describe.]

**Physiology**, fiz-i-ol′o-ji, *n.* the science of the functions of living beings—a branch of biology.— *adjs.* **Physiolog′ic, Physiolog′ical.**—*adv.* **Phy-siolog′ically.**—*n.* **Physiol′ogist.** [Lit. ' the

science of nature,' Gr. *physis*, nature, *logos*, science.]

**Physique**, fiz-ēk′, *n.* the physical structure or natural constitution of a person. [Fr., from root of **Physical.**]

**Phytology**, fī-tol′o-ji, *n.* the *science* of *plants:* botany.—*adj.* **Phytolog′ical.**—*n.* **Phytol′ogist.** [Gr. *phyton*, a plant, *logos*, discourse, science.]

**Piacular**, pī-ak′ū-lar, *adj.* serving to *appease*, expiatory: requiring expiation: atrociously bad. [L. *piaculum*, sacrifice—*pio*,expiate—*pius*,pious.]

**Pianist**, pi-a′nist, *n.* one who plays on the piano-forte, or one well skilled in it.

**Piano**, pi-ä′no, *adv.* (*mus.*) *softly.*—*adv.* **Pianis′-simo,** very softly. [It. *piano* (superl. *pianis-simo*), plain, smooth—L. *planus*, plain. Doublet **Plain.**]

**Pianoforte**, pi-ä′no-fōr′tā, (generally shortened to) **Piano**, pi-a′no, *n.* a musical instrument with wires struck by little hammers moved by keys, so as to produce both *soft* and *strong* sounds. [It. *piano* (see **Piano**, above), and *forte*, strong —L. *fortis*, strong. See **Force.**]

**Piastre**, pi-as′tér, *n.* a silver coin used in Turkey and other countries, of varying value. [Fr.—It. *piastra*, from same root as **Plaster.**]

**Piazza**, pi-az′a, *n.* a *place* or square surrounded by buildings: a walk under a roof supported by pillars. [It. (Fr. *place*)—L. *platea*, a broad street. See **Place,** its doublet.]

**Pibroch**, pē′brok, *n.* the martial music of the Scottish bagpipe. [Gael. *piobaireachd*, pipe-music —*piobair*, a piper—*piob*, a pipe, bagpipe. Cf. **Pipe.**]

**Pica**, pī′ka, *n.* a printing type, used as a standard of measurement by printers. [See **Pie,** a book.]

**Pick**, pik, *v.t.* to prick with a sharp-pointed instrument: to peck, as a bird: to pierce: to open with a pointed instrument, as a lock: to pluck or gather, as flowers, &c.: to separate from: to clean with the teeth: to gather: to choose: to select: to call: to seek, as a quarrel: to steal. —*v.i.* to do anything nicely: to eat by morsels. —*n.* any sharp-pointed instrument: choice.—*n.* **Pick′er.** [A.S. *pycan* (Ger. *picken*)—Celt., as Gael. *pioc*, to pick, W. *pigo.* Cf. the allied **Pike.**]

**Pickaxe**, pik′aks, *n.* a *picking* tool used in digging. [A popular corr. of M.E. *pikois*—O. Fr. *picois*(Fr. *pic*), of same Celt. origin as **Pick,** *v.t.*]

**Picket**, pik′et, *n.* a pointed stake used in fortification: a small outpost or guard.—*v.t.* to fasten to a stake, as a horse: to post as a vanguard. [Fr. *piquet*, dim. of *pic*, a pickaxe. See **Pickaxe.**]

**Pickle**, pik′l, *n.* a liquid in which substances are preserved: anything pickled: a disagreeable position.—*v.t.* to season or preserve with salt, vinegar, &c. [Dut. *pekel*, pickle, brine.]

**Picklock**, pik′lok, *n.* an instrument for *picking locks.*

**Pickpocket**, pik′pok-et, *n.* one who *picks* or steals from other people's *pockets.*

**Picnic**, pik′nik, *n.* a short excursion into the country by a pleasure-party, taking their own provisions: an entertainment in the open air, towards which each person contributes.—*v.i.* to go on a picnic:—*pr.p.* pic′nicking; *pa.t.* and *pa.p.* pic′nicked. [Prob. from E. *pick*, to eat by morsels, with the rhyming addition *nick* (perh. a weakened form of **Knack,** which see).]

**Pictorial**, pik-tōr′i-al, *adj.* relating to pictures: illustrated by pictures.—*adv.* **Pictor′ially.**

**Picture**, pik′tūr, *n.* a *painting:* a likeness in colours: a drawing: painting: a resemblance:

an image.—*v.t.* to paint, to represent by painting : to form an ideal likeness of : to describe vividly. [L. *pictura—pingo, pictus*, Sans. *pinj.* See Paint.]

**Picturesque**, pik-tūr-esk', *adj.* like a *picture* : fit to make a picture : natural.—*adv.* **Pictur-esque'ly.**—*n.* **Picturesque'ness.** [It. *pittoresco —pittura*, a picture—L. *pictura*. See **Picture.**]

**Piddle**, pid'l, *v.i.* to *peddle* or deal in trifles : to trifle. [A weakened form of **Peddle.**]

**Pie**, pī, *n.* a magpie : (*print.*) type mixed or unsorted. [Fr.—L. *pica*, akin to *picus*, a woodpecker.]

**Pie**, pī, *n.* a book which ordered the manner of performing divine service. [Fr.—L. *pica*, lit. magpie, from its old black-letter type on white paper resembling the colours of the magpie.]

**Pie**, pī, *n.* a quantity of meat or fruit baked within a crust of prepared flour. [Ety. dub. ; perh. from Ir. and Gael. *pighe*, pie.]

**Piebald**, pī'bawld, *adj.* of various colours in patches. [For *pie-balled*, lit. 'streaked like the magpie,' from **Pie** (a magpie), and W. *bal*, a streak on a horse's forehead. See **Bald.**]

**Piece**, pēs, *n.* a part of anything : a single article : a separate performance : a literary or artistic composition : a gun : a coin : a person (slightingly). —*v.t.* to enlarge by adding a piece : to patch.— *v.i.* to unite by a coalescence of parts : to join. —*n.* **Piec'er.** [Fr. *pièce* (It. *pezza*), perh. conn. with Bret. *pez*, W. *peth.*]

**Pieceless**, pēs'les, *adj.* not made of pieces : entire.

**Piecemeal**, pēs'mēl, *adj.* made of *pieces* or parts : single.—*adv.* in pieces or fragments : by pieces : gradually. [**Piece**, and **Meal**, a portion.]

**Piecework**, pēs'wurk, *n.*, *work* done by the *piece* or job. [various colours : spotted.

**Pied**, pīd, *adj.* variegated like a mag-*pie* : of

**Pier**, pēr, *n.* the mass of *stone*-work between the openings of a building, also that supporting an arch, bridge, &c. : a mass of stone or wood work projecting into the sea : a wharf. [M. E. *pere*—Fr. *pierre*, a stone—L. *petra*—Gr. *petra*, a rock.]

**Pierce**, pērs, *v.t.* or *v.i.* to thrust or make a hole through : to enter, or force a way into : to touch or move deeply : to dive into, as a secret.— *n.* **Pierc'er.** [Fr. *percer*, of doubtful origin.]

**Pierceable**, pērs'a-bl, *adj.* capable of being pierced. [between windows. [See **Pier.**]

**Pierglass**, pēr'glas, *n.* a *glass* hung in the space

**Piet**, pī'et, *n.* a *pie* or magpie. [A form of **Pie.**]

**Pietism**, pī'et-izm, *n.* the doctrine and practice of the pietists.

**Pietist**, pī'et-ist, *n.* one marked by strong devotional or religious feeling : a name first applied to a sect of German religious reformers at the end of the 17th century, marked by their devotional feeling.—*adj.* **Pietist'ic.**

**Piety**, pī'et-i, *n.* the quality of being pious : reverence for the Deity, parents, friends, or country : sense of duty : dutiful conduct. [Fr. *piété*—L. *pietas*. Doublet **Pity.**]

**Pig**, pig, *n.* a young swine : an oblong mass of unforged metal, as first extracted from the ore, so called because it is made to flow when melted in channels called *pigs*, branching from a main channel called the *sow.*—*v.i.* to bring forth pigs : to live together like pigs :—*pr.p.* pigg'ing ; *pa.t.* and *pa.p.* pigged. [A.S. *pecg*, cog. with Dut. *bigge, big*, a pig. Cf. Ice. *pika*, Dan. *pige*, a girl.]

**Pigeon**, pij'un, *n.* (*lit.*) that which pipes or chirps : a well-known bird, the dove. [Fr.—L. *pipio*,

*-onis*, a young bird or pigeon, from *pipio*, to chirp. An imitative word. See **Pipe.**]

**Pigeon-hearted**, pij'un-härt'ed, *adj.* with a *heart* like a *pigeon's* : timid : fearful.

**Pigeon-hole**, pij'un-hōl, *n.* a *hole* or niche in which pigeons lodge in a dovecot : a division of a case for papers, &c.

**Pigeon-livered**, pij'un-liv'ėrd, *adj.* with a *liver* like a *pigeon's* : timid : cowardly.

**Piggery**, pig'ėr-i, *n.* a place where *pigs* are kept.

**Piggin**, pig'in, *n.* a small wooden vessel. [Gael. *pigean*, dim. of *pigeadh* or *pige*, a pot.]

**Piggish**, pig'ish, *adj.* belonging to or like pigs.

**Pig-iron**, pig'-ī'urn, *n.*, *iron* in *pigs* or rough bars.

**Pigment**, pig'ment, *n.*, *paint* : any substance for colouring : that which gives the iris of the eye its various colours.—*adj.* **Pigment'al.** [L. *pigmentum—pingo*, to paint. See **Picture.**]

**Pigmy.** Same as **Pygmy.**

**Pigtail**, pig'tāl, *n.* the hair of the head tied behind in the form of a pig's tail : a roll of twisted tobacco. [Pig and Tail.]

**Pike**, pīk, *n.* a weapon with a shaft and spearhead, formerly used by foot-soldiers : a voracious fresh-water fish (so called from its pointed snout). [Celt., as Gael. *pic*, a pike, W. *pig*, a point ; cf. L. *s-pica*, a spike. **Beak, Peak, Pick, Picket** are all from the same root, of which the fundamental idea is something 'pointed,' 'sharp.']

**Piked**, pīkt, *adj.* ending in a point.

**Pikeman**, pīk'man, *n.* a *man* armed with a *pike*.

**Pikestaff**, pīk'staf, *n.* the *staff* or shaft of a *pike* : a staff with a pike at the end.

**Pilaster**, pi-las'tėr, *n.* (*arch.*) a square *pillar* or column, usually set within a wall. [Fr. *pilastre*, It. *pilastro*—L. *pīla*, a pillar. See **Pile**, a pillar.]

**Pilastered**, pi-las'tėrd, *adj.* furnished with pilasters or inserted pillars.

**Pilchard**, pil'chärd, *n.* a sea-fish like the herring, but thicker and rounder, caught chiefly on the Cornish coast. [Prob. from Celt. (as in Ir. *pilseir*), with excrescent *d.*]

**Pile**, pīl, *n.* a *roundish* mass : a heap : combustibles for burning, esp. dead bodies : a large building : a heap of shot or shell : (*electricity*) a form of battery.—*v.t.* to lay in a pile or heap : to collect in a mass : to heap up : to fill above the brim. [Fr.—L. *pīla*, a ball.]

**Pile**, pīl, *n.* a *pillar* : a large stake driven into the earth to support foundations.—*v.i.* to drive piles into. [A.S. *pil*—L. *pīla*, a pillar.]

**Pile**, pīl, *n.* a *hairy* surface : the nap on cloth. [L. *pilus*, a hair.]

**Pileate**, pī'le-āt, **Pileated**, pī'le-āt-ed, *adj.* having the form of a cap or hat. [L. *pileatus—pileus*, Gr. *pilos*, hair wrought into felt.]

**Pile-driver**, pīl'-drīv'ėr, **Pile-engine**, pīl'-en'jin, *n.* an engine for *driving* down *piles*.

**Piles**, pīlz, *n.pl.* hemorrhoids, which see. [L. *pīla*, a ball.]

**Pilfer**, pil'fėr, *v.i.* to steal small things.—*v.t.* to steal by petty theft. [From O. Fr. *pelfre*, booty. See **Pelf.**]

**Pilfering**, pil'fėr-ing, *n.* petty theft.

**Pilgrim**, pil'grim, *n.* one who travels to a distance to visit a sacred place : a wanderer. [Fr. *pèlerin* (for *pelegrin* ; It. *pellegrino, peregrino*) —L. *peregrinus*, foreigner, stranger—*pereger*, a traveller—*per*, through, and *ager*, land, E. **Acre.**]

**Pilgrimage**, pil'grim-āj, *n.* the journey of a pilgrim : a journey to a shrine or other sacred place.

**Pill**, pil, *n.* a *little ball* of medicine : anything nauseous. [Contr. of Fr. *pilule*—L. *pilula*, dim. of *pīla*, a ball.]

**Pill**, pil, *v.t.* to rob or plunder. [Fr. *piller*—L. *pilare*, to plunder. Cf. **Compile**.]    [&c.

**Pill**, another spelling of **Peel**, *v.t.* and *v.i.* to strip,

**Pillage**, pil′āj, *n.* plunder : spoil, esp. taken in war.—*v.t.* to plunder or spoil.—*n.* **Pill′ager.** [Fr., from *piller*. See **Pill**, *v.*]

**Pillar**, pil′ar, *n.* (*arch.*) a detached support, differing from a column in that it is not necessarily cylindrical, or of classical proportions : anything that sustains. [O. Fr. *piler* (Fr. *pilier*)—Low L. *pilare*—L. *pīla*, a pillar.]

**Pillared**, pil′ard, *adj.* supported by a *pillar* : having the form of a pillar.

**Pillau**, pil-law′, *n.* a Turkish dish, made of boiled rice and mutton fat.

**Pillion**, pil′yun, *n.* a cushion for a woman behind a horseman : the cushion of a saddle. [Ir. *pilliun*, Gael. *pillean*, a pad, a pack-saddle—*peall*, a skin or mat, akin to L. *pellis*, skin, E. **Fell**, a skin.]

**Pillory**, pil′or-i, *n.* a wooden frame, supported by an upright *pillar* or post, and having holes through which the head and hands of a criminal were put as a punishment.—*v.t.* to punish in the pillory :—*pa.t.* and *pa.p.* pill′oried. [Fr. *pilori* : ety. dub. ; perh. from root of **Pillar**.]

**Pillow**, pil′ō, *n.* a cushion filled with feathers for resting the head on : any cushion.—*v.t.* to lay on for support. [A.S. *pyle*, M. E. *pilwe*—L. *pulvinus*.]

**Pillow-case**, pil′ō-kās, *n.* a *case* for a *pillow*.

**Pillowy**, pil′ō-i, *adj.* like a pillow : soft.

**Pilose**, pi-lōs′, **Pilous**, pī′us, *adj.*, *hairy*.—*n.* **Pilos′ity.**

**Pilot**, pī′lut, *n.* one who conducts ships in and out of a harbour, along a dangerous coast, &c. : a guide.—*v.t.* to conduct as a pilot. [Fr. *pilote*—Dut. *piloot*, from *peilen*, to sound, and *loot* (Ger. *loth*, E. **Lead**), a sounding-lead.]

**Pilotage**, pī′lut-āj, *n.* the act of piloting : the fee or wages of pilots.      [cloth for overcoats.

**Pilot-cloth**, pī′lut-kloth, *n.* a coarse, stout kind of

**Pilot-fish**, pī′lut-fish, *n.* a fish of the mackerel family, so called from its having been supposed to *guide* sharks to their prey.

**Pimenta**, pi-men′ta, **Pimento**, pi-men′to, *n.* Jamaica pepper : the tree producing it. [Port. *pimenta*—L. *pigmentum*, paint, juice of plants.]

**Pimp**, pimp, *n.* one who procures gratifications for the lust of others : a pander.—*v.i.* to procure women for others : to pander. [Fr. *pimper*, a nasalised form of *piper*, to pipe, hence, to decoy, to cheat.]

**Pimpernel**, pim′per-nel, **Pimpinella**, pim-pi-nel′a, *n.* a plant having a double series of small leaves. [Fr. *pimprenelle* (It. *pimpinella*), either a corr. of a L. form *bipennula*, double-winged, dim. of *bi-pennis*—*bis*, twice, and *penna*, feather, wing ; or from a dim. of L. *pampinus*, a vine-leaf.]

**Pimple**, pim′pl, *n.* a *pustule* : a small swelling.—*adjs.* **Pim′pled, Pim′ply**, having pimples. [A.S. *pipel*, nasalised from L. *papula*, a pustule (cf. **Papilla**) ; cf. W. *pwmp*, a knob.]

**Pin**, pin, *n.* a sharp-pointed instrument. esp. for fastening articles together : anything that holds parts together : a peg used in musical instruments for fastening the strings : anything of little value.—*v.t.* to fasten with a pin : to fasten : to inclose :—*pr.p.* pin′ning ; *pa.t.* and *pa.p.* pinned. [M. E. *pinne*, like Celt. *pinne*, and Ger. *penn*, from L. *pinna* or *penna*, a feather, a pen, a peg.]

**Pinafore**, pin′a-fōr, *n.* a loose covering of cotton or linen over a child's dress, orig. only *pinned* to its *front*.

**Pincase**, pin′kās, **Pincushion**, pin′koosh-un, *n.* a *case* or cushion for holding *pins*.

**Pincers**. Same as **Pinchers**.

**Pinch**, pinsh, *v.t.* to gripe hard : to squeeze : to squeeze the flesh so as to give pain : to nip : to distress : to gripe.—*v.i.* to act with force : to bear or press hard : to live sparingly.—*n.* a close compression with the fingers : what can be taken up by the compressed fingers : a gripe : distress : oppression. [Fr. *pincer* (It. *pizzare*), from a root seen in Dut. *pitsen*, to pinch.]

**Pinchbeck**, pinsh′bek, *n.* a yellow alloy of five parts of copper to one of zinc. [From the name of the inventor, Christopher Pinchbeck, in the 18th century.]

**Pincher**, pinsh′er, *n.* one who or that which pinches.

**Pinchers**, pinsh′erz, **Pincers**, pin′serz, *n.* an instrument for seizing anything, esp. for drawing out nails, &c. [See **Pinch**.]

**Pinchingly**, pinsh′ing-li, *adv.* in a pinching manner.

**Pindaric**, pin-dar′ik, *adj.* after the style and manner of *Pindar*, a Greek lyric poet.—*n.* a Pindaric ode : an irregular ode.

**Pinder**, pind′er, **Pinner**, pin′er, *n.* one who *impounds* stray cattle. [From A.S. *pyndan*, to shut up—*pund*. Cf. **Pen**, *v.*, and **Pound**, to shut up.]

**Pine**, pīn, *n.* a northern cone-bearing, resinous tree, furnishing valuable timber. [A.S. *pin*—L. *pīnus* (for *pic-nus*), 'pitch-tree'—*pix*, *picis*, pitch. Cf. **Pitch**, *n.*]

**Pine**, pīn, *v.i.* to waste away under pain or mental distress. [Lit. to 'suffer *pain*,' A.S. *pīnan*, to torment, from *pín*, pain—L. *pœna*. See **Pain**.]

**Pine-apple**, pīn′-ap′l, *n.* a tropical plant, and its fruit, shaped like a *pine*-cone. [**Pine** and **Apple**.]      [raised.

**Pinery**, pīn′er-i, *n.* a place where *pine*-apples are

**Pinfold**, pin′fold, *n.* a pound for cattle. [For *pind-fold* = **Pound-fold**.]

**Pinion**, pin′yun, *n.* a *wing* : the joint of a wing most remote from the body : a smaller wheel with 'leaves' or teeth working into others.—*v.t.* to confine the wings of : to cut off the pinion' to confine by binding the arms. [Fr. *pignon*—L. *pinna* (= *penna*), wing. See **Pen**, *n.*]

**Pink**, pingk, *v.t.* to stab or pierce. [Either through A.S. *pyngan*, from L. *pungo*, to prick ; or acc. to Skeat, a nasalised form of **Pick**.]

**Pink**, pingk, *n.* a plant with beautiful flowers : a shade of light-red colour like that of the flower : the minnow, from the colour of its abdomen in summer : that which is supremely excellent.—*v.t.* to work in eyelet holes : to cut in small scollops or angles. [Prob. a nasalised form of Celt. *pic*, a point, the flower being so called from the finely *pointed* or notched edges of the petals. See **Pike**.]

**Pink-eyed**, pingk′-īd, *adj.* having *small* eyes : having the eyes half-shut.

**Pinking-iron**, pingk′ing-ī′urn, *n.* a tool for *pinking* or scolloping. [**Pinking** and **Iron**.]

**Pin-money**, pin′-mun′i, *n.*, *money* allowed to a wife for private expenses, orig. to buy *pins*.

**Pinnace**, pin′ās, *n.* a small vessel with oars and sails : a boat with eight oars. [Lit. a '*pine*-wood boat,' Fr. *pinasse*—It. *pinassa*—L. *pinus*, a pine. See **Pine**, *n.*]

**Pinnacle**, pin′a-kl, *n.* a slender turret : a high point like a spire.—*v.t.* to build with pinnacles. [Fr. *pinacle*—Low L. *pinna-cu-lum*, double dim. from L. *pinna*, a feather.]

**Pinnate**, pin'āt, *adj.* (*bot.*) shaped like a *feather:* (*zool.*) furnished with fins.—*adv.* **Pinn'ately.** [L. *pinnatus*, from *pinna* (= *penna*), a feather.]

**Pinner**, pin'er, *n.* one who *pins* or fastens : a pin-maker : the lappet of a head-dress flying loose.

**Pin-point**, pin'-point, *n.* the *point* of a *pin*: a trifle.

**Pint**, pīnt, *n.* a measure of capacity = ½ quart or 4 gills : (*med.*) 12 ounces. [Lit. 'a measure *painted*'—i.e. indicated by a mark upon the vessel ; Fr. *pinte*—Sp. *pinta*, mark, pint, from L. *pingo*, to paint. See **Paint**.]

**Pintle**, pin'tl, *n.* a *little pin* : a long iron bolt : the bolt hanging the rudder of a ship. [Dim. of **Pin**.]

**Piny**, pīn'i, *adj.* abounding with *pine*-trees.

**Pioneer**, pī-o-nēr', *n.* a soldier who clears the road before an army, sinks mines, &c. : one who goes before to prepare the way.—*v.t.* to act as pioneer to. [Fr. *pionnier*—*pion*, a foot-soldier —Low L. *pedo, pedonis*, a foot-soldier—L. *pes, pedis*, a foot. See **Pawn**, in chess.]

**Pious**, pī'us, *adj.*, *devout* : having reverence and love for the Deity : proceeding from religious feeling.—*adv.* **Pi'ously.** [Fr. *pieux*—L. *pius*.]

**Pip**, pip, *n.* a disease of fowls, also called *roup.* [Fr. *pépie* (It. *pipita*), a corr. of L. *pituita*, rheum ; akin to Gr. *ptyō*, to spit.]

**Pip**, pip, *n.* the seed of fruit. [Orig. *pippin* or *pepin*—Fr. *pépin* ; ety. unknown.]

**Pip**, pip, *n.* a spot on cards. [Corr. of prov. *pick*, —Fr. *pique*, a spade, at cards. See **Pike**.]

**Pipe**, pīp, *n.* a musical wind instrument consisting of a long tube : any long tube : a tube of clay, &c. with a bowl at one end for smoking tobacco : a cask containing two hhds.—*v.i.* to play upon a pipe : to whistle.—*v.t.* to play on a pipe : to call with a pipe, as on board ships.— *n.* **Pip'er.** [A.S. *pipe*—imitative of the sound ; as are Celt. *pib*, a pipe, Dut. *pijp* ; and the L. *pipire*, to chirp, Gr. *pipizo*.]

**Pipeclay**, pīp'klā, *n.* white *clay* used for making tobacco *pipes* and fine earthenware.

**Piping**, pīp'ing, *adj.* uttering a weak, shrill, *piping* sound, like the sick : sickly : feeble : boiling.

**Pipkin**, pip'kin, *n.* a small earthen pot. [Dim. of **Pipe**.]

**Pippin**, pip'in, *n.* a kind of apple. [Prob. from **Pip**, seed of fruit.]

**Piquant**, pik'ant, *adj.* stimulating to the taste.— *adv.* **Piq'uantly.**—*n.* **Piq'uancy.** [Fr. *piquant*, pr.p. of Fr. *piquer*, to prick.]

**Pique**, pēk, *n.* an offence taken : wounded pride : spite : nicety : punctilio.—*v.t.* to wound the pride of : to offend : to pride or value (one's self) : —*pr.p.* piq'uing ; *pa.t.* and *pa.p.* piqued. [Fr. *pique*, a pike, pique. See **Pick** and **Pike**.]

**Piquet.** Same as **Picket**.

**Piquet**, pi-ket', *n.* a game at cards. [Said to be named from its inventor.]

**Piracy**, pī'ra-si, *n.* the crime of a *pirate* : robbery on the high seas : infringement of copyright.

**Pirate**, pī'rāt, *n.* one who *attempts* to capture ships at sea : a sea-robber : one who steals or infringes a copyright.—*v.t.* to take without permission, as books or writings. [Fr.—L. *pirata* —Gr. *peiratēs*, from *peiraō*, to attempt—*peir-a*, an attempt, cog. with **Ex-per-ience** and **Fare**.]

**Piratical**, pī-rat'ik-al, *adj.* pertaining to a pirate : practising piracy.—*adv.* **Pirat'ically.**

**Pirouette**, pir-oo-et', *n.* a *wheeling* about, esp. in dancing : the turning of a horse on the same ground.—*v.i.* to execute a pirouette. [Fr., prob. dim. of Norm. Fr. *piroue*, a whirligig, cog. with E. *perry*, an old word for a whirlwind (Skeat) ; **cf.** Scot. *pearie*, a pegtop.]

**Piscatorial**, pis-ka-tō'ri-al, **Piscatory**, pis'ka-tor-i, *adj.* relating to *fishes* or fishing.

**Pisces**, pis'ēz, *n.* the *Fishes*, the twelfth sign of the zodiac. [L., pl. of *piscis*, E. **Fish**.]

**Pisciculture**, pis'i-kul-tūr, *n.* the *rearing* of *fish* by artificial methods. [L. *piscis*, fish, and **Culture**.]

**Piscinal**, pis'i-nal or pi-sī'nal, *adj.* belonging to a *fishpond*. [L. *piscinalis*, from *piscina*, a fish-pond.]                                          [**Pisces**.

**Piscine**, pis'īn, *adj.* pertaining to *fishes*. [See

**Piscivorous**, pis-iv'o-rus, *adj.*, *devouring* or feeding on *fishes*. [L. *piscis*, fish, and *voro*, to devour.]

**Pish**, pish, *int.* expressing contempt. [Imitative.]

**Pismire**, piz'mīr, *n.* an ant or emmet. [M. E. *pissemire*—*pisse*, urine, and A.S. *mire*, ant, cog. with Ice. *maurr*, Ir. *moirbh*, and Gr. *murmēx*.]

**Piss**, pis, *v.i.* (*B.*) to discharge urine or make water. [Fr. *pisser ;* imitative.]

**Pistachio**, pis-tā'shi-o, **Pistacia**, pis-tā'shi-a, *n.* a small tree cultivated in S. Europe and in the East : its nut. [It.—L. *pistacium*—Gr. *pista-kion*—Pers. *pista*.]

**Pistil**, pis'til, *n.* (*bot.*) the female organ in the centre of a flower, so called from its likeness to the *pestle* of a mortar. [Fr.—L. *pistillum*. **Pestle** is a doublet.]

**Pistillaceous**, pis-til-lā'shus, *adj.* growing on a *pistil* : pertaining to or having the nature of a pistil.

**Pistillate**, pis'til-lāt, *adj.* having a pistil.

**Pistilliferous**, pis-til-lif'er-us, *adj.* bearing a *pistil* without stamens. [**Pistil**, and *fero*, to bear.]

**Pistol**, pis'tol, *n.* a small hand-gun. [Orig. a dagger, Fr. *pistole*—It. *pistola*, said to be from *Pistoja* (orig. *Pistola*), a town in Italy.]

**Pistole**, pis-tōl', *n.* a Spanish gold coin = about 16 shillings. [Same word as the above, a name jocularly applied to the crowns of Spain, when reduced to a smaller size than the crowns of France.]

**Pistolet**, pis'to-let, *n.* a little pistol.

**Piston**, pis'tun, *n.* a short solid cylinder, used in pumps, &c., fitting and moving up and down within another hollow one. [Lit. the 'pounder,' Fr.—It. *pistone*—*pesto*, to pound—L. *pinso, pistus*. See **Pestle**.]            [*piston* is moved.

**Piston-rod**, pis'tun-rod, *n.* the *rod* by which the

**Pit**, pit, *n.* a hole in the earth : an abyss : the bottomless pit : a hole used as a trap for wild beasts : whatever insnares : the hollow of the stomach : the indentation left by smallpox : the ground-floor of a theatre : the shaft of a mine. —*v.t.* to mark with pits or little hollows : to set in competition :—*pr.p.* pitt'ing ; *pa.t.* and *pa.p.* pitt'ed. [A.S. *pytt*—L. *puteus*, a well.]

**Pitapat**, pit'a-pat, *adv.* with palpitation or quick beating. [A repetition of *pat*.]

**Pitch**, pich, *n.* the solid black shining substance obtained by boiling down common tar.—*v.t.* to smear with pitch. [A.S. *pic*—L. *pix, pic-is* (whence also Ger. *pech*), conn. with Gr. *pissa*. Cf. **Pine**, *n.*]

**Pitch**, pich, *v.t.* (*lit.*) to *pick* or strike with a *pike* : to throw : to fix or set in array : to fix the tone. —*v.i.* to settle, as something pitched : to come to rest from flight : to fall headlong : to fix the choice : to encamp : to rise and fall, as a ship. —*n.* any point or degree of elevation or depression : degree : degree of slope : a descent : (*mus.*) the height of a note : (*mech.*) distance between the centres of two teeth. [A form of **Pick**.]

**Pitcher**, pich′ér, *n.* a vessel for holding water, &c. [O. Fr. *picher*—Low L. *picarium*, a goblet—Gr. *bīkos*, a wine-vessel, an Eastern word. Doublet **Beaker**.]

**Pitcher-plant**, pich′ér-plant, *n.* a tropical *plant*, with vase-shaped leaves holding water like *pitchers*.

**Pitchfork**, pich′fork, *n.* a *fork* for *pitching* hay, &c.

**Pitchpipe**, pich′pīp, *n.* a small *pipe* to *pitch* the voice or tune with.

**Pitchy**, pich′i, *adj.* having the qualities of pitch : smeared with pitch : black like pitch : dark : dismal.

**Piteous**, pit′e-us, *adj.* fitted to excite *pity* : mournful : compassionate : paltry.—*adv.* **Pit′eously.** —*n.* **Pit′eousness.**

**Pitfall**, pit′fawl, *n.* a *pit* slightly covered, so that wild beasts may *fall* into it and be caught.

**Pith**, pith, *n.* the *marrow* or soft substance in the centre of plants : force : importance : condensed substance : quintessence. [A.S. *pitha* ; cog. with Dut. *pit*, marrow.] [energy.

**Pithless**, pith′les, *adj.* wanting pith, force, or

**Pithy**, pith′i, *adj.* full of pith : forcible : strong : energetic.—*adv.* **Pith′ily.**—*n.* **Pith′iness.**

**Pitiable**, pit′i-a-bl, *adj.* deserving pity : affecting : wretched.—*adv.* **Pit′iably.**—*n.* **Pit′iableness.**

**Pitiful**, pit′i-fool, *adj.* compassionate : sad : despicable.—*adv.* **Pit′ifully.**—*n.* **Pit′ifulness.**

**Pitiless**, pit′i-les, *adj.* without pity : unsympathising : cruel.—*adv.* **Pit′ilessly.**—*n.* **Pit′ilessness.** [*pit* or a saw-*pit*.

**Pitman**, pit′man, *n.* a *man* who works in a coal-

**Pitsaw**, pit′saw, *n.* a large *saw*, worked vertically by two men, one standing in a *pit* below.

**Pittance**, pit′ans, *n.* an allowance of food : a dole : a very small portion or quantity. [Fr. *pitance ;* of doubtful origin.]

**Pity**, pit′i, *n.* sympathy with distress : a subject of pity or grief.—*v.t.* to sympathise with :— *pa.t.* and *pa.p.* pit′ied.—**It pitieth them** (*Pr. Bk.*), it causeth pity in them. [Lit. *piety*, O. Fr. *pité* (Fr. *pitié*, It. *pietà*)—L. *pietas*, *pietatis*—*pius*, pious. See **Piety**.]

**Pivot**, piv′ut, *n.* the *pin* on which anything turns : the officer or soldier at the flank on which a company wheels. [Fr. dim. of It. *piva*, a pipe, a peg, a pin—Low L. *pipa*.]

**Pivoting**, piv′ut-ing, *n.* the *pivot*-work in machines.

**Pix**, piks, *n.* Same as **Pyx**.

**Pixy, Pixie**, pik′si, *n.* a small Devonshire fairy.

**Placable**, plā′ka-bl or plak′a-bl, *adj.* that may be *appeased* : relenting : forgiving.—*adv.* **Pla′cably.** —*ns.* **Placabil′ity, Pla′cableness** [L. *placabilis*—*placo*, to appease, akin to *placeo*.]

**Placard**, pla-kärd′ or plak′ard, *n.* anything *broad* and *flat* : a bill stuck upon a wall as an advertisement, &c. [Fr. *placard*, a bill stuck on a wall—*plaque*, plate, tablet ; acc. to Diez, from Dut. *plak*, a piece of flat wood.]

**Placard**, pla-kärd′, *v.t.* to publish or notify by *placards*.

**Place**, plās, *n.* a *broad way* in a city : a space : locality : a town : a residence : existence : rank : office : stead : way : passage in a book.—*v.t.* to put in any place or condition : to settle : to lend : to ascribe.—*n.* **Plac′er.** [Fr.—L. *platea*, a broad street—Gr. *plateia*, a street—*platys*, broad ; akin to E. **Flat**. Cf. **Piazza**.]

**Placeman**, plās′man, *n.* one who has a *place* or office under a government :—*pl.* **Place′men.**

**Placenta**, pla-sen′ta, *n.* the spongy organ connecting the fetus in the womb with the mother :

(*bot.*) the part of a plant to which the seeds are attached :—*pl.* **Placen′tæ.** [Lit. ′a cake,′ L. ; akin to Gr. *plak-ous*, a flat cake, from *plax*, *plak-os*, anything flat and broad.]

**Placental**, pla-sen′tal, *adj.* pertaining to or having a placenta.—*n.* a mammal having a placenta.

**Placid**, plas′id, *adj.* gentle : peaceful.—*adv.* **Plac′idly.**—*ns.* **Placid′ity, Plac′idness.** [L. *placidus*—*placeo*, to please. See **Placable**.]

**Plagiarise**, plā′ji-ar-īz, *v.t.* to *steal* from the writings of another. [plagiarising.

**Plagiarism**, plā′ji-ar-izm, *n.* the act or practice of

**Plagiarist**, plā′ji-ar-ist, *n.* one who plagiarises.

**Plagiary**, plā′ji-ar-i, *n.* one who *steals* the thoughts or writings of others and gives them out as his own.—*adj.* practising literary theft. [Fr. *plagiaire*—L. *plagiarius*, a man-stealer—*plagium*, man-stealing.]

**Plague**, plāg, *n.* any great natural evil : a deadly epidemic or pestilence : anything troublesome. —*v.t.* to infest with disease or calamity : to trouble :—*pr.p.* plāg′uing ; *pa.t.* and *pa.p.* plāgued. [L. *plaga*, a blow, stroke, cog. with Gr. *plēgē*, *plēsso*, to strike.]

**Plague-mark**, plāg′-märk, **Plague-spot**, plāg′-spot, *n.* a mark or spot of *plague* or foul disease.

**Plaice**, plās, *n.* a broad, *flat* fish. [O. Fr. *plaïs* (Fr. *plie*)—L. *platessa*, a flat fish, from same root as **Place**.]

**Plaid**, plad or plād, *n.* a loose outer garment of woollen cloth, chiefly worn by the Highlanders of Scotland. [Gael. *plaide*, a blanket, contr. of *peallaid*, a sheep-skin—*peall*, a skin, cog. with L. *pellis*, E. **Fell**.]

**Plaided**, plad′ed, *adj.* wearing a plaid.

**Plain**, plān, *adj.*, *even : flat* : level : smooth : simple : homely : artless : sincere : evident : mere : not coloured or figured.—*adv.* **Plain′ly.** —*n.* **Plain′ness.** [Fr.—L. *plānus* (for *plac-nus*), akin to **Placenta**. See also **Plank**.]

**Plain**, plān, *n.*, *plain* level land : any *flat* expanse : an open field.

**Plain**, plān, *adv.* honestly : distinctly.

**Plain-dealer**, plān′-dēl′ér, *n.* one who *deals* or speaks his mind *plainly*.

**Plain-dealing**, plān′-dēl′ing, *adj.*, *dealing*, speaking, or acting *plainly* or honestly : open : candid. —*n.* frank and candid speaking or acting : sincerity.

**Plain-hearted**, plān′-härt′ed, *adj.* having a *plain* or honest *heart* : sincere.—*n.* **Plain′-heart′edness.** [*plain*, rough sincerity.

**Plain-spoken**, plān′-spōk′en, *adj.*, *speaking* with

**Plaint**, plānt, *n.* lamentation : complaint : a sad song : (*law*) the exhibiting of an action in writing by a *plaintiff*. [O. Fr. *pleinte* (Fr. *plainte*) —L. *planctus*—*plango*, *planctum*, to beat the breast, &c. in mourning. See **Complain**.]

**Plaintiff**, plānt′if, *n.* a *complainant* : (*English law*) one who commences a suit against another. [Fr. *plaintif*. See **Plaint**.]

**Plaintive**, plānt′iv, *adj.*, *complaining* : expressing sorrow : sad.—*adv.* **Plaint′ively.**—*n.* **Plaint′iveness.** [Same as above word.]

**Plainwork**, plān′wurk, *n.*, *plain* needlework, as distinguished from embroidery.

**Plait**, plāt, *n.* a *fold* : a doubling : a braid.—*v.t.* to fold : to double in narrow folds : to interweave. [O. Fr. *ploit* (Fr. *pli*)—L. *plico*, *plicatum* ; akin to Gr. *plekō*, to fold.]

**Plaiter**, plāt′ér, *n.* one who plaits or braids.

**Plan**, plan, *n.* a drawing of anything on a *plane* or *flat* surface : a ground-plot of a building : a scheme or project : a contrivance.—*v.t.* to make

a sketch of on a flat surface : to form in design :
—*pr.p.* plann'ing ; *pa.t.* and *pa.p.* planned.—*n.*
**Plann'er.** [Fr.—L. *planus*, flat. See **Plain**,
even.]

**Planary,** plăn'ar-i, *adj.* relating to a plane.

**Plane,** plān, *n.* a *level* surface : (*geom.*) an even
superficies.—*adj.*, *plain* : even : level : pertaining to, lying in, or forming a plane.—*v.t.* to
make level. [Fr.—L. *planus.* See **Plain**, even.]

**Plane,** plān, *n.* a carpenter's tool.—*v.t.* to make a
surface (as of wood) level. [Same as above.]

**Planet,** plan'et, *n.* one of the bodies in the solar
system which revolve round the sun. [Fr.
*planète*—Gr. *planētēs*, a wanderer—*planaō*, to
make to wander ; so called because in the
ancient astronomy the planets, among which the
sun and moon were included, seemed to *wander*
about, whilst the other stars seemed fixed.]

**Planetarium,** plan-e-tā'ri-um, *n.* a machine shewing the motions and orbits of the *planets*.

**Planetary,** plan'et-ar-i, *adj.* pertaining to the
*planets* : consisting of or produced by planets :
under the influence of a planet : erratic : revolving.

**Planetoid,** plan'et-oid, *n.* a celestial body having
the *form* or nature of a *planet* : a very small
planet, often called an asteroid. [Gr. *planētēs*,
and *eidos*, form—*eidō*, L. *video*, to see.]

**Plane-tree,** plān'-trē, *n.* a fine tall tree, with large
*broad* leaves. [Fr. *plane*—L. *platanus*—Gr.
*platanos*—*platys*, broad. See **Platane**.]

**Planet-stricken,** plan'et-strik'en, **Planet-struck,**
plan'et-struk, *adj.* (*astrology*) *struck* or affected
by the *planets* : blasted.                            [a *plane*.

**Planisphere,** plan'i-sfēr, *n.* a *sphere* projected on

**Plank,** plangk, *n.* a long, plain piece of timber,
thicker than a board.—*v.t.* to cover with planks.
[L. *planca*, a board, from root of **Plain**, even.]

**Planner,** plan'er, *n.* one who plans or forms a
plan : a projector.

**Plant,** plant, *n.* a sprout : any vegetable production : a child : the tools or material of any trade
or business.—*v.t.* to put into the ground for
growth : to furnish with plants : to set in the
mind : to establish. [A.S. *plante* (Fr. *plante*)
—L. *planta*, a shoot, a plant—nasalised form
of root *plat*, anything flat, 'spread out,' seen in
Gr. *plat-ys*, broad.]

**Plantain,** plan'tān, *n.* an important food-plant of
tropical countries, so called from its *broad* leaf.
[Fr.—L. *plantago*, *plantaginis*, from the root
of **Plant**.]

**Plantation,** plan-tā'shun, *n.* a place *planted* : in
the U.S. a large estate : a colony : introduction.

**Planter,** plant'er, *n.* one who plants or introduces :
the owner of a plantation.

**Plantigrade,** plant'i-grād, *adj.* that walks on the
*sole* of the *foot*.—*n.* a plantigrade animal, as the
bear. [L. *planta*, the sole, *gradior*, to walk.]

**Planting,** plant'ing, *n.* the act of setting in the
ground for growth : the art of forming planta-
tions of trees : a plantation.

**Plash,** plash, a form of **Pleach**.

**Plash,** plash, *n.* a dash of water : a puddle : a
shallow pool.—*v.i.* to dabble in water : to splash.
[From the sound.]                            [puddles : watery.

**Plashy,** plash'i, *adj.* abounding with *plashes* or

**Plaster,** plas'tèr, *n.* something that can be *moulded*
into figures : a composition of lime, water, and
sand for overlaying walls, &c. : (*med.*) an external application spread on cloth, &c.—*adj.*
made of plaster.—*v.t.* to cover with plaster : to
cover with a plaster, as a wound. [A.S. *plaster*,
O. Fr. *plastre*—L. *emplastrum*—Gr. *emplas-
tron*—*em*, upon, *plassō*, to mould, to fashion.]

**Plasterer,** plas'tèr-èr, *n.* one who plasters, or one
who works in plaster.

**Plastering,** plas'tèr-ing, *n.* a covering of plaster :
the plaster-work of a building.

**Plastic,** plas'tik, *adj.*, *moulding:* having power
to give form : capable of being moulded. [Gr.
*plastikos*—*plassō*, to mould.]

**Plasticity,** plas-tis'it-i, *n.* state or quality of
being *plastic*.

**Plat,** *v.t.* Same as **Plait**.

**Plat,** plat, *n.* a piece of ground : a piece of
ground laid out. [A form of **Plot**.]

**Platane,** plat'ān, *n.* the *plane-tree*. [L. *platanus*,
Gr. *platanos*—*platys*, broad, flat.]

**Plate,** plāt, *n.* something *flat* : a thin piece of
metal : wrought gold and silver : household
utensils in gold and silver : a flat dish : an
engraved plate of metal.—*v.t.* to overlay with
a coating of plate or metal : to adorn with
metal : to beat into thin plates.—*n.* **Plate'-glass,**
a fine kind of *glass*, cast in thick *plates*. [O. Fr.
*plate*, fem. of Fr. *plat*, flat—Gr. *platys*, broad.
See **Place**.]

**Plateau,** pla-tō', *n.* a *broad flat* space on an
elevated position : a table-land :—*pl.* **Plateaux'.**
[Fr.—O. Fr. *platel*, dim. of Fr. *plat*. See **Plate**.]

**Platform,** plat'form, *n.* a raised *level* scaffolding :
(*mil.*) an elevated floor for cannon : a statement
of principles to which a body of men declare
their adhesion. [Fr. *plate-forme*, a thing of
'flat form.']

**Platina,** plat'in-a, **Platinum,** plat'in-um, *n.* a
metal of a dim *silvery* appearance. [Sp. *platina*
—*plata*, plate, silver. See **Plate**.]

**Plating,** plāt'ing, *n.* the overlaying with a coating
of *plate* or metal : a thin coating of metal.

**Platitude,** plat'i-tūd, *n.*, *flatness:* that which exhibits dullness : an empty remark.

**Platonic,** pla-ton'ik, **Platonical,** pla-ton'ik-al, *adj.*
pertaining to *Plato*, the Greek philosopher, or
to his philosophical opinions : pure and unmixed
with carnal desires.—*adv.* **Platon'ically.**

**Platonism,** plā'ton-izm, *n.* the philosophical
opinions of *Plato*.—*n.* **Pla'tonist,** a follower of
Plato.

**Platoon,** pla-tōōn', *n.* (*mil.*) orig. a body of soldiers
in a hollow square, now a number of recruits
assembled for exercise : a subdivision of a company. [Lit. 'a *knot* or group of men,' Fr.
*peloton*, a ball, a knot of men—Fr. *pelote*—L.
*pila*, a ball. See **Pellet**.]

**Platter,** plat'er, *n.* a large flat *plate* or dish.

**Plaudit,** plawd'it, *n.*, *applause:* praise bestowed.
[Shortened from L. *plaudite*, praise ye, a call for
applause, 2d pers. pl. imperative of *plaudo*,
*plausum*, to praise.]

**Plauditory,** plawd'it-or-i, *adj.*, *applauding.*

**Plausible,** plawz'i-bl, *adj.* that may be *applauded* :
fitted to gain praise : superficially pleasing : apparently right : popular.—*adv.* **Plaus'ibly.**—*ns.*
**Plaus'ibleness, Plausibil'ity.** [L. *plausibilis*—
*plaudo*, to praise.]

**Play,** plā, *v.i.* to engage in some exercise or in a
*game* : to sport : to trifle : to move irregularly :
to operate : to act in a theatre : to perform on a
musical instrument : to practise a trick : to act
a character : to gamble.—*v.t.* to put in motion :
to perform upon : to perform : to act a sportive
part : to compete with. [A.S. *plega*, a game.]

**Play,** plā, *n.* any exercise for amusement : amusement : a contending for victory : practice in a
contest : gaming : action or use : manner of
dealing, as fair-play : a dramatic composition :
movement : room for motion : liberty of action.

—*n.* Play′bill, a *bill* or advertisement of a *play.*
—*n.* Play′book, a *book* of *plays* or dramas.—*ns.*
Play′fellow, Play′mate, a *fellow* or *mate* in
*play* or amusements.—*n.* Play′thing, any*thing*
for *playing* with: a toy.

Player, plā′er, *n.* one who *plays*: an actor of
plays or dramas: a musician.

Playful, plā′fool, *adj.* given to *play*: sportive.—
*adv.* Play′fully.—*n.* Play′fulness.

Playing-card, plā′ing-kärd, *n.* one of a set of fifty-
two cards used in *playing* games.

Plea, plē, *n.* the defender's answer to the plaintiff's
declaration: an excuse: an apology: urgent
entreaty. [O. Fr. *plait* (Fr. *plaid*)—Low L.
*placitum*, lit. 'what has *pleased* or *seemed good*,'
a decision, a conference, hence, a *pleading*
before a court—L. *placet*, it pleases, seems good
—*placeo*, to please.]

Pleach, plēch, *v.t.* to intertwine the branches of,
as a hedge. [M. E. *plechen*—O. Fr. *plesser*—L.
*plec-tere*, plait, akin to Gr. *plek-ō*, weave. See
Plait and Ply.]

Plead, plēd, *v.i.* to carry on a *plea* or lawsuit: to
argue in support of a cause against another: to
seek to persuade: to admit or deny a charge of
guilt.—*v.t.* to discuss by arguments: to allege
in pleading or defence: to offer in excuse:—
*pa.t.* and *pa.p.* plead′ed, or (less correctly) pled.
—*n.* Plead′er. [Fr. *plaider—plaid*, a plea.
See Plea.]

Pleading, plēd′ing, *adj.* imploring.—*n.pl.* (*law*)
the statements of the two parties in a lawsuit.—
*adv.* Plead′ingly.

Pleasant, plez′ant, *adj., pleasing*: agreeable:
cheerful: gay: trifling.—*adv.* Pleas′antly.—*n.*
Pleas′antness. [Fr. *plaisant*, pr.p. of *plaire.*]

Pleasantry, plez′ant-ri, *n.* anything that promotes
*pleasure*: merriment: lively talk. [Fr. *plai-
santerie—plaisant.*]

Please, plēz, *v.t.* to delight: to satisfy.—*v.i.* to
like: to choose.—*n.* Pleas′er. [O. Fr. *plaisir*
(Fr. *plaire*)—L. *placeo*, to please.]

Pleasing, plēz′ing, *adj.* giving *pleasure*: agreeable: gratifying.—*adv.* Pleas′ingly.

Pleasurable, plezh′ūr-a-bl, *adj.* able to give
*pleasure*: delightful: gratifying.—*adv.* Pleas′-
urably.—*n.* Pleas′urableness.

Pleasure, plezh′ūr, *n.* agreeable emotions: gratification: what the will prefers: purpose: command: approbation.—*v.t.* (*B.*) to give pleasure
to.—*n.* Pleas′ure-boat, a *boat* used for *pleasure*
or amusement.—*n.* Pleas′ure-ground, *ground*
laid out in an ornamental manner for *pleasure.*
[Fr. *plaisir*—L. *placeo.*]

Plebeian, ple-bē′yan, *adj.* pertaining to or consisting of the *common people*: popular: vulgar.
—*n.* orig. one of the common people of ancient
Rome: one of the lower classes. [Fr. *plébéien*—
L. *plebeius—plebs, plebis*, the common people,
conn. with L. *plenus* (Plenary), E. Full, and
lit. sig. a 'crowd,' the 'many.']

Plebiscite, pleb′i-sīt, *n.* a decree passed by the
votes of an entire nation, as in France under
Napoleon III. [Fr.—L. *plebiscitum*, 'decree
of the people,' from *plebs*, the people, and *scitum*,
a decree—*scisco—scio*, to know.]

Pledge, plej, *n.* a security: surety.—*v.t.* to give
as security: to engage for by promise: to invite
to drink by partaking of the cup first: to drink
to the health of.—*n.* Pledg′er. [O. Fr. *plege*
(Fr. *pleige*); ety. dub.]

Pleiads, plē′yadz, Pleiades, plē′ya-dēz, *n.pl.*
(*myth.*) seven daughters of Atlas and Pleione,
after death changed into stars: a group

of seven stars in the shoulder of the constellation Taurus.

Pleiocene, plī′o-sēn, *adj.* (*geol.*) relating to the
strata *more recent* than the miocene or second
tertiary. [Gr. *pleiōn*, more, *kainos*, recent.]

Pleistocene, plīst′o-sēn, *adj.* (*geol.*) pertaining to
the *most recent* tertiary deposits. [Gr. *pleistos*,
most, *kainos*, recent.]

Plenary, plen′ar-i or plē′-, *adj., full*: entire:
complete.—*adv.* Plen′arily.—*n.* Plen′ariness.
[Low L.—L. *ple-nus*, filled, full—*ple-o*, to fill—
Gr. *pim-plē-mi*, akin to Full.]

Plenipotentiary, plen-i-po-ten′shar-i, *adj.* with
*full powers.*—*n.* a negotiator invested with full
powers, esp. a special ambassador or envoy.
[Low L. *plenipotentiarius*—L. *plenus*, and
*potens*, powerful. See Potent.]

Plenitude, plen′i-tūd, *n.* fullness: completeness:
repletion. [L.—*plenus*, full.]

Plenteous, plen′te-us, *adj.* fully sufficient: abundant.—*adv.* Plen′teously.—*n.* Plen′teousness.

Plentiful, plen′ti-fool, *adj.* copious: abundant:
yielding abundance.—*adv.* Plen′tifully.—*n.*
Plen′tifulness.

Plenty, plen′ti, *n.* a *full* supply: abundance.
[O. Fr. *plenté*—L. *plenus*, full.]

Plenum, plē′num, *n.* space considered as in every
part *filled* with matter. [L. See Plenary.]

Pleonasm, plē′o-nazm, *n.* use of *more words* than
are necessary: (*rhet.*) a redundant expression.
[Gr. *pleonasmos—pleiōn*, more, *pleos*, full.]

Pleonastic, plē-o-nas′tik, Pleonastical, plē-o-nas′-
tik-al, *adj.* redundant.—*adv.* Pleonas′tically.
[Gr. *pleonastikos*.]

Plesiosaurus, plē-zi-o-saw′rus, *n.* a gigantic extinct animal, *allied* to the *lizard.* [Gr. *plēsios*,
near to, and *saura*, lizard.]

Plethora, pleth′o-ra, *n.* (*med.*) excessive *fullness*
of blood: over-fullness in any way.—*adj.* Pleth-
or′ic, afflicted with plethora: superabundant:
turgid. [Gr. *plēthōrē*, fullness—*pleos*, full.]

Pleura, plōō′ra, *n.* a delicate serous membrane
which covers the lungs and lines the cavity of
the chest:—*pl.* Pleu′ræ. [Gr., lit. 'a rib,' then
'the side,' then the above membrane.]

Pleurisy, plōō′ri-si, *n.* inflammation of the *pleura.*
[Fr.—L. *pleurisis*—Gr. *pleuritis—pleura.*]

Pleuritic, plōō-rit′ik, Pleuritical, plōō-rit′ik-al,
*adj.* pertaining to or affected with *pleurisy.*

Pleuro-pneumonia, plōō′ro-nu-mō′ni-a, *n.* inflammation of the *pleura* and *lungs.* [Gr. *pleura*,
and *pneumones*, the lungs. See Pneumonia.]

Pliability, plī-a-bil′i-ti, Pliableness, plī′a-bl-nes,
*n.* quality of being pliable or flexible.

Pliable, plī′a-bl, *adj.* easily *bent* or *folded*: supple:
easily persuaded. [See Ply.]

Pliant, plī′ant, *adj.* bending easily: flexible:
tractable: easily persuaded.—*adv.* Pli′antly.
—*n.* Pli′ancy.

Plicate, plī′kāt, Plicated, plī′kāt-ed, *adj.*, folded:
plaited. [L. *plicatus—plico.* See Plait.]

Pliers, plī′erz, *n.pl.* pincers for seizing and *bending.*

Plight, plit, *n.* dangerous condition: condition:
security: pledge: engagement: promise.—*v.t.*
to pledge: to give as security. [A.S. *pliht*, risk
—*plion*, to imperil; cog. with Dut. *pligt*, Ger.
*pflicht*, an obligation.]

Plinth, plinth, *n.* (*arch.*) the lowest *brick*-shaped
part of the base of a column or pedestal: the
projecting face at the bottom of a wall. [L.
*plinthus*—Gr. *plinthos*, a brick; cog. with E.
Flint.]

Pliocene. Same as Pleiocene.

Plod, plod, *v.i.* to travel laboriously: trudge

on steadily : to toil :—*pr.p.* plodd'ing ; *pa.t.* and *pa.p.* plodd'ed. [Orig. 'to wade through pools,' from Ir. *plod*, a pool.]

**Plodder**, plod'ér, *n.* one who plods on : a dull, heavy, laborious man.

**Plodding**, plod'ing, *adj.* laborious, but slow.—*n.* slow movement or study.—*adv.* Plodd'ingly.

**Plot**, plot, *n.* a small piece of ground.—*v.t.* to make a plan of :—*pr.p.* plott'ing ; *pa.t.* and *pa.p.* plott'ed. [A.S. *plot*, a patch of land.]

**Plot**, plot, *n.* a complicated scheme : a conspiracy : stratagem : the chain of incidents in the story of a play, &c.—*v.i.* to scheme : to form a scheme of mischief : to conspire.—*v.t.* to devise :—*pr.p.* plott'ing ; *pa.t.* and *pa.p.* plott'ed. [Fr. *complot*, acc. to Diez, from L. *complicitum*, pa.p. of *complico*, to fold together, to complicate.]

**Plotter**, plot'ér, *n.* one who *plots* : a conspirator.

**Plough**, plow, *n.* an instrument for turning up the soil : tillage.—*v.t.* to turn up with the plough : to furrow : to tear : to divide : to run through in sailing.—*n.* Plough'er. [Ice. *plogr* (Dan. *plov*, Ger. *pflug*), perh. conn. with Gr. *ploion*, a ship.]

**Ploughable**, plow'a-bl, *adj.* capable of being *ploughed* : arable.　　　　　[horses in *ploughing*.

**Ploughboy**, plow'boy, *n.* a *boy* who drives or guides

**Ploughman**, plow'man, *n.* a *man* who *ploughs* : a husbandman : a rustic :—*pl.* Plough'men.

**Ploughshare**, plow'shār, *n.* the part of a *plough* which *shears* or cuts the ground. [Plough and A.S. *scear*, a share of a plough, a shearing—*sceran*, to cut. See Shear.]

**Plover**, pluv'ér, *n.* a well-known wading bird. [Lit. the *rain*-bird, Fr. *pluvier*—L. *pluvia*, rain, cog. with Flow ; so called because associated with rainy weather.]

**Plow**, plow, old spelling of Plough.

**Pluck**, pluk, *v.t.* to *pull* away : to snatch : to strip.—*n.* a single act of plucking. [A.S. *pluccian* ; akin to Dut. *plukken*, Ger. *pflücken*.]

**Pluck**, pluk, *n.* the heart, liver, and lungs of an animal, perh. so called because *plucked* out after it is killed : hence heart, courage, spirit.

**Plucky**, pluk'i, *adj.* having pluck or spirit.—*adv.* Pluck'ily.—*n.* Pluck'iness.

**Plug**, plug, *n.* a *block* or *peg* used to stop a hole.—*v.t.* to stop with a plug : to drive plugs into :—*pr.p.* plugg'ing ; *pa.t.* and *pa.p.* plugged. [Dut. *plug*, a bung, a peg (Sw. *plugg*, a peg, Ger. *pflock*) ; most prob. of Celtic origin, as in Ir., Gael., and W. *ploc*. See Block.]

**Plugging**, plug'ing, *n.* the act of stopping with a *plug* : the material of which a *plug* is made.

**Plum**, plum, *n.* a well-known stone fruit of various colours : the tree producing it. [A.S. *plume*—L. *prunum*—Gr. *prounon*. Doublet Prune.]

**Plumage**, plōm'āj, *n.* the whole *feathers* of a bird. [Fr.—*plume*, a feather. See Plume.]

**Plumb**, plum, *n.* a mass of *lead* or other material, hung on a string, to shew the perpendicular position.—*adj.* perpendicular.—*adv.* perpendicularly.—*v.t.* to adjust by a plumb-line : to make perpendicular : to sound the depth of water by a plumb-line. [Fr. *plomb*—L. *plumbum*, lead, prob. akin to Gr. *molybdos* and Ger. *blei*.]

**Plumbago**, plum-bā'go, *n.* a mineral of carbon and iron, used for pencils, &c., wrongly thought to be *lead*, from its resemblance to it, and hence commonly called 'blacklead.' [L.—*plumbum*, lead. See Plumb.]

**Plumbean**, plum'be-an, **Plumbeous**, plum'be-us, *adj.* consisting of or resembling *lead* : stupid.

**Plumber**, plum'ér, *n.* one who works in *lead*.

**Plumbery**, plum'ér-i, *n.* articles of *lead* : the business of a plumber : a place for plumbing.

**Plumbic**, plum'bik, *adj.* pertaining to or obtained from *lead*.　　　　　[working in *lead*, &c.

**Plumbing**, plum'ing, *n.* the art of casting and

**Plumb-line**, plum'-līn, *n.* a *line* attached to a mass of *lead* to shew the perpendicular : a plummet.

**Plumcake**, plum'kāk, *n.* *cake* containing *plums* (raisins) or other fruit.

**Plume**, plōōm, *n.* a *feather* : a feather worn as an ornament : a crest : token of honour : prize of contest.—*v.t.* to sort the feathers of, as a bird : to adorn with plumes : to strip of feathers : to boast (used reflexively). [Fr.—L. *pluma*, a small soft feather ; perh. from the root of Flow and Float.]

**Plummer, Plummery.** See Plumber, Plumbery.

**Plummet**, plum'et, *n.* a weight of *lead* hung at a string, used for ascertaining the direction of the earth's attraction and for sounding depths : a plumb-line. [Fr. *plombet*, dim. of *plomb*, lead. See Plumb.]　　　　[feathery : plume-like.

**Plumose**, plōō'mōs, **Plumous**, plōō'mus, *adj.*,

**Plump**, plump, *adv.* falling straight downward (like *lead*).—*adj.* downright : unqualified.—*v.i.* to fall or sink suddenly.—*v.t.* to cause to sink suddenly.—*adv.* Plump'ly. [A variation of Plumb.]

**Plump**, plump, *adj.* fat and rounded : sleek : in good condition.—*n.* Plump'ness. [From a common Teut. root, seen in Dut. *plomp*, lumpish, clownish, Ger. *plump*.]

**Plump**, plump, *v.t.* to give in the *lump* or undivided (as a vote to one only). See Plump, *adj.* fat.]

**Plumper**, plump'ér, *n.* a vote given to one candidate only when more are to be elected : one who so votes. [Same as above word.]

**Plumpudding**, plum-pood'ing, *n.* *pudding* containing *plums*, raisins, or other fruit.

**Plumule**, plōō'mūl, *n.* (*bot.*) the rudimentary bud of an embryo. [L. *plumula*, dim. of *pluma*. See Plume.]

**Plunder**, plun'dér, *v.t.* to seize the *baggage* or goods of another by force : to pillage.—*n.* that which is seized by force : booty.—*n.* Plun'derer. [Ger. *plündern*, to pillage—*plunder*, trash, baggage ; akin to Low Ger. *plunnen*, rags.]

**Plunge**, plunj, *v.t.* to cast suddenly into water or other fluid : to force suddenly (into) : to baptise by immersion.—*v.i.* to sink suddenly into any fluid : to dive : to rush headlong, as a horse : to rush into any danger.—*n.* act of plunging : act of rushing headlong, as a horse. [Fr. *plonger* (It. *piombare*, to fall like a plumb-line)—L. *plumbum*, lead.]

**Plunger**, plunj'ér, *n.* one who *plunges* : a diver : a long, solid cylinder used as a forcer in pumps.

**Plunging**, plunj'ing, *adj.* rushing headlong : pitching downward.—*n.* the putting or sinking under water, or other fluid : the act of a horse trying to throw its rider.

**Pluperfect**, plōō'pér-fekt, *adj.* (*gram.*) noting that an action happened before some period referred to. [A corr. of L. *plus-quam-perfectum*, (*lit.*) more than or before perfect.]

**Plural**, plōō'ral, *adj.* containing or expressing *more* than one.—*n.* (*gram.*) the form denoting more than one.—*adv.* Plu'rally. [Fr.—L. *pluralis*—*plus*, *pluris*, more.]

**Pluralism**, plōō'ral-izm, *n.* the state of being plural : the holding of more than one ecclesiastical living.

**Pluralist**, plōō'ral-ist, *n.* a clergyman who holds more than one benefice with cure of souls.

**Plurality,** plōō-ral′i-ti, *n.* the state of being plural: a number consisting of more than one : the majority : the holding of more than one benefice with cure of souls.

**Plus,** plus, *n.* the sign ( + ) prefixed to positive quantities, and set between quantities or numbers to be added together. [L. *plus,* more.]

**Plush,** plush, *n.* a variety of cloth woven like velvet, but having its *pile* or *hairy* surface uncropped. [Fr. *peluche,* through Low L., from L. *pilus,* hair. See **Pile,** a hairy surface.]

**Plutocracy,** plōō-tok′ra-si, *n.,* *government* by the *wealthy.* [Gr. *ploutokratia—ploutos,* wealth, and *kratos,* strength, akin to E. **Hard.**]

**Plutonian,** plōō-tō′ni-an, **Plutonic,** plōō-ton′ik, *adj. infernal* : dark : (*geol.*) formed by the agency of heat at a depth below the surface of the earth. [L. (*lit.*) belonging to *Pluto*—Gr. *Ploutōnios—Ploutōn,* Pluto, the god of the nether world.]

**Pluvial,** plōō′vi-al, *adj.* pertaining to *rain* : rainy. [Fr.—L. *pluvialis—pluvia,* rain, akin to **Flow.**]

**Pluvious,** plōō′vi-us, *adj.* rainy. [L. *pluvius.* See **Pluvial.**]

**Ply,** plī, *v.t.* to work at steadily : to urge.—*v.i.* to work steadily : to go in haste : to make regular passages between two ports : (*naut.*) to make way against the wind :—*pa.t.* and *pa.p.* plied.—*n.* a fold : bent : direction. [Fr. *plier,* to bend or fold—L. *plico,* to bend ; Gr. *plekō,* to fold.]

**Pneumatic,** nū-mat′ik, **Pneumatical,** nū-mat′ik-al, *adj.* relating to *air* : consisting of air : moved by air or wind : pertaining to pneumatics. —*adv.* **Pneumat′ically.** [L.—Gr. *pneumatikos —pneum-a, -atos,* wind, air—*pneō,* to blow, to breathe.]

**Pneumatics,** nū-mat′iks, *n.sing.* the science which treats of *air* and other elastic fluids or gases.

**Pneumatologist,** nū-mat-ol′o-jist, *n.* one versed in pneumatology.

**Pneumatology,** nū-mat-ol′o-ji, *n.* the science of elastic *fluids,* or, more generally, of spiritual substances. [Gr. *pneuma,* wind, spirit, and *logos,* science.]

**Pneumonia,** nū-mō′ni-a, *n.* inflammation of the *lungs.* [Gr. from *pneumōn, pneumonis,* the lungs—*pneuma,* air.] [*lungs.*

**Pneumonic,** nū-mon′ik, *adj.* pertaining to the

**Poach,** pōch, *v.t.* to dress eggs by breaking them into boiling water. [Perh. Fr. *pocher,* to put in a pocket—*poche,* pouch, because the yolk is enveloped by the white as in a *pouch.*]

**Poach,** pōch, *v.i.* to intrude on another's preserves in order to steal game.—*v.t.* to steal game.—*n.* **Poach′er,** one who poaches or steals game. [Fr. *pocher,* orig. to pocket—*poche,* pouch. Cf. above word.]

**Pock,** pok, *n.* a small elevation of the skin containing matter, as in smallpox.—*ns.* **Pock′mark, Pock′pit,** the mark, pit, or scar left by a *pock.* [A.S. *poc,* a pustule ; cog. with Ger. *pocke,* Dut. *pok.* The correct pl. form was *pocks,* erroneously spelt *pox,* and treated as sing.]

**Pocket,** pok′et, *n.* a *little pouch* or bag, esp. one attached to a dress.—*v.t.* to put in the pocket : to take stealthily :—*pr.p.* pock′eting ; *pa.t.* and *pa.p.* pock′eted.—*n.* **Pock′et-book,** a *book* for holding papers carried in the *pocket.*—*n.* **Pock′et-mon′ey,** *money* carried in the *pocket* for ordinary expenses. [Fr. *pochette,* dim. of *poche,* pouch.]

**Pod,** pod, *n.* the covering of the seed of plants, as the pea or bean.—*v.i.* to fill, as a pod : to produce pods :—*pr.p.* podd′ing ; *pa.t.* and *pa.p.* podd′ed.

[Allied to **Pad,** anything stuffed, and to Dan. *pude,* a cushion, from a root meaning 'bag,' anything 'swollen out.' See **Pudding.**]

**Poem,** pō′em, *n.* a composition in verse. [Lit. 'anything made,' Fr. *poème*—L. *poema*—Gr. *poiēma—poieō,* to do or make.]

**Poesy,** pō′e-si, *n.* the art of *composing poems* : poetry : a poem. [Fr. *poësie*—L. *poesis*—Gr. *poiēsis—poieō,* to do or make.]

**Poet,** pō′et, *n.* the author of a poem : one skilled in making poetry : one with a strong imagination :—*fem.* **Po′etess.** [Lit. 'a maker,' Fr. *poète* —L. *poeta*—Gr. *poiētēs—poieō,* to do or make.]

**Poetaster,** pō′et-as-tėr, *n.* a *petty poet* : a writer of contemptible verses. [Freq. of **Poet.**]

**Poetic,** po-et′ik, **Poetical,** po-et′ik-al, *adj.* pertaining or suitable to *poetry* : expressed in poetry : marked by poetic language : imaginative.—*adv.* **Poet′ically,** in a poetic manner.

**Poetics,** po-et′iks, *n.sing.* the branch of criticism which relates to *poetry.* [verses.

**Poetise,** pō′et-īz, *v.i.* to write as a *poet* : to make

**Poetry,** pō′et-ri, *n.* the art of expressing in melodious words the creations of feeling and imagination : utterance in song : metrical composition. [O. Fr. *poeterie.*]

**Poignancy,** poin′an-si, *n.* state of being *poignant.*

**Poignant,** poin′ant, *adj.,* *stinging, pricking* : sharp : penetrating : acutely painful : satirical : pungent.—*adv.* **Poign′antly.** [Fr. *poignant,* pr.p. of O. Fr. *poindre,* to sting—L. *pungo,* to sting, to prick. See **Point** and **Pungent.**]

**Point,** point, *n.* that which *pricks* or *pierces* : anything coming to a sharp end : the mark made by a sharp instrument : (*geom.*) that which has neither length, breadth, nor thickness : a mark shewing the divisions of a sentence : (*mus.*) a dot at the right hand of a note, to raise its value one-half : a very small space : a moment of time : a small affair : a single thing : a single assertion : the precise thing to be considered : anything intended : exact place : degree : that which stings, as the *point* of an epigram : a lively turn of thought : that which awakens attention : a peculiarity :—*pl.* the switch on a railway. [Fr. (*pl. punta*)—L. *punctum—pungo*—root *pug.* See **Poignant.**]

**Point,** point, *v.t.* to give a *point* to : to sharpen : to aim : to direct one's attention : to punctuate, as a sentence : to fill the joints of with mortar, as a wall.—*v.i.* to direct the finger towards an object : to shew game by looking, as a dog.— **Point out** (*B.*) to assign.

**Point-blank,** point′-blank′, *adj.* aimed directly at the mark : direct.—*adv.* directly. [Lit. the *white spot* in the butt at which archers aimed, from Fr. *point-blanc,* white point. See **Blank.**]

**Pointed,** point′ed, *adj.* having a sharp *point* : sharp : direct : personal : keen : telling : (*arch.*) having arches sharply pointed, Gothic.—*adv.* **Point′edly.**—*n.* **Point′edness.**

**Pointer,** point′ėr, *n.* that which *points* : a dog trained to point out game.

**Pointing,** point′ing, *n.* the marking of divisions in writing by *points* or marks : act of filling the crevices of a wall with mortar.

**Pointless,** point′les, *adj.* having *no point* : blunt : dull : wanting keenness or smartness.

**Pointsman,** points′man, *n.* a *man* who has charge of the *points* or switches on a railway.

**Poise,** poiz, *v.t.* to balance : to make of equal weight : to examine.—*n.* weight : balance : equilibrium : that which balances, a regulating power : the weight used with steelyards. [O.

Fr. *poiser*, Fr. *peser*—L. *penso*, inten. of *pendo*, to hang, to weigh.]

**Poison**, poi′zn, *n.* any substance having injurious or deadly effects: anything malignant or infectious: that which taints or destroys moral purity.—*v.t.* to infect or to kill with poison: to taint: to mar: to imbitter: to corrupt.—*n.* **Poi′soner.** [Lit. a *potion* or *draught*, Fr.—L. *potio*, a draught—*poto*, to drink. Doublet **Potion.**]

**Poisonous**, poi′zn-us, *adj.* having the quality of *poison*: destructive: impairing soundness or purity.—*adv.* **Poi′sonously.**—*n.* **Poi′sonousness.**

**Poke**, pōk, *n.* a bag: a pouch. [Prob. from Celt., as Ir. *poc*, a bag. Cf. **Pouch, Pock.**]

**Poke**, pōk, *v.t.* to thrust or push against with something pointed: to search for with a long instrument: to thrust at with the horns.—*v.i.* to grope or feel.—*n.* act of pushing or thrusting: a thrust. [Ir. *poc*, a blow, Gael. *puc*, to push.]

**Poker**, pōk′er, *n.* an iron rod for *poking* or stirring the fire.

**Polar**, pō′lar, *adj.* pertaining to or situated near either of the poles: pertaining to the magnetic poles.—**Polar circle**, a parallel of latitude encircling each of the poles at a distance of 23° 28′ from the pole; the north polar being called the arctic, the south, the antarctic circle.

**Polarisation**, pō-lar-i-zā′shun, *n.* (*opt.*) a particular modification of rays of light, by the action of certain media or surfaces, so that they cannot be reflected or refracted again in certain directions: state of having polarity.

**Polarise**, pō′lar-īz, *v.t.* to give *polarity* to.—*n.* **Po′lariser**, that which polarises or gives polarity to.

**Polarity**, pō-lar′it-i, *n.* a property in certain bodies by which they arrange themselves in certain directions, or point, as it were, to given poles.

**Pole**, pōl, *n.* that on which anything turns, as a pivot or axis: one of the ends of the axis of a sphere, esp. of the earth: (*physics*) one of the two points of a body in which the attractive or repulsive energy is concentrated, as a magnet.—**Poles of the heavens**, the two points in the *heavens* opposite to the *poles* of the earth.—*n.* **Pole-star**, a *star* at or near the *pole* of the heavens. [Fr.—L. *polus*—Gr. *polos*—*pelō*, to be in motion.]

**Pole**, pōl, *n.* a *pale* or *pile*: a long piece of wood: an instrument for measuring: a measure of length, 5½ yards; in square measure, 30¼ yards.—*n.* **Poleaxe**, an *axe* fixed on a *pole*. [A.S. *pál* (Ger. *pfahl*)—L. *palus*, a stake. Doublet **Pale.**]

**Pole**, pōl, *n.* a native of Poland.

**Polecat**, pōl′kat, *n.* a kind of weasel, which emits a disagreeable odour, called also the **Fitchet** and **Foumart**. [M. E. *polcat*, ety. of *Pole*-unknown. See **Cat.**]

**Polemic**, po-lem′ik, **Polemical**, po-lem′ik-al, *adj.* given to disputing: controversial.—*adv.* **Polem′ically.** [Lit. 'warlike,' Gr. *polemos*, war.]

**Polemic**, po-lem′ik, *n.* a disputant.—*n.sing.* **Polem′ics**, contest or controversy: (*theol.*) the history of ecclesiastical controversy.

**Polenta**, po-len′ta, *n.* pudding made of the flour of maize. [It.—L. *polenta*, peeled barley.]

**Police**, po-lēs′, *n.* the system of regulations of a city, town, or district, for the preservation of order and enforcement of law: the internal government of a state: (short for *police-force*) the civil officers for preserving order, &c.—*n.* **Police′man.** [Fr.—L. *politia*—Gr. *politeia*,

the condition of a state—*politeuō*, to govern a state—*politēs*, a citizen—*polis*. a city, from root of *polys*, many, E. **Full.**]

**Policy**, pol′i-si, *n.* the art or manner of governing a nation: a system of official administration: dexterity of management: prudence: cunning: in Scotland, the pleasure-grounds around a mansion. [O. Fr. *policie* (Fr. *police*)—L. &c. See **Police.**]

**Policy**, pol′i-si, *n.* a warrant for money in the funds: a writing containing a contract of insurance. [Fr. *police*, a policy—L. *polyptychum*, a register—Gr. *polyptychon*, a writing folded into leaves—*polys*, many, *ptyx*, *ptychos*, fold, leaf.]

**Polish**, pōl′ish, *adj.* relating to Poland or its people.

**Polish**, pol′ish, *v.t.* to make smooth and glossy by rubbing: to refine: to make elegant.—*v.i.* to become smooth and glossy.—*n.* **Pol′isher.** [Fr. *polir*, *polissant*—L. *polio*, to make to shine.]

**Polite**, po-līt′, *adj.*, *polished*: smooth: refined: well-bred: obliging.—*adv.* **Polite′ly.**—*n.* **Polite′ness.** [L. *politus*, pa.p. of *polio*.]

**Politic**, pol′i-tik, *adj.* pertaining to *policy*: well-devised: judicious: skilled in political affairs: prudent: discreet: cunning.—*adv.* **Pol′iticly.** [Fr. *politique*—Gr. *politikos*—*politēs*, a citizen.]

**Political**, po-lit′ik-al, *adj.* pertaining to *polity* or government: pertaining to nations: derived from government.—*adv.* **Polit′ically.**—**Political Economy**, the science which treats of the production, distribution, and consumption of wealth.

**Politician**, pol-i-tish′an, *n.* one versed in or devoted to *politics*: a man of artifice and cunning.

**Politics**, pol′i-tiks, *n.sing.* the art or science of *government*: the management of a political party: political affairs.

**Polity**, pol′i-ti, *n.* the constitution of the *government* of a state: civil constitution.

**Polka**, pōl′ka, *n.* a dance of Bohemian origin: also its tune. [Bohem. *pulka*, half, from the half-step prevalent in it; also given from Slav. *polka*, a Polish woman.]

**Poll**, pol, *n.* a familiar name, often a parrot. [Contr. of *Polly*, a form of *Molly* = *Mary*.]

**Poll**, pōl, *n.* the round part of the head, esp. the back of it: a register of heads or persons: the entry of the names of electors who vote for civil officers, such as members of parliament: an election of civil officers: the place where the votes are taken.—*v.t.* to remove the top: to cut: to clip: to lop, as the branches of a tree: to enter one's name in a register: to bring to the poll as a voter.—*n.* **Poll′er.** [O. Dut. *polle*, *bol*, a ball, top, Ice. *kollr*, top, head. Cf. **Kill.**]

**Pollack**, pol′ak, **Pollock**, pol′uk, *n.* a sea-fish of the cod family, resembling the whiting. [Celt., as in Gael. *pollag*, a whiting.] [off.

**Pollard**, pol′ard, *n.* a tree *polled* or with its top cut

**Pollen**, pol′en, *n.* the fertilising powder contained in the anthers of flowers: fine flour. [L. 'fine flour.']

**Pollock**. See **Pollack.**

**Poll-tax**, pōl′-taks, *n.* a *tax* by the poll or head—*i.e.* on each person.

**Pollute**, pol-lōōt′, *v.t.* to soil: to defile: to make foul: to taint: to corrupt: to profane: to violate.—*n.* **Pollut′er.** [Lit. 'to overflow,' L. *polluo*, *pollutus*—*pol*, sig. towards, and *luo*, to wash.]

**Pollution**, pol-lōō′shun, *n.* act of *polluting*: state of being polluted: defilement: impurity. [L.]

**Polo**, pō′lo, *n.* a military game, devised by the British officers in India, in which a ball is played between two goals by men on horseback.

**Polony,** po-lō′ni, *n.* a dry sausage made of meat partly cooked. [A corr. of *Bologna sausage.*]

**Poltroon,** pol-trōōn′, *n.* an idle, lazy fellow : a coward : a dastard : one without courage or spirit.—*adj.* base, vile, contemptible. [Lit. 'one who lies in bed,' Fr. *poltron*—It. *poltro* (for *polstro*), orig. a bed, from Ger. *polster,* a bolster. See Bolster.]

**Poltroonery,** pol-trōōn′ér-i, *n.* the spirit of a *poltroon* : laziness : cowardice : want of spirit. [Fr. *poltronnerie.*]

**Polverine,** pol′vèr-īn or -in, *n.* the *dust* or calcined ashes of a plant, used in glass-making. [It. *polverino*—L. *pulvis, pulveris,* dust.]

**Polyandrian,** pol-i-an′dri-an, *adj.* having many or more than twenty stamens. [Gr. *polys,* many, and *anēr, andros,* a man.]

**Polyandry,** pol-i-an′dri, *n.* the practice of the woman having more husbands than one at the same time ; cf. Polygamy. [Gr., from *polys,* many, and *anēr, andros,* a husband.]

**Polyanth,** pol′i-anth, **Polyanthus,** pol-i-an′thus, *n.* a kind of primrose bearing *many flowers.* [Gr., from *polys,* many, and *anthos,* a flower.]

**Polycotyledon,** pol-i-kot-i-lē′don, *n.* a plant having *many cotyledons* or seed-lobes.—*adj.* **Polycotyle′donous.** [Gr. *polys,* many, and Cotyledon.]

**Polygamist,** pol-ig′a-mist, *n.* one who practises or advocates *polygamy.*

**Polygamy,** pol-ig′a-mi, *n.* the having more than one wife at the same time.—*adj.* **Polyg′amous.** [Fr.—L.—Gr. *polygamia—polys,* many, and *gamos,* a marriage. Cf. Bigamy.]

**Polyglot,** pol′i-glot, *adj.* having or containing *many languages.*—*n.* a book in several languages, esp. a Bible of this kind. [From Gr. *polys,* many, and *glotta,* the tongue, language.]

**Polygon,** pol′i-gon, *n.* a figure of *many angles,* or with more than four.—*adjs.* **Polyg′onal, Polyg′onous.** [L.—Gr. *polygōnon—polys,* many, and *gōnia,* a corner. See Knee.]

**Polyhedron,** pol-i-hē′dron, *n.* a solid body with *many bases* or sides.—*adjs.* **Polyhe′dral, Polyhe′drous.** [Gr. *polys,* many, and *hedra,* a base —*hed,* akin to E. Sit.]

**Polynomial,** pol-i-nō′mi-al, *n.* an algebraic quantity of *many names* or terms.—*adj.* of many names or terms. [A hybrid, from Gr. *polys,* many, and L. *nomen,* a name.]

**Polyp, Polype,** pol′ip, **Polypus,** pol′i-pus, *n.* something with *many feet* or roots : an aquatic animal of the radiate kind, with many arms : a tumour growing in the nose, &c. :—*pl.* **Polypes,** pol′ips, **Polypi,** pol′i-pī.—*adj.* **Pol′ypous.** [Gr. *polypous—polys,* many, and *pous,* E. Foot.]

**Polypetalous,** pol-i-pet′al-us, *adj.* with *many petals.* [Gr. *polys,* many, and Petalous.]

**Polypode,** pol′i-pōd, *n.* an animal with *many feet.* [Gr. *polypous—polys,* many, *pous, podos,* a foot.]

**Polypus.** See Polyp.

**Polysyllable,** pol′i-sil-a-bl, *n.* a word of *many* or more than three *syllables.*—*adjs.* **Polysyllab′ic, Polysyllab′ical.** [Gr. *polys,* many, and Syllable.]

**Polytechnic,** pol-i-tek′nik, *adj.* comprehending *many arts.* [Gr. *polys,* many, *technē,* an art.]

**Polytheism,** pol′i-thē-izm, *n.* the doctrine of a *plurality* of *gods.*—*adjs.* **Polytheist′ic, Polytheist′ical.**—*n.* **Pol′ytheist,** a believer in many gods. [Gr. *polys,* many, and *theos,* a god.]

**Pomace,** po-mās′ or pum′as, *n.* the substance of *apples* or similar fruit. [Low L. *pomacium*—L. *pomum,* fruit such as apples, &c.]

**Pomaceous,** po-mā′shus, *adj.* relating to, consisting of, or resembling *apples* : like pomace.

**Pomade,** po-mād′, **Pomatum.** po-mā′tum, *n.* (*orig.*) an ointment made from *apples*: any greasy composition for dressing the hair. [Fr. *pommade*—It. *pomada, pommata,* lip-salve—L. *pomum,* an apple.]

**Pomegranate,** pōm′gran-āt or pum′-, *n.* a tree bearing *fruit* like the orange, with numerous *grains* or seeds. [Through the O. Fr. from L. *pomum,* and *granatum,* having many grains—*granum,* a grain. See Grain.]

**Pommel,** pum′el, *n.* a knob or ball : the knob on a sword-hilt : the high part of a saddle-bow.—*v.t.* to beat as with a pommel, or anything thick or heavy : to bruise :—*pr.p.* pomm′elling ; *pa.t.* and *pa.p.* pomm′elled. [Lit. 'anything round like an apple,' O. Fr. *pomel* (Fr. *pommeau*), dim. of L. *pomum,* an apple.]

**Pomp,** pomp, *n.* pageantry : ceremony : splendour : ostentation : grandeur. [Lit. 'a sending,' then 'a showy procession,' Fr. *pompe*—L. *pompa*—Gr. *pompē—pempō,* to send.]

**Pompous,** pomp′us, *adj.* displaying *pomp* or grandeur : grand : magnificent : dignified : boastful.—*adv.* **Pomp′ously.**—*ns.* **Pomp′ousness, Pompos′ity.**

**Pond,** pond, *n.* a pool of standing water. [From A.S. *pyndan,* to shut in, thus a doublet of **Pound,** an inclosure.]

**Ponder,** pon′dèr, *v.t.* to *weigh* in the mind : to think over : to consider.—*n.* **Pon′derer.** [Lit. to 'weigh,' L. *pondero—pondus, ponderis,* a weight. See Pound, a weight.]

**Ponderable,** pon′dèr-a-bl, *adj.* that may be *weighed* : having sensible weight.—*n.* **Ponderabil′ity.**

**Ponderous,** pon′dèr-us, *adj., weighty* : massive : forcible : important.—*adv.* **Pon′derously.**

**Ponderousness,** pon′dèr-us-nes, **Ponderosity,** pon-dèr-os′i-ti, *n.* weight : heaviness.

**Poniard,** pon′yard, *n.* a small dagger for stabbing. —*v.t.* to stab with a poniard. [Fr. *poignard* —*poing,* fist (It. *pugno*)—L. *pugnus.*]

**Pontage,** pont′aj, *n.* a *toll* paid on *bridges.* [Low L. *pontagium*—L. *pons, pontis,* a bridge, a nasalised form of the root of Path.]

**Pontiff,** pon′tif, *n.* (*orig.*) a Roman high-priest : in the R. Cath. Church, the Pope. [Fr. *pontife*—L. *pontifex, pontificis—pons, pont-is,* a bridge, and *facio,* to make or do, the original meaning being obscure.]

**Pontific,** pon-tif′ik, **Pontifical,** pon-tif′ik-al, *adj.* of or belonging to a *pontiff* or the Pope : splendid : magnificent.—*n.* a book of ecclesiastical ceremonies.—*n.* **Pontif′icals,** the dress of a priest, bishop, or Pope. [Fr.—L. *pontificalis.*]

**Pontificate,** pon-tif′i-kāt, *n.* the dignity of a *pontiff* or high-priest : the office and dignity or reign of a Pope. [Fr.—L. *pontificatus.*]

**Pontoon,** pon-tōōn′, *n.* a portable floating vessel used in forming a bridge for the passage of an army : a bridge of boats : a lighter. [Fr. *ponton* —L. *pons,* a bridge. See Pontage.]

**Pony,** pō′ni, *n.* a *small* horse. [Gael. *ponaidh.*]

**Poodle,** pōō′dl, *n.* a small dog with long silky hair. [Ger. *pudel*; akin to Low Ger. *pudeln,* to waddle.]

**Pooh,** pōō, *int.* of disdain. [Imitative.]

**Pool,** pōōl, *n.* a small body of water. [A.S. *pōl* (Dut. *poel,* Ger. *pfuhl*)—Celt. *poll, pwll*; akin to L. *palus,* a marsh, Gr. *pēlos,* mud.]

**Pool,** pōōl, *n.* the receptacle for the stakes in certain games : the stakes themselves : a variety of play at billiards. [Fr. *poule,* orig. a hen (the stakes being jocularly compared to eggs in a nest)—L. *pullus,* a young animal, E. Foal.]

**Poop,** pōōp, *n.* the hinder part of a ship: a deck above the ordinary deck in the after-part of a ship.—*v.t.* to strike the stern. [Fr. *poupe*—L. *puppis,* the poop.]

**Poor,** pōōr, *adj.* without means: needy: spiritless: depressed: (*B.*) humble: contrite: wanting in appearance: lean: wanting in strength: weak: wanting in value: inferior: wanting in fertility: sterile: wanting in fitness, beauty, or dignity: trifling: paltry: dear (endearingly). — *adv.* **Poor′ly.**—*n.* **Poor′ness.** [O. Fr. *poure, povre* (Fr. *pauvre*)—L. *pau-per = pauca pariens,* producing or providing little, from *paucus,* little, and *pario,* to produce.]

**Poorhouse,** pōōr′hows, *n.* a *house* established at the public expense for the benefit of the *poor.*

**Poor-laws,** pōōr′-lawz, *n., laws* relating to the support of the *poor.* [of the *poor.*

**Poor-rate,** pōōr′-rāt, *n.* a *rate* or tax for the support

**Poor-spirited,** pōōr-spir′it-ed, *adj.. poor* or mean in *spirit:* cowardly: base.—*n.* **Poor-spir′itedness.**

**Pop,** pop, *v.i.* to make a sharp, quick sound: to dart: to move quickly.—*v.t.* to thrust suddenly: to bring suddenly to notice:—*pr.p.* **pop′ping;** *pa.t.* and *pa.p.* **popped.**—*n.* a sharp, quick sound or report.—*adv.* suddenly. [From the sound.]

**Pope,** pōp, *n.* the bishop of Rome, head of the R. Cath. Church : a kind of perch. [A.S. *pápa* —L. *papa,* a father. See **Papa.**]

**Popedom,** pōp′dom, *n.* office, dignity, or jurisdiction of the *Pope.* [A.S. *pápedóm.*]

**Popery,** pōp′ér-i, *n.* the religion of which the *Pope* is the head : Roman Catholicism.

**Popinjay,** pop′in-jā, *n.* (*orig.*) a parrot : a mark like a parrot, put on a pole to be shot at : a fop or coxcomb. [Lit. the 'babbling cock,' Fr. *papegai,* from the imitative root *pap* or *bab,* to chatter, and Fr. *gau*—L. *gallus,* a cock.]

**Popish,** pōp′ish, *adj.* relating to the *Pope* or *Popery:* taught by Popery.—*adv.* **Pop′ishly.**

**Poplar,** pop′lar, *n.* a tree common in the northern hemisphere, of rapid growth, and having soft wood. [O. Fr. *poplier* (Fr. *peuplier*)—L. *pōpulus.*]

**Poplin,** pop′lin, *n.* a fabric made of silk and worsted. [Fr. *popeline.* Ety. unknown.]

**Poppy,** pop′i, *n.* a plant having large showy flowers, from one species of which opium is obtained. [A.S. *popig*—L. *papaver.*]

**Populace,** pop′ū-lās or -las, *n.* the common *people.* [Fr.—It. *popolazzo*—L. *populus.* See **People.**]

**Popular,** pop′ū-lar, *adj.* pertaining to the *people:* pleasing to or prevailing among the people : easily comprehended : inferior : vulgar.—*adv.* **Pop′ularly.** [Fr. *populaire*—L. *popularis*— *ropulus.*] [suitable to the people.

**Popularise,** pop′ū-lar-īz, *v.t.* to make *popular* or

**Popularity,** pop-ū-lar′i-ti, *n.* quality or state of being *popular* or pleasing to the people.

**Populate,** pop′ū-lāt, *v.t.* to *people:* to furnish with inhabitants. [L. *populor, populatus*— *populus.*] [the inhabitants of any place.

**Population,** pop-ū-lā′shun, *n.* act of *populating:*

**Populous,** pop′ū-lus, *adj.* full of *people:* numerously inhabited.—*adv.* **Pop′ulously.**—*n.* **Pop′ulousness.**

**Porcelain,** pors′lān, *n.* a fine kind of earthenware, white, thin, and semi-transparent. [Fr. *porcelaine*—It. *porcellana,* the Venus' shell (which porcelain resembles in transparency)—L. *porcella,* a young sow (which the shell was thought to resemble in form), dim. from *porcus,* a pig.]

**Porch,** pōrch, *n.* a covered way or entrance : a portico at the *entrance* of churches and other buildings : the public porch in the forum of Athens where Zeno the Stoic taught : (*fig.*) the Stoic philosophy. [Fr. *porche* (It. *portico*)—L. *porticus,* from *porta,* a gate, entrance. See **Port,** a gate.]

**Porcine,** por′sīn, *adj.* pertaining to *swine.* [L. *porcinus*—*porcus,* a swine.]

**Porcupine,** por′kū-pīn, *n.* a rodent quadruped, covered with spines or quills. [Lit. the spiny hog,' M. E. *porkepyn*—O. Fr. *porc espin*—L. *porcus,* a pig, and *spina,* a spine.]

**Pore,** pōr, *n.* (*anat.*) a minute *passage* in the skin for the perspiration : an opening between the molecules of a body. [Fr.—L. *porus*—Gr. *poros;* akin to **Fare** and **Ferry.**]

**Pore,** pōr, *v.i.* to look with steady attention on : to study closely. [Perh. akin to **Peer,** to peep.]

**Poriform,** pōr′i-form, *adj.* in the *form* of a pore.

**Pork,** pork, *n.* the flesh of *swine.* [Fr. *porc*—L. *porcus,* a hog ; cog. with W. *porch* and E. **Farrow.** See **Farrow.**] [pork.

**Porker,** pork′èr, *n.* a *young hog:* a pig fed for

**Porosity,** pō-ros′i-ti, *n.* quality of being *porous.*

**Porous,** pōr′us, *adj.* having *pores.*—*adv.* **Por′ously.** [porphyry.

**Porphyrise,** por′fir-īz, *v.t.* to cause to resemble

**Porphyritic,** por-fir-it′ik, **Porphyraceous,** por-fir-ā′shus, *adj.* resembling or consisting of *porphyry.*

**Porphyry,** por′fir-i, *n.* a very hard, variegated rock, of a *purple* and white colour, used in sculpture. [Through Fr. and L., from Gr. *porphyrites*—*porphyra,* purple. Cf. **Purple.**]

**Porpoise,** por′pus, **Porpess,** por′pes, *n.* a gregarious kind of whale, from 4 to 8 feet long, caught for its oil and flesh. [Lit. the hog-fish,' O. Fr. *porpeis*—L. *porcus,* a hog, and *piscis,* a fish, from its hog-like appearance in the water.]

**Porridge,** por′ij, *n.* a kind of pudding usually made by slowly stirring oatmeal amongst boiling water : a kind of broth. [M. E. *porree,* through O. Fr., from Low L. *porrata,* broth made with *leeks*—L. *porrum,* a leek. The affix -*idge* (= -*age*) arose through confusion with **Pottage.**]

**Porringer,** por′in-jèr, *n.* a small dish for *porridge.* [*Porriger,* with inserted *n.* Cf. **Passenger.**]

**Port,** port, *n.,* bearing : demeanour : carriage of the body : the left side of a ship.—*v.t.* to put (as the helm) to the left side of a ship (*lit.* to 'carry') : to hold, as a musket, in a slanting direction upward across the body. [Fr.—L. *porto,* to carry, cog. with **Fare.**]

**Port,** pōrt, *n.* a *harbour:* a haven or safe station for vessels. [A.S.—L. *portus;* akin to *porta,* a gate.]

**Port,** pōrt, *n.* a *gate* or *entrance:* a porthole : lid of a porthole. [Fr. *porte*—L. *porta,* from root of **Fare.**]

**Port,** pōrt, *n.* a dark purple wine from *Oporto* in Portugal. [*Oporto* = (*lit.*) 'the port.']

**Portable,** pōrt′a-bl, *adj.* that may be *carried:* not bulky or heavy.—*n.* **Port′ableness.** [See **Port,** bearing.] [price of carriage.

**Portage,** pōrt′āj, *n.* act of *carrying:* carriage :

**Portal,** pōrt′al, *n.* a *small gate:* any entrance : (*arch.*) the arch over a gate : the lesser of two gates. [O. Fr. (Fr. *portail*)—Low L. *portale.*]

**Port-crayon,** pōrt-krā′on, *n.* a metallic handle for *holding* a *crayon.* [L. *porto,* to carry. **Crayon.**]

**Portcullis,** port-kul′is, *n.* a *sliding door* of cross timbers pointed with iron, hung over a gateway, so as to be let down in a moment to keep out an enemy. [Fr. *portecoulisse,* from *porte,* a gate, and L. *cōlo,* to filter, to slide. See **Colander.**]

**Porte,** pŏrt, *n.* the Turkish government, so called from the 'High Gate,' the chief office of the Ottoman government. [See **Port,** a gate.]

**Portend,** por-tend', *v.t.* to indicate the future by signs: to betoken: presage. [Lit. 'to stretch towards,' L. *portendo, portentus—pro,* forth, and *tendo,* to stretch. See **Tend,** to stretch.]

**Portent,** por'tent, *n.* that which *portends* or foreshows: an evil omen. [O. Fr.—L.]

**Portentous,** por-tent'us, *adj.* serving to *portend:* foreshadowing ill.—*adv.* **Portent'ously.**

**Porter,** pŏrt'ėr, *n.* a *door*-keeper or *gate*-keeper: one who waits at the door to receive messages.—*fem.* **Port'eress** or **Port'ress.** [See **Port,** a gate.]

**Porter,** pŏrt'ėr, *n.* one who *carries* burdens for hire: a dark-brown malt liquor—so called because it was a favourite drink with London *porters.*

**Porterage,** pŏrt'ėr-āj, *n.* charge made by a *porter.*

**Portfolio,** pŏrt-fō'li-ō, *n.* a portable case for keeping loose papers, drawings, &c.: a collection of such papers: the office of a minister of state. [From L. *porto,* to carry, and **Folio,** a sheet of paper; cf. Fr. *portefeuille.*]

**Porthole,** pŏrt'hōl, *n.* a *hole* or *opening* in a ship's side for light and air, or for pointing a gun through. [**Port,** a gate, and **Hole.**]

**Portico,** pŏr'ti-kō, *n.* (*arch.*) a range of columns in the front of a building:—*pl.* **Porticoes** or **Porticos,** pŏr'ti-kōz. [It.—L. *porticus.* Doublet **Porch.**] [tico.

**Porticoed,** pŏr'ti-kōd, *adj.* furnished with a por-

**Portion,** pŏr'shun, *n.* a *part:* an allotment: dividend: the part of an estate descending to an heir: a wife's fortune.—*v.t.* to divide into portions: to allot a share: to furnish with a portion. [Fr.—L. *portio, portionis,* akin to *pars,* a part, and Gr. *porō,* to share.]

**Portioned,** pŏr'shund, *adj.* having a portion or endowment. [assigns shares.

**Portioner,** pŏr'shun-ėr, *n.* one who portions or

**Portionist,** pŏr'shun-ist, *n.* one who has an academical allowance or *portion:* the incumbent of a benefice which has more than one rector or vicar. [dowry, or property.

**Portionless,** pŏr'shun-les, *adj.* having no portion,

**Portly,** pŏrt'li, *adj.* having a dignified *port* or mien: corpulent.—*n.* **Port'liness,** state of being portly. [See **Port,** bearing.]

**Portmanteau,** pŏrt-man'tō, *n.* a bag for carrying apparel, &c. on journeys. [Lit. 'a cloak-carrier,' Fr. *porter,* to carry, *manteau,* a cloak, mantle.]

**Portrait,** pŏr'trāt, *n.* the likeness of a person: description in words. [See **Portray.**]

**Portraiture,** pŏr'trāt-ūr, *n.* the drawing of *portraits,* or describing in words.

**Portray,** por-trā', *v.t.* to paint or draw the likeness of: to describe in words.—*n.* **Portray'er.** [Fr. *portraire*—L.—*pro,* forth, *traho,* to draw.]

**Pose,** pōz, *n.* a position: an attitude.—*v.i.* to assume an attitude. [Fr.—*poser,* to place—Low L. *pausare,* to cease, to make to cease—L. *pausa,* pause—Gr. *pausis.* See **Pause.** Between Fr. *poser,* and L. *ponere, positum,* there has been great confusion, which has influenced the derivatives of both words.]

**Pose,** pōz, *v.t.* to puzzle: to perplex by questions: to bring to a stand. [M. E. *apposen,* a corr. of **Oppose,** which in the schools meant to 'argue against.'] [puzzle.

**Poser,** pōz'ėr, *n.* one who or that which *poses:* a

**Position,** po-zish'un, *n., place,* situation: attitude: state of affairs: the ground taken in argument or a dispute: principle laid down: place in society. [Fr.—L.—*pono, positus,* to place.]

**Positive,** poz'it-iv, *adj.* definitely *placed* or *laid down:* clearly expressed: actual: not admitting any doubt or qualification: decisive: settled by arbitrary appointment: dogmatic: fully assured: certain: (*gram.*) noting the simple form of an adjective: (*math.*) to be added.—*n.* that which is *placed* or laid down: that which may be affirmed: reality.—*adv.* **Pos'itively.**—*n.* **Pos'itiveness.** [Fr.—L. *positivus,* fixed by agreement, from *pono.* See **Position.**]

**Positivism,** poz'it-iv-izm, *n.* a system of philosophy originated by Comte, a French philosopher (1798–1857), which, rejecting all inquiry into causes whether efficient or final, deals only with what is *positive,* or simply seeks to discover the laws of phenomena.

**Positivist,** poz'it-iv-ist, *n.* a believer in positivism.

**Possess,** poz-zes', *v.t.* to have or hold as an owner: to have the control of: to inform: to seize: to enter into and influence. [L. *possideo, possessus.*]

**Possession,** poz-zesh'un, *n.* act of possessing: the thing possessed: property: state of being possessed, as by an evil spirit.

**Possessive,** poz-zes'iv, *adj.* pertaining to or denoting possession.—*adv.* **Possess'ively.**

**Possessor,** poz-zes'or, *n.* one who possesses: owner: proprietor: occupant.

**Possessory,** poz-zes'or-i, *adj.* relating to a possessor or possession: having possession.

**Posset,** pos'et, *n.* hot *milk curdled* with wine or acid. [W. *posel,* curdled milk, Ir. *pusoid.*]

**Possibility,** pos-i-bil'i-ti, *n.* state of being *possible:* that which is possible: a contingency.

**Possible,** pos'i-bl, *adj.* that is *able* to be or happen: that may be done: not contrary to the nature of things.—*adv.* **Poss'ibly.** [Fr.—L. *possibilis—possum,* to be able—*potis,* able, and *esse,* to be.]

**Post,** pōst, *n.* a piece of timber fixed in the ground, generally as a support to something else: a pillar.—*v.t.* to fix on or to a post, that is, in a public place: to expose to public reproach. [A.S. *post*—L. *postis,* a doorpost, from *pono,* to place.]

**Post,** pōst, *n.* a *fixed* place, as a military station: a fixed place or stage on a road: an office: one who travels by stages, esp. carrying letters, &c.: a public letter-carrier: an established system of conveying letters: a size of writing-paper, double that of common note-paper (so called from the water-mark, a *postman's* horn).—*v.t.* to set or station: to put in the post-office: (*book-k.*) to transfer to the ledger.—*v.i.* to travel with posthorses, or with speed.—*adv.* with posthorses: with speed. [Fr. *poste,* from L. *pono, positus,* to place.]

**Postage,** pōst'āj, *n.* money paid for conveyance of letters, &c. by *post* or mail. [mail-service.

**Postal,** pōst'al, *adj.* belonging to the *post*-office or

**Postboy,** pōst'boy, *n.* a boy that rides posthorses, or who carries letters.

**Postcard,** pōst'kärd, *n.* a stamped card on which a message may be sent by post.

**Postchaise,** pōst'shāz, *n.* a *chaise* or carriage with four wheels for the conveyance of those who travel with *post*horses.

**Postdate,** pōstdāt', *v.t.* to *date* after the real time. [L. *post,* after, and **Date.**]

**Post-diluvial,** pōst-dil'ū'vi-al, **Post-dilu'vian,** *adj.* being or happening *after* the *deluge.*—*n.* **Post-dilu'vian,** one who has lived since the deluge. [L. *post,* after, and **Diluvial, Diluvian.**]

**Posterior,** pos-tē'ri-or, *adj., coming after:* later:

hind or hinder.—*n.pl.* **Poste'riors**, short for *posterior parts.*—*n.* **Posterior'ity.**—*adv.* **Poste'riorly.** [L., comp. of *posterus*, coming after—*post*, after.]

**Posterity**, pos-ter'it-i, *n.* those *coming after*: succeeding generations: a race. [Fr.—L.—*posterus*. See **Posterior.**]

**Postern**, pōst'ern, *n.* (*orig.*) a *back* door or gate: a small private door.—*adj.* back: private. [O. Fr. *posterne*, *posterle*—L. *posterula*, a dim. from *posterus.* See **Posterior.**]

**Postfix**, pōst'fiks, *n.* a letter, syllable, or word *fixed* to or put *after* another word, an affix.—**Postfix'**, *v.t.* to add to the end of another word. [L. *post*, after, and **Fix.**]

**Posthaste**, pōst-hāst', *n.*, *haste* in travelling like that of a *post.*—*adv.* with haste or speed.

**Posthorse**, pōst'hors, *n.* a horse kept for posting.

**Posthumous**, post'ū-mus, *adj.* born *after* the father's death: published after the death of the author.—*adv.* **Post'humously.** [L. *posthumus*, *postumus*, superl. of *posterus*, coming after—*post*, after.]

**Postil**, pos'til, *n.* (*orig.*) a note in the margin of the Bible, so called because written *after* the text or *other words*: a marginal note: in R. Cath. Church, a homily read after the gospel.—*v.* to make such notes. [O. Fr. *postille* (It. *postilla*)—Low L. *postilla*—L. *post illa* (*verba*), after those (words).]

**Postillion**, pōs-til'yun, *n.* a *post*boy, one who guides posthorses, or horses in any carriage, riding on one of them. [Fr. *postillon*—*poste.*]

**Postman**, pōst'man, *n.* a post or courier: a letter-carrier. [post-office on a letter.

**Postmark**, pōst'märk, *n.* the mark or stamp of a

**Postmaster**, pōst'mas-tėr, *n.* the manager or superintendent of a post-office: one who supplies posthorses.—*n.* **Postmaster-General**, the chief officer of the post-office department.

**Post-meridian**, pōst-me-rid'i-an, *adj.* coming *after* the sun has crossed the *meridian*: in the afternoon (written P.M.). [L. *post*, after, and **Meridian.**]

**Post-mortem**, pōst-mor'tem, *adj.*, *after death.* [L. *post*, after, and *mortem*, accus. of *mors*, death.]

**Post-obit**, pōst-ō'bit, *n.* a bond payable with unusual interest *after* the *death* of an individual from whom the person granting it has expectations. [L. *post*, after. See **Obit.**]

**Post-office**, pōst'-of'is, *n.* an *office* for receiving and transmitting letters by *post.* [as a letter.

**Postpaid**, pōst'pād, *adj.* having the *postage paid*,

**Postpone**, pōst-pōn', *v.t.* to *put* off to an *after*-period: to defer: to delay. [L. *postpono*, *-positus*—*post*, after, *pono*, to put.]

**Postponement**, pōst-pōn'ment, *n.* act of *putting* off to an *after*-time: temporary delay.

**Post-prandial**, pōst-pran'di-al, *adj.*, *after dinner.* [From L. *post*, after, and *prandium*, a repast.]

**Postscript**, pōst'skript, *n.* a part added to a letter *after* the signature: an addition to a book after it is finished. [L., from *post*, after, and *scriptum*, written, pa.p. of *scribo*, to write.]

**Post-town**, pōst'-town, *n.* a *town* with a *post-office.*

**Postulant**, pos'tū-lant, *n.* a candidate. [See **Postulate.**]

**Postulate**, pos'tū-lāt, *v.t.* to assume without proof: to take without positive consent.—*n.* a position assumed as self-evident: (*geom.*) a self-evident problem. [L. *postulo*, *-atus*, to demand —*posco*, to ask urgently.]

**Postulatory**, pos'tū-la-tor-i, *adj.* assuming or assumed without proof as a *postulate.*

**Posture**, pos'tūr, *n.* the *placing* or position of the body: attitude: state or condition: disposition. —*v.t.* to place in a particular manner. [Fr.— L. *positura*—*pono*, *positum*, to place.]

**Posy**, pō'zi, *n.* a verse of *poetry*: a motto: an inscription on a ring: a motto sent with a bouquet: a bouquet. [Corr. of **Poesy.**]

**Pot**, pot, *n.* a metallic vessel for various purposes, esp. cooking: a drinking vessel: an earthen vessel for plants: the quantity in a pot.—*v.t.* to preserve in pots: to put in pots:—*pr.p.* pott'ing; *pa.t.* and *pa.p.* pott'ed.—**To go to pot**, to go to ruin, orig. said of old metal, to go into the melting-pot. [M. E. *pot*, from the Celt., as Ir. *pota*, Gael. *poit*, W. *pot*.]

**Potable**, pō'ta-bl, *adj.* that may be *drunk*: liquid. —*n.* something drinkable.—*n.* **Po'tableness.** [Fr.—L. *potabilis*—*pōto*, to drink.]

**Potash**, pot'ash, *n.* a powerful alkali, obtained from the ashes of plants. [Lit. 'pot ashes.']

**Potassa**, po-tas'a, *n.* Latinised form of **Potash.**

**Potassium**, po-tas'i-um, *n.* the metallic base of potash. [From **Potassa.**]

**Potation**, po-tā'shun, *n.* a *drinking*: a draught. [L. *potatio*—*pōt-o*, *-atus*, to drink.]

**Potato**, po-tā'to, *n.* one of the tubers of a plant almost universally cultivated for food: the plant itself:—*pl.* **Pota'toes**. [Sp. *patata*, *batate*, orig. a Haytian word.] [drink.

**Poteen**, po-tēn', *n.* Irish whisky. [Ir. *poitin*, I

**Potency**, pō'ten-si, *n.* power.

**Potent**, pō'tent, *adj.* strong: powerful: having great authority or influence.—*adv.* **Po'tently.** [L. *potens*—*potis*, able, *esse*, to be.]

**Potentate**, pō'ten-tāt, *n.* one who is *potent*: a prince: a sovereign. [Fr. *potentat*—Low L. *potentatus*, pa.p. of *potento*, to exercise power.]

**Potential**, po-ten'shal, *adj.*, *powerful*, efficacious: existing in possibility, not in reality: (*gram.*) expressing power, possibility, liberty, or obligation.—*n.* the name for a function of great importance in the mathematical theory of attractions, also in electricity.—*adv.* **Poten'tially.** *n.*—**Potential'ity.**

**Pother**, poth'ėr, *n.* bustle: confusion.—*v.t.* to puzzle: to perplex: to tease.—*v.i.* to make a pother. [A variant of **Potter.**]

**Potherb**, pot'hėrb or pot'ėrb, *n.* an *herb* or vegetable used in *cooking.*

**Pothook**, pot'hook, *n.* a *hook* on which *pots* are hung over the fire: a letter or character formed like a pothook: an ill-formed or scrawled letter.

**Pothouse**, pot'hows, *n.* a low drinking-house.

**Potion**, pō'shun, *n.* a *draught*: a liquid medicine: a dose. [Fr.—L. *potio*—*pōto*, to drink. Doublet **Poison.**] [provided for dinner.

**Potluck**, pot'luk, *n.* whatever may chance to be

**Potsherd**, pot'shėrd, *n.* fragment of a pot. [**Pot**, and A.S. *sceard*, a shred—*sceran*, to divide.]

**Pottage**, pot'āj, *n.* anything cooked in a *pot*: a thick soup of meat and vegetables. [Fr. *potage* —*pot.* See **Pot.**]

**Potter**, pot'ėr, *n.* one whose trade is to make *pots*, or earthenware.

**Potter**, pot'ėr, *v.i.* to be fussily engaged about trifles.—*n.* **Pott'erer.** [Freq. of prov. *pote*, to push. See **Pother** and **Put.**]

**Pottery**, pot'ėr-i, *n.* earthenware *pots* or vessels: a place where earthenware is manufactured.

**Pottle**, pot'l, *n.* a *little pot*: a measure of four pints: a small basket for fruit. [Dim. of **Pot.**]

**Potwalloper**, pot-wol'op-ėr, *n.* a voter in certain English boroughs where every one who boiled a pot was entitled to vote. [Lit. 'pot-boiler,' the latter part of the word being from an O. Low Ger. *wallen*, to boil, E. **Well**.]

**Pouch**, powch, *n.* a *poke*, *pocket*, or *bag*: the bag or sac of an animal.—*v.t.* to put into a pouch. [Fr. *poche*. See **Poke**, a bag.]

**Poult**, pōlt, *n.* a *little hen* or *fowl*, a chicken. [Fr. *poulet*, dim. of *poule*, hen, fowl—L. *pullus*, the young of any animal; cog. with **Foal**. Doublet **Pullet**.]

**Poulterer**, pōlt′ėr-ėr, *n.* one who deals in *fowls*.

**Poultice**, pōl′tis, *n.* a soft composition of meal, bran, &c. applied to sores.—*v.t.* to dress with a poultice. [Lit. ' porridge,' L. *pultes*, pl. of *puls*, *pultis*, Gr. *poltos*, porridge.]

**Poultry**, pōl′ri, *n.* domestic fowls. [See **Poult**.]

**Pounce**, powns, *v.i.* to fall (upon) and seize with the claws: to dart suddenly (upon).—*n.* a hawk's claw. [Orig. to *pierce*, to stamp holes in for ornament; through Romance forms, from L. *pungo*, *punctus*. Doublet **Punch**, *v.*]

**Pounce**, powns, *n.* a fine powder for preparing a surface for writing on: coloured powder sprinkled over holes pricked in paper as a pattern.—*v.t.* to sprinkle with pounce, as paper or a pattern. —*n.* **Pounce′-box**, a *box* with a perforated lid for sprinkling *pounce*. [Orig. powdered *pumice*-stone, Fr. *ponce*, pumice—L. *pumex*, *pumicis*. Doublet **Pumice**.]

**Pound**, pownd, *n.* a *weight* of 12 oz. troy, or 16 oz. avoir.: a sovereign or 20s., also represented by a note (*B*.)=about £4. [A.S. *pund*—L. *pondo*, by weight, *pondus*, a weight—*pendo*, to weigh.]

**Pound**, pownd, *v.t.* to *shut up* or confine, as strayed animals.—*n.* an inclosure in which strayed animals are confined. [M. E. *pond*—A.S. *pund*, inclosure. Doublet **Pond**.]

**Pound**, pownd, *v.t.* to *beat*, to *bruise*: to bray with a pestle.—*n.* **Pound′er**. [M. E. *pounen*—A.S. *punian*, to beat; -*d* excrescent.]

**Poundage**, pownd′āj, *n.* a charge made for each *pound*. [*ing* stray cattle.

**Poundage**, pownd′āj, *n.* a charge made for *pound*-

**Pounder**, pownd′ėr, *n.* he or that which has so many *pounds*.

**Pour**, pōr, *v.t.* to cause to flow: to throw with force: to send forth: to give vent to: to utter. —*v.i.* to flow: to issue forth: to rush. [Celt., as W. *bwrw*, to throw, Gael. *purr*, to push.]

**Pourtray**. Same as **Portray**.

**Pout**, powt, *v.i.* to push out the lips, in contempt or displeasure: to look sulky: to hang or be prominent.—*n.* a fit of sulleness. [Ety. dub.: cf. prov. Fr. *pot*, *pout*, lip, Fr. *bouder*, to pout: W. *pwdu*, pout.]

**Pouter**, powt′er, *n.* one who pouts: a variety of pigeon, having its breast inflated.

**Pouting**, powt′ing, *n.* childish sulleness.

**Poutingly**, powt′ing-li, *adv.* in a pouting or sullen manner.

**Poverty**, pov′ėr-ti, *n.* the state of being *poor*: necessity: want: meanness: defect. [O. Fr. *poverte* (Fr. *pauvreté*)—L. *paupertas*, -*tatis*—*pauper*, poor. See **Poor**.]

**Powder**, pow′dėr, *n.*, *dust*: any substance in fine particles: gunpowder: hair-powder.—*v.t.* to reduce to powder: to sprinkle with powder: to salt.—*v.i.* to crumble into powder. [M. E. *poudre*—Fr.—L. *pulvis*, *pulveris*, dust.]

**Powdered**, pow′dėrd, *adj.* reduced to powder: sprinkled with powder: salted.

**Powdery**, pow′dėr-i, *adj.* resembling or sprinkled with powder: dusty: friable.

**Power**, pow′ėr, *n.*, *strength*: energy: faculty of the mind: any agency: moving force of anything: rule: authority: influence: ability: capacity: a ruler: a divinity: the result of the continued multiplication of a quantity by itself any given number of times: (*optics*) magnifying strength: (*obs.*) a great many. [M. E. *poër*—O. Fr. (Fr. *pouvoir*)—Low L. *pot-ere*, to be able, L. *posse* (*pot-esse*). See **Potent**.]

**Powerful**, pow′ėr-fool, *adj.* having great power: mighty: intense: forcible: efficacious.—*adv.* **Pow′erfully**.—*n.* **Pow′erfulness**.

**Powerless**, pow′ėr-les, *adj.* without power: weak: impotent.—*adv.* **Pow′erlessly**.—*n.* **Pow′erlessness**. [Written for *pocks*, pl. of **Pock**.]

**Pox**, poks, *n.* pustules: an eruptive disease.

**Practicability**, prak-ti-ka-bil′i-ti, *n.* state or quality of being practicable.

**Practicable**, prak′tik-a-bl, *adj.* that may be *practised*, used, or followed: that may be done: passable.—*adv.* **Prac′ticably**.

**Practical**, prak′tik-al, *adj.* that can be put in *practice*: useful: applying knowledge to some useful end.—*adv.* **Prac′tically**.—*n.* **Prac′ticalness**.

**Practice**, prak′tis, *n.* a *doing*: the habit of doing anything: frequent use: performance: method: medical treatment: exercise of any profession: a rule in arithmetic. [M. E. *praktike*—O. Fr. *practique*—Gr. *praktikos*, fit for doing—*prassō*, *praxō*, to do.]

**Practise**, prak′tis, *v.t.* to put in *practice* or do habitually: to perform: to exercise, as a profession: to use or exercise: to commit.—*v.i.* to have or to form a habit: to exercise any employment or profession: to try artifices.—*n.* **Prac′tiser**. [From the noun.]

**Practitioner**, prak-tish′un-ėr, *n.* one who *practises* or is engaged in the exercise of any profession, esp. medicine or law. [Older form *practician*—O. Fr. *practicien*.]

**Præmunire**, prem-ū-nī′re, *n.* the offence of disregard or contempt of the king and his government, especially the offence of intro lucing papal or other foreign authority into England: the writ founded on such an offence: the penalty incurred by the offence. [A corr. of *præmonere*, to forewarn, to cite.]

**Prætor**, prē′tor, *n.* a magistrate of ancient Rome, next in rank to the consuls.—*n.* **Præ′torship**. [Lit. ' one who goes before,' L. *prætor* for *præitor*—*præ*, before, *eo*, *itum*, to go.]

**Prætorial**, pre-tō′ri-al, **Prætorian**, pre-tō′ri-an, *adj.* pertaining to a *prætor* or magistrate: authorised or exercised by the prætor: judicial.

**Prætorium**, pre-tō′ri-um, *n.* the official residence of the Roman *prætor*, proconsul, or governor in a province: the general's tent in a camp: the council of officers who attended the general and met in his tent.

**Pragmatic**, prag-mat′ik, **Pragmatical**, prag-mat′ik-al, *adj.* over-active, officious, meddlesome.—*adv.* **Pragmat′ically**.—**Pragmatic Sanction**, a special decree issued by a sovereign, such as that passed by the Emperor Charles VI. of Germany, securing the crown to Maria Theresa, and which led to the war so called in 1741. [Orig. *fit for action*, Fr.—L.—Gr. *pragmatikos* —*pragma*—*pragmatos*, deed—*prassō*, to do.]

**Prairie**, prā′ri, *n.* an extensive *meadow* or tract of land, level or rolling, without trees, and covered with tall coarse grass. [Fr.—Low L. *prataria*, meadow-land—L. *pratum*, a meadow.]

**Praise**, prāz, *n.* the expression of the *price* or *value* in which any person or thing is held: commendation : tribute of gratitude : a glorifying, as in worship : reason of praise.—*v.t.* to express estimation of : to commend : to honour : to glorify, as in worship. [O. Fr. *preis* (Fr. *prix*)—L. *pretium*, price, value. See Price.]

**Praiseworthy**, prāz′wur-*thi*, *adj.*, *worthy of praise* : commendable.—*n.* **Praise′worthiness.**

**Prance**, prans, *v.i.* to strut about in a showy or warlike manner : to ride showily : to bound gaily, as a horse. [Another form of **Prank**.]

**Prancing**, prans′ing, *adj.* riding showily : springing or bounding gaily.—*adv.* **Pranc′ingly.**

**Prank**, prangk, *v.t.* to display or adorn showily. [Closely akin to *prink*, which is a nasalised form of **Prick**.]

**Prank**, prangk, *n.* a sportive action : a mischievous trick. [Same word as the above.]

**Prate**, prāt, *v.i.* to talk idly : to tattle : to be loquacious.—*v.t.* to speak without meaning.—*n.* trifling talk. [Scand. and Low Ger., as Dan. *prate*, Dut. *praaten*, to tattle.]

**Prater**, prāt′er, *n.* one who prates or talks idly.

**Prating**, prāt′ing, *adj.*, *talking* idly or unmeaningly.—*n.* idle talk.—*adv.* **Prat′ingly.**

**Prattle**, prat′l, *v.i.* to *prate* or talk much and idly : to utter child's talk.—*n.* empty talk. [Freq. of **Prate**.]

**Prattler**, prat′ler, *n.* one who *prattles*, as a child.

**Prawn**, prawn, *n.* a small crustacean animal like the shrimp. [Ety. unknown.]

**Praxis**, praks′is, *n.*, *practice* : an example for exercise. [Gr.—*prassō*, *praxō*, to do.]

**Pray**, prā, *v.i.* to *ask* earnestly : to entreat : to petition or address God.—*v.t.* to ask earnestly and reverently, as in worship : to supplicate :—*pr.p.* prāy′ing ; *pa.t.* and *pa.p.* prāyed. [O. Fr. *preier* (Fr. *prier*)—L. *precor—prex, prec-is*, a prayer, akin to Sans. *pracch*, Ger. *fragen*, to ask.]

**Prayer**, prār, *n.* the act of *praying* : entreaty : the words used : solemn address to God : a formula of worship.

**Prayerful**, prār′fool, *adj.*, *full* of or given to *prayer* : devotional.—*adv.* **Pray′erfully.**—*n.* **Pray′erfulness.**

**Prayerless**, prār′les, *adj.* without or not using prayer.—*adv.* **Pray′erlessly.**—*n.* **Pray′erlessness.**

**Praying**, prā′ing, *n.* the act of making a *prayer* : a prayer made.—*adj.* given to prayer.

**Preach**, prēch, *v.i.* to pronounce a public discourse on sacred subjects : to discourse earnestly : to give advice in an offensive or obtrusive manner.—*v.t.* to publish in religious discourses : to teach publicly. [Fr. *prêcher* (It. *predicare*)—L. *prædico, -atum*, to proclaim—*præ*, before, *dico*, to proclaim, akin to *dico*, to say. See Diction.]

**Preacher**, prēch′er, *n.* one who discourses publicly on religious matters.

**Preaching**, prēch′ing, *n.* the act of preaching : a public religious discourse.

**Preamble**, prē-am′bl or prē′am-bl, *n.* preface : introduction. [Lit. that which 'goes before,' Fr. *préambule*—L. *præ*, before, *ambulo*, to go.]

**Pre-audience**, prē-aw′di-ens, *n.* right of *previous audience* or hearing : precedence at the bar among lawyers. [L. *præ*, before, and Audience.]

**Prebend**, preb′end, *n.* the share of the estate of a cathedral or collegiate church *allowed* to a member of a cathedral church. [L. *præbenda*, a payment to a private person from a public source—*præbeo*, to allow.] [*end.*

**Prebendal**, pre-bend′al, *adj.* relating to a *prebend.*

**Prebendary**, preb′end-ar-i, *n.* an ecclesiastic who

enjoys a *prebend* : an officiating or residentiary canon.—*n.* **Preb′endaryship.**

**Precarious**, pre-kā′ri-us, *adj.* uncertain, because depending on the will of another : held by a doubtful tenure.—*adv.* **Preca′riously.**—*n.* **Preca′riousness.** [Lit. 'obtained by prayer or entreaty,' L. *precarius—precor*, to pray. See Pray.]

**Precaution**, pre-kaw′shun, *n.*, *caution* or care *before*hand : a preventive measure.—*v.t.* to warn or advise beforehand. [Fr.—L. *præ*, before. See Caution.]

**Precautionary**, pre-kaw′shun-ar-i, *adj.* containing or proceeding from *precaution.*

**Precede**, pre-sēd′, *v.t.* to *go before* in time, rank, or importance. [Fr. *précéder*—L. *præcedo—præ*, before, *cedo*, go. See Cede.]

**Precedence**, pre-sēd′ens, **Precedency**, pre-sēd′-en-si, *n.* the act of *going before* in time : priority : the state of being before in rank, or the place of honour : the foremost place in ceremony. [Fr.—L.]

**Precedent**, pre-sēd′ent, *adj.*, *going before* : anterior.—*adv.* **Preced′ently.** [Fr.—L. *præcedens, -entis*, pr.p. of *præcedo.*]

**Precedent**, pres′e-dent, *n.* that which may serve as an example or rule in the future : a parallel case in the past. [Lit. 'foregoing.' See above word.]

**Precedented**, pres′e-dent-ed, *adj.* having a *precedent* : warranted by an example.

**Preceding**, pre-sēd′ing, *adj.*, *going before* in time, rank, &c. : antecedent : previous : former.

**Precentor**, pre-sen′tor, *n.* that leads in music : the leader of a choir : the leader of the psalmody in the Scotch Church.—*n.* **Precen′torship.** [L. *præ*, before, *cantor*, a singer—*canto.* See Chant.]

**Precept**, prē′sept, *n.* rule of action : a commandment : principle, or maxim : (*law*) the written warrant of a magistrate. [Fr. *précepte*—L. *præceptum—præceptus*, pa.p. of *præcipio*, to take beforehand, to give rules to—*præ*, before, and *capio.* See Capable.]

**Preceptive**, pre-sept′iv, *adj.* containing or giving *precepts* : directing in moral conduct : didactic.

**Preceptor**, pre-sept′or, *n.* one who delivers *precepts* : a teacher : an instructor : the head of a school.—*adj.* **Precepto′rial.**—*n.* **Precept′ress.**

**Preceptory**, pre-sept′or-i, *n.* giving *precepts.*—*n.* a religious house or college of the Knights Templar.

**Precession**, pre-sesh′un, *n.* the act of *going before.*

**Precinct**, prē′singkt, *n.* limit or boundary of a place : a territorial district or division : limit of jurisdiction or authority. [Lit. 'girt about,' 'encompassed,' L. *præcinctus*, pa.p. of *præcingo*—*præ*, before, and *cingo*, to gird.]

**Precious**, presh′us, *adj.* of great *price* or worth : costly : highly esteemed : worthless, contemptible (in irony) : (*B.*) valuable because of its rarity.—*adv.* **Prec′iously.**—*n.* **Prec′iousness.** [O. Fr. *precios* (Fr. *précieux*)—L. *pretiosus—pretium*, price. See Price.]

**Precipice**, pres′i-pis, *n.* a very steep place : any steep descent. [Fr.—L. *præcipitium—præceps, præcipitis*, headlong—*præ*, before, and *caput, capitis*, the head. See Head.]

**Precipitable**, pre-sip′i-ta-bl, *adj.* (*chem.*) that may be *precipitated.*—*n.* **Precipitabil′ity.**

**Precipitance**, pre-sip′i-tans, **Precipitancy**, pre-sip′i-tan-si, *n.* quality of being *precipitate* : haste in resolving or executing a purpose.

**Precipitant**, pre-sip′i-tant, *adj.*, *falling headlong* :

rushing down with velocity: hasty: unexpectedly brought on.—*adv.* **Precip'itantly.** [Pr.p. of L. *præcipito.* See **Precipitate.**]

**Precipitate,** pre-sip'i-tāt, *v.t.* to *throw head-foremost*: to urge with eagerness: to hurry rashly: to hasten: (*chem.*) to throw to the bottom, as a substance in solution or suspension.—*adj. falling*, flowing, or rushing *headlong*: lacking deliberation: overhasty: (*med.*) ending soon in death.—*n.* (*chem.*) a substance *precipitated.* [L. *præcipito, -atus—præceps.* See **Precipice.**]

**Precipitately,** pre-sip'i-tāt-li, *adv.* in a *precipitate* manner: headlong.

**Precipitation,** pre-sip-i-tā'shun, *n.* act of *precipitating*: great hurry: rash haste: rapid movement.

**Precipitous,** pre-sip'i-tus, *adj.* like a *precipice*: very steep: hasty: rash.—*adv.* **Precip'itously.** —*n.* **Precip'itousness.** [O. Fr. *precipiteux*— L. *præceps.* See **Precipice.**]

**Précis,** prā-sē', *n.* a *precise* or abridged statement: an abstract: summary. [Fr.]

**Precise,** pre-sīs', *adj.* definite: exact: not vague: adhering too much to rule: excessively nice.— *adv.* **Precise'ly.**—*n.* **Precise'ness.** [Fr. *précis* —L. *præcisus,* pa.p. of *præcido—præ,* before, and *cædo,* to cut. See **Cæsura.**]

**Precisian,** pre-sizh'an, *n.* an over-*precise* person.

**Precision,** pre-sizh'un, *n.* quality of being *precise*: exactness: accuracy.

**Preclude,** pre-klōōd', *v.t.* to hinder by anticipation: to keep back: to prevent from taking place. [L. *præcludo, -clusus—præ,* before, and *claudo,* to shut. See **Clause.**]

**Preclusion,** pre-klōō'zhun, *n.* act of *precluding* or hindering: state of being precluded.

**Preclusive,** pre-klōō'siv, *adj.* tending to *preclude*: hindering beforehand.—*adv.* **Preclu'sively.**

**Precocious,** pre-kō'shus, *adj.* having the mind developed very early: premature: forward.— *adv.* **Preco'ciously.**—*ns.* **Preco'ciousness, Precoc'ity.** [Orig. 'ripe before the natural time,' formed from L. *præcox, præcocis—præ,* before, and *coquo,* to cook, to ripen. See **Cook.**]

**Precognition,** prē-kog-nish'un, *n., cognition,* knowledge, or examination *before*hand: (*Scots law*) an examination as to whether there is ground for prosecution. [L. *præ,* before, and **Cognition.**]

**Preconceive,** prē-kon-sēv', *v.t.* to *conceive* or form a notion of *before*hand. [L. *præ,* before, and **Conceive.**]—*n.* [*ceiving:* previous opinion.

**Preconception,** prē-kon-sep'shun, *n.* act of *precon-*

**Preconcert,** prē-kon-sèrt', *v.t.* to *concert* or settle *before*hand. [L. *præ,* before, and **Concert,** *v.*]

**Precursor,** pre-kur'sor, *n.* a *forerunner*: one who or that which indicates approach. [L.—*præ,* before, and *cursor—curro,* to run. See **Course.**]

**Precursory,** pre-kur'sor-i, *adj., forerunning*: indicating something to follow.

**Predaceous,** pre-dā'shus, *adj.* living by *prey*: predatory. [It. *predace*—L. *præda,* booty, prey.] [ing.

**Predal,** prē'dal, *adj.* pertaining to *prey*: plunder-

**Predatory,** pred'a-tor-i or prē'da-tor-i, *adj., plundering*: characterised by plundering: hungry: ravenous.—*adv.* **Pred'atorily.** [L. *prædor, -atus,* to plunder—*præda,* booty. See **Prey.**]

**Predecease,** prē-de-sēs', *n.,* decease or *death before* something else.—*v.t.* to die before. [L. *præ,* before, and **Decease.**]

**Predecessor,** prē-de-ses'or, *n.* one who has *pre*ceded another in any office. [L. *præ,* before,

and *decessor—decedo, decessus,* to withdraw— *de,* away, and *cedo.* See **Cede.**]

**Predestinarian,** pre-des-tin-ā'ri-an, *adj.* pertaining to *predestination.*—*n.* one who holds the doctrine of predestination. [See **Predestine.**]

**Predestinate,** pre-des'tin-āt, *v.t.* to *determine* before*hand: to preordain by an unchangeable purpose. [See **Predestine.**]

**Predestination,** pre-des-tin-ā'shun, *n.* act of *pre*destinating: (*theol.*) the doctrine that God has from all eternity immutably fixed whatever is to happen.

**Predestinator,** pre-des'tin-ā-tor, *n.* one who *pre*destinates or foreordains: a predestinarian.

**Predestine,** pre-des'tin, *v.t.* to *destine* or decree before*hand: to foreordain. [L. *prædestino, -atus—præ,* before, and *destino.* See **Destine.**]

**Predeterminate,** prē-de-tèr'min-āt, *adj., deter*mined before*hand.—*n.* **Predetermina'tion.**

**Predetermine,** prē-de-tèr'min, *v.t.* to *determine* before*hand. [L. *præ,* before, and **Determine.**]

**Predial,** prē'di-al, *adj.* consisting of land or *farms*: growing from land. [Fr. *prédial*—L. *prædium* (for *præ-hendium*), an estate. See **Prehensile.**]

**Predicable,** pred'i-ka-bl, *adj.* that may be *predi*cated or affirmed of something: attributable.— *n.* anything that can be predicated.—*n.* **Predicability,** quality of being predicable.

**Predicament,** pre-dik'a-ment, *n.* (*logic*) one of the classes or categories which include all *pre*dicables: condition: an unfortunate or trying position. [Low L. *predicamentum.*]

**Predicate,** pred'i-kāt, *v.t.* to affirm one thing of another.—*n.* (*logic* and *gram.*) that which is stated of the subject. [L. *prædico, -atus,* to proclaim, thus a doublet of **Preach.**]

**Predication,** pred-i-kā'shun, *n.* act of *predicating*: assertion.

**Predicative,** pred'i-kāt-iv, *adj.* expressing *predi*cation or affirmation.

**Predict,** pre-dikt', *v.t.* to *declare* or tell before*hand: to prophesy. [L. *prædictus,* pa.p. of *prædico,* from *præ,* before, and *dico,* to say.]

**Prediction,** pre-dik'shun, *n.* act of *predicting*: that which is predicted or foretold: prophecy.

**Predictive,** pre-dikt'iv, *adj., foretelling*: prophetic.

**Predilection,** prē-di-lek'shun, *n.* a *choosing* before*hand: favourable prepossession of mind: partiality. [L. *præ,* before, and *dilectio, -onis,* choice, from *diligo, dilectus,* to love—*dis,* apart, and *lego,* to choose.]

**Predispose,** prē-dis-pōz', *v.t.* to *dispose* or incline before*hand. [L. *præ,* before, and **Dispose.**]

**Predisposition,** prē-dis-po-zish'un, *n.* state of being *predisposed* or previously inclined.

**Predominance,** pre-dom'in-ans, **Predominancy,** pre-dom'in-an-si, *n.* condition of being *predom*inant: superiority: ascendency.

**Predominant,** pre-dom'in-ant, *adj., ruling*: ascendant.—*adv.* **Predom'inantly.**

**Predominate,** pre-dom'in-āt, *v.t.* to *dominate* or rule *over*.—*v.i.* to be dominant over: to surpass in strength or authority: to prevail. [L. *præ,* over, and **Dominate.**]

**Pre-eminence,** pre-em'i-nens, *n.* state of being *pre-eminent*: superiority in excellence. [Fr. —L.]

**Pre-eminent,** pre-em'i-nent, *adj., eminent above* others: surpassing others in good or bad qualities: outstanding.—*adv.* **Pre-em'inently.** [L. *præ,* before, and **Eminent.**]

**Pre-emption,** pre-em'shun, *n.* right of *purchasing*

*before* others. [L. *præ*, before, and *emptio*, a buying—*emo*, *emptus*, to buy.]

**Preen,** prēn, *v.t.* to compose and arrange as birds do their feathers. [Same as **Prune**, *v.*]

**Pre-engage,** prē-en-gāj′, *v.t.* to *engage before*-hand.—*n.* **Pre-engage′ment.** [L. *præ*, before, and **Engage**.]

**Pre-establish,** prē-es-tab′lish, *v.t.* to *establish before*hand.—*n.* **Pre-estab′lishment.** [L. *præ*, before, and **Establish**.]

**Pre-exist,** prē-egz-ist′, *v.i.* to *exist before*hand.—*n.* **Pre-exist′ence.** [L. *præ*, before, and **Exist**.]

**Pre-existent,** prē-egz-ist′ent, *adj.*, *existent* or *existing before*hand.

**Preface,** pref′ās or -as, *n.* something *spoken before*: the introduction to a book, &c.—*v.t.* to introduce with a preface. [Fr. *préface*—L. *præfatio*—*præ*, before, and *for, fatus*, to speak. See **Fate.**]

**Prefatory,** pref′a-tor-i, *adj.* pertaining to a *preface*: introductory.—*adv.* **Pref′atorily.**

**Prefect,** prē′fekt, *n.* one *placed* in authority *over* others: a commander: a governor, esp. of a province in France.—*ns.* **Pre′fecture, Pre′fectship,** his office or jurisdiction. [Fr. *préfet*—L. *præfectus,* pa.p. of *præficio*—*præ*, over, and *facio*, to make, to place. See **Fact.**]

**Prefer,** pre-fėr′, *v.t.* to esteem above another: to regard or hold in higher estimation: to choose or select: to promote: to exalt: to offer or present, as a prayer: to place in advance:—*pr.p.* prefer′ring; *pa.t.* and *pa.p.* preferred′. [Lit. 'to place before,' Fr. *préférer*—L. *præfero*—*præ*, before, and *fero*, E. **Bear.**]

**Preferable,** pref′ėr-a-bl, *adj.* worthy to be *preferred* or chosen: more desirable, or excellent: of better quality.—*adv.* **Pref′erably.**—*n.* **Pref′erableness.** [Fr.]

**Preference,** pref′ėr-ens, *n.* the act of *preferring*: estimation above another: the state of being preferred: that which is preferred: choice.—*adj.* **Preferential,** pref-ėr-en′shal, having a preference.

**Preferment,** pre-fėr′ment, *n.* the act of *preferring*: the state of being advanced: advancement to a higher position: promotion: superior place.

**Prefigurative,** pre-fig′ū-ra-tiv, *adj.* shewing by *previous figures*, types, or similitudes.

**Prefigure,** pre-fig′ūr, *v.t.* to *figure before*hand: to suggest by antecedent representation or by types.—*ns.* **Prefig′urement, Prefigura′tion.** [L. *præ*, before, and **Figure.**]

**Prefix,** pre-fiks′, *v.t.* to *fix* or put *before*, or at the beginning. [L. *præ*, before, and **Fix.**]

**Prefix,** prē′fiks, *n.* a letter, syllable, or word *fixed* or put at the beginning of another word.

**Pregnancy,** preg′nan-si, *n.* state of being *pregnant* or with young: fertility: unusual capacity.

**Pregnant,** preg′nant, *adj.* with child or young: fruitful: abounding with results: full of signification: implying more than is actually expressed: full of promise.—*adv.* **Preg′nantly.** [Lit. 'bringing forth,' O. Fr.—L. *prægnans, -antis*—*præ*, before, and *-gnans*, pr.p. of the obs. verb of which *gnatus* (see **Natal**) is the pa.p.]

**Prehensible,** pre-hen′si-bl, *adj.* that may be *seized.* [See **Prehensile.**]

**Prehensile,** pre-hen′sil, *adj.*, *seizing*: adapted for seizing or holding. [From L. *prehensus,* pa.p. of *pre-hendo*, to seize, from *præ*, before, and root of **Get.**]

**Prehension,** pre-hen′shun, *n.* a *seizing* or taking hold. [L. *prehensio, -onis*.]

**Prehistoric,** prē-his-tor′ik, *adj.* relating to a time *before* that treated of in *history.* [L. *præ*, before, and **Historic**.]

**Prejudge,** pre-juj′, *v.t.* to *judge* or decide upon *before* hearing the whole case: to condemn unheard.—*n.* **Prejudg′ment.** [L. *præ*, before, and **Judge**.]

**Prejudicate,** pre-jōō′di-kāt, *v.t.* to *judge before*-hand: to prejudge.—*v.i.* to decide without examination.—*n.* **Prejudica′tion.** [L. *præjudico, -atum*—*præ*, before, and *judico*, to judge.]

**Prejudicative,** pre-jōō′di-kāt-iv, *adj.* forming a *judgment* or opinion *before*hand.

**Prejudice,** prej′ū-dis, *n.* a *judgment* or opinion formed *before*hand or without due examination: a prejudgment: unreasonable prepossession for or against anything: bias: injury or wrong of any kind: disadvantage: mischief.—*v.t.* to fill with prejudice: to prepossess: to bias the mind of: to injure or hurt. [L. *præjudicium*—*præ*, before, and *judicium*, judgment. See **Judge**.]

**Prejudicial,** prej-ū-dish′al, *adj.* disadvantageous: injurious: mischievous: tending to obstruct.—*adv.* **Prejudi′cially.** [Orig. 'resulting from *prejudice*.']

**Prelacy,** prel′a-si, *n.* the office of a *prelate*: the order of bishops or the bishops collectively: episcopacy.

**Prelate,** prel′āt, *n.* a superior clergyman having authority over others, as a bishop: a church dignitary.—*n.* **Prel′ateship.** [Lit. 'one placed over others,' Fr. *prélat*—L. *prelatus*—*præ*, before, and *latus*, borne. See **Elate**.]

**Prelatic,** pre-lat′ik, **Prelatical,** pre-lat′ik-al, *adj.* pertaining to *prelates* or *prelacy*.—*adv.* **Prelat′ically.**

**Prelatist,** prel′at-ist, *n.* an upholder of *prelacy*.

**Prelect,** pre-lekt′, *v.i.* to *read before* or in presence of others: to read a discourse: to lecture. [L. *prælego*—*præ*, before, and *lego, lectum*, to read.]                            [*read* to others.

**Prelection,** pre-lek′shun, *n.* a *lecture* or discourse

**Prelector,** pre-lek′tor, *n.* one who *prelects*: a lecturer.

**Prelibation,** prē-lī-bā′shun, *n.* a *tasting before*-hand, foretaste. [L. *prælibatio*—*præ*, before, and *libo, -atus*, to taste.]

**Preliminary,** pre-lim′in-ar-i, *adj.* introductory: preparatory: preceding the main discourse or business.—*n.* that which precedes: introduction.—*adv.* **Prelim′inarily.** [L. *præ*, before, and *liminaris*, relating to a threshold—*limen, liminis*, a threshold. Cf. **Limit**.]

**Prelude,** prel′ūd, *n.* a short piece of music *before* a longer piece: a preface: a forerunner. [Lit. 'anything played before,' Fr.—Late L. *præludium*—L. *præ*, before, *ludere*, to play.]

**Prelude,** pre-lūd′, *v.t.* to *play before*: to precede, as an introduction. [From above word.]

**Prelusive,** pre-lū′siv, *adj.* of the nature of a *prelude*: introductory.

**Premature,** prem′a-tūr or prē-ma-tūr′, *adj.*, *mature before* the proper time: happening before the proper time: too soon believed, unauthenticated (as a report).—*adv.* **Prem′aturely.** —*ns.* **Prematur′ity, Prem′atureness.** [L. *præmaturus*—*præ*, before, and *maturus*, ripe.]

**Premeditate,** pre-med′i-tāt, *v.t.* to *meditate upon before*hand: to design previously.—*v.i.* to deliberate beforehand.—*n.* **Premedita′tion.** [L. *præmeditor, -atus*—*præ*, before, and *meditor*, to meditate.]

**Premier,** prēm′yėr or prem′-, *adj.*, *prime* or *first*: chief: (*her.*) most ancient.—*n.* the first or chief:

the prime-minister.—*n.* **Prem'iership.** [Fr.—L. *prim-arius,* of the first rank—*prim-us,* first; cf. **Prime.**]

**Premise,** prem'is, *n.* that which is *premised:* a proposition antecedently supposed or proved for after-reasoning: (*logic*) one of the two propositions in a syllogism from which the conclusion is drawn: the thing set forth in the beginning of a deed:—*pl.* a building and its adjuncts.

**Premise,** pre-mīz', *v.t.* to *send* or state *before* the rest: to make an introduction: to lay down propositions for subsequent reasonings. [Fr.—L. (*sententia*) *præmissa* (a sentence) put before—*præ,* before, and *mitto, missus,* to send. Cf. **Mission.**]

**Premiss,** prem'is, *n.* Same as **Premise.**

**Premium,** prē'mi-um, *n.* a reward: a prize: a bounty: payment made for insurance: the difference in value above the original price or par of stock (opposed to **Discount**): anything offered as an incentive. [L. *premium—præ,* above, and *emo,* to take, to buy.]

**Premonish,** pre-mon'ish, *v.t.* to *admonish* or warn *before*hand.—*n.* **Premoni'tion.** [From *pre,* before, and *monish,* a corr. form through O. Fr., from L. *moneo,* to warn. See **Admonish, Monition.**]

**Premonitive,** pre-mon'it-iv, **Premonitory,** pre-mon'it-or-i, *adj.* giving *warning* or notice *before*hand.—*adv.* **Premon'itorily.**

**Premonitor,** pre-mon'it-or, *n.* one who or that which gives *warning before*hand.

**Prentice,** pren'tis, *n.* short for **Apprentice.**

**Preoccupancy,** pre-ok'ū-pan-si, *n.* the act or the right of occupying beforehand.

**Preoccupy,** pre-ok'ū-pī, *v.t.* to *occupy* or take possession of *before*hand: to occupy beforehand or by prejudices.—*n.* **Preoccupa'tion.** [L. *præ,* before, and **Occupy.**]

**Preordain,** prē-or-dān', *v.t.* to *ordain,* appoint, or determine *before*hand.—*n.* **Preordina'tion.** [L. *præ,* before, and **Ordain.**]

**Prepaid,** pre-pād', *adj., paid before*hand.

**Preparation,** prep-ar-ā'shun, *n.* the act of *preparing:* previous arrangement: the state of being prepared or ready: that which is prepared or made ready: (*anat.*) a part of any animal body preserved as a specimen. [Fr.—L. *præparatio.*]

**Preparative,** pre-par'a-tiv, *adj.* having the power of *preparing* or making ready: fitting for anything.—*n.* that which prepares: preparation.

**Preparatory,** pre-par'a-tor-i, *adj., preparing for:* previous: introductory: preparative.

**Prepare,** pre-pār', *v.t.* to *make ready before*hand: to fit for any purpose: to make ready for use: to adapt: to form: to set or appoint: to provide: to equip.—*n.* **Prepar'er.** [Fr.—L. *præparo—præ,* before, and *paro,* to make ready.]

**Prepared,** pre-pārd', *adj.* made ready: ready.—*adv.* **Prepar'edly.**—*n.* **Prepar'edness.**

**Prepay,** pre-pā', *v.t.* to *pay before* or in advance.—*n.* **Prepay'ment.** [L. *præ,* before, and **Pay.**]

**Prepense,** pre-pens', *adj.* premeditated: intentional, chiefly in the phrase 'malice prepense.'—*adv.* **Prepense'ly.** [Lit. 'weighed before-hand,' through the Fr., from L. *præ,* before, and *pendo, pensum,* to weigh.]

**Preponderant,** pre-pon'dèr-ant, *adj., outweighing:* superior in weight, power, or influence.—*adv.* **Prepon'derantly.**—*n.* **Prepon'derance.**

**Preponderate,** pre-pon'dèr-āt, *v.t.* to *outweigh:* to incline to one side: to exceed in power or influence.—*n.* **Preponderā'tion.** [L. *præ,* before,

and *pondero, -atus,* to weigh, from *pondus,* a weight.]

**Preposition,** prep-o-zish'un, *n.* a word *placed before* a noun or pronoun to show its relation to some other word of the sentence.—*adj.* **Preposi'tional.**—*adv.* **Preposi'tionally.** [Fr.—L. *præpositio—præ,* before, and *pono, positum,* to place or put; so called because orig. *præfixed* to the verb, in order to modify its meaning.]

**Prepossess,** pre-poz-zes', *v.t.* to *possess before*hand: to preoccupy, as the mind: to bias or prejudice. [L. *præ,* before, **Possess.**]

**Prepossessing,** pre-poz-zes'ing, *adj.* tending to *prepossess* in one's favour: giving a favourable impression.—*adv.* **Prepossess'ingly.**

**Prepossession,** pre-poz-zesh'un, *n., previous possession:* preconceived opinion or impression.

**Preposterous,** pre-pos'tèr-us, *adj.* contrary to nature or reason: wrong: absurd: foolish.—*adv.* **Prepos'terously.**—*n.* **Prepos'terousness.** [Lit. 'having that *first* which ought to be *last,*' L. *præposterus—præ,* before, *posterus,* after—*post,* after.]

**Prerogative,** pre-rog'a-tiv, *n.* an exclusive or peculiar privilege. [Lit. 'privilege of voting first, or before others,' Fr.—L. *prærogativus,* that is asked before others for his opinion or vote —*præ,* before, *rogo, -atum,* to ask.]

**Presage,** pres'āj, *n.* something that indicates a future event.—*adj.* **Presage'ful.** [Lit. 'something perceived beforehand,' Fr. *présage—*L. *præsagium—præsagio—præ,* before, *sagio,* to perceive quickly. See **Sagacious.**]

**Presage,** pre-sāj', *v.t.* to forebode: to indicate something to come: to prophesy.—*n.* **Presag'er.**

**Presbyopia,** pres-bi-ō'pi-a, *n.* long-sightedness. [Gr. *presbys,* old, and *ops, opos,* the eye.]

**Presbyter,** prez'bi-tèr, *n.* (in the Eng. Church) one of the second order of the ministry: a member of a presbytery. [Lit. 'elder,' L.—Gr. *presbyteros,* comp. of *presbys,* old. Cf. **Priest.**]

**Presbyterian,** prez-bi-tē'ri-an, **Presbyterial,** prez-bi-tē'ri-al, *adj.* pertaining to or consisting of *presbyters:* pertaining to Presbytery or that form of church government in which all the clergy or presbyters are equal:—opp. to **Episcopacy.**—*n.* **Presbyte'rian,** an adherent of this form of church government.

**Presbyterianism,** prez-bi-tē'ri-an-izm, *n.* the form of church government of Presbyterians.

**Presbytery,** prez'bi-tèr-i, *n.* (*orig.*) a council of *presbyters* or elders: a church court consisting of the ministers and one elder, a layman, from each church within a certain district: (*arch.*) that part of the church reserved for the officiating priests.

**Prescience,** prē'shi-ens, *n., knowledge* of events *before*hand: foresight. [Fr.]

**Prescient,** prē'shi-ent, *adj., knowing* things *before*hand. [L. *præsciens, -entis,* pr.p. of *præscio,* to foreknow—*præ,* before, *scio,* to know.]

**Prescribe,** pre-skrīb', *v.t.* to lay down for direction: to appoint: (*med.*) to give directions for, as a remedy.—*n.* **Prescrib'er.** [L. *præscribo, -scriptum—præ,* before, *scribo,* to write.]

**Prescript,** prē'skript, *n.* something *prescribed:* direction: model prescribed.

**Prescriptible,** pre-skript'i-bl, *adj.* that may be *prescribed* for.—*n.* **Prescriptibil'ity.**

**Prescription,** pre-skrip'shun, *n.* act of *prescribing* or directing: (*med.*) a written direction for the preparation of a medicine: a recipe: (*law*) custom continued until it has the force of law. [Fr.—L. *præscriptio.*]

**Prescriptive**, pre-skript′iv, *adj.* consisting in or acquired by custom or immemorial use. [L.]

**Presence**, prez′ens, *n.* state of being *present* (opp. of **Absence**): situation within sight, &c.: approach face to face: the person of a superior: the persons assembled before a great person: mien: personal appearance: calmness, readiness, as of mind. [Fr.—L. *præsentia—præsens.* See **Present**, *adj.*]

**Presence-chamber**, prez′ens-chām′bėr, *n.* the *chamber* or room in which a great personage receives company.

**Present**, prez′ent, *adj.* being in a certain place (opp. to **Absent**): now under view or consideration: being at this time: not past or future: ready at hand: attentive: not absent-minded: (*gram.*) denoting time just now, or making a general statement.—*n.* present time.—**At present**, at the present time, now. [Lit. 'being before or near,' Fr.—L. *præsens, præsens—præ*, before, and *sens*, being, cog. with Sans. *sant*, being, and **Sooth**.]

**Present**, pre-zent′, *v.t.* to *set before*, to introduce: to exhibit to view: to offer: to put into the possession of another: to make a gift of: to appoint to a benefice: to lay before for consideration: to point, as a gun before firing.—*adj.* **Present′able.**—*n.* **Present′er**. [Fr.—L. *præsento—præsens.* See **Present**, *adj.*]

**Present**, prez′ent, *n.* that which is *presented* or given, a gift.

**Presentation**, prez-en-tā′shun, *n.* act of *presenting*: a setting: representation: the right of presenting to a benefice. [L. *præsentatio.*]

**Presentee**, prez-en-tē′, *n.* one who is *presented* to a benefice.

**Presentiment**, pre-sen′ti-ment, *n.* a *sentiment* or perceiving *before*hand: previous opinion: a conviction of something unpleasant to happen. [O. Fr.—L. *præsentire.* See **Sentiment**.]

**Presently**, prez′ent-li, *adv.* without delay: after a little. [Orig. 'at present,' now.]

**Presentment**, pre-zent′ment, *n.* act of *presenting*: the thing presented or represented: (*law*) information taken of an offence by a grand-jury from observation: accusation presented by a grand-jury.

**Preservation**, prez-ėr-vā′shun, *n.* act of *preserving*: state of being preserved.

**Preservative**, pre-zėrv′a-tiv, **Preservatory**, pre-zėrv′a-tor-i, *adj.* tending to *preserve*: having the quality of preserving.—*n.* that which preserves: a preventive of injury or decay.

**Preserve**, pre-zėrv′, *v.t.* to keep from injury: to defend: to keep in a sound state: to season for preservation: to keep up, as appearances.—*n.* that which is preserved, as fruit, &c.: a place for the protection of animals, as game, &c.—*n.* **Preserv′er**. [Fr. *préserver*—L. *præ*, beforehand, *servo*, to preserve.]

**Preside**, pre-zīd′, *v.i.* to direct or control, esp. at a meeting: to superintend. [Lit. 'to sit before' or 'above,' Fr. *présider*—L. *præsideo—præ*, before, *sedeo*, E. **Sit**.]

**Presidency**, prez′i-den-si, *n.* the office of a *president*, or his dignity, term of office, jurisdiction, or residence.

**President**, prez′i-dent, *n.* one who *presides* over a meeting: a chairman: the chief officer of a college, institution, &c.: an officer elected to the supreme executive of a province or nation.—*n.* **Pres′identship**. [Fr.—L. *præsidens, -entis*, pr.p. of *præsideo.*]

**Presidential**, prez-i-den′shal, *adj.*, *presiding* over: pertaining to a president.

**Presignify**, pre-sig′ni-fī, *v.t.* to signify beforehand. [L. *præ*, before, and **Signify**.]

**Press**, pres, *v.t.* to squeeze or crush strongly: to hug: to drive with violence: to bear heavily on: to distress: to urge: to inculcate with earnestness.—*v.i.* to exert pressure: to push with force: to crowd: to go forward with violence: to urge with vehemence and importunity: to exert a strong influence.—*n.* **Press′er**. [Fr. *presser*—L. *presso—premo, pressus*, to squeeze.]

**Press**, pres, *n.* an instrument for squeezing bodies: a printing-machine: the art or business of printing and publishing: act of urging forward: urgency: a crowd: a closet for holding articles.—**The Press**, the literature of a country, esp. newspapers.—**Press of Sail**, as much sail as can be carried.

**Press**, pres, *v.t.* (*orig.*) to engage men by *prest* or earnest-money for the public service: to carry men off by violence to become soldiers or sailors.—*n.* **Press′-money**, earnest-money. [Corr. from old form *prest*, from O. Fr. *prester* (Fr. *prêter*), to lend—L. *præsto*, to stand before, to offer—*præ*, before, and *sto*, E. **Stand**.]

**Pressfat**, pres′fat, *n.* (*B.*) the *vat* of an olive or wine *press* for collecting the liquor.

**Pressgang**, pres′gang, *n.* a gang or body of sailors under an officer empowered to impress men into the navy. [See **Press**, to carry men off, &c.]

**Pressingly**, pres′ing-li, *adv.* **Press′ingly.**

**Pressing**, pres′ing, *adj.* urgent: importunate: forcing.

**Pressure**, presh′ūr, *n.* act of *pressing*: a squeezing: the state of being pressed: impulse: constraining force: that which presses or afflicts: difficulties: urgency: (*physics*) the action of force on something resisting it. [O. Fr.—L. *pressura—premo.*]

**Prestidigitation**, pres′ti-dij′it-ā-shun, also **Prestig′iation**, *n.* sleight of hand.—*n.* **Pres′tidig′itator** and **Prestig′iator**, one who practises such.

**Prestige**, pres′tij or pres′tēzh, *n.* influence arising from past conduct or from reputation. [Orig. 'illusion' or 'deception,' Fr.—L. *præstigium—præsti(n)guo*, to obscure, to deceive.]

**Presumable**, pre-zūm′a-bl, *adj.* that may be *presumed*.—*adv.* **Presum′ably.**

**Presume**, pre-zūm′, *v.t.* to take as true without examination or proof: to take for granted.—*v.i.* to venture beyond what one has ground for: to act forwardly. [Lit. 'to take beforehand,' Fr. *présumer*—L. *præsumo—præ*, before, *sumo, sub*, under, and *emo*, to take, to buy.]

**Presuming**, pre-zūm′ing, *adj.* venturing without permission: unreasonably bold.—*adv.* **Presum′ingly.**

**Presumption**, pre-zum′shun, *n.* act of *presuming*: supposition: strong probability: confidence grounded on something not proved: forward conduct: (*law*) assuming the truth of certain facts from circumstantial evidence. [Through O. Fr., from L. *præsumptio, -onis.*]

**Presumptive**, pre-zump′tiv, *adj.*, *presuming*: grounded on probable evidence: (*law*) proving circumstantially.—*adv.* **Presump′tively.**

**Presumptuous**, pre-zump′tū-us, *adj.* full of *presumption*: bold and confident: founded on presumption: wilful.—*adv.* **Presump′tuously.**—*n.* **Presump′tuousness.** [L. *præsumptuosus.*]

**Presuppose**, pre-sup-pōz′, *v.t.* to *suppose before* other things: to assume.—*n.* **Presupposi′tion.** [L. *præ*, before, and **Suppose**.]

**Pretence**, pre-tens′, *n.* something *pretended*: appearance or show: pretext: assumption: claim.

**Pretend**, pre-tend′, *v.t.* to hold out as a cloak for

something else : to offer something feigned : to affect to feel.—*v.i.* to put in a claim.—*n.* **Pretend′er.** [Lit. 'to stretch out before one,' Fr. *prétendre*—L. *prætendo*—*præ*, before, *tendo*, *tentum*, *tensum*, to stretch.]

**Pretension,** pre-ten′shun, *n.* something *pretended* : false or fictitious appearance : claim.

**Pretentious,** pre-ten′shus, *adj.* marked by or containing *pretence* : presumptuous : arrogant.

**Preterimperfect,** prē-tėr-im-pėr′fekt, *adj.* implying that an event was happening at a certain time. [L. *præter*, beyond, and **Imperfect.**]

**Preterit, Preterite,** pret′ėr-it, *adj.*, *gone by* : *past* : noting the *past* tense.—*n.* the past tense. [L. *præteritus*—*præter*, beyond, and *eo*, *itum*, to go.] [ing by : omission.

**Pretermission,** prē-tėr-mish′un, *n.* the act of pass-

**Pretermit,** prē-tėr-mit′, *v.t.* to pass by : to omit : —*pr.p.* prētermitt′ing ; *pa.t.* and *pa.p.* prētermitt′ed. [L. *præter*, past, and *mitto*, to send.]

**Preternatural,** prē-tėr-nat′ū-ral, *adj.*, *beyond* what is *natural* : extraordinary.—*adv.* **Preternat′urally.** [L. *præter*, beyond, and **Natural.**]

**Preterperfect,** prē-tėr-pėr′fekt, *adj.* denoting the *perfect* tense. [L. *præter*, more than, and **Perfect.**]

**Preterpluperfect,** prē-tėr-ploo′pėr-fekt, *adj.* denoting the *pluperfect* tense. [L. *præter*, beyond, and **Pluperfect.**]

**Pretext,** prē′tekst or pre-tekst′, *n.* an ostensible motive or reason put forward in order to conceal the real one : a pretence. [Lit. 'something *woven* in front,' L. *prætextum*—*prætexo* —*præ*, before, *texo*, to weave.]

**Pretor,** &c. See **Prætor,** &c.

**Prettily,** pret′i-li, *adv.* in a *pretty* manner : pleasingly : elegantly : neatly.

**Pretty,** pret′i, *adj.* tasteful : pleasing : neat : beautiful without dignity : small : affected : (in contempt) fine.—*n.* **Prett′iness.** [A.S. *prættig*, tricky—*prætt*, trickery ; prob. from the Celt., as W. *praith*, a deed.]

**Pretty,** pret′i, *adv.* in some degree : moderately.

**Pretypify,** pre-tip′i-fī, *v.t.* to represent *before*-hand in a *type*. [L. *præ*, before, and **Typify.**]

**Prevail,** pre-vāl′, *v.i.* to be *very powerful* : to have influence or effect : to overcome : to gain the advantage : to be in force : to succeed. [Fr. *prévaloir*—L. *prævaleo*—*præ*, before or above others, and *valeo*, to be powerful.]

**Prevailing,** pre-vāl′ing, *adj.* having great power : efficacious : most general.

**Prevalence,** prev′al-ens, **Prevalency,** prev′al-en-si, *n.* the state of being *prevalent* : preponderance : superiority : influence : efficacy.

**Prevalent,** prev′al-ent, *adj.*, *prevailing* : having great power : victorious : most common.—*adv.* **Prev′alently.**

**Prevaricate,** pre-var′i-kāt, *v.i.* to shift about from side to side, to evade the truth : to quibble. [Lit. 'to spread the legs apart in walking,' L. *prævaricor*, *-atus*—*præ*, inten., and *varicus*, straddling—*varus*, bent, straddling.]

**Prevarication,** prē-var-i-kā′shun, *n.* the act of quibbling to evade the truth.

**Prevaricator,** pre-var′i-kāt-or, *n.* one who *prevaricates* to evade the truth : a quibbler.

**Prevent,** pre-vent′, *v.t.* to hinder : to obviate. [Lit. and orig. 'to come or go before,' L. *præventus*, pa.p. of *prævenio*—*præ*, before, and *venio*, to come.]

**Preventable,** pre-vent′a-bl, *adj.* that may be *prevented* or hindered.

**Prevention,** pre-ven′shun, *n.* act of preventing :

anticipation : obstruction. [Lit. 'a coming before.']

**Preventive,** pre-vent′iv, *adj.* tending to *prevent* or hinder : preservative.—*n.* that which prevents : a preservative.

**Previous,** prē′vi-us, *adj.*, *going before* : former. —*adv.* **Pre′viously.** [Lit. 'on the way before,' L. *prævius*—*præ*, before, and *via*, a way.]

**Prewarn,** pre-wawrn′, *v.t.* to *warn before*hand. [L. *præ*, before, and **Warn** ; a hybrid word, a quite unnecessary synonym of the correct form **Forewarn.**]

**Prey,** prā, *n.* booty : plunder : that which is or may be seized to be devoured.—*v.i.* to plunder : to seize and devour : to waste or impair gradually : to weigh heavily (followed by *on* or *upon*). [O. Fr. *praie* (Fr. *proie*)—L. *præda*.]

**Price,** prīs, *n.* that at which anything is *prized*, *valued*, or *bought* : excellence : recompense.—*v.t.* to set a value on. [O. Fr. *pris* (Fr. *prix*)— L. *pretium*, akin to Gr. *priamai*, to buy. See **Prize,** *v.*] [without value : worthless.

**Priceless,** prīs′les, *adj.* beyond *price* : invaluable :

**Prick,** prik, *n.* a sharp *point* : a puncture : a sting : remorse.—*v.t.* to pierce with a prick : to erect any pointed thing : to fix by the point : to put on by puncturing : to mark or make by pricking : to incite : to pain :—*pa.t.* and *pa.p.* pricked. [A.S. *pricu*, a point, a dot, cog. with Ger. *prick-eln*, Dut. *prikk-el*, a prickle.]

**Pricker,** prik′ėr, *n.* that which *pricks* : a sharp-pointed instrument : light-horseman.

**Prickle,** prik′l, *n.* a *little prick* : a sharp point growing from the bark of a plant. [liness

**Prickly,** prik′li, *adj.* full of *prickles*.—*n.* **Prick′**-

**Prickly-pear,** prik′li-pār, *n.* a class of plants, generally covered with clusters of strong hairs or *prickles*, and bearing fruit like the *pear*.

**Pride,** prīd, *n.* state or feeling of being *proud* : extreme self-esteem : haughtiness : noble self-esteem : that of which men are proud : that which excites boasting.—*v.t.* to take pride : to value (followed by a reciprocal pron.). [A.S. *pryte*—*prut*, proud. See **Proud.**]

**Priest,** prēst, *n.* one who officiates in sacred offices : one above a deacon and below a bishop : a clergyman.—*fem.* **Priest′ess.** [A.S. *preóst* (O. Fr. *prestre*, Fr. *prêtre*), contr. of L. *presbyter*, an elder or presbyter. Doublet **Presbyter.**]

**Priestcraft,** prēst′kraft, *n.* priestly policy : the *craft* or schemes of *priests* to gain wealth or power.

**Priesthood,** prēst′hood, *n.* the office or character of a *priest* : the priestly order.

**Priestly,** prēst′li, *adj.* pertaining to or resembling a *priest*.—*n.* **Priest′liness.**

**Priest-ridden,** prēst′-rid′en, *adj.*, *ridden* or controlled entirely by *priests*.

**Prig,** prig, *n.* a pert fellow who gives himself airs of superior wisdom. [Ety. unknown.]

**Prig,** prig, *n.* a thief. [Ety. dub.]

**Prim,** prim, *adj.* exact and precise in manner : affectedly nice.—*v.t.* to deck with great nicety : to form with affected preciseness :—*pr.p.* prim′ming ; *pa.t.* and *pa.p.* primmed.—*adv.* **Prim′ly.**— *n.* **Prim′ness.** [O. Fr. *prim*, fem. *prime*—L. *primus*, *prima*, first.]

**Primacy,** prī′ma-si, *n.* the office or dignity of a *primate* or archbishop.

**Prima-donna,** prē′ma-don′a, *n.* the *first* or leading *female* singer in an opera. [Lit. 'first lady' —It.—L. *prima domina*.]

**Primage,** prīm′āj, *n.* an allowance to the captain

of a vessel by the shipper or consignee of goods for loading the same. [See **Prime**, first.]

**Primal**, prī'mal, *adj.*, *first* : original.

**Primary**, prī'mar-i, *adj.*, *first*, original : chief : primitive.—*n.* that which is highest in rank or importance.—*adv.* **Pri'marily.**

**Primate**, prī'māt, *n.* the *first* or highest dignitary in a church : an archbishop.—*n.* **Pri'mateship.**

**Prime**, prīm, *adj.*, *first*, in order of time, rank, or importance : chief : excellent : original : early.—*n.* the beginning : the dawn : the spring : the best part : the height of perfection. [L. *prīmus* (for *pro-i-mus*), cog. with A.S. *for-ma*. Cf. **Former** and **Prior**.]

**Prime**, prīm, *v.t.* to put powder on the nipple of a firearm : to lay on the first coating of colour.—*v.i.* to serve for the charge of a gun. [See **Prime**, *adj.*]

**Prime-minister**, prīm-min'is-tèr, *n.* the *first* or chief *minister* of state. [See **Premier**.]

**Prime-number**, prīm-num'bèr, *n.* a *first number*, *i.e.* one divisible only by itself or unity.

**Primer**, prim'èr or prīm'-, *n.* a *first* book : a work of elementary religious instruction : a first reading-book : an elementary introduction to any subject. [Orig. a small prayer-book.]

**Primeval**, prī-mē'val, *adj.* belonging to the *first ages* : original : primitive. [L. *primævus—primus*, first, and *ævum*, an age. See **Age**.]

**Priming**, prīm'ing, *n.* the *first* coating of colour : the powder in the nipple of a firearm.

**Primitive**, prim'i-tiv, *adj.* belonging to the beginning, or to the *first* times : original : ancient : antiquated : old-fashioned : not derived.—*n.* a primitive word, or one not derived from another.—*adv.* **Prim'itively.**—*n.* **Prim'itiveness.** [Fr.—L. *primitivus*, an extension of *primus*.]

**Primogenial**, prī-mo-jē'ni-al, *adj.*, *first born* or made : primary : constituent. [L. *primus*, first, and *geno, genitus*, to beget. See **Genus**.]

**Primogenitor**, prī-mo-jen'i-tor, *n.* the *first begetter* or father : a forefather.

**Primogeniture**, prī-mo-jen'i-tūr, *n.* state of being *born first* of the same parents : (*law*) the right of inheritance of the eldest born.

**Primordial**, prī-mor'di-al, *adj.*, *first* in *order* : original : existing from the beginning.—*n.* first principle or element. [L. *primus*, first, and *ordo*, order.]

**Primrose**, prim'rōz, *n.* an *early* spring flower common in woods and meadows. [Lit. the 'first rose,' Fr. *prime rose*—L. *prima rosa* : see **Prime** and **Rose**. Historically, this form took the place of M. E. *primerole*, which is traced through O. Fr. *primerole* and Low L. diminutive forms to L. *primus*.]

**Prince**, prins, *n.* one of highest rank : a sovereign : son of a king or emperor : the chief of any body of men.—*fem.* **Princess**, prin'ses. [Lit. 'one taking the first place,' Fr.—L. *princeps—primus*, first, *capio*, to take.]

**Princedom**, prins'dum, *n.* the estate, jurisdiction, sovereignty, or rank of a prince.

**Princely**, prins'li, *adj.*, *princelike* : becoming a prince : grand : august : regal.—*adv.* in a prince-like manner.—*n.* **Prince'liness.**

**Principal**, prin'si-pal, *adj.* taking the *first* place : highest in character or importance : chief.—*n.* a principal person or thing : a head, as of a school or college : one who takes a leading part : money on which interest is paid : (*arch.*) a main beam or timber : (*law*) the perpetrator of a crime, or an abettor : (*music*) an organ stop.—*adv.* **Prin'cipally.** [L. *principalis*.]

**Principality**, prin-si-pal'i-ti, *n.* the territory of a *prince* or the country which gives title to him : obs. (*B.*) a prince, a power.

**Principle**, prin'si-pl, *n.* a fundamental truth : a law or doctrine from which others are derived : an original faculty of the mind : a settled rule of action : (*chem.*) a constituent part.—*v.t.* to establish in principles : to impress with a doctrine. [L. *principium*, beginning—*princeps*.]

**Print**, print, *v.t.* to *press* or *impress* : to mark by pressure : to impress letters on paper, &c. : to publish.—*v.i.* to practise the art of printing : to publish a book.—*n.* a *mark* or character made by *impression* : the impression of types in general : a copy : an engraving : a newspaper : a printed cloth : calico : that which impresses its form on anything : a cut, in wood or metal : (*arch.*) a plaster-cast in low relief. [Shortened from O. Fr. *empreindre, empreint*—L. *imprimo—in*, into, and *premo*, to press.]

**Printer**, print'èr, *n.* one who prints, especially books, newspapers, &c.

**Printing**, print'ing, *n.* act, art, or practice of printing. [printing.

**Prior**, prī'or, *adj.*, *former* : previous : coming before in time.—*n.* the head of a priory.—*fem.* **Pri'oress.** [L. *prior*, former, earlier, comp. from a positive form *pro-*, in front. See **Prime**.]

**Priorate**, prī'or-āt, **Priorship**, prī'or-ship, *n.* the government or office of a *prior*.

**Priority**, prī-or'i-ti, *n.* state of being *prior* or first in time, place, or rank : preference.

**Priory**, prī'or-i, *n.* a convent of either sex, under a *prior* or *prioress*, and next below an abbey.

**Prism**, prizm, *n.* (*geom.*) a solid whose ends are similar, equal, and parallel planes, and whose sides are parallelograms : (*optics*) a solid glass, triangular-shaped body. [Lit. 'anything sawn,' L.—Gr. *prism-a, -atos*, from *prizō*, to saw.]

**Prismatic**, priz-mat'ik, **Prismatical**, priz-mat'i-kal, *adj.* resembling or pertaining to a *prism* : formed by a prism.—*adv.* **Prismat'ically.**

**Prismoid**, priz'moid, *n.* a figure in the form of a prism. [**Prism**, and Gr. *eidos*, form.]

**Prison**, priz'n, *n.* a building for the confinement of criminals, &c. : a gaol : any place of confinement. [Fr.—L. *prensio, -onis*, for *prehensio*, a seizing—*pre-hendo, -hensus*, to seize, from obs. *hendo*. See **Get**.] [prison : a captive.

**Prisoner**, priz'n-èr, *n.* one arrested or confined in

**Pristine**, pris'tin, *adj.* as at *first* : former : belonging to the beginning or earliest time : ancient. [O. Fr.—L. *pristinus*, from *pris-* (= *prius*, earlier), and *-tenus*, stretching.]

**Privacy**, prī'va-si or priv'-, *n.* state of being *private* or retired from company or observation : a place of seclusion : retreat : retirement : secrecy.

**Private**, prī'vāt, *adj.* apart from the state : not invested with public office : peculiar to one's self : belonging to an individual person or company : not public : retired from observation : secret : not publicly known : not holding a commission.—*n.* a common soldier.—*adv.* **Pri'vately.**—*n.* **Pri'vateness.** [Lit. 'cut off from others,' L. *privatus*, pa.p. of *privo*, to separate—*privus*, single. Doublet **Privy**.]

**Privateer**, prī-va-tēr', *n.* an armed *private* vessel commissioned to seize and plunder an enemy's ships.—*v.i.* to cruise in a privateer : to fit out privateers.

**Privation**, prī-vā'shun, *n.* state of being *deprived* of something, esp. of what is necessary for comfort : destitution : hardship : absence of any quality. [Fr. See under **Private**.]

**Privative**, priv'a-tiv, *adj.* causing *privation* : consisting in the absence of something.—*n.* that which is privative or depends on the absence of something else: (*logic*) a term denoting the absence of a quality: (*gram.*) a prefix denoting absence or negation.—*adv.* **Priv′atively.** [L.]

**Privet,** priv′et, *n.* a half-evergreen European shrub much used for hedges. [Ety. unknown.]

**Privilege,** priv′i-lej, *n.* a peculiar advantage: a right not general: prerogative.—*v.t.* to grant a privilege to: to exempt. [Fr.—L. *privilegium,* lit. 'a law regarding only a single person'—*privus,* single, and *lex, legis,* a law.]

**Privily,** priv′i-li, *adv., privately:* secretly.

**Privity,** priv′i-ti, *n.* joint knowledge of something *private* or confidential: knowledge implying concurrence:—*pl.* secret parts.

**Privy,** priv′i, *adj., private:* pertaining to one person: for private uses: secret: appropriated to retirement: admitted to the knowledge of something secret.—*n.* (*law*) a person having an interest in an action: a necessary-house.—*n.* **Privy-council,** the *private council* of a sovereign to advise in the administration of government.—*n.* **Privy-councillor,** a member of the privy-council.—*n.* **Privy-purse,** the *purse* or money for the *private* or personal use of the sovereign.—*n.* **Privy seal** or **signet,** the seal used by or for the king in subordinate matters, or those which are not to pass the great seal. [Fr. *privé*—L. *privatus.* See **Private.**]

**Prize,** prīz, *n.* that which is *taken* or gained by competition: anything taken from an enemy in war: a captured vessel: that which is won in a lottery: anything offered for competition: a reward. [Fr. *prise—pris,* taken, pa.p. of *prendre*—L. *pre(he)ndo.* See **Prison.**]

**Prize,** prīz, *v.t.* to set a *price* on: to value: to value highly. [Fr. *priser*—O. Fr. *pris,* price (Fr. *prix*)—L. *pretium,* price, value.]

**Prize-court,** prīz′-kōrt, *n.* a *court* for judging regarding *prizes* made on the high seas.

**Prize-fighter,** prīz′-fīt′ėr, *n.* a boxer who *fights* publicly for a *prize.*—*n.* **Prize′-fight′ing.**

**Prize-money,** prīz′-mun′i, *n.* share of the *money* or proceeds from any *prizes* taken from an enemy.

**Proa,** prō′a, *n.* a small Malay sailing-vessel. [Malay *prau.*]

**Probability,** prob-a-bil′i-ti, *n.* quality of being *probable:* appearance of truth: that which is probable: chance.

**Probable,** prob′a-bl, *adj.* having more evidence for than against: giving ground for belief: likely.—*adv.* **Prob′ably.** [Orig. 'that may be proved,' Fr.—L. *probabilis—probo, probatus,* to prove—*probus,* good, excellent. See **Prove.**]

**Probate,** prō′bāt, *n.* the *proof* before competent authority that an instrument, purporting to be the will of a person deceased, is indeed his lawful act: the official copy of a will, with the certificate of its having been proved: the right or jurisdiction of proving wills. [L. *probatum,* proved. See **Probable.**]

**Probation,** pro-bā′shun, *n.* act of *proving:* any proceeding to elicit truth, &c.: trial: time of trial: moral trial: novitiate. [Fr.—L.]

**Probational,** pro-bā′shun-al, **Probationary,** pro-bā′shun-ar-i, *adj.* relating to probation or trial.

**Probationer,** pro-bā′shun-ėr, *n.* one who is on probation or trial: (*Scotland*) one licensed to preach, but not ordained to a pastorate.

**Probative,** prō′ba-tiv, **Probatory,** prō′ba-tor-i, *adj.* serving for *proof* or trial: relating to proof.

**Probe,** prōb, *n.* an instrument for *proving* or examining a wound, &c.: that which tries or probes.—*v.t.* to examine with or as with a *probe:* to examine thoroughly. [L. *probo,* to prove.]

**Probity,** prob′i-ti, *n.* uprightness: honesty. [Fr.—L. *probitas—probus,* good, excellent.]

**Problem,** prob′lem, *n.* a matter difficult of settlement or solution: (*geom.*) a proposition in which something is required to be done. [Lit. 'a question *thrown* or put *forward*,' Fr.—L.—Gr. *problēma, -atos—pro,* before, and *ballō,* to throw.]

**Problematic,** prob-lem-at′ik, **Problematical,** prob-lem-at′ik-al, *adj.* of the nature of a problem: questionable: doubtful.—*adv.* **Problemat′ically.**

**Proboscis,** pro-bos′is, *n.* the trunk of some animals, as the elephant, for conveying food to the mouth. [L.—Gr.—*proboskis,* a trunk, lit. 'front-feeder' —*pro,* in front, and *boskō* (L. *pasco*), to feed.]

**Procedure,** pro-sēd′ūr, *n.* the act of *proceeding:* progress: process: conduct.

**Proceed,** pro-sēd′, *v.i.* to *go forward:* to advance: to issue: to be produced: to prosecute. [Fr. *procéder*—L. *procedo—pro,* before, and *cedo,* cessum, to go.]

**Proceeding,** pro-sēd′ing, *n.* a *going forth* or *forward:* progress: step: operation: transaction.

**Proceeds,** prō′sēdz, *n.pl.* the money *proceeding* or arising from anything: rent: produce.

**Process,** pros′es or prō′-, *n.* a *going forward:* gradual progress: operation: the whole proceedings in an action or prosecution: series of measures: a projection on a bone. [Fr. *procès*— L. *processus.*]

**Procession,** pro-sesh′un, *n.* the act of *proceeding:* a train of persons in a formal march. [Fr.—L.]

**Processional,** pro-sesh′un-al, *adj.* pertaining to a *procession:* consisting in a procession.—*n.* a book of the processions of the Romish Church.

**Proclaim,** pro-klām′, *v.t.* to publish: to announce officially.—*n.* **Proclaim′er.** [Fr. *proclamer*— L. *proclamo—pro,* out, and *clamo,* to cry. See **Claim.**]

**Proclamation,** prok-la-mā′shun, *n.* the act of *proclaiming:* official notice given to the public.

**Proclivity,** pro-kliv′i-ti, *n.* an *inclining forwards:* tendency: inclination: aptitude. [L. *proclivitas —proclivus,* having a slope forwards—*pro,* forwards, and *clivus,* a slope. See **Decline.**]

**Proconsul,** pro-kon′sul, *n.* a Roman officer having the power *of* a *consul* without his office: the governor of a province. [L.—*pro,* instead of, and **Consul.**]

**Proconsular,** pro-kon′sū-lar, *adj.* pertaining to or under the government of a *proconsul.*

**Proconsulate,** pro-kon′sū-lāt, **Proconsulship,** pro-kon′sul-ship, *n.* the office or term of office of a *proconsul.*

**Procrastinate,** pro-kras′ti-nāt, *v.t.* to *put off* till some future time: to postpone.—*n.* **Procras′tinator.** [Lit. 'to put off till the morrow,' L. —*pro,* forward, off, and *crastinus,* of to-morrow —*cras,* to-morrow, and *tenus,* stretching.]

**Procrastination,** pro-kras-ti-nā′shun *n.* a putting off till a future time: dilatoriness.

**Procreate,** prō′kre-āt, *v.t.* to generate: to propagate. [L. *procre-o, -atus—pro,* forth, and *creo,* to produce. See **Create.**]

**Procreation,** prō-kre-ā′shun, *n.* the act of *procreating:* generation: production. [Fr.—L.]

**Procreative,** prō′kre-ā-tiv, *adj.* having the power to *procreate:* generative: productive.—*n.* **Pro′creativeness.** [a father

**Procreator,** prō′kre-ā-tor, *n.* one who *procreates:*

**Procrustean,** pro-krus′te-an, *adj.* reducing by violence to strict conformity to a measure or model : from *Procrustes*, a fabled robber of ancient Greece, who stretched or cut a piece off the legs of his captives, so as to fit them to an iron bed, on which he laid them. [Gr. *prokroustēs* (*lit.*) 'the stretcher.']

**Proctor**, prok′tor, *n.* a *procurator* or manager for another : an attorney in the spiritual courts : an official in the English universities who attends to the morals of the students and enforces obedience to university regulations.—*n.* **Proc′torship**. [Contr. of Procurator.]

**Proctorial**, prok-tō′ri-al, *adj.* pertaining to a *proctor:* magisterial.

**Procumbent**, pro-kum′bent, *adj., leaning forwards :* lying down or on the face : (*bot.*) trailing. [L. *pro*, forward, *cumbo*, to lie down.]

**Procurable**, pro-kūr′a-bl, *adj.* that may be *procured.*

**Procuration**, prok-ūr-ā′shun, *n.* the act of managing another's affairs : the instrument giving power to do this : a sum paid by incumbents to the bishop or archdeacon on visitations.

**Procurator**, prok′ūr-ā-tor, *n.* one who *takes care of* or attends to a thing for another : a governor of a province under the Roman emperors.—*n.* **Proc′uratorship**. [L. See Procure. Cf. **Proctor**.]

**Procure**, pro-kūr′, *v.t.* to obtain : to cause : to attract. [Fr. *procurer*—L. *procuro*, to take care of, to manage—*pro*, in behalf of, and *curo*, *-atus*, to care for.]

**Procurement**, pro-kūr′ment, *n.* the act of *procuring:* management : agency.

**Procurer**, pro-kūr′er, *n.* one who *procures:* a pimp : a pander.—*fem.* **Proc′uress**.

**Prodigal**, prod′i-gal, *adj.* wasteful : lavish : profuse.—*n.* one who throws away from him : a waster : a spendthrift.—*adv.* **Prod′igally**, wastefully. [Lit. 'driving forth or away,' Fr.—L. *prodigus*—*prodigo*, to drive away, squander—*pro*, forth or away, and *ago*, to drive.]

**Prodigality**, prod-i-gal′i-ti, *n.* state or quality of *being prodigal:* extravagance : profusion.

**Prodigious**, pro-dij′us, *adj.* like a *prodigy:* astonishing : enormous : monstrous.—*adv.* **Prodig′iously**.—*n.* **Prodig′iousness**. [Fr. *prodigieux*—L. *prodigiosus*. See Prodigy.]

**Prodigy**, prod′i-ji, *n.* a portent : anything extraordinary : a wonder : a monster. [Fr. *prodige*—L. *prodigium*, a prophetic sign.]

**Produce**, pro-dūs′, *v.t.* to *lead* or *bring forward:* to bear : to exhibit : to yield : to cause : (*geom.*) to extend.—*n.* **Produc′er**. [L. *produco*, *-ductus*—*pro*, forward, and *duco*, to lead. See **Duke**.]

**Produce**, prod′ūs, *n.* that which is *produced :* product, proceeds.

**Producible**, pro-dūs′i-bl, *adj.* that may be *produced :* that may be generated or made : that may be exhibited.—*n.* **Produc′ibleness**.

**Product**, prod′ukt, *n.* that which is *produced :* work : composition : effect : (*arith.*) the result of numbers multiplied together.

**Production**, pro-duk′shun, *n.* the act of *producing:* that which is produced : fruit : product.

**Productive**, pro-duk′tiv, *adj.* having the power to *produce :* generative : fertile : efficient.—*adv.* **Produc′tively**.—*n.* **Produc′tiveness**.

**Proem**, prō′em, *n.* an *introduction :* a prelude : a preface.—*adj.* **Proem′ial**. [Fr. *proème*—L. *prooemium*—Gr. *prooimion*—*pro*, before, and *oi-mos*, a way—root *i-*, to go.]

**Profanation**, prof-a-nā′shun, *n.* the act of *profaning:* desecration : irreverence to what is holy. [Fr.—L.]

**Profane**, pro-fān′, *adj.* unholy : impious : impure : common : secular.—*adv.* **Profane′ly**.—*n.* **Profane′ness**. [Lit. 'before the temple,' outside of it, common, Fr.—L. *profanus*—*pro*, before, and *fanum*, a temple. See **Fane**.]

**Profane**, pro-fān′, *v.t.* to violate anything holy : to abuse anything sacred : to put to a wrong use : (*B.*) to pollute : to debase.—*n.* **Profan′er**.

**Profanity**, pro-fan′i-ti, *n.* irreverence : that which is profane : profane language. [L.]

**Profess**, pro-fes′, *v.t.* to own freely : to declare in strong terms : to announce publicly one's skill in. [Fr. *profès*, professed, said of a member of a religious order—L. *professus*, perf.p. of *profiteor*—*pro*, publicly, *fateor*, to confess. See **Confess**.]

**Professed**, pro-fest′, *adj., openly declared :* avowed : acknowledged.—*adv.* **Profess′edly**.

**Profession**, pro-fesh′un, *n.* the act of *professing:* open declaration : an employment not mechanical and requiring some degree of learning : calling, known employment : the collective body of persons engaged in any profession : entrance into a religious order. [Fr.]

**Professional**, pro-fesh′un-al, *adj.* pertaining to a profession.—*n.* one who makes his living by an art, as opposed to an amateur who practises it merely for pastime.—*adv.* **Profess′ionally**.

**Professor**, pro-fes′or, *n.* one who *professes :* one who publicly practises or teaches any branch of knowledge : a public and authorised teacher in a university.—*adj.* **Professo′rial**.—*n.* **Profess′orship**.

**Proffer**, prof′er, *v.t.* to *bring forward :* to propose : to offer for acceptance.—*n.* an offer made : a proposal.—*n.* **Proff′erer**. [Fr. *proférer*—L. *profero*—*pro*, forward, and *fero*, E. **Bear**.]

**Proficience**, pro-fish′ens, **Proficiency**, pro-fish′en-si, *n.* state of being *proficient :* improvement in anything.

**Proficient**, pro-fish′ent, *adj.* competent : thoroughly qualified.—*n.* one who has made considerable advancement in anything : an adept.—*adv.* **Profic′iently**. [L. *proficiens*, *-entis*, pr.p. of *proficere*, to make progress—*pro*, forward, and *facio*, to make.]

**Profile**, prō′fil, *n.* an *outline :* a head or portrait in a side-view : the side-face : the outline of any object without foreshortening.—*v.t.* to draw in profile. [It. *profilo* (Fr. *profil*)—L. *pro*, and *filum*, a thread, outline.]

**Profit**, prof′it, *n.* gain : the gain resulting from the employment of capital : advantage : benefit : improvement.—*v.t.* to benefit or be of advantage to : to improve.—*v.i.* to gain advantage : to receive profit : to improve : to be of advantage : to bring good. [Fr.—L. *profectus*, progress, advance—*proficio*, *profectum*, to make progress. See **Proficient**.]

**Profitable**, prof′it-a-bl, *adj.* yielding or bringing *profit* or gain : lucrative : productive : advantageous : beneficial.—*adv.* **Prof′itably**.—*n.* **Prof′itableness**.

**Profiting**, prof′it-ing, *n., profit*, gain, or advantage : (*B.*) progress or proficiency.

**Profitless**, prof′it-les, *adj.* without profit, gain, or advantage.

**Profligacy**, prof′li-gas-i, **Profligateness**, prof′li-gāt-nes, *n.* the state or quality of being *profligate :* a profligate or vicious course of life.

**Profligate**, prof′li-gāt, *adj.* abandoned to vice : without virtue or decency : dissolute : prodigal.—*n.* one leading a profligate life : one shamelessly vicious.—*adv.* **Prof′ligately**. [Lit, 'dashed down,' L. *profligatus*, pa.p. of *profligo*—*pro*, and *fligo*, to dash, E. **Blow**, *n.*]

**Profound**, pro-fownd', *adj.* far below the surface: low: very deep: intense: abstruse: mysterious: occult: intellectually deep: penetrating deeply into knowledge.—*n.* the sea or ocean. [Lit. 'deep,' Fr. *profond*—L. *profundus*—*pro*, forward, downward, and *fundus*, E. **Bottom**.]

**Profoundly**, pro-fownd'li, *adv.* deeply: with deep knowledge or insight: with deep concern.

**Profoundness**, pro-fownd'nes, **Profundity**, pro-fund'it-i, *n.* the state or quality of being *profound*: depth of place, of knowledge, &c.

**Profuse**, pro-fūs', *adj.* liberal to excess: lavish: extravagant: prodigal.—*adv.* **Profuse'ly**. [L. *profusus*, pa.p. of *profundo*—*pro*, forth, and *fundo*, to pour. See **Fuse**, *v.*]

**Profuseness**, pro-fūs'nes, **Profusion**, pro-fū'zhun, *n.* state of being *profuse*: rich abundance: extravagance: prodigality.

**Progenitor**, pro-jen'it-or, *n.* a forefather: an ancestor. [Fr.—L.—*pro*, before, and *genitor*, a parent, from root *gan* in *gigno*, *genitus*, to beget.]

**Progeny**, proj'en-i, *n.* that which is brought forth: descendants: race: children.

**Prognosis**, prog-nō'sis, *n.*, foreknowledge: (med.) the act or art of foretelling the course of a disease from the symptoms: the opinion thus formed. [Gr.—*pro*, before, *gignōskō*, root *gna*, to know.]

**Prognostic**, prog-nos'tik, *n.* a foreshowing: an indication: a presage.—*adj.* foreknowing: foreshowing: indicating what is to happen by signs or symptoms. [Through O. Fr. (Fr. *pronostic*) from Gr. *prognostikon*.]

**Prognosticate**, prog-nos'ti-kāt, *v.t.* to foreshow: to foretell: to indicate as future by signs.

**Prognostication**, prog-nos-ti-kā'shun, *n.* the act of *prognosticating* or foretelling something future by present signs: a foretoken or previous sign.

**Prognosticator**, prog-nos'ti-kā-tor, *n.* a predictor of future events, esp. a weather prophet.

**Programme**, **Program**, prō'gram, *n.* a public notice in writing: an outline of any forthcoming proceeding: a preliminary outline. [Lit. 'something written publicly,' Fr.—L.—Gr. *programma*—*pro*, before, and *graphō*, to write.]

**Progress**, prog'res, *n.* a going forward: advance: improvement: proficiency: course: passage: procession: a journey of state: a circuit. [Fr.—L. *progressus*—*progredior*, to go forward—*pro*, forward, and *gradior*, to go.]

**Progress**, pro-gres', *v.i.* to go forward: to make progress: to proceed: to advance: to improve.

**Progression**, pro-gresh'un, *n.* motion onward: progress: regular and gradual advance: increase or decrease of numbers or magnitudes according to a fixed law: (music) a regular succession of chords or movement in harmony.—*adj.* **Progression'al**. [Fr.]

**Progressive**, pro-gres'iv, *adj.*, progressing or moving forward: advancing gradually: improving.—*adv.* **Progress'ively**.—*n.* **Progress'iveness**.

**Prohibit**, pro-hib'it, *v.t.* to hinder: to check or repress: to prevent: to forbid: to interdict by authority. [Lit. 'to hold in front,' L. *prohibeo*, *prohibitum*—*pro*, before, and *habeo*, to have. See **Have**.]

**Prohibition**, prō-hi-bish'un, *n.* the act of *prohibiting*, forbidding, or interdicting: an interdict.

**Prohibitive**, pro-hib'it-iv, **Prohibitory**, pro-hib'it-or-i, *adj.* that prohibits or forbids: forbidding.

**Project**, proj'ekt, *n.* a plan: a scheme: contriv-

ance. [Lit. 'a thing cast forward,' O. Fr. (Fr. *projet*)—L. *projectum*—*pro*, before, and *jacio*, to throw.]

**Project**, pro-jekt', *v.t.* to contrive or devise: to exhibit (as in a mirror): to draw: to exhibit in relief.—*v.i.* to shoot forward: to jut out: to be prominent.

**Projectile**, pro-jek'til, *adj.*, projecting or throwing forward: impelling or impelled forward.—*n.* a body projected by force, esp. through the air.

**Projection**, pro-jek'shun, *n.* the act of *projecting*: that which juts out: a plan or design: a delineation: a representation of any object on a plane.

**Projector**, pro-jek'tor, *n.* one who projects or forms schemes.

**Prolate**, prō'lāt, *adj. extended*: elongated in the direction of the line of the poles, as a spheroid. [L. *prolatus*, pa.p. of *profero*, to bring forward or extend—*pro*, forth, and *fero*, to bear.]

**Prolegomena**, pro-leg-om'en-a, *n.pl.* an introduction to a treatise. [Gr. 'things said before.']

**Prolepsis**, pro-lep'sis, *n.* a taking beforehand or anticipation: (rhet.) a figure by which objections are anticipated and answered: the dating of an event before its proper time.—*adjs.* **Prolep'tic**, **Prolep'tical**.—*adv.* **Prolep'tically**. [Gr. *prolambano*, *prolēpsomai*—*pro*, before, and *lambanō*, to take.]

**Proletarian**, pro-le-tā'ri-an, *adj.* belonging to the poorest labouring class: having little or no property: plebeian: vulgar.—*n.* **Proleta'riat**, the lowest class. [L. *proletarius* (in ancient Rome) a citizen of the sixth and lowest class, who served the state not with his property, but with his *children*—*proles*, offspring.]

**Prolific**, pro-lif'ik, **Prolifical**, pro-lif'ik-al, *adj.* producing offspring: fruitful: productive: (bot.) applied to a flower from which another is produced.—*n.* **Prolif'icness**. [Fr. *prolifique*—L. *proles* (for *pro-oles*), offspring (root *ol*, as in *olesco*, to grow), and *facio*, to make.]

**Prolix**, pro-liks' or prō'-, *adj.* tedious, lengthy, minute.—*adv.* **Prolix'ly**.—*ns.* **Prolix'ity**, **Prolix'ness**. [Fr. *prolixe*—L. *prolixus* (lit.) 'having flowed beyond bounds,' from *pro*, forward, and *-lixus*, from *liquor*, to flow. See **Liquid**.]

**Prolocutor**, pro-lok'ū-tor, *n.* the speaker or chairman of a convocation. [L.—*pro*, before, and *loquor*, *locutus*, to speak.]

**Prologue**, prol'og or prō'-, *n.* a preface: the introductory verses before a play. [Fr.—L.—Gr. *prologos*—*pro*, before, *logos*, speech.]

**Prolong**, pro-long', *v.t.* to lengthen out: to continue. [Fr. *prolonger*—L. *prolongo*—*pro*, forwards, *longus*, long.]

**Prolongate**, pro-long'gāt, *v.t.* to lengthen.—*n.* **Prolonga'tion**.

**Promenade**, prom-e-näd' or -nad', *n.* a walk for pleasure, show, or exercise: a place for walking.—*v.i.* to walk for amusement, show, or exercise. [Fr.—from (*se*) *promener*, to walk—L. *promino*, to drive forwards—*pro*, forwards, and *mino*, to drive.]

**Promethean**, pro-mē'the-an, *adj.* pertaining to *Prometheus*: life-giving, like the fire which (in the Greek myth) Prometheus stole from heaven.

**Prominent**, prom'i-nent, *adj.* projecting: conspicuous: principal: eminent: distinguished.—*adv.* **Prom'inently**.—*ns.* **Prom'inence**, **Prom'inency**. [Lit. 'jutting out,' Fr.—L. *promineo*, to jut forth—*pro*, forth, and *mineo*, to jut.]

**Promiscuous**, pro-mis'kū-us, *adj.*, mixed: confused: collected together without order: indiscriminate.—*adv.* **Promis'cuously.**—*n.* **Promis'-cuousness.** [L. *promiscuus*—*pro*, inten., and *misceo*, to mix.]

**Promise,** prom'is, *n.* an engagement to do or not to do something: expectation or that which affords expectation.—*v.t.* to make an engagement to do or not to do something: to afford reason to expect: to assure: to engage to bestow.—*ns.* **Prom'iser, Prom'isor.** [Lit. 'a sending forward,' Fr. *promesse*—L. *promissa, promitto,* to send forward—*pro,* forward, and *mitto,* to send. See **Mission.**]

**Promising,** prom'is-ing, *adj.* affording ground for hope or expectation.—*adv.* **Prom'isingly.**

**Promissory,** prom'is-or-i, *adj.* containing a *promise* of some engagement to be fulfilled.

**Promontory,** prom'on-tor-i, *n.* a headland or high cape. [L. *promontorium*—*pro,* forward, and *mons, montis,* a mountain.]

**Promote,** pro-mōt', *v.t.* to *move forward:* to advance: to further: to encourage: to raise to a higher position: to elevate.—*n.* **Promot'er.**—*adj.* **Promo'tive.** [L. *promotus,* pa.p. of *promoveo*—*pro,* forward, and *moveo,* to move.]

**Promotion,** pro-mō'shun, *n.* the act of *promoting:* advancement: encouragement: preferment.

**Prompt,** promt, *adj.* prepared: ready: acting with alacrity: cheerful: unhesitating.—*adv.* **Prompt'ly.**—*n.* **Prompt'ness.** [Lit. 'brought forward,' Fr.—L. *promptus*—*prōmo,* to bring forward—*pro,* forth, and *emo,* to bring or take.]

**Prompt,** promt, *v.t.* to incite: to move to action: to assist a speaker when at a loss for words: to suggest.—*n.* **Prompt'er.**

**Promptitude,** promt'i-tūd, *n., promptness :* readiness: quickness of decision and action. [Fr.]

**Promulgate,** pro-mul'gāt, *v.t.* to publish: to proclaim.—*n.* **Prom'ulgator.** [L. *promulgo, -atus.* Ety. unknown.]

**Promulgation,** prō-mul-gā'shun, *n.* act of promulgating: publication: open declaration.

**Prone,** prōn, *adj.* with the face downward: bending forward: headlong: disposed: inclined.—*adv.* **Prone'ly.**—*n.* **Prone'ness.** [O. Fr.—L. *pronus ;* cog. with Gr. *prēnēs,* prone.]

**Prong,** prong, *n.* the spike of a fork or similar instrument. [Nasalised form of Prov. E. *prog,* to prick—W. *procio ;* cf. Gael. *brog,* to goad, and *brog,* an awl, and E. **Brooch.** See also **Pang.**]

**Pronominal,** pro-nom'i-nal, *adj.* belonging to or of the nature of a *pronoun.*—*adv.* **Pronom'inally.**

**Pronoun,** prō'nown, *n.* a word used *instead of a noun.* [L. *pro,* for, and **Noun.**]

**Pronounce,** pro-nowns', *v.t.* to utter: to speak distinctly: to utter formally: to utter rhetorically: to declare.—*n.* **Pronoun'cer.** [Fr. *prononcer*—L. *pronuncio*—*pro,* forth, and *nuncio,* to announce—*nuncius,* a messenger. See **Nuncio.**]

**Pronounceable,** pro-nowns'a-bl, *adj.* capable of being pronounced. [ciation.

**Pronouncing,** pro-nowns'ing, *adj.* giving pronun-

**Pronunciation,** pro-nun-si-ā'shun, *n.* act or mode of *pronouncing:* utterance.

**Proof,** prōōf, *n.* that which *proves :* test : experiment : any process to discover or establish a truth : that which convinces : demonstration : evidence : condition of having been proved : firmness of mind : a certain strength of alcoholic spirits : (*print.*) an impression taken for correction, also 'proof-sheet :' an early impression of an engraving :—*pl.* **Proofs.**—*adj.* (*lit.*) *proved:* firm in resisting. [M. E. *preef*—Fr. *preuve*—L. *probo,* to prove. See **Prove.**]

**Proofless,** prōōf'les, *adj.* wanting proof or evidence.

**Prop,** prop, *n.* a support : a stay.—*v.t.* to support by something under or against : to sustain :—*pr.p.* **propp'ing** ; *pa.t.* and *pa.p.* **propped.** [Allied to Sw. *propp,* Ger. *pfropf,* a stopper ; also to Ir. *propa,* prop, Gael. *prop.*]

**Propagandism,** prop-a-gand'izm, *n.* practice of *propagating* tenets or principles. [From the Congregatio de *propagandâ* Fide (L.), 'Society for propagating the Faith,' founded at Rome in 1622.]

**Propagandist,** prop-a-gand'ist, *n.* one who devotes himself to propagandism.

**Propagate,** prop'a-gāt, *v.t.* to multiply plants by *layers* : to extend : to produce : to impel forward in space, as sound : to spread : to extend the knowledge of.—*v.i.* to be produced or multiplied : to have young.—*n.* **Prop'agator.** [L. *propago, -atus,* conn. with *pro-pag-eo, pro-pag-o,* a layer, from root of **Pack** and **Pact,** Gr. *pēg-numi.*]

**Propagation,** prop-a-gā'shun, *n.* act of propagating : the spreading or extension of anything.

**Propel,** pro-pel', *v.t.* to *drive forward :* to urge onward by force :—*pr.p.* **propell'ing** ; *pa.t.* and *pa.p.* **propelled'.** [L. *pro,* forward, *pello,* to drive.]

**Propeller,** pro-pel'ér, *n.* one who or that which propels : a screw for propelling a steamboat : a vessel thus propelled.

**Propensity,** pro-pens'i-ti, *n.* inclination : disposition. [Lit. 'a hanging forwards ;' L. *propensus,* pa.p. of *propendo,* to hang forwards—L. *pro,* forward, *pendeo,* to hang.]

**Proper,** prop'ér, *adj., one's own :* naturally or essentially belonging : peculiar : belonging to only one of a species (as a name) : natural : suitable : correct : just : right : becoming : (*B.*) comely, pretty.—*adv.* **Prop'erly.** [Fr. *propre,* —L. *proprius,* one's own, akin to *prope,* near.]

**Property,** prop'ér-ti, *n.* that which is *proper* to anything : a peculiar or essential quality : a quality : that which is one's own : an estate : right of possessing, employing, &c. : ownership : —*pl.* articles required by actors in a play. [O. Fr. *propreté :* a doublet of **Propriety.**]

**Prophecy,** prof'e-si, *n.* a declaration of something to come : a prediction : public interpretation of Scripture : instruction : (*B.*) also, a book of prophecies. [Lit. a *speaking for* another, O. Fr. *prophecie*—L. *prophetia*—Gr. *prophēteia*—*pro-phētēs.* See **Prophet.**]

**Prophesy,** prof'e-sī, *v.t.* to foretell : to predict.—*v.i.* (*B.*) to exhort : to expound religious subjects :—*pa.t.* and *pa.p.* **proph'esīed.** [*s* has been arbitrarily substituted for *c,* to distinguish the *v.* from the *n.*]

**Prophet,** prof'et, *n.* one who proclaims or interprets the will of God : one who announces things to come : one who predicts or foretells events : (*B.*) one inspired by God to teach :—*pl.* the writings of the prophets.—*fem.* **Proph'etess.** [Fr. — L. *propheta* — Gr. *prophētēs,* (*lit.*) one who *speaks for* another, esp. for a divine power ; hence one who delivers an oracle revealing future events or otherwise announcing the divine will—*pro,* before, in behalf of, and *phē-mi,* to speak. See **Fame.**]

**Prophetic,** pro-fet'ik, **Prophetical,** pro-fet'ik-al, *adj.* containing *prophecy :* foreseeing or foretelling events.—*adv.* **Prophet'ically.**

**Propinquity,** pro-ping'kwi-ti, *n., nearness* in time, place, or blood : proximity. [L. *propinquitas*—*propinquus,* near—*prope,* near.]

**Propitiable**, pro-pish'i-a-bl, *adj.* that may be *propitiated*.

**Propitiate**, pro-pish'i-āt, *v.t.* to make *propitious*: to render favourable.—*v.i.* to make propitiation: to atone.—*n.* **Propi'tiator**. [L. *propitio*, *propitiatum*.]

**Propitiation**, pro-pish-i-ā'shun, *n.* act of *propitiating*: (*theol.*) that which propitiates: atonement.

**Propitiatory**, pro-pish'i-a-tor-i, *adj.* having power to *propitiate*: expiatory.—*n.* the Jewish mercy-seat.

**Propitious**, pro-pish'us, *adj.* favourable: disposed to be gracious or merciful.—*adv.* **Propi'tiously**.—*n.* **Propi'tiousness**. [L. *propitius*—*prope*, near.]

**Proportion**, pro-pōr'shun, *n.* the relation of one thing to another in regard to magnitude: mutual fitness of parts: symmetrical arrangement: (*math.*) the identity or equality of ratios: the 'rule of three,' in which three terms are given to find a fourth: equal or just share.—*v.t.* to adjust: to form symmetrically. [L. *proportio*—*pro*, in comparison with, and *portio*, *portionis*, part, share. See **Portion**.]

**Proportionable**, pro-pōr'shun-a-bl, *adj.* that may be *proportioned*.—*adv.* **Propor'tionably**.

**Proportional**, pro-pōr'shun-al, *adj.* having a due *proportion*: relating to proportion: (*math.*) having the same or a constant ratio.—*n.* (*math.*) a number or quantity in a proportion.—*adv.* **Propor'tionally**.—*n.* **Proportional'ity**.

**Proportionate**, pro-pōr'shun-āt, *adj.* adjusted according to a *proportion*: proportional.—*adv.* **Propor'tionately**.

**Proposal**, pro-pōz'al, *n.* anything *proposed*: a scheme or design: terms or conditions proposed.

**Propose**, pro-pōz', *v.t.* to *put forward* or offer for consideration, &c.—*v.i.* to make a proposal: to make an offer of marriage.—*n.* **Propos'er**. [Fr.—prefix *pro-*, and *poser*, to place. See **Pose**, *n.*]

**Proposition**, prop-o-zish'un, *n.* a *placing before*: offer of terms: the act of stating anything: that which is stated: (*gram.* and *logic*) a complete sentence, or one which affirms or denies something: (*math.*) a theorem or problem to be demonstrated or solved. [Fr.—L. *propositio*. See **Propound**.]

**Propositional**, prop-o-zish'un-al, *adj.* pertaining to or of the nature of a *proposition*: considered as a proposition.

**Propound**, pro-pownd', *v.t.* to offer for consideration: to exhibit.—*n.* **Propound'er**. [Orig. *propone*, from L.—*pro*, forth, and *pono*, to place.]

**Proprietary**, pro-prī'e-tar-i, *adj.* belonging to a *proprietor*.—*n.* a proprietor: an owner.

**Proprietor**, pro-prī'e-tor, *n.* one who has anything as his *property*: an owner.—*fem.* **Propri'etress**.—*n.* **Propri'etorship**.

**Propriety**, pro-prī'e-ti, *n.* state of being *proper* or right: agreement with established principles or customs: fitness: accuracy: *peculiar* right of *possession*, *property*. [Fr.—L. *proprietas*—*proprius*, one's own. See **Proper**.]

**Propulsion**, pro-pul'shun, *n.* act of *propelling*.

**Propulsive**, pro-pul'siv, *adj.* tending or having power to *propel*.

**Prorogation**, prō-ro-gā'shun, *n.* act of *proroguing*.

**Prorogue**, pro-rōg', *v.t.* to continue from one session to another (said of parliament):—*pr.p.* prorōg'uing; *pa.t.* and *pa.p.* prorōgued'. [Fr.—L. *prorogo*, *-atum*—*pro*, forward, and *rogo*, to ask.]

**Prosaic**, pro-zā'ik, **Prosaical**, pro-zā'ik-al, *adj.*

pertaining to prose: like prose.—*adv.* **Prosa'ically**. [See **Prose**.]

**Proscenium**, pro-sē'ni-um, *n.* the *front* part of the *stage*. [L.—Gr. *proskēnion*—*pro*, before, *skēnē*, the stage.]

**Proscribe**, pro-skrīb', *v.t.* to publish the names of persons to be punished: to banish: to prohibit: to denounce, as doctrine.—*n.* **Proscrib'er**. [L. *proscribo*—*pro*, before, publicly, and *scribo*, *scriptum*, to write.]

**Proscription**, pro-skrip'shun, *n.* the act of *proscribing* or dooming to death, or outlawry: utter rejection. [Fr.—L.]

**Proscriptive**, pro-skrip'tiv, *adj.* pertaining to or consisting in *proscription*.

**Prose**, prōz, *n.* the direct, *straightforward* arrangement of words, free from poetical measures: ordinary spoken and written language: all writings not in verse.—*adj.* pertaining to prose: not poetical: plain: dull.—*v.i.* to write prose: to speak or write tediously.—*n.* **Pros'er**. [Fr.—L. *prosa*, for *prorsa*—*prorsus*, straightforward—*pro*, forward, *verto*, *versum*, to turn.]

**Prosecute**, pros'e-kūt, *v.t.* to *follow onwards* or pursue, in order to reach or accomplish: to continue: to pursue by law.—*v.i.* to carry on a legal prosecution. [L. *prosequor*—*pro*, onwards, and *sequor*, *secutus*, to follow. See **Sequence**.]

**Prosecution**, pros-e-kū'shun, *n.* the act of *prosecuting*: pursuit: a civil or criminal suit.

**Prosecutor**, pros'e-kūt-or, *n.* one who *prosecutes* or pursues any plan or business: one who carries on a criminal suit.—*fem.* **Pros'ecutrix**.

**Proselyte**, pros'e-līt, *n.* one who *has come* over to a religion or opinion: a convert. [Fr.—L.—Gr. *prosēlytos*—*proserchomai*, to come to—*pros*, to, and *erchomai*, *ēlython*, to come.]

**Proselytise**, pros-e-līt-īz', *v.t.* to make *proselytes*.

**Proselytism**, pros'e-lit-izm, *n.* the act of *proselytising* or of making converts.

**Prosodial**, pros-ō'di-al, **Prosodical**, pros-od'ik-al, *adj.* pertaining to *prosody*: according to the rules of prosody.—*adv.* **Prosod'ically**.

**Prosodian**, pros-ō'di-an, **Prosodist**, pros'o-dist, *n.* one skilled in *prosody*.

**Prosody**, pros'o-di, *n.* that part of grammar which treats of quantity, accent, and the laws of verse or versification. [Fr.—L. *prosodia*, Gr. *prosōdia*, a song sung to music, an accompanying song—*pros*, to, and *odē*, a song.]

**Prosopopœia**, pros-o-po-pē'ya, *n.* a rhetorical figure by which inanimate objects are spoken of as *persons*: personification. [Gr. *prosōpopoiia*—*prosōpon*, a person, and *poieō*, to make.]

**Prospect**, pros'pekt, *n.* a *looking forward*: a view: object of view: a scene: expectation.—*n.* **Prospect'ing**, searching a district for gold or silver mines with a view to further operations. [L. *prospectus*—*prospicio*, *prospectum*, to look forward—*pro*, forward, and *specio*, to look.]

**Prospection**, pro-spek'shun, *n.* the act of *looking forward* or of providing for future wants.

**Prospective**, pro-spek'tiv, *adj.*, looking forward: acting with foresight: relating to the future: distant.—*adv.* **Prospec'tively**. [Fr.—L.]

**Prospectus**, pro-spek'tus, *n.* the outline of any plan submitted for public approval, particularly of a literary work or of a company or joint-stock concern.

**Prosper**, pros'pėr, *v.t.* to make fortunate or happy: (*B.*) to make to prosper.—*v.i.* to be successful: to succeed.

**Prosperity**, pros-per'i-ti, *n.* the state of being *prosperous*: success: good-fortune.

**Prosperous**, pros'pėr-us, *adj.*, *according to hope* : in accordance with one's wishes : favourable : successful.—*adv.* **Pros'perously.** [L. *prosper*, *prosperus—pro*, in accordance with, and *spes*, hope.]

**Prostitute**, pros'ti-tūt, *v.t.* to expose for sale for bad ends : to sell to wickedness or lewdness : to devote to any improper purpose.—*adj.* openly devoted to lewdness : sold to wickedness.—*n.* a female who indulges in lewdness, esp. for hire : a base hireling. [L. *prostituo, -utum—pro*, before, *statuo*, to place.]

**Prostitution**, pros-ti-tū'shun, *n.* the act or practice of *prostituting* : lewdness for hire : the life of a lewd woman : the being devoted to infamous purposes. [either himself or another.

**Prostitutor**, pros'ti-tūt-or, *n.* one who prostitutes

**Prostrate**, pros'trāt, *adj.*, *thrown forwards* on the ground : lying at length : lying at mercy : bent in adoration.—*v.t.* to throw forwards on the ground : to lay flat : to overthrow : to sink totally : to bow in humble reverence. [L. *pro*, forwards, and *sterno, stratum*, to throw on the ground.]

**Prostration**, pros-trā'shun, *n.* act of *throwing down* or laying flat : act of falling down in adoration : dejection : complete loss of strength.

**Prosy**, prōz'i, *adj.* like dull *prose* : dull and tedious in discourse or writing.—*adv.* **Pros'ily.** —*n.* **Pros'iness.**

**Protean**, prō'te-an or pro-tē'an, *adj.* readily assuming different shapes, *like Proteus*, the sea-god, fabled to have the power of changing himself into an endless variety of forms.

**Protect**, pro-tekt', *v.t.* to *cover in front* : to cover over : to defend : to shelter. [L. *pro*, in front, and *tego, tectum*, akin to Gr. *stegō*, to cover.]

**Protection**, pro-tek'shun, *n.* act of *protecting* : state of being protected : preservation : defence : guard : refuge : security : passport.

**Protectionist**, pro-tek'shun-ist, *n.* one who favours the *protection* of trade by law.

**Protective**, pro-tekt'iv, *adj.* affording *protection* : defensive : sheltering.

**Protector**, pro-tekt'or, *n.* one who *protects* from injury or oppression : a guardian : a regent :— *fem.* **Protect'ress**, **Protect'rix.**—*n.* **Protect'orship.**

**Protectoral**, pro-tekt'or-al, **Protectorial**, pro-tek-tō'ri-al, *adj.* pertaining to a *protector* or regent.

**Protectorate**, pro-tekt'or-āt, *n.* government by a *protector* : the authority assumed by a superior.

**Protégé**, pro-tā-zhā', *n.* one under the *protection* of another : a pupil : a ward :—*fem.* **Protégée'.** [Fr., pa.p. of *protéger*, to protect—L. *protego*.]

**Protein**, prō'te-in, *n.* the supposed common radical of the group of bodies which form the most essential articles of food, albumen, fibrine, &c. [Gr. *prōtos*, first, and suffix -*in*.]

**Protest**, pro-test', *v.i.* to bear *witness before* others : to declare openly : to give a solemn declaration of opinion.—*v.t.* to make a solemn declaration of : to note, as a bill of exchange, from non-acceptance or non-payment.—*n.* **Protest'er.** [Fr.—L. *protestor, -atus—pro*, before, *testor—testis*, a witness.]

**Protest**, prō'test, *n.* a solemn or formal *protesting* or declaration, esp. one in writing by the minority of a body, expressing dissent : the attestation by a notary-public of an unpaid or unaccepted bill.

**Protestant**, prot'es-tant, *adj. protesting*: pertaining to the faith of those who protest against the Church of Rome.—*n.* (*orig.*) one of those who,

in 1529, protested against an edict of Charles V. and the Diet of Spires : one who protests against the Church of Rome. [religion.

**Protestantism**, prot'es-tant-izm, *n.* the *Protestant*

**Protestation**, prot-es-tā'shun, *n.* the act of *protesting* : a solemn declaration : a declaration of dissent : a declaration in pleading.

**Protocol**, prō'to-kol, *n.* the *first* copy of any document : the rough draught of an instrument or transaction. [Fr. *protocole*—Low L. *protocollum*—late Gr. *prōtokollon*, the first leaf glued to the rolls of papyrus and to notarial documents —Gr. *prōtos*, first, and *kolla*, glue.]

**Protomartyr**, prō'to-mär'tėr, *n.* St Stephen the *first* Christian *martyr* : the first who suffers in any cause. [Gr. *prōtos*, first, and **Martyr**.]

**Protophyte**, prō'to-fīt, *n.* the *first* or lowest order of *plants*. [Gr. *prōtos*, first, and *phyton*, a plant —*phyō*, to cause to grow.]

**Protoplasm**, prō'to-plazm, *n.* a homogeneous, structureless substance, forming the physical basis of life, endowed with contractility, with a chemical composition allied to that of albumen. [Gr. *prōtos*, first, and *plasma*, form—*plassō*, to form.]

**Prototype**, prō'to-tīp, *n.* the *first* or original *type* or model after which anything is copied : an exemplar : a pattern. [Fr.—L.—Gr., from *prōtos*, first, and *typos*, a type.]

**Protozoan**, prō-to-zō'an, *n.* one of the *first* or lowest class of *animals*. [Gr. *prōtos*, first, and *zōon*, an animal.]

**Protozoic**, prō-to-zō'ik, *adj.* pertaining to the *protozoans* : containing remains of the earliest life of the globe.

**Protract**, pro-trakt', *v.t.* to *draw out* or lengthen in time : to prolong : to draw to a scale. [L. —*pro*, forth, and *traho*, to draw.]

**Protraction**, pro-trak'shun, *n.* act of *protracting* or prolonging : the delaying the termination of a thing : the plotting or laying down of the dimensions of anything on paper.

**Protractive**, pro-trakt'iv, *adj.*, *drawing out* in time : prolonging : delaying.

**Protractor**, pro-trakt'or, *n.* one who or that which *protracts* : a mathematical instrument for laying down angles on paper, used in surveying, &c.

**Protrude**, pro-trōōd', *v.t.* to *thrust* or push *forwards* : to drive along : to put out.—*v.i.* to be thrust forward or beyond the usual limit. [L. *protrudo—pro*, forwards, and *trudo*, to thrust.]

**Protrusion**, pro-trōō'zhun, *n.* the act of *thrusting forward* or beyond the usual limit : the state of being protruded. [*Protrusus*, pa.p. of *protrudo*. See **Protrude**.] [pelling *forward*.

**Protrusive**, pro-trōō'siv, *adj., thrusting* or impelling

**Protuberance**, pro-tūb'ér-ans, *n.* a *swelling forward* or *forth* : a prominence : a tumour.

**Protuberant**, pro-tūb'ér-ant, *adj., swelling*: prominent.—*adv.* **Protub'erantly.**

**Protuberate**, pro-tūb'ér-āt, *v.i.* to *swell* or bulge out. [L. *protubero, -atus—pro*, forward, *tuber*, a swelling. See **Tuber**.]

**Proud**, prowd (*comp.* **Proud'er** (*superl.* **Proud'est**), *adj.* hav ing excessive self-esteem : arrogant : haughty : daring : grand : ostentatious.—*adv.* **Proud'ly.** [M. E. *prud*—A.S. *prút*. Cf. **Pride**.]

**Proud-flesh**, prowd'-flesh, *n.* a growth or excrescence of *flesh* in a wound. [**Proud** and **Flesh**.]

**Provable**, prōōv'a-bl, *adj.* that may be *proved*.— *adv.* **Prov'ably.**—*n.* **Prov'ableness.**

**Prove**, prōōv, *v.t.* to *try* by experiment or by a test or standard : to try by suffering : to establish or ascertain as truth by argument or other evidence: to demonstrate: to ascertain the genuineness of: to experience or suffer: (*math.*) to ascertain the correctness of any result.—*v.i.* to make trial: to turn out: to be shewn afterwards. —*n.* **Prov'er.** [O. Fr. *prover* (Fr. *prouver*), which, like A.S. *profian* and Ger. *proben* is from L. *probo—probus,* excellent.]

**Proven,** prov'n, (*Scots law*) same as **Proved,** *pa.p.* of **Prove.**

**Provender,** prov'en-dėr, *n.* dry food for beasts, as hay or corn: esp. a mixture of meal and cut straw or hay. [M. E. *provende*—Fr.—L. *præbenda.* See **Prebend,** in Late L. a daily allowance of food.]

**Proverb,** prov'ėrb, *n.* a short familiar sentence, forcibly expressing a well-known truth or moral lesson: a byword:—*pl.* a book of the Old Testament. [Fr. *proverbe*—L. *proverbium—pro,* publicly, and *verbum,* a word.]

**Proverbial,** pro-vėrb'i-al, *adj.* pertaining to *proverbs:* mentioned in or resembling a proverb: widely spoken of.—*adv.* **Proverb'ially.**

**Provide,** pro-vīd', *v.t.* to make ready *before*hand: to prepare: to supply.—*v.i.* to procure supplies or means of defence: to take measures: to bargain previously.—*n.* **Provid'er.** [Lit. 'to foresee,' L. *provideo—pro,* before, *video,* to see. Doublet **Purvey.** See **Vision.**]

**Providence,** prov'i-dens, *n.* timely preparation: (*theol.*) the foresight and care of God over all his creatures: God, considered in this relation: prudence in managing one's affairs. [Fr.—L. *providentia.*]

**Provident,** prov'i-dent, *adj.* providing for the future: cautious: prudent: economical.—*adv.* **Prov'idently.** [L. *provid-ens, -entis,* pr.p. of *provideo.* See **Provide.** Doublet **Prudent.**]

**Providential,** prov-i-den'shal, *adj., effected by* or proceeding from divine *providence.*—*adv.* **Providen'tially.**

**Province,** prov'ins, *n.* a portion of an empire or state: the district over which one has jurisdiction: a region: a business or duty: one's business or calling: a department of knowledge. [Fr.—L. *provincia.* Ety. unknown.]

**Provincial,** pro-vin'shal, *adj.* relating to a *province:* belonging to a division of a country: characteristic of the inhabitants of a province: rude: unpolished.—*n.* an inhabitant of a province or country district: (in the R. Cath. Church) the superintendent of the heads of the religious houses in a *province.*—*adv.* **Provin'cially.**

**Provincialism,** pro-vin'shal-izm, *n.* mode of speech peculiar to a *province* or country district: a peculiarity of dialect.

**Provision,** pro-vizh'un, *n.* act of *providing:* that which is provided or prepared: measures taken beforehand: preparation: previous agreement: a store of food: provender.—*v.t.* to supply with provisions or food. [Fr.—L.—*provisus,* pa.p. of *provideo.* See **Provide.**]

**Provisional,** pro-vizh'un-al, *adj., provided* for an occasion: temporary.—*adv.* **Provis'ionally.**

**Proviso,** pro-vī'zō, *n.* a *provision* or condition in a deed or other writing: the clause containing it: any condition :—*pl.* **Provisos,** provī'zōz. [From the L. phrase *proviso quod,* it being provided that.]

**Provisory,** pro-vī'zor-i, *adj.* containing a *proviso* or condition: conditional: making temporary provision: temporary.—*adv.* **Provi'sorily.**

**Provocation,** prov-o-kā'shun, *n.* act of *provoking:* that which provokes. [Fr.—L. *provocatus,* pa.p. of *provoco.* See **Provoke.**]

**Provocative,** pro-vō'ka-tiv, *adj.* tending to *provoke* or excite.—*n.* anything provocative.

**Provoke,** pro-vōk', *v.t.* to *call forth:* to excite to action: to excite with anger: to offend: (*B.*) to challenge.—*adv.* **Provok'ingly.** [Fr. *provoquer* —L.—*pro,* forth, *voco,* to call. See **Vocal.**]

**Provost,** prov'ust, *n.* the dignitary *set over* a cathedral or collegiate church: the head of a college: (*Scotland*) the chief magistrate of certain classes of burghs, answering to *mayor* in England.—*n.* **Lord Provost,** the style of the chief magistrates of Edinburgh, Glasgow, Perth, and Aberdeen.—*n.* **Provost-Marshal** (*army*) an officer with special powers for enforcing discipline: (*navy*) an officer having charge of prisoners. [Lit. 'one placed over others,' O. Fr. *provost* (Fr. *prévôt*)—L. *præpositus,* pa.p. of *præpono—præ,* over, *pono,* to place.] [*provost.*

**Provostship,** prov'ust-ship, *n.* the office of a

**Prow,** prow, *n.* the *fore*part of a ship. [Fr. *proue* (It. *prua*)—L. *prora*—Gr.—*pro,* before.]

**Prowess,** prow'es or prō'es, *n.* bravery, esp. in war: valour. [Fr. *prouesse,* from O. Fr. *prou* (Fr. *preux*), valiant, prob. from L. *pro,* for the good of. Cf. **Prude.**]

**Prowl,** prowl, *v.i.* to rove in search of *prey* or plunder.—*n.* **Prowl'er.** [O. Fr., as if *proieler,* from Fr. *proie*—L. *præda,* prey. See **Prey.**]

**Proximate,** proks'i-māt, *adj., nearest* or *next:* having the most intimate connection: near and immediate.—*adv.* **Prox'imately.** [L. *proximus,* next, superl. of obs. *propis,* near.]

**Proximity,** proks-im'it-i, *n.* immediate nearness. [Fr.—L.]

**Proximo,** proks'i-mo, *adj.* (*in*) the next (*month*). [L. *proximo*—L. *proximus,* next.]

**Proxy,** proks'i, *n.* the agency of one who acts for another: one who acts for another, or the writing by which he is deputed. [Lit. 'the office of procurator,' from obs. E. *procuracy,* from **Procurator.**]

**Prude,** prŏŏd, *n.* a woman of affected modesty. [Fr.—O. Fr. *prode,* fem. of *prod,* excellent, from L. *probus,* good, virtuous.]

**Prudence,** prŏŏ'dens, *n.* quality of being *prudent:* wisdom applied to practice: caution. [Fr.—L.]

**Prudent,** prŏŏ'dent, *adj.* (*lit.*) *provident* or foreseeing: cautious and wise in conduct: careful: discreet: dictated by forethought: frugal.— *adv.* **Pru'dently.** [Fr.—L. *prūdens, prūdentis,* contr. of *providens,* pr.p. of *provideo,* to foresee. See **Provide.**]

**Prudential,** prŏŏ-den'shal, *adj.* proceeding from or dictated by *prudence.*—*adv.* **Pruden'tially.**

**Prudery,** prŏŏd'ėr-i, *n.* manners of a *prude.*

**Prudish,** prŏŏd'ish, *adj.* like a *prude:* affectedly modest or reserved.—*adv.* **Prud'ishly.**

**Prune,** prŏŏn, *v.t.* to trim, as trees or branches, by lopping off superfluous parts: to divest of anything superfluous.—*n.* **Prun'er.** [Lit. 'to propagate,' older form *proin,* prob. from Fr. *provigner,* to propagate by slips—*provin,* a shoot—L. *propag-o, -inis.* See **Propagate.**]

**Prune,** prŏŏn, *n.* a *plum,* esp. a dried plum. [Fr. —L. *prunum*—Gr. *prounon.*]

**Prunella,** prŏŏ-nel'a, **Prunello,** prŏŏ-nel'ō, *n.* a strong, woollen stuff, generally *black.* [Prob. Latinised form of Fr. *prunelle,* a sloe, dim. of Fr. *prune.* See **Prune,** *n.*]

**Prurience,** prŏŏ'ri-ens, **Pruriency,** prŏŏ'ri-en-si, *n.* state of being *prurient.*

**Prurient,** prŏŏ'ri-ent, *adj., itching* or uneasy with desire. [L. *pruriens,* pr.p. of *prurio,* to itch.]

**Pry,** prī, *v.i.* to *peer* or peep into that which is closed: to inspect closely: to try to discover

with curiosity :—*pa.t.* and *pa.p.* pried.—*adv.*
**Pry′ingly.** [M. E. *piren.* Doublet **Peer,** to look narrowly.]

**Psalm,** säm, *n.* a sacred song.—**The Psalms,** one of the books of the Old Testament. [L. *psalmus* —Gr. *psalmos* (*lit.*) a *twitching* or *twanging* the strings of a harp, from *psallō,* to twang.]

**Psalmist,** säm′ist or sal′mist, *n.* a composer of *psalms,* applied to David and the writers of the Scriptural psalms. [L.—Gr.]

**Psalmodic,** sal-mod′ik, **Psalmodical,** sal-mod′ik-al, *adj.* pertaining to *psalmody.*

**Psalmodist,** sal′mod-ist, *n.* a singer of *psalms.*

**Psalmody,** säm′o-di or sal′mo-di, *n.* the singing of *psalms:* psalms collectively. [Gr. *psalmōdia,* singing to the harp—*psalmos* (see **Psalm**), and *ōdē,* a song (see **Ode**).]

**Psalter,** sawl′tėr, *n.* the book of Psalms, esp. when separately printed : in the R. Cath. Church, a series of 150 devout sentences : a rosary of 150 beads, according to the number of the psalms. [O. Fr. *psaltier*—L. *psalterium.*]

**Psaltery,** sawl′tėr-i, *n.* a stringed instrument of the Jews. [O. Fr. *psalterie* (Fr. *psaltérion*)— L. *psalterium*—Gr. *psalterion.* Cf. **Psalm.**]

**Pseudonym,** sū′do-nim, *n.* a *fictitious name* assumed, as by an author.—*adj.* **Pseudo′nym- ous,** bearing a fictitious name. [Fr.—Gr. *pseud-ēs,* false, and *onoma,* E. **Name.**]

**Pshaw,** shaw, *int.* a term of contempt. [Imitative.]

**Psychical,** sī′kik-al, *adj.* pertaining to the *soul,* or living principle in man. [L. *psychicus*—Gr. *psychikos*—*psychē,* the soul—*psychō,* to breathe.]

**Psychologic,** sī-ko-loj′ik, **Psychological,** sī-ko- loj′ik-al, *adj.* pertaining to *psychology.*—*adv.* **Psycholog′ically.** [*psychology.*]

**Psychologist,** sī-kol′o-jist, *n.* one who studies *psychology.*

**Psychology,** sī-kol′o-ji, *n.* the science which classifies and analyses the phenomena of the human mind. [Gr. *psychē,* the soul, and *logos,* a treatise.]

**Ptarmigan,** tär′mi-gan, *n.* a species of grouse with feathered toes inhabiting the tops of mountains. [Gael. *tarmachan.*]

**Puberty,** pū′bėr-ti, *n.* the age of full development : early manhood or womanhood. [Fr. *puberté*— L. *pubertas, -tatis*—*pubes,* the signs of man- hood, from root of **Pupil.**]

**Pubescence,** pū-bes′ens, *n.* state of one arrived at *puberty :* (*bot.*) the soft, short hair on plants.

**Pubescent,** pū-bes′ent, *adj.* arriving at *puberty :* (*bot.* and *zool.*) covered with soft, short hair. [L. *pubesc-ens, -entis,* pr.p. of *pubesco,* to arrive at *puberty*—*pubes.* See **Puberty.**]

**Public,** pub′lik, *adj.* of or belonging to the people : pertaining to a community or a nation : general : common to all : generally known.—*n.* the people : the general body of mankind : the people, inde- finitely.—*adv.* **Pub′licly.** [Fr.—L. *publicus* —*populus,* the people. Cf. **People.**]

**Publican,** pub′lik-an, *n.* the keeper of an inn or public-house : (*orig.*) a farmer-general of the Roman *public* revenue : a tax-collector. [L.]

**Publication,** pub-li-kā′shun, *n.* the act of *publish- ing* or making public : a proclamation : the act of printing and sending forth to the public, as a book : that which is published as a book, &c.

**Public-house,** pub′lik-hows, *n.* a *house* open to the *public :* a house of public entertainment.

**Publicist,** pub′li-sist, *n.,* one who writes on, or is skilled in *public* law, or current political topics.

**Publicity,** pub-lis′i-ti, *n.* the state of being *public* or open to the knowledge of all : notoriety.

**Public-spirited,** pub′lik-spir′it-ed, *adj.* having a

spirit actuated by regard to the *public* interest : with a regard to the public interest.—*adv.* **Pub′- lic-spir′itedly.**—*n.* **Pub′lic-spir′itedness.**

**Publish,** pub′lish, *v.t.* to make *public :* to divulge or reveal : to announce : to proclaim : to send forth to the public : to print and offer for sale : to put into circulation. [Fr.—L. *publico, -ātus* —*publicus.*]

**Publisher,** pub′lish-ėr, *n.* one who makes *public* or proclaims : one who publishes books.

**Puce,** pūs, *adj.* brownish-purple. [Lit. flea- coloured ; Fr. *puce*—L. *pulex, pulicis,* a flea.]

**Puck,** puk, *n.* a goblin or mischievous sprite : a celebrated fairy. [M. E. *pouke*—Celt., as Ir. *puca,* W. *bwg ;* conn. with Ice. *pūki.* See the parallel forms **Pug, Bug.**]

**Pucker,** puk′ėr, *v.t.* to gather into folds : to wrinkle.—*n.* a fold or wrinkle. [Lit. 'to gather into the form of a *poke.*' See **Poke,** a bag, and **Pock.**]

**Pudding,** pood′ing, *n.* an intestine filled with meat, a sausage : a soft kind of food, of flour, milk, eggs, &c. [Prob. Celt., as W. *poten,* Ir. *putog—pot,* a bag ; Ger. *pudding,* Fr. *boudin,* L. *botulus,* are prob. all related words.]

**Puddle,** pud′l, *n.* a small *pool* of muddy water : a mixture of clay and sand.—*v.t.* to make muddy : to make impervious to water with clay : to con- vert into bar or wrought iron.—*v.i.* to make a dirty stir. [M. E. *podel* (for *plod-el*)—Celt. *plod,* a pool, conn. with **Flood** and **Flow.**]

**Puddler,** pud′lėr, *n.* one who turns cast-iron into wrought-iron by *puddling.*

**Puddling,** pud′ling, *n.* the act of rendering imper- vious to water by means of clay : the process of converting cast iron to bar or wrought iron.

**Puerile,** pū′ėr-īl, *adj.* pertaining to *children :* childish : trifling : silly.—*adv.* **Pu′erilely.** [Fr. *puéril*—L. *puerilis—puer,* a child. Cf. **Foal.**]

**Puerility,** pū-ėr-il′i-ti, *n.* quality of being *puerile :* that which is puerile : a childish expression.

**Puerperal,** pū-ėr′pėr-al, *adj.* relating to *childbirth.* [L. *puerpera,* bearing children—*puer,* a child, and *pario,* to bear. Cf. **Foal** and **Parent.**]

**Puff,** puf, *v.i.* to blow in puffs or whiffs : to swell or fill with air : to breathe with vehemence : to blow at, in contempt : to bustle about.—*v.t.* to drive with a puff : to swell with a wind : to praise in exaggerated terms.—*n.* a sudden, forcible breath : a sudden blast of wind : a gust or whiff : a fungous ball containing dust : any- thing light and porous, or swollen and light : a kind of light pastry : an exaggerated expression of praise.—*n.* **Puff′er.**—**Puff up** (*B.*) to inflate. [Imitative ; cog. with Ger. *puff-en,* &c.]

**Puffery,** puf′ėr-i, *n., puffing* or extravagant praise.

**Puffin,** puf′in, *n.* a water-fowl having a short, thick, projecting beak like that of a parrot. [Named either from its swelling beak or its round belly. See **Puff.**]

**Puffy,** puf′i, *adj.,* puffed out with air or any soft matter : tumid : bombastic.—*adv.* **Puff′ily.**—*n.* **Puff′iness.**

**Pug,** pug, *n.* a monkey : a small kind of dog : any small animal (in familiarity or contempt). [Lit. 'an imp ;' a corr. of **Puck.**] [*tive.*]

**Pugh,** pōō, *int.* of contempt or disdain. [Imita-

**Pugilism,** pū′jil-izm, *n.* the art of boxing or fight- ing with the *fists.*—*adj.* **Pugilist′ic.** [From L. *pugil,* a boxer—root *pug,* whence E. *pugnus,* E. **Fist.**]

**Pugilist,** pū′jil-ist, *n.* one who fights with his *fists.*

**Pugnacious,** pug-nā′shus, *adj.* fond of *fighting :* combative : quarrelsome.—*adv.* **Pugna′ciously.**

—*n.* **Pugnac'ity.** [L. *pugnax, pugnacis*—*pugno*, to fight—*pugnus*, E. **Fist.**]

**Puisne,** pū'ni, *adj. (law)* inferior in rank, applied to certain judges in England. [Lit. 'born after,' O. Fr. (Fr. *puîné*), from *puis*—L. *post*, after, and *né*, pa.p. of *naître*—L. *nascor, natus*, to be born. Doublet of **Puny.**]

**Puissant,** pū'is-ant or pū-is'ant, *adj.*, *potent* or *powerful*: strong: forcible.—*adv.* **Pu'issantly.** —*n.* **Pu'issance.** [Fr. (It. *possente*), from L. *potens*, powerful, modified by the influence of L. *posse*, to be able. Cf. **Potent** and **Possible.**]

**Puke,** pūk, *v.i.* to spew: vomit. [A form of **Spew.**]

**Pule,** pūl, *v.i.* to *pipe* or chirp: to cry, whimper, or whine, like a child.—*n.* **Pul'er.** [From Fr. *piauler*, like It. *pigolare*, L. *pipilo*, and *pipo*, to pipe, formed from the sound.]

**Pull,** pool, *v.t.* to draw or try to draw: to draw forcibly: to tear: to pluck.—*v.i.* to give a pull: to draw.—*n.* the act of pulling: a struggle or contest. [A.S. *pullian*, conn. with Low Ger. *pulen*, to pluck.]

**Pullet,** pool'et, *n.* a *young hen.* [Fr. *poulette*, dim. of *poule*, a hen—Low L. *pulla*, a hen, fem. of L. *pullus*, a young animal, cog. with **Foal.** **Poult** is a doublet.]

**Pulley,** pool'i, *n.* a wheel turning about an axis, and having a groove in which a cord runs, used for raising weights:—*pl.* **Pull'eys.** [M. E. *poleyn*, from A.S. *pullian*: acc. to others, from Fr. *poulain*—Low L. *pullanus*—*pullus* (E. **Foal**): acc. to Diez, from Fr. *poulie*, which is from E. **Pull.**]

**Pulmonary,** pul'mon-ar-i, *adj.* pertaining to or affecting the *lungs.* [L. *pulmonarius*—*pulmo, pulmonis*, a lung—Gr. *pleumōn, pneumōn*, lung —root *pnu*, to breathe.]

**Pulmonic,** pul-mon'ik, *adj.* pertaining to or affecting the *lungs.*—*n.* a medicine for disease of the lungs: one affected by disease of the lungs.

**Pulp,** pulp, *n.* the soft fleshy part of bodies: marrow: the soft part of plants, esp. of fruits: any soft mass.—*v.t.* to reduce to pulp: to deprive of pulp: to separate the pulp. [Fr. *pulpe*—L. *pulpa*, perh. conn. with root of **Palpable.**]

**Pulpit,** pool'pit, *n.* a platform for speaking from: an elevated or inclosed place in a church where the sermon is delivered: a desk.—*adj.* belonging to the pulpit. [Fr.—L. *pulpitum*, a stage. Ety. unknown.]

**Pulpous,** pulp'us, *adj.* consisting of or resembling *pulp*: soft.—*n.* **Pulp'ousness.**

**Pulpy,** pulp'i, *adj.* like *pulp*: soft.—*n.* **Pulp'iness.**

**Pulsate,** pul'sāt, *v.i.* to throb. [L. *pulso, pulsatus*, to beat, freq. of *pello, pulsus*, to drive.]

**Pulsatile,** pul'sat-il, *adj.* that may be *beaten*: played by beating: acting by pulsation.

**Pulsation,** pul-sā'shun, *n.* a *beating* or throbbing: a motion of the pulse: any measured beat: a vibration. [L. *pulsatio.*]

**Pulsative,** pul'sa-tiv, **Pulsatory,** pul'sa-tor-i, *adj.*, *beating* or throbbing.

**Pulse,** puls, *n.* a *beating*: a throb: a vibration: the beating of the heart and the arteries. [Fr. *pouls*—L. *pulsus*—*pello, pulsus.* See **Pulsate.**]

**Pulse,** puls, *n.* grain or seed of beans, pease, &c. [L. *puls*, porridge (Gr. *poltos*). Cf. **Poultice.**]

**Pulseless,** puls'les, *adj.* having no pulsation.

**Pulverable,** pul'vėr-a-bl, **Pulverisable,** pul'vėr-īz-a-bl, *adj.* that may be reduced to fine powder. [L. *pulvis, pulveris*, powder.]

**Pulverise,** pul'vėr-īz, *v.t.* to reduce to *dust* or fine powder.—*n.* **Pulverisa'tion.** [Fr.—Late L. *pulverizo*—*pulvis.*]

**Pulverous,** pul'vėr-us, *adj.* consisting of or like *dust* or powder. [L. *pulvereus.*]

**Puma,** pū'ma, *n.* a carnivorous animal, of the cat kind, of a reddish-brown colour without spots, called also the American lion. [Peruvian *puma.*]

**Pumice,** pū'mis, *n.* a hard, light, spongy, volcanic mineral.—*adj.* **Pumi'ceous,** of or like pumice. [A.S. *pumic(-stan)*, pumice(-stone)—L. *pumex, pumicis*, for *spumex*—*spuma*, foam—*spuo.* See **Spume,** and **Pounce,** a fine powder.]

**Pummel.** Same as **Pommel.**

**Pump,** pump, *n.* a machine for raising water and other fluids.—*v.t.* to raise with a pump: to draw out information by artful questions.—*v.i.* to work a pump: to raise water by pumping.—*n.* **Pump'er.** [Fr. *pompe*—Ger. *pumpe* (for *plumpe*), from the sound of splashing in water. See **Plump.**]

**Pump,** pump, *n.* a thin-soled shoe used in dancing. [Fr. *pompe.* So called from being used on *showy* occasions. See **Pomp.**]

**Pumpkin,** pump'kin, **Pompion,** pump'yun, *n.* a plant of the gourd family and its fruit. [A corr. of Fr. *pompon*—L. *pepō, -onis*—Gr. *pepōn*, ripe, so called because not eaten until ripe.]

**Pun,** pun, *v.t.* to play upon words similar in sound but different in meaning:—*pr.p.* punn'ing; *pa.t.* and *pa p.* punned.—*n.* a play upon words. [Lit. 'to hammer or torture words,' an old form of **Pound,** to beat, from A.S. *punian.*]

**Punch,** contr. of **Punchinello.** [Through the influence of prov. E. *punch*, thick, fat.]

**Punch,** punsh, *n.* a beverage of *five* ingredients, spirit, water, sugar, lemon-juice, and spice. [Hindi *panch*, five—Sans. *panchan*, cog. with E. **Five.**]

**Punch,** punsh, *v.t.* to *prick* or pierce with something sharp: to perforate with a steel tool.— *n.* a tool for stamping or perforating, a kind of awl. [A curtailed form of **Puncheon,** a tool.]

**Punch,** punsh, *v.t.* to strike or hit, esp. on the head.—*n.* a stroke or blow. [Prob. a corr. of **Punish.**]

**Puncheon,** punsh'un, *n.* a steel tool with one end for stamping or perforating metal plates. [O. Fr. *poinson*, a bodkin, a puncheon—L. *punctio, -onis.* a pricking—*pungo, punctus*, to prick.]

**Puncheon,** punsh'un, *n.* a *cask*: a liquid measure of 84 gallons. [O. Fr. *poinson*, a cask; perh. from the above, so called from the brand stamped on it. Cf. **Hogshead.**]

**Punchinello,** punsh-i-nel'o, **Punch,** punsh, *n.* the short, humpbacked figure of a puppet-show: a buffoon. [A corr. of It. *pulcinello*, dim. of *pulcino*, a young chicken, a child—L. *pullus*, a young animal. See **Pullet** and **Foal.**]

**Punctate,** pungk'tāt, **Punctated,** pungk'tāt-ed, *adj.*, *pointed*: (*bot.*) punctured: full of small holes. [Formed from L. *punctum*, a point— *pungo, punctus*, to prick.]

**Punctilio,** pungk-til'yo, *n.* a nice point in behaviour or ceremony: nicety in forms. [Lit 'a little point,' Sp. *puntillo*, dim. of *punto*, point —L. *punctum*, point.]

**Punctilious,** pungk-til'yus, *adj.* attending to *little points* or matters: very nice or exact in behaviour or ceremony: exact or punctual to excess.—*adv.* **Punctil'iously.**—*n.* **Punctil'iousness.**

**Punctual,** pungk'tū-al, *adj.* observant of nice *points*, punctilious: exact in keeping time and appointments: done at the exact time.—*n.* **Punc'tualist.**—*adv.* **Punc'tually.** [Fr. *ponctuel*—L. *punctum*, a point.]

**Punctuality**, pungk-tū-al′i-ti, *n.* quality or state of being *punctual*: the keeping the exact time of an appointment.

**Punctuate**, pungk′tū-āt, *v.t.* to mark with *points*: to divide sentences by certain marks.

**Punctuation**, pungk-tū-ā′shun, *n.* the act or art of dividing sentences by *points* or marks.

**Puncture**, pungk′tūr, *n.* a *pricking*: a small hole made with a sharp point.—*v.t.* to prick: to pierce with a pointed instrument. [L. *punctura* —*pungo*.] [*dita—pand*, to pile up.]

**Pundit**, pun′dit, *n.* a learned man. [Sans. *pan-*

**Pungent**, pun′jent, *adj.*, *pricking* or acrid to taste or smell: keen: sarcastic.—*adv.* **Pun′gently.** —*n.* **Pun′gency.** [L. *pungens*, *-entis*, pr.p. of *pungo*. See **Poignant**.]

**Punish**, pun′ish, *v.t.* to exact a *penalty*: to cause loss or pain for a fault or crime: to chasten.— *n.* **Pun′isher.** [Fr. *punir*, *punissant*—L. *punire* —*pœna*, penalty. See **Pain**.] [ished.

**Punishable**, pun′ish-a-bl, *adj.* that may be pun-

**Punishment**, pun′ish-ment, *n.* loss or *pain* inflicted for a crime or fault.

**Punitive**, pūn′i-tiv, *adj.* pertaining to punishment.

**Punkah**, pung′ka. *n.* a large *fan* consisting of a light framework covered with cloth and suspended from the ceiling of a room. [Hind. *pankhâ*, a fan.] [in punning.

**Punster**, pun′stėr, *n.* one who *puns* or is skilled

**Punt**, punt, *n.* a ferry-boat: a flat-bottomed boat. —*v.t.* to propel, as a boat, by pushing with a pole against the bottom of a river. [A.S.—L. *ponto*, a punt, a pontoon—*pons*, *pontis*. See **Pontage** and **Pontoon**.]

**Puny**, pū′ni, *adj.* (*comp.* **Pu′nier**, *superl.* **Pu′niest**), small: feeble: inferior in size or strength. [Lit. 'born after or late.' Doublet of **Puisne**.]

**Pup**, pup, *v.t.* to bring forth *puppies*, as a bitch: —*pr.p.* pupp′ing; *pa.t.* and *pa.p.* pupped. [Short for **Puppy**.]

**Pupa**, pū′pa, **Pupe**, pūp or pū′pē, *n.* an insect inclosed in a case before its full development: a chrysalis:—*pl.* **Pupæ**, pū′pē, **Pupes**, pū′pēs. [L. *pupa*, a girl, a doll, fem. of *pupus*, a boy, a child.]

**Pupil**, pū′pil, *n.* a *little boy* or *girl*: one under the care of a tutor: a scholar: a ward: (*law*) one under puberty. [Fr. *pupille*—L. *pupillus*, *pupilla*, dims. of *pupus*, boy, *pupa*, girl.]

**Pupil**, pū′pil, *n.* the apple of the eye, so called from the *baby*-like figures seen on it. [Same as above word.]

**Pupilage**, pū′pil-āj, *n.* state of being a *pupil*.

**Pupillary**, **Pupilary**, pū′pil-ar-i, *adj.* pertaining to a *pupil* or ward, or to the pupil of the eye.

**Puppet**, pup′et, *n.* a small *doll* or image moved by wires in a show: one entirely under the control of another.—*n.* **Pupp′et-show**, a mock *show* or drama performed by *puppets*. [O. Fr. *poupette*, dim. from L. *pupa*.]

**Puppy**, pup′i, *n.* a *doll*: a conceited young man: a whelp.—*n.* **Pupp′yism**, conceit in men. [Fr. *toupée*, a doll or puppet—L. *pupa*. Cf. **Pupa**.]

**Pur.** See **Purr**.

**Purblind**, pur′blīnd, *adj.* nearly *blind*: nearsighted.—*adv.* **Pur′blindly.**—*n.* **Pur′blindness.** [For *pure-blind*, *i.e.* wholly blind; the meaning has been modified, prob. through some confusion with the word *to pore*.] [chased.

**Purchasable**, pur′chas-a-bl, *adj.* that may be pur-

**Purchase**, pur′chās, *v.t.* (*lit.*) to *chase* or *seek for*: to acquire: to obtain by paying: to obtain by labour, danger, &c.: (*law*) to sue out or

procure.—*n.* act of purchasing: that which is purchased: any mechanical power or advantage in raising or moving bodies.—*n.* **Pur′chaser.** [Fr. *pourchasser*, to seek eagerly, pursue—*pour* (L. *pro*), for, *chasser*, to chase. See **Chase**.]

**Pure**, pūr, *adj.* (*comp.* **Pur′er**, *superl.* **Pur′est**), clean, unsoiled: unmixed: not adulterated: real: free from guilt or defilement: chaste: modest: mere: that and that only.—*adv.* **Pure′ly.**—*n.* **Pure′ness.** [Fr. *pur*—L. *purus*— root *pu*, to make clean; conn. with E. **Fire**, L. *puto*, and its derivatives.]

**Purgation**, pur-gā′shun, *n.* a *purging*: (*law*) the clearing from imputation of guilt. [Fr.—L. *purgatio*.]

**Purgative**, pur′ga-tiv, *adj.*, *cleansing*: having the power of evacuating the intestines.—*n.* a medicine that evacuates. [L. *purgativus*.]

**Purgatorial**, pur-ga-tō′ri-al, *adj.* pertaining to *purgatory*.

**Purgatory**, pur′ga-tor-i, *adj.*, *purging* or cleansing: expiatory.—*n.* according to R. Catholic and some eastern religions, a place or state in which souls are after death *purified* from venial sins. [Fr. *purgatoire*—L. *purgatorius*. See **Purge**.]

**Purge**, purj, *v.t.* to *make pure*: to carry off whatever is impure or superfluous: to clear from guilt: to evacuate, as the bowels: to clarify, as liquors.—*v.i.* to become pure by clarifying: to have frequent evacuations. [Fr. *purger*—L. *purgo* (for *pur-igo*)—*purus*, pure, and *ago*, to do or make.]

**Purging**, purj′ing, *n.* act of *cleansing* or clearing.

**Purification**, pūr-i-fi-kā′shun, *n.* act of *purifying*: (*B.*) the act of cleansing ceremonially by removing defilement. [Fr.—L. *purificatio*.]

**Purificatory**, pūr-if′i-ka-tor-i, *adj.* tending to *purify* or cleanse.

**Purify**, pūr′i-fī, *v.t.* to *make pure*: to free from guilt or uncleanness: to free from improprieties or barbarisms, as language.—*v.i.* to become pure:—*pa.t.* and *pa.p.* pūr′ifīed.—*n.* **Pur′ifier.** [Fr. *purifier*—L. *purifico*—*purus*, pure, *facio*, to make.]

**Purism**, pūr′izm, *n.*, *pure* or immaculate conduct or style: the doctrine of a purist.

**Purist**, pūr′ist, *n.* one who is excessively *pure* or nice in the choice of words.

**Puritan**, pūr′i-tan, *n.* one professing great *purity* in religious life: one of a religious party in the time of Elizabeth and the Stuarts marked by rigid purity in doctrine and practice.—*adj.* pertaining to the Puritans.

**Puritanic**, pūr-i-tan′ik, **Puritanical**, pūr-i-tan′ik-al, *adj.* like a Puritan: rigid: exact.

**Puritanism**, pūr′i-tan-izm, *n.* the notions or practice of Puritans.

**Purity**, pūr′i-ti, *n.* condition of being *pure*.

**Purl**, purl, *v.i.* to flow with a murmuring sound: to ripple.—*n.* a soft murmuring sound, as of a stream among stones: an eddy or ripple. [Prob. freq. of **Purr**; cf. Sw. *porla*, Ger. *perlen*, to bubble.]

**Purl**, purl, *v.t.* to fringe with a waved edging, as lace: (*knitting*) to invert stitches. [Contr. of *purfle*—Fr. *pourfiler*—*pour* (L. *pro*), and *filer*, to twist threads, from *fil*, a thread. Cf. **File**, a line, &c.]

**Purl**, purl, *n.* ale warmed and spiced. [Prob. from Fr. *perle*, a pearl, from the small pearl-like bubbles rising on its surface. See **Pearl**.]

**Purlieu**, pur′lū, *n.* the borders or environs of any place: (*orig.*) the grounds on the borders of a forest. [Acc. to Skeat, a corr. of O. Fr. *puralee* (a mere translation of L. *perambulatio*), land severed from a royal forest by perambulation—O. Fr. *pur* (= L. *pro*), and *allee*, a going. See Alley.]

**Purloin**, pur-loin', *v.t.* to steal: to plagiarise.—*n.* **Purloin'er**. [Lit. 'to carry away to a long distance;' M. E. *purlongen*—O. Fr. *purloignier*—L. *prolongo*. See Prolong.]

**Purple**, pur'pl, *n.* a very dark-red colour: a purple dress or robe, orig. worn only by royalty: a robe of honour.—*adj.* red tinged with blue: blood-red: bloody.—*v.t.* to dye purple: to clothe with purple. [M. E. *purpre*—O. Fr. *porpre* (Fr. *pourpre*)—L. *purpura*—Gr. *porphyra*. See Porphyry.]

**Purposeless**, pur'pos-les, *adj.* without purpose or effect: aimless.                [intentionally.

**Purport**, pur'port, *n.* design: signification.—*v.i.* to mean. [Lit. 'that which is carried or conveyed,' O. Fr. *pur* (Fr. *pour*)—L. *pro*, for, and Fr. *porter*—L. *porto*, to carry.]

**Purpose**, pur'pos, *n.* that which a person *sets before* himself as an end: aim: intention: effect.—*v.t.* to intend.—*v.i.* to have an intention. [O. Fr. *purposer*, form of *proposer* (see Propose), influenced by Fr. *propos* (—L. *ponere*), to place.]

**Purposely**, pur'pos-li, *adv.* with purpose or design.

**Purr, Pur**, pur, *v.i.* to utter a murmuring sound, as a cat.—*n.* (also **Purr'ing**) the low, murmuring sound of a cat. [From the sound.]

**Purse**, purs, *n.* a small bag for money, orig. made of *skin*: a sum of money: a treasury.—*v.t.* to put into a purse: to contract as the mouth of a purse: to contract into folds. [O. Fr. *borse* (Fr. *bourse*)—Low L. *bursa*—Gr. *byrsa*, a skin, a hide.]

**Purse-proud**, purs'-prowd, *adj.* proud of one's *purse* or wealth: insolent from wealth.—*n.* **Purse'-pride**.

**Purser**, purs'er, *n.* an officer who has charge of the provisions, clothing, and accounts of a ship, now termed a 'paymaster.'—*n.* **Purs'ership**.

**Purslane, Purslain**, purs'lān, *n.* an annual plant, frequently used in salads. [It. *porcellana*, from L. *portulaca*.]

**Pursuance**, pur-sū'ans, *n.* the act of *pursuing* or following out: process: consequence.

**Pursuant**, pur-sū'ant, *adj.* done *pursuing* or seeking any purpose: hence, agreeable.

**Pursue**, pur-sū', *v.t.* to *follow onwards* in order to overtake: to chase: to prosecute: to seek: to imitate: to continue.—*n.* **Pursu'er**, one who pursues: (*Scots law*) a plaintiff. [O. Fr. *porsuir* (Fr. *poursuivre*)—L. *prosequor*, *-secutus*—*pro*, onwards, *sequor*, to follow.]

**Pursuit**, pur-sūt', *n.* the act of *pursuing*, following, or going after: endeavour to attain: occupation.

**Pursuivant**, pur'swi-vant, *n.* a *pursuer* or follower: a state messenger: an attendant on the heralds: one of four junior officers in the Heralds' College. [Fr. *poursuivant*.]

**Pursy**, purs'i, *adj.*, pushed out: puffy: fat and short: short-breathed.—*n.* **Purs'iness**. [O. Fr. *pourcif* (Fr. *poussif*), orig. *poulsif*, broken-winded—O. Fr. *pourcer* (Fr. *pousser*), to push. See Push.]

**Purtenance**, pur'ten-ans, *n.* that which *pertains* or belongs to: (*B.*) the intestines of an animal. [Short for Appurtenance.]

**Purulence**, pū'roo-lens, **Purulency**, pū'roo-len-si, *n.* the forming of *pus* or matter: pus.

**Purulent**, pū'roo-lent, *adj.* consisting of, full of, or resembling *pus* or matter.—*adv.* **Pu'rulently**.

**Purvey**, pur-vā', *v.t.* to *provide*, esp. with conveniences: to procure.—*v.i.* to provide: to buy in provisions. [O. Fr. *porvoir* (Fr. *pourvoir*)—L. *provideo*. See Provide.]

**Purveyance**, pur-vā'ans, *n.* the act of *purveying*: procuring of victuals: the royal prerogative of pre-emption, now abolished.

**Purveyor**, pur-vā'or, *n.* one who *provides* victuals: an officer who formerly exacted provisions for the use of the king's household: a procurer.

**Pus**, pus, *n.* that which has become *putrid*: white matter of a sore. [L. *pus, puris*, matter; akin to Gr. *pyon*, and Sans. root *puy*, to become putrid.]

**Puseyism**, pū'zi-izm, *n.* a name given collectively to the principles of Dr *Pusey* and other Oxford divines, as put forth in a series of pamphlets called 'Tracts for the Times.'—*n.* **Pu'seyite**, one supposed to hold certain views attributed to Dr Pusey.

**Push**, poosh, *v.t.* to *thrust* or *beat* against: to drive by pressure: to press forward: to urge.—*v.i.* to make a thrust: to make an effort: to press against: to burst out.—*n.* a thrust: an impulse: assault: effort: exigence. [Fr. *pousser*—L. *pulso*, freq. of *pello, pulsum*, to beat.]

**Pushing**, poosh'ing, *adj.*, pressing forward in business: enterprising: vigorous.

**Pusillanimous**, pū-sil-an'i-mus, *adj.* having a *little mind*: mean-spirited: cowardly.—*adv.* **Pusillan'imously**.—*ns.* **Pusillan'imousness, Pusillanim'ity**. [L. *pusillanimis—pusillus*, very little (—*pusus*, dim. of *puer*, a boy), and *animus*, the mind.]

**Puss**, poos, *n.* a familiar name for a *cat*: a hare, in sportsmen's language. [Dut. *poes*, puss; Ir. and Gael. *pus*, a cat: prob. imitative of a cat's spitting.]

**Pussy**, poos'i, *n.* a dim. of Puss.

**Pustular**, pus'tū-lar, **Pustulous**, pus'tū-lus, *adj.* covered with *pustules*.

**Pustulate**, pus'tū-lāt, *v.t.* to form into *pustules*.

**Pustule**, pus'tūl, *n.* a small pimple containing *pus*. [Fr.—L. *pustula—pus*.]

**Put**, poot, *v.t.* to *push* or *thrust*: to drive into action: to throw suddenly, as a word: to set, lay, or deposit: to bring into any state: to offer: to propose: to apply: to oblige: to incite: to add.—*v.i.* to place: to turn :—*pr.p.* putting (poot'-); *pa.t.* and *pa.p.* put. [A.S. *potian*; prob. from the Celt., as Gael. *put*, W. *pwtio*.]

**Putative**, pū'ta-tiv, *adj.*, supposed: reputed. [Fr.—L. *putativus—puto, putatus*, to suppose.]

**Putrefaction**, pū-tre-fak'shun, *n.* the act or process of *putrefying*: rottenness: corruption.

**Putrefactive**, pū-tre-fak'tiv, *adj.* pertaining to or causing *putrefaction*.—*n.* **Putrefac'tiveness**.

**Putrefy**, pū'tre-fī, *v.t.* to make *putrid* or rotten: to corrupt.—*v.i.* to become putrid: to rot :—*pa.t.* and *pa.p.* pū'trefied. [Putrid, and L. *facio, factum*, to make.]

**Putrescent**, pū-tres'ent, *adj.*, becoming putrid: pertaining to putrefaction.—*n.* **Putres'cence**.

**Putrid**, pū'trid, *adj.*, stinking: rotten: corrupt.—*ns.* **Putrid'ity, Pu'tridness**. [Fr. *putride*—L. *putridus—puter, putris*, rotten—*puteo*, akin to Gr. *puthō*, Sans. *puy*, to stink. See Pus.]

**Putty**, put'i, *n.* an oxide of tin, or of lead and tin, used in polishing glass, &c.: a cement, of whiting and linseed-oil, used in glazing windows.—*v.t.* to fix or fill up with putty :—*pa.t.* and *pa.p.* putt'ied. [O. Fr. *potée*, properly that which is contained in a pot [Fr. *pot*].]

**Puzzle**, puz'l, *n.* perplexity: something to try the ingenuity, as a toy or riddle.—*v.t.* to pose: to perplex.—*v.i.* to be bewildered.—*n.* **Puzz′ler.** [From M. E. *opposaile* (E. *opposal*), an objection or question put by an examiner—Fr. *opposer.* See **Oppose.**]

**Puzzling,** puz′ling, *adj., posing:* perplexing.

**Pyebald.** See **Piebald.**

**Pygarg,** pī′gärg, *n.* a kind of antelope. [Lit. 'the *white-rumped* animal,' Gr. *pygargos—pygē,* rump, *argos,* white.]

**Pygmean,** pig-mē′an, **Pygmy,** pig′mi, *adj.* pertaining to or like a *pygmy:* dwarfish: diminutive.

**Pygmy,** pig′mi, *n.* one of a fabulous dwarfish race of antiquity: a dwarf: any diminutive thing. [Fr. *pygmē*—L. *Pygmæi*—Gr. *Pygmaioi,* the Pygmies, fabled to be of the length of a (Gr.) *pygmē*=13½ inches (measured from the elbow to the knuckles)—*pygmē,* fist, L. *pugnus.*]

**Pylorus,** pi-lō′rus, *n.* the lower opening of the stomach leading to the intestines.—*adj.* **Pylor′ic.** [Lit. 'gate-keeper,' L.—Gr. *pylōros—pylē,* an entrance, and *ouros,* a guardian.]

**Pyramid,** pir′a-mid, *n.* a solid figure on a triangular, square, or polygonal base, with triangular sides meeting in a point :—*pl.* 'the pyramids' or great monuments of Egypt : a game played on a billiard table. [L.—Gr. *pyramis, pyramidos.* Ety. unknown ; prob. Egyptian.]

**Pyramidal,** pi-ram′i-dal, **Pyramidic,** pir-a-mid′ik, **Pyramidical,** pir-a-mid′ik-al, *adj.* having the form of a *pyramid.*—*advs.* **Pyram′idally, Pyramid′ically.**

**Pyre,** pīr, *n.* a pile of wood, &c. to be set on *fire* at a funeral. [L. *pyra*—Gr. *pyra—pyr,* E. **Fire.**]

**Pyrites,** pir-ī′tēz, *n.* a native compound of sulphur with other metals, so called because it strikes *fire* when struck against steel.—*adjs.* **Pyrit′ic, Pyrit′ical.** [L.—Gr. *pyr,* E. **Fire.**]

**Pyrogenous,** pir-oj′en-us, *adj.* produced by *fire.* [Gr. *pyrogenēs—pyr,* fire, and *gen,* root of *gignomai,* to produce.]

**Pyrometer,** pir-om′e-tėr, *n.* an instrument for *measuring* the temperature of bodies under fierce heat.—*adjs.* **Pyromet′ric, Pyromet′rical.** [Gr. *pyr,* fire. and *metron,* a measure.]

**Pyrotechnic,** pir-o-tek′nik, **Pyrotechnical,** pir-o-tek′nik-al, *adj.* pertaining to *fireworks.* [Gr. *pyr,* fire, and *technikos,* artistic—*technē,* art.]

**Pyrotechnics,** pir-o-tek′niks, **Pyrotechny,** pir′o-tek-ni, *n.* the *art* of making *fireworks.* [Gr. *pyr,* fire, and *technikos,* artistic—*technē,* art.]

**Pyrotechnist,** pir′o-tek-nist, *n.* one skilled in *pyrotechny.*

**Pyrrhonist,** pir′ro-nist, *n.* one who holds the tenets of *Pyrrho,* who taught universal scepticism : a sceptic.—*n.* **Pyrrhonism,** scepticism.

**Pythagorean,** pi-thag-o-rē′an, *adj.* pertaining to *Pythagoras,* a celebrated Greek philosopher, or to his philosophy.—*n.* a follower of Pythagoras.—*n.* **Pythag′orism,** his doctrines.

**Pythian,** pith′i-an, *adj.* pertaining to the *Pythoness :* noting one of the four national festivals of ancient Greece, in honour of Apollo.

**Pythoness,** pith′on-es, *n.* the priestess of the oracle of Apollo at *Pytho,* the oldest name of Delphi, in Greece : a witch.

**Pythonic,** pi-thon′ik, *adj.* pretending to foretell future events like the Pythoness.

**Pythonism,** pith′on-izm, *n.* the art of predicting events by divination.—*n.* **Pyth′onist.**

**Pyx,** piks, *n.* in the R. Cath. Church, the sacred *box* in which the host is kept after consecration : at the Mint, the box containing sample coins.— *v.t.* to test the weight and fineness of, as the coin deposited in the pyx.—**Trial of the Pyx,** final trial by weight and assay of the gold and

silver coins of the United Kingdom, prior to their issue from the Mint. [L. *pyxis,* a box— Gr. *pyxis—pyxos* (L. *buxus*), the box-tree, box-wood—*pyk-nos,* dense—root, *pak,* to bind. Cf. **Box,** a tree, &c., and **Pact.**]

# Q

**Quack,** kwak, *v.i.* to cry like a duck : to boast : to practise as a quack.—*v.t.* to doctor by quackery.—*n.* the cry of a duck : a boastful pretender to skill which he does not possess, esp. medical skill : a mountebank.—*adj.* pertaining to quackery : used by quacks. [An imitative word, seen also in Ger. *quaken,* Dut. *kwaken,* Gr. *koax,* a croak.] [of a *quack,* esp. in medicine.

**Quackery,** kwak′ėr-i, *n.* the pretensions or practice

**Quacksalver,** kwak′sal-vėr, *n.* a *quack* who deals in *salves,* ointments, &c. : a quack generally.

**Quadragesima,** kwod-ra-jes′i-ma, *n.* Lent, or the *forty* days of fast before Easter. [L.—*quadragesimus,* fortieth—*quadraginta,* forty—*quatuor,* four. See **Four.**]

**Quadragesimal,** kwod-ra-jes′i-mal, *adj.* belonging to or used in Lent.

**Quadrangle,** kwod′rang-gl, *n.* a square surrounded by buildings : (*geom.*) a plane figure having *four* equal sides and *angles.* [Fr.—L. *quadrangulum—quatuor,* four, and *angulus,* an angle.]

**Quadrangular,** kwod-rang′gū-lar, *adj.* of the form of a quadrangle.—*adv.* **Quadrang′ularly.**

**Quadrant,** kwod′rant, *n.* (*geom.*) the *fourth part* of a circle, or an arc of 90° : an instrument consisting of the *quadrant* of a circle graduated in degrees, used for taking altitudes. [L. *quadrans,* from *quatuor,* four.]

**Quadrantal,** kwod-rant′al, *adj.* pertaining to, equal to, or included in a *quadrant.*

**Quadrate,** kwod′rāt, *adj., squared :* having four equal sides and four right angles : divisible into four equal parts : (*fig.*) balanced : exact : suited. —*n.* a square or *quadrate* figure.—*v.i.* to square or agree with : to correspond. [L. *quadratus,* pa.p. of *quadro,* to square, from *quatuor,* four.]

**Quadratic,** kwod-rat′ik, *adj.* pertaining to, containing or denoting a *square.*

**Quadrature,** kwod′ra-tūr, *n.* a *squaring :* (*geom.*) the finding, exactly or approximately, of a square that shall be equal to a given figure of some other shape : the position of a heavenly body when 90° distant from another.

**Quadrennial,** kwod-ren′yal, *adj.* comprising *four years:* once in four years.—*adv.* **Quadrenn′ially.** [L. *quadrennis—quatuor,* four, *annus,* a year.]

**Quadrilateral,** kwod-ri-lat′ėr-al, *adj.* having *four sides.*—*n.* (*geom.*) a plane figure having four sides. [L. *quadrilaterus—quatuor,* four, and *latus, lateris,* a side.]

**Quadriliteral,** kwod-ri-lit′er-al, *adj.* of *four letters.* [L. *quatuor,* four, and *litera,* a letter.]

**Quadrille,** ka-dril′ or kwa-dril′, *n.* a game at cards played by *four* : a dance made up of sets of dancers containing *four* couples each. [Fr.; from It. *quadriglia*—L. *quadra,* a square— *quatuor,* four.]

**Quadrillion,** kwod-ril′yun, *n.* a *million* raised to the *fourth* power, represented by a unit with 24 ciphers. [Coined from L. *quater,* four times, on the model of **Million.**]

**Quadrinomial,** kwod-ri-nō′mi-al, *adj.* (*math.*) consisting of *four divisions* or terms.—*n.* an expression of four terms. [From L. *quatuor*, four, and Gr. *nomē*, a division—*nemō*, to distribute.]

**Quadroon**, kwod-rōōn', *n.* the offspring of a mulatto and a white person. [Fr. *quarteron*—L. *quatuor*, four ; so called because their blood is *one-fourth* black.]

**Quadruped**, kwod'roo-ped, *n.* a *four-footed* animal. [L. *quatuor*, four, and *pes, pedis*, a foot.]

**Quadrupedal**, kwod-rōō'pe-dal, *adj.* having four feet.

**Quadruple**, kwod'roo-pl, *adj., fourfold.—n.* four times the quantity or number.—*v.t.* to increase fourfold. [Fr.—L. *quadruplus—quatuor*, four.]

**Quadruplicate**, kwod-rōō'pli-kāt, *adj.* made *fourfold.—v.t.* to make fourfold : to double twice.—*n.* Quadruplica'tion. [L. *quadruplicatus—quatuor*, four, and *plico, plicatus*, to fold.]

**Quaff**, kwaf, *v.t.* to drink in large draughts.—*v.i.* to drink largely.—*n.* Quaff'er. [Scot. *queff, quaich*, a small drinking-cup ; from Ir. and Gael. *cuach*, a cup.]

**Quagga**, kwag'a, *n.* a quadruped of South Africa, like the ass in form and the zebra in colour. [Hottentot *quagga, guacha*.]

**Quaggy**, kwag'i. *adj.* of the nature of a *quagmire*: shaking or yielding under the feet.

**Quagmire**, kwag'mīr, *n.* wet, boggy ground that yields under the feet. [Obs. *Quag*, same as Quake, and Mire.]

**Quail**, kwāl, *v.i.* to cower : to fail in spirit. [A.S. *cwelan*, to suffer, to die ; Ger. *qual*, torment.]

**Quail**, kwāl, *n.* a migratory bird like the partridge, common in Asia, Africa, and S. Europe. [O. Fr. *quaille, caille*—Low L. *quaquila*—O. Flem. *quakele*, from root of Quack.]

**Quaint**, kwānt. *adj.* neat : unusual : odd : whimsical.—*adv.* Quaint'ly.—*n.* Quaint'ness. [Lit. 'known, famous, remarkable,' O. Fr. *cointe*, neat, acquainted—L. *cognitus*, known.]

**Quake**, kwāk, *v.i.* to tremble, esp. with cold or fear :—*pr.p.* quāk'ing ; *pa.t.* and *pa.p.* quāked. —*n.* a shake : a shudder.—*adv.* Quak'ingly. [A.S. *cwacian* ; allied to Quick.]

**Quaker**, kwāk'ėr, *n.* one of the Society of Friends, a religious sect founded by George Fox, born in 1624. [A nickname first given them by Judge Bennet at Derby, because Fox bade him and those present tremble at the word of the Lord. This is Fox's own statement in his *Journal.*]

**Quakerism**, kwāk'ėr-izm, *n.* the tenets of the *Quakers.*

**Qualification**, kwol-i-fi-kā'shun, *n.* that which *qualifies* : a quality that fits a person for a place, &c. : abatement.

**Qualify**, kwol'i-fī, *v.t.* to render capable or suitable : to furnish with legal power : to limit by modifications : to soften : to abate : to reduce the strength of : to vary.—*n.* Qual'ifier. [Fr. *qualifier*, from L. *qualis*, of what sort, and *facio*, to make.]

**Qualitative**, kwol'i-tā-tiv, *adj.* relating to *quality* : (*chem.*) determining the nature of components.

**Quality**, kwol'i-ti, *n.* that which makes a thing *what* it is : property : peculiar power : acquisition : character : rank : superior birth or character. [Fr.—L. *qualitas, qualitatis.*]

**Qualm**, kwäm, *n.* a sudden attack of illness : a scruple, as of conscience. [A.S. *cwealm*, pestilence, death ; Ger. *qualm*, a disposition to vomit, vapour ; Sw. *qvalm*, a suffocating heat ; allied to Quail, *v.*]

**Qualmish**, kwäm'ish, *adj.* affected with *qualm*, or a disposition to vomit, or with slight sickness.

**Quandary**, kwon-dā'ri, *n.* a state of *difficulty* or

uncertainty : a hard plight. [Prob. a corr. of M. E. *wandreth*, from Ice. *vandrædi*, difficulty. trouble.]

**Quantitative**, kwon'ti-tā-tiv, *adj.* relating to *quantity* : measurable in quantity : (*chem.*) determining the relative proportions of components.

**Quantity**, kwon'ti-ti, *n.* the *amount* of anything : bulk ; size : a determinate amount : a sum or bulk : a large portion : (*logic*) the extent of a conception : (*gram.*) the measure of a syllable : (*music*) the relative duration of a tone : (*math.*) anything which can be increased, divided, or measured. [Fr.—L. *quantitas, quantitatis— quantus*, how much—*quam*, how.]

**Quantum**, kwon'tum, *n.* quantity : amount. [L. *quantum*, neut. of *quantus*, how great, how much.]

**Quarantine**, kwor-an-tēn, *n.* the time, orig. *forty* days, during which a ship suspected to be infected with a contagious disease, is obliged to forbear intercourse with the shore.— *v.t.* to prohibit from intercourse from fear of infection. [Fr. *quarante*—L. *quadraginta*, forty —*quatuor*, four.]

**Quarrel**, kwor'el, *n.* an angry dispute : a breach of friendship : a brawl.—*v.i.* to dispute violently : to fight : to disagree :—*pr.p.* quarr'elling ; *pa.t.* and *pa.p.* quarr'elled.—*n.* Quarr'eller. [M. E. *querele*—Fr. *quereile*—L. *querela— queror*, to complain.]

**Quarrelsome**, kwor'el-sum, *adj., disposed to quarrel:* brawling : easily provoked.—*n.* Quarr'elsomeness.

**Quarry**, kwor'i, *n.* a place where stones are dug for building or other purposes.—*v.t.* to dig or take from a quarry :—*pa.t.* and *pa.p.* quarr'ied. [Lit. 'a place where stones are *squared*,' O. Fr. *quarriere* (Fr. *carrière*)—Low L. *quadraria—* L. *quadrus*, square. See Quadrant.]

**Quarry**, kwor'i, *n.* the *entrails* of the *game* given to the dogs after the chase : the object of the chase : the game a hawk is pursuing or has killed : a heap of dead game. [M. E. *querré*— O. Fr. *coree* (Fr. *curée*)—Low L. *corata*, the intestines or inwards of a slain animal, so called because including the heart, from L. *cor, cordis*, the heart ; but acc. to Littré, through O. Fr. *cuirée*, from *cuir*, the skin (—L. *corium*), in which these parts were thrown to the dogs.]

**Quarryman**, kwor'i-man, **Quarrier**, kwor'i-ėr, *n.* a *man* who works in a *quarry.*

**Quart**, kwort or kwawrt, *n.* the *fourth* part of a gallon, or two pints : a vessel containing two pints. [Fr.—L. *quartus*, fourth—*quatuor*, four.]

**Quartan**, kwor'tan, *adj.* occurring every *fourth* day, as an intermittent fever or ague. [Fr.— L. *quartanus*, of or belonging to the fourth.]

**Quarter**, kwor'tėr, *n.* a *fourth* part : the fourth part of a cwt. = 28 lbs. avoirdupois : 8 bushels (dry measure) : the fourth part of a chaldron of coal—of the year—of the moon's period—of a carcass (including a limb)—of the horizon : a cardinal point : a region of a hemisphere : a division of a town, &c. : place of lodging, as for soldiers, esp. in *pl.* : mercy granted to a disabled antagonist, prob. from the idea of the captor sending the prisoner to his quarter or lodging : (*naut.*) the part of a ship's side between the mainmast and the stern.—*v.t.* to divide into *four* equal parts : to divide into parts or compartments : to furnish with quarters : to lodge : to furnish with entertainment : (*her.*) to bear as an appendage to the hereditary arms. [Fr. *quartier*; from L. *quartarius—quartus*, fourth.]

**Quarter-day,** kwor'tėr-dā, *n.* the last *day* of a *quarter*, on which rent or interest is paid.

**Quarter-deck,** kwor'tėr-dek, *n.* the part of the deck of a ship abaft the mainmast.

**Quarterly,** kwor'tėr-li, *adj.* relating to a *quarter* : consisting of or containing a fourth part : once a quarter of a year.—*adv.* once a quarter.—*n.* a periodical published every quarter of a year.

**Quartermaster,** kwor'tėr-mas-tėr, *n.* an officer who looks after the *quarters* of the soldiers, and attends to the supplies : (*naut.*) a petty officer who attends to the helm, signals, &c.

**Quartern,** kwor'tėrn, *n.* the *fourth* of a pint : a gill : (in dry measure) the fourth part of a peck, or of a stone.—**Quartern-loaf,** a loaf of 4 lbs., because orig. made of a *quarter* stone of flour.

**Quarter-sessions,** kwor'tėr-sesh'uns, *n.pl.* county or borough *sessions* held *quarterly*.

**Quarter-staff,** kwor'tėr-staf, *n.* a long *staff* or weapon of defence, grasped at a *quarter* of its length from the end and at the middle.

**Quartette, Quartet,** kwor-tet', *n.* anything in *fours* : a musical composition of four parts, for voices or instruments : a stanza of four lines.

**Quarto,** kwor'tō, *adj.* having the sheet folded into *four* leaves.—*n.* a book of a quarto size :—*pl.* **Quartos,** kwor'tōz.

**Quartz,** kworts, *n.* a mineral composed of pure silica : rock-crystal.—*adj.* **Quartzose,** kworts'ōs, or like quartz. [From Ger. *quarz.*]

**Quash,** kwosh, *v.t.* to crush : to subdue or extinguish suddenly and completely : to annul or make void. [O. Fr. *quasser*, Fr. *casser*—L. *quasso,* inten. of *quatio,* to shake ; prob. from the sound.]

**Quassia,** kwash'i-a, *n.* a South American tree, the bitter wood and bark of which are used as a tonic, so called from a negro named *Quassy* who first discovered its properties.

**Quaternary,** kwa-tėr'nar-i, *adj.* consisting of *four* : by fours : a term applied to strata more recent than the upper tertiary.—*n.* the number four. [L. *quaternarius.*]

**Quaternion,** kwa-tėr'ni-on, *n.* the number *four* : a file of four soldiers. [L. *quaternio.*]

**Quaternions,** kwa-tėr'ni-ons, *n.* a kind of calculus or method of mathematical investigation invented by Sir W. R. Hamilton of Trinity College, Dublin. [So called because *four* independent quantities are involved.]

**Quatrain,** kwot'rān or kä'trān, *n.* a stanza of *four* lines rhyming alternately. [Fr.]

**Quaver,** kwä'vėr, *v.i.* to *shake* : to sing or play with tremulous modulations.—*n.* a vibration of the voice : a note in music, ♪ = ½ a crotchet or ¼ of a semibreve. [From the sound, allied to **Quiver.**]

**Quay,** kē, *n.* a wharf for the loading or unloading of vessels. [Fr. *quai*—Celt., as in W. *cae,* an inclosure, barrier, Bret. *kae.*]

**Quayage,** kē'āj, *n.* payment for use of a quay.

**Quean,** kwēn, *n.* a saucy girl or young woman : a woman of worthless character. [Same as **Queen.**]

**Queasy,** kwē'zi, *adj.* sick, squeamish : inclined to vomit : causing nausea : fastidious.—*adv.* **Quea'sily.**—*n.* **Quea'siness.** [Norw. *kveis,* sickness after a debauch, Ice. *kveisa,* pains in the stomach.]

**Queen,** kwēn, *n.* the wife of a king : a female sovereign : the best or chief of her kind. [Lit. 'a woman,' A.S. *cwen* ; Ice. *kvan, kona,* O. Ger. *quena,* Gr. *gynē,* Russ. *jena,* Sans. *jani,* all from root *gan,* 'to produce,' from which are **Genus, Kin, King,** &c.]

**Queenly,** kwēn'li, *adj.* like a *queen* : becoming or suitable to a queen.

**Queen-mother,** kwēn-muth'ėr, *n.* a *queen*-dowager, the *mother* of the reigning king or queen.

**Queen's Bench.** Same as **King's Bench.**

**Queer,** kwēr, *adj.* odd : singular : quaint.—*adv.* **Queer'ly.**—*n.* **Queer'ness.** [Low Ger. *queer,* across, oblique ; Ger. *quer.*]

**Queerish,** kwēr'ish, *adj.,* *rather queer* : somewhat singular.

**Quell,** kwel, *v.t.* to crush : subdue : to allay.—*n.* **Quell'er.** [A.S. *cwellan,* to kill, akin to **Quail,** *v.*]

**Quench,** kwensh, *v.t.* to put out : to destroy : to check : to allay. [A.S. *cwencan,* to quench, *cwincan,* O. Ger. *kwinka,* to waste away ; akin to **Wane.**] [*quenched* or extinguished.

**Quenchable,** kwensh'a-bl, *adj.* that may be

**Quenchless,** kwensh'les, *adj.* that cannot be *quenched* or extinguished : irrepressible.

**Querimonious,** kwer-i-mōn'yus, *adj.,* *complaining* : discontented.—*adv.* **Querimon'iously.**—*n.* **Querimon'iousness.** [L. *querimonia,* a complaining—*queror,* to complain.]

**Quern,** kwėrn, **Kern,** kėrn, *n.* a handmill for *grinding* grain. [A.S. *cwyrn, cweorn* ; Ice. *kvern,* Goth. *qwairnus* ; Sans. *churn,* to grind ; prob. connected with **Churn.**]

**Querulous,** kwer'ū-lus, *adj., complaining* : discontented.—*adv.* **Quer'ulously.**—*n.* **Quer'ulousness.**

**Query,** kwē'ri, *n.* an *inquiry* or *question* : the mark of interrogation.—*v.t.* to inquire into : to question : to doubt of : to mark with a query.—*v.i.* to question :—*pa.t.* and *pa.p.* quē'ried.—*n.* **Que'rist.** [L. *quære,* imperative of *quæro,* to inquire.] [*quæsitum,* to inquire.

**Quest,** kwest, *n.* the act of *seeking* : search : pursuit : request or desire.

**Question,** kwest'yun, *n.* a *seeking* : an inquiry : an examination : an investigation : dispute : doubt : a subject of discussion.—*v.t.* to ask questions of : to examine by questions : to inquire of : to regard as doubtful : to have no confidence in.—*v.i.* to ask questions : to inquire.—*n.* **Quest'ioner.** [Fr.—L. *quæstio—quæro, quæsitum.*]

**Questionable,** kwest'yun-a-bl, *adj.* that may be *questioned* : doubtful : uncertain : suspicious.—*adv.* **Quest'ionably.**—*n.* **Quest'ionableness.**

**Questionary,** kwest'yun-ar-i, *adj., asking questions.*

**Questionist,** kwest'yun-ist, *n.* a *questioner.*

**Questor,** kwest'or, *n.* a Roman magistrate who had charge of the money affairs of the state : a treasurer.—*n.* **Quest'orship.** [L. *quæstor,* contr. of *quæsitor—quæro.*]

**Queue,** kū, *n.* a *tail*-like twist of hair formerly worn at the back of the head. [See **Cue.**]

**Quibble,** kwib'l, *n.* a turning away from the point in question into matters irrelevant or insignificant : an evasion, a pun : a petty conceit.—*v.i.* to evade a question by a play upon words : to cavil : to trifle in argument : to pun.—*n.* **Quibb'ler.** [From M. E. *quib,* a form of **Quip.**]

**Quick,** kwik, *adj., living, moving* : lively : speedy : rapid : nimble : ready.—*adv.* without delay : rapidly : soon.—*n.* a living animal or plant : the living : the living flesh : the sensitive parts.—*adv.* **Quick'ly.**—*n.* **Quick'ness.** [A.S. *cwic* ; Ice. *kvikr,* Prov. Ger. *queck,* Goth. *qwius,* living ; allied to L. *vivo, victum,* Gr. *bioō,* Sans. *jiv,* to live.]

**Quicken,** kwik'n, *v.t.* to make *quick* or *alive* : to revive : to reinvigorate : to cheer : to excite : to sharpen : to hasten.—*v.i.* to become alive : to move with activity.—*n.* **Quick′ener.** [A.S. *cwician.*]

**Quicklime**, kwik′līm, *n.* recently burnt lime, caustic or unslaked : carbonate of lime without its carbonic acid.

**Quicksand**, kwik′sand, *n.*, *sand* easily *moved*, or readily yielding to pressure : anything treacherous.

**Quickset**, kwik′set, *n.* a *living* plant *set* to grow for a hedge, particularly the hawthorn.—*adj.* consisting of living plants.

**Quicksighted**, kwik′sīt-ed, *adj.* having quick or sharp sight : quick in discernment.

**Quicksilver**, kwik′sil-vėr, *n.* the common name for fluid mercury, so called from its great *mobility* and its *silver* colour.

**Quid**, kwid, *n.* something chewed or kept in the mouth, esp. a piece of tobacco. [A corr. of **Cud**.]

**Quiddity**, kwid′i-ti, *n.* the essence of anything : any trifling nicety : a cavil : a captious question. [Low L. *quidditas*—L. *quid*, what.]

**Quidnunc**, kwid′nungk, *n.* one always on the lookout for news : one who pretends to know all occurrences. [L. ′What now?′]

**Quiescence**, kwī-es′ens, *n.* state of being *quiescent* or at rest : rest of mind : silence.

**Quiescent**, kwī-es′ent, *adj.* being *quiet*, *resting* : still : unagitated : silent.—*adv.* **Quies′cently.** [L. *quiescens, -entis*, pr.p. of *quiesco*, to rest. See **Quiet**.]

**Quiet**, kwī′et, *adj.* at *rest* : calm : smooth : peaceable : gentle, inoffensive.—*n.* the state of being at rest : repose : calm : stillness : peace.—*v.t.* to bring to rest : to stop motion : to calm or pacify : to lull : to allay. [L. *quietus—quiesco* ; akin to L. *cubo*, Gr. *keimai*, Sans. *çi*, to lie.]

**Quietism**, kwī′et-izm, *n.*, *rest* of the mind : mental tranquillity : apathy : the doctrine that religion consists in repose of the mind and passive contemplation of the Deity.—*n.* **Qui′etist**, one who believes in this doctrine.

**Quietly**, kwī′et-li, *adv.* in a *quiet* manner : without motion or alarm : calmly : silently : patiently.

**Quietness**, kwī′et-nes, **Quietude**, kwī′et-ūd, *n.* rest : repose : freedom from agitation or alarm : stillness : peace : silence.

**Quietus**, kwī-ē′tus, *n.* a final settlement or discharge. [L., at rest, quiet.]

**Quill**, kwil, *n.* the reed-pen : the feather of a goose or other bird used as a pen : a pen : anything like a quill : the spine, as of a porcupine : the reed on which weavers wind their thread : the instrument for striking the strings of certain instruments : the tube of a musical instrument. —*v.t.* to plait with small ridges like quills : to wind on a quill. [Orig. a stalk, the stalk of a cane or reed, and lit. anything pointed, tapering, Fr. *quille*, a peg—O. Ger. *kegil* or *chegil*, Ger. *kegel*, a cone-shaped object, ninepin.]

**Quillet**, kwil′et, *n.* a trick in argument : a petty quibble. [A corr. of L. *quidlibet*, ′what you will.′]

**Quilt**, kwilt, *n.* a bed-cover of two cloths sewed together with something soft between them : a thick coverlet.—*v.t.* to make into a quilt : to stitch together with something soft between : to sew like a quilt. [O. Fr. *cuilte* (Fr. *couette*)—L. *culcita*, a cushion, mattress. See **Counterpane**.]

**Quinary**, kwī′nar-i, *adj.* consisting of or arranged in *fives*. [L. *quinarius—quinque*, five.]

**Quince**, kwins, *n.* a fruit with an acid taste and pleasant flavour, much used in making preserves

and tarts. [O. Fr. *coignasse* (Fr. *coing*), It. *cotogna*—L. *cydonium*—Gr. *Cydōnia*, a town in Crete, where it abounds.]

**Quinine**, kwin′īn, *n.* an alkaline substance, obtained from the bark of the *Cinchona* tree, much used in medicine in the treatment of agues and fevers. [Fr.—Peruvian *kina*, bark.]

**Quinquagesima**, kwin-kwa-jes′i-ma, *adj.*, *fiftieth*, applied to the Sunday 50 days before Easter. [L. *quinquaginta*, fifty—*quinque*, five.]

**Quinquangular**, kwin-kwang′gū-lar, *adj.* having *five* angles. [L. *quinque*, five, and **Angular**.]

**Quinquennial**, kwin-kwen′yal, *adj.* occurring once in *five years* : lasting five years. [L. *quinquennalis—quinque*, five, and *annus*, a year.]

**Quinsy**, kwin′zi, *n.* inflammatory sore throat. [M. E. and O. Fr. *squinancie* (Fr. *esquinancie*) —Gr. *kynanchē*, ′dog-throttling′—*kyōn*, a dog, and *anchō*, to press tight, to throttle.]

**Quintain**, kwin′tān, *n.* a post with a ′turning and loaded top or cross-piece, to be tilted at. [Fr. —L. *quintana, quintus*, fifth, from the position of the place of recreation in the Roman camp.]

**Quintal**, kwin′tal, *n.* a *hundred*weight, either 112 or 100 pounds according to the scale. [Through Fr. and Sp. *quintal*, from Arab. *quintar*, weight of 100 pounds—L. *centum*, a hundred.]

**Quintessence**, kwin-tes′ens, *n.* the pure essence of anything : a solution of an essential oil in spirit of wine. [Fr.—L. *quinta essentia*, fifth essence, orig. applied to ether, which was supposed to be purer than fire, the highest of the four ancient elements. See **Essence**.]

**Quintillion**, kwin-til′yun, *n.* the *fifth* power of a *million*, or a unit with 30 ciphers annexed. [L. *quintus*, fifth, and **Million**.]

**Quintuple**, kwin′tū-pl, *adj.*, *fivefold* : (*music*) having five crotchets in a bar.—*v.t.* to make fivefold. [Fr.—L. *quintuplex—quintus*, fifth, *plico*, to fold.]

**Quip**, kwip, *n.* a sharp sarcastic turn, a jibe : a quick retort. [W. *chwip*, a quick turn, *chwipio*, to move briskly.]

**Quire**, kwīr, *n.* a collection of paper consisting of twenty-four sheets, each having a single fold. [O. Fr. *quaier* (Fr. *cahier*), prob. from Low L. *quaternum*, a *quarto* sheet, from *quatuor*, four.]

**Quire**, kwīr, old form of **Choir**.

**Quirk**, kwėrk, *n.* a quick *turn* : an artful evasion : a quibble : a taunt or retort : a slight conceit. [Obs. E. *quirk*, to turn ; prob. from a Celtic imitative root seen in W. *chwiori*, to turn briskly ; by some conn. with **Queer** and **Thwart**.]

**Quirkish**, kwėrk′ish, *adj.* consisting of quirks.

**Quit**, kwit, *v.t.* to release from obligation, accusation, &c. : to acquit : to depart from : to give up : to clear by full performance :—*pr.p.* quitt′ing ; *pa.t.* and *pa.p.* quitt′ed.—*adj.* (*B.*) set free : acquitted : released from obligation.—**To be quits**, to be even with one.—**To quit one′s self** (*B.*) to behave. [Fr. *quitter*, through Low L. *quietare*, from L. *quietus*, quiet. See **Quiet**.]

**Quite**, kwīt, *adv.* completely : wholly : entirely. [Merely a form of **Quit, Quiet**.]

**Quit-rent**, kwit′-rent, *n.* (*law*) a *rent* on manors by which the tenants are *quit* or discharged from other service.

**Quittance**, kwit′ans, *n.* a *quitting* or discharge from a debt or obligation : acquittance.

**Quiver**, kwiv′ėr, *n.* a case for arrows. [O. Fr. *cuivre* ; from O. Ger. *kohhar* (Ger. *köcher*) ; cog. with A.S. *cocer*.]

**Quiver**, kwiv′ėr, *v.i.* to *shake* with slight and tremulous motion : to tremble : to shiver. [M. E.

**cwiver**, brisk—A.S. *cwifer*, seen in adv. *cwifer-lice*, eagerly; cf. Dut. *kuiveren*. See **Quick** and **Quaver**.]

**Quivered**, kwiv´érd, *adj.* furnished with a *quiver*: sheathed, as in a quiver.

**Quixotic**, kwiks-ot´ik, *adj.* like Don *Quixote*, the knight-errant in the novel of Cervantes: romantic to absurdity.—*adv.* **Quixot´ically**.

**Quixotism**, kwiks´ot-izm, *n.* romantic and absurd notions, schemes, or actions like those of Don *Quixote*.

**Quiz**, kwiz, *n.* a riddle or enigma: one who quizzes another: an odd fellow.—*v.t.* to puzzle: to banter or make sport of: to examine narrowly and with an air of mockery.—*v.i.* to practise derisive joking:—*pr.p.* quizz´ing; *pa.t.* and *pa.p.* quizzed. [Said to have originated in a wager that a new word of no meaning would be the talk and puzzle of Dublin in twenty-four hours, when the wagerer chalked the letters *q u i z* all over the town with the desired effect.]

**Quoif**, koif, *n.* a cap or hood.—*v.t.* to cover or dress with a quoif. [Same as **Coif**.]

**Quoin**, koin, *n.* (*arch.*) a wedge used to support and steady a stone: an external angle, esp. of a building: (*gun.*) a wedge of wood or iron put under the breech of heavy guns or the muzzle of siege mortars to raise them to the proper level: (*print.*) a wedge used to fasten the types in the forms. [Same as **Coin**.]

**Quoit**, koit, *n.* a heavy flat ring of iron for throwing at a distant point in play. [Perh. from O. Fr. *coiter*, to drive, press, which may be from L. *coactare—cogere*, to force. See **Cogent**.]

**Quondam**, kwon´dam, *adj.* that was formerly: former. [L., formerly.]

**Quorum**, kwō´rum, *n.* a number of the members of any body sufficient to transact business. [The first word of a commission formerly issued to certain justices, *of whom* (quorum) a certain number had always to be present when the commission met.]

**Quota**, kwō´ta, *n.* the part or share assigned to each. [It.—L. *quotus*, of what number—*quot*, how many.]

**Quotable**, kwōt´a-bl, *adj.* that may be *quoted*.

**Quotation**, kwo-tā´shun, *n.* act of quoting: that which is quoted: the current price of anything.

**Quote**, kwōt, *v.t.* to repeat the words of any one: to adduce for authority or illustration: to give the current price of.—*n.* **Quot´er**. [Lit. to say 'how many', from O. Fr. *quoter*, to number—Low L. *quotare*, to divide into chapters and verses—L. *quotus*.]

**Quoth**, kwōth or kwuth, *v.t.*, *say*, *says*, or *said*—used only in the 1st and 3d persons present and past, and always followed by its subject. [A.S. *cwethan*, pt.t. *cwæth*, to say.]

**Quotidian**, kwo-tid´i-an, *adj.*, *every day*: occurring daily.—*n.* anything returning daily: (*med.*) a kind of ague that returns daily. [Fr.—L. *quotidianus—quot*, as many as, and *dies*, a day.]

**Quotient**, kwō´shent, *n.* (*math.*) the number which shews *how often* one number is contained in another. [Fr.; from L. *quotiens, quoties*, how often—*quot*.]

### R

**Rabbet**, rab´et, *n.* a groove cut in the edge of a plank so that another may fit into it.—*v.* to groove a plank thus. [Fr. *raboter*, to plane.]

**Rabbi**, rab´i or rab´ī, **Rabbin**, rab´in, *n.* Jewish title of a doctor or expounder of the law:—*pl.* **Rabbis** (rab´īz), **Rabb´ins**. [Lit. 'my master,' Gr.—Heb. *rabt—rab*, great, a chief.]

**Rabbinic**, rab-bin´ik, **Rabbinical**, rab-bin´ik-al, *adj.* pertaining to the *rabbis* or to their opinions, learning, and language.

**Rabbinism**, rab´in-izm, *n.* the doctrine or teaching of the *rabbis*: a rabbinic expression.

**Rabbinist**, rab´in-ist, *n.* one who adheres to the Talmud and traditions of the *rabbis*.

**Rabbit**, rab´it, *n.* a small rodent burrowing animal of the hare family: a cony. [M. E. *rabet*, dim. of a root seen in Dut. *robbe*.]

**Rabble**, rab´l, *n.* a disorderly, noisy crowd: a mob: the lowest class of people. [Allied to Dut. *rabbelen*, to gabble, Prov. Ger. *rabbeln*.]

**Rabid**, rab´id, *adj.*, *raving*: furious: mad.—*adv.* **Rab´idly**.—*n.* **Rab´idness**. [L. *rabies*, rage.]

**Rabies**, rā´bi-ēs, *n.* the disease (esp. of dogs) from which hydrophobia is communicated. [L. 'madness.']

**Raca**, rā´ka, *adj.*, *worthless*:—a term of reproach used by the Jews. [Chaldee *reka*, worthless.]

**Raccoon**, **Racoon**, ra-kōōn´, *n.* a carnivorous animal of N. America, valuable for its fur. [A corr. of Fr. *raton*, dim. of *rat*, a rat.]

**Race**, rās, *n.* family: the descendants of a common ancestor: a breed or variety: a herd: peculiar flavour or strength, as of wine, showing its *kind*. [Fr. (It. *razza*)—O. Ger. *reiza*, a line; prob. modified by the influence of L. *radix*, a root.]

**Race**, rās, *n.* a *running*: rapid motion: trial of speed: progress: movement of any kind: course of action: a rapid current: a canal to a water-wheel.—*v.i.* to run swiftly: to contend in running. [A.S. *ræs*, race, stream, cog. with Ice. *rás*, rapid course, Sans. *rish*, to flow.]

**Racecourse**, rās´kōrs, *n.* the *course* or path over which *races* are run.

**Racehorse**, rās´hors, *n.* a *horse* bred for *racing*.

**Raceme**, ra-sēm´, *n.* a *cluster*: (*bot.*) a flower cluster, as in the currant. [Fr.—L. *racemus*, akin to Gr. *rax, ragos*, a berry, a grape. Doublet **Raisin**.]

**Racemed**, ra-sēmd´, *adj.* having *racemes*.

**Racer**, rās´ér, *n.* one who races: a racehorse.

**Rack**, rak, *n.* an instrument for racking or extending: an engine for stretching the body in order to extort a confession: a framework on which articles are arranged: the grating above a manger for hay: (*mech.*) a straight bar with teeth to work with those of a wheel: (*fig.*) extreme pain, anxiety, or doubt.—*v.t.* to stretch forcibly: to strain: to stretch on the rack or wheel: to torture: to exhaust. [Conn. with M. E. *rechen*—A.S. *racan*, to reach, and cog. with Ger. *recken*, Goth. *rakjan*. See **Reach**.]

**Rack**, rak, *n.* thin or broken clouds, *drifting* across the sky. [Ice. *rek*, drift—*reka*, to drive, E. **Wreak**.]

**Rack**, rak, *v.t.* to strain or draw off from the lees, as wine. [O. Fr. *raqué*, ety. unknown.]

**Racket**, rak´et, *n.* a strip of wood with the ends together, covered with network, and having a handle—used in tennis: a snow-shoe.—*v.t.* to strike, as with a racket. [Fr. *raquette*—Sp. *raqueta*—Ar. *rahat*, the palm of the hand.]

**Racket**, rak´et, *n.* a clattering noise. [Gael. *racaid—rac*, to cackle.]

**Rack-rent**, rak´-rent, *n.* an annual rent stretched to the full value of the thing rented or nearly so.

**Racoon**. See **Raccoon**.

**Racy**, rā´si, *adj.* having a strong flavour showing

its *origin*: rich : exciting to the mind by strongly characteristic thought or language : spirited.— *adv.* Ra´cily.—*n.* Ra´ciness. [From Race, a family.]

Raddle, rad´l, *v.t.* to interweave.—*n.* a hedge formed by interweaving the branches of trees. [A.S. *wræd*, a wreath or band.]

Radial, rā´di-al, *adj.* shooting out like a *ray* or *radius*: pertaining to the radius of the fore-arm.

Radiance, rā´di-ans, Radiancy, rā´di-an-si, *n.* quality of being *radiant*: brilliancy : splendour.

Radiant, rā´di-ant, *adj.* emitting *rays* of light or heat : issuing in rays : beaming with light : shining.—*n.* (*optics*) the luminous point from which light emanates : (*geom.*) a straight line from a point about which it is conceived to revolve.—*adv.* Ra´diantly. [L. *radians*, -*antis*, pr.p. of *radio*, *radiatum*, to radiate—*radius*.]

Radiate, rā´di-āt, *v.i.* to emit *rays* of light : to shine : to proceed in direct lines from any point or surface.—*v.t.* to send out in rays. [L. *radio*, -*atum*.]

Radiation, rā-di-ā´shun, *n.* act of radiating : the emission and diffusion of rays of light or heat.

Radical, rad´i-kal, *adj.* pertaining to the *root*, or origin : original : reaching to the principles : implanted by nature : not derived : serving to originate : (*bot.*) proceeding immediately from the root : (*politics*) ultra-liberal, democratic.— *n.* a root : a primitive word or letter : one who advocates radical reform, a democrat : (*chem.*) the base of a compound.—*adv.* Rad´ically.— *n.* Rad´icalness. [See Radix.]

Radicalism, rad´i-kal-izm, *n.* the principles or spirit of a *radical* or democrat.

Radicle, rad´i-kl, *n.* a *little root*: the part of a seed which in growing becomes the root.

Radish, rad´ish, *n.* an annual the root of which is eaten raw as a salad. [Lit. a 'root,' Fr. *radis*, through Prov. *raditz*, from L. *radix*, *radicis*. Cf. Radix.]

Radius, rā´di-us, *n.* (*geom.*) a straight line from the centre to the circumference of a circle : any-thing like a radius, as the spoke of a wheel : (*anat.*) the exterior bone of the arm : (*bot.*) the ray of a flower :—*pl.* Radii, rā´di-ī. [Lit. 'a rod, or ray,' L. See Ray, a line of light.]

Radix, rā´diks, *n.* a *root*: a primitive word : the base of a system of logarithms. [L. *radix*, *radic-is*. See Root, and Wort, a plant.]

Raffle, raf´l, *n.* a kind of lottery in which all the stakes are *seized* or taken by the winner.—*v.i.* to try a raffle.—*n.* Raff´ler. [Fr. *rafle*, a certain game of dice—Fr. *rafler*, to sweep away, from Ger. *raffeln*, freq. of *raffen* (A.S. *reafian*), to seize.]

Raft, raft, *n.* a collection of pieces of timber fastened together for a support on the water : planks conveyed by water.—*n.* Rafts´man, one who guides a raft. [Ice. *raptr* (pron. *raftr*), a rafter.]

Rafter, raft´ėr, *n.* an inclined beam supporting the roof of a house.—*v.t.* to furnish with rafters. [A.S. *ræfter*, a beam ; Ice. *raptr* (*raftr*), a beam ; Dan. *raft*, a pole.]

Rag, rag, *n.* a fragment of cloth : anything rent or worn out. [A.S. *raggie*, rough, cog. with Sw. *ragg*, rough hair, and Rug.]

Ragamuffin, rag-a-muf´in, *n.* a low disreputable person. [Ety. dub.]

Rage, rāj, *n.*, *violent excitement*: enthusiasm : rapture : anger excited to fury.—*v.i.* to be furious with anger : to exercise fury, to ravage : to pre-

vail fatally, as a disease : to be violently agitated, as the waves. [Fr. (Sp. *rabia*)—L. *rabies*—*rabo*, to rave ; akin to Sans. *rabh*, to be agitated, enraged.]

Ragged, rag´ed, *adj.* torn or worn into rags : having a rough edge : wearing ragged clothes : intended for the very poor : (*B.*) rugged.—*adv.* Ragg´edly.—*n.* Ragg´edness.

Raggee, rag-gē´, *n.* a species of millet, grown in Southern India.

Raging, rāj´ing, *adj.* acting with *rage*, violence, or fury.—*adv.* Ragingly.

Ragoût, ra-gōō´, *n.* a stew of meat with kitchen herbs, the French equivalent of Irish stew. [Fr.—*ragoûter*, to restore the appetite—L. *re*, again, Fr. *à* (= *ad*), to, and *goût*—L. *gustus*, taste.]

Ragstone, rag´stōn, Ragg, rag, *n.* an impure lime-*stone*, so called from its *ragged* fracture.

Ragwort, rag´wurt, *n.* a large coarse weed with a yellow flower, so called from its *ragged* leaves. [Rag, and A.S. *wyrt*, a plant.]

Raid, rād, *n.* a hostile or predatory invasion. [Lit. 'a *riding* into an enemy's country,' Scand., as Ice. *reidh*. See Ride. Doublet Road.]

Rail, rāl, *n.* a bar of timber or metal extending from one support to another, as in fences, stair-cases, &c. : a barrier : one of the iron bars on which railway carriages run : (*arch.*) the hori-zontal part of a frame and panel.—*v.t.* to in-close with rails. [Low Ger. *regel*, Ger. *riegel*, from the root of Ger. *reihe*, a row.]

Rail, rāl, *v.i.* to brawl : to use insolent language. [Fr. *railler*, like Span. *rallar*, to scrape, from L. *rallum*, a hoe for scraping a ploughshare—*rado*, to scrape. See Rase.]

Rail, rāl, *n.* a genus of wading birds with a harsh cry. [Fr. *râle* (Ger. *ralle*)—*râler*, to make a rattle in the throat, from the root of Rattle.]

Railing, rāl´ing, *n.* a fence of posts and *rails*: material for rails.

Raillery, rāl´ėr-i, *n.* railing or mockery : banter : good-humoured irony. [Fr. *raillerie*—*railler*. See Rail, to brawl.]

Railroad, rāl´rōd, Railway, rāl´wā, *n.* a *road* or way laid with iron *rails* on which carriages run.

Raiment, rā´ment, *n.* that in which one is *arrayed* or dressed : clothing in general. [Contr. of obs. *Arraiment*—Array.]

Rain, rān, *n.* water from the clouds : to fall from the clouds : to drop like rain.—*v.t.* to pour like rain. [A.S. *regn*, *rén*, rain ; cog. with Dut. and Ger. *regen*, and Scand. *regn*.]

Rainbow, rān´bō, *n.* the brilliant-coloured *bow* or arch seen when *rain* is falling opposite the sun.

Rain-gauge, rān´-gāj, *n.* a *gauge* or instrument for measuring the quantity of *rain* that falls.

Rainy, rān´i, *adj.* abounding with *rain*: showery.

Raise, rāz, *v.t.* to cause to *rise*: to lift up : to set upright : to originate or produce : to bring to-gether : to cause to grow or breed : to produce : to give rise to : to exalt : to increase the strength of : to excite : to recall from death : to cause to swell, as dough. [M. E. *reisen*, from Ice. *reisa*, causal of *risa*, to rise. See Rise and Rear.]

Raisin, rā´zn, *n.* a dried ripe grape. [Fr. (Prov. *razim*, Sp. *racimo*)—L. *racemus*, a bunch of grapes. Doublet Raceme.]

Rajah, rā´ja or rä´ja, *n.* a native prince or king in Hindustan. [From Sans. *rajan*, a king, cog. with L. *rex*.]

Rake, rāk, *n.* an instrument with teeth or pins for smoothing earth, &c.—*v.t.* to scrape with some-thing toothed : to draw together : to gather with

difficulty : to level with a rake : to search diligently over : to pass over violently : (*naut.*) to
fire into, as a ship, lengthwise.—*v.i.* to scrape,
as with a rake : to search minutely : to pass with
violence. [A.S. *raca*, a rake ; cog. with Ger.
*rechen*, Ice. *reka*, a shovel, from the root of
Goth. *rikan* (*rak*), to collect, L. and Gr.
*lego*.]

**Rake**, rāk, *n.* a rascal.   [Contr. of **Rakehell**.]

**Rake**, rāk, *n.* (*naut.*) the projection of the stem
and stern of a ship beyond the extremities of the
keel : the inclination of a mast from the perpendicular. [From the Scand. *raka*, to reach (A.S.
*racan*).   Doublet **Reach**.]

**Rakehell**, rāk′hel, *n.* a rascal or villain : a debauchee. [Corr. of M. E. *rakel, rakle ;* cog. with
Prov. Sw. *rakkel*, a vagabond, Ice. *reikall*, unsettled, from *reika*, to wander, and Prov. E.
*rake*, to wander.]

**Rakish**, rāk′ish, *adj.* having a *rake* or inclination
of the masts.—*adv.* **Rak′ishly**.

**Rakish**, rāk′ish, *adj.* like a *rake :* dissolute :
debauched.—*adv.* **Rak′ishly**.

**Rally**, ral′i, *v.t.* to gather again : to collect and
arrange, as troops in confusion : to recover.—
*v.i.* to reassemble, esp. after confusion : to recover wasted strength :—*pa.t.* and *pa.p.* rallied
(ral′id).—*n.* act of rallying : recovery of order.
[Lit. ' to *re-ally*,' Fr. *rallier*—L. *re*, again, *ad*,
to, and *ligo*, to bind.   See **Ally**, *v.*]

**Rally**, ral′i, *v.t.* to attack with *raillery :* to banter.—*v.i.* to exercise raillery :—*pa.t.* and *pa.p.*
rall′ied.   [Fr. *railler*.   A variant of **Rail**, *v.i.*]

**Ram**, ram, *n.* a male sheep : (*astr.*) Aries (L., the
ram), one of the signs of the zodiac : an engine
of war for battering, with a head like that of a
ram : a hydraulic engine, called water-ram : a
ship of war armed with a heavy iron beak for
running down a hostile vessel.—*v.t.* to thrust
with violence, as a ram with its head : to force
together : to drive hard down :—*pr.p.* ramm′ing ;
*pa.t.* and *pa.p.* rammed. [A.S. *ram, rom ;*
cog. with Ger. *ramm*, Sans. *ram*, to sport.]

**Ramble**, ram′bl, *v.i.* to go from place to place
without object : to visit many places : to be
desultory, as in discourse.—*n.* a roving from
place to place : an irregular excursion.—*n.*
**Ram′bler**.   [Freq. of **Roam**.]

**Rambling**, ram′bling, *adj.* moving about irregularly : unsettled : desultory.

**Ramification**, ram-i-fi-kā′shun, *n.* division or
separation into *branches :* a branch : a division
or subdivision : (*bot.*) manner of producing
branches.

**Ramify**, ram′i-fī, *v.t.* to *make* or divide into
*branches*.—*v.i.* to shoot into branches : to be
divided or spread out :—*pa.t.* and *pa.p.* ram′i-
fied.   [Fr. *ramifier*—L. *ramus*, a branch,
*facio*, to make.]

**Ramose**, ra-mōs′, **Ramous**, rā′mus, *adj.*, *branchy :*
(*bot.*) branched as a stem or root.

**Ramp**, ramp, *v.i.* to *climb* or *creep*, as a plant : to
leap or bound.—*n.* a leap or bound. [Fr. *ramper*,
to creep, to clamber ; from the Teut., Low Ger.
*rappen*, Ger. *raffen*, to snatch, as with the claws.]

**Rampant**, ramp′ant, *adj.*, *ramping* or overgrowing
usual bounds : overleaping restraint : (*her.*)
standing on the hind-legs.—*adv.* **Ramp′antly**.
—*n.* **Ramp′ancy**, state of being rampant. [Fr.,
pr.p. of *ramper*, to creep, to climb.]

**Rampart**, ram′part, *n.* that which *defends* from
assault or danger : (*fort.*) a mound or wall
surrounding a fortified place. [Fr. *rempart*
(orig. *rempar*)—*remparer*, to defend—*re*, again,

*em*, to (= *en*), in, and *parer*, to defend—L. *paro*,
to prepare.   See **Parapet, Parry**.]

**Ramrod**, ram′rod, *n.* a *rod* used in *ramming*
down the charge in a gun.

**Ran**, *pa.t.* of **Run**.

**Rancid**, ran′sid, *adj.* having a *putrid* smell, as
old oil : sour.—*adv.* **Ran′cidly**.   [L. *rancidus*,
putrid.]

**Rancidness**, ran′sid-nes, **Rancidity**, ran-sid′i-ti,
*n.* the quality of being *rancid :* a musty smell,
as of oil.

**Rancorous**, rang′kur-us, *adj.* spiteful : malicious :
virulent.—*adv.* **Ran′corously**.

**Rancour**, rang′kur, *n.* deep-seated enmity : spite :
virulence. [Fr.—L. *rancor*, rancidness, an old
grudge—*ranceo*, to be rancid.]

**Random**, ran′dum, *adj.* done or uttered at hazard :
left to chance.—*adv.* **At random**, without direction : by chance. [O. Fr. *randon*, urgency,
haste ; of doubtful origin.]

**Rang**, rang, *pa.t.* of **Ring**.

**Range**, rānj, *v.t.* to *rank* or set in a *row :* to
place in proper order : to rove or pass over : to
sail in a direction parallel to.—*v.i.* to be placed
in order : to lie in a particular direction : to rove
at large : to sail or pass near.—*n.* a row or rank :
a class or order : a wandering : room for passing
to and fro : space occupied by anything moving :
capacity of mind : extent of acquirements : the
horizontal distance to which a shot is carried :
the long cooking-stove of a kitchen : (*B.*) a
chimney-rack. [Fr. *ranger*, to range—*rang*, a
rank.   Cf. **Rank**.]

**Ranger**, rānj′ér, *n.* a rover : a dog that beats the
ground : an officer who superintends a forest or
park.—*n.* **Rang′ership**.

**Ranine**, rā′nin, *adj.* pertaining to or like a *frog*.
[L. *rana*, a frog.]

**Rank**, rangk, *n.* a row or line, esp. of soldiers
standing side by side : class or order : grade or
degree : station : high social position.—*v.t.* to
place in a line : to range in a particular class :
to place methodically.—*v.i.* to be placed in a
rank : to have a certain degree of elevation or
distinction.—**The ranks**, the order of common
soldiers.—**Rank and file**, the whole body of
common soldiers. [Fr. *rang* (E. **Ring**)—O.
Ger. *hring* or *hrinc*.   Cf. **Harangue**.]

**Rank**, rangk, *adj.* growing high and luxuriantly :
coarse from excessive growth : raised to a high
degree : excessive : causing strong growth : very
fertile : strong scented : strong tasted : rancid :
strong.—*adv.* **Rank′ly**.—*n.* **Rank′ness**. [A.S.
*ranc*, fruitful, rank ; Dan. *rank*, lank, slender ;
a nasalised form of the root of **Rack**.]

**Rankle**, rangk′l, *v.i.* to be inflamed : to fester :
to be a source of disquietude or excitement : to
rage. [From **Rank**, *adj.*]

**Ransack**, ran′sak, *v.t.* to search thoroughly : to
plunder. [Lit. ' to search a house,' Ice. *rann-
saka—rann*, a house, and *sak* (*sækja*), to **Seek**.]

**Ransom**, ran′sum, *n.* price paid for redemption
from captivity or punishment : release from
captivity.—*v.t.* to redeem from captivity, punishment, or ownership.—*n.* **Ran′somer**. [Lit.
' redemption ' or ' buying back,' Fr. *rançon* (It.
*redenzione*)—L. *redemptio*.   See **Redemption**.]

**Ransomless**, ran′sum-les, *adj.* without ransom :
incapable of being ransomed.

**Rant**, rant, *v.i.* to use violent or extravagant
language : to be noisy in words.—*n.* boisterous,
empty declamation. [O. Dut. *ranten*, to rave :
cog. with Low Ger. *randen*, Ger. *ranzen*, and
prob. with O. Ger. *razi, raze*, violent.]

**Ranter**, rant′ėr, *n.* a noisy talker : a boisterous preacher.

**Ranunculus**, ra-nun′kū-lus, *n.* a genus of plants, including the crowfoot, buttercup, &c., so called by Pliny because some grow where *frogs* abound :—*pl.* **Ranun′culuses.** [L., dim. of *ranula*, a little frog, itself a dim. of *rana*, a frog.]

**Rap**, rap, *n.* a sharp blow : a knock.—*v.t.* and *v.i.* to strike with a quick blow : to knock :—*pr.p.* rapp′ing ; *pa.t.* and *pa.p.* rapped. [Scand., as Dan. *rap*; imitative of the sound.]

**Rap**, rap, *v.t.* to *seize* and carry off : to transport out of one's self : to affect with rapture :—*pr.p.* rapp′ing ; *pa.p.* rapped or rapt. [Scand., as Ice. *hrapa*, to rush headlong, cog. with Ger. *raffen*, to snatch.]

**Rapacious**, ra-pā′shus, *adj., seizing* by violence : given to plunder : ravenous : greedy of gain.—*adv.* **Rapa′ciously.**—*n.* **Rapa′ciousness.** [L. *rapax, rapacis—rapio, raptum*, to seize and carry off ; akin to Gr. *harp-azō*, to seize.]

**Rapacity**, ra-pas′i-ti, *n.* the quality of being *rapacious* : ravenousness : extortion.

**Rape**, rāp, *n.* the act of *seizing* by force : violation of the chastity of a female. [M. E. *rape*, haste, from **Rap**, to seize, influenced by L. *rapere*, to snatch.]

**Rape**, rāp, *n.* a plant nearly allied to the *turnip*, cultivated for its herbage and oil-producing seeds. [O. Fr. *rabe* (Fr. *rave*)—L. *rapa, rapum*; cog. with Gr. *rapys*, the turnip.]

**Rapecake**, rāp′kāk, *n., cake* made of the refuse, after the oil has been expressed from the rape-seed.

**Rape-oil**, rāp′-oil, *n., oil* obtained from rape-seed.

**Raphaelism**, raf′a-el-izm, *n.* the principles of painting introduced by *Raphael*, the Italian painter, 1483–1520.—*n.* **Raphaelite**, raf′a-el-īt, one who follows the principles of Raphael.

**Rapid**, rap′id, *adj.* hurrying along : very swift : speedy.—*n.* that part of a river where the current is more rapid than usual (gen. in *pl.*).—*adv.* **Rap′idly.**—*n.* **Rap′idness.** [Fr. *rapide*—L. *rapidus—rapio*. See **Rapacious**.]

**Rapidity**, ra-pid′i-ti, *n.* quickness of motion or utterance : swiftness : velocity.

**Rapier**, rā′pi-ėr, *n.* a light sword with a straight, narrow blade (generally four-sided), used only in thrusting. [Fr. *rapière*, of unknown origin.]

**Rapine**, rap′in, *n.* act of *seizing* and carrying away forcibly : plunder : violence. [Fr.—L. *rapina—rapio*. Doublet **Ravine**.]

**Rapparee**, rap-ar-ē′, *n.* a wild Irish plunderer. [Ir. *rapaire*, a noisy fellow, a thief.]

**Rappee**, rap-pē′, *n.* a moist, coarse kind of snuff. [Fr. *râpé*, rasped, grated—*râper*, to rasp. See **Rasp**.]

**Rapper**, rap′ėr, *n.* one who raps : a door-knocker.

**Rapt**, rapt, *adj.* raised to rapture : transported : ravished. [Lit. 'carried away,' from **Rap**, to seize, influenced by L. *rapere*, to snatch.]

**Raptorial**, rap-tō′ri-al, *adj., seizing* by violence, as a bird of prey. [L. *raptor*, a snatcher—*rapere*.]

**Rapture**, rap′tūr, *n. seizing* and carrying away : extreme delight : transport : ecstasy. [L. *rapio, raptus*, to seize.]

**Rapturous**, rap′tūr-us, *adj., seizing* and carrying away : ecstatic : transporting.—*adv.* **Rap′turously.**

**Rare**, rār, *adj.* (*comp.* **Rar′er**, *superl.* **Rar′est**), *thin* : of a loose texture : not dense : uncommon :

excellent : extraordinary.—*adv.* **Rare′ly.**—*n.* **Rare′ness.** [Fr.—L. *rārus*, rare, thin.]

**Rarefaction**, rar-e-fak′shun or rā-re-fak′shun, *n.* act of *rarefying* : expansion of aëriform bodies. [Fr.—L. See **Rarefy**.]

**Rarefy**, rar′e-fī or rā′re-fī, *v.t.* to make rare, thin, or less dense : to expand a body.—*v.i.* to become thin and porous :—*pa.t.* and *pa.p.* rar′efied. [Fr. *raréfier*—L. *rarus*, rare, *facio, factum*, to make.]

**Rarity**, rār′i-ti or rar′i-ti, *n.* state of being rare : thinness : subtilty : something valued for its scarcity : uncommonness.

**Rascal**, ras′kal, *n.* a tricking, dishonest fellow : a knave : a rogue. [Lit. 'the scrapings and refuse of anything,' Fr. *racaille*, the scum of the people—*racler*, O. Fr. *rascler*, to scrape, through a supposed L. form *rasiculare*, from *rasus*, scraped. See **Rase**.]

**Rascality**, ras-kal′i-ti, *n.* mean trickery or dishonesty : fraud : the mob. [base.

**Rascally**, ras′kal-i, *adj.* mean : vile : worthless :

**Rase**, rāz, *v.t.* to *scratch* or blot out : to efface : to cancel : to level with the ground : to demolish : to ruin (in this sense **Raze** is generally used). [Fr. *raser*—L. *rado, rasum*, to scrape.]

**Rash**, rash, *adj.* (*comp.* **Rash′er**, *superl.* **Rash′est**), *hasty* : sudden : headstrong : incautious.—*adv.* **Rash′ly.**—*n.* **Rash′ness.** [Dan. and Sw. *rask*; Ger. *rasch*, rapid.]

**Rash**, rash, *n.* a slight eruption on the body. [O. Fr. *rasche* (Fr. *rache*)—L. *rado, rasum*, to scrape, to scratch. Cf. **Rase**.]

**Rasher**, rash′ėr, *n.* a thin slice of broiled bacon, prob. so called because *rashly* or quickly roasted.

**Rasorial**, ra-zō′ri-al, *adj.* belonging to an order of birds which *scrape* the ground for their food, as the hen. [Low L. *rasor, rasoris*, a scraper—L. *rado, rasum*, to scrape. See **Rase**.]

**Rasp**, rasp, *v.t.* to rub with a coarse file.—*n.* a file.—*n.* **Rasp′er**. [O. Fr. *rasper* (Fr. *râper*)—O. Ger. *raspón*; akin to Dut. *raspen*, to scrape together.]

**Raspberry**, raz′ber-i, *n.* a kind of bramble, whose fruit has a rough outside like a *rasp*.

**Rasure**, rā′zhūr, *n.* act of *scraping*, shaving, or erasing : obliteration : an erasure. [Fr.—L. See **Rase**.]

**Rat**, rat, *n.* an animal of the mouse kind, but larger and more destructive. [A.S. *ræt*, cog. with Ger. *ratte*, Gael. *radan*, prob. allied to L. *rodo*, to gnaw.]

**Rat**, rat, *v.i.* to desert one's party and join their opponents for gain or power, as *rats* are said to leave a falling house :—*pr.p.* ratt′ing ; *pa.t.* and *pa.p.* ratt′ed.

**Ratable**, rāt′a-bl, *adj.* that may be rated or set at a certain value : subject to taxation.—*ns.* **Ratabil′ity**, **Rat′ableness**, quality of being ratable.—*adv.* **Rat′ably.**

**Ratafia**, rat-a-fē′a, *n.* a spirituous liquor flavoured with fruit. [Fr.—Malay *araq-tâfia*, from Ar. *araq* (see **Arrack**), and Malay *tâfia*, rum.]

**Ratch**, rach, *n.* a *rack* or bar with teeth into which a click drops : the wheel which makes a clock strike. [A weakened form of **Rack**.]

**Ratchet**, rach′et, *n.* a bar acting on the teeth of a ratchet-wheel : a click or pall.

**Ratchet-wheel**, rach′et-hwēl, *n.* a *wheel* having teeth for a *ratchet*.

**Rate**, rāt, *n.* a *ratio* or proportion : allowance : standard : value : price : the class of a ship : movement, as fast or slow : a tax.—*v.t.* to calculate : to estimate : to settle the relative rank, scale, or position of.—*v.i.* to make an estimate : to be placed in a certain class. [O. Fr.—L. *reor, ratus,* to calculate, to think.]

**Rate,** rāt, *v.t.* to *tax* one with a thing : to scold : to chide. [*pays a rate or tax.*]

**Ratepayer,** rāt′pā-ėr, *n.* one who is assessed and pays.

**Rath, Rathe,** rāth, *adj.* early, soon. [A.S. *hrædh,* cog. with O. Ger. *hrad,* quick.]

**Rather,** rä*th*′ėr, *adv.* more willingly : in preference : especially : more so than otherwise : on the contrary : somewhat. [Lit. 'sooner,' A.S. *rathor,* comp. of **Rath,** early.]

**Ratification,** rat-i-fi-kā′shun, *n.* act of ratifying or confirming : confirmation.

**Ratify,** rat′i-fī, *v.t.* to approve and sanction : to settle :—*pa.t.* and *pa.p.* rat′ified. [Fr. *ratifier* —L. *ratus,* fixed by calculation—*reor, ratus,* to calculate, and *facio,* to make. See **Rate,** *n.*]

**Ratio,** rā′shi-o, *n.* the relation of one thing to another. [L. *ratio,* calculation, reason, the faculty which calculates—*reor, ratus.* Doublets **Ration, Reason.**]

**Ratiocination,** rash-i-os-i-nā′shun, *n.* the act or process of *reasoning :* deducing conclusions from premises.—*adj.* **Ratio′cinative.** [Fr.—L. *ratiocinatio*—*ratiocinor, -atus,* to calculate, to reason.]

**Ration,** rā′shun, *n.* the *rate* of provisions distributed to a soldier or sailor daily : an allowance. [Fr.—L. *ratio.* See **Ratio.**]

**Rational,** rash′un-al, *adj.* pertaining to the *reason :* endowed with reason : agreeable to reason : sane : intelligent : judicious : (*arith.* and *alg.*) noting a quantity which can be exactly expressed by numbers : (*geog.*) noting the plane parallel to the sensible horizon of a place, and passing through the earth's centre. [See **Ratio.**]

**Rationale,** rash-i-o-nā′le, *n.* an account of, with *reasons :* an account of the principles of some opinion.

**Rationalise,** rash′un-al-īz, *v.t.* to interpret like a rationalist.—*v.i.* to rely entirely or unduly on reason.

**Rationalism,** rash′un-al-izm, *n.* the religious system or doctrines of a rationalist.

**Rationalist,** rash′un-al-ist, *n.* one guided in his opinions solely by *reason :* esp. one so guided in regard to religion.

**Rationalistic,** rash-un-al-ist′ik, **Rationalistical,** rash-un-al-ist′ik-al, *adj.* pertaining to or in accordance with the principles of rationalism.

**Rationality,** rash-un-al′i-ti, *n.* quality of being rational : possession or due exercise of reason : reasonableness.

**Ratline, Ratlin,** rat′lin, **Rattling,** rat′ling, *n.* one of the small *lines* or ropes traversing the shrouds and forming the steps of the rigging of ships. [Prob. 'rat-line,' *i.e.* for the rats to climb by.]

**Rattan,** rat-an′, *n.* a genus of palms having a smooth, reed-like stem reaching hundreds of feet in length : a walking-stick made of rattan : stems of this palm used as a raft. [Malay *rōtan.*]

**Ratten,** rat′n, *v.t.* to take away a workman's tools for not paying his contribution to the trades-union, or for having in any way offended the union. [Prov. E. and Scot. *ratten,* a rat—Fr. *raton*—Low L. *rato.* Cf. **Rat,** *v.i.*]

**Rattle,** rat′l, *v.i.* to produce rapidly the sound *rat :* to clatter : to speak eagerly and noisily.— *v.t.* to cause to make a rattle or clatter : to stun with noise.—*n.* a sharp noise rapidly repeated : a clatter : loud empty talk : a toy or instrument for rattling. [A.S. *hratele,* cog. with Ger. *rasseln,* Dut. *ratelen ;* Gr. *krotalon.*]

**Rattlesnake,** rat′l-snāk, *n.* a poisonous *snake*

having a number of hard, bony rings loosely jointed at the end of the tail, which make a *rattling* noise.

**Ravage,** rav′āj, *v.t.* to lay waste : to destroy : to pillage.—*n.* devastation : ruin : plunder. [Fr.— *ravir*—L. *rapio,* to carry off by force.]

**Ravager,** rav′āj-ėr, *n.* he or that which lays waste : a plunderer.

**Rave,** rāv, *v.i.* to be *rabid* or mad : to be wild or raging, like a madman : to talk irrationally : to utter wild exclamations. [O. Fr. *raver* (Fr. *rêver*), to dream, to be delirious—L. *rabies,* madness. A doublet of **Rage.**]

**Ravel,** rav′el, *v.t.* to untwist or unweave : to confuse, entangle.—*v.i.* to be untwisted or unwoven :—*pr.p.* rav′elling ; *pa.t.* and *pa.p.* rav′elled. [Dut. *ravelen,* to ravel, to talk confusedly.]

**Ravelin,** rav′lin, *n.* a detached work with two embankments raised before the counterscarp. {Fr. ; It. *rivellino,* perh. from L. *re,* back, and *vallum,* a rampart.]

**Raven,** rāv′n, *n.* a kind of crow, noted for its croak and plundering habits.—*adj.* black, like a raven. [A.S. *hræfn ;* cog. with Ice. *hrafn,* Dut. *raaf :* so called from its cry.]

**Raven,** rav′n, *v.t.* to obtain by violence : to devour with great eagerness or voracity.—*v.i.* to prey with rapacity.—*n.* prey : plunder. [M.E. *ravine,* plunder—O. Fr. *ravine,* rapidity, impetuosity—L. *rapina.* See **Rapine.**]

**Ravening,** rav′n-ing, *n.* (*B.*) eagerness for plunder.

**Ravenous,** rav′n-us, *adj.* voracious, like a *raven :* devouring with rapacity : eager for prey or gratification.—*adv.* **Rav′enously.**—*n.* **Rav′enousness.**

**Ravin** (*B.*) same as **Raven,** to obtain by violence.

**Ravine,** ra-vēn′, *n.* a long, deep hollow, worn away by a torrent : a deep, narrow mountain-pass. [Fr.—L. *rapina.* See **Rapine.**]

**Ravish,** rav′ish, *v.t.* to *seize* or *carry away* by violence : to have sexual intercourse with by force : to fill with ecstasy.—*n.* **Rav′isher.** [Fr. *ravir.*]

**Ravishment,** rav′ish-ment, *n.* act of *ravishing :* abduction : rape : ecstatic delight : rapture.

**Raw,** raw, *adj.* not altered from its natural state : not cooked or dressed : not prepared : not mixed : not covered : sore : unfinished : bleak.—*adv.* **Raw′ly.**—*n.* **Raw′ness.** [A.S. *hreáw,* cog. with Dut. *raauw,* Ice. *hrar,* Ger. *roh,* akin to L. *crudus,* raw.] [*bones.*

**Rawboned,** raw′bōnd, *adj.* with little flesh on the

**Ray,** rā, *n.* a line of light or heat proceeding from a point : intellectual light : apprehension. [Fr. *raie*—L. *radius,* a rod, staff, a beam of light.]

**Ray,** rā, *n.* a class of fishes including the skate, thornback, and torpedo. [Fr. *raie*—L. *raia.*]

**Rayah,** rā′yah, *n.* a non-Mohammedan subject of Turkey who pays the capitation tax. [Ar. *raiyah,* a herd, a peasant—*raya,* to pasture, to feed.]

**Raze,** rāz, *v.t.* to lay level with the ground : to overthrow : to destroy. [A form of **Rase.**]

**Razor,** rā′zor, *n.* a knife for *shaving.*

**Razor-strop,** rā′zor-strop, *n.* a strop for razors.

**Reach,** rēch, *v.t.* to *stretch* or *extend :* to attain or obtain by stretching out the hand : to hand over : to extend to : to arrive at : to gain : to include.—*v.i.* to be extended so as to touch : to stretch out the hand : to try to obtain.—*n.* act or power of reaching : extent : extent of force : penetration : artifice : contrivance : a straight portion of a stream. [A.S. *ræcan ;* Ger. *reichen,* to reach.]

**React**, rē-akt′, *v.i.* to act again : to return an impulse : to act mutually upon each other. [L. *re*, again, and **Act**.]

**Reaction**, rē-ak′shun, *n.*, *action back* upon or *resisting* other action : mutual action : backward tendency from revolution, reform, or progress.

**Reactionary**, rē-ak′shun-ar-i, *adj.* for or implying reaction.

**Read**, rēd, *v.t.* to utter aloud written or printed words : to peruse : to comprehend : to study.—*v.i.* to perform the act of reading : to practise much reading : to appear in reading :—*pa.t.* and *pa.p.* read (red). [A.S. *rædan*, to discern, interpret, read ; Ger. *rathen*, to advise.]

**Read**, red, *adj.* versed in books : learned.

**Readable**, rēd′a-bl, *adj.* that may be read : worth reading : interesting.—*adv.* **Read′ably**.—*n.* **Read′ableness**.

**Readdress**, rē-ad-dres′, *v.t.* to address again or a second time. [L. *re*, again, and **Address**.]

**Reader**, rēd′ėr, *n.* one who reads : one who reads prayers in a church, or lectures on scientific subjects : one who reads or corrects proofs : one who reads much : a reading-book.—*n.* **Read′ership**, the office of a reader.

**Readily**, **Readiness**. See under **Ready**.

**Reading**, rēd′ing, *adj.* addicted to reading.—*n.* act of reading : perusal : study of books : public or formal recital : the way in which a passage reads : an interpretation of a passage or work.

**Reading-book**, rēd′ing-book, *n.* a *book* of exercises in *reading*.

**Reading-room**, rēd′ing-rōōm, *n.* a room with papers, &c. resorted to for reading.

**Readjourn**, rē-ad-jurn′, *v.t.* to adjourn again or a second time. [L. *re*, again, and **Adjourn**.]

**Readjust**, rē-ad-just′, *v.t.* to adjust or put in order again. [L. *re*, again, and **Adjust**.]

**Readmission**, rē-ad-mish′un, *n.* act of readmitting : state of being readmitted.

**Readmit**, rē-ad-mit′, *v.t.* to admit again. [L. *re*, again, and **Admit**.]

**Ready**, red′i, *adj.* prepared at the moment : prepared in mind : willing : not slow or awkward : dexterous : prompt : quick : present in hand : at hand : near : easy : on the point of.—*adv.* in a state of readiness or preparation.—*adv.* **Read′ily**.—*n.* **Read′iness**. [A.S. *ræde* ; Scot. *red*, to set to rights, to put in order, Ger. *be-reit*, ready. Conn. with **Raid**, **Ride**.]

**Ready-made**, red′i-mād, *adj.* made and ready for use : not made to order. [**Ready** and **Made**.]

**Reagent**, rē-ā′jent, *n.* a substance that *reacts* on and detects the presence of other bodies : a test. [L. *re*, again, and **Agent**.]

**Real**, rē′al, *adj.* actually existing : not counterfeit or assumed : true : genuine : (*law*) pertaining to things fixed, as lands or houses. [Lit. relating to the *thing*, Low L. *realis*—L. *res*, a thing.]

**Real**, rē′al, *n.* a Spanish coin, 100 of which = £1 sterling. [Sp.—L. *regalis*, royal.]

**Realisable**, rē′al-īz-a-bl, *adj.* that may be realised.

**Realisation**, rē-al-i-zā′shun, *n.* act of realising or state of being realised.

**Realise**, rē′al-īz, *v.t.* to *make real* : to bring into being or act : to accomplish : to convert into real property : to obtain, as a possession : to feel strongly : to comprehend completely : to bring home to one's own experience.

**Realism**, rē′al-izm, *n.* the medieval doctrine that general terms stand for *real* existences (opp. to **Nominalism**) : the tendency to accept and to represent things as they really are (opp. to **Idealism**) : the doctrine that in external percep-

tion the objects immediately known are *real* existences.—*n.* **Re′alist**, one who holds the doctrine of *realism*.—*adj.* **Realistic**, rē-al-ist′ik, pertaining to the realists or to realism.

**Reality**, rē-al′i-ti, *n.* that which is real and not imaginary : truth : verity : (*law*) the fixed, permanent nature of real property.

**Really**, rē′al-li, *adv.* in reality : actually : in truth.

**Realm**, relm, *n.* a *regal* or *royal* jurisdiction : kingdom : province : country. [O. Fr. *realme*, through a Low L. form *regalimen*, from L. *regalis*, royal. See **Regal**.]

**Realty**, rē′al-ti, *n.* Same as **Reality** in *law*.

**Ream**, rēm, *n.* a quantity of paper consisting of 20 quires. [O. Fr. *raime* (Fr. *rame*)—Sp. *resma*—Arab. *rizmat* (pl. *rizam*), a bundle.]

**Reanimate**, rē-an′i-māt, *v.t.* to restore to life : to infuse new life or spirit into : to revive.—*n.* **Reanima′tion**. [L. *re*, again, and **Animate**.]

**Reap**, rēp, *v.t.* to cut down, as grain : to clear off a crop : to gather : to receive as a reward.—*n.* **Reap′er**. [A.S. *ripan*, to pluck ; cog. with Goth. *raupjan*, Ger. *raufen*.]

**Reappear**, rē-ap-pēr′, *v.i.* to appear again or a second time. [L. *re*, again, and **Appear**.]

**Rear**, rēr, *n.* the back or hindmost part : the last part of an army or fleet.—*n.* **Rear-ad′miral**, an officer of the third rank, who commands the *rear* division of a fleet.—*n.* **Rear′-guard**, troops which *protect* the *rear* of an army.—*n.* **Rear′-rank**, the *hindermost rank* of a body of troops.—*n.* **Rear′-ward**, (*B.*) **Rere′ward**, the *rear-guard*. [O. Fr. *riere*—L. *retro*, behind, from *re*, back, and suffix *tro*, denoting motion.]

**Rear**, rēr, *v.t.* (*orig.*) to *raise* : to bring up to maturity : to educate : to stir up.—*v.i.* to rise on the hind-legs, as a horse. [A.S. *ræran*, to raise, the causal of **Rise**.]

**Rearmouse**. Same as **Reremouse**.

**Reason**, rē′zn, *n.* that which supports or justifies an act, &c. : a motive : proof : excuse : cause : the faculty of the mind by which man draws conclusions, and determines right and truth : the exercise of reason : just view of things : right conduct : propriety : justice.—*v.i.* to exercise the faculty of reason : to deduce inferences from premises : to argue : to debate : (*B.*) to converse.—*v.t.* to examine or discuss : to debate : to persuade by reasoning.—*n.* **Rea′soner**.—**By reason of**, on account of : in consequence of. [Lit. 'a calculation,' Fr. *raison*—L. *ratio*, *rationis*—*reor*, *ratus*, to calculate, to think.]

**Reasonable**, rē′zun-a-bl, *adj.* endowed with reason : rational : acting according to reason : agreeable to reason : just : not excessive : moderate.—*adv.* **Rea′sonably**.—*n.* **Rea′sonableness**.

**Reasoning**, rē′zun-ing, *n.* act of reasoning : that which is offered in argument : course of argument.

**Reassemble**, rē-as-sem′bl, *v.t.* and *v.i.* to assemble or collect again. [L. *re*, again, and **Assemble**.]

**Reassert**, rē-as-sėrt′, *v.t.* to assert again. [L. *re*, again, and **Assert**.]

**Reassurance**, rē-a-shōōr′ans, *n.* repeated assurance : a second assurance against loss.

**Reassure**, rē-a-shōōr′, *v.t.* to assure anew : to give confidence to : to insure an insurer. [L. *re*, again, and **Assure**.]

**Reave**, rēv, *v.t.* to take away by violence :—*pa.t.* and *pa.p.* reft. [A.S. *reafian*, to rob, (*lit.*) 'to strip'—*reaf*, clothing, spoil ; cog. with Ger. *rauben*. See **Rob**.]

**Rebaptise**, rē-bap-tīz′, *v.t.* to baptise again or a second time. [L. *re*, again, and **Baptise**.]

**Rebatement**, re-bāt'ment, *n.* deduction : diminution. [Fr. *rebattre*, to beat back—L. *re*, back, *battuo*, to beat.]

**Rebel**, reb'el, *n.* one who rebels.—*adj.* rebellious. [Fr.—L. *rebellis*, making war afresh, insurgent—*re*, again, and *bellum*, war.]

**Rebel**, re-bel', *v.i.* to renounce authority, or to take up arms against it : to oppose any lawful authority :—*pr.p.* rebell'ing ; *pa.t.* and *pa.p.* rebelled'.

**Rebellion**, re-bel'yun, *n.* act of rebelling : open opposition to lawful authority : revolt.

**Rebellious**, re-bel'yus, *adj.* engaged in rebellion.

**Rebound**, re-bownd', *v.i.* to bound or start back : to be reverberated.—*v.t.* to drive back : to reverberate.—*n.* act of rebounding. [L. *re*, back, and **Bound**.]

**Rebuff**, re-buf', *n.* a beating back : sudden resistance : sudden check : defeat : unexpected refusal.—*v.t.* to beat back : to check : to repel violently : to refuse. [It. *ribuffo*, a reproof—It. *ri* (= L. *re*), back, and *buffo*, a puff, of imitative origin.]

**Rebuild**, rē-bild', *v.t.* to build again : to renew.

**Rebuke**, re-būk', *v.t.* to check with reproof : to chide or reprove : (*B.*) to chasten.—*n.* direct reproof : reprimand : (*B.*) chastisement : reproach : persecution.—*n.* **Rebuk'er**. [O. Fr. *re-bouquer* (Fr. *reboucher*), from *re*, back, *bouque* (Fr. *bouche*), the mouth—L. *bucca*, the cheek.]

**Rebus**, rē'bus, *n.* an enigmatical representation of a word or phrase *by* pictures of *things* : (*her.*) a coat of arms bearing an allusion to the name of the person :—*pl.* **Re'buses**. [Lit. ' by things,' L , from *res, rei*, a thing.]

**Rebut**, re-but', *v.t.* to *butt* or drive *back* : (*law*) to oppose by argument or proof.—*v.i.* (*law*) to return an answer :—*pr.p.* rebutt'ing ; *pa.t.* and *pa.p.* rebutt'ed. [Fr. *rebuter—re*, back, and O. Fr. *bouter*. See **Butt**.]

**Rebutter**, re-but'ér, *n.* that which rebuts : a plaintiff's answer to a defendant's rejoinder.

**Recalcitrant**, re-kal'si-trant, *adj.* showing repugnance or opposition. [Lit. ' kicking back,' L. *recalcitrans, -antis—re*, back, *calcitro, -atum*, to kick—*calx, calcis*, the heel.]

**Recalcitrate**, re-kal'si-trāt, *v.t.* or *v.i.* to express repugnance. [Lit. ' to kick back.']

**Recall**, re-kawl', *v.t.* to call back : to command to return : to revoke : to call back to mind : to remember.—*n.* act of recalling or revoking.

**Recant**, re-kant', *v.t.* to withdraw (a former declaration) : to retract.—*v.i.* to revoke a former declaration : to unsay what has been said.—*n.* **Recant'er**. [Lit. ' to sound or sing back,' L. *re*, back, and **Cant**.]

**Recantation**, rē-kan-tā'shun, *n.* act of recanting : a declaration contradicting a former one.

**Recapitulate**, rē-ka-pit'ū-lāt, *v.t.* to *go over again the heads* or chief points of anything. [L. *recapitulo, -atum—re*, again, and *capitulum*, dim. of *caput*, the head.]

**Recapitulation**, rē-ka-pit-ū-lā'shun, *n.* act of recapitulating : a summary of main points.

**Recapitulatory**, rē-ka-pit'ū-la-tor-i, *adj.* repeating again : containing recapitulation.

**Recapture**, rē-kap'tūr, *v.t.* to capture back or retake, esp. a prize from a captor.—*n.* act of retaking : a prize retaken. [L. *re*, back, and **Capture**.]

**Recast**, rē-kast', *v.t.* to cast or throw again : to cast or mould anew : to compute a second time. [L. *re*, again, and **Cast**.]

**Recede**, re-sēd', *v.i.* to *go* or *fall back* : to retreat : to give up a claim.—*v.t.* to cede back, as to a former possessor. [L. *recedo, recessus—re*, back, and *cedo*, to go. See **Cede**.]

**Receipt**, re-sēt', *n.* act of *receiving* : place of receiving : power of holding : a written acknowledgment of anything received : that which is received : a recipe.—*v.t.* to give a receipt for : to sign. [M. E. *receit*—O. Fr. *recete* (Fr. *recette*)—L. *recipio*.]

**Receivable**, re-sēv'a-bl, *adj.* that may be *received*.

**Receive**, re-sēv', *v.t.* to take what is offered, &c. : to accept : to embrace with the mind : to assent to : to allow : to give acceptance to : to give admittance to : to welcome or entertain ; to hold or contain : (*law*) to take goods knowing them to be stolen : (*B.*) to bear with, to believe in. [O. Fr. *recever* (Fr. *recevoir*)—L. *recipio, receptum—re*, back, and *capio*, to take.]

**Receiver**, re-sēv'ér, *n.* one who receives : (*chem.*) a vessel for receiving and condensing in distillation, or for containing gases : the glass vessel of an air-pump in which the vacuum is formed.

**Recension**, re-sen'shun, *n.* act of reviewing or revising : review, esp. critical revisal of a text : a text established by critical revision. [L. *recensio, recenseo—re*, again, *censeo*, to value, estimate.]

**Recent**, rē'sent, *adj.* of late origin or occurrence : not long parted from : fresh : modern : (*geol.*) subsequent to the existence of man.—*adv.* **Re'cently**.—*n.* **Re'centness**. [Fr.—L. *recens, recentis*.]

**Receptacle**, re-sep'ta-kl, *n.* that into which anything is *received* or contained : (*bot.*) the basis of a flower. [From **Receive**.]

**Receptibility**, re-sep-ti-bil'i-ti, *n.* possibility of *receiving* or of being received.

**Reception**, re-sep'shun, *n.* act of *receiving* : admission : state of being received : a receiving or manner of receiving for entertainment : welcome.

**Receptive**, re-sep'tiv, *adj.* having the quality of *receiving* or containing : (*phil.*) capable of receiving impressions.—*n.* **Receptiv'ity**, quality of being receptive.

**Recess**, re-ses', *n.* a *going back* or withdrawing : retirement : state of being withdrawn : seclusion : remission of business : part of a room formed by a receding of the wall : private abode. [See **Recede**.]

**Recession**, re-sesh'un, *n.* act of receding : a ceding [or giving back.

**Recipe**, res'i-pē, *n.* a medical prescription : any formula for the preparation of a compound :—*pl.* **Recipes**, res'i-pēz. [Lit. *take*, the first word of a medical prescription, L., imperative of *recipio*.]

**Recipient**, re-sip'i-ent, *n.* one who receives.

**Reciprocal**, re-sip'ro-kal, *adj.* acting in return : mutual : given and received.—*n.* that which is reciprocal : (*math.*) unity divided by any quantity. [L. *reciprocus*, perh. from *reque proque*, backward and forward—*re*, back, *pro*, forward, *que*, and.] [interchangeably.

**Reciprocally**, re-sip'ro-kal-li, *adv.* mutually : in-

**Reciprocate**, re-sip'ro-kāt, *v.t.* to give and receive mutually : to requite. [L. *reciproco, reciprocatum*.] [of acts : alternation.

**Reciprocation**, re-sip-ro-kā'shun, *n.* interchange

**Reciprocity**, res-i-pros'i-ti, *n.* mutual obligations : action and reaction.

**Recital**, re-sīt'al, *n.* act of *reciting* : rehearsal : that which is recited : a narration.

**Recitation**, res-i-tā'shun, *n.* act of *reciting* : a public reading : rehearsal.

**Recitative**, res-i-ta-tēv', *adj.* pertaining to musical

*recitation :* in the style of recitation.—*n.* language delivered in the sounds of the musical scale : a piece of music for recitation.

**Recite,** re-sīt′, *v.t.* to read aloud from paper, or repeat from memory : to narrate : to recapitulate.—*n.* **Recit′er.** [Fr.—L. *re,* again, and *cito, citatum,* to call, from *cieo,* to move.]

**Reck,** rek, *v.t.* to *care for :* to regard. [A.S. *recan,* from a root seen in O. Ger. *ruoch,* care, Ger. *ruchlos,* regardless, wicked.]

**Reckless,** rek′les, *adj., careless :* heedless of consequences.—*adv.* **Reck′lessly.**—*n.* **Reck′lessness.**

**Reckling,** rek′ling, *n.* a reckless person.

**Reckon,** rek′n, *v.t.* to count : to place in the number or rank of : to account : to esteem.—*v.i.* to calculate : to charge to account : to make up accounts : to settle : to pay a penalty.—*n.* **Reck′oner.** [A.S. *ge-recenian,* to explain, cog. with Dut. *rekenen,* Ger. *rechnen.*]

**Reckoning,** rek′n-ing, *n.* an *account* of time : settlement of accounts, &c. : charges for entertainment : (*naut.*) a calculation of the ship's position : (*B.*) estimation.

**Reclaim.** re-klām′, *v.t.* to demand the return of : to regain : to bring back from a wild or barbarous state, or from error or vice : to bring into a state of cultivation : to bring into the desired condition : to make tame or gentle : to reform.—*v.i.* to cry out or exclaim. [Fr.—L. *re,* again, and *clamo,* to cry out.]

**Reclaimable,** re-klām′a-bl, *adj.* that may be *re-claimed,* or reformed.—*adv.* **Reclaim′ably.**

**Reclamation,** rek-la-mā′shun, *n.* act of *reclaiming :* state of being reclaimed : demand : recovery.

**Recline,** re-klīn′, *v.t.* to *lean* or *bend backwards :* to lean to or on one side.—*v.i.* to lean : to rest or repose. [L. *reclino*—*re,* back, *clino,* to bend.]

**Recluse,** re-klōōs′, *adj.* secluded : retired : solitary.—*n.* one shut up or secluded : one who lives retired from the world : a religious devotee living in a single cell, generally attached to a monastery. [Fr.—L. *reclusus,* pa.p. of *recludo,* to open, also to shut away—*re,* away, undoing, and *claudo,* to shut.]

**Recognisable,** rek-og-nīz′a-bl, *adj.* that may be recognised or acknowledged.

**Recognisance,** re-kog′ni-zans or re-kon′i-zans, *n.* a *recognition :* an avowal : a profession : a legal obligation entered into before a magistrate to do, or not do, some particular act.

**Recognise,** rek′og-nīz, *v.t.* to *know again :* to recollect : to acknowledge. [L. *recognosco*—*re,* again, and *cognosco,* to know. See **Know.**]

**Recognition,** rek-og-nish′un, *n.* act of *recognising :* state of being recognised : recollection : avowal.

**Recoil,** re-koil′, *v.t.* to start back : to rebound : to return : to shrink from.—*n.* a starting or springing back : rebound. [Fr. *reculer*—L. *re,* back, and Fr. *cul,* the hinder part—L. *culus.*]

**Recollect,** re-ol-lekt′, *v.t.* to remember : to recover composure or resolution (with reflex. pron.). [L. *re,* again, and **Collect.**]

**Recollect,** rē-kol-lekt′, *v.t.* to collect again.

**Recollection,** rek-ol-lek′shun, *n.* act of recollecting or remembering : the power of recollecting : memory : that which is recollected.

**Recommence,** rē-kom-mens′, *v.t.* to commence again.—*n.* **Recommence′ment.** [L. *re,* again, and **Commence.**]

**Recommend,** rek-om-mend′, *v.t.* to commend to another : to bestow praise on : to introduce favourably : to give in charge : to advise. [L. *re,* again, and **Commend.**]

**Recommendable,** rek-om-mend′a-bl, *adj.* that may be recommended : worthy of praise.

**Recommendation,** rek-om-men-dā′shun, *n.* act of recommending : act of introducing with commendation. [recommends : commendatory.]

**Recommendatory,** rek-om-mend′a-tor-i, *adj.* that recommends.

**Recommit,** rē-kom-mit′, *v.t.* to commit again : particularly, to send back to a committee.—*ns.* **Recommit′ment, Recommitt′al.** [L. *re,* again, and **Commit.**]

**Recompense,** rek′om-pens, *v.t.* to return an equivalent for anything : to repay or requite : to reward : to compensate : to remunerate.—*n.* that which is returned as an equivalent : repayment : reward : compensation : remuneration. [Lit. 'to weigh out in return,' Fr. *récompenser*—L. *re,* again, and *compenso.* See **Compensate.**]

**Recompose,** rē-kom-pōz′, *v.t.* to compose again or anew : to form anew : to soothe or quiet. [L. *re,* again, and **Compose.**]

**Reconcilable,** rek-on-sīl′a-bl, *adj.* that may be reconciled : that may be made to agree : consistent.

**Reconcile,** rek′on-sīl, *v.t.* to restore to friendship or union : to bring to agreement : to bring to contentment : to pacify : to make consistent : to adjust or compose.—*n.* **Rec′onciler.** [Lit. 'to bring into counsel again,' Fr. *réconcilier*—L. *re,* again, and *concilio, -atum,* to call together—*con,* together, *calo,* Gr. *kaleō,* to call.]

**Reconciliation,** rek-on-sil-i-ā′shun, **Reconcilement,** rek′on-sīl-ment, *n.* act of reconciling : state of being reconciled : renewal of friendship : atonement : the bringing to agreement things at variance.

**Recondite,** rek′on-dīt or re-kon′dit, *adj.* secret : profound. [Lit. 'put together out of the way,' L. *reconditus,* pa.p. of *recondo,* to put away—*re,* and *condo,* to put together—*con,* together, and *do,* to put.]

**Reconnaissance,** re-kon′ā-sans or -zäns, *n.* the act of *reconnoitring :* a survey or examination : the examination of a tract of country with a view to military or engineering operations. [Fr. Doublet **Recognisance.**]

**Reconnoitre,** rek-on-noi′tėr, *v.t.* to survey or examine : to survey with a view to military operations. [Lit. 'to recognise,' O. Fr. *reconoistre* (Fr. *reconnaître*)—L. *recognosco.* See **Recognise.**]

**Reconsider,** rē-kon-sid′ėr, *v.t.* to consider again : to review.—*n.* **Reconsidera′tion.** [L. *re,* again, and **Consider.**]

**Reconstruct,** rē-kon-strukt′, *v.t.* to construct again : to rebuild.—*n.* **Reconstruc′tion.** [L. *re,* again, and **Construct.**]

**Reconvey,** rē-kon-vā′, *v.t.* to transfer back to a former owner. [L. *re,* again, and **Convey.**]

**Record,** re-kord′, *v.t.* to write anything formally, to preserve evidence of it : to register or enrol : to celebrate. [Fr. *recorder*—L. *recordo, recordor,* to call to mind—*re,* again, and *cor, cordis,* E. **Heart.**]

**Record,** rek′ord, *n.* a register : a formal writing of any fact or proceeding : a book of such writings.

**Recorder,** re-kord′ėr, *n.* one who records or registers : the chief judicial officer in some towns.—*n.* **Record′ership,** his office.

**Recount,** rē-kownt′, *v.t.* to count again.

**Recount,** re-kownt′, *v.t.* to tell over again : to narrate the particulars of : to detail. [Fr. *re-conter*—*re,* and *conter,* to tell, akin to *compter,* to count. See **Count,** *v.t.*]

**Recoup,** rē-kōōp′, *v.t.* to make good : to indemnify.

[Lit. to cut a piece off, to secure a piece, Fr. *recouper*, to cut again—*re*, and *couper*, to cut, *coup*, a stroke, blow, through Low L. *colpus*, L. *colaphus*, from Gr. *kolaphos*, a blow.]

**Recourse**, re-kōrs′, *n.* a going to for aid or protection. [Lit. 'a running back,' Fr. *recours*—L. *recursus*—*re*, back, and *curro*, *cursum*, to run.]

**Recover**, re-kuv′er, *v.t.* to get possession of again: to make up for : to retrieve : to cure : to revive : to bring back to any former state : to obtain as compensation : to obtain for injury or debt.—*v.i.* to regain health : to regain any former state : (*law*) to obtain a judgment. [Lit. 'to take again,' Fr. *recouvrer*—L. *recuperare*—*re*, again, and *capio*, to take.]

**Recoverable**, re-kuv′er-a-bl, *adj.* that may be recovered or regained : capable of being brought to a former condition.

**Recovery**, re-kuv′er-i, *n.* the act of recovering : the act of regaining anything lost : restoration to health or to any former state : the power of recovering anything.

**Recreancy**, rek′re-an-si, *n.* the quality of a recreant : a yielding, mean, cowardly spirit.

**Recreant**, rek′re-ant, *adj.* cowardly : false : apostate : renegade.—*n.* a mean-spirited wretch : an apostate : a renegade. [O. Fr. pr.p. of *recroire*, to change belief—Low L. (*se*) *re-credere*, to be vanquished in judicial combat and forced to confess one's self wrong—L. *re*, denoting change, *credo*, to believe.]

**Recreate**, rē-kre-āt′, *v.t.* to create again or anew. —*n.* **Recrea′tion**. [L. *re*, again, and **Create**.]

**Recreate**, rek′re-āt, *v.t.* to revive : to reanimate : to cheer or amuse : to refresh : to delight.—*v.i.* to take recreation.

**Recreation**, rē-kre-ā′shun, *n.* a creating again : a new creation.

**Recreation**, rek-re-ā′shun, *n.* the act of recreating or state of being recreated : refreshment after toil, sorrow, &c. : diversion : amusement : sport.

**Recreative**, rek′re-āt-iv, *adj.* serving to recreate or refresh : giving relief in weariness, &c. : amusing.

**Recriminate**, re-krim′in-āt, *v.t.* to criminate or accuse in return.—*v.i.* to charge an accuser with a similar crime. [L. *re*, in return, and **Criminate**.]

**Recrimination**, re-krim-in-ā′shun, *n.* the act of recriminating or returning one accusation by another : a counter-charge or accusation.

**Recriminative**, re-krim′in-āt-iv, **Recriminatory**, re-krim′in-a-tor-i, *adj.* recriminating or retorting accusations or charges.

**Recruit**, re-krōōt′, *v.i.* to obtain fresh supplies : to recover in health, &c. : to enlist new soldiers. —*v.t.* to repair : to supply : to supply with recruits.—*n.* the supply of any want : a newly enlisted soldier.—*ns.* **Recruit′er**, **Recruit′ment**. [Lit. 'to grow again,' Fr. *recruter*, from *re* and *croître*—L. *recresco*—*re*, again, and *cresco*, to grow.]

**Recruiting**, re-krōōt′ing, *adj.* obtaining new supplies : enlisting recruits.—*n.* the business of obtaining new supplies or enlisting new soldiers.

**Rectangle**, rekt′ang-gl, *n.* a four-sided figure with *right angles*. [L. *rectus*, right, and *angulus*, an angle.]                              [angles.

**Rectangled**, rekt-ang′gld, *adj.* having right

**Rectangular**, rekt-ang′gul-ar, *adj.*, *right-angled*.

**Rectifiable**, rek′ti-fi-a-bl, *adj.* that may be rectified or set right.

**Rectification**, rek-ti-fi-kā′shun, *n.* the act of recti-

fying or setting right : the process of refining any substance by repeated distillation.

**Rectifier**, rek′ti-fī-er, *n.* one who rectifies or corrects : one who refines a substance by repeated distillation.

**Rectify**, rek′ti-fī, *v.t.* to make *straight* or *right* : to adjust : to correct or redress : to refine by distillation :—*pa.t.* and *pa.p.* rec′tified. [L. *rectus*, straight, right, and *facio*, to make.]

**Rectilineal**, rek-ti-lin′e-al, **Rectilinear**, rek-ti-lin′e-ar, *adj.* bounded by *straight lines* : straight. [L. *rectus*, straight, right, and *linea*, a line.]

**Rectitude**, rek′ti-tūd, *n.*, *uprightness* : correctness of principle or practice : integrity. [Fr.—L. *rectitudo*—*rectus*, straight, E. **Right**.]

**Rector**, rek′tor, *n.* a *ruler* : the parson of an unimpropriated parish who receives the tithes : (*Scot.*) the head master of a public school : the chief elective officer of some universities, as in France and Scotland : the title given by the Jesuits to the heads of their religious houses.—*ns.* **Rec′torate**, **Rec′torship**. [L.—*rego*, *rectum*, to rule ; akin to Sans. *raj*, to govern.]

**Rectoral**, rek′tor-al, **Rectorial**, rek-tō′ri-al, *adj.* pertaining to a rector or to a rectory.

**Rectory**, rek′tor-i, *n.* the province or mansion of a *rector*.

**Rectum**, rek′tum, *n.* the lowest part of the large intestine. [From L. *rectus*, straight.]

**Recumbent**, re-kum′bent, *adj.*, *lying back* : reclining : idle.—*adv.* **Recum′bently**.—*ns.* **Recum′bence**, **Recum′bency**. [L. *recumbo*—*re*, back, and *cumbo*, *cubo*, to lie down.]

**Recuperative**, re-kū′per-a-tiv, **Recuperatory**, re-kū′per-a-tor-i, *adj.* tending to recovery. [L. *recuperativus*—*recupero*, to recover. See **Recover**.]

**Recur**, re-kur′, *v.i.* to return to the mind : to have recourse : to resort : to happen at a stated interval :—*pr.p.* recur′ring ; *pa.t.* and *pa.p.* recurred′. [L. *recurro*—*re*, back, and *curro*, to run. See **Current**.]

**Recurrent**, re-kur′ent, *adj.* returning at intervals. —*ns.* **Recurr′ence**, **Recurr′ency**.

**Recurvate**, re-kur′vāt, *v.t.* to curve or bend back.

**Recusancy**, re-kūz′an-si, *n.* state of being a recusant : nonconformity.

**Recusant**, re-kūz′ant or rek′-, *adj.* refusing to acknowledge the supremacy of the sovereign in religious matters.—*n.* one who refuses to acknowledge the supremacy of the sovereign in religious matters : a nonconformist. [Fr.—pr.p. of L. *recuso*—*re*, against, and *causa*, a cause. See **Cause**.]

**Red**, red, *adj.* (*comp.* **Redd′er**, *superl.* **Redd′est**) of a colour like blood.—*n.* one of the primary colours, of several shades, as scarlet, pink, &c.— *adv.* **Red′ly**.—*n.* **Red′ness**. [A.S. *reád*, cog. with Ice. *raudh-r*, Ger. *roth*, L. *ruf-us*, Gr. *e-rythros*, Celt. *ruadh*, *rhudd*.]

**Redaction**, re-dak′shun, *n.* the act of arranging in systematic order, esp. literary materials : the digest so made. [Fr.—L. *redactus*, pa.p. of *redigo*, to bring back, to get together.]

**Redan**, re-dan′, *n.* (*fort.*) the simplest form of field-work, consisting of two faces which form a salient angle towards the enemy, serving to cover a bridge or causeway. [Fr., for O. Fr. *redent*. See **Redented**.]

**Redbreast**, red′brest, *n.* a favourite song-bird, so called from the *red* colour of its *breast*, the robin.

**Red chalk**, **Red clay**. See **Reddle**.

**Red-deer**, red′-dēr, *n.* a species of *deer* which is *reddish*-brown in summer : the common stag.

**Redden,** red'n, *v.t.* to make red.—*v.i.* to grow red : to blush.

**Reddish,** red'ish, *adj.* somewhat red : moderately red.—*n.* **Redd'ishness.**

**Reddition,** red-dish'un, *n.* a *giving back* or *returning* of anything : surrender : a rendering of the sense : explanation. [Fr.—L. *redditi-o, -onis—redditus,* pa.p. of *reddo,* to restore. See **Render.**]

**Redditive,** red'di-tiv, *adj., returning* an answer.

**Reddle,** red'l, *n.* a soft clay iron ore of a reddish colour, also called **Red clay** or **Red chalk.**

**Redeem,** re-dēm', *v.t.* to ransom : to relieve from captivity at a price : to rescue : to pay the penalty of : to atone for : to perform, as a promise : to improve : to recover, as a pledge. [Lit. 'to buy back,' Fr. *rédimer*—L. *redimo*—*red,* back, and *emo,* to buy, orig. to take.]

**Redeemable,** re-dēm'a-bl, *adj.* that may be redeemed.—*n.* **Redeem'ableness.**

**Redeemer,** re-dēm'ėr, *n.* one who redeems or ransoms : Jesus Christ, the Saviour of the world.

**Redeliver,** rē-de-liv'ėr, *v.t.* to deliver back or again : to liberate a second time.—*n.* **Redeliv'erance.** [L. *re,* back or again, and **Deliver.**]

**Redelivery,** rē-de-liv'ėr-i, *n.* the act of delivering back : a second delivery or liberation.

**Redemption,** re-dem'shun, *n.* act of redeeming or *buying back* : ransom : release : the deliverance of mankind from sin and misery by Christ. [Fr.—L.—*redemptus,* pa.p. of *redimo.* See **Redeem.** Doublet **Ransom.**]

**Redemptive,** re-demp'tiv, *adj.* pertaining to redemption : serving or tending to redeem.

**Redemptory,** re-demp'tor-i, *adj.* serving to redeem : paid for ransom.

**Redented,** re-dent'ed, *adj.* formed like the teeth of a saw. [O. Fr. *redent,* a double notching or jagging—L. *re,* again, and *dens, dentis,* a tooth.]

**Red-hand,** red'hand, *n.* a *bloody hand* : (*her.*) a sinister hand, erect, open, and 'couped,' the distinguishing badge of baronets.—*adv.* in the very act, as if with *red* or bloody *hands.*

**Red-heat,** red'-hēt, *n.* heat amounting to redness.

**Red-hot,** red'-hot, *adj.* heated to redness.

**Redintegration,** red-in-te-grā'shun, *n., restoration to integrity* or to a *whole* or sound state : renovation. [L. *redintegratio.*]

**Red-lead,** red'-led, *n.* a preparation of *lead* of a fine *red* colour used in painting, &c.

**Red-letter,** red'-let'ėr, *adj.* having *red letters* : auspicious or fortunate, as a day, so called from the holidays or saints' days being indicated by *red letters* in the old calendars.

**Redolent,** red'o-lent, *adj., diffusing odour* or fragrance : scented.—*ns.* **Red'olence, Red'olency.** [Fr.—L. *redol-ens, -entis—red, re,* off, again, and *oleo,* to emit an odour. See **Odour** and **Olfactory.**]

**Redouble,** re-dub'l, *v.t.* to double again or repeatedly : to increase greatly : to multiply.—*v.i.* to become greatly increased : to become twice as much. [Fr. *re-doubler.* See **Double.**]

**Redoubt,** re-dowt', *n.* (*fort.*) a field-work inclosed on all sides, its ditch not flanked from the parapet. [Fr. *redoute, réduit,* a redoubt, retreat—It. *ridotto*—L. *reductus,* retired. See **Reduce.**]

**Redoubtable,** re-dowt'a-bl, *adj.* terrible to foes : valiant. [O. Fr. (Fr. *redoutable*), to be feared—O. Fr. *redoubter* (Fr. *redouter*), to fear greatly—L. *re,* back, and *dubito,* to doubt. See **Doubt.**]

**Redound,** re-downd', *v.i.* to be sent back by reaction : to result. [Lit. 'to roll back as a wave,' Fr. *rédonder*—L. *redundo*—*re,* back, and *undo,* to surge—*unda,* a wave.]

**Redraft,** rē-draft', *n.* a second draft or copy : a new bill of exchange which the holder of a protested bill draws on the drawer or indorsers, for the amount of the bill, with costs and charges. [L. *re,* again, and **Draft.**]

**Redress,** re-dres', *v.t.* to set right : to relieve from : to make amends to.—*n.* relief : reparation. [Fr. *redresser—re,* again, and *dresser.* See **Dress.**]

**Redressible,** re-dres'i-bl, *adj.* that may be redressed.

**Redressive,** re-dres'iv, *adj.* affording redress.

**Redshank,** red'shank, *n.* an aquatic bird of the snipe family, with *legs* of a bright *red* colour.

**Red-tape,** red-tāp', *n.* the *red tape* used in public, and esp. government offices, for tying up documents, &c. : applied satirically to the intricate system of routine in vogue there : official formality.—*adj.* pertaining to official formality.

**Red-tapism,** red-tāp'izm, *n.* the system of routine in government and other public offices.—*n.* **Red-tap'ist,** a great stickler for routine.

**Reduce,** re-dūs', *v.t.* to bring into a lower state : to lessen : to impoverish : to subdue : to arrange : (*arith.* and *alg.*) to change numbers or quantities from one denomination into another. [Lit. 'to bring back,' L. *reduco, reductum—re,* back, and *duco,* to lead. See **Duke.**]

**Reducible,** re-dūs'i-bl, *adj.* that may be reduced.

**Reduction,** re-duk'shun, *n.* act of reducing or state of being reduced : diminution : subjugation : a rule for changing numbers or quantities from one denomination to another. [Fr.—L.]

**Redundance,** re-dun'dans, **Redundancy,** re-dun'dan-si, *n.* quality of being redundant or superfluous : that which is redundant.

**Redundant,** re-dun'dant, *adj.* exceeding what is necessary : superfluous, in words or images.—*adv.* **Redun'dantly.** [Lit. 'overflowing like waves,' Fr.—L. *redund-ans, -antis,* pr.p. of *redundo.* See **Redound.**]

**Reduplicate,** re-dū'plik-āt, *v.t.* to duplicate or double again : to multiply : to repeat.—*adj.* doubled.—*n.* **Reduplica'tion.** [L. *re,* again, and **Duplicate.**]

**Re-echo,** rē-ek'o, *v.t.* to echo back.—*v.i.* to give back echoes : to resound.—*n.* the echo of an echo. [L. *re,* back, and **Echo.**]

**Reed,** rēd, *n.* the largest of the British grasses, common at the sides of rivers, lakes, &c. : a musical pipe anciently made of a reed : the mouth-tube of a musical instrument : the part of a loom by which the threads are separated. [A.S. *hreod ;* Dut. and Ger. *riet.*]

**Reeded,** rēd'ed, *adj.* covered with reeds : formed with reed-like ridges or channels.

**Reedy,** rēd'i, *adj.* abounding with reeds : resembling or sounding as a reed.

**Reef,** rēf, *n.* a chain of rocks lying at or near the surface of the water. [Ice. *rif,* Dan. *rev ;* conn. with **Rive,** and so lit. the 'cleft' or 'riven.']

**Reef,** rēf, *n.* a portion of a sail.—*v.t.* to reduce the exposed surface of, as a sail. [Dut. *rif,* reef.]

**Reefy,** rēf'i, *adj.* full of reefs.

**Reek,** rēk, *n.* smoke : vapour.—*v.i.* to emit smoke or vapour : to steam. [A.S. *rec ;* Ice. *reykr,* Ger. *rauch,* Dut. *rook,* smoke.]

**Reeky,** rēk'i, *adj.* full of reek : smoky : soiled with steam or smoke : foul.

**Reel,** rēl, *n.* a lively Scottish dance. [Gael. *righil.*]

**Reel,** rēl, *n.* a *rolling* or turning frame for winding yarn, &c.—*v.t.* to wind on a reel. [A.S. *reol, hreol.*]

**Reel**, rēl, *v.i.* to stagger: to vacillate.

**Re-elect**, rē-e-lekt', *v.t.* to elect again.—*n.* **Re-election**. [L. *re*, again, and **Elect**.]

**Re-eligible**, rē-el'i-ji-bl, *adj.* capable of re-election.—*n.* **Re-eligibil'ity.**

**Re-embark**, rē-em-bärk', *v.t.* to embark or put on board again.—*n.* **Re-embarka'tion.** [L. *re*, again, and **Embark**.]

**Re-enact**, rē-en-akt', *v.t.* to enact again.—*n.* **Re-enact'ment.** [L. *re*, again, and **Enact**.]

**Re-enforce, Re-enforcement.** Same as **Reinforce, Reinforcement.**

**Re-enter**, rē-en'tėr, *v.t.* and *v.i.* to enter again or anew.—**Re-entering angle**, an angle pointing inwards. [L. *re*, again, and **Enter**.]

**Re-entry**, rē-en'tri, *n.* an entering again: the resuming a possession lately lost.

**Reermouse.** See **Reremouse.**

**Re-establish**, rē-es-tab'lish, *v.t.* to establish again.—*n.* **Re-estab'lishment.** [L. *re*, again, and **Establish**.]

**Reeve**, rēv, *n.* a steward or other officer (now used only in composition, as in **Sheriff**). [M. E. *reve*—A.S. *gerefa*; Ger. *graf*; all from Low L. *grafio, graphio*—Gr. *graphō*, to write.]

**Reeve**, rēv, *v.t.* to pass the end of a rope through any hole, as the channel of a block:—*pa.t.* and *pa.p.* reeved, also rove (*naut.*). [See **Reef**, *v.*]

**Re-examine**, rē-egz-am'in, *v.t.* to examine again or anew. [L. *re*, again, and **Examine**.]

**Refection**, re-fek'shun, *n.* refreshment: a meal or repast. [Fr.—L. *refectio*—*reficio, refectum*— *re*, again, and *facio*, to make.]

**Refectory**, re-fek'tor-i, *n.* the place where refections or meals are taken: (*orig.*) a hall in convents or monasteries where meals were taken.

**Refer**, re-fėr', *v.t.* to submit to another person or authority: to assign: to reduce.—*v.i.* to have reference or recourse: to relate: to allude:—*pr.p.* referr'ing; *pa.t.* and *pa.p.* referred'. [Fr. *référer*—L. *refero*, to carry away or back—*re*, back, and *fero*, to bear.]

**Referable**, ref'ėr-a-bl, **Referrible**, re-fėr'i-bl, *adj.* that may be referred or considered in connection with something else: that may be assigned or considered as belonging or related to.

**Referee**, ref-ėr-ē', *n.* one to whom anything is referred: an arbitrator, umpire, or judge.

**Reference**, ref'ėr-ens, *n.* the act of referring: a submitting for information or decision: relation: allusion: one who or that which is referred to: (*law*) the act of submitting a dispute for investigation or decision.

**Referrible.** Same as **Referable.**

**Refine**, re-fīn', *v.t.* to separate from extraneous matter: to reduce to a fine or pure state: to purify: to clarify: to polish: to make elegant: to purify the manners, morals, &c.—*v.i.* to become fine or pure: to affect nicety: to improve in any kind of excellence.—*n.* **Refin'er.** [L. *re*, denoting change of state, and **Fine**; cf. Fr. *raffiner* (*re-affiner*), It. *raffinare.*]

**Refinement**, re-fīn'ment, *n.* act of refining or state of being refined: purification: separation from what is impure, &c.: cultivation: elegance: polish: purity: an excessive nicety.

**Refinery**, re-fīn'ėr-i, *n.* a place for refining.

**Refining**, re-fīn'ing, *n.* the act or process of refining or purifying, particularly metals.

**Refit**, re-fit', *v.t.* to *fit* or prepare *again*.—*n.* **Refit'ment.** [L. *re*, again, and **Fit**.]

**Reflect**, re-flekt', *v.t.* to *bend back*: to throw back after striking upon any surface, as light, &c.—*v.i.* to be thrown back, as light, heat, &c.: to revolve in the mind: to consider attentively or deeply: to ponder: to cast reproach or censure. [L. *reflecto, reflexum*—*re*, and *flecto*, to bend or turn.]

**Reflecting**, re-flekt'ing, *adj.*, *throwing back* light, heat, &c.: given to reflection: thoughtful.

**Reflection**, re-flek'shun, *n.* the act of reflecting: the sending back of light, heat, &c.: the state of being reflected: that which is reflected: the action of the mind by which it is conscious of its own operations: attentive consideration: contemplation: censure or reproach.

**Reflective**, re-flekt'iv, *adj.* reflecting: considering the operations of the mind: exercising thought or reflection: (*gram.*) reciprocal.—*adv.* **Reflect'ively.**—*n.* **Reflect'iveness.**

**Reflector**, re-flekt'or, *n.* one who or that which reflects: a mirror or polished reflecting surface.

**Reflex**, rē'fleks, *adj.*, *bent* or *turned back*: reflected: (*physiology*) said of certain movements which take place independent of the will, being sent back from a nerve-centre in answer to a stimulus from the surface: (*paint.*) illuminated by light reflected from another part of the same picture.—*n.* reflection: light reflected from an illuminated surface.

**Reflexible**, re-fleks'i-bl, **Reflectible**, re-flekt'i-bl, *adj.* that may be reflected or *thrown back*.—*n.* **Reflexibil'ity.**

**Reflexive**, re-fleks'iv, *adj.*, *turned backward*: reflective: respecting the past: turning back on itself.—*adv.* **Reflex'ively.**

**Refluent**, ref'lōō-ent, *adj.*, *flowing back*: ebbing. [L. *refluens, -entis*, pr.p. of *refluo*—*re*, back, and *fluo, fluxum*, to flow.]

**Reflux**, rē'fluks, *adj.*, *flowing* or returning *back*: reflex.—*n.* a flowing back: ebb.

**Reform**, re-form', *v.t.* to form again or anew: to transform: to make better: to remove that which is objectionable from: to repair or improve: to reclaim.—*v.i.* to become better: to abandon evil: to be corrected or improved.—*n.* a forming anew: change, amendment, improvement: an extension or better distribution of Parliamentary representation. [L. *re*, again, *formo*, to shape, from *forma*. See **Form**, *n.*]

**Reformation**, rē-for-mā'shun, *n.* the act of forming again.

**Reformation**, ref-or-mā'shun, *n.* the act of reforming: amendment: improvement: the great religious change of the 16th century, when the Protestants separated from the R. Cath. Church.

**Reformative**, re-form'a-tiv, *adj.* forming again or anew: tending to produce reform.

**Reformatory**, re-form'a-tor-i, *adj.* reforming: tending to produce reform.—*n.* an institution for reclaiming youths and children who have been convicted of crime.

**Reformed**, re-formd', *adj.* formed again or anew: changed: amended: improved: denoting the churches formed after the Reformation, esp. those that separated from Luther on matters of doctrine and discipline: Protestant.

**Reformer**, re-form'ėr, *n.* one who reforms: one who advocates political reform: one of those who took part in the Reformation of the 16th century.

**Refract**, re-frakt', *v.t.* to *break back* or open: to break the natural course, or bend from a direct line, as rays of light, &c. [L. *refringo, refrac-*

*tum—re*, back, and *frango*, to break.   See **Fraction**.]

**Refraction**, re-frak'shun, *n.* the act of refracting: the change in the direction of a ray of light, heat, &c. when it enters a different medium.

**Refractive**, re-frakt'iv, *adj.* refracting: pertaining to refraction.—*n.* **Refract'iveness**.

**Refractory**, re-frakt'or-i, *adj.*, *breaking* through rules: unruly: unmanageable: obstinate: perverse: difficult of fusion, as metals, &c.—*adv.* **Refract'orily**.—*n.* **Refract'oriness**.

**Refrain**, re-frān', *n.* a phrase or verse recurring at the end of each division of a poem: the burden of a song. [Fr.—O. Fr. *refraindre* —L. *refringo* (*refrango*).]

**Refrain**, re-frān', *v.t.* to curb: to restrain.—*v.i.* to keep from action: to forbear. [Fr. *refréner* —L. *refreno—re*, and *frenum*, a bridle.]

**Refrangible**, re-fran'ji-bl, *adj.* that may be *refracted* or turned out of a direct course, as rays of light, heat, &c.—*n.* **Refrangibil'ity**.

**Refresh**, re-fresh', *v.t.* to make *fresh again*: to allay heat: to give new strength, spirit, &c. to: to revive after exhaustion: to enliven: to restore. [L. *re*, again, and **Fresh**.]

**Refreshment**, re-fresh'ment, *n.* the act of refreshing: new strength or spirit after exhaustion: that which refreshes, as food or rest.

**Refrigerant**, re-frij'er-ant, *adj.* making *cold*: cooling: refreshing.—*n.* that which cools.

**Refrigerate**, re-frij'er-āt, *v.t.* to make *cold*: to cool: to refresh.—*n.* **Refrigera'tion**. [Fr.—L. *re*, denoting change of state, and *frigero*, *-atum*, to cool, from *frigus*, cold.  See **Frigid**.]

**Refrigerative**, re-frij'er-a-tiv, **Refrigeratory**, re-frij'er-a-tor-i, *adj.*, *cooling*: refreshing.

**Refrigerator**, re-frij'er-ā-tor, *n.* an apparatus for preserving food by keeping it at a low temperature: an ice-safe.

**Refrigeratory**, re-frij'er-a-tor-i, *n.* a *cooler*: a vessel or apparatus for cooling, used in brewing, &c.

**Reft**, reft, *pa.t.* and *pa.p.* of **Reave**.

**Refuge**, ref'ūj, *n.* that which affords shelter or protection: an asylum or retreat: a resource or expedient. [Lit. 'a fleeing back,' Fr.—L. *refugium—re*, back, and *fugio*, to flee.]

**Refugee**, ref-ū-jē', *n.* one who flees for refuge to another country, esp. from religious persecution or political commotion.

**Refulgence**, re-ful'jens, **Refulgency**, re-ful'jen-si, *n.* state of being refulgent: brightness: brilliance.

**Refulgent**, re-ful'jent, *adj.* casting a flood of light: shining: brilliant.—*adv.* **Reful'gently**. [L. *refulgens*, *-entis*, pr.p. of *refulgeo—re*, intens., *fulgeo*, to shine.]

**Refund**, re-fund', *v.t.* to repay: to restore: to return what has been taken. [Lit. 'to pour back,' L. *refundo*, *refusum—re*, back, and *fundo*, to pour.]

**Refusal**, re-fūz'al, *n.* denial of anything requested: rejection: the right of taking in preference to others.

**Refuse**, re-fūz', *v.t.* to reject: to deny, as a request, &c.—*v.i.* to decline acceptance: not to comply. [Fr. *refuser*, prob. due to confusion of L. *refuto*, to drive back, and *recuso*, to make an objection against.]

**Refuse**, ref'ūs, *adj.*, *refused*: worthless.—*n.* that which is rejected or left as worthless: dross.

**Refutable**, re-fūt'a-bl, *adj.* that may be refuted or disproved.—*adv.* **Refut'ably**.—*n.* **Refutabil'ity**.

**Refutation**, ref-ū-tā'shun, *n.* the act of refuting or disproving.

**Refutatory**, re-fūt'a-tor-i, *adj.* tending to refute: refuting.

**Refute**, re-fūt', *v.t.* to repel: to oppose: to disprove. [Lit. 'to pour back,' Fr. *réfuter*—L. *refuto—re*, back, and base *fud*, root of *fundo*, *futilis*.]

**Regain**, rē-gān', *v.t.* to gain back or again: to recover. [L. *re*, back, and **Gain**.]

**Regal**, rē'gal, *adj.* belonging to a *king*: kingly: royal.—*adv.* **Re'gally**. [Fr.—L. *regalis—rex*, a king, from *rego*, to rule.]

**Regal**, rē'gal, or **Rigole**, rig'ol, *n.* a small portable organ used to support treble voices. [Fr.—It.— L. *regalis*.  See **Regal**, *adj.*]

**Regale**, re-gāl', *v.t.* to entertain in a sumptuous manner: to refresh: to gratify.—*v.i.* to feast.— *n.* a regal or magnificent feast. [Fr. *régaler*— Sp. *regalar*—L. *regelare*, to thaw; or from Fr. and It. *gala*, good cheer.  See **Gala**.]

**Regalement**, re-gāl'ment, *n.* the act of regaling: entertainment: refreshment.

**Regalia**, re-gā'li-a, *n.pl.* the ensigns of royalty: the crown, sceptre, &c., esp. those used at a coronation: the rights and privileges of kings. [Lit. 'royal things,' neuter pl. of *regalis*.]

**Regality**, re-gal'i-ti, *n.* state of being regal: royalty: sovereignty.

**Regard**, re-gärd', *v.t.* to observe particularly: to hold in respect or affection: to pay attention to: to keep or observe: to esteem: to consider. —*n.* (orig.) look, gaze: attention with interest: observation: respect: affection: repute: relation: reference.—*n.* **Regard'er**. [Fr. *regarder* —re, and *garder*, to keep, look after.  See **Guard**.]

**Regardful**, re-gärd'fool, *adj.* full of regard: taking notice: heedful: attentive.—*adv.* **Regard'fully**.

**Regardless**, re-gärd'les, *adj.* without regard: not attending: negligent: heedless.—*adv.* **Regard'lessly**.—*n.* **Regard'lessness**.

**Regatta**, re-gat'a, *n.* a race of yachts: any rowing or sailing match. [Orig. a grand fête and contest of the gondoliers at Venice, It. *regatta* or *rigatta*—It. *riga*, a row—O. Ger. *riga*, Ger. *reihe*, a row.]

**Regelation**, rē-jel-ā'shun, *n.* the act of freezing anew. [L. *re*, again, and *gelatio*, freezing.  See **Gelatin**.]

**Regency**, rē'jen-si, *n.* the office, jurisdiction, or dominion of a regent: a body intrusted with vicarious government.

**Regenerate**, re-jen'er-āt, *v.t.* to generate or produce anew: (*theol.*) to renew the heart and turn it to the love of God.—*adj.* regenerated: renewed.—*ns.* **Regen'erateness**, **Regen'eracy**, state of being regenerate. [L. *regenero*, *-atum*, to bring forth again—re, again, *genero*, to beget, bring forth.  See **Generate**.]

**Regeneration**, rē-jen-ėr-ā'shun, *n.* act of regenerating: state of being regenerated: (*theol.*) *new birth*: the change from a carnal to a Christian life.

**Regenerative**, re-jen'er-āt-iv, *adj.* pertaining to regeneration.—*adv.* **Regen'eratively**.

**Regent**, rē'jent, *adj.* invested with interim sovereign authority.—*n.* one invested with interim authority: one who rules for the sovereign. [Fr.—L. *regens*, *-entis*, pr.p. of *rego*, to rule.]

**Regentship**, rē'jent-ship, *n.* office of a regent: deputed authority.

**Regicide**, rej'i-sīd, *n.* the *murderer* of a *king*:

the murder of a king.—*adj*. **Regici'dal**. [**Fr**.; from L. *rex, regis,* a king, and *caedo,* to kill.]

**Regime**, rā-zhēm′, *n.* mode of *ruling* one's diet: form of government: administration. [**Fr.**—L. *regimen—rego,* to rule.]

**Regimen**, rej′i-men, *n., rule* prescribed: orderly government: any regulation for gradually producing benefit: (*med.*) rule of diet: (*gram.*) the government of one word by another: words governed. [L.]

**Regiment**, rej′i-ment, *n.* a body of soldiers *ruled* or commanded by a colonel, and consisting of a number of companies or troops.

**Regimental**, rej-i-ment′al, *adj.* relating to a regiment:—*n.pl.* the uniform of a regiment.

**Region**, rē′jun, *n.* a portion of land: country: district. [L. *regio, regionis—rego,* to rule, direct, mark a boundary.]

**Register**, rej′is-tèr, *n.* a written record, regularly kept: the book containing the register: that which registers or records: that which regulates, as the damper of a furnace or stove: a stop or range of pipes on the organ, &c.: the compass of a voice or of a musical instrument.—*v.t.* to enter in a register: to record. [Fr. *registre* (It. and Sp. *registro*)—Low L. *registrum,* for L. *regestum—re,* back, and *gero,* to carry.]

**Registrar**, rej′is-trar, *n.* one who keeps a register. —*n.* **Reg'istrarship**, office of a registrar.

**Registration**, rej-is-trā′shun, *n.* act of registering.

**Registry**, rej′is-tri, *n.* act of registering: place where a register is kept: facts recorded.

**Regnancy**, reg′nan-si, *n.* condition of being *regnant* or reigning: reign: predominance.

**Regnant**, reg′nant, *adj., reigning* or *ruling*: predominant: exercising regal authority. [L. *regnans, regnantis,* pr.p. of *regno—rego,* to rule.]

**Regress**, rē′gres, *n.* a *going* or passage *back*: return: power of returning.—*v.i.* to go back: to return to a former place or state. [L. *regressus—re,* back, and *gradior, gressus,* to step, go.]

**Regression**, re-gresh′un, *n.* act of *going back* or *returning.*

**Regressive**, re-gres′iv, *adj., going back*: returning.

**Regret**, re-gret′, *v.t.* to grieve at: to remember with sorrow :—*pr.p.* regrett′ing; *pa.t.* and *pa.p.* regrett′ed.—*n.* sorrow for anything: concern: remorse. [Fr. *regretter—re-,* and Goth. *gretan,* A.S. *grætan,* to weep.]

**Regretful**, re-gret′fool, *adj.* full of regret—*adv.* **Regret'fully**.

**Regular**, reg′ū-lar, *adj.* according to *rule* or established custom: governed by rule: uniform: orderly: periodical: level, unbroken: instituted according to established forms: (*geom.*) having all the sides and angles equal: belonging to the permanent army: as opp. to 'secular' in the R. Cath. Church, denoting monks, friars, &c. under a monastic rule.—*n.* a soldier belonging to the permanent army.—*adv.* **Reg'ularly**. [L. *regularis—regula,* a rule—*rego,* to rule.]

**Regularity**, reg-ū-lar′i-ti, *n.* quality of being regular: conformity to rule: method: uniformity

**Regulate**, reg′ū-lāt, *v.t.* to make *regular*: to adjust by rule: to subject to rules or restrictions: to put in good order.

**Regulation**, reg-ū-lā′shun, *n.* act of regulating: state of being regulated: a rule or order prescribed: precept: law.

**Regulative**, reg′ū-la-tiv, *adj.* tending to regulate.

**Regulator**, reg′ū-lā-tor, *n.* one who or that which regulates: a lever which regulates the motion of a watch, &c.: anything that regulates motion.

**Regulus**, reg′ū-lus, *n.* an intermediate and impure product in the smelting of metallic ores. [Lit. 'little king,' L.; a name given by the alchemists.]

**Rehabilitate**, rē-ha-bil′i-tāt, *v.t.* (*law*) to reinstate, restore to former privileges. [Fr. *réhabiliter*—L. *re,* again, *habeo,* to have.]

**Rehearsal**, re-hèrs′al, *n.* act of rehearsing: recital: recital before public representation.

**Rehearse**, re-hèrs′, *v.t.* to repeat what has already been said: to narrate: to recite before a public representation.—*n.* **Rehears'er**. [Lit. 'to harrow again,' O. Fr. *rehercer—re,* again, *herce* (Fr. *herse*), a harrow. See **Hearse**.]

**Reign**, rān, *n.* rule: dominion: royal authority: supreme power: influence: time during which a sovereign rules.—*v.t.* to rule: to have sovereign power: to be predominant. [Fr. *règne* —L. *regnum—rego,* to rule.]

**Reimburse**, rē-im-burs′, *v.t.* to refund: to pay an equivalent to for loss or expense. [Fr. *rembourser—re,* back, and *embourser,* to put in a purse, from *bourse,* a purse. See **Purse**.]

**Reimbursement**, rē-im-burs′ment, *n.* act of *reimbursing* or repaying.

**Rein**, rān, *n.* the strap of a bridle: an instrument for curbing or governing: government.—*v.t.* to govern with the rein or bridle: to restrain or control.—**To give the reins to**, to leave unchecked. [O. Fr. *reine* (Fr. *rêne*), through Late L. *retina,* from *retineo,* to hold back.]

**Reindeer**, rān′dēr, *n.* a kind of deer in the north, valuable for the chase and for domestic uses. [Ice. *hreinn,* O. Sw. *ren*—Lapp. *reino,* pasture (Skeat), and E. **Deer**.]

**Reinforce**, rē-in-fōrs′, *v.t.* to enforce again: to strengthen with new force or support.—*n.* **Reinforce'ment**, the act of reinforcing: additional force or assistance, esp. of troops. [L. *re,* again, and **Enforce**.]

**Reinless**, rān′les, *adj.* without rein or restraint.

**Reins**, rānz, *n.pl.* the *kidneys*: the lower part of the back over the kidneys: (*B.*) the inward parts: the heart. [Fr.—L. *renes*; Gr. *phrēn,* the midriff.]

**Reinstate**, rē-in-stāt′, *v.t.* to place in a former state. [L. *re,* again, and **Instate**.]

**Reinstatement**, rē-in-stāt′ment, *n.* act of reinstating: re-establishment.

**Reinvest**, rē-in-vest′, *v.t.* to invest again or a second time.—*n.* **Reinvest'ment**, act of *reinvesting*: a second investment. [L. *re,* again, and **Invest**.]

**Reinvigorate**, rē-in-vig′or-āt, *v.t.* to invigorate again. [L. *re,* again, and **Invigorate**.]

**Reissue**, rē-ish′ōō, *v.t.* to issue again.—*n.* a second issue. [L. *re,* again, and **Issue**.]

**Reiterate**, re-it′er-āt, *v.t.* to iterate or repeat again: to repeat again and again.—*adj.* **Reit'erative**. [L. *re,* again, and **Iterate**.]

**Reiteration**, rē-it-èr-ā′shun, *n.* act of reiterating.

**Reject**, re-jekt′, *v.t.* to throw away: to refuse: to renounce. [Lit. 'to throw back,' L. *rejicio, rejectum—re,* back, and *jacio,* to throw.]

**Rejection**, re-jek′shun, *n.* act of rejecting: refusal.

**Rejoice**, re-jois′, *v.i.* to feel and express *joy again and again*: to be glad: to exult or triumph.— *v.t.* to make joyful: to gladden. [Fr. *réjouir —re,* again, and *jouir,* to enjoy—*joie,* joy. See **Joy**.]

**Rejoicing**, re-jois′ing, *n.* act of being joyful: expression, subject, or experience of joy.

**Rejoicingly**, re-jois′ing-li, *adv.* with joy or exultation.

**Rejoin**, re-join', v.t. to join again : to unite what is separated : to meet again.—v.i. to answer to a reply. [L. re, again, and **Join**.]

**Rejoinder**, re-join'dèr, n. an answer joined on to another, an answer to a reply : (law) the defendant's answer to a plaintiff's 'replication.'

**Rejuvenescent**, re-jōō-ven-es'ent, adj., growing young again. [L. re, again, and **Juvenescent**.]

**Rekindle**, rē-kin'dl, v.t. to kindle again : to set on fire or arouse anew. [L. re, again, and **Kindle**.]

**Relapse**, re-laps', v.i. to slide, sink, or fall back : to return to a former state or practice.—n. a falling back into a former bad state. [L. relabor, relapsus—re, back or again, labor, to slip or slide.]

**Relate**, re-lāt', v.t. to describe : to tell : to ally by connection or kindred.—v.i. to have reference : to refer. [Lit. 'to bring back,' L. refero, relatum—re-, back, fero, to carry.]

**Related**, re-lāt'ed, adj. allied or connected by kindred or blood.

**Relation**, re-lā'shun, n. act of relating or telling : recital : that which is related : mutual connection betwen two things : resemblance : connection by birth or marriage.—n. **Rela'tionship**.

**Relational**, re-lā'shun-al, adj. having relation : having kindred.

**Relative**, rel'a-tiv, adj. having relation : respecting : not absolute or existing by itself : considered as belonging to something else : (gram.) expressing relation.—n. that which has relation to something else : a relation : (gram.) a pronoun which relates to something before, called its antecedent.—adv. **Rel'atively**.—n. **Relativ'ity**.

**Relax**, re-laks', v.t. to loosen one thing away from another : to slacken : to make less close : to make less severe : to relieve from attention or effort : to divert : to loosen, as the bowels : to make languid.—v.i. to become less close : to become less severe : to attend less. [L. relaxo, -atum—re-, away from, laxo, to loosen—laxus, loose, slack.]

**Relaxation**, re-laks-ā'shun, n. act of relaxing : state of being relaxed : remission of application.

**Relay**, re-lā', n. a supply of horses to relieve others on a journey. [Fr. relais—re- and laier, a byform of laisser, so that relay is a doublet of **Release**.]

**Release**, re-lēs', v.t. to let loose from : to set free : to discharge from : to relieve : to let go, as a claim : to give up a right to.—n. a setting free : discharge or acquittance : the giving up of a right or claim. [O. Fr. relaisser—re- and laisser—L. laxo. See **Relay**.]

**Relegate**, rel'e-gāt, v.t. to send away, to consign : to exile.—n. **Relega'tion**. [L. relego, -atum—re-, away, lego, to send. See **Legate**.]

**Relent**, re-lent', v.i. to slacken, to soften or grow less severe : to grow tender : to feel compassion. [Fr. ralentir, to retard—O. Fr. alentir—L. lentus, pliant, flexible.]

**Relentless**, re-lent'les, adj. without relenting : without tenderness or compassion : merciless.—adv. **Relent'lessly**.—n. **Relent'lessness**.

**Relevance**, rel'e-vans, **Relevancy**, rel'e-van-si, n. state of being relevant : pertinence : applicability.

**Relevant**, rel'e-vant, adj. bearing upon or applying to the purpose : pertinent : related. [Fr., pr.p. of relever, to raise again, relieve. See **Relieve**.]

**Reliable**, re-lī'a-bl, adj. that may be relied upon.

—adv. **Reli'ably**.—ns. **Reliabil'ity**, **Reli'ableness**.

**Reliance**, re-lī'ans, n. trust : confidence.

**Relic**, rel'ik, n. that which is left after loss or decay of the rest : a corpse : in R. Cath. Church, the body or other memorial of a saint : a memorial. [Fr. relique—L. reliquiæ—reliquo, relictum, to leave behind. See **Relinquish**.]

**Relict**, rel'ikt, n. a woman left behind her husband, a widow. [L. relicta—relinquo. See **Relinquish**.]

**Relief**, re-lēf', n. the removal of any evil : release from a post or duty : that which relieves or mitigates : aid : (fine art) the projection of a sculptured design from its ground. [Same as **Relievo**.]

**Relieve**, re-lēv', v.t. to remove from that which weighs down or depresses : to lessen : to ease : to help : to release : (fine art) to set off by contrast : (law) to redress. [Fr. relever, to raise again—L. relevo—re-, again, levo, to raise—levis, light.]

**Relievo**, **Rilievo**, re-lē'vo, n. See **Alto-relievo**, **Bass-relief**.

**Religion**, re-lij'un, n. the performance of our duties of love and obedience towards God : piety : any system of faith and worship. [Lit. 'restraint,' L. religio, -onis—re-, back, and ligo, to bind.]

**Religionist**, re-lij'un-ist, n. one attached to a religion.

**Religious**, re-lij'us, adj. pertaining to religion : concerned with or set apart to religion : pious : godly : in R. Cath. Church, bound to a monastic life : strict.—adv. **Relig'iously**. [L. religiosus.]

**Relinquish**, re-ling'kwish, v.t. to abandon : to give up : to renounce a claim to.—n. **Relin'quishment**, act of relinquishing or giving up. [O. Fr. relinquir—L. relinquo, relictum—re-, away from, linquo, to leave.]

**Reliquary**, rel'i-kwar-i, n. a small chest or casket for holding relics. [Fr. reliquaire. See **Relic**.]

**Relique**, re-lēk', n. a relic.

**Relish**, rel'ish, v.t. to like the taste of : to be pleased with.—v.i. to have an agreeable taste : to give pleasure.—n. an agreeable peculiar taste or quality : enjoyable quality : power of pleasing : inclination or taste for : appetite : just enough to give a flavour : a sauce. [O. Fr. relecher, to lick or taste again, from re and lecher—O. Ger. lecchon (Ger. lecken), E. lick. See **Lecher** and **Lick**.]

**Reluctance**, re-luk'tans, **Reluctancy**, re-luk'tan-si, n. state of being reluctant : unwillingness.

**Reluctant**, re-luk'tant, adj., struggling or striving against : unwilling : disinclined.—adv. **Reluc'tantly**. [L. reluct-ans, -antis, pr.p. of reluctor—re-, against, luctor, to struggle.]

**Rely**, re-lī', v.i. to rest or repose : to have full confidence in :—pa.t. and pa.p. relied'. [Prob. from re-, back, and **Lie**, to rest.]

**Remain**, re-mān', v.i. to stay or be left behind : to continue in the same place : to be left after or out of a greater number : to continue in an unchanged form or condition : to last.—n.pl. **Remains'**, a corpse : the literary productions of one dead. [O. Fr. remanoir, remaindre—L. remaneo—re, back, maneo, akin to Gr. menō, to stay.]

**Remainder**, re-mān'dèr, n. that which remains or is left behind after the removal of a part : an interest in an estate to come into effect after a certain other event happens. [See **Remain**.]

**Remand**, re-mand', v.t. to recommit or send

back. [L. *remando*—*re*-, back, *mando*, to order. See **Command.**]

**Remark**, re-märk', *v.t.* to *mark* or take notice of: to express what one thinks or sees: to say.—*n.* words regarding anything: notice. [Fr. *re-marquer*—*re*-, intensive, *marquer*, to mark. See **Mark.**]

**Remarkable**, re-märk'a-bl, *adj.* deserving *remark* or notice: distinguished: famous: that may excite admiration or wonder: strange: extra-ordinary.—*adv.* **Remark'ably.**—*n.* **Remark'-ableness.**

**Remediable**, re-mē'di-a-bl, *adj.* that may be remedied: curable.—*adv.* **Reme'diably.**—*n.* **Reme'diableness.**

**Remedial**, re-mē'di-al, *adj.* tending to remedy or remove.—*adv.* **Reme'dially.**

**Remedy**, rem'e-di, *n.* any medicine, appliance, or particular treatment that cures disease: that which counteracts any evil or repairs any loss. —*v.t.* to remove, counteract, or repair:—*pa.t.* and *pa.p.* rem'edied. [L. *remedium*—*re*-, back, again, *medeor*, to restore, cure.]

**Remember**, re-mem'bėr, *v.t.* to keep in mind: (*B.*) to meditate on: to bear in mind with gratitude and reverence: to attend to. [O. Fr. *remember* (Fr. *remémorer*)—L. *rememoro*—*re*-, again, *memoro*, to call to mind—*memor*, mindful. See **Memoir.**]

**Remembrance**, re-mem'brans, *n.* memory: that which serves to bring to or keep in mind: a memorial: the power of remembering: the length of time during which a thing can be remembered. [Fr.]

**Remembrancer**, re-mem'brans-ėr, *n.* that which *reminds*: a recorder: an officer of exchequer.

**Remind**, re-mīnd', *v.t.* to bring to the *mind* of *again*: to bring under the notice or consideration of. [L. *re*, again, and **Mind.**]

**Reminiscence**, rem-i-nis'ens, *n.* recollection: an account of what is remembered: the recurrence to the mind of the past. [Fr.—L. *reminiscentia*, recollections—*reminiscor*, to recall to mind—*re*-, and root *men*, whence *mens*, the mind. See **Mention.**]

**Remiss**, re-mis', *adj.*, *remitting* in attention, &c.: negligent: not punctual: slack: not vigorous. —*adv.* **Remiss'ly.**—*n.* **Remiss'ness.**

**Remissible**, re-mis'i-bl, *adj.* that may be *remitted* or pardoned.—*n.* **Remissibil'ity.**

**Remission**, re-mish'un, *n.* slackening: abatement: relinquishment of a claim: release: pardon.

**Remissive**, re-mis'iv, *adj.*, *remitting*: forgiving.

**Remit**, re-mit', *v.t.* to relax: to pardon: to resign: to transmit, as money, &c.: to put again in custody.—*v.i.* to abate in force or violence:—*pr.p.* remitt'ing; *pa.t.* and *pa.p.* remitt'ed.—*n.* **Remitt'er.** [Lit. 'to let go back,' L. *remitto*, *remissus*—*re*-, back, and *mitto*, to send.]

**Remittal**, re-mit'al, *n.* a remitting: surrender.

**Remittance**, re-mit'ans, *n.* that which is remitted: the sending of money, &c. to a distance: also the sum or thing sent.

**Remittent**, re-mit'ent, *adj.* increasing and remitting or abating alternately, as a disease.

**Remnant**, rem'nant, *n.* that which *remains behind* after a part is removed, &c.: remainder: a fragment. [Contr. of O. Fr. *remainant*, pr.p. of *remaindre*. See **Remain.**]

**Remodel**, rē-mod'l, *v.t.* to model or fashion anew. [L. *re*, again, and **Model.**]

**Remonstrance**, re-mon'strans, *n.* strong statement of reasons against an act: expostulation.

**Remonstrant**, re-mon'strant, *adj.* inclined to remonstrate.—*n.* one who remonstrates.

**Remonstrate**, re-mon'strāt, *v.i.* to set forth strong reasons against a measure. [Lit. 'to point out again and again,' L. *re*-, again, and *monstro*, to point out.]

**Remorse**, re-mors', *n.* the gnawing pain or anguish of guilt. [Lit. 'a biting again,' O. Fr. *remors* (Fr. *remords*)—Low L. *remorsus*—L. *remordeo*, *remorsum*, to bite again—*re*-, again, and *mordeo*, to bite.]      [*adv.* **Remorse'fully.**

**Remorseful**, re-mors'fool, *adj.* full of remorse.—

**Remorseless**, re-mors'les, *adj.* without remorse: cruel.—*adv.* **Remorse'lessly.**—*n.* **Remorse'-lessness.**

**Remote**, re-mōt', *adj.*, *moved back* to a distance in time or place: far: distant: primary, as a cause: not agreeing: not related.—*adv.* **Re-mote'ly.**—*n.* **Remote'ness.** [See **Remove.**]

**Remould**, rē-mōld', *v.t.* to mould or shape anew. [L. *re*, again, and **Mould.**]

**Remount**, rē-mownt', *v.t.* and *v.i.* to mount again. [L. *re*, again, and **Mount.**]

**Removable**, re-mōōv'a-bl, *adj.* that may be removed.—*n.* **Removabil'ity.**

**Removal**, re-mōōv'al, *n.* the act of taking away: displacing: change of place.

**Remove**, re-mōōv', *v.t.* to put from its place: to take away: to withdraw.—*v.i.* to go from one place to another.—*n.* any indefinite distance: a step in any scale of gradation: a dish to be changed while the rest remain. [L. *removeo*, *remotus*—*re*, away, *moveo*, to move. See **Move.**]

**Remunerable**, re-mū'nėr-a-bl, *adj.* that may be remunerated: worthy of being rewarded.

**Remunerate**, re-mū'nėr-āt, *v.t.* to render an equivalent for any service: to recompense. [L. *remuner-o*, *-atus*—*re*-, in return, *munero*, to give something—*munus*, *muneris*, a service, a gift.]      [recompense: requital.

**Remuneration**, re-mū-nėr-ā'shun, *n.* reward:—

**Remunerative**, re-mū'nėr-a-tiv, *adj.* fitted to remunerate: lucrative: yielding due return.

**Renaissance**, re-nās'ans, *n.* the period (in the 15th century) at which the revival of arts and letters took place, marking the transition from the middle ages to the modern world.—*adj.* relating to the foregoing. [Lit. second or new birth, Fr.; see **Renascent.**]

**Renal**, rē'nal, *adj.* pertaining to the *reins* or kidneys. [L. *renalis*—*renes*, *renum* (only in pl.).

**Renard**, ren'ard, *n.* a fox, so called in fables and in poetry. [Fr.—O. Ger. *Reinhard*, *Reginhart*, 'strong in counsel,' the name of the fox in a celebrated German epic poem.]

**Renascent**, re-nas'ent, *adj.* rising again into being.—*n.* **Renas'cence**, the same as **Renaissance.** [L. *renascens*, *-entis*, pr.p. of *renascor* —*re*-, again, and *nascor*, to be born.]

**Rencounter**, ren-kownt'ėr, **Rencontre**, räng-kong'tr, *n.* a meeting in contest: a casual combat: a collision. [Fr. *rencontre*—L. *re*-, against, and root of **Encounter.**]

**Rend**, rend, *v.t.* to tear asunder with force: to split:—*pa.t.* and *pa.p.* rent. [A.S. *rendan*, to tear.]

**Render**, ren'dėr, *v.t.* to give up: to make up: to deliver: to cause to be: to translate into another language: to perform.—*n.* a surrender: a payment of rent. [Fr. *rendre*—L. *reddo*—*re*-, away, and *do*, to give.]

**Rendering**, ren'dėr-ing, *n.* the act of rendering: version: translation.

**Rendezvous**, ren'de-vōō or räng'-, *n.* an appointed

place of meeting, esp. for troops or ships: a place for enlistment.—*v.i.* to assemble at any appointed place. [Fr. *rendez vous*, render yourselves—*rendre*. See **Render**.]

**Renegade**, ren′e-gād, **Renegado**, ren-e-gā′do, *n.* one faithless to principle or party: an apostate: a deserter. [Sp. *renegado*—Low L. *renegatus*—L. *re-*, inten., and *nego*, *negatus*, to deny.]

**Renew**, re-nū′, *v.t.* to make new again: to renovate: to transform to new life: to revive: to begin again: to make again: to invigorate.—*v.i.* to be made new: to begin again. [L. *re*, again, and **New**.]

**Renewable**, re-nū′a-bl, *adj.* that may be renewed.

**Renewal**, re-nū′al, *n.* renovation: regeneration: restoration.

**Rennet**, ren′et, *n.* the prepared inner membrane of a calf's stomach, used to make milk *run* together or coagulate. [From A.S. *rennan*, to cause to run; and cog. with Ger. *rensal*, (melk-)*rinse*.]

**Rennet**, ren′et, *n.* a sweet kind of apple. [Fr. *reinette*, *rainette*, dim. of *raine*, a frog—L. *rana*; so called from its spotted rind.]

**Renounce**, re-nowns′, *v.t.* to disclaim: to disown: to reject publicly and finally: to forsake.—*v.i.* to neglect to follow suit at cards. [L. *renuntio*, —*re-*, away, and *nuntio*, *-atus*, to announce—*nuntius*, a messenger.]

**Renouncement**, re-nowns′ment, *n.* act of renouncing, disclaiming, or rejecting.

**Renovate**, ren′o-vāt, *v.t.* to *renew* or *make new again*: to restore to the original state.—*n.* **Ren′ovator**. [L. *re-*, again, and *novo*, *-atus*, to make new—*novus*, new. See **New**.]

**Renovation**, ren-o-vā′shun, *n.* renewal: state of being renewed.

**Renown**, re-nown′, *n.* a great *name*: celebrity. [Fr. *renom*—L. *re-*, again, *nomen*, a name.]

**Renowned**, re-nownd′, *adj.* celebrated: illustrious: famous. [break: tear.

**Rent** rent, *n.* an opening made by *rending*: fissure:

**Rent**, rent, *n.* annual payment in return for the use of property held of another, esp. houses and lands.—*v.t.* to hold or occupy by paying rent: to let for a rent.—*v.i.* to be let for rent. [Fr. *rente*—*rendre*, to give back. See **Render**.]

**Rent**, rent, *pa.t.* and *pa.p.* of **Rend**.

**Rental**, rent′al, *n.* a schedule or account of *rents*, with the tenants' names, &c.: a rent-roll: rent.

**Renter**, rent′er, *n.* one who holds by paying rent for.

**Rent-roll**, rent′-rōl, *n.* a *roll* or account of *rents*: a rental or schedule of rents.

**Renunciation**, re-nun-si-ā′shun, *n.* disowning: rejection: abandonment. [See **Renounce**.]

**Repaid**, re-pād′, *pa.t.* and *pa.p.* of **Repay**.

**Repair**, re-pār′, *v.i.* to betake one's self to: to go: to resort.—*n.* a retreat or abode. [Fr. *repaire*, a haunt—L. *repatrio*, to return to one's country —*re-*, back, *patria*, native country.]

**Repair**, re-pār′, *v.t.* to restore after injury: to make amends for: to mend.—*n.* restoration after injury or decay: supply of loss. [Fr. *ré-parer*—L. *reparo*—*re-*, again, *paro*, to prepare.]

**Repairer**, re-pār′er, *n.* one who restores or amends.

**Reparable**, rep′ar-a-bl, *adj.* that may be *re-paired*.—*adv.* **Rep′arably**.

**Reparation**, rep-ar-ā′shun, *n.*, *repair*: supply of what is wasted: amends.

**Reparative**, re-par′a-tiv, *adj.* amending defect or injury.—*n.* that which restores to a good state: that which makes amends.

**Repartee**, rep-ar-tē′, *n.* a smart, ready, and witty reply. [Fr. *repartie*—*repartir*, to go back

again—*re-*, back, and *partir*, to set out—L. *partior*, to divide. Cf. the E. **Sally**.]

**Repast**, re-past′, *n.* a meal: the food taken: victuals. [Low L. *repastus* (whence Fr. *repas*) —L. *re-*, intensive, and *pastus*, food, feeding—*pasco*, *pastus*, to feed.]

**Repay**, re-pā′, *v.t.* to *pay back*: to make return for: to recompense: to pay again or a second time. [L. *re*, and **Pay**.]

**Repayable**, re-pā′a-bl, *adj.* that is to be *repaid*.

**Repayment**, re-pā′ment, *n.* act of repaying: the money or thing repaid.

**Repeal**, re-pēl′, *v.t.* to revoke by authority, as a law: to abrogate.—*n.* a revoking or annulling.—*n.* **Repeal′er**, one who repeals: one who seeks for a repeal. [Fr. *rappeler*—*re-*, back, and *appeler*—L. *appello*, to call. See **Appeal**.]

**Repealable**, re-pēl′a-bl, *adj.* that may be repealed.

**Repeat**, re-pēt′, *v.t.* to do again: to speak again, to iterate: to quote from memory: to rehearse. —*v.i.* to strike the hours, as a watch: to recur. —*n.* (*mus.*) a mark directing a part to be repeated. [Fr. *répéter*—L. *repeto*, *repetitus*—*re-*, again, and *peto*, to attack, seek.]

**Repeatedly**, re-pēt′ed-li, *adv.* many times repeated: again and again: frequently.

**Repeater**, re-pēt′er, *n.* one who or that which repeats: a decimal in which the same figure or figures are continually repeated: a watch that strikes again the previous hour at the touch of a spring.

**Repel**, re-pel′, *v.t.* to *drive back*: to repulse: to check the advance of.—*v.i.* to act with opposing force: (*med.*) to check or drive inwards:—*pr.p.* repell′ing; *pa.t.* and *pa.p.* repelled′.—*n.* **Repell′er**. [L. *repello*—*re-*, off, back, and *pello*, to drive.]

**Repellent**, re-pel′ent, *adj.*, *driving back*: able or tending to repel.—*n.* that which repels.

**Repent**, re-pent′, *v.i.* to regret or sorrow for what one has done or left undone: to change from past evil: (*theol.*) to feel such sorrow for sin as produces newness of life.—*v.t.* to remember with sorrow. [Fr. *repentir*—*re-*, and O. Fr. *pentir*— L. *pænitēre*, to cause to repent, from *pænio*, *punio*, to punish. See **Punish**.]

**Repentance**, re-pent′ans, *n.* sorrow for what has been done or left undone: contrition for sin, producing newness of life.

**Repentant**, re-pent′ant, *adj.*, *repenting* or sorry for past conduct: showing sorrow for sin.

**Repercussion**, rē-pėr-kush′un, *n.* a *striking* or driving *back*: reverberation: (*mus.*) frequent repetition of the same sound. [L. *repercussio*—*re-*, back, *percutio*—*per*, through, *quatio*, to strike.] [causing to reverberate.

**Repercussive**, rē-pėr-kus′iv, *adj.*, *driving back*:

**Repertory**, rep′ėr-tor-i, *n.* a place where things are kept to be *brought forth again*: a treasury: a magazine. [Fr.—L. *repertorium*—*reperio*, to find—*re-*, again, and *pario*, to bring forth.]

**Repetition**, rep-e-tish′un, *n.* act of *repeating*: recital from memory.

**Repine**, re-pīn′, *v.i.* to *pine again* or continue to pine (*at* or *against*): to fret one's self: to feel discontent: to murmur: to envy.—*adv.* **Repin′-ingly**.—*n.* **Repin′er**. [L. *re*, again, and **Pine**, *v.*]

**Replace**, re-plās′, *v.t.* to *place back*: to put again in a former place, condition, &c.: to repay: to provide a substitute for: to take the place of. [L. *re*, back, again, and **Place**.]

**Replacement**, re-plās′ment, *n.* act of *replacing*.

**Replenish**, re-plen′ish, *v.t.* to *fill again*: to fill completely: to stock abundantly.—*n.* **Replen′-**

**ishment.** [O. Fr. *replenir*, from *replein*, full—L. *re-*, again, and *plenus*, full.   See **Full**.]

**Replete,** re-plēt', *adj.* full: completely filled. [L. *repletus*, pa.p. of *repleo*—*re-*, again, and *pleo*, to fill.]                          [(*med.*) fullness of blood.

**Repletion,** re-plē'shun, *n.* superabundant fullness:

**Replevin,** re-plev'in, *n.* an action for *replevying*.

**Replevy,** re-plev'i, *v.t.* (*law*) to recover goods distrained upon giving a *pledge* or security to try the right to them at law.—*adj.* **Replev'iable.** [O. Fr. *replevir*—*re-*, back, and *plevir*, to pledge.  See **Pledge**.]

**Replica,** rep'li-ka, *n.* (*paint.*) a copy of a picture done by the same hand that did the original. [It.—L. *replico*.  See **Reply**.]

**Replication,** rep-li-kā'shun, *n.* a reply: (*law*) the plaintiff's answer to a plea. [See **Reply**.]

**Reply,** re-plī', *v.t.* and *v.i.* to answer:—*pa.t.* and *pa.p.* replied'.—*n.* an answer.—*n.* **Repli'er.** [Fr. *répliquer*—L. *replico, -atus*—*re-*, back, and *plico*, to fold.]

**Report,** re-pōrt', *v.t.* to *bring back*, as an answer or account of anything: to give an account of: to relate: to circulate publicly: to write down or take notes of, esp. for a newspaper.—*v.i.* to make a statement: to write an account of occurrences. —*n.* a statement of facts: description: a formal or official statement, esp. of a judicial opinion or decision: rumour: sound: noise: (*B.*) reputation.—*n.* **Report'er,** one who reports, esp. for a newspaper. [L. *reporto*—*re-*, back, and *porto*, to carry.]

**Repose,** re-pōz', *v.t.* to lay at rest: to compose: to place in trust (with *on* or *in*).—*v.i.* to rest: to sleep: to rest in confidence (with *on* or *upon*): to lie.—*n.* a lying at rest: sleep: quiet: rest of mind: (*fine art*) that harmony which gives rest to the eye. [Fr. *reposer*—*re-*, back, and *poser*. See **Pose,** *n.*]

**Reposit,** re-poz'it, *v.t.* to lodge, as for safety.

**Repository,** re-poz'i-tor-i, *n.* a place where anything is laid up for safe keeping.

**Repossess,** rē-poz-zes', *v.t.* to possess again. [L. *re*, again, and **Possess**.]

**Reprehend,** rep-re-hend', *v.t.* to blame: to reprove. [L. *reprehendo, -hensus*—*re-*, inten., and *prehendo*, to lay hold of.  See **Hand**.]

**Reprehensible,** rep-re-hen'si-bl, *adj.* worthy of being reprehended or blamed.—*adv.* **Reprehen'sibly.**                                [sure.

**Reprehension,** rep-re-hen'shun, *n.* reproof: cen-

**Reprehensive,** rep-re-hen'siv, *adj.* containing reproof: given in reproof.

**Represent,** rep-re-zent', *v.t.* to exhibit the image of: to serve as a sign of: to personate or act the part of: to stand in the place of: to bring before the mind: to describe. [L. *represento, -atum*—*re-*, again, and *præsento*, to place before.  See **Present,** *v.*]               [represented.

**Representable,** rep-re-zent'a-bl, *adj.* that may be

**Representation,** rep-re-zen-tā'shun, *n.* act of representing or exhibiting: that which represents: an image: picture: dramatic performance: part performed by a representative: statement.

**Representative,** rep-re-zent'a-tiv, *adj.* representing: showing a likeness: bearing the character or power of others: presenting the full character of a class.—*n.* one who stands for another, a deputy, delegate: (*law*) an heir. [Fr.]

**Repress,** re-pres', *v.t.* to check or restrain. [L. *re*, back, and **Press**.]                       [straint.

**Repression,** re-presh'un, *n.* act of repressing: re-

**Repressive,** re-pres'iv, *adj.* tending or able to repress.—*adv.* **Repress'ively.**

**Reprieve,** re-prēv', *v.t.* to delay the execution of a criminal: to give a respite to.—*n.* a suspension of a criminal sentence: interval of ease or relief. [Lit. to disapprove or disallow (the sentence passed), O. Fr. *repruver* (Fr. *réprouver*)—L. *reprobo*.  See **Reprove**.]

**Reprimand,** rep'ri-mand or -mand', *n.* a severe reproof.—*v.t.* to chide: to reprove severely: to administer reproof publicly or officially. [Fr. *réprimande*—L. *reprimendum*—*reprimo, repressum*, to press back—*re-*, and *primo*, to press.]

**Reprint,** re-print', *v.t.* to print again: to print a new impression of.—*n.* **Re'print,** another impression of. [L. *re*, again, and **Print**.]

**Reprisal,** re-prīz'al, *n.* a *seizing back* or in retaliation: (*war*) the retaking of goods captured by an enemy: anything seized in retaliation: that which is seized for injury inflicted. [Fr. *représaille*—It. *ripresaglia*—*ripreso* (Fr. *reprise*), retaken—L. *re-pre(he)ndere*, to seize again.  See **Apprehend** and **Get**.]

**Reproach,** re-prōch', *v.t.* to cast in one's teeth: to censure severely: to upbraid: to revile: to treat with contempt.—*n.* the act of reproaching: reproof: censure: blame in opprobrious language: disgrace: an object of scorn. [Lit. to *bring* (some offence) *back* or *near* to one, Fr. *reprocher* —*re-*, and *proche*, near—L. *propius*, comp. of *prope*, near.]

**Reproachable,** re-prōch'a-bl, *adj.* deserving reproach: opprobrious.—*adv.* **Reproach'ably.**

**Reproachful,** re-prōch'fool, *adj.* full of reproach or blame: abusive: scurrilous: bringing reproach: shameful: disgraceful.—*adv.* **Reproach'fully.**

**Reprobate,** rep'ro-bāt, *adj.* condemned: base: given over to sin: depraved: vile: (*B.*) that will not stand proof or trial.—*n.* an abandoned or profligate person.—*v.t.* to disapprove: to censure: to disown. [L. *reprobatus*, pa.p. of *reprobo*.  See **Reprove**.]

**Reprobation,** rep-ro-bā'shun, *n.* the act of reprobating: rejection: the act of abandoning to destruction: state of being so abandoned.

**Reproduce,** rē-pro-dūs', *v.t.* to produce again: to form anew. [L. *re*, again, and **Produce**.]

**Reproduction,** rē-pro-duk'shun, *n.* the act of producing new organisms.                       [produce.

**Reproductive,** rē-pro-dukt'iv, *adj.* tending to re-

**Reproof,** re-proōf', *n.* a *reproving* or blaming: rebuke: censure: reprehension.

**Reprovable,** re-proōv'a-bl, *adj.* deserving reproof, blame, or censure.—*adv.* **Reprov'ably.**

**Reprove,** re-proōv', *v.t.* to condemn: to chide: to censure: (*B.*) to disprove or refute.—*n.* **Reprov'er.** [Fr. *réprouver*—L. *reprobo*, the opposite of *approbo* (see **Approve**)—*re-*, off, away, rejection, and *probo*, to try or prove.  See **Prove**.]

**Reptile,** rep'til or -tīl, *adj.* moving or *crawling* on the belly or with very short legs: grovelling: low.—*n.* an animal that moves or crawls on its belly or with short legs: a grovelling, low person. [L. *reptilis*—*repo, serpo*, Gr. *herpō*, Sans. *srip*, to creep.]

**Reptilian,** rep-til'yan, *adj.* belonging to reptiles.

**Republic,** re-pub'lik, *n.* a commonwealth: a form of government without a monarch, in which the supreme power is vested in representatives elected by the people. [Fr. *république*—L. *respublica,* 'common weal.'  See **Public**.]

**Republican,** re-pub'lik-an, *adj.* belonging to a republic: agreeable to the principles of a republic. —*n.* one who advocates a republican form of government: a democrat.

**Republicanism,** re-pub'lik-an-izm, *n.* the principles

of republican government : attachment to republican government.

**Republish**, rē-pub′lish, *v.t.* to publish again or anew.—*n.* **Republica′tion**. [L. *re*, again, and **Publish**.]

**Repudiate**, re-pū′di-āt, *v.t.* to reject : to disclaim : to disavow.—*n.* **Repu′diator**. [L. *repudio*, *repudiatus*—*repudium*, a putting away—*re-*, away, and *pudēre*, to be ashamed.]

**Repudiation**, re-pū-di-ā′shun, *n.* the act of repudiating : rejection : the state of being repudiated. [L. *repudiatio*, *-onis*.]

**Repugnance**, re-pug′nans, *n.* the state of being repugnant : resistance : aversion : reluctance. [L. *repugnantia*. See **Repugnant**.]

**Repugnant**, re-pug′nant, *adj.* hostile : adverse : contrary : distasteful.—*adv.* **Repug′nantly**. [L. *repugno*—*re-*, against, and *pugno*, to fight.]

**Repulse**, re-puls′, *v.t.* to *drive back* : to repel : to beat off.—*n.* the state of being repulsed or driven back : the act of repelling : refusal. [L. *repulsus*, pa.p. of *repello*—*re-*, off, back, and *pello*, to drive. See **Pulsate**.]

**Repulsion**, re-pul′shun, *n.* act of repulsing or driving back : state of being repelled : power by which bodies or their particles repel each other.

**Repulsive**, re-puls′iv, *adj.* that repulses or drives off : repelling : cold, reserved, forbidding.—*adv.* **Repuls′ively**.—*n.* **Repuls′iveness**.

**Repurchase**, rē-pur′chās, *v.t.* to purchase or buy back or again.—*n.* the act of buying again : that which is bought again. [L. *re*, again, **Purchase**.]

**Reputable**, rep′ūt-a-bl, *adj.* in good repute or esteem : respectable : honourable : consistent with reputation.—*adv.* **Rep′utably**.—*n.* **Rep′utableness**.

**Reputation**, rep-ū-tā′shun, *n.* state of being held in repute : estimation : character as established in public opinion : credit : fame. [Fr.—L. *reputatio*, consideration—*re-putare*, to think over.]

**Repute**, re-pūt′, *v.t.* to account or estimate : to hold.—*n.* estimate : established opinion : character. [L. *reputo*, *-atum*—*re-*, again, and *puto*, to reckon, to count.] [estimation.

**Reputedly**, re-pūt′ed-li, *adv.* in common *repute* or

**Request**, re-kwest′, *v.t.* to ask for earnestly : to entreat : to desire.—*n.* petition : prayer : desire : demand : that which is requested : a want : the state of being desired. [L. *requisitum*, pa.p. of *requiro*—*re-*, away, and *quæro*, to seek.]

**Requiem**, rē′kwi-em or rek′-, *n.* a hymn or mass sung for the *quiet* or rest of the soul of the dead : a grand musical composition in honour of the dead. [L., acc. of *requies*—(*re-*, intensive, and *quies*, rest) ; so called from the words *Requiem æternam dona eis, Domine*, 'Give eternal rest to them, O Lord !' which are repeated in the service.]

**Requirable**, re-kwīr′a-bl, *adj.* that may be required : fit or proper to be required.

**Require**, re-kwīr′, *v.t.* to ask : to demand : to need : to exact : to direct. [L. *requiro*.]

**Requirement**, re-kwīr′ment, *n.* the act of requiring : that which is required : claim : demand.

**Requisite**, rek′wi-zit, *adj., required* : needful : indispensable.—*n.* that which is required : anything necessary or indispensable.

**Requisition**, rek-wi-zish′un, *n.* the act of *requiring* : an application : a demand : a written request or invitation.—*n.* **Requisi′tionist**, one who makes a requisition. [L. *requisitio*.]

**Requital**, re-kwīt′al, *n.* the act of requiting : payment in return : recompense : reward.

**Requite**, re-kwīt′, *v.t.* to give *back* so as to be

quits : to repay : to pay in return. [L. *re*, back, and **Quit**.]

**Reredos**, rēr′dos, *n.* the wall of a church *behind* the altar : an ornamental screen there placed. [Fr. *arrière*, behind—L. *ad*, and *retro*, and Fr. *dos*, back—L. *dorsum*.]

**Reremouse**, rēr′mows, *n.* a bat. [Lit. 'the mouse that moves' or agitates the air with its wings. A.S. *hreremus*—*hreran*, to move, and *mus*, a mouse.]

**Rereward**. Same as **Rearward**.

**Rescind**, re-sind′, *v.t.* to *cut away* or off : to annul : to repeal : to reverse. [L. *rescindo*, *rescissum*—*re-*, and *scindo*, to cut. See **Scissors**.]

**Rescission**, re-sizh′un, *n.* the act of *rescinding* : the act of annulling or repealing.—*adj.* **Resciss′ory**.

**Rescript**, rē′skript, *n.* the official answer of a pope or an emperor to any legal question ; an edict or decree. [Lit. 'that which is written in return,' L. *rescriptum*—*re-*, back, *scribo*, *scriptum*, to write.]

**Rescue**, res′kū, *v.t.* to free from danger or violence : to deliver : to liberate.—*n.* the act of rescuing : deliverance from violence or danger : forcible release from arrest or imprisonment :—*pr.p.* res′cūing ; *pa.t.* and *pa.p.* res′cūed. [M. E. *rescous*—O. Fr. *rescousse*—O. Fr. *rescourre*—L. *re*, away, and *excutere*, to shake out—*ex*, out, and *quatio*, to shake.]

**Research**, re-sėrch′, *n.* a careful search : diligent examination or investigation : scrutiny. [L. *re*, inten., and **Search**.]

**Resemblance**, re-zem′blans, *n.* the state of resembling : similitude : likeness : similarity : that which is similar.

**Resemble**, re-zem′bl, *v.t.* to be *similar* to : to have the likeness of : to possess similar qualities or appearance : to compare : to make like. [Fr. *ressembler*—*re-*, and *sembler*, to seem—L. *simulo*, to make like—*similis*, like. Cf. **Assimilate** and **Assemble**.]

**Resent**, re-zent′, *v.t.* (*orig.*) to take well : to take ill : to consider as an injury or affront : to be indignant at : to express indignation. [Fr. *ressentir*, from L. *re-*, in return, and *sentio*, to perceive, to feel.]

**Resentful**, re-zent′fool, *adj.* full of or prone to resentment.—*adv.* **Resent′fully**.

**Resentment**, re-zent′ment, *n.* the act of resenting : displeasure : anger : indignation : wrath.

**Reservation**, rez-ėr-vā′shun, *n.* the act of *reserving* or *keeping back* : the withholding from a statement of a word or clause necessary to convey its real meaning : something withheld : a clause, proviso, or limitation by which something is reserved.

**Reserve**, re-zėrv′, *v.t.* to *keep back* : to keep for future or other use : to retain.—*n.* that which is *reserved* : that which is kept for future use : a part of an army or a fleet reserved to assist those engaged in action : that which is kept back in the mind : mental concealment : absence of freedom in words or actions : caution. [L. *reservo*—*re-*, back, and *servo*, to save, to keep.]

**Reserved**, re-zėrvd′, *adj.* characterised by reserve : not free or frank in words or behaviour : shy : cold.—*adv.* **Reserv′edly**.—*n.* **Reserv′edness**.

**Reservoir**, rez-ėr-vwor′, *n.* a place where anything is *reserved* or kept in store : a place where water is collected and stored for use. [Fr.]

**Reset**, rē-set′, *v.t.* to set again or anew.

**Reset**, re-set′, *v.t.* (*Scot.*) to receive and hide, as stolen goods. [Perh. a corr. of **Receipt**.]

fāte, fär ; mē, hèr ; mīne ; mōte ; mūte ; mōōn ; *then*.

**Reside**, re-zīd', *v.i.* to remain *sitting*: to dwell permanently: to abide: to live: to inhere. [L. *resideo—re-*, back, and *sedeo*, to sit.]

**Residence**, rez'i-dens, *n.* act of residing or of dwelling in a place: place where one resides.

**Residency**, rez'i-den-si, *n.* residence: the official dwelling of a government officer in India.

**Resident**, rez'i-dent, *adj.*, *residing* or dwelling in a place for some time: residing in the place of his duties.—*n.* one who resides: a public minister at a foreign court.

**Residential**, rez-i-den'shal, *adj.* residing: having actual residence.

**Residentiary**, rez-i-den'shar-i, *adj.*, *residing.*—*n.* one who keeps a certain residence, esp. an ecclesiastic.

**Residual**, re-zid'ū-al, *adj.* remaining as residue.

**Residuary**, re-zid'ū-ar-i, *adj.* pertaining to the residue: receiving the remainder.

**Residue**, rez'i-dū, *n.* that which is *left behind* after a part is taken away: the remainder. [L. *residuum*, from *resideo*, to remain behind. See Reside.]

**Residuum**, re-zid'ū-um, *n.*, *residue*: that which is left after any process of purification. [L.]

**Resign**, re-zīn', *v.t.* to yield up to another: to submit calmly. [L. *resigno, -atus*, to unseal, to annul, to give back—*re*, sig. reversal, *signo*, to mark, to seal—*signum*, a mark.]

**Resignation**, rez-ig-nā'shun, *n.* act of resigning or giving up: state of being resigned or quietly submissive: acquiescence: patience. [Fr.—Low L.—L. *resigno.*]

**Resilience**, re-zil'i-ens, **Resiliency**, re-zil'i-en-si, *n.* act of *springing back* or rebounding.

**Resilient**, re-zil'i-ent, *adj.*, *springing back* or rebounding. [L. *resili-ens, -entis*, pr.p. of *re-silio—re-*, back, and *salio*, to leap or spring.]

**Resin**, rez'in, *n.* an inflammable substance, which exudes from trees. [Fr. *résine*—L. *resīna.*]

**Resinous**, rez'in-us, *adj.* having the qualities of or resembling resin.—*adv.* **Res'inously.**—*n.* **Res'-inousness.**

**Resiny**, rez'in-i, *adj.* like resin.

**Resist**, re-zist', *v.t.* to strive against: to oppose.—*v.i.* to make opposition. [L. *resisto—re-*, against, and *sisto*, to stand.]

**Resistance**, re-zist'ans, *n.* act of resisting: opposition: (*mech.*) the power of a body which acts in opposition to the impulse of another.

**Resistible**, re-zist'i-bl, *adj.* that may be resisted.—*adv.* **Resist'ibly.**—*n.* **Resistibil'ity.**

**Resistless**, re-zist'les, *adj.* irresistible.—*adv.* **Resist'lessly.**—*n.* **Resist'lessness.**

**Resolute**, rez'o-lūt, *adj.*, *resolved*: determined: having a fixed purpose: constant in pursuing a purpose.—*adv.* **Res'olutely.**—*n.* **Res'oluteness.**

**Resolution**, rez-o-lū'shun, *n.* act of *resolving*: analysis: solution: state of being resolved: fixed determination: steadiness: that which is resolved: formal proposal in a public assembly.

**Resolvable**, re-zolv'a-bl, *adj.* that may be resolved or reduced to its elements.—*adv.* **Resolv'ably.**

**Resolve**, re-zolv', *v.t.* to separate into parts: to analyse: to free from doubt or difficulty: to explain: to decide: to fix by resolution or formal declaration: (*math.*) to solve: (*med.*) to disperse, as a tumour: (*music*) to carry a discord into a concord.—*v.i.* to determine.—*n.* anything resolved or determined: resolution: fixed purpose. [L. *resolvo, resolutum—re*, inten., and *solvo*, to loose.]

**Resolved**, re-zolvd', *adj.* fixed in purpose.—*adv.* **Resolv'edly.**—*n.* **Resolv'edness.**

**Resonance**, rez'o-nans, *n.* act of *resounding*: the returning of sound by reflection or by the production of vibrations in other bodies.

**Resonant**, rez'o-nant, *adj.*, *sounding back*: returning sound. [L. *resono—re-*, back, and *sono*, to sound.]

**Resort**, re-zort', *v.i.* to go: to betake one's self: to have recourse: to apply.—*n.* act of resorting: a place much frequented: a haunt: resource. [Fr. *ressortir*, lit. 'to obtain again,' from *re-* and L. *sortiri*, to cast lots, to obtain—*sors, sortis*, a lot.]

**Resound**, re-zownd', *v.t.* to *sound back*: to echo: to praise or celebrate with sound: to spread the fame of.—*v.i.* to be sent back or echoed: to echo: to sound loudly: to be much mentioned. [L. *re*, back, and Sound.]

**Resource**, re-sōrs', *n.* a source of help: an expedient:—*pl.* means of raising money: means of any kind. [Fr. *ressource*—O. Fr. *resors*, from *resordre*—L. *re-surgere*, to rise again.]

**Respect**, re-spekt', *v.t.* to esteem for merit: to honour: to relate to.—*n.* act of esteeming highly: regard: expression of esteem: deportment arising from esteem: relation: reference: (*B.*) good-will: partiality. [Lit. 'to look back upon,' L. *respicio, respectum—re*, back, and *specio*, to look.]

**Respectable**, re-spekt'a-bl, *adj.* worthy of respect or regard: moderate in excellence or number: not mean or despicable.—*adv.* **Respect'ably.**—*n.* **Respectabil'ity**, state or quality of being respectable.

**Respectful**, re-spekt'fool, *adj.* full of respect: marked by civility.—*adv.* **Respect'fully.**

**Respective**, re-spekt'iv, *adj.* having *respect* or reference *to*: relative: relating to a particular person or thing: particular.—*adv.* **Respect'ively.**

**Respirable**, re-spīr'a-bl, *adj.* that may be *breathed*: fit for respiration.—*n.* **Respirabil'ity**, quality of being respirable.

**Respiration**, res-pi-rā'shun, *n.* the function of breathing.

**Respirator**, res'pi-rā-tor, *n.* a network of fine wire for respiring or breathing through.

**Respiratory**, re-spīr'a-tor-i, *adj.* pertaining to or serving for respiration.

**Respire**, re-spīr', *v.i.* to *breathe again* and *again*: to breathe: to take rest.—*v.t.* to breathe ou'. [L. *respiro—re-*, sig. repetition, continuance, and *spiro, -atum*, to breathe.]

**Respite**, res'pit, *n.* temporary cessation of anything: pause: interval of rest: (*law*) temporary suspension of the execution of a criminal.—*v.t.* to grant a respite to: to relieve by a pause: to delay. [O. Fr. *respit* (Fr. *répit*)—L. *respectus.* Doublet Respect.]

**Resplendence**, re-splen'dens, **Resplendency**, re-splen'den-si, *n.* state of being resplendent.

**Resplendent**, re-splen'dent, *adj.* very splendid: shining brilliantly: very bright.—*adv.* **Resplen'dently.** [L. *resplendeo—re-*, inten., and *splendeo*, to shine.]

**Respond**, re-spond', *v.i.* to answer or reply: to correspond to or suit: to be answerable. [L. *respondeo, responsum—re-*, back, and *spondeo*, to promise. See Sponsor.]

**Respondent**, re-spond'ent, *adj.* answering: corresponding to expectation.—*n.* one who answers, esp. in a lawsuit: one who refutes objections.

**Response**, re-spons', *n.* a reply: an oracular answer: the answer made by the congregation to the priest during divine service: reply to an objection in a formal disputation. [See Respond.]

**Responsibility**, re-spon-si-bil′i-ti, *n*. state of being *responsible*: what one is responsible for.

**Responsible**, re-spon′si-bl, *adj*. liable to be called to account or render satisfaction: answerable: capable of discharging duty.—*adv*. **Respon′sibly**.

**Responsions**, re-spon′shuns, *n*. the first of the three examinations for the B.A. degree at Oxford, familiarly called 'smalls.' [See **Respond**.]

**Responsive**, re-spon′siv, *adj*. inclined to *respond*: answering: correspondent.—*adv*. **Respon′sively**.

**Rest**, rest, *n*. cessation from motion or disturbance: peace: quiet: sleep: the final sleep or death: place of rest: that on which anything rests; a pause of the voice in reading: (*music*) an interval of silence and its mark.—**At rest**, applied to a body, means, having no velocity with respect to that on which the body stands.—*v.i.* to cease from action or labour: to be still: to repose: to sleep: to be dead: to be supported: to lean or trust: to be satisfied: to come to an end.—*v.t.* to lay at rest: to quiet: to place on a support. [A.S.; Ger. *rast*, Dut. *rust*.]

**Rest**, rest, *n*. that which *remains* after the separation of a part: remainder: others.—*v.i.* to remain. [Fr. *reste*—L. *resto*, to remain—*re-*, back, and *sto*, to stand.]

**Restaurant**, res′to-rang or res′to-rant, *n*. a house for the sale of refreshments. [Fr.—*restaurer*, to restore. See **Restore**.]

**Restitution**, res-ti-tū′shun, *n*. act of restoring what was lost or taken away. [L. *restitutio*—*restituo*, to set up again—*re-*, again, and *statuo*, to make to stand. See **Statue**.]

**Restive**, rest′iv, *adj*. unwilling to go forward: obstinate.—*adv*. **Rest′ively**.—*n*. **Rest′iveness**. [O. Fr. *restif*, Fr. *rétif*—*reste*. See **Rest**, that which remains.]

**Restless**, rest′les, *adj*. in continual motion: uneasy: passed in unquietness: seeking change or action: unsettled: turbulent.—*adv*. **Rest′lessly**.—*n*. **Rest′lessness**. [From **Rest**, cessation from motion.]

**Restoration**, res-to-rā′shun, *n*. act of restoring: replacement: recovery: revival: reparation.

**Restorative**, re-stōr′a-tiv, *adj*., *able or tending to restore*, especially to strength and vigour.—*n*. a medicine that restores.—*adv*. **Restor′atively**.

**Restore**, re-stōr′, *v.t.* to repair: to replace: to return: to bring back to its former state: to revive: to cure.—*n*. **Restor′er**. [Fr. *restaurer* —L. *restauro*—*re-*, again, and root *sta*, to stand.]

**Restrain**, re-strān′, *v.t.* to hold back: to check: to hinder: to limit. [O. Fr. *restraindre*—L. *restringo*, *restrictum*—*re-*, back, and *stringo*, to draw or bind tightly.]

**Restraint**, re-strānt′, *n*. act of restraining: state of being restrained: want of liberty: limitation: hinderance.

**Restrict**, re-strikt′, *v.t.* to limit: to confine: to repress. [See under **Restrain**.]

**Restriction**, re-strik′shun, *n*. act of restricting: limitation: confinement.

**Restrictive**, re-strikt′iv, *adj*. having the *power* or tendency to *restrict*.—*adv*. **Restrict′ively**.

**Result**, re-zult′, *v.i.* to issue (in): to follow as a consequence.—*n*. consequence: conclusion: decision. [Fr.—L. *resulto*—*resilio*. See **Resilient**.]

**Resultant**, re-zult′ant, *adj*., *resulting* from combination.—*n*. (*physics*) a force compounded of two or more forces.

**Resumable**, re-zūm′a-bl, *adj*. liable to be taken back again, or taken up again.

**Resume**, re-zūm′, *v.t.* to *take back* what has been given: to take up again: to begin again after interruption. [L. *resumo*—*re-*, back, *sumo*, *sumptum*, to take. See **Sumptuary**.]

**Resumption**, re-zump′shun, *n*. act of resuming or taking back again.

**Resurgent**, re-sur′jent, *adj*., *rising again*, or from the dead. [L. *re-*, again, and *surgo*, *surrectum*, to rise.]

**Resurrection**, rez-ur-rek′shun, *n*. the *rising again* from the dead: the life thereafter.

**Resuscitate**, re-sus′i-tāt, *v.t.* to revive: to revivify.—*v.i.* to revive: to awaken and come to life again. [L. *re-*, again, and *suscito*—*sus*, from *subs*, for *sub*, from beneath, and *cito*, to put into quick motion—*cieo*, to make to go.]

**Resuscitation**, re-sus-i-tā′shun, *n*. act of reviving from a state of apparent death: state of being revivified.

**Resuscitative**, re-sus′i-tāt-iv, *adj*. tending to *resuscitate*: reviving: revivifying: reanimating.

**Retail**, re-tāl′, *v.t.* to sell in small parts: to deal out in small portions: to tell in broken parts, or at second-hand.—*n*. **Retail′er**. [Fr. *re-tailler*, to cut again—*re-*, again, and *tailler*, to cut. See **Detail**.]

**Retail**, rē′tāl, *n*. the sale of goods in small quantities.

**Retain**, re-tān′, *v.t.* to keep in possession: to detain: to employ by a fee paid. [Fr.—L. *retineo*—*re-*, back, and *teneo*, to hold. See **Tenure**.]

**Retainable**, re-tān′a-bl, *adj*. that may be retained.

**Retainer**, re-tān′ėr, *n*. one who is retained or kept in service: a dependent: a fee paid to a lawyer to defend a cause.

**Retaliate**, re-tal′i-āt, *v.t.* to *return like for like*: to repay.—*v.i.* to return like for like. [L. *re-talio*, *-atum*—*re-*, in return, *talio*, *-onis*, for like—*talis*, of such a kind.]

**Retaliation**, re-tal-i-ā′shun, *n*. act of retaliating: the return of like for like: retribution.

**Retaliative**, re-tal′i-a-tiv, **Retaliatory**, re-tal′i-a-tor-i, *adj*. returning like for like.

**Retard**, re-tärd′, *v.t.* to keep back: to delay: to defer. [Fr.—L. *retardo*—*re-*, inten., and *tardo*, to make slow—*tardus*, slow. See **Tardy**.]

**Retardation**, rē-tar-dā′shun, *n*. delay: hinderance: obstacle.

**Retch**, rech, *v.i.* to try to vomit: to strain. [A.S. *hræcan*, to hawk, cog. with Ice. *hrækja*, to vomit.]

**Retention**, re-ten′shun, *n*. act or power of *retaining*: memory: restraint: custody.

**Retentive**, re-tent′iv, *adj*. having power to *retain*. —*adv*. **Retent′ively**.—*n*. **Retent′iveness**.

**Retiary**, rē′shi-ar-i, *adj*., *netlike*: constructing a web to catch prey: provided with a net. [L. *retiarius*, a gladiator who fights with a net—*rete*, a net.]

**Reticence**, ret′i-sens, **Reticency**, ret′i-sen-si, *n*. concealment by *silence*: reserve in speech.

**Reticent**, ret′i-sent, *adj*. concealing by silence: reserved in speech. [L. *reticens*, *-entis*, pr.p. of *reticeo*—*re-*, and *taceo*, to be silent.]

**Reticular**, re-tik′ū-lar, *adj*. having the form of *network*: formed with interstices.

**Reticulate**, re-tik′ū-lāt, **Reticulated**, re-tik′ū-lāt-ed, *adj*., *netted*: having the form or structure of a net: having veins crossing like network.— *n*. **Reticula′tion**.

**Reticule**, ret′i-kūl, **Reticle**, ret′i-kl, *n*. a little *network* bag: a lady's workbag. [L. *reticulum*, dim. of *rete*, a net.]

**Retiform**, ret'i-form, *adj.* having the *form* or structure of a *net*. [L. *rete*, and *forma*, form.]

**Retina**, ret'i-na, *n.* the innermost coating of the eye, consisting of a fine *network* of optic nerves. [From L. *rete*, a net.]

**Retinue**, ret'i-nū, *n.* the body of retainers who follow a person of rank : a suite. [See **Retain**.]

**Retire**, re-tīr', *v.i.* to draw back : to retreat : to recede.—*v.t.* to withdraw : to cause to retire. [Fr. *retirer*—*re-*, back, and *tirer*, from a Teut. root seen in Goth. *tairan*, Ger. *zerren*, E. **Tear**.]

**Retirement**, re-tīr'ment, *n.* act of retiring or withdrawing from society or from public life : state of being retired : solitude : privacy.

**Retort**, re-tort', *v.t.* to throw back : to return.—*v.i.* to make a sharp reply.—*n.* a ready and sharp reply : a witty answer : a vessel used in distillation, properly a spiral tube. [Fr.—L. *retortum*, pa.p. of *retorqueo*—*re-*, back, and *torqueo*, to twist. See **Torture**.]

**Retouch**, rē-tuch', *v.t.* to improve, as a picture, by new touches.—*n.* the re-application of the artist's hand to a work. [L. *re*, again, and **Touch**.]

**Retrace**, rē-trās', *v.t.* to trace back : to go back by the same course : to renew the outline of. [L. *re*, back, and **Trace**.]

**Retract**, re-trakt', *v.t.* to retrace or draw back : to recall : to recant.—*v.i.* to take back what has been said or granted.—*n.* **Retracta'tion**. [L. *re-traho, retractum*—*re-*, back, and *traho*, to draw.]

**Retractile**, re-trakt'il, *adj.* that may be *drawn back*, as claws.

**Retraction**, re-trak'shun, *n.* act of retracting or drawing back : recantation.

**Retractive**, re-trakt'iv, *adj.* able or ready to retract.—*adv.* **Retract'ively**.

**Retreat**, re-trēt', *n.* a *drawing back* or retracing one's steps : retirement : place of privacy : a place of security : a shelter : (*mil.*) the act of retiring in order from before the enemy, or from an advanced position : the signal for retiring from an engagement or to quarters.—*v.i.* to draw back : to retire, esp. to a place of shelter or security : to retire before an enemy or from an advanced position. [O. Fr. *retret* (Fr. *re-traite*)—L. *retractus*, pa.p. of *retraho*.]

**Retrench**, re-trensh', *v.t.* to cut off or away : to render less : to curtail.—*v.i.* to live at less expense : to economise. [O. Fr. *retrencher* (Fr. *retrancher*)—*re-*, and *trencher*, to cut, which, acc. to Littré, is from L. *truncare*, to cut off, maim.]

**Retrenchment**, re-trensh'ment, *n.* cutting off : lessening or abridging : reduction : (*fort.*) a work within another for prolonging the defence.

**Retribution**, re-tri-bū'shun, *n.* repayment : suitable return : reward or punishment. [L. *retributio*—*retribuo*, to give back—*re-*, back, and *tribuo*, to give. See **Tribute**.]

**Retributive**, re-trib'ū-tiv, *adj.* repaying : rewarding or punishing suitably.

**Retrievable**, re-trēv'a-bl, *adj.* that may be *recovered*.—*adv.* **Retriev'ably**.

**Retrieve**, re-trēv', *v.t.* to recover : to recall or bring back : to bring back to a former state : to repair.—*n.* **Retriev'al**. [O. Fr. *retruver*, Fr. *re-trouver*—*re-*, again, and *trouver*, to find. Cf. **Contrive** and (for the vowel change) **Reprieve**.]

**Retriever**, re-trēv'ér, *n.* a kind of dog trained to find and fetch game that has been shot, and to recover anything lost. [See **Retrieve**.]

**Retrocession**, rē-tro-sesh'un, *n.* a *going back* : a giving back. [L. *retrocessus*—*retrocedo*, to go back, to yield—*retro*, back, and *cedo*, to go.]

**Retrograde**, rē'tro-grād, *adj.*, *going backward* : falling from better to worse : (*biology*) becoming less highly organised.—*v.i.* to go backwards.—*n.* **Retrograda'tion**. [L. *retrogradus*—*retro*, backward, and *gradior, gressus*, to go.]

**Retrogression**, rē-tro-gresh'un, *n.* a *going backward* : a decline in quality or merit.—*adj.* **Retrogress'ive**.—*adv.* **Retrogress'ively**. [See **Retrograde**.]

**Retrospect**, rē'tro-spekt, *n.* a *looking back* : a contemplation of the past. [L. *retrospectus*, pa.p. of *retrospicio*—*retro*, back, and *specio*, to look.]

**Retrospection**, rē-tro-spek'shun, *n.* the act or faculty of *looking back* on the past.—*adj.* **Retrospect'ive**.—*adv.* **Retrospect'ively**.

**Return**, re-turn', *v.i.* to come back to the same place or state : to answer : to retort.—*v.t.* to bring or send back : to transmit : to give back : to repay : to give back in reply : to report : to give an account.—*n.* the act of going back : revolution : periodic renewal : the act of bringing or sending back : restitution : repayment : the profit on capital or labour : a reply : a report or account, esp. official :—*pl.* a light tobacco. [Fr. *retourner*—*re-*, back, and *tourner*, to turn—L. *tornare*. See **Turn**.]

**Returnable**, re-turn'a-bl, *adj.* that may be returned or restored.

**Reunion**, rē-ūn'yun, *n.* a union after separation : an assembly. [Fr. *réunion*—*re-*, and *union*. See **Union**.]

**Reunite**, rē-ū-nīt', *v.t.* to join after separation : to reconcile after variance.—*v.i.* to become united again : to join again. [L. *re*, again, and **Unite**.]

**Reveal**, re-vēl', *v.t.* to *unveil* : to make known : to disclose. [Fr. *révéler*—L. *revelo*—*re-*, reversal, and *velo*, to veil—*velum*, a veil. See **Veil**.]

**Reveille**, rā-vel'yā, *n.* the sound of the drum or bugle at daybreak to *awaken* soldiers. [Lit. 'awake,' imperative of Fr. *réveiller*, to awake—*re-*, again, and *veiller*—L. *vigilare*, to watch. See **Vigil**.]

**Revel**, rev'el, *v.i.* to feast in a riotous or noisy manner : to carouse :—*pr.p.* rev'elling ; *pa.t.* and *pa.p.* rev'elled.—*n.* a riotous or tumultuous feast : carousal.—*n.* **Rev'eller**. [O. Fr. *reveler*—L. *rebellare*, to rebel. See **Rebel** ; prob. influenced also by Fr. *réveiller* (see **Reveille**), and *rêve* (see **Rave**).]

**Revelation**, rev-e-lā'shun, *n.* the act of *revealing* or making known : that which is revealed : the revealing divine truth : that which is revealed by God to man : the Apocalypse or last book of the New Testament. [Fr.—L. *revelatio*—*revelo*. See **Reveal**.]

**Revelry**, rev'el-ri, *n.* riotous or noisy festivity.

**Revenge**, re-venj', *v.t.* to punish or injure in return : to avenge.—*n.* the act of revenging : injury inflicted in return : a malicious injuring in return for an offence or injury received : the passion for retaliation.—*n.* **Reveng'er**. [O. Fr. *revenger, revencher* (Fr. *revancher*)—L. *re-*, in return, and *vindico*, to lay claim to. See **Vindicate** and **Vengeance**.]

**Revengeful**, re-venj'fool, *adj.* full of revenge or a desire to inflict injury in return : vindictive : malicious.—*adv.* **Revenge'fully**.

**Revengement**, re-venj'ment, *n.* (*B.*) revenge.

**Revenue**, rev'en-ū, *n.* the receipts or rents from any source : return : income : the income of a state. [Lit. 'that which comes back,' Fr.

*revenue*, pa.p. of *revenir*, to return—L. *revenire*
—*re*-, back, *venio*, to come.]

**Reverberate**, re-vèr'bèr-āt, *v.t.* to send back, as
sound : to echo : to reflect : to drive from side
to side, as flame.—*v.i.* to echo : to resound : to
bound back : to be repelled.—*n.* **Reverbera'-
tion.** [Lit. 'to beat back,' L. *re*-, back, and
*verber-o*, *-atus*, to beat—*verber*, a lash.]

**Reverberatory**, re-vèr'bèr-a-tor-i, *adj.* that rever-
berates : returning or driving back.

**Revere**, re-vēr', *v.t.* to regard with respectful
awe : to venerate. [Fr. *révérer*—L. *revereor*—
*re*-, intensive, and *vereor*, to feel awe, akin to
Gr. *horaō*, O. Ger. *warten*, E. **Ward**.]

**Reverence**, rev'èr-ens, *n.* fear arising from high
respect : respectful awe : veneration : honour :
an act of revering or obeisance : a bow or courtesy : a title of the clergy.—*v.t.* to regard with
reverence : to venerate or honour. [See **Revere**.]

**Reverend**, rev'èr-end, *adj.* worthy of reverence :
a title of the clergy : (*B.*) awful, venerable.
[Fr.—L. *reverendus*—*revereor*. See **Revere**.]

**Reverent**, rev'èr-ent, *adj.* shewing reverence :
submissive : humble.—*adv.* **Rev'erently.**

**Reverential**, rev-èr-en'shal, *adj.* proceeding from
reverence : respectful : submissive.—*adv.* **Re-
veren'tially.**

**Reverie, Revery**, rev'èr-i, *n.* an irregular train of
thoughts or fancies in meditation : voluntary
inactivity of the external senses to the impressions of surrounding objects during wakefulness. [Lit. 'a dreaming,' Fr., from *rêver*, to
dream. See **Rave**.]

**Reversal**, re-vèrs'al, *n.* the act of reversing : a
change : an overthrowing or annulling.

**Reverse**, re-vèrs', *v.t.* to place in the contrary order
or position : to change wholly : to overthrow : to
change by an opposite decision : to annul.—*n.*
that which is reversed : the opposite : the back,
esp. of a coin : change : misfortune.—*adj.* turned
backward : having an opposite direction. [L.
*reversus*, pa.p. of *reverto*, to turn back—*re*-,
back, and *verto*, to turn.]

**Reversible**, re-vèrs'i-bl, *adj.* that may be reversed.

**Reversion**, re-vèr'shun, *n.* the act of *reverting* or
returning : that which reverts or returns : the
return or future possession of any property after
some particular event : the right to future possession. [L. *reversio*.]

**Reversionary**, re-vèr'shun-ar-i, *adj.* relating to a
reversion : to be enjoyed in succession.

**Revert**, re-vèrt', *v.t.* to turn or drive *back* : to
*reverse*.—*v.i.* to return : to fall back : to refer
back : to return to the original owner or his
heirs. [L. *reverto*.]                    [be reverted.

**Revertible**, re-vèrt'i-bl, *adj.* that may revert or

**Revery.** Same as **Reverie.**

**Review**, re-vū', *v.t.* to re-examine : to revise : to
examine critically : to inspect, as a body of
troops.—*n.* a viewing again : a reconsideration :
a careful or critical examination : a critique : a
periodical with critiques of books, &c. : the
inspection of a body of troops or a number of
ships. [Fr. *revue*, pa.p. of *revoir*—L. *re*-,
again, and *video*. See **View**.]          [review.

**Reviewer**, re-vū'èr, *n.* an inspector : a writer in a

**Revile**, re-vīl', *v.t.* to reproach : to calumniate.—
*n.* **Revil'er.** [L. *re*, and **Vile**.]

**Revindicate**, rē-vin'di-kāt, *v.t.* to vindicate again :
to reclaim. [L. *re*, again, and **Vindicate**.]

**Revisal**, re-vīz'al, **Revision**, re-vizh'un, *n.* review :
re-examination.

**Revise**, re-vīz', *v.t.* to review and amend.—*n.*
review : a second proof-sheet.—*n.* **Revis'er.**

[Fr. *reviser*—L. *re*-, back, and *viso*, to look at
attentively, inten. of *video*, to see.]

**Revisit**, rē-viz'it, *v.t.* to visit again. [L. *re*, again,
and **Visit**.]

**Revival**, re-vīv'al, *n.* recovery from languor,
neglect, depression, &c. : renewed performance
of, as of a play : renewed interest in or attention to : a time of religious awakening.—*n.*
**Reviv'alist**, one who promotes religious re-
vivals.—*n.* **Reviv'alism.**

**Revive**, re-vīv', *v.i.* to *return* to *life*, vigour, or
fame : to recover from neglect, oblivion, or depression.—*v.t.* to restore to life again : to re-
awaken in the mind : to recover from neglect or
depression : to bring again into public notice, as
a play.—*n.* **Reviv'er.** [L. *re*-, again, and *vivo*,
to live. See **Vivid**.]

**Revivify**, re-viv'i-fī, *v.t.* to cause to revive : to
reanimate.—*n.* **Revivifica'tion.**

**Revocable**, rev'o-ka-bl, *adj.* that may be revoked.
—*ns.* **Rev'ocableness**, **Revocabil'ity**.—*adv.*
**Rev'ocably.**                              [reversal.

**Revocation**, rev-o-kā'shun, *n.* a recalling : repeal :

**Revoke**, re-vōk', *v.t.* to annul by *recalling* : to
repeal : to reverse : to neglect to follow suit (at
cards). [L. *revoco*—*re*-, back, and *voco*, to call.
See **Voice**.]

**Revolt**, re-vōlt', *v.i.* to renounce allegiance : to
be grossly offended.—*v.t.* to cause to rise in
revolt : to shock.—*n.* a rebellion.—*n.* **Revolt'er**.
[Fr.—It. *rivolta*—*ri*, against, and *volta*, a turning—L. *volvere*, to turn.]

**Revolting**, re-vōlt'ing, *adj.* causing a turning
away from : shocking.—*adv.* **Revolt'ingly.**

**Revolute**, rev'ol-ūt, *adj.* rolled backward.

**Revolution**, rev-ol-ū'shun, *n.* act of *revolving* :
motion round a centre : course which brings to
the same point or state : space measured by a
revolving body : extensive change in the government of a country : a revolt. [See **Revolve**.]

**Revolutionary**, rev-ol-ū'shun-ar-i, *adj.* pertaining
to or tending to a revolution in government.

**Revolutionise**, rev-ol-ū'shun-īz, *v.t.* to cause a
revolution or entire change of anything.

**Revolutionist**, rev-ol-ū'shun-ist, *n.* one who promotes or favours a revolution.

**Revolve**, re-volv', *v.i.* to *roll back* : to roll round
on an axis : to move round a centre.—*v.t.* to
cause to turn : to consider. [L. *revolvo*, *revo-
lutum*—*re*-, back, and *volvo*, to roll.]

**Revolver**, re-volv'èr, *n.* that which revolves : a
firearm which, by means of revolving barrels,
can fire more than once without reloading.

**Revulsion**, re-vul'shun, *n.* disgust : the diverting
of a disease from one part to another. [Lit. 'a
tearing away,' L. *revulsio*—*revello*, *revulsum*, to
tear off or away—*re*-, away, and *vello*, to tear.]

**Revulsive**, re-vul'siv, *adj.* tending to revulsion.

**Reward**, re-wawrd', *n.* that which is given *in
return* for good or evil : recompense : retribution : the fruit of one's own labour.—*v.t.*
to give in return : to requite, whether good or
evil : to punish : (*B.*) to recompense. [O. Fr.
*reswarder*, from *re* and the Teut. root of **Ward**
or **Guard**.]

**Reynard**, rā'nard, *n.* Same as **Renard**.

**Rhapsodic**, rap-sod'ik, **Rhapsodical**, rap-sod'ik-al,
*adj.* pertaining to, consisting of, or resembling
rhapsody.—*adv.* **Rhapsod'ically.**

**Rhapsodist**, rap'so-dist, *n.* one who recites or
sings rhapsodies : one who composes verses extempore : one who speaks or writes disjointedly.

**Rhapsody**, rap'so-di, *n.* any wild unconnected
composition : a part of an epic poem for recita-

tion at one time. [Fr.—Gr. *rhapsōdia*, lit. 'a stringing together of songs'—*rhaptō*, to sew, and *ōdē*, a song.] [*Rhine.* [L. *Rhenus.*]

**Rhenish**, ren'ish, *adj.* pertaining to the river Rhine.

**Rhetoric**, ret'o-rik, *n.* the art of *speaking* with propriety, elegance, and force. [Fr.—Gr. *rhētorikē*—*rhētōr*, a public speaker—*rheō*, to speak.]

**Rhetorical**, re-tor'ik-al, *adj.* pertaining to rhetoric: oratorical.—*adv.* **Rhetor'ically.**

**Rhetorician**, ret-o-rish'an, *n.* one who teaches the art of rhetoric: an orator.

**Rheum**, rōōm, *n.* the *flow* or discharge from the lungs or nostrils caused by cold: increased action of any organ, esp. of the mucous glands. [L.—Gr. *rheuma*—*rheō*, to flow.]

**Rheumatic**, rōō-mat'ik, **Rheumatical**, rōō-mat'ik-al, *adj.* pertaining to, or affected with rheumatism.

**Rheumatism**, rōōm'a-tizm, *n.* a painful affection of the muscles, so named from a notion that the pain was caused by *rheum* or humour flowing through the part affected.

**Rheumy**, rōōm'i, *adj.* full of or causing rheum.

**Rhinoceros**, rī-nos'er-os, *n.* a very large animal allied to the elephant, having a very thick skin, and one or two *horns* on the nose. [L.—Gr. *rhinokerōs*—*rhin*, *rhinos*, nose, *keras*, a horn.]

**Rhododendron**, rō-do-den'dron, *n.* a genus of plants having evergreen leaves, and large beautiful flowers like *roses*. [Lit. 'the rose-tree,' Gr. *rhodon*, a rose, and *dendron*, a tree.]

**Rhodomontade.** See **Rodomontade.**

**Rhomb**, romb, **Rhombus**, rom'bus, *n.* a quadrilateral figure having its sides equal, but its angles not right angles. [L.—Gr. *rhombos*—*rhembō*, to turn round and round.]

**Rhombic**, rom'bik, *adj.* shaped like a rhomb.

**Rhomboid**, rom'boid, *n.* a figure of the *form* of a *rhomb*: a quadrilateral figure having only its opposite sides and angles equal. [Gr. *rhombos*, and *eidos*, form.] [of a rhomboid.

**Rhomboidal**, rom-boid'al, *adj.* having the shape

**Rhubarb**, rōō'barb, *n.* a plant, the stalks of which are much used in cooking and the root in medicine, so called because brought orig. from the banks of the *Rha* or Volga. [Fr. *rhubarbe*—Low L. *rha-barbarum*—L. *Rhâ*, the Volga, *barbarus*, foreign.]

**Rhumb**, rum, *n.* (*orig.*) a meridian, especially the principal meridian of a map: any vertical circle, hence any point of the compass. [Fr. *rumb*, a byform of *rhombe*, through L., from Gr. *rhombos.* See **Rhomb.**]

**Rhumb-line**, rum'-līn, *n.* a line which cuts all the meridians at the same angle.

**Rhyme**, rīm, *n.* (*orig.*) words arranged in numbers or verses: the correspondence of sounds at the ends of verses: poetry.—*v.i.* to correspond in sound: to make rhymes or verses.—*v.t.* to put into rhyme.—*ns.* **Rhym'er, Rhym'ster.** [Properly *rime* (the *hy* being due to the influence of *Rhythm*)—A.S. *rim*, number, cog. with O. Ger. *rīm* (Ger. *reim*).]

**Rhythm**, rithm, *n.*, *flowing* motion: metre: regular recurrence of accents: harmony of proportion. [L. *rhythmus*—Gr. *rhythmos*—*rheō*, *rheusomai*, to flow.]

**Rhythmic**, rith'mik, **Rhythmical**, rith'mik-al, *adj.* having or pertaining to rhythm or metre.—*adv.* **Rhyth'mically.**

**Rib**, rib, *n.* one of the bones from the backbone which encircle the chest: anything like a rib in form or use: a piece of timber which helps to form or strengthen the side of a ship: a vein of

a leaf: a prominence running in a line: (*arch.*) a moulding or projecting band on a ceiling.—*v.t.* to furnish or inclose with ribs: to form with rising lines :—*pr.p.* ribb'ing ; *pa.t.* and *pa.p.* ribbed. [A.S., cog. with Ger. *rippe.*]

**Ribald**, rib'ald, *n.* a loose, low character.—*adj.* low: base: mean. [O. Fr. *ribalt* (Fr. *ribaud*, It. *ribaldo*)—O. Ger. *ribe*, a prostitute, and suffix -*ald.*] [and vulgar scurrility.

**Ribaldry**, rib'ald-ri, *n.* obscenity: filthiness: low

**Ribbing**, rib'ing, *n.* an arrangement of ribs.

**Ribbon**, rib'on, **Riband**, **Ribband**, rib'and, *n.* a fillet or strip of silk: a narrow strip.—*v.t.* to adorn with ribbons. [O. Fr. *riban* (Fr. *ruban*), perh. from Dut. *ring-band*, necktie, collar (Diez), or from Dut. *rij* (Ger. *reihe*), a row, and Band.]

**Rice**, rīs, *n.* one of the most useful and extensively cultivated of grains, like oats when ripe. [Fr. *riz* (It. *riso*)—L. and Gr. *oryza*—Ar. *rozz*, (with art.) *ar rozz.*]

**Rice-paper**, rīs-pā'pėr, *n.* a white smooth paper, made by the Chinese from the pith of a plant. [So called because formerly supposed to be made from *rice.*]

**Rich**, rich (*comp.* **Rich'er**, *superl.* **Rich'est**), *adj.* abounding in possessions: wealthy: valuable: sumptuous: fertile: full of agreeable or nutritive qualities: bright, as a colour: full of harmonious sounds: full of beauty.—*adv.* **Rich'ly.** [A.S. *rice*, rule (as *ric* in *bishopric*), having rule, having means or wealth, rich ; cog. with Ger. *reich*, empire, also rich, Goth. *reiks*, L. *rex*, a king, Sans. *raj-an*, to rule. The fundamental idea is that of power shewn in stretching out the hand, guiding, obtaining, as in E. **Reach**, Gr. *o-reg-ō*, to reach after, L. *reg-ere*, to keep straight or guide, Sans. *arg-*, to obtain. Through the idea of 'keeping straight,' the root is conn. also with E. **Right**, Ger. *recht*, L. *rectus.*]

**Riches**, rich'ez, *n.pl.* (in B. sometimes *n. sing.*), wealth : richness : abundance. [M. E. *richesse* (n.sing.)—Fr. *richesse.*]

**Richness**, rich'nes, *n.* wealth : abundance : fruitfulness : value : costliness : abundance of imagery.

**Rick**, rik, *n.* a pile or heap, as of hay. [A.S. *hreāc*, cog. with Ice. *hraukr.*]

**Rickets**, rik'ets, *n.sing.* a disease of children, characterised by softness and curvature of the bones. [From the Prov. E. verb (*w*)*rick* (Sw. *vricka*), to twist, whose nasalised form is **Wring**, and freq. **Wriggle.**]

**Rickety**, rik'et-i, *adj.* affected with rickets : feeble.

**Ricochet**, rik'o-shā or -shet, *n.* rebound along the ground, as of a ball fired at a low elevation : the skipping of a flat stone on the surface of water. [Fr. ; ety. unknown.]

**Ricochet**, rik-o-shet', *v.t.* to fire at with guns at a low elevation, so as to make the balls skip on the ground :—*pr.p.* ricochet'ing ; *pa.t.* and *pa.p.* ricochet'ed.

**Rid**, rid, *v.t.* to free : to deliver : to remove by violence : to clear : to disencumber :—*pr.p.* ridd'ing ; *pa.t.* and *pa.p.* ridd. [A.S. *hreddan*, to snatch away ; Ger. *retten.*]

**Riddance**, rid'ans, *n.* act of ridding or freeing.

**Riddle**, rid'l, *n.* an obscure description of something which the hearer is asked to name : a puzzling question : an enigma.—*v.i.* to make riddles : to speak obscurely.—*v.t.* to solve, as a riddle. [A.S. *redels*—*rædan*, to guess, to read —*ræd*, counsel, cog. with Dut. *raad*, Ger. *rath.*]

**Riddle**, rid'l, *n.* a large *sieve* for separating coarser materials from finer.—*v.t.* to separate with a riddle, as grain from chaff : to make full of holes like a riddle, as with shot. [A.S. *hriddel—hridrian*, to sift; Ger. *rädel*, a riddle—*räden*, to sift.]

**Ride**, rīd, *v.i.* to be borne, as on horseback or in a carriage : to practise riding : to float, as a ship at anchor.—*v.t.* to rest on so as to be carried :—*pa.t.* rōde ; *pa.p.* ridd'en.—*n.* act of riding : an excursion on horseback or in a vehicle : the course passed over in riding : a district inspected by an excise officer. [A.S. *rídan* ; Ice. *reida*, to move, Ger. *reiten*, to move along, L. (from Celt.) *rheda*, a carriage. See **Road**.]

**Rider**, rīd'er, *n.* one who rides on a horse : one who manages a horse : an addition to a document after its completion, on a separate piece of paper : an additional clause.

**Ridge**, rij, *n.* the *back* or top of the back : anything like a back, as a long range of hills : an extended protuberance : the earth thrown up by the plough between the furrows : the upper horizontal timber of a roof.—*v.t.* to form into ridges : to wrinkle. [A.S. *hrycg* ; Prov. E. and Scot. *rig* ; Ice. *hryggr*, Ger. *rücken*, the back.]

**Ridgy**, rij'i, *adj.* having, or rising in ridges.

**Ridicule**, rid'i-kūl, *n.* wit exposing one to *laughter* : derision : mockery.—*v.t.* to laugh at : to expose to merriment : to deride : to mock. [L. *ridiculus*, exciting laughter—*rideo*, to laugh.]

**Ridiculous**, ri-dik'ū-lus, *adj.* deserving or exciting ridicule : laughable : absurd.—*adv.* **Ridic'ulously.**—*n.* **Ridic'ulousness.** [L. *ridiculosus*—*ridiculus*.]

**Riding**, rīd'ing, *adj.* used to ride or travel : suitable for riding on, as a horse.—*n.* a road for riding on : a district visited by an excise officer.—*n.* **Rid'ing-habit, Rid'ing-skirt,** the long upper *habit*, garment, or *skirt* worn by ladies when *riding*.

**Riding**, rīd'ing, *n.* one of the *three* divisions of the county of York. [A corr. of A.S. *thrithing*, *thriding*, a third part—*thry, thri,* three.]

**Rife**, rīf, *adj.* prevailing : abundant.—*adv.* **Rife'ly.**—*n.* **Rife'ness.** [A.S. *rif*, prevalent ; cog. with Dut. *rijf*, Ice. *rīfr*, liberal.]

**Riff-raff**, rif'-raf, *n.* sweepings : refuse : the rabble, the mob. [A reduplication of obs. *raff*, sweepings, conn. with **Raffle**, **Rifle**, *v.* to rob.]

**Rifle**, rī'fl, *v.t.* to carry off by force : to strip, to rob.—*n.* **Ri'fler.** [Fr. *rifler, rafler*; from Teut., as Ger. *raffen*, to snatch away. See **Raffle**.]

**Rifle**, rī'fl, *v.t.* to *groove* spirally, as a gun-barrel.—*n.* a musket with a barrel spirally grooved. [Allied to Low Ger. *gerifelde*, rifled, grooved, and Ger. *riefeln*, to channel—*riefe*, a channel, a groove.]

**Rifleman**, rī'fl-man, *n.* a man armed with a rifle.

**Rift**, rift, *n.* an opening *riven* or split in anything : a cleft or fissure.—*v.t.* to rive : to cleave.—*v.i.* to split : to burst open. [From **Rive**.]

**Rig**, rig, *v.t.* to clothe, to dress : to put on : (*naut.*) to fit with sails and tackling :—*pr.p.* rigg'ing ; *pa.t.* and *pa.p.* rigged.—*n.* sails and tackling. [Ice. *rigga*, to bandage, to put on sails—*riga*, to be stiff.]

**Rig**, rig, *n.* (*Scotch*) a ridge. [A form of **Ridge**.]

**Rigging**, rig'ing, *n.* tackle : the system of cordage which supports a ship's masts and extends the sails. [See **Rig**, *v.t.*]

**Right**, rīt, *adj.*, *straight* : most direct : upright : erect : according to truth and justice : according to law : true : correct : just : fit : proper : exact : most convenient : well performed : most dexterous, as the hand : on the right hand : on the right

hand of one looking towards the mouth of a river : (*math.*) upright from a base : containing 90 degrees.—*adv.* **Right'ly.**—*n.* **Right'ness.** [A.S. *riht, ryht*; Ger. *recht*, L. *rectus—rego*, to guide. See **Rich**.]

**Right**, rīt, *adv.* in a straight or direct line : in a right manner : according to truth and justice : correctly : very : in a great degree.

**Right**, rīt, *n.* that which is right or correct : truth : justice : virtue : freedom from error : what one has a just claim to : privilege : property : the right side.—*v.t.* to make right or straight : to set upright : to do justice to.—*v.i.* to recover the proper position.

**Righteous**, rīt'yus or rī'chus, *adj.* living and acting according to *right* and justice : free from guilt or sin : equitable : merited.—*adv.* **Right'eously**, (*Litany*) justly.—*n.* **Right'eousness.** [Lit. 'in a right way,' A.S. *rihtwis—riht*, and *wis*, a way or manner. The form *righteous* is due to the influence of such words as *bounteous, plenteous*, &c.]

**Rightful**, rīt'fool, *adj.* having right : according to justice.—*adv.* **Right'fully.**—*n.* **Right'fulness.**

**Rigid**, rij'id, *adj.* not easily bent : stiff : severe : strict.—*adv.* **Rig'idly.**—*n.* **Rig'idness.** [L. *rigidus—rigeo*, to be stiff with cold ; akin to *frigeo* and to Gr. *rigeō*, to shiver with cold.]

**Rigidity**, ri-jid'it-i, *n.* the quality of resisting change of form : stiffness of manner.

**Rigmarole**, rig'-ma-rōl, *n.* a repetition of foolish words : a long story. [A corr. of *ragman-roll*, a document with a long list of names, or with numerous seals pendent.]

**Rigorous**, rig'ur-us, *adj.* exercising rigour : allowing no abatement : marked by severity : harsh : scrupulously accurate : very severe.—*adv.* **Rig'orously.**—*n.* **Rig'orousness.**

**Rigour**, rig'ur, *n.* the quality of being rigid or severe : stiffness of opinion or temper : strictness : severity of climate : (*med.* spelt **Rigor**) a sense of chilliness attended by a shivering. [L. *rigor—rigeo*.]

**Rilievo.** See **Relievo**.

**Rill**, ril, *n.* a small murmuring brook : a streamlet.—*v.i.* to flow in small streams. [Prob. a Celt. word, akin to Fr. *rigole*, and W. *rhigol*, a furrow, a small trench.]

**Rim**, rim, *n.* a raised margin : a border : a brim.—*v.t.* to put a rim to :—*pr.p.* rimm'ing ; *pa.t.* and *pa.p.* rimmed. [A.S. *rima*; ety. unknown.]

**Rime**, rīm, *n.* hoar-frost : frozen dew.—*adj.* **Rim'y.** [A.S. *hrim*; Dut. *rijm*, O. Ger. *hrifo*, Ger. *reif*.]

**Rind**, rīnd, *n.* the external covering, as the skin of fruit, the bark of trees, &c. [A.S. *rind, rhind*, Ger. *rinde*; prob. from a Teut. root seen in Goth. *rindan* (O. Ger. *rintan*), to surround.]

**Rinderpest**, rin'der-pest, *n.* a malignant and contagious *disease of cattle*. [Ger. 'cattle-plague.']

**Ring**, ring, *n.* a circle : a small hoop, usually of metal, worn on the finger as an ornament : a circular area for races, &c. : a circular group of persons.—*v.t.* to encircle : to fit with a ring. [A.S. *hring*; Ice. *hring-r*, Ger. Dan. and Sw. *ring*. Cf. **Rink** and **Circus**.]

**Ring**, ring, *v.i.* to sound as a bell when struck : to tinkle : to practise the art of ringing bells : to continue to sound : to be filled with report.—*v.t.* to cause to sound, as a metal : to produce by ringing :—*pa.t.* rang, rung ; *pa.p.* rung.—*n.* a sound, esp. of metals : the sound of many voices : a chime of many bells. [A.S. *hringan*, cog. with Ice. *hringia*, to ring bells, *hringla*, to clink, Dan. *ringle*, to tinkle.]

**Ringdove**, ring'duv, *n.* the cushat or wood-*pigeon*; so called from a white *ring* or line on the neck.

**Ringleader**, ring'lēd-ėr, *n.* the head of a riotous body. [Orig. the *leader* in the *ring* of a dance.]

**Ringlet**, ring'let, *n.* a *little ring*: a curl, esp. of hair.

**Ring-ousel**, ring'-ōō'zl, *n.* a species of thrush, with a white band on the breast. [See Ousel.]

**Ring-straked**, ring'-strākt, *adj.* (*B.*) streaked with rings.

**Ringworm**, ring'wurm, *n.* a skin disease in which itchy pimples appear in *rings*, as if caused by a *worm*.

**Rink**, ringk, *n.* the area where a race is run, or games are played.—*n.* **Skat'ing-rink**, a place artificially prepared for skating. [Simply a variant of **Ring**, a circle.]

**Rinse**, rins, *v.t.* to cleanse by introducing water: to cleanse with clean water. [O. Fr. *rinser* (Fr. *rincer*)—Ice. *hreinsa*; Ger. and Dut. *rein*, pure.]

**Riot**, rī'ot, *n.* uproar: tumult: a disturbance of the peace: excessive feasting: luxury.—*v.i.* to brawl: to raise an uproar: to run to excess in feasting, behaviour, &c.: to be highly excited.—*n.* **Ri'oter**. [Fr. *riotte*; ety. dub.]

**Riotous**, rī'ot-us, *adj.* engaging in riot: seditious: tumultuous: luxurious: wanton.—*adv.* **Ri'otously**.—*n.* **Ri'otousness**.

**Rip**, rip, *v.t.* to divide by cutting or *tearing*: to cut open: to take out by cutting or tearing: to tear up for search or alteration:—*pr.p.* ripping; *pa.t.* and *pa.p.* ripped.—*n.* a tear: a rent: a place torn. [A.S. *rypan*; Dan. *rippe*, akin to **Reap**.]

**Riparian**, rip-ā'ri-an, *adj.* belonging to a *river-bank*. [L. *ripa*, a river-bank.]

**Ripe**, rīp, *adj.* ready for harvest: arrived at perfection: fit for use: developed to the utmost: finished: ready: resembling ripe fruit.—*adv.* **Ripe'ly**.—*n.* **Ripe'ness**. [A.S. *rípe*, conn. with *rip*, harvest; cog. with Dut. *rijp*, Ger. *reif*, akin to A.S. *rípan*, E. **Reap**.]

**Ripen**, rīp'en, *v.i.* to grow ripe: to approach or reach perfection.—*v.t.* to make ripe: to bring to perfection. [A.S. *rípian*; Ger. *reifen*.]

**Ripple**, rip'l, *n.* the little waves on the surface of running water: a little wave.—*v.t.* to cause a ripple in.—*v.i.* to curl on the surface, as running water. [Allied to Ger. *rippeln*, Low Ger. *reppen*, to move.]

**Ripple**, rip'l, *v.t.* to pluck the seeds from stalks of flax by drawing them through an iron comb.—*n.* the comb for rippling. [Low Ger. *repel*, machine for breaking flax, Ger. *riffel*, a flax-comb.]

**Rise**, rīz, *v.i.* to move from a lower to a higher position: to ascend: to grow upward: to swell in quantity or extent: to take an upright position: to leave the place of rest: to tower up: to appear above the horizon: to break forth: to appear: to have its source: to increase in size, value, &c.: to become excited or hostile: to break forth into commotion or insurrection: to increase in rank, fortune, or fame: to come to mind: to close a session: (*B.*) to ascend from the grave:—*pa.t.* rōse; *pa.p.* risen (riz'n).—*n.* act of rising: ascent: degree of elevation: a steep: origin: increase: advance: (*mus.*) elevation of the voice. [A.S. *rísan*, cog. with Ice. *rísa*, Goth. *reisan*, Ger. *reisen*; intransitive form of **Raise**.]

**Risible**, riz'i-bl, *adj.* capable of exciting *laughter*: laughable: amusing.—*adv.* **Ris'ibly**.—*n.* **Risibil'ity**, quality of being risible. [L. *risibilis*, from *rideo*, *risum*, to laugh.]

**Rising**, rīz'ing, *n.* act of rising: resurrection: (*B.*) a tumour.

**Risk**, risk, *n.* hazard: chance of loss or injury.—*v.t.* to expose to hazard: to venture. [Fr. *risque* (It. *risico*)—Sp. *risco*, a rock—L. *reseco*, to cut off—*re*, off, *seco*, to cut. The connection is, an abrupt precipice, hence danger.]

**Rissole**, ris'ōl, *n.* fish or meat minced and fried with bread crumbs and egg. [Fr., perh. from the Teut., as Dan. *riste*, to roast.]

**Rite**, rīt, *n.* a religious usage or ceremony. [Fr. *rite*—L. *ritus*.]

**Ritual**, rit'ū-al, *adj.* consisting of or prescribing *rites*.—*n.* manner of performing divine service, or a book containing it: the body of rites employed in the church.—*adv.* **Rit'ually**. [L. *ritualis*. See **Rite**.]

**Ritualism**, rit'ū-al-izm, *n.* system of rituals or prescribed forms of religion: the observance of them: the name given to the great increase of ceremonial in religious worship which has taken place in a large section of the Church of England.

**Ritualist**, rit'ū-al-ist, *n.* one skilled in or devoted to a ritual: one of the party in favour of ritualism in the Church of England.—*adj.* **Ritualist'ic**, pertaining to the ritual.

**Rival**, rī'val, *n.* one pursuing the same object as another: one who strives to equal or excel another: a competitor.—*adj.* having the same claims: standing in competition.—*v.t.* to stand in competition with: to try to gain the same object as another: to try to equal or excel:—*pr.p.* rī'valling; *pa.t.* and *pa.p.* rī'valled. [Lit. one who lives on the opposite side *of a river*, and contends sometimes for the use of it, Fr.—L. *rivalis*—*rivus*, a brook. See **Rivulet**.]

**Rivalry**, rī'val-ri, *n.* act of rivalling: competition: emulation.

**Rive**, rīv, *v.t.* to tear asunder: to split.—*v.i.* to be split asunder:—*pa.t.* rīved; *pa.p.* rīved, riv'en. [A.S. *reófan*; Dan. *rive*.]

**River**, riv'ėr, *n.* a large running stream of water. [Fr. *rivière* (It. *riviera*, shore, river)—Low L. *riparia*, a shore district—L. *ripa*, a bank.]

**Rivet**, riv'et, *n.* a bolt of metal fastened by being hammered at both ends.—*v.t.* to fasten with a rivet: to make firm or immovable:—*pr.p.* riv'eting; *pa.t.* and *pa.p.* riv'eted. [Fr., acc. to Diez from the root of Ice. *rífa*, Dan. *rive*, Ger. *reiben*, E. **Rive**.]

**Rivulet**, riv'ū-let, *n.* a *small river* or stream: a brook. [L. *rivulus*, dim. of *rivus*, a stream, akin to Sans. *sru*, Gr. *rheō*, to flow.]

**Roach**, rōch, *n.* a fresh-water fish of a silvery colour. [Dut. *roch*, Ger. *roche*, Dan. *rokke*.]

**Road**, rōd, *n.* a highway: an open way for passengers and traffic: (*B.*) a plundering excursion. [A.S. *rád*, a riding—*rád*, pa.t. of *rídan*, **Ride**.]

**Road**, rōd, **Roadstead**, rōd'sted, **Roads**, rōdz, *n.* a place where ships *ride* at anchor.

**Roadster**, rōd'stėr, *n.* (*naut.*) a vessel riding at anchor in a *road*: a horse fitted for travelling.

**Roadway**, rōd'wā, *n.* the *way* or part of a *road* or street travelled by carriages.

**Roam**, rōm, *v.i.* to rove about: to ramble.—*v.t.* to wander over. [Prob. formed from **Roamer**.]

**Roamer**, rōm'ėr, *n.* a wanderer. [Usually derived from O. Fr. *romier*, one who makes a pilgrimage to Rome (Sp. *romero*, It. *romeo*)—L. *Roma*, Rome.]

**Roan,** rōn, *adj.* having a bay or dark colour, with spots of gray and white : of a mixed colour, with a decided shade of red.—*n.* a roan colour : a roan horse : grained sheepskin leather. [Fr. *rouan* (It. *roano*) ; ety. unknown.]

**Roan-tree, Rowan-tree,** rō′an-trē, *n.* the mountain-ash. [So called either from the colour of its stem (see **Roan**), or it is a corr. of **Rune,** from its use in divination. See **Rune.**]

**Roar,** rōr, *v.i.* to utter a full, loud sound : to cry, as a beast : to cry aloud : to bawl.—*n.* a full, loud sound : the cry of a beast : an outcry of mirth, esp. of laughter. [A.S. *rārian,* O. Ger. *reran,* Ger. *röhren,* to cry as a stag, to bellow ; influenced also by an old verb *hroren,* the Ger. *rühren,* to move (cf. **Uproar**).]

**Roaring,** rōr′ing, *n.* act or sound of roaring : a disease of horses causing them to *roar* in breathing.

**Roast,** rōst, *v.t.* to cook before a fire : to parch by exposure to heat : to heat to excess : to dissipate the volatile parts of by heat.—*n.* that which is roasted. [O. Fr. *rostir* (Fr. *rôtir*)—O. Ger. *röstan* (whence Ger. *rösten*), to roast.]

**Rob,** rob, *n.* the juice of ripe fruit mixed with honey or sugar. [Fr.—Ar. *robb,* purified sirup of boiled fruit.]

**Rob,** rob, *v.t.* to take away from by force or theft : to plunder : to steal : to deprive: (*B.*) to withhold what is due :—*pr.p.* robb′ing ; *pa.t.* and *pa.p.* robbed.—*n.* **Robb′er,** one who robs. [O. Fr. *rober*—Ger. *rauben,* A.S. *reafian.*]

**Robbery,** rob′ér-i, *n.* theft from the person, aggravated by violence or intimidation : plundering.

**Robe,** rōb, *n.* a gown or outer garment : a dress of dignity or state : a rich dress.—*v.t.* to dress, as with a robe : to clothe. [Fr. ; from O. Ger. *roubon* (Ger. *rauben*), E. **Rob**; applied to clothes, because they were so frequently stolen.]

**Robin,** rob′in, **Robin-redbreast,** rob′in-red′brest, *n.* a singing bird with a reddish breast. [A familiar form of *Robert*: cf. *Jack*-daw, *Mag*-pie.]

**Robust,** rō-bust′, *adj.* of great strength or vigour : requiring strength.—*adv.* **Robust′ly.**—*n.* **Robust′ness.** [Fr.—L. *robustus*—*robur,* oak.]

**Roc,** rok, *n.* an enormous bird in Persian folk-tales. [Pers. *rukh.*]

**Rochet,** roch′et, *n.* a surplice with narrow sleeves worn by bishops. [Fr., dim. of Low L. *roccus*—O. Ger. *roc* (A.S. *rocc,* Ger. *rock*), a coat.]

**Rock,** rok, *n.* a large mass of stone : (*geol.*) a natural deposit of sand, earth, or clay : that which has the firmness of a rock : (*B.*) defence. [Fr. *roc, roche*; prob. Celt., as in Gael. *roc,* W. *rhwg,* a projection.]

**Rock,** rok, *n.* a distaff. [Dut. *rokken,* Ice. *rockr.*]

**Rock,** rok, *v.t.* to *move* backward and forward : to lull to sleep.—*v.i.* to be moved backward and forward : to totter. [Teut., as Ice. *rugga,* Ger. *rücken,* to move.]

**Rocker,** rok′ér, *n.* the curved support on which a cradle or rocking-chair rocks.

**Rockery,** rok′ér-i, *n.* Same as **Rockwork.**

**Rocket,** rok′et, *n.* a firework which is projected through the air, used for making signals in war, and for saving life at sea by conveying a line over a stranded vessel. [It. *rocchetta,* from root of *rock,* a distaff, because its thick upper end is like a distaff.]        [*rocks.*

**Rock-pigeon,** rok-pij′un, *n.* a *pigeon* inhabiting

**Rocksalt,** rok′sawlt, *n., salt* in *rock*-like masses.

**Rockwork,** rok′wurk, *n.* (*arch.*) masonry in imitation of masses of rock: (*hort.*) a pile of earth covered with stones with plants growing between.

**Rocky,** rok′i, *adj.* full of rocks : resembling a rock : hard : unfeeling.—*n.* **Rock′iness.**

**Rococo,** rokō′ko, *n.* a term applied to a debased style of architecture prevailing in the 18th century, marked by endless multiplication of ornamental details. [Formed from Fr. *rocaille,* rockwork.]

**Rod,** rod, *n.* a long twig : a slender stick : anything long and slender : an instrument of correction : an emblem of power or authority : a pole or perch (5½ yards) : (*fig.*) punishment : authority : oppression : (*B.*) race or tribe. [A.S. ; Dut. *roede,* Ger. *ruthe*; akin to L. *rudis,* a rod, and Sans. *ridh,* to grow. See **Rood.**]

**Rode,** rōd, *pa.t.* of **Ride.**

**Rodent,** rō′dent, *adj., gnawing.* [L. *rodens, rodentis,* pr.p. of *rodo,* to gnaw.]

**Rodomontade,** rod-ō-mont-ād′, *n.* vain boasting, like that of *Rodomonte* in the *Orlando Furioso* of Ariosto.—*v.i.* to boast or bluster.

**Roe,** rō, *n.* the eggs or spawn of fishes. [Ice. *hrogn,* Ger. *rogen.*]

**Roe,** rō, *n.* a species of deer, smaller than the fallow-deer : also the female deer.

**Roebuck,** rō′buk, *n.* the male of the roe, having usually one front antler and two hinder ones. [A.S. *rah*; Ger. *reh,* Ice. *ra.*]

**Rogation,** ro-gā′shun, *n.* an *asking*: supplication. —**Rogation-days,** the three days before the festival of Ascension, being days of special supplication. [L., from *rogo,* to ask.]

**Rogue,** rōg, *n.* a dishonest person : a knave : a mischievous or frolicsome person : (*law*) a vagrant. [Fr. *rogue,* proud ; either from Bret. *rok,* proud, or acc. to Diez, from Ice. *hrokr,* proud, haughty.]       [chievousness : waggery.

**Roguery,** rōg′ér-i, *n.* knavish tricks : fraud : mis-

**Roguish,** rōg′ish, *adj.* knavish : mischievous : waggish.—*adv.* **Rog′uishly.**—*n.* **Rog′uishness.**

**Roister,** roist′ér, *v.i.* to bluster, swagger, bully. —*n.* **Roist′erer.** [Fr. *rustre,* a rough, rude fellow—O. Fr. *ruste*—L. *rusticus,* rustic.]

**Rôle,** rōl, *n.* the part performed by an actor in a play : any important part played in public life. [Fr., the part of each actor being written on a *roll* of paper. See **Roll.**]

**Roll,** rōl, *v.i.* to turn like a *wheel* : to turn on an axis : to be formed into a roll or cylinder : to move, as waves : to be tossed about : to move tumultuously : to be hurled : to rock, or move from side to side : to wallow : to spread under a roller : to sound as a drum beaten rapidly.— *v.t.* to cause to roll : to turn on an axis : to wrap round on itself : to inwrap : to drive forward : to move upon wheels : to press with a roller : to beat rapidly, as a drum.—*n.* act of rolling : that which rolls : a roller : that which is rolled up : hence parchment, paper, &c. wound into a circular form : a document : a register : a kind of fancy bread : the continued sound of a drum. [O. Fr. *roeller* (Fr. *rouler*)— Low L. *rotulare*—L. *rotula,* a little wheel— *rota,* a wheel.]

**Roll-call,** rōl′-kawl, *n.* the calling of the roll or list of names, as in the army.

**Roller,** rōl′ér, *n.* that which rolls : a cylinder used for rolling, grinding, &c. : a long broad bandage :—*pl.* heavy waves.

**Rollicking,** rol′ik-ing, *adj.* careless, swaggering. [Prob. a form of **Roll,** with allusion to **Frolic.**]

**Rolling,** rōl′ing, *adj.* moving on *wheels* : used in rolling.—*n.* **Roll′ing-pin,** a cylindrical pin or piece of wood for rolling paste.—*n.* **Roll′ing-press,** a press of two cylinders for rolling or calendering cloth.—*n.* **Roll'ing-stock**, the *stock* or store of engines, carriages, &c. of a railway.

**Romaic**, ro-mā'ik, *n.* modern Greek, the language of the descendants of the Eastern *Romans.* [Fr. *Romaïque;* from modern Gr. *Rōmaikos*—L. *Roma.*]

**Roman**, rō'man, *adj.* pertaining to Rome or to the Romans: pertaining to the Roman Catholic religion: papal: (*print.*) noting the letters commonly used, as opposed to Italics: written in letters (used by the Romans, as IV.), not in figures (as 4).—*n.* a native or citizen of Rome. [L. *Romanus*—*Roma*, Rome.]

**Roman Catholic**, rō'man kath'ol-ik, *adj.* denoting the Christians *throughout the world* who recognise the spiritual supremacy of the Pope or Bishop of *Rome.*—*n.* a member of the Roman Catholic Church.

**Romance**, ro-mans', *n.* the dialects in S. Europe which sprung from a corruption of the *Roman* or Latin language: a tale written in these dialects: any fictitious and wonderful tale: a fictitious narrative in prose or verse which passes beyond the limits of real life.—*adj.* belonging to the dialects called *Romance.*—*v.i.* to write or tell romances: to talk extravagantly.—*n.* **Roman'cer.** [O. Fr. *romans*—Low L. adv. (*loqui*) *romanice* (to speak) in the *Roman* or Latin tongue—L. *Romanicus*, Roman.]

**Romanesque**, rō-man-esk', *n.* that which pertains to *romance:* (*arch.*) the debased style adopted in the later Roman empire: the dialect of Languedoc and other districts of the south of France. [Fr.; L. *romanesco*—*Romanicus.*]

**Romanise**, rō'man-īz, *v.t.* to convert to the *Roman* Catholic religion.—*v.i.* to conform to *Roman* Catholic opinions or practices.

**Romanism**, rō'man-izm, *n.* the tenets of the Roman Catholic Church.

**Romanist**, rō'man-ist, *n.* a Roman Catholic.

**Romantic**, ro-man'tik, *adj.* pertaining to or resembling *romance:* fictitious: extravagant: wild: fantastic.—*adv.* **Roman'tically.**—*n.* **Roman'ticness.**

**Romanticism**, ro-man'ti-sizm, *n.* in literature, the revolt from a classical to a medieval style. [So called because the latter was orig. imitated from *Romance* models.]

**Romish**, rōm'ish, *adj.* belonging to *Rome,* or to the Roman Catholic Church.

**Romp**, romp, *v.i.* to play noisily: to skip about in play.—*n.* a girl who romps: rude frolic. [A form of **Ramp.**]

**Rompish**, romp'ish, *adj.* fond of *romping* or noisy play.—*adv.* **Romp'ishly.**—*n.* **Romp'ishness.**

**Rondeau**, ron'dō, *n.* a little poem in three parts, of which the first two or three words are repeated at the end of the second and third part, and which thus ends as it began. [Fr., from *rond*, round. See **Round.**]

**Rondo**, ron'dō, *n.* the same as **Rondeau.** [It. form of the same word.]

**Rood**, rōōd, *n.* the fourth part of an acre, or forty perches, so called from the *rod* used in measuring: a figure of Christ's cross, and often of the crucifix, in R. Cath. churches. [Same as **Rod.**]

**Roof**, rōōf, *n.* the top covering of a house or building: a vault or arch, or the inner side of it: a house or dwelling.—*v.t.* to cover with a roof: to shelter. [A.S. *hróf;* Dut. *roef.*]

**Roofing**, rōōf'ing, *n.* covering with a roof: materials for a roof: the roof itself.

**Roofless**, rōōf'les, *adj.* without a roof: having no house or home: unsheltered.

**Rook**, rook, *n.* a kind of crow, so called from its *croak.* [A.S. *hróc;* Goth. *hrukjan,* to croak. See **Crow.**]

**Rook**, rook, *n.* a castle or piece used in playing chess. [Fr. *roc;* from Pers. *rokh,* a camel with a *tower* for archers.]

**Rookery**, rook'ėr-i, *n.* a group of trees to which *rooks* resort to build their nests.

**Room**, rōōm, *n., space:* a chamber: extent of place: space unoccupied: freedom to act: fit occasion: place of another: stead: (*B.*) a seat. [A.S. and Ice. *rum;* Ger. *raum.*]

**Roomy**, rōōm'i, *adj.* having ample room: wide: spacious.—*adv.* **Room'ily.**—*n.* **Room'iness.**

**Roost**, rōōst, *n.* a pole or support on which a bird rests at night: a number of fowls resting together.—*v.i.* to sit or sleep on a roost. [A.S. *hrost;* Dut. *roest.*]

**Root**, rōōt, *n.* the part of a plant which is fixed in the earth, and which draws up sap from the soil: an edible root: anything like a root: the bottom: a word from which others are derived: the cause or occasion of anything: (*math.*) the factor of a quantity which multiplied by itself produces that quantity: the value of the unknown quantity in an equation.—*v.i.* to *fix the root:* to be firmly established.—*v.t.* to plant in the earth: to implant deeply. [Ice. and Sw. *rot;* Dan. *rod;* akin to L. *radix,* Gr. *riza,* a root, Sans. *ruh,* to grow.]

**Root**, rōōt, *v.t.* to turn up with the *snout,* as swine.—*v.i.* to turn up the earth with the snout. [A.S. *wrotian*—*wrot,* a snout; Dut. *wroeten.*]

**Rootlet**, rōōt'let, *n.* a *little root:* a radicle.

**Rope**, rōp, *n.* a thick twisted cord.—*v.i.* to extend into a thread, as by a glutinous quality.—*adj.* **Rop'y.**—*adv.* **Rop'ily.**—*n.* **Rop'iness.** [A.S. *ráp;* cog. with Ice. *reip,* Dut. *reep,* Ger. *reif.*]

**Rope-dancer**, rōp'-dans-ėr, *n.* one who performs acrobatic feats on a rope.

**Roper**, rōp'ėr, *n.* a maker of ropes.

**Ropery**, rōp'ėr-i, *n.* a place where ropes are made.

**Ropewalk**, rōp'wawk, *n.* a long narrow shed used for the spinning of ropes.

**Rorqual**, ror'kwal, *n.* a genus of whales of the largest size. [Norw.]

**Rosaceous**, ro-zā'shus, *adj.* (*bot.*) pertaining to the *rose* family: having the petals arranged like those of the rose. [L. *rosaceus.*]

**Rosary**, rō'zar-i, *n.* the string of beads by which Roman Catholics count their prayers. [Low L. *rosarium* (lit. a *rose-bed*), a book of *roses* or choice extracts, an anthology, esp. a series of prayers.]

**Rose**, *pa.t.* of **Rise.**

**Rose**, rōz, *n.* a plant of many species with a beautiful flower, generally *red:* a rosette: a perforated nozzle of a pipe, &c.: pink, the colour of the rose. [A.S. *rose*—L. *rosa,* akin to Gr. *rodon;* prob. akin to *erythros,* red.]

**Roseal**, rōz'e-al, *adj.* like a rose in smell or colour.

**Roseate**, rōz'e-āt, *adj.,* rosy: full of roses: blooming: red.

**Rosemary**, rōz'mar-i, **Rosmarin**, roz'ma-rēn, *n.* a small fragrant evergreen shrub of a pungent taste, once used as an emblem of fidelity. [M. E. *rosemaryne*—L. *ros-marinus,* 'sea-spray,' from its usually growing on the sea-coast —*ros,* dew, *marinus*—*mare,* the sea.]

**Rosette**, ro-zet', *n.* an imitation of a *rose* by means of a ribbon: (*arch.*) a rose-shaped ornament. [Fr., dim. of *rose.*] [*rose-leaves.*

**Rose-water**, rōz'-waw'tėr, *n., water* distilled from

**Rose-window**, rōz'-wind'ō, *n.* a circular *window*

with its compartments branching from a centre, like a *rose*.

**Rosewood**, rōz′wood, *n.* the *wood* of a Brazilian tree having a fragrance like that of *roses*.

**Rosin**, roz′in, *n.* the solid left after distilling off the oil from crude turpentine.—*v.t.* to rub or cover with rosin. [A form of **Resin**.]

**Rosiny**, roz′in-i, *adj.* like or containing *rosin*.

**Roster**, ros′ter, *n.* the list of persons liable to a certain duty. [Prob. Prov. Ger. *roster*—Ger. *register*, a list. See **Register**.]

**Rostral**, ros′tral, *adj.* like a *rostrum* or *beak*.

**Rostrate**, ros′trāt, **Rostrated**, ros′trāt-ed, *adj.*, *beaked*. [shape of a *beak*.

**Rostriform**, ros′tri-form, *adj.* having the *form* or **Rostrum**, ros′trum, *n.* in ancient Rome, an erection for public speakers in the Forum, adorned with the *beaks* or heads of ships taken in war : the platform from which a speaker addresses his audience. [L., lit. 'the beak'—*rodo, rosum*, to gnaw.]

**Rosy**, rōz′i, *adj.* like a rose : red : blooming : blushing : charming.—*n.* **Ros′iness.**

**Rot**, rot, *v.i.* to putrefy : to become decomposed. —*v.t.* to cause to rot : to bring to corruption :— *pr.p.* rott′ing ; *pa.t.* and *pa.p.* rott′ed.—*n.* decay : putrefaction : a disease of the potato : a decay (called **Dry-rot**) which attacks timber : a fatal distemper in sheep. [A.S. *rotian*, cog. with Ice. *rotna*.]

**Rotary**, rō′tar-i, *adj.* turning round like a *wheel* : rotatory. [L. *rota*, a wheel, akin to Sans. *ratha*, a chariot, and Ger. *rad*, a wheel.]

**Rotate**, rō′tāt, *v.t.* to turn anything round like a *wheel* : to cause to turn.—*v.i.* to turn round like a wheel. [L. *roto, rotatus*—*rota*.]

**Rotation**, ro-tā′shun, *n.* a turning round like a *wheel* : series or appropriate succession, as of crops. [Fr.—L. *rotatio*.]

**Rotatory**, rō′ta-tor-i, *adj.* turning round like a *wheel* : going in a circle : following in succession.

**Rote**, rōt, *n.* the frequent and mechanical repetition of words without knowledge of the meaning. [M. E. *rote*, to hum a tune—A.S. *hrutan*, to r̄oar ; cf. Scot. *rout*, to bellow, O. Fr. *rote*, a hurdy-gurdy.]

**Rotten**, rot′n, *adj.* putrefied : corrupt : decomposed : unsound : treacherous.—*n.* **Rott′enness.**

**Rottenstone**, rot′n-stōn, *n.* a soft stone used in a state of powder to polish soft metals and glass. [See **Rotten** and **Stone**.]

**Rotund**, ro-tund′, *adj.* round : spherical.—*ns.* **Rotund′ness, Rotund′ity.** [L. *rotundus*—*rota*. See **Rotary**.]

**Rotunda**, ro-tund′a, **Rotundo**, ro-tund′o, *n.* a *round* building. [Fr. *rotonde*, It. *rotondo*.]

**Rouble.** Same as **Ruble**.

**Roué**, rōō′ā, *n.* a fashionable profligate : a rake : a debauchee. [Lit. ' one broken on the *wheel*,' a name given by Philippe, Duke of Orléans, Regent of France 1715–23, to his dissolute companions, Fr., pa.p. of *rouer*—*roue*—L. *rota*, a wheel.]

**Rouge**, rōōzh, *n.* a *red* paint used to colour the cheeks or lips.—*v.t.* to colour with rouge. [Fr. (It. *roggio, robbio*)—L. *rubeus*, red. See **Ruby**.]

**Rouge-et-noir**, rōōzh′-ā-nwawr′, *n.* a game at cards played at a table, marked with four diamond-shaped spots, two red and two black. [Fr. ' red-and-black.']

**Rough**, ruf, *adj.* not smooth : uneven : uncut : unpolished : unfinished : boisterous : tempestuous : violent : harsh : severe : rude : coarse : disordered in appearance.—*adv.* **Rough′ly.—**

*n.* **Rough′ness.** [A.S. *ruh*, rough, cog. with Ger. *rauch, rauh*, Dut. *ruig*.] [horse.

**Rough**, ruf, *v.t.* to make rough : to break in a **Roughen**, ruf′n, *v.t.* to make rough.—*v.i.* to become rough.

**Rough-rider**, ruf′-rīd′er, *n.* one who *rides rough* or untrained horses : a horse-breaker.

**Roulette**, rōōl-et′, *n.* a little ball or roller : a game of chance played with a small ball on a circle divided into red and black spaces. [Fr.—*rouler*, to roll, from the balls rolling. See **Roll**.]

**Round**, rownd, *adj.* circular : globular : cylindrical : whole : complete : plump : large : smooth : flowing : open : plain : positive : bold : brisk.— *adv.* in a round manner : on all sides : from one side or party to another : circularly.—*prep.* around : on every side of : all over.—*n.* that which is round : a circle or globe : a series of actions : the time of such a series : a turn : routine : revolution : cycle : an accustomed walk : a step of a ladder : a song or dance having a frequent return to the same point : a volley or general discharge of firearms : that in which a whole company takes part.—*v.t.* to make round : to surround : to go round : to complete : to make full and flowing.—*v.i.* to grow or become round or full : to go round.—*adj.* **Round′ish**, somewhat round. [O. Fr. *round, roond* (Fr. *rond*)— L. *rotundus*—*rota*, a wheel. See **Rotary**.]

**Roundabout**, rownd′a-bowt, *adj.* encircling : circuitous : indirect.—*n.* a horizontal revolving wheel on which children ride.

**Roundel**, rownd′el, *n.* anything of a *round* form or figure : a circle : a roundelay. [O. Fr. *rondel* (Fr. *rondeau*), dim. of *rond*. See **Round**.]

**Roundelay**, rownd′e-lā, *n.* a *round* : a song or dance in which parts are repeated. [Same as above, modified by influence of E. **Lay**.]

**Roundhead**, rownd′hed, *n.* a Puritan, so called in the time of Charles I. from the Puritan fashion of having the hair cut close to the head.

**Roundhouse**, rownd′hows, *n.* in ships, a cabin or house on the after-part of the quarter-deck.

**Roundly**, rownd′li, *adv.* in a round manner : fully : completely : boldly : openly : plainly.

**Roundness**, rownd′nes, *n.* quality of being round, globular, or cylindrical : cylindrical form : fullness : smoothness of flow : plainness : boldness.

**Roundrobin**, rownd-rob′in, *n.* a petition with the signatures in the form of a circle or *round ribbon*, so as not to show who signed first. [Fr. *rond ruban*, round ribbon.]

**Roup**, rowp, *n.* a sale by auction.—*v.* to sell by auction. [A Scotch word.]

**Rouse**, rowz, *v.t.* to *raise* up : to stir up : to awaken : to excite : to put into action : to startle or start, as an animal.—*v.i.* to awake : to be excited to action. [Prob. from the root of **Rose**, pa.t. of **Rise**. See also **Raise**.]

**Rouse**, rowz, *n.* a carousal. [Perh. akin to Ger. *rausch*, drunkenness, perh. short for **Carouse**.]

**Rout**, rowt, *n.* a tumultuous crowd, a rabble : a large party : a fashionable evening assembly. [O. Fr. *route*, a band, division—Low L. *rupta*, thing broken—L. *rumpo, ruptus*, to break.]

**Rout**, rowt, *n.* the defeat of an army or body of troops : the disorder of troops defeated.—*v.t.* to put to disorderly flight : to defeat and throw into confusion : to conquer. [O. Fr. *route*— L. *ruptus, rupta*, pa.p. of *rumpo*, to break. See **Rupture**.]

**Route**, rōōt, *n.* a course to be traversed : a line of march : road : track. [Fr.—L. *rupta* (*via*), ' a *broken* way.']

**Routine**, rōōt-ēn′, *n.* course of duties : regular course of action. [Fr.]

**Rove**, rōv, *v.t.* (*lit.*) to *rob* : to wander over like robbers.—*v.i.* to wander about : to ramble : to range. [A byform of **Reave**, modified by influence of Dut. *roven*, to plunder. See **Rob**.]

**Rover**, rōv′ėr, *n.* one who roves : a robber or pirate : a wanderer : an inconstant person.

**Row**, rō, *n.* a line : a rank : persons or things in a line. [A.S. *rawa ;* Ger. *reihe*, Dut. *rij*.]

**Row**, rō, *v.t.* to impel with an oar : to transport by rowing.—*v.i.* to work with the oar : to be moved by oars.—*n.* an excursion in a rowing-boat.—*n.* **Row′er**. [A.S. *rowan ;* Ger. *rudern*, Ice. *roa*.]      [a corr. of **Rout**, a rabble.]

**Row**, row. *n.* a noisy squabble : uproar. [Prob.

**Rowan-tree**, rō′an-trē, *n.* See **Roan-tree**.

**Rowdy**, row′di, *adj.* noisy and turbulent.—*n.* **Row′dyism**. [Short for *rowdydow*, an expression formed on the basis of **Row**, uproar, and **Rout**, a rabble.]

**Rowel**, row′el, *n.* the *little wheel* in a spur, with sharp points : a little flat wheel or ring on horses' bits. [Fr. *rouelle*—Low L. *rotella*, dim. of L. *rota*, a wheel.]

**Rowlock**, rō′lok or rul′uk, *n.* a contrivance on the wale of a boat, to hold the oar in rowing. [**Row**, *v.* and **Lock**.]

**Royal**, roy′al, *adj.*, *regal*, *kingly :* magnificent : illustrious : magnanimous : enjoying the favour or patronage of the sovereign.—*adv.* **Roy′ally**. [Fr.—L. *regalis*. See **Regal**.]

**Royal**, roy′al, *n.* a large kind of paper : a sail above the topgallant sail : one of the soldiers of the 1st British regiment of foot : one of the shoots of a stag's head.

**Royalism**, roy′al-izm, *n.* attachment to *kings* or to kingly government.

**Royalist**, roy′al-ist, *n.* an adherent of royalism.

**Royalty**, roy′al-ti, *n.*, *kingship :* the character, state, or office of a king : majesty : the person of the king or sovereign : fixed sums paid to the crown or other proprietor, as on the produce of a mine, &c. : kingdom.

**Rub**, rub, *v.t.* to move something over (the surface of) with pressure or friction : to clean : to polish : to wipe : to scour : to erase or beat out : to touch hard.—*v.i.* to move along with pressure : to grate : to fret:—*pr.p.* rubb′ing ; *pa.t.* and *pa.p.* rubbed.—*n.* the act of rubbing : that which rubs : a collision : an obstruction : difficulty : a pinch : a joke. [Gael. *rub*, W. *rhwbio*, to rub, to grind.]

**Rubber**, rub′ėr, *n.* caoutchouc : a coarse file : a contest of three games at cards.

**Rubbish**, rub′ish, *n.* waste matter : the fragments of ruinous buildings : any mingled mass : nonsense.—*adj.* **Rubb′ishy**. [From **Rub**.]

**Rubble**, rub′l, *n.* the upper fragmentary decomposed matter of a mass of rock : water-worn stones : small, undressed stones used in coarse masonry. [From **Rub**.]

**Rubescent**, rōō-bes′ent, *adj.* tending to a *red* colour. [L. *rubesco*, to grow red—*ruber*, red.]

**Rubicund**, rōō′bi-kund, *adj.* inclining to *ruby* or *redness :* ruddy.—*n.* **Rubicun′dity**.

**Ruble**, rōō′bl, *n.* a Russian silver coin equal in value to 100 copper copecks, worth about 3s. [Russ. *rubl*, a piece cut off—*rubitj*, to cut.]

**Rubric**, rōō′brik, *n.* the title of a statute : the directions for the service, in Prayer-books, formerly in *red* letter : an ecclesiastical injunction : a thing definitely settled.—*adjs.* **Ru′brical**, **Ru′bric**. [L. *rubrica*, red earth, hence the title of a law (because written in red)—*ruber*, red.]

**Ruby**, rōō′bi, *n.*, *redness :* anything red : a precious stone of a red colour.—*adj.* having the colour of the ruby : red.—*v.t.* to make red :—*pa.t.* and *pa.p.* ru′bied. [Fr. *rubis ;* from L. *rubeus*—*ruber*, red.]

**Rudder**, rud′ėr, *n.* the instrument by which a ship is *rowed* or steered, which originally was an *oar* working at the stern. [A.S. *rother ;* Ger. *ruder*, an oar. See **Row**, *v.t.*]

**Ruddy**, rud′i (*comp.* **Rudd′ier**, *superl.* **Rudd′iest**), *adj.* of a *red* colour : of the colour of the skin in high health.—*adv.* **Rudd′ily**.—*n.* **Rudd′iness**. [M. E. *rude*, the colour of the face, from root of **Red**.]

**Rude**, rōōd (*comp.* **Rud′er**, *superl.* **Rud′est**), *adj.* crude : uncultivated : barbarous : rough : harsh : ignorant : uncivil.—*adv.* **Rude′ly**.—*n.* **Rude′ness**. [Fr.—L. *rudis ;* conn. with **Crude**.]

**Rudiment**, rōōd′i-ment, *n.* anything in its *rude* or first state : a first principle or element.

**Rudimental**, rōōd-i-ment′al, **Rudimentary**, rōōd-i-ment′ar-i, *adj.* pertaining to, consisting in, or containing rudiments or first principles : initial.

**Rue**, rōō, *n.* a plant used in medicine, having a bitter taste and strong smell. [Fr. *rue*—L. *ruta* —Gr. *rhytē*.]

**Rue**, rōō, *v.t.* to be sorry for : to lament :—*pr.p.* rūe′ing ; *pa.t.* and *pa.p.* rūed. [A.S. *hreowan*, to be sorry for—*hreow*, sorrow ; Ger. *reue*, O. Ger. *hriuwa*, mourning.]

**Rueful**, rōō′fool, *adj.*, *sorrowful :* piteous.—*adv.* **Rue′fully**.—*n.* **Rue′fulness**.

**Ruff**, ruf, *n.* an ornament of frills formerly worn round the neck : anything plaited : a species of wading bird, the male of which has the neck surrounded in the breeding season with a *ruff* of long feathers.—*fem.* **Reeve**.—*v.t.* to ruffle : to trump at whist instead of following suit. [Prob. a form of **Rough**.]

**Ruffian**, ruf′i-an, *n.* a brutal, boisterous fellow : a robber : a murderer.—*adj.* brutal : boisterous. [Fr. *rufien ;* It. *rufiano*, prob. from a root *ruf*, seen in Prov. Ger. *ruffer*, *ruffeln*, to pander.]

**Ruffianism**, ruf′i-an-izm, *n.* conduct of a ruffian.

**Ruffianly**, ruf′i-an-li, *adj.* like a ruffian : violent.

**Ruffle**, ruf′l, *v.t.* to make like a *ruff* : to wrinkle : to form into plaits : to form with ruffles : to disorder : to agitate.—*v.i.* to grow rough : to flutter.—*n.* a plaited article of dress : agitation : a low roll of the drum. [See **Ruff**.]

**Ruffler**, ruf′lėr, *n.* a swaggerer, a bully.

**Rufous**, rōō′fus, *adj.*, *reddish* or brownish-red : having reddish hair. [L. *rufus*, akin to *ruber*, red.]

**Rug**, rug, *n.* a coarse, *rough* woollen cloth or coverlet : a soft, woolly mat. [From root of **Rough**.]

**Rugged**, rug′ed, *adj.*, *rough :* uneven : shaggy : sour : stormy : grating to the ear.—*adv.* **Rugg′edly**.—*n.* **Rugg′edness**. [M. E. *rogge*, to shake, Scot. *rug*, to tear, from Scand. *rugga*.]

**Rugose**, rōō′gōs, **Rugous**, rōō′gus, *adj.*, *wrinkled :* full of wrinkles. [L. *rugosus*—*ruga*, a wrinkle.]

**Ruin**, rōō′in, *n.* a *rushing* or *falling down* violently : destruction : overthrow : that which destroys : the remains of a building demolished or decayed (usually in *pl.*).—*v.t.* to demolish : to destroy : to defeat : to impoverish. [Fr.—L. *ruina*—*ruo*, to rush or tumble down.]

**Ruinous**, rōō′in-us, *adj.* fallen to ruins : decayed : pernicious.—*adv.* **Ru′inously**.

**Rule**, rōōl, *n.* government : a principle : a standard : a statute : a maxim : order : an instrument used in drawing lines.—*v.t.* to govern : to manage : to settle as by a rule : to establish by decision : to determine, as a court : to mark with lines.—*v.i.* to exercise power : to decide : to lay down and settle : to stand or range, as prices. [O. Fr. *reule*, Fr. *règle*—L. *regula*—*rego*, to keep straight, to rule.]

**Ruler,** rōōl′ėr, *n.* a sovereign : a governor : an instrument used in drawing lines.

**Ruling,** rōōl′ing, *adj.* predominant : prevailing.

**Rum,** rum, *n.* a kind of spirit distilled from the fermented juice of the sugar-cane, or from molasses. [Prob. a West Indian word.]

**Rumble,** rum′bl, *n.* a seat for servants behind a carriage. [Ety. dub.]

**Rumble,** rum′bl, *v.i.* to make a confused noise from rolling heavily.—*n.* a low, heavy continued sound. [Teut., found in Dut. *rommelen, rummeln,* from the sound.] [sound.

**Rumbling,** rum′bling, *n.* a low, heavy, continued

**Ruminant,** rōō′mi-nant, *adj.* having the power of *ruminating* or chewing the cud.—*n.* an animal that chews the cud, as the ox, &c.

**Ruminate,** rōō′mi-nāt, *v.i.* to chew the cud : to meditate.—*v.t.* to chew over again : to muse on. [L. *rumino, -atum—rumen,* the throat, gullet.]

**Rumination,** rōō-mi-nā′shun, *n.* act of chewing the cud : calm reflection.

**Rummage,** rum′āj, *v.t.* and *v.i.* to search narrowly by turning things over : to clear a ship's hold of goods.—*n.* a careful search. [Orig. a naut. term, M. E. *rume,* to clear a space—A.S. *rum.* room, or from Dut. *ruim,* a ship's hold. See **Room.**]

**Rummer,** rum′ėr, *n.* a large drinking-glass. [Dut. *roemer,* Ger. *römer,* perh. from Low L. *romarius,* a glass of *Roman* ware.]

**Rumour,** rōō′mur, *n.* flying report : a current story.—*v.t.* to report : to circulate by report. [L. *rumor,* a noise ; conn. with *raucus,* hoarse, *rudo,* to bray, Sans. *ru,* to sound.]

**Rump,** rump, *n.* the end of the backbone of an animal with the parts adjacent. [Ice. *rumpr,* Ger. *rumpf,* Dut. *rompe.*]

**Rumple,** rum′pl, *v.t.* to crush out of shape : to make uneven.—*n.* a fold or wrinkle. [A.S. *hrympelle,* a fold ; Dut. *rompelen,* to fold.]

**Run,** run, *v.i.* to move swiftly : to pass quickly on the ground : to flee : to go, as ships, &c. : to have course in any direction : to flow : to dart : to turn : to extend : to pierce : to melt : to be busied : to become : to be in force : to discharge matter, as a sore : to press, esp. for immediate payment.—*v.t.* to cause to move swiftly : to force forward : to push : to cause to pass : to fuse : to discharge, as a sore : to pursue in thought : to incur :—*pr.p.* runn′ing ; *pa.t.* ran ; *pa.p.* run.—*n.* act of *running* : course : flow : discharge from a sore : distance sailed : voyage : continued series : general reception : prevalence : popular clamour : an unusual pressure, as on a bank, for payment of notes. [A.S. *rennan ;* Ger. *rennen,* Ice. *renna,* to run.]

**Runagate,** run′a-gāt, *n.* a vagabond : renegade. [A corr. of **Renegade,** but modified both in form and meaning by **Run.**]

**Runaway,** run′a-wā, *n.* one who *runs away* from danger or restraint : a fugitive.—*adj.* fleeing from danger or restraint : done by or in flight.

**Rune,** rōōn, *n.* one of the characters forming the earliest alphabet of the Teutonic nations. [A.S. *run,* a secret, mysterious talk, mysterious writing ; applied to the old Teutonic written characters from their use in divination. The word is found in M. E. *rounen,* to whisper, and is cog.

with Ice. *run,* with O. Ger. *runa,* a secret, whispering, Goth. *runa,* secret.]

**Rung,** rung, *pa.t.* and *pa.p.* of **Ring.**

**Runic,** rōōn′ik, *adj.* relating to *runes,* to the ancient Teutonic nations, or to their language.

**Runner,** run′ėr, *n.* one who or that which runs : a racer : a messenger : a rooting stem that runs along the ground : the moving stone of a mill : a rope to increase the power of a tackle.

**Running,** run′ing, *adj.* kept for the race : successive : continuous : flowing : easy : discharging matter.—*n.* act of moving swiftly : that which runs or flows : a discharge from a wound.

**Rupee,** rōō-pē′, *n.* the standard silver coin of India, once valued at 2*s.,* now fallen to 1*s.* 2*d.* [Hind. *rupiyah*—Sans. *rupya,* silver.]

**Rupture,** rup′tūr, *n.* the act of *breaking* or bursting : the state of being broken : a breach of the peace : (*med.*) the protrusion of any of the viscera.—*v.t.* to break or burst : to part by violence.—*v.i.* to suffer a breach. [Fr.—Low L. *ruptura*—L. *rumpo, ruptum,* to break.]

**Rural,** rōōr′al, *adj.* of or belonging to the *country* : suiting the country : rustic : pertaining to agriculture.—*adv.* Rur′ally.—*n.* Rural dean, an ecclesiastic under the bishop and archdeacon, with the peculiar care of the clergy of a district. [Fr.—L. *ruralis—rus, ruris,* the country.] [become rural.

**Ruralise,** rōōr′al-īz, *v.t.* to render rural.—*v.i.* to

**Ruse,** rōōz, *n.* a turning or doubling, as of animals to get out of the way of dogs : a trick : fraud. [Fr. *ruser,* to turn, O. Fr. *reüser,* to get out of the way ; prob. from L. *recusare,* to decline.]

**Rush,** rush, *v.i.* to move with a shaking, rustling noise, as the wind : to move forward violently : to enter rashly and hastily.—*n.* a rushing or driving forward. [A.S. *hriscian,* to shake, Ger. *rauschen,* to make a noise.]

**Rush,** rush, *n.* a plant with a round stem and no leaves, common in wet ground. [A.S. *risce,* like Ger. *risch,* from L. *ruscum.*]

**Rushy,** rush′i, *adj.* full of or made of rushes.

**Rusk,** rusk, *n.* a kind of light hard cake : a kind of light soft cake or sweetened biscuit. [Acc. to Mahn, prob. from Low Ger. *rusken,* to crackle.]

**Russet,** rus′et, *adj., rusty* or *reddish*-brown : coarse : rustic.—*n.* a coarse homespun dress.— *adj.* Russ′e⁣ty. [Dim. of Fr. *rousse*—L. *russus,* red ; said to be from *rubeo,* to be red, like *jussus,* from *jubeo.*]

**Russeting,** rus′et-ing, *n.* an apple of a *russet* colour and rough skin.

**Rust,** rust, *n.* the *reddish*-brown coating on iron exposed to moisture : anything resembling rust : a disease of cereals and grasses, showing itself in brown or orange spots on the leaves, caused by small fungi.—*v.i.* to become rusty : to become dull by inaction.—*v.t.* to make rusty : to impair by time and inactivity. [A.S. ; Ger. *rost.*]

**Rustic,** rus′tik, *adj.* pertaining to the *country* : rural : rude : awkward : simple : coarse : artless : unadorned.—*adv.* Rus′tically. [Fr.—L. *rusticus—rus,* the country.]

**Rusticate,** rus′ti-kāt, *v.t.* to send into the *country* : to banish for a time from a town or college.— *v.i.* to live in the country.—*n.* Rustica′tion. [L. *rusticor, rusticatus—rus.*]

**Rusticity,** rus-tis′i-ti, *n., rustic* manners : simplicity : rudeness. [Fr. *rusticité*—L. *rusticitas.*]

**Rustle,** rus′l, *v.i.* to make a soft, whispering sound, as silk, straw, &c.—*n.* a quick succession of small sounds, as that of dry leaves : a rustling. [A.S. *hristlan ;* Ger. *rasseln :* perh. from the sound.]

**Rustling**, rus′ling, *n.* a quick succession of small sounds, as of dry leaves.

**Rusty**, rust′i, *adj.* covered with *rust*: impaired by inactivity: dull.—*adv.* **Rust′ily**.—*n.* **Rust′iness**.

**Rut**, rut, *n.* a track left by a wheel.—*v.t.* to form ruts in :—*pr.p.* rutt′ing ; *pa.t.* and *pa.p.* rutt′ed. [Fr. *route*. See **Route**.]

**Rut**, rut, *n.* the copulation of animals, esp. of deer.—*v.t.* to cover in copulation.—*v.i.* to lust, said of animals :—*pr.p.* rutt′ing ; *pa.p.* rutt′ed. [Fr. *rut*—L. *rugitus*—*rugio*, to roar.]

**Ruthless**, rooth′les, *adj.*, *without pity* or tenderness : insensible to misery : cruel.—*adv.* **Ruth′lessly**.—*n.* **Ruth′lessness**. [Obs. *ruth*, pity—**Rue**, *v.*]

**Rye**, rī, *n.* a genus of grasses allied to wheat and barley, one species of which is cultivated as a grain. [A.S. *ryge*; Ice. *rugr*, Ger. *roggen*, W. *rhyg*.]

**Ryegrass**, rī′gras, *n.* a variety of *grass* like *rye*, cultivated for pasture and fodder.

**Ryot**, rī′ut, *n.* a Hindu cultivator or peasant. [From Ar. *raaya*, to pasture.]


# S

**Sabaism**, sā′ba-izm. Same as **Sabianism**.

**Sabaoth**, sa-bā′oth, *n.pl.*, *armies*, used only in the *B.* phrase, *the Lord of Sabaoth*. [Heb. *tzebaoth*, pl. of *tzaba*, an army—*tzaba*, to go forth.]

**Sabbatarian**, sab-a-tā′ri-an, *n.* one who observes the seventh day of the week as the *Sabbath*: a very strict observer of the Sabbath.—*adj.* pertaining to the Sabbath or to Sabbatarians.—*n.* **Sabbata′rianism**. [L. *sabbatarius*—*Sabbata*. See **Sabbath**.]

**Sabbath**, sab′ath, *n.* among the Jews, the seventh day of the week, set apart for *rest* from work : among Christians, the first day of the week, in memory of the resurrection of Christ: among the ancient Jews, the seventh year, when the land was left fallow. [Lit. *rest*, L. *Sabbata*—Heb. *Shabbath*, rest.]

**Sabbatic**, sab-at′ik, **Sabbatical**, sab-at′ik-al, *adj.* pertaining to or resembling the *Sabbath* : enjoying or bringing rest. [Low L. *sabbaticus*.]

**Sabianism**, sā′bi-an-izm, **Sabaism**, sā′ba-izm, *n.* the worship of the *host* of heaven, *i.e.* heavenly bodies, angels, &c., as well as the Deity. [Prob. from Heb. *tzaba*, an army, a host.]

**Sable**, sā′bl, *n.* an animal of the weasel kind found in N. Europe and N. Asia, valuable for its glossy black fur : its fur. [O. Fr. *sable*, through Low L. *sabelus*, from Russ. *sóbol*.]

**Sable**, sā′bl, *adj.* of the colour of the sable′s fur: black : dark : made of the fur of the sable.

**Sabre**, sā′br, *n.* a heavy one-edged sword, slightly curved towards the point, used by cavalry.—*v.t.* to wound or kill with a sabre. [Fr. *sabre*—Ger. *säbel*, prob. from the Slav., as Russ. *sabla*, Polish *szabla*.]

**Sabre-tache**, sab′ėr-tash, *n.* an ornamental leather case worn by cavalry officers at the left side, suspended from the sword-belt. [Fr. *sabre-tache*, from *sabre*, and Ger. *tasche*, a pocket.]

**Sac**, sak, *n.* (*nat. hist.*) a sack or bag for a liquid. [Fr. form of **Sack**, a bag.]

**Saccharine**, sak′a-rin, *adj.* pertaining to or having the qualities of *sugar*. [Fr. *saccharin*—L. *saccharum*, sugar. See **Sugar**.]

**Saccharometer**, sak-ar-om′e-tėr, *n.* an instrument for *measuring* the quantity of *saccharine* matter in a liquid. [Gr. *sakcharon*, sugar, and *metron*, a measure.]

**Sacerdotal**, sas-ėr-dōt′al, *adj.*, *priestly*.—*adv.* **Sacerdot′ally**. [L.—*sacer-dos*, a priest—*sacer*, sacred, and prob. either *do*, to give, or root *dhā*, to do. See **Sacred**.]

**Sacerdotalism**, sas-ėr-dōt′al-izm, *n.* the spirit of the *priesthood* : devotion to priestly interests.

**Sachel**. Same as **Satchel**. [Indian tribe.

**Sachem**, sā′kem, *n.* one of the chiefs of a N. Amer.

**Sack**, sak, *n.* a large bag of coarse cloth, for holding grain, flour, &c. : the contents of a sack : a loose upper garment or cloak.—*v.t.* to put into a sack. [A.S. *sac*, *sacc*, a word common to all European tongues, perh. orig. Semitic, as Heb. *sak*, a coarse cloth or garment.]

**Sack**, sak, *v.t.* to plunder : to ravage.—*n.* the plunder or devastation of a town : ravage. [Fr. *sac*, a sack, plunder (*saccager*, to sack) ; cf. Dut. *sacken*, to put in sacks, to plunder (from the use of a sack in removing plunder).]

**Sack**, sak, *n.* the old name of a *dry* Spanish wine. [O. E. *seck*—Fr. *sec* (Sp. *seco*)—L. *siccus*, dry.]

**Sackbut**, sak′but, *n.* the name of the trombone when first brought to England : (*B.*) a kind of lyre or stringed instrument. [Fr. *saquebute*; of uncertain origin.]

**Sackcloth**, sak′kloth, *n.*, *cloth* for *sacks* : coarse cloth formerly worn in mourning or penance.

**Sacking**, sak′ing, *n.* cloth of which *sacks* are made : the coarse cloth or canvas that supports a bed.

**Sacking**, sak′ing, *n.* the storming and pillaging of a town.

**Sacrament**, sak′ra-ment, *n.* one of the solemn religious rites in the Christian Church, esp. the Lord's Supper. [L. *sacramentum*, a sacred thing—*sacro*, to consecrate—*sacer*, sacred.]

**Sacramental**, sak-ra-ment′al, *adj.* belonging to or constituting a sacrament.—*adv.* **Sacrament′ally**.

**Sacred**, sā′kred, *adj.*, *set apart* or dedicated, esp. to God : made holy : proceeding from God : religious : entitled to respect or veneration : inviolable.—*adv.* **Sa′credly**.—*n.* **Sa′credness**. [M. E. *sacre*, to set apart, consecrate, pa.p. *sa-cred*—Fr. *sacré*—L. *sacer*, from root *sa*, akin to *sanus*, sound, Gr. *sōs*, safe. Cf. **Whole** and **Holy**.]

**Sacrifice**, sak′ri-fīz, *v.t.* to offer up, esp. on the altar of a divinity : to destroy or give up for something else : to devote or destroy with loss or suffering : to kill.—*v.i.* to make offerings to God.—*n.* **Sac′rificer**. [L. *sacrifico*—*sacer*, sacred, and *facio*, to make, to do.]

**Sacrifice**, sak′ri-fīs, *n.* act of sacrificing or offering to a deity, esp. a victim on an altar : that which is sacrificed or offered : destruction or loss of anything to gain some object : that which is given up, destroyed, or lost for some end.

**Sacrificial**, sak-ri-fish′al, *adj.* relating to or consisting in sacrifice : performing sacrifice. [L. *sacrificialis*.]

**Sacrilege**, sak′ri-lej, *n.* profanation of a sacred place or thing : the breaking into a place of worship and stealing therefrom. [Lit. the crime of *stealing sacred* things, Fr. *sacrilège*—L. *sacrilegium*—*sacer*, sacred, and *lego*, to gather, to steal.]

**Sacrilegious**, sak-ri-lē′jus, *adj.* polluted with sacrilege : profane : violating sacred things.—*adv.* **Sacrile′giously**.—*n.* **Sacrile′giousness**. [L. *sacrilegus*.]

**Sacrist**, sā′krist, *n.* a person in a *sacred* place or cathedral who copies out music for the choir and takes care of the books : a sacristan. [Low L. *sacrista*—L. *sacer*.]

**Sacristan**, sak′rist-an, *n.* an officer in a cnurch who has charge of the *sacred* vessels and other movables: a sexton. [Low L. *sacristanus*—L. *sacer*.]

**Sacristy**, sak′rist-i, *n.* an apartment in a church where the *sacred* utensils, vestments, &c. are kept: vestry. [Low L. *sacristia*—L. *sacer*.]

**Sad**, sad (*comp.* **Sadd′er**, *superl.* **Sadd′est**), *adj.* heavy: serious: cast down: calamitous.—*adv.* **Sad′ly**.—*n.* **Sad′ness**. [A.S. *sæd*, sated, weary, with cog. words in all the Teut. tongues and in L. *satur*, full.]

**Sadden**, sad′n, *v.t.* to make sad.—*v.i.* to grow sad.

**Saddle**, sad′l, *n.* a seat or pad, generally of leather, for a horse's back: anything like a saddle, as a saddle of mutton (the two loins undivided), &c.—*v.t.* to put a saddle on: to load. [A.S. *sadel*. Cog. words are in all the Teut. tongues, and even in Slav. *sedlo*, Celt. *sadell*, and Finn. *satula*.]

**Saddler**, sad′lėr, *n.* a maker of saddles.

**Saddlery**, sad′lėr-i, *n.* occupation of a saddler: materials for saddles: articles sold by a saddler.

**Sadducean**, sad-ū-sē′an, *adj.* of or relating to the Sadducees.

**Sadducee**, sad′ū-sē, *n.* one of a Jewish school or party who denied the resurrection, the existence of spirits, and a future state.—*n.* **Sadduceeism**, sad-ū-sē′izm. [Gr. *Saddoukaios*; Heb. *Zedukim*.]

**Sadly, Sadness.** See under **Sad**.

**Safe**, sāf, *adj.* unharmed: free from danger or injury: secure: securing from danger or injury: no longer dangerous.—*adv.* **Safe′ly**.—*n.* **Safe′ness**. [Fr. *sauf*—L. *salvus*; allied to Gr. *holoos*, Sans. *sarva*, whole, entire, and Goth. *sēls*.]

**Safe**, sāf, *n.* a chest or closet for money, &c., safe against fire, thieves, &c., generally of iron: a chest or cupboard for meats.

**Safe-conduct**, sāf′-kon′dukt, *n.* a writing, passport, or guard granted to a person, to enable him to travel with safety. [See **Safe**, *adj.* and **Conduct**.]

**Safeguard**, sāf′gärd, *n.* he or that which *guards* or renders *safe:* protection: a guard, passport, or warrant to protect a traveller.

**Safety**, sāf′ti, *n.* freedom from danger or loss: close custody.

**Safety-fuse**, sāf′ti-fūz, *n.* a waterproof woven tube inclosing an inflammable substance which burns at a regular rate. [See **Safety** and **Fuse**, *n.*]

**Safety-lamp**, sāf′ti-lamp, *n.* a *lamp* surrounded by wire-gauze, used for *safety* in mines.

**Safety-valve**, sāf′ti-valv, *n.* a *valve* in the top of a steam-boiler, which lets out the steam when the pressure is too great for *safety*.

**Safflower**, saf′flowr, *n.* a plant of Asia and S. Europe, whose flowers yield a red dye. [Corr. of **Saffron Flower**.]

**Saffron**, saf′run, *n.* a bulbous plant of the crocus kind with deep-yellow flowers: a colouring substance prepared from its flowers.—*adj.* having the colour of saffron: deep yellow. [Fr. *safran* (It. *zafferano*)—Ar. *za′farân*, the plant having been cultivated by the Moors in Spain.]

**Saga**, sā′ga, *n.* a Scandinavian legend. [Ice. *saga*—*segja*, E. **Say**. Doublet **Saw**, a saying.]

**Sagacious**, sa-gā′shus, *adj.* keen or quick in perception or thought: acute: discerning and judicious: wise.—*adv.* **Saga′ciously**.—*n.* **Saga′ciousness**. [L. *sagax, sagacis*—*sag-io*, to perceive quickly or keenly.]

**Sagacity**, sa-gas′i-ti, *n.* acuteness of perception or thought: acute practical judgment: shrewdness. [L. *sagacitas*—*sagax*. See **Sagacious**.]

**Sage**, sāj, *n.* an aromatic garden herb, so called

from its supposed healing virtue. [Fr. *sauge* (It. *salvia*)—L. *salvia*—*salvus*, safe, sound.]

**Sage**, sāj, *adj.* discriminating, discerning, wise: well judged.—*n.* a sage or wise man: a man of gravity and wisdom.—*adv.* **Sage′ly**.—*n.* **Sage′ness**. [Fr. *sage* (It. *saggio, savio*) from a L. *sapius* (seen in *ne-sapius*), wise—*sapio*, to taste, discriminate, be wise.]

**Sagittal**, saj′it-al, *adj.* of or like an *arrow*. [L. *sagitta*, an arrow.]

**Sagittarius**, saj-i-tā′ri-us, *n.* the *Archer*, one of the signs of the zodiac. [L.—*sagitta*, an arrow.]

**Sago**, sā′go, *n.* a dry starch produced from the pith of several palms in the E. India Islands, &c., used for food. [Papuan name for the sago-palm.]

**Said**, sed, *pa.t.* and *pa.p.* of **Say**.

**Sail**, sāl, *n.* a sheet of canvas, &c. spread to catch the wind, by which a ship is driven forward: a ship or ships: a trip in a vessel.—*v.i.* to be moved by sails: to go by water: to begin a voyage: to glide or float smoothly along.—*v.t.* to navigate: to pass in a ship: to fly through. [A.S. *segel*, and found in nearly all the Teut. tongues.]

**Sailcloth**, sāl′kloth, *n.* a strong *cloth* for *sails*.

**Sailer**, sāl′ėr, *n.* he who or that which *sails*, mainly limited to ships and boats.

**Sailing**, sāl′ing, *n.* act of sailing: motion of a vessel on water: art of directing a ship's course.

**Sailor**, sāl′or, *n.* one who sails in or navigates a ship: a seaman.

**Sainfoin**, sān′foin, *n.* a leguminous fodder-plant. [Fr. *sain*, wholesome, and *foin*, hay—L. *sanum fœnum*.]

**Saint**, sānt, *n.* a *sanctified* or holy person: one eminent for piety: one of the blessed in heaven: one canonised by the R. Cath. Church. [Fr.—L. *sanctus*, holy—*sancio*, to render sacred.]

**Sainted**, sānt′ed, *adj.* made a saint: holy: sacred: gone to heaven.

**Saintlike**, sānt′līk, **Saintly**, sānt′li, *adj.* like or becoming a saint.—*n.* **Saint′liness**.

**Sake**, sāk, *n.* cause: account: regard. [Lit. 'dispute,' 'cause,' A.S. *sacu* (with cog. words in all the Teut. tongues)—*sacan*, to strive, Goth. *sakan*. **Seek** is a doublet.]

**Salaam, Salam**, sa-läm′, *n.* a word of salutation in the East, chiefly among Mohammedans: homage. [Lit. 'peace,' Ar. *salam*, Heb. *shalôm*.]

**Salacious**, sal-ā′shi-us, *adj.* lustful: lecherous. [L. *salax*—*salio*, to leap.]

**Salad**, sal′ad, *n.* raw herbs cut up and seasoned with *salt*, vinegar, &c. [Fr. *salade* (It. *salato*), lit. salted—L. *sal*, salt.]

**Salæratus**, sal-ē-rā′tus, *n.* a mixture of carbonate of soda and salt, used in baking. [See **Salt** and **Aerate**.]

**Salam.** See **Salaam**.

**Salamander**, sal′a-man-dėr, *n.* a genus of reptiles allied to the frog, once supposed able to live in fire. [Fr. *salamandre*—L. and Gr. *salamandra*.]

**Salamandrine**, sal-a-man′drin, *adj.* pertaining to or resembling a salamander: enduring fire.

**Sal-ammoniac**, sal-am-mōn′i-ak, *n.* chloride of ammonium, a salt of a sharp, acrid taste. [From L. *sal*, salt, and **Ammoniac**.]

**Salaried**, sal′a-rid, *adj.* receiving a salary.

**Salary**, sal′a-ri, *n.* a recompense for services: wages. [Lit. 'salt-money,' O. Fr. *salarie* (Fr. *salaire*, It. *salario*)—L. *salarium*, money given to Roman soldiers for salt—*sal*, salt.]

**Sale**, sāl, *n.* act of *selling:* the exchange of anything for money: power or opportunity of selling: demand: public showing of goods to sell: auction. [Ice. and O. Ger. *sala*. See **Sell**.]

**Saleable**, sāl′a-bl, *adj.* that may be *sold*: in good demand.—*n.* **Sale′ableness.**—*adv.* **Sale′ably.**

**Salep**, sal′ep, *n.* the dried tubers of the *Orchis mascula*: the food prepared from it. [Ar.]

**Salesman**, sālz′man, *n.* a *man* who *sells* goods.

**Salic**, sal′ik, *adj.* denoting a law, as in France, by which males alone can succeed to the throne. [Fr. *salique*, prob. from the Salian Franks, among whom this law existed.]

**Salient**, sā′li-ent, *adj.*, *leaping* or springing: (*fort.*) projecting outwards, as an angle: prominent: (*geom.*) denoting any angle less than two right angles.—*adv.* **Sa′liently**, pr.p. of *salio*, to leap.] [L. *saliens*, -*entis*,

**Salify**, sal′i-fī, *v.t.* to combine with an acid in order to make a *salt*:—*pa.t.* and *pa.p.* sal′ified. —*adj.* **Salifi′able.** [L. *sal*, salt, and *facio*, to make.]

**Saline**, sā′līn or sal-īn′, *adj.* consisting of or containing *salt*: partaking of the qualities of salt. —*n.* a salt-spring.—*n.* **Saline′ness.** [Fr.—L. *salinus*—*sal*, salt.]

**Saliva**, sa-lī′va, *n.* the spittle: the fluid secreted by the glands of the mouth, and used to mix with the food and aid digestion. [It. and L., allied to Gr. *sialon*, saliva, and to **Slaver.**]

**Salival**, sa-lī′val, **Salivary**, sal′i-var-i, *adj.* pertaining to, secreting, or containing saliva.

**Salivate**, sal′i-vāt, *v.t.* to produce an unusual amount of saliva. [*saliva*.

**Salivation**, sal-i-vā′shun, *n.* an unusual flow of saliva.

**Sallow**, sal′ō, *n.* a tree or low shrub of the *willow* kind. [Scot. *saugh*, A.S. *sealh*; cog. with Ger. *sahl* (whence Fr. *saule*), L. *salix*, Gr. *helikē*.]

**Sallow**, sal′ō, *adj.* of a pale, yellowish colour.— *n.* **Sall′owness.** [A.S. *salu*, cog. with Dut. *zaluw*, O. Ger. *salo*.]

**Sally**, sal′i, *n.* a *leaping* or bursting out: a sudden rushing forth of troops to attack besiegers: excursion: outburst of fancy, wit, &c.: levity. —*v.i.* to rush out suddenly:—*pa.t.* and *pa.p.* sall′ied. [Fr. *saillie*—*saillir* (It. *salire*)—L. *salio*, to leap, spring.]

**Sally-port**, sal′i-pōrt, *n.* a *port*, gate, or passage, by which a garrison may make a *sally*.

**Salmagundi**, sal-ma-gun′di, *n.* a mixture of chopped meat and other ingredients: a medley. [Fr. *salmigondis*; ety. unknown.]

**Salmon**, sam′un, *n.* a well-known fish, living mostly in the sea, but ascending rivers to spawn. [O. Fr. *saulmon*—L. *salmo*, perh. from *salio*, to leap, from its *leaping* obstacles on its way from the sea.]

**Salmon-trout**, sam′un-trowt, *n.* a *trout* like the *salmon*, but smaller and thicker in proportion.

**Saloon**, sa-lōōn′, *n.* a spacious and elegant *hall*, or apartment for the reception of company, works of art, or for refreshment, &c.: a main cabin. [Fr. *salon*—*salle*; from O. Ger. *sal*, a dwelling, Ger. *saal*.]

**Saloop**, sa-lōōp′, *n.* a drink composed of sassafras tea, with sugar and milk. [A form of **Salep.**]

**Salsify**, sal′si-fi, *n.* a biennial plant with an eatable root like the carrot or parsnip. [Fr.—It. *sassefrica*.]

**Salt**, sawlt, *n.* a well-known substance used for seasoning, found either in the earth or obtained by evaporation from sea-water: anything like salt: seasoning: piquancy: (*chem.*) a combination of an acid with a base.—*adj.* containing *salt*: tasting of salt: overflowed with or growing in salt water: pungent.—*adj.* **Salt′ish**, somewhat salt.—*adv.* **Salt′ly.**—*n.* **Salt′ness.** [A.S. *sealt*, *salt*; with cog. forms in all the

Teut. and nearly all the Slav. tongues, and in L. *sal*, Gr. *hals*, Sans. *sara*.]

**Salt**, sawlt, *v.t.* to sprinkle or season with salt.

**Saltant**, sal′tant, *adj.*, *leaping*: dancing. [L. *saltans*, pr.p. of *salto*, -*atum*, inten. of *salio*, to leap.]

**Saltation**, sal-tā′shun, *n.* a *leaping* or jumping: beating or palpitation. [L. *saltatio*—*salio*.]

**Saltatory**, sal′ta-tor-i, *adj.*, *leaping*, dancing: having the power of or used in leaping or dancing.

**Saltcellar**, sawlt′sel-ar, *n.* a small hollow vessel for holding *salt*. [**Cellar**, a corr. of M. E. *saller* —Fr. *salière*, salt-box—L. *salarium* (*vas*), vessel for salt—*sal*. **Salt** has been unnecessarily prefixed.]

**Saltire** or **Saltier**, sal′tēr, *n.* (*her.*) a diagonal cross, also called a St Andrew's Cross, from the belief that he suffered martyrdom on such a cross. [O. Fr. *saulteur* (Fr. *sautoir*)—Low L. *saltatorium*, an instrument to help in mounting a horse—L. *salto*, to leap.]

**Saltpan**, sawlt′pan, *n.* a *pan*, basin, or pit where *salt* is obtained or made.

**Saltpetre**, sawlt-pē′tėr, *n.* a salt consisting of nitric acid and potash: nitre. [Lit. 'salt-rock,' **Salt**, and L. and Gr. *petra*, a rock.]

**Salubrious**, sa-lōō′bri-us, *adj.*, *healthful*: favourable to health.—*adv.* **Salu′briously.**—*n.* **Salu′brity.** [L. *salubris*—*salus*, *salutis*, health, akin to **Safe.**]

**Salutary**, sal′ū-tar-i, *adj.* belonging to *health*: promoting health or safety: wholesome: beneficial.—*n.* **Sal′utariness.** [L., from *salus*, health.] [which is said in saluting.

**Salutation**, sal-ū-tā′shun, *n.* act of saluting: that

**Salute**, sa-lūt′, *v.t.* to address with kind wishes: to greet with a kiss, bow, &c.: to honour by a discharge of cannon, striking colours, &c.—*n.* act of saluting: greeting, a kiss: a discharge of cannon in honour of any one. [Lit. 'to wish health to,' L. *saluto*, -*atum*, from *salus*, *salutis*.]

**Salvage**, sal′vāj, *n.* money paid to those who assist in *saving* a ship or goods at sea: the goods and materials saved. [Fr., from L. *salvo*, -*atum*, to save.]

**Salvation**, sal-vā′shun, *n.* act of *saving*: preservation: (*theol.*) the saving of man from eternal misery: (*B.*) deliverance from enemies.

**Salve**, säv, *n.* (*B.*) an ointment: anything to cure sores. [A.S. *sealf*; Dan. *salve*, Ger. *salbe*.]

**Salver**, sal′vėr, *n.* a plate on which anything is presented. [Found in Sp. *salvilla*, a salver— Low L. *salva*, a testing, trial—L. *salvo*, to save; from the practice of tasting food as a guarantee against poison.]

**Salvo**, sal′vō, *n.* an exception: a reservation. [L. *salvo jure*, one's right being safe, an expression used in reserving rights.]

**Salvo**, sal′vō, *n.* a military or naval salute with guns: a simultaneous and concentrated discharge of artillery:—*pl.* **Salvos**, sal′vōz. [Fr. *salve*—L. *salve*, a form of salutation—root of *salus*. See **Safe**, *adj.*]

**Sal-volatile**, sal-vo-lat′i-le, *n.* a solution of carbonate of ammonia. [L., 'volatile salt.']

**Samaritan**, sa-mar′i-tan, *adj.* pertaining to *Samaria*, in Palestine.—*n.* an inhabitant of Samaria: the language of Samaria.

**Same**, sām, *adj.* identical: of the like kind or degree: similar: mentioned before.—*n.* **Same′ness.** [A.S.: Goth. *samana*: akin to L. *similis*, like, Gr. *homos*, Sans. *samas*.]

**Samite**, sā′mīt, *n.* a kind of silk stuff. [O. Fr.—

Low L. *examitum*, from Gr. *hex*, six, and *mitos*, thread.]

**Samphire**, sam′fīr or sam′fẽr, *n.* an herb found chiefly on rocky cliffs near the sea, used in pickles and salads. [Lit. 'the herb of St Peter,' corr. from Fr. *Saint Pierre*, Saint Peter.]

**Sample**, sam′pl, *n.* a specimen : a part to show the quality of the whole.—*v.t.* to make up samples of. [Short for *esample*, from O. Fr. *essample*—L. *exemplum*. Doublet **Example**.]

**Sampler**, sam′plẽr, *n.* one who makes up *samples*. [Used in compounds, as *wool-sampler* ; from **Sample**.]

**Sampler**, sam′plẽr, *n.* a pattern of work : ornamental needle-work. [Formed from L. *exemplar*.]

**Sanable**, san′a-bl, *adj.* able to be made sane or sound : curable.—*n.* **Sanabil′ity**. [L. *sanabilis*—*sano*, *-atum*, to heal. See **Sane**.]

**Sanative**, san′a-tiv, *adj.* tending or able to *heal* : healing.—*n.* **San′ativeness**.

**Sanatorium**, san-a-to′ri-um, *n.* a place for restoring to *health*, a health-station. [health.

**Sanatory**, san′a-tor-i, *adj.*, *healing* : conducive to

**Sanctification**, sangk-ti-fi-kā′shun, *n.* act of sanctifying : state of being sanctified.

**Sanctify**, sangk′ti-fī, *v.t.* to *make sacred* or *holy* : to set apart to sacred use : to free from sin or evil : to make the means of holiness : to secure from violation :—*pa.t.* and *pa.p.* sanc′tified.— *n.* **Sanc′tifier**. [Fr.—L. *sanctifico*, *-atum*—*sanctus*, sacred, *facio*, to make.]

**Sanctimonious**, sangk-ti-mō′ni-us, *adj.* having sanctity : holy : devout : affecting holiness.— *adv.* **Sanctimo′niously**.—*n.* **Sanctimo′niousness**.

**Sanctimony**, sangk′ti-mun-i, *n.* devoutness : appearance of sanctity. [L., from *sanctus*, holy. See **Saint**.]

**Sanction**, sangk′shun, *n.* act of ratifying, or giving authority to : confirmation : support.—*v.t.* to give validity to : to authorise : to countenance. [Fr.—L. *sanctio*.]

**Sanctity**, sangk′ti-ti, *n.* quality of being *sacred* or *holy* : purity : godliness : inviolability.

**Sanctuary**, sangk′tū-ar-i, *n.* a *sacred* place : a place for the worship of God : the most sacred part of the Temple of Jerusalem : the Temple itself : the part of a church round the altar : an inviolable asylum : refuge. [See **Sanctify**.]

**Sanctum**, sangk′tum, *n.* a sacred place : a private room. [L., 'holy.']

**Sand**, sand, *n.* fine particles of crushed or worn rocks :—*pl.* lands covered with sand : a sandy beach : moments of time, from the use of sand in the hour-glass.—*v.t.* to sprinkle with sand. [A.S. ; cog. with Ger. *sand*, Ice. *sand-r*.]

**Sandal**, san′dal, *n.* a kind of shoe consisting of a sole bound to the foot by straps : a loose slipper. [Fr.—L. *sandalium*—Gr. *sandalon*, prob. from Pers. *sandal*, a kind of shoe.]

**Sandalled**, san′dald, *adj.* wearing *sandals*.

**Sandalwood**, san′dal-wood, *n.* a wood, remarkable for its fragrance, brought from the E. Indies and islands of the Pacific. [Fr.—Port. *sandalo*—Ar. *sandal*—Sans. *tschandana*, and **Wood**.]

**Sandeel**, sand′ēl, *n.* a small *eel*-like fish, which buries itself in the *sand* when the tide retires.

**Sanderling**, sand′ẽr-ling, *n.* a small wading bird which feeds on the insects in sea-*sands*.

**Sandglass**, sand′glas, *n.* a *glass* instrument for measuring time by the running of *sand*.

**Sandheat**, sand′hēt, *n.* the *heat* of warm *sand* in chemical operations.

**Sandiver**, san′di-vẽr, *n.* the saline scum which forms on glass during its first fusion : glass-gall. [Said to be a corr. of Fr. *sel de verre*, 'salt of glass.']

**Sand-martin**, sand′-mär′tin, *n.* the smallest of British swallows, which builds its nest in *sandy* river-banks and gravel-pits. [See **Martin**.]

**Sand-paper**, sand′-pā′pẽr, *n.*, *paper* covered with a kind of *sand* for smoothing and polishing.

**Sandpiper**, sand′pī-pẽr, *n.* a wading-bird of the snipe family, which frequents *sandy* river-banks, distinguished by its clear *piping* note.

**Sandstone**, sand′stōn, *n.*, *stone* composed of consolidated *sand*.

**Sandwich**, sand′wich, *n.* two slices of bread with ham, &c. between, said to be named after an Earl of *Sandwich* ; hence armour-plating made up of two plates of iron with a plate of wood between, or *vice versâ*.

**Sandy**, sand′i, *adj.* consisting of or covered with *sand* : loose : of the colour of sand.—*n.* **Sand′iness**.

**Sane**, sān, *adj.*, *sound* in mind or body : healthy : not disordered in intellect.—*n.* **Sane′ness**. [L. *sanus*, akin to Gr. *saos*, *sōs*, sound.]

**Sang**, *pa.t.* of **Sing**.

**Sanguinary**, sang′gwin-ar-i, *adj.*, *bloody* : attended with much bloodshed : bloodthirsty.—*adv.* **San′guinarily**.—*n.* **San′guinariness**. [Fr. See **Sanguine**.]

**Sanguine**, sang′gwin, *adj.* abounding with *blood* : ardent : hopeful : confident.—*adv.* **San′guinely**.—*n.* **San′guineness**. [L. *sanguineus*—*sanguis*, *sanguinis*, blood, prob. from root *sag*, *sak*, to drop, flow, as in A.S. *suc-an*, Ger. *saugen*, E. **Suck**.]

**Sanguineous**, sang-gwin′e-us, *adj.*, *sanguine* : resembling or constituting blood.

**Sanhedrim**, san′he-drim, *n.* the highest council of the Jews, consisting of seventy members with the high-priest. [Lit. 'a sitting together,' Heb. *sanhedrin*, from Gr. *synedrion*—*syn*, together, and *hedra*, a seat.]

**Sanitary**, san′i-tar-i, *adj.* pertaining to, tending, or designed to promote *health*. [From **Sanity**.]

**Sanity**, san′i-ti, *n.* state of being *sane* : soundness of mind or body. [L. *sanitas*—*sanus*. See **Sane**.]

**Sanskrit**, sans′krit, *n.* the ancient language of the Hindus. [Lit. the 'perfect' language, from Sans. *sam*, with (Gr. *hama*), and *krita*, done, perfected, from *kri*, root of L. *creo*. See **Create**.]

**Sap**, sap, *n.* the vital juice of plants : (*bot.*) the part of the wood next to the bark. [A.S. *sæp* ; Low Ger. *sapp*, juice, Ger. *saft* ; all borrowed from L. *sapa*, new wine boiled thick.]

**Sap**, sap, *v.t.* to destroy by *digging* underneath : to undermine.—*v.i.* to proceed by undermining : *pr.p.* sapp′ing ; *pa.t.* and *pa.p.* sapped.—*n.* an approach dug to a fortification under cover of gabions.—*n.* **Sapp′er**, one who saps. [Fr. *saper*, from Low L. *sappa*, a pick.]

**Sapid**, sap′id, *adj.*, *well-tasted* : savoury : that affects the taste. [Fr.—L. *sapidus*—*sapio*, to taste.]

**Sapidity**, sa-pid′i-ti, *n.* savouriness.

**Sapience**, sā′pi-ens, *n.* discernment : wisdom : knowledge. [Fr. See **Sapient**.]

**Sapient**, sā′pi-ent, *adj.*, *wise* : discerning : sagacious.—*adv.* **Sa′piently**. [L. *sapiens*, *sapientis*, *pr.p.* of *sapio*, to taste, to be wise, akin to Gr. *saphēs*, clear, distinct.]

**Sapless**, sap′les, *adj.* wanting sap : not juicy.

**Sapling**, sap'ling, n. a young tree, so called from being full of sap.

**Saponaceous**, sap-o-nā'shus, adj., soapy: soap-like. [Fr. saponacé—L. sapo, saponis, Gr. sapōn, both borrowed from the ancient Celts or Germans. See Soap.]

**Sapphic**, saf'ik, adj. pertaining to Sappho, a Grecian poetess: denoting a kind of verse said to have been invented by Sappho.

**Sapphire**, saf'ir or saf'īr, n. a highly brilliant precious stone, inferior only to the diamond. [Fr.—L. sapphirus—Gr. sappheiros—Ar. safir, Heb. sappir, fair, from shaphar, to shine.]

**Sapphirine**, saf'ir-in, adj. made of or like sapphire.

**Sappy**, sap'i, adj. abounding with sap: juicy.—n. Sapp'iness.

**Saracen**, sar'a-sen, n. a name applied in the middle ages to the Mohammedans.—adjs. Saracen'ic, Saracen'ical. [L. Saracenus—Ar. sharkeyn, eastern people, first applied to some tribes of Bedouins in E. Arabia.]

**Sarcasm**, sär'kazm, n. a bitter sneer: a satirical remark in scorn or contempt. [Fr.—L. sarcasmus—Gr. sarkasmos—sarkazō, to tear flesh like dogs, to speak bitterly—sarx, sarkos, flesh.]

**Sarcastic**, sär-kas'tik, **Sarcastical**, sär-kas'tik-al, adj. containing sarcasm: bitterly satirical.—adv. Sarcas'tically.

**Sarcenet**, särs'net, n. a very thin fine silk. [O. Fr., from Low L. sericinus, silken—L. sericum, silk—L. seres, Gr. sēres, a people of E. Asia, from whom the ancients got their first silk.]

**Sarcophagous**, sär-kof'a-gus, adj., flesh-eating: feeding on flesh.

**Sarcophagus**, sär-kof'a-gus, n. a kind of lime-stone used by the Greeks for coffins, and so called because it was thought to consume the flesh of corpses: any stone receptacle for a corpse. [L.—Gr. sarkophagus—sarx, sarkos, flesh, and phagō, to eat.]

**Sardine**, sär'din, n. a small fish of the herring family, abundant about the island of Sardinia, potted with olive oil for export. [Fr. (It. sardina)—L. sarda, sardina—Gr. sardinē.]

**Sardine**, sär'din, **Sardius**, sär'di-us, n. a name of the cornelian stone.—adj. relating to the sardius. [Fr. sardoine—L. sardonyx—Gr. sardonyx.]

**Sardonic**, sär-don'ik, adj. forced, heartless, or bitter, said of a laugh. [Fr.—L. sardonius, sardonicus—Gr. sardanios, referred to sardonion, a plant of Sardinia (Gr. Sardō), which was said to screw up the face of the eater, but more prob. from Gr. sairō, to grin.]

**Sardonyx**, sär'don-iks, n. a reddish-yellow variety of chalcedony, said to have been found orig. at Sardis in Asia Minor, and to be so called because its colour resembles that of the flesh under the nail. [Gr.—Sardios, Sardian, and onyx, a nail.]

**Sarsaparilla**, sär-sa-pa-ril'a, **Sarsa**, sär'sa, n. a twining shrub like the bramble, found chiefly in Mexico, used in medicine. [Sp. zarzaparilla—zarza, bramble, and parilla, a little vine, and so sig. 'a thorny vine.']

**Sash**, sash, n. a band, riband, or scarf worn as a badge or ornament. [Pers. shash, a turban, perh. from Heb. shesh, fine cloth.]

**Sash**, sash, n. a case or frame for panes of glass.—v.t. to furnish with sashes. [Fr. châsse, chassis—L. capsa, the receiving thing, a case—capio, to take. See Case, a covering.]

**Sassafras**, sas'a-fras, n. a kind of laurel, the wood of which has a pungent taste, and is much used in medicine, so called because formerly used to break or dissolve stone in the bladder. [Fr.—L. saxifraga—saxum, a stone, and frango, to break. See Saxifrage.]

**Sat**, sat, pa.t. and pa.p. of Sit.

**Satan**, sā'tan, n. the enemy of men: the devil: the chief of the fallen angels. [Heb. satan, enemy—satan, Ar. shatana, to be adverse.]

**Satanic**, sa-tan'ik, **Satanical**, sa-tan'ik-al, adj. pertaining to or like Satan: devilish.

**Satchel**, sach'el, n. a small sack or bag, esp. for papers, books, &c. [Older form sachel, dim. of Sack; cf. L. saccellus, dim. of saccus.]

**Sate**, sāt, v.t. to satisfy or give enough: to glut. [A.S. sæd; L. satio, -atum—satis, enough.]

**Satellite**, sat'el-līt, n. an obsequious follower: one of the bodies which revolve round some of the planets. [L. satelles, satellitis, an attendant.]

**Satiable**, sā'shi-a-bl, adj. that may be satiated.

**Satiate**, sā'shi-āt, v.t. to satisfy or give enough: to gratify fully: to glut.—adj. glutted.—n. Satia'tion. [L. satio—satis, enough.]

**Satiety**, sa-tī'e-ti, n. state of being satiated: surfeit.

**Satin**, sat'in, n. a closely woven glossy silk. [Fr. (It. setino)—Low L. setinus, adj., from L. seta, hair.]

**Satinet**, sat'i-net, n. a thin species of satin: a cloth with a cotton warp and woollen weft.

**Satinwood**, sat'in-wood, n. a beautiful ornamental wood from E. and W. Indies, having a texture like satin.

**Satiny**, sat'in-i, adj. like or composed of satin.

**Satire**, sat'īr or sat'ėr, n. a species of poetry, exposing and turning to ridicule vice or folly: severity of remark: ridicule. [Fr.—L. satira, satura (lanx, a dish, understood), a dish full of various kinds of fruit, food composed of various ingredients, a medley; hence applied to a dramatic piece in which dancing, music, and words were intermixed, afterwards to satire in its present sense—satur, full, akin to satis, enough.]

**Satiric**, sa-tir'ik, **Satirical**, sa-tir'ik-al, adj. pertaining to or conveying satire: sarcastic: abusive.—adv. Satir'ically.

**Satirise**, sat'ir-īz, v.t. to make the object of satire: to censure severely.—n. Sat'irist, a writer of satire.

**Satisfaction**, sat-is-fak'shun, n. state of being satisfied: gratification: comfort: that which satisfies: amends: atonement: payment: conviction.

**Satisfactory**, sat-is-fak'tor-i, adj., satisfying: giving content: making amends or payment: atoning: convincing.—adv. Satisfac'torily.—n. Satisfac'toriness.

**Satisfy**, sat'is-fī, v.t. to give enough to: to supply fully: to please fully: to discharge: to free from doubt: to convince.—v.i. to give content: to supply fully: to make payment:—pa.t. and pa.p. sat'isfied. [Fr. satisfaire—L. satis, enough, and facio, to make.]

**Satrap**, sā'trap or sat'rap, n. a Persian viceroy or ruler of one of the greater provinces.—fem. Sa'trapess.—n. Sat'rapy, the government of a satrap. [Gr. satrapēs, from the Persian, lit. 'chief of a district.']

**Saturable**, sat'ū-ra-bl, adj. that may be saturated.

**Saturate**, sat'ū-rāt, v.t. to fill: to unite with till no more can be received: to fill to excess. [L. saturo, -atum—satur, full, akin to satis, enough.]

**Saturation**, sat-ū-rā'shun, n. act of saturating: state of being saturated: the state of a body when quite filled with another.

**Saturday,** sat'ur-dā, *n.* the seventh or last *day* of the week, dedicated by the Romans to *Saturn*. [A.S. *Sæter-dæg, Sætern-dæg,* day of Saturn—L. *Saturnus.*]

**Saturn,** sat'urn or sā'-, *n.* the ancient Roman god of agriculture : one of the planets. [L. *Saturnus—sero, satum,* to sow.]

**Saturnalia,** sat-ur-nā'li-a, *n.pl.* the annual festival in honour of *Saturn*, a time of unrestrained license and enjoyment.

**Saturnalian,** sat-ur-nā'li-an, *adj.* pertaining to the *Saturnalia* : riotously merry : dissolute.

**Saturnian,** sa-turn'i-an, *adj.* pertaining to *Saturn*, whose fabulous reign was called ' the golden age :' happy : pure : simple : denoting the verse in which the oldest Latin poems were written.

**Saturnine,** sat'ur-nīn, *adj.* grave : gloomy : phlegmatic :—because the astrologers said that those born under the planet *Saturn* were so disposed.

**Satyr,** sat'èr or sā'tèr, *n.* a silvan deity, represented as part man and part goat, and extremely wanton. [L. *satyrus—*Gr. *satyros.*]

**Satyric,** sa-tir'ik, *adj.* pertaining to *satyrs*.

**Sauce,** saws, *n.* a liquid seasoning for food, consisting of *salt*, &c. : a relish : impudence.—*v.t.* to put sauce in to relish : to make poignant : to treat with bitter or pert language. [Fr.—L. *salio, salsum,* to salt—*sal*, salt. See **Salt.**]

**Saucepan,** saws'pan, *n.* a *pan* in which *sauce* or any small thing is boiled.

**Saucer,** saws'ér, *n.* the shallow platter for a tea or coffee cup : (*orig.*) a small vessel to hold *sauce*.

**Saucy,** saws'i, *adj.* (*comp.* **Sauc'ier,** *superl.* **Sauc'iest**) sharp : pungent : insolent : impudent.—*adv.* **Sauc'ily.**—*n.* **Sauc'iness.** [From **Sauce.**]

**Saunter,** sawn'tér or sän'tér, *v.i.* to wander about idly : to loiter.—*n.* a sauntering : a place for sauntering.—*n.* **Saun'terer.** [Said to be from Fr. *sainte terre,* holy land, to make a pilgrimage to the *Holy Land.*]

**Saurian,** saw'ri-an, *n.* a reptile or animal covered with scales, as the *lizard*.—*adj.* pertaining to or of the nature of a saurian. [Gr. *saura, sauros,* the lizard.]

**Sausage,** saws'āj, *n.* a gut stuffed with chopped meat *salted* and seasoned. [Fr. *saucisse*, through Low L. *salcitia,* from root of **Sauce.**]

**Sauterne,** sō-tèrn', *n.* a kind of white wine produced at *Sauterne,* in France.

**Savage,** sav'āj, *adj.* wild : uncivilised : fierce : cruel : brutal.—*n.* a human being in a wild state : a brutal person : a barbarian.—*adv.* **Sav'agely.**—*ns.* **Sav'ageness, Sav'agery.** [Lit. living in the *woods*, Fr. *sauvage*, O. Fr. *salvage*—L. *silvaticus,* pertaining to the woods—*silva*, a wood.]

**Savanna, Savannah,** sa-van'a, *n.* one of the vast *meadows* in the west of N. America. [Sp. *savana, sabana,* bed-sheet, a meadow—L. *sabanum—*Gr. *sabanon,* a linen cloth.]

**Save,** sāv, *v.t.* to bring *safe* out of evil : to rescue : to reserve : to spare.—*v.i.* to be economical.—*prep.* except.—*n.* **Sav'er.** [Fr. *sauver*—L. *salvo—salvus.* See **Safe.**]

**Save-all,** sāv'-awl, *n.* a contrivance intended to *save* anything from being wasted.

**Saveloy,** sav'e-loy, *n.* a kind of sausage made of meat chopped and seasoned, orig. of *brains*. [Fr. *cervelas,* a saveloy, *cervelle,* brains—L. *cerebellum.*]

**Saving,** sāv'ing, *adj.* disposed to *save* or be eco-

nomical : incurring no loss, preserving from wrong : (*theol.*) securing salvation.—*prep.* excepting.—*adv.* **Sav'ingly.**—*n.* **Sav'ingness.**

**Saving,** sāv'ing, *n.* that which is *saved* :—*pl.* earnings.

**Savings-bank,** sāv'ingz-bangk, *n.* a *bank* in which *savings* are deposited at interest.

**Saviour,** sāv'yur, *n.* one who *saves* from evil.—**The Saviour,** Jesus Christ, the Redeemer of men.

**Savory,** sā'vor-i, *n.* an aromatic kitchen herb. [From **Savour.**]

**Savour,** sā'vur, *n.*, *taste* : odour : scent : (*B.*) reputation.—*v.i.* to have a particular taste or smell : to be like. [Fr. *saveur*—L. *sapor—sapio,* to taste.]

**Savoury,** sā'vur-i, *adj.* having savour or relish : pleasant.—*adv.* **Sa'vourily.**—*n.* **Sa'vouriness.**

**Savoy,** sa-voy', *n.* a kind of cabbage brought orig. from *Savoy,* in France.

**Saw,** saw, *pa.t.* of See.

**Saw,** saw, *n.* an instrument for *cutting*, formed of a blade, band, or disc of thin steel, with a toothed edge.—*v.t.* to cut with a saw.—*v.i.* to use a saw : to be cut with a saw : *pa.t.* sawed ; *pa.p.* sawed or sawn. [A.S. *saga*; cog. with Ger. *säge,* and allied to L. *seco,* to cut.]

**Saw,** saw, *n.* a saying : a proverb. [A.S. *sagu—sagian, secgan,* to say. Doublet **Saga.** See also **Say.**]

**Sawdust,** saw'dust, *n.*, *dust*, or small pieces of wood, &c. made in *sawing*.

**Sawfish,** saw'fish, *n.* a *fish* allied to the shark, so called from the *saw*-like form of its snout.

**Sawmill,** saw'mil, *n.* a *mill* for *sawing* timber.

**Sawpit,** saw'pit, *n.* a *pit* where wood is *sawed*.

**Sawyer,** saw'yér, *n.* one who *saws* timber.

**Saxifrage,** saks'i-frāj, *n.* a genus of alpine plants formerly used for *dissolving stone* in the bladder. [Fr.—L. *saxum,* a stone, and *frango,* to break.]

**Saxon,** saks'un, *n.* one of the people of N. Germany who conquered England in the 5th and 6th centuries : the language of the Saxons.—*adj.* pertaining to the Saxons, their language, country, or architecture. [A.S. *Seaxe—seax,* O. Ger. *sahs,* a knife, a short sword ; so called from the *short sword* which they carried.]

**Saxonism,** saks'on-izm, *n.* a Saxon idiom.

**Say,** sā, *v.t.* to utter in words : to speak : to declare : to state : to answer.—*v.i.* to speak : to relate : to state :—*pa.t.* and *pa.p.* said (sed).—*n.* something said : a remark : a speech. [A.S. *sagian, secgan* ; cog. with Ice. *segja,* Ger. *sagen.* See **Saw,** a saying.]

**Saying,** sā'ing, *n.* something *said* : an expression : a maxim.

**Scab,** skab, *n.* a crust over a sore : a disease of sheep, resembling the mange. [A.S. *sceb* ; Dan. *scab,* Ger. *schabe* ; L. *scabies,* from *scabo,* Ger. *schaben,* to scratch ; akin to **Shave.**]

**Scabbard,** skab'ard, *n.* the case in which the blade of a sword is kept. [M. E. *scauberk,* prob. from Ice. *skafa,* chisel, and *biarga,* Ger. *bergen,* to hide.]

**Scabbed,** skab'ed, *adj.* affected or covered with scabs : diseased with the scab.—*n.* **Scabb'edness.**

**Scabby,** skab'i, *adj.*, *scabbed.*—*n.* **Scabb'iness.**

**Scaffold,** skaf'old, *n.* a temporary platform for exhibiting or for supporting something : for the execution of a criminal.—*v.t.* to furnish with a scaffold : to sustain. [O. Fr. *eschafault,* Fr. *échafaud* (It. *catafalco*) ; from a Romance word, found in Sp. *catar,* to view, and *falco,* It. *palco,* a scaffold, from Ger. *balke*, a beam. Doublet **Catafalque**.]

**Scaffolding**, skaf'old-ing, *n.* a *scaffold* of wood for supporting workmen while building: materials for scaffolds : (*fig.*) a frame : framework.

**Scalable**, skāl'a-bl, *adj.* that may be scaled or climbed.

**Scald**, skawld, *v.t.* to burn with hot liquid : to expose to a boiling liquid.—*n.* a burn caused by hot liquid.—**Scalding hot**, so hot as to scald. [O. Fr. *eschalder*, Fr. *échauder*—L. *excaldo*, to bathe in warm water, from *calidus*, warm, hot.]

**Scald, Skald**, skald, *n.* one of the ancient Scandinavian poets. [Ice. and Sw. *skald*.]

**Scale**, skāl, *n.* a ladder : series of steps : a graduated measure : (*music*) a series of all the tones : the order of a numeral system : gradation : proportion : series.—*v.t.* to mount, as by a ladder : to ascend. [L. *scala*, a ladder (for *scandla*), from *scando*, to mount, Sans. *skand*, to ascend.]

**Scale**, skāl, *n.* one of the small, thin plates on a fish or reptile : a thin layer.—*v.t.* to clear of scales : to peel off in thin layers.—*v.i.* to come off in thin layers. [A.S. *scealu*, the scale of a fish ; Ger. *schale*, shell (whence Fr. *écaille*, a fish-scale). Doublets **Shell** and **Skull**.]

**Scale**, skāl, *n.* the dish of a balance : a balance—chiefly in pl. :—*pl.* **Scales**. Libra, one of the signs of the zodiac. [A.S. *scalu*, a balance. It is simply a form of **Scale**, a thin plate.]

**Scaled**, skāld, *adj.* having scales.

**Scalene**, ska-lēn', *adj.* (*geom.*) having three unequal sides.—*n.* a scalene triangle. [Lit. 'limping,' Fr.—L. *scalenus*—Gr. *skalēnos*, uneven, from root of *skazō*, to limp.]

**Scall**, skawl, *n.* (*B.*) a scab : scabbiness. [A.S. *scalu*, scale ; simply a form of **Scale**, a thin plate.]

**Scallop**, skol'up, *n.* a bivalvular *shell*-fish, having the edge of its shell in the form of a series of curves : one of a series of curves in the edge of anything.—*v.t.* to cut the edge or border into scallops or curves. [O. Fr. *escalope* ; from Ger. *schale*, shell. See **Scale**, a shell.]

**Scalp**, skalp, *n.* the skin of the head on which the hair grows : the skin of the top of the head torn off as a token of victory by the N. American Indians.—*v.t.* to cut the scalp from. [Prob. from Ice. *skal*, a skull, modified by confusion with L. *scalpo*, to cut ; akin to **Scale**, a shell, and **Shell**.]

**Scalpel**, skalp'el, *n.* a *small* surgical *knife* for dissecting and operating. [L. *scalpellum*, dim. of *scalprum*, a knife—*scalpo*, to cut.]

**Scaly**, skāl'i, *adj.* covered with *scales* : like scales : (*bot.*) formed of scales.—*n.* **Scal'iness**.

**Scammony**, skam'o-ni, *n.* a cathartic gum-resin obtained from a species of convolvulus in Asia Minor. [Gr. *skamōnia*.]

**Scamp**, skamp, *n.* a vagabond : a mean fellow.—*v.t.* in phrase to *scamp work*, to do it dishonestly, without thoroughness. [From **Scamper**.]

**Scamper**, skamp'ėr, *v.i.* to run with speed and trepidation. [Lit. 'to quit the field,' O. Fr. *escamper*—L. *ex*, out of, from, and *campus*, field ; cf. **Decamp**.]

**Scan**, skan, *v.t.* to count the feet or measures in a verse : to examine carefully : to scrutinise :—*pr.p.* scann'ing ; *pa.t.* and *pa.p.* scanned. [Lit. 'to climb,' Fr. *scander*, to scan—L. *scando*, *scansum*, Sans. *skand*, to ascend.]

**Scandal**, skan'dal, *n.* something said which is false and injurious to reputation : disgrace :

opprobrious censure. [*Orig.* offence, Fr. *scandale*—L. *scandalum*—Gr. *skandalon*, a snare laid for an enemy, a stumbling-block.]

**Scandalise**, skan'dal-īz, *v.t.* to give *scandal* or offence to : to shock : to reproach : to disgrace.

**Scandalous**, skan'dal-us, *adj.* giving *scandal* or offence : calling forth condemnation : openly vile : defamatory.—*adv.* **Scan'dalously**.—*n.* **Scan'dalousness**.

**Scandinavian**, skan-di-nā'vi-an, *adj.* of Scandinavia, the peninsula divided into Norway and Sweden. The Scandinavian languages are Icelandic, Danish, Swedish, and Norwegian. [Latinised form of the native name ; the termination -*avia*, sig. 'island,' being the same as the Goth. *avi*, Ice. *ey* (as in *Orkn-ey*), A.S. *ig*.]

**Scansion**, skan'shun, *n.* act of *scanning* or counting the measures in a verse.

**Scansorial**, skan-sō'ri-al, *adj.*, *climbing* : formed for climbing. [From L. *scando*, *scansum*. See **Scan**.]

**Scant**, skant, *adj.* not full or plentiful : scarcely sufficient : deficient. [Ice. *skammt*, short, narrow.]

**Scantling**, skant'ling, *n.* a little piece : a piece or quantity cut for a particular purpose : a certain proportion. [Fr. *échantillon*, a sample—O. Fr. *cant*, edge, corner. See **Cant**, an edge.]

**Scanty**, skant'i, *adj., scant* : not copious or full : hardly sufficient : wanting extent : narrow : small.—*adv.* **Scant'ily**.—*n.* **Scant'iness**.

**Scapegoat**, skāp'gōt, *n.* a *goat* on which, once a year, the Jewish high-priest confessed the sins of the people, and which was then allowed *to escape* into the wilderness. [**Escape** and **Goat**.]

**Scapegrace**, skāp'grās, *n.* a graceless harebrained fellow. [Lit. 'one who has *escaped grace*.']

**Scapement**. Same as **Escapement**.

**Scapular**, skap'ū-lar, *adj.* pertaining to the *shoulder*. [Fr.—Low L. *scapularis*—L. *scapulæ*, the shoulder-blades.]

**Scapular**, skap'ū-lar, **Scapulary**, skap'ū-lar-i, *n.* an ornament worn by some R. C. orders, consisting of two woollen bands, one of which crosses the *shoulders*, and the other the breast.

**Scar**, skär, *n.* the mark left by a wound or sore : any mark or blemish.—*v.t.* to mark with a scar.—*v.i.* to become scarred :—*pr.p.* scarr'ing ; *pa.t.* and *pa.p.* scarred. [Fr. *escarre*—L. *eschara*—Gr. *eschara*, a fireplace, a scab on a wound produced by burning.]

**Scar**, skär, *n.* a precipitous bank or rock. [A Scand. word, as Ice. *sker*, from the root of **Shear**, *v.*, and **Shore**, the coast.]

**Scaramouch**, skar'a-mowch, *n.* a buffoon : a bragging, cowardly fellow. [Fr., through It., from O. Ger. *skerman*, to fight. See **Skirmish**.]

**Scarce**, skārs, *adj.* not plentiful : not equal to the demand : rare : not common.—*adv.* **Scarce'ly**. (*B.*) **Scarce**.—*n.* **Scarce'ness**. [Lit. 'picked out,' O. Fr. *escars* (Fr. *échars*), niggardly—Low L. *scarpsus* = *ex-carpsus*, for L. *excerptus*, pa.p. of *excerpo*—*ex*, out of, and *carpo*, to pick.]

**Scarcity**, skārs'i-ti, *n.* state of being *scarce* : deficiency : rareness.

**Scare**, skār, *v.t.* to drive away by frightening : to strike with sudden terror. [Scot. *skair*, to take fright, conn. with Ice. *skjarr*, shy, timid, Ger. (*sich*) *scheren*, to make off.]

**Scarecrow**, skār'krō, *n.* anything set up to *scare* away *crows* or other birds : a vain cause of terror.

**Scarf**, skärf, *n.* a light piece of dress worn loosely on the shoulders or about the neck : a light handkerchief for the neck :—*pl.* **Scarfs**. [Fr.

*écharpe*, a scarf, a girdle, orig. the pocket which a pilgrim bore suspended from his neck (cf. **Scrip**), from O. Ger. *scherbe*, a pocket.]

**Scarf**, skärf, *v.t.* to join two pieces of timber endwise, so that they may be used as one.—*n*.

**Scarf'ing**. [Sw. *skarfa*, Dan. *skarve*, to join together; Ger. *scharben*, to cut small, A.S. *scearfe*, a fragment. The fundamental idea is that of pointing, cutting, and so piecing together; conn. with **Shear**, *v.*]

**Scarfskin**, skärf'skin, *n.* the *scurf* or surface *skin*: the cuticle or outer skin of animals. [A.S. *sceorf*, scurf, and **Skin**. See **Scurf**.]

**Scarification**, skar-i-fi-kā'shun, *n.* act of scarifying.

**Scarify**, skar'i-fī, *v.t.* to *scratch* or slightly cut the skin: to make small cuts with a lancet, so as to draw blood:—*pa.t.* and *pa.p.* scar'if'ied. [Fr. *scarifier*—L. *scarifico*, *-atum*—Gr. *skariphaomai*—*skariphos*, an etching tool.]

**Scarlatina**, skär-la-tē'na, **Scarlet-fever**, skär'let-fē'vèr, *n.* a contagious *fever*, known by the *scarlet* flush which accompanies it.

**Scarlet**, skär'let, *n.* a bright-red colour: scarlet cloth.—*adj.* of the colour called scarlet. [O. Fr. *escarlate* (Fr. *écarlate*), through Low L. *scarlatum*—Pers. *sakirlat*, perh. from Gr. *Sikelia*, Sicily, which during the Arab domination had a large cotton and silk manufacture.]

**Scarlet-runner**, skär'let-run'ér, *n.* a plant with *scarlet* flowers which *runs* up any support.

**Scarp**, skärp. Same as **Escarp**. [Fr. *escarpe*, through It. *scarpa*, from O. Ger. *scarp* (Ger. *scharf*), E. **Sharp**.]

**Scath**, **Scathe**, skäth, *n.* damage, injury.—*v.t.* to injure. [A.S. *sceatha*, an enemy, cog. with Ger. *schade*, injury.]          [damage, injury.]

**Scathless**, skäth'les or skath'les, *adj.* without *scath*, injury.

**Scatter**, skat'ér, *v.t.* to disperse in all directions: to throw loosely about: to strew: to sprinkle.—*v.i.* to be dispersed or dissipated. [A.S. *scateran*, *scaterian*. See **Shatter**.]

**Scavenger**, skav'en-jèr, *n.* one who cleans the streets. [Orig. *scavager*, an inspector of goods for sale, and also of the streets; from obs. E. *scavage*, duty on goods for sale—A.S. *sceawian*, to inspect, E. **Show**.]

**Scene**, sēn, *n.* (*orig.*) the *stage* of a theatre on which the actors perform: a picture of the place of an action: a large painted view: place of action, occurrence, or exhibition: the part of a play acted without change of place: a series of events connected and exhibited: a number of objects presented to the view at once: spectacle: view: a display of strong feeling between two or more persons. [Fr. *scène*—L. *scena*—Gr. *skēnē*, a covered place, a booth, a stage.]

**Scenery**, sēn'èr-i, *n.* the painted representation on a stage: the appearance of anything presented to the eye: general aspect of a landscape.

**Scenic**, sen'ik or sē'nik, *adj.* pertaining to *scenery*: dramatic: theatrical.

**Scenographic**, sēn-o-graf'ik, **Scenographical**, sēn-o-graf'ik-al, *adj.* drawn in perspective.—*adv.* **Scenograph'ically**.

**Scenography**, sē-nog'ra-fi, *n.* the art of perspective: representation in perspective. [Gr. *skēnē*, a scene, and *graphō*, to write, delineate.]

**Scent**, sent, *v.t.* to discern by the sense of smell: to perfume.—*n.* odour: sense of smell: chase followed by the scent: course of pursuit. [Fr. *sentir*—L. *sentio*, lit. ' to discern by the senses.' See **Sense**.]

**Sceptic**, skep'tik, **Sceptical**, skep'tik-al, *adj.* doubting: hesitating to admit the certainty of

doctrines or principles: (*theol.*) doubting or denying the truth of revelation.—*n.* **Scep'tic**, one who is sceptical: (*theol.*) one who doubts or denies the existence of God or the truths of revelation.—*adv.* **Scep'tically**. [L. *scepticus*—Gr. *skeptikos*, thoughtful, reflective—*skeptomai*, to look about, to consider.]

**Scepticism**, skep'ti-sizm, *n.* doubt: the doctrine that no facts can be certainly known: (*theol.*) doubt of the existence of God or the truth of revelation.

**Sceptre**, sep'tèr, *n.* the staff or baton borne by kings as an emblem of authority: royal power. [L. *sceptrum*—Gr. *skēptron*, a staff to *lean* upon—*skēptō*, to lean.]

**Sceptred**, sep'trd, *adj.* bearing a sceptre.

**Schedule**, shed'ūl, *n.* a piece of paper containing some writing: a list, inventory, or table.—*v.t.* to place in a schedule or list. [O. Fr. *schedule* (Fr. *cédule*)—L. *schedula*, dim. of *scheda*, a strip of papyrus, Gr. *schedē*, anything formed by cleaving, a leaf, from L. *scindo*, Gr. *schizō*, to cleave.]

**Scheik**. Same as **Sheik**.

**Scheme**, skēm, *n.* plan: something contrived to be done: purpose: plot: a combination of things by design: an illustrative diagram.—*v.t.* to plan: to contrive.—*v.i.* to form a plan or scheme.—*n.* **Schem'er**. [Fr.—L. *schema*—Gr. *schēma*, form or shape—*echō*, *schēsō*, to have or hold.]                               [intriguing.

**Scheming**, skēm'ing, *adj.* given to forming schemes.

**Schism**, sizm, *n.* a separation in a church, from diversity of opinion. [L. *schisma*—Gr. *schizō*, to split.]

**Schismatic**, siz-mat'ik, **Schismatical**, siz-mat'ik-al, *adj.* tending to, or of the nature of *schism*.—*n.* **Schismat'ic**, one who separates from a church on account of difference of opinion.—*adv.* **Schismat'ically**. [L. *schismaticus*—Gr. *schismatikos*—*schisma*.]

**Schist**, shist, *n.* (*geol.*) a kind of rock *splitting* into thin layers: slate-rock. [Fr. *schiste*—Gr. *schistos*—*schizō*, to split.]

**Schistic**, shist'ik, **Schistous**, shist'us, **Schistose**, shist-ōs', *adj.* like schist: having a slaty structure.

**Scholar**, skol'ar, *n.* a pupil: a disciple: a student: one who has received a learned education: a man of learning: in the English universities, an undergraduate partly supported from the revenues of a college. [L. *scholaris*, belonging to a *school*—*schola*. See **School**.]

**Scholarly**, skol'ar-li, *adj.* like or becoming a scholar.

**Scholarship**, skol'ar-ship, *n.* the character of a scholar: learning: in the English universities, maintenance for a scholar.

**Scholastic**, sko-las'tik, *adj.* pertaining to a *scholar* or to schools: scholar-like: pertaining to the schoolmen: excessively subtle.—*n.* one who adheres to the method or subtleties of the schools of the middle ages. [Fr.—L. *scholasticus*—Gr. *scholastikos*—*scholazō*, to have leisure, to attend school—*scholē*, leisure. Cf. **School**.]

**Scholiast**, skō'li-ast, *n.* a writer of *scholia*. [Gr. *scholiastēs*—*scholion*, a scholium.]

**Scholiastic**, skō-li-ast'ik, *adj.* pertaining to a *scholiast* or to scholia.

**Scholium**, skō'li-um, *n.* one of the marginal notes of the old critics on the ancient classics: (*math.*) an explanation added to a problem:—*pl.* **Scho'lia**, **Scho'liums**. [Low L.—Gr. *scholion*, a short note or comment—*scholē*, leisure.]

**School**, skōōl, *n.* a place for instruction : an institution of learning, esp. for children : the pupils of a school : exercises for instruction : the disciples of a particular teacher, or those who hold a common doctrine.—*v.t.* to educate in a school : to instruct : to admonish. [L. *schola*—Gr. *scholē*, leisure, a lecture, a school.]

**Schoolman**, skōōl'man, *n.* one of the philosophers and divines of the second half of the middle-ages.

**Schoolmaster**, skōōl'mas-tèr, *n.* the *master* or teacher of a *school* : (*B.*) a pedagogue.—*fem.* **School'mistress.**

**Schooner**, skōōn'èr, *n.* a sharp-built, swift-sailing vessel, generally two-masted, rigged either with fore-and-aft sails on both masts, or with square top and top-gallant sails on the foremast. [Coined in New England from the Prov. Eng. *scoon* (Scot. *scon*), to make a flat stone skip along the surface of water.]

**Sciatic**, sī-at'ik, **Sciatical**, sī-at'ik-al, *adj.* pertaining to or affecting the *hip*. [Low L. *sciaticus*—Gr. *ischion*, the hip-joint.]

**Sciatica**, sī-at'ik-a, *n.* a rheumatic affection of the *hip-joint* : a neuralgic affection of the sciatic nerve. [Low L. *sciatica*—Gr. *ischion*.]

**Science**, sī'ens, *n., knowledge* (systematised) : truth ascertained : pursuit of knowledge or truth for its own sake : knowledge arranged under general truths and principles : that which refers to abstract principles, as distinguished from 'art.' [Fr.—L. *scientia*—*sciens*, *-entis*, pr.p. of *scio*, to know.]

**Scientific**, sī-en-tif'ik, **Scientifical**, sī-en-tif'ik-al, *adj.* producing or containing *science* : according to or versed in science.—*adv.* **Scientif'ically.** [Fr. *scientifique*—L. *scientia*, science, *facio*, to make.] [esp. natural science.

**Scientist**, sī'ent-ist, *n.* one who studies science,

**Scimitar**, sim'i-tar, *n.* a short, single-edged curved sword, broadest at the point end, used by the Turks and Persians. [Prob. through Sp. *cimitarra*, from Basque *cime-terra*, something 'with a fine edge.']

**Scintillate**, sin'til-lāt, *v.i.* to throw out *sparks* : to sparkle. [L. *scintilla*, a spark.]

**Scintillation**, sin-til-lā'shun, *n.* act of throwing out sparks : shining with a twinkling light.

**Sciolism**, sī'ol-izm, *n.* superficial *knowledge*. [L. *sciolus*, dim. of *scius*, knowing—*scio*, to know.]

**Sciolist**, sī'ol-ist, *n.* one who knows anything superficially : a pretender to science.

**Scion**, sī'un, *n.* a *cutting* or twig for grafting : a young member of a family. [Fr. (for *secion*) —L. *sectio*, a cutting—*seco*, to cut.]

**Scirrhous**, skir'rus, *adj.*, *hardened* : proceeding from *scirrhus*.

**Scirrhus**, skir'rus, *n.* (*med.*) a *hardened* gland forming a tumour : a hardening, esp. that preceding cancer. [Gr. *skiros*, hard.]

**Scissors**, siz'urz, *n.pl.* a *cutting* instrument consisting of two blades fastened at the middle. [Formerly written *cisors*—O. Fr. *cisoires*, conn. with Fr. *ciseaux*, scissors, from Late L. *cisorium*, a cutting instrument—L. *cædo*, to cut.]

**Sclave, Sclavonian**, &c. See **Slav, Slavonic.**

**Sclerotic**, skle-rot'ik, *adj.*, *hard*, *firm*, noting the outer membrane of the eyeball.—*n.* the outermost membrane of the eyeball. [From Gr. *sklēros*, hard.]

**Scoff**, skof, *v.i.* to mock : to treat with scorn.—*v.i.* to show contempt or scorn.—*n.* an expression of scorn or contempt.—*n.* **Scoff'er.** [Dan. *skuffe*, to delude, allied to Fris. *schof*.]

**Scold**, skōld, *v.i.* to rail in a loud and violent manner : to find fault.—*v.t.* to chide rudely : to rebuke in words.—*n.* a rude, clamorous woman. —*n.* **Scold'er.** [Low Ger. *schelden*, Ger. *schelten*, to brawl, to scold.]

**Scollop.** Same as **Scallop.**

**Sconce**, skons, *n.* a bulwark : a small fort : a protective headpiece, hence the head, the skull. [O. Fr. *sconcer*, *esconcer*, to conceal, to withdraw—L. *abscondere*.]

**Sconce**, skons, *n.* the part of a candlestick for the candle : a hanging candlestick with a mirror to reflect the light. [O. Fr. *esconse*—Low L. *absconsa*, *sconsa*, orig. a dark-lantern—L. *absconsa candela*, a hidden light—*abscondo*, to hide, *candela*, a light.]

**Scoop**, skōōp, *v.t.* to lift up, as water, with something hollow : to empty with a ladle : to make hollow : to dig out.—*n.* anything hollow for scooping : a large hollow shovel or ladle : a place hollowed out : a sweeping stroke. [Cog. with Dan. *skuffe*, Ger. *schüppe*, prob. from the same root as **Shovel.**]

**Scope**, skōp, *n.* that which one *sees*, space as far as one can see : room or opportunity for free outlook : space for action : the end before the mind : intention. [L. *scopos*—Gr. *skopos*—*skopeō*, *skeptomai*, to look, to view.]

**Scorbutic**, skor-bū'tik, **Scorbu'tical**, -al, *adj.* pertaining to, resembling, or diseased with scurvy. [Late Low L. *scorbuticus*—*scorbutus*, scurvy, prob. from O. Dut. *schore* (Dut. *scheur*), a break, rent, and *bot*, bone, from the wasted appearance of the limbs of a person afflicted with scurvy.]

**Scorch**, skorch, *v.t.* to burn slightly : to roast highly : to affect painfully with heat.—*v.i.* to be burned on the surface : to be dried up. [Lit. 'to strip the bark off,' O. Fr. *escorchæ*, from Low L. *excorticare*—L. *cortex*, *corticis*, bark. See **Cork.**]

**Score**, skōr, *n.* a mark or *notch* for keeping count : a line drawn : the number twenty, once represented by a larger notch : a reckoning : account : reason : the original draught of a musical composition with all the parts, or its transcript.—*v.t.* to mark with notches or lines : to furrow.—*n.* **Scor'er.** [A.S. *scor*, cog. with Ice. *skor*; akin to A.S. *sceran*, E. **Shear.**]

**Scoria**, skō'ri-a, *n., dross* or slag left from metal or ores after being under fire :—*pl.* **Scoriæ**, skō'ri-ā, volcanic ashes. [L.—Gr. *skōria*.]

**Scorn**, skorn, *n.* disdain caused by a mean opinion : extreme contempt : object of contempt.—*v.t.* to hold in extreme contempt : to disdain : (*B.*) **To laugh to scorn**, to deride.—**To think scorn**, to disdain or despise. [O. Fr. *escorner* (It. *scornare*), lit. 'to take the *horns off*,' to humble, to insult, from L. *excornis*, hornless, from *ex*, without, and *cornua*, horns.]

**Scorner**, skorn'èr, *n.* one who scorns : (*B.*) one who scoffs at religion.

**Scornful**, skorn'fool, *adj.* full of scorn : contemptuous : disdainful.—*adv.* **Scorn'fully.**

**Scorpion**, skor'pi-un, *n.* an insect with claws like the lobster, and armed with a poisonous sting in its tail : one of the signs of the zodiac : (*B.*) a whip with points like a scorpion's tail. [Fr.—L. *scorpio*—Gr. *skorpios*.]

**Scot**, skot, *n.* a native of Scotland. [A Celtic word, ety. dub.]

**Scotch**, skoch, **Scottish**, skot'ish, **Scots**, skots, *adj.* pertaining to *Scotland*, its people, or language.—*ns.* **Scotch'man, Scots'man,** a native of Scotland.

**Scotch**, skoch, *v.t.* to cut or wound slightly. [Ety. dub.]

**Scoter**, skō′tėr, *n.* a species of marine duck with dark plumage, also called the 'surf duck.'

**Scot-free**, skot′-frē, *adj.*, *free* from *scot* (*obs.*) or payment: untaxed: unhurt, safe.—**Scot and lot**, a *scot* or tax originally assessed according to the *lot* or ability of the payer. [A.S. *scot*, *sceot* (cog. with Ger. *schosz*)—*sceotan*, to shoot, to throw down as payment. See **Shoot**.]

**Scotticism**, skot′i-sizm, *n.* a Scotch idiom.

**Scoundrel**, skown′drel, *n.* a low, worthless fellow: a rascal: a man without principle.—*n.* **Scoun′drelism**, baseness, rascality. [It. *scondaruolo*, a coward—*scondere*, to hide—L. *abs-condere*. See **Abscond**.]

**Scour**, skowr, *v.t.* to clean by rubbing with something rough: to cleanse from grease, dirt, &c.: to remove by rubbing: to pass quickly over: to range.—*n.* **Scour′er**. [O. Fr. *escurer*, Fr. *écurer*; Ger. *scheuern*; prob. both from Low L. *scurare*, to sweep—L. *ex-curare*.]

**Scourge**, skurj, *n.* a whip made of leather thongs: an instrument of punishment: a punishment: means of punishment.—*v.t.* to whip severely: to punish in order to correct.—*n.* **Scourg′er**. [Fr. *escourgée*, *écourgée*—L. (*scutica*) *excoriata*, (a whip) made of leather—*corium*, leather.]

**Scout**, skowt, *n.* one sent out to bring in tidings, observe the enemy, &c.: a college servant at Oxford. [O. Fr. *escoute*—*escouter* (It. *ascoltare*)—L. *auscultare*, to listen—*auricula*, *auris*, the ear.]

**Scout**, skowt, *v.t.* to sneer at: to reject with disdain. [Acc. to Wedgwood, Scot. *scout*, to pour forth a liquid forcibly.]

**Scowl**, skowl, *v.i.* to wrinkle the brows in displeasure: to look sour or angry: to look gloomy.—*n.* the wrinkling of the brows when displeased: a look of sullenness, anger, or discontent. [Cog. with Dan. *skule*, Dut. *schuilen*; perh. conn. with A.S. *sceol*, squint, Ger. *schel*, squinting, Scot. *skelly*, to squint.]

**Scrabble**, skrab′l, *v.i.* (*B.*) to scrape or make unmeaning marks: to scrawl. [Freq. of **Scrape**.]

**Scrag**, skrag, *n.* anything thin or lean and rough: the bony part of the neck. [Gael. *sgreag*, parched.]

**Scragged**, skrag′ed, **Scraggy**, skrag′i, *adj.* lean and rough: uneven: rugged.—*ns.* **Scragg′edness**, **Scragg′iness**.—*adv.* **Scragg′ily**.

**Scramble**, skram′bl, *v.i.* to struggle to seize something before others: to catch at or strive for rudely: to move on all-fours.—*n.* act of scrambling.—*n.* **Scram′bler**. [Prov. E. *scramb*, to rake together with the hands, or *scramp*, to snatch at; nearly allied to **Scrabble** and **Scrape**.]

**Scrap**, skrap, *n.* a small piece: an unconnected extract.—**Scrap′-book**, *n.* a blank *book* for scraps or extracts, prints, &c. [From **Scrape**.]

**Scrape**, skrāp, *v.t.* to make a harsh or grating noise on: to rub with something sharp: to remove by drawing a sharp edge over: to collect by laborious effort: to save penuriously.—*n.* a perplexing situation: difficulty. [A.S. *screopan*; Ice. *skrapa*, to creak, grate: from the sound.]

**Scraper**, skrāp′ėr, *n.* an instrument used for *scraping*, esp. the soles of shoes.

**Scraping**, skrāp′ing, *n.* that which is scraped off.

**Scratch**, skrach, *v.t.* to rub or mark the surface with something pointed, as the nails: to tear or to dig with the claws.—*v.i.* to use the nails or claws in tearing or digging.—*n.* a mark or tear made by scratching: a slight wound: the line in a prize-ring up to which boxers are led, hence test, trial, as in phrase, 'to come up to the scratch.' [Allied to Ger. *kratzen*, Dut. *krassen*, to scratch, *s* being intrusive.]

**Scratcher**, skrach′ėr, *n.* a bird which scratches for food, as a hen.

**Scrawl**, skrawl, *v.t.* and *v.i.* to scrape, mark, or write irregularly, or hastily.—*n.* irregular or hasty writing.—*n.* **Scrawl′er**. [Akin to Dut. *schravelen*, *schrafelen*, to scrape.]

**Scream**, skrēm, *v.i.* to cry out with a shrill cry, as in fear or pain: to shriek.—*n.* a shrill, sudden cry, as in fear or pain: a shriek. [An imitative word, found in Sw. *skrümma*, to fear; cf. **Creak**, **Crack**, **Screech**, **Shriek**.]

**Screech**, skrēch, *v.i.* to shriek or utter a harsh, shrill, and sudden cry.—*n.* a harsh, shrill, and sudden cry. [An imitative word, found in Gael. *sgreach*, Scot. *skreigh*. See **Scream**.]

**Screech-owl**, skrēch′-owl, *n.* a kind of *owl*, so called from its *screeching* cry.

**Screen**, skrēn, *n.* that which shelters from danger or observation: a partition in churches: a coarse riddle for sifting coal, &c.—*v.t.* to shelter or conceal: to pass through a coarse riddle. [O. Fr. *escren* (Fr. *écran*); of uncertain origin.]

**Screw**, skrōō, *n.* a cylinder with a spiral groove or ridge on either its outer or inner surface, used as a fastening and as a mechanical power: a screw-propeller.—*v.t.* to apply a screw to: to press with a screw: to twist: to oppress by extortion: to force: to squeeze. [Low Ger. *schruve*, Ice. *skrufa*, Ger. *schraube*, whence prob. Fr. *écrou*.]

**Screw-driver**, skrōō′-drīv′ėr, *n.* an instrument for *driving* or turning *screw*-nails.

**Screw-jack**, skrōō′-jak. Same as **Jackscrew**.

**Screw-nail**, skrōō′-nāl, *n.* a *nail* made in the form of a *screw*.

**Screw-propeller**, skrōō′-pro-pel′ėr, *n.* a *screw* or spiral-bladed wheel at the stern of steam-vessels for *propelling* them: a steamer so propelled.

**Screw-steamer**, skrōō′-stēm′ėr, *n.* a *steamer* propelled by a *screw*.

**Scribble**, skrib′l, *v.t.* to *scratch* or write carelessly: to fill with worthless writing.—*v.i.* to write carelessly: to scrawl.—*n.* **Scribb′ler**. [O. Fr. *escrivailler*, to scribble—*escrire*, L. *scribere*, to write, akin to Gr. *graphō*, to scratch.]

**Scribe**, skrīb, *n.* a *writer*: a public or official writer: a clerk, amanuensis, secretary: (*B.*) a copyist or expounder of the law. [Fr.—L. *scriba*—*scribo*, *scribere*, to write.]

**Scrimmage**, skrim′āj, *n.* a skirmish: a general fight. [Prob. a corr. of **Skirmish**.]

**Scrimp**, skrimp, *v.t.* to make too small or short: to limit or shorten.—*adj.* short, scanty. [Scot. *scrimp*, scanty; Ger. *schrumpfen*, to shrink.]

**Scrip**, skrip, *n.* that which is *written*: a piece of paper containing writing: a certificate of stock or shares in any joint-stock company subscribed or allotted. [L. *scriptum*, pa.p. of *scribo*.]

**Scrip**, skrip, *n.* a small bag or wallet. [Ice. *skreppa*; conn. with **Scarf**.]

**Script**, skript, *n.* (*print.*) type like *written* letters. [L. *scriptum*—*scribo*, to write.]

**Scriptural**, skript′ūr-al, *adj.* contained in *Scripture*: according to Scripture: biblical.—*adv.* **Script′urally**.—*n.* **Script′uralness**.

**Scripture**, skript′ūr, *n.* sacred writing: the Bible. —**The Scriptures**, the Bible. [Lit. a *writing*, L. *scriptura*—*scribo*, to write.]

**Scrivener**, skriv'en-ėr, *n.* a *scribe* or *writer*: a copyist: one who draws up contracts, &c.: one who receives the money of others to lay it out at interest. [O. Fr. *escrivain* (Fr. *écrivain*)—Low L. *scribanus*, L. *scriba*, a scribe—*scribo*.]

**Scrofula**, skrof'ū-la, *n.* a disease characterised by chronic swellings of the glands in various parts of the body, esp. the neck, tending to suppurate: the king's-evil. [L. *scrofulæ*—*scrofa*, a sow, from the belief that swine were subject to a disease of this kind.]

**Scrofulous**, skrof'ū-lus, *adj.* pertaining to, resembling, or affected with *scrofula*.

**Scroll**, skrōl, *n.* a *roll* of paper or parchment: a writing in the form of a roll: a rough draught of anything: a schedule: (*arch.*) a spiral ornament: the volute of the Ionic and Corinthian capitals. [O. Fr. *escrol*, Fr. *écrou*; of uncertain origin.]

**Scrub**, skrub, *v.t.* to rub hard, esp. with something rough.—*v.i.* to be laborious and penurious:—*pr.p.* scrubb'ing; *pa.t.* and *pa.p.* scrubbed.—*n.* one who works hard and lives meanly: anything small or mean: a worn-out brush: low underwood.—*n.* **Scrubb'or.** [Low Ger. *schrubben*, Dan. *skrubbe*, to rub or scrub: conn. with **Scrape.**]

**Scrubby**, skrub'i, *adj.* laborious and penurious: mean: small: stunted in growth.

**Scruple**, skrōō'pl, *n.* a small weight (20 grains, or ⅓ drachm): a very small quantity: reluctance to decide or act, as from motives of conscience: difficulty.—*v.i.* to hesitate in deciding or acting. [Fr. *scrupule*—L. *scrupulus.* dim. of *scrupus*, a rough, sharp stone, anxiety.]

**Scrupulous**, skrōō'pū-lus, *adj.* having scruples, doubts, or objections: conscientious: cautious: exact.—*adv.* **Scru'pulously.** [L. *scrupulosus.*]

**Scrupulousness**, skrōō'pū-lus-nes, **Scrupulosity**, skrōō-pū-los'i-ti, *n.* state of being *scrupulous*: doubt: niceness: precision.

**Scrutineer**, skrōō-ti-nēr', *n.* one who makes a *scrutiny*, or minute search or inquiry.

**Scrutinise**, skrōō'ti-nīz, *v.t.* to search minutely or closely: to examine carefully or critically: to investigate.

**Scrutiny**, skrōō'ti-ni, *n.* careful or minute inquiry: critical examination: an examination of the votes given at an election for the purpose of correcting the poll. [L. *scrutinium—scrutor*, to search even to the rags—*scruta*, Gr. *grytē*, rags, trash.]

**Scud**, skud, *v.i.* to run quickly: (*naut.*) to run before the wind in a gale:—*pr.p.* scudd'ing; *pa.t.* and *pa.p.* scudd'ed.—*n.* act of moving quickly: loose, vapoury clouds driven swiftly along. [A.S. *scudan*; Ger. *schüttern.*]

**Scuffle**, skuf'l, *v.i.* to struggle closely: to fight confusedly.—*n.* a struggle in which the combatants grapple closely: any confused contest. [A.S. *scufan*, to shove: Dan. *skuffe*, Sw. *skuffa*, to shove or push, *skuff*, a blow, a thrust. See **Shove, Shuffle.**]

**Sculk.** Same as **Skulk.**

**Scull**, skul, *n.* a short, light oar: a small boat: a cock-boat.—*v.t.* to impel by sculls: to propel by working an oar from side to side of the stern, without raising the blade from the water.—*n.* **Scull'ing.** [Scand. *skol*, to splash.]

**Sculler**, skul'ėr, *n.* one who sculls: a small boat rowed by two sculls pulled by one man.

**Scullery**, skul'ėr-i, *n.* the place for *dishes* and other kitchen utensils. [O. Fr. *esculier—escuelle* —L. *scutella*, a salver—*scutula*, dim. of *scutra*, a dish.]

**Scullion**, skul'yun, *n.* a servant in the *scullery*: a servant for drudgery-work.

**Sculptor**, skulp'tor, *n.* one who *carves* figures.—*fem.* **Sculp'tress.** [ture.

**Sculptural**, skulp'tūr-al, *adj.* belonging to sculp-

**Sculpture**, skulp'tūr, *n.* the art of *carving* figures in wood, stone, &c.: carved-work.—*v.t.* to carve: to form, as a piece of sculpture. [Fr.—L. *sculptura—sculpo, sculptum*, to carve, to cut, Gr. *glyphō*, to carve.]

**Scum**, skum, *n.*, *foam* or *froth*: the extraneous matter rising to the surface of liquids, esp. when boiled or fermented: refuse.—*v.t.* to take the scum from: to skim :—*pr.p.* scumm'ing; *pa.t.* and *pa.p.* scummed.—*n.* **Scumm'er.** [Ice. *skum*; Ger. *schaum*, foam, froth.]

**Scupper**, skup'ėr, *n.* a hole in the side of a ship to carry off water from the deck. [O. Fr. *escupir*; origin dubious.]

**Scurf**, skurf, *n.* the crust or flaky matter formed on the skin: anything adhering to the surface. [A.S. *scurf*, cog. with Ice. *skurfa*, from a root seen in A.S. *sceorfian*, to scrape, scratch; allied to **Scrub, Scrape.**]

**Scurfy**, skurf'i, *adj.* having scurf: like scurf.—*n.* **Scurf'iness.**

**Scurrile**, skur'ril, *adj.*, *buffoon-like*: jesting: foul-mouthed: low. [L. *scurrilis—scurra*, an elegant town-bred man, a buffoon.]

**Scurrility**, skur-ril'it-i, *n.* buffoonery: low or obscene jesting: indecency of language: vulgar abuse. [L. *scurrilitas.*]

**Scurrilous**, skur'ril-us, *adj.* using scurrility, or the language of a buffoon: indecent: vile: vulgar: opprobrious: grossly abusive.—*adv.* **Scur'rilously.** [meanly, basely.

**Scurvily**, skurv'i-li, *adv.* in a scurvy manner:

**Scurviness**, skurv'i-nes, *n.* state of being scurvy: meanness.

**Scurvy**, skurv'i, *n.* a disease marked by livid spots on the skin and general debility. [From **Scurf.**]

**Scurvy**, skurv'i, *adj.*, *scurfy*: affected with scurvy: vile, vulgar, contemptible. [From **Scurf.**]

**Scutage**, skū'tāj, *n.* a pecuniary fine or tax, instead of personal service, which a vassal or tenant owed to his lord, sometimes levied by the crown in feudal times. [From L. *scutum*, a shield.]

**Scutcheon.** Same as **Escutcheon.**

**Scutiform**, skū'ti-form, *adj.* having the *form* of a *shield*. [L. *scutum*, a shield, and **Form.**]

**Scuttle**, skut'l, *n.* a shallow basket: a vessel for holding coal. [A.S. *scutel*, O. Fr. *escuelle*—L. *scutella*, a salver—*scutula*, dim. of *scutra*, a dish. See **Scullery.**]

**Scuttle**, skut'l, *n.* the openings or *hatchways* of a ship: a hole through the hatches or in the side or bottom of a ship.—*v.t.* to cut holes through any part of a ship: to sink a ship by cutting holes in it. [O. Fr. *escoutille*, a hatchway, from O. Ger. *scoz*, Ger. *schoosz*, bosom, a lap.]

**Scuttle**, skut'l, *v.i.* to *scud* or run with haste: to hurry.—*n.* a quick run. [From **Scud.**]

**Scythe**, sīth, *n.* a kind of sickle: an instrument with a large curved blade for mowing grass, &c.—*v.t.* to cut with a scythe, to mow. [A.S. *sithe*; Ice. *sigd*, Low Ger. *sigde*, a sickle, akin to L. *securis*, an axe, *seco*, to cut.]

**Sea**, sē, *n.* the great mass of salt water covering the greater part of the earth's surface: any great expanse of water less than an ocean: the ocean: the swell of the sea in a tempest: a wave: any large quantity of liquid : any rough or agitated place or element.—**At sea**, away from land : on the ocean.—**Half-seas over**, half-drunk.—**High seas**, the open sea.—**To go to sea**, to become a sailor. [A.S. *sæ ;* Ger. *see*, Goth. *saivs*, lake, Ice. *sior*, Sans. *sava*, water.]

**Sea-anemone**, sē'-a-nem'o-nē, *n.* a kind of polyp, like an *anemone*, found on rocks on the *sea*-coast.

**Seaboard**, sē'bōrd, *n.* the *border* or shore of the *sea*. [Sea, and Fr. *bord*, border, the shore.]

**Seacoast**, sē'kōst, *n.* the *coast* or shore of the *sea :* the land adjacent to the sea.

**Seafaring**, sē'fār-ing, *adj., faring* or going to *sea :* belonging to a seaman. [Sea and Fare.]

**Seagage**, sē'gāj, *n.* the depth a vessel sinks in the water. [Sea and Gage.] [*sea*.

**Seagirt**, sē'gèrt, *adj., girt* or surrounded by the

**Sea-going**, sē'-gō'ing, *adj.* sailing on the deep sea, as opposed to coasting or river (vessels).

**Seagreen**, sē'grēn, *adj., green* like the sea.

**Seahorse**, sē'hors, *n.* the walrus : the hippopotamus or river-horse : the hippocampus.

**Seakale**, sē'kāl, *n.* a kind of *kale* or cabbage found on sandy shores of the *sea*.

**Seaking**, sē'king, *n.* a name sometimes given to the leaders of the early Scandinavian piratical expeditions. [Based on a false ety. of Viking, which see.]

**Seal**, sēl, *n.* an engraved stamp for impressing the wax which closes a letter, &c. : the wax or other substance so impressed : that which makes fast or secure : that which authenticates or ratifies : assurance.—*v.t.* to fasten with a seal : to set a seal to : to mark with a stamp : to make fast : to confirm : to keep secure.—**Great seal**, the state seal of the United Kingdom. [A.S. *sigle* (Ger. *siegel*, It. *sigillo*) ; all from L. *sigillum*, dim. of *signum*, a mark or sign.]

**Seal**, sēl, *n.* a marine animal valuable for its skin and oil. [A.S. *seolh ;* Ice. *selr*, O. Ger. *selah*.]

**Seal-engraving**, sēl'-en-grāv'ing, *n.* the art of engraving seals.

**Sea-level**, sē'-lev'el, *n.* the *level* or surface of the *sea*. [letters, &c.

**Sealing-wax**, sēl'ing-waks, *n., wax* for *sealing*

**Seam**, sēm, *n.* that which is *sewed :* the line formed by the sewing together of two pieces : a line of union : a vein or stratum of metal, ore, coal, &c. : (*geol.*) a thin layer between thicker strata.—*v.t.* to unite by a seam : to sew : to make a seam in. [A.S. *seám*, from *seówian*, to sew ; Ice. *saumr*, Ger. *saum*, a seam.]

**Seaman**, sē'man, *n.* a *man* who assists in the navigation of ships at *sea :* a sailor.

**Seamanship**, sē'man-ship, *n.* the art of navigating ships at sea.

**Seamark**, sē'märk, *n.* any *mark* or object on land serving as a guide to those at *sea :* a beacon.

**Seamew**, sē'mū, *n.* a species of gull.

**Seamless**, sēm'les, *adj., without* a *seam :* woven throughout.

**Seamstress**, sēm'stres or sem'-, *n.* one who sews. [From Seam ; doublet Sempstress.]

**Seamy**, sēm'i, *adj.* having a seam or seams.

**Sean**, sēn, *n.* a drag-net : a seine. [See Seine.]

**Séance**, sā'ängs, *n.* a sitting, as of some public body : a sitting for consideration or inquiry. [Fr., from L. *sedeo*, to sit.]

**Seapiece**, sē'pēs, *n.* a *piece* or picture representing a scene at *sea*.

**Seaport**, sē'pōrt, *n.* a *port* or harbour on the *sea*-shore : a town near such a harbour.

**Sear**, sēr, *v.t.* to *dry up :* to burn to dryness on the surface : to scorch : to cauterise : to render callous or insensible.—*adj.* dry, withered. [A.S. *searian ;* O. Ger. *soren*, to dry, Low Ger. *soor*, *sear*.]

**Search**, sèrch, *v.t.* to look round to find : to seek : to examine : to inspect : to explore : to put to the test.—*v.i.* to seek for : to make inquiry.—*n.* the act of seeking or looking for : examination : inquiry : investigation : pursuit. [M. E. *serchen, cerchen*—O. Fr. *cercher* (Fr. *chercher*) —L. *circare*, to go about—*circus*, a circle. See Circle.]

**Searcher**, sèrch'ér, *n.* a seeker : an inquirer or [examiner.

**Searching**, sèrch'ing, *adj.* looking over closely : penetrating : trying : severe.—*adv.* Search'-ingly.

**Search-warrant**, sèrch'-wor'ant, *n.* a legal *warrant* authorising a *search* for stolen goods, &c.

**Seared**, sērd, *adj., dried up :* burned : hardened.

**Searoom**, sē'rōōm, *n., room* or space at *sea* for a ship to drive about without running ashore.

**Seasalt**, sē'salt, *n.* common salt obtained from sea-water by evaporation. [monster.

**Sea-serpent**, sē'-sèr'pent, *n.* a fabulous sea-

**Seashore**, sē'shōr, *n.* the land adjacent to the sea.

**Seasick**, sē'sik, *adj.* affected with *sickness* through the rolling of a vessel at *sea*.—*n.* Sea'-sick'ness.

**Seaside**, sē'sīd, *n.* the land *beside* the sea.

**Season**, sē'zn, *n.* one of the four periods of the year : the usual or proper time : any particular time : any period of time.—*v.t.* to mature : to prepare for use : to accustom : to fit for the taste : to give relish to : to mingle : to moderate.—*v.i.* to become seasoned or matured : to grow fit for use : to become inured.—*n.* Sea'soner. [Fr. *saison*—L. *satio, -onis*, a sowing, seedtime.]

**Seasonable**, sē'zn-a-bl, *adj.* happening in due season : occurring in good, suitable, or proper time : timely : opportune.—*adv.* Sea'sonably. —*n.* Sea'sonableness.

**Seasoning**, sē'zn-ing, *n.* that which is added to food to give it greater relish : anything added to increase enjoyment. [See Season.]

**Seat**, sēt, *n.* that on which one *sits :* a chair, bench, &c. : the place where one sits : site : a place where anything is established : post of authority : station : abode : a mansion.—*v.t.* to place on a seat : to cause to sit down : to place in any situation, site, &c. : to establish : to fix : to assign a seat to. [A.S. *sæte—sitan*, E. Sit, which see.] [*sea*, the narwhal.

**Sea-unicorn**, sē'-ū'ni-korn, *n.* the *unicorn* of the

**Sea-urchin**, sē'-ur'chin, *n.* the sea-hedgehog. [So called from its spines.]

**Seaward**, sē'ward, *adj., towards* the *sea*.—*adv.* towards or in the direction of the sea.

**Seaweed**, sē'wēd, *n.* a *weed* or plant of the *sea*.

**Seaworthy**, sē'wur-thi, *adj., worthy* or fit for *sea*. —*n.* Sea'worthiness.

**Secant**, sē'kant, *adj., cutting :* dividing into two parts.—*n.* a line that cuts another : a straight line from the centre of a circle to one extremity of an arc, produced till it meets the tangent to the other extremity. [L. *secans, secantis*, pr.p. of *seco*, to cut.]

**Secede**, se-sēd', *v.i.* to *go away :* to separate one's self : to withdraw from fellowship or association. [L. *secedo, secessum—se*, away, and *cedo*, to go. See Cede.]

**Seceder**, se-sēd'ér, *n.* one who secedes : one of a body of Presbyterians who seceded from the Church of Scotland about 1733.

**Secession**, se-sesh′un, *n.* the act of *seceding :* withdrawal : departure.

**Seclude**, se-klōōd′, *v.t.* to *shut apart :* to keep apart. [L. *secludo, seclusum—se,* apart, and *claudo,* to shut.]

**Seclusion**, se-klōō′zhun, *n.* the act of *secluding :* a shutting out : the state of being secluded or apart : separation : retirement : privacy : solitude.

**Second**, sek′und, *adj.* immediately *following* the first : the ordinal of two : next in position : inferior.—*n.* one who or that which follows or is second : one who attends another in a duel or a prize-fight : a supporter : the 60th part of a minute of time, or of a degree.—*v.t.* to follow : to act as second : to assist : to encourage : to support the mover of a question or resolution. [Fr.—L. *secundus—sequor, secutus,* to follow. See **Sequence.**]

**Secondarily**, sek′und-ar-i-li, *adv.* in a secondary manner or degree : (*B.*) secondly.

**Secondary**, sek′und-ar-i, *adj., following* or coming after the first : second in position : inferior : subordinate : deputed.—*n.* a subordinate : a delegate or deputy. [L. *secundarius.*]    [ports.

**Seconder**, sek′und-ėr, *n.* one who seconds or supports.

**Second-hand**, sek′und-hand, *adj.* received as it were from the *hand* of a *second* person : not new : that has been used by another.

**Secondly**, sek′und-li, *adv.* in the second place.

**Second-sight**, sek′und-sīt, *n.* a *second* or additional *sight :* power of seeing things future or distant.

**Secrecy**, sē′kre-si, *n.* the state of being *secret :* separation : concealment : retirement : privacy : fidelity to a secret : the keeping of secrets.

**Secret**, sē′kret, *adj.* put *apart* or *separate :* concealed from notice : removed from sight : unrevealed : hidden : secluded : retired : private : keeping secrets : reserved.—*n.* that which is concealed : anything unrevealed or unknown : privacy. [Fr.—L. *secretus,* from *secerno, secretum—se,* apart, and *cerno,* to separate.]

**Secretarial**, sek-re-tā′ri-al, *adj.* pertaining to a secretary or his duties.

**Secretary**, sek′re-tar-i, *n.* one employed to write for another : a public officer intrusted with the affairs of a department of government, or of a company, &c.—*n.* **Sec′retaryship.** [Lit. ′one who is intrusted with secrets,′ a confidant, Fr. *secrétaire*—Low L. *secretarius.* See **Secret.**]

**Secrete**, se-krēt′, *v.t.* to put *apart* or make *secret :* to hide : to conceal : to produce from the circulating fluids, as the blood in animals, the sap in vegetables. [L. *secerno, secretum.*]

**Secretion**, se-krē′shun, *n.* the act of secreting or separating from a circulating fluid : that which is secreted.

**Secretive**, se-krēt′iv, *adj.* tending to or causing secretion : given to secrecy or to keeping secrets. —*adv.* **Secret′ively.**—*n.* **Secret′iveness.**

**Secretly**, sē′kret-li, *adv.* in a secret manner : privately : unknown to others : inwardly.

**Secretness**, sē′kret-nes, *n.* the state of being secret.

**Secretory**, se-krēt′or-i, *adj.* performing the office of secretion.

**Sect**, sekt, *n.* a body of men who unite in holding some particular views, esp. in religion and philosophy : those who dissent from an established church. [Fr. *secte*—L. *secta,* a way, a way of thinking, hence a school of philosophy—*seco, sectum,* to cut off.]

**Sectarian**, sek-tā′ri-an, *adj.* pertaining to or peculiar to a *sect.*—*n.* one of a sect.

**Sectarianism**, sek-tā′ri-an-izm, *n.* quality or character of a sectarian : devotion to a sect.

**Sectary**, sek′tar-i, *n.* one of a *sect :* a dissenter.

**Sectile**, sek′til, *adj.* that may be *cut* with a knife. [L.—*seco,* to cut.]

**Section**, sek′shun, *n.* act of *cutting :* a division : a portion : the plan of any object cut through, as it were, to show its interior : the line formed by the intersection of two surfaces : the surface formed when a solid is cut by a plane.

**Sectional**, sek′shun-al, *adj.* pertaining to a section or distinct part.—*adv.* **Sec′tionally.**

**Sector**, sek′tur, *n.* that which *cuts :* that which is cut off : a portion of a circle between two radii and the intercepted arc : a mathematical instrument for finding a fourth proportional.

**Secular**, sek′ū-lar, *adj.* pertaining to an *age* or *generation :* coming or observed only once in a century : (*geol.*) gradually becoming appreciable in the course of ages : pertaining to the present world, or to things not spiritual : not bound by monastic rules.—*n.* a layman : an ecclesiastic not bound by monastic rules.—*adv.* **Sec′ularly.** [L. *secularis—seculum,* an age, a generation.]

**Secularise**, sek′ū-lar-īz, *v.t.* to make secular : to convert from spiritual to common use.—*n.* **Secularisa′tion.**

**Secularist**, sek′ū-lar-ist, *n.* one who, discarding religious belief and worship, applies himself exclusively to the things of this life.—*n.* **Sec′ularism.**    [or worldly : worldliness.

**Secularity**, sek-ū-lar′i-ti, *n.* state of being secular

**Securable**, se-kūr′a-bl, *adj.* that may be secured.

**Secure**, se-kūr′, *adj., without care* or anxiety, careless, so in *B.:* free from fear or danger : safe : confident : incautious.—*v.t.* to make safe : to render certain : to guarantee : to fasten.— *adv.* **Secure′ly.**—*n.* **Secure′ness.** [L. *se* (for *sine*), without, *cura,* care. See **Care.**]

**Security**, se-kūr′i-ti, *n.* state of being secure : freedom from fear : carelessness : protection : certainty : a pledge :—*pl.* bonds or certificates in evidence of debt or property.

**Sedan**, se-dan′, *n.* a covered chair for one, carried by two men. [Invented at *Sedan,* in France.]

**Sedate**, se-dāt′, *adj.* quiet : serene : serious.— *adv.* **Sedate′ly.**—*n.* **Sedate′ness.** [Lit. ′seated,′ ′settled,′ L. *sedatus—sedo, sedatum,* to seat, to compose, akin to *sedeo,* Sans. *sad,* to sit.]

**Sedative**, sed′a-tiv, *adj.* tending to make sedate or composed : moderating : allaying irritation or pain.—*n.* a medicine that allays irritation or pain.

**Sedentary**, sed′en-tar-i, *adj., sitting* much : passed chiefly in sitting : requiring much sitting : inactive.—*adv.* **Sed′entarily.**—*n.* **Sed′entariness.** [L. *sedentarius—sedeo,* to sit.]

**Sederunt**, sed-ē′runt, *n.* (*Scotland*) the sitting of a court. [L. ′they sat′—*sedeo,* to sit.]

**Sedge**, sej, *n.* a kind of flag or coarse grass growing in swamps and rivers. [Older form *seg*— A.S. *secg;* from root of *Saw,* instrument for cutting, the sedge being so called from its sharp, sword-like leaves. Cf. **Gladiolus.**]

**Sedged**, sejd, *adj.* composed of sedge or flags.

**Sedgy**, sej′i, *adj.* overgrown with sedge.

**Sediment**, sed′i-ment, *n.* that which *settles* at the bottom of a liquid : dregs. [L. *sedimentum— sedeo,* to sit, to settle.]

**Sedimentary**, sed-i-ment′ar-i, *adj.* pertaining to, consisting of, or formed by sediment.

**Sedition**, se-dish′un, *n.* insurrection : any offence against the state next to treason. [Lit. ′a going away,′ L. *seditio—se,* away, and *eo, itum,* Sans. *i,* to go.]

**Seditious**, se-dish′us, *adj.* pertaining to sedition : of the nature of or tending to excite sedition :

turbulent.—*adv.* **Sedi'tiously.**—*n.* **Sedi'tious-ness.**

**Seduce,** se-dūs', *v.t.* to *draw aside* from rectitude: to entice: to corrupt.—*n.* **Sedu'cer.** [L. *seduco*—*se,* aside, and *duco, ductum,* to lead, to draw. See **Duct.**]

**Seducement,** se-dūs'ment, *n.* act of seducing or drawing aside: allurement.

**Seduction,** se-duk'shun, *n.* act of seducing or enticing from virtue: crime of fraudulently depriving an unmarried woman of her chastity.

**Seductive,** se-duk'tiv, *adj.* tending to seduce or draw aside.—*adv.* **Seduc'tively.**

**Sedulous,** sed'ū-lus, *adj.* diligent: constant.—*adv.* **Sed'ulously.**—*n.* **Sed'ulousness.** [Lit. ' sitting constantly,' L. *sedulus*—*sedeo,* to sit.]

**See,** sē, *n.* the *seat* or jurisdiction of a bishop or archbishop. [O. Fr. *se,* sied—L. *sedes*—*sedeo,* to sit. See **Sit.**]

**See,** sē, *v.t.* to perceive by the eye: to observe: to discover: to remark: to experience: to visit.—*v.i.* to look or inquire: to discern: to understand: to be attentive:—*pa.t.* saw; *pa.p.* seen.—*int.* look! behold!—*n.* **Se'er.**—**To see to,** to look after: (*B.*) to behold. [A.S. *seon, sehvan;* cog. with Ger. *sehen.*]

**Seed,** sēd, *n.* the thing *sown:* the substance produced by plants and animals from which new plants and animals are generated: first principle: original: descendants.—*v.i.* to produce seed. [A.S. *sæd*—*sáwan,* E. **Sow;** cog. with Ice. *sádh,* Ger. *saat.*] [*seed.*

**Seedbud,** sēd'bud, *n.* the *bud* or germ of the

**Seedcake,** sēd'kāk, *n.* a sweet *cake* containing aromatic *seeds.*

**Seedling,** sēd'ling, *n.* a *plant* reared from the *seed.*

**Seedlobe,** sēd'lōb, *n.* the *lobe* or leaf of a plant which nourishes the growing point or *seed.*

**Seedsman,** sēds'man, *n.* one who deals in *seeds:* a sower:—*pl.* **Seeds'men.** [*seed.*

**Seedtime,** sēd'tīm, *n.* the *time* or season for sowing

**Seedy,** sēd'i, *adj.* abounding with seed: run to seed: having the flavour of seeds: worn out: shabby.—*adv.* **Seed'ily.**—*n.* **Seed'iness.**

**Seeing,** sē'ing, *n., sight:* vision.—*conj.* since.

**Seek,** sēk, *v.t.* to go in search of: to look for: to try to find or gain: to ask for: to solicit.—*v.i.* to make search or inquiry: to try: to use solicitation: (*B.*) to resort to:—*pa.t.* and *pa.p.* sought.—*n.* **Seek'er.** [A.S. *sécan,* cog. with Ger. *suchen,* E. **Sake.**]

**Seem,** sēm, *v.i.* to appear: to have a show: to look.—*v.t.* (*B.*) to befit.—*n.* **Seem'er.** [A.S. *séman,* to place together, to adapt or fit; conn. with **Same,** and Ger. *ziemen,* to be suitable.]

**Seeming,** sēm'ing, *adj., apparent:* specious.—*n.* appearance: semblance.—*adv.* **Seem'ingly.**—*n.* **Seem'ingness.**

**Seemly,** sēm'li, *adj.* (comp. **Seem'lier,** superl. **Seem'liest**), becoming: suitable: decent.—*adv.* in a decent or suitable manner.—*n.* **Seem'liness.**

**Seen,** sēn, *pa.p.* of See.

**Seer,** sē'r, *n.* one who fore*sees* events: a prophet.

**Seesaw,** sē'saw, *n.* motion to and fro, as in the act of *sawing:* a play among children, in which two seated at opposite ends of a board supported in the centre move alternately up and down.—*adj.* moving up and down, or to and fro.—*v.i.* to move backwards and forwards. [Prob. a reduplication of **Saw.**]

**Seethe,** sēth, *v.t.* to *boil:* to cook in hot liquid.—*v.i.* to be boiling: to be hot:—*pa.t.* seethed or sod; *pa.p.* seethed or sodd'en. [A.S. *seóthan,* cog. with Ice. *sjódha,* and Ger. *sieden.*]

**Segment,** seg'ment, *n.* a part *cut off:* a portion: (*geom.*) the part of a circle cut off by a straight line: the part of a sphere cut off by a plane. [L. *seco,* to cut.]

**Segregate,** seg're-gāt, *v.t.* to separate from others.—*n.* **Segrega'tion.** [Lit. ' to set *apart* from a *flock,*' L. *segrego, -atus—se,* apart, and *grex, gregis,* a flock.]

**Seidlitz,** sīd'litz, *adj.* saline water of or from Seidlitz in Bohemia, also a saline aperient powder.

**Seignior,** sēn'yur, *n.* a title of honour and address in Europe to *elders* or superiors: the lord of a manor.—**Grand Seignior,** the Sultan of Turkey.—*adj.* **Seignorial,** se-nō'ri-al. [Fr. *seigneur*—L. *senior—senex,* old. In Low L. *senior* sometimes = *dominus,* lord. Doublet **Sire.**]

**Seigniory,** sēn'yur-i, *n.* the power or authority of a *seignior* or lord: a manor.

**Seine,** sēn, *n.* a large net for catching fish. [Fr.—L. *sagena*—Gr. *sagēnē.*]

**Seismic,** sīs'mic, belonging to an *earthquake.*

**Seismology,** sīs-mol'o-ji, *n.* the science of earthquakes. [Gr. *seismos,* an earthquake, and *logos.*]

**Seize,** sēz, *v.t.* to take possession of forcibly: to take hold of: to grasp: to apprehend.—*n.* **Seiz'er.**—*adj.* **Seiz'able.** [Fr. *saisir* (Prov. *sazir,* to take possession of)—O. Ger. *sazjan,* to set, Ger. *be-setzen,* E. **Beset.**]

**Seizin,** sēz'in, *n.* the taking possession of an estate of freehold: the thing possessed.

**Seizure,** sē'zhōōr, *n.* act of *seizing:* capture: grasp: the thing seized.

**Selah,** sē'la, *n.* in the Psalms, a word denoting *silence* or a pause in the musical performance of the song. [Heb.]

**Seldom,** sel'dum, *adv., rarely:* not often. [A.S. *seldum;* Ice. *sialdan,* Ger. *selten,* rare.]

**Select,** se-lekt', *v.t.* to *pick out* from a number by preference: to choose: to cull.—*adj., picked out:* nicely chosen: choice.—*n.* **Select'ness.** [L. *seligo, selectum—se,* aside, and *lego,* Gr. *legō,* to gather, to pick out.]

**Selection,** se-lek'shun, *n.* act of selecting: things selected: a book containing select pieces.

**Selenium,** sel-ē'ni-um, *n.* an elementary substance allied to sulphur. [Coined from Gr. *selēnē,* the moon, like *tellurium* from L. *tellus.*]

**Selenography,** sel-en-og'raf-i, *n.* description of the moon. [Gr. *selēnē,* and *graphō,* to write.]

**Self,** self, *n.* one's own person: one's personal interest: selfishness:—*pl.* **Selves** (selvz).—*adj.* very: particular: one's own. [A.S. *self, silf,* cog. with Ger. *selbe,* Goth. *silba.*]

**Self-denial,** self-de-nī'al, *n.* the denial of one's self: the not gratifying one's own appetites or desires.

**Self-evident,** self-ev'i-dent, *adj.* evident of itself or without proof: that commands assent.

**Self-existent,** self-egz-ist'ent, *adj.* existing of or by himself, independent of any other being.—*n.* **Self-exist'ence.**

**Selfish,** self'ish, *adj.* chiefly or wholly regarding one's own self: void of regard to others.—*adv.* **Self'ishly.**—*n.* **Self'ishness.**

**Self-possession,** self-poz-zesh'un, *n.* the possession of one's self or faculties in danger: calmness.

**Self-righteous,** self-rīt'yus, *adj.* righteous in one's own estimation.—*n.* **Self-right'eousness.**

**Selfsame,** self'sām, *adj.* the very same.

**Self-sufficient,** self-suf-fish'ent, *adj.* confident in one's own sufficiency: haughty.—*n.* **Self-suffi'-ciency.** [*will.*

**Self-willed,** self'-wild, *adj.* governed by one's own

**Sell**, sel, *v.t.* to deliver in exchange for something paid as equivalent : to betray for money.—*v.i.* to have commerce : to be sold :—*pa.t.* and *pa.p.* sōld.—*n.* **Sell′er**. [A.S. *sellan*, to give, with cog. words in all the Teut. tongues, as Ice. *selja*, O. Ger. *sellen*, Goth. *saljan*, to offer in sacrifice.]

**Seltzer**, selt′zėr, *adj.* denoting a mineral water brought from Lower *Selters*, a village of Nassau, in Germany.

**Selvage**, sel′vāj, **Selvedge**, sel′vej, *n.* that part of cloth which forms an *edge* of *itself* without hemming : a border. [From Self and Edge.]

**Selves**, selvz, *pl.* of Self.

**Semaphore**, sem′a-fōr, *n.* a contrivance for *conveying signals*, consisting of a mast with arms turned on pivots by means of cords or levers.—*adjs.* **Semaphor′ic**, **Semaphor′ical**. [Gr. *sēma*, a sign, and *pherō*, to bear.]

**Semblance**, sem′blans, *n.*, *likeness* : appearance : figure. [Fr.—*sembler*, to seem—L. *similo*, to make like—*similis*, like.]

**Semibreve**, sem′i-brēv, *n.* a musical note, ◖, half the length of a *breve*. [L. *semi*, half, **Breve**.]

**Semicircle**, sem′i-sėrk-l, *n.*, *half* a *circle* : the figure bounded by the diameter of a circle and half the circumference.—*adj.* **Semicir′cular**. [L. *semi*, half, and **Circle**.]

**Semicircumference**, sem-i-sėr-kum′fėr-ens, *n.* *half* the *circumference* of a circle. [L. *semi*, half, and **Circumference**.]

**Semicolon**, sem′i-kō-lon, *n.* the point ( ; ) showing a division greater than the comma. [Lit. 'half a colon,' L. *semi*, half, and **Colon**.]

**Semidiameter**, sem-i-dī-am′e-tėr, *n.*, *half* the *diameter* of a circle : a radius. [L. *semi*, half, and **Diameter**.]

**Semifluid**, sem-i-flōō′id, *adj.*, *half* or imperfectly *fluid*. [L. *semi*, half, and **Fluid**.]

**Seminal**, sem′in-al, *adj.* pertaining to *seed* : radical : rudimental. [L. *semen*, *seminis*, seed —*sero*, to sow.]

**Seminary**, sem′in-ar-i, *n.* a place of education : (*lit.*) a place where *seed* is sown.

**Semination**, sem-i-nā′shun, *n.* act of *sowing* : natural dispersion of seed.

**Semiquaver**, sem′i-kwā-vėr, *n.* a musical note, ♪ *half* the length of a *quaver*. [L. *semi*, half, and **Quaver**.]

**Semitic**, sem-it′ik, *adj.* pertaining to the great family of languages that includes Hebrew and Arabic. [Derived from *Shem* in Genesis x. 21.]

**Semitone**, sem′i-tōn, *n.*, *half* a *tone* : one of the lesser intervals of the musical scale, as from B to C.—*adj.* **Semiton′ic**. [L. *semi*, half, and **Tone**.]

**Semi-transparent**, sem′i-trans-pā′rent, *adj.*, *half* or imperfectly *transparent*.—*n.* **Sem′i-transpa′rency**. [L. *semi*, half, and **Transparent**.]

**Semivocal**, sem-i-vō′kal, *adj.* pertaining to a semivowel. [L. *semi*, half, and **Vocal**.]

**Semivowel**, sem-i-vow′el, *n.* a *half vowel* : a letter with a half-vowel sound, as *m*. [L. *semi*, half, and **Vowel**.]

**Semolina**, sem-o-lē′na, *n.* the particles of fine hard wheat which do not pass into flour in milling. [From It. *semola*—L. *simila*, the finest wheat flour.]

**Sempiternal**, sem-pi-tėr′nal, *adj.*, *everlasting* : endless. [L. *sempiternus*—*semper*, ever, and *æternus*. See **Eternal**.]

**Sempster**, sem′stėr, **Sempstress**, sem′stres, *n.* a woman who *sews*. [See **Seamstress**.]

**Senary**, sen′ar-i, *adj.* containing *six* : of or belonging to six. [L. *senarius*—*seni*, six each—*sex*, six.]

**Senate**, sen′āt, *n.* a legislative or deliberative body, esp. the upper house of a national legislature. [L. *senatus* (*lit.*) a council of *elders*—*senex*, *senis*, old, an old man.]                [**Sen′atorship**]

**Senator**, sen′a-tur, *n.* a member of a senate.—*n.*

**Senatorial**, sen-a-tō′ri-al, *adj.* pertaining to or becoming a senate or a senator.—*adv.* **Senato′rially**.

**Send**, send, *v.t.* to *cause to go* : to cause to be conveyed : to despatch : to commission : to diffuse : to bestow.—*v.i.* to despatch a message or messenger :—*pa.t.* and *pa.p.* sent.—*n.* **Send′er**. [A.S. *sendan* ; Ice. *senda* ; Goth. *sandjan* ; prob. allied to Sans. *sadh*, to go away.]

**Sendal**, sen′dal, *n.* a thin silk or linen. [O. Fr.— Low L. *sindalum*—L. *sindon*—Gr. *sindōn*, a fine cloth from India.]

**Seneschal**, sen′esh-al, *n.* a steward.—*n.* **Sen′eschalship**. [Lit. 'the *senior* or *oldest* of the servants,' Fr. *sénéchal*—Low L. *siniscalcus*, from a Teut. root *sin* found in Goth. *sini-sta*, oldest (cog. with L. *senex*, *senis*, old), and Goth. *skalks*, O. Ger. *scalc*, a servant.]

**Senile**, sē′nīl, *adj.* pertaining to *old age* or attendant on it : aged.—*n.* **Senility**, se-nil′i-ti. [L. *senilis*—*senex*, *senis*, old.]

**Senior**, sēn′yur, *adj.*, *elder* : older in office.—*n.* one older than another : one older in office : an aged person.—*n.* **Seniority**, sēn-i-or′i-ti. [L., comp. of *senex*.]

**Senna**, sen′a, *n.* the dried, purgative leaflets of several species of cassia. [Ar. *sena*.]

**Sennight**, sen′it, *n.* contracted from *seven night* : a week. [See **Fortnight**.]

**Sensation**, sen-sā′shun, *n.* perception by the *senses* : feeling excited by external objects, by the state of the body, or by immaterial objects : a state of excited feeling.—*adj.* **Sensa′tional**.

**Sensationalism**, sen-sā′shun-al-izm, *n.* the doctrine that our ideas originate solely in *sensation*, and that there are no innate ideas.—*n.* **Sensa′tionalist**, a believer in sensationalism.

**Sense**, sens, *n.* a faculty by which objects are perceived : perception : discernment : understanding : power or soundness of judgment : reason : opinion : conviction : import :—*pl.* **The senses**, or **five senses**, sight, hearing, smell, taste, and touch. [Fr.—L. *sensus*—*sentio*, to discern by the senses.]

**Senseless**, sens′les, *adj.* without *sense* : incapable of feeling : wanting sympathy : foolish.—*adv.* **Sense′lessly**.—*n.* **Sense′lessness**.

**Sensibility**, sens-i-bil′i-ti, *n.* state or quality of being sensible : actual feeling : capacity of feeling : susceptibility : acuteness of feeling : delicacy.

**Sensible**, sens′i-bl, *adj.* capable of being perceived by the *senses* or by the mind : capable of being affected : easily affected : delicate : intelligent : judicious : cognisant : aware.—*n.* **Sens′ibleness**.—*adv.* **Sens′ibly**.

**Sensitive**, sens′i-tiv, *adj.* having *sense* or feeling : susceptible to sensations : easily affected : pertaining to or depending on sensation.—*adv.* **Sens′itively**.—*ns.* **Sens′itiveness**, **Sensitiv′ity**. —**Sens′itive plant**, a *plant*, the leaves of which are so *sensitive* that they close when touched.

**Sensorial**, sen-sō′ri-al, *adj.* pertaining to the sensorium.

**Sensorium**, sen-sō′ri-um, **Sensory**, sen′sor-i, *n.* the organ which receives the impressions made on the *senses*.

**Sensual**, sen'shōō-al, *adj.* pertaining to, affecting, or derived from the *senses*, as distinct from the mind : not intellectual or spiritual : given to the pleasures of sense : voluptuous : lewd.—*adv.* **Sen'sually.**—*n.* **Sen'sualness.** [Fr.—L. *sensualis.*] [to debase by carnal gratification.

**Sensualise**, sen'shōō-al-īz, *v.t.* to make sensual :

**Sensualism**, sen'shōō-al-izm, *n.* sensual indulgence : the doctrine that all our knowledge is derived originally from the senses.

**Sensualist**, sen'shōō-al-ist, *n.* one given to sensualism or sensual indulgence : a debauchee : a believer in the doctrine of sensualism.

**Sensuality**, sen-shōō-al'i-ti, *n.* indulgence in sensual pleasures : lewdness.

**Sensuous**, sen'shōō-us, *adj.* pertaining to *sense* : full of passion : connected with sensible objects.

**Sentence**, sent'ens, *n.* opinion : a judgment pronounced on a criminal by a court or judge : a maxim : (*gram.*) a number of words containing a complete thought.—*v.t.* to pronounce judgment on : to condemn. [Fr.—L. *sententia* (*lit.*) what one *thinks*—*sentio*, to feel, to think.]

**Sentential**, sen-ten'shal, *adj.* pertaining to a *sentence* : comprising sentences.—*adv.* **Senten'tially.**

**Sententious**, sen-ten'shus, *adj.* abounding with *sentences* or maxims : short and pithy in expression : bombastic, or affected in speech.—*adv.* **Senten'tiously.**—*n.* **Senten'tiousness.**

**Sentient**, sen'shi-ent, *adj.*, *discerning* by the *senses* : having the faculty of perception and sensation.—*n.* **Sen'tience.** [Pr.p. of L. *sentio*, to feel.]

**Sentiment**, sen'ti-ment, *n.* a thought occasioned by *feeling* : opinion : judgment : sensibility : feeling : a thought expressed in words : a maxim : a toast. [From L. *sentio*, to feel.]

**Sentimental**, sen-ti-ment'al, *adj.* having or abounding in *sentiments* or reflections : having an excess of sentiment or feeling : affectedly tender.—*adv.* **Sentiment'ally.**

**Sentimentalism**, sen-ti-ment'al-izm, **Sentimentality**, sen-ti-men-tal'i-ti, *n.* quality of being sentimental : affectation of fine feeling.

**Sentimentalist**, sen-ti-ment'al-ist, *n.* one who affects *sentiment* or fine feeling.

**Sentinel**, sen'ti-nel, *n.* one who keeps watch by pacing to and fro a little path : a sentry. [Fr. *sentinelle ;* of doubtful origin.]

**Sentry**, sen'tri, *n.* a *sentinel* : a soldier on guard to observe the approach of danger. [A corr. of **Sentinel.**] [*sentry.*

**Sentry-box**, sen'tri-boks, *n.* a *box* to shelter a

**Separable**, sep'ar-a-bl, *adj.* that may be separated or disjoined.—*adv.* **Sep'arably.**—*n.* **Separability.**

**Separate**, sep'ar-āt, *v.t.* to divide : to part : to withdraw : to set apart for a certain purpose.—*v.i.* to part : to withdraw from each other : to become disunited.—*adj.* separated : divided : apart from another : distinct.—*adv.* **Sep'arately.** [L. *separo, separatus* (*lit.*) to *put aside* or by itself—*se*, aside, and *paro*, to put, to prepare.]

**Separation**, sep-ar-ā'shun, *n.* act of separating or disjoining : state of being separate : disunion.

**Separatism**, sep'ar-a-tizm, *n.* act of separating or withdrawing, esp. from an established church.

**Separatist**, sep'ar-a-tist, *n.* one who separates or withdraws, esp. from an established church : a dissenter.

**Sepia**, sē'pi-a, *n.* a fine brown pigment prepared from the 'ink' of the *cuttle-fish:* Indian or China ink. [L.—Gr., the cuttle-fish.]

**Sepoy**, sē'poy, *n.* a native soldier, whether Hindu or Mohammedan, in the British army in India. [Hind. *sipahi*, a soldier, (*lit.*) a bowman, the *spahi* of Turkish and Algerian armies, from *sip*, a bow and arrow.]

**Sept**, sept, *n.* in Ireland, a subdivision of a tribe. [Probably a corr. of **Sect.**]

**September**, sep-tem'bėr, *n.* the ninth *month* of the year. [L. *septem*, seven, and *ber = fer*, Sans. *bhar*, to carry, bear. It was the *seventh* month of the old Roman year, which began in March.]

**Septenary**, sep'ten-ar-i, *adj.* consisting of *seven*. [L. *septenarius*—*septem*, seven.]

**Septennial**, sep-ten'yal, *adj.* lasting *seven years:* happening every seven years.—*adv.* **Septenn'ially.** [L. *septennis*—*septem*, seven, *annus*, a year.]

**Septic**, sep'tik, *adj.* promoting *putrefaction.*—*n.* a substance that promotes the putrefaction of bodies. [Gr. *sēptikos*—*sēpō*, to make putrid.]

**Septuagenarian**, sep-tū-a-jen-ā'ri-an, *n.* a person *seventy* years old.

**Septuagenary**, sep-tū-aj'en-ar-i, *adj.* consisting of *seventy.*—*n.* one 70 years old. [L. *septuagenarius*—*septuageni*, seventy each—*septem*, seven.]

**Septuagesima**, sep-tū-a-jes'i-ma, *n.* the third Sunday before Lent—the *seventieth* day before Easter. [L. *septuagesimus*—*septem*, seven.]

**Septuagesimal**, sep-tū-a-jes'i-mal, *adj.* consisting of *seventy:* counted by seventies.

**Septuagint**, sep'tū-a-jint, *n.* the Greek version of the Old Testament, said to have been made by *seventy* translators at Alexandria about 300 years B.C. [L. *septuaginta*—*septem*, seven.]

**Sepulchral**, se-pul'kral, *adj.* pertaining to a sepulchre, or to monuments erected for the dead : (*fig.*) deep, hollow, as tone.

**Sepulchre**, sep'ul-kėr, *n.* a place of *burial:* tomb. [Fr.—L. *sepulchrum*—*sepelio, sepultus*, to bury.]

**Sepulture**, sep'ul-tūr, *n.* act of *burying* the dead : interment : burial.

**Sequel**, sē'kwel, *n.* that which *follows:* succeeding part : result : consequence. [Fr.—L. *sequela* —*sequor*, Gr. *hepomai*, to follow.]

**Sequence**, sē'kwens, *n.* state of being *sequent* or following : order of succession : that which follows : consequence : (*music*) a regular succession of similar chords. [L. *sequor*, to follow.]

**Sequent**, sē'kwent, *adj.* following : succeeding.

**Sequester**, se-kwes'tėr, *v.t.* to separate : to withdraw from society : to set apart : (*law*) to place anything contested into the hands of a third person till the dispute is settled : to hold the property of another till the profits pay the demands : to take possession of the estate of a bankrupt in order to distribute it among the creditors.—*v.i.* (*law*) to renounce any interest in the estate of a husband. [Low L. *sequestro, -atum*—L. *sequester*, a depositary, from *sequi*, to follow.]

**Sequestered**, se-kwes'tėrd, *adj.* retired, secluded.

**Sequestrate**, se-kwes'trāt, *v.t.* to *sequester.*

**Sequestration**, sek-wes-trā'shun, *n.* act of *sequestering*, esp. the seizure of any one's property for the use of the state during dispute, or for the benefit of creditors : state of being separated : seclusion from society.

**Sequestrator**, sek-wes-trā'tor, *n.* one who *sequesters* another's property : one to whom property is committed during dispute.

**Sequin**, sē'kwin, *n.* a gold Venetian coin of the 13th c. = 9s. 4d. [Fr.—It. *zecchino*—*zecca*, the mint.]

**Seraglio**, se-ral'yō, *n.* the palace of the Turkish Sultan, esp. the part in which the women are kept. [It. *serraglio—serrare*, to lock up, from L. *sera*, a door-bar, which came to be used for Pers. *serai*, a palace.]

**Seraph**, ser'af, *n.* an angel of the highest rank :— *pl.* **Seraphs**, ser'afs, **Seraphim**, ser'af-im. [Heb., lit. 'a prince of heaven,' akin to *sar*, a prince, in pl. angels.]

**Seraphic**, se-raf'ik, **Seraphical**, se-raf'ik-al, *adj.* pertaining to or becoming a *seraph* : angelic : pure : sublime : refined.—*adv.* **Seraph'ically.**

**Sere.** Same as **Sear.**

**Serenade**, ser-e-nād', *n.* evening music in the open air : music performed by a gentleman under a lady's window at night : a piece of music for such an occasion.—*v.t.* to entertain with a serenade. [Fr.—It. *serenata*, from Prov. *serena*, even-song—L. *serus*, late.]

**Serene**, se-rēn', *adj.* calm : unclouded : undisturbed : unruffled : a form of address used to the princes of Germany and their families.—*adv.* **Serene'ly.** [L. *serenus*, clear.]

**Serenity**, se-ren'i-ti, *n.* state or quality of being *serene* : clearness : calmness : peace.

**Serf**, sèrf, *n.* a slave attached to the soil and sold with it. [Fr.—L. *servus*, a slave. See **Serve.**]

**Serfdom**, sèrf'dom, *n.* condition of a serf.

**Serge**, sèrj, *n.* a cloth made of twilled worsted or *silk*. [Fr.—L. *serica*, silk, from *Seres*, the Chinese.]

**Sergeancy**, sär'jen-si, **Sergeantship**, sär'jent-ship, *n.* office of a sergeant.

**Sergeant**, sär'jent, *n.* a non-commissioned officer next above a corporal.—*n.* **Sergeant-major**, the highest non-commissioned officer, employed to assist the adjutant. [Lit. 'a servant,' Fr. *sergent* —L. *serviens, -entis,* pr.p. of *servio*, to serve. See **Serve.**]

**Serial**, sē'ri-al, *adj.* pertaining to or consisting of a *series* : appearing periodically.—*n.* a tale or other composition appearing in successive parts, as in a periodical. [order.]

**Serially**, sē'ri-al-li, *adv.* in a *series* or regular

**Seriate**, sē'ri-āt, *adj.* arranged in a *series*.

**Series**, sē'ri-ēz, *n.sing.* and *pl.* a succession of things *connected* by some likeness : sequence : order : (*math.*) a progression of numbers or quantities according to a certain law. [L.— *sero, sertus*, to join, akin to Gr. *eirō*, to fasten, Sans. *sarat*, thread. See **Sermon, Serried.**]

**Serious**, sē'ri-us, *adj.* solemn : in earnest : important : attended with danger.—*adv.* **Se'ri-ously.**—*n.* **Se'riousness.** [L. *serius*, akin to *severus*, severe.]

**Serjeant.** sär'jent, *n.* a lawyer of the highest rank. —*n.* **Serjeant-at-arms**, an officer who attends the king, the lord-high-steward, &c. : an officer of a legislative body for keeping order, &c. [Same as **Sergeant.**]

**Sermon**, sèr'mun, *n.* a discourse on a text of Scripture. [L. *sermo, sermonis*, from *sero*, to join or bind together, to compose.]

**Serous**, sē'rus, *adj.* resembling *serum* : thin : watery.—*n.* **Seros'ity.**

**Serpent**, sèr'pent, *n.* a reptile without feet which moves by means of its ribs and scales : a person subtle or malicious : one of the constellations : (*music*) a bass wind-instrument, so called from its form. [Lit. 'the creeping animal,' L. *serpens, -entis,* pr.p. of *serpo*, to creep, akin to Gr. *herpō*, L. *repo*, and Sans. *srip*, to creep.]

**Serpentine**, sèr'pen-tīn, *adj.* resembling a *serpent* : winding : spiral : crooked.—*n.* a mineral of a green, black, or red colour, sometimes spotted like a *serpent's* skin.

**Serrate**, ser'rāt, **Serrated**, ser'rāt-ed, *adj.* notched or cut like a *saw*. [L. *serratus—serra*, a saw.]

**Serration**, ser-rā'shun, *n.* state of being serrated.

**Serried**, ser'rid, *adj.* crowded : pressed together. [P.a.p. of obs. v. *serry*, to press together—Fr. *serrer*, to crowd (It. *serrare*, to lock up)—L. *sera*, a door-bar, conn. with *sero*, to join together.]

**Serum**, sē'rum, *n.* the watery part of curdled milk : whey : the thin fluid which separates from the blood when it coagulates. [L.; prob. akin to Gr. *oros*, serum, and Sans. *saras*, water.]

**Servant**, sèrv'ant, *n.* one who is in the service of another : a domestic : (*B.*) a slave : one of low condition or spirit : a word of civility. [Fr., pr.p. of *servir*, to serve—L. *servire.* Doublet **Sergeant.**]

**Serve**, sèrv, *v.i.* to be a *servant* to : to work for and obey : to discharge the duties of an office : to attend or wait : to be sufficient : to suit.—*v.t.* to work for : to be in the employment of : to obey : to be subservient or subordinate to : to wait upon at table, &c. : to do duty for : to treat.—**Serve up**, to bring to table.—**Serve out**, to deal or distribute. [Fr. *servir*—L. *servio*, from *servus*, a slave, perh. conn. with *sero*, to bind together. See **Series.**]

**Server**, sèrv'èr, *n.* one who serves : a salver.

**Service**, sèrv'is, *n.* condition or occupation of a *servant* : a working for another : duty required in any office : military or naval duty : office of devotion : a musical composition for devotional purposes : labour, assistance, or kindness to another : benefit : profession of respect : order of dishes at table, or a set of them.—*n.* **Serv'ice-book**, a *book* of forms of religious *service* : a prayer-book. [Fr.—L. *servitium.*]

**Serviceable**, sèrv'is-a-bl, *adj.* able or willing to serve : advantageous : useful.—*adv.* **Serv'ice-ably.**—*n.* **Serv'iceableness.**

**Servile**, sèrv'īl, *adj.* pertaining to a *slave* or *servant* : slavish : meanly submissive : cringing.— *adv.* **Serv'ilely.**

**Servility**, sèr-vil'i-ti, *n.* state or quality of being servile : slavery : obsequiousness.

**Servitor**, sèrv'i-tor, *n.* one who serves : a servant : a follower or adherent.

**Servitude**, sèrv'i-tūd, *n.* state of being a *slave* : slavery : state of slavish dependence. [Fr.—L.]

**Sesame**, ses'a-me, **Sesamum**, ses'a-mum, *n.* an annual herb of Southern Asia, whose seed yields a valuable oil. [Gr.]

**Sesquipedalian**, ses-kwi-pe-dā'li-an, *adj.* containing a *foot and a half* : often humorously said of a very long word. [L. *sesqui-pedalis—sesqui*, one half more, and *pes, ped-is*, E. **Foot.**]

**Session**, sesh'un, *n.* the *sitting* or assembly of a court or public body : the time it sits : the period of time between the meeting and prorogation of Parliament : (*Scotland*) the lowest ecclesiastical court of a Presbyterian church.—**Court of Session**, the supreme civil court of Scotland. [Fr.—L. *sessio, sessionis*, from *sessum*, pa.p. of *sedeo*, E. **Sit.**]

**Sesspool.** Same as **Cesspool.**

**Set**, set, *v.t.* to *make* to *sit* : to place : to fix : to put in a condition : to render motionless : to determine beforehand : to obstruct : to plant : to fix in metal : to assign, as a price : to put in order for use : to sharpen : to spread, as sails : to pitch, as a tune : to adapt music to : to adorn with something fixed : to stud : to point, as a dog.—

*v.i.* to sink below the horizon : to decline : to plant : to become fixed : to congeal : to have a certain direction in motion : to point out game : to apply (one's self) :—*pr.p.* set'ting ; *pa.t.* and *pa.p.* set.—**To set aside,** to put away, to omit or reject :—**at naught,** to despise :—**by** (*B.*), to value or esteem :—**forth,** to exhibit : to publish : (*B.*) to set off to advantage : to set out on a journey :—**forward** (*B.*), to further, promote :—**in,** to put in the way : to begin :—**off,** to adorn : to place against as an equivalent :—**on** (*B.*), to attack :—**to,** to affix. [A.S. *settan,* cog. with Ger. *setzen,* Ice. *setja.* Goth. *satjan ;* being the weak causative of the Goth. root-verb *sittan,* E. **Sit.**]

**Set,** set, *adj.* (*lit.*) *seated,* so in *B.* : fixed : firm : determined : regular : established.—*n.* a number of things similar or suited to each other, *set* or used together : a number of persons associated : direction.

**Set-off,** set'-of, *n.* a claim set up against another : a counterbalance.

**Seton,** sē'tn, *n.* a passage made by a needle under the skin, through which threads of *silk* are drawn to cause irritation and discharge. [Fr. *séton* (It. *setone*)—Low L. *seto*—L. *seta,* a bristle. See **Satin.**]

**Settee,** set-tē', *n.* a long *seat* with a back.

**Setter,** set'ẽr, *n.* one who sets, as words to music : a dog which *sets* or crouches when it sees the game.

**Setting,** set'ing, *n.* act of setting : direction of a current of wind : the hardening of plaster : that which sets or holds, as the mounting of a jewel.

**Settle,** set'l, *v.t.* to *set* or place in a fixed state : to fix : to establish in a situation or business : to render quiet, clear, &c. : to decide : to free from uncertainty : to quiet : to compose : to fix by gift or legal act : to adjust : to liquidate or pay : to colonise.—*v.i.* to become fixed or stationary : to fix one's residence : to grow calm or clear : to sink by its own weight : to sink to the bottom : to cease from agitation : to adjust differences or accounts. [M. E. *setlen*—A.S. *setlan.*]

**Settle,** set'l, *n.* a long bench with a high back for *sitting* on : (*B.*) also, a platform lower than another part. [M. E. *setel*—A.S. *setl,* from *sittan,* to sit ; cog. with Ger. *sessel.*]

**Settlement,** set'l-ment, *n.* act of settling : state of being settled : payment : arrangement : a colony newly settled : a sum newly settled on a woman at her marriage.

**Settler,** set'lẽr, *n.* one who settles : a colonist.

**Seven,** sev'n, *adj.* and *n.* six and one. [A.S. *seofon ;* cog. with Dut. *zeven,* Ger. *sieben,* Goth. *sibun,* Gr. *hepta,* L. *septem,* Sans. *saptan.*]

**Sevenfold,** sev'n-fōld, *adj.* folded seven times : multiplied seven times. [A.S. *seofon-feald.* See **Seven** and **Fold.**]

**Seventeen,** sev'n-tēn, *adj.* and *n., seven* and *ten.* [A.S. *seofontine—seofon,* and *tin,* ten.]

**Seventeenth,** sev'n-tēnth, *adj.* and *n.* the *seventh* after the *tenth.* [A.S. *seofonteotha—seofon,* and *teotha,* tenth.]

**Seventh,** sev'nth, *adj.* last of *seven,* next after the sixth.—*n.* one of seven equal parts.—*adv.* **Sev'enthly.** [A.S. *seofotha.*]

**Seventieth,** sev'n-ti-eth, *adj.* last of *seventy* : the ordinal of 70.—*n.* a seventieth part.

**Seventy,** sev'n-ti, *adj.* and *n., seven* times *ten.* [A.S. *seofontig—seofon,* seven, and *tig,* ten.]

**Sever,** sev'ẽr, *v.t.* to separate with violence : to cut apart : to divide : (*B.*) to keep distinct.—*v.i.* to make a separation or distinction : to be

rent asunder. [Fr. *sevrer,* to wean (It. *sevrare, sceverare*)—L. *separo.* Doublet **Separate.**]

**Several,** sev'ẽr-al, *adj.* distinct : particular : different : various : consisting of a number : sundry.—*adv.* **Sev'erally.** [Lit. 'separate,' O. Fr.—L. *se¡aro.* See **Separate, Sever.**]

**Sev·ance,** sev'ẽr-ans, *n.* act of severing : separation.

**Severe,** se-vēr', *adj.* serious : grave : austere : strict : not mild : strictly adhering to rule : sharp : distressing : inclement : searching : difficult to be endured.—*adv.* **Severe'ly.** [Fr. *sévère*—L. *severus,* akin to Gr. *seb-omai,* to worship, Sans. *sêv.*]

**Severity,** se-ver'i-ti, *n.* quality of being severe : gravity : harshness : exactness : inclemency.

**Sew,** sō, *v.t.* to join or fasten together with a needle and thread.—*v.i.* to practise sewing.—*n.* **Sew'er.** [A.S. *seowian, siwian,* cog. with O. Ger. *siuwen,* and Goth. *siujan ;* also conn. with L. *su-o,* and Sans. root *siv.*]

**Sewage,** sū'āj, *n.* refuse carried off by *sewers.*

**Sewer,** sū'ẽr, *n.* an underground passage for *draining* off water and filth. [Lit. 'a drainer,' from an obs. verb *sew,* to drain—O. Fr. *essuer* (Fr. *essuyer,* It. *asciugare*)—Late L. *exsucare* —L. *ex,* out of, and *sucus,* moisture.]

**Sewerage,** sū'ẽr-āj, *n.* the whole sewers of a city : drainage by sewers.

**Sewing,** sō'ing, *n.* act of sewing : what is sewed.

**Sex,** seks, *n.* the distinction between male and female : the characteristics by which an animal or plant is male or female.—**The Sex,** womankind. [Lit. 'a division or *section,*' Fr. *sexe*— L. *sexus,* from the root of *seco,* to cut. See **Sect.**]                        [*sixty* years old.

**Sexagenarian,** seks-a-jen-ā'ri-an, *n.* a person

**Sexagenary,** seks-aj'en-ar-i or seks'a-jen-ar-i, *adj.* designating the number *sixty.*—*n.* a sexagenarian : something containing sixty. [L. *sexaginta,* sixty—*sex,* six.]

**Sexagesima,** seks-a-jes'i-ma, *n.* the second Sunday before Lent, being about the *sixtieth* day before Easter. [L. *sexagesimus,* sixtieth.]

**Sexagesimal,** seks-a-jes'i-mal, *adj.* pertaining to the number *sixty* : proceeding by sixties.

**Sexennial,** seks-en'yal, *adj.* lasting *six years* : happening once in six years.—*adv.* **Sexenn'ially.** [L. *sex,* six, and *annus,* a year.]

**Sextant,** seks'tant, *n.* (*math.*) the *sixth* part of a circle : an optical instrument having an arc = the sixth part of a circle, and used for measuring angular distances. [Fr.—L. *sextans, -antis,* a sixth—*sex,* six.]

**Sexton,** seks'tun, *n.* an officer who has charge of a church, attends the clergyman, digs graves, &c.—*n.* **Sex'tonship,** his office. [A corr. of **Sacristan.**]

**Sextuple,** seks'tū-pl, *adj., sixfold* : (*music*) having six parts. [Fr.—L. *sextus,* sixth, and *-plus,* akin to *plenus,* E. **Full.**]

**Sexual,** seks'ū-al, *adj.* pertaining to *sex* : distinguishing or founded on the sex : relating to the distinct organs of the sexes.—*adv.* **Sex'ually.**

**Sexuality,** seks-ū-al'i-ti, *n.* state or quality of being sexual.

**Shabby,** shab'i, *adj.* threadbare or worn, as clothes : having a look of poverty : mean in look or conduct : low : paltry.—*adv.* **Shabb'ily.** —*n.* **Shabb'iness.** [*Adj.* from *shab,* an old by-form of **Scab** : cog. with Ger. *schäbig,* scabby, threadbare. Doublet **Scabby.**]

**Shackles,** shak'lz, *n.pl.* a chain to confine the limbs : handcuffs : fetters : anything that hinders free action.—*v.t.* **Shack'le,** to fetter : to tie the limbs of: to confine. [A.S. *sceacul, scacul*, a shackle; cog. with O. Dut. *shakel*, a link of a chain, Ice. *skökull*, the pole of a cart.]

**Shad**, shad, *n.* a fish of the herring family. [A.S. *sceadda*—L. *squatus*. See **Skate**.]

**Shade**, shād, *n.* partial darkness: interception of light: obscurity: a shady place: protection: shelter: a screen: degree of colour: a very minute change: (*paint.*) the dark part of a picture: the soul separated from the body: a ghost.—*v.t.* to screen from light or heat: to shelter: to mark with gradations of colour: to darken.—*v.i.* to act as a shade.—*n.* **Shad'er**. [A.S. *scead, sceádu*, cog. with Ger. *schatte, schatten;* perh. conn. with Gr. *skia*, shadow, *skotos*, darkness, and with root *ska*, to cover.]

**Shadow**, shad'ō, *n.*, *shade* caused by an object: shade: darkness: shelter: security: favour: the dark part of a picture: an inseparable companion: a mystical representation: faint appearance: something only in appearance.—*v.t.* to shade: to cloud or darken: to shade, as a painting: to represent faintly.—*adj.* **Shad'owless**. [Doublet of **Shade**.]

**Shadowing**, shad'ō-ing, *n.*, *shading:* gradation of light and colour.

**Shadowy**, shad'ō-i, *adj.* full of shadow: dark: obscure: typical: unsubstantial.

**Shady**, shād'i, *adj.* having or in shade: sheltered from light or heat.—*adv.* **Shad'ily**.—*n.* **Shad'iness**.

**Shaft**, shaft, *n.* anything long and straight, as the stem of an arrow, &c.: the part of a column between the base and capital: the stem of a feather: the entrance to a mine: a pole of a carriage. [A.S. *sceaft*, cog. with Ger. *schaft*, prob. from root of **Shape**.]

**Shafted**, shaft'ed, *adj.* having a shaft or handle.

**Shag**, shag, *n.* that which is rough or bushy: woolly hair: cloth with a rough nap: a kind of tobacco cut into shreds. [A.S. *sceacga*, a head of hair, prob. from a Scand. root seen in Ice. *skegg*, beard, *skagi*, cape (in Shetland, *skaw*).]

**Shaggy**, shag'i, *adj.* covered with rough hair or wool: rough: rugged.—*n.* **Shagg'iness**.

**Shagreen**, sha-grēn', *n.* a kind of leather made from horse's, ass's, or camel's skin: shark-skin. —*adj.* also **Shagreened'**, made of or covered with shagreen. [Fr. *chagrin*—Turk. *ságrī*, the back of an ass or mule. Cf. **Chagrin**, which is the same word.]

**Shah**, shä, *n.* the monarch of Persia. [Pers. *shah*, [a king.]

**Shake**, shāk, *v.t.* to move with quick, short motions: to agitate: to make to tremble: to threaten to overthrow: to cause to waver: to make afraid: to give a tremulous note to.—*v.i.* to be agitated: to tremble: to shiver: to lose firmness:—*pa.t.* shook, (*B.*) shāked; *pa.p.* shāk'en.—*n.* a rapid tremulous motion: a trembling or shivering: a concussion: a rent in timber, rock, &c.: (*music*) a rapid repetition of two notes. [A.S. *scacan*, cog. with Ice. *shaka*, and perh. akin to Ger. *schaukeln*, to make to swing. Cf. **Shock**.]

**Shaker**, shāk'er, *n.* one of a small communistic religious sect in America, so nicknamed from a peculiar *dance* forming part of their religious service.

**Shakespearean** or **-ian**, **Shakspearean** or **-ian**, shāk-spēr'e-an, *adj.* pertaining to or in the style of Shakespeare, or to his works.

**Shako**, shak'ō, *n.* a kind of military cap. [Hun.]

**Shaky**, shāk'i, *adj.* in a shaking condition: feeble: unsteady: full of cracks or clefts.—*n.* **Shak'iness**.

**Shale**, shāl, *n.* a rock of a slaty structure, often found in the coal-measures. [Doublet of **Scale** and **Shell**.]

**Shall**, shal, *v.i.* to be under obligation: used in the future tense of the verb. [Orig. 'to owe,' A.S. *sceal*, to be obliged, Ger. *soll*, Goth. *skal*, Ice. *skal*, to be in duty bound: acc. to Grimm orig. the pa.t. of a root-verb *skilan*, to kill, thus lit. sig. 'I have slain,' hence 'I am liable for the fine or *wer-gild.*']

**Shalloon**, shal-lōōn', *n.* a light kind of woollen stuff said to have been first made at *Châlons* in France.

**Shallop**, shal'op, *n.* a large schooner-rigged boat with two masts. [Fr. *chaloupe*—Dut. *sloep*. Doublet **Sloop**.]

**Shalot, Shallot**, sha-lot', *n.* a kind of onion with a flavour like that of garlic. [Short for **Eschalot**.]

**Shallow**, shal'ō, *n.* a sandbank: a flat place over which the water is not deep: a shoal.—*adj.* not deep: not profound: not wise: trifling.—*n.* **Shall'owness**. [Conn. with **Shoal**, and perh. with **Shelf**.]

**Shalt**, shalt, 2d per. sing. of **Shall**.

**Shaly**, shāl'i, *adj.* pertaining to or having the qualities of shale.

**Sham**, sham, *n.* a pretence: that which deceives expectation: imposture.—*adj.* pretended: false. —*v.t.* to pretend: to feign: to impose upon.—*v.i.* to make false pretences:—*pr.p.* shamm'ing; *pa.t.* and *pa.p.* shammed. [From root of **Shame**.]

**Shamble**, sham'bl, *v.i.* to walk with an awkward, unsteady gait.—*adj.* **Sham'bling**. [Conn. with **Scamper**?]

**Shambles**, sham'blz, *n.pl.* a slaughter-house. [Lit. *stalls* on which butchers exposed their meat for sale, A.S. *scamel* (Ger. *schämel*), a bench—Low L. *scamellum*, for L. *scabellum*, dim. of *scamnum*, a bench.]

**Shame**, shām, *n.* the feeling caused by the exposure of that which ought to be concealed, or by a consciousness of guilt: the cause of shame: dishonour: (*B.*) the parts of the body which modesty requires to be concealed.—*v.t.* to make ashamed: to cause to blush: to cover with reproach. [A.S. *sceamu, scamu*, modesty; cog. with Ger. *scham*, prob. from a root-verb *skiman*, to become red, seen in **Shimmer**.]

**Shamefaced**, shām'fāst (properly **Shamefast**, shām'fast), *adj.* very modest or bashful: easily confused.—*adv.* **Shame'facedly**.—*n.* **Shame'facedness**, modesty. [For M. E. *shamefast* —A.S. *sceam-fæst*—*sceamu*, modesty, *fæst*, fast, perfectly, very.]

**Shameful**, shām'fool, *adj.* disgraceful: raising shame in others: indecent.—*adv.* **Shame'fully**. —*n.* **Shame'fulness**.

**Shameless**, shām'les, *adj.* immodest: done without shame: audacious.—*adv.* **Shame'lessly**.— *n.* **Shame'lessness**.

**Shammy**, sham'i, **Shamoy**, sham'oy, *n.* leather orig. prepared from the skin of the *chamois*, but now from that of the deer, goat, &c. [A corr. of **Chamois**.]

**Shampoo**, sham-pōō', *v.t.* to squeeze and rub the body, in connection with the hot bath: to wash thoroughly with soap and water, as the head. —*n.* **Shampoo'er**. [Hind. *tshampua*, to squeeze.]

**Shamrock**, sham'rok, *n.* a species of clover, the national emblem of Ireland. [A Celt. word; Ir. *seamrog*, Gael. *seamrag*.]

**Shank**, shangk, *n.* the leg below the knee to the foot : the long part of any instrument, as of an anchor between the arms and ring. [A.S. *sceanca*, the bone of the leg, the leg ; cog. with O. Ger. *scincho* (Ger. *schinken*, *schenkel*).]

**Shanty**, shant'i, *n.* a mean dwelling or hut, so called in Ireland. [Perh. from Ir. *sean*, old, and *tig*, a house.]

**Shapable**, shāp'a-bl, *adj.* that may be shaped.

**Shape**, shāp, *v.t.* to *form* : to fashion : to adapt to a purpose : to regulate : to direct : to conceive :—*pa.p.* shāped, (*B.*) shāp'en.—*n.* form or figure : external appearance : that which has form or figure : an appearance : particular nature : expression, as in words. [A.S. *sceapian*, *scapan*, cog. with Goth. *skapjan*, Ger. *schaffen*, Ice. *skapa*, to form ; prob. conn. with **Ship, Shaft, Shift**.]

**Shapeless**, shāp'les, *adj.* having no shape or regular form : wanting symmetry.—*n.* **Shape'-lessness**.

**Shapely**, shāp'li, *adj.* having shape or a regular form : symmetrical.—*n.* **Shape'liness**.

**Share**, shār, *n.* a part *shorn* or cut off : a portion : dividend : one of a number of equal portions of anything.—*v.t.* to divide into parts : to partake with others.—*v.i.* to have a part : to receive a dividend.—*n.* **Shar'er**. [A.S. *scearu*—*sceran*, E. **Shear** ; cog. with Ger. *schar*, *schaar*, a division.]

**Share**, shār, *n.* the iron blade of a plough which *shears* or cuts the ground. [M.E. *schar*—A.S. *scear*—*sceran*, E. **Shear** ; cog. with Ger. *schar*, *schaar*, a division, also a ploughshare. Cf. above word.]

**Shareholder**, shār'hōld-ėr, *n.* one who *holds* or owns a *share* in a joint fund or property.

**Shark**, shärk, *n.* a large voracious fish with large sharp teeth. [Ety. dub. ; perh. from L. *carcharus*—Gr. *karcharos*, sharp-pointed, having sharp teeth.]

**Sharp**, shärp, *adj.* having a thin, cutting edge or fine point : peaked or ridged : affecting the senses as if pointed or cutting : severe : keen : of keen or quick perception : pungent : biting : sarcastic : eager : fierce : impetuous : shrill.—*n.* an acute sound : (*music*) a note raised a semitone : the character ♯, directing this.—*adv.* **Sharp'ly**. *n.*—**Sharp'ness**. [A.S. *scearp* ; cog. with Ice. *skarp-r*, Ger. *scharf* ; from a root *skarp* seen in A.S. *sceorfan*, to split, *sceran*, to **Shear** ; conn. with L. *sarp-ere*, to prune, Gr. *harp-ē*. Cf. also **Scarf** and **Escarp**.]

**Sharpen**, shärp'n, *v.t.* to make sharp or keen : to give edge or point to : to make pungent or painful : to make severe : to make eager, active, or acute.—*v.i.* to grow sharp. [cheat.

**Sharper**, shärp'ėr, *n.* a trickster : a swindler : a

**Sharp-set**, shärp'-set, *adj.* eager : keen : ravenous.

**Sharp-sighted**, shärp'-sīt'ed, *adj.* having acute *sight* : shrewd : discerning : [*wit*) sagacious.

**Sharp-witted**, shärp'-wit'ed, *adj.* having an acute

**Shatter**, shat'ėr, *v.t.* to break so that the pieces are *scattered* : to break or dash to pieces : to crack : to disorder : to render unsound.—*n.* a fragment. [A doublet of **Scatter**.]

**Shave**, shāv, *v.t.* to cut off the hair with a razor : to pare closely : to make smooth by paring : to cut in thin slices : to skim along the surface : to strip :—*pa.p.* shāved or shāv'en. [A.S. *scafan;* Dut. *schaven*, to rub, to shave, Ger *schaben*, L. *scabo*, to scrape, Gr. *skaptō*, to dig. See **Shape**.]

**Shaveling**, shāv'ling, *n.* a monk or friar (in contempt), from his *shaven* crown.

**Shaver**, shāv'ėr, *n.* one who shaves : a barber : a sharp dealer : a plunderer.

**Shaving**, shāv'ing, *n.* the act of shaving : that which is shaved or pared off.

**Shaw**, shaw, *n.* a thicket, a small wood. [M.E. *shawe*, *showe;* Ice. *skógr*, Dan. *skov*.]

**Shawl**, shawl, *n.* a cloth of wool, cotton, silk, or hair, used, particularly by women, as a covering for the shoulders : a kind of mantle.—*v.t.* to wrap in a shawl. [From the Pers. word *shal*, a fine cloth (Ger. *shawl*, Fr. *châle* are from the E. word).]

**She**, shē, *pron. fem.* the female understood or previously mentioned : sometimes used as a noun for female. [Orig. the fem. of the def. art. in A.S.—viz. *seó* or *sia*, which in the 12th century began to replace *heó*, the old fem. pron.]

**Sheaf**, shēf, *n.* a quantity of things, esp. the stalks of grain, *shoved* together and bound : any bundle or collection :—*pl.* **Sheaves**, shēvz.—*v.t.* to bind in sheaves.—*v.i.* to make sheaves. [A.S. *sceaf*, Ger. *schaub*—A.S. *sceofan*, Ger. *schieben*, to shove.]

**Sheafy**, shēf'i, *adj.* consisting of *sheaves*.

**Shear**, shēr, *v.t.* to cut or clip : to clip with shears or any other instrument.—*v.i.* to separate :—*pa.t.* sheared, (*obs.*) shore ; *pa.p.* sheared or shorn.—*n.* **Shear'er**. [A.S. *sceran;* Ice. *skera*, to clip, Ger. *scheren*, to shave, to separate.]

**Shearling**, shēr'ling, *n.* a sheep only once *sheared*.

**Shears**, shērz, *n.pl.* an instrument for *shearing* or cutting, consisting of two blades that meet each other : anything like shears : an apparatus for raising heavy weights, consisting of upright spars fastened together at the top and furnished with tackle.

**Sheath**, shēth, *n.* a case for a sword or other long instrument : a scabbard : any thin defensive covering : a membrane covering a stem or branch : the wing-case of an insect. [A.S. *sceath*, *scæth;* cog. with Ger. *scheide*, a sheath, Ice. *skeid-ir;* from the root of **Shed**, to separate.]

**Sheathe**, shēth, *v.t.* to put into a *sheath* : to cover with a sheath or case : to inclose in a lining.

**Sheathing**, shēth'ing, *n.* that which *sheathes*, esp. the covering of a ship's bottom.

**Sheave**, shēv, *n.* the wheel of a pulley over which the rope runs. [M.E. *shefe*, *shive*, allied to Low Ger. *schive*, Ger. *scheibe*, a flat, thin piece of anything.]

**Shebeen**, she-bēn', *n.* a place where intoxicating drinks are privately and unlawfully sold. [Ir.]

**Shechinah**, she-kī'na, *n.* See **Shekinah**.

**Shed**, shed, *v.t.* to scatter : to throw out : to pour : to spill.—*v.i.* to let fall :—*pr.p.* shedd'ing ; *pa.t.* and *pa.p.* shed.—*n.* **Shedd'er**. [A.S. *sceddan;* cog. with Ger. *schütten*, to pour.]

**Shed**, shed, *v.t.* to part, separate. [A.S. *sceadan;* cog. with Ger. *scheiden*. See **Watershed**.]

**Shed**, shed, *n.* that which *shades* : a slight erection, usually of wood, for shade or shelter : an outhouse : a hut. [From **Shade**.]

**Sheen**, shēn, *n.* that which *shines* : brightness or splendour. [From **Shine**.]

**Sheep**, shēp, *n.sing.* and *pl.* the well-known animal covered with wool : a silly fellow (in contempt). [A.S. *sceap;* Dut. *schaap*, Ger. *schaf*.]

**Sheepcot**, shēp'kot, *n.* a *cot* or inclosure for *sheep*.

**Sheepfold**, shēp'fōld, *n.* a *fold* or inclosure for *sheep* : a flock of sheep.

**Sheepish**, shēp'ish, *adj.* like a sheep : bashful :

foolishly diffident.—*adv.* **Sheep´ishly.**—*n.* **Sheep´ishness.**

**Sheepmaster,** shēp´mas-tèr, *n.* (*B.*) a *master* or owner of *sheep.*

**Sheepshearer,** shēp´shēr-èr, *n.* one who *shears sheep.*

**Sheepshearing,** shēp´shēr-ing, *n.* the *shearing* or removing the fleece of *sheep:* the time of shearing the sheep.

**Sheepwalk,** shēp´wawk, *n.* the place where the *sheep walk* and pasture : sheep-pasture.

**Sheer,** shēr, *adj.* pure : unmingled : simple : without a break, perpendicular.—*adv.* clear : quite : at once. [A.S. *scír* ; Ice. *skírr*, bright, clear, Ger. *schier*, Goth. *skeirs*, clear.]

**Sheer,** shēr, *v.i.* to *deviate* from the line of the proper course, as a ship : to turn aside.—*n.* the deviation from the straight line, or the longitudinal curve or bend of a ship's deck or sides. [From **Shear,** *v.i.*]

**Sheers,** shērz, *n.* Same as **Shears.**

**Sheet,** shēt, *n.* a large, thin piece of anything : a large, broad piece of cloth in a bed : a large, broad piece of paper : a sail : the rope fastened to the leeward corner of a sail to *extend* it to the wind.—*v.t.* to cover with or as with a sheet. [Lit. 'that which is *shot* or spread out,' A.S. *sceát, scete*, from *sceotan*, to shoot, to extend, Ger. *schote*, the sheet (*naut.*).]

**Sheet-anchor,** shēt´-ang´kor, *n.* the largest anchor of a ship, *shot* or thrown out in extreme danger : chief support : last refuge. [See **Sheet.**]

**Sheeting,** shēt´ing, *n.* cloth used for bed-*sheets.*

**Sheet-lightning,** shēt´-līt´ning, *n.*, *lightning* appearing in *sheets* or having a broad appearance.

**Sheik,** shēk, *n.* a man of eminence, a lord, a chief. [Lit. 'an elder,' Ar. *sheikh—shâkha*, to be old.]

**Shekel,** shek´l, *n.* a Jewish *weight* (about half an ounce avoirdupois) and coin (about 2*s.* 6*d.* sterling). [Heb., from *shakal*, to weigh.]

**Shekinah,** she-kī´na, *n.* the Divine presence which *rested* like a cloud or visible light over the mercy-seat. [Heb., from *shakan*, to rest.]

**Shelf,** shelf, *n.* a board fixed on a wall, &c. for laying things on : a flat layer of rock : a ledge : a shoal : a sandbank :—*pl.* **Shelves** (shelvz).—*adj.* **Shelf´y.** [M. E. *scelfe*—A.S. *scylfe—scelan*, to separate, to split ; cog. with Scotch *skelve* and Ger. *schelfe*, a shell or husk.]

**Shell,** shel, *n.* a hard covering of some animals : any framework : a rough kind of coffin : an instrument of music : a bomb.—*v.t.* to break off the shell : to remove the shell from : to take out of the shell : to throw shells or bombs upon : to bombard.—*v.i.* to fall off like a shell : to cast the shell. [Lit. 'something thin like a *scale*,' A.S. *scell*, cog. with Ice. *skell*, Ger. *schale*. Doublet **Scale.**]

**Shellac, Shell-lac,** shel´lak, *n.* lac prepared in thin plates. [See **Lac,** a resinous substance.]

**Shellfish,** shel´fish, *n.* a *fish* or an aquatic animal with an external *shell.*

**Shellproof,** shel´prōōf, *adj.*, *proof* against or able to resist *shells* or bombs.

**Shellwork,** shel´wurk, *n.*, *work* composed of or adorned with *shells.*

**Shelly,** shel´i, *adj.* full of or made of shells.

**Shelter,** shel´tèr, *n.* that which *shields* or protects : a refuge : a retreat, a harbour : one who protects, a guardian : the state of being covered or protected : protection.—*v.t.* to cover or shield : to defend : to conceal.—*v.i.* to take shelter. [Prob. from the M. E. *sheld* (E. **Shield**), through the influence of M. E. *scheltrone* (from A.S.

*scildtruma*, a covering composed of shields, a line of soldiers).]

**Shelve,** shelv, *v.t.* to furnish with shelves : to place on a shelf : to put aside.—*v.i.* to slope like a shelf.

**Shelving,** shelv´ing, *n.* the furnishing with shelves : the act of placing on a shelf : shelves or materials for shelves. [shallow.

**Shelvy,** shelv´i, *adj.* full of shelves or shoals :

**Shemitic.** Same as **Semitic.**

**Shepherd,** shep´èrd, *n.* one who *herds sheep :* a swain : a pastor.—*fem.* **Shep´herdess.** [A.S. *sceap-hirde.* See **Sheep** and **Herd.**]

**Sherbet,** shèr´bet, *n.* a *drink* of water and fruit juices, sweetened and flavoured. [Arab. *sherbet*, a drink, from *shariba*, to drink, perh. conn. with L. *sorbeo*, to sip : other forms are **Shrub** and **Sirup.**]

**Sherd,** shèrd, *n.* (*B.*) a *shred*, a fragment.

**Sheriff,** sher´if, *n.* the governor of a *shire :* an officer in a county who executes the law.—*n.* **Sher´iffship.** [M. E. *shir-reeve*—A.S. *scir-gerefa—scir* (E. **Shire**), and *gerefa*, a governor, cog. with Ger. *graf*, a count, E. **Reeve** ; cf. **Landgrave** and **Margrave.**]

**Sheriffalty,** sher´if-al-ti, **Sheriffdom,** sher´if-dum, *n.* the office or jurisdiction of a *sheriff.*

**Sherry,** sher´i, *n.* a dry wine of an amber colour, obtained principally from *Xeres* in Spain. [Formerly *sherris.*]

**Shew,** shō. Same as **Show.**

**Shewbread,** shō´bred. Same as **Showbread.**

**Shibboleth,** shib´bo-leth, *n.* (*B.*) a word used as a test by the Gileadites to detect the Ephraimites, who could not pronounce the *sh :* the criterion or watchword of a party. [Heb. an ear of corn ; or a stream, from *shabal*, to grow, to flow.]

**Shield,** shēld, *n.* a broad plate worn for defence on the left arm : defence : a person who protects : an escutcheon.—*v.t.* to defend. [A.S. *scyld—scyldan*, to defend ; cog. with Ger. *schild*, Ice. *skiöld-r*, protection.]

**Shieldless,** shēld´les, *adj.* without a shield : defenceless.

**Shift,** shift, *v.t.* to change : to put out of the way : to dress in fresh clothes.—*v.i.* to change about : to remove : to change one's clothes : to resort to expedients for some purpose.—*n.* a change : a contrivance : an artifice : last resource : a chemise (orig. sig. a *change* of linen). —*n.* **Shift´er.** [A.S. *sciftan*, to divide, to order ; cog. with Ice. *skipta*, to divide, to change ; conn. with **Equip.**]

**Shiftless,** shift´les, *adj.* destitute of shifts or expedients : unsuccessful, for want of proper means.

**Shillalah,** shil-lā´la, **Shillaly,** shil-lā´li, *n.* an oak sapling : a cudgel. [Said to be named from an Irish wood, famous for its oaks.]

**Shilling,** shil´ing, *n.* an English silver coin = 12 pence. [Lit. 'the *ringing* (coin),' A.S. *scilling*, cog. with Ger. *schilling* ; the root is seen in O. Ger. *scëllan*, Ger. *schallen*, to sound, to ring.]

**Shimmer,** shim´èr, *v.i.* to gleam : to glisten.—*n.* **Shimm´er.** [A.S. *scymrian—scimian*, to shine —*scima*, lustre, brightness, cog. with Ger. *schimmern.*]

**Shin,** shin, *n.* the large bone of the leg or the fore-part of it. [A.S. *scina*, the shin (esp. in the compound *scin-ban*, shin-bone), cog. with Dut. *scheen*, Ger. *schien.*]

**Shine,** shīn, *v.i.* to beam with steady radiance : to glitter : to be bright or beautiful : to be eminent : —*pa.t.* and *pa.p.* shone (shon), (*B.*) *pa.t.* and *pa.p.* shīned.—*n.* brightness : splendour : fair weather. [A.S. *scinan*; Goth. *skeinan*, Ger. *scheinen*; conn. with root of **Shimmer**.]

**Shingle**, shing′gl, *n.* wood sawed or split thin, used instead of slates or tiles, for covering houses: the coarse gravel on the shores of rivers or of the sea.—*v.t.* to cover or roof with shingles. [Orig. *shindle* (cog. with Ger. *schindel*)—*scindula*, a late form of L. *scandula*, perh. from *scindo*, to split.]

**Shingles**, shing′glz, *n.* an eruptive disease which often spreads round the body like a *belt*. [A corr. of L. *cingulum*, a belt or girdle—*cingo*, to gird.]

**Shingly**, shing′gli, *adj.* abounding with *shingle*.

**Shining**, shīn′ing, *adj.* scattering light: bright: resplendent: conspicuous.—*n.* effusion or clearness of light: brightness.

**Shiny**, shīn′i, *adj.*, *shining*: diffusing light: bright: splendid: unclouded.

**Ship**, ship, *n.* a vessel having three masts, with tops and yards to each: generally, any large vessel.—*v.t.* to put on board a ship: to engage for service on board a ship: to receive on board ship: to fix in its place.—*v.i.* to engage for service on shipboard:—*pr.p.* shipp′ing; *pa.t.* and *pa.p.* shipped.—*n.* **Shipp′er.**—*n.* **Ship-of-the-line**, one of the large war-ships of the royal navy. [Lit. 'a vessel;' A.S. *scip*, cog. with Goth. *skip*, Ice. *skip*, Ger. *schiff*; conn. with E. **Shape**, and with Gr. *skap-tō*, to dig, *skaph-os*, the hull of a ship, a ship, and L. *scapha*, a boat. Doublet **Skiff**.]

**Shipboard**, ship′bōrd, *n.* the *board* or deck of a *ship*.—*adv.* upon or within a ship.

**Ship-broker**, ship′-brōk′ėr, *n.* a *broker* who effects sales, insurances, &c. of *ships*.

**Ship-chandler**, ship′-chand′lėr, *n.* a *chandler* or dealer in cordage, canvas, and other *ship* furniture.

**Shipman**, ship′man, *n.* (*B.*) a *man* who manages a *ship*: a sailor.—*pl.* **Ship′men.** [A.S. *scip-mann*.] [tain of a *ship*.

**Shipmaster**, ship′mas-tėr, *n.* the *master* or cap-

**Shipmate**, ship′māt, *n.* a *mate* or companion in the same *ship*.

**Shipment**, ship′ment, *n.* act of putting on board ship: embarkation: that which is shipped.

**Ship-money**, ship′-mun′i, *n.*, *money* for providing *ships* for the service of the king in time of war, raised at intervals in England 1007—1640.

**Shipping**, ship′ing, *adj.* relating to ships.—*n.* ships collectively: tonnage.—**To take shipping**, (*B.*) to embark.

**Ship's-husband**, ship′s-huz′band, *n.* the owner's agent in the management of a ship.

**Shipwreck**, ship′rek, *n.* the *wreck* or destruction of a *ship*: destruction.—*v.t.* to destroy on the sea: to make to suffer wreck. [*ships*.

**Shipwright**, ship′rīt, *n.* a *wright* who constructs

**Shipyard**, ship′yärd, *n.* a *yard* where *ships* are built or repaired.

**Shire**, shīr, *n.* a *division* of the kingdom under a sheriff: a county. (When added to the name of a county the *i* is pronounced as in *hill*.) [A.S. *scir*, a division—*sceran*, to shear, to cut. See **Share** and **Shear**.]

**Shirk**, shėrk, *v.t.* to avoid, get off or slink away from. [A form of vulgar *shark*, to play the thief, to shift for a living, from **Shark**, the fish.]

**Shirt**, shėrt, *n.* a short garment worn next the body by men.—*v.t.* to cover as with a shirt. [Cog. with Ice. *skyrta*, Ger. *schurz*, an apron; conn. with **Short** and **Skirt**.]

**Shirting**, shėrt′ing, *n.* cloth for *shirts*.

**Shist**, &c. See **Schist**, &c.

**Shittah**, shit′a, **Shittim**, shit′im, *n.* a precious wood used in the construction of the Jewish Tabernacle and its furniture, supposed to be a species of acacia. [Heb. *shittah*, pl. *shittim*.]

**Shiver**, shiv′ėr, *n.* a splinter, or small piece into which a thing breaks by sudden violence.—*v.t.* to shatter.—*v.i.* to fall into shivers. [From root of **Sheave**; allied to Ger. *schiefer*, a splinter.]

**Shiver**, shiv′ėr, *v.i.* to shake or tremble: to shudder.—*v.t.* to cause to shake in the wind, as sails. [An imitative word; allied to O. Dut. *schoeveren*, to shake, prov. Ger. *schubbern*.]

**Shivery**, shiv′ėr-i, *adj.* easily falling into *shivers* or fragments: cohering loosely.

**Shoal**, shōl, *n.* a great multitude of fishes swimming together.—*v.i.* to crowd. [A.S. *scolu*, a company—L. *schola*, a school. See **School**.]

**Shoal**, shōl, *n.* a *shallow*: a place where the water of a river, sea, or lake is not deep: a sandbank.—*adj.* shallow.—*v.i.* to grow shallow: to come upon shallows. [From root of **Shallow**.]

**Shoaly**, shōl′i, *adj.* full of shoals or shallows: not deep.—*n.* **Shoal′iness.**

**Shoar**, shōr, *n.* a prop. Same as **Shore**, a prop.

**Shock**, shok, *n.* a violent *shake*: a sudden dashing of one thing against another: violent onset: an offence.—*v.t.* to shake by violence: to offend: to disgust: to dismay. [Prob. through Fr. *choc*, a dashing, from O. Ger. *schoc*, shock; allied to **Shake**.]

**Shock**, shok, *n.* a *heap* or pile of sheaves of corn. [Ger. *schock*, Dut. *schokke*, a heap.]

**Shock-headed**, shok′-hed′ed, *adj.* having a thick and bushy head of hair. [From Prov. E. *shock*, a rough dog; a form of **Shag**.]

**Shocking**, shok′ing, *adj.* giving a *shock* or shake from horror or disgust: highly offensive.—*adv.* **Shock′ingly.**

**Shod**, shod, *pa.t.* and *pa.p.* of **Shoe**.

**Shoddy**, shod′i, *n.* (*orig.*) the waste *shed* or thrown off in spinning wool: now applied to the wool of old woven fabrics reduced to the state in which it was before being spun and woven, and thus fit for re-manufacture. [From **Shed**, to part.]

**Shoe**, shōō, *n.* a covering for the foot: a rim of iron nailed to the hoof of an animal to keep it from injury: anything in form or use like a shoe:—*pl.* **Shoes** (shōōz).—*v.t.* to furnish with shoes: to cover at the bottom:—*pr.p.* shoe′ing; *pa.t.* and *pa.p.* shod. [A.S. *sco*, *sceo*; Goth. *skohs*, Ger. *schuh*.] [*shoes* or boots.

**Shoeblack**, shōō′blak, *n.* one who *blacks* and cleans

**Shoehorn**, shōō′horn, *n.* a curved piece of *horn* or metal used in putting on a *shoe*.

**Shone**, shon. *pa.t.* and *pa.p.* of **Shine**.

**Shook**, shook, *pa.t.* of **Shake**.

**Shoon**, shōōn, *n.*, *old pl.* of **Shoe**. [A.S. *sceón*. See **Shoe**.]

**Shoot**, shōōt, *v.t.* to *dart*: to let fly with force: to discharge from a bow or gun: to strike with a shot: to thrust forward: to send forth new parts, as a plant.—*v.i.* to perform the act of shooting: to be driven along: to fly, as an arrow: to jut out: to germinate: to advance:—*pa.t.* and *pa.p.* shot.—*n.* act of shooting: a young branch.—*n.* **Shoot′er.** [A.S. *sceotan*; cog. with Dut. *schieten*, Ger. *schiessen*, to dart.]

**Shooting**, shōōt′ing, *n.* act of discharging firearms or an arrow: sensation of a quick pain: act or practice of killing game.

**Shooting-box**, shōōt′ing-boks, *n.* a small house in the country for use in the shooting season.

**Shooting-star**, shōōt′ing-stär, *n.* a meteor, so called from its quick, darting motion.

**Shop**, shop, *n.* a building in which goods are sold by retail : a place where mechanics work.—*v.i.* to visit shops for the purpose of buying :—*pr.p.* shopp′ing ; *pa.p.* shopped. [A.S. *sceoppa*, a treasury (influenced by O. Fr. *eschoppe*, a stall —Ger. *schoppen*, a shed).]

**Shop-lifting**, shop′-lift′ing, *n.*, *lifting* or stealing anything from a *shop*.—*n.* **Shop′-lift′er.**

**Shop-walker**, shop′-wawk′er, *n.* one who *walks* in a *shop* and sees the customers attended to.

**Shore**, shōr, *n.* the coast or land adjacent to the sea, a river, or lake. [Lit. the place where the land is *cut* or broken off, A.S. *score*—*sceran*, to shear, to divide.]

**Shore**, shōr, *n.* a prop or support for the side of a building, or to keep a vessel in dock steady on the slips.—*v.t.* to prop.—*n.* **Shor′er**. [Allied to O. Dut. *schore*, and conn. with **Shear**.]

**Shoreless**, shōr′les, *adj.* having no shore or coast : of indefinite or unlimited extent.

**Shorn**, shorn, *pa.p.* of **Shear**.

**Short**, short, *adj.* (*comp.* **Short′er**, *superl.* **Short′est**), not long in time or space : near at hand : scanty : insufficient : narrow : abrupt : brittle. —*adv.* not long.—*n.* **Short′ness**. **In short**, in a few words. [A.S. *sceort*, cog. with O. Ger. *scurz*, prob. conn. with **Shear**. The Dut. and Scand. *kort*, Ger. *kurz*, are borrowed from L. *curtus*. See **Curt**.]

**Shortcoming**, short′kum-ing, *n.* act of *coming* or falling *short* of produce or result : neglect of or failure in duty.

**Short-dated**, short′-dāt′ed, *adj.* having *short* or little time to run from its *date*, as a bill.

**Shorten**, short′n, *v.t.* to make short : to deprive : to make friable.—*v.i.* to become short or shorter : to contract.

**Shorthand**, short′hand, *n.* an art by which writing is made shorter and easier, so as to keep pace with speaking.

**Short-lived**, short′-līvd, *adj.*, *living* or lasting only for a *short* time.

**Shortly**, short′li, *adv.* in a *short* time : in a brief manner : quickly : soon.

**Short-sighted**, short′-sīt′ed, *adj.* having *sight* extending but a *short* distance : unable to see far : of weak intellect : heedless.—*n.* **Short′sight′edness**.

**Short-winded**, short′-wind′ed, *adj.* affected with *shortness* of *wind* or breath.

**Shot**, *pa.t.* and *pa.p.* of **Shoot**.

**Shot**, shot, *n.* act of *shooting* : a marksman : a missile : flight of a missile or the distance passed by it : small globules of lead : (*gun.*) solid projectiles generally.—*v.t.* to load with shot :—*pr.p.* shott′ing ; *pa.p.* shott′ed.

**Should**, shood, *pa.t.* of **Shall**. [A.S. *sceolde*, pa.t. of *sceal*. See **Shall**.]

**Shoulder**, shōl′der, *n.* the joint which connects the human arm or the foreleg of a quadruped with the body : the flesh and muscles about the shoulder : the upper joint of the foreleg of an animal cut for market : a prominence : (*fig.*) that which sustains.—*v.t.* to push with the shoulder or violently : to take upon the shoulder. [A.S. *sculdor* ; Ger. *schulter*, Dut. *schouder*.]

**Shoulder-belt**, shōl′der-belt, *n.* a *belt* that passes across the *shoulder*.

**Shoulder-blade**, shōl′der-blād, *n.* the broad, flat, *blade*-like bone of the *shoulder*.

**Shoulder-knot**, shōl′der-not, *n.* a *knot* worn as an ornament on the *shoulder*.

**Shout**, showt, *n.* a loud and sudden outcry of joy, triumph, or courage.—*v.i.* to utter a shout.—*v.t.* to utter with a shout : to cry.—*n.* **Shout′er**. [Either merely imitative, or a by-form of **Scout**, as being the sentinel's challenge.]

**Shove**, shuv, *v.t.* to drive along : to push before one.—*v.i.* to push forward : to push off.—*n.* act of shoving : a push. [A.S. *sceofan*, cog. with Dut. *schuiven*, Ger. *schieben*.]

**Shovel**, shuv′l, *n.* an instrument with a broad blade, and a handle for *shoving* and lifting.—*v.t.* to lift up and throw with a shovel : to gather in large quantities.—*v.i.* to use a shovel :—*pr.p.* shov′elling ; *pa.t.* and *pa.p.* shov′elled. [From **Shove** ; cog. with Ger. *schaufel*.]

**Show**, shō, *v.t.* to present to view : to enable to perceive or know : to inform : to teach : to guide : to prove : to explain : to bestow.—*v.i.* to appear : to look :—*pa.p.* shōwn or shōwed.—*n.* act of showing : display : a sight or spectacle : parade : appearance : plausibility : pretence.—*n.* **Show′er**. [A.S. *sceawian* ; Dut. *schouwen*, Ger. *schauen*, Goth. *us-scawjan* ; probably allied to **See**.]

**Showbill**, shō′bil, *n.* a *bill* for *showing* or advertising the price, merits, &c. of goods.

**Showbread**, shō′bred, *n.* among the Jews, the twelve loaves of *bread shown* or presented before the Lord in the sanctuary.

**Shower**, show′er, *n.* a fall of rain or hail, of short duration : a copious and rapid fall.—*v.t.* to wet with rain : to bestow liberally.—*v.i.* to rain in showers. [A.S. *scur* ; Ice. *skur*, O. Ger. *scur* (Ger. *schauer*) ; perh. orig. sig. 'a raincloud.']

**Showery**, show′er-i, *adj.* abounding with showers.

**Showy**, shō′i, *adj.* making a show ; cutting a dash : ostentatious : gay.—*adv.* **Show′ily**.—*n.* **Show′iness**.

**Shrapnel**, shrap′nel, *n.* (*gun.*) a shell filled with musket-balls, called after its inventor, Col. Shrapnel.

**Shred**, shred, *n.* a long, narrow piece cut or torn off : a strip or fragment.—*v.t.* to cut or tear into shreds. [A.S. *screade* ; Ger. *schrot*, Scot. *screed*.]

**Shrew**, shrōō, *n.* a brawling troublesome woman : a scold. [Prob. closely connected with Dut. *schreeuwen*, Low Ger. *schrauen*, Ger. *schreien*, to brawl.]

**Shrewd**, shrōōd, *adj.* of an acute judgment : (*obs.*) malicious, wicked, cunning. — *adv.* **Shrewd′ly**.—*n.* **Shrewd′ness**. [Lit. 'having the nature of a *shrew*.']

**Shrewish**, shrōō′ish, *adj.* having the qualities of a *shrew* : peevish and troublesome : clamorous. —*adv.* **Shrew′ishly**.—*n.* **Shrew′ishness**.

**Shrewmouse**, shrōō′mows, *n.* a harmless little animal like the *mouse*, which burrows in the ground. [A.S. *screawa*, and **Mouse**.]

**Shriek**, shrēk, *v.i.* to utter a shriek : to scream.— *n.* the shrill outcry caused by terror or anguish. [Ice. *skrika*. See **Scream** and **Screech**.]

**Shrievalty**, shrēv′al-ti, *n.* Same as **Sheriffalty**.

**Shrift**, shrift, *n.* confession made to a priest : absolution—especially of a dying man. [From **Shrive**.]

**Shrike**, shrīk, *n.* a bird which preys on insects and small birds, impaling its prey on thorns, hence called the Butcher Bird. [Lit. the 'shrieking' bird, Ice. *skrikja*. Cf. **Shriek**.]

**Shrill**, shril, *adj.* piercing : sharp : uttering an acute sound.—*adv.* **Shril′ly**.—*n.* **Shrill′ness**. [Allied to Low Ger. *schrell*, Ger. *schrill*, and conn. with Ger. *schreien*, to cry.]

**Shrimp**, shrimp, *n.* a *small* shellfish, about two inches long, much esteemed as food. [Prov. E. *shrimp*, anything very small ; conn. with A.S.

*scrymman*, to wither, and Ger. *schrumpfen*, to shrivel.]

**Shrine**, shrīn, *n.* a place in which sacred things are deposited : a sacred place : an altar.—*v.t.* to enshrine. [Lit. 'a chest for *written* papers,' A.S. *scrin*, O. Fr. *escrin*—L. *scrinium*—*scribo*, to write.]

**Shrink**, shringk, *v.i.* to contract : to wither : to occupy less space : to become wrinkled by contraction : to recoil, as from fear, disgust, &c.— *v.t.* to cause to shrink or contract :—*pa.t.* shrank, shrunk ; *pa.p.* shrunk, shrunk'en.—*n.* act of shrinking : contraction : withdrawal or recoil. [A.S. *scrincan* ; akin to Ger. *schränken*, to place obliquely or crosswise : perh. also conn. with **Shrug**.]

**Shrive**, shrīv, *v.t.* to hear at confession.—*v.i.* to receive confession (said of a priest) :—*pa.t.* shrōve or shrived ; *pa.p.* shriv'en. [A.S. *scrifan*, to write, to prescribe penance—L. *scribo*.]

**Shrivel**, shriv'l, *v.i.* and *v.t.* to contract into wrinkles :—*pr.p.* shriv'elling ; *pa.t.* and *pa.p.* shriv'elled. [Ety. dub.; perh. conn. with A.S. *screpa*, to become dry, and obs. E. *rivel*, to shrink, to wither.]

**Shroud**, shrowd, *n.* the dress of the dead : that which clothes or covers :—*pl.* a set of ropes from the mast-heads to a ship's sides, to support the masts.—*v.t.* to inclose in a shroud : to cover : to hide : to shelter. [A.S. *scrud*, cog. with Ice. *skrudh*, clothing.]

**Shrove-tide**, shrōv'-tīd, *n.* the *time* at which *confession* used to be made, the time immediately before Lent.—*n.* **Shrove-Tues'day**, the day before Ash-Wednesday. [M. E. *schrof* (pa.t. of *schriven*)—A.S. *scraf* (pa.t. of *scrifan*). See **Shrive** and **Tide**.]

**Shrub**, shrub, *n.* a low, dwarf tree : a woody plant with several stems from the same root. [A.S. *scrobb*, perh. conn. with prov. E. *shruff*, light rubbish wood, and with the root of **Shrivel**.]

**Shrub**, shrub, *n.* a drink or liquor of lemon-juice, spirit, sugar, and water. [A corr. of **Sherbet**.]

**Shrubbery**, shrub'ėr-i, *n.* a collection of shrubs.

**Shrubby**, shrub'i, *adj.* full of shrubs : like a shrub : consisting of shrubs or brush.

**Shrug**, shrug, *v.t.* to draw up : to contract.—*v.i.* to draw up the shoulders :—*pr.p.* shrug'ging ; *pa.t.* and *pa.p.* shrugged.—*n.* a drawing up of the shoulders. [Ety. dub. ; perh. conn. with **Shrink**.]

**Shrunk**, *pa.t.* and *pa.p.* of **Shrink**.

**Shudder**, shud'ėr, *v.i.* to tremble from fear or horror.—*n.* a trembling from fear or horror. [Dut. *schuddern*, *schudden*, Ger. *schaudern*, to shudder.]

**Shuffle**, shuf'l, *v.t.* to change the positions of : to confuse : to remove or introduce by purposed confusion.—*v.i.* to change the order of cards in a pack : to shift ground : to evade fair questions : to move by shoving the feet along.—*n.* act of shuffling : an evasion or artifice.—*n.* **Shuff'ler.** [A by-form of **Scuffle**, thus conn. with **Shove** and **Shovel**.]

**Shun**, shun, *v.t.* to avoid : to keep clear of : to neglect :—*pr.p.* shun'ning ; *pa.t.* and *pa.p.* shunned. [A.S. *scunian*, *sceonian* ; akin to Dut. *schuinen*, to slope.]

**Shunt**, shunt, *v.t.* to turn off upon a siderail.—*n.* a short siderail for allowing the main-line to be kept free.—*n.* **Shunt'ing.** [M. E. *shunten* ; a form of **Shun**.]

**Shut**, shut, *v.t.* to close, as a door : to forbid entrance into : to contract or close.—*v.i.* to close

itself :—*pr.p.* shutt'ing ; *pa.t.* and *pa.p.* shut. [A.S. *scyttan*, conn. with **Shoot**, from the shooting forward of the bar.]

**Shutter**, shut'ėr, *n.* one who or that which shuts : a close cover for a window or aperture.

**Shuttle**, shut'l, *n.* an instrument used for *shooting* the thread of the woof between the threads of the warp in weaving. [A.S. *scytel*, *sceathel*— *sceotan*, E. **Shoot** ; cog. with Dan. and Sw. *skyttel*.]

**Shuttlecock**, shut'l-kok, *n.* a cork stuck with feathers, like a *cock, shot,* struck, or driven with a battledore.

**Shy**, shī, *adj.* timid : reserved : cautious : suspicious.—*v.i.* to start aside, as a horse from fear : —*pa.t.* and *pa.p.* shīed.—*adv.* **Shy'ly** or **Shi'ly.** —*n.* **Shy'ness.** [A.S. *sceoh* ; Ger. *scheu*.]

**Sibilant**, sib'i-lant, *adj.* making a *hissing* sound. *n.* a sibilant letter. [L. *sibilo*, to hiss ]

**Sibilation**, sib-i-lā'shun, *n.* a *hissing* sound.

**Sibyl**, sib'il, *n.* (*lit.*) she that tells the *will* of *Zeus* or *Jupiter* : a pagan prophetess. [L.—Gr. *sibylla*, Doric Gr. *sio-bolla*—*Dios*, Doric *Sios*, genitive of *Zeus*, and *boulē*, Doric *bolla*, counsel.]

**Sibylline**, sib'il-īn, *adj.* pertaining to, uttered, or written by *sibyls* : prophetical.

**Sick**, sik, *adj.* affected with disease : ill : inclined to vomit : disgusted : used by the sick.—*n.* **Sick'ness**, *pl.* (*B.*) **Sick'nesses**, diseases. [A.S. *sioc* ; Ger. *siech*, Goth. *siuks*.]

**Sicken**, sik'n, *v.t.* to make sick : to disgust.—*v.i.* to become sick : to be disgusted : to become disgusting or tedious : to become weak.

**Sickish**, sik'ish, *adj.* somewhat sick.—*adv.* **Sick'-ishly.**—*n.* **Sick'ishness**

**Sickle**, sik'l, *n.* a hooked instrument for *cutting* grain. [A.S. *sicel* ; Ger. *sichel*, Low Ger. *sekel* ; all from a rustic L. *secula*—*seco*, to cut.]

**Sickly**, sik'li, *adj.* inclined to *sickness* : unhealthy : somewhat sick : weak : languid : producing disease.—*n.* **Sick'liness.**

**Side**, sīd, *n.* the edge or border of anything : the surface of a solid : a part of a thing as seen by the eye : region : part : the part of an animal between the hip and shoulder : any party, interest, or opinion opposed to another : faction : line of descent.—*adj.* being on or toward the side : lateral : indirect.—*v.i.* to embrace the opinion or cause of one party against another. [A.S. *side*, cog. with Ice. *sida*, Ger. *seite*.]

**Sidearms**, sīd'ärmz, *n.pl., arms* or weapons worn on the *side,* as a sword or bayonet.

**Sideboard**, sīd'bōrd, *n.* a piece of furniture on one *side* of a dining-room for holding dishes, &c.

**Sidebox**, sīd'boks, *n.* a *box* or seat at the *side* of a theatre.

**Sided**, sīd'ed, *adj.* having a side.

**Sideling**, sīd'ling, *adj.* inclining to a *side:* sloping.

**Sidelong**, sīd'long, *adj.* oblique : not straight.— *adv.* in the direction of the side : obliquely.

**Sidereal**, sī-dē're-al, *adj.* relating to a *star* or *stars:* starry : (*astr.*) measured by the apparent motion of the stars. [L. *sidus, sideris,* a star.]

**Side-saddle**, sīd'-sad'l, *n.* a *saddle* for women.

**Sideways**, sīd'wāz, **Sidewise**, sīd'wīz, *adv.* toward or on one side : inclining : laterally.

**Siding**, sīd'ing, *n.* a short line of rails on which wagons are shunted from the main-line.

**Sidle**, sī'dl, *v.i.* to go or move *side*-foremost.

**Siege**, sēj, *n.* a *sitting* down with an army round or before a fortified place to take it by force: a continued endeavour to gain possession. [Orig. a 'seat,' Fr. *siége,* seat (It. *seggia, sedia*)—L. *sedes,* a seat—*sedeo,* E. **Sit**.]

**Sienna,** si-en′a, *n.* a fine orange-red pigment used in painting. [From **Sienna** in Italy.]

**Sierra,** sē-er′ra, *n.* a ridge of mountains, the summits of which resemble the teeth of a saw. [Sp., from L. *serra*, a saw.]

**Siesta,** si-es′ta, *n.* a short sleep taken about mid-day or after dinner. [Sp.—L. *sexta* (*hora*), the *sixth* (hour) after sunrise, the hour of noon.]

**Sieve,** siv, *n.* a vessel with a bottom of woven hair or wire to separate the fine part of anything from the coarse. [A.S. *sife*; cog. with Ger. *sieb*. **Sift** is a derivative.]

**Sift,** sift, *v.t.* to separate with or as with a *sieve*: to examine closely.—*n.* **Sift′er.** [A.S. *siftan*—*sife* (see **Sieve**); cog. with Ger. *sichten*.]

**Sigh,** sī, *v.i.* to inhale and respire with a long, deep, and audible breathing, as in grief: to sound like sighing.—*v.t.* to express by sighs.—*n.* a long, deep, audible respiration. [A.S. *sican*: from the sound.]

**Sight,** sīt, *n.* act of *seeing*: view: faculty of seeing: that which is seen: a spectacle: space within vision: examination: a small opening for looking through at objects: a piece of metal on a gun to guide the eye in taking aim. —*v.t.* to catch sight of. [A.S. *ge-siht*; O. Ger. *siht*, Ger. *sicht*, from root of **See**.]

**Sighted,** sīt′ed, *adj.* having sight.

**Sightless,** sīt′les, *adj.* wanting sight: blind.— *adv.* **Sight′lessly.**—*n.* **Sight′lessness.**

**Sightly,** sīt′li, *adj.* pleasing to the sight or eye: comely.—*n.* **Sight′liness.**

**Sign,** sīn, *n., mark, token*: proof: that by which a thing is known or represented: a word, gesture, or mark, intended to signify something else: a remarkable event: an omen: a miracle: a memorial: something set up as a notice in a public place: (*math.*) a mark showing the relation of quantities or an operation to be performed: (*med.*) a symptom: (*astr.*) one of the twelve parts of the zodiac.—*v.t.* to represent or make known by a sign: to attach a signature to. [Fr. *signe*—L. *signum*.]

**Signal,** sig′nal, *n.* a *sign* for giving notice, generally at a distance: token: the notice given.— *v.t.* and *v.i.* to make signals to: to convey by signals:—*pr.p.* sig′nalling; *pa.t.* and *pa.p.* sig′nalled.—*adj.* having a sign: remarkable: notable: eminent.—*n.* **Sig′nalling.**—*adv.* **Sig′nally.** [Fr.]           [nent: to signal.

**Signalise,** sig′nal-īz, *v.t.* to make signal or emi-

**Signature,** sig′na-tūr, *n.* a *sign* or *mark*: the name of a person written by himself: (*music*) the flats and sharps after the clef to show the key. [Fr.—Low L. *signatura*.]

**Signboard,** sīn′bōrd, *n.* a *board* with a *sign* telling a man's occupation or articles for sale.

**Signet,** sig′net, *n.* the privy-seal: (*B.*) a seal. [From **Sign**.]

**Significance,** sig-nif′i-kans, *n.* that which is signified: meaning: importance: moment.

**Significant,** sig-nif′i-kant, *adj., signifying*: expressive of something: standing as a sign.— *adv.* **Signif′icantly.**

**Signification,** sig-ni-fi-kā′shun, *n.* act of signifying: that which is signified: meaning.

**Significative,** sig-nif′i-kāt-iv, *adj., signifying*: denoting by a sign: having meaning: expressive.

**Signify,** sig′ni-fī, *v.t.* to make known by a *sign* or by words: to mean: to indicate or declare: to have consequence:—*pa.t.* and *pa.p.* sig′nified. [L. *significo, -atus—signum*, and *facio*, to make.]

**Signior, Signor,** sēn′yur, *n.* an Italian word of address equivalent to Sir, Mr. [It. *signore*. See **Seignior**.]

**Sign-manual,** sīn-man′ū-al, *n.* (*lit.*) a *sign* made by one's own *hand*: the royal signature, usually only the initial of the sovereign's name, with R. for *Rex* (L. 'king'), or *Regina* (L. 'queen'). [**Sign** and **Manual**.]

**Signora,** sēn-yō′ra, *n.* feminine of **Signor.**

**Signpost,** sīn′pōst, *n.* a *post* on which a *sign* is hung: a direction-post.

**Silence,** sī′lens, *n.* state of being silent: absence of sound or speech: muteness: cessation of agitation: calmness: oblivion.—*v.t.* to cause to be silent: to put to rest: to stop.—*int.* be silent!

**Silent,** sī′lent, *adj.* free from noise: not speaking: habitually taciturn: still: not pronounced.—*adv.* **Si′lently.** [L. *silens, -entis*, pr.p. of *sileo*, to be silent.]

**Silex,** sī′leks, *n., silica,* as found in nature, occurring as flint, quartz, rock-crystal, &c. [L. *silex, silicis,* flint.]

**Silhouette,** sil′oo-et, *n.* a shadow-outline of the human figure or profile filled in of a dark colour. [From *Silhouette,* a French minister of finance in 1759, after whom everything cheap was named, from his excessive economy in financial matters.]

**Silica,** sil′i-ka, *n.* pure *silex* or flint, the most abundant solid constituent of our globe.

**Siliceous, Silicious,** si-lish′us, *adj.* pertaining to, containing, or resembling *silex* or flint.

**Silk,** silk, *n.* the delicate, soft thread produced by certain caterpillars: thread or cloth woven from it.—*adj.* pertaining to or consisting of silk. [A.S. *seolc*—L. *sericum*—Gr. *sērikon,* neut. of adj. *Sērikos,* pertaining to the *Sēres—Sēr,* a native of China, whence silk was first obtained.]

**Silken,** silk′n, *adj.* made of silk: dressed in silk: resembling silk: soft: delicate.     [*silks.*

**Silk-mercer,** silk′-mèr′sèr, *n.* a *mercer* or dealer in

**Silk-weaver,** silk′-wēv′èr, *n.* a *weaver* of *silk* stuffs.     [which produces *silk.*

**Silkworm,** silk′wurm, *n.* the *worm* or caterpillar

**Silky,** silk′i, *adj.* like silk in texture: soft: smooth: glossy.—*n.* **Silk′iness.**

**Sill,** sil, *n.* the timber or stone at the foot of a door or window: the lowest piece in a window-frame. [A.S. *syll,* cog. with Ice. *syila,* Ger. *schwelle,* conn. with **Swell**.]

**Sillabub,** sil′a-bub, *n.* a liquor made of wine or cider mixed with milk and sweetened. [Perh. from *slabbering* it up quickly.]

**Silly,** sil′i, *adj.* simple: harmless: foolish: witless: imprudent: absurd: stupid.—*adv.* **Sill′ily.** —*n.* **Sill′iness.** [Orig. 'happy,' 'blessed,' and so 'innocent,' 'simple,' A.S. *sælig*; cog. with Ger. *selig,* and Goth. *sels,* good.]

**Silt,** silt, *n.* that which is left by *straining*: sediment: the sand, &c. left by water. [Prov. E. *sile,* allied to Low Ger. *sielen,* Sw. *sila,* to let water off, to strain.]

**Silurian,** si-lōō′ri-an, *adj.* belonging to *Siluria,* the country of the *Silures,* the ancient inhabitants of part of Wales and England: applied to the strata below the old red sandstone, which are found best developed in that district.

**Silvan,** sil′van, *adj.* pertaining to *woods*: woody: inhabiting woods. [Fr.—L. *silva*; cf. Gr. *hylē,* a wood.]

**Silver,** sil′vèr, *n.* a soft white metal, capable of a high polish: money made of silver: anything having the appearance of silver.—*adj.* made of silver: resembling silver: white: bright: precious: gentle.—*v.t.* to cover with silver: to make like silver: to make smooth and bright: to make silvery. [A.S. *silfer, seolfer*, cog. with Ice. *silfr*, and Ger. *silber*.]

**Silvering**, sil'vėr-ing, *n*. the operation of covering with silver : the silver so used.

**Silverling**, sil'vėr-ling, *n*. (*B*.) a *small silver* coin.

**Silversmith**, sil'vėr-smith, *n*. a *smith* who works in *silver*.

**Silvery**, sil'vėr-i, *adj*. covered with silver : resembling silver : white : clear, soft, mellow.

**Similar**, sim'i-lar, *adj*., *like :* resembling : uniform : (*geom*.) exactly corresponding in shape, without regard to size.—*adv*. Sim'ilarly.—*n*. Similar'ity. [Fr. *similaire*—L. *similis*, like, same.]

**Simile**, sim'i-le, *n*. something *similar :* similitude : (*rhet*.) a comparison to illustrate anything.

**Similitude**, si-mil'i-tūd, *n*. the state of being *similar* or *like :* resemblance : comparison : simile : (*B*.) a parable. [Fr.—L. *similitudo*.]

**Simious**, sim'i-us, *adj*. pertaining to or resembling an *ape* or *monkey :* monkey-like. [From L. *simius*, an ape—*simus*, flat-nosed.]

**Simmer**, sim'ėr, *v.i*. to boil with a gentle, hissing sound. [From the sound.]

**Simoniac**, si-mō'ni-ak, *n*. one guilty of *simony*.

**Simoniacal**, sim-o-nī'ak-al, *adj*. pertaining to, guilty of, or involving *simony*.

**Simony**, sim'on-i, *n*. the crime of buying or selling ecclesiastical preferment, so named from *Simon Magus* who thought to purchase the gift of the Holy Spirit with money, Acts viii.

**Simoom**, si-mōōm', **Simoon**, si-mōōn', *n*. a destructive hot wind which blows in Northern Africa and Arabia and the adjacent countries from the interior deserts. [Ar. *semûm—semm*, to poison.]

**Simper**, sim'pėr, *v.i*. to smile in a silly affected manner.—*n*. a silly or affected smile. [Prob. conn. with **Simmer**.]

**Simple**, sim'pl, *adj*. single : undivided : resisting decomposition : elementary : homogeneous : open : unaffected : undesigning : true : clear : straightforward : artless : guileless : unsuspecting : credulous : not cunning : weak in intellect : silly.—*n*. something not mixed or compounded : a medicinal herb. [Lit. 'one-fold,' Fr.—L. *simplus—sim-* (L. *semel*, Gr. *hama*, Sans. *sam*), once, and root of *plico*, to fold.]

**Simpleness**, sim'pl-nes, *n*. the state or quality of being simple : artlessness : simplicity : folly.

**Simpleton**, sim'pl-tun, *n*. a *simple* person : a weak or foolish person.

**Simplicity**, sim-plis'i-ti, *n*. the state or quality of being *simple :* singleness : want of complication : openness : clearness : freedom from excessive adornment : plainness : sincerity : artlessness : credulity, silliness, folly. [L. *simplicitas*.]

**Simplify**, sim'pli-fī, *v.t*. to make simple : to render less difficult : to make plain :—*pa.t*. and *pa.p*. sim'plified.—*n*. Simplifica'tion. [L. *simplex*, simple, and *facio*, to make.]

**Simply**, sim'pli, *adv*. in a simple manner : artlessly : foolishly : weakly : plainly : considered by itself : alone : merely : solely.

**Simulate**, sim'ū-lāt, *v.t*. to imitate : to counterfeit : to pretend : to assume the appearance of without the reality.—*n*. Sim'ulator. [L. *simulatus*, pa.p. of *simulo*, to make (something) *similar* to (another thing)—*similis*, like.]

**Simulation**, sim-ū-lā'shun, *n*. the act of simulating or putting on what is not true.

**Simultaneous**, sim-ul-tān'e-us, *adj*. acting, existing, or happening at the *same time*.—*adv*. Simultan'eously. [Low L. *simultaneus*—L. *simul*, at the same time, akin to *similis*, like.]

**Sin**, sin, *n*. wilful violation of law : neglect of duty : neglect of the laws of morality and religion : wickedness : iniquity.—*v.i*. to commit sin : to violate or neglect the laws of morality or religion : to do wrong :—*pr.p*. sinn'ing ; *pa.t*. and *pa.p*. sinned. [A.S. *synn*, cog. with Ice. *syn-d*, Ger. *sünde ;* prob. from a root seen in Goth. *sunja*, truth, and *syn-jon*, to vindicate (both from *sun-is*, true), also in Ice. *syn*, denial. Prob. it thus orig. meant 'a thing to be cleared up or accounted for,' 'an act as to which one must justify one's self,' 'a deed involving responsibility or guilt,' hence 'a crime.']

**Since**, sins, *adv*. from the time that : past : ago.—*prep*. after : from the time of.—*conj*. seeing that : because : considering. [M. E. *sin, sith, sithence ;* A.S. *sith-than*, lit. 'after that,' from *sith*, late (Ger. *seit*), and *than*, dative case of the article.]

**Sincere**, sin-sēr', *adj*. clean : pure : (*B*.) unadulterated : being in reality what it is in appearance : unfeigned : frank : honest : true.—*adv*. Sincere'ly. [Fr.—L. *sincerus*, clean, generally derived from *sine*, without, and *cera*, wax : better from *sim-*, single, and the root of Ger. *schier*, E. **Sheer**. See **Simple, Single**.]

**Sincerity**, sin-sėr'i-ti, *n*. state or quality of being *sincere :* honesty of mind : freedom from pretence.

**Sinciput**, sin'si-put, *n*. the forepart of the head from the forehead to the vertex. [L., lit. 'half a head'—*semi*, half, and *caput*, the head.]

**Sine**, sīn, *n*. a straight line drawn from one extremity of an arc perpendicular to the diameter that passes through the other extremity ⌒.. *sinus*, a curve.]

**Sinecure**, sī'ne-kūr, *n*. an ecclesiastical benefice *without* the *cure* or care of souls : an office with salary but without work.—*n*. Si'necurist, one who holds a sinecure. [L. *sine*, without, and *cura*, care.]

**Sinew**, sin'ū, *n*. that which joins a muscle to a bone, a tendon : muscle, nerve : that which supplies vigour.—*v.t*. to bind as by sinews : to strengthen. [A.S. *sinu*, cog. with Ice. *sin*, Ger. *sehne*.]

**Sinewy**, sin'ū-i, *adj*. furnished with sinews : consisting of, belonging to, or resembling sinews : strong : vigorous.

**Sinful**, sin'fool, *adj*. full of or tainted with sin : iniquitous : wicked : depraved : criminal : unholy.—*adv*. Sin'fully.—*n*. Sin'fulness.

**Sing**, sing, *v.i*. to utter melodious sounds : to make a small, shrill sound : to relate in verse.—*v.t*. to utter musically : to chant : to celebrate or relate in verse :—*pa.t*. sang or sung ; *pa.p*. sung. [A.S. *singan*, cog. with Ger. *singen*, Goth. *siggvan ;* cf. Gael. *seinn*, Sans. *svan*.]

**Singe**, sinj, *v.t*. to burn on the surface : to scorch :—*pr.p*. singe'ing ; *pa.t*. and *pa.p*. singed.—*n*. a burning of the surface : a slight burn. [M. E. *sengen* (cog. with Ger. *sengen*)—A.S. *be-sengan*, the causative of **Sing**, from the singing noise produced by scorching.]

**Singer**, sing'ėr, *n*. one who sings : one whose occupation is to sing.

**Singing**, sing'ing, *n*. the act or art of singing.

**Singing-master**, sing'ing-mas'tėr, *n*. a *master* who teaches *singing*.

**Single**, sing'gl, *adj*. consisting of *one* only : individual : separate : alone : unmarried : not combined with others : unmixed : having one only on each side : straightforward : sincere : simple : pure.—*v.t*. to separate : to choose one from others : to select from a number. [L. *sin-gulus*, one to each, separate, akin to *sem-el*, once, Gr. *ham-a*. See **Simple, Sincere.**]

**Single-hearted,** sing'gl-härt'ed, *adj.* having a *single* or sincere *heart*: without duplicity.

**Single-minded,** sing'gl-mīnd'ed, *adj.* having a *single* or sincere *mind*: upright.

**Singleness,** sing'gl-nes, *n.* state of being *single* or alone: freedom from deceit: sincerity: simplicity.

**Singlestick,** sing'gl-stik, *n.* a *single stick* or cudgel used in fighting: a fight or game with singlesticks.

**Singletree,** sing'gl-trē, *n.* The same as **Swingle-tree.**

**Singly,** sing'gli, *adv.* one by one: particularly: alone: by one's self: honestly: sincerely.

**Singsong,** sing'song, *n.* bad singing: drawling.

**Singular,** sing'gū-lar, *adj.* alone: (*gram.*) denoting one person or thing: single: not complex or compound: standing alone: rare: unusual: uncommon: extraordinary: strange: odd: (*B.*) particular. [L. *singularis*.]

**Singularity,** sing-gū-lar'i-ti, *n.* the state of being singular: peculiarity: anything curious or remarkable: particular privilege or distinction.

**Singularly,** sing'gū-lar-li, *adv.* in a singular manner: peculiarly: strangely: so as to express one or the singular number.

**Sinister,** sin'is-tėr, *adj., left*: on the left hand: evil: unfair: dishonest: unlucky: inauspicious. [L.]

**Sinistral,** sin'is-tral, *adj.* belonging or inclining to the *left*: reversed.—*adv.* **Sin'istrally.**

**Sinistrous,** sin'is-trus, *adj.* on the *left* side: wrong: absurd: perverse.—*adv.* **Sin'istrously.**

**Sink,** singk, *v.i.* to fall to the bottom: to fall down: to descend lower: to fall gradually: to fall below the surface: to enter deeply: to be impressed: to be overwhelmed: to fail in strength.—*v.t.* to cause to sink: to put under water: to keep out of sight: to suppress: to degrade: to cause to decline or fall: to plunge into destruction: to make by digging or delving: to pay absolutely: to lower in value or amount: to lessen:—*pa.t.* sank and sunk; *pa.p.* sunk, sunk'en.—*n.* a drain to carry off dirty water: a box or vessel connected with a drain for receiving dirty water.—*n.* **Sink'er.** [A.S. *sencan*, cog. with Ger. *sinken*, Goth. *siggquan*, Ice. *sökkva*, to fall to the bottom.]

**Sinless,** sin'les, *adj.* without sin: innocent: pure: perfect.—*adv.* **Sin'lessly.**—*n.* **Sin'lessness.**

**Sinner,** sin'ėr, *n.* one who sins: an offender or criminal: (*theol.*) an unregenerate person.

**Sin-offering,** sin'-of'ėr-ing, *n.* an *offering* for or sacrifice in expiation of *sin.*

**Sinter,** sin'tėr, *n.* a name given to rocks precipitated in a crystalline form from mineral waters. [Ger., 'iron sparks.']

**Sinuate,** sin'ū-āt, *adj., curved*: (*bot.*) with a waved margin.—*v.t.* to bend in and out.—*n.* **Sinua'tion.** [L. *sinuatus*, pa.p. of *sinuo*, to bend.]

**Sinuosity,** sin-ū-os'i-ti, *n.* quality of being sinuous: a bend or series of bends and turns.

**Sinuous,** sin'ū-us, **Sinuose,** sin'ū-ōs, *adj., bending* in and out: winding: undulating.—*adv.* **Sin'uously.** [L. *sinuosus*—*sinus*, a bending.]

**Sinus,** sī'nus, *n.* a *bending*: a fold: an opening: a bay of the sea: a recess in the shore: (*anat.*) a cavity wider in the interior than at the entrance: a venous canal: (*med.*) a cavity containing pus. [L. *sinus*, a bending, a curve.]

**Sip,** sip, *v.t.* to *sup* or drink in small quantities: to draw into the mouth: to taste: to drink out of.—*v.i.* to drink in small quantities: to drink by the lips:—*pr.p.* sipp'ing; *pa.t.* and *pa.p.* sipped.

—*n.* the taking of a liquor with the lips: a small draught taken with the lips. [A.S. *súpan*, cog. with Ger. *saufen;* conn. with **Sop, Soup, Sup.**]

**Siphon,** sī'fun, *n.* a bent tube for drawing off liquids from one vessel into another. [Fr.—Gr. *siphōn*—*siphlos*, hollow.]

**Sippet,** sip'et, *n.* a small sop.

**Sir,** sėr, *n.* a word of respect used in addressing a man: the title of a knight or baronet. [Lit. 'senior' or 'elder,' O. Fr. *sire*, through O. Fr. *sendre*, from L. *senior*, an elder, comp. of *senex*, old. Cf. the parallel forms **Sire, Senior, Seignior, Signor.**]

**Sire,** sīr, *n.* (*lit.*) a 'senior' or father: one in the place of a father, as a sovereign: the male parent of a beast, esp. of a horse:—*pl.* (*poetry*) ancestors.—*v.t.* to beget, used of animals. [See above word.]

**Siren,** sī'ren, *n.* (*myth.*) one of certain fabulous nymphs in S. Italy who enticed mariners to destruction by sweet music: a fascinating woman: any one insidious and deceptive: an eel-like, amphibious animal, with only one pair of feet.—*adj.* pertaining to or like a siren: fascinating. [L. *siren*—Gr. *seirēn*, lit. an 'entangler'—*seira*, a cord, a band.]

**Sirene,** sī'rēn, *n.* a musical instrument for determining the number of pulses per second in a given note. [Same word as above.]

**Sirius,** sir'i-us, *n.* the Dogstar. [L.—Gr. *seirios*, scorching; cf. Sans. *surya*, the sun.]

**Sirloin,** sėr'loin, *n.* a *loin* of beef. [Fr. *surlonge*—*sur* (—L. *super*, above), and *longe* (see **Loin**). The first syllable has been modified by confusion with E. **Sir.**]

**Sirname,** sėr'nām, *n.* [A corruption of **Surname.**]

**Sirocco,** si-rok'o, *n.* a hot, oppressive wind, from the south-*east* in S. Italy and adjoining parts. [It. *sirocco*, Sp. *siroco*, Ar. *schoruq*—*scharq*, the east.]

**Sirrah,** sėr'a, *n.* sir, used in anger or contempt. [M. E. *sirrha*—*sir, ha*: or from Ir. *sirreach*, poor.]

**Sirup,** sir'up, *n.* a solution of sugar in water, simple, flavoured, or medicated. [Fr. *sirop*—Low L. *sirupus*—Ar. *sharûb, sharbat*, a drink. See **Sherbet** and **Shrub.**]

**Siskin,** sis'kin, *n.* a migratory song-bird, resembling the green canary. [Dan. *sisgen*, Sw. *siska*.]

**Sister,** sis'tėr, *n.* a female born of the same parents: a female closely allied to or associated with another.—*n.* **Sister-in-law,** a husband's or wife's sister, or a brother's wife. [M. E. *susten*—A.S. *sweoster*, cog. with Dut. *suster*, Ger. *schwester*, Slav. *sestra*, L. *soror* (for *sosor*, orig. *sostor*), Sans. *svasri, svasâr* (orig. *svastâr*).]

**Sisterhood,** sis'tėr-hood, *n.* (*orig.*) *state* of being a *sister*, the duty of a sister: a society of females.

**Sisterlike,** sis'tėr-līk, **Sisterly,** sis'tėr-li, *adj. like* or becoming a *sister*: kind: affectionate.

**Sit,** sit, *v.i.* to rest on the haunches: to perch, as birds: to rest: to remain: to brood: to occupy a seat, esp. officially: to be officially engaged: to blow from a certain direction, as the wind.—*v.t.* to keep the seat upon: to seat:—*pr.p.* sitt'ing; *pa.t.* and *pa.p.* sat.—*n.* **Sitt'er.**—**Sit out,** to sit during.—**Sit up,** to rise from a lying to a sitting position. [A.S. *sittan*, cog. with Ger. *sitzen*, L. *sed-eo*, Gr. *hed-os*, a seat, *hezo-mai*, to sit. Cf. **Seat** and **Set.**]

**Site,** sīt, *n.* the place where anything is *set down* or fixed: situation: a place chosen for any particular purpose. [Fr.—L. *situs*—*situm*, pa. p. of *sino*, to set down. Cf. **Situate.**]

**Sith**, sith, *adv. (B.)* since. [A.S. *sidh*; cog. with Goth. *seidhu*, Ger. *seit*. See **Since**.]

**Sitting**, sit'ing, *n.* state of resting on a seat: a seat: the act or time of resting in a posture for a painter to take a likeness: an official meeting to transact business: uninterrupted application to anything for a time: the time during which one continues at anything: a resting on eggs for hatching.

**Situate**, sit'ū-āt, **Situated**, sit'ū-āt-ed, *adj.*, set or permanently fixed: placed with respect to other objects: residing. [Low L. *situatus*—L. *situo*, to place—*situs*, a site, situation.]

**Situation**, sit-ū-ā'shun, *n.* the place where anything is *situated*: position: temporary state: condition: office: employment.

**Six**, siks, *adj.* and *n.* five and one: a figure denoting six units (6, or VI.). [A.S. *six, sex*; cog. with Scand. *sex*, Goth. *saihs*, Ger. *sechs*, Gael. *se*; also with L. *sex*, Gr. *hex*, Pers. *shesh*, Sans. *shash*.] [times.

**Sixfold**, siks'fōld, *adj.*, folded or multiplied *six*

**Sixpence**, siks'pens, *n.* a silver coin = *six pence.*

**Sixteen**, siks'tēn, *adj.* and *n.*, *six* and *ten.*

**Sixteenth**, siks'tēnth, *adj.* and *n.* the *sixth* after the *tenth.*

**Sixth**, siksth, *adj.* the last of six: the ordinal of six.—*n.* the sixth part: (*music*) an interval of four tones and a semitone, or six intervals. [A.S. *sixta.*]

**Sixthly**, siksth'li, *adv.* in the sixth place.

**Sixtieth**, siks'ti-eth, *adj.* and *n.* the *sixth tenth:* the ordinal of sixty. [A.S. *sixteogeotha.*]

**Sixty**, siks'ti, *adj.* and *n.*, *six* times *ten.* [A.S. *sixtig.*]

**Sizar**, sīz'ar, *n.* in University of Cambridge, orig. one who served out the *sizes* or rations: one of the lowest rank of students. [From **Size**, orig. a '*fixed* quantity.']

**Size**, sīz, *n.* extent of volume or surface: magnitude.—*v.t.* to arrange according to size. [Orig. a 'fixed quantity,' contr. of **Assize**, which see.]

**Size**, sīz, **Sizing**, sīz'ing, *n.* a kind of weak glue, used as varnish: any gluey substance.—**Size**, *v.t.* to cover with size. [W. *syth*, stiffening. glue —*syth*, stiff.] [iness.

**Sizy**, sīz'i, *adj.*, size-like: glutinous.—*n.* **Siz'**

**Skald**, *n.* See **Scald**, a poet.

**Skate**, skāt, *n.* a kind of sandal or frame of wood with a steel ridge under it for moving on ice.—*v.i.* to slide on skates.—*ns.* **Skat'er, Skat'ing.** [Dut. *schaats*; cf. also Dan. *sköite.*]

**Skate**, skāt, *n.* a large flat fish belonging to the Ray family, with spikes or thorns on the back. [M. E. *schate* (Ice. *skata*)—L. *squatus*; cf. **Shad**.]

**Skathe.** Same as **Scathe.**

**Skean**, skēn, *n.* a dagger. [Gael. *sgian*, a knife.]

**Skein**, skān, *n.* a knot or number of knots of thread or yarn. [O. Fr. *escaigne*; Gael. *sgeinn*.]

**Skeleton**, skel'e-tun, *n.* the bones of an animal separated from the flesh and preserved in their natural position: the framework or outline of anything. [Gr. *skeleton* (*sōma*), a dried (body) —*skeletos*, dried—*skellō*, to dry, to parch.]

**Skeleton-key**, skel'e-tun-kē, *n.* a *key* for picking locks, without the inner bits, and so like a *skeleton.*

**Skeptic.** Same as **Sceptic.**

**Skerry**, sker'i, *n.* a rocky isle. [Ice.]

**Sketch**, skech, *n.* a first draft of any plan or painting: an outline.—*v.t.* to make a rough draft of: to draw the outline: to give the principal points of.—*v.i.* to practise sketching.

[Lit. 'something made offhand,' Fr. *esquisse*, influenced by Dut. *schets*, from L. *schedius*, made offhand—Gr. *schedios*, sudden—*schedon*, near—*echō, scheō*, to have.]

**Sketchy**, skech'i, *adj.* containing a *sketch* or outline: incomplete.—*adv.* **Sketch'ily.**—*n.* **Sketch'iness.**

**Skew**, skū, *adj.* oblique: intersecting a road, river, &c. not at right angles, as a bridge.—*adv.* awry: obliquely. [Ice. *skeifr*, Dan. *skjev*; conn. with **Shy**.]

**Skewer**, skū'ėr, *n.* a pin of wood or iron for keeping meat in form while roasting.—*v.t.* to fasten with skewers. [Prov. E. *skiver*, prob. the same as **Shiver**, a splint of wood.]

**Skid**, skid, *n.* a piece of timber hung against a ship's side to protect it from injury: a sliding wedge or drag to check the wheel of a wagon on a steep place: a slab put below a gun to keep it off the ground.—*v.t.* to check with a skid. [A.S. *scíde*, a piece split off, a billet of wood—*scídan*, to cleave.] [Ship.]

**Skiff**, skif, *n.* a small light boat. [A doublet of **Ship**.]

**Skilful**, skil'fool, *adj.* having or displaying skill: dexterous.—*adv.* **Skil'fully.**—*n.* **Skil'fulness.**

**Skill**, skil, *n.* knowledge of anything: dexterity in practice.—*(B.) v.i.* to understand. [Lit. separation,' 'discrimination,' prob. first from the Scand., as Ice. *skil*, and *skilja* (verb), cog. with A.S. *scylan*, to separate.]

**Skilled**, skild, *adj.* having skill: skilful: expert.

**Skillet**, skil'et, *n.* a small metal vessel with a long handle, used for boiling water, in cooking, &c. [Prob. from O. Fr. *escuellette*, dim. of *escuelle* (Fr. *écuelle*)—L. *scutella*, dim. of *scutra*, a dish. See **Scullery**.]

**Skim**, skim, *v.t.* to clear off *scum*: to take off by skimming: to brush the surface of lightly.— *v.i.* to pass over lightly: to glide along near the surface:—*pr.p.* skimm'ing; *pa.t.* and *pa.p.* skimmed. [A by-form of **Scum**.]

**Skimmer**, skim'ėr, *n.* a utensil for skimming milk.

**Skim-milk**, skim'-milk, *n.*, *skimmed milk*: milk from which the cream has been skimmed.

**Skin**, skin, *n.* the natural outer covering of an animal body: a hide: the bark or rind of plants, &c.—*v.t.* to cover with skin: to cover the surface of: to strip the skin from, to peel.— *v.i.* to be covered with a skin:—*pr.p.* skinn'ing; *pa.t.* and *pa.p.* skinned.—*n.* **Skinn'er.** [A.S. *scinn*, cog. with Ice. *shinn*, skin, Ger. *schinden*, to flay.]

**Skin-deep**, skin'-dēp, *adj.* as *deep* as the *skin* only: superficial.

**Skinflint**, skin'flint, *n.* one who takes the smallest gains, who would, as it were, even *skin* a *flint:* a very niggardly person.

**Skinny**, skin'i, *adj.* consisting of skin or of skin only: wanting flesh.—*n.* **Skinn'iness.**

**Skip**, skip, *v.i.* to leap: to bound lightly and joyfully: to pass over.—*v.t.* to leap over: to omit:—*pr.p.* skipp'ing; *pa.t.* and *pa.p.* skipped. —*n.* a light leap: a bound: the omission of a part. [Either Celt., conn. with W. *cip*, a sudden effort, and Gael. *sgiab*, to move suddenly, or Teut., conn. with Ice. *skopa*, to run.]

**Skipper**, skip'ėr, *n.* the master of a merchantship. [Lit. 'a shipper or sailor,' Dut. *schipper*, Dan. *skipper*. See **Ship**.]

**Skipping-rope**, skip'ing-rōp, *n.* a *rope* used in *skipping.*

**Skirmish**, skėr'mish, *n.* an irregular fight between two small parties: a contest.—*v.i.* to fight slightly or irregularly. [M. E. *scarmish*—Fr.

*escarmouche*—O. Ger. *skerman*, to fight, Ger. *schirmen*.]

**Skirmisher**, skėr′mish-ėr, *n.* a soldier belonging to troops dispersed to cover front or flank, and prevent surprises.

**Skirt**, skėrt, *n.* the part of a garment below the waist : a woman's garment like a petticoat : the edge of any part of the dress : border : margin : extreme part.—*v.t.* to border : to form the edge of.—*v.i.* to be on the border : to live near the extremity. [A doublet of **Shirt.** Cf. **Skiff** and **Ship.**]

**Skittish**, skit′ish, *adj.* unsteady, light-headed, easily frightened : hasty : volatile, changeable : wanton.—*adv.* **Skitt′ishly.**—*n.* **Skitt′ishness.** [M. E. *sket*—Ice. *skjotr*, quick, hasty, conn. with root of **Shoot.**]

**Skittles**, skit′lz, *n.pl.* a game in which wooden pins are *shot* or knocked down with a wooden ball. [From root of **Skittish.**]

**Skulk**, skulk, *v.i.* to sneak out of the way : to lurk.—*n.* **Skulk′er.** [Scand., as Dan. *skulke*, to sneak, conn. with Ice. *skjol*, cover, hiding-place : also with E. **Scowl.**]

**Skull**, skul, *n.* the bony case that incloses the brain : the head. [Ice. and Dan. *skal*, a shell ; conn. with **Shell** and **Scale**, a thin plate. The fundamental idea is that of a thin plate or case, with which a body is covered, or in which anything is contained.]    [to the *skull* or head.

**Skullcap**, skul′kap, *n.* a *cap* which fits closely

**Skunk**, skungk, *n.* a small N. American carnivorous quadruped allied to the otter and weasel, which defends itself by emitting a most offensive fluid. [Contr. from the Indian *seganku*.]

**Sky**, skī, *n.* the apparent canopy over our heads : the heavens : the weather. [Dan., Sw., and Ice. *sky*, a cloud ; akin to A.S. *scua*, Gr. *skia*, a shadow, Sans. *sku*, to cover.]

**Sky-blue**, skī′-blōō, *adj.*, *blue* like the *sky.*

**Skyey**, skī′i, *adj.* like the sky : ethereal.

**Skylark**, skī′lärk, *n.* a species of *lark* that mounts high towards the *sky* and sings on the wing.

**Skylarking**, skī′lärk-ing, *n.* running about the rigging of a ship in sport : frolicking. [From **Sky**, and **Lark**, a game.]

**Skylight**, skī′līt, *n.* a window in a roof or ceiling towards the *sky* for the admission of *light.*

**Sky-rocket**, skī′-rok′et, *n.* a *rocket* that ascends high towards the *sky* and burns as it flies.

**Skysail**, skī′sāl, *n.* the *sail* above the ʼ royal.ʼ

**Sky-scraper**, skī′-skrāp′ėr, *n.* a skysail of a triangular shape.

**Skyward**, skī′ward, *adv.*, *toward* the *sky.*

**Slab**, slab, *n.* a thin slip of anything, esp. of stone, having plane surfaces : a piece sawed from a log. [W. *yslab*, *llab*, a thin slip.]

**Slabber**, slab′ėr, *v.i.* to *slaver :* to let the saliva fall from the mouth : to drivel.—*v.t.* to wet by saliva.—*n.* **Slabb′erer.** [Allied to Low Ger. and Dut. *slabbern*, from the sound. Doublet **Slaver.**]

**Slack**, slak, *adj.* lax or loose : not firmly extended or drawn out : not holding fast : weak : not eager or diligent : inattentive : not violent or rapid : slow.—*adv.* in a slack manner : partially : insufficiently.—*adv.* **Slack′ly.**—*n.* **Slack′ness.** [A.S. *sleac*, cog. with Sw. *slak*, Ice. *slakr.*]

**Slack**, slak, **Slacken**, slak′n, *v.i.* to become loose or less tight : to be remiss : to abate : to become slower : to fail or flag.—*v.t.* to make less tight : to loosen : to relax : to remit : to abate : to withhold : to use less liberally : to check : (*B.*) to delay.

**Slag**, slag, *n.* vitrified cinders from smelting-works,

&c. : the scoriæ of a volcano. [Low Ger. *slagge*, Ger. *schlacke*—*schlagen*, to cast off, Ice. *slagga*, to flow over.]

**Slaggy**, slag′i, *adj.* pertaining to or like slag.

**Slain**, slān, *pa.p.* of **Slay.**

**Slake**, slāk, *v.t.* to quench : to extinguish : to mix with water.—*v.i.* to go out : to become extinct. [Lit. to *slacken* or make less active ; it is simply a form of **Slack.**]

**Slam**, slam, *v.t.* or *v.i.* to shut with violence and noise :—*pr.p.* slamm′ing ; *pa.t.* and *pa.p.* slammed.—*n.* the act of slamming : the sound so made. [From the sound.]

**Slander**, slan′dėr, *n.* a false or malicious report : defamation by words : calumny.—*v.t.* to defame : to calumniate.—*n.* **Slan′derer.** [M. E. *sclaunder*—Fr. *esclandre*—L. *scandalum*—Gr. *skandalon.* See **Scandal.**]

**Slanderous**, slan′dėr-us, *adj.* given to or containing slander : calumnious.—*adv.* **Slan′derously.**

**Slang**, slang, *n.* low language. [Ety. dub.]

**Slant**, slant, *adj.*, *sloping :* oblique : inclined from a direct line.—*n.* a slope.—*v.t.* to turn in a sloping direction.—*v.i.* to slope. [Scot. *sclent*, Prov. E. *slen*, to slope, allied to Sw. *slinta*, to slide.]

**Slantly**, slant′li, **Slantwise**, slant′wīz, *adv.* in a *sloping*, oblique, or inclined manner.

**Slap**, slap, *n.* a blow with the hand or anything flat.—*v.t.* to give a slap to :—*pr.p.* slapp′ing ; *pa.t.* and *pa.p.* slapped.—*adv.* with a slap : suddenly, violently. [Allied to Low Ger. *slappe*, Ger. *schlappe :* from the sound.]

**Slapdash**, slap′dash, *adv.* in a bold, careless way. [From **Slap** and **Dash.**]

**Slash**, slash, *v.t.* to cut by *striking* with violence and at random : to make long cuts.—*v.i.* to strike violently and at random with an edged instrument.—*n.* a long cut : a cut at random : a cut in cloth to shew colours through the openings. [Ice. *slasa*, to strike : from the sound.]

**Slate**, slāt, *n.* a well-known stone which *splits* into thin plates : a rock or stone of a slaty structure : a piece of slate for roofing, or for writing upon.—*v.t.* to cover with slate.—*n.* **Sla′ter.** [M. E. *sclat*—O. Fr. *esclat*, from O. Ger. *skleizan*, Ger. *schleissen*, to split.]

**Slate-pencil**, slāt′-pen′sil, *n.* a *pencil* of soft *slate*, or for writing on slate.

**Slating**, slāt′ing, *n.* the act of covering with *slates :* a covering of slates : materials for slating.

**Slattern**, slat′ėrn, *n.* a woman *sluttish* and negligent of her dress : an untidy woman. [Allied to Low Ger. *sluddern*, Dut. *slodderen*, to hang and flap ; prob. from the flapping sound of loose, untidy clothing : conn. with **Slut.**]

**Slatternly**, slat′ėrn-li, *adj.* like a slattern : negligent of person : slovenly : dirty : sluttish.—*adv.* negligently : untidily.

**Slaty**, slāt′i, *adj.* resembling slate : having the nature or properties of slate.

**Slaughter**, slaw′tėr, *n.* a *slaying* or killing : a great destruction of life : carnage : butchery.—*v.t.* to slay : to kill for the market : to destroy by violence (as numbers) : to massacre.—*n.* **Slaugh′terer.** [Ice. *slatr*, prob. influenced by A.S. *sleaht :* both are from root of **Slay.**]

**Slaughterhouse**, slaw′tėr-hows, *n.* a *house* where beasts are *slaughtered* or killed for the market.

**Slaughterman**, slaw′tėr-man, *n.* a *man* employed in *slaughtering*, killing, or butchering animals.

**Slaughterous**, slaw′tėr-us, *adj.* given to slaughter : destructive : murderous.

**Slav**, **Slave**, släv, *n.* the name of the peoples inhabiting E. Europe.—*adj.* **Slav′ic.** [Lit. ʼthe *speaking* men,' from Polish *slowo*, a word, in contrast to *niemiez*, the 'dumb,' 'unintelligible,' applied by the Poles to the Germans. Cf. **Barbarian.**]

**Slave**, slāv, *n.* a captive in servitude: any one in bondage: a serf: one who labours like a slave: a drudge: one wholly under the will of another: one who has lost all power of resistance.—*v.i.* to work like a slave: to drudge. [Orig. a *Slav* made captive by the Teutons, Fr. *esclave*—Ger. *sclave*, from **Slav**, the national name. During the early wars of the Germans against the Slavs, many of the latter were captured and reduced to servitude.]

**Slaver**, slāv′ėr, *n.* a ship employed in the *slave*-trade.

**Slaver**, slāv′ėr, *n.*, *spittle* or *saliva* running from the mouth.—*v.i.* to let the saliva run out of the mouth.—*v.t.* to smear with saliva.—*n.* **Slav′erer.** [A form of **Slabber.**]

**Slavery**, slāv′ėr-i, *n.* the state of being a *slave:* serfdom: the state of being entirely under the will of another: bondage: drudgery.

**Slave-trade**, slāv′-trād, *n.* the *trade* of buying and selling *slaves*.

**Slave-trader**, slāv′-trād′ėr, *n.* a *trader* in *slaves*.

**Slavish**, slāv′ish, *adj.* of or belonging to slaves: becoming slaves: servile: mean: base: laborious.—*adv.* **Slav′ishly.**—*n.* **Slav′ishness.**

**Slavonic**, sla-von′ik, **Sclavonic**, skla-von′ik, **Slavonian**, sla-vōn′yan, **Sclavonian**, skla-vōn′yan, *adj.* of or belonging to the *Slavs*, or their language.

**Slay**, slā, *v.t.* to *strike:* to kill: to put to death: to destroy:—*pa.t.* slew (sl$\bar{\text{oo}}$); *pa.p.* slāin.—*n.* **Slay′er.** [A.S. *slean;* Ice. *slá*, Goth. *slahan*, Ger. *schlagen*, to strike.]

**Sled**, sled, **Sledge**, slej, *n.* a carriage made for *sliding* upon snow: a sleigh. [Low Ger. *slede*, Ice. *sledi;* from a root seen in A.S. *slidan*, to slide.]

**Sledge**, slej, *n.* an instrument for *striking:* a large heavy hammer used chiefly by ironsmiths. [A.S. *slecge*—*slean*, to strike, slay (cf. Ger. *schlägel*, a beater—*schlagen*). See **Slay.**]

**Sleek**, slēk, *adj.*, *smooth:* glossy: soft: not rough.—*adv.* **Sleek′ly.**—*n.* **Sleek′ness.** [Ger. *schlicht*, Ice. *slikja*, to smooth or polish; perh. akin to **Slight.**]

**Sleep**, slēp, *v.i.* to take rest by relaxation: to become unconscious: to slumber: to rest: to be motionless or inactive: to remain unnoticed: to live thoughtlessly: to be dead: to rest in the grave:—*pa.t.* and *pa.p.* slept.—*n.* the state of one who or that which sleeps: slumber: rest.—**On sleep** (*B.*) asleep. [A.S. *slæpan;* Ger. *schlafen*, Goth. *slepan*, from O. Ger. *slaf*, relaxed, Ice. *slapa*, to hang loose.]

**Sleeper**, slēp′ėr, *n.* one who sleeps: a horizontal timber supporting a weight, rails, &c.

**Sleepless**, slēp′les, *adj.* without sleep: unable to sleep.—*adv.* **Sleep′lessly.**—*n.* **Sleep′lessness.**

**Sleep-walker**, slēp′-wawk′ėr, *n.* one who *walks* while *asleep:* a somnambulist.—*n.* **Sleep′-walk′ing.**

**Sleepy**, slēp′i, *adj.* inclined to sleep: drowsy: dull: lazy.—*adv.* **Sleep′ily.**—*n.* **Sleep′iness.**

**Sleet**, slēt, *n.* rain mingled with snow or hail.—*v.i.* to hail or snow with rain mingled. [Prob. allied to Low Ger. *slate*, *slote*, hail, Ger. *schlosze.*] [*n.* **Sleet′iness.**

**Sleety**, slēt′i, *adj.* consisting of or bringing sleet.—

**Sleeve**, slēv, *n.* the part of a garment which *covers* the arm.—*v.t.* to furnish with sleeves. [A.S. *slefe*, a sleeve; cog. with Ger. *schlauf.*]

**Sleigh**, slā, *n.* Same as **Sledge.**

**Sleight**, slīt, *n.* cunning: dexterity: an artful trick.—*n.* **Sleight-of-hand**, legerdemain. [Ice. *slægth*, cunning, *slægr*, sly.]

**Slender**, slen′dėr, *adj.*, *thin* or narrow: feeble: inconsiderable: simple.—*adv.* **Slen′derly.**—*n.* **Slen′derness.** [O. Dut. *slinder*, thin, conn. with Dut. *slenderen*, Ger. *schlendern*, to saunter.]

**Slept**, slept, *pa.t.* and *pa.p.* of **Sleep.**

**Sleuth-hound**, sl$\bar{\text{oo}}$th-hownd, *n.* a dog that tracks game by the scent, a bloodhound. See **Slot.**

**Slew**, sl$\bar{\text{oo}}$, *pa.t.* of **Slay.**

**Slice**, slīs, *v.t.* to *slit* or divide into thin pieces.—*n.* a thin broad piece: a broad knife for serving fish. [O. Fr. *esclisse*—O. Ger. *sleizan*, to split, E. **Slit.**] [broad, flat knife.

**Slicer**, slīs′ėr, *n.* one who or that which slices: a

**Slid**, slid, *pa.t.* and *pa.p.* of **Slide.**

**Slidden**, slid′n, *pa.p.* of **Slide.**

**Slide**, slīd, *v.i.* to *slip* or glide: to pass along smoothly: to fall.—*v.t.* to thrust along: to slip:—*pa.t.* slid; *pa.p.* slid or slidd′en.—*n.* a smooth passage: the fall of a mass of earth or rock: a smooth declivity: a slider: (*music*) two notes sliding into each other. [A.S. *slidan*, to slide; Dut. *slidderen*, to slip.]

**Slider**, slīd′ėr, *n.* one who or that which slides: the part of an instrument or machine that slides.

**Sliding-scale**, slīd′ing-skāl, *n.* a *scale* of duties which *slide* or vary according to the value or market prices: a sliding-rule.

**Slight**, slīt, *adj.* weak: slender: of little value: trifling: small: negligent: not decided.—*adv.* **Slight′ly.**—*n.* **Slight′ness.** [Orig. 'plain, smooth;' found in Low Ger. *sligt*, Ger. *schlicht*, plain, smooth. See **Sleek.**]

**Slight**, slīt, *v.t.* to disregard, as of little value: to neglect.—*n.* neglect: disregard.—*adv.* **Slight′ingly.** [From **Slight**, *adj.*]

**Slily**, slī′li, *adv.* See under **Sly.**

**Slim**, slim, *adj.* (*comp.* **Slimm′er**, *superl.* **Slimm′est**), weak: slender: slight. [Orig. 'vile, worthless;' found in Low Ger. *slim*, Ger. *schlimm.*]

**Slime**, slīm, *n.* glutinous mud: (*B.*) prob. bitumen. [A.S. *slim*, cog. with Ger. *schleim.*]

**Slimy**, slīm′i, *adj.* abounding with or consisting of *slime;* glutinous.—*n.* **Slim′iness.**

**Sling**, sling, *n.* an instrument consisting of a strap and two cords, for throwing stones to a great distance, by *whirling* it rapidly *round:* a throw: a hanging bandage for a wounded limb: a rope with hooks, used in hoisting and lowering weights.—*v.t.* to throw with a sling: to hang so as to swing: to move or swing by means of a rope: to cast:—*pa.t.* and *pa.p.* slung.—*n.* **Sling′er.**—*n.pl.* **Sling′stones** (*B.*) stones thrown from a sling. [A.S. *slingan*, to turn in a circle, cog. with Ger. *schlingen*, to move or twine round.]

**Slink**, slingk, *v.i.* to creep or crawl away, as if ashamed; to sneak:—*pa.t.* and *pa.p.* slunk. [A.S. *slincan;* Low Ger. *sliken*, Ger. *schleichen.*]

**Slip**, slip, *v.i.* to slide or glide along: to move out of place: to escape: to err: to slink: to enter by oversight.—*v.t.* to cause to slide: to convey secretly: to omit: to throw off: to let loose: to escape from: to part from the branch or stem:—*pr.p.* slipp′ing; *pa.t.* and *pa.p.* slipped.—*n.* act of slipping: that on which anything may slip: an error: an escape: a twig: a strip: a leash: a sloping bank for ship-building: anything easily slipped on. [A.S. *slipan;* Sw. *slipa*, Dut. *slippen*, to glide.]

**Slip-knot**, slip'-not, *n.* a *knot* which *slips* along the rope or line around which it is made.

**Slipper**, slip'ėr, *n.* a loose shoe easily *slipped* on.

**Slippered**, slip'ėrd, *adj.* wearing slippers.

**Slippery**, slip'ėr-i, *adj.* apt to slip away : smooth : not affording firm footing or confidence : unstable : uncertain.—*n.* **Slipp'eriness.**

**Slipshod**, slip'shod, *adj.*, *shod* with *slippers*, or shoes down at the heel like slippers : careless.

**Slit**, slit, *v.t.* to cut lengthwise : to split : to cut into strips :—*pr.p.* slitt'ing ; *pa.t.* and *pa.p.* slit. —*n.* a long cut : a narrow opening. [A.S. *slítan ;* Ice. *slíta*, to tear.]

**Sloe**, slō, *n.* a small *sour* wild plum, the fruit of the blackthorn. [A.S. *sla*, Dut. *sleeuwe*, a sloe —*sleeuw*, sour.]

**Slogan**, slō'gan, *n.* a war-cry among the ancient Highlanders of Scotland. [Gael., contracted from *sluagh-ghairm*, an army-cry.]

**Sloop**, slōōp, *n.* a light boat : a one-masted cutter-rigged vessel. [Dut. *sloepe*. See **Shallop.**]

**Slop**, slop, *n.* water carelessly spilled : a puddle : mean liquor or liquid food :—*pl.* dirty water.— *v.t.* to soil by letting a liquid fall upon :—*pr.p.* slopp'ing ; *pa.p.* slopped. [Acc. to Wedgwood, imitative of the sound of dashing water.]

**Slope**, slōp, *n.* any incline down which a thing may *slip :* a direction downward.—*v.t.* to form with a slope, or obliquely.—*v.i.* to be inclined.—*adv.* in a sloping manner. [From *slopen*, ᴅa.p. of A.S. *slúpan.*]

**Sloppy**, slop'i, *adj.* wet : muddy.—*n.* **Slopp'iness.**

**Slops**, slops, *n.pl.* any loose lower garment, that *slips* on easily, esp. trousers : ready-made clothing, &c. [From **Slip.**]

**Slot**, slot, *n.* a broad, flat, wooden bar which *locks* or holds together larger pieces. [Allied to Low Ger. *slot*, Dut. *slot*, a lock.]

**Slot**, slot, *n.* the *track* of a deer. [Ice. *sloth*, track, path ; Scot. *sleuth*, track by the scent.]

**Sloth**, slōth or sloth, *n.* laziness : sluggishness : a quadruped which lives on trees, so named from its *slow* movement when on the ground. [Lit. 'slowness,' A.S. *slǽwth, slewth—slaw*, slow. See **Slow.**]

**Slothful**, slōth'fool or sloth'-, *adj.* given to sloth : inactive : lazy.—*adv.* **Sloth'fully.**—*n.* **Sloth'fulness.**

**Slouch**, slowch, *n.* a hanging down loosely of the head or other part : clownish gait : a clown.— *v.i.* to hang down : to have a clownish look or gait.—*v.t.* to depress. [Allied to **Slack, Slow, Slug.**]

**Slough**, slow, *n.* a *hollow* filled with *mud :* a soft bog or marsh. [A.S. *slog*, a hollow place ; perh. from Gael. *slugaid*, W. *yslwch*, a deep miry place.]

**Slough**, sluf, *n.* the cast-off skin of a serpent : the dead part which separates from a sore.—*v.i.* to come away as a slough : to be in the state of sloughing. [Allied to O. Ger. *sluch*, Ger. *schlauch*, the cast-off skin of the serpent.]

**Sloughy**, slow'i, *adj.* full of sloughs : miry.

**Sloughy**, sluf'i, *adj.* like or containing slough.

**Sloven**, sluv'n, *n.* a man carelessly or dirtily dressed :—*fem.* **Slut.** [Dut. *slof*, Low Ger. *sluf*, slow, indolent.]

**Slovenly**, sluv'en-li, *adj.* like a sloven : negligent of neatness or cleanliness : disorderly : done in an untidy manner.—*adv.* **Slov'enliness.**

**Slow**, slō, *adj.* not swift : late : behind in time : not hasty : not ready : not progressive.—*adv.* **Slow'ly.**—*n.* **Slow'ness.** [A.S. *slaw*, slow, lazy ; cog. with Dut. *slee*, Ice. *sliofr*, blunt.]

**Slow-worm**, slō'-wurm, *n.* a species of *worm*, so called from the *slowness* of its motion.

**Sludge**, sluj, *n.* soft mud or mire. [A form of **Slush.**]

**Slug**, slug, *n.* a heavy, *lazy* fellow : a snail very destructive to vegetation. [From M. E. *slugge*, lazy ; conn. with **Slack.**]

**Slug**, slug, *n.* a cylindrical or oval piece of metal for firing from a gun. [From root of **Slay.**]

**Sluggard**, slug'ard, *n.* one habitually idle or inactive.

**Sluggish**, slug'ish, *adj.* habitually lazy : slothful : having little motion : having little or no power.— *adv.* **Slugg'ishly.**—*n.* **Slugg'ishness.**

**Sluice**, slōōs, *n.* a sliding gate in a frame for *shutting off* or regulating the flow of water : the stream which flows through it : that through which anything flows : a source of supply. [Like Dut. *sluis*, Ger. *schleuse*, from O. Fr. *escluse* (Fr. *écluse*)—Low L. *exclusa* (*aqua*), a sluice, lit. '(water) shut out,' pa.p. of L. *ex-cludo*. See **Exclude.**] [Ety. dub.]

**Slum**, slum, *n.* a low street or neighbourhood.

**Slumber**, slum'bėr, *v.i.* to *sleep* lightly : to sleep : to be in a state of negligence or inactivity.—*n.* light sleep : repose.—*n.* **Slum'berer.** [With intrusive *b* from A.S. *slumerian ;* to slumber— *sluma*, slumber, cog. with Ger. *schlummern*.]

**Slumberous**, slum'bėr-us, *adj.* inviting or causing slumber : sleepy.

**Slump**, slump, *v.i.* to fall or sink suddenly into water or mud. [From the sound.]

**Slump**, slump, *v.t.* to throw into a lump or mass. [A corr. of **Lump.**]

**Slung**, *pa.t.* and *pa.p.* of **Sling.**

**Slunk**, *pa.t.* and *pa.p.* of **Slink.**

**Slur**, slur, *v.t.* to soil : to contaminate : to disgrace : to pass over lightly : to conceal : (*music*) to sing or play in a gliding manner :—*pr.p.* slurr'ing ; *pa.t.* and *pa.p.* slurred.—*n.* a stain : slight reproach : (*music*) a mark showing that notes are to be sung to the same syllable. [Prob. orig. 'to draw or touch in a careless way,' found in Low Ger. *slüren*, Dut. *sleuren*, to drag along the ground.]

**Slush**, slush, *n.* liquid mud : melting snow.—*adj.* **Slush'y.** [Prob. conn. with **Slough** ; cf. Dan. *slaske*, to dabble.]

**Slut**, slut, *n.* (fem. of **Slov'en**), a dirty, untidy woman, used sometimes in contempt. [Dan. *slutte*, Bav. *schlütt*, an uncleanly person.]

**Sluttish**, slut'ish, *adj.* resembling a slut : dirty : careless.—*adv.* **Slutt'ishly.**—*n.* **Slutt'ishness.**

**Sly**, slī, *adj.* dexterous in doing anything so as to be unobserved : cunning : wily : secret : done with artful dexterity.—*adv.* **Sly'ly** or **Sli'ly.**—*n.* **Sly'ness.** [Prob. from Scand. *slœg-r ;* cf. Ger. *schlau*.]

**Smack**, smak, *n.* taste : flavour : a pleasing taste : a small quantity : a taste.—*v.i.* to make a noise with the lips, as after tasting : to have a taste : to have a quality. [A.S. *smœc ;* Dut. *smak :* from the sound made by the lips.]

**Smack**, smak, *n.* a small vessel used chiefly in the coasting and fishing trade. [From A.S. *snacc* (Dut. *smak*, Ger. *schmacke*), perh. from Ice. *snák-r*, E. **Snake.**]

**Small**, smawl, *adj.*, *little* in quantity or degree : minute : not great : unimportant : of little worth or ability : short : having little strength : gentle. —*n.* **Small'ness.** [A.S. *smœl ;* O. Ger. *smal* (Ger. *schmal*).]

**Smallpox**, smawl'poks, *n.* a contagious, feverish disease, characterised by *small pox* or eruptions on the skin. [See **Pock**, of which it is a mistaken form.]

**Smalt**, smawlt, *n.* glass *melted*, tinged blue by cobalt, and pulverised when cold. [Low L. *smaltum*—O. Ger. *smalzjan* (Ger. *schmelzen*), to melt. See **Smelt**, *v.* and **Melt**.]

**Smart**, smärt, *n.* quick, stinging pain of body or mind.—*v.i.* to feel a smart: to be punished.—*adj.* causing a smart: pricking: severe: sharp: vigorous: acute: witty: vivacious.—*adv.* **Smart′ly.**—*n.* **Smart′ness.** [M. E. *smerte*; cog. with Dut. *smerte*, Ger. *schmerz*; perh. also conn. with L. *mord-eo*, to bite, Sans. *mard*.]

**Smart-money**, smärt′-mun′i, *n.*, *money* required of a person in order that he may *smart* or be punished by its loss for being set free from military service or the like: money allowed to soldiers and sailors for wounds received.

**Smash**, smash, *v.t.* to break in pieces violently: to crush.—*n.* act of smashing.—*n.* **Smash′er.** [Prob. imitative, and perh. also influenced by **Mash**.]

**Smatter**, smat′ėr, *v.i.* to talk superficially: to have a superficial knowledge.—*n.* **Smatt′erer.** [M. E. *smateren*, to rattle, to chatter; cog. with Ger. *schmettern*, to rattle, to jabber, to shatter; perh. from the root of **Smite**.]

**Smattering**, smat′ėr-ing, *n.* a superficial knowledge.

**Smear**, smēr, *v.t.* to overspread with anything sticky or oily, as *grease*: to daub. [A.S. *smerian*—*smeru*, fat, grease, cog. with Ger. *schmeer*, grease, Ice. *smjör*, butter.]

**Smell**, smel, *v.i.* to affect the nose: to have odour: to use the sense of smell.—*v.t.* to perceive by the nose:—*pa.t.* and *pa.p.* smelled or smelt.—*n.* the quality of bodies which affects the nose: odour: perfume: the sense which perceives this quality. [Allied to Low Ger. *smellen*, to smoke; so Ger. *riechen*, to smell, from *rauch*, smoke.]

**Smelling-bottle**, smel′ing-bot′l, *n.* a *bottle* containing a *smelling* substance for stimulating the nose and reviving the spirits.

**Smelt**, smelt, *n.* a fish of the salmon or trout family, having a cucumber-like *smell*. [A.S.]

**Smelt**, smelt, *v.t.* to *melt* ore in order to separate the metal.—*n.* **Smelt′er.** [Allied to Dut. *smelten*; prob. conn. with **Melt**.]

**Smeltery**, smelt′ėr-i, *n.* a place for smelting.

**Smew**, smū, *n.* a kind of duck which appears in Britain only in winter. [Ety. unknown.]

**Smile**, smīl, *v.i.* to express pleasure by the countenance: to express slight contempt: to look joyous: to be favourable.—*n.* act of smiling: the expression of the features in smiling: favour. [Dan. *smile*, Sw. *smila*; conn. with E. **Smirk**, L. *mirus*, wonderful, Sans. *smi*, to smile.]

**Smirch**, smirch, *v.* to besmear, dirty. [A weakened form of *smer-k*, from M. E. *smeren*, to smear.]

**Smirk**, smėrk, *v.i.* to *smile* affectedly: to look affectedly soft.—*n.* an affected smile. [A.S. *smercian*; akin to **Smile**.]

**Smite**, smīt, *v.t.* to strike with the fist, hand, or weapon: to beat: to kill: to overthrow in battle: to affect with feeling: (*B.*) to blast: to afflict.—*v.i.* to strike:—*pa.t.* smōte; *pa.p.* smitt′en.—*n.* **Smit′er.** [A.S. *smitan*; cog. with Dut. *smijten*, Ger. *schmeissen*.]

**Smith**, smith, *n.* one who forges with the hammer: a worker in metals: one who makes anything. [A.S., cog. with Ger. *schmied*.]

**Smithery**, smith′ėr-i, *n.* the workshop of a *smith*: work done by a smith.

**Smithy**, smith′i, *n.* the workshop of a *smith*.

**Smitten**, smit′n, *pa.p.* of **Smite**.

**Smock**, smok, *n.* a woman's shift: a smock-frock. [A.S. *smoc*, perh. from A.S. *smeogan*, Ger. *schmiegen*, to creep; and so lit. sig. 'a garment *crept* into.']

**Smock-frock**, smok′-frok, *n.* a loose shirt of fine linen worn over the other clothes. [**Smock** and **Frock**.]

**Smoke**, smōk, *n.* the vapour from a burning body.—*v.i.* to emit smoke: to draw in and puff out the smoke of tobacco: to raise smoke by moving rapidly: (*B.*) to burn: to rage.—*v.t.* to apply smoke to: to dry, scent, or medicate by smoke: to inhale the smoke of: to use in smoking: to try to expel by smoking.—**On a smoke** (*B.*) smoking, or on fire. [A.S. *smoca*; cog. with Low Ger. and Dut. *smook*, Ger. *schmauch*; perh. conn. with the root of **Smack**.]

**Smoker**, smōk′ėr, *n.* one who smokes tobacco: one who dries by smoking.

**Smoky**, smōk′i, *adj.* giving out smoke: like smoke: filled, or subject to be filled, with smoke: tarnished or noisome with smoke.—*adv.* **Smok′ily.**—*n.* **Smok′iness.**

**Smooth**, smōōth, *adj.* having an even surface: not rough: evenly spread: glossy: gently flowing: easy: regular: unobstructed: bland: mild.—*v.t.* to make smooth: to palliate: to soften: to calm: to ease.—*n.* (*B.*) the smooth part.—*adv.* **Smooth′ly.**—*n.* **Smooth′ness.** [Lit. 'yielding to the hammer,' A.S. *smoethe*; cog. with Low Ger. *smoedig*, and with Ger. *schmeidig*, *ge-schmeidig*, soft; from same root as **Smith**.]

**Smoothing-iron**, smōōth′ing-ī′urn, *n.* an instrument of *iron* for *smoothing* clothes.

**Smooth-tongued**, smōōth′-tungd, *adj.* having a *smooth tongue*: flattering.

**Smote**, smōt, *pa.t.* of **Smite**.

**Smother**, smuth′ėr, *v.t.* to suffocate by excluding the air: to conceal.—*v.i.* to be suffocated or suppressed: to smoulder.—*n.* smoke: thick floating dust. [Closely conn. with A.S. *smorian* (cog. with Ger. *schmoren*, to stew); perh. from the same root as **Smear**.]

**Smoulder**, smōl′dėr, *v.i.* to burn slowly or without vent. [Conn. with **Smother**, also influenced by **Smell**.]

**Smug**, smug, *adj.* neat, prim, spruce: affectedly smart. [From the Scand., as Dan. *smuk*, handsome; cf. A.S. *smeag*, fine.]

**Smuggle**, smug′l, *v.t.* to import or export without paying the legal duty: to convey secretly.—*n.* **Smugg′ling.** [Low Ger. *smuggeln*, cog. with Ger. *schmuggeln*; from a root found in Dut. *smuigen*, to do secretly.]

**Smuggler**, smug′lėr, *n.* one who smuggles: a vessel used in smuggling.

**Smut**, smut, *n.* a spot of dirt, soot, &c.: foul matter, as soot: a disease of corn by which the ear becomes a soot-like powder: obscene language.—*v.t.* to soil with smut: to blacken or tarnish.—*v.i.* to gather smut: to be turned into smut:—*pr.p.* smutt′ing; *pa.t.* and *pa.p.* smutt′ed. [Cog. with Sw. *smuts*, Ger. *schmutz*, prob. from root of **Smite**. Cf. **Smutch**.]

**Smutch**, smuch, *v.t.* to blacken, as with soot.—*n.* a dirty mark. [From **Smut**.]

**Smutty**, smut′i, *adj.* stained with smut.—*adv.* **Smutt′ily.**—*n.* **Smutt′iness.**

**Snack**, snak, *n.* a share: a slight, hasty meal. [A form of **Snatch**.]

**Snaffle**, snaf′l, *n.* a bridle which crosses the nose and has a slender mouth-bit without branches. [Perh. an extension of **Snap**.]

# Snag

**Snag**, snag, *n.* a sharp protuberance: a short branch: a projecting tooth or stump. [Akin to Gael. and Ir. *snaigh*, to cut down, to prune.]

**Snagged**, snag'ed, **Snaggy**, snag'i, *adj.* full of snags.

**Snail**, snāl, *n.* a slimy creeping mollusc, with or without a shell. [Lit. 'the *crawling* animal,' A.S. *snegl, snægl*; Ger. *schnecke*; conn. with **Snake** and **Sneak**.]

**Snake**, snāk, *n.* a kind of serpent. [Lit. 'the *creeping* animal,' A.S. *snaca*, prob. from *snican*, to creep; Ice. *snák-r*. Cf. **Snail** and **Sneak**.]

**Snap**, snap, *v.t.* to break short or at once: to bite, or catch at suddenly: to crack.—*v.i.* to break short: to try to bite:—*pr.p.* snapp'ing; *pa.t.* and *pa.p.* snapped.—*n.* act of snapping, or the noise made by it: a small catch or lock. [Allied to Ice. *snapa*, Dut. *snappen*, Ger. *schnappen*. See **Snip.**]

**Snapdragon**, snap'drag-un, *n.* a plant, so called because the lower lip of the corolla when parted shuts with a *snap* like a *dragon's* jaw: a play in which raisins are snatched from burning brandy, also the raisins so taken.

**Snappish**, snap'ish, *adj.* inclined to snap: eager to bite: sharp in reply.—*n.* **Snapp'ishness.**

**Snare**, snār, *n.* a running noose of string or wire, &c. for catching an animal: a trap: that by which any one is entrapped.—*v.t.* same as **Insnare.**—*n.* **Snar'er.**—*adj.* **Snar'y.** [A.S. *snear*, cord, snare; cog. with Ger. *schnur*, Goth. *snorjo*; also conn. with L. *nervus*, Gr. *neuron*, string, nerve.]

**Snarl**, snärl, *v.i.* to growl as a surly dog: to speak in a surly manner.—*n.* **Snarl'er.** [Prob. imitative; Low Ger. *snarren*, Ger. *schnarren*; conn. with E. **Snore.**]

**Snatch**, snach, *v.t.* to seize quickly: to take without permission: to seize and carry away.—*v.i.* to try to seize hastily.—*n.* a hasty catching or seizing: a short time of exertion: a small piece or fragment. [M.E. *snecchen*; cog. with Dut. *snakken*, and with Prov. E. *sneck*, a bolt; also conn. with **Snap.**]

**Sneak**, snēk, *v.i.* to *creep* or steal away privately or meanly: to behave meanly.—*n.* a mean, servile fellow.—*adj.* **Sneak'ing.**—*adv.* **Sneak'ingly.** [A.S. *snican*, to creep; Dan. *snige*. See **Snake.**]

**Sneer**, snēr, *v.i.* to show contempt by the expression of the face, as by turning up the nose: to insinuate contempt.—*n.* an indirect expression of contempt.—*n.* **Sneer'er.**—*adj.* **Sneer'ing.**—*adv.* **Sneer'ingly.** [Imitative; conn. with **Snarl.**]

**Sneeze**, snēz, *v.i.* to eject air rapidly and audibly through the nose.—*n.* a sneezing. [M.E. *nesin, hneosen* (the A.S. is *fneosan*), cog. with Ice. *hniosa*, Ger. *niesen*.]

**Sniff**, snif, *v.t.* to draw in with the breath through the nose.—*v.i.* to *snuff* or draw in air sharply through the nose: to snuff: to scent. [From the root of **Snuff.**]

**Snip**, snip, *v.t.* to cut off at once with scissors: to cut off the nib of: to cut off:—*pr.p.* snipp'ing; *pa.t.* and *pa.p.* snipped.—*n.* a single cut with scissors: a clip or small shred. [Allied to Dut. *snippen*, Ger. *schnippen*; closely conn. with **Snap.**]

**Snipe**, snīp, *n.* a bird which frequents marshy places. [Prob. so called from its long *bill*; Dut. *snip*, Ger. *schnepfe*; conn. with Ger. *schneppe*, E. **Neb.**]

**Snivel**, sniv'l, *v.i.* to run at the nose: to cry, as a

# Snug

child:—*pr.p.* sniv'elling; *pa.t.* and *pa.p.* sniv'elled.—*adj.* **Sniv'elling.** [A.S. *snofel*, mucus from the nose; akin to **Sniff, Snuff.**]

**Sniveller**, sniv'l-ėr, *n.* one prone to snivelling: one who cries for slight causes.

**Snob**, snob, *n.* a vulgar person, esp. one who apes gentility: (*orig.*) a shoemaker.—*adj.* **Snobb'ish.** —*n.* **Snobb'ishness.**—*adv.* **Snobb'ishly.** [Prov. E.]

**Snood**, snōōd, *n.* the fillet which binds a maiden's hair. [A.S. *snod*, prob. orig. Celtic.]

**Snooze**, snōōz, *v.i.* to doze: to slumber.—*n.* a quiet nap. [From root of **Sneeze.**]

**Snore**, snōr, *v.i.* to breathe roughly and hoarsely in sleep.—*n.* a noisy breathing in sleep.—*n.* **Snor'er.** [From the root of **Snarl**, influenced by imitation of the sound.]

**Snort**, snort, *v.i.* to force the air with violence and noise through the nostrils, as horses.—*n.* **Snort'ing.**—*n.* **Snort'er.** [Extension of **Snore.**]

**Snot**, snot, *n.* mucus of the nose.—*adj.* **Snott'y.** [A.S., and in other Teut. tongues; conn. with **Snout.**]

**Snout**, snowt, *n.* the projecting nose of a beast, as of a swine. [Low Ger. *snute*; cog. with Dut. *snuit*, Ger. *schnauze.*]

**Snow**, snō, *n.* frozen moisture which falls from the atmosphere in light, white flakes.—*v.i.* to fall in snow. [A.S. *snaw* (cog. with Goth. *snaivs*, Ger. *schnee*, L. *nix, nivis*)—*snivian*, to snow (cog. with Ger. *schneien*, L. *ningo*, Gr. *niphō*).]

**Snow-blindness**, snō'-blīnd'nes, *n.*, *blindness* caused by the reflection of light from *snow*.

**Snowdrift**, snō'drift, *n.* a bank of snow *drifted* together by the *wind*.

**Snowdrop**, snō'drop, *n.* a bulbous-rooted plant with beautiful *drop*-like flowers, which often come forth before the *snow* has disappeared.

**Snowline**, snō'līn, *n.* the *line* upon a mountain that marks the limit of perpetual *snow*.

**Snowplough**, snō'plow, *n.* a machine like a *plough* for clearing roads and railways from *snow*. [prevent sinking in the *snow.*]

**Snowshoe**, snō'shōō, *n.* a great flat *shoe* worn to

**Snowslip**, snō'slip, *n.* a mass of *snow* which *slips* down a mountain's side.

**Snowy**, snō'i, *adj.* abounding or covered with snow: white, like snow: pure: spotless.

**Snub**, snub, *v.t.* to check: to reprimand:—*pr.p.* snubb'ing; *pa.t.* and *pa.p.* snubbed. [Dan. *snubbe* (*af*), to nip (off), and Ice. *snubba* (lit. 'to cut short'), to chide.]

**Snub-nose**, snub'-nōz, *n.* a short or flat nose. [See under **Snub.**]

**Snuff**, snuf, *v.i.* to draw in air violently and noisily through the nose: to sniff.—*v.t.* to draw into the nose: to smell: to take off the snuff of (as a candle).—*n.* powdered tobacco or other substance for snuffing: the charred part of a candle-wick. [Cog. with Dut. *snuffen*, Ger. *schnaufen*, Sw. *snufva*. See **Sniff, Snivel.**]

**Snuff-box**, snuf'-boks, *n.* a *box* for *snuff*.

**Snuff-dishes**, snuf'-dish'ez, *n.pl.* (*B.*) *dishes* for the *snuff* of the lamps of the tabernacle.

**Snuffer**, snuf'ėr, *n.* one who snuffs:—*pl.* an instrument for taking the snuff off a candle.

**Snuffle**, snuf'l, *v.i.* to breathe hard through the nose. [Freq. of **Snuff.**]

**Snuffy**, snuf'i, *adj.* soiled with or smelling of *snuff*.

**Snug**, snug, *adj.* lying close and warm: comfortable: not exposed to view or notice: being in good order: compact.—*adv.* **Snug'ly.**—*n.* **Snug'ness.** [Scand., as Ice. *snögg-r*, short-haired, smooth; perh. conn. with E. **Sneak.**]

**So,** sō, *adv.* and *conj.* in this manner or degree: thus: for like reason: in such manner or degree: in a high degree: as has been stated: on this account: be it so: provided that: in case that. [A.S. *swā*, Ice. and Goth. *svā*; whence E. and Ger. *so* (*sva* being changed to *sua*, and the *u* coalescing with the *a* to form *o*).]

**Soak,** sōk, *v.t.* to steep in a fluid: to wet thoroughly: to drench: to draw in by the pores. —*v.i.* to be steeped in a liquid: to enter into pores.—*n.* **Soak'er.** [A.S. *socian*; conn. with **Suck.**]

**Soap,** sōp, *n.* a compound of oils or fats with soda or potash, used in washing.—*v.t.* to rub or wash with soap. [A.S. *sápe*, from the root of *sipan*, to drip; cog. with Ger. *seife*; conn. also with L. *sebum*, fat (L. *sapo* is borrowed from the Teut.)]

**Soapstone,** sōp'stōn, *n.* a soft kind of magnesian rock having a *soapy* feel, also called **Steatite.**

**Soapy,** sōp'i, *adj.* like soap: having the qualities of soap: covered with soap.—*n.* **Soap'iness.**

**Soar,** sōr, *v.i.* to mount into the *air:* to fly aloft: to rise to a height. [O. Fr. *es-sor-er*, to balance in air (Fr.; to air or dry, as linen; cf. *es-sor*, flight of birds, and It. *sor-are*, to flutter, to soar)—L. *ex*, out of, and *aura*, air.]

**Sob,** sob, *v.i.* to sigh in a convulsive manner, with tears:—*pr.p.* sobb'ing; *pa.t.* and *pa.p.* sobbed. —*n.* a short, convulsive sigh. [Conn. with A.S. *seofian*, to sigh, Ger. *seuf-z-en*, and E. **Sigh.**]

**Sober,** sō'bėr, *adj.* not drunk: temperate, esp. in the use of liquors: not mad: not wild or passionate: self-possessed: sedate: grave: calm: regular.—*v.t.* to make sober: to free from intoxication.—*adv.* **So'berly.**—*n.* **So'berness.** [Fr. *sobre*—L. *sobrius*, conn. with Gr. *sōphrōn*, of sound mind, and *sōs* (for *saos*), sound, L. *sanus.*]

**Sobriety,** so-brī'et-i, *n.* state or habit of being *sober:* calmness: gravity. [Fr. *sobriété*—L. *sobrietas.* See **Sober.**]

**Sobriquet,** sō'bri-kā, *n.* a contemptuous nickname: an assumed name. [Fr.; ety. dub.; acc. to Diez, perh. comp. of Fr. *sot*, simple, and O. Fr. *briquet*, a young ass, a simpleton.]

**Socage,** sok'āj, *n.* a tenure of lands in England, for which the service is fixed and determinate in quality. [A.S. *soc*, a right of holding a court; from *hlaford-socn*, seeking a lord—*secan*, to seek.] [*ciable:* good-fellowship.

**Sociability,** sō-sha-bil'i-ti, *n.* quality of being so-

**Sociable,** sō'sha-bl, *adj.* inclined to *society:* fit for company: companionable: affording opportunities for intercourse.—*adv.* **So'ciably.**—*n.* **So'ciableness.** [Fr.—L. *sociabilis*—*socio*, to associate—*socius*, a companion.]

**Social,** sō'shal, *adj.* pertaining to *society* or companionship: relating to men united in a society: inclined for friendly intercourse: consisting in mutual converse: convivial.—*adv.* **So'cially.**—*ns.* **Social'ity, So'cialness.** [L. *socialis*—*socius*, a companion.] [state: to render social.

**Socialise,** sō'shal-īz, *v.t.* to reduce to a social

**Socialism,** sō'shal-izm, *n.* the name given to schemes for regenerating society by a more equal distribution of property, and esp. by substituting the principle of association for that of competition.—*n.* **So'cialist,** an adherent of socialism.

**Society,** so-sī'e-ti, *n.* a number of persons *asso-ciated* for a common interest: a community or partnership: the civilised body of mankind: persons who associate: a religious or ecclesiastical body. [L. *societas*—*socius*, a companion.]

**Socinian,** so-sin'i-an, *adj.* pertaining to *Socinus*, who in the 16th century denied the doctrine of the Trinity, the deity of Christ, &c.—*n.* **Socin'-ianism,** the doctrines of Socinus.

**Sociology,** sō-shi-ol'o-ji, *n.* the science that treats of the conditions and development of human society, including ethics, politics, political economy, &c.—*adj.* **Sociolog'ical.** [A hybrid from L. *socius*, a companion, and Gr. *logos*, science.]

**Sock,** sok, *n.* a kind of half-stocking: comedy. [Orig. a low-heeled light shoe, worn by actors of comedy, A.S. *socc*—L. *soccus.*]

**Socket,** sok'et, *n.* a hollow into which something is inserted: the hollow of a candlestick. [From **Sock.**]

**Socratic,** so-krat'ik, **Socratical,** so-krat'ik-al, *adj.* pertaining to *Socrates*, a celebrated Greek philosopher, to his philosophy, or to his manner of teaching, which was by a series of questions leading to the desired result.—*adv.* **Socrat'-ically.**

**Sod,** sod, *n.* any surface of earth grown with grass, &c.: turf.—*adj.* consisting of sod.—*v.t.* to cover with sod. [Low Ger. *sode*, Ger. *sode*; perh. connected with *sod*, pa.t. of **Seethe**, and thus orig. sig. 'fuel for making the pot *boil.*']

**Sod,** sod, *pa.t.* of **Seethe.**

**Soda,** sō'da, *n.* oxide of the metal sodium. [Sp. *soda* (It. *soda*, Fr. *soude*)—L. *solida*, firm, because found in hard masses.]

**Soda-water,** sō'da-waw'tėr, *n.*, *water* containing *soda* charged with carbonic acid.

**Sodden,** sod'n, obs. *pa.p.* of **Seethe.**

**Soddy,** sod'i, *adj.* covered with sod: turfy.

**Sodium,** sō'di-um, *n.* a yellowish-white metal, the base of *soda.*

**Sodomite,** sod'om-īt, *n.* an inhabitant of *Sodom:* one guilty of sodomy.—*adj.* **Sodomit'ical.**—*adv.* **Sodomit'ically.**

**Sodomy,** sod'om-i, *n.* unnatural lust, so called because imputed to the inhabitants of *Sodom.*

**Sofa,** sō'fa, *n.* a long seat with stuffed bottom, back, and arms. [Fr.—Ar. *suffa*—*saffa*, to arrange or set in order.]

**Soft,** soft, *adj.* easily yielding to pressure: easily cut or acted upon: malleable: not rough to the touch: smooth: pleasing or soothing to the senses: easily yielding to any influence: mild: gentle: effeminate: gentle in motion: easy: free from lime or salt, as water.—*adv.* gently: quietly.—*adv.* **Soft'ly.**—*n.* **Soft'ness.** [A.S. *sefte*; cog. with Dut. *saft*, Ger. *sanft.*]

**Soften,** sof'n, *v.t.* to make soft or softer.—*v.i.* to grow soft or softer.—*n.* **Soft'ener.**

**Soil,** soil, *n.* the ground: the mould on the surface of the earth which nourishes plants: country. [Fr. *sol*—L. *solum*, conn. with *solidus*, solid. It has been much confused with the following word.]

**Soil,** soil, *n.* dirt: dung: foulness: a spot or stain. —*v.t.* to make dirty: to stain: to manure.—*v.i.* to take a soil: to tarnish. [Fr. *souille*, wallowing-place—L. *suillus*, piggish—*sus*, a pig, a hog.]

**Soirée,** swä'rā, *n.* an *evening* party: a public meeting with refreshments. [Fr.—*soir*, evening (Prov. *sera*)—L. *serus*, late.]

**Sojourn,** sō'jurn, *v.i.* to stay for a *day:* to dwell for a time.—*n.* a temporary residence.—*n.* **So'journer.** [Fr. *séjourner*—L. *sub*, and Low L. *jornus*—L. *diurnus*, relating to day—*dies*, a day.]

**Solace,** sol'ās, *n.*, *consolation*, *comfort* in distress: relief.—*v.t.* to comfort in distress: to console:

to allay. [O. Fr.—L. *solatium*—*solor, -atus*, to comfort in distress.] [*sula*.]

**Solan-goose**, sō′lan-gōōs, *n.* the gannet. [Ice.

**Solar**, sō′lar, *adj.* pertaining to the *sun*: measured by the progress of the sun : produced by the sun. [L. *solaris*—*sol*, the sun.]

**Sold**, sōld, *pa.t.* and *pa.p.* of **Sell**. [A.S. *sealde, seald*.]

**Solder**, sol′der, *v.t.* to unite two metallic surfaces by a fusible metallic cement : to cement.—*n.* a metallic cement for uniting metals. [Lit. 'to make *solid*,' O. Fr. *solder, solder* (Fr. *souder*) —L. *solidare*, to make solid—*solidus*, solid.]

**Soldier**, sōl′jér, *n.* a man engaged in military service : a private, as distinguished from an officer : a man of much military experience or of great valour. [Lit. 'one who serves for *pay*,' M. E. *souldier*—O. Fr. *soldier* (Fr. *soldat*)—L. *solidus*, a piece of money, the pay of a soldier.]

**Soldierlike**, sōl′jér-līk, **Soldierly**, sōl′jér-li, *adj.*, like a *soldier*: martial : brave.

**Soldiership**, sōl′jér-ship, *n.*, *state* or quality of being a *soldier*: military qualities : martial skill. [body of military men.

**Soldiery**, sōl′jér-i, *n.*, *soldiers* collectively : the

**Sole**, sōl, *n.* the *lowest part* or under side of the foot : the foot : the bottom of a boot or shoe : the bottom of anything.—*v.t.* to furnish with a sole. [A.S. *solea*—*solum*, the lowest part. See **Soil**, the ground.]

**Sole**, sōl, *n.* a genus of flat-fish which keep on or near the *bottom* of the sea. [Fr. *sole*—L. *solea*.]

**Sole**, sōl, *adj.*, *alone*: only : being or acting without another : single : (*law*) unmarried.—*n.* **Sole′-ness**. [L. *solus*, alone. Cf. **Solo**.]

**Solecism**, sol′e-sizm, *n.* a breach of syntax : any absurdity or impropriety. [Fr. *solécisme*—L. *solœcismus*—Gr. *soloikismos*—*soloikos*, speaking incorrectly, awkward ; said to come from the corruption of the Attic dialect among the Athenian colonists of *Soloi* in Cilicia, but this is very improb. (Liddell and Scott).]

**Solecist**, sol′e-sist, *n.* one who commits *solecisms*.

**Solecistic**, sol-e-sist′ik, **Solecist′ical**, -al, *adj.* pertaining to or involving a *solecism*: incorrect : incongruous.—*adv.* **Solecist′ically**.

**Solely**, sōl′li, *adv.*, *alone*: only : singly.

**Solemn**, sol′em, *adj.* (*lit.*) taking place *every year*, said esp. of religious ceremonies : attended with religious ceremonies, pomp, or gravity : impressing with seriousness : awful : devout : having the appearance of gravity : devotional : attended with an appeal to God, as an oath : serious.—*adv.* **Sol′emnly**.—*n.* **Sol′emness**. [Fr. *solennel*, It. *solenne*, L. *sollemnis, solennis*—Oscan *sollus*, all, every, L. *annus*, a year. See **Solid**.]

**Solemnise**, sol′em-nīz, *v.t.* to perform religiously or solemnly *once a year*, or periodically : to celebrate : to render grave.—*ns.* **Sol′emniser, Solemnisa′tion**.

**Solemnity**, so-lem′ni-ti, *n.* a *solemn* religious ceremony : a ceremony adapted to inspire with awe : reverence : seriousness : affected gravity.

**Sol-fa**, sōl-fä′, *v.i.* to sing the notes of the gamut, do, re, mi, *fa, sol*, &c. :—*pr.p.* sol-fa′ing.

**Solfeggio**, sol-fej′i-o, *n.* (*music*) an exercise on the notes of the scale as represented by do, re, mi, &c. [It.]

**Solicit**, so-lis′it, *v.t.* to ask earnestly : to petition : to seek or try to obtain. [Fr. *solliciter*—L. *sollicito*—*sollicitus*. See **Solicitous**.]

**Solicitant**, so-lis′it-ant, *n.* one who *solicits*.

**Solicitation**, so-lis-i-tā′shun, *n.* a *soliciting*: earnest request : invitation. [L. *sollicitatio*.]

**Solicitor**, so-lis′it-or, *n.* one who asks earnestly : one who is legally qualified to act for another in a court of law, esp. in Chancery : a lawyer. —*n.* **Solicitor-general**, in Eng. the second law-officer of the crown. [Fr. *solliciteur*—*solliciter*. See **Solicit**.

**Solicitous**, so-lis′it-us, *adj.*, *soliciting* or earnestly asking or desiring : very desirous : anxious : careful.—*adv.* **Solic′itously**. [Lit. 'thoroughly moved,' L. *sollicitus*—*sollus* (see **Solemn**), and *citus*, pa.p. of *cieo*.]

**Solicitude**, so-lis′i-tūd, *n.* state of being *solicitous*: anxiety or uneasiness of mind : trouble. [Fr. *sollicitude*—L. *sollicitudo*.]

**Solid**, sol′id, *adj.* having the parts firmly adhering : hard : compact : full of matter : not hollow : strong : having length, breadth, and thickness (opp. to a mere surface) : cubic : substantial : weighty.—*n.* a substance having the parts firmly adhering together : a firm, compact body, opposed to fluid.—*adv.* **Sol′idly**.—*n.* **Sol′idness**. [L. *solidus*, akin to O. Lat. *sollus*, Gr. *holos*, whole, Sans. *sarvas*, all. Cf. **Solemn**.]

**Solidarity**, sol-i-dar′i-ti, *n.* the being made *solid* or *compact*: the being bound : a *consolidation*, or oneness of interests. [Fr. *solidarité*—*solidaire*, jointly and severally liable—*solide*—L. *solidus*.] [solid or hard.

**Solidification**, so-lid-i-fi-kā′shun, *n.* act of making

**Solidify**, so-lid′i-fī, *v.t.* to make solid or compact. —*v.i.* to grow solid : to harden :—*pa.p.* solid′i-fied. [Fr. *solidifier*—L. *solidus, facio*, to make.]

**Solidity**, so-lid′i-ti, *n.* a being *solid*: fullness of matter : strength or firmness, moral or physical : soundness : (*geom.*) the solid content of a body.

**Soliloquise**, so-lil′o-kwīz, *v.i.* to *speak* to *one's self* or utter a *soliloquy*.

**Soliloquy**, so-lil′o-kwe, *n.* a *talking* when *solitary* or to one's self : a discourse of a person, not addressed to any one. [L. *soliloquium*—*solus*, alone, and *loqui*, to speak.]

**Soliped**, sol′i-ped, *n.* an animal with a *single* or uncloven *hoof* on each foot. [L. *solus*, alone, *pes, pedis*, a foot.]

**Solitaire**, sol-i-tār′, *n.* a recluse or one who lives *alone*: a game played by *one* person with a board and balls : an ornament worn singly on the neck or wrist.

**Solitary**, sol′i-tar-i, *adj.* being the *sole* person present : alone or lonely : single : living alone : without company : remote from society : retired : gloomy.—*n.* one who lives alone : a recluse or hermit.—*adv.* **Sol′itarily**.—*n.* **Sol′itariness**. [Fr. *solitaire*—L. *solitarius*—*solus*, alone.]

**Solitude**, sol′i-tūd, *n.* a being *alone*: a lonely life : want of company : a lonely place or desert. [Fr.—L. *solitudo*—*solus*, alone.]

**Solmisation**, sol-mi-zā′shun, *n.*, *sol-faïng*: a recital of the notes of the gamut, do, re, mi, &c.

**Solo**, sō′lo, *n.* a musical piece performed by *only one* voice or instrument :—*pl.* **So′los**.—*n.* **So′-loist**. [It.—L. *solus*, alone.]

**Solstice**, sol′stis, *n.* that point in the ecliptic where the *sun* is farthest from the equator, and seems to *stand* still : the time when the sun reaches this point. [Fr.—L. *solstitium*—*sol*, the sun, and *sisto*, to make to stand—*sto*, to stand.]

**Solstitial**, sol-stish′al, *adj.* pertaining to or happening at a *solstice*, especially at the north one.

**Solubility**, sol-ū-bil′i-ti, *n.* capability of being *dissolved* in a fluid.

**Soluble**, sol′ū-bl, *adj.* capable of being *solved* or *dissolved* in a fluid. [L. *solubilis*. See **Solve**.]

**Solution**, sol-ū′shun, *n.* act of *solving* or *dissolving*, esp. a solid by a fluid : the separating of the parts of any body : the preparation resulting from dissolving a solid in a liquid : explanation : removal of a doubt : construction or solving of a problem. [L. *solutio—solvo, solutum,* to loosen.]

**Solvable**, solv′a-bl, *adj.* capable of being *solved* or explained : capable of being paid.—*n.* **Solvability.** [Fr.—L. *solvo,* to dissolve, pay.]

**Solve**, solv, *v.t.* to *loosen* or *separate* the parts of : to clear up or explain : to remove.—*n.* **Solv′er.** [L. *solvo,* to loosen, prob. from *se,* aside, and *luo,* to loosen.]      [able to pay all debts.

**Solvency**, solv′en-si, *n.* state of being *solvent,* or

**Solvent**, solv′ent, *adj.* having power to *solve* or *dissolve :* able to pay all debts.—*n.* anything that *dissolves* another. [L. *solvens, -entis,* pr.p. of *solvo,* to loosen, to pay.]

**Sombre,** som′bèr, *adj.* dull : gloomy : melancholy.—*n.* **Som′breness.** [Lit. 'under a shade,' Fr. *sombre—*Sp. *sombra,* a shade—L. *sub,* under, *umbra,* a shade.]

**Some,** sum, *adj.* denoting an indefinite number or quantity : certain, in distinction from others : moderate or in a certain degree : about. [A.S. *sum ;* Goth. *sums,* Ice. *sumr.*]

**Somebody,** sum′bod-i, *n., some* or any *body* or person : a person of importance.

**Somehow,** sum′how, *adv.* in some way or other.

**Somersault,** sum′er-sawlt, **Somerset,** sum′ér-set, *n.* a *leap* in which a person turns with his heels *over* his head. [Corr. of Fr. *soubresaut,* It. *soprassalto—*L. *supra,* over, *saltus,* a leap—*salio,* to leap.]

**Something,** sum′thing, *n.* an indefinite thing or event : a portion, an indefinite quantity.—*adv.* in some degree.      [at one time or other.

**Sometime,** sum′tīm, *adv.* at a time not fixed : once :

**Sometimes,** sum′tīmz, *adv.* at certain times : now and then : at one time : (*B.*) once.

**Somewhat,** sum′hwot, *n.* an unfixed quantity or degree.—*adv.* in some degree. [**Some** and **What.**]

**Somewhere,** sum′hwār, *adv.* in some place : in one place or another. [**Some** and **Where.**]

**Somewhither,** sum′hwi*th*-èr, *adv.* to some place.

**Somnambulate,** som-nam′bū-lāt, *v.i.* to *walk* in *sleep.—n.* **Somnambula′tion.** [L. *somnus,* sleep, and *ambulo, -atum,* to walk.]

**Somnambulism,** som-nam′bū-lizm, *n.* act or practice of *walking* in *sleep.*

**Somnambulist,** som-nam′bū-list, *n.* a *sleep-walker.*

**Somniferous,** som-nif′ér-us, *adj., bringing* or causing *sleep.* [L. *somnus,* sleep, and *fero,* to bring.]

**Somnolence,** som′no-lens, **Somnolency,** som′no-len-si, *n., sleepiness :* inclination to sleep. [L. *somnolentia—somnus,* sleep.]

**Somnolent,** som′no-lent, *adj., sleepy* or inclined to sleep. [L. *somnolentus.*]

**Son,** sun, *n.* a male child or descendant : any young male person spoken of as a child : a term of affection generally : a disciple : a native or inhabitant : the produce of anything. [A.S. *sunu ;* Ger. *sohn,* Russ. *sün ;* Sans. *sūnu—su,* to beget, bring forth ; conn. with Gr. *huios,* a son.]

**Sonata,** so-nä′ta, *n.* a musical composition for one or more instruments, consisting of three or more movements or divisions. [It.—L. *sono,* to sound.]

**Song,** song, *n.* that which is *sung :* a short poem or ballad : the melody to which it is adapted : a poem, or poetry in general : the notes of birds : a mere trifle : (*B.*) an object of derision.

[A.S. *song, sang ;* Ger. *ge-sang,* Goth. *saggus,* Ice. *söngr ;* from root of **Sing.**]

**Songster,** song′stèr, *n.* a *singer* or one skilled in singing ; esp. a bird that sings.—*fem.* **Song′stress.** [A.S. *sangestre,* from **Song.**]

**Son-in-law,** sun′-in-law, *n.* the husband of one's daughter.

**Sonnet,** son′et, *n.* a *short song* or poem of fourteen lines, with varying rhymes. [Fr.—It. *sonetto,* dim. of *sone,* a sound, song—L. *sonus,* a sound.]

**Sonneteer,** son-et-ēr′, *n.* a composer of *sonnets.*

**Sonorous,** so-nō′rus, *adj., sounding* when struck : giving a clear, loud sound : high sounding.—*adv.* **Sono′rously.—*n.*** **Sono′rousness.** [L. *sonorus—sonor* or *sonus,* a sound—*sono,* to sound. See **Sound.**]

**Sonship,** sun′ship, *n.* state or character of a son.

**Soon,** sōōn, *adv.* immediately or in a short time : without delay : early : readily : willingly. [A.S. *sona,* cog. with Goth. *suns,* immediately, soon.]

**Soot,** soot, *n.* the black powder condensed from smoke. [A.S. and Ice. *sót ;* Dan. *sood.*]

**Sooth,** sōōth, *n.* truth, reality.—*adj.* true : pleasing. [A.S. *soth,* true ; Ice. *sannr,* true, Goth. *sunis :* conn. with Gr. *eteos,* Sans. *satyas,* true.]

**Soothe,** sōōth, *v.t.* to please with soft words : to flatter : to soften.—*adv.* **Sooth′ingly.** [Lit. 'to please any one by agreeing with him, by receiving his words as *true,*' A.S. *gesodhian,* to soothe, *gesoth,* a flatterer—*soth,* true.]

**Soothsay,** sōōth′sā, *v.i.* to foretell.—*ns.* **Sooth′sayer, Sooth′saying.** [Lit. 'to *say* or tell the *truth.*']

**Sooty,** soot′i, *adj.* producing, consisting of, containing, or like *soot.—n.* **Soot′iness.** [A.S. *sotig.*]

**Sop,** sop, *n.* anything dipped or *soaked,* esp. in *soup,* to be eaten : anything given to satisfy.—*v.t.* to steep in liquor :—*pr.p.* sopp′ing ; *pa.t.* and *pa.p.* sopped. [A.S. *sop* (in *sopcoppa,* a soup-cup, dish), from *supan,* to sip, soak ; Ice. *soppa,* broth, soup. See **Sup, Soup.**]

**Sophism,** sof′izm, *n.* a specious fallacy. [Fr. *sophisme—*Gr. *sophisma—sophizō,* to make wise —*sophos,* cleverness.]

**Sophist,** sof′ist, *n.* one of a class of public teachers in Greece in the fifth century B.C. : a captious or fallacious reasoner. [Lit. and orig. 'a wise or clever man,' Gr. *sophistēs—sophos,* wise.]

**Sophistic,** so-fist′ik, **Sophistical,** so-fist′ik-al, *adj.* pertaining to a sophist or to sophistry : fallaciously subtle.—*adv.* **Sophist′ically.** [Gr. *sophistikos.*]

**Sophisticate,** so-fist′i-kāt, *v.t.* to render sophistical, or unsound : to corrupt by mixture.

**Sophistication,** so-fist-i-kā′shun, *n.* act of sophisticating, adulterating, or injuring by mixture.

**Sophistry,** sof′ist-ri, *n.* specious but fallacious reasoning.

**Soporiferous,** sop-or-if′ér-us, *adj., bringing,* causing, or tending to cause *sleep :* sleepy. [L. *sopor, soporis,* sleep, and *fero,* to bring.]

**Soporific,** sop-or-if′ik, *adj., making* or causing *sleep.—n.* anything that causes sleep. [Fr. *soporifique—*L. *sopor,* sleep, and *facio,* to make.]

**Soppy,** sop′i, *adj.,* soppy or soaked in liquid.

**Sopranist,** so-prä′nist, *n.* a singer of *soprano.*

**Soprano,** so-prä′no, *n.* the *highest* kind of female voice : air :—*pl.* **Sopra′nos** or **Sopra′ni.** [Lit. 'superior,' It., from *sopra—*L. *supra* or *super,* above.]

**Sorcerer,** sor′sèr-ér, *n.* one who practises *sorcery :* an enchanter : a magician.—*fem.* **Sor′ceress.**

[Fr. *sorcier*—Low L. *sortiarius*—L. *sors, sortis*, a lot.]

**Sorcery,** sor′sẽr-i, *n.* divination by the assistance of evil spirits : enchantment : magic. [Lit. 'casting lots,' O. Fr. *sorcerie*—L. *sortior*, to cast lots—*sors, sortis*, a lot.]

**Sordid,** sor′did, *adj.* vile : mean : meanly avaricious.—*adv.* **Sor′didly.**—*n.* **Sor′didness.** [Fr. *sordide*—L. *sordidus*—*sordeo*, to be dirty.]

**Sore,** sōr, *n.* a *wound* : an ulcer or boil : (*B.*) grief, affliction.—*adj.* wounded : tender : susceptible of pain : easily pained or grieved : (*B.*) severe.—*adv.* (*B.*) same as **Sore′ly.**—*n.* **Sore′ness.** [A.S. *sar*, a wound ; cog. with Ger. *sehr* (*orig.* painfully), very, Ice. *sar*, wound, sore, pain. See **Sorry.**]

**Sorely,** sōr′li, *adv.* in a sore manner : grievously.

**Sorrel,** sor′el, *n.* a plant of a *sour* taste, allied to the dock. [Fr. *surelle*—*sur*, sour ; from Ger. *sauer*, A.S. *sur*, sour.]

**Sorrel,** sor′el, *adj.* of a *reddish-brown* colour.— *n.* a sorrel or reddish-brown colour. [Fr. *saure*, sorrel ; of uncertain origin.]

**Sorrow,** sor′ō, *n.* pain of mind : grief : affliction. —*v.i.* to feel sorrow or pain of mind : to grieve. [A.S. *sorg, sorh* ; cog. with Ger. *sorge,* Ice. *sorg,* and perhaps allied to **Sore.**]

**Sorrowful,** sor′ō-fool, *adj.* full of sorrow : causing, showing, or expressing sorrow : sad : dejected. —*adv.* **Sor′rowfully.**—*n.* **Sor′rowfulness.**

**Sorry,** sor′i, *adj.* grieved for something past : melancholy : poor : worthless.—*adv.* **Sorr′ily.** —*n.* **Sorr′iness.** [A.S. *sarig,* wounded, sorrowful ; O. Dut. *sorigh ;* conn. with **Sore,** but has come to be regarded as the adj. of **Sorrow.**]

**Sort,** sort, *n.* a number of persons or things having like qualities : class, kind, or species : order or rank : manner.—*v.t.* to separate into lots or classes : to put together : to select.—*v.i.* to be joined with others of the same *sort* : to associate : to suit.—*n.* **Sort′er.**—**Out of sorts,** out of order : unwell. [Lit. 'lot,' Fr. *sorte*—L. *sors, sortis,* a lot—*sero,* to join.]

**Sortie,** sor′tē, *n.* the *issuing* of a body of troops from a besieged place to attack the besiegers [Fr.—*sortir,* to go out, to issue.]

**Sot,** sot, *n.* one stupefied by drinking : a habitual drunkard. [Old Fr. *sot,* perh. of Celt. origin.]

**Soteriology,** sō-tē-ri-ol′o-ji, *n.* (*theol.*) the doctrine of salvation by Jesus Christ. [Gr. *sōtērios,* saving, *sōtēr,* saviour, and *logos,* discourse.]

**Sottish,** sot′ish, *adj.* like a sot : foolish : stupid with drink.—*adv.* **Sott′ishly.**—*n.* **Sott′ishness.**

**Sou,** sōō, *n.* a French copper coin = $\frac{1}{20}$th of a franc. [Fr. *sou ;* It. *soldo*—L. *solidus,* a coin.]

**Souchong,** sōō-shong′, *n.* a fine sort of black tea.

**Sough,** sōōch (*ch* guttural), *v.i.* to whistle or sigh, as the wind.—*n.* a sighing of the wind. [From the sound.]

**Sought,** sawt, *pa.t.* and *pa.p.* of **Seek.**

**Soul,** sōl, *n.* that part of man which thinks, feels, desires, &c. : the seat of life and intellect : life : essence : internal power : energy or grandeur of mind : a human being, a person. [M. E. *saule* —A.S. *sawol ;* Ger. *seele,* Goth. *saivala.*]

**Souled,** sōld, *adj.* full of soul or feeling.

**Soulless,** sōl′les, *adj.* without a soul or nobleness of mind : mean : spiritless.

**Sound,** sownd, *adj.* safe whole, entire : perfect : healthy, strong : pref .wnd : correct : orthodox : weighty.—*adv.* **Sound′ly.**—*n.* **Sound′ness.** [A.S. *sund, gesund ;* cog. with Ger. *gesund,* allied to L. *sanus,* sound, Gr. *saos, sōs,* safe and sound.]

**Sound,** sownd, *n.* a narrow passage of water : a

strait. [A.S. *sund,* a swimming, a narrow arm of the sea, from *svimman,* to swim ; cog. with Ger. *sund,* a strait.]

**Sound,** sownd, *n.* the air or *swimming* bladder of a fish. [A.S. *sund,* swimming.]

**Sound,** sownd, *v.i.* to make a *noise* : to utter a voice : to spread.—*v.t.* to cause to make a noise : to utter audibly : to direct by a sound or audible signal : to publish audibly.—*n.* the impression produced on the ear by the vibrations of air : noise : report : empty or meaningless noise. [M. E. *sounen*—Fr. *sonner*—L. *sono ;* cog. with O. Ger. *svana,* Sans. *svan,* to sound.]

**Sound,** sownd, *v.t.* to measure the depth of, esp. with a line and plummet : to probe : to try to discover a man's secret wishes, &c. : to test : to introduce an instrument into the bladder to examine it.—*v.i.* to use the line and lead in ascertaining the depth of water.—*n.* an instrument to discover stone in the bladder. [Fr. *sonder,* to sound ; acc. to Diez, from Low L. *subundare,* to put under the wave—L. *sub,* under, *unda,* a wave.]

**Sounding,** sownd′ing, *n.* the ascertaining the depth of water :—*pl.* any part of the ocean where a sounding-line will reach the bottom.

**Soup,** sōōp, *n.* the juice or liquid obtained by boiling, seasoned, and often mixed with vegetables. [Fr. *soupe ;* from Ger. *suppe,* soup, cog. with E. **Sup.**]

**Sour,** sowr, *adj.* having a pungent, acid taste : turned, as milk : rancid : crabbed or peevish in temper : bitter.—*adv.* **Sour′ly.**—*n.* **Sour′ness.** [A.S. *sur ;* Ger. *sauer,* Ice. *surr.*]

**Sour,** sowr, *v.t.* to make sour or acid : to make cross, peevish, or discontented.—*v.i.* to become sour or acid : to become peevish or crabbed.

**Source,** sōrs, *n.* that from which anything *rises* or originates : origin : the spring from which a stream flows. [Fr. *source,* from *sourdre* (It. *sorgere*)—L. *surgo,* to raise up, to rise.]

**Souse,** sows, *n.* pickle made of salt : anything steeped in pickle : the ears, feet, &c. of swine pickled.—*v.t.* to steep in pickle : to plunge into water.—*v.i.* to fall on suddenly. [Written also *sonce,* a form of **Sauce.**]

**South,** sowth, *n.* the direction in which the sun appears at noon to the people N. of the Tropic of Cancer : any land opposite the N.—*adj.* lying towards the south.—*adv.* towards the south. [A.S. *sudh ;* Ger. *süd* (whence Fr. *sud*), Ice. *sudr,* prob. from root of **Sun.**]

**South-east,** sowth-ēst′, *n.* the direction equally distant from the *south* and *east.*

**South-east,** sowth-ēst′, **South-easterly,** sowth-ēst′ẽr-li, **South-eastern,** sowth-ēst′ẽrn, *adj.* pertaining to, in the direction of, or coming from the *south-east.*

**Southerly,** su*th*′ẽr-li, **Southern,** su*th*′ẽrn, *adj.* pertaining to, situated in, or proceeding from or towards the *south.*—*superl.* **South′ernmost, Southmost,** sowth′most, *most southern,* furthest towards the south.

**Southernwood,** su*th*′ẽrn-wood, *n.* an aromatic plant of *Southern* Europe, closely allied to wormwood.        [the *south.*

**Southward,** sowth′ward or su*th*′ard, *adv., toward*

**South-west,** sowth-west′, *n.* the direction equally distant from the *south* and *west.*

**South-west,** sowth-west′, **South-westerly,** sowth-west′ẽr-li, **South-western,** sowth-west′ẽrn, *adj.* pertaining to, proceeding from, or lying in the direction of the *south-west.*

**Southwester,** sow-west′ẽr, *n.* a storm or gale

from the south-west : a painted canvas hat with a broad flap behind for the neck.

**Souvenir**, sōōv′nēr, *n.* a remembrancer. [Fr. (It. *sovvenire*)—L. *subvenire*, to come up, to come to mind—*sub*, under, from under, and *venio*, *venire*, to come.]

**Sovereign**, sov′ėr-in, *adj.*, *supreme:* possessing supreme power or dominion : superior to all others : utmost.—*n.* a supreme ruler : a monarch : a gold coin = 20*s.* [M. E. *soveraine*—Fr. *souverain*—Low L. *superanus*—L. *super*, *supra*, above.]

**Sovereignty**, sov′ėr-in-ti, *n.* supreme power : dominion. [Fr. *souveraineté*.]

**Sow**, sow, *n.* a female pig : an oblong piece of metal larger than a pig. [A.S. *su*, *sugu*; cog. with Ger. *sau*, Ice. *syr*; L. *sus*, Gr. *hys*; conn. with **Swine**.]

**Sow**, sō, *v.t.* to scatter seed that it may grow : to plant by strewing : to scatter seed over : to spread.—*v.i.* to scatter seed for growth :—*pa.p.* sown and sowed.—*n.* **Sow′er**. [A.S. *sawan*; Ger. *säen*, Ice. *sa*, Goth. *saian*; akin to L. *sero* (for *seso*). See **Seed**.]

**Spa**, spaw, *n.* a place where there is a mineral spring of water. [From *Spa*, a famous watering-place in Belgium.]

**Space**, spās, *n.* extension as distinct from material substances : room : largeness : distance between objects : interval between lines or words in books : quantity of time : distance between two points of time : a short time : interval.—*v.t.* to make or arrange intervals between. [Fr. *espace* —L. *spatium*, from root *spa*, Sans. *spha*, to draw, as in Gr. *spaō*, Ger. *spannen*.]

**Spacious**, spā′shus, *adj.* having large *space* : large in extent : roomy : wide.—*adv.* **Spa′ciously**.—*n.* **Spa′ciousness**. [Fr. *spacieux*—L. *spatiosus*.]

**Spade**, spād, *n.* a broad *blade* of iron with a handle, used for digging.—*v.t.* to dig with a spade. [A.S. *spadu*; cog. with Ger. *spaten*, L. *spatha*, Gr. *spathē*, any broad blade.]

**Spake**, spāk, old *pa.t.* of **Speak**.

**Span**, span, *n.* the space from the end of the thumb to the end of the little-finger when the fingers are *extended* : nine inches : the spread of an arch between its abutments : a space of time.—*v.t.* to measure by spans : to measure : to embrace :— *pr.p.* spann′ing ; *pa.t.* and *pa.p.* spanned. [A.S. *spann*—*spannan* ; cog. with Ger. *spannen*, L. *pando* (for *spando*). See **Space**.]

**Span**, span, *n.* a yoke of horses or oxen. [Borrowed from Dut. ; from the same root as above word.]

**Spandrel**, span′drel, *n.* the irregular triangular space between the *span* or curve of an arch and the inclosing right angle. [From **Span**.]

**Spangle**, spang′gl, *n.* a small, thin plate or boss of shining metal : anything sparkling and brilliant, like a spangle.—*v.t.* to adorn with spangles. —*v.i.* to glitter. [A.S. *spange*, a clasp, perh. prob. conn. with **Span** ; cog. with Ger *spange*, Ice. *spöng*.]

**Spaniard**, span′yard, *n.* a native of *Spain*.

**Spaniel**, span′yel, *n.* a kind of dog, usually liver and white coloured, and with large pendent ears, once supposed to be of *Spanish* origin. [O. Fr. *espagneul* (Fr. *épagneul*), Spanish.]

**Spanish**, span′ish, *adj.* of or pertaining to *Spain*. —*n.* the language of Spain.

**Spanker**, spang′kėr, *n.* the after-sail of a ship or barque, so called from its *flapping* in the breeze. [From Prov. E. *spank*, to flap, to move quickly.]

**Spar**, spär, *n.* a rafter : a general term for masts,

yards, booms, and gaffs, &c. [Ice. *sparri*, Dut. *spar* ; prob. conn. with **Bar**.]

**Spar**, spär, *n.* a mineral which is perfectly crystalline. [A.S. *spær(-stan)*, gypsum, perh. from the *spar* or *spear* form it assumes ; cf. Ger. *spar* (-*kalk*).]

**Spar**, spär, *v.i.* to box with the hands : to fight with showy action : to dispute :—*pr.p.* sparr′ing ; *pa.t.* and *pa.p.* sparred.—*n.* **Sparr′er**. [O. Fr. *esparer*, Fr. *éparer*, to kick out, from root of **Parry**.]

**Spare**, spär, *v.t.* to use frugally : to do without : to save from any use : to withhold from : to treat tenderly : to part with willingly.—*v.i.* to be frugal : to forbear : to be tender : to forgive. [A.S. *sparian* ; cog. with Ger. *sparen* ; allied also to L. *par-co* (for *spar-co*).]

**Spare**, spär, *adj.*, *sparing :* frugal : scanty : lean : superfluous.—*n.* **Spare′ness**.

**Sparerib**, spär′rib, *n.* a piece of meat consisting of the *ribs* with a *spare* or small amount of flesh.

**Sparing**, spär′ing, *adj.* scarce : scanty : saving.

**Spark**, spärk, *n.* a small particle of fire shot off from a burning body : any small shining body or light : a small portion of anything active or vivid. [A.S. *spearca*, a spark ; Dut. *spark*, *sperk*.]

**Sparkle**, spärk′l, *n.* a little spark : lustre.—*v.i.* to emit sparks : to shine : to glitter. [Dim. of **Spark**.] [glittering : brilliant : lively.

**Sparkling**, spärk′ling, *adj.* giving out *sparks :*

**Sparrer**. See under **Spar**, to box.

**Sparrow**, spar′ō, *n.* a well-known small bird. [A.S. *spearwa* ; cog. with Goth. *sparva*, Ice. *spörr*, Ger. *sper-ling*.]

**Sparrow-bill**, spar′ō-bil, *n.* a small shoe-nail, so called from its shape.

**Sparrow-hawk**, spar′ō-hawk, *n.* a small species of *hawk* destructive to *sparrows*, &c. [A.S. *spear-hafoc*.]

**Sparry**, spär′i, *adj.* consisting of or like *spar*.

**Sparse**, spärs, *adj.* thinly *scattered*.—*adv.* **Sparse′ly**.—*n.* **Sparse′ness**. [L. *sparsum*, pa.p. of *spargo*, to scatter ; allied to Gr. *speirō*, to sow.]

**Spartan**, spär′tan, *adj.* of or pertaining to *Sparta* in Greece : hardy : fearless.

**Spasm**, spazm, *n.* an irregular, violent, and involuntary *drawing* or contraction of the muscles— less violent than a convulsion. [Fr. *spasme*—L. *spasmus*—Gr. *spasmos*—*spaō*, to draw.]

**Spasmodic**, spaz-mod′ik, **Spasmodical**, spaz-mod′-ik-al, *adj.* relating to or consisting in *spasms :* convulsive.—*n.* **Spasmod′ic**, a medicine for removing spasms.

**Spat**, spat, *pa.t.* of **Spit**, to throw from the mouth.

**Spat**, spat, *n.* the spawn or young, *spit* or thrown *out* by shellfish. [From root of **Spit**.]

**Spatter**, spat′ėr, *v.t.* to *spit* or throw out upon : to scatter about : to sprinkle with dirt or anything moist : to defame. [Freq. from **Spat**, pa.t. of **Spit**.]

**Spatter-dashes**, spat′ėr-dash′ez, *n.pl.* coverings for the legs, to keep them clean from water and mud, a kind of gaiters.

**Spatula**, spat′ū-la, **Spattle**, spat′l, *n.* a little spade : a broad kind of knife for spreading plasters. [L. *spatula*, *spathula*, dim. of *spatha*, any broad blade—Gr. *spathē*. See **Spade**.]

**Spavin**, spav′in, *n.* a swelling near the joints of horses, producing lameness, and causing them to lift their feet like a *sparrow-hawk*. [O. Fr. *espavain*, Fr. *éparvin*—*éparvier*, a sparrow-hawk—O. Ger. *sparwari*, E. **Sparrow**.]

**Spavined**, spav'ind, *adj.* affected with *spavin*.

**Spawn**, spawn, *n.* the eggs of fish or frogs when ejected : offspring.—*v.t.* to produce, as fishes and frogs do their eggs : to bring forth.—*v.i.* to deposit eggs, as fishes or frogs : to issue, as off-spring. [Ety. dub.]    [the *spawn* is ejected.

**Spawner**, spawn'ėr, *n.* the female fish, from which

**Speak**, spēk, *v.i.* to utter words or articulate sounds : to say : to talk : to converse : to sound. —*v.t.* to pronounce : to converse in : to address : to declare : to express by signs :—*pa.t.* spōke or spāke ; *pa.p.* spōk'en. [A.S. *specan* (for *spre-can*) : cog. with Dut. *spreken*, Ger. *sprechen*.]

**Speaker**, spēk'ėr, *n.* one who speaks : the person who presides in a deliberative or legislative body, as the House of Commons.—*n.* **Speak'ership**.

**Speaking-trumpet**, spēk'ing-trum'pet, *n.* an instrument somewhat resembling a trumpet, used for intensifying the sound of the voice, so as to convey it to a greater distance.

**Spear**, spēr, *n.* a long weapon used in war and hunting, made of a pole pointed with iron : a lance with barbed prongs used for catching fish. —*v.t.* to pierce or kill with a spear. [A.S. *spere* ; cog. with Ger. *speer*, W. *yspēr*, L. *sparus* : prob. further conn. with **Spar** and **Spire**.]

**Spearman**, spēr'man, *n.* a *man* armed with a *spear*.

**Spearmint**, spēr'mint, *n.* a species of *mint* having *spear*-shaped leaves.

**Special**, spesh'al, *adj.* of a *species* or sort : particular : distinctive : uncommon : designed for a particular purpose : confined to a particular subject.—*adv.* **Spe'cially**.

**Specialise**, spesh'al-īz, *v.t.* to determine in a *special* manner.—*n.* **Specialisa'tion**.

**Specialist**, spesh'al-ist, *n.* one who devotes himself to a *special* subject.

**Speciality**, spesh-i-al'i-ti, *n.* the *special* or particular mark of a person or thing : a special occupation or object of attention. [Fr.—L.]

**Specialty**, spesh'al-ti, *n.* something *special* : a special contract : that for which a person is distinguished.

**Specie**, spē'shi, *n.* gold and silver coin, because *visible* wealth, and not merely representing it, as bills and notes do. [Cf. next word.]

**Species**, spē'shēz, *n.* a group of individuals having common marks or characteristics :—subordinate to a **Genus**. [L. (*lit.*) 'that which is *seen*,' then a form, a particular sort—*specio*, to look.]

**Specific**, spe-sif'ik, **Specifical**, spe-sif'ik-al, *adj.* pertaining to or constituting a *species* : that *specifies* : precise : infallible.—*adv.* **Specif'ically**.

**Specific**, spe-sif'ik, *n.* a remedy which has a *special* power in a particular disease : an infallible remedy.

**Specification**, spes-i-fi-kā'shun, *n.* act of *specify-ing* : a statement of particulars.

**Specify**, spes'i-fī, *v.t.* to make *special* : to mention particularly :—*pa.t.* and *pa.p.* spec'ified. [Low L. *specifico*—L. *species*, and *facio*, to make.]

**Specimen**, spes'i-men, *n.* a portion of anything to *show* the kind and quality of the whole : a sample.

**Specious**, spē'shus, *adj.* that *looks* well at first sight : showy : plausible.—*adv.* **Spe'ciously**.— *n.* **Spe'ciousness**.

**Speck**, spek, *n.* a *spot* : a blemish.—*v.t.* to spot. [A.S. *specca* ; Low Ger. *spaak*.]

**Speckle**, spek'l, *n.* a *little speck* or spot in anything different in substance or colour from the thing itself.—*v.t.* to mark with speckles.

**Spectacle**, spek'ta-kl, *n.* a *sight* : show : exhibi-tion :—*pl.* glasses to assist the sight.—*adj.* **Spec-**

**tac'ular**. [L. *specta-culum*—*specto*, *spectatum*, intens. of *spec-io*, to look at.]

**Spectacled**, spek'ta-kld, *adj.* wearing spectacles.

**Spectator**, spek-tā'tur, *n.* one who *looks on*.—*fem.* **Specta'tress**.

**Spectral**, spek'tral, *adj.* relating to, or like a *spectre*.             [seen.' Doublet **Spectrum**.]

**Spectre**, spek'tėr, *n.* a ghost. [Lit. 'something

**Spectroscope**, spek'tro-skōp, *n.* an instrument for forming and *examining spectra* of luminous bodies, so as to determine their composition. [**Spectrum**, and Gr. *skopeō*, to look at.]

**Spectrum**, spek'trum, *n.* the image of something seen continued after the eyes are closed : the colours of light separated by a prism, and ex-hibited as spread out on a screen :—*pl.* **Spec'tra**. [Lit. 'something seen,' from L. *spec-io*, to see. Doublet **Spectre**.]

**Specular**, spek'ū-lar, *adj.* resembling a *speculum* : having a smooth reflecting surface. [L.]

**Speculate**, spek'ū-lāt, *v.i.* to *look* at or into with the mind : to consider : to theorise : to traffic for great profit.—*n.* **Spec'ulator**. [L. *speculatus*, pa.p. of *speculor*—*specula*, a look-out—*spec-io*, to look.]

**Speculation**, spek-ū-lā'shun, *n.* act of speculating : mental view : contemplation : theory : the buy-ing goods, &c. to sell them at an advance.

**Speculative**, spek'ū-lāt-iv, *adj.* given to specula-tion or theory : ideal : pertaining to speculation in business, &c.—*adv.* **Spec'ulatively**.

**Speculum**, spek'ū-lum, *n.* (*opt.*) a reflector usually made of polished metal : (*surgery*) an instrument for bringing into view parts otherwise hidden : —*pl.* **Spec'ula**. [Lit. 'a *looking*-glass,' L.— *spec-io*, to look.]

**Sped**, sped, *pa.t.* and *pa.p.* of **Speed**.

**Speech**, spēch, *n.* that which is *spoken* : language : the power of speaking : oration : any declaration of thoughts : mention. [A.S. *spæc*, *spræc* ; Ger. *sprache*. See **Speak**.]

**Speechless**, spēch'les, *adj.* destitute or deprived of the power of speech.—*n.* **Speech'lessness**.

**Speed**, spēd, *n.* quickness, velocity : success.— *v.i.* to move quickly : to succeed : to fare.—*v.t.* to despatch quickly : to hasten, as to a conclu-sion : to execute : to aid : to make prosperous : —*pr.p.* speed'ing ; *pa.t.* and *pa.p.* sped. [A.S. *spéd* ; cog. with Dut. *spœd*, speed, Ger. *sputen*, to speed.]

**Speedy**, spēd'i, *adj.* hasty : quick : nimble.—*adv.* **Speed'ily**.—*n.* **Speed'iness**.

**Spell**, spel, *n.* any form of words supposed to possess magical power.—*adj.* **Spell'bound**. [A.S. *spell*, a narrative or tale ; cog. with Goth. *spill*, Ice. *spiall*, a tale.]

**Spell**, spel, *v.t.* to tell or name the letters of : to name, write, or print the proper letters of.—*v.i.* to form words with the proper letters :—*pr.p.* spell'ing ; *pa.t.* and *pa.p.* spelled, spelt. [Same word as above, modified by O. Fr. *espeler* (Fr. *épeler*)—O. Ger. *spellon*, to tell, Goth. *spillon*.]

**Spell**, spel, *v.t.* to take another's place at work.— *n.* a turn at work : a short period :—*pr.p.* spell'ing ; *pa.t.* and *pa.p.* spelled. [A.S. *spelian*, to act for another, perh. conn. with A.S. *spilian*, Ger. *spielen*, to play.]

**Spelling**, spel'ing, *n.* act of spelling or naming the letters of words : orthography.

**Spelling-book**, spel'ing-book, *n.* a *book* for teach-ing to *spell*.—*n.* **Spell'ing-bee**, a competition in spelling.

**Spelt**, spelt, *n.* a kind of corn : also called German wheat. [A.S. (Ger. *spelt*)—L. *spelta*.]

**Spelter,** spel´tėr, *n.* zinc. [Allied to Dut. *spiauter.* See **Pewter.**]

**Spencer,** spens´ėr, *n.* a short over-jacket worn by men or women, named after a Lord *Spencer* who introduced it or made it fashionable.

**Spencer,** spens´ėr, *n.* (in ships and barques) a fore-and-aft sail abaft the fore and main masts. [Ety. unknown.]

**Spend,** spend, *v.t.* to expend or weigh out : to give for any purpose : to consume : to waste : to pass, as time.—*v.i.* to make expense : to be dissipated :—*pr.p.* spend´ing ; *pa.t.* and *pa.p.* spent. —*n.* **Spend´er.** [A.S. *ā-spendan,* for -*spendan* —L. *expendo* or *dispendo,* to weigh out.]

**Spendthrift,** spend´thrift, *n.* one who *spends* the savings of *thrift* : a prodigal. [See **Spend** and **Thrift.**]

**Spent,** spent, *pa.t.* and *pa.p.* of **Spend.**

**Sperm,** spėrm, *n.* animal seed : spawn of fishes or frogs : spermaceti. [Lit. 'that which is *sown*,' Late L.—Gr. *sperm-a, sperm-atos—speirō,* to sow.]

**Spermaceti,** spėr-ma-sē´ti, *n.* a waxy matter from the head of the sperm-whale. [L. (*lit.*) 'the *sperm* of the *whale*'—*sperma* (see **Sperm**), and *cētus,* a whale—Gr. *kētos.*]

**Spermatic,** spėr-mat´ik, **Spermatical,** spėr-mat´-ik-al, *adj.* pertaining to or consisting of *sperm* or seed : seminal.

**Sperm-oil,** spėrm´-oil, *n., oil* from the *sperm-whale.*

**Sperm-whale,** spėrm´-hwāl, *n.* a species of *whale* from which *sperm* or spermaceti is obtained.

**Spew, Spue,** spū, *v.t.* and *v.i.* to vomit : to eject with loathing. [A.S. *spīwan* ; cog. with Dut. *spuwen,* Ger. *speien* ; also conn. with L. *spuo,* Gr. *ptyō,* and with **Spit.**]

**Sphere,** sfēr, *n.* a *ball* or *globe* : an orb : circuit of motion : province or duty : rank : (*geom.*) a surface every point of which is equidistant from one and the same point, called the centre.—*adj.* **Spher´al.** [Fr.—L. *sphaera*—Gr. *sphaira.*]

**Spheric,** sfer´ik, **Spherical,** sfer´ik-al, *adj.* pertaining to or like a *sphere.*—*adv.* **Spher´ically.**

**Sphericity,** sfer-is´i-ti, *n.* state or quality of being spherical : roundness.

**Spheroid,** sfēr´oid, *n.* a body or figure having the *form* of a *sphere,* but not quite round. [Fr. *sphéroïde*—Gr. *sphaira,* and *eidos,* form.]

**Spheroidal,** sfēr-oid´al, *adj.* having the form of a spheroid.

**Spherule,** sfer´ūl, *n.* a little sphere.

**Sphincter,** sfingk´tėr, *n.* (*anat.*) a muscle that contracts or shuts an orifice or opening which it surrounds. [Gr., 'that which binds tight'— *sphinggō,* to bind tight.]

**Sphinx,** sfingks, *n.* (*ancient myth.*) a monster with the head of a woman and the body of a lioness, that proposed riddles to travellers, and *strangled* those who could not solve them. [Lit. 'the throttler,' Gr.—*sphinggō, sphingxō,* to squeeze, akin to L. *fīgo,* to fix.]

**Spice,** spīs, *n.* an aromatic vegetable used for seasoning food, formerly one of the most valuable *kinds* of merchandise : a small quantity.—*v.t.* to season with spice : to tincture. [O. Fr. *espice* (Fr. *épice*)—Late L. *species,* kinds of goods, spices—L. *species,* a particular kind, &c. (see **Species**). Cf. the use of Ger. *materialien* (*lit.* 'materials'), to signify drugs.]

**Spicery,** spīs´ėr-i, *n.* spices in general : a repository of spices.

**Spick,** spik, *n.* a nail : *obs.* save in the phrase **Spick and span new,** *i.e.* as new as a spike just made and a chip just split. [Prov. form of **Spike,** a nail.]

**Spicy,** spīs´i, *adj.* producing or abounding with spices : fragrant : pungent.—*adv.* **Spic´ily.**—*n.* **Spic´iness.**

**Spider,** spī´dėr, *n.* an animal remarkable for spinning webs to take its prey. [Lit. 'the spinner,' for *spinder,* from **Spin** ; cf. Dan. *spinder,* O. Ger. *spinna,* Ger. *spinne.*]

**Spigot,** spig´ut, *n.* a *spike,* or *pointed* piece of wood for stopping a small hole in a cask. [Gael. *spiocaid,* W. *yspigod* ; conn. with root of **Spike,** a nail.]

**Spike,** spīk, *n.* an ear of corn : (*bot.*) an inflorescence, of which the flowers are sessile, or issue directly from a simple undivided axis. [From L. *spica,* an ear of corn.]

**Spike,** spīk, *n.* a small pointed rod : a large nail.— *v.t.* to set with spikes : to stop the vent of with a spike. [A.S. *spicing,* cog. with Ger. *spieker* ; conn. with **Spike,** an ear of corn, and **Spoke,** *n.*]

**Spikelet,** spīk´let, *n.* a little spike.

**Spikenard,** spīk´närd, *n.* a highly aromatic oil or balsam obtained from an Indian plant, the *Nardus,* with *spike*-shaped blossoms : the plant itself. [L. *spica nardi.* See **Nard.**]

**Spiky,** spīk´i, *adj.* furnished with *spikes* : having a sharp point.

**Spill,** spil, *v.t.* to allow to run out of a vessel : to shed : to waste.—*v.i.* to be shed : to be allowed to fall, be lost, or wasted :—*pa.t.* and *pa.p.* spilled, spilt.—*n.* **Spill´er.** [A.S. *spillan* ; cog. with Dut. *spillen,* Ice. *spilla,* to destroy ; also conn. with **Split.**]

**Spill,** spil, **Spile,** spīl, *n.* a small peg or pin to stop a hole. [Lit. 'a splinter,' Dut. *spil,* Ger. *spille,* conn. with E. **Spindle.**]

**Spin,** spin, *v.t.* to draw out and twist into threads : to draw out a thread as spiders do : to draw out tediously : to cause to whirl rapidly.—*v.i.* to practise the art or trade of spinning, to perform the act of spinning : to issue in a small or thread-like current : to whirl :—*pr.p.* spin´ing ; *pa.t.* and *pa.p.* spun.—*n.* **Spinn´er.** [A.S. *spinnan,* cog. with Dut. and Ger. *spinnen* ; closely conn. with **Span.**]

**Spinach, Spinage,** spin´āj, *n.* an esculent vegetable with jagged or *spiny* leaves. [It. *spinace* —Low L. *spinaceus*—*spina,* a thorn.] [bone.

**Spinal,** spīn´al, *adj.* pertaining to the *spine* or back-

**Spindle,** spin´dl, *n.* the pin from which the thread is *spun* or twisted : a pin on which anything turns : the fusee of a watch. [A.S. *spinl* (from **Spin**) ; cog. with Ger. *spindel.* Cf. **Spill,** *n.*]

**Spine,** spīn, *n.* a thorn : a thin, pointed spike, esp. in fishes : the backbone of an animal. [O. Fr. *espine* (Fr. *épine*)—L. *spina,* a thorn, conn. with root of **Spike,** a nail, applied to the backbone because of its sharp-pointed projections.]

**Spinet,** spin´et or spin-et´, *n.* (*mus.*) an old-fashioned keyed instrument like the harpsichord. [It. *spinetta* (Fr. *épinette*), dim. of *spina*—L. *spina,* a thorn ; so called from the pointed quills used in playing on it.]

**Spinning,** spin´ing, *adj.* used in spinning.

**Spinose,** spi´nōs, **Spinous,** spi´nus, *adj.* full of spines : thorny.

**Spinster,** spin´stėr, *n.* (*law*) an unmarried female. [Lit. 'a woman who *spins.*']

**Spiny,** spīn´i, *adj.* full of spines : thorny : troublesome : perplexed.—*n.* **Spin´iness.**

**Spiracle,** spir´a-kl, *n.* a *breathing* hole : any minute passage. [L. *spiraculum,* formed as a double dim. from *spiro,* to breathe.]

**Spiral,** spīr′al, *adj.* pertaining to or like a *spire*: winding like the thread of a screw.—*n.* a spiral line: a curve which continually recedes from a centre about which it revolves: a screw.

**Spirally,** spīr′al-li, *adv.* in a spiral form or direction.

**Spire,** spīr, *n.* a winding line like the threads of a screw: a curl: a wreath: a tapering body: a steeple. [L. *spira*—Gr. *speira*, anything wound round or upon a thing; akin to *eirō*, to fasten together in rows.]

**Spirit,** spir′it, *n.* vital force: the soul: a ghost: mental disposition: enthusiasm: real meaning: chief quality: a very lively person: any volatile, inflammable liquid obtained by distillation, as brandy:—*pl.* intellectual activity: liveliness: persons with particular qualities of mind: mental excitement: spirituous liquors.—**Holy Spirit.** See under **Holy**.—**The Spirit,** the Holy Spirit: the human spirit under the influence of the Holy Spirit.—*v.t.* to take away suddenly or secretly, as by a spirit. [L. *spiritus,* a breath—*spiro,* to breathe.]

**Spirited,** spir′it-ed, *adj.* full of spirit, life, or fire: animated.—*adv.* **Spir′itedly.**—*n.* **Spir′itedness.**

**Spiritism,** spir′it-izm, *n.* See under **Spiritualism.**

**Spiritless,** spir′it-les, *adj.* without spirit, cheerfulness, or courage: dejected: dead.—*adv.* **Spir′itlessly.**

**Spirit-rapper,** spir′it-rap′ėr, *n.* a spiritualist who professes that spirits convey intelligence to him by raps or knocks.

**Spiritual,** spir′it-ū-al, *adj.* consisting of *spirit*: having the nature of a spirit: immaterial: relating to the mind: intellectual: pertaining to the soul: holy: divine: relating to sacred things: not lay or temporal.—*adv.* **Spir′itually.**

**Spiritualise,** spir′it-ū-al-īz, *v.t.* to make *spiritual*: to imbue with spirituality: to refine: to free from sensuality: to give a spiritual meaning to.

**Spiritualism,** spir′it-ū-al-izm, *n.* a being spiritual: the philosophical doctrine that nothing is real but soul or spirit: the doctrine that spirit has a real existence apart from matter: the belief that certain peculiar phenomena (as rapping, table-turning, &c.) are directly due to the influence of departed *spirits,* invoked by a 'medium' (in this sense better called **Spiritism**).

**Spiritualist,** spir′it-ū-al-ist, *n.* one who has a regard only for *spiritual* things: one who holds the doctrine of spiritualism (or spiritism).

**Spirituality,** spir-it-ū-al′i-ti, *n.* state of being *spiritual*: essence distinct from matter.

**Spirituous,** spir′it-ū-us, *adj.* possessing the qualities of *spirit*: containing spirit: volatile.

**Spirt,** spėrt. Same as **Spurt.**

**Spiry,** spīr′i, *adj.* of a *spiral* form: wreathed: tapering like a spire or a pyramid: abounding in spires.

**Spit,** spit, *n.* an iron prong on which meat is roasted.—*v.t.* to pierce with a spit:—*pr.p.* spitt′ing; *pa.t.* and *pa.p.* spitt′ed. [A.S. *spitu*; Dut. *spit,* Ger. *spiesz.*]

**Spit,** spit, *v.t.* to throw out from the mouth: to eject with violence.—*v.i.* to throw out saliva from the mouth:—*pr.p.* spitt′ing; *pa.t.* spit, spat; *pa.p.* spit. [A.S. *spittan*; Ice. *spyta,* Ger. *spützen.* These are all extensions of **Spew.**]

**Spite,** spīt, *n.* grudge: lasting ill-will: hatred.—*v.t.* to vex: to thwart: to hate. [Short for **Despite.**]

**Spiteful,** spīt′fool, *adj.* full of spite: desirous to vex or injure: malignant.—*adv.* **Spite′fully.**—*n.* **Spite′fulness.**

**Spitted,** spit′ed (*B.*) *pa.p.* of **Spit,** to throw out from the mouth.

**Spittle,** spit′l, *n.* the moist matter *spit* or thrown from the mouth: saliva.

**Spittoon,** spit-tōōn′, *n.* a vessel for receiving *spittle.*

**Splash,** splash, *v.t.* to spatter with water or mud.—*v.i.* to dash about water or any liquid.—*n.* water or mud thrown on anything. [Like **Plash,** an imitative word.]

**Splashboard,** splash′bōrd, *n.* a *board* to keep those in a vehicle from being *splashed* with mud.

**Splashy,** splash′i, *adj., splashing*: wet and muddy: full of dirty water.

**Splay,** splā, *v.t.* (*arch.*) to slope or slant: to dislocate, as the shoulder-bone.—*adj.* turned outward, as in *splay-foot.* [A contr. of **Display.**]

**Spleen,** splēn, *n.* a spongy gland near the large extremity of the stomach, supposed by the ancients to be the seat of anger and melancholy: hence, spite: ill-humour: melancholy. [M. E. *splen*—L.—Gr. *splēn*; cog. with L. *lien* (for *p-lien*), Sans. *plihan.*]

**Splendent,** splen′dent, *adj.* splendid or *shining*: bright. [L., pr.p. of *splendeo,* to shine.]

**Splendid,** splen′did, *adj.* magnificent: famous: illustrious: heroic.—*adv.* **Splen′didly.** [Lit. 'shining,' L. *splendidus—splendeo,* to shine.]

**Splendour,** splen′dur, *n.* the appearance of anything *splendid*: brilliance: magnificence.

**Splenetic,** sple-net′ik or splen′e-tik, **Splenetical,** sple-net′ik-al, *adj.* affected with *spleen*: peevish: melancholy.—*n.* **Splen′etic,** a splenetic person.—*adv.* **Splenet′ically.**

**Splenic,** splen′ik, *adj.* pertaining to the *spleen.*

**Splenitis,** sple-nī′tis, *n.* inflammation of the spleen.

**Splice,** splīs, *v.t.* to unite two ends of a rope by interweaving the strands.—*n.* act of splicing: joint made by splicing. [Lit. 'to split in order to join;' a form of **Split**; allied to Dut. *splitsen.*]

**Splint,** splint, *n.* a small piece of wood *split* off: (*med.*) a thin piece of wood, &c. for confining a broken or injured limb: a hard excrescence on the shank-bone of a horse.—*v.t.* to confine with splints. [A nasalised form of **Split.**]

**Splinter,** splint′ėr, *n.* a piece of wood or other substance *split* off.—*v.t.* and *v.i.* to split into splinters.

**Splintery,** splint′ėr-i, *adj.* made of or like *splinters.*

**Split,** split, *v.t.* to cleave lengthwise: to tear asunder violently: to divide: to throw into discord.—*v.i.* to divide or part asunder: to be dashed to pieces:—*pr.p.* splitt′ing; *pa.t.* and *pa.p.* split.—*n.* a crack or rent lengthwise. [Allied to Dut. *splijten,* Ger. *spleiszen.* Cf. **Splice** and **Splint.**]

**Splutter,** splut′ėr, *v.i.* to eject drops of saliva while speaking: to scatter ink upon a paper, as a bad pen. [By-form of **Sputter.**]

**Spoil,** spoil, *v.t.* to take by force: to plunder.—*v.i.* to practise robbery.—*n.* that which is taken by force: plunder: pillage: robbery.—*n.* **Spoil′er,** a plunderer. [Prob. short for *despoile*—O. Fr. *despoiler* (Fr. *dépouiller*)—L. *despoliare*—*de-,* and *spolio*—*spolium,* spoil.]

**Spoil,** spoil, *v.t.* to corrupt: to mar: to make useless.—*v.i.* to decay: to become useless.—*n.* **Spoil′er,** a corrupter. [Same as above word.]

**Spoke,** spōk, *pa.t.* of **Speak.**

**Spoke,** spōk, *n.* one of the bars from the nave to the rim of a wheel. [A.S. *spaca*; cog. with Ger. *speiche*; conn. with **Spike,** a small pointed rod.]

**Spoken,** spōk′n, *pa.p.* of **Speak.**

**Spokeshave,** spōk′shāv, *n.* a plane for dressing the *spokes* of wheels. [Cf. **Shaving.**]

**Spokesman,** spōks'man, *n.* (*B.*) one who *speaks* for another, or for others.

**Spoliate,** spō'li-āt, *v.t.* to *spoil*: to plunder: to pillage.—*v.i.* to practise robbery. [L. *spoliatus,* pa.p. of *spolio—spolium,* spoil.] [bery.

**Spoliation,** spō-li-ā'shun, *n.* act of *spoiling*: rob-

**Spondaic,** spon-dā'ik, *adj.* pertaining to or consisting of *spondees.*

**Spondee,** spon'dē, *n.* in classical poetry, a foot of two long syllables, as *bēllō.* [Fr.—L. *spondēus* (*pes*)—Gr. *spondeios* (*pous*), (a foot) of two syllables, so called because much used in the slow solemn hymns sung at a *spondē* or drink-offering—*spendō.* See **Sponsor.**]

**Sponge,** spunj, *n.* the porous framework of an animal, found attached to rocks, &c. under water, remarkable for its power of sucking up water: an instrument for cleaning cannon after a discharge: the heel of a horse's shoe.—*v.t.* to wipe with a sponge: to wipe out with a sponge: to wipe out completely: to destroy.—*v.i.* to suck in, as a sponge: to gain by mean tricks. [A.S., O. Fr. *esponge* (Fr. *éponge*)—L. *spongia*—Gr. *spongia, sponggos.* Doublet **Fungus.**]

**Spongecake,** spunj'kāk, *n.* a very light cake.

**Spongy,** spunj'i, *adj.* like a *sponge*: of an open texture: soft and porous: wet and soft: capable of imbibing fluids.—*n.* **Spong'iness.**

**Sponsal,** spon'sal, *adj.* pertaining to a *betrothal,* a marriage, or a spouse. [L.—*sponsus,* a betrothal—*spondeo, sponsus,* to promise solemnly. See **Sponsor.**]

**Sponsor,** spon'sur, *n.* one who *promises* solemnly for another: a surety: a godfather or godmother.—*n.* **Spon'sorship.** [L.—*spondeo, sponsus,* to promise solemnly, akin to Gr. *spendō,* to pour a libation, *spondai,* a solemn treaty. Cf. **Spouse.**] [*sponsor,* or sponsorship.

**Sponsorial,** spon-sō'ri-al, *adj.* pertaining to a

**Spontaneity,** spon-ta-nē'i-ti, *n.* state or quality of being *spontaneous.*

**Spontaneous,** spon-tā'ne-us, *adj.* of one's *free-will*: involuntary: acting by its own impulse or natural law: produced of itself or without interference.—*adv.* **Sponta'neously.** [L. *spontaneus—sponte,* of one's own accord—*spondeo.*]

**Spool,** spool, *n.* a hollow cylinder for winding yarn upon.—*v.t.* to wind on spools. [Low Ger.; Ger. *spule.*]

**Spoon,** spoon, *n.* an instrument for supping liquids. [Lit. 'a *chip* of wood,' A.S. *spon*: Ger. *span,* a chip, Ice. *spann,* a chip, a spoon.]

**Spoonbill,** spoon'bil, *n.* a wading bird like the heron, with a long *bill* rounded at the end like a spoon. [As if fed on *spoon*-meat.]

**Spooney,** spoon'i, *adj.* silly, weakly affectionate.

**Spoonful,** spoon'fool, *n.* as much as a *spoon* contains when *full*: a small quantity.

**Spoor,** spoor, *n.* track or trail of an animal, esp. when hunted as game. [Dut. *spoor,* a track, cog. with Scot. *speir,* to ask.]

**Sporadic,** spo-rad'ik, *adj., scattered*—a term specially applied to solitary cases of a disease usually epidemic. [Gr. *sporadikos—sporas, sporados,* scattered—*speirō,* to sow.]

**Spore,** spōr, *n.* a minute grain which serves as a *seed* in flowerless plants like the fern. [Gr. *sporos,* a sowing, seed—*speirō,* to sow.]

**Sporran,** spor'an, *n.* an ornamental pouch worn in front of the kilt by the Highlanders of Scotland. [Gael. *sporan.*]

**Sport,** spōrt, *v.i.* to play: to frolic: to practise field diversions: to trifle.—*v.t.* to amuse: **to make merry**: to represent playfully.—*n.* that which amuses or makes merry: play: mirth: jest: contemptuous mirth: anything for playing with: a toy: idle jingle: field diversion. [Short for **Disport.**]

**Sportful,** spōrt'fool, *adj.* full of sport: merry: full of jesting.—*adv.* **Sport'fully.**—*n.* **Sport'fulness.**

**Sporting,** spōrt'ing, *adj.* relating to or engaging in *sports.*—*adv.* **Sport'ingly.**

**Sportive,** spōrt'iv, *adj.* inclined to *sport*: playful: merry.—*adv.* **Sport'ively.**—*n.* **Sport'iveness.**

**Sportsman,** spōrts'man, *n.* one who practises, or one skilled in field-*sports.*—*n.* **Sports'manship,** practice or skill of a sportsman.

**Spot,** spot, *n.* a mark made by a drop of wet matter: a blot: a discoloured place: a small part of a different colour: a small extent of space: any particular place: something that soils: a stain on character or reputation.—*v.t.* to mark with drops of wet: to stain: to discolour: to taint: to tarnish, as reputation:—*pr.p.* spot'ting; *pa.t.* and *pa.p.* spott'ed. [M. E. *spat,* Scot. and Dut. *spat,* prob. from the root of **Spit,** to throw out from the mouth.]

**Spotless,** spot'les, *adj.* without a spot: untainted: pure.—*adv.* **Spot'lessly.**—*n.* **Spot'lessness.**

**Spotted,** spot'ed, **Spotty,** spot'i, *adj.* marked with *spots* or discoloured places.

**Spousal,** spowz'al, *adj.* pertaining to a *spouse,* or to marriage: nuptial: matrimonial.—*n.* usually in *pl.* nuptials: marriage.

**Spouse,** spowz, *n.* a husband or wife. [Lit. 'one *promised* in marriage,' 'a betrothed person,' O. Fr. *espous* (Fr. *époux,* fem. *épouse*)—L. *sponsus,* pa.p. of *spondeo,* to promise, to promise in marriage. Cf. **Espouse** and **Sponsor.**]

**Spout,** spowt, *v.t.* to throw out, as from a pipe.—*v.i.* to issue with violence, as from a pipe.—*n.* the projecting mouth of a vessel from which a stream issues: a pipe for conducting a liquid. [Allied to Dut. *spuiten,* Ice. *spyta,* from root of **Spit,** to throw out.]

**Sprang,** *pa.t.* of **Spring.**

**Sprat,** sprat, *n.* a seafish like the herring, but much smaller. [M. E. *sprotte*: Dut. *sprot,* Ger. *sprotte.*]

**Sprawl,** sprawl, *v.i.* to toss or kick about the limbs: to stretch the body carelessly when lying: to spread ungracefully.—*n.* **Sprawl'er.** [Akin to Low Ger. *spaddeln,* Dan. *sprælle,* to toss about the limbs.]

**Spray,** sprā, *n.* small particles of water driven by the wind, as from the top of waves, &c. [From A.S. *spregan,* to pour.]

**Spray,** sprā, *n.* a small shoot of a tree. [Akin to A.S. *sprec,* Ice. *sprek,* a twig. Doublet **Sprig.**]

**Spread,** spred, *v.t.* to scatter abroad or in all directions: to stretch: to extend: to overlay: to shoot out, as branches: to circulate, as news: to cause to affect numbers, as a disease: to diffuse: to set with provisions, as a table.—*v.i.* to extend or expand in all directions: to be extended or stretched: to be propagated or circulated:—*pa.t.* and *pa.p.* spread.—*n.* extent: compass: expansion of parts. [A.S. *sprædan*; Dut. *spreiden,* Ger. *spreiten.*]

**Spree,** sprē, *n.* a merry frolic: a drunken frolic. [Prov. E. *adj. sprag, spry, spree,* M. E. *sprac,* from Ice. *sprækr,* lively.]

**Sprig,** sprig, *n.* a small shoot or twig.—*v.t.* to

embroider with representations of twigs :—*pr.p.* sprigg'ing ; *pa.t.* and *pa.p.* sprigged. [Doublet of **Spray**.]

**Sprightly**, sprīt'li, *adj.*, *spirit-like* : airy : full of life : lively : brisk.—*n.* **Spright'liness**. [From *spright*, a corr. of **Spirit**. Cf. **Sprite**.]

**Spring**, spring, *v.i.* to bound : to leap : to rush hastily : to move suddenly by elastic force : to start up suddenly : to break forth : to appear : to issue : to come into existence : (*B.*) to rise, as the sun.—*v.t.* to cause to spring up : to start : to produce quickly : to contrive on a sudden : to explode, as a mine : to open, as a leak : to crack, as a mast :—*pa.t.* sprung, sprang ; *pa.p.* sprung. —*n.* a leap : a flying back with elastic force : elastic power : an elastic body : any active power : that by which action is produced : cause or origin : a source : an outflow of water from the earth : (*B.*) the dawn : the time when plants begin to spring up and grow, the vernal season —March, April, May : a starting of a plank in a vessel : a crack in a mast. [A.S. *springan* ; Ger. *springen*.]

**Springbok**, spring'bok, *n.* a sort of South African antelope, larger than a roebuck. [Dut. for ' spring-buck,' from its leaping motion.]

**Springe**, sprinj, *n.* a snare with a *spring*-noose : a gin.—*v.t.* to catch in a springe. [Prov. E. *springle*—**Spring** ; cf. Ger. *sprenkel*—*springen*.]

**Springer**, spring'er, *n.* a kind of dog allied to the spaniel, useful for *springing* game in copses.

**Spring-tide**, spring'-tīd, *n.* a *tide* which *springs* or rises higher than ordinary tides, after new and full moon.

**Springy**, spring'i, *adj.* pertaining to or like a *spring* : elastic : nimble : abounding with springs or fountains.—*n.* **Spring'iness**.

**Sprinkle**, spring'kl, *v.t.* to scatter in small drops or particles : to scatter on : to baptise with a few drops of water : to purify.—*v.i.* to scatter in drops.—*n.* **Sprin'kle** or **Sprink'ling**, a small quantity sprinkled.—*n.* **Sprink'ler**. [Freq. formed from A.S. *sprengan*, the causative of **Spring** ; cf. Ger. *sprenkeln*.]

**Sprit**, sprit, *n.* (*naut.*) a spar set diagonally to extend a fore-and-aft sail. [A.S. *spreot*, a pole ; Dut. and Ger. *spriet*, a bowsprit ; conn. with **Sprout**.] [corr. of **Spirit**. Cf. **Sprightly**.]

**Sprite**, sprīt, *n.* a *spirit* : a shade : a ghost.

**Sprout**, sprowt, *n.* a germ or young shoot :—*pl.* young shoots from old cabbages.—*v.i.* to shoot : to push out new shoots. [M. E. *sprute*—A.S. *spreotan* (Ger. *spriessen*) ; cog. with Dut. *spruit*. Cf. **Sprit** and **Spruce-beer**.]

**Spruce**, sprōōs, *adj.* smart : neat.—*adv.* **Spruce'ly**. —*n.* **Spruce'ness**. [Prob. from O. Fr. *preus* (Fr. *preux*), gallant.]

**Spruce-beer**, sprōōs'-bēr, *n.*, *beer* flavoured with a decoction of the young *shoots* of the spruce-fir. [Ger. *sprossen-bier* (lit. ' *beer* made of *sprouts*') —*sprossen*, young shoots of trees—*spriesszen*, E. **Sprout**.]

**Spruce-fir**, sprōōs'-fèr, *n.* a genus of firs whose shoots were used for making *spruce*-beer. [See above word.]

**Sprung**, *pa.t.* and *pa.p.* of **Spring**.

**Spud**, spud, *n.* a narrow spade with a short handle. [From root of **Spade**.]

**Spue**. Same as **Spew**.

**Spume**, spūm, *n.* scum or froth *spewed* or thrown up by liquids : foam.—*v.i.* to throw up scum : to foam. [L. *spuma*—*spuo*, E. **Spew**.]

**Spumous**, spūm'us, **Spumy**, spūm'i, *adj.* consisting of *spume* or froth : frothy : foamy.

**Spun**, *pa.t.* and *pa.p.* of **Spin**.

**Spunk**, spungk, *n.* a piece of wood easily set on fire. [Prob. the same word as *spunge*, **Sponge** ; cf. Ir. *sponc*, tinder, sponge.]

**Spur**, spur, *n.* an instrument on a horseman's heels, with sharp points for goading the horse : that which goads or instigates : something projecting : the hard projection on a cock's leg : a small range of mountains extending laterally from a larger range.—*v.t.* to urge on with spurs : to urge onward : to impel : to put spurs on.—*v.i.* to press forward : to travel in great haste :—*pr.p.* spurr'ing ; *pa.t.* and *pa.p.* spurred. [A.S. *spura*, *spora* ; Ice. *spori*, Ger. *spor-n* ; akin to **Spar** and **Spear**.]

**Spurge**, spurj, *n.* a class of acrid plants with a milky juice, used for taking off warts. [O. Fr. *espurge* (Fr. *épurge*)—L. *expurgare*, to purge— *ex*, off, *purgo*, to clear. See **Purge**.]

**Spurious**, spūr'i-us, *adj.* illegitimate : bastard : not genuine : false.—*adv.* **Spur'iously**.—*n.* **Spur'iousness**. [L. *spurius*.]

**Spurn**, spurn, *v.t.* to drive away as with the foot : to kick : to reject with disdain.—*n.* disdainful rejection. [A.S. *spurnan*, an extension of **Spur**.]

**Spurt**, spurt, *v.t.* to spout, or send out in a sudden stream, as water.—*v.i.* to gush out suddenly in a small stream : to flow out forcibly or at intervals. —*n.* a sudden or violent gush of a liquid from an opening : a jet : a sudden and short effort. [Like **Spirt**, formed by transposition from *sprit* (Ger. *spritzen*), conn. with **Sprit** and **Sprout**.]

**Spur-wheel**, spur'-hwēl, *n.* (*mech.*) a *wheel* with the cogs on the face of the edge like a *spur*.

**Sputter**, sput'er, *v.i.* to *spit* in small drops, as in rapid speaking : to throw out moisture in scattered drops : to speak rapidly and indistinctly. —*v.t.* to throw out with haste and noise : to utter hastily and indistinctly.—*n.* moist matter thrown out in particles. [Like **Spatter**, from the stem of **Spit** and **Spout**.]

**Spy**, spī, *n.* one sent into an enemy's country or camp to find out their strength, &c. : one who keeps a watch on others : one who secretly conveys information.—*v.t.* to see : to discover, generally at a distance : to discover by close search : to inspect secretly :—*pa.t.* and *pa.p.* spied. [O. Fr. *espie*—O. Fr. *speha* ; cog. with L. *specio*, Sans. *spac*.] [telescope.

**Spyglass**, spī'glas, *n.* a *glass* for *spying* : a small

**Squabble**, skwob'l, *v.i.* to dispute in a noisy manner : to wrangle.—*n.* a noisy, petty quarrel : a brawl.—*n.* **Squabb'ler**. [Akin to Low Ger. *kabbeln*, to quarrel, and Prov. Ger. *schwabbeln*, to jabber.]

**Squad**, skwod, *n.* a small body of men assembled for drill. [Fr. *escouade* (It. *squadra*)—L. *exquadrare*, to make square. See **Squadron**.]

**Squadron**, skwod'run, *n.* a body of cavalry, consisting of two troops, or 120 to 200 men : a section of a fleet, commanded by a flag-officer. [Orig. a *square* of troops, Fr. *escouade* (It. *squadra*). See **Square**.]

**Squalid**, skwol'id, *adj.*, *stiff* with dirt : filthy.— *adv.* **Squal'idly**.—*n.* **Squal'idness**. [L. *squalidus*—*squaleo*, to be stiff ; akin to Gr. *skellō*, to dry.]

**Squall**, skwawl, *v.i.* to cry out violently.—*n.* a loud cry or scream : a violent gust of wind. [Ice. *svala* ; Ir. and Gael. *sgal*, to shriek ; an imitative word ; cf. **Squeal**.]

**Squally**, skwawl'i, *adj.* abounding or disturbed with *squalls* or gusts of wind : gusty.

**Squalor**, skwol'or, *n.* state of being *squalid*: dirtiness: filthiness. [L.]

**Squander**, skwon'dėr, *v.t.* to spend lavishly or wastefully.—*n.* **Squan'derer**. [Ety. dub.; perh. a nasalised form of Prov. E. *squatter*, to splash, to disperse; allied to E. **Scatter**.]

**Square**, skwār, *adj.* having *four* equal sides and angles: forming a right angle: having a straight front or an outline formed by straight lines.— *n.* that which is square: a square figure: a four-sided space inclosed by houses: a square body of troops: the length of the side of any figure squared: an instrument for measuring right angles: (*arith.*) the product of a quantity multiplied by itself.—*v.t.* to form like a square: to form with four equal sides and angles: (*arith.*) to multiply by itself: (*naut.*) to place at right angles with the keel.—*n.* **Square'ness**. [O. Fr. esquarre (Fr. équerre)—L. *ex-quadrare*, to square—*quadrus*, conn. with *quattuor*, four. Cf. **Squad** and **Quarry**.]

**Squash**, skwosh, *v.t.* to beat or press into pulp: to crush flat.—*n.* a sudden fall or shock of soft bodies: anything soft and easily crushed, anything soft or unripe. [Conn. with **Quash**.]

**Squat**, skwot, *v.i.* to sit down upon the hams or heels: to cower, as an animal: to settle on new land without title:—*pr.p.* squatt'ing; *pa.t.* and *pa.p.* squatt'ed. [Prov. E. *quat*, to squat; prob. a Romance word; cf. It. *quatto*, cowering, Fr. *(se) cacher*, to crouch down, to hide one's self, both from L. *coactus*, pa.p. of *cogo—co-*, together, and *ago*, to drive.]

**Squatter**, skwot'ėr, *n.* a settler on new land without title: one who leases pasture-land from the government, in Australia and New Zealand. [See **Squat**.]

**Squaw**, skwaw, *n.* (*in America*) an Indian woman, *esp.* a wife.

**Squeak**, skwēk, *v.i.* to utter a shrill and usually short cry.—*n.* a sudden, shrill cry. [Imitative; cf. Sw. *sqväka*, to croak, Ger. *quieken*, to squeak.]

**Squeal**, skwēl, *v.i.* to utter a shrill and prolonged sound. [Imitative; cf. Sw. *sqväla*, to cry out.]

**Squeamish**, skwēm'ish, *adj.* sickish at stomach: easily disgusted or offended: fastidious in taste. —*adv.* **Squeam'ishly**.—*n.* **Squeam'ishness**. [Akin to Ice. *sveim-r*, stir, Ger. *schweim-en*, to become giddy or faint, conn. with **Swim**; prob. also influenced by *qualmish* (see **Qualm**).]

**Squeeze**, skwēz, *v.t.* to crush or press between two bodies: to embrace closely: to force through a small hole: to cause to pass.—*v.i.* to push between close bodies: to press: to crowd.—*n.* act of squeezing: pressing between bodies. [M. E. *queisen*—A.S. *cwisan*; akin to Ger. *quetschen*.]

**Squib**, skwib, *n.* a paper tube filled with combustibles, thrown up into the air burning and bursting: a petty lampoon. [Ety. unknown.]

**Squill**, skwil, *n.* a genus of plants (including the bluebell) allied to the lily, an African species of which is used in medicine. [Fr. *squille*—L. *squilla, scilla*—Gr. *skilla*.]

**Squint**, skwint, *adj.* looking obliquely: having the vision distorted.—*v.i.* to look obliquely: to have the vision distorted.—*v.t.* to cause to squint.— *n.* act or habit of squinting: an oblique look: distortion of vision. [Prob. allied to Dut. *schuin*, oblique; cf. **Wink**, and Fr. *guigner*, to squint.]

**Squire**, skwīr, *n.* Short for **Esquire**.

**Squirrel**, skwir'el, *n.* a nimble, reddish-brown, rodent animal with a bushy tail. [Lit. 'shadow-tail,' O. Fr. *esquirel* (Fr. *écureuil*)—Low L.

*scuriolus*, dim. of L. *sciurus*—Gr. *skiouros—skia*, shade, *oura*, tail.]

**Squirt**, skwėrt, *v.t.* to throw out water in a stream from a narrow opening.—*n.* a small instrument for squirting: a small, quick stream. [Allied to Low Ger. *swirtjen*, O. Sw. *squättra*, to scatter. Cf. **Squander**.]

**Stab**, stab, *v.t.* to wound with a pointed weapon: to wound: to injure secretly, or by falsehood or slander.—*v.i.* to give a stab or a mortal wound: —*pr.p.* stabb'ing; *pa.t.* and *pa.p.* stabbed.—*n.* a wound with a pointed weapon: an injury given secretly. [Orig. 'to pierce with a *staff* or stake.' See **Staff**.]

**Stability**, sta-bil'i-ti, *n.* state of being *stable*: firmness: steadiness: immovability. [Fr.—L.]

**Stable**, stā'bl, *adj.* that *stands* firm: firmly established: durable: firm in purpose or character: constant.—*adv.* **Sta'bly**.—*n.* **Sta'bleness**. [Fr.—L. *stabilis—sto*, E. **Stand**.]

**Stable**, stā'bl, *n.* a building for horses and cattle. —*v.t.* to put or keep in a stable.—*v.i.* to dwell in a stable. [O. Fr. *estable* (Fr. *étable*)—L. *stabulum—sto*, E. **Stand**.]

**Stabling**, stā'bling, *n.* act of putting into a *stable*: accommodation for horses and cattle.

**Stablish**, stab'lish, *v.t.* old form of **Establish**.

**Staccato**, stak-kä'to, *adj.* (*mus.*) giving a clear *distinct* sound to each note. [It., from *staccare*, for *distaccare*, to separate, from root of **Tack**.]

**Stack**, stak, *n.* (*lit.*) that which *sticks* out: a large pile of hay, corn, wood, &c.: a number of chimneys standing together.—*v.t.* to pile into a stack or stacks. [Dan. *stak*, Ice. *stak-r*; conn. with **Stake**, **Stick**, and **Stock**.]

**Stackyard**, stak'yärd, *n.* a *yard* for *stacks*.

**Stadium**, stā'di-um, *n.* a Greek measure of length = 606¾ English feet:—*pl.* **Sta'dia**. [L.—Gr. *stadion*.]

**Staff**, staf, *n.* a stick carried for support or defence: a prop: a long piece of wood: pole: a flagstaff: the long handle of an instrument: a stick or ensign of authority: the five lines and spaces for music: a stanza (the previous meanings have *pl.* **Staffs** or **Staves**, stāvz): an establishment of officers acting together in an army, esp. that attached to the commander: a similar establishment of persons in any undertaking (the last two meanings have *pl.* **Staffs**, stafs). [A.S. *stæf*; cog. with Ice. *staf-r*, Ger. *stab*.]

**Stag**, stag, *n.* the *male* deer, esp. one of the red deer.—*fem.* **Hind**. [Ice. *stegg-r*, a male bird, Yorkshire *steg*, a gander, Scot. *stag, staig*, a young horse; prob. from root *stig*, to mount.]

**Stage**, stāj, *n.* an elevated platform, esp. in a theatre: theatre: theatrical representations: any place of exhibition or performance: a place of rest on a journey or road: distance between places: degree of progress. [O. Fr. *estage* (Fr. *étage*), a story of a house, through a L. form *staticus*, from *sto*, E. **Stand**.]

**Stagecoach**, stāj'kōch, *n.* a *coach* that runs regularly with passengers from *stage* to *stage*.

**Stage-player**, stāj'-plā'ėr, *n.* a *player* on the *stage*.

**Stagger**, stag'ėr, *v.i.* to reel from side to side: to begin to give way: to begin to doubt: to hesitate.—*v.t.* to 'cause to reel': to cause to doubt or hesitate: to shock. [Ice. *stakra*, to totter, O. Dut. *staggeren*.]

**Staggers**, stag'ėrz, *n.* a disease of horses.

**Staghound**, stag'hownd, *n.* a *hound* used in hunting the *stag* or deer.

**Staging**, stāj′ing, *n.* a *stage* or structure for workmen in building.

**Stagnant**, stag′nant, *adj.*, *stagnating*: not flowing: motionless: impure from being motionless: not brisk: dull.—*adv.* **Stag′nantly.** [L. *stagnans*, *-antis*, pr.p. of *stagno*. See **Stagnate**.]

**Stagnate**, stag′nāt, *v.i.* to cease to flow: to become dull or motionless. [L. *stagno*, *stagnatus—stagnum*, a pool.]

**Stagnation**, stag-nā′shun, *n.* act of *stagnating*: state of being stagnant or motionless: dullness.

**Staid**, stād, *adj.* steady: sober: grave.—*adv.* **Staid′ly.**—*n.* **Staid′ness.** [From **Stay**.]

**Stain**, stān, *v.t.* to tinge or colour: to give a different colour to: to dye: to mark with guilt or infamy: to bring reproach on: to sully: to tarnish.—*n.* a discoloration: a spot: taint of guilt: cause of reproach: shame. [Short for **Distain**.]

**Stainless**, stān′les, *adj.* without or free from *stain*.

**Stair**, stār, *n.* (*orig.*) a series of steps for ascending to a higher level: one of such steps: a flight of steps, only in *pl.* [A.S. *stæger—stigan*, to ascend, Ger. *steigen*, Ice. *stigi*, a ladder. See **Stile**, a step, and **Sty**.]

**Staircase**, stār′kās, *n.* a *case* or flight of *stairs* with balusters, &c.

**Stake**, stāk, *n.* a strong *stick* pointed at one end: one of the upright pieces of a fence: a post to which an animal is tied, esp. that to which a martyr was tied to be burned: martyrdom: anything pledged in a wager.—*v.t.* to fasten, or pierce with a stake: to mark the bounds of with stakes: to wager: to hazard. [A.S. *staca —stecan*. See **Stick**.]

**Stalactic**, sta-lak′tik, **Stalactitic**, sta-lak-tit′ik, *adj.* having the form or properties of a *stalactite*.

**Stalactite**, sta-lak′tīt, *n.* a cone of carbonate of lime, hanging like an icicle, in a cavern, formed by the *dripping* of water containing carbonate of lime. [Fr.—Gr. *stalaktos*, dropping—*stalazō*, to drip, to drop.]

**Stalagmite**, sta-lag′mīt, *n.* a cone of carbonate of lime on the floor of a cavern, formed by the *dripping* of water from the roof. [Fr.—Gr. *stalagmos*, a dropping—*stalazō*, to drip.]

**Stalagmitic**, sta-lag-mit′ik, *adj.* having the form of *stalagmites*.

**Stale**, stāl, *adj.* too long kept: tainted: vapid or tasteless from age: beer: not new: worn out by age: decayed: no longer fresh: trite.—*n.* **Stale′ness.** [Prov. E. *stale*, conn. with O. Dut. *stel*, old.]

**Stale**, stāl, *v.i.* to make water, as beasts. [Ger. *stallen—stall*, a stable, A.S. *steall* (see **Stall**).]

**Stalk**, stawk, *n.* the stem of a plant: the stem on which a flower or fruit grows: the stem of a quill. [An extension of A.S. *stel* (cf. Ice. *stilkr*, Dan. *stilk*), cog. with Ger. *stiel*, which is allied to, perh. borrowed from, L. *stilus*, a stake, a pale, further conn. with Gr. *stelechos*.]

**Stalk**, stawk, *v.i.* to walk as on stilts: to walk with long, slow steps: to walk behind a stalking-horse: to pursue game by approaching behind covers.—*v.t.* to approach secretly in order to kill, as deer.—*n.* **Stalk′er.** [A.S. *stealcian—stealc*, high, elevated; Dan. *stalke*, to walk with long steps.]

**Stalking-horse**, stawk′ing-hors, *n.* a *horse* behind which a sportsman hides while *stalking* game: a mask or pretence.

**Stall**, stawl, *n.* a place where a horse or other animal *stands* and is fed: a division of a stable for a single animal: a stable: a bench or table on which articles are exposed for sale: the fixed seat of a church dignitary in the choir: a reserved seat in a theatre.—*v.t.* to put or keep in a stall. [A.S. *steall*, Ice. *stall-r*, Ger. *stall*; conn. with Ger. *stellen*, and Gr. *stellō*.]

**Stallage**, stawl′āj, *n.* liberty of erecting *stalls* in a fair or market: rent paid for this liberty.

**Stall-feed**, stawl′-fēd, *v.t.* to *feed* and fatten in a *stall* or stable.

**Stallion**, stal′yun, *n.* a horse not castrated. [Lit. 'a horse kept in the *stall*,' Fr. *estalon* (Fr. *étalon*), through Low L. from O. Ger. *stall* (see **Stall**).]

**Stalwart**, stawl′wart, *adj.* stout: strong: sturdy. [Lit. 'worth stealing,' A.S. *stæl-worth*. See **Steal** and **Worthy**.]

**Stamen**, stā′men, *n.* (*pl.* **Sta′mens**) one of the male organs of a flower which produce the pollen: —*pl.* **Stam′ina**, the principal strength of anything: the firm part of a body which supports the whole. [Lit. 'a thread,' L. *stamen* (pl. *stamina*), the warp in an upright loom, hence, a thread—*sto*, E. **Stand**; like Gr. *stēmōn*, from *stēnai*, to stand.]

**Stammer**, stam′er, *v.i.* to halt in one's speech: to falter in speaking: to stutter.—*v.t.* to utter with hesitation.—*n.* hesitation in speech: defective utterance.—*ns.* **Stamm′erer, Stamm′ering.**—*adv.* **Stamm′eringly.** [A.S. *stamor*, stammering; cog. with Low Ger. *stammern*.]

**Stamp**, stamp, *v.i.* to *step* or plant the foot firmly down.—*v.t.* to strike with the sole of the foot, by thrusting it down: to impress with some mark or figure: to imprint: to fix deeply: to coin: to form: (*B.*) to pound.—*n.* the act of stamping: the mark made by pressing something on a soft body: an instrument for making impressions on other bodies: that which is stamped: an official mark put on things chargeable with duty, as proof that the duty is paid: an instrument for cutting materials into a certain shape by a downward pressure: cast: form: character: a heavy hammer worked by machinery for crushing metal ores.—*ns.* **Stamp′er, Stamp′ing.** [Low Ger. *stampen*, Ice. *stappa*, to stamp; cog. with Gr. *stemph-*, Sans. *stambh*: a nasalised form of **Step**.]

**Stampede**, stam-pēd′, *n.* a sudden fright seizing on large bodies of horses or other cattle, causing them to *stamp* and run: flight caused by panic. [Sp. *estampeda*; from root of **Stamp**.]

**Stanch**, stänsh, *v.t.* to stop the flowing of, as blood.—*v.i.* (*B.*) to cease to flow.—*adj.* constant: trusty: zealous: sound: firm.—*adv.* **Stanch′ly.** —*n.* **Stanch′ness.** [O. Fr. *estanchier* (Fr. *étancher*)—Low L. *stancare*, to stanch—L. *stagno*, *stagnare*, to be or make stagnant. See **Stagnant**.]

**Stanchion**, stan′shun, *n.* an upright iron bar of a window or screen: (*naut.*) an upright beam used as a support. [O. Fr. *estançon—estancer*, to stop, to stay. See **Stencil**.]

**Stand**, stand, *v.i.* to cease to move: to be stationary: to occupy a certain position: to stagnate: to be at rest: to be fixed in an upright position: to have a position or rank: to be in a particular state: to maintain an attitude: to be fixed or firm: to keep one's ground: to remain unimpaired: to endure: to consist: to depend or be supported: to offer one's self as a candidate: to have a certain direction: to hold a course at sea.—*v.t.* to endure: to sustain: to suffer: to abide by:—

*pa.t.* and *pa.p.* stood.—*n.* **Stand'er.**—**Stand against,** to resist :—**by,** to support :—**fast,** to be unmoved :—**for,** to be a candidate for : (*naut.*) to direct the course towards :—**out,** to project :—**to** (*B.*) to agree to :—**up,** to rise from a sitting posture :—**upon** (*B.*) to attack :—**with,** to be consistent. [A.S. *standan,* Goth. *standan,* Ice. *standa,* O. Ger. *stân* (for *stantan*), whence Ger. *stehen;* from a root seen in Gr. *hi-sta-nai,* to place, L. *sta-re,* to stand, Sans. *sthâ.*]

**Stand,** stand, *n.* a place where one *stands* or remains for any purpose : a place beyond which one does not go : an erection for spectators : something on which anything rests : a stop : a difficulty : resistance.—*n.* **Standstill,** a stop.

**Standard,** stand'ard, *n.* that which *stands* or is fixed, as a rule : the upright post of a truss : that which is established as a rule or model : a staff with a flag : an ensign of war : one of the two flags of a cavalry regiment (not dragoons) : (*hort.*) a standing tree, not supported by a wall. —*adj.* according to some standard : legal : usual : having a fixed or permanent value. [A.S.—O. Fr. *estendard* (Fr. *étendard*), which is either from the Teut. root found in Ger. *stehen,* E. **Stand,** or from L. *ex-tendere,* to stretch out.]

**Standing,** stand'ing, *adj.* established : settled : permanent : fixed : stagnant : being erect.—*n.* continuance : existence : place to stand in : position in society.

**Standish,** stand'ish, *n.* a *standing dish* for pen and ink. [**Stand** and **Dish.**]

**Stannary,** stan'ar-i, *adj.* of or relating to *tin mines* or works.—*n.* a tin mine. [L. *stannum,* tin.]                                                           [from *tin.*

**Stannic,** stan'ik, *adj.* pertaining to or procured

**Stanza,** stan'za, *n.* (*poetry*) a series of lines or verses connected with and adjusted to each other : a division of a poem containing every variation of measure in the poem. [It. *stanza,* a stop—L. *stans,* pr.p. of *sto,* to stand.]

**Staple,** stâ'pl, *n.* (*orig.*) a *settled* mart or market : the principal production or industry of a district or country : the principal element : the thread of textile fabrics : unmanufactured material : a loop of iron for holding a pin, bolt, &c.—*adj.* established in commerce : regularly produced for market. [A.S. *stapul* and *staffel,* a prop, a table ; Ger. *stapel,* a heap, mart ; L. *stabilis,* fixed. See **Stable.**]

**Stapler,** stâ'plèr, *n.* a dealer.

**Star,** stär, *n.* one of the bright bodies in the heavens, except the sun and moon : one of the heavenly bodies shining by their own light, and which keep the same relative position in the heavens : a representation of a star worn as a badge of rank or honour : a person of brilliant or attractive qualities : (*print.*) an asterisk (*).—*v.t.* to set with stars : to bespangle.—*v.i.* to shine, as a star : to attract attention :—*pr.p.* starr'ing; *pa.t.* and *pa.p.* starred.—**Star of Bethlehem,** *n.* a garden plant of the lily family, so called from the likeness of its white *star*-like flowers to old drawings of the star of Nativity (Matt. ii. 2, 9, 10). [M. E. *sterre*—A.S. *steorra,* cog. with Ger. *stern,* L. *stella* (for *sterula*), Gr. *astèr,* Sans. *stri,* pl. *star-as.*]

**Starboard,** stär'bôrd, *n.* the right-hand side of a ship, to one looking toward the bow.—*adj.* pertaining to or lying on the right side of a ship. [Lit. 'the steering side,' A.S. *steorbord—steoran,* E. **Steer,** and *bord,* a board, the side of a ship. See **Board, Larboard,** and cf. the Ger. *steuerbord.*]

**Starch,** stärch, *adj.* stiff, precise.—*n.* stiffness : formality. [Simply a form of **Stark.**]

**Starch,** stärch, *n.* a glistering white powder, forming when wet a sort of gum much used for *stiffening* cloth.—*v.t.* to stiffen with starch.—*n.* **Starch'er.** [Lit. 'that which makes *stark* or stiff;' a special use of the *adj.* **Stark**; cf. Ger. *stärke,* starch—*stark,* strong.]

**Star-chamber,** stär'-chäm'bėr, *n.* a tribunal with a civil and criminal jurisdiction, which met in the old council chamber of the palace of Westminster, abolished in the reign of Charles I. [Said to have been so named either from the gilt stars on the ceiling, or from the Jewish bonds (called *starrs,* from Heb. *shetar*) which were kept in the room where the council met.]

**Starched,** stärcht, *adj.* stiffened with *starch*: stiff: formal.—*adv.* **Starch'edly.**—*n.* **Starch'edness.**                                        [stiff: precise.

**Starchy,** stärch'i, *adj.* consisting of or like *starch*:

**Stare,** stär, *v.i.* to look at with a *fixed* gaze, as in horror, astonishment, &c. : to look fixedly.—*v.t.* to influence by gazing.—*n.* a fixed look. [A.S. *starian,* from a Teut. root seen in Ger. *starr,* fixed, rigid ; also in E. **Stern.**]

**Starfish,** stär'fish, *n.* a marine animal usually in the form of a five-rayed *star.*

**Star-gazer,** stär'-gäz'ėr, *n.* one who *gazes* at the *stars:* an astrologer : an astronomer.

**Stark,** stärk, *adj.,* *stiff*: gross : absolute : entire. —*adv.* absolutely : completely.—*adv.* **Stark'ly.** [A.S. *stearc,* hard, strong, cog. with Ice. *sterk-r,* Ger. *stark.* Doublet **Starch.**]

**Starling,** stär'ling, *n.* a bird about the size of the blackbird : (*arch.*) a ring of piles supporting the pier of a bridge. [Formed as a dim. from the obs. *stare*—A.S. *stär,* cog. with Ger. *staar,* L. *stur-nus,* Gr. *psar.*]

**Starred,** stärd, *adj.* adorned or studded with *stars.*

**Starry,** stär'i, *adj.* abounding or adorned with *stars:* consisting of or proceeding from the stars : like or shining like the stars.—*n.* **Starr'iness.**

**Start,** stärt, *v.i.* to move suddenly aside : to wince : to deviate : to begin.—*v.t.* to cause to move suddenly : to disturb suddenly : to rouse suddenly from concealment : to set in motion : to call forth : to invent or discover : to move suddenly from its place : to loosen : to empty : to pour out.—*n.* a sudden movement : a sudden motion of the body : a sudden rousing to action : an unexpected movement : a sally : a sudden fit : a quick spring : the first motion from a point or place : the outset. [Ice. *sterta;* closely akin to Dut. and Low Ger. *storten,* to plunge, Ger. *stürzen.*]

**Startle,** stärt'l, *v.i.* to start or move suddenly : to feel sudden alarm.—*v.t.* to excite suddenly : to shock : to frighten.—*n.* sudden alarm or surprise. [Extension of **Start.**]

**Starvation,** stär-vä'shun, *n.* act of *starving:* state of being starved.

**Starve,** stärv, *v.i.* to die of hunger or cold : to suffer extreme hunger or want : to be in want of anything necessary.—*v.t.* to kill with hunger or cold : to destroy by want : to deprive of power. [A.S. *steorfan,* cog. with Dut. *sterven,* Ger. *sterben,* to die, orig. prob. 'to work one's self to death,' the Ice. *starf,* work, pains, and *starfa,* to work, to take pains, being from the same root.]

**Starveling,** stärv'ling, *adj.* hungry : lean : weak. —*n.* a thin, weak, pining animal or plant. [See **Starve.**]

**State,** stät, *n.* position : condition : situation : circumstances at any time : the whole body of people under one government : the public : the civil power : estate, one of the orders or classes of men forming the body politic (as nobles, clergy, commonalty) : a body of men united by profession : rank, quality : pomp : dignity : —*pl.* the bodies constituting the legislature of a country.—*adj.* belonging to the state : public : royal : ceremonial : pompous : magnificent.—*v.t.* to set forth : to express the details of : to set down fully and formally : to narrate : to set in order : to settle. [Lit. 'a standing,' O. Fr. *estat* (Fr. *état*)—L. *status*, from *sto, statum*, E. **Stand.**]

**Stated**, stāt'ed, *adj., settled* : established : fixed : regular.—*adv.* **Stat'edly.**

**Stately**, stāt'li, *adj.* showing *state* or dignity : majestic : grand.—*n.* **State'liness.**

**Statement**, stāt'ment, *n.* the act of stating : that which is stated : a narrative or recital.

**State-paper**, stāt'-pā'pėr, *n.* an official *paper* or document relating to affairs of *state.*

**State-prisoner**, stāt'-priz'n-ėr, *n.* a *prisoner* confined for offences against the *state.*

**Stateroom**, stāt'rōōm, *n.* a *stately room* in a palace or mansion : principal room in the cabin of a ship.

**Statesman**, stāts'man, *n.* a *man* acquainted with the affairs of the *state* or of government : one skilled in government : one employed in public affairs : a politician.—*n.* **States'manship.**

**Statesmanlike**, stāts'man-līk, *adj., like* a *statesman.*

**Static**, stat'ik, **Statical**, stat'ik-al, *adj.* pertaining to *statics* : pertaining to bodies at rest or in equilibrium : resting : acting by mere weight.

**Statics**, stat'iks, *n.* the science which treats of the action of force in maintaining rest or preventing change of motion. [Gr. *statikē* (*epistēmē*, science, being understood)—*histēmi*, cog. with E. **Stand.**]

**Station**, stā'shun, *n.* the place where a person or thing *stands* : post assigned : position : office : situation : occupation : business : state : rank : condition in life : the place where railway trains come to a stand : a district or branch police-office.—*v.t.* to assign a station to : to set : to appoint to a post, place, or office. [Lit. 'a standing,' Fr.—L. *statio—sto.* See **Stand.**]

**Stationary**, stā'shun-ar-i, *adj.* pertaining to a *station* : *standing* : fixed : settled : acting from or in a fixed position (as an engine) : not progressing or retrogressing : not improving.

**Stationer**, stā'shun-ėr, *n.* one who sells paper and other articles used in writing. [Orig. a bookseller, from occupying a *stall* or *station* in a market-place.]

**Stationery**, stā'shun-ėr-i, *adj.* belonging to a stationer.—*n.* the articles sold by stationers.

**Statist**, stā'tist, *n.* a statesman, a politician.

**Statistic**, sta-tist'ik, **Statistical**, sta-tist'ik-al, *adj.* pertaining to or containing *statistics.*—*adv.* **Statist'ically.** [science of *statistics.*

**Statistician**, stat-ist-ish'an, *n.* one skilled in the

**Statistics**, sta-tist'iks, *n.* a collection of facts and figures regarding the condition of a people, class, &c. : the science which treats of the collection and arrangement of statistics. [Coined (as if from a form *statistikē*) from the Gr. *statizō*, to set up, establish.]

**Statuary**, stat'ū-ar-i, *n.* the art of carving *statues* : a statue or a collection of statues : one who makes statues : one who deals in statues. [L. *statuarius.*]

**Statue**, stat'ū, *n.* a likeness of a living being carved out of some solid substance : an image. [Lit. 'that which is made to stand or is set up,' Fr.—L. *statua—statuo*, to cause to stand—*sto.*]

**Statuesque**, stat-ū-esk', *adj.* like a *statue.* [Fr.]

**Statuette**, stat-ū-et', *n.* a small *statue.* [Fr.]

**Stature**, stat'ūr, *n.* the height of any animal. [L. *statura.*]

**Status**, stā'tus, *n., state* : condition : rank. [L.]

**Statutable**, stat'ūt-a-bl, *adj.* made by *statute* : according to statute.—*adv.* **Stat'utably.**

**Statute**, stat'ūt, *n.* a law expressly enacted by the legislature (as distinguished from a customary law or law of use and wont) : a written law : the act of a corporation or its founder, intended as a permanent rule or law. [L. *statutum*, that which is *set up—statuo.*]

**Statutory**, stat'ūt-or-i, *adj.* enacted by *statute* : depending on statute for its authority. [&c.

**Staunch, Staunchly, Staunchness.** See **Stanch.**

**Stave**, stāv, *n.* one of the pieces of which a cask is made : a staff or part of a piece of music : a stanza.—*v.t.* to break a stave or the staves of : to break : to burst : to drive off, as with a staff : to delay :—*pa.t.* and *pa.p.* stāved or stōve. [By-form of **Stab** and **Staff.**]

**Stay**, stā, *v.i.* to remain : to abide for any time : to continue in a state : to wait : to cease acting : to dwell : to trust.—*v.t.* to cause to stand : to stop : to restrain : to delay : to prevent from falling : to prop : to support :—*pa.t.* and *pa.p.* staid, stayed.—*n.* continuance in a place : abode for a time : stand : stop : a fixed state : (*B.*) a stand-still : prop : support : (*naut.*) a large strong rope running from the head of one mast to another mast ('fore-and-aft' stay), or to the side of the ship ('back '-stay) :—*pl.* a kind of stiff inner waistcoat worn by women. [O. Fr. *esteir* —L. *stare*, to stand.]

**Stead**, sted, *n.* the place which another had or might have. [Lit. 'a standing-place,' A.S. *stede*, from root of **Stand** ; cog. with Ger. *statt.*]

**Steadfast**, sted'fast, *adj.* firmly fixed or established : firm : constant : resolute : steady.—*adv.* **Stead'fastly.**—*n.* **Stead'fastness.**

**Steady**, sted'i, *adj.* (*comp.* **Stead'ier**, *superl.* **Stead'iest**), *firm in standing* or in place : fixed : stable : constant : resolute : consistent : regular : uniform.—*adv.* **Stead'ily.**—*n.* **Stead'iness.**

**Steady**, sted'i, *v.t.* to make *steady* : to make or keep firm :—*pa.t.* and *pa.p.* stead'ied.

**Steak**, stāk, *n.* a slice of meat (esp. beef) broiled, or for broiling. [M. E. *steike*, prob. from Ice. *steik, steikja*, to broil.]

**Steal**, stēl, *v.t.* to take by theft, or feloniously : to take away without notice : to gain or win by address or by gradual means.—*v.i.* to practise theft : to take feloniously : to pass secretly : to slip in or out unperceived :—*pa.t.* stōle ; *pa.p.* stōl'en.—*n.* **Steal'er.** [A.S. *stelan* ; cog. with Ger *stehlen* ; further conn. with Gr. *stereo,* to rob, Sans. *stēnas,* a thief.]

**Stealth**, stelth, *n.* the act of *stealing* : a secret manner of bringing anything to pass.

**Stealthy**, stelth'i, *adj.* done by *stealth* : unperceived : secret.—*adv.* **Stealth'ily.**—*n.* **Stealth'iness.**

**Steam**, stēm, *n.* the vapour into which water is changed when heated to the boiling-point, water in the gaseous state : the mist formed by condensed vapour : any exhalation.—*v.i.* to rise or pass off in steam or vapour : to move by steam. —*v.t.* to expose to steam. [A.S. *steam* ; cog. with Dut. *stoom*, Fris. *stoame.*]

**Steamboat**, stēm'bōt, **Steamship**, stēm'ship, **Steam-vessel**, stēm'-ves'el, *n.* a *boat, ship,* or *vessel* propelled by *steam.*

**Steam-engine**, stēm'-en'jin, *n.* an *engine* or

machine which changes heat into useful work through the medium of *steam*.

**Steamer**, stēm′ér, *n.* a vessel moved by *steam*: a vessel in which articles are steamed.

**Steamy**, stēm′i, *adj.* consisting of or like *steam*: full of steam or vapour.

**Stearine**, stē′a-rin, *n.* the solid substance of beef and mutton suet. [Gr. *stear*, *steatos*, suet—*stēnai*, aorist inf. of *histēmi*, to make to stand.]

**Steatite**, stē′a-tīt, *n.* soapstone, a soft magnesian rock, soapy and unctuous to the touch. [Gr. *steatites*—*stear*. See Stearine.]

**Steed**, stēd, *n.* a horse or stallion, esp. a spir′ted horse. [A.S. *steda*, from the root of Stan.l.]

**Steel**, stēl, *n.* iron combined with carbon for making edged tools: any instrument of steel: an instrument of steel for sharpening knives on: extreme hardness: a chalybeate medicine.—*adj.* made of steel.—*v.t.* to overlay or edge with steel: to harden: to make obdurate. [A.S. *styl*; cog. with Ice. *stal*, Ger. *stahl*.]

**Steelyard**, stil′yärd, *n.* a weighing machine, in which a single weight is moved along a graduated beam. [Orig. the *yard* in London where *steel* was sold by German merchants.]

**Steep**, stēp, *adj.* rising or descending with great inclination: precipitous.—*n.* a precipitous place: a precipice.—*adv.* Steep′ly.—*n.* Steep′ness.—Steep′en, *v.i.* to become steep. [A.S. *steap*.]

**Steep**, stēp, *v.t.* to dip or soak in a liquid: to imbue.—*n.* something steeped or used in steeping: a fertilising liquid for seed. [M. E. *stopen*; prob. conn. with Steep, *adj.*]

**Steeple**, stēp′l, *n.* a tower of a church or building, ending in a point. [A.S. *stepel*; conn. with Steep, *adj.*, and with Staple.]

**Steeplechase**, stēp′l-chās, *n.* a chase or race, over all obstacles, direct toward a distant object, orig. a *steeple*.

**Steer**, stēr, *n.* a young ox, esp. a castrated one from two to four years old. [A.S. *steor*; Ger. *stier*; akin to L. *taurus*, Gr. *tauros*, Sans. *sthūra*, Ice. *thior*, Celt. *tarbh*.]

**Steer**, stēr, *v.t.* to direct with the helm: to guide: to govern.—*v.i.* to direct a ship in its course: to be directed: to move. [A.S. *steoran*; cog. with Ger. *steuern*, Ice. *styra*, to guide.]

**Steerage**, stēr′āj, *n.* act or practice of *steering*: the effect of a rudder on the ship: an apartment in the forepart of a ship for passengers paying a lower rate of fare.

**Steersman**, stērz′man, *n.* a *man* who *steers* a ship.

**Stellar**, stel′ar, **Stellary**, stel′ar-i, *adj.* relating to the *stars*: starry. [L. *stellaris*—*stella*, a star.] [*star*: radiated.

**Stellate**, stel′āt, **Stellated**, stel′āt-ed, *adj.* like a

**Stellular**, stel′ū-lar, *adj.* formed like *little stars*: [From L. *stellula*, dim. of *stella*, a star.]

**Stellulate**, stel′ū-lāt, *adj.* (*bot.*) like a *little star*.

**Stem**, stem, *n.* the part of a tree between the ground and the branches: the little branch supporting the flower or fruit: a race or family: branch of a family. [A.S. *stefn*, *stemm*, cog. with Ger. *stamm*. The root is found in A.S. *stæf*, Ger. *stab*; see Staff.]

**Stem**, stem, *n.* the prow of a ship: a curved piece of timber at the prow to which the two sides of a ship are united.—*v.t.* to cut, as with the stem: to resist or make progress against: to stop, to check:—*pr.p.* stemm′ing; *pa.t.* and *pa.p.* stemmed. [Same word as above, the trunk of a tree forming the forepart of a primitive ship.]

**Stench**, stensh, *n.*, *stink*: bad odour or smell. [A.S. *stenc*; Ger. *stank*. See Stink.]

**Stencil**, sten′sil, *n.* a plate of metal, &c. with a pattern cut out, which is impressed upon a surface by drawing a brush with colour over it.—*v.t.* to print or paint by means of a stencil:—*pr.p.* sten′cilling; *pa.t.* and *pa.p.* sten′cilled. [O. Fr. *estance* (Fr. *étançon*), a support—Low L. *stantia*—L. *sto*, E. Stand.]

**Stenography**, sten-og′ra-fi, *n.* art of *writing* very quickly by means of *abbreviations*: shorthand.—*n.* Stenog′rapher.—*adjs.* Stenograph′ic, Stenograph′ical. [Gr. *stenos*, narrow, and *graphō*, to write.]

**Stentorian**, sten-tō′ri-an, *adj.* very loud or powerful, like the voice of *Stentor*, a herald mentioned by Homer. [L. *stentoreus*—Gr.—*Stentōr*, Stentor.]

**Step**, step, *n.* a pace: the distance crossed by the foot in walking or running: a small space: degree: one remove in ascending or descending a stair: round of a ladder: footprint: manner of walking: proceeding: action:—*pl.* walk: a self-supporting ladder with flat steps.—*v.i.* to advance or retire by pacing: to walk: to walk slowly or gravely.—*v.t.* to set, as a foot: to fix as a mast:—*pr.p.* step′ping; *pa.t.* and *pa.p.* stepped. [A.S. *stæpe*; Ger. *stapfe*.]

**Step-child**, step′-chīld, *n.* one who stands in the relation of a child through the marriage of a parent. [A.S. *steop*, Ger. *stief*, orig. an adj. sig. *bereft*, and Child.]—So **Step′-broth′er**, **Step′-daugh′ter**, **Step′-fa′ther**, **Step′-moth′er**, **Step′-sis′ter**, **Step′-son**.

**Steppe**, step, *n.* one of the vast uncultivated plains in the S.E. of Europe and in Asia. [Russ. *stepj*.]

**Stepping-stone**, step′ing-stōn, *n.* a *stone* for *stepping* on to raise the feet above the water or mud.

**Stereographic**, ster-e-o-graf′ik, **Stereographical**, ster-e-o-graf′ik-al, *adj.* pertaining to *stereography*: made according to stereography: delineated on a plane.—*adv.* Stereograph′ically.

**Stereography**, ster-e-og′ra-fi, *n.* the art of *showing solids* on a plane. [Gr. *stereos*, hard, solid, and *graphō*, to write.]

**Stereoscope**, ster′e-o-skōp, *n.* an optical contrivance by which two flat pictures of the same object are *seen* having an appearance of *solidity* and reality.—*n.* Stereos′copy. [Gr. *stereos*, solid, and *skopeō*, to see.]

**Stereoscopic**, ster-e-o-skop′ik, **Stereoscopical**, ster-e-o-skop′ik-al, *adj.* pertaining to the *stereoscope*.

**Stereotype**, ster′e-o-tīp, *n.* a *solid* metallic plate for printing, cast from an impression of movable *types*, taken on some plastic substance: art of making or printing with such plates.—*adj.* pertaining to or done with stereotypes.—*v.t.* to make a stereotype of: to print with stereotypes. [Gr. *stereos*, solid, and Type.]

**Stereotyper**, ster′e-o-tīp-ér, *n.* one who makes *stereotype* plates.

**Sterile**, ster′il, *adj.* unfruitful: barren: destitute of ideas or sentiment. [Fr.—L. *sterilis*, akin to Gr. *stereos*, hard, and to *steira*, a barren cow, Sans. *stari*.]

**Sterility**, ster-il′i-ti, *n.* quality of being *sterile*: unfruitfulness: barrenness.

**Sterling**, stėr′ling, *adj.* a designation of British money: pure: genuine: of good quality. [Orig. the name of a penny; prob. from the *Easterlings*, the early E. name for the merchants from North Germany, noted for the purity of their money, and said to have perfected the British coin.]

**Stern**, stėrn, *adj.* severe of countenance, manner,

or feeling : austere : harsh : unrelenting : stead-fast.—*adv.* **Stern'ly.**—*n.* **Stern'ness.** [Orig. 'rigid,' A.S. *sterne*, from the root of **Stare** ; conn. with M. E. *stur*, Scot. *stour*, Ger. *starr*.]

**Stern,** stèrn, *n.* the hindpart of a vessel.—*n.* **Stern'post,** the aftermost timber of a ship that supports the rudder. [Lit. 'the part of a ship where it is *steered* ;' cf. Ice. *stjórn*, a steering.]

**Sternmost,** stèrn'mōst, *adj.* furthest *astern*.

**Sternsheets,** stèrn'shēts, *n.* the part of a boat between the *stern* and the rowers.

**Sternum,** stèr'num, *n.* the breastbone.—*adj.* **Ster'nal.** [L.—Gr. *sternon*, the chest.]

**Sternutatory,** stèr-nū'ta-tor-i, *adj.* that causes *sneezing*.—*n.* a substance that causes sneezing. [From L. *sternuto*, *-atum*, to sneeze.]

**Stertorous,** stèr'to-rus, *adj.*, *snoring*.—*adv.* **Ster'torously.** [Fr. *stertoreux*—L. *sterto*, to snore.]

**Stethoscope,** steth'o-skōp, *n.* the tube used in auscultation. [Lit. 'the chest-examiner,' Gr. *stēthos*, the breast, *skopeō*, to see, examine.]

**Stethoscopic,** steth-o-skop'ik, **Stethoscopical,** steth-o-skop'ik-al, *adj.* pertaining to or performed by the *stethoscope*.

**Stevedore,** stēv'e-dōr, *n.* one whose occupation is to load and unload vessels. [A corr. of Sp. *estivador*, a wool-packer—*estivar*, to stow, to pack wool—L. *stipare*, to press together.]

**Stew,** stū, *v.t.* to boil slowly with little moisture. —*v.i.* to be boiled slowly and gently.—*n.* meat stewed. [Lit. 'to put into a *stove*,' O. Fr. *estuver*, Fr. *étuve*, stove—Low L. *stuba*. See **Stove.**]

**Steward,** stū'ard, *n.* one who manages the domestic concerns of a family or institution : one who superintends another's affairs, esp. an estate or farm : the manager of the provision department, &c. at sea : a manager at races, games, &c. [M. E. *stiward*—A.S. *sti-weard*—*stiga*, E. **Sty,** and **Ward.**]

**Stewardess,** stū'ard-es, *n.* a female steward : a female who waits on ladies on shipboard.

**Stewardship,** stū'ard-ship, *n.* office of a steward : management.

**Stick,** stik, *v.t.* to stab : to thrust in : to fasten by piercing : to fix in : to set with something pointed : to cause to adhere—*v.i.* to hold to : to remain : to stop : to be hindered : to hesitate, to be embarrassed or puzzled : to adhere closely in affection :—*pa.t.* and *pa.p.* **stuck.** [A.S. *stician* ; cog. with Dut. *steken*, Ger. *stechen* ; from the same root as Gr. *stizō.* See **Sting.**]

**Stick,** stik, *n.* a small shoot or branch cut off a tree : a staff or walking-stick : anything in the form of a stick. [A.S. *stycce*, cog. with Ice. *stykki*, Ger. *stück* ; from the root of **Stick,** *v.t.*]

**Stickle,** stik'l, *v.i.* to interpose between combatants : to contend obstinately. [See **Stickler.**]

**Stickleback,** stik'l-bak, *n.* a small river-fish, so called from the *spines* on its *back*. [Prov. E. *stickle*—A.S. *sticel* (dim. of **Stick**), a spine, cog. with Ger. *stachel*, and **Back.**]

**Stickler,** stik'lèr, *n.* a second or umpire in a duel : an obstinate contender, esp. for something trifling. [Orig. one of the seconds in a duel, who were placed with *sticks* or staves to interpose occasionally.]

**Sticky,** stik'i, *adj.* that sticks or adheres : adhesive : glutinous.—*n.* **Stick'iness.**

**Stiff,** stif, *adj.* not easily bent : rigid : not liquid : rather hard than soft : not easily overcome : obstinate : not natural and easy : constrained : formal.—*adv.* **Stiff'ly.**—*n.* **Stiff'ness.** [A.S.

*stif* ; cog. with Ger. *steif* ; prob. conn. with L. *stipo*, to cram.]

**Stiffen,** stif'n, *v.t.* to *make stiff*.—*v.i.* to become stiff : to become less impressible or more obstinate. [obstinate : contumacious.

**Stiff-necked,** stif'-nekt, *adj.* (*lit.*) *stiff* in the *neck* :

**Stifle,** stī'fl, *v.t.* to stop the breath of by foul air or other means : to suffocate : to extinguish : to suppress the sound of : to destroy. [Prob. from **Stiff,** and so 'to make *stiff* ;' but influenced by *stive*, M. E. form of E. **Stew.**]

**Stigma,** stig'ma, *n.* a brand : a mark of infamy : (*bot.*) the top of a pistil :—*pl.* **Stig'mas** or **Stig'-mata.** [Lit. 'the mark of a pointed instrument,' L.—Gr.—root *stig*, to be sharp (Sans. *tig*), seen also in L. *-stinguo*, *-stigo*, and in E. **Stick, Sting.**]

**Stigmata,** stig'ma-ta, *n.* the marks of the wounds on Christ's body, or marks resembling them, said to have been miraculously impressed on the bodies of saints.

**Stigmatic,** stig-mat'ik, **Stigmatical,** stig-mat'ik-al, *adj.* marked or branded with a *stigma*: giving infamy or reproach.—*adv.* **Stigmat'ically.**

**Stigmatise,** stig'ma-tīz, *v.t.* to brand with a *stigma*. [Gr. *stigmatizo*. See **Stigma.**]

**Stile,** stīl, *n.* a *step* or set of steps for *climbing* over a wall or fence. [A.S. *stigel*, a step—*stig-an*, akin to Ger. *steigen*, to mount.]

**Stile,** stīl, *n.* the pin of a dial. Same as **Style.**

**Stiletto,** sti-let'o, *n.* a *little style* or dagger with a round pointed blade : a pointed instrument for making eyelet holes :—*pl.* **Stilett'os.**—*v.t.* to stab with a stiletto :—*pr.p.* stilett'oing ; *pa.t.* and *pa.p.* stilett'oed. [It., dim. of *stilo*, a dagger— L. *stilus*. See **Style.**]

**Still,** stil, *adj.* silent : motionless : calm.—*v.t.* to quiet : to silence : to appease : to restrain.—*adv.* always : nevertheless : after that.—*n.* **Still'ness.** [A.S. *stille*, fixed, firm ; Dut. *stille*, Ger. *still* ; from the root of **Stall.**]

**Still,** stil, *v.t.* to cause to fall by *drops* : to distil. —*n.* an apparatus for distilling liquids. [L. *stillo*, to cause to drop—*stilla*, a drop, or simply a contr. for **Distil**, like **Sport** from **Disport.**]

**Still-born,** stil'-bawrn, *adj.* dead when born.

**Still-life,** stil'-līf, *n.* the class of pictures representing inanimate objects.

**Still-room,** stil'-rōōm, *n.* an apartment where liquors, preserves, and the like, are kept : a housekeeper's pantry.

**Stilly,** stil'i, *adj.*, *still* : quiet : calm.

**Stilly,** stil'li, *adv.* silently : gently.

**Stilt,** stilt, *n.* a *support* of wood with a rest for the foot, used in walking.—*v.t.* to raise on stilts : to elevate by unnatural means. [Low Ger. and Dut. *stelte*, a stilt: Sw. *stylta*, a support.]

**Stimulant,** stim'ū-lant, *adj.*, *stimulating* : increasing or exciting vital action.—*n.* anything that stimulates or excites: a stimulating medicine. [See **Stimulus.**]

**Stimulate,** stim'ū-lāt, *v.t.* to *prick* with anything sharp : to incite : to instigate.—*n.* **Stimula'tion.**

**Stimulative,** stim'ū-lāt-iv, *adj.* tending to *stimulate*.—*n.* that which stimulates or excites.

**Stimulus,** stim'ū-lus, *n.* a goad : anything that rouses the mind, or that excites to action : a stimulant :—*pl.* **Stim'uli.** [L. *stimulus* (for *stig-mulus*)—Gr. *stizō*, to prick. See **Stigma.**]

**Sting,** sting, *v.t.* to stick anything sharp into, to pain acutely :—*pa.t.* and *pa.p.* **stung.**—*n.* the sharp-pointed weapon of some animals : the thrust of a sting into the flesh : anything that causes acute pain : the point in the last verse of an epigram. [A.S. *sting-an*; cog. with Ice. *stinga*, Gr. *stizō*, to prick (whence **Stigma**).]

**Stingy**, stin′ji, *adj.* niggardly : avaricious.—*adv.* **Stin′gily**.—*n.* **Stin′giness.** [Ety. unknown.]

**Stink**, stingk, *v.i.* to *smell* : to give out a strong, offensive smell :—*pa.t.* stank; *pa.p.* stunk.—*n.* a disagreeable smell. [A.S. *stincan*; Ger. *stinken*, to smell.]

**Stinkpot**, stingk′pot, *n.* an earthen jar or *pot* charged with a *stinking*, combustible mixture, and used in boarding an enemy's vessel.

**Stint**, stint, *v.t.* to *shorten* : to limit : to restrain. —*n.* limit : restraint : proportion allotted. [A.S. *astyntan*, from **Stunt**.]

**Stipend**, stī′pend, *n.* a salary paid for services: settled pay. [L. *stipendium—stips* (akin to L. *stipo*, to crowd or press together, and therefore orig. 'small coin in heaps'), a donation, and *pendo*, to weigh out.]

**Stipendiary**, stī-pend′i-ar-i, *adj.* receiving *stipend.* —*n.* one who performs services for a salary.

**Stipulate**, stip′ū-lāt, *v.i.* to contract : to settle terms.—*n.* **Stip′ulator.** [L. *stipulor, -atus,* prob. from O. L. *stipulus,* firm, conn. with *stipo,* to press firm.]      [a contract.

**Stipulation**, stip-ū-lā′shun, *n.* act of *stipulating:*

**Stir**, stėr, *v.t.* to move : to rouse : to instigate.— *v.i.* to move one's self : to be active : to draw notice :—*pr.p.* stirr′ing ; *pa.t.* and *pa.p.* stirred. —*n.* tumult : bustle.—*n.* **Stirr′er.** [A.S. *styrian*; Dut. *storen*, Ger. *stören*, to drive; conn. with **Steer**, *v.*]

**Stirrup**, stir′up, *n.* a ring or hoop suspended by a *rope* or strap from the saddle, for a horseman's foot while *mounting* or riding. [A.S. *stigerap* —*stigan,* to mount, and *rap,* a rope.]

**Stitch**, stich, *n.* a pass of a needle and thread : an acute pain.—*v.t.* to sew so as to show a regular line of stitches : to sew or unite.—*v.i.* to practise stitching. [A.S. *stice,* a prick, stitch ; Ger. *sticken,* to embroider : conn. with **Stick**.]

**Stitchwort**, stich′wurt, *n.* a genus of slender plants, including the chickweed, so called because once believed to cure 'stitch' in the side.

**Stithy**, stith′i, *n.* an *anvil* : a smith's shop. [Ice. *stedhi,* Sw. *stad,* an anvil.]

**Stiver**, stī′vėr, *n.* a Dutch coin, worth one penny sterling. [Dut. *stuiver.*]

**Stoat**, stōt, *n.* a kind of weasel, called the ermine when in its winter dress. [Ety. unknown.]

**Stoccado**, stok-äd′o, *n.* a thrust in fencing. [It. *stoccata,* a thrust—*stocco* a rapier, stake—Ger. *stock,* a stick. See **Stick, Stock**.]

**Stock**, stok, *n.* something *stuck* or thrust in : the stem of a tree or plant : a post : a stupid person : the part to which others are attached : the original progenitor : family : a fund : capital : shares of a public debt : store : cattle :—*pl.* **Stocks,** an instrument in which the legs of criminals are confined : the frame for a ship while building : the public funds.—*v.t.* to store : to supply : to fill. [A.S. *stocc,* a stick ; cog. with Dut. *stoc,* Ger. *stock.* For the root see **Stick**.]

**Stock**, stok, *n.* a favourite garden-flower. [Orig. called stock-gillyflower, to distinguish it from the stemless clove-pink, called the *gillyflower,* which see.]

**Stockade**, stok-ād′, *n.* a breastwork formed of *stakes* fixed in the ground.—*v.t.* to surround or fortify with a stockade. [Fr. *estocade—estoc—* Ger. *stock,* a stick.]

**Stockbroker**, stok′brōk-ėr, *n.* a *broker* who deals in *stock* or shares.

**Stockdove**, stok′duv, *n.* a species of pigeon, be-

lieved at one time to be the *stock* of the tame *dove* : or the *dove* that lives on *trees* or in the woods.

**Stock-exchange**, stok′-eks-chānj′, *n.* the place where *stocks* are *exchanged,* or bought and sold.

**Stockfish**, stok′fish, *n.* a general term for cod, ling, tusk, and other fishes used in a dried state.

**Stockholder**, stok′hold-ėr, *n.* one who *holds stock* in the public funds, or in a company.

**Stocking**, stok′ing, *n.* a close covering for the foot and leg. [Probably a cover for the *stocks* or stumps.]

**Stock-jobbing**, stok′-job′ing, *n., jobbing* or speculating in *stocks.*—*n.* **Stock′-jobb′er.**

**Stock-still**, stok′-stil, *adj.,* *still* as a *stock* or post.

**Stoic**, stō′ik, *n.* a disciple of the ancient philosopher Zeno who taught under a *porch* at Athens : one indifferent to pleasure or pain. [L. *Stoicus* —Gr. *Stōikos—stoa,* a porch.]

**Stoic**, stō′ik, **Stoical**, stō′ik-al, *adj.* pertaining to the *Stoics,* or to their opinions : indifferent to pleasure or pain.—*adv.* **Sto′ically.**—*n.* **Sto′icalness.**

**Stoicism**, stō′i-sizm, *n.* the doctrines of the *Stoics :* indifference to pleasure or pain.

**Stoke**, stōk, *v.i.* to *stick,* stir, or tend a fire.—*n.* **Stok′er.** [From **Stock**.]

**Stole**, stōl, *pa.t.* of **Steal.**

**Stole**, stōl, *n.* a long *robe* or *garment* reaching to the feet : a long, narrow scarf with fringed ends worn by a priest. [A.S. *stol*—L. *stola*—Gr. *stolē,* a robe, a garment—*stellō,* to array.]

**Stolen**, stōl′en, *pa.p.* of **Steal.**

**Stolid**, stol′id, *adj.* dull : heavy : stupid : foolish. [L. *stolidus ;* from a root *star,* seen also in Gr. *stereos,* firm.]

**Stolidity**, sto-lid′i-ti, *n.* state of being *stolid :* dullness of intellect. [L. *stoliditas—stolidus.*]

**Stomach**, stum′ak, *n.* the strong muscular bag into which the food passes when swallowed, and where it is principally digested : the cavity in any animal for the digestion of its food : appetite.—*v.t.* to resent, (*orig.*) to bear on the stomach : to brook or put up with. [L. *stomachus* —Gr. *stomachos,* orig. the throat, gullet ; then, the orifice of the stomach ; and later, the stomach itself—*stoma,* a mouth.]

**Stomacher**, stum′a-chėr, *n.* an ornament or support for the *stomach* or breast, worn by women.

**Stomachic**, sto-mak′ik, **Stomachical**, sto-mak′ik-al, *adj.* pertaining to the *stomach* : strengthening or promoting the action of the stomach.— **Stomach′ic,** *n.* a medicine for the stomach.

**Stone**, stōn, *n.* a hard mass of earthy or mineral matter : a precious stone or gem : a tombstone : a concretion formed in the bladder : a hard shell containing the seed of some fruits : a standard weight of 14 lbs. avoirdupois : torpor and insensibility.—*v.t.* to pelt with stones : to free from stones : to wall with stones.—**Stone′-blind,** *adj.* as blind as a stone, perfectly blind. [A.S. *stan,* cog. with Ger. *stein,* Gr. *stia.*]

**Stonechat**, stōn′chat, **Stonechatter**, stōn-chat′ėr, *n.* a little bird, allied to the robin, so called from its *chattering* and perching on large *stones.*

**Stonecutter**, stōn′kut-ėr, *n.* one whose occupation is to *cut* or hew *stone.*

**Stone-fruit**, stōn′-frōot, *n.* a *fruit* with its seeds inclosed in a *stone* or hard kernel.

**Stone's-cast**, stōnz′-kast, **Stone's-throw**, stōnz′-thrō, *n.* the distance which a *stone* may be *cast* or *thrown* by the hand.

**Stoneware**, stōn′wār, *n.* a coarse kind of potter's *ware* baked as hard as a *stone* and glazed.

**Stony**, stōn'i, *adj.* made of or resembling *stone* : abounding with stones : hard : pitiless : obdurate : (*B.*) rocky.                          [*stod.*]

**Stood**, stood, *pa.t.* and *pa.p.* of **Stand**. [A.S.

**Stool**, stōōl, *n.* a seat without a back : the seat used in evacuating the bowels : the act of evacuating the bowels. [A.S. *stol*, Ger. *stuhl* ; akin to Ger. *stellen*, to set, to place ; also to **Still**, *adj.*, **Stall**, **Stand**.]

**Stoop**, stōōp, *v.i.* to bend the body : to lean forward : to submit : to descend from rank or dignity : to condescend : to swoop down on the wing, as a bird of prey.—*v.t.* to cause to incline downward.—*n.* the act of stooping : inclination forward : descent : condescension : a swoop. [A.S. *stupian* ; O. Dut. *stoepen*, Ice. *stupa* ; akin to **Steep** and **Stop**.]

**Stop**, stop, *v.t.* to stuff or close up : to obstruct : to render impassable : to hinder : to intercept : to restrain : to apply musical stops to : to regulate the sounds of a stringed instrument by shortening the strings with the fingers.—*v.i.* to cease going forwards : to cease from any motion or action : to leave off : to be at an end :—*pr.p.* stopp'ing ; *pa.t.* and *pa.p.* stopped.—*n.* act of *stopping* : state of being stopped : hinderance : obstacle : interruption : (*music*) one of the ventholes in a wind instrument, or the place on the wire of a stringed instrument, by the stopping or pressing of which certain notes are produced : a mark used in punctuation. [Lit. 'to stuff with *tow*,' M. E. *stoppen*—O. Fr. *estouper* (Ice. *stoppa*, Ger. *stopfen*, to stuff) ; all from L. *stupa*, the coarse part of flax, tow.]

**Stopcock**, stop'kok, *n.* a short pipe in a cask, &c. opened and *stopped* by a *cock* or key.

**Stoppage**, stop'āj, *n.* act of *stopping* : state of being stopped : an obstruction.

**Stopper**, stop'ér, *n.* one who *stops* : that which closes a vent or hole, as the cork or glass mouthpiece for a bottle : (*naut.*) a short rope for making something fast.—*v.t.* to close or secure with a stopper.

**Stopple**, stop'l, *n.* that which *stops* or closes the mouth of a vessel : a cork or plug.—*v.t.* to close with a stopple.

**Storage**, stōr'āj, *n.* the placing in a *store* : the safe keeping of goods in a store : the price paid or charged for keeping goods in a store.

**Storax**, stō'raks, *n.* a fragrant gum-resin produced on several species of trees growing round the Mediterranean Sea. [L. and Gr. *styrax*.]

**Store**, stōr, *n.* a hoard or quantity gathered : abundance : a storehouse : any place where goods are sold :—*pl.* supplies of provisions, ammunition, &c. for an army or a ship.—*v.t.* to gather in quantities : to supply : to lay up in store : to hoard : to place in a warehouse. [O. Fr. *estoire*. provisions—L. *instauro*, to provide.]

**Storehouse**, stōr'hows, *n.* a *house* for *storing* goods of any kind : a repository : a treasury.

**Storied**, stō'rid, *adj.* told or celebrated in a *story* : having a history : interesting from the stories belonging to it.

**Stork**, stork, *n.* a wading bird nearly allied to the heron. [A.S. *storc* ; Ger. *storch*.]

**Stork's-bill**, storks'-bil, *n.* a kind of geranium, with the fruit like the *bill* of a *stork*. [See **Pelargonium**.]

**Storm**, storm, *n.* a *stir* or violent commotion of the air producing wind, rain, &c. : a tempest : violent agitation of society : commotion : tumult : calamity : (*mil.*) an assault.—*v.i.* to raise a tempest : to blow with violence : to be in a violent passion.—*v.t.* to attack by open force : to assault. [A.S. ; Ice. *stormr* ; from root of **Stir**.]

**Stormy**, storm'i, *adj.* having many storms : agitated with furious winds : boisterous : violent : passionate.—*n.* **Storm'iness**.

**Story**, stō'ri, *n.* a *history* or narrative of incidents (so in *B.*) : a little tale : a fictitious narrative. [O. Fr. *estoire*. It is simply a short form of **History**.]

**Story**, also **Storey**, stō'ri, *n.* a division of a house reached by one flight of stairs : a set of rooms on the same floor or level. [Ety. dub. ; perh. from **Store**, and orig. sig. 'storehouse.']

**Stout**, stowt, *adj.* strong : robust : corpulent : resolute : proud : (*B.*) stubborn.—*n.* a name for porter.—*adv.* **Stout'ly**—*n.* **Stout'ness** : (*B.*) stubbornness. [Allied to O. Fr. *estout*, bold, Dut. *stout*, and Ger. *stolz*, bold, stout ; perh. from the root of **Stilt**.]

**Stove**, stōv, *n.* an apparatus with a fire for warming a room, cooking, &c.—*v.t.* to heat or keep warm. [Orig. 'a hothouse,' allied to Low Ger. *stove*, O. Ger. *stupa* (Ger. *stube*, room) ; cf. also It. *stufa*, Fr. *étuve*—Low L. *stuba* ; but whether the Low L. word is from the O. Ger., or *vice versâ*, is doubtful. Cf. **Stew**.]

**Stow**, stō, *v.t.* to place : to arrange : to fill by packing things in. [Partly from M. E. *stouwen*, to bring to a stand, partly from M. E. *stowen*, to place—*stow*, a place—A.S. *stow* ; cf. Dut. *stuwen*, to stow, to push, Ger. *stauen*.]

**Stowage**, stō'āj, *n.* act of *stowing* or placing in order : state of being laid up : room for articles to be laid away.

**Straddle**, strad'l, *v.i.* to *stride* or part the legs wide : to stand or walk with the legs far apart. —*v.t.* to stand or sit astride of.—*n.* act of striding. [Freq. formed from A.S. *strad*, pa.t. of *stridan*, E. **Stride**.]

**Straggle**, strag'l, *v.i.* to wander from the course : to ramble : to stretch beyond proper limits : to be dispersed. [Freq. formed partly from *stray*, partly from A.S. *strak*, pa.t. of *strican*, to go, to proceed, E. **Strike**.]

**Straggler**, strag'lér, *n.* one who *straggles* or goes from the course : a wandering fellow : a vagabond.

**Straight**, strāt, *adj.* direct : being in a right line : not crooked : nearest : upright.—*adv.* immediately : in the shortest time.—*adv.* **Straight'ly**. —*n.* **Straight'ness**. [Lit. 'stretched,' A.S. *streht*, pa.p. of *streccan*, E. **Stretch**, influenced also by **Strait**.]

**Straighten**, strāt'n, *v.t.* to make *straight*.

**Straightforward**, strāt-for'ward, *adj.* going *forward* in a *straight* course : honest : open : downright.—*adv.* **Straightfor'wardly**.

**Straightway**, strāt'wā, *adv.* directly : immediately : without loss of time. [See **Straight** and **Way**.]

**Strain**, strān, *v.t.* to *stretch tight* : to draw with force : to exert to the utmost : to injure by overtasking : to make tight : to constrain, make uneasy or unnatural : to filter.—*v.i.* to make violent efforts : to pass through a filter.—*n.* the act of straining : a violent effort : an injury inflicted by straining : a note, sound, or song. [O. Fr. *straindre*—L. *stringo*, to stretch tight. See **String** and **Strong**.]

**Strain**, strān, *n.* race : stock : generation : descent. [M. E. *strend*—A.S. *strynd*, stock— *strynan*, to beget.]

**Strainer**, strān'ér, *n.* one who or that which

strains : an instrument for filtration : a sieve, colander, &c.

**Strait**, strāt, *adj.* difficult : distressful : (*obs.* strict, rigorous : narrow, so in *B.*).—*n.* a narrow pass in a mountain, or in the ocean between two portions of land : difficulty : distress. [O. Fr. *estreit, estroit* (Fr. *étroit*)—L. *strictus*, pa.p. of *stringo*, to draw tight. Doublet **Strict**.]

**Straiten**, strāt'n, *v.t.* to make *strait* or narrow : to confine : to draw tight : to distress : to put into difficulties.

**Straitlaced**, strāt'lāst, *adj.* rigid or narrow in opinion. [Lit. ' *laced strait* or tight with stays.']

**Straitly**, strāt'li, *adv.* narrowly : (*B.*) strictly.

**Straitness**, strāt'nes, *n.* state of being *strait* or narrow : strictness : (*B.*) distress or difficulty.

**Strand**, strand, *n.* the margin or beach of the sea or of a lake.—*v.t.* to run aground.—*v.i.* to drift or be driven ashore. [A.S., Ger. *strand*, Ice. *strönd*, border, shore.]

**Strand**, strand, *n.* one of the *strings* or parts that compose a rope.—*v.t.* to break a strand. [Allied to O. Ger. *streno* (Ger. *strähn*), string, rope, with excrescent -*d*.]

**Strange**, strānj, *adj.* foreign : belonging to another country : not formerly known, heard, or seen : not domestic : new : causing surprise or curiosity : marvellous : unusual : odd.—*adv.* **Strange'ly**.—*n.* **Strange'ness**. [O. Fr. *estrange* (Fr. *étrange*)—L. *extraneus*—*extra*, beyond.]

**Stranger**, strānj'ėr, *n.* a foreigner : one from home : one unknown or unacquainted : a guest or visitor : one not admitted to communion or fellowship. [O. Fr. *estrangier*. See **Strange**.]

**Strangle**, strang'gl, *v.t.* to *draw tight* the throat so as to prevent breathing and destroy life : to choke : to hinder from birth or appearance : to suppress.—*n.* **Strang'ler**. [O. Fr. *estrangler* (Fr. *étrangler*)—L. *strangulo, -atum*—Gr. *stranggō*, to draw tight. Cf. **Strangury**.]

**Strangulated**, strang'gū-lāt-ed, *adj.* having the circulation stopped by compression.

**Strangulation**, strang-gū-lā'shun, *n.* act of *strangling* : (*med.*) compression of the throat and partial suffocation in hysterics.

**Strangury**, strang'gū-ri, *n.* painful retention of, or difficulty in discharging *urine*. [L. *stranguria*—Gr. *strangx*, a drop, from *stranggō*, to squeeze, conn. with L. *stringo* (see **Strain**) ; and *ouron*, urine.]

**Strap**, strap, *n.* a narrow strip of cloth or leather : a razor-strop : (*arch.*) an iron plate secured by screw-bolts, for connecting two or more timbers. —*v.t.* to beat or bind with a strap : to strop :— *pr.p.* strapp'ing ; *pa.t* and *pa.p* strapped.—*adj.* **Strapp'ing**, tall, handsome. [Orig. *strop*, from A.S. *stropp*, cog. with Dut. *strop* ; allied to L. *struppus* ; cf. Gr. *strephō*, to twist.]

**Strata**, strā'ta, *pl.* of **Stratum**.

**Stratagem**, strat'a-jem, *n.* a piece of *generalship* : an artifice, esp. in war : a plan for deceiving an enemy or gaining an advantage. [L.—Gr. *stratēgēma*—*stratēgos*, a general—*stratos*, an army, and *agō*, to lead.]

**Strategic**, stra-tej'ik, **Strategical**, stra-tej'i-kal, *adj.* pertaining to or done by *strategy*.—*adv.* **Strateg'ically**.

**Strategist**, strat'e-jist, *n.* one skilled in strategy.

**Strategy**, strat'e-ji, *n.*, *generalship*, or the art of conducting a campaign and manoeuvring an army.

**Strath**, strath, *n.* (*in Scotland*) an extensive valley through which a river runs. [Gael.]

**Stratification**, strat-i-fi-kā'shun, *n.* act of *strati-*

*fying* : state of being stratified : process of being arranged in layers.

**Stratiform**, strat'i-form, *adj.*, *formed* like *strata*.

**Stratify**, strat'i-fī, *v.t.* to *form* or lay in *strata* or layers :—*pr.p.* strat'ifying ; *pa.t.* and *pa.p.* strat'if ied. [Fr. *stratifier*—L. *stratum*, and *facio*, to make.]

**Stratum**, strā'tum, *n.* a bed of earth or rock formed by natural causes, and consisting usually of a series of layers : any bed or layer :—*pl.* **Strata**, strā'ta. [L.—*sterno, stratum*, to spread out.]

**Stratus**, strā'tus, *n.* a form of cloud occurring in a horizontal layer. [L. See **Stratum**.]

**Straw**, straw, *n.* the stalk on which corn grows, and from which it is thrashed : a quantity of them when thrashed : anything worthless. [A.S. *streaw*, Ger. *stroh*, from the root of **Strew**.]

**Strawberry**, straw'ber-i, *n.* a plant and its *berry* or fruit, which is highly esteemed—prob. so called from its *strewing* or spreading along the ground. [A.S. *streaw-berie*.]

**Strawed** (*B.*) for strewed, *pat.* and *pa.p.* of **Strew**.

**Strawy**, straw'i, *adj.* made of or like *straw*.

**Stray**, strā, *v.i.* to wander : to go from the inclosure, company, or proper limits : to err : to rove : to deviate from duty or rectitude.—*n.* a domestic animal that has strayed or is lost. [O. Fr. *estraier*, perh. from *estrai*—L. *strata*, E. **Street** ; perh. influenced by **Strew**.]

**Streak**, strēk, *n.* a line or long mark different in colour from the ground : (*min.*) the appearance presented by the surface of a mineral when scratched.—*v.t.* to form streaks in : to mark with streaks. [A.S. *stric, strica*, a stroke, line ; cog. with Ger. *strich* ; from root of **Strike**.]

**Streaky**, strēk'i, *adj.* marked with *streaks* : striped.

**Stream**, strēm, *n.* a current of water, air, or light, &c. : anything flowing out from a source : anything forcible, flowing, and continuous : drift : tendency.—*v.i.* to flow in a stream : to pour out abundantly : to be overflown with : to issue in rays : to stretch in a long line. [A.S. *stream* ; Ger. *strom*, Ice. *straum-r*.]

**Streamer**, strēm'ėr, *n.* an ensign or flag *streaming* or flowing in the wind : a luminous beam shooting upward from the horizon.

**Streamlet**, strēm'let, *n.* a little stream.

**Streamy**, strēm'i, *adj.* abounding with streams : flowing in a stream.

**Street**, strēt, *n.* a road in a town lined with houses, broader than a lane. [A.S. *stret* (Dut. *straat*, Ger. *strasze*, It. *strada*)—L. *strata* (*via*), a paved (way), from *sterno*, E. **Strew**.]

**Strength**, strength, *n.* quality of being *strong* : power of any kind, active or passive : force : vigour : solidity or toughness : power to resist attack : excellence : intensity : brightness : validity : vigour of style or expression : security : amount of force : potency of liquors : a fortification. [A.S.—*strang*, E. **Strong**.]

**Strengthen**, strength'n, *v.t.* to make *strong* or stronger : to confirm : to encourage : to increase in power or security.—*v.i.* to become stronger.

**Strenuous**, stren'ū-us, *adj.* active : vigorous : urgent : zealous : bold.—*adv.* **Stren'uously**.— *n.* **Stren'uousness**. [L. *strenuus*, akin to Gr. *strēnēs*, strong, hard.]

**Stress**, stres, *n.* force : pressure : urgency : strain : violence, as of the weather : (*mech.*) force exerted in any direction or manner between two bodies. [Short for **Distress**.]

**Stretch**, strech, *v.t.* to extend : to draw out : to

expand : to reach out : to exaggerate, strain, or carry further than is right.—*v.i.* to be drawn out : to be extended : to extend without breaking.—*n.* act of stretching : effort : struggle : reach : extension : state of being stretched : utmost extent of meaning : course. [A.S. *strec'can—strac*, strong, violent, cog. with Ger. *strack*, straight, right out.]

**Stretcher**, strech'ér, *n.* anything used for *stretching :* a frame for carrying the sick or dead : a footboard for a rower.

**Strew**, strōō, *v.t.* to spread by scattering : to scatter loosely :—*pa.p.* strewed or strewn. [A.S. *streowian ;* allied to Ger. *streuen,* L. *sterno* (perf. *stravi*), Gr. *storennymi,* Sans. *stri.*]

**Striated**, strī'āt-ed, *adj.* marked with *striæ* or small channels running parallel to each other. —*n.* **Stria'tion.** [L. *striatus,* pa.p. of *strio,* to furrow—*stria,* a furrow.]

**Stricken**, strik'n (*B.*) *pa.p.* of **Strike.**—**Stricken in years,** advanced in years.

**Strict**, strikt, *adj.* exact : extremely nice : observing exact rules : severe : restricted : thoroughly accurate.—*adv.* **Strict'ly.**—*n.* **Strict'ness.** [Orig. 'drawn tight,' L. *strictus,* pa.p. of *stringo,* to draw tight. Cf. **Strain** and **Strangle.**]

**Stricture**, strik'tūr, *n.* (*med.*) a morbid *contraction* of any passage of the body : an unfavourable criticism : censure : critical remark.

**Stride**, strīd, *v.i.* to walk with long steps.—*v.t.* to pass over at a step :—*pa.t.* strōde (*obs.* strid) : *pa.p.* stridd'en.—a long step. [A.S. *-stridan* (in *be-stridan,* bestride), prob. conn. with A.S. *stridh,* strife, Ger. *streit,* from the idea of ' stretching,' ' straining.']

**Strident**, strī'dent, *adj., creaking,* grating, harsh. [L. *stridens, -entis,* pr.p. of *strideo,* to creak.]

**Strife**, strīf, *n.* contention for superiority : struggle for victory : contest : discord. [M. E. *strif*—O. Fr. *e-strif.* See **Strive.**]

**Strike**, strīk, *v.t.* to give a blow to : to hit with force : to dash : to stamp : to coin : to thrust in : to cause to sound : to let down, as a sail : to ground upon, as a ship : to punish : to affect strongly : to affect suddenly with alarm or surprise : to make a compact or agreement : (*B.*) to stroke.—*v.i.* to give a quick blow : to hit : to dash : to sound by being struck : to touch : to run aground : to pass with a quick effect : to dart : to lower the flag in token of respect or surrender : to give up work in order to secure higher wages or the redress of some grievance :—*pa.t.* struck ; *pa.p.* struck (*obs.* strick'en).—*n.* act of striking for higher wages : (*geol.*) vertical or oblique direction of strata, being at right angles to the dip.—*n.* **Strik'er.—To strike off,** to erase from an account : to print.—**To strike out,** to efface : to bring into light : to form by sudden effort.—**To strike hands** (*B.*) to become surety for any one. [Prob. orig. sig. ' to draw,' A.S. *strican ;* Ger. *streichen,* to move, to strike.]

**Striking,** strik'ing, *adj.* affecting : surprising : forcible : impressive : exact.—*adv.* **Strik'ingly.**

**String,** string, *n.* a small cord or a slip of anything for tying : a ribbon : nerve, tendon : the chord of a musical instrument : a cord on which things are filed : a series of things.—*v.t.* to supply with strings : to put in tune : to put on a string : to make tense or firm : to take the strings off :—*pa.t.* and *pa.p.* strung. [A.S. *streng ;* cog. with Dut. *streng,* Ice. *streng-r,* Ger. *strang ;* conn. with L. *stringo,* to draw tight, Gr. *stranggō.* Cf. **Strangle.**]

**Stringed,** stringd, *adj.* having strings.

**Stringency,** strin'jen-si, *n.* state or quality of being *stringent :* severe pressure.

**Stringent,** strin'jent, *adj., binding* strongly : urgent.—*adv.* **Strin'gently.** [L. *stringens, -entis,* pr.p. of *stringo.* See **Strict.**]

**Stringy,** string'i, *adj.* consisting of *strings* or small threads : fibrous : capable of being drawn into strings.—*n.* **String'iness.**

**Strip,** strip, *v.t.* to pull off in strips or stripes : to tear off : to deprive of a covering : to skin : to make bare : to expose : to deprive : to make destitute : to plunder.—*v.i.* to undress :—*pr.p.* stripp'ing ; *pa.t.* and *pa.p.* stripped.—*n.* same as **Stripe,** a long narrow piece of anything. [A.S. *strypan,* allied to Ger. *streifen.*]

**Stripe,** strīp, *n.* a blow, esp. one made with a lash, rod, &c.: a wale or discoloured mark made by a lash or rod : a line, or long narrow division of a different colour from the ground.—*v.t.* to make stripes upon : to form with lines of different colours. [Allied to Low Ger. *stripe,* Ger. *streif ;* belonging to the stem of **Strip.**]

**Stripling,** strip'ling, *n.* a youth : one yet growing. [Dim. of **Strip,** as being a strip from the main stem.]

**Strive,** strīv, *v.i.* to make efforts : to endeavour earnestly : to labour hard : to struggle : to contend : to aim :—*pa.t.* strōve ; *pa.p.* striv'en.—*n.* **Striv'er.** [O. Fr. *e-strive-r,* from the root of Ger. *streben,* Dut. *streven.* Cf. **Strife.**]

**Stroke,** strōk, *n.* a blow : a sudden attack : calamity : the sound of a clock : a dash in writing : the sweep of an oar in rowing : the movement of the piston of a steam-engine : the touch of a pen or pencil : a masterly effort. [From A.S. *strac,* pa.t. of *strican,* E. **Strike** ; cf. Ger. *streich,* a stroke.]

**Stroke,** strōk, *v.t.* to rub gently in one direction : to rub gently in kindness.—*n.* **Strok'er.** [A.S. *stracian,* from the root of **Stroke,** *n.* ; cf. Ger. *streichen, streicheln.*]

**Strokesman,** strōks'man, *n.* the aftermost rower, whose *stroke* leads the rest.

**Stroll,** strōl, *v.i.* to ramble idly or leisurely : to wander on foot.—*n.* a leisurely walk : a wandering on foot.—*n.* **Stroll'er.** [Ety. unknown.]

**Strong,** strong, *adj.* firm : having physical power : hale, healthy : able to endure : solid : well fortified : having wealth or resources : moving with rapidity : impetuous : earnest : having great vigour, as the mind : forcible : energetic : affecting the senses, as smell and taste, forcibly : having a quality in a great degree : intoxicating : bright : intense : well established.—*adv.* **Strong'ly.** [A.S. *strang, strong ;* Ice. *strang-r,* Ger. *streng,* tight, strong ; from root of **String.**]

**Stronghold,** strong'hōld, *n.* a place *strong* to *hold* out against attack : a fastness or fortified place : a fortress.

**Strop,** strop, *n.* a strip of leather, or of wood covered with leather, &c. for sharpening razors. —*v.t.* to sharpen on a strop :—*pr.p.* stropp'ing ; *pa.t.* and *pa.p.* stropped. [Older form of **Strap.**]

**Strophe,** strōf'e, *n.* in the ancient drama, the song sung by the chorus while dancing towards one side of the orchestra, to which its reverse the antistrophe answers.—*adj.* **Stroph'ic.** [Lit. ' a turning,' Gr. *strophē—strephō,* to turn, twist.]

**Strove,** strōv, *pa.t.* of **Strive.**

**Strow,** strō. Same as **Strew** :—*pa.p.* strōwed or strōwn.

**Struck,** struk, *pa.t.* and *pa.p.* of **Strike.**

**Structure,** strukt'ūr, *n.* manner of *building :* construction : a building, esp. one of large size : arrangement of parts or of particles in a substance : manner of organisation.—*adj.* **Struct'-ural.** [L. *structura—struo, structum*, to build.]

**Struggle,** strug'l, *v.i.* to make great efforts with contortions of the body : to make great exertions : to contend : to labour in pain : to be in agony or distress.—*n.* a violent effort with contortions of the body : great labour : agony. [Ety. dub.]

**Strum,** strum, *v.t.* to play on (as a musical instrument) in a coarse, noisy manner :—*pr.p.* strumm'-ing ; *pa.t.* and *pa.p.* strummed. [From the sound.]

**Strumpet,** strum'pet, *n.* a prostitute.—*adj.* like a strumpet : inconstant : false. [Prob. from L. *stuprata*, pa.p. of *stupro*, to debauch.]

**Strung,** strung, *pa.t.* and *pa.p.* of **String.**

**Strut,** strut, *v.i.* to walk in a pompous manner : to walk with affected dignity :—*pr.p.* strutt'ing ; *pa.t.* and *pa.p.* strutt'ed.—*n.* a proud step or walk : affectation of dignity in walking. [Allied to Ger. *strotzen*, to be swollen or puffed up, Low Ger. *strutt*, sticking out.]

**Strychnia,** strik'ni-a, **Strychnine,** strik'nin, *n.* a poisonous alkaloid obtained from the seeds of nux vomica. [L. *strychnus*—Gr. *strychnos*, a kind of nightshade.]

**Stub,** stub, *n.* the stump left after a tree is cut down.—*v.t.* to take the stubs or roots of from the ground :—*pr.p.* stubb'ing ; *pa.t.* and *pa.p.* stubbed. [A.S. *styb*, cog. with Ice. *stubbr* ; akin to L. *stipes*, Gr. *stypos*, a stem, a stake.]

**Stubbed,** stubd, *adj.* short and thick like a *stub* or stump : blunt : obtuse.—*n.* **Stubb'edness.**

**Stubble,** stub'l, *n.* the *stubs* or stumps of corn left when the stalk is cut. [Dim. of **Stub.**]

**Stubborn,** stub'orn, *adj.* immovably fixed in opinion : obstinate : persevering : steady : stiff : inflexible : hardy : not easily melted or worked.—*adv.* **Stubb'ornly.**—*n.* **Stubb'ornness.** [Lit. 'fixed like a *stub*.']      [thick, and strong.

**Stubby,** stub'i, *adj.* abounding with *stubs* : short,

**Stucco,** stuk'o, *n.* a plaster of lime and fine sand, &c. used for decorations, &c. : work done in stucco.—*v.t.* to face or overlay with stucco : to form in stucco. [It. *stucco* ; from O. Ger. *stucchi*, a crust, a shell.]

**Stuck,** stuk, *pa.t.* and *pa.p.* of **Stick.**

**Stud,** stud, *n.* a collection of breeding horses and mares : the place where they are kept. [A.S. *stod, stodhors*, a stallion ; cog. with Ger. *stute*, a mare ; prob. conn. with **Stand.** See **Stallion, Steed.**]

**Stud,** stud, *n.* a nail with a large head : an ornamental double-headed button.—*v.t.* to adorn with studs or knobs : to set thickly, as with studs :—*pr.p.* studd'ing ; *pa.t.* and *pa.p.* studd'-ed. [A.S. *studu*, a post, nail, 'something fixed,' from root of **Stand.**]

**Student,** stū'dent, *n.* one who *studies*, a scholar : one devoted to learning : a man devoted to books.            [stallion.

**Studhorse,** stud'hors, *n.* a breeding-horse :

**Studied,** stud'id, *adj.* qualified by or versed in *study :* learned : planned with study or deliberation : premeditated.

**Studio,** stū'di-o, *n.* the *study* or workshop of an artist :—*pl.* **Stu'dios.** [It.]

**Studious,** stū'di-us, *adj.* given to *study :* thoughtful : diligent : careful (with *of*) : studied : deliberately planned.—*adv.* **Stu'diously.**—*n.* **Stu'-diousness.**

**Study,** stud'i, *v.t.* to bestow pains upon : to apply the mind to : to examine closely, in order to learn thoroughly : to form and arrange by thought : to con over.—*v.i.* to apply the mind

closely to a subject : to try hard : to muse : to apply the mind to books :—*pa.t.* and *pa.p.* stud'ied.—*n.* a setting of the mind upon a subject : application to books, &c. : absorbed attention : contrivance : any object of attentive consideration : any particular branch of learning : a place devoted to study. [O. Fr. *estudier*, Fr. *étudier*—L. *studeo*, to be eager or zealous ; perh. akin to Gr. *spoudē*, haste.]

**Stuff,** stuf, *n.* materials of which anything is made : textile fabrics, cloth, esp. when woollen : worthless matter : (*B.*) household furniture, &c.—*v.t.* to fill by crowding : to fill very full : to press in : to crowd : to cause to bulge out by filling : to fill with seasoning, as a fowl : to fill the skin of a dead animal, so as to reproduce its living form.—*v.i.* to feed gluttonously. [O. Fr. *estoffe*, Fr. *étoffe*—L. *stuppa*, the coarse part of flax, tow, oakum.]

**Stultification,** stul-ti-fi-kā'shun, *n.* act of *stultifying* or making foolish.

**Stultify,** stul'ti-fī, *v.t.* to make a *fool* of : to cause to appear foolish : to destroy the force of one's argument by self-contradiction :—*pa.t.* and *pa.p.* stul'tified. [L. *stultus*, foolish, *facio*, to make.]

**Stumble,** stum'bl, *v.i.* to strike the feet against something : to trip in walking : (fol. by *upon*) to light on by chance : to slide into crime or error.—*v.t.* to cause to trip or stop : to puzzle.—*n.* a trip in walking or running : a blunder : a failure. [Akin to vulgar E. *stump*, to walk with heavy steps, and to O. Dut. *stomelen*, also to E. **Stamp.**]

**Stumbling-block,** stum'bling-blok, **Stum'bling-stone,** -stōn, *n.* a *block* or *stone* over which one would be likely to *stumble :* a cause of error.

**Stump,** stump, *n.* the part of a tree left in the ground after the trunk is cut down : the part of a body remaining after a part is cut off or destroyed : one of the three sticks forming a wicket in cricket.—*v.t.* to reduce to a stump : to cut off a part of : to knock down the wickets in cricket when the batsman is out of his ground. [Allied to Low Ger. *stump*, Dut. *stomp*.]

**Stump-orator,** stump-or'a-tor, *n.* one who harangues the multitude from a temporary platform, as the *stump* of a tree : a speaker who travels about the country, and whose appeals are mainly to the passions of his audience.

**Stun,** stun, *v.t.* to stupefy or astonish with a loud noise, or with a blow : to surprise completely : to amaze :—*pr.p.* stunn'ing ; *pa.t.* and *pa.p.* stunned. [A.S. *stunian*, to strike against, to stun (cog. with Ger. *staunen*), but prob. modified by confusion with O. Fr. *estonner*, Fr. *étonner*. See **Astonish.**]

**Stung,** stung, *pa.t.* and *pa.p.* of **Sting.**

**Stunk,** stungk, *pa.p.* of **Stink.**

**Stunt,** stunt, *v.t.* to hinder from growth. [A.S. *stunt*, blunt, stupid ; Ice. *stuttr*, short, stunted.]

**Stupefaction,** stū-pi-fak'shun, *n.* the act of *making stupid* or senseless : insensibility : stupidity.

**Stupefactive,** stū-pi-fak'tiv, *adj.* causing stupefaction or insensibility.

**Stupefy,** stū'pi-fī, *v.t.* to *make stupid* or senseless : to deaden the perception : to deprive of sensibility :—*pa.t.* and *pa.p.* stū'pefied. [L. *stupeo*, to be struck senseless, *facio*, to make.]

**Stupendous,** stū-pen'dus, *adj.* to be wondered at for its magnitude : wonderful, amazing, astonishing.—*adv.* **Stupen'dously.**—*n.* **Stupen'dous-ness.** [L. *stupendus*.]

**Stupid,** stū'pid, *adj.* struck *senseless :* insensible : deficient or dull in understanding : formed or done without reason or judgment: foolish: un-skilful.—*adv.* **Stu′pidly.**—*ns.* **Stupid′ity, Stu′-pidness.** [Fr.—L. *stupidus.*]

**Stupor,** stū′por, *n.* the state of being struck *sense-less*: suspension of sense either complete or par-tial: insensibility, intellectual or moral: exces-sive amazement or astonishment.

**Sturdy,** stur′di, *adj.* (*comp.* **Stur′dier,** *superl.* **Stur′diest**), stubborn or obstinate: resolute: firm: forcible: strong: robust: stout.—*adv.* **Stur′dily.**—*n.* **Stur′diness.** [Lit. 'stunned,' O. Fr. *estourdi,* pa.p. of *estourdir* (Fr. *étourdir*), It. *stordire,* to stun; prob. from L. *torpidus,* stupefied.]

**Sturgeon,** stur′jun, *n.* a large cartilaginous sea-fish yielding caviare and isinglass, and used for food. [Fr. *esturgeon,* from O. Ger. *sturio,* Ger. *stör.*]

**Stutter,** stut′ér, *v.i.* to hesitate in speaking: to stammer.—*n.* the act of stuttering: a hesitation in speaking. [M. E. *stutten*—Ice. *stauta;* cog. with Ger. *stottern,* Low Ger. *stöten;* an imita-tive word.]

**Stutterer,** stut′ér-ér, *n.* one who stutters.

**Stuttering,** stut′ér-ing, *adj.* hesitating in speak-ing: stammering.—*adv.* **Stutt′eringly.**

**Sty,** stī, *n.* a small inflamed tumour on the eyelid. [Lit. *anything risen,* A.S. *stigend,* from *stigan,* Goth. *steigan,* Sans. *stigh,* to step up.]

**Sty,** stī, *n.* an inclosure for swine: any place ex-tremely filthy. [A.S. *stige* (Ger. *steige*), from same root as **Sty** above, and lit. sig. the place where beasts *go up,* and lie.]

**Stygian,** stij′i-an, *adj.* (*myth.*) relating to *Styx,* the river of Hades, over which departed souls were ferried: hellish. [L.—Gr. *stygeō,* to hate.]

**Stylar,** stīl′ar, *adj.* pertaining to the *pin* of a dial. [See **Style.**]

**Style,** stīl, *n.* anything long and pointed, esp. a pointed tool for engraving or writing: (*fig.*) manner of writing, mode of expressing thought in language: the distinctive manner peculiar to an author: characteristic or peculiar mode of expression and execution (in the fine arts): title: mode of address: practice, esp. in a law-court: manner: form: fashion: mode of reckoning time: the pin of a dial: (*bot.*) the middle portion of the pistil, between the ovary and the stigma.—*v.t.* to entitle in addressing or speaking of: to name or designate. [Fr.—L. *stilus,* for *stiglus,* from root found in Gr. *stizō,* to puncture. See **Stigma.**]

**Stylish,** stīl′ish, *adj.* displaying *style*: fashion-able: showy: pretending to style.—*adv.* **Styl′-ishly.**—*n.* **Styl′ishness.**

**Styptic,** stip′tik, *adj.,* *contracting* or drawing to-gether: astringent: that stops bleeding.—*n.* an astringent medicine. [Fr.—L. *stypticus*—Gr. *styptikos*—*styphō,* to contract.]

**Suasion,** swā′zhun, *n.* the act of *persuading* or *advising*: advice. [Fr.—L. *suasio*—*suadeo,* to advise.]

**Suasive,** swā′siv, *adj.* tending to *persuade*: per-suasive.—*adv.* **Sua′sively.**—*n.* **Sua′siveness.**

**Suave,** swāv, *adj.* pleasant: agreeable.—*adv.* **Suave′ly.**—*n.* **Suavity** (swav′it-i). [Fr.—L. *suavis,* sweet. See **Sweet.**]

**Subacid,** sub-as′id, *adj.* somewhat *acid* or sour. [L. *sub,* under, and **Acid.**]

**Subaltern,** sub′al-tèrn, *adj.* inferior: subordinate. —*n.* a subordinate: an officer in the army under the rank of captain. [Lit. 'under another,' L. *sub,* under, and *alternus,* one after the other— *alter,* the other.]

**Subalternate,** sub-al-tèrn′āt, *adj.* succeeding by *turns*: subordinate.—*n.* **Subalterna′tion.**

**Subaqueous,** sub-ā′kwe-us, *adj.* lying *under water.* [L. *sub,* under, and **Aqueous.**]

**Subdivide,** sub-di-vīd′, *v.t.* to *divide* into *smaller* divisions: to divide again.—*v.i.* to be subdivided: to separate. [L. *sub,* under, and **Divide.**]

**Subdivision,** sub-di-vizh′un, *n.* the act of *subdivid-ing*: the part made by subdividing.

**Subdual,** sub-dū′al, *n.* the act of subduing.

**Subdue,** sub-dū′, *v.t.* to conquer: to bring under dominion: to render submissive: to tame: to soften.—*adj.* **Subdu′able.**—*n.* **Subdu′er.** [O. Fr. *subduzer*—L. *sub,* under, and *ducere,* to lead.]

**Subeditor,** sub-ed′i-tur, *n.* an *under* or assistant *editor.* [L. *sub,* under, and **Editor.**]

**Subfamily,** sub′fam-i-li, *n.* a *subordinate family*: a division of a family. [L. *sub,* under, and **Family.**]

**Subgenus,** sub-jē′nus, *n.* a *subordinate genus*: a division of a genus. [L. *sub,* under, and **Genus.**]

**Subjacent,** sub-jā′sent, *adj., lying under* or below: being in a lower situation. [L. *subjacens*—*sub,* under, and *jaceo,* to lie.]

**Subject,** sub′jekt, *adj.* under the power of another: liable, exposed: subordinate: subservient.—*n.* one under the power of another: one under allegiance to a sovereign: that on which any operation is performed: that which is treated or handled: (*anat.*) a dead body for dissection: (*art*) that which it is the object of the artist to express: that of which anything is said: topic: matter, materials. [Fr. *sujet*—L. *subjectus*— *sub,* under, and *jacio,* to throw.]

**Subject,** sub-jekt′, *v.t.* to *throw* or bring *under*: to bring under the power of: to make subordi-nate or subservient: to subdue: to enslave: to expose or make liable to: to cause to undergo.

**Subjection,** sub-jek′shun, *n.* the act of *subjecting* or subduing: the state of being subject to another.

**Subjective,** sub-jekt′iv, *adj.* relating to the *sub-ject*: derived from one's own consciousness: denoting those states of thought or feeling of which the mind is the conscious subject, opposed to *objective.*—*adv.* **Subject′ively.**—*n.* **Subject′-iveness.**

**Subjectivity,** sub-jek-tiv′i-ti, *n.* state of being *sub-jective*: that which is treated subjectively.

**Subjoin,** sub-join′, *v.t.* to *join under*: to add at the end or afterwards: to affix or annex. [L. *sub,* under, and **Join.**]

**Subjugate,** sub′joo-gāt, *v.t.* to bring *under* the *yoke*: to bring under power or dominion: to conquer.—*ns.* **Sub′jugator, Subjuga′tion.** [Fr. *subjuguer*—L. *sub,* under, and *jugum,* a yoke.]

**Subjunctive,** sub-jungk′tiv, *adj.* subjoined: added to something: denoting that mood of a verb which expresses condition, hypothesis, or contingency.—*n.* the subjunctive mood. [L. *sub,* under, and *jungo,* to join. See **Join.**]

**Subkingdom,** sub-king′dum, *n.* a *subordinate kingdom*: a division of a kingdom: a sub-division. [L. *sub,* under, and **Kingdom.**]

**Sublease,** sub-lēs′, *n.* an *under-lease* or lease by a tenant to another. [L. *sub,* under, and **Lease.**]

**Sublet,** sub-let′, *v.t.* to *let* or lease, as a tenant, to another. [L. *sub,* under, and **Let.**]

**Sublieutenant,** sub-lef-ten′ant, *n.* the lowest com-missioned officer in the army and navy: in the army, it has taken the place of Ensign.

**Sublimate,** sub′lim-āt, *v.t.* to *lift up on high*: to elevate: to refine and exalt: to purify by raising

by heat into vapour which again becomes solid.
—*n.* the product of sublimation. [L. *sublimo,*
*sublimatum.*]

**Sublimation,** sub-lim-ā'shun, *n.* the act of *sub-
limating* or purifying by raising into vapour by
heat and condensing by cold : elevation : exaltation.

**Sublime,** sub-līm', *adj.* high : lofty : majestic :
awakening feelings of awe or veneration.—*n.*
that which is sublime : the lofty or grand in
thought or style : the emotion produced by
sublime objects.—*v.t.* to exalt : to dignify, to
ennoble : to improve : to purify, to bring to a
state of vapour by heat and condense again by
cold.—*v.i.* to be sublimed or sublimated. [L.
*sublimis,* of which ety. dub. ; perh. *sub-limen,*
up to the lintel.]

**Sublimely,** sub-līm'li, *adv.* in a sublime manner :
loftily : with elevated conceptions.

**Sublimity,** sub-lim'i-ti, *n.* loftiness : elevation :
grandeur : loftiness of thought or style : nobleness of nature or character : excellence.

**Sublunar,** sub-lōōn'ar, **Sublunary,** sub'lōōn-ar-i,
*adj., under* the *moon :* earthly : belonging to
this world. [L. *sub,* under, and **Lunar.**]

**Submarine,** sub-ma-rēn', *adj., under* or in the
*sea.* [L. *sub,* under, and **Marine.**]

**Submerge,** sub-mėrj', **Submerse,** sub-mėrs', *v.t.*
to *plunge under* water : to overflow with water :
to drown.—*v.i.* to plunge under water.—*ns.*
**Submerg'ence, Submer'sion.** [L. *submergo,*
*-mersum—sub,* under, *mergo,* to plunge.]

**Submersed,** sub-mėrst', *adj.* being or growing
*under water :* submerged.

**Submiss,** sub-mis', *adj.* (*obs.*) cast down, prostrate.
—*adv.* **Submiss'ly** (*obs.*), humbly, now **Submissively.**

**Submission,** sub-mish'un, *n.* act of *submitting* or
yielding : acknowledgment of inferiority or of a
fault : humble behaviour : resignation.

**Submissive,** sub-mis'iv, *adj.* willing or ready to
*submit :* yielding : humble : obedient.—*adv.*
**Submiss'ively.**—*n.* **Submiss'iveness.**

**Submit,** sub-mit', *v.t.* to refer to the judgment of
another: to surrender to another.—*v.i.* to yield
one's self to another : to surrender : to yield
one's opinion : to be subject :—*pr.p.* submitt'ing;
*pa.t.* and *pa.p.* submitt'ed. [L. *submitto—sub,*
under, *mitto, missum,* to send.]

**Subordinate,** sub-or'di-nāt, *adj., lower in order,*
rank, nature, power, &c. : descending in a
regular series.—*adv.* **Subor'dinately.** [L. *sub,*
under—*ordo, ordinis,* order.]

**Subordinate,** sub-or'di-nāt, *n.* one in a *lower
order* or rank : an inferior.—*v.t.* to place in a
lower order : to consider of less value : to make
subject.

**Subordination,** sub-or-di-nā'shun, *n.* act of *sub-
ordinating* or placing in a lower order : state of
being subordinate : inferiority of rank or position.

**Suborn,** sub-orn', *v.t.* to procure privately or indirectly : to cause to commit a perjury.—*n.*
**Suborn'er.** [L. *suborno—sub,* under, *orno,* to
adorn, to supply.]

**Subornation,** sub-or-nā'shun, *n.* act of suborning
or causing a person to take a false oath : crime
of procuring any one to do a bad action.

**Subpœna,** sub-pē'na, *n.* a writ commanding the
attendance of a person in court *under a penalty.*
—*v.t.* to serve with a writ of subpœna. [L. *sub,*
under, and *pœna,* punishment.]

**Subscribe,** sub-skrīb', *v.t.* to *write underneath :*
to give consent to something written, or to attest
by writing one's name underneath : to sign one's

name : to promise to give by writing one's signature.—*v.i.* to promise a certain sum by setting
one's name to a paper : to enter one's name
for anything.—*n.* **Subscrib'er.** [L. *subscribo—
sub,* under, and *scribo, scriptum,* to write.]

**Subscription,** sub-skrip'shun, *n.* act of *subscrib-
ing :* a name subscribed : a paper with signatures : consent by signature : sum subscribed.

**Subsection,** sub-sek'shun, *n.* an *under section* or
division : a subdivision. [L. *sub,* under, **Section.**]

**Subsequent,** sub'se-kwent, *adj., following* or
coming *after.—adv.* **Sub'sequently.** [L. *sub-
sequens, -entis,* pr.p. of *subsequor—sub,* under,
after, *sequor,* to follow.]

**Subserve,** sub-sėrv', *v.t.* to serve subordinately or
instrumentally : to help forward. [L. *subservio
—sub,* under, *servio,* to serve.]

**Subservience,** sub-sėrv'i-ens, **Subserviency,** sub-
sėrv'i-en-si, *n.* state of being *subservient :* anything that promotes some purpose.

**Subservient,** sub-sėrv'i-ent, *adj., subserving :*
serving to promote : subject : submissive.—*adv.*
**Subserv'iently.**

**Subside,** sub-sīd', *v.i.* to settle *down :* to settle at
the bottom : to fall into a state of quiet : to sink.
[L. *subsido—sub,* down, and *sido,* to sit.]

**Subsidence,** sub-sīd'ens, **Subsidency,** sub-sīd'en-
si, *n.* act or process of *subsiding,* settling, or
sinking.

**Subsidiary,** sub-sid'i-ar-i, *adj.* furnishing a *subsidy,* help, or additional supplies : aiding.—*n.*
one who or that which aids or supplies : an
assistant.      [*sidy :* to purchase the aid of.

**Subsidise,** sub'si-dīz, *v.t.* to furnish with a *sub-*

**Subsidy,** sub'si-di, *n.* assistance : aid in money : a
sum of money paid by one state to another for
assistance in war. [L. *subsidium,* orig. troops
stationed behind in reserve, aid—*sub,* under,
and *sido,* to sit.]

**Subsist,** sub-sist', *v.i.* to have existence : to have
the means of living. [L. *subsisto,* to stand still
—*sub,* under, *sisto,* to stand, be fixed.]

**Subsistence,** sub-sist'ens, *n.* state of being *subsistent :* real being : means of supporting life :
livelihood.          [real being : inherent.

**Subsistent,** sub-sist'ent, *adj., subsisting :* having

**Subsoil,** sub'soil, *n.* the *under soil :* the bed or
stratum of earth which lies immediately beneath
the surface soil. [L. *sub,* under, and **Soil.**]

**Substance,** sub'stans, *n.* that in which qualities
or attributes exist : that which constitutes anything what it is : the essential part : body :
matter : property. [L. *substantia—substo,* to
stand under—*sub,* under, and *sto,* to stand.]

**Substantial,** sub-stan'shal, *adj.* belonging to or
having *substance :* actually existing : real : solid :
material : having property or estate.—*adv.* **Sub-
stan'tially.**—*n.* **Substantial'ity.** [Fr. *sub-
stantiel*—L. *substantialis.*]

**Substantials,** sub-stan'shalz, *n.pl.* essential parts.

**Substantiate,** sub-stan'shi-āt, *v.t.* to make *substantial :* to prove or confirm.

**Substantive,** sub'stan-tiv, *adj.* expressing *existence :* real : of real, independent importance.—
*adv.* **Sub'stantively.**

**Substantive,** sub'stan-tiv, *n.* (*gram.*) the part of
speech denoting something that *exists :* a noun.

**Substitute,** sub'sti-tūt, *v.t.* to put in place of
another.—*n.* one who or that which is put in
place of another. [L. *substituo, substitutum—
sub,* under, and *statuo,* to set, place.]

**Substitution,** sub-sti-tū'shun, *n.* act of *substituting* or putting in place of another.—*adj.* **Sub-
stitu'tional.** [L. *substitutio.*]

**Substratum**, sub-strā'tum, *n.* an *under stratum* or *layer:* the substance in which qualities exist. [L. *sub*, under, and **Stratum**.]

**Substructure**, sub-strukt'ūr, *n.* an *under structure* or *building:* foundation. [L. *sub*, and **Structure**.]

**Subtend**, sub-tend', *v.t.* to *extend under* or be opposite to. [L. *sub*, under, and **Tend**.]

**Subterfuge**, sub'tėr-fūj, *n.* that to which one resorts for escape or concealment: an artifice to escape censure or an argument: evasion. [Fr.—L. *subterfugio*, to escape secretly—*subter*, under, secretly, and *fugio*, to flee.]

**Subterranean**, sub-ter-rān'e-an, **Subterraneous**, sub-ter-rān'e-us, *adj.*, *under the earth* or ground. [L. *sub*, under, and *terra*, the earth.]

**Subtil**, **Subtilly**. See under **Subtle**.

**Subtile**, sub'til, *adj.* delicately constructed: fine: thin or rare: piercing: shrewd.—*adv.* **Sub'tilely.**—*n.* **Sub'tileness.** [Lit. 'woven fine,' L. *subtilis—sub*, under, fine, and *tela*, a web.]

**Subtilise**, sub'til-īz, *v.t.* to make *subtile*, thin, or rare: to spin into niceties.—*v.i.* to make nice distinctions: to refine in argument. [Fr. *subtiliser*.]

**Subtilty**, sub'til-ti, *n.* state or quality of being *subtile:* fineness: extreme acuteness: cunning.

**Subtle**, sut'l (*B.*, **Sub'til**), *adj.*, *subtile* in a fig. sense: insinuating: sly: artful: cunningly devised.—*adv.* **Subt'ly** (*B.*, **Sub'tilly**).—*n.* **Subt'leness.** [Contr. of **Subtile**.]

**Subtlety**, sut'l-ti, *n.* quality of being *subtle:* artfulness: shrewdness: extreme acuteness.

**Subtract**, sub-trakt', *v.t.* to *take away* a part from the rest: to take one number or quantity from another to find their difference. [L. *sub*, under, and *traho*, *tractum*, to draw away.]

**Subtraction**, sub-trak'shun, *n.* the act or operation of *subtracting:* the taking of a less number or quantity from a greater. [L. *subtractio*.]

**Subtractive**, sub-trak'tiv, *adj.*, *subtracting:* tending to subtract or lessen.

**Subtrahend**, sub'tra-hend, *n.* the sum or number to be *subtracted* from another. [L. *subtrahendus*.]

**Suburb**, sub'urb, **Suburbs**, sub'urbz, *n.* the district which is *near*, but beyond the walls of a city: the confines. [L. *suburbium—sub*, under, near, and *urbs*, a city.]

**Suburban**, sub-urb'an, *adj.* situated or living in the *suburbs*. [L. *suburbanus*.]

**Subvention**, sub-ven'shun, *n.* act of coming to relief, support: a government aid or subsidy. [L. *sub*, under, and *venio*, *ventum*, to come.]

**Subversion**, sub-vėr'shun, *n.* act of *subverting* or overthrowing from the foundation: entire overthrow: ruin. [L. *subversio*.]

**Subversive**, sub-vėr'siv, *adj.* tending to *subvert*, overthrow, or destroy.

**Subvert**, sub-vėrt', *v.t.* to *turn* as from *beneath* or upside down: to overthrow from the foundation: to ruin utterly: to corrupt.—*n.* **Subvert'er.** [L. *sub*, under, and *verto*, *versum*, to turn.]

**Succedaneum**, suk-se-dā'ne-um, *n.* one who or that which comes in the place of another: a substitute. [L. *succedaneus—succedo*.]

**Succeed**, suk-sēd', *v.t.* to *come* or *follow up* or in order: to follow: to take the place of.—*v.i.* to follow in order: to take the place of: to obtain one's wish or accomplish what is attempted: to end with advantage. [L. *succedo—sub*, up, from under, and *cedo*, to go.]

**Success**, suk-ses', *n.* act of *succeeding* or state of having succeeded: the prosperous termination of anything attempted. [L. *successus—succedo*.]

**Successful**, suk-ses'fool, *adj.* resulting in *success:* having the desired effect or termination: prosperous.—*adv.* **Success'fully.**

**Succession**, suk-sesh'un, *n.* act of *succeeding* or following after: series of persons or things following each other in time or place: series of descendants: race: (*agri.*) rotation, as of crops: right to take possession. [L. *successio*.]

**Successional**, suk-sesh'un-al, *adj.* existing in a regular *succession* or order.

**Successive**, suk-ses'iv, *adj.* following in *succession* or in order.—*adv.* **Success'ively.**

**Successor**, suk-ses'or, *n.* one who *succeeds* or comes after: one who takes the place of another. [L.]

**Succinct**, suk-singkt', *adj.* short: concise.—*adv.* **Succinct'ly.**—*n.* **Succinct'ness.** [Lit. 'girded up,' L. *succinctus—sub*, up, and *cingo*, to gird.]

**Succory**, suk'or-i, *n.* a form of **Chicory.**

**Succour**, suk'ur, *v.t.* to assist: to relieve.—*n.* aid: relief.—*n.* **Succ'ourer.** [L. *succurro*, to run up to—*sub*, up, and *curro*, to run.]

**Succulent**, suk'ū-lent, *adj.* full of juice or moisture. — *n.* **Succ'ulence.**—*adv.* **Succ'ulently.** [L. *succulentus—succus*, juice, the thing sucked up—*sugo*, to suck.]

**Succumb**, suk-kumb', *v.i.* to *lie* down *under:* to sink under: to yield. [L. *sub*, under, *cumbo*, to lie down.]

**Such**, such, *adj.* of the like kind: of that quality or character mentioned: denoting a particular person or thing, as in *such and such:* (*B.*) **Such like = Such.** [Lit. 'so like,' A.S. *swelc*, *swilc*, from *swa*, so, and *lic*, like, cog. with Goth. *sva-leiks*. See **So** and **Like**.]

**Suck**, suk, *v.t.* to draw in with the mouth: to draw milk from with the mouth: to imbibe: to drain.—*v.i.* to draw with the mouth: to draw the breast: to draw in.—*n.* act of sucking: milk drawn from the breast.—*n.* **Suck'er.** [A.S. *sucan*, *sugan*; Ger. *saugen*; allied to L. *sugo*, *suctum*, Sans. *chush*, to suck; from the sound.]

**Suckle**, suk'l, *v.t.* to *give suck* to: to nurse at the breast. [Dim. of **Suck**.]

**Suckling**, suk'ling, *n.* a young child or animal being *suckled* or nursed at the breast.

**Suction**, suk'shun, *n.* act or power of *sucking:* act of drawing, as fluids, by exhausting the air.

**Sudatory**, sū'da-tor-i, *adj.*, *sweating*.—*n.* a sweating-bath. [L. *sudatorius—sudo*, *sudatum*, akin to Sans. *svid*, to sweat, and to **Sweat**.]

**Sudden**, sud'en, *adj.* unexpected: hasty: abrupt. —*adv.* **Sudd'enly.**—*n.* **Sudd'enness.** [A.S. *soden*—Fr. *soudain*—L. *subitaneus*, sudden—*subitus*, coming stealthily—*sub*, up, and *eo*, *itum*, akin to Sans. *i*, to go.]

**Sudorific**, sū-dor-if'ik, *adj.*, *causing sweat*.—*n.* a medicine producing sweat. [L. *sudor*, sweat, and *facio*, to make.]

**Suds**, sudz, *n.pl.*, *seething* or boiling water mixed with soap. [From pa.p. of *seothan*, to seethe, cog. with Ger. *sod—sieden*. See **Seethe**.]

**Sue**, sū, *v.t.* to prosecute at law.—*v.i.* to make legal claim: to make application: to entreat: to demand. [M. E. *suen*—O. Fr. *suir* (Fr. *suivre*) —L. *sequor*, *secutus*, akin to Sans. *sach*, to follow.]

**Suet**, sū'et, *n.* the hard *fat* of an animal, particularly that about the kidneys.—*adj.* **Su'ety.** [O. Fr. *seu* (Fr. *suif*)—L. *sebum*, fat.]

**Suffer**, suf'ėr, *v.t.* to undergo: to endure: to be

affected by: to permit.—*v.i.* to feel pain or punishment: to sustain loss: to be injured.—*n.* **Suff'erer.** [L. *suffero—sub*, under, and *fero*, to bear.]                                    [allowable.

**Sufferable,** suf'ėr-a-bl, *adj.* that may be *suffered.*

**Sufferance,** suf'ėr-ans, *n.* state of *suffering:* endurance: permission: toleration.

**Suffering,** suf'ėr-ing, *n.* distress, loss, or injury.

**Suffice,** suf-fīs', *v.i.* to be enough: to be equal to the end in view.—*v.t.* to satisfy. [L. *sufficio*, to take the place of, to meet the need of—*sub*, under, and *facio*, to make.]

**Sufficiency,** suf-fish'en-si, *n.* state of being *sufficient:* competence: ability: capacity: conceit.

**Sufficient,** suf-fish'ent, *adj.*, *sufficing:* enough: equal to any end or purpose: competent.—*adv.* **Suffi'ciently.**

**Suffix,** suf'iks, *n.* a particle added to the root of a word.—**Suffix'**, *v.t.* to add a letter or syllable to a word to mark different notions and relations. [L. *sub*, under, after, and *figo*, to fix.]

**Suffocate,** suf'o-kāt, *v.t.* to choke by stopping the breath: to stifle. [L. *suffoco—sub*, under, and *fauces*, the throat.]

**Suffocation,** suf-fo-kā'shun, *n.* act of *suffocating:* state of being suffocated.

**Suffragan,** suf'ra-gan, *adj.* assisting.—*n.* an assistant bishop. [Lit. 'voting for.']

**Suffrage,** suf'rāj, *n.* a *vote:* united voice, as of a nation, or a congregation in prayer. [L. *suffragium—suffragor*, to vote for.]

**Suffuse,** suf-fūz', *v.t.* to *pour underneath:* to overspread or cover, as with a fluid. [L. *sub*, underneath, and *fundo, fusum*, to pour.]

**Suffusion,** suf-fū'zhun, *n.* act or operation of *suffusing:* state of being suffused: that which is suffused.

**Sugar,** shoog'ar, *n.* a sweet substance obtained chiefly from a kind of cane.—*v.t.* to sprinkle, or mix with sugar: to compliment. [Fr. *sucre*—Low L. *zucara*—Arab. *sokkar*—Pers. *schakar*, Sans. *çarkara*, sugar, orig. grains of sand, applied to sugar because occurring in grains.]

**Sugar-cane,** shoog'ar-kān, *n.* the *cane* or plant from which *sugar* is chiefly obtained.

**Sugary,** shoog'ar-i, *adj.* sweetened with, tasting of or like *sugar:* fond of sweets.

**Suggest,** sug-jest', *v.t.* to introduce indirectly to the thoughts: to hint. [L. *sub*, under, from under, and *gero, gestum*, to carry.]

**Suggestion,** sug-jest'yun, *n.* act of *suggesting:* hint: proposal.

**Suggestive,** sug-jest'iv, *adj.* containing a *suggestion* or hint.—*adv.* **Suggest'ively.**

**Suicidal,** sū-i-sī'dal, *adj.* pertaining to or partaking of the crime of *suicide.*—*adv.* **Suici'dally.**

**Suicide,** sū'i-sīd, *n.* one who *falls* or dies by his *own* hand: self-murder. [Coined from L. *sui*, of himself, and *cædo*, to kill.]

**Suit,** sūt, *n.* act of *suing:* an action at law: a petition: a series: a set: a number of things of the same kind or made to be used together, as clothes or armour: courtship.—*v.t.* to fit: to become: to please.—*v.i.* to agree: to correspond.

**Suitable,** sūt'a-bl, *adj.* that *suits:* fitting: agreeable to: adequate.—*adv.* **Suit'ably.**—*ns.* **Suitabil'ity, Suit'ableness.**

**Suite,** swēt, *n.* a train of *followers* or attendants: a regular set, particularly of rooms. [Fr., from **Sue.**]

**Suitor,** sūt'or, *n.* one who *sues* in love or law: a petitioner: a wooer.

**Sulcate,** sul'kāt, **Sulcated,** sul'kāt-ed, *adj.*, *furrowed:* grooved. [L. *sulcus*, a furrow.]

**Sulk,** sulk, *v.i.* to be sullen.—**Sulks,** *n.* a fit of sullenness.

**Sulky,** sulk'i, *adj.* silently sullen.—*n.* **Sulk'iness.** [A.S. *solcen*, slow: or perh. for *sulty*—O. Fr. *soltif*, sullen, solitary. Compare **Sullen.**]

**Sullen,** sul'en, *adj.* gloomily angry and silent: malignant: dark: dull.—*adv.* **Sull'enly.**—*n.* **Sull'enness** [Lit. 'solitary, dull,' O. Fr. *solain*—L. *solus*, alone. See **Sole,** *adj.*]

**Sully,** sul'i, *v.t.* to *soil:* to spot: to tarnish.—*v.i.* to be soiled:—*pa.t.* and *pa.p.* sull'ied.—*n.* spot: tarnish. [Fr. *souiller.* See **Soil,** v.]

**Sulphate,** sul'fāt, *n.* a salt formed by *sulphuric* acid with a base.                              [acid.

**Sulphite,** sul'fīt, *n.* a salt formed by *sulphurous*

**Sulphur,** sul'fur, *n.* a yellow mineral substance, very brittle, fusible, and inflammable: brimstone. [L.; said to be conn. with Sans. *çulvari.*]

**Sulphurate,** sul'fur-āt, *v.t.* to combine with or subject to the action of *sulphur.*

**Sulphureous,** sul-fū're-us, *adj.* consisting of, containing, or having the qualities of *sulphur.*

**Sulphuret,** sul'fū-ret, *n.* a combination of *sulphur* with an alkali, earth, or metal.

**Sulphuretted,** sul'fū-ret-ed, *adj.* having *sulphur* in combination.

**Sulphuric,** sul-fū'rik, *adj.* pertaining to or obtained from *sulphur:* denoting a certain well-known strong acid, formerly called oil of vitriol.

**Sulphurous,** sul'fur-us, *adj.* pertaining to, resembling, or containing *sulphur:* denoting the pungent acid given out when sulphur is burned in air.

**Sultan,** sul'tan, *n.* the supreme head of the Ottoman empire.—*n.* **Sul'tanship.** [Ar. *sultan*, power, prince—*salita*, to be strong; allied to Heb. *shalat*, to rule.]

**Sultana,** sul-tä'na or sul-tä'na, *n.* the wife or queen of a *sultan:* a small kind of raisin.

**Sultry,** sul'tri, *adj.*, *sweltering:* very hot and oppressive: close.—*n.* **Sul'triness.** [Another form is *sweltry*, from root of **Swelter.**]

**Sum,** sum, *n.* the amount of two or more things taken together: the whole of anything: a quantity of money: a problem in arithmetic: chief points: substance or result of reasoning: summary: height: completion.—*v.t.* to collect into one amount or whole: to count: to bring into a few words:—*pr.p.* summ'ing; *pa.t.* and *pa.p.* summed. [L. *summa—summus, supremus*, highest, superl. of *superus*, on high—*super*, above.]

**Summarise,** sum'ar-īz, *v.t.* to present in a *summary* or briefly.

**Summary,** sum'ar-i, *adj.*, *summed up* or condensed: short: brief: compendious: done by a short method.—*n.* an abstract, abridgment, or compendium.—*adv.* **Summ'arily.**

**Summation,** sum-ā'shun, *n.* act of *summing* or forming a total amount: an aggregate.

**Summer,** sum'ėr, *n.* the second and warmest season of the year—June, July, August.—*v.i.* (*B.*) to pass the summer. [A.S. *sumor*, with cog. words in most Teut. tongues. The root is perh. found in Ir. *samh*, sun.]

**Summer-house,** sum'ėr-hows, *n.* a *house* in a garden used in *summer:* a house for summer residence.

**Summerset.** Same as **Somersault.**

**Summit,** sum'it, *n.* the *highest* point or degree: the top. [L. *summitas—summus, supremus.*]

**Summon,** sum'un, *v.t.* to call with authority: to command to appear, esp. in court: to rouse to exertion.—*n.* **Summ'oner.** [L. *summoneo—sub*, secretly, and *moneo*, to warn.]

**Summons**, sum′unz, *n.* a *summoning* or an authoritative call : a call to appear, esp. in court.

**Sumpter**, sump′tèr, *n.* a horse for carrying *packs* or burdens. [With inserted *p* from Fr. *sommier* —L. *sagmarius*—L. and Gr. *sagma*, a pack-saddle—Gr. *sattō*, to pack.]

**Sumptuary**, sumpt′ū-ar-i, *adj.* pertaining to or regulating *expense*, as in **Sumptuary Laws**, which sought to curtail the expensive habits of the citizens. [L. *sumptuarius*—*sumo*, *sumptum*, to take, contr. of *sub*, up, *emo*, to buy.]

**Sumptuous**, sumpt′ū-us, *adj.* costly : magnificent. —*adv.* **Sumpt′uously**.—*n.* **Sumpt′uousness**.

**Sun**, sun, *n.* the body which is the source of light and heat to our planetary system : a body which forms the centre of a system of orbs : that which resembles the sun in brightness or value. —*v.t.* to expose to the sun's rays :—*pr.p.* sunn′ing ; *pa.t.* and *pa.p.* sunned. [A.S. *sunne* ; Ice. *sunna*, Goth. *sunno* ; an old word, of unknown ety.]

**Sunbeam**, sun′bēm, *n.* a *beam* or ray of the *sun*.

**Sunburned**, sun′burnd, **Sunburnt**, sun′burnt, *adj.*, *burned* or discoloured by the *sun*.

**Sunday**, sun′dā, *n.* the first *day* of the week, so called because anc. dedicated to the *sun* or its worship.

**Sunder**, sun′dèr, *v.t.* to *separate* : to divide : (*B.*) **In sunder**, asunder. [A.S. *sundrian*, to separate ; *sunder*, separate ; Ice. *sundr*, asunder.]

**Sundry**, sun′dri, *adj.*, *separate* : more than one or two : several : divers.—*n.pl.* **Sun′dries**.

**Sunfish**, sun′fish, *n.* a *fish* whose body resembles the forepart of a larger fish cut short off, supposed to be so called from its nearly *circular* form.

**Sunflower**, sun′flow-èr, *n.* a plant so called from its *flower*, which is a large disk with yellow rays.

**Sung**, sung, *pa.t.* and *pa.p.* of **Sing**.

**Sunk**, sungk, **Sunken**, sungk′n, *pa.p.* of **Sink**.

**Sunless**, sun′les, *adj.* without the sun : deprived of the sun or its rays : shaded : dark.

**Sunny**, sun′i, *adj.* pertaining to, coming from, or like the *sun* : exposed to, warmed, or coloured by the sun's rays.—*n.* **Sun′iness**.

**Sunrise**, sun′rīz, **Sunrising**, sun′rīz-ing, *n.* the *rising* or first appearance of the *sun* above the horizon : the time of this rising : the east.

**Sunset**, sun′set, **Sunsetting**, sun′set-ing, *n.* the *setting* or going down of the *sun* : the west.

**Sunshine**, sun′shīn, *n.* the *shining* light of the *sun* : the place on which he *shines* : warmth.

**Sunshine**, sun′shīn, **Sunshiny**, sun′shīn-i, *adj.* bright with sunshine : pleasant : bright like the sun.

**Sunstroke**, sun′strōk, *n.* (*lit.*) a *stroke* of the sun or its heat : a nervous disease, from exposure to the sun.

**Sunward**, sun′ward, *adv.*, *toward* the sun.

**Sup**, sup, *v.t.* to take into the mouth, as a liquid. —*v.i.* to eat the evening meal : (*B.*) to sip :— *pr.p.* supp′ing ; *pa.t.* and *pa.p.* supped.—*n.* a small mouthful, as of a liquid. [A.S. *supan* ; Ice. *supa*, Ger. *saufen*, to drink.]

**Superabound**, sū-pėr-ab-ownd′, *v.i.* to *abound exceedingly* : to be more than enough. [L. *super*, above, and **Abound**.]

**Superabundant**, sū-pėr-ab-und′ant, *adj.*, *abundant to excess* : more than enough : copious.— *adv.* **Superabund′antly**.—*n.* **Superabund′ance**.

**Superadd**, sū-per-ad′, *v.t.* to *add over* and *above*. —*n.* **Superaddi′tion**. [L. *super*, above, and **Add**.]

**Superannuate**, sū-pėr-an′ū-āt, *v.t.* to impair or disqualify by living *beyond* the *years* of service or by old age : to pension on account of old age or infirmity. [L. *super*, above, and *annus*, a year.]

**Superannuation**, sū-pėr-an-ū-ā′shun, *n.* state of being *superannuated*.

**Superb**, sū-pèrb′, *adj.* proud : magnificent : stately : elegant.—*adv.* **Superb′ly**. [L. *superbus*, haughty, proud—*super*, above.]

**Supercargo**, sū-pėr-kär′go, *n.* an officer or person in a merchant-ship placed *over* the *cargo* and superintending all the commercial transactions of the voyage. [L. *super*, over, and **Cargo**.]

**Superciliary**, sū-pėr-sil′i-ar-i, *adj.*, *above* the *eyebrow*. [From L. *super*, above, and *cilium*, the eyelid.]

**Supercilious**, sū-pėr-sil′i-us, *adj.* lofty with pride : disdainful : dictatorial : overbearing.—*adv.* **Supercil′iously**.—*n.* **Supercil′iousness**. [L. *superciliosus*—*supercilium*, an eyebrow—*super*, above, and *cilium*, eyelid, akin to Gr. *kyla*, the parts under the eyes.]

**Supereminent**, sū-pėr-em′i-nent, *adj.*, *eminent* in a *superior* degree : excellent beyond others.— *adv.* **Superem′inently**.—*n.* **Superem′inence**. [L. *super*, above, and **Eminent**.]

**Supererogation**, sū-pėr-er-ō-gā′shun, *n.* doing more than duty requires or is necessary for salvation.—*adj.* **Supererog′atory**. [Lit. 'paying over and above,' L. *super*, above, and *erogo*, *-atum*, to pay out—*ex*, out of, and *rogo*, to ask.]

**Superexcellent**, sū-pėr-ek′sel-lent, *adj.*, *excellent above* others, or in an uncommon degree.—*n.* **Superex′cellence**. [L. *super*, above, **Excellent**.]

**Superficial**, sū-pėr-fish′al, *adj.* pertaining to or being on the *surface* : shallow : slight : containing only what is apparent and simple : not learned.—*adv.* **Superfi′cially**.—*ns.* **Superfi′cialness**, **Superficial′ity**. [From **Superficies**.]

**Superficies**, sū-pėr-fish′ēz, *n.* the *upper face* or surface : the outer face or part of a thing. [L. —*super*, above, and *facies*, face.]

**Superfine**, sū′pėr-fīn, *adj.*, *fine above* others : finer than ordinary. [L. *super*, above, and **Fine**.]

**Superfluity**, sū-pėr-flōō′i-ti, *n.* a *superfluous* quantity or more than enough : state of being superfluous : superabundance.

**Superfluous**, sū-pėr′floo-us, *adj.* more than enough : unnecessary or useless.—*adv.* **Super′fluously**. [L. *superfluus*—*super*, above, and *fluo*, to flow.]

**Superhuman**, sū-pėr-hū′man, *adj.*, *above* what is *human* : divine. [L. *super*, above, and **Human**.]

**Superimpose**, sū-pėr-im-pōz′, *v.t.* to *impose* or lay *above*. [L. *super*, above, and **Impose**.]

**Superincumbent**, sū-pėr-in-kum′bent, *adj.*, *lying above*. [L. *super*, above, and **Incumbent**.]

**Superinduce**, sū-pėr-in-dūs′, *v.t.* to *bring in over and above* something else. [L. *super*, above, and *induco*—*in*, in, and *duco*, to bring.]

**Superintend**, sū-pėr-in-tend′, *v.t.* to have the oversight or charge of : to control. [Lit. ' to be *intent over* anything,' L. *super*, above, and *intendo* —*in*, on, and *tendo*, to stretch.]

**Superintendence**, sū-pėr-in-tend′ens, *n.* oversight : direction : management.

**Superintendent**, sū-pėr-in-tend′ent, *adj.*, *superintending*.—*n.* one who superintends : overseer.

**Superior**, sū-pē′ri-or, *adj.*, *upper* : higher in place, rank, or excellence : surpassing others : beyond the influence of.—*n.* one superior to others : the chief of a monastery, &c. and of certain churches and colleges. [L., comp. of *superus*, high—*super*, above.]

**Superiority**, sū-pē-ri-or'i-ti, *n.* quality or state of being *superior*: pre-eminence: advantage.

**Superlative**, sū-pėr'la-tiv, *adj.*, *carried above* others or to the highest degree: superior to all others: most eminent: (*gram.*) expressing the highest degree of a quality.—*n.* (*gram.*) the superlative or highest degree of adjectives and adverbs.—*adv.* **Super'latively.** [L. *superlativus—superlatus*, pa.p. of *superfero—super*, above, *fero*, to carry.]

**Supernal**, sū-pėr'nal, *adj.* that is *above* or in a higher place or region: relating to things above: celestial. [L. *supernus—super*, above.]

**Supernatural**, sū-pėr-nat'ū-ral, *adj.*, *above* or beyond the powers of *nature*: not according to the usual course of nature: miraculous: spiritual.—*adv.* **Supernat'urally.** [L. *super*, above, and **Natural.**]

**Supernaturalism**, sū-pėr-nat'ū-ral-izm, *n.* the belief in the influence of the supernatural in the world.

**Supernumerary**, sū-pėr-nūm'ėr-ar-i, *adj.*, *over and above* the *number* stated, or which is usual or necessary.—*n.* a person or thing beyond the usual, necessary, or stated number. [L. *supernumerarius—super*, over, and *numerus*, a number.]

**Superpose**, sū-pėr-pōz', *v.t.* to *place over* or upon. [L. *super*, over, and Fr. *poser* (see **Pose**, *n.*).]

**Superposition**, sū-pėr-po-zish'un, *n.* act of *superposing*: state of being superposed: that which is above anything.

**Superscribe**, sū-pėr-skrīb', *v.t.* to *write* or engrave *over*, on the outside or top: to write the name on the outside or cover of. [L. *super*, over, above, and *scribo, scriptum*, to write.]

**Superscription**, sū-pėr-skrip'shun, *n.* act of *superscribing*: that which is written or engraved above or on the outside.

**Supersede**, sū-pėr-sēd', *v.t.* to *sit* or be *above* or superior to: to make useless by superior power: to come in the room of: to displace. [L. *super*, above, and *sedeo, sessum*, to sit.]

**Superstition**, sū-pėr-stish'un, *n.* excessive reverence or fear: excessive exactness in religious opinions or practice: false worship or religion: an ignorant and irrational belief in supernatural agency: belief in what is absurd, without evidence. [L. *superstitio*, excessive religious belief—*super*, over, above, and *sto*, to stand; it orig. meant a '*standing* still *over* or by a thing,' in fear, wonder, dread.]

**Superstitious**, sū-pėr-stish'us, *adj.* pertaining to or proceeding from *superstition*: showing or given to superstition: over-exact.—*adv.* **Supersti'tiously.**

**Superstructure**, sū-pėr-strukt'ūr, *n.* a *structure above* or on something else: anything erected on a foundation. [L. *super*, above, and **Structure.**]

**Supervene**, sū-pėr-vēn', *v.i.* to *come above* or upon: to occur, or take place. [L. *super*, above, and *venio, ventum*, to come.]

**Supervention**, sū-pėr-ven'shun, *n.* act of *supervening* or taking place.

**Supervisal**, sū-pėr-vīz'al, **Supervision**, sū-pėr-vizh'un, *n.* act of *supervising*: inspection: control.

**Supervise**, sū-pėr-vīz', *v.t.* to *oversee*: to superintend. [L. *super*, over, and *video, visum*, to see.]      [an overseer: an inspector.

**Supervisor**, sū-pėr-vīz'or, *n.* one who supervises:

**Supine**, sū-pīn', *adj.*, *lying* on the *back*: leaning backward: negligent: indolent.—*n.* sū'pīn (*Latin gram.*) name given to the verbal form in

*um* and *u* (so called perh. because though furnished with case-endings, it rests or falls back on the verb).—*adv.* **Supine'ly.**—*n.* **Supine'ness.** [L. *supinus—sub*, under, below; cf. Gr. *hyptios*, from *hypo*.]

**Supper**, sup'ėr, *n.* a meal taken at the close of the day. [Lit. 'taking of *soup*,' Fr. *souper—soupe*; from Ger. *suppe*. See **Soup** and **Sup.**]

**Supperless**, sup'ėr-les, *adj.* without supper.

**Supplant**, sup-plant', *v.t.* to displace by stratagem: to take the place of: to undermine.—*n.* **Supplant'er.** [L. *supplanto*, to trip up one's heels—*sub*, under, *planta*, the sole of the foot.]

**Supple**, sup'l, *adj.* pliant: lithe: yielding to the humour of others: fawning.—*v.t.* to make supple: to make soft or compliant.—*v.i.* to become supple.—*n.* **Supp'leness.** [Fr. *souple*—L. *supplex*, bending the knees—*sub*, under, and *plico*, to fold. See **Pliant.**]

**Supplement**, sup'le-ment, *n.* that which *supplies* or fills up: any addition by which defects are supplied.—*v.t.* to supply or fill up: to add to. [L. *supplementum—suppleo*, to fill up.]

**Supplemental**, sup-ple-ment'al, **Supplementary**, sup-ple-ment'ar-i, *adj.* added to *supply* what is wanting: additional.

**Suppliant**, sup'li-ant, *adj.*, *supplicating*: asking earnestly: entreating.—*n.* a humble petitioner.—*adv.* **Supp'liantly.** [Fr. *suppliant*, pr.p. of *supplier*—L. *supplico*.]

**Supplicant**, sup'li-kant, *adj.*, *supplicating*: asking submissively.—*n.* one who supplicates or entreats earnestly. [L. *supplicans*, pr.p. of *supplico*.]

**Supplicate**, sup'li-kāt, *v.t.* to entreat earnestly: to address in prayer. [L. *supplico, -atum—supplex*, kneeling down—*sub*, under, and *plico*, to fold.]

**Supplication**, sup-li-kā'shun, *n.* act of *supplicating*: earnest prayer or entreaty. [L. *supplicatio*.]

**Supplicatory**, sup'li-ka-tor-i, *adj.* containing *supplication* or entreaty: humble.

**Supply**, sup-plī', *v.t.* to *fill up*, esp. a deficiency: to add what is wanted: to furnish: to fill a vacant place: to serve instead of:—*pa.t.* and *pa.p.* supplied'. [Fr.—L. *suppleo—sub*, up, and *pleo*, to fill.]

**Supply**, sup-plī', *n.* act of supplying: that which is supplied or which supplies a want: amount of food or money provided (used generally in *pl.*).

**Support**, sup-pōrt', *v.t.* to *bear up*: to endure or sustain: to keep up as a part or character: to make good: to defend: to represent: to supply with means of living: to uphold by countenance, patronise: to follow on same side as a speaker.—*n.* act of supporting or upholding: that which supports, sustains, or maintains: maintenance. [L. *sub*, up, and *porto*, to bear.]

**Supportable**, sup-pōrt'a-bl, *adj.* capable of being supported: endurable: capable of being maintained.—*adv.* **Support'ably.**

**Supporter**, sup-pōrt'ėr, *n.* one who or that which supports: an adherent: a defender: (*her.*) a figure on each side of the escutcheon.

**Supposable**, sup-pōz'a-bl, *adj.* that may be supposed.

**Suppose**, sup-pōz', *v.t.* to lay down, assume, or state as true: to imagine.—*n.* **Suppos'er.** (Lit. 'to place under,' Fr. *supposer*—L. *sub*, under, and Fr. *poser*, to place (see **Pose**, *n.*).)

**Supposition**, sup-po-zish'un, *n.* act of *supposing*: that which is supposed: assumption. [Fr.—L.]

**Supposititious**, sup-poz-i-tish'us, *adj.* put by trick in *the place of another*: spurious: imaginary.

[L. *supposititius—suppono*, to put in the place of another—*sub*, under, and *pono*, to place.]

**Suppress**, sup-pres′, *v.t.* to *press* or put *down* : to crush : to keep in : to retain or conceal : to stop. —*n.* **Suppress′or**. [L. *suppressum*, pa.p. of *supprimo—sub*, down, under, and *premo* (see **Press**).]

**Suppression**, sup-presh′un, *n.* act of *suppressing*: stoppage : concealment.

**Suppressive**, sup-pres′iv, *adj.* tending to *suppress*: subduing.

**Suppurate**, sup′ū-rāt, *v.i.* to gather *pus* or matter. [L. *sub*, under, and *pus*, *pur-is* (see **Pus**).]

**Suppuration**, sup-ū-rā′shun, *n.* act or process of suppurating or producing pus : matter.

**Suppurative**, sup′ū-rāt-iv, *adj.* tending to suppurate : promoting suppuration.—*n.* a medicine that promotes suppuration.

**Supramundane**, sū-pra-mun′dān, *adj.*, *above the world*. [L. *supra*, above, and **Mundane**.]

**Supremacy**, sū-prem′a-si, *n.* state of being *supreme*: highest authority or power. [Coined from **Supreme**, on the model of **Primacy**.]

**Supreme**, sū-prēm′, *adj.*, *highest*: greatest : most excellent.—*adv.* **Supreme′ly**. [L. *supremus*, superl. of *superus*, high—*super*, above.]

**Surcease**, sur-sēs′, *v.i.* to *cease*.—*v.t.* to cause to cease.—*n.* cessation. [Fr. *sursis*, pa.p. of *sur-seoir*, to leave off—L. *super-sedere*, to sit over, to refrain from. Cf. **Assize**, **Assess**. Doublet **Supersede**.]

**Surcharge**, sur-chärj′, *v.t.* to *overcharge* or overload.—*n.* an excessive load. [Fr. *sur*—L. *super*, over, and **Charge**.]

**Surd**, surd, *adj.* (*alg.*) involving surds : produced by the action of the speech organs on the breath (not the voice), as the 'hard' sounds *k*, *t*, *p*, *f*, &c. —*n.* (*alg.*) a quantity inexpressible by rational numbers, or which has no root. [Lit. 'deaf,' L. *surdus*; allied to Sans. *svar*, heavy.]

**Sure**, shōōr, *adj.*, *secure*: fit to be depended on : certain : strong : confident beyond doubt.— *advs.* **Sure**, **Sure′ly**. [Fr. *sûr*—L. *securus*. Doublet **Secure**.]

**Suretiship**, shōōr′ti-ship, *n.* state of being *surety*: obligation of one person to answer for another.

**Surety**, shōōr′ti, *n.* state of being *sure*: certainty : he or that which makes sure : security against loss : one who becomes bound for another. [Doublet **Security**.]

**Surf**, surf, *n.* the foam made by the dashing of waves.—*adj.* **Surf′y**. [Ety. very dub. ; perh. from **Surge**; under influence of L. *sorbeo*, to suck in.]

**Surface**, sur′fās, *n.* the exterior part of anything. [Fr. (*lit.*) the 'upper face,' from *sur*—L. *super*, and *face*—L. *facies*. See **Face**. Doublet **Superficies**.]

**Surfeit**, sur′fit, *v.t.* to fill to satiety and disgust. —*n.* excess in eating and drinking : sickness or satiety caused by overfulness. [Fr. *surfait*, overdone—L. *super*, and *factum*.]     [tony.

**Surfeiting**, sur′fit-ing, *n.* eating overmuch : glut-

**Surge**, surj, *n.* the *rising* or swelling of a large wave.—*v.i.* to rise high : to swell. [Through O. Fr. forms from L. *surgo*, to rise. See **Source**.]

**Surgeon**, sur′jun, *n.* one who treats injuries or diseases by *operating* upon them with the *hand*. [From *serurgien*, an O. Fr. form of Fr. *chirurgien* (whence E. **Chirurgeon**), which see.]

**Surgeoncy**, sur′jun-si, *n.* the office or employment of a *surgeon* in the army or navy.

**Surgery**, sur′jėr-i, *n.* act and art of treating

diseases by manual operations : a place for surgical operations.

**Surgical**, sur′jik-al, *adj.* pertaining to *surgeons*, or to *surgery*: done by surgery.—*adv.* **Sur′gically**.

**Surgy**, surj′i, *adj.* full of surges or waves: billowy.

**Surloin**, the preferable form of **Sirloin**.

**Surly**, sur′li, *adj.* morose : uncivil : tempestuous. —*adv.* **Sur′lily**.—*n.* **Sur′liness**. [From A.S. *sur*, sour, and *lic*, *lice*, like ; Wedgwood thinks it a modification of *sir-ly*, for *sirlike*, arrogant.]

**Surmise**, sur-mīz′, *n.* suspicion : conjecture.—*v.t.* to imagine : to suspect. [O. Fr. *surmise*, accusation—*surmettre*, to accuse—L. *super*, upon, *mitto*, to send, to put.]

**Surmount**, sur-mownt′, *v.t.* to *mount above*: to surpass.—*adj.* **Surmount′able**, that may be surmounted. [Fr.—*sur* (L. *super*), and *monter* (see **Mount**).]

**Surname**, sur′nām, *n.* a *name over and above* the Christian name : the family name.—*v.t.* to call by a surname. [Formed from Fr. *sur*—L. *super*, over and above, and E. **Name**, on the analogy of Fr. *sur-nom*.]

**Surpass**, sur-pas′, *v.t.* to *pass beyond*: to exceed : to excel. [Fr. *surpasser*, from *sur*—L. *super*, beyond, and *passer* (see **Pass**).]

**Surpassable**, sur-pas′a-bl, *adj.* that may be surpassed or excelled.

**Surplice**, sur′plis, *n.* a white outer garment worn by the clergy. [Fr. *surplis*—Low L. *super-pellicium*, an over-garment. See **Pelisse**.]

**Surplus**, sur′plus, *n.* the *overplus*: excess above what is required. [Fr., from *sur*—L. *super*, over, and *plus*, more.]

**Surplusage**, sur′plus-āj, *n.*, *overplus*.

**Surprise**, sur-prīz′, *n.* act of taking unawares : the emotion caused by anything sudden : amazement.—*v.t.* to come upon suddenly or unawares : to strike with wonder or astonishment : to confuse. [Fr.—*surpris*, pa.p. of *sur-prendre*—L. *super*, and *prehendo*, to take, catch. See **Get**.]

**Surprising**, sur-prīz′ing, *adj.* exciting surprise : wonderful : unexpected.—*adv.* **Surpris′ingly**.

**Surrender**, sur-ren′dėr, *v.t.* to *render* or deliver *over* : to resign.—*v.i.* to yield up one's self to another.—*n.* act of yielding, or giving up to another. [O. Fr. *surrendre*, from *sur*, over—L. *super*, and *rendre* (see **Render**).]

**Surreptitious**, sur-rep-tish′us, *adj.* done by stealth or fraud.—*adv.* **Surrepti′tiously**. [Lit. ' *seized* in an *underhand* manner,' L., from *surripio*, *surreptum—sub*, under, and *rapio*, to seize.]

**Surrogate**, sur′ro-gāt, *n.* a substitute : the deputy of an ecclesiastical judge. [Lit. ' one *asked* to act in the *place* of another,' L. *surrogo*, *surrogatum—sub*, in the place of, and *rogo*, to ask.]

**Surround**, sur-rownd′, *v.t.* to go *round about*: to encompass. [Fr. *sur*—L. *super*, about, and **Round**.]

**Surtout**, sur-tōō′, *n.* a close-bodied frock-coat. [Fr.—Low L. *super-totus*, a garment worn *over all* others.]

**Surveillance**, sur-vel′yans, *n.* a being *vigilant* or watchful : inspection. [Fr.—*surveiller—sur*, over—L. *super*, and *veiller*, to watch—L. *vigilare*. See **Vigil**.]

**Survey**, sur-vā′, *v.t.* to *see* or look *over*: to inspect : to superintend : to examine : to measure and estimate, as land. [O. Fr. *surveoir*—L. *super*, over, and *videre*, to see.]

**Survey**, sur′vā. *n.*, *oversight*: view : examination : the measuring of land, or of a country.

**Surveyor**, sur-vā'or, *n.* an overseer : a measurer of land.—*n.* **Survey'orship.**

**Survival**, sur-vīv'al, *n.* a *surviving* or living after.

**Survive**, sur-vīv', *v.t.* to *live beyond* : to outlive.—*v.i.* to remain alive. [Fr.—L. *super*, beyond, and *vivere*, to live.]

**Survivor**, sur-vīv'or, *n.* one who survives or lives after another.—*n.* **Surviv'orship.**

**Susceptibility**, sus-sep-ti-bil'i-ti, *n.* quality of being susceptible : capability : sensibility.

**Susceptible**, sus-sep'ti-bl, *adj.* capable of receiving anything : impressible : disposed to admit.—*adv.* **Suscep'tibly.** [Fr.—L. *suscipio, susceptum*, to take up, to undergo—*sub*, from beneath, up, and *capio*, to take.]

**Susceptive**, sus-sep'tiv, *adj.* capable of receiving or admitting : readily admitting.

**Suspect**, sus-pekt', *v.t.* to mistrust : to imagine to be guilty : to doubt : to conjecture. [L. *suspicio, suspectum*, to look at secretly—*sub*, from beneath, up, and *specio*, to look at.]

**Suspend**, sus-pend', *v.t.* to *hang* one thing *beneath* another : to make to depend on : to make to stop for a time : to delay : to debar.—*n.* **Suspend'er.** [L. *suspendo*—*sub*, beneath, *pendo, pensum*, to hang.]

**Suspense**, sus-pens', *n.* state of being *suspended* : act of withholding the judgment : uncertainty : indecision : stop betwixt two opposites.

**Suspension**, sus-pen'shun, *n.* act of *suspending* : interruption ; delay : temporary privation of office or privilege : a conditional withholding.

**Suspensory**, sus-pens'or-i, *adj.* that *suspends* : doubtful.—*n.* that which suspends : a bandage.

**Suspicion**, sus-pish'un, *n.* act of *suspecting* : the imagining of something without evidence or on slender evidence : mistrust.

**Suspicious**, sus-pish'us, *adj.* full of *suspicion* : showing suspicion : inclined to suspect : liable to suspicion : doubtful.—*adv.* **Suspi'ciously.**—*n.* **Suspi'ciousness.**

**Sustain**, sus-tān', *v.t.* to *hold up* : to bear : to maintain : to relieve : to prove : to sanction : to prolong.—*n.* **Sustain'er.** [L. *sustineo*—*sub*, from beneath, up, and *teneo*, to hold.]

**Sustainable**, sus-tān'a-bl, *adj.* that may be sustained. [maintenance : provisions.

**Sustenance**, sus'ten-ans, *n.* that which *sustains* :

**Sustentation**, sus-ten-tā'shun, *n.* that which *sustains* : support : maintenance.

**Sutler**, sut'lér, *n.* a person who follows an army and sells liquor or provisions : a camp-hawker. [O. Dut. *soeteler*, a small trader—*soetelen*, to do mean work ; Ger. *sudler*, a dabbler—*sudeln*, to do dirty work.]

**Sutling**, sut'ling, *adj.* pertaining to *sutlers* : engaged in the occupation of a sutler.

**Suttee**, sut-tē', *n.* formerly in India, the sacrifice of a widow on the funeral pile of her husband : the widow so sacrificed. [Sans. *çuddhi*, voluntary sacrifice.]

**Sutural**, sūt'ūr-al, *adj.* relating to a *suture*.

**Suture**, sūt'ūr, *n.* (*med.*) the *sewing* together of a wound : the seam uniting the bones of the skull : (*bot.*) the seam at the union of two margins in a plant. [L. *sutura*—*suo*, to sew.]

**Sutured**, sūt'ūrd, *adj.* having or united by sutures.

**Suzerain**, sōō'ze-rān, *n.* a feudal lord : supreme or paramount ruler. [Lit. 'one who is *above*,' Fr. *sus*—Late L. *susum*, for *sursum* = *sub-versum*, above ; the termination in imitation of Fr. *souverain*, E. **Sovereign.**]

**Suzerainty**, sōō'ze-rān-.i, *n.* the dominion of a *suzerain* : paramount authority.

**Swab**, swob, *n.* a mop for cleaning or drying floors or decks.—*v.t.* to clean or dry with a swab :—*pr.p.* swabb'ing ; *pa.t.* and *pa.p.* swabbed. [Prob. orig. from the splashing movement of water, and so conn. with **Sweep.**]

**Swabber**, swob'ér, *n.* one who uses a *swab* : an officer who sees that the ship is kept clean.

**Swaddle**, swod'l, *v.t.* to *swathe* or bind tight with clothes, as an infant. [A.S. *swethel*, a swaddling-band ; an extension of **Swathe**, to bind.]

**Swaddling-band**, swod'ling-band, **Swaddling-cloth**, swod'ling-kloth, *n.* a *band* or *cloth* formerly used for *swaddling* an infant :—*pl.* (*B.*) **Swaddling-clothes.**

**Swagger**, swag'ér, *v.i.* to *sway* or *swing* the body in bluster : to brag noisily : to bully.—*n.* boastfulness : insolence of manner.—*n.* **Swagg'erer.** [From the root of **Sway, Swing.**]

**Swain**, swān, *n.* a young man : a peasant : a country lover. [A.S. *swan*, a servant ; Ice. *sveinn*, young man, servant, Dan. *svend*, servant ; perh. conn. with root of **Son.**]

**Swallow**, swol'ō, *n.* a migratory bird with long wings, which seizes its insect food on the wing. [A.S. *swalewe* ; cog. with Ger. *schwalbe*.]

**Swallow**, swol'ō, *v.t.* to receive through the gullet into the stomach : to ingulf : to absorb : to occupy : to exhaust. [A.S. *swelgan*, to swallow ; cog. with Ger. *schwelgen* ; conn. with **Swill.**]

**Swam**, swam, *pa.t.* of **Swim.**

**Swamp**, swomp, *n.* wet, *spongy* land : low ground filled with water.—*v.t.* to sink in, or as in a swamp : to overset, or cause to fill with water, as a boat. [Closely conn. with Low Ger. and Scand. *svamp*, which, with A.S. *swamm* and Ger. *schwamm*, signify 'sponge' and 'mushroom ;' all from the root of **Swim.**]

**Swampy**, swomp'i, *adj.* consisting of swamp : wet and spongy.

**Swan**, swon, *n.* a web-footed bird like the duck and goose. [A.S. ; cog. with Ger. *schwan*, Dut. *zwaan* ; from L. *sono*, to sound, Sans. *svan*.]

**Sward**, swawrd, *n.* the grassy surface of land : green turf.—*v.t.* to cover with sward. [Orig. the 'skin of bacon,' A.S. *sweard* ; cog. with Ger. *schwarte*, thick, hard hide, Ice. *svördr*, the skin (esp. of the head), the sward or surface of the earth.] [covered with sward.

**Swarded**, swawrd'ed, **Swardy**, swawrd'i, *adj.*

**Sware**, swār (*B.*) *pa.t.* of **Swear.**

**Swarm**, swawrm, *n.* a body of *humming* or buzzing insects : a cluster of insects, esp. of bees : a great number : throng.—*v.i.* to gather as bees : to appear in a crowd : to throng : to abound : to breed multitudes. [A.S. *swearm* ; Ger. *schwarm* ; from the same root as Ger. *schwirren*, Sans. *svr*, to sound.]

**Swarthy**, swawrth'i, *adj.* of a blackish complexion : dark-skinned : tawny.—*adv.* **Swarth'ily.**—*n.* **Swarth'iness.** [A.S. *sweart* ; cog. with Ice. *svart-r*, Ger. *schwarz*, black ; conn. also with L. *sordidus*, dirty.]

**Swath**, swawth, *n.* a line of grass or corn cut by the scythe : the sweep of a scythe. [A.S. *swathe* ; Dut. *zwade*, also a scythe, which may have been the original meaning.]

**Swathe**, swāth, *v.t.* to bind with a band or bandage.—*n.* a bandage. [A.S. *be-swéthian*. Cf. **Swaddle.**]

**Sway**, swā, *v.t.* to *swing* or wield with the hand : to incline to one side : to influence by power or moral force : to govern.—*v.i.* to incline to one side : to govern : to have weight or influence.—*n.* the sweep of a weapon : that which moves

with power : preponderance : power in governing : influence or authority inclining to one
side. [Prob. Scand., as Ice. *sveigja*, Dan. *svaie*,
to sway, *sveie*, to bend ; akin to **Swing** and
**Wag**.]

**Swear**, swār, *v.i.* to affirm, calling God to witness :
to give evidence on oath : to utter the name of
God or of sacred things profanely.—*v.t.* to utter,
calling God to witness : to administer an oath
to : to declare on oath :—*pa.t.* swōre ; *pa.p.*
sworn.—*n.* **Swear′er.** [A.S. *swerian* ; cog.
with Dut. *zweren*, Ger. *schwören*. Cf. **Answer**.]

**Sweat**, swet, *n.* the moisture from the skin :
labour : drudgery.—*v.i.* to give out sweat or
moisture : to toil.—*v.t.* to give out, as sweat :
to cause to sweat. [A.S. *swat* ; cog. with Low
Ger. *sweet*, Ger. *schweiss* ; further conn. with L.
*sudor*, Gr. *hidrōs*, Sans. *svedas*.]

**Sweaty**, swet′i, *adj.* wet with sweat : consisting
of sweat : laborious.—*n.* **Sweat′iness.**

**Swede**, swēd, *n.* a native of Sweden.

**Swedish**, swēd′ish, *adj.* pertaining to Sweden.

**Sweep**, swēp, *v.t.* to wipe or rub over with a
brush or broom : to carry along or off by a long
brushing stroke or force : to destroy or carry off
at a stroke : to strike with a long stroke : to
carry with pomp : to drag over : to pass rapidly
over.—*v.i.* to pass swiftly and forcibly : to pass
with pomp : to move with a long reach :—*pa.t.*
and *pa.p.* swept.—*n.* act of sweeping : extent of
a stroke, or of anything turning or in motion :
direction of a curve : a chimney-sweeper.—*n.*
**Sweep′er.** [A.S. *swapan* ; cog. with Low Ger.
*swepen*, Ger. *schweifen*. Cf. E. **Swab**, **Swoop**,
and **Swift**.]

**Sweepings**, swēp′ingz, *n.pl.* things collected by
sweeping : rubbish.

**Sweepstakes**, swēp′stāks, *n.* all the money or
other things staked or won at a horserace, or
in gaming. [So called because the winner
*sweeps* up all the *stakes* or deposits.]

**Sweet**, swēt, *adj.* pleasing to the taste or senses :
tasting like sugar : fragrant : melodious : beautiful : fresh, as opp. to salt or to sour : not stale,
sour, or putrid : mild : obliging.—*n.* a sweet
substance : a term of endearment :—*pl.* sweetmeats.—*adv.* **Sweet′ly.**—*n.* **Sweet′ness.** [A.S.
*swet*, cog. with Ger. *süss*, Gr. *hēdys*, L. *suavis*,
sweet, Sans. *svad*, to taste.]

**Sweetbread**, swēt′bred, *n.* the pancreas of an
animal used for food, so called from its *sweetness* and resemblance to *bread*.

**Sweet-brier**, swēt′-brī′ėr, *n.* a thorny shrub of the
rose kind resembling the *brier*, having a *sweet*
smell.

**Sweeten**, swēt′n, *v.t.* to make *sweet* : to make
pleasing, mild, or kind : to increase the agreeable qualities of : to make pure and healthy.—
*n.* **Sweet′ener.**      [that which sweetens.]

**Sweetening**, swēt′n-ing, *n.* act of sweetening :

**Sweetheart**, swēt′härt, *n.* a lover or mistress.
[Simply from **Sweet** and **Heart** ; an expression
found in Chaucer.]

**Sweetish**, swēt′ish, *adj.* somewhat sweet to the
taste.—*n.* **Sweet′ishness.**

**Sweetmeat**, swēt′mēt, *n.* confections made wholly
or chiefly of sugar. [**Sweet** and **Meat**.]

**Sweet-pea**, swēt′-pē, *n.* a *pea* cultivated for its
*sweet* fragrance and beauty.

**Sweet-potato**, swēt′-po-tā′to, *n.* a plant common in
tropical countries, having tubers like the *potato*,
which are *sweet* and highly esteemed as food.

**Sweet-william**, swēt-wil′yam, *n.* a species of
pink of many colours and varieties.

**Swell**, swel, *v.i.* to grow larger : to expand : to
rise into waves : to heave : to be inflated : to
bulge out : to grow louder : to be bombastic, to
strut : to become elated, arrogant, or angry : to
grow upon the view : to grow louder, as a note.
—*v.t.* to increase the size of : to aggravate : to
increase the sound of : to raise to arrogance :—
*pa.p.* swelled or swollen (swōln).—*n.* act of
swelling : increase in size or sound : a gradual
rise of ground : a wave : the waves or tides of
the sea, esp. after a storm : a strutting foppish
fellow, a dandy. [A.S. *swellan* ; cog. with Ger.
*schwellen*, Ice. *svella*.]

**Swelling**, swel′ing, *adj.* (*B.*) inflated, proud,
haughty.—*n.* protuberance : a tumour : a rising,
as of passion : (*B.*) inflation by pride.

**Swelter**, swelt′ėr, *v.i.* to be faint, or oppressed
with heat. [A.S. *sweltan*, to die ; Ice. *svelta*,
to hunger.]

**Swept**, swept, *pa.t.* and *pa.p.* of **Sweep**.

**Swerve**, swėrv, *v.i.* to turn, depart from any line,
duty, or custom : to incline. [A.S. *hweorfan* ;
Dut. *swerven* ; conn. with **Warp**.]

**Swift**, swift, *adj.* moving quickly : fleet : rapid :
speedy : ready.—*n.* a *swiftly* flying bird of the
swallow tribe. [A.S.—*swifan*, to move quickly,
Ice. *svifa*, to glide. See **Swivel**.]

**Swiftly**, swift′li, *adv.* with swiftness : rapidly.

**Swiftness**, swift′nes, *n.* quality of being swift :
quickness : fleetness : rapidity : speed.

**Swill**, swil, *v.t.* or *v.i.* to drink greedily or largely.
—*n.* a large draught of liquor : the liquid mixture given to swine.—*n.* **Swill′er.** [A.S. *swilian*,
conn. with **Swallow**.]

**Swim**, swim, *v.i.* to float, as opp. to sink : to move
on or in water : to be borne along by a current :
to glide along with a waving motion : to be
dizzy : to be drenched : to overflow : to abound.
—*v.t.* to pass by swimming : to make to swim
or float :—*pr.p.* swimm′ing ; *pa.t.* swam ; *pa.p.*
swam or swum.—*n.* act of swimming : any motion
like swimming : air-bladder of a fish. [A.S.
*swimman*, cog. with Ger. *schwimmen*.]

**Swimmer**, swim′ėr, *n.* one who swims ; a web-
footed aquatic bird.

**Swimming**, swim′ing, *n.* the act of floating or
moving on or in the water : dizziness.

**Swimmingly**, swim′ing-li, *adv.* in a gliding manner, as if *swimming* : smoothly : successfully.

**Swindle**, swin′dl, *v.t.* to cheat under the pretence
of fair dealing.—*n.* the act of swindling or
defrauding. [Lit. 'to make dizzy,' Dut. *zwen-
delen*, from the root of A.S. *swindan*, to become
weak, Ger. *schwinden*, to disappear ; conn.
with **Swoon**.]

**Swindler**, swin′dlėr, *n.* one who defrauds by
imposition : a cheat or rogue.

**Swine**, swīn, *n.*, *sing.* and *pl.* a well-known
quadruped with bristly skin and long snout, fed
for its flesh : a pig : pigs collectively. [A.S.
*swin*, cog. with Ger. *schwein*, O. Ger. *suin*, L.
*sus*, Gr. *hys*.]

**Swing**, swing, *v.i.* to sway or wave to and fro, as
a body hanging in air : to vibrate : to practise
swinging : to turn round at anchor : to be
hanged.—*v.t.* to move to and fro : to cause to
wave or vibrate : to whirl, to brandish :—*pa.t.*
and *pa.p.* swung.—*n.* the act of swinging :
motion to and fro : a waving motion : anything
suspended for swinging in : the sweep or compass of a swinging body : power of anything
swinging : free course. [A.S. *swingan*, Ger.
*schwingen*, to swing ; allied to **Wag**. **Sway**.]

**Swingle-tree**, swing′gl-trē, **Single-tree**, sing′gl-trē, *n.* the cross-piece of a carriage, plough, &c., to which the traces of a harnessed horse are fixed. [From **Swing.**]

**Swinish**, swīn'ish, *adj.* like or befitting swine: gross: brutal.—*adv.* **Swin'ishly.**—*n.* **Swin'-ishness.**

**Swirl**, swėrl, *v.i.* to sweep along with a whirling motion.—*n.* whirling motion, as of wind or water. [Imitative like **Whirl.**]

**Swiss**, swis, *adj.* of or belonging to Switzerland. —*n.* a native of Switzerland: the language of Switzerland.

**Switch**, swich, *n.* a small flexible twig: a movable rail for transferring a carriage from one line of rails to another.—*v.t.* to strike with a switch: to transfer a carriage from one line of rails to another by a switch. [Low Ger. *zwukse, swutsche.*]

**Swivel**, swiv'l, *n.* something fixed in another body so as to *turn round* in it: a ring or link that turns round on a pin or neck: a small cannon turning on a swivel. [A.S. *swifan,* to move quickly, to turn round. See **Swift.**]

**Swollen**, swōln, *pa.p.* of **Swell.**

**Swoon**, swōōn, *v.i.* to faint: to fall into a fainting-fit.—*n.* the act of swooning: a fainting-fit. [A.S. and O. Ger. *swindan,* to become weak, to fail.]

**Swoop**, swōōp, *v.t.* to sweep down upon: to take with a sweep: to catch while on the wing: to catch up.—*v.i.* to descend with a sweep.—*n.* the act of swooping: a seizing as a bird on its prey. [A form of **Sweep.**]

**Swop**, swop, *v.t.* to exchange, to barter:—*pr.p.* swopp'ing; *pa.t.* and *pa.p.* swopped.—*n.* an exchange.

**Sword**, sōrd, *n.* an offensive weapon with a long blade, sharp upon one or both edges, for cutting or thrusting: destruction by the sword or by war: war: the emblem of vengeance or justice, or of authority and power. [A.S. *sweord,* cog. with Ice. *sverd,* Ger. *schwert.*]

**Sword-bayonet**, sōrd'-bā'on-et, *n.* a *bayonet* shaped somewhat like a *sword,* and used as one.

**Swordcane**, sōrd'kān, **Swordstick**, sōrd'stik, *n.* a *cane* or *stick* containing a *sword.*

**Swordfish**, sōrd'fish, *n.* a large sea-*fish* having the upper jaw elongated so as to resemble a *sword.*

**Swordsman**, sōrdz'man, *n.* a *man* skilled in the use of the *sword.*—*n.* **Swords'manship.**

**Swore, Sworn.** See **Swear.**

**Sybarite**, sib'a-rīt, *n.* an inhabitant of *Sybaris,* a Greek town in ancient Italy, noted for the effeminacy and luxury of its inhabitants: one devoted to luxury.—*adjs.* **Sybarit'ic, Sybarit'ical.**

**Sycamine**, sik'a-mīn, *n.* (*B.*) supposed to be the [black mulberry tree.]

**Sycamore**, sik'a-mōr, *n.* the fig-mulberry, growing in Egypt and other Eastern countries: in Britain, applied to a large maple, and in America, to the plane-tree. [Gr. *sykomoros—sykon,* a fig, and *moron,* the black mulberry.]

**Sycophancy**, sik'o-fan-si, **Sycophantism**, sik'o-fant-izm, *n.* the behaviour of a *sycophant*: mean tale-bearing: obsequious flattery: servility.

**Sycophant**, sik'o-fant, *n.* a common informer: a servile flatterer. [Gr. *sykophantēs,* usually said to mean one who informed against persons exporting figs from Attica, or plundering the sacred fig-trees; but more prob., one who brings figs to light by shaking the tree, hence one who makes rich men yield up their fruit by informations and other vile arts—*sykon,* a fig, and *phainō,* to bring to light, to show.]

**Sycophantic**, sik-o-fant'ik, **Sycophant'ical,** -ik-al, **Sycophant'ish,** -ish, *adj.* like a *sycophant*: obsequiously flattering: parasitic.

**Syllabic,** sil-lab'ik, **Syllab'ical,** -ik-al, *adj.* consisting of a *syllable* or syllables.—*adv.* **Syllab'ically.**—*n.* **Syllabica'tion.**

**Syllabicate,** sil-lab'i-kāt, *v.t.* to form into *sylla-*

**Syllabify,** sil-lab'i-fī, *v.t.* to form into *syllables*:—*pa.t.* and *pa.p.* syllab'ified.—*n.* **Syllabifica'tion.** [**Syllable,** and L. *facio,* to make.]

**Syllable,** sil'a-bl, *n.* several letters *taken together* so as to form one sound: a word or part of a word uttered by a single effort of the voice: a small part of a sentence. [L. *syllaba*—Gr. *syllabē—syn,* with, together, and *lab,* root of *lambanō,* to take.]

**Syllabub,** sil'a-bus, *n.* Same as **Sillabub.**

**Syllabus,** sil'a-bus, *n.* an abstract or compendium: a table of contents. [L.]

**Syllogise,** sil'o-jīz, *v.i.* to reason by *syllogisms.*

**Syllogism,** sil'o-jizm, *n.* logical form of every argument, consisting of three propositions, of which the first two are called the premises, and the last, which follows from them, the conclusion. [Gr. *syllogismos—syllogizomai—syn,* together, *logizomai,* to reckon—*logos,* speech, reckoning.]

**Syllogistic,** sil-o-jis'tik, **Syllogistical,** sil-o-jis'-tik-al, *adj.* pertaining to a *syllogism*: in the form of a syllogism.—*adv.* **Syllogis'tically.**

**Sylph,** silf, *n.* an imaginary being inhabiting the air: a fairy. [Fr. *sylphe,* of Celtic origin; but cf. Gr. *silphē,* a kind of beetle.]

**Sylphid,** silf'id, *n.* a *little sylph.* [Dim. of **Sylph.**]

**Sylvan.** A wrong form of **Silvan.**

**Symbol,** sim'bol, *n.* a sign by which one knows a thing: an emblem: that which represents something else: a figure or letter representing something: (*theol.*) a creed, compendium of doctrine, or a typical religious rite, as the Eucharist. [Gr. *symbolon,* from *symballō,* to put together, to compare, infer, conclude—*syn,* together, and *ballō,* to throw.]

**Symbolic,** sim-bol'ik, **Symbolical,** sim-bol'ik-al, *adj.* pertaining to or of the nature of a *symbol*: representing by signs: emblematic: figurative: typical.—*adv.* **Symbol'ically.**

**Symbolise,** sim'bol-īz, *v.i.* to be *symbolical*: to resemble in qualities.—*v.t.* to represent by symbols.

**Symboliser,** sim'bol-īz-ėr, **Symbolist,** sim'bol-ist, *n.* one who uses *symbols.*

**Symbolism,** sim'bol-izm, *n.* representation by *symbols* or signs: a system of symbols: use of symbols: (*theol.*) the science of symbols or creeds.

**Symmetrical,** sim-met'rik-al, *adj.* having *symmetry* or due proportion in its parts: harmonious.—*adv.* **Symmet'rically,** with symmetry.

**Symmetrise,** sim'e-trīz, *v.t.* to make *symmetrical.*

**Symmetry,** sim'e-tri, *n.* the state of one part being of the same *measure with,* or proportionate to another: due proportion: harmony or adaptation of parts to each other. [L. and Gr. *symmetria—syn,* together, and *metron,* a measure.]

**Sympathetic,** sim-pa-thet'ik, **Sympathetical,** sim-pa-thet'ik-al, *adj.* showing or inclined to *sympathy*: feeling with another: able to sympathise: compassionate: produced by sympathy. —*adv.* **Sympathet'ically.**

**Sympathise,** sim'pa-thīz, *v.i.* to have *sympathy*: to feel with or for another: to be compassionate.

**Sympathy,** sim'pa-thi, *n., feeling with* another: like feeling: an agreement of inclination, feeling, or sensation: compassion: pity: tenderness. [Gr. *sympatheia*—*syn*, with, and root of Pathos, Patient.]

**Symphonious**, sim-fō'ni-us, *adj.*, *agreeing* or harmonising in *sound*: accordant: harmonious.

**Symphonist**, sim'fo-nist, *n.* a composer of *symphonies*.

**Symphony**, sim'fo-ni, *n.* an *agreeing* together in *sound*: unison, consonance, or harmony of sound : a musical composition for a full band of instruments : an instrumental introduction or termination to a vocal composition. [Gr. *symphōnia*—*syn*, together, *phōnē*, a sound.]

**Symposium**, sim-pō'zi-um, *n.* a *drinking together*: a banquet with philosophic conversation : a merry feast. [L.—Gr. *symposion*—*syn*, together, *posis*, a drinking—*pinō*, to drink.]

**Symptom**, simp'tum, *n.* that which attends and indicates the existence of something else, not as a cause but as a constant effect : (*med.*) that which indicates disease. [Gr. *symptōma*—*syn*, with, *piptō*, to fall.]

**Symptomatic**, simp-tom-at'ik, **Symptomat'ical**, -al, *adj.* pertaining to *symptoms* : indicating the existence of something else : (*med.*) proceeding from some prior disorder.—*adv.* **Symptomat'ically.**

**Synæresis**, sin-er'e-sis, *n.* the *taking* or pronouncing of two vowels *together*, or making one of them silent. [Gr. *synairesis*—*syn*, together, *haireō*, to take. See **Diæresis.**]

**Synagogue**, sin'a-gog, *n.* an *assembly* of Jews for worship : a Jewish place of worship. [Fr.—Gr. *synagōgē*—*syn*, together, *agō*, to lead.]

**Synchronal**, sing'kro-nal, **Synchronous**, sing'kro-nus, *adj.* happening or being at the *same time* : simultaneous : lasting for the same time. [Gr. *syn*, together, *chronos*, time.]

**Synchronism**, sing'kro-nizm, *n.*, *concurrence* of events *in time* : the tabular arrangement of contemporary events, &c. in history. [Gr. *synchronismos*—*synchronizō*, to agree in time.]

**Syncopate**, sing'ko-pāt, *v.t.* to *cut away* so as to bring other parts *together* : to contract, as a word, by taking away letters from the middle : (*music*) to unite by a slur the last note of a bar to the first note of the next. [Low L. *syncopo*, *-atum*—L. *syncope*—Gr. *syn*, together, *koptō*, to cut off.] [ing.

**Syncopation**, sin-ko-pā'shun, *n.* act of syncopat-

**Syncope**, sing'ko-pe, *n.* the omission of letters from the middle of a word, as *ne'er* for *never* : (*med.*) a fainting-fit, an attack in which the breathing and circulation become faint : (*music*) syncopation. [L.—Gr. *syngkopē.*]

**Syndic**, sin'dik, *n.* one who helps in a court of *justice* : an advocate : a government official : a magistrate : one chosen to transact business for others. [L. *syndicus*—Gr. *syndikos*—*syn*, with, *dikē*, justice.]

**Syndicate**, sin'dik-āt, *n.* a body of syndics : a council : the office of a syndic : a body of men chosen to watch the interests of a company, or to manage a bankrupt's property.

**Synecdoche**, sin-ek'do-ke, *n.* a figure of speech by which a part is made to *comprehend* the whole, or the whole is put for a part. [Gr. *synekdochē*—*syn*, together, *ekdechomai*, to receive.] [by or implying *synecdoche*.

**Synecdochical**, sin-ek-dok'ik-al, *adj.* expressed

**Synod**, sin'od, *n.* a *meeting*: an ecclesiastical council : among Presbyterians, a church court consisting of several presbyteries. [A.S. *sinod*—L. *synodus*—Gr. *synodos*—*syn*, together, *hodos*, a way.]

**Synodic**, sin-od'ik, **Synod'ical**, -al, *adj.* pertaining to a *synod*: done in a synod.—*adv.* **Synod'ically.**

**Synonym**, **Synonyme**, sin'o-nim, *n.* a *name* or word having the same meaning *with* another : one of two or more words which have the same meaning. [Gr. *synōnymon*—*syn*, with, *onoma*, a name.]

**Synonymous**, sin-on'i-mus, *adj.* pertaining to *synonyms*: expressing the same thing : having the same meaning.—*adv.* **Synon'ymously.**

**Synonymy**, sin-on'i-mi, *n.* the quality of being *synonymous*: a rhetorical figure by which synonymous words are used. [Gr. *synōnymia*.]

**Synopsis**, sin-op'sis, *n.* a *view* of the whole *together*: a collective or general view of any subject :—*pl.* **Synop'ses.** [Gr. *synopsis*—*syn*, with, together, *opsis*, a view—root *op*, to see.]

**Synoptic**, sin-op'tik, **Synop'tical**, -al, *adj.* affording a general *view* of the whole.—*adv.* **Synop'tically.**

**Syntactic**, sin-tak'tik, **Syntac'tical**, -al, *adj.* pertaining to *syntax*: according to the rules of syntax.—*adv.* **Syntac'tically.**

**Syntax**, sin'taks, *n.* (*gram.*) the correct arrangement of words in sentences. [Gr. *syntaxis*—*syn*, together, *tassō*, *taxō*, to put in order.]

**Synthesis**, sin'the-sis, *n.* a *putting together*, a making a whole out of parts : the combination of separate elements of thought into a whole, or reasoning from principles previously established to a conclusion, as opp. to *analysis* : (*gram.*) the uniting of ideas into a sentence : (*med.*) the reunion of parts that have been divided : (*chem.*) the uniting of elements to form a compound :—*pl.* **Syn'theses** (-sēz). [Gr. *synthesis*—*syn*, with, together, *thesis*, a placing—*tithēmi*, to place.]

**Synthetic**, sin-thet'ik, **Synthet'ical**, -al, *adj.* pertaining to *synthesis*: consisting in synthesis or composition.—*adv.* **Synthet'ically.**

**Syphilis**, sif'i-lis, *n.* an infectious venereal disease.—*adj.* **Syphilit'ic.** [Ety. unknown.]

**Syphon**, **Syren.** Same as **Siphon**, **Siren.**

**Syringe**, sir'inj, *n.* a tube with a piston, by which liquids are sucked up and ejected : a tube used by surgeons for injecting, &c.—*v.t.* to inject or clean with a syringe. [Gr. *syringx*, a reed, a pipe.]

**Syrup.** Same as **Sirup.**

**System**, sis'tem, *n.* anything formed of parts *placed together* : an assemblage of bodies as a connected whole : an orderly arrangement of objects according to some common law or end : regular method or order : a full and connected view of some department of knowledge : the universe. [Gr. *systēma*—*syn*, together, *histēmi*, to place.]

**Systematic**, sis-te-mat'ik, **Systemat'ical**, -al, *adj.* pertaining to or consisting of *system* : formed or done according to system : methodical.—*adv.* **Systemat'ically.**

**Systematise**, sis'tem-a-tīz, *v.t.* to reduce to a *system*.—*n.* **Sys'tematiser.**

**Systole**, sis'to-le, *n.* a *bringing together* or contraction of the heart for expelling the blood : (*gram.*) the shortening of a long syllable. [Gr. *systolē*—*syn*, together, *stello*, to set, place.]

**T**

**Tabard**, tab'ard, *n.* a military garment of the 15th and 16th centuries, now worn by heralds. [O. Fr. ; Low L. *tabardum* ; perh. conn. with L. *tapes*, tapestry, coverlet. See **Tapestry.**]

**Tabbinet**, tab′i-net, *n.* a more delicate kind of *tabby* resembling damask, used for window-curtains.

**Tabby**, tab′i, *n.* a coarser kind of waved or watered silk : an artificial stone, a mixture of shells, gravel, stones, and water.—*adj.* brindled : diversified in colour.—*v.t.* to water or cause to look wavy :—*pa.t.* and *pa.p.* tabb′ied. [Fr. *tabis*—Ar. *atabi*, a kind of rich, waved silk.]

**Taber**, *v.i.* (*B.*). Same as **Tabour**.

**Tabernacle**, tab′er-na-kl, *n.* (*B.*) the movable building carried by the Jews through the desert, and used as a temple : a place of worship or sacred place : in R. Cath. Church, the place in which the consecrated elements of the Eucharist are kept.—*v.i.* to dwell : to abide for a time. [L. *taberna-cu-lum*, double dim. of *taberna*, a hut, shed of boards ; conn. with **Table**. See **Tavern**.]

**Tabid**, tab′id, *adj.*, *wasted* by disease.—*n.* **Tab′idness**. [L. *tabidus*—*tabeo*, to waste away.]

**Tablature**, tab′la-tūr, *n.* something *tabular* : a painting on a wall or ceiling : a picture in general : (*anat.*) a division of the skull into two tables. [Fr., from L. *tabula*, a board, plank.]

**Table**, tā′bl, *n.* a smooth, flat slab or board, with legs, used as an article of furniture : supply of food, entertainment : the company at a table : the board for backgammon or draughts : a surface on which something is written or engraved : that which is cut or written on a flat surface : an inscription : a condensed statement : syllabus or index : (*B.*) a writing tablet.—*v.t.* to make into a table or catalogue : to lay on the table, *i.e.* to postpone consideration of. [Fr. *table*—L. *tabula*, a board, plank.]

**Table-d′hôte**, ta′bl-dōt, *n.* a meal for several persons at the same hour and at fixed prices. [Fr., ' table of the host,' from the landlord presiding at the head of his own table.]

**Tableland**, tā′bl-land, *n.* an extensive flat of elevated *land*, like a *table* : a plateau.

**Tablet**, tab′let, *n.* a *small table* or flat surface : something flat on which to write, paint, &c. : a confection in a flat square form. [Dim. of **Table**.] [meals.

**Table-talk**, tā′bl-tawk, *n.*, *talk* at *table* or at meals.

**Table-turning**, tā′bl-turn′ing, *n.* movements of tables or other objects, attributed by spiritualists to the agency of spirits.

**Taboo, Tabu**, ta-bōō′, *n.* an institution among the Polynesians by which certain things are consecrated : prohibition or interdict.—*v.t.* to forbid approach to : to forbid the use of :—*pr.p.* taboo′ing ; *pa.t.* and *pa.p.* tabooed′. [Polynesian *tabu* or *tapu*.]

**Tabor, Tabour**, tā′bor, *n.* a small drum, played with one stick.—*v.i.* to play on a tabor : to beat lightly and often. [O. Fr. (Fr. *tambour*)—Pers. *'tambūr*, a kind of cithern. Cf. **Tambourine**.]

**Tabouret**, tab′o-ret, **Tabret**, tab′ret, *n.* a *small tabour* or drum. [Dim. of **Tabour**.]

**Tabular**, tab′ū-lar, *adj.* of the form of or pertaining to a *table* : having a flat surface : arranged in a *table* or schedule : having the form of laminæ or plates.

**Tabulate**, tab′ū-lāt, *v.t.* to reduce to *tables* or synopses : to shape with a flat surface.

**Tache**, tash, *n.* (*B.*) a fastening or catch. [Same as **Tack**.]

**Tacit**, tas′it, *adj.* implied, but not expressed by words.—*adv.* **Tac′itly**. [L. *tacitus*, pa.p. of *taceo*, to be silent, to pass over in silence.]

**Taciturn**, tas′i-turn, *adj.* habitually *tacit* or silent : not fond of talking : reserved in speech.—*adv.* **Tac′iturnly**. [L. *taciturnus*—*tacitus*.]

**Taciturnity**, tas-i-turn′i-ti, *n.* habitual silence : reserve in speaking. [L. *taciturnitas*.]

**Tack**, tak, *n.* a short, sharp nail, with a broad head : the course of a ship in reference to the position of her sails : a lease.—*v.t.* to attach or fasten, esp. in a slight manner, as by tacks.—*v.i.* to change the course or *tack* of a ship by shifting the position of the sails. [Lit. that which attaches, from a root widely spread in the Teut. (as Ger. *zacke*), Celt. (as Gael. *tac*), and Romance tongues ; conn. with **Attach**, **Attack**, and **Take**. Cf. **Tag**.]

**Tackle**, tak′l, *n.* the ropes, rigging, &c. of a ship : tools, weapons : ropes, &c. for raising heavy weights : a pulley.—*v.t.* to harness : (*prov.*) to seize or take hold of. [Dut. and Low Ger. *takel*; conn. with **Tack** and **Take**.]

**Tackling**, tak′ling, *n.* furniture or apparatus belonging to the masts, yards, &c. of a ship : harness for drawing a carriage : tackle or instruments. [From **Tackle**.]

**Tacksman**, taks′man, *n.* a tenant or lessee.

**Tact**, takt, *n.* adroitness in managing the feelings of persons dealt with : nice perception in seeing and doing exactly what is best in the circumstances. [Lit. 'touch,' 'feeling,' L. *tactus*—*tango*, *tactum*, to touch. Cf. **Take**.]

**Tactic**, tak′tik, **Tactical**, tak′tik-al, *adj.* pertaining to *tactics*.—*adv.* **Tac′tically**.

**Tactician**, tak-tish′an, *n.* one skilled in *tactics*.

**Tactics**, tak′tiks, *n.sing.* the science or art of manœuvring military and naval forces in the presence of the enemy : way or method of proceeding. [Gr. *taktikē* (*technē*, art, understood), art of arranging men in a field of battle—*tasso*, *taxō*, to arrange.]

**Tactile**, tak′til, *adj.* that may be *touched* or felt. [L. *tango*, to touch. See **Tact**.]

**Taction**, tak′shun, *n.* act of *touching* : touch.

**Tactual**, tak′tū-al, *adj.* relating to or derived from the sense of *touch*.

**Tadpole**, tad′pōl, *n.* a young toad or frog in its first state, having a tail. [M. E. *tadde*, E. **Toad**, and **Poll**, head.]

**Tafferel**, taf′er-el, **Taffrail**, taf′rāl, *n.* the upper part of a ship's stern timbers, which is flat like a table. [Dut. *tafereel*, a panel—*tafel*, a table.]

**Taffeta**, taf′e-ta, **Taffety**, taf′e-ti, *n.* (*orig.*) silk stuff plainly *woven* : a thin, glossy silk stuff, having a wavy lustre. [It. *taffetà*—Pers. *tâftah*, woven.]

**Tag**, tag, *n.* a *tack* or *point* of metal at the end of a string : any small thing *tacked* or attached to another : anything mean.—*v.t.* to fit a *tag* or point to : to tack, fasten, or hang to :—*pr.p.* tagg′ing ; *pa.t.* and *pa.p.* tagged.—*n.* and *adj.* **Tag′rag**, the rabble, or denoting it. [A weaker form of **Tack**.]

**Tail**, tāl, *n.* the end of the backbone of an animal, generally hanging loose, and *hairy* : anything resembling a tail in appearance, position, &c. : the back, lower, or hinder part of anything : anything long and hanging, as a catkin, train of a comet, &c. [A.S. *tægel*; Ger. *zagel*; Goth. *tagl*, hair.]

**Tail**, tāl, *n.* (*law*) the term applied to an estate which is *cut* off or limited to certain heirs. [Fr. *taille*, cutting. See **Entail** and **Retail**.]

**Tailor**, tāl′ur, *n.* one whose business is to *cut* out and make men's clothes.—*fem.* **Tail′oress**.—*v.i.* to work as a tailor.—*n.* **Tail′oring**, the business or work of a tailor. [Fr. *tailleur—tailler*, to cut. Cf. above word.]

**Tailpiece**, tāl′pēs, *n.* a *piece* at the *tail* or end, esp. of a series, as of engravings.

**Taint**, tānt, *v.t.* to *tinge*, *moisten*, or impregnate with anything noxious : to infect : to stain.—*v.i.* to be affected with something corrupting.—*n.* a *stain* or tincture : infection or corruption : a spot : a moral blemish. [O. Fr. *taint*, Fr. *teint*, pa.p. of *teindre*, to dye—L. *tingo, tinctum*, to wet or moisten. See **Tinge**.]

**Take**, tāk, *v.t.* to lay hold of : to get into one's possession : to catch : to capture : to captivate : to receive : to choose : to use : to allow : to understand : to agree to : to become affected with.—*v.i.* to catch : to have the intended effect : to gain reception, to please : to move or direct the course of : to have recourse to :—*pa.t.* took ; *pa.p.* tāk′en.—*n.* **Tak′er.** [A.S. *tacan* ; perh. first from Ice. *taka* ; conn. with L. *ta*(*n*)*g-o*, *te-tig-i*, to touch, and with E. **Tack**.]

**Taking**, tāk′ing, *adj.* captivating : alluring.—*adv.* **Tak′ingly.**

**Talc**, talk, *n.* a mineral occurring in thin flakes, of a white or green colour, and a soapy feel. [Fr. *talc* (Ger. *talk*)—Ar. *'talaq*.]

**Talcky**, talk′i, **Talcous**, talk′us, *adj.* containing, consisting of, or like *talc.*

**Tale**, tāl, *n.* a narrative or story : a fable : what is *told* or counted off : number : reckoning. [A.S. *tal*, a reckoning, a tale ; Ger. *zahl*, a number.]

**Tale-bearer**, tāl′-bār′ėr, *n.* one who maliciously *bears* or tells *tales* or gives information.

**Tale-bearing**, tāl′-bār′ing, *adj.* given to *bear* or tell *tales*, or officiously to give information.—*n.* act of telling secrets.

**Talent**, tal′ent, *n.* (*B.*) a weight or sum of money = 94 lbs. avoir. and £340 or £396 : (*now fig.*) faculty : natural or special gift : special aptitude : eminent ability. [L. *talentum*—Gr. *talanton*, a weight, a talent, from *tlaō, talaō*, to bear, weigh ; akin to L. *tollo*, Ger. *dulden*, Scot. *thole*.]         [mental gifts.

**Talented**, tal′ent-ed, *adj.* possessing *talents* or

**Talisman**, tal′is-man, *n.* a species of charm engraved on metal or stone, to which wonderful effects are ascribed : (*fig.*) something that produces extraordinary effects :—*pl.* **Tal′ismans.** [Fr.—Ar. *telsam*—Late Gr. *telesma*, consecration, incantation—Gr. *teleō*, to consecrate.]

**Talismanic**, tal-is-man′ik, *adj.* pertaining to or having the properties of a *talisman* : magical.

**Talk**, tawk, *v.i.* to speak familiarly : to prattle : to reason.—*n.* familiar conversation : that which is uttered in familiar intercourse : subject of discourse : rumour.—*n.* **Talk′er.** [Prob. freq. of Ice. *tala*, to talk, which is cog. with E. **Tell**.]

**Talkative**, tawk′a-tiv, *adj.* given to much *talking* : prating.—*adv.* **Talk′atively.**—*n.* **Talk′ativeness.**

**Tall**, tawl, *adj.* high, esp. in stature : lofty : long : sturdy : bold : courageous.—*n.* **Tall′ness.** [Ety. very dub. ; perh. conn. with W. *tal, talau*, to make or grow large.]

**Tallow**, tal′ō, *n.* the fat of animals melted : any coarse, hard fat.—*v.t.* to grease with tallow. [A.S. *telg, tælg* ; Ger. *talg*, Ice. *tolg*.]

**Tally**, tal′i, *n.* a stick *cut* or notched to match another stick, used to mark numbers or keep accounts by : anything made to suit another.—*v.t.* to score with corresponding notches : to make to fit.—*v.i.* to correspond : to suit :—*pa.t.* and *pa.p.* tall′ied. [Fr. *taille* (It. *taglia*)—L. *talea*, a cutting. See **Tail** (*law*).]

**Tally-ho**, tal′i-hō, *int.* the huntsman's cry betokening that a fox has gone away.

**Tallyshop**, tal′i-shop, *n.* a *shop* where goods are sold to be paid by instalments, the seller having one account-book which *tallies* with the buyer's.

**Talmud**, tal′mud, *n.* the body of Hebrew laws, comprising the written law and the traditions and comments of the Jewish doctors.—*adjs.* **Talmud′ic**, **Talmud′ical.** [Heb. *talmud*, oral teaching, instruction—*lamad*, to learn.]

**Talon**, tal′on, *n.* the claw of a bird of prey. [Fr. *talon*, through Low L., from L. *talus*, the heel.]

**Tamable**, tām′a-bl, *adj.* that may be *tamed.*—*n.* **Tam′ableness.**

**Tamarind**, tam′a-rind, *n.* an E. Indian tree, with a sweet, pulpy fruit, in pods. [*Tamarindus*, Latinised from Ar. *tamr hindi*, 'Hindu date.']

**Tamarisk**, tam′ar-isk, *n.* a genus of shrubs with small white or pink flowers. [L. *tamariscus*.]

**Tambour**, tam′bōōr, *n.* a small, shallow *drum* : a small, drum-like, circular frame, for embroidering : a rich kind of gold and silver embroidery.—*v.t.* to embroider on a tambour. [Fr. *tambour*, from root of **Tabour**.]

**Tambourine**, tam-bōō-rēn′, *n.* a shallow *drum* with one skin and bells, and played on with the hand. [Fr. *tambourin*, dim. of *tambour.*]

**Tame**, tām, *adj.* having lost native wildness and shyness : domesticated : gentle : spiritless : without vigour : dull.—*v.t.* to reduce to a domestic state : to make gentle : to reclaim : to civilise.—*adv.* **Tame′ly.**—*n.* **Tame′ness.** [A.S. *tam*, cog. with Ger. *zahm* ; further conn. with L. *domo*, Gr. *damao*, Sans. *dam.*]

**Tamer**, tām′ėr, *n.* one who *tames.*

**Tamper**, tam′pėr, *v.i.* to try the *temper* of : to try little experiments without necessity : to meddle : to practise secretly and unfairly. [A by-form of **Temper**.]

**Tan**, tan, *n.* bark bruised and broken for tanning : a yellowish-brown colour.—*v.t.* to convert skins and hides into leather by steeping in vegetable solutions containing tannin : to make brown or tawny.—*v.i.* to become tanned :—*pr.p.* tann′ing ; *pa.t.* and *pa.p.* tanned. [Fr. ; prob. from Ger. *tanne*, fir ; acc. to others, from Bret. *tarn*, oak. Cf. **Tawny**.]

**Tandem**, tan′dem, *adv.* applied to the position of horses harnessed singly one before the other instead of abreast.—*n.* a team of horses (usually two) so harnessed. [Originated in university slang, in a play on the L. adv. *tandem*, at length.]

**Tang**, tang, *n.* a strong or offensive *taste*, esp. of something extraneous : relish : taste. [From root of **Taste**.]

**Tang**, tang, *n.* the tapering part of a knife or tool which goes into the haft. [A by-form of **Tong** in **Tongs**.]        [a contact or touching.

**Tangency**, tan′jen-si, *n.* state of being *tangent* :

**Tangent**, tan′jent, *n.* a line which *touches* a curve, and which when produced does not cut it. [L. *tangens, -entis*, pr.p. of *tango*, to touch.]

**Tangential**, tan-jen′shal, *adj.* of or pertaining to a *tangent* : in the direction of a tangent.

**Tangibility**, tan-ji-bil′i-ti, *n.* quality of being *tangible* or perceptible to the touch.

**Tangible**, tan′ji-bl, *adj.* perceptible by the *touch* : capable of being possessed or realised.—*adv.* **Tan′gibly.** [L. *tangibilis*—*tango.*]

**Tangle**, tang′gl, *n.* a knot of things united confusedly : an edible seaweed.—*v.t.* to unite together confusedly : to interweave : to insnare. [Goth. *tagl*, hair, Ger. *tang*, seaweed.]

**Tank,** tangk, *n.* a large basin or cistern : a reservoir of water. [O. Fr. *estanc* (Fr. *étang*)—L. *stagnum*, a pool of standing water. See **Stagnate.**]

**Tankard,** tangk′ard, *n.* a large vessel for holding liquors : a drinking-vessel with a lid. [**Tank,** with suffix -*ard.*]

**Tanner,** tan′ėr, *n.* one who *tans.*

**Tannery,** tan′ėr-i, *n.* a place for *tanning.*

**Tannic,** tan′ik, *adj.* of or from *tan.*

**Tannin,** tan′in, *n.* an astringent vegetable substance found largely in oak-bark or gall-nuts, of great use in *tanning.* [Fr. *tannin.*]

**Tansy,** tan′zi, *n.* a bitter, aromatic plant, with small yellow flowers, common on old pasture, also a pudding or cake flavoured with it. [Lit. ' the immortal plant,' Fr. *tanaisie*, through late L., from Gr. *athanasia*, immortality.]

**Tantalise,** tan′ta-līz, *v.t.* to tease or torment, by presenting something to excite desire, but keeping it out of reach. [From *Tantalus*, a Gr. mythical personage, who was made to stand up to his chin in water, with branches of fruit hung over his head, the water receding when he wished to drink, and the fruit when he desired to eat.]

**Tantamount,** tan′ta-mownt, *adj., amounting to so much* or to the same : equivalent : equal in value or meaning. [Fr. *tant*—L. *tantum*, so much, so great, and **Amount.**]

**Tap,** tap, *n.* a gentle blow or touch, esp. with something small.—*v.t.* to strike with something small : to touch gently.—*v.i.* to give a gentle knock :—*pr.p.* tapp′ing ; *pa.t.* and *pa.p.* tapped. [From Fr. *tape*—O. Ger. (Ger. *tappe*, a pat with the hand).]

**Tap,** tap, *n.* a hole or short pipe through which liquor is drawn : a place where liquor is drawn. —*v.t.* to pierce, so as to let out fluid : to open a cask and draw off liquor : to broach a vessel :— *pr.p.* tapp′ing ; *pa.t.* and *pa.p.* tapped. [A.S. *täppa* ; cog. with Dut., Ger. *zapfen* ; conn. with **Tip** and **Top.**]

**Tape,** tāp, *n.* a narrow *fillet* or band of wovenwork, used for strings, &c. [A.S. *täppe*, a fillet ; conn. with **Tapestry.**]

**Taper,** tā′pėr, *n.* a small wax-candle or light. [A.S. *tapur, taper.*]

**Taper,** tā′pėr, *adj.* narrowed towards the point, like a *taper :* long and slender.—*v.i.* to become gradually smaller towards one end.—*v.t.* to make to taper. [thinner.

**Tapering,** tā′pėr-ing, *adj.* growing gradually

**Tapestry,** tap′es-tri, *n.* a kind of woven hangings or fabric of wool and silk, with wrought figures. —*v.t.* to adorn with tapestry. [Fr. *tapisserie*— *tapis*, a carpet—L. *tapete*, a carpet, tapestry— Gr. *tapēs, -ētis*—Pers. *tabseh.*]

**Tapeworm,** tāp′wurm, *n.* a *tape*-like *worm*, often of great length, found in the intestines.

**Tapioca,** tap-i-ō′ka, *n.* the glutinous and granular substance obtained from the roots of the Cassava plant of Brazil. [The Brazilian name.]

**Tapir,** tā′pir, *n.* a thick-skinned, short-necked animal, having a short flexible proboscis, found in Sumatra and S. America. [The Brazilian name.] [served from the *tap* or cask.

**Taproom,** tap′rōōm, *n.* a *room* where beer is

**Taproot,** tap′rōōt, *n.* a root of a plant or tree striking directly downward without dividing, and tapering towards the end, as that of the carrot. [liquor : a publican.

**Tapster,** tap′stėr, *n.* one who *taps* or draws off

**Tar,** tär, *n.* a viscous, liquid, resinous substance of a dark colour, obtained from pine-trees : a sailor, so called from his tarred clothes.—*v.t.* to smear with tar :—*pr.p.* tarr′ing ; *pa.t.* and *pa.p.* tarred. [A.S. *teru,* cog. with Low Ger. *tēr.*]

**Tarantula,** tar-an′tū-la, *n.* a kind of poisonous spider found in S. Italy. [It. *tarantola*—L. *Tarentum*, a town in S. Italy where the spider abounds.]

**Taraxacum,** tar-aks′a-kum, *n.* the root of the dandelion, used in medicine. [A botanical Latin word, coined from Gr. *taraxis*, trouble, and *akeomai*, to cure.]

**Tardy,** tär′di, *adj., slow*, late, sluggish : out of season.—*adv.* Tar′dily.—*n.* Tar′diness. [Fr. *tardif—tard*—L. *tardus*, slow.]

**Tare,** tär, *n.* a plant, like the vetch, sometimes cultivated for fodder. [O. E. *tarefitch*, the wild vetch.]

**Tare,** tär, *n.* the weight of the vessel or package in which goods are contained : an allowance made for it. [Fr.—It. *tara*—Ar. *tarah*, thrown away.]

**Target,** tär′get, *n.* a small buckler or shield : a mark to fire at. [O. Fr. *targette* (Fr. *targe*)— O. Ger. *zarga*, cog. with A.S. *targe.*]

**Targeteer,** tär-get-ēr′, *n.* one armed with a *target.*

**Tariff,** tar′if, *n.* a list of the duties, &c. fixed by law on merchandise : a list of charges, fees, or prices. [Fr.—Arab. *ta'rif*, information, from *'arafa*, to explain, inform.] [Ice. *tiörn.*]

**Tarn,** tärn, *n.* a small lake among the mountains.

**Tarnish,** tär′nish, *v.t.* to soil by exposure to the air, &c. : to diminish the lustre or purity of.— *v.i.* to become dull : to lose lustre. [Lit. ' to cover,' ' to darken,' Fr. *ternir*, pr.p. *ternissant* ; *terne*, dull, wan—O. Ger. *tarni*, covered, A.S. *dernian*, to cover, darken.]

**Tarpaulin,** tär-paw′lin, **Tarpauling,** tär-paw′ling, *n.* a *tarred pall* or cover of coarse canvas. [From **Tar,** and prov. E. *pauling*, a covering for a cart, M. E. *pall*, a sort of cloth, connected with **Pall.**] [like *tar.*

**Tarry,** tär′i, *adj.* consisting of, covered with, or

**Tarry,** tar′i, *v.i.* to be *tardy* or slow : to loiter or stay behind : to delay :—*pa.t.* and *pa.p.* tarr′ied. [M. E. *tarien*—O. Fr. *targier, targer* (Fr. *tarder*)—L. *tardus*, slow, modified by confusion with A.S. *tirian*, to irritate, vex. See **Tardy.**]

**Tart,** tärt, *adj.* sharp or sour to the taste : (*fig.*) sharp : severe.—*adv.* Tart′ly.—*n.* Tart′ness. [Lit. ' tearing,' A.S. *teart—tearan*, to tear.]

**Tart,** tärt, *n.* a small pie, containing fruit or jelly. [Fr. *tarte, tourte*—L. *tortus*, twisted, pa.p. of *torqueo*, to twist.]

**Tartan,** tär′tan, *n.* a woollen stuff, checked with various colours, worn in the Scottish Highlands. [Fr. *tiretaine*, linsey-woolsey ; Sp. *tiritana, tiritaira*, a sort of thin silk.]

**Tartar,** tär′tar, *n.* a salt which forms on the sides of casks containing wine (when pure, called *cream of tartar*) : a concretion which sometimes forms on the teeth. [Fr. *tartre*—Low L. *tartarum*—Ar. *dourd.*]

**Tartar,** tär′tar, *n.* a native of *Tartary* in Asia : an irritable person, or one too strong for his assailant.

**Tartareous,** tär-tā′re-us, **Tartarous,** tär′tar-us, *adj.* consisting of or resembling *tartar.*

**Tartaric,** tär-tar′ik, *adj.* pertaining to or obtained from *tartar.*

**Tartarus,** tär′ta-rus, *n.* (*ancient myth.*) the lower world generally, but esp. the place of punishment for the wicked. [L.—Gr. *tartaros*, prob. from the sound, to express something terrible.]

**Tartish,** tärt′ish, *adj.* somewhat *tart.*

**Task,** task, *n.* a set amount of work, esp. of study, given by another : work : drudgery.—*v.t.* to impose a task on : to burden with severe work.—*n.* **Task′er.—To take to task,** to reprove. [Lit. 'a tax,' O. Fr. *tasque*—Low L. *tasca, taxa*—L. *taxo,* to rate, tax. See **Tax.**]

**Taskmaster,** task′mas-tėr, *n.* a *master* who imposes a *task* : one whose office is to assign tasks.

**Tassel,** tas′el, *n.* a hanging ornament consisting of a bunch of silk or other material. [O. Fr. *tassel,* an ornament of a square shape, attached to the dress—L. *taxillus,* dim. of *talus,* a die.]

**Tasselled,** tas′eld, *adj.* adorned with *tassels.*

**Tastable,** tāst′a-bl, *adj.* that may be *tasted.*

**Taste,** tāst, *v.t.* to try or perceive by the touch of the tongue or palate : to try by eating a little : to eat a little of : to partake of : to experience.—*v.i.* to try or perceive by the mouth : to have a flavour of.—*n.* **Tast′er.** [O. Fr. *taster,* Fr. *tâter,* as if from *taxitare*—L. *taxo,* to touch repeatedly, to estimate—root of *tango,* to touch.]

**Taste,** tāst, *n.* the act or sense of *tasting*: the sensation caused by a substance on the tongue : the sense by which we perceive the flavour of a thing : the quality or flavour of anything : a small portion : intellectual relish or discernment : the faculty by which the mind perceives the beautiful : nice perception : choice, predilection.

**Tasteful,** tāst′fool, *adj., full* of *taste* : having a high relish : showing good taste.—*adv.* **Taste′fully.—*n.* Taste′fulness.**

**Tasteless,** tāst′les, *adj., without taste* : insipid.—*adv.* **Taste′lessly.—*n.* Taste′lessness.**

**Tasty,** tāst′i, *adj.* having a good *taste* : possessing nice perception of excellence : in conformity with good taste.—*adv.* **Tast′ily.**

**Tatter,** tat′ėr, *n.* a *torn piece* : a loose hanging rag. [Ice. *tetr, tetur,* a torn garment.]

**Tattle,** tat′l, *n.* trifling talk or chat.—*v.i.* to talk idly or triflingly : to tell tales or secrets.—*n.* **Tatt′ler.** [M. E. *tater,* like Low Ger. *tateln,* an imitative word.]

**Tattoo,** tat-tōō′, *n.* a beat of drum and a bugle-call to warn soldiers to repair to their quarters, orig. to *shut* the *taps* or drinking-houses against the soldiers. [Dut. *taptoe*—*tap,* a tap, and *toe,* which is the prep., E. *to,* Ger. *zu,* in the sense of shut.]

**Tattoo,** tat-tōō′, *v.t.* to mark permanently (as the skin) with figures, by pricking in colouring matter.—*n.* marks or figures made by pricking colouring matter into the skin. [Prob. a reduplication of the Polynesian word *ta,* to strike.]

**Taught,** tawt, *pa.t.* and *pa.p.* of **Teach.**

**Taunt,** tawnt, *v.t.* to reproach or upbraid with severe or insulting words : to censure sarcastically.—*n.* **Taunt′er.—*adv.* Taunt′ingly.** [Fr. *tancer,* to scold ; O. Sw. *tanta,* to reproach, *tant,* mockery.]

**Taunt,** tawnt, *n.* upbraiding, sarcastic, or insulting words : a bitter reproach.

**Taurus,** taw′rus, *n.* the *Bull,* one of the signs of the zodiac.—*adj.* **Tau′rīne.** [L. *taurus,* Gr. *tauros,* a bull.]

**Taut, Taught,** tawt, *adj.* tightly drawn. [A form of **Tight.**]

**Tautologic,** taw-to-loj′ik, **Tautological,** taw-to-loj′ik-al, *adj.* containing *tautology.*—*adv.* **Tautolog′ically.**

**Tautologise,** taw-tol′o-jīz, *v.i.* to use *tautology*: to repeat the same thing in different words.—*n.* **Tautol′ogist.**

**Tautology,** taw-tol′o-ji, *n.* needless repetition of the *same* thing in different *words.* [Gr. *tautologia*—*tauto,* the same, *logos,* word.]

**Tavern,** tav′ėrn, *n.* a licensed house for the sale of liquors with accommodation for travellers : an inn. [Fr. *taverne*—L. *taberna,* orig. 'a hut of boards,' from root of *tabula,* a board.]

**Taw,** taw, *n.* a marble chosen to be played with. [Lit. a thing which one employs one's-self about ; from **Taw,** *v.t.*]

**Taw,** taw, *v.t.* to *prepare* and dress, as skins into white leather. [A.S. *tawian,* to work hard, to prepare ; O. Ger. *zauen,* to do.]

**Tawdry,** taw′dri, *adj.* showy without taste : gaudily dressed.—*adv.* **Taw′drily.—*n.* Taw′driness.** [Said to be corr. from *St Audrey* = *St Ethelreda,* at whose fair laces and gay toys were sold.]

**Tawny,** taw′ni, *adj.* of the colour of things *tanned,* a yellowish brown.—*n.* **Taw′niness.** [Dut. *tanig ;* Fr. *tanné,* pa.p. of *tanner,* to tan. See **Tan.**]

**Tax,** taks, *n.* a rate imposed on property or persons for the benefit of the state : anything imposed : a burdensome duty.—*v.t.* to lay a tax on : to burden : to accuse. [Fr. *taxe,* a tax—L. *taxo,* to handle, value, charge—root of *tango,* to touch. See **Task.**]    [to be *taxed.*

**Taxable,** taks′a-bl, *adj.* capable of being or liable

**Taxation,** taks-ā′shun, *n.* act of *taxing.* [L. *taxatio.*]

**Taxidermy,** taks′i-dėr-mi, *n.* the art of *preparing* and stuffing the *skins* of animals.—*n.* **Tax′idermist.** [Fr.—Gr. *taxis,* arrangement, and *derma,* a skin.]

**Tea,** tē, *n.* the dried leaves of a shrub in China and Japan : an infusion of the leaves in boiling water : any vegetable infusion. [From South Chinese *te,* the common form being *tscha.*]

**Teach,** tēch, *v.t.* to *show:* to impart knowledge to : to guide the studies of : to exhibit so as to impress upon the mind : to impart the knowledge of : to accustom : to counsel.—*v.i.* to practise giving instruction:—*pa.t.* and *pa.p.* taught (tawt). [A.S. *tæcan,* to show, teach ; Ger. *zeigen,* to show; allied to L. *doceo,* to teach, Gr. *deiknumi,* to show.]

**Teachable,** tēch′a-bl, *adj.* capable of being *taught*: apt or willing to learn.—*n.* **Teach′ableness.**

**Teacher,** tēch′ėr, *n.* one who *teaches* or instructs.

**Teak,** tēk, *n.* a tree in the E. Indies and Africa, also its wood, remarkable for its hardness and durability. [Malabar *theka, tekka.*]

**Teal,** tēl, *n.* a web-footed waterfowl allied to the duck, but smaller. [Dut. *teling, taling.*]

**Team,** tēm, *n.* a number of animals moving together or in order : two or more oxen or other animals harnessed to the same vehicle. [A.S. *team,* offspring, anything following in a row, from root of **Teem.**]

**Teamster,** tēm′stėr, *n.* one who drives a *team.*

**Tear,** tēr, *n.* a drop of the fluid from the eyes: anything like a tear. [A.S. *tear, tæher ;* Goth. *tagr ;* cog. with L. *lacrima* (for O. L. *dacrima*), Gr. *dakru.*]

**Tear,** tār, *v.t.* to draw asunder or separate with violence : to make a violent rent in : to lacerate.—*v.i.* to move or act with violence : to rage :—*pa.t.* tōre, (*B.*) tāre ; *pa.p.* tōrn.—*n.* something torn, a rent.—*n.* **Tear′er.** [A.S. *teran ;* cog. with Ger. *zehren,* also with Gr. *derō,* to flay, Sans. *dri,* to split.]

**Tearful,** tēr′fool, *adj.* abounding with or shedding *tears* : weeping.—*adv.* **Tear′fully.—*n.* Tear′fulness.**

---

**Tearless**, tēr′les, *adj., without tears:* unfeeling.

**Tease**, tēz, *v.t.* to comb or card, as wool: to scratch, as cloth : to raise a nap : to vex with importunity, jests, &c. : to torment, irritate. [A.S. *tǽsan*, to pluck, tease ; Dut. *teezen*, to pick ; Ger. *zeisen*, to pluck, pull.]

**Teasel**, tēz′l, *n.* a plant, with large burs or heads covered with stiff, hooked awns, which are used in *teasing* or raising a nap on cloth.—*v.t.* to raise a nap on with the teasel :—*pr.p.* teas′eling ; *pa.t.* and *pa.p.* teas′eled.—*n.* **Teas′eler**. [A.S. *tǽsl*.]

**Teat**, tēt, *n.* the nipple of the female breast through which the young *suck* the milk. [A.S. *tit* ; cog. with Ger. *zitze*, W. *teth*, Gr. *titthē*, the nipple, a nurse—*thaō*, to suckle ; Sans. *dhe*, to suck.]

**Teazle**, tēz′l. Same as **Teasel**.

**Technic**, tek′nik, **Technical**, tek′nik-al, *adj.* pertaining to *art*, esp. the useful arts: belonging to a particular art or profession.—*adv.* **Tech′nically**. [Gr. *technikos*—*technē*, art, akin to *tekō*, to produce, bring forth.]

**Technicality**, tek-ni-kal′i-ti, *n.* state or quality of being *technical :* that which is technical.

**Technics**, tek′niks, *n.pl.* the doctrine of *arts* in general : the branches that relate to the arts.

**Technological**, tek-no-loj′ik-al, *adj.* relating to *technology*.

**Technology**, tek-nol′o-ji, *n.* a *discourse* or *treatise* on the *arts :* an explanation of terms employed in the arts.—*n.* **Technol′ogist**, one skilled in technology. [Gr. *technē*, and *logos*, a discourse.]

**Ted**, ted, *v.t.* to *spread* or turn, as new-mown grass, for drying :—*pr.p.* tedd′ing ; *pa.t.* and *pa.p.* tedd′ed. [W. *tedu*, to stretch out, *teddu*, to spread.]

**Tedious**, tē′di-us, *adj., wearisome:* tiresome from length or slowness : irksome : slow.—*adv.* **Te′diously**.—*n.* **Te′diousness**. [L. *tædiosus*.]

**Tedium**, tē′di-um, *n., wearisomeness :* irksomeness. [L. *tædium—tædet*, it wearies.]

**Teem**, tēm, *v.i.* to bring forth or produce : to bear or be fruitful: to be pregnant: to be full or prolific. [A.S. *tyman*, to produce.]

**Teens**, tēnz, *n.pl.* the years of one's age from thir*teen* to nine*teen*.

**Teeth**. See **Tooth**.

**Teething**, tēth′ing, *n.* the first growth of teeth, or the process by which they make their way through the gums.

**Teetotaler**, tē-tō′tal-ėr, *n.* one pledged to entire abstinence from intoxicating drinks.—*adj.* **Tee-to′tal.**—*n.* **Teeto′talism**. [Prob. from a stammering pronunciation of the word **Total** by a lecturer advocating the temperance cause.]

**Tegument**, teg′ū-ment, *n.* an **Integument**. [L. *tegumentum—tego*, to cover.] [**mentary**.

**Tegumentary**, teg-ū-ment′ar-i, *adj.* See **Tegu-**

**Teinds**, tēndz, *n.pl.* the Scotch form of **Tithes**.

**Telegram**, tel′e-gram, *n.* a message sent by *telegraph*. [Gr. *tēle*, at a distance, and *gramma*, that which is written—*graphō*, to write.]

**Telegraph**, tel′e-graf, *n.* an apparatus for giving signals from a distance, esp. by means of electricity or magnetism.—*v.t.* to convey or announce by telegraph. [Lit. 'the distant writer,' Fr. *télégraphe*—Gr. *tēle*, at a distance, and *graphō*, to write.]

**Telegraphic**, tel-e-graf′ik, *adj.* pertaining to or communicated by a telegraph. [telegraph.

**Telegraphist**, te-leg′ra-fist, *n.* one who works a

**Telegraphy**, tel-eg′ra-fi, *n.* the science or art of constructing or using telegraphs.

**Teleology**, tel-e-ol′o-ji, *n.* the doctrine of the final causes of things,—*adj.* **Teleolog′ical**. [From Gr. *telos*, issue, and *logos*, a discourse.]

**Telephone**, tel′e-fōn, *n.* an instrument for reproducing *sound* at a *distance* by means of electricity.—*adj.* **Telephon′ic**. [Gr. *tēle*, far, and *phōnē*, a sound.]

**Telescope**, tel′e-skōp, *n.* an optical instrument for *viewing* objects at a *distance*. [Fr.—Gr. *tēle*, at a distance, and *skopeō*, to see.]

**Telescopic**, tel-e-skop′ik, *adj.* pertaining to, performed by, or like a *telescope :* seen only by a telescope.—*adv.* **Telescop′ically**.

**Tell**, tel, *v.t.* to *number* or give an account of : to utter : to narrate : to disclose : to inform : to discern : to explain.—*v.i.* to give an account : to produce or take effect :—*pa.t.* and *pa.p.* tōld. [A.S. *tellan* ; Ice. *telia*, Dan. *tale*, Ger. *zählen*, to number. The fundamental idea is prob. to 'arrange in order.']

**Teller**, tel′ėr, *n.* one who *tells* or *counts :* a clerk whose duty it is to receive and pay money.

**Tell-tale**, tel′-tāl, *n.* one who *tells tales :* one who officiously tells the private concerns of others.

**Telluric**, tel-lū′rik, *adj.* pertaining to or proceeding from the *earth :* of or from tellurium. [L. *tellus, telluris*, the earth.]

**Tellurium**, tel-lū′ri-um, *n.* an element by some classed as a metal, brittle and crystalline, chiefly found in a gold ore associated with selenium.

**Temerity**, te-mer′i-ti, *n., rashness :* unreasonable contempt for danger. [Fr. *témérité*—L. *temeritas—temere*, by chance, rashly.]

**Temper**, tem′pėr, *v.t.* to mix in due proportion : to modify by mixture : to moderate : to soften : to bring to a proper degree of hardness, as a metal.—*n.* due mixture or balance of different or contrary qualities: state of a metal as to hardness, &c. : constitution of the body : state of mind, esp. with regard to feelings : passion : calmness or moderation. [A.S. *temprian*—L. *tempero*, to combine properly—*tempus*, perh. from root *tem*, to cut, and so sig. a bit cut off, portion of time.]

**Temperament**, tem′pėr-a-ment, *n.* state with respect to the predominance of any quality : internal constitution or state : disposition. [L. *temperamentum—tempero*.]

**Temperance**, tem′pėr-ans, *n.* moderation, esp. in the appetites and passions. [L. *temperantia*.]

**Temperate**, tem′pėr-āt, *adj.* moderate in degree of any quality, esp. in the appetites and passions : calm : cool : abstemious.—*adv.* **Tem′perately**. —*n.* **Tem′perateness**.

**Temperature**, tem′pėr-a-tūr, *n.* constitution : proportion : degree of any quality, esp. of heat or cold : state of a body with respect to sensible heat. [L. *temperatura—tempero*.]

**Tempest**, tem′pest, *n.* wind rushing with great velocity, usually with rain or snow : a violent storm : any violent commotion. [Lit. 'a portion of time,' 'a season,' then weather, bad weather, O. Fr. *tempeste*—L. *tempestas*, a season, tempest—*tempus*, time.]

**Tempestuous**, tem-pest′ū-us, *adj.* resembling or pertaining to a *tempest :* very stormy : turbulent. —*adv.* **Tempest′uously**.—*n.* **Tempest′uousness**.

**Templar**, tem′plar, *n.* one of a religious and military order, founded in the 12th century for the protection of the Holy Sepulchre and pilgrims going thither : a student or lawyer living in the **Temple**, London. [Orig. called 'Poor Soldiers of the Temple of Solomon,' from their having acquired the church and convent of the *Temple*.]

**Temple**, tem'pl, *n*. (*lit.*) 'a small space cut off' or 'marked out,' esp. for religious purposes: an edifice erected to a deity or for religious purposes: a place of worship: in London, two inns of court, once occupied by the Knights *Templars*. [L. *templum*, prob. for *temulum*, a space marked out, dim. of *tempus*, a piece cut off. See **Temper**.]

**Temple**, tem'pl, *n*. the flat portion of either side of the head above the cheekbone. [O. Fr. *temple*—L. *tempus*, a portion of time, the fit time, pl. *tempora*, properly the right place, the fatal spot, the place where a blow is fatal.]

**Temporal**, tem'por-al, *adj*. pertaining to the *temples*. [L. *temporalis*.]

**Temporal**, tem'por-al, *adj*. pertaining to *time*, esp. to this life or world, opposed to *eternal*: worldly, secular, or civil, opposed to *sacred* or *ecclesiastical*.—*adv.* **Tem'porally**. [Fr.—L. *tempus*, time.]

**Temporality**, tem-por-al'i-ti, *n*. what pertains to *temporal* welfare :—*pl.* secular possessions, revenues of an ecclesiastical proceeding from lands, tithes, and the like.

**Temporary**, tem'por-ar-i, *adj*. for a *time* only: transient.—*adv.* **Tem'porarily**.—*n.* **Tem'porariness**.

**Temporise**, tem'por-īz, *v.i.* to comply with the *time* or *occasion* : to yield to circumstances.

**Tempt**, temt, *v.t.* to put to trial : to test : to try to persuade, esp. to evil : to entice. [Lit. to *stretch* or try the strength of, O. Fr. *tempter*, Fr. *tenter*—L. *tento*, an inten. of *tendo*, to stretch.]

**Temptation**, tem-tā'shun, *n*. act of *tempting*: state of being tempted : that which tempts : enticement to evil : trial.

**Tempter**, temt'ėr, *n*. one who tempts, esp. the devil.—*fem.* **Tempt'ress**.

**Tempting**, temt'ing, *adj*. adapted to tempt or entice.—*adv.* **Tempt'ingly**.

**Ten**, ten, *adj*. twice five.—*n*. a figure denoting ten units, as 10 or x. [A.S. *ten*, *tyn*; Ger. *zehn*, W. *deg*, L. *decem*, Gr. *deka*, Russ. *desjat*, Sans. *daçan*.]

**Tenable**, ten'a-bl, *adj*. capable of being *retained*, kept, or defended.—*n.* **Ten'ableness**. [Fr. *tenable*, from *tenir*—L. *teneo*, to hold.]

**Tenacious**, te-nā'shus, *adj*., *retaining* or *holding fast*: apt to stick: stubborn.—*adv.* **Tena'ciously**.—*n.* **Tena'ciousness**. [L. *tenax*—*teneo*.]

**Tenacity**, te-nas'i-ti, *n*. quality of being *tenacious*: the quality of bodies which makes them stick to others. [L. *tenacitas*—*tenax*.]

**Tenancy**, ten'an-si, *n*. a temporary *holding* of land or property.

**Tenant**, ten'ant, *n*. one who *holds* or possesses land or property under another : one who has, on certain conditions, temporary possession of any place.—*v.t.* to hold as a tenant. [Fr. *tenant*—L. *tenens*, pr.p. of *teneo*, to hold.]

**Tenantable**, ten'ant-a-bl, *adj*. fit to be *tenanted* : in a state of repair suitable for a tenant.

**Tenantless**, ten'ant-les, *adj*. without a *tenant*.

**Tenantry**, ten'ant-ri, *n*. the body of *tenants* on an estate.

**Tench**, tensh, *n*. a fresh-water fish, of the carp family, very tenacious of life. [O. Fr. *tenche*, Fr. *tanche*—L. *tinca*.]

**Tend**, tend, *v.t.* to accompany as assistant or protector : to take care of. [Contracted from **Attend**.]

**Tend**, tend, *v.i.* to *stretch*, *aim at*, or move in a certain direction : to be directed to any end or purpose : to contribute. [Fr. *tendre*—L. *tendo*, Gr. *teinō*, to stretch, aim.]

**Tendency**, tend'en-si, *n*. direction, object, or result to which anything *tends*: inclination : drift. [Fr. *tendance*—L. *tendens*, pr.p. of *tendo*.]

**Tender**, tend'ėr, *n*. a small vessel that *attends* a larger with stores, &c. : a carriage attached to locomotives, to supply fuel and water.

**Tender**, tend'ėr, *v.t.* to *stretch out* or offer for acceptance.—*n*. an offer or proposal, esp. of some service : the thing offered.

**Tender**, ten'dėr, *adj*. soft, delicate : easily impressed or injured : not hardy : fragile : weak and feeble : easily moved to pity, love, &c. : careful not to injure (followed by *of*) : unwilling to cause pain : apt to cause pain : expressive of the softer passions : compassionate.—*adv.* **Ten'derly**.—*n.* **Ten'derness**. [Fr. *tendre*—L. *tener*; conn. with L. *tendo*, Gr. *teinō*, to stretch, and therefore lit. sig. 'that may be stretched.']

**Tender-hearted**, ten'dėr-härt'ed, *adj*. having great *tenderness* of *heart* : full of feeling.

**Tendon**, ten'don, *n*. a hard, strong cord or bundle of fibres by which a muscle is attached to a bone. [Fr. *tendon*—L. *tendo*, to stretch ; Gr. *tenōn*—*teinō*, to stretch.]

**Tendril**, ten'dril, *n*. a slender, spiral shoot of a plant by which it attaches itself for support.—*adj*. clasping or climbing. [From Fr. *tendre*—L. *tener*, tender.]

**Tenebrous**, ten'e-brus, *adj*., *dark*: gloomy. [L. *tenebrosus*—*tenebræ*, darkness.]

**Tenement**, ten'e-ment, *n*. anything *held* or that may be held by a *tenant* : a dwelling or habitation, or part of it, used by one family.—*adj*. **Tenement'al**.

**Tenet**, ten'et, *n*. any opinion, principle, or doctrine which a person *holds* or maintains as true. [L. *tenet*, he holds—*teneo*, to hold.]

**Tenfold**, ten'fōld, *adj*., *ten* times *folded*: ten times more. [**Ten** and **Fold**.]

**Tennis**, ten'is, *n*. a game in which a ball is kept continually in motion by being driven to and fro with rackets. [Prob. from O. Fr. *teneis* (Fr. *tenez*), 'catch !' imper. of *ten-ir*, to hold—L. *ten-ēre*.]

**Tenon**, ten'un, *n*. a projection at the end of a piece of wood inserted into the socket or mortise of another, to *hold* the two together.—*v.t.* to fit with tenons. [Fr. *tenon*—*ten-ir*, to hold—L. *ten-ēre*.]

**Tenor**, ten'ur, *n*. continuity of state : general run or currency : purport : the higher of the two kinds of voices usually belonging to adult males : the part next above the bass in a vocal quartette : one who sings tenor. [L. *tenor*, a holding on—*teneo*, to hold.]

**Tense**, tens, *n*. the form of a verb to indicate the *time* of the action. [Lit. 'time,' O. Fr. *tens* (Fr. *temps*)—L. *tempus*, time.]

**Tense**, tens, *adj*., *strained* to stiffness : rigid.—*adv.* **Tense'ly**.—*n.* **Tense'ness**. [L. *tensus*, pa.p. of *tendo*, to stretch. See **Tend**, *v.i.*]

**Tensile**, ten'sil, **Tensible**, ten'si-bl, *adj*. capable of being *stretched*.

**Tension**, ten'shun, *n*. act of *stretching*: state of being stretched or strained : strain : effort. [L.]

**Tensity**, ten'si-ti, *n*., *tenseness*: state of being tense.

**Tensor**, ten'sor, *n*. a muscle that stretches. [L. the 'extender' or 'stretcher.']

**Tent**, tent, *n*. a portable lodge or shelter, gen. of

canvas *stretched* on poles : a plug or roll of lint used to dilate a wound or opening in the flesh. —*v.t.* to probe : to keep open with a tent. [Fr. *tente*—Low L. *tenta*—L *tendo*, to stretch. See **Tend**, *v.i.* and **Tense**, *adj.*]

**Tentacle**, ten'ta-kl, *n.* a threadlike organ of certain insects for *feeling* or motion.—*adj.* **Tentac'ular**. [Fr. *tentacule*—L. *tento*, to feel—*tendo*, to stretch. Cf. **Tent**.]

**Tentation**, ten-tā'shun, *n.* old form of **Temptation**.

**Tentative**, ten'ta-tiv, *adj.*, *trying*: experimental. [Fr. Late L.—L. *tento*, to handle, try. See **Tentacle**.]

**Tented**, tent'ed, *adj.* covered with *tents*.

**Tenter**, tent'ėr, *n.* a machine for *extending* or *stretching* cloth on by hooks.—*v.t.* to stretch on hooks.—**To be on tenterhooks**, to be on the stretch : to be in suspense or anxiety. [See **Tent**.]

**Tenth**, tenth, *adj.* the last of *ten*: next in order after the ninth.—*n.* one of ten equal parts.

**Tenthly**, tenth'li, *adv.* in the *tenth* place.

**Tenuity**, ten-ū'i-ti, *n.*, *thinness*: smallness of diameter : slenderness : rarity. [L. *tenuitas*—*tenuis*, thin, slender—root of Gr. *teinō*, L. *ten-do*, to stretch. Cf. **Thin**.]

**Tenure**, ten'ūr, *n.* a *holding* or manner of holding by a *tenant*, esp. lands or tenements. [Fr. *tenure*—Low L. *tenura*—L. *teneo*, to hold.]

**Tepefaction**, tep-e-fak'shun, *n.* act of *making tepid* or lukewarm.

**Tepefy**, tep'e-fī, *v.t.* to *make tepid* or moderately warm :—*pa.t.* and *pa.p.* tep'efīed. [L. *tepefacio*—*tepeo*, to be warm, and *facio*, to make.]

**Tepid**, tep'id, *adj.* moderately warm : lukewarm. —*ns.* **Tepid'ity**, **Tep'idness**. [L. *tepidus*—*tepeo*, to be warm, Sans. *tap*.]

**Teraphim**, ter'a-fim, *n.pl.* (*B.*) idols, images, or household gods, consulted as oracles. [Heb.]

**Terce**, tėrs, *n.* Same as **Tierce**.

**Terebinth**, ter'e-binth, *n.* the turpentine-tree.— *adj.* **Terebinth'ine**. [L.—Gr.]

**Teredo**, te-rē'do, *n.* the ship-worm, a worm very destructive in boring into wood. [L.—Gr. *terēdōn*, from *teirō*, to wear away.]

**Tergiversation**, tėr-ji-vėr-sā'shun, *n.* a shuffling or shifting : subterfuge : fickleness of conduct. [Lit. 'a *turning* of the *back*,' L., from *tergum*, the back, and *versor*, to turn.]

**Term**, tėrm, *n.* any *limited* period : the time for which anything lasts : the time during which the courts of law are open : certain days on which rent is paid : that by which a thought is expressed, a word or expression : a condition or arrangement (gen. in *pl.*) : (*alg.*) a member of a compound quantity.—*v.t.* to apply a term to : to name or call. [Fr. *terme*—L. *terminus*, a boundary, Gr. *terma;* further conn. with L. *trans*, E. **Through**. Doublet **Terminus**.]

**Termagant**, tėr'ma-gant, *n.* a boisterous, bold woman.—*adj.* boisterous : brawling : tumultuous. [*Termagant* or *Tervagant*, a supposed Mohammedan false god, represented in the old plays and moralities as of a most violent character.]

**Terminable**, tėr'min-a-bl, *adj.* that may be *limited*: that may *terminate* or cease.

**Terminal**, tėr'min-al, *adj.* pertaining to or growing at the *end* or extremity. [L. *terminalis*.]

**Terminate**, tėr'min-āt, *v.t.* to set a *limit* to : to set the boundary : to put an end to : to finish.— *v.i.* to be limited : to end either in space or time : to close. [L. *terminus*.]

**Termination**, tėr-min-ā'shun, *n.* act of terminating or ending : limit : end : result : the ending of words as varied by their signification.

**Terminational**, tėr-min-ā'shun-al, *adj.* pertaining to or forming a termination.

**Terminative**, tėr'min-āt-iv, *adj.* tending to terminate or determine : absolute.

**Terminology**, tėr-min-ol'o-ji, *n.* doctrine of *terms:* the terms used in any art, science, &c. [L. *terminus*, and Gr. *logos*, discourse. See **Term**.]

**Terminus**, tėr'min-us, *n.* the end or extreme point : one of the extreme points of a railway :— *pl.* **Ter'minī**. [L. 'a boundary.' Doublet **Term**.]

**Tern**, tėrn, *n.* a long-winged aquatic fowl allied to the gull. [Allied to Dan. *terne*, sea-swallow, Ice. *therna*.]

**Ternary**, tėr'nar-i, *adj.* proceeding by or consisting of *threes*.—*n.* the number three. [L. *ternarius*—*terni*, three each—*tres*, three.]

**Ternate**, tėr'nāt, *adj.*, *threefold*, or arranged in threes. [See **Ternary**.]

**Terrace**, ter'ās, *n.* a raised level bank of *earth :* any raised flat place : the flat roof of a house.— *v.t.* to form into a terrace. [Fr. *terrasse*—It. *terrazzo*—L. *terra*, the earth.]

**Terra-cotta**, ter'a-kot'a, *n.* a composition of clay and sand used for statues, hardened like bricks by fire. [Lit. 'baked clay,' It.—L. *terra*, earth, and *cocta*, pa.p. of *coquo*, L. **Cook**.]

**Terraqueous**, ter-ā'kwe-us, *adj.* consisting of *land* and *water*. [Coined from L. *terra*, earth, *aqua*, water.]

**Terreen**, ter-ēn', *n.* Less common form of **Tureen**.

**Terrene**, ter-ēn', *adj.* pertaining to the *earth :* earthy : earthly. [L. *terrenus*—*terra*, the earth.]

**Terrestrial**, ter-es'tri-al, *adj.* pertaining to or existing on the *earth :* earthly : representing the earth. [L. *terrestris*—*terra*, the earth.]

**Terrible**, ter'i-bl, *adj.* fitted to excite *terror* or awe : awful : dreadful.—*adv.* **Terr'ibly**. [L. *terribilis*—*terreo*, to frighten.]

**Terribleness**, ter'i-bl-nes, *n.* state of being *terrible:* terror, dread.

**Terrier**, ter'i-ėr, *n.* a dog that pursues animals to their *earth* or burrow : a hole or burrow where foxes, rabbits, &c. secure themselves. [Fr. *terrier*—*terre*, the earth—L. *terra*.]

**Terrific**, ter-rif'ik, *adj.* creating or *causing terror:* fitted to terrify : dreadful. [L. *terrificus*.]

**Terrify**, ter'i-fī, *v.t.* to *cause terror* in : to frighten greatly : to alarm :—*pa.t.* and *pa.p.* terr'ifīed. [L. *terreo*, and *facio*, to make.]

**Territorial**, ter-i-tō'ri-al, *adj.* pertaining to *territory :* limited to a district.—*adv.* **Territo'rially**.

**Territory**, ter'i-tor-i, *n.* the extent of *land* around or belonging to a city or state : domain : in the United States, a portion of the country not yet admitted as a State into the Union, and still under a provisional government. [L. *territorium*—*terra*, the earth, land.]

**Terror**, ter'ur, *n.* extreme fear : an object of fear or dread. [L. *terror*—*terreo*, to frighten.]

**Terrorism**, ter'ur-izm, *n.* a state of *terror :* a state which impresses terror : an organised system of intimidation.

**Terse**, tėrs, *adj.* compact or concise, with smoothness or elegance : neat.—*adv.* **Terse'ly**.—*n.* **Terse'ness**. [L. *tersus*, lit. 'rubbed' or 'wiped clean'—*tergeo*, *tersum*, to rub clean, akin to *stringo*, to draw tight.]

**Tertian**, tėr'shi-an, *adj.* occurring every *third* day.—*n.* an ague or fever with paroxysms every third day. [L. *tertianus*—*tertius*, third—*tres*, three.]

**Tertiary**, tėr'shi-ar-i, *adj.* of the *third* degree, order, or formation : pertaining to the series of sedimentary rocks or strata lying above the chalk and other secondary strata, and abounding in organic remains. [L. *tertiarius—tertius*.]

**Tesselate**, tes'el-āt, *v.t.* to form into *squares* or lay with checkered work. [L.—*tessella*, dim. of *tessera*, a square piece—Gr. *tessara*, four.]

**Tesselation**, tes-el-ā'shun, *n.* tesselated or mosaic work : the operation of making it.

**Test**, test, *n.* a pot in which metals are tried and refined : any critical trial : means of trial : (*chem.*) anything used to distinguish substances or detect their presence, a reagent : standard : proof : distinction.—*v.t.* to put to proof : to examine critically. [O. Fr. *test*—L. *testa*, a piece of baked clay, an earthen pot.]

**Testable**, test'a-bl, *adj.* capable of being given by *will*. [L. *testabilis*.]

**Testaceous**, tes-tā'shus, *adj.* consisting of or having a hard *shell*. [L. *testaceus—testa*, baked clay, a shell. See **Test**.]

**Testament**, tes'ta-ment, *n.* that which *testifies*, or in which an attestation is made : the solemn declaration in writing of one's will : a will : one of the two great divisions of the Bible. [L. —*testor*, to be a witness—*testis*, a witness.]

**Testamentary**, tes-ta-ment'ar-i, *adj.* pertaining to a *testament* or *will* : bequeathed or done by will. [L. *testatus*, pa.p. of *testor*.]

**Testate**, tes'tāt, *adj.* having made and left a *will*.

**Testator**, tes-tā'tor, *n.* one who leaves a *will*.—*fem.* **Testā'trix**. [L.]

**Tester**, tes'tèr, *n.* a flat canopy, esp. over the *head* of a bed. [O. Fr. *teste* (Fr. *tête*), the head —L. *testa*, an earthen pot, hence a hard shell, the skull.]

**Tester**, tes'tèr, *n.* a sixpence. [O. Fr. *teston—teste* (Fr. *tête*), the head, from the sovereign's head on the coin.]

**Testicle**, tes'ti-kl, *n.* a gland which secretes the seminal fluid in males : one of the stones. [L. *testiculus*, dim. of *testis*, a testicle.]

**Testiculate**, tes-tik'ū-lāt, **Testiculated**, tes-tik'ū-lāt-ed, *adj.* shaped like a *testicle*.

**Testify**, tes'ti-fī, *v.i.* to *bear witness* : to make a solemn declaration : to protest or declare a charge (with *against*).—*v.t.* to bear witness to : to affirm or declare solemnly or on oath :—*pa.t.* and *pa.p.* tes'tifīed.—*n.* **Tes'tifier**. [L. *testificor* —*testis*, a witness, and *facio*, to make.]

**Testimonial**, tes-ti-mō'ni-al, *adj.* containing *testimony*.—*n.* a writing or certificate bearing testimony to one's character or abilities : a sum of money raised by subscription and presented in any form to a person as a token of respect.

**Testimony**, tes'ti-mo-ni, *n.* evidence : declaration to prove some fact : proof : (*B.*) the two tables of the law : the whole divine revelation. [L. *testimonium—testor*, to witness.]

**Testy**, tes'ti, *adj.*, *heady* : easily irritated : fretful : peevish.—*adv.* **Tes'tily**.—*n.* **Tes'tiness**. [From O. Fr. *teste* (Fr. *tête*), the head. See **Tester**.]

**Tetanus**, tet'a-nus, *n.* spasm of the voluntary muscles : lockjaw.—*adj.* **Tetan'ic**. [L.—Gr.—*tetanos*, stretched—*teinō*, to stretch.]

**Tether**, te*th*'èr, *n.* a rope or chain for tying a beast, while feeding, within certain limits.—*v.t.* to confine with a tether : to restrain within certain limits. [M. E. *tedir*, found in Low Ger. *tider*, Ice. *tiodhr* ; conn. with **Tie**.]

**Tetragon**, tet'ra-gon, *n.* a figure of *four angles*. —*adj.* **Tetrag'onal**. [Gr. *tetragōnon—tetra*, four, *gōnia*, an angle.]

**Tetrahedral**, tet-ra-hē'dral, *adj.* having *four sides* : bounded by four triangles.

**Tetrahedron**, tet-ra-hē'dron, *n.* a solid figure

inclosed by *four bases* or triangles. [Gr. *tetra*, four, and *hedra*, a seat, a base.]

**Tetrarch**, tet'rärk, *n.* (under the Romans) the *ruler* of the *fourth* part of a province : a subordinate prince.—*ns.* **Tet'rarchate**, **Tet'rarchy**. [Gr.—*tetra*, four, and *archēs*, a ruler.]

**Tetrarchate**, te-trärk'āt, *n.* office or jurisdiction of a *tetrarch* : the fourth part of a province.

**Tetrasyllabic**, tet-ra-sil-lab'ik, *adj.* consisting of *four syllables*.

**Tetrasyllable**, tet'ra-sil-a-bl, *n.* a word of *four syllables*. [Gr. *tetra*, four, and **Syllable**.]

**Tetter**, tet'èr, *n.* a popular name for several eruptive diseases of the skin. [A.S. *teter*.]

**Teutonic**, tū-ton'ik, *adj.* belonging to the race so called, including Germans, Scandinavians, English, &c. ; also their language. [L.—*Teut-o*, -*onis* (O. Ger. *Diot-o*), lit. 'one of the *people*'—O. Ger. *diot*, the people (A.S. *theod*), whence also Ger. *Deut-sch*, German, E. *Dut-ch*. See **Dutch**.]

**Text**, tekst, *n.* the original words of an author : that on which a comment is written : a passage of Scripture. [Lit. 'something *woven*,' L. *textus—texo*, *textus*, to weave.]

**Text-book**, tekst'-book, *n.* a *book* containing the leading principles of a science. [Orig. a *book* with wide spaces for comments on the *text*.]

**Text-hand**, tekst'-hand, *n.* a large *hand* in writing ; so called because it was the practice to write the *text* of a book in large hand.

**Textile**, tekst'il, *adj.*, *woven* : capable of being woven. [L. *textilis—texo*, *textum*, to weave.]

**Textual**, tekst'ū-al, *adj.* pertaining to or contained in the *text* : serving for a text.—*adv.* **Text'ually**.

**Textualist**, tekst'ū-al-ist, *n.* one ready in citing Scripture *texts* ; one who adheres to the text.

**Texture**, tekst'ūr, *n.* anything *woven*, a web : manner of weaving or connecting : disposition of the parts of a body. [L. *textura—texo*.]

**Thaler**, tä'lèr, *n.* a dollar, in Germany a silver coin worth about 3s. [Ger. See **Dollar**.]

**Than**, *th*an, *conj.* a word placed after the comparative of an adjective or adverb between the things compared. [A.S. *thonne* ; cog. with Ger. *dann*, *denn* ; from stem of **The**. See **Then**.]

**Thane**, thān, *n.* a dignitary under the Anglo-Saxons and Danes, who prob. held the same rank as a baron does now.—*n.* **Thane'dom**. [A.S. *thegn*, a servant, nobleman ; cog. with Ice. *thegn*, a man, warrior, O. Ger. *degen*, a soldier, servant, Gr. *teknon*, child ; from the root of A.S. *thihan*, Ger. (*ge-*)*deihen*, to thrive.]

**Thank**, thangk, *v.t.* to express gratitude for a favour.—*n.* (usually in *pl.*) expression of gratitude for favour received. [A.S. *thanc*, will, thanks ; cog. with Ger. *dank* ; from the root of **Think**, the root idea being 'a movement of mind or feeling.']

**Thankful**, thangk'fool, *adj.*, *full of thanks* : grateful.—*adv.* **Thank'fully**.—*n.* **Thank'fulness**.

**Thankless**, thangk'les, *adj.* unthankful : not expressing thanks for favours : not gaining thanks.

**Thank-offering**, thangk'-of'èr-ing, *n.* an *offering* made to express *thanks* for mercies received.

**Thanksgiver**, thangks'giv-èr, *n.* one who *gives thanks*, or acknowledges a favour.

**Thanksgiving**, thangks'giv-ing, *n.* act of *giving thanks* : a public acknowledgment of divine goodness and mercy : a day set apart for this.

**Thankworthy**, thangk'wur-*th*i, *adj.*, *worthy* of or deserving *thanks*.

**That**, *th*at, *pron. demons.* and *rel.*—as a *demons.*

(*pl.* **Those**) it points out a person or thing: the former or more distant thing: not this but the other: as a *rel.*, who or which.—*conj.* used to introduce a clause: because: for: in order that. [A.S. *thæt*, neut. of the article *se* or *the*; cog. with Ger. *das*, *dasz*; further conn. with Gr. *to*, Sans. *tat*. See **The**.]

**Thatch**, thach, *v.t.* to cover, as a roof, with straw, reeds, &c.—*n.* straw, &c. used to cover the roofs of buildings and stacks.—*n.* **Thatch'er**. [A.S. *theccan*, to cover; cog. with Ger. *decken*, L. *tego*, Gr. *stegō*, to cover. See **Deck** and **Tile**.]

**Thatching**, thach'ing, *n.* the act or art of covering with thatch: the materials used for thatching.

**Thaumaturgy**, thaw'ma-tur-ji, *n.* the art of *working wonders* or miracles.—*adjs.* **Thaumatur'gic**, -al. [Gr. *thauma*, a wonder, and *ergon*, work.]

**Thaw**, thaw, *v.i.* to melt or grow liquid, as ice: to become so warm as to melt ice.—*v.t.* to cause to melt.—*n.* the melting of ice or snow by heat: the change of weather which causes it. [A.S. *thawan*; cog. with Ger. *thauen*, to thaw, to fall in dew.]

**The**, *th*e or (when emphatic) *th*ē, demons. pron. usually called the *definite article*, used to denote a particular person or thing: also to denote a species. [A.S. *se*, *the*, nom. masc. sing. See **That**.]

**The**, *th*e, *adv.* used before comparatives, as, 'the more the better.' [A.S. *thī*, by that, by that much, the instrumental case of **The**, demons. pron.]

**Theatre**, thē'a-tėr, *n.* a place where public representations, chiefly dramatic or musical, are *seen*: any place rising by steps like the seats of a theatre: a building adapted for scholastic exercises, anatomical demonstrations, &c.: scene of action. [Gr. *theatron*—*theaomai*, to see.]

**Theatric**, thē-at'rik, **Theatrical**, thē-at'rik-al, *adj.* relating or suitable to a *theatre*, or to actors: pompous. [ances.

**Theatricals**, thē-at'rik-alz, *n.pl.* dramatic perform-

**Thee**, *th*ē, *pron.* objective of **Thou**. [A.S. *the*, dative and accus. of *thu* (see **Thou**.)]

**Theft**, theft, *n.* act of *thieving*. [A.S. *theofth*, *thyfth*.] [—*thé*, tea.]

**Theine**, thē'in, *n.* the active principle of *tea*. [Fr.

**Their**, *th*ār, *poss. adj. pron.* of or belonging to them. [A.S. *thara*, gen. pl. of the definite article (replaced the older *hira*).]

**Theirs**, *th*ārz, *poss.* of **They**. [**Their**, with the sing. poss. suffix *-s*.]

**Theism**, thē'izm, *n.* belief in the existence of *God* with or without a belief in a special revelation. [Coined from Gr. *theos*, God.]

**Theist**, thē'ist, *n.* one who believes in *God*.

**Theistic**, thē-ist'ik, **Theistical**, thē-ist'ik-al, *adj.* pertaining to *theism*, or to a *theist*: according to the doctrines of theists.

**Them**, *th*em, *pron.* objective of **They**. [A.S. *thām*, dative pl. of the definite article (this replaced the older *him* or *heom*).]

**Theme**, thēm, *n.* a subject set or proposed for discussion, or on which a person speaks or writes. [Fr. *thème*—L. *thema*—Gr. *tithēmi*, to place, set. See **Thesis**.]

**Themselves**, *th*em-selvz', *pron.*, *pl.* of **Himself**, **Herself**, and **Itself**. [See **Them** and **Self**.]

**Then**, *th*en, *adv.* or *that* time: afterward: immediately: at another time: in that case: therefore. [A.S. *thanne*, *thonne*, *thenne*, accus. sing. from the stem of **The**. Doublet **Than**.]

**Thence**, *th*ens, *adv.* from that *time* or place: for

that reason. [M. E. *thenne-s*—*thenne* (see **Then**), with the gen. ending *-s*. Cf. **Hence** and **Whence**.]

**Thenceforth**, *th*ens'fōrth, *adv.* from that time forth or forward. [**Thence** and **Forth**.]

**Thenceforward**, *th*ens-for'ward, *adv.* from that time forward or onward.

**Theocracy**, thē-ok'ra-si, *n.* a *government* in which the chiefs of the state are considered as the immediate ministers of *God* or of the gods, or belong to a sacerdotal race: the state thus governed.—*adjs.* **Theocrat'ic**, **Theocrat'ical**. [Gr. *theokratia*—*theos*, God, and *krateō*, to rule.]

**Theodicy**, thē-od'i-si, *n.* a justification of God's dealings with man. [Gr. *theos*, God, and *dikē*, justice.]

**Theodolite**, thē-od'o-līt, *n.* an instrument used in land-surveying for measuring angles. [Ety. unknown.]

**Theogonist**, thē-og'o-nist, *n.* a writer on *theogony*.

**Theogony**, thē-og'o-ni, *n.* the part of heathen mythology which taught the *birth* and *genealogy* of the *gods*. [Gr. *theogonia*—*theos*, God, and *gonē*, *genos*, race—*genō*, to beget. See **Genesis** and **Genus**.]

**Theologian**, thē-o-lō'ji-an, *n.* one well versed in *theology*: a professor of divinity: a divine.

**Theologic**, thē-o-loj'ik, **Theological**, thē-o-loj'ik-al, *adj.* pertaining to *theology* or divinity.—*adv.* **Theolog'ically**. [Gr. *theologikos*.]

**Theologise**, thē-ol'o-jīz, *v.t.* to render *theological*.—*v.i.* to make a system of theology.

**Theologist**, thē-ol'o-jist, *n.* a student in the science of *theology*: a theologian.

**Theology**, thē-ol'o-ji, *n.* the *science* which treats of God, and of man's duty to him. [Gr. *theologia*—*theos*, God, and *logos*, a treatise.]

**Theorem**, thē'o-rem, *n.* a proposition to be proved. [Gr. *theōrēma*, 'a thing viewed'—*theōreō*, to view. See **Theory**.]

**Theoretic**, thē-o-ret'ik, **Theoretical**, thē-o-ret'ik-al, *adj.* pertaining to *theory*: not practical: speculative.—*adv.* **Theoret'ically**.

**Theorise**, thē'o-rīz, *v.i.* to form a *theory*: to form opinions solely by theories: to speculate.—*n.* **The'oriser**. [theory and speculation.

**Theorist**, thē'o-rist, *n.* a *theoriser*: one given to

**Theory**, thē'o-ri, *n.* an explanation, or system of anything: an exposition of the abstract principles of a science or art: speculation as opposed to practice. [L.—Gr. *theōria*. See **Theorem**.]

**Theosophy**, thē-os'o-fi, *n.*, *divine wisdom*, or knowledge obtained by direct intercourse with God and superior spirits: immediate divine illumination or inspiration. [Gr. *theosophia*—*theos*, God, and *sophos*, wisdom.]

**Therapeutic**, ther-a-pū'tik, *adj.* pertaining to the *healing* art: curative. [Gr. *therapeuō*, to take care of, to heal, to nurse.]

**Therapeutics**, ther-a-pū'tiks, *n.sing.* that part of medicine concerned with the treatment and cure of diseases.

**There**, *th*ār, *adv.* in that place (opposed to **Here**): it is used to begin sentences when the subject comes after the verb.—**Thereabout'** or **-abouts'**, *adv.* about or near that place: near that number, quantity, or degree.—**Thereaft'er**, *adv.* after or according to that.—**Thereat'**, *adv.* at that place or occurrence: on that account.—**Thereby'**, *adv.* by that means: in consequence of that.—**Therefore** (*th*ėr'fur). *adv.* for that or this reason: consequently.—**Therefrom'**, *adv.* from that or this.—**Therein'**, *adv.* in that or this place, time, or thing.—**Thereof** (*th*ār-of'), *adv.*

of that or this.—**Thereon**', *adv.* on that or this.—
**Thereto**', **Thereunto**', *adv.* to that or this.—
**Thereupon**', *adv.* upon or in consequence of
that or this: immediately.—**Therewith**', *adv.*
with that or this. [A.S. *tha-r* or *thæ-r*; conn.
with the stem of **The**. The *-re* is prob. short
for *der* (cf. Sans. *ta-tra*, there).]

**Thermal**, thèr'mal, *adj.* pertaining to *heat*: warm.
[Gr. *thermos*, hot—*thermē*, heat—*therō*, to heat.]

**Thermo-dynamics**, thèr'mo-di-nam'iks, *n.* the
branch of physics which treats of *heat* as a
mechanical agent. [Gr. *thermos*—*thermē*, heat,
and *dynamikos*—*dynamis*, force.]

**Thermo-electricity**, thèr'mo-e-lek-tris'i-ti, *n.* elec-
*tricity* developed by the unequal *heating* of
bodies.

**Thermometer**, thèr-mom'e-tèr, *n.* an instrument
for *measuring* the variations of sensible *heat* or
temperature. [Gr. *thermē*, heat, and *metron*, a
measure.]

**Thermometric**, thèr-mo-met'rik, **Thermometri-
cal**, thèr-mo-met'rik-al, *adj.* pertaining to or made
with a *thermometer*.—*adv.* **Thermomet'rically**.

**Thermo-pile**, thèr'mo-pīl, *n.* a thermo-electric
battery used as a thermometer. [Gr. *thermē*,
heat, and **Pile**, a roundish mass.]

**Thesaurus**, the-saw'rus, *n.* a *treasury* or repository, esp. of knowledge: a lexicon or cyclopædia. [L.—Gr. *thēsauros*—*tithēmi*, to place.]

**These**, thēz, *demon. pron.*, *pl.* of **This**. [A.S.
*thas*, old pl. of *thes*, this. Doublet **Those**.]

**Thesis**, the'sis, *n.* a *position* or that which is *set
down* or advanced for argument: a subject for
a scholastic exercise: an essay on a theme:—*pl.*
**Theses** (the'sēz). [L.—Gr. *ti-thē-mi*, to set.
See **Theme**.]

**Theurgy**, the'ur-ji, *n.* that kind of magic which
affects to work by supernatural agency, as distinguished from natural magic and necromancy.
—*adjs.* **Theur'gic**, **Theur'gical**. [Lit. 'the
work of a god,' Gr. *theourgia*—*theos*, god, and
*ergō*, to work.]

**Thew**, thū, *n.* (used chiefly in *pl.*), muscle or
strength: sinews. [Perhaps a form of **Thigh**.]

**They**, thā, *pers. pron.*, *pl.* of **He**, **She**, or **It**.
[From A.S. *thā*, nom. pl. of the definite article,
which replaced the older *hi*, *heo*. See **The**.]

**Thick**, thik, *adj.* dense: imperfectly mobile: compact: not transparent or clear: misty: dull:
crowded: closely set: abundant: frequent, in
quick succession: having great depth or circumference.—*adv.* closely: frequently: fast: to a
great depth.—*adv.* **Thick'ly**.—*n.* **Thick'ness**.
[A.S. *thicce*; cog. with Ger. *dick*; from root of
A.S. *thihan*, to thrive. See **Thane**.]

**Thicken**, thik'n, *v.t.* to make thick or close: to
strengthen.—*v.i.* to become thick or obscure:
to crowd or press. [A.S. *thiccian*.]

**Thicket**, thik'et, *n.* a collection of trees or shrubs
*thickly* or closely set: close wood or copse.

**Thick-headed**, thik'hed'ed, *adj.* having a *thick
head* or skull: stupid.

**Thickish**, thik'ish, *adj.* somewhat thick.

**Thief**, thēf, *n.* one who steals or takes unlawfully
what is not his own. [A.S. *theof*; cog. with
Ice. *thiof-r*, and Ger. *dieb*.] [A.S. *theofian*.]

**Thieve**, thēv, *v.i.* to practise *theft*: to steal.

**Thievery**, thēv'èr-i, *n.* the practice of thieving.

**Thievish**, thēv'ish, *adj.*, given to, or like *theft* or
stealing: acting by stealth: secret: sly.—*adv.*
**Thiev'ishly**.—*n.* **Thiev'ishness**.

**Thigh**, thī, *n.* the thick fleshy part of the leg from
the knee to the trunk. [A.S. *theoh*; Ice. *thio*,
O. Ger. *diech*, seen in Ger. *dickbein*, thigh.]

**Thimble**, thim'bl, *n.* a metal cover for the finger,
used in sewing. [Lit. 'a thumb-piece;' an extension of **Thumb**.]

**Thimble-rig**, thim'bl-rig, *n.* a sleight-of-hand trick
in which the performer conceals, or pretends to
conceal, a pea or small ball under one of three
thimble-like cups.—*v.i.* to cheat by such means.
—*n.* **Thim'ble-rig'ger**. [From colloquial use
of **Rig**, in the sense of a trick, a wanton trick.]

**Thin**, thin, *adj.* having little thickness: slim:
lean: freely mobile: small: fine: not close or
crowded: not full or well grown.—*adv.* not
thickly or closely: in a scattered state.—*v.t.* to
make thin: to make less close or crowded: to
make rare or less thick or dense:—*pr.p.* thinn'-
ing; *pa.t.* and *pa.p.* thinned.—*adv.* **Thin'ly**.—*n.*
**Thin'ness**. [Lit. 'extended' or 'stretched out,'
A.S. *thyn*; cog. with Ice. *thunn-r*, Ger. *dünn*;
L. *tenuis*, Celt. *tanas*, Sans. *tanus*, from the
root *tan*, stretch. See **Tend** and **Thunder**.]

**Thine**, thīn, *pron.* (possessive form of **Thou**), belonging to thee: thy. [A.S. *thin*; Ger. *dein*.]

**Thing**, thing, *n.* an inanimate object: an event:
a part. [A.S.; Ice. *thing*, Ger. *ding*; the root
idea being 'a lawsuit,' hence 'a cause,' 'an
affair;' cf. the connection of Ger. *sache* and E.
**Sake**; and of Fr. *chose* and L. *causa*.]

**Think**, thingk, *v.i.* to exercise the mind: to revolve ideas in the mind: to judge: to form or
hold as an opinion: to consider: to purpose or
design.—*v.t.* to imagine: to judge: to believe
or consider:—*pa.t.* and *pa.p.* thought.—*n.*
**Think'er**. [A.S. *thencan*, *thyncan*; cog. with
Ger. *denken*, from root of **Thank**.]

**Thinnish**, thin'ish, *adj.* somewhat thin.

**Third**, thèrd, *adj.* the last of *three*.—*n.* one of
*three* equal parts. [A.S. *thridda*. See **Three**.]

**Thirdly**, thèrd'li, *adv.* in the *third* place.

**Thirst**, thèrst, *n.* the uneasiness caused by want
of drink: vehement desire for drink: eager
desire for anything.—*v.i.* to feel thirst: to
desire vehemently. [A.S. *thurst*, *thyrst*; cog.
with Ger. *durst*, from a Teut. root sig. 'dry;'
conn. also with Gr. *ters-omai*, L. *torr-eo*, to
dry, Sans. *trish*, to thirst.]

**Thirsty**, thèrst'i, *adj.* suffering from *thirst*: dry:
parched: vehemently desiring.—*adv.* **Thirst'ily**.
—*n.* **Thirst'iness**. [A.S. *thurstig*.]

**Thirteen**, thèr'tēn, *adj.* and *n.*, *three* and *ten*.

**Thirteenth**, thèr'tēnth, *adj.* and *n.* the last of
*thirteen*. [A.S. *threoteotha*—*threo*, three, and
*teotha*, tenth.]

**Thirtieth**, thèr'ti-eth, *adj.* the last of *thirty*.—*n.*
a thirtieth part. [A.S. *thritigotha*.]

**Thirty**, thèr'ti, *adj.* and *n.* *three* times *ten*. [A.S.
*thritig*—*threo*, three, and *tig*, ten.]

**This**, this, *demons. pron.* or *adj.* denoting a person or thing near, just mentioned, or about to be
mentioned: (*B.*) the last past:—*pl.* **These**.
[A.S. *this*, the neut. of the adj. pron. *thes* (m.),
*theos* (f.), *this* (n.); Ice. *thessi*, Ger. *dieser*.]

**Thistle**, this'l, *n.* a genus of prickly plants. [A.S.
*thistel*; Ger. *distel*.]

**Thistly**, this'li, *adj.* overgrown with *thistles*.

**Thither**, thith'èr, *adv.* to that place: to that end
or result. [A.S. *thider*; from the stem of **The**.]

**Thitherward**, thith'èr-ward, *adv.* toward that
place. [A.S. *thider-weard*.]

**Thole**, **Thowl**, thōl, **Thowel**, thō'el, *n.* a pin in
the side of a boat to keep the oar in place.
[A.S. *thol*; Ger. *dulle*, Ice. *tholl-r*.]

**Thong**, thong, *n.* a piece or strap of leather to
*fasten* anything. [A.S. *thwang*, *thwong*, from
the same root as Ger. *zwang*, constraining

power—*zwingen*, to constrain ; cf. the connection of *band*, *bind*, and *bond*.]

**Thoracic**, tho-ras′ik, *adj.* pertaining to the *thorax* or breast.

**Thorax**, thō′raks, *n.* the part of the body between the neck and belly : the chest. [Lit. 'a breastplate,' L.—Gr.]

**Thorn**, thorn, *n.* a sharp, woody spine on the stem of a plant : a spine : a plant having spines or thorns : anything prickly or troublesome. [A.S.; Ice. *thorn*, Ger. *dorn*; Slav. *tarn*.]

**Thornback**, thorn′bak, *n.* a species of ray or skate which has *thorns* or spines in its *back*.

**Thorny**, thorn′i, *adj.* full of *thorns* : prickly : troublesome : harassing. [A.S. *thorniht*.]

**Thorough**, thur′ō, *adj.* passing *through* or to the end : complete : entire.—(*obs.*) *prep.* through.— *adv.* Thor′oughly.—*n.* Thor′oughness. [A.S. *thurh*, from a root *tar*, 'to go beyond,' seen in L. *tra-ns*. The longer form of **Through**.]

**Thorough-bass**, thur′ō-bās, *n.* (*music*) a *bass* part all *through* a piece, with figures placed over the notes to indicate the harmony to be played to each.

**Thoroughbred**, thur′ō-bred, *adj.* *thoroughly* or completely *bred* : bred from a dam and sire of the best blood, as a horse, and having the qualities supposed to depend thereon.

**Thoroughfare**, thur′ō-fār, *n.* a *fare* or passage for going *through* : a public way or street : right of passing through. [See **Fare**.]

**Thorough-going**, thur′ō-gō′ing, *adj.*, *going through* or to the end : going all lengths : complete.

**Thorough-paced**, thur′ō-pāst, *adj.*, *thoroughly* or perfectly *paced* or trained : complete.

**Thorp**, thorp, *n.* a homestead : a hamlet. [A.S. *thorpe*; Goth. *thaurp*, Ger. *dorf*; allied to L. *turba*, a crowd.]

**Those**, thōz, *pron.*, *pl.* of **That**. [From A.S. *thas*, the old pl. of *thes*, this. See **This**. Doublet **These**.]

**Thou**, thow, *pron.* of the second person sing., the person addressed (now gen. used only in solemn address). [A.S. *thu;* cog. with Goth. *thu*, Gr. *tu*, L. *tu*, Sans. *tva-m*.]

**Though**, thō, *conj.* admitting : allowing : even if : notwithstanding. [Lit. 'on that' (condition), A.S. *theah;* cog. with Goth. *thau-h*, Ice. *thō*, Ger. *doch;* from the stem of **The**.]

**Thought**, thawt, *pa.t.* and *pa.p.* of **Think**. [A.S. *theahte*, *theaht*.]

**Thought**, thawt, *n.* the act of *thinking:* reasoning : deliberation : that which one thinks : idea : fancy : consideration : opinion : meditation : design : care. [A.S. *ge-thoht;* Ice. *thott-r*, O. Ger. *ge-dacht*. See **Think**.]

**Thoughtful**, thawt′fool, *adj.*, *full* of *thought:* employed in meditation : attentive : considerate : promoting serious thought : favourable to meditation.—*adv.* Thought′fully.—*n.* Thought′fulness.

**Thoughtless**, thawt′les, *adj.*, *without thought* or care : careless : inattentive : stupid : dull.—*adv.* Thought′lessly.—*n.* Thought′lessness.

**Thousand**, thow′zand, *adj.* denoting *ten hundred:* proverbially, denoting any great number.—*n.* the number ten hundred : any large number. [A.S. *thusend;* Ger. *tausend*, Goth. *thusundi;* found also in Slav. and Lithuanian, and prob. thence derived.]

**Thousandfold**, thow′zand-fōld, *adj.*, *folded* a *thousand* times : multiplied by a thousand.

**Thousandth**, thow′zandth, *adj.* the last of a *thousand* or of any great number.—*n.* one of a thousand or of any great number.

**Thowel, Thowl.** See **Thole**.

**Thraldom, Thralldom**, thrawl′dum, *n.* the condition of a *thrall* or slave : slavery : bondage.

**Thrall**, thrawl, *n.* a *slave*, *serf:* slavery : servitude. [A.S. *thrall;* Ice. *thrœll*, a slave ; prob. a dim. from A.S. *threagan*, to chide, to vex ; acc. to Trench, from **Thrill**, from the practice of boring the ear of a slave in token of servitude.]

**Thrash**, thrash, *v.t.* to beat out grain from the straw : to beat soundly.—*n.* Thrash′er. [A.S. *therscan;* cog. with Ger. *dreschen*.]

**Thrashing**, thrash′ing, *n.* the act of beating out grain from the straw : a sound beating or drubbing.

**Thrashing-floor**, thrash′ing-flōr, *n.* a *floor* on which grain is *thrashed*.

**Thread**, thred, *n.* a very thin line of any substance *twisted* and drawn out : a filament of any fibrous substance : a fine line of yarn : anything resembling a thread : the prominent spiral part of a screw : something continued in long course : the uniform tenor of a discourse.—*v.t.* to pass a thread through the eye of (as a needle) : to pass or pierce through, as a narrow way. [Lit. 'something twisted,' A.S. *thred* (cog. with Ice. *thrad-r*, Ger. *draht*), from *thrawan*, to wind (E. **Throw**, to twist), Ger. *drehen*.]

**Threadbare**, thred′bār, *adj.* worn to the *bare* or naked *thread:* having the nap worn off : hackneyed : used till its novelty or interest is gone.

**Thready**, thred′i, *adj.* like thread : slender : containing or consisting of thread.

**Threat**, thret, *n.* declaration of an intention to inflict punishment or other evil upon another : menace. [See **Threaten**.]

**Threaten**, thret′n, *v.t.* to declare the intention of inflicting punishment or other evil upon another : to terrify by menaces : to present the appearance of coming evil, or of something unpleasant. [A.S. *threatian*, to threaten ; cog. with Ger. *ver-drieszen*, Goth. *thriutan*, to vex.]

**Threatening**, thret′n-ing, *adj.* indicating a *threat* or menace : indicating something approaching or impending.—*adv.* Threat′eningly.

**Three**, thrē, *adj.* and *n.* two and one. [A.S. and Ice. *thri*, Celt. *tri*, Goth. *threis*, Ger. *drei*, L. *tres*, Gr. *treis*, Sans. *tri*.]

**Threefold**, thrē′fōld, *adj.*, *folded thrice:* thrice repeated : consisting of three. [folds.

**Threeply**, thrē′plī, *adj.* having *three plies* or

**Threescore**, thrē′skōr, *adj.*, *three* times a *score*, sixty.

**Threnody**, thren′o-di, *n.* an *ode* or song *of lamentation*. [Gr. *thrēnōdia*, from *thrēnos*, a lament (—*threomai*, to cry aloud), and *odē*, a song.]

**Thresh**, thresh. Same as **Thrash**.

**Threshold**, thresh′ōld, *n.* a piece of wood or stone under the door of a house : door : entrance : the place or point of entering. [Lit. 'the piece of *wood beaten* by the feet,' M. E. *threshwold*— A.S. *therscwald*—*therscan*, to thresh, *wald*, wood.]

**Threw**, thrōō, *pa.t.* of **Throw**.

**Thrice**, thrīs, *adv.*, *three times*. [M. E. *thries*— **Three**, with a genitive termination.]

**Thrift**, thrift, *n.* state of *thriving:* frugality : prosperity : increase of wealth : gain : a plant so called, of several species. [See **Thrive**.]

**Thriftless**, thrift′les, *adj.*, *not thrifty:* extravagant : not thriving.—*adv.* Thrift′lessly.—*n.* Thrift′lessness.

**Thrifty**, thrift′i, *adj.* (comp. **Thrift′ier**, superl. **Thrift′iest**) showing *thrift* or economy : thriving by frugality.—*adv.* Thrift′ily.—*n.* Thrift′iness.

**Thrill**, thril, *v.t.* to pierce : to affect strongly.

—*v.i.* to pierce, as something sharp : to cause a tingling, shivering feeling to run through the body : to feel a sharp, shivering sensation.—*n.* a thrilling sensation. [A.S. *thyrlian*, to bore a hole ; Ger. *drillen*, to drill a hole. See **Drill**, to pierce.]

**Thrilling**, thril'ing, *adj.* causing to thrill.

**Thrive**, thrīv, *v.i.* to prosper : to increase in goods : to be successful : to grow : to flourish :—*pa.t.* thrōve and thrīved ; *pa.p.* thriv'en. [Ice. *thrifa*, to care, *thrif*, care, good success.]

**Thrivingly**, thrī'ving-li, *adv.* in a *thriving* or prosperous manner.

**Throat**, thrōt, *n.* the forepart of the neck, in which are the gullet and windpipe : an entrance : a narrow part of anything. [A.S. *throte* ; Ger. *drossel*, the throat, gullet.]

**Throb**, throb, *v.i.* to *beat* or palpitate, as the heart or pulse, with more than usual force :—*pr.p.* throbb'ing ; *pa.t.* and *pa.p.* throbbed.—*n.* a beat or strong pulsation. [Sw. *drabba*, to knock ; akin to L. *trepido*, to tremble.]

**Throe**, thrō, *n.*, *suffering*, pain : agony : the pains of childbirth. [A.S. *threa*, suffering—*threowan*, to suffer.]

**Throne**, thrōn, *n.* a chair of state richly ornamented and covered with a canopy : seat of a bishop in his church : sovereign power and dignity.—*v.t.* to place on a royal seat : to exalt :—*pr.p.* thrōn'ing ; *pa.t.* and *pa.p.* thrōned. [L. *thronus*—Gr. *thronos*, a seat—*thraō*, to set.]

**Throng**, throng, *n.* a large number of people *pressed* or *crowded together* : a crowd : a great multitude.—*v.t.* to press or crowd : to annoy with numbers.—*v.i.* to crowd together : to come in multitudes. [A.S. *thrang—thringan*, to press.]

**Throstle**, thros'l, *n.* the song-*thrush* or mavis. [A.S. *throstle* ; cog. with Ger. *drossel*, L. *turdus*, a thrush.]

**Throttle**, throt'l, *n.* the *throat* or windpipe.—*v.t.* to choke by pressure on the windpipe. [Dim. of **Throat**.]

**Through**, thrōō, *prep.* from end to end, or from side to side of : between the sides of : over the whole extent of : among : from beginning to end : by means of : in consequence of.—*adv.* from one end or side to the other : from beginning to end : to the end or purpose. [A.S. *thurh* ; cog. with Ger. *durch*, W. *trw*, Sans. *taras*—root *tar*, to cross (L. *trans*, across).] [**Thoroughly**.]

**Throughly**, thrōō'li, *adv.* (*obs.*) same as **Throughout**, thrōō-owt', *prep.*, *through* to the *out*side : in every part of : from one end to the other.—*adv.* in every part : everywhere.

**Throve**, thrōv, *pa.t.* of **Thrive**.

**Throw**, thrō, *v.t.* to hurl : to fling : to wind or twist together, as yarn : to form on a wheel, as pottery : to venture at dice : to put off : to put on or spread carelessly : to cast down in wrestling.—*v.i.* to cast or hurl : to cast dice :—*pa.t.* threw (thrōō) ; *pa.p.* thrōwn.—*n.* the act of throwing : a cast, esp. of dice : the distance to which anything may be thrown : a violent effort.—*n.* Throw'er. [A.S. *thrawan*, to turn, to twist ; cog. with Ger. *drehen*, to twist, L. *terere*, *torquere*.]

**Thrum**, thrum, *n.* the *end* of a weaver's thread : coarse yarn.—*v.t.* to furnish with thrums : to fringe : to insert short pieces of rope-yarn in a mat or piece of canvas : to play rudely or monotonously on an instrument with the fingers :—*pr.p.* thrumm'ing ; *pa.t.* and *pa.p.* thrummed. [Ice. *thröm* ; Ger. *trumm*, a piece, end, fragment.]

**Thrummy**, thrum'i, *adj.* made of or like *thrums*.

**Thrush**, thrush, *n.* a little bird remarkable for its power of song. [See **Throstle**.]

**Thrush**, thrush, *n.* an inflammatory and suppurating affection in the feet of horses : a disease of the mouth and throat occurring chiefly in early infancy.

**Thrust**, thrust, *v.t.* to push or drive with force.—*v.i.* to make a push, esp. with a pointed weapon : to squeeze in : to intrude :—*pa.t.* and *pa.p.* thrust.—*n.* a stab : an assault. [Ice. *thrysta*, to press.]

**Thug**, thug, *n.* one of a class of professional robbers and assassins, in India, numerous up till 1830.—*ns.* **Thuggee'** and **Thugg'ism**, the practice and superstition of the Thugs. [Sans. *thag*, cheat, knave.]

**Thumb**, thum, *n.* the short, thick finger of the hand : the corresponding member in other animals.—*v.t.* to handle awkwardly : to play or soil with the thumb or fingers.—*v.i.* to finger.—**By rule of thumb**, in a rough and ready practical manner, found by experience to be convenient. [With intrusive *b* from A.S. *thuma* ; cog. with Ice. *thumall* ; conn. with L. *tumeo*, Sans. *taumi*, to grow large.]

**Thumbkin**, thum'kin, **Thumbscrew**, thum'skrōō, *n.* an old instrument of torture for compressing the *thumb* by means of a *screw*.

**Thummim**, thum'im, *n.pl.*, *perfections*. [Heb., pl. of *tom*, perfection. See **Urim**.]

**Thump**, thump, *n.* a heavy blow.—*v.t.* to beat with something heavy.—*v.i.* to strike or fall with a dull, heavy blow.—*n.* Thump'er. [From the sound, like **Bump**.]

**Thunder**, thun'dėr, *n.* the deep rumbling sound after a flash of lightning : any loud noise : an alarming denunciation.—*v.i.* to make thunder : to sound as thunder.—*v.t.* to give out with noise and terror : to publish a denunciation.—*n.* Thun'derer.—*adjs.* Thun'dery, Thun'derous. [With intrusive *d* from A.S. *thunor* ; cog. with Ger. *donner*, Ice. *dunr*, L. *tonitru* (—*tono*). The root is *tan*, found in L. *tendo*, Gr. *teinō*, Ger. *dehnen*, to stretch, from the *stretching* or straining of the god in hurling the thunderbolt.]

**Thunderbolt**, thun'dėr-bōlt, *n.* a *bolt* or shaft of lightning preceding a peal of *thunder* : anything sudden and irresistible : a daring or irresistible hero : ecclesiastical denunciation.

**Thunderstruck**, thun'dėr-struk, *adj.*, *struck* by *lightning* : astonished : struck dumb.

**Thurible**, thūr'i-bl, *n.* a censer of metal for burning *frankincense*. [L. *thuribulum*—*thus*, *thuris*, frankincense ; akin to Gr. *thuos*, a sacrifice.]

**Thurifer**, thūr'i-fėr, *n.* the server who *carries* the *thurible*. [L. *thus*, *thuris*, and *fero*, to bear.]

**Thursday**, thurz'dā, *n.* the fifth *day* of the week, so called because orig. sacred to *Thor*, the old Saxon god of thunder. [A.S. *thunres dæg—thuner*, thunder, and *dæg*, day ; Ice. *thorsdag-r*, Thor's day, Ger. *donnerstag*.]

**Thus**, *th*us, *adv.* in *this* or that manner : to this degree or extent. [A.S., prob. an instrumental case of **This**.]

**Thwack**, thwak, *v.t.* to strike with something blunt and heavy, to thrash.—*n.* a heavy blow. [Imitative.]

**Thwart**, thwawrt, *adj.*, *cross* : being crosswise.—*v.t.* to cross : to oppose : to defeat.—*n.* the bench for rowers placed *athwart* the boat.—*adv.* Thwart'ly. [Ice. *thvert* ; cog. with A.S. *thweorh*, Ger. *quer*. See **Queer**.]

**Thy**, *th*ī, *poss. adj.*, *thine*, of or pertaining to thee. [Short for **Thine**.]

**Thyme**, tīm, *n.* an aromatic herb. [L. *thymum* —Gr. *thyō*, to fill with sweet smells, to burn in sacrifice.]      [grant.

**Thymy**, tīm′i, *adj.* abounding with *thyme*: fra-

**Thyself**, *thī*-self′, *pron.*, thou or thee, in person—used for emphasis. [**Thy** and **Self**.]

**Tiara**, tī-ā′ra, *n.* the lofty ornamental head-dress of the ancient Persians : a head-dress : the mitre of the Jewish high-priest : the pope's triple crown. —*adj.* **Tia′raed**, wearing a *tiara*. [Fr. *tiare*, through L., from Gr. *tiara*.]

**Tibia**, tib′i-a, *n.* the large shinbone. [L., the shin-bone, hence, a flute (orig. made of bone).]

**Tibial**, tib′i-al, *adj.* pertaining to the *tibia* : pertaining to a pipe or flute.

**Tic**, tik, *n.* a convulsive motion of certain muscles, esp. of the face. [Fr., from the likeness of the motion to a ticking sound.]

**Tic-douloureux**, tik-dōō-lōō-rōō′, *n.* painful, convulsive motion of a nerve, usually in the face. [Fr. *tic* (see **Tic**), and *douloureux*, painful.]

**Tick**, tik, *n.* the popular name for several species of large mites which infest dogs, sheep, &c. [M. E. *tike*, cog. with Dut. *teek*, Ger. *zecke*.]

**Tick**, tik, *n.* the case or cover in which feathers &c. are put for bedding.—**Ticken**, tik′en, **Ticking**, tik′ing, *n.* the cloth of which a tick is made. [Allied to Dut. *tijk*, and Ger. *zieche* ; all from L. *theca*—Gr. *thēkē*, a case, that in which anything is put—*ti-thē-mi*, to put.]

**Tick**, tik, *v.i.* to make a small, quick noise : to beat, as a watch. [Imitative ; as are Dut. *tikk-en* and Ger. *tick-en*.]

**Tick**, tik, *v.i.* to run upon score : to get or give credit.—*n.* credit : trust. [Prob. a contr. of **Ticket**.]

**Ticket**, tik′et, *n.* a marked card : a token of any right or debt, as for admission, &c.—*v.t.* to mark by a ticket.—**Ticket-of-leave**, a license to be at large, granted to a convict for good conduct. [Short for Fr. *étiquette*, a label, lit. ' something *stuck* on,' from Ger. *stechen*, E. **Stick**.]

**Tickle**, tik′l, *v.t.* to *touch lightly* and cause to laugh : to please by slight gratification.—*v.i.* to feel titillation or tickling.—*n.* **Tick′ler**. [Dim. of **Tick**, *v.*, in the sense ' to touch lightly.']

**Ticklish**, tik′lish, *adj.* easily tickled : easily affected : nice : critical.—*adv.* **Tick′lishly**.—*n.* **Tick′lishness**.

**Tidal**, tīd′al, *adj.* pertaining to *tides* : flowing and ebbing periodically.

**Tide**, tīd, *n.*, *time* : season : the regular flux and reflux or rising and falling of the sea : course : a tide, time, or season : commotion : turning-point.—*v.t.* to drive with the stream.—*v.i.* to pour a tide or flood : to work in or out of a river or harbour with the tide. [A.S., cog. with Ger. *zeit*, time. Cf. **Tidings**.]

**Tidegauge**, tīd′gāj, *n.* an instrument for registering the state of the tide continuously.

**Tideless**, tīd′les, *adj.* having no tides.

**Tidemill**, tīd′mil, *n.* a *mill* moved by *tide*-water : a mill for clearing lands of tide-water.

**Tide-table**, tīd′-tā′bl, *n.* a *table* giving the time of high *tide* at any place.

**Tide-waiter**, tīd′-wāt′ér, *n.* an officer who *waits* the arrival of vessels, to secure the payment of the duties.      [the *tide* sets.

**Tideway**, tīd′wā, *n.* the *way* or channel in which

**Tidings**, tīd′ingz, *n.pl.* news : intelligence. [Lit. ' things that betide,' from Ice. *tidh-indi—tidh*, time ; cf. Ger. *zeit-ung*, news, from *zeit*. See **Tide** and **Betide**.]

**Tidy**, tī′di, *adj.* neat : in good order.—*n.* a cover

for chairs, &c. : a child's pinafore.—*v.t.* to make neat : to put in good order :—*pa.t.* and *pa.p.* tī′died. [M. E. *tidi* (*lit.*) ' timely,' in good condition, beautiful, from A.S. *tid*, time, E. **Tide** ; cf. Ger. *zeit-ig*, ' timely,' mature.]

**Tie**, tī, *v.t.* to *bind :* to fasten with a cord : to unite : to constrain : (*music*) to unite notes with a tie :—*pr.p.* ty′ing ; *pa.t.* and *pa.p.* tied (tīd).—*n.* a knot : a bond : an equality in numbers, as of votes, or of ' points ' in a game : (*music*) a curved line drawn over two or more notes on the same degree of the stave, signifying that the second note is not to be sounded separately, but is to sustain the first. [A.S. *tian*, to tie, perh. from the root of A.S. *teon*, to draw, Ger. *ziehen*.]

**Tier**, tēr, *n.* a *row* or *rank*, especially when several rows are placed one above another. [A.S. *tier*.]

**Tierce**, tērs, *n.* a cask containing one-*third* of a pipe, that is 42 gallons : a sequence of *three* cards of the same colour : a third, in music : a thrust, in fencing. [Fr.—L. *tertia* (*pars*), a third (part)—*ter*, three times—*tres*, three.]

**Tiffin**, tif′in, *n.* the East Indian name for lunch. [From Prov. E. *tiff*, a draught of beer.]

**Tiger**, tī′gér, *n.* a fierce animal of the cat kind, nearly as large as a lion.—*fem.* **Ti′gress**. [Fr. *tigre*—L. *tigris*—Gr.]

**Tigerish**, tī′gér-ish, *adj.* like a *tiger* in disposition.

**Tight**, tīt, *adj.* close : compact : not leaky : fitting closely : not loose.—*adv.* **Tight′ly**.—*n.* **Tight′ness**. [From A.S. *thihan*, to thrive ; cog. with Ger. *dicht*. See **Tie** and **Thick**.]

**Tighten**, tīt′n, *v.t.* to make tight or tighter : to straiten.

**Tilbury**, til′ber-i, *n.* a kind of gig. [Said to be so named from its first maker.]

**Tile**, tīl, *n.* a piece of baked clay used for *covering* roofs, floors, &c. : a tube of baked clay used in drains.—*v.t.* to cover with tiles.—*n.* **Til′er**. [A.S. *tigol*—L. *tegula—tego*, to cover.]

**Tilery**, tīl′ér-i, *n.* a place where *tiles* are made.

**Tiling**, tīl′ing, *n.* a roof of *tiles* : tiles in general.

**Till**, til, *n.* a money box or drawer in a desk or counter. [From A.S. *tilian*, to tell, count.]

**Till**, til, *prep.* to the time of.—*adv.* to the time when : to the degree that. [A.S. *til*—Scand. ; from the same root as A.S. *til*, suitable, *tilian*, to gain, to get, and Ger. *ziel*, end, limit.]

**Till**, til, *v.t.* to cultivate.—*n.* **Till′er**. [A.S. *tilian*, to till—*til*, an end, a limit ; cog. with Ger. *zielen*, to aim, to arrange.]

**Tillage**, til′āj, *n.* act or practice of *tilling :* husbandry : a place tilled.

**Tiller**, til′ér, *n.* the *handle* or lever for turning a rudder. [Prov. E. *tiller*, the handle of a spade ; perh. from Dut. *tillen*, to lift.]

**Tilt**, tilt, *n.* the canvas *covering* of a cart or wagon : an awning in a boat.—*v.t.* to cover with an awning. [A.S. *teld—teldan*, to cover ; cog. with Ger. *zelt*.]

**Tilt**, tilt, *v.i.* to ride against another and thrust with a lance : to thrust or fight with a lance or rapier : to fall into a sloping posture.—*v.t.* to point or thrust with, as a lance : to slant : to raise one end of : to forge with a tilt-hammer.—*n.* a thrust : in the middle ages, an exercise in which combatants rode against each other with lances : inclination forward.—*n.* **Tilt′er**. [A.S. *tealt*, tottering ; Ice. *tölta*, to trot ; Ger. *zelter*.]

**Tilth**, tilth, *n.* cultivation : cultivated land. [From **Till**, *v.t.*]

**Tilt-hammer**, tilt′-ham′ér, *n.* a heavy *hammer*

used in ironworks, which is *tilted* or lifted by means of projections on the axis of a wheel.

**Timber,** tim´bér, *n.* wood for *building* purposes : the trunk of a tree : material for any structure : one of the larger pieces of the framework of a house, ship, &c.—*v.t.* to furnish with timber or beams. [A.S. *timber*, building, wood ; Ger. *zimmer*, an apartment, building ; from root *dam*, seen in L. *domus*, Gr. *domos*, a house, and *demō*, to build, and Sans. *dama*.]

**Timbre,** tim´bér, *n.* tone or character of a musical sound. [Fr.—L. *tympanum*, a drum.]

**Timbrel,** tim´brel, *n.* a musical instrument somewhat like a *tambourine*. [Through It. *timburello*, from root of **Tabor**.]

**Time,** tīm, *n.* a point at which or period during which things happen : a season or proper time : an opportunity : absolute duration : an interval : past time : the duration of one's life : allotted period : repetition of anything or mention with reference to repetition : musical measure : hour of travail : the state of things at any period, usually in *pl.* : the history of the world, as opposed to eternity : addition of a thing to itself. —**At times,** at distinct intervals : occasionally. —**In time, Time enough,** in good season : sufficiently early.—**The time being,** the present time.—*v.t.* to do at the proper season : to regulate as to time : (*music*) to measure.—*v.i.* to keep or beat time. [A.S. *tima* ; cf. Ice. *timi* ; Celt. *tim* ; and **Tide**.]

**Time-honoured,** tīm´-on´urd, *adj., honoured* for a long *time* : venerable on account of antiquity.

**Time-keeper,** tīm´-kēp´ér, *n.* a clock, watch, or other instrument for *keeping* or marking *time* : one who keeps the time of workmen.

**Timely,** tīm´li, *adj.* in good *time* : sufficiently early.—*adv.* early, soon.—*n.* **Time´liness.**

**Timeous,** tīm´us, *adj.* in good *time* : seasonable.

**Timeously,** tīm´us-li, *adv.* in good *time.*

**Timepiece,** tīm´pēs, *n.* a *piece* of machinery for keeping *time*, esp. a clock for a mantel-piece.

**Time-server,** tīm´-sérv´ér, *n.* one who *serves* or meanly suits his opinions to the *times.*

**Time-table,** tīm´-tā´bl, *n.* a *table* or list showing the *times* of certain things, as trains, steamers, &c. [*time.*

**Timeworn,** tīm´worn, *adj., worn* or decayed by

**Timid,** tim´id, *adj., fearful* : wanting courage : faint-hearted.—*adv.* **Tim´idly.**—*n.* **Tim´idness.** [L. *timidus*—*timeo*, to fear.]

**Timidity,** ti-mid´i-ti, *n.* quality or state of being *timid* : want of courage or boldness.

**Timorous,** tim´or-us, *adj.* full of *fear* : timid : indicating fear.—*adv.* **Tim´orously.**—*n.* **Tim´orousness.**

**Tin,** tin, *n.* a silvery-white, non-elastic, easily fusible, and malleable metal.—*v.t.* to cover or overlay with tin or tinfoil :—*pr.p.* tinn´ing ; *pa.t.* and *pa.p.* tinned. [A.S. ; cog. with Ice. *tin*, Ger. *zinn*.]

**Tinctorial,** tingk-tōr´i-al, *adj.* giving a *tinge* or containing colour : colouring.

**Tincture,** tingk´tūr, *n.* a *tinge* or shade of colour : a slight taste added to anything : (*med.*) a solution of any substance in or by means of spirit of wine.—*v.t.* to tinge : to imbue : to mix with anything foreign. [L. *tinctura*, from root of **Tinge**.]

**Tinder,** tin´dér, *n.* anything used for *kindling* fire from a spark. [A.S. *tender* ; Ice. *tundr*, Ger. *zunder*. The root is found in A.S. *tendan*, Ger. *zünden*, to kindle.]

**Tine,** tīn, *n.* the spike of a fork or harrow, &c.— **Tined,** *adj.* furnished with spikes. [M. E.

*tind,* a prickle ; cog. with Ice. *tind-r*, a tooth, a prickle ; and prob. conn. with **Tooth**.]

**Tinfoil,** tin´foil, *n., tin* in thin leaves. [From **Tin**, and **Foil**, a leaf.]

**Tinge,** tinj, *v.t.* to *tint* or *colour :* to mix with something : to give in some degree the qualities of a substance.—*n.* a small amount of colour or taste infused into another substance. [L. *tingo, tinctum ;* conn. with Gr. *tenggō*, to wet, to stain, Sans. *tuc-.*]

**Tingle,** ting´gl, *v.i.* to feel a thrilling sensation, as in hearing a shrill sound : to feel a sharp, thrilling pain. [Like *tinkle*, an imitative word.]

**Tinker,** tingk´ér, *n.* a mender of brazen or tin kettles, pans, &c. [*Tink*, to make a sharp, shrill sound ; Scot. *tinkler—tinkle ;* also given = a worker in tin.]

**Tinkle,** tingk´l, *v.i.* to make small sharp sounds : to clink : to jingle : to hear small sharp sounds. —*v.t.* to cause to make quick, sharp sounds.—*n.* a sharp clinking sound. [Dim. of *tink*, a sharp, quick sound ; an imitative word.]

**Tinsel,** tin´sel, *n.* something *sparkling* or shining : a stuff for ornamental dresses consisting of cloth overlaid with a thin coating of gold or silver : anything showy, of but little value : anything having a false lustre.—*adj.* like tinsel : gaudy : superficial.—*v.t.* to adorn with or as with tinsel : to make glittering or gaudy :—*pr.p.* tin´selling ; *pa.t.* and *pa.p.* tin´selled. [Fr. *étincelle*—L. *scintilla*, a spark.]

**Tint,** tint, *n.* a slight *tinge* distinct from the principal colour.—*v.t.* to give a slight colouring to. [From root of **Tinge**.]

**Tintinnabulation,** tin-tin-ab-ū-lā´shun, *n.* the tinkling sound of bells. [L. *tintinnabulum*, a bell—*tintinnare*, dim. of *tinnio*, to jingle, to ring ; an imitative word.]

**Tiny,** tī´ni, *adj.* (*comp.* **Ti´nier,** *superl.* **Ti´niest**) *thin ;* very small. [Prob. from the word **Thin** in its Scand. forms, as Dan. *tynd.*]

**Tip,** tip, *n.* the *top* or point of anything small : the end.—*v.t.* to form a point to : to cover the tip or end of :—*pr.p.* tipp´ing ; *pa.t.* and *pa.p.* tipped. [Dut. *tip ;* Ger. *zipf-el*, end, point : a dim. of **Top**.]

**Tippet,** tip´et, *n.* the *tip* or cape of a coat.

**Tipple,** tip´l, *v.i.* to drink in small quantities : to drink strong liquors often or habitually.— *v.t.* to drink, as strong liquors, to excess.—*n.* **Tipp´ler.** [An extension of *tip*, to tilt up a vessel in drinking.]

**Tipstaff,** tip´staf, *n.* a *staff tipped* with metal, or an officer who carries it : a constable.

**Tipsy,** tip´si, *adj.* intoxicated.—*adv.* **Tip´sily.**— *n.* **Tip´siness.** [From stem of **Tipple**.]

**Tiptoe,** tip´tō, *n.* the *tip* or end of the *toe.*

**Tirade,** ti-rād´, *n.* a strain of censure or reproof. [Fr.—*tirer*, to draw, from the O. Ger. *zeran*, E. **Tear**.]

**Tire,** tīr, *n., attire,* apparel : furniture : (*B.*) a head-dress.—*v.t.* (*B.*) to dress, as the head. [A.S. *tir*, glory, adornment ; cog. with Ger. *zier*, ornament, honour, and Lat. (*decus*) *decoris.* See **Attire**.]

**Tire,** tīr, *n.* the hoop of iron that *ties* or binds the fellies of wheels. [From **Tie**.]

**Tire,** tīr, *v.t.* to harass, to vex : to exhaust the strength of : to weary.—*v.i.* to become weary : to be fatigued : to have the patience exhausted. [A.S. *tirian*, to vex, from root of **Tear**.]

**Tired,** tīrd, *adj.* wearied : fatigued.—*n.* **Tired´ness.**

**Tiresome,** tīr´sum, *adj.* that *tires :* fatiguing : tedious.—*adv.* **Tire´somely.**—*n.* **Tire´someness.**

**Tissue**, tish′ū, *n*. cloth inter*woven* with gold or silver, or with figured colours : (*anat*.) the substance of which organs are composed : a connected series.—*v.t.* to form, as tissue : to interweave : to variegate. [Fr. *tissu*, 'woven,' pa.p. of an obs. Fr. verb, from L. *texere*, to weave.]

**Titan**, tī′tan, **Titanic**, tī-tan′ik, *adj*. relating to the *Titans*, giants of mythology : enormous in size or strength. [anything small, and **Bit**.]

**Titbit**, tit′bit, *n*. a choice little bit. [Obs. E. *tit*.

**Tithe**, tīth, *n*. a *tenth* part : the $\frac{1}{10}$ of the produce of land and stock allotted to the clergy.—*v.t.* to tax to a $\frac{1}{10}$. [A.S. *teotha*; cog. with Ger. *zehnte—zehn*. Doublet **Tenth**.]

**Tither**, tīth′er, *n*. one who collects *tithes*.

**Tithing**, tīth′ing, *n*. an old Saxon district containing *ten* householders, each responsible for the behaviour of the rest. [See **Tithe**.]

**Titillate**, tit′il-lāt, *v.t.* to tickle. [L. *titillo, titillatum*.]

**Titillation**, tit-il-lā′shun, *n*. act of titillating : state of being titillated : a pleasant feeling.

**Titlark**, tit′lärk, *n*. a singing bird with a greenish back and head, found in marshes and moors : a small bird (cf. **Titling**). [Lit. 'a little lark,' obs. E. *tit*, Ice. *tita*, anything small, and **Lark**.]

**Title**, tī′tl, *n*. an inscription set over or at the beginning of a thing by which it is known : a name of distinction : that which gives a just right to possession : the writing that proves a right : (*B*.) a sign.—*v.t.* to name. [O. Fr.—L. *titulus*.]

**Titled**, tī′tld, *adj*. having a *title*.

**Title-deed**, tī′tl-dēd, *n*. a *deed* or document that proves a *title* or just right to exclusive possession.

**Title-page**, tī′tl-pāj, *n*. the *page* of a book containing its *title* and usually the author's name.

**Titling**, tīt′ling, *n*. the hedge-sparrow. [Dim. from obs. E. *tit*, anything small.]

**Titmouse**, tit′mows, *n*. a genus of little birds, which feed on insects, &c. :—*pl*. **Titmice**, tit′-mīs. [*Tit*, anything small (cf. **Titling**), and A.S. *mase*, cog. with Ger. *meise*, a small bird.]

**Titter**, tit′er, *v.i.* to laugh with the tongue striking the teeth : to laugh restrainedly : to giggle.—*n*. a restrained laugh. [Imitative; cf. Ger. *zittern*, to tremble.] [of *tit*.]

**Tittle**, tit′l, *n*. a small particle : an iota. [Dim.

**Tittle-tattle**, tit′l-tat′l, *n*. idle, empty talk. [Cf. **Tittle** (above) and **Titter**.]

**Titular**, tit′ū-lar, *adj*. existing in name or *title* only : nominal : having the title without the duties of an office.—*adv*. **Tit′ularly**.

**Titulary**, tit′ū-lar-i, *adj*. consisting in or pertaining to a *title*.—*n*. one having the title of an office whether he performs its duties or not.

**To**, tōō, *prep*. in the direction of : in order to : as far as : in accordance with : sign of the infinitive mood : (*B*.) sometimes = for.—**To and fro**, backwards and forwards. [A.S.; Ger. *zu*, Goth. *du*; Celt. and Slav. *do*.]

**Toad**, tōd, *n*. an amphibious reptile, like the frog, wrongly believed to emit poison. [A.S. *tade*.]

**Toadeater**, tōd′ēt-ėr, *n*. a fawning sycophant : (*orig*.) a mountebank's assistant, whose duty was to swallow or pretend to swallow any kind of garbage. [Said to be a version of Fr. *avaler des couleuvres*, to swallow adders, to put up with all sorts of indignities without resentment.]

**Toadstool**, tōd′stōōl, *n*. a poisonous kind of mushroom.

**Toady**, tōd′i, *n*. a mean hanger-on and flatterer.—*v.t.* to fawn as a sycophant :—*pa.t.* and *pa.p.* toad′ied. [Short for **Toadeater**.]

**Toadyism**, tōd′i-izm, *n*. the practice of a toady.

**Toast**, tōst, *v.t.* to *dry* and *scorch* at the fire.—*n*. bread toasted : a slice of such dipped in liquor. [O. Fr. *toster*—L. *tostus*, roasted, pa.p. of *torreo*.]

**Toast**, tōst, *v.t.* to name when a health is drunk : to drink to the health of.—*v.i.* to drink toasts.—*n*. the person or thing named whose health is to be drunk. [From the *toast* formerly put in liquor.]

**Toaster**, tōst′ėr, *n*. one who or that which *toasts*.

**Toastmaster**, tōst′mas-tėr, *n*. the *master* and announcer of *toasts* at public dinners.

**Tobacco**, to-bak′ō, *n*. a narcotic plant, a native of America, whose dried leaves are used for smoking, chewing, and in snuff. [Through Sp. *tabaco*, from the Indian name for the pipe.]

**Tobacconist**, to-bak′o-nist, *n*. one who sells or manufactures tobacco. [Orig. 'a tobaccosmoker.'] [smoking *tobacco*.

**Tobacco-pipe**, to-bak′o-pīp, *n*. a *pipe* used for

**Toboggan**, tō-bog′gan, *n*. a kind of sled turned up at both ends, much used in Canada for sliding down snow-covered slopes.—*v*. to slide down over snow on such. [A native word.]

**To-brake**, tōō-brāk, *v.t.* (*B*.) broke in pieces. [Prefix **To-**, asunder, and **Break**.]

**Tocsin**, tok′sin, *n*. an alarm-bell, or the ringing of it. [Lit. 'that which is *struck* to give a *signal* or alarm,' Fr.—O. Fr. *toquer* (Fr. *toucher*, E. **Touch**), and O. Fr. *sein*—L. *signum*, E. **Sign**.]

**To-day**, too-dā′, *n*., *this* or the present *day*. [**To**, a corr. of *the* or *this*, and **Day**.]

**Toddle**, tod′l, *v.i.* to walk with short feeble steps, as a child.—*adj*. **Todd′ling**. [Prob. a by-form of **Totter**.]

**Toddy**, tod′i, *n*. the fermented juice of various palms of the East Indies : a mixture of whisky, sugar, and hot water. [Hindustani.]

**Toe**, tō, *n*. one of the five small members at the point of the foot : the corresponding member of a beast's foot : the front of an animal's hoof.—*adj*. **Toed**, tōd, having toes. [A.S. *ta*; Ice. *tā*, Ger. *zehe*, allied to *dic*, to point, in L. *digitus*, Gr. *daktylos*, a finger, a toe.]

**Toffee**, **Toffy**, tof′i, *n*. a hard-baked sweetmeat, made of sugar and butter. [Ety. unknown.]

**Toga**, tō′ga, *n*. the mantle of a Roman citizen. [L.—*tego*, to cover.]

**Togated**, tō′gāt-ed, **Toged**, tōgd, *adj*. dressed in a *toga* or gown. [L. *togatus*—**Toga**.]

**Together**, too-geth′er, *adv*., *gathered to* one place : in the same place, time, or company : in or into union : in concert. [A.S. *togædere*—*to*, to, and *gaderian*, E. **Gather**.]

**Toil**, toil, *n*. a net or snare. [Lit. 'a web,' Fr. *toile*, cloth—L. *tela*, from *texo*, to weave.]

**Toil**, toil, *v.i.* to labour : to work with fatigue.—*n*. labour, esp. of a fatiguing kind.—*n*. **Toil′er**. [Another form of **Till**, *v.t.*]

**Toilet**, **Toilette**, toil′et, *n*. a dressing-table : mode or operation of dressing. [Fr. *toilette*, dim. of *toile*, cloth, thus sig. lit. 'little-cloth,' then, table-cover, dressing-table. Cf. **Toil**, *n*.]

**Toilsome**, toil′sum, *adj*. full of fatigue : wearisome.—*adv*. **Toil′somely**.—*n*. **Toil′someness**.

**Tokay**, tō-kā′, *n*. a white wine with an aromatic taste, produced at *Tokay* in Hungary.

**Token**, tō′kn, *n*. a *mark* : something representing another thing or event : a sign : a memorial of friendship : a coin issued by a private person or civic authority redeemable in current money. [A.S. *tacen*; Ger. *zeichen*, a mark; from the root of Gr. *deiknymi*, L. *dico*, to say, A.S. *tihan*.]

**Told**, tōld, *pa.t.* and *pa.p.* of **Tell**.

**Tolerable**, tol′ér-a-bl, *adj*. that may be *tolerated* or endured : moderately good or agreeable : not contemptible.—*adv.* Tol'erably.—*n.* Tol'erable-ness. [of offensive persons or opinions.

**Tolerance**, tol'ėr-ans, *n.* the *tolerating* or enduring

**Tolerant**, tol'ėr-ant, *adj.*, *tolerating :* enduring : indulgent : favouring toleration.

**Tolerate**, tol'ėr-āt, *v.t.* to *bear :* to endure : to allow by not hindering. [L. *tolero, -atum,* from *tol,* root of *tollo,* to lift up, to bear. Cf. **Talent.**]

**Toleration**, tol-ėr-ā'shun, *n.* act of *tolerating :* allowance of what is not approved : liberty given to a minority to hold and express their own political or religious opinions, and to be admitted to the same civil privileges as the majority.

**Toll**, tōl, *n.* a *tax* for the liberty of passing over a bridge or road, selling goods in a market, &c. : a portion of grain taken by a miller for grinding. [A.S., which (with Dut. *tol,* and Ger. *zoll*) is from L. *telonium*—Gr. *telōnion,* a tollbooth, from *telos,* a tax.]

**Toll**, tōl, *v.i.* to sound, as a large bell.—*v.t.* to cause to sound, as a bell : to strike, or signal by striking.—*n.* the sound of a bell when tolling. [Imitative.]

**Tollbar**, tōl'bär, *n.* a movable *bar* across a road, &c. to stop passengers liable to *toll.*

**Tollbridge**, tōl'brij, *n.* a *bridge* where *toll* is taken.

**Tollgate**, tōl'gāt, *n.* a *gate* where *toll* is taken.

**Tollhouse**, tōl'hows, *n.* the *house* of a *toll*-gatherer.

**Tomahawk**, tom'a-hawk, *n.* a light war-hatchet of the N. American Indians, either wielded or thrown.—*v.t.* to cut or kill with a tomahawk. [The Indian name slightly modified.]

**Tomato**, to-mā'to, *n.* a plant, native to S. America, but much cultivated in the south of Europe for its fleshy fruit, called also the 'love-apple.' [Sp., from the native American.]

**Tomb**, tōōm, *n.* a pit or vault in the earth, in which a dead body is placed : a tombstone. [Fr. *tombe,* through Late L. *tumba,* from Gr. *tymbos.*]

**Tomboy**, tom'boi, *n.* a wild romping girl. [From **Tom,** for Thomas, and **Boy.**]

**Tombstone**, tōōm'stōn, *n.* a *stone* erected over a *tomb* to preserve the memory of the dead.

**Tomcat**, tom'kat, *n.* a *male cat,* esp. when full grown. [**Tom,** a common male name, and **Cat.**]

**Tome**, tōm, *n.* part of a book : a volume of a large work : a book. [Lit. 'a piece *cut* off,' Fr.—L.—Gr. *tomos,* from root of *temnō,* to cut.]

**Tomfool**, tom'fōōl, *n.* a great fool : a trifling fellow.—**Tom'foolery,** *n.* foolish trifling or jesting : buffoonery. [Cf. **Tomtit.**]

**To-morrow**, too-mor'ō, *n.* the morrow after this. [**To,** a corr. of *the* or *this,* and **Morrow.**]

**Tomtit**, tom'tit, *n.* the *tit*mouse. [**Tom,** a common name like Jack, and **Tit,** as in **Titmouse.** Cf. **Tomcat** and **Tomfool.**]

**Ton**, tun, *n.* (*lit.*) a *barrel,* hence a barrel-full : 20 cwt. or 2240 lbs. avoir. [A.S. *tunne,* a vat tub ; Ger. *tonne,* O. Ger. *tunna,* cask.]

**Tone**, tōn, *n.* the character of a sound : quality of the voice : harmony of the colours of a painting, also its characteristic expression as distinguished by its colour : character or style : state of mind : mood : a healthy state of the body.—*v.t.* to utter with an affected tone : to intone. [L. *tonus*—Gr. *tonos,* a sound—*teinō,* to stretch. See **Thunder.**]

**Toned**, tōnd, *adj.* having a *tone* (in compounds).

**Tongs**, tongz, *n.pl.* a domestic instrument, consisting of two jointed pieces or shafts of metal, used for lifting. [A.S. *tange ;* Ice. *taung,* Ger.

*zange,* from a root seen in A.S. *ge-tingan,* to press, push.]

**Tongue**, tung, *n.* the fleshy organ in the mouth, used in tasting, swallowing, and speech : power of speech : manner of speaking : speech : discourse : a language : anything like a tongue in shape : the catch of a buckle : the pointer of a balance : a point of land. [A.S. *tunge ;* Ice. *tunga,* Ger. *zunge,* the tongue ; L. *lingua* (old form *dingua*), Sans. *jihvā.*]

**Tongued**, tungd, *adj.* having a tongue.

**Tongueless**, tung'les, *adj.* having no tongue : mute.

**Tongue-tied**, tung'-tīd, *adj.* having an impediment, as if the *tongue* were *tied :* unable to speak freely.

**Tonic**, ton'ik, *adj.* relating to *tones* or sounds : (*med.*) giving tone and vigour to the system : giving or increasing strength.—*n.* a medicine which gives tone and vigour to the system.

**Tonic solfa**, ton'ik sōl-fä', *n.* a modern system of musical notation, in which the notes are indicated by letters, and time and accent by dashes and colons.

**To-night**, too-nīt', *n.*, *this night :* the night after the present day.

**Tonnage**, tun'āj, *n.* the weight in *tons* of goods in a ship : the cubical content of a ship : a duty on ships, estimated per ton.

**Tonsil**, ton'sil, *n.* one of two glands at the root of the tongue, so named from its shape.—**Tonsilitis**, ton-sil-ī'tis, *n.* inflammation of the tonsils. [L. *tonsilla,* a stake, a tonsil, dim. of *tonsa,* an oar.]

**Tonsile**, ton'sil, *adj.* that may be *clipped.* [L. *tonsilis*—*tondeo, tonsum,* to clip, to shear.]

**Tonsure**, ton'shōōr, *n.* act of *clipping* the hair, or of shaving the head : the corona worn by priests as a mark of their order. [L. *tonsura,* a shearing—*tondeo.*]

**Tontine**, ton-tēn', *n.* a kind of life-annuity increasing as the subscribers die : a loan raised with the benefit of survivorship. [From *Tonti,* a Neapolitan, its inventor.]

**Too**, tōō, *adv.* over : more than enough : likewise. [A form of **To,** sig. lit. 'added to.']

**Took**, took, *pa.t.* and obs. *pa.p.* of **Take.**

**Tool**, tōōl, *n.* an instrument used by workmen : one who acts as the mere instrument of another. [A.S. *tol,* perh. from the root of **Tow.**]

**Tooth**, tōōth, *n.* one of the small bones in the jaws, used in biting and chewing : the taste or palate : anything toothlike : a prong : one of the projections on a saw or wheel :—*pl.* **Teeth.**—*v.t.* to furnish with teeth : to cut into teeth. [A.S. *toth* (for *tonth*) ; cog. with Goth. *tunthus,* L. *dens, dent-is,* Gr. *o-dous, o-dont-os,* Sans. *danta, dant,* prob. the part. of *ad,* E. **Eat.**]

**Toothache**, tōōth'āk, *n.* an *ache* or pain in a *tooth.*

**Toothed**, tōōtht, *adj.* having *teeth :* (*bot.*) having toothlike projections on the edge, as a leaf.

**Toothpick**, tōōth'pik, *n.* an instrument for *picking* out anything in the *teeth.*

**Toothsome**, tōōth'sum, *adj.* pleasant to the taste.

**Top**, top, *n.* the highest part of anything : the upper end or surface : the upper part of a plant : the crown of the head : the highest place or rank : the chief or highest person : (*naut.*) a small platform at the head of the lower mast.—*v.t.* to cover on the top : to tip : to rise above : to surpass : to rise to the top of : to take off the top of :—*pr.p.* topp'ing ; *pa.t.* and *pa.p.* topped. [A.S. ; Ger. *zopf.*]

**Top**, top, *n.* a child's toy, shaped like a pear, and set or kept whirling round by means of a string or a whip. [Prob. same as above word, and sig. orig. 'a *pointed* piece of wood.']

**Topaz**, tō′paz, *n.* a precious stone having brilliant colours, generally yellowish. [Gr. *topazos*.]

**Top-dressing**, top′-dres′ing, *n.* a *dressing* of manure laid on the *top* or surface of land.

**Tope**, tōp, *n.* one of the monumental shrines of the Buddhists. [Corr. from Sans. *stupa*, a heap.]

**Toper**, tō′pėr, *n.* a drunkard. [From *tope*, an obs. *v.* 'to drink hard,' from the phrase *to top off*, sig. 'to drink off at one draught.']

**Topgallant**, top′gal-ant, *adj.* applied to the mast and sail next above the topmast and topsail and below the royal mast.

**Top-heavy**, top′-hev′i, *adj.* having the *top* or upper part too *heavy* for the lower.

**Topic**, top′ik, *n.* a subject of discourse or argument: a matter. [Gr. *ta topika*, the general principles of argument—*topos*, a place.]

**Topical**, top′ik-al, *adj.* pertaining to a place: local: relating to a topic or subject.

**Topically**, top′i-kal-li, *adv.* with reference to a particular *place* or *topic*.

**Topmast**, top′mast, *n.* the second *mast*, or that immediately *above* the lower mast.

**Topmost**, top′mōst, *adj.* next the *top*: highest.

**Topographer**, to-pog′raf-ėr, *n.* one who *describes* a *place*, &c.: one skilled in topography.

**Topographic**, top-o-graf′ik, **Topographical**, top-o-graf′ik-al, *adj.* pertaining to *topography*.

**Topography**, to-pog′raf-i, *n.* the *description* of a *place*: a particular account of the superficial features of a tract of country: the art of describing places. [Gr. *topos*, a place, *graphō*, to describe.]

**Topple**, top′l, *v.i.* to fall forward: to tumble down. [Extension of **Top**, sig. orig. 'to fall top foremost.']

**Topsail**, top′sāl, *n.* a *sail* across the *topmast*.

**Topsyturvy**, top′si-tur-vi, *adv.* bottom upwards. [Acc. to Wedgwood, for *topsi′ to′er way*, corr. of 'topside the other way.']

**Torch**, torch, *n.* a light formed of *twisted* tow dipped in pitch or other inflammable material: a large candle or flambeau. [Fr. *torche*—L. *tortum*, pa.p. of *torqueo*, to twist.]

**Tore**, tōr, *pa.t.* of **Tear**.

**Torment**, tor′ment, *n.* torture: anguish: that which causes pain. [Lit. 'twisting pain,' L. *torqueo*, to twist.]

**Torment**, tor-ment′, *v.t.* to torture: to put to extreme pain, physical or mental: to distress: to afflict.

**Tormentingly**, tor-ment′ing-li, *adv.* in a *torment*ing manner.

**Tormentor**, tor-ment′or, *n.* one who or that which *torments*: (*B.*) a torturer, an executioner.

**Torn**, tōrn, *pa.p.* of **Tear**: (*B.*) stolen.

**Tornado**, tor-nā′do, *n.* a violent hurricane, frequent in tropical countries. [Lit. 'a *turning* or whirling,' Sp.—*tornar*—Low L. *tornare*. See **Turn**.]

**Torpedo**, tor-pē′do, *n.* a species of eel having the power of giving an electric shock when touched so as to produce *torpor* or numbness, the cramp-fish: a submarine apparatus for destroying shipping by explosion. [L.—*torpeo*, to be stiff.]

**Torpescent**, tor-pes′ent, *adj.*, becoming torpid or numb.—*n.* **Torpes′cence**. [L., pr.p. of *torpesco*, to become stiff—*torpeo*, to be stiff.]

**Torpid**, tor′pid, *adj.*, stiff, numb: having lost the power of motion and feeling: sluggish.—*adv.* **Tor′pidly.**—*n.* **Tor′pidness**. [L. *torpidus*—*torpeo*.]

**Torpidity**, tor-pid′i-ti, **Torpitude**, tor′pi-tūd, *n.*

state of being torpid: numbness: dullness: stupidity.

**Torpor**, tor′por, *n.* numbness: inactivity: dullness: stupidity. [L.—*torpeo*.]

**Torque**, tork, *n.* a necklace of metal rings interlaced. [L. *torques*—*torqueo*, to twist. Cf. **Tor′sion**.]

**Torrefaction**, tor-e-fak′shun, *n.* act of *torrefying*: state of being torrefied.

**Torrefy**, tor′e-fī, *v.t.* to scorch: to parch:—*pa.t.* and *pa.p.* torr′efied. [L. *torreo*, to dry, to burn, *facio*, to make. Cf. **Torrid**.]

**Torrent**, tor′ent, *n.* a rushing stream: a strong or turbulent current. [L. *torrens, -entis*, boiling, pr.p. of *torreo*, to dry, to burn. See **Torrid**.]

**Torrid**, tor′id, *adj.*, *burning* or parching: violently hot: dried with heat.—*n.* **Torr′idness**. [L. *torridus—torreo*, to burn, parch. See **Thirst**.]

**Torsion**, tor′shun, *n.* act of *twisting* or turning a body: the force with which a thread or wire tends to return when twisted. [L. *torsio—torqueo, tortum*, to twist.]

**Torsion-balance**, tor′shun-bal′ans, *n.* an instrument for measuring very minute forces by a delicate horizontal bar or needle, suspended by a very fine thread or wire.

**Torso**, tor′sō, *n.* the trunk of a statue without head or limbs:—*pl.* **Tor′sos**. [It.—L. *thyrsus*, a stalk, stem of a plant—Gr. *thyrsos*.] [L.]

**Tortile**, tor′til, *adj.*, *twisted*: wreathed: coiled.

**Tortoise**, tor′tis, *n.* a reptile from which the head, neck, tail, and limbs protrude, so called either from its *crooked* feet or *winding* motion. [O. Fr. *tortis*, from L. *tortus*, twisted. Cf. **Turtle**.]

**Tortoiseshell**, tor′tis-shel, *n.* the *shell* of a species of turtle—turtles being formerly confounded with *tortoises*.—*adj.* of the colour of the foregoing. [ing. [L.]

**Tortuose**, tor′tū-ōs, *adj.*, *twisted*: wreathed: wind-

**Tortuosity**, tor-tū-os′i-ti, *n.* state of being *tortuous*.

**Tortuous**, tor′tū-us, *adj.*, *twisted*, winding: (*fig.*) deceitful.—*adv.* **Tor′tuously.**—*n.* **Tor′tuousness**. [From L. *torqueo, tortum*, to twist.]

**Torture**, tor′tūr, *n.* a putting to the rack or severe pain to extort a confession, or as a punishment: extreme pain: anguish of body or mind.—*v.t.* to put to torture or to the rack: to put to extreme pain: to annoy: to vex.—*n.* **Tor′turer**. [Late L. *tortura*, lit. 'a twisting,' hence torment—*torqueo*. Cf. **Torsion**.]

**Tory**, tō′ri, *n.* applied to a Conservative in English politics. [Ir. *toiridhe*, lit. 'pursuer;' first applied to the Irish bog-trotters and robbers, next, about 1680, to the hottest asserters of the royal prerogative.]

**Toryism**, tō′ri-izm, *n.* the principles of the *Tories*.

**Toss**, tos, *v.t.* to throw up suddenly or violently: to cause to rise and fall: to make restless: to agitate.—*v.i.* to be tossed: to be in violent commotion: to tumble about: to fling.—*n.* act of throwing upward: a throwing up of the head.—*n.* **Toss′er**.—**Toss up**, to throw a coin into the air and wager on which side it will fall. [Celt., as W. *tosiaw*, to jerk, *tos*, a quick jerk.]

**Tost**, tost, a form of **Tossed**, *pa.p.* of **Toss**.

**Total**, tō′tal, *adj.*, *whole*: complete: undivided.— *n.* the whole: the entire amount.—*adv.* **To′tally**. [Fr.—Low L. *totalis*—L. *totus*, whole.]

**Totality**, tō-tal′i-ti, *n.* the *whole* sum, quantity, or amount.

**Totem**, tō′tem, *n.* among the North American Indians, an animal or vegetable regarded as the protector of a tribe.

**Totter**, tot′ėr, *v.i.* to shake as if about to fall: to

be unsteady : to stagger : to shake.—*n.* **Tott′erer.** [Prob. imitative.]

**Toucan,** tōō′kan, *n.* a genus of S. American birds, with a very large bill. [Fr.—Brazilian.]

**Touch,** tuch, *v.t.* to come in contact with : to perceive by feeling : to reach : to relate to : to handle or treat gently or slightly : to move or soften : to influence.—*v.i.* to be in contact with : to speak of anything slightly.—*n.* act of touching : a movement on a musical instrument : sense of feeling : an affection or emotion : a little : (*music*) resistance of the keys of an instrument to the fingers. [Fr. *toucher* (It. *toccare*), from Ger. *zucken*, to move, to draw.]

**Touchhole,** tuch′hōl, *n.* the small hole of a cannon through which the fire is communicated to the charge.

**Touching,** tuch′ing, *adj.* affecting : moving : pathetic.—*prep.* concerning : with regard to.—*adv.* **Touch′ingly.**

**Touch-needle,** tuch′-nē′dl, *n.* a small bar or *needle* of gold for testing articles of the same metal by comparing the streaks they make on a *touch-stone* with those made by the needle.

**Touchstone,** tuch′stōn, *n.* a kind of compact basalt or *stone* for testing gold or silver by the streak of the *touch-needle* : any test.

**Touchwood,** tuch′wood, *n.* decayed *wood* requiring only to be *touched* by fire to burn.

**Tough,** tuf, *adj.* not easily broken : firm : stiff : sticky : tenacious : able to endure hardship.—*adv.* **Tough′ly.**—*n.* **Tough′ness.** [A.S. *toh* ; cog. with Ger. *zähe*.] [*tough.*]

**Toughen,** tuf′n, *v.t.* or *v.i.* to make or become

**Toughish,** tuf′ish, *adj.* rather tough.

**Tour,** tōōr, *n.* a *turn* or circle : a going round : a journey in a circuit : a prolonged journey : a ramble. [Fr.—L. and Gr. *tornos*, a turn. Cf. **Turn.**]

**Tourist,** tōōr′ist, *n.* one who makes a *tour.*

**Tourmaline,** tōōr′ma-lin, *n.* a beautiful mineral used for jewellery. [From *Tourmali*, in Ceylon, whence a variety of the stone was first brought.]

**Tournament,** tōōr′na-ment, **Tourney,** tōōr′ni, *n.* a mock-fight in which combatants, generally on horseback, fought to show their skill in arms, so called probably from the rapid *turning* of their horses. [O. Fr. *tournéement* ; and Fr. *tournoi* —*tournoyer*—L. *torno*, to turn.]

**Tourniquet,** tōōr′ni-ket, *n.* a bandage which is tightened by *turning* a screw to check a flow of blood, used chiefly in amputations. [Fr.—*tourner*—L. *torno*, to turn.]

**Tout,** towt, *v.i.* to look out for custom in an obtrusive way.—*n.* **Tout′er.** [A.S. *totian*, to look out.]

**Tow,** tō, *v.t.* to tug or pull a vessel through the water with a rope.—*n.* orig. a rope for towing with : the coarse part of flax or hemp. [A.S. *teohan, teon.* Cf. **Tug.**]

**Towage,** tō′āj, *n.* act of *towing* : money for towing.

**Toward,** tō′ard, **Towards,** tō′ardz, *prep.* in the direction of : with a tendency to.—*adv.* nearly : in a state of preparation. [A.S. *toweard—to*, to, and *ward*, sig. direction. Cf. **Forward, Forwards.**]

**Toward,** tō′ward, **Towardly,** tō′ward-li, *adj.* ready to do or learn : apt.—*ns.* **To′wardness, To′wardliness.**

**Towboat,** tō′bōt, *n.* a *boat* that is *towed*, or one used for towing other vessels.

**Towel,** tow′el, *n.* a cloth for wiping the skin after it is *washed*, and for other purposes. [Fr. *touaille*—O. Ger. *twehele* (Ger. *quehle*)—O. Ger. *duahan*, Goth. *thwahan*, to wash. Cf. **Doily.**]

**Towelling,** tow′el-ing, *n.* cloth for *towels.*

**Tower,** tow′ėr, *n.* a lofty building, standing alone or forming part of another : a fortress.—*v.i.* to rise into the air : to be lofty. [A.S. *tur, tor* (Ger. *thurm*, Fr. *tour*), from L. *turris*, a tower.]

**Towered,** tow′ėrd, *adj.* having towers.

**Towering,** tow′ėr-ing, *adj.* very high : elevated.

**Towery,** tow′ėr-i, *adj.* having towers : lofty.

**Towline,** tō′līn, *n.* a *line* used in *towing.*

**Town,** town, *n.* a place larger than a village, not a city : the inhabitants of a town. [A.S. *tun*, an inclosure, town ; Ice. *tun*, Ger. *zaun*, a hedge.]

**Townclerk,** town′klärk, *n.* a *clerk* who keeps the records of a *town.*

**Towncrier,** town′krī-ėr, *n.* one who *cries* or makes public proclamations in a *town.*

**Townhall,** town′hawl, *n.* a public *hall* for the official business of a *town.*

**Townhouse,** town′hows, *n.* a *house* or building for transacting the public business of a *town* : a house in town as opposed to one in the country.

**Townsfolk,** townz′fōk, *n.* the *folk* or people of a *town.*

**Township,** town′ship, *n.* the territory or district of a *town* : the corporation of a town : a district.

**Townsman,** townz′man, *n.* an *inhabitant* or fellow-inhabitant of a *town.* [**Town** and **Man.**]

**Towntalk,** town′tawk, *n.* the general *talk* of a *town* : the subject of common conversation.

**Toxicology,** toks-i-kol′o-ji, *n.* the science of poisons.—**Toxicol′ogist,** *n.* one versed in toxicology. —*adj.* **Toxicolog′ical.** [Gr. *toxikon*, arrow-poison—*toxikos*, for the bow—*toxon*, a bow, *logos*, discourse.]

**Toy,** toy, *n.* a child's plaything : a trifle : a thing only for amusement or look : a matter of no importance : sport.—*v.i.* to trifle : to dally amorously. [Dut. *tooi*, ornaments.]

**Toyish,** toy′ish, *adj.* given to *toying* or trifling : playful : wanton.—*adv.* **Toy′ishly.**—*n.* **Toy′ishness.**

**Trace,** trās, *n.* a mark left : footprint :—*pl.* the straps by which a vehicle is drawn.—*v.t.* to follow by tracks or footsteps : to follow with exactness : to sketch.—*n.* **Trac′er.** [Fr.—L. *tractus*, pa.p. of *traho*, to draw.]

**Traceable,** trās′a-bl, *adj.* that may be traced.—*n.* **Trace′ableness.**—*adv.* **Trace′ably.**

**Tracery,** trās′ėr-i, *n.* ornamentation *traced* in flowing outline : certain ornamental stonework.

**Trachea,** tra-kē′a, *n.* the windpipe or tube which conveys air to the lungs, so called from its *roughness*, it being formed of rings of gristle :—*pl.* **Trache′æ.**—*adj.* **Trache′al.** [L. *trachīa*—Gr. *trachys*, *tracheia*, rough.]

**Tracheotomy,** trak-e-ot′o-mi, *n.* the operation of making an opening in the *trachea.* [**Trachea**, and the root of Gr. *temno*, to cut (see **Tome**).]

**Tracing,** trās′ing, *n.* act of one who *traces* : act of copying by marking on thin paper the lines of a pattern placed beneath : the copy so produced.

**Track,** trak, *v.t.* to follow by marks or footsteps : to tow.—*n.* a mark left : footprint : a beaten path : course.—**Track′less,** *adj.* without a path : untrodden.—**Track′road,** *n.* a towing-path. [Fr. *traquer*, to beat a wood, to hunt, orig. to draw a net round a wood to catch the game in it, from Dut. *trekken*, to draw.]

**Tract,** trakt, *n.* something *drawn out* or extended : continued duration : a region : a short treatise. [L., from the pa.p. of *traho*, to draw.]

**Tractability,** trakt-a-bil′it-i, *n.* quality or state of being *tractable* : docility.

**Tractable,** trakt′a-bl, *adj.* easily *drawn*, man-

aged, or taught : docile.—*n.* **Tract'ableness.**—
*adv.* **Tract'ably.** [L. *tracto*, freq. of *traho*.]

**Tractarian**, trakt-ār'i-an, *n.* one of the writers of
the Oxford *Tracts* with which Puseyism originated.—*n.* **Tractar'ianism.**

**Tractile**, trakt'il, *adj.* that may be *drawn* out.

**Traction**, trak'shun, *n.* act of *drawing* or state of
being drawn.

**Tractive**, trakt'iv, *adj.* that *draws* or pulls.

**Tractor**, trakt'or, *n.* that which *draws*.

**Trade**, trād, *n.* buying and selling : commerce :
occupation : men engaged in the same occupation.—*v.i.* to buy and sell : to act merely for
money.—*v.t.* to traffic with.—*n.* **Trad'er.** [Ety.
dub. ; prob. from Fr. *traite*, transport of goods
—L. *tracto*, freq. of *traho*, to draw.]

**Trademark**, trād'mark, *n.* any name or distinctive device warranting goods for sale as the
production of any individual or firm.

**Tradesman**, trādz'man, *n.* a common name for a
shopkeeper : a mechanic :—*fem.* **Trades'woman.**

**Trades-union**, trādz'-ūn'yun, *n.* a *union* among
those of the same *trade* to maintain their rights.

**Tradewinds**, trād'windz, *n. winds* in and near
the torrid zone, so called from their great service
to *trade*.

**Tradition**, tra-dish'un, *n.* the handing down of
opinions or practices to posterity unwritten. [L.
*trans*, over, and *do*, to give.]

**Traditional**, tra-dish'un-al, **Traditionary**, tra-
dish'un-ar-i, *adj.* delivered by *tradition*.—*advs.*
**Tradi'tionally, Tradi'tionarily.**

**Traditionist**, tra-dish'un-ist, *n.* one who adheres
to *tradition*.

**Traduce**, tra-dūs', *v.t.* to calumniate : to defame.
—*n.* **Tradu'cer.** [L. *traduco*, to lead along, to
make a public show of—*trans*, across, *duco* to
lead.]

**Traffic**, traf'ik, *n.* commerce : large trade : the
business done on a railway, &c.—*v.i.* to trade :
to trade meanly.—*v.t.* to exchange :—*pr.p.*
traff'icking ; *pa.t.* and *pa.p.* traff'icked.—*n.*
**Traff'icker.** [Fr. *trafic*—It. *traffico*, prob.
from L. *trans*, across, and *facere*, to make.]

**Tragedian**, tra-jē'di-an, *n.* an actor of *tragedy*.

**Tragedy**, traj'e-di, *n.* a species of drama in which
the action and language are elevated, and the
catastrophe sad : any mournful and dreadful
event. [Lit. 'goat-song,' so called either from
the old dramas being exhibited when a *goat* was
sacrificed, or from a *goat* being the prize, or because the actors were dressed in *goat*-skins, L.
*tragœdia*, from Gr. *tragōdia*—*tragos*, a he-
goat, *aoidos*, *ōdos*, a singer—*aeidō*, *adō*, to sing.]

**Tragic**, traj'ik, **Tragical**, traj'ik-al, *adj.* pertaining to *tragedy* : sorrowful : calamitous.—*adv.*
**Trag'ically.**—*n.* **Trag'icalness.** [L.—Gr.]

**Tragi-comedy**, traj'i-kom'e-di, *n.* a dramatic piece
in which grave and comic scenes are blended.
—*adjs.* **Trag'i-com'ic, Trag'i-com'ical.**—*adv.*
**Trag'i-com'ically.**

**Trail**, trāl, *v.t.* to draw along the ground : to hunt
by tracking.—*v.i.* to be drawn out in length : to
run or climb as a plant.—*n.* anything drawn out
in length : track followed by the hunter. [O. Fr.
*trailler*, to hunt by tracking—L. *traho*, to draw.]

**Train**, trān, *v.t.* to *draw* along : to allure : to
educate : to discipline : to tame for use, as animals : to cause to grow properly : to prepare
men for athletic feats or horses for the race.—*n.*
that which is drawn along after something else :
the part of a dress which trails behind the
wearer : a retinue : a series : process : a line of
gunpowder to fire a charge : a line of carriages

on a railway.—*n.* **Train'er,** one who prepares
men for athletic feats, horses for a race, or the
like. [Fr. *trainer*, through Low L. forms from
L. *traho*, to draw.]

**Trainband**, trān'band, *n.* a *band* of men *trained*
to bear arms, though not regular soldiers.

**Train-bearer**, trān'-bār'ér, *n.* one who *bears* or
holds up a *train*, as of a robe or gown.

**Train-oil**, trān'-oil, *n.* whale *oil* extracted from the
blubber by boiling. [Train- here is the Ger.
and Scand. *tran*, train-oil.]

**Trait**, trā or trāt, *n.* a *drawing*: a touch: a
feature [Fr.—L. *tractus*, from the pa.p. of
*traho*, to draw.]

**Traitor**, trā'tur, *n.* one who, being trusted, *be-*
*trays* : one guilty of treason : a deceiver.—*fem.*
**Trait'ress.** [Fr. *traître*—L. *traditor*—*trado*,
to give up.]

**Traitorous**, trā'tur-us, *adj.* like a *traitor* : perfidious : treasonable.—*adv.* **Trai'torously.**]

**Trajectory**, tra-jekt'or-i, *n.* the curve described
by a body (as a planet or a projectile) under the
action of given forces. [From L. *trajicio*,
*-jectum*—*trans*, across, *jacio*, to throw.]

**Trammel**, tram'el, *n.* a net used in fowling and
fishing : shackles for making a horse amble :
anything that confines.—*v.t.* to shackle : to con
fine : —*pr.p.* tramm'elling ; *pa.t.* and *pa.p.*
tramm'elled. [Fr. *tramail*, a net—Low L.
*tremaculum* (*lit.*) 'of three meshes,' from L.
*tres*, three, and *macula*, a mesh. See **Mail**,
defensive armour.]

**Tramontane**, tra-mon'tān, *adj.* lying *beyond* the
*mountains* (orig. the Alps), from Rome : foreign :
uncivilised. [L. *trans*, beyond, *mons, montis*,
a mountain.]

**Tramp**, tramp, *v.t.* to tread.—*n.* a foot-journey :
a vagrant. [An extension of **Trap**, **Trip**; cf.
Ger. *trampen*.]

**Trample**, tramp'l, *v.t.* to tread under foot : to
treat with pride, to insult.—*v.i.* to tread in contempt : to tread forcibly and rapidly.—*n.*
**Tramp'ler.** [Extension of **Tramp**.]

**Tramroad**, tram'rōd, **Tramway**, tram'wā, *n.* a
road or way for carriages or wagons to run
along easily. [Prob. simply a way or track
made of beams, from Prov. E. *tram*, a beam,
which is prob. from Ice. *tramm*, a beam.]

**Trance**, trans, *n.* a state in which the soul appears
to be absent from the body, or to be rapt in
visions : catalepsy. [Fr. *transe*—*transir*, to be
chilled—L. *trans-ire*, to go across, in Late L. to
pass away, to die.]

**Tranquil**, trang'kwil, *adj., quiet* : peaceful.—*adv.*
**Tran'quilly.** [L. *tranquillus*.]

**Tranquillise**, trang'kwil-īz, *v.t.* to make tranquil.

**Tranquillity**, trang-kwil'it-i, **Tranquilness**,
trang'kwil-nes, *n.* state of being tranquil :
quietness.

**Transact**, trans-akt', *v.t.* to carry through or
manage : to perform.—*v.i.* to manage anything.
—*n.* **Transact'or.** [L. *transactum*, pa.p. of
*transigo*—*trans*, through, and *ago*, to carry on.
See **Act**.]

**Transaction**, trans-ak'shun, *n.* act of *transacting*:
management of any affair : an affair.

**Transalpine**, trans-alp'in, *adj., beyond* the *Alps*
(in regard to Rome). [L. *transalpinus*—*trans*,
beyond, and *Alpinus*, of the Alps.]

**Transatlantic**, trans-at-lan'tik, *adj., beyond* the
*Atlantic* Ocean.

**Transcend**, tran-send', *v.t.* to rise above : to surmount : to surpass : to exceed. [L. *trans*, beyond, *scando*, to climb.]

**Transcendent**, tran-send'ent, *adj., transcending:* superior or supreme in excellence: surpassing others: beyond human knowledge.—*adv.* **Transcend'ently.**—*n.* **Transcend'ence.**

**Transcendental**, tran-send-ent'al, *adj., transcending:* supereminent, surpassing others: concerned with what is independent of experience: vague.—*adv.* **Transcendent'ally.**

**Transcendentalism**, tran-send-ent'al-izm, *n.* the investigation of what is *a priori* in human knowledge, or independent of experience: that which is vague and illusive in philosophy.—*n.* **Transcendent'alist.**

**Transcribe**, tran-skrīb', *v.t.* to *write over* from one book into another: to copy.—*n.* **Transcrib'er.** [L. *transcribo, -scriptum—trans,* over, *scribo,* to write.] [*scribed:* a copy.

**Transcript**, tran'skript, *n.* that which is *transcribed:* a transcript: a copy.

**Transcription**, tran-skrip'shun, *n.* the act of *copying:* a transcript: a copy.

**Transept**, tran'sept, *n.* one of the wings or cross-aisles of a church, at right angles to the nave. [L. *trans,* across, and *septum,* an inclosure—*sepes,* a hedge.]

**Transfer**, trans-fèr', *v.t.* to *carry* or bring *over:* to convey to another place: to remove: to transport:—*pr.p.* transferr'ing; *pa.t.* and *pa.p.* transferred'.—*n.* **Transferr'er.** [L. *trans,* across, *fero,* to carry.]

**Transfer**, trans'fèr, *n.* the act of *transferring:* the conveyance of anything from one person or place to another: that which is transferred.

**Transferable**, trans-fer'a-bl, **Transferrible**, transfer'i-bl, *adj.* that may be *transferred* or conveyed from one place or person to another.—*ns.* **Transferabil'ity**, **Transferribil'ity.**

**Transferee**, trans-fèr-ē', *n.* the person to whom a thing is *transferred.*

**Transference**, trans'fèr-ens, *n.* the act of *transferring* or conveying from one person or place to another: passage from one place to another.

**Transfiguration**, trans-fig-ūr-ā'shun, *n.* a *change* of *form.*—**The Transfiguration**, the supernatural change in the appearance of Christ, described in Matt. xvii.: a feast of the R. C. Church, on 6th August, in commemoration of it.

**Transfigure**, trans-fig'ūr, *v.t.* to *change* the *figure* or form of: to change the appearance of. [L. *trans,* across, denoting change, and **Figure.**]

**Transfix**, trans-fiks', *v.t.* to pierce *through.* [L. *trans,* through, and **Fix.**]

**Transform**, trans-form', *v.t.* to *change* the shape of: to change into another substance: to change the disposition.—*v.i.* to be changed in form or substance. [L. *trans,* across, and **Form.**]

**Transformation**, trans-for-mā'shun, *n.* change of form or substance.

**Transfuse**, trans-fūz', *v.t.* to *pour out* into another vessel: to cause to pass from one to another: to cause to be imbibed.—*n.* **Transfu'sion.** [L. *trans,* over, and *fundo, fusum,* to pour.]

**Transgress**, trans-gres', *v.t.* to pass beyond a limit: to break, as a law.—*v.i.* to offend by violating a law: to sin. [L. *trans,* across, *gradior, gressus,* to step.]

**Transgression**, trans-gresh'un, *n.* the act of *transgressing:* violation of a law or command: offence: fault: crime: sin.

**Transgressor**, trans-gres'or, *n.* one who *transgresses:* one who violates a law or command: a sinner.

**Tranship** or **Trans-ship**, trans-ship', *v.t.* to *transfer* to another *ship.*—*n.* **Trans-ship'ment.** [L. *trans,* across, and **Ship.**]

**Transient**, tran'shent, *adj.* passing: of short duration: not lasting: momentary.—*adv.* **Tran'siently.**—*n.* **Tran'sientness.** [L. *transiens—trans,* across, and *eo, itum,* to go.]

**Transit**, trans'it, *n.* a passing over: conveyance: (*astr.*) the passage of a heavenly body over the meridian of a place: the passage of a planet over the sun's disc.

**Transition**, tran-sizh'un, *n.* passage from one place or state to another: change: (*music*) a change of key.—**Transi'tional**, *adj.* containing or denoting transition.

**Transitive**, trans'i-tiv, *adj.* passing over: having the power of passing: (*gram.*) denoting a verb which has an object.—*adv.* **Trans'itively.**—*n.* **Trans'itiveness.** [L. *transitivus.*]

**Transitory**, trans'i-tor-i, *adj., going* or passing *away:* lasting for a short time: speedily vanishing.—*adv.* **Trans'itorily.**—*n.* **Trans'itoriness.**

**Translate**, trans-lāt', *v.t.* to remove to another place: to render into another language: to explain.—*n.* **Translat'or.** [L. *trans,* over, *fero, latum,* to carry.]

**Translation**, trans-lā'shun, *n.* the act of *translating:* removal to another place: the rendering into another language: a version.

**Translucent**, trans-lōō'sent, *adj., shining through:* allowing light to pass, but not transparent: clear.—*adv.* **Translu'cently.**—*ns.* **Translu'cence**, **Translu'cency.** [L. *translucens—trans,* across, and *luceo,* to shine—*lux, lucis,* light.]

**Transmarine**, trans-ma-rēn', *adj.,* across or *beyond* the *sea.* [L. *trans,* across, and **Marine.**]

**Transmigrate**, trans'mi-grāt, *v.i.* to *migrate* or remove *across,* esp. to another country: to pass into another body or state.—*n.* **Trans'migrator.** [L. *trans,* across, and **Migrate.**]

**Transmigration**, trans-mi-grā'shun, *n.* the act of *removing* to another country: the passing into another state: the passage of the soul after death into another body.

**Transmigratory**, trans-mī'gra-tor-i, *adj., passing* to *another* place, body, or state.

**Transmissible**, trans-mis'i-bl, *adj.* that may be *transmitted* or passed from one to another: capable of being transmitted through any body or substance.—*n.* **Transmissibil'ity.**

**Transmission**, trans-mish'un, **Transmittal**, transmit'al, *n.* act of *transmitting:* the sending from one place or person to another: passage through.

**Transmit**, trans-mit', *v.t.* to *send across* to another person or place: to suffer to pass through:—*pr.p.* transmitt'ing; *pa.t.* and *pa.p.* transmitt'ed.—*n.* **Transmitt'er.** [L. *trans,* across, and *mitto, missum,* to send.]

**Transmutable**, trans-mūt'a-bl, *adj.* that may be *transmuted* or changed into a different form, nature, or substance.—*adv.* **Transmut'ably.**—*ns.* **Transmut'ableness**, **Transmutabil'ity.**

**Transmutation**, trans-mūt-ā'shun, *n.* a changing into a different form, nature, or substance.

**Transmute**, trans-mūt', *v.t.* to *change* to *another* form or substance. [L. *trans,* over, *muto,* to change.]

**Transom**, tran'sum, *n.* a thwart beam or lintel, esp. the horizontal mullion or crossbar of a window: in ships, the beam across the sternpost to strengthen the afterpart. [L. *trans,* across, and *sumo,* to take.]

**Transom-window**, tran'sum-win'dō, *n.* a *window* divided into two parts by a transom.

**Transparency**, trans-pär'en-si, *n.* the quality of being *transparent:* clearness: that which is transparent: a picture on semi-transparent material seen by means of light shining through.

**Transparent**, trans-pār'ent, *adj.* that may be distinctly seen through: clear.—*adv.* **Transpar'ently**.—*n.* **Transpar'entness**. [L. *trans*, through, and *pareo*, to appear.]

**Transpierce**, trans-pērs', *v.t.* to *pierce through*: to permeate. [L. *trans*, through, and **Pierce**.]

**Transpiration**, tran-spi-rā'shun, *n.* act or process of *transpiring*: exhalation through the skin.

**Transpire**, tran-spīr', *v.t.* to *breathe* or pass *through* the pores of the skin.—*v.i.* to exhale: to become public: (erroneously for) to occur. [L. *trans*, through, and *spiro*, to breathe.]

**Transplant**, trans-plant', *v.t.* to remove and *plant* in another place: to remove.—*n.* **Transplanta'tion**. [L. *trans*, across, and **Plant**.]

**Transport**, trans-pōrt', *v.t.* to *carry across* or from one place to another: to banish: to carry away by violence of passion or pleasure. [L. *trans*, across, and *porto*, to carry.]

**Transport**, trans'port, *n.*, *carriage* from one place to another: a vessel for conveyance: the conveyance of troops and their necessaries by land or sea: ecstasy. [*carried across*.]

**Transportable**, trans-pōrt'a-bl, *adj.* that may be transported.

**Transportation**, trans-pōr-tā'shun, *n.* removal: banishment.

**Transposal**, trans-pōz'al, *n.* act of *transposing*: a change of place or order.

**Transpose**, trans-pōz', *v.t.* to put each in the place of the other: to change, as the order of words, or the key in music. [Fr.—L. *trans*, across, and Fr. *poser* (see **Pose**, *n.*).]

**Transposition**, trans-po-zish'un, *n.* act of *transposing* or of putting one thing in place of another: state of being transposed: a change of the order of words: (*music*) a change of key into a higher or lower scale.

**Trans-ship**, &c. See **Tranship**, &c.

**Transubstantiate**, tran-sub-stan'shi-āt, *v.t.* to *change* to *another substance*. [L. *trans*, across, *substantia*, a substance.]

**Transubstantiation**, tran-sub-stan-shi-ā'shun, *n.* a *change* into *another substance:* the Roman Catholic doctrine that the bread and wine in the Eucharist are changed into Christ's body and blood.

**Transverse**, trans-vèrs', *adj.*, *turned* or lying *across*. [L. *trans*, across, *verto*, *versum*, to turn.]

**Transversely**, trans-vèrs'li, *adv.* in a *transverse* or cross *direction*.

**Trap**, trap, *n.* an instrument for *snaring* animals: an ambush: a stratagem: a contrivance for hindering the passage of foul air from a wastepipe, &c.—*v.t.* to catch in a trap:—*pr.p.* trapp'ing; *pa.t.* and *pa.p.* trapped.—*n.* **Trapp'er**. [A.S. *träppe*; cog. with O. Ger. *trapo*, a snare (whence Fr. *trappe*, by which the E. word has been modified).]

**Trap**, trap, *n.* a term loosely applied to many rocks of volcanic origin, so called because lying often in *steps* or terraces.—*adj.* **Trapp'ean**. [Sw. *trapp—trappa*, stairs.]

**Trap**, trap, *v.t.* to *drape* or adorn with gay *clothes:* to ornament:—*pr.p.* trapp'ing; *pa.t.* and *pa.p.* trapped. [Fr. *drap*—Low L. *drappus*, cloth. Cf. **Drab**, **Drape**.]

**Trapan**, tra-pan', *v.t.* to *trap* or to insnare:—*pr.p.* trapann'ing; *pa.t.* and *pa.p.* trapanned'.—*n.* a snare: a stratagem.—*n.* **Trapann'er**. [From **Trap**, instrument for snaring.]

**Trap-door**, trap'-dōr, *n.* a *door* in a floor shutting like the catch of a *trap*.

**Trapeze**, tra-pēz', **Trapezium**, tra-pē'zi-um, *n.* a plane figure having four unequal sides, no two of which are parallel: one of the wrist bones: a swing used in gymnastics. [Gr. *trapezion*, dim. of *trapeza*, a table: contr. either from *tri-peza*, three-legged, or from *tetra-peza*, four-legged.]

**Trapeziform**, tra-pēz'i-form, *adj.* having the *form* of a *trapeze*. [*Trapeze*, and **Form**.]

**Trapezoid**, trap'e-zoid, *n.* a plane four-sided figure *like* a *trapezium*, having two of its opposite sides parallel. [Gr. *trapeza*, and *eidos*, form.]

**Trapezoidal**, trap-e-zoid'al, *adj.* having the form of a *trapezoid*.

**Trappings**, trap'ingz, *n.pl.* gay *clothes:* ornaments, esp. those put on horses. [See **Trap**, to *drape* or adorn.]

**Trash**, trash, *v.t.* to crop: to strip off leaves.—*n.* refuse: matter unfit for food. [Prob. a form of **Thrash**.]

**Trashy**, trash'i, *adj.* like *trash:* worthless.

**Trass**, tras, *n.* a volcanic earth used as a hydraulic cement. [A form of **Terrace**, prob. through the Dutch.]

**Travail**, trav'āl, *n.* excessive labour: toil: labour in childbirth.—*v.i.* to labour: to suffer the pains of childbirth. [Fr.—Prov. *travar*, Fr. *en-traver*, to fetter, to embarrass—L. *trabes*, a beam, which was pierced with holes to confine the feet, esp. of horses. See **Turmoil**.]

**Trave**, trāv, *n.* a *beam:* a wooden frame to confine unruly horses while being shod. [It. *trave;* Sp. *trabe*—L. *trabs*, *trabis*, Gr. *trapēx*, a beam.]

**Travel**, trav'el, *v.i.* to walk: to journey: to pass: to move.—*v.t.* to pass: to journey over:—*pr.p.* trav'elling; *pa.t.* and *pa.p.* trav'elled.—*n.* act of passing from place to place: journey: labour:—*pl.* an account of a journey. [A form of **Travail**.]

**Traveller**, trav'el-èr, *n.* one who *travels:* a wayfarer: one who travels for a mercantile house: a ring that slides along a rope or spar.

**Traversable**, trav'èrs-a-bl, *adj.* that may be *traversed* or denied.

**Traverse**, trav'èrs, *adj.*, *turned* or lying *across:* denoting a method of cross-sailing.—*n.* anything laid or built across: something that crosses or obstructs: a turn: (*law*) a plea containing a denial of some fact alleged by an opponent: a work for protection from the fire of an enemy.—*v.t.* to cross: to pass over: to survey: (*law*) to deny what an opponent has alleged.—*v.i.* (*fencing*) to oppose a movement: to direct a gun to the right or left of its position.—*n.* **Trav'erser**. [L. *trans*, across, and *verto*, *versum*, to turn.]

**Traverse-table**, trav'èrs-tā'bl, *n.* a *table* or platform for shifting carriages to other rails.

**Travesty**, trav'es-ti, *adj.* having on the *vesture* or dress of *another:* disguised so as to be ridiculous.—*n.* a kind of burlesque in which the original characters are preserved, the situations parodied.—*v.t.* to turn into burlesque. [Fr. *travestir*, to disguise—L. *trans*, over, *vestio*, to clothe.]

**Trawl**, trawl, *v.i.* to fish by *trailing* or dragging a bag-net called a trawl along the bottom of the sea. [A form of **Trail**.]

**Trawler**, trawl'èr, *n.* one who or that which *trawls:* a small fishing-vessel used in trawling.

**Tray**, trā, *n.* a shallow *trough*-like vessel: a salver. [A form of **Trough**.]

**Treacherous**, trech'er-us, *adj.* full of *treachery:* faithless.—*adv.* **Treach'erously**.—*n.* **Treach'erousness**.

**Treachery**, trech'ér-i, *n.* faithlessness. [O. Fr. *trecherie* (Fr. *tricherie*)—*trecher* (Fr. *tricher*)—Dut. *trekken*, to draw. **Trick** is a doublet.]

**Treacle**, trē′kl, *n.* the sirup which is drained from sugar in the making. [Orig. 'an antidote against the bite of poisonous animals,' O. Fr. *triacle*—L. *theriacum*—Gr. *thēriaka* (*pharmaka*), antidotes against the bites of wild beasts —*thērion*, a wild beast.]

**Tread**, tred, *v.i.* to set the foot : to walk or go : to copulate, as fowls.—*v.t.* to walk on : to press with the foot : to trample in contempt : to subdue :—*pa.t.* trod ; *pa.p.* trod or trodd′en.—*n.* pressure with the foot : a step.—*n.* **Tread′er.** [A.S. *tredan* ; cog. with Ice. *troda*, Ger. *treten.*]

**Treadle**, **Treddle**, tred′l, *n.* the part of any machine which the foot *treads* on and moves.

**Tread-mill**, tred′-mil, *n.* a *mill* worked by *treading* or stepping from one to another of the steps of a cylindrical wheel, used chiefly as an instrument of prison discipline.

**Treason**, trē′zn, *n.* a *betraying* of the government or an attempt to overthrow it : treachery : disloyalty. [O. Fr. *traïson*, Fr. *trahison*—*trahir* —L. *trado*, to give up, betray.]

**Treasonable**, trē′zn-a-bl, *adj.* pertaining to, consisting of, or involving treason.—*adv.* **Trea′sonably.**

**Treasure**, trezh′ūr, *n.* wealth stored up : riches : a great quantity collected : great abundance : anything much valued.—*v.t.* to hoard up : to collect for future use : to value greatly. [Fr. *trésor*—L. *thesaurus*—Gr. *thēsauros*. See **Thesaurus**.]

**Treasurer**, trezh′ūr-ėr, *n.* one who has the care of a *treasure* or treasury : one who has charge of collected funds.—*n.* **Treas′urership.**

**Treasure-trove**, trezh′ūr-trōv, *n.*, *treasure* or money *found* in the earth, of which the owner is unknown. [**Treasure**, and *trové*, pa.p. of O. Fr. *trover*, to find. See **Trover**.]

**Treasury**, trezh′ūr-i, *n.* a place where treasure is deposited : the department of a government which has charge of the finances.

**Treat**, trēt, *v.t.* to *handle* in a particular manner : to discourse on : to entertain, as with food or drink, &c. : to manage in the application of remedies : to use.—*v.i.* to handle a subject in writing or speaking : to negotiate : to give an entertainment.—*n.* an entertainment. [A.S. *treahtigean*, Fr. *traiter*—L. *tractare*, to handle, manage—*traho*, *tractum*, to draw.]

**Treatise**, trēt′iz, *n.* a written composition in which a subject is *treated* or handled : a formal essay.

**Treatment**, trēt′ment, *n.* the act or manner of *treating*: management : behaviour to any one : way of applying remedies.

**Treaty**, trēt′i, *n.* the act of *treating* to form an agreement : a formal agreement between states.

**Treble**, treb′l, *adj.*, *triple*: threefold : (*music*) denoting the treble, that plays or sings the treble. —*n.* the highest of the four principal parts in the musical scale.—*v.t.* to make three times as much. —*v.i.* to become threefold :—*pa.p.* treb′led (-ld). —*adv.* **Treb′ly.** [O. Fr. form of **Triple**.]

**Treddle.** See **Treadle**.

**Tree**, trē, *n.* a plant having a single trunk, woody, branched, and of a large size : anything like a tree : wood, as in the compounds *axle-tree, saddle-tree*, &c. : (*B.*) a cross. [A.S. *treow*; Goth. *triu*, Ice. *tré*, Gr. *drus*, Sans. *dru*.]

**Treenail**, trē′nāl, *n.* a long *wooden* pin or *nail* to fasten the planks of a ship to the timbers.

**Trefoil**, trē′foil, *n.* a *three-leaved* plant as the white and red clover : (*arch.*) an ornament like trefoil. [L. *trifolium*—*tres*, three, and *folium*, a leaf.]

**Trellis**, trel′is, *n.* a structure of cross-barred or lattice work, for supporting plants, &c. [Fr. *treillis*—Low L. *tralicium* (*translicium*), crossed threads—L. *trans*, across, and *licium*, a thread.]

**Trellised**, trel′ist, *adj.* having a *trellis*, or formed as a trellis.

**Tremble**, trem′bl, *v.i.* to shake, as from fear, cold, or weakness : to shiver : to shake, as sound.—*n.* **Trem′bler.**—*adv.* **Trem′blingly.** [Fr. *trembler* —L. *tremulus*, trembling—*tremo*, to shake, akin to Gr. *treō*, Sans. *tras*, to tremble.]

**Tremendous**, tre-men′dus, *adj.* such as astonishes or terrifies by its force or greatness : dreadful.— *adv.* **Tremen′dously.** [Lit. 'that is to be trembled at,' L. *tremendus*.]       [quivering. [L.]

**Tremor**, trem′or, *n.* a *trembling*, shaking, or **Tremulous**, trem′ū-lus, *adj.*, *trembling*: affected with fear : shaking : quivering.—*adv.* **Trem′ulously.**—*n.* **Trem′ulousness.**

**Trench**, trensh, *v.t.* to *cut* or dig a ditch : to dig deeply with the spade or plough.—*v.i.* to encroach.—*n.* a long narrow cut in the earth : (*fort.*) an excavation to interrupt the approach of an enemy : the excavated approaches made by besiegers. [O. Fr. *trencher*, Fr. *trancher*, acc. to Littré from L. *truncare*, to maim, to cut off —*truncus*, maimed.]

**Trenchant**, trensh′ant, *adj.*, *cutting*: sharp : severe.

**Trencher**, trensh′ėr, *n.* a wooden plate formerly used for *cutting* meat on at meals : the table : food : pleasures of the table. [Fr. *tranchoir*.]

**Trench-plough**, trensh′-plow, *n.* a *plough* for *trenching* or turning up the land more deeply than usual.—*v.t.* to plough with a trench-plough.

**Trend**, trend, *v.i.* to tend, to run, to go in a particular direction.—*n.* tendency. [Perh. a corr. of **Tend**.]

**Trental**, trent′al, *n.* a R. C. office for the dead, of *thirty* masses for *thirty* days after the person's death. [Low L. *trentale*—It. *trenta*, L. *triginta*, thirty.]

**Trepan**, tre-pan′, *v.t.* to insnare :—*pr.p.* trepann′-ing ; *pa.t.* and *pa.p.* trepanned′. [Same as **Trapan**, of which it is an erroneous spelling.]

**Trepan**, tre-pan′, *n.* (*surg.*) a small cylindrical saw used in perforating the skull.—*v.t.* to remove a circular piece of the skull with a trepan, in order to relieve the brain from pressure or irritation. [Lit. 'a borer,' Fr.—It. *trapano*, through Low L.—Gr. *trypănon*—*trypaō*, to bore.]

**Trephine**, tre-fīn′, *n.* the modern *trepan*, having a little sharp borer called the centre pin.—*v.t.* to perforate with the trephine. [Dim. of **Trepan**.]

**Trepidation**, trep-i-dā′shun, *n.* a state of confused hurry or alarm : an involuntary trembling. [L. *trepido*, *-atum*, to hurry with alarm—*trepidus*, restless, alarmed, from the root of Gr. *trepō*, to turn (in flight).]

**Trespass**, tres′pas, *v.i.* to *pass over* a limit or boundary : to enter unlawfully upon another's land : to inconvenience by importunity : to intrude : to injure or annoy another : to sin.—*n.* act of trespassing : any injury to another's person or property : a sin.—*n.* **Tres′passer.** [O. Fr. *trespasser* (Fr. *trépasser*)—L. *trans*, across, and *passer* (see **Pass**).]

**Trespass-offering**, tres′pas-of′ėr-ing, *n.* an *offering* in expiation of a *trespass* or sin.

**Tress**, tres, *n.* a lock or curl of hair : a ringlet (esp. in *pl.*). [Fr. *tresse*, through It. *treccia*, from Gr. *tricha*, threefold—*tris*, three times.]

**Tressed**, trest, *adj.*, *having tresses*: formed into tresses or ringlets : curled.

**Tressel**, **Trestle**, tres′l, *n.* a movable support

fastened to a top-piece: the frame of a table. [O. Fr. *trestel* (Fr. *tréteau*): ety. dub.; perh. through a Low L. dim. from L *transtrum*, a beam, a bench.]

**Tret**, tret, *n.* an allowance to purchasers of 4 lbs. on every 104 lbs. for waste. [Norm. *trett*, deduction, Fr. *trait*—O. Fr. *traire*—L. *trahere*, to draw.]

**Triad**, trī′ad, *n.* the union of *three*. [L. *trias*, *triadis*—Gr. *trias*, *triados*—*treis*, E. **Three**.]

**Trial**, trī′al, *n.* a *trying*: the act of trying: examination by a test: the state of being tried: suffering: temptation: judicial examination: attempt.

**Triangle**, trī′ang-gl, *n.* (*math.*) a plane figure with *three angles* and three sides: (*music*) an instrument of steel in the form of a triangle. [Fr.—L. *triangulum*—*tres*, three, and *angulus*, an angle. See **Angle**.]

**Triangled**, trī′ang-gld, *adj.* having *three angles*.

**Triangular**, trī-ang′gū-lar, *adj.* having *three angles*.—*adv.* **Trian′gularly**.

**Triangulate**, trī-ang′gū-lāt, *v.t.* to survey by means of a series of *triangles*.

**Triangulation**, trī-ang-gū-lā′shun, *n.* act of *triangulating*: the series of triangles so used.

**Trias**, trī′as, *n.* (*geol.*) the oldest group of the Secondary strata, formerly associated with the Permian rocks under the name of the New Red Sandstone.—*adj.* **Trias′sic**. [So called by the German geologists, because the group is separable into three distinct formations, from Gr. *trias*, union of three. Cf. **Triad**.]

**Tribe**, trīb, *n.* a race or family from the same ancestor: a body of people under one leader: a number of things having certain common qualities.—*adj.* **Trib′al**. [L. *tribus*, 'a third part,' orig. applied to one of the three cantons or divisions forming the ancient Roman people, from *tri-*, root of *tres*, E. **Three**, and root *bhu*, E. **Be**.]

**Tribrach**, trī′brak, *n.* (*poetry*) a foot of *three short* syllables. [L.—Gr. *tri-*, root of *treis*, E. **Three**, and *brachys*, short.]

**Tribulation**, trib-ū-lā′shun, *n.* severe affliction: distress. [L. *tribulatio*—*tribulo*, to press or afflict—*tribulum*, a sledge for rubbing out corn —*tero*, to rub, grind.]

**Tribunal**, tri-bū′nal, *n.* the bench on which a judge and his associates sit to administer justice: court of justice. [L.]

**Tribune**, trib′ūn, *n.* a magistrate elected by the Roman plebeians to defend their rights: the raised platform from which speeches were delivered.—*n.* **Trib′uneship**. [L. *tribunus*, orig. 'the representative of a tribe'—*tribus*, a tribe. See **Tribe**.]

**Tributary**, trib′ū-tar-i, *adj.* paying *tribute*: subject: yielding supplies of anything: paid in tribute.—*n.* one who pays tribute: a stream which contributes water to another. — *adv.* **Trib′utarily**.

**Tribute**, trib′ūt, *n.* a fixed amount *paid* at certain intervals by one nation to another for peace or protection: a personal contribution: acknowledgment, or homage paid. [L. *tributum*—*tribuo*, to assign, give, pay—*tribus*, a tribe. See **Tribe**.]

**Trice**, trīs, *n.* a very short time: an instant. [Perh. from *thrice*, while one can count *three*; or from Sp. *tris*, noise of breaking glass (cf. Scot. 'in a *crack*').]

**Tricennial**, trī-sen′yal, *adj.* pertaining to *thirty years*: occurring every thirty years. [L. *tri-*

*cennium*, thirty years—*triginta*, thirty, and *annus*, a year.]

**Tricentenary**, trī-sen′ten-ar-i, *n.* a space of *three hundred years*. [L. *trecenti*, three hundred—*tres*, three, and *centum*, a hundred.]

**Trichina**, tri-kī′na, *n.* a parasitic worm, which in its mature state infests the intestinal canal, and in its larval state the muscular tissue of man and certain animals, esp. the hog:—*pl.* **Trichī′næ**. [Gr. *trichinos*, small like a hair—*thrix*, *trichos*, hair.]

**Trichiniasis**, tri-kin-ī′a-sis, *n.* the disease caused by the presence of trichinæ in the body.

**Trick**, trik, *v.t.* to dress, to decorate. [Celt. *trec*, ornament, *treciaw*, to adorn.]

**Trick**, trik, *n.* any fraud or stratagem to deceive: a clever contrivance to puzzle, amuse, or annoy: a particular habit or manner: a parcel of cards falling to a winner at one turn.—*v.t.* to deceive, to cheat.—*ns.* **Trick′er**, **Trick′ster**. [O. Fr. *tricer*, *trecher*, to beguile, from Dut. *trekken*, to draw. See **Treachery**.]

**Trickery**, trik′ér-i, *n.* act or practice of playing *tricks*: artifice: stratagem: imposition.

**Trickish**, trik′ish, *adj.* addicted to *tricks*: artful in making bargains.

**Trickle**, trik′l, *v.i.* to flow gently or in a small stream. [Scot. *trinkle*; Ger. *tröpfeln*—*tropfen*, to fall in drops.]

**Tricolor**, **Tricolour**, trī′kul-ur, *n.* the national flag of France, of *three colours*, red, white, and blue, in vertical stripes. [Fr. *tricolore*—L. *tres*, three, and *color*, colour.]

**Tricoloured**, trī′kul-urd, *adj.* having *three colours*.

**Tricycle**, trī′sik-l, *n.* a velocipede with three wheels. [Gr. *tri-*, root of *treis*, E. **Three**, and *kyklos*, E. **Cycle**. Cf. **Bicycle**.]

**Trident**, trī′dent, *n.* the *three-pronged* spear or sceptre of Neptune, god of the ocean: any three-toothed instrument. [Fr.—L. *tres*, three, and *dens*, *dentis*, E. **Tooth**.]

**Trident**, trī′dent, **Tridented**, trī′dent-ed, *adj.* having *three teeth* or *prongs*.

**Triennial**, trī-en′yal, *adj.* continuing *three years*: happening every third year.—*adv.* **Trienn′ially**. [L. *triennis*—*tres*, three, and *annus*, a year.]

**Trifle**, trī′fl, *v.i.* to act or talk lightly: to indulge in light or silly amusements: to waste or spend idly or unprofitably.—*n.* anything of little value: a light kind of dish.—*n.* **Trī′fler**. [O. Fr. *trufle*, perh. conn. with O. Dut. *treyfelen*, to play; or perh. only another form of **Truffle**.]

**Trifling**, trī′fling, *adj.* like a *trifle*: of small value or importance: trivial.—*adv.* **Trī′flingly**.

**Trifoliate**, trī-fō′li-āt, *adj.*, *three-leaved*. [L. *tres*, three, and *folium*, leaf.]

**Triform**, trī′form, *adj.* having a *triple form*. [L. *triformis*—*tres*, three, and *forma*, form.]

**Trig**, trig, *adj.* full: trim, neat. [Ety. dub.]

**Trigger**, trig′ér, *n.* a catch which when *pulled* looses the hammer of a gun in firing: a catch to hold a wheel when driving on steep ground. [Either from Dut. *trekker*—*trekken*, to pull (cf. **Trick**, *n.*); or from Ger. *drücker*.]

**Triglyph**, trī′glif, *n.* a *three-grooved* tablet at equal distances along the frieze in Doric architecture. [L. *triglyphus*—Gr. *triglyphos*—*treis*, three, and *glyphō*, to hollow out, to carve.]

**Triglyphic**, trī-glif′ik, **Triglyphical**, trī-glif′ik-al, *adj.* consisting of or pertaining to *triglyphs*: containing three sets of characters or sculptures.

**Trigonometrical**, trig-o-no-met′rik-al, *adj.* pertaining to *trigonometry*: done by the rules of trigonometry.—*adv.* **Trigonomet′rically**.

**Trigonometry**, trig-o-nom'e-tri, *n.* the branch of mathematics which treats of the relations between the sides and angles of triangles. [Lit. 'the measurement of triangles'—Gr. *trigōnon*, a triangle, and *metron*, a measure.]

**Trihedral**, trī-hē'dral, *adj.* having *three* equal *sides*.

**Trihedron**, trī-hē'dron, *n.* a figure having *three* equal *bases* or sides. [Gr. *treis*, three, and *hedra*, a seat, base.]

**Trilateral**, trī-lat'ér-al, *adj.* having *three sides.*—*adv.* Trilat'erally. [L. *tres*, three, *latus*, side.]

**Trilingual**, trī-ling'gwal, *adj.* consisting of *three* tongues or languages. [L. *tres*, three, and *lingua*, tongue.]

**Triliteral**, trī-lit'ér-al, *adj.* consisting of *three* letters. [L. *tres*, three, and *litera*, a letter.]

**Trill**, tril, *v.t.* and *v.i.* to *shake*: to utter with a tremulous vibration: to trickle or flow in a small stream.—*n.* a quaver or tremulous vibration. [Fr. *triller*—It. *trillare*, to shake; imitative.]

**Trillion**, tril'yun, *n.* a *million* raised to the *third* power, or multiplied twice by itself (1,000,000,000,000,000,000). [Fr.—L. *tres*, three, and Low L. *millio*, a million. See **Million**.]

**Trilobite**, trī'lob-īt, *n.* one of an order of fossil crustacea. [Gr. *tri*, thrice, and *lobos*, a lobe.]

**Trilogy**, tril'o-ji, *n.* a series of *three* dramas, each complete in sense, yet mutually related as parts of one great historical piece. [Gr. *trilogia*—*tri*, *tris*, thrice, and *logos*, speech, discourse.]

**Trim**, trim, *adj.* in good order: nice.—*v.t.* to make trim: to put in due order: to dress: to decorate: to clip: to reduce to proper form: to arrange for sailing.—*v.i.* to balance or fluctuate between parties:—*pr.p.* trimm'ing; *pa.t.* and *pa.p.* trimmed.—*n.* dress: ornaments: state of a ship as to sailing qualities.—*adv.* Trim'ly.—*n.* Trim'ness. [A.S. *trum*, firm, *trymian*, to strengthen, set in order.]

**Trimeter**, trim'e-tér, *n.* a division of a verse consisting of *three measures.*—*adjs.* Trim'eter, Trimet'rical. [Gr. *trimetros*—*treis*, three, and *metron*, measure.]

**Trimmer**, trim'ér, *n.* one who *trims*: one who fluctuates between parties, a timeserver.

**Trimming**, trim'ing, *n.* that which *trims*: ornamental parts, esp. of a garment, dish, &c.

**Trimonthly**, trī'munth-li, *adj.* every three months.

**Trinitarian**, trin-i-tār'i-an, *adj.* pertaining to the *Trinity*, or to the doctrine of the Trinity.—*n.* one who holds the doctrine of the Trinity.—Trinitar'ianism, *n.* the tenets of Trinitarians.

**Trinity**, trin'i-ti, *n.* the union of *three* in *one* Godhead: the persons of the Godhead. [L. *trinitas*, three—*trini*, three each—*tres*, three.]

**Trinity-Sunday**, trin'i-ti-sun'dā, *n.* the *Sunday* next after Whitsunday, the Festival of the Holy *Trinity*.

**Trinket**, tringk'et, *n.* a small ornament for the person: anything of little value. [Ety. dub.; perh. nasalised from *tricket*, a dim. of **Trick**.]

**Trinomial**, trī-nō'mi-al, *adj.* (*math.*) consisting of *three* names or terms connected by the sign plus or minus.—*n.* a trinomial quantity. [L. *tres*, three, and *nomen*, name.]

**Trio**, trī'o, *n.* three united: (*music*) a composition for three performers. [It.—L. *tres*, three.]

**Trip**, trip, *v.i.* to move with short, light steps: to stumble and fall: to err: to fail.—*v.t.* to cause to stumble by striking one's feet from under him: to overthrow by taking away support: to catch:—*pr.p.* tripp'ing; *pa.t.* and *pa.p.* tripped.—*n.* a light, short step: a catch by which an antag-

onist is thrown: a false step: a mistake: a short voyage or journey. [Allied to Low Ger. *trippen*, and Ger. *trippeln*; cf. also W. *tripiaw*.]

**Tripartite**, trip'ar-tīt, *adj.*, *divided* into *three parts*: having three corresponding parts: relating to three parties.—Triparti'tion, *n.* a division into three. [L. *ter*, thrice, and *partitus*, pa.p. of *partio*, to divide—*pars*, a part.]

**Tripe**, trīp, *n.* entrails: the large stomach of ruminating animals prepared for food. [Fr., ety. dub.; prob. from Celt. *tripa*.]

**Tripedal**, trip'e-dal, *adj.* having *three feet*. [L. *tres*, three, and *pes, pedis*, E. **Foot**.]

**Tripetalous**, trī-pet'al-us, *adj.* (*bot.*) having *three* petals or flower-*leaves*. [Gr. *treis*, three, and *petalon*, a leaf. See **Petal**.]

**Triphthong**, trif'thong or trip'thong, *n.* a combination of *three* vowels to form one *sound.*—*adj.* Triphthon'gal. [Fr. *triphthongue*—Gr. *treis*, three, and *phthongos*, sound.]

**Triple**, trip'l, *adj.* consisting of three united: three times repeated.—*v.t.* to treble.—*adv.* Trip'ly. [Fr.—L. *tri-plus* (*lit.*) 'thrice-full'—*tri-*, root of *tres*, E. **Three**, and *-plus*, akin to *plenus*, E. **Fill**. Cf. **Double**.]

**Triplet**, trip'let, *n.*, *three* of a kind or three united: three lines rhyming together: (*music*) a group of three notes occupying the time of two, indicated by a slur and the figure 3.

**Triplicate**, trip'li-kāt, *adj.*, *threefold*: made thrice as much.—*n.* a third copy or thing corresponding to two others of the same kind. [L. *ter*, thrice, and *plico*, to fold. Cf. **Duple**, **Duplicate**.]

**Triplication**, trip-li-kā'shun, *n.* act of making *threefold* or adding three together.

**Tripod**, trī'pod, *n.* anything on *three feet* or legs, as a stool, &c. [Gr. *tripous, tripodos*—*tri*, *treis*, three, *pous*, E. **Foot**.]

**Tripos**, trī'pos, *n.* a university examination for honours at Cambridge: a tripos paper. [From a tripod being frequently given as a prize at the Grecian games. See **Tripod**.]

**Tripping**, trip'ing, *n.* the act of *tripping*: a light kind of dance.

**Trippingly**, trip'ing-li, *adv.* in a *tripping* manner: with a light, quick step.

**Triptote**, trip'tōt, *n.* a noun used in *three cases* only. [Fr.—Gr. *triptōton*—*tri*, *treis*, three, thrice, *ptōtos*, falling—*piptō*, to fall.]

**Triptych**, trip'tik, *n.* a set of tablets consisting of *three leaves*, each painted with a distinct subject, but joined together by hinges, and capable of being folded so as to present a new face. [Gr. *tri*, thrice, *ptyx, ptychos*, a fold, a leaf—*ptyssō*, to fold.]

**Trireme**, trī'rēm, *n.* a galley or vessel with *three* banks or rows of *oars*. [Fr.—L. *triremis*—*tri*, *tres*, three, *remus*, an oar.]

**Trisect**, trī-sekt', *v.t.* to *cut* or divide into *three* equal parts. [L. *tri*, thrice, *seco, sectum*, to cut.]

**Trisection**, trī-sek'shun, *n.* the division of anything, as an angle, into *three* equal parts.

**Trisyllabic**, tris-sil-lab'ik, Trisyllab'ical, -al, *adj.* pertaining to a *trisyllable*: consisting of three syllables.—*adv.* Trisyllab'ically.

**Trisyllable**, tris-sil'a-bl, *n.* a word of *three* *syllables*. [Gr. *tri-*, three, and **Syllable**.]

**Trite**, trīt, *adj.*, *worn* out by use: used till its novelty and interest are lost: hackneyed.—*adv.* Trite'ly.—*n.* Trite'ness. [It. *trito*—L. *tritus*, rubbed, pa.p. of *tero*, to rub. See **Try**.]

**Triton**, trī'ton, *n.* (*myth.*) a marine demi-god, one of the trumpeters of Neptune, his trumpet being a wreathed univalve shell : a genus of molluscs with a wreathed univalve shell. [Gr. *Trīton.*]

**Triturable**, trit'ū-ra-bl, *adj.* that may be reduced to a fine powder by *grinding*.

**Triturate**, trit'ū-rāt, *v.t.* to *rub* or grind to a fine powder.—*n.* **Tritura'tion**. [Late L. *trituro, -atum*—L. *tero*, to rub.]

**Triumph**, trī'umf, *n.* in ancient Rome, a solemn procession in honour of a victorious general : joy for success : victory.—*v.i.* to celebrate a victory with pomp : to rejoice for victory : to obtain victory : to be prosperous : (with *over*) to insult a person upon an advantage gained.—*n.* **Tri'umpher**. [L. *triumphus;* akin to Gr. *thriambos*, a hymn to Bacchus.]

**Triumphal**, trī-umf'al, *adj.* pertaining to *triumph:* used in celebrating victory.

**Triumphant**, trī-umf'ant, *adj.* celebrating or rejoicing for a *triumph* : expressing joy for success : victorious.—*adv.* **Triumph'antly**. [L. *triumphans, -antis,* pr.p. of *triumpho,* to celebrate a triumph—*triumphus.*]

**Triumvir**, trī-um'vir, *n.* one of *three men* in the same office or government :—*pl.* **Trium'viri**, **Trium'virs**. [L.—*trium-,* from *tres,* three, and *vir,* a man.]

**Triumvirate**, trī-um'vi-rāt, *n.* an association of *three men* in office or government, or for any political ends. [L.]

**Triune**, trī'ūn, *adj.* being *three* in one. [Coined from L. *tri-,* root of *tres,* three, and *unus,* one.]

**Trivet**, triv'et, *n.* a stool or other thing supported on *three feet* : a movable iron frame in a kitchen fire-grate for supporting kettles, &c. [For *trevet*—Fr. *trépied,* a tripod—L. *tripes, tripedis* —*tres,* three, *pes,* a foot. Cf. **Tripod**.]

**Trivial**, triv'i-al, *adj.* that may be found anywhere, common : of little importance : trifling. —*adv.* **Triv'ially**.—*n.* **Triv'ialness**. [L. *trivialis (lit.)* 'to be found at the *cross-roads* or public streets'—*trivium,* a place where three ways meet—*tres,* three, *via,* a way.]

**Trochaic**, tro-kā'ik, **Trocha'ical**, -al, *adj.* consisting of *trochees*.—**Trocha'ic**, *n.* a trochaic verse or measure.

**Trochee**, trō'kē, *n.* a metrical foot of two syllables, so called from its *tripping* or joyous character : in L. verse, consisting of a long and a short, as *nūmen:* in E. verse, of an accented and unaccented syllable, as *trī'pod.* [Fr. *trochée*—Gr. *trochaios (pous,* foot, understood), running, tripping—*trochos,* a running—*trechō,* to run.]

**Trod**, **Trodd'en**, *pa.t.* and *pa.p.* of **Tread**.

**Troglodyte**, trog'lo-dīt, *n.* the Greek name for certain ancient tribes on the Nile, now a general term for all savage cave-dwellers. [Fr.—Gr. *trōglodytēs*—*trōglē,* a cave, and *dyō,* to enter.]

**Trojan**, trō'jan, *adj.* pertaining to ancient *Troy*.— *n.* an inhabitant of ancient Troy : an old soldier.

**Troll**, trōl, *v.t.* to move circularly : to sing the parts of in succession, as of a catch or round.— *v.i.* to roll : to move or turn about : to sing a catch.—*n.* a song, the parts of which are sung in succession : a round.—*n.* **Troll'er**. [Perh. from Fr. *trôler,* to lead about—Celt. root seen in W. *trolis,* to twist, to roll.]

**Troll**, trōl, *v.i.* to fish, esp. for pike, with a rod of which the line runs on a reel near the handle. [A form of **Trawl**.]

**Trollop**, trol'up, *n.* a loitering, slatternly woman : a woman negligently dressed : a draggle-tail. [From **Troll**, in the sense of running about.]

**Trombone**, trom'bōn, *n.* a deep-toned brass musical wind instrument of the *trumpet* kind.

[It. ; augmentative of *tromba*, a trumpet. See **Trump**, a trumpet.]

**Troop**, trōōp, *n.* a *crowd* or collection of people : a company : soldiers taken collectively, an army, usually in *pl.* : a small body of cavalry corresponding to a company of infantry.—*v.i.* to collect in numbers : to march in a company, or in haste. [Fr. *troupe,* prob. through Low L. forms, from L. *turba,* a crowd.]

**Trooper**, trōōp'ér, *n.* a private cavalry soldier.

**Trope**, trōp, *n.* (*rhet.*) a word or expression *changed* from its proper sense for life or emphasis, a figure of speech. [Fr.—L. *tropus*— Gr. *tropos*—*trepō,* to turn.]

**Trophied**, trō'fid, *adj.* adorned with *trophies*.

**Trophy**, trō'fi, *n.* a memorial of a victory, consisting of a pile of arms erected on the field of battle : anything taken from an enemy and preserved as a memorial of victory : something that is evidence of victory. [Fr. *trophée*—L. *tropæum* — Gr. *tropaion*—*tropē,* a turning — *trepō,* to turn, to turn to flight.]

**Tropic**, trop'ik, *n.* one of the two circles on the celestial sphere, 23° 28′ on each side of the equator, where the sun *turns,* as it were, after reaching its greatest declination north or south : one of two circles on the terrestrial globe corresponding to these :—*pl.* the regions lying between the tropics. [Through L. *tropicus,* from Gr. *tropikos,* relating to a turning—*tropos,* a turning (see **Trope**).]

**Tropic**, trop'ik, **Tropical**, trop'ik-al, *adj.* pertaining to the *tropics:* being within or near the tropics.—*adv.* **Trop'ically**.

**Tropical**, trop'ik-al, *adj.* (*rhet.*) pertaining to a *trope:* changed from its proper or original sense : figurative.—*adv.* **Trop'ically**.

**Tropological**, trō-po-loj'ik-al, *adj.* expressed or varied by *tropes* or figures.

**Tropology**, trō-pol'o-ji, *n.* a *tropical* or figurative mode of speech. [Gr. *tropos,* and *logos,* discourse.]

**Trot**, trot, *v.i.* to go, lifting the feet quicker and higher than in walking : to walk or move fast : to run.—*v.t.* to ride at a trot :—*pr.p.* trott'ing ; *pa.t.* and *pa.p.* trott'ed.—*n.* the pace of a horse or other quadruped when trotting.—*n.* **Trott'er**. [Fr. *trotter,* through various forms from a L. form *tolutare,* for *ire tolutim,* to go on a trot, (*lit.*) 'by a *lifting,*' from root *tol,* to lift.]

**Troth**, troth, *n., truth,* confidence : faith : fidelity. [A.S. *treowth*—*treow,* faith, trust. See **Truth**.]

**Troubadour**, trōō'ba-dōōr, *n.* one of a class of poets from the 11th to the 13th century, chiefly in France. [Fr., from Prov. *trobador*—*trobar* (Fr. *trouver*), to find—L. *turbare,* to throw into disorder (in searching for a thing), hence, to find. See **Trover**.]

**Trouble**, trub'l, *v.t.* to put into a confused state : to agitate : to disturb : to annoy : to busy or engage overmuch.—*n.* disturbance : affliction : uneasiness : that which disturbs or afflicts.—*n.* **Troub'ler**. [Fr. *troubler,* O. Fr. *tourbler*—Low L. *turbulo*—L. *turbare,* to disturb—*turba,* a crowd, tumult.]

**Troublesome**, trub'l-sum, *adj.* causing or giving *trouble* or inconvenience : vexatious : importunate.—*adv.* **Troub'lesomely**.—*n.* **Troub'lesomeness**.

**Troublous**, trub'lus, *adj.* full of *trouble* or disorder : agitated : tumultuous.

**Trough**, trof, *n.* a long, hollow vessel for water or other liquid : a long tray : a long narrow channel. [A.S. *trog;* Ger. *trog.*]

**Trounce**, trowns, *v.t.* to punish or beat severely.

[O. Fr. *tronçonner*, to cut—L. *truncus*, maimed. See **Trench**.]

**Trousers**, trow'zèrz, *n.pl.* long breeches: a garment worn by males on the lower limbs and *trussed* or fastened up at the waist. [O. Fr. *trousses*, breeches worn by pages—Fr. *trousse* (see **Truss**).]

**Trousseau**, trōō-sō', *n.* the lighter articles of a bride's outfit. [Fr., lit. 'a little bundle,' from *trousse*, a bundle (see **Truss**).]

**Trout**, trowt, *n.* a common name for fresh-water fish of the salmon family : the *Salmo Fario*, or Common Trout, much sought after by anglers. [Fr. *truite*, A.S. *truht*—L. *tructa*, *tructus*—Gr. *trōktēs*, a sea-fish with sharp teeth—*trōgō*, to gnaw.]

**Trover**, trōv'èr, *n.* (*law*) the gaining possession of goods. [O. Fr. *trover*, to find (Fr. *trouver*)—L. *turbare*, to throw into disorder (in searching for a thing), hence, to find—*turba*, confusion. Cf. **Treasure-Trove** and **Troubadour**.]

**Trow**, trō, *v.i.* to hold as true : (*B.*) to trust : to believe : to think. [A.S. *treow-ian ;* Ice. *trua*, Ger. *trau-en*. See **True**, **Trust**.]

**Trowel**, trow'el, *n.* a tool used in spreading mortar, and in gardening. [Fr. *truelle*—L. *trulla*, dim. of *trua*, a ladle.]

**Trowsers**. Same as **Trousers**.

**Troy, Troy-weight**, troi'-wāt, *n.* the system of weights used in England for gold, silver, and precious stones. [A corr. of Fr. (*livre*, pound) *d'octroi*, of authority—*octroi*, from L. *auctoritas*, authority, and sig. orig. 'anything *authorised*,' then 'a tax.']

**Truant**, trōō'ant, *n.* an idler : a boy who, idly or without excuse, absents himself from school.—*adj.* wandering from duty : loitering : idle.—*ns.* **Tru'ancy, Tru'antship.** [Fr. *truand*—Low L. *trutanus*—Celt. root *tru*, wretched.]

**Truce**, trōōs, *n.* a temporary peace or suspension of hostilities between two armies or between states : cessation. [Lit. 'a true agreement,' M. E. *treows*, *trewes*, an extension of **True**. See also **Truth**.]

**Truck**, truk, *v.t.* to *exchange* or barter.—*v.i.* to traffic by exchange.—*n.* exchange of goods : barter. [Fr. *troquer*—Sp. *trocar*, perh. a corr. of L. *trans*, across or over, and *vicis*, change.]

**Truck**, truk, *n.* a wheel : a railway wagon for heavy articles : a platform running on wheels : a small wooden cap at the top of a mast or flag-staff. [Perh. a corr. of Gr. *trochos*, a wheel—*trechō*, to run.]

**Truckage**, truk'āj, *n.* the practice of *exchanging* or bartering goods. [See **Truck**, *v.*]

**Truckage**, truk'āj, *n.* charge for carrying articles on a *truck*. [See **Truck**, *n.*]

**Truckle**, truk'l, *v.i.* to yield meanly to the demands of another.—*ns.* **Truck'ler, Truck'ling.** [Extension of **Truck**, *v.*]

**Truckle**, truk'l, *n.* a small wheel or caster. [Dim. of **Truck**, *n.*]

**Truckle-bed**, truk'l-bed, *n.* a low bed on wheels that may be pushed under another. [See **Truck**, *n.*]

**Truck-system**, truk'-sis'tem, *n.* the practice of paying workmen in goods instead of money. [See **Truck**, *v.*]

**Truculent**, truk'ū-lent, *adj.* very fierce : barbarous : cruel : inspiring terror.—*adv.* **Truc'ulently.**—*n.* **Truc'ulence.** [L. *truculentus*—*trux*, wild, fierce.]

**Trudge**, truj, *v.i.* to travel on foot : to travel with labour or effort : to march heavily on. [Allied to **Tread** and **Trot**, and influenced by **Drudge**.]

**True**, trōō, *adj.* agreeing with fact : worthy of belief or confidence : certain : trusty : genuine : exact : straight : right : rightful.—*n.* **True'ness.** [A.S. *treowe ;* cog. with Ice. *trur*, Ger. *treu ;* from the root of **Trow**. See **Trust**.]

**Truffle**, truf'l, *n.* a round underground fungus used in cookery.—**Truffled**, *adj.* cooked with *truffles*. [O. Fr. *truffle* (Fr. *truffe*), a corr. of L. *tuber* (see **Tuber**).]

**Truism**, trōō'izm, *n.* a plain or self-evident *truth.*

**Trull**, trul, *n.* a drab : a vagrant woman of loose habits. [Allied to Ger. *trulle ;* conn. with Scand. *troll*, demon, goblin, monster.]

**Truly**, trōō'li, *adv.* according to *truth :* in fact or reality : exactly : justly : faithfully : sincerely : honestly.

**Trump**, trump, *n.* a trumpet. [Prob. through Fr. *trompe*, from It. *tromba*, which, acc. to Diez, is the L. *tuba*, with inserted *r* and *m.*]

**Trump**, trump, *n.* a card of the leading suit that *triumphs* or wins : one of the suit of cards which takes any other.—*v.i.* to play a trump card.—*v.t.* to play a trump card upon.—**To trump up**, to devise, forge. [From **Triumph**.]

**Trumpery**, trump'èr-i, *n.* falsehood : boastful or empty talk : things of no value : trifles.—*adj.* worthless. [Fr. *tromperie*—*tromper*, to deceive, lit. 'to blow a trumpet (in order to attract the public),' a custom of quacks, &c. See **Trump**, a trumpet.]

**Trumpet**, trump'et, *n.* a wind instrument of music with a ringing and clear tone, used chiefly in war and in military music : (*fig.*) one who praises.—*v.t.* to publish by trumpet : to proclaim : to sound the praises of. [Fr. *trompette*, dim. of *trompe*. See **Trump**, a trumpet.]

**Trumpeter**, trump'et-èr, *n.* one who sounds on the *trumpet* the regimental calls and signals : one who proclaims, praises, or denounces : a kind of pigeon, also a S. American wading-bird.

**Trumpet-fish**, trump'et-fish, *n.* a sea-fish so named from its *trumpet*-like or tubular muzzle.

**Trumpet-tongued**, trump'et-tungd, *adj.* having a voice or *tongue* loud as a *trumpet.*

**Truncate**, trungk'āt, *v.t.* to cut off : to lop : to maim.—*n.* **Trunca'tion.** [L. *trunco, -atum*—*truncus.* See **Trunk**.]

**Truncheon**, trun'shun, *n.* a short staff : a cudgel : a baton or staff of authority.—*v.t.* to beat with a truncheon : to cudgel. [Fr. *tronçon*—*tronc* (see **Trunk**).]

**Trundle**, trun'dl, *n.* anything round : a wheel : a truck.—*v.t.* to roll, as on wheels.—*v.i.* to roll : bowl along. [A.S. *trendel*, a circle, wheel, Ger. *trändeln*, to dawdle.]

**Trundle-bed**, trun'dl-bed, *n.* a *bed* moving on *trundles* or low wheels : a truckle-bed.

**Trunk**, trungk, *n.* the *stem* of a *tree :* the body of an animal apart from the limbs : the main body of anything : anything long and hollow : the proboscis of an elephant : the shaft of a column : a chest for clothes.—**Trunked**, trungkt, *adj.* having a trunk. [Fr. *tronc*—L. *truncus*, the stem or bole of a tree.]

**Trunk-hose**, trungk'-hōz, *n.* large hose or breeches formerly worn over the lower part of the body and the upper part of the legs.

**Trunk-line**, trungk'-līn, *n.* the main *line* of a railway, canal, &c.

**Trunnion**, trun'yun, *n.* one of the knobs on each side of a gun, on which it rests on the carriage. [Fr. *trognon*, a stalk—*tronc*, a stump—L. *truncus.*]

**Truss**, trus, *n.* a bundle : timbers fastened together for supporting a roof: in ships, the rope or iron for keeping the lower yard to the mast: (*med.*) a bandage used in ruptures.—*v.t.* to bind up: to pack close: to furnish with a truss. [Fr. *trousse*—*trousser*, O. Fr. *trosser*, orig. *torser*, to bind together—L. *tortus*, pa.p. of *torqueo*, to twist.]

**Trust**, trust, *n.* confidence in the *truth* of anything: a resting on the integrity, friendship, &c. of another: faith: hope: credit (esp. sale on credit or on promise to pay): he or that which is the ground of confidence: that which is given or received in confidence: charge: (*law*) an estate managed for another.—*adj.* held in trust.—*v.t.* to place trust in: to believe: to give credit to: to sell upon credit: to commit to the care of.— *v.i.* to be confident or confiding.—*n.* **Trust′er**. [Closely conn. with Ice. *traust*, trust, Goth. *trausti*, security, Ger. *trost*, consolation; from root of **Trow** and **True**.]

**Trustee**, trus-tē′, *n.* one to whom anything is *intrusted*: one to whom the management of a property is committed in *trust* for the benefit of others.—*n.* **Trustee′ship**.

**Trustful**, trust′fool, *adj.* full of *trust*: trusting: worthy of trust: faithful.

**Trustworthy**, trust′wur-*th*i, *adj.*, *worthy* of trust or confidence: trusty.—*n.* **Trust′worthiness**.

**Trusty**, trust′i, *adj.* (*comp.* **Trust′ier**, *superl.* **Trust′iest**), that may be *trusted*: deserving confidence: honest: strong: firm.—*n.* **Trust′i-ness**.—*adv.* **Trust′ily**.

**Truth**, trōōth, *n.* that which is *true* or according to the facts of the case: agreement with reality: true state of things, or facts: practice of speaking or disposition to speak the truth: fidelity: a true statement: an established principle: in the fine arts, a faithful adherence to nature.— **Of a truth** (*B.*), truly. [A.S. *treowth*, *trywth*, a derivative of **True**. Doublet **Troth**.]

**Truthful**, trōōth′fool, *adj.*, *full* of *truth*: according to or adhering to truth: reliable.—*adv.* **Truth′fully**.—*n.* **Truth′fulness**.

**Try**, trī, *v.t.* to test: to sift: to prove by experiment: to purify: to examine judicially: to examine carefully: to experience: to attempt: to use as means: to put to severe trial, cause suffering to.—*v.i.* to endeavour: to make an effort :—*pa.t.* and *pa.p.* tried (trīd).—*n.* **Tri′er**. [Fr. *trier*, to pick out, to cull (the grain from the straw), from an assumed L. *tritare*—*tero*, *tritum*, to rub. See **Trite**.]

**Trying**, trī′ing, *adj.* making trial or proof of: adapted to try: searching: severe.

**Trysail**, trī′sāl, *n.* a reduced sail used by small craft, instead of their mainsail, in a storm: a small fore-and-aft sail set with a boom and gaff.

**Tryst**, trīst, *n.* an appointment to meet: appointed place of meeting. [Conn. with **Trust**.]

**Tsar**, tsär, *n.* better form of **Czar**.

**Tsetse**, tset′sē, *n.* a dipterous insect of South Africa, whose bite is fatal to the ox, horse, and dog.

**Tub**, tub, *n.* a two-handed open wooden vessel: a vessel made of staves and hoops: a small cask: anything like a tub: the quantity a tub holds. [Low Ger. *tubbe*, Dut. *tobbe*.]

**Tube**, tūb, *n.* a pipe: a long, hollow cylinder for the conveyance of fluids, &c.: a canal.—*v.t.* to furnish with a tube. [Fr.—L. *tubus*.]

**Tuber**, tū′bėr, *n.* a knob in roots: a rounded, fleshy underground stem, as in the potato. [L., 'a swelling,' from root of L. *tumeo*, to swell. Cf. **Tumid**.]

**Tubercle**, tū′bėr-kl, *n.* a small *tuber* or swelling: a pimple: a small knob on leaves: a small mass of diseased matter frequently found in the lungs. —**Tu′bercled**, *adj.* having tubercles. [L. *tuber-culum*. dim. of **Tuber**.]

**Tubercular**, tū-bėr′kū-lar, **Tuberculous**, tū-bėr′-kū-lus, *adj.* pertaining to *tubercles*: pimpled: affected with or caused by tubercles.

**Tuberous**, tū′bėr-us, **Tuberose**, tū′bėr-ōs, *adj.* having or consisting of *tubers*: knobbed.—*n.* **Tuberos′ity**.

**Tubing**, tūb′ing, *n.* a length of *tube*: tubes collectively: materials for tubes.

**Tubular**, tūb′ū-lar, *adj.* having the form of a *tube* or pipe: consisting of a tube or pipe.

**Tubulated**, tūb′ū-lāt-ed, **Tubulous**, tūb′ū-lus, *adj.* having the form of a *tube* or pipe: having a small tube: containing or composed of small tubes. [dim. of *tubus*.]

**Tubule**, tūb′ūl, *n.* a small *tube* or pipe. [L. *tubulus*.]

**Tuck**, tuk, *v.t.* to *draw* or press *in* or together: to fold under: to gather up: to inclose by pressing clothes closely around.—*n.* a horizontal fold in a garment. [Low Ger. *tucken*, Ger. *zucken*, to draw in, to shrug ; conn. with **Tow** and **Tug**.]

**Tucker**, tuk′ėr, *n.* a piece of cloth *tucked* or drawn over the bosom, worn by women and children.

**Tuesday**, tūz′dā, *n.* the third day of the week. [A.S. *Tiwes dæg* (*lit.*) 'the *day* of *Tiw*' (the god of war) = Dan. *die*(*n*)*s-tag*; cf. L. *dies Martis*. *Tiw* (Ice. *Tyr*, O. Ger. *Zio*) is conn. with Gr. *Zeus*, *Dios*, and L. *deus*, *divus*.]

**Tufa**, tū′fa, **Tuff**, tuf, *n.* a rock formed from the ash or powder from a volcano: also applied to any light, porous rock. [It. *tufo*, Fr. *tuf*—L. *tofus*.]

**Tuft**, tuft, *n.* a number of small things in a knot: a cluster: a dense head of flowers.—*v.t.* to separate into tufts: to adorn with tufts.—*adjs.* **Tuft′ed**, **Tuft′y**. [Fr. *touffe*, from the Teut., as Low Ger. *topp*, Ger. *zopf*. See **Top**.]

**Tuft-hunter**, tuft′-hunt′ėr, *n.* one over-eager to form acquaintance with persons of rank or consequence: a mean hanger-on of the great. [From the *tuft* or tassel in the cap worn by noblemen at the English universities.]

**Tug**, tug, *v.t.* to *pull* with effort: to drag along.— *v.i.* to pull with great effort :—*pr.p.* tugg′ing; *pa.t.* and *pa.p.* tugged.—*n.* a strong pull: a steam-vessel for towing ships. [A.S. *teon*, *teohan*, pl. of pa.t. *tugon*; closely conn. with **Tuck** and **Tow**, *v.*]

**Tuition**, tū-ish′un, *n.* care over a young person: teaching. [Lit. 'a looking to,' 'taking care of,' L. *tuitio*—*tueor*, *tuitus*, to see, to look to.]

**Tulip**, tū′lip, *n.* a bulbous garden-plant with beautiful flowers. [Fr. *tulipe*—Port. *tulipa*, from Pers. and Turk. *tulbend*, *dulbend* (whence E. **Turban**), from the fancied resemblance of the flower to a turban folded round the head.]

**Tulle**, tool, *n.* a delicate kind of silk net or lace. [Fr.; so named from the town of *Tulle*, in the south-west of France.]

**Tumble**, tum′bl, *v.i.* to fall: to come down suddenly and violently: to roll: to twist the body, as a mountebank.—*v.t.* to throw headlong : to turn over: to throw about while examining.—*n.* act of tumbling: a fall: a rolling over. [From a Teut. root seen in Dan. *tumle*—Ice. *tumla* (A.S. *tumbian*); and from which also are the Fr. *tomber* and It. *tombolare*.]

**Tumbler**, tum′blėr, *n.* one who *tumbles*: a large drinking-glass, so called because formerly, having a pointed base, it could not be set down without *tumbling*: a domestic pigeon, so called from its *tumbling* on the wing.

**Tumbrel**, tum′brel, **Tumbril**, tum′bril, *n.* a cart with two wheels for conveying the tools of pioneers, artillery stores, &c. [O. Fr. *tomberel* (Fr. *tombereau*)—Fr. *tomber*, to fall, because the body of the cart could be tumbled without unyoking. Cf. **Tumble**.]

**Tumefaction**, tū-me-fak′shun, *n.* act of *tumefying*: tumour: swelling.

**Tumefy**, tū′me-fī, *v.t.* to cause to swell.—*v.i.* to swell: to rise in a tumour :—*pa.t.* and *pa.p.* tū′mefīed. [L. *tumefacio*—*tumeo*, to swell, and *facio*, to make.]

**Tumid**, tū′mid, *adj.*, *swollen* or enlarged: inflated: falsely sublime: bombastic.—*adv.* **Tu′midly.**—*n.* **Tu′midness.** [L. *tumidus*—*tumeo*, to swell.]

**Tumour, Tumor**, tū′mor, *n.* a diseased *swelling* of any part of the body. [L.—*tumeo*, to swell.]

**Tumular**, tū′mū-lar, *adj.* formed in a *heap*: consisting in a heap. [Formed from L. *tumulus*, a heap. From **Tumulus**.]

**Tumulous**, tū′mū-lus, *adj.* full of *mounds* or hillocks. [From **Tumulus**.]

**Tumult**, tū′mult, *n.* uproar of a multitude: violent agitation with confused sounds. [L. *tumultus*, from root of *tumeo*, to swell.]

**Tumultuary**, tū-mult′ū-ar-i, **Tumultuous**, tū-mult′ū-us, *adj.* full of *tumult*: disorderly: agitated: noisy.—*adv.* **Tumult′uously.**—*n.* **Tumult′uousness.**

**Tumulus**, tū′mū-lus, *n.* a mound of earth over a grave: a barrow :—*pl.* **Tu′mulī.** [L., 'a heap' —*tumeo*, to swell.]

**Tun**, tun, *n.* (*orig.*) a large *cask*: then a measure of capacity for liquids = 2 pipes, 4 hogsheads, or 252 gallons. [A.S. *tunne*, with similar forms in all the Teut., Romance, and Celt. tongues, the common source prob. being the L. *tina*, a wine-vessel. Doublet **Ton**.]

**Tune**, tūn, *n.* (*mus.*) a melodious succession of notes or chords in a particular key: the relation of notes and intervals to each other causing melody: state of giving the proper sound : harmony : a melody or air.—*v.t.* to cause to produce the proper sounds.—*adj.* **Tun′able.** [A variation of **Tone**, prob. partly due to the influence of A.S. *dyne*, E. **Din**.]

**Tuneful**, tūn′fool, *adj.* full of tune or harmony : melodious : musical.—*adv.* **Tune′fully.**

**Tuneless**, tūn′les, *adj.* without tune or melody.

**Tuner**, tūn′ėr, *n.* one who *tunes* or adjusts the sounds of musical instruments.

**Tungsten**, tung′sten, *n.* a very heavy metal. [Sw. *tungsten—tung*, heavy ; *sten*, stone.]

**Tunic**, tū′nik, *n.* a loose frock worn by females and boys: in R. Cath. Church, a long under-garment worn by the officiating clergy : (*anat.*) a membrane that covers some organ: (*bot.*) a covering, as of a seed: (*mil.*) the coat at present worn by English soldiers on full-dress occasions. [Fr. *tunique*—L. *tunica*, an under-garment worn in ancient Rome by both sexes.]

**Tunicate**, tū′nik-āt, **Tunicated**, tū′nik-āt-ed, *adj.* (*bot.*) covered with a *tunic* or with layers. [L.]

**Tunicle**, tū′ni-kl, *n.* a *little tunic*: a kind of long robe. [L. *tunicula*, dim. of *tunica*, a tunic.]

**Tuning-fork**, tūn′ing-fork, *n.* a steel two-pronged instrument, designed when set in vibration to give a musical sound of a certain pitch.

**Tunnel**, tun′el, *n.* a passage cut through a hill or under a river, &c.—*v.t.* to make a passage through: to hollow out :—*pr.p.* tunn′elling; *pa.t.* and *pa.p.* tunn′elled. [An extension of

**Tun** ; on the model of Fr. *tonnelle*, an arbour, (*lit.*) 'a *tun*-shaped vault,' dim. of *tonne*, a tun. See also **Ton**.]

**Tunny**, tun′i, *n.* a very large fish of the mackerel family, fished chiefly on the Mediterranean coasts. [Lit. 'the *darting* fish,' L. *thunnus*, Gr. *thynnos*—*thynō*, to dart or rush along.]

**Tup**, tup, *n.* a ram. [Conn. with Low Ger. *toppen*, Ger. *tupfen*, to touch.]

**Turanian**, tūr-ān′yan, *adj.* a name sometimes used to include all the languages of Europe and Asia not Aryan or Semitic, with the exception of Chinese and its cognate dialects. [From *Turan*, a name given (in contrast to Iran ′or Persia) to the region lying north of that country.]

**Turban**, tur′ban, *n.* a head-covering worn by eastern nations, consisting of a cap with a sash wound round it : a circular head-dress worn by ladies : the whole whorls of a shell. [Earlier forms *turbant, tulipant* (Fr. *turban*), through Port. *turbante*, from Pers. *dulbend*, a piece of muslin wound round the head. Cf. **Tulip**.]

**Turbaned**, tur′band, *adj.* wearing a *turban*.

**Turbary**, turb′ar-i, *n.* the right of digging peat: a place where peat is dug. [From *turba*, the Low L. form of **Turf**.]

**Turbid**, tur′bid, *adj.* disordered : having the sediment disturbed : muddy: thick.—*adv.* **Tur′bidly.**—*n.* **Tur′bidness.** [L. *turbidus—turba*, confusion, tumult.]

**Turbot**, tur′bot, *n.* a large, flat, round fish, esteemed a delicacy. [Fr., a dim. formed from L. *turbo*, a spinning-top, from the likeness of the fish to a top ; cf. the Gr. *rhombos*, sig. a top, also a turbot.]

**Turbulent**, tur′bū-lent, *adj.*, *tumultuous*, disturbed : in violent commotion : disposed to disorder: restless : producing commotion.—*ns.* **Tur′bulence, Tur′bulency.**—*adv.* **Tur′bulently.** [L. *turbulentus—turba*, tumult, a crowd.]

**Tureen**, tū-rēn′, *n.* a large dish for holding soup at table. [Lit. 'an earthenware¹ dish,' Fr. *terrine*—L. *terra*, earth.]

**Turf**, turf, *n.* the surface of land matted with the roots of grass, &c. : a cake of turf cut off : sod: peat : race-ground : horseracing :—*pl.* **Turfs.**—*v.t.* to cover with turf or sod. [A.S. *turf* ; Ice. *torf* ; perh. conn. with Sans. *dûrvâ*, millet-grass.]

**Turfy**, turf′i, *adj.* abounding with, made of, or covered with *turf*: having the nature or appearance of turf.—*n.* **Turf′iness.**

**Turgent**, tur′jent, *adj.*, *swelling* : rising into a tumour : inflated: bombastic.—*adv.* **Tur′gently.** [L. *turg-ens, -entis*, pr.p. of *turgeo*, to swell.]

**Turgescent**, tur-jes′ent, *adj.*, *swelling* : growing big.—*ns.* **Turgesc′ence, Turgesc′ency.** [L. *turgesco—turgeo*, to swell.]

**Turgid**, tur′jid, *adj.*, *swollen* : extended beyond the natural size: pompous : bombastic.—*adv.* **Tur′gidly.**—*ns.* **Tur′gidness, Turgid′ity.** [L. *turgidus—turgeo*, to swell.]

**Turk**, turk, *n.* a native of *Turkey*.—*adj.* **Turk′ish.**

**Turkey**, turk′i, *n.* a large gallinaceous bird, a native of America, so called because erroneously supposed to have come from *Turkey*.

**Turkey-red**, turk′i-red, *n.* a fine durable red dye, obtained from madder, but now mostly prepared chemically, first produced in *Turkey*.

**Turkey-stone**, turk′i-stōn, *n.* a kind of oilstone brought from *Turkey*, and used for hones.

**Turkis**, turk′is, *n.* an older spelling of **Turquoise**.

**Turkish-bath**, turk′ish-bäth, *n.* a kind of hot-air bath in which the patient, after being sweated, is rubbed down, and conducted through a series of cooling chambers until he regains his normal temperature.

**Turmeric,** tur'mėr-ik, *n.* the root of an E. Indian plant, used as a yellow dye, in curry-powder, and as a chemical test for the presence of alkalies. [Ety. unknown.]

**Turmoil,** tur'moil, *n.* harassing labour: disturbance. [Perh. from the L. *tremo,* to shake, modified by the influence of **Turn** and **Moil**.]

**Turmoil,** tur-moil', *v.t.* to harass with commotion: to weary.—*v.i.* to be disquieted or in commotion.

**Turn,** turn, *v.i.* to whirl round: to hinge: to depend: to issue: to take a different direction or tendency: to become by a change: to be turned in a lathe: to sour: to become giddy: to be nauseated: to change from ebb to flow or from flow to ebb: to become inclined in the other direction.—*v.t.* to cause to revolve: to reverse: to change the position or the direction of: to make to nauseate, or make giddy: direct the mind to: infatuate or make mad: to cause to return with profit: to transfer: to convert: to form in a lathe: to shape.—*n.* act of turning: new direction, or tendency: a walk to and fro: change: a winding: a bend: form: manner: opportunity, convenience: act of kindness or malice.—*n.* **Turn'er.—By turns,** one after another, alternately. [A.S. *tyrnan;* Ger. *turnen;* Fr. *tourner;* all from L. *tornare,* to turn in a lathe—*tornus,* a turner's wheel—Gr. *tornos.*]

**Turncoat,** turn'kōt, *n.* one who *turns* his *coat,* that is, abandons his principles or party.

**Turnery,** turn'ėr-i, *n.* art of *turning* or of shaping by a lathe: things made by a turner.

**Turning,** turn'ing, *n.* a winding: deviation from the proper course: turnery:—*pl.* chips.

**Turning-point,** turn'ing-point, *n.* the *point* on which a question *turns,* and which decides the case: a grave and critical period.

**Turnip,** tur'nip, *n.* a plant having a solid bulbous root used as food. [From A.S. *næpe*—L. *napus,* with the prefix *tur-,* a corr. of *terræ,* ' of the earth.']

**Turnkey,** turn'kē, *n.* one who *turns* the *keys* in a prison: a warder.

**Turnpike,** turn'pīk, *n.* a gate set across a road to stop those liable to toll: a turnpike-road. [Orig. a frame consisting of two crossbars armed with *pikes,* and *turning* on a post.]

**Turnpike-road,** turn'pīk-rōd, *n.* a *road* on which *turnpikes* or toll-gates are established.

**Turnsole,** turn'sōl, *n.* a plant so called because its flowers turn towards the sun. [Fr.—*tourner* (see **Turn**) and *sol,* for *soleil*—L. *sol,* the sun.]

**Turnspit,** turn'spit, *n.* one who *turns* a *spit:* a person engaged in some menial occupation: (formerly) a dog employed to turn a spit.

**Turnstile,** turn'stīl, *n.* a revolving frame in a foot-path which prevents the passage of cattle.

**Turn-table,** turn'-tā'bl, *n.* Same as **Traverse-table.**

**Turpentine,** tur'pen-tīn, *n.* the resinous juice of the *terebinth* and other trees. [Fr. *térébenthine* —L. *terebinthina (resina),* (the resin) of the terebinth.]

**Turpitude,** tur'pi-tūd, *n.* baseness: extreme depravity or wickedness: vileness of principles and actions. [L. *turpitudo*—*turpis,* foul, base; conn. with Sans. root *tarp,* to be ashamed.]

**Turquoise,** tur'koiz, *n.* a bluish-green mineral from Persia, valued as a gem. [Fr. (lit. ' Turkish '), so called because first brought from Turkey. Doublet **Turkish.**]

**Turret,** tur'et, *n.* a *small tower* on a building and

rising above it. [O. Fr. *touret* (Fr. *tourelle*), dim. of Fr. *tour,* a tower. See **Tower.**]

**Turreted,** tur'et-ed, *adj.* furnished with *turrets:* formed like a tower.

**Turret-ship,** tur'et-ship, *n.* an ironclad *ship* of war, whose guns are placed in one or more revolving *turrets* placed on deck.

**Turtle,** tur'tl, **Turtle-dove,** tur'tl-duv, *n.* a species of pigeon of a very tender and affectionate disposition. [A.S. *turtle;* Ger. *turtel,* Fr. *tourtereau, tourterelle;* all from the L. name *turtur,* an imitation of the bird's note; cf. Heb. *tôr.*]

**Turtle,** tur'tl, *n.* the sea-*tortoise,* a family of reptiles having their back covered by a horny case, the flesh of some of the species being considered a great delicacy. [A corr. of **Tortoise,** under influence of **Turtle** (above).]

**Tuscan,** tus'kan, *adj.* of or belonging to *Tuscany* in Italy: denoting one of the five orders of architecture, the oldest and simplest. [L.]

**Tush,** tush, *int.* pshaw! be silent! an exclamation of scorn or impatience. [Cf. Ger. *tuschen, vertuschen,* to hush up.]

**Tusk,** tusk, *n.* a long, pointed tooth on either side of the mouth of certain rapacious animals.—*adjs.* **Tusk'ed, Tusk'y.** [A.S. *tusc, tux.*]

**Tussle,** tus'el, *n.* a struggle. [A.S. *tæsan,* to pluck, hence related to **Tease,** and perh. **Tassel,** a teased-out knot of wool.]

**Tussock,** tus'ok, *n.* a tuft of grass or twigs. [From obs. *tur,* a lock of hair, which is of Celt. origin.]

**Tut,** tut, *int.* an exclamation of checking or rebuke. [Cf. Ice. and Gael. *tut.*]

**Tutelage,** tū'tel-āj, *n.,* *guardianship:* state of being under a guardian. [Formed from the L. *tutela*—*tutor,* to guard—*tueor,* to see, to look to. Cf. **Tuition** and **Tutor.**]

**Tutelar,** tū'te-lar, **Tutelary,** tū'te-lar-i, *adj.* protecting: having the charge of a person or place. [L. *tutelaris*—*tutela.* See **Tutelage.**]

**Tutor,** tū'tor, *n.* one who *looks to* or takes care of: one who has charge of the education of another: one who hears the lessons of and examines students: a teacher.—*fem.* **Tu'toress.**—*v.t.* to instruct: to treat with authority or sternness. —*n.* **Tu'torship.** [L. ' a guardian '—*tueor, tuitus,* to look to. Cf. **Tuition** and **Tutelage.**]

**Tutorage,** tū'tor-āj, *n.* the office or authority of a *tutor:* education, as by a tutor.

**Tutorial,** tū-tō'ri-al, *adj.* belonging to or exercised by a *tutor.*

**Twaddle,** twod'l, *v.i.* to talk in a silly manner.—*n.* silly talk.—*n.* **Twadd'ler.** [Earlier form *twattle,* an imitative word; cf. **Tattle, Twitter.**]

**Twain,** twān, *n., two.* [A.S. *twegen,* two, Ice. *tveir.* See **Two** and **Between.**]

**Twang,** twang, *n.* a sharp, quick sound, as of a tight string when pulled and let go: a nasal tone of voice.—*v.i.* to sound as a tight string pulled and let go: to sound with a quick, sharp noise. —*v.t.* to make to sound with a twang. [Imitative.]

**'Twas,** twoz, contr. of *it was.*

**Tweak,** twēk, *v.t.* to twitch, to pull: to pull with sudden jerks.—*n.* a sharp pinch or twitch. [A.S. *twiccian;* Ger. *zwicken.* By-form **Twitch.**]

**Tweed,** twēd, *n.* a kind of woollen *twilled* cloth of various patterns, much used for men's suits. [From a mistaken reading of ' tweels ' upon an invoice, not, as supposed, from the Tweed valley, where the manufacture commenced.]

**Tweezers,** twēz'ėrz, *n.sing.* nippers: small pincers for pulling out hairs, &c. [Obs. *tweeze,* a surgeon's case of instruments—Fr. *étuis,* pl. of *étui,* a case, a box; prob. influenced also by **Tweak.**]

**Twelfth,** twelfth, *adj.* the last of *twelve.*—*n.* one of twelve equal parts. [A.S. *twelfta—twelf.*]

**Twelfth-day,** twelfth'-dā, **Twelfth'-tide,** -tīd, *n.* the *twelfth day* after Christmas, the Epiphany.

**Twelve,** twelv, *adj.* ten and two.—*n.* the number next after eleven: the figures representing twelve. [A.S. *twelf* (Ger. *zwölf,* and Goth. *twa-lif*), that is, 'two and ten' (for *twa-* see **Two,** and for *-lif* see **Eleven.**)]

**Twelvemonth,** twelv'munth, *n., twelve months:* a year.

**Twentieth,** twen'ti-eth, *adj.* the last of *twenty.*—*n.* one of twenty equal parts. [A.S. *twentigtha.*]

**Twenty,** twen'ti, *adj., twice ten:* nineteen and one: an indefinite number.—*n.* the number next after nineteen: the figures representing twenty. [A.S. *twentig,* for *twantig,* from *twa,* two, *tig* (Goth. *tigus*), ten; L. *(d)viginti,* Sans. *vin-shati.*]

**Twice,** twīs, *adv., two times:* once and again: doubly. [O. E. *twies,* A.S. *twiwa—twa,* two.]

**Twig,** twig, *n.* a small shoot or branch of a tree. [A.S. *twig;* cog. with Ger. *zweig;* from the root of **Two.**]

**Twiggy,** twig'i, *adj.* abounding in *twigs* or shoots.

**Twilight,** twī'līt, *n.* the faint light after sunset and before sunrise: an uncertain view.—*adj.* of twilight: faintly illuminated: obscure. [Lit. '*tween light,*' A.S. *twi-,* from *twa,* E. **Two,** and **Light.**]

**Twill,** twil, or **Tweel,** twēl, *n.* an appearance of diagonal lines in cloth, caused by making the weft pass over one and under *two* or more threads of the warp: a fabric with a twill.—*v.t.* to weave with a twill. [Developed from the root of **Two** (A.S. *twa*); cf. Ger. *zwillich,* ticking—*zwei,* two.]

**Twin,** twin, *n.* one of *two* born at a birth: one very like another.—*adj.* being one of two born at a birth: very like another.—*v.i.* to be born at the same birth: to bring forth two at once: to be paired or suited:—*pr.p.* twinn'ing; *pa.p.* twinned.—**The Twins,** the constellation Gemini. [A.S. *twinn,* double—**Two;** Ice. *tvennr.*]

**Twine,** twīn, *n.* a cord composed of *two* or more threads twisted together: a twist.—*v.t.* to wind, as two threads together: to twist together: to wind about.—*v.i.* to unite closely: to bend: to make turns: to ascend spirally round a support. [A.S. *twin,* double-thread (cog. with Dut. *twijn*)—*twa,* E. **Two.**]

**Twinge,** twinj, *v.t.* to *twitch* or pinch: to affect with a sharp, sudden pain.—*v.i.* to have or suffer a sudden, sharp pain, like a twitch.—*n.* a twitch: a pinch: a sudden, sharp pain. [M. E. *twengen,* cog. with Ger. *zwingen,* to constrain. Cf. **Thong.**]

**Twinkle,** twing'kl, *v.i.* to shine with a trembling, sparkling light: to sparkle: to open and shut the eyes rapidly: to quiver.—*n.* **Twink'ler.** [A.S. *twinclian,* a nasalised form of *twiccian,* with the freq. termination *-le.* See **Twitch.**]

**Twinkle,** twing'kl, **Twinkling,** twing'kling, *n.* a quick motion of the eye: the time occupied by a wink: an instant.

**Twirl,** twėrl, *v.t.* to turn round rapidly, esp. with the fingers.—*v.i.* to turn round rapidly: to be whirled round.—*n.* a whirl: a rapid circular motion. [A.S. *thwiril;* cog. with Ger. *quirl, querl,* a stirring-spoon—O. Ger. *tuirl;* from the root of **Queer** and **Thwart.**]

**Twist,** twist, *v.t.* to twine: to unite or form by winding together: to form from several threads: to encircle with something: to wreathe: to wind spirally: to turn from the true form or meaning: to insinuate.—*v.i.* to be united by winding.—*n.* that which is twisted: a cord: a single thread: manner of twisting: a contortion: a small roll of tobacco.—*n.* **Twist'er.** [A.S. *twist,* cloth of double thread—*twa,* E. **Two;** contrast Dut. *twist,* Ger. *zwist,* discord—*zwei,* **Two.**]

**Twit,** twit, *v.t.* to remind of some fault, &c. :—*pr.p.* twitt'ing; *pa.t.* and *pa.p.* twitt'ed.—*n.* **Twitt'er.** [A.S. *æt-witan,* to reproach—*æt,* against, *witan* (Scot. *wyte,* Ger. *ver-weisen*), to blame; closely conn. with root of **Wit.**]

**Twitch,** twich, *v.t.* to pull with a sudden jerk: to pluck: to snatch.—*n.* a sudden, quick pull: a spasmodic contraction of the muscles.—*n.* **Twitch'er.** [A.S. *twiccian,* to pluck; cog. with Ger. *zwicken,* and prob. influenced by **Touch.** By-form **Tweak.**]

**Twitter,** twit'ėr, *n.* a tremulous broken sound: a slight trembling of the nerves.—*v.i.* to make a succession of small tremulous noises: to feel a slight trembling of the nerves. [Allied to Ger. *zwitschern,* Sw. *qvittra,* prob. imitative; cf. **Titter.**]

**Twittering,** twit'ėr-ing, *n.* act of *twittering:* the sound of twittering: nervous excitement.

**Twittingly,** twit'ing-li, *adv.* in a *twitting* manner.

**Two,** tōō, *adj.* one and one.—*n.* the sum of one and one: a figure representing two. [A.S. *twa;* cog. with Ger. *zwei,* Goth. *twai;* also with Gr. *dyō,* L. *duo,* Sans. *dva,* Celt. *da, do.*]

**Two-edged,** tōō'-ejd, *adj.* having *two edges.*

**Twofold,** tōō'fōld, *adj., folded twice:* multiplied by two: double.—*adv.* doubly. [of Japan.]

**Tycoon,** tī-kōōn', *n.* formerly the political sovereign

**Tympanal,** tim'pan-al, **Tympanic,** tim-pan'ik, *adj.* like a *drum:* pertaining to the tympanum.

**Tympanitis,** tim-pan-ī'tis, *n.* inflammation of the membrane of the ear.

**Tympanum,** tim'pan-um, *n.* (*anat.*) the membrane which separates the external from the internal ear, often called the *drum* of the ear: (*arch.*) the triangular space between sloping and horizontal cornices, or in the corners or sides of an arch: the panel of a door. [L.—Gr. *tympanon, typanon,* a kettledrum—*typtō,* to strike.]

**Type,** tīp, *n.* a mark or figure *struck* or stamped upon something: an emblem or figure of something to come: a raised letter, &c. in metal or wood used in printing: the whole types used in printing: a model in nature made the subject of a copy: (*nat. hist.*) that which combines best the characteristics of a group: (*med.*) the order in which the symptoms of a disease exhibit themselves.—*adj.* **Typ'al.** [Fr.—L. *typus,* Gr. *typos—typtō,* to strike.] [casts printers' *type.*

**Typefounder,** tīp'fownd-ėr, *n.* one who *founds* or

**Type-metal,** tīp'-met'al, *n., metal* used for making *types,* a compound of lead and antimony.

**Typhoid,** tī'foid, *adj.* pertaining to a form of enteric fever, which is very *similar* in some of its symptoms to *typhus.* [Gr. *typhōdēs—typhos,* and *eidos,* likeness. See **Typhus.**]

**Typhoon,** tī-fōōn', *n.* a violent hurricane which occurs in the Chinese seas. [Chin. *tei-fun,* 'hot wind.']

**Typhous,** tī'fus, *adj.* relating to *typhus.*

**Typhus,** tī'fus, *n.* a very fatal kind of continued fever, often occurring as an epidemic. [Through Late L. from Gr. *typhos,* smoke, hence stupor arising from fever—*typhō,* to smoke, from the root of L. *fumus* (see **Fume**), and E. **Damp.**]

---

fāte, fär; mē, hér; mīne; mōte; mūte; mōōn; *then.*     

*Words in* UN *not found below are to be explained by prefixing* not, *or want of, to the simple word.*

**Typic**, tip´ik, **Typical**, tip´ik-al, *adj.* pertaining to or constituting a *type*: emblematic: figurative: (*nat. hist.*) combining the characteristics of a group.—*adv.* **Typ´ically**. [Late L.—Gr. *typikos—typos,* a type.]

**Typify**, tip´i-fī, *v.t.* to *make* a *type* of: to represent by an image or resemblance: to prefigure:—*pa.t.* and *pa.p.* typ´ified. [L. *typus,* type, *facio,* to make.]

**Typographer**, tī-pog´raf-èr, *n.* a printer.

**Typographic**, tip-o-graf´ik, **Typograph´ical**, -al, *adj.* pertaining to *typography* or printing.—*adv.* **Typograph´ically.**

**Typography**, tī-pog´raf-i, *n.* the art of printing: (*orig.*) the art of representing by *types* or symbols. [Gr. *typos,* type, *graphō,* to write.]

**Typology**, tī-pol´o-ji, *n.* the doctrine of Scripture types or figures. [Gr. *typos,* a type, and *logos,* a discourse.]

**Tyrannic**, tī-ran´ik, **Tyrann´ical**, -al, **Tyrannous**, tir´an-us, *adj.* pertaining to or suiting a *tyrant*: unjustly severe: imperious: despotic.—*advs.* **Tyrann´ically**, **Tyr´annously** [L.—Gr.]

**Tyrannise**, tir´an-īz, *v.i.* to act as a *tyrant*: to rule with oppressive severity.

**Tyranny**, tir´an-i, *n.* the government or authority of a *tyrant*: absolute monarchy cruelly administered: oppression: cruelty. [L.—Gr. *tyrannis.*]

**Tyrant**, tī´rant, *n.* one who uses his power oppressively: (*orig.*) an absolute monarch. [O. Fr. *tirant* (Fr. *tyran*)—L. *tyrannus*—Gr. *tyrannos,* Doric for *koiranos—kyros, kyrios,* a lord, master.]

**Tyrian**, tir´i-an, *adj.* being of a deep purple colour, like the dye formerly prepared at *Tyre.*

**Tyro**, tī´ro, *n.* one learning any art: one not well acquainted with a subject:—*pl.* **Ty´ros**. [L. *tiro,* a young recruit.]

## U

**Ubiquitous**, ū-bik´wi-tus, *adj.* being *everywhere.*

**Ubiquity**, ū-bik´wi-ti, *n.* existence *everywhere* at the same time: omnipresence. [Fr. *ubiquité,* formed from L. *ubīque,* everywhere.]

**Udal**, ū´dal, *adj.* applied to land held solely by uninterrupted succession, under no feudal superior.—*ns.* **U´dal,** a freehold estate, **U´daller,** a holder of such. [Ice. *odhal,* a homestead. See **Allodial.**]

**Udder**, ud´ėr, *n.* the milk-vessel of a female (esp. of a lower animal). [A.S. *úder;* cog. with Ger. *euter;* also conn. with L. *uber,* Gr. *outhar,* Sans. *ûdhar.*]

**Ugly**, ug´li, *adj.* offensive to the eye: deformed: hateful: ill-natured.—*n.* **Ug´liness**. [Ice. *ugglígr,* frightful, *uggr,* fear, akin to Goth. *ogan,* and A.S. *oge,* fear.]

**Uhlan**, ū´lan, *n.* one of a kind of light cavalry, famous esp. in the Prussian army. [Polish *ulan,* orig. a light Tartar horseman—Turk. *oghlan,* a young man.]

**Ukase**, ū-kās´, *n.* a Russian imperial decree having the force of law. [Russian, from a Slav. root sig. 'to point out.']

**Ulcer**, ul´sėr, *n.* a dangerous sore, discharging matter. [Fr. *ulcère*—L. *ulcus, ulceris,* Gr. *helkos,* a wound.]

**Ulcerate**, ul´sėr-āt, *v.i.* to be formed into an ulcer. —*v.t.* to affect with an ulcer or ulcers.

**Ulceration**, ul-sėr-ā´shun, *n.* process of forming into an ulcer: an ulcer. [L. *ulceratio.*]

**Ulcerous**, ul´sėr-us, *adj.* of the nature of an ulcer.

**Ulna**, ul´na, *n.* the larger of the two bones of the forearm.—*adj.* **Ul´nar.** [L. *ulna,* cog. with E. **Ell,** which see.]

**Ulterior**, ul-tē´ri-or, *adj.* on the *further* side: beyond: further: remoter. [L. *ulterior,* comp. of *ulter,* that is beyond or on the other side.]

**Ultimate**, ul´ti-māt, *adj., furthest*: last: incapable of further division.—*adv.* **Ul´timately.** [L. *ultimus,* the last, superl. of *ulter.*]

**Ultimatum**, ul-ti-mā´tum, *n.* the *last* or final proposition or terms for a treaty:—*pl.* **Ultima´ta.** [Low L., from L. *ultimus,* last.]

**Ultimo**, ul´ti-mo, *adj., in the last* (month). [L.]

**Ultramarine**, ul-tra-ma-rēn´, *adj.* situated *beyond* the *sea.*—*n.* the most beautiful and durable skyblue colour, so called either from its intense blue, or from the *lapis lazuli,* from which it is made, being brought from Asia, beyond the sea. [L. *ultra,* beyond, and **Marine.**]

**Ultramontane**, ul-tra-mon´tān, *adj.* being *beyond* the *mountains* (i. e. the Alps): orig. used in Italy of the French, Germans, &c.; afterwards applied by the northern nations to the Italians, hence its present meaning—viz., holding or denoting extreme views as to the Pope's rights and supremacy. [L. *ultra,* beyond, *montanus,* belonging to a mountain—*mons, montis,* a mountain.]

**Ultramontanism**, ul-tra-mon´tan-izm, *n.* ultramontane or extreme views as to the Pope's rights. [holds to ultramontanism.]

**Ultramontanist**, ul-tra-mon´tan-ist, *n.* one who

**Ultramundane**, ul-tra-mun´dān, *adj.* being *beyond* the *world,* or beyond the limits of our system. [L. *ultra,* beyond, and **Mundane.**]

**Umbel**, um´bel, *n.* a form of flower in which a number of stalks, each bearing a flower, radiate from one centre. [L. *umbella,* dim. of *umbra,* a shade. Doublet **Umbrella.**]

**Umbelliferous**, um-bel-lif´ėr-us, *adj., bearing* or producing *umbels.* [L. *umbella,* and *fero,* to bear.]

**Umber**, um´bėr, *n.* a brown pigment.—**Um´bered,** *adj.* tinged with umber. [So called because orig. obtained from *Umbria,* in Italy.]

**Umbilic**, um-bil´ik, **Umbilical**, um-bil´ik-al, *adj.* pertaining to the *navel.* [L. *umbilĭcus,* the navel, akin to Gr. *omphalos,* the navel, the centre.]

**Umbrage**, um´brāj, *n.* suspicion of injury: offence. [O. Fr. *umbraige* (Fr. *ombrage*)—L. *umbra,* a shadow.]

**Umbrageous**, um-brāj´us, *adj., shady* or forming a shade.—*adv.* **Umbra´geously.**—*n.* **Umbra´geousness.** [Fr. *ombrageux*—L. *umbraticus —umbra.*]

**Umbrella**, um-brel´a, *n.* a familiar covered sliding frame carried in the hand, as a screen from rain or sunshine. [Lit. 'a little shade,' It. *ombrella,* L. *umbella—umbra.* Doublet **Umbel.**]

**Umpire**, um´pīr, *n.* a third person called in to decide a dispute: an arbitrator. [M. E. *impier, nompere—impair,* and *non-pair,* unlike, hence a third party, who gives his casting vote—L. *impar,* uneven.]

**Unaccountable**, un-ak-kownt´a-bl, *adj.* not accountable or to be accounted for: not responsible.—**Unaccount´ably,** *adv.* inexplicably.

**Unadvised**, un-ad-vīzd´, *adj.* not advised: not prudent or discreet: rash.—*adv.* **Unadvis´edly.**

**Unanimity**, ū-na-nim´i-ti, *n.* state of being unanimous. [L. *unanimitas.*]

**Unanimous**, ū-nan´i-mus, *adj.* of *one mind*: agreeing in opinion or will: done with the agreement

*Words in* UN *not found below are to be explained by prefixing* not, *or* want of, *to the simple word.*

of all.—*adv.* **Unan'imously.** [L. *unus*, one, and *animus*, mind.]

**Unassuming,** un-as-sūm'ing, *adj.* not assuming : not forward or arrogant : modest.

**Unavailing,** un-a-vāl'ing, *adj.* not availing, or of no avail or effect : useless.

**Unaware,** un-a-wār', **Unawares,** un-a-wārz', *adv.* without being or making aware : suddenly : unexpectedly.

**Unbar,** un-bär', *v.t.* to remove a bar or hinderance : to unfasten : to open.

**Unbelief,** un-be-lēf', *n.* want of belief : disbelief, esp. in divine revelation.

**Unbeliever,** un-be-lēv'er, *n.* one who does not believe, esp. in divine revelation : an incredulous person. [divine revelation.

**Unbelieving,** un-be-lēv'ing, *adj.* not believing, esp.

**Unbend,** un-bend', *v.t.* to free from being in a bent state : to make straight : to free from strain or exertion : to set at ease.

**Unbending,** un-bend'ing, *adj.* not bending : unyielding : resolute.—*adv.* **Unbend'ingly.**

**Unbias,** un-bī'as, *v.t.* to free from bias or prejudice.

**Unbiased,** un-bī'ast, *adj.* free from bias or prejudice : impartial.

**Unbind,** un-bīnd', *v.t.* to remove a band from : to loose : to set free.

**Unblushing,** un-blush'ing, *adj.* not blushing : without shame : impudent. [open.

**Unbolt,** un-bōlt', *v.t.* to remove a bolt from : to

**Unbosom,** un-booz'um, *v.t.* to disclose what is in the bosom or mind : to tell freely.

**Unbound,** un-bownd', *adj.* not bound : loose : wanting a cover.

**Unbounded,** un-bownd'ed, *adj.* not bounded or limited : boundless : having no check or control.

**Unbrace,** un-brās', *v.t.* to undo the braces or bands of : to loose or relax.

**Unbridled,** un-brī'dld, *adj.* unrestrained : licentious. [Lit. 'loosed from the bridle.']

**Unbuckle,** un-buk'l, *v.t.* to loose from buckles : to unfasten.

**Unburden,** un-bur'dn, **Unburthen,** un-bur'*th*n, *v.t.* to take a burden off : to free the mind from any weight or anxiety.

**Unbutton,** un-but'on, *v.t.* to loose the buttons of.

**Uncage,** un-kāj', *v.t.* to set free from a cage.

**Uncase,** un-kās', *v.t.* to take out of a case : to free from a covering. [slavery.

**Unchain,** un-chān', *v.t.* to free from chains or

**Unchurch,** un-church', *v.t.* to deprive of the rights of a church.

**Uncial,** un'shal, *adj.* applied to large round characters used in ancient MSS. [Lit. 'an *inch* long,' L., from *uncia*, a twelfth part, an inch. See **Inch.**]

**Unciform,** un'si-form, *adj.*, *hook*-shaped.—**Un'cinate,** *adj.*, *hooked* at the end. [L. *uncus*, a hook—root *angk*, bent. See **Anchor** and **Angle.**]

**Uncircumcision,** un-sèr-kum-sizh'un, *n.* want of circumcision : (*B.*) those who are not circumcised.

**Unclasp,** un-klasp', *v.t.* to loose the clasp of.

**Uncle,** ung'kl, *n.* the brother of one's father or mother. [O. Fr. (Fr. *oncle*)—L. *avunculus*, extension of *avus*, a grandfather; cf. Lith. *avynas*, uncle.]

**Unclean,** un-klēn', *adj.* not clean : foul : (*B.*) ceremonially impure : sinful : lewd.

**Uncloak,** un-klōk', *v.t.* to take the cloak off.

**Unclose,** un-klōz', *v.t.* to make not close, to open.

**Unclosed,** un-klōzd', *adj.* open.

**Unclothe,** un-klō*th*', *v.t.* to take the clothes off : to make naked. [to unwind.

**Uncoil,** un-koil', *v.t.* to open out from being coiled :

**Unconscionable,** un-kon'shun-a-bl, *adj.* not conformable to *conscience* : unreasonable : inordinate.

**Unconstitutional,** un-kon-sti-tū'shun-al, *adj.* not constitutional : contrary to the constitution.—*adv.* **Unconstitu'tionally.**

**Uncouple,** un-kup'l, *v.t.* to loose from being coupled : to disjoin : to set loose.

**Uncouth,** un-kōōth', *adj.* awkward or ungraceful, esp. in manners or language.—*adv.* **Uncouth'ly.** —*n.* **Uncouth'ness.** [Lit. and orig. 'unknown,' A.S. *uncudh*—*un-*, not, and *cudh*, for *gecudh*, known—*cunnan*, to know. Cf. the history of **Barbarian,** also of **Outlandish.**]

**Uncover,** un-kuv'er, *v.t.* to remove the cover : to lay open.—*v.i.* to take off the hat.

**Unction,** ung'shun, *n.* an *anointing* : that which is used for anointing : ointment : that quality in language which raises emotion or devotion : warmth of address : divine or sanctifying grace. —**Extreme Unction** (in the R. C. Church), the sacrament of anointing persons with consecrated oil in their last hours. [L. *unctio—ungo*, *unctum*, to anoint. Cf. **Anoint.**]

**Unctuosity,** ungt-ū-os'i-ti, *n.* state or quality of being unctuous : oiliness : greasiness.

**Unctuous,** ung'tū-us, *adj.* oily : greasy. [Formed from L. *unctus*, greased (see **Unction**).]

**Uncurl,** un-kurl', *v.t.* to loose from curls or ringlets.—*v.i.* to relax from a curled state.

**Undated,** un'dāt-ed, *adj.*, *waved* or *wavy* : rising and falling in waves. [L. *undatus*, pa.p. of *undo*, to rise in waves—*unda*, a wave.]

**Undaunted,** un-dänt'ed, *adj.* not daunted : bold : intrepid.

**Undeceive,** un-de-sēv', *v.t.* to free from *deception* or mistake.

**Under,** un'dèr, *prep.* in a lower position than : beneath : below : less than : in subjection, subordination, oppression, liability, &c. : during the time of : undergoing.—*adv.* in a lower degree or condition : in subjection : below : less.—*adj.* lower in position, rank, or degree : subject : subordinate. — **Under way,** moving : having commenced a voyage. [A.S. *under*; cog. with Goth. *undar*, Ice. *undir*, Ger. *unter*; and with L. *inter*, Sans. *antar*, among, within. It is made up of **In**, and the comparative suffix seen also in **After, Further**.]

**Underbred,** un'dèr-bred, *adj.* of inferior breeding or manners. [**Under** and **Breed.**]

**Underclay,** un'dèr-klā, *n.* the bed of clay almost always found under coal-seams, considered as the soil in which grew the plants that formed the coal.

**Undercurrent,** un'dèr-kur-ent, *n.* a current under the surface of the water.

**Underdone,** un-dèr-dun', *adj.* done less than is requisite : insufficiently cooked.

**Underdrain,** un'dèr-drān, *n.* a drain under the surface of the ground.

**Undergird,** un-dèr-gird', *v.t.* to gird or bind under or below : to gird round the bottom.

**Undergo,** un-dèr-gō', *v.t.* to go under or be subjected to : to endure or suffer : to pass through : to sustain without sinking.

**Undergraduate,** un-dèr-grad'ū-āt, *n.* a student who has not taken his first *degree*.

**Underground,** un'dèr-grownd, *adj.* and *adv.* under the surface of the ground.

**Undergrowth,** un'dèr-grōth, *n.* shrubs or low woody *plants* growing *under* or among trees : coppice wood.

**Underhand,** un'dèr-hand, *adj.* and *adv.* secretly : by secret means : by fraud. [Lit. 'done with the *hand* underneath.']

*Words in* UN *not found below are to be explained by prefixing* not, *or want of,* to the simple word.

**Underlay,** un-dér-lā′, *v.t.* to lay under or support by something laid under.

**Underlie,** un-dér-lī′, *v.t.* to lie under or beneath.

**Underline,** un-dér-līn′, *v.t.* to draw a line under or below, as a word.

**Underling,** un′dér-ling, *n.* an *under* or inferior person or agent : a sorry mean fellow. [**Under,** and the dim. affix -*ling.*]

**Undermine,** un-dér-mīn′, *v.t.* to form mines under, in order to destroy : to destroy secretly the foundation or support of anything.

**Undermost,** un′dér-mōst, *adj.* lowest in place or condition.

**Underneath,** un-dér-nēth′, *adv.* beneath : below : in a lower place.—*prep.* under : beneath. [**Under,** and A.S. *neothan,* beneath. See **Nether.**]

**Underplot,** un′dér-plot, *n.* a plot under or subordinate to the main plot in a play or tale : a secret scheme.                    [or beneath : to support.

**Underprop,** un-dér-prop′, *v.t.* to prop from under

**Underrate,** un-dér-rāt′, *v.t.* to rate under the value.—**Un′derrate,** *n.* a price less than the worth.

**Undersell,** un-dér-sel′, *v.t.* to sell under or cheaper than another : to defeat fair trade, by selling for too small a price.

**Underset,** un-dér-set′, *v.t.* to set under : to prop. —**Undersett′er,** *n.* (*B.*) prop, support.

**Undershot,** un-dér-shot, *adj.* moved by water passing under the wheel.

**Undersign,** un-dér-sīn′, *v.t.* to sign or write one's name under or at the foot of.

**Understand,** un-dér-stand′, *v.t.* to comprehend : to have just ideas of : to know thoroughly : to be informed of : to learn : to suppose to mean : to mean without expressing : to imply.—*v.i.* to have the use of the intellectual faculties : to be informed : to learn. [A.S. *understandan* (*lit.*) 'to stand under or in the midst of a thing.' **Under** has here its primary sense of among, between, as in L. *inter*; its force is the same as *dis* in distinguish, discern. Cf. L. *intelligo* (= *inter-lego*), to choose between.]

**Understand′ed** (*Pr. Bk.*) used for **Understood.**

**Understanding,** un-dér-stand′ing, *n.* the act of comprehending : the faculty or the act of the mind by which it understands or thinks : the power to understand : knowledge : exact comprehension : agreement of minds : harmony.—*adj.* (*B.*) knowing, skilful.

**Understate,** un-dér-stāt′, *v.t.* to state or represent under or below the truth.

**Undertake,** un-dér-tāk′, *v.t.* to take under one's management : to take upon one's self : to attempt.—*v.i.* to take upon one's self : to be bound.

**Undertaker,** un-dér-tāk′ér, *n.* one who *undertakes :* one who manages funerals.

**Undertaking,** un-dér-tāk′ing, *n.* that which is *undertaken :* any business or project engaged in.

**Undertone,** un′dér-tōn, *n.* an under or low tone.

**Undervaluation,** un-dér-val-ū-ā′shun, *n.* an undervaluing : rate below the worth.

**Undervalue,** un-dér-val′ū, *v.t.* to value under the worth : to esteem lightly.—*n.* a value or price under the real worth : low rate or price.

**Underwent,** un-dér-went′, *pa.t.* of **Undergo.**

**Underwood,** un′dér-wood, *n.* low wood or trees growing under large ones : coppice.

**Underwrite,** un-dér-rīt′, *v.t.* to write under something else : to subscribe : to subscribe one's name to for insurance.—*v.i.* to practise insuring.

**Underwriter,** un′dér-rīt-ér, *n.* one who insures, as shipping, so called because he *underwrites* his name for a certain amount to the conditions of the policy.

**Undo,** un-doo′, *v.t.* to reverse what has been done : to bring to naught : to loose : to open : to unravel : to impoverish : to ruin, as in reputation.

**Undoing,** un-doo′ing, *n.* the reversal of what has been done : ruin.

**Undress,** un-dres′, *v.t.* to take off the dress or clothes : to strip.—**Undress,** un′dres, *n.* a loose dress : the plain dress worn by soldiers when off duty.

**Undulate,** un′dū-lāt, *v.t.* to *wave,* or to move like waves : to cause to vibrate.—*v.i.* to wave : to vibrate. [Low L. *undulo, -atum*—L. *unda,* a wave.]                    [waving motion or vibration.

**Undulation,** un-dū-lā′shun, *n.* an undulating : a

**Undulatory,** un′dū-la-tor-i, *adj.* moving like *waves :* relating to the theory of light which considers its transmission as wave-motion in a medium filling space.

**Unduly,** un-dū′li, *adv.* not according to duty or propriety : improperly.

**Unearth,** un-érth′, *v.t.* to take out of, drive, or draw from the earth or a burrow, as a fox or badger : to uncover.

**Uneasiness,** un-ēz′i-nes, *n.* state of being uneasy or not at ease : want of ease : disquiet.

**Uneasy,** un-ēz′i, *adj.* not at ease : restless : feeling pain : constrained.

**Unevenness,** un-ēv′n-nes, *n.* quality of being not even : want of an even surface : want of smoothness or uniformity.                    [ing : to unfix.

**Unfasten,** un-fas′n, *v.t.* to loose, as from a fasten-

**Unfetter,** un-fet′ér, *v.t.* to take the fetters from : to set at liberty.

**Unfit,** un-fit′, *adj.* unsuitable.—*v.t.* to disqualify.

**Unfix,** un-fiks′, *v.t.* to make not fixed : to loose the fixing of : to unsettle.

**Unflagging,** un-flag′ing, *adj.* not flagging or drooping : maintaining strength or spirit.

**Unfold,** un-fōld′, *v.t.* to open the folds of : to release from a fold : to spread out : to tell.

**Unfurl,** un-furl′, *v.t.* to loose from being furled : to unfold : to spread.

**Ungainly,** un-gān′li, *adj.* awkward : clumsy : uncouth.—*n.* **Ungain′liness.** [M. E. *un-geinliche*—Ice. *gegn* (A.S. *gegn,* Scot. *gane*), which sig. orig. 'direct towards' or 'ready' (as a road), came to mean 'serviceable,' and then 'kind,' 'good.' Cf. **Again** and **Gainsay.**]

**Ungird,** un-gérd′, *v.t.* to free from a girdle or band : to unbind.

**Unguent,** ung′gwent, *n.* ointment. [L. *unguentum*—*unguo, ungo,* to anoint. Cf. **Unction.**]

**Unhallowed,** un-hal′ōd, *adj., unholy:* profane : very wicked.                    [let go.

**Unhand,** un-hand′, *v.t.* to take the hands off : to

**Unharness,** un-här′nes, *v.t.* to take the harness off : to disarm.                    [render unstable.

**Unhinge,** un-hinj′, *v.t.* to take from the hinges : to

**Unhook,** un-hook′, *v.t.* to loose from a hook.

**Unhorse,** un-hors′, *v.t.* to cause to come off, or to throw from a horse.                    [a house or shelter.

**Unhouse,** un-howz′, *v.t.* to deprive of or drive from

**Unicorn,** ū′ni-korn, *n.* a fabulous animal with *one* horn : (*B.*) prob. the bison. [L. *unus,* E. **One,** and *cornu,* E. **Horn.**]

**Uniform,** ū′ni-form, *adj.* having *one* or the same *form :* having always the same manner or character : consistent with itself : agreeing with another.—*n.* a dress or livery of the same kind for persons who belong to the same body, as of a soldier.—*adv.* **U′niformly.** [L. *unus,* one, and **Form.**]

*Words in* UN *not found below are to be explained by prefixing* not, *or* want of, *to the simple word.*

**Uniformity,** ū-ni-form′i-ti, *n.* state of being uniform : agreement with a pattern or rule : sameness : likeness between the parts of a whole.

**Unify,** ū′ni-fī, *v.t.* to *make* into *one.*—*n.* **Unifica′-tion.** [L. *unus,* one, and *facio,* to make.]

**Uniliteral,** ū-ni-lit′ér-al, *adj.* consisting of *one letter* only. [L. *unus,* one, and *litera,* a letter.]

**Union,** ūn′yun, *n.* a *uniting* : that which is united or made one : a body formed by the combination of parts : concord : harmony in colour : agreement between parts : a combination as among workmen for class protection : several parishes united for joint support and management of their poor, also the workhouse for such : (*pl.*) textile fabrics made up of more than one kind of fibre.—**The Union,** the legislative incorporation of England and Scotland in 1707, or of Ireland with both in 1801.—**Union-jack,** the national flag adopted by Great Britain and Ireland, consisting of a union of the crosses of St George, St Andrew, and St Patrick. [Fr. *union*—L. *unio, -onis*—*unus,* E. **One.**]

**Unique,** ū-nēk′, *adj., single* or alone in any quality : without a like or equal. [Fr.—L. *unicus*—*unus.*]

**Unison,** ū′ni-son, *n.,* oneness or agreement of *sound* : concord : harmony. [L. *unus,* one, and *sonus,* a sound. See **Sound.**]

**Unisonance,** ū-nis′o-nans, *n.* state of being *unisonant* : accordance of sounds.

**Unisonant,** ū-nis′o-nant, **Unisonous,** ū-nis′o-nus, *adj.* being in *unison.* [L. *unus,* one, and *sonans,* pr.p. of *sono,* to sound.]

**Unit,** ū′nit, *n., one* : a single thing or person : the least whole number : anything taken as one : any known determinate quantity by constant application of which any other quantity is measured. [L. *unitum,* pa.p. of *unio,* to unite —*unus,* E. **One.**]

**Unitarian,** ū-ni-tā′ri-an, *n.* one who asserts the *unity* of the Godhead as opposed to the Trinity, and ascribes divinity to God the Father only. —*adj.* pertaining to Unitarians or their doctrine. [From L. *unitas,* unity—*unus,* one.]

**Unitarianism,** ū-ni-tā′ri-an-izm, *n.* the doctrines or principles of a Unitarian.

**Unite,** ū-nīt′, *v.t.* to make *one:* to join two or more into one : to join : to make to agree or adhere.—*v.i.* to become one : to grow or act together.—**Unit′edly,** *adv.* in union : together.

**Unity,** ū′ni-ti, *n.,* oneness : state of being one or at one : agreement : the arrangement of all the parts to one purpose or effect : harmony : (*math.*) any quantity taken as one.—**The Unities** (of *place, time,* and *action*), the three canons of the classical drama ; that the scenes should be at the same place, that all the events should be such as might happen within a single day, and that nothing should be admitted not directly relevant to the development of the plot. [Fr. *unité*—L. *unitas*—*unus.*]

**Univalve,** ū′ni-valv, *adj.* having one valve or shell only.—*n.* a shell of one valve only : a mollusc whose shell is composed of a single piece.

**Universal,** ū-ni-vėr′sal, *adj.* comprehending, affecting, or extending to the whole : comprising all the particulars.—*adv.* **Univer′sally.** [L. *universalis*—*universus.* See **Universe.**]

**Universalism,** ū-ni-vėr′sal-izm, *n.* the doctrine or belief of *universal* salvation, or the ultimate salvation of all mankind.—**Univer′salist,** *n.* a believer in universalism.

**Universality,** ū-ni-vėr-sal′i-ti, *n.* state or quality of being *universal.* [L.]

**Universe,** ū′ni-vėrs, *n.* the *whole* system of created

things : all created things viewed as one whole : the world. [L. *universum* (*lit.*) 'turned into one,' 'combined into one whole'—*unus,* one, *verto, versum,* to turn.]

**University,** ū-ni-vėr′si-ti, *n.* a corporation of teachers or assemblage of colleges for teaching the higher branches of learning, and having power to confer degrees. [Orig. 'any community or association,' L. *universitas,* a corporation—*universus.*]

**Univocal,** ū-niv′o-kal, *adj.* having *one voice* or meaning only : having unison of sounds. [L. *univocus*—*unus,* one, *vox, vocis,* a voice.]

**Unkempt,** un′kemt, *adj., uncombed* : unpolished. [Prefix *un-,* and A.S. *cemban,* to comb—*camb,* E. **Comb.**]

**Unkennel,** un-ken′el, *v.t.* to drive from a kennel or hole : to rouse from secrecy or retreat.

**Unknit,** un-nit′, *v.t.* to separate or loose what is knit or knotted : to open.

**Unknot,** un-not′, *v.t.* to free from knots : to untie.

**Unlace,** un-lās′, *v.t.* to loose from being laced : to loose the dress of.

**Unlade,** un-lād′, *v.t.* to *unload* : to take out the cargo of. [been *learned.*

**Unlearn,** un-lėrn′, *v.t.* to forget or lose what has

**Unless,** un-les′, *conj.* at or for less : if not : supposing that not. [Lit. 'on less ;' cf. the Fr. *à moins.*] [from a gun.

**Unlimber,** un-lim′bėr, *v.t.* to remove the limbers

**Unload,** un-lōd′, *v.t.* to take the load from : to discharge : to disburden. [to open.

**Unlock,** un-lok′, *v.t.* to unfasten what is locked :

**Unloose,** un-lōōs′, *v.t.* to make loose : to set free. [A.S. *onlesan* ; intensive of **Loose.**]

**Unmake,** un-māk′, *v.t.* to destroy the make or form and qualities of.—**Unmade′,** *adj.* not made.

**Unman,** un-man′, *v.t.* to deprive of the powers of a man, as courage, &c. : to deprive of men.

**Unmask,** un-mask′, *v.t.* to take a mask or any disguise off : to expose.—*v.i.* to put off a mask.

**Unmeaning,** un-mēn′ing, *adj.* having no meaning : without intelligence.—*n.* **Unmean′ingness.**

**Unmoor,** un-mōōr′, *v.t.* to loose from being moored or anchored. [ing from.

**Unmuffle,** un-muf′l, *v.t.* to take a muffle or cover-

**Unmuzzle,** un-muz′l, *v.t.* to take a muzzle off.

**Unnerve,** un-nėrv′, *v.t.* to deprive of nerve, strength, or vigour : to weaken.

**Unpack,** un-pak′, *v.t.* to take out of a pack : to open. [or equal.

**Unparalleled,** un-par′al-leld, *adj.* without parallel

**Unpeople,** un-pē′pl, *v.t.* to deprive of people.

**Unpin,** un-pin′, *v.t.* to loose what is pinned.

**Unpretending,** un-pre-tend′ing, *adj.* not pretending or making pretence : modest.

**Unravel,** un-rav′l, *v.t.* to take out of a ravelled state : to unfold or explain : to separate.—*v.i.* to be disentangled. [or body.

**Unrest,** un-rest′, *n.* want of rest : disquiet of mind

**Unrig,** un-rig′, *v.t.* to strip of rigging.

**Unrobe,** un-rōb′, *v.t.* to take a robe off : to undress.

**Unroll,** un-rōl′, *v.t.* to roll down : to open out.

**Unroof,** un-rōōf′, *v.t.* to strip the roof off.

**Unroot,** un-rōōt′, *v.t.* to tear up by the roots.

**Unruly,** un-rōō′li, *adj.* regardless of restraint or law.—*n.* **Unru′liness.** [From A.S. *row,* peace ; Scand. *ro,* Ger. *ruhe* ; modified by **Rule.**]

**Unsaddle,** un-sad′l, *v.t.* to take the saddle off : to throw from the saddle. [to retract.

**Unsay,** un-sā′, *v.t.* to recall what has been said :

**Unscathed,** un-skāth′, *adj.* not harmed or injured. [From *un,* not, and **Scathe,** harm.]

# Unscrew            Urgency

*Words in* UN *not found below are to be explained by prefixing* not, *or want of,* to the simple word.

**Unscrew**, un-skrōō′, *v.t.* to loose from screws : to unfasten.      [what is sealed.

**Unseal**, un-sēl′, *v.t.* to remove the seal of : to open

**Unsearchable**, un-sėrch′a-bl, *adj.* not capable of being found out by searching : mysterious.—*n.* **Unsearch′ableness.**—*adv.* **Unsearch′ably.**

**Unseat**, un-sēt′, *v.t.* to throw from or deprive of a seat.

**Unsettle**, un-set′l, *v.t.* to move from being settled : to make uncertain.—*v.i.* to become unfixed.

**Unsex**, un-seks′, *v.t.* to deprive of sex : to make unmanly or unwomanly.

**Unshackle**, un-shak′l, *v.t.* to loose from shackles : to set free.

**Unship**, un-ship′, *v.t.* to take out of a ship or other vessel : to remove from the place where it is fixed or fitted.      [to the eye : ugly.

**Unsightly**, un-sīt′li, *adj.* not sightly or pleasing

**Unstop**, un-stop′, *v.t.* to *free* from a *stopper :* to free from hinderance.

**Unstring**, un-string′, *v.t.* to take the strings off : to relax or loosen.

**Unthread**, un-thred′, *v.t.* to draw out a thread from : to loose the threads.

**Unthrifty**, un-thrift′i, *adj.* not thrifty : without thriftiness.—*adv.* **Unthrift′ily** —*n.* **Unthrift′iness.**      [bind : to loosen.

**Untie**, un-tī′, *v.t.* to loose from being tied : to un-

**Until**, un-til′, *prep.* till : to : as far as (used mostly with respect to time).—*adv.* till : up to the time that. [A.S. *on*, in, and Till, *prep.*]      [tired.

**Untiring**, un-tīr′ing, *adj.* not tiring or becoming

**Unto**, un′too, *prep.*, *to.* [A.S. *on*, in, and To.]

**Untoward**, un-tō′ard, **Untowardly**, un-tō′ard-li, *adj.* not easily guided : froward : awkward : inconvenient.—*adv.* **Unto′wardly.**—*n.* **Unto′wardness.**

**Untruth**, un-trooth′, *n.* falsehood : a lie.

**Untune**, un-tūn′, *v.t.* to put out of tune : to disorder or confuse.

**Untwine**, un-twīn′, *v.t.* to untwist : to open.

**Untwist**, un-twist′, *v.t.* to open what is twisted.

**Unwarp**, un-wawrp′, *v.t.* to change from being warped.      [fatigable.]—*adv.* **Unwea′riedly.**

**Unwearied**, un-wē′rid, *adj.* not tiring : inde-

**Unweave**, un-wēv′, *v.t.* to undo what is *woven.*

**Unwept**, un-wept′, *adj.* not mourned.

**Unwieldy**, un-wēl′di, *adj.* not easily moved or handled. [See Wield.]

**Unwind**, un-wīnd′, *v.t.* to wind down or off.

**Unwittingly**, un-wit′ing-li, *adv.* without knowledge : ignorantly. [See Wit.]

**Unworthy**, un-wur*th*′i, *adj.* not worthy : worthless : unbecoming.

**Unwrap**, un-rap′, *v.t.* to open what is wrapped or folded.      [disjoin.

**Unyoke**, un-yōk′, *v.t.* to loose from a yoke : to

**Up**, up, *adv.* toward a higher place : aloft : on high : from a lower to a higher position, as out of bed, above the horizon, &c. : in a higher position : in a condition of elevation, advance, excitement, &c. : as far as : completely.—*prep.* from a lower to a higher place on or along.— Used *substantively*, as in the *ups* and *downs* of life. [A.S. *up*, *uppe*; Ger. *auf*; L. *sub*, Gr. *hypo*; allied to Over, Above.]

**Upas**, ū′pas, *n.* the juice of the upas-tree of the Philippine Islands : a vegetable poison. [Malay, ' poison.']      [to sustain.

**Upbear**, up-bār′, *v.t.* to bear up : to raise aloft :

**Upbind**, up-bīnd′, *v.t.* to bind up.

**Upbraid**, up-brād′, *v.t.* to charge with something wrong or disgraceful : to reproach : to reprove severely. [A.S. *upgebredan*, to cry out against

—*up*, and *gebredan*, Ice. *bregda*, to charge, reproach.]

**Upbraiding**, up-brād′ing, *n.* a charging with something wrong : act of reproaching.

**Upheave**, up-hēv′, *v.t.* to heave or lift up.—**Upheav′al**, *n.* the raising of surface formations by the action of internal forces.

**Uphill**, up′hil, *adj.* ascending : difficult.

**Uphold**, up-hōld′, *v.t.* to hold up : to sustain : to countenance : to defend : to continue without failing.—*n.* **Uphold′er.**

**Upholsterer**, up-hōl′stėr-ėr, *n.* one who supplies furniture, beds, &c. [Formerly *upholdster*, and *upholster*, a corr. of Upholder.]

**Upholstery**, up-hōl′stėr-i, *n.* furniture, &c. supplied by *upholsterers.*

**Upland**, up′land, *n.*, *upper* or high *land*, as opposed to meadows, river-sides, &c.—*adj.* high in situation : pertaining to uplands.

**Uplift**, up-lift′, *v.t.* to lift up or raise aloft.

**Upmost.** See Upper.

**Upon**, up-on′, *prep.* same as On. [Up and On.]

**Upper**, up′ėr, *adj.* (*comp.* of Up), *further up :* higher in position, dignity, &c. : superior.— *super.* **Upp′ermost, Up′most.** [For affix *-most*, see Aftermost, Foremost.]      [tage.

**Upperhand**, up′ėr-hand, *n.* superiority : advan-

**Uppermost.** See Upper.

**Upright**, up′rīt, *adj.* right or straight up : in an erect position : adhering to rectitude : honest : just.—*adv.* **Up′rightly.**—*n.* **Up′rightness.**

**Uproar**, up′rōr, *n.* noise and tumult : bustle and clamour. [Dut. *oproer*, from *op*, up, and *roeren* (Ger. *rühren*, A.S. *hreran*), to stir; corr. from a supposed connection with Roar.]

**Uproarious**, up-rōr′i-us, *adj.* making or accompanied by great *uproar.*—*adv.* **Uproar′iously.**

**Uproot**, up-rōōt′, *v.t.* to tear up by the roots.

**Upset**, up-set′, *v.t.* to turn upside down : to overthrow.—*adj.* **Up′set**, *n.* an overturn.—*adj.* relating to what is *set up* for sale, in phrase **Up′set price**, the sum at which anything is started at a public sale. [Lit. ' to set up.']

**Upshot**, up′shot, *n.* final issue : end. [Lit. ' what is shot up or turns out.']

**Upside**, up′sīd, *n.* the *upper side.*—**Upside-down**, *adv.* with the upper part undermost : in complete confusion.

**Upstart**, up′stärt, *n.* one who has suddenly *started up* or risen from low life to wealth, &c.—*adj.* suddenly raised.

**Upward**, up′ward, *adj.* directed *up* or to a higher place.—**Up′ward, Up′wards**, *advs.* toward a higher direction. [Up, and *ward*, sig. direction.]

**Urban**, ur′ban, *adj.* of or belonging to a *city.* [L. *urbanus*—*urbs*, a city.]

**Urbane**, ur-bān′, *adj.* pertaining to or influenced by a *city :* civilised : refined : courteous.

**Urbanity**, ur-ban′i-ti, *n.* the quality of being *urbane :* refinement : politeness. [L. *urbanitas.*]

**Urchin**, ur′chin, *n.* a *hedgehog :* a child, used jocosely. [M. E. *urchon*, O. Fr. *eriçon*, Fr. *hérisson ;* from L. *ericius*, a hedgehog.]

**Ureter**, ū-rē′tėr, *n.* the duct which conveys the urine from the kidneys to the bladder. [Gr.— *ouron*, urine.]

**Urethra**, ū-rē′thra, *n.* the canal leading from the bladder to the external orifice. [Gr.—*ouron*, urine.]

**Urge**, urj, *v.t.* to *press* in any way : to drive : to press earnestly : to provoke. [L. *urgeo*, to press, to drive.]

**Urgency**, ur′jen-si, *n.* quality of being *urgent :* earnest asking : pressing necessity.

**Urgent**, ur′jent, *adj., urging:* pressing with importunity : calling for immediate attention : earnest.—*adv.* **Ur′gently.** [L. *urgens*, pr.p. of *urgeo.*]

**Urim**, ū′rim, and **Thummim**, thum′im, *ns.pl.* a part of the high-priest's breastplate among the ancient Jews, the nature of which is not distinctly understood. [Lit. 'lights and perfections,' Heb. *urim*, prob. pl. of *ur, ōr*, light, and *thummim*, pl. of *tom*, perfection.]

**Urinal**, ū′rin-al, *n.* a vessel for *urine :* a convenience for discharging urine. [L. *urinal—urina.*]

**Urinary**, ū′rin-ar-i, *adj.* pertaining to or like *urine.*

**Urine**, ū′rin, *n.* the fluid which is separated by the kidneys from the blood, and conveyed to the bladder. [Fr.—L. *urina ;* cog. with Gr. *ouron*, Ger. *harn*, Sans. *vari*, water.]

**Urn**, urn, *n.* a kind of vase used for various purposes : a vessel in which the ashes of the dead were anciently deposited. [L. *urna*, a waterpot, an urn, prop. a 'vessel of *burnt* clay,' from *uro*, to burn.]

**Ursine**, ur′sin, *adj.* of or resembling a *bear.* [L. —*ursus*, a bear.]

**Us**, us, *pron.* the objective case of **We.** [A.S.]

**Usable**, ūz′a-bl, *adj.* that may be *used.*

**Usage**, ūz′āj, *n.* act or mode of *using :* treatment : practice : custom. [Fr.—Low L.—L. *usus.*]

**Use**, ūz, *v.t.* to put to some purpose : to avail one's self of : to habituate : to treat or behave toward.—*v.i.* to be accustomed. [Fr. *user*—L. *utor, usus*, to use.]

**Use**, ūs, *n.* act of *using* or putting to a purpose : convenience : employment : need : advantage : practice : custom. [L. *usus—utor.*]

**Useful**, ūs′fool, *adj.* full of *use* or advantage : able to do good : serviceable.—*adv.* **Use′fully.**—*n.* **Use′fulness.**

**Useless**, ūs′les, *adj.* having no *use :* answering no good purpose or the end proposed.—*adv.* **Use′lessly.**—*n.* **Use′lessness.**

**Usher**, ush′ér, *n.* one whose business it is to introduce strangers or to walk before a person of rank : an under-teacher or assistant.—*v.t.* to introduce : to forerun.—*n.* **Ush′ership.** [O. Fr. *ussier*, Fr. *huissier*—L. *ostiarius*, a doorkeeper —*ostium*, a door.]

**Usual**, ū′zhū-al, *adj.* in *use :* occurring in ordinary use : common.—*adv.* **U′sually.** [L. *usualis.*]

**Usufruct**, ū′zū-frukt, *n.* the *use* and *profit*, but not the property, of a thing : liferent. [L.]

**Usurer**, ū′zhōō-rèr, *n.* (*orig.* and in *B.*) a moneylender for interest : one who practises usury.

**Usurp**, ū-zurp′, *v.t.* to take possession of by force without right.—*n.* **Usurp′er.** [Fr.—L. *usurpo*, perh. contr. from *usu-rapio*, to seize to one's own use—*usus*, use, and *rapio*, to seize.]

**Usurpation**, ū-zur-pā′shun, *n.* act of *usurping :* unlawful seizure and possession. [L. *usurpatio.*]

**Usury**, ū′zhōō-ri, *n.* the taking of more than legal interest on a loan : (*orig.*) interest generally. —*adj.* **Usu′rious.** [Lit. 'a using,' L. *usura— utor, usus*, to use.]

**Utensil**, ū-ten′sil, *n.* an instrument or vessel *used* in common life. [Fr. *ustensile*—L. *utensilis*, fit for use—*utor*, to use.]

**Uterine**, ū′tér-in, *adj.* pertaining to the *womb :* born of the same mother by a different father. [Fr. *utérin*—L. *uterinus—uterus*, the womb.]

**Utilise**, ū′til-īz, *v.t.* to make *useful :* to put to profitable use.—*n.* **Utilisa′tion.** [Fr. *utiliser*— L. *utor.*]

**Utilitarian**, ū-til-i-tā′ri-an, *adj.* consisting in or

pertaining to *utility*, or to utilitarianism.—*n.* one who holds utilitarianism.

**Utilitarianism**, ū-til-i-tā′ri-an-izm, *n.* the doctrine which holds that the standard of morality is *utility* or the happiness of mankind.

**Utility**, ū-til′i-ti, *n., usefulness.* [Fr.—L.—*utilis*, useful—*utor*, to use.]

**Utmost**, ut′mōst, *adj., outmost :* furthest out : most distant : last : in the greatest degree : highest.—*n.* the greatest that can be : the greatest effort. [A.S. *utemest—utema*, superl. of *ut*, out, and superl. suffix, -*st.* For mistaken form -*most*, see **Aftermost, Foremost.**]

**Utopian**, ū-tō′pi-an, *adj.* imaginary : fanciful : chimerical. [From *Utopia*, lit. 'nowhere '—Gr. *ou*, not, and *topos*, place, an imaginary island represented by Sir T. More as enjoying perfection in politics, laws, &c.]

**Utter**, ut′ér, *adj.* furthest out : extreme : total : perfect.—*adv.* **Utt′erly.** [A.S. *utor*, outer, extreme—*ut*, out.]

**Utter**, ut′ér, *v.t.* to circulate : to publish abroad : to speak.—*n.* **Utt′erer.** [Lit. 'to send out or forth,' from **Utter**, *adj.*] [expressed.

**Utterable**, ut′ér-a-bl, *adj.* that may be *uttered* or

**Utterance**, ut′ér-ans, *n.* act of *uttering :* manner of speaking : pronunciation : expression.

**Uttermost**, ut′ér-mōst, *adj.* furthest *out :* utmost. —*n.* the greatest degree. [Same as **Utmost**, the *r* being intrusive, and *t* being doubled on the analogy of **Utter.**]

**Uvula**, ū′vū-la, *n.* the fleshy conical body suspended from the palate over the back part of the tongue.—*adj.* **U′vular.** [Coined from L. *uva*, a bunch of grapes.]

**Uxorious**, ugz-ō′ri-us, *adj.* excessively or submissively fond of a *wife.*—*adv.* **Uxo′riously.**—*n.* **Uxo′riousness.** [L. *uxorius—uxor*, a wife.]


# V

**Vacancy**, vā′kan-si, *n. emptiness:* leisure : that which is vacant or unoccupied : emptiness of thought : empty space : void or gap between bodies : a situation unoccupied.

**Vacant**, vā′kant, *adj., empty :* exhausted of air : free : not occupied by an incumbent or possessor : not occupied with study, &c. : thoughtless.— *adv.* **Va′cantly.** [Fr.—L. *vacans, -antis*, pr.p. of *vaco*, to be empty.]

**Vacate**, va-kāt′, *v.t.* to leave empty : to quit possession of. [L. *vaco, -atum*, to be empty.]

**Vacation**, va-kā′shun, *n.* a *vacating* or making void, or invalid : freedom from duty, &c. : recess : break in the sittings of law-courts : school and college holidays. [L.]

**Vaccinate**, vak′sin-āt, *v.t.* to inoculate with the *cowpox* as a preventive against smallpox.— *n.* **Vaccina′tion.** [Formed from L. *vaccinus*, of a cow. See **Vaccine.**]

**Vaccine**, vak′sin, *adj.* pertaining to or derived from *cows.* [L. *vaccīnus—vacca*, a cow, akin to Sans. *vashā*, cow—*vash*, to bellow.]

**Vacillate**, vas′il-āt, *v.i.* to sway to and fro : to waver : to be unsteady.—*n.* **Vacilla′tion.** [L. *vacillo, -atum.*]

**Vacuity**, va-kū′it-i, *n., emptiness :* space unoccupied, or not visibly occupied : void. [L. *vacuitas —vacuus*, empty—*vaco*, to be empty.]

**Vacuum**, vak′ū-um, *n.* a *vacant* or *empty* space : a space empty or devoid of all matter :—*pl.* **Vac′ua.** [L., neut. of *vacuus*, empty.]

**Vagabond**, vag′a-bond, *adj., wandering :* having

no settled home : driven to and fro : unsettled. —*n.* one who wanders without any settled habitation : a wandering, idle fellow.—*n.* **Vag'-abondage**. [Fr.—L.—*vagor, vagari*, to wander —*vagus*, wandering. See **Vague**.]

**Vagary**, va-gār′i, *n.* a *wandering* of the thoughts : a wild freak : a whim.

**Vagrancy**, vā′gran-si, *n.* the state of being a *vagrant* : life and habits of a vagrant.

**Vagrant**, vā′grant, *adj.*, *wandering* without any settled dwelling : unsettled.—*n.* one who has no settled home : an idle or disorderly person : a beggar. [L. *vag-ans, -antis*, pr.p. of *vagor*, to wander ; with *r* intruded.]

**Vague**, vāg, *adj.* unsettled : indefinite : uncertain. —*adv.* **Vague′ly**.—*n.* **Vague′ness**. [Fr.—L. *vagus*, wandering.]

**Vail**, vāl. Same as **Veil**.

**Vail**, vāl, *v.t.* to let fall.—*v.i.* to yield. [Contr. of M. E. *availen*—O. Fr. *avaler*, to descend— Fr. *à val*—L. *ad vallem*, down a valley.]

**Vails**, vālz, *n.pl.* money given to servants. [A contr. of **Avail**, to profit.]

**Vain**, vān, *adj.* unsatisfying : fruitless : unreal : conceited : showy : vacant, worthless, so in *B.* —*adv.* **Vain′ly**.—**In vain**, ineffectually : to no purpose or end : with levity or profanity. [Fr. *vain*—L. *vanus*, empty. Cf. **Vaunt**.]

**Vainglorious**, vān-glō′ri-us, *adj.* given to *vain-glory* : proceeding from vanity.—*adv.* **Vain-glo′riously**.

**Vainglory**, vān-glō′ri, *n.*, *vain* or empty *glory* in one's own performances : pride above desert.

**Valance**, val′ans, *n.* hanging drapery for a bed, &c. —*v.t.* to decorate with such. [Prob. through Norm. Fr. *valaunt*, from Fr. *avalant*, slipping down (see **Avalanche**) ; or from *Valencia* (Fr. *Valence*) in Spain.]

**Vale**, vāl, *n.* a tract of low ground, esp. between hills : a valley. [Fr. *val*—L. *vallis*, a vale.]

**Valediction**, val-e-dik′shun, *n.* a farewell. [L. *valedico, -dictum—vale*, farewell, *dico*, to say.]

**Valedictory**, val-e-dik′tor-i, *adj.*, *saying farewell* : farewell : taking leave.

**Valency**, val′en-si, *n.* (*chem.*) the combining power of an element, or the proportion in which it forms a combination with another. [From L. *valeo*.]

**Valentine**, val′en-tīn, *n.* a lover or sweetheart chosen on *St Valentine's* day, 14th Feb. : a love-letter sent on that day. [Perhaps from the notion that on this day birds began to pair.]

**Valerian**, val-ē′ri-an, *n.* the plant *all-heal*, the root of which is used in medicine. [Coined from L. *valere*, to be strong.]

**Valet**, val′et, *n.* a servant : a man-servant, esp. one who attends on a gentleman's person. [Fr. —O. Fr. *varlet*. See **Varlet, Vassal**.]

**Valetudinarian**, val-e-tūd-in-ār′i-an, **Valetudinary**, val-e-tū′din-ar-i, *adj.* belonging to ill health : sickly : weak.—*n.* a person of ill or weak health. [L. *valetudinarius—valetudo*, state of health, bad health—*valeo*, to be strong.]

**Valetudinarianism**, val-e-tūd-in-ār′i-an-izm, *n.* the condition of a valetudinarian : weak health.

**Valhalla**, val-hal′la, *n.* (in Scandinavian *myth.*) the palace of immortality for the souls of heroes slain in battle. [Ice. *valhöll*, 'the hall of the slain'—*valr*, the slain, conn. with A.S. *wæl*, slaughter, and Ice. *höll*, E. **Hall**.]

**Valiant**, val′yant, *adj.*, *strong* : brave : intrepid in danger : heroic.—**Do val′iantly** (*B.*) to behave gallantly.—*adv.* **Val′iantly** (*Apocrypha*) by force.—*n.* **Val′iantness** (*B.*) courage, bravery. [Fr. *vaillant*—L. *valens, valentis*,

pr.p. of *valeo*, to be strong. See **Valetudinarian**.]

**Valid**, val′id, *adj.*, *strong* : having sufficient strength or force : founded in truth : sound : conclusive : (*law*) executed with the proper formalities : legal : rightful.—*adv.* **Val′idly**.— *n.* **Valid′ity**. [L. *validus*—*valeo*, to be strong.]

**Valise**, va-lēs′, *n.* a *travelling-bag*, generally of leather, opening at the side : a portmanteau. [Fr.—It. *valigia*, through Low L. forms from L. *vidulus*, a travelling-bag.]

**Valley**, val′i, *n.* a *vale* or low land between hills or mountains : a low, extended plain, usually watered by a river :—*pl.* **Vall′eys**. [Fr. *vallée*, an extension of *val* (see **Vale**).]

**Valorous**, val′ur-us, *adj.* possessing or showing *valour* : intrepid : courageous.—*adv.* **Val′orously**.

**Valour**, val′ur, *n.* the quality of being *valiant* : that which enables one to encounter danger fearlessly : intrepidity : courage : bravery. [O. Fr. —Low L. *valor*—L. *valeo*, to be strong.]

**Valuable**, val′ū-a-bl, *adj.* having *value* or worth : costly : deserving esteem.—*n.* **Val′uableness**.

**Valuation**, val-ū-ā′shun, *n.* the act of *valuing* : value set upon a thing : estimated worth.

**Valuator**, val′ū-āt-ur, *n.* one who sets a *value* upon : an appraiser.

**Value**, val′ū, *n.*, *worth* : that which renders anything useful or estimable : the degree of this quality : efficacy : importance : excellence : price : precise meaning.—*v.t.* to estimate the worth of : to rate at a price : to esteem : to prize. [O. Fr., prop. the fem. of Fr. *valu*, pa.p. of *valoir*, to be worth—L. *valeo*.]

**Valueless**, val′ū-les, *adj.* of *no value* or worth.

**Valve**, valv, *n.* one of the leaves of a *folding-door* : a cover to an aperture which opens in one direction and not in the other : one of the pieces or divisions which form a shell.—*adj.* **Valv′ular**. [Fr.—L. *valvæ*, a folding-door.]

**Valved**, valvd, *adj.* having or composed of valves.

**Vamp**, vamp, *n.* the upper leather of a boot or shoe.—*v.t.* to repair with a new vamp : to patch old with new : give a new face to (with *up*). [Corr. of Fr. *avant-pied*, the fore-part of the foot—*avant*, before (see **Van**, the front), and *pied*, L. *pes, pedis*, E. **Foot**.]

**Vampire**, vam′pīr, *n.* in the superstition of Eastern Europe, a ghost which sucks the blood of its sleeping victim : one who lives upon others : a blood-sucker : a large species of blood-sucking bat in S. America. [Fr.—Servian *wampir*.]

**Van**, van, *n.* the *front* : the front of an army or a fleet. [Fr. *avant*—L. *ab*, from, by, and *ante*, before.] [See **Fan**.]

**Van**, van, *n.* a *fan* for grain, &c. [Fr.—L. *vannus*.]

**Van**, van, *n.* a large covered wagon for goods, &c. [Short for **Caravan**.]

**Vandal**, van′dal, *n.* one of a fierce race in N. Germany who sacked Rome in 455 : any one hostile to arts or literature : a barbarian.—**Van′dal, Vandal′ic**, *adj.* barbarous : rude.—**Van′dalism**, *n.* hostility to arts or literature.

**Vane**, vān, *n.* a flag or banner : a thin slip of wood or metal at the top of a spire, &c. to show which way the wind blows : a weather-cock : the thin web of a feather. [Older form *fane*—A.S. *fana* ; Goth. *fana*, cloth, Ger. *fahne* ; akin to L. *pannus*, and Gr. *penos*, a cloth.]

**Vanguard**, van′gärd, *n.* the *guard* in the *van* of an army : the part of an army preceding the main body : the first line.

**Vanilla,** van-il′a, *n.* the dried aromatic *sheath*-like pod or fruit of a tropical orchid, a favourite confection. [Latinised from Fr. *vanille*—Sp. *vainilla*—*vaina*—L. *vagina*, a sheath.]

**Vanish,** van′ish, *v.i.* to pass away from a place, leaving it vacant or *empty*: to disappear: to be annihilated or lost. [L. *vanesco*, to pass away—*vanus*, empty. See **Vain.**]

**Vanity,** van′it-i, *n.* the quality of being *vain*: worthlessness: empty pride: conceit: idle show: uncertainty: vain pursuit: empty pleasure: fruitless desire.—**Vanity-fair,** the world. [Fr.—L. *vanitas*—*vanus*.]

**Vanquish,** vangk′wish, *v.t.* to conquer: to defeat in any contest: to confute.—*n.* **Van′quisher.** [Fr. *vaincre* (pa.t. *vainquis*)—L. *vincere*, to conquer. See **Victor.**]

**Vantage,** van′tāj, *n.* Same as **Advantage.**

**Vapid,** vap′id, *adj.* having the spirit evaporated: spiritless: insipid.—*adv.* **Vap′idly.**—*ns.* **Vap′idness, Vapid′ity.** [L. *vapidus.* See **Vapour.**]

**Vaporise,** vap′or-īz or vā′por-īz, *v.t.* to convert into *vapour.*—*v.i.* to pass off in vapour.—*n.* **Vaporisa′tion.**

**Vaporous,** vā′pur-us, *adj.* full of or like *vapour*: vain: unreal: affected with the vapours.

**Vapour,** vā′pur, *n.* the gas, generally invisible, into which most liquids and solids are convertible by heat: (*physics*) the condition of a body when it becomes gas by heat: water in the atmosphere: anything vain or transitory:—*pl.* a disease of nervous weakness in which a variety of strange images float before the mind.—*v.i.* to pass off in vapour: to evaporate: to boast: to brag. [L. *vapor*, allied to Gr. *kapnos*, smoke, and L. *vappa*, flat or vapid wine.]

**Vapourer,** vā′pur-ėr, *n.* one who vapours, a boaster.

**Vapoury,** vā′pur-i, *adj.* full of *vapour*: affected with the vapours: peevish.

**Variable,** vā′ri-a-bl, *adj.* that may be *varied*: changeable: liable to change: unsteady.—*n.* (*math.*) a quantity subject to continual increase or decrease: a quantity which may have an infinite number of values in the same expression.—*adv.* **Va′riably.**—*ns.* **Va′riableness, Variabil′ity.** [Fr.—L. *variabilis.* See **Vary.**]

**Variance,** vā′ri-ans, *n.* state of being *varied*: an alteration: a change of condition: difference that arises from or produces dispute.—**At variance,** in disagreement. [L. *varius*, speckled, mottled, varied.]

**Variant,** vā′ri-ant, *n.* a variety.

**Variation,** vā-ri-ā′shun, *n.* a varying: a change: change from one to another: successive change: the extent to which a thing varies: (*gram.*) change of termination: (*mus.*) a manner of singing or playing the same air with various changes in time, rhythm, or key. [Fr.—L. *variatio.* See **Vary.**]

**Varicose,** var′i-kōz, **Varicous,** var′i-kus, *adj.* permanently *dilated* or enlarged, as a vein. [L. *varicosus*, full of dilated veins—*varix*, a dilated vein—*varus*, bent, crooked.]

**Variegate,** vā′ri-e-gāt, *v.t.* to mark with *different* colours.—*n.* **Variega′tion.** [L. *variegatus*—*varius*, various, *ago*, to make.]

**Variety,** va-rī′e-ti, *n.* the quality of being *various*: difference: a collection of different things: one of a number of things nearly allied to each other: one or more individuals of a species, which, owing to accidental causes, differ from the normal form in minor points. [L. *varietas*—*varius*, various.]

**Variorum,** va-ri-o′rum, *adj.* a term applied to an edition of some work in which the notes *of various* commentators are inserted. [From the full Latin 'editio cum notis *variorum.*']

**Various,** vā′ri-us, *adj.*, *varied*, different: several: unlike each other: changeable: uncertain: variegated.—*adv.* **Va′riously.** [L. *varius.*]

**Varlet,** vär′let, *n.* a footman: a low fellow: a scoundrel. [Orig. 'a vassal or squire, attendant on a lord,' Fr. *varlet*, formerly *vaslet*, from a dim. of Low L. *vassalis* (see **Vassal**). Doublet **Valet.**]

**Varnish,** vär′nish, *v.t.* to cover with a liquid to give a glossy surface to: to give a fair appearance to.—*n.* a sticky liquid which dries and forms a hard, lustrous coating: palliation. [Fr. *vernisser*, through Low L. from L. *vitrum*, glass.]

**Vary,** vā′ri, *v.t.* to make *different*: to alter: to change to something else: to make of different kinds.—*v.i.* to alter or be altered: to be or become different: to change in succession: to deviate (with *from*): to disagree:—*pa.t.* and *pa.p.* vā′ried. [Fr. *varier*—L. *variare*—*varius.*]

**Vascular,** vas′kū-lar, *adj.* of or relating to the *vessels* of animal and vegetable bodies.—*n.* **Vascular′ity.** [Fr. *vasculaire*—L. *vasculum*, dim. of *vas*, a vessel.]

**Vase,** vāz or väz, *n.* a vessel anciently used for domestic purposes, and in offering sacrifices: an ornamental vessel generally of an antique pattern: a sculptured, vase-like ornament. [Fr.—L. *vasum* or *vas.*]

**Vassal,** vas′al, *n.* one who holds land from and renders homage to a superior. [Fr.—Low L. *vassalis*—W. *gwas*, a youth, servant.]

**Vassalage,** vas′al-āj, *n.* state of being a *vassal*: dependence: subjection.

**Vast,** vast, *adj.* of great extent: very great in amount.—*n.* **Vast′ness.** [Fr. *vaste*—L. *vastus*, waste, vast; perh. akin to *vacuus*, empty.]

**Vastly,** vast′li, *adv.* to a *vast* extent or degree.

**Vat,** vat, *n.* a large *vessel* or tank, esp. one for holding liquors. [Older form *fat*—A.S. *fæt*—Dut. *vat* (Ice. *fat*, Ger. *fass*), from the root of Ger. *fassen*, to hold, to contain: nowise conn. with L. *vas.*]

**Vatican,** vat′i-kan, *n.* an assemblage of buildings in Rome, including one of the pope's palaces: used to mean the papal authority. [Fr. (It. *Vaticano*)—from L. *Mons Vaticanus*, a hill in Rome.]

**Vaticinate,** vat-is′i-nāt, *v.t.* to *prophesy.* [L. *vaticin-or*, *-atus*, to prophesy—*vates*, a seer.]

**Vaticination,** vat-is-i-nā′shun, *n.* prophecy: prediction.

**Vaudeville,** vōd′věl, *n.* a lively or satirical song: a short dramatic piece interspersed with such. [From *vau* (*val*) *de Vire*, in Normandy, where they were first composed about 1400 A.D.]

**Vault,** vawlt, *n.* an arched roof: a chamber with an arched roof, esp. one underground: a cellar: anything vault-like: the bound of a horse: a jump.—*v.t.* to shape as a vault: to arch: to roof with an arch: to form vaults in.—*v.i.* to curvet or leap, as a horse: to leap: to exhibit feats of leaping or tumbling. [Lit. 'a turn,' O. Fr. *volte* (Fr. *voûte*), from L. *volutum*, pa.p. of *volvo*, to roll, to turn. Doublet **Volute.**]

**Vaulted,** vawlt′ed, *adj.* arched: concave overhead: covered with an arch or vault.

**Vaulter,** vawlt′ėr, *n.* one who *vaults* or leaps.

**Vaunt,** vawnt or vänt, *v.i.* to make a *vain* display: to boast.—*v.t.* to make a vain display of: to boast of.—*n.* vain display: boast.—*n.* **Vaunt′er.** [Fr. *vanter*—Low L. *vanitare*—L. *vanitas*, vanity—*vanus*, vain. See **Vain.**]

**Veal**, vēl, *n.* the flesh of a *calf.* [O. Fr. *veel* (Prov. *vedel*)—L. *vitellus*, dim. of *vitulus*, Gr. *italos*, a calf. Cf. **Vellum.**]

**Vector**, vek′tor, *n.* (*math.*) any directed quantity, as a straight line in space, involving both its direction and magnitude.

**Veda**, vē′dä, *n.* name given to the four oldest sacred books of the Hindus :—*pl.* **Vedas**, vē′däz. [Sans. *veda*, knowledge—*vid*, to know, E. **Wit.**]

**Vedette**, ve-det′, *n.* a mounted sentry at the outposts of an army to *watch* an enemy. [Fr.—It. *vedetta*, for *veletta* — *veglia*, L. *vigilia*, a watch.]

**Veer**, vēr, *v.i.* to change direction, as the wind.— *v.t.* to turn : to direct to a different course. [Lit. ' to describe a circle,' Fr. *virer*, prob. from L. *viriæ*, armlets, bracelets.]

**Vegetable**, vej′e-ta-bl, *n.* an organised body without sensation and voluntary motion, nourished by roots fixed in the ground : a plant for the table.—*adj.* belonging to plants : consisting of or having the nature of plants : derived from vegetables.—**Vegetable marrow**, the fruit of a species of gourd, so called from its *marrow*-like appearance. [L. *vegetabilis*, prop. ' animating ' —*vegeto* (see **Vegetable**).]

**Vegetal**, vej′e-tal, *adj.* of the nature of a *vegetable :* pertaining to the vital functions of plants and animals, as growth, reproduction, &c. [Fr. —L. *vegetus*, prop. ' animated.' See **Vegetable.**]

**Vegetarian**, vej-e-tā′ri-an, *n.* one who holds that *vegetables* are the only proper food for man.— *adj.* pertaining to vegetarianism.—**Vegeta′rianism**, *n.* the theory and practice of a vegetarian.

**Vegetate**, vej′e-tāt, *v.i.* to *grow* by roots and leaves : to sprout : to lead an idle, unthinking life. [From L. *vegeto*, -*atum*, to quicken—*vegeo*, to be lively, akin to *vigeo*, to be vigorous (cf. **Vigour**).]

**Vegetation**, vej-e-tā′shun, *n.* process of growing as a plant : vegetable growth : plants in general.

**Vegetative**, vej′e-tāt-iv, *adj.* growing, as plants : producing growth in plants.

**Vehemence**, vē′e-mens, *n.* the quality of being *vehement :* violence : great ardour or fervour.

**Vehement**, vē′e-ment, *adj.* passionate : furious : very eager or urgent.—*adv.* **Ve′hemently.** [Fr. — L. *vehemens*, usually derived from *ve*, out of, and *mens*, mind ; but acc. to Vanicek, from L. *veho*, to carry, bear away.]

**Vehicle**, vē′i-kl, *n.* any kind of *carriage* or conveyance : that which is used to convey : (*med.*) a substance in which a medicine is taken. [L. *vehiculum*—*veho*, to carry, from root of E. **Wagon.**]     [serving as a *vehicle.*

**Vehicular**, ve-hik′ū-lar, *adj.* pertaining to or

**Veil**, vāl, *n.* a *curtain :* anything that hides an object : a piece of muslin or thin cloth worn by ladies to shade or hide the face : a cover : a disguise.—*v.t.* to cover with a veil : to cover : to conceal.—**To take the veil**, to become a nun (the veil symbolising the union with Christ). [O. Fr. *veile* (Fr. *voile*)—L. *velum*, a curtain, a sail, from the root of **Wool.**]

**Vein**, vān, *n.* (*anat.*) one of the vessels or tubes which convey the blood back to the heart : (*bot.*) one of the small branching ribs in a leaf : (*geol.* and *mining*) a seam of a different mineral through a rock : a fissure or cavity : a streak in wood or stone : a train of thought : a course : tendency or turn of mind : humour.—*v.t.* to form veins or the appearance of veins in. [Fr. *veine*—L. *vena*, perh. from root of *veho*, to carry.]

**Veliferous**, vel-if′ér-us, *adj.* carrying sails. [L. *velifer*—*velum*, a sail, and *fero*, to bear.]

**Vellum**, vel′um, *n.* a finer kind of parchment prepared from the skin of *calves*, kids, or lambs. [Fr. *vélin*—Low L. (*charta*, paper, understood) *vitulina*, of a calf—L. *vitulus*. See **Veal.**]

**Velocipede**, ve-los′i-ped or -pēd, *n.* a light carriage for one person, orig. moved by striking the toes on the road, now with a treddle. [Lit. ' swiftfoot,' Fr.—L. *velox*, *velocis*, swift, and *pes*, *pedis*, E. **Foot.**]

**Velocity**, ve-los′i-ti, *n.*, *swiftness :* speed : rate of change of position of a point per unit of time. [L. *velocitas*—*velox*, swift.]

**Velvet**, vel′vet, *n.* a cloth made from silk, with a close shaggy pile : a similar cloth made of cotton. —*adj.* made of velvet : soft like velvet.—*n.* **Velveteen′.** [From Low L. *velluetum*, Fr. *velu*, shaggy—Low L. *villutus*—L. *villus*, shaggy hair. Cf. **Wool.**]

**Velveting**, vel′vet-ing, *n.* the soft pile of *velvet :* velvet goods.             [soft.

**Velvety**, vel′vet-i, *adj.* made of or like *velvet :*

**Venal**, vē′nal, *adj.* that may be *sold* or got for a price : held for sale : mercenary.—*adv.* **Ve′nally.** [Fr.—L. *venalis*—*venus*, sale.]

**Venality**, ve-nal′i-ti, *n.* quality of being *venal :* prostitution of talents or services for a reward.

**Venation**, ve-na′shun, *n.* the way in which the *leaves* of plants are arranged. [L. *vena*, a leaf.]

**Vend**, vend, *v.t.* to give for *sale*, to *sell :* to give for money : to make an object of trade.—*ns.* **Vend′er**, **Vend′or.** [Fr. *vendre*—L. *vendere*— *venus*, sale (see **Venal**), and *do*, to give.]

**Vendible**, vend′i-bl, *adj.* that may be *sold :* that may be disposed of as an object of trade.—*adv.* **Vend′ibly.**—*n.* **Vend′ibleness.**

**Veneer**, ve-nēr′, *v.t.* to overlay or face with another wood.—*n.* a thin leaf of a valuable wood for overlaying an inferior. [A corr. of Fr. *fournir*, to furnish. See **Furnish.**]

**Veneering**, ve-nēr′ing, *n.* the act or art of overlaying an inferior wood with thin leaves of a more valuable kind : the thin leaf thus laid on.

**Venerable**, ven′er-a-bl, *adj.* that may be *venerated :* worthy of veneration, reverence, or honour : rendered sacred by religious or other associations : aged.—*adv.* **Ven′erably.**—*n.* **Ven′erableness.**

**Venerate**, ven′er-āt, *v.t.* to honour or reverence with religious awe : to reverence : to regard with the greatest respect. [L. *veneror*, -*atus*—*venus*, love ; allied to Sans. *van*, to love.]

**Veneration**, ven-er-ā′shun, *n.* the act of *venerating :* the state of being venerated : the highest degree of respect and reverence : respect mingled with reverence and awe : awe.

**Venereal**, ve-nēr′i-al, *adj.* pertaining to or arising from sexual intercourse : exciting desire for sexual intercourse : curing venereal diseases. [L. *venereus*—*Venus*, *Veneris*, the goddess of love ; conn. with L. *veneror*. See **Venerate.**]

**Venery**, ven′er-i, *n.* sexual intercourse.

**Venery**, ven′er-i, *n.* the act or exercise of *hunting :* the sports of the chase. [Fr. *vénerie*, from O. Fr. *vener*—L. *venor*, to hunt. Cf. **Venison.**]

**Venesection**, vē-ne-sek′shun, *n.* the *section* or cutting open of a *vein* for letting blood : bloodletting. [L. *vena*, a vein, and **Section.**]

**Venetian**, ve-nē′shan, *adj.* of or belonging to *Venice.*—*n.* a native or inhabitant of Venice.— **Venetian-blind**, a blind for windows formed of thin slips of wood, so hung as to admit of being set either edgewise or overlapping. [Ancient name, *Venetia*.]

**Vengeance**, venj'ans, *n.* the infliction of punishment upon another, in return for an injury or offence: retribution. [Fr. *venger*—L. *vindico*, to avenge. See **Revenge** and **Vindicate**.]

**Vengeful**, venj'fool, *adj.* vindictive: retributive: revengeful.—*adv.* **Venge'fully**.

**Venial**, vē'ni-al, *adj.* pardonable: excusable: allowed.—*adv.* **Ve'nially**. — *ns.* **Ve'nialness**, **Venial'ity**. [L. *venialis*, pardonable (in Late L.)—*venia*, favour, pardon: akin to **Venerate**.]

**Venison**, ven'i-zn or ven'zn, *n.* the flesh of animals taken in *hunting*, esp. the deer. [Fr. *venaison* —L. *venatio*, a hunting, game—*venor*, to hunt.]

**Venom**, ven'um, *n.* any drink, juice, or liquid injurious or fatal to life: poison: spite: malice. [Fr. *venin* (It. *veneno*)—L. *venenum*.]

**Venomous**, ven'um-us, *adj.* poisonous: spiteful: mischievous.—*adv.* **Ven'omously**.

**Venous**, vē'nus, *adj.* pertaining to or contained in *veins*. veined. [L. *venosus*—*vena*, a vein.]

**Vent**, vent, *n.* a small opening to let air, &c. escape: the flue of a chimney: discharge: escape: passage to notice: publication: the anus of birds and fishes: (*mil.*) the opening at the breech of a firearm through which fire is conveyed to the charge, the touch-hole.—*v. t.* to give a vent or opening to: to let out, as at a vent: to allow to escape: to publish: to pour forth. [Fr.—L. *ventus*, E. **Wind**.]

**Ventilate**, ven'ti-lāt, *v. t.* to fan with *wind*: to open to the free passage of air: to cause fresh air to pass through: to expose to examination and discussion: to make public. [L. *ventilo*, *-atum*—*ventulus*, dim. of *ventus*, E. **Wind**.]

**Ventilation**, ven-ti-lā'shun, *n.* act or art of *ventilating*: state of being ventilated: free exposure to air: supply of air: act of examining and making public: public exposure. [L. *ventilatio*.]

**Ventilator**, ven'ti-lāt-ur, *n.* that which ventilates: a contrivance for introducing fresh air.

**Ventral**, ven'tral, *adj.* belonging to the *belly*. [L. *ventralis*—*venter*, the belly.]

**Ventricle**, ven'tri-kl, *n.* a small cavity within an animal body, as in the heart or brain.—*adj.* **Ventric'ular**. [L. *ventriculus*, dim. of *venter*.]

**Ventriloquise**, ven-tril'o-kwīz, *v.i.* to practise ventriloquism.—**Ventril'oquist**, *n.* one who practises ventriloquism.

**Ventriloquism**, ven-tril'o-kwizm, **Ventriloquy**, ven-tril'o-kwi, *n.* the act or art of speaking so that the voice seems to come from a distance or from some other person.—*adj.* **Ventriloq'uial**. [L. *ventriloquus*, speaking from the belly—*venter*, the belly, and *loquor*, to speak.]

**Venture**, vent'ūr, *n.* that which may *come*: chance: luck: hazard: that which is put to hazard (esp. goods sent by sea at the sender's risk): an undertaking whose issue is uncertain or dangerous.—*v.t.* to send on a venture: to expose to hazard: to risk.—*v.i.* to make a venture: to run a risk: to dare.—**At a venture** (*B.*) at random.—*adjs.* **Vent'urous**, **Vent'uresome**. — *adv.* **Vent'urously**. — *n.* **Vent'urousness**. [Short for **Adventure**.]

**Venue**, ven'ū, *n.* in law, the place where an action is laid. lit. the place to which the jury are summoned to *come*. [Fr.—L. *ven-ire*, to come.]

**Venus**, vē'nus, *n.* (Latin *myth.*) the goddess of love: beauty and love deified: the most brilliant of the planets, second in order from the sun. [From the root of **Venerate**.]

**Veracious**, ve-rā'shus, *adj.* *truthful*: true.—*adv.*

**Vera'ciously**. [L. *verax*, *veracis*—*verus*, true. See **Very**.]

**Veracity**, ve-ras'it-i, *n.* the quality of being *veracious*: habitual truthfulness: truth.

**Veranda**, **Verandah**, ve-ran'da, *n.* a kind of *covered* balcony or open portico, with a roof sloping beyond the main building, supported by light pillars. [Port.—Sans. *varanda*—*vri*, to cover.]

**Verb**, vérb, *n.* (*gram.*) the part of speech which affirms what a thing does or is done to, or in what state it exists. [Lit. 'the word,' Fr. *verbe*—L. *verbum*; from root of Gr. *erō*, to say, to speak.]

**Verbal**, vérb'al, *adj.* relating to or consisting in *words*: spoken (as opposed to written): exact in words: attending to words only: word for word: derived directly from a verb.—*n.* a part of speech, a noun derived from a verb.—*adv.* **Verb'ally**.—*n.* **Verb'alist**. [L. *verbalis*.]

**Verbalise**, vérb'al-īz, *v.t.* to turn into a *verb*.

**Verbalism**, vérb'al-izm, *n.* something expressed in *words* or orally.

**Verbena**, ver-bē'na, *n.* a genus of plants cultivated for their fragrance or beauty: vervain. [L. *verbenæ*, leaves, twigs, and branches of laurel, myrtle, &c.]

**Verbiage**, vérb'i-āj, *n.* abundance of *words*: wordiness: verbosity. [See **Verb**.]

**Verbose**, vér-bōs', *adj.* containing more *words* than are necessary: wordy: diffuse.—*adv.* **Verbose'ly**.—*ns.* **Verbose'ness**, **Verbos'ity**.

**Verdant**, vér'dant, *adj.*, *green*: fresh (as grass or foliage): flourishing: inexperienced: ignorant.—*adv.* **Ver'dantly**.—*n.* **Ver'dancy**. [Fr. *verdoyant*—L. *viridans*, *-antis*, pr.p. of *virido*, to grow green—*viridis*, green—*vireo*, to be green.]

**Verdict**, vér'dikt, *n.* the finding of a jury on a trial: decision: opinion pronounced. [Lit. 'a true saying,' Low L.—L. *vere*, truly, and *dictum*, a saying.]

**Verdigris**, vér'di-gris, *n.* the rust of copper, brass, or bronze: a bluish-green paint got artificially from copper-plates. [A corr. of O. Fr. *verderis* —Low L. *viride æris*, 'the green of brass' (which was the name the alchemists gave it). The *-g-* has slipped in through the influence of **Grease**. See **Verdant** and **Ore**.]

**Verdure**, vérd'ūr, *n.*, *greenness*: freshness of growth. [See **Verdant**.]

**Verge**, vérj, *n.* a slender green branch, a twig: a rod, staff, or mace, or anything like them, used as an emblem of authority: extent of jurisdiction (esp. of the lord-steward of the royal household). [L. *virga*, from the root of *virgo*, a virgin. See **Verge**, *v.*]

**Verge**, vérj, *v.i.* to *bend* or incline: to tend downward: to slope: to tend: to border upon.—*n.* edge: brink. [L. *vergo*, to bend.]

**Verger**, vérj'ér, *n.* one who carries a *verge* or emblem of authority: the beadle of a cathedral church: a pew-opener or attendant in church.

**Verifiable**, ver'i-fī-a-bl, *adj.* that may be verified, proved, or confirmed.

**Verification**, ver-i-fi-kā'shun, *n.* a verifying or proving to be *true*: the state of being verified.

**Verify**, ver'i-fī, *v.t.* to make out or show to be *true*: to establish the truth of by evidence: to confirm:—*pa.t.* and *pa.p.* ver'ified.—*n.* **Ver'ifier**. [L. *verus*, true, and *facio*, to make.]

**Verily**, ver'i-li, *adv.*, *truly*: certainly: really.

**Verisimilar**, ver-i-sim'i-lar, *adj.*, *truth-like*: likely: probable. [L. *verisimilis*—*verus*, true, and *similis*, like. See **Similar**.]

**Verisimilitude**, ver-i-sim-il'i-tūd, *n.*, *similitude*

or likeness to *truth*: likelihood. [L. *verus*, true, and **Similitude**.]

**Veritable**, ver'i-ta-bl, *adj.*, *true*: according to fact: real: actual.—*adv.* **Ver'itably**.

**Verity**, ver'i-ti, *n.* the quality of being *true* or real: truth (so in *B.*): a true assertion or tenet. [L. *veritas*—*verus*, true. Cf. **Very**.]

**Verjuice**, vėr'jōōs, *n.* the expressed *juice* of *green* or unripe fruit. [Fr. *verjus*—*vert*, green (see **Verdant**), and Fr., L. *jus*, juice.]

**Vermicelli**, vėr-mi-chel'i, *n.* the stiff paste or dough of fine wheat flour made into small *worm*-like or thread-like rolls. [It., pl. of *vermicello* —L. *vermiculus*, dim. of *vermis*, E. **Worm**. Cf. **Vermilion** and **Vermin**.]

**Vermicular**, vėr-mik'ū-lar, **Vermiculate**, vėr-mik'ū-lāt, *adj.* pertaining to or like a *worm* (esp. in its motion). [From L. *vermiculus*, dim. of *vermis*, E. **Worm**.]

**Vermiculate**, vėr-mik'ū-lāt, *v.t.* to form inlaid-work which resembles the motion or track of *worms*.—*n.* **Vermicula'tion**. [L. *vermiculor*, *-atus*—*vermis*.]

**Vermiform**, vėr'mi-form, *adj.* having the form of a *worm*. [L. *vermis*, a worm, and **Form**.]

**Vermifuge**, vėr'mi-fūj, *n.* (*med.*) a substance that *expels* intestinal *worms* from animal bodies. [Fr., from L. *vermis*, E. **Worm**, and *fugo*, to cause to flee, to expel.]

**Vermilion**, vėr-mil'yun, *n.* a scarlet colouring substance obtained from a *little worm* or insect (the cochineal); a bright red colouring substance obtained from sulphur and mercury: any beautiful red colour.—*v.t.* to dye vermilion : to colour a delicate red. [Fr. *vermillon*—*vermeil*—L. *vermiculus*, a little worm, hence (in the Vulgate) the 'scarlet' worm, dim. of *vermis*, E. **Worm**. Cf. **Vermicelli**.]

**Vermin**, vėr'min, *n. sing.* and *pl.* a *worm*: a name for all noxious or mischievous animals or insects (esp. such as are small): noxious persons (in contempt). [Fr. *vermine*—L. *vermis*, E. **Worm**.]

**Vermivorous**, vėr-miv'or-us, *adj.*, *devouring worms*. [L. *vermis*, E. **Worm**, and *voro*, to devour.]

**Vernacular**, vėr-nak'ū-lar, *adj.* native : belonging to the country of one's birth.—*adv.* **Vernac'ularly**. [L. *vernaculus*—*verna*, a slave born in his master's house.]

**Vernal**, vėr'nal, *adj.* belonging to the *spring*: appearing in spring: belonging to youth. [L. *vernalis*—*ver*, spring, cog. with Gr. *ear*, *ēr* (for *f-ēr*).]

**Vernation**, vėr-nā'shun, *n.* the particular manner of arrangement of leaves in the bud. [See **Vernal**.]

**Vernier**, vėr'ni-ėr, *n.* a contrivance for measuring very small intervals, consisting of a short scale made to slide along a graduated instrument. [So called from *Vernier*, of Brussels, its inventor.]

**Versatile**, vėr'sa-til, *adj.* liable to be *turned* in opinion : changeable : unsteady : turning easily from one thing to another. [L. *versatilis*—*verso*, freq. of *verto*, to turn.]

**Versatility**, vėr-sa-til'it-i, *n.* the quality of being *versatile*: changeableness : the faculty of turning easily to new tasks or subjects.

**Verse**, vėrs, *n.* a line of poetry : metrical arrangement and language : poetry : a stanza : a short division of any composition, esp. of the chapters of the Bible, orig. confined to the metrical books, applied first to whole Bible in 1528 : (*mus.*) a portion of an anthem to be performed by a single voice to each part.

[L. *versus*, a line in writing—*verto*, *versum*, to turn.]

**Versed**, vėrst, *adj.* thoroughly acquainted, skilled (followed by *in*) : (*math.*) reversed. [Fr. *versé* —L. *versatus*, pa.p. of *versor*, to turn round.]

**Versicle**, vėrs'i-kl, *n.* a little *verse*. [See **Verse**.]

**Versification**, vėrs-i-fi-kā'shun, *n.* the act, art, or practice of composing metrical *verses*. [L.]

**Versify**, vėrs'i-fī, *v.i.* to make *verses*.—*v.t.* to relate in verse : to turn into verse :—*pa.t.* and *pa.p.* vėrs'if'ied.—*n.* **Vers'ifier**. [L. *versifico*— *versus*, a verse, *facio*, to make.]

**Version**, vėr'shun, *n.* the act of translating or *turning* from one language into another : that which is translated from one language into another: account : statement.

**Verst**, vėrst, *n.* a Russian mile, 3500 ft. in length, or almost two-thirds of an English mile. [Russ.]

**Vertebra**, vėrt'e-bra, *n.* one of the small bones of the spine :—*pl.* **Vertebræ** (vėrt'e-brē), the bones and joints forming the backbone.—*adj.* **Vert'ebral**. [L., 'a joint'—*verto*, to turn.]

**Vertebrate**, vėrt'e-brāt, **Vertebrated**, vėrt'e-brāt-ed, *adj.* furnished with joints: having a backbone.—**Vert'ebrate**, *n.* an animal having an internal skeleton with a backbone. [L. *vertebratus*—*vertebra*.]

**Vertex**, vėrt'eks, *n.* the top or summit : the point of a cone, pyramid, or angle : (*astr.*) the zenith : —*pl.* **Vert'ices**. [L., 'a whirl' or 'eddy,' then 'top' or 'summit'—*verto*, to turn. Cf. **Vortex**.]

**Vertical**, vėrt'ik-al, *adj.* pertaining to the *vertex*: placed in the zenith : perpendicular to the plane of the horizon.—*n.* a vertical line.—*adv.* **Vert'ically**.—*n.* **Vert'icalness**.

**Vertigo**, vėr-tī'go or vėrt'i-go, *n.* a sensation of giddiness : dizziness. [L.—*verto*, to turn.]

**Vervain**, vėr'vān, *n.* a plant of the genus *verbena* [Fr. *verveine*—L. *verbēna*.]

**Verve**, vėrv, *n.* the enthusiasm which animates a poet or artist : animation : energy. [Fr.—Late L. *verva* (*lit.*) 'a sculptured ram's head,' hence 'any artistic fancy'—L. *vervex*, a wether. Cf. **Caprice** and L. *capra*, a goat.]

**Very**, vėr'i, *adj.*, *true*: real (so in *B.*) : actual.— *adv.* in a great degree. [Older form *veray*—O. Fr. *verai* (Fr. *vrai*), from L. *verax*, *veracis*, speaking truly—*verus*, true, which is cog. with A.S. *vær*, Ger. *wahr*.]

**Vesication**, ves-i-kā'shun, *n.* the act or process of raising *blisters* on the skin. [Formed from L. *vesica*, a bladder, a blister.]

**Vesicle**, ves'i-kl, *n.* a *small* bladder or blister : a small cavity in an animal body : (*bot.*) a bladder-like cell. [L. *vesicula*, dim. of *vesica*, a bladder, a blister.]

**Vesicular**, ve-sik'ū-lar, **Vesiculous**, ve-sik'ū-lus, *adj.* pertaining to or full of *vesicles* : full of interstices : having little glands on the surface.

**Vesper**, ves'pėr, *n.* the evening star, Venus : the evening :—*pl.* in R. Cath. Church, the evening service : in Eng. Church, the sixth canonical hour, evensong.—*adj.* pertaining to the evening or to vespers. [Fr. ; Gr. *hesperos*. See **Hesper**.]

**Vessel**, ves'el, *n.* a *vase* or utensil for holding something : a hollow structure made to float on water, used for conveyance, &c. : a tube in which fluids, as blood, &c. are contained : a person considered as an agent of God. [O. Fr. (Fr. *vaisseau*)—L. *vascellum*, dim. of *vas*, a vase. Cf. **Vase**.]

**Vest**, vest, *n.* that which is *put on* as dress : a garment : a waistcoat.—*v.t.* to clothe : to invest :

(*law*) to give fixed right of possession.—*v.i.* to descend or to take effect, as a right. [L. *vestis*; conn. with Gr. *esthēs*, clothing, *henn-ymi*, *hes-o*, to put on, Goth. *ga-vasjan*, to clothe, Sans. root *vas-*.]

**Vesta**, vest'a, *n.* among the Romans, the chaste goddess that presided over the family, in whose temple the sacred fire was continually kept burning: a match or waxlight:—*pl.* **Vest'as.** [Root *vas*, to burn, as in Sans. *vasaras*, day, and Gr. *Hestia*.]

**Vestal**, vest'al, *adj.* pertaining to or consecrated to the service of *Vesta*: chaste: pure.

**Vestibule**, ves'ti-būl, *n.* an open court or porch before a house: a hall next the entrance to a house:*(anat.)* a small bony cavity forming part of the ear. [L. *vestibulum*, from the root *vas*, to dwell.]

**Vestige**, ves'tij, *n.* a *track* or footprint: traces or remains of something. [L. *vestigium—vestīgo*, to track—*ve*, denoting separation, and *stich* (Sans. *stigh*, to ascend), root of Gr. *steichō*, Ger. *steigen*, to go.]

**Vestment**, vest'ment, *n.* something *put on*, a garment: a long outer robe:—*pl.* articles of dress worn by officiating ministers. [L. *vestimentum —vestio*, to clothe—*vestis*, a garment.]

**Vestry**, ves'tri, *n.* a room adjoining a church in which the *vestments* are kept and parochial meetings held: an assembly of the managers of parochial affairs. [L. *vestiarium—vestiarius*, belonging to clothes—*vestis*, a garment.]

**Vesture**, vest'ūr, *n.*, *clothing*: dress: a robe: a garment. [Low L. *vestitura—*L. *vestio*.]

**Vesuvian**, ves-ōōv'i-an, *n.* a kind of match not easily extinguishable, for lighting cigars and the like in the open air. [From the volcano *Vesuvius*.]

**Vetch**, vech, *n.* a genus of plants, mostly climbing, some of which are cultivated for fodder, esp. the tare. [O. Fr. *veche* (Fr. *vesce*)—L. *vicia*.]

**Veteran**, vet'ēr-an, *adj.*, *old*: experienced: long exercised, esp. in military life.—*n.* one long exercised in any service, esp. in war. [L. *veteranus—vetus*, *veteris*, old.]

**Veterinarian**, vet-er-in-ār'i-an, *n.* one skilled in the diseases of domestic animals.

**Veterinary**, vet'er-in-ar-i, *adj.* pertaining to the art of treating the diseases of domestic animals: professing or practising this art. [L. *veterinarius—veterinus*, a contr. of *veheterinus—veho*.]

**Veto**, vē'to, *n.* any authoritative prohibition: the power of rejecting or forbidding:—*pl.* **Vetoes,** vē'tōz.—*v.t.* to reject by a veto: to withhold assent to. [L. *veto*, I forbid.]

**Vex**, veks, *v.t.* to harass (so in *B.*): to torment: to irritate by small provocations. [L. *vexo*, to shake or jolt in carrying, to annoy—*veho*, to carry.]

**Vexation**, veks-ā'shun, *n.* a *vexing*: state of being vexed: trouble: a teasing annoyance: uneasiness. [L. *vexatio—vexo*.]

**Vexatious**, veks-ā'shus, *adj.* causing *vexation* or annoyance: teasing: distressing: harassing: full of trouble.—*adv.* **Vexa'tiously.**—*n.* **Vexa'tiousness.**

**Viaduct**, vī'a-dukt, *n.* a *road* or railway *carried* by a structure over a valley, river, &c. [L. *via*, a way, *duco*, *ductum*, to lead, bring.]

**Vial**, vī'al, *n.* Same as **Phial.**

**Viand**, vī'and, *n.* food, usually in *pl.*: articles for food. [Fr. *viande*—Low L. *vivanda* (for *vivenda*), 'food necessary for life'—L. *vivo*, to live.]

**Viaticum**, vī-at'ik-um, *n.* (*orig.*) provisions for the

*way*: in R. C. Church, the communion given to the dying. [L.—*via*, a way.]

**Vibrate**, vī'brāt, *v.i.* to *shake*, to tremble: to move backwards and forwards: to swing: to pass from one state to another.—*v.t.* to cause to shake: to move to and fro: to measure by moving to and fro: to affect with vibratory motion. [L. *vibro*, *-atum*; cf. Sans. *vip*, to tremble.]

**Vibration**, vī-brā'shun, *n.* a vibrating: state of being vibrated.

**Vibratory**, vī'bra-tor-i, *adj.*, *vibrating*: consisting in vibrations: causing vibrations.

**Vicar**, vik'ar, *n.* one who acts in *place of another*: the incumbent of an impropriated benefice.—*n.* **Vic'arship.**—**Vicar-apostolic**, in R. C. Church, a missionary bishop or priest having powers from the pope.—**Vicar-general**, in the Eng. Church, an officer having powers from the chancellor of a diocese. [L. *vicarius*, supplying the place of another—*vicis*, change, alternation.]                      [a *vicar.*

**Vicarage**, vik'ar-āj, *n.* the benefice or residence of

**Vicarial**, vī-kā'ri-al, *adj.* pertaining to a *vicar*.

**Vicariate**, vī-kā'ri-āt, *adj.* having *vicarious* or delegated power.—*n.* delegated power.

**Vicarious**, vī-kā'ri-us, *adj.* filling the *place of another*: performed or suffered in place of or for the sake of another.—*adv.* **Vica'riously.** [See **Vicar.**]

**Vice**, vīs, *n.* an iron or wooden screw-press, fixed to the edge of a workboard, for holding anything tightly while being filed, &c. [Fr. *vis* (It. *vite*, screw)—L. *vitis*, tendril of a vine, anything of a like spiral form.]

**Vice**, vīs, *n.* a *blemish* or fault: immoral conduct: depravity of manners: a bad trick or habit in a horse. [Fr.—L. *vitium*, a blemish or defect.]

**Vice-admiral**, vīs-ad'mir-al, *n.* one acting in the *place* of or second in command to an *admiral*: a civil officer who exercises Admiralty jurisdiction. [L. *vice*, in the place of—*vicis*, change, and **Admiral.**]                      [*vice-admiral.*

**Vice-admiralty**, vīs-ad'mir-al-ti, *n.* the office of a

**Vice-chancellor**, vīs-chan'sel-or, *n.* one acting for a *chancellor*: a lower judge of Chancery. [L. *vice*, and **Chancellor.**]

**Vicegerency**, vīs-jē'ren-si, *n.* the office or deputed power of a *vicegerent*.

**Vicegerent**, vīs-jē'rent, *adj.*, *acting* in *place* of another, having delegated authority.—*n.* one acting in place of a superior. [L. *vice*, in the place of, and *gerens*, *-entis*, pr.p. of *gero*, to act.]

**Viceregal**, vīs-rē'gal, *adj.* pertaining to a *viceroy* or viceroyalty.

**Viceroy**, vīs'roy, *n.* one representing the royal authority in a dependency, as in India. [Fr. *vice-roi—*L. *vice*, in the place of, and *rex*, king.]

**Viceroyalty**, vīs-roy'al-ti, **Viceroyship**, vīs'roy-ship, *n.* the office or jurisdiction of a *viceroy*.

**Vicinage**, vis'in-āj, *n.*, *neighbourhood*: the places near. [O. Fr. *veisinage—veisin—*L. *vicinus*, neighbouring—*vicus*, a row of houses, Gr. *oikos*, a dwelling.]

**Vicinity**, vi-sin'i-ti, *n.*, *neighbourhood*: nearness: that which is near. [L. *vicinitas—vicinus*.]

**Vicious**, vish'us, *adj.* having a *vice* or defect: corrupt in principles or conduct: depraved: impure, as language or air: given to bad tricks, as a horse.—*adv.* **Vi'ciously.**—*n.* **Vi'ciousness.** [See **Vice**, a blemish.]

**Vicissitude**, vi-sis'i-tūd, *n.*, *change* from one thing to another: change: revolution. [L. *vicissitudo —vicis*, change, turn.]

**Victim**, vik'tim, *n.* a living being offered as a sacrifice: some thing or person destroyed in the pursuit of an object: a person suffering injury. [L. *victima*, prob. from root of *vigeo*, with a superlative ending.] [cheat.

**Victimise**, vik'tim-īz, *v.t.* to make a *victim* of: to

**Victor**, vik'tor, *n.* one who *conquers* on any particular occasion: one who defeats in battle: a winner.—*fem.* **Vic'tress**. [L.—*vinco, victum*, to conquer.]

**Victorious**, vik-tō'ri-us, *adj.* relating to *victory*: superior in contest: having overcome an enemy: producing or indicating victory.—*adv.* **Victo'riously.**

**Victory**, vik'tor-i, *n.* a conquering: success in any contest: a battle gained. [L. *victoria*—*victor.*]

**Victual**, vit'l, *v.t.* to supply with *victuals* or food: to store with provisions:—*pr.p.* **Victualling** (vit'l-ing); *pa.t.* and *pa.p.* **Victualled** (vit'ld).—*n.* **Victualler** (vit'l-er).

**Victuals**, vit'lz (in *B.* **Victual**, vit'l), *n.* that which is necessary for *living*: food for human beings: meat. [Low L. *victualia*—L. *victualis*, relating to living—*vivo, victum*, to live.]

**Vidette.** Same as **Vedette.**

**Vidimus**, vid'i-mus, *n.* an inspection, as of accounts, &c. [L. 'we have seen'—*video*, to see.]

**Vie**, vī, *v.i.* to strive for superiority:—*pr.p.* **vy'ing**; *pa.t.* and *pa.p.* **vīed.** [Prob. corr. of **Envy.**]

**View**, vū, *n.* a *seeing*: sight: reach of the sight: whole extent seen: that which is seen: direction in which a thing is seen: the picture of a scene: a sketch: mental survey: mode of looking at or receiving: opinion: intention.—*v.t.* to see: to look at attentively: to examine intellectually.—*n.* **View'er.** [Fr. *vue*—*vu*, pa.p. of *voir*—L. *vidēre*, to see. See **Vision.**]

**Viewless**, vū'les, *adj.* not to be viewed: invisible.

**Vigil**, vij'il, *n.*, *watching*: keeping awake for religious exercises: the eve before a feast or fast day, orig. kept by watching through the night. [L. *vigilia*—*vigil*, awake, watchful—*vigeo*, to be lively.] [ness : circumspection.

**Vigilance**, vij'il-ans, *n.*, *wakefulness*: watchful-

**Vigilant**, vij'il-ant, *adj.* watchful: on the lookout for danger: circumspect.—*adv.* **Vig'ilantly.** [Lit. 'keeping awake,' L. *vigilans, -antis*, pr.p. of *vigilo*, to keep awake—*vigil*.]

**Vignette**, vi-net', *n.* any small ornamental engraving not inclosed by a definite border: (*orig.*) an ornamental flourish of *vine* leaves and tendrils on manuscripts and books. [Fr.—*vigne*—L. *vinea*, a vine. See **Vine.**]

**Vigorous**, vig'ur-us, *adj.* strong either in mind or body.—*adv.* **Vig'orously.**—*n.* **Vig'orousness.**

**Vigour**, vig'ur, *n.* active strength: physical force: vital strength in animals or plants: strength of mind: energy. [L. *vigor*—*vigeo*, to be strong.]

**Viking**, vī'king, *n.* one of the Scandinavian pirates who in the 9th and 10th centuries ravaged the coasts of Western Europe. [Ice. *vikingr* (*lit.*) 'a creeker'—*vic*, a creek or bay.]

**Vilayet**, vil'ā-yèt, *n.* the name given to the great provinces into which the Ottoman empire is divided. [See **Eyalet.**]

**Vile**, vīl, *adj.* worthless: mean: morally impure: wicked: (*orig.*) 'cheap,' so in *B.*—*adv.* **Vile'ly.** —*n.* **Vile'ness.** [Fr.—L. *vilis*.]

**Vilification**, vil-i-fi-kā'shun, *n.* act of *vilifying*.

**Vilify**, vil'i-fī, *v.t.* to make *vile*: to attempt to degrade by slander: to defame:—*pa.t.* and *pa.p.* vil'if'ied.—*n.* **Vilifi'er.** [L. *vilis, facio*, to make.]

**Villa**, vil'a, *n.* a country residence or seat: a suburban mansion. [L. *villa* (for *vicula*), a

country-house, a farm, dim. of *vicus*, a street, a village, Gr. *oikos*, E. *-wick* (as in *Berwick*).]

**Village**, vil'āj, *n.* any small assemblage of houses, less than a town: (*orig.*) a number of houses inhabited by persons near the residence of a proprietor or farmer. [It. *villaggio*—L. *villa*.]

**Villager**, vil'āj-èr, *n.* an inhabitant of a *village*.

**Villain**, vil'ān or vil'in, *n.* a wicked wretch: a man extremely degraded: a deliberate scoundrel. [Orig. 'a serf attached to a *villa* or farm,' O. Fr. *villain*—Low L. *villanus*—L. *villa*.]

**Villainous**, vil'an-us, *adj.* like or suited to a *villain*: depraved: proceeding from extreme depravity: sorry.—*adv.* **Vill'ainously.**

**Villainy**, vil'an-i, *n.* the act of a *villain*: extreme depravity: an atrocious crime.

**Villein**, another spelling of **Villain** (only in its original meaning).

**Vinaigrette**, vin-ā-gret', *n.* a small box of silver or gold for holding aromatic *vinegar*, used as a smelling-bottle. [Fr.—*vinaigre*. See **Vinegar.**]

**Vincibility**, vin-si-bil'i-ti, *n.* the state or quality of being *vincible*.

**Vincible**, vin'si-bl, *adj.* that may be *conquered*. [L. *vincibilis*—*vinco*, to conquer.]

**Vinculum**, ving'kū-lum, *n.* a *band*: a bond: (*math.*) a horizontal line placed over several quantities to show that they are to be treated as one. [L.—*vincio*, to bind.]

**Vindicable**, vin'di-ka-bl, *adj.* that may be *vindicated* or defended.

**Vindicate**, vin'di-kāt, *v.t.* to lay claim to: to defend: to maintain by force.—*n.* **Vin'dicator.** [Lit. 'to assert authority,' L. *vindico, -atum*—*vis, vim*, power, influence, *dico*, to say, assert.]

**Vindication**, vin-di-kā'shun, *n.* act of *vindicating*: defence: justification: support.

**Vindicative**, vin'di-kāt-iv, *adj.*, *vindicating*: tending to vindicate.

**Vindicatory**, vin'di-ka-tor-i, *adj.* tending to *vindicate*: inflicting punishment.

**Vindictive**, vin-dik'tiv, *adj.* revengeful.—*adv.* **Vindic'tively.**—*n.* **Vindic'tiveness.**

**Vine**, vīn, *n.* the plant from which *wine* is made: the woody climbing plant that produces grapes: (*hort.*) a climbing or trailing plant, or its stem. [O. Fr.—L. *vinea*, a vine—*vinum*, Gr. *oinos*, wine. See **Wine.**]

**Vine-dresser**, vīn'-dres'èr, *n.* one who *dresses* or trims, and cultivates *vines*.

**Vinegar**, vin'e-gar, *n.* an acid liquor got from fermented and vinous liquors. [Lit. 'sour wine,' Fr. *vinaigre*—*vin* (—L. *vinum*, wine), and *aigre* —L. *acer*, sour.]

**Vinery**, vīn'èr-i, *n.* a hothouse for rearing *vines*.

**Vineyard**, vin'yard, *n.* a *yard* or inclosure for rearing *grape-vines*: a plantation of grape-vines.

**Vinous**, vī'nus, *adj.* pertaining to or having the qualities of *wine*. [L. *vinosus*—*vinum*.]

**Vintage**, vint'āj, *n.* the gathering of *grapes*: the yearly produce of grapes: the time of grapegathering. [Fr. *vendange*—L. *vindemia*—*vinum*, wine, grapes, and *demo*, to remove—*de*, out of or away, and *emo*, to take.]

**Vintner**, vint'nèr, *n.* a wine-seller. [O. Fr. *vinetier*—L. *vinitor*, a vine-dresser.]

**Viol**, vī'ol, *n.* an old musical instrument like the violin, having from three to six strings. [Fr. *viole*—It. *viola*—Low L. *vidula*, from L. *vitulari*, to skip like a calf, to make merry—*vitula*, a calf. **Fiddle** is from the same root.]

**Violable**, vī'o-la-bl, *adj.* that may be *violated*, injured, or broken.

**Violate**, vī'o-lāt, *v.t.* to injure: to abuse: to

ravish : to profane : to break forcibly : to transgress.—*n.* Vi′olator. [L. *violo, -atum—vis,* Gr. *is,* strength, force.]

Violation, vī-o-lā′shun, *n.* the act of *violating* or *injuring*: infringement : non-observance : profanation : rape.

Violence, vī′o-lens, *n.* the state or quality of being *violent*: force, physical or moral : unjust force : outrage : profanation : injury : rape.

Violent, vī′o-lent, *adj.* acting with physical *force* or strength : moved by strong feeling : passionate : vehement : outrageous : produced by force : unnatural.—*adv.* Vi′olently. [Fr.—L. *violentus—vis,* force. Cf. Violate.]

Violet, vī′o-let, *n.* a plant of many species, with a flower generally of some shade of blue : the colour of the violet, a bluish or light purple. —*adj.* of the colour of the violet, bluish or light purple. [Fr. *violette,* dim. of O. Fr. *viole*—L. *viola,* Gr. *ion.*]

Violin, vī′o-lin, *n.* a musical instrument of four strings played with a bow : a fiddle. [Fr. *violon* —It. *violone—viola* (see Viol).]

Violist, vī′ol-ist, Violinist, vī′o-lin-ist, *n.* a player on the *viol,* or on the *violin.*

Violoncellist, vē-o-lon-sel′ist or -chel′ist, *n.* a player on the *violoncello.*

Violoncello, vē-o-lon-sel′o or -chel′o, *n.* a large stringed musical instrument, between the violin and the double-bass, held between the knees in playing :—*pl.* Violoncel′los. [It., dim. of *violone,* a bass violin (see Violin).]

Viper, vī′pèr, *n.* a poisonous reptile of the order of snakes, once believed to be the only serpent that *brought forth living* young : any base, malicious person. [L. *vipera* (contr. of *vivipera)—vivus,* living, and *pario,* to bring forth.]

Viperous, vī′pèr-us, *adj.* having the qualities of a *viper*: venomous : malignant. [L. *vipereus.*]

Virago, vi-rā′go, *n.* a man-like woman : a bold, impudent woman : a termagant. [L.—*virgo* (see Virgin).]

Virgin, vèr′jin, *n.* a maiden : a woman who has had no sexual intercourse with man : (*B.*) a person of either sex who has not known sexual intercourse : (*astr.*) Virgo, one of the signs of the zodiac.—*adj.* becoming a maiden : maidenly : pure : chaste : undefiled : fresh. [O. Fr.—L. *virgo, virginis,* from a root *varg,* seen in Sans. *urg,* strength, Gr. *orgaō,* to swell.]

Virginal, vèr′jin-al, *n.* an old keyed musical instrument, prob. so called from being used to accompany hymns to the *Virgin.*

Virginity, vèr-jin′i-ti, *n.* the state of a *virgin.*

Virgo, vèr′go, *n.* the *Virgin,* in the zodiac.

Viridity, vi-rid′i-ti, *n.,* *verdure*: greenness. [L. *viriditas—viridis,* green—*vireo,* to be green. See Verdant.]

Virile, vir′il or -īl, *adj.* of or belonging to a *man* or to the male sex : masculine : manly. [L. *virilis* —*vir,* a man. See Virtue.]

Virility, vir-il′i-ti, *n.* the state or quality of being a *man*: the power of a full-grown male : the power of procreation : manhood. [L. *virilitas.*]

Virtu, vèr′tōō or -tū, *n.* a love of the fine arts : taste for curiosities : objects of art or antiquity. [It. Doublet Virtue.]

Virtual, vèr′tū-al, *adj.* having *virtue* or efficacy : having the efficacy without the material part : in effect though not in fact.—*adv.* Vir′tually.

Virtue, vèr′tū, *n.* excellence : worth : moral excellence : the practice of duty : a moral excellence : female chastity : purity : strength (so in *B.*): force : power : efficacy. [O. Fr.—L. *virtus,*

(*lit.*) 'what is excellent in *man,*' manliness, bravery, moral excellence—*vir,* a man, conn. with Gr. *hērōs,* Sans. *vira,* a hero. See World.]

Virtuoso, vèr-too-ō′zo or -tū-ō′so, *n.* one skilled in the fine arts, in antiquities, curiosities, and the like :—*pl.* Virtuo′si. [See Virtu.]

Virtuous, vèr′tū-us, *adj.* having *virtue* or moral goodness : blameless : righteous : practising duty : being according to the moral law : chaste (of a woman).—*adv.* Vir′tuously.

Virulent, vir′ū-lent, *adj.* full of poison : very active in injury : bitter in enmity : malignant. —*adv.* Vir′ulently.—*n.* Vir′ulence. [From Virus.]

Virus, vīr′us, *n.* a slimy liquid : contagious or poisonous matter (as of ulcers, &c.) : the poison which causes infection : any foul, hurtful matter. [L., cog. with Gr. *ios,* Sans. *visham,* poison.]

Visage, viz′āj, *n.* the face or look.—*adj.* Vis′aged. [Fr., through an assumed form *visaticum,* from L. *visus,* seen—*video,* to see.]

Viscera, vis′ér-a, *n.pl.* the inner parts of the animal body : the entrails. [L. *viscus,* pl. *viscera.*]

Visceral, vis′ér-al, *adj.* pertaining to the *viscera.*

Viscid, vis′id, *adj.* having the qualities of *bird-lime*: sticky : tenacious.—*n.* Viscid′ity. [L. *viscidus—viscus,* Gr. *ixos,* the mistletoe, bird-lime made from mistletoe berries.]

Viscount, vī′kownt, *n.* an officer who formerly supplied the place of the count or earl : a title of nobility next below an earl.—*fem.* Vis′countess. [O. Fr. *viscomte* (Fr. *vicomte*)—Low L. *vice-comes,* from L. *vice,* in place of, and *comes,* a companion. See Count.]

Viscous, vis′kus, *adj.* having the qualities of *bird-lime*: sticky : tenacious.—*n.* Viscos′ity. [L. *viscosus.* See Viscid.]

Visibility, viz-i-bil′i-ti, *n.* state or quality of being *visible,* or perceivable by the eye.

Visible, viz′i-bl, *adj.* that may be *seen*: obvious. —*adv.* Vis′ibly.—*n.* Vis′ibleness. [See Vision.]

Vision, vizh′un, *n.* the act or sense of *seeing*: sight : anything seen : anything imagined to be seen : a divine revelation : an apparition : anything imaginary. [Fr.—L. *visio, visionis—video, visum,* to see—root *vid,* as in Gr. *eidō,* Sans. *vid,* to see. Cf. Wit.]

Visionary, vizh′un-ar-i, *adj.* affected by *visions*: existing in imagination only : not real.—*n.* one who forms impracticable schemes.

Visit, viz′it, *v.t.* to *go to see* or inspect : to attend : to call on : (*B.*) to reward or punish.—*v.i.* to be in the habit of seeing or meeting each other : to keep up acquaintance.—*n.* act of *visiting* or going to see. [Fr. *visiter*—L. *visito,* freq. of *viso,* to go to see, visit—*video,* to see.]

Visitant, viz′i-tant, *n.* one who *visits*: one who is a guest in the house of another.

Visitation, viz-i-tā′shun, *n.* act of *visiting*: examination by authority : retribution.

Visitor, viz′it-ur, *n.* one who *visits*: one who inspects or examines.

Visitorial, viz-it-ō′ri-al, *adj.* belonging to a judicial *visitor,* or one who inspects or examines.

Visor, viz′ur, *n.* a part of a helmet covering the face, movable, and perforated to *see* through : a mask. [Fr. *visière*—L. *video.*]

Visored, viz′urd, *adj.* wearing a *visor*: masked.

Vista, vis′ta, *n.* a *view* or prospect through or as through an avenue : the trees, &c. that form the avenue. [It. *vista,* sight, view—L. *video,* to see.]

Visual, vizh′ū-al, *adj.* belonging to *vision* or sight : used in sight : used for seeing.—*adv.* Vis′ually.

**Vital**, vī'tal, *adj.* belonging or contributing to *life:* containing or necessary to life: important as life: essential.—*adv.* **Vi'tally.** [L. *vitalis*—*vita*, life; conn. with Gr. *bios*, life, and E. **Quick** (which see).]

**Vitalise**, vī'tal-īz, *v.t.* to make *vital* or alive: to give life to or furnish with the vital principle.

**Vitality**, vī-tal'i-ti, *n.* quality of being *vital:* principle or power of life. [L. *vitalitas.*]

**Vitals**, vī'talz, *n.pl.* parts essential to *life.*

**Vitiate**, vish'i-āt, *v.t.* to render faulty or defective: to make less pure: to deprave: to taint.—*n.* **Vitia'tion.** [L. *vitio, -atum*—*vitium* (see **Vice**, a blemish).]

**Vitreous**, vit'ri-us, *adj.*, *glassy:* pertaining to, consisting of, or like glass. [L. *vitrum*, glass.]

**Vitrescent**, vi-tres'ent, *adj.* that may be formed into *glass:* tending to become glass.—*n.* **Vitresc'ence.** [Coined from L. *vitrum*, glass.]

**Vitrifaction**, vit-ri-fak'shun, *n.* act, process, or operation of *vitrifying*, or converting into glass.

**Vitrifiable**, vit'ri-fī-a-bl, *adj.* that may be *vitrified* or turned into glass.

**Vitrify**, vit'ri-fī, *v.t.* to make into *glass.*—*v.i.* to become glass:—*pa.t.* and *pa.p.* vit'rified. [L. *vitrum*, glass, and *facio*, to make.]

**Vitriol**, vit'ri-ol, *n.* the popular name of sulphuric acid: a soluble sulphate of a metal, *green vitriol* = sulphate of iron, *blue vitriol* = sulphate of copper, *white vitriol* = sulphate of zinc. [Fr.—It. *vitriuolo*—L. *vitrum*, glass; prob. so called from its glassy appearance.]

**Vitriolic**, vit-ri-ol'ik, *adj.* pertaining to or having the qualities of *vitriol.*

**Vituperate**, vi-tū'pėr-āt, *v.t.* to find *fault* with: to censure. [L. *vitupero, -atum*—*vitium*, a fault, and *paro*, to set out.]

**Vituperation**, vi-tū-pėr-ā'shun, *n.* act of *vituperating:* blame: censure: abuse. [L. *vituperatio.*]

**Vituperative**, vi-tū'pėr-a-tiv, *adj.* containing *vituperation* or censure.—*adv.* **Vitu'peratively.**

**Vivacious**, vī-vā'shus, *adj.*, *lively* or *long-lived:* active: sportive.—*adv.* **Viva'ciously.**—*n.* **Viva'ciousness.** [L. *vivax, vivacis*—*vivo*, to live.]

**Vivacity**, vī-vas'i-ti, *n.* quality of being *vivacious:* life: animation: liveliness or sprightliness of temper or behaviour. [L. *vivacitas.*]

**Vivid**, viv'id, *adj.*, *lively* or *life-like:* having the appearance of life: forming brilliant images in the mind: striking.—*adv.* **Viv'idly.**—*n.* **Viv'idness.** [L. *vividus*—*vivo*, to live.]

**Vivify**, viv'i-fī, *v.t.* to make *vivid* or alive: to indue with life:—*pa.t.* and *pa.p.* viv'ified. [L. *vivus*, alive, *facio*, to make.]

**Viviparous**, vī-vip'a-rus, *adj.*, *producing* young *alive.* [L., from *vivus*, alive, and *pario*, to produce.]

**Vivisection**, viv-i-sek'shun, *n.* the practice of operating by *cutting* or otherwise on *living* animals, for the purposes of research or demonstration. [L. *vivus*, alive, *sectio*—*seco*, to cut.]

**Vixen**, vik'sen, *n.* a she-fox : an ill-tempered woman. [Fem. of *vox*, the southern E. form of *fox.*]

**Vizard**, viz'ard, *n.* Same as **Visor.**

**Vizier**, viz'yėr, *n.* an oriental minister or councillor of state. [Lit. 'a burden-bearer,' Ar. *wezir, wazir*, a porter—*wazara*, to bear a burden.]

**Vocable**, vō'ka-bl, *n.* that which is sounded with the *voice:* a word: a name. [L. *vocabulum*—*voco*, to call.]

**Vocabulary**, vo-kab'ū-lar-i, *n.* a list of *vocables* or words explained in alphabetical order : a dictionary: any list of words. [Low L. *vocabularium.*]

**Vocal**, vō'kal, *adj.* having a *voice:* uttered or changed by the voice.—*adv.* **Vo'cally.** [L. *vocalis*—*vox, vocis*, a voice, akin to *voco*, to call, Sans. *vach*, to speak.] [ing.

**Vocalisation**, vō-kal-i-zā'shun, *n.* act of *vocalis-*

**Vocalise**, vō'kal-īz, *v.t.* to make *vocal:* to form into voice.

**Vocalist**, vō'kal-ist, *n.* a *vocal* musician, a singer.

**Vocation**, vo-kā'shun, *n.* call or act of *calling:* calling: occupation. [L. *vocatio*—*voco.* See **Vocal.**]

**Vocative**, vok'a-tiv, *adj.* used in *calling.*—*n.* the case of a word when the person or thing is addressed. [L. *vocativus*—*voco.* See **Vocal.**]

**Vociferate**, vo-sif'ėr-āt, *v.i.* to cry with a loud *voice.*—*v.t.* to utter with a loud voice. [L.—*vox, vocis*, voice, and *fero*, to carry.]

**Vociferation**, vo-sif-ėr-ā'shun, *n.* act of *vociferating :* a violent or loud outcry. [L. *vociferatio.*]

**Vociferous**, vo-sif'ėr-us, *adj.* making a loud outcry: noisy.—*adv.* **Vocif'erously.**

**Vogue**, vōg, *n.* mode or fashion at any particular time : practice: popular reception. [Lit. 'way, course,' Fr. *vogue*, course of a ship—*voguer*, to row, from Ger. *wogen*, to move, expressing the movement of a vessel on the water.]

**Voice**, vois, *n.*, *sound* from the mouth : sound given out by anything: utterance or mode of utterance: language: expression : expressed opinion : vote: (*gram.*) mode of inflecting verbs, as being active or passive.—*v.t.* to fit for sounding : to regulate the tone of. [O. Fr. (Fr. *voix*)—L. *vox, vocis.*]

**Voiceless**, vois'les, *adj.* having no *voice* or vote.

**Void**, void, *adj.* unoccupied : empty (so in *B.*): having no binding force : wanting : unsubstantial.—*n.* an empty space.—*v.t.* to make vacant: to quit: to send out: to render of no effect. [O. Fr. *void*—L. *viduus*, bereft—root *vid*, to separate: allied to E. **Widow.**]

**Voidable**, void'a-bl, *adj.* that may be *voided* or evacuated.

**Voidance**, void'ans, *n.* act of *voiding* or emptying: state of being void : ejection.

**Volant**, vō'lant, *adj.*, *flying:* nimble. [L. *volans, -antis*, pr.p. of *volo*, to fly.]

**Volatile**, vol'a-til, *adj.* apt to waste away or fly off by evaporation: flighty: apt to change. [Fr.—L. *volatilis*, flying—*volo*, to fly.]

**Volatileness**, vol'a-til-nes, **Volatility**, vol-a-til'i-ti, *n.* quality of being *volatile:* disposition to evaporate: sprightliness: fickleness.

**Volatilisation**, vol-a-til-i-zā'shun, *n.* act or process of making *volatile* or evaporating.

**Volatilise**, vol'a-til-īz, *v.t.* to make *volatile:* to cause to evaporate.

**Volcanic**, vol-kan'ik, *adj.* pertaining to, produced, or affected by a *volcano.*

**Volcano**, vol-kā'no, *n.* a mountain from which smoke, flame, lava, &c. are thrown. [It. *volcano* —L. *Volcanus* or *Vulcanus*, the god of fire.]

**Volition**, vo-lish'un, *n.* act of *willing* or choosing: the exercise of the will : the power of determining. [Low L. *volitio*—L. *volo*, to will, be willing.]

**Volley**, vol'i, *n.* a *flight* of shot : the discharge of many small-arms at once: an outburst of many at once :—*pl.* **Voll'eys.**—*v.t.* to discharge in a volley. [Fr. *volée*, a flight—*voler*—L. *volo*, to fly.]

**Volt**, vōlt, *n.* a *turn* or bound : a sudden movement or leap to avoid a thrust : a gait of two treads made by a horse going sideways round a centre. [Fr. *volte*—It. *volta*—L. *volvo, volutum*, to turn.]

**Voltaic,** vol-tā'ik, *adj.* pertaining to or originated by *Volta,* an Italian : pertaining to Voltaism.

**Voltaism,** vol'ta-izm, *n.* Same as **Galvanism.**

**Volubility,** vol-ū-bil'i-ti, *n.* state or quality of being *voluble :* fluency of speech.

**Voluble,** vol'ū-bl, *adj.* easy to *roll* or move : flowing smoothly : fluent in speech.—*adv.* **Vol'ubly.** [L. *volubilis—volvo, volutum,* to roll.]

**Volume,** vol'ūm, *n.* a book : space occupied : dimensions : fullness of voice. [Lit. 'a *roll'* or scroll (so in *B.*), Fr.—L. *volumen,* a roll—*volvo, volutum,* to roll.]

**Volumed,** vol'ūmd, *adj.* having the form of a *volume* or roll : of volume or bulk.

**Voluminous,** vo-lū'mi-nus, *adj.* consisting of many *volumes* or books, or of many coils : having written much, as an author.—*adv.* **Volu'minously.**—*n.* **Volu'minousness.**

**Voluntary,** vol'un-tar-i, *adj. willing :* acting by choice : free : proceeding from the will : subject to the will : done by design or without compulsion.—*n.* one who does anything of his own free-will : a piece of music played at will.—*adv.* **Vol'untarily.**—*n.* **Vol'untariness.** [L. *voluntarius —voluntas,* choice—*volo,* to will.]

**Voluntaryism,** vol'un-tar-i-ism, *n.* the system of maintaining the church by *voluntary* offerings, instead of by the aid of the state.

**Volunteer,** vol-un-tēr', *n.* one who enters any service, esp. military, *voluntarily* or of his own free choice.—*adj.* entering into service voluntarily.—*v.t.* to offer voluntarily.—*v.i.* to enter into any service of one's own free-will or without being asked.

**Voluptuary,** vo-lupt'ū-ar-i, *n.* a *voluptuous* person or one excessively given to bodily enjoyments or luxury : a sensualist. [L. *voluptuarius— voluptas,* pleasure.]

**Voluptuous,** vo-lupt'ū-us, *adj.* full of *pleasure :* given to excess of pleasure, esp. sensual.—*adv.* **Volupt'uously.**—*n.* **Volupt'uousness.** [L. *voluptuosus—voluptas,* pleasure, conn. with *volupe,* agreeably, also with Gr. *elp-omai,* to hope, and perh. L. *volo,* to wish.]

**Volute,** vo-lūt', *n.* a kind of *rolled* or spiral scroll used in Greek capitals. [Fr.—L. *volvo, volutum,* to roll.]

**Voluted,** vo-lūt'ed, *adj.* having a *volute.*

**Vomer,** vō'mèr, *n.* the thin flat bone separating the nostrils. [L.]

**Vomit,** vom'it, *v.i.* to *throw up* the contents of the stomach by the mouth.—*v.t.* to throw out with violence.—*n.* matter ejected from the stomach : something that excites vomiting. [L. *vomo, -itum,* to throw up, Gr. *emeō.* See **Emetic.**]

**Vomitory,** vom'i-tor-i, *adj.* causing to *vomit.*—*n.* a vomit or emetic : a door of a large building by which the crowd is let out. [L. *vomitorius.*]

**Voracious,** vo-rā'shus, *adj.* eager to *devour :* greedy : very hungry.—*adv.* **Vora'ciously.** [L. *vorax, voracis—voro,* to devour.]

**Voracity,** vo-ras'i-ti, *n.* quality of being *voracious.*

**Vortex,** vor'teks, *n.* a *whirling* motion of a fluid forming a cavity in the centre : a whirlpool : a whirlwind :—*pl.* **Vor'tices.** [L. *vortex, vertex —vorto, verto,* to turn. Doublet **Vertex.**]

**Vortical,** vor'tik-al, *adj., whirling.*

**Votary,** vō'tar-i, *adj.* bound or consecrated by a *vow.*—*n.* one devoted as by a vow to some service, worship, or way of life.—*fem.* **Vo'taress.** [Low L. *votarius*—L. *voveo, votum,* to vow.]

**Vote,** vōt, *n.* expression of a wish or opinion, as to a matter in which one has interest : that by which a choice is expressed, as a ballot : decision by a majority.—*v.i.* to express the choice by a vote.—*v.t.* to choose by a vote.—*n.* **Vot'er.** [L. *votum,* a wish—*voveo, votum,* to vow.]

**Votive,** vōt'iv, *adj.* given by *vow :* vowed.—*adv.* **Vot'ively.** [L. *votivus—votum,* a vow.]

**Vouch,** vowch, *v.t.* to *call* upon to witness : to maintain by repeated affirmations : to warrant : to attest.—*v.i.* to bear witness : to give testimony. [O. Fr. *voucher, vocher,* to call to defend—L. *voco,* to call.]

**Voucher,** vowch'èr, *n.* one who *vouches* or gives witness : a paper which vouches or confirms the truth of anything, as accounts.

**Vouchsafe,** vowch-sāf', *v.t.* to *vouch* or warrant *safe :* to sanction or allow without danger : to condescend to grant.—*v.i.* to condescend.

**Vow,** vow, *n.* a solemn promise to God : a solemn or formal promise of fidelity or affection.—*v.t.* to give by solemn promise : to devote.—*v.i.* to make vows. [O. Fr. *vou* (Fr. *vœu*)—L. *votum —voveo,* to vow.]

**Vowel,** vow'el, *n.* a simple *vocal* sound : the letter representing such a sound.—*adj.* vocal : pertaining to a vowel. [Fr. *voyelle*—L. *vocalis—vox, vocis,* the voice.]

**Voyage,** voy'āj, *n.* passage by water.—*v.i.* to make a voyage, or to pass by water.—*n.* **Voy'ager.** [Fr.—L. *viaticum,* travelling-money— (Fr. *voie*), L. *via,* a way.]

**Vulcanise,** vul'kan-īz, *v.t.* to combine with sulphur by heat, as caoutchouc. [From L. *Vulcanus,* Vulcan, the god of fire.]

**Vulcanite,** vul'kan-īt, *n.* caoutchouc *vulcanised,* or combined with sulphur.

**Vulgar,** vul'gar, *adj.* pertaining to or used by the *common people,* native : public : common : mean or low : rude.—*n.* the common people.—*adv.* **Vul'garly.**—**Vulgar Fractions,** fractions written in the vulgar or ordinary way. [L. *vulgaris —vulgus,* the people ; conn. with Sans. *varga,* a group.]

**Vulgarise,** vul'gar-īz, *v.t.* to make *vulgar* or rude.

**Vulgarism,** vul'gar-izm, *n.* a *vulgar* phrase.

**Vulgarity,** vul-gar'i-ti, *n.* quality of being *vulgar :* mean condition of life : rudeness of manners.

**Vulgate,** vul'gāt, *n.* an ancient Latin version of the Scriptures, so called from its *common* use in the R. Cath. Church. [L. *vulgatus,* common— *vulgo,* to make common—*vulgus* (see **Vulgar**).]

**Vulnerable,** vul'nér-a-bl, *adj.* capable of being *wounded :* liable to injury.—*ns.* **Vulnerabil'ity, Vul'nerableness.** [L. *vulnerabilis—vulnero,* to wound—*vulnus, vulneris,* a wound, akin to *vello* (cf. **Vulture**).]

**Vulnerary,** vul'nér-ar-i, *adj.* pertaining to *wounds :* useful in healing wounds.—*n.* anything useful in curing wounds. [L. *vulnerarius—vulnus.*]

**Vulpine,** vul'pin, *adj.* relating to or like the *fox :* cunning. [L.—*vulpes,* a fox, Gr. *alōpēx.*]

**Vulture,** vult'ūr, *n.* a large rapacious bird of prey. [L. *vultur ;* perh. from *vello,* to pluck, to tear.]

**Vulturine,** vult'ūr-in, **Vulturish,** vult'ūr-ish, *adj.* like the *vulture :* rapacious.

# W

**Wacke,** wak'e, *n.* German miners' term for a soft, grayish kind of trap-rock.

**Wad,** wod, *n.* a mass of loose matter thrust close together, as hay, tow, &c. : a little mass of paper, tow, or the like to keep the charge in a gun.—*v.t.* to form into a mass : to stuff a wad into :— *pr.p.* wadd'ing ; *pa.t.* and *pa.p.* wadd'ed. [A.S.

*wæd*; Fr. *ouate*; allied to Ger. *watte*, garment, E. **Weed.**]

**Wadding**, wod′ing, *n*. a wad, or the materials for wads : a soft stuff, also sheets of carded cotton for stuffing garments, &c. [See **Wad.**]

**Waddle**, wod′l, *v.i.* to take short steps and move from side to side in walking.—*n.* **Wadd′ler.** [Perh. an extension of **Wade** ; cf. Ger. *wedeln*, to wag.]

**Wade**, wād, *v.i.* to walk through any substance that yields to the feet, as water : to pass with difficulty or labour.—*n.* **Wad′er.** [A.S. *wadan*, Ger. *waten.*]

**Wady**, wod′i, *n.* the dry bed of a torrent : a river-valley. [Ar. *wadi*, a ravine (preserved in the Sp. *guad-*, the first syllable of many Spanish river-names).]

**Wafer**, wā′fèr, *n.* a thin cake, usually round, esp. of bread, used in the Eucharist in the R. Cath. Church : a thin leaf of coloured paste for sealing letters, &c.—*v.t.* to close with a wafer. [O. Fr. *waufre* (Fr. *gaufre*), from Ger. *waffel—wabe*, honeycomb.]

**Waft**, waft or wäft, *v.t.* to bear through a fluid medium, as air or water.—*v.i.* to float.—*n.* a floating body : a signal made by moving something, as a flag, in the air.—*n.* **Waft′er.** [Sw. *vefta*, to fan, waft ; prob. allied to **Wave.**]

**Wag**, wag, *v.t.* and *v.i.* to move from side to side : to shake to and fro :—*pr.p.* wagg′ing ; *pa.t.* and *pa.p.* wagged. [A.S. *wagian*, *wegan* ; conn. with **Weigh** and **Wagon.**]

**Wag**, wag, *n.* a droll, mischievous fellow : a man full of sport and humour : a wit. [Prob. from *wagging* the head in derision.]

**Wage**, wāj, *v.t.* to *pledge* : to engage in as if by pledge : to carry on, esp. of war : to venture. —*n.* a *gage* or stake : that for which one labours : wages. [O. Fr. *wager* (Fr. *gager*), to pledge. A doublet of **Gage.**]

**Wager**, wāj′èr, *n.* that which is *waged* or pledged : something staked on the issue of anything : that on which bets are laid : (*law*) an offer to make oath.—*v.t.* to hazard on the issue of anything.— *v.i.* to lay a wager.—*n.* **Wag′erer.** [O. Fr. *waigiere* (Fr. *gageure*)—**Wage.**]

**Wages**, wāj′ez, *n.pl.* (used as *sing.*), *wage* : that which is paid for services. [Pl. of **Wage.**]

**Waggery**, wag′èr-i, *n.* the tricks or manner of a *wag* : mischievous merriment : pleasantry.

**Waggish**, wag′ish, *adj.* like a *wag* : mischievous or roguish in sport : done in waggery or sport. — *adv.* **Wagg′ishly.**—*n.* **Wagg′ishness.**

**Waggle**, wag′l, *v.i.* and *v.t.* to *wag* or move from side to side. [Freq. of **Wag,** *v.*]

**Wagon, Waggon**, wag′un, *n.* a four-wheeled vehicle for carrying heavy goods. [A.S. *wægen*. See the by-form **Wain.** The ending *-on* is probably due to Romance influence.]

**Wagoner, Waggoner**, wag′un-èr, *n.* one who conducts a *wagon.*

**Wagonette**, wag-un-et′, *n.* a kind of open carriage.

**Wagtail**, wag′tāl, *n.* a small bird, so named from its constantly *wagging* its *tail.*

**Waif**, wāf, *n.* anything found astray without an owner : a worthless wanderer. [Norman Fr. *weif* (O. Fr. *gaif*), Low L. *wayvium*, conn. with **Waive.**]

**Wail**, wāl, *v.i.* to lament or sorrow audibly.—*v.t.* to bemoan : to grieve over.—*n.* a cry of woe : loud weeping. [An imitative word, from the A.S. interj. *wâ, wâ-lâ* (E. **Woe**), Goth. *vai;* cf. Ir. *waill.*]

**Wailing**, wāl′ing, *n.*, *wail*—*adv.* **Wail′ingly.**

**Wain**, wān, *n.* a wagon. [A.S. *wægén, wæn;* Ger. *wagen;* from the root *vah*, to carry, L. *veho.* Doublet **Wagon.**]

**Wainscot**, wān′skot, *n.* the panelled boards on the walls of apartments.—*v.t.* to line with, or as if with, boards or panels. [Lit. ' wall-timber or boards,' A.S. *wag*, *wah*, a wall, and *scot* or *schot*, which also appears in the obs. *shide*, a lath—M. E. *scheden*, to divide (Ger. *scheiden*).]

**Waist**, wāst, *n.* the smallest part of the human trunk, between the ribs and the hips : the middle part of a ship. [From **Wax**, to grow ; cf. Ger. *wuchs—wachsen.*]

**Waistband**, wāst′band, *n.* the *band* or part of a garment which encircles the *waist.*

**Waistcoat**, wāst′kōt, *n.* a short *coat* worn immediately under the coat, and fitting the *waist* tightly.

**Wait**, wāt, *v.i.* to stay in expectation : to remain : to attend (with *on*) : to follow : to lie in ambush.— *v.t.* to stay for : to await.—*n.* ambush, now used only in such phrases as ' to lie in wait,' ' to lay wait.' [O. Fr. *waiter* (Fr. *guetter*), to watch, attend—O. Ger. *wahtan.* See **Wake.**]

**Waiter**, wāt′èr, *n.* one who *waits:* an attending servant : a salver or tray.—*fem.* **Wait′ress.**

**Waits**, wāts, *n.pl.* itinerant musicians who welcome in Christmas. [From **Wait.**]

**Waive**, wāv, *v.t.* to relinquish for the present : to give up claim to : not to insist on a right or claim. [O. Fr. *weiver.* Cf. **Waif.**]

**Wake**, wāk, *v.i.* to cease from sleep : to watch (so in *E.*) : to be roused up, active, or vigilant.—*v.t.* to rouse : to revive : to put in action :—*pa.t.* and *pa.p.* waked or woke. [A.S. *wacan;* Ger. *wachen*, to watch ; allied to **Wait, Watch,** also to *wax*, to grow, and to L. *vigeo*, to be lively, to thrive.]

**Wake**, wāk, *n.* act of *waking:* feast of the dedication of a church, formerly kept by watching all night : sitting up of persons with a corpse.

**Wake**, wāk, *n.* the streak of smooth water left in the track of a ship : hence fig., ' in the wake of,' in the train of : immediately after. [From Fr. *ouaiche*, through the Sp., from L. *aquagium*, a watercourse—*aqua*, water, and *ago*, to lead.]

**Wakeful**, wāk′fool, *adj.* being *awake:* indisposed to sleep : vigilant.—*adv.* **Wake′fully.**—*n.* **Wake′fulness.**

**Waken**, wāk′n, *v.t.* and *v.i.* to *wake* or *awake.*

**Wale**, wāl, *n.* a raised streak left by a stripe : a ridge on the surface of cloth : a plank all along the outer timbers on a ship's side.—*v.t.* to mark with wales. [A.S. *walu*, the mark of a stripe or blow ; Sw. *wal.* See **Goal.**]

**Walk**, wawk, *v.i.* to move along leisurely on foot with alternate steps : to pace : to travel on foot : (*B.*) to conduct one's self : to act or behave : to live : to be guided by.—*v.t.* to pass through or upon : to cause to walk. [A.S. *wealcan*, to roll, turn ; cog. with Ger. *walken*, to full cloth.]

**Walk**, wawk, *n.* act or manner of walking : gait : that in or through which one walks : distance walked over : place for walking : path : high pasture-ground : conduct : course of life.

**Wall**, wawl, *n.* an erection of brick, stone, &c. for a fence or security : the side of a building : (*fig.*) defence, means of security :—*pl.* fortifications.— *v.t.* to inclose with or as with a wall : to defend with walls. [A.S. *weall*, *wall*; Ger. *wall*, both from L. *vallum*, a rampart.]

**Wallet**, wol′et, *n.* a bag for carrying necessaries on a journey : a knapsack : a pocket-book.

[Prob. a corr. of Fr. *mallette*, dim. of *malle*, a bag (see **Mail**, a bag), under influence of **Valise**.]

**Wall-eye**, wawl'-ī, *n.* an eye in which the white part is very large: the popular name for the disease of the eye called *glaucoma*.—**Wall'-eyed**, *adj.* very light gray in the eyes, esp. of horses. [Older form *whally-eyed*—A.S. *hwelan*, to waste away.]

**Wall-flower**, wawl'-flow'èr, *n.* a plant with fragrant yellow *flowers*, found on old *walls*. [*wall*.

**Wall-fruit**, wawl'-frōōt, *n.*, *fruit* growing on a *wall*.

**Wallow**, wol'ō, *v.i.* to *roll* about, as in mire: to live in filth or gross vice. [A.S. *walwian*, Goth. *valvjan*, L. *volvo*. Cf. **Well**, a spring, and **Welter**.]

**Walnut**, wawl'nut, *n.* a tree of America and Asia, the wood of which is much used for furniture and gun-stocks: its nut or fruit. [Lit. the 'foreign nut,' A.S. *wealh*, foreign, E. **Welsh**, and *hnutu*, a nut; Ger. *wallnuss*.]

**Walrus**, wol'rus, *n.* an aquatic animal, allied to the seal, having long canine teeth, also called the Morse or the Sea-horse. [Lit. the 'whale-horse,' Ger. *wallross*—root of **Whale**, and *ross*, a horse.]

**Waltz**, wawlts, *n.* a German national dance performed by two persons with a rapid whirling motion: the music for it.—*v.i.* to dance a waltz. [Lit. the 'revolving dance,' Ger. *walzer*—*walzen*, to roll, conn. with **Wallow** and **Welter**.]

**Wampum**, wom'pum, *n.* the North American Indian name for shells or beads used as money.

**Wan**, won, *adj.* faint: wanting colour: pale and sickly: languid.—*adv.* **Wan'ly**.—*n.* **Wan'ness**. [A.S. *wann*, pale: perh. conn. with **Win**, which orig. meant to suffer, struggle.]

**Wand**, wond, *n.* a long slender rod: a rod of authority, or of conjurers. [Ice. *vöndr*, a shoot of a tree, Dan. *vaand*.]

**Wander**, won'dèr, *v.i.* to ramble with no definite object: to go astray (*lit.* or *fig.*): to leave home: to depart from the subject: to be delirious.—*n.* **Wan'derer**. [A.S. *wandrian*; Ger. *wandern*, allied to **Wend**, and to **Wind**, to turn round.]

**Wane**, wān, *v.i.* to decrease, esp. of the moon, as opp. to *wax*: to decline, to fail.—*n.* decline: decrease. [A.S. *wanian*; from root *wan*, seen in **Wanton**.]

**Want**, wont, *n.* state of being without anything: absence of what is needful or desired: poverty: scarcity: need.—*v.t.* to be destitute of: to need: to feel need of: to fall short: to wish for.—*v.i.* to be deficient: to fall short. [Ice. *vanta*, to be wanting; from root of **Wane**.]

**Wanting**, wont'ing, *adj.* absent: deficient.

**Wanton**, won'tun, *adj.* moving or playing loosely: roving in sport: frisky: wandering from rectitude: licentious: running to excess: unrestrained: irregular.—*adv.* **Wan'tonly**.—*n.* **Wan'tonness**. [M. E. *wantowen*, from *wan*, sig. want, and A.S. *togen*, educated, pa.p. of *teon*, to draw, lead; cf. Ger. *ungezogen*, rude.]

**Wanton**, won'tun, *n.* a *wanton* or lewd person, esp. a female: a trifler.—*v.i.* to ramble without restraint: to frolic: to play lasciviously.

**Wapentake**, wap'n-tāk, *n.* a name in Yorkshire for a district similar to the hundreds of southern counties, so called from the inhabitants being formerly taught the use of arms. [A.S. *wæpengetæc* (*lit.*) 'weapon-taking.' See **Weapon** and **Take**. Cf. **Wapinschaw**.]

**Wapinschaw**, wap'in-shaw, *n.* an exhibition of arms, formerly held periodically in Scotland. [Lit. 'weapon-show.']

**Wapiti**, wap'i-ti, *n.* the North American elk.

**War**, wawr, *n.* a state of opposition or contest: a contest between states carried on by arms: open hostility: the profession of arms.—*v.i.* to make war: to contend: to fight:—*pr.p.* warr'ing; *pa.t.* and *pa.p.* warred. [A.S. *werre*, influenced by O. Fr. *werre* (Fr. *guerre*), which is from O. Ger. *werra*, quarrel.]

**Warble**, wawr'bl, *v.i.* to sing in a quavering way, or with variations: to chirp as birds do.—*v.t.* to sing in a vibratory manner: to utter musically: to carol.—*n.* a quavering modulation of the voice: a song. [O. Fr. *werbler*, to warble, make turns with the voice—Ger. *wirbeln*, to make a turn; akin to **Whirl**.]

**Warbler**, wawr'blèr, *n.* one that *warbles*: a songster: a singing-bird.

**Ward**, wawrd, *v.t.* to guard or take care of: to keep in safety: to fend off.—*v.i.* to act on the defensive.—*n.* act of warding, watch: one whose business is to ward or defend: state of being guarded: means of guarding: one who is under a guardian: a division of a city, hospital, &c.: that which guards a lock or hinders any but the right key from opening it: (*B.*) guard, prison. [A.S. *weardian*; Ger. *warten*, to watch, to watch in order to protect. See **Guard**.]

**Warden**, wawrd'en, *n.* one who *wards* or guards: a keeper, esp. a public officer.—*n.* **Ward'enship**. [O. E. *wardein* (Fr. *gardien*).]

**Warder**, wawrd'èr, *n.* one who *wards* or keeps.

**Wardrobe**, wawrd'rōb, *n.* a room or portable closet for *robes* or clothes: wearing-apparel.

**Wardroom**, wawrd'rōōm, *n.* a room used as a messroom by the officers of a war-ship.

**Wardship**, wawrd'ship, *n.* the office of a *ward* or guardian: state of being under a guardian.

**Ware**, wār, *n.* (used generally in *pl.*), merchandise: commodities: goods. [A.S. *waru*; Ger. *waare*, Ice. *vara*.]

**Ware**, wār, *adj.* in *B.* = aware. [See **Wary**.]

**Ware**, wār, in *B.*, *pa.t.* of **Wear**.

**Warehouse**, wār'hows, *n.* a *house* or store for *wares* or goods.—*v.t.* to deposit in a warehouse.

**Warfare**, wawr'fār, *n.* a carrying on war: military life: war: contest or struggle. [**War** and **Fare**.]

**Warily, Wariness**. See under **Wary**.

**Warlike**, wawr'līk, *adj.*, *like*, fit, or disposed for *war*: belonging to war: soldierly.

**Warlock**, wawr'lok, *n.* a male witch: a wizard. [A.S. *wærloga*, a breaker of an agreement—*wær*, a compact, and *leogan*, to lie, modified by Ice. *vardh-lokk-r*, a magical song.]

**Warm**, wawrm, *adj.* having moderate heat, hot: subject to heat: zealous: easily excited: violent: enthusiastic.—*v.t.* to make warm: to interest: to excite.—*v.i.* to become warm or ardent.—*adv.* **Warm'ly**.—*ns.* **Warm'ness**, **Warm'er**. [A.S. *wearm*; Ger. *warm*; allied to O. L. *formus*, Gr. *thermos*, hot, Sans. *gharma*, heat.]

**Warmth**, wawrmth, *n.* state of being warm.

**Warn**, wawrn, *v.t.* to make *wary* or *aware*: to put on ward or guard: to give notice of danger: to caution against: to admonish. [A.S. *warnian*; Ice. *varna*, to warn, forbid, Ger. *warnen*; allied to **Ward**, **Beware**, **Wary**.]

**Warning**, wawrn'ing, *n.* caution against danger, &c.: admonition: previous notice.

**Warp**, wawrp, *v.t.* to turn: to twist out of shape: to turn from the right or proper course: to pervert: to tow or move with a line attached to buoys, &c.—*v.i.* to be twisted out of a straight direction: to bend: to swerve: to move with a bending motion. [A.S. *weorpan, werpan ;* Goth. *wairpan,* Ger. *werfen,* to cast.]

**Warp,** wawrp, *n.* the threads stretched out length-wise in a loom to be crossed by the woof: a rope used in towing. [A.S. *wearp ;* Ger. *werft.*]

**Warrant,** wor'ant, *v.t.* to guarantee or make secure: to give assurance against harm to: to authorise: to maintain: to assure. [O. Fr. *warantir* (Fr. *garantir*)—O. Ger. *weren,* to give bail for; Ger. *gewähren,* to vouch, warrant; conn. with **Ward, Wary.**]

**Warrant,** wor'ant, *n.* that which *warrants* or authorises: a commission giving authority: a writ for arresting a person: security.

**Warrantable,** wor'ant-a-bl, *adj.* authorised by *warrant* or right: justifiable.—*adv.* **Warr'ant-ably.**—*n.* **Warr'antableness.**

**Warranter,** wor'ant-èr, **Warrantor,** wor'ant-or, *n.* one who *warrants.*

**Warranty,** wor'ant-i, *n.* a legal *warrant* or deed of security: a guarantee: authority.

**Warren,** wor'en, *n.* a piece of ground for *warding* or protecting animals, especially rabbits. [O. Fr. *warenne* (Fr. *garenne*)—Fr. *garer,* from Teut. root of **Ward, Warrant.**]    [soldier.

**Warrior,** wor'i-or, *n.* one engaged in *war:* a

**Wart,** wawrt, *n.* a small, hard excrescence on the skin: a protuberance on trees. [A.S. *wearte ;* Ger. *warze ;* prob. allied to L. *verruca.*]

**Warty,** wawrt'i, *adj.* like a *wart:* overgrown with warts.

**Wary,** wār'i, *adj.* warding or guarding against deception, &c. : cautious.—*adv.* **War'ily.**—*n.* **War'iness.** [M. E. *war*—A.S. *wær,* cautious, conn. with **Ward, Warn.**]

**Was,** woz, used as *pa.t.* of **Be.** [A.S. *wæs, wære*—*wesan,* to remain, be; Goth. *visan,* pa.t. *vas,* to remain; Ice. *vera,* pa.t. *var,* Sans. *vas,* to dwell, live.]

**Wash,** wosh, *v.t.* to cleanse with water: to over-flow: to waste away by the action of water: to cover with a thin coat of metal or paint.—*v.i.* to cleanse with water.—*n.* a washing: the shallow part of a river or arm of the sea: a marsh or fen: alluvial matter: waste liquor, refuse of food, &c. : that with which anything is washed: a lotion: a thin coat of paint, metal, &c. [A.S. *wascan ;* Ice. *vaska,* Ger. *waschen.*]

**Washer,** wosh'èr, *n.* one who *washes:* a flat ring of iron or leather between the nave of a wheel and the linch-pin, under the head of a screw, &c.

**Washy,** wosh'i, *adj.* watery: damp: soft: weak: not solid.

**Wasp,** wosp, *n.* a stinging insect, like the bee, allied to the hornet. [A.S. *wǽps* (Ger. *wespe*); prob. from L. *vespa.*]

**Waspish,** wosp'ish, *adj.* like a *wasp:* having a slender waist like a wasp: quick to resent an affront.—*adv.* **Wasp'ishly.**—*n.* **Wasp'ishness.**

**Wassail,** wos'il, *n.* a festive occasion: a drunken bout: a liquor consisting of ale with roasted apples, sugar, nutmeg, and toast, once much used on festive occasions.—*v.i.* to hold a wassail or merry drinking-meeting. [A.S. *wes hál,* 'may you *be* in *health,*' the salutation used in pledging another, which the Normans trans-ferred to mean 'a carousal.' See **Was** and **Hale,** healthy.] [drinks wassail: a reveller.

**Wassailer,** wos'il-èr, *n.* one who *wassails* or

**Waste,** wāst, *adj.,* empty, desert: desolate: stripped: lying unused: unproductive.—*v.t.* to lay waste or make desolate: to destroy: to wear out gradually: to squander: to diminish: to impair.—*v.i.* to be diminished: to dwindle: to

be consumed. [A.S. *weste,* empty; cog. with Ger. *wüst,* desert, L. *vastus,* empty.]

**Waste,** wāst, *n.* act of *wasting:* useless expendi-ture: loss: destruction: that which is wasted or waste: uncultivated country: desert: refuse.

**Wasteful,** wāst'fool, *adj.* full of *waste:* destruc-tive: lavish.—*adv.* **Waste'fully.**—*n.* **Waste'-fulness.**

**Wasteness,** wāst'nes, *n.* (*B.*) devastation.

**Waster,** wāst'èr, *n.* one who or that which *wastes:* (*B.*) a spendthrift: a destroyer.

**Wasting,** wāst'ing, *n.* (*B.*) devastation.

**Watch,** woch, *n.* act of looking out: close observa-tion: guard: one who watches or those who watch: a sentry: the place where a guard is kept: time of watching, esp. in a ship: a divi-sion of the night: a pocket timepiece. [A.S. *wæcce ;* conn. with **Wake.**]

**Watch,** woch, *v.i.* to look with attention: to keep guard: to look out.—*v.t.* to keep in view: to give heed to: to have in keeping: to guard.

**Watcher,** woch'èr, *n.* one who *watches.*

**Watchful,** woch'fool, *adj.* careful to *watch* or observe: attentive: circumspect: cautious.—*adv.* **Watch'fully.**—*n.* **Watch'fulness.**

**Watchman,** woch'man, *n.* a *man* who *watches* or guards, esp. the streets of a city at night.

**Watchword,** woch'wurd, *n.* the pass-*word* to be given to a *watch* or sentry.

**Water,** waw'tèr, *n.* the fluid which forms the ocean, lakes, and rivers: any collection of it, as the ocean, a lake, river, &c. : urine: lustre of a diamond.—*v.t.* to wet, overflow, or supply with water: to wet and press so as to give a wavy appearance to.—*v.i.* to shed water: to take in water. [A.S. *wæter ;* Dut. *water,* Ger. *wasser ;* Gr. *hydōr,* L. *udus,* wet, *unda,* a wave, Sans. *uda,* water; conn. with **Wet.**]

**Water-carriage,** waw'tèr-kar'ij, *n.,* carriage or conveyance by *water.*

**Waterclock,** waw'tèr-klok, *n.* a *clock* which is made to go by the fall of *water.*

**Water-closet,** waw'tèr-kloz'et, *n.* a *closet* used as a privy, in which the discharges are carried off by *water.*

**Water-colour,** waw'tèr-kul'ur, *n.* a *colour* or pig-ment diluted with *water* and gum, instead of oil.

**Watercourse,** waw'tèr-kōrs, *n.* a *course* or channel for *water.*

**Waterfall,** waw'tèr-fawl, *n.* a *fall* or perpendicu-lar descent of a body of *water:* a cataract or cascade.

**Watergauge** or **Watergage,** waw'tèr-gāj, *n.* an instrument for *gauging* or measuring the quantity of *water.*

**Watering-place,** waw'tèr-ing-plās, *n.* a *place* where *water* may be obtained: a place to which people resort to drink mineral water, or bathe, &c.

**Waterish,** waw'tèr-ish, *adj.* resembling *water:* somewhat watery: thin.

**Water-level,** waw'tèr-lev'el, *n.* the *level* formed by the surface of still *water:* a levelling instru-ment in which water is used.

**Water-lily,** waw'tèr-lil'i, *n.* a *water*-plant like a *lily,* with large floating leaves.

**Waterline,** waw'tèr-līn, *n.* the *line* on a ship to which the *water* rises.

**Water-logged,** waw'tèr-logd, *adj.* rendered *log*-like, or unmanageable, from being filled with *water.*

**Waterman,** waw'tèr-man, *n.* a *man* who plies a boat on *water* for hire: a boatman: a ferryman.

**Watermark,** waw'tèr-märk, *n.* a *mark* showing

the height to which *water* has risen : a tide-mark : a mark wrought into paper.

**Watermill**, waw'tèr-mil, *n.* a *mill* driven by *water*.          [**Watershed.**]

**Water-parting**, waw'tèr-pärt'ing, *n.* Same as **Water-power**, waw'tèr-pow'èr, *n.* the *power* of *water*, employed to move machinery, &c.

**Waterproof**, waw'tèr-prōōf, *adj. proof* against *water:* not permitting water to enter.—*n.* anything with such qualities.—**Wa'terproofing**, *n.* the act of making any substance impervious to water.

**Watershed**, waw'tèr-shed, *n.* the line which separates two river-basins : a district from which several rivers rise. [See **Shed**, to part.]

**Waterspout**, waw'tèr-spowt, *n.* a moving *spout* or column of *water*, often seen at sea, and sometimes on land.

**Water-table**, waw'tèr-tā'bl, *n.* a moulding or other projection in the wall of a building to throw off the water.

**Watertight**, waw'tèr-tīt, *adj.* so *tight* as not to admit *water*, nor let it escape.

**Waterwheel**, waw'tèr-hwēl, *n.* a *wheel* moved by *water:* an engine for raising water.

**Waterwork**, waw'tèr-wurk, *n.* any *work* or engine by which *water* is furnished, as to a town, &c.

**Watery**, waw'tèr-i, *adj.* pertaining to or like *water:* thin or transparent : tasteless : containing or abounding with water.—*n.* **Wa'teriness.**

**Wattle**, wot'l, *n.* a twig or flexible rod : a hurdle : the fleshy excrescence under the throat of a cock or a turkey.—*v.t.* to bind with wattles or twigs : to form by plaiting twigs. [A.S. *watul.*]

**Waul**, wawl, *v.i.* to cry as a cat. [Imitative.]

**Wave**, wāv, *n.* a ridge on the surface of water swaying or moving backwards and forwards : a state of vibration propagated through a system of particles : inequality of surface : a line or streak like a wave.—*v.i.* to move like a wave : to play loosely : to be moved, as a signal : to fluctuate.—*v.t.* to move backwards and forwards : to brandish : to waft or beckon : to raise into inequalities of surface. [M. E. *wawe*—A.S. *wæg;* cog. with Ger. *woge*, Ice. *vogr;* allied to **Vogue, Waver.**]      [turbed.

**Waveless**, wāv'les, *adj., free* from *waves:* undis-

**Wavelet**, wāv'let, *n.* a *little wave.* [Dim. of **Wave.**]      [*waved* towards the four points.

**Wave-offering**, wāv'-of'èr-ing, *n.* (*B.*) an *offering*

**Waver**, wāv'èr, *v.i.* to move to and fro : to shake : to be unsteady or undetermined : to be in danger of falling.—*n.* **Wav'erer.** [An extension of **Wave.**]

**Wavy**, wāv'i, *adj.* full of or rising in *waves:* playing to and fro : undulating.

**Wax**, waks, *n.* a fat-like yellow substance produced by bees, and used by them in making their cells : any substance like it, as that in the ear : the substance used to seal letters :* that used by shoemakers to rub their thread.—*v.t.* to smear or rub with wax.—*adj.* **Wax'en.** [A.S. *weax*, *wæx;* Ice. *vax*, Dut. *was*, Ger. *wachs.*]

**Wax**, waks, *v.i.* to *grow* or *increase*, esp. of the moon, as opp. to *wane:* to pass into another state. [A.S. *weaxan;* Ice. *vaxa*, Ger. *wachsen*, Goth. *wahsjan;* L. *augeo*, to increase, Gr. *auxanō*, Sans. *vaksh*, Zend *ukhs.*]

**Waxcloth**, waks'kloth, *n., cloth* covered with a coating of *wax*, used for table-covers, &c. : a popular name for all oil floorcloths.

**Waxen**, waks'n (*B.*) pa.p. of **Wax**, *grown*.

**Waxwork**, waks'wurk, *n., work* made of *wax*, esp. figures or models formed of *wax*.

**Waxy**, waks'i, *adj.* resembling *wax:* soft : adhesive.

**Way**, wā, *n.* passage : road : length of space : distance : direction : manner of life : advance in life : general manner of acting : means : manner : will.—**By the way**, as we go on.—**Ways and means**, resources of revenue. [A.S. *weg;* Ger. *weg*, L. *via*, Sans. *vaha;* akin to *veho*, to carry ; Gr. *ochos*, a carriage. Cf. **Weigh.**]

**Waybill**, wā'bil, *n.* list of passengers and goods carried by a coach.

**Wayfarer**, wā'fār-èr, *n.* one who *fares* or goes on his *way:* a traveller or passenger.

**Wayfaring**, wā'fār-ing, *adj.* travelling or passing.

**Waylay**, wā-lā' or wā'lā, *v.t.* to *lie* in the *way* for : to watch or lie in ambush for.

**Waymark**, wā'märk, *n.* (*B.*) a guidepost.

**Wayward**, wā'wärd, *adj.* froward : wilful.—*n.* **Way'wardness.** [Prob. originally sig. 'taking one's own way' (cf. the *adj.* **Froward**).]

**Wayworn**, wā'wōrn, *adj.* worn out by travel.

**We**, wē, *pron., pl.* of **I** : I and others. [A.S. ; cog. with Goth. *veis*, Ger. *wir.*]

**Weak**, wēk, *adj.* soft : wanting strength : not able to sustain a great weight : wanting health : easily overcome : feeble of mind : wanting moral force : frail : unsteady : slight or incomplete : having little of the chief ingredient : impressible : inconclusive.—*adv.* **Weak'ly.**—*n.* **Weak'ness.** [A.S. *wac*, pliant—*wican*, to yield ; cog. with Dut. *week*, Ice. *veik-r*, Ger. *weich.*]

**Weaken**, wēk'n, *v.t.* to make *weak* : to reduce in strength or spirit.—*v.i.* to grow weak or weaker. [A.S. *wacian;* Ger. *weichen*. See **Weak.**]

**Weakling**, wēk'ling, *n.* a *weak* or feeble creature.

**Weakly**, wēk'li, *adj., weak* in body or mind.

**Weal**, wēl, *n.* state of being *well* : a sound or prosperous state : welfare. [A.S. *wela*, wealth, bliss ; Ger. *wohl*. See **Well**, *adj.*]

**Weal**, wēl, *n.* A form of **Wale.**

**Weald**, wēld, *n.* a *wood* or forest : a wooded region : an open country. [A.S. *weald*, Ger. *wald*, wood, from the root of **Wild.**]

**Wealden**, wēld'n, *adj.* (*geol.*) pertaining to the upper oolitic series of rocks. [So called because first studied in the *wealds* in S. of England.]

**Wealth**, welth, *n.* large possessions of any kind : riches. [Lit. 'state of being *well* or prosperous;' an extension of **Weal**, state of being well.]

**Wealthiest**, welth'i-est, *adj.* superl. of **Wealthy** (*Pr. Bk.*, Ps. lxxviii. 31) fattest.

**Wealthy**, welth'i, *adj.* rich : (*B.*) prosperous.—*adv.* **Wealth'ily.**—*n.* **Wealth'iness.**

**Wean**, wēn, *v.t.* to *accustom* to do without the breast : to reconcile to the want of anything : to estrange the affections from any object or habit. [A.S. *wenian;* Ice. *venja*, Ger. *gewöhnen*, to accustom, *ent-wöhnen*, to disuse, to wean.]

**Weapon**, wep'un, *n.* any instrument of offence or defence.—*adj.* **Weap'oned.** [A.S. *wæpen;* Goth. *vepna*, arms, Ger. *waffen* and *wappen*.]

**Wear**, wār, *v.t.* to carry on the body : to have the appearance of : to consume by use, time, or exposure : to waste by rubbing : to do by degrees. —*v.i.* to be wasted by use or time : to be spent tediously : to consume slowly : to last under use :—*pa.t.* wōre ; *pa.p.* wōrn.—*n.* **Wear'er.** [Lit. 'to cover,' A.S. *werian;* Ice. *verja*, to cover, Goth. *vasjan.* See **Vest.**]

**Wear**, wār, *n.* act of *wearing:* lessening or injury by use or friction.—**Wear and Tear**, loss by wear or use.      [Prob. a corr. of **Veer**.]

**Wear**, wār, *v.t.* to put a ship on another tack.

**Wear**, wēr, *n.* Another spelling of **Weir.**

**Wearable**, wār′a-bl, *adj.* fit to be worn.

**Wearisome**, wē′ri-sum, *adj.* making *weary*: tedious.—*adv.* **Wea′risomely.**—*n.* **Wea′risomeness.**

**Weary**, wē′ri, *adj.* worn out : having the strength or patience exhausted : tired : causing weariness. —*v.t.* to wear out or make weary : to reduce the strength or patience of : to harass.—*adv.* **Wea′rily.**—*n.* **Wea′riness.** [A.S. *werig.*]

**Weasel**, wē′zl, *n.* a small animal with a slender body and short legs, living on birds, mice, &c. [A.S. *wesle* ; Ger. *wiesel.*]

**Weather**, we*th*′er, *n.* state of the air as to heat or cold, dryness or wetness, &c.—*v.t.* to affect by exposing to the air : to sail to the windward of : to gain or pass, as a promontory or cape : to hold out stoutly against difficulties. [A.S. *weder* ; Ice. *vedhr*, Ger. *wetter.*]

**Weather-beaten**, we*th*′er-bēt′n, *adj.* distressed or seasoned by the weather.

**Weatherbound**, we*th*′er-bownd, *adj.*, *bound* or delayed by bad *weather*.

**Weathercock**, we*th*′er-kok, *n.* a vane (often in the form of a *cock*) to show the direction of the *wind* : anything turning easily and often.

**Weathergage**, we*th*′er-gāj, *n.* a *gage* of or that which shows the *weather* : the position of a ship to the windward of another.

**Weatherside**, we*th*′er-sīd, *n.* the *windward side*.

**Weave**, wēv, *v.t.* to twine threads together : to unite threads in a loom to form cloth : to work into a fabric : to unite by intermixture.—*v.i.* to practise weaving :—*pa.t.* wōve, (rarely) weaved ; *pa.p.* wōv′en.—*n.* **Weav′er.** [A.S. *wefan* ; Ice. *vefa*, Ger. *weben.*]

**Weaving**, wēv′ing, *n.* act or art of forming cloth.

**Web**, web, *n.* that which is *woven* : the fine texture spun by the spider as a snare for flies : a film over the eye : the skin between the toes of waterfowls. [A.S. *webb* ; Ice. *vefr*, Ger. *gewebe* ; from root of **Weave.**]

**Webbed**, webd, *adj.* having the toes united by a *web* or skin.

**Webbing**, web′ing, *n.* a narrow *woven* fabric of hemp, used for chairs, &c.

**Web-footed**, web′-foot′ed, *adj.* having webbed feet.

**Wed**, wed, *v.t.* to marry : to join in marriage : to unite closely.—*v.i.* to marry :—*pr.p.* wedd′ing ; *pa.t.* and *pa.p.* wedd′ed or wed. [A.S. *weddan*, to engage, to marry (Ger. *wetten*, to wager)— *wedd*, a pledge, cog. with Goth. *vadi*, Ger. *wette*, a bet. See **Gage**, and **Wage**, **Wager**.]

**Wedded**, wed′ed, *adj.* married : belonging to marriage. [mony.

**Wedding**, wed′ing, *n.* marriage : marriage cere-

**Wedge**, wej, *n.* a piece of wood or metal, thick at one end and sloping to a thin edge at the other, used in splitting : a mass of metal.—*v.t.* to cleave with a wedge : to force or drive with a wedge : to press closely : to fasten with a wedge. [A.S. *wecg* ; Ice. *veggr*, Ger. *weck*, a wedge ; prob. from the root to **Way, Weigh.**]

**Wedgwood-ware**, wej′wood-wār, *n.* a kind of semi-vitrified pottery much esteemed. [Invented by Josiah *Wedgwood* (1730-95).]

**Wedlock**, wed′lok, *n.* marriage : matrimony. [Lit. ‘state of being wedded,’ A.S. *wedlac*— **Wed**, and -*lac*, ‘a gift,’ ‘sport’. See **Lark**, a game, and **Knowledge**.]

**Wednesday**, wenz′dā, *n.* fourth day of the week. [A.S. *Wōdenes dæg*, ‘the *day* of *Wōden* or Odin,’ the chief Teutonic deity.]

**Wee**, wē, *adj.* small. [Cf. Prov. E. *weeny*, small,

A.S. *hwæne*, Ger. *wenig* ; cf. Scot. a *wheen*, a small number.]

**Weed**, wēd, *n.* any useless plant of small growth : anything useless or troublesome.—*v.t.* to free from weeds : to remove anything hurtful or offensive.—*n.* **Weed′er.** [A.S. *weod*, an herb.]

**Weed**, wēd, *n.* a garment : esp. in *pl.* a widow’s mourning apparel. [A.S. *wæd*, clothing ; O. Ger. *wât*, cloth, corrupted to Ger. -*wand* (as in *lein-wand*) ; from a Teut. root seen in Goth. -*vidan*, ‘to bind.’] [weeds.

**Weedy**, wēd′i, *adj.* consisting of *weeds* : full of

**Week**, wēk, *n.* the space of seven days, esp. from Sunday to Sunday. [A.S. *wice* ; Ice. *vika*, Dut. *week*, Ger. *woche* ; conn. also with L. *vicis*, change.] [Sunday.

**Weekday**, wēk′dā, *n.* any *day* of the *week* except

**Weekly**, wēk′li, *adj.* coming, happening, or done once a *week*.—*adv.* once a week.—*n.* a publication appearing once a week.

**Ween**, wēn, *v.i.* to think or fancy. [A.S. *wenan* —*wen* (Ger. *wahn*), expectation, hope.]

**Weep**, wēp, *v.i.* to express grief by shedding tears : to wail or lament.—*v.t.* to lament : to pour forth :—*pa.t.* and *pa.p.* wept. [A.S. *wepan* ; allied to Goth. *vopjan*, E. **Whoop**.]

**Weeper**, wēp′er, *n.* one who *weeps* : a white border round the sleeve of a *mourning* dress.

**Weeping**, wēp′ing, *adj.* drooping the branches (as it were through grief).

**Weevil**, wēv′il, *n.* a small kind of beetle very destructive to grain. [A.S. *wifel* ; Ger. *wiebel*, Lith. *wabalas* ; from the root of **Weave.**]

**Weft**, weft, *n.* the threads *woven* into and crossing the warp. [A.S. *weft*, for *wefed*, a weak pa.p. of *vefan*, E. **Weave.**]

**Weigh**, wā, *v.t.* to compare by the balance : to find the heaviness of : to be equal to in heaviness : to bear up, to raise, esp. a ship’s anchor : to ponder in the mind : to consider worthy of notice. —*v.i.* to have weight : to be considered of importance : to press heavily. [A.S. *wegan*, to carry, to weigh ; Ger. *wiegen*, to weigh ; L. *veho*, to carry. Cf. **Way, Wain.**]

**Weight**, wāt, *n.* the heaviness of a thing when *weighed*, or the amount which anything weighs : the force with which a body is attracted to the earth, measured by the mass into the acceleration : a mass of metal adjusted to a standard and used for finding weight : anything heavy : a ponderous mass : pressure : importance : power : impressiveness. [A.S. *ge-wiht* ; Ger. *ge-wicht* ; from root of **Weigh.**]

**Weighty**, wāt′i, *adj.* heavy : important : forcible. —*adv.* **Weight′ily.**—*n.* **Weight′iness.**

**Weir**, **Wear**, wēr, *n.* a dam across a river : a fence of stakes for catching fish. [A.S. *wer*, an inclosure—*werian*, to protect ; cf. Ger. *wehr*, a dam—*wehren*, to ward.]

**Weird**, wērd, *n.* a spell or charm.—*adj.* skilled in witchcraft : unearthly. [A.S. *wyrd*, fate—root of *weorthan*, Ger. *werden*, to happen. See **Worth.**]

**Welcome**, wel′kum, *adj.* received with gladness : admitted willingly : causing gladness : free to enjoy.—*n.* kindly reception.—*v.t.* to receive with kindness : to entertain hospitably. [From **Come** and **Will**, influenced also by **Well.**]

**Weld**, weld, *n.* a plant used to colour yellow. [Scot. *wald*, Ger. *wau.*]

**Weld**, weld, *v.t.* to join together as iron or steel by hammering, when softened by heat. [Conn. with A.S. *weallen*, to boil ; Ger. *wallen.*]

**Welfare**, wel′fār, *n.* state of *faring* or doing *well* :

freedom from any calamity, &c.: enjoyment of health, &c.: prosperity.

**Welkin**, wel'kin, *n.* the sky or region of clouds. [A.S. *wolcen, welcn*, cloud, air, sky; Ger. *wolke*, cloud; conn. with **Well**, a spring, the root idea being the 'rolling' (of clouds) in the air.]

**Well**, wel, *n.* a rise of water from the earth: a spring: a pit in the earth whence a supply of water is obtained: an inclosure in a ship's hold round the pumps: the open space in the middle of a staircase.—*v.i.* to issue forth, as water from the earth: to spring.—**Well-spring** (*B.*), *n.* a fountain. [A.S. *well*; Ger. *welle*, a wave. The root is found in A.S. *wealwian*, Goth. *valvjan*, L. *volvere*, to roll.]

**Well**, wel, *adj.* good in condition: fortunate: in health.—*adv.* in a proper manner: rightly: thoroughly: favourably: conveniently.—**Well-fa'voured** (*B.*), good-looking, so as to draw *favour*.—**Well-off, Well-to-do**, easy in circumstances, rich.—**Well-read**, widely acquainted with books. [A.S. *wel*, cog. with Goth. *vaila*, Ger. *wohl*.]

**Welladay**, wel'a-dā, **Wellaway**, wel'a-wā, *int.* alas. [Corr. from M. E. *weylaway*—A.S. *wa la wa*, 'woe, lo! woe.']

**Well-being**, wel'-bē'ing, *n.* state of being *well*.

**Well-born**, wel'-bawrn, *adj.*, *born* of a good or respectable family: not of mean birth.

**Well-bred**, wel'-bred, *adj.*, *bred* or trained *well*: educated to polished manners.

**Wellingtonia**, wel-ing-tōn'i-a, *n.* the largest of existing trees, a native of California. [Named after the Duke of Wellington.]

**Well-nigh**, wel'-nī, *adv.* nearly as well: almost.

**Welsh**, welsh, *adj.* pertaining to *Wales* or its inhabitants.—*n.pl.* the inhabitants of Wales:—*sing.* their language. [A.S. *wälsc* (Ger. *welsch*) —*wealh*, a Welshman; hence a foreigner; acc. to Weigand, from L. *Gallicus*—*Gallus*, a Gaul.]

**Welsh-rabbit**, welsh-rab'it, *n.* cheese melted on toasted bread. [Corr. of *Welsh rare bit.*]

**Welt**, welt, *n.* a kind of *hem* or edging round a shoe.—*v.t.* to furnish with a welt. [W. *gwald*, a hem—*gwal*, a wall, *gwaliaw*, to inclose.]

**Welter**, wel'tėr, *v.i.* to *roll* or wallow about, esp. in dirt. [M. E. *walter*, to roll, Sw. *vältra*; conn. with **Waltz** and **Wallow**.]

**Wen**, wen, *n.* a wart: a fleshy, pulpy tumour. [A.S. *wenn*, a swelling; a wart; Dut. *wen*.]

**Wench**, wensh, *n.* a low, coarse woman: a strumpet.—*v.i.* to frequent the company of wenches or strumpets. [A.S. *wencle*, a maid, prob. a Celt. word; conn. with W. *gweini*, to serve.]

**Wend**, wend, *v.i.* to go: to wind or turn. [A.S. *wendan* (Ger. *wenden*), to turn; the causative of **Wind**, to turn round.] [used as *pa.t.* of **Go**.]

**Went**, went, properly *pa.t.* of **Wend**, but now

**Wept**, wept, *pa.t.* and *pa.p.* of **Weep**.

**Were**, wer, *v.i.* the *pl.* of **Was**, used as *pa.t.* of **Be**. [A.S. *wäre*; Ger. *war*, Ice. *vera*, to be. See **Was**.]

**Wergild**, wer'gild, *n.* (among the Old English and Germans) a fine paid in compensation for a murder or severe injury. [A.S., from *wer*, man (see **Werwolf**), and *gild*, payment—*geldan*, to pay (E. **Yield**).]

**Werwolf**, wer'woolf, *n.* a person supposed to be able to change himself into a *wolf* at pleasure. [Lit. 'man-wolf,' A.S. *wer*, man (Goth. *vair*, L. *vir*), and **Wolf**.]

**Wesleyan**, wes'le-an, *adj.* pertaining to *Wesley*.—*n.* one who adopts Wesleyanism.

**Wesleyanism**, wes'le-an-izm, *n.* the system of doctrine and church polity of the Wesleyan Methodists: Arminian Methodism. [Named from John *Wesley*.]

**West**, west, *n.* the quarter where the sun sets: one of the four chief points of the compass: the countries to the west of Europe.—*adj.* situated towards the west. [A.S. *west*; Ger. *west*.]

**Westerly**, west'ėr-li, *adj.* lying towards the *west*: from the west.—*adv.* towards the west.

**Western**, west'ėrn, *adj.* situated in the *west*: moving towards the west.

**Westward**, west'ward, *adj.* and *adv.*, *towards* the *west*.—**West'wardly**, *adv.* towards the west.

**Wet**, wet, *adj.* containing water: having water on the surface: rainy.—*n.* water or wetness: moisture.—*v.t.* to make wet: to soak with water: to sprinkle:—*pr.p.* wett'ing; *pa.t.* and *pa.p.* wet, (rarely) wett'ed.—**Wet-dock**, *n.* a dock or basin for floating vessels at all states of the tide.—**Wet-nurse**, *n.* a nurse who suckles a child for its mother. [A.S. *wæt*; Ice. *vatr*; from root of **Water**.]

**Wether**, weth'ėr, *n.* a castrated ram. [A.S. *wedher*; Ger. *widder*.]

**Wetness**, wet'nes, *n.* state of being *wet*: moisture: a watery or moist state of the atmosphere.

**Wettish**, wet'ish, *adj.* somewhat *wet*.

**Wey**, wā, *n.* a measure or *weight* different with different articles = 182 lbs. wool, 40 bushels salt or corn, 48 bushels oats, &c. [From **Weigh**.]

**Whack**, hwak. Same as **Thwack**.

**Whale**, hwāl, *n.* the common name of an order of mammalia: the largest of sea-animals. [A.S. *hwel* (Ice. *hvalr*, Ger. *wall-fisch*); perh. from root of A.S. *hwelan*, to rush, to roar.]

**Whalebone**, hwāl'bōn, *n.* an elastic substance like *bone*, from the upper jaw of the *whale*.

**Whaler**, hwāl'ėr, *n.* a ship or a person employed in the *whale*-fishing.

**Whaling**, hwāl'ing, *adj.* connected with *whale*-catching.—*n.* the business of catching whales.

**Wharf**, hworf, *n.* a bank of timber or stone on the shore of a harbour or river for lading and unlading vessels:—*pl.* **Wharfs, Wharves**.—*v.t.* to secure by a wharf. [A.S. *hwearf*—*hweorfan*, to turn; conn. with Ger. *werben* (*lit.*) to turn, and so to seek after, acquire.] [*wharf.*]

**Wharfage**, hworf'āj, *n.* the dues paid for using a

**Wharfinger**, hworf'in-jėr, *n.* one who has the care of or owns a *wharf*.

**What**, hwot, *interrog. pron.* neuter of **Who**: how great: something.—*rel. pron.* = that which.—**What time** (*B.*) = at what time, when. [A.S. *hwæt*, neuter of *hwa*, who; Ger. *was*; allied to L. *quid*. See **Who**.]

**Whatever**, hwot-ev'ėr, *pron.*, *everything which*: being this or that: all that: one thing or another.

**Whatnot**, hwot'not, *n.* a piece of furniture with shelves for books, &c. so called because used to hold *anything*. [ever.

**Whatsoever**, hwot-sō-ev'ėr, *pron.* Same as **What-**

**Wheal**, hwēl, *n.* a **Wale**, which see.

**Wheat**, hwēt, *n.* a well-known grassy plant, also its seed, which furnishes a *white* flour for bread. [A.S. *hwæte*; Ger. *weizen*; allied to **White**, and named from its colour.]

**Wheaten**, hwēt'en, *adj.* made of *wheat*.

**Wheat-fly**, hwēt'-flī, *n.* the name of several *flies* or insects injurious to *wheat*.

**Wheedle**, hwēd'l, *v.t.* to entice by soft words: to flatter.—*ns.* **Wheed'ler, Wheed'ling**. [A.S. *wädlian*, to beg—*wädl*, poverty; Ger. *wedeln*, to wag the tail, as a dog.]

---

fāte, fär; me, hėr; mīne; mōte; mūte; mōōn; *then.*

**Wheel**, hwēl, *n.* a circular frame turning on an axle : an old instrument of torture.—*v.t.* to cause to whirl : to convey on wheels.—*v.i.* to turn round or on an axis : to roll forward. [A.S. *hweol*; Ice. *hjol*.]

**Wheeler**, hwēl'er, *n.* one who *wheels* : the horse nearest the wheels of a carriage.

**Wheelwright**, hwēl'rīt, *n.* a *wright* who makes *wheels* and wheel-carriages.

**Wheeze**, hwēz, *v.i.* to breathe with a *hissing* sound : to breathe audibly or with difficulty.—*n.* **Wheez'ing.** [A.S. *hweosan*; Ice. *hvæsa*, to wheeze, to hiss ; from the sound.]

**Whelk**, hwelk, *n.* a mollusc having a spiral shell. [A.S. *weoloc*, a whelk ; perh. from the root of **Walk** and **Welkin**, and sig. orig. the '*wreathed* creature.']

**Whelm**, hwelm, *v.t.* to *cover* completely : to plunge deep : to overburden. [A.S. *for-welman*, to overwhelm ; Ice. *hvelfa*, to overturn ; allied to Scot. *whummle*, to turn upside down.]

**Whelp**, hwelp, *n.* the young of the dog kind and of lions, &c. : a puppy : a cub : a young man (in contempt).—*v.i.* to bring forth young. [A.S. *hwelp*; Ice. *hvelpr*, Ger. *welf*.]

**When**, hwen, *adv.* at what time ? at which time : at or after the time that : while.—**Whenas** (-'az) (*B.*) when. [A.S. *hwanne*, accus. sing. from the stem of **Who** ; Ger. *wann*, *wenn*. Cf. **Then**.]

**Whence**, hwens, *adv.* from what place : from which things : wherefore. [M.E. *whenne-s*— A.S. *hwanon* (Ger. *wannen*) ; from the stem of **Who**. Cf. **Thence**.]

**Whencesoever**, hwens-so-ev'er, *adv.* from what place, cause, or source *soever*.

**Whenever**, hwen-ev'er, *adv.* at every time when.

**Whensoever**, hwen-so-ev'er, *adv.* at what time soever : whenever.

**Where**, hwār, *adv.* at which place, at what place ? to what place, to which place.—**Whereabout'**, about where : near what ?—**Whereas'**, as or on account of which : since : when in fact : near.— **Whereat'**, at which ; at what ?—**Whereby'**, by which.—**Where'fore**, for which reason : why ?— **Wherein'**, in which : in what ? —**Whereof** (-'of'), of which : of what ?—**Whereon'**, on which : on what ?—**Wheresoev'er**, in what place soever.—**Whereto'**, to which : to what ?—**Whereunto'** (*B.*) whereto : for what purpose ?—**Whereupon'**, upon or in consequence of which.—**Wherev'er**, at whatever place.— **Wherewith'**, with which : with what ?—**Wherewithal'**, same as **Wherewith**. [A.S. *hwa-r* or *hwæ-r*; from stem of **Who**. Cf. **There**.]

**Wherry**, hwer'i, *n.* a shallow, light boat, sharp at both ends for speed. [Prob. a corr. of **Ferry**, influenced by **Whir**.]

**Whet**, hwet, *v.t.* to *sharpen* by rubbing : to make keen : to excite :—*pr.p.* whett'ing ; *pa.t.* and *pa.p.* whett'ed.—*n.* act of sharpening : something that sharpens the appetite.—*n.* **Whett'er.** [A.S. *hwettan*, from A.S. *hwæt*, sharp ; Ger. *wetzen*.]

**Whether**, hweth'er, *interrog. pron.* sig. which of two.—*conj.* which of two alternatives. [A.S. *hwæ-ther*, from the stem of **Who**, with the old compar. suffix *-ther*; cog. with Goth. *hva-thar*, Ger. *we-der*; also with L. *u-teru-s*, Gr. *ko-tero-s*, Sans. *ka-tará*. Cf. **Other** and **Alter**.]

**Whetstone**, hwet'stōn, *n.* a *stone* used for *whetting* or sharpening edged instruments. [A.S. *hwæt-stan*.]

**Whey**, hwā, *n.* the watery part of milk, separated from the curd, esp. in making cheese.—*adjs.* **Whey'ey**, **Whey'ish**, of whey : like whey.

[A.S. *hwæg*; Scot. *whig*, Low Ger. *wey*; prob. conn. with root of **Water**.]

**Which**, hwich, a *relative pron.* used of all but persons : that or those which.—an *interrogative pron.* : (*B.*) = who.—**The which** (*B.*) which. [M. E. *hwuch*, *whilk*—A.S. *hwylc*, from *hwi* (E. **Why**), and *lic*, like ; Goth. *hva-leiks*, Ger. *welch*, *welcher*; also conn. with L. *qualis*. Cf. **Such** and **Each**.]

**Whichever**, hwich-ev'er, **Whichsoever**, hwich-so-ev'er, *pron.* every one which : whether one or other.

**Whiff**, hwif, *n.* a sudden puff of air from the mouth : a slight blast.—*v.t.* to throw out in whiffs : to puff. [W. *chwiff*; imitative.]

**Whiffle**, hwif'l, *v.i.* to turn as if by *whiffs* or gusts of wind : to be fickle : to prevaricate.—*n.* **Whiff'ler.** [Freq. of **Whiff**.]

**Whig**, hwig, *n.* the name (now almost superseded by 'Liberal') of one of the great English political parties.—*adj.* **Whig'gish.** — *adv.* **Whig'gishly.**—*ns.* **Whig'gism, Whig'gery,** Whig principles. [Orig. a nickname of the peasantry in the south-west of Scotland ; perh. from Scot. *whig*, sour milk (see **Whey**), their drink ; perh. from a word *whiggam*, which western drovers used in driving. The name was afterwards applied to the Covenanters, who belonged mostly to the south-west of Scotland ; finally given (in 1679) to the popular party which strove to exclude the Duke of York from the succession, because he was a R. Catholic.]

**While**, hwīl, *n.* a space of time.—*adv.* during the time that : at the same time that, as long as.— *v.t.* to cause to pass without irksomeness (with *away*).—**Whiles**, genitive form of while : (*B.*) while. [A.S. *hvil*; Goth. *hveila*, Ger. *weile*.]

**Whilom**, hwīl'om, *adv.* formerly, once, of old (*obs.*) [A.S. *hwīlum*, *hwīlon* (*lit.*) 'at times,' dative pl. of *hwīl*, a time. See **While**.]

**Whilst**, hwīlst, *adv.* same as **While**. [**Whiles**, genitive form of **While**, with excrescent *-t*. Cf. **Midst**.]

**Whim**, hwim, *n.* a caprice : a fancy. [Perhaps originally Scand., and conn. with Ice. *hvima*, to have the eyes wandering.]

**Whimper**, hwim'per, *v.i.* to cry with a low, *whining* voice. [Scot. *whimmer*, Ger. *wimmern*; perhaps from the root of **Whine**.]

**Whimsey**, hwim'zi, *n.* a *whim* : a freak. [Extension of **Whim**.]

**Whimsical**, hwim'zik-al, *adj.* full of *whims* : having odd fancies : fantastical.—*adv.* **Whim'sically.**—*ns.* **Whim'sicalness, Whimsical'ity.**

**Whin**, hwin, *n.* gorse, furze. [W. *chwyn*, weeds.]

**Whine**, hwīn, *v.i.* to utter a plaintive, shrill cry : to complain in an unmanly way.—*n.* a plaintive cry : an affected nasal tone of complaint.—*n.* **Whin'er.**—*adv.* **Whin'ingly.** [A.S. *hwinan*; cf. Ger. *weinen*, to weep.]

**Whinny**, hwin'i, *adj.* abounding in whins.

**Whinny**, hwin'i, *v.i.* to *neigh* or cry like a horse : —*pa.t.* and *pa.p.* whinn'ied. [Imitative ; cf. L. *hinnio*.]

**Whinstone**, hwin'stōn, *n.* general name for any hard, dark, unstratified rock. [Ety. of **Whin** dub.]

**Whip**, hwip, *n.* that which whips : a lash with a handle for punishing or driving : a driver : one who enforces the discipline of a political party.— *v.t.* to strike with a lash : to drive or punish with lashes : to lash with sarcasm : to sew lightly : to snatch (with *up* or *away*).—*v.i.* to move nimbly :

—*pr.p.* whipp'ing; *pa.t.* and *pa.p.* whipped. [A.S. *hweop*; Gael. *cuip*, a whip; cf. W. *chwip*, a quick turn.]

**Whipcord**, hwip'kord, *n.*, *cord* for making *whips*.

**Whiphand**, hwip'hand, *n.* (*lit.*) the *hand* that holds the *whip*: advantage over.

**Whipper**, hwip'ér, *n.* one who *whips*: an officer who inflicts the penalty of whipping.

**Whipper-in**, hwip'ér-in, *n.* one who keeps the hounds from wandering, and *whips* them *in* to the line of chase: one who enforces the discipline of a party. [ment with the whip or lash.

**Whipping**, hwip'ing, *n.* act of *whipping*: punish-

**Whipping-post**, hwip'ing-pōst, *n.* a *post* to which offenders are tied to be *whipped*.

**Whir**, hwér, *n.* a sound from rapid whirling.—*v.i.* to whirl round with a noise:—*pr.p.* whirr'ing; *pa.t.* and *pa.p.* whirred. [Imitative; cf. Ger. *schwirren*.]

**Whirl**, hwérl, *n.* a turning with rapidity: anything that turns with velocity.—*v.i.* to revolve rapidly.—*v.t.* to turn round rapidly. [Ice. *hvirfill*, Ger. *wirbel*: from the root of A.S. *hweorfan*, to turn. Cf. **Wharf**.]

**Whirligig**, hwèrl'i-gig, *n.* a child's toy which is spun or *whirled* rapidly round.

**Whirlpool**, hwérl'pōol, *n.* a *pool* or place where the water *whirls* round rapidly: an eddy.

**Whirlwind**, hwérl'wind, *n.* a violent aërial current, with a whirling, rotatory, or spiral motion.

**Whisk**, hwisk, *v.t.* to move with a quick motion: to sweep or stir rapidly.—*v.i.* to move nimbly and rapidly.—*n.* a rapid sweeping motion: a small bunch of anything used for a brush: a small instrument for beating or whisking, esp. eggs. [Scand. *viska*, Ger. *wischen*; from the root of **Wash**.]

**Whisker**, hwisk'ér, *n.* he who or that which *whisks*: the hair on the sides of a man's face (esp. in *pl.*): the bristle on the face of a cat, &c. —*adj.* **Whisk'ered**.

**Whisky, Whiskey**, hwisk'i, *n.* a spirit distilled from grain and other materials. [Celt. *uisge*, water; which also appears in A.S., a river name.]

**Whisper**, hwis'pér, *v.i.* to speak with a low sound: to speak very softly: to plot secretly.— *v.t.* to utter in a low voice or under the breath. —*n.* a low, hissing voice or sound: cautious or timorous speaking. [A.S. *hwisprian*; Ger. *wispern*, Ice. *hviskra*: allied to **Whistle**; prob. orig. from an interj. like *pst, hst*.]

**Whisperer**, hwis'pér-ér, *n.* one who whispers: (*B.*) a secret informer.

**Whist**, hwist, *n.* a well-known game at cards. [Orig. *whisk*; ety. dub. Usually, but without good reason, said to be so called from the *silence* it requires.]

**Whistle**, hwis'l, *v.i.* to make a shrill sound by forcing the breath through the lips contracted: to make a like sound with an instrument: to sound shrill.—*v.t.* to form or utter by whistling: to call by a whistle.—*n.* the sound made in whistling: a small wind instrument. [A.S. *hwistlan*; Sw. *hwissla*; cf. **Whisper**.]

**Whit**, hwit, *n.* the smallest particle imaginable: a bit. [By-form of **Wight**, a creature.]

**White**, hwīt, *adj.* of the colour of snow: pale: colourless: pure: unblemished: (*B.*) purified from sin.—*n.* the colour of snow: anything white, as a white man, the mark at which an arrow is shot, the albuminous part of an egg.—*v.t.* to make white.—*n.* **White'ness**. [A.S. *hwit*; Ice. *hvit-r*, Ger. *weiss*; also conn. with Sans. *çvit*, to be white, to shine. See **Wheat**.]

**Whitebait**, hwīt'bāt, *n.* a very small, delicious *white* fish of the herring kind. [-bait = '*food*.']

**Whitefriar**, hwīt'frī-ar, *n.* one of the Carmelite order of *friars*, so called from their *white* dress.

**White-heat**, hwīt'-hēt, *n.* the degree of *heat* at which bodies become *white*.

**Whitelead**, hwīt'led, *n.* a carbonate of *lead* used in painting *white*.

**White-livered**, hwīt'-liv'érd, *adj.* having a pale look, so called because thought to be caused by a *white liver*: cowardly: malicious.

**Whiten**, hwīt'en, *v.t.* to make *white*: to bleach. —*v.i.* to become or turn white.—*n.* **Whit'ener**.

**White-swelling**, hwīt'-swel'ing, *n.* a disease of the joints, esp. the knee.

**Whitewash**, hwīt'wosh, *n.* a *wash*, or mixture of whiting or lime and water, used to *whiten* ceilings, &c.—*v.t.* to cover with whitewash: to give a fair appearance to.

**White-wine**, hwīt'-wīn, *n.* any *wine* of a clear, transparent colour, bordering on *white*.

**Whither**, hwith'ér, *adv.* to what place? to which place: to what. [A.S. *hwæ-der, hwi-der*, from the stem of **Who**, with the locative suffix *-der* or *-ther*, Ice. *tha-thra*, Sans. *ta-tra*. Cf. **Thither, There**.] [ever place.

**Whithersoever**, hwith-ér-so-ev'ér, *adv.* to what-

**Whiting**, hwīt'ing, *n.* a small sea-fish allied to the cod, so called from its *white* colour: ground chalk free from stony matter.

**Whitish**, hwīt'ish, *adj.* somewhat white.—*n.* **Whit'ishness**.

**Whitlow**, hwit'lō, *n.* a painful inflammation, tending to suppurate, in the fingers, mostly under the nails. [Prob. compounded of **White**, and M. E. *low*, flame.]

**Whitsun**, hwit'sun, *adj.* pertaining to or observed at *Whitsuntide*.

**Whitsunday**, hwit'sun-dā, **Whitsuntide**, hwit'-sun-tīd, *n.* the seventh *Sunday* after Easter, commemorating the day of Pentecost, when the converts in the primitive church wore *white* robes.

**Whittle**, hwit'l, *v.t.* to pare or cut with a knife: to cut to an edge.—*n.* a small pocket-knife. [M. E. *th-witel* (which, being confused with **Whet**, dropped the *th-*)—A.S. *thwitan*, to cut.]

**Whiz**, hwiz, *v.i.* to make a *hissing* sound, like an arrow or ball flying through the air:—*pr.p.* whizz'ing; *pa.t.* and *pa.p.* whizzed.—*n.* a hissing sound.—*adv.* **Whizz'ingly**. [Imitative; cf. **Wheeze, Whist**, and **Hiss**.]

**Who**, hōō, *pron.* both *rel.* and *interrog.*, always for persons: what person? which person. [A.S. *hwa*: cog. with Goth. *hva-s*, Ice. *hver*, Ger. *wer*; also with Sans. *kâs*, Gr. *pos*, L. *quis*.]

**Whoever**, hōō-ev'ér, *pron.* every one who: whatever person.

**Whole**, hōl, *adj.* sound, as in health (so in *B.*): unimpaired: containing the total amount, number, &c.: all: not defective: complete.—*n.* the entire thing: a system or combination of parts. —*n.* **Whole'ness**.—*adv.* **Whol'ly**. [M. E. *hool*—A.S. *hal*, healthy; Ice. *heill*, Ger. *heil*; also cog. with Gr. *kalos*, beautiful. By-form **Hale**, *adj.*]

**Wholesale**, hōl'sāl, *n.*, *sale* of goods by the *whole* piece or large quantity.—*adj.* buying and selling in large quantities.

**Wholesome**, hōl'sum, *adj.* healthy: sound: salutary.—*adv.* **Whole'somely**.—*n.* **Whole'-someness**.

**Whom**, hōōm, *pron.* objective case of **Who**. [A.S. *hwam*, which was orig. dative of *wha*, **Who**, and replaced the older accus. *hwone*.]

**Whomsoever,** hōōm-so-ev'ėr, *pron.* objective case of **Whosoever.**

**Whoop,** hwōōp or hōōp, *n.* a loud eager cry.—*v.i.* to give a clear, sharp cry : to shout in scorn, eagerness, &c.—*v.t.* to insult with shouts. [A.S. *wôp—wepan* (pa.t. *weôp*), E. **Weep,** Goth. *vopjan,* to cry out.]

**Whooping-** or **Hooping-cough,** hōōp'ing-kof, *n.* a convulsive *cough* of children, like a *whoop.*

**Whore,** hōr, *n.* a woman who practises unlawful sexual intercourse : a prostitute : a harlot.—**Whoredom,** hōr'dum, *n.* unlawful sexual intercourse.—**Whoremonger,** hōr'mung-gèr, *n.* a lecher : a pander. See **Monger.**—*adj.* **Whor'ish.** —*adv.* **Whor'ishly.**—*n.* **Whor'ishness.** [A.S. *hore ;* Ger. *hure.*]

**Whorl,** hworl, *n.* a number of leaves in a *whirl* or circle round the stem. [By-form of **Whirl.**]

**Whortleberry,** hwor'tl-ber-i, *n.* a widely-spread heath plant with a blue edible berry, called also the **Bilberry.** [Changed (probably through influence of **Wort,** a plant) from *hurtle-berry—* A.S. *heorot-berige* (*lit.*) 'hart-berry.']

**Whose,** hōōz, *pron.* the possessive case of **Who** or **Which.**—**Whosoever** (*B.*) of whomsoever. [M. E. *hwas*—A.S. *hwǽs.*]

**Whoso,** hōō'so, **Whosoever,** hōō-so-ev'ėr, *indefinite relative pron.* every one who : whoever.

**Why,** hwī, *adv.* for *what* cause or reason? on which account : wherefore. [A.S. *hwī, hwý,* instrumental case of *hwa,* E. **Who.** Cf. **How.**]

**Wick,** wik, *n.* the threads of cotton or other substance in a candle or lamp which burn. [A.S. *weoca ;* Ger. *wieke,* a roll of lint.]

**Wicked,** wik'ed, *adj.* evil in principle or practice : deviating from morality : sinful : ungodly : naughty.—*n.* (*B.*) a wicked person.—*adv.* **Wick'edly.**—*n.* **Wick'edness.** [Perh. from A.S. *wican,* to become weak, decay ; see **Weak.** But Grimm connects it with A.S. *wicca,* E. **Witch,** so that the primary meaning would be 'bewitched,' 'accursed,' hence 'perverse.']

**Wicker,** wik'ėr, *n.* a small pliant twig or osier.— *adj.* made of twigs or osiers. [Ety. dub.]

**Wicket,** wik'et, *n.* a small gate : one of three upright rods bowled at in cricket. [O. Fr. *wiket* (Fr. *guichet*), a dim. of O. Scand. *vik,* an inlet.]

**Wide,** wīd, *adj.* extended far : having a considerable distance between : broad : distant.—*adv.* **Wide'ly.**—*n.* **Wide'ness.** [A.S. *wid ;* Ice. *widhr,* Ger. *weit.*]

**Widen,** wīd'n, *v.t.* or *v.i.* to make or grow wide or wider.

**Widgeon,** wid'jun, *n.* a waterfowl allied to the duck, but smaller. [Fr. *vingeon, gingeon.*]

**Widow,** wid'ō, *n.* a woman *without* or bereft of her *husband* by death.—*v.t.* to bereave of a husband : to strip of anything valued. [A.S. *widuwe ;* Ger. *wittwe ;* borrowed from L. *vidua,* bereft of a husband, Sans. *vidhava—vi* (= L. *ve-*), without, and *dhava,* a husband.]

**Widower,** wid'ō-ėr, *n.* a man whose wife is dead.

**Widowhood,** wid'ō-hood, *n.* state of being a widow, or (rarely) of being a widower.

**Width,** width, *n.* wideness.

**Wield,** wēld, *v.t.* to use with full command : to manage : to use.—*n.* **Wield'er.** [A.S. *geweldan—wealdan ;* Goth. *valdan,* Ger. *walten.*]

**Wieldy,** wēld'i, *adj.* capable of being wielded : manageable.

**Wife,** wīf, *n.* a woman : a married woman.—*adj.* **Wife'ly.** [A.S. *wif ;* Ice. *vif,* Ger. *weib.*]

**Wifeless,** wīf'les, *adj.* without a wife.

**Wig,** wig, *n.* an artificial covering of hair for the head. [Short for **Periwig.**]

**Wigged,** wigd, *adj.* wearing a wig.

**Wight,** wīt, *n.* a creature or a person—used chiefly in sport or irony. [A.S. *wiht,* a creature ; Ger. *wicht.* Grimm refers it to a root seen in O. Ger. *wihan* (Ger. *weihen*), to consecrate, orig. to do, to make. See **Whit.**]

**Wight,** wīt, *n.* a hero. [A.S. *wig,* war.]

**Wigwam,** wig'wam, *n.* an Indian hut. [E. corr. of North American word sig. 'in his house.']

**Wild,** wīld, *adj.* being in a state of nature : not tamed or cultivated : uncivilised : desert : unsheltered : violent : licentious.—*n.* an uncultivated region : a forest or desert.—*adv.* **Wild'ly.** —*n.* **Wild'ness.** [A.S. *wilde ;* Ger. *wild ;* conn. with Ger. *wald,* forest, E. **Weald.**] [**wilder.**]

**Wilder,** wild'ėr, *v.t.* to bewilder. [Short for **Be-**

**Wilderness,** wil'dėr-nes, *n.* a *wild* or waste place : an uncultivated region. [A.S. *wildeorness.*]

**Wildfire,** wild'fīr, *n.* a composition of inflammable materials : a kind of lightning flitting at intervals.

**Wilding,** wīld'ing, *n.* that which grows *wild* or without cultivation : a wild crab-apple.

**Wile,** wīl, *n.* a trick : a sly artifice. [A.S. *wil ;* Ice. *vel, væl,* a trick. Doublet **Guile.**]

**Wilful,** wil'fool, *adj.* governed only by one's *will :* done or suffered by design : obstinate.—*adv.* **Wil'fully.**—*n.* **Wil'fulness.**

**Will,** wil, *n.* power of choosing or determining : choice or determination : pleasure : command : arbitrary disposal : feeling towards, as in good or ill will : disposition of one's effects at death : the written document containing such.—*v.i.* to exercise the will : to decree : (*B.*) to be willing. —*v.t.* to determine : to be resolved to do : to command : to dispose of by will. [A.S. *willa ;* Goth. *vilja,* Ger. *wille ;* L. *volo,* to will, Gr. *boulē,* will, purpose.]

**Willing,** wil'ing, *adj.* having the *will* inclined to a thing : desirous : disposed : chosen.—*adv.* **Will'ingly.**—*n.* **Will'ingness.**

**Willow,** wil'ō, *n.* a tree of several species, with slender, pliant branches. [A.S. *wilig ;* Low Ger. *wilge, wichel.*]

**Will-worship,** wil'-wur'ship, *n.* (*B.*) *worship* of what one *wills* or wishes : superstitious observance.

**Wilt,** wilt, 2d pers. sing. of **Will.**

**Wily,** wīl'i, *adj.* full of *wiles* or tricks : using craft or stratagem : artful : sly.—*adv.* **Wil'ily.**— **Wil'iness,** *n.* cunning.

**Wimble,** wim'bl, *v.t.* to whirl, to turn : to bore with a wimble.—*n.* an instrument for boring holes, turned by a handle. [A corr. (with freq. suffix) of **Wind,** to turn. See **Gimlet.**]

**Wimple,** wim'pl, *n.* a hood or veil folded round the neck and face (still a part of a nun's dress) : a flag. [O. Fr. *guimple*—O. Ger. *wimpal,* a light robe (Ger. *wimpel,* a streamer). See **Gimp.**]

**Win,** win, *v.t.* to get by labour : to gain in contest : to allure to kindness, to gain : to obtain the favour of.—*v.i.* to gain the victory : to gain favour :—*pr.p.* winn'ing ; *pa.t.* and *pa.p.* won (wun). [A.S. *winnan,* to suffer, to struggle ; Ice. *vinna,* to accomplish, Ger. *ge-winnen,* to win.]

**Wince,** wins, *v.i.* to shrink or start back : to be affected acutely, as by a sarcasm : to be restive, as a horse uneasy at its rider. [Perh. through O. Fr. from Ger. *wanken,* to shake.]

**Win'cey.** Same as **Linsey-woolsey.**

**Winch,** winsh, *n.* the crank of a wheel or axle.— *v.i.* to wince. [A.S. *wince.*]

**Wind,** wind, *n.* air in motion : breath : flatulence : anything insignificant.—*v.t.* (wīnd) to sound by blowing : (wind) to expose to the wind : to drive hard, so as to put out of breath : to allow to recover wind :—*pr.p.* wīnd'ing and wind'ing ; *pa.p.* wound and wind'ed. [A.S. ; Ice. *vindr*, Ger. *wind*, L. *ventus* ; from root of Gr. *aō*, to blow, Sans. *va*.]

**Wind**, wīnd, *v.t.* to *turn* round, to twist : to coil : to encircle : to change.—*v.i.* to turn completely or often : to turn round something : to twist : to move spirally : to meander :—*pr.p.* wīnd'ing ; *pa.t.* and *pa.p.* wound.—**To wind up**, to bring into small compass : to bring to a final settlement, as the affairs of a company. [A.S. *windan* ; Ger. *winden*, Ice. *vinda*, Goth. *vindan*. Cf. **Wend**.]

**Windage**, wind'āj, *n.* the difference between the size of the bore of a gun and that of the ball or shell. [From **Wind**, the space being filled with air.] [dered from sailing by the *wind*.

**Windbound**, wind'bownd, *adj.*, *bound* or hin-

**Windfall**, wind'fawl, *n.* fruit blown off a tree by the *wind* : any unexpected money or other advantage.

**Windgauge**, wind'gāj, *n.* an instrument for *gauging* or measuring the velocity of the *wind*.

**Winding**, wīnd'ing, *n.* a *turning* : a bend.—*adj.* twisting, or bending.—*adv.* **Wind'ingly**.

**Windlass**, wind'las, *n.* a machine for raising heavy weights, consisting of a revolving cylinder. [Dut. *windas*—*winden*, E. **Wind**, and *as*, an axletree ; so Ice. *wind-ass*, a *wind-ing beam*.]

**Windmill**, wind'mil, *n.* a *mill* driven by the *wind*.

**Window**, wind'ō, *n.* an opening in the wall of a building for air and light : the frame in the opening. [Lit. 'wind-eye,' M. E. *windoge*—Ice. *vindauga*—*vindr*, wind, and *auga*, eye.]

**Windpipe**, wind'pīp, *n.* the *pipe* or passage for the *wind* or breath, to and from the lungs.

**Windward**, wind'ward, *adv.*, *toward* where the *wind* blows from.—*adj.* toward the wind.—*n.* the point from which the wind blows.

**Windy**, wind'i, *adj.* consisting of *wind* : next the wind : tempestuous : empty.—*n.* **Wind'iness**.

**Wine**, wīn, *n.* the fermented juice of the grape : a liquor made from other fruits : (*fig.*) intoxication. [A.S. *win* ; Goth. *vein*, Ger. *wein* ; all from L. *vinum*, which is cog. with Gr. *oinos*, Heb. *yayin*, Ar. *wain*.] [of *wine* : a drunkard.

**Wine-bibber**, wīn'-bib'ér, *n.* a *bibber* or drinker

**Wing**, wing, *n.* the organ of a bird, or other animal or insect, by which it flies : flight : any sidepiece : side of an army, ship, building, &c. : (*fig.*) protection.—*v.t.* to furnish or transport with wings : to supply with side-pieces : to wound in the wing.—**On the wing**, on flight : departing. [Sw. *winge*, Ice. *vængr* ; cf. E. **Swing**.]

**Winged**, wingd, *adj.* furnished with *wings* : swift : wounded in the wing.

**Wink**, wingk, *v.i.* to move the eyelids quickly : to give a hint by winking : to seem not to see, connive at (so in *B.*) : to be dim, to flicker.—*n.* act of winking : a hint given by winking. [A.S. *wincian* ; Ger. *winken*.]

**Winner**, win'ér, *n.* one who *wins* in a contest.

**Winning**, win'ing, *adj.* gaining or adapted to gain favour : attracting.—*n.* what is gained in contest, labour, &c.—*adv.* **Winn'ingly**.

**Winnow**, win'ō, *v.t.* to separate the chaff from the grain by *wind* : to fan : to examine.—*v.i.* to separate chaff from grain.—*n.* **Winn'ower**. [A.S. *windwian*, to expose to the wind—**Wind**.]

**Winsome**, win'sum, *adj.* cheerful : pleasant : attractive. [A.S. *wyn-sum*, pleasant—*wyn*, joy, Ger. *wonne*.]

**Winter**, win'tér, *n.* the cold season of the year : the after-autumn.—*v.i.* to pass the winter.—*v.t.* to feed during winter. [A.S. ; Ger. *winter* ; of uncertain origin ; not connected with **Wind**.]

**Winter-quarters**, win'tér-kwawr'térz, *n.pl.* the *quarters* of an army during *winter* : a winter residence.

**Wintery**, win'tér-i, **Wintry**, win'tri, *adj.* resembling or suitable to *winter* : stormy.

**Wipe**, wīp, *v.t.* to clean by rubbing : to rub off : clear away.—*n.* act of cleaning by rubbing : a sarcasm.—*n.* **Wip'er**. [A.S. *wipian* ; see **Wisp**.]

**Wire**, wīr, *n.* a thread of metal.—*v.t.* to bind or supply with wire : to telegraph. [A.S. *wir* ; Ice. *virr* ; perh. conn. with L. *viriæ*, bracelets.]

**Wiredraw**, wīr'draw, *v.t.* to *draw* into *wire* : to draw or spin out to a great length : to strain or stretch the meaning of anything.

**Wire-puller**, wīr'-pool-er, *n.* one who exercises an influence felt but not seen, as if the actors were his puppets and he *pulled* the *wires* that move them : an intriguer. [strong.

**Wiry**, wīr'i, *adj.* made of or like *wire* : flexible and

**Wis**, wis, *v.* (in the form I **wis**), used as = know. [I *wis* is from A.S. *ge-wis*, certainly (Ger. *ge-wiss*), from root of **Wit**.]

**Wisdom**, wiz'dum, *n.* quality of being *wise* : judgment : right use of knowledge : (*B.*) piety. [A.S.]

**Wise**, wīz, *adj.* having *wit* or knowledge : able to make use of knowledge well : judging rightly : discreet : learned : skilful : dictated by wisdom : containing wisdom.—*adv.* **Wise'ly**. [A.S. *wis* ; Ger. *weise* ; from root of **Wit**.]

**Wise**, wīz, *n.* way, manner. [A.S. *wise* ; Ger. *weise* ; akin to **Wise**, *adj.* and **Wit**. Doublet **Guise**.]

**Wiseacre**, wīz'ā-kér, *n.* one who pretends to great wisdom : a simpleton. [From Ger. *weissager*, a prophet—O. Ger. *wizzago* (A.S. *witiga*).]

**Wish**, wish, *v.i.* to have a desire : to long (so in *B.*) : to be inclined.—*v.t.* to desire or long for : to ask : to invoke.—*n.* desire, longing : thing desired : expression of desire.—*n.* **Wish'er**. [A.S. *wyscan* ; Ger. *wünschen*, Sw. *onska*.]

**Wishful**, wish'fool, *adj.* having a wish or desire : eager.—*adv.* **Wish'fully**.—*n.* **Wish'fulness**.

**Wisp**, wisp, *n.* a small bundle of straw or hay. [Probably connected with **Whisk**.]

**Wist**, wist (*B.*) knew. [A.S. *wiste*, pa.t. of *witan*, to know. See **Wit**.]

**Wistful**, wist'fool, *adj.* full of thought : thoughtful : earnest : eager.—*adv.* **Wist'fully**.—*n.* **Wist'fulness**. [From root of **Wit**.]

**Wit**, wit, *v.i.* (*B.*) to know.—**To wit** (gerundial inf. used as *adv.*) = namely, that is to say. [A.S. *witan*, to know ; Goth. *vitan*, Ger. *wissen* ; conn. also with L. *video* (see **Vision**), Gr. *eidon*, Sans. *vid* (see **Veda**).]

**Wit**, wit, *n.* understanding (so in *B.*) : a mental faculty (chiefly in *pl.*) : the power of combining ideas with a ludicrous effect : the result of this power : one who has wit. [A.S. *witt*—*witan*.]

**Witch**, wich, *n.* a woman regarded as having supernatural or magical power and knowledge.—*v.t.* to bewitch. [A.S. *wicce* ; *wicca*, wizard ; acc. to Grimm, from Goth. *weihan* (Ger. *weihen*), to consecrate, orig. to do, to perform (rites). Cf. L. *facio*, *operari*, and Gr. *erdō*.]

**Witchcraft**, wich'kraft, *n.* the *craft* or practice of *witches* : sorcery : supernatural power.

**Witchery**, wich'ér-i, *n.*, *witchcraft* : fascination.

**Witenagemote**, wit'en-ag-e-mōt', *n.* the supreme council of the Anglo-Saxons. [A.S. *wita*, a wise man, *gemot*, a meeting.]

**With,** *n.* Same as **Withe.**

**With,** with, *prep.* denoting nearness or connection: by: in competition or contrast: on the side of: immediately after: among. [A.S. *widh, wither,* prob. orig. sig. 'placed over against;' Ice. *vidh,* Ger. *wider.* It prob. absorbed the A.S. *mid,* with (Ger. *mit,* Gr. *meta*).]

**Withal,** with-awl', *adv., with all* or the rest : likewise : moreover : (*B.*) *prep.* = with.

**Withdraw,** with-draw', *v.t.* to *draw back* or away : to take back : to recall.—*v.i.* to retire : to go away.—*ns.* **Withdraw'al, Withdraw'ment.** [Prefix *with,* against, back, and **Draw.**]

**Withe, With,** with, *n.* a flexible twig, esp. of *willow:* a band of twisted twigs. [A.S. *widhig;* Ice. *vidhir,* Ger. *weide,* willow : further conn. with Gr. *itys,* L. *vitis,* Sans. *vi,* to tie, to plait.]

**Wither,** with'ér, *v.i.* to fade or become dry in the *weather:* to lose freshness : to shrink : waste.—*v.t.* to cause to dry up : to cause to decay, waste. [A.S. *wedrian;* from root of **Weather.**]

**Withers,** with'érz, *n.pl.* the ridge between the shoulder-bones of a horse. [From *wither,* against (see ety. of **With,** *prep.*).]

**Withhold,** with-hōld', *v.t.* to *hold back:* to keep back. [Prefix *with,* against, back, and **Hold.**]

**Within,** with-in', *prep.* in the *inner* part : inside : in the reach of : not going outside of.—*adv.* in the inner part : inwardly. [Prefix *with,* and **In.**]

**Without,** with-owt', *prep.* outside or *out of :* beyond : not with : in absence of : not having : except.—*adv.* on the outside : out of doors. [Prefix *with,* and **Out.**]

**Withstand,** with-stand', *v.t.* to *stand against :* to oppose or resist. [Prefix *with,* against, and **Stand.**]

**Witless,** wit'les, *adj., wanting wit* or understanding : thoughtless.—*adv.* **Wit'lessly.**—*n.* **Wit'lessness.** [tender to wit.

**Witling,** wit'ling, *n.* one who has *little wit:* a pre-

**Witness,** wit'nes, *n., knowledge* brought in proof : testimony of a fact : that which furnishes proof : one who sees or has personal knowledge of a thing : one who attests.—*v.t.* to have direct knowledge of : to see : to give testimony to.—*v.i.* to give evidence. [A.S. *ge-witness*—**Wit.**]

**Witted,** wit'ed, *adj.* having *wit* or understanding.

**Witticism,** wit'i-sizm, *n.* a *witty* remark : a sentence or phrase affectedly witty : a low kind of wit. [**Witty,** and Ger. affix *-cism.*]

**Wittingly,** wit'ing-li, *adv.* knowingly : by design. [From *witting,* pr.p. of **Wit,** to know.]

**Witty,** wit'i, *adj.* possessed of *wit:* amusing : droll : sarcastic : (*B.*) ingenious.—*adv.* **Witt'ily.** —*n.* **Witt'iness.**

**Wive,** wīv, *v.t.* to take for a wife.—*v.i.* to marry. [A.S. *wifian*—*wif,* E. **Wife.**]

**Wizard,** wiz'ard, *n.* one who practises witchcraft or magic.—*fem.* **Witch.** [Lit. 'a wise man,' O. Fr. *guisc-art*—*guisc* = Ice. *vizk-r* (for *vit-sk-r*), from root of **Wit.**]

**Woad,** wōd, *n.* a plant used as a blue dyestuff. [A.S. *wad;* Ger. *waid;* L. *vitrum.*]

**Woe, Wo,** wō, *n.* grief : misery : a heavy calamity : a curse : an exclamation of grief. [A.S. *(interj.) wa;* Ger. *weh;* L. *væ,* Gr. *ouai.* Cf. **Wail.**]

**Woe-begone,** wō'-be-gon', *adj.* beset with woe. [See under **Begone.**]

**Woe worth.** See **Worth.**

**Woful,** wō'fool, *adj.* sorrowful : bringing calamity : wretched.—*adv.* **Wo'fully.**—*n.* **Wo'fulness.**

**Wold,** wōld, *n.* By-form of **Weald.**

**Wolf,** woolf, *n.* a wild animal of prey allied to the dog : anything very ravenous.—*pl.* **Wolves.**

[A.S. *wulf;* Ger. *wolf;* prob. also allied to L. *vulpes,* a fox.]

**Wolf-dog,** woolf'-dog, *n.* a *dog* of large breed kept to guard sheep, esp. against *wolves.*

**Wolfish,** woolf'ish, *adj.* like a *wolf* either in form or quality : rapacious.—*adv.* **Wolf'ishly.**

**Wolverine,** wool'vèr-ēn, *n.* a name given to the glutton, from its rapacity. [Extension of **Wolf.**]

**Woman,** woom'an, *n.* the female of man : a grown female : a female attendant : —*pl.* **Women** (wim'en). [A.S. *wimman, wifmann,* a compound of *wif,* **Wife,** and **Man;** cf. A.S. *mædenmann,* a virgin, Ger. *weibs-mensch,* a female.]

**Womanhood,** woom'an-hood, *n.* the state, character, or qualities of a *woman.*

**Womanish,** woom'an-ish, *adj.* having the qualities of a woman : feminine.—*adv.* **Wom'anishly.** —*n.* **Wom'anishness.**

**Womankind,** woom'an-kīnd, *n.,* women taken together : the female sex.

**Womanlike,** woom'an-līk, *adj., like* a *woman.*

**Womanly,** woom'an-li, *adj.* like or becoming a *woman:* feminine.—*adv.* in the manner of a woman.—*n.* **Wom'anliness.**

**Womb,** wōōm, *n.* the organ in which the young of mammals are developed, and kept till birth : the place where anything is produced : any deep cavity. [A.S. *wamb;* Ger. *wamme,* paunch.]

**Wombat,** wom'bat, *n.* an Australian marsupial mammal of the opossum family.

**Won,** wun, *pa.t.* and *pa.p.* of **Win.**

**Wonder,** wun'dèr, *n.* the state of mind produced by something new, unexpected, or extraordinary : a strange thing : a prodigy.—*v.i.* to feel wonder : to be amazed (with *at*). [A.S. *wundor;* Ger. *wunder,* Ice. *undr.*]

**Wonderful,** wun'dèr-fool, *adj., full of wonder:* exciting wonder : strange : (*B.*) wonderfully. —*adv.* **Won'derfully.**—*n.* **Won'derfulness.**

**Wondrous,** wun'drus, *adj.* such as may excite wonder : strange.—*adv.* **Won'drously.**

**Wont,** wunt, *adj.* used or accustomed.—*n.* habit. —*v.i.* to be accustomed. [Orig. pa.p. of M. E. *wone,* to dwell—A.S. *wunian* (Ger. *wohnen*).]

**Won't,** wōnt, will not. [Contr. of M. E. *wol not.*]

**Wonted,** wunt'ed, *adj.* accustomed : usual. [See **Wont.**]

**Woo,** wōō, *v.t.* to ask in order to marriage : to court.—*v.i.* to court or make love.—*n.* **Woo'er.** [A.S. *wogian,* to woo, prob. orig. 'to bend;' cf. A.S. *vog, voh,* bent, Goth. *un-vahs,* blameless, (*lit.*) 'not-bent.']

**Wood,** wood, *n.* the solid part of trees : trees cut or sawed : timber : a collection of growing trees. —*v.t.* to supply wood. [A.S. *wudu;* cog. with Ice. *vidh-r,* wood, Ger. *wit,* firewood.]

**Woodbine,** wood'bīn, **Woodbind,** wood'bīnd, *n.* the honeysuckle, so called because it twists and *binds* the *trees* together. [A.S. *wudu-bind.* Cf. **Hopbind.**]

**Woodcoal,** wood'kōl, *n., coal* like *wood* in texture : charcoal : lignite or brown coal.

**Woodcock,** wood'kok, *n.* a bird, allied to the snipe, which frequents *woods.*

**Woodcut,** wood'kut, *n.* an engraving *cut* on *wood:* an impression from it.—*n.* **Wood'cutter.**

**Wooded,** wood'ed, *adj.* supplied with *wood :* covered with wood.

**Wooden,** wood'n, *adj.* made of *wood :* hard : clumsy.

**Wood-engraving,** wood'-en-grāv'ing, *n.* the act or art of *engraving* on *wood :* an engraving on or taken from wood. [*wood.*

**Woodland,** wood'land, *n., land* covered with

**Woodlark**, wood′lärk, *n.* a species of *lark*, found in or near *woods*, singing chiefly on the wing.

**Woodman**, wood′man, *n.* a *man* who cuts down *trees*: a forest officer: a huntsman.

**Woodnymph**, wood′nimf, *n.* a *nymph* or goddess of the *woods*.

**Woodpecker**, wood′pek-èr, *n.* a bird that *pecks* holes in the *wood* or bark of trees for insects.

**Wood-pigeon**, wood′-pij′un, *n.* the wild *pigeon* which lives in *woods*, the ringdove.

**Woodruff**, wood′ruf, *n.* a plant, found in *woods* and shady places, with its leaves in whorls like *ruffs.*

**Woodward**, wood′wawrd, *n.* an officer to *guard* the *woods.*

**Woody**, wood′i, *adj.* abounding with *woods*: pertaining to woods: consisting of wood.

**Woof**, wōōf, *n.* Same as **Weft**. [From pa.t. of **Weave**. Cf. **Weft**.]

**Wool**, wool, *n.* the soft, curly hair of sheep and other animals: short thick hair. [A.S. *wull*; cog. with Goth. *vulla*, Ger. *wolle*.]

**Wool-gathering**, wool′-gath′ẻr-ing, *n.* indulgence of idle fancies.—*adj.* dreamy: listless.

**Wool-grower**, wool′-grō′ẻr, *n.* one who *raises* sheep for the production of *wool.*

**Woollen**, wool′en, *adj.* made of or pertaining to *wool.*

**Woolly**, wool′i, *adj.* consisting of or like *wool*: clothed with wool.—*n.* **Wool′iness.**

**Woolsack**, wool′sak, *n.* the seat of the lord chancellor in the House of Lords, being a large square *sack* of *wool* covered with scarlet.

**Word**, wurd, *n.* an oral or written sign expressing an idea or notion: talk, discourse: signal or sign: message: promise: declaration:—(*pl.*) verbal contention.—**The Word**, the Scripture: (*theol.*) the second person in the Trinity.—*v.t.* to express in words. [A.S. *word*; cog. with Goth. *vaurd*, Ice. *ord*, Ger. *wort*: also conn. with L. *verbum*, a word, Gr. *eirō*, to speak.]

**Wordbook**, wurd′book, *n.* a *book* with a collection of *words*: a vocabulary.

**Wording**, wurd′ing, *n.* act, manner, or style of expressing in *words.*

**Wordy**, wurd′i, *adj.*, full of *words*: using or containing many words.—*adv.* **Word′ily.**—*n.* **Word′iness.**

**Wore**, wōr, *pa.t.* of **Wear**.

**Work**, wurk, *n.* effort directed to an end: the result of *work*: that on which one works: anything made or done: deed: effect: a literary composition: a book: management:—*pl.* (*fort.*) walls, trenches, &c.—*v.i.* to make efforts to attain anything: to perform: to be in action: to be occupied in business or labour: to produce effects: to strain or labour: to ferment.—*v.t.* to make by labour: to bring into any state by action: to effect: to influence: to manage: to solve: to cause to ferment: to embroider:—*pa.t.* and *pa.p.* worked or wrought (rawt).—*n.* **Work′er.** [A.S. *weorc*; Ice. *verk*, Ger. *werk*; further conn. with Gr. *ergon.* Cf. **Organ**.]

**Workable**, wurk′a-bl, *adj.* that may be *worked.*

**Workhouse**, wurk′hows, *n.* a *house* where any *work* or manufacture is carried on: a house of shelter for the poor, who are made to work.

**Workman**, wurk′man, *n.* a *man* who *works* or labours, esp. manually: a skilful artificer.

**Workmanlike**, wurk′man-lik, *adj.*, like a *workman*: becoming a skilful workman: well performed.

**Workmanship**, wurk′man-ship, *n.* the skill of a *workman*: manner of making: work done.

**Workshop**, wurk′shop, *n.* a *shop* where *work* is done.

**World**, wurld, *n.* the earth and its inhabitants: the system of things: present state of existence: any planet or heavenly body: public life or society: business: the public: a secular life: course of life: a very large extent of country, as the 'new world:' very much or a great deal, as a 'world of good:' time, as in the phrase 'world without end' = eternally: possibility, as in 'nothing in the world:' (*B.*) the ungodly. [A.S. *wor-uld*, *weor-uld* (*lit.*) 'a generation of men,' from *wer*, a man, and *-uld*, sig. an age; Ice. *veröld*, O. Ger. *weralt* (Ger. *welt*). Cf. **Wer-wolf**, **Wer-gild**: also **Eld** and **Old**.]

**Worldling**, wurld′ling, *n.* one who is devoted to *worldly* or temporal possessions.

**Worldly**, wurld′li, *adj.* pertaining to the *world*, esp. as distinguished from the world to come: devoted to this life and its enjoyments: bent on gain.—*n.* **World′liness.**

**Worldly-minded**, wurld′li-mīnd′ed, *adj.* having the *mind* set on the present *world.*

**Worm**, wurm, *n.* any small creeping animal: anything that gnaws or torments: remorse: a debased being: anything spiral: the thread of a screw: a spiral pipe used in distilling.—*v.i.* to work slowly or secretly.—*v.t.* to effect by slow and secret means. [A.S. *weorm*, *wyrm*, dragon, snake, creeping animal; cog. with Goth. *vaurms*, a serpent, Ice. *ormr*, Ger. *wurm*; also with L. *vermis.* Cf. **Vermicelli** and **Crimson**.]

**Wormwood**, wurm′wood, *n.* the bitter plant absinthium. [A.S. *werm-od* (Ger. *werm-uth*); from the root of **Warm** (with affix *-od*), because orig. taken to *warm* the body; afterwards corrupted to *worm-wood*, through its use as a vermifuge suggesting a false ety.]

**Wormy**, wurm′i, *adj.* like a *worm*: grovelling: containing a worm: abounding with worms.

**Worn**, wōrn, *pa.p.* of **Wear**.

**Worry**, wur′i, *v.t.* to tear with the teeth: to harass: to tease:—*pa.t.* and *pa.p.* worr′ied.—*n.* trouble, perplexity, vexation. [Conn. with Dut. *worgen*, to strangle; Ger. *würgen*, to choke.]

**Worse**, wurs, *adj.* (used as *comp.* of **Bad**), bad or evil in a greater degree: more sick.—*adv.* bad in a higher degree. [A.S. *wyr-sa*, old comp. from a root *weor*, bad, seen also in O. Ger. *wirser*, Goth. *vairs*.]

**Worship**, wur′ship, *n.* religious service: adoration paid to God: a title of honour: submissive respect.—*v.t.* to respect highly: to treat with civil reverence: to pay divine honours to: to adore or idolise.—*v.i.* to perform acts of adoration: to perform religious service:—*pr.p.* wor′shipping; *pa.t.* and *pa.p.* wor′shipped.—*n.* **Wor′shipper.** [Lit. 'state of having worth or worthiness,' A.S. *weordhscipe*—**Worth**, and affix *-ship*, A.S. *-scipe*.]

**Worshipful**, wur′ship-fool, *adj.*, *worthy* of *worship* or honour, used as a term of respect.

**Worst**, wurst, *adj.* bad or evil in the highest degree.—*n.* the highest degree of badness: the most evil state.—*v.t.* to get the advantage over in a contest: to defeat. [A.S. *wyrrest*, *wyrst*, superl. of root *weor*, bad. See **Worse**.]

**Worsted**, woost′ed or woorst′ed, *n.* twisted thread or yarn spun out of long, combed wool. [From *Worsted*, a village near Norwich in England.]

**Wort**, wurt, *n.* a plant of the cabbage kind. [A.S. *wyrt*; Ger. *wurz*, *wurzel*, a root.]

**Wort**, wurt, *n.* new beer unfermented or in the act of fermentation: the sweet infusion of malt.

[A.S. *wirt, wert*; *würze*, sweet herbs; probably orig. same as above word.]

**Worth**, wurth, *n.* value: that quality which renders a thing valuable: price: moral excellence: importance.—*adj.* equal in value to: deserving of.—(*B.*) *v.i.* be. [Lit. 'being, substance,' A.S. *weorth—weorthan*, to be, connected with **Were**. See next word.]

**Worth**, wurth, in the phrase **Woe worth**, sig. *woe be to.* [A.S. *weorth*, imper. of *weorthan*, to be, Ger. *werden*. See above word.]

**Worthily**, wur'*thi*-li, *adv.* in a *worthy* manner: (*Pr. Bk.*) justly: truly.

**Worthless**, wurth'les, *adj.* of *no worth* or value: having no value, virtue, excellence, &c.: useless.—*adv.* **Worth'lessly**.—*n.* **Worth'lessness**.

**Worthy**, wur'*thi*, *adj.* having *worth*: valuable: deserving: suited to: (*B.*) deserving (either of good or bad).—*n.* a man of eminent worth:—*pl.* **Wor'thies**.—*n.* **Wor'thiness**.

**Wot**, wot, **Wotteth**, wot'eth, *v.t.* (*B.*) *pres.t.* of obs. **wit**, to know. [A.S. *wát* (orig. a perf., signifying 'have' or 'has seen'=Gr. *oida*). used as pres. ind. of *witan*, to know. See **Wit**.]

**Would**, wood, *pa.t.* of **Will**. [A.S. *wolde*, *pa.t.* of *willan*.]

**Wound**, wownd, *pa.t.* and *pa.p.* of **Wind**, to turn.

**Wound**, wōōnd, *n.* a cut or bruise: hurt: injury. —*v.t.* to make a wound: to injure. [A.S. *wund*; Ger. *wunde*, Ice. *und*; conn. with **Wind**, to twist.]

**Wove**, **Woven**, *pa.t.* and *pa.p.* of **Weave**.

**Wrack**, rak, *n.* seaweed cast up on the shore, used for making kelp. [Fr. *varech*, anything cast up by the sea; prob. from root of **Wreak**.]

**Wrack**, rak. By-form of **Wreck**.

**Wraith**, rāth, *n.* a spectre. [Lowland Scotch, probably originally Celtic.]

**Wrangle**, rang'gl, *v.i.* to make a disturbance: to dispute: to dispute noisily or peevishly.—*n.* a noisy dispute. [A freq. from the *pa.t.* of **Wring**.]

**Wrangler**, rang'glėr, *n.* one who *wrangles* or disputes angrily: in the university of Cambridge, one of those who pass the best examination for the degree of B.A.—*n.* **Wrang'lership**.

**Wrap**, rap, *v.t.* to roll or fold together: to infold: to cover by winding something round (often with *up*):—*pr.p.* wrapp'ing; *pa.t.* and *pa.p.* wrapped. —*n.* a wrapper, as a shawl, &c. [M. E. *wrappen*. See **Lap**, *v.t.* to wrap, and **Envelope**.]

**Wrapper**, rap'ėr, *n.* one who or that which *wraps*: a loose outer garment of a woman.

**Wrath**, räth, *n.* violent anger: (*B.*) holy indignation. [A.S. *wrædh*, wrath (*lit.*) 'a twist in the temper.' See **Wroth**.]

**Wrathful**, räth'fool, *adj.*, *full of wrath*: very angry: springing from or expressing wrath.—*adv.* **Wrath'fully**.—*n.* **Wrath'fulness**.

**Wreak**, rēk, *v.t.* to inflict. [A.S. *wrecan*, orig. to drive out, and so to banish, punish, avenge; Ice. *reka*, to drive, pursue, Ger. *rüchen*; conn. with L. *urgeo*, Gr. *eirgo*. See **Wreck** and **Wretch**.]

**Wreath**, rēth, *n.* a chaplet: a garland. [Lit. 'that which is *writhed* or twisted,' A.S. *wrædh —wridhan*, E. **Writhe**.]

**Wreathe**, rēth, *v.t.* to twine about or encircle: — *v.i.* to be interwoven. [See **Wreath**.]

**Wreck**, rek, *n.* destruction: destruction of a ship: ruins of a destroyed ship: remains of anything ruined.—*v.t.* to destroy or disable: to ruin.— *v.i.* to suffer wreck or ruin. [Lit. 'thing cast out and broken,' found in Low Ger. *wrak*, Dut. *wrak*; Ice. *reki*, a thing drifted ashore. See **Wreak**.]

**Wrecker**, rek'ėr, *n.* one who plunders *wrecks*.

**Wren**, ren, *n.* a well-known small bird. [A.S. *wrenna*; cf. the Gael. *dreadhan*, Ir. *drean*.]

**Wrench**, rensh, *v.t.* to *wring* or pull with a twist: to force by violence: to sprain.—*n.* a violent twist: a sprain: an instrument for turning bolts, &c. [A.S. *wrencan*; Ger. *renken*; from **Wring**.]

**Wrest**, rest, *v.t.* to *twist* from by force: to twist from truth or from its natural meaning.—*n.* violent pulling and twisting: distortion.—*n.* **Wrest'er**. [A.S. *wræstan*; Dan. *vriste*; perh. from the root of **Writhe**.]

**Wrestle**, res'l, *v.i.* to contend by grappling and trying to throw the other down: to struggle.— *n.* a bout at wrestling: a struggle between two to throw each other down.—*n.* **Wrest'ler**. [A.S. *wræstlian*; from *wræstan*, E. **Wrest**.]

**Wretch**, rech, *n.* a most miserable person: one sunk in vice: a worthless person. [Lit. 'an outcast,' A.S. *wrecca—wrecan*, E. **Wreak**.]

**Wretched**, rech'ed, *adj.* very miserable: worthless.—*adv.* **Wretch'edly**.—*n.* **Wretch'edness**. [From **Wretch**.]

**Wriggle**, rig'l, *v.i.* to *twist* to and fro.—*v.t.* to move by wriggling.—*n.* **Wrigg'ler**. [Extension of obs. *wrig*, conn. with A.S. *wrigian*. See **Wry**.]

**Wright**, rīt, *n.* a maker (chiefly used in compounds, as ship-*wright*, &c.). [A.S. *wyrhta— worhte*, pa.p. of *weorcan*, E. **Work**.]

**Wring**, ring, *v.t.* to *twist*: to force by twisting: to force or compress: to pain: to extort: to bend out of its position.—*v.i.* to writhe: to twist:— *pa.t.* and *pa.p.* wrung, (*B.*) wringed. [A.S. *wringan*; Ger. *ringen*, to wriggle, twist; allied to **Wriggle**. Cf. **Wrench**.]

**Wrinkle**, ring'kl, *n.* a small ridge on a surface from twisting or shrinking: unevenness.—*v.t.* to contract into wrinkles or furrows: to make rough.—*v.i.* to shrink into ridges. [A.S. *wrincle —wrincan, wringan*, to wring: Dut. *wronckel*, a twisting: dim. of **Wring**.]

**Wrinkly**, ringk'li, *adj.* full of *wrinkles*: liable to be wrinkled.

**Wrist**, rist, *n.* the joint by which the hand is united to the arm. [A.S. *wrist*; Ger. *rist*.]

**Wristband**, rist'band, *n.* the *band* or part of a sleeve which covers the *wrist*.

**Writ**, rit, *n.* a *writing* : (*law*) a written document by which one is summoned or required to do something.—**Holy Writ**, the Scriptures.

**Write**, rīt, *v.t.* to form letters with a pen or pencil: to express in writing: to compose: to engrave: to record: to communicate by letter.— *v.i.* to perform the act of writing: to be employed as a clerk: to compose books: to send letters:—*pr.p.* writ'ing; *pa.t.* wrōte; *pa.p.* writt'en. [A.S. *writan*; Ice. *rita*; the original meaning being 'to scratch' (cf. the cog. Ger. *reissen*, to tear).]

**Writer**, rīt'ėr, *n.* one who *writes*: a scribe or clerk: an ordinary legal practitioner in Scotch country towns: an author.—**Writer to the Signet**, an attorney or solicitor in Scotland.

**Writership**, rīt'ėr-ship, *n.* the office of a *writer*.

**Writhe**, rith, *v.t.* to *turn* to and fro: to *twist* violently: to wrest.—*v.i.* to twist. [A.S. *wridhan*, to twist; Ice. *ridha*; L. *vertere*, Sans. *vrat*. See **Wreath**, **Wrath**, and **Wroth**.]

**Writing**, rīt'ing, *n.* act of forming letters with a pen: that which is written: a document: a book: an inscription:—*pl.* legal deeds: official papers.

**Wrong**, rong, *adj.* not according to rule or right:

not fit or suitable : incorrect : not right or true.
—*n.* whatever is not right or just : any injury
done to another.—*adv.* not rightly.—*v.t.* to do
wrong to : to deprive of some right : to injure.
—*adv.* **Wrong′ly.** [Lit. ' twisted,' from **Wring**;
cf. Fr. *tort*, from L. *tortus*, twisted.]

**Wrongful**, rong′fool, *adj.* wrong : unjust : injurious.—*adv.* **Wrong′fully.**—*n.* **Wrong′fulness.**

**Wrong-headed**, rong′-hed′ed, *adj.*, *wrong* in
*head* or mind : wrong in principle.—*n.* **Wrong′-**
**head′edness.**

**Wrote**, rōt, *pa.t.* of **Write**.

**Wroth**, rawth, *adj.* wrathful. [A.S. *wrædh*,
orig. sig. ' twisted ;' Ice. *reidh-r*, O. Ger. *reid*;
from **Writhe**. Cf. **Wrath** and **Wreath**.]

**Wrought**, rawt, *pa.t.* and *pa.p.* of **Work**. [A.S.
*worhte*, *ge-worht*.]

**Wrung**, rung, *pa.t.* and *pa.p.* of **Wring**.

**Wry**, rī, *adj.*, *writhed*, twisted, or turned to one
side : not in the right direction.—*n.* **Wry′ness.**
[A.S. *wrigian*; cf. **Wriggle** and **Writhe**.]

**Wryneck**, rī′nek, *n.* a *twisted* or distorted *neck*:
a small bird allied to the woodpecker, which
*twists* round its head strangely when surprised.

**Wyvern**, wī′vrn, *n.* an imaginary animal resembling a flying *serpent*. [Fr. *vivre*—L. *viperd*,
a viper. See **Viper**.]

# X

**Xanthine**, zan′thin, *n.* the *yellow* colouring matter
in certain plants, as madder. [Gr. *xanthos*,
yellow.]

**Xanthochroi**, zan-thok′roy, *n.pl.* one of the five
groups of men, according to Huxley and other
ethnologists, comprising the fair whites. [Gr.]

**Xebec**, zē′bek, *n.* a small three-masted vessel much
used by the former corsairs of Algiers. [Sp.—
Turkish *sumbaki*.]

**Xylography**, zī-log′raf-i, *n.* the art of engraving
on wood.—*n.* **Xylog′rapher.**—*adj.* **Xylo-**
**graph′ic.** [Gr. *xylon*, wood, and *grapho*, I write.]

# Y

**Yacht**, yot, *n.* a light swift-sailing vessel, elegantly
fitted up for pleasure-trips or racing. [Dut.
*jagt* (formerly *jacht*), from *jagen*, to chase.]

**Yachter**, yot′ėr, *n.* one engaged in sailing a *yacht*.

**Yachting**, yot′ing, *n.* sailing in a *yacht*.

**Yak**, yak, *n.* a large kind of ox, domesticated in
Central Asia.

**Yam**, yam, *n.* a large root like the potato growing
in tropical countries. [West Indian *ihame*.]

**Yankee**, yang′kē, *n.* a citizen of the New England
States in America : an inhabitant of the United
States. [Perh. a corr. of *English*, or of Fr.
*Anglais*, by the N. American Indians.]

**Yard**, yärd, *n.* an E. measure of 3 feet or 36
inches : a long beam on a mast for spreading
square sails. [A.S. *geard*, *gyrd*, a rod, measure;
Dut. *gard*, Ger. *gerte* ; further conn. with Goth.
*gazds*, a stick, and L. *hasta*, a pole, a spear.]

**Yard**, yärd, *n.* an inclosed place, esp. near a building. [A.S. *geard*, hedge, inclosure ; Goth.
*gards*, Ger. *garten* ; conn. with L. *hortus*, Gr.
*chortos*. See **Court, Cohort**, and **Garden**.]

**Yard-arm**, yärd′-ärm, *n.* either half or *arm* of a
ship's *yard* (right or left) from the centre to the
end.

**Yare**, yār, *adj.* ready, dexterous, quick. [A.S.
*gearu*. Doublet **Gear**.]

**Yarn**, yärn, *n.* spun thread : one of the threads of
a rope : a sailor's story (spun out to some length).
[A.S. *gearn*; Ice. and Ger. *garn*.]

**Yarrow**, yar′ō, *n.* the plant milfoil. [A.S. *gearwe*;
Ger. *garbe*.]

**Yataghan**, yat′a-gan, *n.* a long Turkish dagger,
usually curved.

**Yawl**, yawl, *n.* a small ship's boat, with four or
six oars. [Dut. *jol*. Cf. **Jollyboat**.]

**Yawn**, yawn, *v.i.* to open the jaws involuntarily
from drowsiness : to gape.—*n.* the opening of
the mouth from drowsiness. [A.S. *ganian*,
*gænan*; Scot. *gan-t*, Ger. *gähnen*; conn. with
Gr. *chainō*, L. *hio*, to gape. Cf. **Hiatus**.]

**Yawning**, yawn′ing, *adj.* gaping : opening :
wide : drowsy.—*n.* act of opening wide or gaping.

**Yclept** or **Ycleped**, i-klept′, *pa.p.* called (*obs.*)
[A.S. *clypian*, to call.]

**Ye**, yē, *pron.* the nom. pl. of the 2d person. [A.S.
*ge* ; Dut. *gij*; Gr. *hymeis*, L. *vos*, Sans. *yu-sme*
(= *tu-sma*, 'thou' and 'he').]

**Yea**, yā, *adv.*, *yes*: verily. [A.S. *gea*; Ice., Ger.,
and Goth. *ja*. See **Yes**.]                 [*eanian*.]

**Yean**, yēn, *v.t.* to bring forth young. [A.S.

**Year**, yēr, *n.* the time the earth takes to go round
the sun : 365¼ days or 12 months :—*pl.* age or old
age. [A.S. *gear*; Ger. *jahr*; Ice. *âr*; perh. conn.
with Slav. *jaro*, spring, Gr. *hōra*, season.]

**Yearling**, yēr′ling, *n.* an animal a *year* old.

**Yearly**, yēr′li, *adj.* happening every *year*: lasting
a year.—*adv.* once a year : from year to year.

**Yearn**, yėrn, *v.i.* to feel earnest desire : to feel
uneasiness, as from longing or pity. [A.S.
*geornian—georn*, desirous (Ger. *gern*).]

**Yearning**, yėrn′ing, *n.*, *earnest* desire, tenderness,
or pity.—*adj.* longing.—*adv.* **Yearn′ingly.**

**Yeast**, yēst, *n.* the froth of malt liquors in fermentation : a preparation which raises dough for
bread. [A.S. *gist*; Ger. *gäscht*, *gischt*; from a
Teut. root ' to seethe,' conn. with Gr. *zeo*, Sans.
*yas.*]

**Yeasty**, yēst′i, *adj.* like *yeast*: frothy : foamy.

**Yelk.** Same as **Yolk**.

**Yell**, yel, *v.i.* to *howl* or cry out with a sharp
noise : to scream from pain or terror.—*n.* a sharp
outcry. [A.S. *gellan*; Ger. *gellen*; conn. with
A.S. *galan*, to sing (see **Nightingale**).]

**Yellow**, yel′ō, *adj.* of a bright *gold* colour.—*n.* a
bright golden colour.—*n.* **Yell′owness.** [A.S.
*geolu*; Ger. *gelb*; cog. with L. *helvus*, light
bay, *gilvus*, pale yellow.]

**Yellow-fever**, yel′ō-fē′vėr, *n.* a malignant *fever*
of warm climates, often making the skin *yellow*.

**Yellowhammer**, yel′ō-ham-ėr, *n.* a song-bird, so
named from its *yellow* colour : the yellow bunting.                                       [**Yell′owishness.**

**Yellowish**, yel′ō-ish, *adj.* somewhat *yellow*.—*n.*

**Yelp**, yelp, *v.i.* to utter a sharp bark. [A.S.
*gealp*, a loud sound : Ice. *gialpa*, to make a
noise, Ger. *gelfern*; prob. influenced by **Yell**.]

**Yeoman**, yō′man, *n.* a man of common rank next
below a gentleman : a man of small estate : an
officer of the royal household. [Found in O. Fris.
*gaman*, villager—*ga*, a village (Goth. *gawi*, Ger.
*gau*), and **Man** ; cf. also Bavarian *gäu-man*, a
peasant.]                         [*yeomen* or freeholders.

**Yeomanry**, yō′man-ri, *n.* the collective body of

**Yes**, yes, *adv.* ay : a word of affirmation or consent. [A.S. *gese—gea*, yea, and *se* (for *sie*, *si*),
let it be.]

**Yester**, yes′tėr, *adj.* relating to *yesterday* : last.
[A.S. *gistran*, yesterday ; Ger. *gestern*; conn.
with L. *hesternus*, Gr. *chthes*, Sans. *hyas*.]

**Yesterday**, yes′tėr-dā, *n.* the *day last past*.

**Yesternight**, yes′tėr-nīt, *n.* the *night last past*.

**Yet**, yet, *adv.* in addition : besides : at the same
time : up to the present time : hitherto : even :

however.—*conj.* nevertheless : however. [A.S. *git, gita*, from a root seen also in L. *ja-m.*]

**Yew,** ū, *n.* an evergreen tree, allied to the pine. [A.S. *eow, iw;* Ger. *eibe,* Ir. *iubhar.*]

**Yield,** yēld, *v.t.* to resign : to grant : to give out : to produce : to allow.—*v.i.* to submit : to comply with : to give place.—*n.* amount yielded : product. [A.S. *gildan,* to pay ; Goth. *gildan,* Ger. *gelten,* Ice. *gjalda.* See **Guild.**]

**Yielding,** yēld′ing, *adj.* inclined to give way or comply : compliant.—*adv.* **Yield′ingly.**

**Yoke,** yōk, *n.* that which *joins* together : the frame of wood joining oxen for drawing : any similar frame, as one for carrying pails : a mark of servitude : slavery : (*B.*) a pair or couple.—*v.t.* to put a yoke on : to join together : to enslave. [A.S. *ioc;* Ger. *joch;* L. *jugum,* Gr. *zygon.* From the root of L. *jungo,* Sans. *yudj,* to join.]

**Yoke-fellow,** yōk′-fel′ō, **Yoke-mate,** yōk′-māt, *n.* an associate : a mate or fellow.

**Yolk,** yōk, **Yelk,** yelk, *n.* the *yellow* part of an egg. [A.S. *geolca*—from root of A.S. *geolo,* E. **Yellow.**]

**Yon,** yon, **Yonder,** yon′dėr, *adv.* at a distance within view.—*adj.* being at a distance within view. [A.S. *geon-d,* thither, yonder ; cog. with Ger. *jen-er,* that ; the root being the pronominal stem *ya.*]

**Yore,** yōr, *n.* in old time. [From A.S. *geâra,* formerly, allied to *gear,* E. **Year:** or compounded of *geo,* formerly, and *ær,* E. **Ere.**]

**You,** ū, *pron.* 2d pers. pron. pl., but also used as sing. [Orig. only an objective case ; A.S. *eow ;* O. Ger. *iu,* Ger. *euch.* See **Ye.**]

**Young,** yung, *adj.* not long born : in early life : in the first part of growth : inexperienced.—*n.* the offspring of animals. [A.S. *geong;* Ger. *jung;* also conn. with L. *juvenis,* Sans. *yuvan.*]

**Youngish,** yung′gish, *adj.* somewhat *young.*

**Youngling,** yung′ling, *n.* a *young* person or animal. [A.S. *geong-ling;* Ger. *jüng-ling.*]

**Youngster,** yung′stėr, *n.* a *young* person : a lad. [Orig. fem. ; see *-ster* in list of Affixes.]

**Younker,** yung′kėr, *n.* Same as **Youngster.** [From Dut. *jonker* (from · *jonk-heer,* 'young master' or 'lord'), Ger. *junker.*]

**Your,** ūr, *pron.* poss. of **You;** belonging to you. [A.S. *eower.* See **You.**] [noun.

**Yours,** ūrz, *pron.* poss. of **You,** not followed by a

**Yourself,** ūr-self′, *pron., your* own *self* or person.

**Youth,** yōōth, *n.* state of being *young :* early life : a young person : young persons taken together. [A.S. *geoguth,* from the stem of **Young;** Ger. *jugend,* Goth. *junda.*]

**Youthful,** yōōth′fool, *adj.* pertaining to *youth* or early life : young : suitable to youth : fresh : buoyant, vigorous.—*adv.* **Youth′fully.**—*n.* **Youth′fulness.**

**Yucca,** yuk′a, *n.* a large garden plant of the lily family, familiarly called Adam's needle, native to sub-tropical America. [W. Indian name.]

**Yule,** yōōl, *n.* the old name of Christmas, which was grafted on a heathen festival probably connected with the worship of the sun. [A.S. *geól,* Ice. *jôl;* acc. to Grimm, prob. from the root of **Wheel** (Ice. *hjol*), from the sun's *wheeling* round at midwinter.]

## Z

**Zany,** zā′ni, *n.* a merry-andrew : a buffoon. [Fr. *zani*—It. *zani,* a corr. of *Giovanni,* John. Cf. the use of the names **John** and **Jack.**]

**Zeal,** zēl, *n., boiling* or passionate ardour for anything : enthusiasm. [L. *zelus*—Gr. *zēlos, zēo,* to boil. Cf. **Yeast.**]

**Zealot,** zel′ot, *n.* one full of *zeal :* an enthusiast : a fanatic. [Gr. *zēlōtēs*—*zēlos* (see **Zeal**).]

**Zealous,** zel′us, *adj.* full of *zeal :* warmly engaged or ardent in anything.—*adv.* **Zeal′ously.**

**Zebra,** zē′bra, *n.* an animal of the horse kind, beautifully striped. [Of African origin.]

**Zebu,** zē′bōō, *n.* a kind of ox with long ears and a hump on the shoulders, called also the Indian ox. [E. Indian name.]

**Zemindar,** zem-in-dar′, *n.* Indian name for the landlords who pay the government revenue, as distinguished from the ryots or actual cultivators of the soil. [From an Ar. word, sig. 'land.']

**Zenana** or **Zanana,** ze-nä′na, *n.* that part of a Hindu house set apart for females. [Pers. · belonging to women.']

**Zend,** zend, *n.* the primitive language of the Persians.—**Zend-avesta,** zend′-a-ves′ta, *n.* the sacred books of the ancient Persians, written in Zend.

**Zenith,** zen′ith, *n.* the point of the heavens directly *overhead :* greatest height. [Fr., through It. *zenit,* from Ar. *semt,* short for *semt-ur-râs,* lit. ' way of the head.']

**Zephyr,** zef′ir, *n.* the *west* wind : a soft, gentle breeze. [Gr. *zephyros*—*zophos,* darkness, the dark quarter, the west.]

**Zero,** zē′ro, *n.* cipher : nothing : the point from which a thermometer is graduated. [Fr.—It.—Ar. *sifr.* Doublet **Cipher.**]

**Zest,** zest, *n.* something that gives a relish : relish. [Fr. *zeste,* skin of an orange or lemon used to give a flavour ; perh. from L. *schistus*—Gr. *schistos,* cleft, divided—*schizō,* to cleave.]

**Zigzag,** zig′zag, *adj.* having short, sharp turns.—*v.t.* to form with short turns. [An imitative word ; Fr. *zig-zag,* Ger. *zickzack.*]

**Zinc,** zingk, *n.* a bluish-white metal, somewhat like *tin.* [Ger. *zink,* prob. allied to *zinn,* tin.]

**Zincography,** zing-kog′ra-fi, *n.* art of *printing* from plates of *zinc.* [**Zinc,** and Gr. *graphō,* to write.]

**Zirconium,** zir-kō′ni-um, *n.* one of the rarer metals.

**Zodiac,** zō′di-ak, *n.* an imaginary belt in the heavens, containing the twelve constellations, called signs of the zodiac.—*adj.* **Zodi′acal.** [Lit. 'the circle of animals,' Gr. *zōdiakos,* of animals (*kyklos,* a circle)—*zodion,* dim. of *zōon,* an animal, *zao,* to live.]

**Zone,** zōn, *n.* a *girdle :* one of the five great *belts* into which the surface of the earth is divided. [L. *zona*—Gr. *zōnē,* a girdle—*zōnnymi,* to gird ; akin to **Join, Yoke.**]

**Zoned,** zōnd, *adj.* wearing a *zone* or girdle : having zones or concentric bands.

**Zoologist,** zo-ol′o-jist, *n.* one versed in *zoology.*

**Zoology,** zo-ol′o-ji, *n.* that part of natural history which treats of *animals.*—*adj.* **Zoolog′ical.**—*adv.* **Zoolog′ically.** [Gr. *zōon,* an animal, and *logos,* a discourse.]

**Zoophyte,** zō′o-fīt, *n.* a term now applied to true polyps, as corals, &c. [Lit. 'animal-plant,' Gr. *zōophyton*—*zōon,* an animal, *phyton,* a plant.]

**Zoroastrianism,** zor-ō-as′tri-an-izm, *n.* the national faith of ancient Persia, so named from its founder *Zoroaster.*

**Zouave,** zwäv, *n.* one of a body of infantry in the French army. [Name of an Algerian tribe.]

**Zymotic,** zī-mot′ik, *adj.* denoting all diseases, as cholera, typhus, &c. in which a poison works through the body like a *ferment.* [Gr., from *zymōō,* to ferment—*zymē,* leaven.]

## Abortive

**Abortive**, a-bort′iv, *adj.* rendering abortive.

**Absolve**, ab-zolv′, *v.t.* to finish, accomplish.

**Acquist**, ak-kwist′, *n.* acquisition. [mant.

**Adamantean**, ad-a-man-tē′an, *adj.* hard as adamant.

**Ades**, ā′dēz, *n.* Hades.

**Admonishment**, ad-mon′ish-ment, *n.* admonition.

**Adorn**, a-dorn′, *pa.p.* adorned.

**Adust**, a-dust′, **Adusted**, a-dust′ed, *adj.*, *burned up*: dried up. [L. *adustus*, pa.p. of *aduro*, to burn up—*ad*, inten., and *uro*, to burn.]

**Advice**, ad-vīs′, *n.* deliberation.

**Advise**, ad-vīz′, *v.i.* to consider : to take advice.

**Advised**, ad-vīzd′, *adv.* advisedly.

**Affect**, af-fekt′, *v.i.* to be inclined to : to prefer.

**Afflicted**, af-flikt′ed, *pa.p.* beaten down.

**Ake**, āk, *n.* ache.

**Alchymy**, al′ki-mi, *n.* a mixed metal formerly used for various utensils, hence a trumpet.

**Aloof**, a-lōōf′, *prep.* away or at a distance from.

**Altern**, al-tèrn′, *adj.* alternate.—*adv.* alternately.

**Amarant**, a′mar-ant, *n.* amaranth.

**Ammiral**, am′mi-ral, *n.* admiral : also, a ship.

**Amphisbæna**, am-fis-bē′na, *n.* a serpent that can *go both ways*—forwards or backwards. [L.—Gr. *amphis*, *amphi*, on both sides, *bainō*, to go.]

**Anarch**, an′ärk, *n.* anarchist.

**Appaid**, ap-pād′, *pa.p.* of *Appay*, *v.t.* to *appease* or satisfy.

**Appellant**, ap-pel′ant, *n.* a challenger.

**Arbitrement**, är-bit′re-ment, *n.* arbitrament.

**Arboret**, är′bor-et, *n.* a *small tree* or shrub. [O. Fr.—L. *arbor*, a tree.]

**Arborous**, är′bur-us, *adj.* like an *arbour*.

**Arch-chymic**, ärch-kim′ik, *adj.* of *supreme chemical* powers. [**Arch**, chief, and **Chemic**.]

**Ardor, Ardour**, är′dor, *n.* a bright or effulgent spirit. [counsel. [See **Read**.]

**Aread, Areed, Arreed**, a-rēd′, *v.t.* to *read :* to advise.

**Armoury**, ärm′or-i, *n.* armour.

**Assassinated**, as-as′sin-āt-ed, *pa.p.* taken by treachery: maltreated.

**Astonish**, as-ton′ish, *v.t.* to stun.

**Atheist**, ā′thē-ist, *adj.*, godless.

**Atheous**, ā′thē-us, *adj.*, *without God*, ungodly.

**Attent**, at-tent′, *adj.* attentive.

**Attest**, at-test′, *n.* attestation.

**Attrite**, at-trīt′, *adj.* worn by *rubbing*. [L. *attritus*, pa.p. of *attero*, to rub.]

**Auxiliar**, awg-zil′yar, *adj.* auxiliary.

**Azurn**, ā′zhurn, *adj.*, *azure*, of a blue colour. [See **Azure**.]

**Balk**, bawk, *v.t.* to stop short at, omit.

**Base**, bās, *n.* a skirt which hung down from the waist to the knees of a knight when on horseback. [From **Base**, *adj.*]

**Battailous**, bat′il-us, *adj.* arrayed for *battle*, or appearing to be so. [See **Battle**.]

**Battle**, bat′l, *n.* the body of an army.

**Behemoth**, bē′he-moth, *n.* the elephant.

**Bespake**, be-spāk′, *pa.p.* of **Bespeak**.

**Bespeak**, be-spēk′, *v.t.* to speak, or speak to. [Prefix *be*, and **Speak**.]

**Besprent**, be-sprent′, *adj.*, *sprinkled* over. [M. E.

## Conform

*bespreint, besprengyd*, pa.p. of *besprenge*, A.S. *besprengan*, to besprinkle.]

**Bestead, Bested**, be-sted′, *v.t.* to *place* or dispose : to assist, to serve. [Prefix *be*, **Stead**, place.]

**Biding**, bīd′ing, *n.*, *abiding : '*stay.

**Blanc**, blank, *adj.*, *white*. [A form of **Blank**.]

**Blank**, blank, *v.t.* to make pale, and so confound.

**Bloom**, blōōm, *v.t.* to produce in full *bloom* or beauty.

**Boisterous**, bois′tèr-us, *adj.* strong.

**Budge**, buj, *n.* lamb-skin fur, formerly used as an edging for scholastic gowns.—*adj.* lined with budge : scholastic. [Doublet of **Bag**. See also **Budget** and **Bulge**.]

**Burdenous**, bur′dn-us, *adj.* burdensome.

**Captive**, kap′tiv, *v.t.* to take *captive :* to capture.

**Career**, ka-rēr′, *n.* onset.

**Cataphract**, kat′a-frakt, *n.* a cavalry soldier, horse and man being both in complete armour. [Gr. *kataphraktos*, covered—*kata*, quite, *phrassō*, to inclose.]

**Causey**, kawz′e, *n.* causeway.

**Cedarn**, sē′darn, *adj.* of *cedar*.

**Cerastes**, se-ras′tēz, *n.* a genus of poisonous African serpents, having a *horny* scale over each eye. [L.—Gr. *kerastēs*, horned—*keras*, horn.]

**Chalybean**, ka-lib′e-an, *adj.* forged by the *Chalybes* of Pontus, noted for their preparation of steel : well-tempered. [See **Chalybeate**.]

**Chamberlin**, chām′bėr-lin, *n.* a servant in an inn, in olden times, who united in himself the offices of chambermaid, waiter, and boots. [A form of **Chamberlain**.]

**Champain**, sham-pān′, *adj.* champaign.

**Chariot**, char′i-ot, *v.t.* to convey in a chariot.

**Cieling**, sēl′ing, *n.* Same as **Ceiling**, used here by Milton with allusion to its derivation.

**Civil-suited**, siv′il-sūt′ed, *adj.*, *suited* or attired like a *civilian* or citizen, as opposed to the gay dresses of courtiers, &c. [noise.

**Clamour**, klam′ur, *v.t.* to salute with *clamour* or

**Close**, klōs, *adj.* crafty.

**Commercing**, kom-mèrs′ing, *pr.p.* of *Commerce*, *v.i.* to hold intercourse with.

**Compact**, kom-pakt′, *adj.* composed or made of.

**Compare**, kom-pār′, *n.* comparison. [ment.

**Composure**, kom-pō′zhŭr, *n.* composition : agree-

**Concent**, kon-sent′, *n.* a *singing together :* concert : harmony. [L. *concentus*—*con*, together, and *cano*, *cantum*, to sing.] [*cerns* one.

**Concernment**, kon-sèrn′ment, *n.* that which *con*-

**Concoctive**, kon-kokt′iv, *adj.* having the power of digesting or ripening.

**Condense**, kon-dens′, *adj.*, *dense :* compact : close in texture. [See **Condense**.]

**Conduct**, kon′dukt, *n.* the leading of an army.

**Confine**, kon-fīn′, *v.i.* to have the same boundary with : to border on.

**Conflagrant**, kon-flā′grant, *adj.*, *burning together*. [L. *con*, together, and **Flagrant**.]

**Conform**, kon-form′, *adj.* made like in *form :* assuming the same shape : similar. [Late L. *conformis*—L. *con*, and *forma*, form.]

**Conglobe,** kon-glōb′, *v.t.* or *v.i.* to collect *together* into a *globe* or round mass. [L. *conglobo—con*, together, and *globus*, a globe. See **Globe.**]

**Congratulant,** kon-grat′ū-lant, *adj.*, *congratulating*. [L. *congratulans, -antis*, pr.p. of *congratulor*.]

**Conscience,** kon′shens, *n.* consciousness.

**Consolatory,** kon-sol′a-tor-i, *n.* that which *consoles*: a speech or writing intended for consolation.

**Consort,** kon′sort, *n.*, *concert:* harmony of sounds.

**Consult,** kon-sult′, *n.* a consultation : a council.

**Contrarious,** kon-trā′ri-us, *adj.* showing *contrariety:* repugnant : opposite.

**Converse,** kon-vèrs′, *v.i.* to be alternated or mixed.

**Convict,** kon′vikt, *pa.p.* convicted.

**Convince,** kon-vins′, *v.t.* to convict.

**Counterview,** kown′tèr-vū, *n.* an opposite view : contrast : opposition. [Fr. *contrevue*.]

**Crisped,** krisp′ed, *pa.p.* rippled by the wind.

**Cry,** krī, *n.* a pack (of hounds). [Prob. from **Cry**, a loud sound.]

**Cypres-lawn, Cipres-lawn,** sī′pres-lawn, *n.* crape. [Prob. from root of **Crape.**]

**Dank, The,** dangk, *n.* the waters. [From **Dank**, *adj.*]

**Debel,** de-bel′, *v.t.* to carry on *war* against : to conquer, subdue. [L. *debello*, to carry on war —*de.* and *bellum*, war.]

**Defend,** de-fend′, *v.t.* to forbid.

**Deficience,** de-fish′ens, *n.* deficiency.

**Deform,** de-form′, *adj.* deformed.

**Deject,** de-jekt′, *adj.* dejected, cast down.

**Democratie, -ty,** de-mok′ra-ti, *n.* democracy.

**Demonian,** de-mō′ni-an, *adj.* like a *demon.*

**Deport,** de-port′, *n.* deportment.

**Descry,** de-skrī′, *v.t.* to describe.                    [tion.

**Devoted,** de-vōt′ed, *adj.* doomed to evil or destruc-

**Dight,** dīt, *v.t.* to arrange, array, prepare, adorn : —*pa.t* and *pa.p.* dight, dight′ed. [A.S. *dihtan* —L. *dicto*, to order, to dictate, freq. of *dico*, to say.]                    [mensions.

**Dimensionless,** di-men′shun-les, *adj.*, *without* di-

**Dipsas,** dip′sas, *n.* a serpent whose bite caused intolerable thirst. [Gr.—*dipsa*, thirst.]

**Disally,** dis-al-lī′, *v.t.* to *part*, as an *alliance:* to separate. [L. *dis*, asunder, and **Ally.**]                    [ous.

**Discontinuous,** dis-kon-tin′ū-us, *adj.*, *not continu-*

**Discourse,** dis-kōrs′, *n.* the power of the mind to reason by *running*, as it were, from one fact or reason to another.

**Disespouse,** dis-es-powz′, *v.t.* to release from *espousal* or plighted faith. [L. *dis*, asunder, and **Espouse.**]

**Disglorify,** dis-glō′ri-fī, *v.t.* to deprive of glory. With *dis* as a negative prefix, Milton also forms *disallied* and *disespoused.*

**Disordinate,** dis-or′din-āt, *adj.*, *not ordinate* or in order : irregular. [L. *dis*, neg., and **Ordinate.**]

**Dispense,** dis-pens′, *n.* dispensation.

**Displode,** dis-plōd′, *v.t.* to spread out : to discharge. [L.—*dis*, asunder, *plaudo*, to beat.]

**Dispose,** dis-pōz′, *n.* disposal.                    [pute.

**Disputant,** dis′pū-tant, *adj.* disputing. [See **Dis-**

**Disrelish,** dis-rel′ish, *v.t.* to take away the *relish* or taste for anything.

**Dissent,** dis-sent′, *v.t.* to cause difference.

**Distract,** dis-trakt′, *adj.* distracted.

**Distrest,** dis-trest′, *adj.* distressed.

**Disturb,** dis-turb′, *n.* disturbance.

**Dividual,** di-vid′ū-al, *adj.*, *divided* or shared in common with others.

**Divinely,** di-vīn′li, *adv.* from heaven.                    [potion.

**Drench,** drensh, *v.t.* to dose, as with a sleeping

**Easy,** ēz′i, *adj.* having *ease.*

**Eclipse,** e-klips′, *v.i.* to suffer an eclipse.

**Elevate,** el′e-vāt, *adj.* elevated.

**Ellops, Elops,** el′ops, *n.* a serpent that does not hiss. [Gr., mute.]

**Emblaze,** em-blāz′, *v.t.* to emblazon.

**Embost,** em-bost′, *pa.p.* embossed.

**Embost,** em-bost′, *pa.p.* hid or sheltered in a *bush* or wood. [O. Fr. *embosquer—em* (= L. *in*), and O. Fr. *bosc* or *bosque*, from root of **Bush**, a shrub.]

**Emprise,** em-prīz′, *n.* an *enterprise*, an undertaking. [See **Prison.**]

**Enerve,** ē-nèrv′, *v.t.* to enervate.                    [war.

**Enginery,** en′jin-ri, *n.* engines or instruments of

**Ensanguined,** en-san′gwind, *adj.* covered with *blood.* [Prefix *en*, in, and L. *sanguis, sanguinis*, blood.]                    [venture upon.

**Enterprise,** en′tèr-prīz, *v.t.* to undertake : to

**Envermeil,** en-vér′mil, *v.t.* to give a red colour to. —*adj.* having a red colour. [Fr. *en*, in, *vermeil*, vermilion, red ; from root of **Vermilion.**]

**Err,** er, *v.t.* to mistake.

**Etheroous,** e-thē′rē-us, *adj.* ethereal.

**Evinced,** e-vinst′, *pa.p.* subdued.

**Eyn,** ēn, *n.* old plural of **Eye.**                    [comb, fop.

**Fantastic,** fan-tas′tik, *n.* a *fantastic* person, cox-

**Farfet,** fär′fet, *adj.* far-fetched.

**Feature,** fet′ūr, *n.* a form, thing formed or made.

**Feed,** fēd, *n.* a meal : act of feeding.

**Ferry,** fer′i, *v.t.* to pass over in a boat.

**Fitly,** fit′li, *adv.* in a *fitting* manner.—*superl.* **Fit′liest,** most fitly.

**Flaw,** flaw, *n.* a blast of wind. [L. *flatus—flo*.]

**Fledge,** flej, *adj.* feathered : furnished with wings.

**Flowery-kirtled,** flow′èr-i-kér′tld, *adj.* having *kirtles flowered* or adorned with figures of *flowers.*

**Flown,** flōn, *adj.* overflown.

**Forbiddance,** for-bid′ans, *n.* act of *forbidding:* condition of being forbidden : prohibition.

**Forgery,** fōrj′èr-i, *n.* act of *forging* or working into shape.

**Forgetful,** for-get′fool, *adj.* causing forgetfulness.

**Foughten,** fawt′n, *pa.p.* of **Fight.**

**Founder,** fown′dèr, *v.i.* to fail, to miscarry.— **Night-foundered,** having lost the way by night.

**Frame,** frām, *v.i.* to agree.

**Fraud,** frawd, *n.* error, mistake, crime.

**Fraught,** frawt, *n.* freight.                    [ance.

**Frequence,** frē′kwens, *n.* a crowd, throng, attend-

**Frequent,** frē′kwent, *adj.* full, crowded.

**Frequent,** frē-kwent′, *v.t.* to fill.

**Frier,** frī′èr, *n.* a friar

**Frore,** frōr, *adj.*, *frozen*, frosty. [Short for *froren*, *gefroren*, pa.p. of A.S. *freosan*, to freeze.] See **Freeze.**]

**Fuel,** fū′el, *v.t.* to fill or supply with fuel :—*pr.p.* fū′elling ; *pa.p.* fū′elled.

**Fulmine,** ful′min, *v.i.* to *fulminate*, to thunder.

**Funeral,** fū′nèr-al, *n.* death.

**Fusil,** fū′zil, *adj.* capable of being *melted.* [L. *fusilis—fundo.* See **Fuse**, to melt.]

**Gad,** gad, *v.i.* to rove about : of a vine—to creep in all directions.

**Gan,** gan, a contraction of **Began.**

**Gaudy,** gawd′i, *adj.* holiday, festal.

**Gem,** jem, *v.t.* to form into round knots.

**Glib,** glib, *v.t.* to make glib :—*pr.p.* glibb′ing ; *pa.p.* glibbed.

**Gonfalon,** gon′fa-lon, **Gonfanon,** gon′fa-non, *n.* an ensign or standard. [O. Fr. *gonfanon—*O. Ger. *gund*, war, and *fano*, cloth, flag, seen in Ger. *fahne*, and E. **Vane.**]

**Grand, The,** grand, *n.* the great ones, the grandees.

**Gray-fly, Grey-fly,** grā'-flī, *n.* the trumpet-fly or gadfly.　　　　　　　　　　　　　[for the legs.

**Greves,** grēvz, *n.pl.* a form of **Greaves,** armour

**Gride,** grīd, *v.i.* to cut with a grating sound : to pierce harshly. [M. E. *girden,* to strike as with a rod—*gerde,* softened to *yerde,* E. **Yard.** The word is still used metaphorically in the phrase 'to gird at,' to gibe or sneer at.]

**Grisamber,** gris-am'bèr, *n.* ambergris.

**Groundsell,** grownd'sel, **Groundsill,** grownd'sil, *n.* the *sill* or timber of a building which lies next to the *ground.*

**Grunsel,** grun'sel, *n.* a form of **Groundsel.**

**Gryphon,** grif'un, *n.* a form of **Griffin.**

**Gurge,** gèrj, *n.* a whirlpool. [L. *gurges.* See **Gorge.**]

**Gymnic,** jim'nik, *adj.* pertaining to or performing athletic exercises. [Gr. *gymnikos—gymnos.* See **Gymnastic.**]　　　　　　　　[**Inhabit.**]

**Habitant,** hab'i-tant, *n.* an *inhabitant.* [See

**Hæmony,** hē'mon-i, *n.* a plant, probably so named from *Hæmonia* or Thessaly, the land of magic.

**Handed,** hand'ed, *adj.* with hands joined : hand in hand.

**Harald,** har'ald. Same as **Herald.**

**Harass,** har'as, *n.* devastation.

**Harrowed,** här'ōd, *pa.p.* subdued.

**Haut,** hawt, *adj.* haughty.

**Highth,** hīth, *n.* a form of **Height.**

**Highthen,** hīth'n, *v.t.* a form of **Heighten.**

**Hist,** hist, *v.i.* to come stealing along crying *hist !*

**Hosting,** hōst'ing, *n.* an encounter of two *hosts* : a battle.

**Hutch,** huch, *v.t.* to put in a *hutch* or box.

**Hydrus,** hī'drus, *n.* a hydra or water-snake. [L. —Gr.]

**Idolism,** ī'dul-ism, *n.* the worship of idols.

**Idolist,** ī'dul-ist, *n.* an idolater.

**Illaudable,** il-lawd'a-bl, *adj., not laudable* or praiseworthy. [L. *in,* not, and **Laudable.**]

**Imblaze,** im-blāz', *v.t.* a form of **Emblazon.**

**Imblazonry,** im-blā'zn-ri, *n.* Same as **Emblazonry.**

**Imbost,** im-bost'. Same as **Embost.**

**Imbrute,** im-brōōt', *v.t.* to reduce to the state of a *brute.* [L. *in,* into, and **Brute.**]

**Immanacle,** im-man'a-kl, *v.t.* to put in *manacles* ; to fetter or confine. [L. *in,* into, and **Manacle.**]

**Immedicable,** im-med'i-ka-bl, *adj., not medicable* or able to be healed. [L. *in,* not, and **Medicable.**]

**Immix,** im-miks', *v.t.* to *mix.* [L. *in,* and **Mix.**]

**Imparadise,** im-par'a-dīs, *v.t.* to put in a *paradise* or state of extreme felicity.

**Importune,** im-por-tūn', *adj.* importunate.

**Impregn,** im-prēn', *v.t.* to impregnate.

**Imprese,** im-prēs', *n.* a device or emblem on a shield. [It. *impresa*—L. *imprimo, impressum,* to impress.]

**Incomposed,** in-kom-pōzd', *adj., not composed* : disordered. [L. *in,* not, and **Composed.**]

**Indamage,** in-dam'āj. Same as **Endamage.**

**Individual,** in-di-vid'ū-al, *adj., not* to be *divided.*

**Infamed,** in-fāmd', *adj., not famed* : uncelebrated. [L. *in,* not, and **Famed.**]

**Inform,** in-form', *v.t.* to direct : to animate.

**Ingrateful,** in-grāt'fool, *adj., not grateful* : not pleasing. [L. *in,* not, and **Grateful.**]

**Inhabitation,** in-hab-i-tā'shun, *n.* the whole population of the world.

**Innumerous,** in-nū'mèr-us, *adj.* innumerable.

**Inoffensive,** in-of-fen'siv, *adj.* without obstruction.

**Insphered,** in-sfērd', *adj.* placed in a sphere.

**Instinct,** in-stingkt', *adj.* animated, indued with life : opposed to **Extinct.**

**Instinct,** in-stingkt', *adv.* instinctively.

**Instruct,** in-strukt', *pa.p.* instructed.

**Interrupt,** in-tèr-rupt', *adj.* interrupted : broken. [See **Interrupt.**]

**Interveined,** in-tèr-vānd', *adj.* intersected, as with *veins.* [L. *inter,* between, through, and **Vein.**]

**Intoxicate,** in-toks'i-kāt, *pa.p.* intoxicated.

**Jaculation,** jak-ū-lā'shun, *n.* the act of *darting* or throwing out. [L. *jaculor, -atus,* to throw, as a dart—*jaculum,* a dart—*jacio,* to throw.]

**Kerchiefed,** ker'cheft, *adj.* covered as with a *kerchief.*

**Kist,** kist, a form of **Kissed.**

**Kzar,** zär, *n.* a form of **Czar.**

**Landskip,** land'skip, *n.* landscape.

**Lax,** laks, *adv.* at large, with abundance of room.

**Libbard,** lib'ard, *n.* a form of **Leopard.**

**Limbeck,** lim'bek, *n.* a corr. of **Alembic.**

**Lubbar,** lub'ar, *adj.* Same as **Lubber.**

**Mad,** mad, *v.t.* to make mad :—*pr.p.* madd'ing ; *pa.p.* madd'ed.

**Magnetic,** mag-net'ik, *n.* the magnet.

**Marasmus,** ma-raz'mus, *n.* a *wasting* of flesh without apparent disease. [Gr. *marasmos—marainomai,* to waste away, pass. of *maraino,* to put out or quench.]

**Margent,** mär'jent, *n.* a form of **Margin.**

**Marish,** mar'ish, *n.* a form of **Marsh.**

**Marle,** märl, *n.* a form of **Marl.**

**Matron,** mā'trun, *adj.* matronly.

**Meath,** mēth, *n.* a form of **Mead,** the liquor.

**Meditate,** med'i-tāt, *v.t.* to practise.

**Meteorous,** mē-tē'or-us, *adj.* like a *meteor.*

**Mickle,** mik'l, *adj.* a form of **Much.**

**Middle,** for **Middling.**

**Minim,** min'im, *n.* anything very small.

**Miscreated,** mis-krē-āt'ed, *adj.* wrongly *created* : deformed. [A.S. *mis,* ill, wrongly, and **Create.**]

**Misdeem,** mis-dēm', *v.t.* to *deem* or think wrongly. [A.S. *mis,* ill, wrongly, and **Deem.**]

**Mislike,** mis-līk', *v.t.* to *dislike* : to hate. [A.S. *mis,* wrongly, and **Like.**]

**Misthought,** mis-thawt', *n.* a *wrong notion.* [Pa.p. of *misthink,* to think wrongly—*mis,* wrongly, and **Think.**]

**Mistook,** mis-took', mistaken, *pa.p.* of **Mistake.**

**Moly,** mō'li, *n.* a fabulous herb said by Homer to have been given by Mercury to Ulysses, as a counter-charm against the spells of Circe. [Gr.]

**Murren,** mur'ren, *n.* murrain.

**Murrhine, Myrrhine,** mur'rin or mur'rīn, *adj.* relating to or made of *murrha,* a kind of stone, of which costly vessels were made by the ancients. [L. *murrhinus—murrha.*]

**Nathless,** nath'les, *adv., not the less,* nevertheless. [A.S. *natheless—na,* not, *the* and *less.*]

**Need,** nēd, *v.i.* to be required.

**Night-foundered.** See **Founder,** *v.i.* to fail.

**Nocent,** nō'sent, *adj., hurting* : mischievous. [L. *nocens, -entis, pr.p.* of *noceo,* to hurt.]

**Notion,** nō'shun, *n.* sense, understanding, intellectual power.

**Null,** nul, *v.t.* a form of **Annul.**

**Numbered,** num'bèrd, *adj.* numerous.

**Numerous,** nū'mèr-us, *adj.* measured ; melodious.

**Oary,** ōr'i, *adj.* having the form or use of an *oar.*

**Obdured,** ob-dūrd', *adj.* hardened. [See **Obdurate.**]

**Oblige,** ō-blīj'. *v.t.* to render liable to punishment.

**Obscure,** ob-skūr', *n.* obscurity.　　　　　[quies.

**Obsequy,** ob'se-kwe, *n.* used in sing. See **Obse-**

**Officious,** of-fish'us, *adj.* ministering.

**Omnific,** om-nif'ik, *adj., all-creating.* [Formed from L. *omnis,* all, and *facio,* to do or make.]

**Opacous,** ō-pāk'us, *adj.* opaque.

**Oraculous**, ō-rak'ū-lus, *adj.* oracular.

**Orb**, orb, *n.* the world.

**Orc**, ork, *n.* a kind of whale. [L. *orca*.]

**Orient**, ō'ri-ent, *adj.* splendid.

**Overwatch**, ō-vėr-woch', *v.i.* to *watch* or keep awake over*much*.

**Pale**, pāl, *n.* paleness.

**Paragon**, par'a-gon, *v.t.* to compare, to parallel.

**Paranymph**, par'a-nimf, *n.* one who conducted the bride to the bridegroom on the wedding-day. [Gr. *para*, beside, *nymphē*, a bride.]

**Parl, Parle**, pärl, *n.* parley.

**Passion**, pash'un, *n.* compassion.

**Paven**, pāv'n, a form of **Paved**.

**Pennon**, pen'un, *n.* a pinion, a wing.

**Phrenzy**, fren'zi, *n.* a form of **Frenzy**.

**Plain**, plān, *v.t.* to complain, to lament. [See **Plaint**.]

**Plenipotent**, ple-nip'o-tent, *adj.* possessing *full power*. [Formed from L. *plenus*, full, and *potens*, *-entis*, powerful. See **Potent**.]

**Plume**, ploōm, *v.t.* to place as a plume.

**Pollute**, pol'ūt, *pa.p.* polluted.

**Pontifical**, pon-tif'ik-al, *adj.* pertaining to the building of *bridges*. [See **Pontiff**.]

**Pontifice**, pon'ti-fis, *n.*, *bridge-work*; a bridge.

**Pourlieu**, a form of **Purlieu**.

**Pravity**, prav'i-ti, *n.*, *depravity*, moral perversion. [L. *pravitas—pravus*, crooked.]

**Presentment**, pre-zent'ment, *n.* representation, appearance. [**Prevent**.]

**Prevenient**, pre-vēn'i-ent, *adj.* forestalling. [See **Prick**, prik, *v.i.* to spur onward; to ride forth on horseback. [*mark*.

**Printless**, print'les, *adj.* leaving no *print* or **Procinct**, prō-singkt', *n.* complete preparation for battle. [L. *procinctus—pro*, before (one), and *cingo*, *cinctum*, to gird up the clothes.]

**Profluent**, prof'loō-ent, *adj.*, *flowing forward*. [L. *pro*, forward, and **Fluent**.]

**Propense**, pro-pens', *adj.* inclined : prone. [L. *propensus*, pa.p. of *propendeo—pro*, forward, *pendeo*, *pensum*, to hang.]

**Prowest**, prow'est, *adj.* most valiant. [Superl. of obs. adj. *prow*. See **Prowess**.]

**Punctual**, pungk'tū-al, *adj.* being merely a *point*.

**Purchase**, pur'chās, *n.* what is stolen.

**Pure**, pūr, *n.* purity.

**Purfled**, pur'fld, *pa.p.* of **purfle**, to work with gold *thread* : to embroider : to fringe. [O. Fr. *pourfiler*—Fr. *pour*, for, *fil*—L. *filum*, thread.]

**Purpose**, pur'pos, *n.* discourse : conversation.

**Quit**, kwit, *pa.p.* quitted.

**Realty**, rē'al-ti, *n.* royalty.

**Rebec, Rebeck**, rē'bek, *n.* a kind of fiddle. [O. Fr. *rebec*—It. *ribecca*, also *ribebba*—Pers. *rubab*.]

**Recline**, re-klīn', *adj.* reclining.

**Recorder**, re-kord'ėr, *n.* a kind of flute. [From **Record**.]

**Recure**, rē-kūr', *v.t.* to *cure again* : to heal.

**Religions**, re-lij'uns, *n.pl.* religious rites.

**Remark**, re-märk', *v.t.* to make remarkable : to point out.

**Repeat**, re-pēt', *n.* repetition.

**Respiration**, res-pi-rā'shun, *n.* act of *breathing again* or resuming life : resurrection.

**Retire**, re-tīr', *n.* retirement.

**Revolve**, re-volv', *v.t.* to roll and unroll.

**Rheums**, rōōmz, *n.* rheumatism.

**Robustious**, ro-bust'i-us, *adj.* violent : strong.

**Ruin**, rōō'in, *v.i.* to fall down with ruin and precipitation.—*v.t.* to tumble down.

**Ruinous**, rōō'in-us, *adj.* crashing, like the fall of a house.

**Ruth**, rōōth, *n.* pity : grief for the distress of another. [See **Rue**, *v.*]

**Sadly**, sad'li, *adv.* seriously, soberly, truly.

**Sail-broad**, sāl'-brawd, *adj.*, *broad* or spreading like a *sail*.

**Scape**, skāp, *n.* a freak or prank. [See **Escape**.]

**Sciential**, sī-en'shal, *adj.* producing science. [See **Science**.]

**Scrannel**, skran'l. *adj.* producing a weak, screeching noise. [Imitative ; cf. Scot. *scrannie*, a thin, wrinkled beldame.]

**Scull**, skul, *n.* a form of **Shoal**, a multitude.

**Sdain, Sdeign, Sdein**, sdān, *v.t.* to disdain. [Contr. of **Disdain**, It. *sdegnare*.]

**Sensible**, sens'i-bl, *n.* sense : sensation.

**Sent**, sent, *n.* a form of **Scent**.

**Sentery**, sen'tėr-i, *n.* a form of **Sentry**.

**Septentrion**, sep-ten'tri-on, **Septentrional**, sep-ten'tri-on-al, *adj.* belonging to the north. [L. *septentrio* (esp. used in pl.), the north, the seven stars near the north pole, called Charles's Wain, from *septem*, seven, and *triones*, plough-oxen ; acc. to Max Müller, *trio* represents an original *strio*, a star—Sans. *stri*. See **Star**.]

**Sepulchre**, se-pul'kėr, *v.t.* to put in a *sepulchre*, to bury.

**Serenate**, ser-e-nāt', *n.* a form of **Serenade**.

**Servily**, sėrv'il-i, *adv.* a form of **Servilely**.

**Servitude**, sėrv'i-tūd, **Serviture**, sėrv'i-tūr, *n.* servants.

**Sewer**, sū'ėr, *n.* an officer who set on and removed the dishes at a feast. [M. E. *sewen*, through O. Fr., from L. *sequor*, to follow.]

**Sextile**, seks'til, *n.* (*astrology*) the aspect or position of two planets when distant from each other sixty degrees. [L. *sextus*, sixth—*sex*, six.]

**Shade**, shād, *n.* shadow, companion.

**Shaked**, shākt, *pa.p.* of **Shake**.

**Sheeny**, shēn'i, *adj.*, *shining*, bright.

**Shined**, shīnd, *pa.t.* of **Shine**.

**Shroud**, shrowd, *n.* recess, hiding-place.

**Side**, sīd, *v.t.* to be at the *side* of one, to accompany.

**Sideral**, sid'ėr-al, *adj.* relating to the *stars* : baleful, from a supposed unfavourable influence of the stars. [From root of **Sidereal**.]

**Slope**, slōp, *adj.*, *sloped*. [*copiously*.

**Sluice**, slōōs, *v.t.* to convey by *sluices* : to wet

**Smit**, smit, *pa.t.* and *pa.p.* of **Smite**.

**Smote**, smōt, *pa.p.* of **Smite**.

**Solution**, sol-ū'shun, *n.* termination, decision.

**Sophi**, sō'fi, *n.* a title of the king of Persia. [Pers. *sufi*, wise, pious.]

**Sord**, sōrd, *n.* a form of **Sward**.

**Sovran**, sov'ran, *n.* a form of **Sovereign**.

**Specular**, spek'ū-lar, *adj.* affording a view.

**Speculation**, spek'ū-lā'shun, *n.* a *watching* on a high place.

**Spell**, spel, *v.i.* to read or learn to read. [See **Spell**.]

**Spet**, spet, a form of **Spit**, *v.i.*

**Sphere-metal**, sfėr-met'al, *n.*, *metal* like that of which the celestial *spheres* were anciently supposed to be made.

**Sphery**, sfėr'i, *adj.* belonging to the *spheres*, or the revolving, transparent, spherical shells, in which the sun, moon, and stars were, in ancient times, supposed to be held.

**Spiritous**, spir'it-us, *adj.* like *spirit* : refined : pure.

**Spring**, spring, *n.* that which *springs* from a source ; a race of men : a shoot : a grove of shrubs.

**Square**, skwār, *v.t.* to adjust, accommodate.

**State**, stāt, *n.* canopy : covering :—*pl.* governors, chiefs.

**Stay**, stā, *v t*  to wait for

**Strait**, strāt, *adj*  close, intimate.

**Strength**, strength, *n.* a stronghold.

**Strook**, strook, *pa.t.* and *pa.p.* of **Strike**.

**Strucken**, struk′n, *pa.t.* and *pa.p.* of **Strike**.

**Stub**, stub, *n.* a stalk.

**Suage, Swage**, swāj, *v.t.* or *v.i.* a form of **Assuage**.

**Subscribe**, sub-skrīb′, *v.i.* to consent : to assent.

**Success**, suk-ses′, *n.* issue of anything whether happy or unhappy.

**Summed**, sumd, *pa.p.* said of a hawk when his feathers are full grown.

**Suspect**, sus-pekt′, *pa.p.* suspected.—*n.* suspicion.

**Suspense**, sus-pens′, *adj., suspended*, in suspense. [L. *suspensus*, pa.p. of *suspendo*. See **Suspend**.]

**Sustain**, sus-tān′, *n.* that which sustains, a support.

**Swage**, swāj, *v.t.* a form of **Assuage**.

**Swart**, swawrt, *adj.* a form of **Swarthy**.

**Swindge, Swinge**, swinj, *v.t.* to *swing*, lash or wave to and fro, to beat. [A form of **Swing**.]

**Swinked**, swinkd, *adj.* wearied with *labour*. [A.S. *swincan*, to labour.]

**Synod**, sin′od, *n.* (*astron.*) conjunction.

**Syrtis**, sėr′tis, *n.* a quicksand. [L.—Gr. *syreō*, to draw along.]

**Tempered**, tem′pėrd, *pa.p.* modulated.

**Tempest**, tem-pest′, *v.t.* to agitate, as by a *tempest*.

**Tendance**, tend′ans, *n.*, *attendance*.

**Terrene**, ter-ēn′, *n.* the earth.

**Terrour**, ter′or, *n.* a form of **Terror**.

**Thrones**, thrōnz, *n.pl.* angelic beings.

**Thunderous**, thun′dėr-us, *adj.* producing *thunder*; sounding like thunder.

**Thwart**, thwawrt, *adv.*, *thwartly*.—**Thwart′ing**, twisting, zigzag.

**Tiar**, tī′ar, *n.* a form of **Tiara**.

**Timelessly**, tīm′les-li, *adv.*, *untimely*, before due time or season.

**Tine**, tīn, *v.t.* to kindle. [A.S. *tendan*, whence **Tinder**.]

**Tire**, tīr, *n.* a row or rank. [A form of **Tier**.]

**Torneament**, tor-nē′a-ment, *n.* a form of **Tournament**.

**Torrent**, tor′ent, *adj.* boiling, rushing.

**Torture**, tor′tūr, *n.* an instrument of *torture*.

**To-ruffled**, tōō-ruf′ld, *adj.* ruffled. [A.S. prefix *to-* (here used intensively ; see **To-** in PREFIXES), and **Ruffled**.]

**Trading**, trād′ing, *adj.* frequented by traders : where the trade-winds blow.

**Train**, trān, *n.* allurement : snare.

**Transpicuous**, tran-spik′ū-us, *adj.* that can be *seen through*, transparent. [L. *transpicio—trans*, through, *specio*, to look.]

**Trine**, trīn, **Trinal**, trī′nal, *adj.* threefold.—**Trine**, *n.* a triad : (*astrology*) the aspect of the planets when distant from each other a *third* of the zodiac, or 120°. [Fr.—L. *trinus—tres*, three.]

**Triumph**, trī′umf, *n.* a show, spectacle.

**Tumult**, tū′mult, *v.i.* to cause or make a *tumult* or uproar.

**Turkois**, tur-koiz′, *n.* a form of **Turquoise**.

**Turm**, tėrm, *n.* a troop of soldiers. [It.—L. *turma*.]

**Turney**, tėr′ni, *n.* a form of **Tourney**.

**Unapparent**, un-ap-pär′ent, *adj.*, *not apparent* : dark : invisible.

**Unblenched**, un-blensht′, *adj.* not startled or confounded, unblinded. [See **Blench**.]

**Understood**, un-dėr-stood′, *adj.* secret, concealed.

**Undiscording**, un-dis-kord′ing, *adj.*, *not discording* or making discord.

**Unessential**, un-es-sen′shal, *adj.*, *not essential* or substantial : not necessary.

**Unfounded**, un-fownd′ed, *adj.* without bottom, bottomless. [A.S. *un*, not, and **Found**, to lay the bottom of.]

**Unhappy**, un-hap′i, *adj.* unlucky.

**Unkindly**, un-kīnd′li, *adv.* contrary to *kind* or nature.

**Unnumbered**, un-num′bėrd, *adj.*, *not* to be *numbered*, innumerable.

**Unoriginal**, un-or-ij′in-al, *adj.*, *not original* : without origin, birth, or source.

**Unprevented**, un-pre-vent′ed, *adj.*, *not preceded* by anything.

**Unprincipled**, un-prin′si-pld, *adj.* ignorant of the *principia* or beginnings of virtue.

**Unreproved**, un-re-prōōvd′, *adj.*, *not* liable to *reproof* : blameless.

**Unsphere**, un-sfēr′, *v.t.* to bring out of one's proper *sphere*.

**Unsuspect**, un-sus-pekt′, *adj.* not liable to be suspected.

**Unvalued**, un-val′ūd, *adj.* invaluable.

**Unweeting**, un-wēt′ing, *adj.*, *not weeting* or knowing : ignorant. [A.S. *un*, not, and *witan*, to know. See **Wit**.]

**Unweetingly**, un-wēt′ing-li, *adv.* ignorantly.

**Urge**, urj, *v.t.* to torment.

**Use**, ūz, *v.i.* to frequent, inhabit.

**Vacuous**, vak′ū-us, *adj., empty*. [L. *vacuus—vaco*. See **Vacate**.]

**Van**, van, *n.* a wing. [See **Van = Fan**.]

**Vant-brace** or **-brass**, vant′-bras, *n.* armour for the *arms*. [Fr. *avant*, before, *bras*, the arm.]

**Verdurous**, vėrd′ūr-us, *adj.* covered with *verdure*.

**Vermeil-tinctured**, vėr′mil-tingk′tūrd, *adj.*, *vermilion-tinted* : tinged of a bright-red colour.

**Vernant**, vėr′nant, *adj.* flourishing as in *spring* : vernal. [See **Vernal**.]

**Vigilance**, vij′i-lans, *n.* guard, watch.

**Villatic**, vil-at′ik, *adj.* belonging to a *farm*. [L. *villaticus—villa*, a farm.]

**Virtue-proof**, vėr′tū-prōōf, *adj.*, *proof* against temptation by means of *virtue*.

**Virtuous**, vėr′tū-us, *adj.* of magic *virtue*.

**Volubil**, vol′ū-bil, *adj.* a form of **Voluble**.

**Voyageable**, voy′āj-a-bl, *adj.* capable of being sailed over : navigable.

**Wander**, won′dėr, *v.t.* to travel over, without a certain course : to cause to wander.

**Warp**, wawrp, *v.i.* to turn and wave, like a flock of birds or insects.

**Wasteful**, wāst′fool, *adj.* lying *waste*, desolate.

**Weanling**, wēn′ling, *adj.* newly *weaned*.

**Whereso**, hwär′sō, *adv.* in whatever place.

**Whilere**, hwīl-ār′, *adv.* a little *while before* : recently.

**Whist**, hwist, hushed, *pa.p.* of old verb *Whist*, *Hist*.

**Wide**, wīd, *adv.* to its furthest extent.

**Wilderness**, *n.* a form of **Wildness**.

**Wing**, wing, *v.t.* to fly over.

**Wise**, wīz, *n.* wisdom.

**Won**, wun, *v.i.* to dwell. [A.S. *wunian*. See **Wont**.]

**Wonderous**, wun′dėr-us, *adj.* a form of **Wondrous**.

**Worse**, wurs, *v.t.* to worst.

**Wove**, wōv, **Woven**, wōv′n, *pa.p.* of **Weave**.

**Wreck**, rek, *v.t.* a form of **Wreak**.

**Writ**, rit, *pa.p.* of **Write**.

**Ychained**, i-chānd′, *pa.p.* chained. [*Y* from A.S. *ge-*, a participial prefix.]

**Yeanling**, yēn′ling, *n.* a lamb : a kid.

**Ypointing**, i-point′ing, *adj.* pointing. [*Y* from A.S. *ge-*, a prefix of the past part., wrongly used here by Milton with the pres. part.]

# PREFIXES AND SUFFIXES.

## PREFIXES.

**A-** (A.S.) represents:

(1.) A.S. *on*, on, as a*bed* (from M. E. *on bædde*), among, a*bout*, a*-fishing.*

(2.) A.S. *and-*, over against, close to, as a*long* (from A.S. *and-lang*, i.e., over against in length). [Cog. with Goth. *anda*, Ger. *ent-*, *ant-*, L. **Ante-**, Gr. **Anti-** (which see).]

(3.) A.S. *ā-*, out, out from, as in a*rise* (from A.S. *ārisan*, to rise out of or up), or sig. 'very,' as in a*ghast*. [Cog. with Ger. *er-*, Goth. *us-*, *ur-*.]

(4.) A.S. *of*, of, from, as in a*down* (from A.S. *of dune*, 'from the height'), a*new*, a*kin*; or from *of-*, intensive, as a*thirst*.

(5.) A.S. *ge-*, *y-*, as a*ware* (from M. E. *ywar*—A.S. *gewær*), a*-i-ford*. [Scand.]

(6.) for *at*, old sign of inf., as a*do*. [From the **A-** (L. and Gr.) represents: (1.) L. **Ab-**; (2.) L. **Ad-**; (3.) L. **Ex-**, as in a*bash*, a*mend*; (4.) Gr. **A-** (for **An-**). See these prefixes.

**A-, Ab-, Abs-** (L.), away from, as a*vert*, a*bsolve*, a*vaunt*, a*bstract*. [L. *a, ab, abs* (oldest form *ap*); cog. with Gr. **Apo-**, Sans. *apa*, Ger. *ab*, E. **Off.**]

**Ad-** (L.), to, at, as a*dhere*, a*dapt*. The *d* becomes assimilated to the following consonant, as in a*ccede*, a*ffix*, a*ggregate*, a*llot*, a*nnex*, a*pprove*, a*rrive*, a*ssign*, a*ttract*. [L. *ad*; cog. with Sans. *adhi*, Goth. and E. *at*, Celt. *ar-*.]

**Ambi-, Amb-** (L.), round about, both, as a*mbition*, a*mputate*, a*mbidexter*. [L.; cog. with Gr. **Amphi-**, Sans. *abhi*, around, O. Ger. *umpi* (Ger. *um*).]

**Amphi-** (Gr.), round about, both, as a*mphitheatre*, a*mphibious*. [Cog. with L. **Ambi-, Amb-.**]

**An-** (A.S.), against, in return, as a*nswer*. [A.S. *and-*, Ger. *ant-*, Goth. *and-*.]

**An-, A-** (Gr.), not, without, as a*narchy*, a*tom*, a*mbrosia*. [Gr.; cog. with Sans. *an-, a-*, L. *in-*, E. **Un-, In-**, *not*.]

**Ana-** (Gr.), up, back, as a*nalyse*, a*natomy*, a*neurism*. [Cog. with Goth. *ana*, E. **On.**]

**Ante-** (L.), before, as a*ntecedent*, a*nticipate*, a*ncestor* (for L. *ante-cessor*). [L. *ante*, old form *anti*; conn. with **Anti-**.]

**Anti-** (Gr.), opposite to, against, as a*ntipathy*, a*ntipodes*, a*ntagonist*. [Gr.; conn. with L. **Ante-**, Sans. *anti*, facing, Ger. *ant-* in A*nt*wort, E. *an-* (for *and-*) in **Answer** (see Dict.). Cf. **A-** (A.S.) (2.), above.]

**Apo-** (Gr.), off, from, away, as a*postle*, a*phelion*. [Cog. with L. **Ab-.**] [*æt.*]

**At-** (E.), near, as a*tone*; against, as t*wit*. [A.S.]

**Auto-** (Gr.), self, as a*utograph*, a*utopsy*.

**Be-** (A.S.), by, before, beside, as b*ehalf*; intensive, as b*esprinkle*; privative, as b*ehead*. [A form of **By.** See Dict.] [*dvis*, ablative of *duo*, two.]

**Bis-** (L.), twice, as b*iscuit*, b*iennial*. [Corr. of

**Cata-, Cath-, Cat-** (Gr.), down, downwards, according to, as c*ataract*, c*atholic*, c*atechism*. [Gr. *kata*.]

**Circum-, Circu-** (L.), round about, as c*ircumscribe*, c*ircuit*. [Properly accusative of *circus*, a circle. See **Circle** in Dict.]

**Cis-** (L.), on this side, as c*isalpine*. [From the demons. stem *ki-*, which appears in Gr. *e-kei*, there, and the *-c* of L. *hic, sic*.]

**574**

**Com-, Con-** (L.), together, with, as c*onnect*, c*o*here, c*ollect*, c*orrect*; often intensive, as c*ommotion*. [*Com-* is the old form of L. *cum*, with; cog. with Gr. *syn*, Sans. *sam*. The root, originally signifying 'one,' is seen in L. *sim-ul*, together, Gr. *ham-a*, together, E. *simple* (which see in Dict.).]

**Contra-, Contro-, Counter-** (L.), against, as c*ontradict*, c*ontrovert*, c*ounteract*. [L. *contra* (whence Fr. *contre*), from **Con-**, and *-tra*, from root *tar*, to cross, seen also in **Trans-**.]

**De-** (L., or Fr.—L.), down, from, away, occurs in words derived either directly from L., as d*educe*; or through the Fr. from L., in which case **De-** represents either (1.) O. Fr. *des-* from L. *dis-*, asunder, not, as in d*efeat* (O. Fr. *des-*fait), or (2.) Fr.—L. *de-*, as d*escribe* [*lit.* 'write *down*'], d*ecompose*.

**Dia-** (Gr.), two, through, as d*ialogue* ['a conversation between *two*'], d*iameter*. [Gr. *dia* (from *dyo*, two), sig. dividing into *two*. through.]

**Dis-** (Gr.), two, twice, as d*issyllable*, d*icotyledonous*. [From *dvis*, from root of **Two.**]

**Dis-** (L.), in two, asunder, as d*ispart*, d*iffer*, d*isperse*; negative, as d*isrelish*; privative, as d*islodge*. [*Dis* for *dvis*, from L. *duo*, Gr. *dyo*, Sans. *dvi*, Goth. and E. *two*. See **Two** in Dict.]

**Dys-** (Gr.), ill, difficult, as d*ysentery*, d*yspepsy*. [Cog. with Sans. *dus*, Goth. *tus*, Ger. *zer-*, A.S. **To-**, E. **Two.**]

**E-.** See **Ex-**.

**Ec-** or **Ex-** (Gr.), out of, from, as e*cstasy*, e*xodus*. [Gr. *ex*, cog. with L. *ex*, and Russian *iz*, out.]

**Em-, En-** (Fr.—L.), in, into, as e*nlist*; to make, as e*nlarge*; before *b* and *p*, **En-** changes to **Em-**, as e*mbark*. [Fr. *en*—L. *in*. See **In-** (L.), in, into.]

**En-** (Gr.), in, on, as e*nergy*, e*ndemic*, e*mphasis*. [See **In** in Dict.]

**Enter-** (Fr.), between, among, as e*ntertain*. [Fr. *entre*—L. **Inter-.**]

**Epi-** (Gr.), on, as e*pitaph*; during, as e*phemeral*. [Gr. *epi*; Sans. *api*, L. **Ob-.**]

**Es-** (Fr. or Sp.—L.), out, as e*scape*, e*splanade*. [O. Fr. or Sp. *es*—L. **Ex-.**]

**Eso-** (Gr.), in, into, as e*soteric*. [From Gr. *eis*, into, whose form was prob. orig. *ens*, a strengthened form of **En-** (Gr.).]

**Eu-** (Gr.), well, as e*uphony*, e*ulogy*. [Gr. *eu, eus*, good, for *es-us*, real, from root of **Is** (see Dict.).]

**Ex-** or **E-** (L.), from, out of, as e*xpel*, e*ject*, e*fflux*. [Conn. with Gr. **Ec-** or **Ex-.**]

**Exo-** (Gr.), outside, as e*xotic*. [From **Ex-** (Gr.).]

**Extra-** (L.), on the outside, beyond, as e*xtramural*, e*xtraordinary*. [Contr. of *exterā* (*parte* being understood), ablative feminine of *exterus*, beyond, a compar. form, from **Ex-** (L.).]

**For-** (A.S.), through, thorough, away, so as to be non-existent, or to be destroyed, as f*orswear*, f*orbid*. [A.S. *for-*; Ger. *ver-*, Goth. *fra-*, L. *per-*, Sans. *para*; conn. with **Far** and **From.**]

**For-** (Fr.—L.), as in f*oreclose*, f*orfeit*. [Fr.—L. *foris*, lit. 'out of doors,' used in the sense of 'outside,' 'beyond,' 'amiss.']

# Prefixes.

**Fore-** (A.S.), before, as *fore*tell. [A.S. *fore*; O. Ger. *fora* (Ger. *vor*), Goth. *faura*, L. **Pro-**.]

**Gain-** (A.S.), against, as *gain*say. [A.S. *gegn*, *gean*. See **Against** in Dict.]

**Hemi-** (Gr.), half, as *hemi*sphere. [Gr.; cog. with L. **Semi-**, Sans. *sami-*, O. Ger. *sâmi-*.]

**Hyper-** (Gr.), over, above, beyond, as *hyper*borean, *hyper*critical. [Cog. with **Super-** and **Over-**.]

**Hypo-, Hyp-** (Gr.), under, as *hypo*tenuse. [Cog. with L. **Sub-**, Goth. *uf*, Sans. *upa*.]

**I-, Y-**, as in *I*-wis, *y*clept, hand-*y*-work. [A.S. *ge-*, sign of the past participle passive.]

**In-** (L.), not, as *in*firm. Before *p*, the *n* changes to *m*, as *im*pudent; before *l*, *m*, and *r*, it is assimilated to those consonants, as *il*legal, *im*mature, *ir*regular. [L.; cog. with Gr. **An-**, E. **Un-**.]

**In-** (L.), in, into, as *in*fuse, *il*lumine, *im*pel, *ir*rigate. [See **In** in Dict.]

**In-** (A.S.), in, on, as *in*come, *in*ward; to make, as *im*bitter, lit. to put *into* a state of bitterness. [See **In** in Dict.]

**Inter-** (L.), in the midst of, between, as *inter*val, *intel*lect. [A compar. form, cog. with E. **Under**, and Sans. *antar*, within.]

**Intra-** (L.), in the inside of, within, as *intra*mural. [Contr. of *intera*, ablative feminine of *interus*, inward—**Inter-**.]

**Intro-** (L.), into, within, as *intro*duce. [Contr. of *intro*, ablative masculine of *interus*—**Inter-**.]

**Juxta-** (L.), near, as *juxta*position. [Superlative form, from root of L. *ju(n)go*, to join. See **Join** in Dict.]

**Meta-, Met-** (Gr.), lit. 'in the middle,' hence with; after, as *meth*od (lit. way after); often implies change, as *meta*morphose, *met*onymy. [Gr. *meta*; cog. with A.S. *mid*, Goth. *mith*, Ger. *mit*; Sans. *mithu*, Zend *mat*.]

**Mis-** (A.S. and Scand.), wrong, ill, as *mis*behave, *mis*deed, *mis*lead. [A.S. and Scand. *mis-*, Ger. *miss-*. Cf. **Miss**, *v.t.* in Dict.]

**Mis-** (Fr.—L.), as in *mis*chief. [Fr. *mis-*, for O. Fr. *mes-*, from L. *minus*, less.]

**Mono-, Mon-** (Gr.), single, as *mono*graph. [Gr. *monos*, alone.]

**N-** (A.S.), no, not, as *n*ever. [A.S. *ne*; cog. with O. Ger. and Goth. *ni*, L. *ne*, Sans. *na*.]

**Ne-** (Gr.), not, as *ne*penthe; (L.) not, as *ne*farious, *ne*uter. [Allied to E. **No** (see Dict.).]

**Nec-** (L.), not, as *neg*lect, *neg*ative. [Contr. of *neque*, from *ne*, not, *que*, and.]

**Non-** (L.), not, as *non*sense, *non*age. [From *ne unum*, not one. Cf. E. **Not** in Dict.]

**Ob-** (L.), in the way of, against, as *ob*struct, *o*mit, *oc*cur, *of*fer, *op*pose, *o*stentation. [Cog. with Gr. *epi*, Sans. *api*.]

**Off-** (A.S.), off, from, away, as *off*shoot, *off*set. [A form of **Of**. Cf. **A-, Ab-**, and see **Of** in Dict.]

**On-** (A.S.), on, as *on*set, *on*looker. [See **On** in Dict.]

**Out-** (A.S.), out, beyond, as *out*law, *out*bid. [A.S. *ut*. See **Out** in Dict.]

**Over-** (A.S.), over, above, as *over*arch, *over*seer. [See **Over** in Dict.]

**Pan-** (Gr.), all, as *pan*acea, *pan*theism.

**Para-, Par-** (Gr.), beside, as *para*ble; beyond, wrong, as *para*lyse. [Gr. *para*; akin to Sans. *para*, away, L. *per-*, and E. *for-* in *for*give.]

**Pene-** (L.), almost, as *pen*insula.

**Per-** (L.), through, as *per*mit, *pel*lucid, *pol*lute; thoroughly, as *per*fect. In *per*jure, *per*ish, it is equivalent to E. *for-* in *for*swear †see **For-**, A.S.). [Akin to Gr. **Para-**, beside, Sans. *para*, away, E. *for-*, Ger. *ver-*.]

**Peri-** (Gr.), round, as *peri*meter, *peri*phrasis. [Gr. *peri*; Sans. *peri*, also allied to Gr. *para*.]

**Pol-, Por-** (L.), as *pol*lute, *por*tend. [From **O**. L. *port-*, towards.]

**Post-** (L.), backwards, behind, after, as *post*pone.

**Pour-, Pur-** (Fr.—L.), as *pour*tray, *pur*vey. [Fr. —L. **Pro-**.]

**Pre-** (L.), before, as *pre*dict, *pre*fer. [L. *præ*, akin to L. *pro*.]

**Preter-** (L.), beyond, as *preter*it, *preter*natural, *preter*mit. [L. *præter—præ*, with comparative suffix *-ter*. See **Alter** in Dict.]

**Pro-** (Gr.), before, as *pro*logue, *pro*gramme. [Gr. *pro*; cog. with L. **Pro-**, Sans. *pra*, E. **For** (prep.; see Dict.).]

**Pro-** (L.), before, forth, forward, as *pro*ject; instead of, from the idea of being before, as *pro*noun. [Cog. with **Pro-** (Gr.), which see.]

**Pros-** (Gr.), towards, as *pros*elyte, *pros*ody. [Original form *proti*, an extension of **Pro-** (Gr.); cog. with Sans. *prati*, Slav. *proti*.]

**Pur-.** See under **Pour-**.

**Re-, Red-** (L.), change of place or condition, as in *re*move, *re*union (an assemblage of things or persons formerly apart); hence, change of motion from one direction to the opposite = 'back,' 'again,' as *re*tract, *re*sound, *re*deem.

**Retro-** (L.), back, backwards, as *retro*spect, *retro*grade. [From **Re-**, and the compar. suffix *-ter*.]

**Se-** (L.), without, as *se*cure; aside, as *se*duce. [Old form of **Sine-**.]

**Semi-** (L.), half, as *semi*circle. [L.; cog. with Gr. *hêmi*.]

**Sine-** (L.), without, as *sine*cure. [*Si*, demons. instrumental sig. 'by that,' and *ne*, not.]

**Sub-** (L.), under, from under, after, as *sub*ject, *sus*pect, *suc*ceed, *suf*fuse, *sug*gest, *sum*mon, *sup*port, *sur*prise, *sus*pend, *so*journ. [L. *sub* (which in O. Fr. became *so-*).]

**Subter-** (L.), under, as *subter*fuge. [From **Sub-**, and compar. suffix *-ter*, meaning motion. See **Trans-**.]

**Super-** (L.), over, above, beyond, as *super*structure, *super*natural. [L.; cog. with Sans. *upari*, Gr. *hyper*, Goth. *ufar*, E. **Over**.]

**Supra-** (L.), over, above, as *supra*mundane. [Contr. of ablative fem. of *superus*, above, from **Super-**. Cf. **Superior** in Dict.]

**Sur-** (Fr.), over, as *sur*mount. [Fr., from L. *super*.]

**Syn-** (Gr.), together, with, as *syn*tax, *sys*tem, *syl*lable, *sym*bol. [Cog. with **Com-**.]

**To-** (E.), in *to*-day, *to*gether, *to*ward, here-*to*-fore, is the prep. **To** (see Dict.).

**To-** (A.S.), asunder, as in *to*-brake. [A.S. *to-*, cog. with Gr. **Dys-** (which see); cf. **Dis-** (L.).]

**Trans-** (L.), beyond, across, as *trans*port, *trans*verse. [From root *tar*, to cross; the same root occurs in **Inter-**, **Intro-**, **Preter-**, **Retro-**, **Subter-**.]

**U-** (Gr.), no, not, as *U*topia. [Gr. *ou*, not.]

**Ultra-** (L.), beyond, as *ultra*marine. [From *ulter* (stem of *ulterior*), *ul-* being from root of L. *ille*.]

**Un-** (A.S.), not, as *un*happy, *un*truth; back, as *un*tie. [Cog. with Gr. **An-**, and L. **In-** (negative).]

**Under-** (A.S.), under, below, as *under*prop, *under*sell. [See **Under** in Dict.]

**Up-** (A.S.), up, as *up*hill. [See **Up** in Dict.]

**Vis-, Vice-** (Fr.—L.), in place of, as *vis*count, *vice*roy. [Fr. *vis-*, from L. *vice*, instead of.]

**Wan-** (A.S.), wanting, as *wan*ton. [Cf. **Wane** and **Want** in Dict.]

**With-** (A.S.), against, back, as *with*stand, *with*draw; with, near, as *with*in (this meaning is very rare as prefix). [A.S. *with—wither*. See **With** in Dict.]

**Y-.** See under **I-**.

575

# SUFFIXES.

**-able,** adj. suffix, capable of, as port*able*, laugh-*able*. [L. *-a-b-ili-s*.]

**-ac,** adj. suffix, pertaining to, as elegi*ac*; also used as noun suffix, as mani*ac*. [L. *-acus*, Gr. *-akos*.]

**-aceous,** having the qualities of, as herb*aceous*. [L. *-aceus*.]

**-acious,** full of, as aud*acious*. [L. *-ax, -acis*.]

**-ade,** noun suffix, as escap*ade* [Fr.—It.]; and as crus*ade*, torn*ado* [Sp. *-ade*, original form *-ado*.].

**-age,** ending of abstract nouns, as homag*e*; marks place where, as vicar*age*. [Fr. *-age*, from L. *-aticum*.]

**-ain, -an, -en, -on,** noun suffixes, as vill*ain*, pag*an*, ward*en*, surge*on*. [L. *-anus*.]

**-al,** adj. and noun suffix, as mort*al*, cardin*al*. [L. *-alis*.]                    [humane*. [L. *-an*us.]

**-an, -ain, -ane,** adj. suffix, as hum*an*, cert*ain*,

**-ana,** things belonging to, such as sayings, anecdotes, &c., as Johnsoni*ana*. [L. neuter pl. of adjs. in *-anus*. See **-an.**]

**-ance, -ancy.** See **-nce.**

**-and, -end,** noun suffix, as vi*and*, leg*end*. [L. *-andus, -endus,* gerundial suffix.]

**-aneous,** belonging to, as extr*aneous*. [L. *-aneus.*]

**-ant, -ent,** adj. suffix, as repent*ant*, patien*t*; also sometimes denoting the agent, as serge*ant*, stud*ent*, innoc*ent*. [L. *-ans, -ant-is*, or *-ens, -ent-is*, suffix of pr.p.]

**-ar,** belonging to, as angul*ar*. [L. *-ar-is*, Sans. *-ara*.]                    [agent].

**-ar, -ard, -art.** See under **-er** (marking the

**-ar, -er, -or,** noun suffixes, marking place where, as cell*ar*, lard*er*, man*or* [L. *-arium*]; denoting the agent, as vic*ar*, treasur*er*, chancell*or* [L. *-arius*].

**-ard,** intensive, as drunk*ard*, cow*ard*. [Fr.—Ger. *hart*, E. *Hard*.]

**-ary,** noun suffix, marking place where, as semin*ary* [L. *-arium*]; the agent, as secret*ary*, anti-qu*ary* [L. *-arius*]; with *-an* added, forming an adj. suffix, as unit*ari-an*, agr*ari-an*.

**-asm.** See under **-ism.**

**-ass, -ace,** as cuir*ass*, cutl*ass*, men*ace*, pinn*ace*. [L. *-aceus, -acius*, It. *-accio*, Fr. *-as*.]

**-aster,** dim. and freq. (often implying contempt), as poet*aster*. [Fr. *-astre* (It. *-astro*)—L. *-as-ter*, from Aryan *as-tar*.]

**-ate,** verbal suffix, as navig*ate*, perme*ate*; adj., as desol*ate*, delic*ate*; noun, as leg*ate*, advoc*ate*. [Norm. Fr. *-at*, L. *-atus*, suffix of pa.p.]

**-ble.** See **-able.**

**-ble, -ple,** fold, as dou*ble*, tre*ble*, quadru*ple*. [L. *-plus*, lit. 'full.']

**-ce.** See under **-s,** adverbial suffix.

**-celli, -cello,** dim., as vermi*celli*, violon*cello*. [It., from L. *-cu-lus*. See under **-l.**]

**-ch,** dim., as blot*ch*. [See under **-ock.**]

**-cle, -cule,** dim., as in parti*cle*, animal*cule*, from L. *cu-lus*, which also gives (through It.) **-celli,** **-cello.** [See under **-l.**]

**-cy,** being, or state of being, as clemen*cy*. [Fr. *-cie*—L. *-tia*.]

**-d, -t,** or *-ed*, pa.t. suffix, as love*d*. The *e* in *-ed* is the connecting vowel, omitted when the verb ends in *e*. [A.S. *-de*, 'did,' from *di-de*, pa.t. of **Do.**]

**-d,** pa.p. suffix, as love*d*; in nouns (with passive meaning) as dee*d*, see*d*; in adjs., as feathere*d*, wicke*d*, col*d*; in the form **-th** (or *-t*),
576

in abstract nouns and adjs., as dea*th*, fligh*t*, swif*t*, (with euphonic *-s-*) du*-s-t*, bla*-s-t*. [Orig. *-th*, as in uncou*th*, and from the root of **The, That**; seen also in the L. suffix *-tu-s*, as in no*-tu-s*, Sans. *jna-ta-s*, and in the Gr. suffix *-to-s*.]

**-dom,** dominion, power, as king*dom*; state, as free*dom*; act, as martyr*dom*. [A.S. *dôm*, judgment, dominion, Ger. *-thum*.]

**-dor,** as in corri*dor*, mata*dore*, steve*dore*, battle-*door*. [Sp. *-dor*, L. *-tor*.]

**-ed,** see **-d.**

**-ee,** one who or that which is (passive), as trust*ee*, jubil*ee* [Fr. *-ée*—L. *-atus*, of part. pass.]; Pharis*ee*, Sadduc*ee* [L. *-æu-s*].

**-eer, -ier,** one who, has frequentative meaning, as chariot*eer*. [Fr. *-er, -ier*—L. *arius*.]

**-el,** dim., as dams*el*. [See under **-l.**]

**-en,** dim., as chick*en*, maid*en*. [A.S. *-en*.]

**-en,** fem. suffix, now found only in vix*en*. [A.S. *-en, -n*; Ger. *-in*, Gr. *-ine*, L. *-ina*.]

**-en,** made of, as wood*en*, leath*ern*; orig. sig. belonging to, as heath*en*. [A.S., Goth. *-en, -an*, Ger. *-en, -ein*, Sans. *-um*; a genitive suffix, as in min*e*.]

**-en,** pa. part. as wov*en*, bor*ne*, swor*n*. [A.S. *-n, -ne, -en*; conn. with **-ant, -ent.**]

**-en,** pl. suffix, as ox*en*, ki*ne* (for ky-*en*). [A.S. *-an* (for *-ans*.)]

**-en,** to make, as whit*en*. [Orig. reflexive or passive.]

**-en, -in, -ene,** belonging to, as ali*en*, verm*in*, terr*ene*. [L. *-enus, -ena, -enum*.]

**-ence, -ency.** See **-nce, -ncy.**

**-ent,** belonging to, as differ*ent*. [L. *-ens, -entis*. See **-ant.**]

**-eous,** in right*eous*, corr. of **-wise** (which see); in court*eous*, from O. Fr. *-eis* (from L. *-ensis*).

**-eous,** same as **-ous,** as lign*eous*. [L. *-eus*.]

**-er,** freq. and intens., as glimm*er*, flutt*er*.

**-er,** infinitive suffix, as cov*er*, encount*er*. [Fr. *-re, -ir*, from L. pr. infinitive *-are, -ere, -ire*.]

**-er** marks the agent, as writ*er*; sometimes changed to *-ar*, as li*ar*; with *-i-* or *-y-* prefixed, as cloth*-i-er*, law*-y-er*; with excrescent *-t* or *-d*, as bragg*-ar-t*. [A.S. *-ere*; Ger. *-er*.]

**-er,** more, used in compar. of adjs., as great*er*, mor*e*. [Aryan compar. suffix *-ra*.]

**-er,** noun suffix, as matt*er*, gutt*er*. [Fr. *-iere*—L. *-eria*.]

**-erel,** dim. suffix, as mack*erel*. [See under **-l.**]

**-erie,** place where, as menag*erie*. [Fr., from L. *-arium*. See **-ery.**]

**-erly,** direction to or from, as south*erly*. [From **-ern** and **-ly.**]

**-ern,** adj. suffix, sig. direction, as south*ern* [A.S. *-er-n*]; adj. suffix, sig. belonging to, as mod*ern* [L. *-ernus*]; noun suffix, as cist*ern* [L. *-erna*].

**-ery,** noun suffix, as brew*ery*, witch*ery*, cutl*ery*. [Noun suffix **-y** added to nouns in **-er** (marking agent). See **-ary, -erie, -ory.**]

**-es** or **s,** pl. suffix, as fox*es*, hat*s*. [A.S. *-as*. **-s** is a general pl. suffix, as L. and Gr. *-es*.]

**-escent,** growing, becoming, as conval*escent*. [L. *-esco, -isco, -asco*, Gr. *-askō*, suffix, implying becoming, beginning.]

**-ese,** belonging to, as Japan*ese*. [It. *-ese*, L. *-ensis*.]

**-esque,** partaking of the quality of, as pictur*esque*. [Fr. *-esque* (It. *-esco*)—L. *-iscus*, a by-form of *-icus* (see **-ic**), and conn. with **-ish,** adj. suffix.]

-ess, fem. suffix of nouns, as lion*ess*. [Fr. *-esse*, L. *-issa*, Gr. *-issa* (made up of *-it* or *-id* and *-ya*).]

-ess, -ice, -ise, as prow*ess*, just*ice*, merchand*ise*. [Fr.—L. *-itia*.]

-est, as in harv*est*, earn*est*.

-est, suffix of 2d sing. in verbs, as bring*est*. [A.S. *-ast, -est;* L. *-es, -isti;* Gr. *-si, -sthon.* -s or -st = 2d per. pron., Gr. *sy (su),* L. *tu,* E. **Thou.**]

-est, superl. suffix, formed from the compar. by adding *-t,* as small*est*. [A.S. *-est* (in adjs.), *-ost* (in adverbs) ; L. *-issimus,* Gr. *-istos, -stos, -tatos,* Sans. *-ishta.*]

-et, -ete, noun suffix, marking the agent, as proph*et*, po*et*, athl*ete*. [L. *-ēta,* Gr. *-ētēs.*]

-et, -ette, -ot, dim., as cygn*et*, bill*et*, etiqu*ette*, ball*ot*. [Norm. Fr. *-et, -ot,* Fr. *-et, -ette.*]

-eur. See under -or.

-ever, at any time, as who*ever*, every one who. [See **Ever** in Dict.]

-fare, way, as in welf*are*, chaf*fer*. [See **Fare** in Dict.]

-fast, as in stead*fast*, shame*faced*. [A.S. *fæst,* firm, fast.]

-fold, as four*fold*, mani*fold*. [A.S. *feald.*]

-ful, full of, as delight*ful*. [See **Full,** adj. in Dict.]

-fy, to make, as puri*fy*. [Fr. *-fier*—L. *fic-are,* for *fac-ere,* to make.]

-head, -hood, state, nature, as God*head*, man*hood*. [From A.S. *hád,* Ger. *-heit,* state ; changed into **Hood;** to be distinguished from **Head** of the body.]

-i, pl. suffix of nouns in *-us,* as literat*i* [L. *-i;* conn. with Gr. *-ai, -oi*] ; also pl. suffix of nouns borrowed from It., as banditt*i* [It.—L.].

-ible, adj. suffix, as poss*ible*, flex*ible*. [From L. *-ibilis,* another form of *-abilis.* See -able.]

-ic, adj. suffix, of or belonging to, as gigant*ic*, publ*ic* ; also largely used as noun suffix, as log*ic*, fabr*ic*. [L. *-icus, -ica, -icum,* Gr. *-ikos;* cf. Sans. *-ika.*]

-ical, belonging to, as cub*ical*. [-ic and -al.]

-ice, noun suffix, as chal*ice* [Fr.—L. *-ex, -icis*] ; nov*ice* [Fr.—L. *-icius*]. See another -ice under -ess, -ice, -ise.

-ics, lit. things that belong to a science, as mathemat*ics*. [In imitation of Gr. *-ika,* neuter pl. of adjs. in *-ikos.* See -ic.]

-id, noun suffix, as Nere*id;* also used in coining chemical words, as chlor*ide*, ox*ide*, brom*ide* [L. *-id-,* Gr. *-id-,* Fr. *-ide*] ; also adj. suffix, as tep*id*, ac*id* [L. *-idus*].

-ie, -y, dim., as lass*ie*. [From *-ick,* a weakened form of -ock.]

-ier, one who, as caval*ier*. [Fr. *-ier;* usually appears in form -eer.]

-iff, adj. suffix, fit for, disposed to, as plaint*iff* (orig. adj. = 'complaining'), fugit*ive*, act*ive*, pens*ive*. [Fr.—L. *-ivus.*]

-ile, able, as duct*ile*. [L. *-ilis,* contr. of *-ibilis;* to be distinguished from -ile (below). See -able.]

-ile, belonging to, as Gent*ile*. [L. *-ilis.*]

-im, pl. suffix, as cherub*im*. [Heb. *im.*]

-ina, fem. suffix, as czar*ina*. [See -en, fem.]

-ine, fem. suffix, as hero*ine*. [See -en, fem.]

-ine, -in, noun suffix, as rav*ine*, medic*ine*, cous*in;* much used in chemical compounds, as iod*ine*, glycer*ine*, brom*ine;* also adj. suffix, as div*ine*. [L. *-inus, -ina.*]

-ing, dim., as farth*ing*. [The *-ng* is nasalised from Aryan dim. *-ka* (see -ock).]

-ing, suffix of pr.p., as lov*ing*. [Corr. of A.S. *-inde,* which, as also *-ande* and *-ende,* it replaced. See -nd, also -ant, -ent.]

-ing, suffix of verbal nouns, as learn*ing*. [A.S. *-ung,* Ger. *-ung.*]

-ion, being, state of being, as creat*ion*. [L. *-io, -ionis.*]

-ior, more, term. of comp. degree, as super*ior*. [L. *-ior.* See -er, more.]

-ique, belonging to, as ant*ique*. [Fr.—L. *-iquus;* conn. with -ic, L. *-icus.* See -ac.]

-ise, -ize, to make, as equal*ise*. [Gr. *-izō,* L. *-ire,* Fr. *-iser.*]

-ish, adj. suffix, ethnic, as Ir*ish;* signifying somewhat, as brown*ish;* sometimes implying depreciation, as outland*ish*. [A.S. *-isc.*]

-ish, to make, as establ*ish*. [From Fr. pr.p. suffix *-iss-ant;* chiefly used in words from the Fr. The Fr. *-iss-* is from L. *-esc-,* inceptive.]

-isk, dim., as aster*isk*. [Gr. *-iskos;* conn. with -ish, little. See -ock.]

-ism, -asm, forming abstract nouns sig. condition, system, as ego*ism*, de*ism*, Calvin*ism*, lacon*ism*, pleon*asm*. [L. *-ismus, -asmus*—Gr. *-ismos, -asmos.*]

-ist, denoting the person who holds a doctrine or practises an art, as Calvin*ist*, chem*ist*, novel*ist*. [L. *-ista*—Gr. *-istēs.*]

-ite, born in, belonging to, as Israel*ite*, Jesu*it*. [L. *-ita*—Gr. *-itēs.*]

-ive. See under -iff.

-ix, fem. suffix, as testatr*ix*. [L. *-ix, -icis.* Conn. with -ess, fem. suffix.]

-ize, to make, same as -ise.

-k, freq. or intens., as har*k*, tal*k*.

-kin, dim., as lamb*kin;* son of, as Wil*kin*. [A double dim. suffix from *-k* (see -ock), and *in* (see -en, dim.).]

-kind, kind, race, as man*kind*. [See -kin above, and **Kin** in Dict.]

-l, forming diminutives, appears in connection with various vowels, and from various sources, as in -el, -ule, -er-el, -le, -l-et, -l-ing, -c-le, -c-ule, as dams*el*, glob*ule*, mong*rel*, bund*le*, ham*let*, duck*ling*, foll*icle*, mole*cule*.

-le, noun suffix, as brid*le*, bead*le*, ridd*le*, shov*el*, nai*l*. [A.S. *-el,* Ger. *-el*—Aryan *-ar(-al)*] ; also adj. suffix, as id*le*, fick*le*, britt*le*, mick*le* [A.S. *-el, -ol*—Aryan *-ra*].

-le, freq. and intens., as spark*le*, sett*le*, knee*l*.

-lence, -lency, forming abstract nouns. [L. *-l-entia,* from *-lens.* See -lent.]

-lent, full of, as vio*lent*, viru*lent*. [L. *-l-entus;* also adj. suffix, as tepid, acid.]

-less, free from, wanting, as guilt*less*, god*less*. [A.S. *-leas,* Ger. *-los;* from root of **Loose** and **Lose.**]

-let, dim., as stream*let*. [From -l and -et, dim.]

-like, like, as god*like*. [See **Like** in Dict.]

-ling, dim., as dar*ling;* sometimes implying depreciation, as hire*ling*. [Made up of -l and -ing.]

-ling, -long, adv. suffix, as dark*ling*, side*long*. [A.S. *-lunga, -linga.*]

-lock. [See **Wedlock** and **Knowledge** in Dict.]

-lock, -lick, a plant. [See **Hemlock, Garlic.**]

-ly, adj. and adv. suffix, as man*ly*, on*ly*. [The adj. suffix is from A.S. *lic,* E. **Like** ; adv. is from *lic-e,* dat. of *lic.*]

-m, noun suffix, as bloo*m*, stea*m*, sea*m*, fatho*m* [A.S. *-ma, -m*] ; as real*m*, crime, alu*m*, regi*me* [Fr.—L. *-men*].

-men, that which, state, as regi*men*, acu*men*. [Only in words borrowed from Latin. L. *-men;* Sans. *-man.* See -ment, -mony.]

-ment, as nourish*ment*, establish*ment*, detri*ment*. [L. *-men-tu-m,* Fr. *-ment.* See -men.]

-mony, as testi*mony*, parsi*mony*. [L. *-mon-iu-m, -mon-ia.* See -men.]

-most, suffix of superl. deg., as end*most*. See **Most** in Dict. [In most cases this suffix is not the word *most*, the *m* being part of the root, or an old superl. suffix, and -*ost* the superlative suffix, as in *inmost* = in-*m*-*ost*. See -**est**, superl. suffix.]

-**n**, as mai*n*, wago*n*. [Orig. -*na*, the suffix of passive past participles.]

-**nce**, -**ncy**, forming abstract nouns, as dista*nce*, dece*ncy*. [Fr. -*nce*—L. -*nt-ia*.]

-**nd**, as fie*nd* (*lit.* 'hating'), frie*nd* (*lit.* 'loving'). [A.S. pres.p. suffix.]

-**ness**, abstract idea, as tender*ness*. [A.S. -*nis*, -*nes*, cog. with Ger. -*niss*.]

-**ock**, dim., as hill*ock*. [A.S. -*uca*—Aryan -*ka*. See -**ie** and -**ing**, dim.]

-**om**, old dative suffix, now used as objective, as wh*om*; in adverbs of time, as seld*om*. [A.S. -*um*.]

-**on**, -**eon**, -**ion**, noun suffix, as cap*on*, mas*on*, trunch*eon*, oni*on*, clari*on*. [Fr.—L. -*onem*, -*ionem*.]

-**oon**, noun suffix, often augmentative, as ball*oon*, sal*oon*. [Fr. -*on*, It. -*one*.]

-**or**, -**our**, -**er**, denoting the agent, sometimes directly from L. (see -**tor**), but mostly through Fr. -*eur*, and spelled originally -*our*, as emper*or* (old spelling emper*our*, Fr. emper*eur*—L. *imperatorem*); in others, E. -*er* has supplanted -*eur*, -*our*, as preach*er* (Fr. *prêcheur*—L. *prædicatorem*), while -*or* is at times affixed to E. roots, as sail*or*. In certain abstract nouns from L. -*or*, Fr. -*eur* is still represented by -*our*, as lab*our*, hon*our*, and in a few cases directly retained, as grand*eur*.

-**ory**, belonging to, as prefat*ory* [L. -*orius*]; place where, as purgat*ory* [L. -*orium*].

-**ose**, full of, as verb*ose*. [L. -*osus*. See -**ous**.]

-**ot**, dim., as ball*ot*. [See -**et**, dim.]

-**our**. See -**or**.

-**ous**, adj. suffix, as relig*ious*, cur*ious* [L. -*osus*]; dub*ious*, anx*ious* [L. -*us*].

-**ow**, noun suffix, as shad*ow* [from A.S. -*u*]; swal*low* [from A.S. -*ewe*]; marr*ow* [from A.S. -*h*]; also adj. suffix, as narr*ow* [from A.S. -*u*].

-**ple**. See -**ble**, fold.

-**r**, noun suffix, marking the instrument, as stai*r*, timbe*r*; adj. suffix, as bitte*r*.

-**re**, place, as he*re*. [A.S. -*r*, -*ra*, orig. a locative suffix.]

-**red**, manner, state, as hat*red*, kind*red*. [A.S. -*ræden*; cog. with Ger. -*rath*. See **Read** in Dict.]

-**ric**, dominion, power, region, as bishop*ric*. [A.S. *rice*, power. See **Rich** in Dict.]

-**right**, as up*right*, down*right*. [A.S. *riht*. See **Right** in Dict.]

-**s**, adverbial suffix, as need*s*, alway*s*, on*ce*, hen*ce*, then*ce*, whil-*s*-t, betwi-*x*-t. [A.S. -*es*, gen. suffix.]

-**'s** is the present genitive suffix. [Short for A.S. -*es*—Aryan -*s* or *sya*, orig. a demons. pron. The (') is prob. due to a false notion that this -*s* was a relic of *his*.]

-**s**, -**se**, verbal suffix, to make, as cla-*s*-p, clean*se*, rin*se*.

-**ship**, -**scape**, as friend*ship*, steward*ship*, land-*scape*. [A.S. -*scipe*, shape, form—*scapan*, E. **Shape**; cog. with Ger. -*schaft*.]

-**sis**, action or state, as the*sis*. [Gr. -*sis*.]

**578**

-**some**, full of, as glad*some*, bu*xom*, lis*some* [A S. -*sum*, Ger. -*sam*; a by-form of **Same**.]

-**son**, son, as John*son*. [See **Son** in Dict.]

-**st**. See -**est**, suffix of 2d sing.

-**ster** marks the agent, as malt*ster*, often with depreciation, as game*ster*, pun*ster*. [A.S. -*estre*, a fem. suffix, which now keeps this sense only in spin*ster*.]

-**stress**, fem. suffix, as song*stress*. [From -**ster**, orig. fem. suffix, with the addition of L. -**ess**.]

-**sy**, state, as pleuri*sy*. [Same as -**sis**.]

-**t**. See -**d**.

-**t**, -**te**, adj. and noun suffix, as conven*t*, fac*t*, chas*te*, tribu*te*. [L. -*tus*, pa.p. suffix; cog. with -**d**, pa.p. suffix.]

-**teen**, ten to be added, as four*teen*. [A.S. -*tyne*. Cf. -**ty**, ten to be multiplied.]

-**ter**, noun suffix, as charac*ter*. [Gr. -*ter*, L. -*tor*, Sans. -*tri*; perh. conn. with -*ster*.]

-**ter**, -**ther**, as in af*ter*, hi*ther*. [A.S. -*der*, -*ther*, old comparative suffix. See **Whether** in Dict.]

-**th**, order, as six*th*. [Becomes also -**d**; conn. with L. -*tus*, -*tius*, as in L. quar*tus*, four*th*.]

-**th**, suffix of 3d sing. of verbs, now for the most part softened to -*s*. [A.S. from root -*ta*, which appears in L. -*t*, Gr. -*ti*, -*si*, -*tai*, -*to*, and in **That** and **The** (see Dict.).]

-**th**, -**t**. See under -**d** (pa.p. suffix).

-**ther**, denoting the agent, as fa*ther*, mo*ther*. [From Aryan -*tar*, the agent. Cf. -**tor**.]

-**ther**. See -**ter**, -**ther**.

-**tor**, the agent, as conduc*tor*. [From Aryan -*tar*, the agent. See -**ther**, and cf. -**or**, -**our**, -**er**.]

-**tor-y**, -**sor-y**, place, as dormi*tory*.

-**tude**, forms abstract nouns, as grati*tude*. [L. -*tudo*.]

-**ty**, being or state of being, as digni*ty*; quality, as hones*ty*. [Fr. -*té*—L. -*tas*, -*tat-is*.]

-**ty**, ten to be multiplied, as six*ty*. [A.S. -*tig*; cog. with Ger. -*zig*. Cf. -**teen**.]

-**ule**, little, dim., as glob*ule* [L. -*ulus*]. See under -**l**.

-**um**, neuter term., as medi*um*. [L. -*um*, Gr. -*on*.]

-**uncle**, little, dim., as ped*uncle*. [L. -*un-cu-lus*, A.S. -*incle*; conn. with -**en** and -**cule**, diminutives.]

-**ure**, act of, as capt*ure*; state of being, as verd*ure*. [L. -*ura*.]

-**urnal**, belonging to, as di*urnal*. [L. -*urn*-us and -**al**; conn. with -**ern** (in mod*ern*).]

-**ward**, -**wards**, adj. and adv. suffix sig. direction, as home*ward*, home*wards*. [A.S. -*weard*, gen. -*weardes*, cog. with Ger. -*würts*; conn. with A.S. *weorthan*, to be (see **Worth** in Dict.), and L. *versus*—*verto*, to turn. Cf. **Forward**, **Forwards** in Dict.]

-**way**, -**ways**, adv. suffix, sig. manner, direction, as al*way*, al*ways*, straight*way*. [Cf. -**wise**.]

-**wise**, way, manner, as like*wise*, righte*ous*. [A.S. -*wis*, Ger. -*wiss*. See **Wise**, way, in Dict.]

-**y**, adj. suffix, as spong*y* [from L. -*iosus*]; as joll*y* [Norm. Fr -*if* from L. -*ivus* (cf. -**ive**)]; as sill*y*, dirty, any [A.S. -*ig*; cog. with Ger. -*ig*, Goth. -*ha*, -*ga*, L. -*cu-s*, Gr. -*ko-s*].

-**y**, noun suffix, as stor*y*, Ital*y* [Fr. -*ie*, L. -*ia*]; as jo*y*, remed*y* [from L. -*ium*]; as all*y*, deput*y* [from L. -*atus*]; as progen*y* [from L. -*ies*]; as bod*y* [from A.S. -*ig*].

# TABLE OF DIVISIONS OF THE ARYAN LANGUAGES.

The English language—the offspring of the Anglo-Saxon—is one of the Low German dialects which form part of the Teutonic branch of the Indo-European or Aryan Languages.

The Aryan languages may be divided into six principal branches:

| I. | II. | III. | IV. | V. | VI. |
|---|---|---|---|---|---|
| INDIAN. | PERSIC. | CELTIC. | GRÆCO-LATIN. | TEUTONIC. | SLAVONIC. |

The Teutonic branch is divided into three classes, the Low German, High German, and Scandinavian:

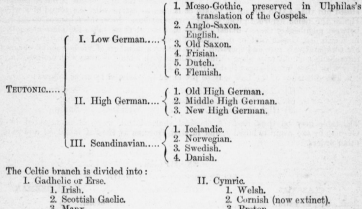

TEUTONIC.....

I. Low German.....
1. Mœso-Gothic, preserved in Ulphilas's translation of the Gospels.
2. Anglo-Saxon. English.
3. Old Saxon.
4. Frisian.
5. Dutch.
6. Flemish.

II. High German....
1. Old High German.
2. Middle High German.
3. New High German.

III. Scandinavian.....
1. Icelandic.
2. Norwegian.
3. Swedish.
4. Danish.

The Celtic branch is divided into:

I. Gadhelic or Erse.
1. Irish.
2. Scottish Gaelic.
3. Manx.

II. Cymric.
1. Welsh.
2. Cornish (now extinct).
3. Breton.

---

## GRIMM'S LAW OF THE INTERCHANGE OF CONSONANT SOUNDS.

The evidence that the group of languages known as the Aryan languages form a family—that is, are all sister-dialects of one common mother-tongue—consists in their grammatical forms being the same, and in their having a great many words in common. In judging whether an individual word in one of these tongues is really the same with a word in another of the tongues, we are no longer guided by mere similarity of sound; on the contrary, identity of sound is generally a presumption that a proposed etymology is wrong. Words are constantly undergoing change, and each language follows its own fashion in making those changes. Corresponding words, therefore, in the several languages must, as a rule, in the long course of ages have come to differ greatly; and these differences follow certain laws which it is possible to ascertain. Unless, then, a proposed identification accord with those laws, it is inadmissible. We are not at liberty to suppose any arbitrary omission of a letter, or substitution of one letter for another, as was the fashion in the old guessing school of etymology.

Of the laws of interchange of sounds in the Indo-European family, the most important is that known as *Grimm's Law*, so called after the famous German philologist who investigated it. It exhibits the relations found to exist between the consonant sounds in three groups of the Aryan languages—namely, (1) the Classical, including Sanskrit, Greek, and Latin; (2) Low German, which we may take Gothic and English as representing; (3) High German, especially Old High German, in which the Law is more consistently carried out than in modern High German.

# Grimm's Law of the Interchange of Consonant Sounds.

The scope of the Law is confined to the interchanges among the following consonant sounds, which are here arranged so as to show their relations to one another:

|  | Sharp. | Flat. | Aspirate. |
|---|---|---|---|
| Labial | p | b | f ($v$) |
| Linguo-dental | t | d | th ($z$) |
| Guttural | k ($c$) | g | ch ($h$) |

The horizontal division into three orders depends on the organ chiefly used in the utterance. The differences between the vertical series are more easily felt than described. Pronounce first *ip* and then *ib*; in the first, the lips are completely closed, and the sound or voice from the larynx abruptly cut off. In the second, the lips are also completely shut, but a muffled voice is continued for a moment; it is produced by the vocal cords being still kept in a state of tension, and the breath continuing to issue through them into the cavity of the mouth for a brief space after the lips are closed. Next pronounce *if*; in this, although the voice-sound abruptly ceases, the lip-aperture is not so completely closed but that a thin stream of breath continues to escape with the sound of a whisper. Hence the name *aspirate* given to such articulations. Now, interchanges do take place between members of these vertical series—that is, one sharp takes the place of another, as in Welsh *p*en, Gaelic *k*in; or in Russian *F*eodor for *Th*eodore. Such instances, however, are comparatively rare and sporadic. It is between members of the horizontal orders that interchanges chiefly take place—that is, labials with labials, dentals with dentals, &c.; and it is with these interchanges that Grimm's Law deals.

The substance of the Law may be presented in a tabular form, as follows:

| | | Sharp. | Flat. | Aspirate. |
|---|---|---|---|---|
| (1) | Classical | Sharp. | Flat. | Aspirate. |
| (2) | Low German | Aspirate. | Sharp. | Flat. |
| (3) | High German | Flat. | Aspirate. | Sharp. |

The table may be thus read: A classical sharp labial, as *p*, is represented in Low German by the aspirate labial *f*, and in High German by the flat labial *b*; and so of the other orders.

## EXAMPLES.

### (A) INTERCHANGE OF LABIALS.

| CLASSICAL. | LOW GERMAN. | O. H. GERMAN. |
|---|---|---|
| Sans., Gr., L. *p*ater | E. *f*ather, Goth. *f*adrs | *v*atar. |
| Gr. *p*teron (peteron) | E. *f*eather | *v*edar, Ger. *f*eder. |
| L. *p*ulex | E. *f*lea, Scot. *f*lech | *v*lo, Ger. *f*loh. |
| L. ra*p*ina | A.S. reaf, E. reave | roub. |
| Gr. kanna*b*is | E. hem*p* | hana*f*, Ger. han*f*. |
| L. fra(n)*g*o | E. *b*reak, Goth. *b*rikan | prechan, Ger. *b*rechen. |
| Gr. *ph*u, L. *f*u | E. *b*e | *p*im (I am). |

### (B) INTERCHANGE OF LINGUO-DENTALS.

| L. *t*enuis | E. *th*in | *d*unni, Ger. *d*ünn. |
|---|---|---|
| L. *t*ectum | E. *th*atch, Goth. *th*ak | *d*ach. |
| Gr. o*d*ont, L. *d*ent | E. *t*ooth, Goth. *t*unthus | zand, Ger. zahn. |
| L. *d*ingua (= lingua) | E. *t*ongue | zunga. |
| Gr. *th*ugatër | E. *d*aughter, Goth. *d*auhtar | tohtar. |
| Gr. *th*ër, L. *f*era | E. *d*eer | tior. |

### (C) INTERCHANGE OF GUTTURALS.

| L. *c*laudus | E. *h*alt | *h*alz. |
|---|---|---|
| Gr. *k*ard-, L. *c*ord- | E. *h*eart | herza. |
| L. o*c*to | E. ei*gh*t, Goth. a*h*tan | a*h*te, Ger. a*ch*t. |
| Gr. *g*onu | E. *k*nee | *ch*nio. |
| L. a*g*er | E. a*c*re, Goth. a*k*rs | a*ch*ar, Ger. a*ck*er. |
| Gr. *ch*ën, L. anser (= *h*anser) | E. *g*oose | *k*ans, Ger. *g*ans. |
| L. *h*ortus | E. *g*arden, Goth. *g*ards | *k*arto, Ger. *g*arten. |

It will be observed that there are a good many exceptions to the Law, especially in the case of the aspirates; the influence of adjoining letters often causes anomalies. The Law holds good oftenest in the beginning of words.

THE following are the more important significant syllables or words that enter into the composition of the names of rivers, mountains, towns, &c. :

**A** (A.S. *eá*, Ice. *-aa*), 'a stream;' as Gret*a*, Thurs*o* ('Thor's stream').

**Abad** (Pers. and Sans.), 'a dwelling;' as Hyder*abad*, Allah*abad*.

**Aber** (Celt.), 'a confluence,' 'an embouchure;' as *Aber*feldy, *Aber*deen, *Aber*ystwith. [Synonymous with **Inver**.]

**All** (Gael.), 'white;' as **Al-ian**, 'white water,' so the rivers *Allen*, *Ellen*, *Aln*, *Lune*, *Allwen*, *Elwin*.

**Ar**, found in many river-names; as *Aire*, *Ayr*, *Aar*, *Arro*, *Arrow*, *Arve*. [Ety. dub., perh. conn. with Sans. *ara*, 'swift,' 'flowing;' perh. with Celt. *garw*, 'violent.']

**Ard** (Celt.), 'high;' as *Ard*och, *Aird*rie, *Ard*rossan, *Ard*glass, *Ard*en, *Ard*ennes.

**Ath** (Ir. and Gael.), 'a ford;' as *Ath*lone, *Ath*truim (now Trim), *Ath*leathain (Broad*ford*), in Skye.

**Auch** (Gael.), **Agh** (Ir.), 'a field;' as *Auch*inleck, *Agh*inver, *Agh*adoe.

**Avon** (Celt.), 'a river;' as *Avon*, *Aven*, *Aisne*, *Inn*, *Ain*, *Vienne*.

**Ay.** See **Ey**.

**Bab** (Ar.), 'a gate;' as *Bab*-el-mandeb, *Bab*-el.

**Bad** (Teut.), 'a bath;' as *Bath*, *Bad*en, Carls*bad*.

**Bally** (Ir. and Gael.), 'a village' or 'town;' as *Bally*more, *Bal*briggan, *Bal*moral.

**Ban** (Celt.), 'white;' as *Ban*na, *Ban*on; the rivers *Ben*, *Bann*, *Bandon*, *Ban*ney, &c.

**Beck** or **Bach** (Teut.), 'a brook;' as Hol*beck*, Lauter*bach*. [See **Beck** in Dict.]

**Beg, Bihan** (Celt.), 'little;' as Bally*beg*, Mor*bihan*.

**Ben** (Gael. and Ir.), 'mountain,' **Pen** (W.), 'headland,' 'hilltop;' as *Ben* Nevis, *Ben* Lomond, The Twelve *Pins*, *Ban*gor; *Pen*, *Pen*nigant, *Pen*zance, *Pen*nine Alps, A*pen*nines, *Pin*dus.

**Berg, Borough** (A.S. *beorh*), 'a hill;' as Ingle*borough*, Flamborough Head, Queens*berry*, Browberg Hill, Königs*berg*, *Berg*en. [From the same root as **Burgh** (below).]

**Beth** (Heb.), 'a house;' as *Beth*el (house of God).

**Blair** (Gael.), 'a plain,' orig. 'a battlefield;' as *Blair* Athole.

**Bottle** or **Battle, Büttel** (Teut.), 'a dwelling;' as New*battle*, Wolfen*büttel*.

**Broad** (E.), as Brad*don, Brad*shaw, Brad*ford.

**Burgh, Borough, Bury** (Teut.), 'a fortified place,' 'a town;' as Edin*burgh*, Peter*borough*, Shrews*bury*, Ham*burg*, Cher*bourg*, Caris*brook*, Bur*gos*. [A.S. *byrig*, E. **Borough** (see Dict.), Ger. *burg*. See also **Barrow**, a mound, in Dict.]

**By** (Scand.), 'a dwelling,' 'a town;' as Der*by*, Rug*by*, Whit*by*, El*bœuf*. [Cf. **Bylaw** in Dict.]

**Caer, Cader** (W.), **Caher** (Ir.), 'fortified inclosure,' as *Caer*leon, *Caer*narvon, *Car*digan, *Car*lisle, *Cader*-Idris, San*quhar*, *Car*lingford.

**Cam** (Celt.), 'crooked;' as *Cam*, *Cam*beck, *Cam*buskenneth, More*cam*be Bay, *Cam*brai.

**Caster, Chester, Cester** (= L. *castra*), 'a camp,' as Don*caster*, *Chester*, Win*chester*, Lei*cester*.

**Cefn** (Celt.), 'a ridge;' as *Cefn*coed, *Chevin*, *Keyn*ton, *Chevin*gton, *Cheviot*, *Cevennes*.

**Cheap** and **Chipping** (A.S. *ceap*), 'price,' 'a market;' as *Chipping*-Norton, *Chep*stow, *Cheap*side, *Copen*hagen (Dan. *Kjöben-havn*, 'merchants' haven'). [See **Cheap** in Dict.]

**Civita** (It.), **Ciudad** (Sp.), 'a city;' as *Civita* Vecchia ('old city'); *Ciudad* Rodrigo ('city of Roderick'). [From L. *civitas*. See **City** in Dict.]

**Clyd** (Celt.), 'warm,' } as *Clyde*, *Clud*en, *Clwyd*,
**Clyth** (Celt.), 'strong,' } *Clyd*, &c.

**Coed** (Celt.), 'a wood;' *Cots*wold Hills, *Chat*moss.

**Coln** (from L. *colonia*), 'a colony;' as Lin*coln*, *Coln*e, Co*logne* (*Köln*). [See **Colony** in Dict.]

**Combe** (A.S.), **Cwm** or **Cum** (Celt.), 'a hollow between hills;' as Wy*combe*, *Comp*ton, The *Coomb*s, *Com*o.

**Craig, Carrick, Crag** (Celt.), 'a rock;' as *Craig*ie, *Crath*ie, *Carrick*, *Carrick*fergus, *Crick*, *Crick*lade, *Croagh*-Patrick. [See **Crag** in Dict.]

**Dal** (Scand.), **Thal** (Ger.), **Dail** and **Dol** (Celt.), 'a dale,' 'a field;' as Liddes*dale*, Ry*dal*, Ken*dal*, Arun*del*, Rhein*thal*; (in Celtic names prefixed) *Dal*ry, *Dal*keith, *Dol*gelly. [See **Dale** and **Dell** in Dict.]

**Den** or **Dean** (Teut.), 'a deep wooded valley;' as Tenter*den*, South*dean*, Hazel*dean*, *Den*holm. [See **Den** in Dict.]

**Don** or **Dan** (derivation not ascertained), 'water;' as the *Don*, Ban*don*, *Dun*, Tyne, Tone; so in the *Dn*iester, *Dn*ieper, *Tan*ais, *Don*etz, *Dwin*a.

**Dour** (Celt.), 'water;' as the *Dour*, *Adour*, *Douro*, *Dore*, Thur, *Doro*, *Adder*, *Der*went, *Dar*win, *Dar*ent. *Dart*, *Dor*chester, *Dor*dogne.

**Drum** and **Drom** (Celt.), 'a backbone,' 'a ridge;' as *Drom*ore, *Drum*mond, Augh*rim*, Leit*rim*.

**Du** (Celt), 'black;' as the *Dou*glas; the rivers *Dul*as, *Doul*as, and prob. *Dee*; *Dub*lin ('dark pool').

**Dun** (Celt.), 'a hill-fortress;' as *Dun*more, *Dum*blane, *Dun*keld, *Dum*barton, *Dum*fries, *Dun*stable, *Dun*mow, *Down*-Patrick, *Don*egal, Mal*don*, Ver*dun*, Ley*den*. [See **Down**, a hill, in Dict.]

**Dysart** (Celt.—L. *desertum*), 'a hermitage;' as *Dysart*, *Dysert*more.

**Ea, Ey** (A.S. *ig*, Ice. *ey*, Norw. and Dan. *ö*. See **Island** in Dict.), 'an island;' as Swan*sea*, *Eton*, Jersey, Rothe*say*, Staff*a*, Faroe.

**Eccles, Egles** (like Fr. *église*, through L., from Gr. *ekklēsia*), 'a church;' as *Eccles*ton, *Eccle*fechan, Terr*egles*.

**Esk** (Gael. and Ir. *easg* [obs.] or *uisge*, W. *wysg*), 'water;' as the *Esk*, *Usk*, *Esky*, *Ise*, *Ease*burn, *Ash*bourne, *Iz*, *Is*is, *Exe*, *Ux*, *Ouse*, *Wisk*, *Wis*, *Is*chia, *Is*ère, *Aisne*, *Ausonne*, *Oise*.

**Fell** (Scand. *fjeld*), 'a mountain;' as Carter*fell*, Goat*fell*, Sna*fel*, Fit*ful* Head (corr. of Hvit-*Fell*, 'white mountain'). [See **Fell** in Dict.]

**Fleet** (Scand. *fleot*, E. *flood*), 'a small river' or 'channel;' as Pur*fleet*; found in Normandy as *fleur*, as Har*fleur* (anciently Harvo*flete*).

**Folk** (A.S.), 'people;' as Nor*folk* ('north people'), Suf*folk* ('south people').

**Garth** (Scand.), 'yard;' **Gorod, Grod, Grade, Grätz** (Slav.), 'inclosure,' 'town;' as Stutt*gart*, Novg*orod* (= Newton), Bel*grade* (= Whitton), König*grätz* (= Kingston). [See **Yard** in Dict.]

**Garw** (Celt.), 'rough;' hence *Gar*onne, *Gar*ioch, *Yar*row, *Yair*, possibly *Garry*.

**Gate** (Teut.), 'a passage' or 'road;' as Canon*gate*, Harrow*gate*, Rei*gate* (= Ridge*gate*), Cat*tegat*. [See **Gate** in Dict.]

**Glen** (Gael.), **Glyn** (W.), 'a narrow valley;' as *Glen*coe, *Glen*garry, *Glyn*neath, *Gla*morgan.

**Gorm** (Gael.), 'blue;' as Cairn*gorm*, king*orn* ('blue point'), corrupted to Kinghorn.

**Gwent** (Celt.), 'a plain;' Latinised into *venta*, as *Venta* Belgarum (now *Win*chester), Caer*went*.

**Gwy**. See **Wy**.

**Hall** (Teut.), 'a stone house;' as Eccles*hall*, Wal*sall;* (in Germany) a *salt*-work, as *Halle*. [See **Hall** in Dict.] [*ham*, Hochheim.

**Ham** (A.S., Ger. *heim*), 'a home;' as Bucking*ham*.

**Hay, Haigh** (Teut.), 'a place surrounded by a *hedge;*' as Rothwell *Haigh*, the *Hague*.

**Hithe** (A.S.), 'haven;' as *Hythe*, Lambeth = Loam-*hithe* (the 'clayey haven').

**Holm** (Scand., &c.), 'an island in a lake or river;' 'a plain near a river;' as Stock*holm*, Flat*holm*.

**Holt** (Teut.), 'a wood;' as Bags*hot*, Alders*hot*, *Hol*stein. [See **Holt** in Dict.]

**Horn** (Teut.), 'a peak;' as Schreck*horn* ('the peak of terror'), Matter*horn* ('meadow-peak').

**Hurst** (A.S. *hyrst*), 'a wood;' as Lynd*hurst*.

**Ing** (A.S.), a suffix denoting *son*, in pl. 'a family' or 'tribe;' as Warr*ing*ton ('the town of the Warrings'), Hadd*ing*ton. [See -*ing* in list of suffixes.]

**Innis** or **Ennis** (Celt.), *inch* in Scotland, an island; as *Inch*colm ('the island of St Columba'); *En*niskillen, *Ennis*more, in Ireland.

**Inver** (Gael.), 'the mouth of a river;' as *Inver*ness, *Inver*aray, *Inner*leithen.

**Kara** (Turk.), 'black;' as *Kara*kum ('black sand'), *Kara* Hissar ('black castle').

**Kenn** (Gael.), **Kin** (Ir.), 'a head;' as *Ken*more, Cantire, *Kin*naird, *Kin*ross, *Kin*sale, *Kent*.

**Kil** (Celt.), L. *cella*, 'a cell,' 'a chapel,' or 'church;' as *Kil*conquhar in Fife, 'the chapel at the head (*cean*) of the fresh-water lake (*iuchair*);' Icolm*kill*, 'the island (*I*) of Columba of the church.'

**Kirk** (North E. and Scand.), **Kirche** (Ger.): as Sel*kirk*, *Kirk*wall, *Kirk*cudbright, *Kirch*heim, Fünf*kirchen*. [See **Church** in Dict.]

**Lax** (Scand.; Ger. *lachs*), 'a salmon;' as Loch *Lax*ford in Sutherland; the *Lax*ay in the Hebrides and in Man; *Lax*weir on the Shannon.

**Leamhan** (Ir. and Gael.; pron. *lavawn*), 'the elm-tree;' as in *Leven*, Lennox, *Laune*.

**Ley** (A.S. *leah*), 'a meadow;' Had*leigh*, Water*loo*.

**Linn** (Celt.), 'a waterfall;' as *Lynn* Regis in Norfolk; Ros*lin*, 'the promontory (*ross*) at the fall.'

**Lis** (Celt.), 'an inclosure,' 'a fort,' 'a garden;' as *Lis*more ('the great inclosure' or 'garden').

**Llan** (W.), 'an inclosure,' 'a church;' as *Llan*daff ('the church on the Taff').

**Low** and **Law** (A.S. *hlaw*), 'a rising ground;' as Houns*low*, Lud*low*, and numerous *laws* in Scotland. [Cog. with Goth. *hlaiw*, and allied to L. *clivus*, a slope, and E. **Lean**, *v*.]

**Magh** (Celt.), 'a plain;' as Ar*magh*, *May*nooth.

**Mark** (Teut.), 'a boundary;' Den*mark*, *Merc*ia, *Murc*ia. [See **March**, a border, in Dict.]

**Mere, Moor** (A.S.), 'a lake' or 'marsh;' as *Mer*sey, Black*more*.

**Mor** (Celt.), 'great;' Ben*more* ('great mountain').

**Mor** (Celt.), 'the sea;' as *Mor*ay, Armo*mor*ica, *Mor*laix, Gla*mor*gan, *Mor*bihan.

**Mull** (Gael.), 'a headland;' as *Mull* of Galloway.

**Ness** or **Naze** (Scand.; see Dict.), 'a nose' or 'promontory;' as Caith*ness*, Sheer*ness*, Cape Gris*nez;* the *Naze*.

**Old, Eld, Alt** (Teut.), 'old;' as *Al*thorp, *El*ton, *Eit*ham, *Ald*bury, *A*bury. [See **Old** in Dict.]

**Patam** (Sans.), 'a city;' Seringa*patam*, *Patn*a.

**Peak, Pike** (conn. with Ger. *spitz*, Fr. *pic* and

*puy*), 'point;' as the *Peak*, the *Pikes* in Cumberland, *Spitz*bergen, *Pic* du Midi, *Puy* de Dôme.

**Peel** (Celt.), 'a stronghold;' as *Peel* in Man, and numerous *peels* on the Border of Scotland.

**Polis** (Gr.), 'a city;' as Greno*ble*, Na*blous*, Na*ples*, Sebasto*pol*.

**Pont** (L.), 'a bridge;' as *Pont*efract, Negro*pont*.

**Poor, Pore** (Sans. *pura*), 'a town;' as Nag*poor*, Cawn*pore*, Singa*pore*.

**Ras** (Ar.), 'a cape;' as *Ras*-al-had.

**Rath** (Ir.), 'a round earthen fort;' as *Rath*more.

**Rhe**, a root found in many languages, meaning 'to flow;' as *Rhine*, Rhone, *Rh*a, *Reno*, *Rye*, *Ray*, *Rhee*, *Wrey*, *Roe*, *Rae*.

**Ridge**, in Scotland **Rigg** (A.S. *hrycg*, Ger. *rücken*), 'a back;' as *Rei*gate, *Rug*eley, Long*ridge*.

**Rin** (Celt.), 'a point of land;' *Rhinns* of Galloway; Pen*rhyn* in Wales, *Ring*send near Dublin.

**Ross** (Celt.), 'a promontory;' Kin*ross*, Mel*rose*, *Ros*neath; in S. Ireland, a wood, as *Ros*common.

**Scale** (Scand.), 'a hut' (Scot. *shieling*; Ice. *skali*); Portin*scale*, and possibly *Shields*, Gala*shiels*.

**Scar** (Scand.), 'a cliff;' *Scar*borough, the *Sker*ries. [*set*, Amble*side*, Sed*litz*.

**Set** (A.S.), 'a seat,' 'a settlement,' Dor*set*, Somer*sex* (

**Sex**, 'Saxons;' as Es*sex* ('East Saxons'), Sus*sex* ('South Saxons').

**Sierra** (Sp.—L. *serra*), 'a saw;' or from Ar. *sehrah*, 'an uncultivated tract.'

**Slievh** (Ir.; allied to L. *clivus*, a slope), 'a mountain;' as *Slievh* Beg.

**South** is found in Suf*folk*, Sus*sex*, *South*ampton, *Suther*land, *Sut*ton, *Sud*bury, *Sud*ley.

**Stan** (Pers.), 'a land;' Hindu*stan*, Afghani*stan*.

**Staple** (A.S.), 'a store;' Dun*stable*, Barn*staple*.

**Stead** (A.S.), **Stadt** (Ger.), 'a town;' as Hamp*stead*, Neu*stadt*.

**Ster** (Scand. *stadhr*), 'a place;' as Ul*ster*.

**Stoke** and **Stow** (A.S.), 'a stockaded place;' as Bristow or Bri*stol*, Tavi*stock*, *Stock*holm.

**Stone**, 'a stone,' 'a rock,' as *Stan*ton, *Staines*, Eddy*stone*, *Stennis*, Franken*stein*.

**Strath** (Gael.), 'a broad valley;' as *Strath*more.

**Street** (L. *stratum*), 'a Roman road;' *Strat*ford, *Strat*ton, *Streat*ham. [See **Street** in Dict.]

**Tain** (Gael.), 'a river;' as the *Tyne*, prob. a form of *Don*.

**Tam** (Celt.), 'still,' 'smooth;' as the *Tham*esis ('smooth Isis'), the *Tema*, *Tame*, *Tamar*, *Tay*.

**Thorpe** (Norse), **Dorf** (Ger.), 'a village;' as Burnham-*Thorpe*, Hey*thorpe*, Düssel*dorf*.

**Toft** (Dan.), 'an inclosure;' as Lowes*toft*, Ive*tot*.

**Ton** (A.S.), 'inclosure,' 'town;' the most common of English local names.

**Tor** (Celt.; found in L. *turris*), 'a tower-like rock;' as the *Tors* in England; Mount *Taur*us.

**Tre** (W.), 'a dwelling;' as *Tre*town, Coven*try* ('convent-dwelling'), Oswes*try*, Uchil*tre*.

**Uchel** (W.), 'high;' **Uachter** (Gael.), 'a height;' as the *Ochil* Hills, *Ochil*tree, *Auchter*arder.

**Wall**, found in many names of places on the Roman wall from Newcastle to Carlisle; as *Wall*send, *Wall*head.

**Weald. Wold** (Ger. *wald*), 'a wood;' *Wal*tham, *Wald*en, the Cots*wolds;* Schwarz*wald* ('Black Forest').

**Well, Ville** (L. *villa*), 'an abode;' as Tanker*ville*, Kettle*well*, Brad*well*, Maxwell*ton*.

**Wick, Wich** (A.S. *wic*, 'a village;' Scand. 'a bay' or 'creek'); as Aln*wick*, Sand*wich*.

**Worth** (A.S. *weorthig*), 'a farm' or 'estate;' as Tam*worth*, Kenil*worth*, Bos*worth*, *Worth*ing.

**Wy** or **Gwy** (W.), 'water;' as the *Wye;* used as affix to many streams, as Con*way*, Med*way*, Sol*way*.

*À bas* (Fr.), down, down with.

*Abbé* (Fr.), the title of a clergyman.

*Ab extra* (L.), from without.

*Ab initio* (L.), from the beginning.

*Abonnement* (Fr.), subscription.

*Ab origine* (L.), from the origin or beginning.

*Ab ovo* (L.), from the egg: from the beginning.

*Abrégé* (Fr.), abridgment.

*Absente reo* (L.), the defendant being absent.

*Ab urbe conditâ* (L.), from the founding of the city (Rome).

*Accessit* (L.), he came near.

*À compte* (Fr.), on account: in part-payment.

*À couvert* (Fr.), under cover: protected.

*Ad aperturam* (*libri*) (L.), as (the book) opens.

*Ad arbitrium* (L.), at pleasure.

*Ad avizandum* (Low L.), to be deliberated upon, (in Scotland) the formula expressing that judgment in a suit is deferred.

*Ad Calendas Græcas* (L.), at the Greek Calends; i.e. never, as the Greeks had no Calends.

*Ad captandum vulgus* (L.), to catch the rabble.

*Ad extremum* (L.), to the extreme.

*Ad finem* (L.), to the end.

*Ad infinitum* (L.), to infinity.

*Ad interim* (L.), in the meanwhile.

*À discrétion* (Fr.), at discretion: without restric- [tion.

*Ad libitum* (L.), at pleasure.

*Ad nauseam* (L.), to disgust.

*Ad referendum* (L.), to be further considered.

*Ad rem* (L.), to the point: to the purpose.

*À droit* (Fr.), to the right.

*Adsum* (L.), I am present, here !

*Ad unguem* (L.), to the nail : nicely.

*Ad unum omnes* (L.), all to a man. [case.

*Ad utrumque paratus* (L.), prepared for either

*Ad valorem* (L.), according to the value.

*Ad vitam aut culpam* (L.), for life or fault—i.e. till some misconduct be proved.

*Æquo animo* (L.), with an equable mind.

*Affaire d'amour* (Fr.), a love affair.

*Affaire d'honneur* (Fr.), an affair of honour.

*Affaire du cœur* (Fr.), an affair of the heart.

*À fond* (Fr.), to the bottom : thoroughly.

*À fortiori* (L.), with stronger reason.

*À gauche* (Fr.), to the left.

*Agenda* (L.), things to be done.

*Agrément* (Fr.), agreeable quality : embellishment.

*À l'abandon* (Fr.), at random, left uncared for.

*À la bonne heure* (Fr.), in good or favourable time.

*À la Française* (Fr.), after the French mode.

*À la mode* (Fr.), acc. to the custom : in fashion.

*À la Tartuffe* (Fr.), like Tartuffe : hypocritically.

*Alere flammam* (L.), to feed the flame.

*Al fresco* (It.), in fresco : in the open air : cool.

*Allez vous en* (Fr.), away with you.

*Allons* (Fr.), let us go : come on : come.

*Alma mater* (L.), lit. a benign mother—applied by graduates to their university.

*À l'outrance* (Fr.), to the utmost.

*Alter ego* (L.), another self.

*Alter idem* (L.), another precisely similar.

*Amende honorable* (Fr.), satisfactory apology : reparation.

*A mensâ et toro* (L.), from bed and board.

*Amor patriæ* (L.), love of country.

*Amour propre* (Fr.), self-love : vanity.

*Analecta* (L.), a collection of literary fragments.

*Anglicè* (L.), in English.

*Anno Domini* (L.), in the year of our Lord.

*Anno mundi* (L.), in the year of the world.

*Anno urbis conditæ* (L.), in the year the city (Rome) was built.

*Annus mirabilis* (L.), year of wonders.

*Ante meridiem* (L.), before noon.

*Aperçu* (Fr.), survey : sketch.

*À point* (Fr.), to a point : exactly right.

*A posteriori* (L.), from the effect to the cause.

*A priori* (L.), from the cause to the effect.

*À propos* (Fr.), to the point : pertinently.

*Aqua vitæ* (L.), water of life : brandy : alcohol.

*Argumentum ad hominem* (L.), an argument to the individual man—that is, to his interests and prejudices.

*Argumentum ad ignorantiam* (L.), argument founded on an adversary's ignorance of facts.

*Argumentum ad invidiam* (L.), an argument appealing to low passions.

*Argumentum ad judicium* (L.), argument appealing to the judgment.

*Argumentum baculinum* (L.), the argument of the cudgel : appeal to force.

*Ariston metron* (Gr.), the middle course is the best : the golden mean.

*Arrière pensée* (Fr.), a mental reservation.

*Ars est celare artem* (L.), true art is to conceal art.

*Ars longa, vita brevis* (L.), art is long, life short.

*Audi alteram partem* (L.), hear the other side.

*Au fait* (Fr.), well acquainted with : expert.

*Au fond* (Fr.), at the bottom.

*Aurea mediocritas* (L.), the golden or happy mean.

*Aura popularis* (L.), the breeze of popular favour.

*Au reste* (Fr.), as for the rest.

*Au revoir* (Fr.), adieu until we meet again.

*Aut Cæsar aut nullus* (L.), either Cæsar or nobody.

*Aux armes* (Fr.), to arms.

*Avant-coureur* (Fr.), a forerunner.

*Avant propos* (Fr.), preliminary matter : preface.

*Avec permission* (Fr.), by consent.

*À verbis ad verbera* (L.), from words to blows.

*À votre santé* (Fr.), to your health.

*Bas bleu* (Fr.), a blue-stocking : a literary woman.

*Beaux esprits* (Fr.), men of wit : gay spirits.

*Beaux yeux* (Fr.), fine eyes. [or genius.

*Bel esprit* (Fr.), a brilliant mind : a person of wit

*Bête noire* (Fr.), a black beast : a bugbear.

*Bis* (L.), twice : repeated.

*Blasé* (Fr.), palled : surfeited.

*Bonâ fide* (L.), in good faith : in reality.

*Bon ami* (Fr.), good friend.

*Bon gré, mal gré* (Fr.), willing or unwilling.

*Bonhomie* (Fr.), good-natured simplicity.
*Bon jour* (Fr.), good-day : good-morning.
*Bonne* (Fr.), a nurse or governess.
*Bonne foi* (Fr.), good faith.
*Bon soir* (Fr.), good-evening.
*Bon-ton* (Fr.), the height of fashion. [liver.
*Bon-vivant* (Fr.), a jovial companion : a good
*Bouillon* (Fr.), soup.
*Breveté* (Fr.), patented.
*Bric-à-brac* (Fr.), odds and ends.
*Brutum fulmen* (L.), a harmless thunderbolt.
*Bundesrath* (Ger.), the Federal Council in the German Empire, consisting of representatives from the individual States.

*Cacoëthes loquendi* (L.), an itch for speaking.
*Cacoëthes scribendi* (L.), an itch for scribbling.
*Café* (Fr.), a coffee-house.
*Canaille* (Fr.), the rabble.
*Cap-à-pie* [pē] (Fr.), from head to foot.
*Caput* (L.), head : chapter.
*Caput mortuum* (L.), the worthless remains.
*Carpe diem* (L.), enjoy the present day : seize the opportunity. [full powers.
*Carte blanche* (Fr.), a blank sheet of instructions :
*Casus belli* (L.), that which involves or justifies war. [arranged according to their subjects.
*Catalogue raisonné* (Fr.), a catalogue of books
*Cavaliere servente* (It.), one who waits with fantastic devotion upon a married lady.
*Cave canem* (L.), beware of the dog, a frequent inscription on Roman thresholds.
*Cedant arma togæ* (L.), let arms yield to the gown—i.e. let military authority yield to the civil power. [the first step is difficult.
*Ce n'est que le premier pas qui coûte* (Fr.), only
*Centum* (L.), a hundred.
*C'est à dire* (Fr.), that is to say. [thing.
*C'est une autre chose* (Fr.), that is quite another
*Ceteris paribus* (L.), other things being equal.
*Chacun à son goût* (Fr.), every one to his taste.
*Chanson* (Fr.), a song.
*Chargé d'affaires* (Fr.), a subordinate diplomatist.
*Chef* (Fr.), the head : the leading person or part.
*Chef de cuisine* (Fr.), head-cook.
*Chef d'œuvre* (Fr.), a masterpiece.
*Chemin de fer* (Fr.), the iron-way, railway.
*Chère amie* (Fr.), a dear friend : a mistress.
*Chevalier d'industrie* (Fr.), lit. a knight of industry : one who lives by persevering fraud.
*Chevaux de frise* (Fr.), in fortification an obstacle consisting of spikes set in a framework of wood.
*Chic* (Fr.), style, easy elegance, adroitness.
*Ci-devant* (Fr.), formerly : former.
*Ci gît* (Fr.), here lies.
*Circulus in probando* (L.), a circle in the proof, using the conclusion as one of the arguments.
*Claqueur* (Fr.), one hired to applaud at a theatre.
*Clôture* (Fr.), closing of a discussion.
*Cogito ergo sum* (L.), I think, therefore I exist.
*Coiffeur* (Fr.), a hairdresser.
*Collectanea* (L.), passages collected from authors.
*Comme il faut* (Fr.), as it should be.
*Compagnon de voyage* (Fr.), a travelling companion.
*Compos mentis* (L.), of a sound mind.
*Compte rendu* (Fr.), an account rendered : report.
*Comptoir* (Fr.), counting-room.
*Con amore* (It.), with love : very earnestly.
*Concierge* (Fr.), the keeper of a prison : porter of a house. [monastery : an associate.
*Confrère* (Fr.), a brother belonging to the same
*Congé d'élire* (Fr.), leave to elect.
*Conseil d'état* (Fr.), a council of state : a privy-council. [morals.
*Contra bonos mores* (L.), against good manners or

*Contre-temps* (Fr.), a mischance.
*Copia verborum* (L.), plenty of words : fluency in speech.
*Coram nobis* (L.), before us.
*Cordon sanitaire* (Fr.), a line of troops to prevent the spreading of contagion or pestilence.
*Corps diplomatique* (Fr.), a diplomatic body.
*Corpus delicti* (L.), the body, substance, or foundation of the offence.
*Couleur de rose* (Fr.), rose colour ; hence, an aspect of beauty and attractiveness.
*Coup de grâce* (Fr.), the finishing stroke.
*Coup de main* (Fr.), a sudden enterprise or effort.
*Coup de soleil* (Fr.), a stroke of the sun.
*Coup d'état* (Fr.), a stroke of policy : a violent measure of state.
*Coup d'œil* (Fr.), a rapid glance of the eye.
*Coupé* (Fr.), the front division of a diligence.
*Coûte que coûte* (Fr.), cost what it may.
*Cui bono?* (L.), for whose benefit is it ?
*Cuisine* (Fr.), kitchen : cooking department.
*Cul de sac* (Fr.), the bottom of the bag : a street or lane that has no outlet.
*Cum grano salis* (L.), with a grain of salt, i.e. with some allowance.
*Cum privilegio* (L.), with privilege.
*Curiosa felicitas* (L.), nice felicity of expression.
*Currente calamo* (L.), with a running or rapid pen.
*Custos rotulorum* (L.), keeper of the rolls.

*Da capo* (It.), from the beginning.
*De bonne grâce* (Fr.), with good grace : willingly.
*De facto* (L.), from the fact : really.
*Dégagé* (Fr.), easy and unconstrained.
*Dei gratiâ* (L.), by the grace of God.
*Déjeuner* (Fr.), breakfast : a fashionable luncheon.
*Déjeûner à la fourchette* (Fr.), a meat breakfast.
*De jure* (L.), from the law : by right.
*Delenda est Carthago* (L.), Carthage must be blotted out, or destroyed.
*De mortuis nil nisi bonum* (L.), say nothing but good of the dead.
*De novo* (L.), anew.
*Deo gratias* (L.), thanks to God.
*Deo volente* (L.), God willing : by God's will.
*De profundis* (L.), out of the depths.
*Dernier ressort* (Fr.), a last resource.
*Désagrément* (Fr.), something disagreeable.
*Desipere in loco* (L.), to jest at the proper time.
*Desunt cetera* (L.), the remainder is wanting.
*De trop* (Fr.), too much, or too many.
*Dies iræ* (L.), day of wrath.
*Dies non* (L.), a day on which judges do not sit.
*Dieu et mon droit* (Fr.), God and my right.
*Die Wacht am Rhein* (Ger.), the watch on the Rhine, a famous German patriotic song.
*Distingué* (Fr.), distinguished : eminent.
*Distrait* (Fr.), absent in thought.
*Divertissement* (Fr.), amusement : sport.
*Dolce far niente* (It.), sweet doing-nothing : sweet idleness.
*Double entendre, Double entente* (Fr.), double meaning : a word or phrase capable of more than one meaning.
*Dramatis personæ* (L.), characters of a drama.
*Droits d'octroi* (Fr.), duties levied on certain articles on their entry into a town.
*Dulce Domum!* (L.), sweetly homeward ! from the song sung by the students of Winchester College at the close of the term.
*Dulce est desipere in loco* (L.), it is pleasant to jest, or revel, at the proper time.
*Dulce et decorum est pro patriâ mori* (L.), it is sweet and glorious to die for one's country.
*Dum spiro, spero* (L.), while I breathe, I hope.

*Dum vivimus, vivamus* (L.), while we live, let us live.

*Eau de Cologne* (Fr.), Cologne water, a perfume.
*Eau de vie* (Fr.), water of life: brandy.
*Ecce homo* (L.), behold the man.
*Editio princeps* (L.), original edition.
*Edition de luxe* (Fr.), a splendid and expensive edition of a book.
*Ego et rex meus* (L.), I and my king.
*El Dorado* (Sp.), the golden land.
*Elève* (Fr.), pupil.
*Embonpoint* (Fr.), in good condition: plump.
*Emeritus* (L.), one retired from active official duties.
*Emigré* (Fr.), an emigrant.
*Empressement* (Fr.), ardour: zeal: interest.
*En ami* (Fr.), as a friend.
*En avant !* (Fr.), forward !
*En déshabillé* (Fr.), in undress.
*En famille* (Fr.), in a domestic state.
*Enfants perdus* (Fr.), lost children: (*mil.*) the forlorn-hope.
*En masse* (Fr.), in a body.
*En passant* (Fr.), in passing: by the way.
*En plein jour* (Fr.), in broad day.
*En rapport* (Fr.), in relation: in connection.
*En règle* (Fr.), in order: according to rules.
*En route* (Fr.), on the way.
*En suite* (Fr.), in company.     [tween two states.
*Entente cordiale* (Fr.), cordial good-will, esp. be-
*Entourage* (Fr.), surroundings: adjuncts.
*En tout* (Fr.), in all: wholly.
*Entrée* (Fr.), entry: a dish served at the commencement of a repast, preparatory to the more substantial fare.
*Entremets* (Fr.), small and dainty dishes set between the principal ones at table.
*Entre nous* (Fr.), between ourselves.
*Entrepôt* (Fr.), a warehouse or magazine.
*En vérité* (Fr.), in truth: verily.
*Errare est humanum* (L.), to err is human.
*Esprit de corps* (Fr.), the animating spirit of a collective body, as of the army or the bar.
*États Généraux* (Fr.), the States-General.
*Et cetera* (L.), and the rest: &c.
*Et hoc genus omne* } (L.), and everything of the
*Et id genus omne* } sort.
*Et sequentes* (L.), and those that follow.
*Et sequentia* (L.), and what follows.
*Et sic de ceteris* (L.), and so of the rest.
*Et tu, Brute !* (L.), and thou also, Brutus !
*Eureka !* (Gr.), I have found it !
*Ex cathedrâ* (L.), from the chair: with high authority.
*Excelsior* (L.), higher: more elevated.
*Exceptio probat regulam* (L.), the exception proves the rule.
*Ex curiâ* (L.), out of court.
*Exempli gratiâ* (L.), by way of example.
*Exequatur* (L.), the writing which recognises a person as consul, &c.
*Exeunt* (L.), they go out.
*Exeunt omnes* (L.), all go out, or retire.
*Ex nihilo nihil fit* (L.), out of nothing, nothing comes.
*Ex officio* (L.), by virtue of his office.
*Ex parte* (L.), on one side only.
*Experto crede* (L.), trust one who has tried, or had experience.
*Exposé* (Fr.), an exposition; recital.
*Extra muros* (L.), beyond the walls.

*Facile princeps* (L.), evidently pre-eminent: the admitted chief.

*Facilis est descensus Averni* (L.), descent to Avernus (or hell) is easy; the road to evil is easy.
*Fainéant* (Fr.), idle.
*Fait accompli* (Fr.), a thing already done.
*Fama clamosa* (L.), a current scandal.
*Fata obstant* (L.), the Fates oppose it.
*Faux pas* (Fr.), a false step: a mistake.
*Fecit* (L.), he made or executed it.
*Feliciter* (L.), happily: successfully.
*Felo de se* (L.), a suicide.
*Femme* (or *fille*) *de chambre* (Fr.), a chambermaid.
*Fête champêtre* (Fr.), a rural festival.     [bonfire.
*Feu de joie* (Fr.), a firing of guns in token of joy : a
*Feuilleton* (Fr.), a small leaf : a supplement to a newspaper, devoted to light, entertaining matter.
*Fiat justitia ruat cœlum* (L.), let justice be done, though the heavens should fall.
*Fidei defensor* (L.), defender of the faith.
*Fides Punica* (L.), Punic faith ; treachery.
*Fidus Achates* (L.), faithful Achates—i.e. a true friend.
*Fils* (Fr.), son.
*Finem respice* (L.), look to the end.
*Flagrante delicto* (L.), in the very act.
*Fra* (It.), brother, friar.
*Fuit Ilium* (L.), Troy has been—i.e. is no more.
*Fulmen brutum* (L.), a harmless thunderbolt.
*Furor loquendi* (L.), a rage for speaking.
*Furor poeticus* (L.), poetical fire.
*Furor scribendi* (L.), a rage for writing.

*Gallicè* (L.), in French.
*Garçon* (Fr.), a boy: a waiter.
*Garde du corps* (Fr.), a body-guard.
*Gardez* (Fr.), take care : be on your guard.
*Genius loci* (L.), the genius of the place.
*Gens d'armes* (Fr.), armed police.
*Gentilhomme* (Fr.), a gentleman.
*Gloria in excelsis* (L.), glory to God in the highest.
*Gloria Patri* (L.), glory be to the Father.
*Gnothi seauton* (Gr.), know thyself.
*Gouvernante* (Fr.), a governess.
*Gradus ad Parnassum* (L.), a step to Parnassus, aid in writing Greek or Latin poetry.
*Grande toilette* (Fr.), full dress.

*Hauteur* (Fr.), haughtiness.
*Hic et ubique* (L.), here and everywhere.
*Hic jacet* (L.), here lies.     [the toil.
*Hic labor, hoc opus est* (L.), this is the labour, this
*Hic sepultus* (L.), here buried.
*Hinc illæ lacrimæ* (L.), hence proceed these tears.
*Hoi polloi* (Gr.), the many : the rabble : the vulgar.
*Homo sum: humani nihil a me alienum puto* (L.), I am a man : I count nothing human indifferent to me.
*Honi soi qui mal y pense* (Fr.), evil to him who evil thinks.
*Hors de combat* (Fr.), out of condition to fight.
*Hortus siccus* (L.), a collection of dried plants.
*Hôtel de ville* (Fr.), a town-hall.     [pital.
*Hôtel Dieu* (Fr.), the house of God, a Paris hos-
*Hôtel garni* (Fr.), hotel with furnished lodgings.
*Humanum est errare* (L.), to err is human.

*Ibidem* (L.), in the same place, thing, or case.
*Ich dien* (Ger.), I serve.
*Idem* (L.), the same.
*Id est* (L.), that is.
*Ignoratio elenchi* (L.), ignorance of the point in question, the logical fallacy of arguing to the wrong point.
*Ignotum per ignotius* (L.), the unknown by the still more unknown.
*Il penseroso* (It.), the pensive man.

# Words and Phrases from Latin, Greek, &c.

*Impedimenta* (L.), luggage in travelling : the baggage of an army. [another.

*Imperium in imperio* (L.), a government within

*In articulo mortis* (L.), at the point of death.

*Index expurgatorius* (L.), a list of prohibited books.

*In esse* (L.), in being.

*In extenso* (L.), at full length.

*In extremis* (L.), at the point of death.

*In formâ pauperis* (L.), as a poor man.

*Infra dignitatem* (L.), below one's dignity.

*In limine* (L.), at the threshold.

*In loco parentis* (L.), in the place of a parent.

*In medias res* (L.), into the midst of things.

*In memoriam* (L.), to the memory of : in memory.

*In nubibus* (L.), in the clouds.

*In pace* (L.), in peace. [tries.

*In partibus infidelium* (L.), in unbelieving coun-

*In petto* (It.), within the breast : in reserve.

*In posse* (L.), in possible existence : in possibility.

*In propriâ personâ* (L.), in person.

*In puris naturalibus* (L.), quite naked.

*In re* (L.), in the matter of.

*In situ* (L.), in its original situation.

*Insouciance* (Fr.), indifference, carelessness.

*In statu quo* (L.), in the former state.

*Inter alia* (L.), among other things.

*Inter nos* (L.), between ourselves.

*Inter pocula* (L.), at one's cups.

*In terrorem* (L.), as a warning.

*Inter se* (L.), among themselves.

*In toto* (L.), in the whole : entirely.

*Intra muros* (L.), within the walls.

*In transitu* (L.), on the passage.

*Invitâ Minervâ* (L.), without genius.

*Ipse dixit* (L.), he himself said it : dogmatism.

*Ipsissima verba* (L.), the very words.

*Ipso facto* (L.), in the fact itself.

*Je ne sais quoi* (Fr.), I know not what.

*Jet d'eau* (Fr.), a jet of water.

*Jeu de mots* (Fr.), a play on words : a pun.

*Jeu d'esprit* (Fr.), a witticism.

*Jupiter Pluvius* (L.), the rain-bringing Jupiter : a rainy day.

*Jure divino* (L.), by divine law.

*Jure humano* (L.), by human law.

*Juste milieu* (Fr.), the golden mean.

*Labore et honore* (L.), by labour and honour.

*Laissez faire* (Fr.), let alone.

*L'allegro* (It.), the merry man.

*Landsturm* (Ger.), the part of the German army consisting of men up to the age of 50 years, who have served in the standing army and the Land-wehr, and who can only be called out in case of invasion.

*Landwehr* (Ger.), 'land-defence,' the part of the German army consisting of those who have recently finished their time in the standing army.

*Lapsus calami* (L.), a slip of the pen.

*Lapsus linguæ* (L.), a slip of the tongue.

*Lapsus memoriæ* (L.), a slip of the memory.

*Lares et penates* (L.), household gods.

*La reyne le veult* (Norm. Fr.), the Queen wills it, the formula expressing the Queen's assent to a bill.

*Laus Deo* (L.), praise to God.

*L'avenir* (Fr.), the future.

*Le beau monde* (Fr.), the fashionable world.

*Le pas* (Fr.), precedence in place or rank.

*Lèse majesté* (Fr.), high-treason.

*Le tout ensemble* (Fr.), all together.

*Lettre de cachet* (Fr.), a sealed letter : a royal warrant. [common law.

*Lex non scripta* (L.), unwritten law—that is, the

*Lex scripta* (L.), statute law.

*Lex talionis* (L.), the law of retaliation.

*Lingua Franca* (It.), the mixed language spoken by Europeans in the East.

*Locum tenens* (L.), one occupying the place : a deputy or substitute.

*Locus classicus* (L.), a classical passage.

*Locus standi* (L.), a place for standing : a right to interfere.

*Lusus naturæ* (L.), a sport or freak of nature.

*Ma chère* (Fr.), my dear.

*Ma foi* (Fr.), upon my faith.

*Magnum bonum* (L.), a great good.

*Magnum opus* (L.), a great work.

*Maison de ville* (Fr.), a town-house.

*Maître d'hôtel* (Fr.), a house-steward.

*Maladie du pays* (Fr.), home-sickness.

*Malâ fide* (L.), with bad faith : treacherously.

*Mal à propos* (Fr.), ill-timed.

*Malgré nous* (Fr.), in spite of us.

*Mandamus* (L.), we command : a writ or com-mand issued by the court of King's Bench.

*Mariage de convenance* (Fr.), marriage from motives of interest rather than of love.

*Materfamilias* (L.), the mother of a family.

*Materia Medica* (L.), medicines collectively, a general term for all substances used as remedies in medicine, also the science of their properties, classification, and use.

*Matériel* (Fr.), material objects used in any de-sign, esp. the baggage and munitions of an army.

*Matinée* (Fr.), a morning or early recital or per-formance.

*Mauvaise honte* (Fr.), false modesty. [fellow.

*Mauvais sujet* (Fr.), a bad subject : a worthless

*Me judice* (L.), I being judge, in my opinion.

*Mélange* (Fr.), a mixture.

*Mêlée* (Fr.), a fight in which the combatants are mingled together : a scuffle : a confused debate.

*Memento mori* (L.), remember death.

*Memorabilia* (L.), things to be remembered.

*Mens sana in corpore sano* (L.), a sound mind in a sound body. [rectitude.

*Mens sibi conscia recti* (L.), a mind conscious of

*Mésalliance* (Fr.), improper association : marriage with one of lower station.

*Messieurs* (Fr.), sirs, gentlemen.

*Meum et tuum* (L.), mine and thine.

*Mirabile dictu* (L.), wonderful to tell.

*Mirabile visu* (L.), wonderful to see.

*Mirabilia* (L.), wonders.

*Mise en scène* (Fr.), the getting up or putting in preparation for the stage.

*Modus* (L.), manner, mode.

*Modus operandi* (L.), manner of operation.

*Mon ami* (Fr.), my friend.

*Mon cher* (Fr.), my dear.

*Monsieur* (Fr.), sir, Mr.

*Mont de piété*, place for lending money to the poor.

*Morceau* (Fr.), a bit : morsel : fragment.

*More majorum* (L.), after the manner of our ancestors.

*More suo* (L.), in his own way.

*Multum in parvo* (L.), much in little.

*Mutatis mutandis* (L.), with necessary changes.

*Née* (Fr.), born : said of a married woman's maiden name.

*Nemine contradicente* (L.), without opposition : no one speaking in opposition.

*Nemine dissentiente* (L.), no one dissenting : with-out a dissenting voice.

*Nemo me impune lacessit* (L.), no one hurts me with impunity—the motto of Scotland.

*Ne plus ultra* (L.), nothing further: the uttermost point.

*Ne sutor ultra crepidam* (L.), let not the shoemaker go beyond his last.

*Nihil ad rem* (L.), nothing to the point.

*Nil desperandum* (L.), never despair.

*N'importe* (Fr.), it matters not.

*Nisi dominus frustra* (L.), unless God be with you, all your toil is vain.

*Nisi prius* (L.), unless previously—a name given to the sittings of juries in civil cases.

*Nitor in adversum* (L.), I strive against opposition.

*Noblesse oblige* (Fr.), rank imposes obligation.

*Nolens volens* (L.), whether he will or not.

*Noli me tangere* (L.), don't touch me.

*Nolle prosequi* (L.), to be unwilling to proceed.

*Nolo episcopari* (L.), I do not wish to be made a bishop. [title : a pseudonym.

*Nom de guerre* (Fr.), a war-name : a travelling

*Nom de plume* (Fr.), a pen-name or literary title.

*Nonchalance* (Fr.), coolness, indifference, carelessness.

*Non compos mentis* (L.), not in sound mind.

*Non mi ricordo* (It.), I don't remember.

*Non multa, sed multum* (L.), not many things, but much.

*Non sequitur* (L.), it does not follow.

*Nosce teipsum* (L.), know thyself.

*Nota bene* (L.), mark well.

*Notanda* (L.), things to be noted.

*Notre Dame* (Fr.), Our Lady.

*Nous avons changé tout cela* (Fr.), we have changed all that.

*Nous verrons* (Fr.), we shall see.

*Novus homo* (L.), a new man, or one who has raised himself from obscurity.

*Obiit* (L.), he, or she, died. [rabble.

*Odi profanum vulgus* (L.), I loathe the profane

*Odium theologicum* (L.), the hatred of divines.

*Œuvres* (Fr.), works.

*On dit* (Fr.), they say : a flying rumour.

*Onus probandi* (L.), the burden of proving.

*Optimates* (L.), men of the first rank.

*Ora pro nobis* (L.), pray for us.

*Ore rotundo* (L.), with round, full voice.

*O ! si sic omnia* (L.), O that he had always done or spoken thus. [manners !

*O tempora ! O mores !* (L.), O the times ! O the

*Otium cum dignitate* (L.), dignified leisure.

*Pace* (L.), by leave of.

*Padrone* (It.), ruler: protector: master.

*Palmam qui meruit ferat* (L.), let him who has won the palm carry it.

*Parergon* (Gr.), something done by the bye.

*Par excellence* (Fr.), by way of eminence.

*Pari passu* (L.), with equal pace : together.

*Particeps criminis* (L.), an accomplice.

*Pas* (Fr.), a step : action : precedence.

*Passim* (L.), everywhere.

*Pâté de foie gras* (Fr.), goose-liver pie.

*Paterfamilias* (L.), the father of a family.

*Patres conscripti* (L.), the conscript fathers : Roman senators.

*Pax vobiscum* (L.), peace be with you.

*Peccavi* (L.), I have sinned.

*Peine forte et dure* (Fr.), strong and severe punishment, a kind of judicial torture.

*Penetralia* (L.), secret recesses.

*Pensée* (Fr.), a thought.

*Per annum* (L.), by the year.

*Per centum* (L.), by the hundred.

*Per contra* (L.), contrariwise.

*Per diem* (L.), by the day.

*Per fas et nefas* (L.), through right and wrong.

*Per saltum* (L.), by a leap or jump.

*Per se* (L.), by himself, itself, &c.

*Personnel* (Fr.), the persons employed in any service as distinguished from the *matériel*.

*Petit* (Fr.), small.

*Petitio principii* (L.), a begging of the question.

*Petit-maître* (Fr.), a fop.

*Pinxit* (L.), painted it.

*Pis aller* (Fr.), the last or worst shift.

*Plebs* (L.), common people.

*Pleno jure* (L.), with full authority.

*Poeta nascitur, non fit* (L.), the poet is born, not made : nature, not study, must form the poet.

*Point d'appui* (Fr.), point of support : prop.

*Pons asinorum* (L.), the asses' bridge.

*Posse comitatus* (L.), the power of the county.

*Poste restante* (Fr.), to remain until called for.

*Post mortem* (L.), after death.

*Pot pourri* (Fr.), a medley or mixture : a ragout of different meats and vegetables.

*Pour passer le temps* (Fr.), to pass away the time.

*Pour prendre congé* (Fr.), to take leave.

*Prescriptum* (L.), a thing prescribed.

*Presto* (It.), quickly.

*Preux chevalier* (Fr.), a brave knight.

*Primâ facie* (L.), on the first view.

*Primo* (L.), in the first place.

*Primum mobile* (L.), the source of motion.

*Pro aris et focis* (L.), for our altars and firesides.

*Pro bono publico* (L.), for the public good.

*Procès-verbal* (Fr.), a written statement.

*Pro et con.* (L.), arguments for or against.

*Profanum vulgus* (L.), the profane rabble.

*Pro formâ* (L.), for the sake of form.

*Projet de loi* (Fr.), a legislative bill.

*Pro memoriâ* (L.), for a memorial.

*Pro patriâ* (L.), for our country.

*Pro ratâ* (L.), in proportion.

*Pro re natâ* (L.), for a special emergency.

*Pro tempore* (L.), for the time being.

*Quantum sufficit* (L.), a sufficient quantity.

*Quasi* (L.), as if : in a manner.

*Quid pro quo* (L.), one thing for another.

*Quid rides ?* (L.), why do you laugh?

*Qui vive ?* (Fr.), who goes there ?—hence, *on the qui vive*, on the alert.

*Quoad sacra* (L.), 'as to things sacred,' applied in Scotland to a district containing a church which is constituted as a parish in ecclesiastical but not in civil matters.

*Quod erat demonstrandum* (L.), which was to be proved or demonstrated.

*Quod erat faciendum* (L.), which was to be done.

*Quod vide* (L.), which see.

*Quo jure* (L.), by what right.

*Quot homines, tot sententiæ* (L.), as many men, so many minds.

*Raison d'être* (Fr.), reason for a thing's existence.

*Rara avis* (L.), a rare bird : a prodigy.

*Realschulen* (Ger.), secondary schools in Germany giving a general practical training.

*Réchauffé* (Fr.), warmed again, as food : hence, stale : old : insipid. [exquisite.

*Recherché* (Fr.), sought out with care : rare :

*Reductio ad absurdum* (L.), a reducing a position to an absurdity.

*Regium donum* (L.), a royal gift.

*Reichstag* (Ger.), the Imperial Diet of Germany.

*Religieuse* (Fr.), a nun. *Religieux* (Fr.), a monk.

*Rem acu tetigisti* (L.), you have touched the thing with a needle—that is, exactly.

*Rentes* (Fr.), funds bearing interest : stocks.

*Requiescat in pace* (L.), may he rest in peace.

*Res angusta domi* (L.), narrow circumstances at home : poverty.

*Res gestæ* (L.), exploits.

*Res judicata* (L.), a case or suit already decided.

*Respice finem* (L.), look to the end.

*Résumé* (Fr.), an abstract or summary.

*Resurgam* (L.), I shall rise again.

*Revenons à nos moutons* (Fr.), let us return to our sheep : let us return to our subject.

*Ruat cœlum* (L.), let the heavens fall.

*Ruse contre ruse* (Fr.), cunning against cunning.

*Ruse de guerre* (Fr.), a stratagem of war.

*Rus in urbe* (L.), the country in town.

*Sanctum sanctorum* (L.), holy of holies.

*Sang-froid* (Fr.), cold blood : coolness.

*Sans cérémonie* (Fr.), without ceremony.

*Sans-culottes* (Fr.), breechless fellows, the ragged or poorest class.                   [without reproach.

*Sans peur et sans reproche* (Fr.), without fear and

*Sans souci* (Fr.), without care.

*Sartor resartus* (L.), the tailor done over.

*Satis verborum* (L.), enough of words.

*Sauve qui peut* (Fr.), save himself who can.

*Savant* (Fr.), a learned man.

*Savoir faire* (Fr.), the knowing how to act : tact.

*Savoir vivre* (Fr.), good-breeding.

*Secundum artem* (L.), according to rule.

*Secundum naturam* (L.), according to nature.

*Secundum ordinem* (L.), in order.

*Semper idem* (L.), always the same.

*Semper paratus* (L.), always ready.

*Seriatim* (L.), in a series.                   [tality.

*Sic itur ad astra* (L.), such is the way to immor-

*Sic passim* (L.), so everywhere.

*Sic transit gloria mundi* (L.), so passes away earthly glory.

*Sic vos non vobis* (L.), thus you toil not for your-selves.                   [cured by like.

*Similia similibus curantur* (L.), like things are

*Sine die* (L.), without a day being appointed, indefinitely.

*Sine quâ non* (L.), an indispensable condition.

*Siste, viator* (L.), stop, traveller.

*Soi-disant* (Fr.), self-called.

*Spero meliora* (L.), I hope for better things.

*Spirituel* (Fr.), intellectual : intelligent : witty.

*Spolia opima* (L.), the richest booty.

*Sponte suâ* (L.), of one's own accord.

*Status quo* (L.), the state in which.

*Stet* (L.), let it stand.

*Suaviter in modo, fortiter in re* (L.), gentle in manner, resolute in deed.

*Sub judice* (L.), under consideration.

*Sub pœnâ* (L.), under a penalty.

*Sub rosâ* (L.), under the rose : privately.

*Sui generis* (L.), of its own kind.

*Summum bonum* (L.), the chief good.

*Suum cuique* (L.), let each have his own.

*Tableau vivant* (Fr.), the representation of some scene by groups of persons.

*Tabula rasa* (L.), a smooth or blank tablet.

*Tædium vitæ* (L.), weariness of life.

*Tant mieux* (Fr.), so much the better.

*Tanto uberior* (L.), so much the richer.

*Tant pis* (Fr.), so much the worse.

*Tapis* (Fr.), the carpet.

*Te Deum* (L.), a hymn of thanksgiving.

*Tempora mutantur, nos et mutamur in illis* (L.), the times are changed, and we with them.

*Tempus fugit* (L.), time flies.

*Terra firma* (L.), solid earth : a safe footing.

*Terra incognita* (L.), an unknown country.

*Tertium quid* (L.), a third something.

*Tête-à-tête* (Fr.), head to head : a private conver-sation.

*Tiers état* (Fr.), the third estate, the Commons.

*Toga virilis* (L.), the garb of manhood.

*To kalon* (Gr.), the beautiful : the chief good.

*Totidem verbis* (L.), in just so many words.

*Toties quoties* (L.), as often as.

*Toto cœlo* (L.), by the whole heavens : diametri-cally opposite.

*Tour de force* (Fr.), a feat of strength or skill.

*Tout-à-fait* (Fr.), entirely.

*Tout-à-vous* (Fr.), wholly yours.

*Tout ensemble* (Fr.), the whole taken together : the broad or general effect.

*Tu quoque, Brute !* (L.), and thou too, Brutus !

*Ubique* (L.), everywhere.

*Ultima ratio regum* (L.), the last argument of kings, war.

*Ultima Thule* (L.), the utmost boundary or limit.

*Ultimus Romanorum* (L.), the last of the Romans.

*Ultra vires* (L.), beyond one's powers.

*Usque ad nauseam* (L.), to disgust.

*Usus loquendi* (L.), current usage of speech.

*Ut infra* (L.), as below.

*Ut supra* (L.), as above.

*Vade mecum* (L.), go with me : a constant com-panion.

*Vale* (L.), farewell.

*Valet de chambre* (Fr.), an attendant : a footman.

*Variæ lectiones* (L.), various readings.

*Variorum notæ* (L.), the notes of various authors.

*Veni, vidi, vici* (L.), I came, I saw, I conquered.

*Verbatim et literatim* (L.), word for word and letter for letter.                   [wise man.

*Verbum sat sapienti* (L.), a word is enough for a

*Versus* (L.), against : toward.

*Vestigia* (L.), tracks : vestiges.

*Vestigia nulla retrorsum* (L.), not a step backward.

*Vexata questio* (L.), a disputed question.

*Viâ* (L.), by way of.

*Via media* (L.), a middle course.

*Vice* (L.), in the place of.

*Vice versâ* (L.), the terms being exchanged.

*Videlicet* (L.), to wit : namely, usually shortened into *viz.*                   [force.

*Vi et armis* (L.), by force and arms : by main

*Vis à vis* (Fr.), opposite : facing.

*Vis inertiæ* (L.), the power of inertia : passive resistance.

*Vivat regina* (L.), long live the queen.

*Vivat rex* (L.), long live the king.

*Vivâ voce* (L.), by the living voice : by oral tes-timony.

*Vive l'empereur* (Fr.), long live the emperor.

*Voilà* (Fr.), behold : there is, or there are.

*Vox, et præterea nihil* (L.), a voice, and nothing more.                   [is the voice of God.

*Vox populi, vox Dei* (L.), the voice of the people

*Vulgò* (L.), commonly.

*Zollverein* (Ger.), the German Customs-League.

# LIST OF ABBREVIATIONS.

**A1.** First-class (of ships).

**A.B.** Able-bodied seaman.

**Abbr.** or **Abbrev.** Abbreviated, or Abbreviation.

**Abp.** Archbishop.

**A.C.,** *ante Christum* (L.) Before Christ.

**Acc.** or **Acct.** Account.

**A.D.,** *anno Domini* (L.) In the year of our Lord.

**A.D.C.** Aide-de-camp.

**Adjt.** Adjutant.

**Ad lib.** or **Ad libit., ad libitum** (L.) At pleasure.

**Æ.** or **Æt., *ætatis*** (L.) Aged.

**A.H.,** *anno Hegiræ* (L.) In the year of the Hegira, or flight of Mohammed.

**Al.** or **Ala.** Alabama.

**A.M., *Artium Magister*** (L.) Master of Arts.

**A.M., *ante meridiem*** (L.) before noon.

**A.M., *anno mundi*** (L.) In the year of the world.

**Anon.** Anonymous.

**Ant.** or **Antiq.** Antiquities.

**App.** Appendix.

**A.R.A.** Associate of the Royal Academy.

**A.R.H.A.** Associate of the Royal Hibernian Academy.

**Ark.** Arkansas.

**A.R.R., *anno regni regis*** or ***reginæ*** (L.) In the year of the king's or queen's reign.

**A.R.S.A.** Associate of the Royal Scottish Academy.

**A.R.S.S., *Antiquariorum Regiæ Societatis Socius*** (L.) Fellow of the Royal Society of Antiquaries.

**A.S.** Anglo-Saxon.

**Asst.** Assistant.

**Att.-gen.** Attorney-general.

**A.U.C., *anno urbis conditæ,*** or *ab urbe conditâ* (L.) In the year from the building of the city—Rome.

**A.V.** Authorised Version, also Artillery Volunteers.

**B.** Born.

**B.A., *Baccalaureus Artium*** (L.) Bachelor of Arts.

**Bart.** or **Bt.** Baronet.

**B.C.** Before Christ.

**B.C.L.** Bachelor of Civil Law.

**B.D.** Bachelor of Divinity.

**Beds.** Bedfordshire.

**Berks.** Berkshire.

**B.L.** Bachelor of Laws.

**Bp.** Bishop.

**Br.** or **Bro.** Brother.

**B.Sc.** See *Sc. B.* [London.

**B.S.L.** Botanical Society of

**Bucks.** Buckinghamshire.

**B.V.** The Blessed Virgin.

**C., Ct., Cent., *centum*** (L.) A hundred.

**C.** Centigrade.

**C.** or **Cap., *caput*** (L.) Chapter.

**C.A.** Chartered Accountant.

**Cal.** California.

**Cam., Camb.** Cambridge.

**Cantab., *Cantabrigiensis*** (L.) Of Cambridge. [terbury.

**Cantuar., *Cantuaria*** (L.) Can-

**Cap., *caput*** (L.) Capital, chapter.

**Caps.** Capitals.

**Capt.** Captain.

**C.B.** Companion of the Bath.

**C.E.** Civil Engineer, also Canada East.

**Cf., *confer*** (L.) Compare.

**Ch.** Church, Chapter.

**Chap.** Chapter.

**Clk.** Clerk.

**C.M.** Certificated Master.

**C.M.** Common Metre.

**C.M., *Chirurgiæ Magister*** (L.) Master in Surgery.

**Col.** Colonel, Column.

**Coll.** College.

**Colloq.** Colloquially.

**Com.** Commander, Commodore, Committee.

**Con., *contra*** (L.) Against.

**Cong.** Congress.

**Conn.** or **Ct.** Connecticut.

**Contr.** Contracted, Contraction.

**Cor. Mem.** Corresponding Member.—*Cor. Sec.* Corresponding Secretary.

**Cr.** Credit, Creditor.

**Crim. Con.** Criminal Conversation, or adultery.

**C.S.** Court of Session, Clerk to the Signet. [of India.

**C.S.I.** Companion of the Star

**C.T.** Certificated Teacher.

**Cur., Curt.** Current — this month.

**C.W.** Canada West.

**Cwt.** A hundredweight ; *c* for *centum* (L.) a hundred, and *wt.* for weight.

**Cyc.** Cyclopædia.

**D.** Died. [penny or pence.

**D., *denarius*** or ***denarii*** (L.) A

**D.C.L.** Doctor of Civil Law.

**D.D., *Divinitatis Doctor*** (L.) Doctor of Divinity.

**Deft.** Defendant.

**Deg.** Degree, Degrees.

**Del.** Delaware, also Delegate.

**Del., *delineavit*** (L.) ' He drew it,' put after the draftsman's name on an engraving.

**D.F.** Defender of the Faith, Dean of the Faculty.

**D.G., *Dei gratiâ*** (L.) By the grace of God.

**D.L.** Deputy Lieutenant.

**D.Lit.** Doctor of Literature.

**D.L.O.** Dead-letter Office.

**Do., *ditto*** (It.) The same.

**Dols.** Dollars.

**Doz.** Dozen.

**Dr.** Debtor, Doctor, Dram.

**D.Sc.** See *Sc.D.*

**D.V., *Deo volente*** (L.) God willing, if God will.

**Dwt.** Pennyweight ; *d* for *denarius* (L.) penny, and *wt.* for weight.

**E.** East.

**Ebor., *Eboracum*** (L.) York.

**E.C.** Eastern Central.

**E.C.** Established Church.

**Eccl., Eccles.** Ecclesiastical.

**Ed.** Editor, Edition.

**Edin.** Edinburgh.

**E.E.** Errors Excepted.

**E.G., *exempli gratiâ*** (L.) For example.

**E.I.** East Indies.

**Emp.** Emperor, Empress.

**Ency., Encyc.** Encyclopædia.

**E.N.E.** East-north-east.

**E.S.E.** East-south-east.

**Esq., Esqr.** Esquire.

**Et al., *et alibi*** (L.) And elsewhere ; or *et alii* or *alia* (L.) And others.

**Etc., *&c., et ceteri*** or ***cetera*** (L.) And others, and so forth.

**Et seq., *et sequentes*** or ***sequentia*** (L.) And the following.

**Ex.** Example, Exception.

**Fahr.** Fahrenheit.

**F.A.S.** Fellow of the Society of Arts, or of Antiquaries.

**F.B.S.E.** Fellow of the Botanical Society of Edinburgh.

**F.C.** Free Church of Scotland.

**Fcp.** Foolscap.

**F.D., *Fidei Defensor*** (L.) Defender of the Faith.

**Fec., *fecit*** (L.) He did it.

**F.E.I.S.** Fellow of the Educational Institute of Scotland.

**F.E.S.** Fellow of the Ethnological or of the Entomological Society.

**F.G.S.** Fellow of the Geological Society.

**Fig.** Figure, Figuratively.

**Flor.** or **Fa.** Florida.

**F.L.S.** Fellow of the Linnæan Society.

**F.M.** Field-marshal.

**Fo., Fol.** Folio.

**F.O.** Field-officer.

**F.P.** Fire-plug.

**F.P.S.** Fellow of the Philological Society.

**F.R.A.S.** Fellow of the Royal Astronomical Society.

589

## List of Abbreviations.

**F.R.C.P.** Fellow of the Royal College of Physicians.

**F.R.C.P.E.** Fellow of the Royal College of Physicians, Edinburgh.

**F.R.C.S.** Fellow of the Royal College of Surgeons.

**F.R.C.S.E.** Fellow of the Royal College of Surgeons, Edinburgh.

**F.R.C.S.I.** Fellow of the Royal College of Surgeons, Ireland.

**F.R.C.S.L.** Fellow of the Royal College of Surgeons, London.

**F.R.G.S.** Fellow of the Royal Geographical Society.

**F.R.H.S.** Fellow of the Royal Horticultural Society.

**F.R.S.** Fellow of the Royal Society.

**F.R.S.E.** Fellow of the Royal Society, Edinburgh.

**F.S.A.** Fellow of the Society of Arts, or of Antiquaries.

**F.S.A.Scot.** Fellow of the Society of Antiquaries of Scotland.  [Society.

**F.S.S.** Fellow of the Statistical

**Ft.** Foot, Feet, Fort.

**F.T.C.D.** Fellow of Trinity College, Dublin.

**F.Z.S.** Fellow of the Zoological Society.

**G.A.** General Assembly.

**G.B.** Great Britain.

**G.C.B.** Grand Cross of the Bath.

**G.C.L.H.** Grand Cross of the Legion of Honour.

**Gen., Genl.** General.

**Gent.** Gentleman, Gentlemen.

**Geo.** Georgia.

**G.P.O.** General Post-office.

**H.** or **Hr.** Hour.

**Hants.** Hampshire.

**H.B.M.** His or Her Britannic Majesty.

**H.C.M.** His or Her Catholic Majesty.

**H.E.I.C.S.** Honourable East India Company's Service.

**Hf.-bd.** Half-bound.

**H.G.** Horse Guards.

**Hhd.** Hogshead.

**H.I.H.** His or Her Imperial Highness.

**H.J.S.,** *hic jacet sepultus* (L.) Here lies buried.

**H.M.** His or Her Majesty.

**H.M.P.,** *hoc monumentum posuit* (L.) Erected this monument.

**H.M.S.** His or Her Majesty's Ship or Service.

**Hon.** Honourable.

**H.P.** Horse-power.

**H.R.H.** His or Her Royal Highness.

**H.R.I.P.,** *hic requiescit in pace* (L.) Here rests in peace.

**H.S.H.** His or Her Serene Highness.

**Ia.,** also **Ind.** Indiana.

**Ib.,** *Ibid., ibidem* (L.) In the same place.

**Id.,** *idem* (L.) The same.

**I.E.,** *id est* (L.) That is.

590

**I.H.S.** for the Greek capitals IHC (a form of Greek Σ), the first three letters of the name Jesus, commonly misread as *Jesus Hominum Salvator* (L.) Jesus Saviour of Men.

**Imp.** Imperial.

**Imp.,** *imperator* (L.) Emperor.

**Incog.,** *incognito* (It.) Unknown.

**In lim.,** *in limine* (L.) At the outset.

**In loc.,** *in loco* (L.) In its place.

**Inst.** Instant—the present month.

**Int.** Interest.

**In trans.,** *in transitu* (L.) On the passage.

**Io.** Iowa.

**I.O.G.T.** Independent Order of Good Templars.

**I.O.U.** I owe you.

**I.P.D.,** *in praesentiâ Dominorum* (L.) In presence of the Lords (of Session).

**I.Q.,** *idem quod* (L.) The same as.

**J.P.** Justice of the Peace.

**Jr., Junr.** Junior.

**Kan.,** also **Ks.** Kansas.

**K.B.** Knight of the Bath, also King's Bench.

**K.C.B.** Knight Commander of the Bath.

**K.G.** Knight of the Garter.

**K.G.C.** Knight of the Grand Cross.

**K.G.C.B.** Knight of the Grand Cross of the Bath.

**K.L.H.** Knight of the Legion of Honour.

**Knt., Kt.** Knight.

**K.P.** Knight of St Patrick.

**K.T.** Knight of the Thistle.

**Ky.** Kentucky.

**L.A.C.** Licentiate of the Apothecaries' Company.

**Lat.** Latitude.

**Lb.,** *libra* (L.) A pound.

**L.C.** Lowercase (in printing).

**L.C.,** *loco citato* (L.) In the place cited.

**L.C.** Lower Canada.

**L.C.B.** Lord Chief-baron.

**L.C.J.** Lord Chief-justice.

**Ld.** Lord.

**Lib.,** *liber* (L.) Book.

**Lieut., Lt.** Lieutenant.

**Linn.** Linnæan, Linnæus.

**Lit.** Literally.

**LL.B.,** *Legum Baccalaureus* (L.) Bachelor of Laws.

**LL.D.,** *Legum Doctor* (L.) Doctor of Laws.

**L.M.** Long Metre.

**Lon., Long.** Longitude.

**Lond.** London.

**Loq.,** *loquitur* (L.) Speaks.

**Lou.** or **La.** Louisiana.

**L.P.** Lord Provost.

**L.S.** Left Side.

**L.S.,** *locus sigilli* (L.) Place of the Seal.

**L.S.D.,** *libræ, solidi, denarii* (L.) Pounds, shillings, pence.

**M., Mons., Monsieur** (Fr.) Mr or Sir.  **MM.** Gentlemen or Sirs.

**M.,** *mille* (L.) A thousand.

**M.** Married.

**M.A.** Master of Arts. See **A.M.**

**Mad., Madm.** Madam.

**Maj.** Major.

**Marq.** Marquis.

**Mass.** Massachusetts.

**M.B.,** *Medicinæ Baccalaureus* (L.) Bachelor of Medicine.

**M.B.,** *Musicæ Baccalaureus* (L.) Bachelor of Music.

**Md.** Maryland.

**M.D.,** *Medicinæ Doctor* (L.) Doctor of Medicine.

**Mdlle., Mlle., Mademoiselle** (Fr.) Miss.

**M.E.** Most Excellent.

**Mem.** Memorandum.

**Mem.,** *memento* (L.) Remember.

**Messrs., Messieurs** (Fr.) Sirs, Gentlemen.

**Mich.** Michigan.

**Minn.** Minnesota.

**Miss.** or **Mis.** Mississippi.

**Mme., Madame** (Fr.) Madam.

**M.N.S.** Member of the Numismatical Society.

**Mo.** Missouri, also Month.

**M.P.** Member of Parliament.

**M.P.S.** Member of the Philological Society.

**M.P.S.** Member of the Pharmaceutical Society.

**Mr.** Master or Mister.

**M.R.A.S.** Member of the Royal Asiatic Society.

**M.R.A.S.** Member of the Royal Academy of Sciences.

**M.R.C.C.** Member of the Royal College of Chemistry.

**M.R.C.P.** Member of the Royal College of Preceptors.

**M.R.C.S.** Member of the Royal College of Surgeons.

**M.R.G.S.** Member of the Royal Geographical Society.

**M.R.I.** Member of the Royal Institution.

**M.R.I.A.** Member of the Royal Irish Academy.

**Mrs.** Mistress.

**M.S.,** *memoriæ sacrum* (L.) Sacred to the Memory.

**MS.** Manuscript.

**MSS.** Manuscripts.

**Mt., Mts.** Mount, Mountains.

**Mus.** Music.

**Mus.B.** Bachelor of Music.

**Mus.D., Doc., Doct.** Doctor of Music.

**N.** North.

**N.B.** North Britain, North British, also New Brunswick.

**N.B.,** *nota bene* (L.) Note well, or take notice.

**N.C.** North Carolina.

**N.E.** North-east.

**Neb.** Nebraska.

**Nem. con.,** *nemine contradicente* (L.) No one contradicting.

**Nem. diss.,** *nemine dissentiente* (L.) No one dissenting.

**N.H.** New Hampshire.

**N.J.** New Jersey.

**N.N.E.** North-north-east.

# List of Abbreviations.

*N.N.W.* North-north-west.

*No., numero* (L.) Number. *Nos.* Numbers.

*Non-con.* Non-content.

*Non obst., non obstante* (L.) Notwithstanding.

*Non pros., non prosequitur* (L.) He does not prosecute.

*Non seq., non sequitur* (L.) It does not follow.

*Notts.* Nottinghamshire.

*N.S.* New Style.

*N.S.* Nova Scotia.

*N.T.* New Testament.

*N.W.* North-west.

*N.Y.* New York.

*Ob., obiit* (L.) Died.

*O.M.* Old Measurement.

*O.S.* Old Style.

*O.T.* Old Testament.

*Oxon., Oxonia* (L.) Oxford.

*Oz.* Ounce.

*P.* Page. *Pp.* Pages.

*Pa.*, also *Penn.* Pennsylvania.

*Par.* Paragraph.

*P.C., Patres Conscripti* (L.) Conscript Fathers.

*P.C.* Privy Councillor.

*Pd.* Paid.

*Per an., per annum* (L.) Per year, by the year.

*Per cent., per centum* (L.) By the hundred.

*Ph.B., Philosophiæ Baccalaureus* (L.) Bachelor of Philosophy.

*Ph.D., Philosophiæ Doctor* (L.) Doctor of Philosophy.

*Phil. Trans.* Philosophical Transactions.

*Pinx., Pxt., pinxit* (L.) He or she painted it.

*P.M., post meridiem* (L.) Afternoon, also Post Master.

*P.O.* Post-office.

*P.O.C.* Peninsular and Oriental Company.

*P.O.O.* Post-office order.

*Pop.* Population.

*P.P.C., pour prendre congé* (Fr.) To take leave.

*P.R., Populus Romanus* (L.) The Roman People.

*P.R.A.* President of the Royal Academy.

*Pres.*, also *Preses.* President.

*Prof.* Professor.

*Pro tem., pro tempore* (L.) For the time being.

*Prox., proximo* (L.) Next.

*P.R.S.* President of the Royal Society.

*P.S., post scriptum* (L.) Postscript, written after.

*P.T.* Post-town.

*P.T.O.* Please turn over.

*Pub. Doc.* Public document.

*Q., Qu.* Query, Question.

*Q.B.* Queen's Bench.

*Q.C.* Queen's Counsel.

*Q.D., quasi dicat* (L.) As if he should say.

*Q.E., quod est* (L.) Which is.

*Q.E.D., quod erat demonstrandum* (L.) Which was to be demonstrated.

*Q.E.F., quod erat faciendum* (L.) Which was to be done.

*Q.E.I., quod erat inveniendum* (L.) Which was to be found out.

*Q.L., quantum libet* (L.) As much as you please.

*Q.M.G.* Quartermaster-general.

*Qr.* Quarter.

*Q.S.* Quarter Sessions.

*Q.S., Quantum suff., quantum sufficit* (L.) A sufficient quantity.

*Qt.* Quart.

*Q.V., quod vide* (L.) Which see.

*R., rex, regina* (L.) King, queen.

*R., recipe* (L.) Take.

*R.A.* Royal Academy, Academician, or Artillery.

*R.C.* Roman Catholic.

*R.E.* Royal Engineers.

*Rec.* Recipe.

*Recd.* Received.

*Recpt.* Receipt.

*Ref. Ch.* Reformed Church.

*Reg. Prof.* Regius Professor.

*Regt.* Regiment.

*Rev., Revd.* Reverend.

*R.H.A.* Royal Horse Artillery.

*R.H.G.* Royal Horse Guards.

*R.I.* Rhode Island.

*R.I.P., requiescat in pace* (L.) May he (or she) rest in peace.

*R.M.* Royal Mail, Royal Marines.

*R.M.A.* Royal Military Asylum.

*R.M.S.* Royal Mail Steamer.

*R.N.* Royal Navy.

*Rom. Cath.* Roman Catholic.

*R.S.A.* Royal Society of Antiquaries, Royal Scottish Academy.

*R.S.D.* Royal Society of Dublin.

*R.S.E.* Royal Society of Edinburgh.

*R.S.L.* Royal Society of London.

*R.S.S.*, also *S.R.S., Regiæ Societatis Socius* (L.) Fellow of the Royal Society.

*Rt. Hon.* Right Honourable.

*Rt. Rev.* Right Reverend.

*Rt. W., Wpful.* Right Worshipful.

*R.V.* Rifle Volunteers.

*S.* South, Saint.

*Sarum.* Salisbury.

*Sc., Scil., scilicet* (L.) To wit, namely, being understood.

*Sc., Sculp., Sculpt., sculpsit* (L.) He or she engraved it.

*S.C.* South Carolina.

*Sc.B., Scientiæ Baccalaureus* (L.) Bachelor of Science.

*Sc.D., Scientiæ Doctor* (L.) Doctor of Science.

*Schr.* Schooner.

*S.E.* South-east.

*Sec., Secy.* Secretary.

*Seq., sequentes* or *sequentia* (L.) The following.

*Serg., Sergt. ; Serj., Serjt.* Sergeant, Serjeant.

*S.M.* Short Metre.

*S.M. Lond. Soc., Societatis Me-* *dicæ Londiniensis Socius* (L.) Member of the London Medical Society.

*Sol.-gen.* Solicitor-general.

*S.P.C.K.* Society for Promoting Christian Knowledge.

*S.P.G.* Society for the Propagation of the Gospel.

*S.P.Q.R., Senatus Populusque Romanus* (L.) The Senate and People of Rome.

*Sq.* Square.

*S.s.* Steamship. [preme Courts.

*S.S.C.* Solicitor before the Su-

*S.S.E.* South-south-east.

*S.S.W.* South-south-west.

*St.* Saint.

*S.T.P., Sanctæ Theologiæ Professor* (L.) Professor of Theology.

*Supp.* Supplement.

*Surv.-gen.* Surveyor-general.

*S.V., sub voce* (L.) Under the word or title.

*S.W.* South-west.

*Tal. qual., talis qualis* (L.) Just as they come, average quantity.

*Ten.* or *Tenn.* Tennessee.

*Text Rec.* The Received Text.

*T.O.* Turn Over.

*Tom.* Tome or volume.

*U.C.* Upper Canada.

*U.K.* United Kingdom.

*Ult., ultimo* (L.) Last.

*U.P.* United Presbyterian.

*U.S., ut supra* (L.) As above.

*U.S.* United States.

*U.S.A.* United States of America.

*V., versus* (L.) Against.

*V., vide* (L.) See.

*Va.* Virginia.

*V.C.* Vice-chancellor.

*V.C.* Victoria Cross.

*Ven.* Venerable. [ample.

*V.G., verbi gratiâ* (L.) For ex-

*Vis., Visc.* Viscount.

*Viz., videlicet* (L.) Namely.

*Vol., Vols.* Volume, Volumes.

*V.R., Victoria Regina* (L.) Queen Victoria.

*V.S.* Veterinary Surgeon.

*Vt.* Vermont.

*Vul.* Vulgate.

*W.* West.

*W.I.* West Indies.

*W.C.* Water-closet.

*W.C.* Western Central.

*Wis.* Wisconsin.

*W.N.W.* West-north-west.

*Wp., Wfl.* Worshipful.

*W.S.* Writer to the Signet.

*W.S.W.* West-south-west.

*X.* or *Xt.* Christ. (*X.* = Gr. *Ch.*)

*Xm., Xmas.* Christmas.

*Xn., Xtian.* Christian.

*Y., Yr.* Year.

*Yd.* Yard.

*Ye.* The, thee.

*Yr.* Your, younger.

*&.* And.

*&c., et cetera* (L.) And so forth.

*4to.* Quarto.

*8vo.* Octavo.

*12mo.* Duodecimo.

# PRONOUNCING VOCABULARY OF SCRIPTURE PROPER NAMES.

[This vocabulary contains all common Scripture Names except monosyllables and dissyllables, the latter being always accented on the first syllable. *Ch* has the sound of *k*, and so has *c*, except when marked ç, to indicate the sound of *s*: *g* is hard, except when marked otherwise.]

A-bad'don.
Ab'a-na.
Ab'a-rim.
A-bed'ne-go.
A-bel-Me-hō'lath.
A-bel-Miz'ra-im.
A-bel-Shit'tim.
A-bi'a.
A-bi'a-thar.
A-bi-e'zer.
Ab'i-gail.
A-bī'hū.
A-bi'jah.
A-bī'jam.
Ab-i-lē'ne.
A-bim'e-lech.
A-bin'a-dab.
A-bī'ram.
Ab'i-shag.
A-bish'a-ī.
A'bra-ham.
Ab'sa-lom.
A-çel'da-ma.
A-chā'ia ('ya).
A-dī'no.
A-don-i-bē'zek.
Ad-o-nī'jah.
Ad-o-nī'ram.
A-don-i-zē'dek.
A-dram'me-lech.
Ad-ra-myt'ti-um.
A'dri-a.
A'dri-el.
A-dul'lam.
Ag'a-bus.
A-grip'pa.
A-has-ū-ē'rus.
A-ha-zī'ah.
A-hī'jah.
A-him'a-az.
A-him'e-lech.
A-hin'o-am.
A-hith'o-phel.
A-hī'tub.
A-hō'li-ab.
A-hol'i-bah.
Aj'a-lon.
Al-ex-an'dri-a.
Al-phæ'us (-fē').
Al-tas'chith.
Am'a-lek-īte.
Am'a-na.
Am'a-sa *or* A-mā'sa.
Am-a-zī'ah.
A-min'a-dab.
Am'mon-īte.
Am'o-rīte.
Am-phip'o-lis.
592

Am'ra-phel.
An'a-kim.
A-nam'me-lech.
An-a-nī'as.
An'a-thoth.
An-dro-nī'cus.
An'ti-och.
An'ti-pas.
An-tip'a-tris.
A-pel'lēs ('lēz).
Ap-ol-lō'ni-a.
A-pol'los.
A-pol'ly-on.
Ap'pi-ī Fō'rum.
Aq'ui-la.
A-rā'bi-an.
Ar'a-rat.
Ar'au'nah.
Ar-che-lā'us.
Arc-tū'rus.
Ar-e-op'a-gus.
Ar'e-tas.
A'ri-el.
Ar-i-ma-thē'a.
A'ri-och.
Ar-is-tar'chus.
Ar-is-to-bū'lus.
Ar-ma-ged'don.
Ar-mē'ni-a.
Ar'o-er.
Ar'te-mas.
A-ru'mah.
As'a-hel.
As'e-nath.
Ash'ke-naz.
Ash'ta-roth.
A-si-a (ā'shi-a).
As'ke-lon.
As-syr'i-a.
Ath-a-lī'ah.
At-ta-lī'a.
Au-gus'tus.
Az-a-rī'ah.
A-zō'tus.

Bā'al-ah.
Bā-al-bē'rith.
Bā'al-gad.
Bā-al-hā'zor.
Bā-al-her'mon.
Bā-al-mē'on.
Bā-al-pē'or.
Bā-al-per'a-zim.
Bā-al-shal'i-sha.
Bā-al-tā'mar.
Bā-al-zē'bub.
Bā-al-zē'phon.
Bā'a-sha.
Bab'y-lon.

Ba-hū'rim.
Ba-rab'bas.
Bar'na-bas.
Bar'sa-bas.
Bar-thol'o-mew.
Bar-ti-mē'us.
Bar-zil'la-ī.
Bath'shē-ba.
Be-el'ze-bub.
Bē-er-la-hāi'roi.
Be-ē'roth.
Bē'er-shē-ba.
Bē'he-moth.
Bē'li-al.
Bel-shaz'zar.
Bel-te-shaz'zar.
Be-nā'iah ('ya).
Ben-hā'dad.
Ben'ja-min.
Be-rē'a.
Ber-nī'çe.
Be-rō'dach-bal'a-dan.
Beth-ab'a-ra.
Beth'a-ny.
Beth-ar'bel.
Beth-a'ven.
Be-thes'da (-thez').
Beth-hō'ron.
Beth'le-hem.
Beth-mā'a-chah.
Beth-pē'or.
Beth'pha-gē (-jē).
Beth-sāi'da.
Beth-shē'mesh.
Be-thū'el.
Be-zal'e-el.
Bi-thyn'i-a.
Bō-a-ner'gēs ('jēz).

Cā'ia-phas ('ya-fas).
Cal'va-ry.
Cā'naan-īte.
Can'da-çē.
Ca-per'na-um.
Cap-pa-dō'ci-a ('shi).
Car'che-mish.
Cen'chre-a (sen').
Ces-a-rē'a (ses-).
Chal-dē'an.
Ched-or-lā'o-mer.
Chem'a-rims.
Cher'eth-ītes.
Chin'ne-reth.
Cho-rā'zin.
Chū-shan-rish-a-thā'im.
Ci-lic-i-a (si-lish'i-a).
Cin'ne-roth (sin').

Clau'di-a.
Clau'di-us.
Clē'o-phas.
Co-los'se.
Co-nī'ah.
Cor-nē'li-us.
Cy-rē'ne (sī-).
Cy-rē'ni-us (sī-).

Dal-ma-nū'tha.
Dal-mā'ti-a ('shi).
Dam'a-ris.
Da-mas'cus.
Dan'i-el.
Da-rī'us.
Deb'o-rah.
De-cap'o-lis.
Del'i-lah.
De-mē'tri-us.
Dī-ā'na *or* Dī-an'a.
Dī-o-nys'i-us (nīzh').
Dī-ot're-phēs (-fēz).
Dru-sil'la.

Ē-bed-mē'lech.
Eb-en-ē'zer.
E'dom-īte.
Ed're-ī.
E-le-ā'leh.
E-le-ā'zar.
El-e-lō'he-Is'ra-el.
El-hā'nan.
E-lī'ab.
E-lī'a-kim.
E-lī'a-shib.
E-lī-ē'zer.
E-lī'hū.
E-lī'jah.
E-lim'e-lech.
El'i-phaz.
E-lī'sha.
E-lish'e-ba.
El'ka-nah.
El'la-sar.
El'na-than.
E-lō'ī.
El'y-mas.
Em'ma-us.
E'ne-as.
En-eg-lā'im.
En-gē'dī.
En-rō'gel.
Ep'a-phras.
E-paph-ro-dī'tus.
Eph'e-sus.
E'phra-im.
Eph'ra-tah.
Ep-i-cū-rē'ans.
E-ras'tus.

Ē-sar-had'don.
Es-drē'lon.
Esh'ta-ol.
E-thi-ō'pi-a.
Eū-nī'çe.
Eū-ō'di-as.
Eū-phrā'tēs ('tēz).
Eū-roc'ly-don.
E̅ū'ty-chus.
E-vil-me-rō'dach.
Ex'o-dus.
E-zē'ki-el.
E-zi-on-gā'ber.

For-tū-nā'tus.

Gab'ba-tha.
Gā'bri-el.
Gad-a-rēnes' (-rēnz').
Ga-lā'ti-a (-lā'shi-a).
Gal'e-ed.
Gal-i-lē'an.
Gal'i-lee.
Gal'li-o.
Ga-mā'li-el.
Ged-a-lī'ah.
Ge-dē'roth.
Ge-hā'zī.
Gem-a-rī'ah.
Ge-nes'a-reth (orje-).
Gen'e-sis (jen').
Ger-ge-sēnes' (-sēnz').
Ger'i-zim.
Geth-sem'a-ne.
Gib'be-thon.
Gib'e-ah.
Gib'e-on.
Gid'e-on.
Gil-bō'a.
Gil'e-ad.
Gir'ga-shīte.
Gol'go-tha.
Go-lī'ath.
Go-mor'rah.

Hab'ak-kuk.
Hach'i-lah.
Had-ad-ē'zer.
Hā-dad-rim'mon.
Hā-gar-ēnes' (-ēnz').
Hag'ga-ī.
Ha-nan'e-el.
Ha-nā'nī.
Han-a-nī'ah.
Ha-rō'sheth.
Hav'i-lah.
Hā-voth-jā'ir.
Haz'a-el.
Heph'zi-bah.

Her-mog′e-nēs (-moj′e-nēz).
He-rō′di-ans.
He-rō′di-as.
He-rō′di-on.
Hez-e-kī′ah.
Hid′de-kel.
Hī-e-rap′o-lis.
Hig-gā′ion (′yon).
Hil-kī′ah.
Ho-sē′a (-zē′).
Ho-shē′a.
Hȳ-me-nē′us.

Ich′a-bod.
I-cō′ni-um.
Id-u-mē′a.
Il-lyr′i-cum.
Im-man′ū-el.
I-sā-iah (ī-zā′ya).
Is-car′i-ot.
Ish-bō′sheth.
Ish′ma-el.
Ish′ma-el-īte.
Is′ra-el (iz′).
Is′ra-el-īte (iz′).
Is′sa-char.
Ith′a-mar.
It′ta-ī.
It-ū-rē′a.

Jā-besh-gil′e-ad.
Jab′ne-el.
Ja-ī′rus.
Jeb′ū-sīte.
Jec-o-nī′ah.
Jed′ū-thun.
Jē-gar-sā-ha-dū′tha.
Je-hō′a-haz.
Je-hō′ash.
Je-hoi′a-chin.
Je-hoi′a-da.
Je-hoi′a-kim.
Je-hon′a-dab.
Je-hō′ram.
Je-hosh′a-phat.
Je-hosh′e-ba.
Je-hō-vah-jī′reh.
Je-hō-vah-nis′sī.
Je-hō-vah-shā′lom.
Jer-e-mī′ah.
Jer′i-chō.
Jer-o-bō′am.
Je-rub′ba-al.
Je-ru′sa-lem.
Jesh′i-mon.
Jesh′ū-run.
Jez′e-bel.
Jez′re-el.
Jo-an′na.
Joch′e-bed.
Jo-hā′nan.
Jon′a-dab.
Jon′a-than.
Josh′ū-a.
Jo-sī′ah.
Joz′a-char.
Jū-dē′a.
Jū′li-us.
Jū′pi-ter.

2 L

Kad′mon-ītes.
Ked′e-moth.
Ken′niz-zītes.
Kē′ri-oth.
Ke-tū′rah.
Kib-roth-hat-tā′a-vah.
Kir-hē′res.
Kir-jath-ā′im.
Kir-jath-ar′ba.
Kir-jath-hū′zoth.
Kir-jath-jē′a-rim.

La-hāi′roi.
La-od-i-çē′a.
La-sē′a.
Laz′a-rus.
Leb′a-non.
Leb-bē′us.
Lem′ū-el.
Le-vī′a-than.
Lib′er-tines (-tinz).
Lib′y-a.
Lo-am′mī.
Lo-rū′ha-mah.
Lu′ci-fer.
Lu-ci-us (lu′shi-us).
Lyc-a-ō′ni-a.
Lyc-i-a (lish′i-a).
Lyd′i-a.
Ly-sā′ni-as.
Lys-i-as (lish′i-as).

Mā′a-cah.
Maç-e-dō′ni-a.
Mach-pē′lah.
Mag′da-la.
Mā′ha-lath.
Mā-ha-nā′im.
Mā-her-shal-al-hash′baz.
Mak-hē′dah.
Mal′a-chī.
Man′a-en.
Ma-nas′seh.
Ma-nō′ah.
Mar-a-nath′a.
Ma-rē′shah.
Mat-ta-nī′ah.
Mat-thī′as (math-).
Maz′za-roth.
Med′e-ba.
Me-gid′do.
Mel-chiz′e-dek.
Mel′i-ta.
Men′a-hem.
Me-phib′o-sheth.
Mer′a-rī.
Mer-a-thā′im.
Mer′i-bah.
Me-rō-dach-bal′a-dan.
Mes-o-po-tā′mi-a.
Mes-sī′ah.
Mē-theg-am′mah.
Me-thū′se-lah.
Mī-cā′iah (′ya).
Mī′cha-el.
Mī-chā′iah (′ya).
Mid′i-an-īte.
Mī-lē′tus.

Mir′i-am.
Mit-y-lē′ne.
Miz′ra-im.
Mō′ab-īte.
Mor′de-cāi.
Mo-rī′ah.
Mys-i-a (mizh′i-a).

Nā′a-man.
Nā′ioth (′yoth).
Nā′o-mī.
Naph′ta-lī.
Na-than′a-el.
Naz-a-rēne′.
Naz′a-reth.
Naz-a-rīte.
Ne-ap′o-lis.
Ne-bā′ioth (′yoth).
Neb-u-chad-nez′zar.
Neb-u-zar-ā′dan.
Neg′i-noth.
Nē-he-mī′ah.
Nē′hi-loth.
Ne-hush′tan.
Neth′i-nims.
Nī-cā′nor.
Nic-o-dē′mus.
Nic-o-lā′i-tans.
Nic′o-las.
Nī-cop′o-lis.
Nin′e-veh.

Ob-a-dī′ah.
Ō-bed-ē′dom.
O′me-ga or O-mē′ga.
O-nes′i-mus.
On-e-siph′o-rus.
O-rī′on.
Oth′ni-el.

Pā-dan-ā′ram.
Pal′es-tīne.
Pam-phyl′i-a.
Par′me-nas.
Par′thi-ans.
Par-vā′im.
Pat′a-ra.
Pek-a-hī′ah.
Pel-a-tī′ah.
Pē′leth-ītes.
Pe-nī′el.
Pe-nū′el.
Per′a-zim.
Pē-rez-uz′zah.
Per′ga-mos.
Per′iz-zīte.
Per-si-a (per′shi-a).
Phal′ti-el.
Phā-raōh-hoph′ra (fā′ro or fā′ra-o).
Phā-raōh-nē′choh.
Phar′i-see.
Phe-nī′çe.
Phe-nic′i-a (-nish′).
Phil-a-del′phi-a.
Phī-lē′mon.
Phī-lē′tus.
Phi-lip′pī.
Phil′is-tine (-tin).
Phin′e-as.
Phryg′i-a (frij′).

Pī-ha-hī′roth.
Pir′a-thon.
Pī-sid′i-a.
Plē′ia-dēs (′ya-dēz).
Pot′i-phar.
Po-tiph′e-rah.
Pris-çil′la.
Proch′o-rus.
Ptol-e-mā′is (tol-).
Pub′li-us.
Pu-tē′o-lī.

Rā′a-mah.
Ra-am′sēs (′sēz).
Rab′sha-kēh.
Ra-gū′el.
Rā-math-ā′im.
Rā-math-lē′hī.
Ra-mē′sēs (′sēz).
Rā-moth-gil′e-ad.
Re-bek′ah.
Rē′chab-ītes.
Rē-ho-bō′am.
Re-hō′both.
Reph′a-im.
Reph′i-dim.
Rhē′gi-um (rē′ji-).

Sa-bā′oth.
Sa-bē′ans.
Sad′du-cees (-sēz).
Sal′a-mis.
Sal-mō′ne.
Sa-lō′mē.
Sa-mā′ri-a.
Sa-mar′i-tan.
Sam-o-thrā′ci-a (-thrā′shi-a).
Sam′ū-el.
San-bal′lat.
Sap-phī′ra (saf-fī′).
Sa-rep′ta.
Scyth′i-an (sith′).
Se-cun′dus.
Se-leū′ci-a (-shi-a).
Sen-nach′e-rib.
Seph′a-rad.
Seph-ar-vā′im.
Ser-a-ī′ah.
Ser′gi-us (ji-).
Shal′i-sha.
Shal-ma-nē′ser (′zer).
Sha-rē′zer.
Shem-a-ī′ah.
Shem′i-nith.
Sheph-a-tī′ah.
Shesh-baz′zar.
Shē′thar-boz′na-ī.
Shib′bo-leth.
Shig-gā′ion (-yun).
Shim′e-ī.
Sho-shan′nim.
Shū′lam-īte.
Sī-lō′am or Sil′o-am.
Sil-vā′nus.
Sim′e-on.
Sī′ri-on.
Sis′e-ra.
Sod′om-ītes.
Sol′o-mon.

Sop′a-ter.
So-sip′a-ter.
Sos′the-nēs (-nēz).
Steph′a-nas.
Suk′ki-ims (-imz).
Su-san′na.
Sy-ē′ne.
Syn′ti-chē.
Syr′a-cūse.
Syr′i-a.
Sȳ-ro-phe-nic-i-an (-nish′i-an).

Tā′a-nach.
Tab′e-rah.
Tab′i-tha.
Ta-hap′a-nēs (-nēz).
Tah′pe-nēs (-nēz).
Tap′pū-ah.
Te-kō′ah.
Ter′a-phim.
Ter′ti-us (-shi-us).
Ter-tul′lus.
Thad-dæ′us (-dē′).
The-oph′i-lus.
Thes-sa-lo-nī′ca.
Thȳ-a-tī′ra.
Tī-bē′ri-as.
Tī-bē′ri-us.
Tig-lath-pi-lē′ser (′zer).
Tim-nath-hē′rēs (′rēz).
Tim′o-thy.
Tir′ha-kah.
Tir′sha-tha.
To-bī′ah.
To-bī′jah.
To-gar′mah.
Trach-o-nī′tis.
Tro-gyl′li-um (-jil′).
Troph′i-mus.
Trȳ-phē′na.
Tū′bal-cāin.
Tych′i-cus.
Tȳ-ran′nus.

U-phar′sin (ū-).
U-rī′ah (ū-).
U-rī′jah (ū-).
Uz-zī′ah.

Zac-chē′us.
Zach-a-rī′ah.
Zach-a-rī′as.
Zal-mun′na.
Zam-zum′mim.
Zar′e-phath.
Zar′e-tan.
Zeb′e-dee.
Ze-bō′im.
Zeb′ū-lun.
Zech-a-rī′ah.
Zed-e-kī′ah.
Ze-lō′phe-had.
Zem-a-rā′im.
Zeph-a-nī′ah.
Zeph′a-thah.
Ze-rub′ba-bel.
Zer-ū-ī′ah.
Zip-pō′rah.

# SELECT LIST OF MYTHOLOGICAL AND CLASSICAL NAMES.

**Achates**, a-kā′tēz, the armour-bearer and faithful friend of Æneas.

**Acheron**, ak′e-ron, a river of the lower world, round which the shades hover.

**Achilles**, a-kil′lēz, the son of Peleus and Thetis, and the bravest of the Greeks in the war against Troy. He was invulnerable, except in his right heel, in which he was mortally wounded, through treachery, by Paris. His quarrel with Agamemnon is the subject of Homer's *Iliad*.

**Actæon**, ak-tē′on, a famous hunter who, having accidentally seen Diana and her nymphs bathing, was changed by the goddess into a stag, and torn to pieces by his own dogs.

**Adonis**, a-dō′nis, a beautiful youth beloved by Venus. He was killed by a wild boar during the chase, and from his blood the anemone sprung. His worship was of Phœnician origin.

**Æacus**, ē′a-kus, one of the judges in Hades.

**Ægeus**, ē-jē′us, a king of Athens who, believing his son Theseus to have perished in his expedition against the Minotaur, threw himself into the sea, hence called the Ægean.

**Æneas**, ē-nē′as, a Trojan prince, son of Anchises and Venus, the ancestral hero of the Romans, and as such the hero of Virgil's *Æneid*.

**Æolus**, ē′o-lus, the god and king of the winds, which he kept inclosed under a mountain.

**Æsculapius**, es-kū-lā′pi-us, son of Apollo, the 'blameless physician' of Homer, killed by Jupiter, to keep men from escaping death altogether, and afterwards deified. His descendants had a secret and hereditary knowledge of the medical art.

**Agamemnon**, ag-a-mem′non, son of Atreus, leader of the Greeks before Troy, murdered on his return home by Ægisthus, with the connivance of his own wife Clytemnestra.

**Aganippe**, ag-a-nip′pē, a fountain at the foot of Mount Helicon, sacred to the Muses.

**Aglaia**, a-glā′i-a, 'the bright one,' one of the Graces.

**Ajax**, ā′jaks, son of Telamon, a Grecian hero in the Trojan war, second only to Achilles in valour. Unsuccessful in his struggle with Ulysses for the armour of Achilles, he killed himself.

**Alcestis**, al-ses′tis, wife of Admetus, died in the stead of her husband, but was brought back to him from the lower world by Hercules.

**Alecto**, a-lek′to, one of the Eumenides or Furies.

**Ammon**, am′mon, a title of Jupiter.

**Amphion**, am-fī′on, a king of Thebes who received from Hermes (Mercury) a lyre, on which he played with such magic skill that the stones moved of their accord and formed the city wall.

**Amphitrite**, am-fi-trī′tē, the wife of Poseidon (Neptune), and mother of Triton.

**Andromache**, an-drom′a-kē, the wife of Hector.

**Andromeda**, an-drom′e-da, the daughter of an Ethiopian king, rescued from a sea-monster by Perseus, who married her.

**Antæus**, an-tē′us, a giant overcome by Hercules.

**Aphrodite**, af-rō-dī′tē, the Greek goddess of love and beauty, the mother of Eros (Cupid), identified with the Roman Venus.

**Apis**, ā′pis, the bull worshipped by the Egyptians.

**Apollo**, a-pol′lo, twin-son with Diana of Jupiter and Latona; the god of prophecy, of song, and of music. See **Phœbus**.

**Arachne**, a-rak′nē, a Lydian maiden who challenged Athena to a trial of skill in spinning, and was by her changed into a spider.

**Ares**, ā′rēz, the Greek form of Mars, god of war.

**Arethusa**, ar-e-thū′sa, one of the Nereids, and the nymph of a celebrated fountain near Syracuse.

**Argus**, ar′gus, the keeper with a hundred eyes, appointed by Hera to watch the cow into which Io had been changed. He was lulled to sleep and killed by Hermes, by command of Zeus. Hera gave his eyes to the tail of the peacock.

**Ariadne**, ar-i-ad′nē, daughter of Minos, king of Crete. She guided Theseus out of the labyrinth of Crete, but was abandoned by him at Naxos, and was afterwards married to Dionysus.

**Arion**, a-rī′on, a famous Greek bard and citharaplayer, who, when cast into the sea by robbers, was carried safe to land by a dolphin which he had charmed by his music.

**Ascanius**, as-kā′ni-us, the son of Æneas.

**Astræa**, as-trē′a, daughter of Zeus and Themis, and the goddess of justice. She lived among men during the golden age.

**Atalanta**, at-a-lant′a, (1) of Bœotia, celebrated for her swiftness, conquered by Hippomenes or by Milanion in running, by the stratagem of dropping three golden apples in the race, and married by him. (2) of Arcadia, a sharer in the Calydonian boar-hunt, passionately loved by Meleager.

**Ate**, ā′tē, the Greek goddess of mischief.

**Athena**, a-thē′na, a Greek goddess, identified with the Roman Minerva.

**Atlantis**, at-lant′is, a great and beautiful island in the Atlantic Ocean, sunk in the sea when its inhabitants became impious.

**Atlas**, at′las, the leader of the Titans in their conflict with Zeus. Being conquered, he was condemned to bear heaven on his head and hands.

**Atropos**, at′ro-pos, 'the inevitable,' one of the Fates.

**Aurora**, aw-rō′ra, the Greek Eos, the goddess of the dawn.

**Avernus**, a-vér′nus, a lake near the entrance to the lower world—the lower world itself.

**Bacchus**, bak′us, the god of wine, son of Jupiter and Semele, daughter of Cadmus.

**Bellerophon**, bel-lér′o-fon, the rider of the winged horse Pegasus, and the destroyer of the Chimæra.

**Bellona**, bel-lō′na, the Roman goddess of war, sister of Mars.

**Briareus**, brī′a-rūs, or **Ægæon**, ē-jē′on, a giant with a hundred arms, the son of Uranus by Gaia. He aided Zeus in his struggle with the Titans.

**Bucephalus**, bū-sef′a-lus, the favourite charger of Alexander the Great.

594

# Select List of Mythological and Classical Names.

**Cacus**, kā′kus, son of Vulcan, a giant and notorious robber. Having stolen the cattle of Hercules, he was killed by him.

**Cadmus**, kad′mus, the mythical founder of Thebes in Bœotia, and the first to introduce alphabetic writing among the Greeks.

**Calchas**, kal′kas, the wisest of the Greek soothsayers at the siege of Troy.

**Calliope**, kal-lī′o-pē, the Muse of epic poetry.

**Calypso**, kal-ip′so, a nymph who inhabited the island of Ogygia, on which Ulysses was shipwrecked. She loved him, and delayed his voyage for seven years.

**Cassandra**, kas-san′dra, a daughter of Priam, king of Troy, beloved by Apollo, who gave her the gift of prophecy, but not of being believed.

**Castor**, kas′tor, and **Pollux**, pol′luks, twin-brothers, the former mortal, the latter immortal, who, from their love to each other, were placed by Jupiter as a constellation in heaven under the name of Gemini, 'the twins.'

**Cecrops**, sē′krops, the first king of Attica, and founder of the Cecropia or citadel at Athens.

**Cerberus**, sėr′bėr-us, the three-headed dog that guarded the entrance to the lower world.

**Ceres**, sē′rēz, the Greek Demeter, goddess of agriculture, especially of corn, sister of Jupiter, and mother of Proserpine.

**Charon**, kā′ron, the son of Erebus, ferried the souls of the dead over the rivers Acheron and Styx, receiving for this service the obolus placed in every corpse's mouth before burial.

**Charybdis**, ka-rib′dis, a dangerous whirlpool between Italy and Sicily, and opposite to Scylla.

**Chiron**, kī′ron, a centaur celebrated for his knowledge of medicine and music, the tutor of Æsculapius, Achilles, and Hercules. Accidentally wounded by one of the poisoned arrows of Hercules, he gave up his immortality, and was changed into the constellation Sagittarius.

**Chloris**, klō′ris, wife of Zephyrus, the Greek goddess of flowers; identical with the Roman Flora.

**Circe**, sir′sē, daughter of Helios and Perse, a sorceress who detained Ulysses on his way home from Troy, converting his men into swine.

**Clio**, klī′o, the Muse of history.

**Clotho**, klō′tho, the spinner of the thread of life, the youngest of the Fates.

**Cocytus**, ko-sī′tus, a river in the lower world.

**Comus**, kō′mus, a god of mirth and joy, represented as a winged youth.

**Corybantes**, kor-i-ban′tes, priests of Cybele or Rhea, in Phrygia, who worshipped her with wild dances to the sound of cymbals.

**Crœsus**, krē′sus, a king of Lydia, of boundless wealth.

**Cupid**, kū′pid, the Greek **Eros**, the god of love, son of Venus, represented as a mischievous boy with arrows, which he aims at gods and men alike.

**Cybele**, sib′e-lē, a goddess originally Phrygian, worshipped at Rome also as Ops.

**Cynthia**, sin′thi-a, Diana, so called from Mount Cynthus, in Delos, her birthplace.

**Cytherea**, sith-ėr-ē′a, Venus, so called from the island of Cythera, where she was worshipped.

**Dædalus**, dē′da-lus, the builder of the Cretan labyrinth, who was shut up by Minos, but escaped by means of artificial wings.

**Damocles**, dam′o-klēz, a flatterer of the tyrant Dionysius. Having lauded highly the happiness of kings, he had his views altered on finding a keen-edged sword suspended by a single horse-hair over his head, as he sat at a banquet.

**Damon**, dā′mon, and **Phintias**, fin′ti-as, two noble Pythagoreans of Syracuse, remembered as models of faithful friendship.

**Danae**, dan′a-ē, the mother of Perseus by Jupiter, visited by the god in a shower of gold, when immured in a tower by her father's order.

**Daphne**, daf′nē, a nymph beloved by Apollo, and turned into a laurel-tree.

**Dejanira**, dej-a-nī′ra, wife of Hercules. Having unwittingly caused his death, she killed herself.

**Delos**, dē′los, the smallest of the Cyclades, a floating island, until Jupiter made it stationary, in order to be a safe resting-place for Latona, and the birthplace of Apollo and Diana.

**Delphi**, del′fī, a small town in Phocis, the Pytho of Homer, celebrated for its oracle of Apollo.

**Deucalion**, dū-kā′li-on, son of Prometheus, with his wife Pyrrha, the sole survivor of the deluge.

**Diana**, dī-ā′na, twin-sister of Apollo, the virgin goddess of the moon and of hunting, identified by the Romans with the Greek Artemis.

**Dido**, dī′do, daughter of the Tyrian king Belus, and the reputed foundress of Carthage. She fell in love with Æneas, the Trojan hero, but not finding her love returned, killed herself.

**Dionysus**, dī-on-ī′sus, the Greek Bacchus.

**Dodona**, do-dō′na, a city of Epirus, famed for an oracle of Jupiter, where the responses were given by the wind rustling through oak-trees.

**Dracon**, drā′kon, the author of the first written code of laws at Athens, in which the penalty of death was attached even to petty crimes.

**Egeria**, e-gēr′i-a, one of the Camenæ or prophetic nymphs of Roman mythology, who dictated to Numa Pompilius his forms of worship.

**Eleusis**, el-ū′sis, a very ancient city of Greece, famous for its mysteries of Ceres.

**Endymion**, en-dim′i-on, a youth celebrated for his beauty, and the perpetual sleep in which he was wrapped by the Moon, in order that she might kiss him without his knowledge.

**Eos**, ē′os. See **Aurora**.

**Erato**, er′a-to, the Muse of amatory poetry.

**Erebus**, er′e-bus, son of Chaos, brother of Nox, the god of darkness, also the lower world.

**Euphrosyne**, ū-fros′i-nē, one of the Graces.

**Europa**, ū-rō′pa, the daughter of Agenor, carried off by Jupiter into Crete under the form of a white bull. The continent of Europe was named after her.

**Eurus**, ū′rus, the east wind.

**Eurydice**, ū-rid′i-sē, the wife of Orpheus. When she died, he followed her to Hades, and by the charms of his lyre won her back from Pluto on condition that he would not look back at her upon the way. This his love made him forget, and she returned to the lower world.  [music.

**Euterpe**, ū-tėr′pē, the Muse of lyric poetry and

**Fates**, three goddesses who determined the birth, life, and death of man—Clotho, Lachesis, and Atropos.

**Flora**, flō′ra, the Roman goddess of flowers.

**Furies**, three goddesses of vengeance—Alecto, Megæra, and Tisiphone.

**Ganymede**, gan′i-mēd, son of Tros, for his beauty carried off from Mount Ida by the eagle of Jupiter to be the cup-bearer of the gods.

**Geryon**, gē′ri-on, a giant king in Spain, whose oxen were carried off by Hercules.

**Glaucus**, glaw′kus, a fisherman who was changed into a sea-god.

**Gorgons**, gor′gons, three female monsters, who turned all they looked upon into stone—Medusa, Euryale, and Stheno.

**Graces**, three attendants of Venus, of great beauty—Aglaia, Thalia, and Euphrosyne.

**Hebe,** hē′bē, the goddess of youth, daughter of Juno, cup-bearer to the gods, and wife of Hercules after he was deified.

**Hecate,** hek′a-tē or hek′āt, a goddess often identified with Diana on earth, Luna in heaven, and Proserpine in the lower world, and therefore represented with three heads.

**Hector,** hek′tor, the son of Priam, king of Troy, and husband of Andromache; the bravest of the Trojans, slain, and dragged three times round the walls of Troy, by Achilles.

**Hecuba,** hek′ū-ba, wife of Priam, and mother of Hector, noted for her misfortunes after the fall of Troy.

**Helena,** hel′e-na, daughter of Jupiter and Leda, sister of Castor, Pollux, and Clytemnestra, wife of Menelaus, and the greatest beauty of her day. She caused the Trojan war by eloping with Paris, son of Priam, king of Troy.

**Helenus,** hel′e-nus, a celebrated soothsayer, son of Priam, king of Troy.

**Helicon,** hel′i-kon, a mountain in Bœotia, sacred to Apollo and the Muses.

**Helle,** hel′lē, a maiden who, while fleeing from her stepmother, was drowned in the strait which, after her, is called the Hellespont.

**Hera,** hē′ra, the Grecian goddess corresponding to the Juno of the Romans.

**Hercules,** her′kū-lēz, the son of Jupiter and Alcmena, one of the most celebrated heroes of antiquity, noted especially for his twelve labours.

**Hermes,** her′mēz, the Greek name of Mercury.

**Hero,** hē′ro, a beautiful priestess of Venus at Sestos, beloved by Leander of Abydos.

**Hesperides,** hes-per′i-dēz, daughters of Hesperus. In their garden were golden apples guarded by a dragon, which was, however, killed by Hercules, who carried off the apples.

**Hesperus,** hes′pėr-us, a son of Aurora, or of Atlas, turned into a star.

**Hippocrene,** hip-po-krē′nē, a fountain near Mount Helicon, sacred to the Muses, and said to have been produced by a stroke of the hoof of the winged horse Pegasus.

**Horæ,** ho′rē, the Hours, daughters of Jupiter and Themis. They controlled the changes of the seasons, and kept watch at the gates of Olympus.

**Hyacinthus,** hī-a-sin′thus, a beautiful lad, beloved by Apollo, and accidentally killed by a blow from his quoit. From his blood sprang the flower that bears his name.

**Hybla,** hib′la, a town in Sicily, the neighbourhood of which was celebrated for its honey.

**Hydra,** hī′dra, a water-serpent with fifty heads, killed by Hercules near the Lernean lake.

**Hygeia,** hī-jē′i-a, the goddess of health, daughter of Æsculapius.

**Hymen,** hī′men, the god of marriage.

**Hymettus,** hi-met′tus, a mountain near Athens, famed for its honey and its marble.

**Hyperion,** hip-e-ri′on, a Titan, son of Uranus (Heaven) and Gaia (the Earth), father of the Sun.

**Iacchus,** i-ak′us, a name of Bacchus.

**Ida,** ī′da, a mountain in Crete, also a mountain-range near Troy.

**Idalia,** i-dā′li-a, a surname of Venus, derived from the town of Idalium in Cyprus, sacred to her.

**Ilium,** il′i-um, a poetical name for Troy.

**Io,** ī′ō, daughter of a king of Argos, loved by Jupiter, and, through fear of Juno, changed into a cow. Juno now tormented her with a gadfly, and she fled from land to land, swimming the Bosporus ('ox-ford'), and at length finding rest in Egypt, where she recovered human form, and was worshipped as Isis.

**Iphigenia,** if-i-jen-ī′a, daughter of Agamemnon. She was to be sacrificed in expiation for an offence of her father against Diana, but was spared by the goddess, who put a hart in her place.

**Iris,** ī′ris, the swift-footed messenger of the gods, the personification of the rainbow.

**Isis,** ī′sis, an Egyptian goddess, by the Greeks identified both with Demeter and with Io.

**Ixion,** iks-ī′on, the son of a king of Thessaly, was chained, for an offence against Juno, to a constantly revolving wheel.

**Janus,** jā′nus, the Roman sun-god, having a face on the front, and another at the back, of his head. His temple in the Forum had two doors opposite each other, which in time of war were open, and in time of peace were shut. The latter happened only thrice in Roman history.

**Jason,** jā′son, the leader of the Argonauts, brought the Golden Fleece from Colchis, with the help of Medea, whom he married.

**Juno,** jū′no, the Greek Hera, daughter of Saturn, sister and wife of Jupiter, and protecting goddess of women.

**Jupiter,** jū′pi-tėr, the chief god among the Romans, son of Saturn, and husband of Juno; corresponding to the Greek Zeus.

**Lachesis,** lak′e-sis, the one of the Fates who determined the lot of life.

**Laocoon,** la-ok′o-on, a Trojan, priest of Apollo, killed, together with his two sons, at the altar by serpents.

**Laodamia,** lā-o-dam-ī′a, wife of Protesilaus. Her husband was killed by Hector before Troy, and she prayed the gods to give him to her for but three hours. The request was granted, and when the time expired, she died with him.

**Latona,** la-tō′na, the mother of Apollo and Diana.

**Leander,** le-an′dėr, a youth of Abydos, who swam across the Hellespont every night to visit Hero of Sestos, until he was drowned in a storm.

**Leda,** lē′da, the wife of Tyndarus, king of Laconia, visited by Jupiter in the form of a swan. By him, she was the mother of Pollux and Helen; by her husband, of Castor and Clytemnestra.

**Lucretia,** lōō-krēsh′i-a, the wife of Collatinus. When dishonoured by Sextus Tarquinius, she killed herself, and thus became the immediate cause of the expulsion of the Tarquins from Rome.

**Luna,** lū′na, the moon-goddess, the Greek Selene.

**Mars,** märz, an old Roman god of war, son of Jupiter and Juno; the Greek Ares.

**Marsyas,** mar′si-as, a satyr who challenged Apollo to a musical contest, with the Muses as judges, and who was flayed alive for his temerity.

**Medea,** me-dē′a, daughter of a king of Colchis. She assisted Jason to obtain the Golden Fleece, afterwards became his wife, and, when deserted by him for another, destroyed her rival and her own children by Jason, and fled to Athens.

**Medusa,** me-dū′sa, one of the Gorgons, killed by Perseus.

**Megæra,** me-gē′ra, one of the Furies.

**Melibœus,** mel-i-bē′us, the name of a shepherd.

**Melpomene,** mel-pom′e-nē, the Muse of tragedy.

**Memnon,** mem′non, a son of Aurora, and king of Æthiopia, who went to aid the Trojans, was slain by Achilles, and, on the funeral pyre, changed, by his mother, into a bird. His marble statue at Thebes, when touched by the first rays of the sun, gave forth a sound like a lute-string.

**Mentor,** men′tor, the faithful friend of Ulysses.

**Mercury,** mėr′kū-ri, son of Jupiter and Maia, a Roman god of commerce and gain, messenger of the gods; identified with the Greek Hermes.

# Select List of Mythological and Classical Names.

**Midas,** mī′das, a Phrygian king who received from Bacchus the power of turning everything he touched to gold. Even his food turning to gold, he escaped starvation only by washing in the Pactolus. He decided in favour of Pan, a musical contest between him and Apollo, who, in revenge, gave Midas an ass's ears.

**Minerva,** min-ėr′va, the Roman goddess of wisdom, identical with the Greek Pallas Athene.

**Minos,** mī′nos, a king and lawgiver of Crete, made after death a judge in the infernal regions.

**Mnemosyne,** nē-mos′i-nē, the mother of the Muses.

**Momus,** mō′mus, the god of mockery and censure.

**Morpheus,** mor′fe-us, the god of dreams.

**Muses,** daughters of Jupiter and Mnemosyne. They were **Calliope,** the Muse of epic poetry; **Clio,** of history; **Erato,** of amatory poetry; **Thalia,** of comedy; **Melpomene,** of tragedy; **Terpsichore,** of dancing; **Euterpe,** of lyric poetry; **Polyhymnia,** of lyric poetry and eloquence; and **Urania,** of astronomy.

**Narcissus,** nar-sis′us, a beautiful youth who fell in love with his own image reflected in a well, and pined away until he was changed into the flower that bears his name.

**Nausicaa,** nä-sik′a-a, the daughter of King Alcinous. When playing at ball with her maidens on the shore, she found the shipwrecked Ulysses, and conducted him to her father's court.

**Nemæan Lion,** ne-mē′an, a lion in the wood of Nemæa, which was destroyed by Hercules.

**Neptune,** nep′tūn, the Poseidon of the Greeks, brother of Jupiter, and chief god of the sea.

**Nestor,** nes′tor, an aged king of Pylos, famous among the Greeks before Troy for his eloquence, wisdom, and foresight.

**Niobe,** nī′o-bē, the wife of Amphion, king of Thebes. Having boasted that she had more children than Latona, her seven sons and seven daughters were killed by Apollo and Diana, and she wept for them until she was turned into stone.

**Nox,** noks, night, the daughter of Chaos.

**Numa,** nū′ma, the second king of Rome, who organised the whole religious ritual of the state.

**Œdipus,** ē′di-pus, a king of Thebes who solved the Sphinx's riddle, whereupon she killed herself.

**Œnone,** ē-nō′ne, a nymph of Mount Ida, beloved by Paris while yet a shepherd.

**Olympus,** o-lim′pus, a mountain on the borders of Thessaly and Macedonia, the seat of the gods.

**Omphale,** om′fa-lē, a Lydian queen whom Hercules served as a slave for a short time. She would amuse herself by wearing his lion's skin and carrying his club, while Hercules donned woman's dress and spun wool.

**Ops,** the wife of Saturn, the Roman goddess of plenty and patroness of husbandry.

**Orestes,** o-res′tēz, son of Agamemnon. He avenged his father's murder by slaying his mother Clytemnestra, and her paramour Ægisthus.

**Orion,** o-rī′on, a celebrated giant and hunter, who at his death was turned into a constellation.

**Orpheus,** or′fūs, a Thracian poet who moved rocks and tamed wild beasts by the music of his lyre.

**Osiris,** o-sī′ris, the chief Egyptian deity, husband of Isis, and the first to introduce civilisation into Egypt.

**Pactolus,** pak-tō′lus, a river in Lydia, said to bring down golden sands, from Midas having washed in it.

**Pæan,** pē′an, a name of Apollo as the healer.

**Pallas,** päl′las, the same as **Athena.**

**Pan,** an Arcadian pastoral god, inventor of the shepherd's flute.

**Pandora,** pan-dō′ra, the first woman, made by Vulcan by command of Jupiter. She brought with her from heaven a box containing all human ills, which feminine curiosity made her open, and out of it they all flew, to afflict mankind, while nothing remained but Hope.

**Parcæ,** par′sē, the Fates.

**Paris,** par′is, son of Priam, king of Troy. Brought up as a shepherd on Mount Ida, there he decided the dispute as to their beauty between Juno, Minerva, and Venus, in favour of the last, who promised him Helen, wife of Menelaus, and the fairest of women. His carrying her off caused the Trojan war, in which he was slain.

**Parnassus,** par-nas′sus, a mountain in Greece sacred to Apollo and the Muses.

**Patroclus,** pa-trok′lus, the dearest friend of Achilles, rashly challenged Hector before Troy, and was killed by him.

**Pegasus,** peg′a-sus, a winged horse which sprang from the blood of Medusa, bore Bellerophon in his struggle with the Chimæra, then flew upwards to heaven. He is called the horse of the Muses.

**Pelops,** pē′lops, son of Tantalus and father of Atreus. When a child, he was served up as food to the gods, but was recalled to life by Jupiter. He became king of Elis, and was so powerful that he gave his name to the whole Greek peninsula.

**Penelope,** pe-nel′o-pē, the wife of Ulysses, celebrated for her constancy during his twenty years' absence. She put off her importunate suitors by promising to marry when she had finished a web she was weaving; but what was woven during the day, she undid at night.

**Perseus,** pėr′sūs, a son of Jupiter, cut off the head of Medusa, and saved Andromeda from a terrible sea-monster.

**Phaethon,** fā′e-thon, a son of Sol. Having obtained leave to drive the chariot of the sun for one day, he upset it, and was hurled by a thunderbolt from Jupiter into the river Po.

**Philomela,** fil-o-mē′la, a daughter of Pandion, king of Athens, changed into a nightingale.

**Phlegethon,** fleg′e-thon, a river of fire in the lower world.

**Phœbe,** fē′bē, a name of Artemis or Diana, as the goddess of the moon, it being regarded as the sister of Phœbus or the Sun.                    [sun.

**Phœbus,** fē′bus, a name of Apollo as god of the

**Phosphorus,** fos′for-us, the Greek name of Lucifer, the morning star.

**Pieria,** pī-ėr′i-a, a district in the north of Greece, one of the earliest seats of the worship of the Muses, who are often styled *Pierides.*

**Pluto,** plū′to, the king of the lower world, brother of Jupiter and Neptune.

**Plutus,** plū′tus, the god of riches.

**Pollux.** See **Castor.**

**Polyhymnia,** pol-i-him′ni-a, the Muse of lyric poetry and eloquence.

**Polyphemus,** pol-i-fē′mus, a one-eyed Cyclops in Sicily, who was blinded by Ulysses while he was sleeping, after having devoured many of the companions of the latter.

**Pomona,** po-mō′na, the goddess of fruit.

**Poseidon,** po-sī′dōn, the Greek god of the sea, identical with the Roman Neptune.

**Priam,** prī′am, the last king of Troy, slain by Pyrrhus.

**Priapus,** prī-ā′pus, son of Bacchus and Venus, the god of fruitfulness, of gardens, &c.

# Select List of Mythological and Classical Names.

**Prometheus**, pro-mē′thŭs, son of Iapetus, and father of Deucalion. He made a man of clay, and put life into him by fire stolen from heaven. For this, Jupiter chained him to a rock, where a vulture preyed continually upon his liver until he was delivered by Hercules.

**Proserpine**, pros′ėr-pin, daughter of Jupiter and Ceres, carried off by Pluto, and made queen of the lower regions.

**Proteus**, prō′te-us, a sea-god who assumed any form he pleased. He tended the seals or sea-calves of Neptune.

**Psyche**, sī′kē, a nymph beloved by Cupid.

**Pygmalion**, pig-mā′li-on, a king of Cyprus who fell in love with the image of a maiden which he himself had made. Venus changed it into a woman, whom he married.

**Pyramus**, pir′a-mus, the devoted lover of Thisbe. Supposing her to be dead, he stabbed himself under a mulberry tree.

**Python**, pī′thon, a serpent killed near Delphi by Apollo, who founded the Pythian games to commemorate the victory.

**Remus**, rē′mus, twin-brother of Romulus, killed by him for laughing at his infant walls.

**Rhadamanthus**, rad-a-man′thus, one of the judges in the lower world.

**Romulus**, rom′yōō-lus, the mythical founder of Rome, son of Mars by Rhea Silvia, exposed at birth in a cradle on the Tiber, and miraculously suckled by a she-wolf.

**Rubico** (Eng. **Rubicon**, rōōb′i-kon), a small stream on the east coast of Italy, the boundary between Italy and Cisalpine Gaul. It was thus the limit of Cæsar's province, and his crossing it at the head of his army at the commencement of the civil war was tantamount to bidding defiance to the laws of the republic.

**Sardanapalus**, sar-dan-a-pāl′us, king of Nineveh, noted for his licentiousness and effeminacy. When hopelessly defeated, he burned himself together with all his treasures.

**Saturn**, sat′urn, an old Roman divinity, the god of agriculture and civilisation, identified by the Romans with the Greek Cronos, and thus the father of Jupiter, by whom he was dethroned.

**Scylla**, sil′la, a rock between Italy and Sicily, opposite Charybdis, very dangerous to passing ships. It was the haunt of Scylla, a fearful monster.

**Semele**, sem′e-lē, the mother, by Jupiter, of Bacchus.

**Semiramis**, sem-ir′a-mis, with her husband Ninus, the mythical founder of Nineveh. She was distinguished for her personal prowess; and after the death of Ninus she reigned alone with great glory.

**Serapis**, se-rā′pis, an Egyptian divinity.

**Silenus**, sī-lē′nus, the companion of Bacchus, represented as being usually drunk, and seated on an ass. When drunk or asleep he would prophesy, if surrounded by a chain of flowers.

**Sinon**, sī′non, a Greek who allowed himself to be taken prisoner by the Trojans, and persuaded them to admit within their city the wooden horse, which was filled with Greek warriors.

**Sisyphus**, sis′i-fus, a wicked king of Corinth, who was punished in the lower world by having to roll to the top of a hill a stone which constantly rolled back again.

**Sol**, the ancient Italian god of the sun, later identified with the Greek Helios, hence often called Titan or Phœbus by the poets.

**Somnus**, som′nus, the god of sleep, said to be son of Night and brother of Death.

598

**Styx**, stiks, a river of the lower world, across which the shades of the departed were ferried.

**Tantalus**, tan′ta-lus, a son of Jupiter, for divulging his father's secrets, was made to stand up to his chin in water, with branches of fruit hung over his head, the water receding when he wished to drink, and the fruit when he desired to eat.

**Tarpeian Rock**, tar-pī′an rok, on the Capitoline hill at Rome, over which criminals were thrown.

**Telemachus**, te-lem′a-kus, the son of Ulysses and Penelope, left Ithaca to search for his father, and found him at home on his return.

**Terminus**, tėr′min-us, the god who guarded boundaries.

**Terpsichore**, tėrp-sik′o-rē, the Muse of dancing.

**Thalia**, tha-lī′a, the Muse of comedy.

**Thersites**, ther-sī′tes, a Greek before Troy famous for his ugliness and scurrility, killed by Achilles.

**Theseus**, thē′sŭs, the great legendary hero of Attica, who killed the Minotaur, and performed various other famous exploits.

**Thespis**, thes′pis, the founder of Greek tragedy.

**Thetis**, thē′tis, a Nereid, mother of Achilles.

**Thisbe**, this′bē, a Babylonian maiden who killed herself beside the body of her lover Pyramus.

**Timon**, tī′mon, a celebrated misanthrope of Athens.

**Timotheus**, tī-mō′the-us, a celebrated musician of Miletus.

**Tiresias**, tī-rē′si-as, a blind soothsayer of Thebes.

**Tisiphone**, tī-sif′o-nē, one of the Furies.

**Titans**, tī′tans, the sons of Titan, helped their father against Jupiter, but were overthrown.

**Tithonus**, tith-ō′nus, the mortal husband of Aurora, endowed by her with immortality, but not eternal youth. In a decrepit old age his immortality became a burden to him, and he was changed into a grasshopper.

**Tityrus**, tit′i-rus, the name of a shepherd.

**Troilus**, trō′i-lus, a son of Priam, king of Troy, slain by Achilles.

**Trophonius**, trof-ō′ni-us, the builder, along with his brother Agamedes, of the temple of Apollo at Delphi. Deified after his death, he imparted oracles in a cave in Bœotia.

**Troy**, a city of Asia Minor, destroyed by the Greeks after a siege of ten years. See **Helena**.

**Tyrtæus**, tir-tē′us, a lame schoolmaster, sent by Athens to Sparta in answer to an appeal for aid, and who, by his inspiriting martial lyrics, led the Spartans on to victory.

**Ulysses**, ū-lis′ēz, a king of Ithaca, famed for his craft and eloquence. His wanderings, for ten years, over many lands and seas, on his way home from Troy, form the subject of the *Odyssey*.

**Urania**, ū-rā′ni-a, the Muse of astronomy.

**Vacuna**, va-kū′na, the goddess of rural leisure.

**Venus**, vē′nus, the goddess of love and beauty.

**Vertumnus**, vėr-tum′nus, the god of the seasons.

**Vesper**, ves′pėr, the same as Hesperus.

**Vesta**, ves′ta, daughter of Saturn, goddess of the household fire and of domestic life. Her priestesses took an oath of virginity, and were charged to keep the sacred fire burning.

**Virginia**, vir-jin′i-a, a Roman girl whom her father Virginius stabbed to death, to save her from the lust of the decemvir Appius Claudius. This led to the expulsion of the decemvirs.

**Vulcan**, vul′kan, the Roman god of fire, son of Jupiter and Juno, confounded with the Greek Hephaistos.

**Zephyrus**, zef′i-rus, the west wind.

**Zeus**, zūs or zē′us, the Greek name of Jupiter.

# THE METRIC OR FRENCH SYSTEM.

## MEASURES OF LENGTH.

The **MÈTRE**, the unit of length, is the ten-millionth part of a line drawn from the Pole to the Equator.

| | | | | | | |
|---|---|---|---|---|---|---|
| 1 Mètre | = | as above. | | | | |
| 1 Décamètre | = | 10 mètres. | | 1 Decimètre | = | $\frac{1}{10}$th of a mètre. |
| 1 Hectomètre | = | 100 " | | 1 Centimètre | = | $\frac{1}{100}$th " |
| 1 Kilomètre | = | 1000 " | | 1 Millimètre | = | $\frac{1}{1000}$th |
| 1 Myriamètre | = | 10,000 " | | | | |

The Greek prefixes (*deca, hecto, kilo, myria*) denote multiplication.
The Latin prefixes (*deci, centi, milli*) denote division.

## SQUARE MEASURE.

The **ARE**, the unit of surface measure, is a square the side of which is ten mètres long.

| | | | | | | |
|---|---|---|---|---|---|---|
| 1 Are | = | 100 Square mètres. | | 1 Déciare | = | $\frac{1}{10}$th of an are. |
| 1 Decare | = | 10 ares. | | 1 Centiare | = | $\frac{1}{100}$th of an are, |
| 1 Hectare | = | 100 " | | | | or, mètre carré (square mètre). |

## MEASURES OF WEIGHT.

The **GRAMME**, the unit of weight, is the *weight* of a cubic centimètre of distilled water at 4° Centigrade.

| | | | | | | |
|---|---|---|---|---|---|---|
| 1 Gramme | = | as above. | | | | |
| 1 Décagramme | = | 10 gram. | | 1 Décigramme | = | $\frac{1}{10}$th of a gram. |
| 1 Hectogramme | = | 100 " | | 1 Centigramme | = | $\frac{1}{100}$th " |
| 1 Kilogramme, or kilo | = | 1000 " | | 1 Milligramme | = | $\frac{1}{1000}$th " |
| 1 Myriagramme | = | 10,000 " | | | | |

$\frac{1}{2}$ kilogramme is called a livre.

## MEASURES OF CAPACITY, DRY AND LIQUID.

The **LITRE**, the unit of the measures of capacity, dry and liquid, is the *volume* of a cubic decimètre.

| | | | | | | |
|---|---|---|---|---|---|---|
| 1 Litre | = | as above. | | 1 Décilitre | = | $\frac{1}{10}$th of a litre. |
| 1 Décalitre | = | 10 litres. | | 1 Centilitre | = | $\frac{1}{100}$th " |
| 1 Hectolitre | = | 100 " | | 1 Millilitre | = | $\frac{1}{1000}$th " |

## MONEY.

| | | | | | | |
|---|---|---|---|---|---|---|
| 1 Franc | = | 100 centimes. | | 1 Décime | = | 10 centimes. |
| | A franc | = 5 grammes | | 1 Sou | = | 5 " |
| | | (4·5 silver, and ·5 alloy). | | | | |

## FRENCH LINEAL MEASURES, &c. = BRITISH.

| French. | British. |
|---|---|
| **LINEAL.** | |
| Millimètre ........... | 0·0394 inch. |
| Centimètre ......... | 0·3937 " ........or less than half an inch. |
| Décimètre ........... | 3·937 inches............nearly 4 inches. |
| Mètre................ | 39·3708 " ............about 3 feet 3 inches. |
| Hectomètre......... | 0·0621 mile............. " $\frac{1}{16}$th of a mile. |
| Kilomètre ........... | 0·6214 " ............8 kilomètres = 5 miles. |
| | |
| **SQUARE.** | |
| Centiare ............ | 1·196 square yard.....or 1$\frac{1}{5}$th square yard. |
| Are................. | 3·954 poles.............40$\frac{1}{2}$ ares = 1 acre. |
| Hectare............. | 2·471 acres .............nearly 2$\frac{1}{2}$ acres. |

## BRITISH LINEAL MEASURES, &c. = FRENCH.

| *British.* | *French.* |
|---|---|
| **LINEAL.** | |
| **Inch** | 25·399 millimètres. |
| **Foot** | 30·479 centimètres. |
| **Yard** | 0·914 mètre. |
| **Chain** [22 yards] | 20·116 mètres. |
| **Furlong** [10 chains] | 201·164 " |
| **Mile** | 1·609 kilomètre..........5 miles = 8 kilomètres, nearly. |
| **SQUARE.** | |
| **Square Foot** | 9·29 square décimètres. |
| **Acre** | 0·405 hectare.........or about 40 ares. |
| **Square mile** | 2·599 square kilomètres .........100 square miles = 260 sq. kilomètres. |

## FRENCH WEIGHTS = BRITISH.

| *French.* | *British.* |
|---|---|
| **Décigramme** | 1·543 grain...................or about 1½ grains. |
| **Gramme** | 15·432 grains...................28⅓ grammes = 1 ounce avoirdupois. |
| **Décagramme** | 0·353 ounce avoirdupois .......about ⅓ of an ounce avoirdupois. |
| **Hectogramme** | 3·527 ounces..................nearly ¼ pound. |
| **Kilogramme** or **kilo** | 2·2046 pounds..............In trade, a kilo is reckoned at 10 per cent. more than 2 pounds. |

## BRITISH WEIGHTS = FRENCH.

| *British.* | *French.* | *British.* | *French.* |
|---|---|---|---|
| **Grain** | ·0064 gramme. | **Pound** (troy) | 373 grammes |
| **Ounce** (avoirdupois) | 28⅓ grammes. | **Cwt** (avoirdupois) | 50·8 kilos. |
| **Pound** | 454 " | **Ton** | 1015 " |

## FRENCH LIQUID AND CORN MEASURES = BRITISH.

| *French.* | *British.* |
|---|---|
| **Litre** | 1·76 pint (imperial).........or about 1¾ pints. |
| **Hectolitre** | 22·01 gallons..................... " 22 gallons. |

## BRITISH LIQUID AND CORN MEASURES = FRENCH.

| *British.* | *French.* | | |
|---|---|---|---|
| **Pint** | 0·568 litre............or more than ½ a litre. | | |
| **Quart** | 1·136 " ................about 1⅛ litres. | | |
| **Gallon** | 4·543 litres............... | " 4½ litres............ | 11 gallons. |
| **Peck** | 9·087 " ............... | " 9 litres. | = 50 litres. |
| **Bushel** ..[8 gallons] | 36·348 " ............... | " 36⅓ litres. | |
| **Quarter** ..[8 bushels] | 2·908 hectolitres.......... | " 3 hectolitres. | |

## MONEY.

| *English.* | *French.* | |
|---|---|---|
| 1 £ | 25 francs 22 centimes, | or about 25 francs. |
| 1 *s.* | 1 franc 26 centimes, | 1¼ franc. |
| 1 *d.* | 10 centimes. | |
| ½ *d.* | 5 centimes, or a 'sou.' | |

A franc is about 9½d. 100 francs = £4, nearly.

A milliard of francs (1,000,000,000) = £40,000,000, nearly.

Edinburgh: Printed by W. & R. Chambers, Limited.